The Norton Anthology
of World Literature

SECOND EDITION

VOLUME F

The Twentieth Century

The Norton Anthology
of World Literature

SECOND EDITION

Sarah Lawall, *General Editor*

PROFESSOR OF COMPARATIVE LITERATURE AND ADJUNCT PROFESSOR OF
FRENCH, UNIVERSITY OF MASSACHUSETTS, AMHERST

Maynard Mack, *General Editor, Emeritus*

LATE OF YALE UNIVERSITY

VOLUME F

The Twentieth Century

W • W • NORTON & COMPANY • *New York* • *London*

Editor: Peter J. Simon
Developmental Editor: Carol Flechner
Associate Managing Editor: Marian Johnson
Production Manager: Diane O'Connor
Editorial Assistant: Isobel T. Evans
Project Editors: Candace Levy, Vivien Reinart, Carol Walker, Will Rigby
Permissions Manager: Nancy Rodwan
Assistant Permissions Manager: Sandra Chin
Text Design: Antonina Krass
Art Research: Neil Ryder Hoos
Maps: Jacques Chazaud

The text of this book is composed in Fairfield Medium
with the display set in Bernhard Modern.
Composition by Binghamton Valley Composition.
Manufacturing by R. R. Donnelley & Sons.
Cover illustration: Romare Bearden, *Sea Nymph*. Private collection. © Romare Bearden
Foundation / Licensed by VAGA, New York, NY.

The Library of Congress has cataloged another edition as follows:

The Norton anthology of world literature / Sarah Lawall, general editor; Maynard
Mack, general editor emeritus.—2nd ed.
   p. cm.
Includes bibliographical references and index.
Contents: v. A. Beginnings to A.D. 100—v. B. A.D. 100–1500—v. C. 1500–1650—v.
D. 1650–1800—v. E. 1800–1900—v. F. The twentieth century.
ISBN 0-393-97764-1 (v.1)—ISBN 0-393-97765-X (v. 2)
   1. Literature—Collections. I. Lawall, Sarah N. II. Mack, Maynard, 1909–

PN6014.N66 2001
808.8—dc21   2001030824

ISBN 0-393-97760-9 (pbk.)

W. W. Norton & Company, Inc., 500 Fifth Avenue, New York, NY 10110
www.wwnorton.com

W. W. Norton & Company Ltd., Castle House, 75/76 Wells Street, London W1T 3QT

1 2 3 4 5 6 7 8 9 0

Contents

Preface

The first edition of the *Norton Anthology of World Literature* to appear in the twenty-first century offers many new works from around the world and a fresh new format that responds to contemporary needs. The global reach of this anthology encompasses important works from Asia and Africa, central Asia and India, the Near East, Europe, and North and South America—all presented in the light of their own literary traditions, as a shared heritage of generations of readers in many countries, and as part of a network of cultural and literary relationships whose scope is still being discovered. With this edition, we institute a shift in title that reflects the way the anthology has grown. The initial *Norton Anthology of World Masterpieces* (1956) aimed to present a broader "Western tradition of world literature" in contrast to previous anthologies confined to English and American works; it focused on the richness and diversity of Western literary tradition, as does the Seventh Edition of 1999. The present volume, which derives from the "Expanded" edition of 1995, contains almost all the texts of the Seventh Edition and also thousands of pages from works around the globe; it now logically assumes the broader title of "World Literature." In altering the current title to *The Norton Anthology of World Literature*, we do not abandon the anthology's focus on major works of literature or a belief that these works especially repay close study. It is their consummate artistry, their ability to express complex signifying structures, that gives access to multiple dimensions of meaning, meanings that are always rooted in a specific setting and cultural tradition but that further constitute, upon comparison, a thought-provoking set of perspectives on the varieties of human experience. Readers familiar with the anthology's two volumes, whose size increased proportionally with the abundance of new material, will welcome the new boxed format, in which each of the earlier volumes is separated into three slim and easily portable smaller books. Whether maintaining the chronological structure of the original boxed set or selecting a different configuration, you will be able to consult a new Web site, developed by Norton specifically for the world-literature anthologies and containing contextual information, audiovisual resources, exploratory analyses, and related material to illustrate and illuminate these compelling texts.

The six volumes represent six consecutive chronological periods from approximately 2500 B.C. to the present. Subsequently, and for pedagogical reasons, our structure is guided by the broad continuities of different cultural traditions and the literary or artistic periods they recognize for themselves. This means that chronology advises but does not dictate the order in which works appear. If Western tradition names a certain time slot "the Renaissance" or "the Enlightenment" (each term implying a shared set of beliefs), that designation has little relevance in other parts of the globe; similarly, "vernacular literature" does not have the same literary-historical status in all traditions; and "classical" periods come at different times in India, China, and Western Europe. We find that it is more useful to start from a tradition's own sense of itself and the specific shape it gives to the community memory embodied as art. Occasionally there are displacements of absolute chronology: Petrarch, for example, belongs chronologically with Boccaccio and Chaucer, and Rousseau is a contemporary of Voltaire. Each can be read as a new and dissonant voice within his own century, a foil and balance for accepted ideas, or he can be considered as part of a powerful new consciousness, along with those indebted to his thought and example. In the first and last volumes of the anthology, for different pedagogical purposes, we have chosen to present diverse cultural traditions together. The first section of the first volume, "The Invention of Writing and the Earliest Literatures," introduces students to the study of world literature with works from three different cultural traditions—Babylonian, Egyptian, Judaic—each among the oldest works that have come down to us in written form, each in its origins reaching well back into a preliterate past, yet directly accessible as an image of human experience and still provocative at the beginning of the twenty-first century. The last volume, *The Twentieth Century*, reminds us that separation in the modern world is no longer a possibility. Works in the twentieth century are demonstrably part of a new global consciousness, itself fostered by advances in communications, that experiences reality in terms of interrelationships, of boundaries asserted or transgressed, and of the creation of personal and social identity from the interplay of sameness and difference. As teachers, we have tried to structure an anthology that is usable, accessible, and engaging in the classroom—that clarifies patterns and relationships for your students, while leaving you free to organize selections from this wealth of material into the themes, genres, topics, and special emphases that best fit your needs.

Changes in this edition have taken several forms. Most visibly, there are many new selections to spark further combinations with works you have already been teaching and to suggest ways of extending your favorite themes with additional geographic, gendered, chronological, or cultural perspectives. Thus the volume on the twentieth-century adds five important Latin American authors who are pivotal figures in their own time and with an established international stature that, in a few cases, is just beginning to be recognized in the United States. In fiction, there is Juan Rulfo, whose landmark novel *Pedro Páramo* is at once an allegory of political power in modern Mexico and a magical narrative that introduced modernist techniques to Latin American fiction, and Clarice Lispector, the innovative Brazilian novelist and short-story writer who writes primarily about women's experience and is internationally known for her descriptions of psychological states of mind. In poetry, the vehicle for political and cultural revolution in so many European and Latin American countries, we introduce the Nicaraguan Rubén Darío, a charismatic diplomat-poet at home in Europe and Latin America who created the image of a Spanish cultural identity that included his own Indian ancestry and counteracted prevailing images of North American dominance. After Darío there is Alfonsina Storni, the Argentinian poet who was as well known in the 1920s and 1930s for her independent journal articles and her feminism as for the intensely personal poetry that assures her reputation today. Finally, the Nobel Prize winner and Chilean activist Pablo Neruda, who reinvigorated the concept of public poet and became the best-known Latin American poet of the twentieth century, is represented by selections from various periods and styles of his work—in particular, the epic vision of human history taken by many to be his crowning achievement, *The Heights of Macchu Picchu.* Works by all five authors add to our representation of Spanish and Latin American literature, but their importance is not limited to regional or cultural representation. Each functions within a broader framework that may be artistic convention; national, ethnic, or class identity; feminist or postcolonial perspectives; or a particular vision of human experience. Each resonates with other works throughout the volume and is an opportunity to enrich your world-literature syllabus with new comparisons and contrasts.

Many of the new selections draw attention to historical circumstances and the texture of everyday life. Biographical tales from records of the ancient Chinese historian Ssu-ma Ch'ien give a glimpse of contemporary attitudes and ideals, as does the dedicated historian's poignant *Letter in Reply to Jen An,* written after his official punishment by castration. Entries in Dorothy Wordsworth's *Grasmere Journals* express the very personal world of the intimate journal, and Virginia Woolf's passionate analysis of the woman writer's position, in *A Room of One's Own,* combines autobiography with essay and fiction. Still other texts focus on specific historical events or issues but employ fictional techniques for greater immediacy. There is a thin line between fiction and autobiography in Tadeusz Borowski's terrifying Holocaust story *Ladies and Gentlemen, to the Gas Chamber.* Nawal El Saadawi's chilling courtroom tale *In Camera* uses the victim's shifting and fragmented perspectives to evoke the harsh realities of twentieth-century political torture and repression. Zhang Ailing's novella of a difficult love, *Love in a Fallen City,* depicts the decline of traditional Chinese society and concludes with the Japanese bombing of Hong Kong in World War II, while Anita Desai's *The Rooftop Dwellers* follows the struggles of a single woman in Delhi to make a career for herself in the face of social disapproval and family pressure. African American realist author Richard Wright describes an adolescent crisis related to specific social images of manliness in *The Man Who Was Almost a Man.* Yet there are always different ways of presenting historical circumstances and dealing with the questions they raise. A play from Renaissance Spain, Lope de Vega's *Fuente Ovejuna,* is a light romantic comedy that draws heavily on dramatic conventions for its humor; it is also set during a famous peasant uprising whose bloodshed, political repercussions, and torture of the entire citizenry are represented in the course of the play. Readers who follow historical and cultural themes throughout the anthology will find much provocative material in these diverse new selections.

In renewing this edition, we have taken several routes: introducing new authors (many previously mentioned); choosing an alternate work by the same author when it resonates with material in other sections or speaks strongly to current concerns; adding small sections to existing larger pieces in order to fill out a theme or narrative line, or to suggest connections with other texts; and grouping several works to bring out new strengths. Three stories by the African writer Bernard Dadié appear here for the first time, as do the romantic adventures of Ludovico Ariosto's epic parody *Orlando Furi-*

oso, an African tale by Doris Lessing—*The Old Chief Mshlanga*—and Alice Munro's complex evocation of childhood memories *Walker Brothers Cowboy*. Among the alternate works by existing authors, we present Gustave Flaubert's great realist novel *Madame Bovary,* James Joyce's Dublin tale *The Dead,* and William Faulkner's *The Bear,* the latter printed in its entirety to convey its full scope as a chronicle of the legacy of slavery in the American South. New plays include Bertolt Brecht's drama *The Good Woman of Setzuan* and William Shakespeare's *Othello* as well as *Hamlet;* each has its own special resonance in world literature. Derek Walcott is represented by a selection of his poetry, including excerpts from the modern epic *Omeros.* Five more magical tales are added to the *Thousand and One Nights* and three new essays from Montaigne, including his memorable *To the Reader.* Six new tales from Ovid (in a new translation by Allen Mandelbaum) round out a set of myths exploring different images of love and gender, themes that reappear in two of the best-known lays of Marie de France, *Lanval* and *Laüstic,* as well as in Boccaccio's famous "Pot of Basil" and the influential tale of patient Griselda and her tyrannical husband, all presented here. From Chaucer, there is the bawdy, popular *Wife of Bath's Tale,* and from the *Heptameron* of Marguerite de Navarre fresh tales of love and intrigue that emphasize the stereotyping of gender roles. To *The Cherry Orchard* by Anton Chekhov, we add his famous tale of uncertain love *The Lady with the Dog.* New selections from Books 4 and 8 of John Milton's *Paradise Lost* depict the drama of Satan's malevolent entry into Paradise, Adam and Eve's innocent conversation, and the angel's warning to Adam. Finally, the poignant tales of Abraham and Isaac and of Jacob and Esau (Genesis 22, 25, 27) are added to the Old Testament selections, as well as the glorious love poetry of the Song of Songs; and Matthew 13 [Why Jesus Teaches in Parables] is included among the selections from the New Testament.

Two founding works of early India, the *Rāmāyana* and the *Mahābhārata,* are offered in greatly increased selections and with new and exceptionally accessible translations. Readers can now follow (in a new translation by Swami Venkatesananda) the trajectory of Rāma's exile and life in the forest, the kidnapping of his wife Sītā, and ensuing magical adventures up to the final combat between Rāma and the demon king Rāvana. A lively narrative of the *Mahābhārata*'s civil war (in a new translation by C. V. Narasimhan) unfolds in sequential excerpts that include two sections of special interest to modern students: the insulted Draupadī's formal accusation of the rulers in the Assembly Hall and the tragic story of the heroic but ill-fated warrior Karna.

To increase our understanding of individual authors' achievement, we join to the Indian Rabindranath Tagore's story *Punishment* a selection of the Bengali poems with which he revolutionized literary style in his homeland, and to the Chinese Lu Xun's two tales, examples of his poetry from *Wild Grass.* Rousseau's *Confessions* gain historical and psychological depth through new passages that shed light on his early years and on the development of his political sympathies.

The epic poetry that acts as the conscience of a community—*The Iliad, The Mahābhārata,* the *Son-Jara,* among others—has long been represented in the anthology. It has been our practice, however, to minimize the presence of lyric poetry in translation, recognizing—as is so cogently argued in the

"Note on Translation," printed at the end of each volume—that the precise language and music of an original poem will never be identical with its translation and that short poems risk more of their substance in the transfer. Yet good translations often achieve a poetry of their own and occupy a pivotal position in a second literary history; thus the Egyptian love songs, the Chinese *Classic of Poetry* (*Book of Songs*), the biblical Song of Songs, and the lyrics of Sappho, Catullus, Petrarch, Rumi, and Baudelaire have all had influence far beyond the range of those who could read the original poems. Some poetry collections—like the Japanese *Man'yōshū* and *Kokinshū*—are recognized as an integral part of the society's cultural consciousness, and others—notably, the European Romantics—embody a sea change in artistic and cultural consciousness.

New to this edition is a series of poetry clusters that complement existing collections and represent a core of important and influential poetry in five different periods. You may decide to teach them as part of a spectrum of poetic expression or as reference points in a discussion of cultural consciousness. Thus a newly translated series of early hymns by the Tamil Śaiva saints exemplifies the early mystical poetry of India, while the multifarious vitality of medieval Europe is recaptured in poems by men and women from Arabic, Judaic, Welsh, Spanish, French, Provençal, Italian, English, and German traditions. Those who have taught English Romantic poetry will find both contrast and comparison in Continental poets from France, Italy, Germany, Spain, and Russia, many of whom possess lasting influence in nineteenth- and twentieth-century literature. Symbolism, whose insights into the relation of language and reality have permeated modern poetry and linguistic theory, is represented by the great nineteenth-century poets Charles Baudelaire, Stéphane Mallarmé, Paul Verlaine, and Arthur Rimbaud. Finally, a cluster of Dada-Surrealist poems that range from slashing, rebellious humor to ecstatic love introduces the free association and dreamlike structures of this visionary movement, whose influence extends around the world and has strong links to modern art and film.

How to choose, as you turn from the library before you to the inevitable constraint of available time? There is an embarrassment of riches, an inexhaustible series of options, to fit whatever course pattern you wish. Perhaps you have already decided to proceed by theme or genre, in chronological order or by a selected comparative principle; or you have favorite titles that work well in the classroom, and you seek to combine them with new pieces. Perhaps you want to create modules that compare ideas of national identity or of bicultural identity and shifting cultural paradigms, that survey images of gender in different times and places or that examine the place of memory in a range of texts. In each instance, you have only to pick and choose among a variety of works from different countries, languages, and cultural backgrounds. If you are teaching the course for the first time or wish to try something different, you may find what you are looking for in the sample syllabi of the *Instructor's Guide* or on the new Web site, which will also contain supporting material such as maps, time lines, and audio pronunciation glossaries, resource links, guides to section materials, various exercises and assignments, and a series of teaching modules related to specific works. Throughout, the editors (who are all practicing teachers) have selected and prepared texts that are significant in their own area of scholarly expertise, meaningful in the larger context of world literature, and, always, delightful, captivating and challenging to students.

Clearly one can parcel out the world in a variety of ways, most notably geopolitical, and there is no one map of world literature. In order to avoid parochialism, some scholars suggest that we should examine cultural activity in different countries at the same period of time. Others attempt to deconstruct prevailing literary assumptions (often selected from Western literary theory) by using history or cultural studies as a framework for examining texts as documents. "Global" literary studies project a different map that depends on one's geopolitical view of global interactions and of the energies involved in the creation and dissemination of literature. *The Norton Anthology of World Literature*, Second Edition, takes a different point of departure, focusing first of all on literary texts—artifacts, if you will, that have a special claim on our attention because they have been read over a great period of time and are cherished by a wide variety of readers. Once such texts have been proposed as objects of knowledge—and enjoyment, and illumination— they are available for any and all forms of analysis. Situating them inside larger forms of textuality—linguistic, historical, or cultural—is, after all, an inevitable part of the meaning-making process. It is the primary task of this anthology, however, to present them as multidimensional objects for discussion and then to let our readers choose when and where to extend the analysis.

From the beginning, the editors of *The Norton Anthology of World Literature* have always balanced the competing—and, we like to think, complementary—claims of teaching and scholarship, of the specialist's focused expertise and the generalist's broader perspectives. The founding editors set the example, which guides their successors. We welcome three new successor editors to this edition: William G. Thalmann, Professor of Classics at the University of Southern California; Lee Patterson, Professor of English at Yale University; and Heather James, Associate Professor of English at the University of Southern California. Two founding editors have assumed Emeritus status: Bernard M. W. Knox, eminent classical scholar and legendary teacher and lecturer; and P. M. Pasinetti, who combines the intellectual breadth of the Renaissance scholar with a novelist's creative intuition. We also pay tribute to the memory of Robert Lyons Danly, translator and astute scholar of Japanese literature, whose lively interventions have been missed since his untimely death in 1995. Finally, we salute the memory of Maynard Mack, General Editor and presiding genius from the first edition through the Expanded Edition of 1995. An Enlightenment scholar of much wisdom, humanity, and gracefully worn knowledge, and a firm believer in the role of great literature—world literature—in illuminating human nature, he was also unstintingly dedicated to this anthology as a teaching enterprise. To him, therefore, and on all counts, we dedicate the first millennial edition of the anthology.

Acknowledgments

Among our many critics, advisers, and friends, the following were of special help in providing suggestions and corrections: Joseph Barbarese (Rutgers University); Carol Clover (University of California, Berkeley); Patrick J. Cook (George Washington University); Janine Gerzanics (University of Southern California); Matthew Giancarlo (Yale University); Kevis Goodman (University of California at Berkeley); Roland Greene (University of Oregon); Dmitri Gutas (Yale University); John H. Hayes (Emory University); H. Mack Horton (University of California at Berkeley); Suzanne Keen (Washington and Lee University); Charles S. Kraszewski (King's College); Gregory F. Kuntz; Michelle Latiolais (University of California at Irvine); Sharon L. James (Bryn Mawr College); Ivan Marcus (Yale University); Timothy Martin (Rutgers University, Camden); William Naff (University of Massachusetts); Stanley Radosh (Our Lady of the Elms College); Fred C. Robinson (Yale University); John Rogers (Yale University); Robert Rothstein (University of Massachusetts); Lawrence Senelick (Boston University); Jack Shreve (Alleghany Community College); Frank Stringfellow (University of Miami); Nancy Vickers (Bryn Mawr College); and Jack Welch (Abilene Christian University).

We would also like to thank the following people who contributed to the planning of the Second Edition: Charles Adams, University of Arkansas; Dorothy S. Anderson, Salem State College; Roy Anker, Calvin College; John Apwah, County College of Morris; Doris Bargen, University of Massachusetts; Carol Barrett, Austin Community College, Northridge Campus; Michael Beard, University of North Dakota; Lysbeth Em Berkert, Northern State University; Marilyn Booth, University of Illinois; George Byers, Fairmont State College; Shirley Carnahan, University of Colorado; Ngwarsungu Chiwengo, Creighton University; Stephen Cooper, Troy State University; Bonita Cox, San Jose State University; Richard A. Cox, Abilene Christian University; Dorothy Deering, Purdue University; Donald Dickson, Texas A&M University; Alexander Dunlop, Auburn University; Janet Eber, County College of Morris; Angela Esterhammer, University of Western Ontario; Walter Evans, Augusta State University; Fidel Fajardo-Acosta, Creighton University; John C. Freeman, El Paso Community College, Valle Verde Campus; Barbara Gluck, Baruch College; Michael Grimwood, North Carolina State University; Rafey Habib, Rutgers University, Camden; John E. Hallwas, Western Illinois College; Jim Hauser, William Patterson College; Jack Hussey, Fairmont State College; Dane Johnson, San Francisco State University; Andrew Kelley, Jackson State Community College; Jane Kinney, Valdosta State University; Candace Knudson, Truman State University; Jameela Lares, University of Southern Mississippi; Thomas L. Long, Thomas Nelson Community College; Sara MacDonald, Sterling College; Linda Macri, University of Maryland; Rita Mayer, San Antonio College; Christopher Morris,

Norwich University; Deborah Nestor, Fairmont State College; John Netland, Calvin College; Kevin O'Brien, Chapman University; Mariannina Olcott, San Jose State University; Charles W. Pollard, Calvin College; Pilar Rotella, Chapman University; Rhonda Sandford, Fairmont State College; Daniel Schenker, University of Alabama at Huntsville; Robert Scotto, Baruch College; Carl Seiple, Kutztown University; Glenn Simshaw, Chemeketa Community College; Evan Lansing Smith, Midwestern State University; William H. Smith, Piedmont College; Floyd C. Stuart, Norwich University; Cathleen Tarp, Fairmont State College; Diane Thompson, Northern Virginia Community College; Sally Wheeler, Georgia Perimeter College; Jean Wilson, McMaster University; Susan Wood, University of Nevada, Las Vegas; Tom Wymer, Bowling Green State University.

Phonetic Equivalents

for use with the Pronouncing Glossaries preceding most
selections in this volume

a as in *cat*
ah as in *father*
ai as in *light*
ay as in *day*
aw as in *raw*
e as in *pet*
ee as in *street*
ehr as in *air*
er as in *bird*
eu as in *lurk*
g as in *good*
i as in *sit*
j as in *joke*
nh a nasal sound (as in French *vin, vɛ̃*)
o as in *pot*
oh as in *no*
oo as in *boot*
oy as in *toy*
or as in *bore*
ow as in *now*
s as in *mess*
ts as in *ants*
u as in *us*
zh as in *vision*

The Norton Anthology
of World Literature

SECOND EDITION

VOLUME F

The Twentieth Century

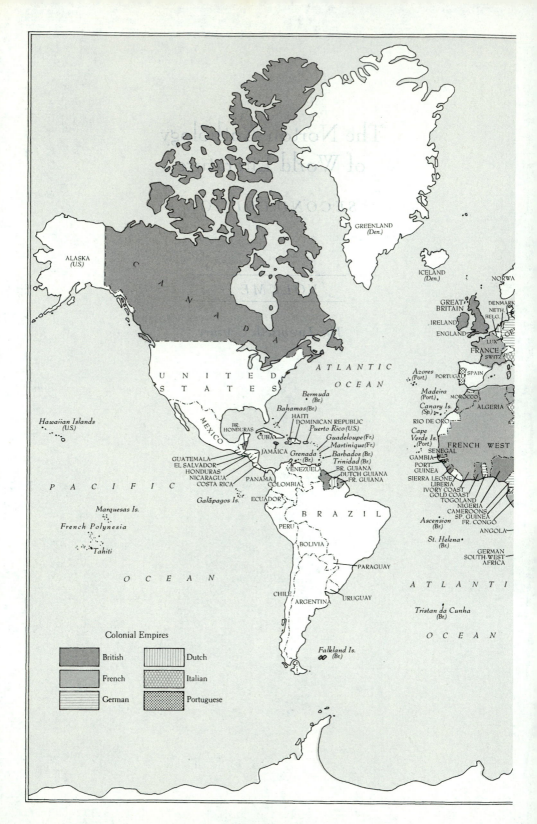

Colonial Empires

British   Dutch
French   Italian
German   Portuguese

GREENLAND (Den.)

ICELAND (Den.)

NORWAY

GREAT BRITAIN
IRELAND
ENGLAND

DENMARK
NETH.
BELG.
LUX.
FRANCE
SWITZ.

Azores (Port.)
PORTUGAL
SPAIN

Madeira (Port.)
Canary Is. (Sp.)
MOROCCO
ALGERIA

RIO DE ORO

Cape Verde Is. (Port.)

FRENCH WEST

SENEGAL
GAMBIA
PORT. GUINEA
SIERRA LEONE
LIBERIA
IVORY COAST
GOLD COAST
TOGOLAND
NIGERIA
CAMEROONS
SP. GUINEA
FR. CONGO

ANGOLA

GERMAN SOUTH-WEST AFRICA

Ascension (Br.)

St. Helena (Br.)

Tristan da Cunha (Br.)

ALASKA (U.S.)

C A N A D A

GREENLAND (Den.)

A T L A N T I C
O C E A N

U N I T E D
S T A T E S

Hawaiian Islands (U.S.)

MEXICO

BR. HONDURAS
GUATEMALA
EL SALVADOR
HONDURAS
NICARAGUA
COSTA RICA
PANAMA

Bermuda (Br.)

Bahamas (Br.)
HAITI
CUBA
DOMINICAN REPUBLIC
Puerto Rico (U.S.)
Guadeloupe (Fr.)
Martinique (Fr.)
JAMAICA
Grenada (Br.)
Barbados (Br.)
Trinidad (Br.)
VENEZUELA
BR. GUIANA
DUTCH GUIANA
FR. GUIANA
COLOMBIA

P A C I F I C

Marquesas Is.

French Polynesia

Tahiti

Galápagos Is.
ECUADOR

PERU

B R A Z I L

BOLIVIA

O C E A N

PARAGUAY

CHILE

ARGENTINA
URUGUAY

Falkland Is. (Br.)

A T L A N T I C

O C E A N

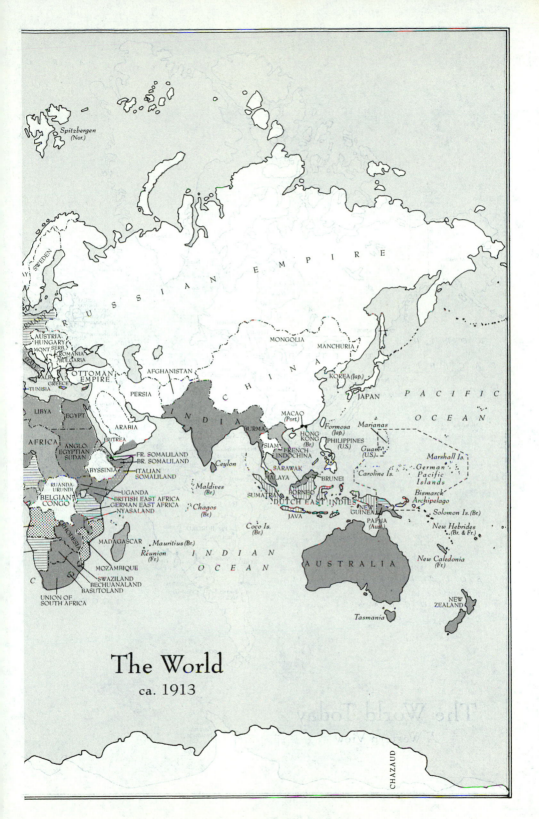

The World

ca. 1913

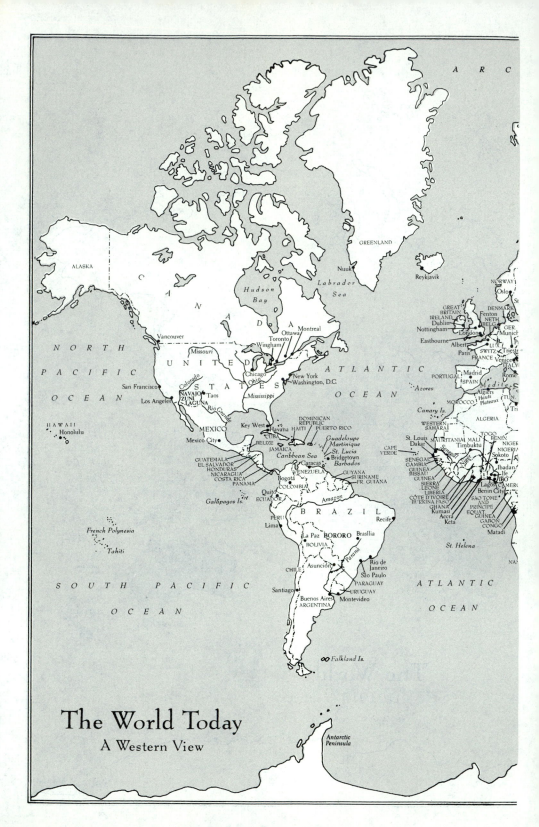

The World Today
A Western View

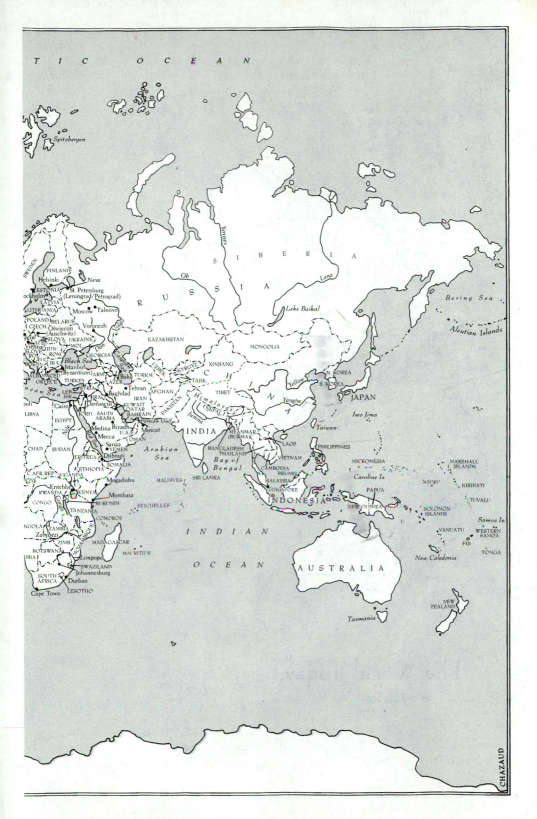

TIC OCEAN

Spitzbergen

SWEDEN
FINLAND
Helsinki   *Neva*
ESTONIA   St. Petersburg
ockholm   (Leningrad/Petrograd)
LATVIA
LITHUANIA   Moscow *Talnovo*
POLAND   BELARUS
CZECH   Voronezh
Oświęcim   UKRAINE
(Auschwitz)   *Don*
SLOVA
Vienna   MOL
SLOVE   ROM
BOS   BUL   *Black Sea*
MACED   Istanbul
GREECE   TURKEY   (Byzantium)
ean Sea   LEB   ISR
oli   SYRIA   Baghdad
LIBYA   IRAQ   IRAN
EGYPT   Damascus
JORD   KUWAIT
SAUDI   QATAR
Medina   Riyadh   U.A.E.
Mecca   OMAN   Muscat
*YEMEN
CHAD   SUDAN
C. AFR. REP.   ETHIOPIA   Djibouti
ONY   UGANDA   SOMALIA
RWANDA   KENYA   Mogadishu
CONGO   Entebbe   Mombasa
BURUNDI
TANZANIA
NGOLA   ZAMBIA   COMOROS
Zambezi   ZIMB
BOTSWANA   MADAGASCAR
IBIA   *Limpopo*   MAURITIUS
SWAZILAND
SOUTH   Johannesburg
AFRICA   Durban
Cape Town   LESOTHO

R U S S I A

KAZAKHSTAN

GEORGIA
ARM   AZER
TURKM.
TURKEY   Tehran
AFGHAN.
PAKISTAN   *Himalayas*
INDIA   NEPAL
Indus   *Jumna*
BANGLADESH
*Arabian
Sea*   THAILAND
*Bay of
Bengal*
MALDIVES   SRI LANKA

SEYCHELLES

*I N D I A N

O C E A N*

S I B E R I A

Ob   *Yenisey*   *Lena*

MONGOLIA

XINJIANG
KYRGYZ
TAJIK
Yellow
TIBET   C H I N A   N. KOREA
Yangtse   S. KOREA

Bering Sea

Aleutian Islands

JAPAN
Iwo Jima
Taiwan

MYANMAR   LAOS
(BURMA)
VIETNAM
CAMBODIA   PHILIPPINES
BRUNEI
MALAYSIA   MICRONESIA
SINGAPORE   *Caroline Is.*
PAPUA
INDONESIA   NEW GUINEA

SOLOMON
ISLANDS

MARSHALL
ISLANDS
NAURU   KIRIBATI
TUVALU

Samoa Is.
VANUATU   WESTERN
SAMOA
FIJI
New Caledonia   TONGA

A U S T R A L I A

Tasmania

NEW
ZEALAND

CHAZAUD

1575

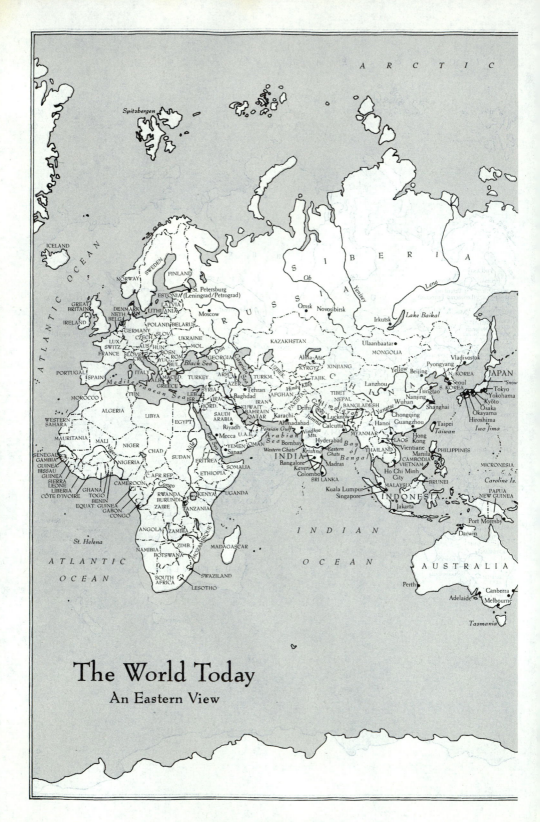

The World Today
An Eastern View

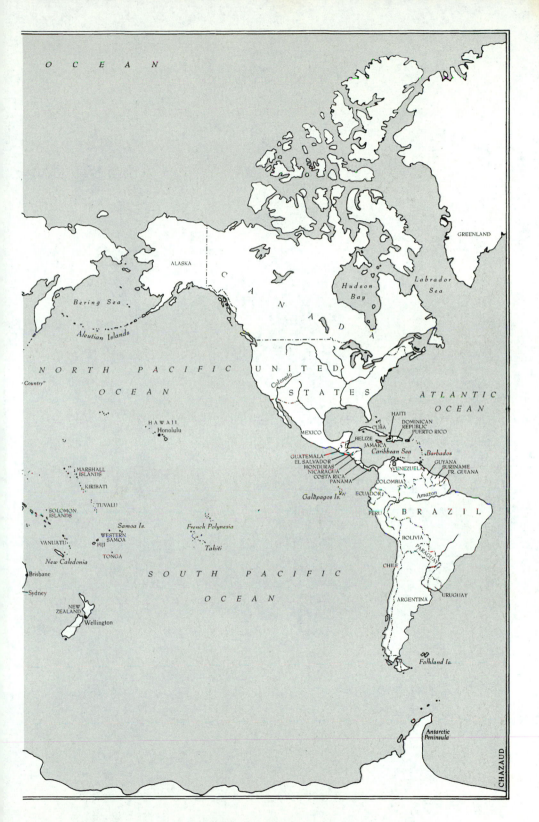

OCEAN

GREENLAND

ALASKA

Labrador Sea

Hudson Bay

C A N A D A

Bering Sea

Aleutian Islands

N O R T H   P A C I F I C

"Country"

O C E A N

U N I T E D

Colorado

S T A T E S

A T L A N T I C

O C E A N

H A W A I I
Honolulu

MEXICO

HAITI

CUBA

DOMINICAN
REPUBLIC
PUERTO RICO

BELIZE

JAMAICA

Caribbean Sea

Barbados

MARSHALL
ISLANDS

KIRIBATI

GUATEMALA
EL SALVADOR
HONDURAS
NICARAGUA
COSTA RICA
PANAMA

VENEZUELA

GUYANA
SURINAME
FR. GUIANA

TUVALU

COLOMBIA

Galápagos Is.

ECUADOR

Amazon

SOLOMON
ISLANDS

PERU

B R A Z I L

Samoa Is.

French Polynesia

BOLIVIA

VANUATU

WESTERN
SAMOA

FIJI

Tahiti

PARAGUAY

New Caledonia

TONGA

CHILE

S O U T H   P A C I F I C

•Brisbane

O C E A N

ARGENTINA

URUGUAY

—Sydney

NEW
ZEALAND

•Wellington

Falkland Is.

*Antarctic
Peninsula*

CHAZAUD

1577

The Modern World:
Self and Other in
Global Context

Modern consciousness in the twentieth century took a remarkable turn. Not because it was "modern" (every period is modern in its own eyes), but because it began for the first time to be truly global. No beckoning frontier, no large area of the globe remained unvisited and mysterious for future explorers to map. Breathtaking advances in technology, transformations of modern states, the rapid spread of international corporations, cultural exchanges occurring rapidly and inevitably as communication and transportation networks linked all sections of the world—all created an era in which the essential reality is interconnectedness rather than isolation. Not that this simplifies matters. Connections bring their own problems, and they are not always welcome. Connections inevitably change the system, disrupt tradition, and confront people with many more choices than they were aware of previously. In many ways, this is the story of the twentieth century as it drew to a close.

These days the terms *modern* and *modernization* reappear everywhere as a key to change. They can be used as a weapon to bring about "progress," or rejected in favor of "tradition," or defined differently according to context and situation. In the West (understood as Europe and North America), modernization has meant industrial progress, a refusal of positivist certainty about the nature of the world, and a desire to transcend narrowly nationalist politics. Elsewhere, modernization has been equated with "Westernization" (especially in technology, industry, political structures, and mass culture) and has been supported or rejected with that understanding.

Modernization has also arrived at different speeds in different parts of the world, growing gradually in Europe out of previous centuries, but coming far more rapidly to non-Western countries, often as a forced change brought about by colonialist politics and economic necessity. Little pockets of Western prosperity around the world—colonial enclaves in China, Africa, India, and South America—drove home the difference between colonizing and colonized societies, and the wealthy Western countries made a tempting model for regions beset by poverty, disease, and social unrest. Political leaders soon equated progress with Westernization, and many sought prosperity by transforming their societies into the closest possible imitation of Europe. Western success, they felt (and were told), was the result not merely of industrialization but also of a whole set of distinctive values and institutions—the concepts of individualism and democracy, attention to literacy and general education, private ownership and a thriving middle class, religious freedom, scientific method, public institutions, and (sometimes) the emancipation of women.

Colonial governments considered it their duty to disseminate these values by setting up school systems where European languages were used instead of local ones, and Western literature and philosophy were taught instead of indigenous culture. As a result, twentieth-century Westernization in many countries not only promised advances in literacy and standard of living but seemed to require the suppression of indigenous traditions, including centuries of literature (much of it oral) as well as languages, philosophy, religion, and models of community life. Works in this volume by Chinua Achebe, Léopold Sédar Senghor, Wole Soyinka, Albert Camus, Naguib Mahfouz, Kojima Nobuo, Derek Walcott, and Lorna Goodison illustrate this conflict of different ways of life. Yet these same works also demonstrate another fact of global existence: that the clash of opposites is also a set of inextricably intermingled experiences, pointing to a fuller understanding of cultural (and multicultural) identity.

Modernism is not the same as modernization. Twentieth-century modernism is a literary and artistic movement with roots in Europe. Even the somewhat earlier *Modernismo* looked to Symbolist poetics for stylistic techniques to revolutionize Spanish-American literature. Modernist works—translated and republished in great numbers—were exported around the globe along with the general expansion of Western culture. Many non-Western writers and intellectuals saw modernist style as the latest image of a progressive Western culture and a technique embodying an "advanced" way of thought. They borrowed artistic forms that were a gradual outgrowth of experimentation and literary evolution in Europe and America and used them as instant models in a new pattern of global crisscrossing that has overlaid narrower lines of literary evolution. In some instances, the militantly new aura of modernist works was prized as a way of rejecting traditional authority, an oblique means of transforming local perceptions. Although a reaction later set in owing to shifts in economic and political power and to a greater acceptance of cultural difference, Western concepts of modernism continue to influence modern literature and literary theory the world over.

THE EUROPEAN ORIGINS OF TWENTIETH-CENTURY MODERNISM

Western modernity evolved out of, and in contrast to, a specific historical situation. This situation differed in other parts of the world, especially in feudal societies without industry, middle class, or a popular press and where artistic tradition supported highly stylized works with mythological subjects. Change followed different lines, therefore, according to whether the immediate past was feudal or democratic and whether the audience favored exquisite craftsmanship or, as in the West, versions of realism. In conservative societies such as China, Japan, and India, the foreign examples that helped usher in modern literature were likely to come from the same European realism against which Western modernism reacted. By the end of the twentieth century, however, Western modernist techniques could be found in literature around the world, usually blended with perspectives drawn from Realism.

In Europe, the idea of modernity was already a source of public debate and widespread anxiety as the Industrial Revolution transformed social, economic, and political life faster, it seemed, than such changes could peacefully be absorbed. Some saw it as a time of decadence and the loss of stable values. Others saw it, more optimistically, as an era in which a progressive Europe would lead the rest of the world to its own pinnacle of achievement (a point of view shared only briefly by the colonized countries). In science, philosophy, social theory, and the arts, the nineteenth century prepared both the evolution and the rebellion of the twentieth.

Scientific Rationalism

By the end of the nineteenth century, unprecedented developments in science had encouraged Westerners to believe that they would soon master all the secrets of the universe. The Enlightenment notion of the world as a machine—something whose parts could be named and seen to function—came back into favor. Discoveries in different fields seemed to make the universe more rational and hence predictable. In chemistry, there was John Dalton's (1766–1844) atomic theory and Dimitri Mendeleyev's (1834–1907) periodic table of elements; in physics, James Maxwell's (1831–1879) field theory unifying the study of electricity, magnetism, and light. The further development of Newtonian ideas made it possible to study the fixed stars, and spectral analysis showed the essential homogeneity of the universe. Technological applications suggested that these discoveries would serve humanity, not master it. Thermodynamics explained the processes of energy transformation, and locomotives and steamships promised rapid transportation throughout the world. Daguerreotype photography (developed by Louis Daguerre [1787–1851]) provided a documentary record. Finally, the history of living nature itself became an object of study when Charles Darwin (1809–1882) examined the evolution of species according to material evidence, without reference to divine laws or purpose.

The enthusiasm for scientific discovery was not confined to scientists. Auguste Comte (1798–1857), a French philosopher known as the founder of "positivism," held that scientific method constituted a total world view in which everything would ultimately be explained, including human society. Comte proposed a science of humanity that would analyze and define the laws governing human society (the first sociology). It became evident, however, that the results of scientific method depended on the objectivity of the scientist's point of view. Count Gobineau (1816–1882) proposed a "scientific" description of society in which there were three races (white, black, and yellow) with innate qualities and in which the white race (predictably, for this white Frenchman) was the superior category. Gobineau's writings laid the groundwork for much "scientific" racism later on, until he himself became a subject of analysis for scientists interested in explaining the history of race prejudice.

In literature, the historian and critic Hippolyte Taine (1828–1893) proposed a science of culture in which each literary work could be categorized as the combined product of its "race, milieu, and time." The novelist Émile Zola offered as scientific justification for his series on the degeneracy of the Rougon-Macquart family an *Introduction to the Study of Experimental Medicine* by Dr. Claude Bernard (1813–1878). Nowadays, it is easier to recognize the preexisting bias that flaws these large explanatory systems and to be cautious of claims of "scientific truth," especially in descriptions of human nature. The enormous wealth created by technology and scientific method, however, offered a powerful incentive for other regions of the world to imitate the Western example.

Western social theorists shared with the philosopher Comte the vision of creating a perfect society by understanding social "laws." Utopian socialists like the French Charles Fourier (1772–1837) and the Comte de Saint-Simon (1760–1825) and the Welsh industrialist Robert Owen (1771–1858) proposed various methods for organizing society and planning its economy. The English philosopher and economist John Stuart Mill (1806–1873) preached the dignity of man, the rights of women, and the possibility of happiness for all. By far the most important and influential theorist was the German Karl Marx (1819–1883), whose *Communist Manifesto* (1848) and *Capital* (1867) proposed a scientific theory of world history driven by broad economic forces. According to Marx, the most basic material needs—food, shelter, and the social relationships enabling group survival—provide an economic foundation from which all other aspects of human culture are derived. His description of modern workers as alienated cogs in the industrial economic machine, no longer owning their own labor, expressed for many the antihuman aspect of modern technological progress. Like his contemporaries, he believed in the power of rational systems to find answers for social ills; he described the division of modern industrial society into the two competing forces of capital and labor (the proletariat) and proposed the theory of dialectical materialism to explain the processes of history.

Reactions to Rationalism

The debate about scientific rationalism was inevitably a debate about knowledge and human values. In the nineteenth century, one of the strongest opponents of positivism and its belief in rational solutions was the German philosopher Friedrich Nietzsche (1844–1900). Nietzsche focused on the individual, not society, and admired only the *Übermensch*, the superhuman being who refused to be bound by the prevailing social paradigms of nationalism, Christianity, faith in science, loyalty to the state, or bourgeois civilized comfort. Nietzsche's distinction between Dionysian (instinctual) and Apollonian (intellectual) forces in human beings, his insistence on the individual's complete freedom (and responsibility) in a world that lacks transcendental law ("God is dead"), and his attack on the unimaginative mediocrity of mass society in the modern industrial world have made him a powerful influence in twentieth-century Western thought. In general, he gave a quasi-philosophical focus to the underlying distrust of rationalist perspectives that was already alive in other parts of the world and had begun to emerge in nineteenth-century Europe with explorations of magic and the occult, theosophy, and the constructed image of an "Eastern" spirituality complementary to the scientific, soulless West.

The shape and intensity of this debate in Europe were dictated for many years by a historical event that turned the younger generations against everything inherited from the recent past: the Great War (World War I, 1914–18). In spite of the confident rationalism of the political leaders of "Papa's Europe" (a term of resentment used by many to describe an authoritarian, patriarchal society that claimed to have all the answers), World War I had for the first time involved the whole continent of Europe and the United States in battle (reaching, with Turkey, into Asia Minor) and was the first "total war" in which modern weapons spared no one, including civilians. Clearly, something was wrong. An entire generation was lost in the trenches, and the survivors emerged resolved to reexamine the bases of certainty, the structures of knowledge, the systems of belief, and the repositories of authority in a society that had allowed such a war to occur. Their reaction would also be reflected in literature, not only in subject matter but—for many—in a new use of language, in new ways of representing our knowledge of the world, and, most especially, new hesitations about subscribing to any single mode of understanding it. They drew on areas beyond the intellect, interrogating modes of human consciousness and feeling in an intellectual attempt to go beyond the self-imposed limitations of previous rationalism.

Several thinkers were particularly important in formulating alternatives to the narrow rationalism of positivist philosophy. The French philosopher Henri Bergson (1859–1941) attacked scientific rationality as artificial and unreal because it froze everything in conceptual space; it ignored the whole dimension of life as it is actually experienced. For Bergson, reality was a fluid, living force (*élan vital*) that could only be apprehended by consciousness. Instead of quantitative and logical inquiry, he proposed intuiting the "immediate data of consciousness" as an alternate, nonscientific means of knowledge. This intuition was not a kind of spiritualism or a meditative philosophy such as Buddhism: Bergson neither ignored nor tried to escape the world of the senses but wished to register its immediate impact with great precision. Authors were not slow to perceive the implications of his prescription for representing reality. Marcel Proust, searching to discover his identity through layers of "lost time," James Joyce, imitating the stream of consciousness in the written flow of words, the later author Tanizaki Jun'ichirō, representing cultural difference as a matter of finely differentiated sensations—all reflect a twentieth-century, Bergsonian change in the way reality is perceived and represented. Bergson himself received the Nobel Prize in literature in 1927, both for the creative imagination shown in his own work and for his literary influence.

Sigmund Freud (1856–1939), the founder of psychoanalysis, was another influential figure. Freud's study of subconscious motives and instinctual drives revealed a level of activity that had been largely ignored outside of literature and was not considered a productive subject for continued "rational" inquiry. His essays and case studies argued that dreams and manias contain their own networks of meaning and that human beings cannot properly be understood without taking into consideration the irrational as well as the rational level of their existence. All are caught up, he suggested, in the process of mediating the same sexual drives and civilizational repressions that caused neurosis in his own patients.

Many of Freud's theories are questioned today (his assumption that every woman considers herself an incomplete man, for example). Some of his psychoanalytic categories seem too rigid. He rejected divergent views, and he ignored the possibility that his own cultural stereotypes influenced both his theories and his view of patients. The mythic images he used to convey some of his basic concepts, like the Oedipus complex, were drawn from a heavily patriarchal Western mythology and are, therefore, less persuasive to societies—India's for example—whose mythology contains strong matriarchal images. Freud's insistence on a fundamental and universally true image of human sexuality has also been interpreted as a defensive reaction against racial and social discord that included anti-Semitism. To prejudice and alienation, he would oppose a grand unifying image. His chief importance, however, lies elsewhere, in his brilliant and even poetic attempts to clarify patterns of human thought and emotion. He focused attention on the way everyday, "rational" behavior is shaped by unconscious impulses and hidden motivations and on the way human beings actually create (and modify) their images of self through engaging in dialogue with others. Freud was indebted to the great poets, and he, like Bergson, was honored as a creative artist when he received the Goethe Prize in 1930.

It is probably impossible for any poet, novelist, or playwright after Freud to write without taking into consideration the psychological undercurrents of human behavior—whether or not the author has read him. Some post-Freudian writers derive themes and images from the idea of subconscious motivations guiding interpersonal relations and social behavior. Others employ a stream-of-consciousness technique very much like Freud's therapeutic tactic of free association. Some exploit the aesthetic possibilities of a surface pattern of apparent intentions concealing a contradictory pattern of repressed desires. Still others exploit the techniques of an otherwise-empty dialogue that creates its own reality through repetition. Freud can even be cited against his own intentions: the Surrealists, while quoting him, completely reverse his aim by pronouncing madness not an illness to be cured, but an insight into a larger reality.

Literature, however, is also a matter of words and not just themes and patterns of consciousness. Different concepts of language have colored literary expression at different times, and twentieth-century literature is no exception. In the early part of the century, the experimental language used in fiction and poetry shows the influence of psychoanalysis and of Symbolist poetics. Its syntax and imagery emulate Freudian free association, the complex inner patterns favored by nineteenth-century Symbolist poetry and the artistic effects of Impressionist or Cubist painting. Later works reflect a change in linguistic theory. Nineteenth-century positivism had assumed that language was an accurate tool for direct reference to reality (a view parodied in "The sun is called a sun because it *looks* like a sun"). In contrast, the Swiss linguist Ferdinand de Saussure (1857–1913) and the Austrian philosopher Ludwig Wittgenstein (1889–1951) emphasized that language is tied to society and usage: descriptions are not "accurate," for they can never grasp absolute reality or give "real" names. All that language can do, as they see it, is to create socially agreed-upon labels ("signifiers" pointing to a "signified"). The sun remains the same gaseous ball whether it is named *sun, soleil,* or *taiyang.* What works in conversation is not the thing itself but the way the label—the word used to describe it—provides a recognizable common ground for different speakers. Language may therefore be described as a "game" played with words—a serious game, since it shapes our vision of reality. Modernist literature shows how words reshape the world we think we know. Thus Wallace Stevens's "moon creeps up / To the bubbling of bassoons," and Gertrude Stein diversifies a carafe into "a kind of glass and a cousin, a spectacle and nothing strange a single hurt color and an arrangement in a system to pointing."

In this perspective, both literature and linguistic systems are seen as *games,* combinations of *pieces* (words) and *rules* (grammar, syntax, and other conventions). Writers stressing the gamelike nature of language combine words and word fragments to exhibit the play of relationships, instead of struggling to find the "right" word dear to Flaubert. Game theory can be frustrating in practice. Samuel Beckett's (1906–1989) tongue-tied characters in *Endgame,* or the endlessly chattering narrators of his novels, make brief conversational sense but finally express very little, unless it be the absurd inexpressibility of the human condition. At its most extreme, this theory leads to a view of all language as an endless networking of associations: a situation in which real communication is impossible. "Reality," instead of becoming more accessible, ultimately disappears inside a web of words.

Yet there are practical conclusions to be drawn from this frustrating prospect. If a work by Borges, Beckett, or Robbe-Grillet persuades us that language determines how we see the world (as well as our own place in it), then we will recognize other shaping uses of language. Not all language games are played by literature. Films have developed their own cinematic language, in which the rapid juxtaposition of different scenes (*montage*) or calculated shifts in camera angle compose a special perspective on reality. Television commercials race through sets of highly associative words and images to persuade you that the sponsor "speaks your language" and is ready to deliver, in that automobile or pair of jeans, the article you really want: wealth, power, cultural identity, or sex appeal. MTV publicity for the latest in music has established its own recognizable style, using fragmented, kaleidoscopic images (derived from Surrealism) to appeal to a younger generation's sense of displacement and discontinuity. The idea of human expression as a set of semiotic strategies—sign systems—has suggested new techniques for criticism and made it possible for readers (or listeners) to identify systems of reference embedded in the written text or alive in oral performance. This emphasis on the shifting play of language is especially appropriate for modernist texts, but it has also created new readings of earlier works and helped redefine the continued appeal of canonical masterpieces. Tradition tells us that such works can bear reading and rereading by different generations, and even different cultures, and always tell us something about ourselves. A semiotic explanation proposes that such works are not exhausted by a single reading or a single audience, because they reach out to the world on many different planes: they achieve their celebrated staying power by bringing together, and making accessible, many systems of meaning.

Theories of linguistic play have not been isolated from concurrent developments in the sciences or from the impact of historical events. Psychology, anthropology, and physics also stressed relationships as they redefined current concepts of human nature and the material world. Gestalt psychology (*Gestalt* is German for "form") after 1912 suggested that the meaning of individual phenomena was not to be found in microscopic analysis of separate pieces but rather in organized wholes. It was the "shape of things" that mattered.

Shapes and the relation of parts were important in structural anthropology, with the anthropologist Claude Lévi-Strauss (born 1908) describing human society as a system of worldviews or "codes" that could be compared from culture to culture. From his early research on the primitive Nambikwara Indians of Brazil to his later comparisons of primitive with modern cultures, Lévi-Strauss has insisted that anthropological knowledge comes only from imaginative participation in the codes governing each society (kinship rules, taboos, habits of social interaction, folkloric imagination). His "structural method" appealed to literary critics as a way to illuminate simultaneously a work's inner structural relationship and its relationships to the individual and culture that produced it.

Even more influential for modern writers was Jungian psychology—based on the work of Carl Gustav Jung (1875–1961)—which claimed that humanity shares a "collective unconscious," a buried level of universal experience tapped by myth, religion, and art. Accordingly, the common experience of our species is revealed in archetypes (master patterns) like the figures of the hero, seer, or Great Mother, the image of the quest, or the process of death and rebirth. Much folklore and ritual poetry (including examples such as Birago Diop's *Mother Crocodile,* Andrew Peynetsa's *The Boy and the Deer*) use variations of such archetypal figures. In retrospect, works such as T. S. Eliot's *The Waste Land* may be seen to incorporate Jungian archetypal images, alluding to a universal level of human experience. In Eliot's case, actual inspiration came from another synthesizing enterprise, James George Frazer's vast masterwork of anthropology, *The Golden Bough* (1890–1915), which profoundly influenced the intellectual climate of Europe and America with its demonstration of the striking resemblances among world mythologies and religions.

The social or "human" sciences were not alone in paying attention to the role played by the perceiver. The "hard" sciences of physics and mathematics were doing the same thing, with results that shocked the general public and intrigued writers and artists. Albert Einstein's theory of relativity (1905) abandoned the concepts of absolute motion and the absolute difference of space and time and, working from pure mathematical logic, proposed that reality should be understood as a four-dimensional continuum (called space-time) that literally could not be expressed either in words or in the old three-dimensional models of Newtonian physics. Since *relativity* implied "relativism" in the popular mind, Einstein's discovery (despite his own religious beliefs) was widely thought to pull the ground out from under any certainty—scientific or religious—about the physical world. Even more disturbing, Werner Heisenberg's "uncertainty principle" (1927) proclaimed that scientific measurement (in this case, the measurement of electrons) was always a matter of statistical approximation, a "probability function" and not an exact description. Ironically, what was scientifically an increasingly *accurate* perception of the nature of things often seemed just the opposite to the general public. People could no longer refer to "self-evident truths" in nature, or go "back to basics," when scientists had just shown that the "basic" world was not what it seemed. Many writers, however, and Proust among the earliest, welcomed what they saw as a richer view of experience and scientific confirmation that reality could be represented in a shifting and fluid perspective.

The world's major religions and philosophies have all had something to say about the nature of reality. They explain the origin and structure of the universe (in ancient Egyptian hymns, the biblical Book of Genesis, the Eleventh Teaching from the *Bhagavad-Gītā,* and the *Popol Vuh*), preach escaping the bonds of the material world for a higher spiritual existence (Buddhism and Hinduism), assert the interpenetration of all existence at all times (Taoism) or the linkage of all forms of life (African and North American indigenous religions), and discuss human mortality. They provide models—differing from culture to culture—that give pattern and meaning to human experience, bridging the gap between things as they appear to us in the details of daily life and dimensions that exceed ordinary measurement.

The modern philosophy that coincides with the rise of Modernism is similarly an inquiry into the reliability of appearances. Ever since Plato, Western philosophers have struggled systematically to understand the relationship between appearance and reality. In the twentieth century, such issues are the central concern of the philosophy known as phenomenology (phenomena are literally *things as they appear*) and its offshoot, existentialism. Both approaches investigate the role of perception in establishing reality. The phenomenology proposed by Edmund Husserl (1859–1938) described all consciousness as consciousness *of* something *by* someone and concluded that every object of study should be imagined in "brackets"—not as a thing in itself but as part of a relationship between perceiver and perceived.

The ethical implications of this view were taken up by the philosophers Martin Heidegger (1889–1976) and Jean-Paul Sartre (1905–1980), who questioned the meaning of existence in a world without preexisting truths, values, or moral laws. Heidegger's profoundly somber vision of the "absurd" condition of human beings, "thrown into the world" without any understanding of their fate, influenced many writers and especially the "theater of the absurd" that flourished after World War II, of which Samuel Beckett and Eugène Ionesco (1912–1994) are the best-known writers. Sartre, who was much more of a social activist, derived from the same absurd freedom an ideal of human "authenticity," which consists in choosing our actions at each point, avoiding the "bad faith" of pretending that others are responsible for our choices, and choosing not just for oneself but "for all" inasmuch as each choice envisages the creation of a new world. This kind of existentialism, with its appealing image of the lonely tragic hero who acts to benefit society without any hope of reward (Sartre portrayed such a hero as Orestes in *The Flies*, based on Aeschylus's *Oresteia*, in Volume A), had tremendous influence on European writers immediately after World War II. Albert Camus, writing at the same time as Sartre, offers in *The Guest* a good example of existentialism's emphasis on freedom, responsibility, and social commitment or "engagement."

Existentialism's popular appeal in the 1940s and 1950s was undoubtedly enhanced by the fact that it was a philosophic attempt to recover clear vision—and a basis for action—in a perplexed and apparently meaningless world. The notion of philosophical absurdity corresponded to a very real confusion caused by the radical historical changes taking place in the first half of the century. By 1950, there had been two world wars, the second of which was truly global, and a sweeping realignment of geopolitical forces that saw the flourishing of Marxism and the establishment of major Communist states. Almost all the old monarchies had been overthrown and colonial empires were being dismantled as the emerging nations of Africa and Asia struggled for independence and self-definition. The wielders of authority became the enormous buck-passing bureaucracies of the modern state, multinational corporations, international governmental organizations, and ethnic alliances. Transportation and telecommunications progressed to an extent only envisaged in earlier ages' science fiction and effectively created but also shrank the global community. The rise of the modern industrial state set up new political, cultural, and economic tensions, the most important of which was a widening gulf between the West and "less developed" countries.

These changes in historical conditions had visible repercussions on modern literature and art. Cultural parochialism—the belief that there is only one correct view of the world (one's own)—was much harder to maintain when people traveled widely and experienced different ways of life. Racial and ethnic stereotypes were challenged, and traditional ideas of identity and social class broken down. Romantic heroism and aristocratic "rank" seemed irrelevant to soldiers who died anonymously in the trenches of World War I or civilians killed at a distance by bombing raids in both wars. The appropriate symbol for modern, impersonal warfare was the Tomb of the Unknown Soldier, first erected in Paris, after World War I, to honor the nameless soldiers who had died defending their country. In literature it was the "common man," not the Romantic hero, whose plight was portrayed. The conventional roles of the sexes also came under examination. Western women achieved civil rights they had been denied for centuries: the right to vote (1920 in the United States), the right to have bank accounts and to own and control their own property, the right to be educated equally with men, and the right to enter professions not previously open to them. When women held many jobs previously thought to be masculine ("Rosie the Riveter" was a famous American poster in World War II), it was no longer possible to pretend that they were incapable of work outside the home. Indeed, it was clear not only that women were quite capable but that they enjoyed taking responsibility in a variety of careers. Later in the century, the image of the emancipated Western woman would be presented as a shocking and even heretical example in traditional Mideastern and African societies; in contrast, the modern Communist Chinese state insisted on women's equality in the workplace. International organizations began to discuss, and women writers to describe, the situation of women in different countries (as do Ingeborg Bachmann, Clarice Lispector, Nawal El Saadawi, and Lorna Goodison, for example). Globally, the nature of the workplace changed as technological advances brought a range of new machines, services, and types of labor. Technology became everywhere part of the modern literary consciousness, inspiring both enthusiasm and fear, and initiating all over again the question of human values in a society where so much could be done (and so many controlled) by the use of machines.

A Century of Isms

The literary and artistic movements of the twentieth century are part of this evolution; they were shaped by it and helped shape it for others. Many flourished in Europe and America and were exported to other parts of the globe, where they flourished or failed according to their relevance for local conditions. The twentieth century has been called by some a "century of isms," or of "vanguardism," reflecting the fact that so many different groups have tried to find an appropriate artistic response to contemporary history. European Expressionism, Dadaism, Surrealism, and Futurism—each worth exploring—are all different ways of expressing the "reality" of the world. Some appear very unreal at first glance, but all reveal an inner (presumably more important) truth than can be shown by documentary detail alone. Thus Expressionists refused the direct representation of reality, or even impressions of it (as in Impressionism), in favor of expressing an inner vision, emotion, or spiritual reality. *The Scream,* a painting by the Norwegian Edvard Munch (1863–1944), evokes a whole realm of spiritual agony, and expressionist writers like the Germans Frank Wedekind (1864–1918) and Gottfried Benn (1886–1956) assert their alienation from an industrial society whose inhumanity repels them. To bring out an underlying psychological distress that "objective" descriptions fail to capture, expressionist writers subordinate conventional (rational) style and let emotion dictate the structure of their works, emphasizing rhythm, disrupted narrative line and broken syntax, and distorted imagery.

Futurism loudly proclaimed its enthusiasm for the dynamic new machine age. F. T. Marinetti (1876–1944) wrote in the first Futurist Manifesto (1908) that "a roaring motor car which seems to run on machine-gun fire is more beautiful than the Winged Victory of Samothrace" (a famous Greek statue). Italian Futurism is still tainted by Marinetti's glorification of terrorism and war and his delighted description (from the pilot's point of view) of bombs bursting below. Russian Futurism was suppressed, along with other experimental art, by the conservative tastes of the government in the USSR. Nonetheless, the Futurists' experiments in typography, in free association, in rapid shifts and breaks of syntax; their manipulation of sounds and word placement for special effects; their harshness and stark vision; and above all their eagerness to depict the new age were widely imitated.

Dada-Surrealism is the best known of the European "isms" and the only one to have followers today. Dada began in Zurich in 1916 as a movement of absolute revolt against Papa's Europe, and the word *dada* is a nonsense word that represents the disgust the Dadaists felt for the traditional middle-class values (patriotism, religion, morality, and rationalism) that they blamed for World War I. Dada set out to subvert authority and break all the rules (including those of art), hoping to liberate the creative imagination. Marcel Duchamp (1887–1968) reversed a series of expectations when he named a piece *Why Not Sneeze, Rrose Sélavy?* (1921): it was a small birdcage filled with what looked like sugar lumps but turned out (when you lifted the heavy cage) to be carved marble cubes. Tristan Tzara (1896–1963) attacked the notion of the inspired genius by giving a recipe for the Dada poem: the "poet" was to cut words out of a newspaper, shake them in a paper bag, and pull them out one at a time. Dada creations were attacks on the mind and emotions; Surrealists emphasized a "revolution of the mind" in which ordinary habits of seeing yielded to a different, "surreal" or "super-real," vision. Freedom from conventional perspectives, they felt, was a first step in reforming society.

Surrealists especially aimed to bring about a fuller awareness of human experience, including both conscious and unconscious states. In France, the Surrealist Manifestoes of 1924 and 1930 proclaimed that Surrealism was a means of expressing "the actual functioning of thought," "the total recuperation of our psychic force by a means that is nothing else than the dizzying descent into ourselves." André Breton, the Surrealist leader, had been a medical intern in a psychiatric clinic during World War

I and was interested in Freud's theories of the unconscious. The Surrealists experimented with various means to liberate the unconscious imagination and reach a sublime state they called "the marvelous." Dream writing, automatic writing (writing rapidly and continuously whatever comes to mind), riddling games, interruption and collage, and chiefly the creation of startling images opened the mind to new possibilities.

The Surrealist image gains its power by forcibly yoking two unrelated elements; it suggests buried connections and possible relationships overlooked by the logical mind. Thus a poem by Paul Éluard, for example, will begin "Earth is blue like an orange, / Never a mistake; words don't lie . . ." and let the reader sort out the connections of shape, color, and distance that may allow such a perspective. The poet's challenge is clear: "words don't lie." Readers faced with the absurdity of "like an orange" will reach for whatever pattern of meaning might exist in a vision that just barely seems to offer such connections. And there it is, a tenuous but consistent structural relationship of similarity or difference—in shape, color, size, and distance from the perceiver. Surrealist language is structured to arouse the free play of the mind, and its antirational and open-ended style foreshadows the emphasis, in later "postmodernist" literature, on word play and radical language games.

Known for its intensity, playfulness, and openness to change, Surrealism has proved to be the most influential and enduring of all these movements, with adherents around the globe. Its impudent rejection of authority and rational thought inspired rebellious writers everywhere, especially in countries where the government linked correct thinking to realistic art. Surrealist themes of liberty, antirationality, and the importance of the unconscious mind, and the preferred Surrealist techniques of collage, constant metamorphosis, and a narrative in which it is hard to distinguish between dream and reality permeate modern literature. They find their way into the explosive sequences of Aimé Césaire and the magical images of Gabriel García Márquez. Surrealist influence has also spread beyond art and literature to advertising, fashion, and MTV, and the term *surrealist* has become a convenient word for unconventional or fantastic works that have no real connection with the movement.

Modernism is the accepted general term for the change in attitudes and artistic strategy that occurred in Europe and America at the beginning of the twentieth century. In its broadest sense, it embraces all the separate movements just described. Taken more narrowly, Modernism refers to a group of Anglo-American writers (many associated with the Imagists, 1908–17) who favored clear, precise images and "common speech" and who thought of the work primarily as an art object produced by consummate craft. James Joyce, Ezra Pound, T. S. Eliot, William Faulkner, and Virginia Woolf are examples of Anglo-American Modernism and of the larger modernism, too. European modernists used language in an exploratory way, redefining the world of art much as the philosophers and scientists had redefined the world of their own disciplines. They disassembled in order to reconstruct, playing with shifting and contradictory appearances to suggest the shifting and uncertain nature of reality (Luigi Pirandello). They broke up the logically developing plot typical of the nineteenth-century novel and offered instead unexpected connections or sudden changes of perspective (Virginia Woolf). They used interior monologues and free association to express the rhythm of consciousness (Joyce, Woolf). They made much greater use of image clusters, thematic associations, and "musical" patterning to supply the basic structures of both fiction and poetry (Marcel Proust, Wallace Stevens, Eliot). They drew attention to style instead of trying to make it invisible or "transparent" (Eliot, Bertolt Brecht). They blended fantasy with reality while representing real historical or psychological dilemmas (Franz Kafka). They raised age-old questions of human identity in terms of contemporary philosophy and psychology (Freud, Proust, Camus). And they explored ancient and non-Western literatures in search of universal themes and fresh modes of expression (Eliot, Pound, Joyce). Whether their style was elaborate or spare, wordy or elliptical, abstract or concrete, modernist works displayed a highly self-conscious use of language, aiming not only to transform the way we see the world but also to change the way we understand language. This aspect of modernism gave it cultural as well as artistic impact, and young writers in other countries frequently adopted modernist techniques as a way to transform their own society's vision. The brilliant linguistic play of Aimé Césaire's *Notebook of a Return to the Native Land,* for example, displayed a dynamic new vision of black identity and Caribbean culture. Yet modernists in the early twentieth century are still close to nineteenth-century thought in one important respect. Their enterprise assumed, through all its fragmentation, a profoundly rich and unified core to human experience. Modernist experiments with perspective and language were carried on inside still-traditional concepts of individual psychological depth and of the art work as a coherent aesthetic whole. The combination of discontinuous, experimental style with a continuing belief in the wholeness of the human personality and of the art work carries with it the stamp of what we call the modernist (as opposed to the "postmodernist") tradition.

MODERNISM EXPANDS AND EVOLVES

The influence of Modernism, or other isms, on non-Western literary developments of the twentieth century has proved more varied. The smaller movements inside Western modernism lost their separate status when exported, becoming merely part of the whole mosaic of twentieth-century Western culture. This mosaic in turn meshed with local priorities such as an emerging national consciousness, religious tradition, or cultural customs, and the entire picture changed in the process. In some cases, Western literary models were adapted to represent the views of a particular national, religious, or ethnic group. In others, exposure to the West inspired a rediscovery of national literary traditions. In yet others, new ideologies of Western origin—social, political, religious, philosophical—had a much greater pollinating effect than any literary movement. While it is impossible to describe the full range of traditions included in this anthology, a few examples will indicate how modernism and modernity were refracted in twentieth-century non-Western civilizations.

Countries like Japan that attempted to reinvent themselves as equals of the materially advanced and economically powerful Western nations undertook a tortuous process of cultural absorption and transformation. Technology transfer and economic integration proved inseparable from institutional change and cultural diffusion. As the Japanese of the late nineteenth century learned the practical aspects of Western civilization—bookkeeping, smelting, cotton spinning, shipbuilding, principles of the joint-stock corporation—their curiosity about the world and their traditional receptivity to foreign ways soon transfigured the fabric of Japanese life.

For intellectuals, including writers, the real issue was not whether modernism offered a superior refraction of reality, although they would take advantage of modernist style when it suited them. More fundamental questions came to the fore. Cultural identity is a theme to which writers like Tanizaki Jun'ichirō return again and again. *In Praise of Shadows* asks what is lost when a nation tries to make itself over in the image of another. Natsume Sōseki, perhaps the most introspective of Japan's modern novelists, frames the same question and concludes that each wave of Westernization hitting Japan is "like sitting at a dinner table and having one dish after another set before us and then taken away so quickly that, far from getting a good taste of each one, we can't even enjoy a clear look at what is being served. A nation, a people, that incurs a civilization like this can only feel a sense of emptiness, a dissatisfaction and anxiety." Yet it was a Western concept, individualism, that Japanese writers saw as the possible salvation. Part and parcel of Japan's modernization was its discovery of the emphasis that Western societies place on human beings as autonomous individual selves. For much of Japanese history, people in this conservative, group-oriented society were thought of as members of a unit (a clan, a fief, a class) who fitted somewhere quite precisely on a Confucian grid of relationships (between ruler and subject, father and son, husband and wife, elder brother and younger, friend and friend). The mesh of these two networks was the source of one's identity: an unproblematic part of a larger whole.

More problematic was the attempt to assert one's newfound ego in a manner that did not infringe on other egos—or to navigate in a culture where individual independence was still uncharted, where support systems that had developed over time in democratic, Judeo-Christian societies for fostering and protecting the individual were completely missing. On the one hand, writers like Kawabata and Tanizaki felt that individualism offered the hope of choosing one's own route through life, colliding with possibilities in a way that would never have been thinkable, and thereby forging one's own personal happiness, the ultimate objective. Tanizaki's essay on Japanese cultural identity is framed as an extended meditation on the values of shadow and light, a style evoking the introspective inquiry of Proust's own search for lost time. On the other hand, many Japanese writers felt that the new intellectuals who asserted their ego in the Western manner were doomed, for they lacked any inherited moral or psychological safeguard against their own destructive self-centeredness.

Modern Japanese novels describe a society mutating so fast that one generation after another must confront the confusion of new freedoms, new relationships, new dynamics, new challenges. In the early years of the century, language itself seemed unstable. Writers felt increasingly dissatisfied with the written medium at their disposal. It had become too florid, or baroque, too removed from everyday speech and, at the same time, both too restrictive and too playful to express the dilemmas of the new age. There was even talk of jettisoning Japanese in favor of English. In the end, through a convoluted process of language reform, literary style was streamlined into a more flexible and colloquial vehicle, producing literature that in its various aspects was the expression of a deeply felt need to grapple with the complexities of contemporary Japanese reality. For the last century, Japanese writers have struggled to assert the authenticity of the individual personality at the same time that they delineated the consequences of the liberation of the self: guilt, betrayal, loneliness, and alienation. Their modernism has as much in common with the realism of Ibsen and Chekhov as it does with the innovative strategies of Proust or Pirandello. Relying on the conceit of an accurate, detailed description of an external reality, combined with psychological appraisal of motivation, they offered their readers a valuable literary compass for situating the bewilderment of identity, self-interest, and "belonging" in a convulsive age of cultural ambiguity.

In twentieth-century China, on the other hand, modernization ended a feudal system that had controlled social and artistic expression for more than two thousand years. The Revolution of 1911 was only the first of many conflicts—revolutions, civil war, or differing programs of social reform, each harshly administered—reflecting the intellectual and political ferment as China emerged from the old Confucian order into the People's Republic of China. (The philosopher Confucius lived between 551 and 479 B.C.) Unchanging, however, was the social importance attributed to writing, which was expected to embody and preserve the core of Chinese cultural identity. This privileged position for literature, visibly different from the Western norm that distinguishes between artistic dedication and social responsibility, could be quite uncomfortable when the ruling powers (as earlier in Russia) enforced political guidelines for writers. The famous speech by Mao Zedong (1893–1976) at the Yan'an Forum on Literature and Art in 1942 warned Chinese writers to think positively and eliminate personal introspection from their work: it was the nation, not the individual, that should be the focus of their attention. The traditional Confucian concept of the ethical artist (like many other Confucian concepts) survives in modern China, although adapted to new circumstances and a greatly changed political scene.

Western readers are generally surprised to find that the Chinese government for thousands of years required literary examinations for any government post. Confucius had proposed an influential model of moral development and related social responsibility, and in 136 B.C., during the Han Dynasty of emperors, Confucianism was proclaimed the state doctrine. The Four Books of Confucian writings were prescribed subjects for the imperial civil service examinations from 1414 until the examinations themselves were abolished in 1905. Confucian principles defined the forms of education and the (mainly literary) examinations, governed the writing of history, prescribed social and family relationships, and extended the rules of family obedience to include obedience to the emperor as head of the "family" state. One of Confucius's followers, Mencius, phrased the five basic human relations of Confucianism as follows: "Between father and son there should be affection, between ruler and minister, there should be righteousness, between husband and wife, there should be attention to their separate functions, between elder and younger brothers, there should be order, and between friends, there should be good faith." The literature favored in traditional China was a subtly disciplined poetry (not fiction, which was thought trivial), and it was written in a refined and elegant classical Chinese whose mastery required years of study.

At the turn of the century, Chinese intellectuals who had traveled abroad began to adapt literary models encountered in Japan, Europe, and America. The most striking change in this first wave of literary modernization had political as well as literary importance: use of the vernacular (popular speech) in both poetry and prose, and depiction of social problems. Lu Xun's *Diary of a Madman* (1918) introduced the use of vernacular prose, and the modernist rhythms of its broken, hallucinated narrative proposed a cannibalistic picture of Confucian society. Poetry in the 1920s was not only written in the vernacular but also rejected classical prosody, which had been used for thousands of years; instead, it experimented with free verse and echoed such diverse writers as Wordsworth, Whitman, Goethe, and Tagore. Playwrights who had read Ibsen and Chekhov dramatized contemporary social problems and the clash of opposed ideas against a realistic background. Romantic and Realist themes co-existed in a broad spectrum of Westernization that aimed not merely to liberate artistic expression but also to represent feelings and social tensions that had not previously found a place in literature. Yet this modern literature was not imitatively "Western" but rather an attempt by a new generation of writers to find different and perhaps fuller ways of expressing Chinese cultural experience. Their actions were never without political implications, both in this original opening up of traditional forms to a variety of different models and in the later turn away from Western examples toward a Marxist literature and political structure that seemed more congenial to China's group-oriented society.

With the formation of a League of Left-Wing Writers in 1930, Mao's proclamations at the Yan'an Forum, and the establishment of the Communist People's Republic of China under his control in 1949, a new conservatism in literature and art returned. Modernism in the Western sense of a liberal, experimental, and individually focused art was thought bourgeois, dilettantish, and antisocial—and was very dangerous to attempt. During the Cultural Revolution, writers and intellectuals who did not actively support socialist realism (the realistic depiction of the Communist state as a workers' paradise and of individuals as representative class figures) were imprisoned and persecuted. Very little was actually published, because little met the approval of the censors. Yet the People's Republic does not represent all Chinese literature, and writers in the Republic of China on Taiwan (some of whom had fled the mainland) followed their own path, writing a variety of prose fiction and founding a "Modernist School" in 1956 that sought a modern Chinese poetry "transplanted" from Europe rather than "inherited" from classical tradition. On the mainland, it was not until 1979 that writers felt free publicly to explore personal themes and use modernist forms. A new cluster of confessional works called "Wound Literature" then emerged, evoking the anguish of young Chinese alienated from their society, while more cautious writers avoided the risk of being declared antisocial by exploring objective forms like the interview, which allows an author to disclaim personal responsibility for what is said. The risk of social disapproval has not disappeared: the campaign against "Spiritual Pollution" in 1983, the expulsion from the party of the prominent writer Liu Binyan in 1987, and the tight control over the translation and publication of minority literatures show otherwise. Yet contemporary Chinese writers are once more part of a worldwide community of artists as they strive to develop a literature that is both characteristically modern and characteristically Chinese.

The situation of modern India is quite different, linguistically and literarily. European trade had been active in India for almost two centuries before British political rule dominated the continent in 1800. Independence from Britain came only in 1947, and by then Western culture and technology had permeated the subcontinent. The civil service and educational system were British, and generations of Indians—the future lawyers, teachers, writers, businesspeople, and government officials—had gone to Europe for university training. English was and remains the common language, the language used in government, although India itself is a mosaic of two hundred regional languages among which are Tamil, Gujarati, Oriya, Hindi, Bengali, Urdu, Kannada, and Sindhi. Some indigenous languages have no written form, and oral literature remains an important element in a society where a large part of the population is still illiterate. Indian works written in English, or translated into English (Indo-Anglian literature), can be read across regional linguistic barriers, and they have consequently come to represent Indian literature to the world outside India. Tagore, for example, who revolutionized Bengali literature, is more widely known abroad for his works in English.

The long-standing political and linguistic link with Europe had foreseeable literary results: first, that Indian intellectuals were educated in the same Western heritage as Europeans, reading in recent literature Wordsworth, Baudelaire, Goethe, and Ibsen; and second, that Western literary forms—tragic drama, the short story, the realistic novel, and personal lyrics, together with the use of the vernacular—edged out the classical Indian traditions of epic, devotional poetry, and oral literature. Realistic novels analyzed Indian social problems, including caste barriers, the position of women, religious strife, and national identity. Personal and autobiographical perspectives, psychological explorations, and depictions of modern society replaced a more impersonal focus on mythological or devotional subjects. Traditional prosody gave way to experiments with new forms, including free verse. Written literature flourished, offering a wide range of perspectives as it adapted European genres to local topics and settings. The performance-oriented Indian tradition, in contrast, moved into the background.

A further result was that the might and prestige of the British empire, and the empire's conviction that Western literature far outshone Indian tradition, encouraged a general belief in the superiority of Western ways and a neglect if not outright suppression of indigenous literature and languages. According to Lord Macaulay (1800–1859) in the nineteenth century, a shelf of European masterworks was worth the whole of Indian art and literature: this attitude informed the education provided in British schools. Reactions, literary as well as political, were inevitable. Premchand (1880–1936), who established the realistic short story in Indian literature, used that form to describe the misery of peasant life under British bureaucracy; the bureaucracy responded by burning his first collection in 1909. Postcolonial writers (those writing after Indian independence) commonly attacked British colonial arrogance and, as part of rejecting capitalist colonialism, turned to Marxism for a vision of social structure that would correspond to the traditionally group-oriented nature of Indian society. Many authors wrote about the difficult position of women in public and private life, and the strain on interpersonal and family relationships, caused by conflicting social paradigms. Others returned to traditional religious themes and imagery in a modern landscape: R. K. Narayan (1906–2001), included satires of Westernized life inside half-realistic, half-mystical narratives set in south India. One of the major self-imposed tasks of postcolonial literature has been to break free of European perspectives, to rediscover Indian traditions in art and literature, and finally to explore the implications of "Indianness" and also cultural ambiguity in a nation with so many competing cultures.

Whether it is a question of "Indianness" versus "Westernness" or of the multicultural identity that is now a global fact of life, Indian literature provides some of the most striking examples. The language of this literature is a hotly debated issue, as it is for African writers. Some critics assert that a truly Indian literature must be written in one of the ethnic languages and that indigenous experience cannot be accurately expressed in the colonizer's tongue. Despite the current government's encouragement of literary and linguistic pluralism, however, most of modern India's regional literature has not reached a wide audience because it is not available in translation—either into European or into other Indian languages. Who is to represent India, and to whom? The purist point of view rejects, perhaps rightly, the notion that Indian culture can be represented as a whole; yet it also denies the authenticity of Indian writers who choose to write in English. Some of these writers (for example, Narayan and Anita Desai) are major artists who ponder the question of "Indianness" in their own terms, whether as an assertion of traditional values or in the somber analysis of unfulfilled personal identities. Perhaps the most poignant example of intertwined literary cultures is Salman Rushdie, born a Muslim in 1947 in Bombay, India, who lived in hiding in England because the modernist style, secular irony, and clashing cultural perspectives of his satiric novel *The Satanic Verses* (1988) caused conservative Muslim clerics to order his death for heresy. Throughout the twentieth century, in one form or another, questions of cultural identity and the challenge of a mixed heritage were part of Indian literary tradition.

In the varied panorama of Middle Eastern countries, modernism and modernization have been linked as two categories of change brought by Western political and economic influence. It is the change of revolution, not evolution, and of a strong (though disputed) push to transform society rapidly in all aspects. The introduction of new generic forms like the novel and the modern short story, and the evolution, or modernization, of the older forms like poetry and drama, meant that Middle Eastern writers ceased to find their themes and forms principally within their own cultural tradition and attempted to internalize and naturalize an imported tradition. Initially, they seemed more drawn by content than form, or, rather, the structural looseness of modern Western poetry made it hard for Middle Eastern poets to see it as poetry at all. They were used to more highly codified forms of poetry, and for a long time they wrote politically engaged poems using traditional rhyme and meter. The link between modernist themes and modernist forms is so strong, however, that few poets now attempt to distinguish between them.

Writers sought an audience within the new middle class, for traditional aristocratic patronage had disappeared. Languages were transformed, sometimes acquiring a new alphabet; literary language became freer, more personal and colloquial; prose fiction, depicting everyday life and social issues, asserted itself in a tradition that had favored poetry and craftsmanship. In some ways, these changes are like those that took place in the West—the development of a new literary language, the recasting of the tradition's myths, the replacement of poetry with prose, the discovery of new heroes and antiheroes—but others are special to the non-Western world in its encounter with Western modernity: for example, the wrenching dislocations experienced by the first generations to be educated in the new learning. To accept Western modernity with its emphasis on the secular world, and its preference for the new, was to engage in a radical transformation of society and, with it, the near annihilation of traditional culture. Such a transformation has been the subject of a series of novels and short stories by the Egyptian writer Naguib Mahfouz (born 1911).

The encounter with European literature divided Middle Eastern intellectuals and writers into two camps: those who believed that the only hope of their respective communities lay in the wholehearted appropriation of Western culture and those who vehemently opposed it. Many in the former group began with the expectation that some essential elements of their native tradition could be maintained, but there were also many who were willing to jettison centuries of accumulated artistic tradition. According to an enthusiastic Turkish formula, citizens should "belong to the Turkish nation, the Moslem religion and European civilization." Modernism flourished in Turkey, where prose writers like Tawfiq al-Hakim (1898–1989) recast traditional subjects in modern form and where vers libre, poetic realism, and surrealism found their way into an increasingly diverse poetry after World War II. The underlying tension is reaffirmed, however, by events in Iran (ancient Persia). Postwar Iranian poetry, inspired by European models, developed both a hermetic, Symbolist-inspired style and a poetry of social action. After the Islamic Revolution of 1979 brought religious traditionalists once more to power, however, the freedom to write in Western modes dwindled sharply and most modernist writers fled the country.

The most striking example of Westernization in the Mideast is surely the transformation of Turkey from a feudal society ruled by a sultan to a modern, thoroughly Westernized state. Kemal Ataturk, president of the Turkish Republic (1923–38), led the Turks into a radical secularization and separation from the past by changing the basis of the Turkish alphabet from Arabic to Latin. His stated intention was to return Turkey to its pre-Islamic roots, but the effect was that within a generation the Turks lost access to the literary tradition of the preceding six centuries and to the Arabic and Persian literature on which it had been nourished. (The same sort of deracination by alphabet reform occurred in the Islamic Republics of the USSR.) A more moderate response, and one that more nearly characterizes the approach of Mideast modernist poets and writers, was that of al-Hakim, who felt that Middle Eastern writers should both appropriate Western classical mythology and recast their own in modern forms. The aesthetic battle has largely been won, and by the modernizers.

It is not possible to discuss modern literature in the Middle East without mentioning Israel, whose political and cultural identity differs sharply from its neighbors'. Israel's past was biblical, not Koranic. Moreover, the first generation of Israeli poets and writers were not only influenced by European literature but had often grown up in that tradition themselves. Yet Israel's poets and writers have faced many of the same dilemmas as other Middle Eastern authors. In language, they have sought to create a new, colloquial idiom to replace the formal, elitist idiom they had inherited: Hebrew had not been used as a colloquial idiom for millennia. In literature, they undertook to give modern form to their inherited tradition (for example, the poems by Yehuda Amichai). They shared with their Middle Eastern counterparts a commitment to use writing as a means of engaging in the discussion the central political questions of the time (A. B. Yehoshua). Some of the most interesting writing in contemporary Israel is produced by writers of a mixed Israeli-Arab heritage who, like their peers in other regions, explore the richness and difficulty of multicultural identity in the modern world.

Modern African literature is probably better known to Western readers than writing from any other part of the globe, for a variety of reasons. The fact that many works were originally written in English, French, and Portuguese made them accessible to a wider audience. The African slave diaspora, which linked ethnic groups in Africa, the United States, and the Caribbean, created a far-flung audience with shared concerns. The colonial education system, which meant that many Europeans taught in African schools and many Africans went to European universities, generated a continuing cultural exchange. Finally, the fascination of European artists and intellectuals at the beginning of the twentieth century with the "otherness" of black African art and civilization became part of the European intellectual and artistic tradition. Many connections exist, but also an unmistakable separation. Black African writers' sense of a distinct, non-European, racially defined identity, a division partly imposed by European colonialism and partly by their own urge to define black culture, permeates the development of modern literature on this continent of mixed African, Arabic, and European heritage. No one can ignore the impact of race on African thought and literature, and the South African writer Nadine Gordimer is keenly aware of her own ambiguously privileged white perspective when she analyzes the shifting overtones of everyday relationships between black and white in a changing Africa.

The importance of "négritude," or consciousness of black identity, can hardly be overestimated. Coined by the Caribbean Aimé Césaire (born 1913) in his *Notebook of a Return to the Native Land* (1939), prefigured by earlier Harlem Renaissance writings about black cultural identity, affirmed and illustrated by Léopold Sédar Senghor (born 1906) in the poems of *Chants d'ombre* (1945) and in a widely influential anthology of 1948, the term is an amalgam of ideas derived from the passionate discussions of black intellectuals gathered in Paris during the 1920s and 1930s. Interpreted differently by different thinkers—as an absolute genetic inheritance or as an oppositional movement linked to specific historical circumstances—négritude provided a counterconcept to colonialist images of Western ethnic and cultural superiority. It crystallized the opposition and offered a positive definition of blackness around which art, literature, and philosophy could rally.

Négritude is most usefully understood as a powerful concept and a reference point rather than as absolute reality. After centuries of intermingled traditions, it is difficult for any society to wrest apart fused layers of cultural identity. (This fact many Indian authors have recognized about their own postcolonial condition, as have Chinese authors after attempting to root out Confucianism.) Senghor has frequently described the two voices, African and French, that resonate in his poetry. His parents came from different African ethnic groups with their own languages; he himself was born in Senegal, when it was still a French colony, and was educated in Paris. There, he absorbed a French literary tradition that would influence his own poetry, but there he also met other black writers and intellectuals, learned about the Harlem Renaissance, studied African cultural history and anthropology, and founded, with Césaire and the Guinean Léon-Gontran Damas (born 1912), the journal *L'Étudiant noir* (The Black Student). Drafted into the French army after graduation, this future president of the independent republic of Senegal spent part of World War II in a German concentration camp, learning German and writing French poems about the African experience of colonialism. Senghor's experience may be the best known, but it is not unique. Birago Diop, Wole Soyinka, Césaire, Chinua Achebe, Derek Walcott, and Kamau Brathwaite also express, in different ways, the interweaving of European and black African or Caribbean identities.

One of the more pressing issues for black African writers has been the use of language. This is not a debate over style, or the language of European modernism with its ruptures, broken images, and stream of consciousness. Such stylistic concerns have less significance here than other social, quasi-existential, themes of personal and cultural identity. The immediate issue is whether to write in the European languages they have learned from childhood—which are now associated with colonialism—or, by translating earlier texts, writing in an African language, or emphasizing performance, to re-create an indigenous artistic tradition. Senghor echoes this tradition when he composes poetry on African themes that is intended to be chanted before a group and accompanied by musical instruments. Some authors follow the example of the Kenyan Ngugi wa Thiongo (born 1938), who chooses now to write in Gikuyu after having made a reputation as a novelist in English; others, like Diop (1906–1992) and Wole Soyinka (born 1934), join to their own work in French and English the translation and adaptation of folk tales; still others, like Achebe and Mariama Bâ, write about African topics in a European language permeated by their own indigenous references and turns of speech. To the extent that this twentieth-century literature is chiefly a *written* literature, exploiting the genres of novel, drama, short story, essay and lyric poetry, the question of language is already compromised by a link with European culture. African tradition (like that of India) emphasized oral and performance-oriented art. Modern African literature, like that of other postcolonial societies, incorporates the dynamism and internal tensions of an evolving society in which indigenous traditions, the colonial heritage, and an ongoing intellectual and artistic ferment coexist as parts of a common history.

In the West, modernism became something wholly different after the mid-century, separating into a profusion of styles and perspectives that express the range and diversity of contemporary cultural experience. With the passage of time, the modernist world no longer seemed "modern" and writers in the latter half of the twentieth century saw their newly canonized predecessors—Joyce, Proust, Eliot, Woolf, Mann, and Stevens, for example—as part of a "high modernism" that championed formal innovation but preserved its roots in mainstream thought. In this view, the high-modernist quest for more profound insight and inclusive vision does not so much break with the past as it continues as idealist Western tradition that reaches back to Homer and the Bible. In seeking to uncover what is essentially human, the argument runs, this idealism fails to take into account the stubborn diversity of human backgrounds and points of view. Nor did the focus on European tradition go unchallenged, as other regions reasserted their own cultural aims. The late twentieth-century writer could not ignore global issues and interrelationships, when events in Asia, Africa, Europe, and the Americas appeared side by side in the daily news, the United Nations had 185 member nations by the end of the century, and—despite the growing use of English as an international business and diplomatic language—over six thousand languages were spoken around the world.

Other political and economic changes had their effect. The first half of the century was marked by two world wars that enlisted forces around the globe in two large alliances, and the Cold War that succeeded World War II also cast global conflict in terms of two superpowers, the United States and the USSR. This relatively monolithic opposition was not to endure. The breakup of colonial empires, the creation of many new nations eager to assert their identity, and the emergence of new centers of trade (Japan, the oil-producing Middle Eastern countries acting together as OPEC) distributed power throughout a more diverse system. Nor were nations necessarily the holders of power, for the second half of the century saw the rise of multinational corporations whose chief loyalty was to business, and of transnational religious movements (like Islamic fundamentalism) that fought to assume authority in formerly secular states. The United Nations provided a forum in which global issues were publicly discussed, and television spread the images around the world. The developing countries of Africa, Asia, and Latin America, possessing many of the world's resources but few industries or corporate structures, called on the former colonial states to share their wealth and expertise. International agencies coordinated aid in the face of environmental catastrophes, epidemics, and famine; crime organizations also operated internationally; and the image of shared global problems moved into the foreground. Thousands of people migrated from poorer countries to seek jobs in wealthier regions, bringing different cultural groups in contact at the same time that they changed local economies. A host of smaller wars, sometimes driven by religious or ethnic allegiances that led to genocide or "ethnic cleansing," forced millions from their homes, and in 1994 the United Nations reported that 1 out of every 114 people in the world had been displaced by military conflict. Individuals were no longer so tied to their native countries; for some, their countries had disappeared in new political arrangements and for others, their simultaneous ties to more than one country created a new dimension of bicultural, hybrid, or "migrant" identity. Mass culture, radio, and television stretched to every part of the globe, often effacing local traditions as they introduced people to a broader horizon. With the disappearance of an old world order, the political picture became at once more fragmented and more interconnected, a situation that was reflected in contemporary literature and art.

After Modernism

How does one move beyond "modernism" in the modern world? The term *postmodernism* was proposed to define an attitude that derived from modernist thought but turned away from it in several important ways. Although the term itself has been debated (and postmodernism's literary demise already announced), to contrast the two concepts illuminates many themes and techniques in twentieth-century literature. Where high modernism evokes a core of profound experience revealed through experiments with form, postmodernist writers reject that profundity: calling something "profound," after all, implies that it is specially true and valuable, and thus reflects the speaker's own judgment. Consequently, postmodernist authors who wish to avoid personalized judgments tend to reject images of depth and profundity and prefer to describe inconclusive surface images. The modernist Wallace Stevens, for example, symbolizes the profound opposition of appearance and reality by describing a joyous wake in *The Emperor of Ice-Cream,* but the postmodernist Alain Robbe-Grillet forestalls any "profound" explanation of *The Secret Room* by offering multiple versions of the same scene. Postmodernists play with language, creating self-reflexive texts that constantly refer to their own composition. Such a style revels in allusions, interruptions, contradictions, and blurred reference, as if to disorient readers hoping to uncover a central meaning. These two descriptive techniques are based on different theoretical principles—on the one hand, the vision of a unified whole dependent on a central motivating principle; on the other, a network of shifting relationships that have no discernible frame or central reference. The line is not easy to draw, however (nor is it necessary to draw one): Luigi Pirandello, Marcel Proust, Bertolt Brecht, and especially Franz Kafka and James Joyce are modernist writers who have also been called precursors of postmodernism. Throughout, the postmodernist attitude claims that modernism's emphasis on profoundly meaningful aesthetic form suggests an image of human experience that is too finished and symmetrical: that our reality is basically "jagged" (Ezra Pound's term) and must be represented in all its incompleteness, diversity, and rough edges.

This shift of artistic sensibility takes to its logical conclusion the modernist's use of fragmentation and discontinuity. Both modernist and postmodernist thinkers are indebted to the evolution of scientific thought in the twentieth century and most of all to its emphasis on randomness and shifting perceptions. The physicist Werner Heisenberg's uncertainty principle (mentioned earlier) stresses the *approximate* nature of any description of reality as well as the fact that the observer's position relative to what is observed changes from moment to moment. The mathematician Kurt Gödel describes the ultimate incompleteness (and, therefore, lack of authority) of all logical systems. A similar emphasis on shifting patterns of perception appears in the later development of Freudian psychoanalysis with the concepts of transference and countertransference. Here, attention is displaced from subconscious and instinctual drives to the concept of dialogue and exchange: therapists no longer "cure" patients of specific psychoses, but engage them in a process of self-definition through interaction with others. Finally, semiotics, literally a science of *signs,* studies the "gamelike" construction of meaning, whether that meaning be located in literary form or in other modes of cultural expression. Cultural semiotics, specifically, investigates the way cultural sign systems (for example, attitudes about gender, race, or knowledge) are part of everything we do or say. Whether or not it is brought to bear on a literary text, semiotics outlines immense networks of potential meaning that reach into all aspects of human experience. It is a philosophy of knowledge that emphasizes relationships instead of a coherent whole, processes instead of stability, internal contradictions instead of symmetry, particulars instead of universals, and, throughout, constant change.

Readers will find that there are certain recurrent strategies in much of this literature, strategies aimed at keeping processes in motion and avoiding any sense of finality. "Me—to play," declares Hamm at the beginning of Samuel Beckett's *Endgame*. In fiction, the implied authorial personality (the coordinating core, for example, of Proust's great novel) is replaced with an anonymous and even self-contradictory narrative viewpoint: the "unnameable" narrator in Beckett's novel of that name, or the impersonal and contradictory narrative perspective of Robbe-Grillet's *The Secret Room*. Just as there is no unified authorial perspective, so individual characters do not develop a consistent psychological identity. Like Hamm and Clov in *Endgame*, such characters exist in a meaningless void, acting and reacting in a permanent present, and located in an ambiguously allusive situation that cannot be defined in external terms. Even the time in which they appear does not seem to have any solid chronological basis: in *Endgame*, we are not sure whether the action of the play concludes or is simply part of a repetitive pattern.

All these strategies actually serve to engage readers in a new and challenging way. By refusing to organize reality in familiar terms—even the most basic terms of time and space—they open a space for other perspectives. Readers confronting a defamiliarized vision of everyday reality may suspect that all representations of reality are similar constructs: this may be a bleak and dispiriting prospect, as in *Endgame*, or it may point to opportunities for change, as in the plays of Bertolt Brecht. Brecht's "alienation techniques" constantly break dramatic illusion, preventing spectators from identifying with characters on stage and encouraging them to interpret scenes in a wider (in this case political) context.

Incompleteness and ambiguity, therefore, do not exclude moral or cultural critiques. Borges, often considered the originator of postmodernism in his labyrinthine, self-reflexive style, uses subtle contrasts to critique cultural and national prejudices in *The Garden of Forking Paths*. The creeping, murkily defined terror of Bachmann's *The Barking* obliquely condemns its agent, the Nazi personality. The elusive daydreams of Clarice Lispector's drunk woman embody considerable personal and social critique. Gabriel García Márquez comes closest to the European "new wave" of radically experimental techniques, with his manipulation of perspective through magical realism, but his focus is clearly the political and cultural reality of Latin America.

Twentieth-century writers draw on various traditions, nonetheless, which is not surprising when we consider that the nineteenth century included the highly distinct Romantic, Realist, and Symbolist movements. Authors as geographically far apart as Richard Wright, Alexander Solzhenitsyn, Tadeusz Borowski, Chinua Achebe, and Alice Munro give their fictions the appearance of documentary reality, whether it be life in a small town, scenes of racial and cultural conflict, or concentration-camp experience during the World War II Holocaust. Their work does not call attention to its own textuality, but uses realistic scenes of daily life to explore social and psychological issues. Kojima Nobuo, Naguib Mahfouz, Zhang Ailing, and Anita Desai also rely on the style of the realistic novel as they lament the difficulty of preserving individual dignity and cultural values in a world of rapidly interpenetrating societies. A. B. Yehoshua explores the identity crisis of modern Israel by depicting, realistically, the interrelationships of Arab and Jewish lives. Extending twentieth-century attempts to recapture and preserve ethnic traditions (for example, the transcription of Inuit songs), Andrew Peynetsa re-creates a Zuni myth, *The Boy and the Deer*; Birago Diop and Bernard Dadié rewrite African folktales; and Leslie Marmon Silko composes, in *Yellow Woman*, a mysterious twentieth-century tale based on Laguna Indian legend.

Faith in a common version of reality gradually fades in the literature of the twentieth century; it is replaced by an increasing awareness of difference and ambiguity, but also of interconnection. More and more, it appears that we will rediscover human nature only by juxtaposing many diverse and composite images. Chinua Achebe describes this impulse to see life from different angles in terms of an old Igbo belief: "Wherever something stands, Something Else will stand beside it. Nothing is absolute." Without diminishing the description of social reality in previous literature, it is possible to say that literature in the twentieth century gave unprecedented recognition to different ethnic, sexual, and cultural identities, both depicted as subject matter and embodied in narrative perspective. In many ways, its pluralism of literary styles and willingness to rethink boundaries correspond to the visible diversity of a new geopolitical age; it reflects, as well, the explorations of uncertainty in modern philosophy and the scientific quest for more precise descriptions of reality. Our understanding of the literary text, both ancient and modern, has taken on new dimensions. What was once a simplified model of world literature has turned out, on examination, to be much more heterogeneous—and even more interesting.

FURTHER READING

Monique Chefdor, Ricardo Quinones, Albert Wachtel, eds., *Modernism: Challenges and Perspectives* (1986), offers valuable essays on international modernism. David Hayman, *Re-Forming the Narrative: Toward a Mechanics of Modernist Fiction* (1987), proposes five tactics that distinguish modernist narrative from earlier fiction. Harry Levin, "What Was Modernism?" (1962, repr. in *Refractions*, 1966), is a survey of modernist writers as humanists and inheritors of the Enlightenment. H. H. Arnason, *History of Modern Art: Painting, Sculpture, Architecture* (1977, illustrated), follows the evolution of the arts in the West from the nineteenth century to the 1960s. Matei Calinescu, *Five Faces of Modernity* (1987), is an informative collection of essays on the aesthetics of modernism, avant-garde, decadence, and kitsch. Morton P. Levitt, *Modernist Survivors: The Contemporary Novel in England, the United States, France, and Latin America* (1987), analyzes the impact of literary modernism and the continuity of humanist values. Detailed analytic surveys of the more radical artistic movements are found in John D. Erickson, *Dada, Poetry, Performance, and Art* (1984), and in Herbert S. Gershman, *The Surrealist Revolution in France* (1974). James F. Knapp, *Literary Modernism and the Transformation of Work* (1988), examines work-related themes in English and American modernist literature and modernism's contradictory attitudes toward a changing economic order. Harry R. Garvin, ed., *Romanticism, Modernism, Postmodernism* (1980), is a collection of essays that attempts to define changing views of the artistic imagination.

Marjorie Perloff, ed., *Postmodern Genres* (1989), collects essays on postmodernism in art and literature. Ihab and Sally Hassan, eds., *Essays in Innovation/Renovation: New Perspectives on the Humanities* (1983), explores change in contemporary Western culture; and Lois Parkinson Zamora and Wendy B. Faris, eds., *Magical Realism: Theory, History, Community* (1997), examines the theoretical and cultural implications of magical-realist style in Latin America and elsewhere. Susan Rubin Suleiman, *Subversive Intent: Gender, Politics, and the Avant-Garde* (1990), analyzes the cultural implications of avant-garde artistic practices. Nancy K. Miller, ed., *The Poetics of Gender* (1986), presents essays on various aspects of feminist criticism. Elise Boulding, *The Underside of History: A View of Women Through Time* (1992), complements traditional histories by drawing attention to the position and contributions of women. Frederick Buell, *National Culture and the New Global System* (1994), analyzes literary examples in a discussion of twentieth-century cultural globalization that moves beyond the concept of "three worlds." Sarah Lawall, ed., *Reading World Literature: Theory, History, Practice* (1994), includes a theoretical introduction to the subject of world literature and twelve essays on specific topics. Janheinz Jahn, *Muntu: African Culture and the Western World*, trans. Marjorie Grene (1990, orig. 1961), is an influential discussion of the interface of two cultures. J. M. Roberts, *History of the World* (1993), is an up-to-date history of world events in a contemporary perspective; its companion volume, *The Twentieth Century* (1999), examines the development of "the first world civilization."

TIME LINE

TEXTS	CONTEXTS
1893 Rabindranath Tagore, **Punishment**	
1895 Higuchi Ichiyō, **Child's Play**	
ca. 1897–1902 Washington Matthews conducts studies of the Navajo **Night Chant**	1899–1902 Boer War in South Africa
	1900 Boxer uprisings in China protest European presence • Max Planck proposes quantum theory, the first step in the discovery of the atom
1902 Joseph Conrad, *Heart of Darkness*	
1903 Henry James, *The Ambassadors*	1903 Wright brothers invent the powered airplane
1905 Sigmund Freud, **Dora (Fragment of an Analysis of a Case of Hysteria)** • Rubén Darío, **Songs of Life and Hope** • F. T. Marinetti, *Futurist Manifesto*	1905 Modern labor movement begins with foundation of International Workers of the World (IWW) • Partition of Bengal based on Hindu and Muslim populations
1907 August Strindberg, *The Ghost Sonata*	1907 Japanese immigration to the United States prohibited
1908 Gertrude Stein, *Three Lives* • Rainer Maria Rilke, **New Poems**	
	1909 Commercial manufacture of plastic begins
	1910 China abolishes slavery • Mexican Revolution (1910–11) • NAACP founded in United States • Post-Impressionist Exhibition in London
	1911 Revolution establishes Chinese Republic after 267 years of Manchu rule
1912 Rabindranath Tagore, **Gitanjali** • Thomas Mann, **Death in Venice**	1912–1913 Balkan wars
1913 Marcel Proust, **Swann's Way,** first volume of *Remembrance of Things Past* (1913–27) • D. H. Lawrence, *Sons and Lovers*	
1914 James Joyce, *Dubliners,* which includes **The Dead**	1914–1918 World War I involves Europe, Turkey, and the United States

Boldface titles indicate works in the anthology.

TIME LINE

TEXTS	CONTEXTS
	1915 Albert Einstein formulates general theory of relativity • First transcontinental phone call, in America
1916 Franz Kafka, ***The Metamorphosis*** • James Joyce, *A Portrait of the Artist as a Young Man*	
1917 T. S. Eliot, ***Prufrock and Other Observations***	**1917** Russian Revolution overthrows Romanov Dynasty
1918 Lu Xun, ***Diary of a Madman***, the first story in modern Chinese vernacular • Tristan Tzara, ***Dada Manifesto***	**1918** Women over 30 given vote in Great Britain
	1918–1920 Global influenza epidemic kills millions
	1919 League of Nations formed (U.S. Senate rejects membership, 1920)
1920 Edith Wharton, *The Age of Innocence*	**1920** Mahatma Gandhi leads India's struggle for independence from Britain
1921 Luigi Pirandello, ***Six Characters in Search of an Author***	**1921–1929** Harlem Renaissance, black literary and artistic movement
1921–1924 Knud Rasmussen documents Inuit culture and collects **Inuit Songs** during the Fifth Thule Expedition	
1922 T. S. Eliot, ***The Waste Land*** • Paris publication of James Joyce, *Ulysses* (imported copies burned in U.S. Post Office) • Rainer Maria Rilke, *Sonnets to Orpheus*	**1922** Turkey becomes a republic • Irish Free State established • USSR formed • Discovery of Egyptian pharaoh Tutankhamen's tomb
1923 Rainer Maria Rilke, *Duino Elegies*	**1923** Earthquakes destroy centers of Tokyo and Yokohama
1924 Thomas Mann, *The Magic Mountain* • André Breton, *First Surrealist Manifesto* • Premchand, ***The Road to Salvation***	**1924** Insecticides first used
1925 *Geriguigatugo* and other tales narrated by Úke Iwágu Úo published in Italian and Bororo	
1926 Franz Kafka, *The Castle* • Paul Éluard, *Capitol of Pain*	

TIME LINE

TEXTS	CONTEXTS
1927 Virginia Woolf, *To the Lighthouse*	
1928 William Butler Yeats, *The Tower*	**1928** Sixty-five states sign Kellogg-Briand antiwar pact in Paris • First Five Year Plan in USSR • Penicillin discovered • First scheduled television broadcasts
1929 William Faulkner, *The Sound and the Fury*	**1929** Stock market crash heralds beginning of world economic crisis; Great Depression lasts until 1937
1932 Zuni Ritual Poetry published by anthropologist Ruth L. Bunzel	
1933 Federico García Lorca, *Blood Wedding*	**1933** Adolf Hitler given dictatorial powers in Germany • Nazis build first concentration camps
1933–1937 Paldo Neruda, ***Residence on Earth***	**1934** Stalin begins purges of Communist Party
1935–1947 Kawabata Yasunari, ***Snow Country***	
1936 Premchand, *The Cow* • Leo Frobenius, *History of African Civilizations*	
1937 Wallace Stevens, *The Man with the Blue Guitar*	
1938 Alfonsina Storni, *Ocher*	
1938–1941 Bertolt Brecht, ***The Good Woman of Setzuan***	
1939 Aimé Césaire, ***Notebook of a Return to the Native Land***	**1939** Germany invades Poland and all Europe is drawn into World War II
1940 Richard Wright, *Native Son*	
	1941 United States and Japan enter World War II
1942 Albert Camus, *The Stranger*	
1943 T. S. Eliot, ***Four Quartets***	
1944 Jorge Luis Borges, ***The Garden of Forking Paths***	

TIME LINE

TEXTS	CONTEXTS
1945 Léopold Sédar Senghor, *Chants d'ombre*	**1945** World War II ends with dropping of atomic bombs on Hiroshima and Nagasaki • United Nations, Arab League founded
	1946 Churchill's "Iron Curtain" speech marks beginning of Cold War • Pan-African Federation formed
1947 Birago Diop, ***Tales of Amadou Koumba***	**1947** Religious massacres accompany partition of India and Pakistan into independent states • Transistor invented
1948 Ezra Pound, *Pisan Cantos* • Tadeusz Borowski, *Farewell to Maria*, which includes ***Ladies and Gentlemen, to the Gas Chamber***	**1948** Creation of Jewish state in Palestine
	1949 Communist People's Republic of China established • Apartheid instituted in South Africa
	1950–1953 Korean War involves North and South Korea, the United Nations, and China
1952 Ralph Ellison, *Invisible Man*	**1952** Revolution in Egypt, which becomes a republic in 1953 • First hydrogen bomb
	1953 Discovery of DNA structure launches modern genetic science
1954 Kojima Nobuo, ***The American School***	
1955 Alain Robbe-Grillet, *The Voyeur* • Juan Rulfo, ***Pedro Páramo***	
1956 Tanizaki Jun'ichirō, *The Key*	**1956** First Congress of Black Writers meets in Paris
1956–1957 Naguib Mahfouz, *The Cairo Trilogy*	
1957 Samuel Beckett, ***Endgame*** • Albert Camus, *Exile and the Kingdom*, which includes ***The Guest***	
1958 Chinua Achebe, ***Things Fall Apart***	**1958** European Common Market established • Algerian War of Independence (1958–62)
1959 Tawfiq al-Hakim, ***The Sultan's Dilemma***	

TIME LINE

TEXTS	CONTEXTS
1960 Marguerite Duras, *Hiroshima mon amour* • Shōno Junzō, *Still Life* • Clarice Lispector, *Family Ties,* which includes **The Daydreams of a Drunk Woman**	**1960–1962** Independence for Belgian Congo, Uganda, Tanganyika, Nigeria
	1961 Soviet astronaut orbits earth
1962 Doris Lessing, *The Golden Notebook* • Alain Robbe-Grillet, *Snapshots,* which includes **The Secret Room**	**1962–1973** United States engaged in Vietnam War
1963 Anna Akhmatova, **Requiem** • Naguib Mahfouz, *God's World,* which includes **Zaabalawi** • Alexander Solzhenitsyn, **Matryona's Home**	
1965 Recorded performance by Andrew Peynetsa of **The Boy and the Deer**	
	1966 Mao Tse-tung's *Cultural Revolution* attacks Confucian tradition and intellectuals in China (1966–69) • First Dakar Arts Festival provides showcase for African culture
1967 Gabriel García Márquez, *One Hundred Years of Solitude*	
1968 Kamau Brathwaite, *Masks* • Alice Munro, *Dance of the Happy Shades,* which includes **Walker Brothers Cowboy**	
	1969 American astronaut is first man on moon
1970 Derek Walcott, *Dream on Monkey Mountain* • A. B. Yehoshua, *Three Days and a Child,* which includes **Facing the Forests** • Gabriel García Márquez, **Death Constant Beyond Love**	
1972 Ingeborg Bachmann, *Three Paths to the Lake,* which includes **The Barking**	

TIME LINE

TEXTS	CONTEXTS
	1973 Arab oil producers cut off shipments to nations supporting Israel; ensuing energy crisis reshapes global economy
1975 Wole Soyinka, ***Death and the King's Horseman***	
1979 Mariama Bâ, *So Long a Letter*	
1980 Mahasweta Devi, ***Breast-Giver*** • Anita Desai, *Clear Light of Day* • Lorna Goodison, *Tamarind Season*	**1980s** Widespread concern as damage to the environment is increasingly documented
1981 Leslie Marmon Silko, *Ceremony* and *Storyteller,* which includes ***Yellow Woman***	
	1983–1984 Famine in Ethiopia • Ethnic and religious riots throughout India
	1986 Nuclear disaster in Chernobyl spreads radiation contamination throughout Europe
	1987 Floods destroy homes of millions in Bangladesh • World stock market crash
	1989 Mikhail Gorbachev restructures the Soviet state • Chinese government shoots thousands of protesters gathered in Tiananmen Square • Berlin Wall demolished
	1990 East and West Germany united
	1991 United States and USSR agree to arms reduction • Economic chaos and nationalist unrest bring end of Soviet Union
	1993 European Community, the West's largest trading unit, formed • World Wide Web established

TIME LINE

TEXTS	CONTEXTS
	1994 Nelson Mandela becomes president of South Africa after first multiracial elections • Israel and PLO sign peace agreement establishing a Palestinian state and begin negotiating its conditions
	1997 Scientists in Scotland create Dolly, the clone of an adult sheep
	1999 A European common currency, the "Euro," is issued
2000 Anita Desai, *Diamond Dust,* which includes *The Rooftop Dwellers*	

THE NIGHT CHANT

Navajo ceremonialism, like Iroquois law and Maya architecture, ranks among the glories of native American achievement. Esteemed for its therapeutic values and duly respected by Western medicine, it has proved a magnet for students of religion and an inexhaustible field for research in the arts and various sciences. Directed primarily toward healing and the restoration of harmony between individuals and the environ- ment, the ceremonies of Mountainway, Beautyway, Enemyway, and Blessingway, to name only a few of the better known, create a spiritual universe of song, prayer, drama, and graphic art, rooted in an oral literature of epic proportions. With its induction of new initiates, its unique all-night sing, and its lofty portrayal of deities, the famous Nightway occupies a place of honor among these "ways," or "chants," and some observers have regarded Nightway as the most important of them all.

Literally rendered "night-way chant," the name is almost always abbreviated to "nightway" in Navajo usage but was called *Night Chant* by its preeminent translator, Washington Matthews (whose Night Chant studies were conducted mainly during the 1890s). It was Matthews who translated the phrase "walk in beauty," often reit- erated by poets and occasionally used as a salutation by speakers of English outside the Navajo community.

The shared quest for *beauty*—a broad term that includes "perfection," "normality," "success," and "well-being"—as exemplified by the Night Chant and other ceremo- nials, is reflected in the remarkable vitality of the Navajo nation and its culture. The Navajo reservation, located in northern Arizona and adjacent New Mexico, is the largest in the contiguous United States; it is the most populous and has the greatest number of native speakers. Farming, sheep ranching, weaving, and silversmithing have long been important industries in the Navajo homeland. The staging of the ceremonials has also been a noteworthy, if small, element in the economy. Ceremo- nialism, at least in theory, provides a livelihood for the specialist, or chanter, who must organize dancers, singers, and other helpers, whose services are paid for by a sponsor, or host.

Although the chant is attended by a large audience of relatives, friends, and visitors, its power is aimed primarily at a single person, usually called "the patient" in anthro- pological writings. Each of the Navajo ceremonials is said to be effective against a particular group of disorders; in the case of the Night Chant, paralytic stroke and ailments of the head. So narrow a view of its virtues, however, is belied by the wide interest it evokes and by the constant demand for performances. In the beginning of the twenty-first century, its practitioners are being called on throughout the winter, with as many as half a dozen Night Chants in progress at any given moment, and bookings for a chant must be made two years in advance. Abbreviated versions may be ordered on shorter notice. Evidently, the chant in its full form is not an emergency therapy; among its more obvious benefits are the prestige it brings to the host who sponsors it and the opportunities it provides for cultural reaffirmation, socializing, and general spiritual revival.

Performed only in fall or winter, the nine-day Night Chant falls into two four-day parts, followed by a climactic ninth-night reprise, the night of nights, in which the long-awaited spirit of thunder is summoned. At this point the ceremony breaks free in a torrent of song continuing unabated until dawn. In part 1 the emphasis is on rites that exorcise evil influences and invoke the distant gods. Part 2 is distinguished by spacious and intricate sand paintings, made of dry pigments sprinkled on the earth. The paintings depict the gods and enable the patient to merge with their divine invul- nerability. Through it all, the ceremonial leader, or chanter, directs the included song recitals and intones the prescribed prayers. The two selections printed here are the prayer to thunder that begins the final night and the last of the Finishing Songs that bring it to a close.

A text of the Night Chant may be read in John Bierhorst, *Four Masterworks of American Indian Literature* (1974). The selections printed here are from Washington Matthews, *The Night Chant: A Navaho Ceremony* (1902). For survey articles on ceremonialism and other Navajo topics, see Alfonso Ortiz, ed., *Southwest*, vol. 10 of *Handbook of North American Indians* (1983). James C. Faris, *The Nightway: A History and a History of Documentation of a Navajo Ceremonial* (1990), brings Night Chant scholarship up to date.

From The Night Chant[1]

Prayer to Thunder[2]

*   *   *

In Tsegíhi,[3]
In the house made of the dawn,
In the house made of the evening twilight,
In the house made of the dark cloud,
In the house made of the he-rain,   5
In the house made of the dark mist,
In the house made of the she-rain,[4]
In the house made of pollen,[5]
In the house made of grasshoppers,
Where the dark mist curtains the doorway,   10
The path to which is on the rainbow,
Where the zigzag lightning stands high on top,
Where the he-rain stands high on top,
Oh, male divinity![6]
With your moccasins of dark cloud, come to us.   15
With your leggings of dark cloud, come to us.
With your shirt of dark cloud, come to us.
With your headdress of dark cloud, come to us.
With your mind enveloped in dark cloud, come to us.
With the dark thunder above you, come to us soaring.   20
With the shapen cloud at your feet, come to us soaring.
With the far darkness made of the dark cloud
    over your head, come to us soaring.
With the far darkness made of the he-rain
    over your head, come to us soaring.
With the far darkness made of the dark mist
    over your head, come to us soaring.
With the far darkness made of the she-rain
    over your head, come to us soaring.   25
With the zigzag lightning flung out on high
    over your head, come to us soaring.

1. Both selections translated by Washington Matthews.   2. In performance each line of the prayer is first recited by the chanter, then repeated by the patient.   3. Pronounced *tsay-gee'-hee*, a distant canyon and site of the *house made of dawn* (line 2), a prehistoric ruin, regarded as the home of deities.   4. Rain without thunder. *He-rain*: rain with thunder.   5. Emblem of peace, of happiness, of prosperity [Translator's note].   6. Thunder, regarded as a bird.

With the rainbow hanging high over your head,
    come to us soaring.
With the far darkness made of the dark cloud on
    the ends of your wings, come to us soaring.
With the far darkness made of the he-rain on
    the ends of your wings, come to us soaring.
With the far darkness made of the dark mist on
    the ends of your wings, come to us soaring.   30
With the far darkness made of the she-rain on
    the ends of your wings, come to us soaring.
With the zigzag lightning flung out on high on
    the ends of your wings, come to us soaring.
With the rainbow hanging high on the ends of
    your wings, come to us soaring.
With the near darkness made of the dark cloud, of
    the he-rain, of the dark mist, and of the
    she-rain, come to us.
With the darkness on the earth, come to us.   35
With these I wish the foam floating on the flowing
    water over the roots of the great corn.
I have made your sacrifice.
I have prepared a smoke[7] for you.
My feet restore for me.
My limbs restore for me.   40
My body restore for me.
My mind restore for me.
My voice restore for me.
Today, take out your spell for me.
Today, take away your spell for me.   45
Away from me you have taken it.
Far off from me it is taken.
Far off you have done it.
Happily I recover.
Happily my interior becomes cool.   50
Happily my eyes regain their power.
Happily my head becomes cool.
Happily my limbs regain their power.
Happily I hear again.
Happily for me *the spell*[8] is taken off.   55
Happily may I walk.
Impervious to pain, may I walk.
Feeling light within, may I walk.
With lively feelings, may I walk.
Happily abundant dark clouds I desire.   60
Happily abundant dark mists I desire.
Happily abundant passing showers I desire.
Happily an abundance of vegetation I desire.
Happily an abundance of pollen I desire.

7. Painted reed filled with native tobacco, offered as a sacrifice.   8. Words added by the translator.

Happily abundant dew I desire.   65
Happily may fair white corn, to the ends of the
      earth, come with you.
Happily may fair yellow corn, to the ends of the
      earth, come with you.
Happily may fair blue corn, to the ends of the
      earth, come with you.
Happily may fair corn of all kinds, to the ends
      of the earth, come with you.
Happily may fair plants of all kinds, to the ends
      of the earth, come with you.   70
Happily may fair goods of all kinds, to the ends
      of the earth, come with you.
Happily may fair jewels of all kinds, to the ends
      of the earth, come with you.
With these before you, happily may they come
      with you.
With these behind you, happily may they come
      with you.
With these below you, happily may they come
      with you.   75
With these above you, happily may they come
      with you.
With these all around you, happily may they
      come with you.
Thus happily you accomplish your tasks.
Happily the old men will regard you.
Happily the old women will regard you.   80
Happily the young men will regard you.
Happily the young women will regard you.
Happily the boys will regard you.
Happily the girls will regard you.
Happily the children will regard you.   85
Happily the chiefs will regard you.
Happily, as they scatter in different directions,
      they will regard you.
Happily, as they approach their homes, they will
      regard you.
Happily may their roads home be on the trail of pollen.
Happily may they all get back.   90
In beauty I walk.
With beauty before me, I walk.
With beauty behind me, I walk.
With beauty below me, I walk.
With beauty above me, I walk.   95
With beauty all around me, I walk.
It is finished in beauty,
It is finished in beauty,
It is finished in beauty,
It is finished in beauty.   100

Finishing Song

From the pond in the white valley—
The young man doubts it—
He takes up his sacrifice,
With that he now heals.
With that your kindred thank you now.   5

From the pools in the green meadow[9]—
The young woman doubts it—
He takes up his sacrifice,[1]
With that he now heals.
With that your kindred thank you now.   10

9. A contrast of landscapes, of the beginning and end of a stream. It rises in a green valley in the mountains and flows down to the lower plains, where it spreads into a single sheet of water. As the dry season approaches, it shrinks, leaving a white saline efflorescence called alkali. The male is associated with the sterile, unattractive alkali flat in the first stanza, while the female is named with the pleasant mountain meadow in the second stanza [adapted from Translator's note].   1. The deity accepts the sacrificial offering (see n. 7, p. 1609) and effects the healing that benefits the patient and his kindred—though young men and young women, with the irreverence of youth, may doubt the truth of the ceremony.

SIGMUND FREUD
1856–1939

Psychoanalysis, for its founder and for those he influenced, was a new cosmology comparable only to the revolutionary discoveries of Nicolaus Copernicus and Charles Darwin. Each changed the way that human beings could think about themselves: Copernicus, by proving the universe did not revolve around Earth; Darwin, by showing that humanity was only one of many evolving biological species; and Sigmund Freud, by offering a model of the unconscious mind and its dependence on drives rooted in sexual desire. Although he was suspicious of philosophers for offering overbroad systems detached from experience, and he always considered himself a scientist, Freud was in fact a system maker whose creative imagination put a personal stamp on everything he wrote. From the early case histories to the later, more speculative, essays on civilization, Freud struggled to understand the nature of human mental activity. Like Proust (to whom he has often been compared), he probed questions of identity, memory, and desire, interrogated personal experience, disclosed his own thought processes, proposed explanations, and constantly reconsidered and revised his ideas. Like fiction writers in general (or at least nineteenth-century fiction writers), Freud imposed a master plot on his scientific inquiries by following a central theme that he tried to bring to a logical conclusion. He himself said that his case histories read like short stories, and he gave the title *The Man Moses, A Historical Novel* to the first draft of *Moses and Monotheism*. The breadth of Freud's appeal may indeed be attributed to the persuasiveness of his prose and to the dramatic power of analytic scenes that are framed in a tight, novel-like structure of plot development and the discovery of answers.

Many of Freud's ideas or terms have entered common usage. The "Freudian slip" (a slip of the tongue that reveals hidden preoccupations), the "Oedipus complex" (a son's rivalry with his father for authority and for his mother's affection), the "Freudian symbol" (an object, especially one linear or curved, that suggests genitalia), the "castration complex," the "death wish," the "repression" of disturbing memories as an unconscious defense mechanism, the "repetition compulsion" that leads people to repeat unpleasant experiences, dreams and "dream work" as the voice of unconscious wishes, free association as a tactic for revealing obsessions, and the multiple forms of narcissism (self-love), all refer to concepts that Freud developed in his work.

Contemporary discussions of personality cannot do without Freud's insights. He did not invent the unconscious, but he focused attention on the strength of its ties to conscious thought. He was the first to interpret dreams as an expression of unconscious impulses. More than that, he described categories by which one could analyze dream structures. Human beings defend themselves from continued contact with painful reality, argued Freud, by transforming the disturbing experience through tactics he called condensation, displacement, representation, symbolization, and a "secondary revision" that retells events in more coherent—and acceptable—form. Interpersonal relationships, he added, were similarly governed by complex buried motivations. Part of the analyst's job was to decipher the underlying pattern suggested by the repressions and revisions of a patient's story. Even in such a controlled medical situation, however, there were two further complications that needed to be taken into account: the "transference" by which a patient sought to make the analyst enact a familiar role in his or her drama, and the "countertransference" that took place when the analyst accepted such a role. In reviewing his first case history (the *"Dora"* case presented here), Freud asserted that he had not yet sufficiently accounted for his patient's transference. Contemporary critics feel that Freud also never recognized his own countertransference, and the fact that he himself had adopted a role in relating to Dora. Such a situation would not have seemed impossible to Freud, who knew how difficult it was to determine motivation and who was constantly on the lookout for blind spots in theory and practice.

Freud's scientism is colored by a deep respect for art and literature. Writers and artists are cited liberally throughout his work; Goethe, Shakespeare, Dostoevsky, da Vinci, and Michelangelo are used as points of departure for individual studies. He named a fundamental psychoanalytic concept after Sophocles' Oedipus. The creative artist, according to Freud, gives aesthetic form to personal "phantasies" or daydreams, but these fantasies are shared—in one form or another—by every human being. Literature and art display the workings of the mind, even if they do not explicate meanings; Freud planned to reverse the order and to formulate scientific insights accompanied by a "detailed description of mental processes such as we are accustomed to find in the works of imaginative writers." If both art and psychoanalysis reveal mental activity, they also have a similar therapeutic value: psychoanalysis clarifies and cures the individual, and artistic creations—the "mental assets of civilization"—are defenses against destructive impulses that, unchecked, lead straight to barbarism. Paradoxically, modern writers who have learned from Freud (for example, Joyce, Kafka, Beckett, Lessing, and others included in this volume) are less intent on the therapeutic possibilities of art than they are on capturing the unconscious in dream scenes, associative language, and the depiction of complexes or madness. In both instances, nonetheless, the aim is to give a fuller representation of human mental activity by taking into account the role played by unconscious desires.

Sigmund Freud (he later changed the name to Sigmund) was born on May 6, 1856, in the small town of Freiberg in Moravia (now Příbor in the Czech Republic). His father was a small-scale wool merchant, some twenty years older than his third wife, Freud's mother, and the family was relatively poor. In 1860, they moved to Vienna, a city that Freud claimed to dislike but where he lived for seventy-nine years until forced to flee by the Nazis.

Sigmund was the oldest of his mother's seven children; she doted on him, and the household revolved around this brilliant son who was expected to achieve great things. He did extremely well in school, graduating from the Gymnasium (academic high school) with impressive grades and beginning his medical studies at the University of Vienna in 1873. Here he had his first serious encounters with anti-Semitism. "I found that I was expected to feel myself inferior and an alien because I was a Jew. I refused absolutely to do the first of these things." Freud later noted that this experience of being considered an outsider, cut off from the "compact majority," taught him to rely on his own judgment and sustained him in later intellectual battles.

In this early period, the young medical student was particularly interested in physiological explanations for human behavior. He studied with the famous physiologist E. W. von Brücke and the brain anatomist Theodor Meynert, receiving his medical degree in 1881. Although he would have preferred a career in research, he prepared for medical practice at the General Hospital so as to be able to support a wife and family. In 1886, he entered private practice as a neurologist and married Martha Bernays after a four-year engagement. Around this time, Freud began to take a greater interest in psychological rather than physiological approaches to brain activity. During the winter of 1885–86 he had studied with the neurologist Jean-Martin Charcot at the Parisian mental hospital of La Salpêtrière. Freud was impressed by Charcot's investigations of hysteria and hypnosis, and he reported on what he had learned when he returned to Vienna. The Viennese medical establishment, however, was shocked by Charcot's ideas (especially the concept of male hysteria). Freud was publicly attacked by his former teacher Meynert and excluded from the laboratories of the General Hospital. In private practice, he continued his work on hysteria, gradually moving from a dependence on medical hypnosis to the use of free association. In 1895 he published (with the Viennese physician Josef Breuer) *Studies on Hysteria*. The book introduced what was called a "cathartic" treatment by which patients would recall, understand, and render harmless painful memories.

Freud felt that hypnosis had only limited value and that its cures were too often temporary; he preferred to explore the broader possibilities of free association. If patients could recall events under hypnosis, he reasoned, they must in fact "know" them at some level of unconscious memory, even if they resisted bringing that material to the surface. Freud's investigation of the selective processes of memory—of what he would call "defense mechanisms" protecting the subject from painful experiences—initiated the study of psychoanalysis proper. He would now describe various defense mechanisms used by individuals to preserve their self-image and sense of well-being. His own self-analysis, undertaken in 1897 after the death of his father, brought forth not only the concept of an Oedipus complex but many other insights into the effects of unconscious processes on conscious behavior and on dreams. *The Interpretation of Dreams*, published in November 1899 (dated 1900), argued that dreams were not random occurrences but had their own coded meaning. Freud included his own "Irma" dream among various examples of the way that dreams censored disturbing material while fulfilling an underlying repressed wish. Interpreting dreams became an important part of his clinical practice and was central to such case histories as *"Dora"* (1905) and *"The Wolfman"* (1918). The influence of unconscious impulses on conscious behavior was also a theme of two other volumes published around the turn of the century: *The Psychopathology of Everyday Life* (1901) and *Jokes and Their Relation to the Unconscious* (1905).

Freud was disappointed at the small response to *The Interpretation of Dreams*, his first major book, and indeed his studies of sexuality attracted far more attention. Contemporary audiences were disconcerted by his clinical descriptions of "normal" and "abnormal" sexual practices, and his recognition of sexual drives in women as well as in men. Even more upsetting was his description of a many-sided or "polymorphously perverse" sexuality in children. Freud was convinced, however, of the causative relation between childhood sexuality, its inevitable channeling and repression, and the adult personality. He continued to explore aspects of human sexuality throughout his work, publishing the controversial *Three Essays on Sexuality* in 1905 and revising and expanding the text through subsequent editions until the sixth and last edition of 1925.

In the last decades of his life, Freud turned to broader speculations and the creation of explanatory structures. With the essay *On Narcissism* (1914), he began to suggest models of the conscious and unconscious mind that included the related concepts of ego, id, super-ego and ego-ideal: very loosely, the ego as rational consciousness; the id as primitive energy ("the dark, inaccessible part of our personality . . . striving to bring about the satisfaction of instinctive needs"); and the super-ego as an internalized ideal image of human behavior, learned from parents and society, that "represents the ethical standards of mankind." An increasingly somber tone accompanied the elaboration of these ideas in *Beyond the Pleasure Principle* (1920), which countered pleasure with a "reality principle" and added the notion of a "death instinct," and in the revised and definitive statement of *The Ego and the Id* (1923). Freud did not content himself with structural models of the individual mind, however, and adapted his theories of mental conflict to larger models of civilization. *Totem and Taboo* (1913), *Group Psychology* (1921), *The Future of an Illusion* (1927), and *Moses and Monotheism* (1938) focused on the relation of individual and group, analyzing particularly the role of religion. Gradually, Freud envisaged an all-encompassing, dialectical scheme in which Eros and Thanatos, the life and death instincts, figured as opposing forces in human beings and in civilization itself. His late study, *Civilization and Its Discontents* (1930), described civilization as a hard-won and not entirely pleasurable prize achieved only through renunciation and control of instinctual desires. The scientific inquiry that began with laboratory studies of cerebral anatomy had emerged in a philosophic essay of grandiose scope and tragic vision. The span of Freud's achievement was noted in the citation for the Goethe Prize awarded that same year: he had "opened access to the driving forces of the soul and thus created the possibility of recognizing the emergence and construction of cultural forms and of curing some of the soul's illnesses."

As the founder of psychoanalysis and a brilliant writer in his own right, Freud was an exceptional innovator whose influence on twentieth-century thought can scarcely be overestimated. He was also a creature of his time, and even those who feel greatly indebted to him recognize the degree to which he shared a traditional nineteenth-century social perspective. Freudian psychology claims universal validity, but its structures are Western and patriarchal: that is, it is based on Western models of a nuclear family, and it is invariably governed by a masculine perspective. Traditional kinship structures in India or Africa, for example, do not respond so readily to the Freudian model. The strongest criticism of Freud's theories of sexuality has come, in fact, from those who note in them the subterranean influence of Victorian gender stereotypes. In Freud's day, women had little control over their own lives: fathers, husbands, or male relatives decided what was best for them. Despite his bold recognition of female sexuality, Freud held conventional views of women's social role. One of the more than nine hundred letters he wrote his fianceé during their four-year engagement reveals his personal attitude: "It seems a completely unrealistic notion to send women into the struggle for existence in the same way as men. Am I to think of my delicate sweet girl as a competitor?" Readers may well feel that both aspects emerge in the *"Dora"* case: on the one hand, an intrepid and imaginative researcher pursuing medical truth through all obstacles and, on the other, a man whose analytic attitude toward his patient is shaped by existing cultural attitudes and by what he thinks is "normal" for a young woman her age.

Dora's real name was Ida Bauer. At age eighteen, she was sent to Freud for treatment after her parents had discovered an apparent suicide letter. Her father, who had previously been Freud's patient, hoped that Freud would bring Dora to reason—which included reconciling her with the "K." family and with Herr K., whom she had accused of propositioning her. Dora was reluctant to undertake the treatment, and she did not welcome Freud's intensifying explanations of what was wrong with her; after eleven weeks she notified him that she would not be coming back. Freud was disappointed not to finish the treatment, especially since his analysis was providing evidence for theories outlined in *The Interpretation of Dreams*. He published his account five years later as a "Fragment of an Analysis of a Case of Hysteria," but this "fragment" continued to occupy his mind and he added footnotes in later editions.

"Dora" is the first of Freud's major case histories, and for many years it was a model for students of psychoanalysis. It has also been called a literary masterwork, a short novel told in the first person in which the narrative point of view is as fascinating as the plot and characters. The author's perspective is personal as well as professional, and he is hurt and even a little vindictive when Dora decides to break off the relationship. His preface observes that Dora may be pained to see her case in print, and he reinforces his argument through numerous footnotes that justify and comment personally on his interpretation of events that themselves recall a romantic novel: there are related love stories, misunderstandings and betrayal, and an unhappy heroine whose destiny is the focus of attention. The author arranges the sequence of events "for the sake of presenting the case in a more connected form." He selects some characters for extended description (the father, Herr K.) while dismissing others equally close (the mother) in a few words. Dramatic tension builds as Freud observes and interprets his subject's every move, concluding triumphantly that "he who has eyes to see and ears to hear, becomes convinced that mortals can keep no secret. If their lips are silent, they gossip with their fingertips; betrayal forces its way through every pore." Freud was not unaware of the literary quality of his case histories: he complained mildly that "it still strikes me myself as strange that the case histories I write should read like short stories and that, as one might say, they lack the serious stamp of science." Yet the stamp of science is also evident in "Dora": it emerges in the narrator's dedication to discovering the truth of mental processes, in the tightly controlled structure he imposes on his quest and—most obviously—in the clinical detail with which he analyzes evidence. Literature and science come together, finally, in Freud's practice of displaying his own tactical strategy as he goes; with "Dora" this laying bare of narrative principles fits both scientific method and modernist literary technique.

In Dora's Case: Freud-Hysteria-Feminism (1985), edited by Charles Bernheimer and Claire Kahane, presents twelve major essays on the "Dora" case, a two-part introduction, and a biographical note. Peter Gay, Freud: A Life for Our Time (1988), is a full, very readable biography by a major cultural historian and Freud scholar. Brief informative biographies are Gerald Levin, Sigmund Freud (1975), and Margaret Muckenhoupt, Sigmund Freud: Explorer of the Unconscious (1997). Madelon Sprengnether, The Spectral Mother: Freud, Feminism, and Psychoanalysis (1990), contains a revisionary discussion of Freud's ambiguous relationship to Dora; Patrick Mahoney, Freud's Dora: A Psychoanalytic, Historical, and Textual Study (1996), also emphasizes Freud's own psychological investment in the case. Malcolm Bowie, Freud, Proust and Lacan: Theory as Fiction (1987), sees the authors as theorists and fiction writers who develop portraits of mental life; chapters on each writer, a chapter comparing Freud and Proust, and a note on translations. Hannah S. Decker, Freud, Dora and Vienna 1900 (1990), describes the cultural context that influenced both Freud and Dora. Paul Robinson, Freud and His Critics (1993), sympathetically cross-examines major attacks on Freud and discusses Freud's place in intellectual history.

From "Dora"
(Fragment of an Analysis of a Case of Hysteria)[1]

I

The Clinical Picture

In my Interpretation of Dreams, published in 1900, I showed that dreams in general can be interpreted, and that after the work of interpretation has

---

1. Translated by Alix and James Strachey. Freud's prefatory remarks have been omitted.

been completed they can be replaced by perfectly correctly constructed thoughts which can be assigned a recognizable position in the chain of mental events. I wish to give an example in the following pages of the only practical application of which the art of interpreting dreams seems to admit. I have already mentioned in my book how it was that I came upon the problem of dreams. The problem crossed my path as I was endeavouring to cure psychoneuroses by means of a particular psychotherapeutic method. For, among their other mental experiences, my patients told me their dreams, and these dreams seemed to call for insertion in the long thread of connections which spun itself out between a symptom of the disease and a pathogenic idea. At that time I learnt how to translate the language of dreams into the forms of expression of our own thought-language, which can be understood without further help. And I may add that this knowledge is essential for the psycho-analyst; for the dream is one of the roads along which consciousness can be reached by the psychical material which, on account of the opposition aroused by its content, has been cut off from consciousness and repressed, and has thus become pathogenic. The dream, in short, is one of the *détours by which repression can be evaded;* it is one of the principal means employed by what is known as the indirect method of representation in the mind. The following fragment from the history of the treatment of a hysterical girl is intended to show the way in which the interpretation of dreams plays a part in the work of analysis. It will at the same time give me a first opportunity of publishing at sufficient length to prevent further misunderstanding some of my views upon the psychical processes of hysteria and upon its organic determinants. I need no longer apologize on the score of length, since it is now agreed that the exacting demands which hysteria makes upon physician and investigator can be met only by the most sympathetic spirit of inquiry and not by an attitude of superiority and contempt. For,

Nicht Kunst und Wissenschaft allein,
Geduld will bei dem Werke sein![2]

If I were to begin by giving a full and consistent case history, it would place the reader in a very different situation from that of the medical observer. The reports of the patient's relatives—in the present case I was given one by the eighteen-year-old girl's father—usually afford a very indistinct picture of the course of the illness. I begin the treatment, indeed, by asking the patient to give me the whole story of his life and illness, but even so the information I receive is never enough to let me see my way about the case. This first account may be compared to an unnavigable river whose stream is at one moment choked by masses of rock and at another divided and lost among shallows and sandbanks. I cannot help wondering how it is that the authorities can produce such smooth and precise histories in cases of hysteria. As a matter of fact the patients are incapable of giving such reports about themselves. They can, indeed, give the physician plenty of coherent information about this or that period of their lives; but it is sure to be followed by another period as to which their communications run dry,

---

2. "Science is not enough, nor art, / In this work patience plays a part" (German). From Goethe's *Faust*, "Witch's Kitchen" 34–35, translated by Walter Kaufmann.

leaving gaps unfilled, and riddles unanswered; and then again will come yet another period which will remain totally obscure and unilluminated by even a single piece of serviceable information. The connections—even the ostensible ones—are for the most part incoherent, and the sequence of different events is uncertain. Even during the course of their story patients will repeatedly correct a particular or a date, and then perhaps, after wavering for some time, return to their first version. The patients' inability to give an ordered history of their life in so far as it coincides with the history of their illness is not merely characteristic of the neurosis. It also possesses great theoretical significance. For this inability has the following grounds. In the first place, patients consciously and intentionally keep back part of what they ought to tell—things that are perfectly well known to them—because they have not got over their feelings of timidity and shame (or discretion, where what they say concerns other people); this is the share taken by *conscious* disingenuousness. In the second place, part of the anamnestic[3] knowledge, which the patients have at their disposal at other times, disappears while they are actually telling their story, but without their making any deliberate reservations: the share taken by *unconscious* disingenuousness. In the third place, there are invariably true amnesias—gaps in the memory into which not only old recollections but even quite recent ones have fallen—and paramnesias,[4] formed secondarily so as to fill in those gaps.[5] When the events themselves have been kept in mind, the purpose underlying the amnesias can be fulfilled just as surely by destroying a connection, and a connection is most surely broken by altering the chronological order of events. The latter always proves to be the most vulnerable element in the store of memory and the one which is most easily subject to repression. Again, we meet with many recollections that are in what might be described as the first stage of repression, and these we find surrounded with doubts. At a later period the doubts would be replaced by a loss or a falsification of memory.[6]

That this state of affairs should exist in regard to the memories relating to the history of the illness is *a necessary correlate of the symptoms and one which is theoretically requisite*. In the further course of the treatment the patient supplies the facts which, though he had known them all along, had been kept back by him or had not occurred to his mind. The paramnesias prove untenable, and the gaps in his memory are filled in. It is only towards the end of the treatment that we have before us an intelligible, consistent, and unbroken case history. Whereas the practical aim of the treatment is to remove all possible symptoms and to replace them by conscious thoughts, we may regard it as a second and theoretical aim to repair all the damages to the patient's memory. These two aims are coincident. When one is reached, so is the other; and the same path leads to them both.

It follows from the nature of the facts which form the material of psychoanalysis that we are obliged to pay as much attention in our case histories

3. Recollected, remembered ("anamnesis": calling to memory).   4. "Memories" blended of fantasy and actual experience.   5. Amnesias and paramnesias stand in a complementary relation to each other. When there are large gaps in the memory there will be few mistakes in it. And conversely, paramnesias can at a first glance completely conceal the presence of amnesias [Freud's note].   6. If a patient exhibits doubts in the course of his narrative, an empirical rule teaches us to disregard such expressions of his judgement entirely. If the narrative wavers between two versions, we should incline to regard the first one as correct and the second as a product of repression [Freud's note].

to the purely human and social circumstances of our patients as to the somatic data and the symptoms of the disorder. Above all, our interest will be directed towards their family circumstances—and not only, as will be seen later, for the purpose of enquiring into their heredity.

The family circle of the eighteen-year-old girl who is the subject of this paper included, besides herself, her two parents and a brother who was one and a half years her senior. Her father was the dominating figure in this circle, owing to his intelligence and his character as much as to the circumstances of his life. It was those circumstances which provided the framework for the history of the patient's childhood and illness. At the time at which I began the girl's treatment her father was in his late forties, a man of rather unusual activity and talents, a large manufacturer in very comfortable circumstances. His daughter was most tenderly attached to him, and for that reason her critical powers, which developed early, took all the more offence at many of his actions and peculiarities.

Her affection for him was still further increased by the many severe illnesses which he had been through since her sixth year. At that time he had fallen ill with tuberculosis and the family had consequently moved to a small town in a good climate, situated in one of our southern provinces. There his lung trouble rapidly improved; but, on account of the precautions which were still considered necessary, both parents and children continued for the next ten years or so to reside chiefly in this spot, which I shall call B——. When her father's health was good, he used at times to be away, on visits to his factories. During the hottest part of the summer the family used to move to a health-resort in the hills.

When the girl was about ten years old, her father had to go through a course of treatment in a darkened room on account of a detached retina. As a result of this misfortune his vision was permanently impaired. His gravest illness occurred some two years later. It took the form of a confusional attack, followed by symptoms of paralysis and slight mental disturbances. A friend of his (who plays a part in the story with which we shall be concerned later on) persuaded him, while his condition had scarcely improved, to travel to Vienna with his physician and come to me for advice. I hesitated for some time as to whether I ought not to regard the case as one of tabo-paralysis,[7] but I finally decided upon a diagnosis of a diffuse vascular affection; and since the patient admitted having had a specific infection before his marriage, I prescribed an energetic course of anti-luetic[8] treatment, as a result of which all the remaining disturbances passed off. It is no doubt owing to this fortunate intervention of mine that four years later he brought his daughter, who had meanwhile grown unmistakably neurotic, and introduced her to me, and that after another two years he handed her over to me for psychotherapeutic treatment.

I had in the meantime also made the acquaintance in Vienna of a sister of his, who was a little older than himself. She gave clear evidence of a severe form of psychoneurosis without any characteristically hysterical symptoms. After a life which had been weighed down by an unhappy marriage, she died of a marasmus[9] which made rapid advances and the symptoms of which were,

7. Paralysis resulting from syphilis attacking the spinal cord and sensory nerves.　8. Antisyphilis.
9. A wasting away of the body.

as a matter of fact, never fully cleared up. An elder brother of the girl's father, whom I once happened to meet, was a hypochondriacal bachelor.

The sympathies of the girl herself, who, as I have said, became my patient at the age of eighteen, had always been with the father's side of the family, and ever since she had fallen ill she had taken as her model the aunt who has just been mentioned. There could be no doubt, too, that it was from her father's family that she had derived not only her natural gifts and her intellectual precocity but also the predisposition to her illness. I never made her mother's acquaintance. From the accounts given me by the girl and her father I was led to imagine her as an uncultivated woman and above all as a foolish one, who had concentrated all her interests upon domestic affairs, especially since her husband's illness and the estrangement to which it led. She presented the picture, in fact, of what might be called the "housewife's psychosis." She had no understanding of her children's more active interests, and was occupied all day long in cleaning the house with its furniture and utensils and in keeping them clean—to such an extent as to make it almost impossible to use or enjoy them. This condition, traces of which are to be found often enough in normal housewives, inevitably reminds one of forms of obsessional washing and other kinds of obsessional cleanliness. But such women (and this applied to the patient's mother) are entirely without insight into their illness, so that one essential characteristic of an "obsessional neurosis" is lacking. The relations between the girl and her mother had been unfriendly for years. The daughter looked down on her mother and used to criticize her mercilessly, and she had withdrawn completely from her influence.

During the girl's earlier years, her only brother (her elder by a year and a half) had been the model which her ambitions had striven to follow. But in the last few years the relations between the brother and sister had grown more distant. The young man used to try so far as he could to keep out of the family disputes; but when he was obliged to take sides he would support his mother. So that the usual sexual attraction had drawn together the father and daughter on the one side and the mother and son on the other.

The patient, to whom I shall in future give the name of "Dora," had even at the age of eight begun to develop neurotic symptoms. She became subject at that time to chronic dyspnoea[1] with occasional accesses in which the symptom was very much aggravated. The first outset occurred after a short expedition in the mountains and was accordingly put down to over-exertion. In the course of six months, during which she was made to rest and was carefully looked after, this condition gradually passed off. The family doctor seems to have had not a moment's hesitation in diagnosing the disorder as purely nervous and in excluding any organic cause for the dyspnoea; but he evidently considered this diagnosis compatible with the aetiology of over-exertion.

The little girl went through the usual infectious diseases of childhood without suffering any lasting damage. As she herself told me—and her words were intended to convey a deeper meaning—her brother was as a rule the first to start the illness and used to have it very slightly, and she would then follow suit with a severe form of it. When she was about twelve she began to suffer from unilateral headaches in the nature of a migraine, and from

---

1. Difficult or labored breathing.

attacks of nervous coughing. At first these two symptoms always appeared together, but they became separated later on and ran different courses. The migraine grew rarer, and by the time she was sixteen she had quite got over it. But attacks of *tussis nervosa*,[2] which had no doubt been started by a common catarrh, continued to occur over the whole period. When, at the age of eighteen, she came to me for treatment, she was again coughing in a characteristic manner. The number of these attacks could not be determined; but they lasted from three to five weeks, and on one occasion for several months. The most troublesome symptom during the first half of an attack of this kind, at all events in the last few years, used to be a complete loss of voice. The diagnosis that this was once more a nervous complaint had been established long since; but the various methods of treatment which are usual, including hydrotherapy and the local application of electricity, had produced no result. It was in such circumstances as these that the child had developed into a mature young woman of very independent judgement, who had grown accustomed to laugh at the efforts of doctors, and in the end to renounce their help entirely. Moreover, she had always been against calling in medical advice, though she had no personal objection to her family doctor. Every proposal to consult a new physician aroused her resistance, and it was only her father's authority which induced her to come to me at all.

I first saw her when she was sixteen, in the early summer. She was suffering from a cough and from hoarseness, and even at that time I proposed giving her psychological treatment. My proposal was not adopted, since the attack in question, like the others, passed off spontaneously, though it had lasted unusually long. During the next winter she came and stayed in Vienna with her uncle and his daughters after the death of the aunt of whom she had been so fond. There she fell ill of a feverish disorder which was diagnosed at the time as appendicitis. In the following autumn, since her father's health seemed to justify the step, the family left the health-resort of B—— for good and all. They first moved to the town where her father's factory was situated, and then, scarcely a year later, settled permanently in Vienna.

Dora was by that time in the first bloom of youth—a girl of intelligent and engaging looks. But she was a source of heavy trials for her parents. Low spirits and an alteration in her character had now become the main features of her illness. She was clearly satisfied neither with herself nor with her family; her attitude towards her father was unfriendly, and she was on very bad terms with her mother, who was bent upon drawing her into taking a share in the work of the house. She tried to avoid social intercourse, and employed herself—so far as she was allowed to by the fatigue and lack of concentration of which she complained—with attending lectures for women and with carrying on more or less serious studies. One day her parents were thrown into a state of great alarm by finding on the girl's writing-desk, or inside it, a letter in which she took leave of them because, as she said, she could no longer endure her life.[3] Her father, indeed, being a man of some

2. Nervous coughing (Latin). 3. As I have already explained, the treatment of the case, and consequently my insight into the complex of events composing it, remained fragmentary. There are therefore many questions to which I have no solution to offer, or in which I can only rely upon hints and conjectures. This affair of the letter came up in the course of one of our sessions, and the girl showed signs of astonishment. "How on earth," she asked, "did they find the letter? It was shut up in my desk." But since she knew that her parents had read this draft of a farewell letter, I conclude that she had herself arranged for it to fall into their hands [Freud's note].

perspicacity, guessed that the girl had no serious suicidal intentions. But he was none the less very much shaken; and when one day, after a slight passage of words between him and his daughter, she had a first attack of loss of consciousness[4]—an event which was subsequently covered by an amnesia—it was determined, in spite of her reluctance, that she should come to me for treatment.

No doubt this case history, as I have so far outlined it, does not upon the whole seem worth recording. It is merely a case of *"petite hystérie"* with the commonest of all somatic[5] and mental symptoms: dyspnoea, *tussis nervosa,* aphonia,[6] and possibly migraines, together with depression, hysterical unsociability, and a *taedium vitae*[7] which was probably not entirely genuine. More interesting cases of hysteria have no doubt been published, and they have very often been more carefully described; for nothing will be found in the following pages on the subject of stigmata of cutaneous sensibility, limitation of the visual field, or similar matters. I may venture to remark, however, that all such collections of the strange and wonderful phenomena of hysteria have but slightly advanced our knowledge of a disease which still remains as great a puzzle as ever. What is wanted is precisely an elucidation of the *commonest* cases and of their most frequent and typical symptoms. I should have been very well satisfied if the circumstances had allowed me to give a complete elucidation of this case of *petite hystérie.* And my experiences with other patients leave me in no doubt that my analytic method would have enabled me to do so.

In 1896, shortly after the appearance of my *Studies on Hysteria* (written in conjunction with Dr. J. Breuer, 1895), I asked an eminent fellow-specialist for his opinion on the psychological theory of hysteria put forward in that work. He bluntly replied that he considered it an unjustifiable generalization of conclusions which might hold good for a few cases. Since then I have seen an abundance of cases of hysteria, and I have been occupied with each case for a number of days, weeks, or years. In not a single one of them have I failed to discover the psychological determinants which were postulated in the *Studies,* namely, a psychical trauma, a conflict of affects, and—an additional factor which I brought forward in later publications—a disturbance in the sphere of sexuality. It is of course not to be expected that the patient will come to meet the physician half-way with material which has become pathogenic for the very reason of its efforts to lie concealed; nor must the enquirer rest content with the first "No" that crosses his path.

In Dora's case, thanks to her father's shrewdness which I have remarked upon more than once already, there was no need for me to look about for the points of contact between the circumstances of the patient's life and her illness, at all events in its most recent form. Her father told me that he and his family while they were at B—— had formed an intimate friendship with a married couple who had been settled there for several years. Frau K. had

---

4. The attack was, I believe, accompanied by convulsions and delirious states. But since this event was not reached by the analysis either, I have no trustworthy recollections on the subject to fall back upon [Freud's note].   5. Physical, relating to the body. *Petite hystérie:* minor hysteria (French).   6. Loss of voice.   7. Boredom, fatigue of life (Latin); see Baudelaire's *ennui.*

nursed him during his long illness, and had in that way, he said, earned a title to his undying gratitude. Herr[8] K. had always been most kind to Dora. He had gone for walks with her when he was there, and had made her small presents; but no one had thought any harm of that. Dora had taken the greatest care of the K.'s two little children, and been almost a mother to them. When Dora and her father had come to see me two years before in the summer, they had been just on their way to stop with Herr and Frau K., who were spending the summer on one of our lakes in the Alps. Dora was to have spent several weeks at the K.'s, while her father had intended to return home after a few days. During that time Herr K. had been staying there as well. As her father was preparing for his departure the girl had suddenly declared with the greatest determination that she was going with him, and she had in fact put her decision into effect. It was not until some days later that she had thrown any light upon her strange behaviour. She had then told her mother—intending that what she said should be passed on to her father—that Herr K. had had the audacity to make her a proposal while they were on a walk after a trip upon the lake. Herr K. had been called to account by her father and uncle on the next occasion of their meeting, but he had denied in the most emphatic terms having on his side made any advances which could have been open to such a construction. He had then proceeded to throw suspicion upon the girl, saying that he had heard from Frau K. that she took no interest in anything but sexual matters, and that she used to read Mantegazza's *Physiology of Love*[9] and books of that sort in their house on the lake. It was most likely, he had added, that she had been over-excited by such reading and had merely "fancied" the whole scene she had described.

"I have no doubt," continued her father, "that this incident is responsible for Dora's depression and irritability and suicidal ideas. She keeps pressing me to break off relations with Herr K. and more particularly with Frau K., whom she used positively to worship formerly. But that I cannot do. For, to begin with, I myself believe that Dora's tale of the man's immoral suggestions is a phantasy that has forced its way into her mind; and besides, I am bound to Frau K. by ties of honourable friendship and I do not wish to cause her pain. The poor woman is most unhappy with her husband, of whom, by the by, I have no very high opinion. She herself has suffered a great deal with her nerves, and I am her only support. With my state of health I need scarcely assure you that there is nothing wrong in our relations. We are just two poor wretches who give one another what comfort we can by an exchange of friendly sympathy. You know already that I get nothing out of my own wife. But Dora, who inherits my obstinacy, cannot be moved from her hatred of the K.'s. She had her last attack after a conversation in which she had again pressed me to break with them. Please try and bring her to reason."

Her father's words did not always quite tally with this pronouncement; for on other occasions he tried to put the chief blame for Dora's impossible behavior on her mother—whose peculiarities made the house unbearable for every one. But I had resolved from the first to suspend my

8. Mr. (German). *Frau:* Mrs. (German).   9. Paolo Mantegazza (1831–1910), author of three books on human sexuality. The *Physiology of Love* (1877) is more romantic and less explicit than, e.g., his *Sexual Relations of Mankind*.

judgement of the true state of affairs till I had heard the other side as well.

* * *

[A brief discussion of trauma theory follows.]

When the first difficulties of the treatment had been overcome, Dora told me of an earlier episode with Herr K., which was even better calculated to act as a sexual trauma. She was fourteen years old at the time. Herr K. had made an arrangement with her and his wife that they should meet him one afternoon at his place of business in the principal square of B—— so as to have a view of a church festival. He persuaded his wife, however, to stay at home, and sent away his clerks, so that he was alone when the girl arrived. When the time for the procession approached, he asked the girl to wait for him at the door which opened on to the staircase leading to the upper story, while he pulled down the outside shutters. He then came back, and, instead of going out by the open door, suddenly clasped the girl to him and pressed a kiss upon her lips. This was surely just the situation to call up a distinct feeling of sexual excitement in a girl of fourteen who had never before been approached. But Dora had at that moment a violent feeling of disgust, tore herself from the man, and hurried past him to the staircase and from there to the street door. She nevertheless continued to meet Herr K. Neither of them ever mentioned the little scene; and according to her account Dora kept it a secret till her confession during the treatment. For some time afterwards, however, she avoided being alone with Herr K. The K.'s had just made plans for an expedition which was to last for some days and on which Dora was to have accompanied them. After the scene of the kiss she refused to join the party, without giving any reason.

In this scene—second in order of mention, but first in order of time—the behaviour of this child of fourteen was already entirely and completely hysterical. I should without question consider a person hysterical in whom an occasion for sexual excitement elicited feelings that were preponderantly or exclusively unpleasurable; and I should do so whether or not the person were capable of producing somatic symptoms. The elucidation of the mechanism of this *reversal of affect* is one of the most important and at the same time one of the most difficult problems in the psychology of the neuroses. In my own judgement I am still some way from having achieved this end; and I may add that within the limits of the present paper I shall be able to bring forward only a part of such knowledge on the subject as I do possess.

In order to particularize Dora's case it is not enough merely to draw attention to the reversal of affect; there has also been a *displacement* of sensation. Instead of the genital sensation which would certainly have been felt by a healthy girl in such circumstances, Dora was overcome by the unpleasurable feeling which is proper to the tract of mucous membrane at the entrance to the alimentary canal—that is by disgust. The stimulation of her lips by the kiss was no doubt of importance in localizing the feeling at that particular place; but I think I can also recognize another factor in operation.[1]

---

1. The causes of Dora's disgust at the kiss were certainly not adventitious, for in that case she could not have failed to remember and mention them. I happen to know Herr K., for he was the same person who had visited me with the patient's father, and he was still quite young and of prepossessing appearance [Freud's note].

The disgust which Dora felt on that occasion did not become a permanent symptom, and even at the time of the treatment it was only, as it were, potentially present. She was a poor eater and confessed to some disinclination for food. On the other hand, the scene had left another consequence behind it in the shape of a sensory hallucination which occurred from time to time and even made its appearance while she was telling me her story. She declared that she could still feel upon the upper part of her body the pressure of Herr K.'s embrace. In accordance with certain rules of symptom-formation which I have come to know, and at the same time taking into account certain other of the patient's peculiarities, which were otherwise inexplicable—such as her unwillingness to walk past any man whom she saw engaged in eager or affectionate conversation with a lady—I have formed in my own mind the following reconstruction of the scene. I believe that during the man's passionate embrace she felt not merely his kiss upon her lips but also the pressure of his erect member against her body. This perception was revolting to her; it was dismissed from her memory, repressed, and replaced by the innocent sensation of pressure upon her thorax, which in turn derived an excessive intensity from its repressed source. Once more, therefore, we find a displacement from the lower part of the body to the upper. On the other hand, the compulsive piece of behaviour which I have mentioned was formed as though it were derived from the undistorted recollection of the scene: she did not like walking past any man who she thought was in a state of sexual excitement, because she wanted to avoid seeing for a second time the somatic sign which accompanies it.

It is worth remarking that we have here three symptoms—the disgust, the sensation of pressure on the upper part of the body, and the avoidance of men engaged in affectionate conversation—all of them derived from a single experience, and that it is only by taking into account the interrelation of these three phenomena that we can understand the way in which the formation of the symptoms came about. The disgust is the symptom of repression in the erotogenic oral zone, which, as we shall hear, had been over-indulged in Dora's infancy by the habit of sensual sucking. The pressure of the erect member probably led to an analogous change in the corresponding female organ, the clitoris; and the excitation of this second erotogenic zone was referred by a process of displacement to the simultaneous pressure against the thorax and became fixed there. Her avoidance of men who might possibly be in a state of sexual excitement follows the mechanism of a phobia, its purpose being to safeguard her against any revival of the repressed perception.

In order to show that such a supplement to the story was possible, I questioned the patient very cautiously as to whether she knew anything of the physical signs of excitement in a man's body. Her answer, as touching the present, was "Yes," but, as touching the time of the episode, "I think not." From the very beginning I took the greatest pains with this patient not to introduce her to any fresh facts in the region of sexual knowledge; and I did this, not from any conscientious motives, but because I was anxious to subject my assumptions to a rigorous test in this case. Accordingly, I did not call a thing by its name until her allusions to it had become so unambiguous that there seemed very slight risk in translating them into direct speech. Her answer was always prompt and frank: she knew about it already. But the question of *where* her knowledge came from was a riddle which her memories were unable to solve. She had forgotten the source of all her information on this subject.

If I may suppose that the scene of the kiss took place in this way, I can arrive at the following derivation for the feelings of disgust.[2] Such feelings seem originally to be a reaction to the smell (and afterwards also to the sight) of excrement. But the genitals can act as a reminder of the excretory functions; and this applies especially to the male member, for that organ performs the function of micturition[3] as well as the sexual function. Indeed, the function of micturition is the earlier known of the two, and the *only* one known during the pre-sexual period. Thus it happens that disgust becomes one of the means of affective expression in the sphere of sexual life. The Early Christian Father's *"inter urinas et faeces nascimur"*[4] clings to sexual life and cannot be detached from it in spite of every effort at idealization. I should like, however, expressly to emphasize my opinion that the problem is not solved by the mere pointing out of this path of association. The fact that this association *can* be called up does not show that it actually *will* be called up. And indeed in normal circumstances it will not be. A knowledge of the paths does not render less necessary a knowledge of the forces which travel along them.

I did not find it easy, however, to direct the patient's attention to her relations with Herr K. She declared that she had done with him. The uppermost layer of all her associations during the sessions, and everything of which she was easily conscious and of which she remembered having been conscious the day before, was always connected with her father. It was quite true that she could not forgive her father for continuing his relations with Herr K. and more particularly with Frau K. But she viewed those relations in a very different light from that in which her father wished them to appear. In her mind there was no doubt that what bound her father to this young and beautiful woman was a common love-affair. Nothing that could help to confirm this view had escaped her perception, which in this connection was pitilessly sharp; *here there were no gaps to be found in her memory.* Their acquaintance with the K.'s had begun before her father's serious illness; but it had not become intimate until the young woman had officially taken on the position of nurse during that illness, while Dora's mother had kept away from the sick-room. During the first summer holidays after his recovery things had happened which must have opened every one's eyes to the true character of this "friendship." The two families had taken a suite of rooms in common at the hotel. One day Frau K. had announced that she could not keep the bedroom which she had up till then shared with one of her children. A few days later Dora's father had given up his bedroom, and they had both moved into new rooms—the end rooms, which were only separated by the passage, while the rooms they had given up had not offered any such security against interruption. Later on, whenever she had reproached her father about Frau K., he had been in the habit of saying that he could not understand her hostility and that, on the contrary, his children had every reason for being grateful to Frau K. Her mother, whom she has asked for an expla-

2. Here, as in all similar cases, the reader must be prepared to be met not by one but by several causes—by *overdetermination* [Freud's note]. In other words, a single symptom may express or be *determined* by different intertwined causes.   3. Urination.   4. We are born between urine and feces (Latin).

nation of this mysterious remark, had told her that her father had been so unhappy at that time that he had made up his mind to go into the wood and kill himself, and that Frau K., suspecting as much, had gone after him and had persuaded him by her entreaties to preserve his life for the sake of his family. Of course, Dora went on, she herself did not believe this story; no doubt the two of them had been seen together in the wood, and her father had thereupon invented this fairy tale of his suicide so as to account for their rendezvous.[5]

When they had returned to B——, her father had visited Frau K. every day at definite hours, while her husband was at his business. Everybody had talked about it and had questioned her about it pointedly. Herr K. himself had often complained bitterly to her mother, though he had spared her herself any allusions to the subject—which she seemed to attribute to delicacy of feeling on his part. When they had all gone for walks together, her father and Frau K. had always known how to manage things so as to be alone with each other. There could be no doubt that she had taken money from him, for she spent more than she could possibly have afforded out of her own purse or her husband's. Dora added that her father had begun to make handsome presents to Frau K., and in order to make these less conspicuous had at the same time become especially liberal towards her mother and herself. And, while previously Frau K. had been an invalid and had even been obliged to spend months in a sanatorium for nervous disorders because she had been unable to walk, she had now become a healthy and lively woman.

Even after they had left B—— for the manufacturing town, these relations, already of many years' standing, had been continued. From time to time her father used to declare that he could not endure the rawness of the climate, and that he must do something for himself; he would begin to cough and complain, until suddenly he would start off to B——, and from there write the most cheerful letters home. All these illnesses had only been pretexts for seeing his friend again. Then one day it had been decided that they were to move to Vienna and Dora began to suspect a hidden connection. And sure enough, they had scarcely been three weeks in Vienna when she heard that the K.'s had moved there as well. They were in Vienna, so she told me, at that very moment, and she frequently met her father with Frau K. in the street. She also met Herr K. very often, and he always used to turn round and look after her; and once when he had met her out by herself he had followed her for a long way, so as to make sure where she was going and whether she might not have a rendezvous.

On one occasion during the course of the treatment her father again felt worse, and went off to B—— for several weeks; and the sharp-sighted Dora had soon unearthed the fact that Frau K. had started off to the same place on a visit to her relatives there. It was at this time that Dora's criticisms of her father were the most frequent: he was insincere, he had a strain of falseness in his character, he only thought of his enjoyment, and he had a gift for seeing things in the light which suited him best.

I could not in general dispute Dora's characterization of her father; and there was one particular respect in which it was easy to see that her

---

5. This is the point of connection with her own pretence at suicide, which may thus be regarded as the expression of a longing for a love of the same kind [Freud's note].

reproaches were justified. When she was feeling embittered she used to be overcome by the idea that she had been handed over to Herr K. as the price of his tolerating the relations between her father and his wife; and her rage at her father's making such a use of her was visible behind her affection for him. At other times she was quite well aware that she had been guilty of exaggeration in talking like this. The two men had of course never made a formal agreement in which she was treated as an object for barter; her father in particular would have been horrified at any such suggestion. But he was one of those men who know how to evade a dilemma by falsifying their judgement upon one of the conflicting alternatives. If it had been pointed out to him that there might be danger for a growing girl in the constant and unsupervised companionship of a man who had no satisfaction from his own wife, he would have been certain to answer that he could rely upon his daughter, that a man like K. could never be dangerous to her, and that his friend was himself incapable of such intentions, or that Dora was still a child and was treated as a child by K. But as a matter of fact things were in a position in which each of the two men avoided drawing any conclusions from the other's behaviour which would have been awkward for his own plans. It was possible for Herr K. to send Dora flowers every day for a whole year while he was in the neighbourhood, to take every opportunity of giving her valuable presents, and to spend all his spare time in her company, without her parents noticing anything in his behaviour that was characteristic of love-making.

When a patient brings forward a sound and incontestable train of argument during psycho-analytic treatment, the physician is liable to feel a moment's embarrassment, and the patient may take advantage of it by asking: "This is all perfectly correct and true, isn't it? What do you want to change in [it] now that I've told it you?" But it soon becomes evident that the patient is using thoughts of this kind, which the analysis cannot attack, for the purpose of cloaking others which are anxious to escape from criticism and from consciousness. A string of reproaches against other people leads one to suspect the existence of a string of self-reproaches with the same content. All that need be done is to turn back each particular reproach on to the speaker himself. There is something undeniably automatic about this method of defending oneself against a self-reproach by making the same reproach against some one else. A model of it is to be found in the *tu quoque*[6] arguments of children; if one of them is accused of being a liar, he will reply without an instant's hesitation: "You're another." A grown-up person who wanted to throw back abuse would look for some really exposed spot in his antagonist and would not lay the chief stress upon the same content being repeated. In paranoia the projection of a reproach on to another person without any alteration in its content and therefore without any consideration for reality becomes manifest as the process of forming delusions.

Dora's reproaches against her father had a "lining" or "backing" of self-reproaches of this kind with a corresponding content in every case, as I shall show in detail. She was right in thinking that her father did not wish to look too closely into Herr K.'s behaviour to his daughter, for fear of being dis-

---

6. You too! (Latin).

turbed in his own love-affair with Frau K. But Dora herself had done precisely the same thing. She had made herself an accomplice in the affair, and had dismissed from her mind every sign which tended to show its true character. It was not until after her adventure by the lake that her eyes were opened and that she began to apply such a severe standard to her father. During all the previous years she had given every possible assistance to her father's relations with Frau K. She would never go to see her if she thought her father was there; but, knowing that in that case the children would have been sent out, she would turn her steps in a direction where she would be sure to meet them, and would go for a walk with them. There had been some one in the house who had been anxious at an early stage to open her eyes to the nature of her father's relations with Frau K., and to induce her to take sides against her. This was her last governess, an unmarried woman, no longer young, who was well-read and of advanced views.[7] The teacher and her pupil were for a while upon excellent terms, until suddenly Dora became hostile to her and insisted on her dismissal. So long as the governess had any influence she used it for stirring up feeling against Frau K. She explained to Dora's mother that it was incompatible with her dignity to tolerate such an intimacy between her husband and another woman; and she drew Dora's attention to all the obvious features of their relations. But her efforts were vain. Dora remained devoted to Frau K. and would hear of nothing that might make her think ill of her relations with her father. On the other hand she very easily fathomed the motives by which her governess was actuated. She might be blind in one direction, but she was sharp-sighted enough in the other. She saw that the governess was in love with her father. When he was there, she seemed to be quite another person: at such times she could be amusing and obliging. While the family were living in the manufacturing town and Frau K. was not on the horizon, her hostility was directed against Dora's mother, who was then her more immediate rival. Up to this point Dora bore her no ill-will. She did not become angry until she observed that she herself was a subject of complete indifference to the governess, whose pretended affection for her was really meant for her father. While her father was away from the manufacturing town the governess had no time to spare for her, would not go for walks with her, and took no interest in her studies. No sooner had her father returned from B—— than she was once more ready with every sort of service and assistance. Thereupon Dora dropped her.

The poor woman had thrown a most unwelcome light on a part of Dora's own behaviour. What the governess had from time to time been to Dora, Dora had been to Herr K.'s children. She had been a mother to them, she had taught them, she had gone for walks with them, she had offered them a complete substitute for the slight interest which their own mother showed in them. Herr K. and his wife had often talked of getting a divorce; but it never took place, because Herr K., who was an affectionate father, would not give up either of the two children. A common interest in the children had from the first been a bond between Herr K. and Dora. Her preoccupation

---

7. This governess used to read every sort of book on sexual life and similar subjects, and talked to the girl about them, at the same time asking her quite frankly not to mention their conversations to her parents, as one could never tell what line they might take about them. For some time I looked upon this woman as the source of all Dora's secret knowledge, and perhaps I was not entirely wrong in this [Freud's note].

with his children was evidently a cloak for something else that Dora was anxious to hide from herself and from other people.

The same inference was to be drawn both from her behaviour towards the children, regarded in the light of the governess's behaviour towards herself, and from her silent acquiescence in her father's relations with Frau K.— namely, that she had all these years been in love with Herr K. When I informed her of this conclusion she did not assent to it. It is true that she at once told me that other people besides (one of her cousins, for instance—a girl who had stopped with them for some time at B——) had said to her: "Why you're simply wild about that man!" But she herself could not be got to recollect any feelings of the kind. Later on, when the quantity of material that had come up had made it difficult for her to persist in her denial, she admitted that she might have been in love with Herr K. at B——, but declared that since the scene by the lake it had all been over. In any case it was quite certain that the reproaches which she made against her father of having been deaf to the most imperative calls of duty and of having seen things in the light which was most convenient from the point of view of his own passions—these reproaches recoiled on her own head.[8]

Her other reproach against her father was that his ill-health was only a pretext and that he exploited it for his own purposes. This reproach, too, concealed a whole section of her own secret history. One day she complained of a professedly new symptom, which consisted of piercing gastric pains. "Whom are you copying now?" I asked her, and found I had hit the mark. The day before she had visited her cousins, the daughters of the aunt who had died. The younger one had become engaged, and this had given occasion to the elder one for falling ill with gastric pains, and she was to be sent off to Semmering.[9] Dora thought it was all just envy on the part of the elder sister; she always got ill when she wanted something, and what she wanted now was to be away from home so as not to have to look on at her sister's happiness.[1] But Dora's own gastric pains proclaimed the fact that she identified herself with her cousin, who, according to her, was a malingerer. Her grounds for this identification were either that she too envied the luckier girl her love, or that she saw her own story reflected in that of the elder sister, who had recently had a love-affair which had ended unhappily. But she had also learned from observing Frau K. what useful things illnesses could become. Herr K. spent part of the year in travelling. Whenever he came back, he used to find his wife in bad health, although, as Dora knew, she had been quite well only the day before. Dora realized that the presence of the husband had the effect of making his wife ill, and that she was glad to be ill so as to be able to escape the conjugal duties which she so much detested. At this point in the discussion Dora suddenly brought in an allusion to her own alternations between good and bad health during the first years of her girl-hood at B——; and I was thus driven to suspect that her states of health were to be regarded as depending upon something else, in the same way as Frau K.'s. (It is a rule of psycho-analytic technique that an internal connec-

---

8. The question then arises: If Dora loved Herr K., what was the reason for her refusing him in the scene by the lake? Or at any rate, why did her refusal take such a brutal form, as though she were embittered against him? And how could a girl who was in love feel insulted by a proposal which was made in a manner neither tactless nor offensive? [Freud's note].   9. A fashionable health resort in the mountains near Vienna.   1. An event of everyday occurrence between sisters [Freud's note].

tion which is still undisclosed will announce its presence by means of a contiguity—a temporal proximity—of associations; just as in writing, if "a" and "b" are put side by side, it means that the syllable "ab" is to be formed out of them.) Dora had had a very large number of attacks of coughing accompanied by loss of voice. Could it be that the presence or absence of the man she loved had had an influence upon the appearance and disappearance of the symptoms of her illness? If this were so, it must be possible to discover some coincidence or other which would betray the fact. I asked her what the average length of these attacks had been. "From three to six weeks, perhaps." How long had Herr K.'s absences lasted? "Three to six weeks, too," she was obliged to admit. Her illness was therefore a demonstration of her love for K., just as his wife's was a demonstration of her *dislike*. It was only necessary to suppose that her behaviour had been the opposite of Frau K.'s and that she had been ill when he was absent and well when he had come back. And this really seemed to have been so, at least during the first period of the attacks. Later on it no doubt became necessary to obscure the coincidence between her attacks of illness and the absence of the man she secretly loved, lest its regularity should betray her secret. The length of the attacks would then remain as a trace of their original significance.

I remembered that long before, while I was working at Charcot's[2] clinic, I had seen and heard how in cases of hysterical mutism writing operated vicariously in the place of speech. Such patients were able to write more fluently, quicker, and better than others did or than they themselves had done previously. The same thing had happened with Dora. In the first days of her attacks of aphonia "writing had always come specially easy to her." No psychological elucidation was really required for this peculiarity, which was the expression of a physiological substitutive function enforced by necessity; it was noticeable, however, that such an elucidation was easily to be found. Herr K. used to write to her at length while he was travelling and to send her picture post-cards. It used to happen that she alone was informed as to the date of his return, and that his arrival took his wife by surprise. Moreover, that a person will correspond with an absent friend whom he cannot talk to is scarcely less obvious than that if he has lost his voice he will try to make himself understood in writing. Dora's aphonia, then, allowed of the following symbolic interpretation. When the man she loved was away she gave up speaking; speech had lost its value since she could not speak to *him*. On the other hand, writing gained in importance, as being the only means of communication with him in his absence.

Am I now going on to assert that in every instance in which there are periodical attacks of aphonia we are to diagnose the existence of a loved person who is at times away from the patient? Nothing could be further from my intention. The determination of Dora's symptoms is far too specific for it to be possible to expect a frequent recurrence of the same accidental aetiology. But, if so, what is the value of our elucidation of the aphonia in the present case? Have we not merely allowed ourselves to become the victims of a *jeu d'esprit*?[3] I think not. In this connection we must recall the question which has so often been raised, whether the symptoms of hysteria

2. Jean-Martin Charcot (1825–1893), French neurologist famous for his research on hysteria and hypnosis. Freud worked at his clinic from 1885 to 1886.   **3.** Play of the mind (French, literal trans.); mental acrobatics.

are of psychical or of somatic origin, or whether, if the former is granted, they are necessarily *all* of them psychically determined. Like so many other questions to which we find investigators returning again and again without success, this question is not adequately framed. The alternatives stated in it do not cover the real essence of the matter. As far as I can see, every hysterical symptom involves the participation of *both* sides. It cannot occur without the presence of a certain degree of *somatic compliance* offered by some normal or pathological process in or connected with one of the bodily organs. And it cannot occur more than once—and the capacity for repeating itself is one of the characteristics of a hysterical symptom—unless it has a psychical significance, a *meaning*. The hysterical symptom does not carry this meaning with it, but the meaning is lent to it, soldered to it, as it were; and in every instance the meaning can be a different one, according to the nature of the suppressed thoughts which are struggling for expression. However, there are a number of factors at work which tend to make less arbitrary the relations between the unconscious thoughts and the somatic processes that are at their disposal as a means of expression, and which tend to make those relations approximate to a few typical forms. For therapeutic purposes the most important determinants are those given by the fortuitous psychical material; the clearing-up of the symptoms is achieved by looking for their psychical significance. When everything that can be got rid of by psychoanalysis has been cleared away, we are in a position to form all kinds of conjectures, which probably meet the facts, as regards the somatic basis of the symptoms—a basis which is as a rule constitutional and organic. Thus in Dora's case we shall not content ourselves with a psycho-analytic interpretation of her attacks of coughing and aphonia; but we shall also indicate the organic factor which was the source of the "somatic compliance" that enabled her to express her love for a man who was periodically absent. And if the connection between the symptomatic expression and the unconscious mental content should strike us as being in this case a clever *tour de force,* we shall be relieved to hear that it succeeds in creating the same impression in every other case and in every other instance.

I am prepared to be told at this point that there is no very great advantage in having been taught by psycho-analysis that the clue to the problem of hysteria is to be found not in "a peculiar instability of the molecules of the nerves" or in a liability to "hypnoid states"—but in a "somatic compliance." But in reply to the objection I may remark that this new view has not only to some extent pushed the problem further back, but has also to some extent diminished it. We have no longer to deal with the *whole* problem, but only with the portion of it involving that particular characteristic of hysteria *which differentiates it* from other psychoneuroses. The mental events in all psychoneuroses proceed for a considerable distance along the same lines before any question arises of the "somatic compliance" which may afford the unconscious mental processes a physical outlet. When this factor is not forthcoming, something other than a hysterical symptom will arise out of the total situation; yet it will still be something of an allied nature, a phobia, perhaps, or an obsession—in short, a psychical symptom.

I now return to the reproach of malingering which Dora brought against her father. It soon became evident that this reproach corresponded to self-reproaches not only concerning her earlier states of ill-health but also concerning the present time. At such points the physician is usually faced by the task of guessing and filling in what the analysis offers him in the shape only of hints and allusions. I was obliged to point out to the patient that her present ill-health was just as much actuated by motives and was just as tendentious as had been Frau K.'s illness, which she had understood so well. There could be no doubt, I said, that she had an aim in view which she hoped to gain by her illness. That aim could be none other than to detach her father from Frau K. She had been unable to achieve this by prayers or arguments; perhaps she hoped to succeed by frightening her father (there was her fare-well letter), or by awakening his pity (there were her fainting-fits), or if all this was in vain, at least she would be taking her revenge on him. She knew very well, I went on, how much he was attached to her, and that tears used to come into his eyes whenever he was asked after his daughter's health. I felt quite convinced that she would recover at once if only her father were to tell her that he had sacrificed Frau K. for the sake of her health. But, I added, I hoped he would not let himself be persuaded to do this, for then she would have learned what a powerful weapon she had in her hands, and she would certainly not fail on every future occasion to make use once more of her liability to ill-health. Yet if her father refused to give way to her, I was quite sure she would not let herself be deprived of her illness so easily.

I will pass over the details which showed how entirely correct all of this was, and I will instead add a few general remarks upon the part played in hysteria by the *motives of illness*. A *motive* for being ill is sharply to be distinguished as a concept from a *liability* to being ill—from the material out of which symptoms are formed. The motives have no share in the formation of symptoms, and indeed are not present at the beginning of the illness. They only appear secondarily to it; but it is not until they have appeared that the disease is fully constituted. Their presence can be reckoned upon in every case in which there is real suffering and which is of fairly long standing. A symptom comes into the patient's mental life at first as an unwelcome guest; it has everything against it; and that is why it may vanish so easily, apparently of its own accord, under the influence of time. To begin with there is no use to which it can be put in the domestic economy of the mind; but very often it succeeds in finding one secondarily. Some psychical current or other finds it convenient to make use of it, and in that way the symptom manages to obtain a *secondary function* and remains, as it were, anchored fast in the patient's mental life. And so it happens that any one who tries to make him well is to his astonishment brought up against a powerful resistance, which teaches him that the patient's intention of getting rid of his complaint is not so entirely and completely serious as it seemed. Let us imagine a workman, a bricklayer, let us say, who has fallen off a house and been crippled, and now earns his livelihood by begging at the street-corner. Let us then suppose that a miracle-worker comes along and promises him to make his crooked leg straight and capable of walking. It would be unwise, I think, to look forward to seeing an expression of peculiar bliss upon the man's features. No doubt at the time of the accident he felt he was extremely unlucky, when he realized that he would never be able to do any more work and would have to starve or live upon charity. But since then the very thing which in the first instance threw him out of employment has become his source of income: he lives by his disablement. If that is taken from him he may become totally helpless. He has in the meantime forgotten his trade and lost his habits of industry; he has grown accustomed to idleness, and perhaps to drink as well.

The motives for being ill often begin to be active even in childhood. A little girl in her greed for love does not enjoy having to share the affection of her parents with her brothers and sisters; and she notices that the whole of their affection is lavished on her once more whenever she arouses their anxiety by falling ill. She has now discovered a means of enticing out her parents' love, and will make use of that means as soon as she has the necessary psychical material at her disposal for producing an illness. When such a child has grown up to be a woman she may find all the demands she used to make in her childhood countered owing to her marriage with an inconsiderate husband, who may subjugate her will, mercilessly exploit her capacity for work, and lavish neither his affection nor his money upon her. In that case ill-health will be her one weapon for maintaining her position. It will procure her the care she longs for; it will force her husband to make pecuniary sacrifices for her and to show her consideration, as he would never have done while she was well; and it will compel him to treat her with solicitude if she recovers, for otherwise a relapse will threaten. Her state of ill-health will have every appearance of being objective and involuntary—the very doctor who treats her will bear witness to the fact; and for that reason she will not need to feel any conscious self-reproaches at making such successful use of a means which she had found effective in her years of childhood.

And yet illnesses of this kind *are* the result of intention. They are as a rule levelled at a particular person, and consequently vanish with that person's departure. The crudest and most commonplace views on the character of hysterical disorders—such as are to be heard from uneducated relatives or nurses—are in a certain sense right. It is true that the paralysed and bedridden woman would spring to her feet if a fire were to break out in her room, and that the spoiled wife would forget all her sufferings if her child were to fall dangerously ill or if some catastrophe were to threaten the family circumstances. People who speak of the patients in this way are right except upon a single point: they overlook the psychological distinction between what is conscious and what is unconscious. This may be permissible where children are concerned, but with adults it is no longer possible. That is why all these asseverations that it is "only a question of willing" and all the encouragements and abuse that are addressed to the patient are of no avail. An attempt must first be made by the roundabout methods of analysis to convince the patient herself of the existence in her of an intention to be ill.

It is in combating the motives of illness that the weak point in every kind of therapeutic treatment of hysteria lies. This is quite generally true, and it applies equally to psycho-analysis. Destiny has an easier time of it in this respect: it need not concern itself either with the patient's constitution or with his pathogenic material; it has only to take away a motive for being ill, and the patient is temporarily or perhaps even permanently freed from his illness. How many fewer miraculous cures and spontaneous disappearances of symptoms should we physicians have to register in cases of hysteria, if we were more often given a sight of the human interests which the patient keeps hidden from us! In one case, some stated period of time has elapsed; in a second, consideration for some other person has ceased to operate; in a third, the situation has been fundamentally changed by some external event—and the whole disorder, which up till then had shown the greatest obstinacy, vanishes at a single blow, apparently of its own accord, but really because it has been deprived of its most powerful motive, one of the uses to which it has been put in the patient's life.

Motives that support the patient in being ill are probably to be found in all fully developed cases. But there are some in which the motives are purely internal—such as desire for self-punishment, that is, penitence and remorse. It will be found much easier to solve the therapeutic problem in such cases than in those in which the illness is related to the attainment of some external aim. In Dora's case that aim was clearly to touch her father's heart and to detach him from Frau K.

None of her father's actions seemed to have embittered her so much as his readiness to consider the scene by the lake as a product of her imagination. She was almost beside herself at the idea of its being supposed that she had merely fancied something on that occasion. For a long time I was in perplexity as to what the self-reproach could be which lay behind her passionate repudiation of this explanation of the episode. It was justifiable to suspect that there was something concealed, for a reproach which misses the mark gives no lasting offence. On the other hand, I came to the conclusion that Dora's story must correspond to the facts in every respect. No sooner had she grasped Herr K.'s intention than, without letting him finish what he had to say, she had given him a slap in the face and hurried away. Her behaviour must have seemed as incomprehensible to the man after she had left him as to us, for he must long before have gathered from innumerable small signs that he was secure of the girl's affections. In our discussion of Dora's second dream we shall come upon the solution of this riddle as well as upon the self-reproach which we have hitherto failed to discover.

As she kept on repeating her complaints against her father with a wearisome monotony, and as at the same time her cough continued, I was led to think that this symptom might have some meaning in connection with her father. And apart from this, the explanation of the symptom which I had hitherto obtained was far from fulfilling the requirements which I am accustomed to make of such explanations. According to a rule which I had found confirmed over and over again by experience, though I had not yet ventured to erect it into a general principle, a symptom signifies the representation—the realization—of a phantasy with a sexual content, that is to say, it signifies a sexual situation. It would be better to say that at least *one* of the meanings of a symptom is the representation of a sexual phantasy, but that no such limitation is imposed upon the content of its other meanings. Any one who takes up psycho-analytic work will quickly discover that a symptom has more than one meaning and served to represent several unconscious mental processes simultaneously. And I should like to add that in my estimation a single unconscious mental process or phantasy will scarcely ever suffice for the production of a symptom.

An opportunity very soon occurred for interpreting Dora's nervous cough in this way by means of an imagined sexual situation. She had once again been insisting that Frau K. only loved her father because he was *"ein ver-*

mögender Mann."[4] Certain details of the way in which she expressed herself (which I pass over here, like most other purely technical parts of the analysis) led me to see that behind this phrase its opposite lay concealed, namely, that her father was *"ein unvermögender Mann."*[5] This could only be meant in a sexual sense—that her father, as a man, was without means, was impotent. Dora confirmed this interpretation from her conscious language; whereupon I pointed out the contradiction she was involved in if on the one hand she continued to insist that her father's relation with Frau K. was a common love-affair, and on the other hand maintained that her father was impotent, or in other words incapable of carrying on an affair of such a kind. Her answer showed that she had no need to admit the contradiction. She knew very well, she said, that there was more than one way of obtaining sexual gratification. (The source of this piece of knowledge, however, was once more untraceable.) I questioned her further, whether she referred to the use of organs other than the genitals for the purpose of sexual intercourse, and she replied in the affirmative. I could then go on to say that in that case she must be thinking of precisely those parts of the body which in her case were in a state of irritation,—the throat and the oral cavity. To be sure, she would not hear of going so far as this in recognizing her own thoughts; and indeed, if the occurrence of the symptom was to be made possible at all, it was essential that she should not be completely clear on the subject. But the conclusion was inevitable that with her spasmodic cough, which, as is usual, was referred for its exciting stimulus to a tickling in her throat, she pictured to herself a scene of sexual gratification *per os*[6] between the two people whose love-affair occupied her mind so incessantly. A very short time after she had tacitly accepted this explanation her cough vanished—which fitted in very well with my view; but I do not wish to lay too much stress upon this development, since her cough had so often before disappeared spontaneously.

This short piece of the analysis may perhaps have excited in the medical reader—apart from the scepticism to which he is entitled—feelings of astonishment and horror; and I am prepared at this point to look into these two reactions so as to discover whether they are justifiable. The astonishment is probably caused by my daring to talk about such delicate and unpleasant subjects to a young girl—or, for that matter, to any woman who is sexually active. The horror is aroused, no doubt, by the possibility that an inexperienced girl could know about practices of such a kind and could occupy her imagination with them. I would advise recourse to moderation and reasonableness upon both points. There is no cause for indignation either in the one case or in the other. It is possible for a man to talk to girls and women upon sexual matters of every kind without doing them harm and without bringing suspicion upon himself, so long as, in the first place, he adopts a particular way of doing it, and, in the second place, can make them feel convinced that it is unavoidable. A gynaecologist, after all, under the same conditions, does not hesitate to make them submit to uncovering every possible part of their body. The best way of speaking about such things is to be

---

4. A man of means (German).   5. A man without means. *Unvermögend* means literally "unable" and is commonly used in the sense of both "not rich" and "impotent."   6. Orally (Latin).

dry and direct; and that is at the same time the method furthest removed from the prurience with which the same subjects are handled in "society," and to which girls and women alike are so thoroughly accustomed. I call bodily organs and processes by their technical names, and I tell these to the patient if they—the names, I mean—happen to be unknown to her. *J'appelle un chat un chat.*[7] I have certainly heard of some people—doctors and lay-men—who are scandalized by a therapeutic method in which conversations of this sort occur, and who appear to envy either me or my patients the titillation which, according to their notions, such a method must afford. But I am too well acquainted with the respectability of these gentry to excite myself over them. I shall avoid the temptation of writing a satire upon them. But there is one thing that I will mention: often, after I have for some time treated a patient who had not at first found it easy to be open about sexual matters, I have had the satisfaction of hearing her exclaim: "Why, after all, your treatment is far more respectable than Mr. X.'s conversation!"

No one can undertake the treatment of a case of hysteria until he is convinced of the impossibility of avoiding the mention of sexual subjects, or unless he is prepared to allow himself to be convinced by experience. The right attitude is: *"pour faire une omelette il faut casser des œufs."*[8] The patients themselves are easy to convince; and there are only too many opportunities of doing so in the course of the treatment. There is no necessity for feeling any compunction at discussing the facts of normal or abnormal sexual life with them. With the exercise of a little caution all that is done is to translate into conscious ideas what was already known in the unconscious; and, after all, the whole effectiveness of the treatment is based upon our knowledge that the affect attached to an unconscious idea operates more strongly and, since it cannot be inhibited, more injuriously than the affect attached to a conscious one. There is never any danger of corrupting an inexperienced girl. For where there is no knowledge of sexual processes even in the unconscious, no hysterical symptom will arise; and where hysteria is found there can no longer be any question of "innocence of mind" in the sense in which parents and educators use the phrase. With children of ten, of twelve, or of fourteen, with boys and girls alike, I have satisfied myself that the truth of this statement can invariably be relied upon.

As regards the second kind of emotional reaction, which is not directed against me this time, but against my patient—supposing that my view of her is correct—and which regards the perverse nature of her phantasies as horrible, I should like to say emphatically that a medical man has no business to indulge in such passionate condemnation. I may also remark in passing that it seems to me superfluous for a physician who is writing upon the aberrations of the sexual instincts to seize every opportunity of inserting into the text expressions of his personal repugnance at such revolting things. We are faced by a fact; and it is to be hoped that we shall grow accustomed to it, when we have put our own tastes on one side. We must learn to speak without indignation of what we call the sexual perversions—instances in which the sexual function has extended its limits in respect either to the part of the body concerned or to the sexual object chosen. The uncertainty in

---

7. I call a cat a cat (French, literal trans.), i.e., call a spade a spade.   8. You can't make an omelet without breaking eggs (French).

regard to the boundaries of what is to be called normal sexual life, when we take different races and different epochs into account, should in itself be enough to cool the zealot's ardour. We surely ought not to forget that the perversion which is the most repellent to us, the sensual love of a man for a man, was not only tolerated by a people so far our superiors in cultivation as were the Greeks, but was actually entrusted by them with important social functions. The sexual life of each one of us extends to a slight degree—now in this direction, now in that—beyond the narrow lines imposed as the standard of normality. The perversions are neither bestial nor degenerate in the emotional sense of the word. They are a development of germs all of which are contained in the undifferentiated sexual disposition of the child, and which, by being suppressed or by being diverted to higher, asexual aims—by being "sublimated"—are destined to provide the energy for a great number of our cultural achievements.

* * *

[A discussion follows of the difference between psychoneuroses and perversions, of Dora's thumb sucking, and of the possibility for symptoms to change in meaning.]

Dora's incessant repetition of the same thoughts about her father's relations with Frau K. made it possible to derive still further important material from the analysis.

A train of thought such as this may be described as excessively intense, or better *reinforced*, or "supervalent" in Wernicke's[9] sense. It shows its pathological character in spite of its apparently reasonable content, by the single peculiarity that no amount of conscious and voluntary effort of thought on the patient's part is able to dissipate or remove it. A normal train of thought, however intense it may be, can eventually be disposed of. Dora felt quite rightly that her thoughts about her father required to be judged in a special way. "I can think of nothing else," she complained again and again. "I know my brother says we children have no right to criticize this behaviour of Father's. He declares that we ought not to trouble ourselves about it, and ought even to be glad, perhaps, that he has found a woman he can love, since Mother understands him so little. I can quite see that, and I should like to think the same as my brother, but I can't. I can't forgive him for it."[1]

Now what is one to do in the face of a supervalent thought like this, after one has heard what its conscious grounds are and listened to the ineffectual protests made against it? Reflection will suggest that *this excessively intense train of thought must owe its reinforcement to the unconscious.* It cannot be resolved by any effort of thought, either because it itself reaches with its root down into unconscious, repressed material, or because another unconscious thought lies concealed behind it. In the latter case, the concealed thought is usually the direct contrary of the supervalent one. Contrary thoughts are always closely connected with each other and are often paired off in such a way that *the one thought is excessively conscious while its counterpart is repressed and unconscious.* This relation between the two thoughts is an effect of the process of repression. For repression is often achieved by means

9. Carl Wernicke (1848–1905), German neurologist.   1. A supervalent thought of this kind is often the only symptom, beyond deep depression, of a pathological condition which is usually described as "melancholia," but which can be cleared up by psycho-analysis like a hysteria [Freud's note].

of an excessive reinforcement of the thought contrary to the one which is to be repressed. This process I call *reactive* reinforcement, and the thought which asserts itself with excessive intensity in consciousness and (in the same way as a prejudice) cannot be removed I call a *reactive thought*. The two thoughts then act towards each other much like the two needles of an astatic galvanometer. The reactive thought keeps the objectionable one under repression by means of a certain surplus of intensity; but for that reason it itself is "damped" and proof against conscious efforts of thought. So that the way to deprive the excessively intense thought of its reinforcement is by bringing its repressed contrary into consciousness.

We must also be prepared to meet with instances in which the supervalence of a thought is due not to the presence of one only of these two causes but to a concurrence of both of them. Other complications, too, may arise, but they can easily be fitted into the general scheme.

Let us now apply our theory to the instance provided by Dora's case. We will begin with the first hypothesis, namely, that her preoccupation with her father's relations to Frau K. owed its obsessive character to the fact that its root was unknown to her and lay in the unconscious. It is not difficult to divine the nature of that root from her circumstances and her conduct. Her behaviour obviously went far beyond what would have been appropriate to filial concern. She felt and acted more like a jealous wife—in a way which would have been comprehensible in her mother. By her ultimatum to her father ("either her or me"), by the scenes she used to make, by the suicidal intentions she allowed to transpire—by all this she was clearly putting herself in her mother's place. If we have rightly guessed the nature of the imaginary sexual situation which underlay her cough, in that phantasy she must have been putting herself in Frau K.'s place. She was therefore identifying herself both with the woman her father had once loved and with the woman he loved now. The inference is obvious that her affection for her father was a much stronger one than she knew or than she would have cared to admit: in fact, that she was in love with him.

I have learnt to look upon unconscious love relations like this (which are marked by their abnormal consequences)—between a father and a daughter, or between a mother and a son—as a revival of germs of feeling in infancy. I have shown at length elsewhere at what an early age sexual attraction makes itself felt between parents and children, and I have explained that the legend of Oedipus is probably to be regarded as a poetical rendering of what is typical in these relations. Distinct traces are probably to be found in most people of an early partiality of this kind—on the part of a daughter for her father, or on the part of a son for his mother; but it must be assumed to be more intense from the very first in the case of those children whose constitution marks them down for a neurosis, who develop prematurely and have a craving for love. At this point certain other influences, which need not be discussed here, come into play, and lead to a fixation of this rudimentary feeling of love or to a reinforcement of it; so that it turns into something (either while the child is still young or not until it has reached the age of puberty) which must be put on a par with a sexual inclination and which, like the latter, has the forces of the libido at its command. The external circumstances of our patient were by no means unfavourable to such an assumption. The nature of her disposition had always drawn her towards her father, and his numerous illnesses were bound to have increased her affection for him. In some of these illnesses he would allow no one but her to discharge the lighter duties of nursing. He had been so proud of the early growth of her intelligence that he had made her his confidante while she was still a child. It was really she and not her mother whom Frau K.'s appearance had driven out of more than one position.

When I told Dora that I could not avoid supposing that her affection for her father must at a very early moment have amounted to her being completely in love with him, she of course gave me her usual reply: "I don't remember that." But she immediately went on to tell me something analogous about a seven-year-old girl who was her cousin (on her mother's side) and in whom she often thought she saw a kind of reflection of her own childhood. This little girl had (not for the first time) been the witness of a heated dispute between her parents, and, when Dora happened to come in on a visit soon afterwards, whispered in her ear: "You can't think how I hate that person!" (pointing to her mother), "and when she's dead I shall marry Daddy." I am in the habit of regarding associations such as this, which bring forward something that agrees with the content of an assertion of mine, as a confirmation from the unconscious of what I have said. No other kind of "Yes" can be extracted from the unconscious; there is no such thing at all as an unconscious "No."[2]

For years on end she had given no expression to this passion for her father. On the contrary, she had for a long time been on the closest terms with the woman who had supplanted her with her father, and she had actually, as we know from her self-reproaches, facilitated this woman's relations with her father. Her own love for her father had therefore been recently revived; and, if so, the question arises to what end this had happened. Clearly as a reactive symptom, so as to suppress something else—something, that is, that still exercised power in the unconscious. Considering how things stood, I could not help supposing in the first instance that what was suppressed was her love of Herr K. I could not avoid the assumption that she was still in love with him, but that, for unknown reasons, since the scene by the lake her love had aroused in her violent feelings of opposition, and that the girl had brought forward and reinforced her old affection for her father in order to avoid any further necessity for paying conscious attention to the love which she had felt in the first years of her girlhood and which had now become distressing to her. In this way I gained an insight into a conflict which was well calculated to unhinge the girl's mind. On the one hand she was filled with regret at having rejected the man's proposal, and with longing for his company and all the little signs of his affection; while on the other hand these feelings of tenderness and longing were combated by powerful forces, amongst which her pride was one of the most obvious. Thus she had succeeded in persuading herself that she had done with Herr K.—that was the advantage she derived from this typical process of repression; and yet she

2. There is another very remarkable and entirely trustworthy form of confirmation from the unconscious, which I had not recognized at the time this was written: namely, an exclamation on the part of the patient of "I didn't think that," or "I didn't think of that." This can be translated point-blank into: "Yes, I was unconscious of that" [Freud's note, added 1923].

was obliged to summon up her infantile affection for her father and to exaggerate it, in order to protect herself against the feelings of love which were constantly pressing forward into consciousness. The further fact that she was almost incessantly a prey to the most embittered jealousy seemed to admit of still another determination.[3]

My expectations were by no means disappointed when this explanation of mine was met by Dora with a most emphatic negative. The "No" uttered by a patient after a repressed thought has been presented to his conscious perception for the first time does no more than register the existence of a repression and its severity; it acts, as it were, as a gauge of the repression's strength. If this "No," instead of being regarded as the expression of an impartial judgement (of which, indeed, the patient is incapable), is ignored, and if work is continued, the first evidence soon begins to appear that in such a case "No" signifies the desired "Yes." Dora admitted that she found it impossible to be as angry with Herr K. as he had deserved. She told me that one day she had met Herr K. in the street while she was walking with a cousin of hers who did not know him. The other girl had exclaimed all at once: "Why, Dora, what's wrong with you? You've gone as white as a sheet!" She herself had felt nothing of this change of colour; but I explained to her that the expression of emotion and the play of features obey the unconscious rather than the conscious, and are a means of betraying the former.[4] Another time Dora came to me in the worst of tempers after having been uniformly cheerful for several days. She could give no explanation of this. She felt so contrary today, she said; it was her uncle's birthday, and she could not bring herself to congratulate him, she did not know why. My powers of interpretation were at a low ebb that day; I let her go on talking, and she suddenly recollected that it was Herr K.'s birthday too—a fact which I did not fail to use against her. And it was then no longer hard to explain why the handsome presents she had had on her own birthday a few days before had given her no pleasure. One gift was missing, and that was Herr K.'s, the gift which had plainly once been the most prized of all.

Nevertheless Dora persisted in denying my contention for some time longer, until, towards the end of the analysis, the conclusive proof of its correctness came to light.

I must now turn to consider a further complication to which I should certainly give no space if I were a man of letters engaged upon the creation of a mental state like this for a short story, instead of being a medical man engaged upon its dissection. The element to which I must now allude can only serve to obscure and efface the outlines of the fine poetic conflict which we have been able to ascribe to Dora. This element would rightly fall a sacrifice to the censorship of a writer, for he, after all, simplifies and abstracts when he appears in the character of a psychologist. But in the world of reality, which I am trying to depict here, a complication of motives, an accumulation and conjunction of mental activities—in a word, over-

---

3. We shall come upon this [in a moment] [Freud's note].   4. Compare the lines: "Ruhing mag ich Euch erscheinen, / Ruhig gehen sehn" [Freud's note]: "Quietly can I watch your coming, / Quietly watch you go" (German). Freud refers to a scene at the beginning of "Ritter Toggenburg," a ballad of love between brother and sister by Friedrich von Schiller (1759–1805) in which the sister hides her emotion from her tearful brother as he departs for the Crusades.

determination—is the rule. For behind Dora's supervalent train of thought which was concerned with her father's relations with Frau K. there lay concealed a feeling of jealousy which had that lady as its *object*—a feeling, that is, which could only be based upon an affection on Dora's part for one of her own sex. It has long been known and often been pointed out that at the age of puberty boys and girls show clear signs, even in normal cases, of the existence of an affection for people of their own sex. A romantic and sentimental friendship with one of her school-friends, accompanied by vows, kisses, promises of eternal correspondence, and all the sensibility of jealousy, is the common precursor of a girl's first serious passion for a man. Thenceforward, in favourable circumstances, the homosexual current of feeling often runs completely dry.

*   *   *

[Examples follow of Dora's estrangement from her governess and Frau K.]

I then found that the young woman[5] and the scarcely grown girl had lived for years on a footing of the closest intimacy. When Dora stayed with the K.'s she used to share a bedroom with Frau K., and the husband used to be quartered elsewhere. She had been the wife's confidante and adviser in all the difficulties of her married life. There was nothing they had not talked about. Medea[6] had been quite content that Creusa should make friends with her two children; and she certainly did nothing to interfere with the relations between the girl and the children's father. How Dora managed to fall in love with the man about whom her beloved friend had so many bad things to say is an interesting psychological problem. We shall not be far from solving it when we realize that thoughts in the unconscious live very comfortably side by side, and even contraries get on together without disputes—a state of things which persists often enough even in the conscious.

When Dora talked about Frau K., she used to praise her "adorable white body" in accents more appropriate to a lover than to a defeated rival. Another time she told me, more in sorrow than in anger, that she was convinced the presents her father had brought her had been chosen by Frau K., for she recognized her taste. Another time, again, she pointed out that, evidently through the agency of Frau K., she had been given a present of some jewellery which was exactly like some that she had seen in Frau K.'s possession and had wished for aloud at the time. Indeed, I can say in general that I never heard her speak a harsh or angry word against the lady, although from the point of view of her supervalent thought she should have regarded her as the prime author of her misfortunes. She seemed to behave inconsequently; but her apparent inconsequence was precisely the manifestation of a complicating current of feeling. For how had this woman to whom Dora was so enthusiastically devoted behaved to her? After Dora had brought forward her accusation against Herr K., and her father had written to him and had asked for an explanation, Herr K. had replied in the first instance by protesting sentiments of the highest esteem for her and by proposing that he should come to the manufacturing town to clear up every misunderstand-

---

5. Frau K.   6. In Euripides' play *Medea* (431 B.C.), the sorceress Medea takes revenge on her unfaithful husband, Jason, by killing their two children and the king's daughter Creusa, whom Jason had planned to marry after discarding his wife.

ing. A few weeks later, when her father spoke to him at B——, there was no longer any question of esteem. On the contrary, Herr K. spoke of her with disparagement, and produced as his trump card the reflection that no girl who read such books and was interested in such things could have any title to a man's respect. Frau K., therefore, had betrayed her and had calumniated her; for it had only been with her that she had read Mantegazza and discussed forbidden topics. It was a repetition of what had happened with the governess: Frau K. had not loved her for her own sake but on account of her father. Frau K. had sacrificed her without a moment's hesitation so that her relations with her father might not be disturbed. This mortification touched her, perhaps, more nearly and had a greater pathogenic effect than the other one, which she tried to use as a screen for it,—the fact that she had been sacrificed by her father. Did not the obstinacy with which she retained the particular amnesia concerning the sources of her forbidden knowledge point directly to the great emotional importance for her of the accusation against her upon that score, and consequently to her betrayal by her friend?

I believe, therefore, that I am not mistaken in supposing that Dora's supervalent train of thought, which was concerned with her father's relations with Frau K., was designed not only for the purpose of suppressing her love for Herr K., which had once been conscious, but also to conceal her love for Frau K., which was in a deeper sense unconscious. The supervalent train of thought was directly contrary to the latter current of feeling. She told herself incessantly that her father had sacrificed her to this woman, and made noisy demonstrations to show that she grudged her the possession of her father; and in this way she concealed from herself the contrary fact, which was that she grudged her father Frau K.'s love, and had not forgiven the woman she loved for the disillusionment she had been caused by her betrayal. The jealous emotions of a woman were linked in the unconscious with a jealousy such as might have been felt by a man. These masculine or, more properly speaking, *gynaecophilic*[7] currents of feeling are to be regarded as typical of the unconscious erotic life of hysterical girls.

II

The First Dream

Just at a moment when there was a prospect that the material that was coming up for analysis would throw light upon an obscure point in Dora's childhood, she reported that a few nights earlier she had once again had a dream which she had already dreamt in exactly the same way on many previous occasions. A periodically recurrent dream was by its very nature particularly well calculated to arouse my curiosity; and in any case it was justifiable in the interests of the treatment to consider the way in which the dream worked into the analysis as a whole. I therefore determined to make an especially careful investigation of it.

Here is the dream as related by Dora: "*A house was on fire.*[8] *My father was standing beside my bed and woke me up. I dressed quickly. Mother wanted to*

7. Woman-loving. 8. In answer to an inquiry Dora told me that there had never really been a fire at their house [Freud's note].

stop and save her jewel-case; but Father said: 'I refuse to let myself and my two children be burnt for the sake of your jewel-case.' We hurried downstairs, and as soon as I was outside I woke up."

As the dream was a recurrent one, I naturally asked her when she had first dreamt it. She told me she did not know. But she remembered having had the dream three nights in succession at L—— (the place on the lake where the scene with Herr K. had taken place), and it had now come back again a few nights earlier, here in Vienna.[9] My expectations from the clearing-up of the dream were naturally heightened when I heard of its connection with the events at L——. But I wanted to discover first what had been the exciting cause of its recent recurrence, and I therefore asked Dora to take the dream bit by bit and tell me what occurred to her in connection with it. She had already had some training in dream interpretation from having previously analysed a few minor specimens.

"Something occurs to me," she said, "but it cannot belong to the dream, for it is quite recent, whereas I have certainly had the dream before."

"That makes no difference," I replied. "Start away! It will simply turn out to be the most recent thing that fits in with the dream."

"Very well, then. Father has been having a dispute with Mother in the last few days, because she locks the dining-room door at night. My brother's room, you see, has no separate entrance, but can only be reached through the dining-room. Father does not want my brother to be locked in like that at night. He says it will not do: something might happen in the night so that it might be necessary to leave the room."

"And that made you think of the risk of fire?"

"Yes."

"Now, I should like you to pay close attention to the exact words you used. We may have to come back to them. You said that 'something might happen in the night so that it might be necessary to leave the room.'"[1]

But Dora had now discovered the connecting link between the recent exciting cause of the dream and the original one, for she continued:

"When we arrived at L—— that time, Father and I, he openly said he was afraid of fire. We arrived in a violent thunderstorm, and saw the small wooden house without any lightning-conductor. So his anxiety was quite natural."

What I now had to do was to establish the relation between the events at L—— and the recurrent dreams which she had had there. I therefore said: "Did you have the dream during your first nights at L—— or during your last ones? in other words, before or after the scene in the wood by the lake of which we have heard so much?" (I must explain that I knew that the scene had not occurred on the very first day, and that she had remained at L—— for a few days after it without giving any hint of the incident.)

Her first reply was that she did not know, but after a while she added: "Yes. I think it was after the scene."

9. The content of the dream makes it possible to establish that it in fact occurred *for the first time* at L—— [Freud's note].   1. I laid stress on these words because they took me aback. They seemed to have an ambiguous ring about them. Are not certain physical needs referred to in the same words? Now, in a line of associations ambiguous words (or, as we may call them, "switch-words") act like points at a junction. If the points are switched across from the position in which they appear to lie in the dream, then we find ourselves on another set of rails; and along this second track run the thoughts which we are in search of but which still lie concealed behind the dream [Freud's note].

So now I knew that the dream was a reaction to that experience. But why had it recurred there three times? I continued my questions: "How long did you stop on at L—— after the scene?"

"Four more nights. On the following day I went away with Father."

"Now I am certain that the dream was an immediate effect of your experience with Herr K. It was at L—— that you dreamed it for the first time, and not before. You have only introduced this uncertainty in your memory so as to obliterate the connection in your mind. But the figures do not quite fit in to my satisfaction yet. If you stayed at L—— for four nights longer, the dream might have occurred four times over. Perhaps this was so?"

She no longer disputed by contention; but instead of answering my question she proceeded:[2] "In the afternoon after our trip on the lake, from which we (Herr K. and I) returned at midday, I had gone to lie down as usual on the sofa in the bedroom to have a short sleep. I suddenly awoke and saw Herr K. standing beside me. . . ."

"In fact, just as you saw your father standing beside your bed in the dream?"

"Yes. I asked him sharply what it was he wanted there. By way of reply he said he was not going to be prevented from coming into his own bedroom when he wanted; besides, there was something he wanted to fetch. This episode put me on my guard, and I asked Frau K. whether there was not a key to the bedroom door. The next morning I locked myself in while I was dressing. That afternoon, when I wanted to lock myself in so as to lie down again on the sofa, the key was gone. I was convinced that Herr K. had removed it."

"Then here we have the theme of locking or not locking a room which appeared in the first association to the dream and also happened to occur in the exciting cause of the recent recurrence of the dream.[3] I wonder whether the phrase 'I dressed quickly' may not also belong to this context?"

"It was then that I made up my mind not to stop on with the K.'s without Father. On the subsequent mornings I could not help feeling afraid that Herr K. would surprise me while I was dressing: so I always dressed very quickly. You see, Father lived at the hotel, and Frau K. used always to go out early so as to go on expeditions with him. But Herr K. did not annoy me again."

"I understand. On the afternoon of the day after the scene in the wood you formed your intention of escaping from his persecution, and during the second, third, and fourth nights you had time to repeat that intention in your sleep. (You already knew on the second afternoon—before the dream, therefore—that you would not have the key on the following morning to lock yourself in with while you were dressing; and you could then form the design of dressing as quickly as possible.) But your dream recurred each night, for the very reason that it corresponded to an intention. An intention remains in existence until it has been carried out. You said to yourself, as it were: 'I shall have no rest and I can get no quiet sleep until I am out of this house.'

2. This was because a fresh piece of material had to emerge from her memory before the question I had put could be answered [Freud's note].   3. I suspected, though I did not as yet say so to Dora, that she had seized upon this element on account of a symbolic meaning which it possessed. "Zimmer" ["room"] in dreams stands very frequently for "Frauenzimmer" [a slightly derogatory word for "woman"; literally, "women's apartments"]. The question whether a woman is "open" or "shut" can naturally not be a matter of indifference. It is well known, too, what sort of "key" effects the opening in such a case [Freud's note].

In your account of the dream you turned it the other way and said: '*As soon as I was outside I woke up.*'"

At this point I shall interrupt my report of the analysis in order to compare this small piece of dream-interpretation with the general statements I have made upon the mechanism of the formation of dreams. I argued in my book, *The Interpretation of Dreams* (1900), that every dream is a wish which is represented as fulfilled, that the representation acts as a disguise if the wish is a repressed one, belonging to the unconscious, and that except in the case of children's dreams only an unconscious wish or one which reaches down into the unconscious has the force necessary for the formation of a dream. I fancy my theory would have been more certain of general acceptance if I had contented myself with maintaining that every dream had a meaning, which could be discovered by means of a certain process of interpretation; and that when the interpretation had been completed the dream could be replaced by thoughts which would fall into place at an easily recognizable point in the waking mental life of the dreamer. I might then have gone on to say that the meaning of a dream turned out to be of as many different sorts as the processes of waking thought; that in one case it would be a fulfilled wish, in another a realized fear, or again a reflection persisting on into sleep, or an intention (as in the instance of Dora's dream), or a piece of creative thought during sleep, and so on. Such a theory would no doubt have proved attractive from its very simplicity, and it might have been supported by a great many examples of dreams that had been satisfactorily interpreted, as for instance by the one which has been analysed in these pages.

But instead of this I formulated a generalization according to which the meaning of dreams is limited to a single form, to the representation of *wishes,* and by so doing I aroused a universal inclination to dissent. I must, however, observe that I did not consider it either my right or my duty to simplify a psychological process so as to make it more acceptable to my readers, when my researches had shown me that it presented a complication which could not be reduced to uniformity until the inquiry had been carried into another field. It is therefore of special importance to me to show that apparent exceptions—such as this dream of Dora's, which has shown itself in the first instance to be the continuation into sleep of an intention formed during the day—nevertheless lend fresh support to the rule which is in dispute.

Much of the dream, however, still remained to be interpreted, and I proceeded with my questions: "What is this about the jewel-case that your mother wanted to save?"

"Mother is very fond of jewellery and had had a lot given her by Father."

"And you?"

"I used to be very fond of jewellery too, once; but I have not worn any since my illness.—Once, four years ago" (a year before the dream), "Father and Mother had a great dispute about a piece of jewellery. Mother wanted to be given a particular thing—pearl drops to wear in her ears. But Father does not like that kind of thing, and he brought her a bracelet instead of the drops. She was furious, and told him that as he had spent so much money on a present she did not like he had better just give it to some one else."

"I dare say you thought to yourself you would accept it with pleasure."

"I don't know.[4] I don't in the least know how Mother comes into the dream; she was not with us at L—— at the time."[5]

"I will explain that to you presently. Does nothing else occur to you in connection with the jewel-case? So far you have only talked about jewellery and have said nothing about a case."

"Yes, Herr K. had made me a present of an expensive jewel-case a little time before."

"Then a return-present would have been very appropriate. Perhaps you do not know that 'jewel-case' is a favourite expression for the same thing that you alluded to not long ago by means of the reticule you were wearing—for the female genitals, I mean."

"I knew you would say that."[6]

"That is to say, you knew that it *was* so.—The meaning of the dream is now becoming even clearer. You said to yourself: 'This man is persecuting me; he wants to force his way into my room. My "jewel-case" is in danger, and if anything happens it will be Father's fault.' For that reason in the dream you chose a situation which expresses the opposite—a danger from which your father is *saving* you. In this part of the dream everything is turned into its opposite; you will soon discover why. As you say, the mystery turns upon your mother. You ask how she comes into the dream? She is, as you know, your former rival in your father's affections. In the incident of the bracelet, you would have been glad to accept what your mother had rejected. Now let us just put 'give' instead of 'accept' and 'withhold' instead of 'reject.' Then it means that you were ready to give your father what your mother withheld from him; and the thing in question was connected with jewellery. Now bring your mind back to the jewel-case which Herr K. gave you. You have there the starting-point for a parallel line of thoughts, in which Herr K. is to be put in the place of your father just as he was in the matter of standing beside your bed. He gave you a jewel-case; so you are to give him your jewel-case. That was why I spoke just now of a 'return-present.' In this line of thoughts your mother must be replaced by Frau K. (You will not deny that she, at any rate, was present at the time.) So you are ready to give Herr K. what his wife withholds from him. That is the thought which has had to be repressed with so much energy, and which has made it necessary for every one of its elements to be turned into its opposite. The dream confirms once more what I had already told you before you dreamt it—that you are summoning up your old love for your father in order to protect yourself against your love for Herr K. But what do all these efforts show? Not only that you are afraid of Herr K., but that you are still more afraid of yourself, and of the temptation you feel to yield to him. In short, these efforts prove once more how deeply you loved him."[7]

4. The regular formula with which she confessed to anything that had been repressed [Freud's note].
5. This remark gave evidence of a complete misunderstanding of the rules of dream-interpretation, though on other occasions Dora was perfectly familiar with them. This fact, coupled with the hesitancy and meagreness of her associations with the jewel-case, showed me that we were here dealing with material which had been very intensely repressed [Freud's note].   6. A very common way of putting aside a piece of knowledge that emerges from the repressed [Freud's note].   7. I added: "Moreover, the re-appearance of the dream in the last few days forces me to the conclusion that you consider that the same situation has arisen once again, and that you have decided to give up the treatment—to which, after all, it is only your father who makes you come." The sequel showed how correct my guess had been. At this point my interpretation touches for a moment upon the subject of "transference"—a theme which is of the highest practical and theoretical importance, but into which I shall not have much further opportunity of entering in the present paper [Freud's note].

Naturally Dora would not follow me in this part of the interpretation. I myself, however, had been able to arrive at a further step in the interpretation, which seemed to me indispensable both for the anamnesis of the case and for the theory of dreams. I promised to communicate this to Dora at the next session.

The fact was that I could not forget the hint which seemed to be conveyed by the ambiguous words already noticed—*that it might be necessary to leave the room; that an accident might happen in the night.* Added to this was the fact that the elucidation of the dream seemed to me incomplete so long as a particular requirement remained unsatisfied; for, though I do not wish to insist that this requirement is a universal one, I have a predilection for discovering a means of satisfying it. A regularly formed dream stands, as it were, upon two legs, one of which is in contact with the main and current exciting cause, and the other with some momentous event in the years of childhood. The dream sets up a connection between those two factors—the event during childhood and the event of the present day—and it endeavours to re-shape the present on the model of the remote past. For the wish which creates the dream always springs from the period of childhood; and it is continually trying to summon childhood back into reality and to correct the present day by the measure of childhood. I believed that I could already clearly detect those elements of Dora's dream which could be pieced together into an allusion to an event in childhood.

I opened the discussion of the subject with a little experiment, which was, as usual, successful. There happened to be a large match-stand on the table. I asked Dora to look round and see whether she noticed anything special on the table, something that was not there as a rule. She noticed nothing. I then asked her if she knew why children were forbidden to play with matches.

"Yes; on account of the risk of fire. My uncle's children are very fond of playing with matches."

"Not only on that account. They are warned not to 'play with fire,' and a particular belief is associated with the warning."

She knew nothing about it.—"Very well, then; the fear is that if they do they will wet their bed. The antithesis of 'water' and 'fire' must be at the bottom of this. Perhaps it is believed that they will dream of fire and then try and put it out with water. I cannot say exactly. But I notice that the antithesis of water and fire has been extremely useful to you in the dream. Your mother wanted to save the jewel-case so that it should not be *burnt*; while in the dream-thoughts it is a question of the 'jewel-case' not being *wetted*. But fire is not only used as the contrary of water, it also serves directly to represent love (as in the phrase 'to be *consumed* with love'). So that from 'fire' one set of rails runs by way of this symbolic meaning to thoughts of love; while the other set runs by way of the contrary 'water,' and, after sending off a branch line which provides another connection with 'love' (for love also makes things wet), leads in a different direction. And what direction can that be? Think of the expressions you used: that *an accident might happen in the night,* and that *it might be necessary to leave the room.* Surely the allusion must be to a physical need? And if you transpose the accident into childhood what can it be but bed-wetting? But what is usually done to prevent children from wetting their bed? Are they not woken up in the night out of their sleep, *exactly as your father woke you up in the dream?* This, then, must be the actual occurrence which enabled you to substitute your father for Herr K., who really woke you up out of your sleep. I am accordingly driven to conclude that you were addicted to bed-wetting up to a later age than is usual with children. The same must also have been true of your brother; for your father said: '*I refuse to let my two children* go to their destruction. . . . ' Your brother has no other sort of connection with the real situation at the K.'s; he had not gone with you to L——. And now, what have your recollections to say to this?"

"I know nothing about myself," was her reply, "but my brother used to wet his bed up till his sixth or seventh year; and it used sometimes to happen to him in the daytime too."

I was on the point of remarking to her how much easier it is to remember things of that kind about one's brother than about oneself, when she continued the train of recollections which had been revived: "Yes. I used to do it too, for some time, but not until my seventh or eighth year. It must have been serious, because I remember now that the doctor was called in. It lasted till a short time before my nervous asthma."

"And what did the doctor say to it?"

"He explained it as nervous weakness: it would soon pass off, he thought; and he prescribed a tonic."[8]

The interpretation of the dream now seemed to me to be complete.[9] But Dora brought me an addendum to the dream on the very next day. She had forgotten to relate, she said, that each time after waking up she had smelt smoke. Smoke, of course, fitted in well with fire, but it also showed that the dream had a special relation to myself; for when she used to assert that there was nothing concealed behind this or that, I would often say by way of rejoinder: "There can be no smoke without fire!" Dora objected, however, to such a purely personal interpretation, saying that Herr K. and her father were passionate smokers—as I am too, for the matter of that. She herself had smoked during her stay by the lake, and Herr K. had rolled a cigarette for her before he began his unlucky proposal. She thought, too, that she clearly remembered having noticed the smell of smoke on the three occasions of the dream's occurrence at L——, and not for the first time at its recent reappearance. As she would give me no further information, it was left to me to determine how this addendum was to be introduced into the texture of the dream-thoughts. One thing which I had to go upon was the fact that the smell of smoke had only come up as an addendum to the dream, and must therefore have had to overcome a particularly strong effort on the part of repression. Accordingly it was probably related to the thoughts which were the most obscurely presented and the most successfully repressed in the dream, to the thoughts, that is, concerned with the temptation to show herself willing to yield to the man. If that were so, the addendum to the dream could scarcely mean anything else than the longing for a kiss, which, with a smoker, would necessarily smell of smoke. But a kiss had passed between

---

8. This physician was the only one in whom she showed any confidence, because this episode showed her that he had not penetrated her secret. She felt afraid of any other doctor about whom she had not yet been able to form a judgement, and we can now see that the motive of her fear was the possibility that he might guess her secret [Freud's note].   9. The essence of the dream might perhaps be translated into words such as these: "The temptation is so strong. Dear Father, protect me again as you used to in my childhood, and prevent my bed from being wetted!" [Freud's note].

Herr K. and Dora some two years further back, and it would certainly have been repeated more than once if she had given way to him. So the thoughts of temptation seemed in this way to have harked back to the earlier scene, and to have revived the memory of the kiss against whose seductive influence the little "thumb-sucker" had defended herself at the time, by the feeling of disgust. Taking into consideration, finally, the indications which seemed to point to there having been a transference on to me—since I am a smoker too—I came to the conclusion that the idea had probably occurred to her one day during a session that she would like to have a kiss from me. This would have been the exciting cause which led her to repeat the warning dream and to form her intention of stopping the treatment. Everything fits together very satisfactorily upon this view; but owing to the characteristics of "transference" its validity is not susceptible of definite proof.

I might at this point hesitate whether I should first consider the light thrown by this dream on the history of the case, or whether I should rather begin by dealing with the objection to my theory of dreams which may be based on it. I shall take the former course.

The significance of enuresis in the early history of neurotics is worth going into thoroughly. For the sake of clearness I will confine myself to remarking that Dora's case of bed-wetting was not the usual one. The disorder was not simply that the habit had persisted beyond what is considered the normal period, but, according to her explicit account, it had begun by disappearing and had then returned at a relatively late age—after her sixth year. Bed-wetting of this kind has, to the best of my knowledge, no more likely cause than masturbation, a habit whose importance in the aetiology of bed-wetting in general is still insufficiently appreciated. In my experience, the children concerned have themselves at one time been very well aware of this connection, and all its psychological consequences follow from it as though they had never forgotten it. Now, at the time when Dora reported the dream, we were engaged upon a line of enquiry which led straight towards an admission that she had masturbated in childhood. A short while before, she had raised the question of why it was that precisely she had fallen ill, and, before I could answer, had put the blame on her father. The justification for this was forthcoming not out of her unconscious thoughts but from her conscious knowledge. It turned out, to my astonishment, that the girl knew what the nature of her father's illness had been. After his return from consulting me she had overheard a conversation in which the name of the disease had been mentioned. At a still earlier period—at the time of the detached retina—an oculist who was called in must have hinted at a luetic aetiology;[1] for the inquisitive and anxious girl overheard an old aunt of hers saying to her mother: "He was ill before his marriage, you know," and adding something which she could not understand, but which she subsequently connected in her mind with improper subjects.

Her father, then, had fallen ill through leading a loose life, and she assumed that he had handed on his bad health to her by heredity. I was careful not to tell her that, as I have already mentioned, I too was of the opinion that the offspring of luetics were very specially predisposed to severe

---

1. Syphilitic origin.

neuropsychoses. The line of thought in which she brought this accusation against her father was continued in her unconscious material. For several days on end she identified herself with her mother by means of slight symptoms and peculiarities of manner, which gave her an opportunity for some really remarkable achievements in the direction of intolerable behaviour. She then allowed it to transpire that she was thinking of a stay she had made at Franzensbad,[2] which she had visited with her mother—I forget in what year. Her mother was suffering from abdominal pains and from a discharge (a catarrh) which necessitated a cure at Franzensbad. It was Dora's view—and here again she was probably right—that this illness was due to her father, who had thus handed on his venereal disease to her mother. It was quite natural that in drawing this conclusion she should, like the majority of laymen, have confused gonorrhoea and syphilis, as well as what is contagious and what is hereditary. The persistence with which she held to this identification with her mother almost forced me to ask her whether she too was suffering from a venereal disease; and I then learnt that she was afflicted with a catarrh (leucorrhoea)[3] whose beginning, she said, she could not remember.

I then understood that behind the train of thought in which she brought these open accusations against her father there lay concealed as usual a *self-accusation*. I met her half-way by assuring her that in my view the occurrence of leucorrhoea in young girls pointed primarily to masturbation, and I considered that all the other causes which were commonly assigned to that complaint were put in the background by masturbation.[4] I added that she was now on the way to finding an answer to her own question of why it was that precisely she had fallen ill—by confessing that she had masturbated, probably in childhood. Dora denied flatly that she could remember any such thing. But a few days later she did something which I could not help regarding as a further step towards the confession. For on that day she wore at her waist—a thing she never did on any other occasion before or after—a small reticule of a shape which had just come into fashion; and, as she lay on the sofa and talked, she kept playing with it—opening it, putting a finger into it, shutting it again, and so on. I looked on for some time and then explained to her the nature of a "symptomatic act." I give the name of symptomatic acts to those acts which people perform, as we say, automatically, unconsciously, without attending to them, or as if in a moment of distraction. They are actions to which people would like to deny any significance, and which, if questioned about them, they would explain as being indifferent and accidental. Closer observation, however, will show that these actions, about which consciousness knows nothing or wishes to know nothing, in fact give expression to unconscious thoughts and impulses, and are therefore most valuable and instructive as being manifestations of the unconscious which have been able to come to the surface. There are two sorts of conscious attitudes possible towards these symptomatic acts. If we can ascribe inconspicuous motives to them we recognize their existence; but if no such pretext can be found for conscious use we usually fail altogether to notice that we have performed them. Dora found no difficulty in producing a motive: "Why

---

2. A famous health resort, or "bath," of mineral springs in the northwest Czech Republic, now called Františkovy Lázany. 3. Genital discharge. 4. This is an extreme view which I should no longer maintain today [Freud's note, added 1923].

should I not wear a reticule like this, as it is now the fashion to do?" But a justification of this kind does not dismiss the possibility of the action in question having an unconscious origin. Though on the other hand the existence of such an origin and the meaning attributed to the act cannot be conclusively established. We must content ourselves with recording the fact that such a meaning fits in quite extraordinarily well with the situation as a whole and with the programme laid down by the unconscious.

On some other occasion I will publish a collection of these symptomatic acts as they are to be observed in the healthy and in neurotics. They are sometimes very easy to interpret. Dora's reticule, which came apart at the top in the usual way, was nothing but a representation of the genitals, and her playing with it, her opening it and putting her finger in it, was an entirely unembarrassed yet unmistakable pantomimic announcement of what she would like to do with them—namely, to masturbate. A very entertaining episode of a similar kind occurred to me a short time ago. In the middle of a session the patient—a lady who was no longer young—brought out a small ivory box, ostensibly in order to refresh herself with a sweet. She made some efforts to open it, and then handed it to me so that I might convince myself how hard it was to open. I expressed my suspicion that the box must mean something special, for this was the very first time I had seen it, although its owner had been coming to me for more than a year. To this the lady eagerly replied: "I always have this box about me; I take it with me wherever I go." She did not calm down until I had pointed out to her with a laugh how well her words were adapted to quite another meaning. The box—*Dose*, πυξις[5]—, like the reticule and the jewel-case, was once again only a substitute for the shell of Venus, for the female genitals.

There is a great deal of symbolism of this kind in life, but as a rule we pass it by without heeding it. When I set myself the task of bringing to light what human beings keep hidden within them, not by the compelling power of hypnosis, but by observing what they say and what they show, I thought the task was a harder one than it really is. He that has eyes to see and ears to hear may convince himself that no mortal can keep a secret. If his lips are silent, he chatters with his finger-tips; betrayal oozes out of him at every pore. And thus the task of making conscious the most hidden recesses of the mind is one which it is quite possible to accomplish.

* * *

[Freud continues and comments on the previous material, including its relationship to *dyspnoea* (breathing difficulties) as another symptom of distress.]

I suspect that we are here concerned with unconscious processes of thought which are twined around a pre-existing structure of organic connections, much as festoons of flowers are twined around a wire; so that on another occasion one might find other lines of thought inserted between the same points of departure and termination. Yet a knowledge of the thought-connections which have been effective in the individual case is of a value which cannot be exaggerated for clearing up the symptoms. It is only because the analysis was prematurely broken off that we have been obliged in Dora's

---

5. Box, in German and Greek, respectively.

case to resort to framing conjectures and filling in deficiencies. Whatever I have brought forward for filling up the gaps is based upon other cases which have been more thoroughly analysed.

The dream from the analysis of which we have derived this information corresponded, as we have seen, to an intention which Dora carried with her into her sleep. It was therefore repeated each night until the intention had been carried out; and it reappeared years later when an occasion arose for forming an analogous intention. The intention might have been consciously expressed in some such words as these: "I must fly from this house, for I see that my virginity is threatened here; I shall go away with my father, and I shall take precautions not to be surprised while I am dressing in the morning." These thoughts were clearly expressed in the dream; they formed part of a mental current which had achieved consciousness and a dominating position in waking life. Behind them can be discerned obscure traces of a train of thought which formed part of a contrary current and had consequently been suppressed. This other train of thought culminated in the temptation to yield to the man, out of gratitude for the love and tenderness he had shown her during the last few years, and it may perhaps have revived the memory of the only kiss she had so far had from him. But according to the theory which I developed in my *Interpretation of Dreams* such elements as these are not enough for the formation of a dream. On that theory a dream is not an intention represented as having been carried out, but a wish represented as having been fulfilled, and, moreover, in most cases a wish dating from childhood. It is our business now to discover whether this principle may not be contradicted by the present dream.

The dream does in fact contain infantile material, though it is impossible at a first glance to discover any connections between that material and Dora's intention of flying from Herr K.'s house and the temptation of his presence. Why should a recollection have emerged of her bed-wetting when she was a child and of the trouble her father used to take to teach the child clean habits? We may answer this by saying that it was only by the help of the train of thought that it was possible to suppress the other thoughts which were so intensely occupied with the temptation to yield or that it was possible to secure the dominance of the intention which had been formed of combating those other thoughts. The child decided to fly *with* her father; in reality she fled *to* her father because she was afraid of the man who was pursuing her; she summoned up an infantile affection for her father so that it might protect her against her present affection for a stranger. Her father was himself partly responsible for her present danger, for he had handed her over to this strange man in the interests of his own love-affair. And how much better it had been when that same father of hers had loved no one more than her, and had exerted all his strength to save her from the dangers that had then threatened her! The infantile, and now unconscious, wish to put her father in the strange man's place had the potency necessary for the formation of a dream. If there were a past situation similar to a present one, and differing from it only in being concerned with one instead of with the other of the two persons mentioned in the wish, that situation would become the main one in the dream. But there *had* been such a situation. Her father had once stood beside her bed, just as Herr K. had the day before, and had woken her up, with a kiss perhaps, as Herr K. may have meant to do. Thus her intention of flying from the house was not in itself capable of producing a dream; but it became so by being associated with another intention which was founded upon infantile wishes. The wish to replace Herr K. by her father provided the necessary motive power for the dream. Let me recall the interpretation I was led to adopt of Dora's rein- forced train of thought about her father's relations with Frau K. My inter- pretation was that she had at that point summoned up an infantile affection for her father so as to be able to keep her repressed love for Herr K. in its state of repression. This same sudden revulsion in the patient's mental life was reflected in the dream.

✳   ✳   ✳

[Freud connects passages from *The Interpretation of Dreams* with Dora's case.]

I add a few remarks which may help towards the synthesis of this dream. The dream-work began on the afternoon of the day after the scene in the wood, after Dora had noticed that she was no longer able to lock the door of her room. She then said to herself: "I am threatened by a serious danger here," and formed her intention of not stopping on in the house alone but of going off with her father. This intention became capable of forming a dream, because it succeeded in finding a continuation in the unconscious. What corresponded to it there was her summoning up her infantile love for her father as a protection against the present temptation. The change which thus took place in her became fixed and brought her into the atti- tude shown by her supervalent train of thought—jealousy of Frau K. on her father's account, as though she herself were in love with him. There was a conflict within her between a temptation to yield to the man's pro- posal and a composite force rebelling against that feeling. This latter force was made up of motives of respectability and good sense, of hostile feel- ings caused by the governess's disclosures (jealousy and wounded pride, as we shall see later), and of a neurotic element, namely, the tendency to a repudiation of sexuality which was already present in her and was based on her childhood history. Her love for her father, which she summoned up to protect her against the temptation, had its origin in this same childhood history.

Her intention of flying to her father, which, as we have seen, reached down into the unconscious, was transformed by the dream into a situation which presented as fulfilled the wish that her father would save her from the danger. In this process it was necessary to put on one side a certain thought which stood in the way; for it was her father himself who had brought her into the danger. The hostile feeling against her father (her desire for revenge), which was here suppressed, was, as we shall discover, one of the motive forces of the second dream.

According to the necessary conditions of dream-formation the imagined situation must be chosen so as to reproduce a situation in infancy. A special triumph is achieved if a recent situation, perhaps even the very situation which is the exciting cause of the dream, can be transformed into an infantile one. This has actually been achieved in the present case, by a purely chance disposition of the material. Just as Herr K. had stood beside her sofa and woken her up, so her father had often done in her childhood. The whole trend of her thoughts could be most aptly symbolized by her substitution of her father for Herr K. in that situation.

* * *

[Freud continues to analyze images of wetness, the jewel-case, and locked doors in relation to Dora's dream and her family situation.]

III

The Second Dream

A few weeks after the first dream the second occurred, and when it had been dealt with the analysis was broken off. It cannot be made as completely intelligible as the first, but it afforded a desirable confirmation of an assumption which had become necessary about the patient's mental state, it filled up a gap in her memory, and it made it possible to obtain a deep insight into the origin of another of her symptoms.

Dora described the dream as follows: "*I was walking about in a town which I did not know. I saw streets and squares which were strange to me.[6] Then I came into a house where I lived, went to my room, and found a letter from Mother lying there. She wrote saying that as I had left home without my parents' knowledge she had not wished to write to me to say that Father was ill. 'Now he is dead, and if you like[7] you can come.' I then went to the station and asked about a hundred times: 'Where is the station?' I always got the same answer: 'Five minutes.' I then saw a thick wood before me which I went into, and there I asked a man whom I met. He said to me: 'Two and a half hours more.'[8] He offered to accompany me. But I refused and went alone. I saw the station in front of me and could not reach it. At the same time I had the usual feeling of anxiety that one has in dreams when one cannot move forward. Then I was at home. I must have been travelling in the meantime, but I know nothing about that. I walked into the porter's lodge, and enquired for our flat. The maidservant opened the door to me and replied that Mother and the others were already at the cemetery.*"[9]

It was not without some difficulty that the interpretation of this dream proceeded. In consequence of the peculiar circumstances in which the analysis was broken off—circumstances connected with the content of the dream—the whole of it was not cleared up. And for this reason, too, I am not equally certain at every point of the order in which my conclusions were reached. I will begin by mentioning the subject-matter with which the current analysis was dealing at the time when the dream intervened. For some time Dora herself had been raising a number of questions about the connection between some of her actions and the motives which presumably underlay them. One of these questions was "Why did I say nothing about the scene by the lake for some days after it had happened?" Her second question was: "Why did I then suddenly tell my parents about it?" Moreover,

---

6. To this she subsequently made an important addendum: "*I saw a monument in one of the squares*" [Freud's note].   7. To this came the addendum: "*There was a question-mark after this word, thus: 'like?' *" [Freud's note].   8. In repeating the dream she said: "*Two hours*" [Freud's note].   9. In the next session Dora brought me two addenda to this: "*I saw myself particularly distinctly going up the stairs,*" and "*After she had answered I went to my room, but not the least sadly, and began reading a big book that lay on my writing-table*" [Freud's note].

her having felt so deeply injured by Herr K.'s proposal seemed to me in general to need explanation, especially as I was beginning to realize that Herr K. himself had not regarded his proposal to Dora as a mere frivolous attempt at seduction. I looked upon her having told her parents of the episode as an action which she had taken when she was already under the influence of a morbid craving for revenge. A normal girl, I am inclined to think, will deal with a situation of this kind by herself.

I shall present the material produced during the analysis of this dream in the somewhat haphazard order in which it recurs to my mind.

She was wandering about alone in a strange town, and saw streets and squares. Dora assured me that it was certainly not B———, which I had first hit upon, but a town in which she had never been. It was natural to suggest that she might have seen some pictures or photographs and have taken the dream-pictures from them. After this remark of mine came the addendum about the monument in one of the squares and immediately afterwards her recognition of its source. At Christmas she had been sent an album from a German health-resort, containing views of the town; and the very day before the dream she had looked this out to show it to some relatives who were stopping with them. It had been put in a box for keeping pictures in, and she could not lay her hands on it at once. She had therefore said to her mother: *"Where is the box?"*[1] One of the pictures was of a square with a monument in it. The present had been sent to her by a young engineer, with whom she had once had a passing acquaintance in the manufacturing town. The young man had accepted a post in Germany, so as to become sooner self-supporting; and he took every opportunity of reminding Dora of his existence. It was easy to guess that he intended to come forward as a suitor one day, when his position had improved. But that would take time, and it meant waiting.

The wandering about in a strange town was overdetermined. It led back to one of the exciting causes from the day before. A young cousin of Dora's had come to stay with them for the holidays, and Dora had had to show him round Vienna. This cause was, it is true, a matter of complete indifference to her. But her cousin's visit reminded her of her own first brief visit to Dresden. On that occasion she had been a stranger and had wandered about, not failing, of course, to visit the famous picture gallery. Another [male] cousin of hers, who was with them and knew Dresden, had wanted to act as a guide and take her round the gallery. *But she declined and went alone,* and stopped in front of the pictures that appealed to her. She remained *two hours* in front of the Sistine Madonna, rapt in silent admiration. When I asked her what had pleased her so much about the picture she could find no clear answer to make. At last she said: "The Madonna."

There could be no doubt that these associations really belonged to the material concerned in forming the dream. They included portions which reappeared in the dream unchanged ("she declined and went alone" and "two hours"). I may remark at once that "pictures" was a nodal point in the network of her dream-thoughts (the pictures in the album, the pictures at Dresden). I should also like to single out, with a view to subsequent investigation,

---

1. In the dream she said: *"Where is the station?"* The resemblance between the two questions led me to make an inference which I shall go into presently [Freud's note].

the theme of the "Madonna," of the virgin mother. But what was most evident was that in this first part of the dream she was identifying herself with a young man. This young man was wandering about in a strange place, he was striving to reach a goal, but he was being kept back, he needed patience and must wait. If in all this she had been thinking of the engineer, it would have been appropriate for the goal to have been the possession of a woman, of herself. But instead of this it was—a station. Nevertheless, the relation of the question in the dream to the question which had been put in real life allows us to substitute *"box"* for "station."² A box and a woman: the notions begin to agree better.

She asked quite a hundred times. . . . This led to another exciting cause of the dream, and this time to one that was less indifferent. On the previous evening they had had company, and afterwards her father had asked her to fetch him the brandy: he could not get to sleep unless he had taken some brandy. She had asked her mother for the key of the sideboard; but the latter had been deep in conversation, and had not answered her, until Dora had exclaimed with the exaggeration of impatience: "I've asked you *a hundred times* already where the key is." As a matter of fact, she had of course only repeated the question about *five times.*³

"Where is the *key?*" seems to me to be the masculine counterpart to the question "Where is the *box?*" They are therefore questions referring to—the genitals.

Dora went on to say that during this same family gathering some one had toasted her father and had expressed the hope that he might continue to enjoy the best of health for many years to come, etc. At this a strange quiver passed over her father's tired face, and she had understood what thoughts he was having to keep down. Poor sick man! who could tell what span of life was still to be his?

This brings us to the *contents of the letter* in the dream. Her father was dead, and she had left home by her own choice. In connection with this letter I at once reminded Dora of the farewell letter which she had written to her parents or had at least composed for their benefit. This letter had been intended to give her father a fright, so that he should give up Frau K.; or at any rate to take revenge on him if he could not be induced to do that. We are here concerned with the subject of her death and of her father's death. (Cf. "cemetery" later on in the dream.) Shall we be going astray if we suppose that the situation which formed the facade of the dream was a phantasy of revenge directed against her father? The feelings of pity for him which she remembered from the day before would be quite in keeping with this. According to the phantasy she had left home and gone among strangers, and her father's heart had broken with grief and with longing for her. Thus she would be revenged. She understood very clearly what it was that her father needed when he could not get to sleep without a drink of brandy.⁴ We will make a

---

2. *Schachtel,* the word which was used for "box" by Dora in her question, is a depreciatory term for "woman." 3. In the dream the number five occurs in the mention of the period of "five minutes." In my book on the interpretation of dreams I have given several examples of the way in which numbers occurring in the dream-thoughts are treated by dreams. We frequently find them torn out of their true context and inserted into a new one [Freud's note]. 4. There can be no doubt that sexual satisfaction is the best soporific, just as sleeplessness is almost always the consequence of lack of satisfaction. Her father could not sleep because he was debarred from sexual intercourse with the woman he loved. (Compare in this connection the phrase discussed just below: "I get nothing out of my wife") [Freud's note].

note of Dora's *craving for revenge* as a new element to be taken into account in any subsequent synthesis of her dream-thoughts.

But the contents of the letter must be capable of further determination. What was the source of the words "if you like"? It was at this point that the addendum of there having been a question-mark after the word "like" occurred to Dora, and she then recognized these words as a quotation out of the letter from Frau K. which had contained the invitation to L——, the place by the lake. In that letter there had been a question-mark placed, in a most unusual fashion, in the very middle of a sentence, after the intercalated words "if you would like to come."

So here we were back again at the scene by the lake and at the problems connected with it. I asked Dora to describe the scene to me in detail. At first she produced little that was new. Herr K.'s exordium had been somewhat serious; but she had not let him finish what he had to say. No sooner had she grasped the purport of his words than she had slapped him in the face and hurried away. I enquired what his actual words had been. Dora could only remember one of his pleas: "You know I get nothing out of my wife." In order to avoid meeting him again she had wanted to get back to L—— on foot, by walking round the lake, and *she had asked a man whom she met how far it was*. On his replying that it was *"Two and a half hours,"* she had given up her intention and had after all gone back to the boat, which left soon afterwards. Herr K. had been there too and had come up to her and begged her to forgive him and not to mention the incident. But she had made no reply.—Yes. The *wood* in the dream had been just like the wood by the shore of the lake, the wood in which the scene she had just described once more had taken place. But she had seen precisely the same thick wood the day before, in a picture at the Secessionist[5] exhibition. In the background of the picture there were *nymphs*.[6]

At this point a certain suspicion of mine became a certainty. The use of *"Bahnhof"*[7] and *"Friedhof"* to represent the female genitals was striking enough in itself, but it also served to direct my awakened curiosity to the similarity formed *"Vorhof"*[8]—an anatomical term for a particular region of the female genitals. This might have been no more than mistaken ingenuity. But now, with the addition of "nymphs" visible in the background of a "thick wood," no further doubts could be entertained. Here was a symbolic geography of sex! "Nymphae," as is known to physicians though not to laymen (and even by the former term is not very commonly used), is the name given to the labia minora, which lie in the background of the "thick wood" of the pubic hair. But any one who employed such technical names as "vestibulum" and "nymphae" must have derived this knowledge from books, and not from popular ones either, but from anatomical text-books or from an encyclopae-dia—the common refuge of youth when it is devoured by sexual curiosity. If this interpretation were correct, therefore, there lay concealed behind the

5. The Vienna Secessionists were a group of recognized *art nouveau* artists—led by painter Gustav Klimt (1862–1918)—who withdrew from established art societies to show their own work.   6. Here for the third time we come upon "picture" (views of towns, the Dresden gallery), but in a much more significant connection. Because of what appears in the picture (the wood, the nymphs), the *"Bild"* ["picture"] is turned into a *"Weibsbild"* [literally, "picture of a woman"—a somewhat derogatory expression for "woman"] [Freud's note].   7. "Station"; literally, "railway-court." *"Friedhof"*: "Cemetery"; literally, "peace-court." Moreover, a "station" is used for purposes of *"Verkehr"* ["traffic," "intercourse," "sexual intercourse"]: this fact determines the psychical coating in a number of cases of railway phobia [Freud's note].   8. Fore court (German, literal trans.); vestibulum.

first situation in the dream a phantasy of defloration, the phantasy of a man seeking to force an entrance into the female genitals.[9]

I informed Dora of the conclusions I had reached. The impression made upon her must have been forcible, for there immediately appeared a piece of the dream which had been forgotten: *"she went calmly to her room, and began reading a big book that lay on her writing-table."* The emphasis here was upon the two details "calmly" and "big" in connection with "book." I asked whether the book was in encyclopaedia *format,* and she said it was. Now children never read about forbidden subjects in an encyclopaedia *calmly.* They do it in fear and trembling, with an uneasy look over their shoulder to see if some one may not be coming. Parents are very much in the way while reading of this kind is going on. But this uncomfortable situation had been radically improved, thanks to the dream's power of fulfilling wishes. Dora's father was dead, and the others had already gone to the cemetery. She might calmly read whatever she chose. Did not this mean that one of her motives for revenge was a revolt against her parents' constraint? If her father was dead she could read or love as she pleased.

At first she would not remember ever having read anything in an encyclopaedia; but she then admitted that a recollection of an occasion of the kind did occur to her, though it was of an innocent enough nature. At the time when the aunt she was so fond of had been so seriously ill and it had already been settled that Dora was to go to Vienna, a *letter* had come from another uncle, to say that they could not go to Vienna, as a boy of his, a cousin of Dora's therefore, had fallen dangerously ill with appendicitis. Dora had thereupon looked up in the encyclopaedia to see what the symptoms of appendicitis were. From what she had then read she still recollected the characteristic localization of the abdominal pain.

I then remembered that shortly after her aunt's death Dora had had an attack of what had been alleged to be appendicitis. Up till then I had not ventured to count that illness among her hysterical productions. She told me that during the first few days she had had high fever and had felt the pain in her abdomen that she had read about in the encyclopaedia. She had been given cold fomentations but had not been able to bear them. On the second day her period had set in, accompanied by violent pains. (Since her health had been bad, the periods had been very irregular.) At that time she used to suffer continually from constipation.

It was not really possible to regard this state as a purely hysterical one. Although hysterical fever does undoubtedly occur, yet it seemed too arbitrary to put down the fever accompanying this questionable illness to hysteria instead of to some organic cause operative at the time. I was on the point of abandoning the track, when she herself helped me along it by producing her last addendum to the dream: *"she saw herself particularly distinctly going up the stairs."*

9. The phantasy of defloration formed the second component of the situation. The emphasis upon the difficulty of getting forward and the anxiety felt in the dream indicated the stress which the dreamer was so ready to lay upon her virginity—a point alluded to in another place by means of the Sistine Madonna. These sexual thoughts gave an unconscious ground-colouring to the wishes (which were perhaps merely kept secret) concerned with the suitor who was waiting for her in Germany. We have already recognized the phantasy of revenge as the first component of the same situation in the dream. The two components do not coincide completely, but only in part. We shall subsequently come upon the traces of a third and still more important train of thought [Freud's note].

I naturally required a special determinant for this. Dora objected that she would anyhow have had to go upstairs if she had wanted to get to her flat, which was on an upper floor. It was easy to brush aside this objection (which was probably not very seriously intended) by pointing out that if she had been able to travel in her dream from the unknown town to Vienna without making a railway journey she ought also to have been able to leave out a flight of stairs. She then proceeded to relate that after the appendicitis she had not been able to walk properly and had dragged her right foot. This state of things had continued for a long time, and on that account she had been particularly glad to avoid stairs. Even now her foot sometimes dragged. The doctors whom she had consulted at her father's desire had been very much astonished at this most unusual after-effect of an appendicitis, especially as the abdominal pains had not recurred and did not in any way accompany the dragging of the foot.[1]

Here, then, we have a true hysterical symptom. The fever may have been organically determined—perhaps by one of those very frequent attacks of influenza that are not localized in any particular part of the body. Nevertheless it was now established that the neurosis had seized upon this chance event and made use of it for an utterance of its own. Dora had therefore given herself an illness which she had read up about in the encyclopaedia, and she had punished herself for dipping into its pages. But she was forced to recognize that the punishment could not possibly apply to her reading the innocent article in question. It must have been inflicted as the result of a process of displacement, after another occasion of more guilty reading had become associated with this one; and the guilty occasion must lie concealed in her memory behind the contemporaneous innocent one.[2] It might still be possible, perhaps, to discover the nature of the subjects she had read about on that other occasion.

What, then, was the meaning of this condition, of this attempted simulation of a perityphlitis?[3] The remainder of the disorder, the dragging of one leg, was entirely out of keeping with perityphlitis. It must, no doubt, fit in better with the secret and possibly sexual meaning of the clinical picture; and if it were elucidated might in its turn throw light on the meaning which we were in search of. I looked about for a method of approaching the puzzle. Periods of time had been mentioned in the dream; and time is assuredly never a matter of indifference in any biological event. I therefore asked Dora when this attack of appendicitis had taken place; whether it had been before or after the scene by the lake. Every difficulty was resolved at a single blow by her prompt reply: "Nine months later." The period of time is sufficiently characteristic. Her supposed attack of appendicitis had thus enabled the patient with the modest means at her disposal (the pains and the menstrual flow) to realize a phantasy of *childbirth*.[4] Dora was naturally aware of the

---

1. We must assume the existence of some somatic connection between the painful abdominal sensations known as "ovarian neuralgia" and locomotor disturbances in the leg on the same side; and we must suppose that in Dora's case the somatic connection had been given an interpretation of a particularly specialized sort, that is to say, that it had been overlaid with and brought into the service of a particular psychological meaning. The reader is referred to my analogous remarks in connection with the analysis of Dora's symptom of coughing and with the relation between catarrh and loss of appetite [Freud's note].   2. This is quite a typical example of the way in which symptoms arise from exciting causes which appear to be entirely unconnected with sexuality [Freud's note].   3. Appendicitis.   4. I have already indicated that the majority of hysterical symptoms, when they have attained their full pitch of development, represent an imagined situation of sexual life—such as a scene of sexual intercourse, pregnancy, childbirth, confinement, etc. [Freud's note].

significance of this period of time, and could not dispute the probability of her having, on the occasion under discussion, read up in the encyclopaedia about pregnancy and childbirth. But what was all this about her dragging her leg? I could now hazard a guess. That is how people walk when they have twisted a foot. So she had made a "false step": which was true indeed if she could give birth to a child nine months after the scene by the lake. But there was still another requirement upon the fulfilment of which I had to insist. I am convinced that a symptom of this kind can only arise where it has an *infantile* prototype. All my experience hitherto has led me to hold firmly to the view that recollections derived from the impressions of later years do not possess sufficient force to enable them to establish themselves as symptoms. I scarcely dared hope that Dora would provide me with the material that I wanted from her childhood, for the fact is that I am not yet in a position to assert the general validity of this rule, much as I should like to be able to do so. But in this case there came an immediate confirmation of it. Yes, said Dora, once when she was a child she had twisted the same foot; she had slipped on one of the steps as she was going *downstairs*. The foot—and it was actually the same one that she afterwards dragged—had swelled up and had to be bandaged and she had had to lie up for some weeks. This had been a short time before the attack of nervous asthma in her eighth year.

The next thing to do was to turn to account our knowledge of the existence of this phantasy: "If it is true that you were delivered of a child nine months after the scene by the lake, and that you are going about to this very day carrying the consequences of your false step with you, then it follows that in your unconscious you must have regretted the upshot of the scene. In your unconscious thoughts, that is to say, you have made an emendation in it. The assumption that underlies your phantasy of childbirth is that on that occasion something took place,[5] that on that occasion you experienced and went through everything that you were in fact obliged to pick up later on from the encyclopaedia. So you see that your love for Herr K. did not come to an end with the scene, but that (as I maintained) it has persisted down to the present day—though it is true that you are unconscious of it."—And Dora disputed the fact no longer.[6]

The labour of elucidating the second dream had so far occupied two hours. At the end of the second session, when I expressed my satisfaction at the result, Dora replied in a depreciatory tone: "Why, has anything so very remarkable come out?" These words prepared me for the advent of fresh revelations.

She opened the third session with these words: "Do you know that I am here for the last time to-day?"—"How can I know, as you have said nothing to me about it?"—"Yes. I made up my mind to put up with it till the New

---

5. The phantasy of defloration is thus found to have an application to Herr K., and we begin to see why this part of the dream contained material taken from the scene by the lake—the refusal, two and a half hours, the wood, the invitation to L—— [Freud's note]. 6. I may here add a few supplementary interpretations to those that have already been given: The *"Madonna"* was obviously Dora herself; in the first place because of the "adorer" who had sent her the pictures, in the second place because she had won Herr K.'s love chiefly by the motherliness she had shown towards his children, and lastly because she had had a child though she was still a girl (this being a direct allusion to the phantasy of childbirth). Moreover, the notion of the "Madonna" is a favourite counter-idea in the mind of girls who feel themselves oppressed by imputations of sexual guilt,—which was the case with Dora [Freud's note].

Year.[7] But I shall wait no longer than that to be cured."—"You know that you are free to stop the treatment at any time. But for to-day we will go on with our work. When did you come to this decision?"—"A fortnight ago, I think."—"That sounds just like a maidservant or a governess—a fortnight's warning."—"There was a governess who gave warning with the K.'s, when I was on my visit to them that time at L——, by the lake."—"Really? You have never told me about her. Tell me."

"Well, there was a young girl in the house, who was the children's govern- ess; and she behaved in the most extraordinary way to Herr K. She never said good morning to him, never answered his remarks, never handed him anything at table when he asked for it, and in short treated him like thin air. For that matter he was hardly any politer to her. A day or two before the scene by the lake, the girl took me aside and said she had something to tell me. She then told me that Herr K. had made advances to her at a time when his wife was away for several weeks; he had made violent love to her and had implored her to yield to his entreaties, saying that he got nothing from his wife, and so on."—"Why, those are the very words he used afterwards, when he made his proposal to you and you gave him the slap in his face."—"Yes. She had given way to him, but after a little while he had ceased to care for her, and since then she hated him."—"And this governess had given warn- ing?"—"No. She meant to give warning. She told me that as soon as she felt she was thrown over she had told her parents what had happened. They were respectable people living in Germany somewhere. Her parents said that she must leave the house instantly; and, as she failed to do so, they wrote to her saying that they would have nothing more to do with her, and that she was never to come home again."—"And why had she not gone away?"—"She said she meant to wait a little longer, to see if there might not be some change in Herr K. She could not bear living like that any more, she said, and if she saw no change she should give warning and go away."—"And what became of the girl?"—"I only know that she went away."—"And she did not have a child as a result of the adventure?"—"No."

Here, therefore (and quite in accordance with the rules), was a piece of material information coming to light in the middle of the analysis and helping to solve problems which had previously been raised. I was able to say to Dora: "Now I know your motive for the slap in the face with which you answered Herr K.'s proposal. It was not that you were offended at his sug- gestions; you were actuated by jealousy and revenge. At the time when the governess was telling you her story you were still able to make use of your gift for putting on one side everything that is not agreeable to your feelings. But at the moment when Herr K. used the words 'I get nothing out of my wife'—which were the same words he had used to the governess—fresh emo- tions were aroused in you and tipped the balance. 'Does he dare,' you said to yourself, 'to treat me like a governess, like a servant?' Wounded pride added to jealousy and to the conscious motives of common sense—it was too much.[8] To prove to you how deeply impressed you were by the governess's story, let me draw your attention to the repeated occasions upon which you have identified yourself with her both in your dream and in your conduct.

7. It was December 31st [Freud's note]. 8. It is not a matter of indifference, perhaps, that Dora may have heard her father make the same complaint about his wife, just as I myself did from his own lips. She was perfectly well aware of its meaning [Freud's note].

You told your parents what happened—a fact which we have hitherto been unable to account for—just as the governess wrote and told *her* parents. You give me a fortnight's warning, just like a governess. The letter in the dream which gave you leave to go home is the counterpart of the governess's letter from her parents forbidding her to do so."

"Then why did I not tell my parents at once?"

"How much time did you allow to elapse?"

"The scene took place on the last day of June; I told my mother about it on July 14th."

"Again a fortnight, then—the time characteristic for a person in service. Now I can answer your question. You understood the poor girl very well. She did not want to go away at once, because she still had hopes, because she expected that Herr K.'s affections would return to her again. So that must have been your motive too. You waited for that length of time so as to see whether he would repeat his proposals; if he had, you would have concluded that he was in earnest, and did not mean to play with you as he had done with the governess."

"A few days after I had left he sent me a picture post-card."[9]

"Yes, but when after that nothing more came, you gave free rein to your feelings of revenge. I can even imagine that at that time you were still able to find room for a subsidiary intention, and thought that your accusation might be a means of inducing him to travel to the place where you were living."—"As he actually offered to do at first," Dora threw in.—"In that way your longing for him would have been appeased"—here she nodded assent, a thing which I had not expected—"and he might have made you the amends you desired."

"What amends?"

"The fact is, I am beginning to suspect that you took the affair with Herr K. much more seriously than you have been willing to admit so far. Had not the K.'s often talked of getting a divorce?"

"Yes, certainly. At first she did not want to, on account of the children. And now she wants to, but he no longer does."

"May you not have thought that he wanted to get divorced from his wife so as to marry you? And that now he no longer wants to because he has no one to replace her? It is true that two years ago you were very young. But you told me yourself that your mother was engaged at seventeen and then waited two years for her husband. A daughter usually takes her mother's love-story as her model. So you too wanted to wait for him, and you took it that he was only waiting till you were grown up enough to be his wife. I imagine that this was a perfectly serious plan for the future in your eyes. You have not even got the right to assert that it was out of the question for Herr K. to have had any such intention; you have told me enough about him that points directly towards his having such an intention. Nor does his behaviour at L—— contradict this view. After all, you did not let him finish his speech and do not know what he meant to say to you. Incidentally, the scheme would by no means have been so impracticable. Your father's relations with Frau K.—and it was probably only for this reason that you lent them your support

---

9. Here is the point of contact with the engineer, who was concealed behind the figure of Dora herself in the first situation in the dream [Freud's note].

for so long—made it certain that her consent to a divorce could be obtained; and you can get anything you like out of your father. Indeed, if your temptation at L—— had had a different upshot, this would have been the only possible solution for all the parties concerned. And I think that is why you regretted the actual event so deeply and emended it in the phantasy which made its appearance in the shape of the appendicitis. So it must have been a bitter piece of disillusionment for you when the effect of your charges against Herr K. was not that he renewed his proposals but that he replied instead with denials and slanders. You will agree that nothing makes you so angry as having it thought that you merely fancied the scene by the lake. I know now—and this is what you do not want to be reminded of—that you *did* fancy that Herr K.'s proposals were serious, and that he would not leave off until you had married him."

Dora had listened to me without any of her usual contradictions. She seemed to be moved; she said good-bye to me very warmly, with the heartiest wishes for the New Year, and—came no more. Her father, who called on me two or three times afterwards, assured me that she would come back again, and said it was easy to see that she was eager for the treatment to continue. But it must be confessed that Dora's father was never entirely straightforward. He had given his support to the treatment so long as he could hope that I should "talk" Dora out of her belief that there was something more than a friendship between him and Frau K. His interest faded when he observed that it was not my intention to bring about that result. I knew Dora would not come back again. Her breaking off so unexpectedly, just when my hopes of a successful termination of the treatment were at their highest, and her thus bringing those hopes to nothing—this was an unmistakable act of vengeance on her part. Her purpose of self-injury also profited by this action. No one who, like me, conjures up the most evil of those half-tamed demons that inhabit the human breast, and seeks to wrestle with them, can expect to come through the struggle unscathed. Might I perhaps have kept the girl under my treatment if I myself had acted a part, if I had exaggerated the importance to me of her staying on, and had shown a warm personal interest in her—a course which, even after allowing for my position as her physician, would have been tantamount to providing her with a substitute for the affection she longed for? I do not know. Since in every case a portion of the factors that are encountered under the form of resistance remains unknown, I have always avoided acting a part, and have contented myself with practising the humbler arts of psychology. In spite of every theoretical interest and of every endeavour to be of assistance as a physician, I keep the fact in mind that there must be some limits to the extent to which psychological influence may be used, and I respect as one of these limits the patient's own will and understanding.

Nor do I know whether Herr K. would have done any better if it had been revealed to him that the slap Dora gave him by no means signified a final "No" on her part, but that it expressed the jealousy which had lately been roused in her, while her strongest feelings were still on his side. If he had disregarded that first "No," and had continued to press his suit with a passion which left room for no doubts, the result might very well have been a triumph of the girl's affection for him over all her internal difficulties. But I think she might just as well have been merely provoked into satisfying her craving for revenge upon him all the more thoroughly. It is never possible to calculate towards which side the decision will incline in such a conflict of motives: whether towards the removal of the repression or towards its reinforcement. Incapacity for meeting a *real* erotic demand is one of the most essential features of a neurosis. Neurotics are dominated by the opposition between reality and phantasy. If what they long for the most intensely in their phantasies is presented to them in reality, they none the less flee from it; and they abandon themselves to their phantasies the most readily where they need no longer fear to see them realized. Nevertheless, the barrier erected by repression can fall before the onslaught of a violent emotional excitement produced by a real cause; it is possible for a neurosis to be overcome by reality. But we have no general means of calculating through what person or what event such a cure can be effected.

IV

Postscript

It is true that I have introduced this paper as a fragment of an analysis; but the reader will have discovered that it is incomplete to a far greater degree than its title might have led him to expect. It is therefore only proper that I should attempt to give a reason for the omissions—which are by no means accidental.

A number of the results of the analysis have been omitted, because at the time when work was broken off they had either not been established with sufficient certainty or they required further study before any general statement could be made about them. At other points, where it seemed to be permissible, I have indicated the direction along which some particular solution would probably have been found to lie. I have in this paper left entirely out of account the technique, which does not at all follow as a matter of course, but by whose means alone the pure metal of valuable unconscious thoughts can be extracted from the raw material of the patient's associations. This brings with it the disadvantage of the reader being given no opportunity of testing the correctness of my procedure in the course of this exposition of the case. I found it quite impracticable, however, to deal simultaneously with the technique of analysis and with the internal structure of a case of hysteria: I could scarcely have accomplished such a task, and if I had, the result would have been almost unreadable. The technique of analysis demands an entirely separate exposition, which would have to be illustrated by numerous examples chosen from a very great variety of cases and which would not have to take the results obtained in each particular case into account. Nor have I attempted in this paper to substantiate the psychological postulates which will be seen to underlie my descriptions of mental phenomena. A cursory attempt to do so would have effected nothing; an exhaustive one would have been a volume in itself. I can only assure the reader that I approached the study of the phenomena revealed by observation of the psychoneuroses without being pledged to any particular psychological system, and that I then proceeded to adjust my views until they seemed adapted for giving an account of the collection of facts which had been observed. I take no pride in having avoided speculation; the material for my hypotheses was collected by the most extensive and laborious series of observations. The decidedness of my attitude on the subject of the unconscious is perhaps specially likely to cause offence, for I handle unconscious ideas, unconscious trains of thought, and unconscious impulses as though they were no less valid and unimpeachable psychological data than conscious ones. But of this I am certain—that any one who sets out to investigate the same region of phenomena and employs the same method will find himself compelled to take up the same position, however much philosophers may expostulate.

Some of my medical colleagues have looked upon my theory of hysteria as a purely psychological one, and have for that reason pronounced it *ipso facto* incapable of solving a pathological problem. They may perhaps discover from this paper that their objection was based upon their having unjustifiably transferred what is a characteristic of the technique on to the theory itself. It is the therapeutic technique alone that is purely psychological; the theory does not by any means fail to point out that neuroses have an organic basis—though it is true that it does not look for that basis in any pathological anatomical changes, and provisionally substitutes the conception of organic functions for the chemical changes which we should expect to find but which we are at present unable to apprehend. No one, probably, will be inclined to deny the sexual function the character of an organic factor, and it is the sexual function that I look upon as the foundation of hysteria and of the psychoneurosis in general. No theory of sexual life will, I suspect, be able to avoid assuming the existence of some definite sexual substances having an excitant action. Indeed, of all the clinical pictures which we meet with in clinical medicine, it is the phenomena of intoxication and abstinence in connection with the use of certain chronic poisons that most closely resemble the genuine psychoneuroses.

But, once again, in the present paper I have not gone fully into all that might be said today about "somatic compliance," about the infantile germs of perversion, about the erotogenic zones, and about our predisposition towards bisexuality; I have merely drawn attention to the points at which the analysis comes into contact with these organic bases of the symptoms. More than this could not be done with a single case. And I had the same reasons that I have already mentioned for wishing to avoid a cursory discussion of these factors. There is a rich opportunity here for further works, based upon the study of a large number of analyses.

Nevertheless, in publishing this paper, incomplete though it is, I had two objects in view. In the first place, I wished to supplement my book on the interpretation of dreams by showing how an art, which would otherwise be useless, can be turned to account for the discovery of the hidden and repressed parts of mental life. (Incidentally, in the process of analysing the two dreams dealt with in the paper, the technique of dream-interpretation, which is similar to that of psycho-analysis, has come under consideration.) In the second place, I wished to stimulate interest in a whole group of phenomena of which science is still in complete ignorance today because they can only be brought to light by the use of this particular method. No one, I believe, can have had any true conception of the complexity of the psychological events in a case of hysteria—the juxtaposition of the most dissimilar tendencies, the mutual dependence of contrary ideas, the repressions and displacements, and so on. The emphasis laid by Janet[1] upon the *"idée fixe"* which becomes transformed into a symptom amounts to no more than an extremely meagre attempt at schematization. Moreover, it is impossible to avoid the suspicion that, when the ideas attaching to certain excitations are incapable of becoming conscious, those excitations must act upon one another differently, run a different course, and manifest themselves differently from those other excitations which we describe as "normal" and which have ideas attaching to them of which we become conscious. When once things have been made clear up to this point, no obstacle can remain in the way of an understanding of a therapeutic method which removes neurotic symptoms by transforming ideas of the former kind into normal ones.

I was further anxious to show that sexuality does not simply intervene, like a *deus ex machina,* on one single occasion, at some point in the working of the processes which characterize hysteria, but that it provides the motive power for every single symptom, and for every single manifestation of a symptom. The symptoms of the disease are nothing else than *the patient's sexual activity.* A single case can never be capable of proving a theorem so general as this one; but I can only repeat over and over again—for I never find it otherwise—that sexuality is the key to the problem of the psychoneuroses and of the neuroses in general. No one who disdains the key will ever be able to unlock the door. I still await news of the investigations which are to make it possible to contradict this theorem or to limit its scope. What I have hitherto heard against it have been expressions of personal dislike or disbelief. To these it is enough to reply in the words of Charcot: "Ça n'empêche pas d'exister."[2]

Nor is the case of whose history and treatment I have published a fragment in these pages well calculated to put the value of psycho-analytic therapy in its true light. Not only the briefness of the treatment (which hardly lasted three months) but another factor inherent in the nature of the case prevented results being brought about such as are attainable in other instances, where the improvement will be admitted by the patient and his relatives and will approximate more or less closely to a complete recovery. Satisfactory results of this kind are reached when the symptoms are maintained solely by the internal conflict between the impulses concerned with sexuality. In such cases the patient's condition will be seen improving in proportion as he is helped towards a solution of his mental problems by the translation of pathogenic into normal material. The course of events is very different when the symptoms have become enlisted in the service of external motives, as had happened with Dora during the two preceding years. It is surprising, and might easily be misleading, to find that the patient's condition shows no noticeable alteration even though considerable progress has been made with the work of analysis. But in reality things are not as bad as they seem. It is true that the symptoms do not disappear while the work is proceeding; but they disappear a little while later, when the relations between patient and physician have been dissolved. The postponement of recovery or improvement is really only caused by the physician's own person.

I must go back a little, in order to make the matter intelligible. It may be

---

1. Pierre Janet (1859–1947), French psychologist and neurologist.   2. That doesn't mean it doesn't exist (French).

safely said that during psycho-analytic treatment the formation of new symptoms is invariably stopped. But the productive powers of the neurosis are by no means extinguished; they are occupied in the creation of a special class of mental structures, for the most part unconscious, to which the name of *"transferences"* may be given.

What are transferences? They are new editions or facsimiles of the impulses and phantasies which are aroused and made conscious during the progress of the analysis; but they have this peculiarity, which is characteristic for their species, that they replace some earlier person by the person of the physician. To put it another way: a whole series of psychological experiences are revived, not as belonging to the past, but as applying to the person of the physician at the present moment. Some of these transferences have a content which differs from that of their model in no respect whatever except for the substitution. These then—to keep to the same metaphor—are merely new impressions or reprints. Others are more ingeniously constructed; their content has been subjected to a moderating influence—to *sublimation,* as I call it—and they may even become conscious, by cleverly taking advantage of some real peculiarity in the physician's person or circumstances and attaching themselves to that. These, then, will no longer be new impressions, but revised editions.

If the theory of analytic technique is gone into, it becomes evident that transference is an inevitable necessity. Practical experience, at all events, shows conclusively that there is no means of avoiding it, and that this latest creation of the disease must be combated like all the earlier ones. This happens, however, to be by far the hardest part of the whole task. It is easy to learn how to interpret dreams, to extract from the patient's associations his unconscious thoughts and memories, and to practise similar explanatory arts; for these the patient himself will always provide the text. Transference is the one thing the presence of which has to be detected almost without assistance and with only the slightest clues to go upon, while at the same time the risk of making arbitrary inferences has to be avoided. Nevertheless, transference cannot be evaded, since use is made of it in setting up all the obstacles that make the material inaccessible to treatment, and since it is only after the transference has been resolved that a patient arrives at a sense of conviction of the validity of the connections which have been constructed during the analysis.

Some people may feel inclined to look upon it as a serious objection to a method which is in any case troublesome enough that it itself should multiply the labours of the physician by creating a new species of pathological mental products. They may even be tempted to infer from the existence of transferences that the patient will be injured by analytic treatment. Both these suppositions would be mistaken. The physician's labours are not multiplied by transference; it need make no difference to him whether he has to overcome any particular impulse of the patient's in connection with himself or with some one else. Nor does the treatment force upon the patient, in the shape of transference, any new task which he would not otherwise have performed. It is true that neuroses may be cured in institutions from which psycho-analytic treatment is excluded, that hysteria may be said to be cured not by the method but by the physician, and that there is usually a sort of blind dependence and a permanent bond between a patient and the physician who has removed his symptoms by hypnotic suggestion; but the scientific explanation of all these facts is to be found in the existence of "transferences" such as are regularly directed by patients on to their physicians. Psycho-analytic treatment does not *create* transferences, it merely brings them to light, like so many other hidden psychical factors. The only difference is this—that spontaneously a patient will only call up affectionate and friendly transferences to help towards his recovery; if they cannot be called up, he feels the physician is "antipathetic" to him, and breaks away from him as fast as possible and without having been influenced by him. In psycho-analysis, on the other hand, since the play of motives is different, all the patient's tendencies, including hostile ones, are aroused; they are then turned to account for the purposes of the analysis by being made conscious, and in this way the transference is constantly being destroyed. Transference, which seems ordained to be the greatest obstacle to psycho-analysis, becomes its most powerful ally, if its presence can be detected each time and explained to the patient.

I have been obliged to speak of transference, for it is only by means of this factor that I can elucidate the peculiarities of Dora's analysis. Its great merit, namely, the unusual clarity which makes it seem so suitable as a first introductory publication, is closely bound up with its great defect, which led to its being broken off prematurely. I did not succeed in mastering the transference in good time. Owing to the readiness with which Dora put one part of the pathogenic material at my disposal during the treatment, I neglected the precaution of looking out for the first signs of transference, which was being prepared in connection with another part of the same material—a part of which I was in ignorance. At the beginning it was clear that I was replacing her father in her imagination, which was not unlikely, in view of the difference between our ages. She was even constantly comparing me with him consciously, and kept anxiously trying to make sure whether I was being quite straightforward with her, for her father "always preferred secrecy and roundabout ways." But when the first dream came, in which she gave herself the warning that she had better leave my treatment just as she had formerly left Herr K.'s house, I ought to have listened to the warning myself. "Now," I ought to have said to her, "it is from Herr K. that you have made a transference on to me. Have you noticed anything that leads you to suspect me of evil intentions similar (whether openly or in some sublimated form) to Herr K.'s? Or have you been struck by anything about me or got to know anything about me which has caught your fancy, as happened previously with Herr K?" Her attention would then have been turned to some detail in our relations, or in my person or circumstances, behind which there lay concealed something analogous but immeasurably more important concerning Herr K. And when this transference had been cleared up, the analysis would have obtained access to new memories, dealing, probably, with actual events. But I was deaf to this first note of warning, thinking I had ample time before me, since no further stages of transference developed and the material for the analysis had not yet run dry. In this way the transference took me unawares, and, because of the unknown quantity in me which reminded Dora of Herr K., she took her revenge on me as she wanted to take her revenge on him, and deserted me as she believed herself to have been deceived and deserted by him. Thus she *acted out* an essential part of her recollections and phantasies instead of reproducing it in the treatment. What this unknown quantity was I naturally cannot tell. I suspect that it had to do with money, or with jealousy of another patient who had kept up relations with my family after her recovery. When it is possible to work transferences into the analysis at an early stage, the course of the analysis is retarded and obscured, but its existence is better guaranteed against sudden and overwhelming resistances.

In Dora's second dream there are several clear allusions to transference. At the time she was telling me the dream I was still unaware (and did not learn until two days later) that we had only *two hours* more work before us. This was the same length of time which she had spent in front of the Sistine Madonna, and which (by making a correction and putting "two hours" instead of "two and a half hours") she had taken as the length of the walk which she had not made round the lake. The striving and waiting in the dream, which related to the young man in Germany, and had their origin in her waiting till Herr K. could marry her, had been expressed in the transference a few days before. The treatment, she had thought, was too long for her; she would never have the patience to wait so long. And yet in the first few weeks she had had discernment enough to listen without making any such objections when I informed her that her complete recovery would require perhaps a year. Her refusing in the dream to be accompanied, and preferring to go alone, also originated from her visit to the gallery at Dresden, and I was myself to experience them on the appointed day. What they meant was, no doubt: "Men are all so detestable that I would rather not marry. This is my revenge."[3]

If cruel impulses and revengeful motives, which have already been used in the patient's ordinary life for maintaining her symptoms, become transferred on to the physician during treatment, before he has had time to detach them from himself by tracing them back to their sources, then it is not to be wondered at if the patient's condition is unaffected by his therapeutic efforts. For how could the patient take a more effective revenge than by demonstrating upon her own person the helplessness and incapacity of the physician? Nevertheless, I am not inclined to put too low a value on the therapeutic results even of such a fragmentary treatment as Dora's.

It was not until fifteen months after the case was over and this paper composed that I had news of my patient's condition and the effects of my treatment. On a date which is not a matter of complete indifference, on the first of April (times and dates, as we know, were never without significance for her), Dora came to see me again: to finish her story and to ask for help once more. One glance at her face, however, was enough to tell me that she was not in earnest over her request. For four or five weeks after stopping the treatment she had been "all in a muddle," as she said. A great improvement had then set in; her attacks had become less frequent and her spirits had risen. In May of that year one of the K.'s two children (it had always been delicate) had died. She took the oppor-

3. The longer the interval of time that separates me from the end of this analysis, the more probable it seems to me that the fault in my technique lay in this omission: I failed to discover in time and to inform the patient that her homosexual (gynaecophilic) love for Frau K. was the strongest unconscious current in her mental life. I ought to have guessed that the main source of her knowledge of sexual matters could have been no one but Frau K.—the very person who later on charged her with being interested in those same subjects. Her knowing all about such things and, at the same time, her always pretending not to know where her knowledge came from was really too remarkable. I ought to have attacked this riddle and looked for the motive of such an extraordinary piece of repression. If I had done this, the second dream would have given me my answer [Freud's note].

tunity of their loss to pay them a visit of condolence, and they received her as though nothing had happened in the last three years. She made it up with them, she took her revenge on them, and she brought her own business to a satisfactory conclusion. To the wife she said: "I know you have an affair with my father"; and the other did not deny it. From the husband she drew an admission of the scene by the lake which he had disputed, and brought the news of her vindication home to her father. Since then she had not resumed her relations with the family.

After this she had gone on quite well till the middle of October, when she had had another attack of aphonia which had lasted for six weeks. I was surprised at this news, and, on my asking her whether there had been any exciting cause, she told me that the attack had followed upon a violent fright. She had seen some one run over by a carriage. Finally she came out with the fact that the accident had occurred to no less a person than Herr K. himself. She had come across him in the street one day; they had met in a place where there was a great deal of traffic; he had stopped in front of her as though in bewilderment, and in his abstraction he had allowed himself to be knocked down by a carriage. She had been able to convince herself, however, that he escaped without serious injury. She still felt some slight emotion if she heard any one speak of her father's affair with Frau K., but otherwise she had no further concern with the matter. She was absorbed in her work, and had no thoughts of marrying.

She went on to tell me that she had come for help on account of a right-sided facial neuralgia, from which she was now suffering day and night. "How long has it been going on?" "Exactly a fortnight."[4] I could not help smiling; for I was able to show her that exactly a fortnight earlier she had read a piece of news that concerned me in the newspaper. (This was in 1902.) And this she confirmed.

Her alleged facial neuralgia was thus a self-punishment—remorse at having once given Herr K. a box on the ear, and at having transferred her feelings of revenge on to me. I do not know what kind of help she wanted from me, but I promised to forgive her for having deprived me of the satisfaction of affording her a far more radical cure for her troubles.

Years have again gone by since her visit. In the meantime the girl has married, and indeed—unless all the signs mislead me—she has married the young man who came into her associations at the beginning of the analysis of the second dream.[5] Just as the first dream represented her turning away from the man she loved to her father—that is to say, her flight from life into disease—so the second dream announced that she was about to tear herself free from her father and had been reclaimed once more by the realities of life.

4. For the significance of this period of time and its relation to the theme of revenge, see the analysis of the second dream [Freud's note].   5. In the editions of 1909, 1912, and 1921 the following footnote appeared at this point: "This, as I afterwards learnt, was a mistaken notion."

RABINDRANATH TAGORE
1861–1941

One of the great intellectuals of the twentieth century, Rabindranath Tagore is the preeminent figure in the history of modern literature in Bengali, the language of the state of West Bengal in eastern India, and of the neighboring nation of Bangladesh. Based on the enthusiastic reception in the West of *Gitanjali* (Song Offerings, 1912), a volume of his poetry in English translation, Tagore won the Nobel Prize for literature in 1913. By the end of his life, he had written more than fifty collections of poetry and composed and set to music over two thousand songs. Both poetry and songs (the latter include the national anthems of India and Bangladesh) continue to be cherished by Bengali audiences, and the Nobel Prize led to the translation of Tagore's poetry into many European and Asian languages. However, poetry was only one manifestation of Tagore's multifaceted genius. In the period during which India emerged from colonial domination to independent nationhood, Tagore pioneered or brought to maturity the major forms of modern Bengali literature, including the novel, the essay, the short story, and drama. His literary activity was organically related to social, artistic, and humanitarian projects aimed at fostering humanism and the spirit of international understanding.

Tagore was born into an illustrious Hindu family from Calcutta, the capital of British India in the nineteenth century. The Tagores were pioneers of the Bengal Renaissance, a movement led by Bengali intellectuals who were in many ways shaped by English education, but who at the same time reacted with profound ambivalence to colonial rule and the imposition of Western cultural norms on Indians. Through their writings and through the institutions they founded, the leaders of the Renaissance sought to refashion Indian society to meet the challenges of the modern world; but they wished to do so without losing the moorings that the highest values and ideals of traditional Indian culture provide. Tagore's father, Debendranath Tagore, was one of the first leaders of the Brahmo Samaj, a major Hindu social reform organization that was founded on just such a blend of Western and Indian ideas.

Each of Debendranath Tagore's fourteen children made significant contributions to Bengali literature and culture. None of them, however, equaled Rabindranath, the youngest, in breadth and importance of achievement. Rabindranath Tagore founded Shantiniketan, a school, and Visva-Bharati, an international university, as alternatives to colonial education. He traveled widely in Europe, Asia, and America, speaking out against the evils of colonialism, wars based on narrow nationalism, and abuses of human rights all over the world. When Mahatma Gandhi led the Indian people in their nonviolent (and ultimately successful) struggle for freedom from British colonial rule in the period between the two world wars, Tagore stood by Gandhi and his movement but pointed out the dangers of focusing on exclusively nationalistic goals, arguing instead for a new world order based on transnational ideals. In all of Tagore's writings, as in the poems and the short story presented here, we discern the universalistic humanism that informed his public life, combined with a profound sense of beauty.

The 1912 collection *Gitanjali* consists of Tagore's own prose translations of his poetry, mainly of songs and poems he had written when he was grieving over the deaths of his wife, two of his young children, and his father, whom he had lost in quick succession. It is unfortunate that Tagore's international reputation as a poet rests in the main on the *Gitanjali* collection and on others that followed soon after, also translated by the author. The *Gitanjali* poems do not convey the impressive range and variety of Tagore's poetry, nor do the prose translations do justice to the poetic qualities of his writing. In fact, the early translations, along with W. B. Yeats's characterization of the *Gitanjali* poems in his preface to the first edition of the collection, led to the mistaken perception of Tagore's poetry as a combination of a vague romantic lyricism and an equally vague Eastern mysticism. However, recent translations from a greater range of Tagore's poetry have been more successful in conveying the concreteness and vigor of Tagore's poems, their accessibility to the modern reader, and the complexity of their stance toward the material and spiritual planes of experience.

It would not be an exaggeration to say that Tagore almost single-handedly brought Bengali poetry into the modern age. Although he drew upon earlier lyric traditions in Sanskrit and Bengali with great sensitivity, from the very beginning his poems were distinguished by their intensely personal voice and innovative use of language, meter, rhythm, and imagery. Tagore constantly experimented with the Bengali language, investing words with a creative tension between rich, older associations and new shades of meaning. He invented new meters and rhythms, pressing diverse sources into service, ranging from Sanskrit poetry to nursery rhymes. Equally fascinated by music and poetry, he often crossed the boundary between lyric and true song. While in his early work Tagore moved easily between intricately structured lyric verse and longer poems with a very loose structure, in his later poems he often abandoned meter altogether, writing what he called "prose poems." Poem 20 from the collection *On My Birthday*, written in a period when the poet had begun to try his hand at painting, reflects Tagore's preoccupation, in the later part of his career, with language as pure form, devoid of all extrinsic meaning, similar to the focus on line and color in his paintings.

A deep sense of the relationship between human beings and nature is an intrinsic aspect of Indian lyricism (e.g., Kālidāsa, vol. B, p. 1267, and the Bengali Vaiṣṇava poets, vol. B, p. 2390). This essential relationship takes new forms of expression in Tagore's poetry. Tagore's innate sensitivity to nature was deepened by the long stretches of time he spent in rural Bengal. Shantiniketan, the school that he established in 1901 and on whose campus he lived, is situated in Bolpur, a rural enclave near Calcutta. In his poems, the landscapes of Bengal—the vast sky, the boats and paddies of the riverine plains of East Bengal, trees, flowers, and changing seasons—are both subject matter and the ground for mystical experience.

Though in tune with specific Indian mystical traditions such as those of the Bengali Vaiṣṇavas (vol. B, p. 2390) and the itinerant Bāul singers of Bengal, Tagore's mysticism is an expression of a unique personal philosophy, one that rejects all creeds, and is founded on his idea of a "deity of life" or "life-god" (*jīban-debatā*). In the poet's mystical religion, the divine (which is beyond gendered identity) is continuously in creative interplay with mundane life, human beings and nature, continually manifesting itself as both part of and separate from life in the world. Forever seeking contact with this life-god, human beings can experience its presence only as "Personality"—that is, the universal and the eternal spirit manifested as and rooted in the specific, the individual, the concrete, and the local. Some of these ideas are drawn from the *Upaniṣads*, ancient Indian mystical texts that formed the basis of the philosophy of the Brahmo Samaj. But the philosophy of the "deity of life" is Tagore's own and finds unique and varied expression in his poems. It is as much at the center of the description of the clerk Haripada's miserable life in a Calcutta lane (*Flute Music*) as in the surreal landscapes of *A Stressful Time* or *The Golden Boat*. In many poems, as in the magnificent *I Won't Let You Go*, precisely observed details of mundane life—a little girl tries to stop her father from leaving her, a wife lists the foods that she has packed for her husband's journey—become the springboard for a passionate meditation on a cosmos that is at once divine and human.

A different aspect of Tagore's humanism is revealed in his fiction. Bengali prose fiction emerged in the late nineteenth century as a result of the impact of English education and Western literary forms. Tagore's elder contemporary Bankim Chandra Chatterjee (1838–1894) wrote historical romances modeled on the novels of Sir Walter Scott, but he also used the novel as a vehicle for social critique and nationalist propaganda. Concern about social issues, especially the need for the emancipation of Bengali women from oppressive cultural practices, dominates Tagore's major novels, beginning with *Cokher bali* (Speck in the Eye) and *Naṣṭanīṛ* (The Broken Nest), published serially in 1901. Here, as well as in his more than one hundred short stories, his preoccupation with the emotional and psychological lives of his characters and his passionate championship of the integrity of the individual strike a new note in Bengali literature.

Tagore's short stories are the first major examples of the genre in any Indian language. Between 1891 and 1895, forty-four of his stories appeared in Bengali periodicals, the majority of them in the monthly journal *Sādhanā* (Endeavor), edited by members of the Tagore family. The rest were written in the 1920s. *Punishment* (*Śāsti*, 1893) belongs to the earlier stories, which were inspired by Tagore's experience of rural Bengal during the decade he spent there as manager of the family estates in Shelidah in the province of East Bengal (now the independent nation of Bangladesh). The characters in Tagore's major fiction tend to be drawn from the Bengali middle class, which he knew well; but a number of these early stories are about the peasants and villagers with whom he came in contact during the Shelidah years. Here the great Padma River and the agricultural landscape of eastern Bengal become the focus of the love of nature and the lyrical, romantic sensibility that are characteristic of the writer's works.

The stories of this period are by no means idyllic pictures of village life. In *Punishment*, Tagore's sensitive portrayal of the complex relationships obtaining among the members of the low-caste Rui family and between them and the upper-class rural society that exploits them, suggests both realism and a sense of tragedy. The transactions among Chandara, the proud and beautiful young woman, her husband, the farm-laborer Chidam, and landlord Ramlochan Chakravarti, "pillar of the village," reveal Tagore's intimate understanding of the ways in which economic, social, and patriarchal oppression are intrinsically linked and of the ability of the oppressed to resist even the most powerful forms of oppression. However, as in his other stories and novels, his real interest in *Punishment* is in delineating the psychological ramifications of social and familial relationships. Chandara is a typical Tagore protagonist, representing the power and dignity of the human will in the face of societal degradation. And yet Tagore's world is a tragic one, populated by individuals who, trapped in what he called the "dreary desert sand of dead habit," are ultimately unable to transcend the tyranny of institutions.

Amiya Chakravarty, ed., *A Tagore Reader* (1961), and Krishna Dutta and Andrew Robinson, *Rabindranath Tagore: An Anthology* (1997), offer excellent introductions to the full range of Tagore's writing. Krishna Kripalani's *Rabindranath Tagore: A Biography* (1962) can be supplemented with the perspectives offered in *Rabindranath Tagore: The Myriad-minded Man* (1995), by Krishna Dutta and Andrew Robinson. Two histories of Bengali literature, Dushan Zbavitel's *Bengali Literature* (1976) and Asit Kumar Bandhyopadhyay's *Modern Bengali Literature* (1986), provide information about the context of Tagore's achievement. Tagore's own translations of his poetry are represented in *Collected Poems and Plays* (1936). For other translations, especially of hitherto untranslated poems, see William Radice, *Rabindranath Tagore: Selected Poems* (1985), and Ketaki Kushari Dyson, *I Won't Let You Go* (1993). William Radice, *Rabindranath Tagore: Selected Short Stories* (1991), offers translations of thirty of Tagore's early short stories, including some of his best-known ones. For a comparison of Tagore's short stories with those of later Bengali writers on the themes of oppression and resistance, see Kalpana Bardhan, ed. and trans., *Of Women, Outcastes, Peasants, and Rebels: A Selection of Bengali Short Sories* (1990).

PRONOUNCING GLOSSARY

The following list uses common English syllables and stress accents to provide rough equivalents of selected words whose pronunciation may be unfamiliar to the general reader.

Baiśakh: *bai'-shahk*

Barobau: *baroh'-bau*

Caitra: *chai'-truh*

Chandara: *chuhn'-duh-rah*

Chidam Rui: *chee'-duhm roo'-yee*

Choṭobau: *choh'-toh-bau*

Dukhiram Rui: *doo-khee'-rahm roo'-yee*

Ganesh: *guh-naysh'*

Ganga: *guhn'-gah*

Gitanjali: *gee-tahn'-juh-lee*

Kashi Majumdar: *kah'-shee muh'-joom-dahr*

Mahabharat: *muh-hah-bah'ruht*

Rabindranath Tagore: *ruh-been'-druh-naht tuh'-gohr'*

Radha: *rah'-dah*

Ram: *rahm*

Ramlochan Chakravarti: *rahm'-loh-chuhn chuhk'-ruh-vuhr-tee*

Santiniketan: *shahn'-tee-nee-kay-tuhn*

Ṭhākur: *thah'-koor*

Visva-bharati: *veesh'-vuh-bah'-ruh-tee*

zamindar: *zuh-meen'-dahr*

From GITANJALI

[The song that I came to sing remains unsung to this day][1]

The song that I came to sing remains unsung to this day.

    I have spent my days in stringing and in unstringing my instrument.

    The time has not come true, the words have not been rightly set; only there is the agony of wishing in my heart.

    The blossom has not opened; only the wind is sighing by.

    I have not seen his face, nor have I listened to his voice; only I have heard his gentle footsteps from the road before my house.   5

    The livelong day has passed in spreading his seat on the floor; but the lamp has not been lit and I cannot ask him into my house.

    I live in the hope of meeting with him; but this meeting is not yet.

[Where the mind is without fear and the head is held high][2]

Where the mind is without fear and the head is held high;

    Where knowledge is free;

    Where the world has not been broken up into fragments by narrow domestic walls;

---

1. Translated by Rabindranath Tagore. In this poem, Tagore draws on the convention in Indian secular and mystical poetry of a woman who sings of her sorrow at being parted from her lover, as she waits for his return.   2. Translated by Rabindranath Tagore.

Where words come out from the depth of truth;
Where tireless striving stretches its arms toward perfection;   5
Where the clear stream of reason has not lost its way into the dreary desert
sand of dead habit;
Where the mind is led forward by thee into ever-widening thought and
action—
Into that heaven of freedom, my Father,[3] let my country awake.

[Deliverance is not for me in renunciation][4]

Deliverance is not for me in renunciation. I feel the embrace of freedom in
a thousand bonds of delight.
    Thou ever pourest for me the fresh draught of thy wine of various colors
and fragrance, filling this earthen vessel to the brim.
    My world will light its hundred different lamps with thy flame and place
them before the altar of thy temple.
    No, I will never shut the doors of my senses. The delights of sight and
hearing and touch will bear thy delight.
    Yes, all my illusions will burn into illumination of joy, and all my desires
ripen into fruits of love.   5

From THE CRESCENT MOON

On the Seashore[5]

On the seashore of endless worlds children meet.
    The infinite sky is motionless overhead and the restless water is boisterous.
On the seashore of endless worlds the children meet with shouts and dances.
    They build their houses with sand, and they play with empty shells. With
withered leaves they weave their boats and smilingly float them on the vast
deep. Children have their play on the seashore of worlds.
    They know not how to swim, they know not how to cast nets. Pearl-fishers
dive for pearls, merchants sail in their ships, while children gather pebbles
and scatter them again. They seek not for hidden treasures, they know not
how to cast nets.
    The sea surges up with laughter, and pale gleams the smile of the sea-
beach. Death-dealing waves sing meaningless ballads to the children, even
like a mother while rocking her baby's cradle. The sea plays with children,
and pale gleams the smile of the sea-beach.   5
    On the seashore of endless worlds children meet. Tempest roams in the

---

3. "Father" most likely refers to god, in keeping with the theology of the Brahmo Samaj, the religious
organization headed by Tagore's father.   4. Translated by Rabindranath Tagore. In this poem, Tagore
passionately rejects the ascetic stream in Indian religion, extolling its life-embracing aspects instead.
5. Translated by Rabindranath Tagore. This is an example of a poem about childhood, a favored theme in
Tagore's writing, that is combined with enigmatic, surrealistic imagery.

pathless sky, ships are wrecked in the trackless water, death is abroad and children play. On the seashore of endless worlds is the great meeting of children.

From THE GARDENER

[At midnight the would-be ascetic announced][6]

At midnight the would-be ascetic announced:
    "This is the time to give up my home and seek for God. Ah, who has held me so long in delusion here?"
    God whispered, "I," but the ears of the man were stopped.
    With a baby asleep at her breast lay his wife, peacefully sleeping on one side of the bed.
    The man said, "Who are ye that have fooled me so long?"   5
    The voice said again, "They are God," but he heard it not.
    The baby cried out in its dream, nestling close to its mother.
    God commanded, "Stop, fool, leave not thy home," but still he heard not.
    God sighed and complained, "Why does my servant wander to seek me, forsaking me?"

[Sudās, the gardener, plucked from his tank . . .][7]

Sudās, the gardener, plucked from his tank the last lotus left by the ravage of winter and went to sell it to the King at the palace gate.
    There he met a traveler who said to him, "Ask your price for the last lotus,—I shall offer it to Lord Buddha."
    Sudās said, "If you pay one golden *māshā* it will be yours."
    The traveler paid it.
    At that moment the King came out and he wished to buy the flower, for he was on his way to see Lord Buddha, and he thought, "It would be a fine thing to lay at his feet the lotus that bloomed in winter."   5
    When the gardener said he had been offered a golden *māshā* the King offered him ten, but the traveler doubled the price.
    The gardener, being greedy, imagined a greater gain from him for whose sake they were bidding. He bowed and said, "I cannot sell this lotus."
    In the hushed shade of the mango grove beyond the city wall Sudās stood before Lord Buddha, on whose lips sat the silence of love and whose eyes beamed peace like the morning star of the dew-washed autumn.

---

6. Translated by Rabindranath Tagore. In addition to the theme of the rejection of asceticism, in this poem there seems to be an allusion to the legend of Prince Siddhartha, who left his wife and child to become Buddha, the Enlightened One.   7. Translated by Rabindranath Tagore. This is one of Tagore's retellings of legends from the life of the Buddha.

Sudās looked in his face and put the lotus at his feet and bowed his head
to the dust.

Buddha smiled and asked, "What is your wish, my son?"   10
Sudās cried, "The least touch of your feet."

From ŚONĀR TARĪ

I Won't Let You Go[8]

The carriage stands at the door. It is midday.
The autumn sun is gradually gathering strength.
The noon wind blows the dust on the deserted
village path. Beneath a cool peepul[9]
an ancient, weary beggar-woman sleeps   5
on a tattered cloth. All is hushed and still
and shines brilliantly—like a sun-lit night.
Only in my home there's neither siesta nor rest.

Ashwin's[1] gone. The Puja vacation's[2] ended.
I've to return to the far-off place where I work.   10
Servants, busybodies, shout and fuss
with ropes and strings, tying packages sprawled
in this room and that, all over the house.
The lady of the house, her heart heavy as a stone,
her eyes moist, nevertheless has no time   15
to shed tears, no, not a minute: she has
too much to organise, rushes about,
extremely busy, and though there already is
too much baggage, she reckons it's not enough.
'Look,' I say, 'what on earth shall I do with these—   20
so many stewpots, jugs, bowls, casseroles,
bedclothes, bottles, boxes? Let me take
a few and leave the rest behind.'

       Nobody pays
the slightest attention to what I say. 'You might   25
suddenly feel the need for this or that
and where then would you find it far from home?
Golden moong beans, long-grain rice, betel leaves,
areca-nuts;[3] in that bowl, covered, a few blocks
of date-palm molasses; firm ripe coconuts;   30
two containers of fine mustard oil;
dried mango, mango-cakes; milk—two seers—
and in these jars and bottles your medicines.

8. Translated by Ketaki Kushari Dyson. *Śonār Tarī*: "The Golden Boat."   9. A variety of fig tree, *ficus religiosa*, related to the Indian banyan tree; it is sacred to Buddhists and Hindus.   1. The sixth month in the Bengali calendar, corresponding to mid-September to mid-October. In Bengal, autumn follows the rainy season.   2. Bengalis celebrate *Durga puja*, the festival of the Goddess Durga, for several days in the autumn month of Ashwin.   3. *Betel leaves* and *areca nuts* are chewed, together with spices and condiments in a digestive preparation called *pan*.

Some sweet goodies I've left inside this bowl.
For goodness's sake, do eat them, don't forget them.'   35
I realise it would be useless to argue with her.
There it is, my luggage, piled high as a mountain.
I look at the clock, then look back at the face
of my beloved, and gently say, 'Bye then.'
Quickly she turns her face away, head bent,   40
and pulls the end of her sari[4] over her eyes
to hide her tears, for tears are inauspicious.

By the front door sits my daughter, four years old,
low in spirits, who, on any other day,
would have had her bath well completed by now,   45
and with two mouthfuls of lunch would have succumbed
to drowsiness in her eyelids, but who, today,
neglected by her mother, has neither bathed
nor lunched yet. Like a shadow she has
kept close to me all morning, observing   50
the fuss of the packing, silent, wide-eyed.
Weary now, and sunk in some thought of hers,
she sits by the front door quietly, without a word.
'Goodbye then, poppet,' when I say,
she simply replies, sad-eyed, her face grave: 55
'I won't let you go.' That is all.
She sits where she is, makes not the slightest attempt
to either hold my arm or close the door,
but only with her heart's right, given by love,
proclaims her stand: 'I won't let you go.'   60
Yet in the end the time comes when, alas,
she has to let me go.

　　　　Foolish girl, my
daughter, who gave you the strength
to make such a statement, so bold, so self-assured—
'I won't let you go'? Whom will you,   65
in this universe, with two little hands
hold back, proud girl, and against whom fight,
with that tiny weary body of yours by the door,
that stock of love in your heart your only arms?   70
Nervously, shyly, urged by our pain within,
we can but express our innermost desire,
just say, 'I do not wish
to let you go.' But who can
say such a thing as 'I won't let you go'!   75
Hearing such a proud assertion of love
from your little mouth, the world, with a mischievous smile,
dragged me from you, and you, quite defeated,
sat by the door like a picture, tears in your eyes.
All I could do was mop my own eyes and leave.   80

4. The garment of Indian women, it is a long piece of cloth draped around the body, with one end left to hang loosely over the shoulder.

On either side of the road as I move on
fields of autumn, bent by the weight of their crops,
bask in the sun; trees, indifferent to others,
stand on either side; staring all day
at their own shadows. Full, autumnal,   85
Ganga[5] flows rapidly. In the blue heavens
white cloudlets lie like delicate new-born calves,
fully satisfied with their mother's milk
and blissfully asleep. I sigh,
looking at the earth, stretching to the horizon,   90
weary of the passing epochs, bare in the brilliant sun.

In what a profound sadness are sky and earth
immersed! The further I go,
the more I hear the same piteous note:
'I won't let you go!' From the earth's edge   95
to the outermost limits of the blue heavens rings
this perennial cry, without beginning, without end:
'I won't let you go! I won't let you go!' That's what
they all say—'I won't let you go!' Mother earth,
holding the littlest grass-stalk to her breast,   100
says with all her power: 'I won't let you go!'
And in a lamp about to go out, someone seems
to pull the dying flame from darkness's grasp,
saying a hundred times, 'Ah, I won't let you go!'
From heaven to earth in this infinite universe   105
this is the oldest statement, the deepest cry—
'I won't let you go!' And yet, alas,
we have to let go of everything, and they go.
Thus it has been since time without beginning.
In creation's torrent, carrier of deluging seas,   110
they all rush past with fierce velocity,
eyes burning, eager arms outstretched,
moaning, calling—'Won't, won't let you go!'—
filling the shores of the cosmos with their clamour.
'Won't, won't let you go,' declares the rear wave   115
to the front wave, but none listens
or responds.

      From all directions today
that sad heart-rending wail reaches my ears,
ringing without pause, and in my daughter's voice: 120
a cry of the cosmos quite as importunate
as a child's. Since time began
all it gets it loses. Yet its grasp
of things hasn't slackened, and in the pride
of undiminished love, like my daughter of four,   125
ceaselessly it sends out this cry: 'I won't let you go!'
Face wan, tears streaming,

5. I.e., the Ganges, sacred river of the Hindus.

its pride is shattered each hour, every minute.
Yet such is love, it never concedes defeat
and in a choked voice rebelliously repeats: 130
'I won't let you go!' Each time it loses,
each time it blurts, 'How can what I
love be ever alienated from me?
Is there anything in this whole universe
as full of yearning, as superlative,   135
as mighty, as boundless as my desire?'
So saying, it arrogantly proclaims:
'I won't let you go', only to see at once
its cherished treasure blown away by a breath
like trivial dry dust, whereupon   140
eyes overflowing, like a tree uprooted,
it collapses on the ground, pride crushed, head bent.
Yet this remains love's plea:
'I won't let the Creator break His promise to me.
A great pledge, sealed and signed, to me was given,   145
a charter of rights in perpetuity.'
Thus, though thin and frail, and face to face
with almighty death, it says, swollen with pride,
'Death, you don't exist!' What cheek!
Death sits, smiling. And that eternal love,   150
so death-tormented, for ever in a flutter
with restless anxiety, has quite overpowered
this infinite universe, like the dampness of tears.
suffusing sad eyes. A weary hope against hope
has drawn a mist of dejection over the whole   155
universe. Yes, I think I see
two hapless imploring arms lie quietly,
encircling the world, in a vain attempt
to bind it in its embrace, like a still reflection
lying in a flowing stream—some illusion   160
of a cloud charged with raindrops and tears.

Wherefore today I can hear
so much yearning in the rustling of the trees,
as the noonday's hot wind, idly unmindful, plays
meaningless games with dry leaves, and as the day wanes,   165
lengthening the shadows under the peepul trees.
The cosmos is a field where the infinite's flute
plays a pastoral lament. And she sits and listens,
earth, her hair down, and it fills her with longing,
there, in the far cornfields, by Ganga's borders,   170
a golden cloth-end, sunlight-yellow, drawn
over her breast. Her eyes are still
fixed on the far blue sky, and she says nothing.
Yes, I've seen her pale face,
no different from the face of my daughter of four,   175
so quiet, so hurt, and nearly lost in the door-edge

[Calcutta, October 29, 1892]

The Golden Boat[6]

Clouds rumbling in the sky; teeming rain.
I sit on the river-bank, sad and alone.
The sheaves lie gathered, harvest has ended,
The river is swollen and fierce in its flow.
As we cut the paddy[7] it started to rain.   5

One small paddy-field, no one but me—
Flood-waters twisting and swirling everywhere.
Trees on the far bank   smear shadows like ink
On a village painted on deep morning grey.
On this side a paddy-field, no one but me.   10

Who is this, steering close to the shore,
Singing? I feel that he is someone I know.
The sails are filled wide, he gazes ahead,
Waves break helplessly against the boat each side.
I watch and feel I have seen his face before.   15

Oh to what foreign land do you sail?
Come to the bank and moor your boat for a while.
Go where you want to,   give where you care to,
But come to the bank a moment, show your smile—
Take away my golden paddy when you sail.   20

Take it, take as much as you can load.
Is there more? No, none, I have put it aboard.
My intense labour   here by the river—
I have parted with it all, layer upon layer:
Now take me as well, be kind, take me aboard.   25

No room, no room, the boat is too small.
Loaded with my gold paddy, the boat is full.
Across the rain-sky   clouds heave to and fro,
On the bare river-bank, I remain alone—
What I had has gone: the golden boat took all.   30

From KALPANĀ

A Stressful Time[8]

Though the evening's coming with slow and languid steps,
    all music's come to a halt, as if at a cue,

---

6. Translated by William Radice. This is one of Tagore's most famous poems, and one whose meaning has been hotly debated ever since it was published. *Sonār Tarī*: "The Golden Boat."   7. Rice is being harvested.   8. Translated by Ketaki Kushari Dyson. *Kalpanā*: "Imagination."

in the endless sky there's none else to fly with you,
   and weariness is descending on your breast,
though a great sense of dread throbs unspoken,   5
   and all around you the horizon is draped,
      yet bird, o my bird,
        already blind, don't fold your wings yet.

No, this is no susurrus of a forest,
   but the sea swelling with a slumber-snoring thunder.   10
No, this is no grove of kunda⁹ flowers,
   but crests of foam heaving with fluid palaver.
Where's that shore, dense with blossoms and leaves?
   Where's that nest, branch that offers shelter?
      Yet bird, o my bird,   15
        already blind, don't fold your wings yet.

Ahead of you still stretches a long, long night;
   the sun has gone to sleep behind a mountain.
The universe—it seems to hold its breath,
   sitting quietly, counting the passing hours.   20
And now on the dim horizon a thin curved moon,
   swimming against obscurity, appears.
      Bird, o my bird,
        already blind, don't fold your wings yet.

Above you the stars have spread their fingers,   25
   as in a mime, with a meaning in their gaze.
Below you death—deep, leaping, restless—
   snarls at you in a hundred thousand waves.
But on a far shore some are pleading with you.
   'Come, come': their wailing prayer says.   30
      So bird, o my bird,
        already blind, don't fold your wings yet.

Ah, there's no fear, no bonds of love's illusion;
   there's no hope, for hope is mere deceit.
There's no speech, no useless lamentation,   35
   neither home nor flower-strewn nuptial sheet.
You've only your wings, and painted in deepest black,
   this vast firmament where dawn's direction's lost.
      Then bird, o my bird,
        already blind, don't fold your wings yet.   40

[Calcutta, April 27, 1897]

---

9. A variety of white jasmine.

From NAIBEDYA[1]

No. 88

This I must admit: how one becomes two
is something I haven't understood at all.
How anything ever happens or one becomes what one is,
how anything stays in a certain way, what we mean
by words like *body, soul, mind:* I don't fathom,   5
but I shall always observe the universe
quietly, without words.

       How can I
even for an instant understand the beginning, the end,
the meaning, the theory—of something outside of which   10
I can never go? Only this I know—
that this thing is beautiful, great, terrifying,
various, unknowable, my mind's ravisher.

This I know, that knowing nothing, unawares,
the current of the cosmos's awareness flows towards you.   15

From SMARAN[2]

No. 5

No, no, she's no longer in my house!
I've looked in every corner. Nowhere to be found!
In my house, Lord, there's such precious little space—
what goes away from it cannot be retraced.
But your house is infinite, all-pervasive,   5
and it's there, Lord, I've come to look for her.
Here I stand, beneath this evening sky,
and look at you, tears streaming from my eyes.
There's a place from where no face, no bliss,
no hope, no thirst can ever be snatched from us.   10
It's there I've brought my devastated heart,
so you can drown, drown, drown it in that source.
Elixir of deathlessness no longer in my house—
may I recover its touch in the universe!

---

1. Translated by Ketaki Kushari Dyson. *Naibedya:* "Offering."   2. Translated by Ketaki Kushari Dyson. This is one of a series of poems Tagore wrote at the death of his wife, Mrinalini, in 1902. Tagore's own translation of this poem is included in *Gitanjali Smaran:* "Remembering."

Hide-and-Seek[3]

If I played a naughty trick on you, Mum,
   and flowered as a champa[4] on a champa tree,   4
and at sunrise, upon a branch,
   had a good play among the young leaves,
then you'd lose, and I'd be the winner,   5
for you wouldn't recognise me.
   You'd call, 'Khoka,[5] where are you?'
      I'd just smile quietly.

All jobs you do in the morning
   I'd watch with my eyes wide open.   10
After your bath, damp hair loose on your back,
   you'd walk this way, under the champa tree.
From here you'd go to the chapel
and smell flowers from afar—
   you wouldn't know that it was   15
      the smell of your Khoka's body in the air.

At noontime, when everyone's had their lunch,
   you'd sit down, the *Mahabharat*[6] in your hands.
Through the window the tree's shade
   would fall on your back, on your lap.   20
I'd bring my little shadow close to you
and sway it softly on your book—
   you wouldn't know that it was
      your Khoka's shadow moving before your eyes.

In the evening you'd light a lamp   25
   and go to the cow-shed, Mum.
Then would I, my flower-play done,
   fall down plonk on the ground.
Once again I'd become your little boy,
go up to you and say, 'Tell me a story.'   30
   You'd say, 'Naughty! Where have you been all day?'
      I'd say, 'I'm not telling you that!'

[Rainy season 1903?]

3. Translated by Ketaki Kushari Dyson. The poem is one of a series Tagore composed for his children in 1903, not long after the death of his wife. He wrote it at the hill resort of Almora, where he had taken his second daughter, Renuka (Rani), who had contracted tuberculosis. Rani died soon after their return. 4. Also called *champak,* this is a strongly scented yellow flower. 5. "Little boy," often used as a form of address for little boys. 6. Ancient Indian epic about the war between the Pāṇḍava and Kaurava princes.

From SHESH SAPTAK

No. 27[7]

Under the cascading stream
      I place my little pitcher
and sit
  all morning,
     sari-end tucked into waist,   5
    dangling my legs
      on a mossy slippery stone.

In an instant the pitcher fills
  and after that it just overflows.
    Curling with foam, the water falls,—   10
    nothing to do, no hurry at all,—
  the flowing water has its holiday play
     in the light of the sun
  and my own play leaps with it
    from my brimming mind.   15
The green-forest-enamelled valley's
      cup of blue sky.
Bubbling over its mountain-bordered rim,
   falls the murmuring sound
     In their dawn sleep   20
      the village girls hear its call.
  The water's sound
    crosses the violet-tinted forest's bounds
    and descends to where the tribal people come
      for their market day,   25
     leaving the tracks of the Terai[8] villages,
climbing the curves of the winding uphill path,
   with the ting-a-ling-a-ling
    of the bells of their bullocks
  carrying packs of dry twigs on their backs.   30

  Thus I while away
the day's first part.
  Red's the colour
   of the morning's young sunshine;
    then it grows white.   35
  Herons fly over the mountains
    towards the marshes.
  A white kite flies alone
  within the deep blue,
   like a silent meditative verse   40
    in the far-away mind
of the peak with its face upturned.

Around noon
  they send me word from home.

---

7. Translated by Ketaki Kushari Dyson. *Shesh Saptak:* "Last Octave."   8. Foothills of the Himalayas.

They are cross with me and say, 45
   'Why are you late?'
I say nothing in reply.
Everyone knows
   that to fill a pitcher it doesn't take long.
   Wasting time which overflows with no work— 50
   who can explain to them the strange passion for that?

24[9]

Take the last song's diminuendo with you.
Speak the last word as you go.

Darkness falls,
there's little time.
In the dim twilight
the farer loses his way.

The sun's last rays now fade from the western sky.
From the tamal[1] grove comes the last peacock-cry.

Who is she who searches the unknown
and for the last time opens my garden-gate?

[1939?]

From PUNASHCHA

Flute Music[2]

Kinugoala Lane[3]
   A two-storey house
   Ground-floor room, bars for windows
   Next to the road.
   On the rotting walls patches of peeling plaster, 5
   The stains of damp and salt.
   A picture label from a bale of cloth
   Stuck on the door shows
   Elephant-headed Ganesh, Bringer of Success.[4]
Apart from me the room has another denizen, 10
   Living rent-free:
   A lizard.

9. Translated by Ketaki Kushari Dyson. 1. A dark-leafed tree with a dark-colored bark. 2. Translated by Krishna Dutta and Andrew Robinson. The absence of rhyme and Tagore's use of short lines, laconic phrases, and colloquial and ironic language fit the subject matter of this poem. *Punashcha:* "Yet Once More" or "Postscript." 3. "Kinu the Milkman's Lane." 4. The elephant-headed Hindu god of good fortune.

The difference between it and me is simple—
It never lacks food.

I earn twenty-five rupees a month,   15
    As a junior clerk in a trading office,
    Eat at the Duttas' house,
    Tutor their boy in exchange.
Then it's off to Sealdah Station
    To spend the evening.   20
    Saves the expense of lighting.
Engines chuffing,
    Whistles screeching,
        Passengers rushing,
            Coolies yelling,   25
                It's half-past ten
When I head for my lonely, silent, gloomy room.

My aunt's village on the Dhaleshwari River.[5]
    Her brother-in-law's daughter
Was all set for marriage to my unfortunate self.   30
Surely the signs were auspicious, I have proof—[6]
    For when the moment came, I ran away.
The girl was saved from me
    And I from her.
She never came to this room, but she's never away from my mind,   35
    Wearing a Dacca sari, vermilion in her parting.[7]

Monsoon lours,
    Tram fares go up,
    Often my wages get cut.
In nooks and corners of the lane   40
There pile up and rot
    Mango skins and stones, jackfruit peelings,
    Fish-gills,
    Corpses of kittens,
    And who knows what other trash!   45
The state of my umbrella is like
    The state of my wage packet,
        Full of holes.

My office clothes resemble
    The thoughts of a Vaishnava guru,[8]   50
    Oozing and lachrymose.
The dark presence of the rains
    Hangs in my moist room
    Like a trapped beast
        Stunned and still.   55

5. A river flowing through Assam and the eastern part of Bengal, now Bangladesh.   6. Hindu marriages are arranged by the two families concerned and are performed at an auspicious time, calculated by astrologers, to ensure good luck for the bride and groom.   7. Dacca, capital of Bangladesh, is famed for its muslin cloth and saris. Bengali women wear vermilion where their hair is parted as a sign of their married status and good fortune for their husbands.   8. Tagore mocks the false piety of religious gurus (teachers), referring here to a member of the Vaishnava sect, devoted to the worship of the Hindu god Viṣṇu.

Day and night I feel that the world
    Is half-dead, and I am strapped to its back.

At a bend in the lane lives Kanta Babu,
    Long hair nattily groomed,
        Wide-eyed   60
            Refined of manner.
He loves to play the cornet.
Frequently the notes come floating
    Through the lane's stinking air.
    Sometimes at dead of night   65
    Or in the half-light before dawn,
    Sometimes in the afternoons
    When light and shadow coruscate.

Suddenly one evening
He begins to play in Shindhu Baroa raga,[9]   70
    And the whole sky rings
    With the yearning of the ages.
Then in a flash I grasp
    That the entire lane is a dreadful lie,
    Insufferable, like the ravings of a drunk.   75
Suddenly my mind sees
    That Akbar the emperor[1]
    And Haripada the clerk
    Are not different.
    Torn umbrella and royal parasol fuse   80
    In the pathos of the fluting melody[2]
    Pointing towards one heaven.

    The music is true, the key
To that endless twilit witching
    Where flows the River Dhaleshwari   85
    Its banks fringed with dark *tamal* trees,[3]
    Where
    In a courtyard
    She is waiting,
    Wearing a Dacca sari, vermilion in her parting.   90

9. The complex melodic scale-pattern of classical Indian music. Each *raga* has its characteristic phrases, ornaments, and mood associations.   1. Akbar (1556–1605), third and most illustrious of the Mughal emperors of India.   2. For Haripada, the sound of Kanta Babu's cornet is magically transformed into that of a flute, with its ancient association with pastoral landscapes and especially with the flute-playing cowherd god Krishna and the myth of his love play with herdswomen on the banks of the river Jamuna. 3. See note 8, selection 13 above.

From BANA-BĀṆĪ

In Praise of Trees[4]

O Tree, life-founder, you heard the sun
Summon you from the dark womb of earth
At your life's first wakening; your height
Raised from rhythmless rock the first
Hymn to the light; you brought feeling to harsh,   5
Impassive desert.
                Thus, in the sky,
By mixed magic, blue with green, you flung
The song of the world's spirit at heaven
And the tribe of stars. Facing the unknown,
You flew with fearless pride the victory   10
Banner of the life-force that passes
Again and again through death's gateway
To follow an endless pilgrim-road
Through time, through changing resting-places,
In ever new mortal vehicles.   15
Earth's reverie snapped at your noiseless
Challenge: excitedly she recalled
Her daring departure from heaven—
A daughter of God leaving its bright
Splendour, ashy-pale, dressed in humble   20
Ochre-coloured garments, to partake
Of the joy of heaven fragmented
Into time and place, to receive it
More deeply now that she would often
Pierce it with stabs of grief   25
                O valiant
Child of the earth, you declared a war
To liberate her from that fortress
Of desert. The war was incessant—
You crossed ocean-waves to establish,
With resolute faith, green seats of power   30
On bare, inaccessible islands;
You bewitched dust, scaled peaks, wrote on stone
In leafy characters your battle
Tales; you spread your code over trackless
Wastes.   35
           Sky, earth, sea were expressionless
Once, lacking the festival magic
Of the seasons. Your branches offered
Music its first shelter, made the songs
In which the restless wind—colouring   40
With kaleidoscopic melody
Her invisible body, edging
Her shawl with prismatic tune—first knew

---

4. Translated by William Radice. This meditative poem was written in 1926, two years before Tagore established an annual tree-planting festival at Santiniketan. *Bana-bāṇī*: "The Message of the Forest."

Herself. You were first to describe
On earth's clay canvas, by absorbing
Plastic power from the sun, a living   45
Image of beauty. You processed light's
Hidden wealth to give colour to light.
When celestial dancing-nymphs shook
Their bracelets in the clouds, shattering
Those misty cups to rain down freshening   50
Nectar, you filled therewith your vessels
Of leaf and flower to clothe the earth
With perpetual youth.
                            O profound,
Silent tree, by restraining valour
With patience, you revealed creative   55
Power in its peaceful form. Thus we come
To your shade to learn the art of peace,
To hear the word of silence; weighed down
With anxiety, we come to rest
In your tranquil blue-green shade, to take   60
Into our souls life rich, life ever
Juvenescent, life true to earth, life
Omni-victorious. I am certain
My thoughts have borne me to your essence—
Where the same fire as the sun's ritual   65
Fire of creation quietly assumes
In you cool green form. O sun-drinker,
The fire with which[5]—by milking hundreds
Of centuries of days of sunlight—
You have filled your core, man has received   70
As your gift, making him world-mighty,
Greatly honoured, rival to the gods:
His shining strength, kindled by your flame,
Is the wonder of the universe
As it cuts through daunting obstacles.   75
Man, whose life is in you, who is soothed
By your cool shade, strengthened by your power,
Adorned by your garland—O tree, friend
Of man, dazed by your leafy flutesong
I speak today for him as I make   80
    This verse-homage,
As I dedicate this offering
    To you.

---

5. Tagore evokes the fire sacrifice of the Vedas (ancient Hindu scriptures), and the Vedic Aryan worship of the sun and fire as divinities, a practice that continues in Hinduism.

From MAHŪĀ

Last Honey[6]

End of the year, of spring;[7] wind, renouncing the world, leaves
   The empty harvested fields with a farewell call to the bees—

     Come, come; Caitra[8] is going, shedding her leaves;
Earth spreads out her robe for summer languor beneath the trees;
But *sajne*[9]-tresses dangle and mango-blossoms are not all shed,   5
   And edging the woods *ākanda* lays its welcoming bed.
   Come, come; in the drought there'll be nothing of these
But the dance of their withered wraiths in the barren night, so come,
                                 bees.

I hear the song of the closing year like a flute in the rustling leaves,
So smear your wings with pollen's chronicle before its fragrance
                                flees.   10
   Take all you can from flowers that summer heat will strew;
   Cram the old year's honey into the hives of the new.
   Come, come; do not delay, new year bees—
Look what a wealth of parting gifts has been laid on the year as she
                                 leaves.

   The fierce, destructive heat of Baiśākh[1] will quickly seize   15
The *dolan-cā̃pā* buds that tremble now in the Caitra breeze.
   Finish all that they have to give, let nothing stay;
As the season ends let everything go in an orgy of giving away.
   Come, thieves of hidden honey; come now, bees—
The year has chosen to marry death and wants to give all as she
                                 leaves.   20

From JANMA-DINĒ

On My Birthday—20[2]

Today I imagine the words of countless
Languages to be suddenly fetterless—
After long incarceration
In the fortress of grammar, suddenly up in rebellion.
Maddened by the stamp-stamping   5
Of unmitigated regimented drilling.

---

6. Translated by William Radice. One of a series of poems on love, written by Tagore at the request of readers who wished to present these poems as wedding gifts to their friends. *Mahūā*: the name of a flower. 7. Unlike the calendars of many other regions of India, which begin with the month of Caitra—mid-March to mid-April and hence the spring season—the Bengali year *ends* with this month, making way for the new year, the month of Baiśākh, and the hot, dry summer. 8. The last month of the Bengali calendar, corresponding to the period mid-March to mid-April. 9. *Sajne, ākanda,* and *dolan-cā̃pā* (line 16) are various spring flowers. 1. The first month of the Bengali calendar, corresponding to the period mid-April to mid-May. 2. Translated by William Radice. One of a series of poems that Tagore wrote in 1940, the penultimate year of his life; many of the other poems in this collection were written from the poet's sickbed. Though rhymed, the poem has a free rhythm and lines of varying length. *Janma-dinē:* "On My Birthday."

They have jumped the constraints of sentence
To seek free expression in a world rid of intelligence,
Snapping the chains of sense in sarcasm
And ridicule of literary decorum.   10
Liberated thus, their queer
Postures and cries appeal only to the ear.
They say, 'We who were born of the gusty tuning
Of the earth's first outbreathing
Came into our own as soon as the blood's beat   15
Impelled man's mindless vitality to break into dance in his throat.
We swelled his infant voice with the babble
Of the world's first poem, the original prattle
Of existence. We are kin to the wild torrents
That pour from the mountains to announce   20
The month of Śrāban:[3] we bring to human habitations
Nature's incantations—'
The festive sound of leaves rustling in forests,
The sound that measures the rhythm of approaching tempests,
The great night-ending sound of day-break—   25
From these sound-fields man has captured words, curbed them like a
                                                         breakneck
Stallion in complex webs of order
To enable him to pass on his messages to the distant lands of the
                                                         future.
By riding words that are bridled and reined
Man has quickened   30
The pace of time's slow clocks:
The speed of his reason has cut through material blocks,
Explored recalcitrant mysteries;
With word-armies
Drawn into battle-lines he resists the perpetual assault of imbecility.   35
But sometimes they slip like robbers into realms of fantasy,
Float on ebbing waters
Of sleep, free of barriers,
Lashing any sort of flotsam and jetsam into metre.
From them, the free-roving mind fashions   40
Artistic creations
Of a kind that do not conform to an orderly
Universe—whose threads are tenuous, loose, arbitrary,
Like a dozen puppies brawling,
Scrambling at each other's necks to no purpose or meaning: 45
Each bites another—
They squeal and yelp blue murder,
But their bites and yelps carry no true import of enmity,
Their violence is bombast, empty fury.
In my mind I imagine words thus shot of their meaning,   50
Hordes of them running amuck all day,
As if in the sky there were nonsense nursery syllables booming—
Horselum, bridelum, ridelum, into the fray.

---

3. The fourth Bengali month, mid-July to mid-August, second month of the rainy season or monsoon.

Punishment[1]

I

When the brothers Dukhiram Rui and Chidam Rui went out in the morning with their heavy farm-knives, to work in the fields, their wives would quarrel and shout. But the people near by were as used to the uproar as they were to other customary, natural sounds. When they heard the shrill screams of the women, they would say, "They're at it again"—that is, what was happening was only to be expected: it was not a violation of Nature's rules. When the sun rises at dawn, no one asks why; and whenever the two wives in this *kuri*-caste[2] household let fly at each other, no one was at all curious to investigate the cause.

Of course this wrangling and disturbance affected the husbands more than the neighbours, but they did not count it a major nuisance. It was as if they were riding together along life's road in a cart whose rattling, clattering, unsprung wheels were inseparable from the journey. Indeed, days when there was no noise, when everything was uncannily silent, carried a greater threat of unpredictable doom.

The day on which our story begins was like this. When the brothers returned home at dusk, exhausted by their work, they found the house eerily quiet. Outside, too, it was extremely sultry. There had been a sharp shower in the afternoon, and clouds were still massing. There was not a breath of wind. Weeds and scrub round the house had shot up after the rain: the heavy scent of damp vegetation, from these and from the waterlogged jute-fields, formed a solid wall all around. Frogs croaked from the milkman's pond behind the house, and the buzz of crickets filled the leaden sky.

Not far off the swollen Padma[3] looked flat and sinister under the mounting clouds. It had flooded most of the grain-fields, and had come close to the houses. Here and there, roots of mango and jackfruit trees on the slipping bank stuck up out of the water, like helpless hands clawing at the air for a last fingerhold.

That day, Dukhiram and Chidam had been working near the zamindar's office. On a sandbank opposite, paddy[4] had ripened. The paddy needed to be cut before the sandbank was washed away, but the village people were busy either in their own fields or in cutting jute: so a messenger came from the office and forcibly engaged the two brothers. As the office roof was leaking in places, they also had to mend that and make some new wickerwork panels: it had taken them all day. They couldn't come home for lunch; they just had a snack from the office. At times they were soaked by the rain; they were not paid normal labourers' wages; indeed, they were paid mainly in insults and sneers.

When the two brothers returned at dusk, wading through mud and water, they found the younger wife, Chandara, stretched on the ground with her sari[5] spread out. Like the sky, she had wept buckets in the afternoon, but had now given way to sultry exhaustion. The elder wife, Radha, sat on the verandah sullenly: her eighteen-month son had been crying, but when the brothers came in they saw him lying naked in a corner of the yard, asleep.

---

1. Translated by William Radice.   2. In Bengal, a low caste originally of bird catchers, but by the 19th century, general laborers.   3. A major river in what is now Bangladesh.   4. The rice crop. *Zamindar*: landlord.   5. A long strip of cloth draped around the body, Indian women's traditional clothing.

Dukhiram, famished, said gruffly, "Give me my food."

Like a spark on a sack of gunpowder, the elder wife exploded, shrieking out, "Where is there food? Did you give me anything to cook? Must I earn money myself to buy it?"

After a whole day of toil and humiliation, to return—raging with hunger—to a dark, joyless, foodless house, to be met by Radha's sarcasm, especially her final jibe, was suddenly unendurable. "What?" he roared, like a furious tiger, and then, without thinking, plunged his knife into her head. Radha collapsed into her sister-in-law's lap, and in minutes she was dead.

"What have you done?" screamed Chandara, her clothes soaked with blood. Chidam pressed his hand over her mouth. Dukhiram, throwing aside the knife, fell to his knees with his head in his hands, stunned. The little boy woke up and started to wail in terror.

Outside there was complete quiet. The herd-boys were returning with the cattle. Those who had been cutting paddy on the far sandbanks were crossing back in groups in a small boat—with a couple of bundles of paddy on their heads as payment. Everyone was heading for home.

Ramlochan Chakravarti, pillar of the village, had been to the post office with a letter, and was now back in his house, placidly smoking. Suddenly he remembered that his sub-tenant Dukhiram was very behind with his rent: he had promised to pay some today. Deciding that the brothers must be home by now, he threw his chadar[6] over his shoulders, took his umbrella, and stepped out.

As he entered the Ruis' house, he felt uneasy. There was no lamp alight. On the dark verandah, the dim shapes of three or four people could be seen. In a corner of the verandah there were fitful, muffled sobs: the little boy was trying to cry for his mother, but was stopped each time by Chidam.

"Dukhi," said Ramlochan nervously, "are you there?"

Dukhiram had been sitting like a statue for a long time; now, on hearing his name, he burst into tears like a helpless child.

Chidam quickly came down from the verandah into the yard, to meet Ramlochan. "Have the women been quarelling again?" Ramlochan asked. "I heard them yelling all day."

Chidam, all this time, had been unable to think what to do. Various impossible stories occurred to him. All he had decided was that later that night he would move the body somewhere. He had never expected Ramlochan to come. He could think of no swift reply. "Yes," he stumbled, "today they were quarrelling terribly."

"But why is Dukhi crying so?" asked Ramlochan, stepping towards the verandah.

Seeing no way out now, Chidam blurted, "In their quarrel, *Choṭobau* struck at *Baṛobau*'s[7] head with a farm-knife."

When immediate danger threatens, it is hard to think of other dangers. Chidam's only thought was to escape from the terrible truth—he forgot that a lie can be even more terrible. A reply to Ramlochan's question had come instantly to mind, and he had blurted it out.

---

6. In Bengal, a sheet of cloth draped around the shoulders, usually worn by men but sometimes by women.
7. "Elder Daughter-in-Law"; members of a family address each other by kinship terms. *Choṭobau*: "Younger Daughter-in-Law."

"Good grief," said Ramlochan in horror. "What are you saying? Is she dead?"

"She's dead," said Chidam, clasping Ramlochan's feet.

Ramlochan was trapped. *"Rām, Rām,"*[8] he thought, "what a mess I've got into this evening. What if I have to be a witness in court?" Chidam was still clinging to his feet, saying, *"Thākur,*[9] how can I save my wife?"

Ramlochan was the village's chief source of advice on legal matters. Reflecting further he said, "I think I know a way. Run to the police station: say that your brother Dukhi returned in the evening wanting his food, and because it wasn't ready he struck his wife on the head with his knife. I'm sure that if you say that, she'll get off."

Chidam felt a sickening dryness in his throat. He stood up and said, *"Thākur,* if I lose my wife I can get another, but if my brother is hanged, how can I replace him?" In laying the blame on his wife, he had not seen it that way. He had spoken without thought; now, imperceptibly, logic and awareness were returning to his mind.

Ramlochan appreciated his logic. "Then say what actually happened," he said. "You can't protect yourself on all sides."

He had soon, after leaving, spread it round the village that Chandara Rui had, in a quarrel with her sister-in-law, split her head open with a farm-knife. Police charged into the village like a river in flood. Both the guilty and the innocent were equally afraid.

II

Chidam decided he would have to stick to the path he had chalked out for himself. The story he had given to Ramlochan Chakravarti had gone all round the village; who knew what would happen if another story was circulated? But he realized that if he kept to the story he would have to wrap it in five more stories if his wife was to be saved.

Chidam asked Chandara to take the blame on to herself. She was dumbfounded. He reassured her: "Don't worry—if you do what I tell you, you'll be quite safe." But whatever his words, his throat was dry and his face was pale.

Chandara was not more than seventeen or eighteen. She was buxom, well-rounded, compact and sturdy—so trim in her movements that in walking, turning, bending or climbing there was no awkwardness at all. She was like a brand-new boat: neat and shapely, gliding with ease, not a loose joint anywhere. Everything amused and intrigued her; she loved to gossip; her bright, restless, deep black eyes missed nothing as she walked to the *ghāt,*[1] pitcher on her hip, parting her veil slightly with her finger.

The elder wife had been her exact opposite: unkempt, sloppy and slovenly. She was utterly disorganized in her dress, housework, and the care of her child. She never had any proper work in hand, yet never seemed to have time for anything. The younger wife usually refrained from comment, for at the mildest barb Radha would rage and stamp and let fly at her, disturbing everyone around.

8. God's name, repeated to express great emotion.   9. "Master" or "lord," term of address for gods and upper-class (Brahmin) men. *Tagore* is an anglicized form of *Thākur.*   1. Steps leading down to a pond or river; meeting place, especially for women, who go there to get water or to wash clothes.

Each wife was matched by her husband to an extraordinary degree. Dukhiram was a huge man—his bones were immense, his nose was squat, in his eyes and expression he seemed not to understand the world very well, yet he never questioned it either. He was innocent yet fearsome: a rare combination of power and helplessness. Chidam, however, seemed to have been carefully carved from shiny black rock. There was not an inch of excess fat on him, not a wrinkle or dimple anywhere. Each limb was a perfect blend of strength and finesse. Whether jumping from a riverbank, or punting a boat, or climbing up bamboo-shoots for sticks, he showed complete dexterity, effortless grace. His long black hair was combed with oil back from his brow and down to his shoulders—he took great care over his dress and appearance. Although he was not unresponsive to the beauty of other women in the village, and was keen to make himself charming in their eyes, his real love was for his young wife. They quarrelled sometimes, but there was mutual respect too: neither could defeat the other. There was a further reason why the bond between them was firm: Chidam felt that a wife as nimble and sharp as Chandara could not be wholly trusted, and Chandara felt that all eyes were on her husband—that if she didn't bind him tightly to her she might one day lose him.

A little before the events in this story, however, they had a major row. Chandara had noticed that when her husband's work took him away for two days or more, he brought no extra earnings. Finding this ominous, she also began to overstep the mark. She would hang around by the *ghāt*, or wander about talking rather too much about Kashi Majumdar's middle son.

Something now seemed to poison Chidam's life. He could not settle his attention on his work. One day his sister-in-law rounded on him: she shook her finger and said in the name of her dead father, "That girl runs before the storm. How can I restrain her? Who knows what ruin she will bring?"

Chandara came out of the next room and said sweetly, "What's the matter, *Didi?*"[2] and a fierce quarrel broke out between them.

Chidam glared at his wife and said, "If I ever hear that you've been to the *ghāt* on your own, I'll break every bone in your body."

"The bones will mend again," said Chandara, starting to leave. Chidam sprang at her, grabbed her by the hair, dragged her back to the room and locked her in.

When he returned from work that evening he found that the room was empty. Chandara had fled three villages away, to her maternal uncle's house. With great difficulty Chidam persuaded her to return, but he had to surrender to her. It was as hard to restrain his wife as to hold a handful of mercury; she always slipped through his fingers. He did not have to use force any more, but there was no peace in the house. Ever-fearful love for his elusive young wife wracked him with intense pain. He even once or twice wondered if it would be better if she were dead: at least he would get some peace then. Human beings can hate each other more than death.

It was at this time that the crisis hit the house.

When her husband asked her to admit to the murder, Chandara stared at him, stunned; her black eyes burnt him like fire. Then she shrank back, as

2. "Elder Sister," respectful form of address for Bengali women.

if to escape his devilish clutches. She turned her heart and soul away from him. "You've nothing to fear," said Chidam. He taught her repeatedly what she should say to the police and the magistrate. Chandara paid no attention—sat like a wooden statue whenever he spoke.

Dukhiram relied on Chidam for everything. When he told him to lay the blame on Chandara, Dukhiram said, "But what will happen to her?" "I'll save her," said Chidam. His burly brother was content with that.

III

This was what he instructed his wife to say: "The elder wife was about to attack me with the vegetable-slicer. I picked up a farm-knife to stop her, and it somehow cut into her." This was all Ramlochan's invention. He had generously supplied Chidam with the proofs and embroidery that the story would require.

The police came to investigate. The villagers were sure now that Chandara had murdered her sister-in-law, and all the witnesses confirmed this. When the police questioned Chandara, she said, "Yes, I killed her."

"Why did you kill her?"

"I couldn't stand her any more."

"Was there a brawl between you?"

"No."

"Did she attack you first?"

"No."

"Did she ill-treat you?"

"No."

Everyone was amazed at these replies, and Chidam was completely thrown off balance. "She's not telling the truth," he said. "The elder wife first—"

The inspector silenced him sharply. He continued according to the rules of cross-examination and repeatedly received the same reply: Chandara would not accept that she had been attacked in any way by her sister-in-law. Such an obstinate girl was never seen! She seemed absolutely bent on going to the gallows; nothing would stop her. Such fierce, passionate pride! In her thoughts, Chandara was saying to her husband, "I shall give my youth to the gallows instead of to you. My final ties in this life will be with them."

Chandara was arrested, and left her home for ever, by the paths she knew so well, past the festival carriage, the market-place, the *ghāt*, the Majumdars' house, the post office, the school—an ordinary, harmless, flirtatious, fun-loving village wife; leaving a shameful impression on all the people she knew. A bevy of boys followed her, and the women of the village, her friends and companions—some of them peering through their veils, some from their doorsteps, some from behind trees—watched the police leading her away and shuddered with embarrassment, fear and contempt.

To the Deputy Magistrate, Chandara again confessed her guilt, claiming no ill-treatment from her sister-in-law at the time of the murder. But when Chidam was called to the witness-box he broke down completely, weeping, clasping his hands and saying, "I swear to you, sir, my wife is innocent." The magistrate sternly told him to control himself, and began to question him. Bit by bit the true story came out.

The magistrate did not believe him, because the chief, most trustworthy, most educated witness—Ramlochan Chakravarti—said: "I appeared on the scene a little after the murder. Chidam confessed everything to me and clung to my feet saying, 'Tell me how I can save my wife.' I did not say anything one way or the other. Then Chidam said, 'If I say that my elder brother killed his wife in a fit of fury because his food wasn't ready, then she'll get off.' I said, 'Be careful, you rogue: don't say a single false word in court—there's no worse offence than that.' " Ramlochan had previously prepared lots of stories that would save Chandara, but when he found that she herself was bending her neck to receive the noose, he decided, "Why take the risk of giving false evidence now? I'd better say what little I know." So Ramlochan said what he knew—or rather said a little more than he knew.

The Deputy Magistrate committed the case to a sessions trial.[3] Meanwhile in fields, houses, markets and bazaars, the sad or happy affairs of the world carried on; and just as in previous years, torrential monsoon rains fell on to the new rice-crop.

Police, defendant and witnesses were all in court. In the civil court opposite hordes of people were waiting for their cases. A Calcutta lawyer had come on a suit about the sharing of a pond behind a kitchen; the plaintiff had thirty-nine witnesses. Hundreds of people were anxiously waiting for hair-splitting judgements, certain that nothing, at present, was more important. Chidam stared out of the window at the constant throng, and it seemed like a dream. A *koel*-bird[4] was hooting from a huge banyan tree in the compound: no courts or cases in *his* world!

Chandara said to the judge, "Sir, how many times must I go on saying the same thing?"

The judge explained, "Do you know the penalty for the crime you have confessed?"

"No," said Chandara.

"It is death by the hanging."

"Then please give it to me, sir," said Chandara. "Do what you like—I can't take any more."

When her husband was called to the court, she turned away. "Look at the witness," said the judge, "and say who he is."

"He is my husband," said Chandara, covering her face with her hands.

"Does he not love you?"

"He loves me greatly."

"Do you not love him?"

"I love him greatly."

When Chidam was questioned, he said, "I killed her."

"Why?"

"I wanted my food and my sister-in-law didn't give it to me."

When Dukhiram came to give evidence, he fainted. When he had come round again, he answered, "Sir, I killed her."

"Why?"

"I wanted a meal and she didn't give it to me."

After extensive cross-examination of various other witnesses, the judge concluded that the brothers had confessed to the crime in order to save the

---

3. A trial that is settled through a special court *sessions* in one continuous sitting.　4. Common Indian songbird.

younger wife from the shame of the noose. But Chandara had, from the police investigation right through to the sessions trial, said the same thing repeatedly—she had not budged an inch from her story. Two barristers did their utmost to save her from the death-sentence, but in the end were defeated by her.

Who, on that auspicious night when, at a very young age, a dusky, diminutive, round-faced girl had left her childhood dolls in her father's house and come to her in-laws' house, could have imagined these events? Her father, on his deathbed, had happily reflected that at least he had made proper arrangements for his daughter's future.

In gaol,[5] just before the hanging, a kindly Civil Surgeon asked Chandara, "Do you want to see anyone?"

"I'd like to see my mother," she replied.

"Your husband wants to see you," said the doctor. "Shall I call him?"

"To hell with him,"[6] said Chandara.

5. Jail.   6. "Death to him" (literal trans.); an expression usually uttered in jest.

WILLIAM BUTLER YEATS
1865–1939

William Butler Yeats is not only the main figure in the Irish literary renaissance but also the twentieth century's greatest poet in the English language. His sensuously evocative descriptions and his fusion of concrete historical examples with an urgent metaphysical vision stir readers around the world. Years after the poet's death, the Nigerian Chinua Achebe borrowed three words from one of his lines as the title of a novel, *Things Fall Apart*—confident that his audience would immediately recognize the source. If the English language has a Symbolist poet, it is once again Yeats for his constant use of allusive imagery and large symbolic structures. Yeats's symbolism is not that of Baudelaire, Mallarmé, or other continental predecessors, however, for the European Symbolists did not share the Irish poet's fascination with occult wisdom and large historical patterns. Yeats adopted a cyclical model of history for which the rise and fall of civilizations are predetermined inside a series of interweaving evolutionary spirals. With this cyclical model, he created a private mythology that allowed him to come to terms with both personal and cultural pain and helped to explain—as symptoms of Western civilization's declining spiral—the plight of contemporary Irish society and the chaos of European culture around World War I. Yeats shares with writers like Rilke and T. S. Eliot the quest for larger meaning in a time of trouble and the use of symbolic language to give verbal form to that quest.

Yeats was born in a Dublin suburb on June 13, 1865, the oldest of four children born to John Butler and Susan Pollexfen Yeats. His father, a cosmopolitan Anglo-Irishman who had turned from law to painting, took over Yeats's education when he found that, at age nine, the boy could not read. J. B. Yeats was a highly argumentative religious skeptic who alternately terrorized his son and awakened his interest in poetry and the visual arts, inspiring at one and the same time both rebellion against scientific rationalism and belief in the higher knowledge of art. His mother's strong ties to her home in County Sligo (where Yeats spent many summers and school holidays) introduced him to the beauties of the Irish countryside and the Irish folklore and supernatural legends that appear throughout his work. Living alternately in Ireland and England for much of his youth, Yeats became part of literary society in both countries and—though an Irish nationalist—was unable to adopt a narrowly patriotic point of view. Even the failed Easter Rebellion of 1916, which he celebrated in *Easter 1916,* and the revolutionary figures who were beloved friends took their place in a larger mythic historical framework. By the end of his life, he had abandoned all practical politics and devoted himself to the reality of personal experience inside a mystic view of history.

For many, it is Yeats's mastery of images that defines his work. From his early use of symbols as private keys, or dramatic metaphors for complex personal emotions, to the immense cosmology of his last work, he continued to create a highly visual poetry whose power derives from the dramatic interweaving of specific images. Symbols such as the Tower, Byzantium, Helen of Troy, the opposition of sun and moon, birds of prey, the blind man, and the fool recur frequently and draw their meaning not from inner connections established inside the poem (as for the French Symbolists) but from an underlying myth based on occult tradition, Irish folklore, history, and Yeats's own personal experience. Symbols as Yeats used them, however, make sense in and among themselves: the "gyre," or spiral unfolding of history, is simultaneously the falcon's spiral flight; and the sphinxlike beast slouching blank-eyed toward Bethlehem in *The Second Coming* is a comprehensible horror capable of many explicit interpretations but resistant to all and, therefore, the more terrifying. Even readers unacquainted with Yeats's mythic system will respond to images precisely expressing a situation or state of mind (for example, golden Byzantium for intellect, art, wisdom— all that "body" cannot supply) and to a visionary organization that proposes shape and context for twentieth-century anxieties.

The nine poems included here cover the range of Yeats's career, which embraced several periods and styles. Yeats had attended art school and planned to be an artist before he turned fully to literature in 1886, and his early works show the influence of the Pre-Raphaelite school in art and literature. Pre-Raphaelitism called for a return to the sensuous representation and concrete particulars found in Italian painting before Raphael (1483–1520), and Pre-Raphaelite poetry evoked a poetic realm of luminous supernatural beauty described in allusive and erotically sensuous detail. Rossetti's *Blessed Damozel,* yearning for her beloved "from the gold bar of heaven," has eyes "deeper than the depth / Of waters stilled at even; / She had three lilies in her hand, / And the stars in her hair were seven." The Pre-Raphaelite fascination with the medieval past (William Morris wrote a *Defense of Guenevere,* King Arthur's adulterous wife) combined with Yeats's own interest in Irish legend, and in 1889 a long poem describing a traveler in fairyland (*The Wanderings of Oisin*) established his reputation and won Morris's praise. The musical, evocative style of Yeats's Pre-Raphaelite period is well shown in *The Lake Isle of Innisfree* (1890), with its hidden "bee-loud glade" where "peace comes dropping slow" and evening, after the "purple glow" of noon, is "full of the linnet's wings." Another poem from the same period, *When You Are Old,* pleads his love for the beautiful actress and Irish nationalist Maud Gonne, whom he met in 1889 and who repeatedly refused to marry him. From the love poems of his youth to his old age, when *The Circus Animals' Desertion* described her as prey to fanaticism and hate, Yeats returned again and again to examine his feelings for this woman, who personified love, beauty, and Irish nationalism along with hope, frustration, and despair.

Yeats's family moved to London in 1887, where he continued an earlier interest in mystical philosophy by taking up theosophy under its Russian interpreter Madame Blavatsky. Madame Blavatsky claimed mystic knowledge from Tibetan monks and preached a doctrine of the Universal Oversoul, individual spiritual evolution through cycles of incarnation, and the world as a conflict of opposites. Yeats was taken with her grandiose cosmology, although he inconveniently wished to test it by experiment and analysis and was ultimately expelled from the society in 1890.

He found a more congenial literary model in the works of William Blake, which he coedited in 1893 with F. J. Ellis. Yeats's interest in large mystical systems later waned but never altogether disappeared, and traces may be seen in the introduction that he wrote in 1916 for *Gitanjali,* a collection of poems by the Indian author Rabindranath Tagore.

Several collections of Irish folk and fairy tales and a book describing Irish traditions (*The Celtic Twilight,* 1893) demonstrated a corresponding interest in Irish national identity. In 1896 he had met Lady Gregory, an Irish nationalist who invited him to spend summers at Coole Park, her country house in Galway, and who worked closely with him (and later J. M. Synge) in founding the Irish National Theatre (later the Abbey Theatre). Along with other participants in what was once called the Irish literary renaissance, he aimed to create "a national literature that made Ireland beautiful in the memory . . . freed from provincialism by an exacting criticism." To this end, he wrote *Cathleen ni Houlihan* (1902), a play in which the title character personifies Ireland, which became immensely popular with Irish nationalists. He also established Irish literary societies in Dublin and Ireland, promoted and reviewed Irish books, and lectured and wrote about the need for Irish community. In 1922 he was elected senator of the Irish Free State, serving until 1928.

Gradually, Yeats became embittered by the split between narrow Irish nationalism and the free expression of Irish culture. He was outraged at the attacks on Synge's *Playboy of the Western World* (1907) for its supposed derogatory picture of Irish culture, and he commented scathingly in *Poems Written in Discouragement* (1913, reprinted in *Responsibilities,* 1914) on the inability of the Irish middle class to appreciate art or literature. When he celebrates the abortive Easter uprisings of 1916, it is with a more universal, aesthetic view; "A terrible beauty is born" in the self-sacrifice that leads even a "drunken, vainglorious lout" to be "transformed utterly" by political martyrdom. Except for summers at Coole Park, Yeats in his middle age was spending more time in England than in Ireland. He began his *Autobiographies* in 1914, and wrote symbolic plays intended for small audiences on the model of the Japanese *nō* theater. There is a change in the tone of his works at this time, a new precision and epigrammatic quality that is partly owing to his disappointment with Irish nationalism and partly to the new tastes in poetry promulgated by his friend Ezra Pound and by T. S. Eliot after the example of John Donne and the metaphysical poets.

Yeats's marriage in 1917 to Georgie Hyde-Lees provided him with much-needed stability and also an impetus to work out a larger symbolic scheme. He interpreted his wife's experiments with automatic writing (writing whatever comes to mind, without correction or rational intent) as glimpses into a hidden cosmic order and gradually evolved a total system, which he explained in *A Vision* (1925). The wheel of history takes twenty-six thousand years to turn; and inside that wheel civilizations evolve in roughly two-thousand-year *gyres,* spirals expanding outward until they collapse at the beginning of a new gyre, which will reverse the direction of the old. Human personalities fall into different types within the system, and both gyres and types are related to the different phases of the moon. Yeats's later poems in *The Tower* (1928), *The Winding Stair* (1933), and *Last Poems* (1939) are set in the context of this system. Even when it is not literally present, it suggests an organizing pattern that resolves contraries inside an immense historical perspective. *Leda and the Swan,* on one level an erotic retelling of a mythic rape, also foreshadows the Trojan War—brute force mirroring brute force. In the two poems on the legendary city of Byzantium, Yeats admired an artistic civilization that "could answer all my questions" but that was also only a moment in history. Byzantine art, with its stylized perspectives and mosaics made by arranging tiny colored pieces of stone, was the exact opposite of the Western tendency to imitate nature, and it provided a kind of escape, or healing distance, for the poet. The idea of an inhuman, metallic, abstract beauty separated "out of nature" by art expresses a mystic and Symbolist quest for an invulnerable world distinct from the ravages of time. This world was to be found in an idealized Byzantium, where the poet's body would be transmuted into "such a form as Grecian goldsmiths make / Of hammered gold and gold enamelling / To keep a drowsy Emperor awake; / Or set upon a golden bough to sing / To lords and ladies of Byzantium / Of what is past, or passing, or to come." At the end of *Among School Children*, the sixty-year-old "public man" compensates for the passing of youth by dreaming of pure "Presences" that never fade. Yeats had often adopted the persona of the old man for whom the perspectives of age, idealized beauty, or history were ways to keep human agony at a distance. In *Lapis Lazuli*, the tragic figures of history transcend their roles by the calm "gaiety" with which they accept their fate; the ancient Chinamen carved in the poem's damaged blue stone climb toward a vantage point where they stare detachedly down on the world's tragedies: "Their eyes mid many wrinkles, their eyes, / Their ancient, glittering eyes, are gay."

But the world is still there, its tragedies still take place, and Yeats's poetry is always aware of the physical and emotional roots from which it sprang. Whatever the wished-for distance, his poems are full of passionate feelings, erotic desire and disappointment, delight in sensuous beauty, horror at civil war and anarchy, dismay at degradation and change. By the time of his death on January 28, 1939, Yeats had rejected his Byzantine identity as the golden songbird and sought out "the brutality, the ill breeding, the barbarism of truth." "The Wild Old Wicked Man" replaced earlier druids or ancient Chinamen as spokesman, and in *The Circus Animals' Desertion* Yeats described his former themes as so many circus animals put on display. No matter how much these themes embodied "pure mind," they were based in "a mound of refuse or the sweepings of a street . . . the foul rag-and-bone shop of the heart"— the rose springing from the dunghill. Yeats's poetry, which draws its initial power from the mastery of images and verbal rhythm, continues to resonate in the reader's mind for this attempt to come to terms with reality, to grasp and make sense of human experience in the transfiguring language of art.

Edward Malins presents a brief introduction with biography, illustrations, and maps in *A Preface to Yeats* (1994). Richard Ellmann, *The Identity of Yeats* (1964), is an excellent discussion of Yeats's work as a whole. Norman A. Jeffares has revised his major study, *A New Commentary on the Collected Poems of W. B. Yeats* (1983); a useful reference work is Lester I. Conner, *A Yeats Dictionary: Persons and Places in the Poetry of William Butler Yeats* (1998). Jeffares's *W. B. Yeats: A New Biography* (1989) takes into account new information about the poet. Recent biographies are R. F. Foster, *W. B. Yeats: A Life*, 2 vols. (1997–99), a full and balanced study, and Terence Brown, *The Life of W. B. Yeats: A Critical Biography* (1999), which emphasizes the evolution of his work within personal and social contexts. Elizabeth Cullingford, *Gender and History in Yeats's Love Poetry* (1993), examines aesthetic form and cultural perspectives in the love lyrics; Deirdre Toomey, *Yeats and Women* (1997), discusses Yeats's relations with women and the women in his poetry; and Marjorie Elizabeth Howes, *Yeats's Nations: Gender, Class, and Irishness* (1996), stresses political and social views. Essay collections include Harold Bloom, ed., *William Butler Yeats* (1986), and Richard J. Finneran, ed., *Critical Essays on W. B. Yeats* (1986). Essays in Deborah Fleming, ed., *Learning the Trade: Essays on W. B. Yeats and Contemporary Poetry* (1993), discuss Yeats's imprint on various contemporary poets; and contributions to Leonard Orr, ed., *Yeats and Postmodernism* (1991), approach Yeats from different postmodernist perspectives.

PRONOUNCING GLOSSARY

The following list uses common English syllables and stress accents to provide rough equivalents of selected words whose pronunciation may be unfamiliar to the general reader.

Callimachus: *ca-li'-mah-cus*

Cuchulain: *coo-hu'-lin*

gyre: *jai-er*

Quattrocento: *kwah-troh-chen'-toh*

When You Are Old[1]

When you are old and gray and full of sleep,
And nodding by the fire, take down this book,
And slowly read, and dream of the soft look
Your eyes had once, and of their shadows deep;

How many loved your moments of glad grace,   5
And loved your beauty with love false or true,
But one man loved the pilgrim soul in you,
And loved the sorrows of your changing face;

And bending down beside the glowing bars,
Murmur, a little sadly, how Love fled   10
And paced upon the mountains overhead
And hid his face amid a crowd of stars.

Easter 1916[1]

I have met them at close of day
Coming with vivid faces
From counter or desk among grey
Eighteenth-century houses.
I have passed with a nod of the head   5
Or polite meaningless words,
Or have lingered awhile and said
Polite meaningless words,
And thought before I had done
Of a mocking tale or a gibe   10
To please a companion
Around the fire at the club,
Being certain that they and I
But lived where motley is worn:
All changed, changed utterly: 15
A terrible beauty is born.

That woman's[2] days were spent
In ignorant good-will,
Her nights in argument
Until her voice grew shrill.   20
What voice more sweet than hers
When, young and beautiful,
She rode to harriers?
This man had kept a school
And rode our wingèd horse;   25

1. An adaptation of a love sonnet by the French Renaissance poet Pierre de Ronsard (1524–1585), which begins similarly ("Quand vous serez bien vieille") but ends by asking the beloved to "pluck the roses of life today." 1. On Easter Sunday 1916, Irish nationalists began an unsuccessful rebellion against British rule, which lasted throughout the week and ended in the surrender and execution of its leaders. 2. Constance Gore-Booth (1868–1927), later Countess Markiewicz, an ardent nationalist.

This other his helper and friend[3]
Was coming into his force;
He might have won fame in the end,
So sensitive his nature seemed,
So daring and sweet his thought.   30
This other man[4] I had dreamed
A drunken, vainglorious lout.
He had done most bitter wrong
To some who are near my heart,
Yet I number him in the song;   35
He, too, has resigned his part
In the casual comedy;
He, too, has been changed in his turn,
Transformed utterly:
A terrible beauty is born.   40

Hearts with one purpose alone
Through summer and winter seem
Enchanted to a stone
To trouble the living stream.
The horse that comes from the road,   45
The rider, the birds that range
From cloud to tumbling cloud,
Minute by minute they change;
A shadow of cloud on the stream
Changes minute by minute;   50
A horse-hoof slides on the brim,
And a horse plashes within it;
The long-legged moor-hens dive,
And hens to moor-cocks call;
Minute by minute they live: 55
The stone's in the midst of all.

Too long a sacrifice
Can make a stone of the heart.
O when may it suffice?
That is Heaven's part, our part   60
To murmur name upon name,
As a mother names her child
When sleep at last has come
On limbs that had run wild.
What is it but nightfall?   65
No, no, not night but death;
Was it needless death after all?
For England may keep faith
For all that is done and said.
We know their dream; enough   70
To know they dreamed and are dead;

3. Patrick Pearse (1879–1916) and his friend Thomas MacDonagh (1878–1916), both schoolmasters and leaders of the rebellion and both executed by the British. As a Gaelic poet, Pearse symbolically rode the winged horse of the Muses, Pegasus.   4. Major John MacBride (1865–1916), who had married and separated from Maud Gonne (1866–1953), Yeats's great love.

And what if excess of love
Bewildered them till they died?
I write it out in a verse—
MacDonagh and MacBride   75
And Connolly[5] and Pearse
Now and in time to be,
Wherever green is worn,
Are changed, changed utterly:
A terrible beauty is born.   80

The Second Coming[1]

Turning and turning in the widening gyre[2]
The falcon cannot hear the falconer;
Things fall apart; the centre cannot hold;
Mere anarchy is loosed upon the world,
The blood-dimmed tide is loosed, and everywhere   5
The ceremony of innocence is drowned;
The best lack all conviction, while the worst
Are full of passionate intensity.

Surely some revelation is at hand;
Surely the Second Coming is at hand.   10
The Second Coming! Hardly are those words out
When a vast image out of *Spiritus Mundi*[3]
Troubles my sight: somewhere in sands of the desert
A shape with lion body and the head of a man
A gaze blank and pitiless as the sun,   15
Is moving its slow thighs, while all about it
Reel shadows of the indignant desert birds.
The darkness drops again; but now I know
That twenty centuries of stony sleep
Were vexed to nightmare by a rocking cradle,   20
And what rough beast, its hour come round at last,
Slouches towards Bethlehem to be born?

Leda and the Swan[1]

A sudden blow: the great wings beating still
Above the staggering girl, her thighs caressed
By the dark webs, her nape caught in his bill,
He holds her helpless breast upon his breast.

---

5. James Connolly (1870–1916), labor leader and nationalist executed by the British.   1. The Second Coming of Christ, believed by Christians to herald the end of the world, is transformed here into the prediction of a new birth initiating a new era and terminating the two-thousand-year cycle of Christianity. 2. The cone pattern of the falcon's flight and of historical cycles, in Yeats's vision.   3. World-soul (Latin) or, as *Anima Mundi* in Yeats's *Per Amica Silentia Lunae*, a "great memory" containing archetypal images; recalls C. G. Jung's collective unconscious.   1. Zeus, ruler of the Greek gods, took the form of a swan to rape the mortal Leda; she gave birth to Helen of Troy, whose beauty caused the Trojan War.

How can those terrified vague fingers push   5
The feathered glory from her loosening thighs?
And how can body, laid in that white rush,
But feel the strange heart beating where it lies?

A shudder in the loins engenders there
The broken wall, the burning roof and tower   10
And Agamemnon dead.[2]
                    Being so caught up,
So mastered by the brute blood of the air,
Did she put on his knowledge with his power
Before the indifferent beak could let her drop?

Sailing to Byzantium[1]

1

That is no country for old men. The young
In one another's arms, birds in the trees
—Those dying generations—at their song,
The salmon-falls, the mackerel-crowded seas,
Fish, flesh, or fowl, commend all summer long   5
Whatever is begotten, born, and dies.
Caught in the sensual music all neglect
Monuments of unageing intellect.

2

An aged man is but a paltry thing,
A tattered coat upon a stick, unless   10
Soul clap its hands and sing, and louder sing
For every tatter in its mortal dress,
Nor is there singing school but studying
Monuments of its own magnificence;
And therefore I have sailed the seas and come   15
To the holy city of Byzantium.

3

O sages standing in God's holy fire
As in the gold mosaic of a wall,
Come from the holy fire, perne in a gyre,[2]
And be the singing-masters of my soul.   20
Consume my heart away; sick with desire
And fastened to a dying animal

2. The ruins of Troy and the death of Agamemnon, the Greek leader, whose sacrifice of his daughter Iphigenia to win the gods' favor caused his wife, Clytemnestra (also a daughter of Leda), to assassinate him on his return.   1. The ancient name for modern Istanbul, the capital of the Eastern Roman Empire, which represented for Yeats (who had seen Byzantine mosaics in Italy) a highly stylized and perfectly integrated artistic world where "religious, aesthetic, and practical life were one."   2. I.e., come spinning down in a spiral. *Perne*: a spool or bobbin. *Gyre*: the cone pattern of the falcon's flight and of historical cycles, in Yeats's vision.

It knows not what it is; and gather me
Into the artifice of eternity.

4

Once out of nature I shall never take   25
My bodily form from any natural thing,
But such a form as Grecian goldsmiths make
Of hammered gold and gold enamelling
To keep a drowsy Emperor awake;
Or set upon a golden bough to sing   30
To lords and ladies of Byzantium
Of what is past, or passing, or to come.

Among School Children

1

I walk through the long schoolroom questioning;
A kind old nun in a white hood replies;
The children learn to cipher and to sing,
To study reading-books and history,
To cut and sew, be neat in everything   5
In the best modern way—the children's eyes
In momentary wonder stare upon
A sixty-year-old smiling public man.[1]

2

I dream of a Ledaean[2] body, bent
Above a sinking fire, a tale that she   10
Told of a harsh reproof, or trivial event
That changed some childish day to tragedy—
Told, and it seemed that our two natures blent
Into a sphere from youthful sympathy,
Or else, to alter Plato's parable,   15
Into the yolk and white of the one shell.[3]

3

And thinking of that fit of grief or rage
I look upon one child or t'other there
And wonder if she stood so at that age—
For even daughters of the swan can share   20
Something of every paddler's heritage—
And had that color upon cheek or hair,
And thereupon my heart is driven wild:
She stands before me as a living child.

1. Yeats was elected senator of the Irish Free State in 1922.   2. Beautiful as Leda or as her daughter
Helen of Troy.   3. In Plato's *Symposium*, Socrates explains love by telling how the gods split human
beings into two halves—like halves of an egg—so that each half seeks its opposite throughout life. Yeats
compares the two parts to the yolk and white of an egg.

4

Her present image floats into the mind—   25
Did Quattrocento finger fashion it
Hollow of cheek[4] as though it drank the wind
And took a mess of shadows for its meat?
And I though never of Ledaean kind
Had pretty plumage once—enough of that,   30
Better to smile on all that smile, and show
There is a comfortable kind of old scarecrow.

5

What youthful mother, a shape upon her lap
Honey of generation had betrayed,
And that must sleep, shriek, struggle to escape   35
As recollection or the drug decide,[5]
Would think her son, did she but see that shape
With sixty or more winters on its head,
A compensation for the pang of his birth,
Or the uncertainty of his setting forth?   40

6

Plato thought nature but a spume that plays
Upon a ghostly paradigm of things;
Solider Aristotle played the taws
Upon the bottom of a king of kings;
World-famous golden-thighed Pythagoras[6]   45
Fingered upon a fiddle-stick or strings
What a star sang and careless Muses heard:
Old clothes upon old sticks to scare a bird.

7

Both nuns and mothers worship images,
But those the candles light are not as those   50
That animate a mother's reveries,
But keep a marble or a bronze repose.
And yet they too break hearts—O Presences
That passion, piety, or affection knows,
And that all heavenly glory symbolize—   55
O self-born mockers of man's enterprise;

8

Labor is blossoming or dancing where
The body is not bruised to pleasure soul,
Nor beauty born out of its own despair,

---

4. Italian painters of the 15th century (the *Quattrocento*), such as Botticelli (1444–1510), were known for their delicate figures.   5. Yeats's note to this poem recalls the Greek scholar Porphyry (ca. 234–ca. 305), who associates "honey" with "the pleasure arising from copulation" that engenders children; the poet further describes honey as a drug that destroys the child's " 'recollection' of pre-natal freedom."   6. Three Greek philosophers. Plato (427–337 B.C.) believed that nature was only a series of illusionistic reflections or appearances cast by abstract "forms" that were the only true realities. Aristotle (384–322 B.C.), more pragmatic, was Alexander the Great's tutor and spanked him with the "taws" (leather straps). Pythagoras (582–407 B.C.), a demigod to his disciples and thought to have a golden thigh bone, pondered the relationship of music, mathematics, and the stars.

Nor blear-eyed wisdom out of midnight oil.   60
O chestnut tree, great-rooted blossomer,
Are you the leaf, the blossom, or the bole?
O body swayed to music, O brightening glance,
How can we know the dancer from the dance?

Byzantium[1]

The unpurged images of day recede;
The Emperor's drunken soldiery are abed;
Night resonance recedes, night-walkers' song
After great cathedral gong;
A starlit or a moonlit dome[2] disdains   5
All that man is,
All mere complexities,
The fury and the mire of human veins.

Before me floats an image, man or shade,
Shade more than man, more image than a shade;   10
For Hades' bobbin bound in mummy-cloth
May unwind the winding path;[3]
A mouth that has no moisture and no breath
Breathless mouths may summon;
I hail the superhuman;   15
I call it death-in-life and life-in-death.

Miracle, bird or golden handiwork,
More miracle than bird or handiwork,
Planted on the starlit golden bough,
Can like the cocks of Hades crow,[4]   20
Or, by the moon embittered, scorn aloud
In glory of changeless metal
Common bird or petal
And all complexities of mire or blood.

At midnight on the Emperor's pavement flit   25
Flames that no faggot feeds, nor steel has lit,
Nor storm disturbs, flames begotten of flame,
Where blood-begotten spirits come
And all complexities of fury leave,
Dying into a dance,   30
An agony of trance,
An agony of flame that cannot singe a sleeve.

---

1. The holy city of *Sailing to Byzantium* (p. 1706), seen here as it resists and transforms the blood and mire of human life into its own transcendent world of art. 2. According to Yeat's system in *A Vision* (1925), the first "starlit" phase in which the moon does not shine and the fifteenth, opposing phase of the full moon represent complete objectivity (potential being) and complete subjectivity (the achievement of complete beauty). In between these absolute phases lie the evolving "mere complexities" of human life. 3. Unwinding the spool of fate that leads from mortal death to the superhuman. *Hades*: the realm of the dead in Greek mythology. 4. To mark the transition from death to the dawn of new life.

Astraddle on the dolphin's [5] mire and blood,
Spirit after spirit! The smithies break the flood,
The golden smithies of the Emperor!   35
Marbles of the dancing floor
Break bitter furies of complexity,
Those images that yet
Fresh images beget,
That dolphin-torn, that gong-tormented sea.   40

Lapis Lazuli[1]

For Harry Clifton

I have heard that hysterical women say
They are sick of the palette and fiddle-bow,
Of poets that are always gay,
For everybody knows or else should know
That if nothing drastic is done   5
Aeroplane and Zeppelin will come out,
Pitch like King Billy[2] bomb-balls in
Until the town lie beaten flat.

All perform their tragic play,
There struts Hamlet, there is Lear,   10
That's Ophelia, that Cordelia;[3]
Yet they, should the last scene be there,
The great stage curtain about to drop,
If worthy their prominent part in the play,
Do not break up their lines to weep.   15
They know that Hamlet and Lear are gay;
Gaiety transfiguring all that dread.
All men have aimed at, found and lost;
Black out; Heaven blazing into the head:[4]
Tragedy wrought to its uttermost.   20
Though Hamlet rambles and Lear rages,
And all the drop-scenes drop at once
Upon a hundred thousand stages,
It cannot grow by an inch or an ounce.

On their own feet they came, or on shipboard,   25
Camel-back, horse-back, ass-back, mule-back,
Old civilisations put to the sword.
Then they and their wisdom went to rack:

5. A dolphin rescued the famous singer Arion by carrying him on his back over the sea. Dolphins were associated with Apollo, Greek god of music and prophecy, and in ancient art they are often shown escorting the souls of the dead to the Isles of the Blessed. Here, the dolphin is also flesh and blood, a part of life.
1. A deep blue semiprecious stone. One of Yeats's letters (to Dorothy Wellesley, July 6, 1935) describes a Chinese carving in lapis lazuli that depicts an ascetic and pupil about to climb a mountain:"Ascetic, pupil, hard stone, eternal theme of the sensual east . . . the east has its solutions always and therefore knows nothing of tragedy."   2. A linkage of past and present. According to an Irish ballad, King William III of England "threw his bomb-balls in" and set fire to the tents of the deposed James II at the Battle of the Boyne in 1690. Also a reference to Kaiser Wilhelm II (King William II) of Germany, who sent zeppelins to bomb London during World War I. *Zeppelin*: a long, cylindrical airship, supported by internal gas chambers.
3. Tragic figures in Shakespeare's plays.   4. The loss of rational consciousness making way for the blaze of inner revelation or "mad" tragic vision. Also suggests the final curtain and an air raid curfew.

No handiwork of Callimachus[5]
Who handled marble as if it were bronze,   30
Made draperies that seemed to rise
When sea-wind swept the corner, stands;
His long lamp-chimney shaped like the stem
Of a slender palm, stood but a day;
All things fall and are built again,   35
And those that build them again are gay.

Two Chinamen, behind them a third,
Are carved in Lapis Lazuli,
Over them flies a long-legged bird,[6]
A symbol of longevity;   40
The third, doubtless a serving-man,
Carries a musical instrument.

Every discoloration of the stone,
Every accidental crack or dent,
Seems a water-course or an avalanche,   45
Or lofty slope where it still snows
Though doubtless plum or cherry-branch
Sweetens the little half-way house
Those Chinamen climb towards, and I
Delight to imagine them seated there;   50
There, on the mountain and the sky,
On all the tragic scene they stare.
One asks for mournful melodies;
Accomplished fingers begin to play.
Their eyes mid many wrinkles, their eyes,   55
Their ancient, glittering eyes, are gay.

The Circus Animals' Desertion

1

I sought a theme and sought for it in vain,
I sought it daily for six weeks or so.
Maybe at last, being but a broken man,
I must be satisfied with my heart, although
Winter and summer till old age began   5
My circus animals were all on show,
Those stilted boys, that burnished chariot,
Lion and woman[1] and the Lord knows what.

2

What can I but enumerate old themes?
First that sea-rider Oisin led by the nose   10

---

5. Athenian sculptor (5th century B.C.), famous for a gold lamp in the Erechtheum (temple on the Acropolis) and for using drill lines in marble to give the effect of flowing drapery.   **6.** A crane.   **1.** Yeats enumerates images and themes from his earlier work; here, the sphinx of *The Double Vision of Michael Robartes.*

Through three enchanted islands, allegorical dreams,[2]
Vain gaiety, vain battle, vain repose,
Themes of the embittered heart, or so it seems,
That might adorn old songs or courtly shows;
But what cared I that set him on to ride,   15
I, starved for the bosom of his faery bride?

And then a counter-truth filled out its play,
The Countess Cathleen[3] was the name I gave it;
She, pity-crazed, had given her soul away,
But masterful Heaven had intervened to save it.   20
I thought my dear must her own soul destroy,
So did fanaticism and hate enslave it,
And this brought forth a dream and soon enough
This dream itself had all my thought and love.

And when the Fool and Blind Man stole the bread   25
Cuchulain[4] fought the ungovernable sea;
Heart-mysteries there, and yet when all is said
It was the dream itself enchanted me:
Character isolated by a deed
To engross the present and dominate memory.   30
Players and painted stage took all my love,
And not those things that they were emblems of.

3

Those masterful images because complete
Grew in pure mind, but out of what began?
A mound of refuse or the sweepings of a street,   35
Old kettles, old bottles, and a broken can,
Old iron, old bones, old rags, that raving slut
Who keeps the till. Now that my ladder's gone,
I must lie down where all the ladders start,
In the foul rag-and-bone shop of the heart.   40

2. In *The Wanderings of Oisin* (1889), an early poem in which Yeats describes a legendary Irish hero who wandered in fairyland for 150 years.   3. A play (1892), dedicated to Maud Gonne, in which the countess is saved by heaven after having sold her soul to the Devil in exchange for food for the poor. The figure of Cathleen comes up frequently in Yeats's work and is often taken as a personification of nationalist Ireland.   4. A legendary Irish hero. Yeats is referring to the play *On Baile's Strand* (1904).

RUBÉN DARÍO
1867–1916

Considered by many to be the greatest Spanish-language poet of the twentieth century and the leading figure in Spanish-American *Modernismo*, Rubén Darío was a charismatic figure whose writings transformed Spanish and Latin American letters. Cosmopolitan in his outlook, he fused elements from European and Latin American tradition to create new forms and a new sensibility for Spanish American literature, asserting in the process a Spanish cultural identity that included his own Indian ancestry and would counterbalance current images of a dominant North America. Darío lived half his adult life in Europe and served as a bridge between countries and generations; he himself could not be limited to a single style or location. When two other great writers of the twentieth century, Pablo Neruda and García Lorca, joined in homage to Darío in 1933, they called him "that great Nicaraguan, Argentinian, Chilean, and Spanish poet" whose poetry, "crisscrossed with sounds and dreams . . . stands solidly outside of norms, forms, and schools."

Rubén Darío was born Félix Rubén García y Sarmiento on January 18, 1867, in Metapa, a small town in Nicaragua that later named itself Ciudad Darío (Darío City). The name Darío, which he began using in 1880, was well known in the region as the name of an influential ancestor, Darío Mayorga. His parents, Rosa Sarmiento and Manuel García, had separated after eight months of marriage, and when the boy was three years old he was sent to live with Rosa's aunt Bernarda in the old Spanish city of Léon, Nicaragua. Bernarda and her husband Félix, a retired colonel, raised the boy as their own, and he seems to have considered them his parents until 1880, when his mother made a brief visit. It was at this point that he began signing his work Rubén Darío, instead of Félix Rubén Ramírez. His autobiographical *La vida de Rubén Darío escrita par él misme* (The Life of Rubén Darío Written by Himself, 1912) describes the impression made on him by the old house and the supernatural horror stories told after dinner (they gave him nightmares), as well as his participation in religious festivities and his first attempts—in primary school—to write poetry. When the elderly colonel died after a few years, the loss of his pension mean a sharply reduced income for the family and partial dependence on wealthy relatives.

Darío had already made a name for himself as a child poet who could be counted on for holiday and personal verses, and he read voraciously in the family library, later listing among his favorites Cervantes's *Don Quixote*, Cicero's *De Officiis* (On Duties), *The Arabian Nights*, Madame de Staël's romantic novel *Corinne*, a French horror story by Regnault-Warin called *La Caverna de Strozzi* (The Strozzi Cave), and Spanish classical plays by such authors as Lope de Vega, Calderón, Tirso de Molina, and Juan Ruiz de Alarcón. The three years he spent in a Jesuit school (1878–1880) had a lasting impact on him: here he was taught Latin and Greek, studied mythology, and read widely in Spanish classical literature. Looking back, Darío commented that his literary demon at this time was a Jesuit angel, and he wrote classical poems "dedicated to the sea, to the sun, or to the Virgin Mary." This religious fervor did not last, and Darío later sharply criticized both the Jesuits and Catholicism, but religious themes and classical images continued to permeate his work.

The young poet's next school, in contrast, was directed by the radical José Leonard, who introduced him to anticlerical thinking, nineteenth-century French literature, and the revolutionary Ecuadorian writer Juan Montalvo. Darío began sending articles to the newspapers, thus entering at the age of fourteen on a journalistic career that would make him European correspondent for the Buenos Aires newspaper *La Nación* and diplomatic representative to various European and Latin American countries. In 1886 he traveled to Chile, where he made friends in literary circles, wrote poetry and impressionistic prose, and barely supported himself by working for newspapers. Writings from this Chilean period emerged in *Azul* (Blue, 1888), the book that would launch his reputation as the founder of Spanish-American—and, later, Spanish—Modernism (*Modernismo*). *Blue*'s initial reception was disappointing, however, and only gradually was it recognized as a turning point in Spanish American and Spanish literary history.

Blue's collection of poetry, short stories, and impressionistic sketches marked a new style—one that was far more similar to the jewellike recent French "art for art's sake" literature than to the lengthy rhetorical developments favored by current writers in Spanish. Sentences and phrases were shorter, with rhythmic and stylistic variations; rare, evocative, and musical words were preferred and carefully arranged to achieve the maximum poetic effect. "Words should paint the color of a sound, the aroma of a star; they should capture the very soul of things," he wrote in an early manifesto. Darío also chose foreign and even exotic subjects instead of realistic or naturalist themes, and he wrote with a mixture of sensuality and idealist yearning for supreme beauty that recalled Symbolist poetry. Other writers before him and contemporary authors such as Antonio Machado and Ramon del Valle Inclán, used similarly innovative techniques, but it was Darío who became known as the chief figure of *Modernismo,* which he promoted in his later European travels. Despite the common name "Modernism" and the fact that both movements aimed to revolutionize literary form in the twentieth century, Spanish-American Modernism should not be confused with the broader European and American Modernism personified by James Joyce, Marcel Proust, and Wallace Stevens (see pp. 1941, 1766, 1896, respectively).

In 1891, Nicaragua arranged to send a delegation to Spain for the fourth centennial of the discovery of America, and Ruben Darío was sent as secretary to the delegation. Exhilarated by the two-month stay in Spain and by the warm reception he experienced as a representative of Spanish American letters, he returned home with new confidence in his role as spokesperson for Latin American literature and culture. Darío was not eager to stay in Nicaragua, however, and his admirers arranged for him to be named Colombia's consul to Buenos Aires. He visited New York and Paris in 1893, before taking up his new position in Buenos Aires, where he was quickly surrounded by disciples of Modernismo. This period of relative financial stability ended when Colombia decided to close the consulate in 1894, but the poet was able to support himself through work for *La Nación* and a position as private secretary in the Post Office. In 1896, he published his second major book of poetry, the *Prosas Profanas* (Profane Hymns), a work that was even more deeply influenced by French Symbolism's search for absolute beauty through aesthetic form. From the allegorical figure of the Swan to the poetic quest of "I seek a form . . . ," Darío evoked and interrogated language's ability to express a world of sensuous experience and spiritual yearning.

In 1898, *La Nación* sent Darío abroad to investigate the reaction in Spain to the country's defeat in the recently concluded Spanish-American War. The poet quickly became a figure in Spanish intellectual and literary circles, and he wrote a series of articles on contemporary Spain that reinvigorated national pride by emphasizing the strength and continuity of the Spanish literary tradition in Latin America. Darío's new vision of a larger Spanish tradition, and a Spanish American identity separate from the looming presence of the United States, began to permeate much of his poetry and prose. "Long live Spanish America! / A thousand cubs of the Spanish lion are roaming free," he proclaimed in *To Roosevelt.* Increasingly celebrated as the most important living writer in Spanish, he served as a cultural bridge between Latin America and Spain, focusing attention on younger authors whether they were Modernists or those who would become the famous Spanish "generation of '98." Darío was still correspondent for *La Nación,* however, and the newspaper sent him to Paris in 1900 to cover a great exposition marking the new century. From that time on, he was based in Paris, traveling to Mallorca for his health and throughout Europe and Latin America on various literary or diplomatic missions. Darío's third major collection, *Cantos de vida y esperanza, Los cisnes, y otros poemas* (Songs of Life and Hope, The Swans, and Other Poems), was published in Paris in 1905, the same year the Nicaraguan government named him consul general in Paris. *Songs of Life and Hope* display the poet's accustomed musicality and technical brilliance as well as a new awareness of political and cultural issues and a somber interrogation of his own mortality in poems such as *Lo Fatal* ("Fatality"). In 1907, Darío received a second governmental honor when he was named the Nicaraguan minister to Spain, and he moved immediately to Madrid. Both posts were honorific but paid little, and the poet survived on help from friends and the income from *La Nación.* By 1910, no longer able to afford life in Madrid, he returned to Paris, where he lived until 1914 and the beginning of World War I. On the trip home—despondent, impoverished, and in poor health—Darío undertook a lecture tour to raise money. He was soon taken ill and obliged to return to Nicaragua, where he died two months later on February 6, 1916. After his death, the government (which owed him months of back pay) ordered national mourning and granted him the burial honors of a war minister; the church performed funeral services usually reserved for royal blood; and official messages of condolence were sent to Nicaragua from Spain and the Spanish American countries.

Our selections from Darío's work are taken from *Profane Hymns* and *Songs of Life and Hope,* and represent both his early Modernist style, inspired by French Symbolism, and the later, more philosophical and political poems. The timeless, idealized landscapes of the early poems evoke a wished-for perfection, whether it be the magical swan whose diverse identities are enumerated in *Blazon*; a fairytale dream of escape and completion (*Sonatina*); or melodious dismay that language is not capable of capturing ideal beauty (*I Seek a Form . . .*). Darío's scenes have many dimensions: the swan of *Blazon* is both transcendentally pure and sensually erotic, a divine icon of Symbolist art; the sad princess of *Sonatina* is—unlike Sleeping Beauty—awake and conscious of something missing from her jewellike setting: she yearns obscurely for a lover who may, in another wishful perspective, be the poet himself, conquering death through his verses. Such poetic confidence is lacking in the sonnet *I Seek a Form . . .* , where the speaker is constantly aware of the gap between his intuition of absolute beauty and his ineffectual attempts to capture it in words. The form he seeks may finally be ineffable—embodied not in words, but in the question shaped by a white swan's curved neck.

To Roosevelt was written in the year after the Hays-Varilla Treaty (1903) ceded the Panama Canal zone to the United States. Darío speaks on behalf of Spanish America and indignantly reproaches the United States of President Theodore Roosevelt for its expansionist politics. Throughout the ode, he opposes a Spanish American cultural identity defined by simplicity, piety, poetry, learning, and spiritual nobility to a powerful northern neighbor known for its energy, greed, aggression, and cultural barbarity. The opposition, however, is not absolute: the second line names the American poet Walt Whitman as a counterexample to Roosevelt's predatory Hunter, and the Spanish are described as torturing early Indian rulers for their wealth. With *Leda,* Darío returns to his favorite image and metaphor for art, the swan. The sonnet is divided between an early emphasis on the bird's sheer beauty in the dawn (recalling the perfect imagery of early poems) and an ensuing violent rape scene, which ends with the excitement of the demigod Pan, peeking through the bushes. Darío's art has come down to earth, for this swan is no longer the bird "made of perfume and ermine, / of white light, of silk, and of dreams," whose rape of Leda in *Blazon* was phrased with great metaphorical delicacy. (Compare this to the version by Yeats, p. 1705). Similarly distant from the early Symbolist-inspired poems is *Fatality,* a somber personal statement permeated with the fear of death and the horror of recognizing one's own mortality. The poet ends on a note of existential anguish, mourning the unknowability of the human condition and unable to ignore the ironic contrast between earthly pleasures and their negation in the tomb.

Keith Ellis, *Critical Approaches to Rubén Darío* (1974), offers a detailed discussion of the way Darío's work has been seen in five critical perspectives; it includes a short appendix on Darío's own literary criticism. Charles D. Watland, *Poet-Errant: A Biography of Rubén Darío* (1965), is copiously documented and the only book-length biography in English. Octavio Paz discusses Darío and Modernism in the title essay of his *The Siren and the Seashell* (1970). Cathy Login Jrade, in *Rubén Darío and the Romantic Search for Unity* (1983), situates Darío within the Romantic-Modernist tradition and Pythagorean pantheism. Dolores Ackel Fiore examines Darío's use of mythology in *Rubén Darío in Search of Inspiration: Greco-Roman Mythology in His Stories and Poetry* (1963).

[POEMS][1]

Sonatina

The Princess is sad. What ails the Princess?
Nothing but sighs escape from her lips,
which have lost their smile and their strawberry red.
The Princess is pale in her golden chair,
the keys of her harpsichord gather dust,   5
and a flower, forgotten, droops in its vase.

The garden is bright with the peacocks' triumph,
the duenna[2] prattles of commonplace things,
the clown pirouettes in his crimson and gold;
but the Princess is silent, her thoughts are far-off: 10
the Princess traces the dragonfly course
of a vague illusion in the eastern sky.

Are her thoughts of a prince of Golconda[3] or China?
Of a prince who has halted his silver coach
to see the soft light that glows in her eyes?   15
Of the king of the fragrant isle of roses,
or the lord who commands the clear-shining diamonds,
or the arrogant lord of the pearls of Ormuz?[4]

Alas, the poor Princess, whose mouth is a rose,
would be a swallow or a butterfly;   20
would skim on light wings, or mount to the sun
on the luminous stair of a golden sunbeam;
would greet the lilies with the verses of May,
or be lost in the wind on the thundering sea.

She is tired of the palace, the silver distaff   25
the enchanted falcon, the scarlet buffoon,[5]
the swans reflected on the azure lake.
And the flowers are sad for the flower of the court:
the jasmines of the east, the water lilies of the north,
the dahlias of the west, and the roses of the south.   30

The poor little Princess with the wide blue eyes
is imprisoned in her gold, imprisoned in her tulle,
in the marble cage of the royal palace,
the lofty palace that is guarded by sentries,
by a hundred Negroes with a hundred halberds,[6]   35
a sleepless greyhound, and a monstrous dragon.

Oh to be a butterfly leaving its cocoon!
(The Princess is sad. The Princess is pale.)

---

1. All the selections have been translated by Lysander Kemp.   2. A governess or chaperone in Spanish society.   3. An ancient city in southern India, famous for its diamonds.   4. The strait of Ormuz is a channel linking the Persian Gulf and the Gulf of Oman.   5. Court jester, here dressed in red. *Distaff:* a spinning-wheel attachment. In the fairytale *Sleeping Beauty,* the princess pricks herself while spinning and falls asleep.   6. Weapons combining an ax blade and a spike on a short spear.

Oh adorable vision of gold, ivory, and rose!
Oh to fly to the land where there is a prince—   40
(The Princess is pale. The Princess is sad.)—
more brilliant than daybreak, more handsome than April!

"Hush, Princess, hush," says her fairy godmother;
"the joyous knight who adores you unseen
is riding this way on his wingèd horse,   45
a sword at his waist and a hawk on his wrist,
and comes from far off, having conquered Death,
to kindle your lips with a kiss of true love!"

Blazon[7]

For the Countess of Peralta

The snow-white Olympic[8] swan,
with beak of rose-red agate,
preens his eucharistic[9] wing,
which he opens to the sun like a fan.

His shining neck is curved   5
like the arm of a lyre,
like the handle of a Greek amphora,[1]
like the prow of a ship.

He is the swan of divine origin
whose kiss mounted through fields   10
of silk to the rosy peaks
of Leda's[2] sweet hills.

White king of Castalia's fount,
his triumph illumines the Danube;[3]
Da Vinci was his baron in Italy;   15
Lohengrin[4] is his blond prince.

His whiteness is akin to linen,
to the buds of white roses,
to the diamantine white
of the fleece of an Easter lamb.   20

He is the poet of perfect verses,
and his lyric cloak is of ermine;
he is the magic, the regal bird
who, dying, rhymes the soul in his song.

---

7. Both a heraldic coat of arms and a poem that enumerates various qualities of the beloved.   8. Associated with Mount Olympus, home of the gods in Greek mythology.   9. Like the white wafer used in the Eucharist, the Christian ritual of communion.   1. Large two-handled jar used in ancient Greece for storing wine or oil.   2. In Greek mythology, a nymph raped by Zeus, who had taken the form of a swan; she gave birth to Helen of Troy.   3. A major river in central Europe. *Castalia's fount:* the spring of Castalia on Mount Parnassus, home of the Greek Muses.   4. The "Swan Knight" of Richard Wagner's opera *Lohengrin* (1850). *Da Vinci:* i.e., Leonardo da Vinci (1452–1519), the Renaissance artist and inventor.

This wingèd aristocrat displays   25
white lilies on a blue field;
and Pompadour,[5] gracious and lovely,
has stroked his feathers.

He rows and rows on the lake
where dreams wait for the unhappy,   30
where a golden gondola waits
for the sweetheart of Louis of Bavaria.[6]

Countess, give the swans your love,
for they are gods of an alluring land
and are made of perfume and ermine,   35
of white light, of silk, and of dreams.

I Seek a Form . . .

I seek a form that my style cannot discover,
a bud of thought that wants to be a rose;
it is heralded by a kiss that is placed on my lips
in the impossible embrace of the Venus de Milo.[7]

The white peristyle[8] is decorated with green palms;   5
the stars have predicted that I will see the goddess;
and the light reposes within my soul like the bird
of the moon reposing on a tranquil lake.

And I only find the word that runs away,
the melodious introduction that flows from the flute,[9]   10
the ship of dreams that rows through all space,

and, under the window of my sleeping beauty,[1]
the endless sigh from the waters of the fountain,[2]
and the neck of the great white swan, that questions me.

To Roosevelt[3]

The voice that would reach you, Hunter, must speak
in Biblical tones, or in the poetry of Walt Whitman.[4]

5. The Marquise de Pompadour (1721–64) was the mistress of King Louis XV of France. *White lilies on a blue field:* the fleur-de-lis. The coat of arms of the French kings displayed stylized white lilies on a blue background.   **6.** The mad king of Bavaria (1864–86) who built a fairytale castle and retired from the world; he was Wagner's patron for many years.   **7.** Ancient Greek statue of Venus, goddess of love and beauty, found on the island of Melos; the statue's arms are missing.   **8.** A courtyard surrounded by columns.   **9.** Compare Mallarmé's *The Afternoon of a Faun,* lines 16–20.   **1.** Sleeping Beauty (capitalized in the original).   **2.** Compare Verlaine's *Moonlight,* lines 11–12.   **3.** President of the United States from 1901 to 1909, Theodore Roosevelt was well known as a hunter and as a political expansionist. **4.** American poet (1819–92) and author of *Leaves of Grass* (1855) whose poetry Darío liked and to whom he addressed a poem.

You are primitive and modern, simple and complex;
you are one part George Washington and one part Nimrod.[5]
    You are the United States   5
future invader of our naive America[6]
with its Indian blood, an America
that still prays to Christ and still speaks Spanish.

You are a strong, proud model of your race;
you are cultured and able; you oppose Tolstoy.[7]   10
You are an Alexander-Nebuchadnezzar,[8]
breaking horses and murdering tigers.
(You are a Professor of Energy,
as the current lunatics say).

You think that life is a fire,   15
that progress is an irruption,
that the future is wherever
your bullet strikes.
                        No.

The United States is grand and powerful.
Whenever it trembles, a profound shudder   20
runs down the enormous backbone of the Andes.[9]
If it shouts, the sound is like the roar of a lion.
And Hugo said to Grant:[1] "The stars are yours."
(The dawning sun of the Argentine barely shines;
the star of Chile is rising . . .)[2] A wealthy country,   25
joining the cult of Mammon to the cult of Hercules;[3]
while Liberty, lighting the path
to easy conquest, raises her torch in New York.
But our own America, which has had poets
since the ancient times of Nezahualcóyotl;[4]
which preserved the footprints of great Bacchus,   30
and learned the Panic[5] alphabet once,
and consulted the stars; which also knew Atlantis[6]
(whose name comes ringing down to us in Plato)
and has lived, since the earliest moments of its life,   35
in light, in fire, in fragrance, and in love—
the America of Moctezuma and Atahualpa,[7]
the aromatic America of Columbus,

5. Mighty hunter and king of ancient Assyria (see Genesis 10. 8–12).   6. I.e., Spanish-speaking South America.   7. The Russian count and novelist Leo Tolstoy (1828–1910) in his later works preached piety, morality, and a simple peasant life.   8. A combination of the Macedonian conqueror Alexander the Great (356–323 B.C.) and Nebuchadnezzar (630–562 B.C.), king of Babylon, who destroyed Jerusalem and made its inhabitants slaves.   9. A mountain chain running the length of South America.   1. Ulysses S. Grant (1822–85), Union general in the Civil War and president from 1869 to 1877. *Hugo:* Darío admired the 19th-century French writer Victor Hugo (1802–85).   2. The flags of Argentina and Chile display a sun and a star, respectively.   3. The Greek demigod known for his strength. *Mammon:* in the New Testament, a false god who personified riches and greed.   4. An Aztec ruler and early poet.   5. Belonging to the woodland god Pan, a follower of Bacchus. *Bacchus:* the Greek god of wine and fertility.   6. The lost civilization of Atlantis, described in Plato's dialogues *Timaeus* and *Critias*.   7. Last Inca emperor (1532–33), captured and held for ransom before being strangled by Pizarro's soldiers. *Moctezuma:* Montezuma II (1466–1520), Aztec emperor in Mexico, treacherously slain for his wealth by Spanish invaders.

Catholic America, Spanish America,
the America where noble Cuauhtémoc said: 40
"I am not on a bed of roses"[8]—our America,
trembling with hurricanes, trembling with Love:
O men with Saxon[9] eyes and barbarous souls,
our America lives. And dreams. And loves.
And it is the daughter of the Sun. Be careful.   45
Long live Spanish America!
A thousand cubs of the Spanish lion are roaming free.
Roosevelt, you must become, by God's own will,
the deadly Rifleman and the dreadful Hunter
before you can clutch us in your iron claws.   50

And though you have everything, you are lacking one thing:
                                                                God!

Leda

The swan in shadow seems to be of snow;
his beak is translucent amber in the daybreak;
gently that first and fleeting glow of crimson
tinges his gleaming wings with rosy light.

And then, on the azure waters of the lake,   5
when dawn has lost its colors, then the swan,
his wings outspread, his neck a noble arc,
is turned to burnished silver by the sun.

The bird from Olympus, wounded by love, swells out
his silken plumage, and clasping her in his wings   10
he ravages Leda there in the singing water,
his beak seeking the flower of her lips.

She struggles, naked and lovely, and is vanquished,
and while her cries turn sighs and die away,
the screen of teeming foliage parts and the wild   15
green eyes of Pan[1] stare out, wide with surprise.

Fatality

The tree is happy because it is scarcely sentient;
the hard rock is happier still, it feels nothing:
there is no pain as great as being alive,
no burden heavier than that of conscious life.

---

8. Words spoken to a fellow prisoner by the last Aztec emperor (d. 1525) while he was being tortured by Spanish invaders.   9. Of Germanic or British ancestry; here, North Americans.   1. The horned shepherd god of woods and field.

To be, and to know nothing, and to lack a way,   5
and the dread of having been, and future terrors . . .
And the sure terror of being dead tomorrow,
and to suffer all through life and through the darkness,

and through what we do not know and hardly suspect . . .
And the flesh that tempts us with bunches of cool grapes,   10
and the tomb that awaits us with its funeral sprays,
and not to know where we go,
nor whence we came! . . .

LUIGI PIRANDELLO
1867–1936

"Who am I?" and "What is real?" are the persistent and even agonized questions that underlie Luigi Pirandello's novels, short stories, and plays. The term *Pirandellismo* or "Pirandellism"—coined from the author's name—suggests that there are as many truths as there are points of view. Here are already the basic issues of later existential philosophy as seen in writers like Jean-Paul Sartre and Albert Camus: the difficulty of achieving a sense of identity, the impossibility of authentic communication between people, and the overlapping frontiers of appearance and reality. These dilemmas are dramatic crises in self-knowledge and as such are particularly suited for demonstration in the theater. Indeed, Pirandello is best known as an innovative dramatist who revolutionized European stage techniques to break down comfortable illusions of compartmentalized, stable reality. Instead of the late nineteenth century's "well-made play"—with its neatly constructed plot that packaged real life into a conventional beginning, middle, and end, and its consistent characters remaining safely inaccessible on the other side of the footlights—he offers unpredictable plots and characters whose ambiguity puts into question the solidity of identities assumed in everyday life. It is not easy to know the truth, he suggests, or to make oneself known behind the face or "naked mask" that each of us wears in society. Pirandello's theater readily displays its nature as dramatic illusion: plays exist within plays until one is not sure where the "real" play begins or ends, and characters question their own reality and that of the audience. In their manipulation of ambiguous appearances and tragicomic effects, these plays foreshadow the absurdist theater of Samuel Beckett, Eugène Ionesco, and Harold Pinter, the cosmic irony of Antonin Artaud's "theater of cruelty," and the emphasis on spectacle and illusion in works by Jean Genet. Above all, they insist that the most "real" life is that which changes from moment to moment, exhibiting a fluidity that renders difficult and perhaps impossible any single formulation of either character or situation. This fluidity is a cause of existential anguish because it implies perpetual loss; readers may wish to contrast Pirandello's cosmos of uncertain boundaries with the sense of continuity throughout different dimensions of existence that informs, for example, Wole Soyinka's *Death and the King's Horseman*.

Pirandello was born in Girgenti (now Agrigento), Sicily, on June 28, 1867. His father was a sulfur merchant who intended his son to go into business like himself, but Pirandello preferred language and literature. After studying in Palermo and the University of Rome, he traveled to the University of Bonn in 1888, and in 1891 he received a doctorate in romance philology with a thesis on the dialect of his hometown. In 1894, Pirandello made an arranged marriage with the daughter of a rich sulfur merchant. They lived for ten years in Rome, where he wrote poetry and short stories, until the collapse of the sulfur mines destroyed the fortunes of both families, and he was suddenly forced to earn a living. To add to his misfortunes, his wife became insane with a jealous paranoia that lasted until her death in 1918. The author himself died on December 1, 1936.

Pirandello's early work shows a number of different influences. His poetry was indebted to nineteenth-century Italian predecessors like Giosuè Carducci (1835–1907), and in 1896 he translated Goethe's *Roman Elegies*. Soon, however, he turned to short stories or *novelle* under the influence of a narrative style called *verismo* (realism) exemplified in the work of the Sicilian writer Giovanni Verga (1840–1922). Pirandello wrote hundreds of stories of all lengths and—in his clarity, realism, and psychological acuteness (often including a taste for the grotesque)—is recognized as an Italian master of the story much as was Guy de Maupassant in France. Collections include the 1894 *Love without Love* and an anthology in 1922 titled *A Year's Worth of Stories*.

In such stories, and in his early novels, Pirandello begins to develop his characteristic themes: the questioning of appearance and reality, and problems of identity. In *The Outcast* (1901), an irate husband drives his innocent wife out of the house only to take her back when—without his knowing it—the supposed adultery has actually occurred. The hero of Pirandello's best-known novel, *The Late Mattia Pascal,* tries to create a fresh identity for himself and leave behind the old Mattia Pascal. When things become too difficult he returns to his "late" self and begins to write his life story, an early example of the tendency in Pirandello's works to comment on their own composition. The protagonists in these and other works are visibly commonplace, middle-class citizens, neither heroic nor villainous, but prototypes of the twentieth-century antihero who remains aggressively average while taking the center of the stage.

The questions of identity that obsessed Pirandello (he speaks of them as reflecting the "pangs of my spirit") are explored on social, psychological, and metaphysical levels. He was acquainted with the experimental psychology of his day, and learned from works such as Alfred Binet's *Personality Alterations* (1892) about the existence of a subconscious personality beneath our everyday awareness (a theme Pirandello shares with Proust and Freud). Successive layers of personality, conflicts among the various parts, and the simultaneous existence of multiple perspectives shape an identity that is never fixed but always fluid and changing. This identity escapes the grasp of onlookers and subject alike, and expresses a basic incongruity in human existence that challenges the most earnest attempts to create a unified self. The protagonist of a later novel, *One, None, and a Hundred Thousand* (1925–26), finds that what "he" is depends on the viewpoint of a great number of people. Such incongruity can be tragic or comic—or both at once—according to one's attitude, a topic that Pirandello explored in a 1908 essay, *On Humor,* and that is echoed in the double-edged humor of his plays. The "Pirandellian" themes of ambiguous identity, lack of communication, and deceptive appearance reappear in all the genres, however, reaching a particular intensity in his first dramatic success, *It Is So [If You Think So]* (1917), and in the play included here, *Six Characters in Search of an Author.*

Six Characters in Search of an Author and *Henry IV* established Pirandello's stature as a major dramatist. He directed his own company (the Teatro d'Arte di Roma) from 1924 to 1928 and received the Nobel Prize for Literature in 1934. His later plays, featuring fantastic and grotesque elements, did not achieve the wide popularity of their predecessors. In 1936, he published a collection of forty-three plays as *Naked Masks,* a title conceived in 1918 after Luigi Chiarelli's "grotesque theater." Pirandello's characters are "naked" and vulnerable inside the social roles or masks they put on to survive: Henry IV, trapped for life inside a pretense of insanity, or the Father in *Six Characters,* forced to play out a demeaning role in which, he insists, only part of his true nature is revealed. The term *naked mask* also suggests Pirandello's superb manipulation of theatrical ambiguity—the confusion between the actor and the character portrayed—that ultimately prolongs the confusion of appearance and reality, which is one of his chief themes. Pirandello was famous in twentieth-century theater for his use of the play within a play, a technique of embedded dramatic episodes that maintain a life of their own while serving as foil to the overall or governing plot. Dividing lines are sometimes hard to draw when stage dialogue can be taken as referring to either context—a situation that allows for double meanings at the same time that it reiterates the impossibility of real communication.

Six Characters in Search of an Author combines all these elements in an extraordinarily self-reflexive style. At the very beginning, the Stage Hand's interrupted hammering suggests that the audience has chanced on a rehearsal—of still another play by Pirandello—instead of coming to a finished performance; concurrently, Pirandello's stage dialogue pokes fun at his own reputation for obscurity. Just as the Actors are apparently set to rehearse The Rules of the Game, six unexpected persons come down the aisle seeking the Producer: they are Characters out of an unwritten novel who demand to be given dramatic existence. The play Six Characters is continually in the process of being composed: composed as the interwoven double plot we see on stage, written down in shorthand by the Prompter for the Actors to reproduce, and potentially composed as the Characters' inner drama finally achieves its rightful existence as a work of art. The conflicts between the different levels of the play finally prevent the completion of any but the first work, but it has created a convincing dramatic illusion in the meantime that incorporates the psychological drama of the "six characters" as well as a discussion of the relationship of life and art.

The initial absurdity of the play appears when the six admittedly fictional characters arrive with their claim to be "truer and more real" than the "real" characters they confront. (Of course, to the audience all the actors on stage are equally unreal.) Their greater "truth" is the truth of art with its profound but formally fixed glimpses into human nature. Each Character represents, specifically and in depth, a particular identity created by the author, who later suggested that the Characters should wear masks to distinguish them from the Actors. These masks are not the conventional masks of ancient Greek drama or the Japanese nō theater, nor do they function as the ceremonial masks representing spirits in African ritual, masks that temporarily invest the wearer with the spirit's identity and authority. Instead, they are a theatrical device, a symbol and visual reminder of each character's unchanging essence. The Six Characters are incapable of developing outside their roles and are condemned, in their search for existence, painfully to reenact their essential selves.

Conversely, the fictional characters have a more stable personality than "real" people who are still "nobody," incomplete, open to change and misinterpretation. Characters are "somebody" because their nature has been decided once and for all. Yet there is a further complication to this contrast between real and fictional characters: the Characters have real anxieties in that they want to play their own roles and are disturbed at the prospect of having Actors represent them incorrectly. All human beings, suggests Pirandello, whether fictional or real, are subject to misunderstanding. We even misunderstand ourselves when we think we are the same person in all situations. "We always have the illusion of being the same person for everybody," says the Father, "but it's not true!" When he explains himself as a very human philosopher driven by the Demon of Experiment, his self-image is quite different from the picture held by his vengeful Stepdaughter or the passive Mother who blames him for her expulsion from the house. The Stepdaughter, in turn, appears to love an innocent little sister because she reminds her of an earlier self. It is an entanglement of motives and deceit of mutual understanding that goes beyond the tabloid level of a sordid family scandal and claims a broader scope. Pirandello, in fact, does not intend merely to describe a particular setting or situation; that is the concern of what he calls "historical writers." He belongs to the opposite category of "philosophical writers" whose characters and situations embody "a particular sense of life and acquire from it a universal value."

Six Characters in Search of an Author underwent an interesting evolution to become the play that we see today. First performed in Rome in 1921, where its unsettling plot and characters already scandalized a traditionalist audience, it was reshaped in more radical theatrical form after the remarkable performance produced by Georges Pitoëff in Paris in 1923. Pirandello, who came to Paris somewhat wary of Pitoëff's innovations (he brought on the Characters in a green-lit stage elevator), was soon convinced that the Russian director's stagecraft suggested changes that would enhance the original text. Pitoëff had used his knowledge of technical effects to accentuate the interrelationships of appearance and reality: he extended the stage with several steps leading down into the auditorium (a break in the conventional stage's "fourth wall" that Pirandello was quick to exploit); he underscored the play within a play with rehearsal effects, showing the Stage Hand hammering and the Director arranging suitable props and lighting; he emphasized the division between Characters and Actors by separating groups on stage and dressing the Characters (all except the Little Girl) in black. Pirandello welcomed and expanded on many of these changes. To distinguish even further the Characters from the Actors, he proposed stylized masks as well as black clothes for the former and light-colored summery clothing for the latter. To bring out Madame Pace's grotesque fictionality, he changed her costume from a sober black gown to a garish red silk dress and carrot-colored wool wig. Most striking, however, is the dramatist's development of Pitoëff's steps into a real bridge between the world of the stage and the auditorium, a strategy that allows his Actors (and Characters) to come and go in the "real world" of the audience. Pirandello's revised ending to *Six Characters in Search of an Author* makes a final break with theatrical illusion: with the other characters immobilized on stage, the Stepdaughter races down the steps, through the auditorium, and out into the foyer from which the audience can still hear her distraught laughter.

Pirandello does not hold his audience by uttering grand philosophical truths. There is constant suspense and a process of discovery in *Six Characters*, from the moment that the rehearsal with its complaining Actors and Manager is interrupted and the initial hints of melodrama and family scandal catch our attention in the Stepdaughter's and Mother's complaints. It is a story that could be found in the most sensational papers: an adulterous wife thrust out of her home and supporting herself and her children after her lover's death by sewing, the daughter's turn to prostitution to support the family, the Father's unknowing attempt to seduce his Stepdaughter (interpreted by the latter as the continuation of an old and perverse impulse), and the final drowning and suicide of the two youngest children. Pirandello plays with the sensational aspect of his story by focusing the play on the characters' repeated attempts to portray the seduction scene; Actors and Manager perceive the salable quality of such "human-interest" events and are eager to let the story unfold. The Stepdaughter's protective fondness for her doomed baby sister and her enigmatic reproach to the little Boy ("instead of killing myself, I'd have killed one of those two") hint at the inner plot that is revealed only as the action continues. The interplay of illusion and reality persists to the very end, when the Actors argue about whether the Boy is dead or not, the Producer is terrified as the lights change eerily around the surviving Characters, and the Stepdaughter breaks away from the ending tableau to escape into the audience.

The translation by John Linstrum has been selected on the one hand for its accuracy to the Italian text and its fluent use of contemporary English idiom and on the other for its quality as a performance-oriented script, staged in London in 1979. Readers are encouraged to test the continued liveliness of Pirandello's dialogue by rehearsing their own selection of scenes—or perhaps by relocating them in a contemporary setting. According to director Robert Brustein, whose 1988 production of *Six Characters in Search of an Author* set the action in New York and replaced Madame Pace with a pimp, "Pirandello both encourages and stimulates a pluralism in theater because there can be dozens, hundreds, thousands of productions of *Six Characters*, and every one of them is going to be different."

A good biography and general introduction is found in Susan Bassnett-McGuire, *Pirandello* (1984). Useful introductions are Fiora A. Bassanese, *Understanding Luigi Pirandello* (1997), and Walter Starkie, *Luigi Pirandello, 1867–1936* (1965). Glauco Cambon, ed., *Pirandello: A Collection of Critical Essays* (1967), emphasizes the plays. Richard Sogliuzzo, *Luigi Pirandello, Director* (1982), deals with Pirandello's dramatic theories and practices; it contains a discussion of *Six Characters*. John Louis Di-Gaetani, ed., *A Companion to Pirandello Studies* (1991), and Gian-Paolo Biasin and Manuela Gieri, eds., *Luigi Pirandello: Contemporary Perspectives* (1999), are excellent collections of essays, many of which take up *Six Characters*. Luigi Pirandello, *Pirandello's Love Letters to Marta Abba* (1994), ed. and trans. Benito Ortonolani, illuminates the author's personal life in 1925–36 and his plans to reform the Italian theater.

PRONOUNCING GLOSSARY

The following list uses common English syllables and stress accents to provide rough equivalents of selected words whose pronunciation may be unfamiliar to the general reader.

commedia dell'arte: *com-may'-dee-ah*
    del ar'-tay
Luigi Pirandello: *loo-ee'-jee pee-ran-*
    del'-oh

Pace: *pah'-chay*
Pitoëff: *pee'-toh-eff*

Six Characters in Search of an Author[1]

A Comedy in the Making

THE CHARACTERS

FATHER
MOTHER
STEPDAUGHTER
SON
LITTLE BOY
LITTLE GIRL
MADAME PACE

THE COMPANY

THE PRODUCER
THE STAGE STAFF
THE ACTORS

Act One

When the audience enters, the curtain is already up and the stage is just as it would be during the day. There is no set; it is empty, in almost total darkness. This is so that from the beginning the audience will have the feeling of being present, not at a performance of a properly rehearsed play, but at a performance of a play that happens spontaneously. Two small sets of steps, one on the right and one on the left, lead up to the stage from the auditorium. On the stage, the top is off the PROMPTER's *box and is lying next to it. Downstage, there is a small*

---

1. Translated by John Linstrum. In the Italian editions, Pirandello notes that he did not divide the play into formal acts or scenes. The translator has marked the divisions for clarity, however, according to the stage directions.

table and a chair with arms for the PRODUCER: *it is turned with its back to the audience.*

Also downstage there are two small tables, one a little bigger than the other, and several chairs, ready for the rehearsal if needed. There are more chairs scattered on both left and right for the ACTORS *to one side at the back and nearly hidden is a piano.*

When the houselights go down the STAGE HAND *comes on through the back door. He is in blue overalls and carries a tool bag. He brings some pieces of wood on, comes to the front, kneels down and starts to nail them together.*

The STAGE MANAGER *rushes on from the wings.*

STAGE MANAGER   Hey! What are you doing?

STAGE HAND   What do you think I'm doing? I'm banging nails in.

STAGE MANAGER   Now? [*He looks at his watch.*] It's half-past ten already. The Producer will be here in a moment to rehearse.

STAGE HAND   I've got to do my work some time, you know.

STAGE MANAGER   Right—but not now.

STAGE HAND   When?

STAGE MANAGER   When the rehearsal's finished. Come on, get all this out of the way and let me set for the second act of *The Rules of the Game.*[2]

[*The* STAGE HAND *picks up his tools and wood and goes off, grumbling and muttering. The* ACTORS *of the company come in through the door, men and women, first one then another, then two together and so on: there will be nine or ten, enough for the parts for the rehearsal of a play by Pirandello,* The Rules of the Game, *today's rehearsal. They come in, say their "Good-mornings" to the* STAGE MANAGER *and each other. Some go off to the dressing-rooms; others, among them the* PROMPTER *with the text rolled up under his arm, scatter about the stage waiting for the* PRODUCER *to start the rehearsal. Meanwhile, sitting or standing in groups, they chat together; some smoke, one complains about his part, another one loudly reads something from "The Stage." It would be as well if the* ACTORS *and* ACTRESSES *were dressed in colourful clothes, and this first scene should be improvised naturally and vivaciously. After a while somebody might sit down at the piano and play a song; the younger* ACTORS *and* ACTRESSES *start dancing.*]

STAGE MANAGER [*Clapping his hands to call their attention.*]   Come on, everybody! Quiet please. The Producer's here.

[*The piano and the dancing both stop. The* ACTORS *turn to look out into the theatre and through the door at the back comes the* PRODUCER; *he walks down the gangway between the seats and, calling "Good-morning" to the* ACTORS, *climbs up one of the sets of stairs onto the stage. The* SECRETARY *gives him the post, a few magazines, a script. The* ACTORS *move to one side of the stage.*]

PRODUCER   Any letters?

SECRETARY   No. That's all the post there is. [*Giving him the script.*]

PRODUCER   Put it in the office. [*Then looking round and turning to the* STAGE MANAGER.] I can't see a thing here. Let's have some lights please.

---

2. *Il giuoco delle parti*, written in 1918. The hero, Leone Gala, pretends to ignore his wife Silia's infidelity until the end, when he takes revenge by tricking her lover Guido Venanzi into taking his place in a fatal duel she had engineered to get rid of her husband.

STAGE MANAGER   Right. [*Calling.*] Workers please!
   [*In a few seconds the side of the stage where the* ACTORS *are standing is brilliantly lit with white light. The* PROMPTER *has gone into his box and spread out his script.*]
PRODUCER   Good. [*Clapping hands.*] Well then, let's get started. Anybody missing?
STAGE MANAGER [*Heavily ironic.*]   Our leading lady.
PRODUCER   Not again! [*Looking at his watch.*] We're ten minutes late already. Send her a note to come and see me. It might teach her to be on time for rehearsals. [*Almost before he has finished, the* LEADING ACTRESS's *voice is heard from the auditorium.*]
LEADING ACTRESS   Morning everybody. Sorry I'm late. [*She is very expensively dressed and is carrying a lap-dog. She comes down the aisle and goes up on to the stage.*]
PRODUCER   You're determined to keep us waiting, aren't you?
LEADING ACTRESS   I'm sorry. I just couldn't find a taxi anywhere. But you haven't started yet and I'm not on at the opening anyhow. [*Calling the* STAGE MANAGER, *she gives him the dog.*] Put him in my dressing-room for me will you?
PRODUCER   And she's even brought her lap-dog with her! As if we haven't enough lap-dogs here already. [*Clapping his hands and turning to the* PROMPTER.] Right then, the second act of *The Rules of the Game*. [*Sits in his arm-chair.*] Quiet please! Who's on?
   [*The* ACTORS *clear from the front of the stage and sit to one side, except for three who are ready to start the scene—and the* LEADING ACTRESS. *She has ignored the* PRODUCER *and is sitting at one of the little tables.*]
PRODUCER   Are you in this scene, then?
LEADING ACTRESS   No—I've just told you.
PRODUCER [*Annoyed.*]   Then get off, for God's sake. [*The* LEADING ACTRESS *goes and sits with the others. To the* PROMPTER.] Come on then, let's get going.
PROMPTER [*Reading his script.*]   "The house of Leone Gala. A peculiar room, both dining-room and study."
PRODUCER [*To the* STAGE MANAGER.]   We'll use the red set.
STAGE MANAGER [*Making a note.*]   The red set—right.
PROMPTER [*Still reading.*]   "The table is laid and there is a desk with books and papers. Bookcases full of books and china cabinets full of valuable china. An exit at the back leads to Leone's bedroom. An exit to the left leads to the kitchen. The main entrance is on the right."
PRODUCER   Right. Listen carefully everybody: there, the main entrance, there, the kitchen. [*To the* LEADING ACTOR *who plays Socrates.[3]*] Your entrances and exits will be from there. [*To the* STAGE MANAGER.] We'll have the French windows there and put the curtains on them.
STAGE MANAGER [*Making a note.*]   Right.
PROMPTER [*Reading.*]   "Scene One. Leone Gala, Guido Venanzi, and Filippo, who is called Socrates." [*To* PRODUCER.] Have I to read the directions as well?

---

3. Nickname given to Gala's servant, Philip, in *The Rules of the Game*, the play they are rehearsing.

PRODUCER   Yes, you have! I've told you a hundred times.

PROMPTER [*Reading.*]   "When the curtain rises, Leone Gala, in a cook's hat and apron, is beating an egg in a dish with a little wooden spoon. Filippo is beating another and he is dressed as a cook too. Guido Venanzi is sitting listening."

LEADING ACTOR   Look, do I really have to wear a cook's hat?

PRODUCER [*Annoyed by the question.*]   I expect so! That's what it says in the script. [*Pointing to the script.*]

LEADING ACTOR   If you ask me it's ridiculous.

PRODUCER [*Leaping to his feet furiously.*]   Ridiculous? It's ridiculous, is it? What do you expect me to do if nobody writes good plays any more[4] and we're reduced to putting on plays by Pirandello? And if you can understand them you must be very clever. He writes them on purpose so nobody enjoys them, neither actors nor critics nor audience. [*The ACTORS laugh. Then crosses to LEADING ACTOR and shouts at him.*] A cook's hat and you beat eggs. But don't run away with the idea that that's all you are doing—beating eggs. You must be joking! You have to be symbolic of the shells of the eggs you are beating. [*The ACTORS laugh again and start making ironical comments to each other.*] Be quiet! Listen carefully while I explain. [*Turns back to LEADING ACTOR.*] Yes, the shells, because they are symbolic of the empty form of reason, without its content, blind instinct! You are reason and your wife is instinct: you are playing a game where you have been given parts and in which you are not just yourself but the puppet of yourself.[5] Do you see?

LEADING ACTOR [*Spreading his hands.*]   Me? No.

PRODUCER [*Going back to his chair.*]   Neither do I! Come on, let's get going; you wait till you see the end! You haven't seen anything yet! [*Confidentially.*] By the way, I should turn almost to face the audience if I were you, about three-quarters face. Well, what with the obscure dialogue and the audience not being able to hear you properly in any case, the whole lot'll go to hell. [*Clapping hands again.*] Come on. Let's get going!

PROMPTER   Excuse me, can I put the top back on the prompt-box? There's a bit of a draught.

PRODUCER   Yes, yes, of course. Get on with it.

> [*The STAGE DOORKEEPER, in a braided cap, has come into the auditorium, and he comes all the way down the aisle to the stage to tell the PRODUCER the SIX CHARACTERS have come, who, having come in after him, look about them a little puzzled and dismayed. Every effort must be made to create the effect that the SIX CHARACTERS are very different from the ACTORS of the company. The placings of the two groups, indicated in the directions, once the CHARACTERS are on the stage, will help this: so will using different coloured lights. But the most effective idea is to use masks for the CHARACTERS, masks*]

---

4. The producer refers to the realistic, tightly constructed plays (often French) that were internationally popular in the late 19th century and a staple of Italian theaters at the beginning of the 20th.   5. Leone Gala is a rationalist and an aesthete—the opposite of his impulsive, passionate wife, Silia. By masking his feelings and constantly playing the role of gourmet cook, he chooses his own role and thus becomes his own "puppet."

specially made of a material that will not go limp with perspiration and light enough not to worry the actors who wear them: they should be made so that the eyes, the nose and the mouth are all free. This is the way to bring out the deep significance of the play. The CHAR-ACTERS should not appear as ghosts, but as created realities, timeless creations of the imagination, and so more real and consistent than the changeable realities of the ACTORS. The masks are designed to give the impression of figures constructed by art, each one fixed for-ever in its own fundamental emotion; that is, Remorse for the FATHER, Revenge for the STEPDAUGHTER, Scorn for the SON, Sorrow for the MOTHER. Her mask should have wax tears in the corners of the eyes and down the cheeks like the sculptured or painted weeping Madonna in a church. Her dress should be of a plain material, in stiff folds, looking almost as if it were carved and not of an ordinary material you can buy in a shop and have made up by a dressmaker.

The FATHER is about fifty: his reddish hair is thinning at the tem-ples, but he is not bald: he has a full moustache that almost covers his young-looking mouth, which often opens in an uncertain and empty smile. He is pale, with a high forehead: he has blue oval eyes, clear and sharp: he is dressed in light trousers and a dark jacket: his voice is sometimes rich, at other times harsh and loud.

The MOTHER appears crushed by an intolerable weight of shame and humiliation. She is wearing a thick black veil and is dressed simply in black; when she raises her veil she shows a face like wax, but not suffering, with her eyes turned down humbly.

The STEPDAUGHTER, who is eighteen years old, is defiant, even insolent. She is very beautiful, dressed in mourning as well, but with striking elegance. She is scornful of the timid, suffering, dejected air of her young brother, a grubby LITTLE BOY of fourteen, also dressed in black; she is full of a warm tenderness, on the other hand, for the LITTLE SISTER (GIRL), a girl of about four, dressed in white with a black silk sash round her waist.

The SON is twenty-two, tall, almost frozen in an air of scorn for the FATHER and indifference to the MOTHER: he is wearing a mauve overcoat and a long green scarf round his neck.]

DOORMAN Excuse me, sir.

PRODUCER [*Angrily.*] What the hell is it now?

DOORMAN There are some people here—they say they want to see you, sir.

[*The PRODUCER and the ACTORS are astonished and turn to look out into the auditorium.*]

PRODUCER But I'm rehearsing! You know perfectly well that no-one's allowed in during rehearsals. [*Turning to face out front.*] Who are you? What do you want?

FATHER [*Coming forward, followed by the others, to the foot of one of the sets of steps.*] We're looking for an author.

PRODUCER [*Angry and astonished.*] An author? Which author?

FATHER Any author will do, sir.

PRODUCER But there isn't an author here because we're not rehearsing a new play.

STEPDAUGHTER [*Excitedly as she rushes up the steps.*] That's better still, better still! We can be your new play.

ACTORS [*Lively comments and laughter from the* ACTORS.] Oh, listen to that, etc.

FATHER [*Going up on the stage after the* STEPDAUGHTER.] Maybe, but if there isn't an author here . . . [*To the* PRODUCER.] Unless you'd like to be . . .

> [*Hand in hand, the* MOTHER *and the* LITTLE GIRL, *followed by the* LITTLE BOY, *go up on the stage and wait. The* SON *stays sullenly behind.*]

PRODUCER Is this some kind of joke?

FATHER Now, how can you think that? On the contrary, we are bringing you a story of anguish.

STEPDAUGHTER We might make your fortune for you!

PRODUCER Do me a favour, will you? Go away. We haven't time to waste on idiots.

FATHER [*Hurt but answering gently.*] You know very well, as a man of the theatre, that life is full of all sorts of odd things which have no need at all to pretend to be real because they are actually true.

PRODUCER What the devil are you talking about?

FATHER What I'm saying is that you really must be mad to do things the opposite way round: to create situations that obviously aren't true and try to make them seem to be really happening. But then I suppose that sort of madness is the only reason for your profession.

> [*The* ACTORS *are indignant.*]

PRODUCER [*Getting up and glaring at him.*] Oh, yes? So ours is a profession of madmen, is it?

FATHER Well, if you try to make something look true when it obviously isn't, especially if you're not forced to do it, but do it for a game . . . Isn't it your job to give life on the stage to imaginary people?

PRODUCER [*Quickly answering him and speaking for the* ACTORS *who are growing more indignant.*] I should like you to know, sir, that the actor's profession is one of great distinction. Even if nowadays the new writers only give us dull plays to act and puppets to present instead of men, I'd have you know that it is our boast that we have given life, here on this stage, to immortal works.

> [*The* ACTORS, *satisfied, agree with and applaud the* PRODUCER].

FATHER [*Cutting in and following hard on his argument.*] There! You see? Good! You've given life! You've created living beings with more genuine life than people have who breathe and wear clothes! Less real, perhaps, but nearer the truth. We are both saying the same thing.

> [*The* ACTORS *look at each other, astonished.*]

PRODUCER But just a moment! You said before . . .

FATHER I'm sorry, but I said that before, about acting for fun, because you shouted at us and said you'd no time to waste on idiots, but you must know better than anyone that Nature uses human imagination to lift her work of creation to even higher levels.

PRODUCER All right then: but where does all this get us?

FATHER Nowhere. I want to try to show that one can be thrust into life in many ways, in many forms: as a tree or a stone, as water or a butterfly—or as a woman. It might even be as a character in a play.

PRODUCER [*Ironic, pretending to be annoyed.*] And you, and these other
people here, were thrust into life, as you put it, as characters in a play?

FATHER Exactly! And alive, as you can see.

[*The* PRODUCER *and the* ACTORS *burst into laughter as if at a joke.*]

FATHER I'm sorry you laugh like that, because we carry in us, as I said
before, a story of terrible anguish as you can guess from this woman
dressed in black.

[*Saying this, he offers his hand to the* MOTHER *and helps her up the
last steps and, holding her still by the hand, leads her with a sense
of tragic solemnity across the stage which is suddenly lit by a fantastic
light.*

The LITTLE GIRL *and the* (LITTLE) BOY *follow the* MOTHER: *then
the* SON *comes up and stands to one side in the background: then
the* STEPDAUGHTER *follows and leans against the proscenium arch:
the* ACTORS *are astonished at first, but then, full of admiration for
the "entrance," they burst into applause—just as if it were a performance specially for them.*]

PRODUCER [*At first astonished and then indignant.*] My God! Be quiet all
of you. [*Turns to the* CHARACTERS.] And you lot get out! Clear off! [*Turns
to the* STAGE MANAGER.] Jesus! Get them out of here.

STAGE MANAGER [*Comes forward but stops short as if held back by something
strange.*] Go on out! Get out!

FATHER [*To* PRODUCER.] Oh no, please, you see, we . . .

PRODUCER [*Shouting.*] We came here to work, you know.

LEADING ACTOR We really can't be messed about like this.

FATHER [*Resolutely, coming forward.*] I'm astonished! Why don't you
believe me? Perhaps you are not used to seeing the characters created
by an author spring into life up here on the stage face to face with each
other. Perhaps it's because we're not in a script? [*He points to the*
PROMPTER's *box.*]

STEPDAUGHTER [*Coming down to the* PRODUCER, *smiling and persuasive.*] Believe me, sir, we really are six of the most fascinating characters. But we've been neglected.

FATHER Yes, that's right, we've been neglected. In the sense that the
author who created us, living in his mind, wouldn't or couldn't make us
live in a written play for the world of art.[6] And that really is a crime sir,
because whoever has the luck to be born a character can laugh even at
death. Because a character will never die! A man will die, a writer, the
instrument of creation: but what he has created will never die! And to
be able to live for ever you don't need to have extraordinary gifts or be
able to do miracles. Who was Sancho Panza? Who was Prospero?[7] But
they will live for ever because—living seeds—they had the luck to find
a fruitful soil, an imagination which knew how to grow them and feed
them, so that they will live for ever.

PRODUCER This is all very well! But what do you want here?

FATHER We want to live, sir.

PRODUCER [*Ironically.*] For ever!

---

6. In the 1925 preface to *Six Characters*, Pirandello explains that these characters came to him first as
characters for a novel that he later abandoned. Haunted by their half-realized personalities, he decided to
use the situation in a play.   7. The magician and exiled duke of Milan in Shakespeare's *The Tempest*.
Sancho Panza was Don Quixote's servant in Cervantes's novel *Don Quixote* (1605–15).

FATHER   No, no: only for a few moments—in you.

AN ACTOR   Listen to that!

LEADING ACTRESS   They want to live in us!

YOUNG ACTOR [*Pointing to the* STEPDAUGHTER.]   I don't mind . . . so long as I get her.

FATHER   Listen, listen: the play is all ready to be put together and if you and your actors would like to, we can work it out now between us.

PRODUCER [*Annoyed.*]   But what exactly do you want to do? We don't make up plays like that here! We present comedies and tragedies here.

FATHER   That's right, we know that of course. That's why we've come.

PRODUCER   And where's the script?

FATHER   It's in us, sir. [*The* ACTORS *laugh.*] The play is in us: we are the play and we are impatient to show it to you: the passion inside us is driving us on.

STEPDAUGHTER [*Scornfully, with the tantalising charm of deliberate impudence.*]   My passion, if only you knew! My passion for him! [*She points at the* FATHER *and suggests that she is going to embrace him: but stops and bursts into a screeching laugh.*]

FATHER [*With sudden anger.*]   You keep out of this for the moment! And stop laughing like that!

STEPDAUGHTER   Really? Then with your permission, ladies and gentlemen; even though it's only two months since I became an orphan, just watch how I can sing and dance.

> [*The* ACTORS, *especially the younger, seem strangely attracted to her while she sings and dances and they edge closer and reach out their hands to catch hold of her.*[8] *She eludes them, and when the* ACTORS *applaud her and the* PRODUCER *speaks sharply to her she stays still quite removed from them all.*]

FIRST ACTOR   Very good! etc.

PRODUCER [*Angrily.*]   Be quiet! Do you think this is a nightclub? [*Turns to* FATHER *and asks with some concern.*] Is she a bit mad?

FATHER   Mad? Oh no—it's worse than that.

STEPDAUGHTER [*Suddenly running to the* PRODUCER.]   Yes. It's worse, much worse! Listen please! Let's put this play on at once, because you'll see that at a particular point I—when this darling little girl here— [*Taking the* LITTLE GIRL *by the hand from next to the* MOTHER *and crossing with her to the* PRODUCER.] Isn't she pretty? [*Takes her in her arms.*] Darling! Darling! [*Puts her down again and adds, moved very deeply but almost without wanting to.*] Well, this lovely little girl here, when God suddenly takes her from this poor Mother: and this little idiot here [*Turning to the* LITTLE BOY *and seizing him roughly by the sleeve.*] does the most stupid thing, like the half-wit he is,—then you will see me run away! Yes, you'll see me rush away! But not yet, not yet! Because, after all the intimate things there have been between him and me [*In the direction of the* FATHER, *with a horrible vulgar wink.*] I can't stay with them any longer, to watch the insult to this mother through that supercilious cretin over there. [*Pointing to the* SON.] Look at him! Look at him! Condescending,

---

8. Pirandello uses a contemporary popular song, "Chu-Chin-Chow" from the Ziegfeld Follies of 1917, for the Stepdaughter to display her talents.

stand-offish, because he's the legitimate son, him! Full of contempt for me, for the boy and for the little girl: because we are bastards. Do you understand? Bastards. [*Running to the* MOTHER *and embracing her.*] And this poor mother—she—who is the mother of all of us—he doesn't want to recognise her as his own mother—and he looks down on her, he does, as if she were only the mother of the three of us who are bastards—the traitor. [*She says all this quickly, with great excitement, and after having raised her voice on the word "bastards" she speaks quietly, half-spitting the word "traitor."*]

MOTHER [*With deep anguish to the* PRODUCER.]   Sir, in the name of these two little ones, I beg you . . . [*Feels herself grow faint and sways.*] Oh, my God.

FATHER [*Rushing to support her with almost all the* ACTORS *bewildered and concerned.*]   Get a chair someone . . . quick, get a chair for this poor widow.

[*One of the* ACTORS *offers a chair: the others press urgently around. The* MOTHER, *seated now, tries to stop the* FATHER *lifting her veil.*]

ACTORS   Is it real? Has she really fainted? etc.

FATHER   Look at her, everybody, look at her.

MOTHER   No, for God's sake, stop it.

FATHER   Let them look?

MOTHER [*Lifting her hands and covering her face, desperately.*]   Oh, please, I beg you, stop him from doing what he is trying to do; it's hateful.

PRODUCER [*Overwhelmed, astounded.*]   It's no use, I don't understand this any more. [*To the* FATHER.] Is this woman your wife?

FATHER [*At once.*]   That's right, she is my wife.

PRODUCER   How is she a widow, then, if you're still alive?

[*The* ACTORS *are bewildered too and find relief in a loud laugh.*]

FATHER [*Wounded, with rising resentment.*]   Don't laugh! Please don't laugh like that! That's just the point, that's her own drama. You see, she had another man. Another man who ought to be here.

MOTHER   No, no! [*Crying out.*]

STEPDAUGHTER   Luckily for him he died. Two months ago, as I told you: we are in mourning for him, as you can see.

FATHER   Yes, he's dead: but that's not the reason he isn't here. He isn't here because—well just look at her, please, and you'll understand at once—hers is not a passionate drama of the love of two men, because she was incapable of love, she could feel nothing—except, perhaps a little gratitude (but not to me, to him). She's not a woman; she's a mother. And her drama—and, believe me, it's a powerful one—her drama is focused completely on these four children of the two men she had.

MOTHER   I had them? How dare you say that I had them, as if I wanted them myself? It was him, sir! He forced the other man on me. He made me go away with him!

STEPDAUGHTER [*Leaping up, indignantly.*]   It isn't true!

MOTHER [*Bewildered.*]   How isn't it true?

STEPDAUGHTER   It isn't true, it just isn't true.

MOTHER   What do you know about it?

STEPDAUGHTER   It isn't true. [*To the* PRODUCER.] Don't believe it! Do you know why she said that? She said it because of him, over there. [*Pointing to the* SON.] She tortures herself, she exhausts herself with worry and all because of the indifference of that son of hers. She wants to make him believe that she abandoned him when he was two years old because the Father made her do it.

MOTHER [*Passionately.*] He did! He made me! God's my witness. [*To the* PRODUCER.] Ask him if it isn't true. [*Pointing to the* FATHER.] Make him tell our son it's true. [*Turning to the* STEPDAUGHTER.] You don't know anything about it.

STEPDAUGHTER I know that when my father was alive you were always happy and contented. You can't deny it.

MOTHER No, I can't deny it.

STEPDAUGHTER He was always full of love and care for you. [*Turning to the* LITTLE BOY *with anger.*] Isn't it true? Admit it. Why don't you say something, you little idiot?

MOTHER Leave the poor boy alone! Why do you want to make me appear ungrateful? You're my daughter. I don't in the least want to offend your father's memory. I've already told him that it wasn't my fault or even to please myself that I left his house and my son.

FATHER It's quite true. It was my fault.

LEADING ACTOR [*To other actors.*] Look at this. What a show!

LEADING ACTRESS And we're the audience.

YOUNG ACTOR For a change.

PRODUCER [*Beginning to be very interested.*] Let's listen to them! Quiet! Listen!

> [*He goes down the steps into the auditorium and stands there as if to get an idea of what the scene will look like from the audience's viewpoint.*]

SON [*Without moving, coldly, quietly, ironically.*] Yes, listen to his little scrap of philosophy. He's going to tell you all about the Daemon of Experiment.

FATHER You're a cynical idiot, and I've told you so a hundred times. [*To the* PRODUCER *who is now in the stalls.*] He sneers at me because of this expression I've found to defend myself.

SON Words, words.

FATHER Yes words, words! When we're faced by something we don't understand, by a sense of evil that seems as if it's going to swallow us, don't we all find comfort in a word that tells us nothing but that calms us?

STEPDAUGHTER And dulls your sense of remorse, too. That more than anything.

FATHER Remorse? No, that's not true. It'd take more than words to dull the sense of remorse in me.

STEPDAUGHTER It's taken a little money too, just a little money. The money that he was going to offer as payment, gentlemen.

> [*The* ACTORS *are horrified.*]

SON [*Contemptuously to his stepsister.*] That's a filthy trick.

STEPDAUGHTER A filthy trick? There it was in a pale blue envelope on the little mahogany table in the room behind the shop at Madame Pace's. You know Madame Pace, don't you? One of those Madames who sell so that they can attract poor girls like me from

"Robes et Mantea eir workroom.[9]

decent families i the right to tyrannise over the whole lot of us with

SON   And she's what he was going to pay her: and luckily—now listen

that money no reason to pay it to her.

carefully at it was close!

STEPDAUG angrily.] Shame on you, daughter! Shame!

MOTHE Shame? Not shame, revenge! I'm desperate, desperate to

STEPD ! The room . . . over here the showcase of coats, there the

li the mirror, and the screen, and over there in front of

that little mahogany table with the pale blue envelope and

in it. I can see it all quite clearly. I could pick it up! But you

rn your faces away, gentlemen: because I'm nearly naked! I'm

ning any longer—I leave that to him. [*Pointing at the* FATHER.]

ell you he was very pale, very pale then. [*To the* PRODUCER.]

e me.

ER   I don't understand any more.

ＲＲ   I'm not surprised when you're attacked like that! Why don't you put your foot down and let me have my say before you believe all these horrible slanders she's so viciously telling about me.

STEPDAUGHTER   We don't want to hear any of your long winded fairy-stories.

FATHER   I'm not going to tell any fairy-stories! I want to explain things to him.

STEPDAUGHTER   I'm sure you do. Oh, yes! In your own special way.

[*The* PRODUCER *comes back up on stage to take control.*]

FATHER   But isn't that the cause of all the trouble? Words! We all have a world of things inside ourselves and each one of us has his own private world. How can we understand each other if the words I use have the sense and the value that I expect them to have, but whoever is listening to me inevitably thinks that those same words have a different sense and value, because of the private world he has inside himself too. We think we understand each other: but we never do. Look! All my pity, all my compassion for this woman [*Pointing to the* MOTHER.] she sees as ferocious cruelty.

MOTHER   But he turned me out of the house!

FATHER   There, do you hear? I turned her out! She really believed that I had turned her out.

MOTHER   You know how to talk. I don't . . . But believe me, sir, [*Turning to the* PRODUCER.] after he married me . . . I can't think why! I was a poor, simple woman.

FATHER   But that was the reason! I married you for your simplicity, that's what I loved in you, believing— [*He stops because she is making gestures of contradiction. Then, seeing the impossibility of making her understand, he throws his arms wide in a gesture of desperation and turns back to the* PRODUCER.] No, do you see? She says no! It's terrifying, sir, believe me, terrifying, her deafness, her mental deafness. [*He taps his forehead.*]

---

9. The implication is that Madame Pace (Italian for "peace") runs a call-girl operation under the guise of selling fashionable "dresses and coats."

Affection for her children, oh yes. But deaf, me—... to
the point of desperation.
STEPDAUGHTER Yes, but make him tell you what go—... deaf, deaf, sir, to
has brought us.
FATHER If only we could see in advance all the harm th—... *his cleverness*
the good we think we are doing.
    [*The* LEADING ACTRESS, *who has been growing angr*—... *me from*
    LEADING ACTOR *flirting with the* STEPDAUGHTER, *c*—...
    and snaps at the PRODUCER.]
LEADING ACTRESS Excuse me, are we going to go on with our r—...
PRODUCER Yes, of course. But I want to listen to this first.
YOUNG ACTOR It's such a new idea.
YOUNG ACTRESS It's fascinating.
LEADING ACTRESS For those who are interested. [*She looks meaningf*—...
    at the LEADING ACTOR.]
PRODUCER [*To the* FATHER.] Look here, you must explain yourself more
    clearly. [*He sits down.*]
FATHER Listen then. You see, there was a rather poor fellow working for
    me as my assistant and secretary, very loyal: he understood her in every-
    thing. [*Pointing to the* MOTHER.] But without a hint of deceit, you must
    believe that: he was good and simple, like her: neither of them was capa-
    ble even of thinking anything wrong, let alone doing it.
STEPDAUGHTER So instead he thought of it for them and did it too!
FATHER It's not true! What I did was for their good—oh yes and mine too,
    I admit it! The time had come when I couldn't say a word to either of
    them without there immediately flashing between them a sympathetic
    look: each one caught the other's eye for advice, about how to take what
    I had said, how not to make me angry. Well, that was enough, as I'm
    sure you'll understand, to put me in a bad temper all the time, in a state
    of intolerable exasperation.
PRODUCER Then why didn't you sack this secretary of yours?
FATHER Right! In the end I did sack him! But then I had to watch this
    poor woman wandering about in the house on her own, forlorn, like a
    stray animal you take in out of pity.
MOTHER It's quite true.
FATHER [*Suddenly, turning to her, as if to stop her.*] And what about the
    boy? Is that true as well?
MOTHER But first he tore my son from me, sir.
FATHER But not out of cruelty! It was so that he could grow up healthy
    and strong, in touch with the earth.
STEPDAUGHTER [*Pointing to the* SON *jeeringly.*] And look at the result!
FATHER [*Quickly.*] And is it my fault, too, that he's grown up like this? I
    took him to a nurse in the country, a peasant, because his mother didn't
    seem strong enough to me, although she is from a humble family herself.
    In fact that was what made me marry her. Perhaps it was superstitious
    of me; but what was I to do? I've always had this dreadful longing for a
    kind of sound moral healthiness.
    [*The* STEPDAUGHTER *breaks out again into noisy laughter.*]
    Make her stop that! It's unbearable.
PRODUCER Stop it will you? Let me listen, for God's sake.

[*When the* PRODUCER *has spoken to her, she resumes her previous position . . . absorbed and distant, a half-smile on her lips. The* PRO-DUCER *comes down into the auditorium again to see how it looks from there.*]

FATHER   I couldn't bear the sight of this woman near me. [*Pointing to the* MOTHER.] Not so much because of the annoyance she caused me, you see, or even the feeling of being stifled, being suffocated that I got from her, as for the sorrow, the painful sorrow that I felt for her.

MOTHER   And he sent me away.

FATHER   With everything you needed, to the other man, to set her free from me.

MOTHER   And to set yourself free!

FATHER   Oh, yes, I admit it. And what terrible things came out of it. But I did it for the best, and more for her than for me: I swear it! [*Folds his arms: then turns suddenly to the* MOTHER.] I never lost sight of you did I? Until that fellow, without my knowing it, suddenly took you off to another town one day. He was idiotically suspicious of my interest in them, a genuine interest, I assure you, without any ulterior motive at all. I watched the new little family growing up round her with unbelievable tenderness, she'll confirm that. [*He points to the* STEPDAUGHTER.]

STEPDAUGHTER   Oh yes, I can indeed. I was a pretty little girl, you know, with plaits down to my shoulders and my little frilly knickers showing under my dress—so pretty—he used to watch me coming out of school. He came to see how I was maturing.

FATHER   That's shameful! It's monstrous.

STEPDAUGHTER   No it isn't! Why do you say it is?

FATHER   It's monstrous! Monstrous. [*He turns excitedly to the* PRODUCER *and goes on in explanation.*] After she'd gone away [*Pointing to the* MOTHER.] my house seemed empty. She'd been like a weight on my spirit but she'd filled the house with her presence. Alone in the empty rooms I wandered about like a lost soul. This boy here, [*Indicating the* SON.] growing up away from home—whenever he came back to the home—I don't know—but he didn't seem to be mine any more. We needed the mother between us, to link us together, and so he grew up by himself, apart, with no connection to me either through intellect or love. And then—it must seem odd, but it's true—first I was curious about and then strongly attracted to the little family that had come about because of what I'd done. And the thought of them began to fill all the emptiness that I felt around me. I needed, I really needed to believe that she was happy, wrapped up in the simple cares of her life, lucky because she was better off away from the complicated torments of a soul like mine. And to prove it, I used to watch that child coming out of school.

STEPDAUGHTER   Listen to him! He used to follow me along the street; he used to smile at me and when we came near the house he'd wave his hand—like this! I watched him, wide-eyed, puzzled. I didn't know who he was. I told my mother about him and she knew at once who it must be. [MOTHER *nods agreement*.] At first, she didn't let me go to school again, at any rate for a few days. But when I did go back, I saw him standing near the door again—looking ridiculous—with a brown paper bag in his hand. He came close and petted me: then he opened the bag

and took out a beautiful straw hat with a hoop of rosebuds round it—
for me!

PRODUCER   All this is off the point, you know.

SON [*Contemptuously.*]   Yes . . . literature, literature.

FATHER   What do you mean, literature? This is real life: real passions.

PRODUCER   That may be! But you can't put it on the stage just like that.

FATHER   That's right you can't. Because all this is only leading up to the
main action. I'm not suggesting that this part should be put on the stage.
In any case, you can see for yourself, [*Pointing at the* STEPDAUGHTER.]
she isn't a pretty little girl any longer with plaits down to her shoulders.

STEPDAUGHTER   —and with frilly knickers showing under her frock.

FATHER   The drama begins now: and it's new and complex.

STEPDAUGHTER [*Coming forward, fierce and brooding.*]   As soon as my
father died . . .

FATHER [*Quickly, not giving her time to speak.*]   They were so miserable.
They came back here, but I didn't know about it because of the Mother's
stubbornness. [*Pointing to the* MOTHER.] She can't really write you know;
but she could have got her daughter to write, or the boy, or tell me that
they needed help.

MOTHER   But tell me, sir, how could I have known how he felt?

FATHER   And hasn't that always been your fault? You've never known anything about how I felt.

MOTHER   After all the years away from him and after all that had
happened.

FATHER   And was it my fault if that fellow took you so far away? [*Turning
back to the* PRODUCER.] Suddenly, overnight, I tell you, he'd found a job
away from here without my knowing anything about it. I couldn't possibly
trace them; and then, naturally I suppose, my interest in them grew less
over the years. The drama broke out, unexpected and violent, when they
came back: when I was driven in misery by the needs of my flesh, still
alive with desire . . . and it is misery, you know, unspeakable misery for
the man who lives alone and who detests sordid, casual affairs; not old
enough to do without women, but not young enough to be able to go
and look for one without shame! Misery? Is that what I called it. It's
horrible, it's revolting, because there isn't a woman who will give her love
to him any more. And when he realises this, he should do without . . .
It's easy to say though. Each of us, face to face with other men, is clothed
with some sort of dignity, but we know only too well all the unspeakable
things that go on in the heart. We surrender, we give in to temptation:
but afterwards we rise up out of it very quickly, in a desperate hurry to
rebuild our dignity, whole and firm as if it were a gravestone that would
cover every sign and memory of our shame, and hide it from even our
own eyes. Everyone's like that, only some of us haven't the courage to
talk about it.

STEPDAUGHTER   But they've all got the courage to do it!

FATHER   Yes! But only in secret! That's why it takes more courage to talk
about it! Because if a man does talk about it—what happens then?—
everybody says he's a cynic. And it's simply not true; he's just like everybody else; only better perhaps, because he's not afraid to use his intelligence to point out the blushing shame of human bestiality, that man,

the beast, shuts his eyes to, trying to pretend it doesn't exist. And what about woman—what is she like? She looks at you invitingly, teasingly. You take her in your arms. But as soon as she feels your arms round her she closes her eyes. It's the sign of her mission, the sign by which she says to a man, "Blind yourself—I'm blind!"

STEPDAUGHTER   And when she doesn't close her eyes any more? What then? When she doesn't feel the need to hide from herself any more, to shut her eyes and hide her own shame. When she can see instead, dispassionately and dry-eyed this blushing shame of a man who has blinded himself, who is without love. What then? Oh, then what disgust, what utter disgust she feels for all these intellectual complications, for all this philosophy that points to the bestiality of man and then tries to defend him, to excuse him . . . I can't listen to him, sir. Because when a man says he needs to "simplify" life like this—reducing it to bestiality—and throws away every human scrap of innocent desire, genuine feeling, idealism, duty, modesty, shame, then there's nothing more contemptible and nauseating than his remorse—crocodile tears!

PRODUCER   Let's get to the point, let's get to the point. This is all chat.

FATHER   Right then! But a fact is like a sack—it won't stand up if it's empty. To make it stand up, first you have to put in it all the reasons and feelings that caused it in the first place. I couldn't possibly have known that when that fellow died they'd come back here, that they were desperately poor and that the Mother had gone out to work as a dressmaker, nor that she'd gone to work for Madame Pace, of all people.

STEPDAUGHTER   She's a very high-class dressmaker—you must understand that. She apparently has only high-class customers, but she has arranged things carefully so that these high-class customers in fact serve her—they give her a respectable front . . . without spoiling things for the other ladies at the shop who are not quite so high-class at all.

MOTHER   Believe me, sir, the idea never entered my head that the old hag gave me work because she had an eye on my daughter . . .

STEPDAUGHTER   Poor Mummy! Do you know what that woman would do when I took back the work that my mother had been doing? She would point out how the dress had been ruined by giving it to my mother to sew: she bargained, she grumbled. So, you see, I paid for it, while this poor woman here thought she was sacrificing herself for me and these two children, sewing dresses all night for Madame Pace.

[The ACTORS make gestures and noises of disgust.]

PRODUCER [Quickly.]   And there one day, you met . . .

STEPDAUGHTER [Pointing at the FATHER.]   Yes, him. Oh, he was an old customer of hers! What a scene that's going to be, superb!

FATHER   With her, the mother, arriving—

STEPDAUGHTER [Quickly, viciously.]   —Almost in time!

FATHER [Crying out.]   —No, just in time, just in time! Because, luckily, I found out who she was in time. And I took them all back to my house, sir. Can you imagine the situation now, for the two of us living in the same house? She, just as you see her here: and I, not able to look her in the face.

STEPDAUGHTER   It's so absurd! Do you think it's possible for me, sir, after what happened at Madame Pace's, to pretend that I'm a modest little miss, well brought up and virtuous just so that I can fit in with his damned pretensions to a "sound moral healthiness"?

FATHER   This is the real drama for me; the belief that we all, you see, think of ourselves as one single person: but it's not true: each of us is several different people, and all these people live inside us. With one person we seem like this and with another we seem very different. But we always have the illusion of being the same person for everybody and of always being the same person in everything we do. But it's not true! It's not true! We find this out for ourselves very clearly when by some terrible chance we're suddenly stopped in the middle of doing something and we're left dangling there, suspended. We realise then, that every part of us was not involved in what we'd been doing and that it would be a dreadful injustice of other people to judge us only by this one action as we dangle there, hanging in chains, fixed for all eternity, as if the whole of one's personality were summed up in that single, interrupted action. Now do you understand this girl's treachery? She accidentally found me somewhere I shouldn't have been, doing something I shouldn't have been doing! She discovered a part of me that shouldn't have existed for her: and now she wants to fix on me a reality that I should never have had to assume for her: it came from a single brief and shameful moment in my life. This is what hurts me most of all. And you'll see that the play will make a tremendous impact from this idea of mine. But then, there's the position of the others. His . . . [Pointing to the SON.]

SON [Shrugging his shoulders scornfully.]   Leave me out of it. I don't come into this.

FATHER   Why don't you come into this?

SON   I don't come into it and I don't want to come into it, because you know perfectly well that I wasn't intended to be mixed up with you lot.

STEPDAUGHTER   We're vulgar, common people, you see! He's a fine gentleman. But you've probably noticed that every now and then I look at him contemptuously, and when I do, he lowers his eyes—he knows the harm he's done me.

SON [Not looking at her.]   I have?

STEPDAUGHTER   Yes, you. It's your fault, dearie, that I went on the streets! Your fault! [Movement of horror from the ACTORS.] Did you or didn't you, with your attitude, deny us—I won't say the intimacy of your home—but that simple hospitality that makes guests feel comfortable? We were intruders who had come to invade the country of your "legitimacy"! [Turning to the PRODUCER.] I'd like you to have seen some of the little scenes that went on between him and me, sir. He says that I tyrannised over everyone. But don't you see? It was because of the way he treated us. He called it "vile" that I should insist on the right we had to move into his house with my mother—and she's his mother too. And I went into the house as its mistress.

SON [Slowly coming forward.]   They're really enjoying themselves, aren't they, sir? It's easy when they all gang up against me. But try to imagine what happened: one fine day, there is a son sitting quietly at home and he sees arrive as bold as brass, a young woman like this, who cheekily asks for his father, and heaven knows what business she has with him. Then he sees her come back with the same brazen look in her eye accompanied by that little girl there: and he sees her treat his father—without knowing why—in a most ambiguous and insolent way—asking him for money in a tone that leads one to suppose he really ought to give it, because he is obliged to do so.

FATHER But I was obliged to do so: I owed it to your mother.

SON And how was I to know that? When had I ever seen her before? When had I ever heard her mentioned? Then one day I see her come in with her, [*Pointing at the* STEPDAUGHTER.] that boy and that little girl: they say to me, "Oh, didn't you know? This is your mother, too." Little by little I began to understand, mostly from her attitude. [*Points to* STEP-DAUGHTER.] Why they'd come to live in the house so suddenly. I can't and I won't say what I feel, and what I think. I wouldn't even like to confess it to myself. So I can't take any active part in this. Believe me, sir, I am a character who has not been fully developed dramatically, and I feel uncomfortable, most uncomfortable, in their company. So please leave me out of it.

FATHER What! But it's precisely because you feel like this . . .

SON [*Violently exasperated.*] How do you know what I feel?

FATHER All right! I admit it! But isn't that a situation in itself? This with-drawing of yourself, it's cruel to me and to your mother: when she came back to the house, seeing you almost for the first time, not recognising you, but knowing that you're her own son . . . [*Turning to point out the* MOTHER *to the* PRODUCER.] There, look at her: she's weeping.

STEPDAUGHTER [*Angrily, stamping her foot.*] Like the fool she is!

FATHER [*Quickly pointing at the* STEPDAUGHTER *to the* PRODUCER.] She can't stand that young man, you know. [*Turning and referring to the* SON.] He says that he doesn't come into it, but he's really the pivot of the action! Look here at this little boy, who clings to his mother all the time, fright-ened, humiliated. And it's because of him over there! Perhaps this little boy's problem is the worst of all: he feels an outsider, more than the others do; he feels so mortified, so humiliated just being in the house,—because it's charity, you see. [*Quietly.*] He's like his father: timid; he doesn't say anything . . .

PRODUCER It's not a good idea at all, using him: you don't know what a nuisance children are on the stage.

FATHER He won't need to be on the stage for long. Nor will the little girl—she's the first to go.

PRODUCER That's good! Yes. I tell you all this interests me—it interests me very much. I'm sure we've the material here for a good play.

STEPDAUGHTER [*Trying to push herself in.*] With a character like me you have!

FATHER [*Driving her off, wanting to hear what the* PRODUCER *has de-cided.*] You stay out of it!

PRODUCER [*Going on, ignoring the interruption.*] It's new, yes.

FATHER Oh, it's absolutely new!

PRODUCER You've got a nerve, though, haven't you, coming here and throwing it at me like this?

FATHER I'm sure you understand. Born as we are for the *stage* . . .

PRODUCER Are you amateur actors?

FATHER No! I say we are born for the stage because . . .

PRODUCER   Come on now! You're an old hand at this, at acting!

FATHER   No I'm not. I only act, as everyone does, the part in life that he's chosen for himself, or that others have chosen for him. And you can see that sometimes my own passion gets a bit out of hand, a bit theatrical, as it does with all of us.

PRODUCER   Maybe, maybe . . . But you do see, don't you, that without an author . . . I could give you someone's address . . .

FATHER   Oh no! Look here! You do it.

PRODUCER   Me? What are you talking about?

FATHER   Yes, you. Why not?

PRODUCER   Because I've never written anything!

FATHER   Well, why not start now, if you don't mind my suggesting it? There's nothing to it. Everybody's doing it. And your job is even easier, because we're here, all of us, alive before you.

PRODUCER   That's not enough.

FATHER   Why isn't it enough? When you've seen us live our drama . . .

PRODUCER   Perhaps so. But we'll still need someone to write it.

FATHER   Only to write it down, perhaps, while it happens in front of him—live—scene by scene. It'll be enough to sketch it out simply first and then run through it.

PRODUCER   [Coming back up, tempted by the idea.]   Do you know I'm almost tempted . . . just for fun . . . it might work.

FATHER   Of course it will. You'll see what wonderful scenes will come right out of it! I could tell you what they will be!

PRODUCER   You tempt me . . . you tempt me! We'll give it a chance. Come with me to the office. [Turning to the ACTORS.] Take a break: but don't go far away. Be back in a quarter of an hour or twenty minutes. [To the FATHER.] Let's see, let's try it out. Something extraordinary might come out of this.

FATHER   Of course it will! Don't you think it'd be better if the others came too? [Indicating the other CHARACTERS.]

PRODUCER   Yes, come on, come on. [Going, then turning to speak to the ACTORS.] Don't forget: don't be late: back in a quarter of an hour.

[The PRODUCER and the SIX CHARACTERS cross the stage and go. The ACTORS look at each other in astonishment.]

LEADING ACTOR   Is he serious? What's he going to do?

YOUNG ACTOR   I think he's gone round the bend.

ANOTHER ACTOR   Does he expect to make up a play in five minutes?

YOUNG ACTOR   Yes, like the old actors in the commedia dell'arte![1]

LEADING ACTRESS   Well if he thinks I'm going to appear in that sort of nonsense . . .

YOUNG ACTOR   Nor me!

FOURTH ACTOR   I should like to know who they are.

THIRD ACTOR   Who do you think? They're probably escaped lunatics—or crooks.

YOUNG ACTOR   And is he taking them seriously?

YOUNG ACTRESS   It's vanity. The vanity of seeing himself as an author.

---

1. A form of popular theater beginning in 16th-century Italy; the actors improvised dialogue according to basic comic or dramatic plots and in response to the audience's reaction.

LEADING ACTOR   I've never heard of such a thing! If the theatre, ladies and gentlemen, is reduced to this . . .

FIFTH ACTOR   I'm enjoying it!

THIRD ACTOR   Really! We shall have to wait and see what happens next I suppose.

> [*Talking, they leave the stage. Some go out through the back door, some to the dressing-rooms.*
> *The curtain stays up.*
> *The interval lasts twenty minutes.*]

Act Two

The theatre warning-bell sounds to call the audience back. From the dressing-rooms, the door at the back and even from the auditorium, the ACTORS, *the* STAGE MANAGER, *the* STAGE HANDS, *the* PROMPTER, *the* PROPERTY MAN *and the* PRODUCER, *accompanied by the* SIX CHARACTERS *all come back on to the stage.*
The house lights go out and the stage lights come on again.

PRODUCER   Come on, everybody! Are we all here? Quiet now! Listen! Let's get started! Stage manager?

STAGE MANAGER   Yes, I'm here.

PRODUCER   Give me that little parlour setting, will you? A couple of plain flats and a door flat will do. Hurry up with it!

> [*The* STAGE MANAGER *runs off to order someone to do this immediately and at the same time the* PRODUCER *is making arrangements with the* PROPERTY MAN, *the* PROMPTER, *and the* ACTORS: *the two flats and the door flat are painted in pink and gold stripes.*]

PRODUCER [*To* PROPERTY MAN.]   Go see if we have a sofa in stock.

PROPERTY MAN   Yes, there's that green one.

STEPDAUGHTER   No, no, not a green one! It was yellow, yellow velvet with flowers on it: it was enormous! And so comfortable!

PROPERTY MAN   We haven't got one like that.

PRODUCER   It doesn't matter! Give me whatever there is.

STEPDAUGHTER   What do you mean, it doesn't matter? It was Mme. Pace's famous sofa.

PRODUCER   It's only for a rehearsal! Please, don't interfere. [*To the* STAGE MANAGER.] Oh, and see if there's a shop window, will you—preferably a long, low one.

STEPDAUGHTER   And a little table, a little mahogany table for the blue envelope.

STAGE MANAGER [*To the* PRODUCER.]   There's that little gold one.

PRODUCER   That'll do—bring it.

FATHER   A mirror!

STEPDAUGHTER   And a screen! A screen, please, or I won't be able to manage, will I?

STAGE MANAGER   All right. We've lots of big screens, don't you worry.

PRODUCER [*To* STEPDAUGHTER.]   Then don't you want some coat-hangers and some clothes racks?

STEPDAUGHTER   Yes, lots of them, lots of them.

PRODUCER [*To the* STAGE MANAGER.] See how many there are and have them brought up.

STAGE MANAGER Right, I'll see to it.

[*The* STAGE MANAGER *goes off to do it: and while the* PRODUCER *is talking to the* PROMPTER, *the* CHARACTERS *and the* ACTORS, *the* STAGE MANAGER *is telling the* SCENE SHIFTERS *where to set up the furniture they have brought.*]

PRODUCER [*To the* PROMPTER.] Now you, go sit down, will you? Look, this is an outline of the play, act by act. [*He hands him several sheets of paper.*] But you'll need to be on your toes.

PROMPTER Shorthand?

PRODUCER [*Pleasantly surprised.*] Oh, good! You know shorthand?

PROMPTER I don't know much about prompting, but I do know about shorthand.

PRODUCER Thank God for that anyway! [*He turns to a* STAGE HAND.] Go fetch me some paper from my office—lots of it—as much as you can find!

[*The* STAGE HAND *goes running off and then comes back shortly with a bundle of paper that he gives to the* PROMPTER.]

PRODUCER [*Crossing to the* PROMPTER.] Follow the scenes, one after another, as they are played and try to get the lines down . . . at least the most important ones. [*Then turning to the* ACTORS.] Get out of the way everybody! Here, go over to the prompt side [*Pointing to stage left.*] and pay attention.

LEADING ACTRESS But, excuse me, we . . .

PRODUCER [*Anticipating her.*] You won't be expected to improvise, don't worry!

LEADING ACTOR Then what are we expected to do?

PRODUCER Nothing! Just go over there, listen and watch. You'll all be given your parts later written out. Right now we're going to rehearse, as well as we can. And they will be doing the rehearsal. [*He points to the* CHARACTERS.]

FATHER [*Rather bewildered, as if he had fallen from the clouds into the middle of the confusion on the stage.*] We are? Excuse me, but what do you mean, a rehearsal?

PRODUCER I mean a rehearsal—a rehearsal for the benefit of the actors. [*Pointing to the* ACTORS.]

FATHER But if we are the characters . . .

PRODUCER That's right, you're "the characters": but characters don't act here, my dear chap. It's actors who act here. The characters are there in the script—[*Pointing to the* PROMPTER.] that's when there is a script.

FATHER That's the point! Since there isn't one and you have the luck to have the characters alive in front of you . . .

PRODUCER Great! You want to do everything yourselves, do you? To act your own play, to produce your own play!

FATHER Well yes, just as we are.

PRODUCER That would be an experience for us, I can tell you!

LEADING ACTOR And what about us? What would we be doing then?

PRODUCER Don't tell me you think you know how to act! Don't make me laugh! [*The* ACTORS *in fact laugh.*] There you are, you see, you've made them laugh. [*Then remembering.*] But let's get back to the point! We need to cast the play. Well, that's easy: it almost casts itself. [*To the* SECOND ACTRESS.] You, the mother. [*To the* FATHER.] You'll need to give her a name.

FATHER   Amalia.

PRODUCER   But that's the real name of your wife isn't it? We can't use her real name.

FATHER   But why not? That is her name . . . But perhaps if this lady is to play the part . . . [*Indicating the* ACTRESS *vaguely with a wave of his hand.*] I don't know what to say . . . I'm already starting to . . . how can I explain it . . . to sound false, my own words sound like someone else's.

PRODUCER   Now don't worry yourself about it, don't worry about it at all. We'll work out the right tone of voice. As for the name, if you want it to be Amalia, then Amalia it shall be: or we can find another. For the moment we'll refer to the characters like this: [*To the* YOUNG ACTOR, *the juvenile lead.*] you are The Son. [*To the* LEADING ACTRESS.] You, of course, are The Stepdaughter.

STEPDAUGHTER [*Excitedly.*]   What did you say? That woman is me? [*Bursts into laughter.*]

PRODUCER [*Angrily.*]   What are you laughing at?

LEADING ACTRESS [*Indignantly.*]   Nobody has ever dared to laugh at me before! Either you treat me with respect or I'm walking out! [*Starting to go.*]

STEPDAUGHTER   I'm sorry. I wasn't really laughing at you.

PRODUCER [*To the* STEPDAUGHTER.]   You should feel proud to be played by . . .

LEADING ACTRESS [*Quickly, scornfully.*]   . . . that woman!

STEPDAUGHTER   But I wasn't thinking about her, honestly. I was thinking about me: I can't see myself in you at all . . . you're not a bit like me!

FATHER   Yes, that's right: you see, our meaning . . .

PRODUCER   What are you talking about, "our meaning"? Do you think you have exclusive rights to what you represent? Do you think it can only exist inside you? Not a bit of it!

FATHER   What? Don't we even have our own meaning?

PRODUCER   Not a bit of it! Whatever you mean is only material here, to which the actors give form and body, voice and gesture, and who, through their art, have given expression to much better material than what you have to offer: yours is really very trivial and if it stands up on the stage, the credit, believe me, will all be due to my actors.

FATHER   I don't dare to contradict you. But you for your part, must believe me—it doesn't seem trivial to us. We are suffering terribly now, with these bodies, these faces . . .

PRODUCER [*Interrupting impatiently.*]   Yes, well, the make-up will change that, make-up will change that, at least as far as the faces are concerned.

FATHER   Yes, but the voices, the gestures . . .

PRODUCER   That's enough! You can't come on the stage here as yourselves. It is our actors who will represent you here: and let that be the end of it!

FATHER   I understand that. But now I think I see why our author who saw us alive as we are here now, didn't want to put us on the stage. I don't want to offend your actors. God forbid that I should! But I think that if I saw myself represented . . . by I don't know whom . . .

LEADING ACTOR [*Rising majestically and coming forward, followed by a laughing group of* YOUNG ACTRESSES.] By me, if you don't object.

FATHER [*Respectfully, smoothly.*] I shall be honoured, sir. [*He bows.*] But I think, that no matter how hard this gentleman works with all his will and all his art to identify himself with me . . . [*He stops, confused.*]

LEADING ACTOR Yes, go on.

FATHER Well, I was saying the performance he will give, even if he is made up to look like me . . . I mean with the difference in our appearance . . . [*All the* ACTORS *laugh.*] it will be difficult for it to be a performance of me as I really am. It will be more like—well, not just because of his figure—it will be more an interpretation of what I am, what he believes me to be, and not how I know myself to be. And it seems to me that this should be taken into account by those who are going to comment on us.

PRODUCER So you are already worrying about what the critics will say, are you? And I'm still waiting to get this thing started! The critics can say what they like: and we'll worry about putting on the play. If we can! [*Stepping out of the group and looking around.*] Come on, come on! Is the scene set for us yet? [*To the* ACTORS *and* CHARACTERS.] Out of the way! Let's have a look at it. [*Climbing down off the stage.*] Don't let's waste any more time. [*To the* STEPDAUGHTER.] Does it look all right to you?

SON What! That? I don't recognise it at all.

PRODUCER Good God! Did you expect us to reconstruct the room at the back of Mme. Pace's shop here on the stage? [*To the* FATHER.] Did you say the room had flowered wallpaper?

FATHER White, yes.

PRODUCER Well it's not white: it's striped. That sort of thing doesn't matter at all! As for the furniture, it looks to me as if we have nearly everything we need. Move that little table a bit further downstage. [*A* STAGE HAND *does it. To the* PROPERTY MAN.] Go and fetch an envelope, pale blue if you can find one, and give it to that gentleman there. [*Pointing to the* FATHER.]

STAGE HAND An envelope for letters?

PRODUCER }
FATHER } Yes, an envelope for letters!

STAGE HAND Right. [*He goes off.*]

PRODUCER Now then, come on! The first scene is the young lady's. [*The* LEADING ACTRESS *comes to the centre.*] No, no, not yet. I said the young lady's. [*He points to the* STEPDAUGHTER.] You stay there and watch.

STEPDAUGHTER [*Adding quickly.*] . . . how I bring it to life.

LEADING ACTRESS [*Resenting this.*] I shall know how to bring it to life, don't you worry, when I am allowed to.

PRODUCER [*His head in his hands.*] Ladies, please, no more arguments! Now then. The first scene is between the young lady and Mme. Pace. Oh! [*Worried, turning round and looking out into the auditorium.*] Where is Mme. Pace?

FATHER She isn't here with us.

PRODUCER So what do we do now?

FATHER But she is real. She's real too!

PRODUCER   All right. So where is she?

FATHER   May I deal with this? [*Turns to the* ACTRESSES.] Would each of you ladies be kind enough to lend me a hat, a coat, a scarf or something?

ACTRESSES [*Some are surprised or amused.*]   What? My scarf? A coat? What's he want my hat for? What are you wanting to do with them? [*All the* ACTRESSES *are laughing.*]

FATHER   Oh, nothing much, just hang them up here on the racks for a minute or two. Perhaps someone would be kind enough to lend me a coat?

ACTORS   Just a coat? Come on, more! The man must be mad.

AN ACTRESS   What for? Only my coat?

FATHER   Yes, to hang up here, just for a moment. I'm very grateful to you. Do you mind?

ACTRESSES [*Taking off various hats, coats, scarves, laughing and going to hang them on the racks.*]   Why not? Here you are. I really think it's crazy. Is it to dress the set?

FATHER   Yes, exactly. It's to dress the set.

PRODUCER   Would you mind telling me what you are doing?

FATHER   Yes, of course: perhaps, if we dress the set better, she will be drawn by the articles of her trade and, who knows, she may even come to join us . . . [*He invites them to watch the door at the back of the set.*] Look! Look!

[*The door at the back opens and* MME. PACE *takes a few steps downstage: she is a gross old harridan wearing a ludicrous carroty-coloured wig with a single red rose stuck in at one side, Spanish fashion: garishly made-up: in a vulgar but stylish red silk dress, holding an ostrich-feather fan in one hand and a cigarette between two fingers in the other. At the sight of this apparition, the* ACTORS *and the* PRODUCER *immediately jump off the stage with cries of fear, leaping down into the auditorium and up the aisles. The* STEPDAUGHTER, *however, runs across to* MME. PACE, *and greets her respectfully, as if she were the mistress.*]

STEPDAUGHTER [*Running across to her.*]   Here she is! Here she is!

FATHER [*Smiling broadly.*]   It's her! What did I tell you? Here she is!

PRODUCER [*Recovering from his shock, indignantly.*]   What sort of trick is this?

LEADING ACTOR [*Almost at the same time as the others.*]   What the hell is happening?

JUVENILE LEAD   Where on earth did they get that extra from?

YOUNG ACTRESS   They were keeping her hidden!

LEADING ACTRESS   It's a game, a conjuring trick!

FATHER   Wait a minute! Why do you want to spoil a miracle by being factual? Can't you see this is a miracle of reality, that is born, brought to life, lured here, reproduced, just for the sake of this scene, with more right to be alive here than you have? Perhaps it has more truth than you have yourselves. Which actress can improve on Mme. Pace there? Well? That is the real Mme. Pace. You must admit that the actress who plays her will be less true than she is herself—and there she is in person! Look! My daughter recognised her straight away and went to meet her. Now watch—just watch this scene.

[*Hesitantly, the* PRODUCER *and the* ACTORS *move back to their original places on the stage.*

But the scene between the STEPDAUGHTER *and* MME. PACE *had already begun while the* ACTORS *were protesting and the* FATHER *explaining: it is being played under their breaths, very quietly, very naturally, in a way that is obviously impossible on stage. So when the* ACTORS' *attention is recalled by the* FATHER *they turn and see that* MME. PACE *has just put her hand under the* STEPDAUGHTER's *chin to make her lift her head up: they also hear her speak in a way that is unintelligible to them. They watch and listen hard for a few moments, then they start to make fun of them.*]

PRODUCER   Well?

LEADING ACTOR   What's she saying?

LEADING ACTRESS   Can't hear a thing!

JUVENILE LEAD   Louder! Speak up!

STEPDAUGHTER [*Leaving* MME. PACE *who has an astonishing smile on her face, and coming down to the* ACTORS.]   Louder? What do you mean, "Louder"? What we're talking about you can't talk about loudly. I could shout about it a moment ago to embarrass him [*Pointing to the* FATHER.] to shame him and to get my own back on him! But it's a different matter for Mme. Pace. It would mean prison for her.

PRODUCER   What the hell are you on about? Here in the theatre you have to make yourself heard! Don't you see that? We can't hear you even from here, and we're on the stage with you! Imagine what it would be like with an audience out front! You need to make the scene go! And after all, you would speak normally to each other when you're alone, and you will be, because we shan't be here anyway. I mean we're only here because it's a rehearsal. So just imagine that there you are in the room at the back of the shop, and there's no one to hear you.

[*The* STEPDAUGHTER, *with a knowing smile, wags her finger and her head rather elegantly, as if to say no.*]

PRODUCER   Why not?

STEPDAUGHTER [*Mysteriously, whispering loudly.*]   Because there is someone who will hear if she speaks normally. [*Pointing to* MME. PACE.]

PRODUCER [*Anxiously.*]   You're not going to make someone else appear are you?

[*The* ACTORS *get ready to dive off the stage again.*]

FATHER   No, no. She means me. I ought to be over there, waiting behind the door: and Mme. Pace knows I'm there, so excuse me will you: I'll go there now so that I shall be ready for my entrance.

[*He goes towards the back of the stage.*]

PRODUCER [*Stopping him.*]   No, no wait a minute! You must remember the stage conventions! Before you can go on to that part . . .

STEPDAUGHTER [*Interrupts him.*]   Oh yes, let's get on with that part. Now! Now! I'm dying to do that scene. If he wants to go through it now, I'm ready!

PRODUCER [*Shouting.*]   But before that we must have, clearly stated, the scene between you and her. [*Pointing to* MME. PACE.] Do you see?

STEPDAUGHTER   Oh God! She's only told me what you already know, that my mother's needlework is badly done again, the dress is spoilt and that

I shall have to be patient if I want her to go on helping us out of our mess.

MME. PACE [*Coming forward, with a great air of importance.*]   Ah, yes, sir, for that I do not wish to make a profit, to make advantage.

PRODUCER [*Half frightened.*]   What? Does she really speak like that?
[*All the* ACTORS *burst out laughing.*]

STEPDAUGHTER [*Laughing too.*]   Yes, she speaks like that, half in Spanish, in the silliest way imaginable!

MME. PACE   Ah it is not good manners that you laugh at me when I make myself to speak, as I can, English, señor.

PRODUCER   No, no, you're right! Speak like that, please speak like that, madam. It'll be marvelous. Couldn't be better! It'll add a little touch of comedy to a rather crude situation. Speak like that! It'll be great!

STEPDAUGHTER   Great! Why not? When you hear a proposition made in that sort of accent, it'll almost seem like a joke, won't it? Perhaps you'll want to laugh when you hear that there's an "old señor"[2] who wants to "amuse himself with me"—isn't that right, Madame?

MME. PACE   Not so old . . . but not quite young, no? But if he is not to your taste . . . he is, how you say, discreet!
[*The* MOTHER *leaps up, to the astonishment and dismay of the* ACTORS *who had not been paying any attention to her, so that when she shouts out they are startled and then smilingly restrain her: however she has already snatched off* MME. PACE'*s wig and flung it on the floor.*]

MOTHER   You witch! Witch! Murderess! Oh, my daughter!

STEPDAUGHTER [*Running across and taking hold of the* MOTHER.]   No! No! Mother! Please!

FATHER [*Running across to her as well.*]   Calm yourself, calm yourself! Come and sit down.

MOTHER   Get her away from here!

STEPDAUGHTER [*To the* PRODUCER *who has also crossed to her.*]   My mother can't bear to be in the same place with her.

FATHER [*Also speaking quietly to the* PRODUCER.]   They can't possibly be in the same place! That's why she wasn't with us when we first came, do you see! If they meet, everything's given away from the very beginning.

PRODUCER   It's not important, that's not important! This is only a first run-through at the moment! It's all useful stuff, even if it is confused. I'll sort it all out later. [*Turning to the* MOTHER *and taking her to sit down on her chair.*] Come on, my dear, take it easy; take it easy: come and sit down again.

STEPDAUGHTER   Go on, Mme. Pace.

MME. PACE [*Offended.*]   Oh no, thank-you! I no longer do nothing here with your mother present.

STEPDAUGHTER   Get on with it, bring in this "old señor" who wants to "amuse himself with me"! [*Turning majestically to the others.*] You see, this next scene has got to be played out—we must do it now. [*To* MME. PACE.] Oh, you can go!

MME. PACE   Ah, I go, I go—I go! Most probably! I go!

2. Old gentleman.

[*She leaves banging her wig back into place, glaring furiously at the* ACTORS *who applaud her exit, laughing loudly.*]

STEPDAUGHTER [*To the* FATHER.]   Now you come on! No, you don't need to go off again! Come back! Pretend you've just come in! Look, I'm standing here with my eyes on the ground, modestly—well, come on, speak up! Use that special sort of voice, like somebody who has just come in. "Good afternoon, my dear."

PRODUCER [*Off the stage by now.*]   Look here, who's the director here, you or me? [*To the* FATHER *who looks uncertain and bewildered.*] Go on, do as she says: go upstage—no, no don't bother to make an entrance. Then come down stage again.

[*The* FATHER *does as he is told, half mesmerised. He is very pale but already involved in the reality of his re-created life, smiles as he draws near the back of the stage, almost as if he genuinely is not aware of the drama that is about to sweep over him. The* ACTORS *are immediately intent on the scene that is beginning now.*]

The Scene

FATHER [*Coming forward with a new note in his voice.*]   Good afternoon, my dear.

STEPDAUGHTER [*Her head down trying to hide her fright.*]   Good afternoon.

FATHER [*Studying her a little under the brim of her hat which partly hides her face from him and seeing that she is very young, he exclaims to himself a little complacently and a little guardedly because of the danger of being compromised in a risky adventure.*]   Ah . . . but . . . tell me, this won't be the first time, will it? The first time you've been here?

STEPDAUGHTER   No, sir.

FATHER   You've been here before? [*And after the* STEPDAUGHTER *has nodded an answer.*] More than once? [*He waits for her reply: tries again to look at her under the brim of her hat: smiles: then says.*] Well then . . . it shouldn't be too . . . . May I take off your hat?

STEPDAUGHTER [*Quickly, to stop him, unable to conceal her shudder of fear and disgust.*]   No, don't! I'll do it!

[*She takes it off unsteadily.*
The MOTHER *watches the scene intently with the* SON *and the two smaller children who cling close to her all the time: they make a group on one side of the stage opposite the* ACTORS: *She follows the words and actions of the* FATHER *and the* STEPDAUGHTER *in this scene with a variety of expressions on her face—sadness, dismay, anxiety, horror: sometimes she turns her face away and sobs.*]

MOTHER   Oh God! Oh God!

FATHER [*He stops as if turned to stone by the sobbing: then he goes on in the same tone of voice.*]   Here, give it to me. I'll hang it up for you. [*He takes the hat in his hand.*] But such a pretty, dear little head like yours should have a much smarter hat than this! Would you like to help me choose one, then, from these hats of Madame's hanging up here? Would you?

YOUNG ACTRESS [*Interrupting.*]   Be careful! Those are our hats!

PRODUCER [*Quickly and angrily.*]   For God's sake, shut up! Don't try to be

funny! We're rehearsing! [*Turns back to the* STEPDAUGHTER.] Please go
on, will you, from where you were interrupted.

STEPDAUGHTER [*Going on.*]   No, thank you, sir.

FATHER   Oh, don't say no to me please! Say you'll have one—to please me.
Isn't this a pretty one—look! And then it will please Madame too, you
know. She's put them out here on purpose, of course.

STEPDAUGHTER   No, look, I could never wear it.

FATHER   Are you thinking of what they would say at home when you went
in wearing a new hat? Goodness me! Don't you know what to do? Shall
I tell you what to say at home?

STEPDAUGHTER [*Furiously, nearly exploding.*]   That's not why! I couldn't
wear it because . . . as you can see: you should have noticed it before.
[*Indicating her black dress.*]

FATHER   You're in mourning! Oh, forgive me. You're right, I see that now.
Please forgive me. Believe me, I'm really very sorry.

STEPDAUGHTER [*Gathering all her strength and making herself overcome her
contempt and revulsion.*]   That's enough. Don't go on, that's enough. I
ought to be thanking you and not letting you blame yourself and get
upset. Don't think any more about what I told you, please. And I should
do the same. [*Forcing herself to smile and adding.*] I should try to forget
that I'm dressed like this.

PRODUCER [*Interrupting, turning to the* PROMPTER *in the box and jumping
up on the stage again.*]   Hold it, hold it! Don't put that last line down,
leave it out. [*Turning to the* FATHER *and the* STEPDAUGHTER.] It's going
well! It's going well! [*Then to the* FATHER *alone.*] Then we'll put in there
the bit that we talked about. [*To the* ACTORS.] That scene with the hats
is good, isn't it?

STEPDAUGHTER   But the best bit is coming now! Why can't we get on
with it?

PRODUCER   Just be patient, wait a minute. [*Turning and moving across to
the* ACTORS.] Of course, it'll all have to be made a lot more light-hearted.

LEADING ACTOR   We shall have to play it a lot quicker, I think.

LEADING ACTRESS   Of course: there's nothing particularly difficult in it.
[*To the* LEADING ACTOR.] Shall we run through it now?

LEADING ACTOR   Yes right . . . Shall we take it from my entrance? [*He goes
to his position behind the door upstage.*]

PRODUCER [*To the* LEADING ACTRESS.]   Now then, listen, imagine the
scene between you and Mme. Pace is finished. I'll write it up myself
properly later on. You ought to be over here I think—[*She goes the opposite way.*] Where are you going now?

LEADING ACTRESS   Just a minute, I want to get my hat—[*She crosses to
take her hat from the stand.*]

PRODUCER   Right, good, ready now? You are standing here with your head
down.

STEPDAUGHTER [*Very amused.*]   But she's not dressed in black!

LEADING ACTRESS   Oh, but I shall be, and I'll look a lot better than you
do, darling.

PRODUCER [*To the* STEPDAUGHTER.]   Shut up, will you! Go over there and
watch! You might learn something! [*Clapping his hands.*] Right! Come
on! Quiet please! Take it from his entrance.

[*He climbs off stage so that he can see better. The door opens at the back of the set and the* LEADING ACTOR *enters with the lively, know-ing air of an ageing roué.*[3] *The playing of the following scene by the* ACTORS *must seem from the very beginning to be something quite different from the earlier scene, but without having the faintest air of parody in it.*

Naturally the STEPDAUGHTER *and the* FATHER *unable to see them-selves in the* LEADING ACTOR *and* LEADING ACTRESS, *hearing their words said by them, express their reactions in different ways, by ges-tures, or smiles or obvious protests so that we are aware of their suffering, their astonishment, their disbelief.*

The PROMPTER'*s voice is heard clearly between every line in the scene, telling the* ACTORS *what to say next.*]

LEADING ACTOR   Good afternoon, my dear.

FATHER [*Immediately, unable to restrain himself.*]   Oh, no!

[*The* STEPDAUGHTER, *watching the* LEADING ACTOR *enter this way, bursts into laughter.*]

PRODUCER [*Furious.*]   Shut up, for God's sake! And don't you dare laugh like that! We're never going to get anywhere at this rate.

STEPDAUGHTER [*Coming to the front.*]   I'm sorry, I can't help it! The lady stands exactly where you told her to stand and she never moved. But if it were me and I heard someone say good afternoon to me in that way and with a voice like that I should burst out laughing—so I did.

FATHER [*Coming down a little too.*]   Yes, she's right, the whole manner, the voice . . .

PRODUCER   To hell with the manner and the voice! Get out of the way, will you, and let me watch the rehearsal!

LEADING ACTOR [*Coming down stage.*]   If I have to play an old man who has come to a knocking shop—

PRODUCER   Take no notice, ignore them. Go on please! It's going well, it's going well! [*He waits for the* ACTOR *to begin again.*] Right, again!

LEADING ACTOR   Good afternoon, my dear.

LEADING ACTRESS   Good afternoon.

LEADING ACTOR [*Copying the gestures of the* FATHER, *looking under the brim of the hat, but expressing distinctly the two emotions, first, complacent satisfaction and then anxiety.*]   Ah! But tell me . . . this won't be the first time I hope.

FATHER [*Instinctively correcting him.*]   Not "I hope"—"will it," "will it."

PRODUCER   Say "will it"—and it's a question.

LEADING ACTOR [*Glaring at the* PROMPTER.]   I distinctly heard him say "I hope."

PRODUCER   So what? It's all the same, "I hope" or "isn't it." It doesn't make any difference. Carry on, carry on. But perhaps it should still be a little bit lighter; I'll show you—watch me! [*He climbs up on the stage again, and going back to the entrance, he does it himself.*] Good afternoon, my dear.

LEADING ACTRESS   Good afternoon.

PRODUCER   Ah, tell me . . . [*He turns to the* LEADING ACTOR *to make sure that he has seen the way he has demonstrated of looking under the brim of*

---

3. Dissipated lover.

the hat.] You see—surprise . . . anxiety and self-satisfaction. [*Then, starting again, he turns to the* LEADING ACTRESS.] This won't be the first time, will it? The first time you've been here? [*Again turns to the* LEADING ACTOR *questioningly.*] Right? [*To the* LEADING ACTRESS.] And then she says, "No, sir." [*Again to* LEADING ACTOR.] See what I mean? More subtlety. [*And he climbs off the stage.*]

LEADING ACTRESS   No, sir.

LEADING ACTOR   You've been here before? More than once?

PRODUCER   No, no, no! Wait for it, wait for it. Let her answer first. "You've been here before?"

> [*The* LEADING ACTRESS *lifts her head a little, her eyes closed in pain and disgust, and when the* PRODUCER *says "Now" she nods her head twice.*]

STEPDAUGHTER [*Involuntarily.*]   Oh, my God! [*And she immediately claps her hand over her mouth to stifle her laughter.*]

PRODUCER   What now?

STEPDAUGHTER [*Quickly.*]   Nothing, nothing!

PRODUCER [*To* LEADING ACTOR.]   Come on, then, now it's you.

LEADING ACTOR   More than once? Well then, it shouldn't be too . . . May I take off your hat?

> [*The* LEADING ACTOR *says this last line in such a way and adds to it such a gesture that the* STEPDAUGHTER, *even with her hand over her mouth trying to stop herself laughing, can't prevent a noisy burst of laughter.*

LEADING ACTRESS [*Indignantly turning.*]   I'm not staying any longer to be laughed at by that woman!

LEADING ACTOR   Nor am I! That's the end—no more!

PRODUCER [*To* STEPDAUGHTER, *shouting.*]   Once and for all, will you shut up! Shut up!

STEPDAUGHTER   Yes, I'm sorry . . . I'm sorry.

PRODUCER   You're an ill-mannered little bitch! That's what you are! And you've gone too far this time!

FATHER [*Trying to interrupt.*]   Yes, you're right, she went too far, but please forgive her . . .

PRODUCER [*Jumping on the stage.*]   Why should I forgive her? Her behaviour is intolerable!

FATHER   Yes, it is, but the scene made such a peculiar impact on us . . .

PRODUCER   Peculiar? What do you mean peculiar? Why peculiar?

FATHER   I'm full of admiration for your actors, for this gentleman [*To the* LEADING ACTOR.] and this lady. [*To the* LEADING ACTRESS.] But, you see, well . . . they're not us!

PRODUCER   Right! They're not! They're actors!

FATHER   That's just the point—they're actors. And they are acting our parts very well, both of them. But that's what's different. However much they want to be the same as us, they're not.

PRODUCER   But why aren't they? What is it now?

FATHER   It's something to do with . . . being themselves, I suppose, not being us.

PRODUCER   Well we can't do anything about that! I've told you already. You can't play the parts yourselves.

FATHER   Yes, I know, I know . . .

PRODUCER Right then. That's enough of that. [*Turning back to the* ACTORS.] We'll rehearse this later on our own, as we usually do. It's always a bad idea to have rehearsals with authors there! They're never satisfied. [*Turns back to the* FATHER *and the* STEPDAUGHTER.] Come on, let's get on with it; and let's see if it's possible to do it without laughing.

STEPDAUGHTER I won't laugh any more, I won't really. My best bit's coming up now, you wait and see!

PRODUCER Right: when you say "Don't think any more about what I told you, please. And I should do the same." [*Turning to the* FATHER.] Then you come in immediately with the line "I understand, ah yes, I understand" and then you ask . . .

STEPDAUGHTER [*Interrupting.*] Ask what? What does he ask?

PRODUCER Why you're in mourning.

STEPDAUGHTER No! No! That's not right! Look: when I said that I should try not to think abut the way I was dressed, do you know what he said? "Well then, let's take it off, we'll take it off at once, shall we, your little black dress."

PRODUCER That's great! That'll be wonderful! That'll bring the house down!

STEPDAUGHTER But it's the truth!

PRODUCER The truth! Do me a favour will you? This is the theatre you know! Truth's all very well up to a point but . . .

STEPDAUGHTER What do you want to do then?

PRODUCER You'll see! You'll see! Leave it all to me.

STEPDAUGHTER No. No I won't. I know what you want to do! Out of my feeling of revulsion, out of all the vile and sordid reasons why I am what I am, you want to make a sugary little sentimental romance. You want him to ask me why I'm in mourning and you want me to reply with the tears running down my face that it is only two months since my father died. No. No. I won't have it! He must say to me what he really did say. "Well then, let's take it off, we'll take it off at once, shall we, your little black dress." And I, with my heart still grieving for my father's death only two months before, I went behind there, do you see? Behind that screen and with my fingers trembling with shame and loathing I took off the dress, unfastened my bra . . .

PRODUCER [*His head in his hands.*] For God's sake! What are you saying!

STEPDAUGHTER [*Shouting excitedly.*] The truth! I'm telling you the truth!

PRODUCER All right then, Now listen to me. I'm not denying it's the truth. Right. And believe me I understand your horror, but you must see that we can't really put a scene like that on the stage.

STEPDAUGHTER You can't? Then thanks very much. I'm not stopping here.

PRODUCER No, listen . . .

STEPDAUGHTER No, I'm going. I'm not stopping. The pair of you have worked it all out together, haven't you, what to put in the scene. Well, thank you very much! I understand everything now! He wants to get to the scene where he can talk about his spiritual torments but I want to show you my drama! Mine!

PRODUCER [*Shaking with anger.*] Now we're getting to the real truth of it, aren't we? Your drama—yours! But it's not only yours, you know. It's drama for the other people as well! For him [*Pointing to the* FATHER.]

and for your mother! You can't have one character coming on like you're doing, trampling over the others, taking over the play. Everything needs to be balanced and in harmony so that we can show what has to be shown! I know perfectly well that we've all got a life inside us and that we all want to parade it in front of other people. But that's the difficulty, how to present only the bits that are necessary in relation to the other characters: and in the small amount we show, to hint at all the rest of the inner life of the character! I agree, it would be so much simpler, if each character, in a soliloquy or in a lecture could pour out to the audience what's bubbling away inside him. But that's not the way we work. [*In an indulgent, placating tone.*] You must restrain yourself, you see. And believe me, it's in your own interests: because you could so easily make a bad impression, with all this uncontrollable anger, this disgust and exasperation. That seems a bit odd, if you don't mind my saying so, when you've admitted that you'd been with other men at Mme. Pace's and more than once.

STEPDAUGHTER   I suppose that's true. But you know, all the other men were all him as far as I was concerned.

PRODUCER [*Not understanding.*]   Uum—? What? What are you talking about?

STEPDAUGHTER   If someone falls into evil ways, isn't the responsibility for all the evil which follows to be laid at the door of the person who caused the first mistake? And in my case, it's him, from before I was even born. Look at him: see if it isn't true.

PRODUCER   Right then! What about the weight of remorse he's carrying? Isn't that important? Then, give him the chance to show it to us.

STEPDAUGHTER   But how? How on earth can he show all his long-suffering remorse, all his moral torments as he calls them, if you don't let him show his horror when he finds me in his arms one fine day, after he had asked me to take my dress off, a black dress for my father who had just died: and he finds that I'm the child he used to go and watch as she came out of school, me, a woman now, and a woman he could buy. [*She says these last words in a voice trembling with emotion.*]

   [*The* MOTHER, *hearing her say this, is overcome and at first gives way to stifled sobs: but then she bursts out into uncontrollable crying. Everyone is deeply moved. There is a long pause.*]

STEPDAUGHTER [*As soon as the* MOTHER *has quietened herself she goes on, firmly and thoughtfully.*]   At the moment we are here on our own and the public doesn't know about us. But tomorrow you will present us and our story in whatever way you choose, I suppose. But wouldn't you like to see the real drama? Wouldn't you like to see it explode into life, as it really did?

PRODUCER   Of course, nothing I'd like better, then I can use as much of it as possible.

STEPDAUGHTER   Then persuade my mother to leave.

MOTHER [*Rising and her quiet weeping changing to a loud cry.*]   No! No! Don't let her! Don't let her do it!

PRODUCER   But they're only doing it for me to watch—only for me, do you see?

MOTHER   I can't bear it, I can't bear it!

PRODUCER   But if it's already happened, I can't see what's the objection.

MOTHER   No! It's happening now, as well: it's happening all the time. I'm not acting my suffering! Can't you understand that? I'm alive and here now but I can never forget that terrible moment of agony, that repeats itself endlessly and vividly in my mind. And these two little children here, you've never heard them speak have you? That's because they don't speak any more, not now. They just cling to me all the time: they help to keep my grief alive, but they don't really exist for themselves any more, not for themselves. And she [*Indicating the* STEPDAUGHTER.] . . . she has gone away, left me completely, she's lost to me, lost . . . you see her here for one reason only: to keep perpetually before me, always real, the anguish and the torment I've suffered on her account.

FATHER   The eternal moment, as I told you, sir. She is here [*Indicating the* STEPDAUGHTER.] to keep me too in that moment, trapped for all eternity, chained and suspended in that one fleeting shameful moment of my life. She can't give up her role and you cannot rescue me from it.

PRODUCER   But I'm not saying that we won't present that bit. Not at all! It will be the climax of the first act, when she [*He points to the* MOTHER.] surprises you.

FATHER   That's right, because that is the moment when I am sentenced: all our suffering should reach a climax in her cry. [*Again indicating the* MOTHER.]

STEPDAUGHTER   I can still hear it ringing in my ears! It was that cry that sent me mad! You can have me played just as you like: it doesn't matter! Dressed, too, if you want, so long as I can have at least an arm—only an arm—bare, because, you see, as I was standing like this [*She moves across to the* FATHER *and leans her head on his chest.*] with my head like this and my arms round his neck, I saw a vein, here in my arm, throbbing: and then it was almost as if that throbbing vein filled me with a shivering fear, and I shut my eyes tightly like this, like this and buried my head in his chest. [*Turning to the* MOTHER.] Scream, Mummy, scream. [*She buries her head in the* FATHER's *chest, and with her shoulders raised as if to try not to hear the scream, she speaks with a voice tense with suffering.*] Scream, as you screamed then!

MOTHER [*Coming forward to pull them apart.*]   No! She's my daughter! My daughter! [*Tearing her from him.*] You brute, you animal, she's my daughter! Can't you see she's my daughter?

PRODUCER [*Retreating as far as the footlights while the* ACTORS *are full of dismay.*]   Marvellous! Yes, that's great! And then curtain, curtain!

FATHER [*Running downstage to him, excitedly.*]   That's it, that's it! Because it really was like that!

PRODUCER [*Full of admiration and enthusiasm.*]   Yes, yes, that's got to be the curtain line! Curtain! Curtain!

[*At the repeated calls of the* PRODUCER, *the* STAGE MANAGER *lowers the curtain, leaving on the apron in front, the* PRODUCER *and the* FATHER.]

PRODUCER [*Looking up to heaven with his arms raised.*]   The idiots! I didn't mean now! The bloody idiots—dropping it in on us like that! [*To the* FATHER, *and lifting up a corner of the curtain.*] That's marvellous! Really marvellous! A terrific effect! We'll end the act like that! It's the best tag line I've heard for ages. What a First Act ending! I couldn't have done better if I'd written it myself!

[*They go through the curtain together.*]

Act Three

When the curtain goes up we see that the STAGE MANAGER *and* STAGE HANDS *have struck the first scene and have set another, a small garden fountain.*

From one side of the stage the ACTORS *come on and from the other the* CHARACTERS. *The* PRODUCER *is standing in the middle of the stage with his hand over his mouth, thinking.*

PRODUCER [*After a short pause, shrugging his shoulders.*]   Well, then: let's get on to the second act! Leave it all to me, and everything will work out properly.

STEPDAUGHTER   This is where we go to live at his house [*Pointing to the* FATHER.] In spite of the objections of him over there. [*Pointing to the* SON.]

PRODUCER [*Getting impatient.*]   All right, all right! But leave it all to me, will you?

STEPDAUGHTER   Provided that you make it clear that he objected!

MOTHER [*From the corner, shaking her head.*]   That doesn't matter. The worse it was for us, the more he suffered from remorse.

PRODUCER [*Impatiently.*]   I know, I know! I'll take it all into account. Don't worry!

MOTHER [*Pleading.*]   To set my mind at rest, sir, please do make sure it's clear that I tried all I could—

STEPDAUGHTER [*Interrupting her scornfully and going on.*]   —to pacify me, to persuade me that this despicable creature wasn't worth making trouble about! [*To the* PRODUCER.] Go on, set her mind at rest, because it's true, she tried very hard. I'm having a whale of a time now! You can see, can't you, that the meeker she was and the more she tried to worm her way into his heart, the more lofty and distant he became! How's that for a dramatic situation!

PRODUCER   Do you think that we can actually begin the Second Act?

STEPDAUGHTER   I won't say another word! But you'll see that it won't be possible to play everything in the garden, like you want to do.

PRODUCER   Why not?

STEPDAUGHTER [*Pointing to the* SON.]   Because to start with, he stays shut up in his room in the house all the time! And then all the scenes for this poor little devil of a boy happen in the house. I've told you once.

PRODUCER   Yes, I know that! But on the other hand we can't put up a notice to tell the audience where the scene is taking place, or change the set three or four times in each Act.

LEADING ACTOR   That's what they used to do in the good old days.

PRODUCER   Yes, when the audience was about as bright as that little girl over there!

LEADING ACTRESS   And it makes it easier to create an illusion.

FATHER [*Leaping up.*] An illusion? For pity's sake don't talk about illusions! Don't use that word, it's especially hurtful to us!

PRODUCER [*Astonished.*] And why, for God's sake?

FATHER It's so hurtful, so cruel! You ought to have realised that!

PRODUCER What else should we call it? That's what we do here—create an illusion for the audience . . .

LEADING ACTOR With our performance . . .

PRODUCER A perfect illusion of reality!

FATHER Yes, I know that, I understand. But on the other hand, perhaps you don't understand us yet. I'm sorry! But you see, for and for your actors what goes on here on the stage is, quite rightly, well, it's only a game.

LEADING ACTRESS [*Interrupting indignantly.*] A game! How dare you! We're not children! What happens here is serious!

FATHER I'm not saying that it isn't serious. And I mean, really, not just a game but an art, that tries, as you've just said, to create the perfect illusion of reality.

PRODUCER That's right!

FATHER Now try to imagine that we, as you see us here, [*He indicates himself and the other* CHARACTERS.] that we have no other reality outside this illusion.

PRODUCER [*Astonished and looking at the* ACTORS *with the same sense of bewilderment as they feel themselves.*] What the hell are you talking about now?

FATHER [*After a short pause as he looks at them, with a faint smile.*] Isn't it obvious? What other reality is there for us? What for you is an illusion you create, for us is our only reality. [*Brief pause. He moves towards the* PRODUCER *and goes on.*] But it's not only true for us, it's true for others as well, you know. Just think about it. [*He looks intently into the* PRODUCER's *eyes.*] Do you really know who you are? [*He stands pointing at the* PRODUCER.]

PRODUCER [*A little disturbed but with a half smile.*] What? Who I am? I am me!

FATHER What if I told you that that wasn't true: what if I told you that you were me?

PRODUCER I would tell you that you were mad!

[*The* ACTORS *laugh.*]

FATHER That's right, laugh! Because everything here is a game! [*To the* PRODUCER.] And yet you object when I say that it is only for a game that the gentleman there [*Pointing to the* LEADING ACTOR.] who is "himself" has to be "me," who, on the contrary, am "myself." You see, I've caught you in a trap.

[*The* ACTORS *start to laugh.*]

PRODUCER Not again! We've heard all about this a little while ago.

FATHER No, no. I didn't really want to talk about this. I'd like you to forget about your game. [*Looking at the* LEADING ACTRESS *as if to anticipate what she will say.*] I'm sorry—your artistry! Your art!—that you usually pursue here with your actors; and I am going to ask you again in all seriousness, who are you?

PRODUCER [*Turning with a mixture of amazement and annoyance, to the*

ACTORS.] Of all the bloody nerve! A fellow who claims he is only a character comes and asks me who I am!

FATHER [*With dignity but without annoyance.*] A character, my dear sir, can always ask a man who he is, because a character really has a life of his own, a life full of his own specific qualities, and because of these he is always "someone." While a man—I'm not speaking about you personally, of course, but man in general—well, he can be an absolute "nobody."

PRODUCER All right, all right! Well, since you've asked me, I'm the Director, the Producer—I'm in charge! Do you understand?

FATHER [*Half smiling, but gently and politely.*] I'm only asking to try to find out if you really see yourself now in the same way that you saw yourself, for instance, once upon a time in the past, with all the illusions you had then, with everything inside and outside yourself as it seemed then—and not only seemed, but really was! Well then, look back on those illusions, those ideas that you don't have any more, on all those things that no longer seem the same to you. Don't you feel that not only this stage is falling away from under your feet but so is the earth itself, and that all these realities of today are going to seem tomorrow as if they had been an illusion?

PRODUCER So? What does that prove?

FATHER Oh, nothing much. I only want to make you see that if we [*Pointing to himself and the other* CHARACTERS.] have no other reality outside our own illusion, perhaps you ought to distrust your own sense of reality: because whatever is a reality today, whatever you touch and believe in and that seems real for you today, is going to be—like the reality of yesterday—an illusion tomorrow.

PRODUCER [*Deciding to make fun of him.*] Very good! So now you're saying that you as well as this play you're going to show me here, are more real than I am?

FATHER [*Very seriously.*] There's no doubt about that at all.

PRODUCER Is that so?

FATHER I thought you'd realised that from the beginning.

PRODUCER More real than I am?

FATHER If your reality can change between today and tomorrow—

PRODUCER But everybody knows that it can change, don't they? It's always changing! Just like everybody else's!

FATHER [*Crying out.*] But ours doesn't change! Do you see? That's the difference! Ours doesn't change, it can't change, it can never be different, never, because it is already determined, like this, for ever, that's what's so terrible! We are an eternal reality. That should make you shudder to come near us.

PRODUCER [*Jumping up, suddenly struck by an idea, and standing directly in front of the* FATHER.] Then I should like to know when anyone saw a character step out of his part and make a speech like you've done, proposing things, explaining things. Tell me when, will you? I've never seen it before.

FATHER You've never seen it because an author usually hides all the difficulties of creating. When the characters are alive, really alive and standing in front of their author, he has only to follow their words, the actions that they suggest to him: and he must want them to be what they want to be: and it's his bad luck if he doesn't do what they want! When a character is born he immediately assumes such an independence even of his own author that everyone can imagine him in scores of situations that his author hadn't even thought of putting him in, and he sometimes acquires a meaning that his author never dreamed of giving him.

PRODUCER   Of course I know all that.

FATHER   Well, then. Why are you surprised by us? Imagine what a disaster it is for a character to be born in the imagination of an author who then refuses to give him life in a written script. Tell me if a character, left like this, suspended, created but without a final life, isn't right to do what we are doing now, here in front of you. We spent such a long time, such a very long time, believe me, urging our author, persuading him, first me, then her, [*Pointing to the* STEPDAUGHTER.] then this poor Mother . . .

STEPDAUGHTER   [*Coming down the stage as if in a dream.*]   It's true, I would go, would go and tempt him, time after time, in his gloomy study just as it was growing dark, when he was sitting quietly in an armchair not even bothering to switch a light on but leaving the shadows to fill the room: the shadows were swarming with us, we had come to tempt him. [*As if she could see herself there in the study and is annoyed by the presence of the* ACTORS.] Go away will you! Leave us alone! Mother there, with that son of hers—me with the little girl—that poor little kid always on his own—and then me with him [*Pointing to the* FATHER.] and then at last, just me, on my own, all on my own, in the shadows. [*She turns quickly as if she wants to cling on to the vision she has of herself, in the shadows.*] Ah, what scenes, what scenes we suggested to him! What a life I could have had! I tempted him more than the others!

FATHER   Oh yes, you did! And it was probably all your fault that he did nothing about it! You were so insistent, you made too many demands.

STEPDAUGHTER   But he wanted me to be like that! [*She comes closer to the* PRODUCER *to speak to him in confidence.*] I think it's more likely that he felt discouraged about the theatre and even despised it because the public only wants to see . . .

PRODUCER   Let's go on, for God's sake, let's go on. Come to the point will you?

STEPDAUGHTER   I'm sorry, but if you ask me, we've got too much happening already, just with our entry into his house. [*Pointing to the* FATHER.] You said that we couldn't put up a notice or change the set every five minutes.

PRODUCER   Right! Of course we can't! We must combine things, group them together in one continuous flowing action: not the way you've been wanting, first of all seeing your little brother come home from school and wander about the house like a lost soul, hiding behind the doors and brooding on some plan or other that would—what did you say it would do?

STEPDAUGHTER   Wither him . . . shrivel him up completely.

PRODUCER   That's good! That's a good expression. And then you "can see it there in his eyes, getting stronger all the time"—isn't that what you said?

STEPDAUGHTER   Yes, that's right. Look at him! [*Pointing to him as he stands next to his* MOTHER.]

PRODUCER   Yes, great! And then, at the same time, you want to show the
little girl playing in the garden, all innocence. One in the house and the
other in the garden—we can't do it, don't you see that?

STEPDAUGHTER   Yes, playing in the sun, so happy! It's the only pleasure I
have left, her happiness, her delight in playing in the garden: away from
the misery, the squalor of that sordid flat where all four of us slept and
where she slept with me—with me! Just think of it! My vile, contaminated body close to hers, with her little arms wrapped tightly round my
neck, so lovingly, so innocently. In the garden, wherever she saw me, she
would run and take my hand. She never wanted to show me the big
flowers, she would run about looking for the "little weeny" ones, so that
she could show them to me; she was so happy, so thrilled! [As she says
this, tortured by the memory, she breaks out into a long desperate cry,
dropping her head on her arms that rest on a little table. Everybody is very
affected by her. The PRODUCER comes to her almost paternally and speaks
to her in a soothing voice.]

PRODUCER   We'll have the garden scene, we'll have it, don't worry: and
you'll see, you'll be very pleased with what we do! We'll play all the scenes
in the garden! [He calls out to a STAGE HAND by name.] Hey . . . , let down
a few bits of tree, will you? A couple of cypresses will do, in front of the
fountain. [Someone drops in the two cypresses and a STAGE HAND secures
them with a couple of braces and weights.]

PRODUCER   [To the STEPDAUGHTER.]   That'll do for now, won't it? It'll just
give us an idea. [Calling out to a STAGE HAND by name again.] Hey, . . .
give me something for the sky will you?

STAGE HAND   What's that?

PRODUCER   Something for the sky! A small cloth to come in behind the
fountain. [A white cloth is dropped from the flies.] Not white! I asked for
a sky! Never mind: leave it! I'll do something with it. [Calling out.] Hey
lights! Kill everything will you? Give me a bit of moonlight—the blues
in the batten and a blue spot on the cloth . . . [They do.] That's it! That'll
do! [Now on the scene there is the light he asked for, a mysterious blue
light that makes the ACTORS speak and move as if in the garden in the
evening under a moon. To the STEPDAUGHTER.] Look here now: the little
boy can come out here in the garden and hide among the trees instead
of hiding behind the doors in the house. But it's going to be difficult to
find a little girl to play the scene with you where she shows you the
flowers. [Turning to the LITTLE BOY.] Come on, come on, son, come
across here. Let's see what it'll look like. [But the (LITTLE) BOY doesn't
move.] Come on will you, come on. [Then he pulls him forward and tries
to make him hold his head up, but every time it falls down again on his chest.]
There's something very odd about this lad . . . What's wrong with him? My
God, he'll have to say something sometime! [He comes over to him again,
puts his hand on his shoulder and pushes him between the trees.] Come
a bit nearer: let's have a look. Can you hide a bit more? That's it. Now
pop your head out and look round. [He moves away to look at the effect
and as the BOY does what he has been told to do, the ACTORS watch
impressed and a little disturbed.] Ahh, that's good, very good . . . [He turns
to the STEPDAUGHTER.] How about having the little girl, surprised to see
him there, run across. Wouldn't that make him say something?

STEPDAUGHTER [*Getting up.*] It's no use hoping he'll speak, not as long as that creature's there. [*Pointing to the* SON.] You'll have to get him out of the way first.

SON [*Moving determinedly to one of the sets of steps leading off the stage.*] With pleasure! I'll go now! Nothing will please me better!

PRODUCER [*Stopping him immediately.*] Hey, no! Where are you going? Hang on!

> [*The* MOTHER *gets up, anxious at the idea that he is really going and instinctively raising her arms as if to hold him back, but without moving from where she is.*]

SON [*At the footlights, to the* PRODUCER *who is restraining him there.*] There's no reason why I should be here! Let me go will you? Let me go!

PRODUCER What do you mean there's no reason for you to be here?

STEPDAUGHTER [*Calmly, ironically.*] Don't bother to stop him. He won't go!

FATHER You have to play that terrible scene in the garden with your mother.

SON [*Quickly, angry and determined.*] I'm not going to play anything! I've said that all along! [*To the* PRODUCER.] Let me go will you?

STEPDAUGHTER [*Crossing to the* PRODUCER.] It's all right. Let him go. [*She moves the* PRODUCER's *hand from the* SON. *Then she turns to the* SON *and says.*] Well, go on then! Off you go!

> [*The* SON *stays near the steps but as if pulled by some strange force he is quite unable to go down them: then to the astonishment and even the dismay of the* ACTORS, *he moves along the front of the stage towards the other set of steps down into the auditorium: but having got there, he again stays near and doesn't actually go down them. The* STEPDAUGHTER *who has watched him scornfully but very intently, bursts into laughter.*]

STEPDAUGHTER He can't, you see? He can't! He's got to stay here! He must. He's chained to us for ever! No, I'm the one who goes, when what must happen does happen, and I run away, because I hate him, because I can't bear the sight of him any longer. Do you think it's possible for him to run away? He has to stay here with that wonderful father of his and his mother there. She doesn't think she has any other son but him. [*She turns to the* MOTHER.] Come on, come on, Mummy, come on! [*Turning back to the* PRODUCER *to point her out to him.*] Look, she's going to try to stop him . . . [*To the* MOTHER, *half compelling her, as if by some magic power.*] Come on, come on. [*Then to the* PRODUCER *again.*] Imagine how she must feel at showing her affection for him in front of your actors! But her longing to be near him is so strong that—look! She's going to go through that scene with him again! [*The* MOTHER *has now actually come close to the* SON *as the* STEPDAUGHTER *says the last line: she gestures to show that she agrees to go on.*]

SON [*Quickly.*] But I'm not! I'm not! If I can't get away then I suppose I shall have to stay here; but I repeat that I will not have any part in it.

FATHER [*To the* PRODUCER, *excitedly.*] You must make him!

SON Nobody's going to make me do anything!

FATHER I'll make you!

STEPDAUGHTER Wait! Just a minute! Before that, the little girl has to go to the fountain. [*She turns to take the* LITTLE GIRL, *drops on her knees in front of her and takes her face between her hands.*] My poor little darling, those beautiful eyes, they look so bewildered. You're wondering where you are, aren't you? Well, we're on a stage, my darling! What's a stage? Well, it's a place where you pretend to be serious. They put on plays here. And now we're going to put on a play. Seriously! Oh, yes! Even you . . . [*She hugs her tightly and rocks her gently for a moment.*] Oh, my little one, my little darling, what a terrible play it is for you! What horrible things have been planned for you! The garden, the fountain . . . Oh, yes, it's only a pretend fountain, that's right. That's part of the game, my pretty darling: everything is pretends here. Perhaps you'll like a pretends fountain better than a real one: you can play here then. But it's only a game for the others; not for you, I'm afraid, it's real for you, my darling, and your game is in a real fountain, a big beautiful green fountain with bamboos casting shadows, looking at your own reflection, with lots of baby ducks paddling about, shattering the reflections. You want to stroke one! [*With a scream that electrifies and terrifies everybody.*] No, Rosetta, no! Your mummy isn't watching you, she's over there with that selfish bastard! Oh, God, I feel as if all the devils in hell were tearing me apart inside . . . And you . . . [*Leaving the* LITTLE GIRL *and turning to the* LITTLE BOY *in the usual way.*] What are you doing here, hanging about like a beggar? It'll be your fault too, if that little girl drowns; you're always like this, as if I wasn't paying the price for getting all of you into this house. [*Shaking his arm to make him take his hand out of his pocket.*] What have you got there? What are you hiding? Take it out, take your hand out! [*She drags his hand out of his pocket and to everyone's horror he is holding a revolver. She looks at him for a moment, almost with satisfaction: then she says, grimly.*] Where on earth did you get that? [*The* (LITTLE) BOY, *looking frightened, with his eyes wide and empty, doesn't answer.*] You idiot, if I'd been you, instead of killing myself, I'd have killed one of those two: either or both, the father and the son. [*She pushes him toward the cypress trees where he then stands watching: then she takes the* LITTLE GIRL *and helps her to climb in to the fountain, making her lie so that she is hidden: after that she kneels down and puts her head and arms on the rim of the fountain.*]

PRODUCER That's good! It's good! [*Turning to the* STEPDAUGHTER.] And at the same time . . .

SON [*Scornfully.*] What do you mean, at the same time? There was nothing at the same time! There wasn't any scene between her and me. [*Pointing to the* MOTHER.] She'll tell you the same thing herself, she'll tell you what happened.

> [*The* SECOND ACTRESS *and the* JUVENILE LEAD *have left the group of* ACTORS *and have come to stand nearer the* MOTHER *and the* SON *as if to study them so as to play their parts.*]

MOTHER Yes, it's true. I'd gone to his room . . .

SON Room, do you hear? Not the garden!

PRODUCER It's not important! We've got to reorganize the events anyway. I've told you that already.

SON [*Glaring at the* JUVENILE LEAD *and the* SECOND ACTRESS.] What do you want?

JUVENILE LEAD Nothing. I'm just watching.

SON [*Turning to the* SECOND ACTRESS] You as well! Getting ready to play her part are you? [*Pointing to the* MOTHER.]

PRODUCER That's it. And I think you should be grateful—they're paying you a lot of attention.

SON Oh, yes, thank you! But haven't you realised yet that you'll never be able to do this play? There's nothing of us inside you and you actors are only looking at us from the outside. Do you think we could go on living with a mirror held up in front of us that didn't only freeze our reflection for ever, but froze us in a reflection that laughed back at us with an expression that we didn't even recognise as our own?

FATHER That's right! That's right!

PRODUCER [*To* JUVENILE LEAD *and* SECOND ACTRESS.] Okay. Go back to the others.

SON It's quite useless. I'm not prepared to do anything.

PRODUCER Oh, shut up, will you, and let me listen to your mother. [*To the* MOTHER.] Well, you'd gone to his room, you said.

MOTHER Yes, to his room. I couldn't bear it any longer. I wanted to empty my heart to him, tell him about all the agony that was crushing me. But as soon as he saw me come in . . .

SON Nothing happened. I got away! I wasn't going to get involved. I never have been involved. Do you understand?

MOTHER It's true! That's right!

PRODUCER But we must make up the scene between you, then. It's vital!

MOTHER I'm ready to do it! If only I had the chance to talk to him for a moment, to pour out all my troubles to him.

FATHER [*Going to the* SON *and speaking violently.*] You'll do it! For your Mother! For your Mother!

SON [*More than ever determined.*] I'm doing nothing!

FATHER [*Taking hold of his coat collar and shaking him.*] For God's sake, do as I tell you! Do as I tell you! Do you hear what she's saying? Haven't you any feelings for her?

SON [*Taking hold of his* FATHER.] No I haven't! I haven't! Let that be the end of it!

[*There is a general uproar. The* MOTHER *frightened out of her wits, tries to get between them and separate them.*]

MOTHER Please stop it! Please!

FATHER [*Hanging on.*] Do as I tell you! Do as I tell you!

SON [*Wrestling with him and finally throwing him to the ground near the steps. Everyone is horrified.*] What's come over you? Why are you so frantic? Do you want to parade our disgrace in front of everybody? Well, I'm having nothing to do with it! Nothing! And I'm doing what our author wanted as well—he never wanted to put us on the stage.

PRODUCER Then why the hell did you come here?

SON [*Pointing to the* FATHER.] He wanted to, I didn't.

PRODUCER But you're here now, aren't you?

SON He was the one who wanted to come and he dragged all of us here with him and agreed with you in there about what to put in the play: and that meant not only what had really happened, as if that wasn't bad enough, but what hadn't happened as well.

PRODUCER   All right, then, you tell me what happened. You tell me! Did you rush out of your room without saying anything?

SON [*After a moment's hesitation.*]   Without saying anything. I didn't want to make a scene.

PRODUCER [*Needling him.*]   What then? What did you do then?

SON [*He is now the centre of everyone's agonised attention and he crosses the stage.*]   Nothing . . . I went across the garden . . . [*He breaks off gloomy and absorbed.*]

PRODUCER [*Urging him to say more, impressed by his reluctance to speak.*]   Well? What then? You crossed the garden?

SON [*Exasperated, putting his face into the crook of his arm.*]   Why do you want me to talk about it? It's horrible! [*The MOTHER is trembling with stifled sobs and looking towards the fountain.*]

PRODUCER [*Quietly, seeing where she is looking and turning to the SON with growing apprehension.*]   The little girl?

SON [*Looking straight in front, out to the audience.*]   There, in the fountain . . .

FATHER [*On the floor still, pointing with pity at the MOTHER.*]   She was trailing after him!

PRODUCER [*To the SON, anxiously.*]   What did you do then?

SON [*Still looking out front and speaking slowly.*]   I dashed across. I was going to jump in and pull her out . . . But something else caught my eye: I saw something behind the tree that made my blood run cold: the little boy, he was standing there with a mad look in his eyes: he was standing looking into the fountain at his little sister, floating there, drowned.
[*The STEPDAUGHTER is still bent at the fountain hiding the LITTLE GIRL, and she sobs pathetically, her sobs sounding like an echo. There is a pause.*]

SON [*Continued.*]   I made a move towards him: but then . . .
[*From behind the trees where the LITTLE BOY is standing there is the sound of a shot.*]

MOTHER [*With a terrible cry she runs along with the SON and all the ACTORS in the midst of a great general confusion.*]   My son! My son! [*And then from out of the confusion and crying her voice comes out.*] Help! Help me!

PRODUCER [*Amidst the shouting he tries to clear a space whilst the LITTLE BOY is carried by his feet and shoulders behind the white skycloth.*]   Is he wounded? Really wounded?
[*Everybody except the PRODUCER and the FATHER who is still on the floor by the steps, has gone behind the skycloth and stays there talking anxiously. Then independently the ACTORS start to come back into view.*]

LEADING ACTRESS [*Coming from the right, very upset.*]   He's dead! The poor boy! He's dead! What a terrible thing!

LEADING ACTOR [*Coming back from the left and smiling.*]   What do you mean, dead? It's all make-believe. It's a sham! He's not dead. Don't you believe it!

OTHER ACTORS FROM THE RIGHT   Make-believe? It's real! Real! He's dead!

OTHER ACTORS FROM THE LEFT   No, he isn't. He's pretending! It's all make-believe.

FATHER [*Running off and shouting at them as he goes.*]   What do you mean, make-believe? It's real! It's real, ladies and gentlemen! It's reality! [*And with desperation on his face he too goes behind the skycloth.*]

PRODUCER [*Not caring any more.*]   Make-believe?! Reality?! Oh, go to hell the lot of you! Lights! Lights! Lights!

> [*At once all the stage and auditorium is flooded with light. The* PRO-DUCER *heaves a sigh of relief as if he has been relieved of a terrible weight and they all look at each other in distress and with uncertainty.*]

PRODUCER   God! I've never known anything like this! And we've lost a whole day's work! [*He looks at the clock.*] Get off with you, all of you! We can't do anything now! It's too late to start a rehearsal. [*When the* ACTORS *have gone, he calls out.*] Hey, lights! Kill everything! [*As soon as he has said this, all the lights go out completely and leave him in the pitch dark.*] For God's sake!! You might have left the workers![4] I can't see where I'm going!

> [*Suddenly, behind the skycloth, as if because of a bad connection, a green light comes up to throw on the cloth a huge sharp shadow of the* CHARACTERS, *but without the* LITTLE BOY *and the* LITTLE GIRL. *The* PRODUCER, *seeing this, jumps off the stage, terrified. At the same time the flood of light on them is switched off and the stage is again bathed in the same blue light as before. Slowly the* SON *comes on from the right, followed by the* MOTHER *with her arms raised towards him. Then from the left, the* FATHER *enters.*
>
> *They come together in the middle of the stage and stand there as if transfixed. Finally from the left the* STEPDAUGHTER *comes on and moves towards the steps at the front: on the top step she pauses for a moment to look back at the other three and then bursts out in a raucous laugh, dashes down the steps and turns to look at the three figures still on the stage. Then she runs out of the auditorium and we can still hear her manic laughter out into the foyer and beyond.*
>
> *After a pause the curtain falls slowly.*]

---

4. Working lights.

MARCEL PROUST
1871–1922

Proust's influence in twentieth-century letters is unequaled by that of any other writer. His massive novel sequence, *Remembrance of Things Past* (À la recherche du temps perdu), broke from nineteenth-century tradition to provide the example of a new kind of characterization and narrative line, a monumentally complex and precisely coordinated aesthetic structure, and a concept of the individual's cumulatively created profound identity—much of it buried in the experience of our senses—that has influenced writers everywhere modern Western literature is known. All of these innovations refer to an exploration of time in terms that parallel the influential work of Proust's contemporary, the philosopher Henri Bergson, with its emphasis on experience as duration, or *lived* time (rather than the artificial measurements of clock or calendar), and the importance of intuitive knowledge. Proust's plot refuses the immediate sense of direction given by traditional nineteenth-century novels: it acquires purpose gradually, through the relationship of different themes, and its collective intent appears only at the end, when Marcel's suddenly catalyzed memory grasps the relationship of all parts. Characters are not sketched in fully from the beginning but are revealed piece by piece, evolving inside the different perspectives of individual chapters; even the protagonist is not fully outlined before the end. Proust's novel is a monumental construction coordinated down to its smallest parts not by the development of traditional novel form but by a new structural vision; it suggested the availability of intuitive or nonrational elements as organizational principles in an example that continues to be a reference point for today's writers.

Marcel Proust was born on July 10, 1871, the older of two sons in a wealthy middle-class Parisian family. His father was a well-known doctor and professor of medicine, a Catholic from a small town outside Paris. His mother, a sensitive, scrupulous, and highly educated woman to whom Marcel was devoted, came from an urban Jewish family. Proust fell ill with severe asthma when he was nine and thereafter spent his childhood holidays at a seaside resort in Normandy that became the fictional model for Balbec. In spite of his illness, which limited what he could do, he graduated with honors from the Lycée Condorcet in Paris in 1889 and did a year's military service at Orléans (the fictional Doncières). As a student, Proust had met many young writers and composers, and he began to frequent the salons of the wealthy bourgeoisie and the aristocracy of the Faubourg Saint-Germain (an elegant area of Paris), from which he drew much of the material for his portraits of society. He wrote for Symbolist magazines such as *Le Banquet* and *La Revue blanche* and published a collection of essays, poems, and stories in an elegant book, *Pleasures and Days* (1896), with drawings by Madeleine Lemaire and music by Reynaldo Hahn. In 1899 (with his mother's help since he knew no English), he began to translate the English moralist and art critic John Ruskin.

Proust is known as the author of one work: the enormous, seven-volume exploration of time and consciousness called *Remembrance of Things Past*. As early as 1895, he had begun work on a shorter novel that traced the same themes and autobiographical awareness, but *Jean Santeuil* (published posthumously in 1952) never found a coherent structure for its numerous episodes and Proust abandoned it in 1899. Many episodes from the unfinished manuscript reflected Proust's interest in current events, especially the Dreyfus Affair (1894–1906) that was dividing France around issues of military honor, anti-Semitism, and national security. Themes, ideas, and some episodes from the earlier novel were absorbed into *Remembrance of Things Past*, and it is striking that the major difference (aside from length) between the two works is simply the extremely sophisticated and subtle structure that Proust devised for the later one.

Proust's health started seriously to decline in 1902, and to make matters worse, he lost both parents by 1905. The following year, his asthma worsening, he moved into a cork-lined, fumigated room at 102 Boulevard Haussmann in Paris, where he stayed until forced to move in 1919. From 1907 to 1914, he spent summers in the seacoast town of Cabourg (another source of material for the fictional Balbec), but when in Paris emerged rarely from his apartment and then only late at night for dinners with friends. In 1909 he conceived the structure of his novel as a whole and wrote its first and last chapters together. A first draft was finished by September 1912, but Proust had difficulty finding a publisher and finally published the first volume at his own expense in 1913. Though *Swann's Way* (*Du côté de chez Swann*) was a success, World War I delayed publication of subsequent volumes, and Proust began the painstaking revision and enlargement of the whole manuscript (from fifteen hundred to four thousand pages, and three to seven parts) that was to occupy him until his death on November 18, 1922. *Within a Budding Grove* (À *l'ombre des jeunes filles en fleurs,* or "In the shadow of young girls in flower") won the prestigious Goncourt Prize in 1919, and *The Guermantes Way* (*Le Côté de Guermantes*) followed in 1920–21. The last volume published in Proust's lifetime was *Cities of the Plain II* (*Sodome et Gomorrhe II*, or "Sodom and Gomorrah II," 1922), and the remaining volumes—*The Captive* (*La Prisonnière*, 1923), *The Fugitive* (*Albertine disparue*, or "Albertine disappeared," 1925), and *Time Regained* (*Le Temps retrouvé*, 1927)—were published posthumously from manuscripts on which he had been working. Written almost completely in the first person and based on events in the author's life (although by no means purely autobiographical), the novel is famous both for its evocation of the closed world of Parisian society at the turn of the century and as a meditation on time and human emotions.

When *Swann's Way* appeared in 1913, it was immediately seen as a new kind of fiction. Unlike nineteenth-century novels such as Flaubert's *Madame Bovary*, *Remembrance of Things Past* has no clear and continuous plot line building to a dénouement, nor (until the last volume, published in 1927) could the reader detect a consistent development of the central character, Marcel. Only at the end does the narrator recognize the meaning and value of what has preceded, and when he retells his story it is not from an omniscient, explanatory point of view but rather as a reliving and gradual assessment of Marcel's lifelong experience. Most of the novel sets forth a roughly chronological sequence of events, yet its opening pages swing through recollections of many times and places before settling on the narrator's childhood in Combray. The second section, *Swann in Love* (*Un Amour de Swann*), is a story told about another character and in the third person. Thus the novel proceeds by apparently discontinuous blocks of recollection, all bound together by the central consciousness of the narrator. This was always Proust's plan: he insisted that he had from the beginning a fixed structure and goal for the whole novel that reached down to the "solidity of the smallest parts," and his substantial revisions of the shorter first draft enriched an already existing structure without changing the sequence of scenes and events.

The overall theme of the novel is suggested by a literal translation of its title: "In Search of Lost Time." The narrator, a "Marcel" who suggests but is not identical with the author, is an old man weakened by a long illness who puzzles over the events of his past, trying to find in them a significant pattern. He begins with his childhood, ordered within the comfortable security of accepted manners and ideals in the family home at Combray. In succeeding volumes he goes out into the world, experiences love and disappointment, discovers the disparity between idealized images of places and their crude, sometimes banal reality, and is increasingly overcome by disillusionment with himself and society. Until the end of the novel, Marcel remains a *grand nerveux* (nervous or high-strung person), an extremely sensitive person impelled by the major experiences of his life—love, betrayal, art, separation, and death—to discard his earlier naive perspective and seek out a largely intuited meaning for life.

In the short ending chapter, things suddenly come into focus as Marcel reaches a new understanding of the role of time. Abruptly reliving a childhood experience when he sees a familiar book and recognizing the ravages of time in the aged and enfeebled figures of his old friends, Marcel faces the approach of death with a new sense of existential continuity and realizes that his vocation as an artist lies in giving form to this buried existence. Apparently lost, the past is still alive within us, a part of our being, and memory can recapture it to give coherence and depth to present identity. Marcel has not yet begun to write by the end of the last volume, *Time Regained*, but paradoxically the book that he plans to write is already there: Proust's *Remembrance of Things Past*.

The larger subject of the novel, penetrating its description of society and Marcel's experience, is "that invisible substance called time." Although neither ever claimed any direct connection (and Proust recognized more readily the influence of his philosophy professor, Darlu), Proust echoes the concerns of contemporary philosopher Bergson when he looks to intuition and a sense of lived experience for a way to represent reality. Bergson's opposition of intellect and intuition, his preference for *duration* (everyday lived time) as opposed to abstract or clock time as a means of knowledge, and his distinction between the interactive "social ego" and the individually "profound" or intuitive ego all correspond to themes in Proust. Marcel's awareness of his life in time is created through memory—not rational or "forced" but spontaneous or "involuntary" memory—the chance recollection that wells up from his subconscious mind when he repeats a previous action such as dipping cookies in lime-blossom tea, stumbling on a paving stone, hearing a spoon clatter, or glimpsing a familiar book. Involuntary memory is more powerful because it draws on a buried level of experience where the five senses are still linked. Life thus recalled comes to us in one piece, not separated into different categories for easier intellectual understanding. Sounds are connected with colors (the name *Brabant* with gold), and emotions with the settings in which they were experienced (sorrow with the smell of varnish on the stairway up to bed). Involuntary memory recreates a whole past world in all its concrete reality—and so does art. When Proust attributes such an absolute metaphysical value to art, making it a special means of knowledge and the focus of his book, he joins a special French tradition of "moralist" writers: those who, from Michel de Montaigne to Albert Camus, strive for clear vision and a sense of universal human values.

Proust's style has a unique "architectural" design that coordinates large blocks of material: themes, situations, places, and events recur and are transformed across time. His long sentences and mammoth paragraphs reflect the slow and careful progression of thought among the changing objects of its perception. The ending paragraph of the *Overture* is composed of two long sentences that encompass an enormous range of meditative detail as the narrator not only recalls his childhood world—the old gray house, garden, public square and country roads, Swann's park, the river, the villagers, and indeed the whole town of Combray—but simultaneously compares the suddenly arisen house to a stage set, and the unfolding village itself to the twists and turns of a Japanese flower taking on color and form inside a bowl of water: here, in the narrator's cup of lime-blossom tea. Characters are remembered in different settings and perspectives, creating a "multiple self" who is free to change and still remain the same. Thus Charles Swann appears first as the visitor who often delays the child Marcel's bedtime kiss from his mother, next as an anxious and disappointed lover, and finally as a tragic, dying man rejected by his friends, the Guermantes, in their haste to get to a ball. Marcel's grandmother appears throughout the scenes in Combray, later during a visit to the seaside resort of Balbec, still later in her death agonies when Marcel is unable truly to grieve, and finally as a sudden recollection when Marcel has trouble tying his shoelace in Balbec. Nor is it characters alone who undergo cumulative transformations. The little musical phrase that Marcel first hears as part of a sonata by the composer Vinteuil and that is associated with love in various settings recurs toward the end of the novel as part of a septet and becomes a revelation of the subtle constructions of art. Places overlap in the memory: the imagined and the real Balbec or Venice confront one another, and the church steeples of Vieuxvicq and Martinville are juxtaposed. On a linguistic level, Proust juxtaposes entire social roles and habits of mind through the interaction of different types of speech. When Charles and the Princesse de Guermantes meet in a bourgeois salon, their manner of speaking to each other creates a small "in-group" dialogue of the aristocracy and sets them off from everyone else. The flexibility of Proust's style, representing thought and habits of speech rather than following a superimposed common code, makes him an example of verbal and visionary innovation that is paralleled by other writers of the same period, such as James Joyce and Virginia Woolf, and is enormously influential on later writers of the "new novel" tradition.

The selection printed here, *Overture*, is the first chapter of *Swann's Way*, the first full volume of Proust's novel. "Swann's way" is one of the two directions in which Marcel's family used to take walks from their home in Combray, toward Tansonville, home of Charles Swann, and is associated with various scenes and anecdotes of love and private life. The longer walk toward the estate of the Guermantes (*The Guermantes Way*), a fictional family of the highest aristocracy appearing frequently in the novel, evokes an aura of high society and French history, a more public sphere. Fictional people and places mingle throughout with the real; names that are not annotated are Proust's inventions. The narrator of *Overture* is Marcel as an old man, and the French verb tense used in his recollections (here and throughout all but the final volume) is appropriately the imperfect, a tense of uncompleted action ("I used to . . . I would ask myself").

As the chapter title suggests, *Overture* introduces the work's themes and methods rather like the overture of an opera. All but one of the main characters appear or are mentioned, and the patterns of future encounters are set. Marcel, waiting anxiously for his beloved mother's response to a note sent down to her during dinner, suffers the same agony of separation as does Swann in his love for the promiscuous Odette, or the older Marcel himself for Albertine. The strange world of half-sleep, half-waking with which the novel begins prefigures later awakenings of memory. Long passages of intricate introspection, and sudden shifts of time and space, introduce us to the style and point of view of the rest of the book. The narrator shares the painful anxiety of little Marcel's desperate wait for his mother's bedtime kiss; for though his observations and judgments are tempered with mature wisdom, he is only at the beginning of his progress to full consciousness. The remembrance of things past is a key to further discovery but not an end in itself.

Overture ends with Proust's most famous image, summing up for many readers the world, the style, and the process of discovery of the Proustian vision. Nibbling at a madeleine (a small, rich cookielike pastry) that he has dipped in lime-blossom tea, Marcel suddenly has an overwhelming feeling of happiness. He soon associates this tantalizing, puzzling phenomenon with the memory of earlier times when he sipped tea with his Aunt Leonie. He realizes that there is something valuable about such passive, spontaneous, and sensuous memory, quite different from the abstract operations of reason. Although the Marcel of "Combray" does not yet know it, he will pursue the elusive significance of this moment of happiness until, in *Time Regained*, he can as a complete artist bring it to the surface and link past and present time in a fuller and richer identity.

Roger Shattuck, *Proust* (1974), is a general study including advice on "how to read" Proust; it is still useful although it predates the revised translation used here; George D. Painter, *Marcel Proust: A Biography* (rev. 1996), offers a comprehensive biography. An excellent general study is Germaine Brée, *Marcel Proust and Deliverance from Time* (1969), translated by R. J. Richards and A. D. Truitt. Terence Kilmartin, *A Reader's Guide to Remembrance of Things Past* (1984), is a handbook guide to Proust's characters, to persons referred to in the text, to places, and to themes, all keyed to the revised translation by the translator. Julia Kristeva, *Proust and the Sense of Time* (1993), trans. Stephen Bann, takes a broadly psychoanalytic approach. René Girard, *Proust: A Collection of Critical Essays* (1962); Harold Bloom, ed., *Marcel Proust's Remembrance of Things Past* (1987); and Barbara J. Bucknall, ed., *Critical Essays on Marcel Proust* (1987), are also recommended.

PRONOUNCING GLOSSARY

The following list uses common English syllables and stress accents to provide rough equivalents of selected words whose pronunciation may be unfamiliar to the general reader.

Bathilde: *bah-teeld'*

Charlus: *shar-lews'*

Chartres: *shar'-tr*

Combray: *cohm-bray'*

Corot: *core-oh'*

Duc: *dewk*

Faubourg Saint-Germain: *foh-boor' sanh zhair–manh'*

George Sand: *zhorzh sonh*

Maubant: *moh-bawnh'*

Maulévrier: *moh-lay'-vree-ay'*

Proust: *proost*

Quai d'Orléans: *kay dor-lay-onh*

Saint-Cloud: *sanh—cloo'*

Saint-Loup: *sanh—loo'*

Sévigné: *say-veen-yay'*

Vinteuil: *van-teuh'-ee*

Remembrance of Things Past[1]

Swann's Way. Overture[2]

For a long time I used to go to bed early. Sometimes, when I had put out my candle, my eyes would close so quickly that I had not even time to say to myself: "I'm falling asleep." And half an hour later the thought that it was time to go to sleep would awaken me; I would make as if to put away the book which I imagined was still in my hands, and to blow out the light; I had gone on thinking, while I was asleep, about what I had just been reading, but these thoughts had taken a rather peculiar turn; it seemed to me that I myself was the immediate subject of my book: a church, a quartet, the rivalry between François I and Charles V.[3] This impression would persist for some moments after I awoke; it did not offend my reason, but lay like scales upon my eyes and prevented them from registering the fact that the candle was no longer burning. Then it would begin to seem unintelligible, as the thoughts of a former existence must be to a reincarnate spirit; the subject of my book would separate itself from me, leaving me free to apply myself to it or not; and at the same time my sight would return and I would be astonished to find myself in a state of darkness, pleasant and restful enough for my eyes, but even more, perhaps, for my mind, to which it appeared incomprehensible, without a cause, something dark indeed.

I would ask myself what time it could be; I could hear the whistling of trains, which, now nearer and now farther off, punctuating the distance like the note of a bird in a forest, showed me in perspective the deserted countryside through which a traveller is hurrying towards the nearby station; and the path he is taking will be engraved in his memory by the excitement induced by strange surroundings, by unaccustomed activities, by the conversation he has had and the farewells exchanged beneath an unfamiliar lamp, still echoing in his ears amid the silence of the night, by the imminent joy of going home.

I would lay my cheeks gently against the comfortable cheeks of my pillow, as plump and blooming as the cheeks of babyhood. I would strike a match to look at my watch. Nearly midnight. The hour when an invalid, who has been obliged to set out on a journey and to sleep in a strange hotel, awakened by a sudden spasm, sees with glad relief a streak of daylight showing under his door. Thank God, it is morning! The servants will be about in a minute: he can ring, and someone will come to look after him. The thought of being

---

1. Translated by C. K. Scott Moncrieff and Terence Kilmartin.   2. The opening section of Combray, the first volume of *Swann's Way*.   3. Francis I (1496–1567), king of France, and Charles V (1500–1558), Holy Roman emperor and king of Spain, fought four wars over the empire's expansion in Europe.

assuaged gives him strength to endure his pain. He is certain he heard footsteps: they come nearer, and then die away. The ray of light beneath his door is extinguished. It is midnight; someone has just turned down the gas; the last servant has gone to bed, and he must lie all night in agony with no one to bring him relief.

I would fall asleep again, and thereafter would reawaken for short snatches only, just long enough to hear the regular creaking of the wainscot,[4] or to open my eyes to stare at the shifting kaleidoscope of the darkness, to savour, in a momentary glimmer of consciousness, the sleep which lay heavy upon the furniture, the room, the whole of which I formed but an insignificant part and whose insensibility I should very soon return to share. Or else while sleeping I had drifted back to an earlier stage in my life, now for ever outgrown, and had come under the thrall of one of my childish terrors, such as that old terror of my great-uncle's pulling my curls which was effectually dispelled on the day—the dawn of a new era to me—when they were finally cropped from my head. I had forgotten that event during my sleep, but I remembered it again immediately I had succeeded in waking myself up to escape my great-uncle's fingers, and as a measure of precaution I would bury the whole of my head in the pillow before returning to the world of dreams.

Sometimes, too, as Eve was created from a rib of Adam, a woman would be born during my sleep from some strain in the position of my thighs. Conceived from the pleasure I was on the point of consummating, she it was, I imagined, who offered me that pleasure. My body, conscious that its own warmth was permeating hers, would strive to become one with her, and I would awake. The rest of humanity seemed very remote in comparison with this woman whose company I had left but a moment ago; my cheek was still warm from her kiss, my body ached beneath the weight of hers. If, as would sometimes happen, she had the features of some woman whom I had known in waking hours, I would abandon myself altogether to the sole quest of her, like people who set out on a journey to see with their eyes some city of their desire, and imagine that one can taste in reality what has charmed one's fancy. And then, gradually, the memory of her would dissolve and vanish, until I had forgotten the girl of my dream.

When a man is asleep, he has in a circle round him the chain of the hours, the sequence of the years, the order of the heavenly host. Instinctively, when he awakes, he looks to these, and in an instant reads off his own position on the earth's surface and the time that has elapsed during his slumbers; but this ordered procession is apt to grow confused, and to break its ranks. Suppose that, towards morning, after a night of insomnia, sleep descends upon him while he is reading, in quite a different position from that in which he normally goes to sleep, he has only to lift his arm to arrest the sun and turn it back in its course,[5] and, at the moment of waking, he will have no idea of the time, but will conclude that he has just gone to bed. Or suppose that he dozes off in some even more abnormal and divergent position, sitting in an armchair, for instance, after dinner: then the world will go hurtling out of orbit, the magic chair will carry him at full speed through time and space, and when he opens his eyes again he will imagine that he went to sleep

---

4. The wooden paneling of the walls.   5. If his uplifted arm prevents him from seeing the sunlight, he will think it is still night.

months earlier in another place. But for me it was enough if, in my own bed,
my sleep was so heavy as completely to relax my consciousness; for then I
lost all sense of the place in which I had gone to sleep, and when I awoke
in the middle of the night, not knowing where I was, I could not even be
sure at first who I was; I had only the most rudimentary sense of existence,
such as may lurk and flicker in the depths of an animal's consciousness; I
was more destitute than the cave-dweller; but then the memory—not yet of
the place in which I was, but of various other places where I had lived and
might now very possibly be—would come like a rope let down from heaven
to draw me up out of the abyss of not-being, from which I could never have
escaped by myself: in a flash I would traverse centuries of civilisation, and
out of a blurred glimpse of oil-lamps, then of shirts with turned-down collars,
would gradually piece together the original components of my ego.

Perhaps the immobility of the things that surround us is forced upon them
by our conviction that they are themselves and not anything else, by the
immobility of our conception of them. For it always happened that when I
awoke like this, and my mind struggled in an unsuccessful attempt to discover where I was, everything revolved around me through the darkness:
things, places, years. My body, still too heavy with sleep to move, would
endeavour to construe from the pattern of its tiredness the position of its
various limbs, in order to deduce therefrom the direction of the wall, the
location of the furniture, to piece together and give a name to the house in
which it lay. Its memory, the composite memory of its ribs, its knees, its
shoulder-blades, offered it a whole series of rooms in which it had at one
time or another slept, while the unseen walls, shifting and adapting themselves to the shape of each successive room that it remembered, whirled
round it in the dark. And even before my brain, lingering in cogitation over
when things had happened and what they had looked like, had reassembled
the circumstances sufficiently to identify the room, it, my body, would recall
from each room in succession the style of the bed, the position of the doors,
the angle at which the daylight came in at the windows, whether there was
a passage outside, what I had had in my mind when I went to sleep and
found there when I awoke. The stiffened side on which I lay would, for
instance, in trying to fix its position, imagine itself to be lying face to the
wall in a big bed with a canopy; and at once I would say to myself, "Why, I
must have fallen asleep before Mamma came to say good night," for I was
in the country at my grandfather's, who died years ago; and my body, the
side upon which I was lying, faithful guardians of a past which my mind
should never have forgotten, brought back before my eyes the glimmering
flame of the night-light in its urn-shaped bowl of Bohemian glass that hung
by chains from the ceiling, and the chimney-piece of Siena marble[6] in my
bedroom at Combray, in my grandparents' house, in those far distant days
which at this moment I imagined to be in the present without being able to
picture them exactly, and which would become plainer in a little while when
I was properly awake.

Then the memory of a new position would spring up, and the wall would
slide away in another direction; I was in my room in Mme de Saint-Loup's[7]

6. From central Italy, mottled and reddish in color. *Bohemian glass:* likely to have been ornately engraved.
Bohemia (now part of the Czech Republic) was a major center of the glass industry.   7. Charles Swann's
daughter, Gilberte, who has married Robert de Saint-Loup, a nephew of the Guermantes.

house in the country; good heavens, it must be ten o'clock, they will have finished dinner! I must have overslept myself in the little nap which I always take when I come in from my walk with Mme de Saint-Loup, before dressing for the evening. For many years have now elapsed since the Combray days when, coming in from the longest and latest walks, I would still be in time to see the reflection of the sunset glowing in the panes of my bedroom window. It is a very different kind of life that one leads at Tansonville, at Mme de Saint-Loup's, and a different kind of pleasure that I derive from taking walks only in the evenings, from visiting by moonlight the roads on which I used to play as a child in the sunshine; while the bedroom in which I shall presently fall asleep instead of dressing for dinner I can see from the distance as we return from our walk, with its lamp shining through the window, a solitary beacon in the night.

These shifting and confused gusts of memory never lasted for more than a few seconds; it often happened that, in my brief spell of uncertainty as to where I was, I did not distinguish the various suppositions of which it was composed any more than, when we watch a horse running, we isolate the successive positions of its body as they appear upon a bioscope.[8] But I had seen first one and then another of the rooms in which I had slept during my life, and in the end I would revisit them all in the long course of my waking dream: rooms in winter, where on going to bed I would at once bury my head in a nest woven out of the most diverse materials—the corner of my pillow, the top of my blankets, a piece of a shawl, the edge of my bed, and a copy of a children's paper—which I had contrived to cement together, bird-fashion, by dint of continuous pressure; rooms where, in freezing weather, I would enjoy the satisfaction of being shut in from the outer world (like the sea-swallow which builds at the end of a dark tunnel and is kept warm by the surrounding earth), and where, the fire keeping in all night, I would sleep wrapped up, as it were, in a great cloak of snug and smoky air, shot with the glow of the logs intermittently breaking out again in flame, a sort of alcove without walls, a cave of warmth dug out of the heart of the room itself, a zone of heat whose boundaries were constantly shifting and altering in temperature as gusts of air traversed them to strike freshly upon my face, from the corners of the room or from parts near the window or far from the fireplace which had therefore remained cold;—or rooms in summer, where I would delight to feel myself a part of the warm night, where the moonlight striking upon the half-opened shutters would throw down to the foot of my bed its enchanted ladder, where I would fall asleep, as it might be in the open air, like a titmouse which the breeze gently rocks at the tip of a sunbeam;—or sometimes the Louis XVI room,[9] so cheerful that I never felt too miserable in it, even on my first night, and in which the slender columns that lightly supported its ceiling drew so gracefully apart to reveal and frame the site of the bed;—sometimes, again, the little room with the high ceiling, hollowed in the form of a pyramid out of two separate storeys, and partly walled with mahogany, in which from the first moment, mentally poisoned by the unfamiliar scent of vetiver,[1] I was convinced of the hostility of the

8. An early moving-picture machine that showed photographs in rapid succession.   9. Furnished in late-18th-century style, named for the French monarch of the time and marked by great elegance. The room is that in which Marcel visits Robert de Saint-Loup in *Guermantes Way*.   1. The aromatic root of a tropical grass packaged as a moth repellent.

violet curtains and of the insolent indifference of a clock that chattered on at the top of its voice as though I were not there; in which a strange and pitiless rectangular cheval-glass, standing across one corner of the room, carved out for itself a site I had not looked to find tenanted in the soft plenitude of my normal field of vision;[2] in which my mind, striving for hours on end to break away from its moorings, to stretch upwards so as to take on the exact shape of the room and to reach to the topmost height of its gigantic funnel, had endured many a painful night as I lay stretched out in bed, my eyes staring upwards, my ears straining, my nostrils flaring, my heart beating; until habit had changed the colour of the curtains, silenced the clock, brought an expression of pity to the cruel, slanting face of the glass, disguised or even completely dispelled the scent of vetiver, and appreciably reduced the apparent loftiness of the ceiling. Habit! that skilful but slow-moving arranger who begins by letting our minds suffer for weeks on end in temporary quarters, but whom our minds are none the less only too happy to discover at last, for without it, reduced to their own devices, they would be powerless to make any room seem habitable.

Certainly I was now well awake; my body had veered round for the last time and the good angel of certainty had made all the surrounding objects stand still, had set me down under my bedclothes, in my bedroom, and had fixed, approximately in their right places in the uncertain light, my chest of drawers, my writing-table, my fireplace, the window overlooking the street, and both the doors. But for all that I now knew that I was not in any of the houses of which the ignorance of the waking moment had, in a flash, if not presented me with a distinct picture, at least persuaded me of the possible presence, my memory had been set in motion; as a rule I did not attempt to go to sleep again at once, but used to spend the greater part of the night recalling our life in the old days at Combray with my great-aunt, at Balbec, Paris, Doncières, Venice, and the rest; remembering again all the places and people I had known, what I had actually seen of them, and what others had told me.

At Combray, as every afternoon ended, long before the time when I should have to go to bed and lie there, unsleeping, far from my mother and grandmother, my bedroom became the fixed point on which my melancholy and anxious thoughts were centred. Someone had indeed had the happy idea of giving me, to distract me on evenings when I seemed abnormally wretched, a magic lantern,[3] which used to be set on top of my lamp while we waited for dinner-time to come; and, after the fashion of the master-builders and glass-painters of gothic days, it substituted for the opaqueness of my walls an impalpable iridescence, supernatural phenomena of many colours, in which legends were depicted as on a shifting and transitory window. But my sorrows were only increased thereby, because this mere change of lighting was enough to destroy the familiar impression I had of my room, thanks to which, save for the torture of going to bed, it had become quite endurable. Now I no longer recognised it, and felt uneasy in it, as in a room in some hotel or chalet, in a place where I had just arrived by train for the first time.

---

2. The narrator's room at the fictional seaside resort of Balbec, a setting in *Within a Budding Grove*.   3. A kind of slide projector.

Riding at a jerky trot, Golo,[4] filled with an infamous design, issued from the little triangular forest which dyed dark-green the slope of a convenient hill, and advanced fitfully towards the castle of poor Geneviève de Brabant. This castle was cut off short by a curved line which was in fact the circumference of one of the transparent ovals in the slides which were pushed into position through a slot in the lantern. It was only the wing of a castle, and in front of it stretched a moor on which Geneviève stood lost in contemplation, wearing a blue girdle.[5] The castle and the moor were yellow, but I could tell their colour without waiting to see them, for before the slides made their appearance the old-gold sonorous name of Brabant had given me an unmistakable clue. Golo stopped for a moment and listened sadly to the accompanying patter read aloud by my great-aunt,[6] which he seemed perfectly to understand, for he modified his attitude with a docility not devoid of a degree of majesty, so as to conform to the indications given in the text; then he rode away at the same jerky trot. And nothing could arrest his slow progress. If the lantern were moved I could still distinguish Golo's horse advancing across the window-curtains, swelling out with their curves and diving into their folds. The body of Golo himself, being of the same supernatural substance as his steed's, overcame every material obstacle—everything that seemed to bar his way—by taking it as an ossature[7] and embodying it in himself: even the door-handle, for instance, over which, adapting itself at once, would float irresistibly his red cloak or his pale face, which never lost its nobility or its melancholy, never betrayed the least concern at this transvertebration.

And, indeed, I found plenty of charm in these bright projections, which seemed to emanate from a Merovingian[8] past and shed around me the reflections of such ancient history. But I cannot express the discomfort I felt at this intrusion of mystery and beauty into a room which I had succeeded in filling with my own personality until I thought no more of it than of myself. The anaesthetic effect of habit being destroyed, I would begin to think—and to feel—such melancholy things. The door-handle of my room, which was different to me from all the other door-handles in the world, inasmuch as it seemed to open of its own accord and without my having to turn it, so unconscious had its manipulation become—lo and behold, it was now an astral body[9] for Golo. And as soon as the dinner-bell rang I would hurry down to the dining-room, where the big hanging lamp, ignorant of Golo and Bluebeard[1] but well acquainted with my family and the dish of stewed beef, shed the same light as on every other evening; and I would fall into the arms of my mother, whom the misfortunes of Geneviève de Brabant had made all the dearer to me, just as the crimes of Golo had driven me to a more than ordinarily scrupulous examination of my own conscience.

But after dinner, alas, I was soon obliged to leave Mamma, who stayed talking with the others, in the garden if it was fine, or in the little parlour where everyone took shelter when it was wet. Everyone except my grandmother, who held that "It's a pity to shut oneself indoors in the country,"

4. Villain of a 5th-century legend. He falsely accuses Geneviève de Brabant of adultery. Brabant was a principality in what is now Belgium. 5. Belt. 6. Marcel's great-aunt is reading the story to him as they wait for dinner. 7. Skeleton. 8. The first dynasty of French kings (500–751). 9. Spiritual counterpart of the physical body. According to the doctrine of Theosophy (a spiritualist movement originating in 1875), the astral body survives the death of the physical body. 1. The legendary wife murderer, presumably depicted on another set of slides.

and used to have endless arguments with my father on the very wettest days, because he would send me up to my room with a book instead of letting me stay out of doors. "That is not the way to make him strong and active," she would say sadly, "especially this little man, who needs all the strength and will-power that he can get." My father would shrug his shoulders and study the barometer, for he took an interest in meteorology, while my mother, keeping very quiet so as not to disturb him, looked at him with tender respect, but not too hard, not wishing to penetrate the mysteries of his superior mind. But my grandmother, in all weathers, even when the rain was coming down in torrents and Françoise had rushed the precious wicker armchairs indoors so that they should not get soaked, was to be seen pacing the deserted rain-lashed garden, pushing back her disordered grey locks so that her forehead might be freer to absorb the health-giving draughts of wind and rain. She would say, "At last one can breathe!" and would trot up and down the sodden paths—too straight and symmetrical for her liking, owing to the want of any feeling for nature in the new gardener, whom my father had been asking all morning if the weather were going to improve—her keen, jerky little step regulated by the various effects wrought upon her soul by the intoxication of the storm, the power of hygiene, the stupidity of my upbringing and the symmetry of gardens, rather than by any anxiety (for that was quite unknown to her) to save her plum-coloured skirt from the mudstains beneath which it would gradually disappear to a height that was the constant bane and despair of her maid.

When these walks of my grandmother's took place after dinner there was one thing which never failed to bring her back to the house: this was if (at one of those points when her circular itinerary brought her back, moth-like, in sight of the lamp in the little parlour where the liqueurs were set out on the card-table) my great-aunt called out to her: "Bathilde! Come in and stop your husband drinking brandy!" For, simply to tease her (she had brought so different a type of mind into my father's family that everyone made fun of her), my great-aunt used to make my grandfather, who was forbidden liqueurs, take just a few drops. My poor grandmother would come in and beg and implore her husband not to taste the brandy; and he would get angry and gulp it down all the same, and she would go out again sad and discouraged, but still smiling, for she was so humble of heart and so gentle that her tenderness for others and her disregard for herself and her own troubles blended in a smile which, unlike those seen on the majority of human faces, bore no trace of irony save for herself, while for all of us kisses seemed to spring from her eyes, which could not look upon those she loved without seeming to bestow upon them passionate caresses. This torture inflicted on her by my great-aunt, the sight of my grandmother's vain entreaties, of her feeble attempts, doomed in advance, to remove the liqueur-glass from my grandfather's hands—all these were things of the sort to which, in later years, one can grow so accustomed as to smile at them and to take the persecutor's side resolutely and cheerfully enough to persuade oneself that it is not really persecution; but in those days they filled me with such horror that I longed to strike my great-aunt. And yet, as soon as I heard her "Bathilde! Come in and stop your husband drinking brandy," in my cowardice I became at once a man, and did what all we grown men do when face to face with suffering and injustice: I preferred not to see them; I ran up to the top of the house to cry by myself in a little room beside the schoolroom and beneath the roof, which smelt of orris-root[2] and was scented also by a wild currant-bush which had climbed up between the stones of the outer wall and thrust a flowering branch in through the half-opened window. Intended for a more special and a baser use, this room, from which, in the daytime, I could see as far as the keep[3] of Roussainville-le-Pin, was for a long time my place of refuge, doubtless because it was the only room whose door I was allowed to lock, whenever my occupation was such as required an inviolable solitude: reading or daydreaming, secret tears or sensual gratification. Alas! I little knew that my own lack of will-power, my delicate health, and the consequent uncertainty as to my future, weighed far more heavily on my grandmother's mind than any little dietary indiscretion by her husband in the course of those endless perambulations, afternoon and evening, during which we used to see her handsome face passing to and fro, half raised towards the sky, its brown and wrinkled cheeks, which with age had acquired almost the purple hue of tilled fields in autumn, covered, if she were "going out," by a half-lifted veil, while upon them either the cold or some sad reflection invariably left the drying traces of an involuntary tear.

My sole consolation when I went upstairs for the night was that Mamma would come in and kiss me after I was in bed. But this good night lasted for so short a time, she went down again so soon, that the moment in which I heard her climb the stairs, and then caught the sound of her garden dress of blue muslin, from which hung little tassels of plaited straw, rustling along the double-doored corridor, was for me a moment of the utmost pain; for it heralded the moment which was bound to follow it, when she would have left me and gone downstairs again. So much so that I reached the point of hoping that this good night which I loved so much would come as late as possible, so as to prolong the time of respite during which Mamma would not yet have appeared. Sometimes when, after kissing me, she opened the door to go, I longed to call her back, to say to her "Kiss me just once more," but I knew that then she would at once look displeased, for the concession which she made to my wretchedness and agitation in coming up to give me this kiss of peace always annoyed my father, who thought such rituals absurd, and she would have liked to try to induce me to outgrow the need, the habit, of having her there at all, let alone get into the habit of asking her for an additional kiss when she was already crossing the threshold. And to see her look displeased destroyed all the calm and serenity she had brought me a moment before, when she had bent her loving face down over my bed, and held it out to me like a host[4] for an act of peace-giving communion in which my lips might imbibe her real presence and with it the power to sleep. But those evenings on which Mamma stayed so short a time in my room were sweet indeed compared to those on which we had guests to dinner, and therefore she did not come at all. Our "guests" were usually limited to M. Swann, who, apart from a few passing strangers, was almost the only person who ever came to the house at Combray, sometimes to a neighbourly dinner (but less frequently since his unfortunate marriage, as my family did not care to receive his wife) and sometimes after dinner, uninvited. On those evenings

---

2. A powder then used as a deodorizer for rooms.   3. The best-fortified tower of a medieval castle. *Baser use:* as a toilet.   4. Communion wafer.

when, as we sat in front of the house round the iron table beneath the big chestnut-tree, we heard, from the far end of the garden, not the shrill and assertive alarm bell which assailed and deafened with its ferruginous,[5] interminable, frozen sound any member of the household who set it off on entering "without ringing," but the double tinkle, timid, oval, golden, of the visitors' bell, everyone would at once exclaim "A visitor! Who in the world can it be?" but they knew quite well that it could only be M. Swann. My great-aunt, speaking in a loud voice to set an example, in a tone which she endeavoured to make sound natural, would tell the others not to whisper so; that nothing could be more offensive to a stranger coming in, who would be led to think that people were saying things about him which he was not meant to hear; and then my grandmother, always happy to find an excuse for an additional turn in the garden, would be sent out to reconnoitre, and would take the opportunity to remove surreptitiously, as she passed, the stakes of a rose-tree or two, so as to make the roses look a little more natural, as a mother might run her hand through her boy's hair after the barber has smoothed it down, to make it look naturally wavy.

We would all wait there in suspense for the report which my grandmother would bring back from the enemy lines, as though there might be a choice between a large number of possible assailants, and then, soon after, my grandfather would say: "I can hear Swann's voice." And indeed one could tell him only by his voice, for it was difficult to make out his face with its arched nose and green eyes, under a high forehead fringed with fair, almost red hair, done in the Bressant style,[6] because in the garden we used as little light as possible, so as not to attract mosquitoes; and I would slip away unobtrusively to order the liqueurs to be brought out, for my grandmother made a great point, thinking it "nicer," of their not being allowed to seem anything out of the ordinary, which we kept for visitors only. Although a far younger man, M. Swann was very much attached to my grandfather, who had been an intimate friend of Swann's father, an excellent but eccentric man the ardour of whose feelings and the current of whose thoughts would often be checked or diverted by the most trifling thing. Several times in the course of a year I would hear my grandfather tell at table the story, which never varied, of the behaviour of M. Swann the elder upon the death of his wife, by whose bedside he had watched day and night. My grandfather, who had not seen him for a long time, hastened to join him at the Swanns' family property on the outskirts of Combray, and managed to entice him for a moment, weeping profusely, out of the death-chamber, so that he should not be present when the body was laid in its coffin. They took a turn or two in the park, where there was a little sunshine. Suddenly M. Swann seized my grandfather by the arm and cried, "Ah, my dear old friend, how fortunate we are to be walking here together on such a charming day! Don't you see how pretty they are, all these trees, my hawthorns, and my new pond, on which you have never congratulated me? You look as solemn as the grave. Don't you feel this little breeze? Ah! whatever you may say, it's good to be alive all the same, my dear Amédée!" And then, abruptly, the memory of his dead wife returned to him, and probably thinking it too complicated to inquire into how, at such a time, he could have allowed himself to be carried

5. Ironlike.   6. Close-cropped, like a crew cut; named after a French actor.

away by an impulse of happiness, he confined himself to a gesture which he habitually employed whenever any perplexing question came into his mind: that is, he passed his hand across his forehead, rubbed his eyes, and wiped his glasses. And yet he never got over the loss of his wife, but used to say to my grandfather, during the two years by which he survived her, "It's a funny thing, now; I very often think of my poor wife, but I cannot think of her for long at a time." "Often, but a little at a time, like poor old Swann," became one of my grandfather's favourite sayings, which he would apply to all manner of things. I should have assumed that this father of Swann's had been a monster if my grandfather, whom I regarded as a better judge than myself, and whose word was my law and often led me in the long run to pardon offences which I should have been inclined to condemn, had not gone on to exclaim, "But, after all, he had a heart of gold."

For many years, during the course of which—especially before his marriage—M. Swann the younger came often to see them at Combray, my great-aunt and my grandparents never suspected that he had entirely ceased to live in the society which his family had frequented, and that, under the sort of incognito which the name of Swann gave him among us, they were harbouring—with the complete innocence of a family of respectable innkeepers who have in their midst some celebrated highwayman without knowing it—one of the most distinguished members of the Jockey Club, a particular friend of the Comte de Paris and of the Prince of Wales, and one of the men most sought after in the aristocratic world of the Faubourg Saint-Germain.[7]

Our utter ignorance of the brilliant social life which Swann led was, of course, due in part to his own reserve and discretion, but also to the fact that middle-class people in those days took what was almost a Hindu view of society, which they held to consist of sharply defined castes, so that everyone at his birth found himself called to that station in life which his parents already occupied, and from which nothing, save the accident of an exceptional career or of a "good" marriage, could extract you and translate you to a superior caste. M. Swann the elder had been a stockbroker; and so "young Swann" found himself immured for life in a caste whose members' fortunes, as in a category of tax-payers, varied between such and such limits of income. One knew the people with whom his father had associated, and so one knew his own associates, the people with whom he was "in a position to mix." If he knew other people besides, those were youthful acquaintances on whom the old friends of his family, like my relatives, shut their eyes all the more good-naturedly because Swann himself, after he was left an orphan, still came most faithfully to see us; but we would have been ready to wager that the people outside our acquaintance whom Swann knew were of the sort to whom he would not have dared to raise his hat if he had met them while he was walking with us. Had it been absolutely essential to apply to Swann a social coefficient peculiar to himself, as distinct from all the other sons of other stockbrokers in his father's position, his coefficient would have been rather lower than theirs, because, being very simple in his habits, and having

7. A fashionable area of Paris on the left bank of the Seine; many of the French aristocracy lived there. *Jockey Club*: an exclusive men's club devoted not only to horseracing but to other diversions (such as the opera). The Comte de Paris (1838–1894) was heir apparent to the French throne, in the unlikely event that the monarchy were reinstated. The Prince of Wales became in 1901 King Edward VII of England. The implication is that Swann's social connections were not merely of the highest but of an idle and somewhat hedonistic sort.

always had a craze for "antiques" and pictures, he now lived and amassed his collections in an old house which my grandmother longed to visit but which was situated on the Quai d'Orléans,[8] a neighbourhood in which my great-aunt thought it most degrading to be quartered. "Are you really a connoisseur, now?" she would say to him: "I ask for your own sake, as you are likely to have fakes palmed off on you by the dealers," for she did not, in fact, endow him with any critical faculty, and had no great opinion of the intelligence of a man who, in conversation, would avoid serious topics and showed a very dull preciseness, not only when he gave us kitchen recipes, going into the most minute details, but even when my grandmother's sisters were talking to him about art. When challenged by them to give an opinion, or to express his admiration for some picture, he would remain almost offensively silent, and would then make amends by furnishing (if he could) some fact or other about the gallery in which the picture was hung, or the date at which it had been painted. But as a rule he would content himself with trying to amuse us by telling us about his latest adventure with someone whom we ourselves knew, such as the Combray chemist,[9] or our cook, or our coachman. These stories certainly used to make my great-aunt laugh, but she could never decide whether this was on account of the absurd rôle which Swann invariably gave himself therein, or of the wit that he showed in telling them: "I must say you really are a regular character, M. Swann!"

As she was the only member of our family who could be described as a trifle "common," she would always take care to remark to strangers, when Swann was mentioned, that he could easily, had he so wished, have lived in the Boulevard Haussmann or the Avenue de l'Opéra, and that he was the son of old M. Swann who must have left four or five million francs,[1] but that it was a fad of his. A fad which, moreover, she thought was bound to amuse other people so much that in Paris, when M. Swann called on New Year's Day bringing her a little packet of *marrons glacés*, she never failed, if there were strangers in the room, to say to him: "Well, M. Swann, and do you still live next door to the bonded vaults,[2] so as to be sure of not missing your train when you go to Lyons?" and she would peep out of the corner of her eye, over her glasses, at the other visitors.

But if anyone had suggested to my great-aunt that this Swann, who, in his capacity as the son of old M. Swann, was "fully qualified" to be received by any of the "best people," by the most respected barristers and solicitors[3] of Paris (though he was perhaps a trifle inclined to let this hereditary privilege go by default), had another almost secret existence of a wholly different kind; that when he left our house in Paris, saying that he must go home to bed, he would no sooner have turned the corner than he would stop, retrace his steps, and be off to some salon on whose like no stockbroker or associate of stockbrokers had ever set eyes—that would have seemed to my aunt as extraordinary as, to a woman of wider reading, the thought of being herself

---

8. A beautiful though less fashionable section in the heart of Paris, along the Seine.   9. Pharmacist.
1. Nearly a million dollars in the currency of the day; about two and a quarter million dollars by today's standards. *Boulevard Haussmann* and *Avenue de l'Opéra*: large modern avenues where the wealthy bourgeoisie (or middle class) liked to live.   2. A wine warehouse in southeastern Paris, close to the *Gare de Lyon*, the terminal from which trains depart for the industrial city of Lyon and other destinations in southeastern France. *Marrons glacés*: candied chestnuts, a traditional gift on New Year's Day, then a more common day for exchanging gifts than Christmas.   3. Trial lawyers and lawyers of other kinds.

on terms of intimacy with Aristaeus[4] and of learning that after having a chat with her he would plunge deep into the realms of Thetis, into an empire veiled from mortal eyes, in which Virgil depicts him as being received with open arms; or—to be content with an image more likely to have occurred to her, for she had seen it painted on the plates we used for biscuits at Combray—as the thought of having had to dinner Ali Baba,[5] who, as soon as he finds himself alone and unobserved, will make his way into the cave, resplendent with its unsuspected treasures.

One day when he had come to see us after dinner in Paris, apologising for being in evening clothes, Françoise told us after he had left that she had got it from his coachman that he had been dining "with a princess." "A nice sort of princess,"[6] retorted my aunt, shrugging her shoulders without raising her eyes from her knitting, serenely sarcastic.

Altogether, my great-aunt treated him with scant ceremony. Since she was of the opinion that he ought to feel flattered by our invitations, she thought it only right and proper that he should never come to see us in summer without a basket of peaches or raspberries from his garden, and that from each of his visits to Italy he should bring back some photographs of old masters for me.

It seemed quite natural, therefore, to send for him whenever a recipe for some special sauce or for a pineapple salad was needed for one of our big dinner-parties, to which he himself would not be invited, being regarded as insufficiently important to be served up to new friends who might be in our house for the first time. If the conversation turned upon the princes of the House of France,[7] "gentlemen you and I will never know, will we, and don't want to, do we?" my great-aunt would say tartly to Swann, who had, perhaps, a letter from Twickenham[8] in his pocket; she would make him push the piano into place and turn over the music on evenings when my grandmother's sister sang, manipulating this person who was elsewhere so sought after with the rough simplicity of a child who will play with a collectors' piece with no more circumspection than if it were a cheap gewgaw. Doubtless the Swann who was a familiar figure in all the clubs of those days differed hugely from the Swann created by my great-aunt when, of an evening, in our little garden at Combray, after the two shy peals had sounded from the gate, she would inject and vitalise with everything she knew about the Swann family the obscure and shadowy figure who emerged, with my grandmother in his wake, from the dark background and who was identified by his voice. But then, even in the most insignificant details of our daily life, none of us can be said to constitute a material whole, which is identical for everyone, and need only be turned up like a page in an account-book or the record of a will; our social personality is a creation of the thoughts of other people. Even the simple act which we describe as "seeing someone we know" is to some extent an intellectual process. We pack the physical outline of the person we see with all the notions we have already formed about him, and in the total picture of him which we compose in our minds those notions have certainly the prin-

---

4. Son of the Greek god Apollo. In Virgil's *Fourth Georgic*, Aristaeus seeks help from the sea nymph Thetis.
5. Hero of an *Arabian Nights* tale, a poor youth who discovers a robber's cave filled with treasure.   6. I.e., a "princess" of some shady level of society.   7. The male members of the French royal family, such as the Comte de Paris. The spirit of the times was anti-Royalist, and in fact all claimants to the French throne and their heirs were banished from France by law in 1886.   8. Fashionable London suburb. The French royal family had a house there.

cipal place. In the end they come to fill out so completely the curve of his cheeks, to follow so exactly the line of his nose, they blend so harmoniously in the sound of his voice as if it were no more than a transparent envelope, that each time we see the face or hear the voice it is these notions which we recognise and to which we listen. And so, no doubt, from the Swann they had constructed for themselves my family had left out, in their ignorance, a whole host of details of his life in the world of fashion, details which caused other people, when they met him, to see all the graces enthroned in his face and stopping at the line of his aquiline nose as at a natural frontier; but they had contrived also to put into this face divested of all glamour, vacant and roomy as an untenanted house, to plant in the depths of these undervalued eyes, a lingering residuum, vague but not unpleasing—half-memory and half-oblivion—of idle hours spent together after our weekly dinners, round the card-table or in the garden, during our companionable country life. Our friend's corporeal envelope had been so well lined with this residuum, as well as various earlier memories of his parents, that their own special Swann had become to my family a complete and living creature; so that even now I have the feeling of leaving someone I know for another quite different person when, going back in memory, I pass from the Swann whom I knew later and more intimately to this early Swann—this early Swann in whom I can distinguish the charming mistakes of my youth, and who in fact is less like his successor than he is like the other people I knew at that time, as though one's life were a picture gallery in which all the portraits of any one period had a marked family likeness, a similar tonality—this early Swann abounding in leisure, fragrant with the scent of the great chestnut-tree, of baskets of raspberries and of a sprig of tarragon.

And yet one day, when my grandmother had gone to ask some favour of a lady whom she had known at the Sacré Cœur[9] (and with whom, because of our notions of caste, she had not cared to keep up any degree of intimacy in spite of several common interests), the Marquise de Villeparisis, of the famous house of Bouillon, this lady had said to her:

"I believe you know M. Swann very well; he's a great friend of my nephews, the des Laumes."[1]

My grandmother had returned from the call full of praise for the house, which overlooked some gardens, and in which Mme de Villeparisis had advised her to rent a flat, and also for a repairing tailor and his daughter who kept a little shop in the courtyard, into which she had gone to ask them to put a stitch in her skirt, which she had torn on the staircase. My grandmother had found these people perfectly charming: the girl, she said, was a jewel, and the tailor the best and most distinguished man she had ever seen. For in her eyes distinction was a thing wholly independent of social position. She was in ecstasies over some answer the tailor had made to her, saying to Mamma:

"Sévigné[2] would not have put it better!" and, by way of contrast, of a nephew of Mme de Villeparisis whom she had met at the house:

9. A convent school in Paris, attended by daughters of the aristocracy and the wealthy bourgeoisie. 1. A fictional family. The Marquise de Villeparisis was a member of the Guermantes family. Proust enhances the apparent reality of the Guermantes by relating them to the historical house of Bouillon, a famous aristocratic family tracing its descent from the Middle Ages. 2. The Marquise de Sévigné (1626–1696), known for the lively style of her letters.

"My dear, he is so common!"

Now, the effect of the remark about Swann had been, not to raise him in my great-aunt's estimation, but to lower Mme de Villeparisis. It appeared that the deference which, on my grandmother's authority, we owed to Mme de Villeparisis imposed on her the reciprocal obligation to do nothing that would render her less worthy of our regard, and that she had failed in this duty by becoming aware of Swann's existence and in allowing members of her family to associate with him. "What! She knows Swann? A person who, you always made out, was related to Marshal MacMahon!"[3] This view of Swann's social position which prevailed in my family seemed to be confirmed later on by his marriage with a woman of the worst type, almost a prostitute, whom, to do him justice, he never attempted to introduce to us—for he continued to come to our house alone, though more and more seldom—but from whom they felt they could establish, on the assumption that he had found her there, the circle, unknown to them, in which he ordinarily moved.

But on one occasion my grandfather read in a newspaper that M. Swann was one of the most regular attendants at the Sunday luncheons given by the Duc de X——, whose father and uncle had been among our most prominent statesmen in the reign of Louis-Philippe.[4] Now my grandfather was curious to learn all the smallest details which might help him to take a mental share in the private lives of men like Molé, the Duc Pasquier, or the Duc de Broglie.[5] He was delighted to find that Swann associated with people who had known them. My great-aunt, on the other hand, interpreted this piece of news in a sense discreditable to Swann; for anyone who chose his associates outside the caste in which he had been born and bred, outside his "proper station," automatically lowered himself in her eyes. It seemed to her that such a one abdicated all claim to enjoy the fruits of the splendid connections with people of good position which prudent parents cultivate and store up for their children's benefit, and she had actually ceased to "see" the son of a lawyer of our acquaintance because he had married a "Highness" and had thereby stepped down—in her eyes—from the respectable position of a lawyer's son to that of those adventurers, upstart footmen or stable-boys mostly, to whom, we are told, queens have sometimes shown their favours. She objected, therefore, to my grandfather's plan of questioning Swann, when next he came to dine with us, about these people whose friendship with him we had discovered. At the same time my grandmother's two sisters, elderly spinsters who shared her nobility of character but lacked her intelligence, declared that they could not conceive what pleasure their brother-in-law could find in talking about such trifles. They were ladies of lofty aspirations, who for that reason were incapable of taking the least interest in what might be termed gossip, even if it had some historical import, or, generally speaking, in anything that was not directly associated with some aesthetic or virtuous object. So complete was their negation of interest in anything which seemed directly or indirectly connected with worldly matters that their sense of hearing—having finally come to realise its temporary futil-

3. Marshal of France (1808–1893), elected president of the French Republic in 1873.   4. King of France from 1830 to 1848, father of the Comte de Paris.   5. Duc Achille Charles Leonce Victor de Broglie (1785–1870) had a busy public career that ended in 1851. Comte Louis Mathieu Molé (1781–1855) held various cabinet positions before becoming premier of France in 1836. Duc Etienne Denis de Pasquier (1767–1862) also held important public positions up to 1837. All were active during the reign of Louis-Philippe.

ity when the tone of the conversation at the dinner-table became frivolous or merely mundane without the two old ladies' being able to guide it back to topics dear to themselves—would put its receptive organs into abeyance to the point of actually becoming atrophied. So that if my grandfather wished to attract the attention of the two sisters, he had to resort to some such physical stimuli as alienists adopt in dealing with their distracted patients: to wit, repeated taps on a glass with the blade of a knife, accompanied by a sharp word and a compelling glance, violent methods which these psychiatrists are apt to bring with them into their everyday life among the sane, either from force of professional habit or because they think the whole world a trifle mad.

Their interest grew, however, when, the day before Swann was to dine with us, and when he had made them a special present of a case of Asti, my great-aunt, who had in her hand a copy of the *Figaro* in which to the name of a picture then on view in a Corot exhibition were added the words, "from the collection of M. Charles Swann," asked: "Did you see that Swann is 'mentioned' in the *Figaro*?"[6]

"But I've always told you," said my grandmother, "that he had a great deal of taste."

"You would, of course," retorted my great-aunt, "say anything just to seem different from *us*." For, knowing that my grandmother never agreed with her, and not being quite confident that it was her own opinion which the rest of us invariably endorsed, she wished to extort from us a wholesale condemnation of my grandmother's views, against which she hoped to force us into solidarity with her own. But we sat silent. My grandmother's sisters having expressed a desire to mention to Swann this reference to him in the *Figaro,* my great-aunt dissuaded them. Whenever she saw in others an advantage, however trivial, which she herself lacked, she would persuade herself that it was no advantage at all, but a drawback, and would pity so as not to have to envy them.

"I don't think that would please him at all; I know very well that I should hate to see my name printed like that, as large as life, in the paper, and I shouldn't feel at all flattered if anyone spoke to me about it."

She did not, however, put any very great pressure upon my grandmother's sisters, for they, in their horror of vulgarity, had brought to such a fine art the concealment of a personal allusion in a wealth of ingenious circumlocution, that it would often pass unnoticed even by the person to whom it was addressed. As for my mother, her only thought was of trying to induce my father to speak to Swann, not about his wife but about his daughter, whom he worshipped, and for whose sake it was understood that he had ultimately made his unfortunate marriage.

"You need only say a word; just ask him how she is. It must be so very hard for him."

My father, however, was annoyed: "No, no; you have the most absurd ideas. It would be utterly ridiculous."

But the only one of us in whom the prospect of Swann's arrival gave rise to an unhappy foreboding was myself. This was because on the evenings

6. Leading Parisian newspaper. *Asti:* an Italian white wine. Jean Corot (1796–1875) was a French landscape painter, very popular at the time.

when there were visitors, or just M. Swann, in the house, Mamma did not come up to my room. I dined before the others, and afterwards came and sat at table until eight o'clock, when it was understood that I must go upstairs; that frail and precious kiss which Mamma used normally to bestow on me when I was in bed and just going to sleep had to be transported from the dining-room to my bedroom where I must keep it inviolate all the time that it took me to undress, without letting its sweet charm be broken, without letting its volatile essence diffuse itself and evaporate; and it was precisely on those very evenings when I needed to receive it with special care that I was obliged to take it, to snatch it brusquely and in public, without even having the time or the equanimity to bring to what I was doing the single-minded attention of lunatics who compel themselves to exclude all other thoughts from their minds while they are shutting a door, so that when the sickness of uncertainty sweeps over them again they can triumphantly oppose it with the recollection of the precise moment when they shut the door.

We were all in the garden when the double tinkle of the visitors' bell sounded shyly. Everyone knew that it must be Swann, and yet they looked at one another inquiringly and sent my grandmother to reconnoitre.

"See that you thank him intelligibly for the wine," my grandfather warned his two sisters-in-law. "You know how good it is, and the case is huge."

"Now, don't start whispering!" said my great-aunt. "How would you like to come into a house and find everyone muttering to themselves?"

"Ah! There's M. Swann," cried my father. "Let's ask him if he thinks it will be fine to-morrow."

My mother fancied that a word from her would wipe out all the distress which my family had contrived to cause Swann since his marriage. She found an opportunity to draw him aside for a moment. But I followed her: I could not bring myself to let her out of my sight while I felt that in a few minutes I should have to leave her in the dining-room and go up to my bed without the consoling thought, as on ordinary evenings, that she would come up later to kiss me.

"Now, M. Swann," she said, "do tell me about your daughter. I'm sure she already has a taste for beautiful things, like her papa."

"Come along and sit down here with us all on the verandah," said my grandfather, coming up to him. My mother had to abandon her quest, but managed to extract from the restriction itself a further delicate thought, like good poets whom the tyranny of rhyme forces into the discovery of their finest lines.

"We can talk about her again when we are by ourselves," she said, or rather whispered to Swann. "Only a mother is capable of understanding these things. I'm sure that hers would agree with me."

And so we all sat down round the iron table. I should have liked not to think of the hours of anguish which I should have to spend that evening alone in my room, without being able to go to sleep: I tried to convince myself that they were of no importance since I should have forgotten them next morning, and to fix my mind on thoughts of the future which would carry me, as on a bridge, across the terrifying abyss that yawned at my feet. But my mind, strained by this foreboding, distended like the look which I shot at my mother, would not allow any extraneous impression to enter. Thoughts did indeed enter it, but only on the condition that they left behind them every element of beauty, or even of humour, by which I might have been distracted or beguiled. As a surgical patient, thanks to a local anaesthetic, can look on fully conscious while an operation is being performed upon him and yet feel nothing, I could repeat to myself some favourite lines, or watch my grandfather's efforts to talk to Swann about the Duc d' Audiffret-Pasquier,[7] without being able to kindle any emotion from the one or amusement from the other. Hardly had my grandfather begun to question Swann about that orator when one of my grandmother's sisters, in whose ears the question echoed like a solemn but untimely silence which her natural politeness bade her interrupt, addressed the other with:

"Just fancy, Flora, I met a young Swedish governess today who told me some most interesting things about the co-operative movement in Scandinavia. We really must have her to dine here one evening."

"To be sure!" said her sister Flora, "but I haven't wasted my time either. I met such a clever old gentleman at M. Vinteuil's who knows Maubant[8] quite well, and Maubant has told him every little thing about how he gets up his parts. It's the most interesting thing I ever heard. He's a neighbour of M. Vinteuil's, and I never knew; and he is so nice besides."

"M. Vinteuil is not the only one who has nice neighbours," cried my aunt Céline in a voice that was loud because of shyness and forced because of premeditation, darting, as she spoke, what she called a "significant glance" at Swann. And my aunt Flora, who realised that this veiled utterance was Céline's way of thanking Swann for the Asti, looked at him also with a blend of congratulation and irony, either because she simply wished to underline her sister's little witticism, or because she envied Swann his having inspired it, or because she imagined that he was embarrassed, and could not help having a little fun at his expense.

"I think it would be worth while," Flora went on, "to have this old gentleman to dinner. When you get him going on Maubant or Mme Materna[9] he will talk for hours on end."

"That must be delightful," sighed my grandfather, in whose mind nature had unfortunately forgotten to include any capacity whatsoever for becoming passionately interested in the Swedish co-operative movement or in the methods employed by Maubant to get up his parts, just as it had forgotten to endow my grandmother's two sisters with a grain of that precious salt which one has oneself to "add to taste" in order to extract any savour from a narrative of the private life of Molé or of the Comte de Paris.

"By the way," said Swann to my grandfather, "what I was going to tell you has more to do than you might think with what you were asking me just now, for in some respects there has been very little change. I came across a passage in Saint-Simon[1] this morning which would have amused you. It's in the volume which covers his mission to Spain; not one of the best, little more in fact than a journal, but at least a wonderfully well written journal, which fairly distinguishes it from the tedious journals we feel bound to read morning and evening."

"I don't agree with you: there are some days when I find reading the papers

7. A fictitious nobleman. 8. Actor at the Comédie Française, the French national theater. M. Vinteuil is a fictitious composer and neighbor of the family. 9. Austrian soprano, who took part in the premiere of Wagner's *Ring* cycle at Bayreuth in 1876. 1. The memoirs of the Duc de Saint-Simon (1675–1755) describe court life and intrigue during the reigns of Louis XIV and Louis XV. He was sent to Spain in 1721 to arrange the marriage of Louis XV and the daughter of the king of Spain.

very pleasant indeed," my aunt Flora broke in, to show Swann that she had read the note about his Corot in the *Figaro*.

"Yes," aunt Céline went one better, "when they write about things or people in whom we are interested."

"I don't deny it," answered Swann in some bewilderment. "The fault I find with our journalism is that it forces us to take an interest in some fresh triviality or other every day, whereas only three or four books in a lifetime give us anything that is of real importance. Suppose that, every morning, when we tore the wrapper off our paper with fevered hands, a transmutation were to take place, and we were to find inside it—oh! I don't know; shall we say Pascal's *Pensées*?"[2] He articulated the title with an ironic emphasis so as not to appear pedantic. "And then, in the gilt and tooled volumes which we open once in ten years," he went on, showing that contempt for worldly matters which some men of the world like to affect, "we should read that the Queen of the Hellenes had arrived at Cannes, or that the Princesse de Léon had given a fancy dress ball. In that way we should arrive at a happy medium." But at once regretting that he had allowed himself to speak of serious matters even in jest, he added ironically: "What a fine conversation we're having! I can't think why we climb to these lofty heights," and then, turning to my grandfather: "Well, Saint-Simon tells how Maulévrier had had the audacity to try to shake hands with his sons.[3] You remember how he says of Maulévrier, 'Never did I find in that coarse bottle anything but ill-humour, boorishness, and folly.' "

"Coarse or not, I know bottles in which there is something very different," said Flora briskly, feeling bound to thank Swann as well as her sister, since the present of Asti had been addressed to them both. Céline laughed.

Swann was puzzled, but went on: " 'I cannot say whether it was ignorance or cozenage,' writes Saint-Simon. 'He tried to give his hand to my children. I noticed it in time to prevent him.' "

My grandfather was already in ecstasies over "ignorance or cozenage," but Mlle Céline—the name of Saint-Simon, a "man of letters," having arrested the complete paralysis of her auditory faculties—was indignant:

"What! You admire that? Well, that's a fine thing, I must say! But what's it supposed to mean? Isn't one man as good as the next? What difference can it make whether he's a duke or a groom so long as he's intelligent and kind? He had a fine way of bringing up his children, your Saint-Simon, if he didn't teach them to shake hands with all decent folk. Really and truly, it's abominable. And you dare to quote it!"

And my grandfather, utterly depressed, realising how futile it would be, against this opposition, to attempt to get Swann to tell him the stories which would have amused him, murmured to my mother: "Just tell me again that line of yours which always comforts me so much on these occasions. Oh, yes: 'What virtues, Lord, Thou makest us abhor!'[4] How good that is!"

I never took my eyes off my mother. I knew that when they were at table I should not be permitted to stay there for the whole of dinner-time, and

2. The "Thoughts" of the French mathematician and religious philosopher Blaise Pascal (1623–1662) are comments on the human condition and one of the triumphant works of French classicism. 3. Maulévrier was the French ambassador to Spain. Saint-Simon considered him of inferior birth, and refused to let his own children shake Maulévrier's hand (*Memoirs*, vol. XXXIX). 4. From *Pompey's Death* (line 1072), a tragedy by the French dramatist Pierre Corneille (1606–1684).

that Mamma, for fear of annoying my father, would not allow me to kiss her several times in public, as I would have done in my room. And so I promised myself that in the dining-room, as they began to eat and drink and as I felt the hour approach, I would put beforehand into this kiss, which was bound to be so brief and furtive, everything that my own efforts could muster, would carefully choose in advance the exact spot on her cheek where I would imprint it, and would so prepare my thoughts as to be able, thanks to these mental preliminaries, to consecrate the whole of the minute Mamma would grant me to the sensation of her cheek against my lips, as a painter who can have his subject for short sittings only prepares his palette, and from what he remembers and from rough notes does in advance everything which he possibly can do in the sitter's absence. But to-night, before the dinner-bell had sounded, my grandfather said with unconscious cruelty: "The little man looks tired; he'd better go up to bed. Besides, we're dining late to-night."

And my father, who was less scrupulous than my grandmother or my mother in observing the letter of a treaty, went on: "Yes; run along; off to bed."

I would have kissed Mamma then and there, but at that moment the dinner-bell rang.

"No, no, leave your mother alone. You've said good night to one another, that's enough. These exhibitions are absurd. Go on upstairs."

And so I must set forth without viaticum;[5] must climb each step of the staircase "against my heart," as the saying is, climbing in opposition to my heart's desire, which was to return to my mother, since she had not, by kissing me, given my heart leave to accompany me forth. That hateful staircase, up which I always went so sadly, gave out a smell of varnish which had, as it were, absorbed and crystallised the special quality of sorrow that I felt each evening, and made it perhaps even crueller to my sensibility because, when it assumed this olfactory guise, my intellect was powerless to resist it. When we have gone to sleep with a raging toothache and are conscious of it only as of a little girl whom we attempt, time after time, to pull out of the water, or a line of Molière[6] which we repeat incessantly to ourselves, it is a great relief to wake up, so that our intelligence can disentangle the idea of toothache from any artificial semblance of heroism or rhythmic cadence. It was the converse of this relief which I felt when my anguish at having to go up to my room invaded my consciousness in a manner infinitely more rapid, instantaneous almost, a manner at once insidious and brutal, through the inhalation—far more poisonous than moral penetration—of the smell of varnish peculiar to that staircase.

Once in my room I had to stop every loophole, to close the shutters, to dig my own grave as I turned down the bedclothes, to wrap myself in the shroud of my nightshirt. But before burying myself in the iron bed which had been placed there because, on summer nights, I was too hot among the rep curtains of the four-poster,[7] I was stirred to revolt, and attempted the desperate stratagem of a condemned prisoner. I wrote to my mother begging her to come upstairs for an important reason which I could not put in writing. My fear was that Françoise, my aunt's cook who used to be put in charge of

---

5. The communion wafer and wine given to the dying in Catholic rites. 6. French dramatist (1622–1673). 7. Bed with corner pillars to support a canopy and curtains. *Rep*: a heavy ribbed fabric.

me when I was at Combray, might refuse to take my note. I had a suspicion that, in her eyes, to carry a message to my mother when there was a guest would appear as flatly inconceivable as for the door-keeper of a theatre to hand a letter to an actor upon the stage. On the subject of things which might or might not be done she possessed a code at once imperious, abundant, subtle, and uncompromising on points themselves imperceptible or irrelevant, which gave it a resemblance to those ancient laws which combine such cruel ordinances as the massacre of infants at the breast with prohibitions of exaggerated refinement against "seething the kid in his mother's milk," or "eating of the sinew which is upon the hollow of the thigh."[8] This code, judging by the sudden obstinacy which she would put into her refusal to carry out certain of our instructions, seemed to have provided for social complexities and refinements of etiquette which nothing in Françoise's background or in her career as a servant in a village household could have put into her head; and we were obliged to assume that there was latent in her some past existence in the ancient history of France, noble and little understood, as in those manufacturing towns where old mansions still testify to their former courtly days, and chemical workers toil among delicately sculptured scenes from *Le Miracle de Théophile* or *Les quatre fils Aymon*.[9]

In this particular instance, the article of her code which made it highly improbable that—barring an outbreak of fire—Françoise would go down and disturb Mamma in the presence of M. Swann for so unimportant a person as myself was one embodying the respect she showed not only for the family (as for the dead, for the clergy, or for royalty), but also for the stranger within our gates; a respect which I should perhaps have found touching in a book, but which never failed to irritate me on her lips, because of the solemn and sentimental tones in which she would express it, and which irritated me more than usual this evening when the sacred character with which she invested the dinner-party might have the effect of making her decline to disturb its ceremonial. But to give myself a chance of success I had no hesitation in lying, telling her that it was not in the least myself who had wanted to write to Mamma, but Mamma who, on saying good night to me, had begged me not to forget to send her an answer about something she had asked me to look for, and that she would certainly be very angry if this note were not taken to her. I think that Françoise disbelieved me, for, like those primitive men whose senses were so much keener than our own, she could immediately detect, from signs imperceptible to the rest of us, the truth or falsehood of anything that we might wish to conceal from her. She studied the envelope for five minutes as though an examination of the paper itself and the look of my handwriting could enlighten her as to the nature of the contents, or tell her to which article of her code she ought to refer the matter. Then she went out with an air of resignation which seemed to imply: "It's hard lines on parents having a child like that."

A moment later she returned to say that they were still at the ice stage and that it was impossible for the butler to deliver the note at once, in front of everybody; but that when the finger-bowls were put round he would find a way of slipping it into Mamma's hand. At once my anxiety subsided; it was

8. Refers to the strict dietary laws of Deuteronomy 14.21 and Genesis 32.32, respectively.   9. The four sons of Aymon (French); heroic knights who together rode the magic horse Bayard. Théophile was saved from damnation by the Virgin Mary after having signed a pact with the Devil.

now no longer (as it had been a moment ago) until to-morrow that I had lost my mother, since my little note—though it would annoy her, no doubt, and doubly so because this stratagem would make me ridiculous in Swann's eyes—would at least admit me, invisible and enraptured, into the same room as herself, would whisper about me into her ear; since that forbidden and unfriendly dining-room, where but a moment ago the ice itself—with burned nuts in it—and the finger-bowls seemed to me to be concealing pleasures that were baleful and of a mortal sadness because Mamma was tasting of them while I was far away, had opened its doors to me and, like a ripe fruit which bursts through its skin, was going to pour out into my intoxicated heart the sweetness of Mamma's attention while she was reading what I had written. Now I was no longer separated from her; the barriers were down; an exquisite thread united us. Besides, that was not all: for surely Mamma would come.

As for the agony through which I had just passed, I imagined that Swann would have laughed heartily at it if he had read my letter and had guessed its purpose; whereas, on the contrary, as I was to learn in due course, a similar anguish[1] had been the bane of his life for many years, and no one perhaps could have understood my feelings at that moment so well as he; to him, the anguish that comes from knowing that the creature one adores is in some place of enjoyment where oneself is not and cannot follow—to him that anguish came through love, to which it is in a sense predestined, by which it will be seized upon and exploited; but when, as had befallen me, it possesses one's soul before love has yet entered into one's life, then it must drift, awaiting love's coming, vague and free, without precise attachment, at the disposal of one sentiment to-day, of another to-morrow, of filial piety or affection for a friend. And the joy with which I first bound myself apprentice, when Françoise returned to tell me that my letter would be delivered, Swann, too, had known well—that false joy which a friend or relative of the woman we love can give us, when, on his arrival at the house or theatre where she is to be found, for some ball or party or "first-night" at which he is to meet her, he sees us wandering outside, desperately awaiting some opportunity of communicating with her. He recognises us, greets us familiarly, and asks what we are doing there. And when we invent a story of having some urgent message to give to his relative or friend, he assures us that nothing could be simpler, takes us in at the door, and promises to send her down to us in five minutes. How we love him—as at that moment I loved Françoise—the good-natured intermediary who by a single word has made supportable, human, almost propitious the inconceivable, infernal scene of gaiety in the thick of which we had been imagining swarms of enemies, perverse and seductive, beguiling away from us, even making laugh at us, the woman we love! If we are to judge of them by him—this relative who has accosted us and who is himself an initiate in those cruel mysteries—then the other guests cannot be so very demoniacal. Those inaccessible and excruciating hours during which she was about to taste of unknown pleasures—suddenly, through an unexpected breach, we have broken into them; suddenly we can picture to ourselves, we possess, we intervene upon, we have almost created, one of the moments the succession of which would have composed those hours, a

---

1. I.e., his unhappy love for Odette de Crécy, described in *Swann in Love*.

moment as real as all the rest, if not actually more important to us because our mistress is more intensely a part of it: namely, the moment in which he goes to tell her that we are waiting below. And doubtless the other moments of the party would not have been so very different from this one, would be no more exquisite, no more calculated to make us suffer, since this kind friend has assured us that "Of course, she will be delighted to come down! It will be far more amusing for her to talk to you than to be bored up there." Alas! Swann had learned by experience that the good intentions of a third party are powerless to influence a woman who is annoyed to find herself pursued even into a ballroom by a man she does not love. Too often, the kind friend comes down again alone.

My mother did not appear, but without the slightest consideration for my self-respect (which depended upon her keeping up the fiction that she had asked me to let her know the result of my search for something or other) told Françoise to tell me, in so many words: "There is no answer"—words I have so often, since then, heard the hall-porters in grand hotels and the flunkeys in gambling-clubs and the like repeat to some poor girl who replies in bewilderment: "What! he said nothing? It's not possible. You did give him my letter, didn't you? Very well, I shall wait a little longer." And, just as she invariably protests that she does not need the extra gas which the porter offers to light for her, and sits on there, hearing nothing further except an occasional remark on the weather which the porter exchanges with a bell-hop whom he will send off suddenly, when he notices the time, to put some customer's wine on the ice, so, having declined Françoise's offer to make me some tea or to stay beside me, I let her go off again to the pantry, and lay down and shut my eyes, trying not to hear the voices of my family who were drinking their coffee in the garden.

But after a few seconds I realised that, by writing that note to Mamma, by approaching—at the risk of making her angry—so near to her that I felt I could reach out and grasp the moment in which I should see her again, I had cut myself off from the possibility of going to sleep until I actually had seen her, and my heart began to beat more and more painfully as I increased my agitation by ordering myself to keep calm and to acquiesce in my ill-fortune. Then, suddenly, my anxiety subsided, a feeling of intense happiness coursed through me, as when a strong medicine begins to take effect and one's pain vanishes: I had formed a resolution to abandon all attempts to go to sleep without seeing Mamma, had made up my mind to kiss her at all costs, even though this meant the certainty of being in disgrace with her for long afterwards—when she herself came up to bed. The calm which suc-ceeded my anguish filled me with an extraordinary exhilaration, no less than my sense of expectation, my thirst for and my fear of danger. Noiselessly I opened the window and sat down on the foot of my bed. I hardly dared to move in case they should hear me from below. Outside, things too seemed frozen, rapt in a mute intentness not to disturb the moonlight which, dupli-cating each of them and throwing it back by the extension in front of it of a shadow denser and more concrete than its substance, had made the whole landscape at once thinner and larger, like a map which, after being folded up, is spread out upon the ground. What had to move—a leaf of the chestnut-tree, for instance—moved. But its minute quivering, total, self-contained, finished down to its minutest gradation and its last delicate tremor, did not impinge upon the rest of the scene, did not merge with it, remained circumscribed. Exposed upon this surface of silence which absorbed nothing of them, the most distant sounds, those which must have come from gardens at the far end of the town, could be distinguished with such exact "finish" that the impression they gave of coming from a distance seemed due only to their "pianissimo" execution, like those movements on muted strings so well performed by the orchestra of the Conservatoire[2] that, even though one does not miss a single note, one thinks nonetheless that they are being played somewhere outside, a long way from the concert hall, so that all the old subscribers—my grandmother's sisters too, when Swann had given them his seats—used to strain their ears as if they had caught the distant approach of an army on the march, which had not yet rounded the corner of the Rue de Trévise.[3]

I was well aware that I had placed myself in a position than which none could be counted upon to involve me in graver consequences at my parents' hands; consequences far graver, indeed, than a stranger would have imagined, and such as (he would have thought) could follow only some really shameful misdemeanour. But in the upbringing which they had given me faults were not classified in the same order as in that of other children, and I had been taught to place at the head of the list (doubtless because there was no other class of faults from which I needed to be more carefully protected) those in which I can now distinguish the common feature that one succumbs to them by yielding to a nervous impulse. But such a phrase had never been uttered in my hearing; no one had yet accounted for my temptations in a way which might have led me to believe that there was some excuse for my giving in to them, or that I was actually incapable of holding out against them. Yet I could easily recognise this class of transgressions by the anguish of mind which preceded as well as by the rigour of the punishment which followed them; and I knew that what I had just done was in the same category as certain other sins for which I had been severely punished, though infinitely more serious than they. When I went out to meet my mother on her way up to bed, and when she saw that I had stayed up in order to say good night to her again in the passage, I should not be allowed to stay in the house a day longer, I should be packed off to school[4] next morning; so much was certain. Very well: had I been obliged, the next moment, to hurl myself out of the window, I should still have preferred such a fate. For what I wanted now was Mamma, to say good night to her. I had gone too far along the road which led to the fulfilment of this desire to be able to retrace my steps.

I could hear my parents' footsteps as they accompanied Swann to the gate, and when the clanging of the bell assured me that he had really gone, I crept to the window. Mamma was asking my father if he had thought the lobster good, and whether M. Swann had had a second helping of the coffee-and-pistachio ice. "I thought it rather so-so," she was saying. "Next time we shall have to try another flavour."

"I can't tell you," said my great-aunt, "what a change I find in Swann. He is quite antiquated!" She had grown so accustomed to seeing Swann always in the same stage of adolescence that it was a shock to her to find him

---

2. The national music conservatory in Paris. 3. A street in Combray. 4. I.e., boarding school.

suddenly less young than the age she still attributed to him. And the others too were beginning to remark in Swann that abnormal, excessive, shameful and deserved senescence of bachelors, of all those for whom it seems that the great day which knows no morrow must be longer than for other men, since for them it is void of promise, and from its dawn the moments steadily accumulate without any subsequent partition[5] among offspring.

"I fancy he has a lot of trouble with that wretched wife of his, who lives with a certain Monsieur de Charlus,[6] as all Combray knows. It's the talk of the town."

My mother observed that, in spite of this, he had looked much less unhappy of late. "And he doesn't nearly so often do that trick of his, so like his father, of wiping his eyes and drawing his hand across his forehead. I think myself that in his heart of hearts he no longer loves that woman."

"Why, of course he doesn't," answered my grandfather. "He wrote me a letter about it, ages ago, to which I took care to pay no attention, but it left no doubt as to his feelings, or at any rate his love, for his wife. Hullo! you two; you never thanked him for the Asti," he went on, turning to his sisters-in-law.

"What! we never thanked him? I think, between you and me, that I put it to him quite neatly," replied my aunt Flora.

"Yes, you managed it very well; I admired you for it," said my aunt Céline.

"But you did it very prettily, too."

"Yes; I was rather proud of my remark about 'nice neighbours.' "

"What! Do you call that thanking him?" shouted my grandfather. "I heard that all right, but devil take me if I guessed it was meant for Swann. You may be quite sure he never noticed it."

"Come, come; Swann isn't a fool. I'm sure he understood. You didn't expect me to tell him the number of bottles, or to guess what he paid for them."

My father and mother were left alone and sat down for a moment; then my father said: "Well, shall we go up to bed?"

"As you wish, dear, though I don't feel at all sleepy. I don't know why; it can't be the coffee-ice—it wasn't strong enough to keep me awake like this. But I see a light in the servants' hall: poor Françoise has been sitting up for me, so I'll get her to unhook me while you go and undress."

My mother opened the latticed door which led from the hall to the stair-case. Presently I heard her coming upstairs to close her window. I went quietly into the passage; my heart was beating so violently that I could hardly move, but at least it was throbbing no longer with anxiety, but with terror and joy. I saw in the well of the stair a light coming upwards, from Mamma's candle. Then I saw Mamma herself and I threw myself upon her. For an instant she looked at me in astonishment, not realising what could have happened. Then her face assumed an expression of anger. She said not a single word to me; and indeed I used to go for days on end without being spoken to, for far more venial offences than this. A single word from Mamma would have been an admission that further intercourse with me was within the bounds of possibility, and that might perhaps have appeared to me more terrible still, as indicating that, with such a punishment as was in store for

5. Sharing, as under a will.   6. Brother of the duc de Guermantes.

me, mere silence and black looks would have been puerile. A word from her then would have implied the false calm with which one addresses a servant to whom one has just decided to give notice; the kiss one bestows on a son who is being packed off to enlist, which would have been denied him if it had merely been a matter of being angry with him for a few days. But she heard my father coming from the dressing-room, where he had gone to take off his clothes, and, to avoid the "scene" which he would make if he saw me, she said to me in a voice half-stifled with anger: "Off you go at once. Do you want your father to see you waiting there like an idiot?"

But I implored her again: "Come and say good night to me," terrified as I saw the light from my father's candle already creeping up the wall, but also making use of his approach as a means of blackmail, in the hope that my mother, not wishing him to find me there, as find me he must if she continued to refuse me, would give in and say: "Go back to your room. I will come."

Too late: my father was upon us. Instinctively I murmured, though no one heard me, "I'm done for!"

I was not, however. My father used constantly to refuse to let me do things which were quite clearly allowed by the more liberal charters granted me by my mother and grandmother, because he paid no heed to "principles," and because for him there was no such thing as the "rule of law."[7] For some quite irrelevant reason, or for no reason at all, he would at the last moment prevent me from taking some particular walk, one so regular, so hallowed, that to deprive me of it was a clear breach of faith; or again, as he had done this evening, long before the appointed hour he would snap out: "Run along up to bed now; no excuses!" But at the same time, because he was devoid of principles (in my grandmother's sense), he could not, strictly speaking, be called intransigent. He looked at me for a moment with an air of surprise and annoyance, and then when Mamma had told him, not without some embarrassment, what had happened, said to her: "Go along with him, then. You said just now that you didn't feel very sleepy, so stay in his room for a little. I don't need anything."

"But, my dear," my mother answered timidly, "whether or not I feel sleepy is not the point; we mustn't let the child get into the habit . . ."

"There's no question of getting into a habit," said my father, with a shrug of the shoulders; "you can see quite well that the child is unhappy. After all, we aren't jailers. You'll end by making him ill, and a lot of good that will do. There are two beds in his room; tell Françoise to make up the big one for you, and stay with him for the rest of the night. Anyhow, I'm off to bed; I'm not so nervy as you. Good night."

It was impossible for me to thank my father; he would have been exasperated by what he called mawkishness. I stood there, not daring to move; he was still in front of us, a tall figure in his white nightshirt, crowned with the pink and violet cashmere scarf which he used to wrap around his head since he had begun to suffer from neuralgia, standing like Abraham in the engraving after Benozzo Gozzoli[8] which M. Swann had given me, telling Sarah that she must tear herself away from Isaac. Many years have passed since that

7. Reference to the *ius gentium*, the "law of nations" or natural law supposed to govern international and public relations. Marcel sees the relationship between himself and his mother and grandmother as a social contract; his father is the unpredictable tyrant. 8. Florentine painter (1420–1497) whose frescoes at Pisa contain scenes from the life of the biblical patriarch Abraham.

night. The wall of the staircase up which I had watched the light of his candle gradually climb was long ago demolished. And in myself, too, many things have perished which I imagined would last for ever, and new ones have arisen, giving birth to new sorrows and new joys which in those days I could not have foreseen, just as now the old are hard to understand. It is a long time, too, since my father has been able to say to Mamma: "Go along with the child." Never again will such moments be possible for me. But of late I have been increasingly able to catch, if I listen attentively, the sound of the sobs which I had the strength to control in my father's presence, and which broke out only when I found myself alone with Mamma. In reality their echo has never ceased; and it is only because life is now growing more and more quiet round about me that I hear them anew, like those convent bells which are so effectively drowned during the day by the noises of the street that one would suppose them to have stopped, until they ring out again through the silent evening air.

Mamma spent that night in my room: when I had just committed a sin so deadly that I expected to be banished from the household, my parents gave me a far greater concession than I could ever have won as the reward of a good deed. Even at the moment when it manifested itself in this crowning mercy, my father's behaviour towards me still retained that arbitrary and unwarranted quality which was so characteristic of him and which arose from the fact that his actions were generally dictated by chance expediencies rather than based on any formal plan. And perhaps even what I called his severity, when he sent me off to bed, deserved that title less than my mother's or my grandmother's attitude, for his nature, which in some respects differed more than theirs from my own, had probably prevented him from realising until then how wretched I was every evening, something which my mother and grandmother knew well; but they loved me enough to be unwilling to spare me that suffering, which they hoped to teach me to overcome, so as to reduce my nervous sensibility and to strengthen my will. Whereas my father, whose affection for me was of another kind, would not, I suspect, have had the same courage, for as soon as he had grasped the fact that I was unhappy he had said to my mother: "Go and comfort him."

Mamma stayed that night in my room, and it seemed that she did not wish to mar by recrimination those hours which were so different from anything that I had had a right to expect, for when Françoise (who guessed that something extraordinary must have happened when she saw Mamma sitting by my side, holding my hand and letting me cry unchided) said to her: "But, Madame, what is young master crying for?" she replied: "Why, Françoise, he doesn't know himself: it's his nerves. Make up the big bed for me quickly and then go off to your own." And thus for the first time my unhappiness was regarded no longer as a punishable offence but as an involuntary ailment which had been officially recognised, a nervous condition for which I was in no way responsible: I had the consolation of no longer having to mingle apprehensive scruples with the bitterness of my tears; I could weep henceforth without sin. I felt no small degree of pride, either, in Françoise's presence at this return to humane conditions which, not an hour after Mamma had refused to come up to my room and had sent the snubbing message that I was to go to sleep, raised me to the dignity of a grown-up person, brought me of a sudden to a sort of puberty of sorrow, a manumission of tears. I ought to have been happy; I was not. It struck me that my mother had just made a first concession which must have been painful to her, that it was a first abdication on her part from the ideal she had formed for me, and that for the first time she who was so brave had to confess herself beaten. It struck me that if I had just won a victory it was over her, that I had succeeded, as sickness or sorrow or age might have succeeded, in relaxing her will, in undermining her judgment; a black date in the calendar. And if I had dared now, I should have said to Mamma: "No, I don't want you to, you mustn't sleep here." But I was conscious of the practical wisdom, of what would nowadays be called the realism, with which she tempered the ardent idealism of my grandmother's nature, and I knew that now the mischief was done she would prefer to let me enjoy the soothing pleasure of her company, and not to disturb my father again. Certainly my mother's beautiful face seemed to shine again with youth that evening, as she sat gently holding my hands and trying to check my tears; but this was just what I felt should not have been; her anger would have saddened me less than this new gentleness, unknown to my childhood experience; I felt that I had with an impious and secret finger traced a first wrinkle upon her soul and brought out a first white hair on her head. This thought redoubled my sobs, and then I saw that Mamma, who had never allowed herself to indulge in any undue emotion with me, was suddenly overcome by my tears and had to struggle to keep back her own. When she realised that I had noticed this, she said to me with a smile: "Why, my little buttercup, my little canary-boy, he's going to make Mamma as silly as himself if this goes on. Look, since you can't sleep, and Mamma can't either, we mustn't go on in this stupid way; we must do something; I'll get one of your books." But I had none there. "Would you like me to get out the books now that your grandmother is going to give you for your birthday? Just think it over first, and don't be disappointed if there's nothing new for you then."

I was only too delighted, and Mamma went to fetch a parcel of books of which I could not distinguish, through the paper in which they were wrapped, any more than their short, wide format but which, even at this first glimpse, brief and obscure as it was, bade fair to eclipse already the paintbox of New Year's Day and the silkworms of the year before. The books were *La Mare au Diable*, *François le Champi*, *La Petite Fadette* and *Les Maîtres Sonneurs*.[9] My grandmother, as I learned afterwards, had at first chosen Musset's poems, a volume of Rousseau, and *Indiana*; for while she considered light reading as unwholesome as sweets and cakes, she did not reflect that the strong breath of genius might have upon the mind even of a child an influence at once more dangerous and less invigorating than that of fresh air and sea breezes upon his body. But when my father had almost called her an imbecile on learning the names of the books she proposed to give me,[1] she had journeyed back by herself to Jouy-le-Vicomte to the bookseller's, so that there should be no danger of my not having my present in time (it was a boiling hot day, and she had come home so unwell that the doctor had

9. Novels of idealized country life by the French woman writer George Sand (1806–1876). The titles can be translated as *The Devil's Pool, François the Foundling Discovered in the Fields, Little Fadette,* and *The Master Bellringers.*   1. The works of Alfred de Musset (1810–1857) and Jean-Jacques Rousseau (1712–1778), often romantic and sometimes confessional, and some works by Sand (*Indiana* was a novel of free love), would be thought unsuitable reading for a young child.

warned my mother not to allow her to tire herself so), and had fallen back upon the four pastoral novels of George Sand.

"My dear," she had said to Mamma, "I could not bring myself to give the child anything that was not well written."

The truth was that she could never permit herself to buy anything from which no intellectual profit was to be derived, above all the profit which fine things afford us by teaching us to seek our pleasures elsewhere than in the barren satisfaction of worldly wealth. Even when she had to make someone a present of the kind called "useful," when she had to give an armchair or some table-silver or a walking-stick, she would choose "antiques," as though their long desuetude had effaced from them any semblance of utility and fitted them rather to instruct us in the lives of the men of other days than to serve the common requirements of our own. She would have liked me to have in my room photographs of ancient buildings or of beautiful places. But at the moment of buying them, and for all that the subject of the picture had an aesthetic value, she would find that vulgarity and utility had too prominent a part in them, through the mechanical nature of their reproduction by photography. She attempted by a subterfuge, if not to eliminate altogether this commercial banality, at least to minimise it, to supplant it to a certain extent with what was art still, to introduce, as it were, several "thicknesses" of art: instead of photographs of Chartres Cathedral, of the Fountains of Saint-Cloud, or of Vesuvius, she would inquire of Swann whether some great painter had not depicted them, and preferred to give me photographs of "Chartres Cathedral" after Corot, of the "Fountains of Saint-Cloud" after Hubert Robert, and of "Vesuvius" after Turner,[2] which were a stage higher in the scale of art. But although the photographer had been prevented from reproducing directly these masterpieces or beauties of nature, and had there been replaced by a great artist, he resumed his odious position when it came to reproducing the artist's interpretation. Accordingly, having to reckon again with vulgarity, my grandmother would endeavour to postpone the moment of contact still further. She would ask Swann if the picture had not been engraved, preferring, when possible, old engravings with some interest of association apart from themselves, such, for example, as show us a masterpiece in a state in which we can no longer see it to-day (like Morghen's print of Leonardo's "Last Supper" before its defacement).[3] It must be admitted that the results of this method of interpreting the art of making presents were not always happy. The idea which I formed of Venice, from a drawing by Titian[4] which is supposed to have the lagoon in the background, was certainly far less accurate than what I should have derived from ordinary photographs. We could no longer keep count in the family (when my great-aunt wanted to draw up an indictment of my grandmother) of all the armchairs she had presented to married couples, young and old, which on a first attempt to sit down upon them had at once collapsed beneath the weight of their recipients. But my grandmother would have thought it sordid to concern herself too closely with the solidity of any piece of furniture in which

---

2. The famous volcano near Naples, painted by J. M. W. Turner (1775–1851). The Cathedral of Chartres, painted in 1830 by Corot. The fountains in the old park at Saint-Cloud, outside Paris, painted by Hubert Robert (1733–1809). 3. Leonardo da Vinci's *Last Supper* was the subject of a famous engraving by Morghen, a late-18th-century engraver. The paints in the original fresco had deteriorated rapidly, and a major restoration took place in the 19th century. 4. Venetian painter (1477–1576).

could still be discerned a flourish, a smile, a brave conceit of the past. And
even what in such pieces answered a material need, since it did so in a
manner to which we are no longer accustomed, charmed her like those old
forms of speech in which we can still see traces of a metaphor whose fine
point has been worn away by the rough usage of our modern tongue. As it
happened, the pastoral novels of George Sand which she was giving me for
my birthday were regular lumber-rooms full of expressions that have fallen
out of use and become quaint and picturesque, and are now only to be found
in country dialects. And my grandmother had bought them in preference to
other books, as she would more readily have taken a house with a gothic
dovecot or some other such piece of antiquity as will exert a benign influence
on the mind by giving it a hankering for impossible journeys through the
realms of time.

Mamma sat down by my bed; she had chosen *François le Champi,* whose
reddish cover and incomprehensible title[5] gave it, for me, a distinct personality and a mysterious attraction. I had not then read any real novels. I had
heard it said that George Sand was a typical novelist. This predisposed me
to imagine that *François le Champi* contained something inexpressibly delicious. The narrative devices designed to arouse curiosity or melt to pity,
certain modes of expression which disturb or sadden the reader, and which,
with a little experience, he may recognise as common to a great many novels,
seemed to me—for whom a new book was not one of a number of similar
objects but, as it were, a unique person, absolutely self-contained—simply
an intoxicating distillation of the peculiar essence of *François le Champi.*
Beneath the everyday incidents, the ordinary objects and common words, I
sensed a strange and individual tone of voice. The plot began to unfold: to
me it seemed all the more obscure because in those days, when I read, I
used often to daydream about something quite different for page after page.
And the gaps which this habit left in my knowledge of the story were widened
by the fact that when it was Mamma who was reading to me aloud she left
all the love-scenes out. And so all the odd changes which take place in the
relations between the miller's wife and the boy, changes which only the
gradual dawning of love can explain, seemed to me steeped in a mystery
the key to which (I readily believed) lay in that strange and mellifluous name
of *Champi,* which invested the boy who bore it, I had no idea why, with its
own vivid, ruddy, charming colour. If my mother was not a faithful reader,
she was none the less an admirable one, when reading a work in which she
found the note of true feeling, in the respectful simplicity of her interpretation and the beauty and sweetness of her voice. Even in ordinary life, when
it was not works of art but men and women whom she was moved to pity or
admire, it was touching to observe with what deference she would banish
from her voice, her gestures, from her whole conversation, now the note of
gaiety which might have distressed some mother who had once lost a child,
now the recollection of an event or anniversary which might have reminded
some old gentleman of the burden of his years, now the household topic
which might have bored some young man of letters. And so, when she read
aloud the prose of George Sand, prose which is everywhere redolent of that
generosity and moral distinction which Mamma had learned from my grand-

5. *Champi* ("foundling") is an old French word the child Marcel would not have known.

mother to place above all other qualities in life, and which I was not to teach her until much later to refrain from placing above all other qualities in literature too, taking pains to banish from her voice any pettiness or affectation which might have choked that powerful stream of language, she supplied all the natural tenderness, all the lavish sweetness which they demanded to sentences which seemed to have been composed for her voice and which were all, so to speak, within the compass of her sensibility. She found, to tackle them in the required tone, the warmth of feeling which pre-existed and dictated them, but which is not to be found in the words themselves, and by this means she smoothed away, as she read, any harshness or discordance in the tenses of verbs, endowing the imperfect and the preterite[6] with all the sweetness to be found in generosity, all the melancholy to be found in love, guiding the sentence that was drawing to a close towards the one that was about to begin, now hastening, now slackening the pace of the syllables so as to bring them, despite their differences of quantity, into a uniform rhythm, and breathing into this quite ordinary prose a kind of emotional life and continuity.

My aching heart was soothed; I let myself be borne upon the current of this gentle night on which I had my mother by my side. I knew that such a night could not be repeated; that the strongest desire I had in the world, namely, to keep my mother in my room through the sad hours of darkness, ran too much counter to general requirements and to the wishes of others for such a concession as had been granted me this evening to be anything but a rare and artificial exception. To-morrow night my anguish would return and Mamma would not stay by my side. But when my anguish was assuaged, I could no longer understand it; besides, to-morrow was still a long way off; I told myself that I should still have time to take preventive action, although that time could bring me no access of power since these things were in no way dependent upon the exercise of my will, and seemed not quite inevitable only because they were still separated from me by this short interval.

And so it was that, for a long time afterwards, when I lay awake at night and revived old memories of Combray, I saw no more of it than this sort of luminous panel, sharply defined against a vague and shadowy background, like the panels which the glow of a Bengal light[7] or a searchlight beam will cut out and illuminate in a building the other parts of which remain plunged in darkness: broad enough at its base, the little parlour, the dining-room, the opening of the dark path from which M. Swann, the unwitting author of my sufferings, would emerge, the hall through which I would journey to the first step of that staircase, so painful to climb, which constituted, all by itself, the slender cone of this irregular pyramid; and, at the summit, my bedroom, with the little passage through whose glazed[8] door Mamma would enter; in a word, seen always at the same evening hour, isolated from all its possible surroundings, detached and solitary against the dark background, the bare minimum of scenery necessary (like the decor one sees prescribed on the title-page of an old play, for its performance in the provinces) to the drama of my undressing; as though all Combray had consisted of but two floors joined by a slender

6. The imperfect is the tense of continued and incomplete action in the past, whereas the preterite describes a single completed action. 7. Fireworks. 8. I.e., with glass panes.

staircase, and as though there had been no time there but seven o'clock at night. I must own[9] that I could have assured any questioner that Combray did include other scenes and did exist at other hours than these. But since the facts which I should then have recalled would have been prompted only by voluntary memory, the memory of the intellect, and since the pictures which that kind of memory shows us preserve nothing of the past itself, I should never have had any wish to ponder over this residue of Combray. To me it was in reality all dead.

Permanently dead? Very possibly.

There is a large element of chance in these matters, and a second chance occurrence, that of our own death, often prevents us from awaiting for any length of time the favours of the first.

I feel that there is much to be said for the Celtic belief that the souls of those whom we have lost are held captive in some inferior being, in an animal, in a plant, in some inanimate object, and thus effectively lost to us until the day (which to many never comes) when we happen to pass by the tree or to obtain possession of the object which forms their prison.[1] Then they start and tremble, they call us by our name, and as soon as we have recognised their voice the spell is broken. Delivered by us, they have overcome death and return to share our life.

And so it is with our own past. It is a labour in vain to attempt to recapture it: all the efforts of our intellect must prove futile. The past is hidden somewhere outside the realm, beyond the reach of intellect, in some material object (in the sensation which that material object will give us) of which we have no inkling. And it depends on chance whether or not we come upon this object before we ourselves must die.

Many years had elapsed during which nothing of Combray, save what was comprised in the theatre and the drama of my going to bed there, had any existence for me, when one day in winter, on my return home, my mother, seeing that I was cold, offered me some tea, a thing I did not ordinarily take. I declined at first, and then, for no particular reason, changed my mind. She sent for one of those squat, plump little cakes called "petites madeleines," which look as though they had been moulded in the fluted valve of a scallop shell. And soon, mechanically, dispirited after a dreary day with the prospect of a depressing morrow, I raised to my lips a spoonful of the tea in which I had soaked a morsel of the cake. No sooner had the warm liquid mixed with the crumbs touched my palate than a shudder ran through me and I stopped, intent upon the extraordinary thing that was happening to me. An exquisite pleasure had invaded my senses, something isolated, detached, with no suggestion of its origin. And at once the vicissitudes of life had become indifferent to me, its disasters innocuous, its brevity illusory—this new sensation having had on me the effect which love has of filling me with a precious essence; or rather this essence was not in me, it *was* me. I had ceased now to feel mediocre, contingent, mortal. Whence could it have come to me, this all-powerful joy? I sensed that it was connected with the taste of the tea and the cake, but that it infinitely transcended those savours, could not, indeed, be of the same nature. Whence did it come? What did it mean? How could I seize and apprehend it?

9. Admit.   1. A belief attributed to Druids, the priests of the ancient Celtic peoples.

I drink a second mouthful, in which I find nothing more than in the first, then a third, which gives me rather less than the second. It is time to stop; the potion is losing its magic. It is plain that the truth I am seeking lies not in the cup but in myself. The drink has called it into being, but does not know it, and can only repeat indefinitely, with a progressive diminution of strength, the same message which I cannot interpret, though I hope at least to be able to call it forth again and to find it there presently, intact and at my disposal, for my final enlightenment. I put down the cup and examine my own mind. It alone can discover the truth. But how? What an abyss of uncertainty, whenever the mind feels overtaken by itself; when it, the seeker, is at the same time the dark region through which it must go seeking and where all its equipment will avail it nothing. Seek? More than that: create. It is face to face with something which does not yet exist, to which it alone can give reality and substance, which it alone can bring into the light of day.

And I begin again to ask myself what it could have been, this unremembered state which brought with it no logical proof, but the indisputable evidence, of its felicity, its reality, and in whose presence other states of consciousness melted and vanished. I decide to attempt to make it reappear. I retrace my thoughts to the moment at which I drank the first spoonful of tea. I rediscover the same state, illuminated by no fresh light. I ask my mind to make one further effort, to bring back once more the fleeting sensation. And so that nothing may interrupt it in its course I shut out every obstacle, every extraneous idea, I stop my ears and inhibit all attention against the sounds from the next room. And then, feeling that my mind is tiring itself without having any success to report, I compel it for a change to enjoy the distraction which I have just denied it, to think of other things, to rest and refresh itself before making a final effort. And then for the second time I clear an empty space in front of it; I place in position before my mind's eye the still recent taste of that first mouthful, and I feel something start within me, something that leaves its resting-place and attempts to rise, something that has been embedded like an anchor at a great depth; I do not know yet what it is, but I can feel it mounting slowly; I can measure the resistance, I can hear the echo of great spaces traversed.

Undoubtedly what is thus palpitating in the depths of my being must be the image, the visual memory which, being linked to that taste, is trying to follow it into my conscious mind. But its struggles are too far off, too confused and chaotic; scarcely can I perceive the neutral glow into which the elusive whirling medley of stirred-up colours is fused, and I cannot distinguish its form, cannot invite it, as the one possible interpreter, to translate for me the evidence of its contemporary, its inseparable paramour, the taste, cannot ask it to inform me what special circumstance is in question, from what period in my past life.

Will it ultimately reach the clear surface of my consciousness, this memory, this old, dead moment which the magnetism of an identical moment has travelled so far to importune, to disturb, to raise up out of the very depths of my being? I cannot tell. Now I feel nothing; it has stopped, has perhaps sunk back into its darkness, from which who can say whether it will ever rise again? Ten times over I must essay the task, must lean down over the abyss. And each time the cowardice that deters us from every difficult task, every important enterprise, has urged me to leave the thing alone, to drink my tea and to think merely of the worries of to-day and my hopes for to-morrow, which can be brooded over painlessly.

And suddenly the memory revealed itself. The taste was that of the little piece of madeleine which on Sunday mornings at Combray (because on those mornings I did not go out before mass), when I went to say good morning to her in her bedroom, my aunt Léonie used to give me, dipping it first in her own cup of tea or tisane. The sight of the little madeleine had recalled nothing to my mind before I tasted it; perhaps because I had so often seen such things in the meantime, without tasting them, on the trays in pastry-cooks' windows, that their image had dissociated itself from those Combray days to take its place among others more recent; perhaps because of those memories, so long abandoned and put out of mind, nothing now survived, everything was scattered; the shapes of things, including that of the little scallop-shell of pastry, so richly sensual under its severe, religious folds, were either obliterated or had been so long dormant as to have lost the power of expansion which would have allowed them to resume their place in my consciousness. But when from a long-distant past nothing subsists, after the people are dead, after the things are broken and scattered, taste and smell alone, more fragile but more enduring, more unsubstantial, more persistent, more faithful, remain poised a long time, like souls, remembering, waiting, hoping, amid the ruins of all the rest; and bear unflinchingly, in the tiny and almost impalpable drop of their essence, the vast structure of recollection.

And as soon as I had recognised the taste of the piece of madeleine[2] soaked in her decoction of lime-blossom which my aunt used to give me (although I did not yet know and must long postpone the discovery of why this memory made me so happy) immediately the old grey house upon the street, where her room was, rose up like a stage set to attach itself to the little pavilion opening on to the garden which had been built out behind it for my parents (the isolated segment which until that moment had been all that I could see); and with the house the town, from morning to night and in all weathers, the Square where I used to be sent before lunch, the streets along which I used to run errands, the country roads we took when it was fine. And as in the game wherein the Japanese amuse themselves by filling a porcelain bowl with water and steeping in it little pieces of paper which until then are without character or form, but, the moment they become wet, stretch and twist and take on colour and distinctive shape, become flowers or houses or people, solid and recognisable, so in that moment all the flowers in our garden and in M. Swann's park, and the water-lilies on the Vivonne[3] and the good folk of the village and their little dwellings and the parish church and the whole of Combray and its surroundings, taking shape and solidity, sprang into being, town and gardens alike, from my cup of tea.

2. A small, rich cookielike pastry.   3. The local river.

HIGUCHI ICHIYŌ

1872–1896

During the two and a half centuries that the Japanese people cocooned their islands in self-quarantine, comfortably assuming the world would go on just as it always had, beyond the archipelago philosophical, scientific, and technological developments transformed the face of Europe and almost everywhere that Europeans traveled. Fueled by the Industrial Revolution, trade finally propelled the "opening" of Japan. The U.S. government concluded that if official relations were established between the two countries, American whaling ships, which increasingly strayed into Japanese waters, could take provisions there. Japan, however, was not interested and rebuffed several overtures, until the United States resorted to gunboat diplomacy. In July 1853 a squadron of four ships that must have looked monstrous to a nation accustomed to wooden junks—two clipper ships and two ironclad steamships—sailed into Edo bay only forty miles south of the *shogun*'s capital and refused to leave until Commodore Matthew C. Perry had been accorded the chance to present his country's demands. Japan had little choice but to accede, recognizing superior military force and already uneasy at reports that China, its old mentor, had suffered defeat at the hands of the British in the recent Opium Wars.

Ironically, in a sense, Japan was right back where it had started. A thousand years earlier, it had discovered the material superiority of Chinese civilization and had labored hard to approximate China's achievements. Now, as the original model floundered, Japan struggled to remake itself anew as the equal of another materially advanced civilization. This time it did so less of its own volition than to preserve its independence.

In the process, what began as an attempt to compensate for a late technological start soon recast Japanese society. The government of the *shogun* and his *samurai,* in power since the seventeenth century, fell in favor of a constitutional monarchy, with a representative system of local government and a bicameral legislative assembly. A ministry of education was created to oversee the training of future generations of model citizens, military conscription was instituted, railways were laid, political parties founded, and newspapers began to circulate as an important component of the infrastructure of a modern state. "Advances" could be seen everywhere, from the new brick buildings several stories high to the streetlights and telegraph poles, racetracks and Italian circuses, or the bowler hats and petticoats the fashionable adopted as outward proof they were the equals of Parisians and Londoners. As the city of Tokyo grew into a modern metropolis, pawnshops proliferated and the number of rats was said to have multiplied by eight million. Virtually no certainty of daily life went unchallenged. It was debated, for example, whether Sunday should be observed as a day of rest. To do so might win Japan the approval of Christian nations but at the expense of valuable time lost in the race to catch up with these same adversaries.

When Westernization gripped Japan in the late nineteenth century, therefore, it seemed to carry all before it, including literature. The Japanese were ardent readers of every new translation: *Robinson Crusoe, Aesop's Fables, Hamlet, Around the World in Eighty Days, Crime and Punishment.* Aspiring writers looked to the example of European fiction, particularly products of the movement known as realism, to spark their efforts at crafting a new novel for Japan. After false starts, they began to write works that truthfully reflected the social situation and portrayed the subtlest feelings of contemporary, middle-class characters, ordinary people whose inner selves were drawn from objective and psychologically perceptive observations of real life.

Some of these writers were even fortunate enough to be sent abroad by the Japanese government. Natsume Sōseki (1867–1916), who taught English literature at Tokyo Imperial University before becoming a novelist, spent two years in London. Mori Ōgai (1862–1922), an army doctor and government adviser who translated the works of Shakespeare, Goethe, Rousseau, and others before establishing a separate career writing novels and short stories, spent four years as a foreign student in Leipzig, Munich, Dresden, and Berlin. Sōseki, Ōgai, and others returned to Japan eager to reinvent literature, just as their compatriots were remaking commerce and industry.

Thus the writers who pioneered the creation of the modern Japanese novel were individuals who, for the most part, benefited from the transformations taking place in Japan at the turn of the twentieth century. They were educated at the new Japanese universities, fully exposed to the latest intellectual currents and confident of their powers of articulation. Encouraged by the government to think of themselves as potential leaders of the new Japan, they found ready outlets for their talents and their advanced training. Viewing life as opening onto limitless opportunities, they had become worldly in ways unlike any previous generation in Japan.

From the perspective of European culture, the fact that a class of privileged, educated males should dominate literary ventures is not unusual. From the Japanese perspective, on the other hand, remembering the ranking role that women writers had played (at least intermittently) since the time of *The Pillow Book*, this male initiative in the sphere of cultural modernization could be read as yet another instance of Japanese success in emulating the West. There was, however, one important woman writer in the early years of Japan's modern period, and it would be no exaggeration to say that, in life and in art, she was everything the men were not.

Higuchi Ichiyō, who died at twenty-four from tuberculosis, had a brief, meteoric career that profited from none of the advantages enjoyed by her male counterparts. Her father, a hapless man of peasant stock who worked his way onto the lower rungs of the new Tokyo municipal bureaucracy and managed to purchase the status of a *samurai* less than a year before modernizing reforms did away with the military gentry, died when Ichiyō was seventeen. He left her, her younger sister, and her mother impoverished, for his last undertaking had been a bungled attempt to seize the spirit of the new age as an entrepreneur. He had no head for business, unfortunately, and sank his meager capital into a poorly run and possibly corrupt little enterprise that no sooner swallowed his funds than it went belly up.

The precocious Ichiyō* had been her father's favorite. While the family's straitened circumstances and Ichiyō's gender conspired to prevent her from receiving the Westernized education available to middle-class young men of the time, Ichiyō's father had indulged the budding prodigy as best he could. From an early age he taught her to recite his favorite poems and bought her abridged versions of the classics. When her mother, whose feet were not firmly planted in the modern era, insisted on withdrawing Ichiyō from grade school—too much book learning, she maintained, made a girl unfeminine—Ichiyō's father overrode his wife, at least partially, and enrolled Ichiyō in a poetic conservatory. Here, in a kind of traditional girls' finishing school, Ichiyō was able to cultivate her love of literature through lessons in the composition of classical poetry and lectures on cherished books like *The Tale of Genji*. And here, for a time, she was eventually able to serve as a teaching assistant, until the poverty that followed from her father's death finally forced Ichiyō into a radical break with the family's pretensions to middle-class respectability.

In the dog days of summer 1893, Ichiyō packed up her mother and sister and moved to the fringes of the red-light district. They had pawned everything they owned to open a shop that sold candy and balloons in an alley behind the brothels. Here, in one of the poorest neighborhoods of Tokyo, where very little idea of Western civilization penetrated, Ichiyō discovered the material for great fiction. It was a world modernization had left behind, populated by throwbacks to Japan's secluded centuries: threadbare merchants and day laborers, fortune-tellers and ne'er-do-wells, jugglers and minstrels, and all sorts of hangers-on who eked out a living catering to the so-called "pleasure quarter" on the other side of the ditch. It was, in short, part of

---

*Note that names are given in the Japanese order, with surname first. In the case of writers like Ichiyō, who replace their given names with pen names, Japanese convention designates them by the pen name rather than the surname—hence Ichiyō, not Higuchi.

the untold story of Japan's modern progress, where things had not changed after all and where the upheavals of recent history had left a number of people, like Ichiyō, on the brink of disaster.

Her education, so different from that of male writers, in the end served her well. And so did her isolation from their literary experiments. Ichiyō's grounding in classical Japanese literature made her receptive to the seventeenth-century fiction of Ihara Saikaku (see volume D, p. 588), whose rediscovery led to the publication of his complete works just as Ichiyō moved to her new plebeian neighborhood, coincidentally the same turf that Saikaku had depicted with such brilliance.

Until the move in 1893, when Ichiyō was twenty-one years old, she had published a handful of stories that could best be described as sentimental tales of unrequited love. The pale, well-born characters, whose quivering sensibilities make them sound like refugees from the classical past, were as bogus as Ichiyō's one-time claim to belong to their stratum of society. Now she found characters with blood flowing through their veins, whose struggles she understood as her own. And now life presented true variety, for the environs of the red-light district were a complex realm, a microcosm of contradictory parts. The walled-off pleasure quarter loomed like a stage set, exuding extravagance and ostentation, wit and artifice. Its values colored this rough neighborhood, where people strove to match the fast-talking ways of the courtesans and their stylish suitors, and even the youngest members of the back streets wanted to be cool. It was a part of town, in other words, where luxury, sophistication, and joie de vivre coexisted with sham, naïveté, and the starkest hand-to-mouth struggle to keep going. It may have been the periphery of a modern metropolis, and a tawdry one, but in his tales of prostitutes and moneylenders Saikaku had already anointed it a fit subject for literature.

In *Child's Play*, Ichiyō follows his lead. She recounts the story of a group of adolescents on the verge of adulthood, growing up in the alleyways behind the brothels. When the story begins, they are still children; by the time it ends, they have lost their innocence, and their fates have come into focus. The heroine will become a prostitute, and her best friend, a pawnbroker. Self-consciousness encroaches on their lives, and the new anxieties it brings eat away at their childhood friendships. One by one, entering adolescence as though it were a cave, the once carefree children retreat to their private crannies. The approach of adulthood brings uncertainty, yearning, and loneliness.

Child's Play is a remarkable group portrait that captures with a stunning sense of place a generation at its first moment of disillusionment. It never patronizes its young subjects, nor does it strive to be modern or relevant. (Indeed, the story's language, in the Japanese, is distinctly old-fashioned.) Yet Ichiyō succeeds in a way that male writers of the same period, setting off halfway around the world for literary inspiration, often do not. It is not surprising that this story is sometimes read as an implicit comment on Japan's own troubled passage from the innocence of a simpler time into the precarious world of modernity.

Child's Play made Ichiyō famous. She had already published a dozen stories in various literary magazines, but this is the one that everybody noticed. Mori Ōgai and other leaders of the literary establishment were astonished by the fresh talent of a writer unschooled in Western fiction, and the general public was equally enthusiastic. One member of the newly formed Higuchi Ichiyō Fan Club traveled from Osaka to invite her to address their members. But by now her health was failing. Although Ichiyō managed to write several more stories—also about children or those on the fringes of society, people the successful adult world did not pay much attention to—she died within a year of the publication of *Child's Play*.

For a biography of Ichiyō, with excerpts from her diary and translations of nine short stories, see Robert Lyons Danly, *In the Shade of Spring Leaves* (1992). Recommended novels by Ichiyō's contemporaries include Marleigh Grayer Ryan, trans., *Japan's First Modern Novel: "Ukigumo" of Futabatei Shimei* (1990); Mori Ōgai, *The*

Wild Geese (1959); Natsume Sōseki, *Kokoro* (1957); and Natsume Sōseki, *Grass on the Wayside* (1990). An extensive history of modern Japanese literature can be found in Donald Keene, *Dawn to the West* (1984).

PRONOUNCING GLOSSARY

The following list uses common English syllables to provide rough equivalents of selected words whose pronunciation may be unfamiliar to the general reader.

Chōkichi: *choh-kee-chee*

Daikokuya: *dai-koh-koo-yah*

Higuchi Ichiyō: *hee-goo-chee ee-chee-yoh*

Ihara Saikaku: *ee-hah-rah sai-kah-koo*

Ikueisha: *ee-koo-ay-shah*

Kii: *kee-ee*

kumade: *koo-mah-de*

Mori Ōgai: *moh-ree oh-gai*

Murasaki: *moo-rah-sah-kee*

Natsume Sōseki: *nah-tsoo-me soh-se-kee*

Nobuyuki: *noh-boo-yoo-kee*

Ōmaki: *oh-mah-kee*

Ryūge: *ryoo-ge*

Senzoku: *sen-zoh-koo*

Shōta: *shoh-tah*

Ushimatsu: *oo-shee-mah-tsoo*

Child's Play[1]

It's a long way round to the front of the quarter,[2] where the trailing branches of the willow tree bid farewell to the nighttime revellers and the bawdyhouse lights flicker in the moat, dark as the dye that blackens the smiles of the Yoshiwara beauties.[3] From the third-floor rooms of the lofty houses[4] the all but palpable music and laughter spill down into the side street. Who knows how these great establishments prosper? The rickshaws pull up night and day.

They call this part of town beyond the quarter "in front of Daion Temple." The name may sound a little saintly, but those who live in the area will tell you it's a lively place. Turn the corner at Mishima Shrine and you don't find any mansions, just tenements of ten or twenty houses, where eaves have long begun to sag and shutters only close halfway. It is not a spot for trade to flourish.

Outside the tumble-down houses everyone works madly: cutting up paper into queer little pieces, slopping them with paint, spearing them on funny-looking spits. Whole families, the whole neighborhood is wrapped up in the production of these strange, bright paper skewers. They dry the painted scraps in the morning and assemble them at night. And what are these things that have everyone so preoccupied? "You don't know?" a merchant will reply

---

1. Translated by Robert Lyons Danly.　2. Yoshiwara, the red-light district on the outskirts of Tokyo. Like Storyville in New Orleans before World War II, such red-light districts in Japan were the common adjunct to a social system that sheltered its "respectable" women—virtuous daughters, chaste wives, and good mothers.　3. The prostitutes follow the ancient aristocratic custom of staining their teeth jet black. 4. In contrast to the sorry sight beyond the confines of the quarter—where most of *Child's Play* is set—the three-story buildings within the red-light district itself suggest, for their time (the 1890s), great opulence. Besides Western-style buildings in central Tokyo, structures of more than two stories would still have been rare. The brothels, with their electric lights and gaiety and sheer height, were imposing edifices to the people who lived on the other side of the moat.

in astonishment. "*Kumade* charms! On Otori day,[5] you ought to see the big-wishers buy them up!"

Year in, year out, the minute the New Year pine bough comes down from the front gate, every self-respecting businessman takes up the same sideline, and by summer hands and feet are splattered with paint. They count on the earnings to buy new clothes for the holidays. If the gods grant prosperity to mere purchasers of these charms, the men who make them figure they stand to reap a windfall. Funny thing, no one hears of any rich men dwelling in these parts.

Most of the people here, in fact, have some connection with the quarter. The menfolk do odd jobs at the less dignified houses. You can hear them in the evenings jiggling their shoe-check tags[6] before they leave for work, and you'll see them putting on their jackets when most men take them off. Wives rub good-luck flints behind them to protect their men from harm. Could this be the final parting? It's a dangerous business. Innocent bystanders get killed when there's a brawl in one of the houses. And look out if you ever foil the double suicide of a courtesan and her lover! Yet off the husbands go to risk their lives each night like schoolboys to a picnic.

Daughters, too, are involved in the quarter: here, a serving girl in one of the great establishments; there, an escort plying back and forth between the teahouse and the brothel. They bustle along with their shop's lantern, an advertisement for all to see. But what will become of these girls once they have graduated from their present course of training? To them, the work is something grand and gala, as if they were performing on a fine wooden stage. Then one day before they know it they have reached the age of thirty, trim and tidy in their cotton coats with matching dresses and their sensible dark blue stockings. They carry their little packages under their arms, and we know what *these* are without asking. Stomp, stomp, they go with the heels of their sandals—they're in an awful hurry—and the flimsy drawbridges flop down across the ditch. "We'll leave it here at the back," they say, setting down their bundles, "it's too far round to the front." So they are needle-women now, apparently.

Customs here are indeed a little different. You won't find many women who tie their sashes neatly behind their waists. It's one thing to see a woman of a certain age who favors gaudy patterns, or a sash cut immoderately wide. It's quite another to see these barefaced girls of fifteen or sixteen, all decked out in flashy clothes and blowing on bladder cherries,[7] which everybody knows are used as contraceptives. But that's what kind of neighborhood it is. A trollop who yesterday went by the name of some heroine in *The Tale of Genji* at one of the third-rate houses along the ditch today runs off with a thug. They open a lean-to bar, though neither of them knows the first thing about running a business. They soon go broke. The beauty begins to miss her former calling. Her assets are gone with the chopped-up chicken bones

---

5. There were two or three Otori days each November, when fairs were held at various shrines in Tokyo. The largest shrine was just outside the red-light district. On fair days the side gates to the quarter were thrown open, and women and children were allowed in to see the sights. Otori was written with the character for "bird," the tenth sign of the Chinese zodiac, under which the Otori days always fell. Thus the number of fair days depended on how many days in November fell under the bird sign. Through a pun on the word for "take," a homonym, Otori day became the day of "taking" good luck; hence the sale of *kumade* charms. *Kumade*: "bear's claws"; good-luck charms named for their five-pronged shape.   6. Shoes were removed upon entering a brothel.   7. *Hōzuki*, Chinese lantern plant (or winter cherry), which bears fruit enclosed in an inflated orange-red calyx that resembles a miniature paper lantern.

left from last night's hors d'oeuvres. Unlike the chicken, however, our charmer can still return to her old nest. People around here, for some reason, find this kind of woman more alluring than your ordinary one.

In such a world, how are the children to escape being influenced? Take the autumn festival.[8] Mother Meng would be scandalized at the speed with which they learn to mimic all the famous clowns; why, there's not a one of them who can't do Rohachi and Eiki.[9] They hear their performances praised, and that night the smart alecks repeat their rounds. It starts at the age of seven or eight, this audacity, and by the time they're fifteen! Towels from the evening bath dangle from their shoulders, and the latest song, in a nasal twang of disrespect, dribbles from the corner of their lips. At school, any moment, a proper music class is apt to lapse into the rhythms of the quarter. Athletic meets ring with the songs of geisha[1]—who needs the school cheer? One sympathizes with their teachers, who toil at the Ikueisha, not far from here. It may be a crowded little schoolhouse—a private school, actually[2]— but the students number close to a thousand, and the teachers who are popular there soon become known. In these parts, the very word *school* is synonymous with the Ikueisha.

Listen to them walking home from school: "Your father sure keeps an eye on the teahouse by the bridge!" they shout at the fireman's boy. It's the wisdom of the street. Children know about the quarter. They scramble over garden walls, imitating firemen. "Hey! You broke the spikes on the fence to keep the thieves away!" A two-bit shyster's son begins his prosecution: "Your old man's a 'horse,' isn't he? Isn't he?" The blood rushes to the defendant's face. The poor boy—he'd sooner die than admit his father collected bills for a brothel. And then there are the favorite sons of the big shots of the quarter, who grow up in lodgings at some remove, free to feign a noble birth. They sport the latest prep-school cap, they have a look of leisure, and they wear their European clothes with style and panache. All the same, it's amusing to watch the others curry favor. "Young master, young master," they call them, when "spoiled brat" would do.

Among the many students at the Ikueisha was Nobuyuki of Ryūge Temple.[3] In time, his thick, black hair would be shorn, and he would don the dark robes of a priest. It may well have been his own choice, and then again perhaps he had resigned himself to fate. His father was a cleric, and already like his father Nobu was a scholar. By nature he was a quiet boy. His classmates considered him a wet blanket and they liked to tease him. "Here— this is your line of work," they would laugh, stringing up a dead cat. "How about offering the last rites?" All that was in the past, however; no one made

8. A lively festival in the red-light district. Entertainers would dance through the streets of the quarter, making the rounds of the teahouses and brothels whose patronage they had enjoyed during the year. For several days, the Yoshiwara assumed even more color than usual. Lanterns shaped like morning glories were hung before the brothels. In the evening, festival floats would parade down the main street of the quarter, each float fitted with a stage on which dances and comic skits were performed. The children of the neighborhood took it all in.   9. The late-19th-century Japanese equivalent of popular comedians. Mother Meng was the mother of the Chinese philosopher Mencius (ca. 372–289 B.C.); legend portrays her as meticulous in her child rearing.   1. "Practitioner of arts" (literal trans.); a professional female entertainer hired primarily for companionship during meals or parties for men. She was trained to sing or dance selections from the classical repertoire; she was not a prostitute, although she might have sexual relations with chosen patrons.   2. In this period, when the Japanese government devoted a good deal of attention to developing a modern public secondary school system, it was the public school that was usually superior to the private. The implication is that the Ikueisha is an overcrowded, second-rate school for a down-at-the-heels neighborhood, a point that has significance later in the story.   3. That is, Nobuyuki lives at Ryūge Temple, where his father is the priest.

fun of him now, not even by mistake. He was fifteen and of average height, his dark hair was closely cropped in schoolboy fashion, and yet something about him was different from the others. Although he had the ordinary-sounding name of Fujimoto Nobuyuki, already in his manner were suggestions of the cloth.

The Festival of Senzoku Shrine was set for the twentieth of August, and not a block would there be without a float of its own jostling for glory. Over the ditch and up the side of the embankment they charge: all the young men, pushing, pulling, bent on taking the quarter. The heart beats faster at the mere thought of it. And keep an eye, mind you, on the young ones—once they get wind of what the older boys are up to. Matching kimonos for the whole gang are only the beginning. The saucy things they dream up will give you goose bumps.

The back-street gang, as they preferred to call themselves, had Chōkichi for their leader. He was the fire chief's son—sixteen and full of it. He hadn't walked without his chest puffed out since the day he started policing the fall festival with his father: baton swinging, belt low around the hips, sneering whenever he answered. The firemen's wives all griped among themselves, "If he weren't the chief's boy, he'd never get away with it."

Selfish Chōkichi saw to it that he always got his way. He stretched his side-street influence wider than it really went, until in Shōta, the leader of the main-street gang, Chōkichi knew that he had met his match. Though Shōta was three years younger, he was the son of Tanaka, the pawnbroker; his family had money, he was a likable boy. Chōkichi went to the Ikueisha; Shōta, to a fancy public school. The school songs they sang may have been the same, but Shōta always made a face, as if Chōkichi and his friends at the Ikueisha were poor relations.

With his band of admirers—even some grown-ups numbered among them—for the last two years Shōta's plans for the festival had flowered more luxuriantly than the efforts of Chōkichi's gang. There had been no contest, and, if he lost again this year, all his threats—"Who do you think you're dealing with? Chōkichi from the back streets, that's who!"—would no longer garner even enough members for a swimming team at the Benten Ditch. If it were a matter of strength, he knew he would prevail, but everyone was taken in by Shōta's quiet ways and his good grades. It was mortifying—some of his own gang had gone over on the sly to Shōta's side. Tarokichi and Sangorō, for instance.

Now the festival was only two days away. It looked more and more as if Chōkichi would lose again. He was desperate. If he could just see that Shōta got a little egg on his face, it wouldn't matter if he himself lost an eye or a limb. He wouldn't have to suffer defeat any more if he could recruit the likes of Ushi, the son of the rickshawman, and Ben, whose family made hair ribbons, and Yasuke, the toymaker's boy. Ah, and better still: if he could get Nobu on his side—there was a fellow who'd have a good idea or two.

Near dusk on the evening of the eighteenth, hoping for a chance to persuade Nobu, Chōkichi made his cocky way through the bamboo thicket of the temple. Swatting the mosquitoes that swarmed about his face, he stole up to Nobu's room.

"Nobu? You there? I know people say I'm a roughneck, and maybe I am.

But it's no wonder, with the way they goad me. Listen, Nobu, I've had enough of them—ever since last year when that jerk from Shōta's gang picked a fight with my little brother and they all came running and jumped on him and threw him around. I mean, what do you think of something like that? Beating up a little kid and breaking his festival lantern! And then that Donkey from the dumpling shop, who's so big and awkward he thinks he can go around acting like a grown-up! He comes and starts insulting me to my brother behind my back. You know what he said? 'Think Chōkichi's so smart, huh? And your father's fire chief? Well, your big brother isn't head of anything. He's the tail end—a pig's tail end!' That's what he said! All this time I'm off in the parade, pulling our float. When I heard about it later, though, I was ready to get even! But my father found out, and *I'm* the one who got in trouble. And you remember the year before that, don't you? I went over to the paper shop, where a bunch of kids from the main street were putting on their slapstick.[4] You know what snide things they said to me? 'Doesn't the back street have its own games?' And all the while they're treating Shōta like king. I don't forget these things, Nobu . . . I don't care how much money he has. Who is he, anyway, but the son of a loan shark? I'd be doing the world a favor to get rid of such a creep. This year, no matter how tough I have to be, I'll see to it that Shōta eats his words. That's why, Nobu—come on—for a friend, you've got to help. I know you don't like this kind of rough stuff. But it's to get our honor back! Don't you want to help me smash that snooty Shōta with his stuck-up school songs? You know when they call me a stupid private-schooler, it goes for you too. So come on. Do me this one favor and help us out. Carry one of the lanterns around at the festival. Listen, I'm eating my heart out, this has been bothering me so much. If we lose this time, it'll be the end of me." Chōkichi's broad shoulders trembled with anger.

"But I'm not very strong."

"I don't care whether you're strong or not."

"I don't think I could carry one of the lanterns."

"You don't have to!"

"You'll lose even with me—you don't care?"

"If we lose, we lose. Look, you don't have to do anything. Just so you're on our side. All we have to do is show you off. It'll attract others. Build up our morale. I know I'm not very smart, but you are. So if they start using big words and making fun of us, you can answer right back in Chinese.[5] I feel better already. You're worth the whole lot of them! Thanks, Nobu." It wasn't often you heard Chōkichi speak so softly.

The one the son of a workman, with his boy's belt and his smart straw sandals; the other like a priest in his somber jacket and his purple band— they were the opposite sides of a coin. More often than not, the two boys disagreed. Yet it was true that Nobu's own parents had a soft spot for Chō-kichi. Why, the venerable Head Priest and his wife had heard Chōkichi's first cries as a babe outside the temple gate. And, after all, they did both go to the same school. If people made fun of the Ikueisha to Chōkichi, it reflected on Nobu too. It was a shame that Chōkichi wasn't better liked, but he never had been what you'd call appealing—unlike Shōta, who attracted

---

4. Improvised pantomimes or comic skits. The term is also one of depreciation, meaning "a farce" or "a waste of time." 5. A way to show off being smart.

everyone, even the older boys, for his allies. Nobu wasn't showing any prejudice. If Chōkichi lost, the blame would rest squarely on Shōta. When Chōkichi came to him like this, out of a sense of decency Nobu could hardly
refuse.

"All right. I'm on your side. But you'd better keep the fighting down . . . If
they start things, we won't have any choice. And if that happens, I'll wrap
Shōta around my little finger." Nobu's reticence had already been forgotten.
He opened his desk drawer and showed Chōkichi the prized Kokaji dagger[6]
his father had brought him from Kyōto.

"Say! That'll really cut!" Chōkichi admired.

Look out—careful how you wave that thing.

Undone, her hair would reach her feet. She wore it swept up and pulled into
a heavy-looking roll in the "red bear" style[7]—a frightening name for a
maiden's hairdo, but the latest fashion even among girls of good family. Her
skin was fair and her nose was nicely shaped. Her mouth, a little large perhaps, was firm and not at all unattractive. If you took her features one by
one, it is true, they were not the classic components of ideal beauty. And yet
she was a winsome girl, exuberant, soft-spoken. Her eyes radiated warmth
whenever she looked at you.

"I'd like to see her three years from now!" young men leaving the quarter
would remark when they noticed her returning from the morning bath, her
towel in hand and her neck a lovely white above her orange kimono of boldly
patterned butterflies and birds, her stylish sash wrapped high at the waist
and her lacquered slippers more thickly soled than what one usually saw,
even around here.

Her name was Midori and she was from the Daikokuya.[8] She was born in
Kishū, though, and her words had the slightest southern lilt. It was charming.
There were few who did not enjoy her generous, open nature.

For a child, Midori had a handsome pocketbook, thanks to her sister's
success in the quarter. The great lady's satellites[9] knew how to purchase good
will: "Here Midori, go buy yourself a doll," the manager would say. "It isn't
much, honey," one of the attendant girls would offer, "but it'll buy you a ball,
anyway." No one took these gifts very seriously, and the income Midori
accepted as her due. It was nothing for her to turn round and treat twenty
classmates to matching rubber balls. She had been known to delight her
friend the woman at the paper store by buying up every last shopworn trifle.
The extravagance day after day was certainly beyond the child's age or station. What would become of her? Her parents looked the other way, never
a word of caution.

And wasn't it odd, how the owner of her sister's house would spoil her so?
She was hardly his adopted child, or even a relation. Yet ever since he had
come to their home in the provinces to appraise her older sister, Midori and
her parents had found themselves here at the Daikokuya. They had packed
up their belongings, along with her sister, to seek their fortunes in the city.

What lay behind it all would be difficult to say, but today her parents were

---

6. One with the inscription of Kokaji Munechika, a renowned swordsmith from Kyoto.   7. A popular if
flamboyant hairstyle, consisting of a large chignon and flowered hairpins. It originated in the red-light
district.   8. The name of the brothel where her older sister is a prostitute.   9. The most successful
courtesans, like Midori's sister, had their own attendants.

housekeepers for the gentleman. On the side, her mother took in sewing from the women of the district; her father kept the books at a third-rate house. They saw to it that Midori went to school and that she learned her sewing and her music. The rest of the time she was on her own: lolling around her sister's rooms for half the day, playing in the streets the other half. Her head was full of the sounds of samisen[1] and drum, of the twilight reds and purples of the quarter. New to the city, Midori had bristled when the other girls made fun of her, calling her a country girl for wearing a lavender collar with her lined kimono. She had cried for three days then. Not now, though. It was Midori who would tease when someone seemed uncouth—"What kind of dress is that!"—and no one had quite the nimble wit to return her rebukes.

The festival was to be held on the twentieth, and this year they would have to outdo themselves. Midori's help was needed. "All right. Everyone plan something. We'll take a vote. I'll pay for everything," she responded with her usual generosity. "Don't worry about the cost."

The children were quicker than adults to seize an opportunity. The beneficent ruler seldom comes a second time.

"Let's do a show. We can borrow a shop where everyone can watch us."

"No—that's stupid! Let's build a little shrine to carry around. A good one like they have at Kabata's. Even if it's heavy, it won't matter, once we get it going to a nice beat."

"Yatchoi![2] Yatchoi!" danced a youth already in the mood, his towel twisted into a festive headband.

"What about us?" "You think Midori's going to have any fun just watching while you're all roughhousing?" "Come on, Midori, have them do something else." The girls, it seemed, would prefer to forgo the celebrations for an afternoon of vaudeville.

Shōta's handsome eyes lit up. "Why don't we do a magic lantern show?[3] I have a few pictures at my house. Midori, you can buy the rest. We can use the paper shop. I'll run the lantern, and Sangorō from the back street can be the narrator. What do you say, Midori? Wouldn't that be good?"

"I like it! If Sangorō does the talking, no one will be able to keep from laughing. Too bad we can't put a picture of him in the show."

Everything was decided. Shōta dashed around to get things ready.

By the next day, word of their plans had reached the back street.

The drums, the samisen! Even in a place never wanting for music, the festival is the liveliest time of year. What could rival it but Otori day? Just watch the shrines try to surpass one another in their celebrations.

The back-street and the main-street gangs each had their own matching outfits, Mōka cotton emblazoned with their street names. "But they're not as nice as last year's," some grumbled. Sleeves were tied up with flaxen cords stained yellow from a jasmine dye. The wider the bright ribbons, everyone

1. A three-stringed musical instrument, resembling the lute but with a longer neck. It became the most popular Japanese instrument, with large repertories of narrative and lyrical music, and thus a fixture of both the theater and the red-light district.   2. A shout of encouragement, stirring people to action or marking time when lifting a heavy object, such as a portable shrine carried in festivals.   3. Shadow pictures or shadowgraphs. Cutout pictures of people and animals were held up to a lantern and projected on a wall with accompanying humorous commentary, a popular form of entertainment in the days before motion pictures.

agreed, the better. Children under fifteen or so weren't satisfied until they had accumulated all the trinkets they could carry—Daruma dolls,[4] owls, dogs of papier-mâché. Some had eight or nine, even eleven, dangling from their yellow armbands. It was a sight to see them, bells of all sizes jingling from their backs as they ran along gamely in their stockinged feet.

Shōta stood apart from the crowd. Today he looked unusually dapper. His red-striped jacket and his dark-blue vest contrasted handsomely with his boyish complexion. He wore a pale blue sash wrapped tightly round the waist. A second look revealed it to be the most expensive crepe. The emblems on his collar were exceptional enough to draw attention by themselves. In his headband he had tucked a paper flower. Though his well-heeled feet beat time to the rhythm of the drums, Shōta did not join the ranks of any of the street musicians.

Festival eve had passed without incident. Now at dusk on this once-in-a-year holiday, twelve of the main-street gang were gathered at the paper shop. Only Midori, a long time with her evening toilette, had yet to appear. Shōta was getting impatient.

"What's taking her so long?" He paced in and out the front door. "Sangorō, go and get her. You've never been to the Daikokuya, though, have you? Call her from the garden, and she'll hear you. Hurry up."

"All right. I'll leave my lantern here. Shōta, keep an eye on it; someone might take the candle."

"Don't be such a cheapskate! Stop dawdling."

"I'm off." The boy didn't seem to mind being scolded by his juniors.

"There goes the god of lightning,"[5] someone said, and the girls all burst out laughing at the way he ran. He was short and beefy, and, with no neck to speak of, his bulging head suggested one of those wooden mallets. Protruding forehead, pug nose, big front teeth—no wonder he was called Bucktooth-Sangorō. He was decidedly dark-skinned, but what one noticed even more was the expression on his face, dimpled and affable and ready for the clown's role. His eyebrows were so oddly placed as to suggest the final outcome of a game of pin-the-tail-on-the-donkey. He was an amusing child, without a mean streak in him.

To those who did not know how poor he was, Sangorō shrugged off his everyday cotton clothes. "Couldn't get a matching kimono made in time."

He was the eldest of six children. Their father contrived to feed them all by clinging to the handles of a rickshaw. True, he worked the prosperous street in front of the quarter, lined with the teahouses. But somehow the wheels of his cart never turned a real profit. Fast as they spun, they only kept the family going hand-to-mouth.

"Now that you're thirteen, I'm counting on you to help out, boy," Sangorō's father had told him the year before last. He went to work at the printing shop over in Namiki but, in his lackadaisical way, in ten days he had tired of the job. Seldom did he last more than a month anywhere. From November to January he worked part-time making shuttlecocks for the New Year's games. In summer he helped the iceman near the hospital. Thanks to the comical way he had of soliciting customers, the two of them did a brisk business. A born hawker, the iceman said.

4. Dolls that represent the priest Bodhidarma, the founder of Zen Buddhism.   5. In the Buddhist pantheon, a swift-footed warrior named Idaten who chased down the thief of the Buddha's ashes.

Ever since he had pulled a float last year at the Yoshiwara carnival, his disapproving friends had dubbed him "Mannenchō." He was as bad, they said, as the jesters from that lowliest of slums. But everyone knew Sangorō was a buffoon. No one disliked him; this was his one advantage.

The pawnshop Shōta's people ran was a lifeline for Sangorō and his family, whose gratitude toward the Tanakas was no small thing. True, the daily interest rates they were obliged to pay bordered on the exorbitant; yet without the loans they could scarcely have kept going. How, then, could they begrudge the moneylender his due?

"Sangorō," Shōta and the main-street gang were forever urging him, "come over to our street and play." And how could he refuse Shōta, to whose family they were all indebted? On the other hand, he was born and raised in the back streets, he lived on land belonging to Ryūge Temple, Chōkichi's father owned their house. It wouldn't do to turn his back openly on Chōkichi. When in the end he quietly went over to the main street, the accusing looks were hard for him to bear.

Shōta sat down in the paper shop, tired of waiting for Midori, and began to sing the opening lines of "Secret Love."

"Listen to that!" laughed the shopkeeper's wife. "Singing love songs already—we'll have to keep an eye on this one."

Shōta's ears turned red. "Let's go!" he called to the others in a loud voice he hoped would cover his embarrassment. But as he ran out of the shop, he bumped into his grandmother.

"Shōta—why haven't you come home for dinner? I've been calling and calling, but you're so busy playing you don't even listen. You can all play again after dinner. Thanks," she added in a curt word of parting to the shopkeeper's wife.

Shōta had no choice but to follow her home.

Whenever he left, how lonely it seemed. Only one less person than before, and yet even the grown-ups missed Shōta. It was not that he was boisterous or always cracking jokes, like Sangorō. Such friendliness, though—you don't usually find it in a rich boy.

"But did you see the nasty way his grandmother has?" housewives gossiped on the street corner. "She's sixty-four if she's a day. And her hair done up like a young floozy! At least she doesn't wear all that powder any more."

"You ought to hear her purr and coax to get her loans back. Nothing stops her. You watch—the borrower could die, and she'd be at the funeral to collect. She's the kind who'll try to take her money with her when she goes."

"We can't even hold our heads up to her—that's the power of money."

"Don't you wish you had a little of it?"

"They say she even lends to the big houses in the quarter."

What they wouldn't give to know how much the old crone had.

"How sad it is for one who waits alone by the midnight hearth." The love songs do have a way of putting things.

The breeze felt cool on that summer evening. In the bath Midori had washed the heat of the day away, and now she stood before her full-length mirror getting ready. Her mother took charge of repairing the girl's hairdo. A beauty, even if she did say so, the woman thought, inspecting her daughter from every angle. "You still don't have enough powder on your neck." They had chosen for the occasion a silk kimono in a cool, pale blue. Her straw-colored sash was flecked with gold threads and custom-made to fit her tiny waist. It would be some time, though, before they could begin deciding on the proper sandals.

"Isn't she ready yet?" Sangorō was losing his patience. He had circled the garden wall seven times. How much longer could he go on yawning? The mosquitoes around here were a local specialty; no sooner had he brushed them away than they would buzz back again. A bite on the neck, a bite on the forehead. Just as he had had about all he could take, Midori finally appeared.

"Let's go," she said.

He pulled her sleeve without answering her and began to run.

Midori was soon out of breath. She could feel her heart pounding. "Well, if you're in such a hurry about it, go on ahead."

Sangorō arrived at the paper shop just before her. Shōta, it appeared, had gone home for dinner.

"This isn't going to be any fun. We can't start the lantern show without Shōta," Midori complained, turning to the shopkeeper's wife. "Any checkers? Cut-outs? We'll need *something* to keep us busy till he comes."

"Here we are." The girls immediately began to cut out the paper dolls the shop lady handed them.

The boys, with Sangorō in the lead, replayed entertainments from the Yoshiwara carnival. Their harmony was odd, but they knew the melodies:

> "Come see the thriving quarter—
> The lights, the lanterns under every eave,
> The gaiety of all five streets!"

In fact, they remembered perfectly the songs and dances of a year, two years before. They didn't miss a beat; they had every gesture down. A crowd gathered at the gate outside to watch the ten of them, carried away by their own side show.

"Is Sangorō there?" called a voice from among the onlookers. "Come here a minute, quick." It was Bunji, the hairdresser's boy.

"Just a second," yelled Sangorō without a care.

No sooner did he run through the doorway than someone punched him in the face. "You double-crosser! This'll teach you! Who do you think I am? Chōkichi! I'll make you sorry you ever made fun of us!"

Sangorō was dumbfounded. He tried to escape, but they grabbed him by the collar.

"Kill him! Shōta too! Don't let the chicken get away. And Donkey from the dumpling shop—don't think you're going to get off so easy!"

The uproar swelled like the rising tide. Paper lanterns came crashing down from the eaves.

"Mind the lamp. You mustn't fight in front of the shop." The woman's yell was loud enough, but who was listening?

There were fourteen or fifteen of them in the attack, streamers round the heads, their oversize lanterns swinging. Blows were struck in all directions, things trampled underfoot. The outrage of it! But Shōta—the one they were after—was nowhere to be found.

"Hide him, will you? Where is he? If you don't tell us, you'll answer for it." They closed in around Sangorō, hitting and kicking, until Midori couldn't stand to watch. She pushed her way to the front, past the restraining hand of the shopkeeper's wife.

"What are you taking it out on him for? If you want to fight with Shōta, fight with Shōta. He didn't run away and he's not hiding. He's not here, that's all. This is our place. Why do you have to go sticking your noses in? You're such a creep, Chōkichi. Why don't you leave Sangorō alone? There— you've knocked him down. Now stop it! If you want to hit someone, hit me. Don't try to hold me back," she turned to the shopkeeper's wife, shouting abuse at Chōkichi all the while she tried to free herself.

"Yeah? You're nothing but a whore, just like your sister," Chōkichi shot back. He stepped around from behind the others and grabbed his muddy sandal. "This is all you're worth." He threw it at Midori.

With a splatter, it struck her square on the forehead. She turned white, but the shopkeeper's wife held her back. "Don't. You'll get hurt."

"Serves you right," Chōkichi gloated. "By the way, guess who's joined our side. Nobu from Ryūge Temple! So try and get even any time you want." He left Sangorō lying in the shop's front door. "You fools! *Weak*lings! Cowards! We'll be waiting for you. Be careful when you walk through the back streets after dark."

Just then he heard the sound of a policeman's boots. Someone had squealed on them. "Come on!" As fast as they could, Ushimatsu, Bunji, and the ten or so others all scattered in different directions, crouching in hiding places among the alleyways until the coast was clear.

"Damn you, Chōkichi! You bastard. Damn you! Damn you, Bunji! Damn you, Ushimatsu! Why don't you just kill me? Come on. Just try and kill me. I'm Sangorō—and maybe it's not so easy! Even if you did kill me, even if I turned into a ghost, I'd haunt you for the rest of your lives. Remember that, Chōkichi!" Sangorō began to sob. Hot tears rolled down his cheeks. He looked as if he must be aching. His sleeves were torn. His back and hips were covered with dirt.

The force of his anger, beyond his power to control, kept the others back. But the shopkeeper's wife rushed over to him. "It's all right," she soothed him with a pat and helped him to his feet. She brushed the gravel from his clothes. "Don't be upset. There were just too many of them, the rest of us weren't much help, not even a grown-up could do anything. It wasn't a fair match—don't be ashamed. It's lucky you weren't hurt, but you won't be safe going home alone. I'll feel much better if the policeman takes you; it's a good thing he's come. Officer, let me tell you what happened."

As she finished her account, the policeman reached for the boy's hand in his professional way. "I'll take you home."

"No. I'm all right. I can go by myself." He seemed to cringe with shame.

"There's nothing to be afraid of. I'll just take you as far as your house. Don't worry." He smiled at Sangorō and patted him on the head.

But Sangorō shrank back farther. "If my father hears about the fight, I'll get in terrible trouble. Chōkichi's father owns our house."

"How about if I take you as far as the front gate? I won't say anything to get you into trouble." He managed to coax the downcast Sangorō and led him off toward home.

The others felt relieved. But as they watched the two depart, at the corner leading to the back streets, for some reason Sangorō shook loose and broke into a run.

It was as rare as snow falling from a summer sky, but today Midori couldn't brook the thought of school. She wouldn't eat her breakfast. Should they order something special? It couldn't be a cold, she had no fever. Too much excitement yesterday, probably. "Why don't you stay home?" her mother suggested. "I'll go to the shrine for you."

Midori wouldn't hear of it. It was *her* vow to Tarō-sama[6] for her sister's success. "I'll just go and come right back. Give me some money for the offering."

Off she went to the shrine among the paddy fields. She rang the bell, shaped like the great mouth of a crocodile, and clasped her hands in supplication. And what were they for, these prayers of hers? She walked through the fields with her head downcast, to and from the shrine.

Shōta saw her from a distance and called out as he ran toward her. He tugged at her sleeve, "Midori, I'm sorry about last night."

"That's all right. It wasn't your fault."

"But they were after me. If Grandmother hadn't come, I wouldn't have left. And then they wouldn't have beaten up Sangorō the way they did. I went to see him this morning. He was crying and furious. I got angry just listening to him talk about it. Chōkichi threw his sandal at you, didn't he? Damn him, anyway! There are limits to what even he can get away with. But I hope you're not mad at me, Midori. I didn't run away from him. I gulped my food down as fast as I could and was just on my way back when Grandmother said I had to watch the house while she went for her bath. That's when all the commotion must have started. Honest, I didn't know anything about it." He apologized as if the crime were his, not Chōkichi's. "Does it hurt?" Shōta examined Midori's forehead.

"Well, it's nothing that will leave a scar," Midori laughed. "But listen, Shōta, you mustn't tell anyone. If Mother ever found out, I'd get a real scolding. My parents never lay a hand on me. If they hear a dolt like Chōkichi smeared mud on my face with his filthy sandal—." She looked away.

"Please forgive me. It's all my fault. Please. Come on, cheer up. I won't be able to stand it if you're mad at me." Before they knew it, they had reached the back gate of Shōta's house. "Do you want to come in? No one's home. Grandmother's gone to collect the interest. It's lonely by myself. Come on, I'll show you those prints I told you about the other day. There are all kinds of them." Shōta wouldn't let go of her sleeve until Midori had agreed.

Inside the dilapidated gate was a small garden. Dwarf trees were lined up in their pots and from the eaves hung a tiny trellis of fern with a windbell, Shōta's memento from the holiday market. But who would have picked it for the wealthiest house in the neighborhood? Here alone by themselves lived an old woman and a boy. No one had ever broken in: there were cold, metal locks everywhere, and the neighboring tenements kept an eye on the place.

Shōta went in first and found a spot where the breeze blew. "Over here," he called to Midori, handing her a fan. For a thirteen-year-old, he was rather too sophisticated. He took out one color print after another. They had been in his family for generations, and he smiled when Midori admired them.

---

6. The deity celebrated at the local shrine. Midori prays to him for her sister's continued prosperity.

"Shall I show you a battledore?[7] It was my mother's. She got it when she worked for a rich man. Isn't it funny? It's so big. And look how different people's faces were in those days. I wish she were still alive . . . My mother died when I was three, and my father went back to his own family's place in the country. So I've been here with Grandmother ever since. You're lucky, Midori."

"Look out. You'll get the pictures wet. Boys aren't supposed to cry."

"I guess I'm a sissy. Sometimes I get to thinking about things . . . It's all right now, but in the winter, when the moon is out and I have to make the rounds in Tamachi collecting the interest, sometimes when I walk along the ditch, I sit down on the bank and cry. Not from the cold. I don't know why . . . I just think about things. I've been doing the collecting ever since year before last. Grandmother's getting old. It's not safe for her at night. And her eyes aren't so good any more. She can't see what she's doing when she has to put her seal on the receipts. We've had a lot of different men working for us. But Grandmother says they all take us for fools—when it's only an old lady and a boy they have to answer to. She's just waiting for the day when I'm a little older and we can open the pawnshop again. We'll put the family sign out in front, even if things aren't as good as they used to be. Oh, I know people say Grandmother's stingy. But she's only careful about things for my sake. It really bothers me, to hear them talk that way. I guess the people I collect from over in Tōrishinmachi are pretty bad off, all right. I suppose it's no wonder they say things about her. When I think about it, though, sometimes I just can't help it if I cry. I guess I am a weakling. This morning when I went to see Sangorō, he was sore all over, but he still went right on working so his father wouldn't find out about last night. I didn't know what to say. A boy looks pretty silly when he cries, doesn't he? That's why the back street makes fun of Sangorō." He seemed ashamed at his own unmanliness.

Occasionally their eyes would meet.

"You looked so handsome yesterday, Shōta. It made me wish I were a boy. You were the best dressed of them all."

"I looked good! *You* were beautiful! Everybody said you were prettier than any of the girls in the quarter, even your sister Ōmaki. Boy, I'd be proud if you were my sister! I'd hold my head up with a girl like you alongside me. But I don't have any brothers or sisters. Hey, Midori, what do you say we have our picture taken? I'll wear what I did yesterday and you can put on one of your best striped kimonos, and we'll have Katō in Suidōjiri take our picture! Won't Nobu be jealous! He'll turn white, he'll be so envious—a milquetoast like him wouldn't know how to turn red. Or maybe he'll just laugh at us. Who cares? If Katō takes a big one, he might use our picture in the window! What's the matter? Don't you like the idea? You don't look very excited." The boy's impatience was disarming.

"What if I look funny? You might not like me any more." Her laugh had a beautiful ring, her spirits had obviously improved.

The cool of the morning had given way to the summer sun. It was time for Midori to be going: "Shōta, why don't you come over this evening? We can float candles on the pond and chase the fish. It'll be easy now that the bridge is fixed."

Shōta beamed as he saw her out. What a beauty Midori was.

7. A rectangular-shaped paddle with a handle used to play shuttlecock, a game like badminton.

Nobu of Ryūge Temple and Midori of the Daikokuya both went to school at the Ikueisha. It had all started at the end of last April, at the spring athletic meet in Mizunoya-no-hara. The cherries had fallen and the wisteria was already in bloom in the shade of the new green leaves. They played their games of tug-of-war and catch and jump rope with such ardor that no one seemed to notice the sun going down. But what had come over Nobu? He had lost his usual composure. He stumbled over the root of a pine by the pond and landed hands-first in the red mud.

Midori, who happened to be going by, took one look at his dirty jacket and proffered her crimson handkerchief. "Here, you can wipe it off with this."

There were those, however, who were jealous of this attention from Midori. "For a priest's son, he sure knows how to flirt. Look at him smile when he thanks her! What's he going to do—take her for his wife? If she goes to live at the temple, then she really will be Miss Daikoku:[8] from Midori of the Daikokuya to Daikoku, goddess of the kitchen! That ought to suit a priest."

Nobu couldn't stomach all the talk. He had never been one to enjoy idle gossip and had always shunned tales about others. How, then, could he tolerate it when he found himself the target of the rumors? He began to dread hearing Midori's name. He was snappish whenever anyone mentioned field day. "You're not going to bring that up again, are you?" It never failed to put him in a bad mood. Yet what reason was there, really, for this loss of temper? He knew he would do better feigning indifference. A stoic face, wait it out, he told himself. He could silence his tormentors with a word or two, but the embarrassment was still there. A cold sweat followed every confrontation.

At first, Midori failed to notice any change. On her way home from school one day she called out with her usual friendliness. Nobu trailed behind amid a cluster of people. The blossoms at the roadside had caught her eye, and she waited for him to catch up. "See the pretty flowers, Nobu? I can't reach them. You're tall enough—won't you pick me some?"

She had singled him out from his younger companions. There was no escaping. He cringed at what he knew the others would be saying. Reaching for the nearest branch, without even choosing, he picked the first flower he saw, a token effort. He flung it at her and was gone.

"Well, if that's how he's going to be! Unsociable thing!"

After several of these incidents, it dawned on Midori: Nobu was being mean to her deliberately. He was never rude to any of the others, only her. When she approached, he fled. If she spoke to him, he became angry. He was sullen and self-conscious. Midori had no idea how to please him, and in the end she gave up trying. Let him be perverse; he was no friend of hers. See if she'd speak to him after he'd cut her to the quick. "Hello's" in the street were a thing of the past. It would take important business indeed before she would deign to talk to him. A great river now stretched between them that all boats were forbidden to cross. Each of them walked alone on separate banks of the stream.

---

8. A euphemism for the wife, or mistress, of a Buddhist priest, who until the modern period was expected to be celibate. The sobriquet derived sarcastically from Daikoku, one of the seven gods of good fortune and the patron saint of the pocketbook. Nobu's tormentors are also playing on the name of the brothel where Midori's sister is employed, the Daikokuya, itself no doubt named for the god of prosperity.

From the day after the festival, Midori came to school no more. She could wash the mud from her face, but the shame could not be scrubbed away so easily.

They sat together side by side at school—Chōkichi's gang and the main-street gang—and one might have expected that they could get along. But there had always been a sharp division.

It was the act of a coward to attack a weak, defenseless girl. Everyone knew Chōkichi was as violent and as stupid as they come. But if he hadn't had Nobu backing him, he could never have behaved so brazenly. And that Nobu! In front of others he pretended to be gentle and wise, but a look behind the scenes would reveal that *he* was the one pulling all the strings. Midori didn't care if he was ahead of her in school, or how good his grades were. So what if he was the young master of Ryūge Temple! She, after all, was Midori of the Daikokuya, and not beholden to him in the slightest. She had never borrowed a single sheet of paper. So who were they to call her a tramp, or those other names Chōkichi had used? She wasn't about to be impressed just because Ryūge Temple had a prominent parishioner or two.

What about the patrons her sister Ōmaki had? The banker Kawa, a steady customer for three years now; Yone, from the stock exchange; and that short one, the member of parliament—why, he'd been all set to buy her sister's contract and marry her, till Ōmaki decided she could do without him. And he was somebody! Just ask the lady who ran Ōmaki's house. Go ahead and ask, if you thought she was making it up. Where would the Daikokuya be without her sister? Why do you think even the owner of the house was never curt with Midori and her parents? Just take that porcelain statue of Daikoku, the one he kept in the alcove. Once when she was playing shuttlecock, she knocked over a vase accidentally and smashed the master's favorite statue to smithereens. He was sitting right in the next room drinking. And all he said was, "Midori, you're turning into a little tomboy." Not one word of reproach. Had it been anyone else, you can be sure, he wouldn't have stopped there. The maids were green with envy. No question about it, the child's privileges derived from her sister's position. Midori knew it, too. Her parents were mere caretakers for the master's house, but her sister was Ōmaki of the Daikokuya. She didn't have to take insults from the likes of Chōkichi. And too bad for him if the little priest wanted to be mean to her. Midori had had enough of school. She was born stubborn and she was not about to suffer anyone's contempt. That day she broke her pencils and threw away her ink; she would spend her time playing with her real friends. She wasn't going to need her abacus or her books.

In evening they rush into the quarter, at dawn they leave less cheerfully. It's a lonely ride home, with only dreams of the night before to keep a man company. Getaways are under cover. A hat pulled low, a towel around the face. More than one of these gentlemen would rather that you didn't look. To watch will only make you feel uneasy. That smirk of theirs—not half-pleased with themselves as the sting of their lady's farewell slap sinks in. After all, she wouldn't want him to forget her. Careful when you get to Sakamoto. The vegetable carts come barreling back from the early morning market. Watch out when you hit Crazy Street. Until Mishima Shrine, you won't be safe from those who wander home all gaga and enraptured from the night before. Their faces never look so resolute the morning after. It's rude to say it, but don't they all suggest love's fools? The fishwives seldom hesitate to sum them up. Look, there goes a man with money. But that one over there, he couldn't have a penny to his name.

One need hardly cite the Chinese "Song of Everlasting Sorrow"[9] and the heights to which Yang's daughter rose to see that there are times when daughters are more valuable than sons. Many a princess comes into the world among the shanties of the back street. Today she calls herself "Snow" in one of those swank geisha houses over in Tsukiji, a celebrated beauty whose accomplishments in dance have entertained a nobleman or two. But yesterday she was a mere delinquent and she earned her spending money making playing cards, you know. "What kind of tree does rice grow on?" she asks, as if she'd grown up in the lap of luxury. Around here, of course, she is not the celebrity she used to be. Once they leave, they're soon forgotten. Already she has been eclipsed by the dye-maker's second daughter, Kokichi, a home-grown flower of a girl, whose name you'll hear throughout the park. The lanterns are up these days at The New Ivy, in Senzoku, where that one works.

Night and day, it's the daughters that you hear of. A boy is about as useful as a mutt sniffing round the rubbish. Every shopkeeper's son is a wastrel. At seventeen, the age of insolence, the young men band together. Before they go completely gallant—you don't see any flutes tucked into sashes yet—they join up with a leader whose alias is invariably a solemn, grandiose affair. They deck themselves out with matching scarves and matching paper lanterns. It won't be long now before they learn to gamble and to window-shop the quarter. Bantering with the courtesans will begin to come more easily. Even with the serious ones, the family business is only something for the day. Back from the evening bath they come in kimonos of a rakish cut, sandals dragging. "Hey, did you see the new one? At What's-Its-Name? She looks like the girl at the sewing shop, over in Kanasugi. But, with that funny little nose of hers, she's even uglier." It's the only thing remotely on their minds. They bum tobacco, a piece of tissue at every house.[1] The pats and pinches they exchange with each beauty along the way: *these* are the things that bring a lifetime of renown. Even the sons of perfectly upstanding families decide to style themselves as local toughs. They are forever picking fights around the Gate.[2]

Ah, the power of women. One need hardly say more. In the quarter, prosperity makes no distinctions between the autumn and the spring. Escort lanterns[3] are not in vogue these days, and still the men are carried away. All it takes is the echo of a pair of sandals. Here she comes! The little girl from the teahouse who will take them to their ladies. Clip-clop, clip-clop. The sound mingles with the music of the theater. They hear it and they stream into the quarter. If you ask them what they're after, it's a flowing robe, a scarlet collar, a baroque coiffure, a pair of sparkling eyes and lips with painted smiles. The beauties may in fact have little of the beautiful about them. The minute they are courtesans, they climb the pedestal. Those of you from other parts may find it all a little hard to understand.

---

9. By Po Chü-i (772–846). The poem concerns the immoderate love of the Chinese emperor Hsüan Tsung for his beautiful young consort, Yang Kuei-fei, and the grief into which he is plunged by her death.   1. Borrowing tobacco or a facial tissue was merely an excuse to get into the houses.   2. The main entrance to the red-light district.   3. Carried by women escorting customers from the teahouse to the brothel.

Needless to say, Midori, who spent her days and nights immersed in such a world, soon took on the color of the quarter. In her eyes, men were not such fearsome things. And her sister's calling was nothing to disparage. When Ōmaki was on the verge of leaving for the city, how Midori had cried. Not in her wildest dreams had she hoped to accompany her sister. And now here they were. Who wouldn't envy a sister like Ōmaki? What with her recent success, it was nothing for her to repay all the debts she had ever owed her parents. Midori had no notion of what price Ōmaki might have paid to reign supreme in her profession. To her it was all a game. She knew about the charms and tricks the girls would use. Simpering to summon men they longed for, like mice grabbing cheese. Tapping on the lattice when they made a wish. She knew the secret signals they would use to give their guests a parting pat. She had mastered the special language of the quarter, and she didn't feel the least embarrassed when she used it.

It was all a little sad. She was fourteen. When she caressed her dolls, she could have been a prince's child. But for her, all lessons in manners and morals and the wifely arts were topics to be left at school. What never ceased to capture her attention were the rumors of her sister's suitors—who was in and who was out of favor—the costumes of the serving girls, the bedding gifts that men would lavish on Ōmaki,[4] the teahouse tips for the introduction of a patron. What was bright and colorful was good, and what was not was bad. The child was still too young to exercise discretion. She was always taken with the flower just before her eyes. A headstrong girl by nature, Midori indulged herself by fluttering about in a world that she had fashioned from the clouds.

Crazy Street, Sleepy Street. The half-witted, groggy gentlemen all pass this way as they head home. At the gate to this village of late risers, the sweepers and the sprinklers have already cleaned the streets. But look down main street. They have roosted for the night among the slums of Mannenchō or Yamabushichō, or perhaps Shintanimachi, and now here they come: what for want of any other word one might as well call "entertainers." The singing candy man. The two-bit player. The puppeteers. The jugglers and the acrobats. The dancers with their parasols. The clowns who do the lion dance.[5] Their dress is as varied as their arts, a gauze of silk, a sash of satin. The clowns prefer the cotton prints from Satsuma, with black bands round the waist. Men, pretty women, troupes of five, seven, even ten, and a lonely old man, all skin and bones, who totters as he clutches his battered samisen. And, look, there's a little girl of five or so they've got to do the Kinokuni dance.[6] Over there, with the red ribbons on her sleeves. But none of them stop here. They know where the business is, and they hurry to the quarter. The guest who has lingered at the teahouse, the beauty in a melancholy mood—these are the ones it pays to entertain. The profits are too good to give it up, or to waste time with benefit performances along the way. Not even the most tattered and suspicious-looking beggar would bother to loiter around here.

A lady minstrel passed before the paper shop. Her hat all but concealed

---

4. A courtesan's regular patrons were expected to finance new sets of nightgowns and bedding on each of the five major holidays. These gifts were an expensive proposition, and the display of new bedding—in plain view of every passerby—became a courtesan's demonstration of her status within her world.   5. A popular folk dance for which performers dress as *shishi*, mythical lionlike creatures who ward off evil.   6. Named after a popular song: "Out in the deep blue sea the white sails pass: / The tangerine boats from Kinokuni."

her striking face, yet she sang and played with the bearing of a star. "It's a shame we never get to hear the end of her song," the shopkeeper's wife complained. Midori, bright from her morning bath, was lounging on the shop's front step, watching the parade pass by. She pushed her hair up with her boxwood comb. "Wait here. I'll bring her back!"

The child never mentioned slipping something in the lady's sleeve to coax her to perform but, sure enough, back in tow she came to sing the requested song of thwarted love. "Thank you very much for your patronage," she concluded in her honeyed tone, and even as it echoed they knew that they were not about to hear its likes again.

"To think—a mere child could have arranged it!" bystanders marveled, more impressed with Midori than with the minstrel.

"Wouldn't it be fun to have them all perform?" Midori whispered to Shōta. "The samisen and the flute and the drums! The singers and the dancers! Everything we never get more than just a glimpse of!"

Even for Midori, the proposal was ambitious. "Don't overdo it, girl," Shōta muttered.

"Thus have I heard it spoken," the reverend priest intoned the sutra.[7] As the holy words were carried from the temple by the soft breeze through the pines, they should have blown away all dust within the heart.

But smoke rose from fish broiling in the kitchen. In the cemetery diapers had been seen drying over tombstones. Nothing wrong here in the eyes of the Order, perhaps; those who fancied their clerics above worldly desires, though, found the doings at Ryūge Temple rather too earthly for their tastes.[8]

Here the fortunes of the head priest were as handsome as his stomach. Both had rounded out nicely through the years. The man's glow of well-being beggared description: not the sunny pink of the cherries, not the deep pink of the peach; from the top of his freshly shaven pate to the bottom of his neck, he shone like burnished copper. When he whooped with laughter— bushy, salt-and-pepper eyebrows floating heavenward—the noise of the old man's excess could have toppled Buddha from the altar.

The priest's young wife (she was only in her forties) was not an unattractive woman. Her skin was fair, and she wore her thinning hair in a small, modest bun. She was always cordial when people came to pray. Even the florist's wife outside the temple gate held her tongue where the reverend's wife was concerned—the fruit, you may be sure, of the temple lady's kindliness: a hand-me-down here, a leftover there. At one time, she herself had been among the parishioners. But her husband died young, and, having nowhere to turn, she came to do the sewing at the temple. In exchange for meals, she took over the washing and the cooking. Before long she was out in the graveyard, sweeping away with the best of the groundsmen. The priest was quick to offer his compassion, and quicker still to calculate the advantages. The woman knew full well that the difference in their ages, some twenty years, might make the arrangement appear a bit unseemly. But she had nowhere else to go, and she came to consider the temple a good place to live out her

---

7. A narrative portion of the Buddhist scriptures.   8. Until 1872, with the exception of members of the sect known as Jōdo Shinshū, Buddhist monks were forbidden to marry or to eat fish (or meat, for that matter). By the time of this story, however, these taboos had been abolished for some twenty years. Therefore, the priest of Ryūge Temple was committing no offense against the letter of the law, but the religious practices and attitudes of centuries were slow to die.

days and to meet her end. She learned not to lose too much sleep over prying neighbors.

Some in the congregation found the situation shocking. Soon enough, however, they began to acknowledge that in her heart the woman was a good person, and they ceased to censure her. While she was carrying their first child, Ohana, the priest finally made an honest woman of her. A retired oil dealer over in Sakamoto, one of the parishioners who went in for such things, acted as the go-between—if you want to call it that.

Nobu was their second child. Someday he would do his father proud, but at the moment he was a taciturn, moody boy who preferred to pass the day alone in his room. Ohana, on the other hand, was quite the opposite, a lovely girl with fine skin and a soft, plump little chin. To call her a beauty would be going too far, perhaps, but since adolescence she had had her share of admirers. It seemed a shame to waste such a girl, for she might have been a geisha. Who knows? There may be worlds where even Buddha enjoys the music of the samisen. In this world, at any rate, there was the matter of what others said, and talk they would if the daughter of a temple became an entertainer with her skirt hitched up. What the priest did instead was to establish Ohana in a little tea shop in Tamachi. He put her behind the counter, where she could vend her charm. Young men with no idea in their heads how tea was weighed and measured began to gather at the shop. Seldom was Ohana's empty before midnight.

But his holiness was the busy one. Loans to collect, the shop to oversee, funerals to arrange, not to mention all the sermons every month. When he wasn't flipping through accounts, he was going through the sutras. If things didn't let up, he'd wear himself out, he would sigh as he dragged his flowered cushion onto the veranda, where he fanned himself, half-naked, and enjoyed his nightly hooch.[9] He was a fish-eater, and Nobu was the one he sent over to the main street for the broiled eels that he liked. "The big oily ones, if you please." It galled Nobu. His eyes never left his feet as he trudged over to the Musashiya. If he heard voices at the paper shop across the street, he would keep on going. Then, when the coast was clear, he'd dart into the eel shop. The shame he felt! He would never eat the smelly things.

The reverend was nothing if not practical. There were some who might call him greedy, but that never bothered him a whit. He was neither a timid soul nor an idler: give him a spare moment and he'd set about fashioning kumade charms. On Otori day he would have his wife out peddling them. Whatever doubts she may have had about the venture, they were short-lived once his holiness started to bemoan the killing everybody else made, rank amateurs up and down the street. He soon persuaded his reluctant wife, set up a booth not a stone's throw from the temple gate, and installed her there to sell his charms and good-luck hairpins. She tied her hair back with a headband, just like the vendors and all the young men. In the daytime, she knew enough to stay out of sight and mingle with the crowd, leaving the florist's wife to manage things. But when the sun went down—who would have guessed it?—the woman had a field day. At dusk she took over for herself, quite forgetting what a spectacle she made with her sudden itch for profit. "Everything marked down! Prices slashed!" she barked after a cus-

9. Very potent cheap liquor.

tomer who backed away. Buffeted and dizzy from the throngs, the victim soon lost his powers of appraisal. They had fled along with memory: two days earlier he had come to this very temple as a pilgrim. "Three for only seventy-five sen."[1] But her price left room to negotiate. "How about five for seventy-three?" "Sold!"

There were, of course, all kinds of sharp practices. Even if no one from the congregation heard, Nobu wondered, what would the neighbors think? And his friends? He could just hear them. Ryūge Temple is selling hairpins now. Nobu's mother is out huckstering like a lunatic. Really, didn't they think they ought to stop?

The reverend priest would hear nothing of it. "Knock it off. You don't know what you're talking about." The mere idea sent the man into paroxysms.

Prayers in the morning, accounts at night. His father's face beamed whenever his fingers touched the abacus. It was enough to turn the boy's stomach. Why on earth had the man become a priest?

There was nothing in his upbringing to make Nobu such a gloomy child. He had the same parents as Ohana. They were part of the same cozy, self-contained family. Yet he was the quiet one. Even when he did speak, his opinions were never taken seriously. His father's schemes, his mother's conduct, his sister's education—to Nobu everything they did was a travesty. He had resigned himself to knowing that they would never listen. How unfair it was. His friends found him contrary and perverse, but in fact he was a weakling. If anyone maligned him in the slightest, he would run for the shelter of his room. He was a coward utterly lacking in the courage to defend himself. At school they called him a brain; his family's station was not lowly. No one knew how weak he really was. More than one of his friends considered Nobu something of a cold fish.

The night of the festival Nobu was sent on an errand to his sister's tea shop in Tamachi, and he was late coming home. Not until the next morning did he learn of the fight at the paper shop. When Ushimatsu and Bunji and the others gave him the details, the full impact of Chōkichi's violent ways startled him anew. What was done was done—but in name he was included in the violence, and it rankled. Now people would be blaming him for the trouble.

It was three days before Chōkichi had the nerve to face Nobu. For once he must have felt a little sheepish about the damage he had done. He did not look forward to Nobu's scolding. "I know you're probably angry," he ventured, having waited for the storm to pass. "I couldn't help it, though. Everything got out of hand. I hadn't meant it to happen. You won't hold it against me, will you, Nobu? How were we to know that you'd be gone and Shōta would fly the coop? It's not as though I planned to beat up Sangorō and pick a fight with that tramp Midori. Things just happened. You don't run away once the lanterns start swinging! All we wanted was to show a little muscle, show 'em who's boss. It's my fault, I know. I should have listened to you. But come on Nobu, if you get mad now, how's it going to look? After I've gone around telling everybody you're on *our* side. You can't leave us in the lurch. Okay, so you don't approve of this one thing. You be the leader, and next time we won't botch things up." Gone was the usual swagger.

Nobu couldn't turn his back on Chōkichi. "All right," he sighed. "But

---

1. A unit of currency. One sen equaled one-hundredth of a yen; the yen had a value of approximately fifty cents.

listen—bully the weak ones, and we'll be the ones in disgrace. We're not going to gain anything fighting Sangorō and Midori. If Shōta and his flunkies want to stir up trouble, we can cross that bridge when we come to it. But let's not egg them on." Chōkichi had to promise: no more fights. For a rebuke, it was rather mild.

The innocent one was Sangorō. They had kicked and beaten him to their hearts' content, and he still ached two, three days afterward. He couldn't stand up, he couldn't sit down. Every evening when his father picked up the empty rickshaw and headed for the teahouses, someone would ask him what was wrong with the boy. "Say, your Sangorō looks a little peaked these days," the caterer remarked, almost accusingly. "Somebody give him a pounding?"

Groveling Tetsu they called his father, head always lowered before his betters. It didn't matter who—the landlord or someone with money or the owner of one of the houses in the quarter, where Tetsu pulled his cart—any of them could make the most impossible demands, and the rickshawman would acquiesce. "Indeed, of course, how right you are." Small wonder, then, what his reaction was to the incident with Chōkichi. "He's the landlord's son, isn't he? I don't care if you were right. I won't have you getting into scraps with him. Now go apologize. You ought to know better!" There was no avoiding it. His father made sure that he got down on his knees in front of Chōkichi.

Within a week Sangorō's wounds healed and his temper cooled. He was ready to forget what he'd been angry about. For the price of a carriage ride, he was baby-sitting again for Chōkichi's little brother, walking round with the child on his back and lulling it to sleep with nursery rhymes. Sangorō was sixteen, that age when boys get cocky, but the lumpish figure he cut failed to trouble him. He wandered over to the main street, unconcerned as always. "Hey, Sangorō. Have you forgotten you're a boy?" Midori and Shōta were great ones when it came to teasing. "Some sight you make, with that baby on your back!" It didn't matter, they were still his friends.

In spring the cherry trees blossom in profusion. In summer the lanterns twinkle in memory of the late Tamagiku.[2] In fall the festival streets overflow with rickshaws. Count them: seventy-five down the road within the space of ten minutes. Then the autumn holidays are over. Here and there a red dragonfly bobs above the rice fields. Before long, quail will be calling out along the moat. Mornings and evenings, the breeze blows cold. At the sundries shop, pocket warmers now take the place of mosquito incense. It's sad, somehow, that faint sound of the mortar grinding flour at Tamura's, over by the bridge. The clock at Kadoebi's has a melancholy ring. Fires glow through all four seasons from the direction of Nippori.[3] It's in autumn that one begins to notice them. Smoke rises each time one more soul embarks on the journey to the other shore.

Deftly, a geisha plays on the samisen. The refrain reaches the path along the bank behind the teahouses. A passerby looks up and listens. Not much of a song, really, but moving all the same. "Together we shall spend our night of love." Women who have done time in the quarter will tell you—it's the men who begin visiting in fall who prove to be the truly faithful ones.

Talk, talk: in this neighborhood, there is always grist for gossip. The details

---

2. A celebrated courtesan whose death in 1726 was commemorated with a festival of lanterns, a popular event in the red-light district.   3. A place of cremation.

are tedious, but the stories make the rounds. A blind masseuse, she was only twenty, killed herself. With a handicap like hers, love was out of the question. Well she couldn't stand it any more. Drowned herself in Mizunoya Pond. Then there are the incidents too commonplace to rate a rumor. Missing persons: Kichigorō, the greengrocer, and Takichi, the carpenter. How come? "They picked them up for this," a fellow whispers, and pantomimes a gambler dealing out the cards.

A moment ago there were children there, down the street. "Ring-a-ring-a-rosy, pocket full of posies." Suddenly it's quiet now, before you notice. Only the sound of rickshaws, loud as ever.

It was a lonely night. Just when it seemed the autumn rains would go on and on falling softly, with a roar a downpour came. At the paper shop they were not expecting anyone. The shopkeeper's wife had closed up for the evening. Inside, playing marbles, were Shōta and Midori, as usual, and two or three of the younger ones. All at once, Midori heard something: "Is that a customer? I hear footsteps."

"I don't hear anything," Shōta said. He stopped counting out the marbles. "Maybe someone wants to play."

Who could it be? They heard him come as far as the gate, but after that, not a word, not a sound.

"Boo!" Shōta opened the door and stuck his head out. "Hey, who's there?" He could just make out the back of someone walking along beneath the eaves two or three houses up ahead. "Who is it? Do you want to come in?" He had slipped Midori's sandals on and was about to run after him, in spite of the rain. "Oh, it's him." Shōta cupped his hand above his head, mimicking a bald monk. "No use—we can call him all we want, he won't come."

"Nobu?" Midori asked. "That old priest! I'll bet he came to buy a writing brush and scurried off the minute he heard us. Nasty, stupid, toothless, old-maid Nobu! Just let him come in. I'll tell him what I think. Too bad he ran away. Let me have the sandals. I want a look." This time Midori poked her head out. The rain dripped down from the eaves onto her forehead. It gave her a chill. She pulled back, staring at the shadowy figure as he made his way around the puddles. He was four or five houses away by now, and he seemed to cower in the gaslight. His paper umbrella hugged his shoulders. She looked and looked.

Shōta tapped her on the shoulder. "Midori, what is it?"

"Nothing," she said absent-mindedly, returning to the game. "I hate that little altar boy! He can't even conduct his fights in public. He makes that pious, old-maid face of his and goes sneaking round corners. Isn't he awful? My mother says people who are straightforward are the good ones. She's right, don't you think, Shōta? It's a sure thing Nobu has an evil heart, the way he lurks around."

"But at least he knows what's what. Not like Chōkichi, there's a real moron. The boy's a total ignoramus," Shōta said knowingly.

"Cut it out. You and your big words." Midori laughed and pinched him on the cheek. "Such a serious face! Since when are you so grown up?"

Shōta was not amused. "For your information, it won't be long before I *am* grown up. I'll wear a topcoat with square-cut shoulders like the shopkeeper at Kabata's, and the gold watch Grandmother's put away for me. I'll wear a ring. I'll smoke cigarettes. And for shoes—you're not going to see me in any clogs. Oh, no. I'll wear leather sandals, the good kind, with triple-layered heels and fancy satin straps. Won't I look sharp!"

"You in triple heels and a square-cut overcoat?" Midori couldn't help snickering. "Mm, sure, if you want to look like a walking medicine bottle."

"Oh, quiet. You don't think I've stopped growing, do you? I won't be this short forever."

"Seeing is believing. You know, Shōta," Midori said, pointing a sarcastic finger at the rafters, "even the mice laugh when you keep making these promises." Everyone, the shopkeeper's wife included, shook with laughter.

His eyes spun; Shōta was completely serious. "Midori makes a joke of everything. But everyone grows up, you know. Why is what I say so funny? The day will come when I go walking with my pretty wife. I always like things to be pretty. If I had to marry someone like that pock-marked Ofuku at the cracker shop, or the girl at the firewood store with the bulging forehead—no thank you. I'd send her home. No pockmarks for me!"

"How good of you to come, then," the shop wife laughed. "Haven't you noticed my spots?"

"Oh, but you're old. I'm talking about brides. Once you're old, it doesn't matter."

"I shouldn't have said anything," the woman sighed. "Well, let's see now. There's Oroku at the flower shop. She has a pretty face. And Kii at the fruit stand. And who else? Who else, I wonder? Why, the prettiest one is sitting right next to you. Shōta, who will it be? Oroku with those eyes of hers? Kii and her lovely voice? Tell us who."

"What are you talking about? Oroku, Kii—what's so good about them?" Shōta's face turned scarlet, and he backed away from the light, into a corner.

"Does that mean it's Midori, then?"

"How do I know?" He looked away, tapping out a song against the wall. "The water wheel goes round and round."

Midori and the rest had begun another game of marbles. *Her* face was not flushed in the slightest.

There would have been no problem if he hadn't taken the short cut. But every time Nobu went off to Tamachi he took the path along the ditch. And every time he saw it: the lattice gate, the stone lantern, the thatched fence. The summer bamboo blinds were rolled up now along the veranda. He couldn't help remembering things. Behind the glass windows,[4] her mother would be there, like some latter-day widow of Azechi at her rosary; and she would be there too, straight from the ancient tales, a young Murasaki[5] with her hair bobbed. This was the house of the man who owned the Daikokuya.

Yesterday and today the autumn rains had continued. The winter slip Ohana had requested was ready, and Nobu's mother was anxious for her to

4. This is mentioned to indicate that the house belongs to someone of means. Glass windows were expensive and still relatively rare in Japan in the 1890s. 5. The favorite of the hero of *The Tale of the Genji*. It is the widow of Azechi (Murasaki's grandmother) with whom the young girl lives when Genji discovers her, on a night when the widow is at her prayers; as soon as he spies Murasaki, Genji knows that the child will grow up to be the woman of his dreams. The equation of Midori with the young Murasaki and the passing Nobu with the traveling Genji is an obvious hint at the blossoming, inarticulate love between Nobu and Midori.

have it. She didn't like to ask in such weather, but would he mind taking it to the shop in Tamachi on his way to school? The poor girl was waiting for the package. Diffident Nobu could never say no. He took the bundle under his arm, stepped into his clogs, and started out, clinging to his umbrella as the rain lapped at his feet.

He followed the ditch around the quarter, the same path he always took, but today luck was not with him. Just in front of the Daikokuya, the wind came up. He had to tug to keep his umbrella from flying off. He braced his legs against the wind, when the strap on one of his clogs tore clean away. Now what was he to do?

It was almost enough to make him swear. He had no choice but to try repairing the clog himself. He propped his umbrella against the gate and sought shelter underneath its eaves. Yet how was a fledgling cleric to accomplish this sort of handiwork? He was flustered, and no matter how hard he tried, he couldn't fix it. He grew more and more irritated. From his sleeve he took out the draft of his school composition and tore it up, twisting the strips of paper in hopes of somehow fashioning a new strap. But the confounded storm grew worse again, and his umbrella began to roll away in the wind. This was more than he could tolerate! He reached out to grab the umbrella—but it was just his luck—his sister's package fell from his lap into the mud. There, now he had mud on his sleeve, too.

A pathetic sight he made, without an umbrella and stranded barefoot in the downpour. From the window, Midori saw the sad figure beyond the gate. "Look, someone's broken his sandal. Mother, can I give him something to fix it with?" She found a piece of Yūzen crepe[6] in the sewing drawer and hurried into her clogs. Grabbing an umbrella from the veranda, she dashed out across the stepping stones toward the front gate.

Then she saw who it was. The blood rushed to Midori's head. Her heart pounded as if she had encountered a dreaded fate. She turned to see, was anyone watching? Trembling, she inched her way toward the gate. At that instant Nobu, too, looked around. He was speechless, he felt cold sweat begin to bead. He wanted to kick off the other sandal and run away.

Had Midori been herself, she would have seized on Nobu's predicament to tell him what she thought. She would have sneered at his cowardice and heaped upon him every bit of abuse that he deserved. Didn't he think he owed her an apology? Bossing everyone around from backstage, ruining all the fun at the festival, just because he was angry at Shōta. And letting them beat up helpless Sangorō! He was the one who had incited Chōkichi to call her those names. And what was wrong with being a courtesan, anyway, even if she were one? She didn't owe him anything. With her parents and her sister and the man from the Daikokuya—what did she need to ask favors of a broken-down priest for? He had better stop calling her names. Something to say, was there? Then he could come out in the open, like a man. Any time, any time. She'd meet him. What did he have to say to that? She would have grabbed him by the sleeve and given him a piece of her mind, all right. Nobu would not have had a prayer.

But instead she cringed in the shadows of the gate. She didn't move, her heart throbbed. This was not the old Midori.

---

6. A fabric colored by an elaborate and expensive dying process created by Miyazaki Yūzen of Kyoto.

Whenever he came near the Daikokuya, timorous Nobu hurried past without so much as looking left or right. But today, the unlucky rain, the unlucky wind, and, to make matters worse, the broken sandal strap! There was nothing for it but to stop and make a new one. He was upset enough already, and then he heard the sound of steps on the flagstones—he felt as if ice water had been poured down his back. Even without looking, he knew who it would be. He shivered and his face changed color. He turned away and pretended to be hard at work. But he was panic-stricken. It didn't look as if the clog would ever be of use again.

From the garden, Midori peered at him. How clumsy he was; he could never do anything right. Who ever heard of trying to make a strap out of anything as flimsy as a piece of paper—or straw, is that what he was using? Old ladies, maybe. It would never hold. Oh, and didn't he know he was getting mud all over the bottom of his jacket? There went the umbrella. Why didn't he close it before he propped it up? How it irritated her to watch his fumbling. "Here's some cloth to fix it with." If only she could have said it. Instead, she stood rooted to the spot, hiding, staring. The girl was oblivious to the rain soaking through her sleeves.

Midori's mother, unaware of what was happening, called out. "Midori, the iron's ready. What are you doing out there? Don't you know better than to play in the rain? You'll catch another cold."

"All right, coming." If only Nobu wouldn't hear. Her heart raced, her head seemed to reel. The last thing she could do was open the gate, but she could not turn her back on him, either. What was she to do? There—she hurled the rag outside the lattice without saying anything. Nobu pretended not to notice. Oh! He was his same old nasty self! It crushed her, the tears welled up. Why did he have to be so mean? Why didn't he just tell her what it was? It made her sick. But her mother kept on calling. It was no use. She started for the house. After all, why should she be sentimental? She wasn't going to let him see Midori eat humble pie.

He heard her walk away; his eyes wandered after her. The scarlet scrap of Yūzen silk lay in the rain, its pattern of red maple leaves near enough to touch. Odd, how her one gesture moved him, and yet he could not bring himself to reach out and take the cloth. He stared at it vacantly, and as he looked at it he felt his heart break.

He bungled everything. Nobu sighed and took the cord from his jacket and wrapped it round the clog. It was unsightly and makeshift, but perhaps it would do, perhaps he could stumble along. But all the way to Ohana's? It was a little late to be wondering that, he thought as he stood up, his sister's package tight under his arm. He had only gone two or three steps when he looked back again at the tatter of silk, bright with autumn maples. It was hard for him to leave it there.

"Nobu, what's the matter? Break your strap? What a sight you are!"

Nobu turned around to see who owned the unexpected voice. It was obnoxious Chōkichi, decked out like a young gallant. He had on his best-dress kimono, and he wore his orange sash profligately low on the hips. His new jacket had a fancy black collar, and the umbrella he carried was festooned with the trademark of one of the houses in the quarter. His high clogs were sporting lacquered rain covers—this was something new. What pride there was in the young man's swagger.

"The strap broke, and I was wondering what to do," Nobu answered helplessly. "I'm not very good at these things."

"No, you wouldn't be. It's all right, wear mine. The straps won't give out."

"But what will you do?"

"Don't worry. I'm used to it. I'll just go like this," he said, tucking up the bottom of his kimono. "Feels much better than wearing sandals, anyway." He kicked off his rain clogs.

"You're going to go barefoot? That won't be fair."

"I don't mind. I'm used to going barefoot. Someone like you has soft feet. You could never walk barefoot on the gravel. Come on, wear these," he urged, arranging his sandals obligingly. What a spectacle: Chōkichi was more detested than the plague god himself, and here he was with soft words on his tongue and bushy eyebrows moving solicitously. "I'll take your sandals and toss them in at the back door. Here, let's switch."

Chōkichi took the broken clogs, and they parted, Nobu bound for his sister's in Tamachi and Chōkichi for home before they met again at school.

The silk shred lay abandoned by the gate. Its red maple leaves shimmered in the rain.

This year there were three Otori fair days.[7] Rain had spoiled the second, but today, like the first, was perfect for a festival. Throngs packed Otori Shrine, young men surged into the quarter through the side gates. They say they've come to pay a visit to the shrine. They are pilgrims, but, ah, the roar of young laughter is loud enough to rend the pillars holding up the heavens, to tear away the very cord from which the earth hangs. Front and back of the main street of the quarter look as if they've been reversed. Today, the side drawbridges are down clear around the moat, and the crowds keep pouring in. "Coming through, coming through." What have we here? Some flat-bottomed boat trying to navigate these waves of people? Who will soon forget the excitement in the air? Peals of laughter, incessant chatter echo from the little shops along the ditch. Strains of the samisen rise from the first-class pleasure houses towering several stories in the sky.

Shōta took a holiday from collecting interest. He dropped in at Sangorō's potato stall, and then he visited his friend Donkey at the dumpling shop. "How are you doing? Making any money?" The sweets looked pretty uninviting.

"Shōta! You're just in time. I've run out of bean jam and don't know what to do. I've already put more on to cook, but they keep coming and I don't want to turn them away. What should I do?"

"Don't be stupid. Look what you've got on the sides of the pot. Add some water and some sugar, and you can feed another ten or twenty people. Everybody does it—you won't be the first. Besides, who's going to notice how it tastes in all this commotion? Start selling, start selling." Shōta was already at the sugar bowl.

Donkey's one-eyed mother was filled with admiration. "You've become a real merchant, Shōta. I'm almost afraid of you."

"This? I saw Clammy do the same thing in the alley. It's not my idea." The woman's praise did not go to his head. "Hey, do you know where Midori is?

I've been looking for her since this morning. Where'd she go off to? She hasn't been to the paper shop. I know that. I wonder if she's in the quarter."

"Oh, Midori, she went by a little while ago. I saw her take one of the side bridges into the quarter. Shōta, you should have seen her. She had her hair all done up like this." He made an oafish effort to suggest the splendor of Midori's new grown-up hairdo. "She's really something, that girl!" The boy wiped his nose as he extolled her.

"Yes, she's even prettier than her sister. I hope she won't end up like Ōmaki." Shōta looked down at the ground.

"What do you mean—that would be wonderful! Next year I'm going to open a shop, and after I save some money I'll buy her for a night!" He didn't understand things.

"Don't be such a smart aleck. Even if you tried, she wouldn't have anything to do with you."

"Why? Why should she refuse me?"

"She just would." Shōta flushed as he laughed. "I'm going to walk around for a while. I'll see you later." He went out the gate.

> "Growing up,
> she plays among the butterflies
> and flowers.
> But she turns sixteen,
> and all she knows
> is work and sorrow."[8]

He sang the popular refrain in a voice that was curiously quavering for him, and repeated it again to himself. His sandals drummed their usual ring against the paving stones, as all at once his little figure vanished into the crowd.

Inside the bustling quarter, Shōta found himself swept along into a corner of the compound. It was there he saw Midori. Why, it certainly was Midori of the Daikokuya; she was talking to an attendant from one of the houses, and, just as he had heard, her hair was done up in the glorious *shimada* style[9] of a young woman. And yet she looked shy today. Colored ribbons cascaded from her hair, tortoise-shell combs and flowered hairpins flickered in the sun. The whole effect was as bright and stately as a Kyōto doll. Shōta was tongue-tied. Any other time, he would have rushed over and taken her arm.

"Shōta!" Midori came running up. "If you have shopping to do, Otsuma, why don't you go on ahead? I'll go home with him." She nodded good-by to the lady.

"Oh, you don't want me around, now that you've found another friend, is that it?" Otsuma smiled as she headed down a narrow street of shops. "I'll be off to Kyōmachi, then."

"You look nice, Midori." Shōta tugged at her sleeve. "When did you get that new hairdo? This morning? Why didn't you come and show it to me?" He pretended to be angry.

Midori had difficulty speaking. "I had it done this morning at my sister's.

8. A popular song. 9. The fashionable hairstyle for young, unmarried women and for courtesans. There were many variations, but essentially the larger the chignon, the more youthful or ostentatious the woman. The hairdo is a clear sign that Midori is no longer considered a child. And the fact that it is large (here translated as "glorious") suggests Midori's affinity with the world of prostitutes.

I hate it." Her spirits drooped. She kept her head down; she couldn't bear it
when a passerby would gawk.

When she felt so awkward and unhappy, flattery only sounded like an insult.
People turned to admire her and she thought they were jeering.

"Shōta, I'm going home."

"Why don't you play? Did someone scold you? I bet you had a fight with
your sister."

Midori felt her face color. Shōta was still a child, clearly. Where did one
begin to explain?

They passed the dumpling shop, and Donkey called out theatrically, "You
two sure are friendly." It made her feel like crying.

"Shōta, I don't want to walk with you." She hurried off ahead of him.

She had promised to go with him to the festival, and now here she was,
headed in the opposite direction. "Aren't you going to come?" he yelled,
running after her. "Why are you going home? You might at least explain!"

Midori walked on without answering, hoping to elude him. Shōta was
stunned. He pulled at her sleeve. It was all so strange. Midori's face only
turned a deeper red. "It's nothing, Shōta." But he knew that this was not the
truth.

He followed her in through the gate at her house and onto the veranda.
There was no need to hesitate; he had been coming here to play for years.

"Oh, Shōta," her mother greeted him. "Nice to see you. She's been in a
bad mood all day. I don't know what to do with her. See if you can cheer her
up."

Shōta became quite the grown-up. "Something the matter, is there?"

"No, no." Her mother gave an odd smile. "She'll get over it in no time.
She's just spoiled. I suppose she's been grumpy with her friends, too? I tell
you, sometimes I've had it with that girl." Her mother turned to look at her,
but Midori had gone into the other room. Her sash and her outer kimono
were discarded on the floor and Midori lay face-down underneath a quilt.

Shōta approached her gingerly. "Midori, what is it? Don't you feel well?
Please tell me what's the matter." He held back as he spoke to her. What
should he do? He folded and unfolded his hands in his lap. Midori said
nothing. He could hear her sobbing into her sleeve. Her bangs, too short still
for sweeping up into the great hairdo, were matted with tears. Something
was terribly wrong, but, child that he was, Shōta had no idea what it could
be, or how to console her. He was totally bewildered. "Please tell me what
it is. You've never said anything to me, so how can you be angry with me?"
He looked at her warily.

"Shōta, it isn't you." Midori wiped her eyes.

But when he asked her what it was, then, she couldn't answer. There were
just sad things, vague things. Feelings . . . She couldn't put them into words.
They made her cheeks burn. Nothing she could point to—and yet lately
everything discouraged her. So many thoughts; none of them would ever
have occurred to the Midori of yesterday. This awkwardness all of a sudden!
How was she to explain it? If they would just leave her alone . . . she'd be
happy to spend night and day in a dark room. No one to talk to her, no one
to stare. Even if she felt unhappy, at least she would be spared the embarrassment. If only she could go on playing house forever—with her dolls for
companions, then she'd be happy again. Oh! She hated, hated, hated this

growing up! Why did things have to change? What she would give to go back a year, ten months, seven months, even.

They were the thoughts of someone already old.

She had forgotten that Shōta was there. But he kept on pestering her until she wanted to drive him away. "For God's sake, go home, Shōta. I feel like dying, with you here. All these questions give me a headache. They make me dizzy. I don't want anybody here! Just go *home!*"

She had never treated him so cruelly; Shōta could make no sense of it. He might as well have been groping through a cloud of smoke. "You sure are acting strange, Midori. I don't know why you talk this way. You must be crazy." The regrets were too much for him. He spoke calmly enough, but now his eyes smarted. This wouldn't help matters.

"Go home! Go home, will you! If you don't get out of here, you're not my friend at all. I hate you, Shōta."

"If that's the way you feel, I'm sorry to have bothered you." He darted off through the garden without so much as a farewell to Midori's mother, who had gone to check the water in the bath.

Shōta made a beeline for the paper shop, ducking, dodging his way through the crowds.

Sangorō was there, his holiday stall sold out and the take jingling in his pocket. Shōta burst in upon them just as Sangorō was playing the part of big brother. "Anything you want—it's yours!" The younger ones jumped up and down with glee. "Hey, Shōta! I was looking for you. I made a lot of money today. I'll treat you."

"You idiot. Since when do you treat me? Don't start talking big." These were rough words for Shōta. "That's not what I came here for." He looked dejected.

"What happened? A fight?" Sangorō shoved a half-eaten doughnut into his pocket. "Who was it? Nobu? Chōkichi? Where? The temple? Was it in the quarter? It won't be like the last time! This time, they won't take us by surprise. There's no way we can lose. I'm ready. Let me lead. We can't chicken out, Shōta."

The call to arms only infuriated him. "Take it easy," Shōta snapped. "There was no fight."

"But you came in here as if something terrible had happened. I thought it was a fight. And besides, if you don't do it tonight, we won't have another chance. Chōkichi's losing his right arm."

"Huh?"

"His accomplice, Nobu. Didn't you hear? I just found out. My father was talking with Nobu's mother. Any day now, he's going off to learn how to be a monk. Once he puts those robes on, they'll cover up his fighting arm. Those long, floppy robes—how can he roll up his sleeves in them? But you know what that means. Next year, you'll have the front and the back street to yourself."

"All right, quiet. For a few coins they'll go over to Chōkichi. I could have a hundred like you, and it wouldn't excite me in the least. They can go where they like for all I care. I'll fight my own battles. It was Nobu I wanted to beat. But if he's running off on me, it can't be helped. I thought he was going next year, after he graduated. What a coward—why is he going so soon?"

But it wasn't Nobu he was worried about. Tonight, there were none of the usual songs from Shōta. Midori was on his mind. The throngs of merrymakers passing in the street only left him feeling lonely. What was there to celebrate?

The lamps went on, and Shōta rolled over on his side. Some festival, everything had ended in a mess!

From that day on Midori was a different person. When she had to, she went to her sister's rooms in the quarter, but she never went to play in town. Her friends missed her and came to invite her to join them in the fun again. "Maybe later. You go on ahead." Empty promises, always. She was cool even to Shōta, once her closest friend. She was forever blushing now. It seemed unlikely that the paper shop would see the old dancing and the games a second time.

People were puzzled. Was the girl sick? "No, no. She'll be her old self again," her mother assured them. "She's just having a rest. One of her little vacations." The woman smiled. And yet there seemed to be more to it.

There was praise for Midori now from some quarters. So ladylike, so well-behaved. Yes, but what a shame, others mourned: she was such a delightful, saucy child.

The front street was quiet suddenly, as if a light had gone out. Seldom did Shōta sing his songs any more. At night you could see him with his lantern making the rounds for the interest payments. The shadow moving along the moat looked chilly, somehow. From time to time, Sangorō would join him, and his voice rang out, comical as ever.

Everyone talked about Nobu, but Midori had not heard any of the rumors. The former spitfire was still closeted away somewhere. With all these changes lately, she hardly knew herself. She was timid now, everything embarrassed her.

One frosty morning, a paper narcissus lay inside the gate. No one knew what it was doing there, but Midori took a fancy to it, for some reason, and she put it in a bud vase. It was perfect, she thought, and yet almost sad in its crisp, solitary shape. That same day—she wasn't sure exactly where—Midori heard of Nobu's plans. Tomorrow he was leaving for the seminary. The color of his robes would never be the same.

THOMAS MANN
1875–1955

Thomas Mann's reputation as the great German novelist of the twentieth century represents only part of his stature; by the time of his death, he had become an international figure to whom people looked for statements on art, modern society, and the human condition. Continuing the great nineteenth-century tradition of psychological realism, Mann took as his subject the cultural and spiritual crises of Europe at the turn of the century. His career spanned a time of great change, including as it did the upheaval of two world wars and the visible disintegration of an entire society. Where other modern novelists, such as James Joyce, William Faulkner, and Virginia Woolf, stressed innovative language and style, Mann emphasized instead the society of his time and—inside that society—the universal human conflicts between art and life, sensuality and intellect, individual and social will.

Many of Mann's themes derive from the nineteenth-century German aesthetic tradition in which he grew up. The philosophers Schopenhauer and Nietzsche and the composer Wagner had the most influence on his work: Arthur Schopenhauer (1788–1860) for his vision of the artist's suffering and development; Friedrich Nietzsche (1844–1900) for his portrait of the diseased artist overcoming chaos and decay to produce, through discipline and will, artworks that justify existence; and Richard Wagner (1813–1883) for embodying the complete artist who controlled all aspects of his work: music, lyrics, the very staging of his operas. Mann's well-known use of the verbal *leitmotif* is also borrowed from Wagner, who would use in his operas a recurrent musical theme (the *leitmotif*) associated with a particular person, thing, action, or state of being. In Mann's literary adaptation, evocative phrases, repeated almost without change, link memories throughout the text and establish a cumulative emotional resonance. In the story *Tonio Kröger,* for example, Tonio's dual ancestry is repeatedly suggested by the contrasting phrases of the "dark, fiery mother, who played the piano and mandolin," and the father with his "thoughtful blue eyes" and "wild flower in the buttonhole." Inside the tradition of realistic narration, Mann created a highly organized literary structure with subtly interrelated themes and images that built up rich associations of ideas: in his own words, an "epic prose composition . . . understood by me as spiritual thematic pattern, as a musical complex of associations."

Mann was born in Lübeck, a historic seaport and commercial city in northern Germany, on June 6, 1875. His father was a grain merchant and head of the family firm; his mother came from a German-Brazilian family and was known for her beauty and musical talent. The contrast of Nordic and Latin that plays such a large part in Mann's work begins in his consciousness of his own heritage and is expanded to far-reaching symbolic levels. He disliked the scientific emphasis of his secondary education and left school in 1894 after repeating two years. Rejoining his family in Munich, where they had moved in 1891 after his father's death, he worked as an unpaid apprentice in a fire insurance business but found more interest in university lectures in history, political economy, and art. He decided against a business career after his first published story, *Fallen* (1896), received praise from the noted poet Richard Dehmel, and from 1896 to 1898 lived and wrote in Italy before returning to Munich for a two-year stint as manuscript reader for the satiric weekly *Simplicissimus*. In 1905, he married Katia Pringsheim, with whom he had six children. The short stories collected in *Little Herr Friedemann* (1899) were a success, and enabled Mann to find a publisher for his first major work, *Buddenbrooks* (1901).

Buddenbrooks describes the decline of a prosperous German family through four generations and is to some extent based on the history of the Mann family business. Nonetheless, the elements of autobiography are quickly absorbed into the more universal themes of the inner decay of the German burgher ("bourgeois," or middle-class) tradition and its growing isolation from other segments of society, a decline paralleled in the portrait of a developing artistic sensitivity and its relation to death. Children in the family of the self-confident, aggressive, and disciplined Consul Johann Buddenbrooks become increasingly introspective, hesitant, unhealthy, and artistic. The end of the family comes with young Hanno, a musical genius who is completely absorbed in his piano improvisations and thus prey to the fatal temptation of infinite beauty. In this novel, as in many later works, Mann's fictional world is governed by a tension or dualism between sensuous experience and intellect or will. A diseased and alienated imaginative soul is set against a healthy, gregarious, somewhat obtuse normal citizen; the erratic and poor artist against the disciplined and prosperous burgher; the dark, brown-eyed Latin against the blond, blue-eyed Nordic; warm, unself-conscious feelings against icy intellect; freedom against authority; immorality and decadence against moral respectability; a longing for the eternal and infinite against active participation in everyday life.

There is no recommended resolution of these polarities, for if either overwhelms the other, tragedy must follow. In the seemingly autobiographical *Tonio Kröger*, the protagonist is portrayed as sensitive to the claims of both, and his growing awareness of their combined importance is a sign of maturity. Ideally, the artist must live both extremes at once, in constant lucidity and pain. In *Death in Venice* (1912), the author Gustave Aschenbach suffers and dies for having been unable to keep the balance; in the novel *Doctor Faustus* (1947), the composer Adrian Leverkühn sells his soul to experience both poles. In *Mario and the Magician* (1929), the sadistic hypnotist Cipolla is an artist in his fashion, exercising a fatally corrupt art in which all his psychological insight, cutting intellect, and iron will produce only torment for himself and others. Mann's letters and essays show that he felt deeply involved in the relations of the artist's life to the artwork, but his protagonists have their own identity and symbolize much more than Mann's own artistic career. As artist and craftsman, he always insisted on distinguishing the work of art from its raw material, the emotions and experiences of life. He cultivated objectivity, distance, and irony in his own works, and no character—including the narrator—is immune from the author's critical eye.

Throughout his writings up to and during World War I, Mann established himself as an important spokesman for modern Germany. His early conservatism and defense of an authoritarian nationalist government (*Reflections of a Non-Political Man*, 1918) gave way to an ardent defense of democracy and liberal humanism as the Nazis came to power. Mann's most famous novel, *The Magic Mountain* (1924), is a bildungsroman (a novel of the protagonist's education and development) that uses the isolation of a mountaintop tuberculosis sanitorium to gain perspective on the philosophic issues of twentieth-century Europe. The hero, Hans Castorp, has to decide how to live as he listens to the competing dogmas of the humanist Settembrini and the fanatic antirationalist Naphta, and undergoes a double temptation of oblivion through eroticism (Clavdia Chauchat) and death (symbolized by the isolated sanitorium). The novel ends with Castorp choosing active participation in a world at war; whether or not he survives the trenches is left unresolved, but he has taken charge of his own destiny. *The Magic Mountain* was immensely popular, and its author received the Nobel Prize in 1929. He was so much an international figure when he went into voluntary exile in Switzerland as Hitler came to power in 1933 that the Nazis, stung by his criticism, revoked his citizenship. Moving to America in 1938, he wrote and lectured against Nazism, and in 1944 he became an American citizen.

Mann's later works cover a range of themes. *Joseph, and His Brothers* (1933–45) is a tetralogy on the biblical tale of Joseph, who, abandoned for dead by his brothers, survives and comes to power in Egypt. *Doctor Faustus*, which Mann called "the novel of my epoch, dressed up in the story of a highly precarious and sinful artistic life," portrayed the composer Adrian Leverkühn as a modern Faust who personifies the temptation and corruption of contemporary Germany. Leverkühn makes a pact with the Devil to become aware of the extremes of his own personality, thus enriching his experience and his music. His pieces are rationally composed by using intellectual patterns derived from the twelve-tone row, an avant-garde theory of composition based on a sequence of twelve tones with no previous harmonic relations, instead of the traditional musical scale. His *Lamentation of Doctor Faustus* is a direct challenge in theme and technique to the scale-based tonality of that earlier German masterpiece, Beethoven's Ninth Symphony with its concluding *Ode to Joy*. A somber and compelling work, *Doctor Faustus* symbolizes the negation of life Mann found inherent in Hitler's attempt to reshape German culture. Well after the war, when Mann had moved to Zurich, he published a final, comic picture of the artist-figure as a confidence man who uses his skill and ironic insight to manipulate society (*The Confessions of Felix Krull*, 1954). Mann's last work before his death on August 12, 1955, the *Confessions* recapitulates his familiar themes but in a lighthearted parody of traditional bildungsromans that is a far cry from the moral seriousness of earlier tales.

Mann's most famous novella, *Death in Venice*, was published in 1912, shortly after the writer's own vacation in Venice and two years before World War I. Its sense of impending doom involves the cultural disintegration of the "European soul" (soon to be expressed in the Great War) symbolized by the corruption and death of the writer Gustave Aschenbach during an epidemic. The story pictures a loss of psychological balance, a sickness of the artistic soul to match that of plague-ridden Venice masking its true condition before unsuspecting tourists. Erotic and artistic themes mingle as the respected Aschenbach, escaping a lifetime of laborious creation and self-discipline, allows himself to be swept away by the classical beauty of a young boy until he becomes a grotesque figure, dyeing his hair and rouging his cheeks in a vain attempt to appear young. The issue, however, is not Aschenbach's obsession with Tadzio but rather the way that this fatal love casts light on the artist's whole career.

Aschenbach has laboriously repressed emotions and spontaneity to achieve the disciplined, classical style of a master—and also to earn fame. Plagued by nervous exhaustion at the beginning of the story, he reacts to the sight of a foreign traveler with a "sudden, strange expansion of his inner space" and starts dreaming of exotic, dangerous landscapes. From the tropical swampland and tigers of the Ganges delta to the mountains of a later dream's Dionysiac revels, these visionary landscapes become a metaphor for all the subterranean impulses he has rejected in himself and for his art. Enigmatic figures guide Aschenbach's adventure of the emotions: the traveler, the grotesque old man on the boat, the gondolier, the street singer, and Tadzio himself interpreted as a godlike figure out of Greek myth or culture. Indeed, allusions to ancient myth and literature multiply rapidly as Aschenbach falls under Tadzio's spell and begins to rationalize his fascination as the artist's pursuit of divine beauty. Turning to Plato's *Phaedrus,* a dialogue that combines themes of love with the search for absolute beauty and truth, Aschenbach sketches his own "Platonic" argument as a meditation on the dual nature of the artist. It is the same dualism that was described by Nietzsche in *The Birth of Tragedy* (1872) as the complementary opposition of the Apollonian and Dionysian aspects of art. In serving Apollo, the god of clarity and light, Aschenbach has sacrificed an integral part of his artistic vision. He has developed an "official" note and been anthologized in textbooks, but he has lost spontaneity and joy; he lives with the tension of a clenched fist and suffers from repressed yearnings for freedom and mystic beauty. Aschenbach has betrayed the "dark god" Dionysus, who takes thorough and humiliating vengeance as the writer sinks into a passive, fatalistic acceptance of his feelings and remains to the end in the plague-stricken city. "Who can untangle the riddle of the artist's essence and character?" asks the narrator. *Death in Venice* is a crystallization of Mann's work at its best, displaying the penetrating detail of his social and psychological realism, the power of his tightly interwoven symbolic structure, and the cumulative impact of his artist-hero's fall.

Ignace Feuerlicht, *Thomas Mann* (1969), provides a general biographical introduction. Henry Hatfield, ed., *Thomas Mann: A Collection of Critical Essays* (1964), and Harold Bloom, ed., *Thomas Mann* (1986), present essays on different works and brief biographical information. Terence J. Reed, *Thomas Mann: The Uses of Tradition* (rev. 1996), is an excellent, well-written general study incorporating recent material. Richard Winston, *Thomas Mann: The Making of an Artist 1875–1911* (1981), the first volume of an unfinished study, is a detailed and authoritative presentation by the translator of Mann's diaries and letters.

PRONOUNCING GLOSSARY

The following list uses common English syllables and stress accents to provide rough equivalents of selected words whose pronunciation may be unfamiliar to the general reader.

Bildungsroman: *bil'-doongs-roh-mahn'*

Föhringer Chaussée: *feuh'-rin-jer shoh-say'*

Schwabing: *shva'-bing*

Wagner: *vahg'-ner*

Death in Venice[1]

CHAPTER 1

On a spring afternoon in 19—,[2] a year that for months glowered threateningly over our continent, Gustav Aschenbach—or von[3] Aschenbach, as he had been known officially since his fiftieth birthday—set off alone from his dwelling in Prinzregentenstrasse[4] in Munich on a rather long walk. He had been overstrained by the difficult and dangerous morning's work, which just now required particular discretion, caution, penetration, and precision of will: even after his midday meal the writer had not been able to halt the running on of the productive machinery within him, that "motus animi continuus" which Cicero[5] claims is the essence of eloquence, nor had he been able to obtain the relaxing slumber so necessary to him once a day to relieve the increasing demands on his resources. Thus, he sought the open air right after tea, hoping that fresh air and exercise would restore him and help him to have a profitable evening.

It was early May, and after weeks of cold, wet weather a premature summer had set in. The Englischer Garten,[6] although only beginning to come into leaf, was as muggy as in August and at the end near the city was full of vehicles and people out for a stroll. Increasingly quiet paths led Aschenbach toward Aumeister,[7] where he spent a moment surveying the lively crowd in the beer garden, next to which several hackneys and carriages were lingering; but then as the sun went down he took a route homeward outside the park over the open fields and, since he felt tired and thunder clouds now threatened over Föhring,[8] he waited at the North Cemetery stop for the tram that would take him directly back into the city.

As it happened he found the tram stop and the surrounding area deserted. Neither on the paved Ungererstrasse, whose streetcar-tracks stretched in glistening solitude toward Schwabing, nor on the Föhringer Chaussee[9] was there a vehicle to be seen, nothing stirred behind the fences of the stonemasons' shops, where the crosses, headstones, and monuments for sale formed a second, untenanted graveyard, and the Byzantine architecture of the mortuary chapel across the way lay silent in the glow of the departing day. Its facade was decorated with Greek crosses and hieratic paintings in soft colors; in addition it displayed symmetrically arranged scriptural quotations in gold letters, such as, "They are entering the house of God," or, "May the eternal light shine upon them." Waiting, he found a few moments' solemn diversion in reading these formulations and letting his mind's eye bask in their radiant mysticism, when, returning from his reveries, he noticed a man in the portico, above the two apocalyptic beasts guarding the front steps. The man's not altogether ordinary appearance took his thoughts in a completely different direction.

---

1. Translated by and some notes adapted from Clayton Koelb.   2. In 1911, when the story was written, the "Moroccan crisis" was precipitated when a German gunboat appeared off the coast of Agadir, prompting negotiations between France and Germany over their respective national interests. A series of similar diplomatic crises led to the outbreak of World War I in 1914.   3. From or of. *Von* appears in the names of only nobility. Aschenbach was made an honorary nobleman on his fiftieth birthday.   4. A street in Munich that forms the southern boundary of the Englischer Garten (English Garden). Mann lived in various apartments in this neighborhood.   5. Marcus Tullius Cicero (106–43 B.C.), Roman orator. *Motus animi continuus:* the continuous motion of the spirit (Latin, attributed to Cicero).   6. The English Garden, a nine-hundred-acre public park with diverse attractions that extended from the city to the water meadows of the Isar River.   7. A beer garden in the northern section.   8. A district in Munich.   9. A street. Ungererstrasse is a street that borders the North Cemetery. Schwabing is another district in Munich.

It was not clear whether the man had emerged from the chapel through the bronze door or had climbed the steps up to the entry from the outside without being noticed. Aschenbach, without entering too deeply into the question, inclined to the first assumption. Moderately tall, thin, clean-shaven, and strikingly snub-nosed, the man belonged to the red-haired type and possessed a redhead's milky and freckled complexion. He was clearly not of Bavarian stock, and in any case the wide and straight-brimmed straw hat that covered his head lent him the appearance of a foreigner, of a traveler from afar. To be sure, he also wore the familiar native rucksack strapped to his shoulders and a yellowish Norfolk suit[1] apparently of loden cloth. He had a gray mackintosh over his left forearm, which he held supported against his side, and in his right hand he held a stick with an iron tip, which he propped obliquely against the ground, leaning his hip against its handle and crossing his ankles. With his head held up, so that his Adam's apple protruded nakedly from the thin neck that emerged from his loose sport shirt, he gazed intently into the distance with colorless, red-lashed eyes, between which stood two stark vertical furrows that went rather oddly with his short, turned-up nose. It may be that his elevated and elevating location had something to do with it, but his posture conveyed an impression of imperious surveillance, forti-tude, even wildness. His lips seemed insufficient, perhaps because he was squinting, blinded, toward the setting sun or maybe because he was afflicted by a facial deformity—in any case they were retracted to such an extent that his teeth, revealed as far as the gums, menacingly displayed their entire white length.

It is entirely possible that Aschenbach had been somewhat indiscreet in his half-distracted, half-inquisitive survey of the stranger, for he suddenly realized that his gaze was being returned, and indeed returned so belliger-ently, so directly eye to eye, with such a clear intent to bring matters to a head and force the other to avert his eyes, that Aschenbach, with an awkward sense of embarrassment, turned away and began to walk along the fence, intending for the time being to pay no more attention to the fellow. In a moment he had forgotten about him. But perhaps the man had the look of the traveler about him, or perhaps because he exercised some physical or spiritual influence, Aschenbach's imagination was set working. He felt a sud-den, strange expansion of his inner space, a rambling unrest, a youthful thirst for faraway places, a feeling so intense, so new—or rather so long unused and forgotten—that he stood rooted to the spot, his hands behind his back and his gaze to the ground, pondering the essence and direction of his emotion.

It was wanderlust and nothing more, but it was an overwhelming wander-lust that rose to a passion and even to a delusion. His desire acquired vision, and his imagination, not yet calmed down from the morning's work, created its own version of the manifold marvels and terrors of the earth, all of them at once now seeking to take shape within him. He saw, saw a landscape, a tropical swamp under a vaporous sky, moist, luxuriant, and monstrous, a sort of primitive wilderness of islands, morasses, and alluvial estuaries; saw hairy palm trunks rise up near and far out of rank fern brakes, out of thick, swollen, wildly blooming vegetation; saw wondrously formless trees sink their aerial roots into the earth through stagnant, green-shadowed pools, where exotic

1. A belted suit.

birds, their shoulders high and their bills shaped weirdly, stood motionless in the shallows looking askance amidst floating flowers that were white as milk and big as platters; saw the eyes of a lurking tiger sparkle between the gnarled stems of a bamboo thicket; and felt his heart pound with horror and mysterious desire. Then the vision faded, and with a shake of his head Aschenbach resumed his promenade along the fences bordering the head-stone-makers' yard.

He had regarded travel, at least since he had commanded the financial resources to enjoy the advantages of global transportation at will, as nothing more than a measure he had to take for his health, no matter how much it went against his inclination. Too much taken up with the tasks that his problematic self and the European soul posed for him, too burdened with the obligation of productivity, too averse to distraction to be a success as a lover of the world's motley show, he had quite contented himself with the view of the earth's surface anyone could get without stirring very far from home. He had never even been tempted to leave Europe. Especially now that his life was slowly waning, now that his artist's fear of never getting finished—his concern that the sands might run out of the glass before he had done his utmost and given his all—could no longer be dismissed as pure fancy, his external existence had confined itself almost exclusively to the lovely city that had become his home and to the rustic country house he had built in the mountains where he spent the rainy summers.

Besides, even this impulse that had come over him so suddenly and so late in life was quickly moderated and set right by reason and a self-discipline practiced since early youth. He had intended to keep at the work to which he now devoted his life until he reached a certain point and then move out to the country. The thought of sauntering about the world, of thereby being seduced away from months of work, seemed all too frivolous, too contrary to plan, and ultimately impermissible. And yet he knew all too well why this temptation had assailed him so unexpectedly. He had to admit it to himself: it was the urge to escape that was behind this yearning for the far away and the new, this desire for release, freedom, and forgetfulness. It was the urge to get away from his work, from the daily scene of an inflexible, cold, and passionate service. Of course he loved this service and almost loved the enervating struggle, renewed each day, between his stubborn, proud, so-often-tested will and his growing lassitude, about which no one could be allowed to know and which the product of his toil could not be permitted to reveal in any way, by any sign of failure or of negligence. Yet it seemed reasonable not to overbend the bow and not to stifle obstinately the outbreak of such a vital need. He thought about his work, thought about the place where once again, today as yesterday, he had been forced to abandon it, a passage that would submit, it seemed, neither to patient care nor to surprise attack. He considered it again, sought once more to break through or untangle the logjam, then broke off the effort with a shudder of repugnance. The passage presented no extraordinary difficulty; what disabled him was the malaise of scrupulousness confronting him in the guise of an insatiable perfectionism. Even as a young man, to be sure, he had considered perfectionism the basis and most intimate essence of his talent, and for its sake he had curbed and cooled his emotions, because he knew that emotion inclines one to satisfaction with a comfortable approximation, a half of perfection. Was his enslaved sensitivity now avenging itself by leaving him, refusing to advance his project and give wings to his art, taking with it all his joy, all his delight in form and expression? It was not that he was producing bad work—that at least was the advantage of his advanced years; he felt every moment comfortably secure in his mastery. But, though the nation honored it, he himself was not pleased with his mastery, and indeed it seemed to him that his work lacked those earmarks of a fiery, playful fancy that, stemming from joy, gave more joy to his appreciative audience than did any inner content or weighty excellence. He was fearful of the summer in the country, all alone in the little house with the maid who prepared his meals and the servant who waited on him at table, fearful too of the familiar mountaintops and mountainsides that once more would surround him in his discontented, slow progress. And so what he needed was a respite, a kind of spur-of-the-moment existence, a way to waste some time, foreign air and an infusion of new blood, to make the summer bearable and productive. Travel it would be then—it was all right with him. Not too far, though, not quite all the way to the tigers. One night in a sleeping car and a siesta for three or maybe four weeks in some fashionable vacation spot in the charming south . . .

Such were his thoughts as the noise of the electric tram approached along the Ungererstrasse, and he decided as he got on to devote this evening to studying maps and time tables. Once aboard it occurred to him to look around for the man in the straw hat, his comrade in this excursion that had been, in spite of all, so consequential. But he could get no clear idea of the man's whereabouts; neither his previous location, nor the next stop, nor the tram car itself revealed any signs of his presence.

CHAPTER 2

Gustav Aschenbach, the author of the clear and vigorous prose epic on the life of Frederick the Great;[2] the patient artist who wove together with enduring diligence the novelistic tapestry *Maia*,[3] a work rich in characters and eminently successful in gathering together many human destinies under the shadow of a single idea; the creator of that powerful story bearing the title "A Man of Misery," which had earned the gratitude of an entire young generation by showing it the possibility for a moral resolution that passed through and beyond the deepest knowledge; the author, finally (and this completes the short list of his mature works), of the passionate treatment of the topic "Art and Intellect,"[4] an essay whose power of organization and antithetical eloquence had prompted serious observers to rank it alongside Schiller's "On Naïve and Sentimental Poetry";[5] Gustav Aschenbach, then, was born the son of a career civil servant in the justice ministry in L., a district capital in the province of Silesia. His ancestors had been officers, judges, and government functionaries, men who had led upright lives of austere decency devoted to the service of king and country. A more ardent spirituality had expressed itself once among them in the person of a preacher; more impetuous and sensuous blood had entered the family line in the pre-

2. King Frederick II (1712–1786) started Prussia on its rise to domination of Germany and made his court a prominent European cultural center.   3. In the Hindu religion, the illusory appearance of the world concealing a higher spiritual reality.   4. *Frederick, Maia, A Man of Misery*, and *Art and Intellect* are titles of projects Mann had worked on and abandoned.   5. An influential essay by the German Romantic writer Friedrich Schiller (1759–1805).

vious generation through the writer's mother, the daughter of a Bohemian music director. It was from her that he had in his features the traits of a foreign race. The marriage of sober conscientiousness devoted to service with darker, more fiery impulses engendered an artist and indeed this very special artist.

Since his entire being was bent on fame, he emerged early on as, perhaps not exactly precocious, but nonetheless, thanks to the decisiveness and peculiar terseness of his style, surprisingly mature and ready to go before the public. He was practically still in high school when he made a name for himself. Ten years later he learned how to keep up appearances, to manage his fame from his writing desk, to produce gracious and significant sentences for his necessarily brief letters (for many demands are made on such a successful and reliable man). By the age of forty, exhausted by the tortures and vicissitudes of his real work, he had to deal with a daily flood of mail bearing stamps from countries in every corner of the globe.

Tending neither to the banal nor to the eccentric, his talent was such as to win for his stories both the acceptance of the general public and an admiring, challenging interest from a more discerning audience. Thus he found himself even as a young man obliged in every way to achieve and indeed to achieve extraordinary things. He had therefore never known sloth, never known the carefree, laissez-faire attitude of youth. When he got sick in Vienna around the age of thirty-five, a canny observer remarked about him to friends, "You see, Aschenbach has always lived like this"—and the speaker closed the fingers of his left hand into a fist—"never like this"—and he let his open hand dangle comfortably from the arm of the chair. How right he was! And the morally courageous aspect of it was that, possessing anything but a naturally robust constitution, he was not so much born for constant exertion as he was called to it.

Medical concerns had prevented him from attending school as a child and compelled the employment of private instruction at home. He had grown up alone and without companions, and yet he must have realized early on that he belonged to a tribe in which talent was not so much a rarity as was the bodily frame talent needs to find its fulfillment, a tribe known for giving their best early in life but not for longevity. His watchword, however, was "Endure," and he saw in his novel about Frederick the Great precisely the apotheosis of this commandment, which seemed to him the essence of a selflessly active virtue. He harbored, moreover, a keen desire to live to a ripe old age, for he had long believed that an artistic career could be called truly great, encompassing, indeed truly worthy of honor only if the artist were allotted sufficient years to be fruitful in his own way at all stages of human life.

Since he thus bore the burdens of his talent on slender shoulders and wished to carry those burdens far, he was in great need of discipline. Fortunately for him discipline was his heritage at birth from his paternal side. At forty, at fifty, even at an age when others squander and stray, content to put their great plans aside for the time being, he started his day at an early hour by dousing his chest and back with cold water. Then, placing two tall wax candles in silver candlesticks at the head of his manuscript, he would spend two or three fervently conscientious morning hours sacrificing on the altar of art the powers he had assembled during his sleep. It was forgivable—

indeed it even indicated the victory of his moral force—that uninformed readers mistook the Maiaworld or the epic scroll on which unrolled Frederick's heroic life for the products of single sustained bursts of energy, whereas they actually grew into grandeur layer by layer, out of small daily doses of work and countless individual flashes of inspiration. These works were thoroughly excellent in every detail solely because their creator had endured for years under the pressure of a single project, bringing to bear a tenacity and perseverance similar to that which had conquered his home province,[6] and because he had devoted only his freshest and worthiest hours to actual composition.

If a work of the intellect is to have an immediate, broad, and deep effect, there must be a mysterious affinity, a correspondence between the personal fate of its originator and the more general fate of his contemporaries. People do not know why they accord fame to a particular work. Far from being experts, they suppose they see in it a hundred virtues that would justify their interest; but the real reason for their approval is something imponderable—it is sympathy. Aschenbach had actually stated forthrightly, though in a relatively inconspicuous passage, that nearly everything achieving greatness did so under the banner of "Despite"—despite grief and suffering, despite poverty, destitution, infirmity, affliction, passion, and a thousand obstacles. But this was more than an observation, it was the fruit of experience; no, it was the very formula for his life and his fame, the key to his work. Was it any wonder, then, that it was also the basis for the moral disposition and outward demeanor of his most original fictional characters?

Early on an observant critic had described the new type of hero that this writer preferred, a figure returning over and over again in manifold variation: it was based on the concept of "an intellectual and youthful manliness which grits its teeth in proud modesty and calmly endures the swords and spears as they pass through its body." It was a nice description, ingenious and precise, despite its seemingly excessive emphasis on passivity. For meeting one's fate with dignity, grace under pressure of pain, is not simply a matter of sufferance; it is an active achievement, a positive triumph, and the figure of St. Sebastian[7] is thus the most beautiful image, if not of art in general, then surely of the art under discussion here. Having looked at the characters in Aschenbach's narrated world, having seen the elegant self-discipline that managed right up to the last moment to hide from the eyes of the world the undermining process, the biological decline, taking place within; having seen the yellow, physically handicapped ugliness that nonetheless managed to kindle its smoldering ardor into a pure flame, managed even to catapult itself to mastery in the realm of beauty; or having seen the pale impotence that pulls out of the glowing depths of the spirit enough power to force a whole frivolous people to fall at the feet of the cross, at the feet of that very impotence; or the lovable charm that survives even the empty and rigorous service of pure form; or the false, dangerous life of the born deceiver, with the quick enervation of its longing and with its artfulness—having seen all these human destinies and many more besides, it was easy enough to doubt that there could be any other sort of heroism than that of weakness. In any case,

---

6. As a result of the Seven Years' War (1759–63), Frederick the Great wrested Silesia from Austria. Today, most of Silesia has become a region in southwestern Poland. 7. A 3rd-century Roman martyr whose arrow-pierced body was a popular subject for Renaissance painters.

what kind of heroism was more appropriate to the times than this? Gustav Aschenbach was the poet of all those who work on the edge of exhaustion, of the overburdened, worn down moralists of achievement who nonetheless still stand tall, those who, stunted in growth and short of means, use ecstatic feats of will and clever management to extract from themselves at least for a period of time the effects of greatness. Their names are legion, and they are the heroes of the age. And all of them recognized themselves in his work; they saw themselves justified, exalted, their praises sung. And they were grateful; they heralded his name.

He had been once as young and rough as the times and, seduced by them, had made public blunders and mistakes, had made himself vulnerable, had committed errors against tact and good sense in word and deed. But he had won the dignity toward which, in his opinion, every great talent feels an inborn urge and spur. One could say in fact that his entire development had been a conscious and defiant rise to dignity, beyond any twinge of doubt and of irony that might have stood in his way.

Pleasing the great mass of middle-class readers depends mainly on offering vividly depicted, intellectually undemanding characterizations, but passionately uncompromising youth is smitten only with what is problematic; and Aschenbach had been as problematic and uncompromising as any young man can be. He had pandered to the intellect, exhausted the soil of knowledge, milled flour from his seed corn, revealed secrets, put talent under suspicion, betrayed art. Indeed, while his portrayals entertained, elevated, invigorated the blissfully credulous among his readers, as a youthful artist it was his cynical observations on the questionable nature of art and of the artist's calling that had kept the twenty-year-old element fascinated.

But it seems that nothing so quickly or so thoroughly blunts a high-minded and capable spirit as the sharp and bitter charm of knowledge; and it is certain that the melancholy, scrupulous thoroughness characteristic of the young seems shallow in comparison with the solemn decision of masterful maturity to disavow knowledge, to reject it, to move beyond it with head held high, to forestall the least possibility that it could cripple, dishearten, or dishonor his will, his capacity for action and feeling, or even his passion. How else could one interpret the famous story "A Man of Misery" save as an outbreak of disgust at the indecent psychologism then current? This disgust was embodied in the figure of that soft and foolish semi-villain who, out of weakness, viciousness, and moral impotence, buys a black-market destiny for himself by driving his wife into the arms of a beardless boy, who imagines profundity can justify committing the basest acts. The weight of the words with which the writer of that work reviled the vile announced a decisive turn away from all moral skepticism, from all sympathy with the abyss, a rejection of the laxity inherent in the supposedly compassionate maxim that to understand everything is to forgive everything. What was coming into play here—or rather, what was already in full swing—was that "miracle of ingenuousness reborn" about which there was explicit discussion, not without a certain mysterious emphasis, in one of the author's dialogues published only slightly later. Strange relationships! Was it an intellectual consequence of this "rebirth," of this new dignity and rigor, that just then readers began to notice an almost excessive increase in his sense of beauty, a noble purity, simplicity, and sense of proportion that henceforth gave his works such a palpable, one might say deliberately classical and masterful quality? But moral determination that goes beyond knowledge, beyond analytic and inhibiting perception—would that not also be a reduction, a moral simplification of the world and of the human soul and therefore also a growing potential for what is evil, forbidden, and morally unacceptable? And does form not have two faces? Is it not moral and amoral at the same time—moral insofar as form is the product and expression of discipline, but amoral and indeed immoral insofar as it harbors within itself by nature a certain moral indifference and indeed is essentially bent on forcing the moral realm to stoop under its proud and absolute scepter?

That is as may be. Since human development is human destiny, how could a life led in public, accompanied by the accolades and confidence of thousands, develop as does one led without the glory and the obligations of fame? Only those committed to eternal bohemianism would be bored and inclined to ridicule when a great talent emerges from its libertine chrysalis, accustoms itself to recognizing emphatically the dignity of the spirit, takes on the courtly airs of solitude, a solitude full of unassisted, defiantly independent suffering and struggle, and ultimately achieves power and honor in the public sphere. And how much playfulness, defiance, and indulgence there is in the way talent develops! A kind of official, educative element began in time to appear in Aschenbach's productions. His style in later years dispensed with the sheer audacity, the subtle and innovative shadings of his younger days, and moved toward the paradigmatic, the polished and traditional, the conservative and formal, even formulaic. Like Louis XIV[8]—as report would have it—the aging writer banished from his vocabulary every base expression. About this time it came to pass that the educational authorities began using selected passages from his works in their prescribed textbooks.[9] He seemed to sense the inner appropriateness of it, and he did not refuse when a German prince, newly ascended to the throne, bestowed on the author of *Frederick*, on his fiftieth birthday, a nonhereditary title.

Relatively early on, after a few years of moving about, a few tries at living here and there, he chose Munich as his permanent residence and lived there in bourgeois respectability such as comes to intellectuals sometimes, in exceptional cases. His marriage to a girl from a learned family, entered upon when still a young man, was terminated after only a short term of happiness by her death. A daughter, already married, remained to him. He never had a son.

Gustav Aschenbach was a man of slightly less than middle height, dark-haired and clean shaven. His head seemed a little too big for a body that was almost dainty. His hair, combed back, receding at the top, still very full at the temples, though quite gray, framed a high, furrowed, and almost embossed-looking brow. The gold frame of his rimless glasses cut into the bridge of his full, nobly curved nose. His mouth was large, sometimes relaxed and full, sometimes thin and tense; his cheeks were lean and hollow, and his well-proportioned chin was marked by a slight cleft. Important destinies seemed to have played themselves out on this long-suffering face, which he often held tilted somewhat to one side. And yet it was art alone, not a difficult

---

8. King of France (1638–1715), the "great monarch" of the French classical period. 9. I.e., he received national recognition in the highly centralized German educational system.

and troubled life, that had taken over the task of chiseling these features. Behind this brow was born the scintillating repartee between Voltaire and King Frederick on the subject of war; these eyes, looking tiredly but piercingly through the glasses, had seen the bloody inferno of the field hospitals during the Seven Years' War.[1] Indeed, even on the personal level art provides an intensified version of life. Art offers a deeper happiness, but it consumes one more quickly. It engraves upon the faces of its servants the traces of imaginary, mental adventures and over the long term, even given an external existence of cloistered quietude, engenders in them a nervous sensitivity, an over-refinement, a weariness and an inquisitiveness such as are scarcely ever produced by a life full of extravagant passions and pleasures.

CHAPTER 3

Several obligations of both a practical and a literary nature forced the eager traveler to remain in Munich for about two weeks after his walk in the park. Finally he gave instructions for his country house to be prepared for his moving in within a month's time and, on a day sometime between the middle and end of May, he took the night train to Trieste, where he remained only twenty-four hours and where he boarded the boat to Pola[2] on the morning of the next day.

What he sought was someplace foreign, someplace isolated, but someplace nonetheless easy to get to. He thus took up residence on an Adriatic island, a destination that had been highly spoken of in recent years and lay not far from the Istrian coast. It was populated by locals dressed in colorful rags who spoke in wildly exotic accents, and the landscape was graced by rugged cliffs on the coast facing the open sea. But the rain and oppressive air, the provincial, exclusively Austrian clientele at the hotel, and the lack of the peaceful, intimate relation with the sea that only a soft sandy beach can offer—these things irritated him, denied him a sense of having found the place he was looking for; he was troubled by a pressure within him pushing in a direction he could not quite grasp; he studied ship schedules, he sought about for something; and suddenly the surprising but obvious destination came to him. If you wanted to reach in a single night someplace incomparable, someplace as out of the ordinary as a fairy tale, where did you go? The answer was clear. What was he doing here? He had gone astray. It was over there that he had wanted to go all along. He did not hesitate a moment in remedying his error and gave notice of his departure. A week and a half after his arrival on the island a swift motorboat carried him and his baggage through the early morning mist across the water to the military port, where he landed only long enough to find the gangway leading him onto the damp deck of a ship that was already getting up steam for a trip to Venice.[3]

It was an aged vessel, long past its prime, sooty, and gloomy, sailing under the Italian flag. In a cavernous, artificially lit cabin in the ship's interior—to

1. A global war (1756–63) fought in Europe, North America, and India between European powers. François Marie Arouet de Voltaire (1694–1778), French writer and philosopher, was a guest at the court of Frederick the Great from 1750 until 1753, when he found it wise to leave after a disagreement. 2. Trieste (in Italy) and Pola (or Pula, in Croatia) are major ports at the head of the Adriatic Sea. Until 1919 they were Austrian possessions. 3. An ancient city whose network of bridges and canals links 118 islands in the Gulf of Venice. The Republic of Venice was headed by a doge (duke) and was a cultural, commercial, and political center in Europe from the 14th century.

which Aschenbach had been conducted with smirking politeness by a hunch-backed, scruffy sailor the moment he embarked—sat a goateed man behind a desk. With his hat cocked over his brow and a cigarette butt hanging from the corner of his mouth, his facial features were reminiscent of an old time ringmaster. He took down the passengers' personal information and doled out tickets with the grimacing, easy demeanor of the professional. "To Venice!" He repeated Aschenbach's request, stretching his arm to dip his pen in the congealed remains at the bottom of his slightly tilted inkwell. "To Venice, first class! There, sir, you're all taken care of." He inscribed great letters like crane's feet on a piece of paper, poured blue sand out of a box onto them, poured it back into an earthenware bowl, folded the paper with his yellow, bony fingers, and resumed writing. "What a fine choice for your destination!" he babbled in the meantime. "Ah, Venice, a wonderful city! A city that is irresistible to cultured people both for its history and for its modern charm!" The smooth swiftness of his movements and the empty chatter with which he accompanied them had an anesthetic and diversionary effect, as if he were concerned that the traveler should change his mind about his decision to go to Venice. He hastily took the money and dropped the change on the stained cloth covering the table with the practiced swiftness of a croupier.[4] "Enjoy yourself, sir!" he said with a theatrical bow. "It is an honor to be of service to you. . . . Next, please!" he cried with his arm raised, acting as if he were still doing a brisk business, though in fact there was no one else there to do business with. Aschenbach returned above deck.

With one arm resting on the rail, he observed the passengers on board and the idle crowd loitering on the pier to watch the ship depart. The second-class passengers, both men and women, crouched on the forward deck using boxes and bundles as seats. A group of young people, apparently employees of businesses in Pola, who had banded together in great excitement for an excursion to Italy, formed the social set of the first upper deck. They made no little fuss over themselves and their plans, chattered, laughed, and took complacent enjoyment in their own continual gesturing. Leaning over the railing they called out in fluent and mocking phrases to various friends going about their business, briefcases under their arms, along the dockside street below, while the latter in turn made mock-threatening gestures with their walking sticks at the celebrants above. One of the merrymakers, wearing a bright yellow, overly fashionable summer suit, red tie, and a panama hat with a cockily turned-up brim, outdid all the others in his screeching gaiety. But scarcely had Aschenbach gotten a closer look at him when he realized with something like horror that this youth was not genuine. He was old, no doubt about it. There were wrinkles around his eyes and mouth. The faint carmine of his cheeks was rouge; the brown hair beneath the colorfully banded hat was a wig; his neck was shrunken and sinewy; his clipped mustache and goatee were dyed; the full, yellowish set of teeth he exposed when he laughed was a cheap set of dentures; and his hands, bedecked with signet rings on both forefingers, were those of an old man. With a shudder Aschenbach watched him and his interaction with his friends. Did they not know, had they not noticed that he was old, that he had no right to wear their foppish and colorful clothes, had no right to pretend to be one of their own? They

---

4. Attendant at a gambling table who handles bets and money.

apparently tolerated him in their midst as a matter of course, out of habit, and treated him as an equal, answering in kind without reluctance when he teasingly poked one of them in the ribs. But how could this be? Aschenbach covered his brow with his hand and closed his eyes, which were feeling inflamed from not getting enough sleep. It seemed to him that things were starting to take a turn away from the ordinary, as if a dreamy estrangement, a bizarre distortion of the world were setting in and would spread if he did not put a stop to it by shading his eyes a bit and taking another look around him. Just at this moment he experienced a sensation of motion and, looking up with an unreasoning terror, realized that the heavy and gloomy hulk of the ship was slowly parting company with the stone pier. The engines ran alternately forward and reverse, and inch by inch the band of oily, iridescent water between the pier and the hull of the ship widened. After a set of cumbersome maneuvers the steamer managed to point its bowsprit toward the open sea. Aschenbach went over to the starboard side, where the hunchback had set up a deck chair for him and a steward dressed in a stained tailcoat offered him service.

The sky was gray and the wind was moist. The harbor and the island were left behind, and soon all sight of land vanished beyond the misty horizon. Flakes of coal soot saturated with moisture fell on the scrubbed, never drying deck. No more than an hour later a canvas canopy was put up, since it had started to rain.

Wrapped in his cloak, a book on his lap, the traveler rested, and the hours passed by unnoticed. It stopped raining; the linen canopy was removed. The horizon was unobstructed. Beneath the overcast dome of the sky the immense disk of the desolate sea stretched into the distance all around. But in empty, undivided space our sense of time fails us, and we lose ourselves in the immeasurable. Strange and shadowy figures—the old fop, the goatbeard from below deck—invaded Aschenbach's mind as he rested. They gestured obscurely and spoke the confused speech of dreams. He fell asleep.

At noon they called him to lunch down in the corridorlike dining hall onto which opened the doors of all the sleeping quarters and in which stood a long table. He dined at one end, while at the other the business employees from Pola, including the old fop, had been carousing since ten o'clock with the jolly captain. The meal was wretched and he soon got up. He felt an urgent need to get out, to look at the sky, to see if it might not be brightening over Venice.

It had never occurred to him that anything else could happen, for the city had always received him in shining glory. But the sky and the sea remained overcast and leaden. From time to time a misty rain fell, and he came to the realization that he would approach a very different Venice by sea than the one he had previously reached by land. He stood by the foremast, gazing into the distance, awaiting the sight of land. He remembered the melancholy, enthusiastic poet of long ago who had furnished his dreams with the domes and bell towers rising from these waters. He softly repeated to himself some of those verses in which the awe, joy, and sadness of a former time had taken stately shape[5] and, easily moved by sensations thus already formed, looked

5. The lines are probably from *Sonnets on Venice* (1825) by the German classical poet August Graf Platen (1796–1835): "My eye left the high seas behind / as the temples of [the architect Andrea] Palladio rose from the waters."

into his earnest and weary heart to see if some new enthusiasm or entanglement, some late adventure of feeling might be in store for him, the idle
traveler.

Then the flat coastline emerged on the right; the sea became populated
with fishing boats; the barrier island with its beach appeared. The steamer
soon left the island behind to the left, slipping at reduced speed through the
narrow harbor named after it.[6] They came to a full stop in the lagoon in view
of rows of colorfully wretched dwellings and awaited the arrival of the launch
belonging to the health service.

An hour passed before it appeared. One had arrived and yet had not
arrived; there was no great hurry and yet one felt driven by impatience. The
young people from Pola had come up on deck, apparently yielding to a patriotic attraction to the military trumpet calls resounding across the water from
the public garden. Full of excitement and Asti, they shouted cheers at the
bersaglieri[7] conducting drills over there. It was disgusting, however, to see
the state into which the made-up old coot's false fellowship with the young
people had brought him. His aged brain had not been able to put up the
same resistance to the wine as the younger and more vigorous heads, and he
was wretchedly drunk. His vision blurred; a cigarette dangled from his shaking fingers; he stood swaying tipsily in place, pulled to and fro by intoxication,
barely able to maintain his balance. Since he would have fallen over at the
first step, he dared not move from the spot. Yet he maintained a woeful
bravado, buttonholing everyone who came near; he stammered, blinked, giggled, raised his beringed, wrinkled forefinger in fatuous banter, and ran the
tip of his tongue around the corners of his mouth in an obscenely suggestive
manner. Aschenbach watched him from under a darkened brow and was
once again seized by a feeling of giddiness, as if the world were displaying a
slight but uncontrollable tendency to distort, to take on a bizarre and sneering aspect. It was a feeling, to be sure, that conditions prevented him from
indulging, for just then the engine began anew its pounding, and the ship,
interrupted so close to its destination, resumed its course through the canal
of San Marco.[8]

Once more, then, it lay before him, that most astounding of landing places,
that dazzling grouping of fantastic buildings that the republic presented to
the awed gaze of approaching mariners: the airy splendor of the palace and
the Bridge of Sighs; the pillars on the water's edge bearing the lion and the
saint; the showy projecting flank of the fairy tale cathedral; the view toward
the gate and the great clock.[9] It occurred to him as he raised his eyes that
to arrive in Venice by land, at the railway station, was like entering a palace
by a back door; that one ought not to approach this most improbable of cities
save as he now did, by ship, over the high seas.

The engine stopped, gondolas swarmed about, the gangway was lowered,
customs officials boarded and haughtily went about their duties; disembar-
kation could begin. Aschenbach let it be known that he desired a gondola to
take him and his luggage over to the landing where he could get one of the

6. Both the barrier island and the harbor are called Lido. The island is the site of a famous resort.
7. Elite Italian troops. *Asti:* or asti spumante, a sweet, sparkling Italian wine. 8. Saint Mark's Canal,
named for the patron saint of Venice. 9. A large clock tower built in the late 15th century. *Bridge of
Sighs:* condemned prisoners would walk over this bridge when proceeding to prison from the ducal palace.
Pillars: one is surmounted by a statue of St. Theodore stepping on a crocodile; the second, by a winged
lion, emblem of St. Mark. *Cathedral:* the Church of St. Mark.

little steamboats that ran between the city and the Lido; for it was his intention to take up residence by the sea. His wishes met with acquiescence; a call went down with his request to the water's surface where the gondoliers were quarreling with each other in dialect. He was still prevented from disembarking; his trunk presented problems; only with considerable difficulty could it be pulled and tugged down the ladderlike gangway. He therefore found himself unable for several moments to escape from the importunities of the ghastly old impostor, who, driven by some dark drunken impulse, was determined to bid elaborate farewell to the foreign traveler. "We wish you the happiest of stays," he bleated, bowing and scraping. "Keeping a fond memory of us! Au revoir, excusez, and bonjour,[1] your excellency!" He drooled, he batted his eyes, he licked the corners of his mouth, and the dyed goatee on his elderly chin bristled. "Our compliments," he babbled, two fingertips at his mouth, "our compliments to your beloved, your dearly beloved, your lovely beloved . . ." And suddenly his uppers fell out of his jaw onto his lower lip. Aschenbach took his chance to escape. "Your beloved, your sweet beloved . . ." He heard the cooing, hollow, obstructed sounds behind his back as he descended the gangway, clutching at the rope handrail as he went.

Who would not need to fight off a fleeting shiver, a secret aversion and anxiety, at the prospect of boarding a Venetian gondola for the first time or after a long absence? This strange conveyance, surviving unchanged since legendary times and painted the particular sort of black[2] ordinarily reserved for coffins, makes one think of silent, criminal adventures in a darkness full of splashing sounds; makes one think even more of death itself, of biers and gloomy funerals, and of that final, silent journey. And has anyone noticed that the seat of one of these boats, this armchair painted coffin-black and upholstered in dull black cloth, is one of the softest, most luxurious, most sleep-inducing seats in the world? Aschenbach certainly realized this as he sat down at the gondolier's feet, opposite his luggage lying in a copious pile in the bow. The oarsmen were still quarreling in a rough, incomprehensible language punctuated by threatening gestures. The peculiar quiet of this city of water, however, seemed to soften their voices, to disembody them, to disperse them over the sea. It was warm here in the harbor. Stroked by the mild breath of the sirocco,[3] leaning back into the cushions as the yielding element carried him, the traveler closed his eyes in the pleasure of indulging in an indolence both unaccustomed and sweet. The trip will be short, he thought; if only it could last forever! The gondola rocked softly, and he felt himself slip away from the crowded ship and the clamoring voices.

How quiet, ever more quiet it grew around him! Nothing could be heard but the splashing of the oar, the hollow slap of the waves against the gondola's prow, rising rigid and black above the water with its halberdlike beak—and then a third thing, a voice, a whisper. It was the murmur of the gondolier, who was talking to himself through his clenched teeth in fits and starts, emitting sounds that were squeezed out of him by the labor of his arms. Aschenbach looked up and realized with some astonishment that the lagoon was widening about him and that he was traveling in the direction of the open sea. It seemed, then, that he ought not to rest quite so peacefully but instead make sure his wishes were carried out.

1. Goodbye, excuse me, and good-day (French).   2. Legend explains the gondolas' traditional black through an ancient law forbidding ostentation.   3. A hot wind originating in the Sahara, which becomes humid as it picks up moisture over the Mediterranean.

"I told you to take me to the steamer landing," he said with a half turn toward the stern. The murmur ceased. He received no answer.

"I told you to take me to the steamer landing!" he repeated, turning around completely and looking up into the face of the gondolier, whose figure, perched on the high deck and silhouetted against the dun sky, towered behind him. The man had a disagreeable, indeed brutal-looking appearance; he wore a blue sailor suit belted with a yellow sash, and a shapeless straw hat that was beginning to come unraveled and was tilted rakishly on his head. His facial features and the blond, curly mustache under his short, turned-up nose marked him as clearly not of Italian stock. Although rather slender of build, so that one would not have thought him particularly well suited to his profession, he plied his oar with great energy, putting his whole body into every stroke. Several times he pulled his lips back with the strain, baring his white teeth. His reddish eyebrows puckered, he looked out over his passenger's head and replied in a decisive, almost curt tone of voice: "You are going to the Lido."

Aschenbach responded, "Indeed. But I took the gondola only to get over to San Marco. I want to use the vaporetto."[4]

"You cannot use the vaporetto, sir."

"And why not?"

"Because the vaporetto does not accept luggage."

He was right about that; Aschenbach remembered. He said nothing. But the gruff, presumptuous manner of the man, so unlike the normal way of treating foreigners in this country, was not to be endured. He said, "That is my business. Perhaps I intend to put my luggage in storage. You will kindly turn back."

There was silence. The oar splashed, the waves slapped dully against the bow. And the murmuring and whispering began anew: the gondolier was talking to himself through his clenched teeth.

What to do? Alone at sea with this strangely insubordinate, uncannily resolute person, the traveler saw no way to enforce his wishes. And anyway, if he could just avoid getting angry, what a lovely rest he could have! Had he not wished the trip could last longer, could last forever? The smartest thing to do was to let matters take their course; more important, it was also the most pleasant thing to do. A magic circle of indolence seemed to surround the place where he sat, this low armchair upholstered in black, so gently rocked by the rowing of the autocratic gondolier behind him. The idea that he might have fallen into the hands of a criminal rambled about dreamily in Aschenbach's mind, but it was incapable of rousing his thoughts to active resistance. More annoying was the possibility that all this was simply a device by which to extort money from him. A sense of duty or of pride, the memory, as it were, that one must prevent such things, induced him once more to pull himself together. He asked, "What do you want for the trip?"

And the gondolier, looking out over him, answered, "You will pay."

It was clear what reply was necessary here. Aschenbach said mechanically, "I will pay nothing, absolutely nothing, if you take me where I do not want to go."

"You want to go to the Lido."

"But not with you."

---

4. Little steamboat (Italian); used for public transport.

"I row you well."

True enough, thought Aschenbach, and relaxed. True enough, you row me well. Even if you are just after my money, even if you send me to the house of Aides[5] with a stroke of your oar from behind, you will have rowed me well.

But no such thing occurred. In fact, some company even happened by in the form of a boat filled with musicians, both men and women, who waylaid the gondola, sailing obtrusively right alongside. They sang to the accompaniment of guitars and mandolins and filled the quiet air over the lagoon with the strains of their mercenary tourist lyrics. Aschenbach threw some money in the hat they held out to him, whereupon they fell silent and sailed off. The murmur of the gondolier became perceptible once again as he talked to himself in fits and starts.

And so they arrived, bobbing in the wake of a steamer sailing back to the city. Two municipal officials walked up and down along the landing, their hands behind their backs and their faces turned to the lagoon. Aschenbach stepped from the gondola onto the dock assisted by one of those old men who seemed on hand, armed with a boathook, at every pier in Venice. Since he had no small coins with him, he crossed over to the hotel next to the steamer wharf to get change with which to pay the boatman an appropriate fee. His needs met in the lobby, he returned to find his baggage stowed on a cart on the dock. Gondola and gondolier had disappeared.

"He took off," said the old man with the boathook. "A bad man he was, sir, a man without a license. He's the only gondolier who doesn't have a license. The others telephoned over. He saw that we were on the lookout for him, so he took off."

Aschenbach shrugged his shoulders.

"You had a free ride, sir," the old man said, holding out his hat. Aschenbach threw some coins in it. He gave instructions that his luggage be taken to the Hotel des Bains[6] and then followed the cart along the boulevard of white blossoms, lined on both sides by taverns, shops, and boarding houses, that runs straight across the island to the beach.

He entered the spacious hotel from behind, from the garden terrace, and crossed the great lobby to reach the vestibule where the office was. Since he had a reservation, he was received with officious courtesy. A manager, a quiet, flatteringly polite little man with a black mustache and a French-style frock coat, accompanied him in the elevator to the third floor and showed him to his room. It was a pleasant place, furnished in cherry wood, decorated with highly fragrant flowers, and offering a view of the open sea through a set of tall windows. After the manager had withdrawn and while his luggage was being brought up and put in place in his room, he went up to one of the windows and looked out on the beach. It was nearly deserted in the afternoon lull, and the ocean, at high tide and bereft of sunshine, was sending long, low waves against the shore in a peaceful rhythm.

A lonely, quiet person has observations and experiences that are at once both more indistinct and more penetrating than those of one more gregarious; his thoughts are weightier, stranger, and never without a tinge of sad-

---

5. A Greek spelling of *Hades*, the ruler of the world of the dead in Greek and Roman mythology. The newly dead entered the underworld by paying a coin to the boatman, Charon, who then ferried them across the river Styx. **6.** Bathing hotel (French, literal trans.); a famous seaside hotel.

ness. Images and perceptions that others might shrug off with a glance, a laugh, or a brief conversation occupy him unduly, become profound in his silence, become significant, become experience, adventure, emotion. Loneliness fosters that which is original, daringly and bewilderingly beautiful, poetic. But loneliness also fosters that which is perverse, incongruous, absurd, forbidden. Thus the events of the journey that brought him here—the ghastly old fop with his drivel about a beloved, the outlaw gondolier who was cheated of his reward—continued to trouble the traveler's mind. Though they did not appear contrary to reason, did not really give cause for second thoughts, the paradox was that they were nonetheless fundamentally and essentially odd, or so it seemed to him, and therefore troubling precisely because of this paradox. In the meantime his eyes greeted the sea, and he felt joy in knowing Venice to be in such comfortable proximity. He turned away at last, went to wash his face, gave some instructions to the maid with regard to completing arrangements to insure his comfort, and then put himself in the hands of the green-uniformed elevator operator, who took him down to the ground floor.

He took his tea on the terrace facing the sea, then went down to the shore and walked along the boardwalk for a good distance toward the Hotel Excelsior. When he got back it seemed about time to change for dinner. He did so slowly and precisely, the way he did everything, because he was used to working as he got dressed. Still, he found himself in the lobby a bit on the early side for dinner. There he found many of the hotel's guests gathered, unfamiliar with and affecting indifference to each other, sharing only the wait for the dinner bell. He picked up a newspaper from a table, sat down in a leather chair, and looked over the assembled company. It differed from that of his previous sojourn in a way that pleased him.

A broad horizon, tolerant and comprehensive, opened up before him. All the great languages of Europe melded together in subdued tones. Evening dress, the universal uniform of cultured society, provided a decorous external unity to the variety of humanity assembled here. There was the dry, long face of an American, a Russian extended family, English ladies, German children with French nannies. The Slavic component seemed to predominate. Polish was being spoken nearby.

It came from a group of adolescents and young adults gathered around a little wicker table under the supervision of a governess or companion. There were three young girls who looked to be fifteen to seventeen years old and a long-haired boy of maybe fourteen. Aschenbach noted with astonishment that the boy was perfectly beautiful. His face, pale and gracefully reserved, was framed by honey-colored curls. He had a straight nose and a lovely mouth and wore an expression of exquisite, divine solemnity. It was a face reminiscent of Greek statues from the noblest period of antiquity; it combined perfection of form with a unique personal charm that caused the onlooker to doubt ever having met with anything in nature or in art that could match its perfection. One could not help noticing, furthermore, that widely differing views on child-rearing had evidently directed the dress and general treatment of the siblings. The three girls, the eldest of whom was for all intents an adult, were got up in a way that was almost disfiguringly chaste and austere. Every grace of figure was suppressed and obscured by their uniformly habitlike half-length dresses, sober and slate-gray in color, tailored as if to be deliberately unflattering, relieved by no decoration save white, turned-down collars. Their smooth hair, combed tightly against their heads, made their faces appear nunnishly vacant and expressionless. It could only be a mother who was in charge here, one who never once considered applying to the boy the severity of upbringing that seemed required of her when it came to the girls. Softness and tenderness were the obvious conditions of the boy's existence. No one had yet been so bold as to take the scissors to his lovely hair, which curled about his brows, over his ears, and even further down the back of his neck—as it does on the statue of the "Boy Pulling a Thorn from his Foot."[7] His English sailor suit had puffy sleeves that narrowed at the cuff to embrace snugly the delicate wrists of his still childlike yet delicate hands. The suit made his slim figure seem somehow opulent and pampered with all its decoration, its bow, braidwork, and embroidery. He sat so that the observer saw him in profile. His feet were clad in black patent leather and arranged one in front of the other; one elbow was propped on the arm of his wicker chair with his cheek resting on his closed hand; his demeanor was one of careless refinement, quite without the almost submissive stiffness that seemed to be the norm for his sisters. Was he in poor health? Perhaps, for the skin of his face was white as ivory and stood out in sharp contrast to the darker gold of the surrounding curls. Or was he simply a coddled favorite, the object of a biased and capricious affection? Aschenbach was inclined to suppose the latter. There is inborn in every artistic disposition an indulgent and treacherous tendency to accept injustice when it produces beauty and to respond with complicity and even admiration when the aristocrats of this world get preferential treatment.

A waiter went about and announced in English that dinner was ready. Most of the company gradually disappeared through the glass door into the dining room. Latecomers passed by, arriving from the vestibule or from the elevators. Dinner was beginning to be served inside, but the young Poles still lingered by their wicker table. Aschenbach, comfortably seated in his deep armchair, his eyes captivated by the beautiful vision before him, waited with them.

The governess, a short, corpulent, rather unladylike woman with a red face, finally gave the sign to get up. With her brows raised she pushed back her chair and bowed as a tall lady, dressed in gray and white and richly bejeweled with pearls, entered the lobby. The demeanor of this woman was cool and measured; the arrangement of her lightly powdered hair and the cut of her clothes displayed the taste for simplicity favored by those who regard piety as an essential component of good breeding. She could have been the wife of a highly placed German official. Her jewelry was the only thing about her appearance that suggested fabulous luxury; it was priceless, consisting of earrings and a very long, triple strand of softly shimmering pearls, each as big as a cherry.

The boy and the girls had risen quickly. They bent to kiss their mother's hand while she, with a restrained smile on her well-preserved but slightly tired and rather pointy-nosed face, looked across the tops of their heads at the governess, to whom she directed a few words in French. Then she walked

---

7. A bronze Greco-Roman statue admired for the graceful pose and handsome appearance of the boy it depicts.

to the glass door. The young ones followed her, the girls in the order of their ages, behind them the governess, the boy last of all. For some reason he turned around before crossing the threshold. Since there was no one else left in the lobby, his strangely misty gray eyes met those of Aschenbach, who was sunk deep in contemplation of the departing group, his newspaper on his knees.

What he had seen was, to be sure, in none of its particulars remarkable. They did not go in to dinner before their mother; they had waited for her, greeted her respectfully when she came, and then observed perfectly normal manners going into the dining room. It was just that it had all happened so deliberately, with such a sense of discipline, responsibility, and self-respect, that Aschenbach felt strangely moved. He lingered a few moments more, then went along into the dining room himself. He was shown to his table, which, he noted with a brief twinge of regret, was very far away from that of the Polish family.

Tired but nonetheless mentally stimulated, he entertained himself during the tedious meal with abstract, even transcendent matters. He pondered the mysterious combination of regularity and individuality that is necessary to produce human beauty; proceeded then to the general problem of form and of art; and ultimately concluded that his thoughts and discoveries resembled those inspirations that come in dreams: they seem wonderful at the time, but in the sober light of day they show up as utterly shallow and useless. After dinner he spent some time smoking, sitting, and wandering about in the park, which was fragrant in the evening air. He went to bed early and passed the night in a sleep uninterruptedly deep but frequently enlivened by all sorts of dreams.

The next day the weather had gotten no better. There was a steady wind off the land. Under a pale overcast sky the sea lay in a dull calm, almost as if it had shriveled up, with a soberingly contracted horizon; it had receded so far from the beach that it uncovered several rows of long sandbars. When Aschenbach opened his window, he thought he could detect the stagnant smell of the lagoon.

He was beset by ill humor. He was already having thoughts of leaving. Once years ago, after several lovely weeks here in springtime, just such weather had been visited upon him and had made him feel so poorly that he had had to take flight from Venice like a fugitive. Was he not feeling once again the onset of the feverish listlessness he had felt then, the throbbing of his temples, the heaviness in his eyelids? To change his vacation spot yet again would be a nuisance; but if the wind did not shift soon, he simply could not remain here. He did not unpack everything, just in case. He ate at nine in the special breakfast room between the lobby and the dining room.

In this room prevailed the solemn stillness that great hotels aspire to. The waiters went about on tip-toe. The clink of the tea service and a half-whispered word were all one could hear. Aschenbach noticed the Polish girls and their governess at a table in the corner diagonally across from the door, two tables away. They sat very straight, their ash-blond hair newly smoothed down flat, their eyes red. They wore starched blue linen dresses with little white turned-down collars and cuffs, and they passed a jar of preserves to each other. They had almost finished their breakfast. The boy was not there.

Aschenbach smiled. Well, little Phaeacian, he thought. It seems you, and not they, have the privilege of sleeping to your heart's content. Suddenly cheered, he recited to himself the line:

"Changes of dress, warm baths, and downy beds."[8]

He ate his breakfast at a leisurely pace, received some mail that had been forwarded—delivered personally by the doorman, who entered the room with his braided hat in hand—and opened a few letters while he smoked a cigarette. Thus it happened that he was present for the entrance of the late sleeper they were waiting for over there in the corner.

He came through the glass door and traversed the silent room diagonally over to the table where his sisters sat. His carriage was extraordinarily graceful, not only in the way he held his torso but also in the way he moved his knees and set one white-shod foot in front of the other. He moved lightly, in a manner both gentle and proud, made more lovely still by the childlike bashfulness with which he twice lifted and lowered his eyelids as he went by, turning his face out toward the room. Smiling, he murmured a word in his soft, indistinct speech and took his place, showing his full profile to the observer. The latter was once more, and now especially, struck with amazement, indeed even alarm, at the truly godlike beauty possessed by this mortal child. Today the boy wore a lightweight sailor suit of blue and white striped cotton with a red silk bow on the chest, finished at the neck with a simple white upright collar. And above this collar, which did not even fit in very elegantly with the character of the costume, rose up that blossom, his face, a sight unforgettably charming. It was the face of Eros, with the yellowish glaze of Parian marble,[9] with delicate and serious brows, the temples and ears richly and rectangularly framed by soft, dusky curls.

Fine, very fine, thought Aschenbach with that professional, cool air of appraisal artists sometimes use to cover their delight, their enthusiasm when they encounter a masterpiece. He thought further: Really, if the sea and the sand were not waiting for me, I would stay here as long as you stay. With that, however, he departed, walking past the attentive employees through the lobby, down the terrace steps, and straight across the wooden walkway to the hotel's private beach. There he let a barefoot old man in linen pants, sailor shirt, and straw hat who managed affairs on the beach show him to his rented beach cabana and arrange a table and chair on its sandy, wooden platform. Then he made himself comfortable in his beach chair, which he had pulled through the pale yellow sand closer to the sea.

The beach scene, this view of a carefree society engaged in purely sensual enjoyment on the edge of the watery element, entertained and cheered him as it always did. The gray, smooth ocean was already full of wading children, swimmers, and colorful figures lying on the sandbars with their arms crossed behind their heads. Others were rowing about in little flat-bottomed boats painted red and blue, capsizing to gales of laughter. People sat on the platforms of the cabanas, arranged in a long neat row along the beach, as if they were little verandas. In front of them people played games, lounged lazily, visited and chatted, some dressed in elegant morning clothes and others enjoying the nakedness sanctioned by the bold and easy freedom of the place. Down on the moist, hard sand there were a few individuals strolling about

---

8. A reference to Homer's *Odyssey* 8.249. The Phaeacians were a peaceful, happy people who showed hospitality to the shipwrecked Odysseus.   9. White marble from the island of Paros was especially prized by sculptors in antiquity. Eros was the Greek god of love.

in white beach robes or in loose, brightly colored bathing dresses. To the right some children had built an elaborate sand castle and bedecked it with little flags in the colors of every country. Vendors of mussels, cakes, and fruit knelt and spread their wares before them. On the left, a Russian family was encamped in front of one of the cabanas that were set at a right angle between the others and the sea, thus closing that end of the beach. The family included men with beards and huge teeth; languid women past their prime; a young lady from a Baltic country, sitting at an easel and painting the ocean to the accompaniment of cries of frustration; two affable, ugly children; and an old maid in a babushka, displaying the affectionately servile demeanor of a slave. They resided there in grateful enjoyment, called out endlessly the names of their unruly, giddy children, exchanged pleasantries at surprising length in their few words of Italian with the jocular old man from whom they bought candy, kissed each other on the cheeks, and cared not a whit for anyone who might witness their scene of shared humanity.

Well, then, I will stay, thought Aschenbach. Where could things be better? His hands folded in his lap, he let his eyes roam the ocean's distances, let his gaze slip out of focus, grow hazy, blur in the uniform distances, mistiness of empty space. He loved the sea from the depth of his being: first of all because a hardworking artist needs his rest from the demanding variety of phenomena he works with and longs to take refuge in the bosom of simplicity and enormity; and, second, because he harbors an affinity for the undivided, the immeasurable, the eternal, the void. It was a forbidden affinity, directly contrary to his calling, and seductive precisely for that reason. To rest in the arms of perfection is what all those who struggle for excellence long to do; and is the void not a form of perfection? But while he was thus dreaming away toward the depths of emptiness, the horizontal line of the sea's edge was crossed by a human figure. When he had retrieved his gaze from the boundless realms and refocused his eyes, he saw it was the lovely boy who, coming from the left, was passing before him across the sand. He went barefoot, ready to go in wading, his slim legs bare from the knees down. He walked slowly but with a light, proud step, as if he were used to going about without shoes, and looked around at the row of cabanas that closed the end of the beach. The Russian family was still there, gratefully leading its harmonious existence, but no sooner had he laid eyes on them than a storm cloud of angry contempt crossed his face. His brow darkened, his lips began to curl, and from one side of his mouth emerged a bitter grimace that gouged a furrow in his cheek. He frowned so deeply that his eyes seemed pressed inward and sunken, seemed to speak dark and evil volumes of hatred from their depths. He looked down at the ground, cast one more threatening glance backward, and then, shrugging his shoulders as if to discard something and get away from it, he left his enemies behind.

A sort of delicacy or fright, something like a mixture of respect and shame, caused Aschenbach to turn away as if he had not seen anything; for it is repugnant to a chance witness, if he is a serious person, to make use of his observations, even to himself. But Aschenbach felt cheered and shaken at the same time—that is, happiness overwhelmed him. This childish fanaticism directed against the most harmless, good-natured target imaginable put into a human perspective something that otherwise seemed divinely indeterminate. It transformed a precious creation of nature that had before been no more than a feast for the eyes into a worthy object of deeper sympathy. It endowed the figure of the youngster, who had already shone with significance because of his beauty, with an aura that allowed him to be taken seriously beyond his years.

Still turned away, Aschenbach listened to the boy's voice, his clear, somewhat weak voice, by means of which he was trying to hail from afar his playmates at work on the sand castle. They answered him, calling again and again his name or an affectionate variation on his name. Aschenbach listened with a certain curiosity, unable to distinguish anything more than two melodious syllables—something like Adgio or more frequently Adgiu, with a drawn-out *u* at the end of the cry. The sound made him glad, it seemed to him that its harmony suited its object, and he repeated it softly to himself as he turned back with satisfaction to his letters and papers.

With his small traveling briefcase on his knees, he took his fountain pen and began to attend to various matters of correspondence. But after a mere quarter of an hour he was feeling regret that he should thus take leave in spirit and miss out on this, the most charming set of circumstances he knew of, for the sake of an activity he carried on with indifference. He cast his writing materials aside and turned his attention back to the sea; and not long after, distracted by the voices of the youngsters at the sand castle, he turned his head to the right and let it rest comfortably on the back of his chair, where he could once more observe the comings and goings of the exquisite Adgio.

His first glance found him; the red bow on his breast could not be missed. He was engaged with some others in setting up an old board as a bridge over the moat around the sand castle, calling out advice on proper procedure and nodding his head. There were about ten companions with him, boys and girls, most of an age with him but a few younger, chattering in a confusion of tongues—Polish, French, and even some Balkan languages. But it was his name that most often resounded through it all. He was evidently popular, sought after, admired. One companion, likewise a Pole, a sturdy boy called something like Yashu, who wore a belted linen suit and had black hair slicked down with pomade, seemed to be his closest friend and vassal. With the work on the sand castle finished for the time being, they went off together along the beach, arms about each other, and the one called Yashu gave his beautiful partner a kiss.

Aschenbach was tempted to shake his finger at him. "Let me give you a piece of advice, Kritobulos," he thought and smiled to himself. "Take a year's journey. You will need at least that much time for your recovery."[1] And then he breakfasted on large, fully ripe strawberries that he obtained from a peddler. It had gotten very warm, although the sun had not managed to pierce the layer of mist that covered the sky. Lassitude seized his spirit, while his senses enjoyed the enormous, lulling entertainment afforded by the quiet sea. The task of puzzling out what name it was that sounded like Adgio struck the serious man as a fitting, entirely satisfying occupation. With the help of a few Polish memories he determined that it was probably Tadzio he had

1. Recalling Socrates' advice to Kritoboulos when the latter kissed Alcibiades' handsome son (Xenophon's *Memorabilia* 1.3).

heard, the nickname for Tadeusz. It was pronounced Tadziu in the form used for direct address.

Tadizo was taking a swim. Aschenbach, who had lost sight of him for a moment, spotted his head and then his arm, which rose as it stroked. He was very far out; the water apparently stayed shallow for a long way. But already his family seemed to be getting concerned about him, already women's voices were calling to him from the cabanas, shouting out once more this name that ruled over the beach almost like a watchword and that possessed something both sweet and wild in its soft consonants and drawn-out cry of *uuu* at the end. "Tadziu! Tadziu!" He turned back; he ran through the sea with his head thrown back, beating the resisting water into a foam with his legs. The sight of this lively adolescent figure, seductive and chaste, lovely as a tender young god, emerging from the depths of the sky and the sea with dripping locks and escaping the clutches of the elements—it all gave rise to mythic images. It was a sight belonging to poetic legends from the beginning of time that tell of the origins of form and of the birth of the gods. Aschenbach listened with his eyes closed to this mythic song reverberating within him, and once again he thought about how good it was here and how he wanted to stay.

Later on Tadzio lay on the sand, resting from his swim, wrapped in a white beach towel that was drawn up under his right shoulder, his head resting on his bare arm. Even when Aschenbach refrained from looking at him, instead reading a few pages in his book, he almost never forgot who was lying nearby or forgot that it would cost him only a slight turn of his head to the right to bring the adorable sight back into view. It almost seemed to him that he was sitting here with the express purpose of keeping watch over the resting boy. Busy as he might be with his own affairs, he maintained his vigilant care for the noble human figure not far away on his right. A paternal kindness, an emotional attachment filled and moved his heart, the attachment that someone who produces beauty at the cost of intellectual self-sacrifice feels toward someone who naturally possesses beauty.

After midday he left the beach, returned to the hotel, and took the elevator up to his room. There he spent a considerable length of time in front of the mirror looking at his gray hair and his severe, tired face. At the same time he thought about his fame and about the fact that many people recognized him on the street and looked at him with respect, all on account of those graceful, unerringly accurate words of his. He called the roll of the long list of successes his talent had brought him, as many as he could think of, and even recalled his elevation to the nobility. He then retired to the dining room for lunch and ate at his little table. As he was entering the elevator when the meal was over, a throng of young people likewise coming from lunch crowded him to the back of the swaying little chamber. Tadzio was among them. He stood very close by, so close in fact that for the first time Aschenbach had the opportunity to view him not from a distance like a picture but minutely, scrutinizing every detail of his human form. Someone was talking to the boy, and while he was answering with his indescribably sweet smile they reached the second floor, where he got off, backing out, his eyes cast down. Beauty breeds modesty, Aschenbach thought and gave urgent consideration as to why. He had had occasion to notice, however, that Tadzio's teeth were not a very pleasing sight. They were rather jagged and pale and had no luster of health but rather a peculiar brittle transparency such as one sometimes sees in anemics. He is very sensitive, he is sickly, thought Aschenbach. He will probably not live long. And he refrained from trying to account for the feeling of satisfaction and reassurance that accompanied this thought.

He passed a couple of hours in his room and in the afternoon took the vaporetto across the stagnant-smelling lagoon to Venice. He got off at San Marco, took tea in the piazza,[2] and then, following his habitual routine in Venice, set off on a walk through the streets. It was this walk, however, that initiated a complete reversal of his mood and his plans.

The air in the little streets was odiously oppressive, so thick that the smells surging out of the dwellings, shops, and restaurants, a suffocating vapor of oil, perfume, and more, all hung about and failed to disperse. Cigarette smoke hovered in place and only slowly disappeared. The press of people in the small spaces annoyed rather than entertained him as he walked. The longer he went on, the more it became a torture. He was overwhelmed by that horrible condition produced by the sea air in combination with the sirocco, a state of both nervousness and debility at once. He began to sweat uncomfortably. His eyes ceased to function, his breathing was labored, he felt feverish, the blood pounded in his head. He fled from the crowded shop-lined streets across bridges into the poor quarter. There beggars molested him, and the evil emanations from the canals hindered his breathing. In a quiet piazza, one of those forgotten, seemingly enchanted little places in the interior of the city, he rested on the edge of a well, dried his forehead, and reached the conclusion that he would have to leave Venice.

For the second time, and this time definitively, it became clear that this city in this weather was particularly harmful to his health. To remain stubbornly in place obviously went against all reason, and the prospect of a change in the direction of the wind was highly uncertain. A quick decision had to be made. To return home this soon was out of the question. Neither his summer nor his winter quarters were prepared for his arrival. But this was not the only place with beaches on the ocean, and those other places did not have the noxious extra of the lagoon and its fever-inducing vapors. He recalled a little beach resort not far from Trieste that had been enthusiastically recommended to him. Why not go there and, indeed, without delay, so that yet another change of location would still be worthwhile? He declared himself resolved and stood up. At the next gondola stop he boarded a boat to take him to San Marco through the dim labyrinth of canals, under graceful marble balconies flanked by stone lions, around corners of slippery masonry, past mournful palace facades affixed with business insignia[3] reflected in the garbage-strewn water. He had trouble getting to his destination, since the gondolier was in league with lace and glass factories and made constant efforts to induce him to stop at them to sightsee and buy; and so whenever the bizarre journey through Venice began to weave its magic, the mercenary lust for booty afflicting this sunken queen of cities[4] did what it could to bring the enchanted spirit back to unpleasant reality.

Upon returning to the hotel he did not even wait for dinner but went right

2. A famous public square in front of the church, lined by restaurants and cafés.   3. Once-stately Renaissance homes that now lodge businesses.   4. A major sea power by the 15th century, Venice was called Queen of the Seas.

to the office and declared that unforeseen circumstances compelled him to depart the next morning. With many expressions of regret the staff acknowledged the payment of his bill. He dined and then passed the mild evening reading magazines in a rocking chair on the rear terrace. Before going to bed he did all his packing for the morning's departure.

He did not sleep especially well, as the impending move made him restless. When he opened the windows the next morning the sky was still overcast, but the air seemed fresher and . . . he already started to have second thoughts. Had he been hasty or wrong to give notice thus? Was it a result of his sick and unreliable condition? If he had just put it off a bit, if he had just made an attempt to get used to the Venetian air or to hold out for an improvement in the weather instead of losing heart so quickly! Then, instead of this hustle and bustle, he would have a morning on the beach like the one yesterday to look forward to. Too late. Now he would have to go ahead with it, to wish today what he wished for yesterday. He got dressed and at eight o'clock took the elevator down to breakfast on the ground floor.

The breakfast room was still empty when he entered. A number of individual guests arrived while he sat waiting for his order. With his teacup at his lips he watched the Polish girls and their attendant come in. Severe and morning-fresh, eyes still red, they proceeded to their table in the corner by the window. Immediately thereafter the doorman approached him with hat in hand to tell him it was time to leave. The car was ready, he said, to take him and some other travelers to the Hotel Excelsior, and from there a motor boat would convey them through the company's private canal to the railroad station. Time was pressing, he said. Aschenbach found it not at all pressing. There was more than an hour until the departure of his train. He was annoyed at the habitual hotel practice of packing departing guests off earlier than necessary and informed the doorman that he wanted to finish his breakfast in peace. The man withdrew hesitatingly only to show up again five minutes later. The car simply could not wait longer, he said. Very well, let it go and take his trunks with it, Aschenbach replied with annoyance. As for himself, he preferred to take the public steamer at the proper time and asked that they let him take care of his own arrangements. The employee bowed. Aschenbach, happy to have fended off this nuisance, finished his meal without haste and even had the waiter bring him a newspaper. Time had become short indeed when at last he got up to leave. And it just so happened that at that very moment Tadzio came in through the glass door.

He crossed the path of the departing traveler on his way to his family's table. He lowered his eyes modestly before the gray-haired, high-browed gentleman, only to raise them again immediately in his own charming way, displaying their soft fullness to him. Then he was past. Adieu, Tadzio, thought Aschenbach. I saw you for such a short time. And enunciating his thought as it occurred to him, contrary to his every habit, he added under his breath the words: "Blessings on you." He then made his departure, dispensed tips, received a parting greeting from the quiet little manager in the French frock coat, and left the hotel on foot, as he had arrived. Followed by a servant with his hand luggage, he traversed the island along the boulevard, white with flowers, that led to the steamer landing. He arrived, he took his seat—and what followed was a journey of pain and sorrow through the uttermost depths of regret.

It was the familiar trip across the lagoon, past San Marco, up the Grand Canal. Aschenbach sat on the curved bench in the bow, his arm resting on the railing, his hand shading his eyes. They left the public gardens behind them; the Piazzetta once more revealed its princely splendor, and soon it too was left behind. Then came the great line of palaces, and as the waterway turned there appeared the magnificent marble arch of the Rialto.[5] The traveler looked, and his heart was torn. He breathed the atmosphere of the city, this slightly stagnant smell of sea and of swamp from which he had felt so strongly compelled to flee, breathed it now deeply, in tenderly painful draughts. Was it possible that he had not known, had not considered how desperately he was attached to all this? What this morning had been a partial regret, a slight doubt as to the rightness of his decision, now became affliction, genuine pain, a suffering in his soul so bitter that it brought tears to his eyes more than once. He told himself he could not possibly have foreseen such a reaction. What was so hard to take, actually sometimes down-right impossible to endure, was the thought that he would never see Venice again, that this was a parting forever. Since it had become evident for the second time that the city made him sick, since for the second time he had been forced to run head over heels away, he would have to regard it henceforth as an impossible destination, forbidden to him, something he simply was not up to, something it would be pointless for him to try for again. Yes, he felt that, should he go away now, shame and spite would certainly prevent him from ever seeing the beloved city again, now that it had twice forced him to admit physical defeat. This conflict between the inclination of his soul and the capacity of his body seemed to the aging traveler suddenly so weighty and so important, his physical defeat so ignominious, so much to be resisted at all cost, that he could no longer grasp the ease with which he had reached the decision yesterday, without serious struggle, to acquiesce.

Meanwhile, the steamer was approaching the railway station, and his pain and helplessness were rising to the level of total disorientation. His tortured mind found the thought of departure impossible, the thought of return no less so. In such a state of acute inner strife he entered the station. It was already very late, he had not a moment to lose if he was to catch his train. He wanted to, and he did not want to. But time was pressing, it goaded him onward; he made haste to obtain his ticket and looked about in the bustle of the station for the hotel employee stationed here. This person appeared and announced that the large trunk was already checked and on its way. Already on its way? Yes indeed—to Como.[6] To Como? After a frantic exchange, after angry questions and embarrassed answers, the fact emerged that the trunk had been put together with the baggage of other, unknown travelers in the luggage office at the Hotel Excelsior and sent off in precisely the wrong direction.

Aschenbach had difficulty maintaining the facial expression expected under such circumstances. An adventurous joy, an unbelievable cheerfulness seized his breast from within like a spasm. The hotel employee sped off to see if he could retrieve the trunk and returned, as one might have expected, with no success whatever. Only then did Aschenbach declare that he did not

5. A famous, highly arched bridge over the Grand Canal.   6. A large lake and resort area in northwest Italy.

wish to travel without his luggage and that he had decided to return and await the recovery of the trunk at the Hotel des Bains. Was the company boat still here at the station? The man assured him it was waiting right at the door. With an impressive display of Italian cajolery he persuaded the agent to take back Aschenbach's ticket. He swore he would telegraph ahead, that no effort would be spared to get the trunk back with all due speed, and . . . thus came to pass something very odd indeed. The traveler, not twenty minutes after his arrival at the station, found himself once again on the Grand Canal on his way back to the Lido.

What a wondrous, incredible, embarrassing, odd and dreamlike adventure! Thanks to a sudden reversal of destiny, he was to see once again, within the very hour, places that he had thought in deepest melancholy he was leaving forever. The speedy little vessel shot toward its destination, foam flying before its bow, maneuvering with droll agility between gondolas and steamers, while its single passenger hid beneath a mask of annoyed resignation the anxious excitement of a boy playing hooky. Still from time to time his frame was shaken with laughter over this mischance, which he told himself could not have worked out better for the luckiest person in the world. Explanations would have to be made, amazed faces confronted, but then—so he told himself—all would be well again, a great disaster averted, a terrible error made right, and everything he thought he had left behind would be open to him once more, would be his to enjoy at his leisure. . . . And by the way, was it just the rapid movement of the boat, or could it really be that he felt a strong breeze off the ocean to complete his bliss?

The waves slapped against the concrete walls of the narrow canal that cut through the island to the Hotel Excelsior. A motor bus was waiting there for the returning traveler and conveyed him alongside the curling waves down the straight road to the Hotel des Bains. The little manager with the mustache and the cutaway frock coat came down the broad flight of steps to meet him.

With quiet cajolery the manager expressed his regret over the incident, declared it extremely embarrassing for himself personally and for the establishment, but expressed his emphatic approval of Aschenbach's decision to wait here for the return of his luggage. To be sure, his room was already taken, but another, by no means worse, stood ready. "Pas de chance, monsieur,"[7] said the elevator man with a smile as they glided upwards. And so the fugitive was billeted once again, and in a room that matched almost exactly his previous one in orientation and furnishings.

Tired, numb from the whirl of this strange morning, he distributed the contents of his small suitcase in his room and then sank down in an armchair by the open window. The sea had taken on a light green coloration, the air seemed thinner and purer, the beach with its cabanas and boats seemed more colorful, although the sky was still gray. Aschenbach looked out, his hands folded in his lap, content to be here once more, but shaking his head in reproach at his own fickle mood, his lack of knowledge of his own desires. He sat thus for perhaps an hour, resting and thoughtlessly dreaming. At noon he spied Tadzio, dressed in his striped linen suit with red bow, returning from the shore through the beach barrier and along the wooden walkway to

7. No luck, sir (French).

the hotel. Aschenbach recognized him at once from his high vantage point even before he got a good look at him, and he was just about to form a thought something like: Look, Tadzio, you too have returned! But at that very moment he felt the casual greeting collapse and fall silent before the truth of his heart. He felt the excitement in his blood, the joy and pain in his soul, and recognized that it was because of Tadzio that his departure had been so difficult.

He sat quite still, quite unseen in his elevated location and looked into himself. His features were active; his brows rose; an alert, curious, witty smile crossed his lips. Then he raised his head and with both his arms, which were hanging limp over the arms of his chair, he made a slow circling and lifting movement that turned his palms forward, as if to signify an opening and extending of his embrace. It was a gesture of readiness, of welcome, and of relaxed acceptance.

CHAPTER 4

The god with fiery cheeks[8] now, naked, directed his horses, four-abreast, fire-breathing, day by day through the chambers of heaven, and his yellow curls fluttered along with the blast of the east wind. A silky-white sheen lay on the Pontos,[9] its broad stretches undulating languidly. The sands burned. Under the silvery shimmering blue of the ether there were rustcolored canvas awnings spread out in front of the beach cabanas, and one passed the morning hours in the sharply framed patch of shade they offered. But the evening was also delightful, when the plants in the park wafted balsamic perfumes, the stars above paced out their circuits, and the murmur of the night-shrouded sea, softly penetrating, cast a spell on the soul. Such an evening bore the joyful promise of another festive day of loosely ordered leisure, bejeweled with countless, thickly strewn possibilities of happy accidents.

The guest, whom accommodating mischance kept here, was far from disposed to see in the return of his belongings a reason to depart once more. He had been obliged to get along without a few things for a couple of days and to appear at meals in the great dining room wearing his traveling clothes. Then, when the errant baggage was finally set down once more in his room, he unpacked thoroughly and filled closets and drawers with his things, determined for the time being to stay indefinitely, happy to be able to pass the morning's hours on the beach in his silk suit and to present himself once more at his little table at dinner time wearing proper evening attire.

The benevolent regularity of this existence had at once drawn him into its power; the soft and splendid calm of this lifestyle had him quickly ensnared. What a fine place to stay, indeed, combining the charms of a refined southern beach resort with the cozy proximity of the wondrous, wonder-filled city! Aschenbach was no lover of pleasure. Whenever and wherever it seemed proper to celebrate, to take a rest, to take a few days off, he soon had to get back—it was especially so in his younger days—anxiously and reluctantly back to the affliction of his high calling, the sacred, sober service of his day-to-day life. This place alone enchanted him, relaxed his will, made him happy. Sometimes in the morning, under the canopy of his beach cabana,

8. Helios, Greek god of the sun (later equated with Apollo). 9. The sea (Greek, literal trans.); a figurative reference to the Adriatic Sea.

dreaming away across the blue of the southern sea, or sometimes as well on a balmy night, leaning back under the great starry sky on the cushions of a gondola taking him back home to the Lido from the Piazza San Marco, where he had tarried long—and the bright lights and the melting sounds of the serenade were left behind—he remembered his country home in the mountains, the site of his summertime struggles, where the clouds drifted through the garden, where in the evening fearful thunderstorms extinguished the lights in the house and the ravens he fed soared to the tops of the spruce trees. Then it might seem to him that he had been transported to the land of Elysium[1] at the far ends of the earth, where a life of ease is bestowed upon mortals, where there is no snow, no winter, no storms or streaming rain, but rather always the cooling breath rising from Okeanos,[2] where the days run out in blissful leisure, trouble-free, struggle-free, dedicated only to the sun and its revels.

Aschenbach saw the boy Tadzio often, indeed almost continually; limited space and a regular schedule common to all the guests made it inevitable that the lovely boy was in his vicinity nearly all day, with brief interruptions. He saw, he met him everywhere: in the hotel's public places, on the cooling boat trips to the city and back, in the ostentation of the piazza itself; and often too in the streets and byways a chance encounter would take place. Chiefly, however, it was the mornings on the beach that offered him with delightful regularity an extended opportunity to study and worship the charming apparition. Yes, it was this narrow and constrained happiness, this regularly recurring good fortune that filled him with contentment and joy in life, that made his stay all the more dear to him and caused one sunny day after another to fall so agreeably in line.

He got up early, as he otherwise did under the relentless pressure of work, and was one of the first on the beach when the sun was still mild and the sea lay white in the glare of morning dreams. He gave a friendly greeting to the guard at the beach barrier, said a familiar hello to the barefoot old man who got his place ready, spreading the brown awning and arranging the cabana furniture on the platform, and settled in. Three hours or four were then his in which, as the sun rose to its zenith and grew fearsome in strength and the sea turned a deeper and deeper blue, he could watch Tadzio.

He would see him coming from the left along the edge of the sea, would see him from the back as he appeared from between the cabanas, or sometimes would suddenly discover, not without a happy shudder, that he had missed his arrival and that he was already there, already in the blue and white bathing suit that was now his only article of attire on the beach, that he was already up to his usual doings in sand and sun—his charmingly trivial, lazily irregular life that was both recreation and rest, filled with lounging, wading, digging, catching, resting, and swimming, watched over by the women on the platform who called to him, making his name resound with their high voices: "Tadziu! Tadziu!" He would come running to them gesturing excitedly and telling them what he had done, showing them what he had found or caught: mussels and sea horses, jelly fish, crabs that ran off going sideways. Aschenbach understood not a single word he said, and though it

---

1. Located at the western edge of the Earth, a pleasant otherworld for those heroes favored of the gods.
2. According to Greek mythology, a river encircling the world.

may have been the most ordinary thing in the world it was all a vague harmony to his ear. Thus, foreignness raised the boy's speech to the level of music, a wanton sun poured unstinting splendor over him, and the sublime perspectives of the sea always formed the background and aura that set off his appearance.

Soon the observer knew every line and pose of this noble body that displayed itself so freely; he exulted in greeting anew every beauty, familiar though it had become, and his admiration, the discreet arousal of his senses, knew no end. They called the boy to pay his compliments to a guest who was attending the ladies at the cabana; he came running, still wet from the sea; he tossed his curls, and as he held out his hand he stood on one foot while holding the other up on tiptoe. His body was gracefully poised in the midst of a charming turning motion, while his face showed an embarrassed amiability, a desire to please that came from an aristocratic sense of duty. Sometimes he would lie stretched out with his beach towel wrapped about his chest, his delicately chiseled arm propped in the sand, his chin in the hollow of his hand. The one called Yashu sat crouching by him, playing up to him, and nothing could have been more enchanting than the smiling eyes and lips with which the object of this flattery looked upon his inferior, his vassal. Or he would stand at the edge of the sea, alone, separated from his friends, very near Aschenbach, erect, his hands clasped behind his neck, slowly rocking on the balls of his feet and dreaming off into the blue yonder, while little waves that rolled in bathed his toes. His honey-colored hair clung in circles to his temples and his neck; the sun made the down shine on his upper back; the subtle definition of the ribs and the symmetry of his chest stood out through the tight-fitting material covering his torso; his armpits were still as smooth as those of a statue, the hollows behind his knees shone likewise, and the blue veins showing through made his body seem to be made of translucent material. What discipline, what precision of thought was expressed in the stretch of this youthfully perfect body! But was not the rigorous and pure will that had been darkly active in bringing this divine form into the clear light of day entirely familiar to the artist in him? Was this same will not active in him, too, when he, full of sober passion, freed a slender form from the marble mass of language,[3] a form he had seen with his spiritual eye and that he presented to mortal men as image and mirror of spiritual beauty?

Image and mirror! His eyes embraced the noble figure there on the edge of the blue, and in a transport of delight he thought his gaze was grasping beauty itself, the pure form of divine thought, the universal and pure perfection that lives in the spirit and which here, graceful and lovely, presented itself for worship in the form of a human likeness and exemplar. Such was his intoxication; the aging artist welcomed the experience without reluctance, even greedily. His intellect was in labor, his educated mind set in motion. His memory dredged up ancient images passed on to him in the days of his youth, thoughts not until now touched by the spark of his personal involvement. Was it not written that the sun turns our attention from intellectual to sensuous matters?[4] It was said that the sun numbs and enchants

---

3. The Italian artist Michelangelo Buonarroti (1475–1564) explained that he created his statues by carving away the marble block until the figure within was set free.   4. In section 764E of the *Erotikos* (Dialogue on love) by the Greek essayist Plutarch (46–120).

our reason and memory to such an extent that the soul in its pleasure forgets its ordinary condition; its amazed admiration remains fixed on the loveliest of sun-drenched objects. Indeed, only with the help of a body can the soul rise to the contemplation of still higher things. Amor[5] truly did as mathematicians have always done by assisting slow-learning children with concrete pictures of pure forms: so, too, did the god like to make use of the figure and coloration of human youth in order to make the spiritual visible to us, furnishing it with the reflected glory of beauty and thus making of it a tool of memory, so that seeing it we might then be set aflame with pain and hope.

Those, at any rate, were the thoughts of the impassioned onlooker. He was capable of sustaining just such a high pitch of emotion. He spun himself a charming tapestry out of the roar of the sea and the glare of the sun. He saw the ancient plane tree not far from the walls of Athens,[6] that sacred, shadowy place filled with the scent of willow blossoms, decorated with holy images and votive offerings in honor of the nymphs and of Achelous.[7] The stream flowed in crystal clarity over smooth pebbles past the foot of the wide-branched tree. The crickets sang. Two figures reclined on the grass that gently sloped so that you could lie with your head held up; they were sheltered here from the heat of the day—an older man and a younger, one ugly and one handsome, wisdom at the side of charm. Amidst polite banter and wooing wit Socrates taught Phaedrus about longing and virtue. He spoke to him of the searing terror that the sensitive man experiences when his eye lights on an image of eternal beauty; spoke to him of the appetites of the impious, bad man who cannot conceive of beauty when he sees beauty's image and is incapable of reverence; spoke of the holy fear that overcomes a noble heart when a godlike face or a perfect body appears before him— how he then trembles and is beside himself and scarcely dares turn his eyes upon the sight and honors him who has beauty, indeed would even sacrifice to him as to a holy image, if he did not fear looking foolish in the eyes of others. For beauty, my dear Phaedrus, beauty alone is both worthy of love and visible at the same time; beauty, mark me well, is the only form of spirit that our senses can both grasp and endure. For what should become of us if divinity itself, or reason and virtue and truth were to appear directly to our senses? Would we not be overcome and consumed in the flames of love, as Semele[8] was at the sight of Zeus? Thus beauty is the sensitive man's way to the spirit—just the way, just the means, little Phaedrus. . . . And then he said the subtlest thing of all, crafty wooer that he was: he said that the lover was more divine than the beloved, because the god was in the former and not in the latter—perhaps the tenderest, most mocking thought that ever was thought, a thought alive with all the guile and the most secret bliss of love's longing.

A writer's chief joy is that thought can become all feeling, that feeling can become all thought. The lonely author possessed and commanded at this moment just such a vibrant thought, such a precise feeling: namely, that nature herself would shiver with delight were intellect to bow in homage

5. The god of love (Latin). 6. A reference to the scene and some of the arguments in Plato's dialogue *Phaedrus*. Plato's school, or Academy, was located in a grove of plane trees outside Athens; in the dialogue, the young student Phaedrus tells Socrates of Lysias's speech on love, and Socrates responds with two speeches of his own. 7. A brook or small river in ancient Athens, here personified as a god. 8. The mortal mother of Zeus's son Dionysus. She perished in flames when the king of the gods appeared (at her request) in his divine glory.

before beauty. He suddenly wanted to write. They say, to be sure, that Eros loves idleness; the god was made to engage in no other activity. But at this moment of crisis the excitement of the love-struck traveler drove him to productivity, and the occasion was almost a matter of indifference. The intellectual world had been challenged to profess its views on a certain great and burning problem of culture and of taste, and the challenge had reached him. The problem was well known to him, was part of his experience; the desire to illuminate it with the splendor of his eloquence was suddenly irresistible. And what is more, he wanted to work here in the presence of Tadzio, to use the boy's physical frame as the model for his writing, to let his style follow the lines of that body that seemed to him divine, to carry his beauty into the realm of intellect as once the eagle carried the Trojan shepherd into the ethereal heavens.[9] Never had his pleasure in the word seemed sweeter to him, never had he known so surely that Eros dwelt in the word as now in the dangerous and delightful hours he spent at his rough table under the awning. There with his idol's image in full view, the music of his voice resounding in his ear, he formed his little essay after the image of Tadzio's beauty—composed that page-and-a-half of choice prose that soon would amaze many a reader with its purity, nobility, and surging depth of feeling. It is surely for the best that the world knows only the lovely work and not also its origins, not the conditions under which it came into being; for knowledge of the origins from which flowed the artist's inspiration would surely often confuse the world, repel it, and thus vitiate the effects of excellence. Strange hours! Strangely enervating effort! Strangely fertile intercourse between a mind and a body! When Aschenbach folded up his work and left the beach, he felt exhausted, even unhinged, as if his conscience were indicting him after a debauch.

The next morning as he was about to leave the hotel he chanced to notice from the steps that Tadzio was already on his way to the shore, alone; he was just approaching the beach barrier. He felt first a suggestion, then a compulsion: the wish, the simple thought that he might make use of the opportunity to strike up a casual, cheerful acquaintanceship with this boy who unwittingly had caused such a stir in his mind and heart, speak with him and enjoy his answer and his gaze. The lovely lad sauntered along; he could be easily caught up with; Aschenbach quickened his steps. He reached him on the walkway behind the cabanas, was about to put his hand on his head or on his shoulder, was about to let some word pass his lips, some friendly French phrase. But then he felt his heart beating like a hammer, perhaps only because of his rapid walk, so that he was short of breath and could only have spoken in a trembling gasp. He hesitated, tried to master himself, then suddenly feared he had been walking too long right behind the handsome boy, feared he might notice, might turn around with an inquiring look. He took one more run at him, but then he gave up, renounced his goal, and hung his head as he went by.

Too late! he thought at that moment. Too late! But was it really too late? This step he had failed to take might very possibly have led to something good, to something easy and happy, to a salutary return to reality. But it may

9. The young Trojan prince Ganymede was tending flocks when Zeus, in the form of an eagle, carried him off to Olympus where he became Zeus's lover and the cupbearer to the gods.

have been that the aging traveler did not wish to return to reality, that he was too much in love with his own intoxication. Who can untangle the riddle of the artist's essence and character? Who can understand the deep instinctive fusion of discipline and a desire for licentiousness upon which that character is based? For it is licentiousness to be unable to wish for a salutary return to reality. Aschenbach was no longer inclined to self-criticism. The taste, the intellectual constitution that came with his years, his self-esteem, maturity, and the simplicity of age made him disinclined to analyze the grounds for his behavior or to decide whether it was conscience or debauchery and weakness that caused him not to carry out his plan. He was confused; he feared that someone, if only the custodian on the beach, might have observed his accelerated gait and his defeat; he feared very much looking foolish. And all the while he made fun of himself, of his comically solemn anxiety. "We've been quite confounded," he thought, "and now we're as crestfallen as a gamecock that lets its wings droop during a fight.[1] It must surely be the god himself who thus destroys our courage at the very sight of loveliness, who crushes our proud spirit so deeply in the dust. . . ." His thoughts roamed playfully: he was far too arrogant to be fearful of a mere emotion.

He had already ceased to pay much attention to the extent of time he was allowing himself for his holiday; the thought of returning home did not even cross his mind. He had had an ample amount of money sent to him by mail. His sole source of concern was the possible departure of the Polish family, but he had privately obtained information, thanks to casual inquiries at the hotel barber shop, that the Polish party had arrived only very shortly before he did. The sun tanned his face and hands, the bracing salt air stimulated his emotions. Just as he ordinarily used up all the resources he gathered from sleep, nourishment, or nature on literary work, so now he expended each contribution that sun, leisure, and sea air made to his daily increase in strength in a generous, extravagant burst of enthusiasm and sentiment.

He slept fitfully; the exquisitely uniform days were separated by short nights full of happy restlessness. To be sure he retired early, for at nine o'clock, when Tadzio had left the scene, the day was over as far as he was concerned. At the first glimmer of dawn, however, a softly penetrating pang of alarm awakened him, as his heart remembered its great adventure. No longer able to endure the pillow, he arose, wrapped himself in a light robe against the morning chill, and positioned himself at the open window to await the sunrise. This wonderful occurrence filled his sleep-blessed soul with reverence. Heaven, earth, and sea still lay in the ghostly, glassy pallor of dawn; a fading star still floated in the insubstantial distance. Then a breath of wind arose, a winged message from unapproachable abodes announcing that Eos was arising from the side of her spouse. There became visible on the furthest boundary between sea and sky that first sweet blush of red that reveals creation assuming perceptible form. The goddess was approaching, she who seduced young men, she who had stolen Kleitos and Kephalos and enjoyed the love of handsome Orion in defiance of all the envious Olympians.[2] A strewing of roses began there on the edge of the world, where all

---

1. From the Greek tragedian Phrynichus (512–476 B.C.), quoted in Plutarch's *Erotikos* (762E). 2. Eos, the Greek goddess of dawn, was known for seducing handsome young men, including Kleitos and Kephalos. When she took the hunter Orion for her lover, Artemis, the jealous goddess of the hunt, killed him with her arrows.

shone and blossomed in unspeakable purity. Childlike clouds, transfigured and luminous, hovered like attending Cupids in the rosy bluish fragrance. Purple light fell on the sea, then washed forward in waves. Golden spears shot up from below to the heights of the heavens, and the brilliance began to burn. Silently, with divine ascendancy, glow and heat and blazing flames spun upwards, as the brother-god's sacred chargers, hooves beating, mounted the heavens. The lonely, wakeful watcher sat bathed in the splendor of the god's rays; he closed his eyes and let the glory kiss his eyelids. With a confused, wondering smile on his lips he recognized feelings from long ago, early, exquisite afflictions of the heart that had withered in the severe service that his life had become and now returned so strangely transformed. He meditated, he dreamed. Slowly his lips formed a name, and still smiling, his face turned upward, his hands folded in his lap, he fell asleep once more in his armchair.

The whole day that had thus began in fiery celebration was strangely heightened and mythically transformed. Where did that breath of air come from, the one that suddenly played about his temples and ears so softly and significantly like a whisper from a higher realm? White feathery clouds stood in scattered flocks in the heavens like grazing herds that the gods tend. A stronger wind blew up; Poseidon's[3] steeds reared and ran, and the bulls obedient to the god with the blue-green locks lowered their horns and bellowed as they charged. But amid the boulders on the distant beach the waves hopped up like leaping goats. A magical world, sacred and animated by the spirit of Pan,[4] surrounded the beguiled traveler, and his heart dreamed tender fables. Often, as the sun set behind Venice, he would sit on a bench in the park to watch Tadzio, dressed in white with a colorful sash, delight in playing ball on the smooth, rolled gravel; and it was as if he were watching Hyacinthos, who had to die because two gods loved him.[5] Indeed he felt the painful envy Zephyros felt toward his rival in love, the god who abandoned his oracle, his bow, and his cithara to spend all his time playing with the beautiful boy. He saw the discus, directed by cruel jealousy, strike the lovely head; he too, turned pale as he received the stricken body; and the flower that sprang from that sweet blood bore the inscription of his unending lament. . . .

There is nothing stranger or more precarious than the relationship between people who know each other only by sight, who meet and watch each other every day, even every hour, yet are compelled by convention or their own whim to maintain the appearance of indifference and unfamiliarity, to avoid any word or greeting. There arises between them a certain restlessness and frustrated curiosity, the hysteria of an unsatisfied, unnaturally suppressed urge for acquaintanceship and mutual exchange, and in point of fact also a kind of tense respect. For people tend to love and honor other people so long as they are not in a position to pass judgment on them; and longing is the result of insufficient knowledge.

Some sort of relationship or acquaintance necessarily had to develop between Aschenbach and the young Tadzio, and with a pang of joy the older

3. God of the sea and brother of Zeus in Greek mythology, associated with the horse and the bull.   4. A Greek demigod, half man and half goat, associated with fertility and sexuality.   5. Apollo and Zephyr, god of the west wind, both loved the youth Hyacinthos. When Apollo accidentally killed him in a discus game—Zephyr blew the discus off course—a flower marked with the Greek syllables "ai ai" ("alas!") sprang from the boy's blood. Apollo is an archer and musician as well as the god of the Delphic oracle.

man was able to ascertain that his involvement and attentions were not alto-gether unrequited. For example, what impelled the lovely boy no longer to use the boardwalk behind the cabanas when he appeared on the beach in the morning but instead to saunter by toward his family's cabana on the front path, through the sand, past Aschenbach's customary spot, sometimes unnecessarily close by him, almost touching his table, his chair? Did Aschen-bach's superior emotional energy exercise such an attraction, such a fasci-nation on the tender, unreflecting object of those emotions? The writer waited daily for Tadzio's appearance; sometimes he would act as if he were busy when this event took place and let the lovely one pass by without seem-ing to notice. Sometimes, though, he would look up, and their eyes would meet. Both of them were gravely serious when it happened. In the refined and respectable bearing of the older man nothing betrayed his inner tumult; but in Tadzio's eyes there was the hint of an inquiry, of a thoughtful question. A hesitation became visible in his gait, he looked at the ground, he looked up again in his charming way, and when he was past there seemed to be something in his demeanor saying that only his good breeding prevented him from turning around.

One evening, however, something quite different happened. The Polish children and their governess were missing at the main meal in the large dining room. Aschenbach had taken note of it with alarm. Concerned about their absence, he was strolling in front of the hotel at the bottom of the terrace after dinner, dressed in his evening clothes and a straw hat, when he suddenly saw appear in the light of the arc lamps the nunlike sisters and their attendant, with Tadzio four steps behind. They were apparently return-ing from the steamer landing after having taken their meal for some reason in the city. It must have been cool on the water: Tadzio wore a dark blue sailor's coat with gold buttons and a sailor's hat to go with it. The sun and sea air had not browned him. His skin was the same marble-like yellow color it had been from the beginning. But today he seemed paler than usual, whether because of the cool temperature or because of the pallid moonglow cast by the lamps. His even brows showed in starker contrast, his eyes dark-ened to an even deeper tone. He was more beautiful than words could ever tell, and Aschenbach felt as he often had before the painful truth that words are capable only of praising physical beauty, not of rendering it visible.

He had not been expecting the exquisite apparition: it had come on unhoped for. He had not had time to fortify himself in a peaceful, respectable demeanor. Joy, surprise, and admiration might have been clearly displayed in the gaze that met that of the one he had so missed—and in that very second, it came to pass that Tadzio smiled. He smiled at Aschenbach, smiled eloquently, intimately, charmingly, and without disguise, with lips that began to open only as he smiled. It was the smile of Narcissus[6] leaning over the mirroring water, that deep, beguiled, unresisting smile that comes as he extends his arm toward the reflection of his own beauty—a very slightly distorted smile, distorted by the hopelessness of his desire to kiss the lovely lips of his shadow—a coquettish smile, curious and faintly pained, infatuated and infatuating.

He who had been the recipient of this smile rushed away with it as if it

---

6. A beautiful Greek youth who fell in love with his own image in a pool and drowned trying to reach it. "Tadzio's smile is Narcissus', who sees his own reflection—he sees it in the face of another / he sees his beauty in its effects. Coquettishness and tenderness are also in this smile" [Mann's note].

were a gift heavy with destiny. He was so thoroughly shaken that he was forced to flee the light of the terrace and the front garden and to seek with a hasty tread the darkness of the park in the rear. Strangely indignant and tender exhortations broke forth from him: "You must not smile so! Listen, no one is allowed to smile that way at anyone!" He threw himself on a bench; he breathed in the nocturnal fragrance of the plants, beside himself. Leaning back with his arms hanging at his sides, overpowered and shivering uncontrollably, he whispered the eternal formula of longing—impossible under these conditions, absurd, reviled, ridiculous, and yet holy and venerable even under these conditions—"I love you!"

CHAPTER 5

In the fourth week of his stay on the Lido Gustav Aschenbach made a number of disturbing discoveries regarding events in the outside world. In the first place it seemed to him that as the season progressed toward its height the number of guests at the hotel declined rather than increased. In particular it seemed that the German language ceased to be heard around him: lately his ear could detect only foreign sounds in the dining room and on the beach. He had taken to visiting the barbershop frequently, and in a conversation there one day he heard something that startled him. The barber had mentioned a German family that had just left after staying only a short time; then he added by way of flattering small talk, "But you're staying, sir, aren't you. You're not afraid of the disease." Aschenbach looked at him. "The disease?" he repeated. The man broke off his chatter, acted busy, ignored the question. When Aschenbach pressed the issue, he explained that he knew nothing and tried to change the subject with a stream of embarrassed eloquence.

That was at noon. In the afternoon Aschenbach sailed across to Venice in a dead calm and under a burning sun. He was driven by his mania to pursue the Polish children, whom he had seen making for the steamer landing along with their attendant. He did not find his idol at San Marco. But at tea, sitting at his round wrought-iron table on the shady side of the piazza, he suddenly smelled a peculiar aroma in the air, one that he now felt had been lurking at the edge of his consciousness for several days without his becoming fully aware of it. It was a medicinally sweet smell that put in mind thoughts of misery and wounds and ominous cleanliness. After a few moments' reflection he recognized it; then he finished his snack and left the piazza on the side opposite the cathedral. The odor became stronger in the narrow streets. At the street corners there were affixed printed posters in which the city fathers warned the population about certain illnesses of the gastric system that could be expected under these atmospheric conditions, advising that they should not eat oysters and mussels or use the water in the canals. The euphemistic nature of the announcement was obvious. Groups of local people stood together silently on the bridges and in the piazzas, and the foreign traveler stood among them, sniffing and musing.

There was a shopkeeper leaning in the doorway of his little vaulted quarters among coral necklaces and imitation amethyst trinkets, and Aschenbach asked him for some information about the ominous odor. The man took his measure with a heavy-lidded stare and then hastily put on a cheerful expression. "A precautionary measure, sir," he answered with many a gesture. "A police regulation that we must accept. The weather is oppressive, the sirocco is not conductive to good health. In short, you understand—perhaps they're being too careful. . . ." Aschenbach thanked him and went on. Even on the steamer that took him back to the Lido he could now detect the odor of disinfectant.

Once back at the hotel he went directly to the lobby to have a look at the newspapers. In the ones in foreign languages he found nothing. The German papers mentioned rumors, cited highly varying figures, quoted official denials, and offered doubts about their veracity. This explained the departure of the German and Austrian element. The citizens of other nations apparently knew nothing, suspected nothing, and were not yet concerned. "Best to keep quiet," thought Aschenbach anxiously, as he threw the papers back on the table. "Best to keep it under wraps." But at the same time his heart filled with a feeling of satisfaction over this adventure in which the outside world was becoming involved. For passion, like crime, does not sit well with the sure order and even course of everyday life; it welcomes every loosening of the social fabric, every confusion and affliction visited upon the world, for passion sees in such disorder a vague hope of finding an advantage for itself. Thus Aschenbach felt a dark satisfaction over the official cover-up of events in the dirty alleys of Venice. This heinous secret belonging to the city fused and became one with his own innermost secret, which he was likewise intent upon keeping. For the lovesick traveler had no concern other than that Tadzio might depart, and he recognized, not without a certain horror, that he would not know how to go on living were that to happen.

Recently he had not contented himself with allowing chance and the daily routine to determine his opportunities to see and be near the lovely lad; he pursued him, he lay in wait for him. On Sundays, for example, the Polish family never went to the beach. He guessed that they went to mass at San Marco. He followed speedily, entered the golden twilight of the sanctuary from the heat of the piazza, and found him, the one he had missed so, bent over a prie-dieu[7] taking part in the holy service. He stood in the background on the fissured mosaic floor, in the midst of a kneeling, murmuring crowd of people who kept crossing themselves, and felt the condensed grandeur of the oriental temple weigh voluptuously on his senses. Up in front the priest moved about, conducted his ritual, and chanted away, while incense billowed up and enshrouded the feeble flames of the altar candles. Mixed in with the sweet, heavy, ceremonial fragrance seemed to be another: the smell of the diseased city. But through all the haze and glitter Aschenbach saw how the lovely one up in front turned his head, looked for him, and found him.

When at last the crowd streamed out of the open portals into the shining piazza with its flocks of pigeons, the infatuated lover hid in the vestibule where he lay in wait, staking out his quarry. He saw the Polish family leave the church, saw the children take leave of their mother with great ceremony, saw her make for the Piazzetta on her way home. He ascertained that the lovely one, his cloisterly sisters, and the governess were on their way off to the right, through the clock tower gate, and into the Merceria,[8] and after

7. Pray God (French, literal trans.); a low bench on which to kneel during prayers, with a raised shelf for elbows or book.   8. Commercial district north of the Piazza San Marco.

giving them a reasonable head start he followed. He followed like a thief as they strolled through Venice. He had to stop when they lingered somewhere, had to flee into restaurants or courtyards to avoid them when they turned back. He lost them, got hot and tired as he searched for them over bridges and in dirty cul-de-sacs, and suffered long moments of mortal pain when he saw them coming toward him in a narrow passage where no escape was possible. And yet one cannot really say he suffered. He was intoxicated in head and heart, and his steps followed the instructions of the demon whose pleasure it is to crush under foot human reason and dignity.[9]

At some point or other Tadzio and his party would take a gondola, and Aschenbach, remaining hidden behind a portico or a fountain while they got in, did likewise shortly after they pulled away from the bank. He spoke quickly and in subdued tones to the gondolier, instructing him that a gen- erous tip was in store for him if he would follow that gondola just now rounding the corner—but not too close, as unobtrusively as possible. Sweat trickled over his body as the gondolier, with the roguish willingness of a procurer, assured him in the same lowered tones that he would get service, that he would get conscientious service.

He leaned back in the soft black cushions and glided and rocked in pursuit of the other black, beak-prowed bark, to which his passion held him fastened as if by a chain. Sometimes he lost sight of it, and at those times he would feel worried and restless. But his boatman seemed entirely familiar with such assignments and always knew just how to bring the object of his desire back into view by means of clever maneuvers and quick passages and shortcuts. The air was still, and it smelled. The sun burned heavily through a haze that gave the sky the color of slate. Water gurgled against wood and stone. The cry of the gondolier, half warning and half greeting, received distant answer from out of the silent labyrinth as if by mysterious arrangement. Umbels of flowers hung down over crumbling walls from small gardens on higher ground. They were white and purple and smelled like almonds. Moorish window casings showed their forms in the haze. The marble steps of a church descended into the waters; a beggar crouching there and asserting his misery held out his hat and showed the whites of his eyes as if he were blind; a dealer in antiques stood before his cavelike shop and with fawning gestures invited the passerby to stop, hoping for a chance to swindle him. That was Venice, that coquettish, dubious beauty of a city, half fairy tale and half tourist trap, in whose noisome air the fine arts once thrived luxuriantly and where musicians were inspired to create sounds that cradle the listener and seductively rock him to sleep. To the traveler in the midst of his adventure it seemed as if his eyes were drinking in just this luxury, as if his ears were wooed by just such melodies. He remembered, too, that the city was sick and was keeping its secret out of pure greed, and he cast an even more licentious leer toward the gondola floating in the distance before him.

Entangled and besotted as he was, he no longer wished for anything else than to pursue the beloved object that inflamed him, to dream about him when he was absent and to speak amorous phrases, after the manner of lovers, to his mere shadow. His solitary life, the foreign locale, and his late but deep transport of ecstasy encouraged and persuaded him to allow himself

---

9. Dionysus, originally an Eastern fertility god, worshiped with wild dances in ecstatic rites.

the most bewildering transgressions without timidity or embarrassment. That is how it happened that on his return from Venice late in the evening he had stopped on the second floor of the hotel in front of the lovely one's door, leaned his brow against the hinge in complete intoxication, unable for a protracted period to drag himself away, heedless of the danger of being caught in such an outrageous position.

Still, there were moments when he paused and half came to his senses. How has this come to pass? he wondered in alarm. How did I come to this? Like everyone who has achieved something thanks to his natural talents, he had an aristocratic interest in his family background. At times when his life brought him recognition and success he would think about his ancestors and try to reassure himself that they would approve, that they would be pleased, that they would have had to admire him. Even here and now he thought about them, entangled as he was in such an illicit experience, seized by such exotic emotional aberrations. He thought about their rigorous self-possession, their manly respectability, and he smiled a melancholy smile. What would they say? But then what would they have said about his whole life, a life that had so diverged, one might say degenerated, from theirs, a life under the spell of art that he himself had mocked in the precocity of his youth, this life that yet so fundamentally resembled theirs? He too had done his service, he too had practiced a strict discipline; he too had been a soldier and a man of war, like many of them. For art was a war, a grinding battle that one was just no longer up to fighting for very long these days. It was a life of self-control and a life lived in despite, a harsh, steadfast, abstemious existence that he had made the symbol of a tender and timely heroism. He had every right to call it manly, call it courageous, and he wondered if the love-god who had taken possession of him might be particularly inclined and partial somehow to those who lived such a life. Had not that very god enjoyed the highest respect among the bravest nations of the earth? Did they not say that it was because of their courage that he had flourished in their cities? Numerous war heroes of ages past had willingly borne the yoke imposed by the god, for a humiliation imposed by the god did not count. Acts that would have been denounced as signs of cowardice when done in other circumstances and for other ends—prostrations, oaths, urgent pleas, and fawning behavior—none redounded to the shame of the lover, but rather he more likely reaped praise for them.[1]

Such was the infatuated thinker's train of thought; thus he sought to offer himself support; thus he attempted to preserve his dignity. But at the same time he stubbornly kept on the track of the dirty doings in the city's interior, that adventure of the outside world that darkly joined together with his heart's adventure and nourished his passion with vague, lawless hopes. Obsessed with finding out the latest and most reliable news about the status and progress of the disease, he went to the city's coffee houses and leafed through the German newspapers, which had long since disappeared from the table in the hotel lobby. He read alternating assertions and denials. The number of illnesses and deaths might be as high as twenty, forty, even a hundred or more; but then in the next article or next issue any outbreak of

---

1. A reference to the Athenian code of love as described by Pausanias in Plato's *Symposium*, sections 182d–e and 183b.

the epidemic, if not categorically denied, would be reported as limited to a few isolated cases brought in by foreigners. There were periodic doubts, warnings, and protests against the dangerous game being played by the Italian authorities. Reliable information was simply not available.

The solitary guest was nonetheless conscious of having a special claim on his share in the secret. Though he was excluded, he took a bizarre pleasure in pressing knowledgeable people with insidious questions and forcing those who were part of the conspiracy of silence to utter explicit lies. At breakfast one day in the main dining room, for example, he engaged the manager in conversation. This unobtrusive little person in his French frock coat was going about between the tables greeting everyone and supervising the help. He made a brief stop at Aschenbach's table, too, for a casual chat. Now then why, the guest just happened to ask very casually, why in the world had they been disinfecting Venice for all this time? "It's a police matter," the toady answered, "a measure intended to stop in due and timely fashion any and all unwholesome conditions, any disturbance of the public health that might come about owing to the brooding heat of this exceptionally warm weather." "The police are to be commended," replied Aschenbach. After the exchange of a few more meteorological observations the manager took his leave.

On that very same day, in the evening after dinner, it happened that a little band of street singers from the city performed in the hotel's front garden. They stood, two men and two women, next to the iron lamppost of an arc light and raised their faces, shining in the white illumination, toward the great terrace, where the guests were enjoying this traditional popular entertainment while drinking coffee and cooling beverages. Hotel employees—elevator boys, waiters, and office personnel—stood by listening at the entrances to the lobby. The Russian family, zealous and precise in taking their pleasure, had wicker chairs moved down into the garden so as to be nearer the performers. There they sat in a semi-circle, in their characteristically grateful attitude. Behind the ladies and gentlemen stood the old slave woman in her turbanlike headdress.

The low-life virtuosos were extracting sounds from a mandolin, a guitar, a harmonica, and a squeaky violin. Interspersed among the instrumental numbers were vocals in which the younger of the women blended her sharp, quavering voice with the sweet falsetto of the tenor in a love duet full of yearning. But the chief talent and real leader of the group was clearly the other man, the guitar player, who sang a kind of buffo[2] baritone while he played. Though his voice was weak, he was a gifted mime and projected remarkable comic energy. Often he would move away from the group, his great instrument under his arm, and advance toward the terrace with many a flourish. The audience rewarded his antics with rousing laughter. The Russians in particular, ensconced in their orchestra seats, displayed particular delight over all this southern vivacity and encouraged him with applause and cheers to ever bolder and more brazen behavior.

Aschenbach sat at the balustrade, cooling his lips from time to time with a mixture of pomegranate[3] juice and soda that sparkled ruby-red in his glass. His nerves greedily consumed the piping sounds, the vulgar, pining melodies;

---

2. Comic.   3. A tropical fruit with many seeds, associated in Greek mythology both with Persephone, the queen of Hades, and with the world of the dead.

for passion numbs good taste and succumbs in all seriousness to enticements that a sober spirit would receive with humor or even reject scornfully. His features, reacting to the antics of the buffoon, had become fixed in a rigid and almost painful smile. He sat in an apparently relaxed attitude, and all the while he was internally tense and sharply attentive, for Tadzio stood no more than six paces away, leaning against the stone railing.

He stood there in the white belted suit that he sometimes wore to dinner, a figure of inevitable and innate grace, his left forearm on the railing, his ankles crossed, his right hand supported on his hip. He wore an expression that was not quite a smile but more an air of distant curiosity or polite receptivity as he looked down toward the street musicians. Sometimes he straightened up and, with a lovely movement of both arms that lifted his chest, he would pull his white blouse down through his leather belt. Occasionally, though—as the aging observer noted with triumph and even with horror, his reason staggering—Tadzio would turn his head to look across his left shoulder in the direction of the one who loved him, sometimes with deliberate hesitation, sometimes with sudden swiftness as if to catch him unawares. Their eyes never met, for an ignominious caution forced the errant lover to keep his gaze fearfully in check. The women guarding Tadzio were sitting in the back of the terrace, and things had reached the point that the smitten traveler had to take care lest his behavior should become noticeable and he fall under suspicion. Indeed his blood had nearly frozen on a number of occasions when he had been compelled to notice on the beach, in the hotel lobby, or in the Piazza San Marco that Tadzio was called away from his vicinity, that they were intent on keeping the boy away from him. He felt horribly insulted, and his pride flinched from unfamiliar tortures that his conscience prevented him from dismissing.

In the meantime the guitar player had begun singing a solo to his own accompaniment, a popular ditty in many verses that was quite the hit just then all over Italy. He was adept at performing it in a highly histrionic manner, and his band joined in the refrain each time, both with their voices and all their instruments. He was of a lean build, and even his face was thin to the point of emaciation. He stood there on the gravel in an attitude of impertinent bravura, apart from his fellow performers, his shabby felt hat so far back on his head that a roll of red hair surged forth from beneath the brim, and as he thumped the guitar strings, he hurled his buffooneries toward the terrace above in an insistent recitative. The veins on his brow swelled in response to his exertions. He seemed not to be of Venetian stock, more likely a member of the race of Neapolitan comics, half pimp, half actor, brutal and daring, dangerous and entertaining. The lyrics of his song were as banal as could be, but in his mouth they acquired an ambiguous, vaguely offensive quality because of his facial expressions and his gestures, his suggestive winks and his manner of letting his tongue play lasciviously at the corner of his mouth. His strikingly large Adam's apple protruded nakedly from his scrawny neck, which emerged from the soft collar of a sport shirt worn in incongruous combination with more formal city clothes. His pale, snub-nosed face was beardless and did not permit an easy reckoning of his age; it seemed ravaged by grimaces and by vice. The two defiant, imperious, even wild-looking furrows that stood between his reddish eyebrows went rather oddly with the grin on his mobile lips. What particularly drew the attention of the lonely spectator, however, was his observation that this questionable figure seemed to carry with it its own questionable atmosphere. For every time the refrain began again the singer would commence a grotesque circular march, clowning and shaking the hands of his audience; every time his path would bring him directly underneath Aschenbach's spot, and every time that happened there wafted up to the terrace from his clothes and from his body a choking stench of carbolic acid.[4]

His song finished, he began collecting money. He started with the Russians, who produced a generous offering, and then ascended the steps. As bold as he had been during the performance, just so obsequious was he now. Bowing and scraping, he slithered about between the tables, a smile of crafty submissiveness laying bare his large teeth, and all the while the two furrows between his red eyebrows stood forth menacingly. The guests surveyed with curiosity and some revulsion this strange being who was gathering in his livelihood. They threw coins in his hat from a distance and were careful not to touch him. The elimination of the physical separation between the performer and his respectable audience always tends to produce a certain embarrassment, no matter how pleasurable the performance. The singer felt it and sought to excuse himself by acting servile. He came up to Aschenbach, and with him came the smell, though no one else in the vicinity seemed concerned about it.

"Listen," the lonely traveler said in lowered tones, almost mechanically. "They are disinfecting Venice. Why?" The jester answered hoarsely: "Because of the police. That, sir, is the procedure when it gets hot like this and when the sirocco comes. The sirocco is oppressive. It's not conducive to good health. . . ." He spoke as if he were amazed that anyone could ask such questions, and he demonstrated by pushing with his open palm just how oppressive the sirocco was. "So there is no disease in Venice?" Aschenbach asked very quietly through his closed teeth. The tense muscles in the comedian's face produced a grimace of comic perplexity. "A disease? What sort of disease? Is the sirocco a disease? Do you suppose our police force is a disease? You like to make fun, don't you? A disease! Why on earth? Some preventive measures, you understand. A police regulation to minimize the effects of the oppressive weather . . . ," he gesticulated. "Very well," Aschenbach said once again, briefly and quietly, and he dropped an indecently large coin into the hat. Then he indicated with a look that the man should go. He obeyed with a grin and a bow. But even before he reached the steps two hotel employees intercepted him and, putting their faces very close to his, cross-examined him in whispers. He shrugged, he protested, he swore that he had been circumspect. You could tell. Dismissed, he returned to the garden and, after making a few arrangements with his group by the light of the arc lamp, he stepped forward to offer one parting song.

It was a song the solitary traveler could not remember ever having heard before, an impudent Italian hit in an incomprehensible dialect embellished with a laughing refrain in which the whole group regularly joined, fortissimo. The refrain had neither words nor instrumental accompaniment; nothing was left but a certain rhythmically structured but still very natural-sounding laughter, which the soloist in particular was capable of producing with great

4. A chemical used as a disinfectant.

talent and deceptive realism. Having reestablished a proper artistic distance
between himself and his audience, he had regained all his former impudence.
His artfully artificial laughter, directed impertinently up to the terrace, was
the laughter of scorn. Even before the part of the song with actual lyrics had
come to a close, one could see him begin to battle an irresistible itch. He
would hiccup, his voice would catch, he would put his hand up to his mouth,
he would twist his shoulders, and at the proper moment the unruly laughter
would break forth, exploding in a hoot, but with such realism that it was
infectious. It spread among the listeners so that even on the terrace an
unfounded mirth set in, feeding on nothing but itself. This appeared only to
double the singer's exuberance. He bent his knees, slapped his thighs, held
his sides, fairly split with laughter; but he was no longer laughing, he was
howling. He pointed his finger upwards, as if to say that there could be
nothing funnier than the laughing audience up there, and soon everyone in
the garden and on the veranda was laughing, including the waiters, elevator
boys, and servants lingering in the doorways.

Aschenbach no longer reclined in his chair; he sat upright as if trying to
defend himself or to flee. But the laughter, the rising smell of hospital san-
itation, and the nearness of the lovely boy—all blended to cast a dreamy spell
about him that held his mind and his senses in an unbreakable, inescapable
embrace. In the general confusion of the moment he made so bold as to cast
a glance at Tadzio, and when he did so he was granted the opportunity to
see that the lovely lad answered his gaze with a seriousness equal to his own.
It was as if the boy were regulating his behavior and attitude according to
that of the man, as if the general mood of gaiety had no power over the boy
so long as the man kept apart from it. This childlike and meaningful docility
was so disarming, so overwhelming, that the gray-haired traveler could only
with difficulty refrain from hiding his face in his hands. It had also seemed
to him that Tadzio's habit of straightening up and taking a deep sighing
breath suggested an obstruction in his breathing. "He is sickly; he will probably not live long," he thought once again with that sobriety that sometimes
frees itself in some strange manner from intoxication and longing. Ingenuous
solicitude mixed with a dissolute satisfaction filled his heart.

The Venetian singers had meanwhile finished their number and left,
accompanied by applause. Their leader did not fail to adorn even his departure with jests. He bowed and scraped and blew kisses so that everyone
laughed, which made him redouble his efforts. When his fellow performers
were already gone, he pretended to back hard into a lamppost at full speed,
then crept toward the gate bent over in mock pain. There at last he cast off
the mask of the comic loser, unbent or rather snapped up straight, stuck his
tongue out impudently at the guests on the terrace, and slipped into the
darkness. The audience dispersed; Tadzio was already long gone from his
place at the balustrade. But the lonely traveler remained sitting for a long
time at his little table, nursing his pomegranate drink much to the annoyance
of the waiters. The night progressed; time crumbled away. Many years ago
in his parents' house there had been an hourglass. He suddenly could see
the fragile and portentous little device once more, as though it were standing
right in front of him. The rust-colored fine sand ran silently through the glass
neck, and as it began to run out of the upper vessel a rapid little vortex
formed.

In the afternoon of the very next day the obstinate visitor took a further step in his probing of the outside world, and this time he met with all possible success. What he did was to enter the English travel agency in the Piazza San Marco and, having changed some money at the cash register and having assumed the demeanor of a diffident foreigner, he directed his fateful question to the clerk who was taking care of him. The clerk was a wool-clad Briton, still young, his hair parted in the middle and eyes set close together, possessed of that steady, trustworthy bearing that stands out as so foreign and so remarkable among the roguishly nimble southerners. He began: "No cause for concern, sir. A measure of no serious importance. Such regulations are frequently imposed to ward off the ill effects of the heat and the sirocco. . . ." But when he raised his blue eyes he met the foreigner's gaze. It was a tired and rather sad gaze, and it was directed with an air of mild contempt toward his lips. The Englishman blushed. "That is," he continued in a low voice, somewhat discomfited, "the official explanation, which they see fit to stick to hereabouts. I can tell you, though, that there's a good deal more to it." And then, in his candid and comfortable language, he told the truth.

For some years now Asiatic cholera had shown an increasing tendency to spread and roam. The pestilence originated in the warm swamps of the Ganges delta,[5] rising on the foul-smelling air of that lushly uninhabitable primeval world, that wilderness of islands avoided by humankind where tigers lurk in bamboo thickets. It had raged persistently and with unusual ferocity throughout Hindustan; then it had spread eastwards to China and westwards to Afghanistan and Persia; and, following the great caravan routes, it had brought its horrors as far as Astrakhan and even Moscow. But while Europe was shaking in fear lest the specter should progress by land from Russia westward, it had emerged simultaneously in several Mediterranean port cities, having been carried in on Syrian merchant ships. It had raised its grisly head in Toulon and Malaga, shown its grim mask several times in Palermo and Naples, and seemed now firmly ensconced throughout Calabria and Apulia.[6] The northern half of the peninsula had so far been spared. On a single day in mid-May of this year, however, the terrible vibrioid bacteria had been found on two emaciated, blackening corpses, that of a ship's hand and that of a woman who sold vegetables. These cases were hushed up. A week later, though, there were ten more, twenty more, thirty more, not localized but spread through various parts of the city. A man from the Austrian hinterlands who had come for a pleasant holiday of a few days in Venice died upon returning to his home town, exhibiting unmistakable symptoms. Thus it was that the first rumors of the affliction visited upon the city on the lagoon appeared in German newspapers. In response the Venetian authorities promulgated the assertion that matters of health had never been better in the city. They also immediately instituted the most urgent measures to counter the disease. But apparently the food supply—vegetables, meat, and milk—had been infected, for death, though denied and hushed up, devoured its way through the narrow streets. The early arrival of summer's heat made a lukewarm broth of the water in the canals and thus made conditions for the

5. In India.   6. Regions in southern Italy. Astrakhan, Toulon, Málaga, Palermo, and Naples are seaports in Russia, France, Spain, Sicily, and southern Italy, respectively.

disease's spread particularly favorable. It almost seemed as though the pestilence had been reinvigorated, as if the tenacity and fecundity of its microscopic agitators had been redoubled. Cures were rare; out of a hundred infected eighty died, and in a particularly gruesome fashion, for the evil raged here with extreme ferocity. Often it took on its most dangerous form, commonly known as the "dry type." In such cases the body is unable to rid itself of the massive amounts of water secreted by the blood-vessels. In a few hours' time the patient dries up and suffocates, his blood as viscous as pitch, crying out hoarsely in his convulsions. It sometimes happened that a few lucky ones suffered only a mild discomfort followed by a loss of consciousness from which they would never again, or only rarely, awaken. At the beginning of June the quarantine wards of the Ospedale Civico quietly filled up, space became scarce in both of the orphanages, and a horrifyingly brisk traffic clogged the routes between the docks at the Fondamenta Nuove[7] and San Michele, the cemetery island. But the fear of adverse consequences to the city, concern for the newly opened exhibit of paintings in the public gardens, for the losses that the hotels, businesses, and the whole tourist industry would suffer in case of a panic or a boycott—these matters proved weightier in the city than the love of truth or respect for international agreements. They prompted the authorities stubbornly to maintain their policy of concealment and denial. The highest medical official in Venice, a man of considerable attainments, had angrily resigned his post and was surreptitiously replaced by a more pliable individual. The citizenry knew all about it, and the combination of corruption in high places with the prevailing uncertainty, the state of emergency in which the city was placed when death was striking all about, caused a certain demoralization of the lower levels of society. It encouraged those antisocial forces that shun the light, and they manifested themselves as immoderate, shameless, and increasingly criminal behavior. Contrary to the norm, one saw many drunks at evening time; people said that gangs of rogues made the streets unsafe at night; muggings and even murders multiplied. Already on two occasions it had come to light that alleged victims of the plague had in fact been robbed of their lives by their own relatives who administered poison. Prostitution and lasciviousness took on brazen and extravagant forms never before seen here and thought to be at home only in the southern parts of the country and in the seraglios of the orient.

The Englishman explained the salient points of these developments. "You would do well," he concluded, "to depart today rather than tomorrow. The imposition of a quarantine cannot be more than a few days off." "Thank you," said Aschenbach and left the agency.

The piazza was sunless and sultry. Unsuspecting foreigners sat in the sidewalk cafes or stood in front of the cathedral completely covered with pigeons. They watched as the swarming birds beat their wings and jostled each other for their chance to pick at the kernels of corn offered to them in an open palm. In feverish excitement, triumphant in his possession of the truth, but with a taste of gall in his mouth and a fantastic horror in his heart, the lonely traveler paced back and forth over the flagstones of the magnificent plaza. He considered doing the decent thing, the thing that would cleanse him. Tonight after dinner he could go up to the lady with the pearls and speak to

---

7. New footings (Italian, literal trans.); the new piers. *Ospedale Civico*: city hospital.

her. He planned exactly what he would say: "Permit me, Madame, stranger though I may be, to be of service to you with a piece of advice, a word of warning concerning a matter that has been withheld from you by self-serving people. Depart at once, taking Tadzio and your daughters with you. There is an epidemic in Venice." He could then lay his hand in farewell on the head of that instrument of a scornful deity, turn away, and flee this swamp. But at the same time he sensed that he was infinitely far from seriously wanting to take such a step. It would bring him back to his senses, would make him himself again; but when one is beside oneself there is nothing more abhorrent than returning to one's senses. He remembered a white building decorated with inscriptions that gleamed in the evening light, inscriptions in whose radiant mysticism his mind's eye had become lost. He remembered too that strange figure of the wanderer who had awakened in the aging man a young man's longing to roam in faraway and exotic places. The thought of returning home, of returning to prudence and sobriety, toil and mastery, was so repugnant to him that his face broke out in an expression of physical disgust. "Let them keep quiet," he whispered vehemently. And: "I will keep quiet!" The consciousness of his guilty complicity intoxicated him, just as small amounts of wine will intoxicate a weary brain. The image of the afflicted and ravaged city hovered chaotically in his imagination, incited in him inconceivable hopes, beyond all reason, monstrously sweet. How could that tender happiness he had dreamed of a moment earlier compare with these expectations? What value did art and virtue hold for him when he could have chaos? He held his peace and stayed.

That night he had a terrifying dream—if indeed one can call "dream" an experience that was both physical and mental, one that visited him in the depths of his sleep, in complete isolation as well as sensuous immediacy, but yet such that he did not see himself as physically and spatially present apart from its action. Instead, its setting was in his soul itself, and its events burst in upon him from outside, violently crushing his resistance, his deep, intellectual resistance, passing through easily and leaving his whole being, the culmination of a lifetime of effort, ravaged and annihilated.

It began with fear, fear and desire and a horrified curiosity about what was to come. Night ruled, and his senses were attentive; for from afar there approached a tumult, a turmoil, a mixture of noises: rattling, clarion calls and muffled thunder, shrill cheering on top of it all, and a certain howl with a drawn-out *uuu* sound at the end. All this was accompanied and drowned out by the gruesomely sweet tones of a flute playing a cooing, recklessly persistent tune that penetrated to the very bowels, where it cast a shameless enchantment. But there was a phrase, darkly familiar, that named what was coming: *"The stranger god!"*[8] A smoky glow welled up, and he recognized a mountain landscape like the one around his summer house. And in the fragmented light he could see people, animals, a swarm, a roaring mob, all rolling and plunging and whirling down from the forested heights, past tree-trunks and great moss-covered fragments of rock, overflowing the slope with their bodies, flames, tumult, and reeling circular dance. Women, stumbling over the fur skirts that hung too long from their belts, moaned, threw their heads

8. Dionysus (also Bacchus), whose cult was brought to Greece from Thrace and Phrygia. The dream describes the orgiastic rites of his worship.

back, shook their tambourines on high, brandished naked daggers and torches that threw off sparks, held serpents with flickering tongues by the middle of their bodies, or cried out, lifting their breasts in both hands. Men with horns on their brows, girdled with hides, their own skins shaggy, bent their necks and raised their arms and thighs, clashed brazen cymbals and beat furiously on drums, while smooth-skinned boys used garlanded staves to prod their goats, clinging to the horns so they could be dragged along, shouting with joy, when the goats sprang. And the ecstatic band howled the cry with soft consonants in the middle and a drawn-out *uuu* sound on the end, a cry that was sweet and wild at the same time, like none ever heard before: here it rang in the air like the bellowing of stags in rut; and there many voices echoed it back in anarchic triumph, using it to goad each other to dance and shake their limbs, never letting it fall silent. But it was all suffused and dominated by the deep, beckoning melody of the flute. Was it not also beckoning him, the resisting dreamer, with shameless persistence to the festival, to its excesses, and to its ultimate sacrifice? Great was his loathing, great his fear, sincere his resolve to defend his own against the foreign invader, the enemy of self-controlled and dignified intellect. But the noise and the howling, multiplied by the echoing mountainsides, grew, gained the upper hand, swelled to a madness that swept everything along with it. Fumes oppressed the senses: the acrid scent of the goats, the emanation of panting human bodies, a whiff as of stagnant water—and another smell perceptible through it all, a familiar reek of wounds and raging sickness. His heart pounded with the rhythm of the drum beats, his mind whirled, rage took hold of him and blinded him, he was overcome by a numbing lust, and his soul longed to join in the reeling dance of the god. Their obscene symbol,[9] gigantic, wooden, was uncovered and raised on high, and they howled out their watchword all the more licentiously. With foam on their lips they raved; they stimulated each other with lewd gestures and fondling hands; laughing and wheezing, they pierced each other's flesh with their pointed staves and then licked the bleeding limbs. Now among them, now a part of them, the dreamer belonged to the stranger god. Yes, they were he, and he was they, when they threw themselves on the animals, tearing and killing, devouring steaming gobbets of flesh, when on the trampled moss-covered ground there began an unfettered rite of copulation in sacrifice to the god. His soul tasted the lewdness and frenzy of surrender.

The afflicted dreamer awoke unnerved, shattered, a powerless victim of the demon. He no longer shunned the observant glances of people about him; he no longer cared if he was making himself a target of their suspicions. And in any case they were all departing, fleeing the sickness. Many cabanas now stood empty, the population of the dining room was seriously depleted, and in the city one only rarely saw a foreigner. The truth seemed to have leaked out, and in spite of the stubborn conniving of those with vested interests at stake, panic could no longer be averted. The lady with the pearls nonetheless remained with her family, perhaps because the rumors did not reach her or perhaps because she was too proud and fearless to succumb to them. Tadzio remained, and to Aschenbach, blind to all but his own concerns, it seemed at times that death and departure might very well remove

9. The phallus.

all the distracting human life around them and leave him alone with the lovely one on this island. Indeed, in the mornings on the beach when his gaze would rest heavily, irresponsibly, fixedly on the object of his desire; or at the close of day when he would take up his shameful pursuit of the boy through narrow streets where loathsome death did its hushed-up business; then everything monstrous seemed to him to have a prosperous future, the moral law to have none.

He wished, like any other lover, to please his beloved and felt a bitter concern that it would not be possible. He added youthfully cheerful touches to his dress, took to using jewelry and perfume. Several times a day he took lengthy care getting dressed and then came down to the dining room all bedecked, excited and expectant. His aging body disgusted him when he looked at the sweet youth with whom he was smitten; the sight of his gray hair and his sharp facial features overwhelmed him with shame and hopelessness. He felt a need to restore and revive his body. He visited the barbershop more and more frequently.

Leaning back in the chair under the protective cloth, letting the manicured hands of the chattering barber care for him, he confronted the tortured gaze of his image in the mirror.

"Gray," he said with his mouth twisted.

"A bit," the man replied. "It's all because of a slight neglect, an indifference to externals—quite understandable in the case of important people, but still not altogether praiseworthy, all the less so since just such people ought not to harbor prejudices in matters of the natural and the artificial. If certain people were to extend the moral qualms they have about the cosmetic arts to their teeth, as logic compels, they would give no little offense. And anyway, we're only as old we feel in our hearts and minds. Gray hair can in certain circumstances give more of a false impression than the dye that some would scorn. In your case, sir, you have a right to your natural hair color. Will you allow me to give you back what is rightfully yours?"

"How?" Aschenbach inquired.

So the glib barber washed his customer's hair with two liquids, one clear and one dark, and it turned as black as it had been in youth. Then he rolled it with the curling iron into soft waves, stepped back and admired his handiwork.

"All that's left," he said, "is to freshen up the complexion a bit."

He went about, with ever renewed solicitude, moving from one task to another the way a person does who can never finish anything and is never satisfied. Aschenbach, resting comfortably, was in any case quite incapable of fending him off. Actually he was rather excited about what was happening, watching in the mirror as his brows took on a more decisive and symmetrical arch and his eyes grew in width and brilliance with the addition of a little shadow on the lids. A little further down he could see his skin, previously brown and leathery, perk up with a light application of delicate carmine rouge, his lips, pale and bloodless only a moment a ago, swell like raspberries, the furrows in his cheeks and mouth, the wrinkles around his eyes give way to a dab of cream and the glow of youth. His heart pounded as he saw in the mirror a young man in full bloom. The cosmetic artist finally pronounced himself satisfied and thanked the object of his ministrations with fawning politeness, the way such people do. "A minor repair job," he said as he put a final touch to Aschenbach's appearance. "Now, sir, you can go and fall in love without second thoughts." The beguiled lover went out, happy as in a dream, yet confused and timid. His tie was red, and his broad-brimmed straw hat was encircled by a band of many colors.

A tepid breeze had come up; it rained only seldom and then not hard, but the air was humid, thick, and full of the stench of decay. Rustling, rushing, and flapping sounds filled his ears. He burned with fever beneath his makeup, and it seemed to him that the air was filled with vile, evil wind-spirits, impure winged sea creatures who raked over, gnawed over, and defiled with garbage the meals of their victim.[1] For the sultry weather ruined one's appetite, and one could not suppress the idea that all the food was poisoned with infection.

Trailing the lovely boy one afternoon, Aschenbach had penetrated deep into the maze in the heart of the diseased city. He had lost his sense of direction, for the little streets, canals, bridges, and piazzas in the labyrinth all looked alike. He could no longer even tell east from west, since his only concern had been not to lose sight of the figure he pursued so ardently. He was compelled to a disgraceful sort of discretion that involved clinging to walls and seeking protection behind the backs of passersby, and so he did not for some time become conscious of the fatigue, the exhaustion which a high pitch of emotion and continual tension had inflicted on his body and spirit. Tadzio walked behind the rest of his family. In these narrow streets he would generally let the governess and the nunlike sisters go first, while he sauntered along by himself, occasionally turning his head to assure himself with a quick glance of his extraordinary dawn-gray eyes over his shoulder that his lover was still following. He saw him, and he did not betray him. Intoxicated by this discovery, lured onward by those eyes, tied to the apron string of his own passion, the lovesick traveler stole forth in pursuit of his unseemly hope—but ultimately found himself disappointed. The Polish family had gone across a tightly arched bridge, and the height of the arch had hidden them from their pursuer. When he was at last able to cross, he could no longer find them. He searched for them in three directions—straight ahead and to both sides along the narrow, dirty landing—but in vain. He finally had to give up, too debilitated and unnerved to go on.

His head was burning hot, his body was sticky with sweat, the scruff of his neck was tingling, an unbearable thirst assaulted him, and he looked about for immediate refreshment of any sort. In front of a small greengrocer's shop he bought some fruit, strawberries that were overripe and soft, and he ate them while he walked. A little piazza that was quite deserted and seemed enchanted opened out before him. He recognized it, for it was here that weeks ago he had made his thwarted plan to flee the city. He collapsed on the steps of the well in the very middle of the plaza and rested his head on the stone rim. It was quiet, grass grew between the paving stones, refuse lay strewn about. Among the weathered buildings of varying heights around the periphery was one that looked rather palatial. It had Gothic-arched windows, now gaping emptily, and little balconies decorated with lions. On the ground floor of another there was a pharmacy. Warm gusts of wind from time to time carried the smell of carbolic acid.

He sat there, the master, the artist who had attained to dignity, the author

---

1. "Harpies: hideously thin, they flew swiftly in, fell with insatiable greed on whatever food was there, ate without being satisfied, and *befouled* whatever they left with their *filth*" [Mann's note]. See Virgil's *Aeneid* 3.210–62.

of the "Man of Misery," that exemplary work which had with clarity of form renounced bohemianism and the gloomy murky depths, had condemned sympathy for the abyss, reviled the vile. There he sat, the great success who had overcome knowledge and outgrown every sort of irony, who had accustomed himself to the obligations imposed by the confidence of his large audience. There he sat, the author whose greatness had been officially recognized and whose name bore the title of nobility, the author whose style children were encouraged to emulate—sat there with his eyes shut, though from time to time a mocking and embarrassed look would slip sidelong out from underneath his lids, only to conceal itself again swiftly; and his slack, cosmetically enhanced lips formed occasional words that emerged out of the strange dream-logic engendered in his half-dozing brain.[2]

"For beauty, Phaedrus—mark me well—only beauty is both divine and visible at the same time, and thus it is the way of the senses, the way of the artist, little Phaedrus, to the spirit. But do you suppose, my dear boy, that anyone could ever attain to wisdom and genuine manly honor by taking a path to the spirit that leads through the senses? Or do you rather suppose (I leave the decision entirely up to you) that this is a dangerously delightful path, really a path of error and sin that necessarily leads astray? For you must know that we poets cannot walk the path of beauty without Eros joining our company and even making himself our leader; indeed, heroes though we may be after our own fashion, disciplined warriors though we may be, still we are as women, for passion is our exaltation, and our longing must ever be for love. That is our bliss and our shame. Do you see, then, that we poets can be neither wise nor honorable, that we necessarily go astray, that we necessarily remain dissolute adventurers of emotion? The masterly demeanor of our style is a lie and a folly, our fame and our honor a sham, the confidence accorded us by our public utterly ridiculous, the education of the populace and of the young by means of art a risky enterprise that ought not to be allowed. For how can a person succeed in educating others who has an inborn, irremediable, and natural affinity for the abyss? We may well deny it and achieve a certain dignity, but wherever we may turn that affinity abides. Let us say we renounce analytical knowledge; for knowledge, Phaedrus, has neither dignity nor discipline; it is knowing, understanding, forgiving, formless and unrestrained; it has sympathy for the abyss; it *is* the abyss. Let us therefore resolutely reject it, and henceforth our efforts will be directed only toward beauty, that is to say toward simplicity, grandeur, and a new discipline, toward reborn ingenuousness and toward form. But form and ingenuousness, Phaedrus, lead to intoxication and to desire, might lead the noble soul to horrible emotional outrages that his own lovely discipline would reject as infamous, lead him to the abyss. Yes, they too lead to the abyss. They lead us poets there, I say, because we are capable not of resolution but only of dissolution. And now I shall depart, Phaedrus; but you stay here until you can no longer see me, and then you depart as well."

A few days afterwards Gustav von Aschenbach left the hotel at a later hour than usual, since he was feeling unwell. He was struggling with certain

---

2. Aschenbach adopts the role of Socrates in Plato's *Phaedrus* to examine the role of the artist. Although the Platonic dialogue briefly contrasts inspired art with mere technical perfection, it is chiefly concerned with moral choices and absolute beauty.

attacks of dizziness that were only partly physical and were accompanied by a powerfully escalating sense of anxiety and indecision, a feeling of having no prospects and no way out. He was not at all sure whether these feelings concerned the outside world or his own existence. He noticed in the lobby a great pile of luggage prepared for departure, and when he asked the door-man who was leaving, he received for an answer the aristocratic Polish name he had in his heart been expecting to hear all along. He took it in with no change in the expression on his ravaged face, briefly raising his head as people do to acknowledge casually the receipt of a piece of information they do not need, and asked, "When?" The answer came: "After lunch." He nod-ded and went to the beach.

It was dreary there. Rippling tremors crossed from near to far on the wide, flat stretch of water between the beach and the first extended sandbar. Where so recently there had been color, life, and joy, it was now almost deserted, and an autumnal mood prevailed, a feeling that the season was past its prime. The sand was no longer kept clean. A camera with no pho-tographer to operate it stood on its tripod at the edge of the sea, a black cloth that covered it fluttering with a snapping noise in a wind that now blew colder.

Tadzio and three or four playmates that still remained were active in front of his family's cabana to Aschenbach's right; and, resting in his beach chair approximately halfway between the ocean and the row of cabanas, with a blanket over his legs, Aschenbach watched him once more. Their play was unsupervised, since the women must have been busy with preparations for their departure. The game seemed to have no rules and quickly degenerated. The sturdy boy with the belted suit and the black, slicked-down hair who was called Yashu, angered and blinded by sand thrown in his face, forced Tadzio into a wrestling match, which ended swiftly with the defeat of the weaker, lovely boy. It seemed as if in the last moments before leave-taking the subservient feelings of the underling turned to vindictive cruelty as he sought to take revenge for a long period of slavery. The winner would not release his defeated opponent but instead kneeled on his back and pushed his face in the sand, persisting for so long that Tadzio, already out of breath from the fight, seemed in danger of suffocating. He made spasmodic attempts to shake off his oppressor, lay still for whole moments, then tried again with no more than a twitch. Horrified, Aschenbach wanted to spring to the rescue, but then the bully finally released his victim. Tadzio was very pale; he got up halfway and sat motionless for several minutes supported on one arm, his hair disheveled and his eyes darkening. Then he rose to his feet and slowly walked away. They called to him, cheerfully at first but then with pleading timidity. He paid no attention. The black-haired boy, apparently instantly regretting his transgression, caught up with him and tried to make up. A jerk of a lovely shoulder put him off. Tadzio crossed diagonally down to the water. He was barefoot and wore his striped linen suit with the red bow.

He lingered at the edge of the sea with his head hung down, drawing figures in the wet sand with his toe. Then he went into the shallows, which at their deepest point did not wet his knees, strode through them, and pro-gressed idly to the sandbar. Upon reaching it he stood for a moment, his face turned to the open sea, then began to walk slowly to the left along the narrow stretch of uncovered ground. Separated from the mainland by the broad expanse of water, separated from his mates by a proud mood, he strode forth, a highly remote and isolated apparition with wind-blown hair, wandering about out there in the sea, in the wind, on the edge of the misty boundlessness. Once more he stopped to gaze outward. Suddenly, as if prompted by a memory or an impulse, he rotated his upper body in a lovely turn out of its basic posture, his hand resting on his hip, and looked over his shoulder toward the shore. The observer sat there as he had sat once before, when for the first time he had met the gaze of those dawn-gray eyes cast back at him from that threshold. His head, resting on the back of the chair, had slowly followed the movements of the one who was striding about out there; now his head rose as if returning the gaze, then sank on his chest so that his eyes looked out from beneath. His face took on the slack, intimately absorbed expression of deep sleep. It seemed to him, though, as if the pale and charming psychagogue[3] out there were smiling at him, beckoning to him; as if, lifting his hand from his hip, he were pointing outwards, hovering before him in an immensity full of promise. And, as so often before, he arose to follow him.

Minutes passed before anyone rushed to the aid of the man who had collapsed to one side in his chair. They carried him to his room. And later that same day a respectfully shaken world received the news of his death.

---

3. Leader of souls to the underworld (Greek); a title of the god Hermes.

RAINER MARIA RILKE
1875–1926

Rainer Maria Rilke's search for the "great mysteries" of the universe combines his own intensely personal awareness with a range of broad questions that are ordinarily called religious. Whether his gaze is turned toward the objects and creatures of Earth, which he describes with extraordinary clarity and affection, or toward a higher intuited realm whose enigma remains to be deciphered, he seeks throughout a comprehensive vision of cosmic unity. Rilke absorbs what he sees around him—objects, people, gestures—until they become part of his consciousness and are ready to emerge in the words of a poem. "Looking is such a wonderful thing, about which we as yet know so little," he wrote his wife, Clara; "we are turned completely outward, but just when we are most outward, things seem to happen inside us." The poet's role, he says, is to observe with a fresh sensitivity "this fleeting world, which in some strange way / keeps calling to us," and to bear witness, through language, to the transfiguration of its materiality in human emotions. Rilke writes at a transitional moment in modern European letters: inheritor of the Symbolists in his allusive imagery and intuitions of cosmic order, and modernist in the "thing-centered" concreteness of individual descriptions, he also foreshadows existentialism as he struggles to comprehend the self's relation to the universe. The best-known and most influential German poet of the twentieth century, Rilke has been read and translated outside Europe in countries as far apart as the United States and Japan. He speaks to a variety of cultures and audiences even though he was perhaps the least socially oriented poet of his time.

Born in Prague on December 4, 1875, to German-speaking parents who separated when he was nine, Rilke had an unhappy childhood that included being dressed as a girl when he was young (thus his mother compensated for the earlier loss of a baby daughter) and being sent to military academies, where he was lonely and miserable, from 1886 to 1891. Illness caused his departure from the second academy; and after a year in business school, he worked in his uncle's law firm and studied at the University of Prague. Rilke hoped to persuade his family that he should devote himself to a literary career rather than business or law, and energetically wrote poetry (*Sacrifice to the Lares*, 1895, *Crowned by Dream*, 1896), plays, stories, and reviews. Moving to Munich in 1897, he met and fell in love with a fascinating and cultured older woman, Lou Andreas-Salomé, who would be a constant influence on him throughout his life. He accompanied Andreas-Salomé and her husband to Russia in 1899, where he met Leo Tolstoy and the painter Leonid Pasternak and—swayed by responding to Russian mysticism and the Russian landscape—wrote most of the poems later published as *The Book of Hours: The Book of Monastic Life* (1905) and a Romantic verse tale that became extremely popular, *The Tale of Love and Death of Cornet Christoph Rilke* (1906). After a second trip to Russia, Rilke spent some time at an artists' colony called Worpswede, where he met his future wife, the sculptor Clara Westhoff. They were married in March 1901 and settled in a cottage near the colony where Rilke wrote the second part of *The Book of Hours: The Book of Pilgrimage*. He and Clara separated in the following year, and Rilke moved to Paris where he embarked on a study of the French sculptor Auguste Rodin (1903).

Unhappy in Paris, where he felt lonely and isolated, he fled to Italy in 1903 to write the last section of *The Book of Hours: The Book of Poverty and Death*. Nonetheless, he had found in Paris a new kind of literary and artistic inspiration. He read French writers and especially Baudelaire, whose minutely realistic but strangely beautiful description of a rotting corpse (*A Carcass*) initiated, he felt, "the entire development toward objective expression, which we now recognize in Cézanne." In Rodin, too, he recognized a workmanlike dedication to the technical demands of his craft; an intense concentration on visible, tangible objects; and above all, a belief in art as an essentially religious activity. Although he wrote in distress to his friend Andreas-Salomé, complaining of nightmares and a sense of failure, it is at this time (and with her encouragement) that Rilke began his major work. The anguished, semiautobiographical spiritual confessions of *The Notebooks of Malte Laurids Brigge* (1910) date to this period, as do a series of *New Poems* (1907–08) in which he abandoned his earlier, impressionistic and Romantic style and developed a more intense Symbolic vision focused on objects. The *New Poems* emphasized physical reality, the absolute otherness and "thing-like" nature of what was observed—be it fountain, panther, flower, human being, or the "Archaic Torso of Apollo." "Thing-poems" (*Dinggedichte*), in fact, is a term often used to describe Rilke's writing at this time, with its open emphasis on material description. In a letter to Andreas-Salomé, he described the way that ancient art objects took on a peculiar luster once they were detached from history and seen as "things" in and for themselves: "No subject matter is attached to them, no irrelevant voice interrupts the silence of their concentrated reality . . . no history casts a shadow over their naked clarity—: they *are*. That is all . . . one day one of them reveals itself to you, and shines like a first star."

Such "things" are not dead or inanimate but supremely alive, filled with a strange vitality before the poet's glance: the charged sexuality of the marble torso, the metamorphosis of the Spanish dance in which the dancer's flamelike dress "becomes a furnace / from which, like startled rattlesnakes, the long / naked arms uncoil, aroused and clicking" (*Spanish Dancer*), or the caged panther's circling "like a ritual dance around a center / in which a mighty will stands paralyzed" (*The Panther*). If things are not dead, neither is death unambiguous: when Rilke retells the ancient myth of Orpheus and his lost wife, Eurydice, the dead woman is seen as achieving a new and fuller existence in the underworld. "Deep within herself. Being dead / filled her beyond fulfillment. . . . She was already loosened like long hair, / poured out like fallen rain, / shared like a limitless supply. / She was already root." Themes of the interpenetration of life and death, the visible and invisible world, and creativity itself are taken up in Rilke's next major work, the sequence of ten elegies (mournful lyric poems, usually laments for loss, and generally of medium length) called the *Duino Elegies* (1923), which he was to begin in 1912 while spending the winter in Duino Castle near Trieste.

The composition of the *Duino Elegies* came in two bursts of inspiration separated by ten years. Despite Rilke's increasing reputation and the popularity of his earlier work, he felt frustrated and unhappy. It was not that he lacked friends or activity; back in Paris once more, he corresponded actively and traveled widely, visiting Italy, Flanders, Germany, Austria, Egypt, and Algeria. But social pressures and everyday anxieties kept him overly occupied, and when a patroness, Princess Marie von Thurn und Taxis-Hohenlohe, proposed that he stay by himself in her castle at Duino during the winter of 1911–12, he was delighted.

Completion did not come easily in the following years, however, with the beginning of World War I. After writing the third Duino elegy in Paris in 1913, Rilke left for Munich—never dreaming that his apartment and personal property would soon be confiscated as that of an enemy alien. In April 1915, everything was sold at public auction; that summer, Duino Castle was bombarded and reduced to ruins. Rilke wrote the somber fourth elegy in Munich on November 22 and 23, and the next day was called up for the draft. Three weeks later, at age forty, he was drafted and became a clerk in the War Archives Office in Vienna where he drew precise vertical and horizontal lines on paper until June 1916, when the intercession of friends released him from military service. Rilke composed little after this experience and feared that he would never be able to complete the Duino sequence. In 1922, however, a friend's purchase of the tiny Château de Muzot in Switzerland gave him a peaceful place to retire and write. He not only completed the *Duino Elegies* in Muzot but wrote in addition—as a memorial for the young daughter of a friend—a two-part sequence of fifty-five sonnets, the *Sonnets to Orpheus* (1923).

With the *Duino Elegies* and the *Sonnets to Orpheus*, Rilke's last great works were complete. The melancholy philosophic vision of the early elegies describes an angel of absolute reality, whose self-contained perfection is terrifyingly separate from mortal concerns. In the later elegies and the *Sonnets*, the idea of angelic perfection is balanced by a newly important human role for the human artist, who serves as a bridge between the worlds of Earth and of the angel. To the poet's initial sense of helplessness and alienation, the later poems respond that all creatures need the artist's transforming glance to reach full being. *Elegies* and the *Sonnets* together move toward a more positive celebration of simple things. A sequence of symbolic figures suggests this development from uncertainty to affirmation, as the dominant angel of the *Elegies* gives way to the human poet Orpheus, who in turn retires into the background of the later *Sonnets* before Eurydice, the woman whose passing into the realm of the dead brings her fuller being. With this major affirmation of the essential unity of life and death, Rilke closed his two complementary sequences ("the little rust-colored sail of the Sonnets and the Elegies' gigantic white canvas") and wrote little—chiefly poems in French—over the next few years. Increasingly ill with leukemia, he died on December 29, 1926, as the result of a sudden infection after pricking himself on roses he cut for a friend in his garden.

The four selections from the *New Poems* printed here demonstrate Rilke's acutely visual imagination and the ambivalent objectivity of his "thing-poems." Whether a flamenco dancer, a caged panther, a swan entering the water, or the splendor of an ancient Greek statue, the subject is presented for itself—but it is also suffused with human emotions. These emotions are mixed and cannot be reduced to one meaning: for example, there is a combined sense of relief and yet obscurely terrifying mortality as the swan glides through the water, and the panther's numbed consciousness, contained force, and momentary tension clearly evoke some kind of response from the reader—pity? horror? fear of entrapment? awe?—but Rilke does not define it for us. Steel bars are the only world known by the caged panther, who has so far forgotten his natural habitat as to react only for a moment when an unexpected (and unspecified) image briefly penetrates his consciousness. The Spanish dancer moves with complete mastery through the traditional flamenco dance steps with all the brilliance and triumph of the flame to which she is compared (*flamenco* is derived from *flamear*, to flame). Both the swan's awkward progress on land and its majestic glide upon entering the water are compared in the poem to the passage from life to death. Concurrently, the detailed physical description makes it easy for readers to identify with the frustrations of the initial laborious advance—and the subsequent letting go and release into a new state of indifference and ease. The "archaic torso of Apollo" is not a living being, but a fifth-century B.C. Greek sculpture on display in the Louvre Museum in Paris. This headless marble torso is truly a "thing," a lifeless, even defaced chunk of stone. Yet such is the perfection of its luminous sensuality—descended, the speaker suggests, from the brilliant gaze of its missing head and "ripening" eyes—that it seems impossibly alive, and an inner radiance bursts starlike from the marble. The *human* vitality of this marble torso, a vitality achieved through artistic vision, challenges and puts to shame the observer's own puny existence. Nor is there any place to escape from the lesson, once it is recognized; instead, "You must change your life."

Ultimately, Rilke is celebrating the power of human creativity to refashion the world in its own image. The poet observes reality and creates from it a new form, a new being. For the poet, however, it is a process of making the visible angelically "invisible," and a bridge between two worlds; he "delivers" things by absorbing them into his imagination's inner dimension, asking, as at the end of the ninth *Elegy*, "Earth, isn't this what you want: to arise within us, / *invisible*?" Rilke's poetic journey, from the *New Poems* to the *Elegies* and the *Sonnets to Orpheus*, was an inward journey that created a bridge between two worlds, preserving the most intense moments of human experience by subjecting them to the transfiguring perspective of art.

J. F. Hendry, *The Sacred Threshold: A Life of Rainer Maria Rilke* (1983), and Patricia Pollock Brodsky, *Rainer Maria Rilke* (1988), are brief and readable biographies with numerous citations from Rilke's letters and work. Heinz F. Peters, *Rainer Maria Rilke: Masks and the Man* (1977), is a biographical and thematic study of Rilke's work and influence. Donald Prater, *A Ringing Glass: The Life of Rainer Maria Rilke* (1986), is an excellent account of the poet's life and the conditions in which his work developed and includes extensive quotations from many unpublished letters. William Rose and G. Craig Houston, eds., *Rainer Maria Rilke, Aspects of His Mind and Poetry* (1970), contains an excellent essay by C. M. Bowra on the *New Poems*. William H. Gass, *Reading Rilke: Reflections on the Problems of Translation* (1999), combines biography, philosophy, and reflections on specific translation problems in the *Duino Elegies*.

PRONOUNCING GLOSSARY

The following list uses common English syllables and stress accents to provide rough equivalents of selected words whose pronunciation may be unfamiliar to the general reader.

Dinggedichte: *ding'-ge-dikh-tuh*   Muzot: *moo-tsot'*

FROM NEW POEMS[1]
Archaic Torso of Apollo[2]

We cannot know his legendary head[3]
with eyes like ripening fruit. And yet his torso
is still suffused with brilliance from inside,
like a lamp, in which his gaze, now turned to low,

gleams in all its power. Otherwise   5
the curved breast could not dazzle you so, nor could
a smile run through the placid hips and thighs
to that dark center where procreation flared.

Otherwise this stone would seem defaced
beneath the translucent cascade of the shoulders   10
and would not glisten like a wild beast's fur:

would not, from all the borders of itself,
burst like a star: for here there is no place
that does not see you. You must change your life.

Archaïscher Torso Apollos

Wir kannten nicht sein unerhörtes Haupt,
darin die Augenäpfel reiften. Aber
sein Torso glüht noch wie ein Kandelaber,
in dem sein Schauen, nur zurückgeschraubt,

sich hält und glänzt. Sonst könnte nicht der Bug   5
der Brust dich blenden, und im leisen Drehen
der Lenden könnte nicht ein Lächeln gehen
zu jener Mitte, die die Zeugung trug.

Sonst stünde dieser Stein entstellt und kurz
unter der Schultern durchsichtigem Sturz   10
und flimmerte nicht so wie Raubtierfelle;

und bräche nicht aus allen seinen Rändern
aus wie ein Stern: denn da ist keine Stelle,
die dich nicht sieht. Du mußt dein Leben ändern.

---

1. All selections translated by Stephen Mitchell. 2. The first poem in the second volume of Rilke's *New Poems* (1908), which were dedicated "to my good friend, Auguste Rodin" (the French sculptor, 1840–1917, whose secretary Rilke was for a brief period and on whom he wrote two monographs, in 1903 and 1907). The poem itself was inspired by an ancient Greek statue discovered at Miletus (a Greek colony on the coast of Asia Minor) that was called simply the *Torso of a Youth from Miletus;* since the god Apollo was an ideal of youthful male beauty, his name was often associated with such statues. 3. In a torso, the head and limbs are missing.

The Panther

In the Jardin des Plantes,[1] Paris

His vision, from the constantly passing bars,
has grown so weary that it cannot hold
anything else. It seems to him there are
a thousand bars; and behind the bars, no world.

As he paces in cramped circles, over and over,   5
the movement of his powerful soft strides
is like a ritual dance around a center
in which a mighty will stands paralyzed.

Only at times, the curtain of the pupils
lifts, quietly—. An image enters in,   10
rushes down through the tensed, arrested muscles,
plunges into the heart and is gone.

The Swan

This laboring through what is still undone,
as though, legs bound, we hobbled along the way,
is like the awkward walking of the swan.

And dying—to let go, no longer feel
the solid ground we stand on every day—   5
is like his anxious letting himself fall

into the water, which receives him gently
and which, as though with reverence and joy,
draws back past him in streams on either side;
while, infinitely silent and aware,   10
in his full majesty and ever more
indifferent, he condescends to glide.

Spanish Dancer[1]

As on all its sides a kitchen-match darts white
flickering tongues before it bursts into flame:
with the audience around her, quickened, hot,
her dance begins to flicker in the dark room.

And all at once it is completely fire.   5

1. A zoo in Paris. Rilke also admired, at Rodin's studio, the plaster cast of an ancient statue of a panther.
1. A traditional Spanish dance, the *flamenco* (from *flamear*, to flame).

One upward glance and she ignites her hair
and, whirling faster and faster, fans her dress
into passionate flames, till it becomes a furnace
from which, like startled rattlesnakes, the long
naked arms uncoil, aroused and clicking.[2]   10

And then: as if the fire were too tight
around her body, she takes and flings it out
haughtily, with an imperious gesture,
and watches: it lies raging on the floor,
still blazing up, and the flames refuse to die—.   15
Till, moving with total confidence and a sweet
exultant smile, she looks up finally
and stamps it out with powerful small feet.

2. The dancer accompanies herself with the rhythmic clicking of castanets (worn on the fingers).

WALLACE STEVENS
1879–1955

"A bucket of sand and a wishing lamp," Wallace Stevens once said, was all he needed to "create a world in half a second that would make this one look like a hunk of mud." His poetry invites us into an imaginative world that fuses poignantly sensuous images with the most abstract metaphysics. Stevens himself embodied contrasts: a Hartford insurance executive as well as a major American poet, he was never a part of the contemporary literary scene with its movements and isms. He was acquainted with current New York writers and artists, he collected modern art (which is often reflected in his poems), and later in his career he wrote and lectured about poetry; but it is not through these associations that he joins the mainstream of modern European and American letters. In his work Stevens combines two aspects of modernist tradition. His musical free verse and sensuous, significant imagery recall Symbolism, which he especially admired in the French poet Paul Verlaine. His stress on concrete, physical descriptions inside a philosophical framework is characteristic of "existential" writers such as Jean-Paul Sartre and Albert Camus. More than any other modern poet, Stevens inherited the Symbolists' desire to balance the intertwined concepts of concrete reality and human imagination. Like the Symbolists, too, he finds an ultimate human value in the artist's freedom to create the world anew in a "supreme fiction": *fiction*, because "true" reality can never be ascertained or re-created; *supreme*, because it is the highest aspiration of human creativity. This fiction is not yet the ungraspable "fictionality" of postmodernist writers such as Samuel Beckett and Alain Robbe-Grillet, for it does not dissolve into a series of competing perspectives. Instead, Stevens's modernist poetry holds up the ideal of a supreme artistic transformation whose creation bestows meaning on an otherwise meaningless universe.

Stevens was born in Reading, Pennsylvania, on October 2, 1879, the second of five children. His father was a schoolteacher and then attorney with diverse interests; his mother taught school. He enrolled at Harvard in 1897 as a nondegree student and while at college contributed poems, stories, and sketches to the Harvard *Advocate* (of which he became president) and the Harvard *Monthly*. He also came to know the philosopher and writer George Santayana, whose assertion of a common imaginative essence in religion and poetry appealed greatly to him.

Stevens left Harvard in 1900 to try journalism and then law school in New York; he received his degree and was admitted to the bar in 1904. After working as an attorney for several firms he finally entered the insurance business in 1908. In 1916 he joined a subsidiary of the Hartford Accident and Indemnity Company, becoming vice president of the parent company in 1934 and remaining there until his death in 1955. He dictated business correspondence and poems to the same secretary. In 1922 business affairs took him to Florida, and until 1940 he returned frequently to its warm and lush landscape, which contrasted in his poetry—both physically and emotionally—with the chillier climate of the north.

Stevens married Elsie V. Kachel in 1909, and in 1924 his daughter, Holly, was born; she later edited her father's letters. He published individual poems in little magazines (small avant-garde literary magazines) and was a friend of *Poetry* editor Harriet Monroe and of the poets William Carlos Williams and Marianne Moore. *Harmonium,* his first collection of poetry, appeared in 1923. In following years, Stevens's insurance career occupied most of his time, and he published little poetry until 1936, when *Ideas of Order* appeared. Later volumes included *The Man with the Blue Guitar* (1937), *Parts of a World* (1942), and a collection of prose essays, *The Necessary Angel* (1951). Stevens kept the two parts of his career quite separate but gradually became a well-known and influential poet, winning the Bollingen Prize for poetry in 1949 and the National Book Award in 1951 (for *The Auroras of Autumn*) and 1955 (for *The Collected Poems of Wallace Stevens*). He died of cancer on August 2, 1955.

Stevens's poetry expresses the dualism between reality and imagination, between things as they really are and as we perceive and then shape them. For we can never know reality directly; our five senses see, touch, taste, smell, and hear what is outside us, constructing an image of the world in which we live, but this world also exists separate from us and beyond our image of it. This paradox underlies all Stevens's poetry, which swings between the two poles of the shaping, creative imagination and the material world of which we are only partly aware. The names of real Connecticut towns or the state of Tennessee, an inventory of the trash in a dump, descriptions of coffee and oranges at breakfast, and marred old pieces of furniture inhabit his poems side by side with the most abstract speculations, transformations of everyday scenes, and visions of the edge of space. Poetic artifice—the playful and imaginative use of language—clothes the most mundane observations, as if to assert a relationship between verbal style and the real subject about which it tries to speak. Stevens once said that "it is pleasant to hear the milkman, and yet . . . the imaginative world is the only real world after all," and this balancing of dualities continues throughout his work.

Sunday Morning, one of Stevens's earlier poems, already reflects this dualism on several levels. The opening lines present a contrast between the comfortable self-indulgence of the Sunday morning breakfast table, warmly alive with sun and bright colors, and the traditional Christian dedication of the day to thoughts of human mortality redeemed by Christ's death. The contrast continues in a quasi-dialogue between the poet, who protests any attempt to transcend this world or death, and the woman, who speaks of paradise and some "imperishable bliss." Earth itself is sufficient paradise, says the poet, and "friendlier" than the untouchable sky or supernatural explanations of different religions; death is a necessary part of life's constant renewal and sharpens our awareness of love and beauty while they exist. The wholly natural beauty of the New England landscape at the poem's end, with its acceptance of death and change, suggests to the speaker a more real and human ideal than the unchanging perfection of eternal life.

The softer, more consolatory tone of *Sunday Morning* (which derives in part from Stevens's recollection of his mother's death in 1912) becomes bold and gaudier in *The Emperor of Ice-Cream,* which also deals—but more ironically—with the contrast of life and death. The scene is a wake: a dead woman lies covered with the same sheet on which she once embroidered fantail pigeons. Stevens, however, begins his poem in the kitchen with the festivities in which the survivors are taking part. For the day is devoted not only to the dead but to the living, in whose imperial court the ice cream server is emperor, and the women dressed in their best clothes are handmaidens. Words with erotic overtones (*concupiscent, wenches*) reinforce the scene's essential hedonism, in which the only reality that counts is the pleasure of the moment.

Yet there is another reality, that of the dead woman, who has now become a mere object much like her own furniture, and Stevens painstakingly registers its details. The dresser is made of pine wood and lacks three glass knobs; the dead woman's calloused feet protrude from the too-short embroidered sheet. Such close-up observation puts the woman in a new imaginative context, in a world of lifeless inanimate things whose stillness comments with grim finality on the first stanza's boisterous celebration. The empire of ice cream contains both life and death; people, flowers, and yesterday's newspapers all ultimately come down to the same level of bare physicality. Wisdom lies in accepting the common outcome of all earthly appearances—"Let be be finale of seem"—and in celebrating life while it remains.

Stevens's juxtaposition of reality and our imaginative perception of it is echoed throughout his writing by a dialectic of other oppositions, one idea being raised seemingly only to be challenged and tested by another. Thus the jar on a hill in Tennessee juxtaposes human intellect and aesthetic imagination against the unshaped wilderness of nature, and *Peter Quince at the Clavier* celebrates the immortal presence—in the memory—of a long-dead woman's physical beauty. Such balancing or counterpoint rejects a single perspective and opens up avenues for continued meditation.

Counterpoint is basically a musical term, and Stevens's work is filled with the imagery of musical performance: the harpsichord of *Peter Quince at the Clavier,* the singer in *The Idea of Order at Key West,* and the nightingale and even grackles of *The Man on the Dump.* Other poems speak of a blue guitar (the image taken from a painting by Pablo Picasso), an old horn, a lute, citherns, saxophones, not to mention the "tink and tank and tunk-a-tunk-tunk" of an unnamed instrument (perhaps a banjo). Musical images are used to describe events, such as the tambourinelike rhythm of Susanna's attendants arriving (with the additional musical end rhymes of *tambourines* and *Byzantines*), or emotions, like the erotic intensity of the elders' lustful glance ("The basses of their beings throb / In witching chords") and the comic counterpoint of their quivering nerves pulsing "pizzicati of Hosanna." Even the title of Stevens's book is the name of a musical instrument, *Harmonium,* and he had wanted to name his collected poems *The Whole of Harmonium.*

Music for Stevens was not, however, merely musical images in a poem, or the notion of harmonizing the sounds of words or holding contrasted ideas in counterpoint. It implied for him a supreme, intuited language, the "foreign song" of the gold-feathered bird on the edge of space in *Of Mere Being,* perhaps the same bird that sang to the emperor in Yeats's *Sailing to Byzantium.* The singer, bird or human, is the type of the poet, the "one of fictive music" who creates the world anew through the incantatory power of imagination.

The singer of *The Idea of Order at Key West* is such a poet, embodying imagination at its most ambitious: "She was the single artificer of the world / In which she sang." Nature itself cannot create such a world, for it lacks the igniting spark; while the sea may imitate human gestures and sounds, it cannot truly speak, and makes only "meaningless plungings of water and wind." Imagination is supreme; the singer has "the maker's rage to order words" (*poet* comes from a Greek word meaning "maker"), and her song creates for herself and for her listeners a world of imagination in which lights from the fishing boats seem to map out the night against which they shine.

The luminous beauty of the singer's world is only one of many possible poetic worlds, all of which take their place on the accumulated heap of poetry where the latest artificer sits as *The Man on the Dump.* The trash heap of history is the place to find outworn poetic images, from dewy clichés to the nightingale as traditional symbol for poetry (see Keats's *Ode to a Nightingale*). In a poem filled with the debris of modern times, from old tires to dead cats, Stevens suggests that poetry's philosophical quest to name the "the" of existence cannot employ previous ages' images and ideas but must develop its own, even if they appear only as the grating music of grackles or beatings on an old tin can. Yet all are engaged in the same enterprise, creating what he elsewhere called "supreme fictions" to give meaning to our lives.

Stevens's poetry celebrates the ability of the individual imagination to conceive its own world. Broader social or political themes are pushed to the background, even in texts (such as *The Man on the Dump* or *The Emperor of Ice-Cream*) that derive power from their realistic descriptions. Consequently, the politically minded critics of the 1930s accused the poet of being an escapist, content to be the "single artificer of his own world of mannerism." Stevens responded that to do otherwise was to misunderstand "the spiritual role of the poet," for this role was not to make political statements but to clarify basic issues by illuminating the relations between human subjectivity and a world of objects. Such an explanation may have seemed too philosophical to those seeking an openly committed literature, and Stevens's early work was largely unappreciated. The gaudy exuberance of its images made it seem less serious than the poetry of political commitment and visionary mysticism that Yeats was then writing, or Eliot's evocation in *The Waste Land* of a universal and profound despair. Only after World War II did Americans, and Europeans, realize that Stevens, too, was a master worthy to stand beside his greatest contemporaries.

A good general introduction is Robert Pack, *Wallace Stevens: An Approach to His Poetry* (1958); Tony Sharpe, *Wallace Stevens: A Literary Life* (2000), is a brief and readable biography. Robert Buttel, *Wallace Stevens: The Makings of Harmonium* (1967), discusses Stevens's early and middle work. Many views on Stevens are presented in Marie Borroff, ed., *Wallace Stevens: A Collection of Critical Essays* (1963). Michel Benamou, *Wallace Stevens and the Symbolist Imagination* (1972), is an interesting study of Stevens's themes and style compared with those of French Symbolist poets. Albert Gelpi, *Wallace Stevens: The Poetics of Modernism* (1985), presents seven essays situating Stevens's work in the context of twentieth-century modernism in English. Historical, philosophical, and artistic perspectives are discussed as well as Stevens's influence on contemporary poets. Anthony Whiting, *The Never-Resting Mind: Wallace Stevens' Romantic Irony* (1996), describes Stevens's work in terms of a tension between opposed aspects of Romantic irony. John T. Newcomb, *Wallace Stevens and Literary Canons* (1992), examines the way Stevens's "canonical" reputation evolves in tandem with critical perspectives on American modernism. Glen MacLeod, *Wallace Stevens and Modern Art: From the Armory Show to Abstract Expression* (1993), traces the relations between Stevens's poetics and his understanding of issues in modern art.

Sunday Morning[1]

I

Complacencies of the peignoir, and late
Coffee and oranges in a sunny chair,
And the green freedom of a cockatoo
Upon a rug mingle to dissipate
The holy hush of ancient sacrifice.   5
She dreams a little, and she feels the dark
Encroachment of that old catastrophe,
As a calm darkens among water-lights.

---

1. Although the central figure of the poem is clearly a woman sitting over late breakfast on Sunday morning instead of going to church, Stevens comments that "this is not essentially a woman's meditation on religion and the meaning of life. It is anybody's meditation" (Stevens's *Letters*, p. 250).

The pungent oranges and bright, green wings
Seem things in some procession of the dead, 10
Winding across wide water, without sound.
The day is like wide water, without sound,
Stilled for the passing of her dreaming feet
Over the seas, to silent Palestine,
Dominion of the blood and sepulchre.[2] 15

II

Why should she give her bounty to the dead?
What is divinity if it can come
Only in silent shadows and in dreams?
Shall she not find in comforts of the sun,
In pungent fruit and bright, green wings, or else 20
In any balm or beauty of the earth,
Things to be cherished like the thought of heaven?[3]
Divinity must live within herself:
Passions of rain, or moods in falling snow;
Grievings in loneliness, or unsubdued 25
Elations when the forest blooms; gusty
Emotions on wet roads on autumn nights;
All pleasures and all pains, remembering
The bough of summer and the winter branch.
These are the measures destined for her soul. 30

III

Jove[4] in the clouds had his inhuman birth.
No mother suckled him, no sweet land gave
Large-mannered motions to his mythy mind
He moved among us, as a muttering king,
Magnificent, would move among his hinds,[5] 35
Until our blood, commingling, virginal,[6]
With heaven, brought such requital to desire
The very hinds discerned it, in a star.[7]
Shall our blood fail? Or shall it come to be
The blood of paradise? And shall the earth 40
Seem all of paradise that we shall know?
The sky will be much friendlier then than now,
A part of labor and a part of pain,
And next in glory to enduring love,
Not this dividing and indifferent blue. 45

IV

She says, "I am content when wakened birds,
Before they fly, test the reality
Of misty fields, by their sweet questionings;
But when the birds are gone, and their warm fields

2. Throughout the stanza there are hints of Christ's Crucifixion and the celebration of the Mass.
3. "The poem is simply an expression of paganism" (Stevens's *Letters*, p. 250).   4. Ruler of the gods in Roman myth. Stevens softens the traditional story in which Jove's father, Cronus, swallows the infant shortly after birth.   5. Shepherds.   6. An allusion to the conception of Jesus in the womb of the Virgin Mary.
7. The star over Bethlehem that marked Jesus' birth.

Return no more, where, then, is paradise?"   50
There is not any haunt of prophecy,[8]
Nor any old chimera of the grave,
Neither the golden underground, nor isle
Melodious, where spirits gat them home,[9]
Nor visionary south, nor cloudy palm   55
Remote on heaven's hill, that has endured
As April's green endures; or will endure
Like her remembrance of awakened birds,
Or her desire for June and evening, tipped
By the consummation of the swallow's wings.   60

V

She says, "But in contentment I still feel
The need of some imperishable bliss."
Death is the mother of beauty; hence from her,
Alone, shall come fulfilment to our dreams
And our desires. Although she strews the leaves   65
Of sure obliteration on our paths,
The path sick sorrow took, the many paths
Where triumph rang its brassy phrase, or love
Whispered a little out of tenderness,
She makes the willow shiver in the sun   70
For maidens who were wont to sit and gaze
Upon the grass, relinquished to their feet.
She causes boys to pile new plums and pears
On disregarded plate.[1] The maidens taste
And stray impassioned in the littering leaves.   75

VI

Is there no change of death in paradise?
Does ripe fruit never fall? Or do the boughs
Hang always heavy in that perfect sky,
Unchanging, yet so like our perishing earth,
With rivers like our own that seek for seas   80
They never find, the same receding shores
That never touch with inarticulate pang?
Why set the pear upon those river-banks
Or spice the shores with odors of the plum?
Alas, that they should wear our colors there,   85
The silken weavings of our afternoons,
And pick the strings of our insipid lutes!
Death is the mother of beauty, mystical,
Within whose burning bosom we devise
Our earthly mothers waiting, sleeplessly.   90

---

8. E.g., like the oracle at Delphi.   9. The Elysian Fields, or Isles of the Blessed, where the heroes of Greek myth went after death.   1. "Plate is used in the sense of so-called family plate. Disregarded refers to the disuse into which things fall that have been possessed for a long time. I mean, therefore, that death releases and renews. What the old have come to disregard, the young inherit and make use of" (Stevens's *Letters*, p. 183).

VII

Supple and turbulent, a ring of men
Shall chant in orgy on a summer morn
Their boisterous devotion to the sun,
Not as a god, but as a god might be,
Naked among them, like a savage source.   95
Their chant shall be a chant of paradise,
Out of their blood, returning to the sky;
And in their chant shall enter, voice by voice,
The windy lake wherein their lord delights,
The trees, like serafin,[2] and echoing hills,   100
That choir among themselves long afterward.
They shall know well the heavenly fellowship
Of men that perish and of summer morn.
And whence they came and whither they shall go
The dew upon their feet shall manifest.[3]   105

VIII

She hears, upon that water without sound,
A voice that cries, "The tomb in Palestine
Is not the porch of spirits lingering.[4]
It is the grave of Jesus, where he lay."
We live in an old chaos of the sun,   110
Or old dependency of day and night,
Or island solitude, unsponsored, free,
Of that wide water, inescapable.
Deer walk upon our mountains, and the quail
Whistle about us their spontaneous cries;   115
Sweet berries ripen in the wilderness;
And, in the isolation of the sky,
At evening, casual flocks of pigeons make
Ambiguous undulations as they sink.
Downward to darkness, on extended wings.   120

Peter Quince at the Clavier[1]

I

Just as my fingers on these keys
Make music, so the selfsame sounds
On my spirit make a music, too.

Music is feeling, then, not sound;
And thus it is that what I feel,   5
Here in this room, desiring you,

---

2. Angels of the highest rank.   3. "Life is as fugitive as dew upon the feet of men dancing in dew. Men do not either come from any direction or disappear in any direction. Life is as meaningless as dew" (Stevens's *Letters*, p. 250).   4. I.e., remaining on Earth after the body is dead.   1. General term in the 16th century for a keyboard instrument, such as a harpsichord. In Shakespeare's *A Midsummer Night's Dream*, Peter Quince is the carpenter-playwright who directs his own play about the tragic lovers Pyramus and Thisbe. Both the play and the production amuse the noble audience.

Thinking of your blue-shadowed silk,
Is music. It is like the strain
Waked in the elders by Susanna.[2]

Of a green evening, clear and warm,   10
She bathed in her still garden, while
The red-eyed elders watching, felt

The basses of their beings throb
In witching chords, and their thin blood
Pulse pizzicati of Hosanna.[3]   15

II

In the green water, clear and warm,
Susanna lay.
She searched
The touch of springs,
And found   20
Concealed imaginings.
She sighed,
For so much melody.

Upon the bank, she stood
In the cool   25
Of spent emotions.
She felt, among the leaves,
The dew
Of old devotions.

She walked upon the grass,   30
Still quavering.
The winds were like her maids,
On timid feet,
Fetching her woven scarves,
Yet wavering.   35

A breath upon her hand
Muted the night.
She turned—
A cymbal crashed,
And roaring horns.   40

III

Soon, with a noise like tambourines,
Came her attendant Byzantines.[4]

---

2. In the biblical Apocrypha, a Babylonian woman falsely accused of adultery by lecherous elders who spied on her bathing.   3. A cry of praise to God. *Pizzicati:* notes sounded by plucking a string (as on a violin).   4. Inhabitants of ancient Byzantium, a Christian empire of the Near East. "Somebody once called my attention to the fact that there were no Byzantines in Susanna's time. I hope that that bit of precious pedantry will seem as unimportant to you as it does to me" (Stevens's *Letters,* p. 250).

They wondered why Susanna cried
Against the elders by her side;

And as they whispered, the refrain   45
Was like a willow swept by rain.

Anon,[5] their lamps' uplifted flame
Revealed Susanna and her shame.

And then, the simpering Byzantines
Fled, with a noise like tambourines.   50

IV

Beauty is momentary in the mind—
The fitful tracing of a portal;
But in the flesh it is immortal.
The body dies; the body's beauty lives.
So evenings die, in their green going,   55
A wave, interminably flowing.
So gardens die, their meek breath scenting
The cowl of winter, done repenting.
So maidens die,[6] to the auroral
Celebration of a maiden's choral.[7]   60
Susanna's music touched the bawdy strings
Of those white elders; but, escaping,
Left only Death's ironic scraping.[8]
Now, in its immortality, it plays
On the clear viol[9] of her memory,   65
And makes a constant sacrament of praise.

Anecdote of the Jar

I placed a jar in Tennessee.
And round it was, upon a hill.
It made the slovenly wilderness
Surround that hill.

The wilderness rose up to it,   5
And sprawled around, no longer wild.
The jar was round upon the ground
And tall and of a port[1] in air.

It took dominion everywhere.
The jar was gray and bare.   10
It did not give of bird or bush,
Like nothing else in Tennessee.

5. Soon.   6. As maidens, that is, become women.   7. Choral song.   8. Rasping fiddle music.
9. A stringed instrument of the 16th and 17th centuries, played with a bow; also a pun on *violation*.
1. Dignified bearing, manner.

The Emperor of Ice-Cream[1]

Call the roller of big cigars,
The muscular one, and bid him whip
In kitchen cups concupiscent[2] curds.
Let the wenches dawdle in such dress
As they are used to wear, and let the boys   5
Bring flowers in last month's newspapers.
Let be be finale of seem.[3]
The only emperor is the emperor of ice-cream.

Take from the dresser of deal,[4]
Lacking the three glass knobs, that sheet   10
On which she embroidered fantails[5] once
And spread it so as to cover her face.
If her horny feet protrude, they come
To show how cold she is, and dumb.
Let the lamp affix its beam.   15
The only emperor is the emperor of ice-cream.

The Idea of Order at Key West[1]

She sang beyond the genius of the sea.[2]
The water never formed to mind or voice,
Like a body wholly body, fluttering
Its empty sleeves; and yet its mimic motion
Made constant cry, caused constantly a cry,   5
That was not ours although we understood,
Inhuman, of the veritable ocean.

The sea was not a mask.[3] No more was she.
The song and water were not medleyed sound
Even if what she sang was what she heard.   10
Since what she sang was uttered word by word.
It may be that in all her phrases stirred
The grinding water and the gasping wind;
But it was she and not the sea we heard.

1. "I think I should select from my poems as my favorite 'The Emperor of Ice-Cream.' This wears a deliberately commonplace costume, and yet seems to me to contain something of the essential gaudiness of poetry; that is the reason why I like it" (Stevens's *Letters*, p. 263).   2. Lusty, sensual. "The words 'concupiscent curds' . . . express the concupiscence of life, but, by contrast with the things in relation to them in the poem they express or accentuate life's destitution" (Stevens's *Letters*, p. 500).   3. "The true sense of 'Let be be the finale of seem' is let being become the conclusion or denouement of appearing to be: in short, icecream is an absolute good. The poem is obviously not about icecream, but about being as distinguished from seeming to be" (Stevens's *Letters*, p. 341).   4. Fir or pine wood.   5. Fantail pigeons.
1. Published in *Ideas of Order* (1936). "In 'The Idea of Order at Key West' life has ceased to be a matter of chance. It may be that every man introduces his own order into the life about him. . . . But still there is order. . . . These are tentative ideas for the purposes of poetry" (Stevens's *Letters*, p. 293). Key West is the southernmost of the Florida keys, and Stevens spent midwinter vacations there for almost twenty years.
2. I.e., beyond the power of the sea to respond.   3. The movement of the waves, imitating fluttering sleeves, also emits an inhuman cry. The sea mimics the human body, but without a mind; it is not even as close as the mask worn by actors in ancient Greek drama.

For she was the maker of the song she sang.   15
The ever-hooded, tragic-gestured sea
Was merely a place by which she walked to sing.
Whose spirit is this? we said, because we knew
It was the spirit that we sought and knew
That we should ask this often as she sang.   20

If it was only the dark voice of the sea
That rose, or even colored by many waves;
If it was only the outer voice of sky
And cloud, of the sunken coral water-walled,
However clear, it would have been deep air,   25
The heaving speech of air, a summer sound
Repeated in a summer without end
And sound alone. But it was more than that,
More even than her voice, and ours, among
The meaningless plungings of water and the wind,   30
Theatrical distances, bronze shadows heaped
On high horizons, mountainous atmospheres
Of sky and sea.
             It was her voice that made
The sky acutest at its vanishing.   35
She measured to the hour its solitude.
She was the single artificer of the world
In which she sang. And when she sang, the sea,
Whatever self it had, became the self
That was her song, for she was the maker. Then we,   40
As we beheld her striding there alone,
Knew that there never was a world for her
Except the one she sang and, singing, made.

Ramon Fernandez,[4] tell me, if you know,
Why, when the singing ended and we turned   45
Toward the town, tell why the glassy lights,
The lights in the fishing boats at anchor there,
As the night descended, tilting in the air,
Mastered the night and portioned out the sea,
Fixing emblazoned zones and fiery poles,[5]   50
Arranging, deepening, enchanting night.

Oh! Blessed rage for order, pale Ramon,
The maker's rage to order words of the sea,
Words of the fragrant portals, dimly-starred,
And of ourselves and of our origins,   55
In ghostlier demarcations, keener sounds.

---

4. French critic (1894–1944) who described the way impressionistic techniques in literature impose a subjective order on reality. Stevens had read some of Fernandez's criticism, but denied that he intended any specific reference here.   **5.** As with the geographic zones and poles of the earth. *Emblazoned*: ornamented, usually with heraldic symbols.

The Man on the Dump

Day creeps down. The moon is creeping up.
The sun is a corbeil of flowers the moon Blanche[1]
Places there, a bouquet. Ho-ho . . . The dump is full
Of images. Days pass like papers[2] from a press.
The bouquets come here in the papers. So the sun,   5
And so the moon, both come, and the janitor's poems
Of every day, the wrapper on the can of pears,
The cat in the paper-bag, the corset, the box
From Esthonia:[3] the tiger chest, for tea.

The freshness of night has been fresh a long time.   10
The freshness of morning, the blowing of day, one says
That it puffs as Cornelius Nepos[4] reads, it puffs
More than, less than or it puffs like this or that.
The green smacks in the eye, the dew in the green
Smacks like fresh water in a can, like the sea   15

On a cocoanut—how many men have copied dew
For buttons, how many women have covered themselves
With dew, dew dresses, stones and chains of dew, heads
Of the floweriest flowers dewed with the dewiest dew.
One grows to hate these things except on the dump.   20

Now, in the time of spring (azaleas, trilliams,
Myrtle, viburnums, daffodils, blue phlox),[5]
Between that disgust and this, between the things
That are on the dump (azaleas and so on)
And those that will be (azaleas and so on).   25
One feels the purifying change. One rejects
The trash.

1. A woman's name, etymologically signifying whiteness. *Corbeil:* basket.   2. Newspapers.   3. Or Estonia; a Baltic republic, once part of the Soviet Union.   4. Roman historian (1st century B.C.), now little read, the author of brief anecdotal and highly moralized *Lives of Famous Men*.   5. Spring flowers.

PREMCHAND
(DHANPAT RAI SHRIVASTAVA)
1880–1936

Dhanpat Rai Shrivastava, known by the pen name Premchand, is the towering figure in the history of modern literature in Hindi, the principal language of north India. Hindi fiction owes its development to Premchand's pioneering achievement. Premchand is also the outstanding Hindi writer on peasant life in north India, which has not changed radically since his time, and his novels and short stories are still popular among Hindi readers. Like several other contemporary Indian writers, Premchand was influenced by the socialist and Marxist critique of capitalism and feudal social structure and intended his fiction to serve as social criticism and a catalyst for social change. A prolific essayist and editor of several journals devoted to literature and public affairs, he also made significant contributions to the political and intellectual debates of his time. In the last year of his life Premchand joined Mulk Raj Anand (born 1905) and other Indian writers in the founding of the Progressive Writers Association. Although English-speaking readers are by and large not familiar with Premchand, the social realism of his work, like that of other Hindi writers of the 1930s, earned him an appreciative audience in the erstwhile Communist bloc countries.

Premchand was born in a village near the north Indian city of Benares. Though his family was poor, they belonged to the Hindu Kayastha caste, a community of professional writers, lawyers, and teachers, and he received an excellent education in Persian and Urdu, the dominant languages of literature and administration in nineteenth-century north India. Premchand spent some years as a schoolteacher in various north Indian towns, acquiring a college degree at the same time. Writing, however, remained his first interest. Although he was the author of fourteen novels, his main energy went to the short story form, which he literally introduced into Hindi. By the end of his life, he had published more than three hundred stories in a dozen collections, and his reputation as the foremost exponent of the Hindi short story remained unchallenged well into the 1960s, when the Marxist and Progressive movements in Hindi literature began to wane and Hindi fiction began to be dominated by writers whose main themes were the problems of modernity and alienation in the context of urban life.

Premchand wrote his first stories and novels in Urdu, a form of the Hindi language that, having evolved out of the interaction of medieval Hindi dialects with the Persian language brought by Muslim rulers in India from the twelfth century onward, has a heavily Persian vocabulary and is written in the Persian script. He later produced versions of his stories both in Urdu and in Hindi, which is written in Sanskrit script and has a vocabulary with primarily Sanskrit and Hindu cultural associations. By the 1920s Hindu and Muslim separatist groups succeeded in identifying Urdu exclusively with Muslim culture and in promoting the dissociation of the Hindu majority from Urdu. After 1920, to reach as large as a public as possible, Premchand was forced to publish primarily through Hindi publishing houses and to give up Urdu publication. Throughout his career, however, Premchand condemned the polarization of north Indian communities along linguistic and religious lines and advocated the adoption of Hindustani, a hybrid form of Urdu and Hindi that had been in currency for some centuries, as the national language.

Premchand's fiction reflects the deep influence on the writer of the great political and social movements that swept over India and the world between the 1890s and the 1930s. Inspired by India's anticolonial nationalist movement, Premchand wrote his first short stories on nationalist themes in the form of historical allegory. The British government banned the Urdu story collection *Soz-e-vatan* (Sufferings of the Motherland, 1907) as seditious literature. In the 1920s Premchand participated in Mahatma Gandhi's campaign of nonviolent resistance to British rule, resigning his post in a government school as a gesture of noncooperation. Meanwhile, the focus of his fiction shifted from political issues to social reform in the villages. The main themes of his later novels and short stories—such as *Godan* (Gift of a Cow, 1936), his last and most celebrated novel—are the exploitation of the poor peasants by landowners and other members of the elite classes and of the lower castes by upper-caste Hindus. Both kinds of fiction reflect a synthesis of Western socialism and Gandhian thought.

Premchand's short stories bear the impress of the realism of Tolstoy, Gorki, Anatole France, Chekhov, Galsworthy, and other European writers whom he admired and translated. Dickens, who was widely read in India, appears to have been a major literary model for Premchand's focus on social problems. Among the nineteenth-century English novelists, the Hindi writer admired the moral sensibility of George Eliot, whose novel *Silas Marner* he adapted in Hindi. The particular blend of idealism and social criticism in Premchand's fiction is, however, entirely his own. *Road to Salvation* (*Mukti-marg,* 1924) is representative of Premchand at his best, examining the mechanics of various forms of exploitation with a clear, ironic eye. Neither Buddhu nor Jhingur belongs to the elite classes, who are strategically positioned to exploit those below them in the rigid class and caste hierarchies of rural India. Yet, instead of uniting to resist their oppressors, they destroy each other, thus revealing the insidious power of systemic oppression. In many of Premchand's stories, there is a clear dividing line between the oppressors (brahman priests, landlords, rich men) and the oppressed (usually poor peasants, women, outcastes). But in this story the author indicts the compliant victim as much as the oppressor. Here brahman ritualism and greed are amply satirized, but Buddhu and Jhingur owe their downfall to their own peculiar combination of gullibility and deviousness, which is itself the product of a social structure that stifles the aspirations of the less privileged.

Premchand's fluid, direct, vivid prose is among the features that account for the immediate and enduring appeal of his stories for Hindi readers. In the typical Premchand story, long, moralizing passages are balanced by the colorful idioms of peasant speech, although the author never uses any actual rural dialect. In the best stories, such as *Road to Salvation,* the didactic tone is also offset, and sometimes entirely replaced, by a form of black humor that allows Premchand to make these moving tales of human suffering also extremely effective as social satire.

Peter Gaeffke, *Hindi Literature in the 20th Century* (1978), is the best history of modern Hindi literature. David Rubin, *The World of Premchand* (1969), provides superb translations and an excellent introduction to Premchand's short stories. Gordon Roadarmel, *The Gift of a Cow* (1968), is the best translation of Premchand's monumental novel of peasant life in north India. For a life of Premchand, see Amrit Rai, *Premchand: His Life and Times* (1991). Also useful is Prakash Chandra Gupta, *Premchand* (1968), a brief literary biography. For trends in the Hindi fiction of the 1960s, see Gordon Roadarmel, ed. and trans., *A Death in Delhi* (1972), a volume of short stories.

PRONOUNCING GLOSSARY

The following list uses common English syllables and stress accents to provide rough equivalents of selected words whose pronunciation may be unfamiliar to the general reader.

chappattie: *chuh-pah'-tee*

Dhanpat Rai Shrivastava: *duhn'-puht rah'-yee shree-vahs'-tuh-vah*

ghee: *geeh*

Harihar: *huh'-ree-huhr*

Jhingur: *jeen'-goor*

Lakshmi: *luhksh'-mee*

pan: *pahn*

pandit: *puhn'-deet*

Premchand: *praym'-chuhnd*

Satyanarayan: *suht'-yuh-nah-rah'-yuhn*

Savan: *sah'-vuhn*

The Road to Salvation[1]

1

The pride the peasant takes in seeing his fields flourishing is like the soldier's in his red turban, the coquette's in her jewels or the doctor's in the patients seated before him. Whenever Jhingur looked at his cane[2] fields a sort of intoxication came over him. He had three *bighas* of land which would earn him an easy 600 rupees.[3] And if God saw to it that the rates went up, then who could complain? Both his bullocks were old so he'd buy a new pair at the Batesar fair. If he could hook on to another two *bighas*, so much the better. Why should he worry about money? The merchants were already beginning to fawn on him. He was convinced that nobody was as good as himself—and so there was scarcely anyone in the village he hadn't quarrelled with.

One evening when he was sitting with his son in his lap, shelling peas, he saw a flock of sheep coming towards him. He said to himself, "The sheep path doesn't come that way. Can't those sheep go along the bank? What's the idea, coming over here? They'll trample and gobble up the crop and who'll make good for it? I bet it's Buddhu the shepherd—just look at his nerve! He can see me here but he won't drive his sheep back. What good will it do me to put up with *this?* If I try to buy a ram from him he actually asks for five rupees, and everybody sells blankets for four rupees but he won't settle for less than five."

By now the sheep were close to the cane-field. Jhingur yelled, "*Arrey,*[4] where do you think you're taking those sheep, you?"

Buddhu said meekly, "Chief, they're coming by way of the boundary embankment.[5] If I take them back around it will mean a couple of miles extra."

"And I'm supposed to let you trample my field to save you a detour? Why didn't you take them by way of some other boundary path? Do you think I'm some bull-skinning nobody or has your money turned your head? Turn 'em back!"

"Chief, just let them through today. If I ever come back this way again you can punish me any way you want."

"I told you to get them out. If just one of them crosses the line you're going to be in a pack of trouble."

"Chief," Buddhu said, "if even one blade of grass gets under my sheep's feet you can call me anything you want."

Although Buddhu was still speaking meekly he had decided that it would be a loss of face to turn back. "If I drive the flock back for a few little threats," he thought, "how will I graze my sheep? Turn back today and tomorrow I won't find anybody willing to let me through, they'll all start bullying me."

And Buddhu was a tough man too. He owned 240 sheep and he was able to get eight annas[6] per night to leave them in people's fields to manure them, and he sold their milk as well and made blankets from their wool. He thought, "Why's he getting so angry? What can he do to me? I'm not his servant."

---

1. Translated by David Rubin. 2. Sugarcane, an important crop in north India. 3. The currency of India. *Bigha:* a measure of land equal to one-fifth of an acre. 4. A rough form of address, equivalent to "Hey!" or "Hey you!" 5. A bank or raised stone structure, marking the edge of a field. 6. Sixteen annas made a rupee.

When the sheep got a whiff of the green leaves they became restless and they broke into the field. Beating them with his stick Buddhu tried to push them back across the boundary line but they just broke in somewhere else. In a fury Jhingur said, "You're trying to force your way through here but I'll teach you a lesson!"

Buddhu said, "It's seeing you that's scared them. If you just get out of the way I'll clear them all out of the field."

But Jhingur put down his son and grabbing up his cudgel he began to whack into the sheep. Not even a washerman would have beat his donkey so cruelly. He smashed legs and backs and while they bleated Buddhu stood silent watching the destruction of his army. He didn't yell at the sheep and he didn't say anything to Jhingur, no, he just watched the show. In just about two minutes, with the prowess of an epic hero, Jhingur had routed the enemy forces. After this carnage among the host of sheep Jhingur said with the pride of victory, "Now move on straight! And don't ever think about coming this way again."

Looking at his wounded sheep, Buddhu said, "Jhingur, you've done a dirty job. You're going to regret it."

2

To take vengeance on a farmer is easier than slicing a banana. Whatever wealth he has is in his fields or barns. The produce gets into the house only after innumerable afflictions of nature and the gods. And if it happens that a human enemy joins in alliance with those afflictions the poor farmer is apt to be left nowhere. When Jhingur came home and told his family about the battle, they started to give him advice.

"Jhingur, you've got yourself into real trouble! You knew what to do but you acted as though you didn't. Don't you realize what a tough customer Buddhu is? Even now it's not too late—go to him and make peace, otherwise the whole village will come to grief along with you."

Jhingur thought it over. He began to regret that he'd stopped Buddhu at all. If the sheep had eaten up a little of his crop it wouldn't have ruined him. The fact is, a farmer's prosperity comes precisely from being humble—God doesn't like it when a peasant walks with his head high. Jhingur didn't enjoy the idea of going to Buddhu's house but urged on by the others he set out. It was the dead of winter, foggy, with the darkness settling in everywhere. He had just come out of the village when suddenly he was astonished to see a fire blazing over in the direction of his cane field. His heart started to hammer. A field had caught fire! He ran wildly, hoping it wasn't his own field, but as he got closer this deluded hope died. He'd been struck by the very misfortune he'd set out to avert. The bastard had started the fire and was ruining the whole village because of him. As he ran it seemed to him that today his field was a lot nearer than it used to be, as though the fallow land between had ceased to exist.

When he finally reached his field the fire had assumed dreadful proportions. Jhingur began to wail. The villagers were running and ripping up stalks of millet to beat the fire. A terrible battle between man and nature went on for several hours, each side winning in turn. The flames would subside and almost vanish only to strike back again with redoubled vigour like battle-crazed warriors. Among the men Buddhu was the most valiant fighter; with his dhoti[7] tucked up around his waist he leapt into the fiery gulfs as though ready to subdue the enemy or die, and he'd emerge after many a narrow escape. In the end it was the men who triumphed, but the triumph amounted to defeat. The whole village's sugarcane crop was burned to ashes and with the cane all their hopes as well.

3

It was no secret who had started the fire. But no one dared say anything about it. There was no proof and what was the point of a case without any evidence? As for Jhingur, it had become difficult for him to show himself out of his house. Wherever he went he had to listen to abuse. People said right to his face, "You were the cause of the fire! You ruined us. You were so stuck up your feet didn't touch the dirt. You yourself were ruined and you dragged the whole village down with you. If you hadn't fought with Buddhu would all this have happened?"

Jhingur was even more grieved by these taunts than by the destruction of his crop, and he would stay in his house the whole day.

Winter drew on. Where before the cane-press had turned all night and the fragrance of the crushed sugar filled the air and fires were lit with people sitting around them smoking their hookas,[8] all was desolation now. Because of the cold people cursed Jhingur and, drawing their doors shut, went to bed as soon as it was dark. Sugarcane isn't only the farmers' wealth; their whole way of life depends on it. With the help of the cane they get through the winter. They drink the cane juice, warm themselves from fires made of its leaves and feed their livestock on the cuttings. All the village dogs that used to sleep in the warm ash of the fires died from the cold and many of the livestock too from lack of fodder. The cold was excessive and everybody in the village was seized with coughs and fevers. And it was Jhingur who'd brought about the whole catastrophe, that cursed, murdering Jhingur.

Jhingur thought and thought and decided that Buddhu had to be put in a situation exactly like his own. Buddhu had ruined him and he was wallowing in comfort, so Jhingur would ruin Buddhu too.

Since the day of their terrible quarrel Buddhu had ceased to come by Jhingur's. Jhingur decided to cultivate an intimacy with him; he wanted to show him he had no suspicion at all that Buddhu started the fire. One day, on the pretext of getting a blanket, he went to Buddhu, who greeted him with every courtesy and honour—for a man offers the hooka even to an enemy and won't let him depart without making him drink milk and syrup.

These days Jhingur was earning a living by working in a jute-wrapping mill.[9] Usually he got several days' wages at once. Only by means of Buddhu's help could he meet his daily expenses between times. So it was that Jhingur re-established a friendly footing between them.

One day Buddhu asked, "Say Jhingur, what would you do if you caught the man who burned your cane field? Tell me the truth."

Solemnly Jhingur said, "I'd tell him, 'Brother, what you did was good. You put an end to my pride, you made me into a decent man.' "

---

7. A sheet of cloth wrapped around the waist, worn by men throughout India.   8. A type of clay pipe that has a water reservoir, common all over north India.   9. In north and eastern India, jute or hemp fiber is made into a kind of cloth that is used as wrapping material or made into sacks.

"If I were in your place," Buddhu said, "I wouldn't settle for anything less than burning down his house."

"But what's the good of stirring up hatred in a life that lasts such a little while in all? I've been ruined already, what could I get out of ruining him?"

"Right, that's the way of a decent religious man," Buddhu said, "but when a fellow's in the grip of anger all his sense gets jumbled up."

4

Spring came and the peasants were getting the fields ready for planting cane. Buddhu was doing a fine business. Everybody wanted his sheep. There were always a half dozen men at his door fawning on him, and he lorded it over everybody. He doubled the price of hiring out his sheep to manure the fields; if anybody objected he'd say bluntly, "Look, brother, I'm not shoving my sheep on you. If you don't want them, don't take them. But I can't let you have them for a pice[1] less than I said." The result was that everybody swarmed around him, despite his rudeness, just like priests after some pilgrim.

Lakshmi, goddess of wealth, is of no great size; she can, according to the occasion, shrink or expand, to such a degree that sometimes she can contract her most magnificent manifestation into the form of a few small figures printed on paper. There are times when she makes some man's tongue her throne and her size is reduced to nothing. But just the same she needs a lot of elbow-room for her permanent living quarters. If she comes into somebody's house, the house should grow accordingly, she can't put up with a small one. Buddhu's house also began to grow. A veranda was built in front of the door, six rooms replaced the former two. In short the house was done over from top to bottom. Buddhu got the wood from a peasant, from another the cowdung cakes for the kiln fuel to make the tiles; somebody else gave him the bamboo and reeds for the mats. He had to pay for having the walls put up but he didn't give any cash even for this, he gave some lambs. Such is the power of Lakshmi: the whole job—and it was quite a good house, all in all—was put up for nothing. They began to prepare for a house-warming.

Jhingur was still labouring all day without getting enough to half fill his belly, while gold was raining on Buddhu's house. If Jhingur was angry, who could blame him? Nobody could put up with such injustice.

One day Jhingur went out walking in the direction of the untouchable tanners'[2] settlement. He called for Harihar, who came out, greeting him with *"Ram Ram!"*[3] and filled the hooka. They began to smoke. Harihar, the leader of the tanners, was a mean fellow and there wasn't a peasant who didn't tremble at the sight of him.

After smoking a bit, Jhingur said, "No singing for the spring festival[4] these days? We haven't heard you."

"What festival? The belly can't take a holiday. Tell me, how are you getting on lately?"

"Getting by," Jhingur said. "Hard times mean a hard life. If I work all day

---

1. Coin of the lowest value.   2. Tanners are treated as untouchable, that is, outcastes, by other Hindus because they handle the carcasses and hides of animals, an activity considered ritually polluting.   3. The name of God is repeated as a greeting and also as an expression of deep emotion.   4. The festival of Holi, during which villagers engage in riotous, carnivalesque play.

in the mill there's a fire in my stove. But these days only Buddhu's making money. He doesn't have room to store it! He's built a new house, bought more sheep. Now there's a big fuss about his house-warming. He's sent *pan*[5] to the headmen of all the seven villages around to invite everybody to it."

"When Mother Lakshmi comes men don't see so clearly," Harihar said. "And if you see him, he's not walking on the same ground as you or I. If he talks, it's only to brag."

"Why shouldn't he brag? Who in the village can equal him? But friend, I'm not going to put up with injustice. When God gives I bow my head and accept it. It's not that I think nobody's equal to me but when I hear *him* bragging it's as though my body started to burn. 'A cheat yesterday, a banker today.' He's stepped on us to get ahead. Only yesterday he was hiring himself out in the fields with just a loincloth on to chase crows and today his lamp's burning in the skies."

"Speak," Harihar said, "Is there something I can do?"

"What can you do? He doesn't keep any cows or buffaloes just because he's afraid somebody will do something to them to get at him."

"But he keeps sheep, doesn't he?"

"You mean, 'hunt a heron and get a grouse'?"

"Think about it again."

"It's got to be a plan that will keep him from ever getting rich again."

Then they began to whisper. It's a mystery why there's just as much love among the wicked as malice among the good. Scholars, holy men and poets sizzle with jealousy when they see other scholars, holy men and poets. But a gambler sympathizes with another gambler and helps him, and it's the same with drunkards and thieves. Now, if a Brahman Pandit[6] stumbles in the dark and falls then another Pandit, instead of giving him a hand, will give him a couple of kicks so he won't be able to get up. But when a thief finds another thief in distress he helps him. Everybody's united in hating evil so the wicked have to love one another; while everybody praises virtue so the virtuous are jealous of each other. What does a thief get by killing another thief? Contempt. A scholar who slanders another scholar attains to glory.

Jhingur and Harihar consulted, plotting their course of action—the method, the time and all the steps. When Jhingur left he was strutting—he'd already overcome his enemy, there was no way for Buddhu to escape now.

On his way to work the next day he stopped by Buddhu's house. Buddhu asked him, "Aren't you working today?"

"I'm on my way, but I came by to ask you if you wouldn't let my calf graze with your sheep. The poor thing's dying tied up to the post while I'm away all day, she doesn't get enough grass and fodder to eat."

"Brother, I don't keep cows and buffaloes. You know the tanners, they're all killers. That Harihar killed my two cows, I don't know what he fed them. Since then I've vowed never again to keep cattle. But yours is just a calf, there'd be no profit to anyone in harming that. Bring her over whenever you want."

Then he began to show Jhingur the arrangements for the housewarming. Ghee, sugar, flour and vegetables were all on hand. All they were waiting for was the Satyanarayan ceremony.[7] Jhingur's eyes were popping.

---

5. The betel leaf; a symbol of invitation to auspicious ceremonies.   6. A scholar, a learned brahman. The brahman is the highest of the four Hindu classes (castes, at their most general level).   7. A ceremony in which the god Vishnu is worshiped to ensure prosperity. Feasting the brahmans is an important part of the worship. *Ghee:* clarified butter, used in Indian cooking and as an offering in Hindu fire rituals.

When he came home after work the first thing he did was bring his calf to Buddhu's house. That night the ceremony was performed and a feast offered to the Brahmans. The whole night passed in lavishing hospitality on the priests. Buddhu had no opportunity to go to look after his flock of sheep.

The feasting went on until morning. Buddhu had just got up and had his breakfast when a man came and said, "Buddhu, while you've been sitting around here, out there in your flock the calf has died. You're a fine one! The rope was still around its neck."

When Buddhu heard this it was as though he'd been punched. Jhingur, who was there having some breakfast too, said, "Oh God, my calf! Come on, I want to see her! But listen, I never tied her with a rope. I brought her to the flock of sheep and went back home. When did you have her tied with a rope, Buddhu?"

"God's my witness, I never touched any rope! I haven't been back to my sheep since then."

"If you didn't, then who put the rope on her?" Jhingur said. "You must have done it and forgotten it."

"And it was in your flock," one of the Brahmans said. "People are going to say that whoever tied the rope, that heifer died because of Buddhu's negligence."

Harihar came along just then and said, "I saw him tying the rope around the calf's neck last night."

"Me?" Buddhu said.

"Wasn't that you with your stick over your shoulder tying up the heifer?"

"And you're an honest fellow, I suppose!" Buddhu said. "You saw me tying her up?"

"Why get angry with me, brother? Let's just say you didn't tie her up, if that's what you want."

"We will have to decide about it," one of the Brahmans said. "A cow slaughterer should be stoned[8]—it's no laughing matter."

"Maharaj,"[9] Jhingur said, "the killing was accidental."

"What's that got to do with it?" the Brahman said. "It's set down that no cow is ever to be done to death in any way."

"That's right," Jhingur said. "Just to tie a cow up is a fiendish act."

"In the Scriptures it's called the greatest sin," the Brahman said. "Killing a cow is no less than killing a Brahman."

"That's right," Jhingur said. "The cow's got a high place, that's why we respect her, isn't it? The cow is like a mother. But Maharaj, it was an accident—figure out something to get the poor fellow off."

Buddhu stood listening while the charge of murder was brought against him like the simplest thing in the world. He had no doubt it was Jhingur's plotting, but if he said a thousand times that he hadn't put the rope on the calf nobody would pay any attention to it. They'd say he was trying to escape the penance.

The Brahman, that divinity, also stood to profit from the imposition of a penance. Naturally, he was not one to neglect an opportunity like this. The outcome was that Buddhu was charged with the death of a cow; the Brahman

---

8. The Hindu veneration of the cow has its origins in the pastoral culture of the Vedic Aryans and the importance of the cow in their religious rituals. As Premchand goes on to show, killing a cow is considered among the most heinous sins. 9. "Lord, Sir, Your Majesty" (Hindi). A respectful form of address for men of higher rank than oneself.

had got very incensed about it too and he determined the manner of compensation. The punishment consisted of three months of begging in the streets, then a pilgrimage to the seven holy places,[1] and in addition the price for five cows and feeding 500 Brahmans. Stunned, Buddhu listened to it. He began to weep, and after that the period of begging was reduced by one month. Apart from this he received no favour. There was no one to appeal to, no one to complain to. He had to accept the punishment.

He gave up his sheep to God's care. His children were young and all by herself what could his wife do? The poor fellow would stand in one door after another hiding his face and saying, "Even the gods are banished for cow-slaughter!" He received alms but along with them he had to listen to bitter insults. Whatever he picked up during the day he'd cook in the evening under some tree and then go to sleep right there. He did not mind the hardship, for he was used to wandering all day with his sheep and sleeping beneath trees, and his food at home hadn't been much better than this, but he was ashamed of having to beg, especially when some harridan would taunt him with, "You've found a fine way to earn your bread!" That sort of thing hurt him profoundly, but what could he do?

He came home after two months. His hair was long, and he was as weak as though he were sixty years old. He had to arrange for the money for his pilgrimage, and where's the moneylender who loans to shepherds? You couldn't depend on sheep. Sometimes there are epidemics and you're cleaned out of the whole flock in one night. Furthermore, it was the middle of the hot weather when there was no hope of profit from the sheep. There was an oil-dealer who was willing to loan him money at an interest of two annas per rupee—in eight months the interest would equal the principal. Buddhu did not dare borrow on such terms. During the two months many of his sheep had been stolen. When the children took them to graze the other villagers would hide one or two sheep away in a field or hut and afterwards slaughter them and eat them. The boys, poor lads, couldn't catch a single one of them, and even when they saw, how could they fight? The whole village was banded together. It was an awful dilemma. Helpless, Buddhu sent for a butcher and sold the whole flock to him for 500 rupees. He took 200 and started out on his pilgrimage. The rest of the money he set aside for feeding the Brahmans.

When Buddhu left, his house was burgled twice, but by good fortune the family woke up and the money was saved.

5

It was Savan,[2] month of rains, with everything lush green. Jhingur, who had no bullocks now, had rented out his field to share-croppers. Buddhu had been freed from his penitential obligations and along with them his delusions about wealth. Neither one of them had anything left; neither could be angry with the other—there was nothing left to be angry about.

Because the jute mill had closed down Jhingur went to work with pick and shovel in town where a very large rest-house for pilgrims was being built.

1. Various lists are given of the seven holy places of pilgrimage in the Hindu religion. These invariably include Benares (or Kashi), Hardwar, Rameswaram, and Gaya.   2. The fifth month in the Hindu calendar, marking the season of the monsoon rains, which corresponds to July or August in the Western calendar.

There were a thousand labourers on the job. Every seventh day Jhingur would take his pay home and after spending the night there go back the next morning.

Buddhu came to the same place looking for work. The foreman saw that he was a skinny little fellow who wouldn't be able to do any heavy work so he had him take mortar to the labourers. Once when Buddhu was going with a shallow pan on his head to get mortar Jhingur saw him. *"Ram Ram"* they said to one another and Jhingur filled the pan. Buddhu picked it up. For the rest of the day they went about their work in silence.

At the end of the day Jhingur asked, "Are you going to cook something?"

"How can I eat if I don't?" Buddhu said.

"I eat solid food only once a day," Jhingur said. "I get by just drinking water with ground meal in it in the evenings. Why fuss?"

"Pick up some of those sticks lying around," Buddhu said. "I brought some flour from home. I had it ground there—it costs a lot here in town. I'll knead it on the flat side of this rock. Since you won't eat food I cook I'll get it ready and you cook it."[3]

"But there's no frying pan."

"There are lots of frying pans," Buddhu said. "I'll scour out one of these mortar trays."

The fire was lit, the flour kneaded. Jhingur cooked the chapatties,[4] Buddhu brought the water. They both ate the bread with salt and red pepper. Then they filled the bowl of the hooka. They both lay down on the stony ground and smoked.

Buddhu said, "I was the one who set fire to your cane field."

Jhingur said light-heartedly, "I know."

After a little while he said, "I tied up the heifer and Harihar fed it something."

In the same light-hearted tone Buddhu said, "I know."

Then the two of them went to sleep.

---

3. As a member of a caste somewhat higher in the hierarchy than Buddhu's, Jhingur cannot eat food cooked by Buddhu.   4. Flat unleavened bread made of whole wheat flour, a staple food of north India.

LU XUN
1881–1936

No country in the world has had so long, continuous, and essentially autonomous a culture as China. For the past century Chinese intellectuals have struggled to free themselves from the oppressive weight of their past and to discover a Chinese cultural identity independent of the traditional civilization. This has, in fact, been a central concern throughout modern Chinese literature. The rapid importation of Western fiction, drama, and poetry in the early twentieth century provided a set of literary models quite distinct from those of the Chinese tradition. Rather than finding in the Western models new possibilities of art, however, many Chinese writers sought in them instruments by which to change the culture or a medium by which to analyze the problems posed by China's cultural legacy. Western writers have often had similar aims, but the marginal status of the writer in European civilization has been a helpful counterweight to such grand purposes. By contrast, the centrality of the writer and intellectual has proved to be one of the tenacious assumptions of traditional Chinese culture, and it is ironic that this assumption stands behind the continuing hope of modern Chinese writers to free China of the weight of its traditional civilization.

Modern China has produced many talented writers, on whom critical opinion is divided. There is, however, almost universal agreement on one authentic genius among them: Lu Xun (also romanized Lu Hsün), the pen name of Zhou Shuren. Few writers of fiction have gained so much fame for such a small oeuvre. His reputation rests entirely on twenty-five stories published between 1918 and 1926, gathered into two collections: *Cheering from the Sidelines* and *Wondering Where to Turn*. In addition to this fiction he published a collection of prose poems, *Wild Grass,* and a large number of literary and political essays. His small body of stories gives a ruthlessly bleak portrayal of an entire culture that has failed. Whether the culture had indeed failed is less important than the powerful representation he gives of it and the way in which his representations touched a deep chord of response in Chinese readers. Lu was a controlled ironist and a craftsman whose narrative skill far exceeded that of most of his contemporaries; yet underneath his mastery the reader senses the depth of his anger at traditional culture.

Lu was well prepared to engage traditional culture on its own terms. Born into a Shaoxing family of Confucian scholar-officials, he had a traditional education and became a classical scholar of considerable erudition and a writer of poetry in the classical language. Sometimes he displays this learning in his fiction, but there it is always undercut by irony. He grew up at a time when the traditional education system, based on the Confucian classics, was being supplanted by a modern one; and after the early death of his father in 1896, Lu, like so many young Chinese intellectuals of the period, went abroad to study—first at Tokyo and then in 1904 at Sendai, a remote Japanese university where he studied medicine. Because it was successfully modernizing a traditional culture, Japan attracted many young Chinese intellectuals. At the time, the Russians and Japanese were at war in the former Chinese territory of Manchuria. In a famous anecdote describing his moment of decision to become a writer, Lu tells of seeing a slide of a Chinese prisoner about to be decapitated as a Russian spy. What shocked the young medical student was the apathetic crowd of Chinese onlookers, gathered around to watch the execution. At that moment he decided that it was their dulled spirits rather than their bodies that were in need of healing.

Returning to Tokyo, Lu founded a journal in which he published literary essays and set to work translating Western works of fiction. In 1909 financial difficulties drove him back to China, where he worked as a teacher in Hangzhou. When the Republican revolution came in 1911, he joined the ministry of education, moving north to Peking, where he also taught at various universities. The Republican government was soon at the mercy of the powerful armies competing for regional power, and during this period, perhaps for self-protection, Lu devoted himself to traditional scholarship. One might have expected the revolutionary writer of narrative to write the first history of Chinese fiction, as Lu did; but he also produced an erudite and painstaking textual study of the third-century writer Xi Kang that is still used.

On May 4, 1919, a massive student strike forced the Chinese government not to sign the Versailles Peace Treaty, which would have given Japan effective control over the Chinese province of Shandong. The date gave its name to the May Fourth Movement, a group of young intellectuals who advocated the use of vernacular Chinese in all writing and a repudiation of classical Chinese literature.* Though Lu himself kept out of the May Fourth Movement, it was during this period (1918–26) that he wrote

---

*Written Chinese ranges between two extremes: the "classical" language, which is essentially that of the 4th to 3rd centuries B.C., and the "vernacular," which attempts to represent the spoken language. Poetry and essays tended to be in classical Chinese, while traditional fiction tended to use the vernacular (although there was also fiction in the classical language). In the modern period, poetry and essays also came to be written in vernacular Chinese. Traditional drama used a mixed style; modern drama, the vernacular.

all but one of his short stories. During the last decade of his life, he became a political activist and put his satirical talents at the service of the Left, becoming one of the favorite writers of the Communist leader Mao Zedong.

Diary of a Madman, Lu's earliest story, takes its title from a work by the Russian novelist Gogol. On one level, it is a parable of the way in which Chinese society devours its members, told under the guise of the discovery of a continuing history of literal cannibalism. But the diarist who makes the "discovery" is indeed, as the title tells us, a madman, and his paranoid raving compels the reader to take the point of view of "sane" society, all the while uncomfortably recognizing that the diarist's claims are true in a figurative sense.

Lu's literary anger at Chinese culture was far from a new phenomenon in Chinese fiction. Traditional novels such as *The Travels of Lao Can* had often ruthlessly satirized the falseness and corruption of the social order. But in traditional Chinese satirical fiction, as in most premodern satire worldwide, the capacity to make moral judgments presumed a secure sense of what was right (whether or not such a sense agreed with conventional morality). In Lu's satire, however, the very capacity to judge evil is itself corrupted by that evil, a circularity perfectly embodied in the figure of a cannibalistic society that feeds on itself.

Diary of a Madman opens with a preface in mannered classical Chinese, giving an account of the discovery of the diary. Such ironic use of classical Chinese to suggest a falsely polite world of social appearances was quite common in traditional Chinese fiction; but its presence usually suggested the alternative possibility of immediate, direct, and genuine language, a language of the heart set against a language of society. The diary that follows the preface is indeed immediate, direct, and genuine, but it is also deluded and twisted. The diarist becomes increasingly convinced that everyone around him wants to eat him; from this growing circle of cannibals observed in the present, the diarist then turns to examine old texts, only to discover that the entire history of the culture has been one of secret cannibalism. Beneath society's false politeness, represented by the voice in the preface, he detects a violent bestiality lurking, a hunger to assimilate others, to "eat men."

As the diary progresses, it becomes increasingly clear that the diarist, who sees himself as the potential victim, is no less the mirror of the society he describes, assimilating everyone around him into his own fixed view of the world. His reading of ancient texts to discover evidence of cannibalism is a parody of traditional Confucian scholarship, the distorting discovery of "secret meanings" that only serve to confirm beliefs already held. His is a world entirely closed in on itself, one that survives by feeding on itself and its young, a voracity that gives Lu his famous last line, "Save the children . . ."

In contrast to the tormented diarist of *Diary of a Madman,* the characters in *Upstairs in a Wineshop* have already been eaten and fully digested. It is a bleak tale of deaths and wasted lives. The narrator's friend, after grand hopes in his youth, finds himself back in his hometown, going through the hollow motions of filial duty. Caring for the family graves was an act that had great resonance in Confucian family ritual. To put to rest the worries of his mother, who has heard that the nearby riverbank is encroaching on the grave site, the friend has come to rebury his younger brother, whom he barely remembers. On digging up the grave, he finds that there is nothing left of his brother's body. Nevertheless, having bought a new coffin, he puts some dirt from the old grave in it, reburying it beside his father in a different graveyard and enclosing it in bricks for a better seal. As the friend says, "At least I've done enough to pull the wool over Mother's eyes and set her mind at rest." Even when the past has lost all meaning, leaving neither physical remains nor memory, the narrator's friend still finds himself trapped by its forms, which he carries out scrupulously, moving a grave site to protect a body that no longer exists. This return to a hometown and to the now meaningless rituals of the past is echoed at the very close of the story, when the friend tells the narrator that he has given up teaching Western learning and has gone back to teaching the Chinese classics to his pupils: "That's what their fathers *want* them to be taught." Here, as in many of Lu's stories, the characters seem imprisoned in an unreality perpetuated by friends and family. They belong neither to the traditional world nor to the modern world but to some limbo in between, going through the ancient forms, all the while knowing that they mean nothing.

The final selection is from Lu Xun's collection of prose poems, *Wild Grass*, published in 1927.

Leo Ou-fan Lee, *Voices from the Iron House: A Study of Lu Xun* (1987), is an excellent introduction to Lu Xun's work, placing it in the context of his life and Chinese cultural history, and Lee, *Lu Xun and His Legacy* (1985), is a collection of scholarly articles treating Lu's literary work, his politics, and his influence. William A. Lyell, *Lu Hsün's Vision of Reality* (1976), is also useful.

PRONOUNCING GLOSSARY

The following list uses common English syllables to provide rough equivalents of selected words whose pronunciation may be unfamiliar to the general reader.

Ah-shun: *ah-shwun*	Mao Zedong: *mao dzuh-doong*
Ah-zhao: *ah–jao*	Shaoxing: *shao-shing*
Changfu: *chahng-foo*	Weifu: *way-foo*
Changgeng: *chahng-gung*	Xu Xilin: *shoo shee-lin*
Laofa: *lao-fah*	Zhao: *jao*
Lu Xun: *loo shoon*	Zhou Shuren: *joe shoo-ren*
Luosi: *lwoh-suh*	

Diary of a Madman[1]

There was once a pair of male siblings whose actual names I beg your indulgence to withhold. Suffice it to say that we three were boon companions during our school years. Subsequently, circumstances contrived to rend us asunder so that we were gradually bereft of knowledge regarding each other's activities.

Not too long ago, however, I chanced to hear that one of them had been hard afflicted with a dread disease. I obtained this intelligence at a time when I happened to be returning to my native haunts and, hence, made so bold as to detour somewhat from my normal course in order to visit them. I encountered but one of the siblings. He apprised me that it had been his younger brother who had suffered the dire illness. By now, however, he had long since become sound and fit again; in fact he had already repaired to other parts to await a substantive official appointment.[2]

The elder brother apologized for having needlessly put me to the inconvenience of this visitation, and concluding his disquisition with a hearty smile, showed me two volumes of diaries which, he assured me, would reveal the nature of his brother's disorder during those fearful days.

---

1. The first two selections translated by and with notes adapted from William A. Lyell.   2. When there were too many officials for the number of offices to be filled, a man might well be appointed to an office that already had an incumbent. The new appointee would proceed to his post and wait until said office was vacated. Sometimes there would be a number of such appointees waiting their turns.

As to the lapsus calami[3] *that occur in the course of the diaries, I have altered not a word. Nonetheless, I have changed all the names, despite the fact that their publication would be of no great consequence since they are all humble villagers unknown to the world at large.*

Recorded this 2nd day in the 7th year of the Republic.[4]

1

Moonlight's really nice tonight. Haven't seen it in over thirty years. Seeing it today, I feel like a new man. I know now that I've been completely out of things for the last three decades or more. But I've still got to be *very* careful. Otherwise, how do you explain those dirty looks the Zhao family's dog gave me?

I've got good reason for my fears.

2

No moonlight at all tonight—something's not quite right. When I made my way out the front gate this morning—ever so carefully—there was something funny about the way the Venerable Old Zhao looked at me: seemed as though he was afraid of me and yet, at the same time, looked as though he had it in for me. There were seven or eight other people who had their heads together whispering about me. They were afraid I'd see them too! All up and down the street people acted the same way. The meanest looking one of all spread his lips out wide and actually *smiled* at me! A shiver ran from the top of my head clear down to the tips of my toes, for I realized that meant they already had their henchmen well deployed, and were ready to strike.

But I wasn't going to let that intimidate *me*. I kept right on walking. There was a group of children up ahead and they were talking about me too. The expressions in their eyes were just like the Venerable Old Zhao's, and their faces were iron gray. I wondered what grudge the children had against me that they were acting this way too. I couldn't contain myself any longer and shouted, "Tell me, tell me!" But they just ran away.

Let's see now, what grudge can there be between me and the Venerable Old Zhao, or the people on the street for that matter? The only thing I can think of is that twenty years ago I trampled the account books kept by Mr. Antiquity, and he was hopping mad about it too. Though the Venerable Old Zhao doesn't know him, he must have gotten wind of it somehow. Probably decided to right the injustice I had done Mr. Antiquity by getting all those people on the street to gang up on me. But the children? Back then they hadn't even come into the world yet. Why should they have given me those funny looks today? Seemed as though they were afraid of me and yet, at the same time, looked as though they would like to do me some harm. That really frightens me. Bewilders me. Hurts me.

I have it! Their fathers and mothers have *taught* them to be like that!

3. "The fall of the reed [writing instrument]" (literal trans.); hence, lapses in writing.   4. The Qing Dynasty was overthrown and the Republic of China was established in 1911; thus it is April 2, 1918. The introduction is written in classical Chinese, whereas the diary entries that follow are all in the colloquial language.

3

I can never get to sleep at night. You really have to study something before you can understand it.

Take all those people: some have worn the cangue on the district magistrate's order, some have had their faces slapped by the gentry, some have had their wives ravished by *yamen*[5] clerks, some have had their dads and moms dunned to death by creditors; and yet, right at the time when all those terrible things were taking place, the expressions on their faces were never as frightened, or as savage, as the ones they wore yesterday.

Strangest of all was that woman on the street. She slapped her son and said: "Damn it all, you've got me so riled up I could take a good bite right out of your hide!" She was talking to him, but she was looking at me! I tried, but couldn't conceal a shudder of fright. That's when that ghastly crew of people, with their green faces and protruding fangs, began to roar with laughter. Old Fifth Chen[6] ran up, took me firmly in tow, and dragged me away.

When we got back, the people at home all pretended not to know me. The expressions in their eyes were just like all the others too. After he got me into the study, Old Fifth Chen bolted the door from the outside—just the way you would pen up a chicken or a duck! That made figuring out what was at the bottom of it all harder than ever.

A few days back one of our tenant farmers came in from Wolf Cub Village to report a famine. Told my elder brother the villagers had all ganged up on a "bad" man and beaten him to death. Even gouged out his heart and liver. Fried them up and ate them to bolster their own courage! When I tried to horn in on the conversation, Elder Brother and the tenant farmer both gave me sinister looks. I realized for the first time today that the expression in their eyes was just the same as what I saw in those people on the street.

As I think of it now, a shiver's running from the top of my head clear down to the tips of my toes.

If they're capable of eating people, then who's to say they won't eat *me*?

Don't you see? That woman's words about "taking a good bite," and the laughter of that ghastly crew with their green faces and protruding fangs, and the words of our tenant farmer a few days back—it's perfectly clear to me now that all that talk and all that laughter were really a set of secret signals. Those words were poison! That laughter, a knife! Their teeth are bared and waiting—white and razor sharp! Those people are cannibals!

As I see it myself, though I'm not what you'd call an evil man, still, ever since I trampled the Antiquity family's account books, it's hard to say *what* they'll do. They seem to have something in mind, but I can't begin to guess what. What's more, as soon as they turn against someone, they'll *say* he's evil anyway. I can still remember how it was when Elder Brother was teaching me composition.[7] No matter how good a man was, if I could find a few things

---

5. Local government offices. The petty clerks who worked in them were notorious for relying on their proximity to power to bully and abuse the common people. *Cangue:* a split board, hinged at one end and locked at the other; holes were cut out to accommodate the prisoner's neck and wrists. 6. People were often referred to by their hierarchical position within their extended family. 7. That is, to compose essays in the classical style.

wrong with him he would approvingly underline my words; on the other hand, if I made a few allowances for a bad man, he'd say I was "an extraordinary student, an absolute genius." When all is said and done, how can I possibly guess what people like *that* have in mind, especially when they're getting ready for a cannibals' feast?

You have to *really* go into something before you can understand it. I seemed to remember, though not too clearly, that from ancient times on people have often been eaten, and so I started leafing through a history book to look it up. There were no dates in this history, but scrawled this way and that across every page were the words BENEVOLENCE, RIGHTEOUSNESS, and MORALITY. Since I couldn't get to sleep anyway, I read that history very carefully for most of the night, and finally I began to make out what was written *between* the lines; the whole volume was filled with a single phrase: EAT PEOPLE!

The words written in the history book, the things the tenant farmer said— all of it began to stare at me with hideous eyes, began to snarl and growl at me from behind bared teeth!

Why sure, *I'm* a person too, and they want to eat *me*!

4

In the morning I sat in the study for a while, calm and collected. Old Fifth Chen brought in some food—vegetables and a steamed fish. The fish's eyes were white and hard. Its mouth was wide open, just like the mouths of those people who wanted to eat human flesh. After I'd taken a few bites, the meat felt so smooth and slippery in my mouth that I couldn't tell whether it was fish or human flesh. I vomited.

"Old Fifth," I said, "tell Elder Brother that it's absolutely stifling in here and that I'd like to take a walk in the garden." He left without answering, but sure enough, after a while the door opened. I didn't even budge—just sat there waiting to see what they'd do to me. I *knew* that they wouldn't be willing to set me loose.

Just as I expected! Elder Brother came in with an old man in tow and walked slowly toward me. There was a savage glint in the old man's eyes. He was afraid I'd see it and kept his head tilted toward the floor while stealing sidewise glances at me over the temples of his glasses. "You seem to be fine today," said Elder Brother.

"You bet!" I replied.

"I've asked Dr. He to come and examine your pulse today."

"He's welcome!" I said. But don't think for one moment that I didn't know the old geezer was an executioner in disguise! Taking my pulse was nothing but a ruse; he wanted to feel my flesh and decide if I was fat enough to butcher yet. He'd probably even get a share of the meat for his troubles. I wasn't a *bit* afraid. Even though I don't eat human flesh, I still have a lot more courage than those who do. I thrust both hands out to see how the old buzzard would make his move. Sitting down, he closed his eyes and felt my pulse[8] for a good long while. Then he froze. Just sat there without moving a

8. In Chinese medicine the pulse is taken at both wrists.

muscle for another good long while. Finally he opened his spooky eyes and said: "Don't let your thoughts run away with you. Just convalesce in peace and quiet for a few days and you'll be all right."

Don't let my thoughts run away with me? Convalesce in peace and quiet? If I convalesce till I'm good and fat, they get more to eat, but what do *I* get out of it? How can I possibly be *all right?* What a bunch! All they think about is eating human flesh, and then they go sneaking around, thinking up every which way they can to camouflage their real intentions. They were comical enough to crack *anybody* up. I couldn't hold it in any longer and let out a good loud laugh. Now *that* really felt good. I knew in my heart of hearts that my laughter was *packed* with courage and righteousness. And do you know what? They were so completely subdued by it that the old man and my elder brother both went pale!

But the more *courage* I had, the more that made them want to eat me so that they could get a little of it for free. The old man walked out. Before he had taken many steps, he lowered his head and told Elder Brother, "To be eaten as soon as possible!" He nodded understandingly. So, Elder Brother, you're in it too! Although that discovery seemed unforeseen, it really wasn't, either. My own elder brother had thrown in with the very people who wanted to eat me!

My elder brother is a cannibal!

I'm brother to a cannibal.

Even though I'm to be the victim of cannibalism, I'm *brother* to a cannibal all the same!

5

During the past few days I've taken a step back in my thinking. Supposing that old man wasn't an executioner in disguise but really was a doctor—well, he'd still be a cannibal just the same. In *Medicinal . . . something or other* by Li Shizhen,[9] the grandfather of the doctor's trade, it says quite clearly that human flesh can be eaten, so how can that old man say that *he's* not a cannibal too?

And as for my own elder brother, I'm not being the least bit unfair to him. When he was explaining the classics to me, he said with his very own tongue that it was all right to *exchange children and eat them.* And then there was another time when he happened to start in on an evil man and said that not only should the man be killed, but his *flesh should be eaten* and *his skin used as a sleeping mat*[1] as well.

When our tenant farmer came in from Wolf Cub Village a few days back and talked about eating a man's heart and liver, Elder Brother didn't seem

9. Lived from 1518 to 1593. *Taxonomy of Medicinal Herbs,* a gigantic work, was the most important pharmacopoeia in traditional China.   1. Both italicized expressions are from the *Zuozhuan* (Zuo commentary to the *Spring and Summer Annals,* a historical work that dates from the 3rd century B.C.). In 448 B.C., an officer who was exhorting his own side not to surrender is recorded as having said, "When the army of Chu besieged the capital of Song [in 603 B.C.], the people exchanged their children and ate them, and used the bones for fuel; and still they would not submit to a covenant at the foot of their walls. For us who have sustained no great loss, to do so is to cast our state away" (translated by James Legge, 5.817). It is also recorded that in 551 B.C. an officer boasting of his own prowess before his ruler pointed to two men whom his ruler considered brave and said, "As to those two, they are like beasts, whose flesh I will eat, and then sleep upon their skins" (Legge 5.492).

to see anything out of the way in that either—just kept nodding his head. You can tell from that alone that his present way of thinking is every bit as malicious as it was when I was a child. If it's all right to exchange *children* and eat them, then *anyone* can be exchanged, anyone can be eaten. Back then I just took what he said as explanation of the classics and let it go at that, but now I realize that while he was explaining, the grease of human flesh was smeared all over his lips, and what's more, his mind was filled with plans for further cannibalism.

6

Pitch black out. Can't tell if it's day or night. The Zhao family's dog has started barking again.

Savage as a lion, timid as a rabbit, crafty as a fox . . .

7

I'm on to the way they operate. They'll never be willing to come straight out and kill me. Besides, they wouldn't dare. They'd be afraid of all the bad luck it might bring down on them if they did. And so, they've gotten everyone into cahoots with them and have set traps all over the place so that I'll do *myself* in. When I think back on the looks of those men and women on the streets a few days ago, coupled with the things my elder brother's been up to recently, I can figure out eight or nine tenths of it. From their point of view, the best thing of all would be for me to take off my belt, fasten it around a beam, and hang myself. They wouldn't be guilty of murder, and yet they'd still get everything they're after. Why, they'd be so beside themselves with joy, they'd sob with laughter. Or if they couldn't get me to do that, maybe they could torment me until I died of fright and worry. Even though I'd come out a bit leaner that way, they'd still nod their heads in approval.

Their kind only know how to eat dead meat. I remember reading in a book somewhere about something called the *hai-yi-na*.[2] Its general appearance is said to be hideous, and the expression in its eyes particularly ugly and malicious. Often eats carrion, too. Even chews the bones to a pulp and swallows them down. Just thinking about it's enough to frighten a man.

The *hai-yi-na* is kin to the wolf. The wolf's a relative of the dog, and just a few days ago the Zhao family dog gave me a funny look. It's easy to see that he's in on it too. How did that old man expect to fool *me* by staring at the floor?

My elder brother's the most pathetic of the whole lot. Since he's a human being too, how can he manage to be so totally without qualms, and what's more, even gang up with them to eat me? Could it be that he's been used to this sort of thing all along and sees nothing wrong with it? Or could it be that he's lost all conscience and just goes ahead and does it even though he knows it's wrong?

If I'm going to curse cannibals, I'll have to start with him. And if I'm going to *convert* cannibals, I'll have to start with him too.

---

2. Three Chinese characters are used here for phonetic value only; that is, *hai yi na* is a transliteration into Chinese of the English word *hyena*.

8

Actually, by now even they should long since have understood the truth of this . . .

Someone came in. Couldn't have been more than twenty or so. I wasn't able to make out what he looked like too clearly, but he was all smiles. He nodded at me. His smile didn't look like the real thing either. And so I asked him, "Is this business of eating people right?"

He just kept right on smiling and said, "Except perhaps in a famine year, how could anyone get eaten?" I knew right off that he was one of them—one of those monsters who devour people!

At that point my own courage increased a hundredfold and I asked him, "Is it right?"

"Why are you talking about this kind of thing anyway? You really know how to . . . uh . . . how to pull a fellow's leg. Nice weather we're having."

"The weather *is* nice. There's a nice moon out, too, but I *still* want to know if it's right."

He seemed quite put out with me and began to mumble, "It's not—"

"Not right? Then how come they're still eating people?"

"No one's eating anyone."

"No one's *eating* anyone? They're eating people in Wolf Cub Village this very minute. And it's written in all the books, too, written in bright red blood!"

His expression changed and his face went gray like a slab of iron. His eyes started out from their sockets as he said, "Maybe they are, but it's always been that way, it's—"

"Just because it's always been that way, does that make it *right?*"

"I'm not going to discuss such things with you. If you insist on talking about that, then *you're* the one who's in the wrong!"

I leaped from my chair, opened my eyes, and looked around—but the fellow was nowhere to be seen. He was far younger than my elder brother, and yet he was actually one of them. It must be because his mom and dad taught him to be that way. And he's probably already passed it on to his own son. No wonder that even the children give me murderous looks.

9

They want to eat others and at the same time they're afraid that other people are going to eat them. That's why they're always watching each other with such suspicious looks in their eyes.

But all they'd have to do is give up that way of thinking, and then they could travel about, work, eat, and sleep in perfect security. Think how happy they'd feel! It's only a threshold, a pass. But what do they do instead? What is it that these fathers, sons, brothers, husbands, wives, friends, teachers, students, enemies, and even people who don't know each other *really* do? Why they all join together to hold each other back, and talk each other out of it!

That's it! They'd rather *die* than take that one little step.

10

I went to see Elder Brother bright and early. He was standing in the courtyard looking at the sky. I went up behind him so as to cut him off from the
door back into the house. In the calmest and friendliest of tones, I said,
"Elder Brother, there's something I'd like to tell you."

"Go right ahead." He immediately turned and nodded his head.

"It's only a few words, really, but it's hard to get them out. Elder Brother,
way back in the beginning, it's probably the case that primitive peoples *all*
ate some human flesh. But later on, because their ways of thinking changed,
some gave up the practice and tried their level best to improve themselves;
they kept on changing until they became human beings, *real* human beings.
But the others didn't; they just kept right on with their cannibalism and
stayed at that primitive level.

"You have the same sort of thing with evolution[3] in the animal world. Some
reptiles, for instance, changed into fish, and then they evolved into birds,
then into apes, and then into human beings. But the others didn't want to
improve themselves and just kept right on being reptiles down to this very
day.

"Think how ashamed those primitive men who have remained cannibals
must feel when they stand before *real* human beings. They must feel even
more ashamed than reptiles do when confronted with their brethren who
have evolved into apes.

"There's an old story from ancient times about Yi Ya boiling his son and
serving him up to Jie Zhou.[4] But if the truth be known, people have *always*
practiced cannibalism, all the way from the time when Pan Gu separated
heaven and earth down to Yi Ya's son, down to Xu Xilin,[5] and on down to
the man they killed in Wolf Cub Village. And just last year when they executed a criminal in town, there was even someone with T.B. who dunked a
steamed bread roll in his blood and then licked it off.

"When they decided to eat me, by yourself, of course, you couldn't do
much to prevent it, but why did you have to go and *join* them? Cannibals
are capable of anything! If they're capable of eating me, then they're capable
of eating *you* too! Even within their own group, they think nothing of devouring each other. And yet all they'd have to do is turn back—*change*—and then
everything would be fine. Even though people may say, 'It's always been like
this,' we can still do our best to improve. And we can start today!

"You're going to tell me it can't be done! Elder Brother, I think you're very
likely to say that. When that tenant wanted to reduce his rent the day before
yesterday, wasn't it you who said it couldn't be done?"

3. Charles Darwin's (1809–1892) theory of evolution was immensely important to Chinese intellectuals
during Lu's lifetime and the common coin of much discourse.   4. An early philosophical text, *Guan Zi*,
reports that the famous cook Yi Ya boiled his son and served him to his ruler, Duke Huan of Qi (685–643
B.C.), because the meat of a human infant was one of the few delicacies the duke had never tasted. Ji and
Zhou were the last evil rulers of the Sang (1776–1122 B.C.) and Zhou (1122–221 B.C.) dynasties. The
madman has mixed up some facts here.   5. From Lu's hometown, Shaoxing (1873–1907). After studies
in Japan, he returned to China and served as head of the Anhui Police Academy. When a high Qing official,
En Ming, participated in a graduation ceremony at the academy, Xu assassinated him, hoping that this
would touch off the revolution. After the assassination, he and some of his students at the academy occupied
the police armory and managed, for a while, to hold off En Ming's troops. When Xu was finally captured,
En Ming's personal body guards dug out his heart and liver and ate them. Pan Gu (literally, "Coiled-up
Antiquity") was born out of an egg. As he stood up, he separated heaven and earth. The world as we know
it was formed from his body.

At first he just stood there with a cold smile, but then his eyes took on a murderous gleam. (I had exposed their innermost secrets.) His whole face had gone pale. Some people were standing outside the front gate. The Venerable Old Zhao and his dog were among them. Stealthily peering this way and that, they began to crowd through the open gate. Some I couldn't make out too well—their faces seemed covered with cloth. Some looked the same as ever—smiling green faces with protruding fangs. I could tell at a glance that they all belonged to the same gang, that they were all cannibals. But at the same time I also realized that they didn't all think the same way. Some thought *it's always been like this* and that they really should eat human flesh. Others knew they shouldn't but went right on doing it anyway, always on the lookout for fear someone might give them away. And since that's exactly what I had just done, I knew they must be furious. But they were all *smiling* at me—cold little smiles!

At this point Elder Brother suddenly took on an ugly look and barked, "Get out of here! All of you! What's so funny about a madman?"

Now I'm on to *another* of their tricks: not only are they unwilling to change, but they're already setting me up for their next cannibalistic feast by labeling me a "madman." That way, they'll be able to eat me without getting into the slightest trouble. Some people will even be grateful to them. Wasn't that the very trick used in the case that the tenant reported? Everybody ganged up on a "bad" man and ate him. It's the same old thing.

Old Fifth Chen came in and made straight for me, looking mad as could be. But he wasn't going to shut *me* up! I was going to tell that bunch of cannibals off, and no two ways about it!

"You can change! You can change from the bottom of your hearts! You ought to know that in the future they're not going to allow cannibalism in the world anymore. If you don't change, you're going to devour each other anyway. And even if a lot of you *are* left, a real human being's going to come along and eradicate the lot of you, just like a hunter getting rid of wolves— or reptiles!"

Old Fifth Chen chased them all out. I don't know where Elder Brother disappeared to. Old Fifth talked me into going back to my room.

It was pitch black inside. The beams and rafters started trembling overhead. They shook for a bit, and then they started getting bigger and bigger. They piled themselves up into a great heap on top of my body!

The weight was incredibly heavy and I couldn't even budge—they were trying to kill me! But I knew their weight was an illusion, and I struggled out from under them, my body bathed in sweat. I was still going to have my say. "Change this minute! Change from the bottom of your hearts! You ought to know that in the future they're not going to allow cannibals in the world anymore . . ."

11

The sun doesn't come out. The door doesn't open. It's two meals a day.

I picked up my chopsticks and that got me thinking about Elder Brother. I realized that the reason for my younger sister's death lay entirely with him. I can see her now—such a lovable and helpless little thing, only five at the time. Mother couldn't stop crying, but *he* urged her to stop, probably because he'd eaten sister's flesh himself and hearing mother cry over her like that shamed him! But if he's still capable of feeling shame, then maybe . . .

Younger Sister was eaten by Elder Brother. I have no way of knowing whether Mother knew about it or not.

I think she *did* know, but while she was crying she didn't say anything about it. She probably thought it was all right, too. I can remember once when I was four or five, I was sitting out in the courtyard taking in a cool breeze when Elder Brother told me that when parents are ill, a son, in order to be counted as a really good person, should slice off a piece of his own flesh, boil it, and let them eat it.[6] At the time Mother didn't come out and say there was anything wrong with that. But if it was all right to eat one piece, then there certainly wouldn't be anything wrong with her eating the whole body. And yet when I think back to the way she cried and cried that day, it's enough to break my heart. It's all strange—very, very strange.

12

Can't think about it anymore. I just realized today that I too have muddled around for a good many years in a place where they've been continually eating people for four thousand years. Younger Sister happened to die at just the time when Elder Brother was in charge of the house. Who's to say he didn't slip some of her meat into the food we ate?

Who's to say I didn't eat a few pieces of my younger sister's flesh without knowing it? And now it's my turn . . .

Although I wasn't aware of it in the beginning, now that I *know* I'm some-one with four thousand years' experience of cannibalism behind me, how hard it is to look real human beings in the eye!

13

Maybe there are some children around who still haven't eaten human flesh.

Save the children . . .

April 1918

Upstairs in a Wineshop

While making a trip from north China down into the southeast, I detoured a bit to visit the area where I was born and had grown up. And so it was that I arrived in S-town.[1] It was the midst of winter and a recent snowfall had rendered the landscape bleak and clear. S-town was only ten miles from my home town, less than half a day by boat, and I had once put in a year here teaching school.

6. In traditional literature, stories about such gruesome acts of filial piety were not unusual.   1. Lu spent the years from 1902 to 1909 as a student in Japan. Upon his return to China, he taught physiology and chemistry for a year at the Zhejiang Normal School in Hangzhou, about thirty miles from his native Shaoxing. Then from 1909 to 1911, he was engaged as a teacher and dean of studies in the Shaoxing High School. In many of his writings, "S-town" stands loosely for Shaoxing and its environs. The stories, of course, are fictional and reflect only in an approximate way the actual events of Lu's life.

A comfortable sense of freedom from my normal round of duties gave such impetus to the nostalgia that assailed me that I ended up checking into a place called the Luosi, a hotel that had not been here back in my teaching days. Since S-town wasn't very large to begin with, I quickly made the rounds on foot as I hunted up a few former colleagues I thought might still be around. It turned out, however, that they had long since scattered to who-knows-where. Then I sauntered over to see the school where I had taught. It had so changed, in both name and appearance, that it no longer felt the least bit familiar. Thus, before two hours were out, my initial homecoming enthusiasm had waned completely. I decided that my detour had been a waste of time and rather regretted having come.

The Luosi rented rooms but sold no food. Meals had to be ordered in from the outside, and the one I got was as tasteless as sawdust. Outside my window, withered moss clung to a stain-mottled wall above which there was nothing to relieve the monotonous pallor of the leaden sky, a pallor emphasized by the light snow that had begun dancing in the wind.

Since I hadn't eaten enough lunch and had nothing to occupy my time, my thoughts turned quite naturally to the *Gallon,* a little two-storied wineshop where my face had once been a familiar one. It occurred to me that this new hotel couldn't be far from it. I locked my door, went outside, and headed off to find the *Gallon.* It wasn't that I wanted to get intoxicated, but simply that I wanted to escape, if only for a moment, that awful nothing-to-do feeling that so often besets the traveler.

It was still there too—the same battered old sign, the same cramped and dingy downstairs room. From the manager on down, however, there wasn't a single person I recognized. As far as the *Gallon* was concerned, I had been transformed into a newcomer.

Nonetheless, I walked over to the corner of the room, placed my hand on the bannister, and climbed the stairs I had trod so many times before to the little room on the second floor. Just as I remembered, there were five small tables. The only change was that the latticed window at the rear had been torn out and replaced by a pane of glass.

"A catty of Shaoxing.[2] To eat? Ten fried beancurd cakes, and don't skimp on the hotsauce!" Saying this to the waiter who had followed me up, I made straight for the table under the back window. Since the room was empty, I was free to pick the best seat—a lofty perch by the window from which I could look down on the abandoned courtyard out back. As I think back on it, that yard probably didn't belong to the wineshop. I had gazed down on it many times before, and sometimes in snowy weather just like today's, too. But now, to forgetful eyes that had become accustomed to the scenery of north China, there were things in that courtyard well worth marveling at. Several old plum trees were doggedly blossoming in the midst of the snow as though oblivious to the rigors of winter, and next to a pavilion that had long since collapsed, a camellia showed more than a dozen red blooms against thick, dark green leaves. Fire-bright against the snow, it stood there in all its grandeur, passionate and proud, seeming to scorn the wanderer's willingness to have ventured so far from home. At this point, I suddenly

---

2. Shaoxing is famous for the manufacture of the liquor that bears its name. The local distillery is a present-day tourist attraction. *Catty:* a measure of weight, approximately 1.33 pounds.

recalled how moist the snow is here in my homeland. It glistens brightly and will stick to anything, nothing like the dry powdery snow of north China that flies up and fills the sky with a white mist whenever the wind picks up.

"Wine . . . for . . . the . . . guest," said the waiter slowly as he arranged cup, chopsticks, winepot, bowl, and saucer. The Shaoxing had arrived. I turned back toward the table and poured myself a cup. It occurred to me that while it was true the north wasn't my home, the south wasn't my home anymore either, for I was treated as a guest here too. No matter how the dry snow of the north scattered in the wind, no matter how the moist snow of the south clung to things—none of that had anything to do with me. Somewhat dejected at the thought, I took a very satisfying sip of wine. The flavor was authentic, and the beancurd cakes were done to a turn, but the hotsauce, sad to say, was watery and weak. The people of S-town have never understood what a spicy cuisine is all about.

Perhaps because it was only the afternoon, no aroma of wine permeated the shop. Even after I had downed my third cup, the upstairs was still empty, save for myself and four unoccupied tables. Gazing at the abandoned courtyard outside, I began to feel even more lonely. And yet, I really didn't want anyone to join me either. And so, when I heard footsteps on the stairs, I could not help but feel irritated. I didn't regain my composure until I saw that it was only the waiter. Sitting there alone, I drank two more cups of wine.

The next time, the footsteps were far too slow to be those of the waiter. I was sure that another patron had arrived. I waited until I thought he must have reached the landing and then, somewhat apprehensively, raised my head to get a good look at this alien companion of mine. I rose from my seat with a start. I had never imagined it would prove to be an old friend—that is, if he would still let me call him that. No doubt about it, the man who had come up was an old schoolmate of mine. After graduation, when I was a teacher, he had once been my colleague too. The only thing about him that had really changed was his movement: he had become noticeably sluggish, nothing like the forceful and agile Lü Weifu I had known in years gone by.

"Weifu, is that you? I never expected to meet you here."

"What, can that really be you? Who would have thought . . ."

I invited him to sit down. To my surprise, he actually seemed to hesitate a bit before joining me. My first reaction was simply to consider his behavior a bit odd, but then I began to feel somewhat saddened and even offended. I studied him more closely: same disheveled hair, same long squarish face, but grown old and thin. His spirits seemed subdued too—one might even have said enfeebled. Yes, beneath those thick black brows of his, the life had gone out of his eyes. And yet as he surveyed his present surroundings, the moment he caught sight of the abandoned courtyard, those eyes blazed with that same old flame with which he had once been able to transfix people. I had often seen that look in our school days.

"Well, Weifu," I began enthusiastically, albeit a bit unnaturally, "it must be a good ten years this time. A while back, I heard you were in Jinan,[3] but I was too darned lazy to get a letter off to you."

___
3. Capital of Shandong Province, about five hundred miles north of the two friends' homeland.

"Yes, well it was the same with me too. I'm at Taiyuan[4] now. Been there over two years already. Mother's with me. It was when I came back down here to get her that I discovered you'd long since moved away—disappeared without a trace."

"What are you up to in Taiyuan?"

"Family tutor in a fellow provincial's home."

"And before that?"

"Before that?" He fished a cigarette out of his pocket, put it between his lips, lit it, took a puff, exhaled, and then gazed musing into the cloud of smoke. "Didn't do anything really, except a bunch of stuff that didn't amount to anything. Actually, it's the *same* as having done nothing."

In his turn, he asked me about my own situation since we had last met. While I was setting it out for him, I told the waiter to bring another pair of chopsticks and a cup. I ordered another two catties of Shaoxing and passed my own over to him in the meantime. We had never stood on ceremony in the past, but now when it came to ordering the food, we outdid each other in insisting that "you order what *you* want" until things got so mixed up we couldn't tell who had ordered what. We had to depend on the waiter's reading it back to us to determine that four dishes had in fact been ordered: beans cooked with fennel, jellied meat, fried beancurd, and dried black carp.

"As soon as I got back, I realized what an absurd figure I must cut," he said with a wan smile, holding his cigarette aloft with one hand and grasping his winecup with the other. "When I was a kid, I used to think that bees and flies were absurd and pathetic. I'd watch the way they'd light someplace, get spooked by something, and then fly away. After making a small circle, they'd always come back again and land just exactly where they had been before. Who could have imagined that someday, having made my own small circle, I would fly back too? And who would ever have expected that you would do the same thing? Couldn't you have managed to fly a little farther away?"

"Hard to say. I'm probably no different than you—just made my little circle before coming back," I answered with a smile as wan as his own. "But why have you flown back *this* time?"

"Just to do some more stuff that doesn't amount to anything." He downed a cup of wine with a single gulp, took several drags on his cigarette, and opened his eyes a bit wider. "Doesn't amount to a darned thing really, but I suppose it won't do any harm to tell you about it."

The waiter came upstairs with our order. When he had it all set down, it covered the whole table. Permeated with the warm aroma of cigarette smoke and fried beancurd, the little upstairs room now assumed a lively air. Outside the window, the snow was falling even thicker than before.

"You probably know I had a little brother who died when he was three and was buried out in the countryside. I can't even remember what he looked like now, but according to Mother, he was a lovable little guy who got along very well with me. Down to this very day, her eyes mist up whenever she speaks of him. Well anyway, this spring we got a letter from a cousin saying that the riverbank was eroding fast, and if we didn't do something pretty soon, his grave would slide into the river. As soon as Mother found out— she knows enough characters to read letters—she was worried sick. Couldn't sleep nights. But what could *I* do? No money, no time. I was helpless.

4. Capital of Shanxi Province, more than seven hundred miles northwest of their homeland.

"The situation dragged on and on until finally I was able to take advantage of the New Year's vacation to come back down and rebury him." Draining another cup of wine, Weifu looked out the window. "When would you ever see anything like this up north—flowers blooming in all that snow, the ground underneath not even frozen?

"Well anyway, day before yesterday I bought a little coffin in town (I thought the original must have long since rotted away), picked up some cotton batting and quilts, hired four grave diggers, and set out to rebury him. Suddenly I began to feel very positive about the whole thing. Now I actually *wanted* to dig up the grave, wanted to have a look at the dead bones of the little brother who had once been so close to me. I'd never quite had such feelings before in my entire life.

"When we got to the gravesite, sure enough, the river water had eaten away at the bank until it was less than two feet from the mound. And what a pitiful little grave mound it was, too. No one had added any dirt to it for over two years, and it was pathetically flat. With an air of command, I stood there in the snow, pointed at it, and gave the order: 'Open it up!' Coming from me, such an authoritative command had an incongruous ring, for I'm a very run-of-the-mill kind of man, not at all accustomed to telling people what to do. But the grave diggers didn't seem to find anything in the least odd about my giving commands. They simply started digging.

"Once they had the mound open, I went over and looked inside. As I had expected, the coffin was almost gone—transformed into shreds of rotting wood. Heart beating wildly, I carefully brushed aside what was left of it, so that I might be able to see my brother. To my surprise, however, there was nothing there, absolutely nothing! The quilt he'd been wrapped in, the clothes he'd worn, his skeleton—all gone. I had always heard that the hair is the last part of the body to rot. 'Perhaps there's still some hair left,' I thought to myself as I knelt down and sifted through the dirt around the place where I thought the pillow must have been. Nothing there either. He had disappeared without leaving a trace!"

I noticed that Weifu's eyes were slightly red, but immediately realized that this signaled nothing more than the fact he had had too much to drink. While we were talking, he had eaten next to nothing but had continued to down cup after cup of wine, and must have long since gone through a good catty or more. The alcohol seemed to put new life into him, both physically and spiritually. He was now beginning to resemble the old Weifu I used to know. Swinging around in my chair, I ordered another two catties of wine; then I turned back and, sitting directly across from my old friend, listened in silence as he continued.

"Actually, at that point, I really didn't have to go through with it. I could simply have smoothed the grave over, sold the coffin, and that would have been the end of it. To be sure, trying to get rid of a coffin like that would have looked a bit peculiar, but as long as I didn't ask too much, I'd probably have been able to sell it back to the store where I'd bought it. At the very least, I'd get enough for a drink or two. But I didn't even try.

"Instead, I spread the quilt out in the new coffin just as I had originally planned, took some dirt from the spot where my brother's body had lain, wrapped it in cotton batting, and put the resulting package inside the quilt. Then I had the coffin moved to the graveyard where my father is buried. I had them bury it next to him. This time I had the coffin enclosed in bricks to make a good tight seal. Had to spend most of my day yesterday supervising the workmen. At any rate, it's over and done with, and at least I've done enough to pull the wool over Mother's eyes and set her mind at rest.

"Hey, why are you looking at me like that? Do you blame me for being so different from the old Lü Weifu who lives in your memory? I can understand your feelings. I too can still remember how it was when we were young, how we used to go to the City Temple together and yank the beards off the statues of the gods, and how we'd often argue the whole day about this or that way of reforming China, until we got so worked up we even came to blows. But now, I am as you see me—a man who goes through the motions of living without taking anything seriously. Sometimes it occurs to me that if my friends from back then were to see me now, they'd disown me. But I am what I am." He fished out another cigarette, dangled it between his lips, and lit up.

"I can tell from your eyes that you still have hopes I'll do something to realize some of our old ideals. Though I'm much more insensitive than I used to be, I can still sense some things by the way a man looks at me. And I'm grateful for your faith in me too. But at the same time, it makes me anxious for fear that when all is said and done, I'll let down those old friends who, like you, continue to think well of me to this very day."

He paused in his recitation, took several drags on his cigarette, and then resumed in slow, measured tones: "Only today, just before I came here to the *Gallon*, I did something else that didn't amount to anything, but at least it was something I wanted to do. It had to do with an old neighbor of ours by the name of Changfu. He was the boatman who lived on the east side of our place. Had a daughter named Ah-shun. You probably saw her now and then when you used to come by to see me. But she was so young back then that you probably didn't give her a second glance. Didn't turn into any great beauty when she grew up, either—just an ordinary kind of oval face that was a bit drawn and somewhat on the sallow side. But those *eyes* of hers! And those long lashes! The whites of her eyes were as clear as a cloudless sky at night. And I'm talking about a northern sky on a night when there's no wind. We have nothing to compare to it down here.

"Ah-shun was a very capable girl, too. Lost her mother when she was eleven or so. From then on, the care of her younger brother and younger sister fell entirely on her. And then of course, she had to attend to her father's needs too. She did it all, and she did it well. Knew how to save a penny, too. After she took over the management of the household, the family's finances gradually got onto a better footing. There was hardly a neighbor around who didn't have a good word for Ah-shun. Even Changfu would often say how grateful he was to have a daughter like her.

"Well, at any rate, when I was on the point of setting out to come back down here this time, my mother started thinking about Ah-shun. Funny what long memories old people have. She said she remembered a time when Ah-shun had wanted a red velvet flower to put in her hair. Seemed that she'd seen another girl wearing one and decided that she'd like one too. But she couldn't find any place that sold them. She bawled and bawled until Changfu finally gave her a beating. Went around with red and swollen eyes for a couple of days afterwards.

"Artificial flowers like that come from outside the province and if she couldn't find one even in S-town, then she certainly wouldn't be able to find it anywhere else. As long as I was coming down this way, Mother told me to buy her one somewhere along the way. Well that was one task I didn't mind in the least. As a matter of fact, I rather looked forward to it, for I honestly felt like doing something for Ah-shun myself.

"When I was down here the year before last to pick up Mother and take her back up north with me, I happened by Changfu's place one day and, somehow or other, struck up a conversation with him. The upshot was that he invited me to stay for a snack, a bowl of cereal made out of buckwheat flour. He made a point of telling me they made theirs with white sugar. Think about that: a fisherman who's able to keep white sugar in the house can't be any pauper, that's for sure. As a matter of fact, you could say he must be eating rather well. Changfu kept pressing me to sit down until I couldn't very well say no. But I agreed only on the condition that he give me a small bowl. Well, he wasn't born yesterday and probably knew what I meant, so he said to his daughter: 'Ah-shun, you know these educated people—don't know what a real meal is, so make sure you use a small bowl. And don't hold back on the sugar either!'"

"When she brought it out, I almost fell off my chair. That bowl was huge. There was easily enough in it to keep my mouth on duty the whole day. But then I saw Changfu's bowl and realized that mine really was small by comparison. I'd never eaten buckwheat cereal in my whole life and didn't find it exactly palatable when I tasted it now, but there was no denying it *was* sweet. Looking as casual about it as I could, I downed a few mouthfuls and was just about to set aside my bowl when I happened to catch a glimpse of Ah-shun standing over in the corner. I lost my nerve immediately, for she was watching me with a mixture of fear and hope, probably afraid that she hadn't made it just right, but at the same time hoping that I'd like it. I knew that if I left over half the bowl, she would feel terribly disappointed, and guilty as well.

"Through sheer will power, I widened my throat as much as I could and crammed that cereal down as fast as it would go, almost as fast as Changfu himself. For the first time in my life I understood what a painful thing forced feeding is. For unpleasantness, I could remember nothing that came even close—except, perhaps, once during my childhood when I had to eat a bowl of tapeworm medicine mixed with brown sugar.

"And yet I didn't mind in the least, for when Ah-shun came to take my bowl, that smile of utter satisfaction, which she was doing her best to hold in, more than repaid any discomfort I may have suffered. Though I left feeling so bloated that I couldn't get to sleep that night and had one nightmare after the other, I still wished Ah-shun nothing but the best and hoped that, for her sake, the world would take a turn for the better. Almost immediately, however, I laughed at myself for entertaining such thoughts, for I realized that they were simply vestiges of the old dreams I'd entertained in days gone by. After that, I put her completely out of mind.

"I hadn't known that she'd once gotten a beating over an artificial velvet flower, but hearing my mother bring it up, my experience with the buckwheat cereal came back to mind and the memory of it made me especially diligent on Ah-shun's behalf. I searched the town over in Taiyuan without finding one. It wasn't until I got to—"

Shish! Outside the window, an accumulation of snow that had been weigh-

ing upon a camellia branch, bending it down into an arc, now slid to the
ground as the branch stretched itself straight out, showing off its dark glistening leaves and blood-red blossoms. The leaden sky was even darker now
and you could hear chirping everywhere: dusk was fast approaching and,
unable to find any food on the snow-blanketed ground, birds now hurried
back to their nests for the night.

"—until I got to Jinan," he continued after turning to look out the window,
"that I managed to find velvet flowers. I had no idea whether they were like
the one she'd taken a beating for, but they *were* velvet. And since I didn't
know whether she preferred lighter or darker hues, I bought her a bright red
one and a pale pink one.

"It was only this afternoon, right after lunch, that I went to look her up.
Put off my departure a whole day just to do it. The house was still there, but
as I looked at it, there seemed to be something that wasn't quite right. Dismissing that as my own subjective feeling, I walked closer and saw Changfu's
son and second daughter, Ah-zhao, standing in the doorway. They were both
grown now. Ah-zhao had developed into a young woman who looked nothing
like her elder sister. Looked more like some sort of witch.

"When she saw me coming toward her, she shot inside like a bolt. I learned
from the son that Changfu wasn't at home. 'How about your elder sister?'
He immediately opened his eyes into a wide and angry stare and asked what
business I had with her. He suddenly looked so vicious you would have
thought he was a wild animal ready to pounce on me to tear the flesh from
my body with bared fangs. Trying to smooth things over as best I could, I
left in a hurry. I never have the guts to see things through any more . . .

"You probably don't know this, but I'm much more afraid of calling on
people than I used to be. You see, now that I *know* what a contemptible
wretch I am, I even despise myself. Sure, people may not come right out and
say anything to me, but knowing how they must feel about me, what's the
point in going to see them? Deliberately making them uncomfortable?
Despite all that, I felt this was one task I had to see through. After wracking
my brains for a while, I walked over to the firewood store diagonally across
from their place. Old Granny Laofa was still there. She recognized me and,
much to my surprise, invited me in. After we'd exchanged greetings, I
explained why I had come back to S-town and why I was looking for Changfu.

"She sighed and said, 'Too bad Ah-shun wasn't lucky enough to get to wear
your flowers.' Granny Laofa then told me the whole story, from beginning
to end.

" 'It was probably around spring last year,' she began, 'that Ah-shun began
lookin' all weak and pale. Later on, she took to cryin' a lot. When they asked
her why, she wouldn't say. Sometimes she'd cry the whole night. Finally,
Changfu couldn't take it anymore and blew his top. Cursed her out for stayin'
an old maid too long, and said it was this that was makin' her crazy. Come
fall, somethin' that started out as just a cold ended up gettin' so bad Ah-shun
couldn't even get out of bed. Wasn't till a few days before she died that she
finally told her dad what was really wrong. Said that for a long time she'd
been the way her mother used to be—spittin' up blood and breakin' into
night sweats. She'd hidden it all that time so as not to worry him.

" 'And then one night, her uncle, Changgeng, came round tryin' to borrow
money—he did that a lot. He wouldn't take no for an answer. When Ah-
shun wouldn't give 'im any, Changgeng gave a mean laugh and said, "Don't

get so uppity there. I'm a helluva lot better than the man they've got picked out for *you!*" After that, Ah-shun got really down in the dumps. Such a modest girl she was. Rather than askin' round to get the facts about this man her dad was supposed to have picked out, she just bawled. Changfu finally found out how she'd been taken in by Changgeng and told her the truth about what a fine fellow he'd lined up for her. By then, though, the harm'd been done. You could tell she didn't really believe what her dad said because she came back with: "It's a good thing I'm in the shape I am, 'cause now it don't matter one way or the other."

" 'If the man he'd picked for her wasn't a match for Changgeng, that'd be enough to scare anybody to death! Not even a match for a *chicken thief?* What sort of excuse for a man would that be? I got to see her intended in person when he came to Ah-shun's funeral. Had nice clean clothes and wasn't all that hard to look at either. Tears in his eyes, he told everybody there how he'd poled a boat almost half his life. Scrimped and saved until he'd finally put enough by to buy himself a wife. And then she went and died on 'im. You could tell he was a good man and that all that stuff Changgeng had said was nothin' but a pack of lies. What a pity that Ah-shun should believe that bastard's crap and go lose her life for nothin'.' The old lady finished it all up by telling me: 'If you wanted to put it on anything, you'd have to put it on Ah-shun's bad fate.'

"Well, whatever the case, I was through with my part of it. But what was I to do with the flowers? I asked Granny Laofa if she would give them to Ahzhao. Since Ah-zhao had treated me like a wild wolf or worse, I really didn't *feel* like letting her have them. So then why did I? Because that way I'd be able to tell Mother how delighted she was. What's it all amount to anyway? Right now, all I've got to worry about is muddling through till New Year's is over and then I can go back to teaching my *thus-spoke-the-Master* and *so-states-the-Poetry-Classic.*"[5]

"You're teaching the *classics?* I asked in astonishment.

"Of course. Did you think I was still teaching ABCD?[6] At first I had two students, one studying the *Poetry Classic* and the other doing *The Mencius.*[7] Later on a third one joined us, a girl. She's reading *Maxims for Young Ladies.*[8] I don't even teach mathematics anymore. It's not that I don't want to, it's just that their fathers don't want me to."

"I never expected that you'd actually be teaching that kind of thing."

"That's what their fathers *want* them to be taught. I'm an outsider, so it's all the same to me. What's it all amount to anyway? All I have to do is muddle along as best . . ."

His entire face was flushed now and he seemed slightly inebriated. The gleam in his eyes, however, had subsided. I gave in to a light sigh and for the moment could think of nothing to say. There was a flurry of sound on the staircase as several newcomers crowded their way up. First in line was a short man with bulging jowls. Second, a tall fellow with a conspicuous red nose.

Others followed behind them, stomping up the stairs with such force that

---

5. Translation of the four-character phrase *ziyue shiyun,* a shorthand reference to classical learning. The friends, of course, consider all such erudition reactionary and useless. The *Master* is Confucius. 6. Shorthand for Western learning; the original text prints it in Roman letters.   7. Mencius (372–279 B.C.) is sometimes referred to as the Saint Paul of Confucianism.   8. An anonymous text known in several different versions.

the whole building trembled. I turned and looked at Lü Weifu just as he also turned to look at me. I told the waiter to total up our bill.

"Does it give you enough to get by on?" I asked as I prepared to leave.

"Yes, it . . . To tell the truth, I get twenty a month and don't get by all that well."

"What do you plan on doing after this?"

"After this? I don't know. Just think, not a single one of the hopes and dreams we had back then has worked out, has it? I don't know anything anymore. I don't even know what tomorrow's going to bring, or even the next moment . . ."

The waiter came up and handed me the check. Not nearly so deferential as when I first arrived, he simply threw me a single glance and then, looking utterly uninterested, stood to one side and smoked while I took out the money to pay.

Weifu and I walked out of the wineshop together, but since his hotel lay in the opposite direction to mine, we parted at the door. As I walked off toward the Luosi, with the cold wind and snowflakes blowing against my face, I felt refreshed. Judging from the color of the sky, it was already dusk. Along with the surrounding buildings and streets, I too became woven into a pure white and ever-shifting web of snow.

February 16, 1926

Wild Grass[1]

Special thanks to D. E. Pollard

Epigraph

When I am silent, I am fulfilled; when I am about to speak, I then feel empty.

My past life is dead. At this death I greatly rejoice, because I know from this death that my life once existed. The dead life has decayed. I greatly rejoice, because I know from this decay that my life was not empty.

The soil of life has been cast upon the surface of the land. Tall trees do not grow from it, only wild grass. For this I am to blame.

Wild grass has no deep roots, it bears no pretty flowers, no pretty leaves. But it drinks in dew and water, sucks in the flesh and blood of long dead corpses, and wrests its existence from each and every thing. When it is alive, it is always trampled on, cut down, until it dies and decays.

But I am at ease, joyful. I will laugh; I will sing.

1. Translated by Ng Mau-sang.

Naturally I love my wild grass, but I hate the ground which uses it for decoration.

Under the crust the subterranean fire is blazing. When it erupts, its lava will consume all the wild grass, all the tall trees. Whereupon nothing will be left to decay.

But I am at ease, joyful. I will laugh; I will sing.

Heaven and earth are so still and silent, I cannot laugh or sing. Even if heaven and earth were not so still and silent, perhaps I still would not be able to do so. At this juncture of light and darkness, life and death, past and future, I offer this clump of wild grass before friends and foes, men and beasts, the loving and the unloving as my witness.

For my sake, and for the sake of friends and foes, men and beasts, those loving and unloving, I hope that death and decay will come speedily to this grass. If not, then *I* will not have lived, and this would be an even greater misfortune than death and decay.

Perish, wild grass, and with it, my epigraph.

April 26, 1927

Autumn Night

Through the window I can see two trees in my backyard. The one is a date tree, the other is also a date tree.

The night sky above is strange and distant. Never in my life have I seen such a strange and distant sky. He seems intent on forsaking the world and staying out of people's sight. But now he is winking—with eyes of a few dozen stars, utterly blue, and cold. A smile hovers around his mouth, seeming to him to be very profound, and thereupon he begins to spread frost on the wild flowers and wild grass in my courtyard.

I do not know the names of these flowers and grasses, or what people call them. I remember a plant which put forth a tiny flower—the flower is still in bloom, but she is even tinier, trembling in the cold, dreaming. She dreams of the coming of spring, of autumn, of a skinny poet wiping his tears on her last petal, telling her that autumn may come, winter may come, but eventually spring will come, when butterflies will fly gaily about, and the bees will sing their spring song. Thereupon she smiles, although she has turned red in the piercing cold and remains curled up.

The date trees have shed all their leaves. Some time ago, a boy or two still came to beat them for the dates that others had left behind. Now, not a single one is left, even the leaves have all fallen. The date tree understands the dream of the tiny pink flower, that after autumn spring will come; he also knows the dream of the fallen leaves, that after spring there is still autumn.

He has shed all his foliage, leaving only the trunk; he is relieved from bending under his load of leaves and fruit, and now enjoys stretching himself. But a few boughs are still hanging down, nursing the wounds caused by the poles that struck him for his dates, while the longest and straightest of his boughs are like iron, silently piercing the strange and distant sky, making him wink his wicked eyes; piercing the full moon in the sky, making her go pale with embarrassment.

The wickedly winking sky turns an even deeper, perturbed blue. He seems intent on escaping from men, on avoiding the date tree, leaving only the moon behind. But the moon has secretly hid herself in the east. Only the naked trunk is still like iron, silently piercing the strange and distant sky, determined to pierce it to death, regardless of how and how often he winks his seductive eyes.

With a sharp shriek, a vicious bird of the night flies past.

I suddenly hear a slight tittering in the middle of the night, so soft that it seems not to want to awaken those who are asleep, though the titter echoes across the surrounding air. In the dead of night, there is no one about. I instantly recognize that this laughter is coming from my own mouth. Put to flight by the sound, I go back into my room, and immediately raise the wick of my lamp.

The glass pane of the back window rattles; many insects are still blindly battering against it. Shortly afterwards, a few squeeze in, probably through the holes in the paper covering. Once inside, they knock against the glass lampshade, making yet more rattling sounds. One plunges in from above, and runs into the flame. It is a real flame, I think. But two or three rest panting on the paper lampshade. The lampshade was replaced only last night, its snow-white paper folded in a wave-like pattern, with a sprig of scarlet jasmine painted in one corner.

When the scarlet jasmine blossoms, the date tree will again dream the dream of the tiny pink flower; it will grow lushly and bend in an arc. I hear again the midnight laughter, and immediately cut the train of my thought. I look at these little insects still resting on the snow-white paper—their heads big and tails small, like sunflower seeds, only half the size of a grain of wheat. How lovely and pitiable they are in their emerald hue.

I yawn, and light a cigarette, puffing out the smoke. I stare at the lamp and pay silent tribute to these dainty heroes in emerald green.

JAMES JOYCE
1882–1941

Modernism is synonymous with James Joyce. An Irish writer who spent most of his life outside Ireland and became an international figure, Joyce created a narrative style that changed the way modern novelists were able to write about the world. Writers as widely separated as the American William Faulkner, the Irishman Samuel Beckett, the Colombian Gabriel García Márquez, and the French "new novelists" Alain Robbe-Grillet, Marguerite Duras, and Nathalie Sarraute learned from his literary and linguistic innovations. From *Dubliners* to *Ulysses* and *Finnegans Wake,* Joyce found new ways to explore the daily lives and fragmentary dreams of characters (including his own youthful self) in the parochial Dublin society he had fled. Although he returned to Ireland as the starting point for all three works, he blamed Irish society for its narrowness and "moral paralysis" and repeatedly evoked the broader horizons of European culture and myth. Joyce's best-known contribution to modern literature is the stream-of-consciousness technique that attempts to reproduce the natural flow of thoughts and emotions. Stream-of-consciousness writing does not always seem logical, for thoughts tend to jump around in an arbitrary manner, but it can be very convincing since it gives the reader apparent access to the workings of a character's mind. The aim—and it is a characteristically modernist aim—is to obtain a fuller understanding of human experience by displaying subconscious associations along with conscious thoughts. Joyce's later work exploits these subterranean connections more and more, and his language becomes increasingly playful, as he strives to create a newly meaningful form of writing and to "forge in the smithy of my soul the uncreated conscience of my race."

Born in Dublin on February 2, 1882, to May Murray and John Stanislaus Joyce, he was given the impressive name of James Augustine Aloysius Joyce. His father held a well-paid and easy post in the civil service, and the family was comfortable until 1891, when his job was eliminated with a small pension and he declined to take up more demanding work elsewhere. The Joyce family (there were ten children) moved steadily down the social and economic scale, and life became difficult under the improvident guidance of a man whom Joyce later portrayed as "a drinker, a good fellow, a storyteller, somebody's secretary, something in a distillery, a tax-gatherer, a bankrupt, and at present a praiser of his own past." Joyce attended the well-known Catholic preparatory school of Clongowes Wood College from six to nine years of age, leaving when his family could no longer afford the tuition; two years later, he was admitted as a scholarship student to Belvedere College in Dublin. Both were Jesuit schools, and provided a rigorous Catholic training against which Joyce violently rebelled but which he was never able to forget. In Belvedere College, shaken by a dramatic hell-fire sermon shortly after his first experience with sex, he even thought of becoming a priest; the life of the senses and his vocation as an artist won out, however, and the sermon and his reaction to it became part of *A Portrait of the Artist as a Young Man.* After graduating from Belvedere in 1898, Joyce entered another Irish Catholic institution—University College, Dublin—where he consciously rebelled against Irish tradition and looked abroad for new values. Teaching himself Norwegian to read Henrik Ibsen in the original, he criticized the writers of the Irish Literary Renaissance as provincial and had no interest in joining their ranks. Like the hero of *Portrait*, Stephen Dedalus, he decided in 1902 to escape the stifling conventions of his native country and leave for the Continent.

This first trip did not last long. For six months, he supported himself in Paris by giving English lessons, but when his mother turned seriously ill he was called home. After her death, he taught school for a time in Dublin and then returned to the Continent with Nora Barnacle, a country woman from western Ireland with whom he had two children and whom he married in 1931. The young couple moved to

Trieste, where Joyce taught English in a Berlitz school and where he started writing both the short stories collected as *Dubliners* (1914) and an early version (partially published as *Stephen Hero* in 1944) of *A Portrait of the Artist as a Young Man*. *Dubliners* sketches aspects of life in Dublin as Joyce knew it, which means that the parochiality, piety, and repressive conventions of Irish life are shown stifling artistic and psychological development. Whether it be the young boy who arrives too late at the fair in *Araby*, the poor-aunt laundress of *Clay*, or the frustrated writer Gabriel Conroy of *The Dead*, characters in *Dubliners* dream of a better life against a dismal and impoverishing background whose cumulative effect is one of despair. The style of *Dubliners* is more realistic than Joyce's later fiction, but he is already employing a structure of symbolic meanings and revelatory moments called "epiphanies." The all-blanketing white snow at the end of *The Dead* suggests the chill uniformity of death and Gabriel Conroy's alienation from (or, on another level, unity with) the rest of his world. It is Gabriel who observes the scene and whose suddenly expanded vision of the whole universe being swallowed up in oblivion constitutes an epiphany, a moment when everything fuses and makes sense in a larger spiritual perspective.

A Portrait of the Artist as a Young Man is based on Joyce's life until 1902, but the novel is clearly not a conventional autobiography and the reader recognizes in the first pages a radical experiment in fictional language. From the child's vocabulary and fragmented echoing of his parents' baby talk ("nicens little boy," "baby tuckoo") to the mature rhetoric of the end ("Old father, old artificer, stand me now and ever in good stead"), everything in *Portrait* is introduced sequentially and shaped to make the most powerful cumulative impact. Even Stephen's first naive thoughts prepare for themes developed later on: the importance of sense impressions, from the clammy bed to his mother's smell; the political symbolism of Dante's green and maroon hairbrushes; the bird imagery and threat of punishment on high in Dante's reproach; and the small boy's habit of thinking over things and rephrasing them in poetic language. Events that stand out in the young boy's mind, such as the humiliation of receiving an unfair spanking in school, are described with their full impact because they are not simply first-person (subjective) or third-person (objective) accounts but an imaginative combination of the two. An outside observer with access to all Stephen's feelings follows the course of events. *Portrait*, like *Dubliners*, is still in the tradition of naturalist narrative and specifically of the *Künstlerroman*, or artist-novel, which follows chronologically the career of its artist hero. Its sophisticated symbolism, use of epiphanies, and stress on dramatic dialogue, however, hint at the radical break with narrative tradition that Joyce was preparing in *Ulysses*.

Ulysses (1922) is one of the most celebrated instances of literary censorship. Its serial publication in the New York *Little Review* from 1918 to 1920 was stopped as obscene by the U.S. Post Office after a complaint from the New York Society for the Prevention of Vice. The novel was banned and all available copies were actually burned in England and America until a 1933 decision by Judge Woolsey in a U.S. district court lifted the ban in the United States. The problem was not new: Joyce's realistic descriptions of sensory experience from bedroom to bathroom, his playfully allusive use of language, and his antinationalist and antireligious attitudes had already offended many readers from *Dubliners* (which an Irish printer refused to print on the grounds that it was anti-Irish) to *Portrait* (which was refused as a "work of doubtful character even though it may be a classic"). While Joyce's descriptions have lost none of their pungency, it is hard to imagine a reader who would not be struck also by another side—by the "classical" density and enormous mythic scope of this complex, symbolic, and linguistically innovative novel. Openly referring to an ancient predecessor, the *Odyssey* of Homer ("Ulysses" is the Latin name for the hero Odysseus), *Ulysses* structures numerous episodes to suggest parallels with the Greek epic, and transforms the twenty-year Homeric journey home into the day-long wanderings through Dublin of an unheroic advertising man, Leopold Bloom, and a rebellious young teacher and writer from *Portrait*, Stephen Dedalus.

Bloom is in one sense a perfectly ordinary man, the "common man" of modern society. He comes to no great decisions (whereas Stephen decides to leave Ireland and dedicate himself to art), and his life will continue its uneventful and somewhat downtrodden way. Yet Bloom is the most fully developed character in the book, a man whose dimensions encompass the mythic overtones of the outcast (Ulysses or the Wandering Jew), the psychological tension of a father and husband cut off from family relationships, and (in bathroom, bedroom, and meat market) the most mundane domestic details. The ancient Ulysses was a man of many roles, and so is the modern Bloom. If the *Odyssey* has been described as one of the first voyages of Everyman, *Ulysses* shows Everyman in the twentieth century. According to T. S. Eliot, Joyce's paralleling of ancient myth and modern life is more than literary homage; it is "a way of controlling, of ordering, of giving a shape and significance to the immense panorama of futility and anarchy which is contemporary history."

There is no classical parallel, however, for the language of *Ulysses*, which has long been recognized as a paradigm of modernist style. Its quick shifts in points of view, changes of narrative voice, and blendings of the most exacting realism with hallucinatory scenes that combine memory and distorted current vision are the literary equivalent of cinematic montage. In addition, Joyce abandoned the regular syntax and logical sequences of traditional narrative for a style that tried to represent the flow of thought and emotion in a character's mind. A development of the "interior monologue," this stream of consciousness technique is far looser and freer in its fragmented, punning, freely associating representation of consciousness. Sometimes it is a sleepy jangle in which the relaxed mind lazily plays with sound associations: "Sinbad the Sailor and Tinbad the Tailor and Jinbad the Jailer and Whinbad the Whaler and Ninbad the Nailer and . . ." Sometimes it is more obscure, as in the introduction to a bar scene with its associative, fragmented vision and imitations of different sounds: "Bronze by gold heard the hoofirons, steelyringing Imperthnthn thnthnthn. Chips, picking chips off rocky thumbnail, chips. Horrid! And gold flushed more. A husky fifenote blew. Blew. Blue bloom in on the Gold pinnacled hair." In the famous ending to the novel, it combines passion and response in specific images called up from memory, as his wife, Molly, recalls her first yielding to Bloom: "O that awful deepdown torrent O and the sea the sea crimson sometimes like fire and the glorious sunsets and the figtrees in the Alameda gardens yes and all the queer little streets and pink and blue and yellow houses and the rosegardens and the jessamine and geraniums and cactuses . . . yes and then he asked me would I yes to say yes my mountain flower and first I put my arms around him yes and drew him down to me so he could feel my breasts all perfume yes and his heart was going like mad and yes I said yes I will Yes." The extraordinary thing about Joyce's stream of consciousness technique, as the perspicacious Judge Woolsey commented in his court decision, was that it represents the many layers of experience making up each individual's current consciousness: "Not only what is in the focus of each man's observation of the actual things about him, but also in a penumbral zone residua of past impressions, some recent and some drawn up by association from the domain of the subconscious." Taken to the extreme, it is so completely individualized that a reader who remains outside the personal code cannot break in; at its best, though, it can draw on echoes and clues already present in the text. The complicated inner reference in *Ulysses* provided a glimpse of unparalleled richness into human awareness and set a challenging example for narrative style after Joyce.

After the publication of *Ulysses*, Joyce spent the next seventeen years writing an even more complex work: *Finnegans Wake* (1939). Despite the title, which refers to a ballad in which the bricklayer Tim Finnegan is brought back to life at his wake when somebody spills whisky on him, the novel is the multivoiced, multidimensional dream of Humphrey Chimpden Earwicker: HCE, Here Comes Everybody, Haveth Childers Everywhere, Tristan, Humpty-Dumpty, and Allmen. HCE's dream includes his wife, Anna Earwicker, as Anna Livia Plurabelle, ALP, the voice of the river Liffey, or a suggestion of historical "holy wars," and together they constitute the originating pair of Adam and Eve. *Finnegans Wake* expands on the encyclopedic series of literary and cultural references underlying *Ulysses* and does so in language that has been even more radically broken apart and reassembled. Digressing exuberantly in all directions at once, with complex puns and hybrid words that mix languages, *Finnegans Wake* is—in spite of its cosmic symbolism—a game of language and reference by an artist "hoppy on akkant of his joyicity." Although it has not achieved the wide audience of *Portrait* or *Ulysses,* when Joyce died in Zurich in 1941 he considered it the culmination of his career as a writer.

The Dead is the last and by far the fullest story in *Dubliners,* and it recapitulates many of the volume's themes. In 1906, Joyce wrote to his publisher that the collection would be "a chapter of the moral history of my country," and he further explained that he had chosen Dublin because it was the "centre of paralysis" in Ireland. The city formed a background of blunted hopes and lost dreams: desperately poor, with large slums and many more people than jobs, it stagnated in political, religious, and cultural divisions that color the lives of characters in these stories. The book is arranged, Joyce explained, in an order that represents four aspects of life in the city: "childhood, adolescence, maturity and public life." Individual stories focus on one or a few characters, who may dream of a better life but are eventually frustrated by, or sink voluntarily back into, their shabby reality. Stories often end with a moment of special insight (an epiphany), visible to the reader but not always to the protagonist, that puts events in sharp and illuminating perspective.

Joyce's work draws heavily on real life, including his own; and several aspects of *The Dead* recall—and transmute—elements in his own life. As in other stories, the neighborhood setting is familiar from his youth. The real-life models for Miss Kate and Miss Julia were indeed music teachers (but they were married). Mr. Bartell D'Arcy evokes a contemporary tenor who performed under a similar name. The figure of Gabriel Conroy, who writes reviews for local journals, dislikes Irish nationalism, and prefers European culture, physically resembles photographs of Joyce—a lesser Joyce who might never have had the courage to leave home for Europe. The tale of Gretta's dead admirer, Michael Furey, echoes Nora Barnacle's similar experience. The sources of *Dubliners,* whether personal or social, are all inescapably real: so real, including coarse language and contemporary allusions, that publishers were unwilling to produce the volume for fear of libel or obscenity charges. An Irish publisher went so far as to print a censored version in 1909 but subsequently burned all the copies when he and Joyce had further disputes. In 1914, some nine years after its initial (later retracted) acceptance, *Dubliners* finally appeared.

The Dead is divided into three parts, chronicling the stages of the Misses Morkan's party and also the stages by which Gabriel Conroy moves from the rather pompous, insecure, and externally oriented figure of the beginning to a man who has been forced to reassess himself and human relationships at the end. The party is an annual dinner dance that takes place after the New Year, probably on January 6, the Catholic Feast of the Epiphany (which many have connected with Gabriel's personal epiphany at the end of the story). A jovial occasion, it brings together friends and acquaintances for an evening of music, dancing, sumptuous food, and a formal after-dinner speech that Gabriel delivers. The undercurrents are not always harmonious, however, for small anxieties and personal frictions crop up that both create a realistic picture and suggest tensions in contemporary Irish society: nationalism, religion, poverty, and class differences. Gabriel has a position to maintain, and he is determined to live up to his responsibilities: he is at once cultured speaker and intellectual, carver and master of ceremonies, and the man whom the Misses Morkan expect to take care of occasional problems like alcoholic guests. He is a complex character, both a writer of real imagination (or we would not have the ending scene) and a narcissistic figure who is so used to focusing on himself that he has drawn apart from other people.

Three times in the course of the story Gabriel's self-image is challenged, each time by a woman. Lily, the maidservant in the beginning scene, rebuffs his patronizing questions with a bitter comment about men; immediately, Gabriel worries about his mistake and whether his speech will likewise take the wrong tone for its audience—that is, be above their heads. In the second episode, Miss Ivors's attack on his ignorance of Irish culture shakes him again, for he interprets it as an attempt to make him look ridiculous. Finally, just as Gabriel is thoroughly aroused by watching his wife's graceful figure and hopes to recapture a long-lost intimacy, he finds that she is thinking of a long-dead suitor, Michael Furey. Michael died because, ill, he made her a farewell visit; and Gabriel realizes that his own colorless self will never rival the memory of Furey's passionate devotion. The jovial evening has lost its sparkle; once again, Gabriel looks back in frustration and unhappiness, and this time recognizes signs of death and delusion everywhere. By the end of *The Dead*, he feels his identity "fading out into a grey impalpable world," approaching—in his artistic imagination—a state in which both living and dead are one community, blanketed by the snow that falls throughout the universe in his final vision.

Harry Levin, *James Joyce: A Critical Introduction* (1941), is an excellent and readable general introduction. The standard and detailed biography, with illustrations, is Richard Ellmann, *James Joyce* (1982). Morris Beja, *James Joyce: A Literary Life* (1992), includes recent scholarship. Derek Attridge, ed., *The Cambridge Companion to James Joyce* (1990), and Mary T. Reynolds, ed., *James Joyce: A Collection of Critical Essays* (1993), treat various aspects of the work. Daniel R. Schwarz, ed., *The Dead* (1994), is a useful short book that includes the text and some contextual material, an account of *Dubliners*' history and criticism from the 1950s, and analyses by different authors using five modern critical perspectives. Diverse critical approaches are represented in Alan Roughley, *James Joyce and Critical Theory: An Introduction* (1991); Rosa M. Bollettieri Bosinelli and Harold F. Mosher, eds., *ReJoycing: New Readings of Dubliners* (1998), which contains two essays on *The Dead*; Suzette A. Henke's feminist study *James Joyce and the Politics of Desire* (1990); and the postcolonial perspectives of *Semicolonial Joyce*, edited by Derek Attridge and Marjory Howes (2000). John Wyse Jackson and Bernard McGinley, eds., *Joyce's Dubliners: An Illustrated Edition with Annotations* (1995), is a fascinating, copiously illustrated and documented edition that includes allusions to other works and a capsule essay after each story. David Pierce, *James Joyce's Ireland* (1992), includes contemporary photographs by Dan Harper and uses documents, photographs, and copious quotation to reconstruct Joyce's biography in historical context.

The Dead

Lily, the caretaker's daughter, was literally run off her feet. Hardly had she brought one gentleman into the little pantry behind the office on the ground floor and helped him off with his overcoat than the wheezy hall-door bell clanged again and she had to scamper along the bare hallway to let in another guest. It was well for her she had not to attend to the ladies also. But Miss Kate and Miss Julia had thought of that and had converted the bathroom upstairs into a ladies' dressing-room. Miss Kate and Miss Julia were there, gossiping and laughing and fussing, walking after each other to the head of the stairs, peering down over the banisters and calling down to Lily to ask her who had come.

It was always a great affair, the Misses Morkan's annual dance. Everybody who knew them came to it, members of the family, old friends of the family, the members of Julia's choir, any of Kate's pupils that were grown up enough and even some of Mary Jane's pupils too. Never once had it fallen flat. For years and years it had gone off in splendid style as long as anyone could remember; ever since Kate and Julia, after the death of their brother Pat, had left the house in Stoney Batter and taken Mary Jane, their only niece, to live with them in the dark gaunt house on Usher's Island,[1] the upper part of which they had rented from Mr. Fulham, the cornfactor on the ground floor. That was a good thirty years ago if it was a day. Mary Jane, who was then a little girl in short clothes, was now the main prop of the household for she had the organ[2] in Haddington Road. She had been through the Academy[3] and gave a pupils' concert every year in the upper room of the Antient Concert Rooms. Many of her pupils belonged to better-class families on the Kingstown and Dalkey line.[4] Old as they were, her aunts also did their share. Julia, though she was quite grey, was still the leading soprano in Adam and Eve's, and Kate, being too feeble to go about much, gave music lessons to beginners on the old square[5] piano in the back room. Lily, the caretaker's daughter, did housemaid's work for them. Though their life was modest they believed in eating well; the best of everything: diamond-bone sirloins, three-shilling tea and the best bottled stout.[6] But Lily seldom made a mistake in the orders so that she got on well with her three mistresses. They were fussy, that was all. But the only thing they would not stand was back answers.

Of course they had good reason to be fussy on such a night. And then it was long after ten o'clock and yet there was no sign of Gabriel and his wife. Besides they were dreadfully afraid that Freddy Malins might turn up screwed.[7] They would not wish for worlds that any of Mary Jane's pupils should see him under the influence; and when he was like that it was sometimes very hard to manage him. Freddy Malins always came late but they wondered what could be keeping Gabriel: and that was what brought them every two minutes to the banisters to ask Lily had Gabriel or Freddy come.

—O, Mr. Conroy, said Lily to Gabriel when she opened the door for him, Miss Kate and Miss Julia thought you were never coming. Good-night, Mrs. Conroy.

—I'll engage they did, said Gabriel, but they forgot that my wife here takes three mortal hours to dress herself.

He stood on the mat, scraping the snow from his goloshes, while Lily led his wife to the foot of the stairs and called out:

—Miss Kate, here's Mrs. Conroy.

Kate and Julia came toddling down the dark stairs at once. Both of them kissed Gabriel's wife, said she must be perished alive and asked was Gabriel with her.

—Here I am as right as the mail,[8] Aunt Kate! Go on up. I'll follow, called out Gabriel from the dark.

He continued scraping his feet vigorously while the three women went upstairs, laughing, to the ladies' dressing-room. A light fringe of snow lay like a cape on the shoulders of his overcoat and like toecaps on the toes of his goloshes; and, as the buttons of his overcoat slipped with a squeaking

---

1. Not an island, but an area in western Dublin on the south bank of the river Liffey. Stoney Batter is a street of small shops and a few houses in Dublin.   2. I.e., earned money by playing the organ at church.
3. The Royal Academy of Music.   4. Railway to a fashionable section of Dublin.   5. I.e., upright. *Adam and Eve's:* popular name (taken from a nearby inn) for a Dublin Catholic church.   6. Strong beer.
7. Drunk.   8. Reliable as mail delivery.

noise through the snow-stiffened frieze, a cold fragrant air from out-of-doors escaped from crevices and folds.

—Is it snowing again, Mr. Conroy? asked Lily.

She had preceded him into the pantry to help him off with his overcoat. Gabriel smiled at the three syllables she had given his surname and glanced at her. She was a slim, growing girl, pale in complexion and with hay-coloured hair. The gas in the pantry made her look still paler. Gabriel had known her when she was a child and used to sit on the lowest step nursing a rag doll.

—Yes, Lily, he answered, and I think we're in for a night of it.

He looked up at the pantry ceiling, which was shaking with the stamping and shuffling of feet on the floor above, listened for a moment to the piano and then glanced at the girl, who was folding his overcoat carefully at the end of a shelf.

—Tell me, Lily, he said in a friendly tone, do you still go to school?

—O no, sir, she answered. I'm done schooling this year and more.

—O, then, said Gabriel gaily, I suppose we'll be going to your wedding one of these fine days with your young man, eh?

The girl glanced back at him over her shoulder and said with great bitterness:

—The men that is now is only all palaver[9] and what they can get out of you.

Gabriel coloured as if he felt he had made a mistake and, without looking at her, kicked off his goloshes and flicked actively with his muffler at his patent-leather shoes.

He was a stout tallish young man. The high colour of his cheeks pushed upwards even to his forehead where it scattered itself in a few formless patches of pale red; and on his hairless face there scintillated restlessly the polished lenses and the bright gilt rims of the glasses which screened his delicate and restless eyes. His glossy black hair was parted in the middle and brushed in a long curve behind his ears where it curled slightly beneath the groove left by his hat.

When he had flicked lustre into his shoes he stood up and pulled his waistcoat down more tightly on his plump body. Then he took a coin rapidly from his pocket.

—O Lily, he said, thrusting it into her hands, it's Christmastime, isn't it? Just . . . here's a little. . . .

He walked rapidly towards the door.

—O no, sir! cried the girl, following him. Really, sir, I wouldn't take it.

—Christmas-time! Christmas-time! said Gabriel, almost trotting to the stairs and waving his hand to her in deprecation.

The girl, seeing that he had gained the stairs, called out after him:

—Well, thank you, sir.

He waited outside the drawing-room door until the waltz should finish, listening to the skirts that swept against it and to the shuffling of feet. He was still discomposed by the girl's bitter and sudden retort. It had cast a gloom over him which he tried to dispel by arranging his cuffs and the bows of his tie. Then he took from his waistcoat pocket a little paper and glanced

9. Fancy talk.

at the headings he had made for his speech. He was undecided about the lines from Robert Browning[1] for he feared they would be above the heads of his hearers. Some quotation that they could recognise from Shakespeare or from the Melodies[2] would be better. The indelicate clacking of the men's heels and the shuffling of their soles reminded him that their grade of culture differed from his. He would only make himself ridiculous by quoting poetry to them which they could not understand. They would think that he was airing his superior education. He would fail with them just as he had failed with the girl in the pantry. He had taken up a wrong tone. His whole speech was a mistake from first to last, an utter failure.

Just then his aunts and his wife came out of the ladies' dressing-room. His aunts were two small plainly dressed old women. Aunt Julia was an inch or so the taller. Her hair, drawn low over the tops of her ears, was grey; and grey also, with darker shadows, was her large flaccid face. Though she was stout in build and stood erect her slow eyes and parted lips gave her the appearance of a woman who did not know where she was or where she was going. Aunt Kate was more vivacious. Her face, healthier than her sister's, was all puckers and creases, like a shrivelled red apple, and her hair, braided in the same old-fashioned way, had not lost its ripe nut colour.

They both kissed Gabriel frankly. He was their favourite nephew, the son of their dead elder sister, Ellen, who had married T. J. Conroy of the Port and Docks.[3]

—Gretta tells me you're not going to take a cab back to Monkstown to-night, Gabriel, said Aunt Kate.

—No, said Gabriel, turning to his wife, we had quite enough of that last year, hadn't we? Don't you remember, Aunt Kate, what a cold Gretta got out of it? Cab windows rattling all the way, and the east wind blowing in after we passed Merrion.[4] Very jolly it was. Gretta caught a dreadful cold.

Aunt Kate frowned severely and nodded her head at every word.

—Quite right, Gabriel, quite right, she said. You can't be too careful.

—But as for Gretta there, said Gabriel, she'd walk home in the snow if she were let.

Mrs. Conroy laughed.

—Don't mind him, Aunt Kate, she said. He's really an awful bother, what with green shades for Tom's eyes at night and making him do the dumb-bells, and forcing Eva to eat the stirabout.[5] The poor child! And she simply hates the sight of it! . . . O, but you'll never guess what he makes me wear now!

She broke out into a peal of laughter and glanced at her husband, whose admiring and happy eyes had been wandering from her dress to her face and hair. The two aunts laughed heartily too, for Gabriel's solicitude was a standing joke with them.

—Goloshes! said Mrs. Conroy. That's the latest. Whenever it's wet under-foot I must put on my goloshes. To-night even he wanted me to put them on, but I wouldn't. The next thing he'll buy me will be a diving suit.

Gabriel laughed nervously and patted his tie reassuringly while Aunt Kate nearly doubled herself, so heartily did she enjoy the joke. The smile soon

---

1. English poet (1812–1889), who had a contemporary reputation for obscurity.   2. Thomas Moore's (1779–1852) immensely popular *Irish Melodies,* a collection of poems with many set to old Irish melodies.   3. The Dublin Port and Docks Board, which regulated customs and shipping.   4. A village on Dublin Bay.   5. Porridge.

faded from Aunt Julia's face and her mirthless eyes were directed towards her nephew's face. After a pause she asked:

—And what are goloshes, Gabriel?

—Goloshes, Julia! exclaimed her sister. Goodness me, don't you know what goloshes are? You wear them over your . . . over your boots, Gretta, isn't it?

—Yes, said Mrs. Conroy. Guttapercha[6] things. We both have a pair now. Gabriel says everyone wears them on the continent.

—O, on the continent, murmured Aunt Julia, nodding her head slowly.

Gabriel knitted his brows and said, as if he were slightly angered:

—It's nothing very wonderful but Gretta thinks it very funny because she says the word reminds her of Christy Minstrels.[7]

—But tell me, Gabriel, said Aunt Kate, with brisk tact. Of course, you've seen about the room. Gretta was saying . . .

—O, the room is all right, replied Gabriel. I've taken one in the Gresham.

—To be sure, said Aunt Kate, by far the best thing to do. And the children, Gretta, you're not anxious about them?

—O, for one night, said Mrs. Conroy. Besides, Bessie will look after them.

—To be sure, said Aunt Kate again. What a comfort it is to have a girl like that, one you can depend on! There's that Lily, I'm sure I don't know what has come over her lately. She's not the girl she was at all.

Gabriel was about to ask his aunt some questions on this point but she broke off suddenly to gaze after her sister who had wandered down the stairs and was craning her neck over the banisters.

—Now, I ask you, she said, almost testily, where is Julia going? Julia! Julia! Where are you going?

Julia, who had gone halfway down one flight, came back and announced blandly:

—Here's Freddy.

At the same moment a clapping of hands and a final flourish of the pianist told that the waltz had ended. The drawing-room door was opened from within and some couples came out. Aunt Kate drew Gabriel aside hurriedly and whispered into his ear:

—Slip down, Gabriel, like a good fellow and see if he's all right, and don't let him up if he's screwed. I'm sure he's screwed. I'm sure he is.

Gabriel went to the stairs and listened over the banisters. He could hear two persons talking in the pantry. Then he recognised Freddy Malins' laugh. He went down the stairs noisily.

—It's such a relief, said Aunt Kate to Mrs. Conroy, that Gabriel is here. I always feel easier in my mind when he's here. . . . Julia, there's Miss Daly and Miss Power will take some refreshment. Thanks for your beautiful waltz, Miss Daly. It made lovely time.

A tall wizen-faced man, with a stiff grizzled moustache and swarthy skin, who was passing out with his partner said:

—And may we have some refreshment, too, Miss Morkan?

—Julia, said Aunt Kate summarily, and here's Mr. Browne and Miss Furlong. Take them in, Julia, with Miss Daly and Miss Power.

—I'm the man for the ladies, said Mr. Browne, pursing his lips until his

---

6. A rubberlike substance.   7. *Goloshes* sounds like "golly shoes," which reminds Gretta of the Christy Minstrels, a popular blackface minstrel show.

moustache bristled and smiling in all his wrinkles. You know, Miss Morkan, the reason they are so fond of me is—

He did not finish his sentence, but, seeing that Aunt Kate was out of earshot, at once led the three young ladies into the back room. The middle of the room was occupied by two square tables placed end to end, and on these Aunt Julia and the caretaker were straightening and smoothing a large cloth. On the sideboard were arrayed dishes and plates, and glasses and bundles of knives and forks and spoons. The top of the closed square piano served also as a sideboard for viands and sweets. At a smaller sideboard in one corner two young men were standing, drinking hop-bitters.[8]

Mr. Browne led his charges thither and invited them all, in jest, to some ladies' punch, hot, strong and sweet. As they said they never took anything strong he opened three bottles of lemonade for them. Then he asked one of the young men to move aside, and, taking hold of the decanter, filled out for himself a goodly measure of whisky. The young men eyed him respectfully while he took a trial sip.

—God help me, he said, smiling, it's the doctor's orders.

His wizened face broke into a broader smile, and the three young ladies laughed in musical echo to his pleasantry, swaying their bodies to and fro, with nervous jerks of their shoulders. The boldest said:

—O, now, Mr. Browne, I'm sure the doctor never ordered anything of the kind.

Mr. Browne took another sip of his whiskey and said, with sidling mimicry:

—Well, you see, I'm like the famous Mrs. Cassidy, who is reported to have said: *Now, Mary Grimes, if I don't take it, make me take it, for I feel I want it.*

His hot face had leaned forward a little too confidentially and he had assumed a very low Dublin accent so that the young ladies, with one instinct, received his speech in silence. Miss Furlong, who was one of Mary Jane's pupils, asked Miss Daly what was the name of the pretty waltz she had played; and Mr. Browne, seeing that he was ignored, turned promptly to the two young men who were more appreciative.

A red-faced young woman, dressed in pansy,[9] came into the room, excitedly clapping her hands and crying:

—Quadrilles![1] Quadrilles!

Close on her heels came Aunt Kate, crying:

—Two gentlemen and three ladies, Mary Jane!

—O, here's Mr. Bergin and Mr. Kerrigan, said Mary Jane. Mr. Kerrigan, will you take Miss Power? Miss Furlong, may I get you a partner, Mr. Bergin. O, that'll just do now.

—Three ladies, Mary Jane, said Aunt Kate.

The two young gentlemen asked the ladies if they might have the pleasure, and Mary Jane turned to Miss Daly.

—O, Miss Daly, you're really awfully good, after playing for the last two dances, but really we're so short of ladies to-night.

—I don't mind in the least, Miss Morkan.

—But I've a nice partner for you, Mr. Bartell D'Arcy, the tenor. I'll get him to sing later on. All Dublin is raving about him.

—Lovely voice, lovely voice! said Aunt Kate.

---

8. Unfermented beer.   9. Violet.   1. An intricate square dance for four couples.

As the piano had twice begun the prelude to the first figure Mary Jane led her recruits quickly from the room. They had hardly gone when Aunt Julia wandered slowly into the room, looking behind her at something.

—What is the matter, Julia? asked Aunt Kate anxiously. Who is it?

Julia, who was carrying in a column of table-napkins turned to her sister and said, simply, as if the question had surprised her:

—It's only Freddy, Kate, and Gabriel with him.

In fact right behind her Gabriel could be seen piloting Freddy Malins across the landing. The latter, a young man of forty, was of Gabriel's size and build, with very round shoulders. His face was fleshy and pallid, touched with colour only at the thick hanging lobes of his ears and at the wide wings of his nose. He had coarse features, a blunt nose, a convex and receding brow, tumid and protruded lips. His heavy-lidded eyes and the disorder of his scanty hair made him look sleepy. He was laughing heartily in a high key at a story which he had been telling Gabriel on the stairs and at the same time rubbing the knuckles of his left fist backwards and forwards into his left eye.

—Good-evening, Freddy, said Aunt Julia.

Freddy Malins bade the Misses Morkan good-evening in what seemed an offhand fashion by reason of the habitual catch in his voice and then, seeing that Mr. Browne was grinning at him from the sideboard, crossed the room on rather shaky legs and began to repeat in an undertone the story he had just told to Gabriel.

—He's not so bad, is he? said Aunt Kate to Gabriel.

Gabriel's brows were dark but he raised them quickly and answered:

—O no, hardly noticeable.

—Now, isn't he a terrible fellow! she said. And his poor mother made him take the pledge on New Year's Eve. But come on, Gabriel, into the drawing-room.

Before leaving the room with Gabriel she signalled to Mr. Browne by frowning and shaking her forefinger in warning to and fro. Mr. Browne nodded in answer and, when she had gone, said to Freddy Malins:

—Now, then, Teddy, I'm going to fill you out a good glass of lemonade just to buck you up.

Freddy Malins, who was nearing the climax of his story, waved the offer aside impatiently but Mr. Browne, having first called Freddy Malins' attention to a disarray in his dress,[2] filled out and handed him a full glass of lemonade. Freddy Malins' left hand accepted the glass mechanically, his right hand being engaged in the mechanical readjustment of his dress. Mr. Browne, whose face was once more wrinkling with mirth, poured out for himself a glass of whisky while Freddy Malins exploded, before he had well reached the climax of his story, in a kink of high-pitched bronchitic laughter and, setting down his untasted and overflowing glass, began to rub the knuckles of his left fist backwards and forwards into his left eye, repeating words of his last phrase as well as his fit of laughter would allow him.

Gabriel could not listen while Mary Jane was playing her Academy piece, full of runs and difficult passages, to the hushed drawing-room. He liked

2. That his fly was open.

music but the piece she was playing had no melody for him and he doubted whether it had any melody for the other listeners, though they had begged Mary Jane to play something. Four young men, who had come from the refreshment-room to stand in the doorway at the sound of the piano, had gone away quietly in couples after a few minutes. The only persons who seemed to follow the music were Mary Jane herself, her hands racing along the key-board or lifted from it at the pauses like those of a priestess in momentary imprecation, and Aunt Kate standing at her elbow to turn the page.

Gabriel's eyes, irritated by the floor, which glittered with beeswax under the heavy chandelier, wandered to the wall above the piano. A picture of the balcony scene in *Romeo and Juliet* hung there and beside it was a picture of the two murdered princes[3] in the Tower which Aunt Julia had worked in red, blue and brown wools when she was a girl. Probably in the school they had gone to as girls that kind of work had been taught, for one year his mother had worked for him as a birthday present a waistcoat of purple tabinet,[4] with little foxes' heads upon it, lined with brown satin and having round mulberry buttons. It was strange that his mother had had no musical talent though Aunt Kate used to call her the brains carrier of the Morkan family. Both she and Julia had always seemed a little proud of their serious and matronly sister. Her photograph stood before the pierglass.[5] She held an open book on her knees and was pointing out something in it to Constantine who, dressed in a man-o'-war suit,[6] lay at her feet. It was she who had chosen the names for her sons for she was very sensible of the dignity of family life. Thanks to her, Constantine was now senior curate in Balbriggan and, thanks to her, Gabriel himself had taken his degree in the Royal University. A shadow passed over his face as he remembered her sullen opposition to his marriage. Some slighting phrases she had used still rankled in his memory; she had once spoken of Gretta as being country cute[7] and that was not true of Gretta at all. It was Gretta who had nursed her during all her last long illness in their house at Monkstown.

He knew that Mary Jane must be near the end of her piece for she was playing again the opening melody with runs of scales after every bar and while he waited for the end the resentment died down in his heart. The piece ended with a trill of octaves in the treble and a final deep octave in the bass. Great applause greeted Mary Jane as, blushing and rolling up her music nervously, she escaped from the room. The most vigorous clapping came from the four young men in the doorway who had gone away to the refreshment-room at the beginning of the piece but had come back when the piano had stopped.

Lancers were arranged. Gabriel found himself partnered with Miss Ivors. She was a frank-mannered talkative young lady, with a freckled face and prominent brown eyes. She did not wear a low-cut bodice and the large brooch which was fixed in the front of her collar bore on it an Irish device.

When they had taken their places she said abruptly:

---

3. According to Shakespeare's *Richard III*, the young heirs to the British throne were murdered in the Tower of London by order of their uncle, King Richard III. *Balcony scene:* Shakespeare's *Romeo and Juliet* 2.2. 4. A damasklike fabric. 5. A large mirror. 6. A sailor suit. 7. Unintelligent (not acute).

—I have a crow to pluck[8] with you.

—With me? said Gabriel.

She nodded her head gravely.

—What is it? asked Gabriel, smiling at her solemn manner.

—Who is G. C.? answered Miss Ivors, turning her eyes upon him.

Gabriel coloured and was about to knit his brows, as if he did not understand, when she said bluntly:

—O, innocent Amy! I have found out that you write for *The Daily Express*.[9] Now, aren't you ashamed of yourself?

—Why should I be ashamed of myself? asked Gabriel, blinking his eyes and trying to smile.

—Well, I'm ashamed of you, said Miss Ivors frankly. To say you'd write for a rag like that. I didn't think you were a West Briton.[1]

A look of perplexity appeared on Gabriel's face. It was true that he wrote a literary column every Wednesday in *The Daily Express*, for which he was paid fifteen shillings. But that did not make him a West Briton surely. The books he received for review were almost more welcome than the paltry cheque. He loved to feel the covers and turn over the pages of newly printed books. Nearly every day when his teaching in the college was ended he used to wander down the quays to the second-hand booksellers, to Hickey's on Bachelor's Walk, to Webb's or Massey's on Aston's Quay, or to O'Clohissey's in the by-street. He did not know how to meet her charge. He wanted to say that literature was above politics. But they were friends of many years' standing and their careers had been parallel, first at the University and then as teachers: he could not risk a grandiose phrase with her. He continued blinking his eyes and trying to smile and murmured lamely that he saw nothing political in writing reviews of books.

When their turn to cross[2] had come he was still perplexed and inattentive. Miss Ivors promptly took his hand in a warm grasp and said in a soft friendly tone:

—Of course, I was only joking. Come, we cross now.

When they were together again she spoke of the University question,[3] and Gabriel felt more at ease. A friend of hers had shown her his review of Browning's poems. That was how she had found out the secret: but she liked the review immensely. Then she said suddenly:

—O, Mr. Conroy, will you come for an excursion to the Aran Isles[4] this summer? We're going to stay there a whole month. It will be splendid out in the Atlantic. You ought to come. Mr. Clancy is coming, and Mr. Kilkelly and Kathleen Kearney. It would be splendid for Gretta too if she'd come. She's from Connacht,[5] isn't she?

—Her people are, said Gabriel shortly.

—But you will come, won't you? said Miss Ivors, laying her warm hand eagerly on his arm.

—The fact is, said Gabriel, I have already arranged to go—

—Go where? asked Miss Ivors.

8. A bone to pick; an argument.   9. Conservative Dublin newspaper opposed to Irish independence.
1. An Irishman who supports union with Britain (an insult).   2. A step in the square dance.   3. Controversy over the establishment of Irish Catholic universities to rival the dominant Protestant tradition of Oxford and Cambridge in England, and Trinity College in Dublin.   4. Off the west coast of Ireland, idealized by the nationalists as an example of unspoiled Irish culture and language.   5. The westernmost province of Ireland.

—Well, you know, every year I go for a cycling tour with some fellows and so—

—But where? asked Miss Ivors.

—Well, we usually go to France or Belgium or perhaps Germany, said Gabriel awkwardly.

—And why do you go to France and Belgium, said Miss Ivors, instead of visiting your own land?

—Well, said Gabriel, it's partly to keep in touch with the languages and partly for a change.

—And haven't you your own language to keep in touch with—Irish? asked Miss Ivors.

—Well, said Gabriel, if it comes to that, you know, Irish is not my language.

Their neighbours had turned to listen to the cross-examination. Gabriel glanced right and left nervously and tried to keep his good humour under the ordeal which was making a blush invade his forehead.

—And haven't you your own land to visit, continued Miss Ivors, that you know nothing of, your own people, and your own country?

—O, to tell you the truth, retorted Gabriel suddenly, I'm sick of my own country, sick of it!

—Why? asked Miss Ivors.

Gabriel did not answer for his retort had heated him.

—Why? repeated Miss Ivors.

They had to go visiting together[6] and, as he had not answered her, Miss Ivors said warmly:

—Of course, you've no answer.

Gabriel tried to cover his agitation by taking part in the dance with great energy. He avoided her eyes for he had seen a sour expression on her face. But when they met in the long chain[7] he was surprised to feel his hand firmly pressed. She looked at him from under her brows for a moment quizzically until he smiled. Then, just as the chain was about to start again, she stood on tiptoe and whispered into his ear:

—West Briton!

When the lancers were over Gabriel went away to a remote corner of the room where Freddy Malins' mother was sitting. She was a stout feeble old woman with white hair. Her voice had a catch in it like her son's and she stuttered slightly. She had been told that Freddy had come and that he was nearly all right. Gabriel asked her whether she had had a good crossing. She lived with her married daughter in Glasgow and came to Dublin on a visit once a year. She answered placidly that she had had a beautiful crossing and that the captain had been most attentive to her. She spoke also of the beautiful house her daughter kept in Glasgow, and of all the nice friends they had there. While her tongue rambled on Gabriel tried to banish from his mind all memory of the unpleasant incident with Miss Ivors. Of course the girl or woman, or whatever she was, was an enthusiast but there was a time for all things. Perhaps he ought not to have answered her like that. But she had no right to call him a West Briton before people, even in joke. She had tried to make him ridiculous before people, heckling him and staring at him with her rabbit's eyes.

6. A square dance step.   7. Another square dance step.

He saw his wife making her way towards him through the waltzing couples. When she reached him she said into his ear:

—Gabriel, Aunt Kate wants to know won't you carve the goose as usual. Miss Daly will carve the ham and I'll do the pudding.

—All right, said Gabriel.

—She's sending in the younger ones first as soon as this waltz is over so that we'll have the table to ourselves.

—Were you dancing? asked Gabriel.

—Of course I was. Didn't you see me? What words had you with Molly Ivors?

—No words. Why? Did she say so?

—Something like that. I'm trying to get that Mr. D'Arcy to sing. He's full of conceit, I think.

—There were no words, said Gabriel moodily, only she wanted me to go for a trip to the west of Ireland and I said I wouldn't.

His wife clasped her hands excitedly and gave a little jump.

—O, do go, Gabriel, she cried. I'd love to see Galway again.

—You can go if you like, said Gabriel coldly.

She looked at him for a moment, then turned to Mrs. Malins and said:

—There's a nice husband for you, Mrs. Malins.

While she was threading her way back across the room Mrs. Malins, without adverting to the interruption, went on to tell Gabriel what beautiful places there were in Scotland and beautiful scenery. Her son-in-law brought them every year to the lakes and they used to go fishing. Her son-in-law was a splendid fisher. One day he caught a fish, a beautiful big big fish, and the man in the hotel boiled it for their dinner.

Gabriel hardly heard what she said. Now that supper was coming near he began to think again about his speech and about the quotation. When he saw Freddy Malins coming across the room to visit his mother Gabriel left the chair free for him and retired into the embrasure of the window. The room had already cleared and from the back room came the clatter of plates and knives. Those who still remained in the drawing-room seemed tired of dancing and were conversing quietly in little groups. Gabriel's warm trembling fingers tapped the cold pane of the window. How cool it must be outside! How pleasant it would be to walk out alone, first along by the river and then through the park! The snow would be lying on the branches of the trees and forming a bright cap on the top of the Wellington Monument.[8] How much more pleasant it would be there than at the supper-table!

He ran over the headings of his speech: Irish hospitality, sad memories, the Three Graces, Paris,[9] the quotation from Browning. He repeated to himself a phrase he had written in his review: *One feels that one is listening to a thought-tormented music*. Miss Ivors had praised the review. Was she sincere? Had she really any life of her own behind all her propagandism? There had never been any ill-feeling between them until that night. It unnerved him to think that she would be at the supper-table, looking up at him while he spoke with her critical quizzing eyes. Perhaps she would not be sorry to see him fail in his speech. An idea came into his mind and gave him courage. He would say, alluding to Aunt Kate and Aunt Julia: *Ladies*

8. A tall obelisk in Phoenix Park, celebrating the duke of Wellington (1769–1852). 9. The Trojan prince of Homer's *Iliad*. *Three Graces:* daughters of Zeus and Eurynome in Greek mythology; they embodied (and bestowed) charm.

*and Gentlemen, the generation which is now on the wane among us may have
had its faults but for my part I think it had certain qualities of hospitality, of
humour, of humanity, which the new and very serious and hypereducated
generation that is growing up around us seems to me to lack.* Very good: that
was one for Miss Ivors. What did he care that his aunts were only two ignorant old women?

A murmur in the room attracted his attention. Mr. Browne was advancing
from the door, gallantly escorting Aunt Julia, who leaned upon his arm,
smiling and hanging her head. An irregular musketry of applause escorted
her also as far as the piano and then, as Mary Jane seated herself on the
stool, and Aunt Julia, no longer smiling, half turned so as to pitch her voice
fairly into the room, gradually ceased. Gabriel recognized the prelude. It was
that of an old song of Aunt Julia's—*Arrayed for the Bridal.*[1] Her voice, strong
and clear in tone, attacked with great spirit the runs which embellish the air
and though she sang very rapidly she did not miss even the smallest of the
grace notes. To follow the voice, without looking at the singer's face, was to
feel and share the excitement of swift and secure flight. Gabriel applauded
loudly with all the others at the close of the song and loud applause was
borne in from the invisible supper-table. It sounded so genuine that a little
colour struggled into Aunt Julia's face as she bent to replace in the music-
stand the old leather-bound song-book that had her initials on the cover.
Freddy Malins, who had listened with his head perched sideways to hear her
better, was still applauding when everyone else had ceased and talking ani-
matedly to his mother who nodded her head gravely and slowly in acquiescence. At last, when he could clap no more, he stood up suddenly and hurried
across the room to Aunt Julia whose hand he seized and held in both his
hands, shaking it when words failed him or the catch in his voice proved too
much for him.

—I was just telling my mother, he said, I never heard you sing so well,
never. No, I never heard your voice so good as it is to-night. Now! Would
you believe that now? That's the truth. Upon my word and honour that's the
truth. I never heard your voice sound so fresh and so . . . so clear and fresh,
never.

Aunt Julia smiled broadly and murmured something about compliments
as she released her hand from his grasp. Mr. Browne extended his open hand
towards her and said to those who were near him in the manner of a show-
man introducing a prodigy to an audience:

—Miss Julia Morkan, my latest discovery!

He was laughing very heartily at this himself when Freddy Malins turned
to him and said:

—Well, Browne, if you're serious you might make a worse discovery. All I
can say is I never heard her sing half so well as long as I am coming here.
And that's the honest truth.

—Neither did I, said Mr. Browne. I think her voice has greatly improved.

Aunt Julia shrugged her shoulders and said with meek pride:

—Thirty years ago I hadn't a bad voice as voices go.

—I often told Julia, said Aunt Kate emphatically, that she was simply
thrown away in that choir. But she never would be said by me.

---

1. An English lyric by George Linley, drawn from the first act of Vincenzo Bellini's 1835 opera *I Puritani*
(The Puritans).

She turned as if to appeal to the good sense of the others against a refractory child while Aunt Julia gazed in front of her, a vague smile of reminiscence playing on her face.

—No, continued Aunt Kate, she wouldn't be said or led by anyone, slaving there in that choir night and day, night and day. Six o'clock on Christmas morning! And all for what?

—Well, isn't it for the honour of God, Aunt Kate? asked Mary Jane, twisting round on the piano-stool and smiling.

Aunt Kate turned fiercely on her niece and said:

—I know all about the honour of God, Mary Jane, but I think it's not at all honourable for the pope to turn out the women out of the choirs that have slaved there all their lives and put little whipper-snappers of boys over their heads.[2] I suppose it is for the good of the Church if the pope does it. But it's not just, Mary Jane, and it's not right.

She had worked herself into a passion and would have continued in defence of her sister for it was a sore subject with her but Mary Jane, seeing that all the dancers had come back, intervened pacifically:

—Now, Aunt Kate, you're giving scandal to Mr. Browne who is of the other persuasion.

Aunt Kate turned to Mr. Browne, who was grinning at this allusion to his religion, and said hastily:

—O, I don't question the pope's being right. I'm only a stupid old woman and I wouldn't presume to do such a thing. But there's such a thing as common everyday politeness and gratitude. And if I were in Julia's place I'd tell that Father Healy straight up to his face . . .

—And besides, Aunt Kate, said Mary Jane, we really are all hungry and when we are hungry we are all very quarrelsome.

—And when we are thirsty we are also quarrelsome, added Mr. Browne.

—So that we had better go to supper, said Mary Jane, and finish the discussion afterwards.

On the landing outside the drawing-room Gabriel found his wife and Mary Jane trying to persuade Miss Ivors to stay for supper. But Miss Ivors, who had put on her hat and was buttoning her cloak, would not stay. She did not feel in the least hungry and she had already overstayed her time.

—But only for ten minutes, Molly, said Mrs. Conroy. That won't delay you.

—To take a pick itself, said Mary Jane, after all your dancing.

—I really couldn't, said Miss Ivors.

—I am afraid you didn't enjoy yourself at all, said Mary Jane hopelessly.

—Ever so much, I assure you, said Miss Ivors, but you really must let me run off now.

—But how can you get home? asked Mrs. Conroy.

—O, it's only two steps up the quay.

Gabriel hesitated a moment and said:

—If you will allow me, Miss Ivors, I'll see you home if you really are obliged to go.

But Miss Ivors broke away from them.

—I won't hear of it, she cried. For goodness sake go in to your suppers and don't mind me. I'm quite well able to take care of myself.

2. In 1903, Pope Pius X decreed that all church singers be male.

—Well, you're the comical girl, Molly, said Mrs. Conroy frankly.

—*Beannacht libh*,[3] cried Miss Ivors, with a laugh, as she ran down the staircase.

Mary Jane gazed after her, a moody puzzled expression on her face, while Mrs. Conroy leaned over the banisters to listen for the hall-door. Gabriel asked himself was he the cause of her abrupt departure. But she did not seem to be in ill humour: she had gone away laughing. He stared blankly down the staircase.

At that moment Aunt Kate came toddling out of the supper-room, almost wringing her hands in despair.

—Where is Gabriel? she cried. Where on earth is Gabriel? There's everyone waiting in there, stage to let, and nobody to carve the goose!

—Here I am, Aunt Kate! cried Gabriel, with sudden animation, ready to carve a flock of geese, if necessary.

A fat brown goose lay at one end of the table and at the other end, on a bed of creased paper strewn with sprigs of parsley, lay a great ham, stripped of its outer skin and peppered over with crust crumbs, a neat paper frill round its shin and beside this was a round of spiced beef. Between these rival ends ran parallel lines of side-dishes: two little minsters[4] of jelly, red and yellow; a shallow dish full of blocks of blancmange and red jam, a large green leaf-shaped dish with a stalk-shaped handle, on which lay bunches of purple raisins and peeled almonds, a companion dish on which lay a solid rectangle of Smyrna figs, a dish of custard topped with grated nutmeg, a small bowl full of chocolates and sweets wrapped in gold and silver papers and a glass vase in which stood some tall celery stalks. In the center of the table there stood, as sentries to a fruit-stand which upheld a pyramid of oranges and American apples, two squat old-fashioned decanters of cut glass, one containing port and the other dark sherry. On the closed square piano a pudding in a huge yellow dish lay in waiting and behind it were three squads of bottles of stout and ale and minerals,[5] drawn up according to the colours of their uniforms, the first two black, with brown and red labels, the third and smallest squad white, with transverse green sashes.

Gabriel took his seat boldly at the head of the table and, having looked to the edge of the carver, plunged his fork firmly into the goose. He felt quite at ease now for he was an expert carver and liked nothing better than to find himself at the head of a well-laden table.

—Miss Furlong, what shall I send you? he asked. A wing or a slice of the breast?

—Just a small slice of the breast.

—Miss Higgins, what for you?

—O, anything at all, Mr. Conroy.

While Gabriel and Miss Daly exchanged plates of goose and plates of ham and spiced beef Lily went from guest to guest with a dish of hot floury potatoes wrapped in a white napkin. This was Mary Jane's idea and she had also suggested apple sauce for the goose but Aunt Kate had said that plain roast goose without apple sauce had always been good enough for her and she hoped she might never eat worse. Mary Jane waited on her pupils and saw

---

3. Farewell; blessings on you (Irish).   **4.** Confectioneries shaped to look like cathedrals.   **5.** Carbonated drinks.

that they got the best slices and Aunt Kate and Aunt Julia opened and carried across from the piano bottles of stout and ale for the gentlemen and bottles of minerals for the ladies. There was a great deal of confusion and laughter and noise, the noise of orders and counter-orders, of knives and forks, of corks and glass-stoppers. Gabriel began to carve second helpings as soon as he had finished the first round without serving himself. Everyone protested loudly so that he compromised by taking a long draught of stout for he had found the carving hot work. Mary Jane settled down quietly to her supper but Aunt Kate and Aunt Julia were still toddling round the table, walking on each other's heels, getting in each other's way and giving each other unheeded orders. Mr. Browne begged of them to sit down and eat their suppers and so did Gabriel but they said there was time enough so that, at last, Freddy Malins stood up and, capturing Aunt Kate, plumped her down on her chair amid general laughter.

When everyone had been well served Gabriel said, smiling:

—Now, if anyone wants a little more of what vulgar people call stuffing let him or her speak.

A chorus of voices invited him to begin his own supper and Lily came forward with three potatoes which she had reserved for him.

—Very well, said Gabriel amiably, as he took another preparatory draught, kindly forget my existence, ladies and gentlemen, for a few minutes.

He sat to his supper and took no part in the conversation with which the table covered Lily's removal of the plates. The subject of talk was the opera company which was then at the Theatre Royal. Mr. Bartell D'Arcy, the tenor, a dark-complexioned young man with a smart moustache, praised very highly the leading contralto of the company but Miss Furlong thought she had a rather vulgar style of production. Freddy Malins said there was a negro chieftain[6] singing in the second part of the Gaiety pantomime who had one of the finest tenor voices he had ever heard.

—Have you heard him? he asked Mr. Bartell D'Arcy across the table.

—No, answered Mr. Bartell D'Arcy carelessly.

—Because, Freddy Malins explained, now I'd be curious to hear your opinion of him. I think he has a grand voice.

—It takes Teddy to find out the really good things, said Mr. Browne familiarly to the table.

—And why couldn't he have a voice too? asked Freddy Malins sharply. Is it because he's only a black?

Nobody answered this question and Mary Jane led the table back to the legitimate opera. One of her pupils had given her a pass for *Mignon*.[7] Of course it was very fine, she said, but it made her think of poor Georgina Burns. Mr. Browne could go back farther still, to the old Italian companies that used to come to Dublin—Tietjens, Ilma de Murzka, Campanini, the great Trebelli, Giuglini, Ravelli, Aramburo.[8] Those were the days, he said, when there was something like singing to be heard in Dublin. He told too of how the top gallery of the old Royal used to be packed night after night, of how one night an Italian tenor had sung five encores to *Let Me Like a Soldier Fall*,[9] introducing a high C every time, and of how the gallery boys would

6. Actually, a blackface performer.   7. Popular French opera (1866) by Ambroise Thomas.   8. Famous opera singers.   9. From William V. Wallace's romantic light opera *Maritana* (1845).

sometimes in their enthusiasm unyoke the horses from the carriage of some great *prima donna* and pull her themselves through the streets to her hotel. Why did they never play the grand old operas now, he asked, *Dinorah, Lucrezia Borgia*?[1] Because they could not get the voices to sing them: that was why.

—O, well, said Mr. Bartell D'Arcy, I presume there are as good singers today as there were then.

—Where are they? asked Mr. Browne defiantly.

—In London, Paris, Milan, said Mr. Bartell D'Arcy warmly. I suppose Caruso,[2] for example, is quite as good, if not better than any of the men you have mentioned.

—Maybe so, said Mr. Browne. But I may tell you I doubt it strongly.

—O, I'd give anything to hear Caruso sing, said Mary Jane.

—For me, said Aunt Kate, who had been picking a bone, there was only one tenor. To please me, I mean. But I suppose none of you ever heard of him.

—Who was he, Miss Morkan? asked Mr. Bartell D'Arcy politely.

—His name, said Aunt Kate, was Parkinson. I heard him when he was in his prime and I think he had then the purest tenor voice that was ever put into a man's throat.

—Strange, said Mr. Bartell D'Arcy. I never even heard of him.

—Yes, yes, Miss Morkan is right, said Mr. Browne. I remember hearing of old Parkinson but he's too far back for me.

—A beautiful pure sweet mellow English tenor, said Aunt Kate with enthusiasm.

Gabriel having finished, the huge pudding was transferred to the table. The clatter of forks and spoons began again. Gabriel's wife served out spoonfuls of the pudding and passed the plates down the table. Midway down they were held up by Mary Jane, who replenished them with raspberry or orange jelly or with blancmange and jam. The pudding was of Aunt Julia's making and she received praises for it from all quarters. She herself said that it was not quite brown enough.

—Well, I hope, Miss Morkan, said Mr. Browne, that I'm brown enough for you because, you know, I'm all brown.

All the gentlemen, except Gabriel, ate some of the pudding out of compliment to Aunt Julia. As Gabriel never ate sweets the celery had been left for him. Freddy Malins also took a stalk of celery and ate it with his pudding. He had been told that celery was a capital thing for the blood and he was just then under doctor's care. Mrs. Malins, who had been silent all through the supper, said that her son was going down to Mount Melleray[3] in a week or so. The table then spoke of Mount Melleray, how bracing the air was down there, how hospitable the monks were and how they never asked for a penny-piece from their guests.

—And do you mean to say, asked Mr. Browne incredulously, that a chap can go down there and put up there as if it were a hotel and live on the fat of the land and then come away without paying a farthing?

—O, most people give some donation to the monastery when they leave, said Mary Jane.

---

1. Operas by Giacomo Meyerbeer (1859) and Gaetano Donizetti (1833), respectively.   2. Enrico Caruso (1873–1921).   3. A Trappist abbey whose hospitality included the treatment of wealthy alcoholics.

—I wish we had an institution like that in our Church, said Mr. Browne candidly.

He was astonished to hear that the monks never spoke, got up at two in the morning and slept in their coffins.[4] He asked what they did it for.

—That's the rule of the order, said Aunt Kate firmly.

—Yes, but why? asked Mr. Browne.

Aunt Kate repeated that it was the rule, that was all. Mr. Browne still seemed not to understand. Freddy Malins explained to him, as best he could, that the monks were trying to make up for the sins committed by all the sinners in the outside world. The explanation was not very clear for Mr. Browne grinned and said:

—I like that idea very much but wouldn't a comfortable spring bed do them as well as a coffin?

—The coffin, said Mary Jane, is to remind them of their last end.

As the subject had grown lugubrious it was buried in a silence of the table during which Mrs. Malins could be heard saying to her neighbour in an indistinct undertone:

—They are very good men, the monks, very pious men.

The raisins and almonds and figs and apples and oranges and chocolates and sweets were now passed about the table and Aunt Julia invited all the guests to have either port or sherry. At first Mr. Bartell D'Arcy refused to take either but one of his neighbours nudged him and whispered something to him upon which he allowed his glass to be filled. Gradually as the last glasses were being filled the conversation ceased. A pause followed, broken only by the noise of the wine and by unsettlings of chairs. The Misses Morkan, all three, looked down at the tablecloth. Someone coughed once or twice and then a few gentlemen patted the table gently as a signal for silence. The silence came and Gabriel pushed back his chair and stood up.

The patting at once grew louder in encouragement and then ceased altogether. Gabriel leaned his ten trembling fingers on the tablecloth and smiled nervously at the company. Meeting a row of upturned faces he raised his eyes to the chandelier. The piano was playing a waltz tune and he could hear the skirts sweeping against the drawing-room door. People, perhaps, were standing in the snow on the quay outside, gazing up at the lighted windows and listening to the waltz music. The air was pure there. In the distance lay the park where the trees were weighted with snow. The Wellington Monument wore a gleaming cap of snow that flashed westward over the white field of Fifteen Acres.[5]

He began:

—Ladies and Gentlemen.

—It has fallen to my lot this evening, as in years past, to perform a very pleasing task but a task for which I am afraid my poor powers as a speaker are all too inadequate.

—No, no! said Mr. Browne.

—But, however that may be, I can only ask you to-night to take the will for the deed and to lend me your attention for a few moments while I endeavour to express to you in words what my feelings are on this occasion.

—Ladies and Gentlemen. It is not the first time that we have gathered together under this hospitable roof, around this hospitable board. It is not

---

4. The coffin story is a popular fiction.   5. A section of Phoenix Park used for British military reviews.

the first time that we have been the recipients—or perhaps, I had better say, the victims—of the hospitality of certain good ladies.

He made a circle in the air with his arm and paused. Everyone laughed or smiled at Aunt Kate and Aunt Julia and Mary Jane who all turned crimson with pleasure. Gabriel went on more boldly:

—I feel more strongly with every recurring year that our country has no tradition which does it so much honour and which it should guard so jealously as that of its hospitality. It is a tradition that is unique as far as my experience goes (and I have visited not a few places abroad) among the modern nations. Some would say, perhaps, that with us it is rather a failing than anything to be boasted of. But granted even that, it is, to my mind, a princely failing, and one that I trust will long be cultivated among us. Of one thing, at least, I am sure. As long as this one roof shelters the good ladies aforesaid—and I wish from my heart it may do so for many and many a long year to come—the tradition of genuine warm-hearted courteous Irish hospitality, which our forefathers have handed down to us and which we in turn must hand down to our descendants, is still alive among us.

A hearty murmur of assent ran around the table. It shot through Gabriel's mind that Miss Ivors was not there and that she had gone away discourteously: and he said with confidence in himself:

—Ladies and Gentlemen.

—A new generation is growing up in our midst, a generation actuated by new ideas and new principles. It is serious and enthusiastic for these new ideas and its enthusiasm, even when it is misdirected, is, I believe, in the main sincere. But we are living in a skeptical and, if I may use the phrase, a thought-tormented age: and sometimes I fear that this new generation, educated or hypereducated as it is, will lack those qualities of humanity, of hospitality, of kindly humour which belonged to an older day. Listening tonight to the names of all those great singers of the past it seemed to me, I must confess, that we were living in a less spacious age. Those days might, without exaggeration, be called spacious days: and if they are gone beyond recall let us hope, at least, that in gatherings such as this we shall still speak of them with pride and affection, still cherish in our hearts the memory of those dead and gone great ones whose fame the world will not willingly let die.

—Hear, hear! said Mr. Browne loudly.

—But yet, continued Gabriel, his voice falling into a softer inflection, there are always in gatherings such as this sadder thoughts that will recur to our minds: thoughts of the past, of youth, of changes, of absent faces that we miss here tonight. Our path through life is strewn with many such sad memories: and were we to brood upon them always we could not find the heart to go on bravely with our work among the living. We have all of us living duties and living affections which claim, and rightly claim, our strenuous endeavours.

—Therefore, I will not linger on the past. I will not let any gloomy moralising intrude upon us here to-night. Here we are gathered together for a brief moment from the bustle and rush of our everyday routine. We are met here as friends, in the spirit of good-fellowship, as colleagues, also to a certain extent, in the true spirit of *camaraderie*, and as the guests of—what shall I call them?—the Three Graces of the Dublin musical world.

The table burst into applause and laughter at this sally. Aunt Julia vainly asked each of her neighbours in turn to tell her what Gabriel had said.

—He says we are the Three Graces, Aunt Julia, said Mary Jane.

Aunt Julia did not understand but she looked up, smiling, at Gabriel, who continued in the same vein:

—Ladies and Gentlemen.

—I will not attempt to play to-night the part that Paris played on another occasion.[6] I will not attempt to choose between them. The task would be an invidious one and one beyond my poor powers. For when I view them in turn, whether it be our chief hostess herself, whose good heart, whose too good heart, has become a byword with all who know her, or her sister, who seems to be gifted with perennial youth and whose singing must have been a surprise and a revelation to us all to-night, or, last but not least, when I consider our youngest hostess, talented, cheerful, hard-working and the best of nieces, I confess, Ladies and Gentlemen, that I do not know to which of them I should award the prize.

Gabriel glanced down at his aunts and, seeing the large smile on Aunt Julia's face and the tears which had risen to Aunt Kate's eyes, hastened to his close. He raised his glass of port gallantly, while every member of the company fingered a glass expectantly, and said loudly:

—Let us toast them all three together. Let us drink to their health, wealth, long life, happiness and prosperity and may they long continue to hold the proud and self-won position which they hold in their profession and the position of honour and affection which they hold in our hearts.

All the guests stood up, glass in hand, and, turning towards the three seated ladies, sang in unison, with Mr. Browne as leader:

> *For they are jolly gay fellows,*
> *For they are jolly gay fellows,*
> *For they are jolly gay fellows,*
> *Which nobody can deny.*

Aunt Kate was making frank use of her handkerchief and even Aunt Julia seemed moved. Freddy Malins beat time with his pudding-fork and the singers turned towards one another, as if in melodious conference, while they sang, with emphasis:

> *Unless he tells a lie,*
> *Unless he tells a lie.*

Then, turning once more towards their hostesses, they sang:

> *For they are jolly gay fellows,*
> *For they are jolly gay fellows,*
> *For they are jolly gay fellows,*
> *Which nobody can deny.*

The acclamation which followed was taken up beyond the door of the supper-room by many of the other guests and renewed time after time, Freddy Malins acting as officer with his fork on high.

---

6. Paris was required to judge a beauty contest between the Greek goddesses Hera, Athena, and Aphrodite; see n. 9, p. 1955.

The piercing morning air came into the hall where they were standing so that Aunt Kate said:

—Close the door, somebody. Mrs. Malins will get her death of cold.

—Browne is out there, Aunt Kate, said Mary Jane.

—Browne is everywhere, said Aunt Kate, lowering her voice.

Mary Jane laughed at her tone.

—Really, she said archly, he is very attentive.

—He has been laid on here like the gas, said Aunt Kate in the same tone, all during the Christmas.

She laughed herself this time good-humouredly and then added quickly:

—But tell him to come in, Mary Jane, and close the door. I hope to goodness he didn't hear me.

At that moment the hall-door was opened and Mr. Browne came in from the doorstep, laughing as if his heart would break. He was dressed in a long green overcoat with mock astrakhan cuffs and collar and wore on his head an oval fur cap. He pointed down the snow-covered quay from where the sound of shrill prolonged whistling was borne in.

—Teddy will have all the cabs in Dublin out, he said.

Gabriel advanced from the little pantry behind the office, struggling into his overcoat and, looking round the hall, said:

—Gretta not down yet?

—She's getting on her things, Gabriel, said Aunt Kate.

—Who's playing up there? asked Gabriel.

—Nobody. They're all gone.

—O no, Aunt Kate, said Mary Jane. Bartell D'Arcy and Miss O'Callaghan aren't gone yet.

—Someone is strumming at the piano, anyhow, said Gabriel.

Mary Jane glanced at Gabriel and Mr. Browne and said with a shiver:

—It makes me feel cold to look at you two gentlemen muffled up like that. I wouldn't like to face your journey home at this hour.

—I'd like nothing better this minute, said Mr. Browne stoutly, than a rattling fine walk in the country or a fast drive with a good spanking goer between the shafts.

—We used to have a very good horse and trap at home, said Aunt Julia sadly.

—The never-to-be-forgotten Johnny, said Mary Jane, laughing.

Aunt Kate and Gabriel laughed too.

—Why, what was wonderful about Johnny? asked Mr. Browne.

—The late lamented Patrick Morkan, our grandfather, that is, explained Gabriel, commonly known in his later years as the old gentleman, was a glue-boiler.

—O, now, Gabriel, said Aunt Kate, laughing, he had a starch mill.

—Well, glue or starch, said Gabriel, the old gentleman had a horse by the name of Johnny. And Johnny used to work in the old gentleman's mill, walking round and round in order to drive the mill. That was all very well; but now comes the tragic part about Johnny. One fine day the old gentleman thought he'd like to drive out with the quality to a military review in the park.

—The Lord have mercy on his soul, said Aunt Kate compassionately.

—Amen, said Gabriel. So the old gentleman, as I said, harnessed Johnny and put on his very best tall hat and his very best stock collar and drove out in grand style from his ancestral mansion somewhere near Back Lane,[7] I think.

Everyone laughed, even Mrs. Malins, at Gabriel's manner and Aunt Kate said:

—O now, Gabriel, he didn't live in Back Lane, really. Only the mill was there.

—Out from the mansion of his forefathers, continued Gabriel, he drove with Johnny. And everything went on beautifully until Johnny came in sight of King Billy's[8] statue: and whether he fell in love with the horse King Billy sits on or whether he thought he was back again in the mill, anyhow he began to walk round the statue.

Gabriel paced in a circle round the hall in his goloshes amid the laughter of the others.

—Round and round he went, said Gabriel, and the old gentleman, who was a very pompous old gentleman, was highly indignant. *Go on, sir! What do you mean, sir? Johnny! Johnny! Most extraordinary conduct! Can't understand the horse!*

The peals of laughter which followed Gabriel's imitation of the incident were interrupted by a resounding knock at the hall-door. Mary Jane ran to open it and let in Freddy Malins. Freddy Malins, with his hat well back on his head and his shoulders humped with cold, was puffing and steaming after his exertions.

—I could only get one cab, he said.

—O, we'll find another along the quay, said Gabriel.

—Yes, said Aunt Kate. Better not keep Mrs. Malins standing in the draught.

Mrs. Malins was helped down the front steps by her son and Mr. Browne and, after many manœuvres, hoisted into the cab. Freddy Malins clambered in after her and spent a long time settling her on the seat, Mr. Browne helping him with advice. At last she was settled comfortably and Freddy Malins invited Mr. Browne into the cab. There was a good deal of confused talk, and then Mr. Browne got into the cab. The cabman settled his rug over his knees, and bent down for the address. The confusion grew greater and the cabman was directed differently by Freddy Malins and Mr. Browne, each of whom had his head out through a window of the cab. The difficulty was to know where to drop Mr. Browne along the route and Aunt Kate, Aunt Julia and Mary Jane helped the discussion from the doorstep with cross-directions and contradictions and abundance of laughter. As for Freddy Malins he was speechless with laughter. He popped his head in and out of the window every moment, to the great danger of his hat, and told his mother how the discussion was progressing till at last Mr. Browne shouted to the bewildered cabman above the din of everybody's laughter:

—Do you know Trinity College?

—Yes, sir, said the cabman.

—Well, drive bang up against Trinity College gates, said Mr. Browne, and then we'll tell you where to go. You understand now?

—Yes, sir, said the cabman.

---

7. A shabby street in a run-down area of Dublin.   8. William III, king of England from 1689 to 1702, defeated the Irish nationalists at the Battle of the Boyne.

—Make like a bird for Trinity College.

—Right, sir, cried the cabman.

The horse was whipped up and the cab rattled off along the quay amid a chorus of laughter and adieus.

Gabriel had not gone to the door with the others. He was in a dark part of the hall gazing up the staircase. A woman was standing near the top of the first flight, in the shadow also. He could not see her face but he could see the terracotta and salmonpink panels of her skirt which the shadow made appear black and white. It was his wife. She was leaning on the banisters, listening to something. Gabriel was surprised at her stillness and strained his ear to listen also. But he could hear little save the noise of laughter and dispute on the front steps, a few chords struck on the piano and a few notes of a man's voice singing.

He stood still in the gloom of the hall, trying to catch the air that the voice was singing and gazing up at his wife. There was grace and mystery in her attitude as if she were a symbol of something. He asked himself what is a woman standing on the stairs in the shadow, listening to distant music, a symbol of. If he were a painter he would paint her in that attitude. Her blue felt hat would show off the bronze of her hair against the darkness and the dark panels of her skirt would show off the light ones. *Distant Music* he would call the picture if he were a painter.

The hall-door was closed; and Aunt Kate, Aunt Julia and Mary Jane came down the hall, still laughing.

—Well, isn't Freddy terrible? said Mary Jane. He's really terrible.

Gabriel said nothing but pointed up the stairs towards where his wife was standing. Now that the hall-door was closed the voice and the piano could be heard more clearly. Gabriel held up his hand for them to be silent. The song seemed to be in the old Irish tonality[9] and the singer seemed uncertain both of his words and of his voice. The voice, made plaintive by distance and by the singer's hoarseness, faintly illuminated the cadence of the air with words expressing grief:

> *O, the rain falls on my heavy locks*
> *And the dew wets my skin,*
> *My babe lies cold*[1] . . .

—O, exclaimed Mary Jane. It's Bartell D'Arcy singing and he wouldn't sing all the night. O, I'll get him to sing a song before he goes.

—O do, Mary Jane, said Aunt Kate.

Mary Jane brushed past the others and ran to the staircase but before she reached it the singing stopped and the piano was closed abruptly.

—O, what a pity! she cried. Is he coming down, Gretta?

Gabriel heard his wife answer yes and saw her come down towards them. A few steps behind her were Mr. Bartell D'Arcy and Miss O'Callaghan.

—O, Mr. D'Arcy, cried Mary Jane, it's downright mean of you to break off like that when we were all in raptures listening to you.

---

9. Based on five (and later seven) tones rather than the modern eight-tone scale.   1. From "The Lass of Aughrim," a ballad about a peasant girl seduced by a lord; when she brings her baby to the castle door, the lord's mother imitates his voice and sends her away. Mother and child are drowned at sea, and the repentant lord curses his mother.

—I have been at him all the evening, said Miss O'Callaghan, and Mrs. Conroy too and he told us he had a dreadful cold and couldn't sing.

—O, Mr. D'Arcy, said Aunt Kate, now that was a great fib to tell.

—Can't you see that I'm as hoarse as a crow? said Mr. D'Arcy roughly.

He went into the pantry hastily and put on his overcoat. The others, taken aback by his rude speech, could find nothing to say. Aunt Kate wrinkled her brows and made signs to the others to drop the subject. Mr. D'Arcy stood swathing his neck carefully and frowning.

—It's the weather, said Aunt Julia, after a pause.

—Yes, everybody has colds, said Aunt Kate readily, everybody.

—They say, said Mary Jane, we haven't had snow like it for thirty years; and I read this morning in the newspapers that the snow is general all over Ireland.

—I love the look of snow, said Aunt Julia sadly.

—So do I, said Miss O'Callaghan. I think Christmas is never really Christmas unless we have the snow on the ground.

—But poor Mr. D'Arcy doesn't like the snow, said Aunt Kate, smiling.

Mr. D'Arcy came from the pantry, fully swathed and buttoned, and in a repentant tone told them the history of his cold. Everyone gave him advice and said it was a great pity and urged him to be very careful of his throat in the night air. Gabriel watched his wife who did not join in the conversation. She was standing right under the dusty fanlight and the flame of the gas lit up the rich bronze of her hair which he had seen her drying at the fire a few days before. She was in the same attitude and seemed unaware of the talk about her. At last she turned towards them and Gabriel saw that there was colour on her cheeks and that her eyes were shining. A sudden tide of joy went leaping out of his heart.

—Mr. D'Arcy, she said, what is the name of that song you were singing?

—It's called *The Lass of Aughrim*, said Mr. D'Arcy, but I couldn't remember it properly. Why? Do you know it?

—*The Lass of Aughrim*, she repeated. I couldn't think of the name.

—It's a very nice air, said Mary Jane. I'm sorry you were not in voice tonight.

—Now, Mary Jane, said Aunt Kate, don't annoy Mr. D'Arcy. I won't have him annoyed.

Seeing that all were ready to start she shepherded them to the door where good-night was said:

—Well, good-night, Aunt Kate, and thanks for the pleasant evening.

—Good-night, Gabriel. Good-night, Gretta!

—Good-night, Aunt Kate, and thanks ever so much. Good-night, Aunt Julia.

—O, good-night, Gretta, I didn't see you.

—Good-night, Mr. D'Arcy. Good-night, Miss O'Callaghan.

—Good-night, Miss Morkan.

—Good-night, again.

—Good-night, all. Safe home.

—Good-night. Good-night.

The morning was still dark. A dull yellow light brooded over the houses and the river; and the sky seemed to be descending. It was slushy underfoot;

and only streaks and patches of snow lay on the roofs, on the parapets of the quay and on the area railings. The lamps were still burning redly in the murky air and, across the river, the palace of the Four Courts[2] stood out menacingly against the heavy sky.

She was walking on before him with Mr. Bartell D'Arcy, her shoes in a brown parcel tucked under one arm and her hands holding her skirt up from the slush. She had no longer any grace of attitude but Gabriel's eyes were still bright with happiness. The blood went bounding along his veins; and the thoughts went rioting through his brain, proud, joyful, tender, valorous.

She was walking on before him so lightly and so erect that he longed to run after her noiselessly, catch her by the shoulders and say something foolish and affectionate into her ear. She seemed to him so frail that he longed to defend her against something and then to be alone with her. Moments of their secret life together burst like stars upon his memory. A heliotrope envelope was lying beside his breakfast-cup and he was caressing it with his hand. Birds were twittering in the ivy and the sunny web of the curtain was shimmering along the floor: he could not eat for happiness. They were standing on the crowded platform and he was placing a ticket inside the warm palm of her glove. He was standing with her in the cold, looking in through a grated window at a man making bottles in a roaring furnace. It was very cold. Her face, fragrant in the cold air, was quite close to his; and suddenly she called out to the man at the furnace:

—Is the fire hot, sir?

But the man could not hear her with the noise of the furnace. It was just as well. He might have answered rudely.

A wave of yet more tender joy escaped from his heart and went coursing in warm flood along his arteries. Like the tender fires of stars moments of their life together, that no one knew of or would ever know of, broke upon and illumined his memory. He longed to recall to her those moments, to make her forget the years of their dull existence together and remember only their moments of ecstasy. For the years, he felt, had not quenched his soul or hers. Their children, his writing, her household cares had not quenched all their souls' tender fire. In one letter that he had written to her then he had said: *Why is it that words like these seem to me so dull and cold? Is it because there is no word tender enough to be your name?*

Like distant music these words that he had written years before were borne towards him from the past. He longed to be alone with her. When the others had gone away, when he and she were in their room in the hotel, then they would be alone together. He would call her softly:

—Gretta!

Perhaps she would not hear at once: she would be undressing. Then something in his voice would strike her. She would turn and look at him.

At the corner of Winetavern Street they met a cab. He was glad of its rattling noise as it saved him from conversation. She was looking out of the window and seemed tired. The others spoke only a few words, pointing out some building or street. The horse galloped along wearily under the murky morning sky, dragging his old rattling box after his heels, and Gabriel was

2. The Irish law courts building.

again in a cab with her, galloping to catch the boat, galloping to their honeymoon.

As the cab drove across O'Connell Bridge Miss O'Callaghan said:

—They say you never cross O'Connell Bridge without seeing a white horse.

—I see a white man this time, said Gabriel.

—Where? asked Mr. Bartell D'Arcy.

Gabriel pointed to the statue,[3] on which lay patches of snow. Then he nodded familiarly to it and waved his hand.

—Good-night, Dan, he said gaily.

When the cab drew up before the hotel Gabriel jumped out and, in spite of Mr. Bartell D'Arcy's protest, paid the driver. He gave the man a shilling over his fare. The man saluted and said:

—A prosperous New Year to you, sir.

—The same to you, said Gabriel cordially.

She leaned for a moment on his arm in getting out of the cab and while standing at the curbstone, bidding the others good-night. She leaned lightly on his arm, as lightly as when she had danced with him a few hours before. He had felt proud and happy then, happy that she was his, proud of her grace and wifely carriage. But now, after the kindling again of so many memories, the first touch of her body, musical and strange and perfumed, sent through him a keen pang of lust. Under cover of her silence he pressed her arm closely to his side; and, as they stood at the hotel door, he felt that they had escaped from their lives and duties, escaped from home and friends and run away together with wild and radiant hearts to a new adventure.

An old man was dozing in a great hooded chair in the hall. He lit a candle in the office and went before them to the stairs. They followed him in silence, their feet falling in soft thuds on the thickly carpeted stairs. She mounted the stairs behind the porter, her head bowed in the ascent, her frail shoulders curved as with a burden, her skirt girt tightly about her. He could have flung his arms about her hips and held her still for his arms were trembling with desire to seize her and only the stress of his nails against the palms of his hands held the wild impulse of his body in check. The porter halted on the stairs to settle his guttering candle. They halted too on the steps below him. In the silence Gabriel could hear the falling of the molten wax into the tray and the thumping of his own heart against his ribs.

The porter led them along a corridor and opened a door. Then he set his unstable candle down on a toilet-table and asked at what hour they were to be called in the morning.

—Eight, said Gabriel.

The porter pointed to the tap of the electric-light and began a muttered apology but Gabriel cut him short.

—We don't want any light. We have light enough from the street. And I say, he added, pointing to the candle, you might remove that handsome article, like a good man.

The porter took up his candle again, but slowly for he was surprised by such a novel idea. Then he mumbled good-night and went out. Gabriel shot the lock to.

3. Of Daniel O'Connell (1775–1847), called "The Liberator" by the Irish independence movement.

A ghostly light from the street lamp lay in a long shaft from one window to the door. Gabriel threw his overcoat and hat on a couch and crossed the room towards the window. He looked down into the street in order that his emotion might calm a little. Then he turned and leaned against a chest of drawers with his back to the light. She had taken off her hat and cloak and was standing before a large swinging mirror, unhooking her waist.[4] Gabriel paused for a few moments, watching her, and then said:

—Gretta!

She turned away from the mirror slowly and walked along the shaft of light towards him. Her face looked so serious and weary that the words would not pass Gabriel's lips. No, it was not the moment yet.

—You looked tired, he said.

—I am a little, she answered.

—You don't feel ill or weak?

—No, tired: that's all.

She went on to the window and stood there, looking out. Gabriel waited again and then, fearing that diffidence was about to conquer him, he said abruptly:

—By the way, Gretta!

—What is it?

—You know that poor fellow Malins? he said quickly.

—Yes. What about him?

—Well, poor fellow, he's a decent sort of chap after all, continued Gabriel in a false voice. He gave me back that sovereign I lent him and I didn't expect it really. It's a pity he wouldn't keep away from that Browne, because he's not a bad fellow at heart.

He was trembling now with annoyance. Why did she seem so abstracted? He did not know how he could begin. Was she annoyed, too, about something? If she would only turn to him or come to him of her own accord! To take her as she was would be brutal. No, he must see some ardour in her eyes first. He longed to be master of her strange mood.

—When did you lend him the pound? she asked, after a pause.

Gabriel stove to restrain himself from breaking out into brutal language about the sottish Malins and his pound. He longed to cry to her from his soul, to crush her body against his, to overmaster her. But he said:

—O, at Christmas, when he opened that little Christmas-card shop in Henry Street.

He was in such a fever of rage and desire that he did not hear her come from the window. She stood before him for an instant, looking at him strangely. Then, suddenly raising herself on tiptoe and resting her hands lightly on his shoulders, she kissed him.

—You are a very generous person, Gabriel, she said.

Gabriel, trembling with delight at her sudden kiss and at the quaintness of her phrase, put his hands on her hair and began smoothing it back, scarcely touching it with his fingers. The washing had made it fine and brilliant. His heart was brimming over with happiness. Just when he was wishing for it she had come to him of her own accord. Perhaps her thoughts had been running with his. Perhaps she had felt the impetuous desire that was

---

4. I.e., loosening her waistband.

in him and then the yielding mood had come upon her. Now that she had fallen to him so easily he wondered why he had been so diffident.

He stood, holding her head between his hands. Then, slipping one arm swiftly about her body and drawing her towards him, he said softly:

—Gretta dear, what are you thinking about?

She did not answer nor yield wholly to his arm. He said again, softly:

—Tell me what it is, Gretta. I think I know what is the matter. Do I know?

She did not answer at once. Then she said in an outburst of tears:

—O, I am thinking about that song, *The Lass of Aughrim*.

She broke loose from him and ran to the bed and, throwing her arms across the bed-rail, hid her face. Gabriel stood stock-still for a moment in astonishment and then followed her. As he passed in the way of the cheval-glass he caught sight of himself in full length, his broad, well-filled shirt-front, the face whose expression always puzzled him when he saw it in a mirror and his glimmering gilt-rimmed eyeglasses. He halted a few paces from her and said:

—What about the song? Why does that make you cry?

She raised her head from her arms and dried her eyes with the back of her hand like a child. A kinder note than he had intended went into his voice.

—Why, Gretta? he asked.

—I am thinking about a person long ago who used to sing that song.

—And who was the person long ago? asked Gabriel, smiling.

—It was a person I used to know in Galway when I was living with my grandmother, she said.

The smile passed away from Gabriel's face. A dull anger began to gather again at the back of his mind and the dull fires of his lust began to glow angrily in his veins.

—Someone you were in love with? he asked ironically.

—It was a young boy I used to know, she answered, named Michael Furey. He used to sing that song, *The Lass of Aughrim*. He was very delicate.

Gabriel was silent. He did not wish her to think that he was interested in this delicate boy.

—I can see him so plainly, she said after a moment. Such eyes as he had: big dark eyes! And such an expression in them—an expression!

—O then, you were in love with him? said Gabriel.

—I used to go out walking with him,[5] she said, when I was in Galway. A thought flew across Gabriel's mind.

—Perhaps that was why you wanted to go to Galway with that Ivors girl? he said coldly.

She looked at him and asked in surprise:

—What for?

Her eyes made Gabriel feel awkward. He shrugged his shoulders and said:

—How do I know? To see him perhaps.

She looked away from him along the shaft of light towards the window in silence.

—He is dead, she said at length. He died when he was only seventeen. Isn't it a terrible thing to die so young as that?

—What was he? asked Gabriel, still ironically.

5. I.e., she dated him.

—He was in the gasworks,[6] she said.

Gabriel felt humiliated by the failure of his irony and by the evocation of this figure from the dead, a boy in the gasworks. While he had been full of memories of their secret life together, full of tenderness and joy and desire, she had been comparing him in her mind with another. A shameful consciousness of his own person assailed him. He saw himself as a ludicrous figure, acting as a pennyboy[7] for his aunts, a nervous well-meaning sentimentalist, orating to vulgarians and idealising his own clownish lusts, the pitiable fatuous fellow he had caught a glimpse of in the mirror. Instinctively he turned his back more to the light lest she might see the shame that burned upon his forehead.

He tried to keep up his tone of cold interrogation but his voice when he spoke was humble and indifferent.

—I suppose you were in love with this Michael Furey, Gretta, he said.

—I was great[8] with him at that time, she said.

Her voice was veiled and sad. Gabriel, feeling now how vain it would be to try to lead her whither he had purposed, caressed one of her hands and said, also sadly:

—And what did he die of so young, Gretta? Consumption, was it?

—I think he died for me, she answered.

A vague terror seized Gabriel at this answer as if, at that hour when he had hoped to triumph, some impalpable and vindictive being was coming against him, gathering forces against him in its vague world. But he shook himself free of it with an effort of reason and continued to caress her hand. He did not question her again for he felt that she would tell him of herself. Her hand was warm and moist: it did not respond to his touch but he continued to caress it just as he had caressed her first letter to him that spring morning.

—It was in the winter, she said, about the beginning of the winter when I was going to leave my grandmother's and come up here to the convent. And he was ill at the time in his lodgings in Galway and wouldn't be let out and his people in Oughterard[9] were written to. He was in decline, they said, or something like that. I never knew rightly.

She paused for a moment and sighed.

—Poor fellow, she said. He was very fond of me and he was such a gentle boy. We used to go out together, walking, you know, Gabriel, like the way they do in the country. He was going to study singing only for his health. He had a very good voice, poor Michael Furey.

—Well; and then? asked Gabriel.

—And then when it came to the time for me to leave Galway and come up to the convent he was much worse and I wouldn't be let see him so I wrote a letter saying I was going up to Dublin and would be back in the summer and hoping he would be better then.

She paused for a moment to get her voice under control and then went on:

—Then the night before I left I was in my grandmother's house in Nun's Island,[1] packing up, and I heard gravel thrown up against the window. The

6. A utilities plant that manufactured coal gas. Working there was unhealthy.   7. Errand boy.
8. Close friends.   9. A small village in western Ireland.   1. An island in the western city of Galway, on which is located the Convent of Poor Clares.

window was so wet I couldn't see so I ran downstairs as I was and slipped out the back into the garden and there was the poor fellow at the end of the garden, shivering.

—And did you not tell him to go back? asked Gabriel.

—I implored of him to go home at once and told him he would get his death in the rain. But he said he did not want to live. I can see his eyes as well as well! He was standing at the end of the wall where there was a tree.

—And did he go home? asked Gabriel.

—Yes, he went home. And when I was only a week in the convent he died and he was buried in Oughterard where his people came from. O, the day I heard that, that he was dead!

She stopped, choking with sobs, and, overcome by emotion, flung herself face downward on the bed, sobbing in the quilt. Gabriel held her hand for a moment longer, irresolutely, and then, shy of intruding on her grief, let it fall gently and walked quietly to the window.

She was fast asleep.

Gabriel, leaning on his elbow, looked for a few moments unresentfully on her tangled hair and half-open mouth, listening to her deep-drawn breath. So she had had that romance in her life: a man had died for her sake. It hardly pained him now to think how poor a part he, her husband, had played in her life. He watched her while she slept as though he and she had never lived together as man and wife. His curious eyes rested long upon her face and on her hair: and, as he thought of what she must have been then, in that time of her first girlish beauty, a strange friendly pity for her entered his soul. He did not like to say even to himself that her face was no longer beautiful but he knew that it was no longer the face for which Michael Furey had braved death.

Perhaps she had not told him all the story. His eyes moved to the chair over which she had thrown some of her clothes. A petticoat string dangled to the floor. One boot stood upright, its limp upper fallen down: the fellow of it lay upon its side. He wondered at his riot of emotions of an hour before. From what had it proceeded? From his aunt's supper, from his own foolish speech, from the wine and dancing, the merrymaking when saying good-night in the hall, the pleasure of the walk along the river in the snow. Poor Aunt Julia! She, too, would soon be a shade with the shade of Patrick Morkan and his horse. He had caught that haggard look upon her face for a moment when she was singing *Arrayed for the Bridal*. Soon, perhaps, he would be sitting in that same drawing-room, dressed in black, his silk hat on his knees. The blinds would be drawn down and Aunt Kate would be sitting beside him, crying and blowing her nose and telling him how Julia had died. He would cast about in his mind for some words that might console her, and would find only lame and useless ones. Yes, yes: that would happen very soon.

The air of the room chilled his shoulders. He stretched himself cautiously along under the sheets and lay down beside his wife. One by one they were all becoming shades. Better pass boldly into that other world, in the full glory of some passion, than fade and wither dismally with age. He thought of how she who lay beside him had locked in her heart for so many years that image of her lover's eyes when he had told her that he did not wish to live.

Generous tears filled Gabriel's eyes. He had never felt like that himself towards any woman but he knew that such a feeling must be love. The tears gathered more thickly in his eyes and in the partial darkness he imagined he saw the form of a young man standing under a dripping tree. Other forms were near. His soul had approached that region where dwell the vast hosts of the dead. He was conscious of, but could not apprehend, their wayward and flickering existence. His own identity was fading out into a grey impalpable world: the solid world itself which these dead had one time reared and lived in was dissolving and dwindling.

A few light taps upon the pane made him turn to the window. It had begun to snow again. He watched sleepily the flakes, silver and dark, falling obliquely against the lamplight. The time had come for him to set out on his journey westward. Yes, the newspapers were right: snow was general all over Ireland. It was falling on every part of the dark central plain, on the treeless hills, falling softly upon the Bog of Allen and, farther westward, softly falling into the dark mutinous Shannon[2] waves. It was falling, too, upon every part of the lonely churchyard on the hill where Michael Furey lay buried. It lay thickly drifted on the crooked crosses and headstones, on the spears of the little gate, on the barren thorns. His soul swooned slowly as he heard the snow falling faintly through the universe and faintly falling, like the descent of their last end, upon all the living and the dead.

2. An estuary of the Shannon River, west-southwest of Dublin. The Bog of Allen is southwest of Dublin.

VIRGINIA WOOLF
1882–1941

Virginia Woolf did more than write innovative novels that stand on a par with those of Joyce and Proust; she also explained and exemplified a new kind of prose that she associated with feminine consciousness. Woolf is known for her precise evocations of states of mind—or of mind and body, since she refused to separate the two. She structures her novels according to her protagonists' moments of awareness, and in that way joins Proust and Joyce in their move away from the linear plots and objective descriptions of nineteenth-century realism. In novels like *Mrs. Dalloway* and *The Waves,* blocks of time are rearranged, different points of view juxtaposed, and incomplete perspectives set against each other to create a larger pattern. Alternating modes of narration prevent any single reference point and remind the reader that subjectivity is always at work, in literature and in everyday life. Woolf has an additional role in modernist literary history: she was an ardent feminist who explored—directly in her essays and indirectly in her novels and short stories—the situation of women in society, the construction of gender identity, and the predicament of the woman writer.

She was born Adeline Virginia Stephen on January 25, 1882, one of the four children of the eminent Victorian editor and historian Leslie Stephen and his wife, Julia. The family actively pursued intellectual and artistic interests, and Julia was admired and sketched by some of the most famous Pre-Raphaelite artists. Following the customs of the day, only the sons, Adrian and Thoby, were given formal and university education; Virginia and her sister, Vanessa (the painter Vanessa Bell), were instructed at home by their parents and depended for further education on their father's immense library. Virginia bitterly resented this unequal treatment and the systematic discouragement of women's intellectual development that it implied. Throughout her own work, themes of society's different attitudes toward men and women play a strong role, especially in *A Room of One's Own* (1929) and *Three Guineas* (1938). *A Room of One's Own* examines the history of literature written by women and contains also an impassioned plea that women writers be given conditions equal to those available for men: specifically, the privacy of a room in which to write and economic independence. (At the time Woolf wrote, it was unusual for women to have any money of their own or to be able to devote themselves to a career.) After her mother's death in 1895, Woolf was expected to take over the supervision of the family household, which she did until her father's death in 1904. Of fragile physical health after an attack of whooping cough when she was six, she suffered in addition a nervous breakdown after the death of each parent.

Woolf moved to central London with her sister and brother Adrian after their father's death and took a house in the Bloomsbury district. They soon became the focus of what was later called the Bloomsbury Group, a gathering of writers, artists, and intellectuals impatient with conservative Edwardian society who met regularly to discuss new ideas. It was an eclectic group and included the novelist E. M. Forster, the historian Lytton Strachey, the economist John Maynard Keynes, and the art critics Clive Bell (who married Vanessa) and Roger Fry (who introduced the group to the French painters Édouard Manet and Paul Cézanne). Woolf was not yet writing fiction but contributed reviews to the *Times Literary Supplement*, taught literature and composition at Morley College (an institution with a volunteer faculty that provided educational opportunities for workers), and worked for the adult suffrage movement and a feminist group. In 1912 she married Leonard Woolf, who encouraged her to write and with whom she founded the Hogarth Press in 1917. The press became one of the most respected of the small literary presses and published works by such major authors as T. S. Eliot, Katherine Mansfield, Strachey, Forster, Maxim Gorky, and John Middleton Murry as well as Woolf's own novels and translations of Freud. Over the next two decades she produced her best-known work while coping with frequent bouts of physical and mental illness. Already depressed during World War II and exhausted after the completion of her last novel, *Between the Acts* (1941), she sensed the approach of a serious attack of insanity and the confinement it would entail: in such situations, she was obliged to "rest" and forbidden to read or write. In March 1941, she drowned herself in a river close to her Sussex home.

As a fiction writer, Woolf is best known for her poetic evocations of the way we think and feel. Like Proust and Joyce, she is superbly capable of evoking all the concrete, sensuous details of everyday experience; like them, she explores the structures of consciousness. Her rejection of nineteenth-century realism was not a criticism of the great realist novels like *Madame Bovary*; she turned her attention to more recent and derivative writers. What she really deplored was the microscopic, documentary realism that contemporaries like Arnold Bennett and John Galsworthy drew from the nineteenth-century masters. Their contemporary attitude of scientific objectivity was false, she felt: they claimed to stand outside the scene they described but refused to take into account the fact that there are no neutral observers. Worse, their goal of scientific objectivity often resulted in a mere chronological accumulation of details, the "appalling narrative business of . . . getting from lunch to dinner." Woolf had an explanation for this documentary style: she attributed it to a consciously masculine (or patriarchal) perspective that found security only in logic, order, and the accumulation of knowledge. She proposed, in contrast, a more subjective and, therefore, a more accurate account of experience. Her focus was not so much the object under observation as the way the observer perceived that object: "Let us record the atoms as they fall upon the mind in the order in which they fall, let us trace the pattern, however disconnected and incoherent in appearance, which each sight or incident scores upon the consciousness." Such writing, underwritten by a feminine creative consciousness, would open new avenues for modern literature.

Woolf's writing has been compared with postimpressionist art in the way that it emphasizes the abstract arrangement of perspectives to suggest additional networks of meaning. After two relatively traditional novels, she began to develop a more flexible approach that openly manipulated fictional structure. The continuously developing plot gave way to an organization by juxtaposed points of view; the experience of "real" or chronological time was displaced (although not completely) by a mind ranging ambiguously among its memories; and an intricate pattern of symbolic themes connected otherwise unrelated characters in the same story. All these techniques made new demands on the reader's ability to synthesize and re-create a whole picture. In *Jacob's Room* (1922), a picture of the hero must be assembled from a series of partial points of view. In *The Waves* (1931), the multiple perspective of different characters soliloquizing on their relationship to the dead Percival is broken by ten interludes that together construct an additional, interacting perspective when they describe the passage of a single day from dawn to dusk. Her novels may expand or telescope the sense of time: *Mrs. Dalloway* (1925) focuses apparently on Clarissa Dalloway's preparations for a party that evening but at the same time calls up—at different times, and according to different contexts—her whole life from childhood to her present age of fifty. Problems of identity are a constant concern in these shifting perspectives, and Woolf often portrays the search of unfulfilled personalities for whatever will complete them. Her work is studded with moments of heightened awareness (comparable to Joyce's epiphanies) in which a character suddenly *sees into* a person or situation. With Woolf, this moment is less a matter of mystical insight (as it is with Joyce) than a creation of the mind using all its faculties.

No one can read Woolf without being struck by the importance she gives to the creative imagination. Her major characters display a sensitivity beyond rational logic, and her narrative style celebrates the aesthetic impulse to coordinate many dimensions inside one harmoniously significant whole. Human beings are not complete, Woolf suggests, without exercising their intuitive and imaginative faculties. Like other modernist writers, she is fascinated by the creative process and often makes reference to it in her work. Whether describing the struggles of a painter in *To the Lighthouse* (1927) or of a writer in the story *An Unwritten Novel,* she illustrates the exploratory and the creative work of human imagination. Not all this work is visible in the finished painting or novel: observing, sifting, coordinating, projecting different interpretations and relationships, the mind performs an enormous labor of coordinating consciousness that cannot be captured entirely in any fixed form.

A Room of One's Own itself does not conform to any one fixed form. At once lecture and essay, autobiography and fiction, it originated in a pair of lectures on women and fiction given at Newnham and Girton Colleges (for women) at Cambridge University in 1928. Woolf warns her audience that, instead of defining either women or fiction, she will use "all the liberties and licenses of a novelist" to get at the matter obliquely and leave her auditors to sort out the truth from the "lies [that] will flow from my lips." She will, she claims, retrace the days (that is, the narrator's days) preceding her visit, and lay bare the thought processes leading up to the lecture itself. The lecture, which is now identical with the thought processes leading up to it, is cast in the form of a meditative ramble through various parts of Oxbridge (a compound of Oxford and Cambridge Universities) and London. It includes the famous (and apparently true) anecdote in which she is warned off the university lawn and forbidden entrance to the library because she is a woman; a vivid contrast of the food and living quarters of women and men at Oxbridge; a literary history of English women writers and their socioeconomic situations; a concluding speculation on the androgynous nature of creativity with an exhortation to her young audience to write about the rich yet unrecorded experience of women; and, of course, the central chapters, printed here, that describe her research into definitions of women and offer the celebrated portrait of Judith Shakespeare.

In chapter 2, the narrator heads for the British Museum to locate a comprehensive definition of femininity. To her surprise and mounting anger, she discovers that the thousands of books on the subject written by fascinated men all define women as inferior animals, useful but somewhat alien in nature. Moreover, these same definitions have become prescriptions for generations of young women who learn to see themselves and their place in life accordingly. Raised in poverty and dependence, such women have neither the means nor the self-confidence to write seriously or to become anything other than the Victorian "Angel of the House." What they require, asserts the narrator, is the self-sufficiency brought by an annual income of five hundred pounds. (Woolf had recently inherited such an income.) Chapter 3 pursues similar themes, adding to the five hundred pounds the need for "a room of one's own" and the privacy necessary to follow out an idea. Moving to history, and focusing on the Elizabethan age after a discouraging inspection of Professor Trevelyan's *History of England,* it evokes the career of the "terribly gifted" Judith Shakespeare, William's imaginary sister. Judith has the same literary and dramatic ambitions as her brother, and she too finds her way to London, but she is blocked at each turn by her identity as a woman. Woolf does not belittle William Shakespeare with this contrast; instead, her narrator remarks meaningfully that his work reveals an "incandescent, unimpeded mind."

The bleak portrayals in these chapters are lightened by a great deal of satirical wit and humor, often conveyed by calculated fictional distortion. Woolf uses her novelist's license to subvert and criticize the patriarchal message she describes. The Reading Room of the British Museum, august repository of masculine knowledge about women, is seen as a (bald-foreheaded) dome crowned with the names of famous men. The narrator's scholarly seeming list of feminine characteristics is not only amusingly biased but contradictory and incoherent; it implies that the "masculine" passion for lists and documentation is not the best way to learn about human nature. Professor von X.'s portrait is an open caricature linked to suggestions that his scientific disdain hides repressed fear and anger. *A Room of One's Own* is still famous for its vivid, scathing, and occasionally humorous portrayal of women as objects of male definition and disapproval. Its model of a feminine literary history and its hypothesis of a separate feminine consciousness and manner of writing had substantial influence on writers and literary theory in the latter half of the twentieth century and will continue to do so into the twenty-first.

Phyllis Rose, *Woman of Letters: A Life of Virginia Woolf* (1978), is a valuable biography; Edward Bishop, *Virginia Woolf* (1991), is a recent brief introduction. Two valuable collections of essays on Woolf's writing and her position in the modernist/postmodernist tradition are Patricia Clements and Isobel Grundy, eds., *Virginia Woolf: New Critical Essays* (1983), and Margaret Homans, ed., *Virginia Woolf: A Collection of Critical Essays* (1993). Jane Marcus, *Virginia Woolf and the Language of Patriarchy* (1987), and Rachel Bowlby, *Feminist Destinations and Further Essays on Virginia Woolf* (1997), offer perceptive feminist analyses that include discussion of *A Room of One's Own.* Mark Hussey and Vara Neverow, eds., *Virginia Woolf: Emerging Perspectives* (1994), contains several essays on *A Room of One's Own.* S. P. Rosenbaum, ed., *Virginia Woolf: Women and Fiction* (1992), transcribes and edits two draft manuscripts that are the basis for *A Room of One's Own.* Gillian Beer, *Virginia Woolf: The Common Ground* (1996), offers four useful general essays and four discussions of specific novels. Patricia Ondek Laurence situates Woolf in *The Reading of Silence: Virginia Woolf in the English Tradition* (1991); comparative studies include Richard Pearce, *The Politics of Narration: James Joyce, William Faulkner, and Virginia Woolf* (1991).

From A Room of One's Own

CHAPTER TWO

The scene, if I may ask you to follow me, was now changed. The leaves were still falling, but in London now, not Oxbridge;[1] and I must ask you to imagine a room, like many thousands, with a window looking across people's hats and vans and motor-cars to other windows, and on the table inside the room a blank sheet of paper on which was written in large letters WOMEN AND FICTION, but no more. The inevitable sequel to lunching and dining at Oxbridge seemed, unfortunately, to be a visit to the British Museum. One must strain off what was personal and accidental in all these impressions and so reach the pure fluid, the essential oil of truth. For that visit to Oxbridge and the luncheon and the dinner had started a swarm of questions. Why did men drink wine and women water? Why was one sex so prosperous and the other so poor? What effect has poverty on fiction? What conditions are necessary for the creation of works of art?—a thousand questions at once suggested themselves. But one needed answers, not questions; and an answer was only to be had by consulting the learned and the unprejudiced, who have removed themselves above the strife of tongue and the confusion of body and issued the result of their reasoning and research in books which are to be found in the British Museum. If truth is not to be found on the shelves of the British Museum, where, I asked myself, picking up a notebook and a pencil, is truth?

Thus provided, thus confident and enquiring, I set out in the pursuit of truth. The day, though not actually wet, was dismal, and the streets in the neighborhood of the Museum were full of open coal-holes, down which sacks were showering; four-wheeled cabs were drawing up and depositing on the pavement corded boxes containing, presumably, the entire wardrobe of some Swiss or Italian family seeking fortune or refuge or some other desirable commodity which is to be found in the boarding-houses of Bloomsbury[2] in the winter. The usual hoarse-voiced men paraded the streets with plants on barrows. Some shouted; others sang. London was like a workshop. London was like a machine. We were all being shot backwards and forwards on this plain foundation to make some pattern. The British Museum was another department of the factory. The swing-doors swung open; and there one stood under the vast dome, as if one were a thought in the huge bald forehead which is so splendidly encircled by a band of famous names.[3] One went to the counter; one took a slip of paper; one opened a volume of the catalogue, and . . . . . the five dots here indicate five separate minutes of stupefaction, wonder and bewilderment. Have you any notion how many books are written about women in the course of one year? Have you any notion how many are written by men? Are you aware that you are, perhaps, the most discussed animal in the universe? Here had I come with a notebook and a pencil proposing to spend a morning reading, supposing that at the end of the morning

---

1. A fictional university combining the names of Oxford and Cambridge Universities in England. It was at Cambridge University in October 1928 that Woolf delivered the talks titled "Women and Fiction" that later became *A Room of One's Own*.   2. A residential and academic borough in London, site of the British Museum and various educational institutions.   3. The names of famous men, including Chaucer, Spenser, Shakespeare, Milton, Pope, Wordsworth, Byron, Carlyle, and Tennyson, are painted in a circle around the dome of the Reading Room at the British Museum.

I should have transferred the truth to my notebook. But I should need to be a herd of elephants, I thought, and a wilderness of spiders, desperately referring to the animals that are reputed longest lived and most multitudinously eyed, to cope with all this. I should need claws of steel and beak of brass even to penetrate the husk. How shall I ever find the grains of truth embedded in all this mass of paper, I asked myself, and in despair began running my eye up and down the long list of titles. Even the names of the books gave me food for thought. Sex and its nature might well attract doctors and biologists; but what was surprising and difficult of explanation was the fact that sex—woman, that is to say—also attracts agreeable essayists, light-fingered novelists, young men who have taken the M.A. degree; men who have taken no degree; men who have no apparent qualification save that they are not women. Some of these books were, on the face of it, frivolous and facetious; but many, on the other hand, were serious and prophetic, moral and hortatory. Merely to read the titles suggested innumerable schoolmasters, innumerable clergymen mounting their platforms and pulpits and holding forth with a loquacity which far exceeded the hour usually allotted to such discourse on this one subject. It was a most strange phenomenon; and apparently—here I consulted the letter M—one confined to male sex. Women do not write books about men—a fact that I could not help welcoming with relief, for if I had first to read all that men have written about women, then all that women have written about men, the aloe that flowers once in a hundred years would flower twice before I could set pen to paper. So, making a perfectly arbitrary choice of a dozen volumes or so, I sent my slips of paper to lie in the wire tray, and waited in my stall, among the other seekers for the essential oil of truth.

What could be the reason, then, of this curious disparity, I wondered, drawing cart-wheels on the slips of paper provided by the British taxpayer for other purposes. Why are women, judging from this catalogue, so much more interesting to men than men are to women? A very curious fact it seemed, and my mind wandered to picture the lives of men who spend their time in writing books about women; whether they were old or young, married or unmarried, red-nosed or humpbacked—anyhow, it was flattering, vaguely, to feel oneself the object of such attention, provided that it was not entirely bestowed by the crippled and the infirm—so I pondered until all such frivolous thoughts were ended by an avalanche of books sliding down on to the desk in front of me. Now the trouble began. The student who has been trained in research at Oxbridge has no doubt some method of shepherding his question past all distractions till it runs into its answer as a sheep runs into its pen. The student by my side, for instance, who was copying assiduously from a scientific manual was, I felt sure, extracting pure nuggets of the essential ore every ten minutes or so. His little grunts of satisfaction indicated so much. But if, unfortunately, one has had no training in a university, the question far from being shepherded to its pen flies like a frightened flock hither and thither, helter-skelter, pursued by a whole pack of hounds. Professors, schoolmasters, sociologists, clergymen, novelists, essayists, journalists, men who had no qualification save that they were not women, chased my simple and single question—Why are women poor?—until it became fifty questions; until the fifty questions leapt frantically into mid-stream and were carried away. Every page in my notebook was scribbled over with notes. To show the state of mind I was in, I will read you a few of them, explaining that the page was headed quite simply, WOMEN AND POVERTY, in block letters; but what followed was something like this:

> Condition in Middle Ages of,
> Habits in the Fiji Islands of,
> Worshipped as goddesses by,
> Weaker in moral sense than,
> Idealism of,
> Greater conscientiousness of,
> South Sea Islanders, age of puberty among,
> Attractiveness of,
> Offered as sacrifice to,
> Small size of brain of,
> Profounder sub-consciousness of,
> Less hair on the body of,
> Mental, moral and physical inferiority of,
> Love of children of,
> Greater length of life of,
> Weaker muscles of,
> Strength of affections of,
> Vanity of,
> Higher education of,
> Shakespeare's opinion of,
> Lord Birkenhead's opinion of,
> Dean Inge's opinion of,
> La Bruyère's opinion of,
> Dr. Johnson's opinion of,
> Mr. Oscar Browning's[4] opinion of, . . .

Here I drew breath and added, indeed, in the margin, Why does Samuel Butler[5] say, "Wise men never say what they think of women"? Wise men never say anything else apparently. But, I continued, leaning back in my chair and looking at the vast dome in which I was a single but by now somewhat harassed thought, what is so unfortunate is that wise men never think the same thing about women. Here is Pope:[6]

> *Most women have no character at all.*

And here is La Bruyère:

> Les femmes sont extrêmes; elles sont meilleures ou pires que les hommes—[7]

4. A schoolmaster and later fellow of King's College, Cambridge (1837–1923); anecdotes about his strong opinions (see p. 1995) were published in a 1927 biography. The first earl of Birkenhead, F. E. Smith (1872–1930), a conservative politician who opposed women's suffrage and praised the domestic "true functions of womanhood." William Ralph Inge (1860–1954), dean of St. Paul's Cathedral in London and a religious writer. Jean de La Bruyère (1645–1696), French moralist and author of satirical *Characters* (1688), imitating the Greek writer Theophrastus. Samuel Johnson (1709–1784), author of moral essays and of the famous *A Dictionary of the English Language* (1747).   5. Satirical author (1835–1902) who wrote *Erewhon* (1872) and *The Way of All Flesh* (1903); his *Notebooks* are the source of this statement.   6. Alexander Pope (1688–1744), translator of Homer and author of *An Essay on Man* (1733–34) and the satirical *The Rape of the Lock* (1712–14).   7. Women are extreme; they are better or worse than men (French).

a direct contradiction by keen observers who were contemporary. Are they capable of education or incapable? Napoleon thought them incapable.[8] Dr. Johnson thought the opposite.[9] Have they souls or have they not souls? Some savages say they have none. Others, on the contrary, maintain that women are half divine and worship them on that account.[1] Some sages hold that they are shallower in the brain; others that they are deeper in the consciousness. Goethe honoured them; Mussolini[2] despises them. Wherever one looked men thought about women and thought differently. It was impossible to make head or tail of it all, I decided, glancing with envy at the reader next door who was making the neatest abstracts, headed often with an A or a B or a C, while my own notebook rioted with the wildest scribble of contradictory jottings. It was distressing, it was bewildering, it was humiliating. Truth had run through my fingers. Every drop had escaped.

I could not possibly go home, I reflected, and add as a serious contribution to the study of women and fiction that women have less hair on their bodies than men, or that the age of puberty among the South Sea Islanders[3] is nine—or is it ninety?—even the handwriting had become in its distraction indecipherable. It was disgraceful to have nothing more weighty or respectable to show after a whole morning's work. And if I could not grasp the truth about W. (as for brevity's sake I had come to call her) in the past, why bother about W. in the future? It seemed pure waste of time to consult all those gentlemen who specialise in woman and her effect on whatever it may be—politics, children, wages, morality—numerous and learned as they are. One might as well leave their books unopened.

But while I pondered I had unconsciously, in my listlessness, in my desperation, been drawing a picture where I should, like my neighbour, have been writing a conclusion. I had been drawing a face, a figure. It was the face and the figure of Professor von X. engaged in writing his monumental work entitled *The Mental, Moral, and Physical Inferiority of the Female Sex.*[4] He was not in my picture a man attractive to women. He was heavily built; he had a great jowl; to balance that he had very small eyes; he was very red in the face. His expression suggested that he was labouring under some emotion that made him jab his pen on the paper as if he were killing some noxious insect as he wrote, but even when he had killed it that did not satisfy him; he must go on killing it; and even so, some cause for anger and irritation remained. Could it be his wife, I asked, looking at my picture. Was she in love with a cavalry officer? Was the cavalry officer slim and elegant and

8. Napoleon wrote: "What we ask of education is not that girls should think, but that they should believe. The weakness of women's brains, the instability of their ideas, the place they will fill in society, their need for perpetual resignation, and for an easy and generous type of charity—all this can only be met by religion" (notes written on May 15, 1807, concerning the establishment of a girl's school at Écouen).   9. " 'Men know that women are an overmatch for them, and therefore they choose the weakest or the most ignorant. If they did not think so, they never could be afraid of women knowing as much as themselves.' . . . Injustice to the sex, I think it but candid to acknowledge that, in a subsequent conversation, he told me that he was serious in what he said."—BOSWELL, *The Journal of a Tour to the Hebrides* [Woolf's note].   1. "The ancient Germans believed that there was something holy in women, and accordingly consulted them as oracles."—FRAZER, *Golden Bough* [Woolf's note].   2. Benito Mussolini (1883–1945), Fascist dictator of Italy between 1922 and 1943. Johann Wolfgang von Goethe (1749–1832), German author of *Faust*. "The eternal feminine draws us along" is the last line of *Faust*, Part 2.   3. The native peoples of the islands in the south-central Pacific Ocean were the subject of several anthropological studies in the early twentieth century, including Margaret Mead's widely read *Coming of Age in Samoa* (1928).   4. A fictional portrait, probably based on Otto Weininger's *Sex and Character* (1906), that distinguished between male (productive and moral) and female (negative and amoral) characteristics.

dressed in astrachan?[5] Had he been laughed at, to adopt the Freudian theory, in his cradle by a pretty girl? For even in his cradle the professor, I thought, could not have been an attractive child. Whatever the reason, the professor was made to look very angry and very ugly in my sketch, as he wrote his great book upon the mental, moral and physical inferiority of women. Drawing pictures was an idle way of finishing an unprofitable morning's work. Yet it is in our idleness, in our dreams, that the submerged truth sometimes comes to the top. A very elementary exercise in psychology, not to be dignified by the name of psycho-analysis, showed me, on looking at my notebook, that the sketch of the angry professor had been made in anger. Anger had snatched my pencil while I dreamt. But what was anger doing there? Interest, confusion, amusement, boredom—all these emotions I could trace and name as they succeeded each other throughout the morning. Had anger, the black snake, been lurking among them? Yes, said the sketch, anger had. It referred me unmistakably to the one book, to the one phrase, which had roused the demon; it was the professor's statement about the mental, moral and physical inferiority of women. My heart had leapt. My cheeks had burnt. I had flushed with anger. There was nothing specially remarkable, however foolish, in that. One does not like to be told that one is naturally the inferior of a little man— I looked at the student next me—who breathes hard, wears a ready-made tie, and has not shaved this fortnight. One has certain foolish vanities. It is only human nature, I reflected, and began drawing cart-wheels and circles over the angry professor's face till he looked like a burning bush or a flaming comet—anyhow, an apparition without human semblance or significance. The professor was nothing now but a faggot burning on the top of Hampstead Heath.[6] Soon my own anger was explained and done with; but curiosity remained. How explain the anger of the professors? Why were they angry? For when it came to analysing the impression left by these books there was always an element of heat. This heat took many forms; it showed itself in satire, in sentiment, in curiosity, in reprobation. But there was another element which was often present and could not immediately be identified. Anger, I called it. But it was anger that had gone underground and mixed itself with all kinds of other emotions. To judge from its odd effects, it was anger disguised and complex, not anger simple and open.

Whatever the reason, all these books,[7] I thought, surveying the pile on the desk, are worthless for my purposes. They were worthless scientifically, that is to say, though humanly they were full of instruction, interest, boredom, and very queer facts about the habits of the Fiji Islanders. They had been written in the red light of emotion and not in the white light of truth. Therefore they must be returned to the central desk and restored each to his own cell in the enormous honeycomb. All that I had retrieved from that morning's work had been the one fact of anger. The professors—I lumped them together thus—were angry. But why, I asked myself, having returned the books, why, I repeated, standing under the colonnade among the pigeons and the prehistoric canoes, why are they angry? And, asking myself this ques-

5. Curly lambskin.   6. A public open space in the village of Hampstead, in London.   7. E.g., *Fijian Society, or the Sociology and Psychology of the Fijians* (1921), by Reverend W. Deane, principal of a teachers' training college in Ndávuilévu, Fiji; and *The Hill Tribes of Fiji* (1922), by A. B. Brewster, a colonial functionary, mixed facts with interpretation. Reverend Deane remarks that "the amount of sexual immorality and promiscuous intercourse during the past forty years is appalling." Fiji is an island in the South Pacific (see n. 3, p. 1981).

tion, I strolled off to find a place for luncheon. What is the real nature of what I call for the moment their anger? I asked. Here was a puzzle that would last all the time that it takes to be served with food in a small restaurant somewhere near the British Museum. Some previous luncher had left the lunch edition of the evening paper on a chair, and, waiting to be served, I began idly reading the headlines. A ribbon of very large letters ran across the page. Somebody had made a big score in South Africa. Lesser ribbons announced that Sir Austen Chamberlain was at Geneva.[8] A meat axe with human hair on it had been found in a cellar. Mr. Justice ———— commented in the Divorce Courts upon the Shamelessness of Women. Sprinkled about the paper were other pieces of news. A film actress had been lowered from a peak in California and hung suspended in mid-air. The weather was going to be foggy. The most transient visitor to this planet, I thought, who picked up this paper could not fail to be aware, even from this scattered testimony, that England is under the rule of a patriarchy. Nobody in their senses could fail to detect the dominance of the professor. His was the power and the money and the influence. He was the proprietor of the paper and its editor and sub-editor. He was the Foreign Secretary and the Judge. He was the cricketer; he owned the race-horses and the yachts. He was the director of the company that pays two hundred per cent to its shareholders. He left millions to charities and colleges that were ruled by himself. He suspended the film actress in mid-air. He will decide if the hair on the meat axe is human; he it is who will acquit or convict the murderer, and hang him, or let him go free. With the exception of the fog he seemed to control every-thing. Yet he was angry. I knew that he was angry by this token. When I read what he wrote about women I thought, not of what he was saying, but of himself. When an arguer argues dispassionately he thinks only of the argu-ment; and the reader cannot help thinking of the argument too. If he had written dispassionately about women, had used indisputable proofs to estab-lish his argument and had shown no trace of wishing that the result should be one thing rather than another, one would not have been angry either. One would have accepted the fact, as one accepts the fact that a pea is green or a canary yellow. So be it, I should have said. But I had been angry because he was angry. Yet it seemed absurd, I thought, turning over the evening paper, that a man with all this power should be angry. Or is anger, I won-dered, somehow, the familiar, the attendant sprite on power? Rich people, for example, are often angry because they suspect that the poor want to seize their wealth. The professors, or patriarchs, as it might be more accurate to call them, might be angry for that reason partly, but partly for one that lies a little less obviously on the surface. Possibly they were not "angry" at all; often, indeed, they were admiring, devoted, exemplary in the relations of private life. Possibly when the professor insisted a little too emphatically upon the inferiority of women, he was concerned not with their inferiority, but with his own superiority. That was what he was protecting rather hot-headedly and with too much emphasis, because it was a jewel to him of the rarest price. Life for both sexes—and I looked at them, shouldering their way along the pavement—is arduous, difficult, a perpetual struggle. It calls

---

8. The site of the League of Nations. Chamberlain was the British Foreign Secretary between 1924 and 1929.

for gigantic courage and strength. More than anything, perhaps, creatures of illusion as we are, it calls for confidence in oneself. Without self-confidence we are as babes in the cradle. And how can we generate this imponderable quality, which is yet so invaluable, most quickly? By thinking that other people are inferior to oneself. By feeling that one has some innate superiority—it may be wealth, or rank, a straight nose, or the portrait of a grandfather by Romney[9]—for there is no end to the pathetic devices of the human imagination—over other people. Hence the enormous importance to a patriarch who has to conquer, who has to rule, of feeling that great numbers of people, half the human race indeed, are by nature inferior to himself. It must indeed be one of the chief sources of his power. But let me turn the light of this observation on to real life, I thought. Does it help to explain some of those psychological puzzles that one notes in the margin of daily life? Does it explain my astonishment the other day when Z, most humane, most modest of men, taking up some book by Rebecca West[1] and reading a passage in it, exclaimed, "The arrant feminist! She says that men are snobs!" The exclamation, to me so surprising—for why was Miss West an arrant feminist for making a possibly true if uncomplimentary statement about the other sex?—was not merely the cry of wounded vanity; it was a protest against some infringement of his power to believe in himself. Women have served all these centuries as looking-glasses possessing the magic and delicious power of reflecting the figure of man at twice its natural size. Without that power probably the earth would still be swamp and jungle. The glories of all our wars would be unknown. We should still be scratching the outlines of deer on the remains of mutton bones and bartering flints for sheepskins or whatever simple ornament took our unsophisticated taste. Supermen[2] and Fingers of Destiny would never have existed. The Czar and the Kaiser would never have worn their crowns or lost them. Whatever may be their use in civilized societies, mirrors are essential to all violent and heroic action. That is why Napoleon and Mussolini both insist so emphatically upon the inferiority of women, for if they were not inferior, they would cease to enlarge. That serves to explain in part the necessity that women so often are to men. And it serves to explain how restless they are under her criticism; how impossible it is for her to say to them this book is bad, this picture is feeble, or whatever it may be, without giving far more pain and rousing far more anger than a man would do who gave the same criticism. For if she begins to tell the truth, the figure in the looking-glass shrinks; his fitness for life is diminished. How is he to go on giving judgment, civilising natives, making laws, writing books, dressing up and speechifying at banquets, unless he can see himself at breakfast and at dinner at least twice the size he really is? So I reflected, crumbling my bread and stirring my coffee and now and again looking at the people in the street. The looking-glass vision is of supreme importance because it charges the vitality; it stimulates the nervous system. Take it away and man may die, like the drug fiend deprived of his cocaine. Under the spell of that illusion, I thought, looking out of the window, half

9. George Romney (1734–1802), portrait painter of 18th-century British society.   1. Pseudonym of Cicily Isabel Andrews (1892–1983), British novelist and journalist.   2. Fascist politicians, such as Adolf Hitler (1889–1945) in Germany and Mussolini (1883–1945) in Italy, rationalized their aggressive policies by exploiting and distorting Friedrich Nietzsche's (1844–1900) concept of the *Übermensch*, or superior being (in *Thus Spake Zarathustra*, 1883–85).

the people on the pavement are striding to work. They put on their hats and coats in the morning under its agreeable rays. They start the day confident, braced, believing themselves desired at Miss Smith's tea party; they say to themselves as they go into the room, I am the superior of half the people here, and it is thus that they speak with that self-confidence, that self-assurance, which have had such profound consequences in public life and lead to such curious notes in the margin of the private mind.

But these contributions to the dangerous and fascinating subject of the psychology of the other sex—it is one, I hope, that you will investigate when you have five hundred a year of your own—were interrupted by the necessity of paying the bill. It came to five shillings and ninepence. I gave the waiter a ten-shilling note and he went to bring me change. There was another ten-shilling note in my purse; I noticed it, because it is a fact that still takes my breath away—the power of my purse to breed ten-shilling notes automatically. I open it and there they are. Society gives me chicken and coffee, bed and lodging, in return for a certain number of pieces of paper which were left me by an aunt, for no other reason than that I share her name.

My aunt, Mary Beton, I must tell you, died by a fall from her horse when she was riding out to take the air in Bombay. The news of my legacy reached me one night about the same time that the act was passed that gave votes to women.[3] A solicitor's letter fell into the post-box and when I opened it I found that she had left me five hundred pounds[4] a year for ever. Of the two—the vote and the money—the money, I own, seemed infinitely the more important. Before that I had made my living by cadging odd jobs from newspapers, by reporting a donkey show here or a wedding there; I had earned a few pounds by addressing envelopes, reading to old ladies, making artificial flowers, teaching the alphabet to small children in a kindergarten. Such were the chief occupations that were open to women before 1918. I need not, I am afraid, describe in any detail the hardness of the work, for you know perhaps women who have done it; nor the difficulty of living on the money when it was earned, for you may have tried. But what still remains with me as a worse infliction than either was the poison of fear and bitterness which those days bred in me. To begin with, always to be doing work that one did not wish to do, and to do it like a slave, flattering and fawning, not always necessarily perhaps, but it seemed necessary and the stakes were too great to run risks; and then the thought of that one gift which it was death to hide[5]—a small one but dear to the possessor—perishing and with it myself, my soul—all this became like a rust eating away the bloom of the spring, destroying the tree at its hearts. However, as I say, my aunt died; and whenever I change a ten-shilling note a little of that rust and corrosion is rubbed off; fear and bitterness go. Indeed, I thought, slipping the silver into my purse, it is remarkable, remembering the bitterness of those days, what a change of temper a fixed income will bring about. No force in the world can take from me my five hundred pounds. Food, house and clothing are mine for ever. Therefore not merely do effort and labour cease, but also hatred

3. Women were given the vote in 1918; the voting age was lowered from thirty to twenty-one in 1928. 4. Roughly nineteen thousand dollars today, calculating inflation and exchange rates between the pound and the dollar in 1928 and 1998. Such calculations are ultimately unreliable, however, since the relative cost of specific items (such as bread or rent) varies. 5. From *When I Consider How My Light Is Spent* by John Milton (1608–1673): "And that one talent which is death to hide, / Lodged with me useless."

and bitterness. I need not hate any man; he cannot hurt me. I need not flatter any man; he has nothing to give me. So imperceptibly I found myself adopting a new attitude towards the other half of the human race. It was absurd to blame any class or any sex, as a whole. Great bodies of people are never responsible for what they do. They are driven by instincts which are not within their control. They too, the patriarchs, the professors, had endless difficulties, terrible drawbacks to contend with. Their education had been in some ways as faulty as my own. It had bred in them defects as great. True, they had money and power, but only at the cost of harbouring in their breasts an eagle, a vulture, for ever tearing the liver out and plucking at the lungs— the instinct for possession, the rage for acquisition which drives them to desire other people's fields and goods perpetually; to make frontiers and flags; battleships and poison gas; to offer up their own lives and their children's lives. Walk through the Admiralty Arch[6] (I had reached that monument), or any other avenue given up to trophies and cannon, and reflect upon the kind of glory celebrated there. Or watch in the spring sunshine the stockbroker and the great barrister going indoors to make money and more money and more money when it is a fact that five hundred pounds a year will keep one alive in the sunshine. These are unpleasant instincts to harbour, I reflected. They are bred of the conditions of life; of the lack of civilisation, I thought, looking at the statue of the Duke of Cambridge,[7] and in particular at the feathers in his cocked hat, with a fixity that they have scarcely ever received before. And, as I realised these drawbacks, by degrees fear and bitterness modified themselves into pity and toleration; and then in a year or two, pity and toleration went, and the greatest release of all came, which is freedom to think of things in themselves. That building, for example, do I like it or not? Is that picture beautiful or not? Is that in my opinion a good book or a bad? Indeed my aunt's legacy unveiled the sky to me, and substituted for the large and imposing figure of a gentleman, which Milton recommended for my perpetual adoration, a view of the open sky.

So thinking, so speculating, I found my way back to my house by the river. Lamps were being lit and an indescribable change had come over London since the morning hour. It was as if the great machine after labouring all day had made with our help a few yards of something very exciting and beauti- ful—a fiery fabric flashing with red eyes, a tawny monster roaring with hot breath. Even the wind seemed flung like a flag as it lashed the houses and rattled the hoardings.

In my little street, however, domesticity prevailed. The house painter was descending his ladder; the nursemaid was wheeling the perambulator care- fully in and out back to nursery tea; the coal-heaver was folding his empty sacks on top of each other; the woman who keeps the green-grocer's shop was adding up the day's takings with her hands in red mittens. But so engrossed was I with the problem you have laid upon my shoulders that I could not see even these usual sights without referring them to one centre. I thought how much harder it is now than it must have been even a century ago to say which of these employments is the higher, the more necessary. Is it better to be a coal-heaver or a nursemaid; is the charwoman who has

---

6. A triple arch in Trafalgar Square (London) at the entrance to the Mall, erected in 1910.   7. An equestrian statue of the second duke of Cambridge (1819–1904), cousin of Queen Victoria, in the full dress uniform of a field marshal.

brought up eight children of less value to the world than the barrister who has made a hundred thousand pounds? It is useless to ask such questions; for nobody can answer them. Not only do the comparative values of char-woman and lawyers rise and fall from decade to decade, but we have no rods with which to measure them even as they are at the moment. I had been foolish to ask my professor to furnish me with "indisputable proofs" of this or that in his argument about women. Even if one could state the value of any one gift at the moment, those values will change; in a century's time very possibly they will have changed completely. Moreover, in a hundred years, I thought, reaching my own doorstep, women will have ceased to be the pro-tected sex. Logically they will take part in all the activities and exertions that were once denied them. The nursemaid will heave coal. The shop-woman will drive an engine. All assumptions founded on the facts observed when women were the protected sex will have disappeared—as, for example (here a squad of soldiers marched down the street), that women and clergymen and gardeners live longer than other people. Remove that protection, expose them to the same exertions and activities, make them soldiers and sailors and engine-drivers and dock labourers, and will not women die off so much younger, so much quicker, than men that one will say, "I saw a woman today," as one used to say, "I saw an aeroplane." Anything may happen when womanhood has ceased to be a protected occupation, I thought, opening the door. But what bearing has all this upon the subject of my paper, Women and Fiction? I asked, going indoors.

CHAPTER THREE

It was disappointing not to have brought back in the evening some important statement, some authentic fact. Women are poorer than men because—this or that. Perhaps now it would be better to give up seeking for the truth, and receiving on one's head an avalanche of opinion hot as lava, discoloured as dish-water. It would be better to draw the curtains; to shut out distractions; to light the lamp; to narrow the enquiry and to ask the historian, who records not opinions but facts, to describe under what conditions women lived, not throughout the ages, but in England, say in the time of Elizabeth.[8]

For it is a perennial puzzle why no woman wrote a word of that extraor-dinary literature when every other man, it seemed, was capable of song or sonnet. What were the conditions in which women lived, I asked myself; for fiction, imaginative work that is, is not dropped like a pebble upon the ground, as science may be; fiction is like a spider's web, attached ever so lightly perhaps, but still attached to life at all four corners. Often the attach-ment is scarcely perceptible; Shakespeare's plays, for instance, seem to hang there complete by themselves. But when the web is pulled askew, hooked up at the edge, torn in the middle, one remembers that these webs are not spun in mid-air by incorporeal creatures, but are the work of suffering human beings, and are attached to grossly material things, like health and money and the houses we live in.

I went, therefore, to the shelf where the histories stand and took down one of the latest, Professor Trevelyan's *History of England*.[9] Once more I

8. Queen of England from 1558 to 1603.   9. Published in London in 1926. References are to pages
260–61 and, later, to pages 436–37.

looked up Women, found "position of," and turned to the pages indicated. "Wife-beating," I read, "was a recognised right of man, and was practised without shame by high as well as low. . . . Similarly," the historian goes on, "the daughter who refused to marry the gentleman of her parents' choice was liable to be locked up, beaten and flung about the room, without any shock being inflicted on public opinion. Marriage was not an affair of personal affection, but of family avarice, particularly in the 'chivalrous' upper classes. . . . Betrothal often took place while one or both of the parties was in the cradle, and marriage when they were scarcely out of the nurses' charge." That was about 1470, soon after Chaucer's[1] time. The next reference to the position of women is some two hundred years later, in the time of the Stuarts.[2] "It was still the exception for women of the upper and middle class to choose their own husbands, and when the husband had been assigned, he was lord and master, so far at least as law and custom could make him. Yet even so," Professor Trevelyan concludes, "neither Shakespeare's women nor those of authentic seventeenth-century memoirs, like the Verneys and the Hutchinsons,[3] seem wanting in personality and character." Certainly, if we consider it, Cleopatra must have had a way with her; Lady Macbeth,[4] one would suppose, had a will of her own; Rosalind, one might conclude, was an attractive girl. Professor Trevelyan is speaking no more than the truth when he remarks that Shakespeare's women do not seem wanting in personality and character. Not being a historian, one might go even further and say that women have burnt like beacons in all the works of all the poets from the beginning of time—Clytemnestra, Antigone, Cleopatra, Lady Macbeth, Phèdre, Cressida, Rosalind, Desdemona, the Duchess of Malfi,[5] among the dramatists; then among the prose writers: Millamant, Clarissa, Becky Sharp, Anna Karenina, Emma Bovary, Madame de Guermantes[6]—the names flock to mind, nor do they recall women "lacking in personality and character." Indeed, if woman had no existence save in the fiction written by men, one would imagine her a person of the utmost importance; very various; heroic and mean; splendid and sordid; infinitely beautiful and hideous in the extreme; as great as a man, some think even greater.[7] But

1. Geoffrey Chaucer (1340?–1400), author of *The Canterbury Tales* (1390–1400).   2. The British royal house from 1603–1714 (except for the Commonwealth interregnum of 1649–60).   3. F. P. Verney compiled *The Memoirs of the Verney Family during the Seventeenth Century* (1892–99), and Lucy Hutchinson recounted her husband's life in *Memoirs of the Life of Colonel Hutchinson* (1806).   4. Heroine of Shakespeare's *Macbeth*. Cleopatra (69–30 B.C.), queen of Egypt and heroine of Shakespeare's *Antony and Cleopatra*.   5. Doomed heroine of John Webster's *The Duchess of Malfi* (ca. 1613). Clytemnestra is the heroine of Aeschylus's *Agamemnon* (458 B.C.). Antigone is the eponymous heroine of a 442 B.C. play by Sophocles. Phèdre is the heroine of Jean Racine's *Phèdre* (1677). Cressida, Rosalind, and Desdemona are heroines of Shakespeare's *Troilus and Cressida*, *As You Like It*, and *Othello*, respectively.   6. A character in Marcel Proust's *Remembrance of Things Past* (*The Guermantes Way*, 1920–21). Millamant is the heroine of William Congreve's satirical comedy *The Way of the World* (1700). Clarissa is the eponymous heroine of Samuel Richardson's seven-volume epistolary novel (1747–48). Becky Sharp appears in William Thackeray's *Vanity Fair* (1847–48). Anna Karenina is the title character in a Leo Tolstoy novel (1875–77). Emma Bovary is the heroine of Gustave Flaubert's *Madame Bovary* (1856).   7. "It remains a strange and almost inexplicable fact that in Athena's city, where women were kept in almost Oriental suppression as odalisques or drudges, the stage should yet have produced figures like Clytemnestra and Cassandra, Atossa and Antigone, Phèdre and Medea, and all the other heroines who dominate play after play of the 'misogynist' Euripides. But the paradox of this world where in real life a respectable woman could hardly show her face alone in the street, and yet on the stage woman equals or surpasses man, has never been satisfactorily explained. In modern tragedy the same predominance exists. At all events, a very cursory survey of Shakespeare's work (similarly with Webster, though not with Marlowe or Jonson) suffices to reveal how this dominance, this initiative of women, persists from Rosalind to Lady Macbeth. So too in Racine; six of his tragedies bear their heroines' names; and what male characters of his shall we set against Hermione and Andromaque, Bérénice and Roxane, Phèdre and Athalie? So again with Ibsen; what men shall we match with Solveig and Nora, Hedda and Hilda Wangel and Rebecca West?"—F. L. LUCAS, *Tragedy*, pp. 114–15 [Woolf's note].

this is woman in fiction. In fact, as Professor Trevelyan points out, she was locked up, beaten and flung about the room.

A very queer, composite being thus emerges. Imaginatively she is of the highest importance; practically she is completely insignificant. She pervades poetry from cover to cover; she is all but absent from history. She dominates the lives of kings and conquerors in fiction; in fact she was the slave of any boy whose parents forced a ring upon her finger. Some of the most inspired words, some of the most profound thoughts in literature fall from her lips; in real life she could hardly read, could scarcely spell, and was the property of her husband.

It was certainly an odd monster that one made up by reading the historians first and the poets afterwards—a worm winged like an eagle; the spirit of life and beauty in a kitchen chopping up suet. But these monsters, however amusing to the imagination, have no existence in fact. What one must do to bring her to life was to think poetically and prosaically at one and the same moment, thus keeping in touch with fact—that she is Mrs. Martin, aged thirty-six, dressed in blue, wearing a black hat and brown shoes; but not losing sight of fiction either—that she is a vessel in which all sorts of spirits and forces are coursing and flashing perpetually. The moment, however, that one tries this method with the Elizabethan woman, one branch of illumination fails; one is held up by the scarcity of facts. One knows nothing detailed, nothing perfectly true and substantial about her. History scarcely mentions her. And I turned to Professor Trevelyan again to see what history meant to him. I found by looking at his chapter headings that it meant—

"The Manor Court and the Methods of Open-field Agriculture . . . The Cistercians and Sheep-farming . . . The Crusades . . . The University . . . The House of Commons . . . The Hundred Years' War . . . The Wars of the Roses . . . The Renaissance Scholars . . . The Dissolution of the Monasteries . . . Agrarian and Religious Strife . . . The Origin of English Sea-power . . . The Armada . . ." and so on. Occasionally an individual woman is mentioned, an Elizabeth, or a Mary; a queen or a great lady. But by no possible means could middle-class women with nothing but brains and character at their command have taken part in any one of the great movements which, brought together, constitute the historian's view of the past. Nor shall we find her in any collection of anecdotes. Aubrey[8] hardly mentions her. She never writes her own life and scarcely keeps a diary; there are only a handful of her letters in existence. She left no plays or poems by which we can judge her. What one wants, I thought—and why does not some brilliant student at Newnham or Girton[9] supply it?—is a mass of information; at what age did she marry; how many children had she as a rule; what was her house like; had she a room to herself; did she do the cooking; would she be likely to have a servant? All these facts lie somewhere, presumably, in parish registers and account books; the life of the average Elizabethan woman must be scattered about somewhere, could one collect it and make a book of it. It would be ambitious beyond my daring, I thought, looking about the shelves for books that were not there, to suggest to the students of those famous colleges that they should re-write history, though I own that it often seems a little queer as it is, unreal,

---

8. John Aubrey (1626–1697), author of *Brief Lives*, which includes sketches of his famous contemporaries.
9. Woolf delivered her lectures at Newnham and Girton Colleges for women, which had become part of Cambridge University in 1880 and 1873, respectively.

lop-sided; but why should they not add a supplement to history? calling it, of course, by some inconspicuous name so that women might figure there without impropriety? For one often catches a glimpse of them in the lives of the great, whisking away into the background, concealing, I sometimes think, a wink, a laugh, perhaps a tear. And, after all, we have lives enough of Jane Austen; it scarcely seems necessary to consider again the influence of the tragedies of Joanna Baillie upon the poetry of Edgar Allan Poe; as for myself, I should not mind if the homes and haunts of Mary Russell Mitford[1] were closed to the public for a century at least. But what I find deplorable, I continued, looking about the bookshelves again, is that nothing is known about women before the eighteenth century. I have no model in my mind to turn about this way and that. Here am I asking why women did not write poetry in the Elizabethan age, and I am not sure how they were educated; whether they were taught to write; whether they had sitting-rooms to themselves; how many women had children before they were twenty-one; what, in short, they did from eight in the morning till eight at night. They had no money evidently; according to Professor Trevelyan they were married whether they liked it or not before they were out of the nursery, at fifteen or sixteen very likely. It would have been extremely odd, even upon this showing, had one of them suddenly written the plays of Shakespeare, I concluded, and I thought of that old gentleman, who is dead now, but was a bishop, I think, who declared that it was impossible for any woman, past, present, or to come, to have the genius of Shakespeare. He wrote to the papers about it. He also told a lady who applied to him for information that cats do not as a matter of fact go to heaven, though they have, he added, souls of a sort. How much thinking those old gentlemen used to save one! How the borders of ignorance shrank back at their approach! Cats do not go to heaven. Women cannot write the plays of Shakespeare.

Be that as it may, I could not help thinking, as I looked at the works of Shakespeare on the shelf, that the bishop was right at least in this; it would have been impossible, completely and entirely, for any woman to have written the plays of Shakespeare in the age of Shakespeare. Let me imagine, since facts are so hard to come by, what would have happened had Shakespeare had a wonderfully gifted sister, called Judith,[2] let us say. Shakespeare himself went, very probably—his mother was an heiress—to the grammar school, where he may have learnt Latin—Ovid, Virgil and Horace[3]—and the elements of grammar and logic. He was, it is well known, a wild boy who poached rabbits, perhaps shot a deer, and had, rather sooner than he should have done, to marry a woman in the neighbourhood, who bore him a child rather quicker than was right. That escapade sent him to seek his fortune in London. He had, it seemed, a taste for the theatre; he began by holding horses at the stage door. Very soon he got work in the theatre, became a successful actor, and lived at the hub of the universe, meeting everybody, knowing everybody, practising his art on the boards, exercising his wits in the streets, and even getting access to the palace of the queen. Meanwhile

---

1. Dramatist, poet, and essayist (1787–1855), author of *Rienzi*, a tragedy in blank verse (1828), and *Our Village* (1832), sketches of country life. Austen (1775–1817), author of *Pride and Prejudice* (1813) and other novels. Baillie (1762–1851), poet and dramatist whose *Plays on the Passions* (1798–1812) were famous in her day.   2. The name of Shakespeare's younger daughter.   3. Roman authors. Publius Ovidius Naso (43 B.C.–A.D. 17), author of the *Metamorphoses*. Publius Vergilius Maro (70–19 B.C.), author of the *Aeneid*. Quintus Horatius Flaccus (65–8 B.C.), author of *Odes* and satires.

his extraordinarily gifted sister, let us suppose, remained at home. She was as adventurous, as imaginative, as agog to see the world as he was. But she was not sent to school. She had no chance of learning grammar and logic, let alone of reading Horace and Virgil. She picked up a book now and then, one of her brother's perhaps, and read a few pages. But then her parents came in and told her to mend the stockings or mind the stew and not moon about with books and papers. They would have spoken sharply but kindly, for they were substantial people who knew the conditions of life for a woman and loved their daughter—indeed, more likely than not she was the apple of her father's eye. Perhaps she scribbled some pages up in an apple loft on the sly, but was careful to hide them or set fire to them. Soon, however, before she was out of her teens, she was to be betrothed to the son of a neighbouring wool-stapler. She cried out that marriage was hateful to her, and for that she was severely beaten by her father. Then he ceased to scold her. He begged her instead not to hurt him, not to shame him in this matter of her marriage. He would give her a chain of beads or a fine petticoat, he said; and there were tears in his eyes. How could she disobey him? How could she break his heart? The force of her own gift alone drove her to it. She made up a small parcel of her belongings, let herself down by a rope one summer's night and took the road to London. She was not seventeen. The birds that sang in the hedge were not more musical than she was. She had the quickest fancy, a gift like her brother's, for the tune of words. Like him, she had a taste for the theatre. She stood at the stage door; she wanted to act, she said. Men laughed in her face. The manager—a fat, loose-lipped man—guffawed. He bellowed something about poodles dancing and women acting—no woman, he said, could possibly be an actress. He hinted—you can imagine what. She could get no training in her craft. Could she even seek her dinner in a tavern or roam the streets at midnight? Yet her genius was for fiction and lusted to feed abundantly upon the lives of men and women and the study of their ways. At last—for she was very young, oddly like Shakespeare the poet in her face, with the same grey eyes and rounded brows—at last Nick Greene[4] the actor-manager took pity on her; she found herself with child by that gentleman and so—who shall measure the heat and violence of the poet's heart when caught and tangled in a woman's body?—killed herself one winter's night and lies buried at some cross-roads where the omnibuses now stop outside the Elephant and Castle.[5]

That, more or less, is how the story would run, I think, if a woman in Shakespeare's day had had Shakespeare's genius. But for my part, I agree with the deceased bishop, if such he was—it is unthinkable that any woman in Shakespeare's day should have had Shakespeare's genius. For genius like Shakespeare's is not born among labouring, uneducated, servile people. It was not born in England among the Saxons and the Britons. It is not born today among the working classes. How, then, could it have been born among women whose work began, according to Professor Trevelyan, almost before they were out of the nursery, who were forced to it by their parents and held to it by all the power of law and custom? Yet genius of a sort must have existed among women as it must have existed among the working classes.

4. A fictional character based on Shakespeare's contemporary Robert Greene (1558–1592) and appearing in Woolf's *Orlando*.   5. A popular London pub.

Now and again an Emily Brontë or a Robert Burns[6] blazes out and proves its presence. But certainly it never got itself on to paper. When, however, one reads of a witch being ducked, of a woman possessed by devils, of a wise woman selling herbs, or even of a very remarkable man who had a mother, then I think we are on the track of a lost novelist, a suppressed poet, of some mute and inglorious[7] Jane Austen, some Emily Brontë who dashed her brains out on the moor or mopped and mowed about the highways crazed with the torture that her gift had put her to. Indeed, I would venture to guess that Anon, who wrote so many poems without signing them, was often a woman. It was a woman Edward Fitzgerald,[8] I think, suggested who made the ballads and the folk-songs, crooning them to her children, beguiling her spinning with them, or the length of the winter's night.

This may be true or it may be false—who can say?—but what is true in it, so it seemed to me, reviewing the story of Shakespeare's sister as I had made it, is that any woman born with a great gift in the sixteenth century would certainly have gone crazed, shot herself, or ended her days in some lonely cottage outside the village, half witch, half wizard, feared and mocked at. For it needs little skill in psychology to be sure that a highly gifted girl who had tried to use her gift for poetry would have been so thwarted and hindered by other people, so tortured and pulled asunder by her own contrary instincts, that she must have lost her health and sanity to a certainty. No girl could have walked to London and stood at a stage door and forced her way into the presence of actor-managers without doing herself a violence and suffering an anguish which may have been irrational—for chastity may be a fetish invented by certain societies for unknown reasons—but were none the less inevitable. Chastity had then, it has even now, a religious importance in a woman's life, and has so wrapped itself round with nerves and instincts that to cut it free and bring it to the light of day demands courage of the rarest. To have lived a free life in London in the sixteenth century would have meant for a woman who was poet and playwright a nervous stress and dilemma which might well have killed her. Had she survived, whatever she had written would have been twisted and deformed, issuing from a strained and morbid imagination. And undoubtedly, I thought, looking at the shelf where there are no plays by women, her work would have gone unsigned. That refuge she would have sought certainly. It was the relic of the sense of chastity that dictated anonymity to women even so late as the nineteenth century. Currer Bell, George Eliot, George Sand,[9] all the victims of inner strife as their writings prove, sought ineffectively to veil themselves by using the name of a man. Thus they did homage to the convention, which if not implanted by the other sex was liberally encouraged by them (the chief glory of a woman is not to be talked of, said Pericles,[1] himself a much-talked-of man), that publicity in women is detestable. Anonymity runs in their blood. The desire to be veiled still possesses them. They are not even now as concerned about the health of their fame as men are, and, speaking generally, will pass a tombstone or a signpost without feeling an irresistible desire to

---

6. Scottish poet (1759–1796). Brontë (1818–1848), author of *Wuthering Heights*.   7. A reference to Thomas Grey's line in *Elegy Written in a Country Churchyard* (1751): "Some mute inglorious Milton here may rest."   8. British author (1809–1883), known for his translation from the Persian of the *Rubáiyát of Omar Khayyám* (1859).   9. Pseudonyms of Charlotte Brontë; Mary Ann Evans (1819–1880), author of *Middlemarch* (1871–72); and Lucile-Aurore Dupin (1804–1876), author of *Lélia* (1833), respectively. 1. From the Greek leader Pericles' funeral oration (431 B.C.), as reported in Thucydides' history of the Peloponnesian War (2.35–46).

cut their names on it, as Alf, Bert or Chas. must do in obedience to their instinct, which murmurs if it sees a fine woman go by, or even a dog, Ce chien est à moi.[2] And, of course, it may not be a dog, I thought, remembering Parliament Square, the Sièges Allée[3] and other avenues; it may be a piece of land or a man with curly black hair. It is one of the great advantages of being a woman that one can pass even a very fine negress without wishing to make an Englishwoman of her.

That woman, then, who was born with a gift of poetry in the sixteenth century, was an unhappy woman, a woman at strife against herself. All the conditions of her life, all her own instincts, were hostile to the state of mind which is needed to set free whatever is in the brain. But what is the state of mind that is most propitious to the act of creation, I asked. Can one come by any notion of the state that furthers and makes possible that strange activity? Here I opened the volume containing the Tragedies of Shakespeare. What was Shakespeare's state of mind, for instance, when he wrote Lear and Antony and Cleopatra? It was certainly the state of mind most favourable to poetry that there has ever existed. But Shakespeare himself said nothing about it. We only know casually and by chance that he "never blotted a line."[4] Nothing indeed was ever said by the artist himself about his state of mind until the eighteenth century perhaps. Rousseau[5] perhaps began it. At any rate, by the nineteenth century self-consciousness had developed so far that it was the habit for men of letters to describe their minds in confessions and autobiographies. Their lives also were written, and their letters were printed after their deaths. Thus, though we do not know what Shakespeare went through when he wrote Lear, we do know what Carlyle went through when he wrote the French Revolution; what Flaubert went through when he wrote Madame Bovary; what Keats[6] was going through when he tried to write poetry against the coming of death and the indifference of the world.

And one gathers from this enormous modern literature of confession and self-analysis that to write a work of genius is almost always a feat of prodigious difficulty. Everything is against the likelihood that it will come from the writer's mind whole and entire. Generally material circumstances are against it. Dogs will bark; people will interrupt; money must be made; health will break down. Further, accentuating all these difficulties and making them harder to bear is the world's notorious indifference. It does not ask people to write poems and novels and histories; it does not need them. It does not care whether Flaubert finds the right word or whether Carlyle scrupulously verifies this or that fact. Naturally, it will not pay for what it does not want. And so the writer, Keats, Flaubert, Carlyle, suffers, especially in the creative years of youth, every form of distraction and discouragement. A curse, a cry of agony, rises from those books of analysis and confession. "Mighty poets in their misery dead"—that is the burden of their song. If anything comes through in spite of all this, it is a miracle, and probably no book is born entire and uncrippled as it was conceived.

But for women, I thought, looking at the empty shelves, these difficulties

---

2. This dog is mine (French); from the philosopher Blaise Pascal's *Thoughts* (1657–58). He uses an anecdote about poor children to illustrate a universal impulse to assert property claims.   3. An avenue in Berlin containing statues of Hohenzollern rulers. Parliament Square is in London next to the Houses of Parliament and Westminster Abbey.   4. Ben Jonson's (1572–1637) description of Shakespeare. 5. Jean-Jacques Rousseau (1712–1778), French author of the *Confessions* (1781).   6. John Keats (1795–1821), British poet. Thomas Carlyle (1795–1881), essayist and historian, translator of Goethe and author of *The French Revolution* (1837).

were infinitely more formidable. In the first place, to have a room of her own, let alone a quiet room or a sound-proof room, was out of the question, unless her parents were exceptionally rich or very noble, even up to the beginning of the nineteenth century. Since her pin money, which depended on the good will of her father, was only enough to keep her clothed, she was debarred from such alleviations as came even to Keats or Tennyson[7] or Carlyle, all poor men, from a walking tour, a little journey to France, from the separate lodging which, even if it were miserable enough, sheltered them from the claims and tyrannies of their families. Such material difficulties were formidable; but much worse were the immaterial. The indifference of the world which Keats and Flaubert and other men of genius have found so hard to bear was in her case not indifference but hostility. The world did not say to her as it said to them, Write if you choose; it makes no difference to me. The world said with a guffaw, Write? What's the good of your writing? Here the psychologists of Newnham and Girton might come to our help, I thought, looking again at the blank spaces on the shelves. For surely it is time that the effect of discouragement upon the mind of the artist should be measured, as I have seen a dairy company measure the effect of ordinary milk and Grade A milk upon the body of the rat. They set two rats in cages side by side, and of the two one was furtive, timid and small, and the other was glossy, bold and big. Now what food do we feed women as artists upon? I asked, remembering, I suppose, that dinner of prunes and custard. To answer that question I had only to open the evening paper and to read that Lord Birkenhead is of opinion—but really I am not going to trouble to copy out Lord Birkenhead's opinion upon the writing of women. What Dean Inge says I will leave in peace. The Harley Street specialist may be allowed to rouse the echoes of Harley Street with his vociferations without raising a hair on my head. I will quote, however, Mr. Oscar Browning, because Mr. Oscar Browning was a great figure in Cambridge at one time, and used to examine the students at Girton and Newnham. Mr. Oscar Browning was wont to declare "that the impression left on his mind, after looking over any set of examination papers, was that, irrespective of the marks he might give, the best woman was intellectually the inferior of the worst man." After saying that Mr. Browning went back to his rooms—and it is this sequel that endears him and makes him a human figure of some bulk and majesty—he went back to his rooms and found a stable-boy lying on the sofa—"a mere skeleton, his cheeks were cavernous and sallow, his teeth were black, and he did not appear to have the full use of his limbs. . . . 'That's Arthur' [said Mr. Browning]. 'He's a dear boy really and most high-minded.' " The two pictures always seem to me to complete each other. And happily in this age of biography the two pictures often do complete each other, so that we are able to interpret the opinions of great men not only by what they say, but by what they do.

But though this is possible now, such opinions coming from the lips of important people must have been formidable enough even fifty years ago. Let us suppose that a father from the highest motives did not wish his daughter to leave home and become writer, painter or scholar. "See what Mr. Oscar Browning says," he would say; and there was not only Mr. Oscar Browning; there was the *Saturday Review*; there was Mr. Greg[8]—the "essentials of a

7. Alfred, Lord Tennyson (1809–1892), British poet.   8. William Rathbone Greg (1809–1891), cited from a *Saturday Review* essay titled *Why Are Women Redundant?*

woman's being," said Mr. Greg emphatically, "are that *they are supported by, and they minister to, men*"—there was an enormous body of masculine opinion to the effect that nothing could be expected of women intellectually. Even if her father did not read out loud these opinions, any girl could read them for herself; and the reading, even in the nineteenth century, must have lowered her vitality, and told profoundly upon her work. There would always have been that assertion—you cannot do this, you are incapable of doing that—to protest against, to overcome. Probably for a novelist this germ is no longer of much effect; for there have been women novelists of merit. But for painters it must still have some sting in it; and for musicians, I imagine, is even now active and poisonous in the extreme. The woman composer stands where the actress stood in the time of Shakespeare. Nick Greene, I thought, remembering the story I had made about Shakespeare's sister, said that a woman acting put him in mind of a dog dancing. Johnson repeated the phrase two hundred years later of women preaching. And here, I said, opening a book about music, we have the very words used again in this year of grace, 1928, of women who try to write music. "Of Mlle. Germaine Tailleferre one can only repeat Dr. Johnson's dictum concerning a woman preacher, transposed into terms of music. 'Sir, a woman's composing is like a dog's walking on his hind legs. It is not done well, but you are surprised to find it done at all.' "[9] So accurately does history repeat itself.

Thus, I concluded, shutting Mr. Oscar Browning's life and pushing away the rest, it is fairly evident that even in the nineteenth century a woman was not encouraged to be an artist. On the contrary, she was snubbed, slapped, lectured and exhorted. Her mind must have been strained and her vitality lowered by the need of opposing this, of disproving that. For here again we come within range of that very interesting and obscure masculine complex which has had so much influence upon the woman's movement; that deep-seated desire, not so much that *she* shall be inferior as that *he* shall be superior, which plants him wherever one looks, not only in front of the arts, but barring the way to politics too, even when the risk to himself seems infinitesimal and the suppliant humble and devoted. Even Lady Bessborough,[1] I remembered, with all her passion for politics, must humbly bow herself and write to Lord Granville Leveson-Gower: " . . . notwithstanding all my violence in politics and talking so much on that subject, I perfectly agree with you that no woman has any business to meddle with that or any other serious business, farther than giving her opinion (if she is ask'd)." And so she goes on to spend her enthusiasm where it meets with no obstacle whatsoever upon that immensely important subject, Lord Granville's maiden speech in the House of Commons. The spectacle is certainly a strange one, I thought. The history of men's opposition to women's emancipation is more interesting perhaps than the story of that emancipation itself. An amusing book might be made of it if some young student at Girton or Newnham would collect examples and deduce a theory—but she would need thick gloves on her hands, and bars to protect her of solid gold.

But what is amusing now, I recollected, shutting Lady Bessborough, had to be taken in desperate earnest once. Opinions that one now pastes in a

9. *A Survey of Contemporary Music*, Cecil Gray, p. 246 [Woolf's note]. The statement is originally found in James Boswell's *Life of Johnson* (1791).   1. Henrietta, Countess of Bessborough, who corresponded with Lord Granville George Leveson-Gower (1815–1891), British foreign secretary in William Gladstone's administrations and after him the leader of the Liberal Party.

book labelled cock-a-doodle-dum and keeps for reading to select audiences on summer nights once drew tears, I can assure you. Among your grand-mothers and great-grandmothers there were many that wept their eyes out. Florence Nightingale shrieked aloud in her agony.[2] Moreover, it is all very well for you, who have got yourselves to college and enjoy sitting-rooms—or is it only bed-sitting-rooms?—of your own to say that genius should disregard such opinions; that genius should be above caring what is said of it. Unfor-tunately, it is precisely the men or women of genius who mind most what is said of them. Remember Keats. Remember the words he had cut on his tombstone.[3] Think of Tennyson; think—but I need hardly multiply instances of the undeniable, if very, unfortunate, fact that it is the nature of the artist to mind excessively what is said about him. Literature is strewn with the wreckage of men who have minded beyond reason the opinions of others.

And this susceptibility of theirs is doubly unfortunate, I thought, returning again to my original enquiry into what state of mind is most propitious for creative work, because the mind of an artist, in order to achieve the prodi-gious effort of freeing whole and entire the work that is in him, must be incandescent, like Shakespeare's mind, I conjectured, looking at the book which lay open at *Antony and Cleopatra*. There must be no obstacle in it, no foreign matter unconsumed.

For though we say that we know nothing about Shakespeare's state of mind, even as we say that, we are saying something about Shakespeare's state of mind. The reason perhaps why we know so little of Shakespeare—compared with Donne or Ben Jonson or Milton—is that his grudges and spites and antipathies are hidden from us. We are not held up by some "revelation" which reminds us of the writer. All desire to protest, to preach, to proclaim an injury, to pay off a score, to make the world the witness of some hardship or grievance was fired out of him and consumed. Therefore his poetry flows from him free and unimpeded. If ever a human being got his work expressed completely, it was Shakespeare. If ever a mind was incan-descent, unimpeded, I thought, turning again to the bookcase, it was Shake-speare's mind.

---

2. See *Cassandra*, by Florence Nightingale, printed in *The Cause*, by R. Strachey [Woolf's note]. Nightingale (1820–1910), English nurse and founder of nursing as a profession for women.   3. "Here lies one whose name was writ in water."

FRANZ KAFKA
1883–1924

The predicament of Franz Kafka's writing is, for many, the predicament of modern civilization. Nowhere is the anxiety and alienation of twentieth-century society more visible than in his stories of individuals struggling to prevail against a vast, meaning-less, and apparently hostile system. Identifying that system as bureaucracy, family, religion, language, or the invisible network of social habit is less important than rec-ognizing the protagonists' bewilderment at being placed in impossible situations. Kafka's heroes are driven to find answers in an unresponsive world, and they are required to act according to incomprehensible rules administered by an inaccessible authority; small wonder that they fluctuate between fear, hope, anger, resignation, and despair. Kafka's fictional world has long fascinated contemporary writers, who find in it an extraordinary blend of prosaic realism and nightmarish, infinitely interpretable symbolism. Whether evoking the multilayered bureaucracy of the modern state, the sense of guilt felt by those facing the accusations of authority, or the vulnerability of characters who cannot make themselves understood, Kafka's descriptions are believable because of their scrupulous attention to detail: the flea on a fur collar, the dust under an unmade bed, the creases and yellowing of an old newspaper, or the helplessness of a beetle turned upside down. The sheer *ordinariness* of these details grounds the entire narrative, giving the reader a continuing expectation of reality even when events escape all logic and the situation is at its most hallucinatory. This paradoxical combination has appealed to a range of contemporary writers—each quite different from the other—who have read and absorbed Kafka's lesson: Samuel Beckett, Harold Pinter, Alain Robbe-Grillet, Gabriel García Márquez.

Kafka was born into cultural alienation: Jewish (though not truly part of the Jewish community) in Catholic Bohemia, son of a German-speaking shopkeeper when German was the language of the imposed Austro-Hungarian government, and drawn to literature when his father—a domineering, self-made man—pushed him toward success in business. Nor was he happier at home. Resenting his father's overbearing nature and feeling deprived of maternal love, he nonetheless lived with his parents for most of his life and complained in long letters about his coldness and inability to love (despite numerous liaisons). Kafka took a degree in law to qualify himself for a position in a large accident-insurance corporation, where he worked until illness forced his retirement in 1922. By the time of his death from tuberculosis two years later, he had published a number of short stories and two novellas (*The Metamorphosis*, 1915; *In the Penal Colony*, 1919), but left behind him the manuscripts of three near-complete novels that—considering himself a failure—he asked to have burned. Instead, Kafka's executor, Max Brod, published the novels (*The Trial*, 1925; *The Castle*, 1926; *Amerika*, 1927) and a biography celebrating the genius of his tormented, guilt-ridden friend.

Despite the indubitable fact that Franz Kafka became a respected senior executive, handling claims, litigations, public relations, and his institute's annual reports, and was one of the few top German executives retained when Czechoslovakia came into existence in 1918, his image in the modern imagination is derived from the portraits of inner anguish given in his fiction, diaries, and letters. This "Kafka" is a tormented and sensitive soul, guiltily resentful of his job in a giant bureaucracy, unable to free himself from his family or to cope with the demands of love, physically feeble, and constantly beset by feelings of inferiority and doom in an existence whose laws he can never quite understand. "Before the Law," a parable published in Kafka's lifetime and included in *The Trial*, recounts the archetypal setting of the "Kafka" character: a countryman waits and waits throughout his lifetime for permission to enter a crucial Gate, where the doorkeeper (the first of many) repeatedly refuses him entrance. He tries everything from good behavior to bribes without success. Finally, as the now-aged countryman dies in frustration, he is told that the gate existed only for him, and that it is now being closed. For the countryman (as for Vladimir and Estragon in Beckett's *Waiting for Godot*, and indeed for much modern literature), there is no response. The Law that governs our existence is all-powerful but irrational; at least it is not to be understood by its human suppliants, a lesson that Kafka could have derived equally well from his readings in the Danish philosopher Søren Kierkegaard, in Friedrich Nietzsche, or in the Jewish Talmud.

The combination of down-to-earth, matter-of-fact setting and unreal or nightmarish events is the hallmark of Kafka's style. His characters speak prosaically and react in a commonsense way when such a response (given the situation) is utterly grotesque. A young businessman is changed overnight into a giant beetle (*The Meta-*

morphosis) or charged with undefined crimes and finally executed (*The Trial*); a would-be land surveyor is unable to communicate with the castle that employs him and that keeps sending incomprehensible messages (*The Castle*); a visitor to a penal colony observes a gigantic machine whose function is to execute condemned criminals by inscribing their sentence deeper and deeper into their flesh (*In the Penal Colony*). The term *surrealist* is often attached to this blend of everyday reality and dream configuration, with its implication of psychic undercurrents and cosmic significance stirring beneath the most ordinary-seeming existence. Kafka, however, had no connection with the Surrealists, whose vision of a miraculous level of existence hidden behind everyday life is the obverse of his heroes' vain attempts to maintain control over the impossible and the absurd.

Kafka's stories are not allegories, although many readers have been tempted to find in them an underlying message. A political reading sees them as indictments of faceless bureaucracy controlling individual lives in the modern totalitarian state. The sense of being found guilty by an entire society recalls the traditional theme of the Wandering Jew and predicts for many the Holocaust of World War II (in fact, Kafka's three sisters died in concentration camps). His heroes' self-conscious quest to fit into some meaningful structure, their ceaseless attempts to do the right thing when there is no rational way of knowing what that is, is the very picture of absurdity and alienation that existentialist philosophers and writers examined during and after World War II. The assumption that there is a Law and the presence of protagonists who die in search for purity (*The Hunger Artist*) or in a humble admission of guilt (*The Trial*) allow the stories to be taken as religious metaphors. Kafka's desperately lucid analysis of the way his parents' influence shaped an impressionable child into an unhappy adult (*Letter to My Father*) articulates emotional tangles and parent-child rivalry with an openness and detail that recalls decades of psychoanalytical criticism following Freud. The picture of a sick society where individual rights and sensitivity no longer count and unreasoning torment is visited on the ignorant has been read as an indictment of disintegrating modern culture. Yet no one allegorical interpretation is finally possible, for all these potential meanings overlap as they expand toward social, familial, political, philosophical, and religious dimensions and constitute the richly allusive texture of separate tales by a master storyteller.

The Metamorphosis, Kafka's longest complete work published in his lifetime, is first of all a consummate narrative: the question "What happens next?" never disappears from the moment that Gregor Samsa wakes up to find himself transformed. "It was no dream," no nightmarish fantasy in which Gregor temporarily identified himself with other downtrodden vermin of society. Instead, this grotesque transformation is permanent, a single unshakable fact that renders almost comic his family's calculations and attempts to adjust. "The terror of art," said Kafka in a conversation about *The Metamorphosis*, is that "the dream reveals the reality." This artistic dream, become Gregor's reality, sheds light on the intolerable nature of his former daily existence. The other side of his job is its mechanical rigidity, personal rivalries, and threatening suspicion of any deviation from the norm. Gregor himself is part of this world, as he shows when he fawns on the manager and tries to manipulate him by criticizing their boss.

More disturbing is the transformation that takes place in Gregor's family, where the expected love and support turns into shamed acceptance and animal resentment now that Gregor has let the family down. Mother and sister are ineffectual, and their sympathy is slowly replaced by disgust. Gregor's father quickly reassumes his position of authority and beats the beetle back into his room: first with the businesslike newspaper and manager's cane, and later with a barrage of apples from the family table. Just before his death Gregor has become an "it" whose death is warmly wished by the whole family—and perhaps they are right, in one of Kafka's ironies. The beetle's death brings not remorse but a new lease on life to his family. Weak and passive when Gregor took care of them, they regain strength and vitality under the pressure of earning a living. Mother, father, and sister celebrate Gregor's death with a holiday trip out of town, into the sunshine and open air, where they make plans for the future.

Gregor Samsa may be a pathetic figure, but he is not a tragic one. In his passiveness and unvoiced resentment, his willingness to exist at a surface level of adjustment to job and family, he has become an accomplice in his own fate. His descent into animal consciousness is not a true pilgrimage to inner awareness, even though it involves letting go the trappings of civilization. Rather, it is an obscuring of consciousness that is perfectly represented when he is swept out onto the dustheap at the end. From that point on, it is the family's story, continuing a career that has meant death for Gregor and joyous survival for his family but in which both are reduced to existence on an animal level.

Anthony Thorlby, *Kafka: A Study* (1972), is a brief general introduction. Heinz Politzer, *Franz Kafka: Parable and Paradox* (1966), presents an interesting, readable study of symbolic relationships. Ernest Pawel, *The Nightmare of Reason: A Life of Franz Kafka* (1984), is an excellent modern biography with penetrating descriptions of his family and friends. Max Brod, *Franz Kafka: A Biography* (1960), is an early, admiring biography by a close friend and Kafka's executor. Ronald Gray, ed., *Kafka: A Collection of Critical Essays* (1962), is a useful early collection of essays on different works. Harold Bloom, ed., *Franz Kafka's The Metamorphosis* (1988), collects essays on spiritual, metaphorical, formal, social, and psychoanalytic aspects of *The Metamorphosis*. Jack Murray analyzes the sense of space in *The Landscapes of Alienation: Ideological Subversion in Kafka, Céline, and Onetti* (1991). Kurt Fickert, *End of a Mission: Kafka's Search for Truth in His Last Stories* (1993), interprets the stories as metaphors for an autobiographical quest to resolve personal problems.

The Metamorphosis[1]

I

One morning, upon awakening from agitated dreams, Gregor Samsa found himself, in his bed, transformed into a monstrous vermin. He lay on his hard, armorlike back, and when lifting his head slightly, he could view his brown, vaulted belly partitioned by arching ridges, while on top of it, the blanket, about to slide off altogether, could barely hold. His many legs, wretchedly thin compared with his overall girth, danced helplessly before his eyes.

"What's happened to me?" he wondered. It was no dream. His room, a normal if somewhat tiny human room, lay quietly between the four familiar walls. Above the table, on which a line of fabric samples had been unpacked and spread out (Samsa was a traveling salesman), hung the picture that he had recently clipped from an illustrated magazine and inserted in a pretty gilt frame. The picture showed a lady sitting there upright, bedizened in a fur hat and fur boa, with her entire forearm vanishing inside a heavy fur muff that she held out toward the viewer.

Gregor's eyes then focused on the window, and the dismal weather—rain-drops could be heard splattering on the metal ledge—made him feel quite melancholy.

"What if I slept a little more and forgot all about this nonsense," he thought. But his idea was impossible to carry out, for while he was accustomed to sleeping on his right side, his current state prevented him from

1. Translated by Joachim Neugroschel.

getting into that position. No matter how forcefully he attempted to wrench himself over on his right side, he kept rocking back into his supine state. He must have tried it a hundred times, closing his eyes to avoid having to look at those wriggling legs, and he gave up only when he started feeling a mild, dull ache in his side such as he had never felt before.

"Oh, God," he thought, "what a strenuous profession I've picked! Day in, day out on the road. It's a lot more stressful than the work in the home office, and along with everything else I also have to put up with these agonies of traveling—worrying about making trains, having bad, irregular meals, meeting new people all the time, but never forming any lasting friendships that mellow into anything intimate. To hell with it all!"

Feeling a slight itch on his belly, he slowly squirmed along on his back toward the bedpost in order to raise his head more easily. Upon locating the itchy place, which was dotted with lots of tiny white specks that he could not fathom, he tried to touch the area with one of his legs, but promptly withdrew it, for the contact sent icy shudders through his body.

He slipped back into his former position.

"Getting up so early all the time," he thought, "makes you totally stupid. A man has to have his sleep. Other traveling salesmen live like harem women. For instance, whenever I return to the hotel during the morning to write up my orders, those men are still having breakfast. Just let me try that with my boss; I'd be kicked out on the spot. And anyway, who knows, that might be very good for me. If I weren't holding back because of my parents, I would have given notice long ago, I would have marched straight up to the boss and told him off from the bottom of my heart. He would have toppled from his desk! Besides, it's so peculiar the way he seats himself on it and talks down to the employees from his great height, and we also have to get right up close because he's so hard of hearing. Well, I haven't abandoned all hope; once I've saved enough to pay off my parents' debt to him—that should take another five or six years—I'll go through with it no matter what. I'll make a big, clean break! But for now, I've got to get up, my train is leaving at five A.M."

And he glanced at the alarm clock ticking on the wardrobe. "God Almighty!" he thought. It was six-thirty, and the hands of the clock were calmly inching forward, it was even past the half hour, it was almost a quarter to. Could the alarm have failed to go off? From the bed, you could see that it was correctly set at four o'clock; it must have gone off. Yes, but was it possible to sleep peacefully through that furniture-quaking jangle? Well, fine, he had not slept peacefully, though probably all the more soundly. But what should he do now? The next train would be leaving at seven; and to catch it, he would have to rush like mad, and the samples weren't packed up yet, and he felt anything but fresh or sprightly. And even if he did catch the train, there would be no avoiding the boss's fulminations, for the errand boy must have waited at the five A.M. train and long since reported Gregor's failure to show up. The boy was the director's creature, spineless and mindless. Now what if Gregor reported sick? But that would be extremely embarrassing and suspect, for throughout his five years with the firm he had never been sick even once. The boss was bound to come over with the medical-plan doctor, upbraid the parents about their lazy son, and cut off all objections by referring to the doctor, for whom everybody in the world was in the best of health but work-shy. And besides, would the doctor be all that wrong in this case? Aside from his drowsiness, which was really superfluous after his long sleep, Gregor actually felt fine and was even ravenous.

As he speedily turned all these things over in his mind, but could not resolve to get out of bed—the alarm clock was just striking a quarter to seven—there was a cautious rap on the door near the top end of his bed.

"Gregor," a voice called—it was his mother—"it's a quarter to seven. Didn't you have a train to catch?"

The gentle voice! Gregor was shocked to hear his own response; it was unmistakably his earlier voice, but with a painful and insuppressible squeal blending in as if from below, virtually leaving words in their full clarity for just a moment, only to garble them in their resonance, so that you could not tell whether you had heard right. Gregor had meant to reply in detail and explain everything, but, under the circumstances, he limited himself to saying, "Yes, yes, thank you, Mother, I'm getting up."

Because of the wooden door, the change in Gregor's voice was probably not audible on the other side, for the mother was put at ease by his reassurance and she shuffled away. However, their brief exchange had made the rest of the family realize that Gregor, unexpectedly, was still at home, and the father was already at one side door, knocking weakly though with his fist: "Gregor, Gregor," he called, "what's wrong?" And after a short pause, he admonished him again, though in a deeper voice, "Gregor! Gregor!"

At the other side door, however, the sister plaintively murmured, "Gregor? Aren't you well? Do you need anything?"

Gregor replied to both sides, "I'm ready now," and by enunciating fastidiously with drawn-out pauses between words, he tried to eliminate anything abnormal from his voice. Indeed, the father returned to his breakfast; but the sister whispered, "Gregor, open up, I beg you." However, Gregor had absolutely no intention of opening up; instead, he praised the cautious habit he had developed during his travels of locking all doors at night, even in his home.

For now, he wanted to get up calmly and without being nagged, put on his clothes, above all have breakfast, and only then think about what to do next; for he realized he would come to no sensible conclusion by pondering in bed. He remembered that often, perhaps from lying awkwardly, he had felt a slight ache, which, upon his getting up, had turned out to be purely imaginary, and he looked forward to seeing today's fancies gradually fading away. He had no doubt whatsoever that the change in his voice was nothing but the harbinger of a severe cold, an occupational hazard of traveling salesmen.

Throwing off the blanket was quiet simple; all he had to do was puff himself up a little, and it dropped away by itself. Doing anything else, however, was difficult, especially since he was so uncommonly broad. He would have needed arms and hands to prop himself up, and all he had was the numerous tiny legs that kept perpetually moving every which way but without his managing to control them. If he tried to bend a leg, it first straightened out; and if he finally succeeded in taking charge of it, the other legs meanwhile all kept carrying on, as if emancipated, in extreme and painful agitation. "Just don't dawdle in bed," Gregor told himself.

To start with, he wanted to get out of bed with the lower part of his body;

but this portion, which, incidentally, he had not yet seen and could not properly visualize, proved too cumbersome to move—it went so slowly. And when eventually, having grown almost frantic, he gathered all his strength and recklessly thrust forward, he chose the wrong direction and slammed violently into the lower bedpost, whereupon the burning pain he then felt made him realize that the lower part of his body might be precisely the most sensitive, at least for now.

He therefore first tried to get his upper portion out of the bed, and to do so he cautiously turned his head toward the side of the mattress. This actually proved easy; and eventually, despite its breadth and weight, his body bulk slowly followed the twisting of his head. But when his head was finally looming over the edge of the bed, in the free air, he was scared of advancing any further in this manner; for if he ultimately let himself plunge down like this, only an outright miracle would prevent injury to his head. And no matter what, he must not lose consciousness now of all times; he would be better off remaining in bed.

But when, sighing after repeating this exertion, he still lay there as before, watching his tiny legs battle each other perhaps even more fiercely and finding no way to bring peace and order to this idiosyncratic condition, he again mused that he could not possibly stay there. The most logical recourse would be to make any sacrifice whatsoever if there was even the slightest hope of his freeing himself from the bed. Yet at the same time, he did not neglect to keep reminding himself that a calm, indeed the calmest reflection was far superior to desperate resolves. In such moments, he fixed his eyes as sharply as he could on the window; but unfortunately, little comfort or encouragement could be drawn from the sight of the morning fog, which shrouded even the other side of the narrow street. "Already seven o'clock," he said to himself when the alarm clock struck again, "already seven o'clock and still such a thick fog." And for a short while, he lay quietly, breathing faintly, as if perhaps expecting the silence to restore real and normal circumstances.

But then he told himself, "I absolutely must be out of bed completely before the clock strikes seven-fifteen. Besides, by then someone from work will come to inquire about me, since the office opens before seven." And he now began seesawing the full length of his body at an altogether even rhythm in order to rock it from the bed. If he could get himself to tumble from the bed in this way, then he would no doubt prevent injury to his head by lifting it sharply while falling. His back seemed hard; nothing was likely to happen to it during the landing on the carpet. His greatest misgiving was about the loud crash that was sure to ensue, probably causing anxiety if not terror behind all the doors. Still, this risk had to be run.

By the time Gregor was already sticking halfway out of the bed (this new method was more of a game than a struggle, all he had to do was keep seesawing and wrenching himself along), it occurred to him how easy everything would be if someone lent him a hand. It would take only two strong people (he thought of his father and the maid); they would only have to slip their arms under his vaulted back, slide him out of the bed, crouch down with their burden, and then just wait patiently and cautiously as he flipped over to the floor, where he hoped his tiny legs would have some purpose. Now quite aside from the fact that the doors were locked, should he really call for assistance? Despite his misery, he could not help smiling at the very idea.

By now he was already seesawing so intensely that he barely managed to keep his balance, and so he would have to make up his mind very soon, for it was already ten after seven—when the doorbell rang. "It's someone from the office," he told himself, almost petrified, while his tiny legs only danced all the more hastily. For an instant, there was total hush. "They're not answering," Gregor said to himself, prey to some absurd hope. But then of course, the maid, as usual, strode firmly to the door and opened it. Gregor only had to hear the visitor's first word of greeting and he knew who it was—the office manager himself. Why oh why was Gregor condemned to working for a company where the slightest tardiness aroused the murkiest suspicions? Was every last employee a scoundrel, wasn't there a single loyal and dedicated person among them, a man who, if he failed to devote even a few morning hours to the firm, would go crazy with remorse, becoming absolutely incapable of leaving his bed? Wouldn't it suffice to send an office boy to inquire—if indeed this snooping were at all necessary? Did the office manager himself have to come, did the entire innocent family have to be shown that this was the only person who had enough brains to be entrusted with investigating this suspicious affair? And more because of these agitating reflections than because of any concrete decision, Gregor swung himself out of bed with all his might. There was a loud thud, but not really a crash. His fall was slightly cushioned by the carpet; and also, his back was more pliable than he had thought. Hence the dull thud was not so blatant. However, by not holding his head carefully enough, he had banged it; now he twisted it, rubbing it on the carpet in annoyance and pain.

"Something fell in there," said the office manager in the left-hand room. Gregor tried to imagine whether something similar to what had happened to him today might not someday happen to the office manager. After all, the possibility had to be granted. However, as if in brusque response to this question, the office manager now took a few resolute steps in the next room, causing his patent-leather boots to creak.

From the right-hand room, the sister informed Gregor in a whisper, "Gregor, the office manager is here."

"I know," said Gregor to himself, not daring to speak loudly enough for the sister to hear.

"Gregor," the father now said from the left-hand room, "the office manager has come to inquire why you didn't catch the early train. We have no idea what to tell him. Besides, he would like to speak to you personally. So please open the door. I'm sure he will be kind enough to overlook the disorder in the room."

"Good morning, Mr. Samsa," the office manager was calling amiably.

"He's not well," the mother said to the office manager while the father kept talking through the door, "he's not well, believe me, sir. Why else would Gregor miss a train! I mean, the boy thinks of nothing but his job. I'm almost annoyed that he never goes out in the evening; goodness, he's been back in town for a whole week now, but he's stayed in every single night. He just sits here at the table, quietly reading the newspaper or poring over timetables. The only fun he has is when he does some fretsawing. For instance, he spent two or three evenings carving out a small picture frame; you'd be amazed how pretty it is. It's hanging inside, in his room; you'll see it in a moment when Gregor opens the door. By the way, sir, I'm delighted that you're here; we could never have gotten Gregor to unlock the door by ourselves—he's so stubborn; and he must be under the weather, even though he denied it this morning."

"I'll be right there," said Gregor slowly and deliberately, but not stirring so as not to miss one word of the conversation.

"I can think of no other explanation either, Mrs. Samsa," said the manager, "I do hope it is nothing serious. Though still and all, I must say that for business reasons we businessmen—unfortunately or fortunately, as you will—very often must simply overcome a minor indisposition."

"Well, can the manager come into your room now?" asked the impatient father, knocking on the door again.

"No," said Gregor. In the left-hand room there was an embarrassed silence, in the right-hand room the sister began sobbing.

Why didn't she join the others? She had probably only just gotten out of bed and not yet started dressing. And what was she crying about? Because Gregor wouldn't get up and let the manager in, because he was in danger of losing his job, and because the boss would then go back to dunning Gregor's parents with his old claims? For the time being, those were most likely pointless worries. Gregor was still here and had no intention whatsoever of running out on his family. True, at this moment he was simply lying on the carpet, and no one aware of his condition would have seriously expected him to let in the manager. Indeed, Gregor could hardly be dismissed on the spot for this petty discourtesy, for which he would easily hit on an appropriate excuse later on. He felt it would make far more sense if they left him alone for now instead of pestering him with tears and coaxing. However, the others were in a state of suspense, which justified their behavior.

"Mr. Samsa," the manager now called out, raising his voice, "what is wrong? You are barricading yourself in your room, answering only 'yes' or 'no,' causing your parents serious and unnecessary anxieties, and—I only mention this in passing—neglecting your professional duties in a truly outrageous manner. I am speaking on behalf of your parents and the director of the firm and I am quite earnestly requesting an immediate and cogent explanation. I am dumbfounded, dumbfounded. I believed you to be a quiet, reasonable person, and now you suddenly seem intent on flaunting bizarre moods. This morning the director hinted at a possible explanation for your tardiness—it pertained to the cash collections that you were recently entrusted with—but in fact I practically gave him my word of honor that this explanation could not be valid. Now, however, I am witnessing your incomprehensible stubbornness, which makes me lose any and all desire to speak up for you in any way whatsoever. And your job is by no means rock solid. My original intention was to tell you all this in private, but since you are forcing me to waste my time here needlessly, I see no reason why your parents should not find out as well. Frankly, your recent work has been highly unsatisfactory. We do appreciate that this is not the season for doing a lot of business; still, there is no season whatsoever, there can be no season for doing no business at all, Mr. Samsa."

"But, sir," Gregor exclaimed, beside himself, forgetting everything else in his agitation, "I'll open the door immediately, this very instant. A slight indisposition, a dizzy spell have prevented me from getting up. I am still lying in bed. But now I am quite fresh again. I am getting out of bed this very second. Please be patient for another moment or two! It is not going as well as I expected. But I do feel fine. How suddenly it can overcome a person! Just last night I was quite well, my parents know I was—or rather, last night I did have a slight foreboding. It must have been obvious to anyone else. Just why didn't I report it at the office!? But one always thinks one can get over an illness without staying home. Sir! Please spare my parents! There are no grounds for any of the things you are accusing me of—in fact, no one has ever so much as breathed a word to me. Perhaps you have not seen the latest orders that I sent in. Anyhow, I *will* be catching the eight A.M. train, these several hours of rest have revitalized me. Do not waste any more of your time, sir; I'll be in the office myself instantly—please be kind enough to inform them of this and to give my best to the director!"

And while hastily blurting out all these things, barely knowing what he was saying, Gregor, most likely because of his practice in bed, had managed to get closer to the wardrobe and was now trying to pull himself up against it. He truly wanted to open the door, truly show himself and speak to the office manager; he was eager to learn what the others, who were so keen on his presence now, would say upon seeing him. If they were shocked, then Gregor would bear no further responsibility and could hold his peace. But if they accepted everything calmly, then he like-wise had no reason to get upset, and could, if he stepped on it, actually be in the station by eight. At first, he kept sliding down the smooth side of the wardrobe, but eventually he gave himself a final swing and stood there ignoring the burning pains in his abdomen, distressful as they were. Next he let himself keel over against the back of a nearby chair, his tiny legs clinging to the edges. In this way, he gained control of himself and he kept silent, for now he could listen to the office manager.

"Did you understand a single word of that?" the office manager asked the parents. "He's not trying to make fools of us, is he?!"

"For goodness' sake," the mother exclaimed, already weeping, "he may be seriously ill and we're torturing him. Grete! Grete!" she then shouted.

"Mother?" the sister called from the other side. They were communicating across Gregor's room. "You have to go to the doctor immediately. Gregor is sick. Hurry, get the doctor. Did you hear Gregor talking just now?"

"That was an animal's voice," said the manager, his tone noticeably soft compared with the mother's shouting.

"Anna! Anna!" the father called through the vestibule into the kitchen, clapping his hands, "Get a locksmith immediately!" And the two girls, their skirts rustling, were already dashing through the vestibule (how could the sister have dressed so quickly?) and tearing the apartment door open. No one heard it slamming; they must have left it open, as is common in homes that are struck by disaster.

Gregor, however, had grown much calmer. True, the others no longer understood what he said even though it sounded clear enough to him, clearer than before, perhaps because his ears had gotten used to it. But nevertheless, the others now believed there was something not quite right about him, and they were willing to help. His spirits were brightened by the aplomb and assurance with which their first few instructions had been carried out. He felt included once again in human society and, without really drawing a sharp distinction between the doctor and the locksmith, he expected magnificent and astonishing feats from both. Trying to make his voice as audible as he could for the crucial discussions about to take place, he coughed up a little, though taking pains to do so quite softly, since this noise too might sound different from human coughing, which he no longer felt capable of judging for himself. Meanwhile, the next room had become utterly hushed. Perhaps the parents and the office manager were sitting and whispering at the table, perhaps they were all leaning against the doors and eavesdropping.

Gregor slowly lumbered toward the door, shoving the chair along, let go of it upon arriving, tackled the door, held himself erect against it—the pads on his tiny feet were a bit sticky—and for a moment he rested from the strain. But then, using his mouth, he began twisting the key in the lock. Unfortunately he appeared to have no real teeth—now with what should he grasp the key?—but to make up for it his jaws were, of course, very powerful. They actually enabled him to get the key moving, whereby he ignored the likelihood of his harming himself in some way, for a brown liquid oozed from his mouth, flowing over the key and dripping to the floor.

"Listen," said the office manager in the next room, "he's turning the key." This was very encouraging for Gregor; but everyone should have cheered him on, including the father and the mother. "Attaboy, Gregor!" they should have shouted. "Don't let go, get that lock!" And imagining them all as suspensefully following his efforts, he obliviously bit into the key with all the strength he could muster. In tune with his progress in turning the key, he kept dancing around the lock, holding himself upright purely by his mouth and, as need be, either dangling from the key or pushing it down again with the full heft of his body. It was the sharper click of the lock finally snapping back that literally brought Gregor to. Sighing in relief, he told himself, "So I didn't need the locksmith after all," and he put his head on the handle in order to pull one wing of the double door all the way in.

Since he had to stay on the same side as the key, the door actually swung back quite far without his becoming visible. He had to twist slowly around the one wing, and very gingerly at that, to avoid plopping over on his back before entering the next room. He was still busy performing this tricky maneuver, with no time to heed anything else, when he heard the office manager blurt out a loud "Oh!"—it sounded like a whoosh of wind—and now he also saw him, the person nearest to the door, pressing his hand to his open mouth and slowly shrinking back as if he were being ousted by some unseeable but relentless force. The mother, who, despite the office manager's presence, stood there with her hair still undone and bristling, first gaped at the father, clasping her hands, then took two steps toward Gregor and collapsed, her petticoats flouncing out all around her and her face sinking quite undetectably into her breasts. The father clenched his fist, glaring at Gregor as if trying to shove him back into his room, then peered unsteadily around the parlor before covering his eyes with his hands and weeping so hard that his powerful chest began to quake.

Gregor did not step into the parlor after all; instead he leaned against his side of the firmly bolted second wing of the door, so that only half his body could be seen along with his head, which tilted sideways above it, peeping out at the others. Meanwhile the day had grown much lighter. Across the street, a portion of the endless, grayish black building (it was a hospital) stood out clearly with its regular windows harshly disrupting the façade. The rain was still falling, but only in large, visibly separate drops that were also literally hurled separately to the ground. The breakfast dishes still abundantly covered the table because breakfast was the most important meal of the day for Gregor's father; and he would draw it out for hours on end by reading various newspapers. The opposite wall sported a photograph of Gregor from his military days: it showed him as a lieutenant, hand on sword, with a carefree smile, demanding respect for his bearing and his uniform. The vestibule door was open, and since the apartment door was open too, one could see all the way out to the landing and the top of the descending stairs.

"Well," said Gregor, quite aware of being the only one who had kept calm, "I'll be dressed in a minute, pack up my samples, and catch my train. Would you all, would you all let me go on the road? Well, sir, you can see I am not stubborn and I enjoy working. Traveling is arduous, but I could not live without it. Why, where are you going, sir? To the office? Right? Will you report all this accurately? A man may be temporarily incapacitated, but that is precisely the proper time to remember his past achievements and to bear in mind that later on, once the obstacle is eliminated, he is sure to work all the harder and more intently. After all, I am so deeply obligated to the director, you know that very well. And then, I have to take care of my parents and my sister. I'm in a tight spot, but still I'll work my way out again. So please don't make things more difficult for me than they already are. Put in a good word for me at the office! People don't like a traveling salesman, I know. They think he makes barrels of money and has a wonderful life. They simply have no special reason to examine their prejudice. But you, sir, you have a better notion of what it's all about than the rest of the staff, why, than even— this is strictly between us—a better notion than even the director, who, as owner of the firm, is easily swayed against an employee. You also know very well that a traveling salesman, being away from the office most of the year, can so easily fall victim to gossip, coincidences, and unwarranted complaints, and he cannot possibly defend himself since he almost never finds out about them, except perhaps when he returns from a trip, exhausted, and personally suffers their awful consequences at home without fathoming their inscrutable causes. Sir, please do not leave without saying something to show that you agree with me at least to some small extent!"

But the office manager had already turned away at Gregor's very first words, and he only looked back at him over his twitching shoulder and with gaping lips. Indeed during Gregor's speech, the manager did not halt for even an instant. Rather, without losing sight of Gregor, he retreated toward the door, but only very gradually, as if there were some secret ban on leaving the room. He was already in the vestibule, and to judge by his abrupt movement when he finally pulled his leg out of the parlor, one might have thought he had just burned the sole of his foot. In the vestibule, however, he stretched out his right hand very far, toward the staircase, as if some unearthly redemption were awaiting him there.

Gregor realized he must on no account allow the office manager to leave in this frame of mind; if he did, Gregor's position at the office would be thoroughly compromised. The parents did not quite understand this. During these long years, they had become convinced that he was set up for life at this firm, and besides they were so preoccupied with their immediate problems as to have lost all sense of foresight. Gregor, however, did possess such foresight. The office manager had to be held back, calmed down, cajoled, and finally won over; Gregor's future and that of his family hinged on it! If only the sister had been here! She was intelligent; she had already started to cry when Gregor was still lying calmly on his back. And the office manager, that ladies' man, would certainly have let her take him in hand: she would have shut the apartment door, kept him in the vestibule, and talked him out of his terror. But the sister was not there, so Gregor had to act on his own. Forgetting that he was yet unacquainted with his current powers of movement and also that once again his words had possibly, indeed probably, not been understood, he left the wing of the door and lumbered through the opening. He intended to head toward the office manager, who was ludicrously clutching the banister on the landing with both hands. But Gregor, fumbling for support, yelped as he flopped down upon his many tiny legs. The instant this happened, he felt a physical ease and comfort for the first time that morning. His tiny legs had solid ground underneath, and he was delighted to note that they were utterly obedient—they even strove to carry him off to wherever he wished; and he already believed that the final recovery from all sufferings was at hand. He lay on the floor, wobbling because of his checked movement, not that far from his mother, who seemed altogether self-absorbed. But at that same moment, she unexpectedly leaped up, stretched her arms far apart, splayed her fingers, and cried, "Help! For God's sake, help!" Next she lowered her head as if to see Gregor more clearly, but then, in self-contradiction, she senselessly backed away, forgetting the covered table behind her, hurriedly sat down upon it without thinking, and apparently failed to notice that next to her the large coffeepot had been knocked over and was discharging a torrent of coffee full force upon the carpet.

"Mother, Mother," Gregor murmured, looking up at her. For an instant, the office manager had entirely slipped his mind; on the other hand, Gregor could not help snapping his jaws a few times at the sight of the flowing coffee. This prompted the mother to scream again, flee from the table, and collapse into the father's arms as he came dashing up to her. But Gregor had no time for his parents: the office manager was already on the stairs; with his chin on the banister, he took one final look back. Gregor broke into a run, doing his best to catch up with him. The office manager must have had an inkling of this, for he jumped down several steps at a time and disappeared. However, he did shout, "Ugh!" and his shout rang through the entire stairwell.

Unfortunately, the father, who so far had stayed relatively composed, seemed thoroughly bewildered by the office manager's flight. For, instead of rushing after him or at least not preventing Gregor from pursuing him, the father, with his right hand, grabbed the cane that the office manager, together with a hat and overcoat, had forgotten on a chair and, with his left hand, took a large newspaper from the table. Stamping his feet, he brandished the cane and the newspaper at Gregor in order to drive him back into his room. No pleading from Gregor helped, indeed no pleading was understood; no matter how humbly Gregor turned his head, the father merely stamped his feet all the more forcefully. Across the room, the mother had flung open a window despite the cool weather, and leaning way out, she buried her face in her hands. A strong draft arose between the street and the stairwell, the window curtains flew up, the newspapers rustled on the table, stray pages wafted across the floor. The father charged pitilessly, spewing hisses like a savage. Since Gregor as yet had no practice in moving backwards, it was really slow going. Had he only been permitted to wheel around, he would have been inside his room at once. But he was afraid it would take too long, trying the father's patience even more—and at any moment now the cane in the father's hand threatened to deal the lethal blow to Gregor's back or head. Ultimately, however, Gregor had no choice, for he realized with dismay that he did not even know how to stay the course when backing up. And so, while constantly darting fearful side glances at his father, he began rotating as swiftly as he could, though he was actually very slow. Perhaps the father sensed Gregor's good intention, for he did not interfere—instead, he occasionally even steered the pivoting motion from a distance with the tip of his cane. If only the father would stop that unbearable hissing! It made Gregor lose his head altogether. He had swung around almost fully when, constantly distracted by those hisses, he actually miscalculated and briefly shifted the wrong way. And then, as soon as he finally managed to get his head to the doorway, his body proved too broad to squeeze through all that readily. Naturally, in the father's present mood, it never even remotely crossed his mind to push back the other wing of the door and create a passage wide enough for Gregor. He was obsessed simply with forcing Gregor back into his room as fast as possible. Nor would he ever have stood for the intricate preparations that Gregor needed for hoisting himself on end and perhaps passing through the doorway in that posture. Instead, as if there were no hindrance, the father drove Gregor forward with a great uproar: behind Gregor the yelling no longer sounded like the voice of merely one father. Now it was do or die, and Gregor—come what might—jammed into the doorway. With one side of his body heaving up, he sprawled lopsided in the opening. His one flank was bruised raw, ugly splotches remained on the white door, and he was soon wedged in and unable to budge on his own. The tiny legs on his one side were dangling and trembling in midair and the tiny legs on his other side were painfully crushed against the floor. But now the father gave him a powerful shove from behind—a true deliverance. And Gregor, bleeding heavily, flew far into his room. The door was slammed shut with the cane, and then the apartment was still at last.

II

It was almost dusk by the time Gregor emerged from his comatose sleep. He would certainly have awoken not much later even without being disturbed, for he felt sufficiently well rested; yet it seemed to him as if he had been aroused by fleeting steps and a cautious shutting of the vestibule door. The glow from the electric streetlamps produced pallid spots on the ceiling and the higher parts of the furniture, but down by Gregor it was dark. Slowly, still clumsily groping with his feelers, which he was just learning to appreciate, he lumbered toward the door to see what had been going on. His left side appeared to be one long, unpleasantly tightening scar, and he actually had to limp on his two rows of legs. One tiny leg, moreover, had been badly hurt during that morning's events (it was almost miraculous that only one had been hurt) and it dragged along lifelessly.

Only upon reaching the door did Gregor discover what had actually enticed him: it was the smell of something edible. For there stood a bowl full of fresh milk with tiny slices of white bread floating in it. He practically chortled for joy, being even hungrier now than in the morning, and he promptly dunked his head into the milk until it was nearly over his eyes. Soon, however, he withdrew his head in disappointment. Not only did the bruises on his left side make it difficult for him to eat—he could eat only if his entire wheezing body joined in—but he did not care for the milk, even though it had always been his favorite beverage, which was no doubt why his sister had placed it in his room. As a matter of fact, he turned away from the bowl almost with loathing and crawled back to the middle of the room.

In the parlor, as Gregor could see through the door crack, the gaslight was lit. But while at this time of day his father would usually take up his newspaper, an afternoon daily, and read it in a raised voice to the mother and sometimes also to the sister, not a sound was to be heard. Well, perhaps this practice of reading aloud, which the sister had always told Gregor about and written him about, had recently been discarded altogether. Yet while the entire apartment was hushed, it was anything but deserted.

"My, what a quiet life the family used to lead," Gregor thought to himself, and as he peered into the darkness, he felt a certain pride that he had managed to provide his parents and his sister with such a life in such a beautiful apartment. What if now all calm, all prosperity, all contentment should come to a horrifying end? Rather than lose himself in such ruminations, Gregor preferred to start moving, and so he crept up and down the room.

Once, during the long evening, one side door and then the other was opened a tiny crack and quickly shut again: somebody had apparently felt an urge to come in, but had then thought the better of it. Gregor halted right at the parlor door, determined to somehow bring in the hesitant visitor or at least find out who it was. But the door was not reopened, and Gregor waited in vain. That morning, when the doors had been locked, everybody had wanted to come in; but now that he had opened one door, and the rest had clearly been opened during the day, nobody came, and the keys were on the other side.

It was not until late at night that the light in the parlor was put out. Gregor could easily tell that the parents and the sister had stayed up this long, for, as he could clearly discern, all three of them were tiptoeing off. Since nobody would be visiting Gregor until morning, he had lots of time to reflect undisturbed and to figure out how to restructure his life. But the free, high-ceilinged room where he was forced to lie flat on the floor terrified him without his being able to pinpoint the cause; after all, it was his room and he had been living there for the last five years. Turning half involuntarily and not without a faint sense of embarrassment, he scurried under the settee, where, even though his back was a bit squashed and he could not lift his head, he instantly felt very cozy, regretting only that his body was too broad to squeeze in all the way.

There he remained for the rest of the night, either drowsing and repeatedly yanked awake by his hunger, or else fretting amid vague hopes, all of which, however, led to his concluding that for now he would have to lie low and, by being patient and utterly considerate, help the family endure the inconveniences that, as it happened, he was forced to cause them in his present state.

By early morning—it was still almost night—Gregor had a chance to test the strength of the resolutions he had just made, for the sister, almost fully dressed, opened the vestibule door and suspensefully peered in. She did not find him right away, but when she noticed him under the settee (goodness, he had to be somewhere, he couldn't just have flown away), she was so startled that unable to control herself she slammed the door from the outside. But, apparently regretting her behavior, she instantly reopened the door and tiptoed in as if visiting a very sick patient or even a stranger. Gregor, having pushed his head forward to the very edge of the settee, was watching her. Would she notice that he had barely touched the milk, though by no means for lack of hunger, and would she bring in some other kind of food more to his taste? If she did not do so on her own, he would rather starve to death than point it out to her, even while he felt a tremendous urge to scoot out from under the settee, throw himself at her feet, and beg her for some good food. But the sister, with some surprise, instantly noticed the full bowl, from which only a little milk had splattered all around. She promptly picked up the bowl, though not with her bare hands, but with a rag, and carried it away. Gregor was extremely curious as to what she would replace it with, and all sorts of conjectures ran through his mind. But he would never have hit on what the sister actually did in the goodness of her heart. Hoping to check his likes and dislikes, she brought him a whole array of food, all spread out on an old newspaper. There were old, half-rotten vegetables, some bones left over from supper and coated with a solidified white sauce, a few raisins and almonds, some cheese that Gregor had declared inedible two days ago, dry bread, bread and butter, and salted bread and butter. Furthermore, along with all those things, she brought some water in the bowl, which had probably been assigned to Gregor for good. And sensing that Gregor would not eat in front of her, she discreetly hurried away, even turning the key, just to show him that he could make himself as comfortable as he wished. Gregor's tiny legs whirred as he charged toward the food. His wounds, incidentally, must have healed up by now, he felt no handicap anymore, which was astonishing; for, as he recalled, after he had nicked his finger with a knife over a month ago, the injury had still been hurting the day before yesterday. "Am I less sensitive now?" he wondered, greedily sucking at the cheese, which had promptly exerted a more emphatic attraction on him than any of the other food. His eyes watered with contentment as he gulped down the cheese, the vegetables, and the sauce in rapid succession. By contrast, he did not relish the fresh foods, he could not even stand their smells, and he actually dragged the things he wanted to eat a short distance away. He was already done long since and was simply lazing in the same spot when the sister, to signal that he should withdraw, slowly turned the key. Startled, he jumped up though he was almost dozing, and scuttered back under the settee. However, it took a lot of self-control to remain there even during the few short moments that the sister spent in the room, for his body was slightly bloated from the ample food and he could scarcely breathe in that cramped space. Amid short fits of suffocation, he stared with somewhat bulging eyes while the unsuspecting sister, wielding a broom, swept up not only the leftovers but also the untouched food, as if this too were now unusable; she then hastily dumped everything into a pail, shutting its wooden lid and carrying everything into a pail, shutting its wooden lid and carrying everything out. No sooner had she turned her back than he skulked out from under the settee and began stretching and puffing up.

That was how Gregor received his food every day: once in the morning, when the parents and the maid were still asleep, and the second time after the family lunch, for the parents would then take a brief nap while the sister would send the maid out on some errand. While the parents certainly did not want Gregor to starve either, they may not have endured knowing more about his eating than from hearsay, or the sister may have wished to spare them some—perhaps only slight—grief, for they were really suffering enough as it was.

Gregor could not find out what excuses they had come up with to get the doctor and the locksmith out of the apartment; for since he was not understood, no one, including the sister, assumed that he could understand them. And so, whenever she was in his room, he had to content himself with occasionally hearing her sighs and her appeals to the saints. It was only later, when she had gotten a bit accustomed to everything (naturally there could be no question of her ever becoming fully accustomed), Gregor sometimes caught a remark that was meant to be friendly or might be interpreted as such. "He certainly enjoyed it today," she would say when Gregor had polished off a good portion of the food; while in the opposite event, which was gradually becoming more and more frequent, she would say almost sadly: "Now once again nothing's been touched."

But while Gregor could learn no news directly, he would eavesdrop, picking up a few things from the adjacent rooms, and the instant he heard voices, he would promptly scuttle over to the appropriate door, squeezing his entire body against it. During the early period in particular, no conversation took place that was not somehow about him, even if only in secret. For two whole days, every single meal was filled with discussions about what they ought to do; but even between meals, they kept harping on the same theme, for there were always at least two family members in the apartment, since plainly nobody wished to stay home alone and they could by no means all go out at the same time. Furthermore, on the very first day, the maid—it was not quite clear how much she knew about what had occurred—had implored the mother on bended knees to dismiss her immediately. Then, saying goodbye a quarter hour later, she had tearfully thanked them for the dismissal as if it were the most benevolent deed that they had ever done for her; and without being asked, she had sworn a dreadful oath that she would never breathe a single word to anyone.

So now the sister, together with the mother, also had to do the cooking; but this was not much of a bother, for they ate next to nothing. Over and over, Gregor heard them urging one another to eat, though in vain, receiving no other answer than, "Thanks, I've had enough," or something similar. They may not have drunk anything either. The sister would often ask the father if he would like some beer and she warmly offered to go and get it herself; when he failed to respond, she anticipated any misgivings on his part by saying she could also send the janitor's wife. But then the father would finally utter an emphatic "No," and the subject was no longer broached.

In the course of the very first day, the father laid out their overall financial circumstances and prospects to both the mother and the sister. From time to time, he rose from the table to fetch some document or notebook from his small strongbox, which he had salvaged after the collapse of his business five years earlier. They heard him opening the complicated lock and then shutting it again after removing whatever he had been looking for. The father's explanations were to some extent the first pleasant news that Gregor got to hear since his imprisonment. He had been under the impression that the father had failed to rescue anything from his business—at least, the father had told him nothing to the contrary, nor, admittedly, had Gregor ever asked him. Gregor's sole concern at that time had been to do whatever he could to make the family forget as quickly as possible the business catastrophe that had plunged them all into utter despair. And so he had thrown himself into his job with tremendous fervor, working his way up, almost overnight, from minor clerk to traveling salesman, who, naturally, had an altogether different earning potential and whose professional triumphs were instantly translated, by way of commissions, into cash, which could be placed on the table at home for the astonished and delighted family. Those had been lovely times, and they had never recurred, at least not with that same luster, even though Gregor was eventually earning so much money that he was able to cover and indeed did cover all the expenditures of the family. They had simply grown accustomed to this, both the family and Gregor; they accepted the money gratefully, he was glad to hand it over, but no great warmth came of it. Only the sister had remained close to Gregor; and since she, unlike Gregor, loved music and could play the violin poignantly, he was secretly planning to send her to the conservatory next year regardless of the great expense that it was bound to entail and that would certainly be made up for in some other way. During Gregor's brief stays in the city, the conservatory was often mentioned in his talks with the sister, but only as a lovely dream that could never possibly be realized; nor did the parents care to hear these innocent references. But Gregor's ideas on the subject were very definite and he intended to make the solemn announcement on Christmas Eve.

Such were the thoughts, quite futile in his present condition, that ran through his mind as he clung upright to the door, eavesdropping. Sometimes he was so thoroughly exhausted that he could no longer listen. His head would then inadvertently bump against the door, but he promptly pulled it erect again; for even that slight tap had been heard in the next room, causing everyone to stop talking. "What's he up to now!?" the father would say after a while, obviously turning toward the door, and only then did the interrupted conversation gradually resume.

Gregor now learned precisely enough (for the father would often repeat his explanations, partly because he himself had not dealt with these matters in a long time and partly because the mother did not always understand everything right off) that despite the disaster, some assets, albeit a very tiny sum, had survived from the old days, growing bit by bit because of the untouched interest. Furthermore, since the money that Gregor had brought home every month (keeping only a little for himself) had never been fully spent, it had accumulated into a small principal. Gregor, behind his door, nodded eagerly, delighted at this unexpected thrift and prudence. Actually, he could have applied this surplus toward settling the father's debt to the director, thereby bringing the day when he could have been rid of that job a lot closer; but now, the way the father had arranged things was better, no doubt.

Of course this sum was by no means large enough for the family to live off the interest; it might suffice to keep them going for one, at most two years, and that was all. It was simply money that really should not be drawn on and that ought to be put aside for emergencies, while the money to live on had to be earned. But the father, though still healthy, was an old man, who had not done a lick of work in five years and in any case could not be expected to take on very much. During those five years, his first vacation in an arduous and yet unsuccessful life, he had grown very fat, becoming rather clumsy. And should perhaps the old mother go to work—she, who suffered from asthma, who found it strenuous just walking through the apartment, and who spent every other day on the sofa, gasping for air by the open window? Or should the sister go to work—she, who was still a child at seventeen and should certainly keep enjoying her lifestyle, which consisted of dressing nicely, sleeping late, lending a hand with the housekeeping, going out to a few modest amusements, and above all, playing the violin? At first, whenever the conversation turned to this need to earn money, Gregor would always let go of the door and throw himself on the cool leather sofa nearby, for he felt quite hot with shame and grief.

Often he would lie there all through the long night, not getting a wink of sleep and merely scrabbling on the leather for hours on end. Or else, undaunted by the great effort, he would shove a chair over to the window, clamber up to the sill, and, propped on the chair, lean against the panes, obviously indulging in some vague memory of the freedom he had once found by gazing out the window. For actually, from day to day, even the things that were rather close were growing hazier and hazier; he could no longer even make out the hospital across the street, the all-too-frequent sight of which he used to curse. And if he had not known for sure that he lived on Charlotte Street, a quiet but entirely urban thoroughfare, he might have believed that he was staring at a wasteland in which gray sky and gray earth blurred together indistinguishably. Only twice had the observant sister needed to see the chair standing by the window; now, whenever she tidied up the room she would push the chair back to the window—indeed, from then on she would even leave the inside casement ajar.

If only Gregor could have spoken to her and thanked her for everything she had to do for him, he would have endured her kind actions more readily; but instead they caused him great suffering. Of course, she tried to surmount the overall embarrassment as much as possible, and naturally, as time wore by, she succeeded more and more. However, Gregor too eventually gained a sharper sense of things. Her very entrance was already terrible for him. No sooner had she stepped in than, without even taking time to close the door— careful as she usually was to protect everyone else from seeing Gregor's room—she charged straight over to the window and, as if almost suffocating, yanked it open with hasty hands, lingering there briefly no matter how chilly the weather and inhaling deeply. This din and dashing terrified Gregor twice a day. Throughout her visits he would cower under the settee, fully realizing that she would certainly have preferred to spare him this disturbance if only she had been able to keep the window shut while staying in the same room with him.

Once—something like a month had passed since Gregor's metamorphosis, and there was truly no special reason why the sister should still be alarmed by his appearance—she turned up a bit earlier than usual and caught Gregor staring out the window, motionless and terrifyingly erect. He would not have been surprised if she had refused to come in since his position prevented her from opening the window immediately. But not only did she not come in, she actually recoiled and closed the door; an outsider might have honestly thought that Gregor had meant to ambush her and bite her. Naturally he hid under the settee at once, but then had to wait until noon for his sister to return, and she seemed far more upset than usual. It thus dawned on him that his looks were still unbearable to her and were bound to remain unbearable, which meant that it must have taken a lot of self-control for her not to run away upon glimpsing even the tiny scrap of his body that protruded from under the settee. So one day, hoping to spare her even this sight—the job took him four hours—he got the sheet on his back and lugged it over to the settee, arranging it in such a way that it concealed him entirely, thereby preventing the sister from seeing him even when she stooped down. After all, if she considered the sheet unnecessary, she could have removed it, for it was plain that Gregor could not possibly enjoy cutting himself off so thoroughly. But she left the sheet just as it was, and once, he even believed he caught a grateful glance when he cautiously lifted it a smidgen with his head to see how his sister was taking this innovation.

During the first two weeks, the parents could not get themselves to come into his room, and he often heard them expressing their great appreciation of the sister's efforts, whereas earlier they had often been cross with her for being, they felt, a somewhat useless girl. But now both the father and the mother would frequently wait outside Gregor's door while the sister tidied up inside, and upon reemerging, she promptly had to render a detailed account of what the room looked like, what Gregor had eaten, how he had behaved this time, and whether he was perhaps showing some slight improvement. The mother, incidentally, wanted to visit Gregor relatively soon. At first, the father and the sister tried to reason with her, and Gregor paid very close attention to their arguments, approving of them wholeheartedly. Later, however, the mother had to be held back forcibly, and when she then cried out, "Let me go to Gregor, he's my unhappy son! Don't you understand I have to go to him?" Gregor felt it might be a good idea if she did come in after all—not every day, naturally, but perhaps once a week: she was much better at everything than the sister, who, for all her courage, was still a child and might ultimately have taken on such a demanding task purely out of teenage capriciousness.

Gregor's wish to see his mother came true shortly. During the day, if only out of consideration for his parents, he did not want to appear at the window. On the other hand, he could not creep very far around the few square meters of the floor, he found it hard to lie still even at night, and eating soon gave him no pleasure whatsoever. So, for amusement, he got into the habit of prowling crisscross over the walls and ceiling. He particularly liked hanging from the ceiling. It was quite different from lying on the floor: he could breathe more freely and a faint tingle quivered through his body. In his almost blissful woolgathering up there, Gregor might, to his own surprise, let go and crash down on the floor. But since he naturally now controlled his body far more effectively than before, he was never harmed by that great plunge. The sister instantly noticed the new entertainment that Gregor had found for himself—after all, when creeping, he occasionally left traces of his sticky substance behind. And so, taking it into her head to enable Gregor to crawl over the widest possible area, she decided to remove the obstructive furniture—especially the wardrobe and the desk. However, there was no way she could manage this alone. She did not dare ask her father for help, and the maid would most certainly not have pitched in; for while this girl, who was about sixteen, had been valiantly sticking it out since the cook's departure, she had asked for the special favor of keeping the kitchen door locked all the time and opening it only when specifically called. As a result, the sister had no choice but to approach the mother one day during the father's absence. And indeed, with cries of joyful excitement, the mother came over, although falling silent at the door to Gregor's room. First, naturally, the sister checked inside to make sure everything was in order; only then did she let the mother enter. Gregor had hurriedly pulled the sheet lower and in tighter folds, truly making it look as if it had been tossed casually over the settee. This time, Gregor also refrained from peeping out from under the sheet: he would go without seeing the mother for now and was simply glad that she had come despite everything.

"Come on, he's out of sight," said the sister, evidently leading the mother by the hand. Gregor now heard the two delicate women pushing the very heavy old wardrobe from its place and the sister constantly insisting on doing the major share of the work, ignoring the warnings from the mother, who was afraid she would overexert herself. It took a very long time. After probably just a quarter hour of drudging, the mother said it would be better if they left the wardrobe here. For one thing, it was too heavy—they would not be done before the father's arrival; and if the wardrobe stood in the middle of the room, it would block Gregor's movements in all directions. Secondly, it was not at all certain that they were doing Gregor a favor by removing the furniture. She said that the opposite seemed to be the case, the sight of the bare wall literally made her heart bleed. And why wouldn't Gregor respond in the same way since he was long accustomed to the furniture and would therefore feel desolate in the empty room? "And isn't that," the mother concluded very softly (in fact, she persistently almost whispered, as if, not knowing Gregor's precise whereabouts, she wanted to keep him from hearing the very sound of her voice, convinced as she was that he did not understand the words), "and if we remove the furniture, isn't that like showing him that we've given up all hope of his improvement and that we're callously leaving him to his own devices? I believe it would be best if we tried to keep the room just as it was, so that when Gregor comes back to us he will find that nothing's been changed and it will be much easier for him to forget what happened."

Upon hearing the mother's words, Gregor realized that in the course of these two months the lack of having anyone to converse with, plus the monotonous life in the midst of the family, must have befuddled his mind, for there was no other way to account for how he could have seriously longed to have his room emptied out. Did he really want the warm room, so cozily appointed with heirlooms, transformed into a lair, where he might, of course, be able to creep, unimpeded, in any direction, though forgetting his human past swiftly and totally? By now, he was already on the verge of forgetting, and had been brought up sharply only by the mother's voice after not hearing it for a long time. Nothing should be removed, everything had to remain: he could not do without the positive effects of the furniture on his state of mind. And if the furniture interfered with his senselessly crawling about, then it was a great asset and no loss.

Unfortunately, the sister was of a different mind; in the discussions concerning Gregor, she had gotten into the habit—not without some justification, to be sure—of acting the great expert in front of the parents. So now the mother's advice was again reason enough for the sister to demand that they remove not only the wardrobe and the desk, in line with her original plan, but all the furniture except for the indispensable settee. Her resoluteness was, naturally, prompted not just by childish defiance and the unexpected self-confidence she had recently gained at such great cost. After all, she had observed that while he needed a lot of space to creep around in, Gregor, so far as could be seen, made no use whatsoever of the furniture. Perhaps, however, the enthusiasm of girls her age also played its part—an exuberance that they try to indulge every chance they get. It now inveigled Grete into making Gregor's situation even more terrifying, so she could do even more for him than previously. For most likely no one but Grete would ever dare venture into a room where Gregor ruled the bare walls all alone.

And so she dug in her heels, refusing to give in to the mother, who, apparently quite anxious and uncertain of herself in this room, soon held her tongue and, to the best of her ability, helped the sister push out the wardrobe. Well, Gregor could, if necessary, do without the wardrobe, but the desk had to remain. And no sooner had the squeezing, groaning women shoved the wardrobe through the doorway than Gregor poked his head out from under the settee to judge how he could intervene as cautiously and considerately as possible. But alas, it was precisely the mother who was the first to return while Grete was still in the next room, holding her arms around the wardrobe and rocking it back and forth by herself without, of course, getting it to budge from the spot. The mother, however, was not used to the sight of Gregor—it might sicken her. And so Gregor, terrified, scuttered backwards to the other end of the settee, but was unable to prevent the front of the sheet from stirring slightly. That was enough to catch the mother's eye. She halted, stood still for an instant, then went back to Grete.

Gregor kept telling himself that nothing out of the ordinary was happening, it was just some furniture being moved. But these comings and goings of the women, their soft calls to one another, the scraping of the furniture along the floor was, as he soon had to admit, like a huge rumpus pouring in on all sides. And no matter how snugly he pulled in his head and legs and pressed his body against the floor, he inevitably had to own up that he would not endure the hubbub much longer. They were clearing out his room, stripping him of everything he loved. They had already dragged away the wardrobe, which contained the fretsaw and other tools, and they were now unprying the solidly embedded desk, where he had done his assignments for business college, high school, why, even elementary school—and he really had no time to delve into the good intentions of the two women, whom, incidentally, he had almost forgotten about, for they were so exhausted that they were already laboring in silence, and all that could be heard was the heavy plodding of their feet.

And so, while the women were in the next room, leaning against the desk to catch their breath, he broke out, changing direction four times, for he was truly at a loss about what to rescue first—when he saw the picture of the woman clad in nothing but furs hanging blatantly on the otherwise empty wall. He quickly scrambled up to it and squeezed against the glass, which held him fast, soothing his hot belly. At least, with Gregor now covering it up, this picture would certainly not be carried off by anyone. He turned his head toward the parlor door, hoping to observe the women upon their return.

After granting themselves little rest, they were already coming back; Grete had put her arm around her mother, almost carrying her. "Well, what should we take next?" said Grete, looking around. At this point, her eyes met those of Gregor on the wall. It was no doubt only because of the mother's presence that she maintained her composure. Bending her face toward the mother to keep her from peering about, she said, although trembling and without thinking: "Come on, why don't we go back to the parlor for a moment?" It was obvious to Gregor that she wanted to get the mother to safety and then chase him down from the wall. Well, just let her try! He clung to his picture, refusing to surrender it. He would rather jump into Grete's face.

But Grete's words had truly unnerved the mother, who stepped aside, glimpsed the huge brown splotch on the flowered wallpaper, and cried out in a harsh, shrieking voice before actually realizing that this was Gregor, "Oh God, oh God!" With outspread arms as if giving up everything, she collapsed across the settee and remained motionless.

"Hey, Gregor!" the sister shouted with a raised fist and a penetrating glare. These were her first direct words to him since his metamorphosis. She ran into the next room to get some sort of essence for reviving the mother from her faint. Gregor also wanted to help (there was time enough to salvage the picture later), but he was stuck fast to the glass and had to wrench himself loose. He then also scurried into the next room as if he could give the sister some kind of advice as in earlier times, but then had to stand idly behind her while she rummaged through an array of vials. Upon spinning around, she was startled by the sight of him. A vial fell on the floor and shattered. A sliver of glass injured Gregor's face, and some corrosive medicine oozed from the sliver. Grete, without further delay, grabbed as many vials as she could hold and dashed over to the mother, slamming the door with her foot. Gregor was thus cut off from the mother, who might have been dying because of him; he had to refrain from opening the door lest he frighten away the sister, who had to remain with the mother. There was nothing he could do but wait, and so, tortured by self-rebukes and worries, he began to creep about—he crept over everything, walls, furniture, and ceiling, and finally, in his despair, when the entire room began whirling around him, he plunged down to the middle of the large table.

A short while passed, with Gregor lying there worn out. The entire apartment was still, which was possibly a good sign. Then the doorbell rang. The maid was, naturally, locked up in her kitchen, and so Grete had to go and answer the door. The father had come.

"What's happened?" were his first words; Grete's face must have revealed everything. She replied in a muffled voice, obviously pressing her face into his chest: "Mother fainted, but she's feeling better now. Gregor broke out."

"I expected it," said the father, "I kept telling you both, but you women refuse to listen."

It was clear to Gregor that the father had misinterpreted Grete's all-too-brief statement and leaped to the conclusion that Gregor had perpetrated some kind of violence. That was why he now had to try and placate the father, for he had neither the time nor the chance to enlighten him. He therefore fled to the door of his room, squeezing against it, so that the father, upon entering from the vestibule, could instantly see that Gregor had every intention of promptly returning to his room and that there was no need to force him back. All they had to do was open the door and he would vanish on the spot.

But the father was in no mood to catch such niceties. "Ah!" he roared upon entering, and his tone sounded both furious and elated. Gregor drew his head back from the door and raised it toward the father. He had really not pictured him as he was standing there now; naturally, because of his new habit of creeping around, Gregor had lately failed to concern himself with anything else going on in the apartment and he should actually have been prepared for some changes. And yet, and yet, was this still his father? The same man who used to lie buried in bed, exhausted, whenever Gregor started out on a business trip; who, whenever Gregor came home in the evening, would greet him, wearing a robe, in the armchair; who, being quite incapable of standing up, would only raise his arms as a sign of joy; and who, bundled up in his old overcoat, laboriously shuffled along during rare family strolls on a few Sundays during the year and on the highest holidays, always cautiously planting his cane, trudging a bit more slowly between Gregor and the mother (they were walking slowly as it was), and who, whenever he was about to say anything, nearly always halted and gathered the others around him? But now the father stood quite steady, in a snug blue uniform with gold buttons, such as attendants in banks wear; his heavy double chin unfurled over the high stiff collar of the jacket. From under his bushy eyebrows, the black eyes gazed fresh and alert; the once disheveled hair was now glossy, combed down, and meticulously parted. Removing his cap with its gold monogram, probably that of a bank, and pitching it in an arc the full length of the room over to the settee, he lunged toward Gregor, his face grim, his hands in his trouser pockets, the tails of his long uniform jacket swinging back. He himself most likely did not know what he had in mind; nevertheless he lifted his feet unusually high, and Gregor marveled at the gigantic size of his boot soles. But he did not dwell on this; after all, from the very first day of his new life, he had known that the father viewed only the utmost severity as appropriate for dealing with him. And so now Gregor scooted away, stopping only when the father halted, and skittering forward again the instant the father moved. In this way, they circled the room several times with nothing decisive happening; in fact, because of its slow tempo, the whole business did not even resemble a chase. That was why Gregor kept to the floor for now, especially since he feared that the father might view an escape to the walls or the ceiling as particularly wicked. Nevertheless, Gregor had to admit that he could not endure even this scurrying much longer, because for every step the father took, Gregor had to carry out an endless string of movements. He was already panting noticeably, just as his lungs had never been altogether reliable even in his earlier days. He was just barely staggering along, trying to focus all his strength on running, scarcely keeping his eyes open, feeling so numb that he could think of no other possible recourse than running, and almost forgetting that he was free to use the walls, which, however, were blocked here by intricately carved furniture bristling with sharp points and notches—when all at once a lightly tossed something flew down right next to him, barely missing him, and rolled on ahead of him. It was an apple. Instantly a second one flew after the first. Gregor halted, petrified. Any more running would be useless, for the father was dead set on bombarding him. He had filled his pockets with fruit from the bowl on the sideboard and, not taking sharp aim for the moment, was hurling apple after apple. Those small red apples ricocheted around the floor as if galvanized, colliding with one another. A weakly thrown apple grazed Gregor's back, sliding off harmlessly. Another one, however, promptly following it, actually dug right into his back. Gregor wanted to keep dragging himself along as though this startling and incredible pain would vanish with a change of location, yet he felt nailed to the spot and so he stretched out with all his senses in utter derangement. It was only with his final glance that he saw the door to his room burst open. The mother, wearing only a chemise (for the sister had undressed her to let her breathe more freely while unconscious), hurried out in front of the screaming sister and dashed toward the father. Stumbling over her unfastened petticoats as they glided to the floor one by one, she pressed against the father, flung her arms around his neck in total union with him—but now Gregor's eyesight failed entirely—and, with her hands clutching the back of the father's head, she begged him to spare Gregor's life.

III

Gregor's serious injury, from which he suffered for over a month (since no one had the nerve to remove the apple, it stayed lodged in his flesh as a visible memento), apparently reminded even the father that Gregor, despite his now dismal and disgusting shape, was a member of the family and could not be treated like an enemy. Instead, familial obligations dictated that they swallow their repulsion and endure, simply endure.

Now Gregor's injury may have cost him some mobility, no doubt for good, impelling him to take long, long minutes to shuffle across his room like an old war invalid (there was no question of his creeping up the walls). Still, this worsening of his condition was, to his mind, more than made up for by the fact that every evening the parlor door, which he would watch sharply for one or two hours in advance, was opened, so that he, lying in the darkness of his room and invisible from the parlor, was allowed to see the entire family at the illuminated table and, by general consent as it were, listen to their talks—rather, that is, than eavesdropping as before.

Of course, these were no longer the lively exchanges of earlier days, which Gregor had always somewhat wistfully mused about in the tiny hotel rooms whenever he had wearily collapsed into the damp bedding. Now, the evenings were usually very hushed. The father would doze off in his armchair shortly after supper; the mother and the sister would urge one another to keep still. The mother, hunched way over beneath the light, would be sewing fine lingerie for a fashion boutique; the sister, having found a job as salesgirl, was studying shorthand and French every evening in hopes of perhaps eventually obtaining a better position. Sometimes the father would wake up and, as if unaware that he had been sleeping, would say to the mother: "How long you've been sewing again today!" and doze off again while mother and sister smiled wearily at each other.

In a kind of obstinacy, the father refused to take off his attendant's uniform at home; and while his robe dangled uselessly on the clothes hook, he would slumber in his chair, fully dressed, as if always on duty and at his superior's beck and call even here. And so, despite all the painstaking efforts of mother and sister, the uniform, which had not been brand-new in the first place, grew less and less tidy, and Gregor would often spend entire evenings gazing at this soiled and spotted garment, which shone with its always polished gold buttons, while the old man slept a very uncomfortable and yet peaceful sleep.

The instant the clock struck ten, the mother, by speaking softly to the father, tried to awaken him and talk him into going to bed, for after all, this was no way to get proper sleep, which the father, who had to start work at six A.M., badly needed. But with the obstinacy that had gotten hold of him upon his becoming a bank attendant, he would always insist on remaining at the table a bit longer even though he invariably nodded out and, moreover, could then be coaxed only with the greatest difficulty to trade the chair for the bed. No matter how much the mother and the sister cajoled and gently admonished him, he would shake his head slowly for a quarter of an hour, keeping his eyes shut and refusing to stand up. The mother would tug at his sleeve, whispering honeyed words into his ear, and the sister would leave her homework to help the mother; but none of this had any effect on the father. He would merely sink deeper into his chair. It was only when the women lifted him under his armpits that he would open his eyes, glance to and fro between mother and sister, and say: "What a life. This is my rest in my old days." And supporting himself on the two women, he would ponderously struggle to his feet as if being the greatest burden on himself, let the two women steer him to the door, wave them off upon arriving and trudge on unaided, while the mother hastily discarded her sewing and the daughter her pen in order to run after him and continue being helpful.

Who in this overworked and exhausted family had time to look after Gregor any more than was absolutely necessary? The household was reduced further; the maid was now dismissed after all, and a gigantic bony charwoman with white hair fluttering around her head would come every morning and evening to do the heaviest chores. Everything else was taken care of by the mother along with her great amount of needlework. It even happened that various items of family jewelry, which mother and sister had once blissfully sported at celebrations and festivities, were now being sold off, as Gregor learned in the evenings from the general discussions of the prices they had obtained. Their greatest persistent complaint, though, was that since they could hit on no way of moving Gregor, they could not give up this apartment, which was much too large for their present circumstances. Gregor, however, realized it was not just their consideration for him that held them back, for they could have easily transported him in a suitable crate with a couple of air holes in it. The main obstacle to the family's relocation was their utter despair and their sense of being struck by a misfortune like no one else among their friends and relatives. Whatever the world demands of poor people, they carried out to an extreme: the father fetched breakfast for the minor bank tellers, the mother sacrificed herself to underwear for strangers, the sister, ordered around by customers, ran back and forth behind the counter. But those were the limits of the family's strength. And the injury in Gregor's back started hurting again whenever mother and sister, having returned from getting the father to bed, ignored their work as they huddled together cheek to cheek, and the mother, pointing toward Gregor's room, now said: "Close that door, Grete," so that Gregor was back in the dark, while the women in the next room mingled their tears or peered dry-eyed at the table.

Gregor spent his nights and days almost entirely without sleep. Occasionally he decided that the next time the door opened, he would take over the family's affairs as in the past. Now, after a long absence, the director and the office manager reappeared in his thoughts, the clerks and the trainees, the dim-witted errand boy, two or three friends from other companies, a chambermaid in a provincial hotel, a dear, fleeting memory, a milliner's cashier whom he had courted earnestly but too slowly—they all reappeared, mingling with strangers or forgotten people. Yet rather than helping him and his family, they were all unapproachable, and he was glad when they dwindled away. At other moments, he was in no mood to worry about his family—he was filled with sheer rage at being poorly looked after; and although unable to picture anything that might tempt his appetite, he did try to devise ways of getting into the pantry and, while not hungry, taking what was ultimately his due. No longer paying any heed to what might be a special treat for Gregor, the sister, before hurrying off to work in the morning and after lunch, would use her foot to shove some random food into Gregor's room. Then, in the evening, indifferent as to whether the food had been merely tasted or—most often the case—left entirely untouched, she would sweep it out with a swing of the broom. She would now tidy up the room in the evening, and she could not have done it any faster. Grimy streaks lined the walls, knots of dust and filth littered the floor. In the beginning, when the sister arrived, Gregor would station himself in such particularly offensive corners as if to chide her. But he could have waited there for weeks on end without her making any improvement; she certainly saw the dirt as clearly as he did, but she had simply made up her mind to leave it there. Nevertheless, with a touchiness that aside from being quite novel for her had actually seized hold of the entire family, she made sure that this tidying-up remained her bailiwick. Once, the mother had subjected Gregor's room to a major cleansing, which had required several buckets of water (the great dampness, of course, made Gregor ill, and afterwards he sprawled on the settee, embittered and immobile). But the mother's punishment was not long in coming. For that evening, the instant the sister noticed the change in Gregor's room, she ran, deeply offended, into the parlor, and even though the mother raised her hands beseechingly, the sister had a crying fit. The father was, naturally, startled out of his armchair, and both parents gaped, at first in helpless astonishment, until they too started in: the father upbraided the mother, on his right, for not leaving the cleaning to the sister and he yelled at the sister, on his left, warning her that she would never again be allowed to clean Gregor's room. The mother tried to drag the father, who was beside himself with rage, into the bedroom; the sister, quaking with sobs, kept hammering the table with her little fists; and Gregor hissed loudly in his fury because no one thought of closing his door to shield him from this spectacle and commotion.

But even if the sister, exhausted from her work at the shop, was fed up with looking after Gregor as before, by no means did the mother have to step in to keep Gregor from being neglected. For now the charwoman was here. This old widow, who, with the help of her strong bone structure, must have managed to overcome the worst things in her long life, felt no actual repugnance toward Gregor. While not really snooping, she had once happened to open the door to his room and, at the sight of Gregor, who, completely caught off guard, began scrambling every which way even though no one was chasing him, she had halted in astonishment with her hands folded on her abdomen. Since then, she had never failed to quickly open the door a crack every morning and evening and peep in on him. Initially, she would even summon him with phrases that she must have considered friendly, like "C'mon over, you old dung beetle!" or "Just look at the old dung beetle!" But Gregor refused to respond to such overtures; he stayed motionless in his place as though the door had not been opened. If only they had ordered this charwoman to clean his room daily instead of letting her gratuitously disturb him whenever the mood struck her! Early one morning, when a violent rain, perhaps a sign of the coming spring, was pelting against the windowpanes, the charwoman launched into her phrases again. Gregor felt so bitterly provoked that he charged toward her as if to attack, albeit slowly and feebly. But the charwoman, undaunted, merely heaved up a chair by the door and stood there with her mouth wide open, obviously intending to close it only when the chair in her hand smashed down into Gregor's back. "So that's as far as you're going?" she asked when he shifted away, and she calmly returned the chair to the corner.

Gregor was now eating next to nothing. It was only when he happened to pass the food left for him that he would playfully take a morsel into his mouth, keep it in for hours and hours, and then usually spit it out again. At first, he thought that his anguish about the condition of his room was what kept him from eating, but he very soon came to terms with those very changes. The family had gotten used to storing things here that could not be put anywhere else, and now there were many such items here, for they had rented out one room of the apartment to three boarders. These earnest gentlemen—all three had full beards, as Gregor once ascertained through the crack of the door—were sticklers for order, not only in their room, but also, since they were lodging here, throughout the apartment, especially the kitchen. They could not endure useless, much less dirty refuse. Moreover, they had largely brought in their own household goods. For this reason, many of the family's belongings had become superfluous; but while they had no prospects of selling them, they did not want to throw them out either. All these items wound up in Gregor's room—as did the ash bucket and the garbage can from the kitchen. If anything was unusable at the moment, the charwoman, who was always in a mad rush, would simply toss it into Gregor's room; luckily, he mostly saw only the object in question and the hand that held it. She may have intended to come for these things in her own good time or dump them all out in one fell swoop; but instead, they remained wherever they happened to land, unless Gregor twisted his way through the clutter, making it shift. At first, he had no choice, there being nowhere else for him to crawl; but later on it got to be more and more fun, even if, dead-tired and mournful after such treks, he would lie unstirring for hours on end.

Since the boarders sometimes also ate their supper at home in the common parlor, the door between that room and Gregor's would remain shut on those evenings. But Gregor easily did without the open door—after all, there had been evenings when he had not even taken advantage of it; instead, unnoticed by the family, he had crouched in the darkest nook of his room. Once, however, the charwoman had left the parlor door ajar, and it remained ajar even when the boarders came in that evening and the light was turned on. Settling down at the head of the table, where the father, the mother, and

Gregor had eaten in earlier times, they unfolded their napkins and took hold of their knives and forks. Instantly the mother appeared in the kitchen doorway with a platter of meat and, right behind her, the sister with a heaping platter of potatoes. The steaming food gave off thick fumes. The platters were set down in front of the boarders, who bent over them as if to test the food before eating it; and indeed the man sitting in the middle, and apparently looked up to as an authority by the two others, cut up a piece of meat on the platter, clearly in order to determine whether it was tender enough or should perhaps be sent back to the kitchen. He was satisfied, and so mother and sister, who had been watching in suspense, began to smile with sighs of relief.

The family itself ate in the kitchen. Nevertheless, before heading there, the father would stop off in the parlor, bowing once, with his cap in his hand, and circle the table. The boarders would all rise and mumble something into their beards. Then, by themselves again, they would eat in almost total silence. It struck Gregor as bizarre that amid all the various and sundry noises of eating, he kept making out the noise of their chewing as if he were being shown that one needed teeth for eating and that one could accomplish nothing with even the most wonderful toothless jaws. "I do have an appetite," Gregor told himself, "but not for these foods. How well these boarders eat, and I'm starving to death!"

That very evening (Gregor could not recall hearing it all this time), the sound of the violin came from the kitchen. The boarders had already finished their supper. The middle one had pulled out a newspaper, giving the other two one page each; and now they were leaning back, reading and smoking. When the violin began to play, the boarders pricked up their ears, got to their feet, and tiptoed over to the vestibule doorway, crowding into it and remaining there.

They must have been overheard from the kitchen, for the father called: "Do you gentlemen mind the violin? We can stop it immediately."

"Quite the contrary," said the middle gentleman, "would the young lady care to come and play in this room, which is far more convenient and comfortable?"

"Oh, thank you," called the father as if he were the violinist. The gentlemen came back into the parlor and waited. Soon the father arrived with the music stand, the mother with the sheet music, and the sister with the violin. The sister calmly prepared everything for the playing. The parents, having never rented out rooms before, which was why they were being so overly courteous to the boarders, did not dare sit in their own chairs. The father leaned against the door, slipping his right hand between two buttons of his buttoned-up uniform jacket; the mother, however, was offered a chair by one gentleman and, leaving it where he happened to place it, she sat off to the side, in a corner.

The sister began to play; the father and the mother, on either side, closely followed the motions of her hands. Gregor, drawn to the playing, had ventured a bit further out, so that his head was already sticking into the parlor. He was hardly aware of his recent lack of consideration toward the others, although earlier he had prided himself on being considerate. For now more than ever he had reason to hide, thoroughly coated as he was with the dust that shrouded everything in his room, flurrying about at the vaguest movement. Furthermore, threads, hairs, and scraps of leftover food were sticking to his back and his sides, for he had become much too apathetic to turn over and scour his back on the carpet as he used to do several times a day. And so, despite his present state, he had no qualms about advancing a bit across the spotless parlor floor.

Nor, to be sure, did anyone take any notice of him. The family was engrossed in the violin playing; the boarders, in contrast, their hands in their trouser pockets, had initially placed themselves much too close to the sister's music stand so they could all read the score, which was bound to fluster her. As a result, half muttering with lowered heads, they soon retreated to the window, where they remained, with the father eyeing them uneasily. It now truly seemed more than obvious that their hope of listening to a lovely or entertaining violin recital had been dashed, that they had had enough of the performance, and that it was only out of sheer courtesy that they were allowing themselves to be put upon in their leisure. It was especially the manner in which they all blew their cigar smoke aloft through their mouths and noses that hinted at how fidgety they were. And yet the sister was playing so beautifully. Her face was leaning to the side, her sad, probing eyes were following the lines of notes. Gregor crawled a bit farther out, keeping his head close to the floor, so that their eyes might possibly meet. Was he a beast to be so moved by music? He felt as if he were being shown the path to the unknown food he was yearning for. He was determined to creep all the way over to the sister, tug at her skirt to suggest that she take her violin and come into his room, for no one here would reward her playing as he intended to reward it. He wanted to keep her there and never let her out, at least not in his lifetime. For once, his terrifying shape would be useful to him; he would be at all the doors of his room simultaneously, hissing at the attackers. His sister, however, should remain with him not by force, but of her own free will. She should sit next to him on the settee, leaning down to him and listening to him confide that he had been intent on sending her to the conservatory, and that if the misfortune had not interfered, he would have announced his plan to everyone last Christmas (Christmas was already past, wasn't it?), absolutely refusing to take "no" for an answer. After his declaration, the sister would burst into tears of emotion, and Gregor would lift himself all the way up to her shoulder and kiss her throat, which she had been keeping free of any ribbon or collar since she had first started working.

"Mr. Samsa!" the middle gentleman called to the father and, not wasting another word, pointed his index finger at Gregor, who was slowly edging forward. The violin broke off, the middle gentleman first smiled at his friends, shaking his head, and then looked back at Gregor. The father, instead of driving Gregor out, evidently considered it imperative first to calm the boarders, even though they were not the least bit upset and appeared to find Gregor more entertaining than the violin playing. The father hurried over to them and, with outspread arms, tried to push them into their room while simultaneously blocking their view of Gregor with his body. They now in fact began to grow a bit irate, though there was no telling whether it was due to the father's behavior or to their gradual realization that they had unknowingly had a neighbor like Gregor in the next room. They demanded explanations from the father, raised their arms like him, plucked at their beards, and only very slowly backed away toward their room. Meanwhile the sister had managed to overcome her bewilderment, caused by the abrupt end to her playing, and after a time of holding the violin and the bow in her slackly dangling hands and gazing at the score as if still playing, she suddenly pulled herself together, left the instrument in the mother's lap (she was still in her chair, her lungs heaving violently), and rushed into the next room, toward which the father was more and more forcefully herding the boarders. One could see the blankets and pillows in the beds flying aloft, then being neatly arranged under the sister's practiced hands. Before the gentlemen ever reached the room, she had finished making up the beds and slipped out. The father seemed once again so thoroughly overcome by his obstinacy that he neglected to pay the tenants the respect nevertheless due them. He merely kept shoving until the middle gentleman, who was already in the doorway of the room, brought him to a halt by thunderously stamping his foot. "I hereby declare," said the middle gentleman, raising his hand and looking around for the mother and the sister as well, "that in consideration of the repulsive conditions" (here he abruptly spit on the floor) "prevailing in this apartment and in this family, I am giving immediate notice in regard to my room. Naturally, I will not pay a single penny for the days I have resided here; on the other hand, I will give serious thought to the eventuality of pursuing some sort of claims against you, for which—believe me—excellent grounds can easily be shown." He paused and peered straight ahead as if expecting something. And indeed, his two friends promptly chimed in, saying, "We are giving immediate notice too." Thereupon he grabbed the doorknob and slammed the door with a crash.

The father, groping and staggering along, collapsed into his chair; he looked as if he were stretching out for his usual evening nap, but his head, dangling as if unsupported, revealed that he was anything but asleep. All this while, Gregor had been lying right where the boarders had first spotted him. His frustration at the failure of his plan, and perhaps also the feebleness caused by his persistent hunger, made it impossible for him to move. Dreading with some certainty that at any moment now he would have to bear the blame for the overall disaster, he waited. He was not even startled when the violin, sliding away from the mother's trembling fingers, plunged from her lap with a reverberating thud.

"My dear parents," said the sister, pounding her hand on the table by way of introduction, "things cannot go on like this. You may not realize it, but I do. I will not pronounce my brother's name in front of this monstrosity, and so all I will say is: We must try to get rid of it. We have done everything humanly possible to look after it and put up with it; I do not believe there is anything we can be reproached for."

"She couldn't be more right," said the father to himself. The mother, still struggling to catch her breath and with an insane look in her eyes, began to cough into her muffling hand.

The sister hurried over to the mother and held her forehead. The father, apparently steered to more concrete thoughts by the sister's words, sat bolt upright now, toying with his attendant's cap, which lay on the table, among the borders' leftover supper dishes. Every so often he glanced at Gregor, who kept silent.

"We've got to get rid of it," the sister now said exclusively to the father, for the mother heard nothing through her coughing, "it will kill the both of you, I can see it coming. People who have to work as hard as we do can't also endure this nonstop torture at home. I can't stand it anymore either." And she began sobbing so violently that her tears flowed down to the mother's face, from which she wiped them with mechanical gestures.

"But, child," said the father with compassion and marked understanding, "what should we do?"

The sister merely shrugged her shoulders to convey the perplexity that, in contrast with her earlier self-assurance, had overcome her as she wept.

"If he understood us," said the father, half wondering. The sister, in the thick of her weeping, wildly flapped her hand to signal that this was inconceivable.

"If he understood us," the father repeated, closing his eyes in order to take in the sister's conviction that this was impossible, "then perhaps we might come to some sort of terms with him. But as things are now—"

"It has to go," exclaimed the sister, "that's the only way, Father. You simply have to try and get rid of the idea that it is Gregor. Our real misfortune is that we believed it for such a long time. Just how can that possibly be Gregor? If that were Gregor, he would have realized long ago that human beings can't possibly live with such an animal and he would have left of his own accord. We might have no brother then, but we could go on living and honor his memory. Instead, this animal harries us, it drives out the boarders, it obviously wants to take over the whole apartment and make us sleep in the gutter. Look, Father," she suddenly screamed, "he's starting again!" And in a panic that Gregor could not for the life of him fathom, the sister actually deserted the mother. Literally thrusting away from her chair as if she would rather sacrifice her mother than remain near Gregor, she dashed behind the father, who, made frantic only by the sister's behavior, stood up, half raising his hands to shield her.

Yet Gregor never even dreamed of scaring anyone, least of all his sister. He had merely started wheeling around in order to lumber back to his room, although because of his sickly condition his movements did look peculiar, for he had to execute the intricate turns by repeatedly raising his head and banging it against the floor. He paused and looked around. His good intention seemed to have been recognized; the panic had only been momentary. Now they all gazed at him in dismal silence. The mother, stretching out her legs and pressing them together, sprawled in her chair, her eyes almost shut in exhaustion; the father and the sister sat side by side, she with her arm around his neck.

"Now maybe I can turn around," Gregor thought, resuming his labor. He could not help panting from the strain and he also had to rest intermittently. At least, no one was bullying him, and he was left to his own devices. Upon completing the turn, he headed straight back. Amazed that his room was far away, he could not understand how, given his feebleness, he had come this great distance almost unwittingly. But, absorbed in creeping rapidly, he scarcely noticed that no interfering word or outcry came from his family. It was only upon reaching the door that he turned his head—not all the way for he felt his neck stiffening; nevertheless, he did see that nothing had changed behind him, except that the sister had gotten to her feet. His final look grazed the mother, who was fast asleep by now.

No sooner was he inside his room than the door was hastily slammed, bolted, and locked. Gregor was so terrified by the sudden racket behind him that his tiny legs buckled. It was the sister who had been in such a rush. She had been standing there, waiting, and had then nimbly jumped forward, before Gregor had even heard her coming. "Finally!" she yelled to the parents while turning the key in the lock.

"What now?" Gregor wondered, peering around in the dark. He soon discovered that he could no longer budge at all. He was not surprised, it even struck him as unnatural that he had ever succeeded in moving on these skinny little legs. Otherwise he felt relatively comfortable. His entire body was aching, but it seemed to him as if the pains were gradually fading and would ultimately vanish altogether. He could barely feel the rotting apple in his back or the inflamed area around it, which were thoroughly cloaked with soft dust. He recalled his family with tenderness and love. His conviction that he would have to disappear was, if possible, even firmer than his sister's. He lingered in this state of blank and peaceful musing until the tower clock struck three in the morning. He held on long enough to glimpse the start of the overall brightening outside the window. Then his head involuntarily sank to the floor, and his final breath came feebly from his nostrils.

When the charwoman showed up early that morning (in her haste and sheer energy, and no matter how often she had been asked not to do it, she slammed all the doors so hard that once she walked in no peaceful sleep was possible anywhere in the apartment), and peeked in on Gregor as usual, she at first found nothing odd about him. Having credited him with goodness knows what brain power, she thought he was deliberately lying there so motionless, pretending to sulk. Since she happened to be clutching the long broom, she tried to tickle him from the doorway. This had no effect, and so she grew annoyed and began poking Gregor. It was only upon shoving him from his place but meeting no resistance that she became alert. When the true state of affairs now dawned on the charwoman, her eyes bulged in amazement and she whistled to herself. But instead of dawdling there, she yanked the bedroom door open and hollered into the darkness: "Go and look, it's croaked; it's lying there, absolutely croaked!"

Mr. and Mrs. Samsa sat upright in their matrimonial bed, trying to cope with the shock caused by the charwoman. When they managed to grasp what she meant, the two of them, one on either side, hastily clambered out of bed. Mr. Samsa threw the blanket over his shoulders, while Mrs. Samsa emerged in her nightgown; that was how they entered Gregor's room. Meanwhile, the door to the parlor, where Grete had been sleeping since the arrival of the boarders, had likewise opened; she was fully dressed and her face was pale as if she had not slept.

"Dead?" said Mrs. Samsa, quizzically eyeing the charwoman even though she could have gone to check everything for herself, or could have surmised it without checking.

"You bet," said the charwoman and by way of proof she thrust out the broom and pushed Gregor's corpse somewhat further to the side. Mrs. Samsa made as if to hold back the broom, but then let it be.

"Well," said Mr. Samsa, "now we can thank the Lord." He crossed himself and the three women imitated his example. Grete, her eyes glued to the corpse, said: "Just look how skinny he was. Well, he stopped eating such a long time ago. The food came back out exactly as it went in." And indeed,

Gregor's body was utterly flat and dry; they realized this only now when it was no longer raised on its tiny legs and nothing else diverted their eyes.

"Grete, come into our room for a bit," said Mrs. Samsa, smiling wistfully, and Grete, not without looking back at the corpse, followed her parents into the bedroom. The charwoman closed the door to Gregor's room and opened the window all the way. Though it was still early morning, there was a touch of warmth in the fresh air. It was already late March, after all.

The three boarders stepped out of their room and, astonished, cast about for their breakfast; they had been forgotten. "Where is breakfast?" the middle gentleman peevishly asked the charwoman. But putting her finger on her lips, she hastily and silently beckoned for the gentlemen to come into Gregor's room. And come they did, and with their hands in the pockets of their somewhat threadbare jackets, they stood around Gregor's corpse in the now sunlit room.

Next, the bedroom door opened, and Mr. Samsa, in his livery, appeared with his wife on one arm and his daughter on the other. Their eyes were all slightly tearstained; now and then, Grete pressed her face into the father's arm.

"Leave my home at once!" Mr. Samsa told the three gentlemen, pointing at the door without releasing the women.

"What do you mean?" asked the middle gentleman, somewhat dismayed and with a sugary smile. The two other gentlemen held their hands behind their backs, incessantly rubbing them together as if gleefully looking forward to a grand argument that they were bound to win.

"I mean exactly what I said," replied Mr. Samsa, and with his two companions he made a beeline toward the tenant. The latter at first stood his ground, eyeing the floor as if his thoughts were being rearranged to form a new pattern in his head.

"Well, then we'll go," he said, looking up at Mr. Samsa as if, in a sudden burst of humility, he were requesting sanction even for this decision. Mr. Samsa, with bulging eyes, merely vouchsafed him a few brief nods. Thereupon the gentleman strode right into the vestibule. His two friends, who had been listening for a short while with utterly calm hands, now quite literally hopped after him as if fearing that Mr. Samsa might precede them into the vestibule and might thrust himself between them and their leader. Once in the vestibule, all three boarders pulled their hats from the coat rack, their canes from the umbrella stand, bowed wordlessly, and left the apartment. Impelled by a suspicion that proved to be thoroughly groundless, Mr. Samsa and the two women stepped out on the landing. As they leaned on the banister, they watched the three gentlemen marching down the long stairway slowly but steadily, vanishing on every floor in the regular twist of the staircase, and popping up again several moments later. The lower the gentlemen got, the more the Samsa family lost interest in them, and as a butcher's boy, proudly balancing a basket on his head, came toward the gentlemen and then mounted well beyond them, Mr. Samsa and the women left the banister, and as if relieved, they all returned to their apartment.

They decided to spend this day resting and strolling; not only had they earned this break from work, they absolutely needed it. And so they sat down at the table to write three letters of explanation: Mr. Samsa to his superiors, Mrs. Samsa to her customer, and Grete to her employer. As they were writing, the charwoman came in to tell them she was leaving, for her morning's work was done. The three letter writers at first merely nodded without glancing up; it was only when she kept hovering that they looked up in annoyance. "Well?" asked Mr. Samsa. The charwoman stood beaming in the doorway as if she were about to announce some great windfall for the family, but would do so only if they dragged it out of her. On her hat, the small, almost erect ostrich plume, which had annoyed Mr. Samsa throughout her service here, swayed lightly in all directions. "What can we do for you?" asked Mrs. Samsa, whom the charwoman respected the most.

"Well," the charwoman replied with such friendly chuckling that she had to break off, "listen, you don't have to worry about getting rid of that stuff in the next room. It's all been taken care of."

Mrs. Samsa and Grete huddled over their letters as if to keep writing; Mr. Samsa, aware that the charwoman was on the verge of launching into a blow-by-blow description, resolutely stretched out his arm to ward her off. Not being allowed to tell her story, she suddenly remembered that she was in an awful hurry, and clearly offended, she called out: "So long, everybody." She then vehemently whirled around and charged out of the apartment with a horrible slam of the door.

"She'll be dismissed tonight," said Mr. Samsa, receiving no answer from his wife or his daughter, for the charwoman had ruffled the peace and quiet that they had barely gained. Standing up, the two women went over to the window and remained there, clasped in each other's arms. Mr. Samsa looked back from his chair and silently watched them for a while. Then he exclaimed: "Come on, get over here. Forget about the past once and for all. And show me a little consideration." The women, promptly obeying him, hurried over, caressed him, and swiftly finished their letters.

Then all three of them left the apartment together, which they had not done in months, and took the trolley out to the countryside beyond the town. The streetcar, where they were the only passengers, was flooded with warm sunshine. Leaning back comfortably in their seats, they discussed their future prospects and concluded that, upon closer perusal, these were anything but bad; for while they had never actually asked one another for any details, their jobs were all exceedingly advantageous and also promising. Naturally, the greatest immediate improvement in their situation could easily be brought about by their moving; they hoped to rent a smaller and cheaper apartment, but with a better location and altogether more practical than their current place, which had been found by Gregor. As they were conversing, both Mr. and Mrs. Samsa, upon seeing the daughter becoming more and more vivacious, realized almost in unison that lately, despite all the sorrows that had left her cheeks pale, she had blossomed into a lovely and shapely girl. Lapsing into silence and communicating almost unconsciously with their eyes, they reflected that it was high time they found a decent husband for her. And it was like a confirmation of their new dreams and good intentions that at the end of their ride the daughter was the first to get up, stretching her young body.

ZUNI RITUAL POETRY

Although repeatedly invaded since the 1500s and subjected, in turn, to regulation by Spanish, Mexican, and U.S. authority, Oraibi, Taos, Acoma, Zuni, and the other pueblos of the North American Southwest—the continent's oldest towns north of Mexico—have yet to be conquered in the full sense of the term. Bastions of spiritual and social autonomy, the pueblo communities make a profound impression on the nonnative world by the strength of their traditions in an era of change; and of this there can be no more convincing proof than the ceremonial system of Zuni pueblo with its annual cycle of drama, sacrifice, and oratory. Heard at the winter solstice and again, repeatedly, through the phases of the next twelve moons, the spoken word, to the accompaniment of ritual acts, continues to provide the cohesive bond for a growing community of nearly ten thousand people.

Continuously occupied since at least the 1300s, the Zuni territory in western New Mexico has traditionally supported an agricultural economy, dominated by the town, or pueblo, of Zuni itself, surrounded by outlying seasonal farming villages. The raising of livestock became important during the Spanish and Mexican period (1540–1846), but by the mid-twentieth century most Zuni residents had come to rely either on the thriving silversmithing industry or on jobs in off-reservation communities. Farming as a livelihood gradually became insignificant. Yet the agricultural cycle today still inspires Zuni ceremonialism.

The often-quoted and deeply admired texts for the Zuni ceremonial round were published just once, in 1932—yet plentifully—by the anthropologist Ruth L. Bunzel under the rubric *Zuni Ritual Poetry*. They comprise one of the two most important bodies of native American oratory on record, exceeded in scope and in quantity only by the Aztec orations preserved in the sixteenth-century Florentine Codex.

As the Zuni orations make clear, the purpose of the ceremonial round is to establish a relationship between "daylight people," or ordinary humans, and the so-called raw people, such as deer, bear, the sun, rainstorms, and corn plants, who consume either raw food or the offerings that the daylight people present to them. In a special category of raw people are the *kokkokwe*, ancestral spirits known in English as kachinas, represented during the ceremonies by masked dancers. Dependent on humans for their nurture, the kachinas and other raw people are given offerings that include the feather-decorated willow shafts called prayer sticks or, in Bunzel's translation, "plume wands." In return the raw people grant "seeds," "breath," "life," "light," and all manner of good fortune. The offerings are sacrificed by depositing, or "planting," them at prescribed locations. Since the Zuni hold that sacrifices were established in the ancient time by the raw people, it is natural enough to find kachinas themselves planting wands during the course of the rituals. In effect these are human sacrifices, with the prayer sticks standing in for the people.

As mentioned, the ceremonial year at Zuni begins with the winter solstice. This important event is followed by a series of winter dances and a calendar of prayer-stick offerings coordinated with the reappearances of the moon. The summer solstice, with its urgent prayers for rain, marks a second ceremonial high point, followed again by the repeating schedule of monthly offerings. Ceremonial activity quickens in the fall with the setting of the date for the great Shalako, a ceremony held shortly before the winter solstice. The selections offered here are from the prayers for three of the annual episodes: the winter solstice observances, the Scalp Dance, and the Shalako.

The winter solstice rites span twenty days, with the solstice itself falling in the middle. This "middle," moreover, is regarded as the center of the entire year. On the first day an announcement is made that prayer sticks will be planted ten days hence. The offerings are not prepared, however, until the ninth day, when the Fire Keeper is appointed. On the tenth day, ideally December 21, the offerings are planted, and the Fire Keeper lights the New Year's fire. With this begins a ten-day "fire taboo," during which no fire may be seen outdoors and no ashes may be removed from any house (the ashes accumulating just as stored crops, one hopes, will accumulate later in the year). When the taboo is lifted, the Fire Keeper delivers his prayer, or oration, asking especially for plentiful crops, as in the excerpt printed here.

The Scalp Dance formerly was performed on the return of a victorious war party to purify any warrior who had taken a scalp and to induct the trophy itself into the company of previously won scalps, regarded as rain makers. The dead in general are a source of contamination, threatening to those who have come into contact with them; but having "attained the place of blessed waters," they also have the power to send rain and, by extension, fruitfulness and good fortune. By the 1970s the Scalp Dance, no longer relevant as an occasional observance, had been brought into the annual round as a fall ritual. In the excerpt from the prayer given here, the scalp is envisioned in its role as rain maker and as an agent of blessing.

The Shalako, the most festive of the ceremonials, attracts an international audience of visitors, who arrive at Zuni in time for the grand entrance of the kachinas at the start of eight days of public proceedings. Led by the kachina Sayatasha, the masked party, which includes the troupe of six Shalako (giant kachinas in ten-foot-high bird-like costumes), enters the town and breaks up into small groups, each assigned to a house renovated for the occasion. During the first evening Sayatasha delivers his lengthy "night chant," which includes a house blessing for the benefit of his host. Dances and other rites during the next several days are marked by the presence of the Koyemshi, or clowns, who attend the kachinas and mock them. On the eighth day, with the spectacle finished, the Koyemshi are dismissed from their duties, and the ceremonial year comes to a close.

The ceremonial orations typically request or predict blessings, as can be seen from all the selections presented here. This culminating portion of the "talk" is preceded by a summary of what the speaker has been doing to obtain the desired result, as in the excerpt from the "Shalako House Blessing" (which describes the consecration of the structure and, as a result, the fruitfulness it will one day contain). The avowal of duty is in turn preceded by a statement noting the day or the occasion, making reference to a particular position in the ceremonial year. All three segments—occasion, duty, and result—can be observed in the *Dismissal of the Koyemshi*, presented here in full.

Our selections are from Ruth L. Bunzel, "Zuni Ritual Poetry," *Forty-Seventh Annual Report of the Bureau of American Ethnology* (1932), which includes annotated texts in Zuni and English. Two related works by Bunzel, "Introduction to Zuni Ceremonialism" and "Zuni Katcinas," are in the same volume. Alfonso Ortiz, ed., *Southwest*, vol. 9 of *Handbook of North American Indians* (1979), serves as a guide to the history and culture of Zuni and other pueblos. William M. Clements, *Native American Verbal Art: Texts and Contexts* (1996), includes a discussion of identity and difference in Zuni verbal art and offers an extended bibliography. For recent impressions of Zuni life and Zuni ceremonialism, see Barbara Tedlock, *The Beautiful and the Dangerous* (1992).

PRONOUNCING GLOSSARY

The following list uses common English syllables and stress accents to provide rough equivalents of selected words whose pronunciation may be unfamiliar to the general reader.

Acoma: *ak'-uh-muh*	Oraibi: *oh-righ'-bee*
kachinas: *kuh-chee'-nuhz*	Sayatasha: *sah'-yah-tah-shah*
kokkokwe: *koh'-koh-kway*	Shalako: *shah'-lah-koh*
Koyemshi: *koh'-yaym-shee*	Uwanammi: *oo'-wah-nahm-mee*

From A Prayer at the Winter Solstice[1]

* * *

Perhaps if we are lucky
Our earth mother
Will wrap herself in a fourfold robe
Of white meal,
Full of frost flowers;   5
A floor of ice will spread over the world,
The forests,
Because of the cold will lean to one side,
Their arms will break beneath the weight of snow.
When the days are thus   10
The flesh of our earth mother
Will crack with cold.
Then in the spring when she is replete with living waters
Our mothers,
All different kinds of corn   15
In their earth mother
We shall lay to rest.
With their earth mother's living waters
They will be made into new beings;
Into their sun father's daylight   20
They will come out standing;
Yonder to all directions
They will stretch out their hands calling for rain.
Then with their fresh waters
The rain makers[2] will pass us on our roads.   25
Clasping their young ones in their arms
They will rear their children.
Gathering them[3] into our houses,
Following these toward whom our thoughts bend,
With our thoughts following them,   30
Thus we shall always live.

From The Scalp Dance

* * *

Indeed, the enemy,
Though in his life
He was a person given to falsehood,
He has become one to foretell[1]
How the world will be,   5
How the days will be.

---

1. All selections translated by Ruth L. Bunzel. Text printed in italics was added by Bunzel.   2. Or Uwan-ammi; water spirits who live in all the waters of the earth; cumulus clouds are their houses: mist is their breath [adapted from Translator's note].   3. The corn at harvest.   1. It is expected that the scalp will prove an omen of good fortune.

That during his time,
We may have good days,
Beautiful days,
Hoping for this,   10
We shall keep his days.[2]
Indeed, if we are lucky,
During the enemy's time
Fine rain caressing the earth,
Heavy rain caressing the earth,   15
We shall win.
When the enemy's days are in progress,
The enemy's waters,
We shall win,
His seeds we shall win,   20
His riches we shall win,
His power,
His strong spirit,
His long life,
His old age,   25
In order to win these,
Tirelessly, unwearied,
We shall pass his days.
Now, indeed, the enemy,
Even one who thought himself a man,   30
In a shower of arrows,
In a shower of war clubs,
With bloody head,
The enemy,
Reaching the end of his life,   35
Added to the flesh of our earth mother.

From Shalako

From *Sayatasha's*[1] *Night Chant*

HOUSE BLESSING

* * *

Then my father's rain-filled room
I rooted at the north,
I rooted at the west,
I rooted at the south,
I rooted at the east,[2]   5
I rooted above,
Then in the middle of my father's roof,
With two plume wands joined together,

2. I.e., observe the several days' ritual, which is spoken of as the "enemy's time," "enemy's days," or simply "his time."   1. Long Horn; the kachina's mask has a curved horn on the right side.   2. Consecrating the principal room (*rain-filled room*) of the human host (*father*) by stroking each wall with a torch, a whip, or other instrument.

I consecrated his roof.
This is well; 10
In order that my father's offspring may increase,
I consecrated the center of his roof.
And then also, the center of my father's floor,
With seeds of all kinds,[3]
I consecrated the center of his floor. 15
This is well;
In order that my father's fourth room[4]
May be bursting with corn,
That even in his doorway,
The shelled corn may be scattered before the door, 20
The beans may be scattered before the door,
That his house may be full of little boys,
And little girls,
And people grown to maturity;
That in his house 25
Children may jostle one another in the doorway,
In order that it may be thus,
I have consecrated the rain-filled room
Of my daylight father,
My daylight mother. 30

*   *   *

DISMISSAL OF THE KOYEMSHI[5]

This many are the days,
My children,
Since with their plume wand they appointed us.
Throughout the winter,
And the summer 5
Anxiously we have awaited our time.
Hither toward the south
We have given our fathers plume wands.[6]
For all our ladder descending children[7]
We have been asking for life. 10
Now we have reached the appointed time.
This night
We have fulfilled the thoughts of our fathers.
Always with one thought
We shall live. 15
My children,
This night
Your children,
Your families,

---

3. Male and female wands joined together (representing fertility) are placed in a decorated box suspended from the ceiling; seeds, in a permanent excavation below the floor. Thus the sixfold blessing encompasses the four directions, the zenith, and the nadir.   4. Innermost room.   5. A troupe of ten clowns appearing in dances throughout the year. Their impersonators, appointed at the winter solstice to serve for twelve months, are here dismissed by their leader, or "father" (who calls them *children*), bringing the Shalako to an end.   6. I.e., raw people (*fathers*) have been given *plume wands* in exchange for benefits conferred on humans.   7. Humans; so called since houses in former times were entered through an opening in the roof.

Happily you will pass on their roads.[8]   20
Happily we shall always live.
Even though we say we have fulfilled their thoughts
No indeed
Anxiously awaiting until we shall again come to our
        appointed time
We shall live henceforth.   25
My children,
Thus I have finished my words for you.
To this end, my children:
May you now go happily to your children.
Asking for life from my fathers   30
Yonder on all sides,
Asking for my fathers' life-giving breath,
Their breath of old age,
And into my warm body,
Drawing their breath,   35
I add to your breath.
To this end, my children
May your roads be fulfilled;
May you grow old;
May you be blessed with life.   40

8. Will meet, will join.

INUIT SONGS

The inhospitable central Arctic, directly north and northwest of Hudson Bay, is home to numerous small communities using varieties of one of the world's most far-flung languages: Inuit-Inupiaq, also called Eskimo, spoken across Alaska, Canada, and Greenland from the Bering Strait to the North Atlantic. Known to Europe since the earliest Norse colonization of Greenland, an event memorialized in the Icelandic sagas (ca. A.D. 1000–1300), the Inuit project an image of superhuman survivorship and intense artistry far beyond their native realm. As early as the eighteenth century, their poetry became known to an international audience through the *Volkslieder* (Folksongs, 1778–79) of the German philosopher and critic Johann Gottfried Herder, whose publication of an Inuit father's lament for his dead son ("My joy has gone into darkness and has become hidden in the mountain") gave the world its first taste of a literary tradition eventually to be revealed in depth—not from Greenland but from the central Arctic, the last region of the inhabitable north to be reached by Europe and still today a stronghold of native tradition.

It was Knud Johan Victor Rasmussen, born in Greenland to an Inuit mother, who gave the great singers of the central Arctic their lasting voice. Leader of the Danish-sponsored Fifth Thule Expedition (1921–24), Rasmussen brought a team of distinguished scientists through the heart of the Canadian Arctic, assigning to himself the task of documenting what he termed *intellectual culture*. The results were reported in a series of publications that included texts obtained from several dozen native singers, five of whom are represented in the selections printed here.

Orpingalik, a prominent shaman of Pelly Bay (on the Boothia Peninsula in north-central Canada), gave Rasmussen nearly a hundred songs in the course of a week. In his extensive accompanying testimony, he is revealed as a theorist as well as a poet.

"We will fear to use words," he explained on one occasion, "but it will happen that the words we need will come of themselves. When the words we want to use shoot up of themselves, we get a new song."

Uvlunuaq, wife of Orpingalik, was a gifted singer in her own right. As reported by Rasmussen, "They had a son Igsivalitaq ('the frostbitten one'); a year or two before, this son had murdered a hunting companion in a fit of temper, and now he lived as outlaw in the mountains round Pelly Bay, fearing that the Mounted Police, of whom he had heard tell, would come for him. And his mother had made the following song through sorrow over her son's fate."

Netsit, storyteller and singer of the Umingmaktôrmiut ("Musk Ox People"), accompanied Rasmussen in his travels in the vicinity of Bathurst Inlet (seven hundred miles west of Pelly Bay). Netsit's "Dead Man's Song" is apparently another's composition, since he prefaced it with the statement, "After Aijuk's death, they say, his song was dreamt by Paulinâq."

Uvavnuk, fellow tribeswoman of Orpingalik and Uvlunuaq, died before Rasmussen's arrival. A sometime shaman, whose powers came and went, she composed her song "The Great Sea" in a seizure of ecstasy said to have filled her body with light. At the end of her life, she declared to an assembled audience that she had brought forth all manner of game from the interior of the earth; following her death, the people enjoyed a year of abundance. Her song was performed for Rasmussen by her son Niviatsian, himself a shaman.

Kibkarjuk, an elder woman of the Pâdlermiut ("People of the Dried Willow Branches"), saved her village from starvation during the winter of 1921–22. Having dreamed of a distant, trout-filled lake, she succeeded in locating it after a perilous journey through blizzards, accompanied only by her small adopted son. Nevertheless, she was no longer her husband's favorite wife. In the song included here, she draws on that unhappy circumstance, recalling younger days.

Inuit songs are performed in the communal feasting house to the accompaniment of drumming and dancing. The audience joins in on the refrains, which consist of untranslatable song-syllables (for example, *unaija unaija*). Songs may also enliven the intimacy of a family gathering at home, or they may be sung in private. Orpingalik referred to his own songs as "my companions in solitude."

The translations printed here are from Rasmussen's Danish versions, rather than from the original Inuit. By virtue of his command of both Inuit and Danish, and in view of his consultations with the singers themselves, Rasmussen was uniquely qualified to interpret an obscure diction characterized by word distortions and special vocabulary. A native speaker of Greenland Inuit, he was able to penetrate the subtleties of the Canadian dialects—though not without effort. As one of his informants commented approvingly, upon taking leave, "Your tongue is not so frozen as when you came."

For a fuller selection of Inuit song texts, one may turn to Tom Lowenstein, *Eskimo Poems from Canada and Greenland* (1973), a literary anthology based on the research of Rasmussen. The source works are Knud Rasmussen, *Intellectual Culture of the Hudson Bay Eskimos* (1930), *The Netsilik Eskimos* (1931), and *Intellectual Culture of the Copper Eskimos* (1932). David Damas, ed., *Arctic*, vol. 5 of *Handbook of North American Indians* (1984), provides an indispensable guide to Inuit history and culture.

PRONOUNCING GLOSSARY

The following list uses common English syllables and stress accents to provide rough equivalents of selected words whose pronunciation may be unfamiliar to the general reader.

aji jai ja: *ah-yee' yigh yah*

ejaja-eja: *eh-yah'-yah—eh-yah*

Igsivalitaq: *eeg-see'-vah-lee-tahk*

ija-je-ja: *ee-yah—yeh-yah*

Inuit: *in'-oo-it* Orpingalik: *or-peeng'-ah-leek*
Inupiaq: *in-oo'-pee-ak* unaija: *oo-nigh'-ya*
Kibkarjuk: *keeb'-kahr-yook* Uvavnuk: *oo-vahv'-nook*
Netsit: *nayt'-seet* Uvlunuaq: *oov-loo'-noo-ahk*

ORPINGALIK
flourished 1923

My Breath[1]

This is what I call my song, because it is as important for me to sing it, as it
is to draw breath.

> This is my song: a powerful song.
> Unaija-unaija.[2]
> Since autumn I have lain here,
> helpless and ill,
> as if I were my own child.   5
>
> Sorrowfully, I wish my woman
> to another hut,
> another man for refuge,
> firm and safe as the winter-ice.
> Unaija-unaija.   10
>
> And I wish my woman
> a more fortunate protector,
> now I lack the strength
> to raise myself from bed.
> Unaija-unaija.   15
>
> Do you know yourself?
> How little of yourself you understand!
> Stretched out feebly on my bench,
> my only strength is in my memories.
> Unaija-unaija.   20
>
> Game! Big game,
> chasing ahead of me!
> Allow me to re-live that!
> Let me forget my frailty,
> by calling up the past!   25
> Unaija-unaija.
>
> I bring to mind that great white one,
> the polar bear,

---

1. Translated by Tom Lowenstein. Orpingalik told Rasmussen that this song came to him in a fit of despondency after a long illness.   2. The refrain connotes melancholy and resignation [Translator's note].

approaching with raised hind-quarters,
his nose in the snow—   30
convinced, as he rushed at me,
that of the two of us,
he was the only male!
Unaija-unaija.

Again and again he threw me down: 35
but spent at last,
he settled by a hump of ice,
and rested there,
ignorant that I was going to finish him.
He thought he was the only male around!   40
But I too was a man!
Unaija-unaija.

Nor will I forget that great blubbery one,
the fjord-seal, that I slaughtered
from an ice-floe before dawn,   45
while friends at home
were laid out like the dead,
feeble with hunger,
famished with bad luck.
I hurried home,   50
laden with meat and blubber,
as though I were just running across the ice
to view a breathing-hole.[3]
Yet this had been an old and cunning bull,
who'd scented me at once—   55
but before he had drawn breath,
my spear was sinking
through his neck.

This is how it was.
Now I lie on my bench,   60
too sick to even fetch
a little seal oil for my woman's lamp.
Time, time scarcely seems to pass,
though dawn follows dawn,
and spring approaches the village.   65
Unaija-unaija.

How much longer must I lie here?
How long? How long must she go begging
oil for the lamp,
reindeer-skins for her clothes,   70
and meat for her meal?
I, a feeble wretch:
she, a defenceless woman.
Unaija-unaija.

Do you know yourself?   75
How little of yourself you understand!

3. Hole in the ice where a seal comes up to breathe.

Dawn follows dawn,
and spring is approaching the village.
Unaija-unaija.

UVLUNUAQ
flourished 1923

Song of a Mother[1]

[A young man had killed his hunting companion in a fit of rage. The murderer's mother sang this song to express her grief.]

Ejaja-eja.
A bit of song comes back.
I draw it to me like a friend.
    Ejaja-eja.

I ought, I suppose, to be ashamed   5
of the child I once carried on my back,
when I heard he'd left the settlement.
They're right to tell me so:
I ought to be ashamed.
    Ejaja-eja.   10

I am ashamed:
because he didn't have a mother
who was faultless
as the clear sky,
wise and without folly.   15
Now that he's the butt
of everybody's tongue,
this evil talk will finish him.
    Ejaja-eja.

He has become the burden   20
of my age.
But far from being
properly ashamed,
I'm envious of others
when they break up   25
after feasts, and set off
with crowds of friends
behind them, waving on the ice.
    Ejaja-eja.

I remember one mild spring.   30
We'd camped near Cross-Eye Lake.
Our footsteps sank
with a soft creak

---

1. Translated by Tom Lowenstein.

into half-thawed snow.
I stayed near the men,   35
like a tame animal.
But when the news
about the murder came,
and that he'd fled,
the ground heaved under me   40
like a mountain,
and I stood on its summit,
and I staggered.

NETSIT

flourished 1923

Dead Man's Song[1]

I'm filled with joy
when the day dawns quietly
over the roof of the sky,
    aji, jai ja.

I'm filled with joy   5
when the sun rises slowly
over the roof of the sky,
    aji, jai ja.

But other times, I choke with fear:
a greedy swarm of maggots   10
eats into the hollows
of my collar-bone and eyes,
    aji, jai ja.

I lie here dreaming
how I choked with fear   15
when they shut me
in an ice-hut on the lake,[2]
    aji, jai ja.

And I could not see
my soul would ever free itself   20
and get up to the hunting-grounds
of the sky,
    aji, jai ja.

Fear grew, and grew.
Fear overwhelmed me   25
when the fresh-water ice

---

1. Translated by Tom Lowenstein. "Dreamed by one who is alive" [Rasmussen's note].   2. The dead are often interred by being left in the snow hut in which they have died, it being closed up with a block of snow [Rasmussen's note].

snapped in the cold,
and the booming crack of the frost
grew into the sky,
    aji, jai ja.   30

Life was wonderful
in winter.
But did winter make me happy?
No, I always worried
about hides for boot-soles   35
and for boots:
and if there'd be enough
for all of us.
Yes, I worried constantly,
    aji, jai ja.   40

Life was wonderful
in summer.
But did summer make me happy?
No, I always worried
about reindeer skins and rugs for the platform.[3]   45
Yes, I worried constantly,
    aji, jai ja.

Life was wonderful
when you stood at your fishing-hole
on the ice.   50
But was I happy waiting at my fishing hole?
No, I always worried
for my little hook,
in case it never got a bite.
Yes, I worried constantly,   55
    aji, jai ja.

Life was wonderful
when you danced in the feasting-house.[4]
But did this make me any happier?
No, I always worried   60
I'd forget my song.
Yes, I worried constantly,
    aji, jai ja.

Life was wonderful . . .
And I still feel joy   65
each time the day-break
whitens the dark sky,
each time the sun
climbs over the roof of the sky,
    aji, jai ja.   70

---

3. That is, the sleeping platform within the house.   **4.** Where songs are performed.

UVAVNUK
died before 1921

The Great Sea[1]

The great sea
Has sent me adrift,
It moves me as the weed in a great river,
Earth and the great weather
Move me,   5
Have carried me away
And move my inward parts with joy.

1. Translated by W. Worster.

KIBKARJUK
flourished 1922

Song of the Rejected Woman[1]

[Kibkarjuk remembers when she was her husband's favorite wife, and was
allowed to hunt caribou herself.]

     Inland,
       far inland go my thoughts,
       my mournful thoughts.
To never leave the woman's bench
is too much to endure: 5
I want to wander inland,
     far inland.
       Ija-je-ja.

My thoughts return
to hunting: 10
animals, delightful food!
To never leave the woman's bench
is too much to endure:
I want to wander inland,
     far inland.   15
       Ija-je-ja.

I hunted like
the men:
I carried weapons,
shot a reindeer bull,   20
a reindeer cow and calf,
yes, slew them with my arrows,
with my arrows,
one evening towards winter,

1. Translated by Tom Lowenstein.

as the sky-dusk fell 25
far inland.
   Ija-je-ja.

This is what I think about,
this is what I struggle with,
while inland, under falling snow, 30
the earth turns white,
far inland.
   Ija-je-ja.

TANIZAKI JUN'ICHIRŌ
1886–1965

It would be hard to find a novelist in modern Japan, or anywhere, whose career could rival in distinction and productivity that of Tanizaki Jun'ichirō. No other Japanese writer quite combines popular appeal, fecund imagination, and understanding of the historical moment with such a pitch-perfect style and deadly sense of humor. For all they delight the reader, these qualities are only the most striking in a grab bag of mischievous idiosyncrasies that made Tanizaki, long before the publication of his last novel at the age of seventy-six, Japan's favorite literary curmudgeon. Many critics imply that he should have been Japan's first recipient of the Nobel Prize for Literature, and his admirers may well regret that a mere three years after Tanizaki's death this distinction went to Kawabata Yasunari (p. 2337). With a life's work as rich as Tanizaki's, however, accolades seem irrelevant. Tanizaki built his own monument.

He was born into a merchant family in the heart of the old commercial quarter of Tokyo, where a trace of seventeenth- and eighteenth-century townsman customs still hung in the air like incense. Tanizaki's maternal grandfather was an old-style store-keeper whose printing shop saw the family through some lean times when Tanizaki's father proved an inept rice broker. The experiences and milieu of his childhood seem to have shaped the literary Tanizaki to a profound degree. His youthful world was an unstable mix of financial stringency and the cultured leisure of the secure, old-fashioned bourgeoisie. His mother, a noted beauty used to the comforts and established customs of a prosperous house, took him often to the traditional plays of the *kabuki* theater, whose open, straw-matted stalls and adjoining teahouses later made their way into his fiction. The plays that he watched from these timeworn stalls would have left a child wide-eyed with wonder, for *kabuki* appealed to its audiences through tangled plots and larger-than-life heroes and managed to blend a spectacular compound of drama, music, and dance with lavish costumes, revolving sets, and special effects, including everything from severed heads to fox spirits flying through the air.

His mother also took Tanizaki on outings by rickshaw to see the cherry blossoms and by train to visit the *shogun*'s tomb in nearby Nikko. She would dress him in formal silk kimonos whose patterns, cuts, and fabrics were miniature models of the well-turned-out gentleman. He was taught to recognize fine hand-made paper and to select quality bean jam and other traditional sweets so that he could be dispatched when gift-wrapping or a delicacy was needed.

He learned the songs of the *geisha* houses at his father's knee. And like the children in *Child's Play* (p. 1807), he was allowed to roam through the byways of his downtown neighborhood. He discovered the many bookstores in the area, where he spent his allowance on adventure stories or tales of the *samurai*. On summer evenings, when amateur players gathered in the garden of the local shrine, he would slip out to watch them reenact famous ghost stories or the latest grisly murder.

On other evenings he would overhear his parents quarreling about money. Or he would go to his grandfather's house for a bath. The walk home in the dark seems to have stimulated his growing powers of imagination, in the same way that his parents' arguments exposed him to sexual tension. *Kabuki* theater and the bookshops drew him into the world of fiction, and the neighborhood plays on the shrine grounds were his introduction to violence and manipulation. All these threads—together with his training as an epicure and a tendency to idolize his beautiful, almost archaically cultured mother—would become major themes in his fiction.

So too would the world of darkness that Tanizaki has immortalized in his famous essay *In Praise of Shadows*. The dark held for him a fascination that, if his memoirs are to be believed, went back to his earliest years. He was drawn, for example, to the storehouse at the rear of his grandfather's compound.

> It was located in the farthest reaches of the property: to get to it, one had to pass through the little room where Grandmother sat all day before the brazier; then through a room with a formal alcove, which my uncle used as a study; then along a passage which led ultimately to a separate two-story building. There was usually no one about the storehouse except when something was being put into it, or taken out. For the most part, the place was perfectly quiet. I liked to sneak off there by myself and sit on the cold stone steps where no voices broke the silence and even the noise of the print shop was reduced to a dull and distant hum. I would press my face against the gleaming black double-doors, which were covered with wire netting and closed by a large padlock, and try to peer into the dark interior through the crack between them. I didn't know just what was hidden within, but there was a faint, elegant fragrance like aloes and musk mingled with the inevitable smell of damp and mold.*

These dark, musty depths held the promise of untold mysteries, and they were linked in Tanizaki's mind with relics of the old Japan.

As a young adult Tanizaki shed (temporarily) this childhood fascination, a not uncommon pattern among those young enough to want to rid themselves of youth. He set himself up as a writer of "demonic" fiction, as critics called it: historical tales of sexual obsession and sadomasochism, and stories of what might be called Japan's own version of a "lost generation," pursuing its debauches in the new, modern age. When financial success came, he ensconced his wife and daughter in a house as different from the houses of his youth as it is possible to imagine. He moved to Yokohama, the new port city south of Tokyo where foreigners gathered, and went to work writing screenplays for one of the new motion-picture studios. There he bought a Western-style house in the thick of the foreign settlement in the Bluff area, overlooking the city. It was a swank residence that came equipped with electricity and glass windows as well as the furniture and cook of its former British owners. And there he engaged, to use the words with which he describes one of his fictional characters, "in foreign tastes of the most hair-raising variety." Western foods like roast turkey and kidney pie became staples. He took to wearing brown suits and playing the guitar. He boasted that he went entire days without removing his shoes (violating Japanese custom). He and his wife embraced "social dancing" and gravitated to the bright lights of the foreigners' Christmas balls and New Year's fêtes as moths flying to the flame.

But the dancing stopped when a massive earthquake ripped through the Tokyo-Yokohama area on September 1, 1923. Tanizaki was vacationing in a mountain resort southwest of the epicenter, and his first reaction was a perverse flood of joy. "Good," he later describes himself as thinking. "Now Tokyo will become a decent place!" The

*Paul McCarthy, trans., *Childhood Years* (1988).

old had been leveled, and the new city would be a shiny metropolis of horns and headlights, champagne and high-rises, Turkish baths and showgirls irradiated in the glare of footlights.

In anticipation of this exciting new city, Tanizaki moved temporarily to the Kyoto-Osaka region, hub of the old Japan, where polite classical tradition and antiquated merchant culture merged at a relatively safe remove from the onslaught of the West. Once he had relocated, Tanizaki began to reconsider his youthful enthusiasms. No doubt he was affected by the more conservative environment, for a process now began in which his own, and Japan's, infatuation with the West came into sociological and historical focus.

His first major work, A Fool's Love (1924), portrays his compatriots in the grip of a national obsession. The hero, the fool of the title who narrates the novel and is clearly intended to serve as an emblematic figure, is a country bumpkin new to the big city and riding the escalator of upward mobility. His profession as an electrical engineer, his uncritical admiration of all things European, and even his name, Jōji, which can quickly elide into what sounds like the Japanese pronunciation of "George," place him in the vanguard of modernization. When Jōji meets a bar girl, Naomi, who reminds him of the movie star Mary Pickford, he sees in her the key to his dream of a modern, American sort of life unfettered by Japanese conventions. He installs her in a stylish Western house (not unlike Tanizaki's) and proceeds to squander his savings on piano lessons and Paris fashions. The more Naomi succeeds in replicating the look of an American flapper, the nastier and more demanding she becomes and the more seductive to the masochistic Jōji, who, in cutting himself off from his own past, has surrendered his inherited sense of virtue and, with it, self-worth. He is increasingly unhinged in his confusion of eros with the West. By the end of the book, when his wife has taken a succession of foreign lovers, relegating Jōji to the role of houseboy with occasional privileges, he views this shucking of convention as yet another triumph of modern sophistication. In his fool's mind the material attractions of another culture are mistaken for sexual allure, or perhaps more accurately, the two have fused into an impossible muddle: the novel's metaphor for Japan's modern plight. It is not the West per se that Tanizaki objects to, but the West as it is appropriated and misperceived by the Japanese, objectified and turned into a fetish. The entire nation, he says, is in the throes of a fatal attraction, a predicament entirely of its own making.

It was at this juncture that Tanizaki wrote In Praise of Shadows. One might characterize the piece as an essay on aesthetics, and indeed Tanizaki is as learned and rigorous an aesthete as they come. He would devote many years to rendering The Tale of Genji into modern Japanese. On three separate occasions he produced a translation of this thousand-page classical novel, sinking himself into the courtly world of the eleventh century and reemerging each time with a work of brilliant erudition, impressive for the affinity it displayed for the sensibility of a remote and, to current Japanese readers, alien society. He would also write a considerable body of historical fiction, which, though highly imaginative, demonstrates his love of the arcana of historical scholarship. On almost every page of the essay, this learning is evident. So is the discriminating, antiquarian taste of the serious aesthete. The author of In Praise of Shadows, very much his mother's son, is disappointed when the sliding doors of his new house fail to provide a "mellow softness" or when a moon-viewing party must be canceled lest a recording of "Moonlight Sonata" break the spell.

Yet it would be a serious mistake to read this work solely as a tract on aesthetics. An eloquent and deeply felt paean to the past and to the tastes that are formed by tradition, it is also an argument for reconsidering how far one ought to go in remaking oneself in another's image. Tanizaki had by now recovered a respect for the past as a meaningful, ultimately inescapable component of our lives, however detached they may seem from what has gone before. He had come to appreciate that one cannot discard the cultural legacy one has inherited without in the process ending up empty:

a fool. He chooses architecture as his figure of speech, but when he describes what Japanese houses were like before electric lights and telephones he is talking about the whole of Japanese culture.

In Praise of Shadows has been called perverse. It is certainly idiosyncratic. Virtually everything Tanizaki wrote shows a playful sense of humor, and this essay, for all its seriousness, is no exception. When Tanizaki tells us "the Japanese toilet truly is a place of spiritual repose," even in overcrowded Japan one may assume that the tongue is firmly planted in the cheek. His portrait of Japanese womanhood is also skewed in a peculiarly Tanizakian fashion. It is not that what he says about traditional Japanese standards of feminine beauty is incorrect or exaggerated. Rather, the master story-teller cannot help selecting his words in such a way that the evocation romanticizes women into an ethereal and mysterious composite. He may be criticized for this, and indeed his entire work, repeatedly addressing male desire for a transcendent female, is a ripe target for feminist criticism. Likewise, Tanizaki's fascination with skin color may offend those who misread his blunt language as racism, when in fact his motives are the very opposite: to embrace difference and to insist, even as he overstates, that distinctions—and distance—be allowed to stand. To deprive Tanizaki of his chosen material, especially when he is the first to acknowledge the manipulative aspects of both craft and obsession, would inevitably impoverish an extravagant art. Japan itself, for that matter, and the weight of its traditions have to a certain extent been exoticized by Tanizaki. One could argue that it is all part of a rhetorical strategy.

The vagrant structure of the essay, too, may seem unorthodox. What does Einstein's trip to Japan have to do with it, one might ask. Tanizaki surely does wander, from jade to temples to *sushi* to makeup. The links are sometimes tenuous, and just as we catch the drift of things Tanizaki is apt to circle back to an earlier theme. Yet for all it lacks in logical progression, In Praise of Shadows is a modern example of a hallowed Japanese literary tradition: a twentieth-century version of the discursive essays known as *zuihitsu* that were first practiced by Sei Shōnagon in *The Pillow Book* and Yoshida Kenkō in *Essays in Idleness*. Tanizaki breaks no new ground when he "follows the brush" (or more likely the fountain pen), unconcerned with contriving a structure. But steeped as he was in the Japanese classics, Tanizaki knew intuitively that an essay on the vicissitudes of Japan's pursuit of the West is most effectively expressed in a genre whose very form conveys uncertainty.

Tanizaki's complete works run to twenty-eight volumes, of which In Praise of Shadows is but a tantalizing sample. Altogether, he wrote in an amazing variety of forms: novels, short stories, plays, poetry, movie scripts, essays, criticism, and translations. But his major works all configure themselves around a handful of recurring themes. The world as Tanizaki sees it is composed of worlds constructed. Jōji in A Fool's Love tries to build a world that will have the glamour of an American movie and, therefore, freedom from Japanese propriety. The protagonist of Tanizaki's next major novel, Some Prefer Nettles (1928–29), written shortly before In Praise of Shadows, finds himself drawn like Tanizaki toward the old Japan, away from foreign fads. He observes his father-in-law cultivating a life of obsolete practices, and he begins to understand their attraction for the old man, and thus their reality.

During World War II, Tanizaki sought escape in the writing of an extended novel of manners, The Makioka Sisters (1943–48). Ostensibly, it tells the story of a declining merchant family's frustrated attempts to secure a husband for one of the younger sisters. The bulk of the long novel, however, details the efforts of the four sisters to stage a life for themselves in mimicry of prouder days. Even as he wrote, the progress of the war ensured that his novel would be an elegy, and Tanizaki must have known that this leisurely world of bourgeois elegance he had called into being one last time was in every way now a fiction.

Fiction, manipulation, constructed or imagined worlds, obsession, and desire also mark Tanizaki's postwar novels. The Key (1956) chronicles the sexual fantasies of an aging professor and his wife, told through the medium of their two diaries. They each pretend their diaries are a secret, knowing full well that they write only to be read and to goad the other into a greater sexual frenzy. Writing becomes deceit, and deceit the father of reality. *Diary of a Mad Old Man* (1961–62), the last completed novel from a writer still vigorous in his seventies, records a geriatric urge to satisfy sexual appetites only slightly diminished by age. Before death can defeat him, the septuagenarian concocts elaborate scenarios that allow him to neck with his daughter-in-law or to fondle her lithesome feet. It is no accident that in both of these final works Western consumer goods—Courvoisier, mascara, Polaroid cameras—serve as exotic stimulants, the passport into a world of dreams.

With a wicked sense of humor and an almost religious faith in the power of imagination, Tanizaki knew precisely what he was up to. As his apotheosis of the common privy, so full of delectable hyperbole, amply demonstrates, he was a supremely ironic writer. He was also intensely self-aware. Unlike most of his characters, he understood his need to fashion fictional worlds. And in fact, when—some years after he published *In Praise of Shadows*—an architect he had hired told him, "I've read your essay and I know exactly what you want," Tanizaki is reported to have answered, "No, no. I could never *live* in a house like that."

Tanizaki has been well served in translation. *A Fool's Love* is available in English as *Naomi* (1985), Anthony H. Chambers, trans. Chambers has also translated two novellas in one volume: *The Secret History of Lord Musashi and Arrowroot* (1982). Also in English are Edward G. Seidensticker, trans., *Some Prefer Nettles* (1955) and *The Makioka Sisters* (1957), and Howard Hibbett, trans., *The Key* (1961) and *Diary of a Mad Old Man* (1965). Hibbett, trans., *Seven Japanese Tales* (1963), is a collection of short stories that includes *The Tattooer,* the story that established Tanizaki's reputation, and *A Portrait of Shunkin,* one of his most celebrated works. Also recommended are Paul McCarthy, trans., *A Cat, a Man and Two Women* (1990) and *Childhood Years* (1988), Tanizaki's memoir. Ken K. Ito, *Visions of Desire: Tanizaki's Fictional Worlds* (1991), is an excellent study, and Donald Keene, *Dawn to the West* (1984), a history of modern Japanese literature, has a substantial chapter on Tanizaki.

PRONOUNCING GLOSSARY

The following list uses common English syllables to provide rough equivalents of selected words whose pronunciation may be unfamiliar to the general reader.

Baikō: *bai-koh*

Bunraku: *boon-rah-koo*

Chion'in: *chee-ohn-een*

Hiei: *hee-ay*

Higashiyama: *hee-gah-shee-yah-mah*

Honganji: *hohn-gahn-jee*

Jōji: *joh-jee*

Kairakuen: *kai-rah-koo-en*

Kongo Iwao: *kohn-goh ee-wah-oh*

kotei: *koh-tay*

Kurodani: *koo-roh-dah-nee*

Meiji: *may-jee*

Miyako: *mee-yah-koh*

Natsume Sōseki: *nah-tsoo-me soh-se-kee*

Nyoigatake: *nyoh-ee-gah-tah-kay*

Onoe: *oh-noh-ay*

Saitō Ryoku: *sai-toh ryoh-koo*

Sei Shōnagon: *say shoh-nah-gohn*

shōji: *shoh-jee*

Tanizaki Jun'ichirō: *tah-nee-zah-kee joon-ee-chee-roh*

Waranjiya: *wah-rahn-jee-yah*

Yamamoto Sanehiko: *yah-mah-moh-toh sah-ne-hee-koh*

Yoshida Kenkō: *yoh-shee-dah ken-koh*

zuihitsu: *zoo-ee-hee-tsoo*

In Praise of Shadows[1]

What incredible pains the fancier of traditional architecture must take when he sets out to build a house in pure Japanese style, striving somehow to make electric wires, gas pipes, and water lines harmonize with the austerity of Japanese rooms—even someone who has never built a house for himself must sense this when he visits a teahouse, a restaurant, or an inn. For the solitary eccentric it is another matter; he can ignore the blessings of scientific civilization and retreat to some forsaken corner of the countryside; but a man who has a family and lives in the city cannot turn his back on the necessities of modern life—heating, electric lights, sanitary facilities—merely for the sake of doing things the Japanese way. The purist may rack his brain over the placement of a single telephone, hiding it behind the staircase or in a corner of the hallway, wherever he thinks it will least offend the eye. He may bury the wires rather than hang them in the garden, hide the switches in a closet or cupboard, run the cords behind a folding screen. Yet for all his ingenuity, his efforts often impress us as nervous, fussy, excessively con-trived. For so accustomed are we to electric lights that the sight of a naked bulb beneath an ordinary milk glass[2] shade seems simpler and more natural than any gratuitous attempt to hide it. Seen at dusk as one gazes out upon the countryside from the window of a train, the lonely light of a bulb under an old-fashioned shade, shining dimly from behind the white paper shoji[3] of a thatch-roofed farmhouse, can seem positively elegant.

But the snarl and the bulk of an electric fan remain a bit out of place in a Japanese room. The ordinary householder, if he dislikes electric fans, can simply do without them. But if the family business involves the entertain-ment of customers in summertime, the gentleman of the house cannot afford to indulge his own tastes at the expense of others. A friend of mine, the proprietor of a Chinese restaurant called the Kairakuen, is a thoroughgoing purist in matters architectural. He deplores electric fans and long refused to have them in his restaurant, but the complaints from customers with which he was faced every summer ultimately forced him to give in.

I myself have had similar experiences. A few years ago I spent a great deal more money than I could afford to build a house. I fussed over every last fitting and fixture, and in every case encountered difficulty. There was the shoji: for aesthetic reasons I did not want to use glass, and yet paper alone would have posed problems of illumination and security. Much against my will, I decided to cover the inside with paper and the outside with glass. This required a double frame, thus raising the cost. Yet having gone to all this trouble, the effect was far from pleasing. The outside remained no more than a glass door; while within, the mellow softness of the paper was destroyed by the glass that lay behind it. At that point I was sorry I had not just settled for glass to begin with. Yet laugh though we may when the house is someone else's, we ourselves accept defeat only after having a try at such schemes.

Then there was the problem of lighting. In recent years several fixtures designed for Japanese houses have come on the market, fixtures patterned

---

1. Translated by Thomas J. Harper and Edward G. Seidensticker.   2. Opaque, milky white glass.
3. Sliding doors constructed of a wooden frame and grid covered with translucent paper, or sometimes glass.

after old floor lamps, ceiling lights, candle stands, and the like. But I simply do not care for them, and instead searched in curio shops for old lamps, which I fitted with electric light bulbs.

What most taxed my ingenuity was the heating system. No stove[4] worthy of the name will ever look right in a Japanese room. Gas stoves burn with a terrific roar, and unless provided with a chimney, quickly bring headaches. Electric stoves, though at least free from these defects, are every bit as ugly as the rest. One solution would be to outfit the cupboards with heaters of the sort used in streetcars. Yet without the red glow of the coals, the whole mood of winter is lost and with it the pleasure of family gatherings round the fire. The best plan I could devise was to build a large sunken hearth, as in an old farmhouse. In this I installed an electric brazier, which worked well both for boiling tea water and for heating the room. Expensive it was, but at least so far as looks were concerned I counted it one of my successes.

Having done passably well with the heating system, I was then faced with the problem of bath and toilet. My Kairakuen friend could not bear to tile the tub and bathing area, and so built his guest bath entirely of wood. Tile, of course, is infinitely more practical and economical. But when ceiling, pillars, and paneling are of fine Japanese stock, the beauty of the room is utterly destroyed when the rest is done in sparkling tile. The effect may not seem so very displeasing while everything is still new, but as the years pass, and the beauty of the grain begins to emerge on the planks and pillars, that glittering expanse of white tile comes to seem as incongruous as the proverbial bamboo grafted to wood.[5] Still, in the bath utility can to some extent be sacrificed to good taste. In the toilet somewhat more vexatious problems arise.[6]

Every time I am shown to an old, dimly lit, and, I would add, impeccably clean toilet in a Nara or Kyoto[7] temple, I am impressed with the singular virtues of Japanese architecture. The parlor may have its charms, but the Japanese toilet truly is a place of spiritual repose. It always stands apart from the main building, at the end of a corridor, in a grove fragrant with leaves and moss. No words can describe that sensation as one sits in the dim light, basking in the faint glow reflected from the shoji, lost in meditation or gazing out at the garden. The novelist Natsume Sōseki[8] counted his morning trips to the toilet a great pleasure, "a physiological delight" he called it. And surely there could be no better place to savor this pleasure than a Japanese toilet where, surrounded by tranquil walls and finely grained wood, one looks out upon blue skies and green leaves.

As I have said there are certain prerequisites: a degree of dimness, absolute cleanliness, and quiet so complete one can hear the hum of a mosquito. I love to listen from such a toilet to the sound of softly falling rain, especially if it is a toilet of the Kantō[9] region, with its long, narrow windows at floor level; there one can listen with such a sense of intimacy to the raindrops falling from the eaves and the trees, seeping into the earth as they wash over

---

4. Used as a space heater.   5. That is, putting together two types of material that are not compatible.
6. In the traditional Japanese house the bath and toilet are in separate rooms.   7. Former capitals of Japan, where temples retain their original architectural style.   8. Generally considered by the Japanese to be their greatest 20th-century novelist (1867–1916).   9. Located in the east-central portion of the main island of Japan, which includes Tokyo. Traditional architectural style there differed slightly from that in the older region of Nara, Kyoto, and Osaka to the west.

the base of a stone lantern and freshen the moss about the stepping stones. And the toilet is the perfect place to listen to the chirping of insects or the song of the birds, to view the moon, or to enjoy any of those poignant moments that mark the change of the seasons. Here, I suspect, is where haiku[1] poets over the ages have come by a great many of their ideas. Indeed one could with some justice claim that of all the elements of Japanese architecture, the toilet is the most aesthetic. Our forebears, making poetry of everything in their lives, transformed what by rights should be the most unsanitary room in the house into a place of unsurpassed elegance, replete with fond associations with the beauties of nature. Compared to Westerners, who regard the toilet as utterly unclean and avoid even the mention of it in polite conversation, we are far more sensible and certainly in better taste. The Japanese toilet is, I must admit, a bit inconvenient to get to in the middle of the night, set apart from the main building as it is; and in winter there is always a danger that one might catch cold. But as the poet Saitō Ryokū[2] has said, "elegance is frigid." Better that the place be as chilly as the out-of-doors; the steamy heat of a Western-style toilet in a hotel is most unpleasant.

Anyone with a taste for traditional architecture must agree that the Japanese toilet is perfection. Yet whatever its virtues in a place like a temple, where the dwelling is large, the inhabitants few, and everyone helps with the cleaning, in an ordinary household it is no easy task to keep it clean. No matter how fastidious one may be or how diligently one may scrub, dirt will show, particularly on a floor of wood or tatami matting. And so here too it turns out to be more hygienic and efficient to install modern sanitary facilities—tile and a flush toilet—though at the price of destroying all affinity with "good taste" and the "beauties of nature." That burst of light from those four white walls hardly puts one in a mood to relish Sōseki's "physiological delight." There is no denying the cleanliness; every nook and corner is pure white. Yet what need is there to remind us so forcefully of the issue of our own bodies. A beautiful woman, no matter how lovely her skin, would be considered indecent were she to show her bare buttocks or feet in the presence of others; and how very crude and tasteless to expose the toilet to such excessive illumination. The cleanliness of what can be seen only calls up the more clearly thoughts of what cannot be seen. In such places the distinction between the clean and the unclean is best left obscure, shrouded in a dusky haze.

Though I did install modern sanitary facilities when I built my own house, I at least avoided tiles, and had the floor done in camphor wood. To that extent I tried to create a Japanese atmosphere—but was frustrated finally by the toilet fixtures themselves. As everyone knows, flush toilets are made of pure white porcelain and have handles of sparkling metal. Were I able to have things my own way, I would much prefer fixtures—both men's and women's—made of wood. Wood finished in glistening black lacquer is the very best; but even unfinished wood, as it darkens and the grain grows more subtle with the years, acquires an inexplicable power to calm and sooth. The ultimate, of course, is a wooden "morning glory" urinal[3] filled with boughs of cedar; this is a delight to look at and allows not the slightest sound. I could

---

1. See the headnote for "Matsuo Bashō" (volume D) for a discussion of *haiku*.   2. He also wrote satirical essays and comic fiction and compiled the first collected edition of Higuchi Ichiyō's works.   3. That is, in the shape of a morning glory flower.

not afford to indulge in such extravagances. I hoped I might at least have the external fittings made to suit my own taste, and then adapt these to a standard flushing mechanism. But the custom labor would have cost so much that I had no choice but to abandon the idea. It was not that I objected to the conveniences of modern civilization, whether electric lights or heating or toilets, but I did wonder at the time why they could not be designed with a bit more consideration for our own habits and tastes.

The recent vogue for electric lamps in the style of the old standing lanterns comes, I think, from a new awareness of the softness and warmth of paper, qualities which for a time we had forgotten; it stands as evidence of our recognition that this material is far better suited than glass to the Japanese house. But no toilet fixtures or stoves that are at all tasteful have yet come on the market. A heating system like my own, an electric brazier in a sunken hearth, seems to me ideal; yet no one ventures to produce even so simple a device as this (there are, of course, those feeble electric hibachi,[4] but they provide no more heat than an ordinary charcoal hibachi); all that can be had ready-made are those ugly Western stoves.

There are those who hold that to quibble over matters of taste in the basic necessities of life is an extravagance, that as long as a house keeps out the cold and as long as food keeps off starvation, it matters little what they look like. And indeed for even the sternest ascetic the fact remains that a snowy day is cold, and there is no denying the impulse to accept the services of a heater if it happens to be there in front of one, no matter how cruelly its inelegance may shatter the spell of the day. But it is on occasions like this that I always think how different everything would be if we in the Orient had developed our own science. Suppose for instance that we had developed our own physics and chemistry: would not the techniques and industries based on them have taken a different form, would not our myriads of everyday gadgets, our medicines, the products of our industrial art—would they not have suited our national temper better than they do? In fact our conception of physics itself, and even the principles of chemistry, would probably differ from that of Westerners; and the facts we are now taught concerning the nature and function of light, electricity, and atoms might well have presented themselves in different form.

Of course I am only indulging in idle speculation; of scientific matters I know nothing. But had we devised independently at least the more practical sorts of inventions, this could not but have had profound influence upon the conduct of our everyday lives, and even upon government, religion, art, and business. The Orient quite conceivably could have opened up a world of technology entirely its own.

To take a trivial example near at hand: I wrote a magazine article recently comparing the writing brush with the fountain pen, and in the course of it I remarked that if the device had been invented by the ancient Chinese or Japanese it would surely have had a tufted end like our writing brush. The ink would not have been this bluish color but rather black, something like India ink, and it would have been made to seep down from the handle into the brush. And since we would have then found it inconvenient to write on

4. A metal or porcelain brazier originally containing live coals and used to heat a room.

Western paper, something near Japanese paper—even under mass production, if you will—would have been most in demand. Foreign ink and pen would not be as popular as they are; the talk of discarding our system of writing for Roman letters would be less noisy; people would still feel an affection for the old system. But more than that: our thought and our literature might not be imitating the West as they are, but might have pushed forward into new regions quite on their own. An insignificant little piece of writing equipment, when one thinks of it, has had a vast, almost boundless, influence on our culture.

But I know as well as anyone that these are the empty dreams of a novelist, and that having come this far we cannot turn back. I know that I am only grumbling to myself and demanding the impossible. If my complaints are taken for what they are, however, there can be no harm in considering how unlucky we have been, what losses we have suffered, in comparison with the Westerner. The Westerner has been able to move forward in ordered steps, while we have met superior civilization and have had to surrender to it, and we have had to leave a road we have followed for thousands of years. The missteps and inconveniences this has caused have, I think, been many. If we had been left alone we might not be much further now in a material way than we were five hundred years ago. Even now in the Indian and Chinese countryside life no doubt goes on much as it did when Buddha and Confucius were alive. But we would have gone only in a direction that suited us. We would have gone ahead very slowly, and yet it is not impossible that we would one day have discovered our own substitute for the trolley, the radio, the airplane of today. They would have been no borrowed gadgets, they would have been the tools of our own culture, suited to us.

One need only compare American, French, and German films to see how greatly nuances of shading and coloration can vary in motion pictures. In the photographic image itself, to say nothing of the acting and the script, there somehow emerge differences in national character. If this is true even when identical equipment, chemicals, and film are used, how much better our own photographic technology might have suited our complexion, our facial features, our climate, our land. And had we invented the phonograph and the radio, how much more faithfully they would reproduce the special character of our voices and our music. Japanese music is above all a music of reticence, of atmosphere. When recorded, or amplified by a loudspeaker, the greater part of its charm is lost. In conversation, too, we prefer the soft voice, the understatement. Most important of all are the pauses. Yet the phonograph and radio render these moments of silence utterly lifeless. And so we distort the arts themselves to curry favor for them with the machines. These machines are the inventions of Westerners, and are, as we might expect, well suited to the Western arts. But precisely on this account they put our own arts at a great disadvantage.

Paper, I understand, was invented by the Chinese; but Western paper is to us no more than something to be used, while the texture of Chinese paper and Japanese paper gives us a certain feeling of warmth, of calm and repose. Even the same white could as well be one color for Western paper and another for our own. Western paper turns away the light, while our paper seems to take it in, to envelop it gently, like the soft surface of a first snowfall.

It gives off no sound when it is crumpled or folded, it is quiet and pliant to the touch as the leaf of a tree.

As a general matter we find it hard to be really at home with things that shine and glitter. The Westerner uses silver and steel and nickel tableware, and polishes it to a fine brilliance, but we object to the practice. While we do sometimes indeed use silver for teakettles, decanters, or saké[5] cups, we prefer not to polish it. On the contrary, we begin to enjoy it only when the luster has worn off, when it has begun to take on a dark, smoky patina. Almost every householder has had to scold an insensitive maid who has polished away the tarnish so patiently waited for.

Chinese food is now most often served on tableware made of tin, a material the Chinese could only admire for the patina it acquires. When new it resembles aluminum and is not particularly attractive; only after long use brings some of the elegance of age is it at all acceptable. Then, as the surface darkens, the line of verse etched upon it gives a final touch of perfection. In the hands of the Chinese this flimsy, glittering metal takes on a profound and somber dignity akin to that of their red unglazed pottery.

The Chinese also love jade. That strange lump of stone with its faintly muddy light, like the crystallized air of the centuries, melting dimly, dully back, deeper and deeper—are not we Orientals the only ones who know its charms? We cannot say ourselves what it is that we find in this stone. It quite lacks the brightness of a ruby or an emerald or the glitter of a diamond. But this much we can say: when we see that shadowy surface, we think how Chinese it is, we seem to find in its cloudiness the accumulation of the long Chinese past, we think how appropriate it is that the Chinese should admire that surface and that shadow.

It is the same with crystals. Crystals have recently been imported in large quantities from Chile, but Chilean crystals are too bright, too clear. We have long had crystals of our own, their clearness always moderated, made graver by a certain cloudiness. Indeed, we much prefer the "impure" varieties of crystal with opaque veins crossing their depths. Even of glass this is true; for is not fine Chinese glass closer to jade or agate than to Western glass? Glassmaking has long been known in the Orient, but the craft never developed as in the West. Great progress has been made, however, in the manufacture of pottery. Surely this has something to do with our national character. We do not dislike everything that shines, but we do prefer a pensive luster to a shallow brilliance, a murky light that, whether in a stone or an artifact, bespeaks a sheen of antiquity.

Of course this "sheen of antiquity" of which we hear so much is in fact the glow of grime. In both Chinese and Japanese the words denoting this glow describe a polish that comes of being touched over and over again, a sheen produced by the oils that naturally permeate an object over long years of handling—which is to say grime. If indeed "elegance is frigid," it can as well be described as filthy. There is no denying, at any rate, that among the elements of the elegance in which we take such delight is a measure of the unclean, the unsanitary. I suppose I shall sound terribly defensive if I say that Westerners attempt to expose every speck of grime and eradicate it, while we Orientals carefully preserve and even idealize it. Yet for better or

5. Japanese rice wine.

for worse we do love things that bear the marks of grime, soot, and weather, and we love the colors and the sheen that call to mind the past that made them. Living in these old houses among these old objects is in some mysterious way a source of peace and repose.

I have always thought that hospitals, those for the Japanese at any rate, need not be so sparkling white, that the walls, uniforms, and equipment might better be done in softer, more muted colors. Certainly the patients would be more reposed where they are able to lie on tatami[6] matting surrounded by the sand-colored walls of a Japanese room. One reason we hate to go to the dentist is the scream of his drill; but the excessive glitter of glass and metal is equally intimidating. At a time when I was suffering from a severe nervous disorder, a dentist was recommended to me as having just returned from America with the latest equipment, but these tidings only made my hair stand on end. I chose instead to go to an old-fashioned dentist who maintained an office in an old Japanese house, a dentist of the sort found in small country towns. Antiquated medical equipment does have its drawbacks; but had modern medicine been developed in Japan we probably would have devised facilities and equipment for the treatment of the sick that would somehow harmonize with Japanese architecture. Here again we have to come off the loser for having borrowed.

There is a famous restaurant in Kyoto, the Waranjiya, one of the attractions of which was until recently that the dining rooms were lit by candlelight rather than electricity; but when I went there this spring after a long absence, the candles had been replaced by electric lamps in the style of old lanterns. I asked when this had happened, and was told that the change had taken place last year; several of their customers had complained that candlelight was too dim, and so they had been left no choice—but if I preferred the old way they should be happy to bring me a candlestand. Since that was what I had come for, I asked them to do so. And I realized then that only in dim half-light is the true beauty of Japanese lacquerware revealed. The rooms at the Waranjiya are about nine feet square, the size of a comfortable little tearoom, and the alcove pillars and ceilings glow with a faint smoky luster, dark even in the light of the lamp. But in the still dimmer light of the candlestand, as I gazed at the trays and bowls standing in the shadows cast by that flickering point of flame, I discovered in the gloss of this lacquerware a depth and richness like that of a still, dark pond, a beauty I had not before seen. It had not been mere chance, I realized, that our ancestors, having discovered lacquer, had conceived such a fondness for objects finished in it.

An Indian friend once told me that in his country ceramic tableware is still looked down upon, and that lacquerware is in far wider use. We, however, use ceramics for practically everything but trays and soup bowls; lacquerware, except in the tea ceremony and on formal occasions, is considered vulgar and inelegant. This, I suspect, is in part the fault of the much-vaunted "brilliance" of modern electric lighting. Darkness is an indispensable element of the beauty of lacquerware. Nowadays they make even a white lacquer, but the lacquerware of the past was finished in black, brown, or red, colors built

6. Modular straw mats measuring approximately six by three feet, the customary flooring for a traditional Japanese room. (Wood was used for corridors.) The patients would be lying on bedding called *futon* placed directly on the floor.

up of countless layers of darkness, the inevitable product of the darkness in which life was lived. Sometimes a superb piece of black lacquerware, decorated perhaps with flecks of silver and gold—a box or a desk or a set of shelves—will seem to me unsettlingly garish and altogether vulgar. But render pitch black the void in which they stand, and light them not with the rays of the sun or electricity but rather a single lantern or candle: suddenly those garish objects turn somber, refined, dignified. Artisans of old, when they finished their works in lacquer and decorated them in sparkling patterns, must surely have had in mind dark rooms and sought to turn to good effect what feeble light there was. Their extravagant use of gold, too, I should imagine, came of understanding how it gleams forth from out of the darkness and reflects the lamplight.

Lacquerware decorated in gold is not something to be seen in a brilliant light, to be taken in at a single glance; it should be left in the dark, a part here and a part there picked up by a faint light. Its florid patterns recede into the darkness, conjuring in their stead an inexpressible aura of depth and mystery, of overtones but partly suggested. The sheen of the lacquer, set out in the night, reflects the wavering candlelight, announcing the drafts that find their way from time to time into the quiet room, luring one into a state of reverie. If the lacquer is taken away, much of the spell disappears from the dream world built by that strange light of candle and lamp, that wavering light beating the pulse of the night. Indeed the thin, impalpable, faltering light, picked up as though little rivers were running through the room, collecting little pools here and there, lacquers a pattern on the surface of the night itself.

Ceramics are by no means inadequate as tableware, but they lack the shadows, the depth of lacquerware. Ceramics are heavy and cold to the touch; they clatter and clink, and being efficient conductors of heat are not the best containers for hot foods. But lacquerware is light and soft to the touch, and gives off hardly a sound. I know few greater pleasures than holding a lacquer soup bowl in my hands, feeling upon my palms the weight of the liquid and its mild warmth. The sensation is something like that of holding a plump newborn baby. There are good reasons why lacquer soup bowls are still used, qualities which ceramic bowls simply do not possess. Remove the lid from a ceramic bowl, and there lies the soup, every nuance of its substance and color revealed. With lacquerware there is a beauty in that moment between removing the lid and lifting the bowl to the mouth when one gazes at the still, silent liquid in the dark depths of the bowl, its color hardly differing from that of the bowl itself. What lies within the darkness one cannot distinguish, but the palm senses the gentle movements of the liquid, vapor rises from within forming droplets on the rim, and the fragrance carried upon the vapor brings a delicate anticipation. What a world of difference there is between this moment and the moment when soup is served Western style, in a pale, shallow bowl. A moment of mystery, it might almost be called, a moment of trance.

Whenever I sit with a bowl of soup before me, listening to the murmur that penetrates like the far-off shrill of an insect, lost in contemplation of flavors to come, I feel as if I were being drawn into a trance. The experience must be something like that of the tea master who, at the sound of the kettle, is taken from himself as if upon the sigh of the wind in the legendary pines of Onoe.[7]

It has been said of Japanese food that it is a cuisine to be looked at rather than eaten. I would go further and say that it is to be meditated upon, a kind of silent music evoked by the combination of lacquerware and the light of a candle flickering in the dark. Natsume Sōseki, in *Pillow of Grass,* praises the color of the confection yōkan;[8] and is it not indeed a color to call forth meditation? The cloudy translucence, like that of jade; the faint, dreamlike glow that suffuses it, as if it had drunk into its very depths the light of the sun; the complexity and profundity of the color—nothing of the sort is to be found in Western candies. How simple and insignificant cream-filled chocolates seem by comparison. And when yōkan is served in a lacquer dish within whose dark recesses its color is scarcely distinguishable, then it is most certainly an object for meditation. You take its cool, smooth substance into your mouth, and it is as if the very darkness of the room were melting on your tongue; even undistinguished yōkan can then take on a mysteriously intriguing flavor.

In the cuisine of any country efforts no doubt are made to have the food harmonize with the tableware and the walls; but with Japanese food, a brightly lighted room and shining tableware cut the appetite in half. The dark miso[9] soup that we eat every morning is one dish from the dimly lit houses of the past. I was once invited to a tea ceremony where miso was served; and when I saw the muddy, claylike color, quiet in a black lacquer bowl beneath the faint light of a candle, this soup that I usually take without a second thought seemed somehow to acquire a real depth, and to become infinitely more appetizing as well. Much the same may be said of soy sauce. In the Kyoto-Osaka region a particularly thick variety of soy is served with raw fish, pickles, and greens; and how rich in shadows is the viscous sheen of the liquid, how beautifully it blends with the darkness. White foods too— white miso, bean curd, fish cake, the white meat of fish—lose much of their beauty in a bright room. And above all there is rice. A glistening black lacquer rice cask set off in a dark corner is both beautiful to behold and a powerful stimulus to the appetite. Then the lid is briskly lifted, and this pure white freshly boiled food, heaped in its black container, each and every grain gleaming like a pearl, sends forth billows of warm steam—here is a sight no Japanese can fail to be moved by. Our cooking depends upon shadows and is inseparable from darkness.

I possess no specialized knowledge of architecture, but I understand that in the Gothic cathedral of the West, the roof is thrust up and up so as to place its pinnacle as high in the heavens as possible—and that herein is thought to lie its special beauty. In the temples of Japan, on the other hand, a roof of heavy tiles is first laid out, and in the deep, spacious shadows created by the eaves the rest of the structure is built. Nor is this true only of temples; in the palaces of the nobility and the houses of the common people, what first strikes the eye is the massive roof of tile or thatch and the heavy darkness

7. "A place high in the mountains." Wind blowing through the pines provokes a sense of solitude and loneliness.   8. Made from a sweet bean paste. It is usually made from dark red beans but comes in several colors and flavors, including a jadelike green.   9. Made by mixing steamed soybeans with salt and a fermenting agent; one of the basic flavorings in Japanese cooking.

that hangs beneath the eaves. Even at midday cavernous darkness spreads over all beneath the roof's edge, making entryway, doors, walls, and pillars all but invisible. The grand temples of Kyoto—Chion'in, Honganji—and the farmhouses of the remote countryside are alike in this respect: like most buildings of the past their roofs give the impression of possessing far greater weight, height, and surface than all that stands beneath the eaves.

In making for ourselves a place to live, we first spread a parasol to throw a shadow on the earth, and in the pale light of the shadow we put together a house. There are of course roofs on Western houses too, but they are less to keep off the sun than to keep off the wind and the dew; even from without it is apparent that they are built to create as few shadows as possible and to expose the interior to as much light as possible. If the roof of a Japanese house is a parasol, the roof of a Western house is no more than a cap, with as small a visor as possible so as to allow the sunlight to penetrate directly beneath the eaves. There are no doubt all sorts of reasons—climate, building materials—for the deep Japanese eaves. The fact that we did not use glass, concrete, and bricks, for instance, made a low roof necessary to keep off the driving wind and rain. A light room would no doubt have been more convenient for us, too, than a dark room. The quality that we call beauty, however, must always grow from the realities of life, and our ancestors, forced to live in dark rooms, presently came to discover beauty in shadows, ultimately to guide shadows towards beauty's ends.

And so it has come to be that the beauty of a Japanese room depends on a variation of shadows, heavy shadows against light shadows—it has nothing else. Westerners are amazed at the simplicity of Japanese rooms, perceiving in them no more than ashen walls bereft of ornament. Their reaction is understandable, but it betrays a failure to comprehend the mystery of shadows. Out beyond the sitting room, which the rays of the sun can at best but barely reach, we extend the eaves or build on a veranda, putting the sunlight at still greater a remove. The light from the garden steals in but dimly through paper-paneled doors, and it is precisely this indirect light that makes for us the charm of a room. We do our walls in neutral colors so that the sad, fragile, dying rays can sink into absolute repose. The storehouse, kitchen, hallways, and such may have a glossy finish, but the walls of the sitting room will almost always be of clay textured with fine sand. A luster here would destroy the soft fragile beauty of the feeble light. We delight in the mere sight of the delicate glow of fading rays clinging to the surface of a dusky wall, there to live out what little life remains to them. We never tire of the sight, for to us this pale glow and these dim shadows far surpass any ornament. And so, as we must if we are not to disturb the glow, we finish the walls with sand in a single neutral color. The hue may differ from room to room, but the degree of difference will be ever so slight; not so much a difference in color as in shade, a difference that will seem to exist only in the mood of the viewer. And from these delicate differences in the hue of the walls, the shadows in each room take on a tinge peculiarly their own.

Of course the Japanese room does have its picture alcove, and in it a hanging scroll and a flower arrangement. But the scroll and the flowers serve not as ornament but rather to give depth to the shadows. We value a scroll above all for the way it blends with the walls of the alcove, and thus we consider the mounting quite as important as the calligraphy or painting. Even the greatest masterpiece will lose its worth as a scroll if it fails to blend with the alcove, while a work of no particular distinction may blend beautifully with the room and set off to unexpected advantage both itself and its surroundings. Wherein lies the power of an otherwise ordinary work to produce such an effect? Most often the paper, the ink, the fabric of the mounting will possess a certain look of antiquity, and this look of antiquity will strike just the right balance with the darkness of the alcove and room.

We have all had the experience, on a visit to one of the great temples of Kyoto or Nara, of being shown a scroll, one of the temple's treasures, hanging in a large, deeply recessed alcove. So dark are these alcoves, even in bright daylight, that we can hardly discern the outlines of the work; all we can do is listen to the explanation of the guide, follow as best we can the all-but-invisible brush strokes, and tell ourselves how magnificent a painting it must be. Yet the combination of that blurred old painting and the dark alcove is one of absolute harmony. The lack of clarity, far from disturbing us, seems rather to suit the painting perfectly. For the painting here is nothing more than another delicate surface upon which the faint, frail light can play; it performs precisely the same function as the sand-textured wall. This is why we attach such importance to age and patina. A new painting, even one done in ink monochrome or subtle pastels, can quite destroy the shadows of an alcove, unless it is selected with the greatest care.

A Japanese room might be likened to an inkwash painting, the paper-paneled shoji being the expanse where the ink is thinnest, and the alcove where it is darkest. Whenever I see the alcove of a tastefully built Japanese room, I marvel at our comprehension of the secrets of shadows, our sensitive use of shadow and light. For the beauty of the alcove is not the work of some clever device. An empty space is marked off with plain wood and plain walls, so that the light drawn into it forms dim shadows within emptiness. There is nothing more. And yet, when we gaze into the darkness that gathers behind the crossbeam, around the flower vase, beneath the shelves, though we know perfectly well it is mere shadow, we are overcome with the feeling that in this small corner of the atmosphere there reigns complete and utter silence; that here in the darkness immutable tranquility holds sway. The "mysterious Orient" of which Westerners speak probably refers to the uncanny silence of these dark places. And even we as children would feel an inexpressible chill as we peered into the depths of an alcove to which the sunlight had never penetrated. Where lies the key to this mystery? Ultimately it is the magic of shadows. Were the shadows to be banished from its corners, the alcove would in that instant revert to mere void.

This was the genius of our ancestors, that by cutting off the light from this empty space they imparted to the world of shadows that formed there a quality of mystery and depth superior to that of any wall painting or ornament. The technique seems simple, but was by no means so simply achieved. We can imagine with little difficulty what extraordinary pains were taken with each invisible detail—the placement of the window in the shelving recess, the depth of the crossbeam, the height of the threshold. But for me the most exquisite touch is the pale white glow of the shoji in the study bay; I need only pause before it and I forget the passage of time.

The study bay, as the name suggests, was originally a projecting window built to provide a place for reading. Over the years it came to be regarded as no more than a source of light for the alcove; but most often it serves not so much to illuminate the alcove as to soften the sidelong rays from without, to filter them through paper panels. There is a cold and desolate tinge to the light by the time it reaches these panels. The little sunlight from the garden that manages to make its way beneath the eaves and through the corridors has by then lost its power to illuminate, seems drained of the complexion of life. It can do no more than accentuate the whiteness of the paper. I sometimes linger before these panels and study the surface of the paper, bright, but giving no impression of brilliance.

In temple architecture the main room stands at a considerable distance from the garden; so dilute is the light there that no matter what the season, on fair days or cloudy, morning, midday, or evening, the pale, white glow scarcely varies. And the shadows at the interstices of the ribs seem strangely immobile, as if dust collected in the corners had become a part of the paper itself. I blink in uncertainty at this dreamlike luminescence, feeling as though some misty film were blunting my vision. The light from the pale white paper, powerless to dispel the heavy darkness of the alcove, is instead repelled by the darkness, creating a world of confusion where dark and light are indistinguishable. Have not you yourselves sensed a difference in the light that suffuses such a room, a rare tranquility not found in ordinary light? Have you never felt a sort of fear in the face of the ageless, a fear that in that room you might lose all consciousness of the passage of time, that untold years might pass and upon emerging you should find you had grown old and gray?

And surely you have seen, in the darkness of the innermost rooms of these huge buildings, to which sunlight never penetrates, how the gold leaf of a sliding door or screen will pick up a distant glimmer from the garden, then suddenly send forth an ethereal glow, a faint golden light cast into the enveloping darkness, like the glow upon the horizon at sunset. In no other setting is gold quite so exquisitely beautiful. You walk past, turning to look again, and yet again; and as you move away the golden surface of the paper glows ever more deeply, changing not in a flash, but growing slowly, steadily brighter, like color rising in the face of a giant. Or again you may find that the gold dust of the background, which until that moment had only a dull, sleepy luster, will, as you move past, suddenly gleam forth as if it had burst into flame.

How, in such a dark place, gold draws so much light to itself is a mystery to me. But I see why in ancient times statues of the Buddha were gilt with gold and why gold leaf covered the walls of the homes of the nobility. Modern man, in his well-lit house, knows nothing of the beauty of gold; but those who lived in the dark houses of the past were not merely captivated by its beauty, they also knew its practical value; for gold, in these dim rooms, must have served the function of a reflector. Their use of gold leaf and gold dust was not mere extravagance. Its reflective properties were put to use as a source of illumination. Silver and other metals quickly lose their gloss, but gold retains its brilliance indefinitely to light the darkness of the room. This is why gold was held in such incredibly high esteem.

I have said that lacquerware decorated in gold was made to be seen in the dark; and for this same reason were the fabrics of the past so lavishly woven of threads of silver and gold. The priest's surplice[1] of gold brocade is perhaps the best example. In most of our city temples, catering to the masses as they do, the main hall will be brightly lit, and these garments of gold will seem merely gaudy. No matter how venerable a man the priest may be, his robes will convey no sense of his dignity. But when you attend a service at an old temple, conducted after the ancient ritual, you see how perfectly the gold harmonizes with the wrinkled skin of the old priest and the flickering light of the altar lamps, and how much it contributes to the solemnity of the occasion. As with lacquerware, the bold patterns remain for the most part hidden in darkness; only occasionally does a bit of gold or silver gleam forth.

I may be alone in thinking so, but to me it seems that nothing quite so becomes the Japanese skin as the costumes of the Nō theatre. Of course many are gaudy in the extreme, richly woven of gold and silver. But the Nō actor, unlike the Kabuki[2] performer, wears no white powder. Whenever I attend the Nō I am impressed by the fact that on no other occasion is the beauty of the Japanese complexion set off to such advantage—the brownish skin with a flush of red that is so uniquely Japanese, the face like old ivory tinged with yellow. A robe woven or embroidered in patterns of gold or silver sets it off beautifully, as does a cloak of deep green or persimmon,[3] or a kimono or divided skirt of a pure white, unpatterned material. And when the actor is a handsome young man with skin of fine texture and cheeks glowing with the freshness of youth, his good looks emerge as perfection, with a seductive charm quite different from a woman's. Here, one sees, is the beauty that made feudal lords lose themselves over their boy favorites.

Kabuki costumes, in the history plays and dance dramas, are no less colorful than Nō costumes; and Kabuki is commonly thought to have far greater sexual appeal than Nō. But to the adept the opposite is true. At first Kabuki will doubtless seem the more erotic and visually beautiful; but, whatever they may have been in the past, the gaudy Kabuki colors under the glare of the Western floodlamps verge on a vulgarity of which one quickly tires. And if this is true of the costumes it is all the more true of the makeup. Beautiful though such a face may be, it is after all made up; it has nothing of the immediate beauty of the flesh. The Nō actor performs with no makeup on his face or neck or hands. The man's beauty is his own; our eyes are in no way deceived. And so there is never that disappointment with the Nō actor that we feel upon seeing the unadorned face of the Kabuki actor who has played the part of a woman or handsome young man. Rather we are amazed how much the man's looks are enhanced by the gaudy costume of a medieval warrior—a man with skin like our own, in a costume we would not have thought would become him in the slightest.

I once saw Kongō Iwao play the Chinese beauty Yang Kuei-fei in the Nō

---

1. A loose outer robe, extending to the knees, worn by priests. 2. One of the principal theatrical traditions of Japan, originating in the 17th century. *Kabuki* is gaudier and somewhat more realistic than the older, aristocratic *nō*, which dates from the 14th century, although, in the eyes of today's audiences, it appears almost as stylized. *Nō* is a more austere form of drama. While *kabuki* relies on intricate plots and flamboyant theatrical effects, including trap doors, revolving stages, and elaborate sets, *nō* is performed on a bare stage without sets and with virtually no props. In contrast to the spectacle *kabuki* offers, the luxurious *nō* costumes that Tanizaki mentions (together with masks worn by the main actors) provide the only striking visual feature in the performance. Both *nō* and *kabuki* combine acting with music and dance. In *kabuki* the three elements propel melodramatic or action-packed stories; a *nō* play, however, is essentially a dramatic poem, with minimal action, often depicting remote or supernatural events. Tanizaki refers only to male actors because both theatrical traditions had banned women from the stage, a point he takes up subsequently. 3. Pale to reddish orange.

play *Kōtei*,[4] and I shall never forget the beauty of his hands showing ever so slightly from beneath his sleeves. As I watched his hands, I would occasionally glance down at my own hands resting on my knees. Again, and yet again, I looked back at the actor's hands, comparing them with my own; and there was no difference between them. Yet strangely the hands of the man on the stage were indescribably beautiful, while those on my knees were but ordinary hands. In the Nō only the merest fraction of the actor's flesh is visible— the face, the neck, the hands—and when a mask is worn, as for the role of Yang Kuei-fei, even the face is hidden; and so what little flesh can be seen creates a singularly strong impression. This was particularly true of Kongō Iwao; but even the hands of an ordinary actor—which is to say the hands of an average, undistinguished Japanese—have a remarkable erotic power which we would never notice were we to see the man in modern attire.

I would repeat that this is by no means true only of youthful or handsome actors. An ordinary man's lips will not ordinarily attract us; and yet on the Nō stage, the deep red glow and the moist sheen that come over them give a texture far more sensual than the painted lips of a woman. Chanting may keep the actor's lips constantly moist, but there is more to his beauty than this. Then again, the flush of red in the cheeks of a child actor can emerge with extraordinary freshness—an effect which in my experience is most striking against a costume in which green predominates. We might expect this to be true of a fair-skinned child; yet remarkably the reddish tinge shows to better effect on a dark-skinned child. For with the fair child the contrast between white and red is too marked, and the dark, somber colors of the Nō costume stand out too strongly, while against the brownish cheeks of the darker child the red is not so conspicuous, and costume and face complement each other beautifully. The perfect harmony of the yellow skin with garments of a subdued green or brown forces itself upon our attention as at no other time.

Were the Nō to be lit by modern floodlamps, like the Kabuki, this sense of beauty would vanish under the harsh glare. And thus the older the structure the better, for it is an essential condition of the Nō that the stage be left in the darkness in which it has stood since antiquity. A stage whose floor has acquired a natural gloss, whose beams and backdrop glow with a dark light, where the darkness beneath the rafters and eaves hangs above the actors' heads as if a huge temple bell were suspended over them—such is the proper place for Nō. Its recent ventures into huge auditoriums may have something to recommend them, but in such a setting the true beauty of the Nō is all but lost.

The darkness in which the Nō is shrouded and the beauty that emerges from it make a distinct world of shadows which today can be seen only on the stage; but in the past it could not have been far removed from daily life. The darkness of the Nō stage is after all the darkness of the domestic architecture of the day; and Nō costumes, even if a bit more splendid in pattern and color, are by and large those that were worn by court nobles and feudal lords. I

4. *The Emperor* by Kanze Kojirō Nobumitsu (1435–1516), who also wrote the *nō* play *Dōjōji*. The ghost of a former retainer of the Chinese emperor appears at the sickbed of the emperor's consort (Yang Kuei-fei) and drives away the demon afflicting her. Kongō Iwao (1886–1951), head of the traditional Kongō troupe of *nō* actors.

find the thought fascinating: to imagine how very handsome, by comparison with us today, the Japanese of the past must have been in their resplendent dress—particularly the warriors of the fifteenth and sixteenth centuries. The Nō sets before us the beauty of Japanese manhood at its finest. What grand figures those warriors who traversed the battlefields of old must have cut in their full regalia emblazoned with family crests, the somber ground and gleaming embroidery setting off strong-boned faces burnished a deep bronze by wind and rain. Every devotee of the Nō finds a certain portion of his pleasure in speculations of this sort; for the thought that the highly colored world on the stage once existed just as we see it imparts to the Nō a historical fascination quite apart from the drama.

But the Kabuki is ultimately a world of sham, having little to do with beauty in the natural state. It is inconceivable that the beautiful women of old—to say nothing of the men—bore any resemblance to those we see on the Kabuki stage. The women of the Nō, portrayed by masked actors, are far from real- istic; but the Kabuki actor in the part of a woman inspires not the slightest sense of reality. The failure is the fault of excessive lighting. When there were no modern floodlamps, when the Kabuki stage was lit by the meager light of candles and lanterns, actors must have been somewhat more con- vincing in women's roles. People complain that Kabuki actors are no longer really feminine, but this is hardly the fault of their talents or looks. If actors of old had had to appear on the bright stage of today, they would doubtless have stood out with a certain masculine harshness, which in the past was discreetly hidden by darkness. This was brought home to me vividly when I saw the aging Baikō in the role of the young Okaru.[5] A senseless and extrav- agant use of lights, I thought, has destroyed the beauty of Kabuki.

A knowledgeable Osaka gentleman has told me that the Bunraku puppet theatre was for long lit by lamplight, even after the introduction of electricity in the Meiji era,[6] and that this method was far more richly suggestive than modern lighting. Even now I find the puppets infinitely more real than the actors of female Kabuki parts. But in the dim lamplight, the hard lines of the puppet features softened, the glistening white of their faces muted—a chill comes over me when I think of the uncanny beauty the puppet theatre must once have had.

The female puppets consist only of a head and a pair of hands. The body, legs, and feet are concealed within a long kimono, and so the operators need only work their hands within the costume to suggest movements. To me this is the very epitome of reality, for a woman of the past did indeed exist only from the collar up and the sleeves out; the rest of her remained hidden in darkness. A woman of the middle or upper ranks of society seldom left her house, and when she did she shielded herself from the gaze of the public in the dark recesses of her palanquin.[7] Most of her life was spent in the twilight of a single house, her body shrouded day and night in gloom, her face the only sign of her existence. Though the men dressed somewhat more color- fully than they do today, the women dressed more somberly. Daughters and

---

5. The heroine of the popular play *The Bridegroom's Journey*. Onoe Baikō VI (1870–1934), a *kabuki* actor who specialized in playing women's roles.   6. The period during which Japan embarked on modernization (1868–1912). *Bunraku puppet theater*: contemporaneous with *kabuki* and, in the 18th century, its rival.   7. An enclosed seat mounted on shafts, designed to carry a single passenger.

wives of the merchant class wore astonishingly severe dress. Their clothing was in effect no more than a part of the darkness, the transition between darkness and face.

One thinks of the practice of blackening the teeth.[8] Might it not have been an attempt to push everything except the face into the dark? Today this ideal of beauty has quite disappeared from everyday life, and one must go to an ancient Kyoto teahouse, such as the Sumiya in Shimabara,[9] to find traces of it. But when I think back to my own youth in the old downtown section of Tokyo, and I see my mother at work on her sewing in the dim light from the garden, I think I can imagine a little what the old Japanese woman was like. In those days—it was around 1890—the Tokyo townsman still lived in a dusky house, and my mother, my aunts, my relatives, most women of their age, still blackened their teeth. I do not remember what they wore for everyday, but when they went out it was often in a gray kimono with a small, modest pattern.

My mother was remarkably slight, under five feet I should say, and I do not think that she was unusual for her time. I can put the matter strongly: women in those days had almost no flesh. I remember my mother's face and hands, I can clearly remember her feet, but I can remember nothing about her body. She reminds me of the statue of Kannon in the Chūgūji,[1] whose body must be typical of most Japanese women of the past. The chest as flat as a board, breasts paper-thin, back, hips, and buttocks forming an undeviating straight line, the whole body so lean and gaunt as to seem out of proportion with the face, hands, and feet, so lacking in substance as to give the impression not of flesh but of a stick—must not the traditional Japanese woman have had just such a physique? A few are still about—the aged lady in an old-fashioned household, some few geisha. They remind me of stick dolls, for in fact they are nothing more than poles upon which to hang clothes. As with the dolls their substance is made up of layer upon layer of clothing, bereft of which only an ungainly pole remains. But in the past this was sufficient. For a woman who lived in the dark it was enough if she had a faint, white face—a full body was unnecessary.

I suppose it is hard for those who praise the fleshly beauty we see under today's bright lights to imagine the ghostly beauty of those older women. And there may be some who argue that if beauty has to hide its weak points in the dark it is not beauty at all. But we Orientals, as I have suggested before, create a kind of beauty of the shadows we have made in out-of-the-way places. There is an old song that says "the brushwood we gather—stack it together, it makes a hut; pull it apart, a field once more." Such is our way of thinking—we find beauty not in the thing itself but in the patterns of shadows, the light and the darkness, that one thing against another creates.

A phosphorescent jewel gives off its glow and color in the dark and loses its beauty in the light of day. Were it not for shadows, there would be no

---

8. A cosmetic custom, dating from protohistoric times. A solution of iron filings was used to darken the teeth. In the era of *The Tale of Genji*, women of the court nobility blackened their teeth. The practice, which was thought to strengthen teeth and prevent toothache, was also taken up by male aristocrats and later emulated by members of the *samurai* class. By the beginning of the modern period, married women from all social classes (as well as prostitutes) blackened their teeth. The practice fell out of fashion when the empress abandoned it in 1873, no doubt to align Japanese cosmetic taste with the style of the West. 9. The red-light district. 1. An ancient Buddhist convent in Japan's early capital of Nara. Kannon, a deity in the Buddhist pantheon, was venerated for her compassion.

beauty. Our ancestors made of woman an object inseparable from darkness, like lacquerware decorated in gold or mother-of-pearl. They hid as much of her as they could in shadows, concealing her arms and legs in the folds of long sleeves and skirts, so that one part and one only stood out—her face. The curveless body may, by comparison with Western women, be ugly. But our thoughts do not travel to what we cannot see. The unseen for us does not exist. The person who insists upon seeing her ugliness, like the person who would shine a hundred-candlepower light upon the picture alcove, drives away whatever beauty may reside there.

Why should this propensity to seek beauty in darkness be so strong only in Orientals? The West too has known a time when there was no electricity, gas, or petroleum, and yet so far as I know the West has never been disposed to delight in shadows. Japanese ghosts have traditionally had no feet; Western ghosts have feet, but are transparent. As even this trifle suggests, pitch darkness has always occupied our fantasies, while in the West even ghosts are as clear as glass. This is true too of our household implements: we prefer colors compounded of darkness, they prefer the colors of sunlight. And of silver and copperware: we love them for the burnish and patina, which they consider unclean, unsanitary, and polish to a glittering brilliance. They paint their ceilings and walls in pale colors to drive out as many of the shadows as they can. We fill our gardens with dense plantings, they spread out a flat expanse of grass.

But what produces such differences in taste? In my opinion it is this: we Orientals tend to seek our satisfactions in whatever surroundings we happen to find ourselves, to content ourselves with things as they are; and so darkness causes us no discontent, we resign ourselves to it as inevitable. If light is scarce then light is scarce; we will immerse ourselves in the darkness and there discover its own particular beauty. But the progressive Westerner is determined always to better his lot. From candle to oil lamp, oil lamp to gaslight, gaslight to electric light—his quest for a brighter light never ceases, he spares no pains to eradicate even the minutest shadow.

But beyond such differences in temperament, I should like to consider the importance of the difference in the color of our skin. From ancient times we have considered white skin more elegant, more beautiful than dark skin, and yet somehow this whiteness of ours differs from that of the white races. Taken individually there are Japanese who are whiter than Westerners and Westerners who are darker than Japanese, but their whiteness and darkness is not the same. Let me take an example from my own experience. When I lived on the Bluff in Yokohama[2] I spent a good deal of my leisure in the company of foreign residents, at their banquets and balls. At close range I was not particularly struck by their whiteness, but from a distance I could distinguish them quite clearly from the Japanese. Among the Japanese were ladies who were dressed in gowns no less splendid than the foreigners', and whose skin was whiter than theirs. Yet from across the room these ladies, even one alone, would stand out unmistakably from amongst a group of foreigners. For the Japanese complexion, no matter how white, is tinged by

2. Port city fifteen miles south of Tokyo; in the late 19th and early 20th centuries, it was the site of one of the major foreign enclaves. Tanizaki bought a house in the hilly section known as the Bluff, which was particularly favored by foreigners.

a slight cloudiness. These women were in no way reticent about powdering themselves. Every bit of exposed flesh—even their backs and arms—they covered with a thick coat of white. Still they could not efface the darkness that lay below their skin. It was as plainly visible as dirt at the bottom of a pool of pure water. Between the fingers, around the nostrils, on the nape of the neck, along the spine—about these places especially, dark, almost dirty, shadows gathered. But the skin of the Westerners, even those of a darker complexion, had a limpid glow. Nowhere were they tainted by this gray shadow. From the tops of their heads to the tips of their fingers the whiteness was pure and unadulterated. Thus it is that when one of us goes among a group of Westerners it is like a grimy stain on a sheet of white paper. The sight offends even our own eyes and leaves none too pleasant a feeling.

We can appreciate, then, the psychology that in the past caused the white races to reject the colored races. A sensitive white person could not but be upset by the shadow that even one or two colored persons cast over a social gathering. What the situation is today I do not know, but at the time of the American Civil War, when persecution of Negroes was at its most intense, the hatred and scorn were directed not only at full-blooded Negroes, but at mulattos, the children of mulattos, and even the children of mulattos and whites. Those with the slightest taint of Negro blood, be it but a half, a quarter, a sixteenth, or a thirty-second, had to be ferreted out and made to suffer. Not even those who at a glance were indistinguishable from pure-blooded whites, but among whose ancestors two or three generations earlier there had been a Negro, escaped the searching gaze, no matter how faint the tinge that lay hidden beneath their white skin.

And so we see how profound is the relationship between shadows and the yellow races. Because no one likes to show himself to bad advantage, it is natural that we should have chosen cloudy colors for our food and clothing and houses, and sunk ourselves back into the shadows. I am not saying that our ancestors were conscious of the cloudiness in their skin. They cannot have known that a whiter race existed. But one must conclude that something in their sense of color led them naturally to this preference.

Our ancestors cut off the brightness on the land from above and created a world of shadows, and far in the depths of it they placed woman, marking her the whitest of beings. If whiteness was to be indispensible to supreme beauty, then for us there was no other way, nor do I find this objectionable. The white races are fair-haired, but our hair is dark; so nature taught us the laws of darkness, which we instinctively used to turn a yellow skin white. I have spoken of the practice of blackening the teeth, but was not the shaving of the eyebrows also a device to make the white face stand out? What fascinates me most of all, however, is that green, iridescent lipstick, so rarely used today even by Kyoto geisha. One can guess nothing of its power unless one imagines it in the low, unsteady light of a candle. The woman of old was made to hide the red of her mouth under green-black lipstick, to put shimmering ornaments in her hair; and so the last trace of color was taken from her rich skin. I know of nothing whiter than the face of a young girl in the wavering shadow of a lantern, her teeth now and then as she smiles shining a lacquered black through lips like elfin fires. It is whiter than the whitest white woman I can imagine. The whiteness of the white woman is clear, tangible, familiar, it is not this other-worldly whiteness. Perhaps the latter does not even exist. Perhaps it is only a mischievous trick of light and shadow, a thing of a moment only. But even so it is enough. We can ask for nothing more.

And while I am talking of this whiteness I want to talk also of the color of the darkness that enfolds it. I think of an unforgettable vision of darkness I once had when I took a friend from Tokyo to the old Sumiya teahouse in Kyoto. I was in a large room, the "Pine Room" I think, since destroyed by fire, and the darkness, broken only by a few candles, was of a richness quite different from the darkness of a small room. As we came in the door an elderly waitress with shaven eyebrows and blackened teeth was kneeling by a candle behind which stood a large screen. On the far side of the screen, at the edge of the little circle of light, the darkness seemed to fall from the ceiling, lofty, intense, monolithic, the fragile light of the candle unable to pierce its thickness, turned back as from a black wall. I wonder if my readers know the color of that "darkness seen by candlelight." It was different in quality from darkness on the road at night. It was a repletion,[3] a pregnancy of tiny particles like fine ashes, each particle luminous as a rainbow. I blinked in spite of myself, as though to keep it out of my eyes.

Smaller rooms are the fashion now, and even if one were to use candles in them one would not get the color of that darkness; but in the old palace and the old house of pleasure the ceilings were high, the skirting corridors were wide, the rooms themselves were usually tens of feet long and wide, and the darkness must always have pressed in like a fog. The elegant aristocrat of old was immersed in this suspension of ashen particles, soaked in it, but the man of today, long used to the electric light, has forgotten that such a darkness existed. It must have been simple for specters to appear in a "visible darkness," where always something seemed to be flickering and shimmering, a darkness that on occasion held greater terrors than darkness out-of-doors. This was the darkness in which ghosts and monsters were active, and indeed was not the woman who lived in it, behind thick curtains, behind layer after layer of screens and doors—was she not of a kind with them? The darkness wrapped her round tenfold, twentyfold, it filled the collar, the sleeves of her kimono, the folds of her skirt, wherever a hollow invited. Further yet: might it not have been the reverse, might not the darkness have emerged from her mouth and those black teeth, from the black of her hair, like the thread from the great earth spider?[4]

The novelist Takebayashi Musōan[5] said when he returned from Paris a few years ago that Tokyo and Osaka were far more brightly lit than any European city; that even on the Champs Élysées there were still houses lit by oil lamps, while in Japan hardly a one remained unless in a remote mountain village. Perhaps no two countries in the world waste more electricity than America and Japan, he said, for Japan is only too anxious to imitate America in every way it can. That was some four or five years ago, before the vogue for neon signs. Imagine his surprise were he to come home today, when everything is so much brighter.

---

3. A fullness, abundance; a state of being permeated with something.　　4. A creature from early Japanese folklore thought to live deep beneath the mountains and to emerge to spin a lethal, mesmerizing web in which it entraps human beings and sucks their vital essences.　　5. He was also a translator (1880–1962); his works include *Praise for Marriage* and *Tales of a Mindless Recluse*.

Yamamoto Sanehiko, president of the Kaizō publishing house, told me of something that happened when he escorted Dr. Einstein on a trip to Kyoto. As the train neared Ishiyama,[6] Einstein looked out the window and remarked, "Now that is terribly wasteful." When asked what he meant, Einstein pointed to an electric lamp burning in broad daylight. "Einstein is a Jew, and so he is probably very careful about such things"—this was Yamamoto's interpretation. But the truth of the matter is that Japan wastes more electric light than any Western country except America.

This calls to mind another curious Ishiyama story. This year I had great trouble making up my mind where to go for the autumn moon-viewing. Finally, after much perplexed head-scratching, I decided on the Ishiyama Temple. The day before the full moon, however, I read in the paper that there would be loudspeakers in the woods at Ishiyama to regale the moon-viewing guests with phonograph records of the Moonlight Sonata. I canceled my plans immediately. Loudspeakers were bad enough, but if it could be assumed that they would set the tone, then there would surely be floodlights too strung all over the mountain. I remember another ruined moon-viewing, the year we took a boat on the night of the harvest full moon and sailed out over the lake of the Suma Temple.[7] We put together a party, we had our refreshments in lacquered boxes, we set bravely out. But the margin of the lake was decorated brilliantly with electric lights in five colors. There was indeed a moon if one strained one's eyes for it.

So benumbed are we nowadays by electric lights that we have become utterly insensitive to the evils of excessive illumination. It does not matter all that much in the case of the moon, I suppose, but teahouses, restaurants, inns, and hotels are sure to be lit far too extravagantly. Some of this may be necessary to attract customers, but when the lights are turned on in summer even before dark it is a waste, and worse than the waste is the heat. I am upset by it wherever I go in the summer. Outside it will be cool, but inside it will be ridiculously hot, and more often than not because of lights too strong or too numerous. Turn some of them off and in no time at all the room is refreshingly cool. Yet curiously neither the guests nor the owner seem to realize this. A room should be brighter in winter, but dimmer in summer; it is then appropriately cool, and does not attract insects. But people will light the lights, then switch on an electric fan to combat the heat. The very thought annoys me.

One can endure a Japanese room all the same, for ultimately the heat escapes through the walls. But in a Western-style hotel circulation is poor, and the floors, walls, and ceilings drink in the heat and throw it back from every direction with unbearable intensity. The worst example, alas, is the Miyako Hotel in Kyoto, as anyone who has been in its lobby on a summer's evening should agree. It stands on high ground, facing north, commanding a view of Mount Hiei, Nyoigatake, the Kurodani pagoda, the forests, the green hills of Higashiyama—a splendidly fresh and clean view, all the more disappointing for being so. Should a person of a summer's evening set out to refresh himself among purple hills and crystal streams, to take in the cool breeze that blows through the tower on the heights, he will only find himself

---

6. A town approximately six miles southeast of Kyoto known for its Buddhist temple of the same name.
7. Buddhist temple in Suma, on the Inland Sea; a location made famous by *The Tale of Genji* when its hero is exiled to the coastal town. Suma also figures in the *nō* play *Atsumori*.

beneath a white ceiling dotted with huge milk glass lights, each sending forth a blinding blaze.

As in most recent Western-style buildings, the ceilings are so low that one feels as if balls of fire were blazing directly above one's head. "Hot" is no word for the effect, and the closer to the ceiling the worse it is—your head and neck and spine feel as if they were being roasted. One of these balls of fire alone would suffice to light the place, yet three or four blaze down from the ceiling, and there are smaller versions on the walls and pillars, serving no function but to eradicate every trace of shadow. And so the room is devoid of shadows. Look about and all you will see are white walls, thick red pillars, a garish floor done in mosaic patterns looking much like a freshly printed lithograph—all oppressively hot. When you enter from the corridor the difference in temperature is all too apparent. No matter how cool a breeze blows in, it is instantly transformed to hot wind.

I have stayed at the Miyako several times and think fondly of it. My warnings are given with the friendliest of intentions. It is a pity that so lovely a view, so perfect a place for enjoying the cool of a summer's night, should be utterly destroyed by electric lights. The Japanese quite aside, I cannot believe that Westerners, however much they may prefer light, can be other than appalled at the heat, and I have no doubt they would see immediately the improvement in turning down the lights. The Miyako is by no means the only example. The Imperial Hotel, with its indirect lighting, is on the whole a pleasant place, but in summer even it might be a bit darker.

Light is used not for reading or writing or sewing but for dispelling the shadows in the farthest corners, and this runs against the basic idea of the Japanese room. Something is salvaged when a person turns off the lights at home to save money, but at inns and restaurants there is inevitably too much light in the halls, on the stairs, in the doorway, the gate, the garden. The rooms and the water and stones outside become flat and shallow. There are advantages for keeping warm in the winter, I suppose, but in the summer, no matter to what isolated mountain resort a person flees to escape the heat, he has a disappointment waiting if it is an inn or hotel he is going to. I have found myself that the best way to keep cool is to stay at home, open the doors, and stretch out in the dark under a mosquito net.

I recently read a newspaper or magazine article about the complaints of old women in England. When they were young, they said, they respected their elders and took good care of them; but their own daughters care nothing at all for them, and avoid them as though they were somehow dirty. The morals of the young, they lamented, are not what they once were. It struck me that old people everywhere have much the same complaints. The older we get the more we seem to think that everything was better in the past. Old people a century ago wanted to go back two centuries, and two centuries ago they wished it were three centuries earlier. Never has there been an age that people have been satisfied with. But in recent years the pace of progress has been so precipitous that conditions in our own country go somewhat beyond the ordinary. The changes that have taken place since the Restoration of 1867[8] must be at least as great as those of the preceding three and a half centuries.

---

8. When Japan's modern period began. The *shogun*, the military dictator, abdicated power, and the emperor was restored as an apparent figurehead for the new Western-influenced government.

It will seem odd, I suppose, that I should go on in this vein, as if I too were grumbling in my dotage. Yet of this I am convinced, that the conveniences of modern culture cater exclusively to youth, and that the times grow increasingly inconsiderate of old people. Let me take a familiar example: now that we cannot cross an intersection without consulting a traffic signal, old people can no longer venture confidently out into the streets. For someone sufficiently well-off to be driven about in an automobile there may be no problem, but on those rare occasions when I go into Osaka, it sets every nerve in my body on edge to cross from one side of the street to the other. If the signal is in the middle of the intersection it is easy enough to see it; but it is all but impossible to pick out a stop light that stands off to the side, where no one would ever expect to find it. If the intersection is broad, it is only too easy to confuse the light for facing traffic with the light for crossing traffic. It seemed to me the end of everything when the traffic policeman came to Kyoto. Now one must travel to such small cities as Nishinomiya, Sakai, Wakayama, or Fukuyama for the feel of Japan.

The same is true of food. In a large city it takes a concerted search to turn up a dish that will be palatable to an old person. Not long ago a newspaper reporter came to interview me on the subject of unusual foods, and I described to him the persimmon-leaf sushi made by the people who live deep in the mountains of Yoshino—and which I shall take the opportunity to introduce to you here. To every ten parts of rice one part of saké is added just when the water comes to a boil. When the rice is done it should be cooled thoroughly, after which salt is applied to the hands and the rice molded into bite-size pieces. At this stage the hands must be absolutely free of moisture, the secret being that only salt should touch the rice. Thin slices of lightly salted salmon are placed on the rice, and each piece is wrapped in a persimmon leaf, the surface of the leaf facing inward. Both the persimmon leaves and the salmon should be wiped with a dry cloth to remove any moisture. Then in a rice tub or sushi box, the interior of which is perfectly dry, the pieces are packed standing on end so that no space remains between them, and the lid is put in place and weighted with a heavy stone, as in making pickles. Prepared in the evening, the sushi should be ready to eat the next morning. Though the taste is best on the first day, it remains edible for two or three days. A slight bit of vinegar is sprinkled over each piece with a sprig of bitter nettle just before eating.

I learned of the dish from a friend who had been to Yoshino and found it so exceptionally good that he took the trouble to learn how to make it—but if you have the persimmon leaves and salted salmon it can be made anywhere. You need only remember to keep out every trace of moisture, and to cool the rice completely. I made some myself, and it was very good indeed. The oil of the salmon and the slight hint of salt give just the proper touch of seasoning to the rice, and the salmon becomes as soft as if it were fresh—the flavor is indescribable, and far better than the sushi one gets in Tokyo. I have become so fond of it that I ate almost nothing else this summer. What impressed me, however, was that this superb method of preparing salted salmon was the invention of poor mountain people. Yet a sampling of the various regional cuisines suggests that in our day country people have far more discriminating palates than city people, and that in this respect they enjoy luxuries we cannot begin to imagine.

And so as time goes by, old people give up the cities and retire to the country; and yet there is not much cause for hope there either, for country towns are year by year going the way of Kyoto, their streets strung with bright lights. There are those who say that when civilization progresses a bit further transportation facilities will move into the skies and under the ground, and that our streets will again be quiet, but I know perfectly well that when that day comes some new device for torturing the old will be invented. "Out of our way, old people," we say, and they have no recourse but to shrink back into their houses, to make whatever tidbits they can for themselves, and to enjoy their evening saké as best they can to the accompaniment of the radio.

But do not think that old people are the only ones to find fault. The author of the "Vox Populi Vox Dei" column in the Osaka *Asahi*[9] recently castigated city officials who quite needlessly cut a swath through a forest and leveled a hill in order to build a highway through Minō Park. I was somewhat encouraged;[1] for to snatch away from us even the darkness beneath trees that stand deep in the forest is the most heartless of crimes. At this rate every place of any beauty in Nara or in the suburbs of Kyoto and Osaka, as the price of being turned over to the masses, will be denuded of trees. But again I am grumbling.

I am aware of and most grateful for the benefits of the age. No matter what complaints we may have, Japan has chosen to follow the West, and there is nothing for her to do but move bravely ahead and leave us old ones[2] behind. But we must be resigned to the fact that as long as our skin is the color it is the loss we have suffered cannot be remedied. I have written all this because I have thought that there might still be somewhere, possibly in literature or the arts, where something could be saved. I would call back at least for literature this world of shadows we are losing. In the mansion called literature I would have the eaves deep and the walls dark, I would push back into the shadows the things that come forward too clearly, I would strip away the useless decoration. I do not ask that this be done everywhere, but perhaps we may be allowed at least one mansion where we can turn off the electric lights and see what it is like without them.

---

9. "Morning Sun"; a daily newspaper. *Vox Populi Vox Dei*: "the voice of the people is the voice of God" (Latin); that is, the voice of the people is supreme.   1. Because the editorial shared the author's interest in preservation.   2. A bit of an exaggeration; Tanizaki was forty-eight.

T. S. ELIOT
1888–1965

In poetry and in literary criticism, Thomas Stearns Eliot has a unique position as a writer who not only expressed but helped to define modernist taste and style. He rejected the narrative, moralizing, and frequently "noble" style of late Victorian poetry, employing instead precisely focused and often startling images and an elliptical, allusive, and ironic voice that had enormous influence on modern American poetry. His early essays on literature and literary history helped bring about not only a new appreciation of seventeenth-century "metaphysical" poetry but also a different understanding of the text, no longer seen as the inspired overflow of spontaneous emotion but as a carefully made aesthetic object. Yet much of Eliot's immediate impact was not merely formal but spiritual or philosophical. The search for meaning that pervades his work created a famous picture of the barrenness of modern culture in *The Waste Land* (1922), which juxtaposed images of past nobility and present decay, civilizations near and far, and biblical, mythical, and Buddhist allusions to evoke the dilemma of a composite, anxious, and infinitely vulnerable modern soul. Readers in different countries who know nothing of Eliot's other works are often familiar with *The Waste Land* as a literary-historical landmark representing the cultural crisis in European society after World War I. In many ways, Eliot's combination of spiritual insight and technical innovation carries on the tradition of the Symbolist poet who was both visionary artist and consummate craftsman.

Two countries, England and the United States, claim Eliot as part of their national literature. Born September 26, 1888, to a prosperous and educated family in St. Louis, Eliot went to Harvard University for his undergraduate and graduate education and moved to England only in 1915, where he became a British citizen in 1927. While at Harvard, Eliot was influenced by the anti-Romantic humanist Irving Babbitt and the philosopher and aesthetician George Santayana. He later wrote a doctoral dissertation on the philosophy of F. H. Bradley, whose examination of private consciousness (*Appearance and Reality*) appears in Eliot's own later essays and poems. Eliot also found literary examples that would be important for him in future years: the poetry of Dante and John Donne, and the plays of Elizabethan and Jacobean dramatists. In 1908 he read Arthur Symons's *The Symbolist Movement in Literature* and became acquainted with the French Symbolist poets, whose richly allusive images—as well as highly self-conscious, ironic, and craftsmanlike technique—he would adopt for his own. Eliot began writing poetry while in college and published his first major poem, *The Love Song of J. Alfred Prufrock,* in Chicago's *Poetry* magazine in 1915. When he moved to England, however, he began a many-sided career as poet, reviewer, essayist, editor, and, later, playwright. By the time he received the Nobel Prize for literature in 1948, Eliot was recognized as one of the most influential twentieth-century writers in English.

Eliot's first poems, in 1915, already displayed the evocative yet startling images, abrupt shifts in focus, and combination of human sympathy and ironic wit that would attract and puzzle his readers. The *Preludes* linked the "notion of some infinitely gentle / Infinitely suffering thing" with a harsh fatalism in which "The worlds revolve like ancient women / Gathering fuel in vacant lots." Prufrock's dramatic monologue openly tried to startle readers by asking them to imagine the evening spread out "like a patient etherised upon a table" and by changing focus abruptly between imaginary landscapes, metaphysical questions, drawing-room chatter, literary and biblical allusions, and tones of high seriousness set against the most banal and even sing-song speech. "I grow old . . . I grow old . . . / I shall wear the bottoms of my trousers rolled." The individual stanzas of *Prufrock* are individual scenes, each with its own coherence (for example, the third stanza's yellow fog as a cat). Together, they compose a symbolic landscape sketched in the narrator's mind as a combination of factual observation and subjective feelings: the delicately stated eroticism of the arm "downed with light brown hair," and the frustrated aggression in "I should have been a pair of ragged claws / Scuttling across the floors of silent seas." In its discontinuity, precise yet evocative imagery, mixture of romantic and everyday reference, formal and conversational speech, and in the complex and ironic self-consciousness of its most unheroic hero, *The Love Song of J. Alfred Prufrock* already displays many of the modernist traits typical of Eliot's entire work. Also typical is the theme of spiritual void and of a disoriented protagonist who—at least at this point—does not know how to cope with a crisis that is as much that of modern Western culture as it is his own personal tragedy.

Once established in London, Eliot married, taught briefly before taking a job in the foreign department of Lloyd's Bank (1917–25), and in 1925 joined the publishing firm of Faber & Faber. He wrote a number of essays and book reviews that were published in *The Sacred Wood* (1920) and *Homage to Dryden* (1924) and enjoyed a great deal of influence as assistant editor of the *Egoist* (1917–19) and founding editor of the quarterly *Criterion* from 1922 until it folded in 1939. Eliot helped shape changing literary tastes as much by his essays and literary criticism as by his poetry. Influenced himself by T. E. Hulme's proposal that the time had come for a classical literature of "hard, dry wit" after Romantic vagueness and religiosity and following Imagism's goal of clear, precise physical images phrased in everyday language, he outlined his own definitions of literature and literary history and contributed to a theoretical approach later known as the New Criticism. In his essay *Tradition and the Individual Talent* (1919), Eliot proclaimed that there existed a special level of great works—"masterpieces"—that formed among themselves an "ideal order" of quality even though, as individual works, they expressed the characteristic sensibility of their age. The best poets were aware of fitting into the cumulative "mind of Europe" (for Eliot, the humanistic tradition of Homer, Dante, and Shakespeare) and thus of being to some extent depersonalized in their works. Eliot's "impersonal theory of poetry" emphasizes the medium in which a writer works, rather than his or her inner state; craft and control rather than the Romantic ideal of a spontaneous overflow of private emotion. In a famous passage that compares the creative mind to the untouched catalyst of a chemistry experiment, he insists that the writer makes the art object out of language and the experience of any number of people. "The poet's mind is in fact a receptacle for seizing and storing up numberless feelings, phrases, images, which remain there until all the particles which can unite to form a new compound are present together." Poetry can and should express the whole being—intellectual and emotional, conscious and unconscious. In a review of Herbert Grierson's edition of the seventeenth-century Metaphysical poets (1921), Eliot praised the complex mixture of intellect and passion that characterized John Donne and the other Metaphysicals (and that characterized Eliot himself) and criticized the tendency of English literature after the seventeenth century to separate the language of analysis from that of feeling. His criticism of this "dissociation of sensibility" implied a change in literary tastes: from Milton to Donne, from Tennyson to Gerard Manley Hopkins, from Romanticism to classicism, from simplicity to complexity.

The great poetic example of this change came with *The Waste Land* in 1922. Eliot dedicated the poem to Ezra Pound, who had helped him revise the first draft, with a quotation from Dante praising the "better craftsman." Quotations from, or allusions to, a wide range of sources, including Shakespeare, Dante, Charles Baudelaire, Richard Wagner, Ovid, St. Augustine, Buddhist sermons, folk songs, and the anthropologists Jessie Weston and James Frazer, punctuate this lengthy poem, to which Eliot added explanatory notes when it was first published in book form. *The Waste Land* describes modern society in a time of cultural and spiritual crisis and sets off the fragmentation of modern experience against references (some in foreign languages) to a more stable cultural heritage. The ancient Greek prophet Tiresias is juxtaposed with the contemporary charlatan Madame Sosostris; celebrated lovers like Antony and Cleopatra with a house-agent's clerk who mechanically seduces an uninterested typist at the end of her day; the religious vision of St. Augustine and Buddhist sermons with a sterile world of rock and dry sand where "one can neither stand nor lie nor sit." The modern wasteland could be redeemed if it learned to answer (or perhaps, to ask) the right questions: a situation Eliot symbolized by oblique references to the legend of a knight passing an evening of trial in a Chapel Perilous, and healing a Fisher King by asking the right questions about the Holy Grail and its lance. The series of references (many from literary masterworks) that Eliot integrated into his poem were so many "fragments I have shored against my ruins," pieces of a puzzle whose resolution would bring "shantih," or the peace that passes understanding, but that is still out of reach, as the poem's final lines in a foreign language suggest.

The most influential technical innovation in *The Waste Land* was the deliberate use of fragmentation and discontinuity. Eliot pointedly refused to supply any transitional passages or narrative thread and expected the reader to construct a pattern whose implications would make sense as a whole. This was a direct attack on linear habits of reading, which are here broken up with sudden introductions of a different scene or unexplained literary references, shifts in perspective, interpolation of a foreign language, changes from elegant description to barroom gossip, from Elizabethan to modern scenes, from formal to colloquial language. Eliot's rupture of traditional expectations served several functions. It contributed to the general picture of cultural disintegration that the poem expressed, it allowed him to exploit the Symbolist or allusive powers of language inasmuch as they now carried the burden of meaning, and finally—by drawing attention to its own technique—it exemplified modernist "self-reflexive" or self-conscious style. It is impossible to read a triple shift such as "I remember / Those are pearls that were his eyes. / 'Are you alive, or not? Is there nothing in your head?' "—moving from the narrator's meditative recall to a quotation from Shakespeare and the woman's blunt attack—without noticing the abrupt changes in style and tone. Eliot's "heap of broken images" and "fragments shored against my ruins" also took the shape of fragments of thought and speech, and as such embodied a new tradition of literary language.

The spiritual search of *Prufrock, Gerontion* (1919), and *The Waste Land* entered a new phase for Eliot in 1927, when he became a member of the Anglican Church. *Ash Wednesday* (1930) and a verse play on the death of the English St. Thomas à Becket (*Murder in the Cathedral*, 1935) display the same distress over the human condition but now within a framework of hope for those who have accepted religious discipline. Eliot began writing plays to reach a larger audience, of which the best known are *The Family Reunion* (1939), which recasts the Orestes story from Greek tragedy, and *The Cocktail Party* (1949), a drawing-room comedy that also explored its characters' search for salvation. He is still best known for his poetry, however, and his last major work in that genre is the *Four Quartets*, begun in 1934 and published in its entirety in 1943.

As their title suggests, the *Four Quartets* are divided into sections much like the movement of a musical quartet. Each has five sections, inside which themes are introduced, developed, and resolved, and each has the title of a place. *Little Gidding* is a village in Huntingdonshire, England, that was the home of a seventeenth-century Anglican Catholic religious community of which only a chapel (rebuilt after the English Civil Wars) remained. All the *Quartets* use varying forms of free verse, ranging from the most intense short lyrics to—for the first time—continuous narrative passages of the kind Eliot once disdained. Throughout, the poet ponders the relationship of historical change and eternal order.

Eliot's experiences in World War II as a watchman checking for fires during bombing raids enter into *Little Gidding,* and he uses the chapel in that village as the point of departure for a meditation on the meaning of strife and change in a universe that the mind strives to structure, always imperfectly, by the timeless truths of religion. The *Quartet* opens with a section that is itself divided into three separate movements, first establishing the season of "midwinter spring" with the sun blazing on ice, then the chapel as the goal of any season's journey, and finally the chapel as a place so consecrated by prayer that the dead may communicate with the living. The lyrics opening the second section mourn the place's present decay by all four elements of earth, air, fire, and water and pass on to an imaginary conversation between the poet, wandering after the last bomb and before the all-clear signal, and an anonymous "dead master." The mood is pessimistic, and the dead master (a "compound ghost" with elements of Eliot, the Virgil of Dante's *Divine Comedy*, and W. B. Yeats) prophesies a bitter old age full of remorse and impotent rage at human folly. Their conversation suggests a comparison between the air-raid scene and Dante's *Inferno*, for it echoes the triple-line stanzaic form of *The Divine Comedy* and recalls the Italian poet's own encounter with his former master, Brunetto Latini, in Hell (*Inferno* 15.22–124). The rest of the poem, however, moves forward to a kind of resolution out of time. The third section's beginning rhetoric of logical persuasion ("There are three conditions") introduces the concept of memory expanding our perspectives and enabling us to transcend the narrow commitments of history and civil war. The intense lyrics of the short fourth section propose that the flames of the annunciatory dove (or bomb) may be purgation as well as destruction; and in the final section, as the afternoon draws to a close, the poet ends his meditation on past and present, time and eternity, by asserting his faith in a condition of mind and spirit that combines both *now* and *always*, a transcendental vision that is a "condition of complete simplicity" and "crowned knot of fire."

The poem's conclusion is thus a religious one, moving from the agony of history to an eternal, purifying flame that may recall a similar mystic vision of all-penetrating light at the end of Dante's *Paradiso*. It may seem paradoxical that the poet who is known for expressing the dilemma of modern consciousness and for developing a new poetic style appropriate to twentieth-century experience should resolve that experience in a metaphor of transcendence. From his earliest work, however, Eliot was preoccupied with the spiritual implications of the most mundane reality, and the yoking of concrete with transcendental vision defines at once the range and depth of his modernist style.

Bernard Bergonzi, *T. S. Eliot* (1972), and Tony Sharpe, *T. S. Eliot: A Literary Life* (1991), are brief and readable introductions to the life and works; Lyndall Gordon, *T. S. Eliot: An Imperfect Life* (1998), is a recent, full biography. Martin Scofield, *T. S. Eliot: The Poems* (1988), offers a concise, balanced discussion of the evolution of Eliot's poetry. *The Waste Land* is discussed in Jay Martin, ed., *Twentieth-Century Interpretations of The Waste Land* (1968); Lois A. Cuddy and David H. Hirsch, eds., *Critical Essays on T. S. Eliot's The Waste Land* (1991); and as part of John Mayer, *T. S. Eliot's Silent Voices* (1989), which analyzes themes of awareness and self-consciousness in the early poetry. *Little Gidding* is examined in Steve Ellis, *The English Eliot: Design, Language, and Landscape in Four Quartets* (1991), and Edward Lobb, ed., *Words in Time: New Essays on Eliot's Four Quartets* (1994). John Paul Riquelme, *Harmony of Dissonances: T. S. Eliot, Romanticism, and Imagination* (1991), links Eliot's response to Romanticism with postmodern views. Useful general collections are Linda Wagner, ed., *T. S. Eliot: A Collection of Criticism* (1974), Ronald Bush, ed., *T. S. Eliot: The Modernist in History* (1991), and Harold Bloom, ed., *T. S. Eliot* (1999).

The Love Song of J. Alfred Prufrock

> *S'io credesse che mia risposta fosse*
> *A persona che mai tornasse al mondo,*
> *Questa fiamma staria senza piu scosse.*
> *Ma perciocche giammai di questo fondo*
> *Non torno vivo alcun, s'i'odo il vero,*
> *Senza tema d'infamia ti rispondo.*[1]

Let us go then, you and I,
When the evening is spread out against the sky

---

1. From Dante's *Inferno* 27.61–66, in which the false counselor Guido da Montefeltro, enveloped in flame, explains that he would never reveal his past if he thought the traveler could report it: "If I thought my reply were meant for one / who ever could return into the world, / this flame would stir no more; and yet, since none— / if what I hear is true—ever returned / alive from this abyss, then without fear / of facing infamy, I answer you."

Like a patient etherised upon a table;
Let us go, through certain half-deserted streets,
The muttering retreats   5
Of restless nights in one-night cheap hotels
And sawdust restaurants with oyster-shells:
Streets that follow like a tedious argument
Of insidious intent
To lead you to an overwhelming question . . .   10
Oh, do not ask, "What is it?"
Let us go and make our visit.

    In the room the women come and go
Talking of Michelangelo.[2]

    The yellow fog that rubs its back upon the window-panes,   15
The yellow smoke that rubs its muzzle on the window-panes
Licked its tongue into the corners of the evening,
Lingered upon the pools that stand in drains,
Let fall upon its back the soot that falls from chimneys,
Slipped by the terrace, made a sudden leap,   20
And seeing that it was a soft October night,
Curled once about the house, and fell asleep.

    And indeed there will be time[3]
For the yellow smoke that slides along the street,
Rubbing its back upon the window-panes;   25
There will be time, there will be time
To prepare a face to meet the faces that you meet;
There will be time to murder and create,
And time for all the works and days of hands[4]
That lift and drop a question on your plate;   30
Time for you and time for me,
And time yet for a hundred indecisions,
And for a hundred visions and revisions,
Before the taking of a toast and tea.

    In the room the women come and go   35
Talking of Michelangelo.

    And indeed there will be time
To wonder, "Do I dare?" and, "Do I dare?"
Time to turn back and descend the stair,
With a bald spot in the middle of my hair—   40
(They will say: "How his hair is growing thin!")
My morning coat, my collar mounting firmly to the chin,
My necktie rich and modest, but asserted by a simple pin—
(They will say: "But how his arms and legs are thin!")

---

2. Michelangelo Buonarroti (1475–1564), famous Italian Renaissance sculptor, painter, architect, and poet; here, merely a topic of fashionable conversation.   **3.** Echo of a love poem by Andrew Marvell (1621–1678), *To His Coy Mistress:* "Had we but world enough and time."   **4.** An implied contrast with the more productive agricultural labor of hands in the *Works and Days* of the Greek poet Hesiod (8th century B.C.).

Do I dare   45
Disturb the universe?
In a minute there is time
For decisions and revisions which a minute will reverse.

    For I have known them all already, known them all—
Have known the evenings, mornings, afternoons,   50
I have measured out my life with coffee spoons;
I know the voices dying with a dying fall[5]
Beneath the music from a farther room.
    So how should I presume?

    And I have known the eyes already, known them all—   55
The eyes that fix you in a formulated phrase,
And when I am formulated, sprawling on a pin,
When I am pinned and wriggling on the wall,
Then how should I begin
To spit out all the butt-ends of my days and ways?   60
    And how should I presume?

    And I have known the arms already, known them all—
Arms that are braceleted and white and bare
(But in the lamplight, downed with light brown hair!)
Is it perfume from a dress   65
That makes me so digress?
Arms that lie along a table, or wrap about a shawl.
    And should I then presume?
    And how should I begin?

                . . .

    Shall I say, I have gone at dusk through narrow streets   70
And watched the smoke that rises from the pipes
Of lonely men in shirt-sleeves, leaning out of windows? . . .

    I should have been a pair of ragged claws
Scuttling across the floors of silent seas.

                . . .

    And the afternoon, the evening, sleeps so peacefully!   75
Smoothed by long fingers,
Asleep . . . tired . . . or it malingers,
Stretched on the floor, here beside you and me.
Should I, after tea and cakes and ices,
Have the strength to force the moment to its crisis?   80
But though I have wept and fasted, wept and prayed,
Though I have seen my head (grown slightly bald) brought in upon a
    platter,
I am no prophet[6]—and here's no great matter;
I have seen the moment of my greatness flicker,

5. Recalls Duke Orsino's description of a musical phrase in Shakespeare's *Twelfth Night* (1.1.4): "It has a
dying fall."   6. Salome obtained the head of the prophet John the Baptist on a platter as a reward for
dancing before the tetrarch Herod (Matthew 14.3–11).

And I have seen the eternal Footman hold my coat, and snicker,   85
And in short, I was afraid.

  And would it have been worth it, after all,
After the cups, the marmalade, the tea,
Among the porcelain, among some talk of you and me,
Would it have been worth while,   90
To have bitten off the matter with a smile,
To have squeezed the universe into a ball
To roll it toward some overwhelming question,[7]
To say: "I am Lazarus, come from the dead,[8]
Come back to tell you all, I shall tell you all"—   95
If one, settling a pillow by her head,
  Should say: "That is not what I meant at all.
  That is not it, at all."

  And would it have been worth it, after all,
Would it have been worth while,   100
After the sunsets and the dooryards and the sprinkled streets,
After the novels, after the teacups, after the skirts that trail along
    the floor—
And this, and so much more?—
It is impossible to say just what I mean!
But as if a magic lantern[9] threw the nerves in patterns on a screen: 105
Would it have been worth while
If one, settling a pillow or throwing off a shawl,
And turning toward the window, should say:
  "That is not it at all,
  That is not what I meant, at all."   110

      No! I am not Prince Hamlet, nor was meant to be;
Am an attendant lord, one that will do
To swell a progress,[1] start a scene or two,
Advise the prince; no doubt, an easy tool,
Deferential, glad to be of use,   115
Politic, cautious, and meticulous;
Full of high sentence, but a bit obtuse;
At times, indeed, almost ridiculous—
Almost, at times, the Fool.

  I grow old . . . I grow old . . .   120
I shall wear the bottoms of my trousers rolled.

  Shall I part my hair behind? Do I dare to eat a peach?
I shall wear white flannel trousers, and walk upon the beach.
I have heard the mermaids singing, each to each.

7. Another echo of *To His Coy Mistress*, when the lover suggests rolling "all our strength and all / our sweetness up into one ball" to send against the "iron gates of life."   8. The story of Lazarus, raised from the dead, is told in John 11.1–44.   9. A slide projector.   1. A procession of attendants accompanying a king or nobleman across the stage, as in Elizabethan drama.

I do not think that they will sing to me.   125

I have seen them riding seaward on the waves
Combing the white hair of the waves blown back
When the wind blows the water white and black.

We have lingered in the chambers of the sea
By sea-girls wreathed with seaweed red and brown   130
Till human voices wake us, and we drown.

The Waste Land[1]

"Nam Sibyllam quidem Cumis ego ipse oculis meis vidi in ampulla
pendere, et cum illi pueri dicerent: Σίβυλλα τί θέλεισ; respon-
debat illa: αποθανεῖν θέλω."[2]

For Ezra Pound
il miglior fabbro.[3]

I. *The Burial of the Dead*[4]

April is the cruellest month, breeding
Lilacs out of the dead land, mixing
Memory and desire, stirring
Dull roots with spring rain.
Winter kept us warm, covering   5
Earth in forgetful snow, feeding
A little life with dried tubers.
Summer surprised us, coming over the Starnbergersee[5]
With a shower of rain; we stopped in the colonnade,
And went on in sunlight, into the Hofgarten,[6]   10
And drank coffee, and talked for an hour.
Bin gar keine Russin, stamm' aus Litauen, echt deutsch.[7]
And when we were children, staying at the archduke's,
My cousin's, he took me out on a sled,
And I was frightened. He said, Marie,   15
Marie, hold on tight. And down we went.[8]
In the mountains, there you feel free.
I read, much of the night, and go south in the winter.

1. Eliot provided footnotes for *The Waste Land* when it was first published in book form; these notes are
included here. A general note at the beginning referred readers to the religious symbolism described in
Jessie L. Weston's study of the Grail legend, *From Ritual to Romance* (1920), and to fertility myths and
vegetation ceremonies (especially those involving Adonis, Attis, and Osiris) as described in the *The Golden
Bough* (1890–1918) by the anthropologist Sir James Frazer.   2. Lines from Petronius's *Satyricon* (ca.
A.D. 60) describing the Sibyl, a prophetess shriveled with age and suspended in a bottle. "For indeed I
myself have seen with my own eyes the Sibyl at Cumae, hanging in a bottle, and when those boys would
say to her: 'Sibyl, what do you want?' she would reply: 'I want to die.' "   3. The dedication to Pound,
who suggested cuts and changes in the first manuscript of *The Waste Land*, borrows words used by Guido
Guinizelli to describe his predecessor, the Provençal poet Arnaut Daniel, in Dante's *Purgatorio* (26.117):
he is "the better craftsman."   4. From the burial service of the Anglican Church.   5. A lake near
Munich.   6. A public park.   7. "I am certainly no Russian, I come from Lithuania and am pure
German." German settlers in Lithuania considered themselves superior to the Baltic natives.   8. Lines
8–16 recall *My Past*, the memoirs of Countess Marie Larisch.

What are the roots that clutch, what branches grow
Out of this stony rubbish? Son of man,[9]   20
You cannot say, or guess, for you know only
A heap of broken images, where the sun beats,
And the dead tree gives no shelter, the cricket no relief,[1]
And the dry stone no sound of water. Only
There is shadow under this red rock,   25
(Come in under the shadow of this red rock),
And I will show you something different from either
Your shadow at morning striding behind you
Or your shadow at evening rising to meet you;
I will show you fear in a handful of dust.   30

           Frisch weht der Wind
           Der Heimat zu
           Mein Irisch Kind,
           Wo weilest du?[2]

"You gave me hyacinths first a year ago;   35
"They called me the hyacinth girl."
—Yet when we came back, late, from the Hyacinth garden,
Your arms full, and your hair wet, I could not
Speak, and my eyes failed, I was neither
Living nor dead, and I knew nothing,   40
Looking into the heart of light, the silence.
Oed' und leer das Meer.[3]

    Madame Sosostris,[4] famous clairvoyante,
Had a bad cold, nevertheless
Is known to be the wisest woman in Europe,   45
With a wicked pack of cards.[5] Here, said she,
Is your card, the drowned Phoenician Sailor,
(Those are pearls that were his eyes.[6] Look!)
Here is Belladonna, the Lady of the Rocks,
The lady of situations.   50
Here is the man with three staves, and here the Wheel,

---

9. "Cf. Ezekiel II,i" [Eliot's note]. The passage reads "Son of man, stand upon thy feet, and I will speak unto thee."   **1.** "Cf. Ecclesiastes XII, v" [Eliot's note]. "Also when they shall be afraid of that which is high, and fears shall be in the way, . . . the grasshopper shall be a burden, and desire shall fail."   **2.** "V. *Tristan und Isolde,* I, verses 5–8" [Eliot's note]. A sailor in Richard Wagner's opera sings, "The wind blows fresh / Towards the homeland / My Irish child / Where are you waiting?" (German)   **3.** "Id. III, verse 24" [Eliot's note]. "Barren and empty is the sea" (German) is the erroneous report the dying Tristan hears as he waits for Isolde's ship in the third act of Wagner's opera.   **4.** A fortune-teller with an assumed Egyptian name, possibly suggested by a similar figure in a novel by Aldous Huxley (*Crome Yellow,* 1921). **5.** "I am not familiar with the exact constitution of the Tarot pack of cards, from which I have obviously departed to suit my own convenience. The Hanged Man, a member of the traditional pack, fits my purpose in two ways: because he is associated in my mind with the Hanged God of Frazer, and because I associate him with the hooded figure in the passage of the disciples to Emmaus in Part V. The Phoenician Sailor and the Merchant appear later; also the 'crowds of people,' and Death by Water is executed in Part IV. The Man with Three Staves (an authentic member of the Tarot pack) I associate, quite arbitrarily, with the Fisher King himself" [Eliot's note]. Tarot cards are used for telling fortunes; the four suits (cup, lance, sword, and coin) are life symbols related to the Grail legend; and as Eliot suggests, various figures on the cards are associated with different characters and situations in *The Waste Land.* For example, the *drowned Phoenician Sailor* (line 47) recurs in the merchant from Smyrna (III) and Phlebas the Phoenician (IV). *Belladonna* (line 49)—a poison, hallucinogen, medicine, and cosmetic (in Italian, "beautiful lady"); also an echo of Leonardo da Vinci's painting of the Virgin, *Madonna of the Rocks*—heralds the neurotic society woman amid her jewels and perfumes (II). *The Wheel* (line 51) is the wheel of fortune. The Hanged Man (line 55) becomes the sacrificed fertility god whose death ensures resurrection and new life for his people. **6.** A line from Ariel's song in Shakespeare's *The Tempest* (1.2.398), which describes the transformation of a drowned man.

And here is the one-eyed merchant, and this card,
Which is blank, is something he carries on his back,
Which I am forbidden to see. I do not find
The Hanged Man. Fear death by water.   55
I see crowds of people, walking round in a ring.
Thank you. If you see dear Mrs. Equitone,
Tell her I bring the horoscope myself:
One must be so careful these days.

    Unreal City,[7]   60
Under the brown fog of a winter dawn,
A crowd flowed over London Bridge, so many,
I had not thought death had undone so many.[8]
Sighs, short and infrequent, were exhaled,[9]
And each man fixed his eyes before his feet.   65
Flowed up the hill and down King William Street,
To where Saint Mary Woolnoth kept the hours
With a dead sound on the final stroke of nine.[1]
There I saw one I knew, and stopped him, crying: "Stetson!
"You who were with me in the ships at Mylae![2]   70
"That corpse you planted last year in your garden,
"Has it begun to sprout? Will it bloom this year?
"Or has the sudden frost disturbed its bed?
"Oh keep the Dog far hence, that's friend to men,[3]
"Or with his nails he'll dig it up again!   75
"You! hypocrite lecteur!—mon semblable,—mon frère!"[4]

II. A Game of Chess[5]

    The Chair she sat in, like a burnished throne,[6]
Glowed on the marble, where the glass

---

7. "Cf. Baudelaire: 'Fourmillante cité, cité pleine de rêves, / Où le spectre en plein jour raccroche le passant'" [Eliot's note]. "Swarming city, city full of dreams, / Where the specter in broad daylight accosts the passerby"; a description of Paris from "The Seven Old Men" in *The Flowers of Evil* (1857).   8. "Cf. *Inferno* III, 55–57: 'si lunga tratta / di gente, ch'io non avrei mai creduto / che morte tanta n'avesse disfatta'" [Eliot's note]. "Behind that banner trailed so long a file / of people—I should never have believed / that death could have unmade so many souls"; not only is Dante amazed at the number of people who have died but he is also describing a crowd of people who were neither good nor bad—nonentities denied even the entrance to hell.   9. "Cf. *Inferno* IV, 25–27: 'Quivi, secondo che per ascoltare, / non avea pianto, ma' che di sospiri, / che l'aura eterna facevan tremare'" [Eliot's note]. "Here, so far as I could tell by listening, there was no weeping but so many sighs that they caused the everlasting air to tremble"; the first circle of hell, or limbo, contained the souls of virtuous people who lived before Christ or had not been baptized.   1. "A phenomenon which I have often noticed" [Eliot's note]. The church is in the financial district of London, where King William Street is also located.   2. An "average" modern name (with business associations) linked to the ancient battle of Mylae (260 B.C.), where Rome was victorious over its commercial rival, Carthage.   3. "Cf. the Dirge in Webster's *White Devil*" [Eliot's note]. The dirge, or song of lamentation, sung by Cornelia in John Webster's play (1625), asks to "keep the wolf far thence, that's foe to men," so that the wolf's nails may not dig up the bodies of her murdered relatives. Eliot's reversal of dog for wolf, and friend for foe, domesticates the grotesque scene; it may also foreshadow rebirth since (according to Weston's book), the rise of the Dog Star, Sirius, announced the flooding of the Nile and the consequent return of fertility to Egyptian soil.   4. "V. Baudelaire, Preface to *Fleurs du Mal*" [Eliot's note]. Baudelaire's poem preface, titled "To the Reader," ended "Hypocritical reader!—my likeness!—my brother!" The poet challenges the reader to recognize that both are caught up in the worst sin of all—the moral wasteland of *ennui* ("boredom") as lack of will, the refusal to care one way or the other. 5. Reference to a play, *A Game of Chess* (1627) by Thomas Middleton (1580–1627); see n. 5, p. 2083. Part II juxtaposes two scenes of modern sterility: an initial setting of wealthy boredom, neurosis, and lack of communication, and a pub scene in which similar concerns of appearance, sexual attraction, and thwarted childbirth are brought out more visibly, and in more vulgar language.   6. "Cf. *Antony and Cleopatra*, II, ii, 1.190" [Eliot's note]. A paler version of Cleopatra's splendor as she met her future lover, Antony: "The barge she sat in, like a burnished throne, / Burned on the water."

Held up by standards wrought with fruited vines
From which a golden Cupidon peeped out   80
(Another hid his eyes behind his wing)
Doubled the flames of sevenbranched candelabra
Reflecting light upon the table as
The glitter of her jewels rose to meet it,
From satin cases poured in rich profusion.   85
In vials of ivory and coloured glass
Unstoppered, lurked her strange synthetic perfumes,
Unguent, powdered, or liquid—troubled, confused
And drowned the sense in odours; stirred by the air
That freshened from the window, these ascended   90
In fattening the prolonged candle-flames,
Flung their smoke into the laquearia,[7]
Stirring the pattern on the coffered ceiling.
Huge sea-wood fed with copper
Burned green and orange, framed by the coloured stone,   95
In which sad light a carvèd dolphin swam.
Above the antique mantel was displayed
As though a window gave upon the sylvan scene[8]
The change of Philomel,[9] by the barbarous king
So rudely forced; yet there the nightingale[1]   100
Filled all the desert with inviolable voice
And still she cried, and still the world pursues,
"Jug Jug"[2] to dirty ears.
And other withered stumps of time
Were told upon the walls; staring forms   105
Leaned out, leaning, hushing the room enclosed.
Footsteps shuffled on the stair.
Under the firelight, under the brush, her hair
Spread out in fiery points
Glowed into words, then would be savagely still.   110

        "My nerves are bad to-night. Yes, bad. Stay with me.
Speak to me. Why do you never speak. Speak.
        What are you thinking of? What thinking? What?
I never know what you are thinking. Think."

        I think we are in rats' alley[3]   115
Where the dead men lost their bones.

        "What is that noise?"
                        The wind under the door.[4]

---

7. "Laquearia. V. *Aeneid*, I, 726: dependent lychni laquearibus aureis incensi, et noctem flammis funalia vincunt" [Eliot's note]. "Glowing lamps hang from the gold-paneled ceiling, and the torches conquer night with their flames"; the banquet setting of another classical love scene, in which Dido is inspired with a fatal passion for Aeneas.   8. "Sylvan scene. V. Milton, *Paradise Lost*, IV, 140" [Eliot's note]. Eden as first seen by Satan.   9. "V. Ovid, *Metamorphoses*, VI, Philomela" [Eliot's note]. Philomela was raped by her brother-in-law, King Tereus, who cut out her tongue so that she could not tell her sister, Procne. Later Procne is changed into a swallow and Philomela into a nightingale to save them from the king's rage after they have revenged themselves by killing his son.   1. "Cf. Part III, l.204" [Eliot's note].   2. Represents the nightingale's song in Elizabethan poetry.   3. "Cf. Part III, l.195" [Eliot's note].   4. "Cf. Webster: 'Is the wind in that door still?'" [Eliot's note]. From *The Devil's Law Case* (1623), 3.2.162, with the implied meaning "is there still breath in him?"

"What is that noise now? What is the wind doing?"
                    Nothing again nothing.   120
                                        "Do
"You know nothing? Do you see nothing? Do you remember
"Nothing?"

    I remember
Those are pearls that were his eyes.   125
"Are you alive, or not? Is there nothing in your head?"
                              But

O O O O that Shakespeherian Rag—
It's so elegant
So intelligent   130
"What shall I do now? What shall I do?"
"I shall rush out as I am, and walk the street
"With my hair down, so. What shall we do to-morrow?
"What shall we ever do?"
                              The hot water at ten.   135
And if it rains, a closed car at four.
And we shall play a game of chess,[5]
Pressing lidless eyes and waiting for a knock upon the door.

    When Lil's husband got demobbed,[6] I said—
I didn't mince my words, I said to her myself,
HURRY UP PLEASE ITS TIME[7]   140
Now Albert's coming back, make yourself a bit smart.
He'll want to know what you done with that money he gave you
To get yourself some teeth. He did, I was there.
You have them all out, Lil, and get a nice set,   145
He said, I swear, I can't bear to look at you.
And no more can't I, I said, and think of poor Albert,
He's been in the army four years, he wants a good time,
And if you don't give it him, there's others will, I said.
Oh is there, she said. Something o' that, I said.   150
Then I'll know who to thank, she said, and give me a straight look.
HURRY UP PLEASE ITS TIME
If you don't like it you can get on with it, I said.
Others can pick and choose if you can't.
But if Albert makes off, it won't be for lack of telling.   155
You ought to be ashamed, I said, to look so antique.
(And her only thirty-one.)
I can't help it, she said, pulling a long face,
It's them pills I took, to bring it off, she said.
(She's had five already, and nearly died of young George.)   160
The chemist[8] said it would be all right, but I've never been the same.
You are a proper fool, I said.
Well, if Albert won't leave you alone, there it is, I said,

---

5. "Cf. the game of chess in Middleton's *Women Beware Women*" [Eliot's note]. In this scene, a woman is seduced in a series of strategic steps that parallel the moves of a chess game, which is occupying her mother-in-law at the same time.   **6.** Demobilized, discharged from the army.   **7.** The British bartender's warning that the pub is about to close.   **8.** The druggist, who gave her pills to cause a miscarriage.

What you get married for if you don't want children?
HURRY UP PLEASE ITS TIME   165
Well, that Sunday Albert was home, they had a hot gammon,[9]
And they asked me in to dinner, to get the beauty of it hot—
HURRY UP PLEASE ITS TIME
HURRY UP PLEASE ITS TIME
Goonight Bill. Goonight Lou. Goonight May. Goonight.   170
Ta ta. Goonight. Goonight.
Good night, ladies, good night, sweet ladies, good night, good night.[1]

III. The Fire Sermon[2]

The river's tent is broken: the last fingers of leaf
Clutch and sink into the wet bank. The wind
Crosses the brown land, unheard. The nymphs are departed.   175
Sweet Thames, run softly, till I end my song.[3]
The river bears no empty bottles, sandwich papers,
Silk handkerchiefs, cardboard boxes, cigarette ends
Or other testimony of summer nights. The nymphs are departed.
And their friends, the loitering heirs of city directors;   180
Departed, have left no addresses.
By the waters of Leman I sat down and wept[4] . . .
Sweet Thames, run softly till I end my song,
Sweet Thames, run softly, for I speak not loud or long.
But at my back in a cold blast I hear[5]   185
The rattle of the bones, and chuckle spread from ear to ear.

A rat crept softly through the vegetation
Dragging its slimy belly on the bank
While I was fishing in the dull canal
On a winter evening round behind the gashouse   190
Musing upon the king my brother's wreck
And on the king my father's death before him.[6]
White bodies naked on the low damp ground
And bones cast in a little low dry garret,
Rattled by the rat's foot only, year to year.   195
But at my back from time to time I hear[7]
The sound of horns and motors, which shall bring[8]
Sweeney to Mrs. Porter in the spring.

9. Ham.   1. The popular song for a party's end ("Good Night, Ladies") shifts into Ophelia's last words in *Hamlet* (4.5.72) as she goes off to drown herself.   2. Reference to the Buddha's Fire Sermon (see n. 2, p. 2088), in which he denounced the fiery lusts and passions of earthly experience. "All things are on fire . . . with the fire of passion . . . of hatred . . . of infatuation." Part III describes the degeneration of even these passions in the sterile decadence of the modern Waste Land.   3. "V. Spenser, *Prothalamion*" [Eliot's note]. The line is the refrain of a marriage song by the Elizabethan poet Edmund Spenser (1552?–1599) and evokes a river of unpolluted pastoral beauty.   4. In Psalms 137.1, the exiled Hebrews sit by the rivers of Babylon and weep for their lost homeland. *Waters of Leman:* Lake Geneva (where Eliot wrote much of *The Waste Land*). A *leman* is a mistress or lover.   5. Distorted echo of Andrew Marvell's (1621–1678) poem *To His Coy Mistress:* "But at my back I always hear / Time's wingèd chariot hurrying near."
6. "Cf. *The Tempest* I.ii" [Eliot's note]. Ferdinand, the king's son, believing his father drowned and mourning his death, hears in the air a song containing the line that Eliot quotes earlier at lines 48 and 126.
7. "Cf. Marvell, 'To His Coy Mistress'" [Eliot's note].   8. "Cf. Day, *Parliament of Bees:* 'When of the sudden, listening, you shall hear, / A noise of horns and hunting, which shall bring / Actaeon to Diana in the spring, / Where all shall see her naked skin'" [Eliot's note]. The young hunter Actaeon was changed into a stag, hunted down, and killed when he came upon the goddess Diana bathing. Sweeney is in no such danger from his visit to Mrs. Porter.

O the moon shone bright on Mrs. Porter[9]
And on her daughter   200
They wash their feet in soda water
Et O ces voix d'enfants, chantant dans la coupole![1]

Twit twit twit
Jug jug jug jug jug jug
So rudely forc'd.   205
Tereu[2]

   Unreal City
Under the brown fog of a winter noon
Mr. Eugenides, the Smyrna merchant
Unshaven, with a pocket full of currants   210
C.i.f. London: documents at sight,[3]
Asked me in demotic French
To luncheon at the Cannon Street Hotel
Followed by a weekend at the Metropole.[4]

   At the violet hour, when the eyes and back   215
Turn upward from the desk, when the human engine waits
Like a taxi throbbing waiting,
I Tiresias,[5] though blind, throbbing between two lives,
Old man with wrinkled female breasts, can see
At the violet hour, the evening hour that strives   220
Homeward, and brings the sailor home from sea,[6]
The typist home at teatime, clears her breakfast, lights
Her stove, and lays out food in tins.
Out of the window perilously spread
Her drying combinations touched by the sun's last rays,   225
On the divan are piled (at night her bed)
Stockings, slippers, camisoles, and stays.
I Tiresias, old man with wrinkled dugs
Perceived the scene, and foretold the rest—
I too awaited the expected guest.   230

---

9. "I do not know the origin of the ballad from which these lines are taken: it was reported to me from Sydney, Australia" [Eliot's note]. A song popular among Allied troops during World War I. One version continues lines 199–201 as follows: "And so they oughter / To keep them clean." **1.** "V. Verlaine, *Parsifal*" [Eliot's note]. "And O these children's voices, singing in the dome!" (French); the last lines of a sonnet by Paul Verlaine (1844–1896), which ambiguously celebrates the Grail hero's chaste restraint. In Richard Wagner's opera, Parsifal's feet are washed to purify him before entering the presence of the Grail. **2.** Tereus, who raped Philomela (see line 99); also the nightingale's song. **3.** "The currants were quoted at a price 'carriage and insurance free to London'; and the Bill of Lading etc. were to be handed to the buyer upon payment of the sight draft" [Eliot's note]. **4.** Smyrna is an ancient Phoenician seaport, and early Smyrna merchants spread the Eastern fertility cults. In contrast, their descendant Mr. Eugenides ("Well-born") invites the poet to lunch in a large commercial hotel and a weekend at a seaside resort in Brighton. **5.** "Tiresias, although a mere spectator and not indeed a 'character,' is yet the most important personage in the poem, uniting all the rest. Just as the one-eyed merchant, seller of currants, melts into the Phoenician Sailor, and the latter is not wholly distinct from Ferdinand Prince of Naples, so all the women are one woman, and the two sexes meet in Tiresias. What Tiresias *sees*, in fact, is the substance of the poem. The whole passage from Ovid is of great anthropological interest" [Eliot's note]. The passage then quoted from Ovid's *Metamorphoses* (3.320–38) describes how Tiresias spent seven years of his life as a woman and thus experienced love from the point of view of both sexes. Blinded by Juno, he was recompensed by Jove with the gift of prophecy. **6.** "This may or may not appear as exact as Sappho's lines, but I had in mind the 'longshore' or 'dory' fisherman, who returns at nightfall" [Eliot's note]. The Greek poet Sappho's poem describes how the evening star brings home those whom dawn has sent abroad; there is also an echo of Robert Louis Stevenson's (1850–1894) *Requiem* 1.221: "Home is the sailor, home from the sea."

He, the young man carbuncular, arrives,
A small house agent's clerk, with one bold stare,
One of the low on whom assurance sits
As a silk hat on a Bradford⁷ millionaire.
The time is now propitious, as he guesses,   235
The meal is ended, she is bored and tired,
Endeavours to engage her in caresses
Which still are unreproved, if undesired.
Flushed and decided, he assaults at once;
Exploring hands encounter no defence;   240
His vanity requires no response,
And makes a welcome of indifference.
(And I Tiresias have foresuffered all
Enacted on this same divan or bed;
I who have sat by Thebes below the wall   245
And walked among the lowest of the dead.)⁸
Bestows one final patronising kiss,
And gropes his way, finding the stairs unlit . . .

      She turns and looks a moment in the glass,
Hardly aware of her departed lover;   250
Her brain allows one half-formed thought to pass:
"Well now that's done: and I'm glad it's over."
When lovely woman stoops to folly and⁹
Paces about her room again, alone,
She smoothes her hair with automatic hand,   255
And puts a record on the gramophone.

      "This music crept by me upon the waters"¹
And along the Strand, up Queen Victoria Street.
O City city,² I can sometimes hear
Beside a public bar in Lower Thames Street,   260
The pleasant whining of a mandoline
And a clatter and a chatter from within
Where fishmen lounge at noon: where the walls
Of Magnus Martyr³ hold
Inexplicable splendour of Ionian white and gold.   265

                The river sweats⁴
                Oil and tar

7. A manufacturing town in Yorkshire that prospered greatly during World War I.   8. Tiresias prophesied in the marketplace at Thebes for many years before dying and continuing to prophesy in Hades.
9. "V. Goldsmith, the song in *The Vicar of Wakefield*" [Eliot's note]. "When lovely woman stoops to folly / And finds too late that men betray / What charm can soothe her melancholy, / What art can wash her guilt away?" Oliver Goldsmith (ca. 1730–1774), *The Vicar of Wakefield* (1766).   1. "V. *The Tempest*, as above" [Eliot's note, referring to line 191]. Spoken by Ferdinand as he hears Ariel sing of his father's transformation by the sea, his eyes turning to pearls, his bones to coral, and everything else he formerly was into "something rich and strange."   2. A double invocation: the city of London and the City as London's central financial district (see lines 60 and 207). See also lines 375–76, the great cities of Western civilization.   3. "The interior of St. Magnus Martyr is to my mind one of the finest among Wren's interiors. See *The Proposed Demolition of Nineteen City Churches*: (P. S. King & Son, Ltd)" [Eliot's note]. The architect was Christopher Wren (1632–1723), and the church is located just below London Bridge on Lower Thames Street.
4. "The Song of the (three) Thames-daughters begins beings here. From line 292 to 306 inclusive they speak in turn. V. *Götterdämmerung* III.i.: the Rhine-daughters" [Eliot's note]. In Wagner's opera *The Twilight of the Gods* (1876), the three Rhine-maidens mourn the loss of their gold, which gave the river its sparkling beauty; lines 277–78 here echo the Rhine-maidens' refrain.

The barges drift
With the turning tide
Red sails   270
Wide
To leeward, swing on the heavy spar.
The barges wash
Drifting logs
Down Greenwich reach   275
Past the Isle of Dogs.[5]
       Weialala leia
       Wallala leialala

Elizabeth and Leicester[6]
Beating oars   280
The stern was formed
A gilded shell
Red and gold
The brisk swell
Rippled both shores   285
Southwest wind
Carried down stream
The peal of bells
White towers
       Weialala leia   290
       Wallala leialala

"Trams and dusty trees.
Highbury bore me. Richmond and Kew
Undid me.[7] By Richmond I raised my knees
Supine on the floor of a narrow canoe."   295

"My feet are at Moorgate,[8] and my heart
Under my feet. After the event
He wept. He promised 'a new start.'
I made no comment. What should I resent?'

"On Margate Sands.[9]   300
I can connect
Nothing with nothing.
The broken fingernails of dirty hands.
My people humble people who expect
Nothing.'   305
      la la

---

5. A peninsula opposite Greenwich on the Thames.   6. "V. Froude, *Elizabeth*, vol. I, ch. iv, letter of De Quadra to Philip of Spain: 'In the afternoon we were in a barge, watching the games on the river. (The queen) was alone with Lord Robert and myself on the poop, when they began to talk nonsense, and went so far that Lord Robert at last said, as I was on the spot there was no reason why they should not be married if the queen pleased" [Eliot's note]. Sir Robert Dudley (1532–1588), the earl of Leicester, was a favorite of Queen Elizabeth and at one point hoped to marry her.   7. "Cf. *Purgatorio*, V, 133: 'Ricorditi di me, che son la Pia; / Siena mi fe', disfecemi Maremma' " [Eliot's note]. La Pia, in Purgatory, recalls her seduction: "Remember me, who am La Pia. / Siena made me, Maremma undid me." Eliot's parody substitutes Highbury (a London suburb) and Richmond and Kew, popular excursion points on the Thames.   8. A London slum.   9. A seaside resort on the Thames.

> To Carthage then I came[1]
>
> Burning burning burning burning[2]
> O Lord Thou pluckest me out[3]
> O Lord Thou pluckest   310
>
> burning

IV. Death by Water

Phlebas the Phoenician, a fortnight dead,
Forgot the cry of gulls, and the deep sea swell
And the profit and loss.
                    A current under sea   315
Picked his bones in whispers. As he rose and fell
He passed the stages of his age and youth
Entering the whirlpool.
                    Gentile or Jew
O you who turn the wheel and look to windward,   320
Consider Phlebas, who was once handsome and tall as you.

V. What the Thunder Said[4]

After the torchlight red on sweaty faces
After the frosty silence in the gardens
After the agony in stony places
The shouting and the crying   325
Prison and palace and reverberation
Of thunder of spring over distant mountains
He who was living is now dead[5]
We who were living are now dying
With a little patience   330

    Here is no water but only rock
Rock and no water and the sandy road
The road winding above among the mountains
Which are mountains of rock without water
If there were water we should stop and drink   335
Amongst the rock one cannot stop or think

---

1. "V. St. Augustine's *Confessions*: 'to Carthage then I came, where a cauldron of unholy loves sang all about mine ears' " [Eliot's note]. The youthful Augustine is described. Carthage is also the scene of Dido's faithful love for Aeneas, referred to in line 92.   2. "The complete text of the Buddha's Fire Sermon (which corresponds in importance to the Sermon on the Mount) from which these words are taken, will be found translated in the late Henry Clarke Warren's *Buddhism in Translation* (Harvard Oriental Studies). Mr. Warren was one of the great pioneers of Buddhist studies in the Occident" [Eliot's note]. The Sermon on the Mount is in Matthew 5–7.   3. "From St. Augustine's *Confessions* again. The collocation of these two representatives of eastern and western asceticism, as the culmination of this part of the poem is not an accident" [Eliot's note]. See also Zechariah 3.2, where the high priest Joshua is described as a "brand plucked out of the fire."   4. "In the first part of Part V three themes are employed: the journey to Emmaus, the approach to the Chapel Perilous (see Miss Weston's book) and the present decay of eastern Europe" [Eliot's note]. On their journey to Emmaus (Luke 24.13–34), Jesus' disciples were joined by a stranger who later revealed himself to be the crucified and resurrected Christ. The *thunder* of the title is a divine voice in the Hindu *Upanishads* (see n. 3, p. 2090).   5. Allusions to stages in Christ's Passion: the betrayal, prayer in the garden of Gethsemane, imprisonment, trial, crucifixion, and burial. Despair reigns, for this is death before the Resurrection.

Sweat is dry and feet are in the sand
If there were only water amongst the rock
Dead mountain mouth of carious teeth that cannot spit
Here one can neither stand nor lie nor sit   340
There is not even silence in the mountains
But dry sterile thunder without rain
There is not even solitude in the mountains
But red sullen faces sneer and snarl
From doors of mudcracked houses   345
                          If there were water

   And no rock
   If there were rock
   And also water
   And water   350
   A spring
   A pool among the rock
   If there were the sound of water only
   Not the cicada[6]
   And dry grass singing   355
   But sound of water over a rock
   Where the hermit-thrush[7] sings in the pine trees
   Drip drop drip drop drop drop drop
   But there is no water

   Who is the third who walks always beside you?   360
When I count, there are only you and I together[8]
But when I look ahead up the white road
There is always another one walking beside you
Gliding wrapt in a brown mantle, hooded
I do not know whether a man or a woman   365
—But who is that on the other side of you?

   What is that sound high in the air[9]
Murmur of maternal lamentation
Who are those hooded hordes swarming
Over endless plains, stumbling in cracked earth   370
Ringed by the flat horizon only
What is the city over the mountains
Cracks and reforms and bursts in the violet air
Falling towers
Jerusalem Athens Alexandria   375
Vienna London
Unreal

6. Grasshopper or cricket; see line 23.   7. "The hermit-thrush which I have heard in Quebec Province.
. . . Its 'water-dripping song' is justly celebrated" [Eliot's note].   8. "The following lines were stimulated
by the account of one of the Antarctic expeditions (I forget which, but I think one of Shackleton's): it was
related that the party of explorers, at the extremity of their strength, had the constant delusion that there
was *one more member* than could actually be counted" [Eliot's note]. See also n. 4, p. 2088.   9. Eliot's
note to lines 367–77 refers to Hermann Hesse's *Blick ins Chaos* (Glimpse into Chaos) and a passage that
reads, translated, "Already half of Europe, already at least half of Eastern Europe is on the way to Chaos,
drives drunk in holy madness on the edge of the abyss and sings at the same time, sings drunk and hymn-like,
as Dimitri Karamazov sang [in Dostoevsky's *The Brothers Karamazov*]. The offended bourgeois laughs at
the songs; the saint and the seer hear them with tears."

A woman drew her long black hair out tight
And fiddled whisper music on those strings
And bats with baby faces in the violet light   380
Whistled, and beat their wings
And crawled head downward down a blackened wall
And upside down in air were towers
Tolling reminiscent bells, that kept the hours
And voices singing out of empty cisterns and exhausted wells.   385

    In this decayed hole among the mountains
In the faint moonlight, the grass is singing
Over the tumbled graves, about the chapel
There is the empty chapel, only the wind's home.
It has no windows, and the door swings,   390
Dry bones can harm no one.
Only a cock stood on the rooftree
Co co rico co co rico[1]
In a flash of lightning. Then a damp gust
Bringing rain   395

    Ganga was sunken, and the limp leaves
Waited for rain, while the black clouds
Gathered far distant, over Himavant.[2]
The jungle crouched, humped in silence.
Then spoke the thunder   400
DA
Datta: what have we given?[3]
My friend, blood shaking my heart
The awful daring of a moment's surrender
Which an age of prudence can never retract   405
By this, and this only, we have existed
Which is not to be found in our obituaries
Or in memories draped by the beneficent spider[4]
Or under seals broken by the lean solicitor
In our empty rooms   410
DA
Dayadhvam:[5] I have heard the key
Turn in the door once and turn once only

---

1. European version of the cock's crow: *cock-a-doodle-doo*. The cock crowed in Matthew 26.34 and 74, after Peter had denied Jesus three times.   2. A mountain in the Himalayas. *Ganga:* the river Ganges in India.   3. " 'Datta, dayadhvam, damyata' (Give, sympathise, control). The fable of the meaning of the Thunder is found in the *Brihadaranyaka*—Upanishad 5,1" [Eliot's note]. In the fable, the word *DA*, spoken by the supreme being Prajapati, is interpreted as *Datta* ("to give alms"), *Dayadhvam* ("to sympathise or have compassion"), and *Damyata* ("to have self-control") by gods, human beings, and demons respectively. The conclusion is that when the thunder booms DA DA DA, Prajapati is commanding that all three virtues be practiced simultaneously.   4. "Cf. Webster, *The White Devil*, V, vi: ' . . . they'll remarry / Ere the worm pierce your winding-sheet, ere the spider / Make a thin curtain for your epitaphs' " [Eliot's note].
5. Eliot's note on the command "to sympathize" or reach outside the self, cites two descriptions of helpless isolation. The first comes from Dante's *Inferno* 33.46: as Ugolino, imprisoned in a tower with his children to die of starvation, says "And I heard below the door of the horrible tower being locked up". The second is a modern description by the English philosopher F. H. Bradley (1846–1924) of the inevitably self-enclosed or private nature of consciousness: "My external sensations are no less private to myself than are my thoughts or my feelings. In either case my experience falls within my own circle, a circle closed on the outside; and, with all its elements alike, every sphere is opaque to the others which surround it. . . . In brief, regarded as an existence which appears in a soul, the whole world for each is peculiar and private to that soul" (*Appearance and Reality*).

We think of the key, each in his prison
Thinking of the key, each confirms a prison   415
Only at nightfall, aethereal rumours
Revive for a moment a broken Coriolanus[6]
DA
Damyata: The boat responded
Gaily, to the hand expert with sail and oar   420
The sea was calm, your heart would have responded
Gaily, when invited, beating obedient
To controlling hands
                              I sat upon the shore
Fishing,[7] with the arid plain behind me   425
Shall I at least set my lands in order?
London Bridge is falling down falling down falling down

Poi s'ascose nel foco che gli affina[8]
Quando fiam uti chelidon[9]—O swallow swallow
Le Prince d'Aquitaine à la tour abolie[1]   430
These fragments I have shored against my ruins
Why then Ile fit you. Hieronymo's mad againe.[2]
Datta. Dayadhvam. Damyata.
            Shantih   shantih   shantih[3]

From Four Quartets

Little Gidding[1]

Midwinter spring is its own season
Sempiternal though sodden towards sundown,
Suspended in time, between pole and tropic.
When the short day is brightest, with frost and fire,
The brief sun flames the ice, on pond and ditches,   5
In windless cold that is the heart's heat,
Reflecting in a watery mirror
A glare that is blindness in the early afternoon.
And glow more intense than blaze of branch, or brazier,

---

6. A proud Roman patrician who was exiled and led an army against his homeland. In Shakespeare's play, both his grandeur and his downfall come from a desire to be ruled only by himself.   7. "V. Weston: *From Ritual to Romance*; chapter on the Fisher King" [Eliot's note].   8. Eliot's note quotes a passage in the *Purgatorio* in which Arnaut Daniel (see n. 3, p. 2079) asks Dante to remember his pain. The line cited here, "then he hid himself in the fire which refines them" (*Purgatorio* 26.148), shows Daniel departing in fire which—in Purgatory—exists as a purifying rather than a destructive element.   9. "V. *Pervigilium Veneris*. Cf. Philomela in Parts II and III" [Eliot's note]. "When shall I be as a swallow?" A line from the *Vigil of Venus*, an anonymous late Latin poem, that asks for the gift of song; here associated with Philomela as a swallow, not the nightingale of lines 99–103 and 203–06.   1. "V. Gerard de Nerval, Sonnet *El Desdichado*" [Eliot's note]. The Spanish title means "The Disinherited One," and the sonnet is a monologue describing the speaker as a melancholy, ill-starred dreamer: "the Prince of Aquitaine in his ruined tower." Another line recalls the scene at the end of *Love Song of J. Alfred Prufrock* (p. 2079): "I dreamed in the grotto where sirens swim."   2. "V. Kyd's *Spanish Tragedy*" [Eliot's note]. Thomas Kyd's revenge play (1594) is subtitled "Hieronymo's Mad Againe." The protagonist "fits" his son's murderers into appropriate roles in a court entertainment so that they may all be killed.   3. "Shantih. Repeated as here, a formal ending to an Upanishad. 'The Peace which passeth understanding' is our equivalent to this word" [Eliot's note]. The *Upanishads* comment on the sacred Hindu scriptures, the *Vedas*.   1. A village in Huntingdonshire that housed a religious community in the 17th century. Eliot visited the (rebuilt) chapel on a midwinter day.

Stirs the dumb spirit: no wind, but pentecostal fire[2]   10
In the dark time of the year. Between melting and freezing
The soul's sap quivers. There is no earth smell
Or smell of living thing. This is the spring time
But not in time's covenant. Now the hedgerow
Is blanched for an hour with transitory blossom   15
Of snow, a bloom more sudden
Than that of summer, neither budding nor fading,
Not in the scheme of generation.
Where is the summer, the unimaginable
Zero summer?   20
        If you came this way,
Taking the route you would be likely to take
From the place you would be likely to come from,
If you came this way in may time,[3] you would find the hedges
White again, in May, with voluptuary sweetness.   25
It would be the same at the end of the journey,
If you came at night like a broken king,[4]
If you came by day not knowing what you came for,
It would be the same, when you leave the rough road
And turn behind the pig-sty to the dull façade   30
And the tombstone. And what you thought you came for
Is only a shell, a husk of meaning
From which the purpose breaks only when it is fulfilled
If at all. Either you had no purpose
Or the purpose is beyond the end you figured   35
And is altered in fulfilment. There are other places
Which also are the world's end, some at the sea jaws,
Or over a dark lake, in a desert or a city—
But this is the nearest, in place and time,
Now and in England.   40
        If you came this way,
Taking any route, starting from anywhere,
At any time or at any season,
It would always be the same: you would have to put off
Sense and notion. You are not here to verify,   45
Instruct yourself, or inform curiosity
Or carry report. You are here to kneel
Where prayer has been valid. And prayer is more
Than an order of words, the conscious occupation
Of the praying mind, or the sound of the voice praying.   50
And what the dead had no speech for, when living,
They can tell you, being dead: the communication
Of the dead is tongued with fire beyond the language of the living.
Here, the intersection of the timeless moment
Is England and nowhere. Never and always.   55

2. On the Pentecost day after Christ's resurrection, the apostles saw "cloven tongues like as of fire" (Acts 2.3) and were "filled with the Holy Ghost" (Acts 2.4).   3. When the May (Hawthorne) is in bloom. 4. Charles I, king of England (1600–1649), visited the religious community several times and went there secretly after his final defeat in the English Civil War.

II

Ash on an old man's sleeve
Is all the ash the burnt roses leave.
Dust in the air suspended
Marks the place where a story ended.
Dust inbreathed was a house—   60
The wall, the wainscot and the mouse.
The death of hope and despair,
    This is the death of air.[5]

There are flood and drouth
Over the eyes and in the mouth,   65
Dead water and dead sand
Contending for the upper hand.
The parched eviscerate soil
Gapes at the vanity of toil,
Laughs without mirth.   70
    This is the death of earth.

Water and fire succeed
The town, the pasture and the weed.
Water and fire deride
The sacrifice that we denied.   75
Water and fire shall rot
The marred foundations we forgot,
Of sanctuary and choir.
    This is the death of water and fire.

In the uncertain hour before the morning[6]   80
  Near the ending of interminable night
  At the recurrent end of the unending
After the dark dove[7] with the flickering tongue
  Had passed below the horizon of his homing
  While the dead leaves still rattled on like tin   85
Over the asphalt where no other sound was
  Between three districts whence the smoke arose
  I met one walking, loitering and hurried
As if blown towards me like the metal leaves
  Before the urban dawn wind unresisting.   90
  And as I fixed upon the down-turned face
That pointed scrutiny with which we challenge
  The first-met stranger in the waning dusk
  I caught the sudden look of some dead master

---

5. Allusion to "Fire lives in the death of air," a phrase from the pre-Socratic philosopher Heraclitus (535–475 B.C.) describing how one element (here, fire) lives at the expense of another (here, air).   6. The narrative passage from here to the end of Part II is written in tercets, a form that recalls Dante's use of *terza rima* (triple rhyme) in *The Divine Comedy*. Eliot later commented that this section was "the nearest equivalent to a canto of the *Inferno* or *Purgatorio*" that he could create.   7. A play on the emblem of the Holy Spirit that descended to the apostles at Pentecost and on the then-current German slang for bomb, *Taube* ("dove").

Whom I had known, forgotten, half recalled 95
  Both one and many; in the brown baked features
  The eyes of a familiar compound ghost
Both intimate and unidentifiable.
  So I assumed a double part,[8] and cried
  And heard another's voice cry: "What! are *you* here?" 100
Although we were not. I was still the same,
  Knowing myself yet being someone other—
  And he a face still forming; yet the words sufficed
To compel the recognition they preceded.
  And so, compliant to the common wind, 105
  Too strange to each other for misunderstanding,
In concord at this intersection time
  Of meeting nowhere, no before and after,
  We trod the pavement in a dead patrol.
I said: "The wonder that I feel is easy, 110
  Yet ease is cause of wonder. Therefore speak:
  I may not comprehend, may not remember."
And he: "I am not eager to rehearse
  My thought and theory which you have forgotten.
  These things have served their purpose: let them be. 115
So with your own, and pray they be forgiven
  By others, as I pray you to forgive
  Both bad and good. Last season's fruit is eaten
And the fullfed beast shall kick the empty pail.
  For last year's words belong to last year's language 120
  And next year's words await another voice.
But, as the passage now presents no hindrance
  To the spirit unappeased and peregrine
  Between two worlds become much like each other,
So I find words I never thought to speak 125
  In streets I never thought I should revisit
  When I left my body on a distant shore.
Since our concern was speech, and speech impelled us
  To purify the dialect of the tribe[9]
  And urge the mind to aftersight and foresight, 130
Let me disclose the gifts reserved for age
  To set a crown upon your lifetime's effort.
  First, the cold friction of expiring sense
Without enchantment, offering no promise
  But bitter tastelessness of shadow fruit 135
  As body and soul begin to fall asunder.
Second, the conscious impotence of rage
  At human folly, and the laceration
  Of laughter at what ceases to amuse.

---

8. The role of questioner of souls (after Dante in *The Divine Comedy*) and the role of one interrogating himself.   9. In his epitaph-sonnet for Edgar Allan Poe, *The Tomb of Edgar Poe*, the French poet Stéphane Mallarmé (1842–1898) defines the poet's role as purifying speech by using ordinary language (*the dialect of the tribe*) in a more precise and yet complex way, creating a new structure of interlocking or multiple meanings (see lines 221–24.)

And last, the rending pain of re-enactment   140
    Of all that you have done, and been; the shame
    Of motives late revealed, and the awareness
Of things ill done and done to others' harm
    Which once you took for exercise of virtue.
    Then fools' approval stings, and honour stains.   145
From wrong to wrong the exasperated spirit
    Proceeds, unless restored by that refining fire
    Where you must move in measure, like a dancer.'[1]
The day was breaking. In the disfigured street
    He left me, with a kind of valediction,   150
    And faded on the blowing of the horn.[2]

III

There are three conditions which often look alike
Yet differ completely, flourish in the same hedgerow:
Attachment to self and to things and to persons; detachment
From self and from things and from persons; and, growing between
     them, indifference   155
Which resembles the others as death resembles life,
Being between two lives—unflowering, between
The live and the dead nettle. This is the use of memory:
For liberation—not less of love but expanding
Of love beyond desire, and so liberation   160
From the future as well as the past. Thus, love of a country
Begins as attachment to our own field of action
And comes to find that action of little importance
Though never indifferent. History may be servitude,
History may be freedom. See, now they vanish,   165
The faces and places, with the self which, as it could, loved them,
To become renewed, transfigured, in another pattern.

Sin is Behovely,[3] but
All shall be well, and
All manner of thing shall be well.   170
If I think, again, of this place,
And of people, not wholly commendable,
Of no immediate kin or kindness,
But some of peculiar genius,
All touched by a common genius,   175
United in the strife which divided them;
If I think of a king at nightfall,
Of three men, and more, on the scaffold[4]
And a few who died forgotten
In other places, here and abroad,   180

---

1. In Dante's *Purgatorio* (26.148), fire is seen as a purgative or refining element, and characters are enveloped in flames that move in accord with their bodies.   **2.** The horn that marks the all-clear signal after an air raid; also the disappearance of Hamlet's father's ghost (*Hamlet* 1.2.157): "It faded on the crowing of the cock."   **3.** Inevitable. Lines 168–70 repeat the consoling words of Dame Julian of Norwich, a 14th-century English mystic: "Sin is behovabil, but all shall be well and all manner of thing shall be well."   **4.** Charles I and his chief advisers were executed on the scaffold after the English Civil War.

And of one who died blind and quiet,[5]
Why should we celebrate
These dead men more than the dying?
It is not to ring the bell backward
Nor is it an incantation
To summon the spectre of a Rose.   185
We cannot revive old factions[6]
We cannot restore old policies
Or follow an antique drum.
These men, and those who opposed them
And those whom they opposed   190
Accept the constitution of silence
And are folded in a single party.
Whatever we inherit from the fortunate
We have taken from the defeated
What they had to leave us—a symbol: 195
A symbol perfected in death.
And all shall be well and
All manner of thing shall be well
By the purification of the motive
In the ground of our beseeching.   200

IV

The dove descending breaks the air
With flame of incandescent terror
Of which the tongues declare
The one discharge from sin and error.
The only hope, or else despair   205
    Lies in the choice of pyre or pyre—
    To be redeemed from fire by fire.

Who then devised the torment? Love.
Love is the unfamiliar Name
Behind the hands that wove   210
The intolerable shirt of flame[7]
Which human power cannot remove.
    We only live, only suspire
    Consumed by either fire or fire.   215

V

What we call the beginning is often the end
And to make an end is to make a beginning.
The end is where we start from. And every phrase

---

5. The poet John Milton (1608–1674), who supported Parliament and the Commonwealth in the English
Civil War.   6. Alluding to the factionalisms of history exemplified here in the Wars of the Roses (1555–
85), when Yorkists, whose badge was the white rose, fought Lancastrians, whose badge was a red rose, for
the English throne. The struggle ended in the strong centralized monarchy of the Tudors, whose Tudor
Rose "in-folded" (cf. line 259) the other two. There is also allusion to the discovery, beyond history, of the
vast rose of pure light seen by Dante in the *Paradiso* (30.112ff), evoked in line 261.   7. The shirt,
poisoned with the blood of Nessus the centaur, that Deianeira (unknowingly) gave her husband, Hercules,
to strengthen his love for her. Instead, the shirt so burned Hercules' flesh that he chose death on a funeral
pyre to escape the agony.

And sentence that is right (where every word is at home,
Taking its place to support the others,   220
The word neither diffident nor ostentatious,
An easy commerce of the old and the new,
The common word exact without vulgarity,
The formal word precise but not pedantic,
The complete consort[8] dancing together)   225
Every phrase and every sentence is an end and a beginning,
Every poem an epitaph. And any action
Is a step to the block, to the fire, down the sea's throat
Or to an illegible stone: and that is where we start.
We die with the dying: 230
See, they depart, and we go with them.
We are born with the dead:
See, they return, and bring us with them.
The moment of the rose and the moment of the yew-tree
Are of equal duration. A people without history   235
Is not redeemed from time, for history is a pattern
Of timeless moments. So, while the light fails
On a winter's afternoon, in a secluded chapel
History is now and England.

With the drawing of this Love and the voice of this Calling[9]   240
We shall not cease from exploration
And the end of all our exploring
Will be to arrive where we started
And know the place for the first time.
Through the unknown, remembered gate   245
When the last of earth left to discover
Is that which was the beginning;
At the source of the longest river
The voice of the hidden waterfall
And the children in the apple-tree   250
Not known, because not looked for
But heard, half-heard, in the stillness
Between two waves of the sea.
Quick now, here, now, always[1]—
A condition of complete simplicity   255
(Costing not less than everything)
And all shall be well and
All manner of thing shall be well
When the tongues of flame are in-folded
Into the crowned knot of fire   260
And the fire and the rose are one.

8. Both "harmony" and "company." 9. Line from *The Cloud of Unknowing*, a 14th-century book of Christian mysticism. 1. This same line occurs toward the end of *Burnt Norton*, the first of the *Four Quartets*, where it also follows voices of children hidden in foliage; there is a suggestion of sudden insight gained in a moment of passive openness to illumination.

ANNA AKHMATOVA
1889–1966

The voice of Anna Akhmatova is intensely personal, whether she speaks as lover, wife, and mother or as a national poet commemorating the mute agony of millions. From the subjective love lyrics of her earliest work to the communal mourning of *Requiem* and the many-layered drama of *Poem without a Hero,* she expresses universal themes in terms of individual experience, and historical events through the filter of basic emotions like fear, love, hope, and pain. Akhmatova is one of the great Russian poets of the twentieth century, but she retains a broad sense of European culture, both past and present, and fills her later works with references to Western music, literature, and art that give a startling breadth and scope to her very personalized poetry. Too cosmopolitan and too independent to be tolerated by the authorities, Akhmatova was viciously attacked and her books suppressed (1922–40) because they did not fit the government-approved model of literature: they were too "individualistic" and were not "socially useful." Although she was rehabilitated in the 1960s and eventually achieved recognized status as national poet, Akhmatova was read in secret for a long time, chiefly for the perfection of her early love lyrics. After the death of Joseph Stalin in 1953, however, her collected poems—including poems of the war years and unknown texts written during the periods of enforced silence—brought the full range of her work to public attention.

She was born Anna Andreevna Gorenko on June 11, 1889, in a suburb of the Black Sea port of Odessa and in a traditional society that she described as "Dostoevsky's Russia." Her father was a maritime engineer and her mother an independent woman of populist sympathies who belonged to an early revolutionary group called People's Will. The poet took the pen name of Akhmatova (accented on the second syllable) from her maternal great-grandmother, who was of Tatar descent. Her family soon moved to Tsarskoe Selo ("the Czar's Village"), a small town outside St. Petersburg that had been for centuries the site of the summer palace of the czars, and also—perhaps more important for Akhmatova—a place where the great Romantic poet Alexandr Pushkin wrote his youthful works. She attended the local school at Tsarskoe Selo but completed her degree in Kiev; in 1907, she briefly studied law at the Kiev College for Women before moving to St. Petersburg to study literature.

In Tsarskoe Selo, Akhmatova met Nikolai Gumilyov, whom she married in April 1910. After their marriage, the couple visited Paris during the spring of 1910 and in 1911, meeting many writers and artists, including Amedeo Modigliani, who sketched Akhmatova several times and with whom she recalled wandering around Paris and reading aloud the poetry of Paul Verlaine. It was a time of change in the arts, and when the couple returned to St. Petersburg, Gumilyov helped organize a Poets' Guild that became the core of a new small literary movement, Acmeism, which rejected the romantic, quasi-religious aims of Russian Symbolism and (like Imagism) valued clarity and concreteness and a closeness to things of this Earth. The Symbolist–Acmeist debate went on inside a lively literary and social life, while the three main figures of Acmeism—Akhmatova, Gumilyov, and Osip Mandelstam—gained a reputation as important poets.

Akhmatova's first collection of poems, *Evening,* was published in the spring of 1912; it is an intensely personal collection of lyrics in which the poet describes evening as a time of awakening to love—and grief. There is a new clarity and directness to these traditionally romantic subjects, however, as for the first time in Russian poetry a woman in love expresses and analyzes her own emotions. In October of the same year, her son, Lev Gumilyov, was born; it was his arrest and imprisonment in 1935 that inspired the first poems of the cycle that would become *Requiem.* Lev was ultimately imprisoned for a total of fourteen years as the government sought a way to punish his mother, who would not or could not write according to the approved Socialist Realist style praising the government. Even after she had become a national poet known for her patriotic poetry during World War II, Akhmatova was still criticized by the Stalinist regime as a reactionary "half-harlot, half-nun" who wrote subjective love lyrics without social significance: the love poetry of *Evening*, *Rosary* (1914), and *The White Flock* (1917, published a month before the start of the Russian Revolution).

The White Flock was published during World War I, the destruction of which so shocked Akhmatova that she wrote, "This untimely death is so terrible / I cannot look at God's world." Yet more bloodshed was to follow in the civil war following the Revolution of 1917. Akhmatova refused to flee abroad, as many Russians did. Her marriage with Gumilyov was breaking up, and they divorced in 1918; she remarried an Assyriologist, Vladimir Shileiko, who did not approve of his wife's writing poetry and burned some of her poems (she divorced him in 1928). Akhmatova's political difficulties began in 1922. Although she and Gumilyov were divorced, his arrest and execution for counterrevolutionary activities in 1921 put her own status into question. After 1922 and the publication of *Anno Domini*, she was no longer allowed to publish and was forced into the unwilling withdrawal from public activity that Russians call "internal emigration." Officially forgotten, she was not forgotten in fact; in the schools, her poems were copied out by hand and circulated among students who never heard her name mentioned in a literature class.

Depending on a meager and irregular pension, Akhmatova prepared essays on the life and works of Pushkin, and wrote poems that would not appear until much later. Stalin's "Great Purge" of 1935–38 sent millions of people to prison camps and made the 1930s a time of terror and uncertainty for everyone. It is this fear and misery that is expressed in *Requiem*, as the poet blends references to her own life with an awareness of the common plight. The art critic Nikolai Punin, with whom she lived from 1926 to 1940, was arrested briefly in 1935; Osip Mandelstam, her great friend, was exiled to Voronezh in May 1934 and then sent to a prison camp in 1938, where he died the same year; her son, Lev, was arrested briefly in 1935 and again in 1938, remaining imprisoned until 1941, when he was allowed to enlist in the military. Composing *Requiem* itself was a risky act carried out over several years, and Akhmatova and her friend Lidia Chukovskaya memorized the stanzas to preserve the poem in the absence of written copy. Akhmatova wrote of Mandelstam (perhaps of them all) that "in the room of the poet in disgrace / Fear and the Muse keep watch by turns / And the night comes on / That knows no dawn." A temporary lifting of the ban against her works in 1940 did not last; although she was allowed to publish a new collection, *From Six Books*, the edition was recalled by officials after six months.

It was in 1940 that Akhmatova became interested in larger musical forms and began thinking in terms of cycles of poems instead of her accustomed separate lyrics. She envisaged a larger framework for the core poems of *Requiem* in this year, and wrote the "Dedication" and two epilogues. She also began work on the *Poem without a Hero*, a long and complex verse narrative in three parts that sums up many of her earlier themes: love, death, creativity, the unity of European culture, and the suffering of her people. During World War II the poet was allowed a partial return to public life, addressing women on the radio during the siege of Leningrad (St. Petersburg) in 1941, and writing patriotic lyrics such as the famous *Courage* (published in *Pravda* in 1942), which rallied the Russian people to defend their homeland (and national language) from enslavement. Despite her patriotic activities, she was subject to vicious official attacks after the war. Stalin's minister of culture, Andrei Zhdanov, in the famous Report of 1946 proclaimed the doctrine of Socialist Realism as the official style and attacked Akhmatova's "individualistic" writing as the "poetry of an overwrought upper-class lady who frantically races back and forth between boudoir and chapel." Akhmatova was immediately expelled from the Writer's Union, which meant that she was not officially recognized as a professional writer (and hence could not earn her living as one).

Unable once more to publish her work, she supported herself between 1946 and 1958 by translating poetry from a number of foreign languages. Her son was arrested again in 1949, and hoping to obtain his release, she wrote the kind of adulatory poetry in praise of Stalin that the regime required. The attempt was unsuccessful, and her son remained in prison until 1956. The Stalinist cycle, *In Praise of Peace* (1950), contains such clumsy imitations of socialist-realist poetry that it has been considered a parody: "Where a tank rumbled, there is now a peaceful tractor." Akhmatova later directed that it be omitted from her collected works.

During the slow thaw that followed Stalin's death in 1953, Akhmatova was rehabilitated. Gradually her poems were allowed back into print; an edition of selected poems with added texts was published in 1958, and in the same year she was even elected to an honorary position on the executive council of the Writer's Union. In 1965 a larger collection appeared, *The Flight of Time,* which contained a new series called *The Seventh Book* as well as part of the still-unfinished *Poem without a Hero.* She took an interest in the young writers who flocked to her and supported those who—like Josif Brodsky—were accused by the new order of being a "parasite on the state." Akhmatova's work was already recognized internationally: Robert Frost visited her on his trip to the Soviet Union in 1962, *Requiem* was first published "without her consent" in Munich in 1963 (not until 1987 was the full text published in the Soviet Union), and in 1964 she traveled to Italy to receive the Taormina poetry prize. She was surrounded by admirers when she visited England in 1965 to receive an honorary degree from Oxford University. Her death in 1966 signaled the end of an era in modern Russian poetry, for she was the last of the famous "quartet" that also included Mandelstam, Tsvetaeva, and Pasternak.

Requiem is a lyrical cycle, a series of poems written on a common theme, but it is also a short epic narrative. The story it tells is acutely personal, even autobiographical, but like an epic it also transcends personal significance and describes (as in *The Song of Roland*) a moment in the history of a nation. Akhmatova, who had seen her husband and son arrested and her friends die in prison camps, was only one of millions who had suffered similar losses in the purges of the 1930s. The "Preface," "Dedication," and two epilogues to *Requiem* constitute a framework examining this image of a common fate, while the core of numbered poems develops a more subjective picture and the stages of an individual drama. In the inner poems, Akhmatova blends her separate personal losses—husband, son, and friends—to create a single focus, the figure of a mother grieving for her condemned son. In the frame, the poet identifies herself with the crowd of women with whom she waited for seventeen months outside the Leningrad prison—women who, in turn, represent bereaved women throughout the Soviet Union. The "I" of the speaker throughout remains anonymous, in spite of the fact that she describes her personal emotions in the central poems; her identity is that of a sorrowing mother, and she is distinguished from her fellow-sufferers only by the poetic gift that makes her the "exhausted mouth, / Through which a hundred million scream." *Requiem* is at once a public and a private poem, a picture of individual grief simultaneously linked to a national disaster, and a vision of community suffering that extends past even national disaster into medieval Russian history and Greek mythology. The martyrdom of the Soviet people is consistently pictured in religious terms, from the recurrent mention of crosses and crucifixion to the culminating image of maternal suffering in Mary, the mother of Christ.

The "Dedication" and "Prologue" establish the context for the poem as a whole: the mass arrests in the 1930s after the assassination on December 1, 1934, of Sergei

Kirov, the top Communist Party official in Leningrad. The women waiting outside the Kresty ("Crosses") prison of Leningrad arrive at dawn in the coldest of weather, waiting for news of their loved ones, hoping to be allowed to pass them a parcel or a letter, and fearing the sentence of death or exile to the prison camps of frozen Siberia. Instead of living a natural life where "for someone the sunset luxuriates," these women and the prisoners are forced into a suspended existence of separation and uncertainty in which all values are inverted and the city itself has become only the setting for its prisons. It is a situation before which the great forces of nature bow in silent horror.

With the numbered poems, Akhmatova recounts the growing anguish of a bereaved mother as her son is arrested and sentenced to death. The speaker describes her husband's arrest at dawn, in the midst of the family. Her son was arrested later, and in the rest of the poem she relives her numbed incomprehension as she struggles against the increasing likelihood that he will be condemned to death. Recalling her own carefree adolescence in contrast to her current situation as she weeps outside the prison walls or pleads with Stalin to relent, the mother has a premonition of his fate that pushes her into the temporary relief of insanity and forgetting, and to a desire for her own arrest and death. After sentence is passed, the traumatized mother can speak of his execution only in oblique terms that are at once universal and potentially consoling: by shifting the image of death onto the plane of the Crucifixion and God's will. It is a tragedy that cannot be comprehended or looked at directly, just as, she suggests, at the Crucifixion "No one glanced and no one would have dared" to look at the grieving Mary. In the two epilogues, the grieving speaker returns from religious transcendence to Earth and current history. Here she takes on a newly composite identity, seeing herself not as an isolated sufferer but as reciprocally identified with the women whose fate she has shared. It is their memory she perpetuates by writing *Requiem*, and it is in their memory that she herself lives on. No longer the victim of purely personal tragedy, she has become a bronze statue commemorating a community of suffering, a figure shaped by circumstances into a monument of public and private grief.

Sam Driver, *Anna Akhmatova* (1972), is an excellent introduction to Akhmatova's work and its historical context that stresses the years up to 1922; and Roberta Reeder, *Anna Akhmatova: Poet and Prophet* (1995), is a good recent biography. David Wells, *Anna Akhmatova: Her Poetry* (1996), is a readable, well-documented study that discusses works in chronological order. Amanda Haight, *Anna Akhmatova: A Poetic Pilgrimage* (1976), and Susan Amert, *In a Shattered Mirror: The Later Poetry of Anna Akhmatova* (1992), are perceptive book-length studies. Ronald Hingley, *Nightingale Fever: Russian Poets in Revolution* (1981), discusses Akhmatova, Pasternak, Tsvetaeva, and Mandelstam in the context of Russian literary history and Soviet politics up to the early years of World War II. Wendy Rosslyn, ed., *The Speech of Unknown Eyes: Akhmatova's Readers on Her Poetry* (1990), collects a range of different responses. Sharon Leiter, *Akhmatova's Petersburg* (1983), examines the image of St. Petersburg as a focus for spiritual and historical themes in Akhmatova's poetry. Anna Akhmatova, *My Half Century: Selected Prose*, ed. Ronald Meyer (1992), includes autobiographical material, correspondence, short pieces on other writers, and an essay on Akhmatova's prose.

Requiem[1]

1935–1940

No, not under the vault of alien skies,[2]
And not under the shelter of alien wings—
I was with my people then,
There, where my people, unfortunately, were.

1961

Instead of a Preface

In the terrible years of the Yezhov terror,[3] I spent seventeen months in the
prison lines of Leningrad. Once, someone "recognized" me. Then a woman
with bluish lips standing behind me, who, of course, had never heard me
called by name before, woke up from the stupor to which every one had
succumbed and whispered in my ear (everyone spoke in whispers there):
"Can you describe this?"
And I answered: "Yes, I can."
Then something that looked like a smile passed over what had once been
her face.

April 1, 1957
Leningrad[4]

Dedication

Mountains bow down to this grief,
Mighty rivers cease to flow,
But the prison gates hold firm,
And behind them are the "prisoners' burrows"
And mortal woe.   5
For someone a fresh breeze blows,
For someone the sunset luxuriates—
We[5] wouldn't know, we are those who everywhere
Hear only the rasp of the hateful key
And the soldiers' heavy tread.   10
We rose as if for an early service,
Trudged through the savaged capital
And met there, more lifeless than the dead;
The sun is lower and the Neva[6] mistier,
But hope keeps singing from afar.   15
The verdict . . . And her tears gush forth,
Already she is cut off from the rest,
As if they painfully wrenched life from her heart,
As if they brutally knocked her flat,
But she goes on . . . Staggering . . . Alone . . .   20

---

1. Translated by Judith Hemschemeyer.   2. A phrase borrowed from *Message to Siberia* by the Russian
poet Pushkin (1799–1837).   3. In 1937–38, mass arrests were carried out by the secret police, headed
by Nikolai Yezhov.   4. The prose preface was written after her son had been released from prison and it
was possible to think of editing the poem for publication.   5. The women waiting in line before the
prison gates.   6. The large river that flows through St. Petersburg.

Where now are my chance friends
Of those two diabolical years?
What do they imagine is in Siberia's storms,[7]
What appears to them dimly in the circle of the moon?
I am sending my farewell greeting to them.   25

March 1940

Prologue

That was when the ones who smiled
Were the dead, glad to be at rest.
And like a useless appendage, Leningrad
Swung from its prisons.
And when, senseless from torment,   5
Regiments of convicts marched,
And the short songs of farewell
Were sung by locomotive whistles.
The stars of death stood above us
And innocent Russia writhed   10
Under bloody boots
And under the tires of the Black Marias.[8]

I

They led you away at dawn,
I followed you, like a mourner,
In the dark front room the children were crying,[9]
By the icon shelf the candle was dying.
On your lips was the icon's chill.[1]   5
The deathly sweat on your brow . . . Unforgettable!—
I will be like the wives of the Streltsy,[2]
Howling under the Kremlin towers.

1935

II

Quietly flows the quiet Don,[3]
Yellow moon slips into a home.

He slips in with cap askew,
He sees a shadow, yellow moon.

This woman is ill,   5
This woman is alone,

---

7. Victims of the purges who were not executed were condemned to prison camps in Siberia. Their wives
were allowed to accompany them into exile, although they had to live in towns at a distance from the camps.
8. Police cars for conveying those arrested.   9. Akhmatova's third husband, the art historian Nikolai
Punin, was arrested at dawn while the children (his daughter and her cousin) cried.   1. The icon—a
small religious painting—was set on a shelf before which a candle was kept lit. Punin had kissed the icon
before being taken away.   2. Elite troops organized by Ivan the Terrible around 1550. They rebelled and
were executed by Peter the Great in 1698. Pleading in vain, their wives and mothers saw the men killed
under the towers of the Kremlin.   3. The great Russian river, often celebrated in folk songs. This poem
is modeled on a simple, rhythmic short folk song known as a *chastuska*.

Husband in the grave,[4] son in prison,
Say a prayer for me.

III

No, it is not I, it is somebody else who is suffering.
I would not have been able to bear what happened,
Let them shroud it in black,
And let them carry off the lanterns . . .

                             Night.   5

1940

IV

You should have been shown, you mocker,
Minion of all your friends,
Gay little sinner of Tsarskoye Selo,[5]
What would happen in your life—
How three-hundredth in line, with a parcel,   5
You would stand by the Kresty prison,

Your tempestuous tears
Burning through the New Year's ice.
Over there the prison poplar bends,
And there's no sound—and over there how many   10
Innocent lives are ending now . . .

V

For seventeen months I've been crying out,
Calling you home.
I flung myself at the hangman's[6] feet,
You are my son and my horror.
Everything is confused forever,   5
And it's not clear to me
Who is a beast now, who is a man,
And how long before the execution.
And there are only dusty flowers,
And the chinking of the censer, and tracks   10
From somewhere to nowhere.
And staring me straight in the eyes,
And threatening impending death,
Is an enormous star.[7]

1939

---

4. Akhmatova's first husband, the poet Nikolai Gumilyov, was shot in 1921. 5. Akhmatova recalls her early, carefree, and privileged life in Tsarskoe Selo outside St. Petersburg. 6. Stalin's. Akhmatova wrote a letter to him pleading for the release of her son. 7. The *star*, the *censer*, the foliage, and the confusion between beast and man recall apocalyptic passages in the Book of Revelation (8.5, 7, 10–11 and 9.7–10).

VI

The light weeks will take flight,
I won't comprehend what happened.
Just as the white nights[8]
Stared at you, dear son, in prison

So they are staring again,   5
With the burning eyes of a hawk,
Talking about your lofty cross,
And about death.

1939

VII

THE SENTENCE

And the stone word fell
On my still-living breast.
Never mind, I was ready.
I will manage somehow.

Today I have so much to do: 5
I must kill memory once and for all,
I must turn my soul to stone,
I must learn to live again—

Unless . . . Summer's ardent rustling
Is like a festival outside my window.   10
For a long time I've foreseen this
Brilliant day, deserted house.

June 22, 1939[9]
Fountain House

VIII

TO DEATH

You will come in any case—so why not now?
I am waiting for you—I can't stand much more.
I've put out the light and opened the door
For you, so simple and miraculous.
So come in any form you please,   5
Burst in as a gas shell
Or, like a gangster, steal in with a length of pipe,
Or poison me with typhus fumes.

---

8. In St. Petersburg, because it is so far north, the nights around the summer solstice are never totally dark.   9. The date that her son was sentenced to labor camp.

Or be that fairy tale you've dreamed up,[1]
So sickeningly familiar to everyone— 10
In which I glimpse the top of a pale blue cap[2]
And the house attendant white with fear.
Now it doesn't matter anymore. The Yenisey[3] swirls,
The North Star shines.
And the final horror dims 15
The blue luster of beloved eyes.

August 19, 1939
Fountain House

IX

Now madness half shadows
My soul with its wing,
And makes it drunk with fiery wine
And beckons toward the black ravine.

And I've finally realized 5
That I must give in,
Overhearing myself
Raving as if it were somebody else.

And it does not allow me to take
Anything of mine with me 10
(No matter how I plead with it,
No matter how I supplicate):

Not the terrible eyes of my son—
Suffering turned to stone,
Not the day of the terror, 15
Not the hour I met with him in prison,

Not the sweet coolness of his hands,
Not the trembling shadow of the lindens,
Not the far-off, fragile sound—
Of the final words of consolation. 20

May 4, 1940
Fountain House

1. A denunciation to the police for imaginary crimes, common during the purges as people hastened to protect themselves by accusing their neighbors.   2. The NKVD (secret police) wore blue caps.   3. A river in Siberia along which there were many prison camps.

X

CRUCIFIXION

"Do not weep for Me, Mother,
I am in the grave."

1

A choir of angels sang the praises of that momentous hour,
And the heavens dissolved in fire.
To his Father He said: "Why hast Thou forsaken me!"[4]
And to his Mother: "Oh, do not weep for Me . . ."[5]

1940
Fountain House

2

Mary Magdalene beat her breast and sobbed,
The beloved disciple[6] turned to stone,
But where the silent Mother stood, there
No one glanced and no one would have dared.

1943
Tashkent

Epilogue I

I learned how faces fall,
How terror darts from under eyelids,
How suffering traces lines
Of stiff cuneiform on cheeks,
How locks of ashen-blonde or black   5
Turn silver suddenly,
Smiles fade on submissive lips
And fear trembles in a dry laugh.
And I pray not for myself alone,
But for all those who stood there with me   10
In cruel cold, and in July's heat,
At that blind, red wall.

Epilogue II

Once more the day of remembrance[7] draws near.
I see, I hear, I feel you:

The one they almost had to drag at the end,
And the one who tramps her native land no more,

---

4. Jesus' last words from the Cross (Matthew 27.46).   5. These words and the epigraph refer to a line
from the Russian Orthodox prayer sung at services on Easter Saturday: "Weep not for Me, Mother, when
you look upon the grave." Jesus is comforting Mary with the promise of his resurrection.   6. The apostle
John.   7. In the Russian Orthodox Church, a memorial service is held on the anniversary of a death.

And the one who, tossing her beautiful head,   5
Said: "Coming here's like coming home."

I'd like to name them all by name,
But the list[8] has been confiscated and is nowhere to be found.

I have woven a wide mantle for them
From their meager, overheard words.   10

I will remember them always and everywhere,
I will never forget them no matter what comes.

And if they gag my exhausted mouth
Through which a hundred million scream,

Then may the people remember me   15
On the eve of my remembrance day.

And if ever in this country
They decide to erect a monument to me,

I consent to that honor
Under these conditions—that it stand   20

Neither by the sea, where I was born:
My last tie with the sea is broken,

Nor in the tsar's garden near the cherished pine stump,[9]
Where an inconsolable shade[1] looks for me,

But here, where I stood for three hundred hours,   25
And where they never unbolted the doors for me.

This, lest in blissful death
I forget the rumbling of the Black Marias,

Forget how that detested door slammed shut
And an old woman howled like a wounded animal.   30

And may the melting snow stream like tears
From my motionless lids of bronze,

And a prison dove coo in the distance,
And the ships of the Neva sail calmly on.

March 1940

8. Of prisoners.   9. The gardens and park surrounding the summer palace in Tsarskoe Selo. Akhmatova
writes elsewhere of the stump of a favorite tree in the gardens and of the poet Pushkin, whom she describes
as walking in the park.   1. A ghost; probably the restless spirit of Akhmatova's executed husband, Gumilyov, who had courted her in Tsarskoe Selo.

DADA-SURREALIST POETRY: A SELECTION

Dada-Surrealist poetry was written for the intuitions. Not that it lacks structure or its own inner logic, but it appeals directly to the impulsive, irrational, and unconscious layers of human experience. Part of a social and artistic revolution that began during World War I, flourished as a group movement until World War II, and found adherents around the world in succeeding decades, Dada-Surrealism exploded literary and artistic conventions to liberate the human imagination and catalyze, in each reader or spectator, an unending process of growth. In less than thirty years, Surrealism's challenge to create revolutionary insights, shocking combinations, and unheard-of realities through the power of the imagination had attracted followers in literature and art from Africa to Canada, Denmark to Peru, and Japan to Czechoslovakia. Surrealist reviews sprang up in the Antilles (*Légitime Défense* and *Tropiques*), Mexico (*Dyn*), Chile (*Mandragora*), Romania (*Unu*), Argentina (*Que*), and elsewhere. Many writers, like the Martinican Aimé Césaire, the Senegalese Léopold Sédar Senghor, the Chilean Pablo Neruda, the Greek Odysseus Elytis, the Japanese Kobo Abe, or the Icelandic Haldor Laxness, passed through a period in which they experimented with startling images and combinations of ideas, dreamlike scenes, or "automatic" writing to disclose unconscious associations and impulses. Others, among them the Czech poet Victor Neszval and the Irish "Spike" Milligan, creator of *The Goon Show* on British radio, are specifically associated with Surrealism. There was never a single formula for Surrealist writers, however: such a thought would have been anathema to these consciously anticonventional artists. Instead, Surrealism's influence spread because its ideas suggested ways to revitalize art and literature; and its groups, expositions, and reviews were opportunities to discuss Surrealist principles and to explore, in common, new modes of expression. Dada-Surrealist writers sought to present desire, not discipline; automatic writing, not rationality or grammar; dream worlds, not common sense; marvels (sur-realism), not realism; joyous pursuit of error, not predetermined routes to a goal; and art and poetry as living experience, not as products canonized or hung in museums. Their much-publicized attacks on audience expectations were intended to awaken minds that had been numbed by habit—by the day-to-day routine of work, respectability, and reverence for authority. Games (and they invented many) were perhaps the most authentic expression of Dada-Surrealist attitudes, for games required live participation by several people, an exchange of ideas, and successive moves that always opened new horizons.

It is thus paradoxical that Dada-Surrealism produced written works that became an influential part of literary history, reprinted and anthologized in their turn. This potential paradox was not lost on the group, and quarrels arose if anyone seemed too close to mainstream publication. Yet the major Dada-Surrealist writers were still artists who wished to create new forms, and they found in the movement a fresh vision and different concepts of poetic language. If their printed poetry had found its final shape, unlike a game, it was nonetheless written to launch a second game in the mind of the reader. By proposing startling combinations of images and ideas, and making these combinations attractive, Dada-Surrealist poets guided readers into trying new modes of thought. They created beautiful, unexpected combinations that were rationally impossible but made a strange, intuitive sense in terms of unconscious emotions or desires. In the earlier stages of the movement, they experimented with "automatic" writing: that is, they wrote without exerting conscious or rational control over the free flow of speech, to bring subterranean impulses to the surface. (The genuine automatism of Surrealist poetry is much debated, and some works printed as automatic poems were in fact edited for publication.) Some writers—like Tristan Tzara and Paul Éluard—eventually moved past Surrealism to other styles; others, like Kurt Schwitters and Aimé Césaire, were already working inside a larger framework. Only André Breton, the founding figure of Parisian Surrealism, remained true to its principles (which he usually defined) throughout his life. His own work strongly influenced Joyce Mansour, a younger writer whose macabre work is in many ways an ironic comment on the glorious visions of early Surrealism. Selections from the six writers presented here constitute a brief introduction to Dada-Surrealism but are only a small part of a movement whose influence has been felt worldwide in art and literature.

Tristan Tzara (born in Romania as Samuel Rosenstock) is the best-known figure of Dadaism. His celebrity is in part owing to his own efforts, since Dadaism itself was a decentered movement, and early Dada groups existed in Berlin, Cologne, Hanover (Germany), Zürich, and New York, each with its distinguishing characteristics. In 1916, the German poet Hugo Ball had received permission to set up a literary cabaret in a Zürich bar; called the Cabaret Voltaire, it attracted a group of writers, artists, and performers who were fleeing the war and who were eager to attack conservative cultural institutions. The Cabaret Voltaire was the scene of raucous performances with masks, costumes, simultaneous readings, nonsense poetry, "sound" poetry, and chants with African drums—to mention only a few. Modern "happenings" descend from Dadaist performance art.

Tzara was part of the group, and when the Cabaret closed he became the most aggressive Dada publicist, issuing seven Dadist manifestos that are now themselves considered artistic compositions. His *First Dadaist Manifesto* of 1918 is a violent, nihilist, ironic attack on ready-made ideas ("I am against systems, the most acceptable system is the one of not having any system, on principle"). Throughout the manifesto, Tzara uses nonsense words and aggressive attacks to counteract conventional images of discipline and order: after "IDEAL IDEAL IDEAL" and "KNOWLEDGE KNOWLEDGE KNOWLEDGE" he shouts "BOOMBOOM BOOMBOOM BOOMBOOM." Yet there is both method and artistry in his madness, as can be seen in the concluding section of the *First Dadaist Manifesto, DADAIST DISGUST*, with its insistent rhythms and refrains whose mounting excitement is indicated by increasingly varied print. Tzara has just proclaimed "the opposition of all cosmic faculties" to the causes of this disgust, and he proceeds with a cumulative summary of such oppositions. Dada will abolish conventional ideas and social hierarchies; it will abolish the long view of chronological perspective and live for the spontaneous joy of momentary madness; Dada unites contraries because definitions do not matter; and Dada reaches for freedom, which, in a burst of twisting irrational images, turns out to be LIFE itself. Communicating "life" is the goal and substance of Dadaist poetry, life that explodes past any artificial and socially engineered restraints. Another of Tzara's manifestos, the ironically titled *Proclamation Without Pretention*, contrasts Dadaist spontaneity and willingness to embrace living contradictions with academic "Art," which is concocted by an artistic "druggist" using formulas and logic. Like Verlaine in his *Art of Poetry*, the Dadaist and Surrealist poets were suspicious of Art and Literature insofar as they evoked self-reproducing traditions: poetry, in its etymological sense as *creativity*, was far more important. The wit and humor of this *Proclamation* and its playful typography, not all of which can be reproduced here, make it far more than a conventional manifesto.

Kurt Schwitters, who lived in Hanover, Germany, until the Nazis forced him to flee to England, is best known for his collages and "Merz" constructions. *Merz*, a nonsense word he extracted from a German bank sign, *Commerzbank*, became the artist's term for small and large artworks he constructed out of objects collected at random or obtained as personal mementos. His home in Hanover contained an enormous Merz column that grew outward and up through the ceiling over the years; it was destroyed during World War II. Schwitters's poetry includes, in addition to *Anna Blume*, the *Sonata in Vowels*, a startling and impressive sound poem in which a series of vowels is arranged in sonata form and performed by the artist as a piece of music. *Anna Blume* itself is a happily delirious love lyric that expresses the speaker's delight in both Anna's person and her first name (a palindrome: it is the same forward and backward). A conversational sequence of associations and contradictions, and the humorous parody of a logical syllogism, together create a gently sensual portrait.

When Tzara moved to Paris in 1920, he was welcomed enthusiastically by a group of young French poets that included Paul Éluard (born Eugène Grindel) and André Breton. Both are central figures in French Surrealism. Éluard reached a particularly wide audience with his love lyrics, magical evocations of transfigured landscapes that teach, in the poet's words, "how to see" and "to see otherwise, other things." Poems from *Capital of Pain* (1926) reshape familiar images into new subjective creations: the speaker is so close to his beloved that they seem to be somehow identical; elsewhere, she permeates the natural landscape, and they are again indistinguishable. Various images achieve the shock that the Surrealists prized for its ability to jolt readers out of their habitual ways of seeing: "She is standing on my eyelids," for example, may ultimately evoke the poet dreaming of his beloved but is first of all a startling image. Yet there is usually a kind of inner logic: the irrational (but imaginable) pictures of the second stanza are explained in the last lines, when the poet comments that her effect is to make him speak lyrical nonsense. Éluard's "seeing otherwise" is implicit in variously transfigured scenes that depict, on the one hand, the poet leaving everyday reality behind as he drifts into the rich inner life of dream and, on the other, a subjective moment that is constructed as a fleeting yet inexorable mirror. His visionary poetry, full of metamorphoses, points toward the "marvelous" state that was the Surrealists' poetic goal.

Breton, often called the Pope of Surrealism for his dedication to Surrealist principles and his insistence on doctrinal purity, outlined a series of core beliefs in the first Surrealist *Manifesto* (1924): absolute freedom of imagination, respect for madness as special inner vision, a belief in the revelatory power of dreams and the unconscious, a hatred of clichéd or predictable thinking (and a related fascination with chance), and the power of "mad love" to transcend rationality and project the lover to a sublime or marvelous state *beyond*. Breton is always alert for the moment when reality metamorphoses into Surrealist experience, and in *Vigilance* this alertness is rewarded: the dreaming poet sets his everyday surroundings on fire and observes a gradual change of state in which he himself finally participates. Another version of metamorphosis occurs in *Free Union*, a poem celebrating his wife in a cumulative series of associations that extend, finally, to the four basic elements: earth, air, fire, and water. *Free Union* means both free love and the free union or association of images: this series of apparently random associations with the woman (in imitation of the medieval *blason* or poem of extended comparison) is in fact organized by visual and sonorous associations, one sound or image suggesting another.

With Aimé Césaire and Joyce Mansour, Surrealist poetry takes on a new cast. Césaire is best known for his long poem *Notebook of a Return to the Native Land* (1939), several plays, and the *Discourse on Colonialism* (1950), and as a founder of Négritude. His Surrealist decade begins officially in 1941 when Breton, coming across Césaire's poetry in the journal *Tropiques*, arranges to meet him and becomes a fervent supporter. Césaire's *Miraculous Weapons* (1946) employs Surrealist verbal techniques in explosive scenes that emphasize processes of destruction, liberation, and new birth, all the while evoking the varied landscape of his native Martinique. These poems proceed by sequences of association and opposition, juxtaposing local and cosmic images. A chameleon, a child diving for coins, or a tropical tree appear simultaneously with the voice of thunderbolts, the mythic serpent sun, and a poet-prophet who is an organic part of the miracles he describes. Césaire was interested in liberating unconscious patterns of thought through the Surrealist tactic of automatic writing: *The Virgin Forest* is one such experiment, later separated into three shorter prose poems one of which, *Day and Night,* is printed here.

Joyce Mansour, an Egyptian who lived much of her adult life in Paris, was one of three contemporary poets praised by Breton in a 1960 interview, and she herself dedicated three books to Breton, recognizing his influence. Her work, however, reverses many of the traditional Surrealist themes and attitudes. Where the founding (male) Surrealist poets experience the marvelous through the mad love of a woman, Mansour develops the same visionary erotics in terms of men, and its horizons are not so celebratory. Her materialist, visceral, and predatory vision is focused in terms of this world and its images, not on an expanding, infinitely multiplied cosmos. Mansour's eyes may close, like Éluard's, in a dreamlike vision that contains impossible images, and she too may imagine identity with her partner, but the result is a self-conscious (and, therefore, faintly humorous) landscape of nightmare.

"Surrealism," says Breton, "is based on the belief in the superior reality of certain forms of previously neglected associations, in the omnipotence of dream, in the disinterested play of thought." The Dada-Surrealist attempt to uncover and reproduce such associations, and to use the free play of thought as model for literary creation, is still with us at the beginning of the twenty-first century.

Valuable discussions of Dada include Alan Young, *Dada and After: Extremist Modernism and English Literature* (1981), and John D. Erickson, *Dada: Performance, Poetry, and Art* (1984). Studies of Surrealist poets include Mary Ann Caws, *The Poetry of Dada and Surrealism* (1970), and J. H. Matthews, *Surrealist Poetry in France* (1969), which has a chapter on Mansour. Maurice Nadeau, *History of Surrealism* (1954), trans. Richard Howard, is an early and authoritative history of Surrealism to 1939; it includes an extensive chronology and a selection of Surrealist documents. Herbert S. Gershman, *The Surrealist Revolution in France* (1974), is a good shorter account that also contains a chronology. William S. Rubin, *Dada, Surrealism and Their Heritage* (1968), gives a detailed history of Surrealist art with many superb illustrations; a shorter history is available in Dawn Ades, *Dada and Surrealism* (1974). Marcel Raymond, *From Baudelaire to Surrealism* (1950), trans. G.M., and Anna Balakian, *The Literary Origins of Surrealism* (1947), trace Surrealism's roots in European Romantic and Symbolist poetry. Discussions of Aimé Césaire include Gregson Davis, *Aimé Césaire* (1994), and A. James Arnold, *Modernism and Negritude* (1981).

TRISTAN TZARA
1896–1963

From Dada Manifesto 1918

DADAIST DISGUST[1]

Every product of disgust capable of becoming a negation of the family is *dada*; the whole being protesting in its destructive force with clenched fists: **DADA**; knowledge of all the means rejected up to this point by the timid sex of easy compromise and sociability: DADA; abolition of logic, dance of all those impotent to create: *DADA*; of all hierarchy and social equation installed for the preservation of values by our valets: DADA; each and every object, feelings and obscurities, apparitions and the precise shock of parallel lines, can be means for the combat: DADA; abolition of memory: **DADA**; abolition of archeology: *DADA*; abolition of the prophets: ***DADA***; abolition of the future: DADA; an absolute indisputable belief in each god immediate product of spontaneity: **DADA**; elegant and unprejudicial leap from one har-

---

1. Both Tzara selections translated from the French by Mary Ann Caws. The last section of Tzara's *Dada Manifesto 1918*.

mony to the other sphere; trajectory of a word tossed like a sonorous cry of phonograph record; respecting all individualities in their momentary madness: serious, fearful, timid, ardent, vigorous, determined, enthusiastic; stripping its chapel of every useless awkward accessory; spitting out like a luminous waterfall any unpleasant or amorous thought, or coddling it—with the lively satisfaction of knowing that it doesn't matter—with the same intensity in the bush of his soul, free of insects for the aristocrats, and gilded with archangels' bodies. Freedom: *DADA DADA DADA*, shrieking of contracted pains, intertwining of contraries and of all contradictions, grotesqueries, nonsequiturs: LIFE.

Proclamation Without Pretention[2]

Art goes to sleep for the birth of a new world
"ART"—a *parrot word*—replaced by **DADA**
PLESIAUSAURUS,[3] or handkerchief
The talent WHICH YOU CAN LEARN *makes the poet a druggist*
TODAY *criticism balances no longer launches resemblances*   5
Hypertrophic painters hyperestheticized and hypnotized by the
hyacinths of muezzins of hypocritical appearance
CONSOLIDATE THE EXACT HARVEST OF CALCULATIONS
HYPERDROME[4] OF IMMORTAL GUARANTEES: *There is no importance there*
is no transparency or apparency   10
MUSICIANS BREAK YOUR BLIND INSTRUMENTS on the stage
The **SYRINGE** *is only for my understanding.* **I am writing because**
it is as natural as pissing as being sick
Art needs an operation
Art is a ***PRETENTION*** heated in the TIMIDITY of the urinary   15
basin, **Hysteria** born in the **Studio**

We are seeking **upright pure sober unique** strength we are
seeking **NOTHING** we affirm the **VITALITY** of each instant
the anti-philosophy of **Spontaneous** acrobatic
In this moment I hate the man who whispers before intermission—   20
eau de cologne—bitter theater. CHEERY WIND.
IF EVERYBODY SAYS THE OPPOSITE IT IS BECAUSE THEY ARE RIGHT.
Prepare the geyser actions of our blood—submarine formation
of transchromatic airplanes, cellular metals numbered in the
leap of images
                    above the regulations of the   25
BEAUTIFUL and its control
It is not for the runts who are still worshipping
their navel

2. Published in 1918.   3. A large prehistoric marine reptile.   4. A play on *hyper* (above) and *hippo-* *drome* (a racetrack for horses).

KURT SCHWITTERS

1887–1948

Anna Blume[1]

O beloved of my twenty-seven senses, I
love your!—you ye you your, I your, you my.
—We?
This belongs (by the way) elsewhere.
Who are you, uncounted female? You are   5
—are you? People say you are,—let
them say on, they don't know a hawk from a handsaw.[2]
You wear your hat upon your feet and walk round
on your hands, upon your hands you walk.
Halloo, your red dress, sawn up in white pleats.   10
Red I love Anna Blume, red I love your!—You
ye you your, I your, you my.—We?
This belongs (by the way) in icy fire.
Red bloom, red Anna Blume, what do people say?
Prize question: 1.) Anna Blume has a bird.   15
              2.) Anna Blume is red.
              3.) What colour is the bird?
Blue is the colour of your yellow hair.
Red is the cooing of your green bird.
You simple girl in a simple dress, you dear   20
green beast, I love your! You ye you your,
I your, you my.—We?
This belongs (by the way) in the chest of fires.
Anna Blume! Anna, a-n-n-a, I trickle your
name. Your name drips like softest tallow.   25
Do you know, Anna, do you know already?
You can also be read from behind, and you, you
the loveliest of all, are from behind, as you are from
before: "a-n-n-a".
Tallow trickles caressingly down my back.   30
Anna Blume, you trickle beast, I love your!

---

1. Translated from the German by David Britt. Published in 1919. An English adaptation entitled *Eve Blossom* also exists.   **2.** They don't know how the church tower stands (literally); i.e., they don't know the simplest things.

PAUL ÉLUARD
1895–1952

Woman in Love[1]

She is standing on my eyelids
And her hair is in mine,
She has the shape of my hands,
She has the color of my eyes,
She is engulfed in my shadow   5
Like a stone against the sky.

Her eyes are always open
She does not let me sleep.
Her dreams in broad daylight
Make suns evaporate,   10
Make me laugh, weep and laugh,
And speak without anything to say.

To Be Caught in One's Own Trap

It is a restaurant like the others. Must I believe I resemble no one? Next to me a great woman is beating eggs with her fingers. A passenger places his clothing on a table and avoids me. He is wrong, I don't know any mystery, I don't even know the meaning of the word. I have never looked for anything, never found anything, he is wrong to insist.

The storm that, off and on, leaves the fog turns my eyes and shoulders. Space then has doors and windows. The passenger announces to me I am not the same anymore. Not the same anymore! I gather the fragments of all my wonders. It is the great woman who told me that these are fragments of wonders, these fragments. I throw them in the healthy streams full of birds. The sea, the calm sea is between them like the sky in the light. Colors too, if someone talks to me of colors, I don't look anymore. Talk to me about shapes, I really need cause for concern.

Great woman, talk to me about shapes, or I fall asleep and I lead a rich life, my hands caught in my head and my head in my mouth, in my closed mouth, inward language.

[Nature was caught in the nets of your life]

Nature was caught in the nets of your life.
The tree, your shadow, shows its naked flesh: the sky.
It has the voice of the sand and the gestures of the wind.
And everything you say moves behind you.

---

1. All Éluard selections translated from the French by Lloyd Alexander. The Éluard selections are taken from *Capital of Pain* (1926).

[She is always unwilling to understand, to listen]

She is always unwilling to understand, to listen,
She laughs to hide her fear of herself.
She has always walked beneath the arches of nights
And wherever she went
She left   5
The mark of broken things.

[Unknown, she was my favorite shape]

Unknown, she was my favorite shape,
She who relieved me of the worry of being a man,
And I see her and I lose her and I suffer
My pain, like a little sunlight in cold water.

The Mirror of a Moment

It dissipates day,
It shows men the thin images of appearance,
It robs men of the possibility of amusement.
It is as hard as stone,
Formless stone,   5
The stone of movement and sight,
And its brilliance deforms all armor, all masks.
What the hand has taken does not deign to take the shape of the hand,
What has been understood no longer exists,
The bird was confused with the wind,   10
The sky with its truth,
Man with his reality.

ANDRÉ BRETON
1896–1966

Free Union[1]

Woman of mine with woodfire hair
With thoughts like flashes of heat lightning
With an hourglass waist
Woman of mine with an otterlike waist between the tiger's teeth

1. Both Breton selections translated from the French by Mary Ann Caws. Published in 1932.

Woman of mine with a rosette mouth like a posy of stars of ultimate
    magnitude   5
With teeth like a white mouse's spoor on white earth
With a tongue of rubbed amber and glass
Woman of mine with a tongue like a stabbed communion host
With the tongue of a doll that opens and shuts its eyes
A tongue of incredible stone   10
Woman of mine with eyelashes like the strokes of a child's writing
With eyebrows like the rim of a swallow's nest
Woman of mine with temples of slate on a greenhouse roof
And mist on the window-panes
Woman of mine with champagne shoulders   15
Like a fountain of dolphin heads under ice
Woman of mine with matchstick wrists
Woman of mine with fingers of chance and the ace of hearts
With fingers of mown hay
Woman of mine with armpits of marten and beechnut[2]   20
And of Midsummer Night
Of privet and scalare[3] nests
With arms of sluice and sea foam
And of mingled wheat and mill
Woman of mine with flare legs   25
With movements of clockwork[4] and despair
Woman of mine with calves of eldertree pith
Woman of mine with feet of initials[5]
With feet of keys on a ring with feet of Java sparrows[6] drinking
Woman of mine with a neck of impearled barley[7]   30
Woman of mine with the throat of a golden vale[8]
Of rendezvous in the very bed of the torrent
With breasts of night
Woman of mine with breasts of marine molehills
Woman of mine with breasts of rubied crucible   35
With breasts like the spectre of the rose[9] under the dew
Woman of mine with a belly unfolding like the fan of days
The belly of a giant claw
Woman of mine with the back of a bird in vertical flight
With a quicksilver back   40
A back of light
With a nape of rolled stone and moist chalk
And the drop of a glass just drained
Woman of mine with nacelle hips
With chandelier and arrow-feather hips   45
Like scapes of white peacock plumes
Of imperceptible sway
Woman of mine with buttocks of sandstone and amianthus
Woman of mine with swan's-back buttocks

2. The French word is suggested by the sound of *mown hay* in line 19.   3. A species of tropical fish that includes the angelfish.   4. Word play on a mechanical (*clockwork*) time fuse (*flare*).   5. Also a botanical term for fast-multiplying cells at the tips of roots and branches.   6. Birds of the finch family, often kept in cages. The French word's primary meaning is caulkers (of a boat's seams).   7. A play on pearl barley.   8. A reference to Val-d'Or, a place in Saint-Cloud near Paris, or possibly a town in southwestern Quebec, Canada, where gold was discovered in 1909.   9. A poem by Théophile Gautier (1811–1872), which was the subject of a 1911 ballet by Sergey Diaghilev (1872–1929).

Woman of mine with springtime buttocks 50
With the gladiolus sex
Woman of mine with the placer and platypus sex
Woman of mine with the sex of seaweed and oldtime sweets
Woman of mine with the mirror-like sex
Woman of mine with eyes full of tears 55
With violet-panoplied and magnetic-needle eyes
Woman of mine with savannah eyes
Woman of mine with eyes of water to be drunk in prison
Woman of mine with eyes of wood always under the axe
With water-level eyes the level of air earth and fire 60

Vigilance

In Paris the tower of Saint-Jacques[1] swaying
Like a sunflower
Sometimes runs its brow against the Seine and its shadow glides impercep-
    tibly among the tugs
At that moment on tiptoe in my sleep
I head for the room where I am lying 5
And set fire to it
So that nothing will remain of the consent wrung from me
The furniture then makes way for animals of the same size looking at me
    fraternally
Lions in whose manes the chairs are now burning out
Sharks whose white bellies absorb the last quivering of the sheets 10
At the hour of love and of blue eyelids
I see myself burning in turn I see that solemn hiding place of nothings
Which was once my body
Probed by the patient beaks of the fire-ibises
When all is finished I enter invisible into the ark 15
Taking no heed of the passersby of life whose shuffling steps are heard far
    off
I see the ridges of the sun
Through the hawthorn of the rain
I hear human linen tearing like a great leaf
Under the fingernails of absence and presence who are in collusion 20
All the looms are withering only a piece of perfumed lace remains of them
A shell of lace in the perfect shape of a breast
I touch nothing but the heart of things I hold the thread

---

1. Only the tower remains of the Parisian church of Saint-Jacques-de-la-Boucherie, one of whose patrons was the medieval alchemist Nicolas Flamel (1330–1418). The tower was cherished by the Surrealists for its associations with alchemy.

AIMÉ CÉSAIRE
born 1913

Do Not Have Pity[1]

Smoke on, salt swamps

Rock-painted icons of the unknown
deflect towards me the muted nightfall
of their laughter

smoke on, salt marshes, sea-needle heart   5
dead stars coaxed by marvellous hands dart forth
from the pulp of my eyes
Smoke on smoke on
the thin penumbra of my voice cracks with
flaming red cities   10
and my pure hands irresistibly call forth
at a very far remove from the ancestral heritage
the invincible zeal of acid in the flesh of
life—sea swamps—

like a viper sprung from the blond force of a blinding light.   15

Sun Serpent

Sun serpent: eye beguiling my eye
and the sea squalid with islands, finger joints cracking flame-throwing
roses, and my body lightning-blasted, unharmed,
the water hoists up carcasses of light lost in the gangway without ceremony
haloes of whirling ice encircle the smoking heart of crows   5
our hearts—
the voice of muffled thunderbolts rolling on their forked hinges
diffused by anolis lizards[2] through a landscape of broken glasses
vampire flowers relieving orchids of their spell
elixir of fire at the core   10
fire righteous fire, mango tree of night swaddled with bees
my desire: a contingent of tigers surprised amidst the sulphur
but at its arousal the tin is gilded with childhood layers
and my pebbled body gobbling fish gobbling doves gobbling slumbers . . .
the word Brazil is sugar in the depth of the swamp.   15

Day and Night

the sun the executioner the press of the masses the routine of dying and my
cry of wounded beast—and so it goes even unto the infinity of fevers, the

---

1. All Césaire selections translated from the French by Gregson Davis. From *Miraculous Weapons* (1946). The original title was "Do Not Have Pity for Me," a rebellious echo of the French poet Guillaume Apollinaire's (1880–1918) line "Have pity on me," which ends a description of the modern poet caught between old and new orders (*The Pretty Redhead*). 2. Antillean lizards related to iguanas.

awesome floodgate of death bombarded by my very own aleutian eyes that
from wormy earth search amid earth and worms your eyes of flesh, of sun,
like the black urchin for the coin in the water where flows the never-failing
song of the virgin forest sprung from the silence of the earth, of my very own
aleutian eyes, and so it goes: the lewd leapfrog of hermaphrodite thoughts,
the calls of jaguars, of water-hole, of antelopes, of savannahs with their
branches plucked in the course of their first great adventure: the exquisite
cyathus subtending a beautiful nymph stripped of her leaves amid the milk
of manchineel[3] trees and the accolades of brotherhood leeches.

3. Manzanilla.

JOYCE MANSOUR
1928–1987

[I saw you through my closed eye][1]

I saw you through my closed eye
Climbing the wall frightened of your dreams.
Your feet were losing their footing on the sleepy moss.
Your eyes were holding onto hanging nails.
While I screamed without opening my mouth   5
To open your head to the night.

[I opened your head]

I opened your head
To read your thoughts.
I devoured your eyes
To taste your sight.
I drank your blood   5
To know your wants
And made of your shivering body
My nourishment.

[Men's vices]

Men's vices
are my domain
Their wounds my sweet desserts
I love to chew on their vile thoughts
For their ugliness makes my beauty.   5

1. All Mansour selections translated from the French by Serge Gavronsky. From *Screams* (1953).

[Empty black haunted house]

Empty black haunted house
Our steps precede and follow us.
Rooms crowded with unfinished visions
Of objects beyond reach
Empty empty perverted house.   5
Your head walled in your eyes
That burn indecently blue
Haunt us call us
Fill our mouths.
Eternal inedible bread.   10

ALFONSINA STORNI
1892–1938

Alfonsina Storni is a unique voice in Latin American literature. Independent and outspoken, an international literary figure who was the first woman to be accepted by Argentina's male-dominated literary establishment, her reputation as a feminist has almost overshadowed her work as a poet. The two aspects are strongly connected. She drew on her own life for the substance of her poems, plays, articles, and lectures, and made herself—especially in her early work—a voice for women's experience. Obliged from a young age to be totally self-supporting, an unwed mother at the age of nineteen, she soon acquired a realistic perspective and a sense of outrage at the conventional treatment of women. Her sarcastic indictment of male vanity scandalized readers at the time and continues to be a sore point for many later critics. Storni is best known for three volumes of intensely subjective and emotional lyrics and for the skill with which she uses conversational language to create dramatic situations. In her later poetry, she turns away from subjective lyricism and explores various ways of capturing a reality outside herself.

She was born on May 29, 1892, in the small town of Sala Capriasca, Switzerland, during an extended family vacation that was intended to help her father recover from ill health and depression. Alfonso Storni had moved from Switzerland in 1880 to San Juan, Argentina, where he and his three brothers established a brewery. Initially successful, the business was doing poorly when Alfonsina, her older brother and sister, and her parents returned to Argentina in 1896, and it collapsed in 1900. Humiliated by their loss of prosperity and social position, they moved to the small town of Rosario, where her mother, Paulina, ran a school for a short time from their home. In 1901, the family started a new venture, the Swiss Café, and Alfonsina waited on tables and helped in the kitchen. It was the beginning of real poverty but also a lesson in independence for the once-pampered and privileged child: the café went bankrupt in 1904, and Alfonsina left school in 1906 to help her mother support the family by sewing. When her father died in the same year, she took a new job in a hat factory that paid more money. From that time on, the poet supported herself in a range of positions: actress, cashier, secretary, market researcher, lecturer, and, most of all, drama teacher in a children's theater. Looking back in 1934, Storni remarked that being forced to earn her own living (like a man, she explained, and certainly not like the sheltered women of her time) gave her an intellectual and emotional independence that colored everything she wrote. "My writing has inevitably reflected this, which is my personal truth: I have had to live as a man, so I demand to live by male standards. . . . What I am doing is anticipating the woman of the future, because female standards all depend on the economic system."

She started writing at the age of twelve but was fascinated with the theater and in 1907 joined a traveling acting company. A year was enough to dissuade her from becoming a professional actress, but she retained her interest in the theater, writing plays, teaching drama, and emphasizing dramatic situations in her poetry. In 1911, she earned a limited teaching degree while working as a chorus girl on weekends, and went back to Rosario to teach in a rural elementary school. Here, she fell in love with a married man and became pregnant, leaving for Buenos Aires to avoid the scandal sure to ensue after the birth of her child. Her son, Alejandro, was born when his mother was only nineteen years old, and she cautiously concealed his existence from her new employer. When her first book of poetry was published in 1916, she lost her job nonetheless: *The Restlessness of the Rosebush* was too openly based in her own situation, with its descriptions of sexual love, the pain of loss, and its defiance of social conventions. "I am like the she-wolf. / I broke with the pack," proclaims its best-known poem. She began to make a name for herself as a writer: she received a literary prize, published articles in various journals and newspapers, and became the first woman in Argentina to be part of a literary circle when she joined the group "Nosotros." Storni supported herself by teaching in various elementary schools and subsequently in a children's theater, all the while writing numerous articles (chiefly on women's rights), lecturing on Spanish American women poets, and publishing books of poetry that earned her a reputation for lyricism, emotional intensity, and wit.

Storni's next two collections, *The Sweet Pain* (1918) and *Irremediably* (1919), are similarly focused on the speaker's love and suffering, but these feelings are now part of a larger and more critical perspective. The setting favors images of daily life, and the poet employs everyday language and a tone of disillusionment and outrage. Rows of identical houses in *Squares and Angles* suggest her contempt for the all-embracing conformity of bourgeois life—a life that indiscriminately shapes everything into squares: souls, ideas, and even a tear. One of her best-known poems, *You Want Me White,* scornfully addresses a lover who accepts the double standard by which the woman must be "white" (chaste, pure, inexperienced) while the man pursues a more colorful existence, his soul "entangled / In all the bedrooms." In *Irremediably*'s *Little Bitty Man,* the speaker rebels against being caged like a canary and aims to fly free. Underlying the rebellion of each poem is Storni's recurrent theme that human beings act according to preset cultural images and fail therefore to communicate: "you don't understand me / and never will. / Nor do I understand you." She speaks out for women because, unlike men, they have not been permitted to speak for themselves: *Ancestral Burden,* a poem addressing her mother, evokes the repressed bitterness of generations of women who have mutely endured their assigned roles.

By now a well-known poet, Storni received two important literary prizes when she published her next collection, *Languor* (1920), the third volume in a series that was seen as her record of an ardent love, its disillusionment, and the final renunciation of erotic passion. The prologue to *Languor* announced that she would henceforth abandon subjective poetry, having said all she wished to say about her personal life, and that her future poetry would take a different direction. She became an Argentinian citizen, wrote a novel, *The Swallow*, and joined Anaconda, an important literary group associated with the noted Uruguayan novelist Horacio Quiroga, who became a close friend. The years ahead were difficult ones in Argentina, marked by an economic depression, mass social protests, and a military coup in 1930. Thanks to a friend, however, Storni obtained a position in 1921 teaching drama at the Children's Theater of Lavarden, and in 1923 and 1926 she found additional posts at two other schools; the combination of jobs gave her and her young son a degree of economic security. She entered on a period of increased social and literary activity during which she wrote and produced plays for children and adults, participated in various literary and artistic circles (where she met Federico García Lorca, Pablo Neruda, and other international figures), traveled and lectured in Europe—and was treated several times for fatigue and nervous depression.

The new poetry she had foreseen in *Languor* did not appear until 1925, with the publication of *Ocher*, a collection of complex, sensuous, and occasionally humorous poems that revel in the use of her craft but observe life—and the poet herself—from an ironic distance. "I am useless," proclaims a sonnet that begins with resignation at her failure to bring about change; the poem ends, however, in a powerful evocation of the voluptuous pleasure felt by a warm body in the summer sun. Storni's next major work, *The World of Seven Wells*, appeared nine years later and confirmed the poet's shift toward more objectively phrased and abstract descriptions; the title poem is an extended metaphor for the human head with its seven openings. She continues to use the subjective "I" as an anchor for her creative vision, but, for the first time, she employs free verse and structures poems according to fantastic or dreamlike associations. Her *Portrait of García Lorca*, written two years before his murder, is a disturbing composition in which images of death and violence (echoing similar images in Lorca) overlay different parts of his head, gradually transforming his physical identity until both eyes and eyebrows fuse with the marine horizon. The last collection, *Masks and Clover* (1938), published a few months before her death, moves even further from her initial subjective lyricism. Its fifty-two poems are all "antisonnets": that is, poems that preserve the Petrarchan sonnet's two quatrains and two tercets but lack rhymes; they exploit instead the rhythmic potential of a hendecasyllabic line. Storni foresaw that readers would find these poems harsh and obscure after her earlier emotional lyricism, and she was right. Recent critics, however, have come to prize the poems' tight construction, use of abstract imagery, and innovative perspectives.

The final years of her life were clouded with illness, pain, and the knowledge of terminal illness. She had been diagnosed with cancer in 1935 and operated on in the same year. The operation—a mastectomy—left her shattered, and, when the disease recurred and spread in 1938, she was unwilling to undergo further operations. Images of death and of the sea had permeated *The World of Seven Wells*, and they reappear in *Departure*, given here from an anthology of her poetry that Storni compiled in 1938. On October 25 of that year, in considerable pain, she took her own life by walking into the sea at Mar del Plata, Argentina.

Sonia Jones, *Alfonsina Storni* (1979), is a useful survey of Storni's life and work. Rachel Phillips, *Alfonsina Storni: From Poetess to Poet* (1975), analyzes the evolution of Storni's poetry. Florence Williams Talamantes, ed., *Alfonsina Storni: Argentina's Feminist Poet* (1975), Dorothy Scott Loos, ed., *Alfonsina Storni: Selected Poems* (1986), and Marion Freeman, ed., *Alfonsina Storni: Selected Poems* (1987), offer a range of selections and brief introductions.

[POEMS]

Squares and Angles[1]

Houses in a row, houses in a row,
Houses in a row.
Squares, squares, squares.
Houses in a row.
People now have square souls,   5

---

1. Translated by Florence Williams Talamantes.

Ideas in a row
And an angle on the back.
Yesterday I myself cried a tear.
My God—square.

You Want Me White²

You'd like me to be white as dawn,
You'd like me to be made of foam,
You wish I were mother of pearl,
A lily
Chaste above all others.   5
Of delicate perfume.
A closed bud.

Not one ray of the moon
Should have filtered me,
Not one daisy   10
Should have called me sister.
You want me to be snowy,
You want me to be white,
You want me to be like dawn.

You who have held all the wineglasses   15
In your hand,
Your lips stained purple
With fruit and honey
You who in the banquet
Crowned with young vines   20
Made toasts with your flesh to Bacchus.³
You who in the gardens
Black with Deceit
Dressed in red
Ran to your Ruin.   25

You who keep your skeleton
Well preserved, intact,
I don't know yet
Through what miracles
You want to make me white   30
(God forgive you),
You want to make me chaste
(God forgive you),
You want to make me like dawn!

Run away to the woods;   35
Go to the mountain;

---

2. Translated by Marion Freeman and Mary Crow. *White* here does not refer to race; it means colorless and pure.   3. In Greek and Roman mythology, the god of wine.

Wash your mouth;
Get to know the wet earth
With your hands;
Feed your body   40
With bitter roots;
Drink from the rocks;
Sleep on the white frost;
Renew your tissue
With the salt of rocks and water;   45
Talk to the birds
And get up at dawn.
And when your flesh
Has returned to you,
And when you have put   50
Your soul back into it,
Your soul which was left entangled
In all the bedrooms,
Then, my good man,
Ask me to be white,   55
Ask me to be snowy,
Ask me to be chaste.

Little-Bitty Man[4]

Little bitty man, little bitty man,
let your canary loose that wants to fly away.
I'm that canary, little bitty man,
let me go free.

I was in your cage, little bitty man,   5
little bitty man who gives me a cage.
I say little bitty because you don't understand me
and never will.

Nor do I understand you, but meanwhile
open up the cage, for I want to be free.   10
Little bitty man, I loved you half an hour.
Ask no more of me.

Ancestral Burden[5]

You once told me my father never wept;
You once told me my grandfather never wept;
The men of my race have not wept;
They were of steel.

---

4. Translated by Mary Crow and Marion Freeman.   5. Translated by Florence Williams Talamantes.

Speaking thus you cried a tear 5
And it fell into my mouth . . . More poison
I have never drunk in another glass
So small.

Weak woman, poor woman who understands,
The pain of centuries I knew upon drinking it; 10
Oh, my soul cannot bear
All its burden.

The World of Seven Wells[6]

There above, on the neck,
is balanced the world
of the seven doors:
the human head . . .

Round like two planets: 5
the first nucleus
burns into its center.
The bark is of bone;
over it the clay epidermis
sown
with the thick forest of the hair. 10

From the nucleus
in absolute blue tides
the water of the glance ascends
and opens the tender doors
of the eyes like seas on the land. 15

. . . so calm
those gentle waters of God
that over them
butterflies and insects hover. 20

And the other two doors;
the antennae nestled
in the catacombs where the ears begin;
wells of sound,
snails of mother-of-pearl where 25
the spoken word
and the unspoken word resound;
tubes located to the right and to the left
so that the sea may never be silent,
and the mechanical wing of the worlds 30
may be sounded.

6. Translated by Florence Williams Talamantes.

And the mountain raised
over the equatorial line of the head:
the wax-like nostrils of the nose
through which the color of life   35
begins to grow silent;
the two doors
through which one perceives
—flowers, branches and fruit—
the tempting fragrance of spring.   40

And the crater of the mouth
with raised edges
and dry chapped walls;
the crater which spouts forth
the sulphur of violent words,   45
the dense smoke which comes
from the heart and its turmoil;
the door
of sumptuously worked coral
through which the beast gulps,   50
and the angel sings and smiles
and the human volcano erupts.

There above, on the neck,
is balanced the world
of seven wells: 55
the human head.

And the rosy meadows open
in their valleys of silk:
the mossy cheeks.

And there shines   60
on the curve of the forehead,
a white desert,
the distant light of a dead moon . . .

Portrait of García Lorca[7]

Looking for the roots of wings
his forehead
moves to the right
and to the left.

Over the whirlwind of his face   5
a curtain of death is drawn,
thick and twisted.

7. Translated by Jim Normington.

A wild animal
snarls in his face
trying to destroy him   10
in its rage.

His distant eyes
suggest Grecian eyes . . .

The Andalusian[8] hills
of his cheekbones
and the trembling valley   15
of his mouth
are smothered in climbing vines.[9]

A scream
leaps from his throat
begging   20
for moonlit knives[1]
made of sharp-edged water.

Slice the throat.
From north to south.
From east to west.   25

Let the head fly
(only the head)
wounded by dark
ocean waves.
Let the mane[2] of the satyr[3]   30
fall on him
like bell-shaped flowers
on the face
of an ancient mask.   35

Silence his huge voice
in its nasal passages.

Free him from it
and from his gentle arms
and earthly body.   40

Before throwing
his body into space
force his arched eyebrows
to become bridges
of the Atlantic   45
and Pacific

---

8. Lorca came from Andalusia, a province of Spain.   9. The convolvulus, a twining vine with bell-shaped
flowers.   1. Literally, a knife shaped like a half-moon.   2. Literally, small white snails.   3. In Greek
and Roman mythology, a woodland god.

So that his eyes
like lost ships
can sail,
without ports   50
or shores.

Departure[4]

A road
to the limit:
high golden doors
close it off;
deep galleries;   5
arcades . . .

The air has no weight;
the doors stand by themselves
in the emptiness;
they disintegrate into golden dust;   10
they close, they open;
they go down to the algae
tombs;
they come up loaded with coral.

Patrols,   15
there are patrols of columns;
the doors hide
behind the blue parapets;
water bursts into fields of forget-me-nots;
it tosses up deserts of purple crystals;   20
it incubates great emerald worms;
it plaits its innumerable arms.

A rain of wings,
now;
pink angels   25
dive like arrows
into the sea.
I could walk on them
without sinking.
A path of ciphers   30
for my feet;
columns of numbers
for each step—
submarine.

They carry me: 35
invisible vines

4. Translated by Marion Freeman.

stretch out their hooks
from the horizon.
My neck creaks.
I walk.   40
The water holds its own.
My shoulders open into wings.
I touch the ends of the sky
with their tips.
I wound it.   45
The sky's blood
bathing the sea . . .
poppies, poppies,
there is nothing but poppies.

I grow light: 50
the flesh falls from my bones.
Now.
The sea rises through the channels
of my spine.
Now.   55
The sky rolls through the bed
of my veins.
Now.
The sun! The sun!
Its last rays   60
envelop me,
push me:
I am a spindle
I spin, spin, spin, spin!

WILLIAM FAULKNER
1897–1962

William Faulkner's account of historical change in the American South far transcends regional issues. He writes about the Old South becoming the New, about the clash of generations and ways of life, about racial and family tragedies, and about the opposition of good and evil in almost archetypal terms. His fantastic, sometimes allegorical depictions of events anticipate "magical realist" fiction. Yet Faulknerian style is best known for innovative use of language and for brilliantly extended narrative sentences. Adapting James Joyce's stream of consciousness technique, Faulkner provides insights into his characters' minds that reveal and interpret the same stories they record. With Faulkner, the nineteenth-century Balzacian tradition of the human comedy—the novel as a panorama of society—acquires a new vocabulary and renewed historicity.

William Cuthbert Falkner was born on September 25, 1897, in New Albany, Mississippi, to a prosperous family with many ties to southern history. The eldest of four sons, Faulkner (he adopted this spelling in 1924 for his first book) was named for a great-grandfather who commanded a Confederate regiment in the Civil War, built railroads, and wrote novels. Faulkner's father worked for the family railroad until it was sold in 1902, afterwards moving his family to Oxford and eventually becoming business manager of the University of Mississippi. Faulkner's close acquaintance with southern customs and attitudes, his own experience as the descendant of a once-prosperous and influential family, and his attachment to the region of Lafayette County and the town of Oxford (Yoknapatawpha County and Jefferson in the novels) helped shape themes and setting in his fiction.

Young Faulkner did not like school, although he read widely in his grandfather's library and borrowed books from an older friend, Philip Stone. Leaving high school after two years to work as a bookkeeper in his grandfather's bank, he continued reading and discussing literature with Stone, who introduced him to the French writer Honoré de Balzac's novels and encouraged his writing. In the last six months of 1918 he trained in Canada as a fighter pilot—then a common way of getting more quickly into combat in World War I—but the war ended, and he returned to Oxford to enroll at the university as a special student. While in school, Faulkner published poetry, prose, and drawings in *The Mississippian* and worked on the yearbook but decided to leave the university in November 1920 to work in a New York bookstore. By December 1921 he had returned to Oxford, where he became postmaster at the university; three years later, he was dismissed for irresponsibility. During these years he wrote mainly poetry and seems to have been influenced by the French Symbolists: his first published poem, *L'Après-midi d'un faune,* takes its title from an earlier poem by Stéphane Mallarmé. With Stone's help, Faulkner published his first book, a collection of lyrics called *The Marble Faun* (also the title of a novel by Nathaniel Hawthorne) in 1924.

In 1925, Faulkner spent six months living in New Orleans, where he was attracted to a literary group associated with *The Double Dealer,* a magazine in which he himself published poems, essays, and prose sketches. The group's chief figure was the novelist Sherwood Anderson, author of a series of regional stories published as *Winesburg, Ohio,* who encouraged Faulkner to make fictional use of his southern background and who recommended his first novel (without having read it) to a publisher. After completing *Soldier's Pay* (published in 1926), Faulkner took a freighter to Europe, where he bicycled and hiked through Italy and France and lived for a short while in Paris. At the end of the year he returned to Mississippi, where he wrote his second novel, *Mosquitoes* (1927), a satire on the New Orleans group.

Taking up Anderson's earlier suggestion, Faulkner now embarked on the regional "Yoknapatawpha" (*yok-na-pa-taw'-pha*) series with *Sartoris* (1929), an account of the return home, marriage, and death of wounded veteran Bayard Sartoris. In Yoknapatawpha County, Faulkner created a whole fictional world with characters who reappear from novel to novel (a technique he would have encountered in Balzac's *Comédie humaine*). Here imaginary families such as the Sartorises, Compsons, Sutpens, McCaslins, and Snopeses rise to prosperity or fall into various kinds of weakness, degradation, and death. Individual characters work out destinies that are already half-shaped by family tradition and invisible community pressures. They are caught in close and often incestuous blood relationships and make their way in a world where the values, traditions, and privileges of an old plantation society are yielding to the values of a new mercantile class. A network of family dynasties illustrates this picture of a changing society: the decaying and impoverished Compson family (*The Sound and the Fury,* 1929); two generations of Sutpens rising to great wealth and dying in madness and isolation (*Absalom, Absalom!,* 1936); the McCaslin family with its history of incest, miscegenation, and guilt (*Go Down, Moses,* 1942); and the viciously grasping and ambitious "poor white" Snopes family (*The Hamlet,* 1940; *The Town,* 1957; *The Mansion,* 1959). These are violent works, and the murders, lynchings, and bestialities of all kinds that appear in them account for Faulkner's early American reputation as a lurid local writer. European critics, however—especially the French, who recognized his ability as early as 1931—were quick to recognize mythic overtones and classical and biblical prototypes in these tales of twisted family relationships.

After *Sartoris*, Faulkner, for his next novel, *The Sound and the Fury*, experimented with a new style modeled on the stream-of-consciousness technique of Joyce's *Ulysses*. Here the Compson family's tragedy is told through several different points of view, the first of which is the disconnected and emotionally skewed world of the idiot Benjy. Both *Sartoris* and *The Sound and the Fury* were rejected several times before finally being published in 1929, and Faulkner supported himself during these years chiefly through odd jobs (working on a shrimp trawler, in a lumber mill, at a power plant, and as a carpenter, painter, and paper hanger), and then from his short stories, of which he sold thirty between 1930 and 1932. In 1929 he married Estelle Oldham Franklin, with whom he had one child, Jill, in 1933. Irritated at the difficulty of finding publishers for his serious or experimental works, Faulkner set out to write a best-seller—and succeeded. *Sanctuary*, a novel of the Deep South that described the rape and prostitution of a schoolgirl, murder, perjury, and the lynching of an innocent man, was made into a movie (*The Story of Temple Drake*) and brought its author invitations to work on movie scripts for a variety of Hollywood studios. From 1932 to 1955, the novelist added to his income by working as a film doctor, revising and collaborating on scripts for films such as *To Have and Have Not* and *The Big Sleep*. Although his works continued to receive critical praise, he did not have any commercial successes after *Sanctuary*; in 1945, when he was, according to the French writer and philosopher Jean-Paul Sartre, the idol of young French readers, almost all of his novels were out of print. It took an anthology, *The Portable Faulkner*, in 1946, to reintroduce Faulkner to a wide audience. In 1950 he won the Nobel Prize for Literature and used the prize money to establish the William Faulkner Foundation to assist Latin American writers and award educational scholarships to Mississippi blacks. Five years later he received the Pulitzer Prize and the National Book Award for *A Fable* (1954). Faulkner's last book was a comedy set in Yoknapatawpha County, *The Reivers* (1962). He died of a heart attack in Oxford, Mississippi, on July 6, 1962.

In Faulkner's world, men and women are measured by the breadth of their compassion or the quality of their endurance. Although there are villains, few wholly negative characters appear, and these are seen as grotesque distortions of humanity: the cruel and frustrated Jason Compson, or the impotent rapist Popeye of *Sanctuary*, who "had that vicious depthless quality of stamped tin." Heroes tend to be larger than life, casting their shadow even after death, as does Addie Bundren in *As I Lay Dying* (1930), when Addie's dying wish obliges her family to accompany her coffin across Mississippi in a miniature epic journey through flood and fire. Heroes have the moral endurance of Bayard Sartoris II, who as a boy kills his grandmother's murderer and as a man faces down his father's killer—unarmed—to break the pattern of "honorable revenge"; or the physical endurance of the tall convict in *Old Man*, whose "whole purpose" was "to prove . . . just how much the human body could bear, stand, endure." Yet Faulkner's world is by no means unrelievedly somber. The everyday realism and earthy humor of his works have led to his being called a comic writer, in the broad sense that implies a universal vision encompassing the pettiness as well as the grandeur of human existence. Not all of his characters are heroes. Some are ordinary people whose perseverance and dedication to an idea, a person, or a way of life give them larger significance; some are thoughtful people driven by circumstances to question their own identity and values; some are idiots able only to feel a succession of emotions; some are simply confidence men. Faulkner generally describes such figures from the outside. We see them act, and we may even follow their thoughts in interior monologues, but we are receiving only traces of inner personalities that have already been decided and to which we have no real access.

The "truth" of the novels comes to us through a variety of perspectives and rhetorical strategies. Three different narrators in *Absalom, Absalom!* tell the story of Thomas Sutpen. The four points of view in *The Sound and the Fury* move from Benjy's childish imagined inner monologue to the adult monologues of his nervously suicidal and psychopathic brothers and finally to a third-person narrative focusing on Dilsey, the black woman who has been in charge of family and household and who "endures." Fifty-nine sections of interior monologue in *As I Lay Dying* express the inner relationships of the Bundren family; and six pages of ledger-reading in *Go Down, Moses* explore those of the McCaslins. The convict in *Old Man* possesses a dogged, wilfully limited view of things modeled on simplistic cops-and-robbers stories and adventure tales. A narrative perspective may change tone, as happens at the end of the epic coffin journey in *As I Lay Dying* when the widowed Anse Bundren returns happily from town with a new set of false teeth, a new wife, and a phonograph. Chronology may be broken, as in the time changes represented by two typefaces in Benjy's section of *The Sound and the Fury*; details are exaggerated or distorted; dialect speech emphasizes the presence of the storyteller's art. Throughout, Faulkner's fluid style escapes rigid categories; it is a style of tensions and contradictions, of tragedy and humor, realism and mythic outreach, now short and laconic, now rambling.

One of the most widely read of Faulkner's works is *The Bear*, itself part of a larger volume called *Go Down, Moses*, which the writer called a novel although the first edition was published (apparently without his knowledge) as *Go Down, Moses and Other Stories*. *The Bear* is the fifth of seven chapters in *Go Down, Moses* and has been printed separately both as the well-known tale of the hunt (sections 1–3) and as the larger narrative (1–5), whose scope is chiefly defined by the extraordinary fourth section concerning Ike McCaslin after the hunt. Of this part, Faulkner wrote to his editor that there was "more meat in it than I thought, a section now that I am going to be proud of and which requires careful writing and rewriting to get it exactly right." The larger story broadens and extends the relationship with overall themes in *Go Down, Moses*: the legacy of slavery and incest, the expiation of guilt, and the moral status of owning property (whether land or people). Here Ike McCaslin, reading old family ledgers from the plantation, gradually deciphers his uncles' cryptic annotations to various expenses as well as the death of one Eunice, a slave. Eunice had a daughter, Tomasina, by the slave-owning grandfather, old Carothers McCaslin; when it became obvious that Tomasina was pregnant by the same Carothers McCaslin, her mother committed suicide. The next generation of McCaslins tries in various ways to make amends, but it is Ike who makes expiation the center of his existence. Tracking down Eunice's descendants—his cousins—to pay them their thousand-dollar legacies, he confronts the broader implications of the past: the theft and fragmentation of land that was once a wilderness owned in common and the contamination of this land by the institution of slavery. References to the Bible and moral responsibility fill the long dialogue in which he tries to explain things to his older cousin, McCaslin Edmonds. (The book's title, *Go Down, Moses*, alludes both to the biblical story of Moses rescuing the Israelites from slavery in Egypt and to a well-known Negro spiritual.) Ike decides finally (at twenty-one) to separate himself from the historical taint by renouncing his inheritance; for a while he makes a meager living as a carpenter and then, after a failed marriage, returns to the woods and a solitary life.

The first three sections and the concluding fifth section of *The Bear* introduce the themes of wilderness and lost harmony while describing a bear hunt in Ike's youth. Or rather, several bear hunts: although *The Bear* begins when Ike is sixteen, there are numerous flashbacks to earlier scenes as the youth is initiated into the wilderness. Guided by the part-Chickasaw Sam Fathers, "his spirit's father," he learns to strip himself of civilized defenses (gun, watch, and compass) and see Old Ben himself: "not even a mortal beast but an anachronism indomitable and invincible out of an old dead time . . . apotheosis of the old wild life which the little puny humans swarmed and hacked at in a fury of abhorrence and fear." Part of *The Bear*'s appeal lies in these mythic overtones: the story presents at once a rite of passage for the youth, an archetypal image of the hunt, and a somber tribute to a disappearing natural world.

Stylistically, there is a notable difference between the sections describing the hunt and the more elaborate subjective narrative of section 4. The earlier sections are not as straightforward as the beginning seems to promise, however: "There was a man and a dog too this time." Almost immediately, sentences lengthen to include a range of memories and interpretations that emanate from the boy but are articulated in an expanded, omniscient perspective. Section 4 is heavily internalized, as the twenty-one-year-old Ike carries on a dialogue with his cousin McCaslin Edmonds in which punctuation is for the most part left out, and the two speakers are distinguished only by "and he" and "and McCaslin" at the end of paragraphs. One result of this style, an adaptation of the stream of consciousness technique, is that the reader seems to share Ike's memories and become part of the ongoing debate in his mind. Ike's distress, and the sequence of his reactions as he deciphers, questions, compares, interprets, and finally understands the family ledger, is famously expressed in the rush of a single unbroken sentence of more than eighteen hundred words (pp. 2172–75).

Ike's renunciation has been interpreted in various ways. To many, he is a sacrificial figure who atones for his family's guilt by renouncing an irretrievably tainted inheritance; symbolically, he rejects the exploitative materialism of industrial society and returns to a simpler life in harmony with nature. When an interviewer asked what Ike had gained by his renunciation, Faulkner responded "serenity . . . what would pass for wisdom." Others, however, have felt that Ike is ultimately a failure because he turns his back on life; that his passivity is mistaken and an abandonment of responsibility. Here, Faulkner commented to an overenthusiastic proponent of the first view: "I think a man ought to do more than just repudiate." Either reading vindicates Faulkner's role as a persuasive interpreter of cultural values and chronicler of historical change.

Suggested studies include Michael Millgate, *The Achievement of William Faulkner* (1963), a critical study of the novels and stories with a brief biography in the first chapter; Cleanth Brooks, *William Faulkner: The Yoknapatawpha Country* (1963), a basic literary analysis and study of Faulkner's mythical South in the Yoknapatawpha stories, with a list of Faulkner's fictional characters; and James B. Carothers, *William Faulkner's Short Stories* (1985), an examination of the short stories in the context of the novels. *William Faulkner, The Man and The Artist* (1987), is a vivid narrative biography written by historian Stephen B. Oates. Joseph Blotner is the author of *Faulkner: A Biography* (1974, 2 vols.), the authorized and immensely detailed biography. Doreen Fowler and Ann J. Abadie, eds., *Faulkner and the Craft of Fiction: Faulkner and Yoknapatawpha* (1989), collects useful essays on themes and narrative structures. Francis Lee Utley, Lynn Z. Bloom, and Arthur F. Kinney, eds., *Bear, Man, and God: Eight Approaches to William Faulkner's The Bear* (1971), contains valuable essays on various topics and includes excerpts from Faulkner interviews. *Go Down, Moses* (1994), annotated by Nancy Dew Taylor, offers a detailed and informative series of annotations. James Early, *The Making of Go Down, Moses* (1972), describing earlier versions of *The Bear*, emphasizes themes, linguistic strategies, and conceptions of character. Linda Wagner-Martin, ed., *New Essays on Go Down, Moses* (1996), prints five essays that use modern critical perspectives to discuss tensions of race and gender.

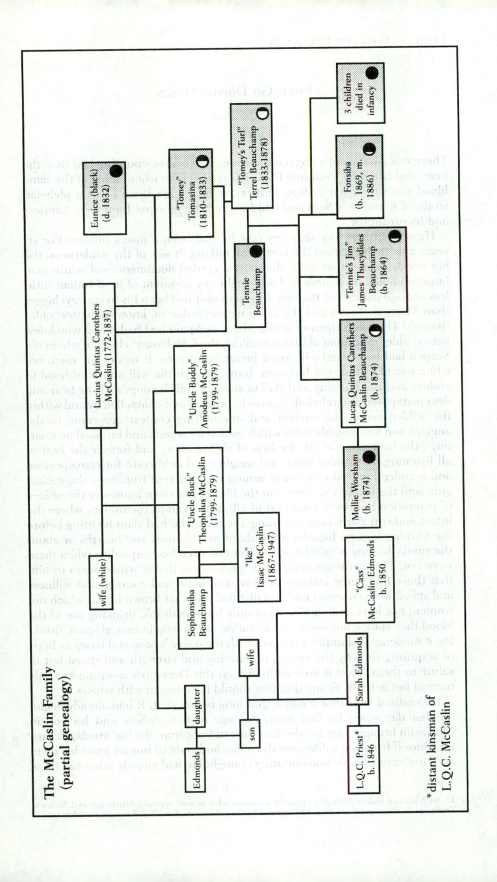

The McCaslin Family
(partial genealogy)

Eunice (black) (d. 1832)

"Tomey" Tomasina (1810–1833)

"Tomey's Turf" Terrel Beauchamp (1833–1878)

3 children died in infancy

Fonsiba (b. 1869, m. 1886)

"Tennie's Jim" James Thucydides Beauchamp (b. 1864)

Tennie Beauchamp

Lucas Quintus Carothers McCaslin Beauchamp (b. 1874)

Lucius Quintus Carothers McCaslin (1772–1837)

"Uncle Buddy" Amodeus McCaslin (1799–1879)

"Uncle Buck" Theophilus McCaslin (1799–1879)

"Ike" Isaac McCaslin (1867–1947)

Sophonsiba Beauchamp

Mollie Worsham (b. 1874)

"Cass" McCaslin Edmonds b. 1850

wife (white)

wife

Sarah Edmonds

Edmonds

daughter

son

L.Q.C. Priest* b. 1846

*distant kinsman of L.Q.C. McCaslin

From Go Down, Moses

The Bear

1

There was a man and a dog too this time. Two beasts, counting Old Ben, the bear, and two men, counting Boon Hogganbeck, in whom some of the same blood ran which ran in Sam Fathers, even though Boon's was a plebeian strain of it and only Sam and Old Ben and the mongrel Lion were taintless and incorruptible.

He was sixteen. For six years now he had been a man's hunter. For six years now he had heard the best of all talking. It was of the wilderness, the big woods, bigger and older than any recorded document:—of white man fatuous enough to believe he had bought any fragment of it, of Indian ruthless enough to pretend that any fragment of it had been his to convey; bigger than Major de Spain and the scrap he pretended to, knowing better; older than old Thomas Sutpen of whom Major de Spain had had it and who knew better; older even than old Ikkemotubbe, the Chickasaw[1] chief, of whom old Sutpen had had it and who knew better in his turn. It was of the men, not white nor black nor red but men, hunters, with the will and hardihood to endure and the humility and skill to survive, and the dogs and the bear and deer juxtaposed and reliefed[2] against it, ordered and compelled by and within the wilderness in the ancient and unremitting contest according to the ancient and immitigable rules which voided all regrets and brooked no quarter;—the best game of all, the best of all breathing and forever the best of all listening, the voices quiet and weighty and deliberate for retrospection and recollection and exactitude among the concrete trophies—the racked guns and the heads and skins—in the libraries of town houses or the offices of plantation houses or (and best of all) in the camps themselves where the intact and still-warm meat yet hung, the men who had slain it sitting before the burning logs on hearths when there were houses and hearths or about the smoky blazing of piled wood in front of stretched tarpaulins when there were not. There was always a bottle present, so that it would seem to him that those fine fierce instants of heart and brain and courage and wiliness and speed were concentrated and distilled into that brown liquor which not women, not boys and children, but only hunters drank, drinking not of the blood they spilled but some condensation of the wild immortal spirit, drinking it moderately, humbly even, not with the pagan's base and baseless hope of acquiring thereby the virtues of cunning and strength and speed but in salute to them. Thus it seemed to him on this December morning not only natural but actually fitting that this should have begun with whisky.

He realised later that it had begun long before that. It had already begun on that day when he first wrote his age in two ciphers and his cousin McCaslin brought him for the first time to the camp, the big woods, to earn for himself from the wilderness the name and state of hunter provided he in his turn were humble and enduring enough. He had already inherited then,

---

1. An American Indian tribe that originally inhabited what is now northern Mississippi and Alabama. Traditionally, all property was owned in common by the tribe.   2. Set off as if in sculptural *bas-relief*.

without ever having seen it, the big old bear with one trap-ruined foot that in an area almost a hundred miles square had earned for himself a name, a definite designation like a living man:—the long legend of corn-cribs broken down and rifled, of shoats and grown pigs and even calves carried bodily into the woods and devoured and traps and deadfalls[3] overthrown and dogs mangled and slain and shotgun and even rifle shots delivered at point-blank range yet with no more effect than so many peas blown through a tube by a child—a corridor of wreckage and destruction beginning back before the boy was born, through which sped, not fast but rather with the ruthless and irresistible deliberation of a locomotive, the shaggy tremendous shape. It ran in his knowledge before he ever saw it. It loomed and towered in his dreams before he even saw the unaxed woods where it left its crooked print, shaggy, tremendous, red-eyed, not malevolent but just big, too big for the dogs which tried to bay it, for the horses which tried to ride it down, for the men and the bullets they fired into it; too big for the very country which was its constricting scope. It was as if the boy had already divined what his senses and intellect had not encompassed yet: that doomed wilderness whose edges were being constantly and punily gnawed at by men with plows and axes who feared it because it was wilderness, men myriad and nameless even to one another in the land where the old bear had earned a name, and through which ran not even a mortal beast but an anachronism indomitable and invincible out of an old dead time, a phantom, epitome and apotheosis of the old wild life which the little puny humans swarmed and hacked at in a fury of abhorrence and fear like pygmies about the ankles of a drowsing elephant;—the old bear, solitary, indomitable, and alone; widowered childless and absolved of mortality—old Priam[4] reft of his old wife and outlived all his sons.

Still a child, with three years then two years then one year yet before he too could make one of them, each November he would watch the wagon containing the dogs and the bedding and food and guns and his cousin McCaslin and Tennie's Jim and Sam Fathers too until Sam moved to the camp to live, depart for the Big Bottom, the big woods. To him, they were going not to hunt bear and deer but to keep yearly rendezvous with the bear which they did not even intend to kill. Two weeks later they would return, with no trophy, no skin. He had not expected it. He had not even feared that it might be in the wagon this time with the other skins and heads. He did not even tell himself that in three years or two years or one year more he would be present and that it might even be his gun. He believed that only after he had served his apprenticeship in the woods which would prove him worthy to be a hunter, would he even be permitted to distinguish the crooked print, and that even then for two November weeks he would merely make another minor one, along with his cousin and Major de Spain and General Compson and Walter Ewell and Boon and the dogs which feared to bay it and the shotguns and rifles which failed even to bleed it, in the yearly pageant-rite of the old bear's furious immortality.

His day came at last. In the surrey with his cousin and Major de Spain and General Compson he saw the wilderness through a slow drizzle of

---

3. Hunters' traps in which a log falls on the animal when it takes the bait. *Shoats:* young pigs.　　4. Ruler of Troy in Homer's *Iliad* who was killed by Achilles' son when the city fell.

November rain just above the ice point as it seemed to him later he always saw it or at least always remembered it—the tall and endless wall of dense November woods under the dissolving afternoon and the year's death, sombre, impenetrable (he could not even discern yet how, at what point they could possibly hope to enter it even though he knew that Sam Fathers was waiting there with the wagon), the surrey moving through the skeleton stalks of cotton and corn in the last of open country, the last trace of man's puny gnawing at the immemorial flank, until, dwarfed by that perspective into an almost ridiculous diminishment, the surrey itself seemed to have ceased to move (this too to be completed later, years later, after he had grown to a man and had seen the sea) as a solitary small boat hangs in lonely immobility, merely tossing up and down, in the infinite waste of the ocean while the water and then the apparently impenetrable land which it nears without appreciable progress, swings slowly and opens the widening inlet which is the anchorage. He entered it. Sam was waiting, wrapped in a quilt on the wagon seat behind the patient and steaming mules. He entered his novitiate to the true wilderness with Sam beside him as he had begun his apprenticeship in miniature to manhood after the rabbits and such with Sam beside him, the two of them wrapped in the damp, warm, negro-rank quilt while the wilderness closed behind his entrance as it had opened momentarily to accept him, opening before his advancement as it closed behind his progress, no fixed path the wagon followed but a channel nonexistent ten yards ahead of it and ceasing to exist ten yards after it had passed, the wagon progressing not by its own volition but by attrition of their intact yet fluid circumambience, drowsing, earless, almost lightless.

It seemed to him that at the age of ten he was witnessing his own birth. It was not even strange to him. He had experienced it all before, and not merely in dreams. He saw the camp—a paintless six-room bungalow set on piles above the spring high-water—and he knew already how it was going to look. He helped in the rapid orderly disorder of their establishment in it and even his motions were familiar to him, foreknown. Then for two weeks he ate the coarse rapid food—the shapeless sour bread, the wild strange meat, venison and bear and turkey and coon which he had never tasted before— which men ate, cooked by men who were hunters first and cooks afterward; he slept in harsh sheetless blankets as hunters slept. Each morning the gray of dawn found him and Sam Fathers on the stand, the crossing, which had been allotted him. It was the poorest one, the most barren. He had expected that; he had not dared yet to hope even to himself that he would even hear the running dogs this first time. But he did hear them. It was on the third morning—a murmur, sourceless, almost indistinguishable, yet he knew what it was although he had never before heard that many dogs running at once, the murmur swelling into separate and distinct voices until he could call the five dogs which his cousin owned from among the others. "Now," Sam said, "slant your gun up a little and draw back the hammers and then stand still."

But it was not for him, not yet. The humility was there; he had learned that. And he could learn the patience. He was only ten, only one week. The instant had passed. It seemed to him that he could actually see the deer, the buck, smoke-colored, elongated with speed, vanished, the woods, the gray solitude still ringing even when the voices of the dogs had died away; from far away across the sombre woods and the gray half-liquid morning there came two shots. "Now let your hammers down,"[5] Sam said.

He did so. "You knew it too," he said.

"Yes," Sam said. "I want you to learn how to do when you didn't shoot. It's after the chance for the bear or the deer has done already come and gone that men and dogs get killed."

"Anyway, it wasn't him," the boy said. "It wasn't even a bear. It was just a deer."

"Yes," Sam said, "it was just a deer."

Then one morning, it was in the second week, he heard the dogs again. This time before Sam even spoke he readied the too-long, too-heavy, man-size gun as Sam had taught him, even though this time he knew the dogs and the deer were coming less close than ever, hardly within hearing even. They didn't sound like any running dogs he had ever heard before even. Then he found that Sam, who had taught him first of all to cock the gun and take position where he could see best in all directions and then never to move again, had himself moved up beside him. "There," he said. "Listen." The boy listened, to no ringing chorus strong and fast on a free scent but a moiling yapping an octave too high and with something more than indecision and even abjectness in it which he could not yet recognise, reluctant, not even moving very fast, taking a long time to pass out of hearing, leaving even then in the air that echo of thin and almost human hysteria, abject, almost humanly grieving, with this time nothing ahead of it, no sense of a fleeing unseen smoke-colored shape. He could hear Sam breathing at his shoulder. He saw the arched curve of the old man's inhaling nostrils.

"It's Old Ben!" he cried, whispering.

Sam didn't move save for the slow gradual turning of his head as the voices faded on and the faint steady rapid arch and collapse of his nostrils. "Hah," he said. "Not even running. Walking."

"But up here!" the boy cried. "Way up here!"

"He do it every year," Sam said. "Once. Ash and Boon say he comes up here to run the other little bears away. Tell them to get to hell out of here and stay out until the hunters are gone. Maybe." The boy no longer heard anything at all, yet still Sam's head continued to turn gradually and steadily until the back of it was toward him. Then it turned back and looked down at him—the same face, grave, familiar, expressionless until it smiled, the same old man's eyes from which as he watched there faded slowly a quality darkly and fiercely lambent, passionate and proud. "He dont care no more for bears than he does for dogs or men neither. He come to see who's here, who's new in camp this year, whether he can shoot or not, can stay or not. Whether we got the dog yet that can bay and hold him until a man gets there with a gun. Because he's the head bear. He's the man." It faded, was gone; again they were the eyes as he had known them all his life. "He'll let them follow him to the river. Then he'll send them home. We might as well go too; see how they look when they get back to camp."

The dogs were there first, ten of them huddled back under the kitchen, himself and Sam squatting to peer back into the obscurity where they

5. I.e., release them. Cocking the hammers prepares the double-barreled shotgun to fire.

crouched, quiet, the eyes rolling and luminous, vanishing, and no sound, only that effluvium which the boy could not quite place yet, of something more than dog, stronger than dog and not just animal, just beast even. Because there had been nothing in front of the abject and painful yapping except the solitude, the wilderness, so that when the eleventh hound got back about mid-afternoon and he and Tennie's Jim held the passive and still trembling bitch while Sam daubed her tattered ear and raked shoulder with turpentine and axle-grease, it was still no living creature but only the wilderness which, leaning for a moment, had patted lightly once her temerity. "Just like a man," Sam said. "Just like folks. Put off as long as she could having to be brave, knowing all the time that sooner or later she would have to be brave once so she could keep on calling herself a dog, and knowing beforehand what was going to happen when she done it."

He did not know just when Sam left. He only knew that he was gone. For the next three mornings he rose and ate breakfast and Sam was not waiting for him. He went to his stand alone; he found it without help now and stood on it as Sam had taught him. On the third morning he heard the dogs again, running strong and free on a true scent again, and he readied the gun as he had learned to do and heard the hunt sweep past on since he was not ready yet, had not deserved other yet in just one short period of two weeks as compared to all the long life which he had already dedicated to the wilderness with patience and humility; he heard the shot again, one shot, the single clapping report of Walter Ewell's rifle. By now he could not only find his stand and then return to camp without guidance, by using the compass his cousin had given him he reached Walter waiting beside the buck and the moiling of dogs over the cast entrails before any of the others except Major de Spain and Tennie's Jim on the horses, even before Uncle Ash arrived with the one-eyed wagon-mule which did not mind the smell of blood or even, so they said, of bear.

It was not Uncle Ash on the mule. It was Sam, returned. And Sam was waiting when he finished his dinner and, himself on the one-eyed mule and Sam on the other one of the wagon team, they rode for more than three hours through the rapid shortening sunless afternoon, following no path, no trail even that he could discern, into a section of country he had never seen before. Then he understood why Sam had made him ride the one-eyed mule which would not spook at the smell of blood, of wild animals. The other one, the sound one, stopped short and tried to whirl and bolt even as Sam got down, jerking and wrenching at the rein while Sam held it, coaxing it forward with his voice since he did not dare risk hitching it, drawing it forward while the boy dismounted from the marred one which would stand. Then, standing beside Sam in the thick great gloom of ancient woods and the winter's dying afternoon, he looked quietly down at the rotted log scored and gutted with claw-marks and, in the wet earth beside it, the print of the enormous warped two-toed foot. Now he knew what he had heard in the hounds' voices in the woods that morning and what he had smelled when he peered under the kitchen where they huddled. It was in him too, a little different because they were brute beasts and he was not, but only a little different—an eagerness, passive; an abjectness, a sense of his own fragility and impotence against the timeless woods, yet without doubt or dread; a flavor like brass in the sudden run of saliva in his mouth, a hard sharp constriction either in his brain or his stomach, he could not tell which and it did not matter; he knew only that for the first time he realised that the bear which had run in his listening and loomed in his dreams since before he could remember and which therefore must have existed in the listening and the dreams of his cousin and Major de Spain and even old General Compson before they began to remember in their turn, was a mortal animal and that they had departed for the camp each November with no actual intention of slaying it, not because it could not be slain but because so far they had no actual hope of being able to. "It will be tomorrow," he said.

"You mean we will try tomorrow," Sam said. "We aint got the dog yet."

"We've got eleven," he said. "They ran him Monday."

"And you heard them," Sam said. "Saw them too. We aint got the dog yet. It wont take but one. But he aint there. Maybe he aint nowhere. The only other way will be for him to run by accident over somebody that had a gun and knowed how to shoot it."

"That wouldn't be me," the boy said. "It would be Walter or Major or——"

"It might," Sam said. "You watch close tomorrow. Because he's smart. That's how come he has lived this long. If he gets hemmed up and has got to pick out somebody to run over, he will pick out you."

"How?" he said. "How will he know. . . ." He ceased. "You mean he already knows me, that I aint never been to the big bottom before, aint had time to find out yet whether I . . ." He ceased again, staring at Sam; he said humbly, not even amazed: "It was me he was watching. I dont reckon he did need to come but once."

"You watch tomorrow," Sam said. "I reckon we better start back. It'll be long after dark now before we get to camp."

The next morning they started three hours earlier than they had ever done. Even Uncle Ash went, the cook, who called himself by profession a camp cook and who did little else save cook for Major de Spain's hunting and camping parties, yet who had been marked by the wilderness from simple juxtaposition to it until he responded as they all did, even the boy who until two weeks ago had never even seen the wilderness, to a hound's ripped ear and shoulder and the print of a crooked foot in a patch of wet earth. They rode. It was too far to walk: the boy and Sam and Uncle Ash in the wagon with the dogs, his cousin and Major de Spain and General Compson and Boon and Walter and Tennie's Jim riding double on the horses; again the first gray light found him, as on that first morning two weeks ago, on the stand where Sam had placed and left him. With the gun which was too big for him, the breech-loader[6] which did not even belong to him but to Major de Spain and which he had fired only once, at a stump on the first day to learn the recoil and how to reload it with the paper shells, he stood against a big gum tree beside a little bayou whose black still water crept without motion out of a cane-brake, across a small clearing and into the cane again, where, invisible, a bird, the big woodpecker called Lord-to-God[7] by negroes, clattered at a dead trunk. It was a stand like any other stand, dissimilar only in incidentals to the one where he had stood each morning for two weeks; a territory new to him yet no less familiar than that other one which after two

---

6. A gun that is loaded behind the barrel (through the breech), as opposed to the earlier muzzle-loader style.   7. The impressively large pileated woodpecker.

weeks he had come to believe he knew a little—the same solitude, the same loneliness through which frail and timorous man had merely passed without altering it, leaving no mark nor scar, which looked exactly as it must have looked when the first ancestor of Sam Fathers' Chickasaw predecessors crept into it and looked about him, club or stone axe or bone arrow drawn and ready, different only because, squatting at the edge of the kitchen, he had smelled the dogs huddled and cringing beneath it and saw the raked ear and side of the bitch that, as Sam had said, had to be brave once in order to keep on calling herself a dog, and saw yesterday in the earth beside the gutted log, the print of the living foot. He heard no dogs at all. He never did certainly hear them. He only heard the drumming of the woodpecker stop short off, and knew that the bear was looking at him. He never saw it. He did not know whether it was facing him from the cane or behind him. He did not move, holding the useless gun which he knew now he would never fire at it, now or ever, tasting in his saliva that taint of brass which he had smelled in the huddled dogs when he peered under the kitchen.

Then it was gone. As abruptly as it had stopped, the woodpecker's dry hammering set up again, and after a while he believed he even heard the dogs—a murmur, scarce a sound even, which he had probably been hearing for a time, perhaps a minute or two, before he remarked it, drifting into hearing and then out again, dying away. They came nowhere near him. If it was dogs he heard, he could not have sworn to it; if it was a bear they ran, it was another bear. It was Sam himself who emerged from the cane and crossed the bayou, the injured bitch following at heel as a bird dog is taught to walk. She came and crouched against his leg, trembling. "I didn't see him," he said. "I didn't, Sam."

"I know it," Sam said. "He done the looking. You didn't hear him neither, did you?"

"No," the boy said. "I—"

"He's smart," Sam said. "Too smart." Again the boy saw in his eyes that quality of dark and brooding lambence as Sam looked down at the bitch trembling faintly and steadily against the boy's leg. From her raked shoulder a few drops of fresh blood clung like bright berries. "Too big. We aint got the dog yet. But maybe some day."

Because there would be a next time, after and after. He was only ten. It seemed to him that he could see them, the two of them, shadowy in the limbo from which time emerged and became time: the old bear absolved of mortality and himself who shared a little of it. Because he recognised now what he had smelled in the huddled dogs and tasted in his own saliva, recognised fear as a boy, a youth, recognises the existence of love and passion and experience which is his heritage but not yet his patrimony, from entering by chance the presence or perhaps even merely the bedroom of a woman who has loved and been loved by many men. *So I will have to see him*, he thought, without dread or even hope. *I will have to look at him*. So it was in June of the next summer. They were at the camp again, celebrating Major de Spain's and General Compson's birthdays. Although the one had been born in September and the other in the depth of winter and almost thirty years earlier, each June the two of them and McCaslin and Boon and Walter Ewell (and the boy too from now on) spent two weeks at the camp, fishing and shooting squirrels and turkey and running coons and wildcats with the dogs at night.

That is, Boon and the negroes (and the boy too now) fished and shot squirrels and ran the coons and cats, because the proven hunters, not only Major de Spain and old General Compson (who spent those two weeks sitting in a rocking chair before a tremendous iron pot of Brunswick stew, stirring and tasting, with Uncle Ash to quarrel with about how he was making it and Tennie's Jim to pour whisky into the tin dipper from which he drank it) but even McCaslin and Walter Ewell who were still young enough, scorned such other than shooting the wild gobblers with pistols for wagers or to test their marksmanship.

That is, his cousin McCaslin and the others thought he was hunting squirrels. Until the third evening he believed that Sam Fathers thought so too. Each morning he would leave the camp right after breakfast. He had his own gun now, a new breech-loader, a Christmas gift; he would own and shoot it for almost seventy years, through two new pairs of barrels and locks and one new stock, until all that remained of the original gun was the silver-inlaid trigger-guard with his and McCaslin's engraved names and the date in 1878. He found the tree beside the little bayou[8] where he had stood that morning. Using the compass he ranged from that point; he was teaching himself to be better than a fair woodsman without even knowing he was doing it. On the third day he even found the gutted log where he had first seen the print. It was almost completely crumbled now, healing with unbelievable speed, a passionate and almost visible relinquishment, back into the earth from which the tree had grown. He ranged the summer woods now, green with gloom, if anything actually dimmer than they had been in November's gray dissolution, where even at noon the sun fell only in windless dappling upon the earth which never completely dried and which crawled with snakes—moccasins and water-snakes and rattlers, themselves the color of the dappled gloom so that he would not always see them until they moved; returning to camp later and later and later, first day, second day, passing in the twilight of the third evening the little log pen enclosing the log barn where Sam was putting up the stock for the night. "You aint looked right yet," Sam said.

He stopped. For a moment he didn't answer. Then he said peacefully, in a peaceful rushing burst, as when a boy's miniature dam in a little brook gives way: "All right. Yes. But how? I went to the bayou. I even found that log again. I—"

"I reckon that was all right. Likely he's been watching you. You never saw his foot?"

"I . . ." the boy said. "I didn't . . . I never thought . . ."

"It's the gun," Sam said. He stood beside the fence, motionless, the old man, son of a negro slave and a Chickasaw chief, in the battered and faded overalls and the frayed five-cent straw hat which had been the badge of the negro's slavery and was now the regalia of his freedom. The camp—the clearing, the house, the barn and its tiny lot with which Major de Spain in his turn had scratched punily and evanescently at the wilderness—faded in the dusk, back into the immemorial darkness of the woods. *The gun*, the boy thought. *The gun.* "You will have to choose," Sam said.

He left the next morning before light, without breakfast, long before Uncle Ash would wake in his quilts on the kitchen floor and start the fire. He had

---

8. Creek or small river.

only the compass and a stick for the snakes. He could go almost a mile before he would need to see the compass. He sat on a log, the invisible compass in his hand, while the secret night-sounds which had ceased at his movements, scurried again and then fell still for good and the owls ceased and gave over to the waking day birds and there was light in the gray wet woods and he could see the compass. He went fast yet still quietly, becoming steadily better and better as a woodsman without yet having time to realise it; he jumped a doe and a fawn, walked them[9] out of the bed, close enough to see them— the crash of undergrowth, the white scut, the fawn scudding along behind her, faster than he had known it could have run. He was hunting right, upwind, as Sam had taught him, but that didn't matter now. He had left the gun; by his own will and relinquishment he had accepted not a gambit, not a choice, but a condition in which not only the bear's heretofore inviolable anonymity but all the ancient rules and balances of hunter and hunted had been abrogated. He would not even be afraid, not even in the moment when the fear would take him completely: blood, skin, bowels, bones, memory from the long time before it even became his memory—all save that thin clear quenchless lucidity which alone differed him from this bear and from all the other bears and bucks he would follow during almost seventy years, to which Sam had said: "Be scared. You cant help that. But dont be afraid. Aint nothing in the woods going to hurt you if you dont corner it or it dont smell that you are afraid. A bear or a deer has got to be scared of a coward the same as a brave man has got to be."

By noon he was far beyond the crossing on the little bayou, farther into the new and alien country than he had ever been, travelling now not only by the compass but by the old, heavy, biscuit-thick silver watch which had been his father's. He had left the camp nine hours ago; nine hours from now, dark would already have been an hour old. He stopped, for the first time since he had risen from the log when he could see the compass face at last, and looked about, mopping his sweating face on his sleeve. He had already relinquished, of his will, because of his need, in humility and peace and without regret, yet apparently that had not been enough, the leaving of the gun was not enough. He stood for a moment—a child, alien and lost in the green and soaring gloom of the markless wilderness. Then he relinquished completely to it. It was the watch and the compass. He was still tainted. He removed the linked chain of the one and the looped thong of the other from his overalls and hung them on a bush and leaned the stick beside them and entered it.

When he realised he was lost, he did as Sam had coached and drilled him: made a cast to cross his backtrack. He had not been going very fast for the last two or three hours, and he had gone even less fast since he left the compass and watch on the bush. So he went slower still now, since the tree could not be very far; in fact, he found it before he really expected to and turned and went to it. But there was no bush beneath it, no compass nor watch, so he did next as Sam had coached and drilled him: made this next circle in the opposite direction and much larger, so that the pattern of the two of them would bisect his track somewhere, but crossing no trace nor mark anywhere of his feet or any feet, and now he was going faster though still not panicked, his heart beating a little more rapidly but strong and

9. Sneaked up without frightening them.

steady enough, and this time it was not even the tree because there was a down log beside it which he had never seen before and beyond the log a little swamp, a seepage of moisture somewhere between earth and water, and he did what Sam had coached and drilled him as the next and the last, seeing as he sat down on the log the crooked print, the warped indentation in the wet ground which while he looked at it continued to fill with water until it was level full and the water began to overflow and the sides of the print began to dissolve away. Even as he looked up he saw the next one, and, moving, the one beyond it: moving, not hurrying, running, but merely keeping pace with them as they appeared before him as though they were being shaped out of thin air just one constant pace short of where he would lose them forever and be lost forever himself, tireless, eager, without doubt or dread, panting a little above the strong rapid little hammer of his heart, emerging suddenly into a little glade and the wilderness coalesced. It rushed, soundless, and solidified—the tree, the bush, the compass and the watch glinting where a ray of sunlight touched them. Then he saw the bear. It did not emerge, appear: it was just there, immobile, fixed in the green and windless noon's hot dappling, not as big as he had dreamed it but as big as he had expected, bigger, dimensionless against the dappled obscurity, looking at him. Then it moved. It crossed the glade without haste, walking for an instant into the sun's full glare and out of it, and stopped again and looked back at him across one shoulder. Then it was gone. It didn't walk into the woods. It faded, sank back into the wilderness without motion as he had watched a fish, a huge old bass, sink back into the dark depths of its pool and vanish without even any movement of its fins.

2

So he should have hated and feared Lion. He was thirteen then. He had killed his buck and Sam Fathers had marked his face with the hot blood, and in the next November he killed a bear. But before that accolade he had become as competent in the woods as many grown men with the same experience. By now he was a better woodsman than most grown men with more. There was no territory within twenty-five miles of the camp that he did not know—bayou, ridge, landmark trees and path; he could have led anyone direct to any spot in it and brought him back. He knew game trails that even Sam Fathers had never seen; in the third fall he found a buck's bedding-place by himself and unbeknown to his cousin he borrowed Walter Ewell's rifle and lay in wait for the buck at dawn and killed it when it walked back to the bed as Sam had told him how the old Chickasaw fathers did.

By now he knew the old bear's footprint better than he did his own, and not only the crooked one. He could see any one of the three sound prints and distinguish it at once from any other, and not only because of its size. There were other bears within that fifty miles which left tracks almost as large, or at least so near that the one would have appeared larger only by juxtaposition. It was more than that. If Sam Fathers had been his mentor and the backyard rabbits and squirrels his kindergarten, then the wilderness the old bear ran was his college and the old male bear itself, so long unwifed and childless as to have become its own ungendered progenitor, was his alma mater.[1]

1. Cherished mother (Latin, literal trans.); one's former school or college.

He could find the crooked print now whenever he wished, ten miles or five miles or sometimes closer than that, to the camp. Twice while on stand during the next three years he heard the dogs strike its trail and once even jump it by chance, the voices high, abject, almost human in their hysteria. Once, still-hunting[2] with Walter Ewell's rifle, he saw it cross a long corridor of down timber where a tornado had passed. It rushed through rather than across the tangle of trunks and branches as a locomotive would, faster than he had ever believed it could have moved, almost as fast as a deer even because the deer would have spent most of that distance in the air; he realised then why it would take a dog not only of abnormal courage but size and speed too ever to bring it to bay. He had a little dog at home, a mongrel, of the sort called fyce by negroes, a ratter, itself not much bigger than a rat and possessing that sort of courage which had long since stopped being bravery and had become foolhardiness. He brought it with him one June and, timing them as if they were meeting an appointment with another human being, himself carrying the fyce with a sack over its head and Sam Fathers with a brace of the hounds on a rope leash, they lay downwind of the trail and actually ambushed the bear. They were so close that it turned at bay although he realised later this might have been from surprise and amazement at the shrill and frantic uproar of the fyce. It turned at bay against the trunk of a big cypress, on its hind feet; it seemed to the boy that it would never stop rising, taller and taller, and even the two hounds seemed to have taken a kind of desperate and despairing courage from the fyce. Then he realised that the fyce was actually not going to stop. He flung the gun down and ran. When he overtook and grasped the shrill, frantically pinwheeling little dog, it seemed to him that he was directly under the bear. He could smell it, strong and hot and rank. Sprawling, he looked up where it loomed and towered over him like a thunderclap. It was quite familiar, until he remembered: this was the way he had used to dream about it.

Then it was gone. He didn't see it go. He knelt, holding the frantic fyce with both hands, hearing the abased wailing of the two hounds drawing further and further away, until Sam came up, carrying the gun. He laid it quietly down beside the boy and stood looking down at him. "You've done seed him twice now, with a gun in your hands," he said. "This time you couldn't have missed him."

The boy rose. He still held the fyce. Even in his arms it continued to yap frantically, surging and straining toward the fading sound of the hounds like a collection of live-wire springs. The boy was panting a little. "Neither could you," he said. "You had the gun. Why didn't you shoot him?"

Sam didn't seem to have heard. He put out his hand and touched the little dog in the boy's arms which still yapped and strained even though the two hounds were out of hearing now. "He's done gone," Sam said. "You can slack off and rest now, until next time." He stroked the little dog until it began to grow quiet under his hand. "You's almost the one we wants," he said. "You just aint big enough. We aint got that one yet. He will need to be just a little bigger than smart, and a little braver than either." He withdrew his hand from the fyce's head and stood looking into the woods where the bear and the hounds had vanished. "Somebody is going to, some day."

---

2. The hunter alternately moves and stops, waiting for prey to pass by.

"I know it," the boy said. "That's why it must be one of us. So it wont be until the last day. When even he dont want it to last any longer."

So he should have hated and feared Lion. It was in the fourth summer, the fourth time he had made one in the celebration of Major de Spain's and General Compson's birthday. In the early spring Major de Spain's mare had foaled a horse colt. One evening when Sam brought the horses and mules up to stable them for the night, the colt was missing and it was all he could do to get the frantic mare into the lot. He had thought at first to let the mare lead him back to where she had become separated from the foal. But she would not do it. She would not even feint toward any particular part of the woods or even in any particular direction. She merely ran, as if she couldn't see, still frantic with terror. She whirled and ran at Sam once, as if to attack him in some ultimate desperation, as if she could not for the moment realise that he was a man and a long-familiar one. He got her into the lot at last. It was too dark by that time to back-track her, to unravel the erratic course she had doubtless pursued.

He came to the house and told Major de Spain. It was an animal, of course, a big one, and the colt was dead now, wherever it was. They all knew that. "It's a panther," General Compson said at once. "The same one. That doe and fawn last March." Sam had sent Major de Spain word of it when Boon Hogganbeck came to the camp on a routine visit to see how the stock had wintered—the doe's throat torn out, and the beast had run down the helpless fawn and killed it too.

"Sam never did say that was a panther," Major de Spain said. Sam said nothing now, standing behind Major de Spain where they sat at supper, inscrutable, as if he were just waiting for them to stop talking so he could go home. He didn't even seem to be looking at anything. "A panther might jump a doe, and he wouldn't have much trouble catching the fawn afterward. But no panther would have jumped that colt with the dam right there with it. It was Old Ben," Major de Spain said. "I'm disappointed in him. He has broken the rules. I didn't think he would have done that. He has killed mine and McCaslin's dogs, but that was all right. We gambled the dogs against him; we gave each other warning. But now he has come into my house and destroyed my property, out of season too. He broke the rules. It was Old Ben, Sam." Still Sam said nothing, standing there until Major de Spain should stop talking. "We'll back-track her tomorrow and see," Major de Spain said.

Sam departed. He would not live in the camp; he had built himself a little hut something like Joe Baker's, only stouter, tighter, on the bayou a quarter-mile away, and a stout log crib where he stored a little corn for the shoat he raised each year. The next morning he was waiting when they waked. He had already found the colt. They did not even wait for breakfast. It was not far, not five hundred yards from the stable—the three-months' colt lying on its side, its throat torn out and the entrails and one ham partly eaten. It lay not as if it had been dropped but as if it had been struck and hurled, and no cat-mark, no claw-mark where a panther would have gripped it while finding its throat. They read the tracks where the frantic mare had circled and at last rushed in with that same ultimate desperation with which she had whirled on Sam Fathers yesterday evening, and the long tracks of dead and terrified running and those of the beast which had not even rushed at her when she advanced but had merely walked three or four paces toward her until she broke, and General Compson said, "Good God, what a wolf!"

Still Sam said nothing. The boy watched him while the men knelt, measuring the tracks. There was something in Sam's face now. It was neither exultation nor joy nor hope. Later, a man, the boy realised what it had been, and that Sam had known all the time what had made the tracks and what had torn the throat out of the doe in the spring and killed the fawn. It had been foreknowledge in Sam's face that morning. *And he was glad,* he told himself. *He was old. He had no children, no people, none of his blood anywhere above earth that he would ever meet again. And even if he were to, he could not have touched it, spoken to it, because for seventy years now he had had to be a negro. It was almost over now and he was glad.*

They returned to camp and had breakfast and came back with guns and the hounds. Afterward the boy realised that they also should have known then what killed the colt as well as Sam Fathers did. But that was neither the first nor the last time he had seen men rationalise from and even act upon their misconceptions. After Boon, standing astride the colt, had whipped the dogs away from it with his belt, they snuffed at the tracks. One of them, a young dog hound without judgment yet, bayed once, and they ran for a few feet on what seemed to be a trail. Then they stopped, looking back at the men, eager enough, not baffled, merely questioning, as if they were asking "Now what?" Then they rushed back to the colt, where Boon, still astride it, slashed at them with the belt.

"I never knew a trail to get cold that quick," General Compson said.

"Maybe a single wolf big enough to kill a colt with the dam right there beside it dont leave scent," Major de Spain said.

"Maybe it was a hant," Walter Ewell said. He looked at Tennie's Jim. "Hah, Jim?"

Because the hounds would not run it, Major de Spain had Sam hunt out and find the tracks a hundred yards farther on and they put the dogs on it again and again the young one bayed and not one of them realised then that the hound was not baying like a dog striking game but was merely bellowing like a country dog whose yard has been invaded. General Compson spoke to the boy and Boon and Tennie's Jim: to the squirrel hunters. "You boys keep the dogs with you this morning. He's probably hanging around somewhere, waiting to get his breakfast off the colt. You might strike him."

But they did not. The boy remembered how Sam stood watching them as they went into the woods with the leashed hounds—the Indian face in which he had never seen anything until it smiled, except that faint arching of the nostrils on that first morning when the hounds had found Old Ben. They took the hounds with them on the next day, though when they reached the place where they hoped to strike a fresh trail, the carcass of the colt was gone. Then on the third morning Sam was waiting again, this time until they had finished breakfast. He said, "Come." He led them to his house, his little hut, to the corn-crib beyond it. He had removed the corn and had made a deadfall of the door, baiting it with the colt's carcass; peering between the logs, they saw an animal almost the color of a gun or pistol barrel, what little time they had to examine its color or shape. It was not crouched nor even standing. It was in motion, in the air, coming toward them—a heavy body crashing with tremendous force against the door so that the thick door jumped and clattered in its frame, the animal, whatever it was, hurling itself against the door again seemingly before it could have touched the floor and got a new purchase to spring from. "Come away," Sam said, "fore he break his neck." Even when they retreated the heavy and measured crashes continued, the stout door jumping and clattering each time, and still no sound from the beast itself—no snarl, no cry.

"What in hell's name is it?" Major de Spain said.

"It's a dog," Sam said, his nostrils arching and collapsing faintly and steadily and that faint, fierce milkiness in his eyes again as on that first morning when the hounds had struck the old bear. "It's the dog."

"*The* dog?" Major de Spain said.

"That's gonter hold Old Ben."

"Dog the devil," Major de Spain said. "I'd rather have Old Ben himself in my pack than that brute. Shoot him."

"No," Sam said.

"You'll never tame him. How do you ever expect to make an animal like that afraid of you?"

"I dont want him tame," Sam said; again the boy watched his nostrils and the fierce milky light in his eyes. "But I almost rather he be tame than scared, of me or any man or any thing. But he wont be neither, of nothing."

"Then what are you going to do with it?"

"You can watch," Sam said.

Each morning through the second week they would go to Sam's crib. He had removed a few shingles from the roof and had put a rope on the colt's carcass and had drawn it out when the trap fell. Each morning they would watch him lower a pail of water into the crib while the dog hurled itself tirelessly against the door and dropped back and leaped again. It never made any sound and there was nothing frenzied in the act but only a cold and grim indomitable determination. Toward the end of the week it stopped jumping at the door. Yet it had not weakened appreciably and it was not as if it had rationalised the fact that the door was not going to give. It was as if for that time it simply disdained to jump any longer. It was not down. None of them had ever seen it down. It stood, and they could see it now—part mastiff, something of Airedale and something of a dozen other strains probably, better than thirty inches at the shoulders and weighing as they guessed almost ninety pounds, with cold yellow eyes and a tremendous chest and over all that strange color like a blued gun-barrel.

Then the two weeks were up. They prepared to break camp. The boy begged to remain and his cousin let him. He moved into the little hut with Sam Fathers. Each morning he watched Sam lower the pail of water into the crib. By the end of that week the dog was down. It would rise and half stagger, half crawl to the water and drink and collapse again. One morning it could not even reach the water, could not raise its forequarters even from the floor. Sam took a short stick and prepared to enter the crib. "Wait," the boy said. "Let me get the gun—"

"No," Sam said. "He cant move now." Nor could it. It lay on its side while Sam touched it, its head and the gaunted body, the dog lying motionless, the yellow eyes open. They were not fierce and there was nothing of petty malevolence in them, but a cold and almost impersonal malignance like some natural force. It was not even looking at Sam nor at the boy peering at it between the logs.

Sam began to feed it again. The first time he had to raise its head so it could lap the broth. That night he left a bowl of broth containing lumps of meat where the dog could reach it. The next morning the bowl was empty and the dog was lying on its belly, its head up, the cold yellow eyes watching the door as Sam entered, no change whatever in the cold yellow eyes and still no sound from it even when it sprang, its aim and co-ordination still bad from weakness so that Sam had time to strike it down with the stick and leap from the crib and slam the door as the dog, still without having had time to get its feet under it to jump again seemingly, hurled itself against the door as if the two weeks of starving had never been.

At noon that day someone came whooping through the woods from the direction of the camp. It was Boon. He came and looked for a while between the logs, at the tremendous dog lying again on its belly, its head up, the yellow eyes blinking sleepily at nothing: the indomitable and unbroken spirit. "What we better do," Boon said, "is to let that son of a bitch go and catch Old Ben and run him on the dog." He turned to the boy his weather-reddened and beetling face. "Get your traps together. Cass says for you to come on home. You been in here fooling with that horse-eating varmint long enough."

Boon had a borrowed mule at the camp; the buggy was waiting at the edge of the bottom. He was at home that night. He told McCaslin about it. "Sam's going to starve him again until he can go in and touch him. Then he will feed him again. Then he will starve him again, if he has to."

"But why?" McCaslin said. "What for? Even Sam will never tame that brute."

"We dont want him tame. We want him like he is. We just want him to find out at last that the only way he can get out of that crib and stay out of it is to do what Sam or somebody tells him to do. He's the dog that's going to stop Old Ben and hold him. We've already named him. His name is Lion."

Then November came at last. They returned to the camp. With General Compson and Major de Spain and his cousin and Walter and Boon he stood in the yard among the guns and bedding and boxes of food and watched Sam Fathers and Lion come up the lane from the lot—the Indian, the old man in battered overalls and rubber boots and a worn sheepskin coat and a hat which had belonged to the boy's father; the tremendous dog pacing gravely beside him. The hounds rushed out to meet them and stopped, except the young one which still had but little of judgment. It ran up to Lion, fawning. Lion didn't snap at it. He didn't even pause. He struck it rolling and yelping for five or six feet with a blow of one paw as a bear would have done and came on into the yard and stood, blinking sleepily at nothing, looking at no one, while Boon said, "Jesus. Jesus.—Will he let me touch him?"

"You can touch him," Sam said. "He dont care. He dont care about nothing or nobody."

The boy watched that too. He watched it for the next two years from that moment when Boon touched Lion's head and then knelt beside him, feeling the bones and muscles, the power. It was as if Lion were a woman—or perhaps Boon was the woman. That was more like it—the big, grave, sleepy-seeming dog which, as Sam Fathers said, cared about no man and no thing; and the violent, insensitive, hard-faced man with his touch of remote Indian blood and the mind almost of a child. He watched Boon take over Lion's feeding from Sam and Uncle Ash both. He would see Boon squatting in the cold rain beside the kitchen while Lion ate. Because Lion neither slept nor ate with the other dogs though none of them knew where he did sleep until in the second November, thinking until then that Lion slept in his kennel beside Sam Fathers' hut, when the boy's cousin McCaslin said something about it to Sam by sheer chance and Sam told him. And that night the boy and Major de Spain and McCaslin with a lamp entered the back room where Boon slept—the little, tight, airless room rank with the smell of Boon's unwashed body and his wet hunting-clothes—where Boon, snoring on his back, choked and waked and Lion raised his head beside him and looked back at them from his cold, slumbrous yellow eyes.

"Damn it, Boon," McCaslin said. "Get that dog out of here. He's got to run Old Ben tomorrow morning. How in hell do you expect him to smell anything fainter than a skunk after breathing you all night?"

"The way I smell aint hurt my nose none that I ever noticed," Boon said.

"It wouldn't matter if it had," Major de Spain said. "We're not depending on you to trail a bear. Put him outside. Put him under the house with the other dogs."

Boon began to get up. "He'll kill the first one that happens to yawn or sneeze in his face or touches him."

"I reckon not," Major de Spain said. "None of them are going to risk yawning in his face or touching him either, even asleep. Put him outside. I want his nose right tomorrow. Old Ben fooled him last year. I dont think he will do it again."

Boon put on his shoes without lacing them; in his long soiled underwear, his hair still tousled from sleep, he and Lion went out. The others returned to the front room and the poker game where McCaslin's and Major de Spain's hands waited for them on the table. After a while McCaslin said, "Do you want me to go back and look again?"

"No," Major de Spain said. "I call," he said to Walter Ewell. He spoke to McCaslin again. "If you do, dont tell me. I am beginning to see the first sign of my increasing age: I dont like to know that my orders have been disobeyed, even when I knew when I gave them that they would be.—A small pair," he said to Walter Ewell.

"How small?" Walter said.

"Very small," Major de Spain said.

And the boy, lying beneath his piled quilts and blankets waiting for sleep, knew likewise that Lion was already back in Boon's bed, for the rest of that night and the next one and during all the nights of the next November and the next one. He thought then: *I wonder what Sam thinks. He could have Lion with him, even if Boon is a white man. He could ask Major or McCaslin either. And more than that. It was Sam's hand that touched Lion first and Lion knows it.* Then he became a man and he knew that too. It had been all right. That was the way it should have been. Sam was the chief, the prince; Boon, the plebeian, was his huntsman. Boon should have nursed the dogs.

On the first morning that Lion led the pack after Old Ben, seven strangers appeared in the camp. They were swampers: gaunt, malaria-ridden men appearing from nowhere, who ran trap-lines for coons or perhaps farmed little patches of cotton and corn along the edge of the bottom, in clothes but little better than Sam Fathers' and nowhere near as good as Tennie's Jim's, with worn shotguns and rifles, already squatting patiently in the cold drizzle in the side yard when day broke. They had a spokesman; afterward Sam

Fathers told Major de Spain how all during the past summer and fall they had drifted into the camp singly or in pairs and threes, to look quietly at Lion for a while and then go away: "Mawnin, Major. We heerd you was aimin to put that ere blue dawg on that old two-toed bear this mawnin. We figgered we'd come up and watch, if you dont mind. We wont do no shooting, lessen he runs over us."

"You are welcome," Major de Spain said. "You are welcome to shoot. He's more your bear than ours."

"I reckon that aint no lie. I done fed him enough cawn to have a sheer[3] in him. Not to mention a shoat three years ago."

"I reckon I got a sheer too," another said. "Only it aint in the bear." Major de Spain looked at him. He was chewing tobacco. He spat. "Hit was a heifer calf. Nice un too. Last year. When I finally found her, I reckon she looked about like that colt of yourn looked last June."

"Oh," Major de Spain said. "Be welcome. If you see game in front of my dogs, shoot it."

Nobody shot Old Ben that day. No man saw him. The dogs jumped him within a hundred yards of the glade where the boy had seen him that day in the summer of his eleventh year. The boy was less than a quarter-mile away. He heard the jump but he could distinguish no voice among the dogs that he did not know and therefore would be Lion's, and he thought, believed, that Lion was not among them. Even the fact that they were going much faster than he had ever heard them run behind Old Ben before and that the high thin note of hysteria was missing now from their voices was not enough to disabuse him. He didn't comprehend until that night, when Sam told him that Lion would never cry on a trail. "He gonter growl when he catches Old Ben's throat," Sam said. "But he aint gonter never holler, no more than he ever done when he was jumping at that two-inch door. It's that blue dog in him. What you call it?"

"Airedale," the boy said.

Lion was there; the jump was just too close to the river. When Boon returned with Lion about eleven that night, he swore that Lion had stopped Old Ben once but that the hounds would not go in and Old Ben broke away and took to the river and swam for miles down it and he and Lion went down one bank for about ten miles and crossed and came up the other but it had begun to get dark before they struck any trail where Old Ben had come up out of the water, unless he was still in the water when he passed the ford where they crossed. Then he fell to cursing the hounds and ate the supper Uncle Ash had saved for him and went off to bed and after a while the boy opened the door of the little stale room thunderous with snoring and the great grave dog raised its head from Boon's pillow and blinked at him for a moment and lowered its head again.

When the next November came and the last day, the day on which it was now becoming traditional to save for Old Ben, there were more than a dozen strangers waiting. They were not all swampers this time. Some of them were townsmen, from other county seats like Jefferson, who had heard about Lion and Old Ben and had come to watch the great blue dog keep his yearly

3. *Sheer:* share (dialect). *Cawn:* corn.

rendezvous with the old two-toed bear. Some of them didn't even have guns and the hunting-clothes and boots they wore had been on a store shelf yesterday.

This time Lion jumped Old Ben more than five miles from the river and bayed and held him and this time the hounds went in, in a sort of desperate emulation. The boy heard them; he was that near. He heard Boon whooping; he heard the two shots when General Compson delivered both barrels, one containing five buckshot, the other a single ball, into the bear from as close as he could force his almost unmanageable horse. He heard the dogs when the bear broke free again. He was running now; panting, stumbling, his lungs bursting, he reached the place where General Compson had fired and where Old Ben had killed two of the hounds. He saw the blood from General Compson's shots, but he could go no further. He stopped, leaning against a tree for his breathing to ease and his heart to slow, hearing the sound of the dogs as it faded on and died away.

In camp that night—they had as guests five of the still terrified strangers in new hunting coats and boots who had been lost all day until Sam Fathers went out and got them—he heard the rest of it: how Lion had stopped and held the bear again but only the one-eyed mule which did not mind the smell of wild blood would approach and Boon was riding the mule and Boon had never been known to hit anything. He shot at the bear five times with his pump gun,[4] touching nothing, and Old Ben killed another hound and broke free once more and reached the river and was gone. Again Boon and Lion hunted as far down one bank as they dared. Too far; they crossed in the first of dusk and dark overtook them within a mile. And this time Lion found the broken trail, the blood perhaps, in the darkness where Old Ben had come up out of the water, but Boon had him on a rope, luckily, and he got down from the mule and fought Lion hand-to-hand until he got him back to camp. This time Boon didn't even curse. He stood in the door, muddy, spent, his huge gargoyle's face tragic and still amazed. "I missed him," he said. "I was in twenty-five feet of him and I missed him five times."

"But we have drawn blood," Major de Spain said. "General Compson drew blood. We have never done that before."

"But I missed him," Boon said. "I missed him five times. With Lion looking right at me."

"Never mind," Major de Spain said. "It was a damned fine race. And we drew blood. Next year we'll let General Compson or Walter ride Katie, and we'll get him."

Then McCaslin said, "Where is Lion, Boon?"

"I left him at Sam's," Boon said. He was already turning away. "I aint fit to sleep with him."

So he should have hated and feared Lion. Yet he did not. It seemed to him that there was a fatality in it. It seemed to him that something, he didn't know what, was beginning; had already begun. It was like the last act on a set stage. It was the beginning of the end of something, he didn't know what except that he would not grieve. He would be humble and proud that he had been found worth to be a part of it too or even just to see it too.

---

4. A repeating shotgun that fires only when a slide below the barrel is pushed in and out (i.e., pumped).

3

It was December. It was the coldest December he had ever remembered. They had been in camp four days over two weeks, waiting for the weather to soften so that Lion and Old Ben could run their yearly race. Then they would break camp and go home. Because of these unforeseen additional days which they had had to pass waiting on the weather, with nothing to do but play poker, the whisky had given out and he and Boon were being sent to Memphis with a suitcase and a note from Major de Spain to Mr Semmes, the distiller, to get more. That is, Major de Spain and McCaslin were sending Boon to get the whisky and sending him to see that Boon got back with it or most of it or at least some of it.

Tennie's Jim waked him at three. He dressed rapidly, shivering, not so much from the cold because a fresh fire already boomed and roared on the hearth, but in that dead winter hour when the blood and the heart are slow and sleep is incomplete. He crossed the gap between house and kitchen, the gap of iron earth beneath the brilliant and rigid night where dawn would not begin for three hours yet, tasting, tongue palate and to the very bottom of his lungs the searing dark, and entered the kitchen, the lamp-lit warmth where the stove glowed, fogging the windows, and where Boon already sat at the table at breakfast, hunched over his plate, almost in his plate, his working jaws blue with stubble and his face innocent of water and his coarse, horse-mane hair innocent of comb—the quarter Indian, grandson of a Chickasaw squaw, who on occasion resented with his hard and furious fists the intimation of one single drop of alien blood and on others, usually after whisky, affirmed with the same fists and the same fury that his father had been the full-blood Chickasaw and even a chief and that even his mother had been only half white. He was four inches over six feet; he had the mind of a child, the heart of a horse, and little hard shoe-button eyes without depth or meanness or generosity or viciousness or gentleness or anything else, in the ugliest face the boy had ever seen. It looked like somebody had found a walnut a little larger than a football and with a machinist's hammer had shaped features into it and then painted it, mostly red; not Indian red but a fine bright ruddy color which whisky might have had something to do with but which was mostly just happy and violent out-of-doors, the wrinkles in it not the residue of the forty years it had survived but from squinting into the sun or into the gloom of cane-brakes where game had run, baked into it by the camp fires before which he had lain trying to sleep on the cold November or December ground while waiting for daylight so he could rise and hunt again, as though time were merely something he walked through as he did through air, aging him no more than air did. He was brave, faithful, improvident and unreliable; he had neither profession job nor trade and owned one vice and one virtue: whisky, and that absolute and unquestioning fidelity to Major de Spain and the boy's cousin McCaslin. "Sometimes I'd call them both virtues," Major de Spain said once. "Or both vices," McCaslin said.

He ate his breakfast, hearing the dogs under the kitchen, wakened by the smell of frying meat or perhaps by the feet overhead. He heard Lion once, short and peremptory, as the best hunter in any camp has only to speak once to all save the fools, and none other of Major de Spain's and Mc-Caslin's dogs were Lion's equal in size and strength and perhaps even in courage, but they were not fools; Old Ben had killed the last fool among them last year.

Tennie's Jim came in as they finished. The wagon was outside. Ash decided he would drive them over to the log-line where they would flag the outbound log-train and let Tennie's Jim wash the dishes. The boy knew why. It would not be the first time he had listened to old Ash badgering Boon.

It was cold. The wagon wheels banged and clattered on the frozen ground; the sky was fixed and brilliant. He was not shivering, he was shaking, slow and steady and hard, the food he had just eaten still warm and solid inside him while his outside shook slow and steady around it as though his stomach floated loose. "They wont run this morning," he said. "No dog will have any nose today."

"Cep Lion," Ash said. "Lion dont need no nose. All he need is a bear." He had wrapped his feet in towsacks and he had a quilt from his pallet bed on the kitchen floor drawn over his head and wrapped around him until in the thin brilliant starlight he looked like nothing at all that the boy had ever seen before. "He run a bear through a thousand-acre ice-house. Catch him too. Them other dogs dont matter because they aint going to keep up with Lion nohow, long as he got a bear in front of him."

"What's wrong with the other dogs?" Boon said. "What the hell do you know about it anyway? This is the first time you've had your tail out of that kitchen since we got here except to chop a little wood."

"Aint nothing wrong with them," Ash said. "And long as it's left up to them, aint nothing going to be. I just wish I had knowed all my life how to take care of my health good as them hounds knows."

"Well, they aint going to run this morning," Boon said. His voice was harsh and positive. "Major promised they wouldn't until me and Ike get back."

"Weather gonter break today. Gonter soft up. Rain by night." Then Ash laughed, chuckled, somewhere inside the quilt which concealed even his face. "Hum up here, mules!" he said, jerking the reins so that the mules leaped forward and snatched the lurching and banging wagon for several feet before they slowed again into their quick, short-paced, rapid plodding. "Sides, I like to know why Major need to wait on you. It's Lion he aiming to use. I aint never heard tell of you bringing no bear nor no other kind of meat into this camp."

Now Boon's going to curse Ash or maybe even hit him, the boy thought. But Boon never did, never had; the boy knew he never would even though four years ago Boon had shot five times with a borrowed pistol at a negro on the street in Jefferson, with the same result as when he had shot five times at Old Ben last fall. "By God," Boon said, "he aint going to put Lion or no other dog on nothing until I get back tonight. Because he promised me. Whip up them mules and keep them whipped up. Do you want me to freeze to death?"

They reached the log-line and built a fire. After a while the log-train came up out of the woods under the paling east and Boon flagged it. Then in the warm caboose the boy slept again while Boon and the conductor and brakeman talked about Lion and Old Ben as people later would talk about Sullivan and Kilrain and, later still, about Dempsey and Tunney.[5] Dozing, swaying as the springless caboose lurched and clattered, he would hear them still talking, about the shoats and calves Old Ben had killed and the cribs he had rifled and the traps and deadfalls he had wrecked and the lead he probably carried under his hide—Old Ben, the two-toed bear in a land where bears with trap-ruined feet had been called Two-Toe or Three-Toe or Cripple-Foot for fifty years, only Old Ben was an extra bear (the head bear, General Compson called him) and so had earned a name such as a human man could have worn and not been sorry.

They reached Hoke's at sunup. They emerged from the warm caboose in their hunting clothes, the muddy boots and stained khaki and Boon's blue unshaven jowls. But that was all right. Hoke's was a sawmill and commissary and two stores and a loading-chute on a sidetrack from the main line, and all the men in it wore boots and khaki too. Presently the Memphis train came. Boon bought three packages of popcorn-and-molasses and a bottle of beer from the news butch[6] and the boy went to sleep again to the sound of his chewing.

But in Memphis it was not all right. It was as if the high buildings and the hard pavements, the fine carriages and the horse cars[7] and the men in starched collars and neckties made their boots and khaki look a little rougher and a little muddier and made Boon's beard look worse and more unshaven and his face look more and more like he should never have brought it out of the woods at all or at least out of reach of Major de Spain or McCaslin or someone who knew it and could have said, "Dont be afraid. He wont hurt you." He walked through the station, on the slick floor, his face moving as he worked the popcorn out of his teeth with his tongue, his legs spraddled and stiff in the hips as if he were walking on buttered glass, and that blue stubble on his face like the filings from a new gun-barrel. They passed the first saloon. Even through the closed doors the boy could seem to smell the sawdust and the reek of old drink. Boon began to cough. He coughed for something less than a minute. "Damn this cold," he said. "I'd sure like to know where I got it."

"Back there in the station," the boy said.

Boon had started to cough again. He stopped. He looked at the boy. "What?" he said.

"You never had it when we left camp nor on the train either." Boon looked at him, blinking. Then he stopped blinking. He didn't cough again. He said quietly:

"Lend me a dollar. Come on. You've got it. If you ever had one, you've still got it. I dont mean you are tight with your money because you aint. You just dont never seem to ever think of nothing you want. When I was sixteen a dollar bill melted off of me before I even had time to read the name of the bank that issued it."[8] He said quietly: "Let me have a dollar, Ike."

"You promised Major. You promised McCaslin. Not till we get back to camp."

<hr>

5. Famous boxing matches. John L. Sullivan (1858–1918), heavyweight boxer who vanquished Jake Kilrain (1859–1937) in a seventy-five-round bare-knuckle championship fight held at a lumber camp in Richburg, Mississippi, on July 8, 1889. William H. ("Jack") Dempsey (1895–1983) tried unsuccessfully to regain his world championship from James J. ("Gene") Tunney (1898–1978) on September 22, 1927, before a large crowd at Chicago's Soldier Field.   6. A vendor of newspapers and snacks on the train.   7. Horse-drawn streetcars.   8. Before 1865, various Mississippi banks and counties issued their own currency.

"All right," Boon said in that quiet and patient voice. "What can I do on just one dollar? You aint going to lend me another."

"You're damn right I aint," the boy said, his voice quiet too, cold with rage which was not at Boon, remembering: Boon snoring in a hard chair in the kitchen so he could watch the clock and wake him and McCaslin and drive them the seventeen miles in to Jefferson to catch the train to Memphis; the wild, never-bridled Texas paint pony which he had persuaded McCaslin to let him buy and which he and Boon had bought at auction for four dollars and seventy-five cents and fetched home wired between two gentle old mares with pieces of barbed wire and which had never even seen shelled corn before and didn't even know what it was unless the grains were bugs maybe and at last (he was ten and Boon had been ten all his life) Boon said the pony was gentled and with a towsack over its head and four negroes to hold it they backed it into an old two-wheeled cart and hooked up the gear and he and Boon got up and Boon said, "All right, boys. Let him go" and one of the negroes—it was Tennie's Jim—snatched the towsack off and leaped for his life and they lost the first wheel against a post of the open gate only at that moment Boon caught him by the scruff of the neck and flung him into the roadside ditch so he only saw the rest of it in fragments: the other wheel as it slammed through the side gate and crossed the back yard and leaped up onto the gallery and scraps of the cart here and there along the road and Boon vanishing rapidly on his stomach in the leaping and spurting dust and still holding the reins until they broke too and two days later they finally caught the pony seven miles away still wearing the hames[9] and the headstall of the bridle around its neck like a duchess with two necklaces at one time. He gave Boon the dollar.

"All right," Boon said. "Come on in out of the cold."

"I aint cold," he said.

"You can have some lemonade."

"I dont want any lemonade."

The door closed behind him. The sun was well up now. It was a brilliant day, though Ash had said it would rain before night. Already it was warmer; they could run tomorrow. He felt the old lift of the heart, as pristine as ever, as on the first day; he would never lose it, no matter how old in hunting and pursuit: the best, the best of all breathing, the humility and the pride. He must stop thinking about it. Already it seemed to him that he was running, back to the station, to the tracks themselves: the first train going south; he must stop thinking about it. The street was busy. He watched the big Norman draft horses, the Percherons;[1] the trim carriages from which the men in the fine overcoats and the ladies rosy in furs descended and entered the station. (They were still next door to it but one.) Twenty years ago his father had ridden into Memphis as a member of Colonel Sartoris' horse in Forrest's[2] command, up Main street and (the tale told) into the lobby of the Gayoso Hotel where the Yankee officers sat in the leather chairs spitting into the tall bright cuspidors and then out again, scot-free—

9. Curved harness pieces that fit around the neck of a horse.   1. Large, powerful farm horses used, like *Norman draft horses,* for heavy labor.   2. Confederate general Nathan Bedford Forrest (1821–1877). It was actually his brother, William, who rode into the Gayoso Hotel in an unsuccessful attempt to capture Union general Stephen Hurlbut. *Horse:* cavalry. In Faulkner's novels, Colonel Sartoris commanded a cavalry unit under General Forrest.

The door opened behind him. Boon was wiping his mouth on the back of his hand. "All right," he said. "Let's go tend to it and get the hell out of here."

They went and had the suitcase packed. He never knew where or when Boon got the other bottle. Doubtless Mr Semmes gave it to him. When they reached Hoke's again at sundown, it was empty. They could get a return train to Hoke's in two hours; they went straight back to the station as Major de Spain and then McCaslin had told Boon to do and then ordered him to do and had sent the boy along to see that he did. Boon took the first drink from his bottle in the wash room. A man in a uniform cap came to tell him he couldn't drink there and looked at Boon's face once and said nothing. The next time he was pouring into his water glass beneath the edge of a table in the restaurant when the manager (she was a woman) did tell him he couldn't drink there and he went back to the washroom. He had been telling the negro waiter and all the other people in the restaurant who couldn't help but hear him and who had never heard of Lion and didn't want to, about Lion and Old Ben. Then he happened to think of the zoo. He had found out that there was another train to Hoke's at three oclock and so they would spend the time at the zoo and take the three oclock train until he came back from the washroom for the third time. Then they would take the first train back to camp, get Lion and come back to the zoo where, he said, the bears were fed on ice cream and lady fingers and he would match Lion against them all.

So they missed the first train, the one they were supposed to take, but he got Boon onto the three oclock train and they were all right again, with Boon not even going to the washroom now but drinking in the aisle and talking about Lion and the men he buttonholed no more daring to tell Boon he couldn't drink there than the man in the station had dared.

When they reached Hoke's at sundown, Boon was asleep. The boy waked him at last and got him and the suitcase off the train and he even persuaded him to eat some supper at the sawmill commissary. So he was all right when they got in the caboose of the log-train to go back into the woods, with the sun going down red and the sky already overcast and the ground would not freeze tonight. It was the boy who slept now, sitting behind the ruby stove while the springless caboose jumped and clattered and Boon and the brake-man and the conductor talked about Lion and Old Ben because they knew what Boon was talking about because this was home. "Overcast and already thawing," Boon said. "Lion will get him tomorrow."

It would have to be Lion, or somebody. It would not be Boon. He had never hit anything bigger than a squirrel that anybody ever knew, except the negro woman that day when he was shooting at the negro man. He was a big negro and not ten feet away but Boon shot five times with the pistol he had borrowed from Major de Spain's negro coachman and the negro he was shooting at outed with a dollar-and-a-half mail-order pistol and would have burned Boon down with it only it never went off, it just went snicksnick-snicksnicksnick five times and Boon still blasting away and he broke a plate-glass window that cost McCaslin forty-five dollars and hit a negro woman who happened to be passing in the leg only Major de Spain paid for that; he and McCaslin cut cards, the plate-glass window against the negro woman's leg. And the first day on stand this year, the first morning in camp, the buck ran right over Boon; he heard Boon's old pump gun go whow. whow. whow.

whow. whow. and then his voice: "God damn, here he comes! Head him! Head him!" and when he got there the buck's tracks and the five exploded shells were not twenty paces apart.

There were five guests in camp that night, from Jefferson: Mr Bayard Sartoris and his son and General Compson's son and two others. And the next morning he looked out the window, into the gray thin drizzle of daybreak which Ash had predicted, and there they were, standing and squatting beneath the thin rain, almost two dozen of them who had fed Old Ben corn and shoats and even calves for ten years, in their worn hats and hunting coats and overalls which any town negro would have thrown away or burned and only the rubber boots strong and sound, and the worn and blueless guns,[3] and some even without guns. While they ate breakfast a dozen more arrived, mounted and on foot: loggers from the camp thirteen miles below and saw-mill men from Hoke's and the only gun among them that one which the log-train conductor carried: so that when they went into the woods this morning Major de Spain led a party almost as strong, excepting that some of them were not armed, as some he had led in the last darkening days of '64 and '65.[4] The little yard would not hold them. They overflowed it, into the lane where Major de Spain sat his mare while Ash in his dirty apron thrust the greasy cartridges into his carbine[5] and passed it up to him and the great grave blue dog stood at his stirrup not as a dog stands but as a horse stands, blinking his sleepy topaz eyes at nothing, deaf even to the yelling of the hounds which Boon and Tennie's Jim held on leash.

"We'll put General Compson on Katie this morning," Major de Spain said. "He drew blood last year; if he'd had a mule then that would have stood, he would have—"

"No," General Compson said. "I'm too old to go helling through the woods on a mule or a horse or anything else any more. Besides, I had my chance last year and missed it. I'm going on a stand this morning. I'm going to let that boy ride Katie."

"No, wait," McCaslin said. "Ike's got the rest of his life to hunt bears in. Let somebody else—"

"No," General Compson said. "I want Ike to ride Katie. He's already a better woodsman than you or me either and in another ten years he'll be as good as Walter."

At first he couldn't believe it, not until Major de Spain spoke to him. Then he was up, on the one-eyed mule which would not spook at wild blood, looking down at the dog motionless at Major de Spain's stirrup, looking in the gray streaming light bigger than a calf, bigger than he knew it actually was—the big head, the chest almost as big as his own, the blue hide beneath which the muscles flinched or quivered to no touch since the heart which drove blood to them loved no man and no thing, standing as a horse stands yet different from a horse which infers only weight and speed while Lion inferred not only courage and all else that went to make up the will and desire to pursue and kill, but endurance, the will and desire to endure beyond all imaginable limits of flesh in order to overtake and slay. Then the dog looked at him. It moved its head and looked at him across the trivial uproar

---

3. Guns whose blued metal parts have lost their color. 4. Toward the end of the Civil War (1860–65).
5. A gun that is somewhat shorter than a rifle.

of the hounds, out of the yellow eyes as depthless as Boon's, as free as Boon's of meanness or generosity or gentleness or viciousness. They were just cold and sleepy. Then it blinked, and he knew it was not looking at him and never had been, without even bothering to turn its head away.

That morning he heard the first cry. Lion had already vanished while Sam and Tennie's Jim were putting saddles on the mule and horse which had drawn the wagon and he watched the hounds as they crossed and cast, snuffing and whimpering, until they too disappeared. Then he and Major de Spain and Sam and Tennie's Jim rode after them and heard the first cry out of the wet and thawing woods not two hundred yards ahead, high, with that abject, almost human quality he had come to know, and the other hounds joining in until the gloomed woods rang and clamored. They rode then. It seemed to him that he could actually see the big blue dog boring on, silent, and the bear too: the thick, locomotive-like shape which he had seen that day four years ago crossing the blow-down,[6] crashing on ahead of the dogs faster than he had believed it could have moved, drawing away even from the running mules. He heard a shotgun, once. The woods had opened, they were going fast, the clamor faint and fading on ahead; they passed the man who had fired—a swamper, a pointing arm, a gaunt face, the small black orifice of his yelling studded with rotten teeth.

He heard the changed note in the hounds' uproar and two hundred yards ahead he saw them. The bear had turned. He saw Lion drive in without pausing and saw the bear strike him aside and lunge into the yelling hounds and kill one of them almost in its tracks and whirl and run again. Then they were in a streaming tide of dogs. He heard Major de Spain and Tennie's Jim shouting and the pistol sound of Tennie's Jim's leather thong as he tried to turn them. Then he and Sam Fathers were riding alone. One of the hounds had kept on with Lion though. He recognised its voice. It was the young hound which even a year ago had had no judgment and which, by the lights of the other hounds anyway, still had none. *Maybe that's what courage is,* he thought. "Right," Sam said behind him. "Right. We got to turn him from the river if we can."

Now they were in cane: a brake.[7] He knew the path through it as well as Sam did. They came out of the undergrowth and struck the entrance almost exactly. It would traverse the brake and come out onto a high open ridge above the river. He heard the flat clap of Walter Ewell's rifle, then two more. "No," Sam said. "I can hear the hound. Go on."

They emerged from the narrow roofless tunnel of snapping and hissing cane, still galloping, onto the open ridge below which the thick yellow river, reflectionless in the gray and streaming light, seemed not to move. Now he could hear the hound too. It was not running. The cry was a high frantic yapping and Boon was running along the edge of the bluff, his old gun leaping and jouncing against his back on its sling made of a piece of cotton plowline. He whirled and ran up to them, wild-faced, and flung himself onto the mule behind the boy. "That damn boat!" he cried. "It's on the other side! He went straight across! Lion was too close to him! That little hound too! Lion was so close I couldn't shoot! Go on!" he cried, beating his heels into the mule's flanks. "Go on!"

---

6. A tangle of trees and branches blown down by a cyclone or tornado.　7. A cane brake is a twenty- to thirty-foot-high thicket of sugarcane, often used by bears as winter shelter.

They plunged down the bank, slipping and sliding in the thawed earth, crashing through the willows and into the water. He felt no shock, no cold, he on one side of the swimming mule, grasping the pommel with one hand and holding his gun above the water with the other, Boon opposite him. Sam was behind them somewhere, and then the river, the water about them, was full of dogs. They swam faster than the mules; they were scrabbling up the bank before the mules touched bottom. Major de Spain was whooping from the bank they had just left and, looking back, he saw Tennie's Jim and the horse as they went into the water.

Now the woods ahead of them and the rain-heavy air were one uproar. It rang and clamored; it echoed and broke against the bank behind them and reformed and clamored and rang until it seemed to the boy that all the hounds which had ever bayed game in this land were yelling down at him. He got his leg over the mule as it came up out of the water. Boon didn't try to mount again. He grasped one stirrup as they went up the bank and crashed through the undergrowth which fringed the bluff and saw the bear, on its hind feet, its back against a tree while the bellowing hounds swirled around it and once more Lion drove in, leaping clear of the ground.

This time the bear didn't strike him down. It caught the dog in both arms, almost loverlike, and they both went down. He was off the mule now. He drew back both hammers of the gun but he could see nothing but moiling spotted houndbodies until the bear surged up again. Boon was yelling something, he could not tell what; he could see Lion still clinging to the bear's throat and he saw the bear, half erect, strike one of the hounds with one paw and hurl it five or six feet and then, rising and rising as though it would never stop, stand erect again and begin to rake at Lion's belly with its fore-paws. Then Boon was running. The boy saw the gleam of the blade in his hand and watched him leap among the hounds, hurdling them, kicking them aside as he ran, and fling himself astride the bear as he had hurled himself onto the mule, his legs locked around the bear's belly, his left arm under the bear's throat where Lion clung, and the glint of the knife as it rose and fell.

It fell just once. For an instant they almost resembled a piece of statuary: the clinging dog, the bear, the man stride its back, working and probing the buried blade. Then they went down, pulled over backward by Boon's weight, Boon underneath. It was the bear's back which reappeared first but at once Boon was astride it again. He had never released the knife and again the boy saw the almost infinitesimal movement of his arm and shoulder as he probed and sought; then the bear surged erect, raising with it the man and the dog too, and turned and still carrying the man and the dog it took two or three steps toward the woods on its hind feet as a man would have walked and crashed down. It didn't collapse, crumple. It fell all of a piece, as a tree falls, so that all three of them, man dog and bear, seemed to bounce once.

He and Tennie's Jim ran forward. Boon was kneeling at the bear's head. His left ear was shredded, his left coat sleeve was completely gone, his right boot had been ripped from knee to instep; the bright blood thinned in the thin rain down his leg and hand and arm and down the side of his face which was no longer wild but was quite calm. Together they prized Lion's jaws from the bear's throat. "Easy, goddamn it," Boon said. "Cant you see his guts are all out of him?" He began to remove his coat. He spoke to Tennie's Jim in that calm voice: "Bring the boat up. It's about a hundred yards down the bank there. I saw it." Tennie's Jim rose and went away. Then, and he could not remember if it had been a call or an exclamation from Tennie's Jim or if he had glanced up by chance, he saw Tennie's Jim stooping and saw Sam Fathers lying motionless on his face in the trampled mud.

The mule had not thrown him. He remembered that Sam was down too even before Boon began to run. There was no mark on him whatever and when he and Boon turned him over, his eyes were open and he said something in that tongue which he and Joe Baker had used to speak together. But he couldn't move. Tennie's Jim brought the skiff up; they could hear him shouting to Major de Spain across the river. Boon wrapped Lion in his hunting coat and carried him down to the skiff and they carried Sam down and returned and hitched the bear to the one-eyed mule's saddle-bow with Tennie's Jim's leash-thong and dragged him down to the skiff and got him into it and left Tennie's Jim to swim the horse and the two mules back across. Major de Spain caught the bow of the skiff as Boon jumped out and past him before it touched the bank. He looked at Old Ben and said quietly: "Well." Then he walked into the water and leaned down and touched Sam and Sam looked up at him and said something in that old tongue he and Joe Baker spoke. "You dont know what happened?" Major de Spain said.

"No, sir," the boy said. "It wasn't the mule. It wasn't anything. He was off the mule when Boon ran in on the bear. Then we looked up and he was lying on the ground." Boon was shouting at Tennie's Jim, still in the middle of the river.

"Come on, goddamn it!" he said. "Bring me that mule!"

"What do you want with a mule?" Major de Spain said.

Boon didn't even look at him. "I'm going to Hoke's to get the doctor," he said in that calm voice, his face quite calm beneath the steady thinning of the bright blood.

"You need a doctor yourself," Major de Spain said. "Tennie's Jim—"

"Damn that," Boon said. He turned on Major de Spain. His face was still calm, only his voice was a pitch higher. "Cant you see his goddamn guts are all out of him?"

"Boon!" Major de Spain said. They looked at one another. Boon was a good head taller than Major de Spain; even the boy was taller now than Major de Spain.

"I've got to get the doctor," Boon said. "His goddamn guts——"

"All right," Major de Spain said. Tennie's Jim came up out of the water. The horse and the sound mule had already scented Old Ben; they surged and plunged all the way up to the top of the bluff, dragging Tennie's Jim with them, before he could stop them and tie them and come back. Major de Spain unlooped the leather thong of his compass from his buttonhole and gave it to Tennie's Jim. "Go straight to Hoke's," he said. "Bring Doctor Crawford back with you. Tell him there are two men to be looked at. Take my mare. Can you find the road from here?"

"Yes, sir," Tennie's Jim said.

"All right," Major de Spain said. "Go on." He turned to the boy. "Take the mules and the horse and go back and get the wagon. We'll go on down the river in the boat to Coon bridge. Meet us there. Can you find it again?"

"Yes, sir," the boy said.

"All right. Get started."

He went back to the wagon. He realised then how far they had run. It was already afternoon when he put the mules into the traces and tied the horse's lead-rope to the tail-gate. He reached Coon bridge at dusk. The skiff was already there. Before he could see it and almost before he could see the water he had to leap from the tilting wagon, still holding the reins, and work around to where he could grasp the bit and then the ear of the plunging sound mule and dig his heels and hold it until Boon came up the bank. The rope of the led horse had already snapped and it had already disappeared up the road toward camp. They turned the wagon around and took the mules out and he led the sound mule a hundred yards up the road and tied it. Boon had already brought Lion up to the wagon and Sam was sitting up in the skiff now and when they raised him he tried to walk, up the bank and to the wagon and he tried to climb into the wagon but Boon did not wait; he picked Sam up bodily and set him on the seat. Then they hitched Old Ben to the one-eyed mule's saddle again and dragged him up the bank and set two skid-poles[8] into the open tail-gate and got him into the wagon and he went and got the sound mule[9] and Boon fought it into the traces, striking it across its hard hollow-sounding face until it came into position and stood trembling. Then the rain came down, as though it had held off all day waiting on them.

They returned to camp through it, through the streaming and sightless dark, hearing long before they saw any light the horn and the spaced shots to guide them. When they came to Sam's dark little hut he tried to stand up. He spoke again in the tongue of the old fathers; then he said clearly: "Let me out. Let me out."

"He hasn't got any fire," Major said. "Go on!" he said sharply.

But Sam was struggling now, trying to stand up. "Let me out, master," he said. "Let me go home."

So he stopped the wagon and Boon got down and lifted Sam out. He did not wait to let Sam try to walk this time. He carried him into the hut and Major de Spain got light on a paper spill from the buried embers on the hearth and lit the lamp and Boon put Sam on his bunk and drew off his boots and Major de Spain covered him and the boy was not there, he was holding the mules, the sound one which was trying again to bolt since when the wagon stopped Old Ben's scent drifted forward again along the streaming blackness of air, but Sam's eyes were probably open again on that profound look which saw further than them or the hut, further than the death of a bear and the dying of a dog. Then they went on, toward the long wailing of the horn and the shots which seemed each to linger intact somewhere in the thick streaming air until the next spaced report joined and blended with it, to the lighted house, the bright streaming windows, the quiet faces as Boon entered, bloody and quite calm, carrying the bundled coat. He laid Lion, blood coat and all, on his stale sheetless pallet bed which not even Ash, as deft in the house as a woman, could ever make smooth.

The sawmill doctor from Hoke's was already there. Boon would not let the doctor touch him until he had seen to Lion. He wouldn't risk giving Lion chloroform. He put the entrails back and sewed him up without it while Major de Spain held his head and Boon his feet. But he never tried to move. He lay there, the yellow eyes open upon nothing while the quiet men

8. They made a ramp of two poles set into the opened back of the wagon.　9. As opposed to the other, one-eyed mule.

in the new hunting clothes and in the old ones crowded into the little airless room rank with the smell of Boon's body and garments, and watched. Then the doctor cleaned and disinfected Boon's face and arm and leg and bandaged them and, the boy in front with a lantern and the doctor and McCaslin and Major de Spain and General Compson following, they went to Sam Fathers' hut. Tennie's Jim had built up the fire; he squatted before it, dozing. Sam had not moved since Boon had put him in the bunk and Major de Spain had covered him with the blankets, yet he opened his eyes and looked from one to another of the faces and when McCaslin touched his shoulder and said, "Sam. The doctor wants to look at you," he even drew his hands out of the blanket and began to fumble at his shirt buttons until McCaslin said, "Wait. We'll do it." They undressed him. He lay there—the copper-brown, almost hairless body, the old man's body, the old man, the wild man not even one generation from the woods, childless, kinless, people-less—motionless, his eyes open but no longer looking at any of them, while the doctor examined him and drew the blankets up and put the stethoscope back into his bag and snapped the bag and only the boy knew that Sam too was going to die.

"Exhaustion," the doctor said. "Shock maybe. A man his age swimming rivers in December. He'll be all right. Just make him stay in bed for a day or two. Will there be somebody here with him?"

"There will be somebody here," Major de Spain said.

They went back to the house, to the rank little room where Boon still sat on the pallet bed with Lion's head under his hand while the men, the ones who had hunted behind Lion and the ones who had never seen him before today, came quietly in to look at him and went away. Then it was dawn and they all went out into the yard to look at Old Ben, with his eyes open too and his lips snarled back from his worn teeth and his mutilated foot and the little hard lumps under his skin which were the old bullets (there were fifty-two of them, buckshot rifle and ball) and the single almost invisible slit under his left shoulder where Boon's blade had finally found his life. Then Ash began to beat on the bottom of the dishpan with a heavy spoon to call them to breakfast and it was the first time he could remember hearing no sound from the dogs under the kitchen while they were eating. It was as if the old bear, even dead there in the yard, was a more potent terror still than they could face without Lion between them.

The rain had stopped during the night. By midmorning the thin sun appeared, rapidly burning away mist and cloud, warming the air and the earth; it would be one of those windless Mississippi December days which are a sort of Indian summer's Indian summer. They moved Lion out to the front gallery, into the sun. It was Boon's idea. "Goddamn it," he said, "he never did want to stay in the house until I made him. You know that." He took a crowbar and loosened the floor boards under his pallet bed so it could be raised, mattress and all, without disturbing Lion's position, and they carried him out to the gallery and put him down facing the woods.

Then he and the doctor and McCaslin and Major de Spain went to Sam's hut. This time Sam didn't open his eyes and his breathing was so quiet, so peaceful that they could hardly see that he breathed. The doctor didn't even take out his stethoscope nor even touch him. "He's all right," the doctor said. "He didn't even catch cold. He just quit."

"Quit?" McCaslin said.

"Yes. Old people do that sometimes. Then they get a good night's sleep or maybe it's just a drink of whisky, and they change their minds."

They returned to the house. And then they began to arrive—the swamp-dwellers, the gaunt men who ran traplines and lived on quinine and coons and river water, the farmers of little corn-and-cotton-patches along the bottom's edge whose fields and cribs and pig-pens the old bear had rifled, the loggers from the camp and the sawmill men from Hoke's and the town men from further away than that, whose hounds the old bear had slain and traps and deadfalls he had wrecked and whose lead he carried. They came up mounted and on foot and in wagons, to enter the yard and look at him and then go on to the front where Lion lay, filling the little yard and overflowing it until there were almost a hundred of them squatting and standing in the warm and drowsing sunlight, talking quietly of hunting, of the game and the dogs which ran it, of hounds and bear and deer and men of yesterday vanished from the earth, while from time to time the great blue dog would open his eyes, not as if he were listening to them but as though to look at the woods for a moment before closing his eyes again, to remember the woods or to see that they were still there. He died at sundown.

Major de Spain broke camp that night. They carried Lion into the woods, or Boon carried him that is, wrapped in a quilt from his bed, just as he had refused to let anyone else touch Lion yesterday until the doctor got there; Boon carrying Lion, and the boy and General Compson and Walter and still almost fifty of them following with lanterns and lighted pine-knots—men from Hoke's and even further, who would have to ride out of the bottom in the dark, and swampers and trappers who would have to walk even, scattering toward the little hidden huts where they lived. And Boon would let nobody else dig the grave either and lay Lion in it and cover him and then General Compson stood at the head of it while the blaze and smoke of the pine-knots streamed away among the winter branches and spoke as he would have spoken over a man. Then they returned to camp. Major de Spain and McCaslin and Ash had rolled and tied all the bedding. The mules were hitched to the wagon and pointed out of the bottom and the wagon was already loaded and the stove in the kitchen was cold and the table was set with scraps of cold food and bread and only the coffee was hot when the boy ran into the kitchen where Major de Spain and McCaslin had already eaten. "What?" he cried. "What? I'm not going."

"Yes," McCaslin said, "we're going out tonight. Major wants to get on back home."

"No!" he said. "I'm going to stay."

"You've got to be back in school Monday. You've already missed a week more than I intended. It will take you from now until Monday to catch up. Sam's all right. You heard Doctor Crawford. I'm going to leave Boon and Tennie's Jim both to stay with him until he feels like getting up."

He was panting. The others had come in. He looked rapidly and almost frantically around at the other faces. Boon had a fresh bottle. He upended it and started the cork by striking the bottom of the bottle with the heel of his hand and drew the cork with his teeth and spat it out and drank. "You're damn right you're going back to school," Boon said. "Or I'll burn the tail off of you myself if Cass dont, whether you are sixteen or sixty. Where in hell do you expect to get without education? Where would Cass be? Where in hell would I be if I hadn't never went to school?"

He looked at McCaslin again. He could feel his breath coming shorter and shorter and shallower and shallower, as if there were not enough air in the kitchen for that many to breathe. "This is just Thursday. I'll come home Sunday night on one of the horses. I'll come home Sunday, then. I'll make up the time I lost studying Sunday night. McCaslin," he said, without even despair.

"No, I tell you," McCaslin said. "Sit down here and eat your supper. We're going out to—"

"Hold up, Cass," General Compson said. The boy did not know General Compson had moved until he put his hand on his shoulder. "What is it, bud?" he said.

"I've got to stay," he said. "I've got to."

"All right," General Compson said. "You can stay. If missing an extra week of school is going to throw you so far behind you'll have to sweat to find out what some hired pedagogue put between the covers of a book, you better quit altogether.—And you shut up, Cass," he said, though McCaslin had not spoken. "You've got one foot straddled into a farm and the other foot straddled into a bank; you aint even got a good hand-hold where this boy was already an old man long before you damned Sartorises and Edmondses invented farms and banks to keep yourselves from having to find out what this boy was born knowing and fearing too maybe but without being afraid, that could go ten miles on a compass because he wanted to look at a bear none of us had ever got near enough to put a bullet in and looked at the bear and came the ten miles back on the compass in the dark; maybe by God that's the why and the wherefore of farms and banks.—I reckon you still aint going to tell what it is?"

But still he could not. "I've got to stay," he said.

"All right," General Compson said. "There's plenty of grub left. And you'll come home Sunday, like you promised McCaslin? Not Sunday night: Sunday."

"Yes, sir," he said.

"All right," General Compson said. "Sit down and eat, boys," he said. "Let's get started. It's going to be cold before we get home."

They ate. The wagon was already loaded and ready to depart; all they had to do was to get into it. Boon would drive them out to the road, to the farmer's stable where the surrey had been left. He stood beside the wagon, in silhouette on the sky, turbaned like a Paythan[1] and taller than any there, the bottle tilted. Then he flung the bottle from his lips without even lowering it, spinning and glinting in the faint starlight, empty. "Them that's going," he said, "get in the goddamn wagon. Them that aint, get out of the goddamn way." The others got in. Boon mounted to the seat beside General Compson and the wagon moved, on into the obscurity until the boy could no longer see it, even the moving density of it amid the greater night. But he could still hear it, for a long while: the slow, deliberate banging of the wooden frame as it lurched from rut to rut. And he could hear Boon even when he could no longer hear the wagon. He was singing, harsh, tuneless, loud.

1. Or Pathan; member of an ethnic group living in parts of Afghanistan and northwest Pakistan.

That was Thursday. On Saturday morning Tennie's Jim left on McCaslin's woods-horse which had not been out of the bottom one time now in six years, and late that afternoon rode through the gate on the spent horse and on to the commissary where McCaslin was rationing[2] the tenants and the wage-hands for the coming week, and this time McCaslin forestalled any necessity or risk of having to wait while Major de Spain's surrey was being horsed and harnessed. He took their own, and with Tennie's Jim already asleep in the back seat he drove in to Jefferson and waited while Major de Spain changed to boots and put on his overcoat, and they drove the thirty miles in the dark of that night and at daybreak on Sunday morning they swapped to the waiting mare and mule and as the sun rose they rode out of the jungle and onto the low ridge where they had buried Lion: the low mound of unannealed earth where Boon's spade-marks still showed and beyond the grave the platform of freshly cut saplings bound between four posts and the blanket-wrapped bundle upon the platform[3] and Boon and the boy squatting between the platform and the grave until Boon, the bandage removed, ripped, from his head so that the long scoriations of Old Ben's claws resembled crusted tar in the sunlight, sprang up and threw down upon them with the old gun with which he had never been known to hit anything although McCaslin was already off the mule, kicked both feet free of the irons and vaulted down before the mule had stopped, walking toward Boon.

"Stand back," Boon said. "By God, you wont touch him. Stand back, McCaslin." Still McCaslin came on, fast yet without haste.

"Cass!" Major de Spain said. Then he said "Boon! You, Boon!" and he was down too and the boy rose too, quickly, and still McCaslin came on not fast but steady and walked up to the grave and reached his hand steadily out, quickly yet still not fast, and took hold the gun by the middle so that he and Boon faced one another across Lion's grave, both holding the gun, Boon's spent indomitable amazed and frantic face almost a head higher than McCaslin's beneath the black scoriations of beast's claws and then Boon's chest began to heave as though there were not enough air in all the woods, in all the wilderness, for all of them, for him and anyone else, even for him alone.

"Turn it loose, Boon," McCaslin said.

"You damn little spindling—" Boon said. "Dont you know I can take it away from you? Dont you know I can tie it around your neck like a damn cravat?"

"Yes," McCaslin said. "Turn it loose, Boon."

"This is the way he wanted it. He told us. He told us exactly how to do it. And by God you aint going to move him. So we did it like he said, and I been sitting here ever since to keep the damn wildcats and varmints away from him and by God—" Then McCaslin had the gun, down-slanted while he pumped the slide, the five shells snicking out of it so fast that the last one was almost out before the first one touched the ground and McCaslin dropped the gun behind him without once having taken his eyes from Boon's.

"Did you kill him, Boon?" he said. Then Boon moved. He turned, he moved like he was still drunk and then for a moment blind too, one hand out as he

---

2. Distributing food and materials.   3. Chickasaw burial customs held that the body of someone dying away from home should be placed on a platform to preserve it from wild animals.

blundered toward the big tree and seemed to stop walking before he reached the tree so that he plunged, fell toward it, flinging up both hands and catching himself against the tree and turning until his back was against it, backing with the tree's trunk his wild spent scoriated face and the tremendous heave and collapse of his chest, McCaslin following, facing him again, never once having moved his eyes from Boon's eyes. "Did you kill him, Boon?"

"No!" Boon said. "No!"

"Tell the truth," McCaslin said. "I would have done it if he had asked me to." Then the boy moved. He was between them, facing McCaslin; the water felt as if it had burst and sprung not from his eyes alone but from his whole face, like sweat.

"Leave him alone!" he cried. "Goddamn it! Leave him alone!"

4

then he was twenty-one. He could say it, himself and his cousin juxtaposed not against the wilderness but against the tamed land which was to have been his heritage,[4] the land which old Carothers McCaslin his grandfather had bought with white man's money from the wild men whose grandfathers without guns hunted it, and tamed and ordered or believed he had tamed and ordered it for the reason that the human beings he held in bondage and in the power of life and death had removed the forest from it and in their sweat scratched the surface of it to a depth of perhaps fourteen inches in order to grow something out of it which had not been there before and which could be translated back into the money he who believed he had bought it had had to pay to get it and hold it and a reasonable profit too: and for which reason old Carothers McCaslin, knowing better, could raise his children, his descendants and heirs, to believe the land was his to hold and bequeath since the strong and ruthless man has a cynical foreknowledge of his own vanity and pride and strength and a contempt for all his get: just as, knowing better, Major de Spain and his fragment of that wilderness which was bigger and older than any recorded deed: just as, knowing better, old Thomas Sutpen, from whom Major de Spain had had his fragment for money: just as Ikkemotubbe, the Chickasaw chief, from whom Thomas Sutpen had had the fragment for money or rum or whatever it was, knew in his turn that not even a fragment of it had been his to relinquish or sell

not against the wilderness but against the land, not in pursuit and lust but in relinquishment, and in the commissary as it should have been, not the heart perhaps but certainly the solar-plexus of the repudiated and relinquished: the square, galleried, wooden building squatting like a portent above the fields whose laborers it still held in thrall '65[5] or no and placarded over with advertisements for snuff and cures for chills and salves and potions manufactured and sold by white men to bleach the pigment and straighten the hair of negroes that they might resemble the very race which for two hundred years had held them in bondage and from which for another hundred years not even a bloody civil war would have set them completely free

himself and his cousin amid the old smells of cheese and salt meat and kerosene and harness, the ranked shelves of tobacco and overalls and bottled

---

4. Ike renounced his inherited property in favor of his first cousin once removed, McCaslin (Cass) Edmonds.   5. Even after the end of the Civil War in 1865, the freed slaves must depend on working in the fields.

medicine and thread and plow-bolts, the barrels and kegs of flour and meal and molasses and nails, the wall pegs dependant with plowlines and plow-collars and hames and trace-chains, and the desk and the shelf above it on which rested the ledgers in which McCaslin recorded the slow outward trickle of food and supplies and equipment which returned each fall as cotton made and ginned[6] and sold (two threads frail as truth and impalpable as equators yet cable-strong to bind for life them who made the cotton to the land their sweat fell on), and the older ledgers clumsy and archaic in size and shape, on the yellowed pages of which were recorded in the faded hand of his father Theophilus and his uncle Amodeus during the two decades before the Civil War, the manumission in title at least of Carothers Mc-Caslin's slaves:

'Relinquish,' McCaslin said. 'Relinquish. You, the direct male descendant of him who saw the opportunity and took it, bought the land, took the land, got the land no matter how, held it to bequeath, no matter how, out of the old grant, the first patent, when it was a wilderness of wild beasts and wilder men, and cleared it, translated it into something to bequeath to his children, worthy of bequeathment for his descendants' ease and security and pride and to perpetuate his name and accomplishments. Not only the male descendant but the only and last descendant in the male line and in the third generation, while I am not only four generations from old Carothers, I derived through a woman and the very McCaslin in my name is mine only by sufferance and courtesy and my grandmother's pride in what that man accomplished whose legacy and monument you think you can repudiate.' and he[7]

'I cant repudiate it. It was never mine to repudiate. It was never Father's and Uncle Buddy's to bequeath me to repudiate because it was never Grand-father's to bequeath them to bequeath me to repudiate because it was never old Ikkemotubbe's to sell to Grandfather for bequeathment and repudiation. Because it was never Ikkemotubbe's fathers' fathers' to bequeath Ikkemo-tubbe to sell to Grandfather or any man because on the instant when Ikke-motubbe discovered, realised, that he could sell it for money, on that instant it ceased ever to have been his forever, father to father to father, and the man who bought it bought nothing.'

'Bought nothing?' and he

'Bought nothing. Because He told in the Book how He created the earth, made it and looked at it and said it was all right, and then He made man.[8] He made the earth first and peopled it with dumb creatures, and then He created man to be His overseer on the earth and to hold suzerainty over the earth and the animals on it in His name, not to hold for himself and his descendants inviolable title forever, generation after generation, to the oblongs and squares of the earth, but to hold the earth mutual and intact in the communal anonymity of brotherhood, and all the fee He asked was pity and humility and sufferance and endurance and the sweat of his face for bread. And I know what you are going to say,' he said: 'That nevertheless Grandfather—' and McCaslin

'—did own it. And not the first. Not alone and not the first since, as your

---

6. I.e., cleaned of its seeds in a machine called the cotton gin. 7. Ike speaks. *And he* and *and McCaslin* indicate the alternation of speakers, an alternation that is held in abeyance from p. 2172 to p. 2175 while Isaac recalls reading and deciphering the family ledgers. 8. The first of a series of references to the biblical Book of Genesis.

Authority states, man was dispossessed of Eden. Nor yet the second and still not alone, on down through the tedious and shabby chronicle of His chosen sprung from Abraham,[9] and of the sons of them who dispossessed Abraham, and of the five hundred years during which half the known world and all it contained was chattel to one city[1] as this plantation and all the life it contained was chattel and revokeless thrall to this commissary store and those ledgers yonder during your grandfather's life, and the next thousand years while men fought over the fragments of that collapse until at last even the fragments were exhausted and men snarled over the gnawed bones of the old world's worthless evening until an accidental egg[2] discovered to them a new hemisphere. So let me say it: That nevertheless and notwithstanding old Carothers did own it. Bought it, got it, no matter; kept it, held it, no matter; bequeathed it: else why do you stand here relinquishing and repudiating? Held it, kept it for fifty years until you could repudiate it, while He—this Arbiter, this Architect, this Umpire—condoned—or did He? looked down and saw—or did He? Or at least did nothing: saw, and could not, or did not see; saw, and would not, or perhaps He would not see—perverse, impotent, or blind: which?' and he

'Dispossessed.' and McCaslin

'What?' and he

'Dispossessed. Not impotent: He didn't condone; not blind, because He watched it. And let me say it. Dispossessed of Eden. Dispossessed of Canaan,[3] and those who dispossessed him dispossessed him dispossessed, and the five hundred years of absentee landlords in the Roman bagnios, and the thousand years[4] of wild men from the northern woods who dispossessed them and devoured their ravished substance ravished in turn again and then snarled in what you call the old world's worthless twilight over the old world's gnawed bones, blasphemous in His name until He used a simple egg to discover to them a new world where a nation of people could be founded in humility and pity and sufferance and pride of one to another. And Grandfather did own the land nevertheless and notwithstanding because He permitted it, not impotent and not condoning and not blind because He ordered and watched it. He saw the land already accursed even as Ikkemotubbe and Ikkemotubbe's father old Issetibbeha and old Issetibbeha's fathers too held it, already tainted even before any white man owned it by what Grandfather and his kind, his fathers, had brought into the new land which He had vouchsafed them out of pity and sufferance, on condition of pity and humility and sufferance and endurance, from that old world's corrupt and worthless twilight as though in the sailfuls of the old world's tainted wind which drove the ships—' and McCaslin

'Ah.'

'—and no hope for the land anywhere so long as Ikkemotubbe and Ikkemotubbe's descendants held it in unbroken succession. Maybe He saw that only by voiding the land for a time of Ikkemotubbe's blood and substituting

9. The Jews.   1. Rome at the height of its power (78 B.C.–3rd century A.D.).   2. An anecdote relates that Christopher Columbus, responding to those who belittled his achievement in discovering the New World, challenged his critics to make an egg stand on end. After they failed, he positioned the egg by first tapping one end to flatten it—showing that the difficult part is to be the first to find the solution.   3. The Bible's Promised Land, "flowing with milk and honey" (Exodus 3.8).   4. Beginning about A.D. 350, northern invaders (including Huns and Vikings) overran Europe and Asia. *Bagnios:* Roman public baths, meeting places, and sometimes brothels.

for it another blood, could He accomplish His purpose. Maybe He knew already what that other blood would be, maybe it was more than justice that only the white man's blood was available and capable to raise the white man's curse, more than vengeance when—' and McCaslin

'Ah.'

'—when He used the blood which had brought in the evil to destroy the evil as doctors use fever to burn up fever, poison to slay poison. Maybe He chose Grandfather out of all of them He might have picked. Maybe He knew that Grandfather himself would not serve His purpose because Grandfather was born too soon too, but that Grandfather would have descendants, the right descendants; maybe He had foreseen already the descendants Grandfather would have, maybe He saw already in Grandfather the seed progenitive of the three generations He saw it would take to set at least some of His lowly people free—' and McCaslin

'The sons of Ham![5] You who quote the Book: the sons of Ham.' and he

'There are some things He said in the Book, and some things reported of Him that He did not say. And I know what you will say now: That if truth is one thing to me and another thing to you, how will we choose which is truth? You dont need to choose. The heart already knows. He didn't have His Book written to be read by what must elect and choose, but by the heart, not by the wise of the earth because maybe they dont need it or maybe the wise no longer have any heart, but by the doomed and lowly of the earth who have nothing else to read with but the heart. Because the men who wrote his Book for Him were writing about truth and there is only one truth and it covers all things that touch the heart.' and McCaslin

'So these men who transcribed His Book for Him were sometime liars.' and he

'Yes. Because they were human men. They were trying to write down the heart's truth out of the heart's driving complexity, for all the complex and troubled hearts which would beat after them. What they were trying to tell, what He wanted said, was too simple. Those for whom they transcribed His words could not have believed them. It had to be expounded in the everyday terms which they were familiar with and could comprehend, not only those who listened but those who told it too, because if they who were that near to Him as to have been elected from among all who breathed and spoke language to transcribe and relay His words, could comprehend truth only through the complexity of passion and lust and hate and fear which drives the heart, what distance back to truth must they traverse whom truth could only reach by word-of-mouth?' and McCaslin

'I might answer that, since you have taken to proving your points and disproving mine by the same text, I dont know. But I dont say that, because you have answered yourself: No time at all if, as you say, the heart knows truth, the infallible and unerring heart. And perhaps you are right, since although you admitted three generations from old Carothers to you, there were not three. There were not even completely two. Uncle Buck and Uncle Buddy. And they not the first and not alone. A thousand other Bucks and

5. Noah's sons were Shem, Ham, and Japheth, described in the Old Testament as ancestors of the various human races. When Ham saw his father's nakedness, Noah cursed and condemned Ham's son, Canaan, to be the perpetual servant of Shem and Japheth (Genesis 9.25–27). Since Ham represented the Canaanite (Mideastern) and African peoples, this passage was often used to justify the exploitation of blacks.

Buddies in less than two generations and sometimes less than one in this land which so you claim God created and man himself cursed and tainted. Not to mention 1865.' and he

'Yes. More men than Father and Uncle Buddy,' not even glancing toward the shelf above the desk, nor did McCaslin. They did not need to. To him it was as though the ledgers in their scarred cracked leather bindings were being lifted down one by one in their fading sequence and spread open on the desk or perhaps upon some apocryphal Bench or even Altar or perhaps before the Throne Itself for a last perusal and contemplation and refreshment of the Allknowledgeable before the yellowed pages and the brown thin ink in which was recorded the injustice and a little at least of its amelioration and restitution faded back forever into the anonymous communal original dust

the yellowed pages scrawled in fading ink by the hand first of his grandfather and then of his father and uncle, bachelors up to and past fifty and then sixty, the one who ran the plantation and the farming of it and the other who did the housework and the cooking and continued to do it even after his twin married and the boy himself was born

the two brothers who as soon as their father was buried moved out of the tremendously-conceived, the almost barn-like edifice which he had not even completed, into a one-room log cabin which the two of them built themselves and added other rooms to while they lived in it, refusing to allow any slave to touch any timber of it other than the actual raising into place the logs which two men alone could not handle, and domiciled all the slaves in the big house some of the windows of which were still merely boarded up with odds and ends of plank or with the skins of bear and deer nailed over the empty frames: each sundown the brother who superintended the farming would parade the negroes as a first sergeant dismisses a company, and herd them willynilly, man woman and child, without question protest or recourse, into the tremendous abortive edifice scarcely yet out of embryo, as if even old Carothers McCaslin had paused aghast at the concrete indication of his own vanity's boundless conceiving: he would call his mental roll and herd them in and with a hand-wrought nail as long as a flenching-knife[6] and suspended from a short deer-hide thong attached to the door-jamb for that purpose, he would nail to the door of that house which lacked half its windows and had no hinged back door at all, so that presently and for fifty years afterward, when the boy himself was big to hear and remember it, there was in the land a sort of folk-tale: of the countryside all night long full of skulking McCaslin slaves dodging the moonlit roads and the Patrol-riders[7] to visit other plantations, and of the unspoken gentlemen's agreement between the two white men and the two dozen black ones that, after the white man had counted them and driven the home-made nail into the front door at sundown, neither of the white men would go around behind the house and look at the back door, provided that all the negroes were behind the front one when the brother who drove it drew out the nail again at daybreak

the twins who were identical even in their handwriting, unless you had specimens side by side to compare, and even when both hands appeared on

---

6. Or flensing knife; a long flaying knife.   7. Groups of four men who rode the countryside to catch slaves who left their plantation without permission.

the same page (as often happened, as if, long since past any oral intercourse, they had used the diurnally advancing pages to conduct the unavoidable business of the compulsion which had traversed all the waste wilderness of North Mississippi in 1830 and '40[8] and singled them out to drive) they both looked as though they had been written by the same perfectly normal ten-year-old boy, even to the spelling, except that the spelling did not improve as one by one the slaves which Carothers McCaslin had inherited and purchased—Roscius and Phoebe and Thucydides and Eunice and their descendants, and Sam Fathers and his mother for both of whom he had swapped an underbred trotting gelding to old Ikkemotubbe, the Chickasaw chief from whom he had likewise bought the land, and Tennie Beauchamp whom the twin Amodeus had won from a neighbor in a poker-game, and the anomaly calling itself Percival Brownlee which the twin Theophilus had purchased, neither he nor his brother ever knew why apparently, from Bedford Forrest while he was still only a slave-dealer and not yet a general (It was a single page, not long and covering less than a year, not seven months in fact, begun in the hand which the boy had learned to distinguish as that of his father:

> Percavil Brownly 26yr Old. cleark @ Bookepper. bought from N. B. Forest at Cold Water[9] 3 Mar 1856 $265. dolars

and beneath that, in the same hand:

> 5 mar 1856 No bookepper any way Cant read. Can write his Name but I already put that down My self Says he can Plough but dont look like it to Me. sent to Feild to day Mar 5 1856

and the same hand:

> 6 Mar 1856 Cant plough either Says he aims to be a Precher so may be he can lead live stock to Crick to Drink

and this time it was the other, the hand which he now recognised as his uncle's when he could see them both on the same page:

> Mar 23th 1856 Cant do that either Except one at a Time Get shut of him

then the first again:

> 24 Mar 1856 Who in hell would buy him

then the second:

> 19th of Apr 1856 Nobody You put yourself out of Market at Cold Water two months ago I never said sell him Free him

the first:

> 22 Apr 1856 Ill get it out of him

the second:

> Jun 13th 1856 How $1 per yr 265$ 265 yrs Wholl sign his Free paper[1]

then the first again:

---

8. Chickasaw and Choctaw lands were sold cheaply to white settlers, starting a boom in land speculation that was known nationally as "Flush Times."   9. I.e., Coldwater, Mississippi.   1. A document attesting the free status of an ex-slave.

> *1 Oct 1856 Mule josephine Broke Leg @ shot Wrong stall wrong niger wrong everything $100. dolars*

and the same:

> *2 Oct 1856 Freed Debit McCaslin @ McCaslin $265. dolars*

then the second again:

> *Oct 3th Debit Theophilus McCaslin Niger 265$ Mule 100$ 365$ He hasnt gone yet Father should be here*

then the first:

> *3 Oct 1856 Son of a bitch wont leave What would father done*

the second:

> *29th of Oct 1856 Renamed him*

the first:

> *31 Oct 1856 Renamed him what*

the second:

> *Chrstms 1856 Spintrius[2]*

) took substance and even a sort of shadowy life with their passions and complexities too as page followed page and year year; all there, not only the general and condoned injustice and its slow amortization but the specific tragedy which had not been condoned and could never be amortized, the new page and the new ledger, the hand which he could now recognise at first glance as his father's:

> *Father dide Lucius Quintus Carothers McCaslin, Callina 1772 Missippy 1837. Dide and burid 27 June 1837*
> *Roskus. rased by Granfather in Callina Dont know how old. Freed 27 June 1837 Dont want to leave. Dide and Burid 12 Jan 1841*
> *Fibby Roskus Wife. bought by granfather in Callina says Fifty Freed 27 June 1837 Dont want to leave. Dide and burd 1 Aug 1849*
> *Thucydus Roskus @ Fibby Son born in Callina 1779. Refused 10acre peace fathers Will 28 Jun 1837 Refused Cash offer $200. dolars from A. @ T. McCaslin 28 Jun 1837 Wants to stay and work it out*

and beneath this and covering the next five pages and almost that many years, the slow, day-by-day accrument of the wages allowed him and the food and clothing—the molasses and meat and meal, the cheap durable shirts and jeans and shoes and now and then a coat against rain and cold—charged against the slowly yet steadily mounting sum of balance (and it would seem to the boy that he could actually see the black man, the slave whom his white owner had forever manumitted by the very act from which the black man could never be free so long as memory lasted, entering the commissary, asking permission perhaps of the white man's son to see the ledger-page which he could not even read, not even asking for the white man's word,

---

2. From a Latin word meaning "male prostitute."

which he would have had to accept for the reason that there was absolutely no way under the sun for him to test it, as to how the account stood, how much longer before he could go and never return, even if only as far as Jefferson seventeen miles away) on to the double pen-stroke closing the final entry:

> 3 Nov 1841 By Cash to Thucydus McCaslin $200. dolars Set Up blaksmith in J. Dec 1841 Dide and burid in J. 17 feb 1854
> Eunice Bought by Father in New Orleans 1807 $650. dolars. Marrid to Thucydus 1809 Drownd in Crick Cristmas Day 1832

and then the other hand appeared, the first time he had seen it in the ledger to distinguish it as his uncle's, the cook and housekeeper whom even McCaslin, who had known him and the boy's father for sixteen years before the boy was born, remembered as sitting all day long in the rocking chair from which he cooked the food, before the kitchen fire on which he cooked it:

> June 21th 1833 Drownd herself

and the first:

> 23 Jun 1833 Who in hell ever heard of a niger drownding him self

and the second, unhurried, with a complete finality; the two identical entries might have been made with a rubber stamp save for the date:

> Aug 13th 1833 Drownd herself

and he thought *But why? But why?* He was sixteen then. It was neither the first time he had been alone in the commissary nor the first time he had taken down the old ledgers familiar on their shelf above the desk ever since he could remember. As a child and even after nine and ten and eleven, when he had learned to read, he would look up at the scarred and cracked backs and ends but with no particular desire to open them, and though he intended to examine them someday because he realised that they probably contained a chronological and much more comprehensive though doubtless tedious record than he would ever get from any other source, not alone of his own flesh and blood but of all his people, not only the whites but the black one too, who were as much a part of his ancestry as his white progenitors, and of the land which they had all held and used in common and fed from and on and would continue to use in common without regard to color or titular ownership, it would only be on some idle day when he was old and perhaps even bored a little since what the old books contained would be after all these years fixed immutably, finished, unalterable, harmless. Then he was sixteen. He knew what he was going to find before he found it. He got the commissary key from McCaslin's room after midnight while McCaslin was asleep and with the commissary door shut and locked behind him and the forgotten lantern stinking anew the rank dead icy air, he leaned above the yellowed page and thought not Why drowned herself, but thinking what he believed his father had thought when he found his brother's first comment: Why did Uncle Buddy think she had drowned herself? finding, beginning to find on the next succeeding page what he knew he would find, only this was still not it because he already knew this:

> *Tomasina called Tomy Daughter of Thucydus @ Eunice Born 1810 dide*
> *in Child bed June 1833 and Burd. Yr stars fell*[3]

nor the next:

> *Turl Son of Thucydus @ Eunice Tomy born Jun 1833 yr stars fell Fathers*
> *will*

and nothing more, no tedious recording filling this page of wages day by day and food and clothing charged against them, no entry of his death and burial because he had outlived his white half-brothers and the books which McCaslin kept did not include obituaries: just *Fathers will* and he had seen that too: old Carothers' bold cramped hand far less legible than his sons' even and not much better in spelling, who while capitalising almost every noun and verb, made no effort to punctuate or construct whatever, just as he made no effort either to explain or obfuscate the thousand-dollar legacy to the son of an unmarried slave-girl, to be paid only at the child's coming-of-age, bearing the consequence of the act of which there was still no definite incontrovertible proof that he acknowledged, not out of his own substance but penalising his sons with it, charging them a cash forfeit on the accident of their own paternity; not even a bribe for silence toward his own fame since his fame would suffer only after he was no longer present to defend it, fling-ing almost contemptuously, as he might a cast-off hat or pair of shoes, the thousand dollars which could have had no more reality to him under those conditions than it would have to the negro, the slave who would not even see it until he came of age, twenty-one years too late to begin to learn what money was. *So I reckon that was cheaper than saying My son to a nigger* he thought. *Even if My son wasn't but just two words. But there must have been love* he thought. *Some sort of love. Even what he would have called love: not just an afternoon's or a night's spittoon* There was the old man, old, within five years of his life's end, long a widower and, since his sons were not only bachelors but were approaching middleage, lonely in the house and doubt-less even bored since his plantation was established now and functioning and there was enough money now, too much of it probably for a man whose vices even apparently remained below his means; there was the girl, hus-bandless and young, only twenty-three when the child was born: perhaps he had sent for her at first out of loneliness, to have a young voice and movement in the house, summoned her, bade her mother send her each morning to sweep the floors and make the beds and the mother acquiescing since that was probably already understood, already planned: the only child of a couple who were not field hands and who held themselves something above the other slaves not alone for that reason but because the husband and his father and mother too had been inherited by the white man from his father, and the white man himself had travelled three hundred miles and better to New Orleans in a day when men travelled by horseback or steamboat, and bought the girl's mother as a wife for

and that was all. The old frail pages seemed to turn of their own accord even while he thought *His own daughter His own daughter. No No Not even him* back to that one where the white man (not even a widower then) who

---

3. The great meteor shower of November 12, 1833.

never went anywhere any more than his sons in their time ever did and who
did not need another slave, had gone all the way to New Orleans and bought
one. And Tomey's Terrel was still alive when the boy was ten years old and
he knew from his own observation and memory that there had already been
some white in Tomey's Terrel's blood before his father gave him the rest of
it; and looking down at the yellowed page spread beneath the yellow glow of
the lantern smoking and stinking in that rank chill midnight room fifty years
later, he seemed to see her actually walking into the icy creek on that Christmas day six months before her daughter's and her lover's (*Her first lover's* he
thought. *Her first*) child was born, solitary, inflexible, griefless, ceremonial,
in formal and succinct repudiation of grief and despair who had already had
to repudiate belief and hope

that was all. He would never need look at the ledgers again nor did he; the
yellowed pages in their fading and implacable succession were as much a
part of his consciousness and would remain so forever, as the fact of his own
nativity:

> *Tennie Beauchamp 21 yrs Won by Amodeus McCaslin from Hubert Beau-
> champ Esqre Possible Strait against three Treys in sigt Not called*[4] *1859
> Marrid to Tomys Turl 1859*

and no date of freedom because her freedom, as well as that of her first
surviving child, derived not from Buck and Buddy McCaslin in the commissary but from a stranger in Washington[5] and no date of death and burial, not
only because McCaslin kept no obituaries in his books, but because in this
year 1883 she was still alive and would remain so to see a grandson by her
last surviving child:

> *Amodeus McCaslin Beauchamp Son of tomys Turl @ Tennie Beauchamp
> 1859 dide 1859*

then his uncle's hand entire, because his father was now a member of the
cavalry command of that man whose name as a slave-dealer he could not
even spell: and not even a page and not even a full line:

> *Dauter Tomes Turl and tenny 1862*

and not even a line and not even a sex and no cause given though the boy
could guess it because McCaslin was thirteen then and he remembered how
there was not always enough to eat in more places than Vicksburg:

> *Child of tomes Turl and Tenny 1863*

and the same hand again and this one lived, as though Tennie's perseverance
and the fading and diluted ghost of old Carothers' ruthlessness had at last
conquered even starvation: and clearer, fuller, more carefully written and
spelled than the boy had yet seen it, as if the old man, who should have been
a woman to begin with, trying to run what was left of the plantation in his
brother's absence in the intervals of cooking and caring for himself and the
fourteen-year-old orphan, had taken as an omen for renewed hope the fact

4. Description of the poker hand with which Amodeus McCaslin won Tennie Beauchamp from Hubert
Beauchamp (pronounced *bee'-chum*).   5. I.e., they were freed under President Abraham Lincoln's
Emancipation Proclamation (1863).

that this nameless inheritor of slaves was at least remaining alive long enough to receive a name:

> *James Thucydus Beauchamp[6] Son of Tomes Turl and Tenny Beauchamp Born 29th december 1864 and both Well Wanted to call him Theophilus but Tride Amodeus McCaslin and Callina McCaslin and both dide so Disswaded Them Born at Two clock A,m, both Well*

but no more, nothing; it would be another two years yet before the boy, almost a man now, would return from the abortive trip into Tennessee with the still-intact third of old Carothers' legacy to his Negro son and his descendants, which as the three surviving children established at last one by one their apparent intention of surviving, their white half-uncles had increased to a thousand dollars each, conditions permitting, as they came of age, and completed the page himself as far as it would ever be completed when that day was long passed beyond which a man born in 1864 (or 1867 either, when he himself saw light) could have expected or himself hoped or even wanted to be still alive; his own hand now, queerly enough resembling neither his father's nor his uncle's nor even McCaslin's, but like that of his grandfather's save for the spelling:

> *Vanished sometime on night of his twenty-first birthday Dec 29 1885. Traced by Isaac McCaslin to Jackson Tenn. and there lost. His third of legacy $1000.00 returned to McCaslin Edmonds Trustee this day Jan 12 1886*

but not yet: that would be two years yet, and now his father's again, whose old commander was now quit of soldiering and slave-trading both; once more in the ledger and then not again and more illegible than ever, almost indecipherable at all from the rheumatism which now crippled him and almost completely innocent now even of any sort of spelling as well as punctuation, as if the four years during which he had followed the sword of the only man ever breathing who ever sold him a negro, let alone beat him in a trade, had convinced him not only of the vanity of faith and hope but of orthography too:

> *Miss sophonsiba[7] b dtr t t @ t 1869*

but not of belief and will because it was there, written, as McCaslin had told him, with the left hand, but there in the ledger one time more and then not again, for the boy himself was a year old, and when Lucas was born six years later, his father and uncle had been dead inside the same twelve-months almost five years; his own hand again, who was there and saw it, 1886, she was just seventeen, two years younger than himself, and he was in the commissary when McCaslin entered out of the first of dusk and said, 'He wants to marry Fonsiba,' like that: and he looked past McCaslin and saw the man, the stranger, taller than McCaslin and wearing better clothes than McCaslin and most of the other white men the boy knew habitually wore, who entered the room like a white man and stood in it like a white man, as though he had let McCaslin precede him into it not because McCaslin's skin was white but simply because McCaslin lived there and knew the way, and who talked

---

6. Tennie's Jim.   7. Also called Fonsiba; daughter of Tomey's Turl and Tennie.

like a white man too, looking at him past McCaslin's shoulder rapidly and keenly once and then no more, without further interest, as a mature and contained white man not impatient but just pressed for time might have looked. 'Marry Fonsiba?' he cried. 'Marry Fonsiba?' and then no more either, just watching and listening while McCaslin and the Negro talked:

'To live in Arkansas, I believe you said.'

'Yes. I have property there. A farm.'

'Property? A farm? You own it?'

'Yes.'

'You don't say Sir, do you?'

'To my elders, yes.'

'I see. You are from the North.'

'Yes. Since a child.'

'Then your father was a slave.'

'Yes. Once.'

'Then how do you own a farm in Arkansas?'

'I have a grant. It was my father's. From the United States. For military service.'

'I see,' McCaslin said. 'The Yankee army.'

'The United States army,' the stranger said; and then himself again, crying it at McCaslin's back:

'Call aunt Tennie! I'll go get her! I'll—' But McCaslin was not even including him; the stranger did not even glance back toward his voice, the two of them speaking to one another again as if he were not even there:

'Since you seem to have it all settled,' McCaslin said, 'why have you bothered to consult my authority at all?'

'I dont,' the stranger said. 'I acknowledge your authority only so far as you admit your responsibility toward her as a female member of the family of which you are the head. I dont ask your permission. I——'

'That will do!' McCaslin said. But the stranger did not falter. It was neither as if he were ignoring McCaslin nor as if he had failed to hear him. It was as though he were making, not at all an excuse and not exactly a justification, but simply a statement which the situation absolutely required and demanded should be made in McCaslin's hearing whether McCaslin listened to it or not. It was as if he were talking to himself, for himself to hear the words spoken aloud. They faced one another, not close yet at slightly less than foils' distance, erect, their voices not raised, not impactive, just succinct:

'——I inform you, notify you in advance as chief of her family. No man of honor could do less. Besides, you have, in your way, according to your lights and upbringing——'

'That's enough, I said,' McCaslin said. 'Be off this place by full dark. Go.' But for another moment the other did not move, contemplating McCaslin with that detached and heatless look, as if he were watching reflected in McCaslin's pupils the tiny image of the figure he was sustaining. 'Yes,' he said. 'After all, this is your house. And in your fashion you have. . . . But no matter. You are right. This is enough.' He turned back toward the door; he paused again but only for a second, already moving while he spoke: 'Be easy. I will be good to her.' Then he was gone.

'But how did she ever know him?' the boy cried. 'I never even heard of him before! And Fonsiba, that's never been off this place except to go to church since she was born——'

'Ha,' McCaslin said. 'Even their parents dont know until too late how seventeen-year-old girls ever met the men who marry them too, if they are lucky.' And the next morning they were both gone, Fonsiba too. McCaslin never saw her again, nor did he, because the woman he found at last five months later was no one he had ever known. He carried a third of the three-thousand-dollar fund in gold in a money-belt, as when he had vainly traced Tennie's Jim into Tennessee a year ago. They—the man—had left an address of some sort with Tennie, and three months later a letter came, written by the man although McCaslin's wife Alice had taught Fonsiba to read and write too a little. But it bore a different postmark from the address the man had left with Tennie, and he travelled by rail as far as he could and then by contracted stage and then by a hired livery rig and then by rail again for a distance: an experienced traveller by now and an experienced bloodhound too and a successful one this time because he would have to be; as the slow interminable empty muddy December miles crawled and crawled and night followed night in hotels, in roadside taverns of rough logs and containing little else but a bar, and in the cabins of strangers and the hay of lonely barns, in none of which he dared undress because of his secret golden girdle like that of a disguised one of the Magi[8] travelling incognito and not even hope to draw him but only determination and desperation, he would tell himself: *I will have to find her. I will have to. We have already lost one of them. I will have to find her this time.* He did. Hunched in the slow and icy rain, on a spent hired horse splashed to the chest and higher, he saw it—a single log edifice with a clay chimney which seemed in process of being flattened by the rain to a nameless and valueless rubble of dissolution in that roadless and even pathless waste of unfenced fallow and wilderness jungle— no barn, no stable, not so much as a hen-coop: just a log cabin built by hand and no clever hand either, a meagre pile of clumsily-cut firewood sufficient for about one day and not even a gaunt hound to come bellowing out from under the house when he rode up—a farm only in embryo, perhaps a good farm, maybe even a plantation someday, but not now, not for years yet and only then with labor, hard and enduring and unflagging work and sacrifice; he shoved open the crazy kitchen door in its awry frame and entered an icy gloom where not even a fire for cooking burned and after another moment saw, crouched into the wall's angle behind a crude table, the coffee-colored face which he had known all his life but knew no more, the body which had been born within a hundred yards of the room that he was born in and in which some of his own blood ran but which was now completely inheritor of generation after generation to whom an unannounced white man on a horse was a white man's hired Patroller wearing a pistol sometimes and a blacksnake whip always; he entered the next room, the only other room the cabin owned, and found, sitting in a rocking chair before the hearth, the man himself, reading—sitting there in the only chair in the house, before that miserable fire for which there was not wood sufficient to last twenty-four hours, in the same ministerial clothing in which he had entered the

8. A reference to the three wise men of the Bible who traveled to Bethlehem bringing gifts for Jesus' birth (Matthew 2.1).

commissary five months ago and a pair of gold-framed spectacles which, when he looked up and then rose to his feet, the boy saw did not even contain lenses, reading a book in the midst of that desolation, that muddy waste fenceless and even pathless and without even a walled shed for stock to stand beneath: and over all, permeant, clinging to the man's very clothing and exuding from his skin itself, that rank stink of baseless and imbecile delusion, that boundless rapacity and folly, of the carpetbagger[9] followers of victorious armies.

'Dont you see?' he cried. 'Dont you see? This whole land, the whole South, is cursed, and all of us who derive from it, whom it ever suckled, white and black both, lie under the curse? Granted that my people brought the curse onto the land: maybe for that reason their descendants alone can—not resist it, not combat it—maybe just endure and outlast it until the curse is lifted. Then your peoples' turn will come because we have forfeited ours. But not now. Not yet. Dont you see?'

The other stood now, the unfrayed garments still ministerial even if not quite so fine, the book closed upon one finger to keep the place, the lenseless spectacles held like a music master's wand in the other workless hand while the owner of it spoke his measured and sonorous imbecility of the boundless folly and the baseless hope: 'You're wrong. The curse you whites brought into this land has been lifted. It has been voided and discharged. We are seeing a new era, an era dedicated, as our founders intended it, to freedom, liberty and equality for all, to which this country will be the new Canaan——'

'Freedom from what? From work? Canaan?' He jerked his arm, comprehensive, almost violent: whereupon it all seemed to stand there about them, intact and complete and visible in the drafty, damp, heatless, negro-stale negro-rank sorry room—the empty fields without plow or seed to work them, fenceless against the stock which did not exist within or without the walled stable which likewise was not there. 'What corner of Canaan is this?'

'You are seeing it at a bad time. This is winter. No man farms this time of year.'

'I see. And of course her need for food and clothing will stand still while the land lies fallow.'

'I have a pension,' the other said. He said it as a man might say I *have grace* or I *own a gold mine*. 'I have my father's pension too. It will arrive on the first of the month. What day is this?'

'The eleventh,' he said. 'Twenty days more. And until then?'

'I have a few groceries in the house from my credit account with the merchant in Midnight who banks my pension check for me. I have executed to him a power of attorney to handle it for me as a matter of mutual——'

'I see. And if the groceries dont last the twenty days?'

'I still have one more hog.'

'Where?'

'Outside,' the other said. 'It is customary in this country to allow stock to range free during the winter for food. It comes up from time to time. But no matter if it doesn't; I can probably trace its footprints when the need——'

'Yes!' he cried. 'Because no matter: you still have the pension check. And

9. Opportunist who packed his belongings in a satchel made of carpet material and came south to make a fortune off the ruin of the Confederacy.

the man in Midnight will cash it and pay himself out of it for what you have already eaten and if there is any left over, it is yours. And the hog will be eaten by then or you still cant catch it, and then what will you do?'

'It will be almost spring then,' the other said. 'I am planning in the spring——'

'It will be January,' he said. 'And then February. And then more than half of March—' and when he stopped again in the kitchen she had not moved, she did not even seem to breathe or to be alive except her eyes watching him; when he took a step toward her it was still not movement because she could have retreated no further: only the tremendous fathomless ink-colored eyes in the narrow, thin, too thin coffee-colored face watching him without alarm, without recognition, without hope. 'Fonsiba,' he said. 'Fonsiba. Are you all right?'

'I'm free,' she said. Midnight was a tavern, a livery stable, a big store (that would be where the pension check banked itself as a matter of mutual elimination of bother and fret, he thought) and a little one, a saloon and a blacksmith shop. But there was a bank there too. The president (the owner, for all practical purposes) of it was a translated Mississippian who had been one of Forrest's men too: and his body lightened of the golden belt for the first time since he left home eight days ago, with pencil and paper he multiplied three dollars by twelve months and divided it into one thousand dollars; it would stretch that way over almost twenty-eight years and for twenty-eight years at least she would not starve, the banker promising to send the three dollars himself by a trusty messenger on the fifteenth of each month and put it into her actual hand, and he returned home and that was all because in 1874 his father and his uncle were both dead and the old ledgers never again came down from the shelf above the desk to which his father had returned them for the last time that day in 1869. But he could have completed it:

> *Lucas Quintus Carothers McCaslin Beauchamp. Last surviving son and child of Tomey's Terrel and Tennie Beauchamp. March 17, 1874*

except that there was no need: not *Lucius Quintus* @c[1] @c @c, but *Lucas Quintus*, not refusing to be called Lucius, because he simply eliminated that word from the name; not denying, declining the name itself, because he used three quarters of it; but simply taking the name and changing, altering it, making it no longer the white man's but his own, by himself composed, himself selfprogenitive and nominate, by himself ancestored, as, for all the old ledgers recorded to the contrary, old Carothers himself was

and that was all: 1874 the boy; 1888 the man, repudiated denied and free; 1895 and husband but no father, unwidowered but without a wife, and found long since that no man is ever free and probably could not bear it if he were; married then and living in Jefferson in the little new jerrybuilt bungalow which his wife's father had given them: and one morning Lucas stood suddenly in the doorway of the room where he was reading the Memphis paper and he looked at the paper's dateline and thought *It's his birthday. He's twenty-one today* and Lucas said: 'Whar's the rest of that money old Carothers left? I wants it. All of it.'

that was all: and McCaslin

---

1. Etc. (as Ike imagines the handwritten entry).

'More men than that one Buck and Buddy to fumble-heed that truth so mazed for them that spoke it and so confused for them that heard yet still there was 1865:' and he

'But not enough. Not enough of even Father and Uncle Buddy to fumble-heed in even three generations not even three generations fathered by Grandfather not even if there had been nowhere beneath His sight any but Grandfather and so He would not even have needed to elect and choose. But He tried and I know what you will say. That having Himself created them He could have known no more of hope than He could have pride and grief but He didn't hope He just waited because He had made them: not just because He had set them alive and in motion but because He had already worried with them so long: worried with them so long because He had seen how in individual cases they were capable of anything any height or depth remembered in mazed incomprehension out of heaven where hell was created too[2] and so He must admit them or else admit His equal somewhere and so be no longer God and therefore must accept responsibility for what He Himself had done in order to live with Himself in His lonely and paramount heaven. And He probably knew it was vain but He had created them and knew them capable of all things because He had shaped them out of the primal Absolute which contained all and had watched them since in their individual exaltation and baseness and they themselves not knowing why nor how nor even when: until at last He saw that they were all Grandfather all of them and that even from them the elected and chosen the best the very best He could expect (not hope mind; not hope) would be Bucks and Buddies and not even enough of them and in the third generation not even Bucks and Buddies but—' and McCaslin

'Ah:' and he

'Yes. If He could see Father and Uncle Buddy in Grandfather He must have seen me too.—an Isaac born into a later life than Abraham's and repudiating immolation: fatherless and therefore safe declining the altar because maybe this time the exasperated Hand might not supply the kid—' and McCaslin

'Escape:' and he

'All right. Escape.—Until one day He said what you told Fonsiba's husband that afternoon here in this room: *This will do. This is enough:* not in exasperation or rage or even just sick to death as you were sick that day: just *This is enough* and looked about for one last time, for one time more since He had created them, upon this land this South for which He had done so much with woods for game and streams for fish and deep rich soil for seed and lush springs to sprout it and long summers to mature it and serene falls to harvest it and short mild winters for men and animals and saw no hope anywhere and looked beyond it where hope should have been, where to East North and West lay illimitable that whole hopeful continent dedicated as a refuge and sanctuary of liberty and freedom from what you called the old world's worthless evening and saw the rich descendants of slavers, females of both sexes, to whom the black they shrieked of was another specimen another example like the Brazilian macaw brought home in a cage by a traveller, passing resolutions about horror and outrage in warm and air-proof

---

2. Because the rebellious angels were cast out of heaven into hell.

halls: and the thundering cannonade of politicians earning votes and the medicine-shows of pulpiteers earning Chatauqua fees,[3] to whom the outrage and the injustice were as much abstractions as Tariff or Silver[4] or Immortality and who employed the very shackles of its servitude and the sorry rags of its regalia as they did the other beer and banners and mottoes redfire and brimstone and sleight-of-hand and musical handsaws: and the whirling wheels which manufactured for a profit the pristine replacements of the shackles and shoddy garments as they wore out and spun the cotton and made the gins which ginned it and the cars and ships which hauled it, and the men who ran the wheels for that profit and established and collected the taxes it was taxed with and the rates for hauling it and the commissions for selling it: and He could have repudiated them since they were his creation now and forever more throughout all their generations until not only that old world from which He had rescued them but this new one too which He had revealed and led them to as a sanctuary and refuge were become the same worthless tideless rock cooling in the last crimson evening except that out of all that empty sound and bootless fury one silence, among that loud and moiling all of them just one simple enough to believe that horror and outrage were first and last simply horror and outrage and was crude enough to act upon that, illiterate and had no words for talking or perhaps was just busy and had no time to, one out of them all who did not bother Him with cajolery and adjuration then pleading then threat and had not even bothered to inform Him in advance what he was about so that a lesser than He might have even missed the simple act of lifting the long ancestral musket down from the deer-horns above the door, whereupon He said *My name is Brown*[5] too and the other *So is mine* and He *Then mine or yours cant be because I am against it* and the other *So am I* and He triumphantly *Then where are you going with that gun?* and the other told him in one sentence one word and He: amazed: Who knew neither hope nor pride nor grief *But your Association, your Committee, your Officers. Where are your Minutes, your Motions, your Parliamentary Procedures?* and the other *I aint against them. They are all right I reckon for them that have the time. I am just against the weak because they are niggers being held in bondage by the strong just because they are white.* So He turned once more to this land which He still intended to save because He had done so much for it—' and McCaslin

'What?' and he

'—to these people He was still committed to because they were his creations—' and McCaslin

'Turned back to us? His face to us?' and he

'—whose wives and daughters at least made soups and jellies for them when they were sick and carried the trays through the mud and the winter too into the stinking cabins and sat in the stinking cabins and kept fires going

3. Money from the Chautauqua Movement, a religiously based adult education program, begun in 1874, that expanded to include traveling programs, which later took on a carnival aspect.   4. In political debates over silver and gold as the basis of the U.S. currency, "sound-money" policies (chiefly northeastern business interests) feared inflation and supported gold, whereas the agricultural South and West supported the increased use of silver. The Bland-Allison Act of 1878 renewed the minting of silver dollars and mandated the increased purchase of silver bullion. *Tariff:* Republicans backed protective tariffs in the 1880 presidential campaign and accused Democrats of not supporting domestic industry.   5. John Brown (1800–1859), a militant abolitionist who was executed for leading an attack on the federal arsenal at Harpers Ferry, Virginia.

until crises came and passed but that was not enough: and when they were very sick had them carried into the big house itself into the company room itself maybe and nursed them there which the white man would have done too for any other of his cattle that was sick but at least the man who hired one from a livery wouldn't have and still that was not enough: so that He said and not in grief either Who had made them and so could know no more of grief than He could of pride or hope: *Apparently they can learn nothing save through suffering, remember nothing save when underlined in blood—*' and McCaslin

'Ashby on an afternoon's ride, to call on some remote maiden cousins of his mother or maybe just acquaintances of hers, comes by chance upon a minor engagement of outposts and dismounts and with his crimson-lined cloak for target leads a handful of troops he never saw before against an entrenched position of backwoods-trained riflemen. Lee's battle-order, wrapped maybe about a handful of cigars and doubtless thrown away when the last cigar was smoked, found by a Yankee Intelligence officer on the floor of a saloon behind the Yankee lines after Lee had already divided his forces before Sharpsburg.[6] Jackson on the Plank Road, already rolled up the flank which Hooker[7] believed could not be turned and, waiting only for night to pass to continue the brutal and incessant slogging which would fling that whole wing back into Hooker's lap where he sat on a front gallery in Chancellorsville[8] drinking rum toddies and telegraphing Lincoln that he had defeated Lee, is shot from among a whole covey of minor officers and in the blind night by one of his own patrols, leaving as next by seniority Stuart[9] that gallant man born apparently already horsed and sabred and already knowing all there was to know about war except the slogging and brutal stupidity of it: and that same Stuart off raiding Pennsylvania hen-roosts when Lee should have known of all of Meade just where Hancock was on Cemetery Ridge: and Longstreet too at Gettysburg[1] and that same Longstreet shot out of saddle by his own men in the dark by mistake just as Jackson was. His face to us? His face to us?' and he

'How else have made them fight? Who else but Jacksons and Stuarts and Ashbys and Morgans and Forrests?[2]—the farmers of the central and middle-west, holding land by the acre instead of the tens or maybe even the hundreds, farming it themselves and to no single crop of cotton or tobacco or cane, owning no slaves and needing and wanting none and already looking toward the Pacific coast, not always as long as two generations there and having stopped where they did stop only through the fortuitous mischance that an ox died or a wagon-axle broke. And the New England mechanics who didn't even own land and measured all things by the weight of water and the cost of turning wheels and the narrow fringe of traders and ship-owners still looking backward across the Atlantic and attached to the continent only by their counting-houses. And those who should have had the alertness to see:

6. The site of a Civil War battle. General Robert E. Lee (1807–1870) led the Confederate Army of Northern Virginia. A copy of Lee's orders for September 9, 1862, was used by a staff member to wrap cigars, which fell out of his pocket and were found by Union soldiers. 7. Joseph Hooker (1814–1879), led the Union Army of the Potomac at Chancellorsville. Thomas J. ("Stonewall") Jackson (1824–1863), general in the Confederate Army. 8. Site of a major Confederate victory. 9. J. E. B. Stuart (1833–1864), Confederate general who was supposed to inform Lee of the Union Army's movements. 1. Site of the bloodiest battle of the Civil War and a significant Union victory. George Gordon Meade (1815–1872) and Winfield Scott Hancock (1824–1886), Union generals whose forces occupied the high ground at Gettysburg (including Cemetery Ridge). James Longstreet (1821–1904), Confederate general. 2. Confederate generals.

the wildcat manipulators[3] of mythical wilderness town-sites; and the astute-ness to rationalise: the bankers who held the mortgages on the land which the first were only waiting to abandon and on the railroads and steamboats to carry them still further west, and on the factories and the wheels and the rented tenements those who ran them lived in; and the leisure and scope to comprehend and fear in time and even anticipate: the Boston-bred (even when not born in Boston) spinster descendants[4] of long lines of similarly-bred and likewise spinster aunts and uncles whose hands knew no callus except that of the indicting pen, to whom the wilderness itself began at the top of tide and who looked, if at anything other than Beacon Hill, only toward heaven—not to mention all the loud rabble of the camp-followers of pio-neers: the bellowing of politicians, the mellifluous choiring of self-styled men of God, the—' and McCaslin

'Here, here. Wait a minute:' and he

'Let me talk now. I'm trying to explain to the head of my family something which I have got to do which I dont quite understand myself, not in justifi-cation of it but to explain it if I can. I could say I dont know why I must do it but that I do know I have got to because I have got myself to have to live with for the rest of my life and all I want is peace to do it in. But you are the head of my family. More. I knew a long time ago that I would never have to miss my father, even if you are just finding out that you have missed your son.—the drawers of bills and the shavers of notes[5] and the schoolmasters and the self-ordained to teach and lead and all that horde of the semi-literate with a white shirt but no change for it, with one eye on themselves and watching each other with the other one. Who else could have made them fight: could have struck them so aghast with fear and dread as to turn shoul-der to shoulder and face one way and even stop talking for a while and even after two years of it keep them still so wrung with terror that some among them would seriously propose moving their very capital into a foreign country lest it be ravaged and pillaged by a people whose entire white male population would have little more than filled any one of their larger cities: except Jackson in the Valley and three separate armies trying to catch him and none of them ever knowing whether they were just retreating from a battle or just running into one and Stuart riding his whole command entirely around the biggest single armed force this continent ever saw in order to see what it looked like from behind and Morgan[6] leading a cavalry charge against a stranded man-of-war. Who else could have declared a war against a power with ten times the area and a hundred times the men and a thousand times the resources, except men who could believe that all necessary to conduct a successful war was not acumen nor shrewdness nor politics nor diplomacy nor money nor even integrity and simple arithmetic but just love of land and courage——'

'And an unblemished and gallant ancestry and the ability to ride a horse,' McCaslin said. 'Dont leave that out.' It was evening now, the tranquil sunset

---

3. Speculators who bought, sold, and rented tracts of land in the Midwest that were originally given to homesteaders under the Homestead Act of 1862 or were acquired by purchasing land warrants given to ex-soldiers under an Act of Congress in 1847.   4. Many members of the activist Boston Female Anti-slavery Society were not born in Boston; Angelina and Sarah Grimké, for example, were born in Charleston, South Carolina. Despite Ike's claim, they were not all spinsters.   5. Bankers and moneylenders, respec-tively.   6. Morgan, leading a group of twelve men disguised as Union soldiers, burned the moored Federal steamboat *Minnetonka*. In 1862, by a forced march in Virginia's Shenandoah Valley, Jackson's small Con-federate army eluded three Union armies sent to destroy them. Stuart, on a scouting mission, circled one hundred thousand Union troops commanded by General McClellan.

of October[7] mazy with windless woodsmoke. The cotton was long since picked and ginned, and all day now the wagons loaded with gathered corn moved between field and crib, processional across the enduring land. 'Well, maybe that's what He wanted. At least, that's what He got.' This time there was no yellowed procession of fading and harmless ledger-pages. This was chronicled in a harsher book and McCaslin, fourteen and fifteen and sixteen, had seen it and the boy himself had inherited it as Noah's grandchildren had inherited the Flood although they had not been there to see the deluge: that dark corrupt and bloody time[8] while three separate peoples had tried to adjust not only to one another but to the new land which they had created and inherited too and must live in for the reason that those who had lost it were no less free to quit it than those who had gained it were:—those upon whom freedom and equality had been dumped overnight and without warning or preparation or any training in how to employ it or even just endure it and who misused it not as children would nor yet because they had been so long in bondage and then so suddenly freed, but misused it as human beings always misuse freedom, so that he thought *Apparently there is a wisdom beyond even that learned through suffering necessary for a man to distinguish between liberty and license;* those who had fought for four years and lost to preserve a condition under which that franchisement was anomaly and paradox, not because they were opposed to freedom as freedom but for the old reasons for which man (not the generals and politicians but man) has always fought and died in wars: to preserve a status quo or to establish a better future one to endure for his children; and lastly, as if that were not enough for bitterness and hatred and fear, that third race even more alien to the people whom they resembled in pigment and in whom even the same blood ran, than to the people whom they did not,—that race threefold in one and alien even among themselves save for a single fierce will for rapine and pillage, composed of the sons of middle-aged Quartermaster lieutenants and Army sutlers[9] and contractors in military blankets and shoes and transport mules, who followed the battles they themselves had not fought and inherited the conquest they themselves had not helped to gain, sanctioned and protected even if not blessed, and left their bones and in another generation would be engaged in a fierce economic competition of small sloven farms with the black men they were supposed to have freed and the white descendants of fathers who had owned no slaves anyway whom they were supposed to have disinherited and in the third generation would be back once more in the little lost county seats as barbers and garage mechanics and deputy sheriffs and mill- and gin-hands and power-plant firemen, leading, first in mufti then later in an actual formalised regalia of hooded sheets and passwords and fiery christian symbols, lynching mobs against the race their ancestors had come to save:[1] and of all that other nameless horde of speculators in human misery, manipulators of money and politics and land, who follow catastrophe and are their own protection as grasshoppers are and need no blessing and sweat no plow or axe-helve and batten and vanish and leave no bones, just as they derived apparently from no ancestry, no mortal flesh, no

7. October 1888.   8. The Reconstruction period (1865–77) following the Civil War.   9. Tradespeople who sell provisions to soldiers.   1. Civilian, or regular dress (*mufti*), was soon replaced by the anonymity of hooded sheets worn by members of the Ku Klux Klan, an anti-black, anti-Catholic, anti-Semitic, and anti-immigrant organization.

act even of passion or even of lust: and the Jew who came without protection too since after two thousand years he had got out of the habit of being or needing it, and solitary, without even the solidarity of the locusts and in this a sort of courage since he had come thinking not in terms of simple pillage but in terms of his great-grandchildren, seeking yet some place to establish them to endure even though forever alien: and unblessed: a pariah about the face of the Western earth which twenty centuries later was still taking revenge on him for the fairy tale with which he had conquered it. McCaslin had actually seen it, and the boy even at almost eighty would never be able to distinguish certainly between what he had seen and what had been told him: a lightless and gutted and empty land where women crouched with the huddled children behind locked doors and men armed in sheets and masks rode the silent roads and the bodies of white and black both, victims not so much of hate as of desperation and despair, swung from lonely limbs: and men shot dead in polling-booths with the still wet pen in one hand and the unblotted ballot in the other: and a United States marshal in Jefferson who signed his official papers with a crude cross, an ex-slave called Sickymo, not at all because his ex-owner was a doctor and apothecary but because, still a slave, he would steal his master's grain alcohol and dilute it with water and peddle it in pint bottles from a cache beneath the roots of a big sycamore tree behind the drug store, who had attained his high office because his half-white sister was the concubine of the Federal A.P.M.:[2] and this time Mc-Caslin did not even say Look but merely lifted one hand, not even pointing, not even specifically toward the shelf of ledgers but toward the desk, toward the corner where it sat beside the scuffed patch on the floor where two decades of heavy shoes had stood while the white man at the desk added and multiplied and subtracted. And again he did not need to look because he had seen this himself and, twenty-three years after the Surrender[3] and twenty-four after the Proclamation, was still watching it: the ledgers, new ones now and filled rapidly, succeeding one another rapidly and containing more names than old Carothers or even his father and Uncle Buddy had ever dreamed of; new names and new faces to go with them, among which the old names and faces that even his father and uncle would have recognised, were lost, vanished—Tomey's Terrel dead, and even the tragic and miscast Percival Brownlee, who couldn't keep books and couldn't farm either, found his true niche at last, reappeared in 1862 during the boy's father's absence and had apparently been living on the plantation for at least a month before his uncle found out about it, conducting impromptu revival meetings among negroes, preaching and leading the singing also in his high sweet true soprano voice and disappeared again on foot and at top speed, not behind but ahead of a body of raiding Federal horse and reappeared for the third and last time in the entourage of a travelling Army paymaster, the two of them passing through Jefferson in a surrey at the exact moment when the boy's father (it was 1866) also happened to be crossing the Square, the surrey and its occupants traversing rapidly that quiet and bucolic scene and even in that fleeting moment and to others beside the boy's father giving an illusion of flight and illicit holiday like a man on an excursion during his wife's

2. Assistant paymaster, not necessarily in the army.   3. The war ended on April 9, 1865, when Lee surrendered to Union general Ulysses S. Grant.

absence with his wife's personal maid, until Brownlee glanced up and saw his late co-master and gave him one defiant female glance and then broke[4] again, leaped from the surrey and disappeared this time for good and it was only by chance that McCaslin, twenty years later, heard of him again, an old man now and quite fat, as the well-to-do proprietor of a select New Orleans brothel; and Tennie's Jim gone, nobody knew where, and Fonsiba in Arkansas with her three dollars each month and the scholar-husband with his lenseless spectacles and frock coat and his plans for the spring; and only Lucas was left, the baby, the last save himself of old Carothers' doomed and fatal blood which in the male derivation seemed to destroy all it touched, and even he was repudiating and at least hoping to escape it;—Lucas, the boy of fourteen whose name would not even appear for six years yet among those rapid pages in the bindings new and dustless too since McCaslin lifted them down daily now to write into them the continuation of that record which two hundred years had not been enough to complete and another hundred would not be enough to discharge; that chronicle which was a whole land in miniature, which multiplied and compounded was the entire South, twenty-three years after surrender and twenty-four from emancipation—that slow trickle of molasses and meal and meat, of shoes and straw hats and overalls, of plow-lines and collars and heel-bolts and buckheads and clevises,[5] which returned each fall as cotton—the two threads frail as truth and impalpable as equators yet cable-strong to bind for life them who made the cotton to the land their sweat fell on: and he

'Yes. Binding them for a while yet, a little while yet. Through and beyond that life and maybe through and beyond the life of that life's sons and maybe even through and beyond that of the sons of those sons. But not always, because they will endure. They will outlast us because they are—' it was not a pause, barely a falter even, possibly appreciable only to himself, as if he couldn't speak even to McCaslin, even to explain his repudiation, that which to him too, even in the act of escaping (and maybe this was the reality and the truth of his need to escape) was heresy: so that even in escaping he was taking with him more of that evil and unregenerate old man who could summon, because she was his property, a human being because she was old enough and female, to his widower's house and get a child on her and then dismiss her because she was of an inferior race, and then bequeath a thousand dollars to the infant because he would be dead then and wouldn't have to pay it, than even he had feared. 'Yes. He didn't want to. He had to. Because they will endure. They are better than we are. Stronger than we are. Their vices are vices aped from white men or that white men and bondage have taught them: improvidence and intemperance and evasion—not laziness: evasion: of what white men had set them to, not for their aggrandisement or even comfort but his own—' and McCaslin

'All right. Go on: Promiscuity. Violence. Instability and lack of control. Inability to distinguish between mine and thine—' and he

'How distinguish, when for two hundred years mine did not even exist for them?' and McCaslin

'All right. Go on. And their virtues—' and he

'Yes. Their own. Endurance—' and McCaslin

4. I.e., broke cover, as hunted animals might do.   5. Metal parts used to join pieces of a plow.

'So have mules:' and he

'—and pity and tolerance and forbearance and fidelity and love of children—' and McCaslin

'So have dogs:' and he

'—whether their own or not or black or not. And more: what they got not only not from white people but not even despite white people because they had it already from the old free fathers a longer time free than us because we have never been free—' and it was in McCaslin's eyes too, he had only to look at McCaslin's eyes and it was there, that summer twilight seven years ago, almost a week after they had returned from the camp before he discovered that Sam Fathers had told McCaslin: an old bear, fierce and ruthless not just to stay alive but ruthless with the fierce pride of liberty and freedom, jealous and proud enough of liberty and freedom to see it threatened not with fear nor even alarm but almost with joy, seeming deliberately to put it into jeopardy in order to savor it and keep his old strong bones and flesh supple and quick to defend and preserve it; an old man, son of a Negro slave and an Indian king, inheritor on the one hand of the long chronicle of a people who had learned humility through suffering and learned pride through the endurance which survived the suffering, and on the other side the chronicle of a people even longer in the land than the first, yet who now existed there only in the solitary brotherhood of an old and childless Negro's alien blood and the wild and invincible spirit of an old bear; a boy who wished to learn humility and pride in order to become skillful and worthy in the woods but found himself becoming so skillful so fast that he feared he would never become worthy because he had not learned humility and pride though he had tried, until one day an old man who could not have defined either led him as though by the hand to where an old bear and a little mongrel dog showed him that, by possessing one thing other, he would possess them both; and a little dog, nameless and mongrel and many-fathered, grown yet weighing less than six pounds, who couldn't be dangerous because there was nothing anywhere much smaller, not fierce because that would have been called just noise, not humble because it was already too near the ground to genuflect, and not proud because it would not have been close enough for anyone to discern what was casting that shadow and which didn't even know it was not going to heaven since they had already decided it had no immortal soul, so that all it could be was brave even though they would probably call that too just noise. *And you didn't shoot,' McCaslin said. 'How close were you?'*

'I dont know,' he said. 'There was a big wood tick just inside his off hind leg. I saw that. But I didn't have the gun then.'

'But you didn't shoot when you had the gun,' McCaslin said. 'Why?' But McCaslin didn't wait, rising and crossing the room, across the pelt of the bear he had killed two years ago and the bigger one McCaslin had killed before he was born, to the bookcase beneath the mounted head of his first buck, and returned with the book and sat down again and opened it. 'Listen,' he said. He read the five stanzas aloud and closed the book on his finger and looked up. 'All right,' he said. 'Listen,' and read again, but only one stanza this time and closed the book and laid it on the table. 'She cannot fade, though thou hast not thy bliss,' McCaslin said: 'Forever wilt thou love, and she be fair.'

'He's talking about a girl,' he said.

'He had to talk about something,' McCaslin said. Then he said, *'He was talking about truth. Truth is one. It doesn't change. It covers all things which touch the heart—honor and pride and pity and justice and courage and love. Do you see now?'* He didn't know. Somehow it had seemed simpler than that, simpler than somebody talking in a book about a young man and a girl he would never need to grieve over because he could never approach any nearer and would never have to get any further away. He had heard about an old bear and finally got big enough to hunt it and he hunted it four years and at last met it with a gun in his hands and he didn't shoot. Because a little dog—But he could have shot long before the fyce covered the twenty yards to where the bear waited, and Sam Fathers could have shot at any time during the interminable minute while Old Ben stood on his hind legs over them. . . . He ceased. McCaslin watched him, still speaking, the voice, the words as quiet as the twilight itself was: *'Courage and honor and pride, and pity and love of justice and of liberty. They all touch the heart, and what the heart holds to becomes truth, as far as we know truth. Do you see now?'* and he could still hear them, intact in this twilight as in that one seven years ago, no louder still because they did not need to be because they would endure: and he had only to look at McCaslin's eyes beyond the thin and bitter smiling, the faint lip-lift which would have had to be called smiling;—his kinsman, his father almost, who had been born too late into the old time and too soon for the new, the two of them juxtaposed and alien now to each other against their ravaged patrimony, the dark and ravaged fatherland still prone and panting from its etherless operation:

'Habet[6] then.—So this land is, indubitably, of and by itself cursed:' and he

'Cursed:' and again McCaslin merely lifted one hand, not even speaking and not even toward the ledgers: so that, as the stereopticon condenses into one instantaneous field the myriad minutia of its scope, so did that slight and rapid gesture establish in the small cramped and cluttered twilit room not only the ledgers but the whole plantation in its mazed and intricate entirety—the land, the fields and what they represented in terms of cotton ginned and sold, the men and women whom they fed and clothed and even paid a little cash money at Christmas-time in return for the labor which planted and raised and picked and ginned the cotton, the machinery and mules and gear with which they raised it and their cost and upkeep and replacement—that whole edifice intricate and complex and founded upon injustice and erected by ruthless rapacity and carried on even yet with at times downright savagery not only to the human beings but the valuable animals too, yet solvent and efficient and, more than that: not only still intact but enlarged, increased; brought still intact by McCaslin, himself little more than a child then, through and out of the debacle and chaos of twenty years ago where hardly one in ten survived,[7] and enlarged and increased and would continue so, solvent and efficient and intact and still increasing so long as McCaslin and his McCaslin successors lasted, even though their surnames might not even be Edmonds then: and he: 'Habet too. Because that's it: not the land, but us. Not only the blood, but the name too; not only its color but

---

6. He has it (Latin, literal trans.); here "he's had it." A phrase shouted at Roman gladiatorial bouts when one fighter landed a winning blow.   7. Few farms survived the Reconstruction intact.

its designation: Edmonds, white, but, a female line, could have no other but the name his father bore; Beauchamp, the elder line and the male one, but, black, could have had any name he liked and no man would have cared, except the name his father bore who had no name—' and McCaslin

'And since I know too what you know I will say now, once more let me say it: And one other, and in the third generation too, and the male, the eldest, the direct and sole and white and still McCaslin even, father to son to son—' and he

'I am free:' and this time McCaslin did not even gesture, no inference of fading pages, no postulation of the stereoptic whole, but the frail and iron thread strong as truth and impervious as evil and longer than life itself and reaching beyond record and patrimony both to join him with the lusts and passions, the hopes and dreams and griefs, of bones whose names while still fleshed and capable even old Carothers' grandfather had never heard: and he: 'And of that too:' and McCaslin

'Chosen, I suppose (I will concede it) out of all your time by Him as you say Buck and Buddy were from theirs. And it took Him a bear and an old man and four years just for you. And it took you fourteen years to reach that point and about that many, maybe more, for Old Ben, and more than seventy for Sam Fathers. And you are just one. How long then? How long?' and he

'It will be long. I have never said otherwise. But it will be all right because they will endure—' and McCaslin

'And anyway, you will be free.—No, not now nor ever, we from them nor they from us. So I repudiate too. I would deny even if I knew it were true. I would have to. Even you can see that I could do no else. I am what I am; I will be always what I was born and have always been. And more than me. More than me, just as there were more than Buck and Buddy in what you called His first plan which failed:' and he

'And more than me:' and McCaslin

'No. Not even you. Because mark. You said how on that instant when Ikkemotubbe realised that he could sell the land to Grandfather, it ceased forever to have been his. All right; go on: Then it belonged to Sam Fathers, old Ikkemotubbe's son. And who inherited from Sam Fathers, if not you? co-heir perhaps with Boon, if not of his life maybe, at least of his quitting it?' and he

'Yes. Sam Fathers set me free.' And Isaac McCaslin, not yet Uncle Ike, a long time yet before he would be uncle to half a county and still father to none, living in one small cramped fireless rented room in a Jefferson board-ing-house where petit juries were domiciled during court terms and itinerant horse- and mule-traders stayed, with his kit of brand-new carpenter's tools and the shotgun McCaslin had given him with his name engraved in silver and old General Compson's compass (and, when the General died, his silver-mounted horn too) and the iron cot and mattress and the blankets which he would take each fall into the woods for more than sixty years and the bright tin coffee-pot

there had been a legacy, from his Uncle Hubert Beauchamp, his godfather, that bluff burly roaring childlike man from whom Uncle Buddy had won Tomey's Terrel's wife Tennie in the poker-game in 1859—'possible strait against three Treys in sigt Not called'—; no pale sentence or paragraph scrawled in cringing fear of death by a weak and trembling hand as a last

desperate sop flung backward at retribution, but a Legacy, a Thing, possessing weight to the hand and bulk to the eye and even audible: a silver cup
filled with gold pieces and wrapped in burlap and sealed with his godfather's
ring in the hot wax, which (intact still) even before his Uncle Hubert's death
and long before his own majority, when it would be his, had become not only
a legend but one of the family lares. After his father's and his Uncle Hubert's
sister's marriage they moved back into the big house, the tremendous cavern
which old Carothers had started and never finished, cleared the remaining
negroes out of it and with his mother's dowry completed it, at least the rest
of the windows and doors and moved into it, all of them save Uncle Buddy
who declined to leave the cabin he and his twin had built, the move being
the bride's notion and more than just a notion and none ever to know if she
really wanted to live in the big house or if she knew before hand that Uncle
Buddy would refuse to move: and two weeks after his birth in 1867, the first
time he and his mother came down stairs, one night and the silver cup sitting
on the cleared dining-room table beneath the bright lamp and while his
mother and his father and McCaslin and Tennie (his nurse: carrying him)—
all of them again but Uncle Buddy—watched, his Uncle Hubert rang one by
one into the cup the bright and glinting mintage and wrapped it into the
burlap envelope and heated the wax and sealed it and carried it back home
with him where he lived alone now without even his sister either to hold him
down as McCaslin said or to try to raise him up as Uncle Buddy said, and
(dark times then in Mississippi) Uncle Buddy said most of the niggers gone
and the ones that didn't go even Hub Beauchamp could not have wanted:
but the dogs remained and Uncle Buddy said Beauchamp fiddled while Nero
fox-hunted[8]

    they would go and see it there; at last his mother would prevail and they
would depart in the surrey, once more all save Uncle Buddy and McCaslin
to keep Uncle Buddy company until one winter Uncle Buddy began to fail
and from then on it was himself, beginning to remember now, and his mother
and Tennie and Tomey's Terrel to drive: the twenty-two miles into the next
county, the twin gateposts on one of which McCaslin could remember the
half-grown boy blowing a fox-horn at breakfast dinner and supper-time and
jumping down to open to any passer who happened to hear it but where
there were no gates at all now, the shabby and overgrown entrance to what
his mother still insisted that people call Warwick because her brother was if
truth but triumphed and justice but prevailed the rightful earl of it, the
paintless house which outwardly did not change but which on the inside
seemed each time larger because he was too little to realise then that there
was less and less in it of the fine furnishings, the rosewood and mahogany
and walnut which for him had never existed anywhere anyway save in his
mother's tearful lamentations and the occasional piece small enough to be
roped somehow onto the rear or the top of the carriage on their return (And
he remembered this, he had seen it: an instant, a flash, his mother's soprano
'Even my dress! Even my dress!' loud and outraged in the barren unswept
hall; a face young and female and even lighter in color than Tomey's Terrel's
for an instant in a closing door; a swirl, a glimpse of the silk gown and the
flick and glint of an ear-ring: an apparition rapid and tawdry and illicit yet

8. A play on the old saying "Nero fiddled while Rome burned."

somehow even to the child, the infant still almost, breathless and exciting and evocative: as though, like two limpid and pellucid streams meeting, the child which he still was had made serene and absolute and perfect rapport and contact through that glimpsed nameless illicit hybrid female flesh with the boy which had existed at that stage of inviolable and immortal adolescence in his uncle for almost sixty years; the dress, the face, the ear-rings gone in that same aghast flash and his uncle's voice: 'She's my cook! She's my new cook! I had to have a cook, didn't I?' then the uncle himself, the face alarmed and aghast too yet still innocently and somehow even indomitably of a boy, they retreating in their turn now, back to the front gallery, and his uncle again, pained and still amazed, in a sort of desperate resurgence if not of courage at least of self-assertion: 'They're free now! They're folks too just like we are!' and his mother: 'That's why! That's why! My mother's house! Defiled! Defiled!' and his uncle: 'Damn it, Sibbey, at least give her time to pack her grip:' then over, finished, the loud uproar and all, himself and Tennie and he remembered Tennie's inscrutable face at the broken shutterless window of the bare room which had once been the parlor while they watched, hurrying down the lane at a stumbling trot, the routed compounder of his uncle's uxory: the back, the nameless face which he had seen only for a moment, the once-hooped dress ballooning and flapping below a man's overcoat, the worn heavy carpet-bag jouncing and banging against her knee, routed and in retreat true enough and in the empty lane solitary young-looking and forlorn yet withal still exciting and evocative and wearing still the silken banner captured inside the very citadel of respectability, and unforgettable.)

the cup, the sealed inscrutable burlap, sitting on the shelf in the locked closet, Uncle Hubert unlocking the door and lifting it down and passing it from hand to hand: his mother, his father, McCaslin and even Tennie, insisting that each take it in turn and heft it for weight and shake it again to prove the sound, Uncle Hubert himself standing spraddled before the cold unswept hearth in which the very bricks themselves were crumbling into a litter of soot and dust and mortar and the droppings of chimney-sweeps,[9] still roaring and still innocent and still indomitable: and for a long time he believed nobody but himself had noticed that his uncle now put the cup only into his hands, unlocked the door and lifted it down and put it into his hands and stood over him until he had shaken it obediently until it sounded then took it from him and locked it back into the closet before anyone else could have offered to touch it, and even later, when competent not only to remember but to rationalise, he could not say what it was or even if it had been anything because the parcel was still heavy and still rattled, not even when, Uncle Buddy dead and his father, at last and after almost seventy-five years in bed after the sun rose, said: 'Go get that damn cup. Bring that damn Hub Beauchamp too if you have to:' because it still rattled though his uncle no longer put it even into his hands now but carried it himself from one to the other, his mother, McCaslin, Tennie, shaking it before each in turn, saying: 'Hear it? Hear it?' his face still innocent, not quite baffled but only amazed and not very amazed and still indomitable: and, his father and Uncle Buddy both gone now, one day without reason or any warning the almost completely

---

9. Or chimney swifts, a sparrow-sized bird with long wings that nests in chimneys.

empty house in which his uncle and Tennie's ancient and quarrelsome great-grandfather (who claimed to have seen Lafayette[1] and McCaslin said in another ten years would be remembering God) lived, cooked and slept in one single room, burst into peaceful conflagration, a tranquil instantaneous sourceless unanimity of combustion, walls floors and roof: at sunup it stood where his uncle's father had built it sixty years ago, at sundown the four blackened and smokeless chimneys rose from a light white powder of ashes and a few charred ends of planks which did not even appear to have been very hot: and out of the last of evening, the last one of the twenty-two miles, on the old white mare which was the last of that stable which McCaslin remembered, the two old men riding double up to the sister's door, the one wearing his fox-horn on its braided deerhide thong and the other carrying the burlap parcel wrapped in a shirt, the tawny wax-daubed shapeless lump sitting again and on an almost identical shelf and his uncle holding the half-opened door now, his hand not only on the knob but one foot against it and the key waiting in the other hand, the face urgent and still not baffled but still and even indomitably not very amazed and himself standing in the half-opened door looking quietly up at the burlap shape become almost three times its original height and a good half less than its original thickness and turning away and he would remember not his mother's look this time nor yet Tennie's inscrutable expression but McCaslin's dark and aquiline face grave insufferable and bemused: then one night they waked him and fetched him still half-asleep into the lamp light, the smell of medicine which was familiar by now in that room and the smell of something else which he had not smelled before and knew at once and would never forget, the pillow, the worn and ravaged face from which looked out still the boy innocent and immortal and amazed and urgent, looking at him and trying to tell him until McCaslin moved and leaned over the bed and drew from the top of the night shirt the big iron key on the greasy cord which suspended it, the eyes saying Yes Yes Yes now, and cut the cord and unlocked the closet and brought the parcel to the bed, the eyes still trying to tell him even when he took the parcel so that was still not it, the hands still clinging to the parcel even while relinquishing it, the eyes more urgent than ever trying to tell him but they never did; and he was ten and his mother was dead too and McCaslin said, 'You are almost halfway now. You might as well open it:' and he: 'No. He said twenty-one:' and he was twenty-one and McCaslin shifted the bright lamp to the center of the cleared dining-room table and set the parcel beside it and laid his open knife beside the parcel and stood back with that expression of old grave intolerant and repudiating and he lifted it, the burlap lump which fifteen years ago had changed its shape completely overnight, which shaken gave forth a thin weightless not-quite-musical curiously muffled clatter, the bright knife-blade hunting amid the mazed intricacy of string, the knobby gouts of wax bearing his uncle's Beauchamp seal rattling onto the table's polished top and, standing amid the collapse of burlap folds, the un-stained tin coffee-pot still brand new, the handful of copper coins and now he knew what had given them the muffled sound: a collection of minutely-folded scraps of paper sufficient almost for a rat's nest, of good linen bond,

1. The Marquis de Lafayette (1757–1834), who fought on the side of the colonists during the American Revolution, traveled through the South in 1825.

of the crude ruled paper such as negroes use, of raggedly-torn ledger-pages and the margins of newspapers and once the paper label from a new pair of overalls, all dated and all signed, beginning with the first one not six months after they had watched him seal the silver cup into the burlap on this same table in this same room by the light even of this same lamp almost twenty-one years ago:

> *I owe my Nephew Isaac Beauchamp McCaslin five (5) pieces Gold which I,O.U constitues My note of hand with Interest at 5 percent.*
> *Hubert Fitz-Hubert Beauchamp*
> *at Warwick 27 Nov 1867*

and he: 'Anyway he called it Warwick:' once at least, even if no more. But there was more:

> *Isaac 24 Dec 1867 I.O.U. 2 pieces Gold H.Fh.B. I.O.U. Isaac 1 piece Gold 1 Jan 1868 H.Fh.B.*

then five again then three then one then one then a long time and what dream, what dreamed splendid recoup, not of any injury or betrayal of trust because it had been merely a loan: nay, a partnership:

> *I.O.U. Beauchamp McCaslin or his heirs twenty-five (25) pieces Gold This & All preceeding constituting My notes of hand at twenty (20) percentum compounded annually. This date of 19th January 1873*
> *Beauchamp*

no location save that in time and signed by the single not name but word as the old proud earl himself might have scrawled Nevile:[2] and that made forty-three and he could not remember himself of course but the legend had it at fifty, which balanced: one: then one: then one: then one and then the last three and then the last chit, dated after he came to live in the house with them and written in the shaky hand not of a beaten old man because he had never been beaten to know it but of a tired old man maybe and even at that tired only on the outside and still indomitable, the simplicity of the last one the simplicity not of resignation but merely of amazement, like a simple comment or remark, and not very much of that:

> *One silver cup. Hubert Beauchamp*

and McCaslin: 'So you have plenty of coppers anyway. But they are still not old enough yet to be either rarities or heirlooms. So you will have to take the money:' except that he didn't hear McCaslin, standing quietly beside the table and looking peacefully at the coffee-pot and the pot sitting one night later on the mantel above what was not even a fireplace in the little cramped icelike room in Jefferson as McCaslin tossed the folded banknotes onto the bed and, still standing (there was nowhere to sit save on the bed) did not even remove his hat and overcoat: and he

'As a loan. From you. This one:' and McCaslin

'You cant. I have no money that I can lend to you. And you will have to

2. Hubert signs with the family name Beauchamp, as might the head of a noble family. His sister, Sophonsiba, liked to claim that he was the true earl of Warwick (England) inasmuch as the rights of a former countess of Warwick, Anne Beauchamp, were set aside upon the death of her husband, Richard Neville (1428–1471).

go to the bank and get it next month because I wont bring it to you:' and he could not hear McCaslin now either, looking peacefully at McCaslin, his kinsman, his father almost yet no kin now as, at the last, even fathers and sons are no kin: and he

'It's seventeen miles, horseback and in the cold. We could both sleep here:' and McCaslin

'Why should I sleep here in my house when you wont sleep yonder in yours?' and gone, and he looking at the bright rustless unstained tin and thinking and not for the first time how much it takes to compound a man (Isaac McCaslin for instance) and of the devious intricate choosing yet unerring path that man's (Isaac McCaslin's for instance) spirit takes among all that mass to make him at last what he is to be, not only to the astonishment of them (the ones who sired the McCaslin who sired his father and Uncle Buddy and their sister, and the ones who sired the Beauchamp who sired his Uncle Hubert and his Uncle Hubert's sister) who believed they had shaped him, but to Isaac McCaslin too

as a loan and used it though he would not have had to: Major de Spain offered him a room in his house as long as he wanted it and asked nor would ever ask any question, and old General Compson more than that, to take him into his own room, to sleep in half of his own bed and more than Major de Spain because he told him baldly why: 'You sleep with me and before this winter is out, I'll know the reason. You'll tell me. Because I don't believe you just quit. It looks like you just quit but I have watched you in the woods too much and I dont believe you just quit even if it does look damn like it:' using it as a loan, paid his board and rent for a month and bought the tools, not simply because he was good with his hands because he had intended to use his hands and it could have been with horses, and not in mere static and hopeful emulation of the Nazarene[3] as the young gambler buys a spotted shirt because the old gambler won in one yesterday, but (without the arrogance of false humility and without the false humbleness of pride, who intended to earn his bread, didn't especially want to earn it but had to earn it and for more than just bread) because if the Nazarene had found carpentering good for the life and ends He had assumed and elected to serve, it would be all right too for Isaac McCaslin even though Isaac McCaslin's ends, although simple enough in their apparent motivation, were and would be always incomprehensible to him, and his life, invincible enough in its needs, if he could have helped himself, not being the Nazarene, he would not have chosen it: and paid it back. He had forgotten the thirty dollars which McCaslin would put into the bank in his name each month, fetched it in to him and flung it onto the bed that first one time but no more; he had a partner now or rather he was the partner: a blasphemous profane clever old dipsomaniac who had built blockade-runners[4] in Charleston in '62 and '3 and had been a ship's carpenter since and appeared in Jefferson two years ago nobody knew from where nor why and spent a good part of his time since recovering from delirium tremens in the jail; they had put a new roof on the stable of the bank's president and (the old man in jail again still celebrating that job) he went to the bank to collect for it and the president said, 'I should

3. Jesus.   4. Ships that ran the blockade of Union ships outside the port of Charleston, South Carolina, during the Civil War.

borrow from you instead of paying you:' and it had been seven months now
and he remembered for the first time, two-hundred-and-ten dollars, and this
was the first job of any size and when he left the bank the account stood at
two-twenty, two-forty to balance, only twenty dollars more to go, then it did
balance though by then the total had increased to three hundred and thirty
and he said, 'I will transfer it now:' and the president said, 'I cant do that.
McCaslin told me not to. Haven't you got another initial you could use and
open another account?' but that was all right, the coins the silver and the
bills as they accumulated knotted into a handkerchief and the coffee-pot
wrapped in an old shirt as when Tennie's great-grandfather had fetched it
from Warwick eighteen years ago, in the bottom of the iron-bound trunk
which old Carothers had brought from Carolina and his landlady said, 'Not
even a lock! And you dont even lock your door, not even when you leave!'
and himself looking at her as peacefully as he had looked at McCaslin that
first night in this same room, no kin to him at all yet more than kin as those
who serve you even for pay are your kin and those who injure you are more
than brother or wife.

and had the wife now, got the old man out of jail and fetched him to the
rented room and sobered him by superior strength, did not even remove his
own shoes for twenty-four hours, got him up and got food into him and they
built the barn this time from the ground up and he married her: an only
child, a small girl yet curiously bigger than she seemed at first, solider perhaps, with dark eyes and a passionate heart-shaped face, who had time even
on that farm[5] to watch most of the day while he sawed timbers to the old
man's measurements: and she: 'Papa told me about you. That farm is really
yours, isn't it?' and he
    'And McCaslin's:' and she
    'Was there a will leaving half of it to him?' and he
    'There didn't need to be a will. His grandmother was my father's sister.
We were the same as brothers:' and she
    'You are the same as second cousins and that's all you ever will be. But I
dont suppose it matters:' and they were married, they were married and it
was the new country, his heritage too as it was the heritage of all, out of the
earth, beyond the earth yet of the earth because his too was of the earth's
long chronicle, his too because each must share with another in order to
come into it and in the sharing they become one: for that while, one: for that
little while at least, one: indivisible, that while at least irrevocable and unre-
coverable, living in a rented room still but for just a little while and that room
wall-less and topless and floorless in glory for him to leave each morning and
return to at night; her father already owned the lot in town and furnished
the material and he and his partner would build it, her dowry from one: her
wedding-present from three, she not to know it until the bungalow was finished and ready to be moved into and he never knew who told her, not her
father and not his partner and not even in drink though for a while he
believed that, himself coming home from work and just time to wash and
rest a moment before going down to supper, entering no rented cubicle since
it would still partake of glory even after they would have grown old and lost
it: and he saw her face then, just before she spoke: 'Sit down:' the two of

5. I.e., the farm where Ike is building a barn, not the McCaslin farm of the next question.

them sitting on the bed's edge, not even touching yet, her face strained and terrible, her voice a passionate and expiring whisper of immeasurable promise: 'I love you. You know I love you. When are we going to move?' and he

'I didn't—I didn't know—Who told you—' the hot fierce palm clapped over his mouth, crushing his lips into his teeth, the fierce curve of fingers digging into his cheek and only the palm slacked off enough for him to answer:

'The farm. Our farm. Your farm:' and he

'I—' then the hand again, finger and palm, the whole enveloping weight of her although she still was not touching him save the hand, the voice: 'No! No!' and the fingers themselves seeming to follow through the cheek the impulse to speech as it died in his mouth, then the whisper, the breath again, of love and of incredible promise, the palm slackening again to let him answer:

'When?' and he

'I—' then she was gone, the hand too, standing, her back to him and her head bent, the voice so calm now that for an instant it seemed no voice of hers that he ever remembered: 'Stand up and turn your back and shut your eyes:' and repeated before he understood and stood himself with his eyes shut and heard the bell ring for supper below stairs and the calm voice again: 'Lock the door:' and he did so and leaned his forehead against the cold wood, his eyes closed, hearing his heart and the sound he had begun to hear before he moved until it ceased and the bell rang again below stairs and he knew it was for them this time and he heard the bed and turned and he had never seen her naked before, he had asked her to once, and why: that he wanted to see her naked because he loved her and he wanted to see her looking at him naked because he loved her but after that he never mentioned it again, even turning his face when she put the nightgown on over her dress to undress at night and putting the dress on over the gown to remove it in the morning and she would not let him get into bed beside her until the lamp was out and even in the heat of summer she would draw the sheet up over them both before she would let him turn to her: and the landlady came up the stairs up the hall and rapped on the door and then called their names but she didn't move, lying still on the bed outside the covers, her face turned away on the pillow, listening to nothing, thinking of nothing, not of him anyway he thought then the landlady went away and she said, 'Take off your clothes:' her head still turned away, looking at nothing, thinking of nothing, waiting for nothing, not even him, her hand moving as though with volition and vision of its own, catching his wrist at the exact moment when he paused beside the bed so that he never paused but merely changed the direction of moving, downward now, the hand drawing him and she moved at last, shifted, a movement one single complete inherent not practiced and one time older than man, looking at him now, drawing him still downward with the one hand down and down and he neither saw nor felt it shift, palm flat against his chest now and holding him away with the same apparent lack of any effort or any need for strength, and not looking at him now, she didn't need to, the chaste woman, the wife, already looked upon all the men who ever rutted and now her whole body had changed, altered, he had never seen it but once and now it was not even the one he had seen but composite of all woman-flesh since man that ever of its own will reclined on its back and opened, and out of it somewhere, without any movement of lips even, the dying and invincible whisper: 'Promise:' and he

'Promise?'

'The farm.' He moved. He had moved, the hand shifting from his chest once more to his wrist, grasping it, the arm still lax and only the light increasing pressure of the fingers as though arm and hand were a piece of wire cable with one looped end, only the hand tightening as he pulled against it. 'No,' he said. 'No:' and she was not looking at him still but not like the other but still the hand: 'No, I tell you. I wont. I cant. Never:' and still the hand and he said, for the last time, he tried to speak clearly and he knew it was still gently and he thought, *She already knows more than I with all the man-listening in camps where there was nothing to read ever even heard of. They are born already bored with what a boy approaches only at fourteen and fifteen with blundering and aghast trembling:* 'I cant. Not ever. Remember:' and still the steady and invincible hand and he said Yes and he thought, *She is lost. She was born lost. We were all born lost* then he stopped thinking and even saying Yes, it was like nothing he had ever dreamed, let alone heard in mere man-talking until after a no-time he returned and lay spent on the insatiate immemorial beach and again with a movement one time more older than man she turned and freed herself and on their wedding night she had cried and he thought she was crying now at first, into the tossed and wadded pillow, the voice coming from somewhere between the pillow and the cachinnation: 'And that's all. That's all from me. If this dont get you that son you talk about, it wont be mine:' lying on her side, her back to the empty rented room, laughing and laughing

5

He went back to the camp one more time before the lumber company moved in and began to cut the timber. Major de Spain himself never saw it again. But he made them welcome to use the house and hunt the land whenever they liked, and in the winter following the last hunt when Sam Fathers and Lion died, General Compson and Walter Ewell invented a plan to corporate themselves, the old group, into a club and lease the camp and the hunting privileges of the woods—an invention doubtless of the somewhat childish old General but actually worthy of Boon Hogganbeck himself. Even the boy, listening, recognised it for the subterfuge it was: to change the leopard's spots when they could not alter the leopard, a baseless and illusory hope to which even McCaslin seemed to subscribe for a while, that once they had persuaded Major de Spain to return to the camp he might revoke himself, which even the boy knew he would not do. And he did not. The boy never knew what occurred when Major de Spain declined. He was not present when the subject was broached and McCaslin never told him. But when June came and the time for the double birthday celebration there was no mention of it and when November came no one spoke of using Major de Spain's house and he never knew whether or not Major de Spain knew they were going on the hunt though without doubt old Ash probably told him: he and McCaslin and General Compson (and that one was the General's last hunt too) and Walter and Boon and Tennie's Jim and old Ash loaded two wagons and drove two days and almost forty miles beyond any country the boy had ever seen before and lived in tents for the two weeks. And the next spring they heard (not from Major de Spain) that he had sold the timber-rights to a Memphis lumber company and in June the boy came to town with McCaslin one Saturday and went to Major de Spain's office—the big, airy, book-lined second-storey room with windows at one end opening upon the shabby hinder purlieus of stores and at the other a door giving onto the railed balcony above the Square, with its curtained alcove where sat a cedar water-bucket and a sugar-bowl and spoon and tumbler and a wicker-covered demijohn of whiskey, and the bamboo-and-paper punkah[6] swinging back and forth above the desk while old Ash in a tilted chair beside the entrance pulled the cord.

"Of course," Major de Spain said. "Ash will probably like to get off in the woods himself for a while, where he wont have to eat Daisy's cooking. Complain about it, anyway. Are you going to take anybody with you?"

"No sir," he said. "I thought that maybe Boon—" For six months now Boon had been town-marshal at Hoke's; Major de Spain had compounded with the lumber company—or perhaps compromised was closer, since it was the lumber company who had decided that Boon might be better as a town-marshal than head of a logging gang.

"Yes," Major de Spain said. "I'll wire him today. He can meet you at Hoke's. I'll send Ash on by the train and they can take some food in and all you will have to do will be to mount your horse and ride over."

"Yes sir," he said. "Thank you." And he heard his voice again. He didn't know he was going to say it yet he did know, he had known it all the time: "Maybe if you . . ." His voice died. It was stopped, he never knew how because Major de Spain did not speak and it was not until his voice ceased that Major de Spain moved, turned back to the desk and the papers spread on it and even that without moving because he was sitting at the desk with a paper in his hand when the boy entered, the boy standing there looking down at the short plumpish grey-haired man in sober fine broadcloth and an immaculate glazed shirt whom he was used to seeing in boots and muddy corduroy; unshaven, sitting the shaggy powerful long-hocked mare with the worn Winchester carbine across the saddle-bow and the great blue dog standing motionless as bronze at the stirrup, the two of them in that last year and to the boy anyway coming to resemble one another somehow as two people competent for love or for business who have been in love or in business together for a long time sometimes do. Major de Spain did not look up again.

"No. I will be too busy. But good luck to you. If you have it, you might bring me a young squirrel."

"Yes sir," he said. "I will."

He rode his mare, the three-year-old filly he had bred and raised and broken himself. He left home a little after midnight and six hours later, without even having sweated her, he rode into Hoke's, the tiny log-line junction which he had always thought of as Major de Spain's property too although Major de Spain had merely sold the company (and that many years ago) the land on which the sidetracks and loading-platforms and the commissary store stood, and looked about in shocked and grieved amazement even though he had had forewarning and had believed himself prepared: a new planing-mill already half completed which would cover two or three

6. A fan.

acres and what looked like miles and miles of stacked steel rails red with the light bright rust of newness and of piled crossties sharp with creosote, and wire corrals and feeding-troughs for two hundred mules at least and the tents for the men who drove them; so that he arranged for the care and stabling of his mare as rapidly as he could and did not look any more, mounted into the log-train caboose with his gun and climbed into the cupola and looked no more save toward the wall of wilderness ahead within which he would be able to hide himself from it once more anyway.

Then the little locomotive shrieked and began to move: a rapid churning of exhaust, a lethargic deliberate clashing of slack couplings traveling backward along the train, the exhaust changing to the deep slow clapping bites of power as the caboose too began to move and from the cupola he watched the train's head complete the first and only curve in the entire line's length and vanish into the wilderness, dragging its length of train behind it so that it resembled a small dingy harmless snake vanishing into weeds, drawing him with it too until soon it ran once more at its maximum clattering speed between the twin walls of unaxed wilderness as of old. It had been harmless once. Not five years ago Walter Ewell had shot a six-point buck from this same moving caboose, and there was the story of the half-grown bear: the train's first trip in to the cutting thirty miles away, the bear between the rails, its rear end elevated like that of a playing puppy while it dug to see what sort of ants or bugs they might contain or perhaps just to examine the curious symmetrical squared barkless logs which had appeared apparently from nowhere in one endless mathematical line overnight, still digging until the driver on the braked engine not fifty feet away blew the whistle at it, whereupon it broke frantically and took the first tree it came to: an ash sapling not much bigger than a man's thigh and climbed as high as it could and clung there, its head ducked between its arms as a man (a woman perhaps) might have done while the brakeman threw chunks of ballast at it, and when the engine returned three hours later with the first load of outbound logs the bear was halfway down the tree and once more scrambled back up as high as it could and clung again while the train passed and was still there when the engine went in again in the afternoon and still there when it came back out at dusk; and Boon had been in Hoke's with the wagon after a barrel of flour that noon when the train-crew told about it and Boon and Ash, both twenty years younger then, sat under the tree all that night to keep anybody from shooting it and the next morning Major de Spain had the log-train held at Hoke's and just before sundown on the second day, with not only Boon and Ash but Major de Spain and General Compson and Walter and Mc-Caslin, twelve then, watching, it came down the tree after almost thirty-six hours without even water and McCaslin told him how for a minute they thought it was going to stop right there at the barrow-pit where they were standing and drink, how it looked at the water and paused and looked at them and at the water again, but did not, gone, running, as bears run, the two sets of feet, front and back, tracking two separate though parallel courses.

It had been harmless then. They would hear the passing log-train some-times from the camp; sometimes, because nobody bothered to listen for it or not. They would hear it going in, running light and fast, the light clatter of the trucks, the exhaust of the diminutive locomotive and its shrill peanut-parcher whistle[7] flung for one petty moment and absorbed by the brooding and inattentive wilderness without even an echo. They would hear it going out, loaded, not quite so fast now yet giving its frantic and toylike illusion of crawling speed, not whistling now to conserve steam, flinging its bitten laboring miniature puffing into the immemorial woodsface with frantic and bootless vainglory, empty and noisy and puerile, carrying to no destination or purpose sticks which left nowhere any scar or stump as the child's toy loads and transports and unloads its dead sand and rushes back for more, tireless and unceasing and rapid yet never quite so fast as the Hand which plays with it moves the toy burden back to load the toy again. But it was different now. It was the same train, engine cars and caboose, even the same enginemen brake-man and conductor to whom Boon, drunk then sober then drunk again then fairly sober once more all in the space of fourteen hours, had bragged that day two years ago about what they were going to do to Old Ben tomorrow, running with its same illusion of frantic rapidity between the same twin walls of impenetrable and impervious woods, passing the old landmarks, the old game crossings over which he had trailed bucks wounded and not wounded and more than once seen them, anything but wounded, bolt out of the woods and up and across the embankment which bore the rails and ties then down and into the woods again as the earth-bound supposedly move but crossing as arrows travel, groundless, elongated, three times its actual length and even paler, different in color, as if there were a point between immobility and absolute motion where even mass chemically altered, changing without pain or agony not only in bulk and shape but in color too, approaching the color of wind, yet this time it was as though the train (and not only the train but himself, not only his vision which had seen it and his memory which remembered it but his clothes too, as garments carry back into the clean edgeless blowing of air the lingering effluvium of a sick-room or of death) had brought with it into the doomed wilderness even before the actual axe the shadow and portent of the new mill not even finished yet and the rails and ties which were not even laid; and he knew now what he had known as soon as he saw Hoke's this morning but had not yet thought into words: why Major de Spain had not come back, and that after this time he himself, who had had to see it one time other, would return no more.

Now they were near. He knew it before the engine-driver whistled to warn him. Then he saw Ash and the wagon, the reins without doubt wrapped once more about the brake-lever as within the boy's own memory Major de Spain had been forbidding him for eight years to do, the train slowing, the slackened couplings jolting and clashing again from car to car, the caboose slowing past the wagon as he swung down with his gun, the conductor leaning out above him to signal the engine, the caboose still slowing, creeping, although the engine's exhaust was already slatting in mounting tempo against the unechoing wilderness, the crashing of draw-bars[8] once more travelling backward along the train, the caboose picking up speed at last. Then it was gone. It had not been. He could no longer hear it. The wilderness soared, musing, inattentive, myriad, eternal, green; older than any mill-shed, longer than any spurline. "Mr Boon here yet?" he said.

---

7. A steam whistle used by peanut vendors to attract business to their roasting machines. 8. Bars that attach railroad-car couplings.

"He beat me in," Ash said. "Had the wagon loaded and ready for me at Hoke's yistiddy when I got there and setting on the front steps at camp last night when I got in. He already been in the woods since fo daylight this morning. Said he gwine up to the Gum Tree and for you to hunt up that way and meet him." He knew where that was: a single big sweet-gum just outside the woods, in an old clearing; if you crept up to it very quietly this time of year and then ran suddenly into the clearing, sometimes you caught as many as a dozen squirrels in it, trapped, since there was no other tree near they could jump to. So he didn't get into the wagon at all.

"I will," he said.

"I figured you would," Ash said, "I fotch you a box of shells." He passed the shells down and began to unwrap the lines from the brake-pole.

"How many times up to now do you reckon Major has told you not to do that?" the boy said.

"Do which?" Ash said. Then he said: "And tell Boon Hogganbeck dinner gonter be on the table in a hour and if yawl want any to come on and eat it."

"In an hour?" he said. "It aint nine oclock yet." He drew out his watch and extended it face-toward Ash. "Look." Ash didn't even look at the watch.

"That's town time. You aint in town now. You in the woods."

"Look at the sun then."

"Nemmine the sun too," Ash said. "If you and Boon Hogganbeck want any dinner, you better come on in and get it when I tole you. I aim to get done in that kitchen because I got my wood to chop. And watch your feet. They're[9] crawling."

"I will," he said.

Then he was in the woods, not alone but solitary; the solitude closed about him, green with summer. They did not change, and, timeless, would not, anymore than would the green of summer and the fire and rain of fall and the iron cold and sometimes even snow

the day, the morning when he killed the buck and Sam marked his face with its hot blood, they returned to camp and he remembered old Ash's blinking and disgruntled and even outraged disbelief until at last McCaslin had had to affirm the fact that he had really killed it: and that night Ash sat snarling and unapproachable behind the stove so that Tennie's Jim had to serve the supper and waked them with breakfast already on the table the next morning and it was only half-past one oclock and at last out of Major de Spain's angry cursing and Ash's snarling and sullen rejoinders the fact emerged that Ash not only wanted to go into the woods and shoot a deer also but he intended to and Major de Spain said, 'By God, if we dont let him we will probably have to do the cooking from now on:' and Walter Ewell said, 'Or get up at midnight to eat what Ash cooks:' and since he had already killed his buck for this hunt and was not to shoot again unless they needed meat, he offered his gun to Ash until Major de Spain took command and allotted that gun to Boon for the day and gave Boon's unpredictable pump gun to Ash, with two buckshot shells but Ash said, 'I got shells:' and showed them, four: one buck, one of number three shot for rabbits, two of bird-shot and told one by one their history and their origin and he remembered not Ash's face alone but Major de Spain's and Walter's and General Compson's too, and Ash's voice: 'Shoot? In course they'll shoot! Genl Cawmpson guv me this un'—the buckshot—'right outen the same gun he kilt

<hr>

9. I.e., snakes are.

that big buck with eight years ago. And this un'—it was the rabbit shell: triumphantly—'is oldern thisyer boy!' And that morning he loaded the gun himself, reversing the order: the bird-shot, the rabbit, then the buck so that the
buckshot would feed first into the chamber, and himself without a gun, he and
Ash walked beside Major de Spain's and Tennie's Jim's horses and the dogs
(that was the snow) until they cast and struck, the sweet strong cries ringing
away into the muffled falling air and gone almost immediately, as if the constant and unmurmuring flakes had already buried even the unformed echoes
beneath their myriad and weightless falling, Major de Spain and Tennie's Jim
gone too, whooping on into the woods; and then it was all right, he knew as
plainly as if Ash had told him that Ash had now hunted his deer and that even
his tender years had been forgiven for having killed one, and they turned back
toward home through the falling snow—that is, Ash said, 'Now whut?' and he
said, 'This way'—himself in front because, although they were less than a mile
from camp, he knew that Ash, who had spent two weeks of his life in the camp
each year for the last twenty, had no idea whatever where they were, until quite
soon the manner in which Ash carried Boon's gun was making him a good deal
more than just nervous and he made Ash walk in front, striding on, talking
now, an old man's garrulous monologue beginning with where he was at the
moment then of the woods and of camping in the woods and of eating in camps
then of eating then of cooking it and of his wife's cooking then briefly of his
old wife and almost at once and at length of a new light-colored woman who
nursed next door to Major de Spain's and if she didn't watch out who she was
switching her tail at he would show her how old was an old man or not if his
wife just didn't watch him all the time, the two of them in a game trail through
a dense brake of cane and brier which would bring them out within a quarter-
mile of camp, approaching a big fallen tree-trunk lying athwart the path and
just as Ash, still talking, was about to step over it the bear, the yearling, rose
suddenly beyond the log, sitting up, its forearms against its chest and its wrists
limply arrested as if it had been surprised in the act of covering its face to pray:
and after a certain time Ash's gun yawed jerkily up and he said, 'You haven't
got a shell in the barrel yet. Pump it:' but the gun already snicked and he said,
'Pump it. You haven't got a shell in the barrel yet:' and Ash pumped the action
and in a certain time the gun steadied again and snicked and he said, 'Pump
it:' and watched the buckshot shell jerk, spinning heavily, into the cane. This
is the rabbit shot: he thought and the gun snicked and he thought: The next is
bird-shot: and he didn't have to say Pump it; he cried, 'Dont shoot! Dont shoot!'
but that was already too late too, the light dry vicious snick! before he could
speak and the bear turned and dropped to all-fours and then was gone and
there was only the log, the cane, the velvet and constant snow and Ash said,
'Now whut?' and he said, 'This way. Come on:' and began to back away down
the path and Ash said, 'I got to find my shells:' and he said, 'Goddamn it,
goddamn it, come on:' but Ash leaned the gun against the log and returned
and stooped and fumbled among the cane roots until he came back and stooped
and found the shells and they rose and at that moment the gun, untouched,
leaning against the log six feet away and for that while even forgotten by both
of them, roared, bellowed and flamed, and ceased: and he carried it now,
pumped out the last mummified shell and gave that one also to Ash and, the
action still open, himself carried the gun until he stood it in the corner behind
Boon's bed at the camp

—; summer, and fall, and snow, and wet and saprife spring in their ordered immortal sequence, the deathless and immemorial phases of the mother who had shaped him if any had toward the man he almost was, mother and father both to the old man born of a Negro slave and a Chickasaw chief who had been his spirit's father if any had, whom he had revered and harkened to and loved and lost and grieved: and he would marry someday and they too would own for their brief while that brief unsubstanced glory which inherently of itself cannot last and hence why glory: and they would, might, carry even the remembrance of it into the time when flesh no longer talks to flesh because memory at least does last: but still the woods would be his mistress and his wife.

He was not going toward the Gum Tree. Actually he was getting farther from it. Time was and not so long ago either when he would not have been allowed here without someone with him, and a little later, when he had begun to learn how much he did not know, he would not have dared be here without someone with him, and later still, beginning to ascertain, even if only dimly, the limits of what he did not know, he could have attempted and carried it through with a compass, not because of any increased belief in himself but because McCaslin and Major de Spain and Walter and General Compson too had taught him at last to believe the compass regardless of what it seemed to state. Now he did not even use the compass but merely the sun and that only subconsciously, yet he could have taken a scaled map and plotted at any time to within a hundred feet of where he actually was; and sure enough, at almost the exact moment when he expected it, the earth began to rise faintly, he passed one of the four concrete markers set down by the lumber company's surveyor to establish the four corners of the plot which Major de Spain had reserved out of the sale, then he stood on the crest of the knoll itself, the four corner-markers all visible now, blanched still even beneath the winter's weathering, lifeless and shockingly alien in that place where dissolution itself was a seething turmoil of ejaculation tumescence conception and birth, and death did not even exist. After two winters' blanketings of leaves and the flood-waters of two springs, there was no trace of the two graves anymore at all. But those who would have come this far to find them would not need headstones but would have found them as Sam Fathers himself had taught him to find such: by bearings on trees: and did, almost the first thrust of the hunting knife finding (but only to see if it was still there) the round tin box manufactured for axle-grease and containing now Old Ben's dried mutilated paw, resting above Lion's bones.

He didn't disturb it. He didn't even look for the other grave where he and McCaslin and Major de Spain and Boon had laid Sam's body, along with his hunting horn and his knife and his tobacco-pipe, that Sunday morning two years ago; he didn't have to. He had stepped over it, perhaps on it. But that was all right. *He probably knew I was in the woods this morning long before I got here,* he thought, going on to the tree which had supported one end of the platform where Sam lay when McCaslin and Major de Spain found them—the tree, the other axle-grease tin nailed to the trunk, but weathered, rusted, alien too yet healed already into the wilderness' concordant generality, raising no tuneless note, and empty, long since empty of the food and tobacco he had put into it that day, as empty of that as it would presently be of this which he drew from his pocket—the twist of tobacco, the new bandanna handkerchief, the small paper sack of the peppermint candy which

Sam had used to love; that gone too, almost before he had turned his back, not vanished but merely translated into the myriad life which printed the dark mold of these secret and sunless places with delicate fairy tracks, which, breathing and biding and immobile, watched him from beyond every twig and leaf until he moved, moving again, walking on; he had not stopped, he had only paused, quitting the knoll which was no abode of the dead because there was no death, not Lion and not Sam: not held fast in earth but free in earth and not in earth but of earth, myriad yet undiffused of every myriad part, leaf and twig and particle, air and sun and rain and dew and night, acorn oak and leaf and acorn again, dark and dawn and dark and dawn again in their immutable progression and, being myriad, one: and Old Ben too, Old Ben too; they would give him his paw back even, certainly they would give him his paw back: then the long challenge and the long chase, no heart to be driven and outraged, no flesh to be mauled and bled—Even as he froze himself, he seemed to hear Ash's parting admonition. He could even hear the voice as he froze, immobile, one foot just taking his weight, the toe of the other just lifted behind him, not breathing, feeling again and as always the sharp shocking inrush from when Isaac McCaslin long yet was not, and so it was fear all right but not fright as he looked down at it. It had not coiled yet and the buzzer had not sounded either, only one thick rapid contraction, one loop cast sideways as though merely for purchase from which the raised head might start slightly backward, not in fright either, not in threat quite yet, more than six feet of it, the head raised higher than his knee and less than his knee's length away, and old, the once-bright markings of its youth dulled now to a monotone concordant too with the wilderness it crawled and lurked: the old one, the ancient and accursed about the earth, fatal and solitary and he could smell it now: the thin sick smell of rotting cucumbers and something else which had no name, evocative of all knowledge and an old weariness and of pariah-hood and of death. At last it moved. Not the head. The elevation of the head did not change as it began to glide away from him, moving erect yet off the perpendicular as if the head and that elevated third were complete and all: an entity walking on two feet and free of all laws of mass and balance and should have been because even now he could not quite believe that all that shift and flow of shadow behind that walking head could have been one snake: going and then gone; he put the other foot down at last and didn't know it, standing with one hand raised as Sam had stood that afternoon six years ago when Sam led him into the wilderness and showed him and he ceased to be a child, speaking the old tongue which Sam had spoken that day without premeditation either: "Chief," he said: "Grandfather."

He couldn't tell when he first began to hear the sound, because when he became aware of it, it seemed to him that he had been already hearing it for several seconds—a sound as though someone were hammering a gun-barrel against a piece of railroad iron, a sound loud and heavy and not rapid yet with something frenzied about it, as the hammerer were not only a strong man and an earnest one but a little hysterical too. Yet it couldn't be on the log-line because, although the track lay in that direction, it was at least two miles from him and this sound was not three hundred yards away. But even as he thought that, he realised where the sound must be coming from: who- ever the man was and whatever he was doing, he was somewhere near the edge of the clearing where the Gum Tree was and where he was to meet Boon. So far, he had been hunting as he advanced, moving slowly and quietly and watching the ground and the trees both. Now he went on, his gun unloaded and the barrel slanted up and back to facilitate its passage through brier and undergrowth, approaching as it grew louder and louder that steady savage somehow queerly hysterical beating of metal on metal, emerging from the woods, into the old clearing, with the solitary gum tree directly before him. At first glance the tree seemed to be alive with frantic squirrels. There appeared to be forty or fifty of them leaping and darting from branch to branch until the whole tree had become one green maelstrom of mad leaves, while from time to time, singly or in twos and threes, squirrels would dart down the trunk then whirl without stopping and rush back up again as though sucked violently back by the vacuum of their fellows' frenzied vortex. Then he saw Boon, sitting, his back against the trunk, his head bent, hammering furiously at something on his lap. What he hammered with was the barrel of his dismembered gun, what he hammered at was the breech of it. The rest of the gun lay scattered about him in a half-dozen pieces while he bent over the piece on his lap his scarlet and streaming walnut face, hammering the disjointed barrel against the gun-breech with the frantic abandon of a madman. He didn't even look up to see who it was. Still hammering, he merely shouted back at the boy in a hoarse strangled voice:

"Get out of here! Dont touch them! Dont touch a one of them! They're mine!"

BERTOLT BRECHT
1898–1956

Bertolt Brecht is a dominant figure in modern drama not only as the author of a half dozen plays that rank as modern classics but as the first master of a powerful new concept of theater. He was dissatisfied with the traditional notion, derived from Aristotle's *Poetics*, that drama should draw its spectators into identification with and sympathy for the characters, and with the realist aesthetic of naturalness and psychological credibility. Brecht saw only harm in such uncritical submission to illusions created on stage. Like Pirandello, he believed that the modern stage should break open the closed world established as a dramatic convention by writers such as Ibsen and Chekhov, whose audiences were to look at the action from a distance, as if it were a slice of real life going on behind an invisible "fourth wall." Unlike Pirandello, however, Brecht did not stress the anguish of individuals in society and the difficulty of knowing who we are; his focus was the community at large and social responsibility. For Brecht, a political activist, the modern audience must not be allowed to indulge in passive emotional identification at a safe distance or in the subjective whirlpool of existential identity crises. His characters are to be seen as members of society, and his audience must be educated and moved to action. The movement called "epic theater," which was born in the 1920s, suited his needs well, and through his plays, theoretical writings, and dramatic productions he developed its basic ideas into one of the most powerful theatrical styles of the twentieth century.

Eugen Berthold Brecht was born in the medieval town of Augsburg, Bavaria, on February 10, 1898. His father was a respected town citizen, director of a paper mill, and a Catholic. His mother, the daughter of a civil servant from the Black Forest, was a Protestant who raised young Berthold in her own faith. (The spelling *Bertolt* was adopted later.) Brecht attended local schools until 1917, when he enrolled in Munich University to study natural science and medicine. He continued his studies while acting as drama critic for an Augsburg newspaper and writing his own plays: *Drums in the Night* (1918) won the Kleist Prize in 1922. In 1918 Brecht was mobilized for a year as an orderly in a military hospital, and he pursued medical studies at Munich until 1921. In 1929 he married Helene Weigel, an actress who worked closely with him and for whom he wrote many leading roles. Together they would direct and make famous the theater group founded for them in 1949 in East Berlin: the Berliner Ensemble.

Moving to Berlin, Brecht worked briefly with the directors Max Reinhardt and Erwin Piscator but was chiefly interested in his own writing. In this pre-Marxist period he is especially concerned with the plight of the individual "common man," pushed around by social and economic forces beyond his control until he loses both identity and humanity. In *A Man's a Man* (1924–25), the timid dock worker Galy Gay is transformed by fright and persuasion into another person, the ferociously successful soldier Jeriah Jip. When the actual Jip turns up at the end of the play, he is given Gay's former papers and forced to assume Gay's old identity. The play teaches that human personalities can be broken down and reassembled like a machine; the only weapon against such mindless manipulation is awareness, an awareness that enables people to understand and control their destiny.

Most of Brecht's plays are didactic, either openly or by implication. After he became a fervent Marxist in the mid-1920s, he considered it even more his moral and artistic duty to encourage the audience to remedy social ills. *The Threepenny Opera* (1928), a ballad opera written with composer Kurt Weill (1900–1950) and modeled on John Gay's *The Beggar's Opera* (1728), satirizes capitalist society from the point of view of outcasts and romantic thieves. Brecht also wrote a number of "lesson" plays intended to set forth Communist doctrine and to instruct the workers of Germany in the meaning of social revolution. The lesson is particularly harsh in *The Measures Taken* (1930), which describes the necessary execution of a young party member who has broken discipline and helped the local poor, thus postponing the revolution. Such drama, however doctrinally pure, was not likely to win adherents to the cause, and the lesson plays were condemned as unattractive and "intellectualist" by the Communist press in Berlin and Moscow.

Brecht's unorthodoxy, his pacifism, his enthusiasm for Marx, and his desire to create an activist popular theater that would embody a Marxist view of art all put him at odds with the rising power of Hitler's National Socialism. He fled Germany for Denmark in 1933, before the Nazis could include him in their purge of left-wing intellectuals; in 1935 he was deprived of his German citizenship. Brecht was to flee several more times as the Nazi invasions expanded throughout Europe: in 1939 he went to Sweden, in 1940 to Finland, and in 1941 to the United States, where he joined a colony of German expatriates in Santa Monica, California, working for the film industry. This was the period of some of his greatest plays: *The Life of Galileo* (1938–39), which attacks society for suppressing Galileo's discovery that the Earth revolves around the sun but also condemns the scientist for not insisting openly on the truth; *Mother Courage and Her Children* (1939), which describes an avaricious peddler who doggedly pursues the profits to be made from war even though her own three children are victims of it; *The Good Woman of Setzuan* (1938–40), printed here, which shows how an instinctively good and generous person can survive in this world only by putting on a mask of hardness and calculation; and *The Caucasian Chalk Circle* (1944–45), an adaptation of the story of the Judgment of Solomon in which the child is given to the servant girl rather than the governor's wife (the implied comparison being between those who do the work of society and those who merely profit from their possessions). In America,

Brecht arranged for the translation of his work into English, and *Galileo,* with Charles Laughton in the title role, was produced in 1947. In the same year, Brecht was questioned by the House Un-American Activities Committee as part of a wide-ranging inquiry into possible Communist activity in the entertainment business. No charges were brought, but he left for Europe the day after being brought before the committee.

After leaving the United States, Brecht worked for a year in Zurich before going to Berlin with his wife to stage *Mother Courage.* The East Berlin government offered the couple positions as directors of their own troupe, the Berliner Ensemble, and Brecht—who had just finished a theoretical work on the theater, *A Little Organon for the Theater* (1949)—turned his attention to the professional role of director. Although the East Berliners subsidized Brecht's work and advertised the artist's presence among them as a tribute to their own political system, they also obliged him to defend some of his plays against charges of political unorthodoxy and indeed to revise them. After 1934, the prevailing Communist Party view had upheld a style called "socialist realism," whose goal was to offer simple messages and to foster identification with revolutionary heroes. Brecht's mind was too keen and questioning, too attracted by irony and paradox, for him to provide the simplistic drama desired or to have a comfortable relation with authority, either of the right or of the left. After settling in East Berlin, he wrote no major new plays but only minor propaganda pieces and adaptations of classical works such as Molière's *Don Juan* and Shakespeare's *Coriolanus.* As an additional measure of protection, he took out Austrian citizenship through his wife's nationality. Brecht died in Berlin on August 14, 1956. Presumably, he would have taken ironic pleasure in the fact that, on February 10, 1998, the one hundredth anniversary of his birth was celebrated throughout a united Germany and included a presidential speech at the Berlin Academy of Arts.

The "epic theater" for which Brecht is known derives its name from a famous essay, *On Epic and Dramatic Poetry,* by Goethe and Schiller, who in 1797 described *dramatic* poetry as pulling the audience into emotional identification, in contrast to *epic* poetry, which by being distanced in the time, place, and nature of the action could be absorbed in calm contemplation. The idea of an epic theater is a paradox: how can a play engage an audience that is still held at a distance? Brecht's solution was to employ many "alienation effects" that were genuinely dramatic but that prevented total identification with the characters and forced spectators to think critically about what was taking place. In this, he echoed the work of the revolutionary Soviet director Vsevolod Meyerhold, whose antirealistic use of masks, pantomime, posters and film projections, song interludes, and direct address to the audience was well known to German audiences in the 1920s. These alienation effects have since become standard production techniques in the modern theater. In spite of Brecht's intentions and frequent revisions, however, the characters and situations of his plays remain emotionally engrossing, especially in his best-known works, such as *The Good Woman of Setzuan.*

Brecht's concept of an epic theater touches on all aspects of the form: dramatic structure, stage setting, music, and the actor's performance. The structure is to be open, episodic, and broken by dramatic or musical interludes. It is a "chronicle" that recounts events in an epic or distanced perspective. Episodes may also be performed independently as self-contained dramatic parables, instead of being organically tied to a centrally developing plot. Skits appear between scenes: in *A Man's a Man,* there is a fantastic interlude in which an elephant is accused of having murdered its mother. Songs break dramatic action and yet crystallize important themes: in *The Good Woman of Setzuan,* "The Song of Defenselessness" presents an outraged Shen Te masking herself and turning into Shui Ta; Yang Sun's lording it over his coworkers is satirized in "The Song of the Eighth Elephant." Sometimes a narrator comments on the action (as in *The Threepenny Opera* and *A Man's a Man*). The alienation effects are also heightened by setting most of the plays in far-away lands (China in *The Good*

Woman of Setzuan, India in *A Man's a Man*, England in *The Threepenny Opera*, the Soviet Union in *The Caucasian Chalk Circle*, Chicago in *Saint Joan of the Stockyards* and *The Resistible Rise of Arturo Ui*) or distant times (the seventeenth century in *Mother Courage*, Renaissance Italy in *Galileo*, or an imagined ghostly afterlife in *The Trial of Lucullus*).

Stagecraft and performance further support Brecht's concept of a critical, intellectualized theater. Events on stage may be announced beforehand by signs or accompanied by projected images during the action itself. Place-names printed on signs are suspended over the actors, and footlights and stage machinery are openly displayed. Masks are used for wicked people (for example, the Shui Ta personality in *The Good Woman of Setzuan*), or soldiers' faces are chalked white to suggest a stylized fear. Songs that interrupt the dramatic action are addressed directly to the audience, sometimes heralded by a sign that Brecht called a "musical emblem." In addition, Brecht described a special kind of acting: actors should "demonstrate" their parts instead of being submerged in them. At rehearsals, Brecht often asked actors to speak their parts in the third person instead of the first. Such constant artificiality injected into all aspects of the performance makes it difficult for the audience to identify completely and unself-consciously with the characters on stage.

Audiences may react emotionally to Brecht's plays and characters, but their reactions are never simple. Brecht's characters are complex and inhabit complex situations. Galileo is both a dedicated scientist who sacrifices his reputation for honesty so as to complete his work, and a weak sensualist who fails to realize how his recantation will affect others' pursuit of scientific knowledge. In *The Good Woman of Setzuan*, the overgenerous Shen Te can survive only by periodically adopting the mask of a harshly practical "cousin," Shui Ta. Mother Courage is both a tragic mother figure and a small-time profiteer who loses her children as she battens on war. Brecht's work teems with such paradoxes at all levels. He is a cynic who deflates religious zeal, militant patriotism, and heroic example as delusions that lead the masses on to futile sacrifice; but he is also a preacher who makes prominent use of traditional biblical language and imagery, and themes of individual sacrifice.

The Good Woman of Setzuan was written between 1938 and 1941, with the collaboration of Margarete Steffin and Ruth Berlau, and with music by Paul Dessau. Painfully drafted while Brecht, his family, Steffin, and Berlau sought refuge in Scandinavia from the Nazis' conquest of Europe, the play is stamped with bitter disillusionment with a world in which it is impossible to be good and survive. The "good woman," Shen Te, is forced to disguise herself as her male "cousin" and alter ego, the cruel Shui Ta, to save herself from a swarm of parasites and opportunists who will not leave her a roof over her head. Appearing alternately as the ruthless Shui Ta and the generous Shen Te, she embodies different ways of being, encounters different responses from the people around her, is gradually contaminated, and recognizes despairingly that she will always need to call on her wicked cousin to survive. The play's setting in China was probably suggested by a 1935 visit to Moscow, where Brecht was impressed by the highly stylized performances of the Chinese actor Mei Lan-fang, one of whose traditional roles was that of the woman warrior who must disguise herself as a man. Brecht had already written a short play and a story that described the way women were subordinated and exploited in traditional patriarchal society, a theme that returns strongly in *The Good Woman of Setzuan*. The opposition of men and women is not absolute, however, for the play contains both good and bad male and female characters. Indeed, the Woman of the English title may be misleading, even if Shen Te represents goodness, for the German title's *Mensch* means literally "person" or "human being" and embraces both genders. For Brecht, the problem of good and evil, and the need to reform a corrupt world, confronts both women and men. As the Epilogue tells the audience: "You write the happy ending to the play!"

Shen Te's story has a larger frame: the state of the universe or, more mundanely, the question of whether the world is so corrupt that affairs cannot be allowed to continue. Her situation arises from a good deed whose counterpart recurs in various world mythologies and also in the Bible: hospitality offered to disguised divine messengers, who reward the giver accordingly. Three Chinese gods visiting Earth in search of good people give Shen Te, a penniless prostitute, a thousand silver dollars in recompense for being the only person in Setzuan to give them lodging. Brecht borrows (as so often) from the Bible: specifically, from the Old Testament story of Sodom and Gomorrah, in which God sends angels down to find ten good people in the debauched city of Sodom so that it may be saved from destruction. But these modern gods are somewhat comic and certainly ineffectual. Wearing old-fashioned clothes and dusty shoes, they have been delegated as the result of a bureaucratic Resolution on high (whose terms they debate); they ignore inconvenient questions and merely repeat the conventional, inapplicable regulations; they are terrified of complications that would disturb the status quo and—in an echo of Nazi slogans about proper order—they persuade themselves at the end that "everything is in order" and leave on a pink cloud despite Shen Te's despairing cries. These caricatured godlets represent the bureaucratic state more than anything else. Their refusal to be involved only reinforces Brecht's underlying thesis that "good" and "evil" are not divine but rather social issues and that the way to reform a corrupt world is for people to unite in common action focused on the common good.

The current translation, by Eric Bentley, Brecht's early translator and collaborator, is a performance-oriented version of the original text of 1941, undertaken with Brecht's approval.

Martin Esslin, *Brecht, The Man and His Work* (1974), John Fuegi, *Brecht and Company: Sex, Politics, and the Making of Modern Drama* (1994), and John Willett, *The Theatre of Bertolt Brecht: A Study from Eight Aspects* (1959), offer biographical and critical perspectives on the author and his work. John Willett, ed. and trans., *Brecht on Theatre: The Development of an Aesthetic* (1964), contains Brecht's own essays and lectures on his theater. Ronald Hayman, *Brecht: A Biography* (1983), offers a detailed view of Brecht's life. Eric Bentley, *The Brecht Commentaries 1943–1986* (1987), offers lively essays by a friend and sometime colleague on the major plays, on Brecht's stagecraft, and on his place in modern culture. The essays in Walter Benjamin, *Understanding Brecht* (1983), provide important insights by a close friend and major intellectual figure into Brecht's work and modern thought. A range of essays on Brecht's work is found in *Bertolt Brecht: Centenary Essays*, edited by Steve Giles and Rodney Livingstone (1998), and *A Bertolt Brecht Reference Companion*, edited by Siegfried Mews (1997), which also contains a bibliography. *The Cambridge Companion to Brecht* (1994), edited by Peter Thompson and Glendyr Sacks, contains an essay on *The Good Person of Szechwan*. Interesting comparative studies include Anthony Tatlow, *The Mask of Evil: Brecht's Response to the Poetry, Theatre and Thought of China and Japan* (1977); Renata Berg-Pan's *Bertolt Brecht and China* (1979); and "Brecht, Feminism, and Chinese Theatre," in the *Brecht Sourcebook*, edited by Carol Martin and Henry Bial (2000), a useful collection of essays grouped by aesthetic theories, practice, and interpretations abroad.

PRONOUNCING GLOSSARY

The following list uses common English syllables and stress accents to provide rough equivalents of selected words whose pronunciation may be unfamiliar to the general reader.

Lin To: *lin taw*	Shu Fu: *shoo foo*
Mi Tzu: *mee'-dzu*	Shui Ta: *shway tah*
Setzuan: *seu-chwan'*	Yang Sun: *yahng sun*
Shen Te: *shun-teu*	Wong: *wahng*

The Good Woman of Setzuan[1]

CHARACTERS

WONG, *a water seller*
THREE GODS
SHEN TE, *a prostitute, later a shopkeeper*
MRS. SHIN, *former owner of Shen Te's shop*
A *family of eight* (HUSBAND, WIFE, BROTHER, SISTER–IN–LAW, GRANDFATHER, NEPHEW, NIECE, BOY)
An UNEMPLOYED MAN
A CARPENTER

MRS. MI TZU, *Shen Te's landlady*
Mr. SHUI TA
YANG SUN, *an unemployed pilot, later a factory manager*
An OLD WHORE
A POLICEMAN
An OLD MAN
An OLD WOMAN, *his wife*
Mr. SHU FU, *a barber*
MRS. YANG, *mother of Yang Sun*
GENTLEMEN, VOICES, PRIEST, WAITER, *children (three), etc.*

Prologue

At the gates of the half-Westernized city of Setzuan. Evening. WONG *the water seller*[2] *introduces himself to the audience.*

WONG   I sell water here in the city of Setzuan. It isn't easy. When water is scarce, I have long distances to go in search of it, and when it is plentiful, I have no income. But in our part of the world there is nothing unusual about poverty. Many people think only the gods can save the situation. And I hear from a cattle merchant—who travels a lot—that some of the highest gods are on their way here at this very moment. Informed sources have it that heaven is quite disturbed at all the complaining.[3] I've been coming out here to the city gates for three days now to bid these gods welcome. I want to be the first to greet them. What about those fellows over there? No, no, they *work*. And that one there has ink on his fingers, he's no god, he must be a clerk from the cement factory. *Those* two are another story. They look as though they'd like to beat you. But gods don't need to beat you, do they? [THREE GODS *appear.*] What about those three? Old-fashioned clothes—dust on their feet—they *must* be gods! [*He throws himself at their feet.*] Do with me what you will, illustrious ones!

FIRST GOD [*With an ear trumpet.*]   Ah! [*He is pleased.*] So we were expected?

WONG [*Giving them water.*]   Oh, yes. And I *knew* you'd come.

FIRST GOD   We need somewhere to stay the night. You know of a place?

WONG   The whole town is at your service, illustrious ones! What sort of a place would you like?

[*The* GODS *eye each other.*]

FIRST GOD   Just try the first house you come to, my son.

1. Translated by Eric Bentley. Setzuan is a province in China; the play's setting is both the capital of Setzuan and, according to a later statement in the play, a generalized location: "wherever man is exploited by man."   2. Water peddlers were common in ancient China.   3. Heaven, in Chinese philosophy, was identical with absolute and transcendental order.

WONG   That would be Mr. Fo's place.

FIRST GOD   Mr. Fo.

WONG   One moment! [*He knocks at the first house.*]

VOICE FROM MR. FO'S.   No!

>   [WONG *returns a little nervously.*]

WONG   It's too bad. Mr. Fo isn't in. And his servants don't dare do a thing without his consent. He'll have a fit when he finds out who they turned away, won't he?

FIRST GOD [*Smiling.*]   He will, won't he?

WONG   One moment! The next house is Mr. Cheng's. Won't he be thrilled!

FIRST GOD   Mr. Cheng

>   [WONG *knocks.*]

VOICE FROM MR. CHENG'S   Keep your gods. We have our own troubles!

WONG [*Back with the* GODS.]   Mr. Cheng is very sorry, but he has a houseful of relations. I think some of them are a bad lot, and naturally, he wouldn't like you to see them.

THIRD GOD   Are we so terrible?

WONG   Well, only with bad people, of course. Everyone knows the province of Kwan is always having floods.

SECOND GOD   Really? How's that?

WONG   Why, because they're so irreligious.

SECOND GOD   Rubbish. It's because they neglected the dam.

FIRST GOD [*To* SECOND.]   Sh! [*To* WONG.] You're still in hopes, aren't you, my son?

WONG   Certainly. All Setzuan is competing for the honor! What happened up to now is pure coincidence. I'll be back. [*He walks away, but then stands undecided.*]

SECOND GOD   What did I tell you?

THIRD GOD   It *could* be pure coincidence.

SECOND GOD   The same coincidence in Shun, Kwan, and Setzuan? People just aren't religious any more, let's face the fact. Our mission has failed!

FIRST GOD   Oh come, we might run into a good person any minute.

THIRD GOD   How did the resolution read? [*Unrolling a scroll and reading from it.*] "The word can stay as it is if enough people are found [*At the word "found" he unrolls it a little more*] living lives worthy of human beings." Good people, that is. Well, what about this water seller himself? *He's* good, or I'm very much mistaken.

SECOND GOD   You're very much mistaken. When he gave us a drink, I had the impression there was something odd about the cup. Well, look! [*He shows the cup to the* FIRST GOD.]

FIRST GOD   A false bottom!

SECOND GOD   The man is a swindler.

FIRST GOD   Very well, count *him* out. That's one man among millions. And as a matter of fact, we only need one on *our* side. These atheists are saying, "The world must be changed because no one can *be* good and *stay* good." No one, eh? I say: let us find one—just one—and we have those fellows where we want them!

THIRD GOD [*To* WONG.]   Water seller, is it so hard to find a place to stay?

WONG   Nothing could be easier. It's just me. I don't go about it right.

THIRD GOD   Really?

>   [*He returns to the others.* A GENTLEMAN *passes by.*]

WONG   Oh dear, they're catching on. [*He accosts the* GENTLEMAN.] Excuse the intrusion, dear sir, but three gods have just turned up. Three of the very highest. They need a place for the night. Seize this rare opportunity—to have real gods as your guests!

GENTLEMAN [*laughing*].   A new way of finding free rooms for a gang of crooks. [*Exit* GENTLEMAN.]

WONG [*shouting at him.*]   Godless rascal! Have you no religion, gentlemen of Setzuan? [*Pause*]. Patience, illustrious ones! [*Pause.*] There's only one person left. Shen Te, the prostitute. She *can't* say no. [*Calls up to a window.*] Shen Te!

[SHEN TE *opens the shutters and looks out.*]

WONG   Shen Te, it's Wong. *They're* here, and nobody wants them. Will you take them?

SHEN TE   Oh, no, Wong, I'm expecting a gentleman.

WONG   Can't you forget about him for tonight?

SHEN TE   The rent has to be paid by tomorrow or I'll be out on the street.

WONG   This is no time for calculation, Shen Te.

SHEN TE   Stomachs rumble even on the Emperor's birthday, Wong.

WONG   Setzuan is one big dung hill!

SHEN TE   Oh, very well! I'll hide till my gentleman has come and gone. Then I'll take them. [*She disappears.*]

WONG   They mustn't see her gentleman or they'll know what she is.

FIRST GOD [*Who hasn't heard any of this.*]   I think it's hopeless.

[*They approach* WONG.]

WONG [*Jumping, as he finds them behind him*].   A room has been found, illustrious ones! [*He wipes sweat off his brow.*]

SECOND GOD   Oh, good.

THIRD GOD   Let's see it.

WONG [*Nervously.*]   Just a minute. It has to be tidied up a bit.

THIRD GOD   Then we'll sit down here and wait.

WONG [*Still more nervous.*]   No, no! [*Holding himself back.*] Too much traffic, you know.

THIRD GOD [*With a smile.*]   Of course, if you *want* us to move.

[*They retire a little. They sit on a doorstep.* WONG *sits on the ground.*]

WONG [*After a deep breath.*]   You'll be staying with a single girl—the finest human being in Setzuan!

THIRD GOD   That's nice.

WONG [*To the audience.*]   They gave me such a look when I picked up my cup just now.

THIRD GOD   You're worn out, Wong.

WONG   A little, maybe.

FIRST GOD   Do people here have a hard time of it?

WONG   The good ones do.

FIRST GOD   What about yourself!

WONG   You mean I'm not good. That's true. And I don't have an easy time either!

[*During this dialogue, a* GENTLEMAN *has turned up in front of Shen Te's House, and has whistled several times. Each time* WONG *has given a start.*]

THIRD GOD [*To* WONG, *softly.*]   Psst! I think he's gone now.

WONG [*Confused and surprised.*] Ye-e-es.

[*The* GENTLEMAN *has left now, and* SHEN TE *has come down to the street.*]

SHEN TE [*softly.*] Wong!

[*Getting no answer, she goes off down the street.* WONG *arrives just too late, forgetting his carrying pole.*]

WONG [*Softly.*] Shen Te! Shen Te! [*To himself.*] So she's gone off to earn the rent. Oh dear, I can't go to the gods *again* with no room to offer them. Having failed in the service of the gods, I shall run to my den in the sewer pipe down by the river and hide from their sight!

[*He rushes off.* SHEN TE *returns, looking for him, but finding the* GODS. *She stops in confusion.*]

SHEN TE You are the illustrious ones? My name is Shen Te. It would please me very much if my simple room could be of use to you.

THIRD GOD Where is the water seller, Miss . . . Shen Te?

SHEN TE I missed him, somehow.

FIRST GOD Oh, he probably thought you weren't coming, and was afraid of telling us.

THIRD GOD [*Picking up the carrying pole.*] We'll leave this with you. He'll be needing it.

[*Led by* SHEN TE, *they go into the house. It grows dark, then light. Dawn. Again escorted by* SHEN TE, *who leads them through the half-light with a little lamp, the* GODS *take their leave.*]

FIRST GOD Thank you, thank you, dear Shen Te, for your elegant hospitality! We shall not forget! And give our thanks to the water seller—he showed us a good human being.

SHEN TE Oh, *I'm* not good. Let me tell you something: when Wong asked me to put you up, I hesitated.

FIRST GOD It's all right to hesitate if you then go ahead! And in giving us that room you did much more than you knew. You proved that good people still exist, a point that has been disputed of late—even in heaven. Farewell!

SECOND GOD Farewell!

THIRD GOD Farewell!

SHEN TE Stop, illustrious ones! I'm not sure you're right. I'd like to be good, it's true, but there's the rent to pay. And that's not all: I sell myself for a living. Even so I can't make ends meet, there's too much competition. I'd like to honor my father and mother and speak nothing but the truth and not covet my neighbor's house. I should love to stay with one man. But how? How is it done? Even breaking a few of your commandments,[4] I can hardly manage.

FIRST GOD [*Clearing his throat.*] These thoughts are but, um, the misgivings of an unusually good woman!

THIRD GOD Good-bye, Shen Te! Give our regards to the water seller!

SECOND GOD And above all: be good! Farewell!

FIRST GOD Farewell!

THIRD GOD Farewell!

4. An allusion to the Decalogue of the Old Testament and specifically to Commandments 4, 6, 8, 9, and 10 (Exodus 20).

[*They start to wave good-bye.*]

SHEN TE   But everything is so expensive, I don't feel sure I can do it!

SECOND GOD   That's not in our sphere. We never meddle with economics.

THIRD GOD   One moment. [*They stop.*] Isn't it true she might do better if she had more money?

SECOND GOD   Come, come! How could we ever account for it Up Above?

FIRST GOD   Oh, there are ways. [*They put their heads together and confer in dumb show. To* SHEN TE, *with embarrassment.*] As you say you can't pay your rent, well, um, we're not paupers, so of course we *insist* on paying for our room. [*Awkwardly thrusting money into her hands.*] There! [*Quickly.*] But don't tell anyone! The incident is open to misinterpretation.

SECOND GOD   It certainly is!

FIRST GOD [*Defensively.*]   But there's no law against it! It was never decreed that a god mustn't pay hotel bills!

[*The* GODS *leave.*]

1

A small tobacco shop. The shop is not as yet completely furnished and hasn't started doing business.

SHEN TE [*To the audience.*]   It's three days now since the gods left. When they said they wanted to pay for the room, I looked down at my hand, and there was more than a thousand silver dollars![5] I bought a tobacco shop with the money, and moved in yesterday. I don't own the building, of course, but I can pay the rent, and I hope to do a lot of good here. Beginning with Mrs. Shin, who's just coming across the square with her pot. She had the shop before me, and yesterday she dropped in to ask for rice for her children. [*Enter* MRS. SHIN. *Both women bow*.] How do you do, Mrs. Shin.

MRS. SHIN   How do you do, Miss Shen Te. You like your new home?

SHEN TE   Indeed, yes. Did your children have a good night?

MRS. SHIN   In that hovel? The youngest is coughing already.

SHEN TE   Oh, dear!

MRS. SHIN   You're going to learn a thing or two in these slums.

SHEN TE   Slums? That's not what you said when you sold me the shop!

MRS. SHIN   Now don't start nagging! Robbing me and my innocent children of their home and then calling it a slum! That's the limit!

[*She weeps.*]

SHEN TE [*Tactfully.*]   I'll get your rice.

MRS. SHIN   And a little cash while you're at it.

SHEN TE   I'm afraid I haven't sold anything yet.

MRS. SHIN [*Screeching.*]   I've got to have it. Strip the clothes from my back and then cut my throat, will you? I know what I'll do: I'll dump my children on your doorstep! [*She snatches the pot out of* SHEN TE's *hands.*]

5. Either official Chinese silver dollars (yuan) or coins from one of the foreign currencies in circulation.

SHEN TE   Please don't be angry. You'll spill the rice.
> [*Enter an elderly* HUSBAND *and* WIFE *with their shabbily dressed* NEPHEW.]

WIFE   Shen Te, dear! You've come into money, they tell me. And we haven't a roof over our heads! A tobacco shop. We had one too. But it's gone. Could we spend the night here, do you think?

NEPHEW [*Appraising the shop.*]   Not bad!

WIFE   He's our nephew. We're inseparable!

MRS. SHIN   And who are these . . . ladies and gentlemen?

SHEN TE   They put me up when I first came in from the country. [*To the audience.*] Of course, when my small purse was empty, they put me out on the street, and they may be afraid I'll do the same to them [*To the newcomers, kindly.*] Come in, and welcome, though I've only one little room for you—it's behind the shop.

HUSBAND   That'll do. Don't worry.

WIFE [*Bringing* SHEN TE *some tea.*]   We'll stay over here, so we won't be in your way. Did you make it a tobacco shop in memory of your first real home? We can certainly give you a hint or two! That's one reason we came.

MRS SHIN [*To* SHEN TE.]   Very nice! As long as you have a few customers too!

HUSBAND   Sh! A customer!
> [*Enter an* UNEMPLOYED MAN, *in rags.*]

UNEMPLOYED MAN   Excuse me. I'm unemployed.
> [MRS. SHIN *laughs.*]

SHEN TE   Can I help you?

UNEMPLOYED MAN   Have you any damaged cigarettes? I thought there might be some damage when you're unpacking.

WIFE   What nerve, begging for tobacco! [*Rhetorically.*] Why don't they ask for bread?

UNEMPLOYED MAN   Bread is expensive. One cigarette butt and I'll be a new man.

SHEN TE [*Giving him cigarettes.*]   That's very important—to be a new man. You'll be my first customer and bring me luck.
> [*The* UNEMPLOYED MAN *quickly lights a cigarette, inhales, and goes off, coughing.*]

WIFE   Was that right, Shen Te, dear?

MRS. SHIN   If this is the opening of a shop, you can hold the closing at the end of the week.

HUSBAND   I bet he had money on him.

SHEN TE   Oh, no, he said he hadn't!

NEPHEW   How d'you know he wasn't lying?

SHEN TE [*Angrily.*]   How do you know he was?

WIFE [*Wagging her head.*]   You're too good, Shen Te, dear. If you're going to keep this shop, you'll have to learn to say no.

HUSBAND   Tell them the place isn't yours to dispose of. Belongs to . . . some relative who insists on all accounts being strictly in order . . .

MRS. SHIN   That's right! What do you think you are—a philanthropist?

SHEN TE [*Laughing.*]   Very well, suppose I ask you for my rice back, Mrs. Shin?

WIFE [*Combatively, at* MRS. SHIN.] So that's *her* rice?
    [*Enter the* CARPENTER, *a small man.*]
MRS. SHIN [*Who, at the sight of him, starts to hurry away.*] See you tomor-
    row, Miss Shen Te! [*Exit* MRS. SHIN.]
CARPENTER Mrs. Shin, it's you I want!
WIFE [*To* SHEN TE.] Has she some claim on you?
SHEN TE She hungry. That's a claim.
CARPENTER Are you the new tenant? And filling up the shelves already?
    Well, they're not yours till they're paid for, ma'am. I'm the carpenter, so
    I should know.
SHEN TE I took the shop "furnishings included."
CARPENTER You're in league with that Mrs. Shin, of course. All right. I
    demand my hundred silver dollars.
SHEN TE I'm afraid I haven't got a hundred silver dollars.
CARPENTER Then you'll find it. Or I'll have you arrested.
WIFE [*Whispering to* SHEN TE.] That relative: make it a cousin.
SHEN TE Can't it wait till next month?
CARPENTER No!
SHEN TE Be a little patient, Mr. Carpenter, I can't settle all claims at once.
CARPENTER Who's patient with me? [*He grabs a shelf from the wall.*] Pay
    up—or I take the shelves back!
WIFE Shen Te! Dear! Why don't you let your . . . cousin settle this affair?
    [*To* CARPENTER.] Put your claim in writing. Shen Te's cousin will see
    you get paid.
CARPENTER [*Derisively.*] Cousin, eh?
HUSBAND Cousin, yes.
CARPENTER I know these cousins!
NEPHEW Don't be silly. He's a personal friend of mine.
HUSBAND What a man! Sharp as a razor!
CARPENTER All right. I'll put my claim in writing. [*Puts shelf on floor, sits
    on it, writes out bill.*]
WIFE [*To* SHEN TE.] He'd tear the dress off your back to get his shelves.
    Never recognize a claim! That's my motto.
SHEN TE He's done a job, and wants something in return. It's shameful
    that I can't give it to him. What will the gods say?
HUSBAND You did your bit when you took *us* in.
    [*Enter the* BROTHER, *limping, and the* SISTER-IN-LAW, *pregnant.*]
BROTHER [*To* HUSBAND *and* WIFE.] So this is where you're hiding out!
    There's family feeling for you! Leaving us on the corner!
WIFE [*Embarrassed, to* SHEN TE.] It's my brother and his wife. [*To them.*]
    Now stop grumbling, and sit quietly in that corner. [*To* SHEN TE.] It can't
    be helped. She's in her fifth month.
SHEN TE Oh yes. Welcome!
WIFE [*To the couple.*] Say thank you. [*They mutter something.*] The cups
    are there. [*To* SHEN TE.] Lucky you bought this shop when you did!
SHEN TE [*Laughing and bringing tea.*] Lucky indeed!
    [*Enter* MRS. MI TZU, *the landlady.*]
MRS. MI TZU Miss Shen Te? I am Mrs. Mi Tzu, your landlady. I hope our
    relationship will be a happy one. I like to think I give my tenants modern,
    personalized service. Here is your lease. [*To the others, as* SHEN TE *reads*

the lease.] There's nothing like the opening of a little shop, is there? A moment of true beauty! [*She is looking around.*] Not very much on the shelves, of course. But everything in the gods' good time! Where are your references, Miss Shen Te?

SHEN TE Do I *have* to have references?

MRS. MI TZU After all, I haven't a notion who you are!

HUSBAND Oh, *we'd* be glad to vouch for Miss Shen Te! We'd go through fire for her!

MRS. MI TZU And who may *you* be?

HUSBAND [*Stammering.*] Ma Fu, tobacco dealer.

MRS. MI TZU Where is your shop, Mr. . . . . Ma Fu?

HUSBAND Well, um, I haven't got a shop—I've just sold it.

MRS. MI TZU I see. [*To* SHEN TE.] Is there no one else that knows you?

WIFE [*Whispering to* SHEN TE.] Your cousin! Your cousin!

MRS. MI TZU This is a respectable house, Miss Shen Te. I never sign a lease without certain assurances.

SHEN TE [*Slowly, her eyes downcast.*] I have . . . a cousin.

MRS. MI TZU On the square? Let's go over and see him. What does he do?

SHEN TE [*As before.*] He lives . . . in another city.

WIFE [*Prompting.*] Didn't you say he was in Shung?

SHEN TE That's right. Shung.

HUSBAND [*Prompting.*] I had his name on the tip of my tongue, Mr. . . .

SHEN TE [*With an effort.*] Mr. . . . Shui . . . Ta.

HUSBAND That's it! Tall, skinny fellow!

SHEN TE Shui Ta!

NEPHEW [*To* CARPENTER.] *You* were in touch with him, weren't you? About the shelves?

CARPENTER [*Surlily.*] Give him this bill. [*He hands it over.*] I'll be back in the morning. [*Exit* CARPENTER.]

NEPHEW [*Calling after him, but with his eyes on* MRS. MI TZU.] Don't worry! Mr. Shui Ta pays on the nail!

MRS. MI TZU [*Looking closely at* SHEN TE.] I'll be happy to make his acquaintance, Miss Shen Te. [*Exit* MRS. MI TZU.]
     [*Pause.*]

WIFE By tomorrow morning she'll know more about you than you do yourself.

SISTER-IN-LAW [*To* NEPHEW.] This thing isn't built to last.
     [*Enter* GRANDFATHER.]

WIFE It's Grandfather! [*To* SHEN TE.] Such a good old soul!
     [*The* BOY *enters.*]

BOY [*Over his shoulder.*] Here they are!

WIFE And the boy, how he's grown! But he always could eat enough for ten.
     [*Enter the* NIECE.]

WIFE [*To* SHEN TE.] Our little niece from the country. There are more of us now than in your time. The less we had, the more there were of us; the more there were of us, the less we had. Give me the key. We must protect ourselves from unwanted guests. [*She takes the key and locks the door.*] Just make yourself at home. I'll light the little lamp.

NEPHEW [*A big joke.*]   I hope her cousin doesn't drop in tonight! The strict Mr. Shui Ta!

[SISTER-IN-LAW *laughs.*]

BROTHER [*Reaching for a cigarette.*]   One cigarette more or less . . .

HUSBAND   One cigarette more or less.

[*They pile into the cigarettes. The* BROTHER *hands a jug of wine round.*]

NEPHEW   Mr. Shui Ta'll pay for it!

GRANDFATHER [*Gravely, to* SHEN TE.]   How do you do?

[SHEN TE, *a little taken aback by the belatedness of the greeting, bows. She has the carpenter's bill in one hand, the landlady's lease in the other.*]

WIFE   How about a bit of a song? To keep Shen Te's spirits up?

NEPHEW   Good idea. Grandfather: you start!

SONG OF THE SMOKE

GRANDFATHER
        I used to think (before old age beset me)
          That brains could fill the pantry of the poor.
        But where did all my cerebration get me?
        I'm just as hungry as I was before.
            So what's the use?
                See the smoke float free
            Into ever colder coldness!
                It's the same with me[6]

HUSBAND   The straight and narrow path leads to disaster
          And so the crooked path I tried to tread.
          That got me to disaster even faster.
          (They say we shall be happy when we're dead.)
            So what's the use?
                See the smoke float free
            Into ever colder coldness!
                It's the same with me

NIECE   You older people, full of expectation,
          At any moment now you'll walk the plank!
        The future's for the younger generation!
        Yes, even if that future is a blank.
            So what's the use?
                See the smoke float free
            Into ever colder coldness!
                It's the same with me.

NEPHEW [*To the* BROTHER.]   Where'd you get that wine?

SISTER-IN-LAW [*Answering for the* BROTHER.]   He pawned the sack of tobacco.

HUSBAND [*Stepping in.*]   What? That tobacco was all we had to fall back on! You pig!

BROTHER   You'd call a man a pig because your wife was frigid! Did you refuse to drink it?

---

6. The refrain in this song is taken from a poem Brecht wrote in the 1920s entitled *The Song of the Opium Den.*

[*They fight. The shelves fall over.*]

SHEN TE [*Imploringly.*] Oh don't! Don't break everything! Take it, take it all, but don't destroy a gift from the gods!

WIFE [*Disparagingly.*] This shop isn't big enough. I should never have mentioned it to Uncle and the others. When *they* arrive, it's going to be disgustingly overcrowded.

SISTER-IN-LAW And did you hear our gracious hostess? She cools off quick!

[*Voices outside. Knocking at the door.*]

UNCLE'S VOICE Open the door!

WIFE Uncle? Is that you, Uncle?

UNCLE'S VOICE Certainly, it's me. Auntie says to tell you she'll have the children here in ten minutes.

WIFE [*To* SHEN TE.] I'll have to let him in.

SHEN TE [*Who scarcely hears her.*]

> The little lifeboat is swiftly sent down
> Too many men too greedily
> Hold on to it as they drown.

1a

Wong's den in a sewer pipe.

WONG [*Crouching there.*] All quiet! It's four days now since I left the city. The gods passed this way on the second day. I heard their steps on the bridge over there. They must be a long way off by this time, so I'm safe. [*Breathing a sigh of relief, he curls up and goes to sleep. In his dream the pipe becomes transparent, and the* GODS *appear. Raising an arm, as if in self-defense.*] I know, I know, illustrious ones! I found no one to give you a room—not in all Setzuan! There, it's out. Please continue on your way!

FIRST GOD [*Mildly.*] But you did find someone. Someone who took us in for the night, watched over us in our sleep, and in the early morning lighted us down to the street with a lamp.

WONG It was . . . Shen Te that took you in?

THIRD GOD Who else?

WONG And I ran away! "She isn't coming," I thought, "she just can't afford it."

GODS [*Singing.*]

> O you feeble, well-intentioned, and yet feeble chap
> Where there's need the fellow thinks there is no goodness!
> When there's danger he thinks courage starts to ebb away!
> Some people only see the seamy side!
> What hasty judgment! What premature desperation!

WONG I'm *very* ashamed, illustrious ones.

FIRST GOD Do us a favor, water seller. Go back to Setzuan. Find Shen Te, and give us a report on her. We hear that she's come into a little money. Show interest in her goodness—for no one can be good for long if goodness is not in demand. Meanwhile we shall continue the search, and find other good people. After which, the idle chatter about the impossibility of goodness will stop!

[*The* GODS *vanish.*]

2

A knocking.

WIFE   Shen Te! Someone at the door. Where is she anyway?

NEPHEW   She must be getting the breakfast. Mr. Shui Ta will pay for it.
   [*The* WIFE *laughs and shuffles to the door. Enter Mr.* SHUI TA *and the* CARPENTER.]

WIFE   Who is it?

SHUI TA   I am Miss Shen Te's cousin.

WIFE   What??

SHUI TA   My name is Shui Ta.

WIFE   Her cousin?

NEPHEW   Her cousin?

NIECE   But that was a joke. She hasn't got a cousin.

HUSBAND   So early in the morning?

BROTHER   What's all the noise?

SISTER-IN-LAW   This fellow says he's her cousin.

BROTHER   Tell him to prove it.

NEPHEW   Right. If you're Shen Te's cousin, prove it by getting the breakfast.

SHUI TA [*Whose regime begins as he puts out the lamp to save oil; loudly, to all present, asleep or awake.*]   Would you all please get dressed! Customers will be coming! I wish to open my shop!

HUSBAND   *Your* shop? Doesn't it belong to our good friend Shen Te?
   [SHUI TA *shakes his head.*]

SISTER-IN-LAW   So we've been cheated. Where *is* the little liar?

SHUI TA   Miss Shen Te has been delayed. She wishes me to tell you there will be nothing she can do—now I am here.

WIFE [*Bowled over.*]   I thought she was good!

NEPHEW   Do you have to believe *him*?

HUSBAND   I don't.

NEPHEW   Then do something.

HUSBAND   Certainly! I'll send out a search party at once. You, you, you, and you, go out and look for Shen Te. [*As the* GRANDFATHER *rises and makes for the door*] Not you, Grandfather, you and I will hold the fort.

SHUI TA   You won't find Miss Shen Te. She has suspended her hospitable activity for an unlimited period. There are too many of you. She asked me to say: this is a tobacco shop, not a gold mine.

HUSBAND   Shen Te never said a thing like that. Boy, food! There's a bakery on the corner. Stuff your shirt full when they're not looking!

SISTER-IN-LAW   Don't overlook the raspberry tarts.

HUSBAND   And don't let the policeman see you.

[The BOY leaves.]

SHUI TA Don't you depend on this shop now? Then why give it a bad name by stealing from the bakery?

NEPHEW Don't listen to him. Let's find Shen Te. She'll give him a piece of her mind.

SISTER-IN-LAW Don't forget to leave us some breakfast.

[BROTHER, SISTER-IN-LAW and NEPHEW leave.]

SHUI TA [To the CARPENTER.] You see, Mr. Carpenter, nothing has changed since the poet, eleven hundred years ago, penned these lines:

> A governor was asked what was needed
> To save the freezing people in the city.
> He replied:
> "A blanket ten thousand feet long
> To cover the city and all its suburbs."[7]

[He starts to tidy up the shop.]

CARPENTER Your cousin owes me money. I've got witnesses. For the shelves.

SHUI TA Yes, I have your bill. [He takes it out of his pocket.] Isn't a hundred silver dollars rather a lot?

CARPENTER No deductions! I have a wife and children.

SHUI TA How many children?

CARPENTER Three.

SHUI TA I'll make you an offer. Twenty silver dollars.

[The HUSBAND laughs.]

CARPENTER You're crazy. Those shelves are real walnut.

SHUI TA Very well, Take them away.

CARPENTER What?

SHUI TA They cost too much. Please take them away.

WIFE Not bad! [And she, too, is laughing.]

CARPENTER [A little bewildered.] Call Shen Te, someone! [To SHUI TA.] She's good!

SHUI TA Certainly. She's ruined.

CARPENTER [Provoked into taking some of the shelves.] All right, you can keep your tobacco on the floor.

SHUI TA [to the HUSBAND.] Help him with the shelves.

HUSBAND [Grins and carries one shelf over to the door where the CARPENTER now is.] Good-bye, shelves!

CARPENTER [To the HUSBAND.] You dog! You want my family to starve?

SHUI TA I repeat my offer. I have no desire to keep my tobacco on the floor. Twenty silver dollars.

CARPENTER [With desperate aggressiveness.] One hundred!

[SHUI TA shows indifference, looks through the window. The HUSBAND picks up several shelves.]

CARPENTER [To HUSBAND.] You needn't smash them against the doorpost, you idiot! [To SHUI TA.] These shelves were made to measure. They're no use anywhere else!

SHUI TA Precisely.

[The WIFE squeals with pleasure.]

---

7. Reference to a poem, The Big Rug, by the classical Chinese poet Po Chü-i (A.D. 772–846).

CARPENTER [*Giving up, sullenly*.] Take the shelves. Pay what you want to pay.

SHUI TA [*Smoothly*.] Twenty silver dollars.

    [*He places two large coins on the table. The* CARPENTER *picks them up*.]

HUSBAND [*Brings the shelves back in*.] And quite enough too!

CARPENTER [*Slinking off*.] Quite enough to get drunk on.

HUSBAND [*Happily*.] Well, we got rid of *him*!

WIFE [*Weeping with fun, gives a rendition of the dialogue just spoken*.] "Real walnut," says he. "Very well, take them away," says his lordship. "I have three children," says he. "Twenty silver dollars," says his lordship. "They're no use anywhere else," says he. "Pre-cisely," said his lordship! [*She dissolves into shrieks of merriment*.]

SHUI TA And now: go!

HUSBAND What's that?

SHUI TA You're thieves, parasites. I'm giving you this chance. Go!

HUSBAND [*Summoning all his ancestral dignity*.] That sort deserves no answer. Besides, one should never shout on an empty stomach.

WIFE Where's that boy?

SHUI TA Exactly. The boy. I want no stolen goods in this shop. [*Very loudly*.] I strongly advise you to leave! [*But they remain seated, noses in the air. Quietly*.] As you wish. [SHUI TA *goes to the door. A* POLICEMAN *appears*. SHUI TA *bows*.] I am addressing the officer in charge of this precinct?

POLICEMAN That's right, Mr., um, what was the name, sir?

SHUI TA Mr. Shui Ta.

POLICEMAN Yes, of course, sir.

    [*They exchange a smile*.]

SHUI TA Nice weather we're having.

POLICEMAN A little on the warm side, sir.

SHUI TA Oh, a little on the warm side.

HUSBAND [*Whispering to the* WIFE.] If he keeps it up till the boy's back, we're done for. [*Tries to signal* SHUI TA.]

SHUI TA [*Ignoring the signal*.] Weather, of course, is one thing indoors, another out on the dusty street!

POLICEMAN Oh, quite another, sir!

WIFE [*To the* HUSBAND.] It's all right as long as he's standing in the doorway—the boy will see him.

SHUI TA Step inside for a moment! It's quite cool indoors. My cousin and I have just opened the place. And we attach the greatest importance to being on good terms with the, um, authorities.

POLICEMAN [*Entering*.] Thank you, Mr. Shui Ta. It *is* cool!

HUSBAND [*Whispering to the* WIFE.] And now the boy *won't* see him.

SHUI TA [*Showing* HUSBAND *and* WIFE *to the* POLICEMAN.] Visitors, I think my cousin knows them. They were just leaving.

HUSBAND [*Defeated*.] Ye-e-es, we were . . . just leaving.

SHUI TA I'll tell my cousin you couldn't wait.

    [*Noise from the street. Shouts of* "Stop, Thief!"]

POLICEMAN What's that?

    [*The* BOY *is in the doorway with cakes and buns and rolls spilling out of his shirt. The* WIFE *signals desperately to him to leave. He gets the idea.*]

POLICEMAN   No, you don't. [*He grabs the* BOY *by the collar.*] Where's all this from?

BOY [*Vaguely pointing.*]   Down the street.

POLICEMAN [*Grimly.*]   So that's it. [*Prepares to arrest the* BOY.]

WIFE [*Stepping in.*]   And *we* knew nothing about it. [*To the* BOY.] Nasty little thief!

POLICEMAN [*Dryly.*]   Can you clarify the situation, Mr. Shui Ta?
    [SHUI TA *is silent.*]

POLICEMAN [*Who understands silence.*]   Aha. You're all coming with me— to the station.

SHUI TA   I can hardly say how sorry I am that *my* establishment . . .

WIFE   Oh, he saw the boy leave not ten minutes ago!

SHUI TA   And to conceal the theft asked a policeman in?

POLICEMAN   Don't listen to her, Mr. Shui Ta, I'll be happy to relieve you of their presence one and all! [*To all three.*] Out!
    [*He drives them before him.*]

GRANDFATHER [*Leaving last, gravely.*]   Good morning!

POLICEMAN   Good morning!
    [SHUI TA, *left alone, continues to tidy up.* MRS. MI TZU *breezes in.*]

MRS. MI TZU   *You're* her cousin, are you? Then have the goodness to explain what all this means—police dragging people from a respectable house! By what right does your Miss Shen Te turn my property into a house of assignation?—Well, as you see, I know all!

SHUI TA   Yes. My cousin has the worst possible reputation: that of being poor.

MRS. MI TZU   No sentimental rubbish, Mr. Shui Ta. Your cousin was a common . . .

SHUI TA   Pauper. Let's use the uglier word.

MRS. MI TZU   I'm speaking of her conduct, not her earnings. But there must have *been* earnings, or how did she buy all this? Several elderly gentlemen took care of it, I suppose. I repeat: this is a respectable house! I have tenants who prefer not to live under the same roof with such a person.

SHUI TA [*Quietly.*]   How much do you want?

MRS. MI TZU [*He is ahead of her now.*]   I beg your pardon.

SHUI TA   To reassure yourself. To reassure your tenants. How much will it cost?

MRS. MI TZU   You're a cool customer

SHUI TA [*Picking up the lease.*]   The rent is high. [*He reads on.*] I assume it's payable by the month?

MRS. MI TZU   Not in her case.

SHUI TA [*Looking up.*] What?

MRS. MI TZU   Six months' rent payable in advance. Two hundred silver dollars.

SHUI TA   Six . . . ! Sheer usury! And where am I to find it?

MRS. MI TZU   You should have thought of that before.

SHUI TA   Have you no heart, Mrs. Mi Tzu? It's true Shen Te acted foolishly, being kind to all those people, but she'll improve with time. I'll see to it she does. She'll work her fingers to the bone to pay her rent, and all the time be as quiet as a mouse, as humble as a fly.

MRS. MI TZU   Her social background . . .

SHUI TA   Out of the depths! She came out of the depths! And before she'll go back there, she'll work, sacrifice, shrink from nothing. . . . Such a tenant is worth her weight in gold, Mrs. Mi Tzu.

MRS. MI TZU   It's silver we were talking about, Mr. Shui Ta. Two hundred silver dollars or . . .

[*Enter the* POLICEMAN.]

POLICEMAN   Am I intruding, Mr. Shui Ta?

MRS. MI TZU   This tobacco shop is well known to the police, I see.

POLICEMAN   Mr. Shui Ta has done us a service, Mrs. Mi Tzu. I am here to present our official felicitations!

MRS. MI TZU   That means less than nothing to me, sir. Mr. Shui Ta, all I can say is: I hope your cousin will find my terms acceptable. Good day, gentlemen. [*Exit.*]

SHUI TA   Good day, ma'am.

[*Pause.*]

POLICEMAN   Mrs. Mi Tzu a bit of a stumbling block, sir?

SHUI TA   She wants six months' rent in advance.

POLICEMAN   And you haven't got it, eh? [SHUI TA *is silent.*] But surely you can get it, sir? A man like you?

SHUI TA   What about a woman like Shen Te?

POLICEMAN   You're not staying, sir?

SHUI TA   No, and I won't be back. Do you smoke?

POLICEMAN   [*Taking two cigars, and placing them both in his pocket.*] Thank you, sir—I see your point, Miss Shen Te—let's mince no words—Miss Shen Te lived by selling herself. "What else could she have done?" you ask. "How else was she to pay the rent?" True. But the fact remains, Mr. Shui Ta, it is not respectable. Why not? A very deep question. But, in the first place, love—love isn't bought and sold like cigars, Mr. Shui Ta. In the second place, it isn't respectable to go waltzing off with some-one that's paying his way, so to speak—it must be for love! Thirdly and lastly, as the proverb has it: not for a handful of rice but for love! [*Pause. He is thinking hard.*] "Well," you may say, "and what good is all this wisdom if the milk's already spilt?" Miss Shen Te is what she is. Is *where* she is. We have to face the fact that if she doesn't get hold of six months' rent pronto, she'll be back on the streets. The question then as I see it—everything in this world is a matter of opinion—the question as I see it is: *how* is she to get hold of this rent? How? Mr. Shui Ta: I don't know. [*Pause.*] I take that back, sir. It's just come to me. A husband. We must find her a husband!

[*Enter a little* OLD WOMAN.]

OLD WOMAN   A good cheap cigar for my husband, we'll have been married forty years tomorrow and we're having a little celebration.

SHUI TA   Forty years? And you still want to celebrate?

OLD WOMAN   As much as we can afford to. We have the carpet shop across the square. We'll be good neighbors, I hope?

SHUI TA   I hope so too.

POLICEMAN   [*Who keeps making discoveries.*]   Mr. Shui Ta, you know what we need? We need capital. And how do we acquire capital? We get married.

SHUI TA [*To* OLD WOMAN.]   I'm afraid I've been pestering this gentleman with my personal worries.

POLICEMAN [*Lyrically.*]   We can't pay six months' rent, so what do we do? We marry money.

SHUI TA   That might not be easy.

POLICEMAN   Oh, I don't know. She's a good match. Has a nice, growing business. [*To the* OLD WOMAN.] What do you think?

OLD WOMAN [*Undecided.*]   Well—

POLICEMAN   Should she put an ad in the paper?

OLD WOMAN [*Not eager to commit herself.*]   Well, if *she* agrees—

POLICEMAN   I'll write it for her. *You* lend us a hand, and *we* write an ad for you! [*He chuckles away to himself, takes out his notebook, wets the stump of a pencil between his lips, and writes away.*]

SHUI TA [*Slowly.*]   Not a bad idea.

POLICEMAN   "What . . . *respectable* . . . man . . . with small capital . . . widower . . . not excluded . . . desires . . . marriage . . . into flourishing . . . tobacco shop?" And now let's add: "Am . . . pretty . . . " No! . . . . "Pre-possessing appearance."

SHUI TA   If you don't think that's an exaggeration?

OLD WOMAN   Oh, not a bit. I've seen her.

> [*The* POLICEMAN *tears the page out of his notebook, and hands it over to* SHUI TA.]

SHUI TA [*With horror in his voice.*]   How much luck we need to keep our heads above water! How many ideas! How many friends! [*To the* POLICE-MAN.] Thank you, sir, I think I see my way clear.

3

Evening in the municipal park. Noise of a plane overhead. YANG SUN, *a young man in rags, is following the plane with his eyes: one can tell that the machine is describing a curve above the park.* YANG SUN *then takes a rope out of his pocket, looking anxiously about him as he does so. He moves toward a large willow. Enter two prostitutes, one old, the other the* NIECE *whom we have already met.*

NIECE   Hello. Coming with me?

YANG SUN [*Taken aback.*]   If you'd like to buy me a dinner.

OLD WHORE   Buy you a dinner! [*To the* NIECE.] Oh, we know him—it's the unemployed pilot. Waste no time on him!

NIECE   But he's the only man left in the park. And it's going to rain.

OLD WHORE   Oh, how do you know?

> [*And they pass by.* YANG SUN *again looks about him, again takes his rope, and this time throws it round a branch of the willow tree. Again he is interrupted. It is the two prostitutes returning—and in such a hurry they don't notice him.*]

NIECE   It's going to pour!

> [*Enter* SHEN TE.]

OLD WHORE   There's that *gorgon* Shen Te! That *drove* your family out into the cold!

NIECE It wasn't her. It was that cousin of hers. She offered to pay for the
  cakes. I've nothing against her.
OLD WHORE I have, though. [*So that* SHEN TE *can hear.*] Now where could
  the little lady be off to? She may be rich now but that won't stop her
  snatching our young men, will it?
SHEN TE I'm going to the tearoom by the pond.
NIECE Is it true what they say? You're marrying a widower—with three
  children?
SHEN TE Yes. I'm just going to see him.
YANG SUN [*His patience at breaking point.*] Move on there! This is a park,
  not a whorehouse!
OLD WHORE Shut your mouth!
      [*But the two prostitutes leave.*]
YANG SUN Even in the farthest corner of the park, even when it's raining,
  you can't get rid of them! [*He spits.*]
SHEN TE [*Overhearing this.*] And what right have you to scold them? [*But
  at this point she sees the rope.*] Oh!
YANG SUN Well, what are you staring at?
SHEN TE That rope. What is it for?
YANG SUN Think! Think! I haven't a penny. Even if I had, I wouldn't spend
  it on you. I'd buy a drink of water.
      [*The rain starts.*]
SHEN TE [*Still looking at the rope.*] What is the rope for? You mustn't!
YANG SUN What's it to you? Clear out!
SHEN TE [*Irrelevantly.*] It's raining.
YANG SUN Well, don't try to come under this tree.
SHEN TE Oh, no. [*She stays in the rain.*]
YANG SUN Now go away. [*Pause.*] For one thing, I don't like your looks,
  you're bowlegged.
SHEN TE [*Indignantly.*] That's not true!
YANG SUN Well, don't show 'em to me. Look, it's raining. You better come
  under this tree.
      [*Slowly, she takes shelter under the tree.*]
SHEN TE Why did you want to do it?
YANG SUN You really want to know? [*Pause.*] To get rid of you! [*Pause.*]
  You know what a flyer is?
SHEN TE Oh yes, I've met a lot of pilots. At the tearoom.
YANG SUN You call *them* flyers? Think they know what a machine is?
  Just 'cause they have leather helmets? They gave the airfield director a
  bribe, that's the way *those* fellows got up in the air! Try one of them
  out sometime. "Go up to two thousand feet," tell him, "then let it fall,
  then pick it up again with a flick of the wrist at the last moment."
  Know what he'll say to that? "It's not in my contract." Then again,
  there's the landing problem. It's like landing on your own backside. It's
  no different, planes are human. Those fools don't understand. [*Pause.*]
  And I'm the biggest fool for reading the book on flying in the Peking
  school and skipping the page where it says: "We've got enough flyers
  and we don't need you." I'm a mail pilot with no mail. You understand
  that?
SHEN TE [*Shyly.*] Yes, I do.
YANG SUN No, you don't. You'd never understand that.

SHEN TE   When we were little we had a crane with a broken wing. He
    made friends with us and was very good-natured about our jokes. He
    would strut along behind us and call out to stop us going too fast for
    him. But every spring and autumn when the cranes flew over the vil-
    lages in great swarms, he got quite restless. [*Pause.*] I understand
    that.
        [*She bursts out crying.*]
YANG SUN   Don't!
SHEN TE [*Quieting down.*]   No.
YANG SUN   It's bad for the complexion.
SHEN TE [*Sniffing.*]   I've stopped.
        [*She dries her tears on her big sleeve. Leaning against the tree, but
        not looking at her, he reaches for her face.*]
YANG SUN   You can't even wipe your own face. [*He is wiping it for her with
    his handkerchief. Pause.*]
SHEN TE [*Still sobbing.*]   I don't know *anything!*
YANG SUN   You interrupted me! What for?
SHEN TE   It's such a rainy day. You only wanted to do . . . *that* because it's
    such a rainy day. [*To the audience.*]
            In our country
            The evenings should never be somber
            High bridges over rivers
            The gray hour between night and morning
            And the long, long winter:
            Such things are dangerous
            For, with all the misery,
            A very little is enough
            And men throw away an unbearable life.
        [*Pause.*]
YANG SUN   Talk about yourself for a change.
SHEN TE   What about me? I have a shop.
YANG SUN [*Incredulous.*]   You have a shop, have you? Never thought of
    walking the streets?
SHEN TE   I did walk the streets. Now I have a shop.
YANG SUN [*Ironically.*]   A gift of the gods, I suppose!
SHEN TE   How did you know?
YANG SUN [*Even more ironical.*]   One fine evening the gods turned up
    saying: here's some money!
SHEN TE [*Quickly.*]   One fine morning.
YANG SUN [*Fed up.*]   This isn't much of an entertainment.
        [*Pause.*]
SHEN TE   I can play the zither a little. [*Pause.*] And I can mimic men.
    [*Pause.*] I got the shop, so the first thing I did was to give my zither away.
    I can be as stupid as a fish now, I said to myself, and it won't matter.
            I'm rich now, I said
            I walk alone, I sleep alone
            For a whole year, I said
            I'll have nothing to do with a man.
YANG SUN   And now you're marrying one! The one at the tearoom by the
    pond?

[SHEN TE *is silent.*]

YANG SUN   What do you know about love?

SHEN TE   Everything.

YANG SUN   Nothing. [*Pause.*] Or d'you just mean you enjoyed it?

SHEN TE   No.

YANG SUN [*Again without turning to look at her, he strokes her cheek with his hand.*]   You like that?

SHEN TE   Yes.

YANG SUN [*Breaking off.*]   You're easily satisfied, I must say. [*Pause.*] What a town!

SHEN TE   You have no friends?

YANG SUN [*Defensively.*]   Yes, I have! [*Change of tone.*] But they don't want to hear I'm still unemployed. "What?" they ask. "Is there still water in the sea?" You have friends?

SHEN TE [*Hesitating.*]   Just a . . . cousin.

YANG SUN   Watch him carefully.

SHEN TE   He only came once. Then he went away. He won't be back. [YANG SUN *is looking away.*] But to be without hope, they say, is to be without goodness!

[*Pause.*]

YANG SUN   Go on talking. A voice is a voice.

SHEN TE   Once, when I was a little girl, I fell, with a load of brushwood. An old man picked me up. He gave me a penny too. Isn't it funny how people who don't have very much like to give some of it away? They must like to show what they can do, and how could they show it better than by being kind? Being wicked is just like being clumsy. When we sing a song, or build a machine, or plant some rice, we're being kind. You're kind.

YANG SUN   You make it sound easy.

SHEN TE   Oh, no. [*Little pause.*] Oh! A drop of rain!

YANG SUN   Where'd you feel it?

SHEN TE   Between the eyes.

YANG SUN   Near the right eye? Or the left?

SHEN TE   Near the left eye.

YANG SUN   Oh, good. [*He is getting sleepy.*] So you're through with men, eh?

SHEN TE [*With a smile.*]   But I'm not bowlegged.

YANG SUN   Perhaps not.

SHEN TE   Definitely not.

[*Pause.*]

YANG SUN [*Leaning wearily against the willow.*]   I haven't had a drop to drink all day, I haven't eaten anything for *two* days. I couldn't love you if I tried.

[*Pause.*]

SHEN TE   I like it in the rain.

[*Enter* WONG *the water seller, singing.*]

THE SONG OF THE WATER SELLER IN THE RAIN

"Buy my water," I am yelling
And my fury restraining

For no water I'm selling
'Cause it's raining, 'cause it's raining!
 I keep yelling: "Buy my water!"
 But no one's buying
 Athirst and dying
 And drinking and paying!
 Buy water!
 Buy water, you dogs!

Nice to dream of lovely weather!
Think of all the consternation
Were there no precipitation
Half a dozen years together!
 Can't you hear them shrieking: "Water!"
 Pretending they adore me?
 They all would go down on their knees before me!
 Down on your knees!
 Go down on your knees, you dogs!

What are lawns and hedges thinking?
What are fields and forests saying?
"At the cloud's breast we are drinking!
And we've no idea who's paying!"
 I keep yelling: "Buy my water!"
 But no one's buying
 Athirst and dying
 And drinking and paying!
 Buy water!
 Buy water, you dogs!

[*The rain has stopped now.* SHEN TE *sees* WONG *and runs toward him.*]

SHEN TE Wong! You're back! Your carrying pole's at the shop.

WONG Oh, thank you, Shen Te. And how is life treating *you*?

SHEN TE I've just met a brave and clever man. And I want to buy him a cup of your water.

WONG [*Bitterly.*] Throw back your head and open your mouth and you'll have all the water you need—

SHEN TE [*Tenderly.*]
 I want *your* water, Wong
 The water that has tired you so
 The water that you carried all this way
 The water that is hard to sell because it's been raining.
I need it for the young man over there—he's a flyer!
 A flyer is a bold man:
 Braving the storms
 In company with the clouds
 He crosses the heavens
 And brings to friends in faraway lands
 The friendly mail!

[*She pays* WONG, *and runs over to* YANG SUN *with the cup. But* YANG SUN *is fast asleep.*]

SHEN TE [*Calling to* WONG, *with a laugh.*]   He's fallen asleep! Despair and rain and I have worn him out!

3a

Wong's den. The sewer pipe is transparent, and the GODS *again appear to* WONG *in a dream.*

WONG [*Radiant*]   I've seen her, illustrious ones! And she hasn't changed!

FIRST GOD   That's good to hear.

WONG   She loves someone.

FIRST GOD   Let's hope the experience gives her the strength to stay good!

WONG   It does. She's doing good deeds all the time.

FIRST GOD   Ah? What sort? What sort of good deeds, Wong?

WONG   Well, she has a kind word for everybody.

FIRST GOD [*Eagerly.*]   And then?

WONG   Hardly anyone leaves her shop without tobacco in his pocket— even if he can't pay for it.

FIRST GOD   Not bad at all. Next?

WONG   She's putting up a family of eight.

FIRST GOD [*Gleefully, to the* SECOND GOD.]   Eight! [*To* WONG.] And that's not all, of course!

WONG   She bought a cup of water from me even thought it was raining.

FIRST GOD   Yes, yes, yes, all these smaller good deeds!

WONG   Even they run into money. A little tobacco shop doesn't make so much.

FIRST GOD [*Sententiously.*]   A prudent gardener works miracles on the smallest plot.

WONG   She hands out rice every morning. That eats up half her earnings.

FIRST GOD [*A little disappointed.*]   Well, as a beginning . . .

WONG   They call her the Angel of the Slums—whatever the carpenter may say!

FIRST GOD   What's this? A carpenter speaks ill of her?

WONG   Oh, he only says her shelves weren't paid for in full.

SECOND GOD [*Who has a bad cold and can't pronounce his n's and m's.*]   What's this? Not paying a carpenter? Why was that?

WONG   I suppose she didn't have the money.

SECOND GOD [*Severely.*]   One pays what one owes, that's in our book of rules! First the letter of the law, then the spirit.

WONG   But it wasn't Shen Te, illustrious ones, it was her cousin. She called *him* in to help.

SECOND GOD   Then her cousin must never darken her threshold again!

WONG   Very well, illustrious ones! But in fairness to Shen Te, let me say that her cousin is a businessman.

FIRST GOD   Perhaps we should inquire what is customary? I find business quite unintelligible. But everybody's doing it. Business! Did the Seven Good Kings do business? Did Kung the Just[8] sell fish?

---

8. The philosopher Confucius (551–479 B.C.). *Seven Good Kings:* legendary wise kings who personified the old order and traditional values.

SECOND GOD   In any case, such a thing must not occur again!
>   [*The* GODS *start to leave.*]
THIRD GOD   Forgive us for taking this tone with you, Wong, we haven't
>   been getting enough sleep. The rich recommend us to the poor, and the
>   poor tell us they haven't enough room.
SECOND GOD   Feeble, feeble, the best of them!
FIRST GOD   No great deeds! No heroic daring!
THIRD GOD   On such a *small* scale!
SECOND GOD   Sincere, yes, but what is actually *achieved*?
>   [*One can no longer hear them.*]
WONG [*Calling after them.*]   I've thought of something, illustrious ones:
>   Perhaps you shouldn't ask—too—much—all—at—once!

4

The square in front of Shen Te's tobacco shop. Besides Shen Te's place, two other
shops are seen: the carpet shop and a barber's. Morning. Outside Shen Te's the
GRANDFATHER, *the* SISTER-IN-LAW, *the* UNEMPLOYED MAN, *and* MRS. SHIN *stand*
waiting.

SISTER-IN-LAW   She's been out all night again.
MRS. SHIN   No sooner did we get rid of that crazy cousin of hers than Shen
>   Te herself starts carrying on! Maybe she does give us an ounce of rice
>   now and then, but can you depend on her? Can you depend on her?
>   [*Loud voices from the barber's.*]
VOICE OF SHU FU   What are you doing in my shop? Get out—at once!
VOICE OF WONG   But sir. They all let me sell . . .
>   [WONG *comes staggering out of the barber's shop pursued by Mr.*
>   SHU FU, *the barber, a fat man carrying a heavy curling iron.*]
SHU FU   Get out, I said! Pestering my customers with your slimy old water!
>   Get out! Take your cup!
>   [*He holds out the cup.* WONG *reaches out for it. Mr.* SHU FU *strikes*
>   *his hand with the curling iron, which is hot.* WONG *howls.*]
SHU FU   You had it coming my man!
>   [*Puffing, he returns to his shop. The* UNEMPLOYED MAN *picks up the*
>   *cup and gives it to* WONG.]
UNEMPLOYED MAN   You can report that to the police.
WONG   My hand! It's smashed up!
UEMPLOYED MAN   Any bones broken?
WONG   I can't move my fingers.
UNEMPLOYED MAN   Sit down. I'll put some water on it.
>   [WONG *sits.*]
MRS. SHIN   The water won't cost you anything.
SISTER-IN-LAW   You might have got a bandage from Miss Shen Te till she
>   took to staying out all night. It's a scandal.
MRS. SHIN [*Despondently.*]   If you ask me, she's forgotten we ever existed!
>   [*Enter* SHEN TE *down the street, with a dish of rice.*]
SHEN TE [*To the audience.*]   How wonderful to see Setzuan in the early

morning! I always used to stay in bed with my dirty blanket over my head afraid to wake up. This morning I saw the newspapers being delivered by little boys, the streets being washed by strong men, and fresh vegetables coming in from the country on ox carts. It's a long walk from where Yang Sun lives, but I feel lighter at every step. They say you walk on air when you're in love, but it's even better walking on the rough earth, on the hard cement. In the early morning, the old city looks like a great heap of rubbish! Nice, though, with all its little lights. And the sky, so pink, so transparent, before the dust comes and muddies it! What a lot you miss if you never see your city rising from its slumbers like an honest old craftsman pumping his lungs full of air and reaching for his tools, as the poet says! [*Cheerfully, to her waiting guests.*] Good morning, everyone, here's your rice! [*Distributing the rice, she comes upon* WONG.] Good morning, Wong, I'm quite lightheaded today. On my way over, I looked at myself in all the shop windows. I'd love to be beautiful.

[*She slips into the carpet shop. Mr.* SHU FU *has just emerged from his shop.*]

SHU FU [*To the audience.*] It surprises me how beautiful Miss Shen Te is looking today! I never gave her a passing thought before. But now I've been gazing upon her comely form for exactly three minutes! I begin to suspect I am in love with her. She is overpoweringly attractive! [*Crossly, to* WONG.] Be off with you rascal!

[*He returns to his shop.* SHEN TE *comes back out of the carpet shop with the* OLD MAN, *its proprietor, and his wife—whom we have already met—the* OLD WOMAN. SHEN TE *is wearing a shawl. The* OLD MAN *is holding up a looking glass for her.*]

OLD WOMAN Isn't it lovely? We'll give you a reduction because there's a little hole in it.

SHEN TE [*Looking at another shawl on the old woman's arm.*] The other one's nice too.

OLD WOMAN [*Smiling.*] Too bad there's no hole in that!

SHEN TE That's right. My shop doesn't make very much.

OLD WOMAN And your deeds eat it all up! Be more careful, my dear . . .

SHEN TE [*Trying on the shawl with the hole.*] Just now, I'm lightheaded! Does the color suit me?

OLD WOMAN You'd better ask a man.

SHEN TE [*To the* OLD MAN.] Does the color suit me?

OLD MAN You'd better ask your young friend.

SHEN TE I'd like to have your opinion.

OLD MAN It suits you very well. But wear it this way: the dull side out.

[SHEN TE *pays up.*]

OLD WOMAN If you decide you don't like it, you can exchange it. [*She pulls* SHEN TE *to one side.*] Has he got money?

SHEN TE [*With a laugh*] Yang Sun? Oh, no.

OLD WOMAN Then how're you going to pay your rent?

SHEN TE I'd forgotten about that.

OLD WOMAN And next Monday is the first of the month! Miss Shen Te, I've got something to say to you. After we [*Indicating her husband.*] got to know you, we had our doubts about that marriage ad. We thought it would be better if you'd let *us* help you. Out of our savings. We reckon we could lend you two hundred silver dollars. We don't need anything in writing—you could pledge us your tobacco stock.

SHEN TE You're prepared to lend money to a person like me?

OLD WOMAN It's folks like you that need it. We'd think twice about lending anything to your cousin.

OLD MAN [*Coming up.*] All settled, my dear?

SHEN TE I wish the gods could have heard what your wife was just saying, Mr. Ma. They're looking for good people who're happy—and helping me makes you happy because you know it was love that got me into difficulties!

[*The old couple smile knowingly at each other.*]

OLD MAN And here's the money, Miss Shen Te.

[*He hands her an envelope.* SHEN TE *takes it. She bows. They bow back. They return to their shop.*]

SHEN TE [*Holding up her envelope.*] Look, Wong, here's six months' rent! Don't you believe in miracles now? And how do you like my new shawl?

WONG For the young fellow I saw you with in the park?

[SHEN TE *nods.*]

MRS. SHIN Never mind all that. It's time you took a look at this hand!

SHEN TE Have you hurt your hand?

MRS. SHIN That barber smashed it with his hot curling iron. Right in front of our eyes.

SHEN TE [*Shocked at herself.*] And I never noticed! We must get you to a doctor this minute or who knows what will happen?

UNEMPLOYED MAN It's not a doctor he should see, it's a judge. He can ask for compensation. The barber's filthy rich.

WONG You think I have a chance?

MRS. SHIN [*With relish.*] If it's really good and smashed. But is it?

WONG I think so. It's very swollen. Could I get a pension?

MRS. SHIN You'd need a witness.

WONG Well, you all saw it. You could all testify.

[*He looks round. The* UNEMPLOYED MAN, *the* GRANDFATHER, *and the* SISTER-IN-LAW *are all sitting against the wall of the shop eating rice. Their concentration on eating is complete.*]

SHEN TE [*To* MRS. SHIN.] You saw it yourself.

MRS. SHIN I want nothing to do with the police. It's against my principles.

SHEN TE [*To* SISTER-IN-LAW.] What about you?

SISTER-IN-LAW Me? I wasn't looking.

SHEN TE [*To the* GRANDFATHER, *coaxingly.*] Grandfather, *you'll* testify, won't you?

SISTER-IN-LAW And a lot of good that will do. He's simple-minded.

SHEN TE [*To the* UNEMPLOYED MAN.] You seem to be the only witness left.

UNEMPLOYED MAN My testimony would only hurt him. I've been picked up twice for begging.

SHEN TE

Your brother is assaulted, and you shut your eyes?
He is hit, cries out in pain, and you are silent?

The beast prowls, chooses and seizes his victim, and you say:
"Because we showed no displeasure, he has spared us."
If no one present will be a witness, I will. I'll say *I* saw it.

MRS. SHIN [*Solemnly.*]   The name for that is perjury.

WONG   I don't know if I can accept that. Though maybe I'll have to. [*Looking at his hand.*] Is it swollen enough, do you think? The swelling's not going down.

UNEMPLOYED MAN   No, no, the swelling's holding up well.

WONG   Yes. It's *more* swollen if anything. Maybe my wrist is broken after all. I'd better see a judge at once.

[*Holding his hand very carefully, and fixing his eyes on it, he runs off.* MRS. SHIN *goes quickly into the barber's shop.*]

UNEMPLOYED MAN [*Seeing her.*]   She is getting on the right side of Mr. Shu Fu.

SISTER-IN-LAW   You and I can't change the world, Shen Te.

SHEN TE   Go away! Go away all of you! [*The* UNEMPLOYED MAN *, the* SISTER-IN-LAW *, and the* GRANDFATHER *stalk off, eating and sulking. To the audience.*]

They've stopped answering
They stay put
They do as they're told
They don't care
Nothing can make them look up
But the smell of food.

[*Enter* MRS. YANG, *Yang Sun's mother, out of breath.*]

MRS. YANG   Miss Shen Te. My son has told me everything. I am Mrs. Yang, Sun's mother. Just think. He's got an offer. Of a job as a pilot. A letter has just come. From the director of the airfield in Peking!

SHEN TE   So he can fly again! Isn't that wonderful!

MRS. YANG [*Less breathlessly all the time.*]   They won't give him the job for nothing. They want five hundred silver dollars.

SHEN TE   We can't let money stand in his way, Mrs. Yang!

MRS. YANG   If only you could help him out!

SHEN TE   I have the shop. I can try! [*She embraces* MRS. YANG.] I happen to have two hundred with me now. Take it. [*She gives her the old couple's money.*] It was a loan but they said I could repay it with my tobacco stock.

MRS. YANG   And they were calling Sun the Dead Pilot of Setzuan! A friend in need!

SHEN TE   We must find another three hundred.

MRS. YANG   How?

SHEN TE   Let me think. [*Slowly.*] I know someone who can help. I didn't want to call on his services again, he's hard and cunning. But a flyer must fly. And I'll make this the last time.

[*Distant sound of a plane.*]

MRS. YANG   If the man you mentioned can do it . . . Oh, look, there's the morning mail plane, heading for Peking!

SHEN TE   The pilot can see us, let's wave!

[*They wave. The noise of the engine is louder.*]

MRS. YANG   You know that pilot up there?

SHEN TE   Wave, Mrs. Yang! I know the pilot who will be up there. He gave
up hope. But he'll do it now. One man to raise himself above the misery,
above us all. [*To the audience.*]

> Yang Sun, my lover:
> Braving the storms
> In company with the clouds
> Crossing the heavens
> And bringing to friends in faraway lands
> The friendly mail!

4a

In front of the inner curtain. Enter SHEN TE *, carrying Shui Ta's mask. She sings.*

THE SONG OF DEFENSELESSNESS

> In our country
> A useful man needs luck
> Only if he finds strong backers
> Can he prove himself useful.
> The good can't defend themselves and
> Even the gods are defenseless.
>
> Oh, why don't the gods have their own ammunition
> And launch against badness their own expedition
> Enthroning the good and preventing sedition
> And bringing the world to a peaceful condition?
>
> Oh, why don't the gods do the buying and selling
> Injustice forbidding, starvation dispelling
> Give bread to each city and joy to each dwelling?
> Oh, why don't the gods do the buying and selling?

[*She puts on Shui Ta's mask and sings in his voice.*]

> You can only help one of your luckless brothers
> By trampling down a dozen others.
>
> Why is it the gods do not feel indignation
> And come down in fury to end exploitation
> Defeat all defeat and forbid desperation
> Refusing to tolerate such toleration?
>
> Why is it?

5

Shen Te's tobacco shop. Behind the counter, Mr. SHUI TA, *reading the paper.*
MRS. SHIN *is cleaning up. She talks and he takes no notice.*

MRS. SHIN   And when certain rumors get about, what *happens* to a little
place like this? It goes to pot. *I* know. So, if you want my advice, Mr.

Shui Ta, find out just what has been going on between Miss Shen Te and that Yang Sun from Yellow Street. And remember: a certain interest in Miss Shen Te has been expressed by the barber next door, a man with twelve houses and only one wife,[9] who, for that matter, is likely to drop off at any time. A certain interest has been expressed. He was even inquiring about her means and, if *that* doesn't prove a man is getting serious, what would?

[*Still getting no response, she leaves with her bucket.*]

YANG SUN'S VOICE   Is that Miss Shen Te's tobacco shop?

MRS. SHIN'S VOICE   Yes, it is, but it's Mr. Shui Ta who's here today.

[SHUI TA *runs to the mirror with the short, light steps of* SHEN TE, *and is just about to start primping, when he realizes his mistake, and turns away, with a short laugh. Enter* YANG SUN. MRS. SHIN *enters behind him and slips into the back room to eavesdrop.*]

YANG SUN   I am Yang Sun. [SHUI TA *bows.*] Is Shen Te in?

SHUI TA   No.

YANG SUN   I guess you know our relationship? [*He is inspecting the stock.*] Quite a place! And I thought she was just talking big. I'll be flying again, all right. [*He takes a cigar, solicits and receives a light from* SHUI TA.] You think we can squeeze the other three hundred out of the tobacco stock?

SHUI TA   May I ask if it is your intention to sell at once?

YANG SUN   It was decent of her to come out with the two hundred but they aren't much use with the other three hundred still missing.

SHUI TA   Shen Te was overhasty promising so much. She might have to sell the shop itself to raise it. Haste, they say, is the wind that blows the house down.

YANG SUN   Oh, she isn't a girl to keep a man waiting. For one thing or the other, if you take my meaning.

SHUI TA   I take your meaning

YANG SUN [*Leering.*]   Uh, huh.

SHUI TA   Would you explain what the five hundred silver dollars are for?

YANG SUN   Want to sound me out? Very well. The director of the Peking airfield is a friend of mine from flying school. I give him five hundred: he gets me the job.

SHUI TA   The price is high.

YANG SUN   Not as these things go. He'll have to fire one of the present pilots—for negligence. Only the man he has in mind isn't negligent. Not easy, you understand. You needn't mention that part of it to Shen Te.

SHUI TA [*Looking intently at* YANG SUN.]   Mr. Yang Sun, you are asking my cousin to give up her possessions, leave her friends, and place her entire fate in your hands. I presume you intend to marry her?

YANG SUN   I'd be prepared to.

[*Slight pause.*]

SHUI TA   Those two hundred silver dollars would pay the rent here for six months. If you were Shen Te wouldn't you be tempted to continue in business?

YANG SUN   What? Can you imagine Yang Sun the flyer behind a counter? [*In an oily voice.*] "A strong cigar or a mild one, worthy sir?" Not in this century!

---

9. Ancient Chinese law permitted a man to have more than one wife.

SHUI TA My cousin wishes to follow the promptings of her heart, and, from her own point of view, she may even have what is called the right to love. Accordingly, she has commissioned me to help you to this post. There is nothing here that I am not empowered to turn immediately into cash. Mrs. Mi Tzu, the landlady, will advise me about the sale.

[Enter MRS. MI TZU.]

MRS. MI TZU Good morning, Mr. Shui Ta, you wish to see me about the rent? As you know it falls due the day after tomorrow.

SHUI TA Circumstances have changed, Mrs. Mi Tzu: my cousin is getting married. Her future husband here, Mr. Yang Sun, will be taking her to Peking. I am interested in selling the tobacco stock.

MRS. MI TZU How much are you asking, Mr. Shui Ta?

YANG SUN Three hundred sil—

SHUI TA Five hundred silver dollars.

MRS. MI TZU How much did she pay for it, Mr. Shui Ta?

SHUI TA A thousand. And very little has been sold.

MRS. MI TZU She was robbed. But I'll make you a special offer if you'll promise to be out by the day after tomorrow. Three hundred silver dollars.

YANG SUN [Shrugging.] Take it, man, take it.

SHUI TA It is not enough.

YANG SUN Why not? Why not? Certainly, it's enough.

SHUI TA Five hundred silver dollars.

YANG SUN But why? We only need three!

SHUI TA [To MRS. MI TZU.] Excuse me. [Takes YANG SUN on one side.] The tobacco stock is pledged to the old couple who gave my cousin the two hundred.

YANG SUN Is it in writing?

SHUI TA No.

YANG SUN [To MRS. MI TZU.] Three hundred will do.

MRS. MI TZU Of course, I need an assurance that Miss Shen Te is not in debt.

YANG SUN Mr. Shui Ta?

SHUI TA She is not in debt.

YANG SUN When can you let us have the money?

MRS. MI TZU The day after tomorrow. And remember: I'm doing this because I have a soft spot in my heart for young lovers! [Exit.]

YANG SUN [Calling after her.] Boxes, jars and sacks—three hundred for the lot and the pain's over! [To SHUI TA.] Where else can we raise money by the day after tomorrow?

SHUI TA Nowhere. Haven't you enough for the trip and the first few weeks?

YANG SUN Oh, certainly.

SHUI TA How much, exactly.

YANG SUN Oh, I'll dig it up, even if I have to steal it.

SHUI TA I see.

YANG SUN Well, don't fall off the roof. I'll get to Peking somehow.

SHUI TA Two people can't travel for nothing.

YANG SUN [Not giving SHUI TA a chance to answer.] I'm leaving her behind. No millstones round my neck!

SHUI TA Oh.

YANG SUN Don't look at me like that!

SHUI TA How precisely is my cousin to live?

YANG SUN Oh, you'll think of something.

SHUI TA A small request, Mr. Yang Sun. Leave the two hundred silver
dollars here until you can show me two tickets for Peking.

YANG SUN You learn to mind your own business, Mr. Shui Ta.

SHUI TA I'm afraid Miss Shen Te may not wish to sell the shop when she
discovers that . . .

YANG SUN You don't know women. She'll want to. Even then.

SHUI TA [A slight outburst.] She is a human being, sir! And not devoid of
common sense!

YANG SUN Shen Te is a woman: she is devoid of common sense. I only
have to lay my hand on her shoulder, and church bells ring.

SHUI TA [With difficulty.] Mr. Yang Sun!

YANG SUN Mr. Shui Whatever-it-is!

SHUI TA My cousin is devoted to you . . . because . . .

YANG SUN Because I have my hands on her breasts. Give me a cigar. [He
takes one for himself, stuffs a few more in his pocket, then changes his
mind and takes the whole box.] Tell her I'll marry her, then bring me the
three hundred. Or let her bring it. One or the other. [Exit.]

MRS. SHIN [Sticking her head out of the back room.] Well, he has your
cousin under his thumb, and doesn't care if all Yellow Street knows
it!

SHUI TA [Crying out.] I've lost my shop! And he doesn't love me! [He runs
berserk through the room, repeating these lines incoherently. Then stops
suddenly, and addresses MRS. SHIN.] Mrs. Shin, you grew up in the gutter,
like me. Are we lacking in hardness? I doubt it. If you steal a penny from
me, I'll take you by the throat till you spit it out! You'd do the same to
me. The times are bad, this city is hell, but we're like ants, we keep
coming, up and up the walls, however smooth! Till bad luck comes. Being
in love, for instance. One weakness is enough, and love is the deadliest.

MRS. SHIN [Emerging from the back room.] You should have a little talk
with Mr. Shu Fu, the barber. He's a real gentleman and just the thing
for your cousin. [She runs off.]

SHUI TA

> A caress becomes a stranglehold
> A sigh of love turns to a cry of fear
> Why are there vultures circling in the air?
> A girl is going to meet her lover.

[SHUI TA sits down and Mr. SHU FU enters with MRS. SHIN.]

SHUI TA Mr. Shu Fu?

SHU FU Mr. Shui Ta.

[They both bow.]

SHUI TA I am told that you have expressed a certain interest in my cousin
Shen Te. Let me set aside all propriety and confess: she is at this moment
in grave danger.

SHU FU Oh, dear!

SHUI TA She has lost her shop, Mr. Shu Fu.

SHU FU The charm of Miss Shen Te, Mr. Shui Ta, derives from the goodness, not of her shop, but of her heart. Men call her the Angel of the Slums.

SHUI TA Yet her goodness has cost her two hundred silver dollars in a single day: we must put a stop to it.

SHU FU Permit me to differ, Mr. Shui Ta. Let us, rather, open wide the gates to such goodness! Every morning, with pleasure tinged by affection, I watch her charitable ministrations. For they are hungry, and she giveth them to eat! Four of them, to be precise. Why only four? I ask. Why not four hundred?[1] I hear she has been seeking shelter for the homeless. What about my humble cabins behind the cattle run? They are at her disposal. And so forth. And so on. Mr. Shui Ta, do you think Miss Shen Te could be persuaded to listen to certain ideas of mine? Ideas like these?

SHUI TA Mr. Shu Fu, she would be honored.

[Enter WONG and the POLICEMAN. Mr. SHU FU turns abruptly away and studies the shelves.]

WONG Is Miss Shen Te here?

SHUI TA No.

WONG I am Wong the water seller. You are Mr. Shui Ta?

SHUI TA I am.

WONG I am a friend of Shen Te's.

SHUI TA An intimate friend, I hear.

WONG [To the POLICEMAN.] You see? [To SHUI TA.] It's because of my hand.

POLICEMAN He hurt his hand, sir, that's a fact.

SHUI TA [Quickly.] You need a sling, I see. [He takes a shawl from the back room, and throws it to WONG.]

WONG But that's her new shawl!

SHUI TA She has no more use for it.

WONG But she bought it to please someone!

SHUI TA It happens to be no longer necessary.

WONG [Making the sling.] She is my only witness.

POLICEMAN Mr. Shui Ta, your cousin is supposed to have seen the barber hit the water seller with a curling iron.

SHUI TA I'm afraid my cousin was not present at the time

WONG But she was, sir! Just ask her! Isn't she in?

SHUI TA [Gravely.] Mr. Wong, my cousin has her own troubles. You wouldn't wish her to add to them by committing perjury?

WONG But it was she that told me to go to the judge!

SHUI TA Was the judge supposed to heal your hand?

[Mr. SHU FU turns quickly around. SHUI TA bows to SHU FU, and vice versa.]

WONG [Taking the sling off, and putting it back.] I see how it is.

POLICEMAN Well, I'll be on my way. [To WONG.] And you be careful. If Mr. Shu Fu wasn't a man who tempers justice with mercy, as the saying is, you'd be in jail for libel. Be off with you!

[Exit WONG followed by POLICEMAN.]

SHUI TA Profound apologies, Mr. Shu Fu.

---

1. An allusion to the biblical miracle of loaves and fishes, when Christ fed five thousand people (Matthew 14.13–21).

SHU FU   Not at all, Mr. Shui Ta. [*Pointing to the shawl.*] The episode is over?

SHUI TA   It may take her time to recover. There are some fresh wounds.

SHUI FU   We shall be discreet. Delicate. A short vacation could be arranged . . .

SHUI TA   First of course, you and she would have to talk things over.

SHU FU   At a small supper in a small, but high-class, restaurant.

SHUI TA   I'll go and find her. [*Exit into back room.*]

MRS. SHIN [*Sticking her head in again.*]   Time for congratulations, Mr. Shu Fu?

SHU FU   Ah, Mrs. Shin! Please inform Miss Shen Te's guests they may take shelter in the cabins behind the cattle run!

   [MRS. SHIN *nods, grinning.*]

SHU FU [*To the audience.*]   Well? What do you think of me, ladies and gentlemen? What could a man do more? Could he be less selfish? More farsighted? A small supper in a small but . . . Does that bring rather vulgar and clumsy thoughts into your mind? Ts, ts, ts. Nothing of the sort will occur. She won't even be touched. Not even accidentally while passing the salt. An exchange of ideas only. Over the flowers on the table—white chrysanthemums, by the way [*He writes down a note of this.*]—yes, over the white chrysanthemums, two young souls will . . . shall I say "find each other"? We shall NOT exploit the misfortune of others. Understanding? Yes. An offer of assistance? Certainly. But quietly. Almost inaudibly. Perhaps with a single glance. A glance that could also—mean more.

MRS. SHIN [*Coming forward.*]   Everything under control, Mr. Shu Fu?

SHU FU   Oh, Mrs. Shin, what do you know about this worthless rascal Yang Sun?

MRS. SHIN   Why, he's the most worthless rascal . . .

SHU FU   Is he really? You're sure? [*As she opens her mouth.*] From now on, he doesn't exist! Can't be found anywhere!

   [*Enter* YANG SUN.]

YANG SUN   What's been going on here?

MRS. SHIN   Shall I call Mr. Shui Ta, Mr. Shu Fu? He wouldn't want strangers in here!

SHU FU   Mr. Shui Ta is in conference with Miss Shen Te. Not to be disturbed!

YANG SUN   Shen Te here? I didn't see her come in. What kind of conference?

SHU FU [*Not letting him enter the back room.*]   Patience, dear sir! And if by chance I have an inkling who you are, pray take note that Miss Shen Te and I are about to announce our engagement.

YANG SUN   What?

MRS. SHIN   You didn't expect that, did you?

   [YANG SUN *is trying to push past the barber into the back room when* SHEN TE *comes out.*]

SHU FU   My dear Shen Te, ten thousand apologies! Perhaps you . . .

YANG SUN   What is it, Shen Te? Have you gone crazy?

SHEN TE [*Breathless.*]   My cousin and Mr. Shu Fu have come to an understanding. They wish me to hear Mr. Shu Fu's plans for helping the poor.

YANG SUN   Your cousin wants to part us.

SHEN TE Yes.

YANG SUN And you've agreed to it?

SHEN TE Yes.

YANG SUN They told you I was bad. [SHEN TE *is silent.*] And suppose I am.
Does that make me need you less? I'm low, Shen Te, I have no money,
I don't do the right thing but at least I put up a fight! [*He is near her
now, and speaks in an undertone.*] Have you no eyes? Look at him. Have
you forgotten already?

SHEN TE No.

YANG SUN How it was raining?

SHEN TE No.

YANG SUN How you cut me down from the willow tree? Bought me water?
Promised me money to fly with?

SHEN TE [*Shakily.*] Yang Sun, what do you want?

YANG SUN I want you to come with me

SHEN TE [*In a small voice.*] Forgive me, Mr. Shu Fu, I want to go with
Mr. Yang Sun.

YANG SUN We're lovers, you know. Give me the key to the shop. [SHEN
TE *takes the key from around her neck.* YANG SUN *puts it on the counter.
To* MRS. SHIN.] Leave it under the mat when you're through. Let's go,
Shen Te.

SHU FU But this is rape! Mr. Shui Ta!!

YANG SUN [*To* SHEN TE.] Tell him not to shout.

SHEN TE Please don't shout for my cousin, Mr. Shu Fu. He doesn't agree
with me, I know, but he's wrong. [*To the audience.*]

> I want to go with the man I love
> I don't want to count the cost
> I don't want to consider if it's wise
> I don't want to know if he loves me
> I want to go with the man I love.

YANG SUN That's the spirit.

[*And the couple leave.*]

5a

In front of the inner curtain. SHEN TE *in her wedding clothes, on the way to her
wedding.*

SHEN TE Something terrible has happened. As I left the shop with Yang
Sun, I found the old carpet dealer's wife waiting on the street, trembling
all over. She told me her husband had taken to his bed—sick with all
the worry and excitement over the two hundred silver dollars they lent
me. She said it would be best if I gave it back now. Of course, I had to
say I would. She said she couldn't quite trust my cousin Shui Ta or even
my fiancé, Yang Sun. There were tears in her eyes. With my emotions in
an uproar, I threw myself into Yang Sun's arms, I couldn't resist him.
The things he'd said to Shui Ta had taught Shen Te nothing. Sinking
into his arms, I said to myself:

To let no one perish, not even oneself
To fill everyone with happiness, even oneself
Is so good
How could I have forgotten those two old people? Yang Sun swept me
away like a small hurricane. But he's not a bad man, and he loves me.
He'd rather work in the cement factory than owe his flying to a crime.
Though, of course, flying *is* a great passion with Sun. Now, on the way
to my wedding, I waver between fear and joy.

6

*The "private dining room" on the upper floor of a cheap restaurant in a poor
section of town. With* SHEN TE: *the* GRANDFATHER, *the* SISTER-IN-LAW, THE
NIECE, MRS. SHIN, *the* UNEMPLOYED MAN. *In a corner, alone, a* PRIEST.[2] *A*
WAITER *pouring wine. Downstage,* YANG SUN *talking to his mother. He wears a
diner jacket.*

YANG SUN   Bad news, Mamma. She came right out and told me she can't
  sell the shop for me. Some idiot is bringing a claim because he lent her
  the two hundred she gave you.
MRS. YANG   What did you say? Of course, you can't marry her now.
YANG SUN   It's no use saying anything to *her.* I've sent for her cousin, Mr.
  Shui Ta. He said there was nothing in writing.
MRS. YANG   Good idea. I'll go out and look for him. Keep an eye on things.
    [*Exit* MRS. YANG. SHEN TE *has been pouring wine.*]
SHEN TE [*To the audience, pitcher in hand.*]   I wasn't mistaken in him.
  He's bearing up well. Though it must have been an awful blow—giving
  up flying. I do love him so. [*Calling across the room to him.*] Sun, you
  haven't drunk a toast with the bride!
YANG SUN   What do we drink to?
SHEN TE   Why, to the future!
YANG SUN   When the bridegroom's dinner jacket won't be a hired one!
SHEN TE   But when the bride's dress will still get rained on sometimes!
YANG SUN   To everything we ever wished for!
SHEN TE   May all our dreams come true!
    [*They drink.*]
YANG SUN [*With loud conviviality.*]   And now, friends, before the wedding
  gets under way, I have to ask the bride a few questions. I've no idea what
  kind of a wife she'll make, and it worries me. [*Wheeling on* SHEN TE.]
  For example. Can you make five cups of tea with three tea leaves?
SHEN TE   No.
YANG SUN   So I won't be getting very much tea. Can you sleep on a straw
  mattress the size of that book? [*He points to the large volume the* PRIEST
  is reading.]
SHEN TE   The two of us?
YANG SUN   The one of you.
SHEN TE   In that case, no.

2. A Buddhist monk or priest.

YANG SUN   What a wife! I'm shocked!
> [*While the audience is laughing, his mother returns. With a shrug of her shoulders, she tells* SUN *the expected guest hasn't arrived. The* PRIEST *shuts the book with a bang, and makes for the door.*]

MRS. YANG   Where are *you* off to? It's only a matter of minutes.

PRIEST [*Watch in hand.*]   Time goes on, Mrs. Yang, and I've another wedding to attend to. Also a funeral.

MRS. YANG [*Irately.*]   D'you think we planned it this way? I was hoping to manage with one pitcher of wine, and we've run through two already. [*Points to empty pitcher. Loudly.*] My dear Shen Te, I don't know where your cousin can be keeping himself!

SHEN TE   My cousin?!

MRS. YANG   Certainly. I'm old-fashioned enough to think such a close relative should attend the wedding.

SHEN TE   Oh, Sun, is it the three hundred silver dollars?

YANG SUN [*Not looking her in the eye.*]   Are you deaf? Mother says she's old-fashioned. And I say I'm considerate. We'll wait another fifteen minutes.

HUSBAND   Another fifteen minutes.

MRS. YANG [*Addressing the company.*]   Now you all know, don't you, that my son is getting a job as a mail pilot?

SISTER-IN-LAW   In Peking, too, isn't it?

MRS. YANG   In Peking, too! The two of us are moving to Peking!

SHEN TE   Sun, tell your mother Peking is out of the question now.

YANG SUN   Your cousin'll tell her. If he agrees. I don't agree.

SHEN TE [*Amazed, and dismayed.*]   Sun!

YANG SUN   I hate this godforsaken Setzuan. What people! Know what they look like when I half close my eyes? Horses! Whinnying, fretting, stamping, screwing their necks up! [*Loudly.*] And what is it the thunder says? They are su-per-flu-ous! [*He hammers out the syllables.*] They've run their last race! They can go trample themselves to death! [*Pause.*] I've got to get out of here.

SHEN TE   But I've promised the money to the old couple.

YANG SUN   And since you always do the wrong thing, it's lucky your cousin's coming. Have another drink.

SHEN TE [*Quietly.*]   My cousin can't be coming.

YANG SUN   How d'you mean?

SHEN TE   My cousin can't be where I am.

YANG SUN   Quite a conundrum!

SHEN TE [*Desperately.*]   Sun, I'm the one that loves you. Not my cousin. He was thinking of the job in Peking when he promised you the old couple's money—

YANG SUN   Right. And that's why he's bringing the three hundred silver dollars. Here—to my wedding.

SHEN TE   He is not bringing the three hundred silver dollars.

YANG SUN   Huh? What makes you think that?

SHEN TE [*Looking into his eyes.*]   He says you only bought one ticket to Peking.
> [*Short pause.*]

YANG SUN   That was yesterday. [*He pulls two tickets part way out of his inside pocket, making her look under his coat.*] Two tickets. I don't want Mother to know. She'll get left behind. I sold her furniture to buy these tickets, so you see . . .

SHEN TE   But what's to become of the old couple?

YANG SUN   What's to become of me? Have another drink. Or do you believe in moderation? If I drink, I fly again. And if you drink, you may learn to understand me.

SHEN TE   You want to fly. But I can't help you.

YANG SUN   "Here's a plane, my darling—but it's only got one wing!"

[*The* WAITER *enters.*]

WAITER   Mrs. Yang!

MRS. YANG   Yes?

WAITER   Another pitcher of wine, ma'am?

MRS. YANG   We have enough, thanks. Drinking makes me sweat.

WAITER   Would you mind paying, ma'am?

MRS. YANG [*To everyone.*]   Just be patient a few moments longer, everyone, Mr. Shui Ta is on his way over! [*To the* WAITER.] Don't be a spoilsport.

WAITER   I can't let you leave till you've paid your bill, ma'am.

MRS. YANG   But they know me here!

WAITER   That's just it.

PRIEST [*Ponderously getting up.*]   I humbly take my leave. [*And he does.*]

MRS. YANG [*To the others, desperately.*]   Stay where you are, everybody! The priest says he'll be back in two minutes!

YANG SUN   It's no good Mamma. Ladies and gentlemen, Mr. Shui Ta still hasn't arrived and the priest has gone home. We won't detain you any longer.

[*They are leaving now*]

GRANDFATHER [*In the doorway, having forgotten to put his glass down.*]   To the bride! [*He drinks, puts down the glass, and follows the others.*]

[*Pause.*]

SHEN TE   Shall I go too?

YANG SUN   You? Aren't you the bride? Isn't this your wedding? [*He drags her across the room, tearing her wedding dress.*] If we can wait, you can wait. Mother calls me her falcon. She wants to see me in the clouds. But I think it may be St. Nevercome's Day before she'll go to the door and see my plane thunder by. [*Pause. He pretends the guests are still present.*] Why such a lull in the conversation, ladies and gentlemen? Don't you like it here? The ceremony is only slightly postponed—because an important guest is expected at any moment. Also because the bride doesn't know what love is. While we're waiting, the bridegroom will sing a little song. [*He does so.*]

THE SONG OF ST. NEVERCOME'S DAY

On a certain day, as is generally known,
    One and all will be shouting: Hooray, hooray!
For the beggar maid's son has a solid-gold throne
    And the day is St. Nevercome's Day
On St. Nevercome's, Nevercome's, Nevercome's Day
    He'll sit on his solid-gold throne

Oh, hooray, hooray! That day goodness will pay!
That day badness will cost you your head!
And merit and money will smile and be funny
While exchanging salt and bread
On St. Nevercome's, Nevercome's, Nevercome's Day
While exchanging salt and bread

And the grass, oh, the grass will look down at the sky
And the pebbles will roll up the stream
And all men will be good without batting an eye
They will make of our earth a dream
On St. Nevercome's, Nevercome's, Nevercome's Day
They will make of our earth a dream

And as for me, that's the day I shall be
A flyer and one of the best
Unemployed man, you will have work to do
Washerwoman, you'll get your rest
On St. Nevercome's, Nevercome's, Nevercome's Day
Washerwoman, you'll get your rest

MRS. YANG   It looks like he's not coming.
[*The three of them sit looking at the door.*]

6a

Wong's den. The sewer pipe is again transparent and again the GODS *appear to* WONG *in a dream.*

WONG   I'm so glad you've come, illustrious ones. It's Shen Te. She's in great trouble from following the rule about loving thy neighbor. Perhaps she's *too* good for this world!
FIRST GOD   Nonsense! You are eaten up by lice and doubts!
WONG   Forgive me, illustrious one, I only meant you might deign to intervene.
FIRST GOD   Out of the question! My colleague here intervened in some squabble or other only yesterday. [*He points to the* THIRD GOD, *who has a black eye.*] The results are before us!
WONG   She had to call on her cousin again. But not even he could help. I'm afraid the shop is done for.
THIRD GOD [*A little concerned.*]   Perhaps we should help after all?
FIRST GOD   The gods help those that help themselves.
WONG   What if we *can't* help ourselves, illustrious ones?
[*Slight pause.*]
SECOND GOD   Try, anyway! Suffering ennobles!
FIRST GOD   Our faith in Shen Te is unshaken!
THIRD GOD   We certainly haven't found any *other* good people. You can see where we spend our nights from the straw on our clothes.
WONG   You might help her find her way by—
FIRST GOD   The good man finds his own way here below!

SECOND GOD   The good woman too.
FIRST GOD   The heavier the burden, the greater her strength!
THIRD GOD   We're only onlookers, you know.
FIRST GOD   And everything will be all right in the end, O ye of little faith!
    [*They are gradually disappearing through these last lines.*]

7

The yard behind Shen Te's shop. A few articles of furniture on a cart. SHEN TE
and MRS. SHIN *are taking the washing off the line.*

MRS. SHIN   If you ask me, you should fight tooth and nail to keep the
    shop.
SHEN TE   How can I? I have to sell the tobacco to pay back the two hun-
    dred silver dollars today.
MRS. SHIN   No husband, no tobacco, no house and home! What are you
    going to live on?
SHEN TE   I can work. I can sort tobacco.
MRS. SHIN   Hey, look, Mr. Shui Ta's trousers! He must have left here stark
    naked!
SHEN TE   Oh, he may have another pair, Mrs. Shin.
MRS. SHIN   But if he's gone for good as you say, why has he left his pants
    behind?
SHEN TE   Maybe he's thrown them away.
MRS. SHIN   Can I take them?
SHEN TE   Oh, no.
    [*Enter Mr.* SHU FU, *running.*]
SHU FU   Not a word! Total silence! I know all. You have sacrificed your
    own love and happiness so as not to hurt a dear old couple who had put
    their trust in you! Not in vain does this district—for all its malevolent
    tongues—call you the Angel of the Slums! That young man couldn't rise
    to your level, so you left him. And now, when I see you closing up the
    little shop, that veritable haven of rest for the multitude, well, I cannot,
    I cannot let it pass. Morning after morning I have stood watching in the
    doorway not unmoved—while you graciously handed out rice to the
    wretched. Is that never to happen again? Is the good woman of Setzuan
    to disappear? If only you would allow *me* to assist you! Now don't say
    anything! No assurances, no exclamations of gratitude! [*He has taken out
    his checkbook.*] Here! A blank check. [*He places it on the cart.*] Just my
    signature. Fill it out as you wish. Any sum in the world. I herewith retire
    from the scene, quietly, unobtrusively, making no claims, on tiptoe, full
    of veneration, absolutely selflessly . . . [*He has gone.*]
MRS. SHIN   Well! You're saved. There's always some idiot of a man. . . .
    Now hurry! Put down a thousand silver dollars and let me fly to the bank
    before he comes to his senses.
SHEN TE   I can pay you for the washing without any check.
MRS. SHIN   What? You're not going to cash it just because you might have
    to marry him? Are you crazy? Men like him *want* to be led by the nose!

Are you still thinking of that flyer? All Yellow Street knows how he treated you!

SHEN TE

When I heard his cunning laugh, I was afraid
But when I saw the holes in his shoes, I loved him dearly.

MRS. SHIN   Defending that good-for-nothing after all that's happened!

SHEN TE [*Staggering as she holds some of the washing.*]   Oh!

MRS. SHIN [*Taking the washing from her, dryly.*]   So you feel dizzy when you stretch and bend? There couldn't be a little visitor on the way? If that's it, you can forget Mr. Shu Fu's blank check: it wasn't meant for a christening present!

[*She goes to the back with a basket. Shen Te's eyes follow* MRS. SHIN *for a moment. Then she looks down at her own body, feels her stomach, and a great joy comes into her eyes.*]

SHEN TE   O joy! A new human being is on the way. The world awaits him. In the cities the people say: he's got to be reckoned with, this new human being! [*She imagines a little boy to be present, and introduces him to the audience.*] This is my son, the well-known flyer!

Say: Welcome
To the conqueror of unknown mountains and unreachable regions
Who brings us our mail across the impassable deserts!

[*She leads him up and down by the hand.*]

Take a look at the world, my son. That's a tree. Tree, yes. Say: "Hello, tree!" And bow. Like this. [*She bows.*] Now you know each other. And, look, here comes the water seller. He's a friend, give him your hand. A cup of fresh water for my little son, please. Yes, it *is* a warm day. [*Handing the cup.*] Oh dear, a policeman, we'll have to make a circle round *him*. Perhaps we can pick a few cherries over there in the rich Mr. Pung's garden. But we mustn't be seen. You want cherries? Just like children with fathers. No, no, you can't go straight at them like that. Don't pull. We must learn to be reasonable. Well, have it your own way. [*She has let him make for the cherries.*] Can you reach? Where to put them? Your mouth is the best place. [*She tries one herself.*] Mmm, they're good. But the policeman, we must run! [*They run.*] Yes, back to the street. Calm now, so no one will notice us. [*Walking the street with her child, she sings.*]

Once a plum—'twas in Japan—
Made a conquest of a man
But the man's turn soon did come
For he gobbled up the plum

[*Enter* WONG, *with a child by the hand. He coughs.*]

SHEN TE   Wong!

WONG   It's about the carpenter, Shen Te. He's lost his shop, and he's been drinking. His children are on the streets. This is one. Can you help?

SHEN TE [*To the child.*]   Come here, little man. [*Takes him down to the footlights. To the audience.*]

You there! A man is asking you for shelter!
A man of tomorrow says: what about today?
His friend the conqueror, whom you know,
Is his advocate!

[*To* WONG.] He can live in Mr. Shu Fu's cabins. I may have to go there myself. I'm going to have a baby. That's a secret—don't tell Yang Sun— we'd only be in his way. Can you find the carpenter for me?

WONG   I knew you'd think of something. [*To the child.*] Good-bye, son, I'm going for your father.

SHEN TE   What about your hand, Wong? I wanted to help, but my cousin . . .

WONG   Oh, I can get along with one hand, don't worry. [*He shows how he can handle his pole with his left hand alone.*]

SHEN TE   But your right hand! Look, take this cart, sell everything that's on it, and go to the doctor with the money . . .

WONG   She's still good. But first I'll bring the carpenter. I'll pick up the cart when I get back [*Exit* WONG.]

SHEN TE [*To the child.*]   Sit down over here, son, till your father comes.
          [*The child sits crosslegged on the ground. Enter the* HUSBAND *and* WIFE, *each dragging a large, full sack.*]

WIFE [*Furtively.*]   You're alone, Shen Te, dear?
          [SHEN TE *nods. The* WIFE *beckons to the* NEPHEW *offstage. He comes on with another sack.*]

WIFE   Your cousin's away? [SHEN TE *nods.*] He's not coming back?

SHEN TE   No. I'm giving up the shop.

WIFE   That's why we're here. We want to know if we can leave these things in your new home. Will you do us this favor?

SHEN TE   Why, yes, I'd be glad to.

HUSBAND [*Cryptically.*]   And if anyone asks about them, say they're yours.

SHEN TE   Would anyone ask?

WIFE [*With a glance back at her husband.*]   Oh, someone might. The police, for instance. They don't seem to like us. Where can we put it?

SHEN TE   Well, I'd rather not get in any more trouble . . .

WIFE   Listen to her! The good woman of Setzuan!
          [SHEN TE *is silent.*]

HUSBAND   There's enough tobacco in those sacks to give us a new start in life. We could have our own tobacco factory!

SHEN TE [*Slowly.*]   You'll have to put them in the back room
          [*The sacks are taken offstage, while the child is alone. Shyly glancing about him, he goes to the garbage can, starts playing with the contents, and eating some of the scraps. The others return.*]

WIFE   We're counting on you, Shen Te!

SHEN TE   Yes. [*She sees the child and is shocked.*]

HUSBAND   We'll see you in Mr. Shu Fu's cabins.

NEPHEW   The day after tomorrow.

SHEN TE   Yes. Now, go. Go! I'm not feeling well.
          [*Exeunt all three, virtually pushed off.*]
                    He is eating the refuse in the garbage can!
                    Only look at his little gray mouth!
          [*Pause. Music.*]
                    As this is the world *my* son will enter
                    I will study to defend him.
                    To be good to you, my son,
                    I shall be a tigress to all others

If I have to.
And I shall have to.
[*She starts to go*]
One more time, then. I hope really the last.
[*Exit* SHEN TE, *taking Shui Ta's trousers.* MRS. SHIN *enters and watches her with marked interest. Enter the* SISTER-IN-LAW *and the* GRANDFATHER.]

SISTER-IN-LAW   So it's true, the shop has closed down. And the furniture's in the back yard. It's the end of the road!

MRS. SHIN [*Pompously.*]   The fruit of high living, selfishness, and sensuality! Down the primrose path to Mr. Shu Fu's cabins—with you!

SISTER-IN-LAW   Cabins? Rat holes! He gave them to us because his soap supplies only went moldy there!
[*Enter the* UNEMPLOYED MAN.]

UNEMPLOYED MAN   Shen Te is moving?

SISTER-IN-LAW   Yes, She was sneaking away.

MRS. SHIN   She's ashamed of herself, and no wonder!

UNEMPLOYED MAN   Tell her to call Mr. Shui Ta or she's done for this time!

SISTER-IN-LAW   Tell her to call Mr. Shui Ta or *we're* done for this time!
[*Enter* WONG *and* CARPENTER, *the latter with a child on each hand.*]

CARPENTER   So we'll have a roof over our heads for a change!

MRS. SHIN   Roof? Whose roof?

CARPENTER   Mr. Shu Fu's cabins. And we have little Feng to thank for it.
[*Feng, we find, is the name of the child already there; his father now takes him. To the other two.*] Bow to your little brother, you two!
[*The* CARPENTER *and the two new arrivals bow to Feng. Enter* SHUI TA.]

UNEMPLOYED MAN   Sst! Mr. Shui Ta!
[*Pause.*]

SHUI TA   And what is this crowd here for, may I ask?

WONG   How do you do, Mr. Shui Ta. This is the carpenter. Miss Shen Te promised him space in Mr. Shu Fu's cabins.

SHUI TA   That will not be possible.

CARPENTER   We can't go there after all?

SHUI TA   All the space is needed for other purposes.

SISTER-IN-LAW   You mean we have to get out? But we've got nowhere to go.

SHUI TA   Miss Shen Te finds it possible to provide employment. If the proposition interests you, you may stay in the cabins.

SISTER-IN-LAW [*With distaste.*]   You mean *work?* Work for Miss Shen Te?

SHUI TA   Making tobacco, yes. There are three bales here already. Would you like to get them?

SISTER-IN-LAW [*Trying to bluster.*]   We have our own tobacco! We were in the tobacco business before you were born!

SHUI TA [*To the* CARPENTER *and the* UNEMPLOYED MAN]   You *don't* have your own tobacco. What about you?
[*The* CARPENTER *and the* UNEMPLOYED MAN *get the point, and go for the sacks. Enter* MRS. MI TZU.]

MRS. MI TZU   Mr. Shui Ta? I've brought you your three hundred silver dollars.

SHUI TA   I'll sign your lease instead. I've decided not to sell.

MRS. MI TZU   What? You don't need the money for that flyer?

SHUI TA   No.

MRS. MI TZU   And you can pay six months' rent?

SHUI TA [*Takes the barber's blank check from the cart and fills it out.*]   Here is a check for ten thousand silver dollars. On Mr. Shu Fu's account. Look. [*He shows her the signature on the check.*] Your six months' rent will be in your hands by seven this evening. And now, if you'll excuse me.

MRS. MI TZU   So it's Mr. Shu Fu now. The flyer has been given his walking papers. These modern girls! In my day they'd have said she was flighty. That poor, deserted Mr. Yang Sun!

[*Exit* MRS. MI TZU. *The* CARPENTER *and the* UNEMPLOYED MAN *drag the three sacks back on the stage.*]

CARPENTER [*To* SHUI TA.]   I don't know why I'm doing this for you.

SHUI TA   Perhaps your children want to eat, Mr. Carpenter.

SISTER-IN-LAW [*Catching sight of the sacks.*]   Was my brother-in-law here?

MRS. SHIN   Yes, he was.

SISTER-IN-LAW   I thought as much. I know those sacks! That's our tobacco!

SHUI TA   Really? I thought it came from my back room! Shall we consult the police on the point?

SISTER-IN-LAW [*Defeated.*]   No.

SHUI TA   Perhaps you will show me the way to Mr. Shu Fu's cabins?

[*Taking Feng by the hand,* SHUI TA *goes off, followed by the* CARPENTER *and his two older children, the* SISTER-IN-LAW, *the* GRANDFATHER, *and the* UNEMPLOYED MAN. *Each of the last three drags a sack. Enter* OLD MAN *and* OLD WOMAN.]

MRS. SHIN   A pair of pants—missing from the clothes line one minute—and next minute on the honorable backside of Mr. Shui Ta.

OLD WOMAN   We thought Miss Shen Te was here.

MRS. SHIN [*Preoccupied.*]   Well, she's not.

OLD MAN   There was something she was going to give us.

WONG   She was going to help me too. [*Looking at his hand.*]   It'll be too late soon. But she'll be back. This cousin has never stayed long.

MRS. SHIN [*Approaching a conclusion.*]   No, he hasn't, has he?

7a

The Sewer Pipe: WONG *asleep. In his dream, he tells the* GODS *his fears. The* GODS *seem tired from all their travels. They stop for a moment and look over their shoulders at the water seller.*

WONG   Illustrious ones. I've been having a bad dream. Our beloved Shen Te was in great distress in the rushes down by the river—the spot where the bodies of suicides are washed up. She kept staggering and holding her head down as if she was carrying something and it was dragging her down into the mud. When I called out to her, she said she had to take your Book of Rules[3] to the other side, and not get it wet, or the ink would all come off. You had talked to her about the virtues, you know, the time she gave you shelter in Setzuan.

THIRD GOD   Well, but what do you suggest, my dear Wong?

WONG   Maybe a little relaxation of the rules, Benevolent One, in view of the bad times.

THIRD GOD   As for instance?

WONG   Well, um, good-will, for instance, might do instead of love?

THIRD GOD   I'm afraid that would create new problems.

WONG   Or, instead of justice, good sportsmanship?

THIRD GOD   That would only mean more work.

WONG   Instead of honor, outward propriety?

THIRD GOD   Still more work! No, no! The rules will have to stand, my dear Wong!

[*Wearily shaking their heads, all three journey on.*]

8

Shui Ta's tobacco factory in Shu Fu's cabins. Huddled together behind bars, several families, mostly women and children. Among these people the SISTER-IN-LAW, *the* GRANDFATHER, *the* CARPENTER, *and his three children. Enter* MRS. YANG *followed by* YANG SUN.

MRS. YANG [*To the audience.*]   There's something I just *have* to tell you: strength and wisdom are wonderful things. The strong and wise Mr. Shui Ta has transformed my son from a dissipated good-for-nothing into a model citizen. As you may have heard, Mr. Shui Ta opened a small tobacco factory near the cattle runs. It flourished. Three months ago— I shall never forget it—I asked for an appointment, and Mr. Shui Ta agree to see us—me and my son. I can see him now as he came through the door to meet us. . . .

[*Enter* SHUI TA, *from a door.*]

SHUI TA   What can I do for you, Mrs. Yang?

MRS. YANG   This morning the police came to the house. We find you've brought an action for breach of promise of marriage. In the name of Shen Te. You also claim that Sun came by two hundred silver dollars by improper means.

SHUI TA   That is correct.

MRS. YANG   Mr. Shui Ta, the money's all gone. When the Peking job didn't materialize, he ran through it all in three days. I know he's a good-for-nothing. He sold my furniture. He was moving to Peking without me. Miss Shen Te thought highly of him at one time.

SHUI TA   What do *you* say, Mr. Yang Sun?

YANG SUN   The money's gone.

SHUI TA [*To* MRS. YANG.]   Mrs. Yang, in consideration of my cousin's

---

3. Reference to neo-Confucianist commentators' rigid and prescriptive interpretation of Confucius's *Analects*, especially regarding the role of women.

incomprehensible weakness for your son, I am prepared to give him another chance. He can have a job—here. The two hundred silver dollars will be taken out of his wages.

YANG SUN   So it's the factory or jail?

SHUI TA   Take your choice.

YANG SUN   May I speak with Shen Te?

SHUI TA   You may not.

      [*Pause.*]

YANG SUN [*Sullenly.*]   Show me where to go.

MRS. YANG   Mr. Shui Ta, you are kindness itself: the gods will reward you! [*To* YANG SUN.] And honest work will make a man of you, my boy. [YANG SUN *follows* SHUI TA *into the factory.* MRS. YANG *comes down again to the footlights.*] Actually, honest work didn't agree with him—at first. And he got no opportunity to distinguish himself till—in the third week—when the wages were being paid . . .

      [SHUI TA *has a bag of money. Standing next to his foreman—the former* UNEMPLOYED MAN—*he counts out the wages. It is Yang Sun's turn.*]

UNEMPLOYED MAN [*Reading.*]   Carpenter, six silver dollars. Yang Sun, six silver dollars.

YANG SUN [*Quietly.*]   Excuse me, sir. I don't think it can be more than five. May I see? [*He takes the foreman's list.*] It says six working days. But that's a mistake, sir. I took a day off for court business. And I won't take what I haven't earned, however miserable the pay is!

UNEMPLOYED MAN   Yang Sun. Five silver dollars. [*To* SHUI TA.] A rare case, Mr. Shui Ta!

SHUI TA   How is it the book says six when it should say five?

UNEMPLOYED MAN   I must've made a mistake, Mr. Shui Ta. [*With a look at* YANG SUN.] It won't happen again.

SHUI TA [*Taking* YANG SUN *aside.*]   You don't hold back, do you? You give your all to the firm. You're even honest. Do the foreman's mistakes always favor the workers?

YANG SUN   He does have . . . friends.

SHUI TA   Thank you. May I offer you any little recompense?

YANG SUN   Give me a trial period of one week, and I'll prove my intelligence is worth more to you than my strength.

MRS. YANG [*Still down at the footlights.*]   Fighting words, fighting words! That evening, I said to Sun: "If you're a flyer, then fly, my falcon! Rise in the world!" And he got to be foreman. Yes, in Mr. Shui Ta's tobacco factory, he worked real miracles.

      [*We see* YANG SUN *with his legs apart standing behind the workers, who are handing along a basket of raw tobacco above their heads.*]

YANG SUN   Faster! Faster! You, there, d'you think you can just stand around, now you're not foreman any more? It'll be your job to lead us in song. Sing!

      [UNEMPLOYED MAN *starts singing. The others join in the refrain.*]

SONG OF THE EIGHTH ELEPHANT

Chang had seven elephants—all much the same—
But then there was Little Brother
The seven, they were wild, Little Brother, he was tame
And to guard them Chang chose Little Brother
    Run faster!
    Mr. Chang has a forest park
    Which must be cleared before tonight
    And already it's growing dark!

When the seven elephants cleared that forest park
Mr. Chang rode high on Little Brother
While the seven toiled and moiled till dark
On his big behind sat Little Brother
    Dig faster!
    Mr. Chang has a forest park
    Which must be cleared before tonight
    And already it's growing dark!

And the seven elephants worked many an hour
Till none of them could work another
Old Chang, he looked sour, on the seven he did glower
But gave a pound of rice to Little Brother
    What was that?
    Mr. Chang has a forest park
    Which must be cleared before tonight
    And already it's growing dark!

And the seven elephants hadn't any tusks
The one that had the tusks was Little Brother
Seven are no match for one, if the one has a gun!
How old Chang did laugh at Little Brother!
    Keep on digging!
    Mr. Chang has a forest park
    Which must be cleared before tonight
    And already it's growing dark!

[Smoking a cigar, SHUI TA strolls by. YANG SUN, laughing, has joined
    in the refrain of the third stanza and speeded up the tempo of the
    last stanza by clapping his hands.]
MRS. YANG   And that's why I say: strength and wisdom are wonderful
    things. It took the strong and wise Mr. Shui Ta to bring out the best in
    Yang Sun. A real superior man is like a bell. If you ring it, it rings, and
    if you don't, it don't, as the saying is.[4]

---

4. A saying by the Chinese philosopher Mo-tzu (470–391 B.C.).

9

Shen Te's shop, now an office with club chairs and fine carpets. It is raining.
SHUI TA, *now fat, is just dismissing the* OLD MAN *and* OLD WOMAN. MRS. SHIN,
in obviously new clothes, looks on, smirking.

SHUI TA   No! I canNOT tell you when we expect her back.

OLD WOMAN   The two hundred silver dollars came today. In an envelope.
There was no letter, but it must be from Shen Te. We want to write and
thank her. May we have her address?

SHUI TA   I'm afraid I haven't got it.

OLD MAN [*Pulling Old Woman's sleeve.*]   Let's be going.

OLD WOMAN   She's got to come back some time!

[*They move off, uncertainly, worried.* SHUI TA *bows.*]

MRS. SHIN   They lost the carpet shop because they couldn't pay their taxes.
The money arrived too late.

SHUI TA   They could have come to me.

MRS. SHIN   People don't like coming to you.

SHUI TA [*Sits suddenly, one hand to his head.*]   I'm dizzy.

MRS. SHIN   After all, you *are* in your seventh month. But old Mrs. Shin
will be there in your hour of trial! [*She cackles feebly.*]

SHUI TA [*In a stifled voice.*]   Can I count on that?

MRS. SHIN   We all have our price, and mine won't be too high for the great
Mr. Shui Ta! [*She opens Shui Ta's collar.*]

SHUI TA   It's for the child's sake. All of this.

MRS. SHIN   "All for the child," of course.

SHUI TA   I'm so fat. People must notice.

MRS. SHIN   Oh no, they think it's 'cause you're rich.

SHIU TA [*More feelingly.*]   What will happen to the child?

MRS. SHIN   You ask that nine times a day. Why, it'll have the best that
money can buy!

SHUI TA   He must never see Shui Ta.

MRS. SHIN   Oh, no. Always Shen Te.

SHUI TA   What about the neighbors? There are rumors, aren't there?

MRS. SHIN   As long as Mr. Shu Fu doesn't find out, there's nothing to
worry about. Drink this.

[*Enter* YANG SUN *in a smart business suit, and carrying a businessman's briefcase.* SHUI TA *is more or less in Mrs. Shin's arms.*]

YANG SUN [*Surprised.*]   I guess I'm in the way.

SHUI TA [*Ignoring this, rises with an effort.*]   Till tomorrow, Mrs. Shin.

[MRS. SHIN *leaves with a smile, putting her new gloves.*]

YANG SUN   Gloves now! She couldn't be fleecing you? And since when did
you have a private life? [*Taking a paper from the briefcase.*] You haven't
been at your best lately, and things are getting out of hand. The police
want to close us down. They say that at the most they can only permit
twice the lawful number of workers.

SHUI TA [*Evasively.*]   The cabins are quite good enough.

YANG SUN   For the workers maybe, not for the tobacco. They're too damp.
We must take over some of Mrs. Mi Tzu's buildings.

SHUI TA   Her price is double what I can pay.

YANG SUN   Not unconditionally. If she has me to stroke her knees she'll come down.

SHUI TA   I'll never agree to that.

YANG SUN   What's wrong? Is it the rain? You get so irritable whenever it rains.

SHUI TA   Never! I will never . . .

YANG SUN   Mrs. Mi Tzu'll be here in five minutes. *You* fix it. And Shu Fu will be with her. . . . What's all that noise?

[*During the above dialogue,* WONG *is heard offstage, calling:* "The good Shen Te, where is she? Which of you has seen Shen Te, good people? Where is Shen Te?" *A knock. Enter* WONG.]

WONG   Mr. Shui Ta, I've come to ask when Miss Shen Te will be back, it's six months now. . . . There are rumors. People say something's happened to her.

SHUI TA   I'm busy. Come back next week.

WONG [*Excited.*]   In the morning there was always rice on her doorstep— for the needy. It's been there again lately!

SHUI TA   And what do people conclude from this?

WONG   That Shen Te is still in Setzuan! She's been . . . [*He breaks off.*]

SHUI TA   She's been what? Mr. Wong, if you're Shen Te's friend, talk a little less about her, that's my advice to you.

WONG   I don't want your advice! Before she disappeared, Miss Shen Te told me something very important—she's pregnant!

YANG SUN   What? What was that?

SHUI TA [*Quickly.*]   The man is lying.

WONG   A good woman isn't so easily forgotten, Mr. Shui Ta.

[*He leaves.* SHUI TA *goes quickly into the back room.*]

YANG SUN [*To the audience.*]   Shen Te pregnant? So that's why. Her cousin sent her away, so I wouldn't get wind of it. I have a son, a Yang appears on the scene, and what happens? Mother and child vanish into thin air! That scoundrel, that unspeakable . . . [*The sound of sobbing is heard from the back room.*] What was that? Someone sobbing? Who was it? Mr. Shui Ta the Tobacco King doesn't weep his heart out. And where does the rice come from that's on the doorstep in the morning? [SHUI TA *returns. He goes to the door and looks out into the rain.*] Where is she?

SHUI TA   Sh! It's nine o'clock. But the rain's so heavy, you can't hear a thing.

YANG SUN   What do you want to hear?

SHUI TA   The mail plane.

YANG SUN   What?!

SHUI TA   I've been told *you* wanted to fly at one time. Is that all forgotten?

YANG SUN   Flying mail is night work. I prefer the daytime. And the firm is very dear to me—after all it belongs to my ex-fiancée, even if she's not around. And she's not, is she?

SHUI TA   What do you mean by that?

YANG SUN   Oh, well, let's say I haven't altogether—lost interest.

SHUI TA   My cousin might like to know that.

YANG SUN   I might not be indifferent—if I found she was being kept under lock and key.

SHUI TA   By whom?

YANG SUN   By you.

SHUI TA   What could you do about it?

YANG SUN   I could submit for discussion—my position in the firm.

SHUI TA   You are now my manager. In return for a more . . . appropriate position, you might agree to drop the inquiry into your ex-fiancée's whereabouts?

YANG SUN   I might.

SHUI TA   What position *would* be more appropriate?

YANG SUN   The one at the top.

SHUI TA   My own? [*Silence.*] And if I preferred to throw you out on your neck?

YANG SUN   I'd come back on my feet. With suitable escort.

SHUI TA   The police?

YANG SUN   The police.

SHUI TA   And when the police found no one?

YANG SUN   I might ask them not to overlook the back room. [*Ending the pretense.*] In short, Mr. Shui Ta, my interest in this young woman has not been officially terminated. I should like to see more of her. [*Into Shui Ta's face.*] Besides, she's pregnant and needs a friend. [*He moves to the door.*] I shall talk about it with the water seller.

[*Exit. SHUI TA is rigid for a moment, then he quickly goes into the back room. He returns with Shen Te's belongings: underwear, etc. He takes a long look at the shawl of the previous scene. He then wraps the things in a bundle, which, upon hearing a noise, he hides under the table. Enter* MRS. MI TZU *and Mr.* SHU FU. *They put away their umbrellas and galoshes.*]

MRS. MI TZU   I thought your manager was here, Mr. Shui Ta. He combines charm with business in a way that can only be to the advantage of all of us.

SHU FU   You sent for us, Mr. Shui Ta?

SHUI TA   The factory is in trouble.

SHU FU   It always is.

SHUI TA   The police are threatening to close us down unless I can show that the extension of our facilities is imminent.

SHU FU   Mr. Shui Ta, I'm sick and tired of your constantly expanding projects. I place cabins at your cousin's disposal; you make a factory of them. I hand your cousin a check; you present it. Your cousin disappears; you find the cabins too small and start talking of yet more—

SHUI TA   Mr. Shu Fu, I'm authorized to inform you that Miss Shen Te's return is now imminent.

SHU FU   Imminent? It's becoming his favorite word.

MRS. MI TZU   Yes, what does it mean?

SHUI TA   Mrs. Mi Tzu, I can pay you exactly half what you asked for your buildings. Are you ready to inform the police that I am taking them over?

MRS. MI TZU   Certainly, if I can take over your manager.

SHU FU   What?

MRS. MI TZU   He's so efficient.

SHUI TA   I'm afraid I need Mr. Yang Sun.

MRS. MI TZU   So do I.

SHUI TA   He will call on you tomorrow.

SHU FU   So much the better. With Shen Te likely to turn up at any moment, the presence of that young man is hardly in good taste.

SHUI TA   So we have reached a settlement. In what was once the good Shen Te's little shop we are laying the foundations for the great Mr. Shui Ta's twelve magnificent super tobacco markets. You will bear in mind that though they call me the Tobacco King of Setzuan, it is my cousin's interests that have been served . . .

VOICES [Off.]   The police, the police! Going to the tobacco shop! Something must have happened!

[Enter YANG SUN, WONG, and the POLICEMAN.]

POLICEMAN   Quiet there, quiet, quiet! [They quiet down.] I'm sorry, Mr. Shui Ta, but there's a report that you've been depriving Miss Shen Te of her freedom. Not that I believe all I hear, but the whole city's in an uproar.

SHUI TA   That's a lie.

POLICEMAN   Mr. Yang Sun has testified that he heard someone sobbing in the back room.

SHU FU   Mrs. Mi Tzu and myself will testify that no one here has been sobbing.

MRS. MI TZU   We have been quietly smoking our cigars.

POLICEMAN   Mr. Shui Ta, I'm afraid I shall have to take a look at that room. [He does so. The room is empty.] No one there, of course, sir.

YANG SUN   But I heard sobbing. What's that?

[He finds the clothes.]

WONG   Those are Shen Te's things. [To crowd.] Shen Te's clothes are here!

VOICES [Off, in sequence.]   Shen Te's clothes!
—They've been found under the table!
—Body of murdered girl still missing!
—Tobacco King suspected!

POLICEMAN   Mr. Shui Ta, unless you can tell us where the girl is, I'll have to ask you to come along.

SHUI TA   I do not know.

POLICEMAN   I can't say how sorry I am, Mr. Shui Ta. [He shows him the door.]

SHUI TA   Everything will be cleared up in no time. There are still judges in Setzuan.

YANG SUN   I heard sobbing!

9a

Wong's den. For the last time, the GODS appear to the water seller in his dream. They have changed and show signs of a long journey, extreme fatigue, and plenty of mishaps. The FIRST no longer has a hat; the THIRD has lost a leg; all three are barefoot.

WONG   Illustrious ones, at last you're here. Shen Te's been gone for months and today her cousin's been arrested. They think he murdered her to get the shop. But I had a dream and in this dream Shen Te said her cousin was keeping her prisoner. You must find her for us, illustrious ones!

FIRST GOD   We've found very few good people anywhere, and even they didn't keep it up. Shen Te is still the only one that stayed good.

SECOND GOD   If she *has* stayed good.

WONG   Certainly she has. But she's vanished.

FIRST GOD   That's the last straw. All is lost!

SECOND GOD   A little moderation, dear colleague!

FIRST GOD [*Plaintively.*]   What's the good of moderation now? If she can't be found, we'll have to resign! The world is a terrible place! Nothing but misery, vulgarity, and waste! Even the countryside isn't what it used to be. The trees are getting their heads chopped off by telephone wires, and there's such a noise from all the gunfire, and I can't stand those heavy clouds of smoke, and—

THIRD GOD   The place is absolutely unlivable! Good intentions bring people to the brink of the abyss, and good deeds push them over the edge. I'm afraid our book of rules is destined for the scrap heap—

SECOND GOD   It's people! They're a worthless lot!

THIRD GOD   The world is too cold!

SECOND GOD   It's people! They're too weak!

FIRST GOD   Dignity, dear colleagues, dignity! Never despair! As for this world, didn't we agree that we only have to find one human being who can stand the place? Well, we found her. True, we lost her again. We must find her again, that's all! And at once!

[*They disappear.*]

10

Courtroom. Groups: SHU FU *and* MRS. MI TZU; YANG SUN *and* MRS. YANG; WONG, *the* CARPENTER, *the* GRANDFATHER, *the* NIECE, *the* OLD MAN, *the* OLD WOMAN; MRS. SHIN, *the* POLICEMAN; *the* UNEMPLOYED MAN, *the* SISTER-IN-LAW.

OLD MAN   So much power isn't good for one man.

UNEMPLOYED MAN   And he's going to open twelve super tobacco markets!

WIFE   One of the judges is a friend of Mr. Shu Fu's.

SISTER-IN-LAW   Another one accepted a present from Mr. Shui Ta only last night. A great fat goose.

OLD WOMAN [*To* WONG]   And Shen Te is nowhere to be found.

WONG   Only the gods will ever know the truth.

POLICEMAN   Order in the court! My lords the judges!

[*Enter the* THREE GODS *in judges' robes. We overhear their conversation as they pass along the footlights to their bench.*]

THIRD GOD   We'll never get away with it, our certificates were so badly forged.

SECOND GOD   My predecessor's "sudden indigestion" will certainly cause comment.

FIRST GOD   But he *had* just eaten a whole goose.

UNEMPLOYED MAN   Look at that! *New* judges.

WONG   New judges. And what good ones!

> [*The* THIRD GOD *hears this, and turns to smile at* WONG. *The* GODS *sit. The* FIRST GOD *beats on the bench with his gavel. The* POLICE-MAN *brings in* SHUI TA, *who walks with lordly steps. He is whistled[5] at.*]

POLICEMAN [*To* SHUI TA.]   Be prepared for a surprise. The judges have been changed.

> [SHUI TA *turns quickly round, looks at them, and staggers.*]

NIECE   What's the matter now?

WIFE   The great Tobacco King nearly fainted.

HUSBAND   Yes, as soon as he saw the new judges.

WONG   Does *he* know who they are?

> [SHUI TA *picks himself up, and the proceedings open.*]

FIRST GOD   Defendant Shui Ta, you are accused of doing away with your cousin Shen Te in order to take possession of her business. Do you plead guilty or not guilty?

SHUI TA   Not guilty, my lord.

FIRST GOD [*Thumbing through the documents of the case.*]   The first witness is the policeman. I shall ask him to tell us something of the respective reputations of Miss Shen Te and Mr. Shui Ta.

POLICEMAN   Miss Shen Te was a young lady who aimed to please, my lord. She liked to live and let live, as the saying goes. Mr. Shui Ta, on the other hand, is a man of principle. Though the generosity of Miss Shen Te forced him at times to abandon half measures, unlike the girl he was always on the side of the law, my lord. One time, he even unmasked a gang of thieves to whom his too trustful cousin had given shelter. The evidence, in short, my lord, proves that Mr. Shui Ta was *incapable* of the crime of which he stands accused!

FIRST GOD   I see. And are there others who could testify along, shall we say, the same lines?

> [SHU FU *rises.*]

POLICEMAN [*Whispering to* GODS.]   Mr. Shu Fu—a very important person.

FIRST GOD [*Inviting him to speak.*]   Mr. Shu Fu!

SHU FU   Mr. Shui Ta is a businessman, my lord. Need I say more?

FIRST GOD   Yes.

SHU FU   Very well, I will. He is Vice President of the Council of Commerce and is about to be elected a Justice of the Peace. [*He returns to his seat.* MRS. MI TZU *rises.*]

WONG   Elected! *He* gave him the job!

> [*With a gesture the* FIRST GOD *asks who* MRS. MI TZU *is.*]

POLICEMAN   Another very important person. Mrs. Mi Tzu.

FIRST GOD [*Inviting her to speak.*]   Mrs. Mi Tzu!

MRS. MI TZU   My lord, as Chairman of the Committee on Social Work, I wish to call attention to just a couple of eloquent facts: Mr. Shui Ta not only has erected a model factory with model housing in our city, he is a regular contributor to our home for the disabled. [*She returns to her seat.*]

---

5. Hissed.

POLICEMAN [*Whispering.*]   And she's a great friend of the judge that ate the goose!

FIRST GOD [*To the* POLICEMAN.]   Oh, thank you. What next? [*To the Court, genially.*] Oh, yes. We should find out if any of the evidence is less favorable to the defendant.

[WONG, *the* CARPENTER, *the* OLD MAN, *the* OLD WOMAN, *the* UNEMPLOYED MAN, *the* SISTER-IN-LAW, *and the* NIECE *come forward.*]

POLICEMAN [*Whispering.*]   Just the riffraff, my lord.

FIRST GOD [*Addressing the "riffraff."*]   Well, um, riffraff—do you know anything of the defendant, Mr. Shui Ta?

WONG   Too much, my lord.

UNEMPLOYED MAN   What don't we know, my lord.

CARPENTER   He ruined us.

SISTER-IN-LAW   He's a cheat.

NIECE   Liar.

WIFE   Thief.

BOY   Blackmailer.

BROTHER   Murderer.

FIRST GOD   Thank you. We should now let the defendant state his point of view.

SHUI TA   I only came on the scene when Shen Te was in danger of losing what I had understood was a gift from the gods. Because I did the filthy jobs which someone had to do, they hate me. My activities were restricted to the minimum, my lord.

SISTER-IN-LAW   He had us arrested!

SHUI TA   Certainly. You stole from the bakery!

SISTER-IN-LAW   Such concern for the bakery! You didn't want the shop for yourself, I suppose!

SHUI TA   I didn't want the shop overrun with parasites.

SISTER-IN-LAW   We had nowhere else to go.

SHUI TA   There were too many of you.

WONG   What about this old couple: Were *they* parasites?

OLD MAN   We lost our shop because of you!

OLD WOMAN   And we gave your cousin money!

SHUI TA   My cousin's fiancé was a flyer. The money had to go to *him*.

WONG   Did you care whether he flew or not? Did you care whether she married him or not? You wanted her to marry someone else! [*He points to* SHU FU.]

SHUI TA   The flyer unexpectedly turned out to be a scoundrel.

YANG SUN [*Jumping up.*]   Which was the reason you made him your manager?

SHUI TA   Later on he improved.

WONG   And when he improved, you sold him to her? [*He points out* MRS. MI TZU.]

SHUI TA   She wouldn't let me have her premises unless she had him to stroke her knees!

MRS. MI TZU   What? The man's a pathological liar. [*To him.*] Don't mention my property to me as long as you live! Murderer! [*She rustles off, in high dudgeon.*]

YANG SUN [*Pushing in.*]   My lord, I wish to speak for the defendant.

SISTER-IN-LAW   Naturally. He's your employer.

UNEMPLOYED MAN   And the worst slave driver in the country.

MRS. YANG   That's a lie! My lord, Mr. Shui Ta is a great man. He . . .

YANG SUN   He's this and he's that, but he is not a murderer, my lord. Just fifteen minutes before his arrest I heard Shen Te's voice in his own back room.

FIRST GOD   Oh? Tell us more!

YANG SUN   I heard sobbing, my lord!

FIRST GOD   But lots of women sob, we've been finding.

YANG SUN   Could I fail to recognize her voice?

SHU FU   No, you made her sob so often yourself, young man!

YANG SUN   Yes. But I also made her happy. Till he [*Pointing at* SHUI TA.] decided to sell her to you!

SHUI TA   Because you didn't love her.

WONG   Oh, no: it was for the money, my lord!

SHUI TA   And what was the money for, my lord? For the poor! And for Shen Te so she could go on being good!

WONG   For the poor? That he sent to his sweatshops? And why didn't you let Shen Te be good when you signed the big check?

SHUI TA   For the child's sake, my lord.

CARPENTER   What about *my* children? What did he do about them? [SHUI TA *is silent.*]

WONG   The shop was to be a fountain of goodness. That was the gods' idea. You came and spoiled it!

SHUI TA   If I hadn't, it would have run dry!

MRS. SHIN   There's a lot in that, my lord.

WONG   What have you done with the good Shen Te, bad man? She *was* good, my lords, she was, I swear it! [*He raises his hand in an oath.*]

THIRD GOD   What's happened to your hand, water seller?

WONG [*Pointing to* SHUI TA.]   It's all his fault, my lord, *she* was going to send me to a doctor— [*To* SHUI TA.] You were her worst enemy!

SHUI TA   I was her only friend!

WONG   Where is she then? Tell us where your good friend is! [*The excitement of this exchange has run through the whole crowd.*]

ALL   Yes, where is she? Where is Shen Te? [*Etc.*]

SHUI TA   Shen Te . . . had to go.

WONG   Where? Where to?

SHUI TA   I cannot tell you! I cannot tell you!

ALL   Why? Why did she have to go away? [*Etc.*]

WONG [*Into the din with the first words, but talking on beyond the others.*]   Why not, why not? Why did she have to go away?

SHUI TA [*Shouting.*]   Because you'd all have torn her to shreds, that's why! My lords, I have a request. Clear the court! When only the judges remain, I will make a confession.

ALL [*Except* WONG, *who is silent, struck by the new turn of events.*]   So he's guilty? He's confessing! [*Etc.*]

FIRST GOD [*Using the gavel.*]   Clear the court!

POLICEMAN   Clear the court!

WONG   Mr. Shui Ta has met his match this time.

MRS. SHIN [*With a gesture toward the judges.*]   You're in for a little surprise.

> [*The court is cleared. Silence.*]

SHUI TA   Illustrious ones!

> [*The* GODS *look at each other, not quite believing their ears.*]

SHUI TA   Yes, I recognize you!

SECOND GOD [*Taking matters in hand, sternly.*]   What have you done with our good woman of Setzuan?

SHUI TA   I have a terrible confession to make: I am she! [*He takes off his mask, and tears away his clothes.* SHEN TE *stands there.*]

SECOND GOD   Shen Te!

SHEN TE   Shen Te, yes. Shui Ta *and* Shen Te. Both.

> Your injunction
> To be good and yet to live
> Was a thunderbolt:
> It has torn me in two
> I can't tell how it was
> But to be good to others
> And myself at the same time
> I could not do it
> Your world is not an easy one, illustrious ones!
> When we extend our hand to a beggar, he tears it off for us
> When we help the lost, we are lost ourselves
> And so
> Since not to eat is to die
> Who can long refuse to be bad?
> As I lay prostrate beneath the weight of good intentions
> Ruin stared me in the face
> It was when I was unjust that I ate good meat
> And hobnobbed with the mighty
> Why?
> Why are bad deeds rewarded?
> Good ones punished?
> I enjoyed giving
> I truly wished to be the Angel of the Slums
> But washed by a foster-mother in the water of the gutter
> I developed a sharp eye
> The time came when pity was a thorn in my side
> And, later, when kind words turned to ashes in my mouth
> And anger took over
> I became a wolf
> Find me guilty, then, illustrious ones,
> But know:
> All that I have done I did
> To help my neighbor
> To love my lover
> And to keep my little one from want
> For your great, godly deeds, I was too poor, too small.

[*Pause.*]

FIRST GOD [*Shocked.*]   Don't go on making yourself miserable, Shen Te!
    We're overjoyed to have found you!
SHEN TE   I'm telling you I'm the bad man who committed all those crimes!
FIRST GOD [*Using—or failing to use—his ear trumpet.*]   The good woman
    who did all those good deeds?
SHEN TE   Yes, but the bad man too!
FIRST GOD [*As if something had dawned.*]   Unfortunate coincidences!
    Heartless neighbors!
THIRD GOD [*Shouting in his ear.*]   But how is she to continue?
FIRST GOD   Continue? Well, she's a strong, healthy girl . . .
SECOND GOD   You didn't hear what she said!
FIRST GOD   I heard every word! She is confused, that's all! [*He begins to
    bluster.*] And what about this book of rules—we can't renounce our rules,
    can we? [*More quietly.*] Should the world be changed? How? By whom?
    The world should *not* be changed! [*At a sign from him, the lights turn
    pink, and music plays.*]
            And now the hour of parting is at hand.
            Dost thou behold, Shen Te, yon fleecy cloud?
            It is our chariot. At a sign from me
            'Twill come and take us back from whence we came
            Above the azure vault and silver stars. . . .
SHEN TE   No! Don't go, illustrious ones!
FIRST GOD
            Our cloud has landed now in yonder field
            From which it will transport us back to heaven.
            Farewell, Shen Te, let not thy courage fail thee. . . .
        [*Exeunt* GODS.]
SHEN TE   What about the old couple? They've lost their shop! What about
    the water seller and his hand? And I've got to defend myself against the
    barber, because I don't love him! And against Sun, because I do love him!
    How? How?
        [*Shen Te's eyes follow the* GODS *as they are imagined to step into a
        cloud, which rises and moves forward over the orchestra and up
        beyond the balcony.*]
FIRST GOD [*From on high.*]   We have faith in you, Shen Te!
SHEN TE   There'll be a child. And he'll have to be fed. I can't stay here.
    Where shall I go?
FIRST GOD   Continue to be good, good woman of Setzuan!
SHEN TE   I need my bad cousin!
FIRST GOD   But not very often!
SHEN TE   Once a week at least!
FIRST GOD   Once a month will be quite enough!
SHEN TE [*Shrieking.*]   No, no! Help!
        [*But the cloud continues to recede as the* GODS *sing.*]

VALEDICTORY HYMN

What rapture, oh, it is to know
    A good thing when you see it
And having seen a good thing, oh,
    What rapture 'tis to flee it

Be good, sweet maid of Setzuan
Let Shui Ta be clever
Departing, we forget the man
Remember your endeavor

Because through all the length of days
Her goodness faileth never
Sing hallelujah! Make Shen Te's
Good name live on forever!

SHEN TE   Help!

Epilogue

You're thinking, aren't you, that this is no right
Conclusion to the play you've seen tonight?
After a tale, exotic, fabulous,
A nasty ending was slipped up on us.
We feel deflated too. We too are nettled
To see the curtain down and nothing settled.
How could a better ending be arranged?
Could one change people? Can the world be changed?
Would new gods do the trick? Will atheism?
Moral rearmament? Materialism?
It is for you to find a way, my friends,
To help good men arrive at happy ends.
You write the happy ending to the play!
There must, there must, there's got to be a way!

FEDERICO GARCÍA LORCA
1898–1936

Although he died young, the poet and playwright Federico García Lorca is the best-known writer of modern Spain and perhaps the most famous Spanish writer since Cervantes. A member of the brilliant "Generation of 1927" (along with Jorgé Guillen, Vicente Aleixandre, Pedro Salinas, and Rafael Alberti), known for the striking imagery and lyric musicality of his work, Lorca is both classical and modern, traditional and innovative, difficult and popular, a voice combining regional and universal themes. The poetry and plays that began as (and always were) personal statements took on larger significance first as the expression of tragic conflicts in Spanish culture and then as poignant laments for humanity—seen especially in the plight of those who are deprived, by society or simply by death, of the fulfillment that could have been theirs. When Lorca was dragged from a friend's house and executed by a Fascist squad on August 19, 1936, his murder outraged the whole European and American literary and artistic community and seemed to symbolize in addition the mindless destruction of humane and cultural values that loomed with the approach of World War II.

Lorca (despite the Spanish practice of using both paternal and maternal last names—correctly "García Lorca"—the author is generally called "Lorca") was born on June 5, 1898, in the small village of Fuentevaqueros, near the Andalusian city of Granada. His father was a prosperous farmer, and his mother, who had been a school-teacher, encouraged him to read widely and develop his musical talent. The composer Manuel de Falla befriended the young musician, who became an expert pianist and guitar player. Lorca began law studies at the University of Granada, where—after several years' absence—he received a degree in 1923. He published a book called *Impressions and Landscapes* (1918) after a trip through Spain but left Granada in 1919 for Madrid, where he entered the Residencia de Estudiantes, a modern college established to provide a cosmopolitan education for Spanish youth. Madrid was not only the capital of Spain but also the center of intellectual and artistic ferment, and the Residencia attracted many of those who would become the most influential writers and artists of their generation (among the latter the artist Salvador Dalí and the film director Luis Buñuel). Lorca soon gained the reputation of a rising young poet from poetry readings and the publication of a few poems in magazines, even before the appearance of his first collection of verse, the *Book of Poems* of 1921. Although he lived at the Residencia almost continuously until 1928, he never seriously pursued a degree but spent his time reading, writing, improvising music and poetry in company with his friends, and producing his first plays.

In these early years, before his departure for New York in 1929, Lorca concentrated on writing poetry, although he was clearly interested in the theater as well. *The Butterfly's Evil Spell* (1920), a fantasy about a cockroach that is hopelessly enchanted by the beauty of a butterfly, was staged in Barcelona; in 1923 Lorca wrote, designed sets for, and directed a puppet play on a theme from Andalusian folklore, *The Girl Who Waters the Sweet Basil Flower and the Inquisitive Prince*, for which de Falla himself arranged the music. Yet the major achievement of this period is the composition of several books of poetry, not all of which were published at the time: the *Book of Poems*; most of the *Songs* (1927); early versions of the poems in the *Poem of the Deep Song*, which was not published as a book until 1931, although several poems were recited at a 1922 Andalusian festival; and the *Gypsy Ballads* (1928), which was an immediate popular success.

The first collection, the *Book of Poems*, introduces themes that will become familiar in later works: death, an innocent or childlike point of view, a closeness to nature that takes the form of animal fables or symbolic meanings attached to images like the pomegranate ("the idea of blood enclosed / In a hard and bitter globe"), and overall a certain witty or ironic distance from the situations he describes. The playful tone never quite covers Lorca's constant preoccupation with death, however: death as the common fate that shadows our most vivid experiences. Speaking to a chorus of questioning children in *The Ballad of the Little Square*, the poet answers that he feels in his mouth only "the savor of the bones / of my great skull."

The *Poem of the Deep Song* marked a return to the gypsy themes and ballads of Lorca's home province of Andalusia, a region known for its mixture of Arab and Spanish culture and for a tradition of wandering gypsy singers who improvised, to guitar accompaniment, rhythmic laments on themes of love and death. The *cante jondo* ("deep song") was an ancient Andalusian ballad form that centered on repeated notes or phrases, and Lorca took full advantage (as he would in the *Lament for Ignacio Sánchez Mejías*) of the haunting quality that could be obtained through this obsessive refrain. The *Songs* written subsequently are noted for their lyricism and for the moments of experience they capture; however, many reach beyond the sensuously precise description of real objects to encompass abstract concepts, psychological states, and clusters of associations—as does the Symbolist poetry Lorca knew. Lorca describes how "the ear of grain keeps intact / its hard yellow laughter," how a little mute boy looks for his voice in a drop of water, and how Narcissus (both youth and flower) is mirrored in a double image in which "over your white eyes flicker / shadows and sleeping fish."

Lorca's next collection, the *Gypsy Ballads*, marks the beginning of his mature verse. Blending classical ballad form with scenes taken directly from contemporary life, the poet expresses, with images of violence and eroticism, the tragic struggle in which innocence, spontaneity, creativity, and freedom are repressed by society and by the inevitable limitations of human nature. In the famous *Ballad of the Spanish Civil Guard,* the militia with their "patent-leather souls" and heads filled with "a vague astronomy / of shapeless pistols" cut down the gypsies in their fantastic city with its banners and "cinnamon towers." The unsuspecting populace, caught in the midst of their festival, are helpless to prevent absolute destruction—the tile roofs become "furrows in the soil," and the burned city itself persists only in the sterile "play of moon and sand" on the poet's brow. A hostile, violent world is pictured here, in which even the wind pursues a young girl with lustful breath and "hot sword," and St. Eulalia's martyrdom and mutilation are described with a mixture of eroticism and horror. These themes are not restricted to poetry: they reoccur in a contemporary play, *Mariana Pineda* (1928), in which Lorca's heroine is executed for refusing to identify a group of revolutionaries (among them the lover who abandoned her).

Impelled by an emotional crisis, Lorca left Spain for New York in 1929 and there wrote a series of poems later published as *Poet in New York* (1940). The collection does not focus exclusively on the city, however, and moves from the poet's youth in Europe to scenes of rural New York and northern Vermont as Lorca tries to come to terms with his own complex personality against a background of psychological, artistic, and social tensions. Blended with the familiar theme of doomed love and death is a tentative exploration of homosexuality, which Lorca could not admit to inside traditional Spanish society and which he expressed only with hesitation and anxiety in this and later works. A large part of the ten-section *Poet in New York* does, however, focus primarily on the city, which is seen as a frightening symbol of the modern industrial West. In a richly varied and densely metaphorical apocalyptic vision, Lorca juxtaposes two ways of life and creates a vision of contrast that, he said, "puts my poetic world in contact with the poetic world of New York." Beginning with a denunciation of the dehumanized commercial city-world of sterile concrete and glass, he moves on to celebrate the only area where the natural world survives: Harlem, with its "garnet violence deaf and dumb in the shadows," and its "great king a prisoner in a janitor's uniform." In the face of this universal despair there are foreshadowings of a coming upheaval when "the Stock Market will be a pyramid of moss" and the oppressed and deprived will unite to proclaim "the reign of the ear of corn." The book's ending sections mark an escape from New York to Havana and (in spite of a continued sense of alienation) to the dancelike harmony of a more primitive life.

From 1930 to his death in 1936, Lorca was extremely active in the theater both as writer and as director (after 1931) of a traveling theatrical group (La Barraca) subsidized by the Spanish Republic. After a series of farces that mixed romantically tragic and comic themes, he presented the tragedies for which he is best known: *Blood Wedding* (1933) and *Yerma* (1934). In 1936 he wrote the posthumously published *The House of Bernarda Alba* (1945). All Lorca's theater, from the early fantasy of *The Butterfly's Evil Spell* to the puppet plays, farces, and last tragedies, rejects the conventionally realistic nineteenth-century drama and employs an openly poetic form that suggests musical patterns, includes choruses, songs, and stylized movement, and may even (as in the fragmentary surrealist drama, *The Audience*) attack the audience itself. The tragic themes of Lorca's poetry emerge here in dramatic form, usually centering on the suffering of individual women whose instinctual fulfillment (through love or children) is denied by fate or social circumstance. In *Blood Wedding,* the Mother's last remaining son dies in a moonlit struggle with Leonardo, who has run away with the son's bride (Leonardo's former betrothed) on their wedding day. Leonardo (who also dies) is a member of the family that has killed the Mother's husband and other sons, and images of approaching death and sensual, frustrated love permeate the whole play. In *Yerma* (the title name also means desert or sterility), the heroine is caught between her own passionate, sensual nature, yearning to love and bear children, and the need—for honor's sake—to remain with a husband who cares only for a well-regulated house. When Yerma realizes the extent of Juan's spiritual as well as sexual sterility, she strangles him and (because she will not remarry) simultaneously kills her only chance to fulfill her natural instincts through bearing children. *The House of Bernarda Alba* (subtitled "A Drama About Women in the Villages of Spain") revolves around the same themes of sterility and frustrated love, as the repressed spinster daughters of the stern matriarch Bernarda Alba (and even the mad grandmother) reveal their common desire to marry a young man. Bernarda, however, upholds the proprieties that hedge in Spanish society; she refuses to let her daughters have visitors, ignores their rivalry over young Pepe el Romano (engaged to the wealthy oldest daughter, Angustias), recommends a painful death for an unwed mother being dragged through the streets, and—when the youngest daughter, Adela, commits suicide over Pepe, who has become her lover—seems chiefly concerned that Adela's body be dressed "as though she were a virgin." The conflict between social custom and individual need takes on mythic proportions in *The House of Bernarda Alba*, where only women appear on a stage that is strangely quarantined and painted white, and where the disturbing male principle represented by Pepe el Romano is reiterated by the noise of a stallion's hooves banging against stable walls.

In 1936, the year of his death, Lorca was revising a series of short lyric poems based on the Arabic forms of *casida* and the *gacela,* a collection eventually published in 1940 as *The Divan at Tamarit* (a "divan" is a poetic collection, and Lorca wrote the poems at a country house called after the ancient place-name of Tamarit). In the previous year, he had published a long elegiac poem on the death of his good friend, the famous bullfighter Ignacio Sánchez Mejías, who had been fatally gored by a bull on August 11, 1934, in Manzanares and died two days later in Madrid. Sánchez Mejías was a cultured man, well-known in literary circles and himself the author of a play, and Lorca's *Lament for Ignacio Sánchez Mejías* celebrates both his friend and the value of human grace and courage in a world where everything ends in death.

Lorca's *Lament* is not only cast as an elegy (a medium-length poem that mourns a death), but also recalls one of the most famous poems of Spanish literature: the *Verses on the Death of His Father* written by the medieval poet Jorge Manrique (1440–1479). Manrique's catalog of his father's noble qualities ("What a friend to his friends!") and his description of individual lives as flowing into the sea of death are echoed by passages in the modern elegy. Yet there is a fundamental difference between the two: while Manrique's elegy stresses religious themes and the prospect of eternal life, Lorca—in grim contrast—rejects such consolation and insists that his friend's death is permanent.

The four parts of the *Lament* incorporate a variety of forms and perspectives, all working together to suggest a progression from the report of death in the precise first line—"At five in the afternoon"—to the end where the dead man's nobility and elegance survive in "a sad breeze through the olive trees." The "deep song" technique of an insistent refrain coloring the whole organizes the first section, *Cogida* [the bull's toss] *and Death*, with its throbbing return to the moment of death. The scene in the arena wavers between an objective report—the boy with the shroud, the coffin on wheels—and the shared agony of the bull's bellowing and wounds burning like suns. Lorca moves in the next ballad section to a personal refusal of Sánchez Mejías's death ("I will not see it!") and a request that images of whiteness cover up this spilled blood; instead, he imagines Ignacio climbing steps to seek dawn and a mystic meeting with his true self but encountering, bewildered, only his broken body. After a tribute to his princely friend, the poet finally admits what he cannot force himself to see: the finality of physical dissolution as moss and grass invade the buried bullfighter's skull.

In *The Laid Out Body,* a series of somber quatrains in regular meter recognizes the inevitability of death and dissolution (Ignacio's "pure shape which had nightingales" is now "filled with depthless holes"), and the fact that the bullfighter will be entombed in unyielding, lifeless stone. In this and the final section, with its rhythmic free verse, Lorca accepts physical death ("even the sea dies!") but preserves, in his poetry, a vision of his noble countryman that surpasses such obliteration. For those who exist only on the unthinking, physical level (the bull, fig tree, household ants, the black satin of his funeral suit), Ignacio has indeed "died for ever." Yet human beings recognize other qualities beyond the physical and in fact shape their estimate of an individual according to these qualities. In life, Sánchez Mejías was known to his friends for "the signal maturity of your understanding . . . your appetite for death and the taste of its mouth." These qualities survive, for a while, in memory. Lorca, echoing the pride with which the Latin poet Horace claimed to perpetuate his subjects in a "monument of lasting bronze," sings of his friend "for posterity" and captures the life and death of Sánchez Mejías in his *Lament*.

Ian Gibson, *Federico García Lorca: A Life* (1989), is an extensive and detailed biography. Carl W. Cobb, *Federico García Lorca* (1967), is a good general biography. Candelas Newton, *Understanding Federico García Lorca* (1995), is a brief general discussion of the work; E. Honig, *García Lorca* (1980), provides a critical introduction in literary historical context; and C. B. Morris, *Son of Andalusia: The Lyrical Landscapes of Federico García Lorca* (1997), offers a more specialized view, with illustrations. Manuel Durán, ed., *Lorca: A Collection of Critical Essays* (1962), is a valuable collection of essays on the poet and his work (mainly the poetry). Manuel Durán and Francesca Colecchia, eds., *Lorca's Legacy* (1991), offer a range of essays and a recent bibliography.

Lament for Ignacio Sánchez Mejías[1]

1. Cogida[2] and Death

At five in the afternoon.
It was exactly five in the afternoon.
A boy brought the white sheet
at five in the afternoon.
A frail of lime[3] ready prepared   5
at five in the afternoon.
The rest was death, and death alone
at five in the afternoon.

The wind carried away the cottonwool[4]
at five in the afternoon.   10
And the oxide scattered crystal and nickel
at five in the afternoon.
Now the dove and the leopard[5] wrestle
at five in the afternoon.
And a thigh with a desolate horn   15
at five in the afternoon.
The bass-string struck up
at five in the afternoon.

---

1. Translated by Stephen Spender and J. L. Gili.   **2.** Harvesting (Spanish, literal trans.); the toss when the bull catches the bullfighter.   **3.** A disinfectant that was sprinkled on the body after death. *Frail:* a basket.   **4.** To stop the blood; the beginning of a series of medicinal, chemical, and inhuman images that emphasize the presence of death.   **5.** Traditional symbols for peace and violence; they wrestle with one another as the bullfighter's thigh struggles with the bull's horn.

Arsenic bells[6] and smoke
at five in the afternoon.
Groups of silence in the corners   20
at five in the afternoon.
And the bull alone with a high heart!
At five in the afternoon.
When the sweat of snow was coming   25
at five in the afternoon,
when the bull ring was covered in iodine
at five in the afternoon,
death laid eggs in the wound
at five in the afternoon.   30
At five in the afternoon.
Exactly at five o'clock in the afternoon.

A coffin on wheels is his bed
at five in the afternoon.
Bones and flutes resound in his ears[7]   35
at five in the afternoon.
Now the bull was bellowing through his forehead
at five in the afternoon.
The room[8] was iridescent with agony
at five in the afternoon.   40
In the distance the gangrene now comes
at five in the afternoon.
Horn of the lily through green[9] groins
at five in the afternoon.
The wounds were burning like suns   45
at five in the afternoon,
and the crowd was breaking the windows[1]
at five in the afternoon.
At five in the afternoon.
Ah, that fatal five in the afternoon!   50
It was five by all the clocks!
It was five in the shade of the afternoon!

2. *The Spilled Blood*

I will not see it!

Tell the moon to come
for I do not want to see the blood   55
of Ignacio on the sand.
I will not see it!

The moon wide open.
Horse of still clouds,
and the grey bull ring of dreams   60

---

6. Bells are rung to announce a death. The *bass-string* of the guitar strums a lament.   7. A suggestion
of the medieval dance of death.   8. The room adjoining the arena where wounded bullfighters are taken
for treatment.   9. Gangrene turns flesh a greenish color. *Lily:* the shape of the wound resembles this
flower.   1. A Spanish idiom for the crowd's loud roar.

with willows in the barreras.[2]
I will not see it!

Let my memory kindle![3]
Warn the jasmines[4]
of such minute whiteness!
I will not see it!

The cow of the ancient world
passed her sad tongue
over a snout of blood
spilled on the sand,
and the bulls of Guisando,[5]
partly death and partly stone,
bellowed like two centuries
sated with treading the earth.
No.
I do not want to see it!
I will not see it!

Ignacio goes up the tiers[6]
with all his death on his shoulders.
He sought for the dawn
but the dawn was no more.   80
He seeks for his confident profile
and the dream bewilders him.
He sought for his beautiful body
and encountered his opened blood.   85
Do not ask me to see it!
I do not want to hear it spurt
each time with less strength:
that spurt that illuminates
the tiers of seats, and spills   90
over the corduroy and the leather
of a thirsty multitude.
Who shouts that I should come near!
Do not ask me to see it!

His eyes did not close   95
when he saw the horns near,
but the terrible mothers
lifted their heads.[7]
And across the ranches,[8]
an air of secret voices rose,   100
shouting to celestial bulls,
herdsmen of pale mist.

65

70

75

2. The barriers around the ring within which the fight takes place and over which a fighter may escape the bull's charge. *Willows:* symbols of mourning.   3. My memory burns within me (literal trans.).   4. The poet calls on (*warn* as "notify") the small white jasmine flowers to come and cover the blood.   5. Carved stone bulls from the Celtic past, a tourist attraction in the province of Madrid.   6. An imaginary scene in which the bullfighter mounts the stairs of the arena.   7. The three Fates traditionally raised their heads when the thread of life was cut.   8. Fighting bulls are raised on the ranches of Lorca's home province of Andalusia.

There was no prince in Seville[9]
who could compare with him,
nor sword like his sword
nor heart so true.   105
Like a river of lions
was his marvellous strength,
and like a marble torso
his firm drawn moderation.
The air of Andalusian Rome   110
gilded his head[1]
where his smile was a spikenard[2]
of wit and intelligence.
What a great torero[3] in the ring!   115
What a good peasant in the sierra![4]
How gentle with the sheaves!
How hard with the spurs!
How tender with the dew!
How dazzling in the fiesta!   120
How tremendous with the final
banderillas[5] of darkness!

But now he sleeps without end.
Now the moss and the grass
open with sure fingers   125
the flower of his skull.
And now his blood comes out singing;
singing along marshes and meadows,
sliding on frozen horns,
faltering soulless in the mist,   130
stumbling over a thousand hoofs
like a long, dark, sad tongue,
to form a pool of agony
close to the starry Guadalquivir.[6]
Oh, white wall of Spain!   135
Oh, black bull of sorrow!
Oh, hard blood of Ignacio!
Oh, nightingale of his veins!
No.
I will not see it!   140
No chalice can contain it,
no swallows[7] can drink it,
no frost of light can cool it,
nor song nor deluge of white lilies,
no glass can cover it with silver.   145
No.
I will not see it!

---

9. Leading city of Andalusia.   1. The image suggests a statue from Roman times, when Andalusia was part of the Roman Empire.   2. A small, white, fragrant flower common in Andalusia; by extension, the bullfighter's white teeth.   3. Bullfighter.   4. Mountainous country. Sánchez Mejías is seen as a good *serrano* or "man of the hills."   5. The multicolored short spears that are thrust in the bull's shoulders to provoke him to attack.   6. A great river that passes through all the major cities of Andalusia. The singing stream of the bullfighter's blood suggests both the river and a nightingale.   7. According to a Spanish legend of the Crucifixion, swallows—a symbol of innocence—drank the blood of Christ on the Cross. The poet is seeking ways of concealing the dead man's blood.

3. *The Laid Out Body*[8]

Stone is a forehead where dreams grieve
without curving waters and frozen cypresses.
Stone is a shoulder on which to bear Time   150
with trees formed of tears and ribbons and planets.[9]

I have seen grey showers move towards the waves
raising their tender riddled arms,
to avoid being caught by the lying stone
which loosens their limbs without soaking the blood.   155

For stone gathers seed and clouds,
skeleton larks and wolves of penumbra:
but yields not sounds nor crystals nor fire,
only bull rings and bull rings and more bull rings without walls.

Now Ignacio the well born lies on the stone.   160
All is finished. What is happening? Contemplate his face:
death has covered him with pale sulphur
and has placed on him the head of a dark minotaur.[1]

All is finished. The rain penetrates his mouth.
The air, as if mad, leaves his sunken chest,   165
and Love, soaked through with tears of snow,
warms itself on the peak of the herd.[2]

What are they saying? A stenching silence settles down.
We are here with a body laid out which fades away,
with a pure shape which had nightingales   170
and we see it being filled with depthless holes.

Who creases the shroud? What he says is not true![3]
Nobody sings here, nobody weeps in the corner,
nobody pricks the spurs, nor terrifies the serpent.
Here I want nothing else but the round eyes   175
to see this body without a chance of rest.

Here I want to see those men of hard voice.
Those that break horses and dominate rivers;
those men of sonorous skeleton who sing
with a mouth full of sun and flint.   180

Here I want to see them. Before the stone.
Before this body with broken reins.
I want to know from them the way out
for this captain strapped down by death.

---

8. Present body (literal trans.); the Spanish expression for a funeral wake, when the body is laid out for
public mourning. The title contrasts with that of the next section: *Absent Soul.*   9. Traditional funeral
imagery carved on gravestones.   1. A monster from Greek myth: half man, half bull.   2. Of the ranch
(literal trans.).   3. Lorca criticizes the conventional pieties voiced by someone standing close to the
shrouded body; the poet prefers a clear-eyed, realistic view of death.

I want them to show me a lament like a river   185
which will have sweet mists and deep shores,
to take the body of Ignacio where it loses itself
without hearing the double panting of the bulls.

Loses itself in the round bull ring of the moon
which feigns in its youth a sad quiet bull: 190
loses itself in the night without song of fishes
and in the white thicket of frozen smoke.

I don't want them to cover his face with handkerchiefs
that he may get used to the death he carries.
Go, Ignacio; feel not the hot bellowing.   195
Sleep, fly, rest: even the sea dies!

4. Absent Soul

The bull does not know you, nor the fig tree,
nor the horses, nor the ants in your own house.
The child and the afternoon do not know you
because you have died for ever.   200

The back of the stone does not know you,
nor the black satin in which you crumble.
Your silent memory does not know you
because you have died for ever.

The autumn will come with small white snails,[4]   205
misty grapes and with clustered hills,
but no one will look into your eyes
because you have died for ever.

Because you have died for ever,
like all the death of the Earth,   210
like all the dead who are forgotten
in a heap of lifeless dogs.[5]

Nobody knows you. No. But I sing of you.
For posterity I sing of your profile and grace.
Of the signal maturity of your understanding.   215
Of your appetite for death and the taste of its mouth.
Of the sadness of your once valiant gaiety.

It will be a long time, if ever, before there is born
an Andalusian so true, so rich in adventure.
I sing of his elegance with words that groan,   220
and I remember a sad breeze through the olive trees.

---

4. Actually, conch shell–shaped horns; the shepherds' horns that sound in the hills each fall as the sheep are driven to new pastures.   5. Dogs as a (typically Continental) image for undignified, inferior creatures.

From Llanto por Ignacio Sánchez Mejías

4. *Alma Ausente*

No te conoce el toro ni la higuera,
ni caballos ni hormigas de tu casa.
No te conoce el niño ni la tarde
porque te has muerto para siempre.

No te conoce el lomo de la piedra,   5
ni el raso negro donde te destrozas.
No te conoce tu recuerdo mudo
porque te has muerto para siempre.

El otoño vendrá con caracolas,
uva de niebla y montes agrupados,   10
pero nadie querrá mirar tus ojos
porque te has muerto para siempre.

Porque te has muerto para siempre,
como todos los muertos de la Tierra,
como todos los muertos que se olvidan   15
en un montón de perros apagados.

No te conoce nadie. No. Pero yo te canto.
Yo canto para luego tu perfil y tu gracia.
La madurez insigne de tu conocimiento.
Tu apetencia de muerte y el gusto de su boca.   20
La tristeza que tuvo tu valiente alegría.

Tardará mucho tiempo en nacer, si es que nace,
un andaluz tan claro, tan rico de aventura.
Yo canto su elegancia con palabras que gimen
y recuerdo una brisa triste por los olivos.   25

TAWFIQ AL-HAKIM
1898–1989

Tawfiq al-Hakim is the master of a genre that he invented: Arabic literary drama.
From the mid-1930s, when he achieved renown as a playwright, until the late 1970s,
he was the premier dramatist of Egypt and of the Arab world. In the course of his
long career, he produced plays in a wide variety of styles, from dramatic pageant to
absurdist drama, and on themes drawn from the Egypt of the pharaohs, classical
Greece, the golden age of Islamic history, and the concerns of the moment. His plays
have been staged throughout the Arab world and, in translation, in the capitals of
Asia, Europe, and America. His great gift has been to give dramatic life to questions
of enduring interest and to shape a language for the stage that is flexible, idiomatic,
and vivid.

To understand the importance of al-Hakim's achievement one needs some knowledge of the nature of traditional Arabic and Middle Eastern literature and the place of drama and the theater within it. Until the modern era, Middle Eastern literature was sharply divided between formal and popular traditions in literary style, genre, and mode of performance. Formal poetry and prose were elegant, learned, richly rhetorical, and highly conventional in their themes. Their subject matter was governed by well-established conventions, and their genres had been fixed in the first few centuries of the classical era—roughly the seventh through thirteenth centuries. Drama was not a genre of classical literature. There were not only no great playwrights in Arabic, Persian or Turkish—there were none at all.

Popular literature found its audiences among the vast majority of the population that could neither read nor write. Its home was in the marketplace and the village square, not in the court or the centers of learning. For the most part, it was transmitted orally rather than in writing. What little we know about it is based on a few popular texts, such as the tales of *The Thousand and One Nights*, that were written down before the modern era. In contrast to formal literature, the essence of popular literature was performance, and its goal was entertainment, not edification. It often shared stories with classical works but cast them in popular language and adapted them to the tastes of ordinary people. Dramatic performance of various kinds seem to have been a familiar and long-standing element within it.

We know from the accounts of European travelers that in eighteenth-century Egypt both farces and puppet plays were widely popular, and elements of this public theatrical tradition may even have survived from pharaonic rituals. Moreover, in the mid-nineteenth century enterprising theatrical producers in Syria and Egypt translated European plays freely into colloquial Arabic and adapted them to local tastes and their own theatrical tradition. Molière, Racine, and Shakespeare, among many others, were introduced to Egyptian audiences this way, although in renderings so free that little of the original work survived. Later, some authors attempted to write or translate plays in formal Arabic to elevate drama to the level of literary art. Their efforts had unfortunate but predictable results. What was acceptable to the educated few put audiences to sleep, and what was popular in the theater was dismissed as burlesque by the arbiters of literary taste. So matters stood until the time of al-Hakim, who took on himself the task of creating a theatrical language that would bridge this gap.

Al-Hakim was born in Alexandria in 1898 to a conservative middle-class Egyptian family that was appalled by his early determination to pursue a literary career. At his father's insistence, he first studied law in Cairo and then went on to Paris to earn a doctorate of law degree. Literature, however, remained his principal interest. He almost failed to receive his law degree because he preferred to spend his time collaborating with a friend in writing musical comedies, and he spent his three years in Paris (1925–28) reading widely in French literature, associating with other writers, and going to the theater. There he made the wonderful discovery that in Europe plays were accepted as a respectable literary form. He returned to Cairo in 1928 without a doctorate, determined to be a writer.

Al-Hakim had begun publishing his work while still in his twenties, but this paid little. Since it was virtually impossible for him, or any other writer, to earn a living from the pen, he was obliged to pursue a parallel career. For a university graduate like himself, the obvious choice was government service, and he first took a job in the Ministry of Legal Affairs as a prosecutor in a village in the Nile delta—an experience he later used in his novel *Maze of Justice* (1937). He left the ministry for the Ministry of Education in 1934 and was subsequently director of social guidance in the Ministry of Social Affairs. He continued to write and publish throughout this period and enjoyed growing success and recognition of his work. In 1943 al-Hakim left government service to pursue writing full time. He also joined the staff of the newspaper *Akhbar al-Yawm* in 1943 and stayed there for eight years. In 1951 he was appointed director of the National Library, and in 1959 he returned to Paris as his country's permanent delegate to UNESCO. During the fall of that year he wrote *The Sultan's*

Dilemma. Later he was appointed a member of the Higher Council for Arts and Letters, and in 1961 he became a member of the board of directors of Egypt's most prestigious newspaper, *Al-Ahram,* a position he held until his retirement.

Al-Hakim is principally known as a dramatist, but he was a prolific writer who did not limit himself to a single form. In the more than fifty years of his productive life he wrote some seventy plays as well as short stories, novels, and several volumes of essays and of autobiography. His productivity was as great and varied as that of his illustrious contemporary, the novelist Naguib Mahfouz, and he helped to shape narrative prose and drama. His novel *The Return of the Spirit,* for example, initiated a vogue for setting novels in the pharaonic period.

The task that al-Hakim set for himself was to create a drama that was sufficiently formal in language and challenging in substance to be regarded as literature and yet close enough to the language of everyday life to be vital and engaging. Classical Arabic, the only language that was acceptable as a vehicle for serious literature, really had no colloquial form. In classical Arabic there was no history of dramatic literature. As for colloquial Arabic, it had many dialects but none that was as close to classical Arabic as spoken English is to even the most literary style of written English and none that was acceptable as a vehicle for literature. With no tradition of dramatic dialogue to draw on, al-Hakim was obliged to invent his own spoken classical language and, more generally, to create his own dramatic tradition from the materials available to him. On the one hand, there was the stuff of classical and popular Arabic literature—materials as varied as the Koran and *The Thousand and One Nights.* Although none of this literature was dramatic in form, it was a rich source of stories and characters, and it was immediately familiar to his audience. The challenge for him was to give these familiar materials dramatic shape, as he does in his play *Muhammad* (1936), in which the great events of the Prophet's life are brought to the stage in a vivid and moving pageant. In other works he responds to traditional materials even more creatively. In his *Shahrazad* (1934), he continues the story of *The Thousand and One Nights* from the point where Shahrazad leaves off, and he explores her marital life with the Shahrayar. He also drew on Egypt's pharaonic past for inspiration, as in his drama *Isis* (1955).

The other source that al-Hakim had available to him was the long and varied dramatic tradition of Europe. Arab dramatists, he argued, must build their craft on the European classics. It was foreign to Egypt and Islam, but it was the obvious school to which Arab dramatists must go, and he wrote eloquently of the need to make the classical Greek theatrical tradition their own. Al-Hakim believed strongly that some sort of synthesis of East and West was inevitable. However, it would not be enough simply to translate classical European drama, to adopt European classics as though they were their own. Rather, the works of the ancient Greek masters must be rethought and recast in the mold of Egyptian culture. In rewriting the classics, al-Hakim was, of course, following the example of modern European dramatists. But while their audiences could hold each new work up against the template of the original, for al-Hakim's audience his plays were completely independent works. And the focus of the transformations he made was not from classic to modern but from European to Middle Eastern. When he wrote his own *King Oedipus* (1949), for example, he made Tiresias the villain of the piece because, he said, as a Muslim and an Arab, he simply could not accept that the gods would inflict so cruel a fate on the heroic Oedipus.

In other works he attempted to combine Eastern and Western elements. In the preface to *The Wisdom of Solomon* (1943), a work in which he anticipates the looming conflict between technology and humane values, he gives a sense of this integration. "This story," he says, "is based on three books: the Koran, the Bible, and *A Thousand and One Nights.* I have followed the same procedure I used in the *Sleepers of Ephesus, Shahrazad,* and *Pygmalion,* and have made use of the old texts and ancient legends to create a picture in my mind . . . nothing more, nothing less." The incorporation of three such disparate works is emblematic of the synthesis he hoped to achieve.

The phrase "a picture in my mind . . . nothing more, nothing less" may seem puzzling at first because we are used to thinking of dramatic texts and dramatic performances as joined, but in Egypt this was and is far from the case. For many years the plays that al-Hakim wrote to create a new dramatic literature were rarely, if ever, performed. There were essentially two reasons for this. First, there was, initially, no audience of theater-goers who were used to watching modern plays that were serious in substance and contemporary in language and sensibility. Second, there were no trained actors. The players who performed in popular farces and burlesques had no formal training and were completely unready and unwilling to present serious drama seriously and in al-Hakim's version of classical Arabic. However, when he published his plays in book form or in newspapers (Egyptian newspapers often publish stories, novels, plays and poems), they found an increasingly appreciative audience. Moreover, once professional actors began to appear in Egypt in the late 1940s, his plays were performed there and in other parts of the Arab world with great success.

The enormous volume of al-Hakim's work, the many styles in which he wrote, and the great disparities between his best efforts and the rest of his work make any comprehensive evaluation all but impossible. Since he was trying to find a middle ground between an elevated poetic rhetoric and vulgar farce, those who criticize his work have tended to cluster around one pole or the other. Because of the moral seriousness with which he took his role as a writer and his love of philosophical questions, his plays often have a philosophical and discursive quality that led some critics to speak of him as an "ivory tower" playwright. Yet many of his plays are immersed in the problems of daily life. *Boss Kuduz's Building* (1948) is an ironic attack on war profiteers. *I Want to Kill* (1957) explores the breakdown of an apparently ideal marriage that has been challenged by the sudden intrusion of violence. While virtually all commentators find something to disagree with in al-Hakim's work, over and over one encounters the judgment that despite these failings, nothing should be allowed to detract from the tremendous status he has in contemporary Arabic letters.

The Sultan's Dilemma is often spoken of as al-Hakim's best work, and in it we see him at his most appealing. It is a comedy with a light touch and charming wit, but one that raises serious and thoughtful questions. In it we encounter a ruler who, when confronted with a dilemma that challenges the basis of his authority, chooses to put his trust in law and does so despite a great deal of encouragement to allow might to make right. Appealing as the message is, it could easily have degenerated into a tedious and soporific polemic. Here it is saved from that by al-Hakim's deft touch. He gives each point of view an individual personality, balances the seriousness of the debate with comic exchanges between the characters, and varies the rhythm by moving the action back and forth between groups and individuals. The result is a drama that manages to be serious without being solemn.

Implausible as the central event of this play is—a sultan who is an unmanumitted slave—it does in fact reflect a historical reality. Slaves have occupied positions of great authority in Islamic societies since the early days of its empire. In the ninth century the Arab caliphs of Baghdad began to introduce Turkish slave soldiers from central Asia as a personal guard. These slaves, often purchased as children and raised in the royal household, depended completely on their masters and so were completely loyal to them. Unlike other groups within the state, they were not distracted by loyalties to tribe, family, region, profession, ethnic group, or a religion other than Islam. The Ottoman Empire (1281–1924), the last great dynasty to rule in the Islamic Middle East before the modern period, reserved the highest offices in both the military and government administration for slaves who were forcibly recruited as youths from the Christian communities in eastern Europe and the Caucasus. Before the Ottomans, Egypt was ruled for two and a half centuries (1250–1517) by a dynasty whose name, *mamluk,* means slave and whose monarchs were, as the play indicates, manumitted slaves. The events of the play are not based on historical fact, however, nor are they an attempt to recreate a plausible kind of pseudo history. This is a fantasy, an artful improvisation. The fact of the Mamluk Dynasty provides al-Hakim with an attractive metaphor, the Sultan as slave, and one whose serious implications he explores. The metaphor also has an unexpectedly modern resonance, since democratic leaders are fond of presenting themselves as servants or slaves of the people they govern. *The Sultan's Dilemma* playfully suggests what might happen if that were literally true.

The opening scene between the executioner and the condemned man establishes that while the play will deal with serious matters, the tone will be light and comic. It makes a connection between the life of ordinary Egyptians and the court since the intervention of the beautiful lady, a woman of doubtful virtue, and her maid set up the dilemma that the Sultan must confront. Had the slave merchant been executed there would be no play. This opening sequence promises us that the play will end happily and that the humorous possibilities of every situation will be exploited. It also introduces the theme of hair-splitting legalism that recurs throughout the play, and by presenting the lady as a woman of shrewdness, compassion, and authority despite her unsavory reputation, it prepares us for the role she plays in the last portion of the play.

The middle portion of the play reveals the dilemma of the title and, in the persons of the vizier and the chief cadi, articulates the two horns of that dilemma. It ends once the Sultan makes his decision, and the remainder of the play follows the working-out of the consequences of his choice. The orderly scenario that the officers of the court have planned turns into chaos because of the unforeseen and unforeseeable intervention of the lady. By trusting himself to the law the Sultan has entered on a course that is, apparently, more open to risk than anyone had anticipated, and again he must choose to continue as he began or fall back on arbitrary violence. The final scenes are in essence a playing-out of the reward he receives for having made the right decision.

There are two good studies of al-Hakim in English: Richard Long, *Tawfiq al Hakim: Playwright of Egypt* (1979), and Paul Starkey, *From the Ivory Tower: A Critical Study of Tawfiq al-Hakim* (1987). Both contain useful bibliographies. In addition, the translation by Denys Johnson-Davies was first published in a collection titled *Fate of a Cockroach: Four Plays of Freedom* (1973). Johnson-Davies has also published a translation of al-Hakim's delightful absurdist play *The Tree Climber* (1966).

PRONOUNCING GLOSSARY

The following list uses common English syllables and stress accents to provide rough equivalents of selected words whose pronunciation may be unfamiliar to the general reader.

adab: *a'-dab*

cadi: *caw'-dee*

Kuduz: *coo-dooz'*

muezzin: *moo-ez'-zin*

Naguib Mahfouz: *nuh-geeb' mah-fooz'*

Tawfiq al-Hakim: *tow-feek' al–ha-keem'*

vizier: *vi-zeer'*

The Sultan's Dilemma[1]

Characters

THE SULTAN	UNKNOWN MAN
THE VIZIER[2]	1ST LEADING CITIZEN
THE CHIEF CADI[3]	2ND LEADING CITIZEN
A BEAUTIFUL LADY	3RD LEADING CITIZEN
HER MAIDSERVANT	1ST MAN IN CROWD
AN EMINENT SLAVE TRADER	2ND MAN IN CROWD
THE CONDEMNED MAN	MOTHER
THE EXECUTIONER	CHILD
THE WINE MERCHANT	TOWNSPEOPLE
THE MUEZZIN	GUARDS
THE SHOEMAKER	SULTAN'S RETINUE

Act One

An open space in the city during the time of the Mamluke Sultans.[4]
On one side there is a mosque with a minaret; on the other, a
tavern. In the centre is a house with a balcony. Dawn is about to
break and silence reigns. A stake has been set up to which a man,
condemned to death, has been tied. His EXECUTIONER *is nearby*
trying to fight off sleep.

CONDEMNED MAN: [*Contemplating the* EXECUTIONER.] Getting sleepy? Of
course you are. Congratulations. Sleep well. You're not awaiting something that will spoil *your* peace of mind.

EXECUTIONER: Quiet!

CONDEMNED MAN: And so—when is it to be?

EXECUTIONER: I told you to be quiet.

CONDEMNED MAN: [*Pleadingly.*] Tell me truly when it's to be? When?

EXECUTIONER: When are you going to stop disturbing me?

CONDEMNED MAN: Sorry. It is, though, something that particularly concerns me. When does this event—a joyous one for you—take place?

EXECUTIONER: At dawn. I've told you this more than ten times. At dawn I'll
carry out the sentence on you. Now do you understand? So let me enjoy
a moment's peace.

CONDEMNED MAN: Dawn? It's still far off, isn't it, Executioner?

EXECUTIONER: I don't know.

CONDEMNED MAN: You don't know?

EXECUTIONER: It's the Muezzin[5] who knows. When he goes up to the minaret of this mosque and gives the call to the dawn prayer, I'll raise my
sword and swipe off your head—those are the orders. Happy now?

CONDEMNED MAN: Without a trial? I haven't yet been put on trial, I haven't
yet appeared before a judge.

EXECUTIONER: That's nothing to do with me.

---

1. Translated by Denys Johnson-Davies.   2. The chief minister of the sultan.   3. Judge.   4. Ruled
in Egypt from 1250 to 1517.   5. Gives the call to prayer at the five daily appointed times.

CONDEMNED MAN: For sure, you have nothing to do with anything except my execution.

EXECUTIONER: At dawn, in furtherance of the Sultan's orders.

CONDEMNED MAN: For what crime?

EXECUTIONER: That's not my affair.

CONDEMNED MAN: Because I said . . .

EXECUTIONER: Quiet! Quiet! Shut your mouth—I have been ordered to cut off your head right away if you utter a word about your crime.

CONDEMNED MAN: Don't be upset, I'll shut my mouth.

EXECUTIONER: You've done well to shut your mouth and leave me to enjoy my sleep. It's in your interest that I should enjoy a quiet and peaceful sleep.

CONDEMNED MAN: In my interest?

EXECUTIONER: Certainly, it's in your interest that I should be completely rested and in excellent health, both in body and mind; because when I'm tired, depressed, and strung up, my hand shakes, and when it shakes I perform my work badly.

CONDEMNED MAN: And what's your work to me?

EXECUTIONER: Fool! My work has to do with your neck. Poor performance means your neck will not be cleanly cut, because a clean cut requires a steady hand and calm mind so that the head may fly off at a single blow, allowing you no time to feel any sensation of pain. Do you understand now?

CONDEMNED MAN: Of course, that's quite right.

EXECUTIONER: You see! Now you must be quite convinced why it is necessary that you should let me rest; also, to bring joy to my heart and raise my morale.

CONDEMNED MAN: Your morale? *Yours?*

EXECUTIONER: Naturally, if I were in your shoes . . .

CONDEMNED MAN: O God, take him at his word! I wish you *were* in my shoes.

EXECUTIONER: What are you saying?

CONDEMNED MAN: Carry on. What would you do if you had the honour and good fortune to be in my shoes?

EXECUTIONER: I'll tell you what I'd do—have you any money?

CONDEMNED MAN: Ah, money! Yes, yes, yes! Money! An apposite[6] thought. As for money, my friend, you may say what you like about that. The whole city knows—and you among them—that I'm one of the very richest of merchants and slave-traders.

EXECUTIONER: No, you have misunderstood me—I'm not talking of a bribe. It's impossible to bribe me—not because of my honesty and integrity, but because, quite frankly, I am unable to save you. All I wanted was to accept your invitation to have a drink—if you should happen to do so. A glass of wine is not a bribe. It would be impolite of me to refuse your invitation. Look! There's a Wine Merchant a stone's throw away from you—his tavern is open all night, because he has customers who visit that whore who lives in the house opposite.

CONDEMNED MAN: A drink? Is that all?

---

6. To the point, appropriate.

EXECUTIONER: That's all.

CONDEMNED MAN: I've got a better and more attractive idea. Let's go up together, you and I, to that beautiful woman. I know her and if we went to her we'd spend the most marvellous night of our lives—a night to fill your heart with joy and gaiety and raise your morale. What do you say?

EXECUTIONER: No, gracious sir.

CONDEMNED MAN: You would accept my invitation to a drink, but refuse my invitation to a party of drinking and fun, beauty and merriment?

EXECUTIONER: In that house? No, my dear condemned friend, I prefer for you to stay as you are: fettered with chains till dawn.

CONDEMNED MAN: What a pity you don't trust me! What if I were to promise you that before the call to dawn prayers I would be back again in chains?

EXECUTIONER: Does a bird return to the snare?

CONDEMNED MAN: Yes, I swear to you on my honour.

EXECUTIONER: *Your* honour? What an oath!

CONDEMNED MAN: You don't believe me.

EXECUTIONER: I believe you so long as you are where you are—and in handcuffs.

CONDEMNED MAN: How can I invite you to have a drink then?

EXECUTIONER: That's easy. I'll go to the tavern and ask him to bring two glasses of his best wine and when he brings them we'll drink them right here. What do you say?

CONDEMNED MAN: But . . .

EXECUTIONER: We're agreed. I'll go—there's no need for you to trouble yourself. Just a minute, with your permission.

[*The* EXECUTIONER *goes to the tavern at the corner of the square and knocks at the door. The* WINE MERCHANT *comes out to him, he whispers something in his ear, and returns to his place.*]

EXECUTIONER: [*To the* CONDEMNED MAN.] Everything necessary has been arranged, and you will see, my dear condemned man, the good result shortly.

CONDEMNED MAN: What good result?

EXECUTIONER: My masterful work. When I drink I'm very precise in my work, but, if I haven't drunk, my work goes all to hell. By way of example I'll tell you what happened the other day. I was charged with the job of executing someone, and I hadn't drunk a thing all that day. Do you know what I did? I gave that poor fellow's neck such a blow that his head flew off into the air and landed far away—not in this basket of mine, but in another basket over there, the basket belonging to the Shoemaker next door to the tavern. God alone knows the trouble we had getting the missing head out of the heaps of shoes and soles.

CONDEMNED MAN: The Shoemaker's basket! What a shameful thing to happen! I beseech you by God not to let my head suffer such a fate.

EXECUTIONER: Don't be afraid. Things are different where you are concerned. The other head belonged to a horribly stingy fellow.

[*The* WINE MERCHANT *appears from his shop carrying two glasses.*]

WINE MERCHANT: [*Moving towards the* CONDEMNED MAN.] This is of course for you—your last wish.

CONDEMNED MAN: No, for the Executioner—it's his cherished wish.

EXECUTIONER: [*To the* WINE MERCHANT.] To bring calm and contentment to my heart.

WINE MERCHANT: And from whom shall I receive payment?

CONDEMNED MAN: From me of course—to bring joy and gladness to his heart.

EXECUTIONER: It is incumbent upon me to accept his warm invitation.

CONDEMNED MAN: And it is incumbent upon me to raise his morale.

WINE MERCHANT: What very good friends you two are!

EXECUTIONER: It is a reciprocated affection.

CONDEMNED MAN: Until dawn breaks.

EXECUTIONER: Don't worry about the dawn now—it is still far off. Come, let's touch glasses.

> [*The* EXECUTIONER *snatches up the two glasses and strikes one against the other, turns, raises a glass, and drinks to the* CONDEMNED MAN.]

EXECUTIONER: Your health!

CONDEMNED MAN: Thank you.

EXECUTIONER: [*After he has drained his glass he holds the other glass up to the* CONDEMNED MAN'*s mouth.*] And now it's your turn, my dear fellow.

CONDEMNED MAN: [*Taking a gulp and coughing.*] Enough. You drink the rest for me.

EXECUTIONER: Is that your wish?

CONDEMNED MAN: The last!

EXECUTIONER: [*Raising the second glass.*] Then I raise my glass to . . .

CONDEMNED MAN: Your masterful work.

EXECUTIONER: God willing! Also to your generosity and kindness, my friend.

WINE MERCHANT: [*Taking the two empty glasses from the* EXECUTIONER.] What's this old slave-trader done? What's his crime? All of us in the city know him—he's no murderer or thief.

CONDEMNED MAN: And yet my head will fall at dawn, just like that of any murderer or thief.

WINE MERCHANT: Why? For what crime?

CONDEMNED MAN: For no reason except that I said . . . .

EXECUTIONER: Quiet! Don't utter a word! Shut your mouth!

CONDEMNED MAN: I've shut my mouth.

EXECUTIONER: And you, Wine Merchant, you've got your glasses, so off with you!

WINE MERCHANT: And my money?

EXECUTIONER: It's he who invited me—and only a dastardly fellow refuses an invitation.

CONDEMNED MAN: To be sure I invited him, and he was good enough to accept my invitation. Your money, Tavern Owner, is here in a purse in my belt. Approach and take what you want.

EXECUTIONER: Allow me to approach on his behalf.

> [*He approaches and takes some money from the* CONDEMNED MAN'*s purse and pays the* WINE MERCHANT.]

EXECUTIONER: Take what you're owed and a bit more that you may know we're generous people.

> [*The* WINE MERCHANT *takes his money and returns to his shop. The* EXECUTIONER *begins humming in a low voice.*]

CONDEMNED MAN: [*Anxiously.*] And now . . .

EXECUTIONER: Now we begin our singing and merrymaking. Do you know, my dear condemned man, that I'm very fond of good singing, a pleasant tune, and fine lyrics? It fills the heart with contentment and joy, with gladness and a delight in life. Sing me something!

CONDEMNED MAN: I? Sing?

EXECUTIONER: Yes. Why not? What's to stop you? Your larynx—thanks be to God—is perfectly free. All you have to do is raise your voice in song and out will come a lovely tune to delight the ear. Come on, sing! Entertain me!

CONDEMNED MAN: God bless us! O God, bear witness!

EXECUTIONER: Come along! Sing to me!

CONDEMNED MAN: Do you really think I'm in the mood for singing at this time?

EXECUTIONER: Did you not just now promise me to bring gladness to my soul and remove the depression from my heart?

CONDEMNED MAN: Are you the one to feel depressed?

EXECUTIONER: Yes, please remove my depression. Overwhelm me with joy! Let me enjoy the strains of ballads and songs! Drown me with melodies and sweet tunes! Listen—I've remembered something. I know by heart a song I composed myself during one night of sleeplessness and woe.

CONDEMNED MAN: Then sing it to me.

EXECUTIONER: I don't have a beautiful voice.

CONDEMNED MAN: And who told you that *my* voice was beautiful?

EXECUTIONER: To me all other people's voices are beautiful—because I don't listen to them, especially if I'm drunk. All I'm concerned with is being surrounded on all sides by singing: the feeling that there is singing all around me soothes my nerves. Sometimes I feel as though I myself would like to sing, but one condition must obtain: that I find someone to listen to me. And if there is someone to listen, let him beware if he does not show admiration and appreciation, for if not . . . if not I become shy and embarrassed and begin to tremble, after which I get very angry. Now, having drawn your attention to the condition, shall I sing?

CONDEMNED MAN: Sing!

EXECUTIONER: And will you admire me and show your appreciation?

CONDEMNED MAN: Yes.

EXECUTIONER: You promise faithfully?

CONDEMNED MAN: Faithfully.

EXECUTIONER: Then I'll sing you my tender song. Are you listening?

CONDEMNED MAN: I'm listening and appreciating.

EXECUTIONER: The appreciation comes at the end. As for now, all you're asked to do is merely to listen.

CONDEMNED MAN: I'm merely listening.

EXECUTIONER: Good. Are you ready?

CONDEMNED MAN: Why? Isn't it you who're going to sing?

EXECUTIONER: Yes, but it's necessary for you to be ready to listen.

CONDEMNED MAN: And am I capable of doing anything else? You have left my ears free—no doubt for that purpose.

EXECUTIONER: Then let's start. This tender song, called *The Flower and the Gardener,* was composed by me. Yes, I composed it myself.

CONDEMNED MAN: I know that.

EXECUTIONER: How odd! Who told you?

CONDEMNED MAN: You told me so yourself just a moment ago.

EXECUTIONER: Really? Really? And now, do you want me to begin?

CONDEMNED MAN: Go ahead.

EXECUTIONER: I'm just about to begin. Listen—but you're not listening.

CONDEMNED MAN: I am listening.

EXECUTIONER: The listening must be done with superlative attention.

CONDEMNED MAN: With superlative attention!

EXECUTIONER: Be careful not to upset me by letting your mind wander and not paying attention.

CONDEMNED MAN: I am paying attention.

EXECUTIONER: Are you ready?

CONDEMNED MAN: Yes.

EXECUTIONER: I don't find you excessively enthusiastic.

CONDEMNED MAN: And how should I behave?

EXECUTIONER: I want you to be burning with enthusiasm. Tell me you absolutely insist that you listen to my singing.

CONDEMNED MAN: I absolutely insist . . .

EXECUTIONER: You say it coldly, with indifference.

CONDEMNED MAN: Coldly?

EXECUTIONER: Yes. I want the insistence to issue forth from the depths of your heart.

CONDEMNED MAN: It comes from the depths of my heart.

EXECUTIONER: I don't sense the warmth of sincerity in your voice.

CONDEMNED MAN: Sincerity?

EXECUTIONER: Yes, it's not apparent from the tone of your voice; it is the tone and timbre of the voice that reveals a person's true feelings, and your voice is cold and indifferent.

CONDEMNED MAN: And so—are you going to sing or aren't you?

EXECUTIONER: I shan't sing.

CONDEMNED MAN: Thanks be to God!

EXECUTIONER: You thank God for my not singing?

CONDEMNED MAN: No, I shall always thank God for your singing and your not singing alike. I don't believe there's anyone who'd object to praising God in all circumstances.

EXECUTIONER: Deep down you're wishing that I won't sing.

CONDEMNED MAN: Deep down? Who but God knows a man's inner thoughts?

EXECUTIONER: Then you want me to sing?

CONDEMNED MAN: If you like.

EXECUTIONER: I'll sing.

CONDEMNED MAN: Sing!

EXECUTIONER: No, I have a condition: implore me first of all to sing. Plead with me.

CONDEMNED MAN: I plead with you.

EXECUTIONER: Say it sensitively, entreatingly.

CONDEMNED MAN: Please—I implore you—by your Lord, by the Lord of all creation. I ask of God, the One, the Conqueror, the Strong and Mighty, to soften your cruel heart and to listen to my request and to be so good and gracious as to sing.

EXECUTIONER: Again!

CONDEMNED MAN: What?

EXECUTIONER: Repeat this pleading!

CONDEMNED MAN: God Almighty! Have mercy upon me! You've killed me
with all this resistance and coyness. Sing if you want to; if not, then, for
God's sake let me be and I'll have nothing to do with it.

EXECUTIONER: Are you angry? I don't want you to be angry. I'll sing so as
to calm you down and remove your feeling of distress. I'll start right away.
[*He coughs, then hums softly preparatory to singing.*]

CONDEMNED MAN: At last!

EXECUTIONER: [*Standing up suddenly.*] If you'd prefer me not to sing, say
so frankly.

CONDEMNED MAN: Heavens above! He's going to start all over again.

EXECUTIONER: Is your patience exhausted?

CONDEMNED MAN: And how!

EXECUTIONER: Am I making you suffer?

CONDEMNED MAN: And how!

EXECUTIONER: Just be patient, my dear fellow. Be patient.

CONDEMNED MAN: This Executioner is really killing me!

EXECUTIONER: What are you saying?

CONDEMNED MAN: I can't stand any more.

EXECUTIONER: You can't stand the waiting. What a poor, pining creature
you are, so consumed with wanting to hear my singing! I'll begin then. I
shan't make you wait any longer. I'll start right away. Listen! Here's my
tender song.

[*He clears his throat, hums, and then sings in a drunken voice.*]

> O flower whose life is but a night,
> Greetings from your admirers!
> Plucked at dawn of day tomorrow,
> The robe of dew from you will fall.
> In a firewood basket you will lie
> And all around my tunes will die.
> In the air the deadly blade will flash
> Shining bright in gardener's hand.
> O flower, whose life is but a night!
> On you be peace, on you be peace!

[*Silence.*]

EXECUTIONER: Why are you silent? Didn't you like it? This is the time to
show admiration and appreciation.

CONDEMNED MAN: Is this your tender song, you ill-omened Executioner?

EXECUTIONER: Please—I'm no Executioner.

CONDEMNED MAN: What do you think you are then?

EXECUTIONER: I'm a gardener.

CONDEMNED MAN: A gardener?

EXECUTIONER: Yes, a gardener. Do you understand? A gardener. I'm a gar-
den-er.

[*A window is opened in the beautiful lady's house, and the* MAID
looks out.]

MAID: What's all this now? What's this uproar when people are asleep? My
mistress has a headache and wishes to sleep undisturbed.

EXECUTIONER: [*Sarcastically.*] Your mistress! [*He laughs derisively.*] Her
mistress!

MAID: I told you to stop that noise.

EXECUTIONER: Take yourself off, server of vice and obscenity.

MAID: Don't insult my mistress! If she wanted to she could have twenty sweepers like you to sweep the dust from under her shoes.

EXECUTIONER: Hold your tongue and take yourself off, you filthiest of creatures!

[*The* LADY *appears at the window behind her servant.*]

LADY: What's happening?

MAID: This drunken executioner is raising a din and hurling abuse at us.

LADY: How dare he!

EXECUTIONER: [*Pointing at the window.*] That's her, in all her splendour— her famous mistress!

LADY: Show a little respect, man!

EXECUTIONER: [*Laughing sarcastically.*] Respect!

LADY: Yes, and don't force me to teach you how to respect ladies.

EXECUTIONER: Ladies? [*He laughs.*] Ladies! She says ladies! Listen and marvel!

LADY: [*To her* MAID.] Go down and give him a lesson in manners.

MAID: [*To the* EXECUTIONER.] Wait for me—if you're a man!

[*The two women disappear from the window.*]

EXECUTIONER: [*To the* CONDEMNED MAN.] What does this . . . this she-devil intend to do? Do you know? She's capable of anything. Good God, did you see how she threatened me?

MAID: [*Emerging from the door of the house, a shoe held high in her hand.*] Come here!

EXECUTIONER: What are you going to do with that shoe?

MAID: This shoe is the oldest and filthiest thing I could find in the house— do you understand? I came across nothing older or filthier befitting that dirty, ugly face of yours.

EXECUTIONER: Now the effect of the glass of lovely wine has really flown from my head. Did you hear the nice polite things she was saying, oh condemned man?

CONDEMNED MAN: Yes.

EXECUTIONER: And you utter not a word?

CONDEMNED MAN: I?

EXECUTIONER: And you remain unmoved?

CONDEMNED MAN: How?

EXECUTIONER: You let her insult me like this and remain silent?

CONDEMNED MAN: And what do you want me to do?

EXECUTIONER: Do something! At least say something!

CONDEMNED MAN: What's it got to do with me?

EXECUTIONER: What lack of gallantry, what flagging resolution! You see her raising the shoe in her hand like someone brandishing a sword and you don't make a move to defend me. You just stand there with shackled hands. You just look on without caring. You listen without concern to my being insulted, humiliated, and abused? By God, this is no way to show chivalry.

CONDEMNED MAN: Truly!

MAID: [*Shaking the shoe in her hand.*] Listen here, man! Leave this poor fellow alone. You face up to me if you've got any courage. Your reckoning is with me. You've behaved very rudely towards us and it's up to you to apologize and ask our forgiveness. Otherwise, by the Lord of Hosts, by the Almighty, by the Omnipotent . . .

EXECUTIONER: [*Gently.*] Steady! Steady!

MAID: Speak! What's your answer?

EXECUTIONER: Let's come to an understanding.

MAID: First, ask for forgiveness.

EXECUTIONER: From whom should I ask forgiveness? From you?

MAID: From my mistress.

EXECUTIONER: Where is she?

LADY: [*Appearing on the threshold of her house.*] Here I am. Has he apologized?

MAID: He will do so, milady.

EXECUTIONER: Yes, milady.

LADY: Good. Then I accept your apology.

EXECUTIONER: Only, milady—would it not be best for the waters to flow back to their usual channels and for things to be as before?

LADY: They are.

EXECUTIONER: I meant for the wine to flow back into the channels of my head.

LADY: What do you mean?

EXECUTIONER: I mean that there is a certain damage that requires repairing. Your efficient servant has removed the intoxication from my head. From where shall I fill the void?

LADY: I shall take upon myself the filling of your head. Take as much drink as you wish from the Wine Merchant at my expense.

EXECUTIONER: Thank you, O bountiful lady. [*The* EXECUTIONER *signals to the* WINE MERCHANT *who is standing by the door of his tavern to bring him a glass.*]

CONDEMNED MAN: [*To the* LADY.] Do you not know me, beautiful lady?

LADY: Of course I know you. From the first instant when they brought you here at nightfall. I caught sight of you from my window and recognized you and it saddened me to see you in shackles, but—but what crime have you committed?

CONDEMNED MAN: Nothing much. All that happened was that I said . . .

EXECUTIONER: [*Shouting.*] Careful! Careful! Shut your mouth!

CONDEMNED MAN: I've shut my mouth.

LADY: Naturally they gave you a trial?

CONDEMNED MAN: No.

LADY: What are you saying? Weren't you given a trial?

CONDEMNED MAN: I wasn't taken to court. I sent a complaint to the Sultan asking that I be given the right to appear before the Chief Cadi, the most just of those who judge by conscience, the most scrupulous adherent to the canonical law, and the most loyal defender of the sanctity of the law. But—here dawn approaches and the Executioner has had his orders to cut off my head when the call to dawn prayers is given.

LADY: [*Looking up at the sky.*] The dawn? The dawn's almost breaking. Look at the sky!

EXECUTIONER: [*In his hand a glass taken from the* WINE MERCHANT.] It's not the sky, my dear lady, that will decide the moment of fate for this condemned man but the minaret of this mosque. I am waiting for the Muezzin.

LADY: The Muezzin. He is surely on his way. Sometimes I stay awake in the morning and I see him at this very moment making for the mosque.

CONDEMNED MAN: Then my hour has come.

LADY: No—not so long as your complaint has not been examined.

CONDEMNED MAN: This Executioner will not await the result of the complaint. Isn't that so, Executioner?

EXECUTIONER: I shall await only the Muezzin. Those are my orders.

LADY: Whose orders? The Sultan's?

EXECUTIONER: Roughly.

CONDEMNED MAN: [Shouting.] Roughly? Is it not then the Sultan?

EXECUTIONER: The Vizier—the orders of the Vizier are the orders of the Sultan.

CONDEMNED MAN: Then I am irretrievably lost.

EXECUTIONER: Just so. No sooner does the Muezzin's call to prayer rise up to the sky than your soul rises with it. This causes me great sadness and distress but work is work. A job's a job.

LADY: [Turning towards the street.] Oh disaster! Here is the Muezzin—he has arrived.

CONDEMNED MAN: The die is cast.

[The MUEZZIN makes his appearance.]

EXECUTIONER: Hurry, O Muezzin—we're waiting for you.

MUEZZIN: Waiting for me? Why?

EXECUTIONER: To give the call to the dawn prayer.

MUEZZIN: Do you want to pray?

EXECUTIONER: I want to carry out my work.

MUEZZIN: What have I to do with your work?

EXECUTIONER: When your voice rises up to the sky the soul of this man will rise with it.

MUEZZIN: God forbid!

EXECUTIONER: Those are the orders.

MUEZZIN: The life of this man hangs on my vocal cords?

EXECUTIONER: Yes.

MUEZZIN: There is no power and no strength save in God!

EXECUTIONER: O Muezzin, hasten to your work so that I may do mine.

LADY: And what's the hurry, kind Executioner? The Muezzin's voice has been affected by the night cold and he is in need of a hot drink. Come into my house, Muezzin. I shall prepare you something which will put your voice to rights.

EXECUTIONER: And the dawn?

LADY: The dawn is in no danger and the Muezzin knows best as to its time.

EXECUTIONER: And my work?

LADY: Your work is in no danger—so long as the Muezzin has not yet called for the dawn prayers.

EXECUTIONER: Do you agree, oh Muezzin?

LADY: He agrees to accepting my little invitation for a short while, for he is among my best friends in the quarter.

EXECUTIONER: And those who have gone to pray in the mosque?

MUEZZIN: There are only two men there. One of them is a stranger to this city and has taken up his abode in the mosque, whilst the other is a beggar who has sought shelter in it from the night cold. All are now deep in sleep and seldom do people pay attention to the call to dawn prayers.

Only those get up whom I wake with a kick so that they may perform their religious duties.

LADY: Most of the people of the quarter live a life of ease and sleep well on into the forenoon.

EXECUTIONER: Are you both meaning to say that the call to dawn prayers won't be given today?

LADY: What we mean is . . . there's no hurry. There is safety in proceeding slowly, remorse in proceeding hastily. Don't worry yourself! The call to the dawn prayer will be given in good time, and in any event you are all right and are not answerable. The Muezzin alone is responsible. Let us go then, oh Muezzin! A cup of coffee will restore your voice.

MUEZZIN: There's no harm in just a little time and just a small cup.

[*The* LADY *enters her house with the* MUEZZIN.]

EXECUTIONER: [*To the* CONDEMNED MAN.] Did you see? Instead of going up into the minaret he went up to the house of the . . . the honoured lady. There's the Muezzin for you!

CONDEMNED MAN: A gallant man! He risks everything. As for you, you against whom no censure or blame will be directed, you who are safely covered by your excuse, who bear no liability, possessed as you are of a pretext, it's you who's raging and storming and becoming alarmed. Calm down a little, my friend! Be forbearing and patient! Put your trust in God! Listen, I've got an idea—an excellent, a brilliant idea. It will calm your nerves and bring joy to your soul. Sing me your tender song once again with that sweet, melodious voice of yours, and I swear to you I'll listen to it with a heart palpitating with enthusiasm and admiration. Come along—sing! I'm listening to you with my very being.

EXECUTIONER: I no longer have any desire to.

CONDEMNED MAN: Why? What's upset you? Is it because you didn't lop off my head?

EXECUTIONER: It's because I failed to carry out my duty.

CONDEMNED MAN: Your duty is to carry out the sentence at the time of the call to the dawn prayer. Yet who gives the call to the dawn prayer? You or the Muezzin?

EXECUTIONER: The Muezzin.

CONDEMNED MAN: And has he done so?

EXECUTIONER: No.

CONDEMNED MAN: Then what fault is it of yours?

EXECUTIONER: Truly it is not my fault.

CONDEMNED MAN: This is what we're all saying.

EXECUTIONER: You're comforting me and making light of things for me.

CONDEMNED MAN: I'm telling the truth.

EXECUTIONER: [*Looking up and down the street and shouting.*] What are these crowds? Good God! It's the Vizier's retinue! It's the Vizier!

CONDEMNED MAN: Don't tremble like that! Calm yourself!

EXECUTIONER: It won't be held against me . . . I'm covered, aren't I?

CONDEMNED MAN: Set your mind at rest! You are covered with a thousand blankets of arguments and excuses.

EXECUTIONER: It's the accursed Muezzin who will pay the harsh reckoning.

[*The* VIZIER *appears surrounded by his guards.*]

VIZIER: [*Shouting.*] How strange! Has this criminal not been executed yet?

EXECUTIONER: We are awaiting the dawn prayer, milord Vizier, in accordance with your orders.

VIZIER: The dawn prayer? We have performed it at the palace mosque in the presence of Our Majesty the Sultan and the Chief Cadi.

EXECUTIONER: It's not my fault, milord Vizier. The Muezzin of this mosque has not yet gone up to the minaret.

VIZIER: How's that? This is unbelievable. Where is this Muezzin?

[*The* MUEZZIN *comes out drunk from the door of the house and tries to hide himself behind the* LADY *and her* MAID.]

EXECUTIONER: [*Catching sight of him and shouting.*] That's him! There he is!

VIZIER: [*To the guards.*] Bring him here! [*They bring him before the* VIZIER.] Are you the Muezzin of this mosque?

MUEZZIN: Yes, milord Vizier.

VIZIER: Why have you not yet given the call to the dawn prayer?

MUEZZIN: Who told you that, milord Vizier? I gave the call to the dawn prayer some time ago . . .

VIZIER: To the dawn prayer?

MUEZZIN: At its due time, just like every day, and there are those who heard me.

LADY: Truly we all heard him give the call to the dawn prayer from up in the minaret.

MAID: Yes, today as is his habit every day at the same time.

VIZIER: But this Executioner claims . . .

LADY: This Executioner was drunk and fast asleep.

MAID: And the sound of his snoring rose up to us and woke us from our sweet slumbers.

VIZIER: [*In astonishment to the* EXECUTIONER.] Is it thus that you carry out my orders?

EXECUTIONER: I swear, I swear, milord Vizier . . .

VIZIER: Enough of that!

[*The* EXECUTIONER *is tongue-tied with bewilderment.*]

CONDEMNED MAN: O Vizier, I would beg you to listen to me. I sent to His Majesty the Sultan a complaint . . .

EXECUTIONER: [*Collecting his wits and shouting.*] I swear, milord Vizier, that I was awake . . .

VIZIER: I told you to keep quiet. [*He turns to the* CONDEMNED MAN.] Yes, your complaint is known to His Majesty the Sultan and he ordered that you be turned over to the Chief Cadi. His Majesty the Sultan will himself attend your trial. This is his noble wish and his irrefutable command. Guards! Clear the square of people and let everyone go home. This trial must take place in complete secrecy.

[*The guards clear the square of people.*]

EXECUTIONER: Milord Vizier . . . [*He tries to explain matters but the* VIZIER *dismisses him with a gesture.*]

[*The* SULTAN *appears with his retinue, accompanied by the* CHIEF CADI.]

CONDEMNED MAN: [*Shouting.*] Your Majesty! Justice! I beg for justice!

SULTAN: Is this the accused?

CONDEMNED MAN: Your Majesty! I have committed no fault or crime!

SULTAN: We shall see.

CONDEMNED MAN: And I haven't been tried yet! I haven't been tried!

SULTAN: You shall be given a fair trial in accordance with your wish, and the Chief Cadi shall be in charge of your trial in our presence. [*The* SULTAN *makes a sign to the* CHIEF CADI *to start the trial, then sits down in a chair which has been brought for him, while the* VIZIER *stands by his side.*]

CADI: [*Sitting on his chair.*] Remove the accused's chains. [*One of the guards undoes the* CONDEMNED MAN's *fetters.*] Approach, man! What is your crime?

CONDEMNED MAN: I have committed no crime.

CADI: What is the charge brought against you?

CONDEMNED MAN: Ask the Vizier that!

CADI: I am asking *you*.

CONDEMNED MAN: I did nothing at all except utter an innocent word in which there is neither danger nor harm.

VIZIER: It's a terrible and sinful word.

CADI: [*To the* CONDEMNED MAN.] What is this word?

CONDEMNED MAN: I don't like to repeat it.

VIZIER: Now you don't like to, but in the middle of the market place and amongst throngs of people . . .

CADI: What is this word?

VIZIER: He said that His Majesty, the great and noble Sultan, is a mere slave.

CONDEMNED MAN: Everyone knows this—it is common knowledge.

VIZIER: Don't interrupt me—and he claimed that he was the slave trader who undertook the sale of our Sultan in his youth to the former Sultan.

CONDEMNED MAN: That's true. I swear it by a sacred oath—and it is a matter of pride to me which I shall treasure for all time.

SULTAN: [*To the* CONDEMNED MAN.] You? You sold me to the late Sultan?

CONDEMNED MAN: Yes.

SULTAN: When was that?

CONDEMNED MAN: Twenty-five years ago, Your Majesty. You were a small boy of six, lost and abandoned in a Circassian village raided by the Mongols.[7] You were extremely intelligent and wise for one of your tender years. I rejoiced in you and carried you off to the Sultan of this country. As the price for you he made me a present of one thousand dinars.[8]

SULTAN: [*Derisively.*] Only a thousand dinars!

CONDEMNED MAN: Of course you were worth more than that but I was new to the trade, not being more than twenty-six years of age. That deal was the beginning of my business—it opened for me the way to the future.

SULTAN: For you and for me!

CONDEMNED MAN: Thanks be to God!

SULTAN: Is it this that merits your death—bringing me to this country? I see the matter quite differently.

VIZIER: He deserves death for his babbling and indiscretion.

SULTAN: I see no great harm in his saying or bruiting[9] abroad the fact that I was a slave. The late Sultan was just that—is not that right, Vizier?

---

7. Mongol armies devastated this region in both the 13th and the 14th centuries. Circassia is a region in the Caucasus Mountains near the Black Sea.   8. Gold coins.   9. Spreading, repeating.

VIZIER: That's right but . . .

SULTAN: Is it not so, Chief Cadi?

VIZIER: Quite so, O Sultan.

SULTAN: The entire family comes from slaves since time immemorial. The Mamluke Sultans were all taken from earliest childhood to the palace, there to be given a strict and hardy upbringing; and later they became rulers, army leaders, and Sultans of countries. I am merely one of those, in no way different from them.

CONDEMNED MAN: Rather are you among the best of them in wisdom and sound judgement, may God preserve you for the good of your subjects.

SULTAN: Even so, I don't remember your face; in fact I don't clearly remember my childhood days in that Circassian village you talk about and in which you say you found me. All I remember is my childhood at the palace under the protection of the late Sultan. He used to treat me as though I were his real son, for he himself had no children. He brought me up and instructed me so that I might take over the rule. I knew for absolute certainty that he was not my father.

CONDEMNED MAN: Your parents were killed by the Mongols.

SULTAN: No one ever talked to me of my parents. I knew only that I had been brought to the palace at a young age.

CONDEMNED MAN: And it was I who brought you there.

SULTAN: Maybe.

CONDEMNED MAN: Therefore, Your Majesty, what is my crime?

SULTAN: By God, I know not. Ask him who accused you.

VIZIER: That's not his real crime.

SULTAN: Is there a real crime?

VIZIER: Yes, Your Majesty. To say that you had been a slave is truly not something shameful, no reason for guilt—all the Mamluk Sultans have been slaves. It's not there that the crime lies. However, a Mamluke Sultan is generally manumitted before ascending the throne.

SULTAN: So what?

VIZIER: So, Your Majesty, this man claims that you have not yet been manumitted,[1] that you are still a slave and that a person bearing such a stigma is not entitled to rule over a free people.

SULTAN: [*To the* CONDEMNED MAN.] Did you really say this?

CONDEMNED MAN: I did not say all that; however, people in the market place always enjoy such gossip and tittle-tattle.

SULTAN: And from where did you learn that I had not been manumitted?

CONDEMNED MAN: It is not I who said so. They ascribe to me every infamous word that is spoken.

SULTAN: But they are nevertheless indulging in gossip and tittle-tattle.

CONDEMNED MAN: Not I.

SULTAN: You or someone else—it no longer matters. The important thing now is that all the people everywhere know that it is all sheer lies—isn't that so, Chief Cadi?

CADI: The fact is, Your Majesty . . .

SULTAN: It's utter falsehood and slander. It's mere fabrication unsupported by logic or common sense. Not yet manumitted? I? I, who was a leader of armies and conquered the Mongols? I, the right-hand man of the late

---

1. Emancipated; freed from slavery.

Sultan, whom he arranged to rule after him? All this, and the Sultan did not think about manumitting me before his death? Is it plausible? Listen, Cadi! All you now have to do is to let the town-criers announce an official denial in the city and publish to the people the text of the document registering my manumission, which is doubtless kept in your strong-rooms, isn't that so?

CADI: [*Combing his fingers through his beard.*] You are saying, Your Majesty . . .

SULTAN: Didn't you hear what I said?

CADI: Yes, but . . .

SULTAN: You were busy playing with your beard.

CADI: Your Majesty!

SULTAN: What? Your Majesty the Sultan is addressing you in clear and simple language requiring no long consideration or deep thought. All it amounts to is that it has become necessary to make public the document. Do you understand?

CADI: Yes.

SULTAN: You're still playing with your beard. Can't you leave it alone—just for a while?

VIZIER: [*Intervening.*] Your Majesty! Would you permit me . . .

SULTAN: What's up with you? You too?

VIZIER: I would ask Your Majesty to . . .

SULTAN: What's all this embarrassment? You and he are as bad as each other.

CADI: It is better to postpone this trial until some other time—when we are on our own, Your Majesty.

VIZIER: Yes, that would be best.

SULTAN: I'm beginning to catch on.

> [*The* VIZIER, *by a sign, orders everyone to move off with the* CON-
> DEMNED MAN, *leaving only himself, the* SULTAN, *and the* CHIEF CADI
> *on stage.*]

SULTAN: Now here we are on our own. What have you to say? I see from your expressions that you have things to say.

CADI: Yes, Your Majesty. You have with your perspicacity realized . . . in actual fact there is no document of your manumission in my strong-rooms.

SULTAN: Perhaps you have not yet received it, though it must be some-where. Isn't that so, Vizier?

VIZIER: In truth, Your Majesty . . .

SULTAN: What?

VIZIER: The truth is that . . .

SULTAN: Speak!

VIZIER: There is no document to prove your having been manumitted.

SULTAN: What are you saying?

VIZIER: The late Sultan collapsed suddenly following a heart attack and departed this life before manumitting you.

SULTAN: What's this you're alleging, you rogue?

VIZIER: I'm certainly a rogue, Your Majesty—and a criminal. I'm wicked, I don't deny it. I should have arranged all this at the time, but this business of manumission did not occur to me. My head was filled with other weighty matters. At that time, Your Majesty, you were far away—in the thick of the fray. No one but myself was present by the dying Sultan's bedside. I forgot this matter under the stress of the situation, the momentous nature of the occasion, and the intensity of my grief. Nothing occupied me at that moment save taking the oath, before the dying man, that I would serve you, Your Majesty, with the very same devotion as that with which I had served him for the whole of his life.

SULTAN: Truly, here and now you have really served me!

VIZIER: I deserve death—I know that. It is an unpardonable crime. The late Sultan could not think of everything or remember everything. It was the very essence of my work to think for him and to remind him of important matters. It was certainly my duty to put before him the matter of manumission, because of its particular seriousness, and to do the necessary legal formalities. But your lofty position, Your Majesty, your influence, your prestige, your great place in people's hearts—all these high attributes caused us to overlook your being a slave; to overlook the necessity for someone of your stature to have such proofs and documents. I swear to God, this matter never occurred to me until after you had ascended the throne, Your Majesty. At that time the whole business became clear to me. I was seized with terror and almost went mad. I would surely have done so, had I not calmed down and pulled myself together, cherishing the hope that this matter would never arise or be revealed.

SULTAN: And now it has arisen and been revealed.

VIZIER: What a tragedy! I did not know that such a man would come along one day with his gossip and tittle-tattle.

SULTAN: For this reason you wanted to close his mouth by handing him over to the executioner?

VIZIER: Yes.

SULTAN: And so bury your fault by burying the man himself?

VIZIER: [With head lowered.] Yes.

SULTAN: And what's the point of that now? Everyone's gossiping now.

VIZIER: If this man's head were cut off and hung up in the square before the people, no tongue would thenceforth dare to utter.

SULTAN: Do you think so?

VIZIER: If the sword is not able to cut off tongues, then what can?

CADI: Will you allow me to say a word, Your Majesty?

SULTAN: I'm listening.

CADI: The sword certainly does away with heads and tongues; it does not, however, do away with difficulties and problems.

SULTAN: What do you mean?

CADI: I mean that the problem will still nevertheless remain, namely that the Sultan is ruling without having been manumitted, and that a slave is at the head of a free people.

VIZIER: Who dares to say this? Whoever does so will have his head cut off.

CADI: That's another question.

VIZIER: It is not necessary for the person ruling to be carrying around documents and proofs. We have the strongest and most striking example of this in the Fatimid dynasty. Every one of us remembers what Al-Mu'izz li-Din Allah Al-Fatimi did.[2] One day he came along claiming he was descended from the Prophet (the prayers of God be upon him), and when

2. The Fatimid Dynasty ruled Egypt from 909 to 1171. Al-Mu'izz ruled from 953 to 975.

the people did not believe him, he went at them with drawn sword and opened up his coffers of gold, saying 'These are my forbears, these my ancestors'. The people kept silent and he reigned and his children reigned after him quietly and peaceably for centuries long.

SULTAN: What do you say about this, Cadi?

CADI: I say that this is correct from the historical point of view but . . . .

SULTAN: But what?

CADI: Then, O illustrious Sultan, you would like to solve your problem by this method?

SULTAN: And why not?

VIZIER: Truly, why not? There is nothing easier than this, especially in this matter of ours. It is sufficient for us to announce publicly that Our Majesty the Sultan has been legally manumitted, that he was manumitted by the late Sultan before his death, and that the documents and proofs are recorded and kept with the Chief Cadi—and death to anyone who dares deny it!

CADI: There is a person who will so deny.

VIZIER: Who's that?

CADI: I.

SULTAN: You?

CADI: Yes, Your Majesty. I cannot take part in this conspiracy.

VIZIER: It is not a conspiracy—it's a plan for saving the situation.

CADI: It is a conspiracy against the law I represent.

SULTAN: The law?

CADI: Yes, Sultan—the law. In the eyes of the civil and religious codes you are only a slave, and a slave—by civil and religious law—is regarded as a thing, a chattel. As the late Sultan, who had the power of life and death over you, did not manumit you before his death, you are thus still a thing, a chattel, owned by someone else, and so you have forfeited the basic qualification for entering into the normal transactions exercised by the rest of free people.

SULTAN: Is this the law?

CADI: Yes.

VIZIER: Take it easy, Chief Cadi! We are not now discussing the view of the law but are looking for a way by which to be free of this law, and the way to be free of it is to assume that manumission has in fact taken place. So long as the matter is a secret between us three, with no one but ourselves knowing the truth, it will be easy to induce the people to believe . . .

CADI: The lie.

VIZIER: The solution rather—it's a more appropriate and suitable word.

CADI: A solution through lying.

VIZIER: And what's the harm in that?

CADI: In relation to you two there is no harm.

VIZIER: And in relation to you?

CADI: In relation to me it's different, for I cannot fool myself and I cannot free myself from the law, being as I am the person who represents it; I cannot break an oath by which I took upon myself to be the trusted servant of the civil and religious law.

SULTAN: You took this upon yourself before me.

CADI: And before God and my conscience.

SULTAN: Which means that you won't go along with us?

CADI: Along this road, no.

SULTAN: You will not join hands with us?

CADI: In this instance, no.

SULTAN: Then in that case you can take yourself off to one side. Don't interfere in anything and leave us to act as we think fit. You thus keep your oath and satisfy your conscience.

CADI: I'm sorry, Your Majesty.

SULTAN: Why?

CADI: Because, having admitted that in the eyes of the law you are lacking the authority to make a contract, I find myself obliged to order that all your actions are null and void.

SULTAN: You're mad—that's impossible!

CADI: I'm sorry but I cannot do other than this so long as . . .

SULTAN: So long as?

CADI: So long as you don't order me to be dismissed from my post, thrown out of the country, or have my head cut off. In this manner I would be freed from my oath and you could suit yourself and do as you pleased.

SULTAN: Is this a threat?

CADI: No, it's a solution.

VIZIER: You're complicating the problem for us, Chief Cadi.

CADI: I am helping you to get out of an impasse.

SULTAN: I've begun to weary of this man.

VIZIER: He knows that we are in his grasp in that he will divulge everything to the people if the least amount of coercion is used on him.

SULTAN: [To the CADI.] The substance of what you say is that you don't want to assist us.

CADI: On the contrary, Your Majesty, I wish very greatly to be of assistance to you, but *not* in this manner.

SULTAN: What do you suggest then?

CADI: That the law be applied.

SULTAN: If *you* applied the law, *I'd* lose my throne.

CADI: Not only that.

SULTAN: Is there something even worse?

CADI: Yes.

SULTAN: What is there then?

CADI: Owing to the fact that in the eyes of the law you are a chattel owned by the late Sultan, you have become part of his inheritance, and as he died without leaving an heir, his estate reverts to the Exchequer.[3] You are thus one of the chattels owned by the Exchequer—an unproductive chattel yielding no profit or return. I, in my additional capacity as Treasurer of the Exchequer, say: it is the custom in such cases to get rid of unprofitable chattels by putting them up for sale at auction, so that the good interests of the Exchequer be not harmed and so that it may utilize the proceeds of the sale in bringing benefit to the people generally and in particular to the poor.

SULTAN: [*Indignantly.*] An unproductive chattel? I?

3. Treasury.

CADI: I am speaking of course strictly from the legal point of view.

SULTAN: Up until now I have obtained no solutions from you. All I have had are insults.

CADI: Insults? I beg your pardon, illustrious Sultan. You know very well how much I revere and admire you and in what high esteem I hold you. You will recollect no doubt that it was I who from the first moment was the one to come forward to pay you homage and proclaim you as the Sultan to rule over our country. What I am doing now is merely to give a frank review of the situation from the point of view of civil and religious law.

SULTAN: The long and short of it is then that I'm a thing and a chattel and not a man or a human being?

CADI: Yes.

SULTAN: And that this thing or chattel is owned by the Exchequer?

CADI: Indeed.

SULTAN: And that the Exchequer disposes of unproductive chattels by putting them up for sale at auction for the public good?

CADI: Exactly.

SULTAN: Oh Chief Cadi, don't you feel, as I do, that this is all extraordinarily bizarre?

CADI: Yes, but . . .

SULTAN: And that there's a great deal of undue exaggeration and extravagance in it all?

CADI: Maybe, but in my capacity as Cadi what concerns me is where the facts stand in relation to the processes of the law.

SULTAN: Listen, Cadi. This law of yours has brought me no solution, whereas a small movement of my sword will ensure that the knot of the problem is severed instantly.

CADI: Then do so.

SULTAN: I shall. What does the spilling of a little blood matter for the sake of the practicability of governing?

CADI: Then you must start by spilling my blood.

SULTAN: I shall do everything I think necessary for safeguarding the security of the State, and I shall in fact start with you. I shall cast you into prison. Vizier! Arrest the Cadi!

VIZIER: Your Majesty, you have not yet listened to his answer to your question.

SULTAN: What question?

VIZIER: The question about the solution he deems appropriate for the problem.

SULTAN: He has answered this question.

VIZIER: What he said was not the solution but a review of the situation.

SULTAN: Is that true, Cadi?

CADI: Yes.

SULTAN: Have you then a solution to this problem of ours?

CADI: [In the same tone.] Yes.

SULTAN: Then speak! What is the solution?

CADI: There is only one solution.

SULTAN: Say! What is it?

CADI: That the law be applied.

SULTAN: Again? Once more?

CADI: Yes—once more and always, for I see no other solution.

SULTAN: Do you hear, Vizier? After this, do you entertain any hope of co-operation with this stubborn old windbag?

VIZIER: Allow me, Your Majesty, to interrogate him a little.

SULTAN: Do as you like!

VIZIER: O Chief Cadi, the question is a subtle one and it requires of you to explain to us clearly and in detail your point of view.

CADI: My point of view is both clear and simple and I can propound it in two words: for the solution of this problem we have before us two alternatives, that of the sword and that of the law. As for the sword, that is none of my concern; as for the law, that is what it behoves me to recommend and on which I can give a legal opinion. The law says: it is only his master, the possessor of the power of life and death over him, who has the right to manumit a slave. In this instance, the master, the possessor of the power of life and death, died without leaving an heir and the ownership of the slave has reverted to the Exchequer. The Exchequer may not manumit him without compensation in that no one has the right to dispose gratis of property or chattels belonging to the State. It is, however, permitted for the Exchequer to make a disposition by sale, and the selling of the property of the State is not valid by law other than by an auction carried out publicly. The legal solution, therefore, is that we should put up His Majesty the Sultan for sale by public auction and the person to whom he is knocked down thereafter manumits him. In this manner the Exchequer is not harmed or defrauded in respect of its property and the Sultan gains his manumission and release through the law.

SULTAN: [To the VIZIER.] Do you hear all this?

VIZIER: [To the CADI.] We put up Our Majesty, the illustrious Sultan, for sale by public auction! This is sheer madness!

CADI: This is the legal and legitimate solution.

SULTAN: [To the VIZIER.] Don't waste time. No answer is left for this stupid and impudent fellow except to chop off his head—and let result what may! And it is I who shall perform this with my own hand. [He draws his sword.]

CADI: It is a great honour for me, Your Majesty, to die by your hand and for me to give up my life for the sake of truth and principles.

VIZIER: Patience, Your Majesty, patience! Don't make a martyr of this man! Such a broken-down old man could not hope for a more splendid death. It will be said that through him you destroyed the civil and religious laws; he will become the living symbol of the spirit of truth and principles— and many a glorious martyr has more effect and influence on the conscience of peoples than a tyrannical king.

SULTAN: [Suppressing his anger.] God's curse . . .

VIZIER: Don't give him this glory, Your Majesty, at the expense of the situation.

SULTAN: Then what's to be done? This man puts us in a dilemma, he makes us choose between two alternatives, both of them painful: the law which shows me up as weak and makes a laughing-stock of me, or the sword which brands me with brutality and makes me loathed.

VIZIER: [Turning to the CADI.] O Chief Cadi! Be tractable and obliging!

Don't be rigid and hard! Meet us half-way, find a compromise and work
with us towards finding a reasonable solution.

CADI: There is no reasonable way out other than the law.

VIZIER: We put the Sultan up for sale by auction?

CADI: Yes.

VIZIER: And the person he's knocked down to buys him?

CADI: He manumits him immediately, at the session for drawing up the
contract—that's the condition.

VIZIER: And who will accept to lose his money in this manner?

CADI: Many people—those who would ransom the Sultan's freedom with
their money.

VIZIER: Then why don't we ourselves undertake this duty—you and I—and
ransom our Sultan secretly with our own money and gain this honour?
Is it not an appropriate idea?

CADI: I'm afraid not. It cannot be secret—the law is specific in that it lays
down that every sale of the properties of the Exchequer must be carried
out publicly and by general auction.

SULTAN: [To the VIZIER.] Don't trouble yourself with him—he's determined
to disgrace us.

VIZIER: [To the CADI.] For the last time, Chief Cadi—is there no stratagem
for extracting us from this impasse?

CADI: A stratagem? I am not the person to ask to look for stratagems.

SULTAN: Naturally! This man looks only for what will provoke and humiliate
us.

CADI: Not I as a person, Your Majesty. I as a person am weak and have
nothing to do with the whole matter. If the matter were in my hands and
depended upon my wishes, I would like nothing better than to extricate
you from this situation in the best manner you could wish.

SULTAN: Poor weak fellow! The matter's not in his hands—in whose hands
then?

CADI: The law's.

SULTAN: Yes, the spectre behind which he hides in order to subjugate me,
impose his will upon me, and show me up before the people in that
laughable, feeble, and ignominious guise.

CADI: I as a person would rather wish for you to appear in the guise of the
glorious ruler.

SULTAN: Do you consider it as being among the characteristics of glory that
a sultan be treated like goods or chattels to be sold in the market?

CADI: It is certainly a characteristic of glory that a sultan should submit to
the law as do the rest of people.

VIZIER: It is truly laudable, Chief Cadi, that the ruler should obey the law
as does the sentenced person, but this entails a great hazard. The politics
of government have their procedures; the ruling of people has other
methods.

CADI: I know nothing of politics or of the business of ruling people.

SULTAN: It's our business—allow us then to exercise it in our own way.

CADI: I have not fettered your hands, Your Majesty. You possess complete
freedom to exercise your rule as you wish.

SULTAN: Fine! I now see what I must do.

VIZIER: What are you going to do, Your Majesty?

SULTAN: Look at this old man! Do you see him carrying a sword on his belt? Of course not. He carries nothing but a tongue in his mouth with which he turns words and phrases. He's good at using the acumen and skill he possesses, but I carry this. [*And he indicates his sword.*] It's not made of wood, it's not a toy. It's a real sword and must be useful for something, must have some reason for its existence. Do you understand what I'm saying? Answer! Why was it ordained that I should carry it? Is it for decoration or for action?

VIZIER: For action.

SULTAN: And you, Cadi—why do you not answer? Answer! Is it for decoration or for action?

CADI: For one or the other.

SULTAN: What are you saying?

CADI: I am saying, for this or for that.

SULTAN: What do you mean?

CADI: I mean that you have a choice, Your Majesty. You can employ it for action, or you can employ it for decoration. I recognize the undoubted strength possessed by the sword, its swift action and decisive effect. But the sword gives right to the strongest, and who knows who will be the strongest tomorrow? There may appear some strong person who will tilt the balance of power against you. As for the law, it protects your rights from every aggression, because it does not recognize the strongest—it recognizes right. And now there's nothing for you to do, Your Majesty, but choose: between the sword which imposes and yet exposes you, and between the law which threatens and yet protects you.

SULTAN: [*Thinking a while.*] The sword which imposes and exposes me, and the law which threatens and protects me?

CADI: Yes.

SULTAN: What talk is this?

CADI: The frank truth.

SULTAN: [*Thinking and repeating over to himself.*] The sword which imposes and exposes? The law which threatens and protects?

CADI: Yes, Your Majesty.

SULTAN: [*To the* VIZIER.] What an accursed old man he is! He's got a unique genius for always landing us in a spot.

CADI: I have done nothing, Your Majesty, except to present to you the two sides of the question; the choice is yours.

SULTAN: The choice? The choice? What is your opinion, Vizier?

VIZIER: It is for you to decide about this, Your Majesty.

SULTAN: As far as I can see, you don't know either.

VIZIER: Actually, Your Majesty, the . . .

SULTAN: The choice is difficult?

VIZIER: Certainly.

SULTAN: The sword which imposes me on all and yet which exposes me to danger, or the law which threatens my wishes yet which protects my rights.

VIZIER: Yes.

SULTAN: You choose for me.

VIZIER: I? No, no, Your Majesty!

SULTAN: What are you frightened of?

VIZIER: Of the consequences—of the consequences of this choice. Should it one day become apparent that I had chosen the wrong course, then what a catastrophe there'd be!

SULTAN: You don't want to bear the responsibility?

VIZIER: I wouldn't dare—it's not my right.

SULTAN: In the end a decision must be made.

VIZIER: No one, Your Majesty, but yourself has the right to decide in this matter.

SULTAN: Truly, there is no one but myself. I cannot escape from that. It's I who must choose and bear the responsibility of the choice.

VIZIER: You are our master and our ruler.

SULTAN: Yes, this is my most fearful moment, the fearful moment for every ruler—the moment of giving the final decision, the decision that will change the course of things, the moment when is uttered that small word which will decide the inevitable choice, the choice that will decide fate.
[He thinks hard as he walks up and down, with the other two waiting for him to speak. Silence reigns for a moment.]

SULTAN: [With head lowered in thought.] The sword or the law? The law or the sword?

VIZIER: Your Majesty, I appreciate the precariousness of your situation.

SULTAN: Yet you don't want to assist me with an opinion?

VIZIER: I cannot. In this situation you alone are the one to decide.

SULTAN: There is, therefore, no getting away from deciding all by myself?

VIZIER: That's so.

SULTAN: The sword or the law? The law or the sword? [He thinks for a while, then raises his head sharply.] Good—I've decided.

VIZIER: Let us have your orders, Your Majesty.

SULTAN: I have decided to choose, to choose . . .

VIZIER: What, Your Majesty?

SULTAN: [Shouting decisively.] The law! I have chosen the law!

CURTAIN

Act Two

The same square. GUARDS *have started to arrange rows of people around a platform that has been set up there. The* WINE MERCHANT's *shop is closed and he is standing talking to the* SHOEMAKER, *who is engrossed in his work at the open door of his shop.*

WINE MERCHANT: How odd of you, Shoemaker! You open your shop and work when today every shop is closed, just like a feast day?

SHOEMAKER: And why should I close it? Is it because they're selling the Sultan?

WINE MERCHANT: You fool—because you'll be watching the most incredible sight in the world!

SHOEMAKER: I can see everything that goes on from here while I work.

WINE MERCHANT: It's up to you. As for me I've closed my shop so that I shan't miss the smallest detail of this wonderful spectacle.

SHOEMAKER: You're making the biggest mistake, my friend. Today's an excellent opportunity for attracting customers. It's not every day you get such crowds gathered outside your shop. It is certain that today many people will suffer from thirst and will yearn for a drop of your drink.

WINE MERCHANT: Do you think so?

SHOEMAKER: It's obvious. Look—here am I, for example, showing off my finest shoes today. [*He points to the shoes hanging up at the door of his shop.*]

WINE MERCHANT: My dear Shoemaker, those who come to buy today have come to buy the Sultan, not your shoes.

SHOEMAKER: Why not? Maybe there are some among the people who are in greater need of my shoes.

WINE MERCHANT: Shut up, say no more! It seems you don't understand what's so extraordinary about this happening, don't realize that it's unique. Do you find a sultan being put up for sale every day?

SHOEMAKER: Listen, friend. I'll talk to you frankly: even were I to have sufficient money to buy the Sultan, by God I wouldn't do it!

WINE MERCHANT: You wouldn't buy him?

SHOEMAKER: Never!

WINE MERCHANT: Allow me to say you're a fool!

SHOEMAKER: No, I'm intelligent and astute. Just tell me what you'd want me to do with a sultan in my shop? Can I teach him this trade of mine? Of course not! Can I entrust him with any work? Certainly not! Then, it's I who'll go on working doubly hard so as to feed him, look after him, and serve him. I swear that that is what would happen. I'd merely be buying a rod for my back, a sheer luxury I couldn't afford. My resources, friend, don't allow me to acquire works of art.

WINE MERCHANT: What nonsense!

SHOEMAKER: And you—would you buy him?

WINE MERCHANT: Can there be any doubt about that?

SHOEMAKER: What would you do with him?

WINE MERCHANT: Many things, very many things, my friend. His mere presence in my shop would be enough to bring along the whole city. It would be enough to ask him to recount to my customers every evening the stories of his battles against the Mongols, the strange things that have happened to him, his voyages and adventures, the countries he has seen, the places he's been to, the deserts he's crossed—wouldn't all that be valuable and enjoyable?

SHOEMAKER: Certainly, you could employ him in that manner but I . . .

WINE MERCHANT: You too could do the same.

SHOEMAKER: How? He knows nothing about repairing shoes or making soles for him to be able to talk about them.

WINE MERCHANT: It's not necessary for him to talk in your shop.

SHOEMAKER: What would he do then?

WINE MERCHANT: If I were in your place I'd know how to employ him.

SHOEMAKER: How? Tell me.

WINE MERCHANT: I'd sit him down in front of the door of the shop in a comfortable chair, I'd put a new pair of shoes on his feet and a placard above his head reading: 'Sultan Shoes Sold Here', and the next day you'd see how the people of the city would flock to your shop and demand your wares.

SHOEMAKER: What a great idea!

WINE MERCHANT: Isn't it?

SHOEMAKER: I'm beginning to admire your ingenuity.

WINE MERCHANT: What do you say then to thinking about buying him together and making him our joint property. I'd release him to you during the day and you could give him to me for the evening?

SHOEMAKER: A lovely dream! But all we own, you and I, isn't enough to buy one of his fingers.

WINE MERCHANT: That's true.

SHOEMAKER: Look! The crowds have begun to arrive and collect.

[*Groups of men, women and children gather together and chat among themselves.*]

FIRST MAN: [*To another man.*] Is it here they'll be selling the Sultan?

SECOND MAN: Yes, don't you see the guards?

FIRST MAN: If only I had money!

SECOND MAN: Shut up! That's for the rich!

CHILD: Mother! Is that the Sultan?

MOTHER: [*To the* CHILD.] No, child, that's one of the guards.

CHILD: Where is the Sultan then?

MOTHER: He hasn't come yet.

CHILD: Has the Sultan got a sword?

MOTHER: Yes, a large sword.

CHILD: And will they sell him here?

MOTHER: Yes, child.

CHILD: When, Mother?

MOTHER: Very soon.

CHILD: Mother! Buy him for me!

MOTHER: What?

CHILD: The Sultan! Buy me the Sultan!

MOTHER: Quiet! He's not a toy for you to play with.

CHILD: You said they'll sell him here. Buy him for me then.

MOTHER: Quiet, child. This is not a game for children.

CHILD: For whom then? For grown-ups?

MOTHER: Yes, it's for grown-ups.

[*The window of the* LADY's *house is opened and the* MAIDSERVANT *looks out.*]

MAID: [*Calling.*] Wine Merchant! Tavern keeper! Have you closed your shop today?

WINE MERCHANT: Yes—haven't I done right? And your mistress? Where is she? Is she still in bed?

MAID: No, she has just got out of her bath to dress.

WINE MERCHANT: She was superb! Her trick with the Executioner worked well.

MAID: Quiet! He's there. I can see him in the crowd. Now he's spotted us.

EXECUTIONER: [*Approaching the* WINE MERCHANT.] God curse you and wine!

WINE MERCHANT: Why? What sin has my wine committed to justify your curse? Didn't it bring joy to your heart that night, stimulate you in your singing, and cause you to see everything around you clear and pure?

EXECUTIONER: [*In tones of anger.*] Clear and pure! Certainly that night I saw everything clear and pure!

WINE MERCHANT: Certainly—do you doubt it?

EXECUTIONER: Shut up and don't remind me of that night.

WINE MERCHANT: I've shut up. Tell me: are you on holiday today?

EXECUTIONER: Yes.

WINE MERCHANT: And your friend the condemned man?

EXECUTIONER: He has been pardoned.

WINE MERCHANT: And you, naturally. No one asked you about that business at dawn?

EXECUTIONER: No.

WINE MERCHANT: Then everything has turned out for the best.

EXECUTIONER: Yes, but I don't like anyone to make a fool of me or play tricks on me.

MAID: Even when it means saving a man's head?

EXECUTIONER: Shut up, you vile woman—you and your mistress.

MAID: Are you continuing to insult us on such a day?

WINE MERCHANT: [To the EXECUTIONER.] Don't upset yourself! This evening I'll bring you a large glass of the best wine—free.

EXECUTIONER: Free?

WINE MERCHANT: Yes, a present from me, to drink to the health . . .

EXECUTIONER: Of whom?

WINE MERCHANT: [Catching sight of the MUEZZIN approaching.] To the health of the brave Muezzin!

EXECUTIONER: That most evil of liars!

MUEZZIN: A liar? Me?

EXECUTIONER: Yes, you claim that I was fast asleep at that hour.

MUEZZIN: And you were drunk!

EXECUTIONER: I'm absolutely convinced that I was awake and alert and that I hadn't slept for a moment up until then.

MUEZZIN: So long as you're absolutely convinced of that . . .

EXECUTIONER: Yes, I didn't sleep at all up until then.

MUEZZIN: Fine!

EXECUTIONER: You mean you agree about that?

MUEZZIN: Yes.

EXECUTIONER: Then it's you who're lying.

MUEZZIN: No!

EXECUTIONER: Then I was sleeping?

MUEZZIN: Yes.

EXECUTIONER: How can you say yes?

MUEZZIN: No!

EXECUTIONER: Make your mind up! Is it yes or is it no?

MUEZZIN: Which do you want?

EXECUTIONER: I want to know whether I was asleep at that time or whether I was awake.

MUEZZIN: What does it matter to you? So long as everything has passed peacefully—your friend the condemned man has been issued with a pardon and no one has asked you about anything. As for me, no one has spoken to me about the matter of that dawn. The question in relation to us all has ended as well as we could hope, so why dig up the past?

EXECUTIONER: Yes, but the question still troubles me since that day. I haven't grasped the situation absolutely clearly. I want to know whether

I really was asleep at that time and whether you really gave the call to the dawn prayer without my being aware of it. In the end you must divulge to me what actually happened for you doubtless know the whole truth. Tell me exactly what happened then. I was in truth a little drunk at the time but . . .

MUEZZIN: Since the matter occupies your mind to such an extent, why should I put you at ease. I prefer to leave you like this, grilling away and turning on the fire of doubt.

EXECUTIONER: May you turn on Hell's Fire, you ruffian of a Muezzin!

MUEZZIN: [Shouting.] Look! Look! The Sultan's retinue has come!

[The RETINUE with the SULTAN at its head appears, followed by the CHIEF CADI, the VIZIER, and the condemned SLAVE TRADER. They walk towards the dais, where the SULTAN seats himself in the middle chair with all around him, while the SLAVE TRADER stands beside him to face the people.]

WINE MERCHANT: [To the EXECUTIONER.] Extraordinary! This is your friend the condemned man. What has brought him here alongside the Sultan?

EXECUTIONER: [Looking at him.] Truly, by God, it's none other than he.

MUEZZIN: No doubt he is the person charged with making the sale—is he not one of the biggest slave traders?

WINE MERCHANT: Do you see, Executioner? His escape, therefore, from your hands was no accident.

EXECUTIONER: How extraordinary! Here he is selling the same sultan twice—once as a child and again now when he's grown up.

MUEZZIN: Quiet! He's about to talk.

SLAVE TRADER: [Clapping his hands.] Quiet, people! I announce to you, in my capacity of slave-trader and auctioneer, that I have been charged with carrying out this sale by public auction for the benefit of the Exchequer. It honours me, first of all, that the Chief Cadi will open these proceedings with a word explaining the conditions of this sale. Let our venerable Chief Cadi now speak.

CADI: O people! The sale to be held before you is not like any other sale: it is of a special kind and this fact has been previously announced to you. This sale must be accompanied by another contract, a contract of man-umission whereby the person who is the highest bidder at the auction may not retain what he has bought but must proceed with the manu-mission at the same session as the contract of sale, that is to say at this present session of ours. There is no need for me to remind you of the law's provision which prevents State employees from participating in any sale by the State. Having said this I leave the Vizier to speak to you about the patriotic character of these proceedings.

SHOEMAKER: [Whispering to the WINE MERCHANT.] Did you hear? The buyer cannot keep what he has bought. This means throwing one's money into the sea.

WINE MERCHANT: [Whispering.] We'll now see what imbecile will come forward.

SLAVE TRADER: Silence! Silence!

VIZIER: Honourable people! You are today present at a great and unique occasion, one of the most important in our history: a glorious Sultan asks for his freedom and has recourse to his people instead of to his sword—

that sharp and mighty sword by which he was victorious in battles against the Mongols and with which he could also have been victorious in gaining his freedom and liberating himself from slavery. But our just and triumphant Sultan has chosen to submit to the law like the lowliest individual amongst his subjects. Here he is seeking his freedom by the method laid down by law. Whoever of you wishes to redeem the freedom of his beloved Sultan, let him come forward to this auction, and whoever of you pays the highest price will have done a goodly act for his homeland and will be remembered for time immemorial.

    [*Cheers from the crowd.*]

VOICE: [*Raised from amongst* THE PEOPLE.] Long live the Sultan!

ANOTHER VOICE: Long live the law!

SLAVE TRADER: Silence, O people!

VIZIER: [*Continuing.*] And now, O noble people, that you know the small and trivial sacrifice your country expects of you for the sake of this high and lofty purpose—the freeing of your Sultan with your money and the passing of that money to the Exchequer so that it may be spent on the poor and those in need—now that your dearly beloved and cherished Sultan has come to you so that you may compete in showing your appreciation of him and liberating him, I declare that the proceedings shall begin.

    [*He indicates to the* SLAVE TRADER *that he should begin, while the crowds cheer.*]

SLAVE TRADER: Silence! Silence! O people of this city, the auction has commenced. I shall not resort to enumerating properties and attributes as is generally resorted to in the markets for the purpose of making people want to acquire the goods, for the subject of this sale is above every description or comment. It is no extravagance or exaggeration to say that he is worth his weight in gold. However, it is not the intention to make things difficult or to inhibit you, but to facilitate matters for you in gauging what is possible. I thus begin the auction with a sum both small and paltry in respect of a sultan: Ten thousand dinars! [*Uproar amongst the crowd.*]

SHOEMAKER: [*To the* WINE MERCHANT.] Ten thousand? Only! What a trifling sum! Look at that great ruby in his turban! By God, it alone is worth a hundred thousand dinars!

WINE MERCHANT: Truly it's a paltry amount—especially when paid for a noble and patriotic end! Ten thousand dinars! It is not seemly. I'm a loyal citizen and this displeases me. [*Shouts.*] Eleven thousand dinars!

SLAVE TRADER: Eleven thousand dinars! Eleven thousand?

SHOEMAKER: [*To the* WINE MERCHANT.] Only eleven thousand dinars? Is that all you have? Then I'll say [*Shouting.*]—twelve thousand dinars!

SLAVE TRADER: Twelve thousand dinars! Twelve thousand . . .

WINE MERCHANT: [*To the* SHOEMAKER.] Are you outbidding me? Then I'll say . . . thirteen thousand dinars!

SLAVE TRADER: Thirteen thousand dinars! Thirteen thousand . . .

    [*An* UNKNOWN MAN *comes forward suddenly, forcing his way through the crowd.*]

UNKNOWN MAN: [*Shouting.*] Fifteen thousand dinars!

SHOEMAKER: Good heavens! Who can this man be?

WINE MERCHANT: A joker of your own ilk without doubt.

SHOEMAKER: And of your ilk too.

SLAVE TRADER: Fifteen thousand dinars! Fifteen thousand! Fifteen thousand!

SHOEMAKER: [*Shouting.*] Sixteen thousand dinars!

SLAVE TRADER: [*Shouting.*] Sixteen thousand dinars! Sixteen!

UNKNOWN MAN: Eighteen thousand dinars!

SHOEMAKER: [*To the* WINE MERCHANT.] In one fell swoop! This fellow's overdoing things!

SLAVE TRADER: Eighteen thousand dinars! Eighteen thousand!

WINE MERCHANT: [*Scrutinizing the* UNKNOWN MAN *closely.*] It seems to me I've seen this man somewhere. Yes, he's one of the well-to-do; he comes to my tavern from time to time and drinks a glass of wine before going up to that beautiful lady.

SHOEMAKER: [*Turning to her window.*] Look! There she is at the window! Glittering in all her cheap finery as though she were some sugar doll! [*Shouts to her.*] You pretty one up in your heights, are you too not a loyal citizen?

LADY: Shut up, you Shoemaker! I am not one to be made fun of in such circumstances. By God, if you don't keep quiet I'll tell on you and they'll put you into prison.

SLAVE TRADER: [*Calling out.*] Eighteen thousand dinars ... at a sum of eighteen thousand ...

[A LEADING CITIZEN *comes forward to the dais.*]

CITIZEN: [*Shouting.*] Nineteen thousand dinars!

UNKNOWN MAN: I bid twenty thousand dinars!

SLAVE TRADER: Twenty thousand dinars! Twenty thousand dinars! Twenty!

CITIZEN: I bid twenty-one thousand dinars!

UNKNOWN MAN: Twenty-two thousand dinars!

[A SECOND LEADING CITIZEN *comes forward.*]

2ND CITIZEN: Twenty-three thousand dinars!

SLAVE TRADER: Twenty-three! Twenty-three!

UNKNOWN MAN: Twenty-five!

SLAVE TRADER: Twenty-five thousand dinars! Twenty-five!

[A THIRD LEADING CITIZEN *comes forward.*]

3RD CITIZEN: Twenty-six!

SLAVE TRADER: [*Shouting.*] Twenty-six thousand dinars! Twenty-six!

UNKNOWN MAN: Twenty-eight!

SLAVE TRADER: [*Shouting.*] Twenty-eight! Twenty-eight thousand dinars!

3RD CITIZEN: Twenty-nine!

SHOEMAKER: [*Whispering to the* WINE MERCHANT.] Are these people really serious about all this?

WINE MERCHANT: It seems so.

SLAVE TRADER: Twenty-nine ... twenty-nine thousand dinars! Twenty-nine!

UNKNOWN MAN: [*Shouting.*] Thirty! I bid thirty thousand dinars!

SLAVE TRADER: Thirty! At a sum of thirty! Thirty thousand dinars!

SHOEMAKER: [*Whispering.*] Thirty thousand dinars to be thrown into the sea! What a madman!

SLAVE TRADER: [*Shouting at the top of his voice.*] Thirty thousand dinars! Thirty! Any better bid? No one? No one bids more than thirty thousand dinars? Is this all I'm offered as a price for our great Sultan?

SULTAN: [*To the* VIZIER.] So this is the height of noble, patriotic, appreciation!

VIZIER: Your Majesty, those present bidding here are mostly the miserly merchants and well-to-do, those whose nature is niggardly, whose one desire is profit, and who begrudge spending money for the sake of a lofty purpose.

SLAVE TRADER: [*Shouting.*] Thirty thousand dinars! Once again I say: Who bids more? No one? No? No? [*The* SLAVE TRADER *exchanges glances with the* VIZIER, *then announces.*] I shall count up to three: One—two—three! That's it! The final price is thirty thousand dinars. [*Cheering from the crowd.*]

WINE MERCHANT: [*To the* SHOEMAKER.] He's a client of mine, the man who won the auction.

SLAVE TRADER: Come forward the winner! Accept congratulations for your good luck! [*The crowds cheer him.*]

VIZIER: I congratulate you, good citizen, and salute you. [*Cheering from the crowd.*]

SLAVE TRADER: [*Shouting.*] Silence! Silence!

VIZIER: [*Continuing what he has to say.*] I salute you, good citizen, in the name of the fatherland and in the name of this loyal and upright people from whom you have your origins, for buying and ransoming the freedom of our great Sultan. This sublime deed of yours will be inscribed for evermore in the pages of the history of this noble people.

[*Cheering from the crowd.*]

SLAVE TRADER: [*Shouting.*] Silence! [*Turns to the* UNKNOWN MAN.] O good citizen, the sum is ready, is it not?

UNKNOWN MAN: Certainly—the sacks of gold are but a few paces away.

SLAVE TRADER: Good. Wait, then, for the venerable Chief Cadi to give his orders.

CADI: The question is decided. The judgement of the law has been carried out. The problem has been solved. Approach, good citizen. Are you able to sign your name?

UNKNOWN MAN: Yes, milord Cadi.

CADI: Sign, then, on these deeds.

UNKNOWN MAN: I hear and obey, milord Cadi.

CADI: [*Presenting him with a document.*] Here—sign here.

UNKNOWN MAN: [*Reading before signing.*] What's this? And that?

CADI: This is the contract of sale.

UNKNOWN MAN: Yes, I'll sign. [*He signs the document.*]

CADI: And this too. [*He presents him with the second document.*]

UNKNOWN MAN: This? What's this?

CADI: This is the deed of manumission.

UNKNOWN MAN: [*Taking a step backwards.*] I'm sorry.

CADI: [*Taken unawares.*] What are you saying?

UNKNOWN MAN: I can't sign this deed.

CADI: Why not? What's this you're saying?

UNKNOWN MAN: I'm saying it's not within my power.

CADI: What's not within your power?

UNKNOWN MAN: To sign the deed of manumission.

CADI: [*In a daze.*] It's not within your power to sign?

UNKNOWN MAN: No, it's not within my power or authority.

CADI: What's the meaning of this? What do you mean by this? You're undoubtedly mad. It's your bounden duty to sign the deed of manumission. That's the condition—the basic condition for the whole of these proceedings.

UNKNOWN MAN: I much regret that I am in no position to do this. This is beyond me, is outside the limits of my authority.

VIZIER: What's this man saying?

CADI: I don't understand.

VIZIER: [To the UNKNOWN MAN.] Why do you refuse to sign the deed of manumission?

UNKNOWN MAN: Because I have not been given permission to do so.

VIZIER: Have not been given permission?

UNKNOWN MAN: [Confirming what he has to say with nods of the head.] I have not been given permission, having been empowered only in respect of the bidding and the contract of sale. Outside this sphere I have no authorization.

CADI: Authorization? Authorization from whom?

UNKNOWN MAN: From the person who appointed me to act for him.

CADI: You are the agent for another person?

UNKNOWN MAN: Yes, milord Cadi.

CADI: Who is this person?

UNKNOWN MAN: I can't say.

CADI: But you must say.

UNKNOWN MAN: No! No, I can't.

VIZIER: You are absolutely required to tell us the person who appointed you to act for him in signing the deed of sale.

UNKNOWN MAN: I cannot divulge his name.

VIZIER: Why?

UNKNOWN MAN: Because I swore an irrevocable oath that I would keep his name a secret.

VIZIER: And why should the person who appointed you be so careful about his name remaining secret?

UNKNOWN MAN: I don't know.

VIZIER: He obviously has a lot of money seeing that he is able to spend this vast sum all at once.

UNKNOWN MAN: These thirty thousand dinars are his whole life's savings.

VIZIER: And he empowered you to put them all into this auction?

UNKNOWN MAN: Yes.

VIZIER: That's the very acme of generosity, the height of noble feeling . . . but why hide his name? Is it modesty? Is it an urgent wish that his bounty should remain hidden and his good deed unknown?

UNKNOWN MAN: Perhaps.

CADI: In such an event he should have given permission to his agent to sign the manumission deed as well.

UNKNOWN MAN: No, he commissioned me to sign only the contract of sale.

CADI: This is evidence of evil intent.

VIZIER: Truly!

SULTAN: [In a sarcastic tone.] It seems that things have become complicated.

CADI: A little, Your Majesty.

VIZIER: This man must speak, otherwise I'll force him to talk.

CADI: Gently, O Vizier, gently. He will talk of his own accord and will answer my questions in friendly fashion. Listen, good man—this person who appointed you, what things does he make in order to earn his living?

UNKNOWN MAN: He makes nothing.

CADI: Has he no trade?

UNKNOWN MAN: They claim he has.

CADI: They claim he has a trade but he does not make anything.

UNKNOWN MAN: That's so.

CADI: Then he's an employee.

UNKNOWN MAN: No.

CADI: He's rich?

UNKNOWN MAN: Fairly so.

CADI: And you're in charge of directing his affairs?

UNKNOWN MAN: That's about it.

CADI: Is he one of the notables?

UNKNOWN MAN: Better than that.

CADI: How's that?

UNKNOWN MAN: The notables visit him but he is unaffected by their visits.

CADI: He's a vizier then?

UNKNOWN MAN: No.

CADI: Has he influence?

UNKNOWN MAN: Yes, on his acquaintances.

CADI: Has he many acquaintances?

UNKNOWN MAN: Yes—many.

CADI: [*Thinking in silence as he passes his fingers through his beard.*] Yes. Yes.

SULTAN: Well finally, O Cadi—have you found a solution to these riddles? Or shall we now spend our time in games of riddles and conundrums?

VIZIER: [*His patience exhausted.*] We must have resort to the use of force, Your Majesty. There is no other choice open to us. That person, cloaked in secrets and concealing his name, who storms into this auction like this must inevitably be planning some suspiciously dangerous plan of action. With your permission, Your Majesty, I shall act in the matter. [*Calling to the* GUARDS.] Take this man off and torture him till he reveals the name of the person who appointed him and connived with him.

UNKNOWN MAN: [*Shouting.*] No! No! No! Don't send me to be tortured! Please! Don't torture me, I implore you!

VIZIER: Then talk!

UNKNOWN MAN: I swore not to.

VIZIER: [*To the* GUARDS.] Take him away!

[*The* GUARDS *surround him.*]

UNKNOWN MAN: No! No! No!

[*The door of the* LADY's *house is opened. She appears and approaches the dais, followed by her* MAID *and slave-girls carrying sacks.*]

LADY: Leave him! Leave him! It is I who appointed him and here are your sacks of gold—full thirty thousand dinars in cash!

[*Commotion among the crowds.*]

SLAVE TRADER: [*Shouting.*] Be quiet! Silence!

VIZIER: Who's this woman?

THE CROWDS: [*Shouting.*] The whore whose house is before us.

VIZIER: Whore!

CROWDS: Yes, a whore well known in the district.

SULTAN: Bravo! Bravo! The crowning touch!

VIZIER: You, O woman, are you she who . . .

LADY: Yes, I am the person who authorized this man to take part in the auction on my account. [*Turning to the* UNKNOWN MAN.] Is that not so?

UNKNOWN MAN: That's the truth, milady.

VIZIER: You? You dare to buy His Majesty?

LADY: And why not? Am I not a citizen and do I not have money? Why then should I not have exactly the same rights as the others?

CADI: Yes, you have this right. The law applies to all. You must also, however, make yourself acquainted with the conditions of this sale.

LADY: That's natural. I know it's a sale.

CADI: A sale with a particular characteristic.

LADY: A sale by public auction.

CADI: Yes, but . . .

VIZIER: Before everything else it's a patriotic action. You are a citizen and I would think you are concerned with the well-being of the fatherland.

LADY: Without doubt.

VIZIER: Then sign this deed.

LADY: What does this deed contain?

VIZIER: Manumission.

LADY: What does that mean.

VIZIER: Don't you know the meaning of manumission?

LADY: Does it mean giving up what I am in possession of?

VIZIER: Yes.

LADY: Giving up the chattel I bought at the auction?

VIZIER: That's it.

LADY: No, I don't want to give it up.

SULTAN: That's just fine!

VIZIER: You shall give it up, woman!

LADY: No.

VIZIER: Don't force me to be tough. You know that I can force you.

LADY: By what means?

VIZIER: [*Pointing to his sword.*] By this.

SULTAN: Resort to the sword now? The time has passed.

VIZIER: She must yield.

LADY: I do yield, oh Vizier—I yield to the law. Is it not in pursuance of the law that I have signed the contract of sale with the State? Is this law therefore respected or not?

SULTAN: Reply, O Chief Cadi.

CADI: Truly, woman, you have signed a contract of sale but it is a conditional contract.

LADY: Meaning?

CADI: Meaning that it's a sale dependent upon a condition.

LADY: What condition?

CADI: Manumission—otherwise the sale itself becomes null and void.

LADY: You mean, O Cadi, that in order for the sale to become valid I must sign the manumission?

CADI: Yes.

LADY: And you likewise mean that I must sign the manumission so that the purchase may become effective?

CADI: Exactly.

LADY: But, milord Cadi, what is a purchase? Is it not owning a thing in return for a price?

CADI: That is so.

LADY: And what is manumission? Is it not the opposite of possession? Is it not yielding up possession?

CADI: Yes.

LADY: Then, O Cadi, you make manumission a condition of possession, that is to say that in order validly to possess the thing sold, the purchaser must yield up that very thing.

CADI: What? What?

LADY: You're saying, in other words, in order to possess something you must yield it up.

CADI: What are you saying? In order to possess you must yield up?

LADY: Or, if you like, in order to possess you must not possess.

CADI: What is this talk?

LADY: This is your condition: in order to buy you must manumit; in order for me to possess I must not possess. Do you find this reasonable?

SULTAN: She is right—neither common sense nor logic can accept this.

CADI: Who taught you this, woman? There is certainly someone learned in the law, some knowing, impudent debauchee who has taught her the things she is saying.

SULTAN: What does it matter? That changes nothing. This is *your* law, O Cadi. Now, you've seen for yourself! With the law there is always some argument that clashes with some other argument, and none is devoid of sense and logic.

CADI: But this is picking holes. This is sophistry. What this woman is saying is mere sophistry.

SULTAN: It's your condition that's sophistry. Selling is selling—that's self-evident. As for the rest, it is binding on no one.

CADI: Yes, Your Majesty. However, this woman took part in the auction being aware of the nature of it and knowing full well the whys and wherefores of it; for her to behave after that in this way is nothing but trickery, deceit, and double-dealing.

SULTAN: If you now want to give her a lesson in morals, that's your affair. As for the law, it no longer has a leg to stand on and you should desist from talking in its name.

CADI: Rather it is my duty, Your Majesty, to protect the law from such creatures who ridicule and make fun of it.

LADY: I would ask you, O Cadi, not to insult me.

CADI: And you, woman, should be ashamed of yourself—aren't you embarrassed at this behaviour of yours?

LADY: Embarrassed and ashamed? Why? Because I bought something the State was selling? Because I refused to be robbed of the thing I bought, the thing I'd paid such a high price for? Here are the sacks of gold, count out what is owing to you and take it!

CADI: I refuse your money, and I thus invalidate this contract.

LADY: For what reason do you invalidate it?

CADI: Because you're a woman of bad reputation and wicked conduct. This money may well have been earned through immorality, so how can it be accepted as money to be paid to the Exchequer and the State?

LADY: This same money of mine has in fact been accepted as payment for dues and taxes, and are not dues and taxes paid to the Exchequer and the State? If that is your opinion, O Cadi, then I shall not pay a single tax to the State from now on.

SULTAN: Accept her money, O Cadi: it's a lot easier and simpler.

CADI: Then you insist on the stand you've taken, woman?

LADY: Certainly. I am not joking with these sacks of gold. I am paying in order to buy and I buy in order to possess. The law gives me this right. A sale is a sale. Possession is possession. Take your due and hand me over what is mine!

VIZIER: How can you want us to hand over to you the Sultan who rules this land, O woman?

LADY: Why then have you put the Sultan up for sale?

SULTAN: What she says is logical. What a woman!

LADY: I shall reply, for the reply is simple. You put him up for sale so that one of the people might buy him. Now I have bought him, having been the highest bidder at the auction—in public, in front of everyone. Here is the required price and all that remains for you to do is to hand over to me the goods purchased.

SULTAN: The goods?

LADY: Yes, and I demand that they be delivered to the house.

SULTAN: Which house?

LADY: My house of course—this house opposite.

SULTAN: [To the CADI.] Do you hear?

CADI: There is no longer any use or point in arguing with a woman of this sort. Your Majesty, I wash my hands of it.

SULTAN: What an excellent solution, Chief Cadi! You land me in this mire and then wash your hands of it.

CADI: I admit my failure—I didn't know I'd be facing this sort of a person.

SULTAN: And then?

CADI: Punish me, Your Majesty. I deserve the most terrible punishment for my bad advice and lack of foresight. Order that my head be cut off!

SULTAN: What's the point of cutting off your head? That head of yours on your shoulders cast me into this plight—will your decapitated head get me out of it?

VIZIER: Leave the matter to me, Your Majesty! I now see clearly what must be done. [He draws his sword.]

SULTAN: No!

VIZIER: But, Your Majesty . . .

SULTAN: I said no. Sheathe your sword!

VIZIER: Listen to me for a moment, Your Majesty.

SULTAN: Sheathe your sword! We have accepted this situation, so let's proceed.

VIZIER: Your Majesty, seeing that the Cadi has failed and is at a loss, let us go back to our own methods.

SULTAN: No, I shall not go back.

VIZIER: By the sword everything is easily accomplished and is solved in the twinkling of an eye.

SULTAN: No, I have chosen the law and I shall continue on that path whatever obstacles I may encounter.

VIZIER: The law?

SULTAN: Yes, and you yourself said so a while ago and expressed it in beautiful terms: 'The Sultan has chosen to submit to the law just like the lowliest individual amongst his subjects.' These fine words deserve that every effort be expended in implementing them.

VIZIER: Do you think, Your Majesty, that the lowliest individual amongst your subjects would agree to accept this situation? Here are the people standing before us; if you will permit me I shall ask them and seek their decision. Do you give me permission?

SULTAN: Do so and show me!

VIZIER: [Addressing the crowd.] O people! You see how this impudent woman treats your august Sultan, are you in agreement with what she has done?

THE PEOPLE: [Shouting.] No!

VIZIER: Are you happy with her insulting behaviour towards our illustrious ruler?

THE PEOPLE: No!

VIZIER: Do you consider it merits punishment?

THE PEOPLE: [Shouting.] Yes!

VIZIER: What is the appropriate punishment for her?

THE PEOPLE: [Shouting.] Death!

VIZIER: [Turning to the SULTAN.] You see, Your Majesty—the people have given their verdict.

LADY: [Turning to THE PEOPLE.] Death for me? Why, O people, do you condemn me to death? What offence have I committed? Is buying an affront and a crime? Have I stolen this money? It is my life's savings. Am I grabbing and making off by force with the thing offered for sale? I have bought it with my own money at a public auction before your very eyes. For what offence do you seek to spill the blood of a weak woman who has bought something at an auction?

VOICES: [Rising from amidst the crowd.] Death to the whore!

OTHER VOICES: [From amongst the crowd.] No, don't kill her!

SULTAN: [To the Vizier.] Do you see?

VIZIER: [To the people.] O people, do you consider that the judgement against her should be put into effect?

VOICES: [Shouting.] Yes!

OTHER VOICES: [Shouting.] No!

SULTAN: Opinions are divided, Vizier.

VIZIER: But the majority, Your Majesty, are on the side of death.

SULTAN: For me that is no justification for killing this woman. You are wanting the excuse of a semi-legal justification for employing the sword.

VIZIER: The death of this woman is essential for getting us out of this predicament.

SULTAN: We now need a lifeless corpse to save us?

VIZIER: Yes, Your Majesty.

SULTAN: Once again I am forced to choose between the mire and blood.

VIZIER: We can no longer force a way out for ourselves other than by the sword.

SULTAN: He who proceeds forwards along a straight line always finds a way out.

VIZIER: Your Majesty means . . .

SULTAN: I mean that there is no retreating, no turning back—do you understand?

VIZIER: I understand, Your Majesty. You wish to go on complying with the law.

SULTAN: Just so. I shall not swerve from what I have chosen, I shall not go back on what I have decided.

VIZIER: And how shall we go on complying with the law with which the Cadi himself has announced his defeat and inability to cope?

SULTAN: He is free to announce his defeat. As for me, I shall not retreat, so let us proceed along the road to its end.

VIZIER: And this woman who blocks the road for us?

SULTAN: Leave her to me. [*He turns to the woman.*] Come here, woman! Approach! Another step—here in front of me! I want to put a few questions to you. Do you permit me?

LADY: I hear and obey, Your Majesty.

SULTAN: First and foremost—who am I?

LADY: Who are you?

SULTAN: Yes, who am I?

LADY: You are the Sultan?

SULTAN: You admit I'm the Sultan?

LADY: Naturally.

SULTAN: Good—and what's the Sultan's job?

LADY: His job is to rule.

SULTAN: You agree that he rules?

LADY: Certainly.

SULTAN: Very good. In as much as you acknowledge all this, how can you demand that the Sultan be handed over to you?

LADY: Because he has become mine by right.

SULTAN: I do not dispute your right. However, I merely wonder at the possibility of your implementing this right. In as much as I am a sultan who rules, how can I carry out the functions of my office if I am handed over to you in your house?

LADY: Nothing is easier or simpler. You are a sultan during the day, therefore I shall lend you to the State for the whole of the day, and in the evening you will return to my house.

SULTAN: I'm afraid you don't understand my work correctly. A sultan is not the owner of a shop who keeps it open during the day and then locks it up at night. He is at the beck and call of the State at any moment. There are urgent and important questions that often require him to hold talks with his men of State in the middle of the night.

LADY: This too is an easy matter, for in my house there is a quiet secluded room where you can work with your men of State.

SULTAN: Do you regard such a set-up as acceptable?

LADY: More than acceptable, I regard it as marvellous!

SULTAN: It is indeed marvellous—a sultan who directs affairs of State from the house of a woman of whom it is said that she . . . please forgive me . . . my apologies.

LADY: Say it! Go on! The word no longer wounds me because of the many torments I have suffered—I have become immune. However, I assure you, O Sultan, that you will experience greater joy in my house than you do in yours.

SULTAN: Possibly, except that a ruler is not proficient in carrying out the functions of government when he does so from the houses of others.

LADY: That is if the ruler is free.

SULTAN: You have scored—I am not free. [*He lowers his head. A moment's silence.*]

LADY: What I admire in you, O Sultan, is your composed and calm attitude in the face of this catastrophe.

SULTAN: [*Raising his head.*] You are admitting then that it is a catastrophe?

LADY: It's self-evident—a great Sultan like you being badly treated in this way.

SULTAN: And is anyone but you badly treating me?

LADY: How right you are! What pride and joy it is to me to hear this from the mouth of a great sultan! It's an honour which merits the payment of all the world's gold. No one in the city after today will dare slight me, for I am treating sultans badly!

VIZIER: [*In a rage.*] Enough, woman! Enough! This is unbearable. She has overstepped all limits of decency. The head of this mischievous and shameless woman must fall!

SULTAN: Calm yourself!

LADY: Yes, calm yourself, O Vizier—and don't interfere in what does not concern you.

VIZIER: How can all this be borne? Patience, Lord! Patience, Lord!

LADY: Yes, have patience, O Vizier, and let the Sultan and me talk. This matter concerns us alone.

SULTAN: That's true.

LADY: Where did we get to, Your Majesty?

SULTAN: I no longer know—it was you who were talking.

LADY: Oh yes, I remember now—we got to where I was saying that it was an honour . . .

SULTAN: For you to treat me badly.

LADY: Rather that I should have the good fortune of enjoying talking to you. In fact, Your Majesty, it's the first time I have seen you at close quarters. People have talked about you so much but I didn't know you were so charming.

SULTAN: Thank you.

LADY: Truly, it's as though we'd been friends for a long time.

SULTAN: Is it your custom to subject your friends to humiliation and ridicule in this manner?

LADY: Not at all—just the opposite.

SULTAN: Then why make an exception of me?

LADY: This in fact is what has begun to upset me. How I would like to bring happiness to your heart and show you reverence and respect! But how? How can I do that! What's the way to do it?

SULTAN: The way's easy.

LADY: By signing this manumission deed?

SULTAN: I would have thought so.

LADY: No, I don't want to let you go. I don't want to give you up. You belong to me. You're mine—mine.

SULTAN: I belong to you and to all the rest of the people.

LADY: I want you to be mine alone.

SULTAN: And my people?

LADY: Your people have not paid gold in order to acquire you.

SULTAN: That's right, but you must know that it's absolutely impossible for me to be yours alone and for me to remain thereafter a sultan. There is only one situation in which it is in order for me to be yours alone.

LADY: What's that?

SULTAN: That I should not be a sultan, that I should give up the throne and relinquish power.

LADY: No, I don't wish that for you—I wish you to remain a sultan.

SULTAN: In that event there must be sacrifice.

LADY: From my side?

SULTAN: Or from my own.

LADY: I should give you up?

SULTAN: Or I should give up the throne?

LADY: It's for me to choose?

SULTAN: Of course it's for you to choose, because all the cards are in your hands.

LADY: Have I all that importance, all that weight?

SULTAN: At this moment, yes.

LADY: This is wonderful!

SULTAN: Certainly.

LADY: Then I now hold all the cards in my hands?

SULTAN: Yes.

LADY: At my pleasure I keep the Sultan in power?

SULTAN: Yes.

LADY: And by a word from me the removal of the Sultan is accomplished?

SULTAN: Yes.

LADY: This is truly wonderful!

SULTAN: Without doubt.

LADY: And who has given me all this authority—money?

SULTAN: The law.

LADY: A word from my mouth can change your destiny and channel your life either to slavery and bondage, or to freedom and sovereignty.

SULTAN: And it is up to you to choose.

LADY: [Thoughtfully.] Between bondage that bestows you upon me, and between freedom which retains you for your throne and your people.

SULTAN: It is up to you to choose.

LADY: The choice is difficult.

SULTAN: I know.

LADY: It is painful to let you go, to lose you for ever; but it is also painful to see you lose your throne, for our country has never had the good fortune to have a sultan with such courage and sense of justice. No, do not give up the rule, do not relinquish the throne! I want you to remain a sultan.

SULTAN: And so?

LADY: I shall sign the deed.

SULTAN: The manumission deed?

LADY: Yes.

CADI: [Hurrying to present the deed.] Here is the deed.

LADY: I have only a final request.

SULTAN: What is it?

LADY: That you give this night to me, Your Majesty—a single night. Honour me by accepting my invitation and be my guest until daybreak. And when the Muezzin gives the call to dawn prayers from this minaret here, I shall sign the deed of manumission and Your Majesty will be free.

CADI: If the Muezzin does give the call to dawn prayers!

LADY: Yes. Is this too much—that I buy with these sacks of gold not the Sultan himself but a single night with him as my guest?

SULTAN: I accept.

VIZIER: But, Your Majesty, who will guarantee that this promise will be kept by such a woman?

SULTAN: I shall. I am the guarantor, I trust what she says.

CADI: Do you take an oath on what you say, woman?

LADY: Yes, I swear. I swear a triple oath by Almighty God. I shall sign the deed of manumission when the Muezzin gives the call to dawn prayers from on top of this minaret.

CADI: I bear witness before God to that. All of us here are witnesses.

SULTAN: As for me, I believe her without an oath.

LADY: And now, O noble Sultan, will you be so good as to honour my humble house with your gracious presence?

SULTAN: With great pleasure!

[*The* SULTAN *rises and follows the* LADY *into her house. Music.*]

CURTAIN

Act Three

[*The same square. One side of the mosque with its minaret is in view, also a side of the* LADY's *house, showing a portion of the room with the window overlooking the square. The time is night. Among the throng are the* VIZIER, *the* SHOEMAKER, *and the* WINE MERCHANT.]

VIZIER: [*In the square, shouting to the* GUARDS.] What are all these crowds waiting for in the middle of the night? Turn the people away! Let everyone go to his home, to his bed!

GUARDS: [*Turning away the crowds.*] To your homes! To your houses!

THE CROWDS: [*Grumbling.*] No! No!

SHOEMAKER: [*Shouting.*] I want to stay here.

WINE MERCHANT: And I too shan't budge from here.

VIZIER: [*To the* GUARDS.] What are they saying?

GUARDS: They refuse to go.

VIZIER: [*Shouting.*] Refuse? What's this nonsense? Make them!

GUARDS: [*Forcefully.*] Everyone to his home! Everyone to his house! Get along! Get along!

SHOEMAKER: I'm already at home. This is my shop.

WINE MERCHANT: I too have my tavern right here before you.

GUARDS: Will you not obey orders? Get going! Get going! [*They push the* WINE MERCHANT *and the* SHOEMAKER.]

SHOEMAKER: There's no reason for violence—please.

WINE MERCHANT: Don't push me about like this!

VIZIER: [*To the* GUARDS.] Bring along those two trouble-makers!

[*The* GUARDS *seize hold of the* SHOEMAKER *and the* WINE MERCHANT *and bring them before the* VIZIER.]

SHOEMAKER: By God, I haven't done anything, milord Vizier.

VIZIER: Why do you refuse to go home?

SHOEMAKER: I don't want to go to bed. I have a strong desire to stay here, milord Vizier—in order to watch.

VIZIER: To watch what?

SHOEMAKER: To watch Our Majesty the Sultan leaving this house.

WINE MERCHANT: I too, milord Vizier—let me watch it.

VIZIER: Really, what affrontery! Today everyone's affrontery has reached the bounds of impudence. Even you and your comrade have the nerve to talk in such terms.

WINE MERCHANT: It's not impudence, milord Vizier, it's a request.

VIZIER: A request?

SHOEMAKER: Yes, milord Vizier, we request that you give us permission to watch.

VIZIER: What insolence! And what have you to do with this matter?

SHOEMAKER: Are we not good citizens? The fate of our Sultan inevitably concerns us.

VIZIER: This does not give you both the right to disobey orders.

SHOEMAKER: We are not disobeying, we are requesting. How can we sleep a wink tonight with the fate of our Sultan in the balance?

VIZIER: In the balance?

SHOEMAKER: Yes, milord—the balance of capricious whims.

VIZIER: What do you mean?

SHOEMAKER: I mean that the outcome is not reassuring.

VIZIER: Why do you think so?

SHOEMAKER: With such a woman one can be certain of nothing.

WINE MERCHANT: We have made a bet between ourselves. He says this woman will break her promise, while I say she will honour it.

VIZIER: A fine thing, indeed—of an important event like this you make a game of having bets!

WINE MERCHANT: We are not alone in this, milord Vizier. Many such as we among these crowds are tonight making bets among themselves. Even the Muezzin and the Executioner have made a bet.

VIZIER: The Executioner: where is the Executioner?

WINE MERCHANT: [*Pointing.*] Over there, milord. He's trying to hide among the people.

VIZIER: [*To the* GUARDS.] Bring him over here.

[*The* GUARDS *bring the* EXECUTIONER *to the* VIZIER.]

EXECUTIONER: [*Frightened.*] It's not my fault, milord Vizier. It's the Muezzin's mistake. It's he who's responsible, it's he who did not give the call to the dawn prayers.

VIZIER: Dawn? What dawn? We're no longer talking about dawn prayers, you idiot. [*The* WINE MERCHANT *and the* SHOEMAKER *laugh.*] Do you dare to laugh in my presence? Get out of my sight! Out! [*The* WINE MERCHANT *and the* SHOEMAKER *take to their heels.*] And now, Executioner—are you busy with bets?

EXECUTIONER: Bets? Who said so, milord?

VIZIER: I want a straight answer to my question.

EXECUTIONER: But, milord, I . . .

VIZIER: Don't be frightened—tell me.

EXECUTIONER: But this bet, milord . . .

VIZIER: I know, I know, and I shall not punish you. Answer this question frankly: will this woman in your opinion break her promise or will she honour it?

EXECUTIONER: But, milord Vizier, I . . .

VIZIER: I told you not to be frightened but to express your opinion without constraint. That's an order and you must obey it.

EXECUTIONER: Your order must be obeyed, milord—in truth I have no trust in this woman.

VIZIER: Why?

EXECUTIONER: Because she's a liar, a cheat, and a swindler!

VIZIER: Do you know her?

EXECUTIONER: I got to know some of her wiles when I was here that day waiting for the dawn in order to carry out the sentence of execution on the slave trader.

VIZIER: A liar, a cheat, and a swindler?

EXECUTIONER: Yes.

VIZIER: And what does such a woman deserve?

EXECUTIONER: Punishment of course.

VIZIER: And what is the punishment you deem suitable for her if she has tricked and lied to our exalted Sultan?

EXECUTIONER: Death, without doubt!

VIZIER: Good. Then be prepared to carry out this sentence at dawn.

EXECUTIONER: [*As though talking to himself.*] Dawn? Yet again?

VIZIER: What are you saying?

EXECUTIONER: I am saying that at dawn I shall be ready to execute the order of milord Vizier.

VIZIER: Yes, if the Muezzin has given the call to the dawn prayer and our Sultan has not emerged from this house a free man . . .

EXECUTIONER: Then I cut off the head of this woman.

VIZIER: Yes, as punishment for the crime of . . .

EXECUTIONER: Lying and cheating.

VIZIER: No.

EXECUTIONER: [*Not understanding.*] No?

VIZIER: [*As though talking to himself.*] No, that is not enough—it is not a crime that merits death. This woman is liable to find some high-sounding phrases in law and logic to justify her action. No, there must be some terrible and serious crime which she will not be able to justify or defend herself against—a crime that will earn her the universal opprobrium of the whole people. We could for instance say she is a spy.

EXECUTIONER: A spy?

VIZIER: Yes, that she's working for the Mongols. Then the people in their entirety will rise up and demand her head.

EXECUTIONER: Yes, an appropriate punishment.

VIZIER: Is that not your opinion?

EXECUTIONER: And I shall raise my voice crying 'Death to the traitor!'

VIZIER: Your voice alone will not suffice. There must be other voices besides yours giving this cry.

EXECUTIONER: There will be other voices.

VIZIER: Do you know whose they'll be?

EXECUTIONER: It won't be difficult to find them.

VIZIER: Witnesses must be got ready.

EXECUTIONER: All that is easy, milord.

VIZIER: I think that such an arrangement can be successful. I'm relying on you if things go badly.

EXECUTIONER: I am your faithful servant, milord Vizier.

[*A part of the room in the* LADY's *house is lit up.*]

VIZIER: Quiet! A light in the window! Let's move away a little.

[*While the room is lit up, the square becomes dark; the* LADY *appears and moves towards the sofa followed by the* SULTAN.]

SULTAN: [*Sitting down.*] Your house is magnificent and your furnishings costly.

LADY: [*Sitting at his feet.*] Yes, I told you just now that my husband was a wealthy merchant who had taste and a passion for poetry and singing.

SULTAN: Were you one of his slave-girls?

LADY: Yes, he bought me when I was sixteen years of age, then gave me my freedom and married me several years before his death.

SULTAN: Your luck was better than mine. With you no one forgot to free you at the proper time.

LADY: My real good luck is your having honoured my house with your presence tonight.

SULTAN: Here I am in your house—what do you intend doing with me tonight?

LADY: Nothing except to allow you to relax a little.

SULTAN: Is that all?

LADY: Nothing more than that. Previously I said to you that at my house there is more joy than at yours. I have beautiful slave-girls who excel at dancing and singing and playing on every musical instrument. Be assured, you will not be bored here tonight.

SULTAN: Until dawn breaks?

LADY: Think not of the dawn now. The dawn is still far off.

SULTAN: I shall do all you demand until dawn breaks.

LADY: I shall ask nothing of you except to converse, to take food, and to listen to singing.

SULTAN: Nothing but that?

LADY: But do you want me to ask of you more than that?

SULTAN: I don't know—you know best.

LADY: Let us then start with conversation—tell me about yourself.

SULTAN: About myself?

LADY: Yes, your story—tell me the story of your life.

SULTAN: You want me to tell you stories?

LADY: Yes, in truth you must have a store of wonderfully entertaining stories.

SULTAN: It is *I* now who must tell stories!

LADY: And why not?

SULTAN: Truly that's how it should be, seeing that it is I who am in the

position of Shahrazad![4] She too had to tell stories throughout the whole
night, awaiting the dawn that would decide her fate.

LADY: [*Laughing.*] And I, then, am the dreadful, awe-inspiring Shahriyar?[5]

SULTAN: Yes—isn't it extraordinary? Today everything is upside down.

LADY: No, you are always the Sultan. As for me, I am she who plays the
role of Shahrazad, always seated at your feet.

SULTAN: A Shahrazad having her apprehensive Shahriyar by the neck until
the morning comes.

LADY: No, rather a Shahrazad who will bring joy and gladness to the heart
of her sultan. You will see now how I shall deal with your anxiety and
misgivings. [*She claps and soothing music issues forth from behind the
screens.*]

SULTAN: [*After listening for a while.*] A delightful performance!

LADY: And I myself shall dance for you. [*She rises and dances.*]

SULTAN: [*After she has finished her dance.*] Delightful! It's all delightful! Do
you do this every night?

LADY: No, Your Majesty. This is an exception. It's just for you, for I myself
have not danced since being manumitted and married. On other nights
it is the slave-girls who do the dancing and singing.

SULTAN: For your clients?

LADY: My guests, rather.

SULTAN: As you will—your guests. Doubtless these guests of yours pay you
a high fee for all this. I now realize how it is you have such wealth.

LADY: My wealth I inherited from my husband. Sometimes I spend on these
nights more than I get back.

SULTAN: Why? For nothing?

LADY: For the sake of art. I am a lover of art.

SULTAN: [*Sarcastically.*] Refined art to be sure!

LADY: You don't believe me. You don't take what I say seriously. So be it.
Think as badly of me as you like—I am not in the habit of defending
myself against other people's assumptions. In people's eyes I am a woman
who behaves badly, and I have reached the stage where I have accepted
this judgement. I have found this convenient—it is no longer in my interests to correct people's opinion. When one has crossed the ultimate
boundaries of wickedness one becomes free, and I am in need of my
freedom.

SULTAN: You too?

LADY: Yes, in order to do what I enjoy.

SULTAN: And what do you enjoy?

LADY: The company of men.

SULTAN: Understood!

LADY: No, you understand wrongly. It's not as you think.

SULTAN: How is it then?

LADY: Do you want lies or the truth?

SULTAN: The truth of course.

LADY: You won't believe the truth, so what's the point of my telling it? A
truth that people don't believe is a useless truth.

SULTAN: Say it in any case.

---

4. The narrator of *The Thousand and One Nights.*   5. The king to whom Shahrazad tells the stories.

LADY: I shall say it purely to amuse you. I enjoy the company of men for their souls, not for their bodies. Do you understand?

SULTAN: No, not exactly.

LADY: I shall elucidate. When I was a young slave-girl of the same age as the slave-girls I have with me now, my master brought me up to love poetry and singing and playing on musical instruments. He used to make me attend his banquets and converse with his guests, who were poets and singers; they also included intellectuals and men of wit and charm. We would spend the night reciting poetry, singing and playing music and conversing, quoting and capping quotations from the masterpieces of literature, and laughing from the depths of our hearts. Those were wonderfully enjoyable nights, but they were also innocent and chaste. Please believe that. My master was a good man and knew no pleasure in life other than these nights—a pleasure without sin, without vulgarity. In this way did he bring me up and educate me. And when I later became his wife he did not wish to deprive me of the pleasure of those nights which used so to enchant me; he therefore allowed me to continue to attend, though from behind silken curtains. That's the whole story.

SULTAN: And after his death?

LADY: After his death I was unable to give up this practice, so I continued to invite my husband's guests. At first I would receive them screened behind the silken curtains, but when the people of the district began spreading gossip at seeing men nightly entering the house of a woman with no husband I found it pointless to continue to be screened behind the curtains. I said to myself: seeing that the people's verdict has pronounced me guilty, let me make myself the judge of my own behaviour.

SULTAN: It is truly extraordinary that your exterior should proclaim so loudly what is not to be found within; your shop window advertises goods that are not to be found inside.

LADY: It is for you to believe or not what I have said to you.

SULTAN: I prefer to believe—it is more conducive to peace of mind.

LADY: Be that as it may, I do not at all intend to change my life and habits. If the road I tread be filled with mire I shall continue to wade through it.

SULTAN: Mire! It's to be found on every road—be sure of that!

LADY: Now you remind me of what I did to you in front of the masses of people.

SULTAN: Truly you rolled me in it properly!

LADY: I was intentionally insolent to you, deliberately vulgar and impudent. Do you know why? Because I imagined you as being quite different. I imagined you as an arrogant sultan, strutting about haughtily and giving yourself airs—like most sultans. You could, in fact, well have been even more conceited and overbearing by reason of the wars you have waged and your victories. People always talk of that fabulous ruby which adorns your turban, that ruby that is without peer in the world, of which it is said that you seized it at sword-point from the head of the Mongol Chief. Yes, your deeds are wondrous and splendid. Thus the picture of you in my mind was synonymous with haughtiness, harshness, and cruelty. But as soon as you talked to me so pleasantly and modestly I was overcome by a certain bewilderment and confusion.

SULTAN: Don't be misled! I am not always so pleasant, nor so modest. There are times when I am more cruel and brutal than the worst of sultans.

LADY: I don't believe that.

SULTAN: That's because you've fallen under the influence of the present circumstances.

LADY: You mean that you are specially pleasant to me? This fills me with great pride, dear Majesty. But wait! Perhaps I have misunderstood. What is it that causes you to be so pleasant to me? Is it personal? Or is it the decision you await from me at daybreak?

SULTAN: I affect being pleasant with you, I put it on, in order to gain your sympathy—isn't that so?

LADY: And no sooner will you achieve your freedom than you'll revert to your true nature and will become the cruel Sultan who pursues revenge in order to atone to himself for his moments of humiliation—and then will come my hour of doom.

SULTAN: It would therefore be wise and far-sighted of you to keep me always in your grasp and power.

LADY: Is that so?

SULTAN: That is absolutely logical, seeing that you have your doubts.

LADY: Have I not the right to doubt?

SULTAN: I don't blame you if you do, for it is I who, quite simply and incautiously, have implanted in you the seeds of doubt by saying what I did about myself.

LADY: [*Regarding him searchingly.*] No.

SULTAN: No? Why?

LADY: I prefer to rely on the womanly instinct that is deep within me. It never deceives me.

SULTAN: And what does your womanly instinct tell you?

LADY: It tells me that you are not that type of man. You are different. I should have realized this from the moment I saw you renouncing the use of the sword.

SULTAN: If only you knew how easy things would have been had I used my sword!

LADY: Do you now regret it?

SULTAN: I am merely talking about how easy it would have been. However, the real victory is in solving the problem by sleight-of-hand.

LADY: And this is the path you are now pursuing?

SULTAN: Yes, but I am not confident about the result.

LADY: Let's suppose the result to be that your hopes are dashed—what will you do then?

SULTAN: I have already told you.

LADY: Give up your throne?

SULTAN: Yes.

LADY: No, I do not believe you would really do that. I'm not so simple or stupid as to believe that or to take it seriously. Even if you wanted to do it not a single person in the country would accept it, or would permit you to embark upon such an action. You would bear a heavy burden by accepting the easy solution and would revert to using the simple expedient.

SULTAN: It has never happened that I have taken a step backwards—not even in the field of battle. I admit that this is wrong from the military point of view, for there are circumstances that make retreat necessary. However, I have never done so. Perhaps luck was on my side; in any event I have adopted this bad practice.

LADY: You're amazing!

SULTAN: The truth is rather that I'm an unimaginative man.

LADY: You?

SULTAN: The proof is that were I possessed of imagination and had envisaged what awaited me at the end of such a road, I would have been stunned.

LADY: Nothing stuns you. You have composure, self-confidence, control over your actions, the ability to do what you want with meticulous precision and resoluteness. You are far from being weak or wily—you're frank, natural, and courageous. There's no more to say.

SULTAN: Are you flattering me? Who should be flattering whom? Once again the situations have been reversed.

LADY: Will you permit me, my dear Sultan?

SULTAN: To do what?

LADY: To ask you a personal question?

SULTAN: Personal? Is not all this that we are engaged in personal?

LADY: I want to ask you about—about your heart, about love.

SULTAN: Love? What love?

LADY: Love—for a woman?

SULTAN: Do you imagine I have the time to occupy myself with such things?

LADY: How strange! Has your heart never opened to love a woman?

SULTAN: Why have you opened your large eyes like this in astonishment? Is it such an important matter?

LADY: But you have definitely known many women?

SULTAN: Certainly—that is the nature of military life. The leader of an army, as you know, every night has some female prisoner, some captive, brought to him. Sometimes there are beautiful women among them. That's all there is to it.

LADY: And not a single particular woman succeeded in attracting your glances?

SULTAN: My glances? You should know that at the end of the day I returned always to my tent with eyes filled with the dust of battle.

LADY: And on the following day? Did you not retain a single memory of those beautiful women?

SULTAN: On the following day I would again mount my steed and think of something else.

LADY: But now you're the Sultan. You certainly have sufficient time for love.

SULTAN: Do you believe so?

LADY: What prevents you?

SULTAN: The problems of government. And this is one of them—this problem that has descended upon my head today so unexpectedly and put me in this fix. Do you consider that such a problem allows one to be in the mood for love?

LADY: [Laughing.] You're right!

SULTAN: You laugh!

LADY: Another question—the last, be sure of that! A very serious question this time, because it relates to me.

SULTAN: To you?

LADY: Yes. Let us assume that I have manumitted you at dawn—you will of course return to your palace.

SULTAN: Of course. I have business awaiting me there.

LADY: And I?

SULTAN: And what about you?

LADY: Will you not think about me after that?

SULTAN: I don't understand.

LADY: You really don't understand what I mean?

SULTAN: You know the language of women is too subtle for me, it is very often obscure.

LADY: You understand me only too well, for you are exceedingly intelligent and astute, and also very sensitive, despite appearances and the impression you like to give. In any case I shall explain my words—here is what I want to know: Will you forget me altogether and erase me from your memory directly you have left here?

SULTAN: I do not think it is possible to erase you altogether from my memory.

LADY: And will you retain a pleasant memory of me?

SULTAN: Certainly!

LADY: Is that all? Does everything for me end just like that?

SULTAN: Are we going over the same ground as before?

LADY: No, I merely wish to ask you: Is this night our last night together?

SULTAN: That's a question which it's difficult to answer.

LADY: Good! Don't answer it now!

    [*The* MAIDSERVANT *appears.*]

MAID: Dinner is served, milady.

LADY: [*Rising to her feet.*] If Your Majesty pleases.

SULTAN: [*Rising to his feet.*] You are a model of kindness and hospitality.

LADY: Rather is it you who do me a kindness.

    [*She leads him into another room to the accompaniment of music. The light in the house is extinguished and a dim light comes on in the square.*]

SHOEMAKER: [*To the* WINE MERCHANT *in a corner of the square.*] Look! They've put out the light.

WINE MERCHANT: [*Looking towards the window.*] That's a good sign!

SHOEMAKER: How?

WINE MERCHANT: Putting out the light means going to bed!

SHOEMAKER: And so?

WINE MERCHANT: And so agreement is complete.

SHOEMAKER: Over what?

WINE MERCHANT: Over everything.

SHOEMAKER: You mean that she'll accept to give him up at dawn?

WINE MERCHANT: Yes.

SHOEMAKER: And so you win the bet.

WINE MERCHANT: Without the slightest doubt.

SHOEMAKER: You're over-optimistic, my friend, to think that such a woman would easily accept throwing her money into the sea.

WINE MERCHANT: Who is to know? I say yes.

SHOEMAKER: And I say no.

WINE MERCHANT: Fine, let us await the dawn.

SHOEMAKER: What time is it now?

WINE MERCHANT: [*Looking at the sky.*] According to the stars it is now approximately midnight.

SHOEMAKER: Dawn is still far-off and I am beginning to feel sleepy.

WINE MERCHANT: Go to bed!

SHOEMAKER: I? Out of the question! The whole city is staying up tonight, so how can I be the only one to sleep? In fact I have more reason than anybody to stay up until dawn in order to witness your defeat.

WINE MERCHANT: My defeat?

SHOEMAKER: Without the slightest doubt.

WINE MERCHANT: We shall see which of us turns out to be the loser.

SHOEMAKER: [*Turning to a corner of the square.*] Look! Over there!

WINE MERCHANT: What?

SHOEMAKER: [*Whispering.*] The Vizier and the Executioner. They look as though they're hatching some plot.

WINE MERCHANT: Quiet!

[*The* VIZIER *walks up and down as he questions the* EXECUTIONER.]

VIZIER: What exactly did you hear from the guards?

EXECUTIONER: I heard them say, milord Vizier, that it was impossible to quell the people and force them to go to bed tonight. The crowds are still standing or squatting in the lanes and alleyways and all are whispering together and gossiping.

VIZIER: Gossiping?

EXECUTIONER: Yes.

VIZIER: And what's all this whispering and gossiping about?

EXECUTIONER: About the business of the Sultan of course and what he's doing tonight in this house.

VIZIER: And what, in your opinion, might he be doing in this house?

EXECUTIONER: Are you asking me, milord Vizier?

VIZIER: Yes, I'm asking you. Are you not one of the people, and does not your opinion represent public opinion? Answer me! What do you imagine the Sultan is doing in this house?

EXECUTIONER: Actually . . . well he's certainly not performing his prayers there!

VIZIER: Are you making fun? Are you being insolent?

EXECUTIONER: Pardon, milord Vizier. I merely wanted to say that this house is not . . . is no saintly place.

VIZIER: Then the gossip in the city is along these lines—that the Sultan is spending the night in a . . . .

EXECUTIONER: A brothel!

VIZIER: What are you saying?

EXECUTIONER: That's what they are saying, milord. I am reporting what I heard.

VIZIER: Is this all that people are mentioning about this important matter? They are forgetting the noble purport, the lofty aim, the sublime concept, the patriotic objective! Even you, as I see it, have forgotten all this.

EXECUTIONER: No, milord Vizier, I have forgotten nothing.

VIZIER: We shall see. Tell me then why the Sultan accepted to enter this house.

EXECUTIONER: In order to . . . to gratify the whore.

VIZIER: Is that all it's about? What a shallow way of looking at things!

EXECUTIONER: Milord Vizier, I was present and I saw and heard everything from the beginning.

VIZIER: And you didn't understand any of it, except for the insignificant and degrading side of the issue. Are there many like you among the people?

EXECUTIONER: Like me they were all present.

VIZIER: And they all made of it what you did as far as I can see. Their talk does not deal with the profound reason, the exalted meaning of all that has happened. Their talk deals merely with what you yourself say: the Sultan is spending the night in a brothel! What a catastrophe! It's this that's the real catastrophe!

[*The* CHIEF CADI *appears.*]

CADI: I haven't slept tonight.

VIZIER: You too?

CADI: Why I too?

VIZIER: The whole of the rest of the city hasn't slept tonight.

CADI: I know that.

VIZIER: And everyone's whispering and gossiping.

CADI: I know that as well.

VIZIER: And do you know what they're saying in the city?

CADI: The worst possible things. The point of interest and excitement for the people is the scandalous side of the affair.

VIZIER: Unfortunately so.

CADI: It's my fault.

VIZIER: And mine too. I should have been more resolute in the defence of my opinion.

CADI: But, on the other hand, how could we have anticipated that woman's intervention?

VIZIER: We should have anticipated everything.

CADI: You're right.

VIZIER: Now the die is cast and we have no power to do anything.

CADI: Yet it is in our power to snatch the Sultan away from this house.

VIZIER: We must wait for the dawn.

CADI: No, now . . . at once!

VIZIER: But the dawn is still far off.

CADI: It must be made to come now—at once!

VIZIER: Who? What?

CADI: The dawn!

VIZIER: My apologies—I don't understand.

CADI: You will shortly. Where's the Muezzin of this mosque?

VIZIER: [*Turning towards the* EXECUTIONER.] The Executioner must know.

EXECUTIONER: He's over there, among the crowds.

CADI: Go and bring him to me.

[*The* EXECUTIONER *returns, and after some whispered conversation hurries off obediently.*]

VIZIER: [*To the* CADI.] It seems you have some plan or other?

CADI: Yes.

VIZIER: May I know it?

CADI: Shortly.

[*The* MUEZZIN *appears, panting.*]

MUEZZIN: Here I am, milord Cadi.

CADI: Come close! I want to talk to you regarding the dawn.

MUEZZIN: The dawn? Be sure, milord Cadi, that I have committed no wrong. This Executioner is accusing me falsely of . . .

CADI: Listen to me well.

MUEZZIN: I swear to you, milord Cadi, that on that day . . .

CADI: Will you stop this nonsensical chattering! I told you to listen to me well. I want you to carry out what I am going to say to the letter. Do you understand?

MUEZZIN: Yes.

CADI: Go and climb up into your minaret and give the call to the dawn prayer.

MUEZZIN: When?

CADI: Now!

MUEZZIN: [*In surprise.*] Now?

CADI: Yes, immediately.

MUEZZIN: The dawn prayer?

CADI: Yes, the dawn prayer. Go and give the call to the dawn prayer. Is what I say clear or not?

MUEZZIN: It's clear, but it's now approximately . . . midnight.

CADI: Let it be!

MUEZZIN: Dawn at midnight?

CADI: Yes! Hurry!

MUEZZIN: Isn't this just a little . . . premature?

CADI: No.

MUEZZIN: [*Whispering to himself.*] I'm at a loss about this dawn—sometimes I'm asked to put it back and sometimes I'm asked to bring it forward.

CADI: What are you saying?

MUEZZIN: Nothing, milord Cadi. I shall go at once to carry out your order.

CADI: Listen! Make sure you tell no one that it was the Cadi who gave you this order.

MUEZZIN: Meaning, milord?

CADI: Meaning that it's you on your own initiative who have acted thus.

MUEZZIN: On my own initiative? I go up into the minaret to give the call to dawn prayers at midnight? Anyone behaving like that *must* be a crazy idiot.

CADI: Leave to me the task of explaining your behaviour at the appropriate time.

MUEZZIN: But, milord, by this action I expose myself to the ridicule of the masses and they'll ask that I be punished.

CADI: And whom will you appear before to be tried? Won't it be before me, the Chief Cadi?

MUEZZIN: And if you disown and abandon me?

CADI: Do not be afraid, that will never happen.

MUEZZIN: And how can I be sure?

CADI: I promise you—have you no faith in my promise?

MUEZZIN: [*Whispering to himself.*] The promises tonight are many—and not a soul is sure of anything.

CADI: What are you saying?

MUEZZIN: Nothing. I'm just asking myself—why should I expose myself to all this danger?

CADI: It's a service you're rendering the State.

MUEZZIN: [*In astonishment.*] The State?

CADI: Yes, I shall tell you about the matter so that you may rest assured. Listen! If you give the call to dawn prayers now, the Sultan will immediately leave this house a free man. That, in a couple of words, is what it's all about. Do you understand now?

MUEZZIN: It's a patriotic act!

CADI: It certainly is. What do you say then?

MUEZZIN: I shall do it immediately. I shall be proud of it the whole of my life. Permit me, milord Cadi, also to tell you something—what I say being strictly between ourselves—which is that I previously told you a small falsehood of this sort in order to save the head of someone who had been condemned to death; so why should I not commit a similar falsehood in order to gain the freedom of Our Majesty the beloved Sultan!

CADI: You're quite right, but I enjoin you to secrecy. Be careful not to let that tongue of yours wag! Hide this pride of yours in your soul, for if you begin to boast of what you have done in these present circumstances the whole business will be ruined. Shut your mouth well if you want your action to bear fruit and be appreciated.

MUEZZIN: I shall shut my mouth.

CADI: Good. Hurry off and do it.

MUEZZIN: As swift as the winds I'll be!

[*The* MUEZZIN *leaves hurriedly.*]

CADI: [*To the* VIZIER.] What do you think?

VIZIER: Do you think a trick like this will put matters right?

CADI: Yes, in the best way possible. Tonight I set about considering every aspect of the matter. I no longer regard myself as having been defeated. I still have in my quiver—or, to be more exact, in the law's quiver—many tricks.

VIZIER: Let us pray to God to make your tricks successful this time. Your personal honour is at stake.

CADI: You will see.

[*The voice of the* MUEZZIN *rings out.*]

MUEZZIN: [*From afar.*] God is great! God is great! Come to prayers! Come to prayers! Come to salvation! Come to salvation!

[*The crowd make their appearance in a state of agitation, astonishment, protest, and anger.*]

THE PEOPLE: [*Shouting.*] The dawn? Now? It's still night—we're in the middle of the night. He's mad! This madman—arrest him! Bring him down, bring him down from on top of the minaret! Bring him down!

VIZIER: [*To the* CADI.] The crowds will fall upon this poor fellow.

CADI: Order your guards to disperse the crowds.

VIZIER: [*Shouting at the* GUARDS.] Clear the square! Clear everyone out of the square!

[*The* GUARDS *chase* THE PEOPLE *away and clear the square, while the* MUEZZIN *continues with his call to prayer. The light goes on in the* LADY'S *room. She appears at the window followed by the* SULTAN.]

LADY: Is it really dawn?

CADI: It is the call to prayers. Come down here at once!

LADY: This is absurd—look at the stars in the sky.

SULTAN: [*Looking at the sky.*] Truly this is most strange.

CADI: [*To the* LADY.] I told you to come down here immediately.

SULTAN: [*To the* LADY.] Let us go down together to see what it's all about.

LADY: Let us go, Your Majesty. [*They leave the room, the light is extinguished, and they are seen coming out of the house.*]

SULTAN: [*Looking at the sky.*] The dawn? At this hour?

VIZIER: Yes, Your Majesty.

SULTAN: This is truly extraordinary. What do you say, Cadi?

CADI: No, Your Majesty, the dawn has not yet broken.

VIZIER: [*Taken aback.*] How's that?

CADI: It's quite obvious—it's still night.

VIZIER: [*To the* CADI *in astonishment.*] But . . .

CADI: But we have all heard the Muezzin give the call to dawn prayers. Did you hear it, woman?

LADY: Yes, I did.

CADI: You admit then that you heard the voice of the Muezzin giving the call to dawn prayers?

LADY: Yes, but . . .

CADI: There is nothing more to be said. As you have admitted this, there is nothing left for you to do but keep your promise. Here is the deed of manumission—you have only to sign.

[*He presents her with the deed.*]

LADY: I promised to sign it at dawn and here you are admitting, O Cadi, that it's still night.

CADI: Not so fast, woman! Your promise is inscribed in my head, word for word. Your exact words were: 'When the Muezzin gives the call to dawn prayers.' The whole matter now comes down to this question: have you or have you not heard the voice of the Muezzin?

LADY: I heard it, but if the dawn's still far off . . . .

CADI: The dawn as such is not in question—the promise related to the voice of the Muezzin as he gave the call to the dawn prayer. If the Muezzin has made a mistake in his calculation or conduct, it is he who is responsible for his mistake—that's his business. It's not ours. You understand?

LADY: I understand—it's not a bad trick!

CADI: The Muezzin will of course be prosecuted for his mistake. This, however, doesn't change the facts, which are that we have all heard the Muezzin giving the call to the dawn prayers from on top of his minaret. And so all the legal consequences deriving therefrom must take their course—immediately! Come along then and sign!

LADY: Is it thus that you interpret my one condition before manumitting the Sultan?

CADI: In the same manner as you interpreted our condition when you purchased the Sultan!

VIZIER: You have fallen into the very same snares of the law. Therefore, submit and sign!

LADY: This is not honest! It's sheer trickery!

VIZIER: Trickery matched by trickery! You began it—and he who begins is the greater offender. You are the last person to object and protest.

SULTAN: [*Shouting.*] Shame! Enough! Enough! Stop this nonsense! Cease this pettiness! She shall not sign. I absolutely refuse that she should sign this way. And you, Chief Cadi, aren't you ashamed of yourself for fooling around with the law like this?

CADI: Milord Sultan . . .

SULTAN: I am disappointed. I am disappointed in you, Chief Cadi. Is this, in your opinion, the law? The expenditure of effort and skill in trickery and fraud!

CADI: Your Majesty, I merely wanted . . .

SULTAN: To rescue me, I know that, but did you think I'd accept being rescued by such methods?

CADI: With such a woman, Your Majesty, we have the right . . .

SULTAN: No, you have no right at all to do this. You have no such right. Maybe it was the right of this woman to indulge in trickery—she cannot be blamed if she did so; maybe she should be the object of indulgence because of her intelligence and skill. As for the Chief Cadi, the representative of justice, the defender of the sanctity of the law, the upright servant of the canonical law, it is one of his most bounden duties to preserve the law's purity, integrity, and majesty, whatever the price. It was you yourself who first showed me the virtue of the law and the respect it must be shown, who told me that it was the supreme power before which I myself must bow. And I have bowed down right to the end in all humility. But did it ever occur to me that I would see you yourself eventually regarding the law in this manner; stripping it of its robe of sanctity so that it becomes in your hands no more than wiles, clauses, words—a mere plaything?

CADI: Let me explain to you, Your Majesty . . .

SULTAN: No, explain nothing. Go now! It's better for you to go home and betake yourself to bed until the morning. As for me I shall respect this lady's situation—in the true sense in which we all understand it. Let us go, milady! Let us return to your house! I am at your disposal.

LADY: No, Your Majesty.

SULTAN: No?

LADY: No, your Chief Cadi wanted to rescue you, and I don't want to be any less loyal than him towards you. You are now free, Your Majesty.

SULTAN: Free?

LADY: Yes, bring the deed of manumission, Chief Cadi, so that I may sign it.

CADI: You'll sign it now?

LADY: Yes, now.

CADI: [*Presenting her with the deed.*] God grant she's telling the truth!

LADY: [*Signing the deed.*] Believe me this time! There's my signature!

CADI: [*Examining the signature.*] Yes, despite everything you're a good woman.

SULTAN: Rather is she one of the most outstanding of women! The people of the city must respect her. That's an order, O Vizier!

VIZIER: I hear and obey, Your Majesty!

CADI: [*Folding up the deed.*] Everything has now been completed, Your Majesty, in first-class fashion.

SULTAN: And without a drop of blood being spilt—that's the important thing.

VIZIER: Thanks to your courage, Your Majesty. Who would imagine that to proceed to the end of this road would require more courage than that of the sword?

CADI: Truly!

SULTAN: Let us give praise to the generosity of this noble lady. Allow me, milady, to address my thanks to you, and I ask that you accept the return of your money to you, for there is no longer any reason why you should lose it. Vizier! Pay her from my private purse the amount which she has lost.

LADY: No, no, Your Majesty. Don't take away this honour from me. There are no riches in the world, in my opinion, to equal this beautiful memory on which I shall live for the whole of my life. With something so paltry I have participated in one of the greatest of events.

SULTAN: Good—as the memory has such significance for you, then keep this memento of it. [*He takes the enormous ruby from his turban.*]

VIZIER: [*Whispering.*] The ruby? The one without peer in the world?

SULTAN: Compared with your goodness, this is accounted a petty thing.
[*He presents her with the ruby.*]

LADY: No, dear Majesty, I don't deserve, am not worthy of this . . . this . . .

SULTAN: [*Starting to leave.*] Farewell, good lady!

LADY: [*With tears in her eyes.*] Farewell, dear Sultan!

SULTAN: [*Noticing her tears.*] Are you crying?

LADY: With joy!

SULTAN: I shall never forget that I was your slave for a night.

LADY: For the sake of principles and the law, Your Majesty! [*She lowers her head to hide her tears.*]

[*Music. The* SULTAN's *cortège moves off.*]

CURTAIN

KAWABATA YASUNARI
1899–1972

At the time he was awarded the Nobel Prize in 1968, Kawabata Yasunari was the patriarch of Japanese letters. One of Japan's most frequently translated novelists, he served as a literary godfather to the country's aspiring writers, both in his official capacity as president of the Japan P.E.N. Club (which included poets, essayists, and novelists) and through countless book reviews and his active interest in fostering new talent. If Kawabata had done nothing more than discover Mishima Yukio he would be well remembered, since the popular and prolific Mishima achieved a fame beyond Japan that all but eclipsed that of his mentor. It was on Kawabata, however, that the Swedish Academy chose to bestow Japan's first Nobel Prize for Literature. He was only the second such Nobel laureate in all of Asia (Rabindranath Tagore of India [p. 1671] having received the prize in 1913), and not until twenty-six years later would he be joined by another Japanese novelist, Ōe Kenzaburō, who received the Nobel Prize in 1994.

In its citation in 1968 the Swedish Academy commended Kawabata's mastery in illuminating "the essence of the Japanese mind." Kawabata was also praised during the presentation ceremonies as a conservator of Japanese tradition: "In the postwar wave of violent Americanization his fiction is a gentle reminder of the necessity of trying to save something of the old Japan's beauty and individuality for the new." Kawabata was acutely aware of "the old Japan's beauty." He spoke of it in his acceptance speech in Stockholm, and he writes of it frequently in his novels, which take as their backdrop such traditions as the tea ceremony, the *geisha* house, and *go*, the ancient game of strategy. Yet it is doubtful that his vision of the old Japan and its beauty corresponded with what the Nobel Prize committee thought it saw. Perhaps the award was in part a gesture toward all Japanese writers, or toward Japan, or toward Asia in general, for the Swedish tribute idealizes Kawabata as it reiterates the Western fantasy of a mysterious Orient (revealed by the writer's ability to extract "the essence of the Japanese mind," whatever that might be) and as it simultaneously rewards Kawabata's work, basically, for being charming. Perhaps Kawabata's frail appearance—so birdlike or, in the words of one critic, suggestive of a doe frightened by headlights—only encouraged the Europeans to view the author and his fiction as gentler and more winsome than either really was. In fact, in the appraisal of his own translator, there is a strain of bitterness and even ugliness that runs through Kawabata's writing. Beauty is seldom present without an aspect of decay, and critics see in his subtle joining of the two Kawabata's great strength.

Other strengths include a magician's ability to fashion weightless texts. Ungrounded by anything but the most elemental structure, they seem to levitate and float at random—between past and present time, action and celebration of the setting, oblique depiction of character and the mystic's sense of the oneness of humanity and nature—until the writer decides, quite arbitrarily it would seem, to bring the text down at its "conclusion." To some, this will appear the badge of modernism; to others, pure Japanese convention. Both views have their justification, and here again it is the joining of the two that makes Kawabata interesting. *Snow Country,* his undisputed masterpiece, is a good example.

The novel is set in a hot-spring resort in the mountains of northwest Japan. In the winter, when cold winds swoop down from Siberia, drawing moisture as they cross the Sea of Japan, they blow into the mountainous spine of the central island and deposit snowfalls of up to fifteen feet. The onslaught continues almost daily from November through April, making the area one of the snowiest regions in the world and making, too, the name *snow country* a very specific appellation. It does not mean just any countryside where snow falls, but a distinct location in Japan west of the central mountain range, where the winters are long and dark, the snow piles up to the eaves, and people live cut off from the world beyond the mountains. Their isolation is broken only by the occasional tourist. Today the interruptions are more than occasional, as holiday skiers flock into the region, but at the time of the novel, in the 1930s, visitors were fewer and as apt to come for the waters and the leisurely seclusion as for the ski runs.

And just as *snow country* has a particular connotation in Japan, so does *hot spring*. The Japanese do not go for "the season" (as it was called when Americans summered in Saratoga or other famous spas), nor do they go for health—nor, it should be added, do they generally go as couples, especially at the time of this novel. A man would visit a hot spring for a brief respite from work and family. (Then as now, husband and wife in Japan led lives surprisingly autonomous by American standards.) He would stay at an inn, soak in its steaming waters, relax, view the local sights (the autumn leaves, perhaps, or the cherry blossoms), and while away the evening hours in the company of *geisha*.

So it is with the protagonist of *Snow Country*. Shimamura is a man whose days are nothing but leisure. A well-heeled dilettante for whom commitment is anathema, Shimamura travels to the snow country in the same manner that he drifts through all of life, in vague search of idle pleasures. Apparently unfettered by the need to earn a living, he cultivates his aesthetic sensibilities; should they turn in the direction of genuine enthusiasm, he scrupulously retreats. Having once been a student of traditional Japanese dance, for example, he has abandoned the avocation after his growing expertise prompted calls for active involvement in the dance world. Instead, he has since taken up the study of Western ballet—pure book learning, however, because he shuns actual performances, which were in any case still safely uncommon in Japan of the 1930s. Shimamura is an intelligent man, quite aware of the dynamics of his peculiar detachment. "It was like being in love with someone he had never seen," the narrator has Shimamura acknowledging. "Nothing could be more comfortable than writing about the ballet from books. A ballet he had never seen was an art in another world. It was an unrivaled armchair reverie, a lyric from some paradise. He called his work research, but it was actually free, uncontrolled fantasy."

His ennui, then, takes Shimamura to the snow country, where he meets a local *geisha*, far livelier than he and less cynical, who falls deeply in love with this enigmatic figure. To appreciate the relation between them one must understand that the hot-spring *geisha* is the sad country cousin of the city *geisha*, who draws on a proud tradition of artistic accomplishment and can expect to be pampered by prosperous patrons. The city *geisha* at this time could still aspire to the repute we might accord a fashion model. The country *geisha*, on the other hand, had to entertain whatever traveler happened to pass through the village. There was sometimes a thin line between performer and prostitute. Chances were that she would drift from one hot spring to another, less and less appreciated with each move, until finally, as Kawabata says, "going pleasantly to seed." Appreciating both the beauty and sadness of this woman, Shimamura develops an attenuated sort of affection, not unlike his aloof attachment to ballet. Their sporadic affair over the course of his three visits to the snow country forms a study in disappointing love, where beauty is wasted and melancholy is the fate of the sensitive soul.

The novel trembles with sensitivity, and it is hard not to take the implied author, that personality we imagine standing behind the work, for Shimamura. Kawabata, the lyrical sensualist, weaves a narrative almost as disengaged as its hero: at once serene and disquieting, sensuous and cold. The narrative itself is sporadic and sometimes riddlelike—a shifting movement of images and allusions, dialogue and description—creating a text that is spare, elliptical, opaque, and, for all its authority, somehow hesitant, as though Kawabata too were avoiding a final commitment.

The tentative, capricious qualities of the novel would appear to have their source in Kawabata's early involvement with European modernism. While still a student at Tokyo University specializing in Japanese literature, Kawabata joined with other literary youths to form a group that called itself the Neosensualist, or New Sensibilities, school. His formal studies of native literature were supplemented by the circle's enthusiastic readings in avant-garde European literature, which its members explored not as scholars so much as for inspiration in their own budding careers as writers. From 1924, the year Kawabata graduated, to 1927 the group of twenty or so published their own magazine, *The Literary Age* (though many of the works most often cited as examples of the New Sensibilities style appeared in other journals). The youthful group took as its mission the elevation of contemporary Japanese literature as art for art's sake, rescuing it from the joint clutches of a drab, confessional, naturalistic movement and the equally flat-footed, if politically engaged, proletarian movement. Just as the European school known as modernism might be better described in the plural, there were various modernisms that influenced the New Sensibilities writers. In the group as a whole, futurism, cubism, expressionism, and Dadaism commanded the most explosive attention, with certain radical members, perhaps jolted by the fermenting compound of nihilism and imaginative liberation, declaring an open "war of utter rebellion against the Japanese language."

The modernist trends insinuated into Kawabata's writing were less belligerent. From Joyce, apparently, he learned that words could be ordered not only in the sequence of historical or narrative time but according to the movement and rhythm of the subjective imagination, the stream of consciousness. From Freud, he was inspired to splinter the naturalistic surface of a text by probing the irrational unconscious forces of the mind and the world of dreams, both sleeping and wakeful. By the Surrealists, he was encouraged to free-associate, seeing art as the juxtaposition of random images whose multiple views and abrupt transitions challenge the reader to forge a coherent meaning from fragmentary forms. In Symbolism, he admired the primacy of suggestion over direct statement and the quest for the luminous image that transformed reality into metaphor. And, in absorbing the spirit of modernism, Kawabata saw literature as style, the writer as introvert, life as a rupture of expected continuities, and all human relations, therefore, as ultimately insubstantial.

The question is, how much of this was really new, or European, and how much had Kawabata inherited from his own tradition? Poetry, imagistic from earliest times in Japan, had always cultivated the art of indirection, with states of mind a principal concern. Nonlinear structure had long marked the country's literature, from diaries and discursive essays known as *zuihitsu* to *nō* plays. The great women writers of the eleventh century, steeped in the Buddhist teaching that the world is evanescent and not to be trusted, had eloquently appraised the consequences both of fickle love and of impossible yearnings. Aestheticism was at the heart of traditional Japanese literature, and so in a way was an element of the surreal. Chikamatsu Monzaemon, the greatest dramatist of Japan's long period of seclusion (1600–1868), posited that "art is something which lies in the slender margin between the real and the unreal." And the coalescing of a text into an unpredictable progression of startling, discontinuous images piloted by thin or abrupt transitions that seem to fling flashes of acute perception into a narrative void was the very essence of the art of Japanese linked verse known as *renga*, dating from the fifteenth century.

Kawabata is often described as a *haiku*-like writer. The crisp, seventeen-syllable poems that communicate a moment of truth or a poignant awakening through the union of incongruous or contrary images do indeed suggest the terse, austere, intuitive style of *Snow Country*. But *haiku* grew out of a form of linked verse, and the elliptical, associative, and unresolved aspects of the novel seem more the offspring of *renga*. This "medieval" literary form would still have been known to most educated Japanese of Kawabata's generation. Lacking a single integrated plot, topic, or point of view, *renga* requires a group of poets who take turns composing verses to form a sequence wherein each verse is linked only to the one immediately preceding and the one immediately following. The result is a continuous stream of images and poetic associations, a vibration of themes at once fragmentary and symphonic.

Whether he consciously emulated *renga* or not, Kawabata clearly found an accumulative, open-ended approach to be congenial. This we know from his curious publishing preferences. Some authors dislike being asked whether they use a number-two pencil or a word processor, but in Kawabata's case writing habits may be considered quite pertinent. Virtually never did he compose a work from start to finish. Serialization (in magazines or, earlier in the century, in newspapers) is hardly uncommon in Japan, but Kawabata's brand of publishing in stages is especially unusual. *Snow Country,* like most of his novels, may be said to have grown organically and slowly. It began life as a short story, which he wrote in 1934 and published in 1935 in a magazine called *Japanese Opinion.* The story bears a resemblance to the first section of the completed novel, set on a train traveling into the snow country, but it lacks the mystery and otherworldliness it would acquire when rewritten as the novel's opening. Initially, Kawabata considered the work finished. He soon changed his mind, however, and incorporated some leftover material into another short story for a different magazine. He would have added the material to the original story, but the deadline had already passed. No doubt he considered the second piece finished as well, until another aspect of the story came to mind. And so it grew, incrementally, stories published here and there over a two-year span, with no indication that they formed a single work of fiction. In 1937 Kawabata combined and revised the disparate parts and published them as a novel.

Two years later he was back again, tinkering. He added two new chapters in 1939 and 1940, revised them, thought some more, became dissatisfied with the ending, and in 1947 finally completed the novel, which was published the following year. This is the form in which *Snow Country* is known today. But even that is not the end of the story's gestation. Indicative of the pride of place he gave the novel in his body of work, shortly before his death twenty-four years later, he distilled the entire novel into a ten-page episode that he called a "palm-sized" short story, a genre of vignette he had invented at the beginning of his career and frequently returned to. We might call these miniatures short shorts or "vest-pocket" stories. Some are no more than three or four paragraphs, but they are yet another reason Kawabata's fiction is habitually compared with *haiku.*

A literary text to Kawabata was a permeable thing. In its shifting boundaries perhaps he discerned an analogue of the Buddhist concept of mutability: life forever fluid and uncertain. Though he cut his teeth on European fiction, as a writer he acknowledged a large debt to Buddhism, whose scriptures he proclaimed "the supreme works of world literature," "incomparably wonderful lyric poems." If for Kawabata a text, like a life, is never finished (for Buddhism holds that death leads to reincarnation), he would seem to be the most "Japanese" of writers, just as the Swedish Academy had classified him.

Yet the indeterminacy of his method of composition may be taken for a theory of literature that is very modern—indeed, in the late twentieth and early twenty-first centuries, postmodern. Reader-response criticism, for example, might construe the ellipses and logical holes in Kawabata or the centrifugal pull of digression as case studies illustrating the theory that a text is seldom self-contained, that in filling in the "gaps" to construct meaning the reader is also a literary producer. Deconstruction, which argues that the meaning of a text is always in play and consequently perpetually deferred, with language itself inherently unstable, might serve to place Kawabata's tentative intentions within a philosophical (albeit skeptical) framework.

If there is a strain of nihilism (a philosophy of skepticism that denies meaningfulness) in this school of literary theory, there is also a trace of it in Kawabata. Despite the evidence that appears everywhere in his fiction—one character even speaks baldly of "the joy of emptiness"—Kawabata denied he was a nihilist. In his acceptance speech at the Nobel ceremonies, he took pains to distinguish his "emptiness" as the nothingness of Zen and Japanese tradition, not the nihilism of the West. It is difficult to tell what to make of Kawabata's address in Stockholm, described by one critic as "a forced march through a blizzard of cherry blossoms." But perhaps what Kawabata meant to say in quoting innumerable ancient poems, in invoking dwarf pines and flower arranging, is simply that the sad, untapped, autumnal feel of empty space in the Japanese aesthetic (think of the rock garden or architecture or *haiku*) signifies not hopelessness or despair—but beauty. Perhaps what he meant to say is that accepting absence or imperfection can bring quietude, and that this is the source of the beautiful.

In the same speech, Kawabata condemned suicide, mindful no doubt of the unusual number of his fellow writers who had died by their own hands. Less than four years later, however, he was to die in the same manner. Perhaps what he expressed in Stockholm was only a kind of hope, which his writings intermittently succeeded in adhering to. There is beauty aplenty in Kawabata. The simplicity of his style summons a range of subtleties, a depth of emotions; his command of imagery and allusion makes poetry of prose. But there is also the ironic detachment, sometimes shading into withdrawal or callousness, that we associate with a nihilist's despair at the futility of human existence.

Kawabata was born in Osaka in 1899 and was orphaned by the age of three. Childhood for him meant becoming "an expert in funerals." His grandmother died when he was seven, his only sister when he was nine, his grandfather when he was fifteen. Bereft of close relations and living mainly in school dormitories, the young Kawabata knew a loneliness that must have seeped into his bones. It surely accounts for the melancholy and rootlessness that color his fiction. Death and decay were already his intimates, soon joined by a first experience of impossible love. His central preoccupations were thus all in place before he published a first story in his early twenties. Though he oscillates between modernist and traditional approaches, the principal themes of his work remained constant for the next fifty years.

His most famous disciple, Mishima Yukio, would call Kawabata "the eternal traveler." From his first important short story, the typical protagonist in Kawabata's fiction is a man away from home. In *The Izu Dancer* (1926) a lonely student sets out on a walking trip on the Izu Peninsula south of Tokyo. The action takes place along the road and in remote inns, where, befriended by a troupe of entertainers, he becomes infatuated with the young dancer of the title. Temporarily dislocated, he is a poor judge of his surroundings; the Izu dancer turns out to be a mere child. A similar displacement marks *The Master of Go* (1954). In this fictionalized account of a 1938 *go* match (a board game of strategy, like chess) the champion and his challenger play out their protracted game sequestered in a series of inns, where they are quite cut off from the rest of the world. When the game is over and they emerge from isolation—the master defeated—tradition itself has been displaced. *Snow Country*, too, takes its protagonist out of his "real" world of family ties and responsibility. In the far-off snow country, Shimamura becomes even more detached and tentative than usual. *The House of the Sleeping Beauties* (1961), one of Kawabata's last novels, is perhaps his darkest and most disturbing statement on the space that another place, away from home, opens as a site for fantasy or a closet life—in this case the desire of an old man to sleep beside young girls who have been drugged into obliviousness.

Kawabata described himself as one drawn to "islands in a distant sea." His novels and short stories were all in one sense or another travels to a distant lodging, a temporary home—isolated, provisional, and sometimes claustrophobic. For all the beauty of the scenery, the perpetual traveler finds in his wanderings only the most fragile sense of place. People are even more fragile. They have a tendency to fade away into the landscape or disappear into a symbol. "Perhaps I was never in touch with reality," Kawabata said after World War II. In the most misanthropic of his stories, *Of Birds and Beasts*, the crotchety hero is made to confront his true nature. "All alone, he came to the arbitrary conclusion: he did not like people." "I have the feeling I have never taken a woman's hand in mine with romantic intentions," Kawabata once said of himself. "And it's not only women I have never taken by the hand.

For me, I wonder if the same isn't true of the whole of life." No writer surpasses Kawabata in capturing a life folding in on itself, so close to beauty yet so estranged.

Even in translation, the eloquent abstinence of Kawabata's style shines through, and it is reasonable to assume that Edward Seidensticker's English versions were influential in bringing Kawabata the Nobel Prize. Especially recommended are *Thousand Cranes* (1959), *The Sound of the Mountain* (1970), *The Master of Go* (1972), *The Izu Dancer and Other Stories* (1974), and *House of the Sleeping Beauties and Other Stories* (1969). A collection of Kawabata's very short pieces has been translated by Lane Dunlop and J. Martin Holman, *Palm-of-the-Hand Stories* (1988). For background on Kawabata, see Seidensticker, "On Kawabata Yasunari" in *This Country, Japan* (1979). There are chapter-length studies of the author in Donald Keene, *Dawn to the West* (1984); Masao Miyoshi, *Accomplices of Silence: The Modern Japanese Novel* (1974); and David Pollack, *Reading against Culture: Ideology and Narrative in the Japanese Novel* (1992).

PRONOUNCING GLOSSARY

The following list uses common English syllables to provide rough equivalents of selected words whose pronunciation may be unfamiliar to the general reader.

Chijimi: *chee-jee-mee*	Mishima Yukio: *mee-shee-mah*
Jizo: *jee-zoh*	*yoo-kee-oh*
Kikumura: *kee-koo-moo-rah*	nagauta: *nah-gah-oo-tah*
Kikuyu: *kee-koo-yoo*	samisen: *sah-mee-sen*
Komako: *koh-mah-koh*	Shimamura: *shee-mah-moo-rah*
kotatsu: *koh-tah-tsoo*	zuihitsu: *zoo-ee-hee-tsoo*

Snow Country[1]

PART ONE

The train came out of the long tunnel into the snow country. The earth lay white under the night sky. The train pulled up at a signal stop.

A girl who had been sitting on the other side of the car came over and opened the window in front of Shimamura. The snowy cold poured in. Leaning far out the window, the girl called to the station master as though he were a great distance away.

The station master walked slowly over the snow, a lantern in his hand. His face was buried to the nose in a muffler, and the flaps of his cap were turned down over his ears.

It's that cold, is it, thought Shimamura. Low, barracklike buildings that might have been railway dormitories were scattered here and there up the frozen slope of the mountain. The white of the snow fell away into the darkness some distance before it reached them.

"How are you?" the girl called out. "It's Yoko."

"Yoko, is it. On your way back? It's gotten cold again."

"I understand my brother has come to work here. Thank you for all you've done."

"It will be lonely, though. This is no place for a young boy."

---

1. Translated by and with notes adapted from Edward G. Seidensticker.

"He's really no more than a child. You'll teach him what he needs to know, won't you."

"Oh, but he's doing very well. We'll be busier from now on, with the snow and all. Last year we had so much that the trains were always being stopped by avalanches, and the whole town was kept busy cooking for them."

"But look at the warm clothes, would you. My brother said in his letter that he wasn't even wearing a sweater yet."

"I'm not warm unless I have on four layers, myself. The young ones start drinking when it gets cold, and the first thing you know they're over there in bed with colds." He waved his lantern toward the dormitories.

"Does my brother drink?"

"Not that I know of."

"You're on your way home now, are you?"

"I had a little accident. I've been going to the doctor."

"You must be more careful."

The station master, who had an overcoat on over his kimono, turned as if to cut the freezing conversation short. "Take care of yourself," he called over his shoulder.

"Is my brother here now?" Yoko looked out over the snow-covered platform. "See that he behaves himself." It was such a beautiful voice that it struck one as sad. In all its high resonance it seemed to come echoing back across the snowy night.

The girl was still leaning out the window when the train pulled away from the station. "Tell my brother to come home when he has a holiday," she called out to the station master, who was walking along the tracks.

"I'll tell him," the man called back.

Yoko closed the window and pressed her hands to her red cheeks.

Three snowplows were waiting for the heavy snows here on the Border Range.[2] There was an electric avalanche-warning system at the north and south entrances to the tunnel. Five thousand workers were ready to clear away the snow, and two thousand young men from the volunteer fire-departments could be mobilized if they were needed.

Yoko's brother would be working at this signal stop, so soon to be buried under the snow—somehow that fact made the girl more interesting to Shimamura.

"The girl"—something in her manner suggested the unmarried girl. Shimamura of course had no way of being sure what her relationship was to the man with her. They acted rather like a married couple. The man was clearly ill, however, and illness shortens the distance between a man and a woman. The more earnest the ministrations, the more the two come to seem like husband and wife. A girl taking care of a man far older than she, for all the world like a young mother, can from a distance be taken for his wife.

But Shimamura in his mind had cut the girl off from the man with her and decided from her general appearance and manner that she was unmarried. And then, because he had been looking at her from a strange angle for so long, emotions peculiarly his own had perhaps colored his judgment.

It had been three hours earlier. In his boredom, Shimamura stared at his left hand as the forefinger bent and unbent. Only this hand seemed to have

2. The mountain range dividing two prefectures.

a vital and immediate memory of the woman he was going to see. The more
he tried to call up a clear picture of her, the more his memory failed him,
the farther she faded away, leaving him nothing to catch and hold. In the
midst of this uncertainty only the one hand, and in particular the forefinger,
even now seemed damp from her touch, seemed to be pulling him back to
her from afar. Taken with the strangeness of it, he brought the hand to his
face, then quickly drew a line across the misted-over window. A woman's eye
floated up before him. He almost called out in his astonishment. But he had
been dreaming, and when he came to himself he saw that it was only the
reflection in the window of the girl opposite. Outside it was growing dark,
and the lights had been turned on in the train, transforming the window into
a mirror. The mirror had been clouded over with steam until he drew that
line across it.

The one eye by itself was strangely beautiful, but, feigning a traveler's
weariness and putting his face to the window as if to look at the scenery
outside, he cleared the steam from the rest of the glass.

The girl leaned attentively forward, looking down at the man before her.
Shimamura could see from the way her strength was gathered in her shoulders that the suggestion of fierceness in her eyes was but a sign of an intentness that did not permit her to blink. The man lay with his head pillowed at
the window and his legs bent so that his feet were on the seat facing, beside
the girl. It was a third-class coach. The pair were not directly opposite Shimamura but rather one seat forward, and the man's head showed in the
window-mirror only as far as the ear.

Since the girl was thus diagonally opposite him, Shimamura could as well
have looked directly at her. When the two of them came on the train, however, something coolly piercing about her beauty had startled Shimamura,
and as he hastily lowered his eyes he had seen the man's ashen fingers clutching at the girl's. Somehow it seemed wrong to look their way again.

The man's face in the mirror suggested the feeling of security and repose
it gave him to be able to rest his eyes on the girl's breast. His very weakness
lent a certain soft balance and harmony to the two figures. One end of his
scarf served as a pillow, and the other end, pulled up tight over his mouth
like a mask, rested on his cheek. Now and then it fell loose or slipped down
over his nose, and almost before he had time to signal his annoyance the girl
gently rearranged it. The process was repeated over and over, automatically,
so often that Shimamura, watching them, almost found himself growing
impatient. Occasionally the bottom of the overcoat in which the man's feet
were wrapped would slip open and fall to the floor, and the girl would quickly
pull it back together. It was all completely natural, as if the two of them,
quite insensitive to space, meant to go on forever, farther and farther into
the distance. For Shimamura there was none of the pain that the sight of
something truly sad can bring. Rather it was as if he were watching a tableau
in a dream—and that was no doubt the working of his strange mirror.

In the depths of the mirror the evening landscape moved by, the mirror
and the reflected figures like motion pictures superimposed one on the other.
The figures and the background were unrelated, and yet the figures, transparent and intangible, and the background, dim in the gathering darkness,
melted together into a sort of symbolic world not of this world. Particularly

when a light out in the mountains shone in the center of the girl's face, Shimamura felt his chest rise at the inexpressible beauty of it.

The mountain sky still carried traces of evening red. Individual shapes were clear far into the distance, but the monotonous mountain landscape, undistinguished for mile after mile, seemed all the more undistinguished for having lost its last traces of color. There was nothing in it to catch the eye, and it seemed to flow along in a wide, unformed emotion. That was of course because the girl's face was floating over it. Cut off by the face, the evening landscape moved steadily by around its outlines. The face too seemed transparent—but was it really transparent? Shimamura had the illusion that the evening landscape was actually passing over the face, and the flow did not stop to let him be sure it was not.

The light inside the train was not particularly strong, and the reflection was not as clear as it would have been in a mirror. Since there was no glare, Shimamura came to forget that it was a mirror he was looking at. The girl's face seemed to be out in the flow of the evening mountains.

It was then that a light shone in the face. The reflection in the mirror was not strong enough to blot out the light outside, nor was the light strong enough to dim the reflection. The light moved across the face, though not to light it up. It was a distant, cold light. As it sent its small ray through the pupil of the girl's eye, as the eye and the light were superimposed one on the other, the eye became a weirdly beautiful bit of phosphorescence on the sea of evening mountains.

There was no way for Yoko to know that she was being stared at. Her attention was concentrated on the sick man, and even had she looked toward Shimamura, she would probably not have seen her reflection, and she would have paid no attention to the man looking out the window.

It did not occur to Shimamura that it was improper to stare at the girl so long and stealthily. That too was no doubt because he was taken by the unreal, otherworldly power of his mirror in the evening landscape.

When, therefore, the girl called out to the station master, her manner again suggesting overearnestness, Shimamura perhaps saw her first of all as rather like a character out of an old, romantic tale.

The window was dark by the time they came to the signal stop. The charm of the mirror faded with the fading landscape. Yoko's face was still there, but for all the warmth of her ministrations, Shimamura had found in her a transparent coldness. He did not clear the window as it clouded over again.

He was startled, then, when a half-hour later Yoko and the man got off the train at the same station as he. He looked around as though he were about to be drawn into something, but the cold air on the platform made him suddenly ashamed of his rudeness on the train. He crossed the tracks in front of the locomotive without looking back again.

The man, clinging to Yoko's shoulder, was about to climb down to the tracks from the platform opposite when from this side a station attendant raised a hand to stop them.

A long freight train came out of the darkness to block them from sight.

The porter from the inn was so well-equipped for the cold that he suggested a fireman. He had on ear flaps and high rubber boots. The woman looking out over the tracks from the waiting-room wore a blue cape with the cowl pulled over her head.

Shimamura, still warm from the train, was not sure how cold it really was. This was his first taste of the snow-country winter, however, and he felt somewhat intimidated.

"Is it as cold as all that?"

"We're ready for the winter. It's always especially cold the night it clears after a snow. It must be below freezing tonight."

"This is below freezing, is it?" Shimamura looked up at the delicate icicles along the eaves as he climbed into the taxi. The white of the snow made the deep eaves look deeper still, as if everything had sunk quietly into the earth.

"The cold here is different, though, that's easy to see. It feels different when you touch something."

"Last year it went down to zero."

"How much snow?"

"Ordinarily seven or eight feet, sometimes as much as twelve or thirteen, I'd say."

"The heavy snows come from now on?"

"They're just beginning. We had about a foot, but it's melted down a good bit."

"It's been melting, has it?"

"We could have a heavy snow almost any time now, though."

It was the beginning of December.

Shimamura's nose had been stopped up by a stubborn cold, but it cleared to the middle of his head in the cold air, and began running as if the matter in it were washing cleanly away.

"Is the girl who lived with the music teacher still around?"

"She's still around. You didn't see her in the station? In the dark-blue cape?"

"So that's who it was. We can call her later, I suppose?"

"This evening?"

"This evening."

"I hear the music teacher's son came back on your train. She was at the station to meet him."

The sick man he had watched in that evening mirror, then, was the son of the music teacher in whose house the woman Shimamura had come to see was living.

He felt a current pass through him, and yet the coincidence did not seem especially remarkable. Indeed he was surprised at himself for being so little surprised.

Somewhere in his heart Shimamura saw a question, as clearly as if it were standing there before him: was there something, what would happen, between the woman his hand remembered and the woman in whose eye that mountain light had glowed? Or had he not yet shaken off the spell of the evening landscape in that mirror? He wondered whether the flowing landscape was not perhaps symbolic of the passage of time.

The hot-spring inn had its fewest guests in the weeks before the skiing season began, and by the time Shimamura had come up from the bath the place seemed to be asleep. The glass doors rattled slightly each time he took a step down the sagging corridor. At the end, where it turned past the office, he saw the tall figure of the woman, her skirts trailing coldly off across the dark floor.

He started back as he saw the long skirts—had she finally become a geisha?[3] She did not come toward him, she did not bend in the slightest movement of recognition. From the distance he caught something intent and serious in the still form. He hurried up to her, but they said nothing even when he was beside her. She started to smile through the thick, white geisha's powder. Instead she melted into tears, and the two of them walked off silently toward his room.

In spite of what had passed between them, he had not written to her, or come to see her, or sent her the dance instructions he had promised. She was no doubt left to think that he had laughed at her and forgotten her. It should therefore have been his part to begin with an apology or an excuse, but as they walked along, not looking at each other, he could tell that, far from blaming him, she had room in her heart only for the pleasure of regaining what had been lost. He knew that if he spoke he would only make himself seem the more wanting in seriousness. Overpowered by the woman, he walked along wrapped in a soft happiness. Abruptly, at the foot of the stairs, he shoved his left fist before her eyes, with only the forefinger extended.

"This remembered you best of all."

"Oh?" The woman took the finger in her hand and clung to it as though to lead him upstairs.

She let go his hand as they came to the *kotatsu*[4] in his room, and suddenly she was red from her forehead to her throat. As if to conceal her confusion, she clutched at his hand again.

"This remembered me?"

"Not the right hand. This." He pushed his right hand into the *kotatsu* to warm it, and again gave her his left fist with the finger extended.

"I know." Her face carefully composed, she laughed softly. She opened his hand, and pressed her cheek against it. "This remembered me?"

"Cold! I don't think I've ever touched such cold hair."

"Is there snow in Tokyo yet?"

"You remember what you said then? But you were wrong. Why else would anyone come to such a place in December?"

"Then": the danger of avalanches was over, and the season for climbing mountains in the spring green had come.

Presently the new sprouts would be gone from the table.

Shimamura, who lived a life of idleness, found that he tended to lose his honesty with himself, and he frequently went out alone into the mountains to recover something of it. He had come down to the hot-spring village after seven days in the Border Range. He asked to have a geisha called. Unfor-

---

3. A woman entertainer at certain restaurants or, sometimes, at traditional Japanese inns. Hired primarily for the companionship during meals or parties that her skills or repartee provides male customers, the *geisha* ("practitioner of the arts") is presumed competent to sing or dance selections from the classic repertoire. A *geisha* is not a prostitute, although she may extend that favor to chosen patrons; in any case, she cuts a more worldly figure than the chaste housewife. The *geisha*'s employment prospects were more viable in prewar Japan, the time of *Snow Country*. Today she represents an expensive museum piece for the moneyed, beyond the reach (or interest) of the average Japanese.   4. A charcoal brazier covered by a wooden frame and a quilt. It resembles a table at which four people can sit. Although it warms little more than the hands and feet, the *kotatsu* was at this time the only heating device in the ordinary Japanese house.

tunately, however, there was a celebration that day in honor of the opening of a new road, the maid said, so lively a celebration that the town's combined cocoon-warehouse[5] and theater had been taken over, and the twelve or thirteen geisha had more than enough to keep them busy. The girl who lived at the music teacher's might come, though. She sometimes helped at parties, but she would have gone home after no more than one or two dances. As Shimamura questioned her, the maid told him more about the girl at the music teacher's: the samisen[6] and dancing teacher had living with her a girl who was not a geisha but who was sometimes asked to help at large parties. Since there were no young apprentice geisha in the town, and since most of the local geisha were at an age when they preferred not to have to dance, the services of the girl were much valued. She almost never came alone to entertain a guest at the inn, and yet she could not exactly be called an amateur—such in general was the maid's story.

An odd story, Shimamura said to himself, and dismissed the matter. An hour or so later, however, the woman from the music teacher's came in with the maid. Shimamura brought himself up straight. The maid started to leave but was called back by the woman.

The impression the woman gave was a wonderfully clean and fresh one. It seemed to Shimamura that she must be clean to the hollows under her toes. So clean indeed did she seem that he wondered whether his eyes, back from looking at early summer in the mountains, might not be deceiving him.

There was something about her manner of dress that suggested the geisha, but she did not have the trailing geisha skirts. On the contrary, she wore her soft, unlined summer kimono with an emphasis on careful propriety. The obi[7] seemed expensive, out of keeping with the kimono, and struck him as a little sad.

The maid slipped out as they started talking about the mountains. The woman was not very sure of the names of the mountains that could be seen from the inn, and, since Shimamura did not feel the urge to drink that might have come to him in the company of an ordinary geisha, she began telling of her past in a surprisingly matter-of-fact way. She was born in this snow country, but she had been put under contract as a geisha[8] in Tokyo. Presently she found a patron who paid her debts for her and proposed to set her up as a dancing teacher, but unfortunately a year and a half later he died. When it came to the story of what had happened since, the story of what was nearest to her, she was less quick to tell her secrets. She said she was nineteen. Shimamura had taken her to be twenty-one or twenty-two, and, since he assumed that she was not lying, the knowledge that she had aged beyond her years gave him for the first time a little of the ease he expected to feel with a geisha. When they began talking of the Kabuki,[9] he found that she knew more about actors and styles than he did. She talked on feverishly, as

5. Raising silkworms was a common source of supplementary income in prewar rural villages, and raw silk was a major Japanese export.   6. The geisha's traditional instrument. It resembles a banjo with a round body, long neck, and three strings, which give off a sharp, plaintive tone once likened by a French observer to the sound of a nerve being plucked.   7. The sash with which a kimono is tied. A woman's obi is wide and stiff; a man's is narrower and usually softer.   8. Debts incurred by parents could be repaid by their daughters becoming geisha. Unless the woman could find a patron willing to pay off the debt for her parents, she was unlikely to earn enough money to escape her situation.   9. One of the major forms of traditional theater, dating from the 17th century. It is characterized by stylized dialogue and stage movements; vivid costumes and makeup; and animated, often violent action, incorporating musical accompaniment and dancing.

though she had been starved for someone who would listen to her, and presently began to show an ease and abandon that revealed her to be at heart a woman of the pleasure quarters[1] after all. And she seemed in general to know what there was to know about men. Shimamura, however, had labeled her an amateur and, after a week in the mountains during which he had spoken to almost no one, he found himself longing for a companion. It was therefore friendship more than anything else that he felt for the woman. His response to the mountains had extended itself to cover her.

On her way to the bath the next afternoon, she left her towel and soap in the hall and came in to talk to him.

She had barely taken a seat when he asked her to call him a geisha.

"Call you a geisha?"

"You know what I mean."

"I didn't come to be asked that." She stood up abruptly and went over to the window, her face reddening as she looked out at the mountains. "There are no women like that here."

"Don't be silly."

"It's the truth." She turned sharply to face him, and sat down on the window sill. "No one forces a geisha to do what she doesn't want to. It's entirely up to the geisha herself. That's one service the inn won't provide for you. Go ahead, try calling someone and talking to her yourself, if you want to."

"You call someone for me."

"Why do you expect me to do that?"

"I'm thinking of you as a friend. That's why I've behaved so well."

"And this is what you call being a friend?" Led on by his manner, she had become engagingly childlike. But a moment later she burst out: "Isn't it fine that you think you can ask me a thing like that!"

"What is there to be so excited about? I'm too healthy after a week in the mountains, that's all. I keep having the wrong ideas. I can't even sit here talking to you the way I would like to."

The woman was silent, her eyes on the floor. Shimamura had come to a point where he knew he was only parading his masculine shamelessness, and yet it seemed likely enough that the woman was familiar with the failing and need not be shocked by it. He looked at her. Perhaps it was the rich lashes of the downcast eyes that made her face seem warm and sensuous. She shook her head very slightly, and again a faint blush spread over her face.

"Call any geisha you like."

"But isn't that exactly what I'm asking you to do? I've never been here before, and I've no idea which geisha are the best-looking."

"What do you consider good-looking?"

"Someone young. You're less apt to make mistakes when they're young. And someone who doesn't talk too much. Clean, and not too quick. When I want someone to talk to, I can talk to you."

"I'll not come again."

"Don't be foolish."

"I said I'll not come again. Why should I come again?"

---

1. A red-light district such as the Yoshiwara, on the outskirts of Tokyo. Its women included not only prostitutes but professional entertainers.

"But haven't I told you it's exactly because I want to be friends with you that I've behaved so well?"

"You've said enough."

"Suppose I were to go too far with you. Very probably from tomorrow I wouldn't want to talk to you. I couldn't stand the sight of you. I've had to come into the mountains to want to talk to people again, and I've left you alone so that I can talk to you. And what about yourself? You can't be too careful with travelers."

"That's true."

"Of course it is. Think of yourself. If it were a woman you objected to, you wouldn't want to see me afterwards. It would be much better for her to be a woman you picked out."

"I don't want to hear any more." She turned sharply away, but presently she added: "I suppose there's something in what you say."

"An affair of the moment, no more. Nothing beautiful about it. You know that—it couldn't last."

"That's true. It's that way with everyone who comes here. This is a hot spring and people are here for a day or two and gone." Her manner was remarkably open—the transition had been almost too abrupt. "The guests are mostly travelers. I'm still just a child myself, but I've listened to all the talk. The guest who doesn't say he's fond of you, and yet you somehow know is—he's the one you have pleasant memories of. You don't forget him, even long after he's left you, they say. And he's the one you get letters from."

She stood up from the window sill and took a seat on the mat below it. She seemed to be living in the past, and yet she seemed to be very near Shimamura.

Her voice carried such a note of immediate feeling that he felt a little guilty, as though he had deceived her too easily.

He had not been lying, though. To him this woman was an amateur. His desire for a woman was not of a sort to make him want this particular woman—it was something to be taken care of lightly and with no sense of guilt. This woman was too clean. From the moment he saw her, he had separated this woman and the other in his mind.

Then too, he had been trying to decide where he would go to escape the summer heat, and it occurred to him that he could bring his family to this mountain hot spring. The woman, being fortunately an amateur, would be a good companion for his wife. He might even have his wife take dancing lessons to keep from getting bored. He was quite serious about it. He said he felt only friendship for the woman, but he had his reasons for thus stepping into shallow water without taking the final plunge.

And something like that evening mirror was no doubt at work here too. He disliked the thought of drawn-out complications from an affair with a woman whose position was so ambiguous; but beyond that he saw her as somehow unreal, like the woman's face in that evening mirror.

His taste for the occidental dance[2] had much the same air of unreality about it. He had grown up in the merchants' section of Tokyo, and he had been thoroughly familiar with the Kabuki theater from his childhood. As a student his interests had shifted to the Japanese dance and the dance-

---

2. That is, Western dance; here, ballet.

drama.[3] Never satisfied until he learned everything about his subject, he had taken to searching through old documents and visiting the heads of various dance schools, and presently he had made friends with rising figures in the dance world and was writing what one might call research pieces and critical essays. It was but natural, then, that he should come to feel a keen dissatisfaction with the slumbering old tradition as well as with reformers who sought only to please themselves. Just as he had arrived at the conclusion that there was nothing for it but to throw himself actively into the dance movement, and as he was being persuaded to do so by certain of the younger figures in the dance world, he abruptly switched to the occidental dance. He stopped seeing the Japanese dance. He gathered pictures and descriptions of the occidental ballet, and began laboriously collecting programs and posters from abroad. This was more than simple fascination with the exotic and the unknown. The pleasure he found in his new hobby came in fact from his inability to see with his own eyes occidentals in occidental ballets. There was proof of this in his deliberate refusal to study the ballet as performed by Japanese. Nothing could be more comfortable than writing about the ballet from books. A ballet he had never seen was an art in another world. It was an unrivaled armchair reverie, a lyric from some paradise. He called his work research, but it was actually free, uncontrolled fantasy. He preferred not to savor the ballet in the flesh; rather he savored the phantasms of his own dancing imagination, called up by Western books and pictures. It was like being in love with someone he had never seen. But it was also true that Shimamura, with no real occupation, took some satisfaction from the fact that his occasional introductions to the occidental dance put him on the edge of the literary world—even while he was laughing at himself and his work.

It might be said that his knowledge was now for the first time in a very great while being put to use, since talk of the dance helped bring the woman nearer to him; and yet it was also possible that, hardly knowing it, he was treating the woman exactly as he treated the occidental dance.

He felt a little guilty, as though he had deceived her, when he saw how the frivolous words of the traveler who would be gone tomorrow seemed to have struck something deep and serious in the woman's life.

But he went on: "I can bring my family here, and we can all be friends."

"I understand that well enough." She smiled, her voice falling, and a touch of the geisha's playfulness came out. "I'd like that much better. It lasts longer if you're just friends."

"You'll call someone, then?"

"Now?"

"Now."

"But what can you say to a woman in broad daylight?"

"At night there's too much danger of getting the dregs no one else wants."

"You take this for a cheap hot-spring town like any other. I should think you could tell just from looking at the place." Her tone was sober again, as though she felt thoroughly degraded. She repeated with the same emphasis as before that there were no girls here of the sort he wanted. When Shimamura expressed his doubts, she flared up, then retreated a step. It was up to

3. *Kabuki* contains complex and energetic dance sequences essential to its dramatic effect.

the geisha whether she would stay the night or not. If she stayed without permission from her house, it was her own responsibility. If she had permission the house took full responsibility, whatever happened. That was the difference.

"Full responsibility?"

"If there should happen to be a child, or some sort of disease."

Shimamura smiled wryly at the foolishness of his question. In a mountain village, though, the arrangements between a geisha and her keeper might indeed still be so easygoing. . . .

Perhaps with the idler's bent for protective coloring, Shimamura had an instinctive feeling for the spirit of the places he visited, and he had felt as he came down from the mountains that, for all its air of bare frugality, there was something comfortable and easy about the village. He heard at the inn that it was indeed one of the more comfortable villages in this harsh snow country. Until the railway was put through, only very recently, it had served mainly as a medicinal spring for farmers in the area. The house that kept geisha would generally have a faded shop curtain that advertised it as a restaurant or a tearoom, but a glance at the old-style sliding doors, their paper panels dark with age, made the passer-by suspect that guests were few. The shop that sold candy or everyday sundries might have its one geisha, and the owner would have his small farm besides the shop and the geisha. Perhaps because she lived with the music teacher, there seemed to be no resentment at the fact that a woman not yet licensed as a geisha was now and then helping at parties.

"How many are there in all?"

"How many geisha? Twelve or thirteen, I suppose."

"Which one do you recommend?" Shimamura stood up to ring for the maid.

"You won't mind if I leave now."

"I mind very much indeed."

"I can't stay." She spoke as if trying to shake off the humiliation. "I'm going. It's all right. I don't mind. I'll come again."

When the maid came in, however, she sat down as though nothing were amiss. The maid asked several times which geisha she should call, but the woman refused to mention a name.

One look at the seventeen- or eighteen-year-old geisha who was presently led in, and Shimamura felt his need for a woman fall dully away. Her arms, with their underlying darkness, had not yet filled out, and something about her suggested an unformed, good-natured young girl. Shimamura, at pains not to show that his interest had left him, faced her dutifully, but he could not keep himself from looking less at her than at the new green on the mountains behind her. It seemed almost too much of an effort to talk. She was the mountain geisha through and through. He lapsed into a glum silence. No doubt thinking to be tactful and adroit, the woman stood up and left the room, and the conversation became still heavier. Even so, he managed to pass perhaps an hour with the geisha. Looking for a pretext to be rid of her, he remembered that he had had money telegraphed from Tokyo. He had to go to the post office before it closed, he said, and the two of them left the room.

But at the door of the inn he was seduced by the mountain, strong with the smell of new leaves. He started climbing roughly up it.

He laughed on and on, not knowing himself what was funny.

When he was pleasantly tired, he turned sharply around and, tucking the skirts of his kimono into his *obi*, ran headlong back down the slope. Two yellow butterflies flew up at his feet.

The butterflies, weaving in and out, climbed higher than the line of the Border Range, their yellow turning to white in the distance.

"What happened?" The woman was standing in the shade of the cedar trees. "You must have been very happy, the way you were laughing."

"I gave it up." Shimamura felt the same senseless laugh rising again. "I gave it up."

"Oh?" She turned and walked slowly into the grove. Shimamura followed in silence.

It was a shrine grove. The woman sat down on a flat rock beside the moss-covered shrine dogs.[4]

"It's always cool here. Even in the middle of the summer there's a cool wind."

"Are all the geisha like that?"

"They're all a little like her, I suppose. Some of the older ones are very attractive, if you had wanted one of them." Her eyes were on the ground, and she spoke coldly. The dusky green of the cedars seemed to reflect from her neck.

Shimamura looked up at the cedar branches. "It's all over. My strength left me—really, it seems very funny."

From behind the rock, the cedars threw up their trunks in perfectly straight lines, so high that he could see the tops only by arching his back. The dark needles blocked out the sky, and the stillness seemed to be singing quietly. The trunk against which Shimamura leaned was the oldest of all. For some reason all the branches on the north side had withered, and, their tips broken and fallen, they looked like stakes driven into the trunk with their sharp ends out, to make a terrible weapon for some god.

"I made a mistake. I saw you as soon as I came down from the mountains, and I let myself think that all the geisha here were like you," he laughed. It occurred to him now that the thought of washing away in such short order the vigor of seven days in the mountains had perhaps first come to him when he saw the cleanness of this woman.

She gazed down at the river, distant in the afternoon sun. Shimamura was a little unsure of himself.

"I forgot," she suddenly remarked, with forced lightness. "I brought your tobacco. I went back up to your room a little while ago and found that you had gone out. I wondered where you could be, and then I saw you running up the mountain for all you were worth. I watched from the window. You were very funny. But you forgot your tobacco. Here."

She took the tobacco from her kimono sleeve and lighted a match for him.

"I wasn't very nice to that poor girl."

"But it's up to the guest, after all, when he wants to let the geisha go."

4. Stone-carved statues that are the guardians of the shrine. Designed to blend into the natural setting, Shinto shrines are typically characterized by large, aged trees; clean, uncluttered grounds; and subdued colors, symbolizing the ritual purity of Shinto. The shrine area exudes a sense of tranquillity and solitude.

Through the quiet, the sound of the rocky river came up to them with a rounded softness. Shadows were darkening in the mountain chasms on the other side of the valley, framed in the cedar branches.

"Unless she were as good as you, I'd feel cheated when I saw you afterwards."

"Don't talk to me about it. You're just unwilling to admit you lost, that's all." There was scorn in her voice, and yet an affection of quite a new sort flowed between them.

As it became clear to Shimamura that he had from the start wanted only this woman, and that he had taken his usual roundabout way of saying so, he began to see himself as rather repulsive and the woman as all the more beautiful. Something from that cool figure had swept through him after she called to him from under the cedars.

The high, thin nose was a little lonely, a little sad, but the bud of her lips opened and closed smoothly, like a beautiful little circle of leeches. Even when she was silent her lips seemed always to be moving. Had they had wrinkles or cracks, or had their color been less fresh, they would have struck one as unwholesome, but they were never anything but smooth and shining. The line of her eyelids neither rose nor fell. As if for some special reason, it drew its way straight across her face. There was something faintly comical about the effect, but the short, thick hair of her eyebrows sloped gently down to enfold the line discreetly. There was nothing remarkable about the outlines of her round, slightly aquiline face. With her skin like white porcelain coated over a faint pink, and her throat still girlish, not yet filled out, the impression she gave was above all one of cleanness, not quite one of real beauty.

Her breasts were rather full for a woman used to the high, binding *obi* of the geisha.

"The sand flies have come out," she said, standing up and brushing at the skirt of her kimono.

Alone in the quiet, they could think of little to say.

It was perhaps ten o'clock that night. The woman called loudly to Shimamura from the hall, and a moment later she fell into his room as if someone had thrown her. She collapsed in front of the table. Flailing with a drunken arm at everything that happened to be on it, she poured herself a glass of water and drank in great gulps.

She had gone out to meet some travelers down from the mountains that evening, men she had been friendly with during the skiing season the winter before. They had invited her to the inn, whereupon they had had a riotous party, complete with geisha, and had proceeded to get her drunk.

Her head waved uncertainly, and she seemed prepared to talk on forever. Presently she remembered herself. "I shouldn't be here. I'll come again. They'll be looking for me. I'll come again later." She staggered from the room.

An hour or so later, he heard uneven steps coming down the long hall. She was weaving from side to side, he could tell, running into a wall, stumbling to the floor.

"Shimamura, Shimamura," she called in a high voice. "I can't see. Shimamura!"

It was, with no attempt at covering itself, the naked heart of a woman calling out to her man. Shimamura was startled. That high, piercing voice must surely be echoing all through the inn. He got up hastily. Pushing her fingers through the paper panel, the woman clutched at the frame of the door, and fell heavily against him.

"You're here." Clinging to him, she sank to the floor. She leaned against him as she spoke. "I'm not drunk. Who says I'm drunk? Ah, it hurts, it hurts. It's just that it hurts. I know exactly what I'm doing. Give me water, I want water. I mixed my drinks, that was my mistake. That's what goes to your head. It hurts. They had a bottle of cheap whisky. How was I to know it was cheap?" She rubbed her forehead with her fists.

The sound of the rain outside was suddenly louder.

Each time he relaxed his embrace even a little, she threatened to collapse. His arm was around her neck so tight that her hair was rumpled against his cheek. He thrust a hand inside the neck of her kimono.

He added coaxing words, but she did not answer. She folded her arms like a bar over the breast he was asking for.

"What's the matter with you." She bit savagely at her arm, as though angered by its refusal to serve her. "Damn you, damn you. Lazy, useless. What's the matter with you."

Shimamura drew back startled. There were deep teeth-marks on her arm.

She no longer resisted, however. Giving herself up to his hands, she began writing something with the tip of her finger. She would tell him the people she liked, she said. After she had written the names of some twenty or thirty actors, she wrote "Shimamura, Shimamura," over and over again.

The delicious swelling under Shimamura's hand grew warmer.

"Everything is all right." His voice was serene. "Everything is all right again." He sensed something a little motherly in her.

But the headache came back. She writhed and twisted, and sank to the floor in a corner of the room.

"It won't do. It won't do. I'm going home. Going home."

"Do you think you can walk that far? And listen to the rain."

"I'll go home barefoot. I'll crawl home."

"You don't think that's a little dangerous? If you have to go, I'll take you."

The inn was on a hill, and the road was a steep one.

"Suppose you try loosening your clothes. Lie down for a little while and you'll feel well enough to go."

"No, no. This is the way. I'm used to it." She sat up straight and took a deep breath, but breathing was clearly painful. She felt a little nauseated, she said, and opened the window behind her, but she could not vomit. She seemed to be holding back the urge to fall down writhing on the floor. Now and then she came to herself. "I'm going home, I'm going home," she said again and again, and presently it was after two.

"Go on to bed. Go on to bed when a person tells you to."

"But what will you do?" Shimamura asked.

"I'll just sit here like this. When I feel a little better I'll go home. I'll go home before daylight." She crawled over on her knees and tugged at him. "Go on to sleep. Pay no attention to me, I tell you."

Shimamura went back to bed. The woman sprawled over the table and took another drink of water.

"Get up. Get up when a person tells you to."

"Which do you want me to do?"

"All right, go to sleep."

"You aren't making much sense, you know." He pulled her into bed after him.

Her face was turned half away, hidden from him, but after a time she thrust her lips violently toward him.

Then, as if in a delirium she were trying to tell of her pain, she repeated over and over, he did not know how many times: "No, no. Didn't you say you wanted to be friends?"

The almost too serious tone of it rather dulled his ardor, and as he saw her wrinkle her forehead in the effort to control herself, he thought of standing by the commitment he had made.

But then she said: "I won't have any regrets. I'll never have any regrets. But I'm not that sort of woman. It can't last. Didn't you say so yourself?"

She was still half numb from the liquor.

"It's not my fault. It's yours. You lost. You're the weak one. Not I." She ran on almost in a trance, and she bit at her sleeve as if to fight back the happiness.

She was quiet for a time, apparently drained of feeling. Then, as if the thought came to her from somewhere in her memory, she struck out: "You're laughing, aren't you? You're laughing at me."

"I am not."

"Deep in your heart you're laughing at me. Even if you aren't now, you will be later." She was choked with tears. Turning away from him, she buried her face in her hands.

But a moment later she was calm again. Soft and yielding as if she were offering herself up, she was suddenly very intimate, and she began telling him all about herself. She seemed quite to have forgotten the headache. She said not a word about what had just happened.

"But I've been so busy talking I haven't noticed how late it is." She smiled a little bashfully. She had to leave before daylight, she said. "It's still dark. But people here get up early." Time after time she got up to look out the window. "They won't be able to see my face yet. And it's raining. No one will be going out to the fields this morning."

She seemed reluctant to go even when the lines of the mountain and of the roofs on its slopes were floating out of the rain. Finally it was time for the hotel maids to be up and about. She retouched her hair and ran, almost fled, from the room, brushing aside Shimamura's offer to see her to the door. Someone might catch a glimpse of the two of them together.

Shimamura went back to Tokyo that day.

"You remember what you said then? But you were wrong. Why else would anyone come to such a place in December? I wasn't laughing at you."

The woman raised her head. Her face where it had been pressed against Shimamura's hand was red under the thick powder, from the eye across the bridge of the nose. It made him think of the snow-country cold, and yet, because of the darkness of her hair, there was a certain warmth in it.

She smiled quietly, as though dazzled by a bright light. Perhaps, as she smiled, she thought of "then," and Shimamura's words gradually colored her whole body. When she bowed her head, a little stiffly, he could see that even her back under her kimono was flushed a deep red. Set off by the color of her hair, the moist sensuous skin was as if laid naked before him. Her hair could not really have been called thick. Stiff like a man's, and swept up into a high Japanese-style coiffure with not a hair out of place, it glowed like some heavy black stone.

Shimamura looked at the hair and wondered whether the coldness that had so startled him—he had never touched such cold hair, he said—might be less the cold of the snow-country winter than something in the hair itself. The woman began counting on her fingers. For some time she counted on.

"What are you counting?" he asked. Still the counting continued.

"It was the twenty-third of May."

"You're counting the days, are you. Don't forget that July and August are two long months in a row."

"It's the hundred-and-ninety-ninth day. It's exactly a hundred and ninety-nine days."

"How did you remember it was the twenty-third of May?"

"All I have to do is look in my diary."

"You keep a diary?"

"It's always fun to read an old diary. But I don't hide anything when I write in my diary, and sometimes I'm ashamed to look at it myself."

"When did you begin?"

"Just before I went to Tokyo as a geisha. I didn't have any money, and I bought a plain notebook for two or three sen[5] and drew in lines. I must have had a very sharp pencil. The lines are all neat and close together, and every page is crammed from top to bottom. When I had enough money to buy a diary, it wasn't the same any more. I started taking things for granted. It's that way with my writing practice, too. I used to practice on newspapers before I even thought of trying good paper, but now I set it down on good paper from the start."

"And you've kept the diary all this time?"

"Yes. The year I was sixteen and this year have been the best. I write in my diary when I'm home from a party and ready for bed, and when I read it over I can see places where I've gone to sleep writing. . . . But I don't write every day. Some days I miss. Way off here in the mountains, every party's the same. This year I couldn't find anything except a diary with a new day on each page. It was a mistake. When I start writing, I want to write on and on."

But even more than at the diary, Shimamura was surprised at her statement that she had carefully catalogued every novel and short story she had read since she was fifteen or sixteen. The record already filled ten notebooks.

"You write down your criticisms, do you?"

"I could never do anything like that. I just write down the author and the characters and how they are related to each other. That is about all."

"But what good does it do?"

"None at all."

---

5. One sen equaled one-hundredth of a yen; the yen had a value of twenty-five to thirty cents before World War II.

"A waste of effort."

"A complete waste of effort," she answered brightly, as though the admission meant little to her. She gazed solemnly at Shimamura, however.

A complete waste of effort. For some reason Shimamura wanted to stress the point. But, drawn to her at that moment, he felt a quiet like the voice of the rain flow over him. He knew well enough that for her it was in fact no waste of effort, but somehow the final determination that it was had the effect of distilling and purifying the woman's existence.

Her talk of novels seemed to have little to do with "literature" in the everyday sense of the word. The only friendly ties she had with the people of this village had come from exchanging women's magazines, and afterwards she had gone on with her reading by herself. She was quite indiscriminate and had little understanding of literature, and she borrowed even the novels and magazines she found lying in the guests' rooms at the inn. Not a few of the new novelists whose names came to her meant nothing to Shimamura. Her manner was as though she were talking of a distant foreign literature. There was something lonely, something sad in it, something that rather suggested a beggar who has lost all desire. It occurred to Shimamura that his own distant fantasy on the occidental ballet, built up from words and photographs in foreign books, was not in its way dissimilar.

She talked on happily too of movies and plays she had never seen. She had no doubt been starved all these months for someone who would listen to her. Had she forgotten that a hundred and ninety-nine days earlier exactly this sort of conversation had set off the impulse to throw herself at Shimamura? Again she lost herself in the talk, and again her words seemed to be warming her whole body.

But her longing for the city had become an undemanding dream, wrapped in simple resignation, and the note of wasted effort was much stronger in it than any suggestion of the exile's lofty dissatisfaction. She did not seem to find herself especially sad, but in Shimamura's eyes there was something strangely touching about her. Were he to give himself quite up to that consciousness of wasted effort, Shimamura felt, he would be drawn into a remote emotionalism that would make his own life a waste. But before him was the quick, live face of the woman, ruddy from the mountain air.

In any case, he had revised his view of her, and he had found, surprisingly, that her being a geisha made it even more difficult for him to be free and open with her.

Dead-drunk that night, she had savagely bitten her half-paralyzed arm in a fit of irritation at its recalcitrance. "What's the matter with you? Damn you, damn you. Lazy, worthless. What's the matter with you?"

And, unable to stand, she had rolled from side to side. "I'll never have any regrets. But I'm not that sort of woman. I'm not that sort of woman."

"The midnight for Tokyo." The woman seemed to sense his hesitation, and she spoke as if to push it away. At the sound of the train whistle she stood up. Roughly throwing open a paper-paneled door and the window behind it, she sat down on the sill with her body thrown back against the railing. The train moved off into the distance, its echo fading into a sound as of the night wind. Cold air flooded the room.

"Have you lost your mind?" Shimamura too went over to the window. The air was still, without a suggestion of wind.

It was a stern night landscape. The sound of the freezing of snow over the land seemed to roar deep into the earth. There was no moon. The stars, almost too many of them to be true, came forward so brightly that it was as if they were falling with the swiftness of the void. As the stars came nearer, the sky retreated deeper and deeper into the night color. The layers of the Border Range, indistinguishable one from another, cast their heaviness at the skirt of the starry sky in a blackness grave and somber enough to communicate their mass. The whole of the night scene came together in a clear, tranquil harmony.

As she sensed Shimamura's approach, the woman fell over with her breast against the railing. There was no hint of weakness in the pose. Rather, against the night, it was the strongest and most stubborn she could have taken. So we have to go through that again, thought Shimamura.

Black though the mountains were, they seemed at that moment brilliant with the color of the snow. They seemed to him somehow transparent, somehow lonely. The harmony between sky and mountains was lost.

Shimamura put his hand to the woman's throat. "You'll catch cold. See how cold it is." He tried to pull her back, but she clung to the railing.

"I'm going home." Her voice was choked.

"Go home, then."

"Let me stay like this a little longer."

"I'm going down for a bath."

"No, stay here with me."

"If you close the window."

"Let me stay here like this a little longer."

Half the village was hidden behind the cedars of the shrine grove. The light in the railway station, not ten minutes away by taxi, flickered on and off as if crackling in the cold.

The woman's hair, the glass of the window, the sleeve of his kimono—everything he touched was cold in a way Shimamura had never known before.

Even the straw mats under his feet seemed cold. He started down to the bath.

"Wait. I'll go with you." The woman followed meekly.

As she was rearranging the clothes he had thrown to the floor outside the bath, another guest, a man, came in. The woman crouched low in front of Shimamura and hid her face.

"Excuse me." The other guest started to back away.

"No, please," Shimamura said quickly. "We'll go next door." He scooped up his clothes and stepped over to the women's bath. The woman followed as if they were married. Shimamura plunged into the bath without looking back at her. He felt a high laugh mount to his lips now that he knew she was with him. He put his face to the hot-water tap and noisily rinsed his mouth.

Back in the room, she raised her head a little from the pillow and pushed her side hair up with her little finger.

"This makes me very sad." She said only that. Shimamura thought for a moment that her eyes were half open, but he saw that the thick eyelashes created the illusion.

The woman, always high-strung, did not sleep the whole night.

It was apparently the sound of the *obi* being tied that awakened Shimamura.

"I'm sorry. I should have let you sleep. It's still dark. Look—can you see me?" She turned off the light. "Can you see me? You can't?"

"I can't see you. It's still pitch dark."

"No, no. I want you to look close. Now. Can you see me?" She threw open the window. "It's no good. You can see me. I'm going."

Surprised anew at the morning cold, Shimamura raised his head from the pillow. The sky was still the color of night, but in the mountains it was already morning.

"But it's all right. The farmers aren't busy this time of the year, and no one will be out so early. But do you suppose someone might be going out into the mountains?" She talked on to herself, and she walked about trailing the end of the half-tied *obi*. "There were no guests on the five-o'clock from Tokyo. None of the inn people will be up for a long while yet."

Even when she had finished tying the *obi*, she stood up and sat down and stood up again, and wandered about the room with her eye on the window. She seemed on edge, like some restless night beast that fears the approach of the morning. It was as though a strange, magical wildness had taken her.

Presently the room was so light that he could see the red of her cheeks. His eye was fastened on that extraordinarily bright red.

"Your cheeks are flaming. That's how cold it is."

"It's not from the cold. It's because I've taken off my powder. I only have to get into bed and in a minute I'm warm as an oven. All the way to my feet." She knelt at the mirror by the bed.

"It's daylight. I'm going home."

Shimamura glanced up at her, and immediately lowered his head. The white in the depths of the mirror was the snow, and floating in the middle of it were the woman's bright red cheeks. There was an indescribably fresh beauty in the contrast.

Was the sun already up? The brightness of the snow was more intense, it seemed to be burning icily. Against it, the woman's hair became a clearer black, touched with a purple sheen.

Probably to keep snow from piling up, the water from the baths was led around the walls of the inn by a makeshift ditch, and in front of the entrance it spread out like a shallow spring. A powerful black dog stood on the stones by the doorway lapping at the water. Skis for the hotel guests, probably brought out from a storeroom, were lined up to dry, and the faint smell of mildew was sweetened by the steam. The snow that had fallen from the cedar branches to the roof of the public bath was breaking down into something warm and shapeless.

By the end of the year, that road would be shut off from sight by the snowstorms. She would have to go to her parties in long rubber boots with baggy "mountain trousers" over her kimono, and she would have a cape pulled around her and a veil over her face. The snow would by then be ten feet deep—the woman had looked down on the steep road from the window of the inn, high on a hill, before daybreak this morning, and now Shimamura was walking down the same road. Diapers hung high beside the road to dry. Under them stretched the vista of the Border Range, the snow on its peaks glowing softly. The green onions in the garden patches were not yet buried in the snow.

Children of the village were skiing in the fields.

As he started into the part of the village that fronted on the highway, he heard a sound as of quiet rain.

Little icicles glistened daintily along the eaves.

"While you're at it, would you mind shoveling a little from ours?" Dazzled by the bright light, a woman on her way back from the bath wiped at her forehead with a damp towel as she looked up at a man shoveling snow from a roof. A waitress, probably, who had drifted into the village a little in advance of the skiing season. Next door was a café with a sagging roof, its painted window flaking with age.

Rows of stones held down the shingles with which most of the houses along the street were roofed. Only on the side exposed to the sun did the round stones show their black surfaces, less a moist black from the melting snow than an ink-stone black, beaten away at by icy wind and storm. The houses were of a kind with the dark stones on their roofs. The low eaves hugging the ground seemed to have in them the very essence of the north country.

Children were breaking off chunks of ice from the drains and throwing them down in the middle of the road. It was no doubt the sparkle of the ice as it went flying off into bits that enchanted them so. Shimamura, standing in the sunlight, found it hard to believe that the ice could be so thick. He stopped for a moment to watch.

A girl of twelve or thirteen stood knitting apart from the rest, her back against a stone wall. Under the baggy "mountain trousers," her feet were bare but for sandals, and Shimamura could see that the soles were red and cracked from the cold. A girl of perhaps two stood on a bundle of firewood beside her patiently holding a ball of yarn. Even the faded, ashen line of reclaimed yarn from the younger girl to the older seemed warmly aglow.

He could hear a carpenter's plane in a ski shop seven or eight doors down the street. Five or six geisha were talking under the eaves opposite. Among them, he was sure, would be the woman, Komako—he had just that morning learned her geisha name[6] from a maid at the inn. And indeed, there she was. She had apparently noticed him. The deadly serious expression on her face set her off from the others. She would of course flush scarlet, but if she could at least pretend that nothing had happened—before Shimamura had time to go further with his thoughts, he saw that she had flushed to the throat. She might better have looked away, but her head turned little by little to follow him, while her eyes were fixed on the ground in acute discomfort.

Shimamura's cheeks too were aflame. He walked briskly by, and immediately Komako came after him.

"You mustn't. You embarrass me, walking by at a time like this."

"I embarrass you—you think I'm not embarrassed myself, with all of you lined up to waylay me? I could hardly make myself walk past. Is it always this way?"

"Yes, I suppose so. In the afternoon."

6. *Geisha* were given professional names, often based on the names of heroines in popular love stories or classical Japanese literature.

"But I'd think you'd be even more embarrassed, turning bright red and then chasing after me."

"What difference does it make?" The words were clear and definite, but she was blushing again. She stopped and put her arm around a persimmon tree beside the road. "I ran after you because I thought I might ask you to come by my house."

"Is your house near here?"

"Very near."

"I'll come if you'll let me read your diary."

"I'm going to burn my diary before I die."

"But isn't there a sick man in your house?"

"How did you know?"

"You were at the station to meet him yesterday. You had on a dark-blue cape. I was sitting near him on the train. And there was a woman with him, looking after him, as gentle as she could be. His wife? Or someone who went from here to bring him home? Or someone from Tokyo? She was exactly like a mother. I was very much impressed."

"Why didn't you say so last night? Why were you so quiet?" Something had upset her.

"His wife?"

Komako did not answer. "Why didn't you say anything last night? What a strange person you are."

Shimamura did not like this sharpness. Nothing he had done and nothing that had happened seemed to call for it, and he wondered if something basic in the woman's nature might not be coming to the surface. Still, when she came at him the second time, he had to admit that he was being hit in a vulnerable spot. This morning, as he glanced at Komako in that mirror reflecting the mountain snow, he had of course thought of the girl in the evening train window. Why then had he said nothing?

"It doesn't matter if there is a sick man. No one ever comes to my room." Komako went in through an opening in a low stone wall.

To the right was a small field, and to the left persimmon trees stood along the wall that marked off the neighboring plot. There seemed to be a flower garden in front of the house, and red carp were swimming in the little lotus pond. The ice had been broken away and lay piled along the bank. The house was old and decayed, like the pitted trunk of a persimmon. There were patches of snow on the roof, the rafters of which sagged to draw a wavy line at the eaves.

The air in the earthen-floored hallway was still and cold. Shimamura was led up a ladder before his eyes had become accustomed to the darkness. It was a ladder in the truest sense of the word, and the room at the top was an attic.

"This is the room the silkworms used to live in. Are you surprised?"

"You're lucky you've never fallen downstairs, drinking the way you do."

"I have. But generally when I've had too much to drink I crawl into the kotatsu downstairs and go off to sleep." She pushed her hand tentatively into the kotatsu, then went below for charcoal. Shimamura looked around at the curious room. Although there was but one low window, opening to the south, the freshly changed paper on the door turned off the rays of the sun brightly. The walls had been industriously pasted over with rice paper, so that the effect was rather like the inside of an old-fashioned paper box; but overhead was only the bare roof sloping down toward the window, as if a dark loneliness had settled itself over the room. Wondering what might be on the other side of the wall, Shimamura had the uneasy feeling that he was suspended in a void. But the walls and the floor, for all their shabbiness, were spotlessly clean.

For a moment he was taken with the fancy that the light must pass through Komako, living in the silkworms' room, as it passed through the translucent silkworms.

The *kotatsu* was covered with a quilt of the same rough, striped cotton material as the standard "mountain trousers." The chest of drawers was old, but the grain of the wood was fine and straight—perhaps it was a relic of Komako's years in Tokyo. It was badly paired with a cheap dresser, while the vermilion sewing-box gave off the luxurious glow of good lacquer. The boxes stacked along the wall behind a thin woolen curtain apparently served as bookshelves.

The kimono of the evening before hung on the wall, open to show the brilliant red under-kimono.

Komako came spryly up the ladder with a supply of charcoal.

"It's from the sickroom. But you needn't worry. They say fire spreads no germs." Her newly dressed hair almost brushed the *kotatsu* as she stirred away at the coals. The music teacher's son had intestinal tuberculosis, she said, and had come home to die.

But it was not entirely accurate to say that he had "come home." He had as a matter of fact not been born here. This was his mother's home. His mother had taught dancing down on the coast even when she was no longer a geisha, but she had had a stroke while she was still in her forties, and had come back to this hot spring to recover. The son, fond of machinery since he was a child, had stayed behind to work in a watch-shop. Presently he moved to Tokyo and started going to night school, and the strain was evidently too much for him. He was only twenty-five.

All this Komako told him with no hesitation, but she said nothing about the girl who had brought the man home, and nothing about why she herself was in this house.

Shimamura felt most uncomfortable at what she did say, however. Suspended there in the void, she seemed to be broadcasting to the four directions.

As he stepped from the hallway, he saw something faintly white through the corner of his eye. It was a samisen box,[7] and it struck him as larger and longer than it should be. He found it hard to imagine her carrying so unwieldy an object to parties. The darkened door inside the hallway slid open.

"Do you mind if I step over this, Komako?" It was that clear voice, so beautiful that it was almost sad. Shimamura waited for an echo to come back.

It was Yoko's voice, the voice that had called out over the snow to the station master the night before.

"No, please go ahead." Yoko stepped lightly over the samisen box, a glass chamber-pot in her hand.

It was clear, from the familiar way she had talked to the station master

7. Komako's mastery of the instrument comes up later in the story.

the evening before and from the way she wore "mountain trousers," that she was a native of this snow country, but the bold pattern of her *obi*, half visible over the trousers, made the rough russet and black stripes of the latter seem fresh and cheerful, and for the same reason the long sleeves of her woolen kimono took on a certain voluptuous charm. The trousers, split just below the knees, filled out toward the hips, and the heavy cotton, for all its natural stiffness, was somehow supple and gentle.

Yoko darted one quick, piercing glance at Shimamura and went silently out over the earthen floor.

Even when he had left the house, Shimamura was haunted by that glance, burning just in front of his forehead. It was cold as a very distant light, for the inexpressible beauty of it had made his heart rise when, the night before, that light off in the mountains had passed across the girl's face in the train window and lighted her eye for a moment. The impression came back to Shimamura, and with it the memory of the mirror filled with snow, and Komako's red cheeks floating in the middle of it.

He walked faster. His legs were round and plump, but he was seized with a certain abandon as he walked along gazing at the mountains he was so fond of, and his pace quickened, though he hardly knew it. Always ready to give himself up to reverie, he could not believe that the mirror floating over the evening scenery and the other snowy mirror were really works of man. They were part of nature, and part of some distant world.

And the room he had only this moment left had become part of that same distant world.

Startled at himself, in need of something to cling to, he stopped a blind masseuse at the top of the hill.

"Could you give me a massage?"

"Let me see. What time will it be?" She tucked her cane under her arm and, taking a covered pocket watch from her *obi*, felt at the face with her left hand. "Two thirty-five. I have an appointment over beyond the station at three-thirty. But I suppose it won't matter if I'm a little late."

"You're very clever to be able to tell the time."

"It has no glass, and I can feel the hands."

"You can feel the figures?"

"Not the figures." She took the watch out again, a silver one, large for a woman, and flicked open the lid. She laid her fingers across the face with one at twelve and one at six, and a third halfway between at three. "I can tell the time fairly well. I may be a minute off one way or the other, but I never miss by as much as two minutes."

"You don't find the road a little slippery?"

"When it rains my daughter comes to call for me. At night I take care of the people in the village, and never come up this far. The maids at the inn are always joking and saying it's because my husband won't let me go out at night."

"Your children are growing up?"

"The oldest girl is twelve." They had reached Shimamura's room, and they were silent for a time as the massaging began. The sound of a samisen came to them from the distance.

"Who would that be, I wonder."

"You can always tell which geisha it is by the tone?"

"I can tell some of them. Some I can't. You must not have to work. Feel how nice and soft you are."

"No stiff muscles on me."

"A little stiff here at the base of the neck. But you're just right, not too fat and not too thin. And you don't drink, do you?"

"You can tell that?"

"I have three other customers with physiques exactly like yours."

"A common sort of physique."

"But when you don't drink, you don't know what it is really to enjoy yourself—to forget everything that happens."

"Your husband drinks, does he?"

"Much too much."

"But whoever it is, she's not much of a musician."

"Very poor indeed."

"Do you play yourself?"

"I did when I was young. From the time I was eight till I was nineteen. I haven't played in fifteen years now. Not since I was married."

Did all blind people look younger than they were? Shimamura wondered.

"But if you learn when you're young, you never forget."

"My hands have changed from doing this sort of work, but my ear is still good. It makes me very impatient to hear them playing. But then I suppose I felt impatient at my own playing when I was young." She listened for a time. "Fumi at the Izutsuya, maybe. The best ones and the worst are the easiest to tell."

"There are good ones?"

"Komako is very good. She's young, but she's improved a great deal lately."

"Really?"

"You know her, don't you? I say she's good, but you have to remember that our standards here in the mountains are not very high."

"I don't really know her. I was on the train with the music teacher's son last night, though."

"He's well again?"

"Apparently not."

"Oh? He's been sick for a long time in Tokyo, and they say it was to help pay the doctors' bills that Komako became a geisha last summer. I wonder if it did any good."

"Komako, you say?"

"They were only engaged. But I suppose you feel better afterwards if you've done everything you can."

"She was engaged to him?"

"So they say. I don't really know, but that's the rumor."

It was almost too ordinary a thing to hear gossip about geisha from the hot-spring masseuse, and that fact had the perverse effect of making the news the more startling; and Komako's having become a geisha to help her fiancé was so ordinary a bit of melodrama that he found himself almost refusing to accept it. Perhaps certain moral considerations—questions of the propriety of selling oneself as a geisha—helped the refusal.

Shimamura was beginning to think he would like to go deeper into the story, but the masseuse was silent.

If Komako was the man's fiancée, and Yoko was his new lover, and the man was going to die—the expression "wasted effort" again came into Shimamura's mind. For Komako thus to guard her promise to the end, for her even to sell herself to pay doctors' bills—what was it if not wasted effort?

He would accost her with this fact, he would drive it home, when he saw her again, he said to himself; and yet her existence seemed to have become purer and cleaner for this new bit of knowledge.

Aware of a shameful danger lurking in his numbed sense of the false and empty, he lay concentrating on it, trying to feel it, for some time after the masseuse left. He was chilled to the pit of his stomach—but someone had left the windows wide open.

The color of evening had already fallen on the mountain valley, early buried in shadows. Out of the dusk the distant mountains, still reflecting the light of the evening sun, seemed to have come much nearer.

Presently, as the mountain chasms were far and near, high and low, the shadows in them began to deepen, and the sky was red over the snowy mountains, bathed now in but a wan light.

Cedar groves stood out darkly by the river bank, at the ski ground, around the shrine.

Like a warm light, Komako poured in on the empty wretchedness that had assailed Shimamura.

There was a meeting at the inn to discuss plans for the ski season. She had been called in for the party afterwards. She put her hands into the kotatsu, then quickly reached up and stroked Shimamura's cheek.

"You're pale this evening. Very strange." She clutched at the soft flesh of his cheek as if to tear it away. "Aren't you the foolish one, though."

She already seemed a little drunk. When she came back from the party she collapsed before the mirror, and drunkenness came out on her face to almost comic effect. "I know nothing about it. Nothing. My head aches. I feel terrible. Terrible. I want a drink. Give me water."

She pressed both hands to her face and tumbled over with little concern for her carefully dressed hair. Presently she brought herself up again and began cleaning away the thick powder with cold cream. The face underneath was a brilliant red. She was quite delighted with herself. To Shimamura it was astonishing that drunkenness could pass so quickly. Her shoulders were shaking from the cold.

All through August she had been near nervous collapse, she told him quietly.

"I thought I'd go mad. I kept brooding over something, and I didn't know myself what it was. It was terrifying. I couldn't sleep. I kept myself under control only when I went out to a party. I had all sorts of dreams, and I lost my appetite. I would sit there jabbing at the floor for hours on end, all through the hottest part of the day."

"When did you first go out as a geisha?"

"In June. I thought for a while I might go to Hamamatsu."

"Get married?"

She nodded. The man had been after her to marry him, but she couldn't like him. She had had great trouble deciding what to do.

"But if you didn't like him, what were you so undecided about?"

"It's not that simple."

"Marriage has so much charm?"

"Don't be nasty. It's more that I want to have everything around me tidy and in order."

Shimamura grunted.

"You're not a very satisfying person, you know."

"Was there something between you and the man from Hamamatsu?"

She flung out her answer: "If there had been, do you think I would have hesitated? But he said that as long as I stayed here, he wouldn't let me marry anyone else. He said he would do everything possible to stand in the way."

"But what could he do from as far away as Hamamatsu? You worried about that?"

Komako stretched out for a time, enjoying the warmth of her body. When she spoke again, her tone was quite casual. "I thought I was pregnant." She giggled. "It seems ridiculous when I look back on it now."

She curled up like a little child, and grabbed at the neck of his kimono with her two fists.

The rich eyelashes again made him think that her eyes were half open.

Her elbow against the brazier, Komako was scribbling something on the back of an old magazine when Shimamura awoke the next morning.

"I can't go home. I jumped up when the maid came to bring charcoal, but it was already broad daylight. The sun was shining in on the door. I was a little drunk last night, and I slept too well."

"What time is it?"

"It's already eight."

"Let's go have a bath." Shimamura got out of bed.

"I can't. Someone might see me in the hall." She was completely tamed. When Shimamura came back from the bath, he found her industriously cleaning the room, a kerchief draped artistically over her head.

She had polished the legs of the table and the edge of the brazier almost too carefully, and she stirred up the charcoal with a practiced hand.

Shimamura sat idly smoking, his feet in the *kotatsu*. When the ashes dropped from his cigarette Komako took them up in a handkerchief and brought him an ashtray. He laughed, a bright morning laugh. Komako laughed too.

"If you had a husband, you'd spend all your time scolding him."

"I would not. But I'd be laughed at for folding up even my dirty clothes. I can't help it. That's the way I am."

"They say you can tell everything about a woman by looking inside her dresser drawers."

"What a beautiful day." They were having breakfast, and the morning sun flooded the room. "I should have gone home early to practice the samisen. The sound is different on a day like this." She looked up at the crystal-clear sky.

The snow on the distant mountains was soft and creamy, as if veiled in a faint smoke.

Shimamura, remembering what the masseuse had said, suggested that she practice here instead. Immediately she telephoned her house to ask for music and a change of clothes.

So the house he had seen the day before had a telephone, thought Shimamura. The eyes of the other girl, Yoko, floated into his mind.

"That girl will bring your music?"

"She might."

"You're engaged to the son, are you?"

"Well! When did you hear that?"

"Yesterday."

"Aren't you strange? If you heard it yesterday, why didn't you tell me?" But her tone showed none of the sharpness of the day before. Today there was only a clean smile on her face.

"That sort of thing would be easier to talk about if I had less respect for you."

"What are you really thinking, I wonder? That's why I don't like Tokyo people."

"You're trying to change the subject. You haven't answered my question, you know."

"I'm not trying to change the subject. You really believed it?"

"I did."

"You're lying again. You didn't really."

"I couldn't quite believe all of it, as a matter of fact. But they said you went to work as a geisha to help pay doctors' bills."

"It sounds like something out of a cheap magazine. But it's not true. I was never engaged to him. People seem to think I was, though. It wasn't to help anyone in particular that I became a geisha. But I owe a great deal to his mother, and I had to do what I could."

"You're talking in riddles."

"I'll tell you everything. Very clearly. There does seem to have been a time when his mother thought it would be a good idea for us to get married. But she only thought it. She never said a word. Both of us knew in a vague sort of way what was on her mind, but it went no farther. And that's all there is to tell."

"Childhood friends."

"That's right. But we've lived most of our lives apart. When they sent me to Tokyo to be a geisha, he was the only one who saw me off. I have that written down on the very first page of my very oldest diary."

"If the two of you had stayed together, you'd probably be married by now."

"I doubt it."

"You would be, though."

"You needn't worry about him. He'll be dead before long."

"But is it right for you to be spending your nights away from home?"

"It's not right for you to ask. How can a dying man keep me from doing as I like?"

Shimamura could think of no answer.

Why was it that Komako said not a word about the girl Yoko?

And Yoko, who had taken care of the sick man on the train, quite as his mother must have when he was very young—how would she feel coming to an inn with a change of kimono for Komako, who was something, Shimamura could not know what, to the man Yoko had come home with?

Shimamura found himself off in his usual distant fantasies.

"Komako, Komako." Yoko's beautiful voice was low but clear.

"Thank you very much." Komako went out to the dressing-room. "You brought it yourself, did you? It must have been heavy."

Yoko left immediately.

The top string snapped as Komako plucked tentatively at the samisen. Shimamura could tell even while she was changing the string and tuning the instrument that she had a firm, confident touch. She took up a bulky bundle and undid it on the *kotatsu*. Inside were an ordinary book of lyrics and some twenty scores. Shimamura glanced curiously at the latter.

"You practice from these?"

"I have to. There's no one here who can teach me."

"What about the woman you live with?"

"She's paralyzed."

"If she can talk she ought to be able to help you."

"But she can't talk. She can still use her left hand to correct mistakes in dancing, but it only annoys her to have to listen to the samisen and not be able to do anything about it."

"Can you really understand the music from only a score?"[8]

"I understand it very well."

"The publishing gentleman[9] would be happy if he knew he had a real geisha—not just an ordinary amateur—practicing from his scores way off here in the mountains."

"In Tokyo I was expected to dance, and they gave me dancing lessons. But I got only the faintest idea of how to play the samisen. If I were to lose that there would be no one here to teach me again. So I use scores."

"And singing?"

"I don't like to sing. I did learn a few songs from my dancing, and I manage to get through them, but newer things I've had to pick up from the radio. I've no idea how near right I am. My own private style—you'd laugh at it, I know. And then my voice gives out when I'm singing for someone I know well. It's always loud and brave for strangers." She looked a little bashful for a moment, then brought herself up and glanced at Shimamura as though signaling that she was ready for him to begin.

He was embarrassed. He was unfortunately no singer.

He was generally familiar with the Nagauta[1] music of the Tokyo theater and dance, and he knew the words to most of the repertoire. He had had no formal training, however. Indeed he associated the Nagauta less with the parlor performance of the geisha than with the actor on the stage.

"The customer is being difficult." Giving her lower lip a quick little bite, Komako brought the samisen to her knee, and, as if that made her a different person, turned earnestly to the lyrics before her.

"I've been practicing this one since last fall."

A chill swept over Shimamura. The goose flesh seemed to rise even to his cheeks. The first notes opened a transparent emptiness deep in his entrails, and in the emptiness the sound of the samisen reverberated. He was startled—or, better, he fell back as under a well-aimed blow. Taken with a feeling almost of reverence, washed by waves of remorse, defenseless, quite deprived of strength—there was nothing for him to do but give himself up to the

---

8. While there is some notation for the samisen, *geisha* usually learn to play the instrument through rote memorization, imitating music they hear performed by a teacher. Komako's reliance solely on written music illustrates her isolation.   9. That is, the publisher of the sheet music Komako is using.   1. "Long songs" (literal trans.); lyric ballads common in *kabuki* plays and popular among *geisha* and amateur students of the samisen.

current, to the pleasure of being swept off wherever Komako would take him.

She was a mountain geisha, not yet twenty, and she could hardly be as good as all that, he told himself. And in spite of the fact that she was in a small room, was she not slamming away at the instrument as though she were on the stage? He was being carried away by his own mountain emotionalism. Komako purposely read the words in a monotone, now slowing down and now jumping over a passage that was too much trouble; but gradually she seemed to fall into a spell. As her voice rose higher, Shimamura began to feel a little frightened. How far would that strong, sure touch take him? He rolled over and pillowed his head on an arm, as if in bored indifference.

The end of the song released him. Ah, this woman is in love with me—but he was annoyed with himself for the thought.

Komako looked up at the clear sky over the snow. "The tone is different on a day like this." The tone had been as rich and vibrant as her remark suggested. The air was different. There were no theater walls, there was no audience, there was none of the city dust. The notes went out crystalline into the clean winter morning, to sound on the far, snowy peaks.

Practicing alone, not aware herself of what was happening, perhaps, but with all the wideness of nature in this mountain valley for her companion, she had come quite as a part of nature to take on this special power. Her very loneliness beat down sorrow and fostered a wild strength of will. There was no doubt that it had been a great victory of the will, even granted that she had had an amount of preparatory training, for her to learn complicated airs from only a score, and presently go through them from memory.

To Shimamura it was wasted effort, this way of living. He sensed in it too a longing that called out to him for sympathy. But the life and way of living no doubt flowed thus grandly from the samisen with a new worth for Komako herself.

Shimamura, untrained in the niceties of samisen technique and conscious only of the emotion in the tone, was perhaps an ideal audience for Komako.

By the time she had begun her third song—the voluptuous softness of the music itself may have been responsible—the chill and the goose flesh had disappeared, and Shimamura, relaxed and warm, was gazing into Komako's face. A feeling of intense physical nearness came over him.

The high, thin nose was usually a little lonely, a little sad, but today, with the healthy, vital flush on her cheeks, it was rather whispering: I am here too. The smooth lips seemed to reflect back a dancing light even when they were drawn into a tight bud; and when for a moment they were stretched wide, as the singing demanded, they were quick to contract again into that engaging little bud. Their charm was exactly like the charm of her body itself. Her eyes, moist and shining, made her look like a very young girl. She wore no powder, and the polish of the city geisha had over it a layer of mountain color. Her skin, suggesting the newness of a freshly peeled onion or perhaps a lily bulb, was flushed faintly, even to the throat. More than anything, it was clean.

Seated rigidly upright, she seemed more demure and maidenly than usual.

This time using a score, she sang a song she had not yet finished memorizing. At the end she silently pushed the plectrum[2] under the strings and let herself fall into an easier posture.

Her manner quickly took on a touch of the seductive and alluring.

Shimamura could think of nothing to say. Komako did not seem to care particularly what he thought of her playing, however. She was quite unaffectedly pleased with herself.

"Can you always tell which geisha it is from the tone of the samisen?"

"That's easy. There aren't twenty of us all together. It depends a little on the style, though. The individual comes out more in some styles than in others."

She took up the samisen again and shifted her weight so that her feet were a little to one side and the instrument rested on the calf of one leg.

"This is the way you hold it when you're small." She leaned toward the samisen as though it were too large for her. "Da-a-ark hair. . . ." Her voice was deliberately childish and she picked out the notes uncertainly.

" 'Dark Hair' was the first one you learned?"

"Uh-uh." She shook her head girlishly, as no doubt she did in the days when she was still too small to hold the samisen properly.

Komako no longer tried to leave before daybreak when she stayed the night.

"Komako," the two-year-old daughter of the innkeeper would call from far down the hall, her voice rising in the mountain-country lilt. The two of them would play happily in the *kotatsu* until nearly noon, when they would go for a bath.

Back from the bath, Komako was combing her hair. "Whenever the child sees a geisha, she calls out 'Komako' in that funny accent, and when she sees a picture of someone with her hair done in the old way, that's 'Komako' too. Children can tell when you like them. Come, Kimi. Let's go play at Komako's." She stood up to leave, then sat down lazily on the veranda. "Eager people from Tokyo already out skiing."

The room looked from high ground directly south over the ski runs at the base of the mountain.

Shimamura glanced up from the *kotatsu*. There were patches of snow on the mountain, and five or six figures in black ski clothes were moving about in the terraced fields. It seemed a trifle silly. The slope was a gentle one, and the walls between the fields were not yet covered with snow.

"They look like students. Is today Sunday? Do you suppose that's fun?"

"They're good, though," Komako said, as if to herself. "Guests are always surprised when a geisha says hello to them on the ski grounds. They don't recognize her for the snow-burn. At night the powder hides it."

"You wear ski clothes?"

She wore "mountain trousers," she said. "But what a nuisance the ski season is. It's all coming again. You see them in the evening at the inn, and they say they'll see you again the next day skiing. Maybe I should give up skiing this year. Good-by. Come along, Kimi. We'll have snow this evening. It's always cold the night before it snows."

2. A pick for plucking the strings of a musical instrument.

Shimamura went out to the veranda. Komako was leading Kimi down the steep road below the ski grounds.

The sky was clouding over. Mountains still in the sunlight stood out against shadowed mountains. The play of light and shade changed from moment to moment, sketching a chilly landscape. Presently the ski grounds too were in shadow. Below the window Shimamura could see little needles of frost like isinglass[3] among the withered chrysanthemums, though water was still dripping from the snow on the roof.

It did not snow that evening. A hailstorm turned to rain.

Shimamura called Komako again the night before he was to leave. It was a clear, moonlit night. At eleven o'clock the air was bitterly cold, but Komako insisted on going for a walk. She pulled him roughly from the *kotatsu*.

The road was frozen. The village lay quiet under the cold sky. Komako hitched up the skirt of her kimono and tucked it into her *obi*. The moon shone like a blade frozen in blue ice.

"We'll go to the station," said Komako.

"You're insane. It's more than a mile each way."

"You'll be going back to Tokyo soon. We'll go look at the station."

Shimamura was numb from his shoulders to his thighs.

Back in his room, Komako sank disconsolately to the floor. Her head was bowed and her arms were deep in the *kotatsu*. Strangely, she refused to go with him to the bath.

Bedding had been laid out with the foot of the mattress inside the *kotatsu*. Komako was sitting forlornly beside it when Shimamura came back from the bath. She said nothing.

"What's the matter?"

"I'm going home."

"Don't be foolish."

"Go on to bed. Just let me sit here for a little while."

"Why do you want to go home?"

"I'm not going home. I'll sit here till morning."

"Don't be difficult."

"I'm not being difficult. I'm not being difficult."

"Then . . . ?"

"I . . . don't feel well."

"Is that all?" Shimamura laughed. "I'll leave you quite to yourself."

"No."

"And why did you have to go out and run all over town?"

"I'm going home."

"There's no need to go home."

"But it's not easy for me. Go on back to Tokyo. It's not easy for me." Her face was low over the *kotatsu*.

Was it sorrow at finding herself about to sink into too deep a relationship with a traveler? Or at having to keep herself under control at so dear a moment? She has come that far, then, Shimamura said to himself. He too was silent for a time.

"Please go back to Tokyo."

"As a matter of fact, I was thinking of going back tomorrow."

---

3. Thin, translucent sheets of mica (an aluminum silicate mineral).

"No! Why are you going back?" She looked up, startled, as though aroused from sleep.

"What can I do for you, no matter how long I stay?"

She gazed at him for a moment, then burst out violently: "You don't have to say that. What reason have you to say that?" She stood up irritably, and threw herself at his neck. "It's wrong of you to say such things. Get up. Get up, I tell you." The words poured out deliriously, and she fell down beside him, quite forgetting in her derangement the physical difficulty she had spoken of earlier.

Some time later, she opened warm, moist eyes.

She picked up the hair ornament that had fallen to the floor.

"You really must go back tomorrow," she said quietly.

As Shimamura was changing clothes to leave on the three-o'clock train the next afternoon, the manager of the inn beckoned Komako into the hall. "Let's see. Suppose we make it about eleven hours," he could hear Komako's answer. They were evidently discussing the bill for her services as a geisha, and the manager perhaps thought it would be unreasonable to charge for the whole sixteen or seventeen hours.

The bill as a matter of fact was computed by the hour—"Left at five," or "Left at twelve"—without the usual charge for overnight services.

Komako, in an overcoat and a white scarf, saw him to the station.

Even when he had finished buying presents to take back to Tokyo, he had some twenty minutes to kill. Walking with Komako in the slightly raised station plaza, he thought what a narrow little valley it was, crowded in among the snowy mountains. Komako's too-black hair was a little touching, a little sad, in the loneliness of the shadowed mountain pocket.

The sun shone dimly on a spot in the mountains far down the river.

"It's melted a good deal since I came."

"Two days of snow, though, and we'll have six feet. Then it snows again, and before long the lights on those poles are out of sight. I'll walk along thinking of you, and I'll find myself strung up on a wire."

"The snow is that deep?"

"They say that in the next town up the line the schoolchildren jump naked from the second floor of the dormitory. They sink out of sight in the snow, and they move around under it as though they were swimming. Look, a snowplow."

"I'd like to see it that deep. But I suppose the inn will be crowded. And there might be danger of slides along the way."

"With you it's not a question of money, is it? Have you always had so much to spend?" She turned to look up at his face. "Why don't you grow a mustache?"

"I've thought of it." Shimamura, freshly shaven, stroked the blue-black traces of his beard. A deep line from the corner of his mouth set off the softness of his cheek. Was that, he wondered, what Komako found attractive? "You always look a little as though you'd just shaved too when you take off that powder."

"Listen! The crows. That frightening way they sometimes have. Where are they, I wonder? And isn't it cold!" Komako hugged herself as she looked up at the sky.

"Shall we go in by the stove?"

A figure in "mountain trousers" came running up the wide road from the main highway into the station plaza. It was Yoko.

"Komako. Yukio—Komako," she panted, clinging to Komako like a child that has run frightened to its mother, "come home. Right away. Yukio's worse. Right away."

Komako closed her eyes, as if from the pain of the assault on her shoulder. Her face was white, but she shook her head with surprising firmness.

"I can't go home. I'm seeing off a guest."

Shimamura was startled. "You needn't see me off."

"It's not right to leave. How do I know you'll come again?"

"I'll come, I'll come."

Yoko seemed not to hear the exchange. "I just called the inn," she went on feverishly, "and they said you were at the station. So I came here. I ran all the way. Yukio is asking for you." She pulled at Komako, but Komako shook her off impatiently.

"Leave me alone."

It was Komako who reeled back, however. She retched violently, but nothing came from her mouth. The rims of her eyes were moist. There was goose flesh on her cheeks.

Yoko stood rigid, gazing at Komako. Her face, like a mask, wore an expression of such utter earnestness that it was impossible to tell whether she was angry or surprised or grieved. It seemed an extraordinarily pure and simple face to Shimamura.

She turned quickly and, without the slightest change of expression, clutched at Shimamura's hand. "I'm sorry, but would you let her go home?" A tense, high-pitched voice assailed him. "Let her go home."

"Of course I'll let her go home. Go on home," he called out to Komako. "Don't be a fool."

"And what say do you have in the matter?" Komako pushed Yoko roughly away from him.

Shimamura tried to signal the taxi waiting in front of the station. Yoko clutched at his arm so tightly that his fingers were numbed. "I'll send her home in a taxi," he said. "Why don't you go on ahead? People will be watching us."

Yoko nodded quickly, and turned away with almost unbelievable alacrity. Why was the girl always so earnest, so sober, Shimamura wondered. But such musings did not seem entirely in keeping with the occasion.

That voice, so beautiful it was almost lonely, lingered in Shimamura's ears as if it were echoing back from somewhere in the snowy mountains.

"Where are you going?" Komako pulled at Shimamura. He had signaled the taxi and was walking toward it. "I won't. I'm not going home."

For an instant Shimamura felt something very near physical revulsion.

"I don't know what there is among the three of you, but the man may be dying even now. She came for you, didn't she, because he wants to see you. Go home like a good girl. You'll regret it all your life if you don't. What if he dies even while you're standing here? Don't be stubborn. Forgive and forget."

"Forgive and forget? You don't understand. You don't understand at all."

"And when they sent you to Tokyo, he was the only one who saw you off, didn't you say? Do you think it's right not to say good-by to the man you yourself said was on the very first page of the very first volume of your diary? This is the very last page of his."

"But I don't want to. I don't want to see a man die."

It could have been the coldest heartlessness or too warm a passion—Shimamura did not know which.

"I'll not be able to write in my diary any more. I'll burn it," she said softly, almost to herself. Her cheeks were flushed. "You're a good, simple person at heart, aren't you? If you really are, I won't mind sending my whole diary to you. You won't laugh at me? You're a good, honest person at heart, I'm sure."

Shimamura was moved by a wave of feeling he could not define himself. He thought he must indeed be the plainest, most honest person in the world. He no longer worried about sending Komako home. She said nothing more.

A porter from the inn came to tell them that the gate to the tracks was open.

Four or five villagers in somber winter dress got on and off the train.

"I'll not go to the platform with you. Good-by." Komako stood inside the closed window of the waiting-room. From the train window it was as though one strange piece of fruit had been left behind in the grimy glass case of a shabby mountain grocery.

The window of the waiting-room was clear for an instant as the train started to move. Komako's face glowed forth, and as quickly disappeared. It was the bright red it had been in the mirror that snowy morning, and for Shimamura that color again seemed to be the point at which he parted with reality.

The train climbed the north slope of the Border Range into the long tunnel. On the far side it moved down a mountain valley. The color of evening was descending from chasms between the peaks. The dim brightness of the winter afternoon seemed to have been sucked into the earth, and the battered old train had shed its bright shell in the tunnel. There was no snow on the south slope.

Following a stream, the train came out on the plain. A mountain, cut at the top in curious notches and spires, fell off in a graceful sweep to the far skirts. Over it the moon was rising. The solid, integral shape of the mountain, taking up the whole of the evening landscape there at the end of the plain, was set off in a deep purple against the pale light of the sky. The moon was no longer an afternoon white, but, faintly colored, it had not yet taken on the clear coldness of the winter night. There was not a bird in the sky. Nothing broke the lines of the wide skirts to the right and the left. Where the mountain swept down to meet the river, a stark white building, a hydroelectric plant perhaps, stood out sharply from the withered scene the train window framed, one last spot saved from the night.

The window began to steam over. The landscape outside was dusky, and the figures of the passengers floated up half-transparent. It was the play of that evening mirror again. The train, probably no more than three or four worn-out, faded, old-fashioned coaches strung together, was not from the same world as the trains one finds on the main lines. The light inside was dim.

Shimamura abandoned himself to the fancy that he had stepped into some unreal conveyance, that he was being borne away in emptiness, cut off from time and place. The monotonous sound of the wheels became the woman's voice.

Her words, though short and broken, were a sign that she was alive in all her vital intensity, and he knew he had not forgotten her from the fact that listening was a trial. But to the Shimamura of that moment, moving away from the woman, the voice was already a distant one that could do no more than sharpen the poignancy of travel.

Would Yukio be breathing his last even now? Komako had for reasons of her own refused to go home; and had she then failed to reach his bedside in time?

There were so few passengers that Shimamura felt a little uneasy.

Besides Shimamura himself, there were only a man, probably in his fifties, and opposite him a red-faced girl. A black shawl was thrown over the full flesh of her shoulders, and her cheeks were a wonderful, fiery red. She leaned slightly forward to catch every word the man said, and she answered him happily. A pair off on a long journey together, Shimamura concluded.

As the train pulled into a station behind which rose the chimneys of spinning-factories, however, the man hastily got up, took a wicker trunk from the baggage rack, and threw it out the window to the platform. "Maybe we'll meet again sometime," he called back to the girl as he hurried from the train.

Shimamura suddenly wanted to weep. He had been caught quite off guard, and it struck him afresh that he had said good-by to the woman and was on his way home.

He had not considered the possibility that the two had simply met on the train. The man was perhaps a traveling salesman.

PART TWO

It was the egg-laying season for moths, Shimamura's wife told him as he left Tokyo, and he was not to leave his clothes hanging in the open. There were indeed moths at the inn. Five or six large corn-colored moths clung to the decorative lantern under the eaves, and in the little dressing-room was a moth whose body was large out of all proportion to its wings.

The windows were still screened from the summer. A moth so still that it might have been glued there clung to one of the screens. Its feelers stood out like delicate wool, the color of cedar bark, and its wings, the length of a woman's finger, were a pale, almost diaphanous green. The ranges of mountains beyond were already autumn-red in the evening sun. That one spot of pale green struck him as oddly like the color of death. The fore and after wings overlapped to make a deeper green, and the wings fluttered like thin pieces of paper in the autumn wind.

Wondering if the moth was alive, Shimamura went over to the window and rubbed his finger over the inside of the screen. The moth did not move. He struck at it with his fist, and it fell like a leaf from a tree, floating lightly up midway to the ground.

In front of the cedar grove opposite, dragonflies were bobbing about in countless swarms, like dandelion floss in the wind.

The river seemed to flow from the tips of the cedar branches.

He thought he would never tire of looking at the autumn flowers that spread a blanket of silver up the side of the mountain.

A White-Russian[4] woman, a peddler, was sitting in the hallway when he came out of the bath. So you find them even in these mountains—He went for a closer look.

She appeared to be in her forties. Her face was wrinkled and dirty, but her skin, where it showed at the full throat and beyond, was a pure, glowing white.

"Where are you from?" Shimamura asked.

"Where am I from? Where am I from?" The woman seemed troubled for an answer. She began to put away her wares, the most ordinary Japanese cosmetics and hair ornaments.

Her skirt, like a dirty sheet wrapped around her, had quite lost the feel of occidental dress, and had taken on instead something of the air of Japan. She carried her wares on her back in a large Japanese-style kerchief. But for all that, she still wore foreign shoes.

The innkeeper's wife stood beside Shimamura watching the Russian leave. The two of them went into the office, where a large woman was seated at the hearth with her back to them. She took her long skirts in her hand as she stood up to go. Her cloak was a formal black.

She was a geisha Shimamura remembered having seen with Komako in an advertising photograph, the two of them on skis with cotton "mountain trousers" pulled over party kimonos. She seemed to be well along in years, plump and to all appearances good-natured.

The innkeeper was warming thick, oblong cakes over the embers.

"Won't you have one?" he asked Shimamura. "You really must have one. The geisha you saw brought them to celebrate the end of her term."

"She's leaving, is she?"

"Yes."

"She looks like a good sort."

"She was very popular. Today she's going the rounds to say good-by."

Shimamura blew on the cake and bit into it. The hard crust, a little sour, gave off a musty smell.

Outside the window, the bright red of ripe persimmons was bathed in the evening sun. It seemed to send out a red glow even to the bamboo of the pothook over the hearth.

"See how long they are." Shimamura looked out in astonishment at the steep path, down which old women were trudging with bundles of autumn grass on their backs. The grass looked to be twice the height of the women, and the tassels were long and powerful.

"It's *kaya* grass."[5]

"*Kaya*, is it?"

"The government railways built a sort of rest-room, I suppose you would call it, for their hot-spring exhibit, and they thatched the teahouse with *kaya* from these mountains. Someone in Tokyo bought it exactly as it was."

"*Kaya*, is it," Shimamura repeated, half to himself. "It's *kaya* then on the mountain? I thought it must be a flower of some sort."

---

4. One who fought against the Bolsheviks in the civil war that followed the Russian Revolution (1917). A number of them fled to Japan after the collapse of the anti-Bolshevik forces.   5. A tall, coarse grass used for thatching.

The first thing that had struck Shimamura's eye as he got off the train was that array of silver-white. High up the mountain, the *kaya* spread out silver in the sun, like the autumn sunlight itself pouring over the face of the mountain. Ah, I am here, something in Shimamura called out as he looked up at it.

But the great strands he saw here seemed quite different in nature from the grasses that had so moved him. The large bundles hid the women carrying them, and rustled against the rocks that flanked the path. And the plumes were long and powerful.

Under the dim light in the dressing-room, Shimamura could see that the large-bodied moth was laying eggs along the black lacquer of the clothes-frame. Moths were beating at the lantern under the eaves.

There was a steady humming of autumn insects, as there had been from before sundown.

Komako was a little late.

She gazed in at him from the hall.

"Why have you come here? Why have you come to a place like this?"

"I've come to see you."

"You don't mean that. I dislike people from Tokyo because they're always lying." She sat down, and her voice was softer. "I'm never going to see anyone off again. I can't describe how it felt to see you off."

"This time I'll go without telling you."

"No. I mean I won't go to the station again."

"What happened to him?"

"He died, of course."

"While you were seeing me off?"

"But that's not the reason. I had no idea I could hate so to see someone off."

Shimamura nodded.

"Where were you on the fourteenth of February? I was waiting for you. But I'll know better than to believe you next time."

The fourteenth of February was the "bird-chasing festival,"[6] a children's festival that had in it the spirit of this snow country. For ten days before the festival the children of the village tramped down the snow with straw boots, and presently, cutting the now boardlike snow into two-foot cubes, they built a snow palace some six yards square and more than ten feet high. Since the New Year was celebrated here early in February, the traditional straw ropes[7] were still strung up over the village doorways. On the fourteenth the children gathered the ropes and burned them in a red bonfire before the snow palace. They pushed and jostled one another on the roof and sang the bird-chasing song,[8] and afterwards, setting out lights, they spent the night in the palace. At dawn on the fifteenth they again climbed to the roof to sing the bird-chasing song.

It was then that the snow was deepest, and Shimamura had told Komako he would come for the festival.

6. An observance in rural agricultural communities lasting from the night of the fourteenth until dawn the next morning. Children and youths ran around the houses of the village singing and banging mallets and sticks, ladles and whisks, and other implements to ensure a fruitful harvest in the coming year by scaring away any birds that might feed on crops.   7. Sacred rope hung at Shinto shrines and elsewhere (especially during holidays) to sanctify the premises. According to the traditional lunar calendar of premodern times, the New Year was usually in early February.   8. One of the various songs sung during the bird-chasing festival.

"I was at home in February. I took a vacation. I was sure you would be here on the fourteenth, and I came back especially. I could have stayed to take care of her longer if I had known."

"Was someone ill?"

"The music teacher. She had pneumonia down on the coast. The telegram came when I was at home, and I went down to take care of her."

"Did she get better?"

"No."

"I'm sorry." Shimamura's words could have been either an expression of sympathy or an apology for the broken promise.

Komako shook her head mildly, and wiped at the table with her handkerchief. "The place is alive with insects." A swarm of tiny winged insects fell from the table to the floor. Several small moths were circling the light.

Moths, how many kinds he could not tell, dotted the screen, floating on the clear moonlight.

"My stomach aches." Komako thrust both hands tight inside her *obi,* and her head fell to Shimamura's knee. "My stomach aches."

Insects smaller than moths gathered on the thick white powder at her neck. Some of them died there as Shimamura watched.

The flesh on her neck and shoulders was richer than it had been the year before. She is just twenty, he told himself.

He felt something warm and damp on his knee.

" 'Komako, go on up and look in the Camellia Room,' they said in the office, very pleased with themselves. I don't like that way they have. I'd been to see Kikuyu off, and I was just ready for a good nap when someone said there had been a call from here. I didn't feel like coming. I had too much to drink last night at Kikuyu's farewell party. They only laughed down in the office and wouldn't tell me who was here. And it was you. It's been a whole year. You're the sort that comes only once a year?"

"I had one of the cakes she left."

"You did?" Komako sat up. Her face was red where it had been pressed against his knee. She seemed very young.

She had seen the old geisha Kikuyu to the second station down the line, she said.

"It's very sad. We used to be able to work things out together, but now it's every geisha for herself. The place has changed. New geisha come in and no one gets along with anyone else. I'll be lonesome without Kikuyu. She was at the center of everything. And she made more money than any of the rest of us. Her people took very good care of her."

Kikuyu had worked out her contract, and she was going home. Would she get married or would she open an inn or restaurant of her own? Shimamura asked.

"Kikuyu is a very sad case. She made a bad marriage, and she came here afterwards." Komako was silent for a time, evidently unsure how much she should tell. She looked out toward the slope below the terraced fields, bright in the moonlight. "You know the new house halfway up the hill?"

"The restaurant—the Kikumura, is it called?"

"That's the one. Kikuyu was supposed to manage the Kikumura, but at the last minute she had a change of heart. It caused all sorts of excitement. She had a patron build the place for her, and then, when she was all ready to move in, she threw it over. She found someone she liked and was going to marry him, but he ran off and left her. Is that what happens when you lose your head over a man? I wonder. She can't very well go back to her old work, and she can't take over the restaurant now that she's turned it down, and she's ashamed to stay here after all that's happened. There's nothing for her to do but start over somewhere else. It makes me very sad to think about Kikuyu. There were all sorts of people—but of course we don't really know the details."

"Men? How many? Five or so?"

"I wonder." Komako laughed softly and turned away. "Kikuyu was weak. A weakling."

"Maybe there was nothing else she could do."

"But isn't it so? You can't go losing your head over every man that likes you." Her eyes were on the floor, and she was stroking her hair meditatively with a hair ornament. "It wasn't easy, seeing her off."

"And what happened to the restaurant?"

"The wife of the man who built it has taken it over."

"An interesting situation. The wife managing the mistress's restaurant."

"But what else could they do? The place was ready to open, and the wife moved in with all her children."

"What about her own house?"

"They left the old woman to take care of it, I hear. The man's a farmer, but he likes to have his fun. He's a very interesting fellow."

"So it would seem. Is he well along in years?"

"He's young. No more than thirty-one or thirty-two."

"The mistress must be older than the wife, then."

"They're both twenty-six."

"The 'Kiku' of 'Kikumura' would be from 'Kikuyu.' And the wife took over the name even?"

"But they couldn't change the name once it was advertised."

Shimamura straightened the collar of his kimono. Komako got up to close the window.

"Kikuyu knew all about you. She told me today you were here."

"I saw her down in the office when she came to say good-by."

"Did she say anything to you?"

"Not a thing."

"Do you know how I feel?" Komako threw open the window she had just shut, and sat down on the sill as if she meant to throw herself out.

"The stars here are different from the stars in Tokyo," Shimamura said after a time. "They seem to float up from the sky."

"Not tonight, though. The moon is too bright. . . . . The snow was dreadful this year."

"I understand there were times when the trains couldn't get through."

"I was almost afraid. The roads weren't open until May, a month later than usual. You know the shop up at the ski grounds? An avalanche went through the second floor of it. The people below heard a strange noise and thought the rats were tearing up the kitchen. There were no rats, though, and when they looked upstairs the place was full of snow and the shutters and all had been carried off. It was just a surface slide, but there was a great deal of talk on the radio. The skiers were frightened away. I said I wouldn't ski any more and I gave my skis away the end of last year, but I went out again after all. Twice, three times maybe. Have I changed?"

"What have you been doing since the music teacher died?"

"Don't you worry about other people's problems. I came back and I was waiting for you in February."

"But if you were down on the coast you could have written me a letter."

"I couldn't. I really couldn't. I couldn't possibly write the sort of letter your wife would see. I couldn't bring myself to. I don't tell lies just because people might be listening." The words came at him in a sudden torrent. He only nodded. "Why don't you turn out the light? You don't have to sit in this swarm of insects."

The moonlight, so bright that the furrows in the woman's ear were clearly shadowed, struck deep into the room and seemed to turn the mats on the floor a chilly green.

"No. Let me go home."

"I see you haven't changed." Shimamura raised his head. There was something strange in her manner. He peered into the slightly aquiline face.

"People say I haven't changed since I came here. I was sixteen then. But life goes on the same, year after year."

Her cheeks still carried the ruddiness of her north-country girlhood. In the moonlight the fine geishalike skin took on the luster of a sea shell.

"But did you hear I'd moved?"

"Since the teacher died? You're not in the silkworms' room any more, then? This time it's a real geisha house?"

"A real geisha house? I suppose it is. They sell tobacco and candy in the shop, and I'm the only geisha they have. I have a real contract, and when I read late in the night I always use a candle to save electricity."

Shimamura let out a loud guffaw.

"The meter, you know. Shouldn't use too much electricity."

"I see, I see."

"But they're very good to me, so good that I sometimes find it hard to believe I'm really hired out as a geisha. When one of the children cries, the mother takes it outside so that I won't be bothered. I have nothing to complain about. Only sometimes the bedding is crooked. When I come home late at night, everything is laid out for me, but the mattresses aren't square one on the other, and the sheet is wrong. I hate it. After they've been so kind, though, I feel guilty making the bed over."

"You'd wear yourself out if you had a house of your own."

"So everyone says. There are four little children, and the place is a terrible clutter. I spend the whole day picking things up. I know everything will be thrown down again as soon as my back is turned, but somehow I can't help myself. I want to be as clean and neat as the place will let me. . . . Do you understand how I feel?"

"I understand."

"If you understand, then tell me. Tell me, if you see how I feel." Again that tense, urgent note came into her voice. "See, you can't. Lying again. You have plenty of money, and you're not much of a person. You don't understand at all." She lowered her voice. "I'm very lonely sometimes. But I'm a fool. Go back to Tokyo, tomorrow."

"It's very well for you to condemn me, but how can you expect me to tell you exactly what I mean?"

"Why can't you? It's wrong of you." Her voice was almost desperate. Then she closed her eyes, and began again as if she had asked herself whether

Shimamura knew her, felt her for what she was, and had answered that he did. "Once a year is enough. You'll come once a year, won't you, while I'm here?"

Her contract was for four years, she said.

"When I was at home, I didn't dream I would ever be a geisha again. I even gave away my skis before I left. And so all I've accomplished, I suppose, has been to give up smoking."

"I remember how much you used to smoke, now that you mention it."

"When guests at parties give me cigarettes, I tuck them away in my sleeve, and I have a fine collection by the time I'm ready to go home."

"But four years—that's a long time."

"It will pass in a hurry."

"Aren't you warm, though." Shimamura took her in his arms as she came to him.

"I've always been warm."

"I suppose the nights will be getting chilly."

"It's five years now since I came here. At first I wondered how I could live in such a place—especially before the railroad came through. And it's going on two years since you first came."

He had come three times in less than two years, and on each new visit he had found Komako's life changed.

Crickets were chirping outside in a noisy chorus.

"I wish they'd be a little quieter." Komako pulled away from Shimamura.

The moths at the window started up as the wind came from the north.

Shimamura knew well enough that the thick eyelashes made her eyes seem half open, and yet he found himself looking again to be sure.

"I'm fatter now that I've stopped smoking."

The fat on her abdomen was heavier, he had noticed.

They had long been apart, but what eluded his grasp when he was away from her was immediately near and familiar when he was beside her again.

"One is bigger than the other." She cupped her breasts lightly in her hands.

"I suppose that's a habit of his—one side only."

"What a nasty thing to say!" Here she was—this was it, he remembered.

"Next time tell him to treat them both alike."

"Alike? Shall I tell him to treat them both alike?" She brought her face gently toward his.

It was a second-floor room, but it seemed to be surrounded by croaking toads. Two and three of them were moving from spot to spot, remarkably long-winded croakers.

Back from the bath, Komako began talking of herself. Her voice was quiet and her manner was completely serene.

The first physical examination she had had here—she thought it would be as when she was an apprentice geisha, and she bared her chest for a tuberculosis check. The doctor laughed, and she burst into tears—such were the intimate details she went into. She talked on as Shimamura encouraged her with questions.

"I'm always exactly on the calendar. Two days less than a month each time."

"I don't suppose it keeps you from your parties?"

"You understand such things, do you?"

Every day she had a bath in the hot spring, famous for its lingering warmth. She walked two miles and more between parties at the old spring and the new, and here in the mountains there were few parties that kept her up late. She was therefore healthy and full-bodied, though she did have a suggestion of the low, bunched-up hips so common with geisha, narrow from side to side and wide from front to back. To Shimamura there was something touching about the fact that such a woman could call him back from afar.

"I wonder if I can have children." And she wondered too if being generally faithful to one man was not the same thing as being married.

That was the first Shimamura had heard of the "one man" in Komako's life. She had known him since she was sixteen, she said. Shimamura thought he understood now the lack of caution that had at first so puzzled him.

She had never liked the man, Komako continued, and had never felt near him, perhaps because the affair had begun when she was down on the coast just after the death of the man who had paid her debts.

"But it's certainly better than average if it's lasted five years."

"I've had two chances to leave him. When I went to work as a geisha here, and when I moved after the music teacher died. But I've never had the will power to do it. I don't have much will power."

The man was still down on the coast. It had not been convenient to keep her there, and when the music teacher came back to these mountains he had left Komako with her. He had been very kind, Komako said, and it made her sad to think that she could not give her whole self to him. He was considerably older than she, and he but rarely came to see her.

"I sometimes think it would be easiest to break away from him if I were to be really bad. I honestly think so sometimes."

"That would never do."

"But I wouldn't be up to it. It's not in my nature. I'm fond of this body I live in. If I tried, I could cut my four years down to two, but I don't strain myself. I take care of myself. Think of all the money I could make if I really tried. But it's enough if the man I have my contract with hasn't lost money at the end of four years. I know about how much it takes each month for an installment on the loan, and interest, and taxes, and my own keep, and I don't strain myself to make more. If it's a party that doesn't seem worth the trouble, I slip off and go home, and they don't call me late at night even from the inn unless an old guest has asked especially for me. If I wanted to be extravagant, I could go on and on, but I work as the mood takes me. That's enough. I've already paid back more than half the money, and it's not a year yet. But even so I manage to spend thirty yen or so on myself every month."

It was enough if she made a hundred yen a month, she said. The month before, the least busy of the year, she had made sixty yen. She had had some ninety parties, more than any other geisha. She received a fixed amount for herself from each party, and the larger number of parties therefore meant relatively more for her and less for the man to whom she was indentured. But she moved busily from one to another as the spirit took her. There was not a single geisha at this hot spring who lost money and had to extend her contract.

Komako was up early the next morning. "I dreamed I was cleaning house for the woman who teaches flower-arranging, and I woke up."

She had moved the little dresser over to the window. In the mirror the mountains were red with autumn leaves, and the autumn sun was bright.

This time it was not Yoko he heard, Yoko calling through the door in that voice so clear he found it a little sad. Komako's clothes were brought rather by the little daughter of the man with whom she had her contract.

"What happened to the girl?" Shimamura asked.

Komako darted a quick glance at him. "She spends all her time at the cemetery. Over there at the foot of the ski course. See the buckwheat field—the white flowers? And the cemetery to the left of it?"

Shimamura went for a walk in the village when Komako had left.

Before a white wall, shaded by eaves, a little girl in "mountain trousers" and an orange-red flannel kimono, clearly brand-new, was bouncing a rubber ball. For Shimamura, there was autumn in the little scene.

The houses were built in the style of the old regime.[9] No doubt they were there when provincial lords passed down this north-country road. The eaves and the verandas were deep, while the latticed, paper-covered windows on the second floor were long and low, no more than a foot or so high. There were reed blinds hanging from the eaves.

Slender autumn grasses grew along the top of an earthen wall. The pale-yellow plumes were at their most graceful, and below each plume narrow leaves spread out in a delicate fountain.

Yoko knelt on a straw mat beside the road, flailing at beans spread out before her in the sunlight.

The beans jumped from their dry pods like little drops of light.

Perhaps she could not see him because of the scarf around her head. She knelt, flailing away at the beans, her knees spread apart in their "mountain trousers," and she sang in that voice so clear it was almost sad, the voice that seemed to be echoing back from somewhere.

> "The butterfly, the dragonfly, the cricket.
> The pine cricket, bell cricket, horse cricket
> Are singing in the hills."

How large the crow is, starting up from the cedar in the evening breeze—so says the poet. Again there were swarms of dragonflies by the cedar grove Shimamura could see from his window. As the evening approached, they seemed to swim about faster, more restlessly.

Shimamura had bought a new guide to these mountains while he was waiting for his train in Tokyo. Thumbing through it, he learned that near the top of one of the Border Range peaks a path threaded its way through beautiful lakes and marshes, and in this watery belt Alpine plants grew in the wildest profusion. In the summer red dragonflies flew calmly about, lighting on a hat or a hand, or the rim of a pair of spectacles, as different from the persecuted city dragonfly as a cloud from a mud puddle.

But the dragonflies here before him seemed to be driven by something. It was as though they wanted desperately to avoid being pulled in with the cedar grove as it darkened before the sunset.

9. The *shogun*'s government during the Edo period (1600–1868).

The western sun fell on distant mountains, and in the evening light he could see how the red leaves were working their way down from the summits.

"People are delicate, aren't they?" Komako had said that morning. "Broken into a pulp, they say, skull and bones and all. And a bear could fall from a higher ledge and not be hurt in the least." There had been another accident up among the rocks, and she had pointed out the mountain on which it had happened.

If man had a tough, hairy hide like a bear, his world would be different indeed, Shimamura thought. It was through a thin, smooth skin that man loved. Looking out at the evening mountains, Shimamura felt a sentimental longing for the human skin.

"The butterfly, the dragonfly, the cricket." A geisha had been singing the song to a clumsy samisen accompaniment as he sat down to an early dinner.

The guidebook gave only the most essential information on routes, schedules, lodgings, costs, and left the rest to the imagination. Shimamura had come down from these mountains, as the new green was making its way through the last of the snow, to meet Komako for the first time; and now, in the autumn climbing season, he found himself drawn again to the mountains he had left his tracks in. Though he was an idler who might as well spend his time in the mountains as anywhere, he looked upon mountain climbing as almost a model of wasted effort. For that very reason it pulled at him with the attraction of the unreal.

When he was far away, he thought incessantly of Komako; but now that he was near her, this sighing for the human skin took on a dreamy quality like the spell of the mountains. Perhaps he felt a certain security, perhaps he was at the moment too intimate, too familiar with her body. She had stayed with him the night before. Sitting alone in the quiet, he could only wait for her. He was sure she would come without his calling. As he listened to the noisy chatter of a group of schoolgirls out on the hiking trip, however, he began to feel a little sleepy. He went to bed early.

Rain fell during the night, one of those quick showers that come in the autumn.

When he awoke the next morning, Komako was sitting primly beside the table, a book open before her. She wore an everyday kimono and cloak.

"Are you awake?" Her voice was soft as she turned to him.

"What are you doing here?"

"Are you awake?"

Shimamura glanced around the room, wondering if she had come in the night without his knowing it. He picked up the watch beside his pillow. It was only six-thirty.

"You're early."

"But the maid has already brought charcoal."

A morninglike steam was rising from the teakettle.

"It's time to get up." She sat beside his pillow, the picture of the proper housewife. Shimamura stretched and yawned. He took the hand on her knee and caressed the small fingers, callused from playing the samisen.

"But it's barely sunrise."

"Did you sleep well by yourself?"

"Very well."

"You didn't grow a mustache after all."

"You did tell me to grow a mustache, didn't you?"

"It's all right. I knew you wouldn't. You always shave yourself nice and blue."

"And you always look as if you'd just shaved when you wash away that powder."

"Isn't your face a little fatter, though? You were very funny asleep, all round and plump with your white skin and no mustache."

"Sweet and gentle?"

"But unreliable."

"You were staring at me, then? I'm not sure I like having people stare at me when I'm asleep."

Komako smiled and nodded. Then, like a glow that breaks into a flame, the smile became a laugh. There was strength in the fingers that took his.

"I hid in the closet. The maid didn't suspect a thing."

"When? How long were you hidden?"

"Just now, of course. When the maid came to bring charcoal." She laughed happily at the prank, and suddenly she was red to the ears. As if to hide her confusion, she began fanning herself with the edge of his quilt. "Get up. Get up, please."

"It's cold." Shimamura pulled the quilt away from her. "Are the inn people up yet?"

"I have no idea. I came in from the back."

"The back?"

"I fought my way up from the cedar grove."

"Is there a path in back?"

"No. But it's shorter."

Shimamura looked at her in surprise.

"No one knows I'm here. I heard someone in the kitchen, but the front door must still be locked."

"You seem to be an early riser."

"I couldn't sleep."

"Did you hear the rain?"

"It rained? That's why the underbrush was wet, then. I'm going home. Go on back to sleep."

But Shimamura jumped vigorously out of bed, the woman's hand still in his. He went over to the window and looked down at the hill she said she had come up. Below the shrubbery, halfway down toward the cedar grove, dwarf bamboo was growing in a wild tangle. Directly below the window were rows of taro[1] and sweet potatoes, onions and radishes. It was a most ordinary garden patch, and yet the varied colors of the leaves in the morning sun made him feel that he was seeing them for the first time.

The porter was throwing feed to the carp from the corridor that led to the bath.

"It's colder, and they aren't eating well," he said as Shimamura passed. Shimamura stood for a moment looking at the feed on the water, dried and crumbled silkworms.

1. A plant grown for its edible, starchy, tuberous rootstocks.

Komako was waiting for him, clean and prim as before, when he came back from the bath.

"It would be good to work on my sewing in a quiet place like this," she said.

The room had evidently been cleaned, and the sun poured in on the deepest corners of the slightly worn matting.

"You sew, do you?"

"What an insulting question. I had to work harder than anyone else in the family. I see now, looking back, that the years when I was growing up were the worst ones of all." She spoke almost to herself, but her voice was tense as she continued: "The maid saw me. She gave me a strange look and asked when I had come. It was very embarrassing—but I couldn't go on hiding in the closet forever. I'm going home. I'm very busy. I couldn't sleep, and I thought I'd wash my hair. I have to wait for it to dry, and then go to the hairdresser's, and if I don't wash it early in the morning I'm never ready for an afternoon party. There's a party here too, but they only told me about it last night. I won't come. I've made other promises. And I won't be able to see you tonight—it's Saturday and I'll be very busy."

She showed no sign of leaving, however.

She decided not to wash her hair after all. She took Shimamura down to the back garden. Her damp sandals and stockings were hidden under the veranda where she had come in.

The dwarf bamboo she said she had fought her way through seemed impassible. Starting down along the garden path toward the sound of the water, they came out on the high river bank. There were children's voices in the chestnut trees. A number of burrs lay in the grass at their feet. Komako stamped them open and took out the fruit. The kernels were small.

Kaya plumes waved on the steep slope of the mountain opposite, a dazzling silver in the morning sun. Dazzling, and yet rather like the fleeting translucence that moved across the autumn sky.

"Shall we cross over? We can see your fiancé's grave."

Komako brought herself to her full height and glared at him. A handful of chestnuts came at his face.

"You're making fun of me."

Shimamura had no time to dodge. The chestnuts lashed at his forehead.

"What possible reason could you have for going to the cemetery?"

"But there's no need to lose your temper."

"I was completely in earnest. I'm not like people who can do exactly as they want and think of no one else."

"And who can do that?" Shimamura muttered weakly.

"Why do you have to call him my fiancé? Didn't I tell you very carefully he wasn't? But you've forgotten, of course."

Shimamura had not forgotten. Indeed, the memory gave the man Yukio a certain weight in his thoughts.

Komako seemed to dislike talking about Yukio. She was not his fiancée, perhaps, but she had become a geisha to help pay doctors' bills. There was no doubt that she had been "completely in earnest."

Shimamura showed no anger even under the barrage of chestnuts. Komako looked curiously at him, and her resistance seemed to collapse. She took his arm. "You're a simple, honest person at heart, aren't you? Something must be making you sad."

"They're watching us from the trees."

"What of it? Tokyo people are complicated. They live in such noise and confusion that their feelings are broken to little bits."

"Everything is broken to little bits."

"Even life, before long. . . . Shall we go to the cemetery?"

"Well. . . ."

"See? You don't really want to go at all."

"But you made such an issue of it."

"Because I've never once gone to the cemetery. I really haven't gone once. I feel guilty sometimes, now that the teacher's buried there too. But I can't very well start going now. I'd only be pretending."

"You're more complicated than I am."

"Why? I'm never able to be completely open with living people, and I want at least to be honest with him now that he's dead."

They came out of the cedar grove, where the quiet seemed to fall in chilly drops. Following the railway along the foot of the ski grounds, they were soon at the cemetery. Some ten weathered old tombstones and a forlorn statue of Jizo,[2] guardian of children, stood on a tiny island of high ground among the paddies. There were no flowers.

Quite without warning, Yoko's head and shoulders rose from the bushes behind the Jizo. Her face wore the usual solemn, masklike expression. She darted a burning glance at the two of them, and nodded a quick greeting to Shimamura. She said nothing.

"Aren't you early, though, Yoko? I thought of going to the hairdresser's. . . ." As Komako spoke, a black squall came upon them and threatened to sweep them from their feet.

A freight train roared past.

"Yoko, Yoko. . . ." A boy was waving his hat in the door of a black freight car.

"Saichiro, Saichiro," Yoko called back.

It was the voice that had called to the station master at the snowy signal stop, a voice so beautiful it was almost lonely, calling out as if to someone who could not hear, on a ship far away.

The train passed, and the buckwheat across the tracks emerged fresh and clean as the blind was lifted. The field of white flowers on red stems was quietness itself.

The two of them had been so startled at seeing Yoko that they had not noticed the approach of the freight train; but the first shock was dispelled by the train.

They seemed still to hear Yoko's voice, and not the dying rumble of the freight train. It seemed to come back like an echo of distilled love.

"My brother," said Yoko, looking after the train. "I wonder if I should go to the station."

"But the train won't wait for you at the station," Komako laughed.

"I suppose not."

"I didn't come to see Yukio's grave."

2. A Buddhist divinity who promised to deliver all people from worldly suffering.

Yoko nodded. She seemed to hesitate a moment, then knelt down before the grave.

Komako watched stiffly.

Shimamura looked away, toward the Jizo. It had three long faces, and, besides the hands clasped at its breast, a pair each to the left and the right.[3]

"I'm going to wash my hair," Komako said to Yoko. She turned and started back along a ridge between the paddies.

It was the practice in the snow country to string wooden or bamboo poles on a number of levels from tree trunk to tree trunk, and to hang rice sheaves head down from them to dry. At the height of the harvest the frames presented a solid screen of rice. Farmers were hanging out rice along the path Shimamura and Komako took back to the village.

A farm girl threw up a sheaf of rice with a twist of her trousered hips, and a man high above her caught it expertly and in one deft sweep of his hand spread it to hang from the frame. The unconscious, practiced motions were repeated over and over.

Komako took one of the dangling sheaves in her hand and shook it gently up and down, as though she were feeling the weight of a jewel.

"See how it's headed. And how nice it is to the touch. Entirely different from last year's rice." She half-closed her eyes from the pleasure. A disorderly flock of sparrows flew low over her head.

An old notice was pasted to a wall beside the road: "Pay for field hands. Ninety sen a day, meals included. Women forty per cent less."

There were rice frames in front of Yoko's house too, beyond the slightly depressed field that separated the house from the road. One set of frames was strung up high in a row of persimmon trees, along the white wall between the garden and the house next door, while another, at right angles to it, followed the line between the field and the garden. With an opening for a doorway at one end, the frames suggested a makeshift little theater covered not with the usual straw mats but with unthreshed rice. The taro in the field still sent out powerful stems and leaves, but the dahlias and roses beyond were withered. The lotus pond with its red carp was hidden behind the screen of rice, as was the window of the silkworm room, where Komako had lived.

Bowing her head sharply, almost angrily, Yoko went in through the opening in the headed rice.

"Does she live alone?" Shimamura asked, looking after the bowed figure.

"I imagine not." Komako's answer was a little tart. "But what a nuisance. I'll not go to the hairdresser's after all. You say things you have no business saying, and we ruin her visit to the cemetery."

"You're only being difficult—is it really so terrible to run into her at the cemetery?"

"You have no idea how I feel. . . . If I have time later, I'll stop by to wash my hair. I may be late, but I'll stop by."

It was three in the morning.

Shimamura was awakened by a slamming as though someone were knocking the doors loose. Komako lay stretched out on top of him.

3. Unlike this statue, the usual representation of Jizo was as a monk with a jewel in one hand and a staff in the other.

"I said I would come and I've come. Haven't I? I said I'd come and I've come, haven't I?" Her chest, even her abdomen, rose and fell violently.

"You're dead-drunk."

"Haven't I? I said I'd come and I've come, haven't I?"

"You have indeed."

"Couldn't see a thing on the way. Not a thing. My head aches."

"How did you manage to get up the hill?"

"I have no idea. Not the slightest." She lay heavily across his chest. He found it a little oppressive, especially when she turned over and arched her back; but, too suddenly awakened, he fell back as he tried to get up. It was an astonishingly hot object that his head came to rest on.

"You're on fire."

"Oh? Fire for a pillow. See that you don't burn yourself."

"I might very well." He closed his eyes and the warmth sank into his head, bringing an immediate sense of life. Reality came through the violent breathing, and with it a sort of nostalgic remorse. He felt as though he were waiting tranquilly for some undefined revenge.

"I said I'd come, and I've come." She spoke with the utmost concentration. "I've come, and now I'm going home. I'm going to wash my hair."

She got to her knees and took a drink of water in great swallows.

"I can't let you go home like this."

"I'm going home. I have some people waiting. Where did I leave my towel?"

Shimamura got up and turned on the light. "Don't!" She hid her face in her hands, then buried it, hands and all, in the quilt.

She had on a bold informal kimono with a narrow undress *obi*, and under it a nightgown. Her under-kimono had slipped down out of sight. She was flushed from drink even to the soles of her bare feet, and there was something very engaging about the way she tried to tuck them out of sight.

Evidently she had thrown down her towel and bath utensils when she came in. Soap and combs were scattered over the floor.

"Cut. I brought scissors."

"What do you want me to cut?"

"This." She pointed at the strings that held her Japanese coiffure in place. "I tried to do it myself, but my hands wouldn't work. I thought maybe I could ask you."

Shimamura separated the hair and cut at the strings, and as he cut she shook the long hair loose. She was somewhat calmer.

"What time is it?"

"Three o'clock."

"Not really! You'll be careful not to cut the hair, won't you?"

"I've never seen so many strings."

The false hair that filled out the coiffure was hot where it touched her head.

"Is it really three o'clock? I must have fallen asleep when I got home. I promised to come for a bath with some people, and they stopped by to call me. They'll be wondering what's happened."

"They're waiting for you?"

"In the public bath. Three of them. There were six parties, but I only got to four. Next week we'll be very busy with people coming to see the maple leaves. Thanks very much." She raised her head to comb her hair, now long and flowing, and she laughed uncertainly. "Funny, isn't it." Unsure what to do with herself, she reached to pick up the false hair. "I have to go. It's not right to keep them waiting. I'll not come again tonight."

"Can you see your way home?"

"Yes."

But she tripped over the skirt of her kimono on the way out.

At seven and again at three in the morning—twice in one short day she had chosen unconventional hours to come calling. There was something far from ordinary in all this, Shimamura told himself.

Guests would soon be coming for the autumn leaves. The door of the inn was being decorated with maple branches to welcome them.

The porter who was somewhat arrogantly directing operations was fond of calling himself a "migrant bird." He and his kind worked the mountain resorts from spring through to the autumn leaves, and moved down to the coast for the winter. He did not much care whether or not he came to the same inn each year. Proud of his experience in the prosperous coast resorts, he had no praise for the way the inn treated its guests. He reminded one of a not-too-sincere beggar as he rubbed his hands together and hovered about prospective guests at the station.

"Have you ever tasted one of these?" he asked Shimamura, picking up a pomegranatelike *akebi*.[4] "I can bring some in from the mountains if you like." Shimamura, back from a walk, watched him tie the *akebi*, stem and all, to a maple branch.

The freshly cut branches were so long that they brushed against the eaves. The hallway glowed a bright, fresh scarlet. The leaves were extraordinarily large.

As Shimamura took the cool *akebi* in his hand, he noticed that Yoko was sitting by the hearth in the office.

The innkeeper's wife was heating *saké*[5] in a brass boiler. Yoko, seated opposite her, nodded quickly in answer to each remark. She was dressed informally, though she did not have on the everyday "mountain trousers." Her plain woolen kimono was freshly washed.

"That girl is working here?" Shimamura asked the porter nonchalantly.

"Yes, sir. Thanks to all of you, we've had to take on extra help."

"You, for instance."

"That's right. She's an unusual type, though, for a girl from these parts."

Yoko worked only in the kitchen, apparently. She was not yet serving at parties. As the inn filled, the voices of the maids in the kitchen became louder, but he did not remember having heard Yoko's clear voice among them. The maid who took care of his room said that Yoko liked to sing in the bath before she went to bed, but that, too, Shimamura had missed.

Now that he knew Yoko was in the house, he felt strangely reluctant to call Komako. He was conscious of an emptiness that made him see Komako's life as beautiful but wasted, even though he himself was the object of her love; and yet the woman's existence, her straining to live, came touching him like naked skin. He pitied her, and he pitied himself.

4. The purple fruit of a deciduous woody vine, which also yields purple flowers.   5. A winelike alcoholic beverage brewed from fermented rice.

He was sure that Yoko's eyes, for all their innocence, could send a probing light to the heart of these matters, and he somehow felt drawn to her too.

Komako came often enough without being called.

When he went to see the maple leaves up the valley, he passed her house. Hearing the automobile and thinking it must be he, she ran out to look—and he did not even glance back, she complained. That was most unfeeling of him. She of course stopped by whenever she came to the inn, and she stopped by too on her way to the bath. When she was to go to a party, she came an hour or so early and waited in his room for the maid to call her. Often she would slip away from a party for a few minutes. After retouching her face in the mirror, she would stand up to leave. "Back to work. I'm all business. Business, business."

She was in the habit of forgetting something she had brought with her, a cloak, perhaps, or the cover to a samisen plectrum.

"Last night when I got home there was no hot water for tea. I hunted through the kitchen and found the left-overs from breakfast. Co-o-old. . . . They didn't call me this morning. When I woke up it was already ten-thirty. I meant to come see you at seven, but it was no good."

Such were the things she talked of. Or she told him of the inn she had gone to first, and the next and the next, and the parties she had been to at each.

"I'll come again later." She had a glass of water before she left. "Or maybe I won't. Thirty guests and only three of us. I'll be much too busy."

But almost immediately she was back.

"It's hard work. Thirty of them and only three of us. And the other two are the very oldest and the very youngest in town, and that leaves all the hard work for me. Stingy people. A travel club of some sort, I suppose. With thirty guests you need at least six geisha. I'll go have a drink and pick a fight with them."

So it was every day. Komako must have wanted to crawl away and hide at the thought of where it was leading. But that indefinable air of loneliness only made her the more seductive.

"The floor always creaks when I come down the hall. I walk very softly, but they hear me just the same. 'Off to the Camellia Room again, Komako?' they say as I go by the kitchen. I never thought I'd have to worry so about my reputation."

"The town's really too small."

"Everyone has heard about us, of course."

"That will never do."

"You begin to have a bad name, and you're ruined in a little place like this." But she looked up and smiled. "It makes no difference. My kind can find work anywhere."

That straightforward manner, so replete with direct, immediate feeling, was quite foreign to Shimamura, the idler who had inherited his money.

"It will be the same, wherever I go. There's nothing to be upset about."

But he caught an echo of the woman underneath the surface nonchalance.

"And I can't complain. After all, only women are able really to love." She flushed a little and looked at the floor.

Her kimono stood out from her neck, and her back and shoulders were like a white fan spread under it. There was something sad about the full flesh under that white powder. It suggested a woolen cloth, and again it suggested the pelt of some animal.

"In the world as it is," he murmured, chilled at the sterility of the words even as he spoke.

But Komako only replied: "As it always has been." She raised her head and added absentmindedly: "You didn't know that?"

The red under-kimono clinging to her skin disappeared as she looked up.

Shimamura was translating Valéry and Alain,[6] and French treatises on the dance from the golden age of the Russian ballet. He meant to bring them out in a small luxury edition at his own expense. The book would in all likelihood contribute nothing to the Japanese dancing world. One could nonetheless say, if pressed, that it would bring aid and comfort to Shimamura. He pampered himself with the somewhat whimsical pleasure of sneering at himself through his work, and it may well have been from such a pleasure that his sad little dream world sprang. Off on a trip, he saw no need to hurry himself.

He spent much of his time watching insects in their death agonies.

Each day, as the autumn grew colder, insects died on the floor of his room. Stiff-winged insects fell on their backs and were unable to get to their feet again. A bee walked a little and collapsed, walked a little and collapsed. It was a quiet death that came with the change of seasons. Looking closely, however, Shimamura could see that the legs and feelers were trembling in the struggle to live. For such a tiny death, the empty eight-mat room[7] seemed enormous.

As he picked up a dead insect to throw it out, he sometimes thought for an instant of the children he had left in Tokyo.

A moth on the screen was still for a very long time. It too was dead, and it fell to the earth like a dead leaf. Occasionally a moth fell from the wall. Taking it up in his hand, Shimamura would wonder how to account for such beauty.

The screens were removed, and the singing of the insects was more subdued and lonely day by day.

The russet deepened on the Border Range. In the evening sun the mountains lighted up sharply, like a rather chilly stone. The inn was filled with maple-viewing guests.

"I don't think I'll come again tonight. Some people from the village are having a party." Komako left, and presently he heard a drum in the large banquet-room, and strident women's voices. At the very height of the festivities he was startled by a clear voice almost at his elbow.

"May I come in?" It was Yoko. "Komako asked me to bring this."

She thrust her hand out like a postman. Then, remembering her manners, she knelt down awkwardly before him. Shimamura opened the knotted bit of paper, and Yoko was gone. He had not had time to speak to her.

"Having a fine, noisy time. And drinking." That was the whole of the message, written in a drunken hand on a paper napkin.

Not ten minutes later Komako staggered in.

---

6. Or Alain-Fournier, pen name of Henri-Alban Fournier (1886–1914), French poet, journalist, and novelist. Paul Valéry (1871–1945), one of the greatest French poets of the 20th century, also critic and essayist.
7. About four yards square.

"Did she bring something to you?"

"She did."

"Oh?" Komako cocked an eye at him in wonderfully high spirits. "I do feel good. I said I'd go order more *saké*, and I ran away. The porter caught me. But *saké* is wonderful. I don't care a bit if the floor creaks. I don't care if they scold me. As soon as I come here I start feeling drunk, though. Damn. Well, back to work."

"You're rosy down to the tips of your fingers."

"Business is waiting. Business, business. Did she say anything? Terribly jealous. Do you know how jealous?"

"Who?"

"Someone will be murdered one of these days."

"She's working here?"

"She brings *saké*, and then stands there staring in at us, with her eyes flashing. I suppose you like her sort of eyes."

"She probably thinks you're a disgrace."

"That's why I gave her a note to bring to you. I want water. Give me water. Who's a disgrace? Try seducing her too before you answer my question. Am I drunk?" She peered into the mirror, bracing both hands against the stand. A moment later, kicking aside the long skirts, she swept from the room.

The party was over. The inn was soon quiet, and Shimamura could hear a distant clatter of dishes. Komako must have been taken off by a guest to a second party, he concluded; but just then Yoko came in with another bit of paper.

"Decided not to go to Sampukan go from here to the Plum Room may stop by on way home good night."

Shimamura smiled wryly, a little uncomfortable before Yoko. "Thank you very much. You've come to help here?"

She darted a glance at him with those beautiful eyes, so bright that he felt impaled on them. His discomfort was growing.

The girl left a deep impression each time he saw her, and now she was sitting before him—a strange uneasiness swept over him. Her too-serious manner made her seem always at the very center of some remarkable occurrence.

"They're keeping you busy, I suppose."

"But there's very little I can do."

"It's strange how often I see you. The first time was when you were bringing that man home. You talked to the station master about your brother. Do you remember?"

"Yes."

"They say you sing in the bath before you go to bed."

"Really! They accuse me of having such bad manners?" The voice was astonishingly beautiful.

"I feel I know everything about you."

"Oh? And have you asked Komako, then?"

"She won't say a thing. She seems to dislike talking about you."

"I see." Yoko turned quickly away. "Komako is a fine person, but she's not been lucky. Be good to her." She spoke rapidly, and her voice trembled very slightly on the last words.

"But there's nothing I can do for her."

It seemed that the girl's whole body must soon be trembling. Shimamura looked away, fearful that a dangerous light would be breaking out on the too-earnest face.

He laughed. "I think I'd best go back to Tokyo soon."

"I'm going to Tokyo myself."

"When?"

"It doesn't matter."

"Shall I see you to Tokyo when I go back?"

"Please do." The seriousness was intense, and at the same time her tone suggested that the matter was after all trivial. Shimamura was startled.

"If it will be all right with your family."

"The brother who works on the railroad is all the family I have. I can decide for myself."

"Have you made arrangements in Tokyo?"

"No."

"Have you talked to Komako, then?"

"To Komako? I don't like Komako. I haven't talked to her."

She looked up at him with moist eyes—a sign perhaps that her defenses were breaking down—and he found in them an uncanny sort of beauty. But at that moment his affection for Komako welled up violently. To run off to Tokyo, as if eloping, with a nondescript woman would somehow be in the nature of an intense apology[8] to Komako, and a penance for Shimamura himself.

"It doesn't frighten you to go off alone with a man?"

"Why should it?"

"It doesn't seem dangerous to go to Tokyo without at least deciding where you will stay and what you might want to do?"

"A woman by herself can always get by." There was a delicious lilt in her speech. Her eyes were fixed on his as she spoke again: "You won't hire me as a maid?"

"Really, now. Hire you as a maid?"

"But I don't want to be a maid."

"What were you in Tokyo before?"

"A nurse."

"You were in a hospital? Or in nursing school?"

"I just thought I'd like to be a nurse."

Shimamura smiled. This perhaps explained the earnestness with which she had taken care of the music teacher's son on the train.

"And you still want to be a nurse?"

"I won't be a nurse now."

"But you'll have to make up your mind. This indecisiveness will never do."

"Indecisiveness? It has nothing to do with indecisiveness." Her laugh threw back the accusation.

Her laugh, like her voice, was so high and clear that it was almost lonely. There was not a suggestion in it of the dull or the simple-minded; but it struck emptily at the shell of Shimamura's heart, and fell away in silence.

"What's funny?"

---

8. In the sense of expressing a deep regret about the course their relationship had taken.

"But there has only been one man I could possibly nurse."

Again Shimamura was startled.

"I could never again."

"I see." His answer was quiet. He had been caught off guard. "They say you spend all your time at the cemetery."

"I do."

"And for the rest of your life you can never nurse anyone else, or visit anyone else's grave?"

"Never again."

"How can you leave the grave and go off to Tokyo, then?"

"I'm sorry. Do take me with you."

"Komako says you're frightfully jealous. Wasn't the man her fiancé?"

"Yukio? It's a lie. It's a lie."

"Why do you dislike Komako, then?"

"Komako." She spoke as if calling to someone in the same room, and she gazed hotly at Shimamura. "Be good to Komako."

"But I can do nothing for her."

There were tears in the corners of Yoko's eyes. She sniffled as she slapped at a small moth on the matting. "Komako says I'll go crazy." With that she slipped from the room.

Shimamura felt a chill come over him.

As he opened the window to throw out the moth, he caught a glimpse of the drunken Komako playing parlor games with a guest. She leaned forward half from her seat, as though to push her advantage home by force. The sky had clouded over. Shimamura went down for a bath.

In the women's bath next door, Yoko was bathing the innkeeper's little daughter.

Her voice was gentle as she undressed the child and bathed it—soothing and agreeable, like the voice of a young mother.

Presently she was singing in that same voice:

> "See, out in back,
> Three pears, three cedars,
> Six trees in all.
> Crows' nests below,
> Sparrows' nests above.
> And what is it they're singing?
> 'Hakamairi itchō, itchō, itchō ya.' "[9]

It was a song little girls sang as they bounced rubber balls. The quick, lively manner in which Yoko rolled off the nonsense-words made Shimamura wonder if he might not have seen the earlier Yoko in a dream.

She chattered on as she dressed the child and led it from the bath, and even when she was gone her voice seemed to echo on like a flute. On the worn floor of the hallway, polished to a dark glow, a geisha had left behind a samisen box, the very embodiment of quiet in the late autumn night. As Shimamura was looking for the owner's name, Komako came out from the direction of the clattering dishes.

---

9. "To the cemetery, a hundred yards, a hundred yards, a hundred yards again" (literal trans.); in imitation of the birds.

"What are you looking at?"

"Is she staying the night?"

"Who? Oh, her. Don't be foolish. You think we carry these with us wherever we go, do you? Sometimes we leave them at an inn for days on end." She laughed, but almost immediately she was breathing painfully and her eyes were screwed tightly shut. Dropping her long skirts, she fell against Shimamura. "Take me home, please."

"You don't have to go, do you?"

"It's no good. I have to go. The rest went on to other parties and left me behind. No one will say anything if I don't stay too long—I had business here. But if they stop by my house on their way to the bath and find me away, they'll start talking."

Drunk though she was, she walked briskly down the steep hill.

"You made that girl weep."

"She does seem a trifle crazy."

"And do you enjoy making such remarks?"

"But didn't you say it yourself? She remembered how you said she would go crazy, and it was then that she broke down—mostly out of resentment, I suspect."

"Oh? It's all right, then."

"And not ten minutes later she was in the bath, singing in fine voice."

"She's always liked to sing in the bath."

"She said very seriously that I must be good to you."

"Isn't she foolish, though? But you didn't have to tell me."

"Tell you? Why is it that you always seem so touchy when that girl is mentioned?"

"Would you like to have her?"

"See? What call is there for a remark like that?"

"I'm not joking. Whenever I look at her, I feel as though I have a heavy load and can't get rid of it. Somehow I always feel that way. If you're really fond of her, take a good look at her. You'll see what I mean." She laid her hand on his shoulder and leaned toward him. Then, abruptly, she shook her head. "No, that's not what I want. If she were to fall into the hands of someone like you, she might not go crazy after all. Why don't you take my load for me?"

"You're going a little too far."

"You think I'm drunk and talking nonsense? I'm not. I would know she was being well taken care of, and I could go pleasantly to seed here in the mountains. It would be a fine, quiet feeling."

"That's enough."

"Just leave me alone." In her flight, she ran into the closed door of the house she lived in.

"They've decided you're not coming home."

"But I can open it." The door sounded old and dry as she lifted it from the groove and pushed it back.

"Come on in."

"But think of the hour."

"Everyone will be asleep."

Shimamura hesitated.

"I'll see you back to the inn, then."

"I can go by myself."

"But you haven't seen my room."

They stepped through the kitchen door, and the sleeping figures of the family lay sprawled before them. The thin mattresses on the floor were covered with cheap striped cloth, now faded, of the sort often used for "mountain trousers." The mother and father and five or six children, the oldest a girl perhaps sixteen, lay under a scorched lampshade. Heads faced in every direction. There was drab poverty in the scene, and yet under it there lay an urgent, powerful vitality.

As if thrown back by the warm breath of all the sleepers, Shimamura started toward the door. Komako noisily closed it in his face, however, and went in through the kitchen. She made no attempt to soften her footsteps. Shimamura followed stealthily past the children's pillows, a strange thrill rising in his chest.

"Wait here. I'll turn on the light upstairs."

"It's all right." Shimamura climbed the stairs in the dark. As he looked back, he saw the candy shop beyond the homely sleeping faces.

The matting was worn in the four rustic rooms on the second floor.

"It's a little large, I have to admit, for just one person." The partitions between the rooms had been taken down, and Komako's bedding lay small and solitary inside the sliding doors, their paper panels yellowed with age, that separated the rooms from the skirting corridor. Old furniture and tools, evidently the property of the family she lived with, were piled in the far room. Party kimonos hung from pegs along the wall. The whole suggested a fox's or badger's lair[1] to Shimamura.

Komako sat down solidly in the slightly raised alcove and offered him the only cushion.

"Bright red." She peered into the mirror. "Am I really so drunk?" She fumbled through the top drawer of the dresser. "Here. My diary."

"As long as this, is it?"

She took up a small figured-paper box filled to the top with assorted cigarettes.

"I push them up my sleeve or inside my *obi* when a guest gives them to me, and some of them are a little smashed. They're clean, though. I make up for wrinkles by having every variety to offer." She stirred up the contents to demonstrate that he could have his choice.

"But I don't have a match. I don't need matches now that I've stopped smoking."

"It's all right. How is the sewing?"

"I try to work at it, but the guests for the maple leaves keep me busy." She turned to put away the sewing that lay in front of the dresser.

The fine-grained chest of drawers and the expensive vermilion-lacquered sewing-box, relics perhaps of her years in Tokyo, were as they had been in the attic that so resembled an old paper box; but they seemed sadly out of place in these dilapidated second-floor rooms.

A thin string ran from Komako's pillow to the ceiling.

"I turn the light out with this when I'm reading." She tugged at the string.

---

1. Both animals were considered to be tricksters with supernatural powers—the fox sinister and the badger comical—and both were thought capable of assuming human form. Traditional belief explained derangement as possession by a fox spirit, and in folklore and popular drama a fox would often appear as a beautiful temptress.

Gentle and subdued, the proper housewife again, she was not quite able even so to hide her discomposure.

"Lonely as the fox's lady out at night, aren't you."

"I really am."

"And do you mean to live here four years?"

"But it's going on a year already. It won't be long."

Shimamura was nervous. He thought he could hear the breathing of the family below, and he had run out of things to talk about. He stood up to leave.

Komako slid the door half shut behind him. She glanced up at the sky. "It's beginning to look like snow. The end of the maple leaves." She recited a line of poetry as she stepped outside: "Here in our mountains, the snow falls even on the maple leaves."[2]

"Well, good night."

"Wait. I'll see you back to the hotel. As far as the door, no farther."

But she followed him inside.

"Go on to bed." She slipped away, and a few minutes later she was back with two glasses filled to the brim with *saké*.

"Drink," she ordered as she stepped into the room. "We're going to have a drink."

"But aren't they asleep? Where did you find it?"

"I know where they keep it." She had quite obviously had herself a drink as she poured from the vat. The earlier drunkenness had come back. With narrowed eyes, she watched the *saké* spill over on her hand. "It's no fun, though, swallowing the stuff down in the dark."

Shimamura drank meekly from the cup that was thrust at him.

It was not usual for him to get drunk on so little; but perhaps he was chilled from the walk. He began to feel sick. His head was whirling, and he could almost see himself going pale. He closed his eyes and fell back on the quilt. Komako put her arms around him in alarm. A childlike feeling of security came to him from the warmth of her body.

She seemed ill at ease, like a young woman, still childless, who takes a baby up in her arms. She raised her head and looked down, as at the sleeping child.

"You're a good girl."

"Why? Why am I good? What's good about me?"

"You're a good girl."

"Don't tease me. It's wrong of you." She looked aside, and she spoke in broken phrases, like little blows, as she rocked him back and forth.

She laughed softly to herself.

"I'm not good at all. It's not easy having you here. You'd best go home. Each time I come to see you I want to put on a new kimono, and now I have none left. This one is borrowed. So you see I'm not really good at all."

Shimamura did not answer.

"And what do you find good in me?" Her voice was a little husky. "The first day I met you I thought I had never seen anyone I disliked more. People just don't say the sort of things you said. I hated you."

Shimamura nodded.

2. The line is from a *kabuki* play.

"Oh? You understand then why I've not mentioned it before? When a woman has to say these things, she has gone as far as she can, you know."

"But it's all right."

"Is it?" They were silent for some moments. Komako seemed to be looking back on herself, and the awareness of a woman's being alive came to Shimamura in her warmth.

"You're a good woman."

"How am I good?"

"A good woman."

"What an odd person." Her face was hidden from him, as though she were rubbing her jaw against an itching shoulder. Then suddenly, Shimamura had no idea why, she raised herself angrily to an elbow.

"A good woman—what do you mean by that? What do you mean?"

He only stared at her.

"Admit it. That's why you came to see me. You were laughing at me. You were laughing at me after all."

She glared at him, scarlet with anger. Her shoulders were shaking. But the flush receded as quickly as it had come, and tears were falling over her blanched face.

"I hate you. How I hate you." She rolled out of bed and sat with her back to him.

Shimamura felt a stabbing in his chest as he saw what the mistake had been. He lay silent, his eyes closed.

"It makes me very sad," she murmured to herself. Her head was on her knees, and her body was bent into a tight ball.

When she had wept herself out, she sat jabbing at the floor mat with a silver hair-ornament. Presently she slipped from the room.

Shimamura could not bring himself to follow her. She had reason to feel hurt.

But soon she was back, her bare feet quiet in the corridor. "Are you going for a bath?" she called from outside the door. It was a high, thin little voice.

"If you want."

"I'm sorry. I've reconsidered."

She showed no sign of coming in. Shimamura picked up his towel and stepped into the hall. She walked ahead of him with her eyes on the floor, like a criminal being led away. As the bath warmed her, however, she became strangely gay and winsome, and sleep was out of the question.

The next morning Shimamura awoke to a voice reciting a Nō play.[3]

He lay for a time listening. Kamoko turned and smiled from the mirror.

"The guests in the Plum Room. I was called there after my first party. Remember?"

"A Nō club out on a trip?"

"Yes."

"It snowed?"

"Yes." She got up and threw open the sliding door in front of the window. "No more maple leaves."

From the gray sky, framed by the window, the snow floated toward them

---

3. Japan's oldest extant theatrical tradition, originating in the 14th century, a highly stylized combination of acting, chanting, and dancing.

in great flakes, like white peonies. There was something quietly unreal about it. Shimamura stared with the vacantness that comes from lack of sleep.

The Nō reciters had taken out a drum.

He remembered the snowy morning toward the end of the year before, and glanced at the mirror. The cold peonies floated up yet larger, cutting a white outline around Komako. Her kimono was open at the neck, and she was wiping at her throat with a towel.

Her skin was as clean as if it had just been laundered. He had not dreamed that she was a woman who would find it necessary to take offense at such a trivial remark, and that very fact lent her an irresistible sadness.

The mountains, more distant each day as the russet of the autumn leaves had darkened, came brightly back to life with the snow.

The cedars, under a thin coating of snow, rose sheer from the white ground to the sky, each cut off sharply from the rest.

The thread was spun in the snow, and the cloth woven in the snow, washed in the snow, and bleached in the snow. Everything, from the first spinning of the thread to the last finishing touches, was done in the snow. "There is Chijimi linen[4] because there is snow," someone wrote long ago. "Snow is the mother of Chijimi."

The Chijimi grass-linen of this snow country was the handwork of the mountain maiden through the long, snowbound winters. Shimamura searched for the cloth in old-clothes shops to use for summer kimonos. Through acquaintances in the dance world, he had found a shop that specialized in old Nō robes, and he had a standing order that when a good piece of Chijimi came in he was to see it.

In the old days, it is said, the early Chijimi fair was held in the spring, when the snow had melted and the snow blinds were taken down from the houses. People came from far and near to buy Chijimi, even wholesalers from the great commercial cities, Edo, Nagoya, and Osaka;[5] and the inns at which they stayed were fixed by tradition. Since the labors of half a year were on display, youths and maidens gathered from all the mountain villages. Sellers' booths and buyers' booths were lined up side by side, and the market took on the air of a festival. With prizes awarded for the best pieces of weaving, it came also to be a sort of competition for husbands. The girls learned to weave as children, and they turned out their best work between the ages of perhaps fourteen and twenty-four. As they grew older they lost the touch that gave tone to the finest Chijimi. In their desire to be numbered among the few outstanding weavers, they put their whole labor and love into this product of the long snowbound months—the months of seclusion and boredom, between October, under the old lunar calendar,[6] when the spinning began, and mid-February of the following year, when the last bleaching was finished.

There may have been among Shimamura's kimonos one or more woven by these mountain maidens toward the middle of the last century.

He still sent his kimonos back for "snow-bleaching." It was a great deal of

---

4. A crepe cloth woven with a stronger thread horizontally and made to shrink so that it would wrinkle. It was prized as a fabric for lightweight kimonos. The connection between Chijimi linen and snow becomes clear below. 5. Three great commercial centers in premodern Japan. Present-day Tokyo was known as Edo until the end of the *shogun*'s rule. 6. Introduced from China and followed until 1873, when, as part of its drive toward modernization, Japan adopted the solar-based Gregorian calendar employed in the West.

trouble to return old kimonos—that had touched the skin of he could not know whom—for rebleaching each year to the country that had produced them; but when he considered the labors of those mountain maidens, he wanted the bleaching to be done properly in the country where the maidens had lived. The thought of the white linen, spread out on the deep snow, the cloth and the snow glowing scarlet in the rising sun, was enough to make him feel that the dirt of the summer had been washed away, even that he himself had been bleached clean. It must be added, however, that a Tokyo shop took care of the details for him, and he had no way of knowing that the bleaching had really been done in the old manner.

From ancient times there were houses that specialized in bleaching. The weavers for the most part did not do their own. White Chijimi was spread out on the snow after it was woven, colored Chijimi bleached on frames while still in thread. The bleaching season came in January and February under the lunar calendar, and snow-covered fields and gardens were the bleaching grounds.

The cloth or thread was soaked overnight in ash water.[7] The next morning it was washed over and over again, wrung, and put out to bleach. The process was repeated day after day, and the sight when, as the bleaching came to an end, the rays of the rising sun turned the white Chijimi blood-red was quite beyond description, Shimamura had read in an old book. It was something to be shown to natives of warmer provinces. And the end of the bleaching was a sign that spring was coming to the snow country.

The land of the Chijimi was very near this hot spring, just down the river, where the valley began to widen out. Indeed it must almost have been visible from Shimamura's window. All of the Chijimi market towns now had railway stations, and the region was still a well-known weaving center.

Since Shimamura had never come to the snow country in midsummer, when he wore Chijimi, or in the snowy season, when it was woven, he had never had occasion to talk of it to Komako; and she hardly seemed the person to ask about the fate of an old folk art.

When he heard the song Yoko sang in the bath, it had come to him that, had she been born long ago, she might have sung thus as she worked over her spools and looms, so exactly suited to the fancy was her voice.

The thread of the grass-linen, finer than animal hair, is difficult to work except in the humidity of the snow, it is said, and the dark, cold season is therefore ideal for weaving. The ancients used to add that the way this product of the cold has of feeling cool to the skin in the hottest weather is a play of the principles of light and darkness. This Komako too, who had so fastened herself to him, seemed at center cool, and the remarkable, concentrated warmth was for that fact all the more touching.

But this love would leave behind it nothing so definite as a piece of Chijimi. Though cloth to be worn is among the most short-lived of craftworks, a good piece of Chijimi, if it has been taken care of, can be worn quite unfaded a half-century and more after weaving. As Shimamura thought absently how human intimacies have not even so long a life, the image of Komako as the mother of another man's children suddenly floated into his mind. He looked around, startled. Possibly he was tired.

---

7. Lye used to bleach or dye fabric.

He had stayed so long that one might wonder whether he had forgotten his wife and children. He stayed not because he could not leave Komako nor because he did not want to. He had simply fallen into the habit of waiting for those frequent visits. And the more continuous the assault became, the more he began to wonder what was lacking in him, what kept him from living as completely. He stood gazing at his own coldness, so to speak. He could not understand how she had so lost herself. All of Komako came to him, but it seemed that nothing went out from him to her. He heard in his chest, like snow piling up, the sound of Komako, an echo beating against empty walls. And he knew that he could not go on pampering himself forever.

He leaned against the brazier, provided against the coming of the snowy season, and thought how unlikely it was that he would come again once he had left. The innkeeper had lent him an old Kyoto teakettle, skillfully inlaid in silver with flowers and birds, and from it came the sound of wind in the pines. He could make out two pine breezes, as a matter of fact, a near one and a far one. Just beyond the far breeze he heard faintly the tinkling of a bell. He put his ear to the kettle and listened. Far away, where the bell tinkled on, he suddenly saw Komako's feet, tripping in time with the bell. He drew back. The time had come to leave.

He thought of going to see the Chijimi country. That excursion might set him on his way toward breaking away from this hot spring.

He did not know at which of the towns downstream he should get off the train. Not interested in modern weaving centers, he chose a station that looked suitably lonesome and backward. After walking for a time he came out on what seemed to be the main street of an old post town.[8]

The eaves pushing out far beyond the houses were supported by pillars along both sides of the street, and in their shade were passages for communication when the snow was deep, rather like the open lean-to the old Edo shopkeeper used for displaying his wares. With deep eaves on one side of each house, the passages stretched on down the street.

Since the houses were joined in a solid block, the snow from the roofs could only be thrown down into the street. One might more accurately say that at its deepest the snow was thrown not down but up, to a high bank of snow in the middle of the street. Tunnels were cut through for passage from one side to the other.

The houses in Komako's hot-spring village, for all of its being a part of this same snow country, were separated by open spaces, and this was therefore the first time Shimamura had seen the snow passages. He tried walking in one of them. The shade under the old eaves was dark, and the leaning pillars were beginning to rot at their bases. He walked along looking into the houses as into the gloom where generation after generation of his ancestors had endured the long snows.

He saw that the weaver maidens, giving themselves up to their work here under the snow, had lived lives far from as bright and fresh as the Chijimi they made. With an allusion to a Chinese poem, Shimamura's old book had pointed out that in harsh economic terms the making of Chijimi was quite impractical, so great was the expenditure of effort that went into even one

---

8. A relay posting station (like a pony express stop) along the main thoroughfares of Japan in the 17th–19th centuries.

piece. It followed that none of the Chijimi houses had been able to hire weavers from outside.

The nameless workers, so diligent while they lived, had presently died, and only the Chijimi remained, the plaything of men like Shimamura, cool and fresh against the skin in the summer. This rather unremarkable thought struck him as most remarkable. The labor into which a heart has poured its whole love—where will it have its say, to excite and inspire, and when?

Like the old post road that was its ancestor, the main street ran without a curve through the straggling village, and no doubt on through Komako's hot spring. The roofs, with rows of stones to weigh down their shingles, were very much like the ones he already knew.

The pillars supporting the deep eaves cast dim shadows across the ground. With his hardly having noticed, afternoon had drawn on toward evening.

There was nothing more to see. He took a train to another village, very much like the first. Again he walked about for a time. Feeling a little chilly, he stopped for a bowl of noodles.

The noodle shop stood beside a river, probably the river that flowed past the hot spring. Shaven-headed Buddhist nuns were crossing a bridge in twos and threes to the far side. All wore rough straw sandals, and some had dome-shaped straw hats tied to their backs. Evidently on their way from a service, they looked like crows hurrying home to their nests.

"Quite a procession of them," Shimamura said to the woman who kept the shop.

"There's a nunnery up in the hills. I suppose they're getting everything done now. It will be next to impossible for them to go out once the heavy snows begin."

The mountain beyond the bridge, growing dark in the twilight, was already covered with snow.

In this snow country, cold, cloudy days succeed one another as the leaves fall and the winds grow chilly. Snow is in the air. The high mountains near and far become white in what the people of the country call "the round of the peaks." Along the coast the sea roars, and inland the mountains roar—"the roaring at the center," like a distant clap of thunder. The round of the peaks and the roaring at the center announce that the snows are not far away. This too Shimamura had read in his old book.

The first snow had fallen the morning he lay in bed listening to the Nō recital. Had the roaring already been heard, then, in the sea and the mountains? Perhaps his senses were sharper, off on a trip with only the company of the woman Komako: even now he seemed to catch an echo of a distant roaring.

"They'll be snowbound too, will they? How many are there?"

"A great many."

"What do they do with themselves, do you suppose, shut up together through the snows? Maybe we could set them to making Chijimi."

The woman smiled vaguely at the inquisitive stranger.

Shimamura went back to the station and waited two hours for a train. The wintry sun set, and the air was so clear that it seemed to burnish the stars. Shimamura's feet were cold.

He arrived back at the hot spring not knowing what he had gone out looking for. The taxi crossed the tracks into the village as usual. A brightly lighted house stood before them as they skirted the cedar grove. Shimamura felt warm and safe again. It was the restaurant Kikumura, and three or four geisha were talking in the doorway.

Komako will be among them—but almost before he had time to frame the thought he saw only Komako.

The driver put on the brakes. Apparently he had heard rumors about the two.

Shimamura turned away from her to look out the rear window. In the light of the stars, the tracks were clear against the snow, surprisingly far into the distance.

Komako closed her eyes and jumped at the taxi. It moved slowly up the hill without stopping. She stood on the running-board, hunched over the door handle.

She had leaped at the car as if to devour it, but for Shimamura something warm had suddenly come near. The impulsive act struck him as neither rash nor unnatural. Komako raised one arm, half-embracing the closed window. Her kimono sleeve fell back from her wrist, and the warm red of the under-kimono, spilling through the thick glass, sank its way into the half-frozen Shimamura.

She pressed her forehead to the window. "Where have you been? Tell me where you've been," she called in a high voice.

"Don't be a fool. You'll get hurt," he shouted back, but they both knew it was only a gentle game.

She opened the door and fell inside the taxi. It had already stopped, however. They were at the foot of the path up the mountain.

"Where have you been?"

"Well. . . ."

"Where?"

"Nowhere in particular."

He noticed with surprise that she had the geisha's way of arranging her skirts.

The driver waited silently. It was a bit odd, Shimamura had to admit, for them to be sitting in a taxi that had gone as far as it could.

"Let's get out." Komako put her hand on his. "Cold. See how cold. Why didn't you take me with you?"

"You think I should have?"

"What a strange person." She laughed happily as she hurried up the stone steps. "I saw you leave. About two . . . a little before three?"

"That's right."

"I ran out when I heard the car. I ran out in front. And you didn't look around."

"Look around?"

"You didn't. Why didn't you look around?"

Shimamura was a little surprised at this insistence.

"You didn't know I was seeing you off, did you?"

"I didn't."

"See?" Laughing happily to herself, she came very near him. "Why didn't you take me along? You leave me behind and you come back cold—I don't like it at all."

Suddenly a fire-alarm was ringing, with the special fury that told of an emergency.

They looked back.

"Fire, fire!"

"A fire!"

A column of sparks was rising in the village below.

Komako cried out two or three times, and clutched at Shimamura's hand.

A tongue of flames shot up intermittently in the spiral of smoke, dipping down to lick at the roofs about it.

"Where is it? Fairly near the music teacher's?"

"No."

"Where, then?"

"Farther up toward the station."

The tongue of flame sprang high over the roofs.

"It's the cocoon-warehouse. The warehouse. Look, look! The cocoon-warehouse is on fire." She pressed her face to his shoulder. "The warehouse, the warehouse!"

The fire blazed higher. From the mountain, however, it was as quiet under the starry sky as a little make-believe fire. Still the terror of it came across to them. They could almost hear the roar of the flames. Shimamura put his arm around Komako's shoulders.

"What is there to be afraid of?"

"No, no, no!" Komako shook her head and burst into tears. Her face seemed smaller than usual in Shimamura's hand. The hard forehead was trembling.

She had burst out weeping at the sight of the fire, and Shimamura held her to him without thinking to wonder what had so upset her.

She stopped weeping as quickly as she had begun, and pulled away from him.

"There's a movie in the warehouse. Tonight. The place will be full of people. . . . People will be hurt. People will burn to death."

They hurried up toward the inn. There was shouting above them. Guests stood on the second- and third-floor verandas, flooded with light from the open doors. At the edge of the garden, withering chrysanthemums were silhouetted against the light from the inn—or the starlight. For an instant he almost thought it was the light from the fire. Several figures stood beyond the chrysanthemums. The porter and two or three others came bounding down the steps.

"Is it the cocoon-warehouse?" Komako called after them.

"That's right."

"Is anyone hurt? Has anyone been hurt?"

"They're getting everyone out. The film caught fire, and in no time the whole place was on fire. Heard it over the telephone. Look!" The porter raised one arm as he ran off. "Throwing children over one after another from the balcony, they say."

"What shall we do?" Komako started off down the stairs after the porter. Several others overtook her, and she too broke into a run. Shimamura followed.

At the foot of the stairs, their uneasiness increased. Only the very tip of the flames showed over the roofs, and the fire-alarm was nearer and more urgent.

"Careful. It's frozen, and you might slip." She stopped as she turned to look back at him. "But it's all right. You don't need to go any farther. I ought to go on myself to see if anyone has been hurt."

There was indeed no reason for him to go on. His excitement fell away. He looked down at his feet and saw that they had come to the crossing.

"The Milky Way. Beautiful, isn't it," Komako murmured. She looked up at the sky as she ran off ahead of him.

The Milky Way. Shimamura too looked up, and he felt himself floating into the Milky Way. Its radiance was so near that it seemed to take him up into it. Was this the bright vastness the poet Bashō[9] saw when he wrote of the Milky Way arched over a stormy sea? The Milky Way came down just over there, to wrap the night earth in its naked embrace. There was a terrible voluptuousness about it. Shimamura fancied that his own small shadow was being cast up against it from the earth. Each individual star stood apart from the rest, and even the particles of silver dust in the luminous clouds could be picked out, so clear was the night. The limitless depth of the Milky Way pulled his gaze up into it.

"Wait, wait," Shimamura called.

"Come on." Komako ran toward the dark mountain on which the Milky Way was falling.

She seemed to have her long skirts in her hands, and as her arms waved the skirts rose and fell a little. He could feel the red over the starlit snow.

He ran after her as fast as he could.

She slowed down and took his hand, and the long skirts fell to the ground. "You're going too?"

"Yes."

"Always looking for excitement." She clutched at her skirts, now trailing over the snow. "But people will laugh. Please go back."

"Just a little farther."

"But it's wrong. People won't like it if I take you to a fire."

He nodded and stopped. Her hand still rested lightly on his sleeve, however, as she walked on.

"Wait for me somewhere. I'll be right back. Where will you wait?"

"Wherever you say."

"Let's see. A little farther." She peered into his face, and abruptly shook her head. "No. I don't want you to."

She threw herself against him. He reeled back a step or two. A row of onions was growing in the thin snow beside the road.

"I hated it." That sudden torrent of words came at him again. "You said I was a good woman, didn't you? You're going away. Why did you have to say that to me?"

He could see her stabbing at the mat with that silver hair-ornament.

"I cried about it. I cried again after I got home. I'm afraid to leave you. But please go away. I won't forget that you made me cry."

A feeling of nagging, hopeless impotence came over Shimamura at the thought that a simple misunderstanding had worked its way so deep into the woman's being.[1] But just then they heard shouts from the direction of the fire, and a new burst of flame sent up its column of sparks.

---

9. A *haiku* poet (1644–1694). The poem alluded to is contained in *The Narrow Road of the Interior* (see p. 629): "Tumultuous seas: / spanning the sky to Sado Isle, / the Milky Way."   1. Komako may be reacting to an earlier conversation (p. 2399), when Shimamura says to her, "You're a good girl" and then corrects himself, perhaps unconsciously, saying "You're a good woman." This slight shift in tone acknowledges the sexual nature of their relationship. At this moment Komako sees that she has been used. Because we are given primarily Shimamura's point of view and virtually never an inside view of how Komako feels, we can only guess at what her expectations may have been.

"Look. See how it's flaming up again."

They ran on, released.

Komako ran well. Her sandals skimmed the frozen snow, and her arms, close to her sides, seemed hardly to move. She was as one whose whole strength is concentrated in the breast—a strangely small figure, Shimamura thought. Too plump for running himself, he was exhausted the more quickly from watching her. But Komako too was soon out of breath. She fell against him.

"My eyes are watering," she said. "That's how cold it is."

Shimamura's eyes too were moist. His cheeks were flushed, and only his eyes were cold. He blinked, and the Milky Way came to fill them. He tried to keep the tears from spilling over.

"Is the Milky Way like this every night?"

"The Milky Way? Beautiful, isn't it? But it's not like this every night. It's not usually so clear."

The Milky Way flowed over them in the direction they were running, and seemed to bathe Komako's head in its light.

The shape of her slightly aquiline nose was not clear, and the color was gone from her small lips. Was it so dim, then, the light that cut across the sky and overflowed it? Shimamura found that hard to believe. The light was dimmer even than on the night of the new moon, and yet the Milky Way was brighter than the brightest full moon. In the faint light that left no shadows on the earth, Komako's face floated up like an old mask. It was strange that even in the mask there should be the scent of the woman.

He looked up, and again the Milky Way came down to wrap itself around the earth.

And the Milky Way, like a great aurora, flowed through his body to stand at the edges of the earth. There was a quiet, chilly loneliness in it, and a sort of voluptuous astonishment.

"If you leave, I'll lead an honest life," Komako said, walking on again. She put her hand to her disordered hair. When she had gone five or six steps she turned to look back at him. "What's the matter? You don't have to stand there, do you?"

But Shimamura stood looking at her.

"Oh? You'll wait, then? And afterwards you'll take me to your room with you."

She raised her left hand a little and ran off. Her retreating figure was drawn up into the mountain. The Milky Way spread its skirts to be broken by the waves of the mountain, and, fanning out again in all its brilliant vastness higher in the sky, it left the mountain in a deeper darkness.

Komako turned into the main street and disappeared. Shimamura started after her.

Several men were pulling a fire-pump down the street to a rhythmical chant. Floods of people poured after them. Shimamura joined the crowd from the side road he and Komako had taken.

Another pump came down the street. He let it pass, and fell in behind it.

It was an old wooden hand-pump, ridiculously small, with swarms of men at the long rope pulling it and other swarms to man it.

Komako too had stopped to let it pass. She spotted Shimamura and ran along beside him. All down the road people who had stood aside fell in again as if sucked up by the pump. The two of them were now no more than part of a mob running to a fire.

"So you came. Always looking for excitement."

"That's right. It's a sad little pump, though, isn't it. The better part of a hundred years old."

"At least. Careful you don't fall."

"It is slippery."

"Come sometime when we have a real blizzard, and the snow drives along the ground all night long. But you won't, of course. Rabbits and pheasants come running inside the house to get out of the storm." Komako's voice was bright and eager. She seemed to take her beat from the chanting voices and the tramping feet around her. Shimamura too was buoyed up by the crowd.

They could hear the sound of the flames now, and tongues of flame leaped up before them. Komako clutched at Shimamura's arm. The low, dark houses along the street seemed to be breathing as they floated up in the light of the fire and faded away again. Water from the pumps flowed along the street. They came against a wall of people. Mixed in with the smoke was a smell like boiling cocoons.

The same standard remarks were taken up in loud voices through the crowd: the fire had started at the projector; children had been thrown one after another from the balcony; no one was hurt; it was lucky there had been no rice or cocoons in the warehouse. And yet a sort of quiet unified the whole fiery scene, as though everyone were voiceless before the flames, as though the heart, the point of reference, had been torn away from each individual. Everyone seemed to be listening to the sound of the fire and the pumps.

Now and then a villager came running up late, and called out the name of a relative. There would be an answer, and the two would call happily back and forth. Only those voices seemed alive and present. The fire-alarm no longer sounded.

Afraid people would be watching, Shimamura slipped away from Komako and stood behind a group of children. The children moved back from the heat. The snow at their feet was melting, while farther on it had already turned to slush from the fire and water, a muddy confusion of footprints.

They were standing in the field beside the cocoon-warehouse. Most of the crowd on the main street had poured into that same open space.

The fire had apparently started near the entrance, and the walls and roof of half the building had burned away. The pillars and beams were still smoldering. It was a wide barn of a building, only shingles and boarded walls and floors, and the inside was fairly free of smoke. Though the roof, soaked from the pumps, did not seem to be burning, the fire continued to spread. A tongue would shoot up from a quite unexpected spot, the three pumps would turn hastily towards it, and a shower of sparks would fly up in a cloud of black smoke.

The sparks spread off into the Milky Way, and Shimamura was pulled up with them. As the smoke drifted away, the Milky Way seemed to dip and flow in the opposite direction. Occasionally a pump missed the roof, and the end of its line of water wavered and turned to a faint white mist, as though lighted by the Milky Way.

Komako had come up to him, he did not know when. She took his hand.

He looked around at her, but said nothing. She gazed at the fire, the pulse of the fire beating on her intent, slightly flushed face. Shimamura felt a violent rising in his chest. Komako's hair was coming undone, and her throat was bare and arched. His fingers trembled from the urge to touch it. His hand was warm, but Komako's was still warmer. He did not know why he should feel that a separation was forcing itself upon them.

Flames shot up again from the pillars and beams at the entrance. A line of water was turned on them. Hissing clouds of steam arose as the framework began to give way.

The crowd gasped as one person. A woman's body had fallen through the flames.

The cocoon-warehouse had a balcony that was little more than a perfunctory recognition of its duties as an auditorium. Since it fell from the balcony, low for a second floor, the body could have taken but a fraction of a second to reach the ground; but the eye had somehow been able to trace its passage in detail. Perhaps the strange, puppetlike deadness of the fall was what made that fraction of a second seem so long. One knew immediately that the figure was unconscious. It made no noise as it struck the ground between the fire that had newly blazed up and the fire that still smoldered beyond. Water had collected inside the building, and no dust arose from the fall.

A line of water from one of the pumps arched down on the smoldering fire, and a woman's body suddenly floated up before it: such had been the fall. The body was quite horizontal as it passed through the air. Shimamura started back—not from fear, however. He saw the figure as a phantasm from an unreal world. That stiff figure, flung out into the air, became soft and pliant. With a doll-like passiveness, and the freedom of the lifeless, it seemed to hold both life and death in abeyance. If Shimamura felt even a flicker of uneasiness, it was lest the head drop, or a knee or a hip bend to disturb that perfectly horizontal line. Something of the sort must surely happen; but the body was still horizontal when it struck the ground.

Komako screamed and brought her hands to her eyes. Shimamura gazed at the still form.

When did he realize that it was Yoko? The gasp from the crowd and Komako's scream seemed to come at the same instant; and that instant too there was a suggestion of a spasm in the calf of Yoko's leg, stretched out on the ground.

The scream stabbed him through. At the spasm in Yoko's leg, a chill passed down his spine to his very feet. His heart was pounding in an indefinable anguish.

Yoko's leg moved very slightly, hardly enough to catch the eye.

Even before the spasm passed, Shimamura was looking at the face and the kimono, an arrow figure against a red ground. Yoko had fallen face up. The skirt of her kimono was pulled just over one knee. There was but that slight movement in her leg after she struck the earth. She lay unconscious. For some reason Shimamura did not see death in the still form. He felt rather that Yoko had undergone some shift, some metamorphosis.

Two or three beams from the collapsing balcony were burning over her head. The beautiful eyes that so pierced their object were closed. Her jaw was thrust slightly out, and her throat was arched. The fire flickered over the white face.

Shimamura felt a rising in his chest again as the memory came to him of the night he had been on his way to visit Komako, and he had seen that mountain light shine in Yoko's face. The years and months with Komako seemed to be lighted up in that instant; and there, he knew, was the anguish.

Komako put her hands to her eyes and screamed, and even as the crowd held its breath in that first gasp she broke away from Shimamura and ran toward the fire.

The long geisha's skirts trailing behind her, she staggered through the pools of water and the charred bits of wood that lay scattered over the ground. She turned and struggled back with Yoko at her breast. Her face was strained and desperate, and beneath it Yoko's face hung vacantly, as at the moment of the soul's flight. Komako struggled forward as if she bore her sacrifice, or her punishment.

The crowd found its various voices again. It surged forward to envelop the two.

"Keep back. Keep back, please." He heard Komako's cry. "This girl is insane. She's insane."

He tried to move toward that half-mad voice, but he was pushed aside by the men who had come up to take Yoko from her. As he caught his footing, his head fell back, and the Milky Way flowed down inside him with a roar.

JORGE LUIS BORGES
1899–1986

Although other modernist writers are known for their formal innovations, it is the Argentinian Jorge Luis Borges who represents, above all, the gamelike or playful aspect of literary creation. The "real world" is only one of the possible realities in Borges's multiple universe, which treats history, fantasy, and science fiction as having equal claim on our attention: since they all can be imagined, they all are perhaps equally real. His is a world of pure thought, in which abstract fictional games are played out when an initial situation or concept is pushed to its elegantly logical extreme. If everything is possible, there is no need for the artificial constraints imposed by conventional artistic attempts to represent reality: no need for psychological consistency, for a realistic setting, or for a story that unfolds in ordinary time and space. The voice telling the story becomes lost inside the setting it creates, just as a drawing by Saul Steinberg or Maurits Escher depicts a pen drawing the rest of the landscape in which it appears. Not unexpectedly, this thorough immersion in the play of subjective imagination appealed to writers such as the French "new novelists," who were experimenting with shifting perspectives and a refusal of objective reality. For a long time, Borges's European reputation outstripped his prestige in his native land.

Borges was born in Buenos Aires, Argentina, on August 24, 1899, to a prosperous family whose ancestors were distinguished in Argentinian history. The family moved early to a large house whose library and garden were to form an essential part of his literary imagination. His paternal grandmother being English, the young Borges knew English as soon as Spanish and was educated by an English tutor until he was nine. Traveling in Europe, the family was caught in Geneva at the outbreak of World War I; Borges attended secondary school in Switzerland and throughout the war, at which time he learned French and German. After the war they moved to Spain, where he associated with a group of young experimental poets known as the Ultraists. When Borges returned home in 1921, he founded his own group of Argentinian Ultraists (their mural-review, *Prisma*, was printed on sign paper and plastered on walls); became close friends with the philosopher Macedonio Fernandez, whose dedication to pure thought and linguistic intricacies greatly influenced his own attitudes; and contributed regularly to the avant-garde review *Martín Fierro*, at that time associated with an apolitical art for art's sake attitude quite at odds with that of the Boedo group of politically committed writers. Although devoted to pure art, Borges also consistently opposed the military dictatorship of Juan Perón and made his political views plain in speeches and nonliterary writings even though they were not included in his fiction. His attitude did not go unnoticed: in 1946, the Perón regime removed him from the librarian's post that he had held since 1938 and offered him a job as a chicken inspector.

During the 1930s, Borges turned to short narrative pieces and in 1935 published a collection of sketches titled *Universal History of Infamy*. His more mature stories— brief, metaphysical fictions whose density and elegance at times approach poetry— came as an experiment after a head injury and operation in 1938. *The Garden of Forking Paths* (1941), his first major collection, introduced him to a wider public as an intellectual and idealist writer, whose short stories subordinated familiar techniques of character, scene, plot, and narrative voice to a central idea, which was often a philosophical concept. This concept was used not as a lesson or dogma but as the starting point of fantastic elaborations to entertain readers within the game of literature.

Borges's imaginative world is an immense labyrinth, a "garden of forking paths" in which images of mazes and infinite mirroring, cyclical repetition and recall, illustrate the effort of an elusive narrative voice to understand its own significance and that of the world. In *Borges and I*, he comments on the parallel existence of two Borgeses: the one who exists in his work (the one his readers know) and the living, fleshly identity felt by the man who sets pen to paper. "Little by little, I am giving over everything to him . . . I do not know which one of us has written this page." Borges has written on the idea (derived from the British philosophers David Hume and George Berkeley) of the individual self as a cluster of different perceptions, and he further elaborates this notion in his fictional proliferation of identities and alternate realities. Disdaining the "psychological fakery" of realistic novels (the "draggy novel of characters"), he prefers writing that is openly artful, concerned with technique for its own sake, and invents its own multidimensional reality.

Stories in *The Garden of Forking Paths*, *Fictions* (1944), and *The Aleph* (1949) develop these themes in a variety of styles. Borges is fond of detective stories (and has written a number of them) in which the search for an elusive explanation, given carefully planted clues, matters more than how recognizable the characters may be. In *Death and the Compass*, a mysterious murderer leaves tantalizing traces that refer to points of the compass and lead the detective into a fatal trap that closes on him at a fourth compass point, symbolized by the architectural lozenges of the house in which he dies. The author composes an art of puzzles and discovery, a grand code that treats our universe as a giant library where meaning is locked away in endless hexagonal galleries (*The Library of Babel*), as an enormous lottery whose results are all the events of our lives (*The Lottery in Babylon*), as a series of dreams within dreams (*The Circular Ruins*), or as a small iridescent sphere containing all of the points in space (*The Aleph*). In *Pierre Menard, Author of the "Quixote,"* the narrator is a scholarly reviewer of a certain fictitious Menard, whose masterwork has been to rewrite *Don Quixote* as if it were created today: not revise it or transcribe it, but actually *reinvent* it word for word. He has succeeded; the two texts are "verbally identical" although Menard's modern version is "more ambiguous" than Cervantes's and thus "infinitely richer."

The imaginary universe of *Tlön, Uqbar, Orbis Tertius* exemplifies the mixture of fact and fiction with which Borges invites us to speculate on the solidity of our own world. The narrator is engaged in tracking down mysterious references to a country called Tlön, whose language, science, and literature are exactly opposite (and perhaps related to) our own. For example, the Tlönians use verbs or adjectives instead of nouns, since they have no concept of objects in space, and their science consists of an association of ideas in which the most astounding theory becomes the truth. In a postscript, the narrator reveals that the encyclopedia has turned out to be an immense scholarly hoax, yet also mentions that strange and unearthly objects—recognizably from Tlön—have recently been found.

The intricate, riddling, mazelike ambiguity of Borges's stories earned him international reputation and influence, to the point that a "style like Borges" has become a recognized term. In Argentina, he was given the prestigious post of Director of the National Library after the fall of Perón in 1955, and in 1961 he shared the International Publishers' Prize with Samuel Beckett. Always nearsighted, he grew increasingly blind in the mid-1950s and was forced to dictate his work. Nonetheless, he continued to travel, teach, and lecture in the company of his wife, Else Astete Milan, whom he married in 1967. Until his death Borges lived in his beloved Buenos Aires, the city he celebrated in his first volume of poetry.

The Garden of Forking Paths begins as a simple spy story purporting to reveal the hidden truth about a German bombing raid during World War I. Borges alludes to documented facts: the geographic setting of the town of Albert and the Ancre River; a famous Chinese novel as Ts'ui Pên's proposed model; the *History of the World War (1914–1918)* published by B. H. Liddell Hart in 1934. Official history is undermined on the first page, however, both by the newly discovered confession of Dr. Yu Tsun and by his editor's suspiciously defensive footnote. Ultimately, Yu Tsun will learn from his ancestor's novel that history is a labyrinth of alternate possibilities (much like the "alternate worlds" of science fiction).

Borges executes his detective story with the traditional carefully planted clues. We know from the beginning that Yu Tsun—even though arrested—has successfully outwitted his rival, Captain Richard Madden; that his problem was to convey the name of a bombing target to his chief in Berlin; that he went to the telephone book to locate someone capable of transmitting his message; and that he had one bullet in his revolver. The cut-off phone call, the chase at the railroad station, and Madden's hasty arrival at Dr. Albert's house provide the excitement and pressure expected in a straightforward detective plot. Quite different spatial and temporal horizons open up halfway through, however. Coincidences—those chance relationships that might well have happened differently—introduce the idea of forking paths or alternate possible routes for history. Both Yu Tsun and Richard Madden are aliens trying to prove their worth inside their respective bureaucracies; the road to Stephen Albert's house turns mazelike always to the left; the only suitable name in the phone book—the man Yu Tsun must kill—is a Sinologist who has reconstructed the labyrinthine text written long ago by Yu Tsun's ancestor. This text, Ts'ui Pên's *The Garden of Forking Paths,* describes the universe as an infinite series of alternative versions of experience. In different versions of the story (taking place at different times), Albert and Yu Tsun are enemies or friends or not even there. The war and Richard Madden appear diminished (although no less real) in such a kaleidoscopic perspective, for they exist in only one of many possible dimensions. Yet Madden hurries up the walk, and current reality returns to demand Albert's death. It may seem as though the vision of other worlds in which Albert continues to exist (or is Yu Tsun's enemy) would soften the murderer's remorse for his deed. Instead, it makes more poignant the narrator's realization that in this dimension no other way could be found.

Useful biographies are James Woodall, *The Man in the Mirror of the Book: A Life of Jorge Luis Borges* (1996), and James Woodall, *Borges: A Life* (1996). George R. McMurray, *Jorge Luis Borges* (1980), and Martin S. Stabb, *Borges Revisited* (1991), are general introductions to the man and his work. Jaime Alazraki, ed., *Critical Essays on Jorge Luis Borges* (1987), assembles articles and reviews (including the 1970 *Autobiographical Essay*), four comparative essays, and a general introduction that offer valuable perspectives on Borges's writing as well as his impact on American writers and critics. Linda S. Maier, *Borges and the European Avant-Garde* (1996), focuses on the European scene. Edna Aizenberg, ed., *Borges and His Successors: The Borgesian Impact on Literature and the Arts* (1990), is a wide-ranging collection of essays describing Borges as the precursor of postmodern fiction and criticism. Anna Maria Barrenechea, *Borges the Labyrinth Maker* (1965), discusses Borges's intricate style, while Daniel Balderston, *Out of Context: Historical Reference and the Representation of Reality in Borges* (1993), focuses on the texts' manipulation of fictional and historical reality. Fernando Sorrentino, *Seven Conversations with Jorge Luis Borges* (1981), is a series of informal, widely ranging interviews from 1972, with a prefaced list of the topics of each conversation. José Eduardo González, *Borges and the Politics of Form* (1998), examines the way Borges's style represents the aesthetic and political views of different cultural periods.

PRONOUNCING GLOSSARY

The following list uses common English syllables and stress accents to provide rough equivalents of selected words whose pronunciation may be unfamiliar to the general reader.

Borges: *bore'-kess*
Hsi P'êng: *shee pung*
Hung Lu Meng: *hoong low mung*

Ts'ui Pên: *tsoo-ay pun*
Yu Tsun: *yew tsoo-en*

The Garden of Forking Paths[1]

On page 22 of Liddell Hart's *History of World War I* you will read that an attack against the Serre-Montauban line by thirteen British divisions (supported by 1,400 artillery pieces), planned for the 24th of July, 1916, had to be postponed until the morning of the 29th. The torrential rains, Captain Liddell Hart comments, caused this delay, an insignificant one, to be sure.

The following statement, dictated, reread and signed by Dr. Yu Tsun, former professor of English at the *Hochschule* at Tsingtao,[2] throws an unsuspected light over the whole affair. The first two pages of the document are missing.

" . . . and I hung up the receiver. Immediately afterwards, I recognized the voice that had answered in German. It was that of Captain Richard Madden. Madden's presence in Viktor Runeberg's apartment meant the end of our anxieties and—but this seemed, *or should have seemed,* very secondary to me—also the end of our lives. It meant that Runeberg had been arrested or murdered.[3] Before the sun set on that day, I would encounter the same fate. Madden was implacable. Or rather, he was obliged to be so. An Irishman at the service of England, a man accused of laxity and perhaps of treason, how could he fail to seize and be thankful for such a miraculous opportunity: the discovery, capture, maybe even the death of two agents of the German Reich?[4] I went up to my room; absurdly I locked the door and threw myself on my back on the narrow iron cot. Through the window I saw the familiar

---

1. Translated by Donald A. Yates.   2. Or Ch'ing-tao; a major port in east China, part of territory leased to (and developed by) Germany in 1898. *Hochschule:* university (German).   3. "A hypothesis both hateful and odd. The Prussian spy Hans Rabener, alias Viktor Runeberg, attacked with drawn automatic the bearer of the warrant for his arrest, Captain Richard Madden. The latter, in self-defense, inflicted the wound which brought about Runeberg's death [Editor's note]." This entire note is by Borges as "Editor." 4. Empire (German).

roofs and the cloud-shaded six o'clock sun. It seemed incredible to me that that day without premonitions or symbols should be the one of my inexorable death. In spite of my dead father, in spite of having been a child in a symmetrical garden of Hai Feng, was I—now—going to die? Then I reflected that everything happens to a man precisely, precisely *now*. Centuries of centuries and only in the present do things happen; countless men in the air, on the face of the earth and the sea, and all that really is happening is happening to me . . . The almost intolerable recollection of Madden's horselike face banished these wanderings. In the midst of my hatred and terror (it means nothing to me now to speak of terror, now that I have mocked Richard Madden, now that my throat yearns for the noose) it occurred to me that that tumultuous and doubtless happy warrior did not suspect that I possessed the Secret. The name of the exact location of the new British artillery park on the River Ancre. A bird streaked across the gray sky and blindly I translated it into an airplane and that airplane into many (against the French sky) annihilating the artillery station with vertical bombs. If only my mouth, before a bullet shattered it, could cry out that secret name so it could be heard in Germany . . . My human voice was very weak. How might I make it carry to the ear of the Chief? To the ear of that sick and hateful man who knew nothing of Runeberg and me save that we were in Stafford shire[5] and who was waiting in vain for our report in his arid office in Berlin, endlessly examining newspapers . . . I said out loud: *I must flee.* I sat up noiselessly, in a useless perfection of silence, as if Madden were already lying in wait for me. Something—perhaps the mere vain ostentation of proving my resources were nil—made me look through my pockets. I found what I knew I would find. The American watch, the nickel chain and the square coin, the key ring with the incriminating useless keys to Runeberg's apartment, the notebook, a letter which I resolved to destroy immediately (and which I did not destroy), a crown, two shillings and a few pence, the red and blue pencil, the handkerchief, the revolver with one bullet. Absurdly, I took it in my hand and weighed it in order to inspire courage within myself. Vaguely I thought that a pistol report can be heard at a great distance. In ten minutes my plan was perfected. The telephone book listed the name of the only person capable of transmitting the message; he lived in a suburb of Fenton,[6] less than a half hour's train ride away.

I am a cowardly man. I say it now, now that I have carried to its end a plan whose perilous nature no one can deny. I know its execution was terrible. I didn't do it for Germany, no. I care nothing for a barbarous country which imposed upon me the abjection of being a spy. Besides, I know of a man from England—a modest man—who for me is no less great than Goethe.[7] I talked with him for scarcely an hour, but during that hour he was Goethe . . . I did it because I sensed that the Chief somehow feared people of my race—for the innumerable ancestors who merge within me. I wanted to prove to him that a yellow man could save his armies. Besides, I had to flee from Captain Madden. His hands and his voice could call at my door at any moment. I dressed silently, bade farewell to myself in the mirror, went downstairs, scrutinized the peaceful street and went out. The station was

---

5. County in west-central England.   6. In Lincolnshire, a county in east England.   7. Johann Wolfgang von Goethe (1749–1832), German poet, novelist, and dramatist; author of *Faust*; often taken as representing the peak of German cultural achievement.

not far from my home, but I judged it wise to take a cab. I argued that in this way I ran less risk of being recognized; the fact is that in the deserted street I felt myself visible and vulnerable, infinitely so. I remember that I told the cab driver to stop a short distance before the main entrance. I got out with voluntary, almost painful slowness; I was going to the village of Ashgrove but I bought a ticket for a more distant station. The train left within a very few minutes, at eight-fifty. I hurried; the next one would leave at nine-thirty. There was hardly a soul on the platform. I went through the coaches; I remember a few farmers, a woman dressed in mourning, a young boy who was reading with fervor the *Annals* of Tacitus,[8] a wounded and happy soldier. The coaches jerked forward at last. A man whom I recognized ran in vain to the end of the platform. It was Captain Richard Madden. Shattered, trembling, I shrank into the far corner of the seat, away from the dreaded window.

From this broken state I passed into an almost abject felicity. I told myself that the duel had already begun and that I had won the first encounter by frustrating, even if for forty minutes, even if by a stroke of fate, the attack of my adversary. I argued that this slightest of victories foreshadowed a total victory. I argued (no less fallaciously) that my cowardly felicity proved that I was a man capable of carrying out the adventure successfully. From this weakness I took strength that did not abandon me. I foresee that man will resign himself each day to more atrocious undertakings; soon there will be no one but warriors and brigands; I give them this counsel: *The author of an atrocious undertaking ought to imagine that he has already accomplished it, ought to impose upon himself a future as irrevocable as the past.* Thus I proceeded as my eyes of a man already dead registered the elapsing of that day, which was perhaps the last, and the diffusion of the night. The train ran gently along, amid ash trees. It stopped, almost in the middle of the fields. No one announced the name of the station. "Ashgrove?" I asked a few lads on the platform. "Ashgrove," they replied. I got off.

A lamp enlightened the platform but the faces of the boys were in shadow. One questioned me, "Are you going to Dr. Stephen Albert's house?" Without waiting for my answer, another said, "The house is a long way from here, but you won't get lost if you take this road to the left and at every crossroads turn again to your left." I tossed them a coin (my last), descended a few stone steps and started down the solitary road. It went downhill, slowly. It was of elemental earth; overhead the branches were tangled; the low, full moon seemed to accompany me.

For an instant, I thought that Richard Madden in some way had penetrated my desperate plan. Very quickly, I understood that that was impossible. The instructions to turn always to the left reminded me that such was the common procedure for discovering the central point of certain labyrinths. I have some understanding of labyrinths: not for nothing am I the great grandson of that Ts'ui Pên who was governor of Yunnan and who renounced worldly power in order to write a novel that might be even more populous than the *Hung Lu Meng*[9] and to construct a labyrinth in which all men would become lost. Thirteen years he dedicated to these heterogeneous tasks, but

---

8. Cornelius Tacitus (55–117), Roman historian whose *Annals* give a vivid picture of the decadence and corruption of the Roman Empire under Tiberius, Claudius, and Nero.   9. *The Dream of the Red Chamber* (1791) by Ts'ao Hsüeh-ch'in; the most famous Chinese novel, a love story and panorama of Chinese family life involving more than 430 characters.

the hand of a stranger murdered him—and his novel was incoherent and no one found the labyrinth. Beneath English trees I meditated on that lost maze: I imagined it inviolate and perfect at the secret crest of a mountain; I imagined it erased by rice fields or beneath the water; I imagined it infinite, no longer composed of octagonal kiosks and returning paths, but of rivers and provinces and kingdoms . . . I thought of a labyrinth of labyrinths, of one sinuous spreading labyrinth that would encompass the past and the future and in some way involve the stars. Absorbed in these illusory images, I forgot my destiny of one pursued. I felt myself to be, for an unknown period of time, an abstract perceiver of the world. The vague, living countryside, the moon, the remains of the day worked on me, as well as the slope of the road which eliminated any possibility of weariness. The afternoon was intimate, infinite. The road descended and forked among the now confused meadows. A high-pitched, almost syllabic music approached and receded in the shifting of the wind, dimmed by leaves and distance. I thought that a man can be an enemy of other men, of the moments of other men, but not of a country: not of fireflies, words, gardens, streams of water, sunsets. Thus I arrived before a tall, rusty gate. Between the iron bars I made out a poplar grove and a pavilion. I understood suddenly two things, the first trivial, the second almost unbelievable: the music came from the pavilion, and the music was Chinese. For precisely that reason I had openly accepted it without paying it any heed. I do not remember whether there was a bell or whether I knocked with my hand. The sparkling of the music continued.

From the rear of the house within a lantern approached: a lantern that the trees sometimes striped and sometimes eclipsed, a paper lantern that had the form of a drum and the color of the moon. A tall man bore it. I didn't see his face for the light blinded me. He opened the door and said slowly, in my own language: "I see that the pious Hsi P'êng persists in correcting my solitude. You no doubt wish to see the garden?"

I recognized the name of one of our consuls and I replied, disconcerted, "The garden?"

"The garden of forking paths."

Something stirred in my memory and I uttered with incomprehensible certainty, "The garden of my ancestor Ts'ui Pên."

"Your ancestor? Your illustrious ancestor? Come in."

The damp path zigzagged like those of my childhood. We came to a library of Eastern and Western books. I recognized bound in yellow silk several volumes of the Lost Encyclopedia, edited by the Third Emperor of the Luminous Dynasty but never printed.[1] The record on the phonograph revolved next to a bronze phoenix. I also recall a *famille rose*[2] vase and another, many centuries older, of that shade of blue which our craftsmen copied from the potters of Persia . . .

Stephen Albert observed me with a smile. He was, as I have said, very tall, sharp-featured, with gray eyes and a gray beard. He told me that he had been a missionary in Tientsin "before aspiring to become a Sinologist."

---

1. The Yung-lo emperor of the Ming ("bright") Dynasty commissioned a massive encyclopedia between 1403 and 1408. A single copy of the 11,095 manuscript volumes was made in the mid-1500s; the original was later destroyed, and only 370 volumes of the copy remain today.   2. Pink family (French); refers to a Chinese decorative enamel ranging in color from an opaque pink to purplish rose. *Famille rose* pottery was at its best during the reign of Yung Chên (1723–1735).

We sat down—I on a long, low divan, he with his back to the window and a tall circular clock. I calculated that my pursuer, Richard Madden, could not arrive for at least an hour. My irrevocable determination could wait.

"An astounding fate, that of Ts'ui Pên," Stephen Albert said. "Governor of his native province, learned in astronomy, in astrology and in the tireless interpretation of the canonical books, chess player, famous poet and calligrapher—he abandoned all this in order to compose a book and a maze. He renounced the pleasures of both tyranny and justice, of his populous couch, of his banquets and even of erudition—all to close himself up for thirteen years in the Pavilion of the Limpid Solitude. When he died, his heirs found nothing save chaotic manuscripts. His family, as you may be aware, wished to condemn them to the fire; but his executor—a Taoist or Buddhist monk—insisted on their publication."

"We descendants of Ts'ui Pên," I replied, "continue to curse that monk. Their publication was senseless. The book is an indeterminate heap of contradictory drafts. I examined it once: in the third chapter the hero dies, in the fourth he is alive. As for the other undertaking of Ts'ui Pên, his labyrinth . . ."

"Here is Ts'ui Pên's labyrinth," he said, indicating a tall lacquered desk.

"An ivory labyrinth!" I exclaimed. "A minimum labyrinth."

"A labyrinth of symbols," he corrected. "An invisible labyrinth of time. To me, a barbarous Englishman, has been entrusted the revelation of this diaphanous mystery. After more than a hundred years, the details are irretrievable; but it is not hard to conjecture what happened. Ts'ui Pên must have said once: *I am withdrawing to write a book*. And another time: *I am withdrawing to construct a labyrinth*. Every one imagined two works; to no one did it occur that the book and the maze were one and the same thing. The Pavilion of the Limpid Solitude stood in the center of a garden that was perhaps intricate; that circumstance could have suggested to the heirs a physical labyrinth. Ts'ui Pên died; no one in the vast territories that were his came upon the labyrinth; the confusion of the novel suggested to me that *it* was the maze. Two circumstances gave me the correct solution of the problem. One: the curious legend that Ts'ui Pên had planned to create a labyrinth which would be strictly infinite. The other: a fragment of a letter I discovered."

Albert rose. He turned his back on me for a moment; he opened a drawer of the black and gold desk. He faced me and in his hands he held a sheet of paper that had once been crimson, but was now pink and tenuous and cross-sectioned. The fame of Ts'ui Pên as a calligrapher had been justly won. I read, uncomprehendingly and with fervor, these words written with a minute brush by a man of my blood: *I leave to the various futures (not to all) my garden of forking paths*. Wordlessly, I returned the sheet. Albert continued:

"Before unearthing this letter, I had questioned myself about the ways in which a book can be infinite. I could think of nothing other than a cyclic volume, a circular one. A book whose last page was identical with the first, a book which had the possibility of continuing indefinitely. I remembered too that night which is at the middle of the Thousand and One Nights when Scheherazade[3] (through a magical oversight of the copyist) begins to relate

3. The narrator of the collection also known as the *Arabian Nights*, a thousand and one tales supposedly told by Scheherazade to her husband, Shahrayar, king of Samarkand, to postpone her execution.

word for word the story of the Thousand and One Nights, establishing the risk of coming once again to the night when she must repeat it, and thus on to infinity. I imagined as well a Platonic, hereditary work, transmitted from father to son, in which each new individual adds a chapter or corrects with pious care the pages of his elders. These conjectures diverted me; but none seemed to correspond, not even remotely, to the contradictory chapters of Ts'ui Pên. In the midst of this perplexity, I received from Oxford the manuscript you have examined. I lingered, naturally, on the sentence: *I leave to the various futures (not to all) my garden of forking paths.* Almost instantly, I understood: 'The garden of forking paths' was the chaotic novel; the phrase 'the various futures (not to all)' suggested to me the forking in time, not in space. A broad rereading of the work confirmed the theory. In all fictional works, each time a man is confronted with several alternatives, he chooses one and eliminates the others; in the fiction of Ts'ui Pên, he chooses—simultaneously—all of them. *He creates,* in this way, diverse futures, diverse times which themselves also proliferate and fork. Here, then, is the explanation of the novel's contradictions. Fang, let us say, has a secret; a stranger calls at his door; Fang resolves to kill him. Naturally, there are several possible outcomes: Fang can kill the intruder, the intruder can kill Fang, they both can escape, they both can die, and so forth. In the work of Ts'ui Pên, all possible outcomes occur; each one is the point of departure for other forkings. Sometimes, the paths of this labyrinth converge: for example, you arrive at this house, but in one of the possible pasts you are my enemy, in another, my friend. If you will resign yourself to my incurable pronunciation, we shall read a few pages."

His face, within the vivid circle of the lamplight, was unquestionably that of an old man, but with something unalterable about it, even immortal. He read with slow precision two versions of the same epic chapter. In the first, an army marches to a battle across a lonely mountain; the horror of the rocks and shadows makes the men undervalue their lives and they gain an easy victory. In the second, the same army traverses a palace where a great festival is taking place; the resplendent battle seems to them a continuation of the celebration and they win the victory. I listened with proper veneration to these ancient narratives, perhaps less admirable in themselves than the fact that they had been created by my blood and were being restored to me by a man of a remote empire, in the course of a desperate adventure, on a Western isle. I remember the last words, repeated in each version like a secret commandment: *Thus fought the heroes, tranquil their admirable hearts, violent their swords, resigned to kill and to die.*

From that moment on, I felt about me and within my dark body an invisible, intangible swarming. Not the swarming of the divergent, parallel and finally coalescent armies, but a more inaccessible, more intimate agitation that they in some manner prefigured. Stephen Albert continued:

"I don't believe that your illustrious ancestor played idly with these variations. I don't consider it credible that he would sacrifice thirteen years to the infinite execution of a rhetorical experiment. In your country, the novel is a subsidiary form of literature; in Ts'ui Pên's time it was a despicable form. Ts'ui Pên was a brilliant novelist, but he was also a man of letters who doubtless did not consider himself a mere novelist. The testimony of his contemporaries proclaims—and his life fully confirms—his metaphysical and mystical interests. Philosophic controversy usurps a good part of the novel. I know that of all problems, none disturbed him so greatly nor worked upon him so much as the abysmal problem of time. Now then, the latter is the only problem that does not figure in the pages of the *Garden*. He does not even use the word that signifies *time*. How do you explain this voluntary omission?"

I proposed several solutions—all unsatisfactory. We discussed them. Finally, Stephen Albert said to me:

"In a riddle whose answer is chess, what is the only prohibited word?"

I thought a moment and replied, "The word *chess*."

"Precisely," said Albert. "*The Garden of Forking Paths* is an enormous riddle, or parable, whose theme is time; this recondite cause prohibits its mention. To omit a word always, to resort to inept metaphors and obvious periphrases, is perhaps the most emphatic way of stressing it. That is the tortuous method preferred, in each of the meanderings of his indefatigable novel, by the oblique Ts'ui Pên. I have compared hundreds of manuscripts, I have corrected the errors that the negligence of the copyists has introduced, I have guessed the plan of this chaos, I have re-established—I believe I have re-established—the primordial organization, I have translated the entire work: it is clear to me that not once does he employ the word 'time.' The explanation is obvious: *The Garden of Forking Paths* is an incomplete, but not false, image of the universe as Ts'ui Pên conceived it. In contrast to Newton and Schopenhauer,[4] your ancestor did not believe in a uniform, absolute time. He believed in an infinite series of times, in a growing, dizzying net of divergent, convergent and parallel times. This network of times which approached one another, forked, broke off, or were unaware of one another for centuries, embraces *all* possibilities of time. We do not exist in the majority of these times; in some you exist, and not I; in others I, and not you; in others, both of us. In the present one, which a favorable fate has granted me, you have arrived at my house; in another, while crossing the garden, you found me dead; in still another, I utter these same words, but I am a mistake, a ghost."

"In every one," I pronounced, not without a tremble to my voice, "I am grateful to you and revere you for your re-creation of the garden of Ts'ui Pên."

"Not in all," he murmured with a smile. "Time forks perpetually toward innumerable futures. In one of them I am your enemy."

Once again I felt the swarming sensation of which I have spoken. It seemed to me that the humid garden that surrounded the house was infinitely saturated with invisible persons. Those persons were Albert and I, secret, busy and multiform in other dimensions of time. I raised my eyes and the tenuous nightmare dissolved. In the yellow and black garden there was only one man; but this man was as strong as a statue . . . this man was approaching along the path and he was Captain Richard Madden.

"The future already exists," I replied, "but I am your friend. Could I see the letter again?"

Albert rose. Standing tall, he opened the drawer of the tall desk; for the

---

4. German philosopher (1788–1860), whose concept of will proceeded from a concept of the self as enduring through time. In *Seven Conversations with Jorge Luis Borges*, Borges also comments on Schopenhauer's interest in the "oneiric [dreamlike] essence of life." Newton (1642–1727), English mathematician and philosopher best known for his formulation of laws of gravitation and motion.

moment his back was to me. I had readied the revolver. I fired with extreme caution. Albert fell uncomplainingly, immediately. I swear his death was instantaneous—a lightning stroke.

The rest is unreal, insignificant. Madden broke in, arrested me. I have been condemned to the gallows. I have won out abominably; I have communicated to Berlin the secret name of the city they must attack. They bombed it yesterday; I read it in the same papers that offered to England the mystery of the learned Sinologist Stephen Albert who was murdered by a stranger, one Yu Tsun. The Chief had deciphered this mystery. He knew my problem was to indicate (through the uproar of the war) the city called Albert, and that I had found no other means to do so than to kill a man of that name. He does not know (no one can know) my innumerable contrition and weariness.

For Victoria Ocampo

ANDREW PEYNETSA
1904?–1976

Among the Zuni of western New Mexico the art of fiction is practiced by the teller of *telapnaawe,* "tales," which may be recited only during the cold months, between the fall and spring equinoxes, and only after the sun has set. *Telapnaawe* are told by both men and women, more often men, either at home or in meetings of the religious and social organizations known as medicine societies. Before the advent of television nearly every older man at Zuni performed *telapnaawe,* though some narrators were recognized as more adept than others. Evidently among the most gifted of his generation was the teller Andrew Peynetsa, who during the mid-1960s together with his clan relative Walter Sanchez performed nearly a hundred stories—including histories, both sacred and secular, as well as the fictional *telapnaawe*—for the benefit of small audiences of which the anthropologist Dennis Tedlock was a regular member. Tedlock preserved these recitals on tape, which were later translated with the help of Andrew's nephew, Joseph Peynetsa. It was on the evening of January 20, 1965, that Andrew Peynetsa—in a recital lasting half an hour—gave his performance of the *telapnaawe* (singular) about the boy and the deer that would measurably influence the study of Native American narratives and would challenge the way one looks at narrative art in general.

Little has been recorded of Andrew Peynetsa's life. The date of his birth is uncertain; he is said to have been seventy-two when he died in 1976. As a child he was schooled in Albuquerque, and he spoke English as well as Zuni. In the 1960s, when most Zunis were turning to silversmithing or were working away from the reservation, Peynetsa continued to devote himself to the traditional Zuni occupation of farming. He was an active medicine society member, a specialist in society liturgy, and a master orator (for oratory, as opposed to narrative, see the headnote "Zuni Ritual Poetry," p. 2031).

The Boy and the Deer is not an original story by Peynetsa. Strictly speaking, there can be no "new" *telapnaawe.* The narrator's contribution lies in the handling of a traditional plot, to which fresh details expressing manners, locale, and even character may be freely added, yielding the typically Zunian style that is as much novelistic as it is traditional, or folkloric.

The earliest Deer Boy tale on record was collected in the 1880s by the flamboyant, controversial Frank Hamilton Cushing, who took up residence at Zuni Pueblo and was accepted into the innermost circles of Zuni society, becoming the first and most famous practitioner of what would come to be called "participant ethnography." Several additional Deer Boy variants were recorded in the 1920s by two well-known anthropologists, Ruth Bunzel and Ruth Benedict. All versions have in common the illegitimate birth of the boy who, abandoned by his human mother, is reared in the hills by a deer mother, is eventually captured by his human kinsmen, and returns, if only briefly, to human society. What made the Peynetsa version distinctive is that it exhibited a new and perhaps extreme theory of translation, as worked out by Tedlock—combined with the widely acknowledged perfection of Peynetsa's art, which made the theory compelling. The translated text was published in Tedlock's *Finding the Center* (1972), a collection that included eight other Zuni stories. *The Boy and the Deer,* however, is the one that has been remembered, repeatedly cited, and reprinted.

Listening and relistening to the recordings he had made, Tedlock came to feel that the live recital with its louds, softs, and calculated silences could not be translated into prose. Further, he would come to disparage prose itself, stating that "prose has no real existence outside the printed page." To avoid creating so lifeless an artifact, Tedlock published the Peynetsa and Sanchez narratives as a kind of poetry, using the poetic "line" to mark the narrator's pauses, adding typographic devices to indicate vocal changes. The result was not without precedent. Anthropologists had been experimenting for a decade or more with new methods for recording and translating texts. It was *Finding the Center,* however, that won an army of converts to the new quest for accuracy; and it may be said that *The Boy and the Deer* stands as a landmark in the development of the interrelated subdisciplines that have been called "ethnopoetics," "the ethnography of speaking" and, encompassing a broader scope, "discourse analysis." The pervading commandment—which has spread beyond anthropology—is to pay close, even minute, attention to human utterance for both its informational and its artistic values.

Yet *The Boy and the Deer* is a haunting story that, in a sense, can survive even the clumsiest paraphrase. It reaches deep into Native American tradition to present the essential conflict between the animal and human worlds, enabling the reader or listener to join with nature in its willingness to serve humanity—and, equally, to join in the guilt of the human community for taking this gift. Expressed in stories of animal-human marriage or, as here, animal-human adoption, the basic theme is common to the Native oral literatures of North, South, and Central America. Its unwritten history no doubt stretches back thousands of years.

This is not to suggest that ancient stories are kept alive for their venerability alone. To be continually re-created they must remain relevant. In an essay titled *An American Indian View of Death* (1975), Tedlock explores this connection between traditional knowledge and contemporary reality, showing how Andrew Peynetsa's version of *The Boy and the Deer* prefigured a tragic incident that occurred at Zuni in the summer of 1966. A young man, while hunting, accidentally killed himself as he bent over his rifle to straighten the sight. He had been holding the barrel with the muzzle toward his chin. The weapon discharged; the bullet entered the boy's chin and lodged in his brain. In Peynetsa's story, with chilling similarity, the boy pulls a yucca blade toward him, piercing his heart. Were these deaths truly accidental? In regard to both story and real-life incident the question became a topic of speculation. Referring to the story, Peynetsa himself commented, after narrating it: "Yes, his mother got blamed, because she sent him to get the yucca; he wasn't just going to do that. Her folks said she shouldn't tell him to get it and that his uncles should go and get it. Probably he had it in his mind to kill himself, that's the way I felt when I was telling it."

By the same token it was decided among the relatives of the teenage boy with the rifle that he had "shortened his road." After his death it was recalled that he had been in a hurry to finish things and to acquire knowledge beyond his years. No one said he had committed suicide; it was merely proposed that he had had in the back of his mind that his life would end prematurely. Yet, just as in Peynetsa's commentary on the fictional story, the web of cause and effect did not involve the victim alone. Each member of the boy's family now remembered something he or she might have done, or refrained from doing, to prevent the outcome. In any case, the victim's fate—if not to the point of death, then beyond that point—had been preordained, not only for the young rifleman but for the fictional deer boy. According to Zuni doctrine, the human being in the afterworld eventually becomes transformed into an animal with which he or she had been associated in life. There is reason to believe, according to Tedlock, that the boy with the rifle would become a deer—just as the deer boy in the story, as Peynetsa phrases it, "entered upon the roads of his elders."

In reading the text as printed here, note that the end of each line indicates a pause, often imperceptible, of a half second or more, depending on the whim of the narrator. A space between lines (with a centered bullet) implies a pause of at least two seconds. A vowel followed by a dash is to be held for about two seconds. Use a hushed voice for words in smaller type, a loud voice for words printed entirely in capital letters. Passages with words raised or lowered are to be chanted: chant raised words about three half tones higher than normal; lowered words, about three half tones lower. Special directions appear in parentheses, for example, "(sharply)." Audience responses are labeled "(audience)." As a final instruction, Tedlock advises the reader not to attempt mechanical accuracy to the point where it interferes with the flow of performance.

Tedlock's *An American Indian View of Death*, mentioned above, is in Dennis Tedlock and Barbara Tedlock, eds., *Teachings from the American Earth* (1975). Further essays, relating to Zuni narrative and to Andrew Peynetsa, are in Dennis Tedlock, *The Spoken Word and the Work of Interpretation* (1983). For earlier versions of the Deer Boy story, see Frank Hamilton Cushing, *Zuñi Folk Tales* (1986); Ruth Bunzel, *Zuni Texts* (1933); and Ruth Benedict, *Zuni Mythology* (1935).

PRONOUNCING GLOSSARY

The following list uses common English syllables and stress accents to provide rough equivalents of selected words whose pronunciation may be unfamiliar to the general reader.

eeso: *eh'-soh*	son'ahchi: *sohn'-ah-chee*
He'shokta: *hay'-shohk-tah*	sonti: *sohn'-tee*
Huututu: *hoo'-too-too*	telapnaawe: *tay'-lahp-nah-way*
Kyaklo: *kyah'-kloh*	telele: *tay-lay-lay*
Pawtiwa: *pow'-tee-wah*	Tísshomahhá: *tees'-shoh-mah-hah'*
Peynetsa: *pay'-nay-tsah*	

The Boy and the Deer[1]

SON'AHCHI.[2]

(*audience*) Ee———so.[3]

SONTI[4] ᴸᴼ———ᴺᴳ ᴬGO.

(*audience*) Ee———so.

THERE WERE ⱽᴵᴸLAGERS AT ᴴᴱ'SHOKTA[5]

---

1. Translated by Dennis Tedlock.   2. Strictly untranslatable, but analogous to "once upon a time."
3. Untranslatable; roughly, "so it was."   4. Analogous to "once long ago."   5. Zuni tales customarily begin by setting the locale. He'shokta is a pueblo ruin about three miles northwest of Zuni.

and
up on the Prairie-Dog Hills
the deer
had their home.

                              •

The daughter of a priest   10
      sit   room   fourth   down   bas
was   ting in a   on the   story   weaving   ket-plaques.[6]
She was always sitting and working in there, and the Sun came up
every day   Sun came up
            when the
the   girl   would sit   working

at the place where he came in.   15
It seems the Sun made her pregnant.
When he made her pregnant
                                                          bel
though she sat in there without knowing any man, her   ly grew large.
She worked o———n for a time
weaving basket-plaques, and   20
her belly grew large, very very large.
When her time was near
she had a pain in her belly.
Gathering all her clothes
she went out and   25
went down to Water's End.

                              •

On she went until
she came to the bank
went on down to the river, and washed her clothes.

                              •

Then   30
having washed a few things, she had a pain in her belly.

                              •

She came out of the river. Having come out she sat down
by a juniper tree and strained her muscles:
the little baby came out.
She dug a hole, put juniper leaves in it   35
then laid the baby there.
She went back into the water
gathered all her clothes
and carefully washed the blood off herself.
She bundled   40
her clothes
put them on her back
and returned to her home at He'shokta.

                              •

And the DEER
who lived on the Prairie-Dog Hills   45
were going down to DRINK, going down to drink at dusk.

6. Ornamental disks of woven yucca and grass fibers.

The Sun had almost set when they went down to drink and the little baby
   was crying.
"Where is the little baby crying?" they said.
It was two fawns on their way down
with their mother   50
who heard him.
The crying was coming from the direction of a tree.
They were going into the water

            •

and there
they came upon the crying.   55
Where a juniper tree stood, the child
was crying.

            •

The deer
the two fawns and their mother went to him.

            •

"Well, why shouldn't we   60
save him?
Why don't you two hold my nipples
so
so he can nurse?" that's what the mother said to her fawns.

            •

The two fawns helped the baby   65
suck their mother's nipple and get some milk.
Now the little boy

            •

was nursed, the little boy was nursed by the deer
o———n until he was full.
Their mother lay down cuddling him the way deer sleep   70
with her two fawns
together
lying beside her
and they SLEPT WITH THEIR FUR AROUND HIM.
They would nurse him, and so they lived on, lived on.   75
As he grew
he was without clothing, NAKED.
His elder brother and sister had fur:
they had fur, but he was NAKED and this was not good.

            •

The deer   80
the little boy's mother
spoke to her two fawns: "Tonight
when you sleep, you two will lie on both sides
and he will lie in the middle.
While you're sleeping   85
I'll go to Kachina Village,[7] for he is without clothing, naked, and
this is not good."

            •

---

7. This lies beneath the surface of the lake and comes to life only at night; it is the home of all the kachinas, the ancestral gods of the Zunis. Kachinas are impersonated by the Zunis in masked dances [Translator's note].

That's what she said to her children, and
there
at the village of He'shokta   90
                                        •
were young men
who went out hunting, and the young men who went out hunting
    looked for deer.
When they went hunting they made their kills around the
    Prairie-Dog Hills.
And their mother went to Kachina Village, she went o——n until
    she reached Kachina Village.
It was filled with dancing kachinas.   95
                                        •
"My fathers, my children, how have you been passing the days?"
    "Happily, our child, so you've come, sit down," they said.
"Wait, stop your dancing, our child has come and must have
    something to say," then the kachinas stopped.
The deer sat down the old lady deer sat down.
A kachina priest spoke to her:
"Now speak.   100
You must've come because you have something to say."
    "YES, in TRUTH
I have come because I have something to SAY.
There in the village of He'shokta is a priest's daughter
who abandoned her child.
We found him   105
we have been raising him.
But he is poor, without clothing, naked, and this
is not good.
So I've come to ask for clothes for him," that's what she said.
"Indeed." "Yes, that's why I've come, to ask for clothes for him."   110
"Well, there is always a way," they said.
Kyaklo
laid out his shirt.
Long Horn put in his kilt and his moccasins.
                                        •
And Huututu[8] put in his buckskin leggings   115
he laid out his bandoleer.[9]
                                        •
And Pawtiwa[1] laid out his macaw headdress.
                                        •
Also they put in the BELLS he would wear on his legs.
                                        •
Also they laid out
                                        •
strands of turquoise beads   120
moccasins.
So they laid it all out, hanks of yarn for his wrists and ankles
they gathered all his clothing.
When they had gathered it his mother put it on her back: "Well, I must GO

8. Kyaklo, Long Horn, and Huututu are kachina priests.   9. Belt worn over the shoulder to support
carried articles.   1. The chief priest.

but when he has grown larger I will return to ask for clothing again." 125
That's what she said. "Very well indeed."
Now the deer went her way.
When she got back to her children they were all sleeping.
When she got there they were sleeping and she
lay down beside them. 130
The little boy, waking up
began to nurse, his deer mother nursed him
and he went back to sleep. So they spent the night and then
(*with pleasure*) the little boy was clothed by his mother.
His mother clothed him. 135

When he was clothed he was no longer cold.
He went around playing with his elder brother and sister, they would
   run after each other, playing.
They lived on this way until he was grown.
And THEN
they went back up to their old home on the Prairie-Dog Hills.
   Having gone up 140
they remained there and would come down only to drink, in
   the evening.
There they lived o———n for a long time

until
from the village
his uncle 145
went out hunting. Going out hunting
he came along
down around
Worm Spring, and from there he went on towards

the Prairie-Dog Hills and came up near the edge of a valley there. 150
When he came to the woods on the Prairie-Dog Hills he looked down and
THERE IN THE VALLEY was the herd of deer. In the herd of deer
there was a little boy going around among them
dressed in white.
He had bells on his legs and he wore a macaw headdress. 155
He wore a macaw headdress, he was handsome, surely it was a boy
a male
a person among them.
While he was looking the deer mothers spotted him.
When they spotted the young man[2] they ran off. 160
There the little boy outdistanced the others.

"Haa———, who could that be?"
That's what his uncle said. "Who
could you be? Perhaps you are a daylight person."[3]
That's what his UNCLE thought and he didn't do ANYTHING
   to the deer. 165
He returned to his house in the evening.

---

2. That is, the little boy's uncle.   3. Living human beings are "daylight people"; all other beings, including animals, some plants, various natural phenomena, and deceased humans (kachinas), are called "raw people," because they do not depend on cooked food [Translator's note].

It was evening
dinner was ready and when they sat down to eat
the young man spoke:
"Today, while I was out hunting   170
when I reached the top
of the Prairie-Dog Hills, where the woods are, when I reached the top,
    THERE in the VALLEY was a HERD OF DEER.
There was a herd of deer

and with them was a LITTLE BOY:
whose child could it be?   175
When the deer spotted me they ran off and he outdistanced them.
He wore bells on his legs, he wore a macaw headdress, he was dressed in white."
That's what the young man was saying
telling his father.
It was one of the boy's OWN ELDERS   180
his OWN UNCLE had found him. (*audience*) Ee——so.
His uncle had found him.

Then
he said, "If
the herd is to be chased, then tell your Bow Priest."[4]   185
That's what the young man said. "Whose child could this be?
PERHAPS WE'LL CATCH HIM."
That's what he was saying.
A girl
a daughter of the priest said "Well, I'll go ask the Bow Priest."   190
She got up and went to the Bow Priest's house.
Arriving at the Bow Priest's house
she entered:
"My fathers, my mothers, how have you been passing the days?"
    "Happily, our child
so you've come, sit down," they said. "Yes.   195
Well, I'm
asking you to come.
Father asked that you come, that's what my father said," that's what
    she told the Bow Priest.
"Very well, I'll come," he said.
The girl went out and went home and after a while the Bow Priest
    came over.   200
He came to their house
while they were still eating.

"My children, how are you
this evening?" "Happy
sit down and eat," he was told.   205
He sat down and ate with them.
When they were finished eating, "Thank you," he said. "Eat plenty,"
    he was told.
He moved to another seat

---

4. In charge of hunting, warfare, and public announcements; he shouts from the top of the highest house [Translator's note].

•

and after a while
the Bow Priest questioned them: 210
"NOW, for what reason have you
summoned ME?
Perhaps it is because of a WORD of some importance that you have
summoned me. You must make this known to me
so that I may think about it as I pass the days," that's what he said.   215
"YES, in truth
today, this very day
my child here
went out to hunt.
Up on the Prairie-Dog Hills, there   220
HE SAW A HERD OF DEER.
But a LITTLE BOY WAS AMONG THEM.
Perhaps he is a daylight person.
Who could it be?
He was dressed in white and he wore a macaw headdress.   225
When the deer ran off he OUTDISTANCED them:
he must be very fast.
That's why my child here said, 'Perhaps
they should be CHASED, the deer should be chased.'
He wants to see him caught, that's what he's thinking.   230
Because he said this
I summoned you," he said. "Indeed."
"Indeed, well

                                            •

perhaps he's a daylight person, what else can he be?
It is said he was dressed in white, what else can he be?"   235
That's what they were saying.
"WHEN would you want to do this?" that's what he said.
The young man who had gone out hunting said, "Well, in four days
so we can prepare our weapons."
That's what he said.   240
"So you should tell your people that in FOUR DAYS there will be
    a deer chase."
That's what
he said. "Very well."

                                            •

(sharply) Because of the little boy the word was given out for
    the deer chase.
The Bow Priest went out and shouted it.   245
When he shouted the VILLAGERS
heard him.
(slowly) "In four days there will be a deer chase.
A little boy is among the deer, who could it be? With luck
you might CATCH him.   250
We don't know who it will be.
You will find a child, then," that's what he SAID as he shouted.

                                            •

Then they went to sleep and lived on with anticipation.
Now when it was the THIRD night, the eve of the chase

the deer   255
spoke to her son
when the deer had gathered:
"My son." "What is it?" he said.
"Tomorrow we'll be chased, the one who found us is your uncle.
When he found us he saw you, and that's why   260

we'll be chased.
They'll come out after you:
your uncles.

(*excited*) The uncle who saw you will ride a spotted horse, and
   HE'LL BE THE ONE who
WON'T LET YOU GO, and   265
your elder brothers, your mothers
no
he won't think of killing them, it'll be you alone
he'll think of, he'll chase.
You won't be the one to get tired, but we'll get tired.   270
It'll be you alone
WHEN THEY HAVE KILLED US ALL
and you will go on alone.
Your first uncle
will ride a spotted horse and a second uncle will ride a white horse.   275
THESE TWO WILL FOLLOW YOU.
You must pretend you are tired but keep on going
and they will catch you.
But WE
MYSELF, your elder SISTER, your elder BROTHER   280
ALL OF US

will go with you.
Wherever they take you we will go along with you."
That's what his deer mother told him that's what she said.
THEN HIS DEER MOTHER TOLD HIM EVERYTHING:
   "AND NOW
I will tell you everything.   285
From here

from this place
where we're living now, we went down to drink. When we went
   down to drink
it was one of your ELDERS, one of your OWN ELDERS   290
your mother who sits in a room on the fourth story down making
   basket-plaques:
IT WAS SHE
whom the Sun had made pregnant.
When her time was near
she went down to Water's End to the bank   295
to wash clothes
and when you were about to come out

she had pains, got out of the water
went to a TREE and there she just DROPPED you.
THAT is your MOTHER. 300
She's in a room on the fourth story down making basket-plaques,
    that's what you'll tell them.

                                    •

THAT'S WHAT SHE DID TO YOU, SHE JUST DROPPED YOU.
When we went down to drink
we found you, and because you have grown up
on my milk 305
and because of the thoughts of your Sun Father, you have grown
    fast.
Well, you
have looked at us
at your elder sister and your elder brother
and they have fur. 'Why don't I have fur like them?' you have
    asked. 310
But that is proper, for you are a daylight person.
That's why I went to Kachina Village to get clothes for you
the ones you were wearing.
You began wearing those when you were small
before you were GROWN. 315
Yesterday I went to get the clothes you're wearing now
the ones you will wear when they chase us. When you've been caught
you must tell these things to your elders.

                                    •

When they bring you in
when they've caught you and bring you in 320
you
you will go inside. When you go inside
your grandfather
a priest
will be sitting by the fire. 'My grandfather, how have you been passing
    the days?' 325
'Happily. As old as I am, I could be a grandfather to anyone, for we
    have many children,' he will say.
'Yes, but truly you are my real grandfather,' you will say.
When you come to where your grandmother is sitting, 'Grandmother
    of mine, how have you been passing the days?' you will say.
'Happily, our child, surely I could be a grandmother to anyone,
    for we have the whole village as our children,' she will say.
Then, with the uncles who brought you in and 330
with your three aunts, you will shake hands.
'WHERE IS MY MOTHER?' you will say.
'Who is your mother?' they will say. 'She's in a room on the
    fourth story down making basket-plaques, tell her to come in,'
    you will say.

                                    •

Your youngest aunt will go in to get her.
When she enters: 335
(sharply) 'There's a little boy who wants you, he says you are
    his mother.'

(*tight*) 'How could that be? I don't know any man, how could I
    have an offspring?'
'Yes, but he wants you,' she will say
and she will force her to come out.
THEN THE ONE WE TOLD YOU ABOUT WILL COME OUT: 340
you will shake hands with her, call her mother. 'Surely we could be
    mothers to anyone, for we have the whole village as our
    CHILDREN,' she will say to you.
'YES, BUT TRULY YOU ARE MY REAL MOTHER.
There, in a room on the fourth story down
you sit and work.
My Sun Father, where you sit in the light   345
my Sun Father
made you pregnant.
When you were about to deliver
it was to Water's End
that you went down to wash. You washed at the bank   350
and when I was about to come out
when it hurt you
you went to a tree and just dropped me there.
You gathered your clothes, put them on your back, and returned
to your house.   355
But my MOTHERS
HERE
found me. When they found me
because it was on their milk
that I grew, and because of the thoughts of my Sun Father   360
I grew fast.
I had no clothing
so my mother went to Kachina Village to ask for clothing.'
THAT'S WHAT YOU MUST SAY."

                                    •

That's what he was told, that's what his mother told him. "And 365
tonight
(*aside*) we'll go up on the Ruin Hills."
That's what the deer mother told her son. "We'll go to the Ruin
    Hills
we won't live here anymore.
(*sharply*) We'll go over there where the land is rough   370
for TOMORROW they will CHASE us.
Your uncles won't think of US, surely they will think of YOU
ALONE. They have GOOD HORSES," that's what
his mother told him. It was on the night before
that the boy   375
was told by his deer mother.
The boy became
so unhappy.
They slept through the night
and before dawn the deer   380
went to the Ruin Hills.

                                    •

They went there and remained, and the VILLAGERS AWOKE.
It was the day of the chase, as had been announced, and the people
   were coming out.
They were coming out, some carrying bows, some on foot and
some on horseback, they kept on this way   385
o———n they went on
past Stone Chief, along the trees, until they got to the Prairie-Dog
   Hills and there were no deer.
Their tracks led straight and they followed them.
Having found the trail they went on until
when they reached the Ruin Hills, there in the valley   390
beyond the thickets there
was the herd, and the
young man and two of his elder sisters were chasing each other
by the edge of the valley, playing together. Playing together
they were spotted.   395
The deer saw the people.
They fled.
Many were the people who came out after them
now they chased the deer.
Now and again they dropped them, killed them.   400
Sure enough the boy outdistanced the others, while his mother
   and his elder sister and brother
still followed their child. As they followed him
he was far in the lead, but they followed on, they were on the run
and sure enough his uncles weren't thinking about killing deer, it
   was the boy they were after.
And ALL THE PEOPLE WHO HAD COME   405
      KILLED THE DEER
                  killed the deer.
                        killed the deer.
Wherever they made their kills they gutted them, put them on
   their backs, and went home.
Two of the uncles
                   •
then
went ahead of the group, and a third uncle   410
(*voice breaking*) dropped his elder sister
his elder brother
his mother.
He gutted them there while the other two uncles went on. As they went ON
the boy pretended to be tired. The first uncle pleaded:
"Tísshomahhá![5]   415
STOP," he said, "Let's stop this contest now."
That's what he was saying as
the little boy kept on running.
As he kept on his bells went telele.
O———n, he went on this way   420
on until

                   •

5. A common interjection; roughly, "oh no!"

the little boy stopped and his uncle, dismounting
caught him.

         •

Having caught him
(*gently*) "Now come with me, get up," he said.   425
His uncle
helped his nephew get up, then his uncle got on the horse.
They went back. They went on
until they came to where his mother and his elder sister and brother were lying
and the third uncle was there. The third uncle was there.   430
"So you've come." "Yes."
The little boy spoke: "This is my mother, this is my
elder sister, this is my elder brother.
They will accompany me to my house.
They will accompany me," that's what the boy said.   435
"Very well."
His uncles put the deer on their horses' backs.
On they went, while the people were coming in coming in, and
    still the uncles didn't arrive, until at nightfall
the little boy was brought in, sitting up on the horse.
It was night and the people, a crowd of people, came out to see the boy as
    he was brought in on the horse through the plaza   440
and his mother and his elder sister and brother
came along also
as he was brought in.
His grandfather came out. When he came out the little boy and his
    uncle dismounted.
His grandfather took the lead with the little boy following, and they
    went up.   445
When they reached the roof his grandfather
made a corn-meal road[6]
and they entered.
His grandfather entered
with the little boy following   450
while his
uncles brought in the deer. When everyone was inside

         •

the little boy's grandfather spoke: "Sit down," and the little boy spoke to his
    grandfather as he came to where he was sitting:
"Grandfather of mine, how have you been passing the days?" that's
    what he said.
"Happily our child   455
surely I could be a grandfather to anyone,[7] for we have the whole village
    as our children." "Yes, but you are my real grandfather," he said.
When he came to where his grandmother was sitting he said the
    same thing.
"Yes, but surely I could be a grandmother to anyone, for we have many
    children." "Yes, but you are my real grandmother," he said.

---

6. In the "long ago," houses were entered through a trap-door in the roof; the boy and his grandfather go up an outside ladder to reach the roof and then down a second ladder into the house. Just before they enter the grandfather makes a "cornmeal road" by sprinkling a handful of cornmeal in front of them, thus treating the boy as an important ritual personage [Translator's note].   7. A priest is everyone's "grandfather."

He looked the way
his uncle had described him, he wore a macaw headdress and
   his clothes were white.   460
He had new moccasins, new buckskin leggings.
He wore a bandoleer and a macaw headdress.
He was a stranger.
He shook hands with his uncles and shook hands with his aunts.
"WHERE IS MY MOTHER?" he said.   465

•

"She's in a room on the fourth story down weaving basket-plaques,"
   he said.
"Tell her to come out."
Their younger sister went in.
"Hurry and come now:
some little boy has come and says you are his mother."   470
(*tight*) "How could that be?
I've never known any man, how could I have an offspring?" she said.
"Yes, but come on, he wants you, he wants you to come out."
Finally she was forced to come out.
The moment she entered the little boy   475
went up to his mother.
"Mother of mine, how have you been passing the days?"
"Happily, but surely I could be anyone's
mother, for we have many children," that's what his mother said.
That's what she said.   480

•

"YES INDEED
but you are certainly my REAL MOTHER.
YOU GAVE BIRTH TO ME," he said.

•

Then, just as his deer mother had told him to do
he told his mother everything: 485

•

"You really are my mother.
In a room on the fourth story down
you sit and work.
As you sit and work
the light comes through your window.   490
My Sun Father
made you pregnant.
When he made you pregnant you
sat in there and your belly began to grow large.   495
Your belly grew large
you
you were about to deliver, you had pains in your belly, you were
   about to give birth to me, you had pains in your belly
you gathered your clothes
and you went down to the bank to wash.
When you got there you   500
washed your clothes in the river.
When I was about to COME OUT and caused you pain
you got out of the water

you went to a juniper tree.
There I made you strain your muscles   505
and there you just dropped me.
When you dropped me
you made a little hole and placed me there.
You gathered your clothes
bundled them together   510
washed all the blood off carefully, and came back here.
When you had gone
my elders here
came down to DRINK
and found me.   515
They found me

                               •

I cried and they heard me.
Because of the milk
of my deer mother here   520
my elder sister and brother here
because of
their milk
I grew.
I had no clothing, I was poor.   525
My mother here went to Kachina Village to ask for my clothing.

That's where
she got my clothing.
That's why I'm clothed. Truly, that's why I was among them
that's why one of you   530
who went out hunting discovered me.
You talked about it and that's why these things happened today."
    (audience) Ee——so.
That's what the little boy said.

                               •

"THAT'S WHAT YOU DID AND YOU ARE MY REAL MOTHER," that's
    what he told his mother. At that moment his mother
embraced him embraced him.
His uncle got angry his uncle got angry.   535
He beat
his kinswoman
he beat his kinswoman.
That's how it happened.
The boy's deer elders were on the floor.   540
His grandfather then
spread some covers
on the floor, laid them there, and put strands of turquoise beads on them.[8]
After a while they skinned them.   545
With this done and dinner ready they ate with their son.

8. Joseph Peynetsa [Andrew Peynetsa's nephew, who helped with the translation] commented: "When the
deer die, they go to Kachina Village. And from there they go to their re-make, transform into another being,
maybe a deer. That's in the prayers the Zunis say for deer, and that's why you have to give them cornmeal
and put necklaces on them, so that they'll come back to your house once again" [Translator's note].

•

They slept through the night, and the next day
the little boy spoke: "Grandfather." "What is it?"
"Where is your quiver?" he said. "Well, it must be hanging in the other
  room," he said.

•

He went out, having been given the quiver, and wandered around.   550
He wandered around, he wasn't thinking of killing deer, he just
  wandered around.
In the evening he came home empty-handed.
They lived on

•

and slept through the night.
After the second night he was wandering around again.   555
The third one came
and on the fourth night, just after sunset, his mother
spoke to him: "I need
the center blades of the yucca plant," she said.
"Which kind of yucca?"   560
"Well, the large yucca, the center blades," that's what his mother said. "Indeed.
Tomorrow I'll try to find it for you," he said.
(aside) She was finishing her basket-plaque and this was for the outer part.
  (audience) Ee——so.
That's what she said.
The next morning, when he had eaten   565
he put the quiver on and went out.
He went up on Big Mountain and looked around until he found
  a large yucca
with very long blades.

•

"Well, this must be the kind you talked about," he said. It was the center
  blades she wanted.
He put down his bow and his quiver, got hold of the center blades, and
  began to pull.
(with strain) He pulled   570

it came loose suddenly
and he pulled it straight into his heart.
There he died.

•

He died and they waited for him but he didn't come.   575

•

When the Sun went down
and he still hadn't come, his uncles began to worry.
They looked for him.
They found his tracks, made torches, and followed him
until they found him with the center blades of the yucca in his heart.   580

•

Their
nephew
was found and they brought him home.
The next day

•

he was buried.   585
Now he entered upon the roads
of his elders.[9]
THIS WAS LIVED LONG AGO. LEE——SEMKONIKYA.[1]

9. The deer.   1. A standard closing, for which Tedlock has proposed the translation: "The word is just so—— short."

PABLO NERUDA
1904–1973

Love poet, nature poet, political poet, and poet of common things, the Nobel prize-winner Pablo Neruda is known equally as Latin America's most important twentieth-century poet and an advocate of justice and equality for the masses. His audience was humanity itself, and he engaged himself as poet and activist in the great issues of the day. Neruda's influence on the younger generation of Spanish and Spanish American literature was immense; for them, as Julio Cortázar wrote, he exemplified not only a newly materialist style and awareness, but also an *American* way of seeing. His America is not the "Saxon America" of the North, however (much as he admired Walt Whitman), but Latin America, which he saw as the essence of humanity and seed of the future. Whatever his varied styles (lyrical, polemic, objective, and prophetic) or subjects (love, daily life, elemental nature, political oppression), he evoked the most basic levels of human emotions and experience. From erotic love in all its sensuality to a passion for natural objects and their place in daily life, Neruda wrote about fundamental interactions. In the second half of his life, after seeing widespread poverty and squalor in the Far East and the savage destruction of the Spanish Civil War, he adopted the role of public poet, emphasizing the common people's struggle for survival and freedom in both ancient and modern times. Neruda possessed a faith in the power of language to represent reality—and to communicate—that is diametrically opposed to the skeptical views of Samuel Beckett and Alain Robbe-Grillet in this volume: for Neruda, "the word fills with meaning" and his *General Song* was the "common book of mankind."

He was born Neftalí Ricardo Reyes y Basoalto, on July 12, 1904, in the small town of Parral, in southern Chile. His mother, a schoolteacher, died a month after his birth, and his father, a railroad worker, moved in 1906 to another town, Temuco, where he remarried and where Neruda had his early schooling. The boy's stepmother was a kind peasant woman whom he loved and called his "guardian angel," but his father was a more distant figure. Their family was among the first white settlers to open up the indigenous lands of the Araucanian Mapuche tribe, a fact that Neruda—who had both Spanish and Indian blood—would recall with mixed feelings.

The young Neftalí Reyes attended school in Temuco, wrote poems in his arithmetic notebook, and read voraciously. Temuco, however, was a frontier town, and the boy's love of literature was not encouraged either at home or at school—with one exception. That exception was the poet Gabriela Mistral, principal of the girls' school at Temuco, who would herself win the Nobel Prize in literature in 1945. She encouraged the young writer and loaned him books: the son of the railroad worker who disapproved of literature read Russian novels, Symbolist poetry (translating Baudelaire), and works by the French science-fiction writer Jules Verne. Already beginning the prolific production that marked his career, he published an article and fourteen poems between 1917 and 1919, and began to win local literary prizes. At fifteen, seeking a pen name that would not be tied to the provinces, he chose the surname of a Czech writer, Jan Neruda, and the given name Pablo, which some have associated with the Evangelist Saint Paul.

In 1921, Neruda traveled to Santiago, the capital of Chile, where he planned to become a French teacher, and entered the Instituto Pedagógico. He earned a small income by writing articles for newspapers and journals, and by doing translations, but he was constantly hungry. He continued to write poetry and to embark on love affairs. In 1924, *Twenty Love Poems and a Song of Despair* was immediately popular and brought him a national reputation. Two women dominate these sensual and erotic poems, women who are concurrently equated with natural forces: "Body of woman, white hills, white thighs." Neruda fuses closeness and distance, intimacy and alienation: he sees his beloved as part of nature and an intimate companion, but he also addresses her as a separate, mysterious Other. It is a continuation of the Romantic fusion of woman and nature, and ends in Romantic separation and loneliness: "My voice tried to find the wind to touch her hearing" (*Tonight I Can Write . . .*). *Twenty Love Poems* established Neruda's reputation as both a love poet and a poet of nature, a reputation he would reinforce in later collections.

Although he published a novel, *The Inhabitant and His Hope*, and a collection of Surrealist-inspired poems, *Venture of the Infinite Man*, in 1926, he was unhappy with his continued poverty and looked for a way to leave Santiago. Like Rubén Darío, he benefited from the Latin American tradition of awarding diplomatic posts to talented artists and in 1927 was appointed Chile's consul to Rangoon, Burma. The next five years, during which he also served in Ceylon, Java, and Singapore, were not comfortable ones, for the poet had only a sketchy knowledge of English and his salary was dependent on the amount of consular work he was able to do. He supplemented his income by writing articles for the Santiago newspaper *La Nación* and, lonely and isolated, appalled at the squalor and misery brought by colonial occupation, started writing the somber poems that would be printed in the first volume of *Residence on Earth (1925–1931)* (1933). The despairing tone of this volume, with its existential uncertainties, distorted images, and focus on private experience, would be repudiated by Neruda in his more public, Marxist phase. According to Argentinian novelist Julio Cortázar, however, *Residence on Earth* had an enormous impact on the younger generation of Spanish American writers: "It required a different dimension of language and, after that, an *American* way of seeing that had not been seen until then." *Walking Around,* a poem from the second volume of *Residence on Earth (1925–1935)* (1935), conveys the collection's existential anguish and the poet's awareness of his surroundings—"It happens that I am tired of being a man"—but later in the poem, the speaker rebels at the scene through which he strides "with fury, with forgetfulness."

Neruda returned to Chile in 1932 and was sent as consul to Buenos Aires the following year. Although he did not care for bureaucratic work, he entered happily into the literary circles of the Argentinian capital, where he also became a friend of the visiting Spanish poet Federico García Lorca (see p. 2267). Their friendship was renewed in 1934 when Neruda went as consul to Spain, and Lorca introduced him to the Madrid audience in 1935 as "an authentic poet, one of those who has tuned his sense to a world which is not ours, and which few people perceive . . . [one of] the great ones." Neruda's fame grew with the publication of the second volume of *Residence on Earth*. It was a time of struggle between the established tradition of "pure poetry," represented by Juan Ramón Jiménez, and a new mode of "impure poetry," in which the poetic "I" was less controlling and remained open to the chaos of external phenomena. Neruda became a founding editor of a new poetry journal, *Green Horse for Poetry*, and published a combative manifesto, *Towards an Impure Poetry*, in the first issue of October 1935. "It is useful, at certain hours of the day and night, to look closely at the world of objects at rest. . . . From them flow the contacts of man with the earth, like an object lesson for all troubled lyricists." The battle continues in *Walking Around,* where he mocks the pure poet's traditional image of the poetic swan (compare Baudelaire, Mallarmé, and Darío in this volume) by describing himself as "a felt swan / navigating on a water of origin and ash"—the urban landscape. The poem's list of randomly encountered objects ("forgotten sets of teeth in a coffee-pot . . . stores full of orthopaedic appliances") contrasts with pure poetry's carefully arranged landscapes and suggests the Surrealists' enthusiasm for unpredictable reality.

Walking Around also demonstrates the poet's conversion to a more activist political stance, influenced by his friends, the radical poets Rafael Alberti and Miguel Hernández. In 1936, civil war broke out in Spain between the Republic and the forces of General Francisco Franco, and Neruda, like artists all over Europe, supported the side of the Republic; he lost his consul's post in consequence. His friend Lorca was dragged from home by Fascist guards and murdered. Neruda traveled, lectured, and set up various organizations (including a review, *Poets of the World Defend the Spanish People*) to aid the Spanish Republic. Maintaining close ties with the Communist party, which had joined the fight against Spanish Fascism, he published in 1937 a new collection of poems, *Spain in My Heart,* that heralded a change in his literary stance. From now on, he would be a public poet, reading his poems aloud and addressing not individuals but a larger community—a community that could be either contemporary (*I'm Explaining a Few Things*) or far removed (the Inca laborers of *The Heights of Macchu Picchu*). In *I'm Explaining a Few Things,* Neruda tells his listeners, who are presumably looking for beauty, philosophy, or an exotic portrait of the Chilean landscape, that things have changed in Spain and there are other topics for poetry. Flames, molten metal, dead children, and the blood of victims have replaced the house, flowers, and thriving marketplace that he once knew. Neruda's repeated exhortation "Come and see the blood in the streets!" illustrates the poet's intention to speak directly to his audience, and to articulate great issues instead of private feelings.

Further consular appointments took Neruda to Paris in 1939, where he was charged with helping refugees from Spain, and to Mexico, where he lived until 1943. Traveling throughout Central and South America, he absorbed images of people and places, and began to imagine a poem that would delineate Latin American identity. The gradual evolution of this plan is illustrated by the career of *The Song of Chile* (1943), which Neruda began in 1938 as a national epic but which was later incorporated as canto 7 of the broader *General Song* (1950). The *General Song* celebrates both Latin American identity and human beings generally, while describing Latin American history—a history that, after October 22, 1943, was anchored for Neruda in the lost Inca city of Macchu Picchu in Peru. (The usual spelling is "Machu Picchu," but Neruda uses "Macchu" throughout.) Climbing the mountain to its stone ruins on that day, the poet had an almost mystical vision of the past linked with vast natural forces and the progress of humanity, a vision that he expressed two years later in the crucial second canto of the *General Song: The Heights of Macchu Picchu.* The *General Song* is divided into fifteen cantos, each with its own subdivisions.

It begins with a description of the land's first inhabitants, focuses on the ancient mountain fortress of Macchu Picchu, continues with a thematic account of subsequent centuries of foreign invaders (including both Spanish Conquistadors and twentieth-century United States corporations), and denounces Latin American leaders who have betrayed their people. At this point, the linear history of Latin America gives way to seven thematically related but otherwise disparate cantos. Neruda now speaks in prophetic tones, invoking America as a whole (meaning Latin America), and he focuses on a variety of topics that include his own memories (*The Fugitive*), exhortations of others (*Let the Railsplitter Awake,* addressing the people of the United States), and a vision of all-embracing elemental life (*The Great Ocean*). The *General Song*'s violent criticism of North American commercial aggression has limited its audience in the United States, but the poem is internationally recognized as a major work of Latin American literature and a remarkable plea for universal justice and equality.

The second canto of the *General Song, The Heights of Macchu Picchu* was published as a separate poem in 1946 and only later integrated into the larger work. Its twelve sections (also called cantos) are divided into two broad movements that express different philosophical attitudes and a turning point in the poet's thought. Throughout the first five cantos, Neruda struggles with the sense of loss and alienation that dominated the first two volumes of his *Residence on Earth*; beginning with Canto VI, he describes his ascent to Macchu Picchu and the vision of a larger community of struggling, suffering human beings that now gives meaning to his hitherto solitary existence. The portion printed here, the second half of *The Heights of Macchu Picchu*, begins with the poet's invocation of the abandoned city after having climbed to its perch on a precipice in the Andes. He invokes the "mother of stone" and of the Latin American people, and bears witness to a lost civilization. Canto IX consists of a sequence of extraordinary metaphors that describe the city in fused images of nature and daily life, of the passage of time and intuited associations that transcend chronology. In Cantos X through XII, Neruda imagines the experience of the people who interest him most: not emperors, but everyday people, the laborers who built Macchu Picchu and knew hunger and fatigue. The geometry of Macchu Picchu's impressive architecture shapes, for him, a "hypotenuse of rough blood and sackcloth," and he calls out for the workers, his brothers, to speak to him of their long-gone suffering. Though they are dead, he imagines their experiences and voice coming to reside in his own flesh and blood, reborn in a brotherhood of the people.

Neruda lived as an exile during much of the time he wrote the *General Song*. He had returned to Chile in 1943, was elected in 1945 to the Chilean Senate as the representative of the Communist party, and worked for the candidacy of the future president, Gabriel González Videla. Two years later, González Videla had turned his back on leftist politics; when Neruda criticized him in an open letter, the government ordered his arrest and he was forced to flee. The conclusion of the *General Song* speaks bitterly of this period and of "my Canto general, written / on the run, singing beneath / the clandestine wings of my country." Celebrated internationally, officially honored in Latin America, Europe, India, and China, Neruda was nonetheless unable to return to Chile until 1952.

In that year, he turned to a different style: an unadorned, direct expression with everyday subject matter such as fire, rain, bread, clothes, a bee, or tomatoes. Focusing on everyday objects was not new for him, nor was the emphasis on nature, but this time he would not use intricate allusions or the *General Song*'s rhetorical grandeur. This new simplicity stemmed from Neruda's commitment to his role as public poet; he felt a responsibility to write for simple people, including those who were just learning to read. "We must go back to what is simply human," he said, and the *Elemental Odes* (1954) respond to this need. The short lines, vivid, realistic images, humorous narrative, and cheerful preparations for a feast in *Ode to the Tomato* create an attractive scene of joyful abundance whose subtle artistry is concealed. Other books of love poetry followed—*The Captain's Verses* (1952) and *One Hundred Sonnets of Love* (1959)—and various autobiographical books, including the five-volume poetic *Notes from Isla Negra* (1964), written from the seacoast home he cherished and filled with unusual objects (shells, carved figureheads, a stuffed horse).

Neruda continued to write prolifically in various styles, publishing one or more books a year; he traveled around the world, lecturing and reading his poetry, and he continued to be politically active. After the election of Salvador Allende as president of Chile in 1970, Neruda was appointed ambassador to Paris, a position he accepted despite having been recently diagnosed as having cancer. In 1971, Neruda was awarded the Nobel Prize for literature, and, in 1972, he returned to Isla Negra, gravely ill. The news at home was not good: political tensions were mounting in Chile, and

Neruda watched the rising unrest daily on television. His friend, President Allende, was assassinated in a military coup on September 11, 1973, and the poet died twelve days later. The first public demonstration against Pinochet's military government took place at Neruda's funeral, a gesture that proved dangerous (his house was sacked afterward) but a fitting tribute to this national poet and representative of the people.

Pablo Neruda, *Memoirs*, translated by Hardie St. Martin (1977), contains much biographical information; Manuel Duran and Margery Safir, *Earth Tones: The Poetry of Pablo Neruda* (1981), is an excellent thematic study that also offers a short biography; *Pablo Neruda*, edited by Harold Bloom (1989), contains nineteen valuable essays and reminiscences by scholars, translators, and those who knew Neruda; John Felstiner, *Translating Neruda: The Way to Macchu Picchu* (1980), describes in detail the process of translating *The Heights of Macchu Picchu* in terms of Neruda's life and perspectives; Louis Poirot, *Pablo Neruda: Absence and Presence* (1990), matches photographs of Neruda, his friends, and his homes with related passages from the poet, his wife, and friends. Also recommended are James Nolan, *Poet-Chief: The Native American Poetics of Walt Whitman and Pablo Neruda* (1994), Salvatore Bizzarro, *Pablo Neruda: All Poets the Poet* (1979), and Enrico Mario Santi, *Pablo Neruda: The Poetics of Prophecy* (1982).

PRONOUNCING GLOSSARY

The following list uses common English syllables and stress accents to provide rough equivalents of selected words whose pronunciation may be unfamiliar to the general reader.

Argüelles: *ar-hweh'-jes*

Castille: *cah-stee'*

Macchu Picchu: *mah'-choo peek'-choo*

Mantur: *mahn-toor*

Pablo Neruda: *pah'-bloh nay-roo'-dah*

Raúl: *rah-ool'*

Urubamba: *oo-roo-bahm'-ba*

Wilkamayu: *vill-kah-mah'-joo*

Wiracocha: *veer-ah-coch'-ah*

Tonight I Can Write . . . [1]

Tonight I can write the saddest lines.

Write, for example, 'The night is shattered
and the blue stars shiver in the distance.'

The night wind revolves in the sky and sings.

Tonight I can write the saddest lines.   5
I loved her, and sometimes she loved me too.

Through nights like this one I held her in my arms.
I kissed her again and again under the endless sky.

She loved me, sometimes I loved her too.
How could one not have loved her great still eyes.   10

Tonight I can write the saddest lines.
To think that I do not have her. To feel that I have lost her.

---

1. Translated by W. S. Merwin.

To hear the immense night, still more immense without her.
And the verse falls to the soul like dew to the pasture.

What does it matter that my love could not keep her.   15
The night is shattered and she is not with me.

This is all. In the distance someone is singing. In the distance.
My soul is not satisfied that it has lost her.

My sight searches for her as though to go to her.
My heart looks for her, and she is not with me.   20

The same night whitening the same trees.
We, of that time, are no longer the same.

I no longer love her, that's certain, but how I loved her.
My voice tried to find the wind to touch her hearing.

Another's. She will be another's. Like my kisses before.   25
Her voice. Her bright body. Her infinite eyes.

I no longer love her, that's certain, but maybe I love her.
Love is so short, forgetting is so long.

Because through nights like this one I held her in my arms
my soul is not satisfied that it has lost her.   30

Though this be the last pain that she makes me suffer
and these the last verses that I write for her.

Walking Around[2]

It happens that I am tired of being a man.
It happens that I go into the tailor's shops and the movies
all shrivelled up, impenetrable, like a felt swan
navigating on a water of origin and ash.

The smell of barber shops makes me sob out loud.   5
I want nothing but the repose either of stones or of wool,
I want to see no more establishments, no more gardens,
nor merchandise, nor glasses, nor elevators.

It happens that I am tired of my feet and my nails
and my hair and my shadow.   10
It happens that I am tired of being a man.

Just the same it would be delicious
to scare a notary with a cut lily
or knock a nun stone dead with one blow of an ear.

2. Translated by W. S. Merwin.

It would be beautiful   15
to go through the streets with a green knife
shouting until I died of cold.

I do not want to go on being a root in the dark,
hesitating, stretched out, shivering with dreams,
downwards, in the wet tripe of the earth,   20
soaking it up and thinking, eating every day.

I do not want to be the inheritor of so many misfortunes.
I do not want to continue as a root and as a tomb,
as a solitary tunnel, as a cellar full of corpses,
stiff with cold, dying with pain.   25

For this reason Monday burns like oil
at the sight of me arriving with my jail-face,
and it howls in passing like a wounded wheel,
and its footsteps towards nightfall are filled with hot blood.

And it shoves me along to certain corners, to certain damp houses,   30
to hospitals where the bones come out of the windows,
to certain cobblers' shops smelling of vinegar,
to streets horrendous as crevices.

There are birds the colour of sulphur, and horrible intestines
hanging from the doors of the houses which I hate,   35
there are forgotten sets of teeth in a coffee-pot,
there are mirrors
which should have wept with shame and horror,
there are umbrellas all over the place, and poisons, and navels.

I stride along with calm, with eyes, with shoes,   40
with fury, with forgetfulness,
I pass, I cross offices and stores full of orthopaedic appliances,
and courtyards hung with clothes on wires,
underpants, towels and shirts which weep
slow dirty tears.   45

I'm Explaining a Few Things[3]

You are going to ask: and where are the lilacs?
and the poppy-petalled metaphysics?
and the rain repeatedly spattering
its words and drilling them full
of apertures and birds?   5

I'll tell you all the news.

3. Translated by Nathaniel Tarn.

I lived in a suburb,
a suburb of Madrid,[4] with bells,
and clocks, and trees.

From there you could look out   10
over Castille's[5] dry face:
a leather ocean.
            My house was called
the house of flowers, because in every cranny
geraniums burst: it was
a good-looking house   15
with its dogs and children.
                  Remember, Raúl?
Eh, Rafael?
            Federico,[6] do you remember
from under the ground
my balconies on which
the light of June drowned flowers in your mouth?
                                Brother, my brother! 20
Everything
loud with big voices, the salt of merchandises,
pile-ups of palpitating bread,
the stalls of my suburb of Argüelles with its statue
like a drained inkwell in a swirl of hake:[7]   25
oil flowed into spoons,
a deep baying
of feet and hands swelled in the streets,
metres, litres, the sharp
measure of life,
                  stacked-up fish,   30
the texture of roofs with a cold sun in which
the weather vane falters,
the fine, frenzied ivory of potatoes,
wave on wave of tomatoes rolling down to the sea.

And one morning all that was burning,   35
one morning the bonfires
leapt out of the earth
devouring human beings—
and from then on fire,
gunpowder from then on,   40
and from then on blood.
Bandits[8] with planes and Moors,
bandits with finger-rings and duchesses,
bandits with black friars spattering blessings
came through the sky to kill children   45

---

4. The capital of Spain.   5. Spain.   6. I.e., the poet Federico García Lorca, who was murdered by the Fascists on August 19, 1936. *Rafael:* his friend, the poet Rafael Alberti.   7. A fish similar to the cod. *Argüelles:* a a busy shopping area in Madrid, near the university.   8. Neruda lists categories of invaders. *Moors:* probably an analogy between the early Muslim invaders of Spain and German and Italian pilots who bombed the village of Guernica in April 1937. *Finger-rings, duchesses, friars* imply a collusion of the wealthy, the aristocracy, and the Church to suppress the people.

and the blood of children ran through the streets
without fuss, like children's blood.

Jackals that the jackals would despise,
stones that the dry thistle would bite on and spit out,
vipers that the vipers would abominate!   50

Face to face with you I have seen the blood
of Spain tower like a tide
to drown you in one wave
of pride and knives!

Treacherous   55
generals:
see my dead house,
look at broken Spain:
from every house burning metal flows
instead of flowers,   60
from every socket of Spain
Spain emerges
and from every dead child a rifle with eyes,
and from every crime bullets are born
which will one day find   65
the bull's eye of your hearts.

And you will ask: why doesn't his poetry
speak of dreams and leaves
and the great volcanoes of his native land?

Come and see the blood in the streets.   70
Come and see
the blood in the streets.
Come and see the blood
in the streets!

Canto General

From *The Heights of Macchu Picchu*[9]

VI

And so I scaled the ladder of the earth
amid the atrocious maze of lost jungles
up to you, Macchu Picchu.
High citadel of terraced stones,
at long last the dwelling of him whom the earth   5
did not conceal in its slumbering vestments.
In you, as in two parallel lines,

9. Translated by Jack Schmitt. *Macchu Picchu*: ancient city of the Incas, situated on a remote precipice in the Andes mountains of Peru; the city escaped the Spanish invaders and was rediscovered in 1911. The Inca empire flourished in the 14th century and was destroyed by Francisco Pizarro in 1532.

the cradle of lightning and man
was rocked in a wind of thorns.

Mother of stone, sea spray of the condors. 10

Towering reef of the human dawn.

Spade lost in the primal sand.

This was the dwelling, this is the site:
here the full kernels of corn rose
and fell again like red hailstones. 15

Here the golden fiber emerged form the vicuña[1]
to clothe love, tombs, mothers,
the king, prayers, warriors.

Here man's feet rested at night
beside the eagle's feet, in the high gory 20
retreats, and at dawn
they trod the rarefied mist with feet of thunder
and touched lands and stones
until they recognized them in the night or in death.

I behold vestments and hands, 25
the vestige of water in the sonorous void,
the wall tempered by the touch of a face
that beheld with my eyes the earthen lamps,
that oiled with my hands the vanished
wood: because everything—clothing, skin, vessels, 30
words, wine, bread—
is gone, fallen to earth.

And the air flowed with orange-blossom
fingers over all the sleeping:
a thousand years of air, months, weeks of air, 35
of blue wind, of iron cordillera,[2]
like gentle hurricanes of footsteps
polishing the solitary precinct of stone.

VII

O remains of a single abyss, shadows of one gorge—
the deep one—the real, most searing death
attained the scale
of your magnitude,
and from the quarried stones, 5
from the spires,
from the terraced aqueducts
you tumbled as in autumn

---

1. A llama-like animal, found in the Andes, that possesses a fine soft fleece.   2. Mountain range.

to a single death.
Today the empty air no longer weeps,   10
no longer knows your feet of clay,
has now forgotten your pitchers that filtered the sky
when the lightning's knives emptied it,
and the powerful tree was eaten away
by the mist and felled by the wind.   15
It sustained a hand that fell suddenly
from the heights to the end of time.
You are no more, spider hands, fragile
filaments, spun web:
all that you were has fallen: customs, frayed   20
syllables, masks of dazzling light.

But a permanence of stone and word:
the citadel was raised like a chalice in the hands
of all, the living, the dead, the silent, sustained
by so much death, a wall, from so much life a stroke   25
of stone petals: the permanent rose, the dwelling:
this Andean reef of glacial colonies.

When the clay-colored hand
turned to clay, when the little eyelids closed,
filled with rough walls, brimming with castles,   30
and when the entire man was trapped in his hole,
exactitude remained hoisted aloft:
this high site of the human dawn:
the highest vessel that has contained silence:
a life of stone after so many lives.   35

VIII

Rise up with me, American[3] love.

Kiss the secret stones with me.
The torrential silver of the Urubamba[4]
makes the pollen fly to its yellow cup.
It spans the void of the grapevine,   5
the petrous plant, the hard wreath
upon the silence of the highland casket.
Come, minuscule life, between the wings
of the earth, while—crystal and cold, pounded air
extracting assailed emeralds—   10
O, wild water, you run down from the snow.

Love, love, even the abrupt night,
from the sonorous Andean flint
to the dawn's red knees,
contemplates the snow's blind child.   15

---

3. For Neruda (and for many Latin Americans), *America* refers to Latin America; North America is called
"Saxon America."   4. The river flowing through the valley below Macchu Picchu, called Wilkamayu by
the Indians.

O, sonorous threaded Wilkamayu,
when you beat your lineal thunder
to a white froth, like wounded snow,
when your precipitous storm
sings and batters, awakening the sky,   20
what language do you bring to the ear recently
wrenched from your Andean froth?

Who seized the cold's lightning
and left it shackled in the heights,
dispersed in its glacial tears,   25
smitten in its swift swords,
hammering its embattled stamens,
borne on its warrior's bed,
startled in its rocky end?

What are your tormented sparks saying?   30
Did your secret insurgent lightning
once journey charged with words?
Who keeps on shattering frozen syllables,
black languages, golden banners,
deep mouths, muffled cries,   35
in your slender arterial waters?

Who keeps on cutting floral eyelids
that come to gaze from the earth?
Who hurls down the dead clusters
that fell in your cascade hands   40
to strip the night stripped
in the coal of geology?

Who flings the branch down from its bonds?
Who once again entombs farewells?

Love, love, never touch the brink   45
or worship the sunken head:
let time attain its stature
in its salon of shattered headsprings,
and, between the swift water and the walls,
gather the air from the gorge,   50
the parallel sheets of the wind,
the cordilleras' blind canal,
the harsh greeting of the dew,
and, rise up, flower by flower, through the dense growth,
treading the hurtling serpent.   55

In the steep zone—forest and stone,
mist of green stars, radiant jungle—
Mantur explodes like a blinding lake
or a new layer of silence.

Come to my very heart, to my dawn,   60
up to the crowned solitudes.
The dead kingdom is still alive.

And over the Sundial the sanguinary shadow
of the condor[5] crosses like a black ship.

IX

Sidereal eagle, vineyard of mist.
Lost bastion, blind scimitar.
Spangled waistband, solemn bread.
Torrential stairway, immense eyelid.
Triangular tunic, stone pollen.   5
Granite lamp, stone bread.
Mineral serpent, stone rose.
Entombed ship, stone headspring.
Moonhorse, stone light.
Equinoctial square, stone vapor.   10
Ultimate geometry, stone book.
Tympanum fashioned amid the squalls.
Madrepore[6] of sunken time.
Rampart tempered by fingers.
Ceiling assailed by feathers.   15
Mirror bouquets, stormy foundations.
Thrones toppled by the vine.
Regime of the enraged claw.
Hurricane sustained on the slopes.
Immobile cataract of turquoise.   20
Patriarchal bell of the sleeping.
Hitching ring of the tamed snows.
Iron recumbent upon its statues.
Inaccessible dark tempest.
Puma hands, bloodstained rock.   25
Towering sombrero, snowy dispute.
Night raised on fingers and roots.
Window of the mists, hardened dove.
Nocturnal plant, statue of thunder.
Essential cordillera, searoof.   30
Architecture of lost eagles.
Skyrope, heavenly bee.
Bloody level, man-made star.
Mineral bubble, quartz moon.
Andean serpent, brow of amaranth.[7]   35
Cupola of silence, pure land.
Seabride, tree of cathedrals.
Cluster of salt, black-winged cherry tree.
Snow-capped teeth, cold thunderbolt.
Scored moon, menacing stone.   40

5. The heights of Macchu Picchu and the smaller Huayna Picchu were said to form the shape of a condor,
a large vulturelike bird seen as the messenger of humanity. *Sundial*: the *intihuatana*, or "hitching post of
the sun," a large altar carved directly out of the granite; its shape and position served to predict the date
of the winter solstice and other periods of importance to agriculture.   6. Coral.   7. An annual plant
with flowers and highly nutritious edible seeds.

Headdresses of the cold, action of the air.
Volcano of hands, obscure cataract.
Silver wave, pointer of time.

X

Stone upon stone, and man, where was he?
Air upon air, and man, where was he?
Time upon time, and man, where was he?
Were you too a broken shard
of inconclusive man, of empty raptor,   5
who on the streets today, on the trails,
on the dead autumn leaves, keeps
tearing away at the heart right up to the grave?
Poor hand, foot, poor life . . .
Did the days of light   10
unraveled in you, like raindrops
on the banners of a feast day,
give petal by petal of their dark food
to the empty mouth?
                  Hunger, coral of mankind,
hunger, secret plant, woodcutters' stump,   15
hunger, did the edge of your reef rise up
to these high suspended towers?

I want to know, salt of the roads,
show me the spoon—architecture, let me
scratch at the stamens of stone with a little stick,   20
ascend the rungs of the air up to the void,
scrape the innards until I touch mankind.

Macchu Picchu, did you put
stone upon stone and, at the base, tatters?
Coal upon coal and, at the bottom, tears?   25
Fire in gold and, within it, the trembling
drop of red blood?
Bring me back the slave that you buried!
Shake from the earth the hard bread
of the poor wretch, show me   30
the slave's clothing and his window.
Tell me how he slept when he lived.
Tell me if his sleep was
harsh, gaping, like a black chasm
worn by fatigue upon the wall.   35
The wall, the wall! If upon his sleep
each layer of stone weighed down, and if he fell beneath it
as beneath a moon, with his dream!
Ancient America, sunken bride,
your fingers too,   40
on leaving the jungle for the high void of the gods,
beneath the nuptial standards of light and decorum,
mingling with the thunder of drums and spears,
your fingers, your fingers too,
which the abstract rose, the cold line, and   45

the crimson breast of the new grain transferred
to the fabric of radiant substance, to the hard cavities—
did you, entombed America, did you too store in the depths
of your bitter intestine, like an eagle, hunger?

XI

Through the hazy splendor,
through the stone night, let me plunge my hand,
and let the aged heart of the forsaken beat in me
like a bird captive for a thousand years!
Let me forget, today, this joy, which is greater than the sea,   5
because man is greater than the sea and its islands,
and we must fall into him as into a well to emerge from the bottom
with a bouquet of secret water and sunken truths.
Let me forget, great stone, the powerful proportion,
the transcendent measure, the honeycombed stones,   10
and from the square let me today run
my hand over the hypotenuse of rough blood and sackcloth.
When, like a horseshoe of red elytra,[8] the frenzied condor
beats my temples in the order of its flight,
and the hurricane of cruel feathers sweeps the somber dust   15
from the diagonal steps, I do not see the swift brute,
I do not see the blind cycle of its claws,
I see the man of old, the servant, asleep in the fields,
I see a body, a thousand bodies, a man, a thousand women,
black with rain and night, beneath the black squall,   20
with the heavy stone of the statue:
Juan Stonecutter, son of Wiracocha[9]
Juan Coldeater, son of a green star,
Juan Barefoot, grandson of turquoise,
rise up to be born with me, my brother.   25

XII

Rise up to be born with me, my brother.

Give me your hand from the deep
zone of your disseminated sorrow.
You'll not return from the bottom of the rocks.
You'll not return from subterranean time.   5
Your stiff voice will not return.
Your drilled eyes will not return.
Behold me from the depths of the earth,
laborer, weaver, silent herdsman:
tamer of the tutelary guanacos:[1]   10
mason of the defied scaffold:
bearer of the Andean tears:
jeweler with your fingers crushed:
tiller trembling in the seed:
potter spilt in your clay: 15

8. An insect's wing cases.   9. Inca rain god who taught the arts of civilization to humanity.   1. Reddish-brown grazing animals related to the llama.

bring to the cup of this new life, brothers,
all your timeless buried sorrows.
Show me your blood and your furrow,
tell me: I was punished here,
because the jewel did not shine or the earth   20
did not surrender the gemstone or kernel on time:
show me the stone on which you fell
and the wood on which you were crucified,
strike the old flintstones,
the old lamps, the whips sticking   25
throughout the centuries to your wounds
and the war clubs glistening red.
I've come to speak through your dead mouths.
Throughout the earth join all
the silent scattered lips   30
and from the depths speak to me all night long,
as if I were anchored with you,
tell me everything, chain by chain,
link by link, and step by step,
sharpen the knives that you've kept,   35
put them in my breast and in my hand,
like a river of yellow lightning,
like a river of buried jaguars,
and let me weep hours, days, years,
blind ages, stellar centuries.   40

Give me silence, water, hope.

Give me struggle, iron, volcanoes.

Cling to my body like magnets.

Hasten to my veins and to my mouth.

Speak through my words and my blood.   45

Ode to the Tomato[2]

The street
drowns in tomatoes:
noon,
summer,
light   5
breaks
in two
tomato
halves,
and the streets   10
run
with juice.

2. Translated by Nathaniel Tarn.

In December[3]
the tomato
cuts loose,
invades   15
kitchens,
takes over lunches,
settles
at rest   20
on sideboards,
with the glasses,
butter dishes,
blue salt-cellars.
It has   25
its own radiance,
a goodly majesty.
Too bad we must
assassinate:
a knife   30
plunges
into its living pulp,
red
viscera,
a fresh,   35
deep,
inexhaustible
sun
floods the salads
of Chile,   40
beds cheerfully
with the blonde onion,
and to celebrate
oil
the filial essence   45
of the olive tree
lets itself fall
over its gaping hemispheres,
the pimento
adds   50
its fragrance,
salt its magnetism—
we have the day's
wedding:
parsley   55
flaunts
its little flags,
potatoes
thump to a boil,
the roasts   60
beat
down the door

3. Summer in Chile.

with their aromas:
it's time!
let's go!   65
and upon
the table,
belted by summer,
tomatoes,
stars of the earth,   70
stars multiplied
and fertile
show off
their convolutions,
canals   75
and plenitudes
and the abundance
boneless,
without husk,
or scale or thorn,   80
grant us
the festival
of ardent colour
and all-embracing freshness.

SAMUEL BECKETT
1906–1989

The sparest, starkest representation of the human condition in all its "absurd" emptiness fills Samuel Beckett's novels and plays. Not that other authors do not concern themselves with the problem of representing reality, but where Pirandello plays with allusions to an elusive identity, Joyce with the stream of consciousness, and Proust with layers of the self reconstituted through affective memory, Beckett's world is haunted—like that of Kafka—by an absence of meaning at the core. Whether expressed by the protagonist's ramblings in the novels *Molloy* (1951), *Malone Dies* (1951), or *The Unnamable* (1953), by the stripped-down dialogue of the plays *Waiting for Godot* (1952) and *Endgame* (1957), or by the telegraphic style of a late novel, *How It Is* (1961), Beckett's characters engage in a desperate attempt to find or to create meaning for themselves. Born into a world without reason, they live out their lives waiting for an explanation that never comes and whose existence may be only a figment of their imagination. In the meantime, human relationships are reduced to the most elemental tensions of cruelty, hope, frustration, and disillusionment around themes of birth, death, human emotions, material obstacles, and unending consciousness. Beckett's comedy of errors is a bitter one and, even in its puns and parodies, draws heavily on what the author has described as "the power of the text to claw."

Like Joyce and Yeats, Beckett was born in Ireland; like Joyce, he chose to live abroad for most of his life. Born near Dublin on April 13, 1906, he was educated in Ireland and received a B.A. from Trinity College in 1927. From 1928 to 1930, he taught English at the École Normale Supérieure in Paris, where he met James Joyce and was for a while influenced by the older novelist's exuberant and punning use of language. Beckett wrote an essay on the early stages of Joyce's *Finnegans Wake* and later helped in the

French translation of part of the book. In 1930 he entered a competition for a poem on the subject of time and won first prize with a ninety-eight-line (and seventeen-footnote) monologue, *Whoroscope,* spoken by the seventeenth-century French physicist and philosopher René Descartes. Beckett returned to Trinity College, where he took an M.A. in 1931, published an essay on Proust, and stayed on the following year to teach French. It was a brief academic career, for he gave up teaching in 1932 and, after living in England, France, and Germany, made Paris his permanent home in 1937. Although two early novels, *Murphy* (1938) and *Watt* (1953), were written in English, Beckett was already turning to French as his preferred language for original composition; in the years after World War II, he wrote almost exclusively in French and only later translated (often with substantial changes) the same texts into English. He said that he wrote in French because it was easier to write "without style"— without the native speaker's temptation to elegance and virtuoso display. Although no generalization holds true for all cases, comparing the French and English versions of the same work often suggests just such a contrast, with the French text closer to basic grammatical forms and, therefore, possessing a harsher, less nuanced focus.

Whether comic or despairing (often both), Beckett's characters ring changes on the Cartesian image of the Rational Man that has been at the base of Western cultural attitudes ever since the philosopher René Descartes moved from specific questions about the physical sciences to the larger question of human existence. Descartes, like Beckett, went back to zero in order not to be led astray by any preconceived assumptions or doctrines. He doubted everything—except that he doubted, which in itself indicated that he was thinking and that since "I think, therefore I am" (*Cogito, ergo sum*). Upon that certainty Descartes erected a logical system for exploring the natural universe and explaining the human condition. Beckett is not so sure that logic allows us to know what we are looking at or to match up our terminology with reality at all. In *Watt,* the protagonist is caught in a peculiar hesitation inasmuch as things, "if they consented to be named, did so as it were with reluctance." He looks at a pot, but "it was not a pot, the more he looked, the more he reflected, the more he felt sure of that, that it was not a pot at all. It resembled a pot, it was almost a pot, but it was not a pot of which one could say, Pot, pot and be comforted." The gentle bewilderment that Watt feels turns bitter and more dangerous in later novels such as the famous trilogy (*Molloy, Malone Dies,* and *The Unnamable*), or in *How It Is,* which refuses to present any image of rational control as it murmurs, free of punctuation, the monologue of an unstructured consciousness inside an accompanying "quaqua [bzzz bzzz] on all sides."

The narrative perspective in the trilogy moves from a series of related monologue stories, in which narrators come more and more to resemble one another, to the ramblings of an "unnamable" speaker who seems to represent them all at the end. In *Molloy,* there are two interlocking points of view, as first Molloy tells of setting out on a bicycle to visit his bedridden mother, a search that takes him months and leads him all over (with many echoes of Homer's *Odyssey*). The last we hear of Molloy is that he is crippled and has lost his bicycle but is determined still to proceed if only by rolling; Moran takes over at that point and describes a corresponding search for Molloy in the course of which he loses his bicycle, is crippled, and ends up frustrated back home. The next novel, *Malone Dies,* is similarly divided between protagonists, even if in the mind of a single narrator: a dying and bedridden Malone writes the diary of his last days and also composes the story of Macmann, who is to die at the same moment as Malone and apparently does so as the novel ends. The last in the trilogy, *The Unnamable,* has no fixed authorial perspective or claim to responsibility. "I'm in words, made of words." Someone (unnamed and—by now—clearly unnamable) is seated in an undefined gray space and time, writing a series of stories that may be the tales of Malone, Malloy, and Moran, or of a new Mahood who also becomes Worm, who may in turn be the narrator writing stories about himself; or it may simply evoke the act of storytelling as it creates fictions of life to establish some mode of reality. In 1949, when the trilogy was just complete, Beckett published a dialogue on modern art that described the artist's disgust with traditional art's "puny exploits . . . doing a little better the same old thing" and his preference for "the expression that there is nothing to express, nothing with which to express, nothing from which to express, no power to express, no desire to express, together with the obligation to express." The disintegration of narrative perspective in Beckett's fiction is one means of denying that there is a knowable "something to express" or an authoritative point of view from which to express "nothing."

How can one possibly make a convincing stage play out of "nothing"? The popularity of Beckett's first performed play, *Waiting for Godot* (French version presented 1953; English, 1955), showed that absurdist theater—with its empty, repetitive dialogue, its grotesquely bare yet apparently symbolic settings, and its refusal to build to a dramatic climax—had meaning even for audiences used to theatrical realism and logically developing plots. These audiences found two clownlike tramps, Vladimir and Estragon (Didi and Gogo), talking, quarreling, falling down, contemplating suicide, and generally filling up time with conversation that ranges from vaudeville patter to metaphysical speculation as they wait under a tree for a Godot who never comes. Instead, the two are joined in the middle of each act by another grotesque pair: the rich Pozzo and his brutally abused servant Lucky, whom he leads around by a rope tied to his neck. The popular interpretation of "Godot" as a diminutive for "God" and of the play as a statement of existential anguish at the inexplicable human condition, is scarcely defused by Beckett's caution that "If by Godot I had meant God, I would have said God." Yet identifying Godot is less important than identifying the ignominious plight on stage as symbolically our own and identifying *with* the characters as they express the anxious, often repugnant but also comic picture of human relationships in an absurd universe.

After the popular success of *Waiting for Godot*, Beckett wrote *Endgame* (French version performed 1957; English, 1958) and a series of stage plays and brief pieces for the radio. The stage plays have the same bare yet striking settings: *Krapp's Last Tape* (1958) presents an old man sitting at a table with his tape recorder, recalling a love affair thirty years past; and *Happy Days* (1961) portrays a married couple in which Winnie, the wife, chatters ceaselessly about her possessions although she is buried up to her waist in the first act and to her neck in the second. When Beckett received the Nobel Prize in literature in 1969, he was recognized as the purest exponent of the twentieth century's chief philosophical dilemma: the notion of the "absurd," or the grotesque contradiction between human attempts to discover meaning in life and the simultaneous conviction that there is no "meaning" available that we have not created ourselves. *Endgame,* often called Beckett's major achievement, is a prime example of this dilemma.

When the curtain rises on *Endgame,* it is as though the world were awaking from sleep. The sheets draping the furniture and central character are taken off, and Hamm sets himself in motion like an actor or chess pawn: "Me . . . to play." Yet we are also near the end for, as the title implies, nothing new will happen; an "endgame" is the final phase of a chess game, the stage at which the end is predictably in sight although the play must still be completed. Throughout, the theme of "end," "finish," "no more" is sounded, even while Hamm notes the passage of time: "Something is taking its course." But time does not lead anywhere; it is either past or present and always barren. The past exists as Nagg's and Nell's memories, as Hamm's story, which may or may not describe Clov's entry into the home, and as a period in which Clov once loved Hamm. The present shows four characters dwindling away, alone in a dead world, caught between visions of dusty hell and dreams of life reborn. In one of the biblical echoes that permeate the play, Hamm and Clov repeatedly evoke the last words of the crucified Jesus in the Gospel according to St. John: "It is finished." But this is not a biblical morality play, and *Endgame* describes a world not of divine creation, but of self-creation. Hamm may be composing and directing the entire performance: a storyteller and playwright with "asides" and "last soliloquy" whose "dialogue" keeps Clov on stage against his will, a mad artist who (when looking out the window onto a flourishing world) can see only dust and ashes, or a magician presiding over an imaginary kingdom who concludes an inner story and unavailing prayer with Prospero's line from Shakespeare's *The Tempest* (4.1.148): "Our revels now are ended." Or he may simply be aware of their lives *as* a performance without any other meaning: Shakespeare's passage continues later: "We are such stuff / As dreams are made on, and our little life / Is rounded with a sleep." The situation at the end of the play is little changed—only barer, as Hamm discards his stick, whistle, and dog, "reckoning closed and story ended." Yet Clov is still waiting to leave as Hamm covers his face, and it is not impossible that the play will resume in precisely the same terms tomorrow.

Endgame, like *Waiting for Godot* (and like Kafka's stories), has been given a number of symbolic interpretations. Some refer to Beckett's love of wordplay: Hamm as Hamm-actor, Hammlet, Hammer, and Nag and Nell as shortened forms of *Nägel* and *nello*, German and Italian words for "nail," which are invoked as crucifixion themes suggesting the martyrdom of humanity. The setting of a boxlike room with two windows is seen as a skull, the seat of consciousness, or (emphasizing the bloody handkerchief and the reference to fontanelles—the soft spot in the skull of a newborn child) as a womb. The characters' isolation in a dead world after an unnamed catastrophe (which may be Hamm's fault) suggests the world after atomic holocaust; or, for those who recall Beckett's fascination with the apathetic figure of Belacqua waiting, in the Purgatory of Dante's *Divine Comedy*, for his punishment to begin, it evokes an image of pre-Purgatorial consciousness. The ashcans in which Hamm has "bottled" his parents, and the general cruelty between characters, are to represent the dustbin of modern Western civilized values. Hamm and Clov represent the uneasy adjustment of soul and body, the class struggle of rich and poor, or the master-slave relationship in all senses (including the slave's acceptance of his victimization). Clearly Beckett has created a structure that accommodates all these readings while authorizing none. He himself said to director Alan Schneider that he was less interested in symbolism than in describing a "local situation," an interaction of four characters in a given set of circumstances, and that the audience's interpretation was its own responsibility.

Beckett both authorized and denied these interpretations. He pruned down an earlier, more anecdotal two-act play to achieve *Endgame*'s skeletal plot and almost anonymous characters, and in doing so created a structure that immediately elicits the reader's instinct to "fill in the blanks." His puns and allusions openly point to a further meaning that *may* be contained in the implied reference, but may also be part of an infinite regress of meaning—expressing the "absurd" itself. Working against too heavy an insistence on symbolic meanings is the fact that the play is also funny—especially when performed on stage. The characters popping out of ashcans, the jerky, repetitive motions with which Clov carries out his master's commands, and the often obscene vaudeville patter accompanied by appropriate gestures all provide a comic perspective that keeps *Endgame* from sinking into tragic despair. The intellectual distance offered by comedy is entirely in keeping with the more somber side of the play, which rejects pathos and constantly drags its characters' escapist fancies down to the minimal facts of survival: food, shelter, sleep, painkiller. Thus it is possible to say that *Endgame* describes—but only among many other things—what it is like to be alive, declining toward death in a world without meaning.

Samuel Beckett, *Endgame: with a Revised Text* (1992), ed. S. E. Gontarski, is a revised text based on productions directed or supervised by Beckett; the attached theatrical notebooks often clarify situations and settings. Arthur N. Athanason, *Endgame: The Ashbin Play* (1993), is a brief introduction; and Alexander Astro, *Understanding Samuel Beckett* (1990), discusses the complete work with interpretations emphasizing cultural and linguistic aspects. Andrew Kennedy, *Samuel Beckett* (1989), provides a compact, comprehensive overview of Beckett's work with separate chapters on the major plays and novels. Richard Begam, *Samuel Beckett and the End of Modernity* (1996), discusses Beckett in the context of postmodernism; Cathleen

Culotta Andonian, ed., organizes *The Critical Response to Samuel Beckett* (1998) in ten sections that represent different stages in the reception of his work. Useful biographies are Deirdre Bair, *Samuel Beckett: A Biography* (1993); Anthony Cronin, *Samuel Beckett: The Last Modernist* (1996); Lois G. Gordon, *The World of Samuel Beckett, 1906–1946* (1996); and James Knowlson, *Damned to Fame: The Life of Samuel Beckett* (1996). Hugh Kenner, *Samuel Beckett: A Critical Study* (1974), is an earlier but still valuable discussion of Beckett's work. Useful essay collections are Jennifer Birkett and Kate Ince, eds., *Samuel Beckett* (2000), and Steven Connor, ed., *Waiting for Godot and Endgame—Samuel Beckett* (1992), which includes eleven essays, of which seven are wholly or partially on *Endgame*.

Endgame[1]

For Roger Blin

CHARACTERS

NAGG
NELL
HAMM
CLOV

Bare interior.
Gray light.
Left and right back, high up, two small windows, curtains drawn.
Front right, a door. Hanging near door, its face to wall, a picture.
Front left, touching each other, covered with an old sheet, two ashbins.
Center, in an armchair on castors, covered with an old sheet, HAMM.
Motionless by the door, his eyes fixed on HAMM, CLOV. *Very red face.*
Brief tableau.

[CLOV *goes and stands under window left. Stiff, staggering walk. He looks up at window left. He turns and looks at window right. He goes and stands under window right. He looks up at window right. He turns and looks at window left. He goes out, comes back immediately with a small step-ladder, carries it over and sets it down under window left, gets up on it, draws back curtain. He gets down, takes six steps (for example) towards window right, goes back for ladder, carries it over and sets it down under window right, gets up on it, draws back curtain. He gets down, takes three steps towards window left, goes back for ladder, carries it over and sets it down under window left, gets up on it, looks out of window. Brief laugh. He gets down, takes one step towards window right, goes back for ladder, carries it over and sets it down under window right, gets up on it, looks out of window. Brief laugh. He gets down, goes with ladder towards ashbins, halts, turns, carries back ladder and sets it down under window right, goes to ashbins, removes sheet covering them, folds it over his arm. He raises one lid, stoops and looks into bin. Brief laugh. He closes lid. Same with other bin. He goes to* HAMM, *removes sheet covering him, folds it over his arm. In a dressing-gown, a stiff toque[2] on his head, a large blood-stained handkerchief over his face, a whistle hanging from his neck, a rug over his knees, thick socks on his feet,* HAMM *seems to be asleep.* CLOV *looks him over. Brief laugh. He goes to door, halts, turns towards auditorium.*]

1. Translated by the author.   2. A fitted cloth hat with little or no brim, sometimes indicating official status, as with a judge's toque.

CLOV [*Fixed gaze, tonelessly.*]   Finished, it's finished, nearly finished, it must be nearly finished. [*Pause.*] Grain upon grain, one by one, and one day, suddenly, there's a heap, a little heap, the impossible heap. [*Pause.*] I can't be punished any more. [*Pause.*] I'll go now to my kitchen, ten feet by ten feet by ten feet, and wait for him to whistle me. [*Pause.*] Nice dimensions, nice proportions, I'll lean on the table, and look at the wall, and wait for him to whistle me.

> [*He remains a moment motionless, then goes out. He comes back immediately, goes to window right, takes up the ladder and carries it out. Pause.* HAMM *stirs. He yawns under the handkerchief. He removes the handkerchief from his face. Very red face. Black glasses.*]

HAMM   Me— [*He yawns.*]—to play.[3] [*He holds the handkerchief spread out before him.*] Old Stancher![4] [*He takes off his glasses, wipes his eyes, his face, the glasses, puts them on again, folds the handkerchief and puts it back neatly in the breast-pocket of his dressing-gown. He clears his throat, joins the tips of his fingers.*] Can there be misery— [*He yawns.*]—loftier than mine? No doubt. Formerly. But now? [*Pause.*] My father? [*Pause.*] My mother? [*Pause.*] My . . . dog? [*Pause.*] Oh I am willing to believe they suffer as much as such creatures can suffer. But does that mean their sufferings equal mine? No doubt. [*Pause.*] No, all is a— [*He yawns.*]—bsolute, [*Proudly.*] the bigger a man is the fuller he is. [*Pause. Gloomily.*] And the emptier. [*He sniffs.*] Clov! [*Pause.*] No, alone. [*Pause.*] What dreams! Those forests! [*Pause.*] Enough, it's time it ended, in the shelter too. [*Pause.*] And yet I hesitate, I hesitate to . . . to end. Yes, there it is, it's time it ended and yet I hesitate to— [*He yawns.*]—to end. [*Yawns.*] God, I'm tired, I'd be better off in bed. [*He whistles. Enter* CLOV *immediately. He halts beside the chair.*] You pollute the air! [*Pause.*] Get me ready, I'm going to bed.

CLOV   I've just got you up.

HAMM   And what of it?

CLOV   I can't be getting you up and putting you to bed every five minutes, I have things to do. [*Pause.*]

HAMM   Did you ever see my eyes?

CLOV   No.

HAMM   Did you never have the curiosity, while I was sleeping, to take off my glasses and look at my eyes?

CLOV   Pulling back the lids? [*Pause.*] No.

HAMM   One of these days I'll show them to you. [*Pause.*] It seems they've gone all white. [*Pause.*] What time is it?

CLOV   The same as usual.

HAMM [*Gesture towards window right.*]   Have you looked?

CLOV   Yes.

HAMM   Well?

CLOV   Zero.

HAMM   It'd need to rain.

CLOV   It won't rain. [*Pause.*]

HAMM   Apart from that, how do you feel?

---

3. Hamm announces that it is his move at the beginning of *Endgame*: the comparison is with a game of chess, of which the "endgame" is the final stage.   4. The handkerchief that stanches his blood.

CLOV   I don't complain.

HAMM   You feel normal?

CLOV [*Irritably.*]   I tell you I don't complain.

HAMM   I feel a little queer. [*Pause.*] Clov!

CLOV   Yes.

HAMM   Have you not had enough?

CLOV   Yes! [*Pause.*] Of what?

HAMM   Of this . . . this . . . thing.

CLOV   I always had. [*Pause.*] Not you?

HAMM [*Gloomily.*]   Then there's no reason for it to change.

CLOV   It may end. [*Pause.*] All life long the same questions, the same answers.

HAMM   Get me ready. [CLOV *does not move.*] Go and get the sheet. [CLOV *does not move.*] Clov!

CLOV   Yes.

HAMM   I'll give you nothing more to eat.

CLOV   Then we'll die.

HAMM   I'll give you just enough to keep you from dying. You'll be hungry all the time.

CLOV   Then we won't die. [*Pause.*] I'll go and get the sheet. [*He goes towards the door.*]

HAMM   No! [CLOV *halts.*] I'll give you one biscuit per day. [*Pause.*] One and a half. [*Pause.*] Why do you stay with me?

CLOV   Why do you keep me?

HAMM   There's no one else.

CLOV   There's nowhere else. [*Pause.*]

HAMM   You're leaving me all the same.

CLOV   I'm trying.

HAMM   You don't love me.

CLOV   No.

HAMM   You loved me once.

CLOV   Once!

HAMM   I've made you suffer too much. [*Pause.*] Haven't I?

CLOV   It's not that.

HAMM [*Shocked.*]   I haven't made you suffer too much?

CLOV   Yes!

HAMM [*Relieved.*]   Ah you gave me a fright! [*Pause. Coldly.*] Forgive me. [*Pause. Louder.*] I said, Forgive me.

CLOV   I heard you. [*Pause.*] Have you bled?

HAMM   Less. [*Pause.*] Is it not time for my pain-killer?

CLOV   No. [*Pause.*]

HAMM   How are your eyes?

CLOV   Bad.

HAMM   How are your legs?

CLOV   BAD.

HAMM   But you can move.

CLOV   Yes.

HAMM [*Violently.*]   Then move! [CLOV *goes to back wall, leans against it with his forehead and hands.*] Where are you?

CLOV   Here.

HAMM   Come back! [CLOV *returns to his place beside the chair.*] Where are you?

CLOV   Here.

HAMM   Why don't you kill me?

CLOV   I don't know the combination of the cupboard. [*Pause.*]

HAMM   Go and get two bicycle-wheels.

CLOV   There are no more bicycle-wheels.

HAMM   What have you done with your bicycle?

CLOV   I never had a bicycle.

HAMM   The thing is impossible.

CLOV   When there were still bicycles I wept to have one. I crawled at your feet. You told me to go to hell. Now there are none.

HAMM   And your rounds? When you inspected my paupers. Always on foot?

CLOV   Sometimes on horse. [*The lid of one of the bins lifts and the hands of* NAGG *appear, gripping the rim. Then his head emerges. Nightcap. Very white face.* NAGG *yawns, then listens.*] I'll leave you, I have things to do.

HAMM   In your kitchen?

CLOV   Yes.

HAMM   Outside of here it's death. [*Pause.*] All right, be off. [*Exit* CLOV. *Pause.*] We're getting on.

NAGG   Me pap!⁵

HAMM   Accursed progenitor!

NAGG   Me pap!

HAMM   The old folks at home! No decency left! Guzzle, guzzle, that's all they think of. [*He whistles. Enter* CLOV. *He halts beside the chair.*] Well! I thought you were leaving me.

CLOV   Oh not just yet, not just yet.

NAGG   Me pap!

HAMM   Give him his pap.

CLOV   There's no more pap.

HAMM   [*To* NAGG.]   Do you hear that? There's no more pap. You'll never get any more pap.

NAGG   I want me pap!

HAMM   Give him a biscuit. [*Exit* CLOV.] Accursed fornicator! How are your stumps?

NAGG   Never mind me stumps.
        [*Enter* CLOV *with biscuit.*]

CLOV   I'm back again, with the biscuit. [*He gives biscuit to* NAGG *who fingers it, sniffs it.*]

NAGG   [*Plaintively.*]   What is it?

CLOV   Spratt's medium.⁶

NAGG   [*As before.*]   It's hard! I can't!

HAMM   Bottle him!
        [CLOV *pushes* NAGG *back into the bin, closes the lid.*]

CLOV   [*Returning to his place beside the chair.*]   If age but knew!

HAMM   Sit on him!

CLOV   I can't sit.

HAMM   True. And I can't stand.

---

5. Food, mush.   6. A common plain cookie.

CLOV   So it is.

HAMM   Every man his speciality. [*Pause.*] No phone calls? [*Pause.*] Don't we laugh?

CLOV [*After reflection.*]   I don't feel like it.

HAMM [*After reflection.*]   Nor I. [*Pause.*] Clov!

CLOV   Yes.

HAMM   Nature has forgotten us.

CLOV   There's no more nature.

HAMM   No more nature! You exaggerate.

CLOV   In the vicinity.

HAMM   But we breathe, we change! We lose our hair, our teeth! Our bloom! Our ideals!

CLOV   Then she hasn't forgotten us.

HAMM   But you say there is none.

CLOV [*Sadly.*]   No one that ever lived ever thought so crooked as we.

HAMM   We do what we can.

CLOV   We shouldn't. [*Pause.*]

HAMM   You're a bit of all right, aren't you?[7]

CLOV   A smithereen.[8] [*Pause.*]

HAMM   This is slow work. [*Pause.*] Is it not time for my pain-killer?

CLOV   No. [*Pause.*] I'll leave you, I have things to do.

HAMM   In your kitchen?

CLOV   Yes.

HAMM   What, I'd like to know.

CLOV   I look at the wall.

HAMM   The wall! And what do you see on your wall? Mene, mene?[9] Naked bodies?

CLOV   I see my light dying.

HAMM   Your light dying! Listen to that! Well, it can die just as well here, *your* light. Take a look at me and then come back and tell me what you think of *your* light. [*Pause.*]

CLOV   You shouldn't speak to me like that. [*Pause.*]

HAMM [*Coldly.*]   Forgive me. [*Pause. Louder.*] I said, Forgive me.

CLOV   I heard you.

[*The lid of* NAGG's *bin lifts. His hands appear, gripping the rim. Then his head emerges. In his mouth the biscuit. He listens.*]

HAMM   Did your seeds come up?

CLOV   No.

HAMM   Did you scratch round them to see if they had sprouted?

CLOV   They haven't sprouted.

HAMM   Perhaps it's still too early.

CLOV   If they were going to sprout they would have sprouted. [*Violently.*] They'll never sprout!

[*Pause.* NAGG *takes biscuit in his hand.*]

HAMM   This is not much fun. [*Pause.*] But that's always the way at the end of the day, isn't it, Clov?

CLOV   Always.

7. You're pretty good, aren't you? (British slang).   8. A tiny bit.   9. From Daniel 5.25: "Mene, mene, tekel, upharsin"; words written by a divine hand on the wall during the feast of Belshazzar, king of Babylon. They predict doom and tell the king "Thou art weighed in the balances, and art found wanting" (Daniel 5.27).

HAMM   It's the end of the day like any other day, isn't it, Clov?
CLOV   Looks like it. [*Pause.*]
HAMM [*Anguished.*]   What's happening, what's happening?
CLOV   Something is taking its course. [*Pause.*]
HAMM   All right, be off. [*He leans back in his chair, remains motionless.* CLOV *does not move, heaves a great groaning sigh.* HAMM *sits up.*] I thought I told you to be off.
CLOV   I'm trying. [*He goes to door, halts.*] Ever since I was whelped.
       [*Exit* CLOV.]
HAMM   We're getting on.
       [*He leans back in his chair, remains motionless.* NAGG *knocks on the lid of the other bin. Pause. He knocks harder. The lid lifts and the hands of* NELL *appear, gripping the rim. Then her head emerges. Lace cap. Very white face.*]
NELL   What is it, my pet? [*Pause.*] Time for love?
NAGG   Were you asleep?
NELL   Oh no!
NAGG   Kiss me.
NELL   We can't.
NAGG   Try.
       [*Their heads strain towards each other, fail to meet, fall apart again.*]
NELL   Why this farce, day after day? [*Pause.*]
NAGG   I've lost me tooth.
NELL   When?
NAGG   I had it yesterday.
NELL [*Elegiac.*]   Ah yesterday!
       [*They turn painfully towards each other.*]
NAGG   Can you see me?
NELL   Hardly. And you?
NAGG   What?
NELL   Can you see me?
NAGG   Hardly.
NELL   So much the better, so much the better.
NAGG   Don't say that. [*Pause.*] Our sight has failed.
NELL   Yes.
       [*Pause. They turn away from each other.*]
NAGG   Can you hear me?
NELL   Yes. And you?
NAGG   Yes. [*Pause.*] Our hearing hasn't failed.
NELL   Our what?
NAGG   Our hearing.
NELL   No. [*Pause.*] Have you anything else to say to me?
NAGG   Do you remember—
NELL   No.
NAGG   When we crashed on our tandem[1] and lost our shanks.
       [*They laugh heartily.*]
NELL   It was in the Ardennes.
       [*They laugh less heartily.*]

1. A bicycle built for two.

NAGG   On the road to Sedan.[2] [*They laugh still less heartily.*] Are you
    cold?

NELL   Yes, perished. And you?

NAGG [*Pause.*]   I'm freezing. [*Pause.*] Do you want to go in?

NELL   Yes.

NAGG   Then go in. [NELL *does not move.*] Why don't you go in?

NELL   I don't know. [*Pause.*]

NAGG   Has he changed your sawdust?

NELL   It isn't sawdust. [*Pause. Wearily.*] Can you not be a little accurate,
    Nagg?

NAGG   Your sand then. It's not important.

NELL   It is important. [*Pause.*]

NAGG   It was sawdust once.

NELL   Once!

NAGG   And now it's sand. [*Pause.*] From the shore. [*Pause. Impatiently.*]
    Now it's sand he fetches from the shore.

NELL   Now it's sand.

NAGG   Has he changed yours?

NELL   No.

NAGG   Nor mine. [*Pause.*] I won't have it! [*Pause. Holding up the biscuit.*]
    Do you want a bit?

NELL   No. [*Pause.*] Of what?

NAGG   Biscuit. I've kept you half. [*He looks at the biscuit. Proudly.*] Three
    quarters. For you. Here. [*He proffers the biscuit.*] No? [*Pause.*] Do you
    not feel well?

HAMM [*Wearily.*]   Quiet, quiet, you're keeping me awake. [*Pause.*] Talk
    softer. [*Pause.*] If I could sleep I might make love. I'd go into the woods.
    My eyes would see . . . the sky, the earth. I'd run, run, they wouldn't
    catch me. [*Pause.*] Nature! [*Pause.*] There's something dripping in my
    head. [*Pause.*] A heart, a heart in my head. [*Pause.*]

NAGG [*Soft.*]   Do you hear him? A heart in his head! [*He chuckles
    cautiously.*]

NELL   One mustn't laugh at those things, Nagg. Why must you always
    laugh at them?

NAGG   Not so loud!

NELL [*Without lowering her voice.*]   Nothing is funnier than unhappiness,
    I grant you that. But—

NAGG [*Shocked.*]   Oh!

NELL   Yes, yes, it's the most comical thing in the world. And we laugh, we
    laugh, with a will, in the beginning. But it's always the same thing. Yes,
    it's like the funny story we have heard too often, we still find it funny,
    but we don't laugh any more. [*Pause.*] Have you anything else to say to
    me?

NAGG   No.

NELL   Are you quite sure? [*Pause.*] Then I'll leave you.

NAGG   Do you not want your biscuit? [*Pause.*] I'll keep it for you. [*Pause.*]
    I thought you were going to leave me.

2. Town in northern France where the French were defeated in the Franco-Prussian War (1870). Ardennes
is a forest in northern France, the scene of bitter fighting in both world wars.

NELL   I am going to leave you.

NAGG   Could you give me a scratch before you go?

NELL   No. [*Pause.*] Where?

NAGG   In the back.

NELL   No. [*Pause.*] Rub yourself against the rim.

NAGG   It's lower down. In the hollow.

NELL   What hollow?

NAGG   The hollow! [*Pause.*] Could you not? [*Pause.*] Yesterday you scratched me there.

NELL   [*Elegiac.*]   Ah yesterday!

NAGG   Could you not? [*Pause.*] Would you like me to scratch you? [*Pause.*] Are you crying again?

NELL   I was trying. [*Pause.*]

HAMM   Perhaps it's a little vein. [*Pause.*]

NAGG   What was that he said?

NELL   Perhaps it's a little vein.

NAGG   What does that mean? [*Pause.*] That means nothing. [*Pause.*] Will I tell you the story of the tailor?

NELL   No. [*Pause.*] What for?

NAGG   To cheer you up.

NELL   It's not funny.

NAGG   It always made you laugh. [*Pause.*] The first time I thought you'd die.

NELL   It was on Lake Como.[3] [*Pause.*] One April afternoon. [*Pause.*] Can you believe it?

NAGG   What?

NELL   That we once went out rowing on Lake Como. [*Pause.*] One April afternoon.

NAGG   We had got engaged the day before.

NELL   Engaged!

NAGG   You were in such fits that we capsized. By rights we should have been drowned.

NELL   It was because I felt happy.

NAGG   [*Indignant.*]   It was not, it was not, it was my story and nothing else. Happy! Don't you laugh at it still? Every time I tell it. Happy!

NELL   It was deep, deep. And you could see down to the bottom. So white. So clean.

NAGG   Let me tell it again. [*Raconteur's voice.*] An Englishman, needing a pair of striped trousers in a hurry for the New Year festivities, goes to his tailor who takes his measurements. [*Tailor's voice.*] "That's the lot, come back in four days, I'll have it ready." Good. Four days later. [*Tailor's voice.*] "So sorry, come back in a week, I've made a mess of the seat." Good, that's all right, a neat seat can be very ticklish. A week later. [*Tailor's voice.*] "Frightfully sorry, come back in ten days. I've made a hash of the crotch." Good, can't be helped, a snug crotch is always a teaser. Ten days later. [*Tailor's voice.*] "Dreadfully sorry, come back in a fortnight, I've made a balls of the fly." Good, at a pinch, a smart fly is a stiff proposition. [*Pause. Normal voice.*] I never told it worse. [*Pause.

---

3. A large lake and tourist resort in northern Italy, near the Swiss border.

Gloomy.] I tell this story worse and worse. [*Pause. Raconteur's voice.*] Well, to make it short, the bluebells are blowing and he ballockses[4] the buttonholes. [*Customer's voice.*] "God damn you to hell, Sir, no, it's indecent, there are limits! In six days, do you hear me, six days, God made the world. Yes Sir, no less Sir, the WORLD! And you are not bloody well capable of making me a pair of trousers in three months!" [*Tailor's voice, scandalized.*] "But my dear Sir, my dear Sir, look— [*Disdainful gesture, disgustedly.*]—at the world— [*Pause.*] and look— [*Loving gesture, proudly.*]—at my TROUSERS!"

> [*Pause. He looks at* NELL *who has remained impassive, her eyes unseeing, breaks into a high forced laugh, cuts it short, pokes his head towards* NELL, *launches his laugh again.*]

HAMM   Silence!

> [NAGG *starts, cuts short his laugh.*]

NELL   You could see down to the bottom.

HAMM [*Exasperated.*]   Have you not finished? Will you never finish? [*With sudden fury.*] Will this never finish? [NAGG *disappears into his bin, closes the lid behind him.* NELL *does not move. Frenziedly.*] My kingdom for a nightman![5] [*He whistles. Enter* CLOV.] Clear away this muck! Chuck it in the sea!

> [CLOV *goes to bins, halts.*]

NELL   So white.

HAMM   What? What's she blathering about?

> [CLOV *stoops, takes* NELL's *hand, feels her pulse.*]

NELL [*To* CLOV.]   Desert!

> [CLOV *lets go her hand, pushes her back in the bin, closes the lid.*]

CLOV [*Returning to his place beside the chair.*]   She has no pulse.

HAMM   What was she drivelling about?

CLOV   She told me to go away, into the desert.

HAMM   Damn busybody! Is that all?

CLOV   No.

HAMM   What else?

CLOV   I didn't understand.

HAMM   Have you bottled her?

CLOV   Yes.

HAMM   Are they both bottled?

CLOV   Yes.

HAMM   Screw down the lids. [CLOV *goes towards door.*] Time enough. [CLOV *halts.*] My anger subsides, I'd like to pee.

CLOV [*With alacrity.*]   I'll go and get the catheter. [*He goes towards door.*]

HAMM   Time enough. [CLOV *halts.*] Give me my pain-killer.

CLOV   It's too soon. [*Pause.*] It's too soon on top of your tonic, it wouldn't act.

HAMM   In the morning they brace you up and in the evening they calm you down. Unless it's the other way round. [*Pause.*] That old doctor, he's dead naturally?

CLOV   He wasn't old.

---

4. "Bollixes," botches.   5. Parody of Shakespeare's *Richard III*, where the defeated king seeks a horse to escape from the battlefield: "A horse! a horse! My kingdom for a horse!" (5.4.7).

HAMM   But he's dead?

CLOV   Naturally. [*Pause.*] *You* ask *me* that? [*Pause.*]

HAMM   Take me for a little turn. [CLOV *goes behind the chair and pushes it forward.*] Not too fast! [CLOV *pushes chair.*] Right round the world! [CLOV *pushes chair.*] Hug the walls, then back to the center again. [CLOV *pushes chair.*] I was right in the center, wasn't I?

CLOV   [*Pushing.*]   Yes.

HAMM   We'd need a proper wheel-chair. With big wheels. Bicycle wheels! [*Pause.*] Are you hugging?

CLOV   [*Pushing.*]   Yes.

HAMM   [*Groping for wall.*]   It's a lie! Why do you lie to me?

CLOV   [*Bearing closer to wall.*]   There! There!

HAMM   Stop! [CLOV *stops chair close to back wall.* HAMM *lays his hand against wall.*] Old wall! [*Pause.*] Beyond is the . . . other hell. [*Pause. Violently.*] Closer! Closer! Up against!

CLOV   Take away your hand. [HAMM *withdraws his hand.* CLOV *rams chair against wall.*] There!

[HAMM *leans towards wall, applies his ear to it.*]

HAMM   Do you hear? [*He strikes the wall with his knuckles.*] Do you hear? Hollow bricks! [*He strikes again.*] All that's hollow! [*Pause. He straightens up. Violently.*] That's enough. Back!

CLOV   We haven't done the round.

HAMM   Back to my place! [CLOV *pushes chair back to center.*] Is that my place?

CLOV   Yes, that's your place.

HAMM   Am I right in the center?

CLOV   I'll measure it.

HAMM   More or less! More or less!

CLOV   [*Moving chair slightly.*]   There!

HAMM   I'm more or less in the center?

CLOV   I'd say so.

HAMM   You'd say so! Put me right in the center!

CLOV   I'll go and get the tape.

HAMM   Roughly! Roughly! [CLOV *moves chair slightly.*] Bang in the center!

CLOV   There! [*Pause.*]

HAMM   I feel a little too far to the left. [CLOV *moves chair slightly.*] Now I feel a little too far to the right. [CLOV *moves chair slightly.*] I feel a little too far forward. [CLOV *moves chair slightly.*] Now I feel a little too far back. [CLOV *moves chair slightly.*] Don't stay there, [*i.e., behind the chair*] you give me the shivers.

[CLOV *returns to his place beside the chair.*]

CLOV   If I could kill him I'd die happy. [*Pause.*]

HAMM   What's the weather like?

CLOV   As usual.

HAMM   Look at the earth.

CLOV   I've looked.

HAMM   With the glass?

CLOV   No need of the glass.

HAMM   Look at it with the glass.

CLOV   I'll go and get the glass.

[*Exit* CLOV.]

HAMM   No need of the glass!

[*Enter* CLOV *with telescope.*]

CLOV   I'm back again, with the glass. [*He goes to window right, looks up at it.*] I need the steps.

HAMM   Why? Have you shrunk? [*Exit* CLOV *with telescope.*] I don't like that, I don't like that.

[*Enter* CLOV *with ladder, but without telescope.*]

CLOV   I'm back again, with the steps. [*He sets down ladder under window right, gets up on it, realizes he has not the telescope, gets down.*] I need the glass. [*He goes towards door.*]

HAMM [*Violently.*]   But you have the glass!

CLOV [*Halting, violently.*]   No, I haven't the glass!

[*Exit* CLOV.]

HAMM   This is deadly.

[*Enter* CLOV *with telescope. He goes towards ladder.*]

CLOV   Things are livening up. [*He gets up on ladder, raises the telescope, lets it fall.*] I did it on purpose. [*He gets down, picks up the telescope, turns it on auditorium.*] I see . . . a multitude . . . in transports . . . of joy.[6] [*Pause.*] That's what I call a magnifier. [*He lowers the telescope, turns towards* HAMM.] Well? Don't we laugh?

HAMM [*After reflection.*]   I don't.

CLOV [*After reflection.*]   Nor I. [*He gets up on ladder, turns the telescope on the without.*] Let's see. [*He looks, moving the telescope.*] Zero . . . [*he looks*] . . . zero . . . [*he looks*] . . . and zero.

HAMM   Nothing stirs. All is—

CLOV   Zer—

HAMM [*Violently.*]   Wait till you're spoke to! [*Normal voice.*] All is . . . all is . . . all is what? [*Violently.*] All is what?

CLOV   What all is? In a word? Is that what you want to know? Just a moment. [*He turns the telescope on the without, looks, lowers the telescope, turns towards* HAMM.] Corpsed. [*Pause.*] Well? Content?

HAMM   Look at the sea.

CLOV   It's the same.

HAMM   Look at the ocean!

[CLOV *gets down, takes a few steps towards window left, goes back for ladder, carries it over and sets it down under window left, gets up on it, turns the telescope on the without, looks at length. He starts, lowers the telescope, examines it, turns it again on the without.*]

CLOV   Never seen anything like that!

HAMM [*Anxious.*]   What? A sail? A fin? Smoke?

CLOV [*Looking.*]   The light is sunk.

HAMM [*Relieved.*]   Pah! We all knew that.

CLOV [*Looking.*]   There was a bit left.

HAMM   The base.

CLOV [*Looking.*]   Yes.

HAMM   And now?

---

6. Echo of Revelation 7.9–10: "After this I beheld, and, lo, a great multitude, which . . . cried with a loud voice, saying, Salvation."

CLOV [*Looking.*]   All gone.

HAMM   No gulls?

CLOV [*Looking.*]   Gulls!

HAMM   And the horizon? Nothing on the horizon?

CLOV [*Lowering the telescope, turning towards* HAMM, *exasperated.*]   What in God's name could there be on the horizon? [*Pause.*]

HAMM   The waves, how are the waves?

CLOV   The waves? [*He turns the telescope on the waves.*] Lead.

HAMM   And the sun?

CLOV [*Looking.*]   Zero.

HAMM   But it should be sinking. Look again.

CLOV [*Looking.*]   Damn the sun.

HAMM   Is it night already then?

CLOV [*Looking.*]   No.

HAMM   Then what is it?

CLOV [*Looking.*]   Gray. [*Lowering the telescope, turning towards* HAMM, *louder.*] Gray! [*Pause. Still louder.*] GRRAY! [*Pause. He gets down, approaches* HAMM *from behind, whispers in his ear.*]

HAMM [*Starting.*]   Gray! Did I hear you say gray?

CLOV   Light black. From pole to pole.

HAMM   You exaggerate. [*Pause.*] Don't stay there, you give me the shivers. [CLOV *returns to his place beside the chair.*]

CLOV   Why this farce, day after day?

HAMM   Routine. One never knows. [*Pause.*] Last night I saw inside my breast. There was a big sore.

CLOV   Pah! You saw your heart.

HAMM   No, it was living. [*Pause. Anguished.*] Clov!

CLOV   Yes.

HAMM   What's happening?

CLOV   Something is taking its course. [*Pause.*]

HAMM   Clov!

CLOV [*Impatiently.*]   What is it?

HAMM   We're not beginning to . . . to . . . mean something?

CLOV   Mean something! You and I, mean something! [*Brief laugh.*] Ah that's a good one!

HAMM   I wonder. [*Pause.*] Imagine if a rational being came back to earth, wouldn't he be liable to get ideas into his head if he observed us long enough. [*Voice of rational being.*] Ah, good, now I see what it is, yes, now I understand what they're at! [CLOV *starts, drops the telescope and begins to scratch his belly with both hands. Normal voice.*] And without going so far as that, we ourselves . . . [*With emotion.*] . . . we ourselves . . . at certain moments . . . [*Vehemently.*] To think perhaps it won't all have been for nothing!

CLOV [*Anguished, scratching himself.*]   I have a flea!

HAMM   A flea! Are there still fleas?

CLOV   On me there's one. [*Scratching.*] Unless it's a crablouse.

HAMM [*Very perturbed.*]   But humanity might start from there all over again! Catch him, for the love of God!

CLOV   I'll go and get the powder.

[*Exit* CLOV.]

HAMM   A flea! This is awful! What a day!
    [*Enter* CLOV *with a sprinkling-tin.*]
CLOV   I'm back again, with the insecticide.
HAMM   Let him have it!
    [CLOV *loosens the top of his trousers, pulls it forward and shakes powder into the aperture. He stoops, looks, waits, starts, frenziedly shakes more powder, stoops, looks, waits.*]
CLOV   The bastard!
HAMM   Did you get him?
CLOV   Looks like it. [*He drops the tin and adjusts his trousers.*] Unless he's laying doggo.
HAMM   Laying! Lying you mean. Unless he's *lying* doggo.
CLOV   Ah? One says lying? One doesn't say laying?
HAMM   Use your head, can't you. If he was laying we'd be bitched.
CLOV   Ah. [*Pause.*] What about that pee?
HAMM   I'm having it.
CLOV   Ah that's the spirit, that's the spirit! [*Pause.*]
HAMM   [*With ardour.*] Let's go from here, the two of us! South! You can make a raft and the currents will carry us away, far away, to other . . . mammals!
CLOV   God forbid!
HAMM   Alone, I'll embark alone! Get working on that raft immediately. Tomorrow I'll be gone for ever.
CLOV   [*Hastening towards door.*] I'll start straight away.
HAMM   Wait! [CLOV *halts.*] Will there be sharks, do you think?
CLOV   Sharks? I don't know. If there are there will be. [*He goes towards door.*]
HAMM   Wait! [CLOV *halts.*] Is it not yet time for my pain-killer?
CLOV   [*Violently.*] No! [*He goes towards door.*]
HAMM   Wait! [CLOV *halts.*] How are your eyes?
CLOV   Bad.
HAMM   But you can see.
CLOV   All I want.
HAMM   How are your legs?
CLOV   Bad.
HAMM   But you can walk.
CLOV   I come . . . and go.
HAMM   In my house. [*Pause. With prophetic relish.*] One day you'll be blind, like me. You'll be sitting there, a speck in the void, in the dark, for ever, like me. [*Pause.*] One day you'll say to yourself, I'm tired, I'll sit down, and you'll go and sit down. Then you'll say, I'm hungry, I'll get up and get something to eat. But you won't get up. You'll say, I shouldn't have sat down, but since I have I'll sit on a little longer, then I'll get up and get something to eat. But you won't get up and you won't get anything to eat. [*Pause.*] You'll look at the wall awhile, then you'll say, I'll close my eyes, perhaps have a little sleep, after that I'll feel better, and you'll close them. And when you open them again there'll be no wall any more. [*Pause.*] Infinite emptiness will be all around you, all the resurrected dead of all the ages wouldn't fill it, and there you'll be like a little bit of grit in the middle of the steppe. [*Pause.*] Yes, one day you'll know what it is,

you'll be like me, except that you won't have anyone with you, because you won't have had pity on anyone and because there won't be anyone left to have pity on. [*Pause.*]

CLOV   It's not certain. [*Pause.*] And there's one thing you forget.

HAMM   Ah?

CLOV   I can't sit down.

HAMM   [*Impatiently.*]   Well you'll lie down then, what the hell! Or you'll come to a standstill, simply stop and stand still, the way you are now. One day you'll say, I'm tired, I'll stop. What does the attitude matter? [*Pause.*]

CLOV   So you all want me to leave you.

HAMM   Naturally.

CLOV   Then I'll leave you.

HAMM   You can't leave us.

CLOV   Then I won't leave you. [*Pause.*]

HAMM   Why don't you finish us? [*Pause.*] I'll tell you the combination of the cupboard if you promise to finish me.

CLOV   I couldn't finish you.

HAMM   Then you won't finish me. [*Pause.*]

CLOV   I'll leave you, I have things to do.

HAMM   Do you remember when you came here?

CLOV   No. Too small, you told me.

HAMM   Do you remember your father?

CLOV   [*Wearily.*]   Same answer. [*Pause.*] You've asked me these questions millions of times.

HAMM   I love the old questions. [*With fervor.*] Ah the old questions, the old answers, there's nothing like them! [*Pause.*] It was I was a father to you.

CLOV   Yes. [*He looks at* HAMM *fixedly.*] You were that to me.

HAMM   My house a home for you.

CLOV   Yes. [*He looks about him.*] This was that for me.

HAMM   [*Proudly.*]   But for me, [*Gesture towards himself.*] no father. But for Hamm, [*Gesture towards surroundings.*] no home. [*Pause.*]

CLOV   I'll leave you.

HAMM   Did you ever think of one thing?

CLOV   Never.

HAMM   That here we're down in a hole. [*Pause.*] But beyond the hills? Eh? Perhaps it's still green. Eh? [*Pause.*] Flora! Pomona! [*Ecstatically.*] Ceres![7] [*Pause.*] Perhaps you won't need to go very far.

CLOV   I can't go very far. [*Pause.*] I'll leave you.

HAMM   Is my dog ready?

CLOV   He lacks a leg.

HAMM   Is he silky?

CLOV   He's a kind of Pomeranian.

HAMM   Go and get him.

CLOV   He lacks a leg.

HAMM   Go and get him! [*Exit* CLOV.] We're getting on.
    [*Enter* CLOV *holding by one of its three legs a black toy dog.*]

7. In Roman mythology, the goddesses of flowers, fruits, and fertility.

CLOV   Your dogs are here. [*He hands the dog to* HAMM *who feels it, fondles it.*]

HAMM   He's white, isn't he?

CLOV   Nearly.

HAMM   What do you mean, nearly? Is he white or isn't he?

CLOV   He isn't. [*Pause.*]

HAMM   You've forgotten the sex.

CLOV [*Vexed.*]   But he isn't finished. The sex goes on at the end. [*Pause.*]

HAMM   You haven't put on his ribbon.

CLOV [*Angrily.*]   But he isn't finished, I tell you! First you finish your dog and then you put on his ribbon! [*Pause.*]

HAMM   Can he stand?

CLOV   I don't know.

HAMM   Try. [*He hands the dog to* CLOV *who places it on the ground.*] Well?

CLOV   Wait! [*He squats down and tries to get the dog to stand on its three legs, fails, lets it go. The dog falls on its side.*]

HAMM [*Impatiently.*]   Well?

CLOV   He's standing.

HAMM [*Groping for the dog.*]   Where? Where is he?

        [CLOV *holds up the dog in a standing position.*]

CLOV   There. [*He takes* HAMM's *hand and guides it towards the dog's head.*]

HAMM [*His hand on the dog's head.*]   Is he gazing at me?

CLOV   Yes.

HAMM [*Proudly.*]   As if he were asking me to take him for a walk?

CLOV   If you like.

HAMM [*As before.*]   Or as if he were begging me for a bone. [*He withdraws his hand.*] Leave him like that, standing there imploring me.

        [CLOV *straightens up. The dog falls on its side.*]

CLOV   I'll leave you.

HAMM   Have you had your visions?

CLOV   Less.

HAMM   Is Mother Pegg's light on?

CLOV   Light! How could anyone's light be on?

HAMM   Extinguished!

CLOV   Naturally it's extinguished. If it's not on it's extinguished.

HAMM   No, I mean Mother Pegg.

CLOV   But naturally she's extinguished! [*Pause.*] What's the matter with you today?

HAMM   I'm taking my course. [*Pause.*] Is she buried?

CLOV   Buried! Who would have buried her?

HAMM   You.

CLOV   Me! Haven't I enough to do without burying people?

HAMM   But you'll bury me.

CLOV   No I won't bury you. [*Pause.*]

HAMM   She was bonny once, like a flower of the field. [*With reminiscent leer.*] And a great one for the men!

CLOV   We too were bonny—once. It's a rare thing not to have been bonny—once. [*Pause.*]

HAMM   Go and get the gaff.

        [CLOV *goes to door, halts.*]

CLOV   Do this, do that, and I do it. I never refuse. Why?

HAMM   You're not able to.

CLOV   Soon I won't do it any more.

HAMM   You won't be able to any more. [*Exit* CLOV.] Ah the creatures, the creatures, everything has to be explained to them.

   [*Enter* CLOV *with gaff.*]

CLOV   Here's your gaff. Stick it up. [*He gives the gaff to* HAMM *who, wielding it like a puntpole, tries to move his chair.*]

HAMM   Did I move?

CLOV   No.

   [HAMM *throws down the gaff.*]

HAMM   Go and get the oilcan.

CLOV   What for?

HAMM   To oil the castors.

CLOV   I oiled them yesterday.

HAMM   Yesterday! What does that mean? Yesterday!

CLOV [*Violently.*]   That means that bloody awful day, long ago, before this bloody awful day. I use the words you taught me. If they don't mean anything any more, teach me others. Or let me be silent. [*Pause.*]

HAMM   I once knew a madman who thought the end of the world had come. He was a painter—and engraver. I had a great fondness for him. I used to go and see him, in the asylum. I'd take him by the hand and drag him to the window. Look! There! All that rising corn! And there! Look! The sails of the herring fleet! All that loveliness! [*Pause.*] He'd snatch away his hand and go back into his corner. Appalled. All he had seen was ashes. [*Pause.*] He alone had been spared. [*Pause.*] Forgotten. [*Pause.*] It appears the case is . . . was not so . . . so unusual.

CLOV   A madman! When was that?

HAMM   Oh way back, way back, you weren't in the land of the living.

CLOV   God be with the days!

   [*Pause.* HAMM *raises his toque.*]

HAMM   I had a great fondness for him. [*Pause. He puts on his toque again.*] He was a painter—and engraver.

CLOV   There are so many terrible things.

HAMM   No, no, there are not so many now. [*Pause.*] Clov!

CLOV   Yes.

HAMM   Do you not think this has gone on long enough?

CLOV   Yes! [*Pause.*] What?

HAMM   This . . . this . . . thing.

CLOV   I've always thought so. [*Pause.*] You not?

HAMM [*Gloomily.*]   Then it's a day like any other day.

CLOV   As long as it lasts. [*Pause.*] All life long the same inanities.

HAMM   I can't leave you.

CLOV   I know. And you can't follow me. [*Pause.*]

HAMM   If you leave me how shall I know?

CLOV [*Briskly.*]   Well you simply whistle me and if I don't come running it means I've left you. [*Pause.*]

HAMM   You won't come and kiss me goodbye?

CLOV   Oh I shouldn't think so. [*Pause.*]

HAMM   But you might be merely dead in your kitchen.

CLOV   The result would be the same.

HAMM   Yes, but how would I know, if you were merely dead in your kitchen?

CLOV   Well . . . sooner or later I'd start to stink.

HAMM   You stink already. The whole place stinks of corpses.

CLOV   The whole universe.

HAMM [*Angrily.*]   To hell with the universe. [*Pause.*] Think of something.

CLOV   What?

HAMM   An idea, have an idea. [*Angrily.*] A bright idea!

CLOV   Ah good. [*He starts pacing to and fro, his eyes fixed on the ground, his hands behind his back. He halts.*] The pains in my legs! It's unbelievable! Soon I won't be able to think any more.

HAMM   You won't be able to leave me. [CLOV *resumes his pacing.*] What are you doing?

CLOV   Having an idea. [*He paces.*] Ah! [*He halts.*]

HAMM   What a brain! [*Pause.*] Well?

CLOV   Wait! [*He meditates. Not very convinced.*] Yes . . . [*Pause. More convinced.*] Yes! [*He raises his head.*] I have it! I set the alarm. [*Pause.*]

HAMM   This is perhaps not one of my bright days, but frankly—

CLOV   You whistle me. I don't come. The alarm rings. I'm gone. It doesn't ring. I'm dead. [*Pause.*]

HAMM   Is it working? [*Pause. Impatiently.*] The alarm, is it working?

CLOV   Why wouldn't it be working?

HAMM   Because it's worked too much.

CLOV   But it's hardly worked at all.

HAMM [*Angrily.*]   Then because it's worked too little!

CLOV   I'll go and see. [*Exit* CLOV. *Brief ring of alarm off. Enter* CLOV *with alarm-clock. He holds it against* HAMM'*s ear and releases alarm. They listen to it ringing to the end. Pause.*] Fit to wake the dead! Did you hear it?

HAMM   Vaguely.

CLOV   The end is terrific!

HAMM   I prefer the middle. [*Pause.*] Is it not time for my pain-killer?

CLOV   No! [*He goes to door, turns.*] I'll leave you.

HAMM   It's time for my story. Do you want to listen to my story.

CLOV   No.

HAMM   Ask my father if he wants to listen to my story.
   [CLOV *goes to bins, raises the lid of* NAGG's, *stoops, looks into it. Pause. He straightens up.*]

CLOV   He's asleep.

HAMM   Wake him.
   [CLOV *stoops, wakes* NAGG *with the alarm. Unintelligible words.* CLOV *straightens up.*]

CLOV   He doesn't want to listen to your story.

HAMM   I'll give him a bon-bon.
   [CLOV *stoops. As before.*]

CLOV   He wants a sugar-plum.

HAMM   He'll get a sugar-plum.
   [CLOV *stoops. As before.*]

CLOV   It's a deal. [*He goes towards door.* NAGG's *hands appear, gripping the rim. Then the head emerges.* CLOV *reaches door, turns.*] Do you believe in the life to come?

HAMM   Mine was always that. [*Exit* CLOV.] Got him that time!

NAGG   I'm listening.

HAMM   Scoundrel! Why did you engender me?

NAGG   I didn't know.

HAMM   What? What didn't you know?

NAGG   That it'd be you. [*Pause.*] You'll give me a sugar-plum?

HAMM   After the audition.

NAGG   You swear?

HAMM   Yes.

NAGG   On what?

HAMM   My honor.
         [*Pause. They laugh heartily.*]

NAGG   Two.

HAMM   One.

NAGG   One for me and one for—

HAMM   One! Silence! [*Pause.*] Where was I? [*Pause. Gloomily.*] It's finished, we're finished. [*Pause.*] Nearly finished. [*Pause.*] There'll be no more speech. [*Pause.*] Something dripping in my head, ever since the fontanelles. [*Stifled hilarity of* NAGG.] Splash, splash, always on the same spot. [*Pause.*] Perhaps it's a little vein. [*Pause.*] A little artery. [*Pause. More animated.*] Enough of that, it's story time, where was I? [*Pause. Narrative tone.*] The man came crawling towards me, on his belly. Pale, wonderfully pale and thin, he seemed on the point of— [*Pause. Normal tone.*] No, I've done that bit. [*Pause. Narrative tone.*] I calmly filled my pipe—the meerschaum, lit it with . . . let us say a vesta, drew a few puffs. Aah! [*Pause.*] Well, what is it *you* want? [*Pause.*] It was an extraordinarily bitter day, I remember, zero by the thermometer. But considering it was Christmas Eve there was nothing . . . extra-ordinary about that. Seasonable weather, for once in a way. [*Pause.*] Well, what ill wind blows you my way? He raised his face to me, black with mingled dirt and tears. [*Pause. Normal tone.*] That should do it. [*Narrative tone.*] No, no, don't look at me, don't look at me. He dropped his eyes and mumbled something, apologies I presume. [*Pause.*] I'm a busy man, you know, the final touches, before the festivities, you know what it is. [*Pause. Forcibly.*] Come on now, what is the object of this invasion? [*Pause.*] It was a glorious bright day, I remember, fifty by the heliometer,[8] but already the sun was sinking down into the . . . down among the dead. [*Normal tone.*] Nicely put, that. [*Narrative tone.*] Come on now, come on, present your petition and let me resume my labors. [*Pause. Normal tone.*] There's English for you. Ah well . . . [*Narrative tone.*] It was then he took the plunge. It's my little one, he said. Tsstss, a little one, that's bad. My little boy, he said, as if the sex mattered. Where did he come from? He named the hole. A good half-day, on horse. What are you insinuating? That the place is still inhabited? No no, not a soul, except himself and the child— assuming he existed. Good. I enquired about the situation at Kov, beyond the gulf. Not a sinner. Good. And you expect me to believe you have left your little one back there, all alone, and alive into the bargain? Come now! [*Pause.*] It was a howling wild day, I remember, a hundred by the

___

8. Literally, a "sun meter." Ordinarily, a telescope used to measure distances between celestial bodies.

anemometer.[9] The wind was tearing up the dead pines and sweeping them . . . away. [*Pause. Normal tone.*] A bit feeble, that. [*Narrative tone.*] Come on, man, speak up, what is you want from me, I have to put up my holly. [*Pause.*] Well to make it short it finally transpired that what he wanted from me was . . . bread for his brat? Bread? But I have no bread, it doesn't agree with me. Good. Then perhaps a little corn? [*Pause. Normal tone.*] That should do it. [*Narrative tone.*] Corn, yes, I have corn, it's true, in my granaries. But use your head. I give you some corn, a pound, a pound and a half, you bring it back to your child and you make him—if he's still alive—a nice pot of porridge, [NAGG *reacts.*] a nice pot and a half of porridge, full of nourishment. Good. The colors come back into his little cheeks—perhaps. And then? [*Pause.*] I lost patience. [*Violently.*] Use your head, can't you, use your head, you're on earth, there's no cure for that! [*Pause.*] It was an exceedingly dry day, I remember, zero by the hygrometer.[1] Ideal weather, for my lumbago. [*Pause. Violently.*] But what in God's name do you imagine? That the earth will awake in spring? That the rivers and seas will run with fish again? That there's manna in heaven still for imbeciles like you? [*Pause.*] Gradually I cooled down, sufficiently at least to ask him how long he had taken on the way. Three whole days. Good. In what condition he had left the child. Deep in sleep. [*Forcibly.*] But deep in what sleep, deep in what sleep already? [*Pause.*] Well to make it short I finally offered to take him into my service. He had touched a chord. And then I imagined already that I wasn't much longer for this world. [*He laughs. Pause.*] Well? [*Pause.*] Well? Here if you were careful you might die a nice natural death, in peace and comfort. [*Pause.*] Well? [*Pause.*] In the end he asked me would I consent to take in the child as well—if he were still alive. [*Pause.*] It was the moment I was waiting for. [*Pause.*] Would I consent to take in the child . . . [*Pause.*] I can see him still, down on his knees, his hands flat on the ground, glaring at me with his mad eyes, in defiance of my wishes. [*Pause. Normal tone.*] I'll soon have finished with this story. [*Pause.*] Unless I bring in other characters. [*Pause.*] But where would I find them? [*Pause.*] Where would I look for them? [*Pause. He whistles. Enter* CLOV.] Let us pray to God.

NAGG   Me sugar-plum!

CLOV   There's a rat in the kitchen!

HAMM   A rat! Are there still rats?

CLOV   In the kitchen there's one.

HAMM   And you haven't exterminated him?

CLOV   Half. You disturbed us.

HAMM   He can't get away?

CLOV   No.

HAMM   You'll finish him later. Let us pray to God.

CLOV   Again!

NAGG   Me sugar-plum!

HAMM   God first! [*Pause.*] Are you right?

CLOV [*Resigned.*]   Off we go.

HAMM [*To* NAGG.]   And you?

9. A wind meter.   1. A moisture meter.

NAGG [*Clasping his hands, closing his eyes, in a gabble.*]   Our Father which
  art—
HAMM   Silence! In silence! Where are your manners? [*Pause.*] Off we go.
  [*Attitudes of prayer. Silence. Abandoning his attitude, discouraged.*] Well?
CLOV [*Abandoning his attitude.*]   What a hope! And you?
HAMM   Sweet damn all! [*To* NAGG.] And you?
NAGG   Wait! [*Pause. Abandoning his attitude.*] Nothing doing!
HAMM   The bastard! He doesn't exist!
CLOV   Not yet.
NAGG   Me sugar-plum!
HAMM   There are no more sugar-plums! [*Pause.*]
NAGG   It's natural. After all I'm your father. It's true if it hadn't been me
  it would have been someone else. But that's no excuse. [*Pause.*] Turkish
  Delight,[2] for example, which no longer exists, we all know that, there is
  nothing in the world I love more. And one day I'll ask you for some, in
  return for a kindness, and you'll promise it to me. One must live with
  the times. [*Pause.*] Whom did you call when you were a tiny boy, and
  were frightened, in the dark? Your mother? No. Me. We let you cry. Then
  we moved you out of earshot, so that we might sleep in peace. [*Pause.*]
  I was asleep, as happy as a king, and you woke me up to have me listen
  to you. It wasn't indispensable, you didn't really need to have me listen
  to you. [*Pause.*] I hope the day will come when you'll really need to have
  me listen to you, and need to hear my voice, any voice. [*Pause.*] Yes, I
  hope I'll live till then, to hear you calling me like when you were a tiny
  boy, and were frightened, in the dark, and I was your only hope. [*Pause.*
  NAGG *knocks on lid of* NELL's *bin. Pause.*] Nell! [*Pause. He knocks louder.
  Pause. Louder.*] Nell! [*Pause.* NAGG *sinks back into his bin, closes the lid
  behind him. Pause.*]
HAMM   Our revels now are ended.[3] [*He gropes for the dog.*] The dog's gone.
CLOV   He's not a real dog, he can't go.
HAMM [*Groping.*]   He's not there.
CLOV   He's lain down.
HAMM   Give him up to me. [CLOV *picks up the dog and gives it to* HAMM.
  HAMM *holds it in his arms. Pause.* HAMM *throws away the dog.*] Dirty brute!
  [CLOV *begins to pick up the objects lying on the ground.*] What are you
  doing?
CLOV   Putting things in order. [*He straightens up. Fervently.*] I'm going to
  clear everything away! [*He starts picking up again.*]
HAMM   Order!
CLOV [*Straightening up.*]   I love order. It's my dream. A world where all
  would be silent and still and each thing in its last place, under the last
  dust. [*He starts picking up again.*]
HAMM [*Exasperated.*]   What in God's name do you think you are doing?
CLOV [*Straightening up.*]   I'm doing my best to create a little order.
HAMM   Drop it!
    [CLOV *drops the objects he has picked up.*]
CLOV   After all, there or elsewhere. [*He goes towards door.*]
HAMM [*Irritably.*]   What's wrong with your feet?

---

2. A sticky sweet candy.   3. Lines spoken by Prospero in Shakespeare's *The Tempest* 4.1.148.

CLOV   My feet?

HAMM   Tramp! Tramp!

CLOV   I must have put on my boots.

HAMM   Your slippers were hurting you? [*Pause.*]

CLOV   I'll leave you.

HAMM   No!

CLOV   What is there to keep me here?

HAMM   The dialogue. [*Pause.*] I've got on with my story. [*Pause.*] I've got
on with it well. [*Pause. Irritably.*] Ask me where I've got to.

CLOV   Oh, by the way, your story?

HAMM   [*Surprised.*]   What story?

CLOV   The one you've been telling yourself all your days.

HAMM   Ah you mean my chronicle?

CLOV   That's the one. [*Pause.*]

HAMM   [*Angrily.*]   Keep going, can't you, keep going!

CLOV   You've got on with it, I hope.

HAMM   [*Modestly.*]   Oh not very far, not very far. [*He sighs.*] There are days
like that, one isn't inspired. [*Pause.*] Nothing you can do about it, just
wait for it to come. [*Pause.*] No forcing, no forcing, it's fatal. [*Pause.*]
I've got on with it a little all the same. [*Pause.*] Technique, you know.
[*Pause. Irritably.*] I say I've got on with it a little all the same.

CLOV   [*Admiringly.*]   Well I never! In spite of everything you were able to
get on with it!

HAMM   [*Modestly.*]   Oh not very far, you know, not very far, but nevertheless, better than nothing.

CLOV   Better than nothing! Is it possible?

HAMM   I'll tell you how it goes. He comes crawling on his belly—

CLOV   Who?

HAMM   What?

CLOV   Who do you mean, he?

HAMM   Who do I mean! Yet another.

CLOV   Ah him! I wasn't sure.

HAMM   Crawling on his belly, whining for bread for his brat. He's offered
a job as gardener. Before— [CLOV *bursts out laughing.*] What is there so
funny about that?

CLOV   A job as gardener!

HAMM   Is that what tickles you?

CLOV   It must be that.

HAMM   It wouldn't be the bread?

CLOV   Or the brat. [*Pause.*]

HAMM   The whole thing is comical, I grant you that. What about having
a good guffaw the two of us together?

CLOV   [*After reflection.*]   I couldn't guffaw again today.

HAMM   [*After reflection.*]   Nor I. [*Pause.*] I continue then. Before accepting
with gratitude he asks if he may have his little boy with him.

CLOV   What age?

HAMM   Oh tiny.

CLOV   He would have climbed the trees.

HAMM   All the little odd jobs.

CLOV   And then he would have grown up.

HAMM   Very likely. [*Pause.*]

CLOV   Keep going, can't you, keep going!

HAMM   That's all. I stopped there. [*Pause.*]

CLOV   Do you see how it goes on.

HAMM   More or less.

CLOV   Will it not soon be the end?

HAMM   I'm afraid it will.

CLOV   Pah! You'll make up another.

HAMM   I don't know. [*Pause.*] I feel rather drained. [*Pause.*] The prolonged
   creative effort. [*Pause.*] If I could drag myself down to the sea! I'd make
   a pillow of sand for my head and the tide would come.

CLOV   There's no more tide. [*Pause.*]

HAMM   Go and see is she dead.
   [CLOV *goes to bins, raises the lid of* NELL's, *stoops, looks into it.
   Pause.*]

CLOV   Looks like it.
   [*He closes the lid, straightens up.* HAMM *raises his toque. Pause. He
   puts it on again.*]

HAMM [*With his hand to his toque.*]   And Nagg?
   [CLOV *raises lid of* NAGG's *bin, stoops, looks into it. Pause.*]

CLOV   Doesn't look like it. [*He closes the lid, straightens up.*]

HAMM [*Letting go his toque.*]   What's he doing? [CLOV *raises lid of* NAGG's
   bin, stoops, looks into it. Pause.]

CLOV   He's crying. [*He closes lid, straightens up.*]

HAMM   Then he's living. [*Pause.*] Did you ever have an instant of happiness?

CLOV   Not to my knowledge. [*Pause.*]

HAMM   Bring me under the window. [CLOV *goes towards chair.*] I want to
   feel the light on my face. [CLOV *pushes chair.*] Do you remember, in the
   beginning, when you took me for a turn? You used to hold the chair too
   high. At every step you nearly tipped me out. [*With senile quaver.*] Ah
   great fun, we had, the two of us, great fun. [*Gloomily.*] And then we got
   into the way of it. [CLOV *stops the chair under window right.*] There
   already? [*Pause. He tilts back his head.*] Is it light?

CLOV   It isn't dark.

HAMM [*Angrily.*]   I'm asking you is it light.

CLOV   Yes. [*Pause.*]

HAMM   The curtain isn't closed?

CLOV   No.

HAMM   What window is it?

CLOV   The earth.

HAMM   I knew it! [*Angrily.*] But there's no light there! The other! [CLOV
   stops the chair under window left. HAMM *tilts back his head.*] That's what
   I call light! [*Pause.*] Feels like a ray of sunshine. [*Pause.*] No?

CLOV   No.

HAMM   It isn't a ray of sunshine I feel on my face?

CLOV   No. [*Pause.*]

HAMM   Am I very white? [*Pause. Angrily.*] I'm asking you am I very white!

CLOV   Not more so than usual. [*Pause.*]

HAMM   Open the window.

CLOV   What for?

HAMM   I want to hear the sea.

CLOV   You wouldn't hear it.

HAMM   Even if you opened the window?

CLOV   No.

HAMM   Then it's not worth while opening it?

CLOV   No.

HAMM   [*Violently.*]   Then open it! [CLOV *gets up on the ladder, opens the window. Pause.*] Have you opened it?

CLOV   Yes. [*Pause.*]

HAMM   You swear you've opened it?

CLOV   Yes. [*Pause.*]

HAMM   Well . . . ! [*Pause.*] It must be very calm. [*Pause. Violently.*] I'm asking you is it very calm!

CLOV   Yes.

HAMM   It's because there are no more navigators. [*Pause.*] You haven't much conversation all of a sudden. Do you not feel well?

CLOV   I'm cold.

HAMM   What month are we? [*Pause.*] Close the window, we're going back. [CLOV *closes the window, gets down, pushes the chair back to its place, remains standing behind it, head bowed.*] Don't stay there, you give me the shivers! [CLOV *returns to his place beside the chair.*] Father! [*Pause. Louder.*] Father! [*Pause.*] Go and see did he hear me.
        [CLOV *goes to* NAGG's *bin, raises the lid, stoops. Unintelligible words.* CLOV *straightens up.*]

CLOV   Yes.

HAMM   Both times?
        [CLOV *stoops. As before.*]

CLOV   Once only.

HAMM   The first time or the second?
        [CLOV *stoops. As before.*]

CLOV   He doesn't know.

HAMM   It must have been the second.

CLOV   We'll never know. [*He closes lid.*]

HAMM   Is he still crying?

CLOV   No.

HAMM   The dead go fast. [*Pause.*] What's he doing?

CLOV   Sucking his biscuit.

HAMM   Life goes on. [CLOV *returns to his place beside the chair.*] Give me a rug. I'm freezing.

CLOV   There are no more rugs. [*Pause.*]

HAMM   Kiss me. [*Pause.*] Will you not kiss me?

CLOV   No.

HAMM   On the forehead.

CLOV   I won't kiss you anywhere. [*Pause.*]

HAMM   [*Holding out his hand.*]   Give me your hand at least. [*Pause.*] Will you not give me your hand?

CLOV   I won't touch you. [*Pause.*]

HAMM   Give me the dog. [CLOV *looks round for the dog.*] No!

CLOV   Do you not want your dog?

HAMM   No.

CLOV   Then I'll leave you.

HAMM   [*Head bowed, absently.*]   That's right.

[CLOV *goes to door, turns.*]

CLOV   If I don't kill that rat he'll die.

HAMM   [*As before.*]   That's right. [*Exit* CLOV. *Pause.*] Me to play. [*He takes out his handkerchief, unfolds it, holds it spread out before him.*] We're getting on. [*Pause.*] You weep, and weep, for nothing, so as not to laugh, and little by little . . . you begin to grieve. [*He folds the handkerchief, puts it back in his pocket, raises his head.*] All those I might have helped. [*Pause.*] Helped! [*Pause.*] Saved. [*Pause.*] Saved! [*Pause.*] The place was crawling with them! [*Pause. Violently.*] Use your head, can't you, use your head, you're on earth, there's no cure for that! [*Pause.*] Get out of here and love one another! Lick your neighbor as yourself![4] [*Pause. Calmer.*] When it wasn't bread they wanted it was crumpets. [*Pause. Violently.*] Out of my sight and back to your petting parties! [*Pause.*] All that, all that! [*Pause.*] Not even a real dog! [*Calmer.*] The end is in the beginning and yet you go on. [*Pause.*] Perhaps I could go on with my story, end it and begin another. [*Pause.*] Perhaps I could throw myself out on the floor. [*He pushes himself painfully off his seat, falls back again.*] Dig my nails into the cracks and drag myself forward with my fingers. [*Pause.*] It will be the end and there I'll be, wondering what can have brought it on and wondering what can have . . . [*He hesitates.*] . . . why it was so long coming. [*Pause.*] There I'll be, in the old shelter, alone against the silence and . . . [*He hesitates.*] . . . the stillness. If I can hold my peace, and sit quiet, it will be all over with sound, and motion, all over and done with. [*Pause.*] I'll have called my father and I'll have called my . . . [*He hesitates.*] . . . my son. And even twice, or three times, in case they shouldn't have heard me, the first time, or the second. [*Pause.*] I'll say to myself, He'll come back. [*Pause.*] And then? [*Pause.*] And then? [*Pause.*] He couldn't, he has gone too far. [*Pause.*] And then? [*Pause. Very agitated.*] All kinds of fantasies! That I'm being watched! A rat! Steps! Breath held and then . . . [*He breathes out.*] Then babble, babble, words, like the solitary child who turns himself into children, two, three, so as to be together, and whisper together, in the dark. [*Pause.*] Moment upon moment, pattering down, like the millet grains of . . . [*He hesitates.*] . . . that old Greek,[5] and all life long you wait for that to mount up to a life. [*Pause. He opens his mouth to continue, renounces.*] Ah let's get it over! [*He whistles. Enter* CLOV *with alarm-clock. He halts beside the chair.*] What? Neither gone nor dead?

CLOV   In spirit only.

HAMM   Which?

CLOV   Both.

HAMM   Gone from me you'd be dead.

CLOV   And vice versa.

---

4. Parody of Jesus' words in the Bible: "Thou shalt love thy neighbor as thyself" (Matthew 19.19).
5. Zeno of Elea, a Greek philosopher active around 450 B.C., known for logical paradoxes that reduce to absurdity various attempts to define *Being*. Aristotle reports that Zeno's paradox on sound questioned: If a grain of millet falling makes no sound, how can a bushel of grains make any sound? (Aristotle's *Physics* 5.250a.19).

HAMM   Outside of here it's death! [*Pause.*] And the rat?

CLOV   He's got away.

HAMM   He can't go far. [*Pause. Anxious.*] Eh?

CLOV   He doesn't need to go far. [*Pause.*]

HAMM   Is it not time for my pain-killer?

CLOV   Yes.

HAMM   Ah! At last! Give it to me! Quick! [*Pause.*]

CLOV   There's no more pain-killer. [*Pause.*]

HAMM [*Appalled.*]   Good . . . ! [*Pause.*] No more pain-killer!

CLOV   No more pain-killer. You'll never get any more pain-killer. [*Pause.*]

HAMM   But the little round box. It was full!

CLOV   Yes. But now it's empty.

> [*Pause.* CLOV *starts to move about the room. He is looking for a place*
> *to put down the alarm-clock.*]

HAMM [*Soft.*]   What'll I do? [*Pause. In a scream.*] What'll I do? [CLOV *sees*
the picture, takes it down, stands it on the floor with its face to the wall,
hangs up the alarm-clock in its place.] What are you doing?

CLOV   Winding up.

HAMM   Look at the earth.

CLOV   Again!

HAMM   Since it's calling to you.

CLOV   Is your throat sore? [*Pause.*] Would you like a lozenge? [*Pause.*] No.
[*Pause.*] Pity. [*He goes, humming, towards window right, halts before it,*
looks up at it.]

HAMM   Don't sing.

CLOV [*Turning towards* HAMM.]   One hasn't the right to sing any more?

HAMM   No.

CLOV   Then how can it end?

HAMM   You want it to end?

CLOV   I want to sing.

HAMM   I can't prevent you.

> [*Pause.* CLOV *turns towards window right.*]

CLOV   What did I do with that steps? [*He looks around for ladder.*] You
didn't see that steps? [*He sees it.*] Ah, about time. [*He goes towards win-*
dow left.] Sometimes I wonder if I'm in my right mind. Then it passes
over and I'm as lucid as before. [*He gets up on ladder, looks out of win-*
dow.] Christ, she's under water! [*He looks.*] How can that be? [*He pokes*
forward his head, his hand above his eyes.] It hasn't rained. [*He wipes the*
pane, looks. Pause.] Ah what a fool I am! I'm on the wrong side! [*He gets*
down, takes a few steps towards window right.] Under water! [*He goes*
back for ladder.] What a fool I am! [*He carries ladder towards window*
right.] Sometimes I wonder if I'm in my right senses. Then it passes off
and I'm as intelligent as ever. [*He sets down ladder under window right,*
gets up on it, looks out of window. He turns towards HAMM.] Any particular
sector you fancy? Or merely the whole thing?

HAMM   Whole thing.

CLOV   The general effect? Just a moment. [*He looks out of window. Pause.*]

HAMM   Clov.

CLOV [*Absorbed.*]   Mmm.

HAMM   Do you know what it is?

CLOV [*As before.*]   Mmm.

HAMM   I was never there. [*Pause.*] Clov!

CLOV [*Turning towards* HAMM, *exasperated.*]   What is it?

HAMM   I was never there.

CLOV   Lucky for you. [*He looks out of window.*]

HAMM   Absent, always. It all happened without me. I don't know what's happened. [*Pause.*] Do you know what's happened? [*Pause.*] Clov!

CLOV [*Turning towards* HAMM, *exasperated.*]   Do you want me to look at this muckheap, yes or no?

HAMM   Answer me first.

CLOV   What?

HAMM   Do you know what's happened?

CLOV   When? Where?

HAMM [*Violently.*]   When! What's happened? Use your head, can't you! What has happened?

CLOV   What for Christ's sake does it matter? [*He looks out of window.*]

HAMM   I don't know.

      [*Pause.* CLOV *turns towards* HAMM.]

CLOV [*Harshly.*]   When old Mother Pegg asked you for oil for her lamp and you told her to get out to hell, you knew what was happening then, no? [*Pause.*] You know what she died of, Mother Pegg? Of darkness.

HAMM [*Feebly.*]   I hadn't any.

CLOV [*As before.*]   Yes, you had. [*Pause.*]

HAMM   Have you the glass?

CLOV   No, it's clear enough as it is.

HAMM   Go and get it.

      [*Pause.* CLOV *casts up his eyes, brandishes his fists. He loses balance, clutches on to the ladder. He starts to get down, halts.*]

CLOV   There's one thing I'll never understand. [*He gets down.*] Why I always obey you. Can you explain that to me?

HAMM   No. . . . Perhaps it's compassion. [*Pause.*] A kind of great compassion. [*Pause.*] Oh you won't find it easy, you won't find it easy.

      [*Pause.* CLOV *begins to move about the room in search of the telescope.*]

CLOV   I'm tired of our goings on, very tired. [*He searches.*] You're not sitting on it? [*He moves the chair, looks at the place where it stood, resumes his search.*]

HAMM [*Anguished.*]   Don't leave me there! [*Angrily* CLOV *restores the chair to its place.*] Am I right in the center?

CLOV   You'd need a microscope to find this— [*He sees the telescope.*] Ah, about time. [*He picks up the telescope, gets up on the ladder, turns the telescope on the without.*]

HAMM   Give me the dog.

CLOV [*Looking.*]   Quiet!

HAMM [*Angrily.*]   Give me the dog!

      [CLOV *drops the telescope, clasps his hands to his head. Pause. He gets down precipitately, looks for the dog, sees it, picks it up, hastens towards* HAMM *and strikes him violently on the head with the dog.*]

CLOV   There's your dog for you!

      [*The dog falls to the ground. Pause.*]

HAMM   He hit me!

CLOV   You drive me mad, I'm mad!

HAMM   If you must hit me, hit me with the axe. [*Pause.*] Or with the gaff, hit me with the gaff. Not with the dog. With the gaff. Or with the axe.
    [CLOV *picks up the dog and gives it to* HAMM *who takes it in his arms.*]

CLOV [*Imploringly.*]   Let's stop playing!

HAMM   Never! [*Pause.*] Put me in my coffin.

CLOV   There are no more coffins.

HAMM   Then let it end! [CLOV *goes towards ladder.*] With a bang! [CLOV *gets up on ladder, gets down again, looks for telescope, sees it, picks it up, gets up ladder, raises telescope.*] Of darkness! And me? Did anyone ever have pity on me?

CLOV [*Lowering the telescope, turning towards* HAMM.]   What? [*Pause.*] Is it me you're referring to?

HAMM [*Angrily.*]   An aside, ape! Did you never hear an aside before? [*Pause.*] I'm warming up for my last soliloquy.

CLOV   I warn you. I'm going to look at this filth since it's an order. But it's the last time. [*He turns the telescope on the without.*] Let's see. [*He moves the telescope.*] Nothing . . . nothing . . . good . . . good . . . nothing . . . goo— [*He starts, lowers the telescope, examines it, turns it again on the without. Pause.*] Bad luck to it!

HAMM   More complications! [CLOV *gets down.*] Not an underplot, I trust.
    [CLOV *moves ladder nearer window, gets up on it, turns telescope on the without.*]

CLOV [*Dismayed.*]   Looks like a small boy!

HAMM [*Sarcastic.*]   A small . . . boy!

CLOV   I'll go and see. [*He gets down, drops the telescope, goes towards door, turns.*] I'll take the gaff. [*He looks for the gaff, sees it, picks it up, hastens towards door.*]

HAMM   No! [CLOV *halts.*]

CLOV   No? A potential procreator?

HAMM   If he exists he'll die there or he'll come here. And if he doesn't . . . [*Pause.*]

CLOV   You don't believe me? You think I'm inventing? [*Pause.*]

HAMM   It's the end, Clov, we've come to the end. I don't need you any more. [*Pause.*]

CLOV   Lucky for you. [*He goes towards door.*]

HAMM   Leave me the gaff.
    [CLOV *gives him the gaff, goes towards door, halts, looks at alarm-clock, takes it down, looks round for a better place to put it, goes to bins, puts it on lid of* NAGG's *bin. Pause.*]

CLOV   I'll leave you. [*He goes towards door.*]

HAMM   Before you go . . . [CLOV *halts near door.*] . . . say something.

CLOV   There is nothing to say.

HAMM   A few words . . . to ponder . . . in my heart.

CLOV   Your heart!

HAMM   Yes. [*Pause. Forcibly.*] Yes! [*Pause.*] With the rest, in the end, the shadows, the murmurs, all the trouble, to end up with. [*Pause.*] Clov. . . . He never spoke to me. Then, in the end, before he went, without my having asked him, he spoke to me. He said . . .

CLOV [*Despairingly.*]   Ah . . . !

HAMM   Something . . . from your heart.

CLOV   My heart!

HAMM   A few words . . . from your heart. [*Pause.*]

CLOV [*Fixed gaze, tonelessly, towards auditorium.*]   They said to me, That's love, yes, yes, not a doubt, now you see how—

HAMM   Articulate!

CLOV [*As before.*]   How easy it is. They said to me, That's friendship, yes, yes, no question, you've found it. They said to me, Here's the place, stop, raise your head and look at all that beauty. That order! They said to me. Come now, you're not a brute beast, think upon these things and you'll see how all becomes clear. And simple! They said to me, What skilled attention they get, all these dying of their wounds.

HAMM   Enough!

CLOV [*As before.*]   I say to myself—sometimes, Clov, you must learn to suffer better than that if you want them to weary of punishing you—one day. I say to myself—sometimes, Clov, you must be there better than that if you want them to let you go—one day. But I feel too old, and too far, to form new habits. Good, it'll never end, I'll never go. [*Pause.*] Then one day, suddenly, it ends, it changes, I don't understand, it dies, or it's me, I don't understand, that either. I ask the words that remain—sleeping, waking, morning, evening. They have nothing to say. [*Pause.*] I open the door of the cell and go. I am so bowed I only see my feet, if I open my eyes, and between my legs a little trail of black dust. I say to myself that the earth is extinguished, though I never saw it lit. [*Pause.*] It's easy going. [*Pause.*] When I fall I'll weep for happiness. [*Pause. He goes towards door.*]

HAMM   Clov! [CLOV *halts, without turning.*] Nothing. [CLOV *moves on.*] Clov!

[CLOV *halts, without turning.*]

CLOV   This is what we call making an exit.

HAMM   I'm obliged to you, Clov. For your services.

CLOV [*Turning, sharply.*]   Ah pardon, it's I am obliged to you.

HAMM   It's we are obliged to each other. [*Pause.* CLOV *goes towards door.*] One thing more. [CLOV *halts.*] A last favor. [*Exit* CLOV.] Cover me with the sheet. [*Long pause.*] No? Good. [*Pause.*] Me to play. [*Pause. Wearily.*] Old endgame lost of old, play and lose and have done with losing. [*Pause. More animated.*] Let me see. [*Pause.*] Ah yes! [*He tries to move the chair, using the gaff as before. Enter* CLOV, *dressed for the road. Panama hat, tweed coat, raincoat over his arm, umbrella, bag. He halts by the door and stands there, impassive and motionless, his eyes fixed on* HAMM, *till the end.* HAMM *gives up.*] Good. [*Pause.*] Discard. [*He throws away the gaff, makes to throw away the dog, thinks better of it.*] Take it easy. [*Pause.*] And now? [*Pause.*] Raise hat. [*He raises his toque.*] Peace to our . . . arses. [*Pause.*] And put on again. [*He puts on his toque.*] Deuce. [*Pause. He takes off his glasses.*] Wipe. [*He takes out his handkerchief and, without unfolding it, wipes his glasses.*] And put on again. [*He puts on his glasses, puts back the handkerchief in his pocket.*] We're coming. A few more squirms like that and I'll call. [*Pause.*] A little poetry. [*Pause.*] You prayed— [*Pause. He corrects himself.*] You CRIED for night; it comes— [*Pause. He corrects himself.*] It FALLS: now cry in darkness. [*He repeats, chanting.*] You cried for night; it falls: now cry in darkness.[6] [*Pause.*] Nicely put, that. [*Pause.*] And now? [*Pause.*] Moments for nothing, now as always, time was never and time is over, reckoning closed and story ended. [*Pause. Narrative tone.*] If he could have his child with him. . . . [*Pause.*] It was the moment I was waiting for. [*Pause.*] You don't want to abandon him? You want him to bloom while you are withering? Be there to solace your last million last moments? [*Pause.*] He doesn't realize, all he knows is hunger, and cold, and death to crown it all. But you! You ought to know what the earth is like, nowadays. Oh I put him before his responsibilities! [*Pause. Normal tone.*] Well, there we are, there I am, that's enough. [*He raises the whistle to his lips, hesitates, drops it. Pause.*] Yes, truly! [*He whistles. Pause. Louder. Pause.*] Good. [*Pause.*] Father! [*Pause. Louder.*] Father! [*Pause.*] Good. [*Pause.*] We're coming. [*Pause.*] And to end up with? [*Pause.*] Discard. [*He throws away the dog. He tears the whistle from his neck.*] With my compliments. [*He throws whistle towards auditorium. Pause. He sniffs. Soft.*] Clov! [*Long pause.*] No? Good. [*He takes out the handkerchief.*] Since that's the way we're playing it . . . [*He unfolds handkerchief.*] . . . let's play it that way . . . [*He unfolds.*] . . . and speak no more about it . . . [*He finishes unfolding.*] . . . speak no more. [*He holds handkerchief spread out before him.*] Old stancher! [*Pause.*] You . . . remain.

    [*Pause. He covers his face with handkerchief, lowers his arms to armrests, remains motionless.*]

    [*Brief tableau.*]

Curtain

6. Parody of a line from the poem *Meditation*, by Baudelaire: "You were calling for evening; it falls; here it is."

BIRAGO DIOP
1906–1992

Although Birago Diop was an accomplished poet and dramatist, his achievement as a writer resides principally in his felicitous renderings of the African folktale and his effective adaptation of an essentially oral mode to a literate medium. His work thus testifies to the productive relationship between orality and literacy that has largely conditioned the modern African imagination. For, in their spirit and essential features, Diop's tales derive from the folktale tradition in Africa and incorporate the formal principles and performance modes associated with this tradition. Diop himself disclaims authorship of these tales. He ascribes them to Amadou Koumba, an old sage and *griot* who recited them to him during a memorable week he spent, in the late 1930s, in the hinterland of the former French West African empire, during one of his many tours of duty as a veterinary officer in the colonial service. Listening to Amadou Koumba brought back to Diop vivid memories of the nightly folktale sessions that formed part of his childhood in the family compound in Dakar and confirmed for him the imaginative scope as well as the profound human import of the tales.

    Given these circumstances, Diop has claimed for himself only the merit of having transcribed and rendered the tales in French. This explains why, in his retelling, they retain a quality of authenticity and bear out his desire to be considered the faithful perpetuator of an age-old tradition. Diop's fidelity to this tradition does not, however, preclude an originality of style that puts his personal seal on the tales, for they emerge in his versions as individual re-creations of a communal resource. They are not "translations" but rather "transpositions" from an African—and specifically Wolof (an ethnic group in central Senegal)—mode of expression into a European one. They represent, in other words, a conscious reworking of folktale elements in a new idiom.

Diop was born in 1906 in Dakar, Senegal, to an influential Wolof family that, though nominally Muslim, had remained firmly rooted in the traditional way of life. He began attending koranic school at the customary age of five, learning the rudiments of Arabic and the sacred texts of Islam. However, at ten, he enrolled on his own at the French school, where he spent the next four years and developed an enduring attachment to the French language and literature, which formed the basis of the curriculum. After completing his primary education in 1921, he was sent to live with a relative in St. Louis, at that time the capital of Senegal, and was admitted the following year to the Lycée Faidherbe as a scholarship student. An old colonial city founded in the late sixteenth century by the French at the mouth of the Senegal River in the far north of the colony, St. Louis in the 1920s was a social and cultural elite center. In its intellectual atmosphere Diop's passion for literature and the arts was further strengthened. He immersed himself while a student at the lycée in classical French literature and began to try his hand at poetry. The influence of the French Romantic and Parnassian poets was predominant in this early work, colored no doubt by a naive exoticism but testifying to a preoccupation with form (indicative of the Parnassians) that was to become a hallmark of his writing. It was also during this period that he encountered the works of the French anthropologists Georges Hardy and Robert Delavignette, both colonial administrators, whose investigations of the indigenous social institutions and the traditional arts had begun to foster a revised image of Africa, one at variance with the received Western opinion of Africa as the "Dark Continent." From his reading of their works, Diop acquired a new reverence for his cultural background.

In 1928, Diop obtained his *baccalauréat* (the high school degree in the French system) and was immediately drafted into the colonial army and attached as an assistant nurse to the military hospital in St. Louis. There he decided to become a doctor, and although he subsequently won a scholarship to study at the University of Toulouse in France, he was refused admission to the faculty of medicine; he decided instead to become a veterinary surgeon. He graduated in 1933 and moved to Paris the same year for advanced studies. This was the first of Diop's many sojourns in Paris, and although it lasted less than a year, it enabled him to meet his compatriot Léopold Sédar Senghor and other French-speaking African and Caribbean intellectuals then promoting the new self-awareness among black people that was to lead to the concept of Négritude, the idea of a collective personality of the black race, and the literary movement by which it came to be sustained. With Senghor and others in the group around him Diop helped found *L'Etudiant noir* (The Black Student), a journal devoted to African cultural renovation and the rehabilitation of the black race. The efforts of the group benefited from a new climate of French appreciation of African culture and from the growing recognition of African art, whose impact on avant-garde European artists had been decisive. These shifts in attitude were complemented by a lively interest in African folklore, of which the success of Blaise Cendrar's *Anthologie Nègre* provided striking evidence. But perhaps more important for Diop was the work of the West Indian novelist René Maran, whose *Batouala* had won the prestigious Prix Goncourt in 1921 and whose last work, *Le Livre de la brousse,* had given a new orientation to the literature of exoticism in French. Maran's integration of the African environment into his novels, with human characters interacting with vegetation and wildlife, could not but recall to his African readers the elements and atmosphere of their traditional tales and must have made a lasting impression on Diop. Moreover, Diop's French education had already made him familiar with the *Fables* of La Fontaine, derived from Aesop, a work peopled by animal characters, representing a wide range of human dispositions and dramatic situations, as in the folktales of his West African homeland.

Diop's appointment as a veterinary officer, on his return to Senegal in 1934, was to determine the direction of his literary career. Because his job required him to travel all over the West African savanna, he came into intimate contact with the daily life of rural folk. The experience gave him a new awareness, as an African assimilated to Western culture, of his antecedents in the indigenous way of life and a fresh insight into the centrality of the imaginative function—of which in oral communities the folktale was the immediate vehicle of expression. His sessions with Amadou Koumba crystallized his resolve to set down in writing the tales he had heard both as a city child and during his travels in the country. Unable to return in 1942 to Senegal from his annual summer vacation in France because of the war and the German occupation, he devoted the next two years to writing poetry and composing the first of his folktale adaptations. This work began to appear in various literary journals, and in 1947 the tales were gathered into a volume and published under the title *Les Contes d'Amadou Khoumba* (The Tales of Amadou Koumba). They were immediately acclaimed by Senghor, who included a poem from the collection in his historic anthology of black writing in French published the following year. The poem, *Souffles* (Breaths), featured as a song interlude in the tale *Sarzan*, remains the best known statement in literature of the mystical conception of the universe in African thought systems:

> Listen more often
> To Things than to Beings
> The voice of fire
> The voice of water
> Listen in the wind
> The sigh of the woods
> The breath of the ancestors
>
> Those who are dead are not dead
> They are in the shadows that lighten around us
> And in the shadows that thicken into darkness
> The dead are not under the ground
> They are in the trees that tremble
> They are in the woods that groan
> They are in the water that flows
> They are in the water that sleeps
> They are in the Hut, they are in the Crowd
> The dead are not dead.

Diop's second collection, *Les Nouveaux Contes d'Amadou Koumba* (New Tales of Amadou Koumba), with an extensive prefatory essay by Senghor, appeared in 1958, and confirmed his special genius. It was followed by *Leurres et lueurs* (1960), which brought together poems Diop had written over a period of some twenty years. Appointed by President Senghor as ambassador to Tunisia at the independence of Senegal in 1960, Diop put together a third collection, *Contes et lavanes* (1963), containing new tales and a selection of Wolof riddles and aphorisms (the *lavanes* of the title). After four years, he gave up his official position to return to private life in Dakar, where he set up a veterinary clinic and began work on his memoirs, two books of which were later published: *La Plume raboutée* (The Splintered Pen) (1978) and *À Rebrousse-temps* (Against the Grain of Time) (1982). With his tales translated into several languages and many of them adapted for the stage, by himself and others,

Diop was esteemed as one of the architects of a modern African literary renaissance. But apart from receiving visitors from all over the world at his clinic, he lived a largely uneventful life until his death in 1992.

The two selections presented here offer a representative view of Diop's themes and of his formal approach to the material he inherited from the oral tradition. The theme of just retribution meted out to vice receives a pointed human application in *The Bone,* through the depiction of an obsessive and ultimately self-destructive character trait. The setting of this tale in a highly integrated community puts in bold relief Mor Lame's willful deviation from shared norms and gives telling effect to the macabre details of the story; the ironic turn of events that concludes the tale underlines the preeminently didactic function of the folktale in the oral tradition. The tale is remarkable for the way the background functions within the narrative to determine its pace and structure, with the stages of Mor Lame's descent to the grave linked to the progression of the day, itself marked by the Muslim prayers prescribed for the faithful from sunrise to sunset.

Mother Crocodile offers a much wider canvas than *The Bone.* Its portrait gallery introduces us to the principal animal characters of Wolof folktales, some of whom, notably Leuk-the-Hare, have whole cycles devoted to them. Diop builds on and extends the traditional folktale's anthropomorphism—which gives animals human traits and contexts—to project a view sympathetic to reclaiming the ancestral heritage. The immediate theme of memory on which the tale revolves illustrates the enduring value of traditional wisdom and refers beyond itself to the human world of heroic and epic narratives in which the broader historical consciousness of traditional societies is grounded. The references in the tale to some dramatic moments of the precolonial period in the West African savanna—evoked as a theater both of human interaction going back to the Middle Ages and of varied forms of socioeconomic and cultural life—affirm the significance of the historical background of the region for the generation of Africans, alienated by Western colonialism from their past, to whom Diop's ideological message is addressed. At the same time, the parallel maintained throughout the tale between the human and animal realms, leading to its grim conclusion, conveys a vivid sense not only of humanity's profound rootage in nature but also of the tragic implications of history, so often manifested at all times and in all places as the violent enactment of human passions.

Although many other African writers have turned to the folktale tradition for inspiration, in this mode the work of Diop remains unequaled. The familiar style of the narrative reproduces the conversational flow of African folktale sessions, highlighted by proverbs and aphorisms and punctuated by songs and refrains sung or chanted by both the narrator and the audience. His concern for structure is reflected in the economy of his narrative style and in the elegance of his French, which can only be captured imperfectly in translation. The diversity of situations in his stories reveals his insight into the many facets of human nature, while his animal characters reinforce with their allegorical implications his seriocomic vision of the human condition. Free from self-consciousness, he captures and transmits the atmosphere of the West African savanna, with its customs and values, and gives to his stories, through the blend of realism and fantasy, the stamp of a specific and deeply felt life. But perhaps the most engaging qualities of Diop's writing are the gentle humor with which these tales are rendered, expressive of his essentially humane outlook and the rich imagination that enabled him to reestablish the folktale as a viable genre in the modern literature of Africa written in European languages.

An extensive secondary literature on Birago Diop exists in French; in her introduction to *Tales of Amadou Koumba* (1989), a selection in English translation from Birago Diop's first two volumes, Dorothy S. Blair offers an admirably succinct account of Diop's life and of his work in relation to its background in the oral tradition.

The following list uses common English syllables to provide rough equivalents of selected words whose pronunciation may be unfamiliar to the general reader.

Assalamou Aleykoum: *ah-sah-lah-moo*   Mor Lame: *mawr lahm*

alay-ee-koom   Ngalam: *en-gah-lahm*

Bafoulabe: *bah-foo-lah-bay*   Ngolo: *en-goh-loh*

Brack-Oualo: *brahk–waloh*   N'Guew: *en-gay-woo*

Brahim Saloum: *brah-heem sah-loom*   Niangal: *nyan-gahl*

Birago Diop: *bee-rah-goh jop*   Peul: *pel*

Diara: *jah-rah*   Samba Lame: *sahm-bah lahm*

Diassigue: *dyah-seeg*   Sa n'diaye: *sah en-dee-aye*

Djoliba: *joh-lee-bah*   Sègue: *seg*

Dougoudougou: *doo-goo-doo-goo*   Serigne: *say-reenh*

griot: *gree-oh*   Thile: *teel*

Kouloubali: *koo-loo-bah-lee*   Thioker: *tyoh-ker*

Lamene: *lah-men*   Thioye: *tyo-ee*

Mame: *mahm*   tong-tong: *tawn–tawn*

Momor: *maw-mawr*   Trarza: *trahr-zah*

The Bone[1]

"If he had his belly behind him, it would drag him into a hole." So runs the saying about the impenitent glutton.[2]

And, when talking about Mor Lame, one would add, "If your greed has not been the end of you, then it is not genuine greed!"

For Mor Lame was both a gourmand and a glutton.

In many of the villages, the cattle stocks, ravaged by the most deadly of plagues ever known in the memory of the elders, were slowly building up again. But in Lamene[3] no man of twenty knew what a horned beast looked like.

It is true that Lamene was not as old as the village of Niangal,[4] where, in times gone by, the traveller found, as he later sang, nothing but:

> Fresh fish for some
> Dried fish for others
> Chicken
> Was not yet
> Quite the fashion![5]

---

1. Translated by Dorothy S. Blair.   2. It is standard procedure to announce the theme of a story with this kind of general observation.   3. A village in north-central Senegal.   4. Another village in north-central Senegal.   5. This song, which dwells on the monotony of the villagers' diet, emphasizes the interest of the meat-sharing ceremony that becomes central to the story.

The thatch on all the huts had been renewed less often, and the fields ploughed less often than in Niangal. But if chicken had been the fashion for quite a long time, beef had been unknown for two generations.

That year the rains had been abundant, the earth bounteous, the locusts absent. The children had not been too carried away by their games and had guarded the young ears quite reasonably against the attacks of impudent millet-eaters.[6]

Many a cudgel had forced Golo[7]-the-Monkey and his tribe to respect the ground-nut[8] crop.

Since several members of his family had lost a paw or two in the traps set by the folk of Lamene, Thile-the-Jackal had deemed it wiser to go elsewhere in search of melons, which, if not juicier than those of Lamene, would at least be easier to gather and a less risky proposition for the picker.

In a word, the crops had been magnificent, undreamed of by the folk of Lamene.

So they had decided to send donkeys laden with millet, maize and ground-nuts down to Ferlo, where the Peul[9] tribes pasture their huge herds. Now these Peul folk hardly ever eat meat, for it is true that one becomes satiated with abundance. As the saying goes, "When gathering is too easy, bending down becomes difficult." However the Peul do not live on milk alone and are only too pleased to have millet, for they never touch harrow or hoe, in order to make a *couscous*[1] to mix with the milk from their cows, fresh, curdled, or sour.

The donkeys had been gone for three moons, driven along the paths towards Ferlo by the strongest young men of Lamene, who had been instructed to bring back with them a fine seven-year-old bull.

The sharing-out of this animal (known as the *Tong-Tong*[2]) among the heads of families would allow the elders of the village, the old folk, and the middle-aged (the majority of whom, alas! were now toothless) to relearn the taste of red meat. The younger ones, who would probably only get the bones to gnaw in the end, would get to know, if not the taste, at least the smell of meat grilling or stewing.

The very day the donkeys and their drivers had set out, Mor Lame had decided in his own mind which morsel he would choose on the occasion of the *Tong-Tong*: a shin-bone, well covered with meat and full of juicy marrow. Every subsequent day he had said to his wife, Awa, "You will cook it very slowly, and for a long time, until it is tender and melts like butter in the mouth. And that day you'll see that no one comes near my hut!"

The day came when the young men of Lamene returned to the village from Ferlo, driving back in their midst a splendid bull with huge horns, a rope attached to its right hind leg, and its tawny coat gleaming in the setting sun.

6. The locusts. *Young ears:* that is, of the millet plant.   7. Monkey (Wolof). Diop usually combines the Wolof and French names of his animal characters.   8. Peanut.   9. The French word for the Fulani people, who are pastoralists. Ferlo is an area in northern Senegal, inhabited mainly by the Fulani; the region is less susceptible to drought than other parts of the country.   1. Steamed grains (usually wheat or millet) as well as the soup or stew that is served with them.   2. A ceremony designed to help the poorer people obtain meat and for religious sacrifices.

From its neck the dewlap, massive as a baobab[3] trunk, hung down to the ground.

At the risk of receiving a kick, which in fact he just avoided, Mor Lame came to feel his shin-bone. After reminding those who were responsible for killing and cutting up the bull at the first cock-crow, that this was the portion he had chosen, he went off to instruct his wife to cook it very slowly, very gently, and for a very long time.

The sharing-out was done as soon as the *assaloumou Aleykoum* had been said at the end of the *Fidjir* prayer.[4]

The children had scarcely begun to scrape off the shreds of the meat still clinging to the carcass, when Mor Lame was already in his hut. After closing and barricading the door, he gave his portion to his wife, saying,

"Cook it slowly, gently, and for a very long time!"

Awa put into the pot everything necessary to stew a shinbone till it melts deliciously in the mouth and makes a rich creamy broth, a juicy sauce fit to accompany a calabash of *couscous*, cooked just right and mixed with just the right quantity of ground baobab seeds to make it easily digestible.

She put the pot on the fire and the lid on the pot.

Mor Lame lay down on his bed of branches and bark-fibres. Awa squatted near the fire, whose smoke blackened the roof of the hut. The aroma of the cooking slowly mounted and gradually drove away the smell of smoke, filling the whole hut and tickling Mor Lame's nostrils.

Mor Lame half rose, leaned on his elbow and asked his wife,

"Where is the bone?"

"The bone is there," replied Awa, lifting the lid and skewering the shin.

"Is it getting softer?"

"It is getting softer."

"Put the lid back and stir up the fire!" ordered Mor Lame.

In Lamene everyone was a fervent believer and no adult ever missed a single prayer. So Moussa was astonished that day not to see Mor Lame, his hut brother, at the *yor-yor* prayer.[5]

He swore that he would taste some of that meat, and went to the home of the man who was his more-than-brother.

Stronger than brotherly love, more rigid than paternal love, "hut fraternity"[6] subjects every man worthy of the name to rules, obligations, and laws which he cannot transgress without falling in everyone's estimation.

When, at the age of twelve, you have mingled the blood of your sex[7] with that of another boy one cold morning on the old mortar-stone set up on the ground; when you have sung the same initiatory songs with him, suffered the same blows, eaten from the same calabashes the same delicious or disgusting food; when in a word you have become a man at the same time as he and in the same hut, you are then the slave of his desires, the servant of

3. A gigantic tree found in the dry areas of the West African savannah; its seeds and leaves are used for cooking.   4. Said at dawn, this is the first of the many prayers that Muslims are obliged to say throughout the day. *Assalamou Aleykoum*: Peace be unto you (Arabic), a standard greeting.   5. Said in the mid-morning.   6. A bond among men of the same age group who underwent the initiation ceremony together. 7. The principal element of the initiation ceremony is circumcision.

his needs, the prisoner of his troubles, for all your life; before everyone—father and mother, uncles and brothers.

The day of the *Tong-Tong*, Moussa intended to use and even abuse this right, which custom and tradition gave him over Mor Lame.

"He shall not eat that bone all by himself! He shall not eat it without me!" he said to himself, as he hammered louder and louder on the fence surrounding Mor Lame's hut, calling to his hut-brother,

"It's me, Mor! It's me, Moussa, your more-than-brother! Let me in!"

At the sound of the knocking and the shouting, Mor Lame got up suddenly and asked,

"Where is the bone?"

"The bone is there."

"Is it getting soft?"

Awa lifted the lid, skewered the shin, and said,

"It's getting soft."

"Put the lid back, stir up the fire, then go out and shut the door!" ordered her husband, as he took up a mat.

He spread his mat in the shade of a flame tree[8] in the middle of the courtyard, and then opened the gate to Moussa.

Cordial, merry greetings there were on the one hand; on the other, grunts and a surly face, like a back-side exposed to the cold morning air.

No one shuts the door in the face of a man who knocks, especially if he is your hut-brother. So Moussa came in and lay down beside Mor Lame, who rested his head on Awa's lap.

Perhaps they might have been able to hear something besides the twitterings of birds, especially the hoarse, peevish chatter of the parrots, if Moussa had not kept up a ceaseless flow of conversation, all by himself.

He talked of the district, of this man and of that, of the good old times of their youth! He revived the memories of their time in the "men's hut," in order to remind Mor Lame discreetly of his duties and obligations, if by chance he had forgotten them, or was inclined to neglect them.

Mor Lame was not in a talkative mood that day, and replied only "yes" and "no" and "perhaps" and "*inch Allah!*"[9] and even more often by those same grunts that had constituted the main part of his greeting.

The shade of the flame tree grew smaller and smaller, and was already exposing the feet of the two hut brothers to the heat of the sun.

Mor Lame beckoned to his wife. As she bent over him, he whispered into her ear,

"Where is the bone?"

"It is over there!"

"Is it soft yet?"

Awa got up, went into the hut; she lifted the lid of the pot, skewered the shin, put the lid back on the pot, came and sat down and then whispered to her husband,

"It's soft!"

---

8. A tall tree with brightly colored flowers.   9. An Arabic expression, equivalent to "God willing."

The sun, having paused a moment at the zenith to see if he should retrace his steps or continue on his way, began to go down towards the west.

The shade of the flame tree stretched out to the east.

The Muezzin called the *Teshar*[1] prayer. Mor Lame and Moussa, with Awa far behind them, performed their devotions; they greeted their guardian angels, asked forgiveness and remission of their sins from the Lord, and then lay down again in the shade of the flame tree, which stretched ever further towards the east.

Another prayer. Then the *izan* prayer,[2] after which the sun, tired of his journey, retired to rest.

As soon as he had lain down for the last time, Mor Lame immediately took his wife aside and asked,

"Where is the bone?"

"The bone is over there."

"Is it soft?"

Awa went into the hut and came back saying,

"It is soft."

"That fellow, Moussa!" said her husband in an undertone, but with rage in his heart. "That dog that won't go away! Awa I'm going to fall ill."

And he did exactly what he said.

Rigid and trembling, he began to sweat like a water-cooler, hung up in the shade of a tamarind tree, shivering like milk which is just coming to the boil.

Assisted by Moussa, who, as a true hut brother, was most sympathetic with Mor Lame's sufferings, Awa carried her husband into another hut from the one where the stew-pot was boiling.

With his wife at the head of his bed and his hut brother at the foot Mor Lame groaned, shivering and sweating. He heard the hours passing until it was midnight.

Weakly he asked Awa,

"Where is the bone?"

"The bone is over there."

"Is it soft?"

"It is soft."

"Leave it there. This dog will not go away. Wife, I am going to die. Then he will be forced to go."

Having said this he pretended to be dead like a corpse already stiff and dry!

"Moussa, your hut brother is dead. Go and fetch Serigne-the-Marabout[3] and the people of the village!"

"No, indeed!" said Moussa most positively. "Never will I abandon my more-than-brother at this hour; nor will I leave you alone with his corpse! The earth is not yet cold; the first cock has not yet crowed. I shall not arouse the whole village. We will watch over him, we two together, as is our duty, we who are—or were—those most dear to him. When the sun rises, the women will pass by here on their way to the well. They will take it upon themselves to inform the people of the village."

1. One of the five required daily prayers. *Muezzin*: calls the faithful to prayer from the mosque's tower.
2. Said individually at the call of the muezzin, as opposed to collective prayers led by the imam (a religious leader) at the mosque.   3. A religious leader, equivalent to *imam*. The term is specific to Islam in French-speaking West Africa.

And Moussa sat down at the feet of the "corpse" with Awa at its head. The earth grew cold; the first cock crew. The sun left his resting-place. Women passed Mor Lame's house, on their way to the well. Intrigued by the unusual silence they went in and learned of the death of Mor Lame. The news spread through Lamene like a whirlwind. Serigne-the-Marabout, the notables and all the men of the village invaded the house.

Awa bent over her husband and whispered in his ear,

"Mor, things are getting too serious. The whole village is here, in your house, come to wash you and wrap you in your shroud and bury you."

"Where is Moussa?" whispered the corpse of Mor Lame.

"Moussa is here."

"Where is the bone?"

"The bone is over there."

"Is it soft?"

"It is soft."

"Then let them wash me!" decreed Mor Lame.

Just as Serigne-the-Marabout was about to wrap him in the white shroud, seven cubits[4] long, Awa came forward and said:

"Serigne, my husband charged me to recite over his dead body a sourate[5] he taught me, so that the Lord would have mercy on him."

The Marabout and his followers retired. Then Awa whispered in her husband's ear,

"Mor, get up! They are going to wrap you in your shroud and they will bury you if you go on pretending to be dead."

"Where is the bone?" inquired Mor's corpse.

"It's over there."

"Is it soft?"

"It is soft."

"And where is Moussa?"

"He is still here."

"Then let them wrap me in my shroud!" decided Mor Lame.

And so it was done.

And then his body was placed on a plank and covered with the coffin which served for all the dead. The holy words were spoken and he was carried to the cemetery.

Women do not accompany a burial to the cemetery, any more than they go into a Mosque.

But Awa suddenly remembered that she had another sourate to say over her husband's body, at the edge of the grave. So she ran after them, and when they had all drawn aside she fell on her knees near the head of the corpse and begged,

"Mor Lame, get up! You are going too far. They are going to bury you now."

"Where is the bone?" asked Mor Lame, through his shroud.

"The bone is at home."

"Is it soft? Is it nice and soft?"

4. The cubit is an ancient measure of length, based on the distance from the elbow to the fingers, about a foot and a half.   5. A verse of the Koran; each one has a name related to different situations in life.

"It is nice and soft."

"And Moussa?"

"Moussa is still here."

"Then let them bury me. I hope he will go away in the end!"

The last prayers were said and the body of Mor Lame was lowered into the grave, lying on the right side.[6]

The first clods of earth were already half covering the departed, when Awa asked once more to be allowed to say a last *sourate*.

"Mor Lame!" she whispered into the grave, "Mor, get up, they are filling up the grave!"

"Where is the bone?" asked Mor Lame, through the sand and his shroud.

"It is at home," answered Awa, through her tears.

"Is it soft?"

"It is soft."

"Where is Moussa?"

"He is still here."

"Let them fill up my grave."

Mor Lame, the glutton, Mor-the-Greedy, was still busy explaining to the Angel of Death, who had come to take him away, and who did not seem to understand that he was not really dead, "Hey! I'm only here on account of a bone!" when Serigne-the-Marabout, with the approval of the elders of the village, who are always of good counsel, decided,

"Moussa, you were the hut brother, the more-than-brother of the late Mor Lame. Awa cannot pass into better hands than yours. As soon as the period of a widow's mourning is over, you will take her for your wife.[7] She will be a good wife to you."

And everybody went their way with many an *"inch Allah!"*

Then Moussa, who was already acting as the master of the house in place of the late Mor Lame, asked Awa,

"Where is the bone?"

"It is here," replied the docile widow.

"Bring it and let us make an end of it."

Mother Crocodile[1]

The most stupid of all animals that fly, walk or swim, that live beneath the ground, in water, or in the air, are undoubtedly crocodiles, which crawl on the earth and walk at the bottom of the water.

"That is not my opinion," said Amadou Koumba. "That is what Golo the monkey says. And although everyone agrees that Golo is the most coarsely spoken of all creatures, since he is their *griot*[2] he sometimes manages to make the most sensible remarks, so some say; or at least to make us believe he has made them, according to others."

So Golo was in the habit of stating to anyone who was prepared to listen

---

6. The position in which Muslims are laid in the grave.   7. A reference to the levirate, a custom by which a man inherited his dead brother's widow. The custom was prevalent in nearly all ancient societies and is still practiced in many traditional societies.   1. Translated by Dorothy S. Blair.   2. A traditional storyteller and oral historian.

to him that crocodiles were the most stupid of all creatures, for no other reason than that they had the best memories.

There is no means of knowing whether Golo intended this to be praise or blame, the expression of envy or contempt. Indeed, as far as memory is concerned, Golo must have arrived late when the Lord was sharing it out. In spite of his great love of mischief, his empty head very quickly forgets the tricks he is continually playing on everyone in turn, to the detriment of his ribs and his hairless posterior. So his opinion of crocodiles might have been expressed one day when he had a bone to pick with Diassigue, the Mother-Crocodile, who might have taken a somewhat rough revenge for a little bit of teasing.

Diassigue had a good memory. It is possible that she had the best memory in the world, for she was content, from her lair in the mud or under the sunny banks of the river, to watch animals, things, and men, and collect the sounds and news the canoes confided to the gossiping fish from the mountains of Fouta-Djallon as far as the Great Sea,[3] where the sun goes down to bathe at the end of the day. She listened to the chatter of the women who came to wash linen, scour calabashes, or draw water at the river. She listened to the donkeys and the camels who came from far off, from north and south, and set down their loads of millet and of rubber, staying long to quench their thirst.[4] The birds came to tell her what the wild ducks whistled as they passed overhead, flying back to the sands.[5]

So Diassigue had a good memory;[6] and much as he deplored this, in his heart of hearts Golo had to admit it. As for her being stupid, Golo's statement was pure exaggeration; in fact he lied like the buffoon that he was. But the saddest part of the whole business was that Diassigue's children, the little crocodiles, began to share the monkey's opinion of their mother, imitating in this the cunning and malicious hare Leuk, whose conscience is as mobile as the pair of old, worn-out slippers which he has been wearing clipped on to his head since the day he took them off to run faster, and which he has used as ears ever since. Thile-the-Jackal, who always tacks from right to left as he runs, even on the bare sand, for fear of some unexpected attack, Thile also thought like Golo, Leuk, and Bouki-the-Hyena, that thief and coward, whose hind-quarters always seem to be sagging beneath a shower of blows, like Thioye-the-Parrot, whose round tongue is always colliding with her fish-hook of a beak which catches all the ill-natured gossip and tittle-tattle that flies around on the four winds. Sègue-the-Panther, with her reputation for double-dealing, might well have shared the opinion of all this common rabble, but she bore Golo too much of a grudge for the thrashings she got from him every time she tried to jump up into the highest branches of a tree to catch him, from which her nose was still bruised.

So Diassigue's own children also began to believe that Golo was speaking the truth. They thought that perhaps their mother really did sometimes talk a lot of nonsense.

When she became weary of the sun's caresses, or tired of watching the moon ceaselessly quenching her thirst in the water half the night through,

---

3. From far inland in Guinea to the Atlantic Ocean off Senegal, a distance of some fifteen hundred miles.
4. Besides providing realistic details of daily life in the region, the passage indicates Diassigue's attentive disposition, an essential factor of her wisdom.   5. The Sahara, immediately to the north and northwest.
6. Symbolic of knowledge derived from accumulated experience.

or bored with watching stupid canoes[7] swim past, with their bellies upward, down the river that travels as fast as they do, then Diassigue would collect her offspring and tell them stories, histories of men, not of crocodiles, for crocodiles have no history.[8] And that is possibly what annoyed them instead of pleasing them—poor little crocodiles.

So Mother-Crocodile would collect her children around her and tell them what she had seen, what her mother had seen and told to her, and what her mother's mother had seen and told to her mother.

The little crocodiles often yawned when she told them of warriors and merchants from Ghana,[9] whom her great-grandmother had seen sailing up and down the rivers in search of slaves and the gold of N'Galam.[1] When she told them of Soumangourou, of Soun Diata Keita[2] and of the empire of Mali. When she told them of the first men with white skin whom her grandmother had seen bowing low to the rising sun after first washing their arms, their faces, their feet, and their hands; of the red colour of the water[3] after the passing of the white men, who had taught the black men to bow down like them to the rising sun. This exceeding red colour of the river had forced her grandmother to leave the Senegal River and go, by way of the Bafing and the Tinkisso, down to the King of Rivers, the Djoliba, the Niger,[4] where she found more white-eared men who had come down from the country of the sands. Her grandmother had seen more wars and corpses there; so many corpses that the greediest of crocodile families could have suffered an attack of indigestion lasting seven times seven moons. There she had seen empires born and kingdoms die.

The little crocodiles yawned when Diassigue told them what her mother had seen and heard: Kouloubali overthrowing the King of the Manding, n'Golo Diara who had lived for three times thirty years and had beaten the Mossi[5] on the eve of his death; when she told them of the Toucouleur Samba Lame, who had been master of the river, master of the Brack-Oualo, master of Damel King of the Cayor and master of the Moors,[6] which makes the Toucouleur fisherfolk even more conceited as they sing his praises over the heads of the little crocodiles and disturb their frolics with their long rods.

When Diassigue spoke the little crocodiles yawned or dreamed of crocodile exploits, of distant banks from which the river washed away gold nuggets and gold dust, and where every year a nubile virgin with fresh young flesh would be offered to the crocodiles. They dreamed of those distant lands, yonder in Pinkou,[7] where the sun was born; lands where crocodiles were

---

7. The epithet extends to the men who row the canoes.   8. An ironic reference to the conventional idea of Africa in Western colonial ideology.   9. The medieval empire in West Africa from which the modern country takes its name.   1. A mine in western Senegal, famous for its high concentration of gold. It has given rise to a Wolof expression denoting any object of high quality.   2. That is, Son-Jara Keita. Soumangourou was Son-Jara's arch-rival (see *The Epic of Son-Jara*, in volume C).   3. An allusion to the conversion by the sword of the West African indigenous populations to Islam by the Arab invaders (*the first men with white skin*). *Bowing low:* Muslins say their prayers with their faces turned to Mecca, in the east. 4. The most important river in West Africa. Apart from its great size, the river has dominated life in the region for centuries, acquiring a legendary quality, hence the epithet "King of Rivers." The Senegal (in the north) serves for much of its length as the border with Mauritania. The Bafing and Tinkisso rivers run through Mali and the Niger Republic, emptying into the Niger.   5. An ethnic group in Burkina Faso and Mali. *Kouloubali:* a Malian surname; the reference is obscure. *N'Golo Diara:* from the context, one of the rulers of the ancient Manding Empire of Mali, thus in the line of Son-Jara.   6. Specifically, the Mauritanians of Arab origin. *The Toucouleur:* originally inhabitants of the Tekrour Empire, now living in Senegal, Mauritania, and Mali. *Brack-Oualo:* the title of the ruler of the Walo kingdom in northern Senegal. The kingdom lasted until the late 19th century, when it was conquered by France.   7. The East (Wolof).

gods, or so they had been told one day by Ibis-the-Pilgrim, the wisest of birds. They dreamed of going down to the vast distant lakes of Macina, to hear the songs of the Bozo[8] oarsmen, and find out whether what Dougou-dougou, the little duck, had told them was true, namely that these songs were more like those of Oualo women, who came down to wash their linen near the crocodile holes, than those of the Somono[9] canoemen, whose ancestors had come from the mountains of the south, on the banks of the Niger, when Diassigue's mother was swimming up the big river.

They dreamed of the Bafing and the Bakoy, the blue river and the white river, which meet down in Bafoulabe[1] to form the river in which they lived. They dreamed of those nuptial places, where, according to the tales the Dog-Fish told, nothing separated the waters of the two rivers, and yet each one kept its own colour for a long, long distance. They would have loved to swim in the waters of the two rivers at the same time; such was the dream of little crocodiles, to have one side of their body in the blue river, one side in the white river, and their back-bone burning in the sun.

They often dreamed of following the same course as their great-grandmother, travelling down from the Senegal River to the Niger, by way of the Bafing and the Tinkisso. The little crocodiles' dreams, like their parents' teeth, never stopped growing. They dreamed of great crocodile exploits, and Diassigue, the Mother-Crocodile, could only tell them tales of men, of wars, of massacres of men by other men . . . .

That is why the little crocodiles were ready to share Golo's opinion of their mother, an opinion which had been passed on to them by Thioker-the-Partridge, the most scandal-mongering of birds.

One morning some crows flew very high above the river croaking:

A naked sun—a sun of gold
A naked sun of an early dawn
Sheds its golden light of morn
On the banks of the river of gold[2]

Diassigue emerged from her hole in the side of the bank and watched the crows fly away.

At midday other crows followed, flying lower, and croaking:

A naked sun—a sun all white
A sun all naked and white
Sheds its silvery light
On the river all white

Diassigue lifted her nose and watched the crows fly away.

At twilight other crows came and perched on the bank and croaked:

A naked sun—a sun all red
A sun all naked and red
Sheds its streams of blood all red
On the river all red.

8. An ethnic group in Mali. Macina is a Muslim state in central Mali.   9. An ethnic group in Mali.
1. A village in Mali, at the confluence of the river Niger and the Senegal River. *Bakoy*: a river in Mali.
2. This song, with its variations marking the onset of war, would normally be taken up by the audience in an oral performance.

Diassigue approached with measured, dignified step, her flabby belly scraping the sand, and asked them the meaning of their migration and their song.

"Brahim Saloum has declared war on Yeli,"[3] the crows told her.

Very upset, Diassigue hurried home.

"Children," she said, "the Emir of Trarza has declared war on the Wolofs. We must get away from here."

The youngest of the crocodile sons asked,

"What difference does it make to us crocodiles if the Wolofs of Walo fight against the Moors of Trarza?"

"My child," replied Mother-Crocodile, "the dry grass can set fire to the green grass.[4] Let us go."

But the little crocodiles would not follow their mother.

As soon as Yeli had crossed the river with his army and had set foot on the north bank, on Ghana territory, he guessed his adversary's intention to draw him as far from the river as possible. In fact, the Moors, who had come right down to the river to hurl defiance at the Walo army, now seemed to flee before the Wolofs. They did not wish to join battle till they were a long way off, far to the north, in the sands, where the black men would be out of sight of the river which made them invisible whenever they bathed or drank from it before the battle. Before pursuing the men of Trarza, Yeli ordered his men to fill all the water-skins that the camels and donkeys carried. They were then forbidden to touch them until the command was given.

For seven days the Walo army pursued the Moors; finally Brahim Saloum halted his warriors, judging the Wolofs to be far enough away from the river to suffer from thirst as soon as they began to fight, and battle was joined.

The most terrible fighting raged for seven days, during which time each Wolof had to choose his Moor and each Moor had to attack his black man. Yeli was engaged in single combat against Brahim Saloum and his five brothers. He killed the Emir on the first day. On each of the succeeding five days he killed one brother. On the seventh day he picked up the son of Brahim Saloum who had been abandoned by the Trarza army on the field of battle. The heir to the Moorish kingdom bore a wound on his right side. Yeli took him back with him to his capital.

All the priests and medicine-men were summoned to care for the young captive prince. But all the attention lavished on him seemed only to aggravate the wound.

Finally there came to the court of Brack-Walo an old, old woman, who prescribed the effective remedy. This remedy was: to apply, three times a day, to the sore place, the fresh brain of a young crocodile.

---

3. The personal name of the king (Brack-Oualo) of Walo. Brahim Saloum was a Mauritanian ruler, later referred to as "the Emir of Trarza."   4. The use of the proverb here conforms to its function in the folktale to bring home its moral; more generally, proverbs function as vehicles of collective wisdom.

LÉOPOLD SÉDAR SENGHOR
born 1906

Léopold Sédar Senghor's poetry takes as its primary subject the encounter between Africa and Europe. The harsh circumstances of this encounter, the conflict between two races and their conceptions of life, together with the pressure of this situation on his personal world, provide the background to his intense exploration of the historical and moral implications of the African and black experience in modern times. But it is essential to see how his concerns become transmuted into an art that takes them beyond their immediate historical reference. For Senghor's poetry reflects the movement of his sensibility beyond the contingencies of a collective and personal history toward a broader vision of humanity.

Senghor was born in Joal, a small fishing village in the Sine-Saloum basin in west-central Senegal, then a colony of France. His father, who was a Serer (the dominant ethnic group of his native region), was a prosperous and influential merchant. His mother was a Peul, one of a pastoral and nomadic people found all over the northern savannah belt of western Africa. This double ethnic ancestry was later to assume a larger meaning for Senghor. As he says in *Prayer of the Senegalese Soldiers:* "I grew up in the heartland of Africa, at the crossroads/Of castes and races and roads." Senghor's early childhood seems to have been a serene and sheltered time within a closely knit pastoral community, and his memory of it has acquired a unique symbolic value in his poetry. Senghor has also indicated that the two most important influences in his childhood were those of his maternal uncle, who gave him his early education in the traditional culture (as was customary in a matrilineal society), and that of the poet Marônne, whose recitations of the traditional oral poetry introduced him to the imaginative uses of language.

Senghor's encounter with the French language did not begin until he was seven, when he was sent to the local elementary school to start his formal education. The following year, his father transferred him to a boarding school run by Catholic missionaries in the nearby village of Ngasobil. After elementary school, Senghor entered the Collège Libermann, a junior seminary in Dakar, now the capital of Senegal, with the intention of becoming a Catholic priest. He abandoned the plan after six years, however, and enrolled in the state secondary school, the Lycée van Vollenhoven, where he distinguished himself as a star pupil, winning the prize in French every year. Obtaining his *baccalauréat* in 1928, he won a state scholarship to continue his education in France. He arrived in Paris in the autumn of the same year and enrolled in the Lycée Louis-le-Grand to prepare for entry into the prestigious École Normale Supérieure. His arrival in Paris brought him in direct contact with French people and French culture and began a relationship marked by conflicting emotions of attachment and discomfort.

The late 1920s and early 1930s were a period of political, social, intellectual, and artistic upheaval in Europe. The troubled state of Europe made a profound impression on the young African scholar, who had previously held a distant and idealized image of the European continent. From the beginning of his sojourn in France, Senghor found himself at the center of a group of African and Caribbean students and intellectuals who had been influenced by radical currents in Western thought, in particular Marxism, as well as by the militant literature of black American writers such as Langston Hughes, Claude McKay, and Countee Cullen, associated with the Harlem Renaissance. This group included Aimé Césaire, a fellow student, with whom Senghor struck up an important friendship. It was through their collaboration that the Négritude movement, with its challenge of the colonial order and passionate concern for the rehabilitation of Africa and the black race, developed. Also inspiring were the Pan-African activities of W. E. B. Du Bois, whose *Souls of Black Folk,* published early in the century, sought to inspire race pride and a sense of African identity among

African Americans and also contributed to the growing racial consciousness of the French-speaking black world.

During this period Senghor became acquainted with the modernist current of Baudelaire and his Symbolist successors. The influence of Baudelaire and Verlaine on Senghor is direct, and his poetry reflects their evocative manner and expressive musicality. To the succeeding Surrealist movement, Senghor's poetry owes little in style and manner, but he does seek to translate into an African register the Surrealist view of life with its appeal to the inner forces of consciousness and quasi-mystical conception of reality. Similarly valuable to Senghor was the poetry of Paul Claudel, whose organic images celebrate the mysteries of the Catholic faith. Claudel's powerful poetic temperament found expression in an ample verse form that allies the movement of modern free verse to the cadences of the Bible, as in the Psalms and other Old Testament books. This verse form, known in French as the *verset,* was taken over by Senghor, who infused into it elements of the oral poetry of traditional Africa. In other French poets as well (such as Charles Péguy and St. John Perse), Senghor found models for his own effort, always, however, shaping what he learned to his own needs.

Senghor's Parisian studies culminated in 1935 with his passing the highly competitive examination for the *agrégation,* the first African to be awarded the degree. This opened up for him a career in the French educational system, and for the next five years, he held various teaching positions, notably at Tours in central France and St. Martin-des-Fossés near Paris, where he began to write the poems later collected in his first volume *Chants d'ombre* (Shadow Songs, 1945). At the outbreak of World War II in 1939, he was drafted as an officer into the French army and saw service on the northern front, where he was taken prisoner by the Germans in 1940. He spent his time during his internment learning German and writing the poems that make up *Hosties noires* (Black Hosts, 1948). In 1942, released on health grounds but confined to Paris, he resumed teaching and in 1944 was appointed professor of African languages at the École Nationale de la France d'Outre-Mer. After the war, he was active in the effort to promote a new understanding of Africa and helped to launch a cultural journal, *Présence Africaine,* founded in Paris in 1947 by his friend and compatriot Alioune Diop, as a vehicle for African and black self-affirmation. The following year, Senghor published the historic *Anthologie de la nouvelle poésie nègre et malgache,* which may be said to have launched Négritude as a movement, due largely to the impact of the prefatory essay, *Orphée noir* (Black Orpheus), by the eminent French philosopher Jean-Paul Sartre. Sartre provided both a critical review of French-speaking black poetry and a philosophical exposition of the concept of Négritude. The publication of *Chants pour Naët* (Songs for Naët, 1948), a collection of love poems dedicated to his first wife, confirmed Senghor's status as a lyric poet of the first order. Meanwhile, his political career had begun with his election in 1946 to the French Constituent Assembly as deputy for Senegal, a career that was to be distinguished by service as a spokesman for Africa in the French parliament under the Fourth Republic and was to culminate in his election to the presidency of Senegal at its independence from France in 1960. Politics and literature thus came to run more or less parallel, as complementary aspects of a life devoted to the African cause.

Senghor's first volume, *Chants d'ombre,* is a kind of mental diary of his experience of cultural exile in Europe. The poems are marked by an acute sense of solitude, the physical separation from his homeland becoming symbolic of a more profound estrangement, that of the soul from its roots. The theme of exile runs through the volume. A complementary aspect of this theme is the poet's nostalgia for his origins. The memory of Africa is colored by its association with his childhood, which becomes transformed into an anterior state of grace. Thus he declares, in the poem *Prayer of the Senegalese Soldiers*: "I have chosen to live near the rebuilt walls of my memory / And from the top of the high ramparts / I remember Joal-of-the-Shades / the face of the land of my blood." This recall of origins signals a movement to a unified experience of the self. But beyond this quest for harmony, the African theme registers the poet's broader affirmation of his antecedents, of a historical and spiritual continuity that forms the basis of his identity. The bond with nature, the living presence of the ancestors, the supernatural as informing principle of visible reality, these are some of the motifs around which Senghor weaves his themes, as a mode of reconnection with his African origins. The historical consciousness is linked in his poetry with a metaphysical conception of human destiny: the individual participating in the life of the community attains to a larger relation with the forces of creation.

Senghor's later volumes develop and amplify this progression from the social and psychological to the imaginative and visionary. Although the political emphasis is more pronounced in *Hosties noires,* the same movement is implied. Through their direct reference to World War II, the poems constitute a commentary on public events and a judgment on the passions behind those events. The critique of Europe and the colonial protest are intertwined; this is conveyed in the title of the volume, which suggests the sacrifice of Africans to the blind fury of the European war. The association also carries religious overtones: that of the collective passion of the black race, conferring on it the nobility of suffering. The African image thus takes on an explicit polemical role in the volume; the opposition between Africa and Europe is not only historical and political but also moral and spiritual. The European war is seen as an apocalypse in which Africa assumes the aspect of a redeeming force and the black poet becomes the prophet of a new hope for humanity. This polemical and limited vision assumes, however, another dimension: at its heart lies a conflict that lends a poignancy to his critique of Europe. The appeal of the humanist ideals of French civilization remains too strong for him and its intellectual and literary traditions run too deeply in his nature to admit of a total and untroubled rejection. His commitment to the African cause produces a singular ambivalence. At the same moment that Senghor reaffirms his African belonging, he also seeks to transcend the antithesis created by the colonial situation and to elaborate a new ideal of unity that would embrace both halves of his awareness. This need lies behind Senghor's idea of a *Civilisation de l'universel,* which has become a key component of his conception of Négritude.

Between 1949 and 1960, Senghor's energies were absorbed by politics and his crusade for the rehabilitation of Africa and its peoples, through a constant stream of essays and lectures in France and other parts of Europe as well as in Africa. His writings during this period, later collected in four volumes under the title *Liberté,* demonstrate a concern for a reassessment of Africa's civilization and values and a redefinition of the African continent's place in the modern world. In 1956, Senghor's collection *Ethiopiques* inaugurated a new direction in his poetry, one less overtly related to the colonial experience. This new direction was confirmed in subsequent volumes: *Nocturnes* (1961), *Elégie des Alizés* (Elegy of the West Wind, 1968), *Lettres d'hivernage* (Letters in the Rainy Season, 1973), and *Elégies Majeures* (1979). The later poetry confirms Senghor's standing as a great lyric poet, turning to a deeper exploration of the poetic self and developing a more complex attitude to the world. The interplay between the elegiac and the lyrical that runs as an undercurrent in the early poems receives in this later work an expanded frame of reference. The tensions of public life are balanced against the comforts of love, the death of individuals and of civilizations, and the assurance of rebirth within the stream of the universal life. If in the early volumes Senghor voices an individual predicament as part of a collective historical plight, in the later poetry, his vision embraces a wider universe of experience.

It is especially in this perspective that Africa reveals its central significance as prime mediator of his vision. Senghor's African beliefs and symbolic schemes give depth of meaning and even a ritual dimension to his poetry. The constant recourse to organic imagery indicates a consciousness formed by an agrarian culture and shows a preoccupation with growth, with a sense of the surge of life in the natural world, characteristic of an animist outlook. The dominant imagery of *night* derives its importance from its association with Africa and blackness. Night carries connotations of peace and meditation, of the propitious presence of the dead, and of the mystic life of the African continent and the universe. It is the organizing symbol of Senghor's poetry, representing for him the authentic mode of the black poet's imagination: "I proclaim the Night more truthful than the day." Africa is envisaged, then, in poetic terms; it becomes an image both of the racial homeland and of humanity's appropriate relation to the universe:

I would choose the poetry of the rivers, the winds, the forests,
The assonance of the plains and streams, choose the rhythm of my naked body's
    blood
Choose the vibrating balaphons and the harmony of chords. . . . I choose my toiling
    black people, my peasant people.

Although a controversial figure in African literary and intellectual circles, Senghor is widely respected as both poet and statesman. When he voluntarily gave up power as president of Senegal in 1980 to go into private life, he left behind an outstanding contribution to the political and social development of Africa and to the continent's cultural and intellectual renaissance. His election to the French Academy in 1983 came as a fitting recognition of one of the foremost modern writers in the French language.

Of the abundant critical literature on Senghor's work in French, little is yet available in English. Sylvia Washington Bâ's *The Concept of Négritude in the Poetry of Léopold Sédar Senghor* (1973) provides the most comprehensive discussion of the work. Both Okechukwu Mezu, *The Poetry of Léopold Sédar Senghor* (1973), and Janice Spleth, *Léopold Sédar Senghor* (1985), present useful overviews. The selections presented here are taken from *The Collected Poetry* (1991), translated by Melvin Dixon, whose introduction is helpful. Also useful are Ellen Conroy Kennedy, *The Négritude Poets* (1989), and Lilyan Kesteloot, *Black Writers in French* (1991). For accounts of Senghor's life and intellectual development, with incidental comments on his poetry, see Jacques Louis Hymans, *Léopold Sédar Senghor: An Intellectual Biography* (1971); and Janet G. Vaillant, *Black, French and African: A Life of Léopold Sédar Senghor* (1990).

PRONOUNCING GLOSSARY

The following list uses common English syllables to provide rough equivalents of selected words whose pronunciation may be unfamiliar to the general reader.

Dyouma: *joom-a*

Guéolowâr: *gayl-wahr*

guimm: *geem*

Ngom: *en-gom*

Nyaout Mbodybe: *en-yah-oot em-boj*

Sine: *seen*

Tamsir Dargui Ndyâye: *tahm-seer dahr-gee enjahee*

Tyâné: *cha-nay*

Woi: *woh-ee*

[Poems]

Letter to a Poet[1]

to Aimé Césaire

To my Brother *aimé*,[2] beloved friend, my bluntly fraternal greetings!
Black sea gulls like seafaring boatmen have brought me a taste
Of your tidings mixed with spices and the noisy fragrance of Southern
    Rivers[3]
And Islands.[4] They showed your influence, your distinguished brow,
The flower of your delicate lips. They are now your disciples,   5
A hive of silence, proud as peacocks. You keep their breathless zeal
From fading until moonrise. Is it your perfume of exotic fruits,
Or your wake of light in the fullness of day?
O, the many plum-skin women in the harem of your mind!

Still charming beyond the years, embers aglow under the ash   10
Of your eyelids, is the music we stretched our hands
And hearts to so long ago. Have you forgotten your nobility?
Your talent to praise the Ancestors, the Princes,
And the Gods, neither flower nor drops of dew?[5]
You were to offer the Spirits the virgin fruits of your garden   15
—You ate only the newly harvested millet blossom
And stole not a petal to sweeten your mouth.
At the bottom of the well of my memory, I touch your face
And draw water to refresh my long regret.
You recline royally, elbow on a cushion of clear hillside,   20
Your bed presses the earth, easing the toil of wetland drums
Beating the rhythm of your song, and your verse
Is the breath of the night and the distant sea.
You praised the Ancestors and the legitimate princes.
For your rhyme and counterpoint you scooped a star from the
    heavens.
    25
At your bare feet poor men threw down a mat of their year's wages,
And women their amber[6] hearts and soul-wrenching dance.

My friend, my friend—Oh, you will come back, come back!
I shall await you under the mahogany tree,[7] the message
Already sent to the woodcutter's boss. You will come back   30
For the feast of first fruits[8] when the soft night
In the sloping sun rises steaming from the rooftops
And athletes,[9] befitting your arrival,
Parade their youthfulness, adorned like the beloved.

---

1. All selections translated by Melvin Dixon.   2. Beloved (French). The poem pays homage to fellow poet Aimé Césaire (p. 2539).   3. Senghor plays here on the poetic resonance of the French administrative term (*Rivières du Sud*) for the area comprising the former French empire in west and central Africa. 4. The Caribbean, where Césaire was born.   5. The conventions of Western lyricism are contrasted with the more pressing social themes of the black poet.   6. A translucent stone, with a brownish yellow hue. 7. Of royal significance.   8. The harvest festival.   9. Wrestlers, the traditional sporting heroes of Senegal.

Night in Sine[1]

Woman, place your soothing hands upon my brow,
Your hands softer than fur.
Above us balance the palm trees, barely rustling
In the night breeze. Not even a lullaby.
Let the rhythmic silence cradle us.   5
Listen to its song. Hear the beat of our dark blood,
Hear the deep pulse of Africa in the mist of lost villages.

Now sets the weary moon upon its slack seabed
Now the bursts of laughter quiet down, and even the storyteller
Nods his head like a child on his mother's back   10
The dancers' feet grow heavy, and heavy, too,
Come the alternating voices of singers.

Now the stars appear and the Night dreams
Leaning on that hill of clouds, dressed in its long, milky pagne.[2]
The roofs of the huts shine tenderly. What are they saying   15
So secretly to the stars? Inside, the fire dies out
In the closeness of sour and sweet smells.

Woman, light the clear-oil lamp. Let the Ancestors
Speak around us as parents do when the children are in bed.
Let us listen to the voices of the Elissa[3] Elders. Exiled like us   20
They did not want to die, or lose the flow of their semen in the sands.
Let me hear, a gleam of friendly souls visits the smoke-filled hut,
My head upon your breast as warm as tasty *dang*[4] steaming from the fire,
Let me breathe the odor of our Dead, let me gather
And speak with their living voices, let me learn to live   25
Before plunging deeper than the diver[5]
Into the great depths of sleep.

Black Woman

Naked woman, black woman
Dressed in your color[1] that is life, in your form that is beauty!
I grew up in your shadow. The softness of your hands
Shielded my eyes, and now at the height of Summer and Noon,
From the crest of a charred hilltop I discover you, Promised Land[2]   5
And your beauty strikes my heart like an eagle's lightning flash.

Naked woman, dark woman
Ripe fruit with firm flesh, dark raptures of black wine,
Mouth that gives music to my mouth

---

1. A river in Senegal. The Serer, Senghor's ethnic group, inhabit the basin formed by the confluence of Sine and Saloum.   2. Printed cloth (French African); here the Milky Way, with which the moon appears to be robed.   3. A village in Guinea Bissau, south of Senegal, where Senghor's ancestors are buried. 4. A cereal meal.   5. The setting moon.   1. A reference to the green vegetation of the African landscape, to which the black woman is assimilated.   2. The analogy with the Israelites in the Old Testament of the Bible confers a religious note on this poem.

Savanna of clear horizons, savanna quivering to the fervent caress   10
Of the East Wind,[3] sculptured tom-tom, stretched drumskin
Moaning under the hands of the conqueror
Your deep contralto voice[4] is the spiritual song of the Beloved.

Naked woman, dark woman
Oil no breeze can ripple, oil soothing the thighs   15
Of athletes and the thighs of the princes of Mali[5]
Gazelle with celestial limbs, pearls are stars
Upon the night of your skin. Delight of the mind's riddles,
The reflections of red gold from your shimmering skin
In the shade of your hair, my despair   20
Lightens in the close suns of your eyes.

Naked woman, black woman
I sing your passing beauty and fix it for all Eternity
before jealous Fate reduces you to ashes to nourish the roots of life.

Prayer to the Masks

Masks![1] O Masks!
Black mask, red mask, you white-and-black masks
Masks of the four cardinal points where the Spirit blows
I greet you in silence!
And you, not the least of all, Ancestor with the lion head.[2]   5
You keep this place safe from women's laughter
And any wry, profane smiles[3]
You exude the immortal air where I inhale
The breath of my Fathers.
Masks with faces without masks, stripped of every dimple   10
And every wrinkle
You created this portrait, my face leaning
On an altar of blank paper[4]
And in your image, listen to me!
The Africa of empires is dying—it is the agony   15
Of a sorrowful princess
And Europe, too, tied to us at the navel.
Fix your steady eyes on your oppressed children
Who give their lives like the poor man his last garment.
Let us answer "present" at the rebirth of the World   20
As white flour cannot rise without the leaven.[5]
Who else will teach rhythm to the world

---

3. The Harmattan, a dry, sharp wind that blows from the Sahara, northeast of Senegal, between November and April.   **4.** An allusion to the vocal register of Marian Anderson (1897–1993), an African American singer famous for her rendering of Negro spirituals.   **5.** The ancient empire of the West African savanna. **1.** Representatives of the spirits of the ancestors. In African belief, the ancestors inhabit the immaterial world beyond the visible, from there offering protection to their living descendants.   **2.** The animal totem of Senghor's family. His father bore the Serer name Diogoye ("Lion"). A totem is an animal or plant that is closely associated with a family, sometimes considered to be a member of the family.   **3.** Ancestral masks are usually kept in an enclosure, a sacred place forbidden to women and uninitiated males. There is also a suggestion here that Senghor will protect them from the patronizing gaze of white people.   **4.** An ironic reference to Senghor's Western education.   **5.** An ingredient (for example, yeast) in baked goods that make them rise; also a biblical image.

Deadened by machines and cannons?
Who will sound the shout of joy at daybreak to wake orphans and the dead?
Tell me, who will bring back the memory of life   25
To the man of gutted hopes?
They call us men of cotton, coffee, and oil
They call us men of death.
But we are men of dance, whose feet get stronger
As we pound upon firm ground.[6]   30

Letter to a Prisoner

Ngom! Champion of Tyâné![1]

It is I who greet you, I your village neighbor, your heart's neighbor.
I send you my white[2] greeting like the dawn's white cry,
Over the barbed wires of hate and stupidity,
And I call you by your name and your honor.   5
My greetings to Tamsia Dargui Ndyâye, who lives off parchments[3]
That give him a subtle tongue and long thin fingers,[4]
To Samba Dyouma, the poet, whose voice is the color of flame[5]
And whose forehead bears the signs of his destiny,
To Nyaoutt Mbodye and to Koli Ngom, your namesake   10
And to all those who, at the hour when the great arms
Are sad like branches beaten by the sun, huddle at night
Shivering around the dish of friendship.

I write you from the solitude of my precious—and closely guarded—
Residence of my black skin. Fortunate are my friends   15
Who know nothing of the icy walls and the brightly lit
Apartments that sterilize every seed on the ancestors' masks
And even the memories of love.
You know nothing of the good white bread, milk, and salt,
Or those substantial dishes that do not nourish,   20
That separate the refined from the boulevard crowds,
Sleepwalkers who have renounced their human identity
Chameleons[6] deaf to change, and their shame locks you
In your cage of solitude.
You know nothing of restaurants and swimming pools   25
Forbidden to noble black blood
And Science and Humanity erecting their police lines
At the borders of negritude.[7]
Must I shout louder? Tell me, can you hear me?
I no longer recognize white men, my brothers,   30

6. A reference to Antaeus, who in Greek mythology drew strength by touching the earth with his feet.
1. A Serer female name. The direct address with which the poem opens is a convention of oral poetry.
Ngom, a comrade in the German prisoner-of-war camp, is addressed by his praise name as a champion
wrestler, whose exploits in the arena bring honor to his beloved, Tyâné. In the poem, Senghor shares his
experience of wartime Paris, to which he has returned after his release from the camp, with the Africans
whom he left behind.   2. Wan, melancholic.   3. Implies intellectual and spiritual nourishment. *Tamsir*: a title for a learned man, equivalent to "doctor."   4. Of the ascetic man of letters.   5. A reference
to Dyouma's golden voice and the passionate content of his lyrics. Oral poets sang or declaimed their
compositions.   6. A reference to those French people who collaborated with the German forces of the
Occupation.   7. Here, a collective term for the black race, in its historical circumstance the world over.

Like this evening at the cinema, so lost were they
Beyond the void made around my skin.[8]

I write to you because my books are white like boredom,
Like misery, like death.
Make room for me around the pot so I can take my place   35
Again, still warm.
Let our hands touch as they reach into the steaming
Rice of friendship. Let the old Serer words
Pass from mouth to mouth like a pipe among friends.
Let Dargui share his succulent fruits,[9] the hay   40
Of every smelly drought! And you, serve us your wise words
As huge as the navel[1] of prodigious Africa.
Which singer this evening will summon the Ancestors around us,
Gathering like a peaceful herd of beasts of the bush?
Who will nestle our dreams under the eyelids of the stars?   45

Ngom! Answer me by the new-moon mail.
At the turn in the road, I shall meet your naked, hesitant words.
Like the fledgling emerging from his cage
Your words are put together so naively; and the learned may mock them,
But they bring me back to the surreal   50
And their milk gushes on my face.
I await your letter at the hour when morning lays death low.
I shall receive it piously like the morning ablution,
Like the dew of dawn.

Paris, June 1942

The Kaya-Magan[1]

(guimm *for* kora[2])

KAYA-MAGAN am I! the first person[3]
King of the black night, the silver night,
King of the night of glass.
Graze my antelopes safe from lions, far from the charm of my voice.
You delight in dotting the silent plains!   5
Here you are each day my flowers, my stars,
Here you are at my joyful feast.
So feed on my abundant breasts, for I, who am the source of joy,
Do not eat. Graze from my strong, manly breasts,
The milk grass[4] gleaming from my chest.   10

---

8. A rare report of Senghor's personal experience of racial discrimination.   9. Of his mind, which is well
stocked with learning and wisdom.   1. Many African children have large navels. Senghor turns this into
a mark of natural strength.   1. King of Gold; legendary founder of the ancient empire of Ghana.   2. A
stringed instrument, which sounds like the harp. It is often played to accompany praise songs to royalty
and nobility. *Guimm:* ode (Serer).   3. As a ruler who takes precedence over his subjects.   4. That is,
milk from grass eaten by cows.

May a thousand stars be lit each night on the Great Square[5]
May twelve thousand bowls ringed with sea serpents[6] be warmed
For my pious subjects, for the fawns of my womb,
The residents of my house and their dependents, the *Guélowârs*[7]
Of the nine fortresses[8] and the villages in the wild bush,   15
For all who have entered by the four carved doors[9]—
The solemn march of my long-suffering people!
Their steps are lost in the sands of Time.[1]
For the whites of the north,[2] the blacks of the south
Of so soft a blue. To say nothing of the red men of the west[3]   20
Or the River herds! Eat and sleep, children of my sap.
Live your lives fully and peace to you who decline.
Even you draw breath from my nostrils.

I say KAYA-MAGAN am I! King of the moon, I join night and day.
I am the Prince of the north, of the south,   25
Prince of the Rising and Setting Sun
The savanna open to a hundred ruts, the mold that melds
Precious metals. Red gold comes from it and the red Man,
Red my delight as King of Gold—I, who have the splendor
Of noon and the feminine tenderness of night.   30
So peck at my curved brow, birds of my serpentine hair.[4]
You can't live on whole milk alone. So nibble the Wiseman's brain,
The master of hieroglyphics in his glass tower.

Graze, fawns of my womb, under my scepter and my crescent moon.[5]
I am the Buffalo that mocks the Lion and his rifles   35
Loaded up to his chin. He'll have to prepare himself
Inside his walls. My empire is Caesar's banished ones,[6]
The great outlaws of reason or instinct
My empire is that of Love, for I am weak for you, woman,
Foreigner with clear eyes,[7] lips of cinnamon apple,   40
And a sex like a burning bush
For I am both sides of a double door, the binary rhythm of space
And the third beat,[8] I am the movement of drums,
The strength of future Africa.
Now sleep, fawns of my womb, sleep under my crescent moon.   45

---

5. The picture is that of a great celebration.   6. Symbols of spiritual insight.   7. Warriors (Wolof).
8. At the nine outposts of the empire; they are manned by the Guélowârs.   9. The gates of the capital
city, which open to the four cardinal points.   1. A double reference: to the hourglass as well as to the
desert origins of the founders of the Ghana Empire.   2. The Moors of Mauritania.   3. People who
have mixed white and black parentage.   4. In some African royal masks, the hair on the king's head is
represented as a knotted serpent, with birds pecking at the forehead, to signify abundance.   5. Symbol
of Islam, the religion of the emperor.   6. Beyond Western civilization.   7. Senghor's French wife.
8. The off beat in music based on syncopated rhythm, as jazz. This expresses Senghor's idea of a third term
transcending the conflict of opposites.

To New York

(for jazz orchestra and trumpet solo)

I

New York! At first I was bewildered by your beauty,
Those huge, long-legged, golden girls.
So shy, at first, before your blue metallic eyes and icy smile,
So shy. And full of despair at the end of skyscraper streets
Raising my owl eyes at the eclipse of the sun.   5
Your light is sulphurous against the pale towers
Whose heads strike lightning into the sky,
Skyscrapers defying storms with their steel shoulders
And weathered skin of stone.
But two weeks on the naked sidewalks of Manhattan—   10
At the end of the third week the fever
Overtakes you with a jaguar's leap
Two weeks without well water or pasture all birds of the air
Fall suddenly dead under the high, sooty terraces.
No laugh from a growing child, his hand in my cool hand.   15
No mother's breast, but nylon legs. Legs and breasts
Without smell or sweat. No tender word, and no lips,
Only artificial hearts paid for in cold cash
And not one book offering wisdom.
The painter's palette yields only coral crystals.   20
Sleepless nights, O nights of Manhattan!
Stirring with delusions while car horns blare the empty hours
And murky streams carry away hygenic loving
Like rivers overflowing with the corpses of babies.

II

Now is the time for signs and reckoning, New York!   25
Now is the time of manna and hyssop.[1]
You have only to listen to God's trombones,[2] to your heart
Beating to the rhythm of blood, your blood.
I saw Harlem teeming with sounds and ritual colors
And outrageous smells—   30
At teatime in the home of the drugstore-deliveryman
I saw the festival of Night begin at the retreat of day.
And I proclaim Night more truthful than the day.
It is the pure hour when God brings forth
Life immemorial in the streets,   35
All the amphibious elements shining like suns.
Harlem, Harlem! Now I've seen Harlem, Harlem!
A green breeze of corn rising from the pavements

---

1. An aromatic herb with religious associations. *Manna:* the food that came down miraculously from Heaven to feed the Israelites when they were wandering in the desert after leaving Egypt.   2. The title of a book of sermons by James Weldon Johnson, written in the idiom of black preachers. The work has become a classic of African American literature.

Plowed by the Dan[3] dancers' bare feet,
Hips rippling like silk and spearhead breasts,   40
Ballets of water lilies and fabulous masks
And mangoes of love rolling from the low houses
To the feet of police horses.
And along sidewalks I saw streams of white rum
And streams of black milk in the blue haze of cigars.   45
And at night I saw cotton flowers snow down
From the sky and the angels' wings and sorcerers' plumes.
Listen, New York! O listen to your bass male voice,
Your vibrant oboe voice, the muted anguish of your tears
Falling in great clots of blood,   50
Listen to the distant beating of your nocturnal heart,
The tom-tom's rhythm and blood, tom-tom blood and tom-tom.

III

New York! I say New York, let black blood flow into your blood.
Let it wash the rust from your steel joints, like an oil of life
Let it give your bridges the curve of hips and supple vines.   55
Now the ancient age returns, unity is restored,
The reconciliation of Lion and Bull and Tree[4]
Idea links to action, the ear to the heart, sign to meaning.
See your rivers stirring with musk alligators[5]
And sea cows[6] with mirage eyes. No need to invent the Sirens. 60
Just open your eyes to the April rainbow
And your ears, especially your ears, to God
Who in one burst of saxophone laughter
Created heaven and earth in six days,
And on the seventh slept a deep Negro sleep.   65

Songs for Signare

(for flutes[1])

A *hand of light*[2] caressed my dark eyelids and your smile rose
Over the mists floating monotonously on my Congo.[3]
My heart has echoed the virgin song of the dawn birds
As my blood used to beat to the white song of sap in my branching arms.
See the bush flower and the star in my hair   5
And the bandana on the brow of the herdsman athlete.[4]
I will take up the flute and play a rhythm for the peace
Of the herds and sitting all day in the shade of your lashes,
Close to the Fimla Springs[5] I shall graze faithfully the golden

---

3. An ethnic group in Ivory Coast, reputed for the vigor of its dances. These lines establish a racial and cultural connection between Africa and black America.   4. Symbolic of suffering, from the Christian Cross. *Lion:* a symbol of the black race. *Bull:* a symbol of the white race.   5. Held in Serer mythology to conserve the memory of the past.   6. Or manatees, credited by the Serer with being able to see into the future.   1. Associated with shepherds in the pastoral tradition.   2. That is, of the beloved. This is a love poem based on the Western pastoral convention.   3. A river in central Africa that flows through dense tropical landscape; here, an image of the poet's state of mind.   4. The poet himself.   5. The source of a stream in Sine-Saloum.

Lowings[6] of your herds. For this morning a hand of light   10
Caressed my dark eyelids, and all day long
My heart has echoed the virgin song of the birds.

Elegy of the Circumcised[1]

Childhood Night,[2] blue Night, gold Night, O Moon!
How often have I invoked you, O Night! while weeping by the road,
Feeling the pain of adulthood. Loneliness! and its dunes all around.
One night during childhood it was a night as black as pitch.
Our backs were bent with fear at the lion's roar,[3] and the shifting   5
Silence in the night bent the tall grass. Branches caught fire
And you were fired with hope! and my pale memory of the Sun
Barely reassured my innocence. I had to die.[4]
I laid my hands on my neck like the virgin who shivers in the throes
Of death. I had to die to the beauty of the song—all things drift   10
Along the thread of death. Look at twilight on the turtledoves' breast,
When blue ringdoves coo and dream sea gulls fly
With their plaintive cries.

Let us die and dance elbow to elbow in a braided garland[5]
May our clothes not impede our steps, but let the gift   15
Of the betrothed girl glow like sparks under the clouds.
Woi![6] The drum furrows the holy silence.
Let us dance, the song whipping the blood, and let the rhythm
Chase away the agony that grabs us by the throat.
Life keeps death away.   20
Let us dance to the refrain of agony, may the night of sex[7]
Rise above our ignorance, above our innocence.
Ah! To die to childhood, let the poem die, the syntax disintegrate,
And all the unimportant words become spoiled.
The rhythm's weight is sufficient, no need for cement words   25
To build the city of tomorrow on rock.
May the Sun rise up from the sea of shadows
Blood![8] The waves are the color of dawn.

But God, I have wailed too much—how many times?
—The transparent childhood nights.   30
The Male-Noon is the time of Spirits, when all form
Gets rid of its flesh, like trees in Europe under the winter sun.
See, the bones are abstract, they obey only the measures
Of the ruler, the compass, the sextant.
Like sand, life slips freely from man's fingers,   35

6. This association of the sound of the cattle with color is an example of synaesthesia.   1. The circumcision rite is the essential element in the initiation ceremony that marks the formal passage of the adolescent to adult status. The ceremony involves the confinement of candidates in the bush for a long period, during which they undergo a series of tests and receive instruction in the history and customs of the land. At the end of this period, on a designated night, they are circumcised one after the other.   2. The night of the circumcision.   3. Simulated, as part of the initiation ceremony, and intended to develop the virtue of courage in the boys.   4. Initiation is the symbolic death of the child who is reborn an adult.   5. The triumphant dance of the initiates after the ceremony.   6. A chant.   7. Initiation also purifies the adolescent, in preparation for sexuality in its creative function.   8. That shed at circumcision, heralding a new birth.

And snowflakes imprison the water's life,
The water snake[9] glides through the vain hands of the reeds.
Lovely Nights, friendly Nights, childhood Nights
Along the salt flats and in the woods, nights throbbing
With presences and with eyelids, full of wings and breaths   40
And living silence, now tell me how many times
Have I cried for you in the bloom of my age?
The poem withers in the midday sun and feeds upon the evening dew,
The tom-tom beats the rhythm of sap in the smell of ripe fruit.
Master of the Initiates,[1] I know I need your knowledge
        to understand   45
The cipher of things, to be aware of my duties as father and *lamarque*,[2]
To measure exactly the scope of my responsibilities, to distribute
The harvest without forgetting any worker or orphan.
The song is not just a charm, it feeds the woolly heads of my flock.
The poem is a snake-bird,[3] the dawn marriage of shadow and light   50
It soars like the Phoenix![4] It sings with wings spread
Over the slaughter of words.

9. A symbol of wisdom and durability.   1. An elder who supervises the ceremony.   2. A word coined by Senghor from the Wolof *lam* and the Greek *archos*, both meaning "landowner." The line refers to the civic and moral obligations taught to the initiates.   3. Or plumed serpent, which is endowed with vision- ary powers. This creature is found in the mythology of many cultures.   4. A mythical bird that is supposed to rise from its own ashes, thus a symbol of regeneration. Like the bird, poetry embodies the force of renewal in nature.

RICHARD WRIGHT
1908–1960

Richard Wright is known internationally for powerful naturalist fiction that describes alienated protagonists trapped in a materialistic and repressive society. He is equally well known for another reason: his novels, short stories, autobiography, and essays made him the twentieth-century's most forceful exponent of African American con- sciousness. From his explosive first novel, *Native Son* (1940), to the political essays of his later years, Wright explored the phenomenon of racism in modern society. Concurrently, he pursued questions of existential identity, wrote about economic inequities, and maintained that his characters' struggle transcended any purely racial or gender definition. Realistic settings, an often hallucinatory narrative, and the vio- lent protest embedded in his works opened new horizons for contemporary readers and new possibilities for young African American writers. Wright himself left the United States during the anti-Communist witch-hunts of the late forties and spent the last fifteen years of his life in Paris. There he was welcomed by writers and intellectuals like the existentialist philosopher Jean-Paul Sartre, the modernist writer Gertrude Stein, and the Swedish sociologist Gunnar Myrdal. He continued to write fiction but devoted much of his time to political and cultural issues, giving lectures and writing polemic essays based on travels in Africa, Asia, and Spain.

   Wright was born in 1908 on a farm near Natchez, Mississippi. His father was a poor and illiterate sharecropper, and his mother taught in black country schools. When Wright was five years old, his father deserted the family, and the family moved several times to be with relatives while Wright's mother worked. A brief period of prosperity in Arkansas ended when they had to flee town after the saloon-keeper uncle with whom they were living was shot by envious whites. After Wright's mother suffered a paralytic stroke in 1919, the family was forced to move to her parents' house in Jackson, Mississippi. Wright's education was irregular, and in many ways he was self-taught: attending segregated black public schools and a Seventh Day Adventist school until ninth grade, he was frequently absent because of family illness or inability to buy books and clothes. The future novelist learned about the larger world from library books that he not only had to acquire by subterfuge but also had to conceal. His grandmother and aunt, strict Seventh Day Adventists, believed fiction immoral and burned any novels or magazines he brought home. The privations and violence of those early years, his rebellion against a fanatically strict religious upbringing, and his long puzzlement over racism—his grandmother appeared white, and as a child he did not feel a part of racial divisions—are described in *Uncle Tom's Children* (1938) and in the autobiographical *Black Boy* (1945).

After graduating from junior high school in 1925, Wright worked two years for an optical company in Memphis. He read widely, exploring many of the European authors praised by contemporary editor and satirist H. L. Mencken, whose scathing critique of American culture astonished and impressed him. Like other black writers of his generation, Wright found in the naturalist tradition of Europe and America a style congenial to what he had to say. He was particularly struck by the direct, factual, and seemingly objective manner of the American novelists Theodore Dreiser and Sinclair Lewis: "All my life had shaped me for the realism, the naturalism of the modern novel." His first-written, posthumously published novel, *Lawd Today* (1963), contains pages of dialogue that read like transcriptions of overheard speech. Later works go beyond this documentary style, as Wright finds affinities with the prose styles of Marcel Proust and the expatriate writer Gertrude Stein, and as he comes into contact with other American writers who show him diverse literary techniques adaptable to his own vision.

In 1927, eager to escape the South, Wright moved to Chicago, one of the northern cities that Southern blacks saw as havens of opportunity and acceptance. Life was not easy in Chicago: he supported himself as a porter, dishwasher, and postal clerk; and when he lost his job in the Depression, he went on relief sweeping streets. Soon he found work with the WPA Federal Writers' Project, one of many federal projects created to help jobless people through the Depression. He wrote guidebooks for the WPA and poems, fiction, and essays on his own; in addition, he read authors like Dostoevsky, Gogol, Baudelaire, Mann, Proust, and T. S. Eliot and works in psychology and sociology. A friend introduced him to the John Reed Club, a Communist literary group, and he became a member of the Party in 1933. He withdrew from the Party in 1942, however, after becoming disillusioned with its emphasis on international political objectives and concurrent disregard for Wright's chief concerns: individualism, black civil rights, and artistic freedom.

Wright's first short-story collection, *Uncle Tom's Children* (1938), is set in the South, and all four stories are concerned with racism. (A new edition in 1940 included a fifth story and an autobiographical essay, *The Ethics of Living Jim Crow.*) The stories are tense with terror, beatings, and murder, and only one (*Fire and Cloud*) gives any sense of even momentary triumph. *Big Boy Leaves Home*, the often-reprinted first story, describes a teenager's flight after three of his friends are killed—one in a horrific scene of tarring, feathering, and burning alive. *Uncle Tom's Children* won first prize in a Federal Writers' Project competition sponsored by *Story* magazine and was named one of the ten best books of the year. Still, Wright was dissatisfied. He felt that something was lacking: "I found that I had written a book which even bankers' daughters could read and weep over and feel good about. I swore that if I ever wrote another book, no one would weep over it; that it would be so hard and deep that they would face it without the consolation of tears." Perhaps he had in mind the philosophical and political dimension of his later novels, starting with *Native Son*; perhaps, like Bertolt Brecht, he felt he could not teach his audience unless he prevented them from identifying too closely with his characters.

With *Native Son,* the account of a black chauffeur in Chicago who kills two women (one white and the other his black girlfriend) and is brought to trial after a lengthy manhunt, Wright finds the "hard and deep" tone he sought. The novel is, on one level, a lurid drama of murder, futile attempts to hide evidence, and eventual discovery; but it is also a dramatic account of poverty in the black ghetto and a psychological portrait of the hatred, fear, and confusion that characterize its violent protagonist, Bigger Thomas. In the lengthy third section, Wright presents a sociological analysis in the words of Bigger's Communist defense lawyer, who almost abandons any effective defense of his client for a lengthy denunciation of the society that made him a criminal. The ending of the novel shows a condemned Bigger surrounded by people who have their own interpretations of his condition, and Bigger himself just beginning to attain a sense of his own identity: "what I wanted, what I am." The novel appeared in 1940 as a Book-of-the-Month Club selection (with some deletions required by the publisher); it quickly broke sales records, and the novelist became a national figure.

Wright's style combines naturalism—that is, realistic description governed by "scientific" principles of environmental influence—and a poetic or symbolic style. Obsessive themes and color associations imply extended networks of meaning: the color white, for example, is always vaguely threatening and recurs in nightmares. The famous opening scene of *Native Son,* in which Bigger kills a monstrous rat invading his family kitchen, establishes a violent, doom-laden atmosphere that prefigures Bigger's own destiny to be hunted like an animal and killed. Realistic narrative often shifts into obsessed imaginings and fantastic dreams that suggest the action of larger psychological or cultural forces.

After his move to Paris in the mid-forties, Wright's work developed more global and universal themes. Now openly anti-Communist, he continued to push for revolutionary reform in *Black Power* (1954, an essay on Ghana), *Pagan Spain* (1956), and the lectures of *White Man, Listen!* (1957). His model for reform, however, was Western and industrial, a perspective that did not appeal to many African writers of the Négritude (black identity) movement. The new novels became more philosophical and even didactic. *Savage Holiday* (1954), using Freudian symbolism (and white characters); *The Outsider* (1957), dramatizing existential themes in a collapsing society; and *The Long Dream* (1958), the first volume of a projected trilogy on black experience, move beyond racial questions to explore the human condition. Some critics have argued that Wright's exile in Europe cut him off from his roots and that the later novels are comparatively weak. Yet all share Wright's great theme in which a protagonist passes through violent crises that force a coming to terms with his or her identity and role in society. This subject, he asserted, is "the main burden of all serious fiction . . . character-destiny and the items, social, political, and personal, of that character-destiny." When Wright died of a heart attack on November 28, 1960, he was in the midst of many unfinished projects, including a book of haiku poetry.

The Man Who Was Almost a Man is drawn from the posthumously published *Eight Men* (1961), a collection of five stories, two radio plays, and an autobiographical essay that were written at different periods. An early version of the story, *Almos' a Man,* was published in 1941 and itself stems from a projected novel about a black boxer, *Tarbaby's Dawn.* Like much of Wright's fiction, *The Man Who Was Almost a Man* derives its setting and themes from the author's experience even though events are altered to fit the requirements of the story. Here racial issues are only hinted at as part of the background, while emphasis is put on the difficult passage from adolescence to maturity and on the vulnerability of fragile personalities to being defined from outside.

Seventeen-year-old Dave Saunders is desperate to be considered a man: his family, coworkers, employer, and the store owner all call him "boy" and remind him that he is only a child. He comes from a strict family that guides his every step. Treated like a child, he responds by seeing adulthood as a matter of power: and power, to Dave, means a gun. With a gun, people would have to respect him; he could "kill anybody, black or white." When Dave's attempts at gun practice turn sour, his adolescent vulnerability is badly hurt as he is ridiculed by his coworkers, betrayed—as he sees it—by his mother, promised a beating by his father, and required to pay for the dead mule with his wages for the next two years. Humiliation tips the balance between accepting responsibility for his actions and running away. It is not as a man that he flees, however, but as an adolescent whose whole sense of identity is now locked up with the gun. Like the railroad tracks stretching ahead, "away to somewhere, somewhere where he could be a man," Dave's escape is presented not as a solution but as a continuation of the same problem.

The Man Who Was Almost a Man is a good example of Wright's ability to combine realistic description with modernist techniques expressing a state of mind. His skillful use of dialect and his knowledgeable description of local scenes and attitudes place the story firmly in its sociohistorical setting. A more poetic approach is used to convey Dave's emotional turmoil: sensual images suggest his quasi-erotic response to the revolver, and an internalized point of view reproduces his startled pain when he shoots the gun and his horror when he realizes that he has just shot Jenny. Time slows down while Dave ineffectually plugs the mule's wounds with earth and watches her die; time slows again, and faces blur, when he is the humiliated focus of the crowd's attention. This blend of narrative realism and modernist manipulation of language typifies Wright's best work and makes The Man Who Was Almost a Man one of his most popular stories.

Michel Fabre, The Unfinished Quest of Richard Wright (rev. ed. 1992), trans. Isabel Barzun, is an excellent and readable biography. Useful essay collections that reprint reviews of Wright's work are Robert J. Butler, ed., The Critical Response to Richard Wright (1995), and Henry Louis Gates Jr. and K. A. Appiah, eds., Richard Wright: Critical Perspectives Past and Present (1993), which contains an essay specifically on the short stories. In addition are Harold Bloom, ed., Richard Wright (1987); Arnold Rampersad, ed., with Bruce Simon and Jeffrey Tucker, Richard Wright: A Collection of Critical Essays (1995); and Richard Macksey and Frank E. Moorer, eds., Richard Wright, A Collection of Critical Essays (1984).

The Man Who Was Almost a Man

Dave struck out across the fields, looking homeward through paling light. Whut's the use talkin wid em niggers in the field? Anyhow, his mother was putting supper on the table. Them niggers can't understan nothing. One of these days he was going to get a gun and practice shooting, then they couldn't talk to him as though he were a little boy. He slowed, looking at the ground. Shucks, Ah ain scareda them even ef they are biggern me! Aw, Ah know whut Ahma do. Ahm going by ol Joe's sto n git that Sears Roebuck catlog n look at them guns. Mebbe Ma will lemme buy one when she gits mah pay from ol man Hawkins. Ahma beg her t gimme some money. Ahm ol ernough to hava gun. Ahm seventeen. Almost a man. He strode, feeling his long loose-jointed limbs. Shucks, a man oughta hava little gun aftah he done worked hard all day.

He came in sight of Joe's store. A yellow lantern glowed on the front porch. He mounted steps and went through the screen door, hearing it bang behind him. There was a strong smell of coal oil and mackerel fish. He felt very

confident until he saw fat Joe walk in through the rear door, then his courage
began to ooze.

"Howdy, Dave! Whutcha want?"

"How yuh, Mistah Joe? Aw, Ah don wanna buy nothing. Ah jus wanted t
see ef yuhd lemme look at tha catlog erwhile."

"Sure! You wanna see it here?"

"Nawsuh. Ah wans t take it home wid me. Ah'll bring it back termorrow
when Ah come in from the fiels."

"You plannin on buying something?"

"Yessuh."

"Your ma lettin you have your own money now?"

"Shucks. Mistah Joe, Ahm gittin t be a man like anybody else!"

Joe laughed and wiped his greasy white face with a red bandanna.

"Whut you plannin on buyin?"

Dave looked at the floor, scratched his head, scratched his thigh, and
smiled. Then he looked up shyly.

"Ah'll tell yuh, Mistah Joe, ef yuh promise yuh won't tell."

"I promise."

"Waal, Ahma buy a gun."

"A gun? Whut you want with a gun?"

"Ah wanna keep it."

"You ain't nothing but a boy. You don't need a gun."

"Aw, lemme have the catlog, Mistah Joe. Ah'll bring it back."

Joe walked through the rear door. Dave was elated. He looked around at
barrels of sugar and flour. He heard Joe coming back. He craned his neck
to see if he were bringing the book. Yeah, he's got it. Gawddog, he's got it!

"Here, but be sure you bring it back. It's the only one I got."

"Sho, Mistah Joe."

"Say, if you wanna buy a gun, why don't you buy one from me? I gotta gun
to sell."

"Will it shoot?"

"Sure it'll shoot."

"Whut kind is it?"

"Oh, it's kinda old . . . a left-hand Wheeler.[1] A pistol. A big one."

"Is it got bullets in it?"

"It's loaded."

"Kin Ah see it?"

"Where's your money?"

"Whut yuh wan fer it?"

"I'll let you have it for two dollars."

"Just two dollahs? Shucks, Ah could buy tha when Ah git mah pay."

"I'll have it here when you want it."

"Awright, suh. Ah be in fer it."

He went through the door, hearing it slam again behind him. Ahma git
some money from Ma n buy me a gun! Only two dollahs! He tucked the
thick catalogue under his arm and hurried.

"Where yuh been, boy?" His mother held a steaming dish of black-eyed
peas.

---

1. The first revolving pistol, patented by Captain Artemus Wheeler in 1818; it was superseded by the Colt
revolver after 1830.

"Aw, Ma, Ah jus stopped down the road t talk wid the boys."

"Yuh know bettah t keep suppah waitin."

He sat down, resting the catalogue on the edge of the table.

"Yuh git up from there and git to the well n wash yosef! Ah ain feedin no hogs in mah house!"

She grabbed his shoulder and pushed him. He stumbled out of the room, then came back to get the catalogue.

"Whut this?"

"Aw, Ma, it's jusa catlog."

"Who yuh git it from?"

"From Joe, down at the sto."

"Waal, thas good. We kin use it in the outhouse."

"Naw, Ma." He grabbed for it. "Gimme ma catlog, Ma."

She held onto it and glared at him.

"Quit hollerin at me! Whut's wrong wid yuh? Yuh crazy?"

"But Ma, please. It ain mine! It's Joe's! He tol me t bring it back t im termorrow."

She gave up the book. He stumbled down the back steps, hugging the thick book under his arm. When he had splashed water on his face and hands, he groped back to the kitchen and fumbled in a corner for the towel. He bumped into a chair; it clattered to the floor. The catalogue sprawled at his feet. When he had dried his eyes he snatched up the book and held it again under his arm. His mother stood watching him.

"Now, ef yuh gonna act a fool over that ol book, Ah'll take it n burn it up."

"Naw, Ma, please."

"Waal, set down n be still!"

He sat down and drew the oil lamp close. He thumbed page after page, unaware of the food his mother set on the table. His father came in. Then his small brother.

"Whutcha got there, Dave?" his father asked.

"Jusa catlog," he answered, not looking up.

"Yeah, here they is!" His eyes glowed at blue-and-black revolvers. He glanced up, feeling sudden guilt. His father was watching him. He eased the book under the table and rested it on his knees. After the blessing was asked, he ate. He scooped up peas and swallowed fat meat without chewing. Buttermilk helped to wash it down. He did not want to mention money before his father. He would do much better by cornering his mother when she was alone. He looked at his father uneasily out of the edge of his eye.

"Boy, how come yuh don quit foolin wid tha book n eat yo suppah?"

"Yessuh."

"How you n ol man Hawkins gitten erlong?"

"Suh?"

"Can't yuh hear? Why don yuh lissen? Ah ast yu how wuz yuh n ol man Hawkins gittin erlong?"

"Oh, swell, Pa. Ah plows mo lan than anybody over there."

"Waal, yuh oughta keep yo mind on whut yuh doin."

"Yessuh."

He poured his plate full of molasses and sopped it up slowly with a chunk of cornbread. When his father and brother had left the kitchen, he still sat and looked again at the guns in the catalogue, longing to muster courage

enough to present his case to his mother. Lawd, ef Ah only had tha pretty
one! He could almost feel the slickness of the weapon with his fingers. If he
had a gun like that he would polish it and keep it shining so it would never
rust. N Ah'd keep it loaded, by Gawd!

"Ma?" His voice was hesitant.

"Hunh?"

"Ol man Hawkins give yuh mah money yit?"

"Yeah, but ain no usa yuh thinking bout throwin nona it erway. Ahm kee-
pin tha money sos yuh kin have cloes t go to school this winter."

He rose and went to her side with the open catalogue in his palms. She
was washing dishes, her head bent low over a pan. Shyly he raised the book.
When he spoke, his voice was husky, faint.

"Ma, Gawd knows Ah wans one of these."

"One of whut?" she asked, not raising her eyes.

"One of these," he said again, not daring even to point. She glanced up at
the page, then at him with wide eyes.

"Nigger, is yuh gone plumb crazy?"

"Aw, Ma—"

"Git outta here! Don yuh talk t me bout no gun! Yuh a fool!"

"Ma, Ah kin buy one fer two dollahs."

"Not ef Ah knows it, yuh ain!"

"But yuh promised me one—"

"Ah don care whut Ah promised! Yuh ain nothing but a boy yit!"

"Ma, ef yuh lemme buy one Ah'll *never* ast yuh fer nothing no mo."

"Ah tol yuh t git outta here! Yuh ain gonna toucha penny of tha money fer
no gun! Thas how come Ah has Mistah Hawkins t pay yo wages t me, cause
Ah knows yuh ain got no sense."

"But, Ma, we needa gun. Pa ain got no gun. We needa gun in the house.
Yuh kin never tell whut might happen."

"Now don yuh try to maka fool outta me, boy! Ef we did hava gun, yuh
wouldn't have it!"

He laid the catalogue down and slipped his arm around her waist.

"Aw, Ma, Ah done worked hard alla summer n ain ast yuh fer nothin, is
Ah, now?"

"Thas whut yuh spose t do!"

"But Ma, Ah wans a gun. Yuh kin lemme have two dollahs outta mah
money. Please, Ma. I kin give it to Pa . . . Please, Ma! Ah loves yuh, Ma."

When she spoke her voice came soft and low.

"Whut yu wan wida gun, Dave? Yuh don need no gun. Yuh'll git in trouble.
N ef yo pa jus thought Ah let yuh have money t buy a gun he'd hava fit."

"Ah'll hide it, Ma. It ain but two dollahs."

"Lawd, chil, whut's wrong wid yuh?"

"Ain nothin wrong, Ma. Ahm almos a man now. Ah wans a gun."

"Who gonna sell yuh a gun?"

"Ol Joe at the sto."

"N it don cos but two dollahs?"

"Thas all, Ma. Jus two dollahs. Please, Ma."

She was stacking the plates away; her hands moved slowly, reflectively.
Dave kept an anxious silence. Finally, she turned to him.

"Ah'll let yuh git tha gun ef yuh promise me one thing."

"Whut's tha, Ma?"

"Yuh bring it straight back t me, yuh hear? It be fer Pa."

"Yessum! Lemme go now, Ma."

She stooped, turned slightly to one side, raised the hem of her dress, rolled down the top of her stocking, and came up with a slender wad of bills.

"Here," she said. "Lawd knows yuh don need no gun. But yer pa does. Yuh bring it right back t me, yuh hear? Ahma put it up. Now ef yuh don, Ahma have yuh pa lick yuh so hard yuh won fergit it."

"Yessum."

He took the money, ran down the steps, and across the yard.

"Dave! Yuuuuuh Daaaaave!"

He heard, but he was not going to stop now. "Naw, Lawd!"

The first movement he made the following morning was to reach under his pillow for the gun. In the gray light of dawn he held it loosely, feeling a sense of power. Could kill a man with a gun like this. Kill anybody, black or white. And if he were holding his gun in his hand, nobody could run over him; they would have to respect him. It was a big gun, with a long barrel and a heavy handle. He raised and lowered it in his hand, marveling at its weight.

He had not come straight home with it as his mother had asked; instead he had stayed out in the fields, holding the weapon in his hand, aiming it now and then at some imaginary foe. But he had not fired it; he had been afraid that his father might hear. Also he was not sure he knew how to fire it.

To avoid surrendering the pistol he had not come into the house until he knew that they were all asleep. When his mother had tiptoed to his bedside late that night and demanded the gun, he had first played possum; then he had told her that the gun was hidden outdoors, that he would bring it to her in the morning. Now he lay turning it slowly in his hands. He broke it, took out the cartridges, felt them, and then put them back.

He slid out of bed, got a long strip of old flannel from a trunk, wrapped the gun in it, and tied it to his naked thigh while it was still loaded. He did not go in to breakfast. Even though it was not yet daylight, he started for Jim Hawkins' plantation. Just as the sun was rising he reached the barns where the mules and plows were kept.

"Hey! That you, Dave?"

He turned. Jim Hawkins stood eying him suspiciously.

"What're yuh doing here so early?"

"Ah didn't know Ah wuz gittin up so early, Mistah Hawkins. Ah wuz fixin t hitch up ol Jenny n take her t the fiels."

"Good. Since you're so early, how about plowing that stretch down by the woods?"

"Suits me, Mistah Hawkins."

"O.K. Go to it!"

He hitched Jenny to a plow and started across the fields. Hot dog! This was just what he wanted. If he could get down by the woods, he could shoot his gun and nobody would hear. He walked behind the plow, hearing the traces creaking, feeling the gun tied tight to his thigh.

When he reached the woods, he plowed two whole rows before he decided to take out the gun. Finally, he stopped, looked in all directions, then untied the gun and held it in his hand. He turned to the mule and smiled.

"Know whut this is, Jenny? Naw, yuh wouldn know! Yuhs jusa ol mule! Anyhow, this is a gun, n it kin shoot, by Gawd!"

He held the gun at arm's length. Whut t hell, Ahma shoot this thing! He looked at Jenny again.

"Lissen here, Jenny! When Ah pull this ol trigger, Ah don wan yuh t run n acka fool now!"

Jenny stood with head down, her short ears pricked straight. Dave walked off about twenty feet, held the gun far out from him at arm's length, and turned his head. Hell, he told himself, Ah ain afraid. The gun felt loose in his fingers; he waved it wildly for a moment. Then he shut his eyes and tightened his forefinger. Bloom! A report half deafened him and he thought his right hand was torn from his arm. He heard Jenny whinnying and galloping over the field, and he found himself on his knees, squeezing his fingers hard between his legs. His hand was numb; he jammed it into his mouth, trying to warm it, trying to stop the pain. The gun lay at his feet. He did not quite know what had happened. He stood up and stared at the gun as though it were a living thing. He gritted his teeth and kicked the gun. Yuh almos broke mah arm! He turned to look for Jenny; she was far over the fields, tossing her head and kicking wildly.

"Hol on there, ol mule!"

When he caught up with her she stood trembling, walling her big white eyes at him. The plow was far away; the traces had broken. Then Dave stopped short, looking, not believing. Jenny was bleeding. Her left side was red and wet with blood. He went closer. Lawd, have mercy! Wondah did Ah shoot this mule? He grabbed for Jenny's mane. She flinched, snorted, whirled, tossing her head.

"Hol on now! Hol on."

Then he saw the hole in Jenny's side, right between the ribs. It was round, wet, red. A crimson stream streaked down the front leg, flowing fast. Good Gawd! Ah wuzn't shootin at tha mule. He felt panic. He knew he had to stop that blood, or Jenny would bleed to death. He had never seen so much blood in all his life. He chased the mule for half a mile, trying to catch her. Finally she stopped, breathing hard, stumpy tail half arched. He caught her mane and led her back to where the plow and gun lay. Then he stooped and grabbed handfuls of damp black earth and tried to plug the bullet hole. Jenny shuddered, whinnied, and broke from him.

"Hol on! Hol on now!"

He tried to plug it again, but blood came anyhow. His fingers were hot and sticky. He rubbed dirt into his palms, trying to dry them. Then again he attempted to plug the bullet hole, but Jenny shied away, kicking her heels high. He stood helpless. He had to do something. He ran at Jenny; she dodged him. He watched a red stream of blood flow down Jenny's leg and form a bright pool at her feet.

"Jenny . . . Jenny," he called weakly.

His lips trembled. She's bleeding t death! He looked in the direction of home, wanting to go back, wanting to get help. But he saw the pistol lying in the damp black clay. He had a queer feeling that if he only did something, this would not be; Jenny would not be there bleeding to death.

When he went to her this time, she did not move. She stood with sleepy, dreamy eyes; and when he touched her she gave a low-pitched whinny and knelt to the ground, her front knees slopping in blood.

"Jenny . . . Jenny . . ." he whispered.

For a long time she held her neck erect; then her head sank, slowly. Her ribs swelled with a mighty heave and she went over.

Dave's stomach felt empty, very empty. He picked up the gun and held it gingerly between his thumb and forefinger. He buried it at the foot of a tree. He took a stick and tried to cover the pool of blood with dirt—but what was the use? There was Jenny lying with her mouth open and her eyes walled and glassy. He could not tell Jim Hawkins he had shot his mule. But he had to tell something. Yeah, Ah'll tell em Jenny started gittin wil n fell on the joint of the plow. . . . But that would hardly happen to a mule. He walked across the field slowly, head down.

It was sunset. Two of Jim Hawkins' men were over near the edge of the woods digging a hole in which to bury Jenny. Dave was surrounded by a knot of people, all of whom were looking down at the dead mule.

"I don't see how in the world it happened," said Jim Hawkins for the tenth time.

The crowd parted and Dave's mother, father, and small brother pushed into the center.

"Where Dave?" his mother called.

"There he is," said Jim Hawkins.

His mother grabbed him.

"Whut happened, Dave? Whut yuh done?"

"Nothin."

"C mon, boy, talk," his father said.

Dave took a deep breath and told the story he knew nobody believed.

"Waal," he drawled. "Ah brung ol Jenny down here sos Ah could do mah plowin. Ah plowed bout two rows, just like yuh see." He stopped and pointed at the long rows of upturned earth. "Then somethin musta been wrong wid ol Jenny. She wouldn ack right a-tall. She started snortin n kickin her heels. Ah tried t hol her, but she pulled erway, rearin n goin in. Then when the point of the plow was stickin up in the air, she swung erroun n twisted herself back on it . . . She stuck herself n started t bleed. N fo Ah could do anything, she wuz dead."

"Did you ever hear of anything like that in all your life?" asked Jim Hawkins.

There were white and black standing in the crowd. They murmured. Dave's mother came close to him and looked hard into his face. "Tell the truth, Dave," she said.

"Looks like a bullet hole to me," said one man.

"Dave, whut yuh do wid the gun?" his mother asked.

The crowd surged in, looking at him. He jammed his hands into his pockets, shook his head slowly from left to right, and backed away. His eyes were wide and painful.

"Did he hava gun?" asked Jim Hawkins.

"By Gawd, Ah tol yuh tha wuz a gun wound," said a man, slapping his thigh.

His father caught his shoulders and shook him till his teeth rattled.

"Tell whut happened, yuh rascal! Tell whut . . ."

Dave looked at Jenny's stiff legs and began to cry.

"Whut yuh do wid tha gun?" his mother asked.

"Whut wuz he doin wida gun?" his father asked.

"Come on and tell the truth," said Hawkins. "Ain't nobody going to hurt you . . ."

His mother crowded close to him.

"Did yuh shoot tha mule, Dave?"

Dave cried, seeing blurred white and black faces.

"Ahh ddinn gggo tt sshooot hher . . . Ah ssswear ffo Gawd Ahh ddin . . . Ah wuz a-tryin t sssee ef the old gggun would sshoot—"

"Where yuh git the gun from?" his father asked.

"Ah got it from Joe, at the sto."

"Where yuh git the money?"

"Ma give it t me."

"He kept worryin me, Bob. Ah had t. Ah tol im t bring the gun right back t me . . . It was fer yuh, the gun."

"But how yuh happen to shoot that mule?" asked Jim Hawkins.

"Ah wuzn shootin at the mule, Mistah Hawkins. The gun jumped when Ah pulled the trigger . . . N fo Ah knowed anythin Jenny was there a-bleedin."

Somebody in the crowd laughed. Jim Hawkins walked close to Dave and looked into his face.

"Well, looks like you have bought you a mule, Dave."

"Ah swear fo Gawd, Ah didn go t kill the mule, Mistah Hawkins!"

"But you killed her!"

All the crowd was laughing now. They stood on tiptoe and poked heads over one another's shoulders.

"Well, boy, looks like yuh done bought a dead mule! Hahaha!"

"Ain tha ershame."

"Hohohohoho."

Dave stood, head down, twisting his feet in the dirt.

"Well, you needn't worry about it, Bob," said Jim Hawkins to Dave's father. "Just let the boy keep on working and pay me two dollars a month."

"Whut yuh wan fer yo mule, Mistah Hawkins?"

Jim Hawkins screwed up his eyes.

"Fifty dollars."

"Whut yuh do wid tha gun?" Dave's father demanded.

Dave said nothing.

"Yuh wan me t take a tree n beat yuh till yuh talk!"

"Nawsuh!"

"Whut yuh do wid it?"

"Ah throwed it erway."

"Where?"

"Ah . . . Ah throwed it in the creek."

"Waal, c mon home. N firs thing in the mawnin git to tha creek n fin tha gun."

"Yessuh."

"Whut yuh pay fer it?"

"Two dollahs."

"Take tha gun n git yo money back n carry it t Mistah Hawkins, yuh hear? N don fergit Ahma lam you black bottom good fer this! Now march yosef on home, suh!"

Dave turned and walked slowly. He heard people laughing. Dave glared, his eyes welling with tears. Hot anger bubbled in him. Then he swallowed and stumbled on.

That night Dave did not sleep. He was glad that he had gotten out of killing the mule so easily, but he was hurt. Something hot seemed to turn over inside him each time he remembered how they had laughed. He tossed on his bed, feeling his hard pillow. *N Pa says he's gonna beat me* . . . He remembered other beatings, and his back quivered. *Naw, naw, Ah sho don wan im t beat me tha way no mo. Dam em all! Nobody ever gave him anything. All he did was work. They treat me like a mule, n then they beat me.* He gritted his teeth. *N Ma had t tell on me.*

Well, if he had to, he would take old man Hawkins that two dollars. But that meant selling the gun. And he wanted to keep that gun. Fifty dollars for a dead mule.

He turned over, thinking how he had fired the gun. He had an itch to fire it again. *Ef other men kin shoota gun, by Gawd, Ah kin!* He was still, listening. *Mebbe they all sleepin now.* The house was still. He heard the soft breathing of his brother. *Yes, now!* He would go down and get that gun and see if he could fire it! He eased out of bed and slipped into overalls.

The moon was bright. He ran almost all the way to the edge of the woods. He stumbled over the ground, looking for the spot where he had buried the gun. *Yeah, here it is.* Like a hungry dog scratching for a bone, he pawed it up. He puffed his black cheeks and blew dirt from the trigger and barrel. He broke it and found four cartridges unshot. He looked around; the fields were filled with silence and moonlight. He clutched the gun stiff and hard in his fingers. But, as soon as he wanted to pull the trigger, he shut his eyes and turned his head. *Naw, Ah can't shoot wid mah eyes closed n mah head turned.* With effort he held his eyes open; then he squeezed. *Blooooom!* He was stiff, not breathing. The gun was still in his hands. *Dammit, he'd done it!* He fired again. *Blooooom!* He smiled. *Blooooom! Blooooom! Click, click.* There! It was empty. If anybody could shoot a gun, he could. He put the gun into his hip pocket and started across the fields.

When he reached the top of a ridge he stood straight and proud in the moonlight, looking at Jim Hawkins' big white house, feeling the gun sagging in his pocket. *Lawd, ef Ah had just one mo bullet Ah'd taka shot at tha house. Ah'd like t scare ol man Hawkins jusa little . . . Jusa enough t let im know Dave Saunders is a man.*

To his left the road curved, running to the tracks of the Illinois Central. He jerked his head, listening. From far off came a faint *hoooof-hoooof*; *hoooof-hoooof*; *hoooof-hoooof.* . . . He stood rigid. *Two dollahs a mont. Les see now . . . Tha means it'll take bout two years. Shucks! Ah'll be dam!*

He started down the road, toward the tracks. *Yeah, here she comes!* He stood beside the track and held himself stiffly. Here she comes, erroun the

ben . . . C mon, yuh slow poke! C mon! He had his hand on his gun; something quivered in his stomach. Then the train thundered past, the gray and
brown box cars rumbling and clinking. He gripped the gun tightly; then he
jerked his hand out of his pocket. Ah betcha Bill wouldn't do it! Ah betcha
. . . The cars slid past, steel grinding upon steel. Ahm ridin yuh ternight, so
hep me Gawd! He was hot all over. He hesitated just a moment; then he
grabbed, pulled atop of a car, and lay flat. He felt his pocket; the gun was
still there. Ahead the long rails were glinting in the moonlight, stretching
away, away to somewhere, somewhere where he could be a man . . .

NAGUIB MAHFOUZ
born 1911

The foremost novelist writing in Arabic traces his roots to the civilization of the
ancient Egyptians, over five thousand years ago. Past and present combine for Naguib
Mahfouz as he interrogates the destiny of his people and their often-traumatic adjustment to modern industrial society. Without Mahfouz, it is said, the turbulent history
of twentieth-century Egypt would never be known. His fictional families and frustrated middle-class clerks have documented the successive stages of Egyptian social
and political life from the time the country cast off foreign rule and became a "postcolonial" society. Time, in fact, is the real protagonist of his novels: the time in which
individuals live and die, governments come and go, and social values are transformed—time, ultimately, as the conqueror that reduces human endeavor to nothing
and forces attention on spiritual truth. Mahfouz's novels and short stories have millions of readers throughout the Arab world, and a growing audience in the West,
because they deal with basic human issues in a realistic social context. Generations
of Arabs have read his works or seen them adapted to film and television, and his
characters have become household words. Mahfouz the craftsman has also wrought
a change in Arabic prose, synthesizing traditional literary style and modern speech to
create a new literary language understood by Arabs everywhere.

Readers of his best-known works, however, will find many similarities with the
nineteenth-century realist novel in Europe. Mahfouz has been called the "Balzac of
Egypt"—a comparison to the great French novelist and panoramic chronicler of society Honoré de Balzac (1799–1850)—and he is well acquainted with the works of
Gustave Flaubert, Leo Tolstoy, and other nineteenth-century novelists. Traditional
Arabic literature has many forms of narrative, but the novel is not one of them; and
contemporary writers like Mahfouz have adapted the Western form to their own
needs. Their readers will find familiar nineteenth-century strategies such as a chronological plot, unified characters, the inclusion of documentary information and realistic details, a panoramic view of society including a strong moral and humanistic
perspective, and—typically if not necessarily—a picture of urban middle-class life.
Among twentieth-century authors Mahfouz might be compared with Alexander Solzhenitsyn for his realist style and analysis of national identity. The Egyptian author
employs allegory much more than do traditionally realist authors, however, and his
most recent work has made use of fragmented and absurdist techniques as well as a
variety of classical Arabic forms. He continues to be preoccupied with individual
experience inside what he calls the "tragedies of society," although his focus is not
restricted to the individualized existentialism of Jean-Paul Sartre or Albert Camus

and embraces a complex of social relationships. Like the nineteenth-century novelists he follows, Mahfouz believes in the social function of art and the concomitant responsibility of the writer. His books have been censored and banned in many Arab countries, and he was blacklisted for several years for supporting Egypt's 1979 peace treaty with Israel.

Naguib Mahfouz was born in Cairo on December 11, 1911, the youngest of seven children in the family of a civil servant. The family moved from their home in the old Jamaliya district to the suburbs of Cairo when the boy was young. He attended government schools and entered the University of Cairo in 1930, graduating in 1934 with a degree in philosophy. These were not quiet years: Egypt, officially under Ottoman rule, had been occupied by the British since 1883 and was declared a British protectorate at the start of World War I in 1914. Mahfouz grew up in the midst of an ongoing struggle for national independence that culminated in a violent uprising against the British in 1919 and the negotiation of a constitutional monarchy in 1923. The consistent focus on Egyptian cultural identity that permeates his work may well have its roots in this early turbulent period. The difficulty of disentangling cultural traditions, however, is indicated by the fact that Mahfouz's first published book was a 1932 translation of an English work on ancient Egypt.

While at the university, Mahfouz made friends with the socialist and Darwinian thinker Salama Musa and began to write articles for Musa's journal Al-Majalla al-Jadida (The modern magazine). In 1938, he published his first collection of stories, Whispers of Madness, and in 1939 the first of three historical novels set in ancient Egypt. He planned at that time to write a set of forty books on the model of the historical romance written by the British novelist Sir Walter Scott (1771–1832). These first novels already included modern references, and few missed the criticism of King Farouk in Radubis (1943) or the analogy in The Struggle for Thebes (1944) between the ancient Egyptian battle to expel Hyksos usurpers and twentieth-century rebellions against foreign rule. In 1945 Mahfouz shifted decisively to the realistic novel and a portrayal of modern society. He focused on the social and spiritual dilemmas of the middle class in Cairo, documenting in vivid detail the life of an urban society that represented modern Egypt.

The major work of this period, and Mahfouz's masterwork in many eyes, is The Cairo Trilogy (1956–57), three volumes depicting the experience of three generations of a Cairo family between 1918 and 1944. Into this story, whose main protagonist Mahfouz has called Time, is woven a social history of Egypt after World War I. Mahfouz's achievement was recognized in the State Prize for literature in 1956, but he himself temporarily ceased to write after finishing the Trilogy in 1952. In that year, an officers' coup headed by Gamal Abdel Nasser overthrew the monarchy and instituted a republic that promised democratic reforms, and there was a change in the panorama of Egyptian society that Mahfouz described. Although the author was at first optimistic about the new order, he soon recognized that not much had changed for the general populace. When he started publishing again in 1959, his works included much open criticism of the Nasser regime.

Although he had become the best-known writer in the Arab world, his works read by millions, Mahfouz like other Arab authors could not make a living from his books. Copyright protection was minimal, and without copyright protection even best-selling authors received only small sums for their books. Until he began writing for motion pictures in the 1960s, he supported himself and his family through various positions in governmental ministries and as a contributing editor for the leading newspaper, Al-Ahram. Attached to the Ministry of Culture in 1954, he adapted novels for film and television and later became director-general of the governmental Cinema Organization. (Cinema, radio, and television are nationalized industries in Egypt.) After his retirement from the civil service in 1971, Mahfouz continued to publish articles and short stories in Al-Ahram, where most of his novels have appeared in serialized form before being issued as paperbacks. When he received the Nobel Prize in 1988, at the age of seventy-seven, he was still publishing a weekly column, "Point of View," in *Al-Ahram.*

Three years after *The Cairo Trilogy* brought him international praise, Mahfouz shocked many readers with a new book, *Children of Gebelawi.* Serialized in *Al-Ahram, Children of Gebelawi* is on the surface another description of a patriarchal family evolving in modern times. The story of the patriarch Gebelawi and his disobedient or ambitious children, however, is also an allegory of religious history. Its personification of God, Adam, and the prophets—among whom science is included as the youngest and most destructive son—and its simultaneous portrayal of the prophets as primarily social reformers rather than religious figures, scandalized orthodox believers. The book was banned throughout the Arab world except in Lebanon, and the Jordan League of Writers attacked Mahfouz as a "delinquent man" whose novels were "plagued with sex and drugs." *Children of Gebelawi* remains unpublished in Egypt to this day.

Mahfouz took up writing short stories again in the early 1960s after concentrating on novels for two decades. His second collection, *God's World* (1963), combined social realism and metaphysical speculation. He also began to move away from an "objective," realistic style toward one that emphasized subjective and mystic awareness, drawing on an Islamic mystical tradition whose comprehensive tolerance is far from (and often opposed by) the rigid beliefs of contemporary Muslim fundamentalists. The perceptions of individual characters govern works such as *The Thief and the Dogs* (1962), the story of a released prisoner who—seeking revenge on his unfaithful wife and the man who betrayed him—is trapped by police dogs and shot; and *Miramar* (1967), in which different points of view describe the disappointed love of a young servant girl, her determination to shape her own career, and the death of a lodger. Mahfouz did not abandon social commentary in his new mode. Individual characters represent particular classes or even (with *Miramar's* servant girl) Egypt itself, and the film made from *Miramar* attracted large audiences for its sharp criticism of the dominant political party, the Arab Socialist Union. In *Mirrors* (1972), brief accounts of fifty-four different characters "mirror" various aspects of contemporary Egyptian society.

Mahfouz's approach changed again in the late 1960s; social commentary in the novels became even more direct, while individual stories grew more fragmented and even absurdist in style. Egypt's defeat by Israel in the June 1967 war had a shattering effect on the nation's self-confidence, and Mahfouz responded to what he saw as the country's spiritual dilemma. Stories written between October and December 1967 and collected in *Under the Bus Shelter* repeatedly show contradictory and incomprehensible events happening to perplexed and frustrated people. An almost cinematic style emerged, emphasizing dialogue over interpretation; some pieces in later collections resemble one-act plays. In the title story of *Under the Bus Shelter,* people waiting for a bus observe beatings, a car crash with several deaths, a couple making love on a corpse, dancing, the rapid construction of a monumental grave in which both corpses and lovers are buried, inaudible speeches, a man who may possibly be the director of the film (if it *is* a film) but may also be a thug, a decapitation, and finally "a group of official-looking men wandering around" whose appearance frightens off the others—until the puzzled observers are shot by a previously apathetic policeman when they ask questions. Several novels in the 1970s and 1980s reveal a similar bleak perspective in a more didactic style; *There Only Remains One Hour* (1982), for example, portrays current events as a sequence of failed efforts to achieve peace and prosperity.

Mahfouz's style continues to evolve in new directions. Among his recent works are adaptations of classical Arabic narrative forms such as the *maqama* (elaborate rhymed trickster tales) or folk narratives like the *Arabian Nights* into imaginative sequences such as *The Nights of "The Thousand and One Nights"* or *The Epic of the Riff-Raff.* While these works disconcerted some adherents of his earlier, realistic style, they are an integral part of the Egyptian writer's attempt to find new ways to express Arabic culture and to comment from a broader, often prophetic perspective on the contemporary scene. That Mahfouz is impelled by a sense of moral purpose is evident throughout his works, and perhaps no more so than in his Nobel Prize acceptance speech in 1988. Speaking first for Arabic letters but also as a representative of the Third World, he addressed the leaders of a Western civilization that has allowed science and technology to outweigh basic human values. "The developed world and the third world are but one family. Each human being bears responsibility towards it by the degree of what he has obtained of knowledge, wisdom, and civilization. . . . In the name of the third world: Be not spectators to our miseries." The "able ones, the civilized ones," he added, perhaps ironically, must be guided by the collective needs of humanity. He continues to defend humanitarian values in Egypt as well. After Islamic fundamentalists pressured the Ministry of Culture into establishing precensorship for books in 1994, Mahfouz attacked this "intellectual terrorism" against the arts; he was later stabbed in the neck and lost the use of his writing hand.

Zaabalawi, a story included in *God's World*, contains many of Mahfouz's predominant themes. Written two years after *Children of Gebelawi*, it echoes the earlier work's religious symbolism in the mysterious character of Zaabalawi himself. It is also a social document: the narrator's quest for Zaabalawi brings him before various representatives of modern Egyptian society inside a realistically described Cairo. *Zaabalawi*, therefore, takes on the character of a social and metaphysical allegory. Its terminally ill narrator seeks to be cured in a quest that implies not only physical healing but also religious salvation. He has already exhausted the resources of medical science and, in desperation, he decides to seek out a holy man whose name he recalls from childhood tales.

In the initial stage of his search, the protagonist is coldly received by a lawyer and a district officer, former acquaintances of Zaabalawi who have become worldly, materialistic, and highly successful. Moreover, these bureaucrats who depend on reason, technology, and businesslike efficiency can do no more than send him to old addresses or draw him city maps. Zaabalawi is still alive, they say, but he is unpredictable and hard to find now that he no longer inhabits his old home—a now-dilapidated mansion in front of which an old bookseller sells used books on mysticism and theology. In contrast, the calligrapher and composer to whom the narrator next turns welcome him as a person. Indeed, the composer reproves him for thinking only of his errand and overlooking the value of getting to know another human being. The relationship among art, human sympathy, and spiritual values is made clear, for Zaabalawi is close to both artists and has provided inspiration for their best works. In the last scene, at the Negma Bar, Mahfouz fuses the realistic description of a hardened drinker with a dream-vision of another, peaceful world. At this stage of the quest, the narrator is not even allowed to state his errand but must place himself on a level with his drunken host before being allowed to speak. When he does sink into oblivion (in stages that suggest a mystic stripping-away of rational faculties), he is rewarded in his dreams by a glimpse of paradise and wakes to find that Zaabalawi has been beside him as he slept. *Zaabalawi* ends as it began—"I have to find Zaabalawi"—but the seeker is now more confident, and the route more clearly marked.

Roger M. A. Allen, *The Arabic Novel: An Historical and Critical Introduction* (1982), is an authoritative introduction that situates Mahfouz in the context of modern Arabic literature and includes a bibliography of works in Arabic and Western languages. The author's own perspective is given in Najib Mahfuz, *Echoes of an Autobiography* (1997), trans. Denys Johnson-Davies. Sasson Somekh, *"Za'balawi"*— Author, Theme and Technique" in *Journal of Arabic Literature* (1970), examines the story as a "double-layered" structure governed by references to Sufi mysticism. Michael Beard and Adnan Haydar, eds., *Naguib Mahfouz: From Regional Fame to Global Recognition* (1993), assembles eleven original essays on themes, individual works, and cultural contexts in Mahfouz's work. Trevor le Gassick, ed., *Critical Perspectives on Naguib Mahfouz* (1991), reprints articles on Mahfouz's work up to the

1970s. Rasheed El-Enany, ed., *Naguib Mahfouz: The Pursuit of Meaning* (1993), is an excellent study that includes biography, analyses of novels, short stories, and plays and a guide for further reading. Comparative studies include Mona Mikhail, *Studies in the Short Fiction of Mahfouz and Idris* (1992), an introductory work juxtaposing themes in Hemingway, Idris, Mahfouz, and Camus; and Sarnia Mehrez, *Egyptian Writers Between History and Fiction: Essays on Naguib Mahfouz, Sonallah Ibrahim, and Gamal al-Ghitani* (1994). Rasheed El-Enany discusses the place of religion in Mahfouz's work in "The Dichotomy of Islam and Modernity in the Fiction of Naguib Mahfouz," in John C. Hawley, ed., *The Postcolonial Crescent: Islam's Impact on Contemporary Literature* (1998).

PRONOUNCING GLOSSARY

The following list uses common English syllables and stress accents to provide rough equivalents of selected words whose pronunciation may be unfamiliar to the general reader.

Hassanein: *hassan-ayn'*

Naguib Mahfouz: *nah-geeb' mah-fooz'*

Qamar: *qa-mar'*

Umm al-Ghulam: *oum al–ghol-am'*

Wanas al-Damanhouri: *wan'-nas ad–dam-an-oo'-ree*

Zaabalawi: *zah-bah-lah'-wee*

Zaabalawi[1]

Finally I became convinced that I had to find Sheikh[2] Zaabalawi.
  The first time I had heard of his name had been in a song:

> Oh what's become of the world, Zaabalawi?
> They've turned it upside down and taken away its taste.

It had been a popular song in my childhood, and one day it had occurred to me to demand of my father, in the way children have of asking endless questions:
"Who is Zaabalawi?"
He had looked at me hesitantly as though doubting my ability to understand the answer. However, he had replied, "May his blessing descend upon you, he's a true saint of God, a remover of worries and troubles. Were it not for him I would have died miserably—"
In the years that followed, I heard my father many a time sing the praises of this good saint and speak of the miracles he performed. The days passed and brought with them many illnesses, for each one of which I was able, without too much trouble and at a cost I could afford, to find a cure, until I became afflicted with that illness for which no one possesses a remedy. When I had tried everything in vain and was overcome by despair, I remembered by chance what I had heard in my childhood: Why, I asked myself, should I not seek out Sheikh Zaabalawi? I recollected my father saying that he had made his acquaintance in Khan Gaafar[3] at the house of Sheikh Qamar, one of those sheikhs who practiced law in the religious courts, and so I took myself off to his house. Wishing to make sure that he was still living there, I made inquiries of a vendor of beans whom I found in the lower part of the house.

---

1. Translated by Denys Johnson-Davies.   2. A title of respect (originally "old man"), often indicating rulership.   3. Gaafar Market, an area of shops.

"Sheikh Qamar!" he said, looking at me in amazement. "He left the quarter ages ago. They say he's now living in Garden City and has his office in al-Azhar Square."[4]

I looked up the office address in the telephone book and immediately set off to the Chamber of Commerce Building, where it was located. On asking to see Sheikh Qamar, I was ushered into a room just as a beautiful woman with a most intoxicating perfume was leaving it. The man received me with a smile and motioned me toward a fine leather-upholstered chair. Despite the thick soles of my shoes, my feet were conscious of the lushness of the costly carpet. The man wore a lounge suit and was smoking a cigar; his manner of sitting was that of someone well satisfied both with himself and with his worldly possessions. The look of warm welcome he gave me left no doubt in my mind that he thought me a prospective client, and I felt acutely embarrassed at encroaching upon his valuable time.

"Welcome!" he said, prompting me to speak.

"I am the son of your old friend Sheikh Ali al-Tatawi," I answered so as to put an end to my equivocal position.

A certain languor was apparent in the glance he cast at me; the languor was not total in that he had not as yet lost all hope in me.

"God rest his soul," he said. "He was a fine man."

The very pain that had driven me to go there now prevailed upon me to stay.

"He told me," I continued, "of a devout saint named Zaabalawi whom he met at Your Honor's. I am in need of him, sir, if he be still in the land of the living."

The languor became firmly entrenched in his eyes, and it would have come as no surprise if he had shown the door to both me and my father's memory.

"That," he said in the tone of one who has made up his mind to terminate the conversation, "was a very long time ago and I scarcely recall him now."

Rising to my feet so as to put his mind at rest regarding my intention of going, I asked, "Was he really a saint?"

"We used to regard him as a man of miracles."

"And where could I find him today?" I asked, making another move toward the door.

"To the best of my knowledge he was living in the Birgawi Residence in al-Azhar," and he applied himself to some papers on his desk with a resolute movement that indicated he would not open his mouth again. I bowed my head in thanks, apologized several times for disturbing him, and left the office, my head so buzzing with embarrassment that I was oblivious to all sounds around me.

I went to the Birgawi Residence, which was situated in a thickly populated quarter. I found that time had so eaten at the building that nothing was left of it save an antiquated façade and a courtyard that, despite being supposedly in the charge of a caretaker, was being used as a rubbish dump. A small, insignificant fellow, a mere prologue to a man, was using the covered entrance as a place for the sale of old books on theology and mysticism.

When I asked him about Zaabalawi, he peered at me through narrow, inflamed eyes and said in amazement, "Zaabalawi! Good heavens, what a

4. An area of Cairo close to the famous mosque and university of al-Azhar.

time ago that was! Certainly he used to live in this house when it was habitable. Many were the times he would sit with me talking of bygone days, and I would be blessed by his holy presence. Where, though, is Zaabalawi today?"

He shrugged his shoulders sorrowfully and soon left me, to attend to an approaching customer. I proceeded to make inquiries of many shopkeepers in the district. While I found that a large number of them had never even heard of Zaabalawi, some, though recalling nostalgically the pleasant times they had spent with him, were ignorant of his present whereabouts, while others openly made fun of him, labeled him a charlatan, and advised me to put myself in the hands of a doctor—as though I had not already done so. I therefore had no alternative but to return disconsolately home.

With the passing of days like motes in the air, my pains grew so severe that I was sure I would not be able to hold out much longer. Once again I fell to wondering about Zaabalawi and clutching at the hope his venerable name stirred within me. Then it occurred to me to seek the help of the local sheikh of the district; in fact, I was surprised I had not thought of this to begin with. His office was in the nature of a small shop, except that it contained a desk and a telephone, and I found him sitting at his desk, wearing a jacket over his striped galabeya.[5] As he did not interrupt his conversation with a man sitting beside him, I stood waiting till the man had gone. The sheikh then looked up at me coldly. I told myself that I should win him over by the usual methods, and it was not long before I had him cheerfully inviting me to sit down.

"I'm in need of Sheikh Zaabalawi," I answered his inquiry as to the purpose of my visit.

He gazed at me with the same astonishment as that shown by those I had previously encountered.

"At least," he said, giving me a smile that revealed his gold teeth, "he is still alive. The devil of it is, though, he has no fixed abode. You might well bump into him as you go out of here, on the other hand you might spend days and months in fruitless searching."

"Even you can't find him!"

"Even I! He's a baffling man, but I thank the Lord that he's still alive!"

He gazed at me intently, and murmured, "It seems your condition is serious."

"Very."

"May God come to your aid! But why don't you go about it systematically?" He spread out a sheet of paper on the desk and drew on it with unexpected speed and skill until he had made a full plan of the district, showing all the various quarters, lanes, alleyways, and squares. He looked at it admiringly and said, "These are dwelling-houses, here is the Quarter of the Perfumers, here the Quarter of the Coppersmiths, the Mouski,[6] the police and fire stations. The drawing is your best guide. Look carefully in the cafés, the places where the dervishes perform their rites, the mosques and prayer-rooms, and the Green Gate,[7] for he may well be concealed among the beggars and be indistinguishable from them. Actually, I myself haven't seen him for years,

5. The traditional Arabic robe, over which this modernized district officer wears a European jacket.
6. The central bazaar. 7. A medieval gate in Cairo.

having been somewhat preoccupied with the cares of the world, and was only brought back by your inquiry to those most exquisite times of my youth."

I gazed at the map in bewilderment. The telephone rang, and he took up the receiver.

"Take it," he told me, generously. "We're at your service."

Folding up the map, I left and wandered off through the quarter, from square to street to alleyway, making inquiries of everyone I felt was familiar with the place. At last the owner of a small establishment for ironing clothes told me, "Go to the calligrapher[8] Hassanein in Umm al-Ghulam—they were friends."

I went to Umm al-Ghulam,[9] where I found old Hassanein working in a deep, narrow shop full of signboards and jars of color. A strange smell, a mixture of glue and perfume, permeated its every corner. Old Hassanein was squatting on a sheepskin rug in front of a board propped against the wall; in the middle of it he had inscribed the word "Allah"[1] in silver lettering. He was engrossed in embellishing the letters with prodigious care. I stood behind him, fearful of disturbing him or breaking the inspiration that flowed to his masterly hand. When my concern at not interrupting him had lasted some time, he suddenly inquired with unaffected gentleness, "Yes?"

Realizing that he was aware of my presence, I introduced myself. "I've been told that Sheikh Zaabalawi is your friend; I'm looking for him," I said.

His hand came to a stop. He scrutinized me in astonishment. "Zaabalawi! God be praised!" he said with a sigh.

"He *is* a friend of yours, isn't he?" I asked eagerly.

"He was, once upon a time. A real man of mystery: he'd visit you so often that people would imagine he was your nearest and dearest, then would disappear as though he'd never existed. Yet saints are not to be blamed."

The spark of hope went out with the suddenness of a lamp snuffed by a power-cut.

"He was so constantly with me," said the man, "that I felt him to be a part of everything I drew. But where is he today?"

"Perhaps he is still alive?"

"He's alive, without a doubt. . . . He had impeccable taste, and it was due to him that I made my most beautiful drawings."

"God knows," I said, in a voice almost stifled by the dead ashes of hope, "how dire my need for him is, and no one knows better than you[2] of the ailments in respect of which he is sought."

"Yes, yes. May God restore you to health. He is, in truth, as is said of him, a man, and more. . . ."

Smiling broadly, he added, "And his face possesses an unforgettable beauty. But where is he?"

Reluctantly I rose to my feet, shook hands, and left. I continued wandering eastward and westward through the quarter, inquiring about Zaabalawi from everyone who, by reason of age or experience, I felt might be likely to help me. Eventually I was informed by a vendor of lupine[3] that he had met him a short while ago at the house of Sheikh Gad, the well-known composer. I

---

8. One who practices the art of decorative lettering (literally "beautiful writing"), which is respected as a fine art in Arabic and Asian cultures. 9. A street in Cairo. 1. God (Arabic). 2. One of the calligrapher's major tasks is to write religious documents and prayers to Allah. 3. Beans.

went to the musician's house in Tabakshiyya,[4] where I found him in a room tastefully furnished in the old style, its walls redolent with history. He was seated on a divan, his famous lute beside him, concealing within itself the most beautiful melodies of our age, while somewhere from within the house came the sound of pestle and mortar and the clamor of children. I immediately greeted him and introduced myself, and was put at my ease by the unaffected way in which he received me. He did not ask, either in words or gesture, what had brought me, and I did not feel that he even harbored any such curiosity. Amazed at his understanding and kindness, which boded well, I said, "O Sheikh Gad, I am an admirer of yours, having long been enchanted by the renderings of your songs."

"Thank you," he said with a smile.

"Please excuse my disturbing you," I continued timidly, "but I was told that Zaabalawi was your friend, and I am in urgent need of him."

"Zaabalawi!" he said, frowning in concentration. "You need him? God be with you, for who knows, O Zaabalawi, where you are."

"Doesn't he visit you?" I asked eagerly.

"He visited me some time ago. He might well come right now; on the other hand I mightn't see him till death!"

I gave an audible sigh and asked, "What made him like that?"

The musician took up his lute. "Such are saints or they would not be saints," he said, laughing.

"Do those who need him suffer as I do?"

"Such suffering is part of the cure!"

He took up the plectrum and began plucking soft strains from the strings. Lost in thought, I followed his movements. Then, as though addressing myself, I said, "So my visit has been in vain."

He smiled, laying his cheek against the side of the lute. "God forgive you," he said, "for saying such a thing of a visit that has caused me to know you and you me!"

I was much embarrassed and said apologetically, "Please forgive me; my feelings of defeat made me forget my manners."

"Do not give in to defeat. This extraordinary man brings fatigue to all who seek him. It was easy enough with him in the old days when his place of abode was known. Today, though, the world has changed, and after having enjoyed a position attained only by potentates, he is now pursued by the police on a charge of false pretenses. It is therefore no longer an easy matter to reach him, but have patience and be sure that you will do so."

He raised his head from the lute and skillfully fingered the opening bars of a melody. Then he sang:

> I make lavish mention, even though I blame myself, of those I love,
> For the stories of the beloved are my wine.[5]

With a heart that was weary and listless, I followed the beauty of the melody and the singing.

"I composed the music to this poem in a single night," he told me when

---

4. A quarter named for the straw trays made and sold there. 5. From a poem by the medieval mystic poet Ibn al-Farid, who represents spiritual ecstasy as a kind of drunkenness.

he had finished. "I remember that it was the eve of the Lesser Bairam.[6] Zaabalawi was my guest for the whole of that night, and the poem was of his choosing. He would sit for a while just where you are, then would get up and play with my children as though he were one of them. Whenever I was overcome by weariness or my inspiration failed me, he would punch me playfully in the chest and joke with me, and I would bubble over with melodies, and thus I continued working till I finished the most beautiful piece I have ever composed."

"Does he know anything about music?"

"He is the epitome of things musical. He has an extremely beautiful speaking voice, and you have only to hear him to want to burst into song and to be inspired to creativity. . . ."

"How was it that he cured those diseases before which men are powerless?"

"That is his secret. Maybe you will learn it when you meet him."

But when would that meeting occur? We relapsed into silence, and the hubbub of children once more filled the room.

Again the sheikh began to sing. He went on repeating the words "and I have a memory of her" in different and beautiful variations until the very walls danced in ecstasy. I expressed my wholehearted admiration, and he gave me a smile of thanks. I then got up and asked permission to leave, and he accompanied me to the front door. As I shook him by the hand, he said, "I hear that nowadays he frequents the house of Hagg Wanas al-Damanhouri. Do you know him?"

I shook my head, though a modicum of renewed hope crept into my heart.

"He is a man of private means," the sheikh told me, "who from time to time visits Cairo, putting up at some hotel or other. Every evening, though, he spends at the Negma Bar in Alfi Street."

I waited for nightfall and went to the Negma Bar. I asked a waiter about Hagg Wanas, and he pointed to a corner that was semisecluded because of its position behind a large pillar with mirrors on all four sides. There I saw a man seated alone at a table with two bottles in front of him, one empty, the other two-thirds empty. There were no snacks or food to be seen, and I was sure that I was in the presence of a hardened drinker. He was wearing a loosely flowing silk galabeya and a carefully wound turban; his legs were stretched out toward the base of the pillar, and as he gazed into the mirror in rapt contentment, the sides of his face, rounded and handsome despite the fact that he was approaching old age, were flushed with wine. I approached quietly till I stood but a few feet away from him. He did not turn toward me or give any indication that he was aware of my presence.

"Good evening, Mr. Wanas," I greeted him cordially.

He turned toward me abruptly, as though my voice had roused him from slumber, and glared at me in disapproval. I was about to explain what had brought me to him when he interrupted in an almost imperative tone of voice that was none the less not devoid of an extraordinary gentleness, "First, please sit down, and, second, please get drunk!"

I opened my mouth to make my excuses but, stopping up his ears with his fingers, he said, "Not a word till you do what I say."

I realized I was in the presence of a capricious drunkard and told myself

---

6. A major Islamic holiday, celebrated for three days to end the month's fasting during Ramadan.

that I should at least humor him a bit. "Would you permit me to ask one question?" I said with a smile, sitting down.

Without removing his hands from his ears he indicated the bottle. "When engaged in a drinking bout like this, I do not allow any conversation between myself and another unless, like me, he is drunk, otherwise all propriety is lost and mutual comprehension is rendered impossible."

I made a sign indicating that I did not drink.

"That's your lookout," he said offhandedly. "And that's my condition!"

He filled me a glass, which I meekly took and drank. No sooner had the wine settled in my stomach than it seemed to ignite. I waited patiently till I had grown used to its ferocity, and said, "It's very strong, and I think the time has come for me to ask you about—"

Once again, however, he put his fingers in his ears. "I shan't listen to you until you're drunk!"

He filled up my glass for the second time. I glanced at it in trepidation; then, overcoming my inherent objection, I drank it down at a gulp. No sooner had the wine come to rest inside me than I lost all willpower. With the third glass, I lost my memory, and with the fourth the future vanished. The world turned round about me and I forgot why I had gone there. The man leaned toward me attentively, but I saw him—saw everything—as a mere meaningless series of colored planes. I don't know how long it was before my head sank down onto the arm of the chair and I plunged into deep sleep. During it, I had a beautiful dream the like of which I had never experienced. I dreamed that I was in an immense garden surrounded on all sides by luxuriant trees, and the sky was nothing but stars seen between the entwined branches, all enfolded in an atmosphere like that of sunset or a sky overcast with cloud. I was lying on a small hummock of jasmine petals, more of which fell upon me like rain, while the lucent spray of a fountain unceasingly sprinkled the crown of my head and my temples. I was in a state of deep contentedness, of ecstatic serenity. An orchestra of warbling and cooing played in my ear. There was an extraordinary sense of harmony between me and my inner self, and between the two of us and the world, everything being in its rightful place, without discord or distortion. In the whole world there was no single reason for speech or movement, for the universe moved in a rapture of ecstasy. This lasted but a short while. When I opened my eyes, consciousness struck at me like a policeman's fist and I saw Wanas al-Damanhouri regarding me with concern. Only a few drowsy customers were left in the bar.

"You have slept deeply," said my companion. "You were obviously hungry for sleep."

I rested my heavy head in the palms of my hands. When I took them away in astonishment and looked down at them, I found that they glistened with drops of water.

"My head's wet," I protested.

"Yes, my friend tried to rouse you," he answered quietly.

"Somebody saw me in this state?"

"Don't worry, he is a good man. Have you not heard of Sheikh Zaabalawi?"

"Zaabalawi!" I exclaimed, jumping to my feet.

"Yes," he answered in surprise. "What's wrong?"

"Where is he?"

"I don't know where he is now. He was here and then he left."

I was about to run off in pursuit but found I was more exhausted than I had imagined. Collapsed over the table, I cried out in despair, "My sole reason for coming to you was to meet him! Help me to catch up with him or send someone after him."

The man called a vendor of prawns and asked him to seek out the sheikh and bring him back. Then he turned to me. "I didn't realize you were afflicted. I'm very sorry. . . ."

"You wouldn't let me speak," I said irritably.

"What a pity! He was sitting on this chair beside you the whole time. He was playing with a string of jasmine petals he had around his neck, a gift from one of his admirers, then, taking pity on you, he began to sprinkle some water on your head to bring you around."

"Does he meet you here every night?" I asked, my eyes not leaving the doorway through which the vendor of prawns had left.

"He was with me tonight, last night and the night before that, but before that I hadn't seen him for a month."

"Perhaps he will come tomorrow," I answered with a sigh.

"Perhaps."

"I am willing to give him any money he wants."

Wanas answered sympathetically, "The strange thing is that he is not open to such temptations, yet he will cure you if you meet him."

"Without charge?"

"Merely on sensing that you love him."

The vendor of prawns returned, having failed in his mission.

I recovered some of my energy and left the bar, albeit unsteadily. At every street corner I called out "Zaabalawi!" in the vague hope that I would be rewarded with an answering shout. The street boys turned contemptuous eyes on me till I sought refuge in the first available taxi.

The following evening I stayed up with Wanas al-Damanhouri till dawn, but the sheikh did not put in an appearance. Wanas informed me that he would be going away to the country and would not be returning to Cairo until he had sold the cotton crop.

I must wait, I told myself; I must train myself to be patient. Let me content myself with having made certain of the existence of Zaabalawi, and even of his affection for me, which encourages me to think that he will be prepared to cure me if a meeting takes place between us.

Sometimes, however, the long delay wearied me. I would become beset by despair and would try to persuade myself to dismiss him from my mind completely. How many weary people in this life know him not or regard him as a mere myth! Why, then, should I torture myself about him in this way?

No sooner, however, did my pains force themselves upon me than I would again begin to think about him, asking myself when I would be fortunate enough to meet him. The fact that I ceased to have any news of Wanas and was told he had gone to live abroad did not deflect me from my purpose; the truth of the matter was that I had become fully convinced that I had to find Zaabalawi.

Yes, I have to find Zaabalawi.

AIMÉ CÉSAIRE
born 1913

Aimé Césaire has been called "Poet of the Black Diaspora." The title draws attention to the dominant reference of Césaire's work, which is to the bitter historical experience of the black population in the New World, especially in the Caribbean—its uprooting, transplantation, and dispossession as part of its enslavement in America and its longing for the lost homeland of Africa. Most striking is the acute race consciousness he displays, responding to the somber experience of domination and devaluation that black people have endured in modern times. It is impossible to understand Césaire's poetry apart from this determining context and its impact on the poet. The collective experience of the black race touched Césaire so directly and profoundly that it constitutes the framework of his poetic destiny. His poetry presents itself as a symbolic mode of working through both a historical predicament and a personal drama.

Césaire was born on June 26, 1913, at Basse-Pointe, in northern Martinique, the second child in a family of modest means; his father was a junior functionary of the French colonial administration and his mother, a dressmaker. The burden of race and the legacy of slavery weighed heavily on the black population in the highly stratified society of colonial Martinique, exerting a pressure that Césaire could not have escaped during his childhood. Apart from this, Césaire's earliest impressions were almost certainly formed by the landscape of his birthplace, on the Atlantic coast of his native island, where the sea is especially forceful, and in the vicinity of the volcano Mont Pélé, amid an abundant tropical vegetation. These features of the physical environment in which he grew up are significant elements of his imaginative universe.

Césaire received his primary education at Basse-Pointe, then went for his secondary education to Fort-de-France, the capital of the colony, where he attended the Lycée Schoelcher, named after the most prominent French abolitionist. After obtaining his *baccalauréat* in 1931, he was awarded a scholarship to continue his studies in France. Shortly after his arrival in Paris that year, and his enrollment at the Lycée Louis-le-Grand in the preparatory class for the École Normale Supérieure, he met Léopold Sédar Senghor (p. 2502) and formed with him a lasting friendship. It was through the close collaboration of the two men over the next few years that what came to be known as the Négritude movement developed. The term itself, which denotes a sense of collective racial identity and common destiny among black people the world over, was coined by Césaire and first appeared in print in his celebrated long poem *Cahier d'un retour au pays natal* (Notebook of a Return to the Native Land), which he was to publish in 1939 and which remains his best-known work.

The meeting with Senghor had a highly personal significance for Césaire. As he was later to remark, "When I met Senghor, I knew I was an African." By introducing Césaire to aspects of African civilization that formed Senghor's own background, Senghor helped free his friend from the negative associations that Africa held for West Indians of his generation. The two men became intellectual companions, with a common passion for Africa. Together they read and discussed the ethnographic literature on Africa that began to appear during this period—notably the works of the French anthropologist Maurice Delafosse and the German cultural historian Leo Frobenius—which emphasized the coherence of African social systems and the value of the continent's indigenous cultures. Through Senghor and in these books, Césaire encountered a positive image of Africa that enabled him to identify with the continent of his ancestors and thus to arrive at self-acceptance as a black person.

Césaire's relationship with Senghor developed within the context of a black awakening that was already under way during the years between the two world wars. In the United States, the activities of W. E. B. Du Bois had given concrete form to the idea of Pan-Africanism as a movement of black solidarity concerned with the bleak situation of black people both in America and on the African continent. By the time of Césaire's arrival in Paris, a strong anticolonial sentiment had developed among African and Caribbean students and intellectuals. This new militancy can be attributed to several factors. Foremost among them was the political, social, and cultural malaise, resulting from World War I, which undermined the claim of Western civilization to moral superiority, a claim consistently used to justify the colonial enterprise. Another factor was the rise of socialism with its explicit challenge to imperialism. Finally, there was the Harlem Renaissance, at its height in the 1920s, which had introduced a strongly affirmative note into black American literature.

This revolution of consciousness among French-speaking black intellectuals prompted Césaire and Senghor to question the premises on which colonial ideology was based: the notion of Africa as a "dark" continent, symbolizing the inferiority of the black race. This they did through the journal *L'Etudiant noir,* founded in 1935 by a group of West Indian and African students. Although devoted exclusively to cultural matters, *L'Etudiant noir* had a pronounced Pan-African orientation, for its aim was to establish connections between the conditions of life and the cultures expressing those conditions in Africa as well as in the American diaspora and to affirm what Césaire termed, in an article in the journal, "the primacy of self."

In the midst of this intense promotion of a new black consciousness, Césaire continued his literary and classical studies. He entered the Ecole Normale Supérieure in 1935, and a year later obtained his first degree, the *Licence-des-Lettres.* The following year, he obtained the *Diplôme d'Etudes Supérieures* (equivalent to the Master's degree), writing a thesis on the South in black American literature. He had also begun to write poetry and was especially drawn to the work of the Surrealists, in particular André Breton, whose aesthetic of spontaneous expression had a special appeal for Césaire. Surrealism offered not only a modern poetic idiom but also an instrument for sounding the depths of his own consciousness and releasing the tension between a mind-set acquired from his Western conditioning and what he considered to be his authentic self, grounded in an African sensibility and disposition. In this spirit, he began to compose *Notebook of a Return to the Native Land* in the autumn of 1936 and completed it in time for publication in the journal *Volontés,* in August 1939, just before the outbreak of World War II. The poem attracted practically no attention at the time but was later to play a determining role in shaping contemporary attitudes in the French-speaking black world and beyond.

Césaire returned to Martinique later in the year, in the early stages of a war that soon saw the collapse of France and the setting up of the Vichy regime, which quickly established its control over the island colony and pursued authoritarian and racist policies. In response to this somber atmosphere, Césaire, now a professor at his old school, founded the journal *Tropiques* with his wife, Suzanne, and a few colleagues. In the articles they wrote for the journal over the four years of its life, they scrutinized the complex social and psychological problems of their island people and undertook to foster in them a new awareness of their potential, a new determination of the collective will.

The first issue of the journal had just appeared, in April 1941, when André Breton, passing through Martinique on his way to voluntary exile in the United States, came on a copy in a local bookshop. Its tone and content made such an impression on him that he asked to meet Césaire and his collaborators and thus became acquainted with the first version of *Notebook,* which had been published earlier in Paris. Later, he arranged the publication of a revised and expanded edition in volume form, along with an English translation. In the preface of this edition, issued in New York in 1947, he hailed Césaire's poem as "the greatest lyrical monument of the age."

Invited in 1944 to deliver a keynote address at a philosophy conference at Port-au-Prince, in Haiti, Césaire chose the subject *poésie et connaissance* (poetry and knowledge), stressing the importance of poetry both as a reflection of the lived conditions of existence and as a privileged insight into the true nature of things. His stay in Haiti lasted seven months, during which he familiarized himself with the life of Toussaint L'Ouverture, hero of the Haitian revolution, whose biography he would publish in 1961, and of Henri Christophe, Toussaint's successor, about whom he wrote a powerful play in the mid-1960s.

In 1945, Césaire was elected mayor of Fort-de-France and, under the banner of the Communist Party, one of the deputies for Martinique in the French Constituent Assembly. His active political career ended only with his retirement from politics in 1993. He has been at the forefront of the ideological battles of French-speaking black intellectuals, carried on through the journal *Présence Africaine*, founded in 1947 by the Senegalese Alioune Diop. He was principal speaker at the two Congresses of Black Writers organized by that journal, the first in Paris in 1956 and the second in Rome in 1959. His *Discourse on Colonialism*, published in 1955, contains a vigorous denunciation of the brutal methods of colonial conquest and remains an outstanding example of polemical literature.

With the active promotion of Breton, Césaire's poems began to appear in the mid-1940s in Surrealist journals. His first collection, *Les Armes miraculeuses* (The Miraculous Arms, 1946), shows the peculiar strength of his poetic imagination and his links to Surrealism. The title asserts his aggressive stance, the dissidence that underlies every image: "And the mines of radium buried deep/in the abyss of my innocences / will burst into grains/in the manger of birds."

The same dissident mood can be observed in his next collection, *Soleil cou coupé* (Solar Throat Slashed, 1948). The title, derived from a poem by Apollinaire (*Lone*), confirms the modernist orientation of the poet's social and metaphysical revolt. The poems are marked by baroque imagery, and a wide range of poetic voices project the turmoil of the poet's inner state. His dark presence in the world predisposes him to a combative role. Playing deliberately on the sinister associations of blackness in Western culture, he assumes the aspect of a primordial force engaged in the revision of an inequitable history:

> A robust bolt of thunder flashes danger
> from the most untouchable brow in the world
> in you all the widowed light
> of twilights of cities stabbed
> by birds from the countryside
> And beware the crow that does not fly it is my head which has broken
> loose of the centrepole of my shoulders
> uttering an ancient screech rending guts disrupting watering holes

In Césaire's next volume *Corps perdu* (Lost Body, 1950), the language is sparer, though still animated by a sense of justified revolt:

> And our faces beautiful
> as the true operative power
> of negation.

Since its republication in volume form, Césaire had been revising *Notebook,* and in 1956 the publishing house of Présence Africaine brought out an enlarged and updated version. The poem quickly established itself as the centerpiece of the literature of Négritude. The most impassioned statement in all literature of the racial sentiment of black people in their historical, social, and cultural relation to the Western world, the poem also became recognized as a masterpiece of modern French poetry, the only *long* poem in the Surrealist tradition. Thus *Notebook* belongs as much to mainstream French literature as to the evolving canon of French-speaking literature in Africa and the Caribbean.

The long opening evocation of the physical and moral misery of the Antilles is an essential part of the process of self-knowledge that is the poem's goal. But the movement of self-recovery it narrates also involves a recognition of the wider world of humanity in need of spiritual renewal: "You know that it is not from hatred of other races / that I demand a digger for this unique race / that what I want / is for universal hunger / for universal thirst." Despite the force of its commitment to a collective social and political cause, the poem's enduring significance resides in its apprehension of a realm of transcendental values. This aspect of the poem is intimated constantly in the imagery that gives a mystic resonance to the experience it dramatizes. It emerges fully in the concluding stanzas of the poem, confirming for us the meaning of the poet's adventure: the turbulent movement through history mirrors the unfolding of his aspiration to a higher mode of being.

In his later work, Césaire combines the sinewy character of his earlier poetry with an opulent and ceremonial style of address, as in the poems of *Ferrements* (1960). The need for more direct communication, evident in this volume, led him next to drama. *The Tragedy of King Christophe* (1963), based on events in Haiti after its independence in the early nineteenth century, confronts the problems of decolonization. The connection hinted at here between the Haitian precedent and the African situation becomes overt in his next play, *Une Saison au Congo* (A Season in the Congo, 1966), which focuses on Patrice Lumumba and his tragic fate in the former Belgian Congo (now Congo). In these plays, the dialogue often assumes heroic dimensions, rising to become a comprehensive meditation on nation building. Césaire returns to the colonial question in *Une tempête* (1969), an adaptation of Shakespeare's *The Tempest,* which examines in contemporary terms the relation between Prospero and Caliban.

Césaire's *moi laminaire* (1982) represents a stock-taking of his poetic and political career. The spareness of the imagery, rooted more than ever in the Caribbean landscape, endows with a lyrical gravity the uncompromising self-reflection undertaken in these poems. The volume thus returns to and confirms the introspective note in Césaire's work, in a complex interaction of personal, historical, and mythical references. Beyond its social and political references, Césaire's poetry expresses a deeply human ideal, a primary vision in which humanity, restored to nature, will find the "rock without dialect, the leaf without keep, the fragile water without femur."

The fullest critical account of Césaire's work is to be found in A. James Arnold, *Négritude and Modernism: The Poetry and Poetics of Aimé Césaire* (1981); Arnold has further developed his views in his introduction to Clayton Eshleman and Annette Smith, trans., *Aimé Césaire: Lyrical and Dramatic Poetry* (1992). Janis Pallister, *Aimé Césaire* (1991), is a useful general discussion of the main themes; while Ronnie Leah Scharfman, *Engagement and the Language of the Subject in the Poetry of Aimé Césaire* (1980), examines the complex psychological mechanisms at work in the poetry. Gregson Davis, *Aimé Césaire* (1997), is an insightful examination of the evolution of Césaire's work; it contains chapters on *Notebook* and the poet's Surrealist period as well as a chronology and a bibliography. The translation of *Notebook* printed here is taken from Clayton Eshleman and Annette Smith, trans., *Aimé Césaire: The Collected Poetry* (1983), which contains, in addition to translations of Césaire's poetry up to the late 1970s, a valuable general introduction.

PRONOUNCING GLOSSARY

The following list uses common English syllables to provide rough equivalents of selected words whose pronunciation may be unfamiliar to the general reader.

grigri: *gree-gree*

jiculi: *jee-koo-lee*

likouala: *lee-koo-ah-la*

patyura: *paht-yur-ah*

Notebook of a Return to the Native Land[1]

At the end of daybreak . . .

Beat it, I said to him, you cop, you lousy pig, beat it, I detest the flunkies of order and the cockchafers of hope. Beat it, evil grigri,[2] you bedbug of a petty monk. Then I turned toward paradises lost for him and his kin, calmer than the face of a woman telling lies, and there, 5
rocked by the flux of a never exhausted thought I nourished the wind, I unlaced the monsters and heard rise, from the other side of disaster,[3] a river of turtledoves and savanna clover which I carry forever in my depths height-deep as the twentieth floor of the most arrogant houses and as a guard against the putrefying force of crepuscular surroundings, surveyed 10
night and day by a cursed venereal sun.

At the end of daybreak burgeoning with frail coves, the hungry Antilles, the Antilles pitted with smallpox, the Antilles dynamited by alcohol, stranded in the mud of this bay, in the dust of this town sinisterly stranded. 15

At the end of daybreak, the extreme, deceptive desolate bedsore on the wound of the waters; the martyrs who do not bear witness; the flowers of blood that fade and scatter in the empty wind like the screeches of babbling parrots; an aged life mendaciously smiling, its lips opened by vacated agonies; an aged poverty rotting under the sun, silently; an 20
aged silence bursting with tepid pustules, the awful futility of our raison d'être.[4]

At the end of daybreak, on this very fragile earth thickness exceeded in a humiliating way by its grandiose future—the volcanoes will explode,[5] the naked water will bear away the ripe sun stains and nothing will be 25
left but a tepid bubbling pecked at by sea birds—the beach of dreams and the insane awakenings.

At the end of daybreak, this town sprawled-flat toppled from its common sense, inert, winded under its geometric weight of an eternally renewed cross, indocile to its fate, mute, vexed no matter what, inca- 30
pable of growing with the juice of this earth, self-conscious, clipped, reduced, in breach of fauna and flora.

At the end of daybreak, this town sprawled-flat . . .

And in this inert town, this squalling throng so astonishingly detoured from its cry as this town has been from its movement, from its meaning, 35
not even worried, detoured from its true cry, the only cry you would have wanted to hear because you feel it alone belongs to this town; because you feel it lives in it in some deep refuge and pride in this inert town, this throng detoured from its cry of hunger, of poverty, of revolt, of hatred, this throng so strangely chattering and mute. 40

1. Translated by Clayton Eshleman and Annette Smith.   2. Charms.   3. That is, Africa before the historical disaster of slavery.   4. Reason for being (French, literal trans.).   5. A reference to Mont Pélee which suddenly erupted in 1902 and destroyed Saint-Pierre, the former capital of Martinique.

In this inert town, this strange throng which does not pack, does not mix: clever at discovering the point of disencasement,[6] of flight, of dodging. This throng which does not know how to throng, this throng, clearly so perfectly alone under this sun, like a woman one thought completely occupied with her lyric cadence, who abruptly challenges a hypothetical rain and enjoins it not to fall; or like a rapid sign of the cross without perceptive motive; or like the sudden grave animality of a peasant, urinating standing, her legs parted, stiff.

In this inert town, this desolate throng under the sun, not connected with anything that is expressed, asserted, released in broad earth daylight, its own. Neither with Josephine, Empress of the French, dreaming way up there above the nigger scum. Nor with the liberator[7] fixed in his whitewashed stone liberation. Nor with the conquistador.[8] Nor with this contempt, with this freedom, with this audacity.

At the end of daybreak, this inert town and its beyond of lepers, of consumption, of famines, of fears squatting in the ravines, fears perched in the trees, fears dug in the ground, fears adrift in the sky, piles of fears and their fumaroles[9] of anguish.

At the end of daybreak, the morne[1] forgotten, forgetful of leaping.

At the end of daybreak, the morne in restless, docile hooves—its malarial blood routs the sun with its overheated pulse.

At the end of daybreak, the restrained conflagration of the morne like a sob gagged on the verge of a bloodthirsty burst, in quest of an ignition that slips away and ignores itself.

At the end of daybreak, the morne crouching before bulimia on the lookout for tuns[2] and mills, slowly vomiting out its human fatigue, the morne solitary and its blood shed, the morne bandaged in shades, the morne and its ditches of fear, the morne and its great hands of wind.

At the end of daybreak, the famished morne and no one knows better than this bastard morne why the suicide choked with a little help from his hypoglossal jamming his tongue backward to swallow it;[3] why a woman seems to float belly up on the Capot River[4] (her chiaroscuro body submissively organized at the command of her navel) but she is only a bundle of sonorous water.

And neither the teacher in his classroom, nor the priest at catechism will be able to get a word out of this sleepy little nigger, no matter how energetically they drum on his shorn skull, for starvation has quick-

6. The point at which two pieces of machinery can be fitted into each other or disconnected.   7. Victor Schoelcher (1804–1893), French abolitionist, whose statue stands in a square in the capital, Fort-de-France. Josephine (1763–1814), the first wife of Napoléon Bonaparte, was born in Martinique into the white settler class; she became empress when Napoléon took the title "emperor of the French" in 1804.   8. Conqueror (Spanish), applied to Cortés, Pizarro, and other adventurers who conquered South America on behalf of Spain. Here, Bélain d'Estambuc, who occupied Martinique in 1635 and claimed it for France.   9. In volcanic regions, ground holes that emit gases and vapors.   1. A little hill or hillock characteristic of Martinican landscape.   2. Casks, in which rum is stored. *Bulimia:* here, excessive hunger. The references are to the economic life of the islands, dominated by the production of sugar and the distillation of rum.   3. Slaves committed suicide by choking on their own tongues. *Hypoglossal:* the nerve under the tongue.   4. A stream in northern Martinique. The passage plays on an allusion to Ophelia, in Shakespeare's *Hamlet,* who floats down river after her suicide by drowning.

sanded his voice into the swamp of hunger (a word-one-single-word and
we-will-forget-about-Queen-Blanche-of-Castille,[5]   a-word-one-single-
word, you-should-see-this-little savage-who-doesn't-know-any-of-The-   80
Ten-Commandments).

for his voice gets lost in the swamp of hunger,
and there is nothing, really nothing to squeeze out of this little brat,
other than a hunger which can no longer climb to the rigging of his
    voice
a sluggish flabby hunger,   85
a hunger buried in the depth of the Hunger of this famished morne.

At the end of daybreak, the disparate stranding,[6] the exacerbated
stench of corruption, the monstrous sodomies of the host and the sacrificing priest, the impassable beakhead frames of prejudice and stupidity, the prostitutions, the hypocrisies, the lubricities, the treasons, the   90
lies, the frauds, the concussions—the panting of a deficient cowardice,
the heave-holess enthusiasm of supernumerary sahibs,[7] the greeds, the
hysterias, the perversions, the clownings of poverty, the cripplings, the
itchings, the hives, the tepid hammocks of degeneracy. Right here the
parade of laughable and scrofulous buboes, the forced feedings of very   95
strange microbes, the poisons without known alexins, the sanies[8] of
really ancient sores, the unforeseeable fermentations of putrescible
species.

At the end of daybreak, the great motionless night, the stars deader
than a caved-in balafon.[9]   100

the teratical[1] bulb of night, sprouted from our vilenesses and our
renunciations.

And our foolish and crazy stunts to revive the golden splashing of
privileged moments, the umbilical cord restored to its ephemeral splendor, the bread, and the wine of complicity, the bread, the wine, the blood   105
of honest weddings.

And this joy of former times making me aware of my present poverty,
a bumpy road plunging into a hollow where it scatters a few shacks; an
indefatigable road charging at full speed a morne at the top of which it
brutally quicksands into a pool of clumsy houses, a road foolishly climb-   110
ing, recklessly descending, and the carcass of wood, which I call "our
house," comically perched on minute cement paws, its coiffure of corrugated iron in the sun like a skin laid out to dry, the main room, the
rough floor where the nail heads gleam, the beams of pine and shadow
across the ceiling, the spectral straw chairs, the grey lamp light, the   115
glossy flash of cockroaches in a maddening buzz . . .

At the end of daybreak, this most essential land restored to my gour-
mandise,[2] not in diffuse tenderness, but the tormented sensual concentration of the fat tits of the mornes with an occasional palm tree as their

---

5. A queen of France in the Middle Ages.   6. The heterogeneous character of the West Indian population.   7. Lord, commander (Hindi).   8. Fluid from a wound. *Scrofulous buboes:* swellings caused by
tuberculosis ("scrofula"). *Alexins:* antidotes.   9. An African musical instrument similar to a xylophone.
1. Monstrous.   2. Here, keen desire.

hardened sprout, the jerky orgasm of torrents and from Trinité to Grand-   120
Rivière,[3] the hysterical grandsuck of the sea.

And time passed quickly, very quickly.

After August and mango trees decked out in all their little moons,
September begetter of cyclones, October igniter of sugar-cane, November who purrs in the distilleries, there came Christmas.   125

It had come in at first, Christmas did, with a tingling of desires, a
thirst for new tenderness, a burgeoning of vague dreams, then with a
purple rustle of its great joyous wings it had suddenly flown away, and
then its abrupt fall out over the village that made the shack life burst
like an overripe pomegranate.   130

Christmas was not like other holidays. It didn't like to gad about the
streets,[4] to dance on public squares, to mount the wooden horses, to use
the crowd to pinch women, to hurl fireworks in the faces of the tamarind
trees. It had agoraphobia,[5] Christmas did. What it wanted was a whole
day of bustling, preparing, a cooking and cleaning spree,   135
endless jitters
about-not-having-enough,
about-running-short,
about-getting-bored,

then at evening an unimposing little church, which would benevolently   140
make room for the laughter, the whispers, the secrets, the love talk, the
gossip and the guttural cacophony of a plucky singer and also boisterous
pals and shameless hussies and shacks up to their guts in succulent
goodies, and not stingy, and twenty people can crowd in, and the street
is deserted, and the village turns into a bouquet of singing, and you are   145
cozy in there, and you eat good, and you drink hearty and there are blood
sausages, one kind only two fingers wide twined in coils, the other broad
and stocky, the mild one tasting of wild thyme, the hot one spiced to an
incandescence, and steaming coffee and sugared anise[6] and milk punch,
and the liquid sun of rums, and all sorts of good things which drive your   150
taste buds wild or distill them to the point of ecstasy or cocoon them
with fragrances, and you laugh, and you sing, and the refrains flare on
and on like coco-palms:

ALLELUIA
KYRIE ELEISON[7] . . . LEISON . . . LEISON   155
CHRISTE ELEISON . . . LEISON . . . LEISON.

And not only do the mouths sing, but the hands, the feet, the buttocks,
the genitals, and your entire being liquefies into sounds, voices, and
rhythm.

At the peak of its ascent, joy bursts like a cloud. The songs don't stop,   160
but now anxious and heavy roll through the valleys of fear, the tunnels
of anguish and the fires of hell.

And each one starts pulling the nearest devil by his tail, until fear
imperceptibly fades in the fine sand lines of dream, and you really live

3. Towns in northern Martinique.   4. As during Carnival (just before Lent).   5. The fear of open
spaces, the opposite of claustrophobia.   6. A liqueur made from aniseed.   7. Lord have mercy (Greek);
a chant from the first part of the Catholic mass.

as in a dream, and you drink and you shout and you sing as in a dream, 165
and doze too as in a dream, with rose petal eyelids, and the day comes
velvety as a sapodilla[8] tree, and the liquid manure smell of the cacao
trees, and the turkeys which shell their red pustules[9] in the sun, and the
obsessive bells, and the rain,
    the bells . . . the rain . . . 170
    that tinkle, tinkle, tinkle . . .

At the end of daybreak, this town sprawled-flat . . .

    It crawls on its hands without the slightest desire to drill the sky with
a stature of protest. The backs of the houses are afraid of the sky truffled
with fire, their feet of the drownings of the soil, they chose to perch 175
shallowly between surprises and treacheries. And yet it advances, the
town does. It even grazes every day further out into its tide of tiled
corridors, prudish shutters, gluey courtyards, dripping paintwork. And
petty hushed-up scandals, petty unvoiced guilts, petty immense hatreds
knead the narrow streets into bumps and potholes where the waste-water 180
grins longitudinally through turds . . .

    At the end of daybreak, life prostrate, you don't know how to dispose
of your aborted dreams, the river of life desperately torpid in its bed,
neither turgid nor low, hesitant to flow, pitifully empty, the impartial
heaviness of boredom distributing shade equally on all things, the air 185
stagnant, unbroken by the brightness of a single bird.

    At the end of daybreak, another little house very bad-smelling in a
very narrow street, a minuscule house which harbors in its guts of rotten
wood dozens of rats and the turbulence of my six brothers and sisters, a
cruel little house whose demands panic the ends of our months and my 190
temperamental father gnawed by one persistent ache, I never knew
which one, whom an unexpected sorcery could lull to melancholy tenderness or drive to towering flames of anger; and my mother whose legs
pedal, pedal, night and day, for our tireless hunger, I was even awakened
at night by these tireless legs which pedal the night and the bitter bite 195
in the soft flesh of the night of a Singer[1] that my mother pedals, pedals
for our hunger and day and night.

    At the end of daybreak, beyond my father, my mother, the shack
chapped with blisters, like a peach tree afflicted with curl,[2] and the thin
roof patched with pieces of gasoline cans, which create swamps of rust 200
in the stinking sordid grey straw pulp, and when the wind whistles, these
odds and ends make a noise bizarre, first like the crackling of frying,
then like a brand dropped into water the smoke of its twigs flying up.
And the bed of boards from which my race arose, my whole entire race
from this bed of boards, with its kerosene case paws, as if it had ele- 205
phantiasis,[3] that bed, and its kidskin, and its dry banana leaves, and its
rags, yearning for a mattress, my grandmother's bed. (Above the bed, in

---

8. A fleshy fruit found in the West Indies.   9. Pimples. The red skin hanging in a fold around the neck
of turkeys seems to be covered with them.   1. An old-model sewing machine that was powered by the
movement of the legs.   2. An infection that attacks the leaves of the peach tree.   3. A disease that
causes swelling of the legs.

a jar full of oil a dim light whose flame dances like a fat cockroach . . .
on the jar in gold letters: MERCI.[4])
   And this rue Paille,[5] this disgrace,   210

an appendage repulsive as the private parts of the village which extends
right and left, along the colonial highway, the grey surge of its shingled
roofs. Here there are only straw roofs, spray browned and wind plucked.

   Everybody despises rue Paille. It's there that the village youth go
astray. It's there especially that the sea pours forth its garbage, its dead   215
cats and its croaked dogs. For the street opens on to the beach, and the
beach alone cannot satisfy the sea's foaming rage.

   A blight this beach as well, with its piles of rotting muck, its furtive
rumps relieving themselves, and the sand is black,[6] funereal, you've
never seen a sand so black, and the scum glides over it yelping, and the   220
sea pummels it like a boxer, or rather the sea is a huge dog licking and
biting the shins of the beach, biting them so fiercely that it will end up
devouring it, the beach and rue Paille along with it.

   At the end of daybreak, the wind of long ago—of betrayed trusts, of
uncertain evasive duty and that other dawn in Europe—arises . . .   225

To go away.
As there are hyena-men and panther-men, I would be a jew-man[7]
a Kaffir-man
   a Hindu-man-from-Calcutta
   a Harlem-man-who-doesn't-vote[8]   230

the famine man, the insult-man, the torture man you can grab anytime,
beat up, kill—no joke, kill—without having to account to anyone, without having to make excuses to anyone
a jew-man
a pogrom[9]-man   235
a puppy
a beggar
but *can* one kill Remorse, perfect as the stupefied face of an English
lady discovering a Hottentot[1] skull in her soup-tureen?

I would rediscover the secret of great communications and great com-   240
bustions. I would say storm. I would say river. I would say tornado. I
would say leaf. I would say tree. I would be drenched by all rains, moistened by all dews. I would roll like frenetic blood on the slow current of
the eye of words turned into mad horses into fresh children into clots
into curfew into vestiges of temples into precious stones remote enough   245
to discourage miners. Whoever would not understand me would not
understand any better the roaring of a tiger.

---

4. Thank you (French); the inscription is presumably addressed to God.   5. Straw Road (French, literal trans.); a street whose houses are roofed with straw.   6. Because of its volcanic origin.   7. Césaire's identification with another persecuted people, extended in the lines below to other minorities.   8. Harlem, the center of black life in New York City, is an appropriate reference for the denial of civil rights to blacks in the United States before corrective legislation in the 1960s. *Kaffir:* a term of contempt formerly applied by whites to black South Africans. Calcutta, India, was noted for its extreme poverty.   9. Organized harassment of Jews, often leading to their massacre.   1. A people of southwest Africa, who were decimated by white invaders in the 19th century.

And you ghosts rise blue from alchemy from a forest of hunted beasts
of twisted machines of a jujube tree of rotten flesh of a basket of oysters
of eyes of a network of straps in the beautiful sisal² of human skin I   250
would have words vast enough to contain you earth taut earth drunk
earth great vulva raised to the sun
earth great delirium of God's mentula³
savage earth arisen from the storerooms of the sea a clump of Cecropia⁴
in your mouth earth whose tumultuous face I can only compare to the   255
virgin and mad forest which were it in my power I would show in guise
of a face to the undeciphering eyes of men all I would need is a mouthful
of jiculi milk⁵ to discover in you always as distant as a mirage—a thousand times more native and made golden by a sun that no prism
divides—the earth where everything is free and fraternal, my earth.   260

To go away. My heart was pounding with emphatic generosities. To
go away . . . I would arrive sleek and young in this land of mine and I
would say to this land whose loam is part of my flesh: "I have wandered
for a long time and I am coming back to the deserted hideousness of
your sores."   265
I would go to this land of mine and I would say to it: "Embrace me
without fear . . . And if all I can do is speak, it is for you I shall speak."
And again I would say:
"My mouth shall be the mouth of those calamities that have no mouth,
my voice the freedom of those who break down in the solitary confine-   270
ment of despair."
And on the way I would say to myself:
"And above all, my body as well as my soul, beware of assuming the
sterile attitude of a spectator, for life is not a spectacle, a sea of miseries
is not a proscenium,⁶ a man screaming is not a dancing bear . . ."   275

And behold here I am!
Once again this life hobbling before me, what am I saying life, *this
death*, this death without sense or piety, this death that so pathetically
falls short of greatness, the dazzling pettiness of this death, this death
hobbling from pettiness to pettiness; these shovelfuls of petty greeds over   280
the conquistador; these shovelfuls of petty flunkies over the great-
savage, these shovelfuls of petty souls over the three-souled Carib,⁷
and all these deaths futile
absurdities under the splashing of my open conscience
tragic futilities lit up by this single noctiluca⁸   285
and I alone, sudden stage of this daybreak when the apocalypse of monsters cavorts then, capsized, hushes
warm election of cinders, of ruins and collapses
—One more thing! only one, but please make it only one: I have no right
to measure life by my sooty finger span; to reduce myself to this little   290
ellipsoidal nothing⁹ trembling four fingers above the line,¹ I a man, to

---

2. A fibrous plant. *Jujube tree:* produces red fruit.   3. Penis, here ascribed to the sun.   4. A tree with
a milky sap.   5. The juice of a tropical plant; it produces a hallucinatory effect.   6. A platform that
serves as a stage for a performance.   7. Indicating the indigenous Carib Indians as well as the descendants of Africans and of Europeans.   8. Light from a glowworm.   9. That is, Martinique, which is
oval-shaped.   1. A reference to Martinique's geographical position close to the equator.

so overturn creation, that I include myself between latitude and
longitude!

At the end of daybreak,
the male thirst and the desire stubborn,   295
here I am, severed from the cool oases of brotherhood
this so modest nothing bristles with hard splinters
this too safe horizon is startled like a jailer.

Your last triumph, tenacious crow of Treason.

What is mine, these few thousand deathbearers who mill in the cal-   300
abash of an island and mine too, the archipelago arched[2] with an
anguished desire to negate itself, as if from maternal anxiety to protect
this impossibly delicate tenuity separating one America from another;
and these loins which secrete for Europe the hearty liquor of a Gulf
Stream,[3] and one of the two slopes of incandescence between which the   305
Equator tightropewalks toward Africa. And my nonfence island, its brave
audacity standing at the stern of this Polynesia, before it, Guadeloupe,
split in two down its dorsal line and equal in poverty to us, Haiti where
negritude rose for the first time[4] and stated that it believed in its humanity and the funny little tail of Florida where the strangulation of a nigger 310
is being completed, and Africa gigantically caterpillaring up to the His-
panic foot of Europe, its nakedness where Death scythes widely.

And I say to myself Bordeaux and Nantes and Liverpool[5] and New
York and San Francisco

not an inch of this world devoid of my fingerprint   315
and my calcaneum[6] on the spines of skyscrapers and my filth in the
glitter of gems!
Who can boast of being better off than I? Virginia.
Tennessee. Georgia. Alabama[7]
monstrous putrefactions of stymied   320
revolts
marshes of putrid blood
trumpets absurdly muted
land red, sanguineous, consanguineous[8] land.

What is also mine: a little   325
cell in the Jura,[9]
a little cell, the snow lines it with white bars
the snow is a jailer mounting
guard before a prison

2. Like a tense bow, an image suggested by the half circle formed by the islands across the Caribbean Sea.
3. An ocean current that flows from the West Indies to the north Atlantic; it has a tempering effect on
the climate of western Europe. *Delicate tenuity*: the thin strip of Central America, protected by the Caribbean from the full force of the Atlantic.   4. A reference to the slave revolt, led by Toussaint L'Ouverture
(c. 1743–1803), which led to the independence of Haiti in 1804. Guadeloupe, the other French West
Indian colony, is now a French department. It lies north of Martinique and is made up of two islands
(Basse-Terre and Grande-Terre). *Polynesia*: in the sense of a group of islands.   5. Bordeaux and Nantes
in France and Liverpool in England were the principal ports from which, in a triangular circuit, the slave
ships sailed out to Africa and, after being loaded with their human cargo, crossed to America, returning
with produce to Europe.   6. Heel, complementary to *fingerprint*.   7. Along with New York and San
Francisco, symbols of the economic exploitation of the black people.   8. Linked by blood; here, that of
the black slave.   9. L'Ouverture was captured by the French and taken to France, to be imprisoned in
the fortress of Joux, in the Jura Mountains, where he eventually died.

What is mine
a lonely man imprisoned in
whiteness
a lonely man defying the white
screams of white death
(TOUSSAINT, TOUSSAINT L'OUVERTURE)

a man who mesmerizes
the white hawk of white death
a man alone in the sterile
sea of white sand
a coon grown old standing up to
the waters of the sky
Death traces a shining circle
above this man
death stars softly above his head
death breathes, crazed, in the ripened
cane field of his arms
death gallops in the prison like
a white horse[1]
death gleams in the dark like the
eyes of a cat
death hiccups like water under the Keys[2]
death is a struck bird
death wanes
death flickers
death is a very shy patyura[3]
death expires in a white pool
of silence.
Swellings of night in the four corners
of this dawn
convulsions of congealed death
tenacious fate
screams erect from mute earth
the splendor of this blood will it not burst open?

330

335

340

345

350

355

360

   At the end of daybreak this land without a stele,[4] these paths without
memory, these winds without a tablet.
   So what?
   We would tell. Would sing. Would howl.
   Full voice, ample voice, you would be our wealth, our spear
pointed.
   Words?
   Ah yes, words!

365

370

Reason, I crown you evening wind.[5]
Your name voice of order?
To me the whip's corolla.[6]
Beauty I call you the false claim of the stone.

375

---

1. Refers both to Baron Samedi, the spirit of death in Haitian folk belief, and the horse of death in Western iconography.   2. Coral reefs in the Caribbean.   3. According to Césaire, a variation on "patira," the name for a peccary found in Paraguay [*Translators' note*].   4. Funeral monuments to military heroes.
5. Boding death.   6. The strands of the whip commonly used on slaves.

But ah! my raucous laughter
smuggled in
Ah! my saltpetre[7] treasure!
Because we hate you
and your reason, we claim kinship   380
with dementia praecox[8] with the flaming madness
of persistent cannibalism

Treasure, let's count:
the madness that remembers[9]
the madness that howls   385
the madness that sees
the madness that is unleashed
And you know the rest

That 2 and 2 are 5[1]
that the forest miaows   390
that the tree plucks the maroons from the fire[2]
that the sky strokes its beard
etc. etc. . . . .

Who and what are we?
A most worthy question!   395

From staring too long at trees I have
become a tree and my long tree
feet have dug in the ground large
venom sacs high cities of bone
from brooding too long on the Congo[3]   400
I have become a Congo resounding with
forests and rivers
where the whip cracks like a great banner
the banner of a prophet
where the water goes   405
likouala-likouala
where the angerbolt hurls its greenish
axe[4] forcing the boars of
putrefaction to the lovely wild edge
of the nostrils.   410

At the end of daybreak the sun which
hacks and spits up its lungs
At the end of daybreak
a slow gait of sand
a slow gait of gauze   415
a slow gait of corn kernels

---

7. Potassium nitrate, used in the manufacture of gunpowder.   8. Schizophrenia.   9. The immediate
reference is to the memory of slavery, but the phrase draws its full meaning from the Surrealist belief in
madness as a form of insight.   1. Deliberately irrational, again as part of the Surrealist convention.
2. Runaway slaves (*maroons*) often made animal sounds as signals to each other. They also hid in the
treetops to escape their pursuers; plays also on the French meaning of *maroon* = chestnut.   3. A river
that flows through dense tropical forests in central Africa.   4. *Angerbolt* refers to the uprising of the
native population, an act that restores the people to harmony with their essential beings (*greenish axe*). The
Likouala River is in the interior of the present-day Congo Republic.

At the end of daybreak
a full gallop of pollen
a full gallop of a slow gait of
little girls   420
a full gallop of hummingbirds[5]
a full gallop of daggers to stave in
the earth's breast

customs angels mounting guard over
prohibitions at the gates of foam   425

I declare my crimes[6] and that there is nothing
to say in my defense.
Dances. Idols. An apostate. I too
I have assassinated God with my laziness with
my words with my gestures   430
with my obscene songs

I have worn parrot plumes
musk cat skins
I have exhausted the missionaries' patience
insulted the benefactors of mankind.   435
Defied Tyre. Defied Sidon.
Worshipped the Zambezi.[7]
The extent of my perversity overwhelms me!

But why impenetrable jungle are you still hiding the raw zero of my
mendacity and from a self-conscious concern for nobility not celebrating   440
the horrible leap of my Pahouin[8] ugliness?

voum rooh oh[9]
voum rooh oh
to charm the snakes to conjure
the dead   445
voum rooh oh
to compel the rain to turn back
the tidal waves
voum rooh oh
to keep the shade from moving   450
voum rooh oh that my own skies
may open

—me on a road, a child, chewing
sugar cane root
—a dragged man on a bloodspattered road   455
a rope around his neck

---

5. Symbols of Césaire's native land.   6. The stereotypes of Africans in colonial ideology are echoed in this ironic confession.   7. A river in southern Africa. The religious practices of Africans were often devalued as animism, of which river worship was a prominent feature. Tyre and Sidon were commercial ports in ancient Phoenicia, often mentioned in history books as early centers of civilization.   8. An ethnic group in present-day Gabon.   9. An incantation, by which Césaire assumes the powers enumerated in this stanza.

—standing in the center of a huge circus,
on my black forehead a crown of daturas[1]
voum rooh
to fly off
than the sorceresses toward other stars
higher than quivering higher
ferocious exultation of forests and
mountains uprooted at the hour
when no one expects it[2]
the islands linked for a thousand years!

voum rooh oh
that the promised times may return
and the bird who knew my name
and the woman[3] who had a thousand names
names of fountain sun and tears
and her hair of minnows[4]
and her steps my climates
and her eyes my seasons
and the days without injury
and the nights without offense
and the stars my confidence
and the wind my accomplice

But who misleads my voice? who grates
my voice? Stuffing my throat
with a thousand bamboo fangs. A thousand
sea urchin stakes. It is you dirty end
of the world. Dirty end of daybreak.
It is you dirty hatred. It is you weight
of the insult and a hundred years of whip
lashes. It is you one hundred years of my
patience, one hundred years of my effort
simply to stay alive
rooh oh
we sing of venomous flowers
flaring in fury-filled prairies;
the skies of love cut with bloodclots;
the epileptic mornings; the white blaze
of abyssal[5] sands, the sinking
of flotsam in nights electrified
with feline smells.

What can I do?

One must begin somewhere.

Begin what?

---

1. A mildly poisonous, hallucinatory plant, with which his brow is decked—as befits his combative role—
instead of the laurels associated with classical tradition.   2. Another reference to the sudden eruption
of Mont Pelée.   3. A guardian goddess, identified with Césaire's vision of Martinique's future. *The bird
who knew my name*: the hummingbird (see n. 5, p. 2553).   4. The woman is now presented as the sea
goddess of folk mythology, with hair made of small fish.   5. Unfathomable.

The only thing in the world 500
worth beginning:
The End of the world of course.

Torte[6]
oh torte of the terrifying autumn
where the new steel and the perennial concrete 505
grow
torte oh torte
where the air rusts in great sheets
of evil glee
where the sanious[7] water scars the great 510
solar cheeks
I hate you

one still sees madras rags[8] around the loins
of women rings in their ears
smiles on their lips babies 515
at their nipples, these for starters:

ENOUGH OF THIS OUTRAGE!

So here is the great challenge and the satanic
compulsion and the insolent
nostalgic drift of April moons,[9] 520
of green fires, of yellow fevers!

Vainly in the tepidity of your throat
you ripen for the twentieth time the same indigent
solace that we are
mumblers of words 525

Words? while we handle
quarters of earth, while we wed
delirious continents, while
we force steaming gates,
words, ah yes, words! but 530
words of fresh blood, words that are
tidal waves and erysipelas[1]
malarias and lava and brush
fires, and blazes of flesh,
and blazes of cities . . . 535

Know this:
the only game I play is the millennium
the only game I play is the Great
Fear[2]

Put up with me. I won't put up with you! 540

6. A kind of crude peasant bread.   7. Pertaining to fluid from a wound.   8. The scarf of fine material
worn around the waist by Martinican women.   9. Often reddish in hue and considered an ill omen.
1. An inflammation of the skin.   2. The year A.D. 1000 was awaited in early Christendom with foreboding (the Great Fear) as the date that would mark the end of the world predicted in the Book of Revelation.

Sometimes you see me with a great display of brains
snap up a cloud too red
or a caress of rain, or a prelude
of wind,
don't fool yourself: 545

I am forcing the vitelline membrane[3] that separates
me from myself,
I am forcing the great waters which girdle me with blood

I and I alone choose
a seat on the last train of the last   550
surge of the last tidal wave

I and I alone
make contact with the latest
anguish

I and oh, only I   555
secure the first
drops of virginal milk through a straw!

And now a last boo:
to the sun (not strong enough to inebriate
my very tough head)   560
to the mealy night with its golden
hatchings of erratic fireflies
to the head of hair trembling at the very
top of the cliff
where the wind leaps in bursts of salty
cavalries   565
I clearly read in my pulse that for me
exoticism is no provender[4]

Leaving Europe utterly twisted with screams
the silent currents of despair
leaving timid Europe which   570
collects and proudly overrates itself
I summon this egotism beautiful
and bold
    and my ploughing reminds me of an implacable cutwater.[5]

So much blood in my memory! In my memory are lagoons. They are   575
covered with death's-heads.
    They are not covered with water lilies.
In my memory are lagoons. No women's loincloths spread out on their
    shores.
My memory is encircled with blood. My memory has a belt of corpses!
and machine gun fire of rum barrels brilliantly sprinkling   580
our ignominious revolts, amorous glances swooning from having
swigged too much ferocious freedom

(niggers-are-all-alike, I-tell-you vices-all-the-vices-believe-you-me
nigger-smell, that's-what-makes-cane-grow

3. Protects the fetus in its mother's womb.   4. Animal feed.   5. The prow of a ship.

remember-the-old-saying: 585
beat-a-nigger, and you feed him)
among "rocking chairs" contemplating the voluptuousness of quirts[6]
I circle about, an unappeased filly

Or else quite simply as they like to think of us!
Cheerfully obscene, completely nuts about jazz to cover their extreme
   boredom 590
I can boogie-woogie, do the Lindy-hop[7] and tap-dance.
And for a special treat the muting of our cries muffled with wah-wah.[8]
Wait . . . Everything is as it should be. My good angel grazes the neon.
I swallow batons. My dignity wallows in puke . . .
   Sun, Angel Sun, curled Angel of the Sun 595
   for a leap beyond the sweet and greenish
treading of the waters of abjection!

   But I approached the wrong sorcerer, on this exorcised earth, cast
adrift from its precious malignant purpose, this voice that cries, little by
little hoarse, vainly, vainly hoarse, 600
   and there remains only the accumulated droppings of our lies—and
they do not respond.
What madness to dream up a marvelous caper above the baseness!
Oh Yes the Whites are great warriors hosannah to the master and to the
nigger-gelder! 605
Victory! Victory, I tell you: the defeated are content!
Joyous stenches and songs of mud!
   By a sudden and beneficent inner revolution, I now honour my
repugnant ugliness.

   On Midsummer Day, as soon as the first shadows fall on the village 610
of Gros-Morne, hundreds of horse dealers gather on rue "De PROFUN-
DIS,"[9] a name at least honest enough to announce an onrush from the
shoals of Death. And it truly is from Death, from its thousand petty local
forms (cravings unsatisfied by Para grass[1] and tipsy bondage to the distilleries) that the astonishing cavalry of impetuous nags surges unfenced 615
toward the great-life. What a galloping! what neighing! what sincere
urinating! what prodigious droppings! "A fine horse difficult to mount!"—
"A proud mare sensitive to the spur"—"A fearless foal superbly
pasterned!"[2]
   And the shrewd fellow whose waistcoat displays a proud watch chain, 620
palms off instead of full udders, youthful mettle and genuine contours,
either the systematic puffiness from obliging wasps, or the obscene
stings from ginger, or the helpful distribution of several gallons of sugared water.[3]

   I refuse to pass off my puffiness for authentic glory. 625
   And I laugh at my former childish fantasies.
   No, we've never been Amazons of the king of Dahomey, nor princes

---

6. Riding whips.   7. A dance named after Charles Lindbergh, who made aviation history in 1927 by
being the first to fly solo across the Atlantic.   8. Sarcastic imitation of the muted trumpet.   9. Out of
the depths (Latin), from a liturgy for the dead. Gros-Morne is north of Fort-de-France.   1. Coarse elephant grass on which the horses are fed.   2. Nobly built.   3. Ways in which the horses have been
doctored to give them a false air of well-being.

of Ghana with eight hundred camels, nor wise men in Timbuktu under
Askia the Great, nor the architects of Djenne, nor Madhis,[4] nor warriors.
We don't feel under our armpit the itch of those who in the old days   630
carried a lance. And since I have sworn to leave nothing out of our
history (I who love nothing better than a sheep grazing his own afternoon
shadow), I may as well confess that we were at all times pretty mediocre
dishwashers, shoeblacks without ambition, at best conscientious sorcerers and the only unquestionable record that we broke was that of endur-   635
ance under the chicote[5] . . .

And this land screamed for centuries that we are bestial brutes; that
the human pulse stops at the gates of the slave compound; that we are
walking compost hideously promising tender cane and silky cotton and
they would brand us with red-hot irons and we would sleep in our excre-   640
ment and they would sell us on the town square and an ell[6] of English
cloth and salted meat from Ireland cost less than we did, and this land
was calm, tranquil, repeating that the spirit of the Lord was in its acts.

We the vomit of slave ships
We the venery of the Calabars[7]   645
what? Plug up our ears?
We, so drunk on jeers and inhaled fog that we rode the roll to death!
Forgive us fraternal whirlwind!

I hear coming up from the hold the enchained curses, the gasps of
the dying, the noise of someone thrown into the sea . . . the baying of a   650
woman in labor . . . the scrape of fingernails seeking throats . . . the
flouts of the whip . . . the seethings of vermin amid the weariness . . .

Nothing could ever lift us toward a noble hopeless adventure.
So be it. So be it.
I am of no nationality recognized by the chancelleries.   655
I defy the craniometer. Homo sum etc.
Let them serve and betray and die
So be it. So be it. It was written in the shape of their pelvis.[8]

And I, and I,
I was singing the hard fist   660
You must know the extent of my cowardice. One evening on the streetcar
facing me, a nigger.
A nigger big as a pongo[9] trying to make himself small on the streetcar bench. He was trying to leave behind, on this grimy bench, his gigantic legs and his trembling famished boxer hands. And everything had left   665

---

4. In Islam, leaders in a holy war. *Amazons:* female warriors in the ancient African kingdom of Dahomey.
Ghana is the medieval West African empire after which the modern state is named. Timbuktu, on the river
Niger, was an outstanding intellectual center in the Middle Ages. Askia the Great was ruler of the African
empire of Songhai from the late 15th to the early years of the 16th century. Djenne, in present-day Mali,
was a university town in the Middle Ages. This passage contains references to aspects of precolonial African
history to which the West Indian has at best an ambiguous connection.   5. Whip.   6. A unit of measure that equals about 45 inches.   7. A coastal town in southeastern Nigeria; a major slave depot.
8. Ironic reference to physiological arguments employed to establish the inferiority of the black race,
notably by the French writer Arthur Gobineau, whose actual words are quoted here. *Craniometer:* an
instrument for measuring the size of skulls, thought to be a factor in the evolution of the brain. *Homo sum:*
I am man (Latin); a quotation from *The Self-Tormentor* by the playwright Terence. The rest of the line
reads, "and I consider nothing human foreign to me."   9. *Pongo* is a genus of anthropoid apes.

him, was leaving him. His nose which looked like a drifting peninsula and even his negritude discolored as a result of untiring tawing.[1] And the tawer was Poverty. A big unexpected lop-eared bat whose claw marks in his face had scabbed over into crusty islands. Or rather, it was a tireless worker, Poverty was, working on some hideous cartouche.[2] One could easily see how that industrious and malevolent thumb had kneaded bumps into his brow, bored two bizarre parallel tunnels in his nose, overexaggerated his lips, and in a masterpiece of caricature, planed, polished and varnished the tiniest cutest little ear in all creation.

He was a gangly nigger without rhythm or measure.

A nigger whose eyes rolled a bloodshot weariness.

A shameless nigger and his toes sneered in a rather stinking way at the bottom of the yawning lair of his shoes.

Poverty, without any question, had knocked itself out to finish him off.

It had dug the socket, had painted it with a rouge of dust mixed with rheum.[3]

It had stretched an empty space between the solid hinge of the jaw and bone of an old tarnished cheek. Had planted over it the small shiny stakes of a two- or three-day beard. Had panicked his heart, bent his back.

And the whole thing added up perfectly to a hideous nigger, a grouchy nigger, a melancholy nigger, a slouched nigger, his hands joined in prayer on a knobby stick. A nigger shrouded in an old threadbare coat. A comical and ugly nigger, with some women behind me sneering at him.

He was COMICAL AND UGLY,[4]

COMICAL AND UGLY for sure.

I displayed a big complicitous smile . . .

My cowardice rediscovered!

Hail to the three centuries which uphold my civil rights and my mini-mized blood!

My heroism, what a farce!

This town fits me to a t.

And my soul is lying down. Lying down like this town in its refuse and mud.

This town, my face of mud.

For my face I demand the vivid homage of spit! . . .

So, being what we are, ours the warrior thrust, the triumphant knee, the well-plowed plains of the future?

Look, I'd rather admit to uninhibited ravings, my heart in my brain like a drunken knee.

My star now, the funereal menfenil.[5]

And on this former dream my cannibalistic cruelties:

(The bullets in the mouth thick saliva
our heart from daily lowness bursts the continents break the fragile bond
of isthmuses

---

1. Working of leather.   2. Portrait sketch.   3. Liquid from the eye.   4. An echo of Baudelaire's poem *The Albatross*. The individual is, of course, without the mystical significance Baudelaire attributes to the ungainly bird.   5. A Caribbean sparrow hawk with black plumage; hence *funereal*.

lands leap in accordance with the fatal division of rivers
and the morne which for centuries kept its scream within itself, it is its
turn to draw and quarter the silence and this people an ever-rebounding
spirit   715
and our limbs vainly disjointed by the most refined tortures
and life even more impetuously jetting from this compost—unexpected
as a soursop amidst the decomposition of jack tree[6] fruit!)

On this dream so old in me my cannibalistic cruelties

I was hiding behind a stupid vanity destiny called me I was hiding behind   720
it and suddenly there was a man on the ground, his feeble defenses
scattered,
his sacred maxims trampled underfoot, his pedantic rhetoric oozing air
through each wound.
There is a man on the ground   725
and his soul is almost naked
and destiny triumphs in watching this soul which defied its metamorphosis in the ancestral slough.

I say that this is right.
My back will victoriously exploit the chalaza[7] of fibers.   730
I will deck my natural obsequiousness with gratitude
And the silver-braided bullshit of the postillion of Havana,[8] lyrical
baboon pimp for the glamour of slavery, will be more than a match for
my enthusiasm.

I say that this is right   735
I live for the flattest part of my soul.
For the dullest part of my flesh!

    Tepid dawn[9] of ancestral heat and fear
I now tremble with the collective trembling that our docile blood sings
in the madrepore.[1]   740

And these tadpoles hatched in me by my prodigious ancestry!
Those who invented neither powder nor compass
those who could harness neither steam nor electricity
those who explored neither the seas nor the sky but who know
in its most minute corners the land of suffering   745
those who have known voyages only through uprootings
those who have been lulled to sleep by so much kneeling
those whom they domesticated and Christianized
those whom they inoculated with degeneracy
tom-toms of empty hands   750
inane tom-toms of resounding sores
burlesque tom-toms of tabetic treason[2]

---

6. Or breadfruit, which provided an important source of nourishment for the slaves. *Soursop:* a tropical
tree with a white fleshy fruit, which has a sharp taste.   7. A whip made of hard fibers.   8. A port city
in Cuba. *Postilion:* a valet employed to welcome newly arrived slaves with a speech in praise of slavery.
9. Announces a new movement in the poem, leading to Césaire's celebration of his race.   1. Coral reef,
symbolizing Martinique and, by extension, the Caribbean region.   2. Ineffectual revolt. *Tabetic:* derives
from the Latin *tabidus,* "wasting away."

Tepid dawn of ancestral heat and fears
overboard with alien riches
overboard with my genuine falsehoods
But what strange pride suddenly illuminates me!   755
let the hummingbird come
let the sparrow hawk come
the breach in the horizon
the cynocephalus   760
let the lotus[3] bearer of the world come
the pearly upheaval of dolphins
cracking the shell of the sea
let a plunge of islands come
let it come from the disappearing of days of dead   765
flesh in the quicklime of birds of prey[4]
let the ovaries of the water come where the future stirs its testicles
let the wolves come who feed in the untamed openings of the body at
the hour when my moon and your sun meet at the ecliptic inn[5]

under the reserve of my uvula[6] there is a wallow of boars   770
under the grey stone of the day there are your eyes which are a shimmering conglomerate of coccinella[7]
in the glance of disorder there is this swallow of mint and broom[8] which
melts always to be reborn in the tidal wave of your light
Calm and lull oh my voice the child who does not know that the map of   775
spring is always to be drawn again
the tall grass will sway gentle ship of hope for the cattle
the long alcoholic sweep of the swell
the stars with the bezels[9] of their rings never in sight will cut the pipes
of the glass organ of evening zinnias   780
coryanthas[1]
will then pour into the rich extremity of my fatigue
and you star[2] please from your luminous foundation draw lemurian
being—of man's unfathomable
sperm the yet undared form   785

carried like an ore in woman's trembling belly!

oh friendly light
oh fresh source of light
those who have invented neither powder nor compass
those who could harness neither steam nor electricity   790
those who explored neither the seas nor the sky but those
without whom the earth would not be the earth
gibbosity[3] all the more beneficent as the bare earth even more earth

---

3. A white flower, symbol of Isis, the ancient Egyptian goddess of the rising sun. Cynocephalus: an African
monkey, with a head resembling a dog's, noted for its great strength.   4. An extremely compressed image
that identifies Césaire's revolt with the action of *birds of prey* or *quicklime* (calcium oxide, which has a
dissolving effect), both of which cleanse the land of dead bodies.   5. The partners fuse into one another
as in an eclipse of the sun or moon.   6. The tissue at the back of the tongue, opening into the throat.
7. Beetles. The passage refers to Césaire's wife, Suzanne, whose bright eyes are compared to the shimmering of a swarm of beetles.   8. Medicinal plants. *Swallow:* a harbinger of spring, associated with the
health-restoring properties of medicinal plants.   9. The upper parts of rings in which the stones are set.
1. Tropical flowers.   2. Perhaps the sun.   3. An ugly swelling.

silo[4] where that which is earthiest about earth ferments and ripens
my negritude[5] is not a stone, its deafness hurled against the clamor of   795
the day
my negritude is not a leukoma[6] of dead liquid over the earth's dead
eye
my negritude is neither tower nor cathedral
it takes root in the red flesh of the soil   800
it takes root in the ardent flesh of the sky
it breaks through the opaque prostration with its upright patience[7]

Eia for the royal Cailcedra![8]
Eia for those who have never invented anything
for those who never explored anything   805
for those who never conquered anything

but yield, captivated, to the essence of all things
ignorant of surfaces but captivated by the motion of all things
indifferent to conquering, but playing the game of the world
truly the eldest sons of the world   810
porous to all the breathing of the world
fraternal locus for all the breathing of the world
drainless channel for all the water of the world
spark of the sacred fire of the world
flesh of the world's flesh pulsating with the very motion of the world!   815
    Tepid dawn of ancestral virtues

Blood! Blood! all our blood aroused by the male heart of the sun
those who know about the femininity of the moon's oily body
the reconciled exultation of antelope and star
those whose survival travels in the germination of grass!   820
Eia perfect circle of the world, enclosed concordance!

Hear the white world
horribly weary from its immense efforts
its stiff joints crack under the hard stars
hear its blue steel rigidity pierce the mystic flesh   825
its deceptive victories tout its defeats
hear the grandiose alibis of its pitiful stumblings

Pity for our omniscient and naive conquerors!

Eia for grief and its udders of reincarnated tears
for those who have never explored anything   830
for those who have never conquered anything

Eia for joy
Eia for love
Eia for grief and its udders of reincarnated tears

and here at the end of this daybreak is my virile prayer that I hear neither   835
the laughter nor the screams, my eyes fixed on this town which I prophesy, beautiful,

---

4. A granary. Here, the black race as the spiritual reservoir of humankind.   5. See p. 2539, above.
6. A film over the eye, caused by infection.   7. A reference to the Cross, symbol of Christ's Passion.
8. A tree typical of the west African savannah, with royal significance. *Eia:* a triumphant cry.

grant me the savage faith of the sorcerer
grant my hands power to mold
grant my soul the sword's temper   840
I won't flinch. Make my head into a figurehead
and as for me, my heart, do not make me into a father nor a brother,
nor a son, but into the father, the brother, the son,
nor a husband, but the lover of this unique people.

Make me resist any vanity, but espouse its genius as the fist the extended   845
arm!

Make me a steward of its blood
make me trustee of its resentment
make me into a man for the ending
make me into a man for the beginning   850
make me into a man of meditation
but also make me into a man of germination

make me into the executor of these lofty works
the time has come to gird one's loins like a brave man[9]—

But in doing so, my heart, preserve me from all hatred   855
do not make me into that man of hatred for whom I feel only hatred
for entrenched as I am in this unique race
you still know my tyrannical love
you know that it is not from hatred of other races
that I demand a digger for this unique race   860
that what I want
is for universal hunger
for universal thirst

to summon it to generate,
free at last, from its intimate closeness   865
the succulence of fruit.

And be the tree of our hands!
it turns, for all, the wounds cut
in its trunk[1]
the soil works for all   870
and toward the branches a headiness of fragrant precipitation!

But before stepping on the shores of future orchards
grant that I deserve those on their belt of sea
grant me my heart while awaiting the earth
grant me on the ocean sterile   875
but somewhere caressed by the promise of the clew-line[2]
grant me on this diverse ocean
the obstinacy of the fierce pirogue[3]
and its marine vigor.
See it advance rising and falling on the pulverized wave   880

9. An echo of God's words to Job: "Gird up now thy loins like a man" (Job 38.3).   1. Like the rubber
tree, which thrives on incisions made in its trunk to produce sap.   2. Rope by which a clew of an upper
square sail is hauled up.   3. A dug-out canoe, in which local fishermen go out to sea.

see it dance the sacred dance before the greyness of the village
see it trumpet from a vertiginous conch[4]

see the conch gallop up to the uncertainty of the morne

and see twenty times over the paddle
vigorously   885
plow the water
the pirogue rears under the attack of the swells
deviates for an instant
tries to escape, but the paddle's rough caress turns it,
then it charges, a shudder runs along the wave's spine,   890
the sea slobbers and rumbles
the pirogue like a sleigh glides onto the sand.

    At the end of this daybreak, my virile prayer:

grant me pirogue muscles on this raging sea
and the irresistible gaiety of the conch of good tidings!   895
Look, now I am only a man, no degradation, no spit perturbs him, now
I am only a man who accepts emptied of anger
(nothing left in his heart but immense love, which burns)

I accept . . . I accept . . . totally, without reservation . . .
my race that no ablution of hyssop[5] mixed with lilies could purify   900
my race pitted with blemishes
my race a ripe grape for drunken feet
my queen of spittle and leprosy
my queen of whips and scrofula
my queen of squasma and chloasma[6] (oh those queens I once loved in   905
the remote gardens of spring against the illumination of all the candles
of the chestnut[7] trees!)
I accept. I accept.
and the flogged nigger saying: "Forgive me master"
and the twenty-nine legal blows[8] of the whip   910
and the four-feet-high cell
and the spiked iron-collar
and the hamstringing of my runaway audacity
and the fleur de lys[9] flowing from the red iron into the fat of my shoulder
and Monsieur VAULTIER MAYENCOURT'S dog house[1] where I   915
barked
six poodle months
and Monsieur BRAFIN
and Monsieur FOURNIOL
and Monsieur de la MAHAUDIERE[2]   920
and the yaws

---

4. A seashell that has a wound-up (vertiginous) shape. It can be made into a horn, which has a trumpeting sound like that of an elephant.   5. An aromatic plant featured in a Latin chant said before High Mass in the Catholic Church.   6. Suggests sickness, possibly derived from the Greek word meaning "paleness." Squasma: scales on the skin.   7. In the French, there is a play on the word marron, which means both chestnut and runaway slave.   8. The limit prescribed by the Code Noir (Black Code), designed to regulate slaveowners' treatment of their slaves.   9. The lily flower (French); the emblem of the Bourbon Dynasty in France, with which recaptured slaves were branded.   1. Mayencourt, a slaveowner, caused the death of one of his slaves by caging him in a dog kennel for six months.   2. Slaveowners involved in an incident in which two slaves committed suicide.

the mastiff[3]
the suicide
the promiscuity
the bootkin[4]   925
the shackles
the rack
the cippus
the head screw[5]

> Look, am I humble enough? Have I enough calluses on my knees?   930
> Muscles on my loins?
> Grovel in mud. Brace yourself in the thick of the mud. Carry.
> Soil of mud. Horizon of mud. Sky of mud.
> Dead of the mud, oh names to thaw in the palm of a feverish
> breathing!   935

Siméon Piquine, who never knew his father or mother; unheard of in
any town hall[6] and who wandered his whole life—seeking a new
name.

Grandvorka—of him I only know that he died, crushed one harvest
evening, it was his job, apparently, to throw sand under the wheels of 940
the running locomotive, to help it across bad spots.

Michel who used to write me signing a strange name. Lucky Michel
address *Condemned District*[7] and you their living brothers Exélie Vêté
Congolo Lemké Boussolongo what healer with his thick lips would suck
from the depths of the gaping wound the tenacious secret of venom?   945

what cautious sorcerer would undo from your ankles the viscous tepidity
of mortal rings?

Presences it is not on your back that I will make my peace with the world

Islands scars of the water
Islands evidence of wounds   950
Islands crumbs
Islands unformed

Islands cheap paper shredded upon the water
Islands stumps skewered side by side on the flaming sword of the Sun
Mulish reason you will not stop me from casting on the waters at the   955
mercy of the currents of my thirst
your form, deformed islands,
your end, my defiance.

Annulose[8] islands, single beautiful hull
And I caress you with my oceanic hands. And I turn you   960
around with the tradewinds of my speech. And I lick you with my seaweed tongues.
And I sail you unfreebootable!

O death your mushy marsh!
Shipwreck your hellish debris! I accept!   965

---

3. A bloodhound, used to hunt down runaway slaves. *Yaws:* a tropical disease that attacks the skin and
bones.   4. Stocks designed to lock in the victim's legs.   5. A form of punishment in which a cord was
wound tightly around the slave's head. *Cippus:* an elevated spot where slaves were whipped.   6. Where
births and deaths are recorded.   7. Indicative of a mood of total despair.   8. Strung out, as in a ceremonial procession.

At the end of daybreak, lost puddles, wandering scents, beached hurricanes, demasted hulls, old sores, rotted bones, vapors, shackled volcanoes, shallow-rooted dead, bitter cry. I accept!

And my special geography too; the world map made for my own use, not tinted with the arbitrary colors of scholars, but with the geometry of   970
my spilled blood, I accept both the determination of my biology, not a prisoner to a facial angle, to a type of hair, to a well-flattened nose, to a clearly Melanian coloring, and negritude, no longer a cephalic index, or plasma, or soma, but measured by the compass of suffering[9]
and the Negro every day more base, more cowardly, more sterile, less   975
profound, more spilled out of himself, more separated from himself, more wily with himself, less immediate to himself,

I accept, I accept it all

and far from the palatial sea that foams beneath the suppurating syzygy[1] of blisters, miraculously lying in the despair of my arms the body of   980
my country, its bones shocked and, in its veins, the blood hesitating like a drop of vegetal milk at the injured point of the bulb . . .

Suddenly now strength and life assail me like a bull and the water of life overwhelms the papilla[2] of the morne, now all the veins and veinlets are bustling with new blood and the enormous breathing lung of   985
cyclones and the fire hoarded in volcanoes and the gigantic seismic pulse which now beats the measure of a living body in my firm conflagration.

And we are standing now, my country and I, hair in the wind, my hand puny in its enormous fist and now the strength is not in us but above us, in a voice that drills the night and the hearing like the penetrance   990
of an apocalyptic wasp.[3] And the voice proclaims that for centuries Europe has force-fed us with lies and bloated us with pestilence,

for it is not true that the work of man is done
that we have no business being on earth that we parasite the world
that it is enough for us to heel to the world   995
whereas the work has only begun
and man still must overcome all the interdictions wedged in the recesses of his fervor and no race has a monopoly on beauty, on intelligence, on strength[4]

and there is room for everyone at the convocation of conquest and we   1000
know now that the sun turns around our earth lighting the parcel designated by our will alone and that every star falls from sky to earth at our omnipotent command.

I now see the meaning of this trial by the sword: my country is the "lance of night" of my Bambara[5] ancestors. It shrivels and its point desperately retreats toward the haft when it is sprinkled with chicken blood   1005

9. Earlier in the 20th century physical anthropologists were interested in the worldwide distribution of various physical traits of humans (some of which are listed here). Others used such data to advance and justify racial theories. *Melanian:* dark. *Cephalic:* relating to the head. *Soma:* body (Greek).   1. The alignment of the sun and the moon; also the movement of the tides.   2. Nipple.   3. An allusion to the plague that descended on the Egyptians before the liberation of the Israelites in Exodus 5–11.   4. A pointed reference to the writings of Gobineau, who argued the superiority of the white race in terms of the qualities stated here.   5. An ethnic group concentrated in present-day Mali. The passage refers to a ritual in which warriors sprinkled human blood on their spears to ensure their effectiveness.

and it says that its nature requires the blood of man, his fat, his liver, his heart, not chicken blood.

And I seek for my country not date hearts, but men's hearts which, in order to enter the silver cities through the great trapezoidal[6] gate, beat 1010 with warrior blood, and as my eyes sweep my kilometers of paternal earth I number its sores almost joyfully and I pile one on top of the other like rare species, and my total is ever lengthened by unexpected mintings of baseness.

And there are those who will never get over not being made in the like- 1015 ness of God but of the devil, those who believe that being a nigger is like being a second-class clerk; waiting for a better deal and upward mobility; those who beat the drum of compromise in front of themselves, those who live in their own dungeon pit; those who drape themselves in proud pseudomorphosis;[7] those who say to Europe: "You see, I *can* bow 1020 and scrape, like you I pay my respects, in short, I am no different from you; pay no attention to my black skin: the sun did it."[8]

And there is the nigger pimp, the nigger askari,[9] and all the zebras shak- ing themselves in various ways to get rid of their stripes in a dew of fresh milk.[1] And in the midst of all that I say right on! my grandfather 1025 dies, I say right on! the old negritude progressively cadavers itself.

No question about it: he was a good nigger. The Whites say he was a good nigger, a really good nigger, massa's good ole darky. I say right on!

He was a good nigger, indeed,
poverty had wounded his chest and back and they had stuffed into his 1030 poor brain that a fatality impossible to trap weighed on him; that he had no control over his own fate; that an evil Lord had for all eternity inscribed Thou Shall Not in his pelvic constitution; that he must be a good nigger; must sincerely believe in his worthlessness, without any perverse curiosity to check out the fatidic hieroglyphs.[2] 1035

He was a very good nigger

and it never occurred to him that he could hoe, burrow, cut anything, anything else really than insipid cane

He was a very good nigger.

And they threw stones at him, bits of scrap iron, broken bottles, but 1040 neither these stones, nor this scrap iron, nor these bottles . . . O peaceful years of God on this terraqueous[3] clod!

and the whip argued with the bombilation[4] of the flies over the sugary dew of our sores.

I say right on! The old negritude 1045
progressively cadavers itself
the horizon breaks, recoils and expands

6. A reference to a four-sided figure that has only two sides parallel; a frequent motif in the architecture of ancient civilizations.   7. A false personality.   8. Adapted from the Song of Solomon (1.6). The words have been attributed to the queen of Sheba.   9. African colonial soldiers in east Africa (Swahili). 1. Recalls the queen of Sheba's description of Solomon's eyes as "washed in milk" (Song of Solomon 5.12). 2. Characters in ancient Egyptian writing. *Fatidic*: pertaining to fate.   3. From the Latin *terra*, "of the earth."   4. Swarming.

and through the shredding of clouds the flashing of a sign[5]
the slave ship cracks everywhere . . . Its belly convulses and resounds
. . . The ghastly tapeworm[6] of its cargo gnaws the fetid guts of the strange   1050
suckling of the sea!

And neither the joy of sails filled like a pocket stuffed with doubloons,
nor the tricks played on the dangerous stupidity of the frigates of order[7]
prevent it from hearing the threat of its intestinal rumblings

In vain to ignore them the captain hangs the biggest loudmouth nigger   1055
from the main yard or throws him into the sea, or feeds him to his
mastiffs

Reeking of fried onions the nigger scum rediscovers the bitter taste of
freedom in its spilled blood

And the nigger scum is on its feet   1060

the seated nigger scum
unexpectedly standing
standing in the hold
standing in the cabins
standing on deck   1065
standing in the wind
standing under the sun
standing in the blood
   standing
      and   1070
       free
standing and no longer a poor madwoman in her maritime freedom and
destitution gyrating in perfect drift[8]
and there she is:
most unexpectedly standing   1075
standing in the rigging
standing at the tiller
standing at the compass
standing at the map
standing under the stars   1080
   standing
      and
       free
and the lustral[9] ship fearlessly advances on the crumbling water.

And now our ignominious plops are rotting away!   1085
by the clanking noon sea
by the burgeoning midnight sun[1]
listen sparrow hawk who holds the keys to the orient
by the disarmed day
by the stony spurt of the rain   1090

---

5. Like the clap of thunder heard when Moses brought down the tablets from Mount Sinai (Genesis 19.1–3).   **6.** A tropical parasite that lives in the intestines of its victims.   **7.** Patrol ships sent out from England to enforce Britain's abolition of slavery. *Doubloons:* old Spanish coins.   **8.** An allusion to the "Ship of Fools" in which the insane were packed off to sea and set adrift. The passage describes the momentary disarray on the ship after being taken over by the victorious slaves.   **9.** Purifying. The slaves have been cleansed by their act of revolt.   **1.** A phenomenon that can be observed at the height of summer in the arctic and antarctic.

listen dogfish that watches over the occident

listen white dog of the north, black serpent of the south that cinches
the sky girdle
There still remains one sea to cross
oh still one sea to cross 1095
that I may invent my lungs
that the prince may hold his tongue
that the queen may lay me
still one old man to murder
one madman to deliver 1100
that my soul may shine bark shine
bark bark bark
and the owl² my beautiful inquisitive angel may hoot.
The master of laughter?
The master of ominous silence? 1105
The master of hope and despair?
The master of laziness? Master of the dance?
 It is I!
and for this reason, Lord,
the frail-necked men 1110
receive and perceive deadly triangular calm³

Rally to my side my dances
you bad nigger dances
the carcan-cracker⁴ dance
the prison-break dance 1115
the it-is-beautiful-good-and-legitimate-to-be-a-nigger-dance
Rally to my side my dances and let the sun bounce on the racket of my
hands

but no the unequal sun is not enough for me
coil, wind, around my new growth 1120
light on my cadenced fingers
to you I surrender my conscience and its fleshy rhythm
to you I surrender the fire in which my weakness smolders
to you I surrender the "chain-gang"
to you the swamps 1125
to you the nontourist of the triangular circuit
devour wind
to you I surrender my abrupt words
devour and encoil yourself
and self-encoiling embrace me with a more ample shudder 1130
embrace me unto furious us
embrace, embrace US
but after having drawn from us blood
drawn by our own blood!
embrace, my purity mingles only with yours 1135
so then embrace

2. Césaire's guardian angel. The owl was also associated with Minerva, the goddess of wisdom in Roman mythology.   3. The Holy Trinity of Christianity was represented as a triangle, a figure associated in Césaire's consciousness with the triangular circuit of the slave trade.   4. A dance of freedom. *Carcan*: an iron collar fixed around the necks of slaves.

like a field of even filagos[5]
at dusk
our multicolored purities
and bind, bind me without remorse   1140
bind me with your vast arms to the luminous clay
bind my black vibration to the very navel of the world
bind, bind me, bitter brotherhood
then, strangling me with your lasso of stars
rise,   1145
Dove[6]
rise
rise
rise
I follow you who are imprinted on my ancestral white cornea.[7]   1150
rise sky licker
and the great black hole where a moon ago I wanted to drown it is there
I will now fish the malevolent tongue of the night in its motionless
veerition![8]

---

5. The causuarina tree, which grows tall and straight.   6. The symbol of Pentecost in Christian iconol-
ogy, from which it has acquired its conventional meaning of peace.   7. The transparent tissue that covers
the front of the eye.   8. Coined on a Latin verb "verri," meaning "to sweep," "to scrape a surface," and
ultimately "to scan" [*Translators' note*].

ALBERT CAMUS
1913–1960

Albert Camus is often linked with the twentieth-century philosopher Jean-Paul Sartre
as an "existentialist" writer, and indeed—as novelist, playwright, and essayist—he is
widely known for his analysis of two concerns basic to existentialism: its distinctive
assessment of the human condition and its search for authentic values. Yet Camus
rejected doctrinaire labels, and Sartre himself suggested that the author was better
placed in the tradition of French "moralist" writers such as Michel de Montaigne and
René Pascal, who analyzed human behavior inside an implied ethical context with its
own standards of good and evil. For Camus, liberty, justice, brotherhood, and happiness were some of these standards, along with the terms *revolt* and *absurd* that
described human nonacceptance of a world without meaning or value. From his
childhood among the very poor in Algiers to his later roles as journalist, Resistance
fighter, internationally famous literary figure, and winner of the Nobel Prize in 1957,
Camus never strayed from an intense awareness of the most basic levels of human
existence or from a sympathy with those—often poor and oppressed—who lived at
that level. "I can understand only in human terms. I understand the things I touch,
things that offer me resistance." He describes the raw experience of life as it is shared
by all human beings, and provides a bond between them. Camus's reaction to the
"absurd," the human condition stripped bare, is, therefore, quite different from Samuel Beckett's retreat into agonized subjectivity; where Beckett is haunted by the fictionality of experience, Camus asserts human consciousness and human solidarity as
the only values there are.

Camus was born on November 7, 1913, into a "world of poverty and light" in
Mondavi, Algeria (then a colony of France). He was the second son in a poor family

of mixed Alsatian-Spanish descent, and his father died in one of the first battles of World War I. The two boys lived together with their mother, uncle, and grandmother in a two-room apartment in the working-class section of the capital city, Algiers. Camus and his brother, Lucien, were raised by their strict grandmother while their mother worked as a cleaning woman to support the family. Images of the Mediterranean landscape, with its overwhelming, sensual closeness of sea and blazing sun, recur throughout his work, as does a profound compassion for those who—like his mother—labor unrecognized and in silence. (Camus's mother was illiterate and was left deaf and with a speech impediment by an untreated childhood illness.)

A passionate athlete as well as scholarship student, Camus completed his secondary education and enrolled as a philosophy student at the University of Algiers before contracting, at seventeen, the tuberculosis that undermined his health and shocked him with its demonstration of the human body's vulnerability to disease and death. Camus later finished his degree, but in the meantime he had gained from his illness a metaphor for everything that opposes and puts limits to human fulfillment and happiness: something he was later to term (after Antonin Artaud) the "plague" that infects bodies, minds, cities, and society. (*The Plague* is the title of his second novel.)

Camus lived and worked as a journalist in Algeria until 1940. He then moved to France when his political commentary (including a famous report on administrative mismanagement during a famine of Berber tribesmen) so embroiled him with the local government that his paper was suspended and he himself refused a work permit. Then as later, however, his work extended far beyond journalism. He published two collections of essays, *The Wrong Side and the Right Side* (1937) and *Nuptials* (1939), started a novel (*A Happy Death*), and founded a collective theater, Le Théâtre du Travail (The Labor Theater), for which he wrote and adapted a number of plays. The theater always fascinated Camus, possibly because it involved groups of people and live interaction between actors and audience. He not only continued to write plays after leaving Algeria (*Cross Purposes*, 1944; *The Just Assassins*, 1950) but was considering directing a new theater shortly before his death. The Labor Theater was a popular theater with performances on the docks in Algiers and was sponsored by the Communist Party, which Camus had joined in 1934. Like many intellectuals of his day, Camus found in the party a promising vehicle for social protest; he was unwilling to abandon either his independence or his convictions, however, and resigned in 1935 when the party line changed and he was asked to give up his support for Algerian nationalism. He left the Labor Theater in 1937 and, with a group of young Algerian intellectuals associated with the publishing house of Charlot, founded a similar but politically independent Team Theater (Théâtre de l'Equipe). During this decade, Camus also began work on his most famous novel, *The Stranger* (1942), the play *Caligula* (1944), and a lengthy essay defining his concept of the "absurd" hero, *The Myth of Sisyphus* (1942).

These three works established Camus's reputation as a philosopher of the absurd: the absurdly grotesque discrepancy between human beings' brief, material existence and their urge to believe in larger meanings—to "make sense" of a world that has no discernible sense. In *The Stranger*, Camus described a thirty-year-old clerk named Meursault who lives a series of "real" events: he attends his mother's funeral, makes love to his mistress, goes swimming, shoots an Arab on the beach, and is tried for murder. These events are described through Meursault's mind, and yet they appear without any connection, as if each one began a new world. They are simply a series of concrete, sensuous *facts* separated from each other and from any kind of human or social meaning. Meursault is finally condemned to death not for murder but for this alienation and for its failure to respond to society's expectations of proper behavior. Just before his execution, when he is infuriated by the prison chaplain's attempt to console him with thoughts of an afterlife, he rises to a new level of existential awareness and an ardent affirmation of life in the here-and-now, the only truly human field of action. Stylistically, much of *The Stranger*'s impact comes from the contrast between the immediacy of the physical experience described and the objective mean-inglessness of that experience. On all levels, the novel reaffirms the importance of life lived moment by moment, in a total awareness that creates whatever meaning exists: the same awareness of his own activity that brings the mythological Sisyphus happiness when eternally pushing uphill the rock that will only roll down again, or the same search for an absolute honesty free of human pretenses that characterizes the mad emperor Caligula.

During World War II, Camus worked in Paris as a reader for the publishing firm of Gallimard, a post that he kept until his death in 1960. At the same time, he was part of the French Resistance and helped edit the underground journal *Combat*. His friendship with the existentialist philosopher Jean-Paul Sartre began in 1944, and after the war he and Sartre were internationally known as uncompromising analysts of the modern conscience. Camus's second novel, *The Plague* (1947), used a descrip-tion of plague in a quarantined city, the Algerian Oran, to symbolize the spread of evil during World War II ("the feeling of suffocation from which we all suffered, and the atmosphere of threat and exile") and also to show the human struggle against physical and spiritual death in all its forms. Not content merely to symbolize his views in fiction, Camus also spoke out in philosophical essays and political statements, and his independent mind and refusal of doctrinaire positions brought him attacks from all sides. In the bitter struggle that brought independence to Algeria in 1962, Camus recognized the claims of both French and Arab Algerians to the land in which they were born. In the quest for social reform, he rejected any ideology that subordinated individual freedom and singled out Communism—the doctrine most reformist intel-lectuals saw as the only active hope—as a particular danger with its emphasis on the deindividualized and inevitable march of history. Camus's open anti-Communism led to a spectacular break with Sartre, whose review *Les Temps Modernes* (Modern Times) condemned *The Rebel* (1951) in bitter personal attacks. The concept of revolt that Camus outlined in *The Rebel* was more ethical than political: he defined revolt as a basic nonacceptance of preestablished limits (whether by death or by oppression) that was shared by all human beings and, therefore, required a reciprocal acceptance and balancing of each person's rights. Such "revolt" was directly opposed to revolutionary nihilism in that it made the rebellious impulse a basis for social tolerance inside the individual's self-assertion; it had no patience for master plans that prescribed patterns of thought or action.

Five years after *The Rebel* was published, Camus produced a very different book in *The Fall* (1956). This novel is a rhetorical tour de force spoken by a fallen lawyer who uses all the tricks of language to confess his weaknesses and yet emerge trium-phant, the omniscient judge of his fellow creatures. If Camus's *Notebooks* reveal in his early works a cycle of Sisyphus or the absurd, and his middle ones a Promethean cycle of revolt, *The Fall* inaugurates a third cycle, that of Nemesis, or judgment. It offers a complex, ironic picture that combines a yearning toward purity with a cynical debunking of all such attempts. The narrator, Clamence, is a composite personality including (among other things) satirized aspects of both Sartre and Camus, but it is impossible to get to the bottom of his character behind the layers of self-consciously manipulated language. The style itself challenges and disorients the reader, who is both included and excluded from a narration that presents Clamence's half of a dia-logue in which "you," the reader, are presumed to be present as the other half.

Camus was a consummate artist as well as moralist, well aware of the opportunities as well as the illusions of his craft. When he received the Nobel Prize in 1957, his acceptance speech emphasized the artificial but necessary "human" order imposed by art on the chaos of immediate experience. The artist is important as *creator*, because he or she shapes a human perspective, allows understanding in human terms, and therefore provides a basis for action. By stressing the gap between art and reality, Camus in effect provides a bridge between them as two poles of human understand-ing. His own works illustrate this act of bridging through their juxtaposition of realistic detail and almost mythic allegorization of human destiny. The symbolism of his titles, from *The Stranger* to the last collection of stories, *Exile and the Kingdom* (1957), repeatedly interprets human destiny in terms of a thematic opposition between the individual's sense of alienation and exile in the world, and simultaneous search for the true realm of human happiness and action.

With *The Guest,* taken from *Exile and the Kingdom,* Camus returns to the landscape of his native Algeria. The colonial context is crucial in this story, not only to explain the real threat of guerrilla reprisal at the end (Camus may be recalling the actual killing of rural schoolteachers in 1954) but to establish the dimensions of a political situation in which the government, police, educational system, and economic welfare of Algeria are all controlled by France. A similar colonial (or newly post-colonial) setting is used to indicate a charged political atmosphere in works by Doris Lessing, Naguib Mahfouz, Chinua Achebe, and Wole Soyinka. The beginning of Camus's story illustrates how French colonial education reproduces French, not local concerns: the schoolteacher's geography lesson outlines the four main rivers of France. The Arab is led along like an animal behind the gendarme Balducci, who rides a horse (here too, Camus may be recalling a humiliation reported two decades before and used to inspire Algerian nationalists). Within this political context, however, he concentrates on quite different issues: freedom, brotherhood, responsibility, and the ambiguity of actions along with the inevitability of choice.

The remote desert landscape establishes a total physical and moral isolation for events in the story. "No one, in this desert . . . mattered," and the schoolteacher and his guest must each decide on his own what to do. When Balducci invades Daru's monastic solitude and tells him that he must deliver the Arab to prison, Daru is outraged to be involved and, indeed, to have responsibility for another's fate. Cursing both the system that tries to force him into complicity and the Arab who has not had enough sense to get away, Daru tries in every way possible to avoid taking a stand. In the morning, however, when the Arab has not in fact run away, the schoolteacher makes up a package of food and money and passes on to the Arab his own freedom of choice. We cannot underestimate the quiet heroism of this act, by which Daru alienates himself from his own people and—unexpectedly—from the Arab's compatriots too; he is, he believes, conveying to a fellow human being the freedom of action, which all people require. This level of common humanity is strongly underlined throughout the whole story as a "sort of brotherhood" and "strange alliance" that comes from having shared food and drink, and slept as equals under the same roof. Such hospitality is also the nomadic "law of the desert" that establishes fellowship between guest and host (a law that Daru refers to when he points out the second road at the end). The host's humane hospitality has placed a new burden and reciprocal responsibility on his guest, one that may explain why the Arab chooses—in apparent freedom—the road to prison. Camus considered "Cain" and "The Law" as titles for this story before settling on *The Guest* (and the title word *l'hôte,* is identical for "guest" and "host" in French). Both guest and host are obliged to shoulder the ambiguous, and potentially fatal, burden of freedom.

Germaine Brée, *Albert Camus* (1964), is an excellent general study; see also *Camus: A Collection of Critical Essays* (1961). Catherine Savage Brosman, *Albert Camus* (2001), is a short introduction and biography. Herbert Lottman, *Albert Camus: A Biography* (1979), and Oliver Todd, *Albert Camus: A Life* (1997), are detailed biographies. English Showalter, *Exiles and Strangers: A Reading of Camus's Exile and the Kingdom* (1984), offers essays on the six stories of Camus's collection and separate comments on translations. Stephen E. Bronner, *Camus: Portrait of a Moralist* (1999), relates art, philosophy, and French and Algerian politics in a brief biographical study.

The Guest[1]

The schoolmaster was watching the two men climb toward him. One was on horseback, the other on foot. They had not yet tackled the abrupt rise leading to the schoolhouse built on the hillside. They were toiling onward, making slow progress in the snow, among the stones, on the vast expanse of the high, deserted plateau. From time to time the horse stumbled. Without hearing anything yet, he could see the breath issuing from the horse's nostrils. One of the men, at least, knew the region. They were following the trail although it had disappeared days ago under a layer of dirty white snow. The schoolmaster calculated that it would take them half an hour to get onto the hill. It was cold; he went back into the school to get a sweater.

He crossed the empty, frigid classroom. On the blackboard the four rivers of France,[2] drawn with four different colored chalks, had been flowing toward their estuaries for the past three days. Snow had suddenly fallen in mid-October after eight months of drought without the transition of rain, and the twenty pupils, more or less, who lived in the villages scattered over the plateau had stopped coming. With fair weather they would return. Daru now heated only the single room that was his lodging, adjoining the classroom and giving also onto the plateau to the east. Like the class windows, his window looked to the south too. On that side the school was a few kilometers from the point where the plateau began to slope toward the south. In clear weather could be seen the purple mass of the mountain range where the gap opened onto the desert.

Somewhat warmed, Daru returned to the window from which he had first seen the two men. They were no longer visible. Hence they must have tackled the rise. The sky was not so dark, for the snow had stopped falling during the night. The morning had opened with a dirty light which had scarcely become brighter as the ceiling of clouds lifted. At two in the afternoon it seemed as if the day were merely beginning. But still this was better than those three days when the thick snow was falling amidst unbroken darkness with little gusts of wind that rattled the double door of the classroom. Then Daru had spent long hours in his room, leaving it only to go to the shed and feed the chickens or get some coal. Fortunately the delivery truck from Tadjid, the nearest village to the north, had brought his supplies two days before the blizzard. It would return in forty-eight hours.

Besides, he had enough to resist a siege, for the little room was cluttered with bags of wheat that the administration left as a stock to distribute to those of his pupils whose families had suffered from the drought. Actually they had all been victims because they were all poor. Every day Daru would distribute a ration to the children. They had missed it, he knew, during these bad days. Possibly one of the fathers or big brothers would come this afternoon and he could supply them with grain. It was just a matter of carrying them over to the next harvest. Now shiploads of wheat were arriving from France and the worst was over. But it would be hard to forget that poverty, that army of ragged ghosts wandering in the sunlight, the plateaus burned to a cinder month after month, the earth shriveled up little by little, literally

---

1. Translated by Justin O'Brien.   2. The Seine, Loire, Rhône, and Gironde rivers. French geography was taught in the French colonies.

scorched, every stone bursting into dust under one's foot. The sheep had died then by thousands and even a few men, here and there, sometimes without anyone's knowing.

In contrast with such poverty, he who lived almost like a monk in his remote schoolhouse, nonetheless satisfied with the little he had and with the rough life, had felt like a lord with his whitewashed walls, his narrow couch, his unpainted shelves, his well, and his weekly provision of water and food. And suddenly this snow, without warning, without the foretaste of rain. This is the way the region was, cruel to live in, even without men—who didn't help matters either. But Daru had been born here. Everywhere else, he felt exiled.

He stepped out onto the terrace in front of the schoolhouse. The two men were now halfway up the slope. He recognized the horseman as Balducci, the old gendarme he had known for a long time. Balducci was holding on the end of a rope an Arab who was walking behind him with hands bound and head lowered. The gendarme waved a greeting to which Daru did not reply, lost as he was in contemplation of the Arab dressed in a faded blue jellaba, his feet in sandals but covered with socks of heavy raw wool, his head surmounted by a narrow, short *chèche*.[3] They were approaching. Balducci was holding back his horse in order not to hurt the Arab, and the group was advancing slowly.

Within earshot, Balducci shouted: "One hour to do the three kilometers from El Ameur!" Daru did not answer. Short and square in his thick sweater, he watched them climb. Not once had the Arab raised his head. "Hello," said Daru when they got up onto the terrace. "Come in and warm up." Balducci painfully got down from his horse without letting go the rope. From under his bristling mustache he smiled at the schoolmaster. His little dark eyes, deep-set under a tanned forehead, and his mouth surrounded with wrinkles made him look attentive and studious. Daru took the bridle, led the horse to the shed, and came back to the two men, who were now waiting for him in the school. He led them into his room. "I am going to heat up the classroom," he said. "We'll be more comfortable there." When he entered the room again, Balducci was on the couch. He had undone the rope tying him to the Arab, who had squatted near the stove. His hands still bound, the *chèche* pushed back on his head, he was looking toward the window. At first Daru noticed only his huge lips, fat, smooth, almost Negroid; yet his nose was straight, his eyes were dark and full of fever. The *chèche* revealed an obstinate forehead and, under the weathered skin now rather discolored by the cold, the whole face had a restless and rebellious look that struck Daru when the Arab, turning his face toward him, looked him straight in the eyes. "Go into the other room," said the schoolmaster, "and I'll make you some mint tea." "Thanks," Balducci said. "What a chore! How I long for retirement." And addressing his prisoner in Arabic: "Come on, you." The Arab got up and, slowly, holding his bound wrists in front of him, went into the classroom.

With the tea, Daru brought a chair. But Balducci was already enthroned on the nearest pupil's desk and the Arab had squatted against the teacher's platform facing the stove, which stood between the desk and the window.

---

3. Scarf; here, wound as a turban around the head. *Jellaba*: a long hooded robe worn by Arabs in North Africa.

When he held out the glass of tea to the prisoner, Daru hesitated at the sight of his bound hands. "He might perhaps be untied." "Sure," said Balducci. "That was for the trip." He started to get to his feet. But Daru, setting the glass on the floor, had knelt beside the Arab. Without saying anything, the Arab watched him with his feverish eyes. Once his hands were free, he rubbed his swollen wrists against each other, took the glass of tea, and sucked up the burning liquid in swift little sips.

"Good," said Daru. "And where are you headed?"

Balducci withdrew his mustache from the tea. "Here, son."

"Odd pupils! And you're spending the night?"

"No. I'm going back to El Ameur. And you will deliver this fellow to Tinguit. He is expected at police headquarters."

Balducci was looking at Daru with a friendly little smile.

"What's this story?" asked the schoolmaster. "Are you pulling my leg?"

"No, son. Those are the orders."

"The orders? I'm not . . ." Daru hesitated, not wanting to hurt the old Corsican.[4] "I mean, that's not my job."

"What! What's the meaning of that? In wartime people do all kinds of jobs."

"Then I'll wait for the declaration of war!"

Balducci nodded.

"O.K. But the orders exist and they concern you too. Things are brewing, it appears. There is talk of a forthcoming revolt. We are mobilized, in a way."

Daru still had his obstinate look.

"Listen, son," Balducci said. "I like you and you must understand. There's only a dozen of us at El Ameur to patrol throughout the whole territory of a small department[5] and I must get back in a hurry. I was told to hand this guy over to you and return without delay. He couldn't be kept there. His village was beginning to stir; they wanted to take him back. You must take him to Tinguit tomorrow before the day is over. Twenty kilometers shouldn't faze a husky fellow like you. After that, all will be over. You'll come back to your pupils and your comfortable life."

Behind the wall the horse could be heard snorting and pawing the earth. Daru was looking out the window. Decidedly, the weather was clearing and the light was increasing over the snowy plateau. When all the snow was melted, the sun would take over again and once more would burn the fields of stone. For days, still, the unchanging sky would shed its dry light on the solitary expanse where nothing had any connection with man.

"After all," he said, turning around toward Balducci, "what did he do?" And, before the gendarme had opened his mouth, he asked: "Does he speak French?"

"No, not a word. We had been looking for him for a month, but they were hiding him. He killed his cousin."

"Is he against us?"[6]

"I don't think so. But you can never be sure."

"Why did he kill?"

"A family squabble, I think. One owed the other grain, it seems. It's not at all clear. In short, he killed his cousin with a billhook. You know, like a sheep, *kreezk!*"

Balducci made the gesture of drawing a blade across his throat and the Arab, his attention attracted, watched him with a sort of anxiety. Daru felt a sudden wrath against the man, against all men with their rotten spite, their tireless hates, their blood lust.

But the kettle was singing on the stove. He served Balducci more tea, hesitated, then served the Arab again, who, a second time, drank avidly. His raised arms made the jellaba fall open and the schoolmaster saw his thin, muscular chest.

"Thanks, kid," Balducci said. "And now, I'm off."

He got up and went toward the Arab, taking a small rope from his pocket.

"What are you doing?" Daru asked dryly.

Balducci, disconcerted, showed him the rope.

"Don't bother."

The old gendarme hesitated. "It's up to you. Of course, you are armed?"

"I have my shotgun."

"Where?"

"In the trunk."

"You ought to have it near your bed."

"Why? I have nothing to fear."

"You're crazy, son. If there's an uprising, no one is safe, we're all in the same boat."

"I'll defend myself. I'll have time to see them coming."

Balducci began to laugh, then suddenly the mustache covered the white teeth.

"You'll have time? O.K. That's just what I was saying. You have always been a little cracked. That's why I like you, my son was like that."

At the same time he took out his revolver and put it on the desk.

"Keep it; I don't need two weapons from here to El Ameur."

The revolver shone against the black paint of the table. When the gendarme turned toward him, the schoolmaster caught the smell of leather and horseflesh.

"Listen, Balducci," Daru said suddenly, "every bit of this disgusts me, and first of all your fellow here. But I won't hand him over. Fight, yes, if I have to. But not that."

The old gendarme stood in front of him and looked at him severely.

"You're being a fool," he said slowly. "I don't like it either. You don't get used to putting a rope on a man even after years of it, and you're even ashamed—yes, ashamed. But you can't let them have their way."

"I won't hand him over," Daru said again.

"It's an order, son, and I repeat it."

"That's right. Repeat to them what I've said to you: I won't hand him over."

Balducci made a visible effort to reflect. He looked at the Arab and at Daru. At last he decided.

"No, I won't tell them anything. If you want to drop us, go ahead; I'll not denounce you. I have an order to deliver the prisoner and I'm doing so. And now you'll just sign this paper for me."

"There's no need. I'll not deny that you left him with me."

"Don't be mean with me. I know you'll tell the truth. You're from hereabouts and you are a man. But you must sign, that's the rule."

Daru opened his drawer, took out a little square bottle of purple ink, the red wooden penholder with the "sergeant-major" pen he used for making models of penmanship, and signed. The gendarme carefully folded the paper and put it into his wallet. Then he moved toward the door.

"I'll see you off," Daru said.

"No," said Balducci. "There's no use being polite. You insulted me."

He looked at the Arab, motionless in the same spot, sniffed peevishly, and turned away toward the door. "Good-by, son," he said. The door shut behind him. Balducci appeared suddenly outside the window and then disappeared. His footsteps were muffled by the snow. The horse stirred on the other side of the wall and several chickens fluttered in fright. A moment later Balducci reappeared outside the window leading the horse by the bridle. He walked toward the little rise without turning around and disappeared from sight with the horse following him. A big stone could be heard bouncing down. Daru walked back toward the prisoner, who, without stirring, never took his eyes off him. "Wait," the schoolmaster said in Arabic and went toward the bedroom. As he was going through the door, he had a second thought, went to the desk, took the revolver, and stuck it in his pocket. Then, without looking back, he went into his room.

For some time he lay on his couch watching the sky gradually close over, listening to the silence. It was this silence that had seemed painful to him during the first days here, after the war. He had requested a post in the little town at the base of the foothills separating the upper plateaus from the desert. There, rocky walls, green and black to the north, pink and lavender to the south, marked the frontier of eternal summer. He had been named to a post farther north, on the plateau itself. In the beginning, the solitude and the silence had been hard for him on these wastelands peopled only by stones. Occasionally, furrows suggested cultivation, but they had been dug to uncover a certain kind of stone good for building. The only plowing here was to harvest rocks. Elsewhere a thin layer of soil accumulated in the hollows would be scraped out to enrich paltry village gardens. This is the way it was: bare rock covered three quarters of the region. Towns sprang up, flourished, then disappeared; men came by, loved one another or fought bitterly, then died. No one in this desert, neither he nor his guest, mattered. And yet, outside this desert neither of them, Daru knew, could have really lived.

When he got up, no noise came from the classroom. He was amazed at the unmixed joy he derived from the mere thought that the Arab might have fled and that he would be alone with no decision to make. But the prisoner was there. He had merely stretched out between the stove and the desk. With eyes open, he was staring at the ceiling. In that position, his thick lips were particularly noticeable, giving him a pouting look. "Come," said Daru. The Arab got up and followed him. In the bedroom, the schoolmaster pointed to a chair near the table under the window. The Arab sat down without taking his eyes off Daru.

"Are you hungry?"

"Yes," the prisoner said.

Daru set the table for two. He took flour and oil, shaped a cake in a frying-pan, and lighted the little stove that functioned on bottled gas. While the cake was cooking, he went out to the shed to get cheese, eggs, dates, and condensed milk. When the cake was done he set it on the window sill to cool, heated some condensed milk diluted with water, and beat up the eggs into an omelette. In one of his motions he knocked against the revolver stuck in his right pocket. He set the bowl down, went into the classroom, and put the revolver in his desk drawer. When he came back to the room, night was falling. He put on the light and served the Arab. "Eat," he said. The Arab took a piece of the cake, lifted it eagerly to his mouth, and stopped short.

"And you?" he asked.

"After you. I'll eat too."

The thick lips opened slightly. The Arab hesitated, then bit into the cake determinedly.

The meal over, the Arab looked at the schoolmaster. "Are you the judge?"

"No, I'm simply keeping you until tomorrow."

"Why do you eat with me?"

"I'm hungry."

The Arab fell silent. Daru got up and went out. He brought back a folding bed from the shed, set it up between the table and the stove, perpendicular to his own bed. From a large suitcase which, upright in a corner, served as a shelf for papers, he took two blankets and arranged them on the camp bed. Then he stopped, felt useless, and sat down on his bed. There was nothing more to do or to get ready. He had to look at this man. He looked at him, therefore, trying to imagine his face bursting with rage. He couldn't do so. He could see nothing but the dark yet shining eyes and the animal mouth.

"Why did you kill him?" he asked in a voice whose hostile tone surprised him.

The Arab looked away.

"He ran away. I ran after him."

He raised his eyes to Daru again and they were full of a sort of woeful interrogation. "Now what will they do to me?"

"Are you afraid?"

He stiffened, turning his eyes away.

"Are you sorry?"

The Arab stared at him openmouthed. Obviously he did not understand. Daru's annoyance was growing. At the same time he felt awkward and self-conscious with his big body wedged between the two beds.

"Lie down there," he said impatiently. "That's your bed."

The Arab didn't move. He called to Daru:

"Tell me!"

The schoolmaster looked at him.

"Is the gendarme coming back tomorrow?"

"I don't know."

"Are you coming with us?"

"I don't know. Why?"

The prisoner got up and stretched out on top of the blankets, his feet toward the window. The light from the electric bulb shone straight into his eyes and he closed them at once.

"Why?" Daru repeated, standing beside the bed.

The Arab opened his eyes under the blinding light and looked at him, trying not to blink.

"Come with us," he said.

In the middle of the night, Daru was still not asleep. He had gone to bed after undressing completely; he generally slept naked. But when he suddenly realized that he had nothing on, he hesitated. He felt vulnerable and the temptation came to him to put his clothes back on. Then he shrugged his shoulders; after all, he wasn't a child and, if need be, he could break his adversary in two. From his bed he could observe him, lying on his back, still motionless with his eyes closed under the harsh light. When Daru turned out the light, the darkness seemed to coagulate all of a sudden. Little by little, the night came back to life in the window where the starless sky was stirring gently. The schoolmaster soon made out the body lying at his feet. The Arab still did not move, but his eyes seemed open. A faint wind was prowling around the schoolhouse. Perhaps it would drive away the clouds and the sun would reappear.

During the night the wind increased. The hens fluttered a little and then were silent. The Arab turned over on his side with his back to Daru, who thought he heard him moan. Then he listened for his guest's breathing, become heavier and more regular. He listened to that breath so close to him and mused without being able to go to sleep. In this room where he had been sleeping alone for a year, this presence bothered him. But it bothered him also by imposing on him a sort of brotherhood he knew well but refused to accept in the present circumstances. Men who share the same rooms, soldiers or prisoners, develop a strange alliance as if, having cast off their armor with their clothing, they fraternized every evening, over and above their differences, in the ancient community of dream and fatigue. But Daru shook himself; he didn't like such musings, and it was essential to sleep.

A little later, however, when the Arab stirred slightly, the schoolmaster was still not asleep. When the prisoner made a second move, he stiffened, on the alert. The Arab was lifting himself slowly on his arms with almost the motion of a sleepwalker. Seated upright in bed, he waited motionless without turning his head toward Daru, as if he were listening attentively. Daru did not stir; it had just occurred to him that the revolver was still in the drawer of his desk. It was better to act at once. Yet he continued to observe the prisoner, who, with the same slithery motion, put his feet on the ground, waited again, then began to stand up slowly. Daru was about to call out to him when the Arab began to walk, in a quite natural but extraordinarily silent way. He was heading toward the door at the end of the room that opened into the shed. He lifted the latch with precaution and went out, pushing the door behind him but without shutting it. Daru had not stirred. "He is running away," he merely thought. "Good riddance!" Yet he listened attentively. The hens were not fluttering; the guest must be on the plateau. A faint sound of water reached him, and he didn't know what it was until the Arab again stood framed in the doorway, closed the door carefully, and came back to bed without a sound. Then Daru turned his back on him and fell asleep. Still later he seemed, from the depths of his sleep, to hear furtive steps around the schoolhouse. "I'm dreaming! I'm dreaming!" he repeated to himself. And he went on sleeping.

When he awoke, the sky was clear; the loose window let in a cold, pure air. The Arab was asleep, hunched up under the blankets now, his mouth open, utterly relaxed. But when Daru shook him, he started dreadfully, staring at Daru with wild eyes as if he had never seen him and such a frightened expression that the schoolmaster stepped back. "Don't be afraid. It's me. You must eat." The Arab nodded his head and said yes. Calm had returned to his face, but his expression was vacant and listless.

The coffee was ready. They drank it seated together on the folding bed as they munched their pieces of the cake. Then Daru led the Arab under the shed and showed him the faucet where he washed. He went back into the room, folded the blankets and the bed, made his own bed and put the room in order. Then he went through the classroom and out onto the terrace. The sun was already rising in the blue sky; a soft, bright light was bathing the deserted plateau. On the ridge the snow was melting in spots. The stones were about to reappear. Crouched on the edge of the plateau, the schoolmaster looked at the deserted expanse. He thought of Balducci. He had hurt him, for he had sent him off in a way as if he didn't want to be associated with him. He could still hear the gendarme's farewell and, without knowing why, he felt strangely empty and vulnerable. At that moment, from the other side of the schoolhouse, the prisoner coughed. Daru listened to him almost despite himself and then, furious, threw a pebble that whistled through the air before sinking into the snow. That man's stupid crime revolted him, but to hand him over was contrary to honor. Merely thinking of it made him smart with humiliation. And he cursed at one and the same time his own people who had sent him this Arab and the Arab too who had dared to kill and not managed to get away. Daru got up, walked in a circle on the terrace, waited motionless, and then went back into the schoolhouse.

The Arab, leaning over the cement floor of the shed, was washing his teeth with two fingers. Daru looked at him and said: "Come." He went back into the room ahead of the prisoner. He slipped a hunting-jacket on over his sweater and put on walking-shoes. Standing, he waited until the Arab had put on his *chèche* and sandals. They went into the classroom and the schoolmaster pointed to the exit, saying: "Go ahead." The fellow didn't budge. "I'm coming," said Daru. The Arab went out. Daru went back into the room and made a package of pieces of rusk, dates, and sugar. In the classroom, before going out, he hesitated a second in front of his desk, then crossed the threshold and locked the door. "That's the way," he said. He started toward the east, followed by the prisoner. But, a short distance from the schoolhouse, he thought he heard a slight sound behind them. He retraced his steps and examined the surroundings of the house, there was no one there. The Arab watched him without seeming to understand. "Come on," said Daru.

They walked for an hour and rested beside a sharp peak of limestone. The snow was melting faster and faster and the sun was drinking up the puddles at once, rapidly cleaning the plateau, which gradually dried and vibrated like the air itself. When they resumed walking, the ground rang under their feet. From time to time a bird rent the space in front of them with a joyful cry. Daru breathed in deeply the fresh morning light. He felt a sort of rapture before the vast familiar expanse, now almost entirely yellow under its dome of blue sky. They walked an hour more, descending toward the south. They reached a level height made up of crumbly rocks. From there on, the plateau sloped down, eastward, toward a low plain where there were a few spindly trees and, to the south, toward outcroppings of rock that gave the landscape a chaotic look.

Daru surveyed the two directions. There was nothing but the sky on the horizon. Not a man could be seen. He turned toward the Arab, who was looking at him blankly. Daru held out the package to him. "Take it," he said. "There are dates, bread, and sugar. You can hold out for two days. Here are a thousand francs too." The Arab took the package and the money but kept his full hands at chest level as if he didn't know what to do with what was being given him. "Now look," the schoolmaster said as he pointed in the direction of the east, "there's the way to Tinguit. You have a two-hour walk. At Tinguit you'll find the administration and the police. They are expecting you." The Arab looked toward the east, still holding the package and the money against his chest. Daru took his elbow and turned him rather roughly toward the south. At the foot of the height on which they stood could be seen a faint path. "That's the trail across the plateau. In a day's walk from here you'll find pasturelands and the first nomads. They'll take you in and shelter you according to their law." The Arab had now turned toward Daru and a sort of panic was visible in his expression. "Listen," he said. Daru shook his head: "No, be quiet. Now I'm leaving you." He turned his back on him, took two long steps in the direction of the school, looked hesitantly at the motionless Arab, and started off again. For a few minutes he heard nothing but his own step resounding on the cold ground and did not turn his head. A moment later, however, he turned around. The Arab was still there on the edge of the hill, his arms hanging now, and he was looking at the schoolmaster. Daru felt something rise in his throat. But he swore with impatience, waved vaguely, and started off again. He had already gone some distance when he again stopped and looked. There was no longer anyone on the hill.

Daru hesitated. The sun was now rather high in the sky and was beginning to beat down on his head. The schoolmaster retraced his steps, at first somewhat uncertainly, then with decision. When he reached the little hill, he was bathed in sweat. He climbed it as fast as he could and stopped, out of breath, at the top. The rock-fields to the south stood out sharply against the blue sky, but on the plain to the east a steamy heat was already rising. And in that slight haze, Daru, with heavy heart, made out the Arab walking slowly on the road to prison.

A little later, standing before the window of the classroom, the schoolmaster was watching the clear light bathing the whole surface of the plateau, but he hardly saw it. Behind him on the blackboard, among the winding French rivers, sprawled the clumsily chalked-up words he had just read: "You handed over our brother. You will pay for this." Daru looked at the sky, the plateau, and, beyond, the invisible lands stretching all the way to the sea. In this vast landscape he had loved so much, he was alone.

KOJIMA NOBUO
born 1915

Kojima Nobuo, a deft satirist, belongs to the generation of writers in Japan who came of age during World War II. Their experiences of war, disastrous defeat, and humiliating occupation inevitably made them connoisseurs of absurdity. Together in particular with Yasuoka Shōtarō (born 1920), Kojima uses irony and ridicule to articulate the postwar pathology of the Japanese antihero: the befuddled ordinary man uprooted by failure, crushed by society, oppressed by go-getters, and so paralyzed by the flux all around him that he surrenders those few privileges still given the Confucian-based head of the household. Now even home denies refuge to the timid and profoundly ineffectual Japanese male. This may surprise American readers whose image of Japan was formed during the prosperous decades of the 1970s and 1980s. Nowhere in the fiction of Kojima will we recognize the dynamos who built Japan's extraordinary postwar economy (unless, of course, we are seeing them with their masks off, neuroses exposed in the empty hours away from their devotions to the Company).

Kojima was born near the town of Gifu in central Japan, the son of a carpenter who made Buddhist altars. An avid reader from childhood, he explored as a student a range of world literature, including British, American, and Russian writers. He would later aver that Gogol, the nineteenth-century Russian satirist, was a particularly important influence; one can also detect the impact of Kafka and Dostoevsky. In 1941 Kojima graduated with a degree in English literature from the prestigious University of Tokyo. His senior thesis, *Thackeray as a Humorist*, foretold his own future as a satirical writer. Throughout his career, he has combined the work of a novelist with teaching, translation, and writing literary criticism. During his tenure as a professor of English literature at Meiji University in Tokyo, he has published a number of scholarly volumes, including literary biography, and translated a baker's half-dozen of American writers (William Saroyan, Sherwood Anderson, Dorothy Parker, Nathaniel Hawthorne, Robert Penn Warren, Irwin Shaw, and Bernard Malamud).

Without doubt, though, it was Kojima's wartime and immediate postwar experiences that most shaped his fiction. Both periods seemed to demonstrate the randomness and futility of life. No sooner had he mastered the English language as a university student and begun to earn his living teaching English after graduating than he found his country and himself at war with virtually every English-speaking nation. In basic training for the army he was promptly ordered to forget the enemy's hateful tongue. He was also taunted—for being a university graduate, for wearing eyeglasses. Army officers made him drink more liquor than he could hold. He was sent to Manchuria, where scouting missions took on the color of childhood games of hide-and-seek. "When we went out on punitive expeditions," he would later write, "I always felt a great sense of futility. Of course, it would be futile to be killed in battle, but it was truly miserable to be scrambling around looking for an enemy. Whenever we went out looking for them, it was always after they had already run away."*

Then orders were reversed, and in 1944 Kojima was assigned to an intelligence unit in Peking, where he was to use his English after all. Here he spent his days intercepting radio communications of the U.S. Air Force and relaying the information to headquarters. On a slow day, or a particularly creative one, by Kojima's own admission, half the "decoded messages" were the products of sheer invention, the author's first fiction. It may even be said that English saved his life. His former battalion, sent to the Philippines not long after he was posted to Peking, was annihilated by General MacArthur's forces in the battle of Leyte at the end of 1944. As the war hurtled to conclusion, his final linguistic duty was to teach his commanding officers to say "I am not a war criminal" and "Would you care for a drink?"

*Van C. Gessel, *The Sting of Life: Four Contemporary Japanese Novelists* (1989) 15.

Not surprisingly, then, English figures in Kojima's early fiction. From his intelligence post in China he returned to a homeland completely devastated. More than three million Japanese had died during the war, almost one million of them civilians. Air raids and two atomic bombs had destroyed all but one of Japan's major cities. Over 30 percent of the Japanese people had lost their homes. Food shortages brought black marketeering and near starvation. Once prosperous families were reduced to trading heirlooms for basic necessities. The yen plummeted to barely a hundredth of its prewar value. Industry hardly existed. Perhaps most shocking of all: five hundred thousand former enemy troops, mostly American, now occupied the country. The Allied Occupation of Japan lasted from 1945 to 1952, first to maintain order and establish a new Japanese government and then to oversee extensive political, social, and economic reforms that would purge Japan of "irresponsible militarism" and refashion the country into an American-style democracy. The commanding presence of General MacArthur—whom some viewed as a latter-day *shogun* in the long tradition of Japan's military dictators, whose victories tolerated the continued existence of a figurehead emperor—seemed, like his many soldiers, to be everywhere, and so did their language.

Kojima might have been expected to benefit from this situation. But as his satiric masterpiece *The American School* (1954) makes patently clear, he views those who use the victors' language as carpetbaggers, or opportunists. The antagonist of the story, Yamada, an unctuous teacher of English dying for approval in defeated, shame-ridden Japan, tries to turn an excursion with his fellow teachers to a model school on one of the new American military bases into a demonstration that he alone, by virtue of his English fluency, is worthy of American respect. But as is often the case with people who must have the approval of others in order to respect themselves, Yamada is pathetic and dangerous because he stands for nothing except catering to those in power. For his foil he chooses Isa, the protagonist, a meek, inadequate colleague who is already quite beleaguered even before Yamada proposes a "demonstration" in front of the Americans. It is Isa's misfortune to despise the very language that he teaches, or to despise the uses to which it is now put by his compatriots. When they speak English, those who don't mind toadying enter a twilight zone of colonialism and opportunity. Their obsequious actions are made painless and unreal by the distancing that a foreign language automatically furnishes. They cease, in short, in Isa's eyes, to be Japanese. Yet, of course, they can never be American. Neither fish nor fowl, they let English transport them to an unreal world of license where they humiliate themselves without feeling any shame.

For its relentless, ironic evocation of the insidious shattering of a principled world and for its implied commentary on both Japan's postwar confusion and its historical tendency, at certain watersheds, to let others set its standards (China in the seventh century, the West in the nineteenth, and the United States in the third quarter of the twentieth), *The American School* won Kojima the Akutagawa Prize, one of his country's highest literary honors. With this work, Kojima consolidated his position as a chronicler of the helpless lot of postwar Japanese intellectuals. From his debut story in 1952, *The Rifle*, the portrait of a soldier who sells his soul to the army, to his most famous novel, *A Close Family* (1965), a record of the exact opposite, and his *Reasons for Parting* (1982), an immense novel hailed as a landmark in modern Japanese fiction, he has continued to bear witness to what he sees as the slow but discernible disintegration of humanity.

Kojima's novels and the bulk of his short fiction remain untranslated. *Stars,* however, from the same year as *The American School,* is included in Van C. Gessel and Tomone Matsumoto, eds., *The Shōwa Anthology: Modern Japanese Short Stories* (1985), a good source for modern and contemporary Japanese short fiction. Howard Hibbett, ed., *Contemporary Japanese Literature: An Anthology of Fiction, Film, and Other Writing Since 1945* (1977), and Yukiko Tanaka and Elizabeth Hanson, eds., *This Kind of Woman: Ten Stories by Japanese Women Writers, 1960–1976* (1982), also are good sources for modern Japanese literature. Works in English by members of Kojima's loose-knit coterie in the 1950s include Van C. Gessel's translation, *Stained Glass Elegies: Stories by Shūsaku Endō* (1984); Kären Wigen Lewis's translation of Yasuoka Shōtarō, *A View by the Sea* (1984); and Kathryn Sparling's translation of Shimao Toshio, *"The Sting of Death" and Other Stories* (1985). Also highly recommended are E. Dale Saunders's translation of Abe Kōbō, *The Woman in the Dunes* (1964), and John Nathan's translation of Ōe Kenzaburō, *A Personal Matter* (1968). For a critical study of Kojima, Yasuoka, Shimao, and Endō, see Van C. Gessel, *The Sting of Life: Four Contemporary Japanese Novelists* (1989).

PRONOUNCING GLOSSARY

The following list uses common English syllables to provide rough equivalents of selected words whose pronunciation may be unfamiliar to the general reader.

Gifu: *gee-foo*

Jizo: *jee-zoh*

Kojima Nobuo: *koh-jee-mah noh-boo-oh*

Meiji: *may-jee*

Michiko: *mee-chee-koh*

Shibamoto: *shee-bah-moh-toh*

Yasuoka Shōtarō: *yah-soo-oh-kah shoh-tah-roh*

The American School[1]

It was past eight-thirty and still the official had not appeared. The teachers had been told to assemble by this hour for their excursion to the American school, and most of them had come twenty minutes or so early. Having made their way to the Prefectural Office[2] through the morning throngs of commuters, all thirty of them were now left sitting here and there on the deserted stairs and around the gravel drive. There was one woman among them. She had apparently gone to some trouble to dress for the occasion; but her high heels, hat, and new plaid suit only made her look more sad and shabby.

As soon as they were all present, the teachers went en masse to the Office of Education on the second floor, only to be driven back down to this place which had not even been mentioned at the organization meeting a week ago. Right after the roll call the chairman of that meeting, an administrator from the Office of Education, had read off a list of instructions. The first was to assemble promptly at the appointed time. The second was to dress impeccably. The latter had created a stir which did not die down until the promulgation of the third point, that they must maintain a solemn silence at all times. Finally, they were to pack a lunch, for they would have to march to and from the school, a total distance of some eight miles; and even teachers had learned to feel proper hunger pangs in the three years since the War.

An American jeep ploughed through the gravel of the driveway, rounded the sharp curve, and came to a stop in front of the prefectural building. A teacher who had been sitting just inside the door jumped to his feet and moved away.

There was one man who had all the while been standing straight as a ramrod. The best-dressed and healthiest-looking of the group, he was conspicuous in an almost disconcerting way. At the previous week's meeting he

---

1. Translated by William F. Sibley.   2. A state-level government office.

had repeatedly raised his hand with questions for the chairman, a man by the name of Shibamoto. "Are we only supposed to observe?" he had inquired at one juncture. "What do you mean?" Shibamoto asked. "I was just wondering," he said, "if we might not give them a demonstration of our oral method." With a slight swagger that accentuated his heavy judo wrestler's build, the official reiterated loudly that the purpose of the excursion was to observe. He added that the Office of Education had gone to considerable lengths to secure permission for the visit. The man, whose name was Yamada, had at last given up this line of questioning.

He seized the floor once again in the commotion that followed the remarks on proper dress. "Quite right, sir," he said. "We must all present a neat appearance, whatever the cost. Any sloppiness would reflect on the profession. Worst of all, it would raise serious doubts about our competence to teach English. They despise us as a defeated people to begin with, and when they see the clothes we wear—I know, because I interpreted for the inspectors when they came to our school—they just look the other way. Not to mention the toilets . . ." His speech was interrupted at this point, and by now everyone was staring at him, with particular attention to his feet. There was scarcely another pair of leather shoes in sight. Undaunted, he resumed as soon as the mutters died down. They should avoid speaking Japanese in front of their hosts, he insisted, in order to display to the fullest extent their command of English. This was greeted by more general muttering, and a shrill outcry from the man sitting next to him: "What nonsense!" Yamada turned to face the heckler. But before he could launch into a longwinded defense of his proposal, Shibamoto called for order with the request that both Mr. Yamada and Mr. Isa refrain from intemperate language.

Isa had once been pressed into service at election time as interpreter for the Occupation inspection team (all elections were to be conducted impartially under the watchful eyes of the authorities). He was taken by jeep from one small village to the next, and was expected to keep his American counterpart informed of what was going on. Still only about thirty years old, he had never had a single conversation in English; occasional attempts at practical application of the language in the classroom had left him tingling with embarrassment; and when word came that the Americans would soon be visiting his school he had feigned illness, lying in bed for several days with an icebag pressed against his forehead, where there was not the slightest trace of fever. Only fear of unknown reprisals at the hands of the Occupation officials had deterred him from a similar stratagem at the time of the elections.

The moment he was packed into the jeep with a Negro soldier, he had turned to the fellow and said, in English: "I am truly very sorry to have kept you waiting." This was met with silence, and when he repeated the words three times over, the soldier only stared at him coldly and uncomprehendingly. The phrase he had prepared several days ago and practiced constantly since was clearly too formal and correct. From then on he limited himself to two words, "stop" and "go." For those five hours he felt as if he were being boiled alive, though outwardly he appeared to be merely loafing on the job. And in either case, the result was that he was of no use to anyone.

As soon as they approached the first polling-place, he fled. He tried to reason with himself, before sneaking off to hide, that it would go still worse with him than if he had refused to come in the first place. But the prospect of being addressed in that unfamiliar language in front of a crowd made his knees quake. By the time the Negro noticed his absence and came back to find him, he was long gone.

Isa was not by nature so craven; indeed, as the jeep drove into the village he had felt a strong impulse to do violence to his keeper. But after they slowed down, it seemed easier to escape, and so he jumped off the rear and made for the wooded slope above the road. On discovering that his passenger had fled, the soldier went after him, partly out of fear at being left alone in these dark hills. Deep in the woods Isa saw the man coming. He called out to him in Japanese: "You'll have to speak our language. Speak Japanese or else! What would you do if someone really said that to you?" As the face of his adversary drew near, a neatly trimmed beard, features strained in an effort to make out the indistinct words, it gave a feeling of loneliness. The beard contributed an incongruously civilized air, and as the face moved still closer it seemed almost to show some understanding of the stream of Japanese that issued forth from behind the trees. Isa babbled on as fast as he could. When the Negro at last realized that the words were not in his language, he threw up his hands and shrugged his shoulders. Seated behind the wheel again, he looked even lonelier than before, as if unaccountably intimidated by this creature who spoke scarcely a word of normal English, and who would lapse without warning into Japanese gibberish. He ceased to pay any attention at all to Isa, and proceeded as though chauffeuring an honored guest around the countryside. A pointless errand on the whole; but at least, it occurred to him, the man might be of some service in helping him deal with hostile natives.

Each time an American jeep drove up, Isa drifted a little away from the prefectural building. Yamada's foolish suggestions at the organization meeting were still fresh in his mind, especially the proposal of a demonstration class, which had aroused in him an instant panic that persisted to this moment. Well, he would simply keep a close watch on Yamada and shut him up if necessary. He had, however, already yielded on one point: he was wearing a pair of black leather civilian shoes. They were an odd match with his khaki uniform, but he had wanted at least to spare himself the embarrassment of army boots. Likewise, having set out with his lunch box in an old army bag, along the way he had taken the box out, folded up the incriminating bag, and stuck it under his arm.

Yamada continued to stand alone surveying the scene expectantly. Whenever a jeep pulled up he would bustle over to explain the situation. "We represent the English teachers of this prefecture," he would begin stiffly. "We are very devoted to the English language. We work very hard to teach the English. We are now utilizing the latest methods of instruction, just like you have in your country."

"If you work so goddam hard, what are you hanging around for at this hour?" one driver replied, reaching down with a look of extreme boredom to hand him a cigarette.

"I do not smoke," said Yamada.

"Are you the chief?"

"Our leader is an official of this prefecture. He is very late for our appointment. Government officials are lazy people. But you must not think that all Japanese are like that."

The soldier, who was black, threw up his hands in disgust. "I am truly very sorry to have kept you waiting," he said, and drove off.

Yamada did not know what to make of this parting remark. The American had perhaps been mocking Japanese officials. He looked at his watch again and muttered to himself. What would their hosts think if they arrived late at the school? Something must be done. He called out to those of his colleagues who were sprawled within earshot, "Will some of you come up to the Education Office with me? If we don't do something we'll be late. They have our names on file at the school. We'll be disgraced. 'What can you expect from a defeated people?' they'll say."

Yamada noticed that Isa, who was sitting only a few feet away, kept his back turned as though preoccupied with some important business. He went over to investigate and found him with his lunch box open on his lap. Isa had been up since three, riding his bicycle to the nearest station, then taking a combination of streetcars and trains until he reached this distant city. He was hungry; rather, he thought he ought to be hungry by now.

Yamada stood for a moment in silent amazement. "This is not time to be eating," he said. "Come with me to the Education Office. If the officials there won't cooperate, we'll speak to the Occupation personnel."

The bare mention of the local Occupation force was enough to upset Isa. He had already noticed the bearded Negro in one of the jeeps, and had seen Yamada accost him. Indeed, it was one reason for beginning his lunch now. This was a high-risk area where he might be addressed in English at any moment. A mouthful of food would, he sensed, offer some defense against any demand that might be made of him. And so he did not answer Yamada, and regretted having challenged him at last week's meeting, thus attracting his attention. Isa had decided not to speak a word in any language today, for if he began by conversing in Japanese he would surely end by having to speak English. The best strategy was a tight-lipped silence that would lead people to believe he was indisposed. Then no one, neither official nor colleague, would think it strange if, when his turn came to talk at the school, he had nothing to say. Without looking up from his lunch he waved his chopsticks in the air by way of a reply.

"What kind of answer is that?" Yamada put his question in both languages and waited for an answer. Isa pretended not to hear. Yamada was given to venting his wrath in English. "Oh, for shame!" he exclaimed, stalking off towards the overdressed instructress, Michiko, who capitulated on the spot and followed him up the stairs.

On their way into the office they bumped into the tardy official. Shibamoto was wearing his Sunday best, which consisted of a long overcoat and a soft felt hat. As he led them out of the building, he blew a whistle to assemble the others. Yamada protested that the whistle would sound a shrill note of unreconstructed militarism; furthermore, for the same reason, they should not march in a solid phalanx.[3] Shibamoto granted his point and ordered the group to fall out. When the command was given to reassemble in loose ranks, Yamada placed himself like a staff adjutant at Shibamoto's side. The rest of

---

3. Soldiers marching in rank and file.

the teachers straggled behind in a long procession, with Isa bringing up the rear.

Shibamoto made a brief announcement: "We received notification that the time for our visit had been changed. Sorry for the inconvenience. They were very pleased with the first group. Try to keep up the good record. Ready?"

It was about four miles to the American school down an asphalt road that ran straight as the crow flies from the outskirts of the city. Strung out like a chain gang, the teachers set out with Shibamoto and Yamada in the lead. Isa, at the other end, made no effort to move up. He found himself walking beside the woman, and this was somehow reassuring. Within ten minutes they had reached the asphalt road. There was an uninterrupted flow of traffic traveling to and fro among the various installations of the large base that stretched out for miles around the school. A sigh rippled through the group at the sight of this long black ribbon which was clearly not made for walking.

Isa watched with secret admiration as Michiko took a pair of sneakers from her cloth bundle and put them on. What foresight! The men around him were all wearing long overcoats, with a sprinkling of army issue such as he himself had on. The poverty revealed in their bulky clothing showed up starkly against the hard pavement. "I don't want you in rows, but do move closer together," Shibamoto cautioned. "You mustn't look so straggly—there are Occupation personnel all around you." Cars and jeeps were in fact flying by, thick and fast, though there was not another pedestrian to be seen anywhere on the forbidding road.

The presence of a single woman in their midst was enough to mitigate the ragged, faintly subversive spectacle created by the twenty-nine men. Before five minutes had gone by, a car coming from the opposite direction pulled up beside Michiko. A soldier stuck his head out the window and spoke to her. "What are you people doing here?" he asked, echoing the question put to them several times in front of the prefectural building. Michiko stated the purpose of their excursion in clear, correct English. "You're an English teacher, are you? Well, you're pretty damn good, I'd say." The soldier thrust some cans of cheese in her hands and drove off.

It was not until Michiko laughed out loud and tugged at his sleeve that Isa turned to face her. With eyes studiously averted from the exchange with the soldier, he had begun to reconsider his choice of companion. Walking beside the woman, he was easy prey for any number of foreign soldiers. He felt the weight of the can that Michiko had stuffed into his pocket while he was staring at the rice paddies below the road. Living in an era when true goodwill was translated into gifts of food, he was naturally pleased and flattered, and especially so for having failed to notice that she had received two cans from the soldier and had to give one away to keep the other. What if he was a little more vulnerable being next to her, he had only to look the other way when the enemy approached, and there were these unexpected benefits.

It had occurred to Michiko as they started down the asphalt road that she had forgotten something. In her rush this morning to change after sending off her son, her only child by the husband she had lost in the War (he too had been a teacher), it must have slipped her mind. She poked around in the cloth bundle and her suspicions were confirmed. Luckily the missing article was one that could be borrowed in a pinch; and at the moment the two cans of cheese plopped into her hands, she had picked Isa as her most likely benefactor.

Tranquilly and with unexpected warmth, the winter sun shone down upon the black surface until the glare began to affect one's eyes. Cars continued to pass by in both directions, and then a jeep drove up, this time from behind, and slowed down almost to the pace of the procession. Two soldiers, one white, one black, leaned out to look the group over. Yamada turned around and waited until the jeep drew up beside him. "Haro[4] boys! What are you doing?" he hailed them.

With a look of mild surprise one of the soldiers asked in return: "Only one woman?" Having verified with their own eyes, without listening to Yamada's reply, that the woman they had passed was the only one, they stopped the jeep in the middle of the road and waited. As Michiko approached they called out to her: "Ojosan![5] Ojosan!" They asked where she was going and told her to get in. Her quick response was livelier than when she spoke in Japanese, her face more expressive, even distinctly feminine. "I'm on a group excursion," she said. "I really can't go ahead by myself."

The soldiers exchanged an approving glance as they inspected the proper Japanese lady from top to bottom. They tore the wrapper from two bars of chocolate and, with a parting nod full of regret, tossed them down to Michiko. She broke one of the bars into pieces and passed them out to a few people around her, this time omitting Isa. Afterward the teachers who had dropped back toward her at this point showed no disposition to move up again.

They had not been marching in close ranks from the outset, and by now the group had split into two separate platoons: Shibamoto, Yamada, and their followers in the lead, Michiko and her attendants in the rear, with a gap of over a hundred yards in between.

It came to Isa by slow degrees that his shoes hurt. Each step brought new pains. He began to regret having worn these ill-fitting genuine leather shoes; and when he reflected that he had put them on to please Yamada, to speak the foreign tongue in the right style—simply to hold down his job—his regrets gave way to anger. The pain grew more and more acute. He struggled to keep up with Michiko, but even this was too much for him. He now noticed with a twinge of envy how smooth and easy her stride had become since she abandoned her high heels for sneakers. No one else, either in his platoon or the group up front, showed signs of suffering from the same problem. He himself had never paid much attention to shoes until this moment. The offending pair, on loan from a colleague, had seemed just right when he first tried them on. A tiny discrepancy was enough, it appeared, to cause a great deal of pain. Isa became suspicious of the colleague who had lent him the shoes. For all he knew, the man could be in league with Yamada.

There was no telling how much farther they had to go, for the view ahead was blocked by a rise in the road. When Isa looked back to see how much ground they had covered he was distressed to find the prefectural building looming still quite large behind them.

About fifteen feet ahead, Michiko stood looking over her shoulder in his

---

4. "Hello." The soldier is making fun of the inability of Japanese to discriminate between the sounds *l* and *r* in the English language.   **5.** A term of address for a young lady, similar to our "Miss."

direction. "Is something wrong?" she asked when at last he caught up with her. At his mumbled reply apropos of shoes her face took on a look of utmost gravity. Having set out in new shoes herself, she had more than an inkling of what she would have endured but for the sneakers. "That will never do. We still have a long way to go. Maybe you should hitch a ride—why don't you stop one of these jeeps?"

Isa's pain yielded to astonishment and terror. What she suggested would not have occurred to him in his wildest dreams. "If it ever came to that!" he muttered as he stumbled forward in an effort to keep up, putting as much weight as possible on his toes to relieve the pinch on his insteps. He hoped to set her mind at ease and avoid further suggestions of drastic remedies, but he soon realized that his awkward gait only made matters worse.

Michiko slackened her pace and walked silently at Isa's side as if to subdue his pain by force of her own calm will. Until now she had found him a tedious companion, thoroughly wrapped up in himself for no apparent reason. But as soon as she began to share in his suffering, faint memories stirred within her of the love, long forgotten, that a woman can also share with a man. She did not, however, lose sight of her objective. She meant to have from him that homely article left behind in her haste. What love she felt for him was bound up with her hopes of getting it, and seemed to emanate like hunger pangs from somewhere near the pit of her empty stomach. While more cars whizzed by she spoke to him again in a soothing tone, as if to stroke his heaving back. "You really ought to get yourself a lift," she said. "Shall I ask for you?"

"No! No thank you! Never mind! I'd sooner go barefoot."

"Now really, I don't see why . . ."

Isa felt like biting his tongue for breaking his vow of silence. Yet had he kept quiet Michiko would no doubt have hailed a jeep immediately, and at her fluent English they would have picked him up without further ado. Then where would he be? No matter how dire his need, the very thought of riding next to a foreigner again made him sick. He remembered all too vividly his day of torture with the black soldier. He had felt as though at any moment he could murder the man, and if it had gone on for another day he surely would have done so, unless, of course, he had first found a way to escape.

The tender feelings which Michiko had summoned up from deep within her subsided in the face of Isa's stubborn refusal. The sweat now trickling down her body served as a nagging reminder of her impure motives. Very well, she thought, she would get what she was after anyway. And even that didn't really matter so much; she could if necessary do without. Resolved to not so much as look back at him, she forged ahead toward Yamada's platoon. The others followed in her wake, leaving Isa far behind.

Up front, Yamada and Shibamoto were trading boasts. Shibamoto, by his own account, had been one of a handful of judo experts in the prefecture before the War disrupted things—a fifth-degree black belt, no less. And contrary to malicious postwar propaganda, devotees of the martial arts were not all war criminals. One had only to consider himself, holder of a prominent post in the administrative section of the prefectural Education Office. Moreover, he taught judo not only to the local police, but to the Occupation personnel themselves, and had in fact got the job through his American supervisor.

Yamada's ears perked up at the mention of Occupation personnel. He was intensely interested in every kind of contact with the Americans, though so far his own had been restricted to interpreting. He had a consuming ambition to study abroad, to which end he schemed and fretted the livelong day.

Eager to establish his credentials with such a well-connected man, Yamada explained that he had conducted any number of demonstration classes at his school; that although they were supposedly professional teachers of English, few of his colleagues made a good showing . . . Yes, said Shibamoto, he had heard about all that. From a leather briefcase the likes of which were seldom seen in these times, Yamada removed a mimeographed schedule of a typical demonstration class, which he happened to have brought along.

"Rook heah, see for yourself," he said, breaking momentarily into English. "I hope sometime soon to hold a teaching seminar here in the city—with the backing of the administrative section, of course. And we would certainly welcome cooperation from the Americans." He handed Shibamoto his card. His name and titles appeared in Japanese script on one side, Roman on the other. "I might not look it now, but I hold a second-degree black belt in fencing," he volunteered.

"Is that so? I suppose you've had some experience in your day," said Shibamoto.

"You bet I have!" Yamada slashed the air with an imaginary sword. "This might not be the time to mention it, but when I was in OTS[6] I got to whet my blade a bit, if you know what I mean."

"It must be hard, cutting off heads."

"Not really. It takes a good arm, a sharp sword, and practice, of course. That's all."

"How many did you polish off?"

"Let's see . . ." Yamada paused and looked around. "About twenty, I guess. Half of them must've been POWs."

"Any Yanks?"

"Naturally."

"How did they compare with the Chinese?"

"Well, there's quite a difference in how they take it. When you come right down to it, they show their lack of what you might call Oriental philosophy."

"You're lucky they never caught up with you."

". . . I was only following orders."

Yamada was suddenly aware of the dangerous turn in the conversation. What had he been saying? He fell silent. Noticing that Shibamoto had removed his overcoat, he hastily took off his own and stuck it under his arm. He looked over his shoulder at the disorderly procession and his taut, swarthy features collapsed into a disdainful grimace.

"What do you think of this mess?" he said to Shibamoto. "If the War were still on and this were a real march. . . ! But what can you expect from a bunch of high school teachers?"

Yamada fixed Isa hawklike in a distant gaze. In this perspective the laggard could not fail to arouse contempt and indignation. While Yamada stood at the side of the road the group straggled by in little clumps, their pace so listless that he wanted to ask with the Americans what business they had on

6. Officers' Training School.

this highway. He made up his mind to stay where he was and wait for Isa to come along. Over the past week he had not forgotten Isa's vague but unmistakable hostility. As he waited, the word "insubordinate" popped into his head. It seemed to furnish a key to understanding this queer fellow. With his own tales of martial valor still ringing in his ears, Yamada became again the company commander he had been until three years before. But for all the brutal self-assurance restored to him in this transformation, he did not bark out a reprimand to Isa, preferring to take him by surprise.

Michiko passed by first. "His shoes pinch," she explained, pointing back at Isa.

"His shoes pinch? Ridiculous!" This went beyond simple insubordination. To dawdle over such an infantile triviality was inexcusable. At this rate he was likely to start whining about his bladder or a sore throat and fall still farther behind. Well, what was the matter with his shoes? Yamada stared at the black blobs of Isa's feet scraping across the asphalt in the distance. He waited till the dusty shoes had shuffled up diffidently under his nose before he spoke. "Are those your shoes?" he snapped, in English.

Isa had not noticed Yamada at the side of the road. His eyes were wide open with the effort of bearing the pain, but he could not see a thing.

"It's your fault this group is in such a shambles. It only takes one straggler like you to throw everyone out of step."

Michiko came back and repeated to Yamada her suggestion that Isa ask for a ride.

"From the Americans?" Yamada's shoulders fell as he studied Isa's feet. Ignoring Michiko, he lashed out again at Isa: "That is out of the question. Mistah Isa, have you no pride? Maybe for ap-pen-di-ci-tis. But for *shoes?*"

Several other teachers had wandered back to see what was holding things up and stood looking over Yamada's shoulder. "He'd do better to go barefoot," one of them said. This solution had occurred to Isa any number of times since the pain began. But each time he had rejected it for fear of being spotted by the Americans, who were sure to question him about his bare feet and force him to ride in a jeep.

Yamada changed his tone. "Try to keep moving, at least. You've got everyone stopped in their tracks wondering what to do about you—Oh, Mr. Shibamoto. What do you think, sir?"

When Yamada failed to return to the front rank, Shibamoto had planted himself at the roadside like a stone Jizo.[7] Once the leaders dropped out, the rest of the procession ground to a halt.

"If this keeps up we'll be late, sir. We'll be disgraced. The main thing is to make sure the Americans don't see him. Oh, for shame!"

"What seems to be the trouble here?" Shibamoto had not yet grasped the cause of Yamada's excitement. When the problem was put to him he proposed that Isa go ahead and remove his shoes. Yamada and a few others would walk along on either side and shield him from the passers-by.

Shibamoto's proposal was duly adopted and Isa was promptly relieved of his suffering. It even struck him that this pavement could have been made for bare feet, which were not, after all, without some resemblance to the rubber tires of a car.

7. A stone statue of the guardian deity of children.

Michiko brooded over the man who was once more walking beside her, though likely soon to lag behind again. Isa seemed as unresponsive as ever, and she made no attempt to speak to him. But his stubborn streak had begun to remind her of her late husband. Surrounded by Yamada and the others, he strode along unshod and full of purpose, a shy but spirited little man in the jaws of adversity. That is what her husband had been when he went off to war.

Her thoughts drifted back to that day when she had struggled to keep up with the column of soldiers bound for the front as they marched the five miles from their base to the station. They had not paused once along the way, pushing ahead at an unrelenting pace that did not allow for last-minute farewells. Her husband marched with clenched teeth and scarcely cast a glance in her direction. The only time he turned his head to face her, he made a curt gesture with his hand as if to drive her away. There had of course been others besides herself, among them aged mothers calling out their son's names as they stumbled after the swift procession.

Michiko had understood her husband's embarrassment then. The feelings of the barefoot man next to her now were no doubt of the same kind. Perhaps she would speak to him once they were at the school. She was suddenly aware again of the high heels pressing through the cloth against her hands like hard little buds about to flower. Yes, after she had changed her shoes at the school she would have a word with him.

Isa showed no sign of faltering, indeed he fairly loped along, with none of the strain that was beginning to tell on the others. He was, however, still shy of foreign eyes, though his fears were very different from Yamada's, and he walked somewhat stooped over. He hurried ahead driven by the desire to reach his destination at the earliest possible moment, and in the happy expectation of freedom from any further need to propel himself. He was too absorbed in the delicate task of simultaneously staying out of sight and rushing forward to reflect that he would still have to move about at the school, and then make the trek back to the city.

Taking but small comfort in Isa's return to the fold and the restoration of some semblance of order, Yamada dwelt on the disgust which the man's every action stirred up in him. He decided the time had come to broach to Shibamoto the subject that had been in the back of his mind all day. "You know, sir," he began, "we really ought to give a demonstration class while we're there. It's a rare opportunity to show them what we can do, and maybe we can get them to evaluate and rank us while we're at it."

Shibamoto was busy surveying the buildings of the American school, which had come into view as soon as they passed the crest in the road. He gave Yamada a doubtful look and did not reply. When Yamada pressed the point by suggesting that he himself could make the request, Shibamoto wearily repeated that their hosts might find the exercise troublesome.

"I don't see why it should be any trouble. It will be our show—a demonstration of what English teachers in this country are capable of. Afterwards we'll let them give us a few pointers, that's all. As a judo expert I'm sure you can see the wisdom of our taking the offensive, so to speak."

This was a thrust that Shibamoto could not parry. He would have to let the man have his way. He had never met such a cocky instructor, he thought, as Yamada announced once again that he would take the bull by the horns.

Isa did not miss a word of this exchange. When he saw Shibamoto weaken, his thoughts turned instinctively to escape. Slipping easily through the loose cordon they had strung around him, he sidled off to the edge of the road and unbuttoned his fly. Yamada was still preoccupied and failed to notice this dereliction; the others were too tired to bother with him.

Just then Michiko was accosted by another jeep. She broke into a cold sweat as she ascertained that the melancholy black face looking down at her wanted to know about Isa, who stood relieving himself up the road. But her fears were set to rest when she heard the soldier ask, "What's with the bare feet?" She explained, and the jeep rumbled off in Isa's direction.

Isa wheeled around in alarm, and at one glance recognized his old adversary. He backed away, stunned by the accuracy of his presentiment that he would see the man again today. When he reached the shoulder of the road he turned and leaped into the field below. Here he was far less protected than he had been on that wooded slope. The soldier was beckoning to him with a miniature package of cigarettes. The next moment Yamada was yelling at him. "He's only trying to do you a favor. What's the matter with you!" Joining forces, the soldier and Yamada clambered into the field. Together they dragged Isa back up to the road and bundled him into the jeep. The vehicle bearing the solitary captive soon vanished in a cloud of sand, and raucous laughter swept through the ranks.

Above the road ahead some crows flocked and veered off to one side as if to clear a path for the car passing far below. Or perhaps they were preparing to scavenge around the American school. Michiko watched this scene and savored a certain relief, accompanied by a quiet, private laugh, at the removal of the burden that Isa had become for her. She no longer imagined that she could understand his excessive timidity, unless, she speculated, he had done something awful during the War.

Isa sat hunched up in the back of the jeep. He quickly averted his eyes from the driver's seat and peered out at the dwindling faces of his colleagues. Although their features were already blurred, he could clearly see that they were laughing. Yet, for all their scorn, their company was far preferable to the predicament that now filled him with despair. The general laughter left little doubt that Yamada would succeed in squeezing out of him some sort of performance in English. As far as he was concerned, it was now all but inevitable; that is, it seemed quite within the realm of possibility, which was for Isa tantamount to inevitability.

On their first encounter the Negro had mistaken Isa's cowed silence for sullen contempt, with overtones of a personal animus against himself. Afterwards he had Isa's credentials checked through the Education Office, without bothering to state the cause of his curiosity; and when the record showed no reason for the man's refusal to speak English, he felt that his suspicions had been confirmed. This unlooked-for second meeting was a stroke of luck: he would have a little revenge for that business in the woods.

The jeep screeched to a halt and Isa found a pistol pointing into his face. Then came the command: "Speak English, man. Let's hear it again. 'I am truly very sorry to have kept you waiting.' "

Isa trembled all over and stammered out the phrase as dictated. Below the trim moustache the mouth of his captor opened in a loud guffaw. The pistol was only a toy, he said. Humming a jazz tune, he started up the engine and drove on.

At the American school the soldier bade Isa a friendly farewell as he climbed out of the jeep. "Maybe we'll meet again," he said, with some appreciation, it appeared, of the karma[8] that had already brought them together twice. Isa felt weak inside at the mere suggestion.

As soon as the jeep was out of sight Isa, still barefoot, ran toward the fence enclosing the school playground. After a few moments' rest he put on his shoes and crouched down to look around. The children at recess on the playground, boys and girls mixed together, ranged from the early grades through junior high school. Even now, in midwinter, they were scampering about in a colorful assortment of light clothes, a sweater here, a blouse and jumper there. Isa retreated into the shadow of one of the buildings to continue his inspection from a less public vantage point.

Along with a sense of relative security, he experienced an overwhelming mental fatigue. He closed his eyes for fear of fainting and felt the tears well up behind his eyelids. At first he could not tell what had brought on his tears, but he knew it was a joy so intense as to be close to sorrow. With his eyes still closed he slowly discerned the source of his bliss in a murmuring of soft voices, sweet and clear as a mountain stream. They seemed to come from another world, perhaps in part because the words made little sense to him.

Isa opened his eyes and saw a cluster of young girls, twelve or thirteen years old, chatting with each other about fifty feet from where he was hiding. He concluded that he and his colleagues were members of a pathetic race which had no place here.

Listening to these mellifluous English voices, he could not account for the fear and horror which the language had always inspired in him. At the same time his own inner voice whispered: It is foolish for Japanese to speak this language like foreigners. If they do, it makes them foreigners, too. And that is a real disgrace.

He pictured clearly to himself the outlandish gestures that Yamada affected when he spoke English. There was no dignity in talking just like a foreigner. But it was equally demeaning to speak a foreign tongue like a Japanese. This was the fate that awaited him today, he knew, if he were called upon to talk at the school. The few times that he had begun his class with a halting goodo-moaning-ebury-body he had afterward flushed crimson and felt himself at the bottom of some dark ravine. No! That was not for him. He would sooner make himself over into a whole new man.

Enrapt with the schoolgirls' merry fugue, Isa did not hear the jeep return. The soldier got out, whistling another tune. Some distance from where Isa remained hidden, he stood leaning over the fence and searched out his son. Having been on urgent business to the barracks that adjoined the school, only after it was finished did he remember Isa's feet. The boy, who looked to be of junior-high-school age, came running to his father, and a few moments later disappeared into the school.

Presently a beautiful tall lady of a type one often sees in American movies appeared before Isa's eyes. With the black boy in tow, she advanced swiftly and purposefully toward the fence. Isa stole off into the shade of a nearby

8. Fate in the Buddhist religion; the outcome of one's actions in previous existences, since Buddhism holds that we are endlessly reborn unless we achieve enlightenment and thus escape the cycle of death and rebirth.

grove, lest she find him crouching there and take him for a thief. He shut his eyes and mentally blocked his ears, to no avail; he could distinctly hear her footsteps and the sound of her voice calling out as she came closer and closer. Although he suspected that her call was meant for him, and had in any case resigned himself by now to being caught, he still did not respond. He kept his head down and his eyes closed until he felt a touch on his shoulders and heard the word ". . . shoes?" At this he stood up and bowed.

When he opened his eyes and saw the lady standing right beside him, he was all but blinded by the look of abundance on her face: features that spoke of an ample diet, material well-being, and pride of race. She was for all that only human, and a fellow schoolteacher as well. So he tried to tell himself, but he could not quite believe it. Next to her—she stood at least a head taller than he—Isa felt weak around the knees, and in reply to her questions he only nodded and bowed. In the end, like a timid servant with his mistress, he allowed himself to be led off toward the school.

Isa caught enough of the cascade of soothing words that poured from her lips like melting snow to realize that he had that meddlesome Negro to thank for his new predicament. "I only want to do something about those feet," the lady said. "I'm not going to poison you." He wanted to say thank you—that much he could manage. But once he had opened his mouth she would expect him to keep up a steady conversation. He had better just play dumb and follow her like a dog.

Isa sank back into despondency when he thought of the interrogation to which, as a solitary Japanese among a horde of foreigners, and an English teacher of sorts, he was sure to be subjected. He was too busy brooding to notice the gaggle of students that trailed behind him as he limped along, until a few sharp words from the lady sent them shouting and laughing back to the playground.

She kept smiling at him and making what sounded like friendly remarks, which required him to play deaf as well as dumb. But he had begun to receive contradictory signals from his conscience. To atone for the appearance of incivility he had given so far, he was tempted to fall down and kiss the lady's feet, or at least the ground beneath them. Caught between these conflicting impulses, Isa took it into his head to carry her books for her. He moved abruptly to her side and, without a word, tried to wrest the heavy books from her arms. He had the appropriate phrase on the tip of his tongue but was too embarrassed to say it. Perplexed by this dumbshow, the lady clutched the books to her breast. When he continued to tug at the books, bowing and grinning abjectly, she eventually guessed his intention and thanked him; but she would not surrender her burden.

It was enough for Isa that she had recognized his gesture. Hereafter, however incompetent he might appear at the school, he would not be considered a barbaric ingrate. As they approached the building, he felt something like the relief of a condemned criminal who had made one last plea for forgiveness from his fellow men.

Since the nurse was not to be found in the dispensary, the schoolmistress led Isa to her own office, where she shut the door firmly and turned the key. Once again Isa had a sinking feeling, such as the toy pistol had produced in him a while ago. "Sit down," said the lady, whose name, he gathered from the sign on the door, was Emily. "We lock the door so we can smoke," she explained. "Even the men do. It sets a bad example for the students, you see."

It took Isa some time to decipher this statement. From the moment he entered the room he kept his eyes glued to the floor and let his ears tune out her speech, which he dimly imagined to be a reproach for his earlier rudeness. In any case the words seemed to have nothing to do with his feet, and it was not until he raised his head, afraid of appearing very rude indeed, that he saw the smoke and half grasped their meaning. Still standing in silence, he traced the upward spiral of smoke with his eyes, the better to extricate himself from Miss Emily's gaze.

Out of the clear blue sky came the order: "Take off your shoes!" Or so he interpreted her sharp utterance. But no sooner was he down to his army socks than she burst out laughing and murmured something about coffee. Then he thought he heard her say, though it made little sense to him, that he should "help himself." When Isa, thoroughly confused, began to pull up his socks, in a single violent motion Miss Emily lunged at him and stripped them off. She gaped at his exposed feet, at first with simple curiosity, then with a look of distress on detecting the raw wound where the skin had been scraped away. "Dear me," she exclaimed, putting out her cigarette.

It was by no means easy for Isa to make such a spectacle of himself in front of a foreign lady, here in this secret room. But so long as he was not obliged to speak, he was resigned to suffering these minor indignities. Nevertheless, he was desperately eager to return to the group, to become again only one among many.

After drinking a cup of coffee by herself, Miss Emily went out into the corridor, locking the door behind her. As she left, Isa understood her to say that she was going to consult with the nurse, which was encouraging—but why had she locked the door? Only then did he finish puzzling out her remark upon entering the room, to the effect that they mustn't let the students see them smoke. Yet that was only part of it, he knew. She was also worried about his wandering around the school on the loose, or still worse, escaping again, like a wounded animal that runs away when one is only trying to help it. As soon as Isa reached this point in his train of thought he felt an irresistible impulse to flee that very moment. He immediately opened the window, jumped out, and started to run.

After a few steps he felt the ground against his bare feet and remembered his shoes. He could not just leave them there, they did not belong to him. As he was hoisting himself back up through the window, the door opened across the room and he found himself face to face with Miss Emily.

While Isa was still lurking behind the trim modern buildings of the American school, Yamada wasted no time in approaching Michiko. In the past he had seen her from a distance conversing with foreigners in a free and easy manner. Since the beginning of today's excursion, when he dragged her off to the Education Office, he had been scheming for a chance to examine her English at first hand. It was not uncommon for members of his profession to test each other's mettle on some trivial pretext, like samurai picking quarrels simply to show off their prowess. Yamada was a past master at this sort of thing. And when he came up against colleagues whose English was better than his own, especially if they were women, he would try to defeat them on other grounds, to browbeat them if need be with the brute strength of his manly will. But in the end he often lost anyway.

Yamada had bided his time while Isa was tagging along beside Michiko, with what seemed to be warm encouragement on her part. Now that that nuisance had been removed, he could proceed with his interrogation. He unleashed a barrage of questions in English that left her scarcely a moment to catch her breath. What schools had she gone to, where did she graduate, had she taken special lessons in conversation, how many American friends did she have????

At first, even Michiko, with her considerable abilities, could not bring herself to reply in kind to her countryman's tirade in a foreign language. She answered only haltingly, and half in Japanese. But when Yamada showed no sign of relenting, she saw what he was up to, and resented his contempt for her sex.

And what, if she might inquire, was the big attraction of English for him? Would he like to try a demonstration class with her sometime? Wasn't it curious that he pronounced certain words with a kind of Boston accent, others in a sort of Southern drawl, which was a little like mixing Kyushu speech with the slow country dialect of Aomori?[9]

Yamada was staggered by the woman's counterattack, delivered in rapid-fire, thoroughly natural English. It was not so much her fluency as the substance of her remarks that defeated him. She was more than a match for him, he conceded; he would have to find some other weakness. In his experience, when dealing with women, food and clothing were the best bet.

"That's a fine outfit you're wearing," he said, lapsing back into Japanese. "Did you get it before the War?"

"Yes," she answered softly. "That is, the material comes from a robe that belonged to my husband. He was killed in the War."

"I'm sorry to hear that. It must be hard for you." Yamada peered shrewdly into Michiko's face as he added: "If you need rice, I can get it fairly cheap."

"That's very kind of you," she said. "May I have your card?"

"And if you'd like a little piecework to do at home, perhaps I could find you something."

"I would certainly appreciate it. Men really are much better at arranging these things, aren't they!"

The procession had at last come to a halt in front of the gate to the school compound. As soon as Yamada noticed the guard looking over their credentials, he burst in with the information that one of their number had preceded them by jeep. Turning back to Michiko, he then announced in English: "I imagine that he is still barefoot, and has concealed himself somewhere behind the school."

"What makes you think that?" asked Michiko.

"Elementary," said Yamada. "The man does not know the language." Lowering his voice, but still speaking English, he suggested that the time had come for her to change her shoes.

Michiko did not need prompting; it had been on her mind all day long. Yet Yamada's sharpness surprised her. He must have been watching her closely since the march began. From now on, she in turn would have to keep an eye on him. Maybe he had Isa pegged, too, she thought. But was it possible that the poor fellow was still slinking around behind some building? She

9. The northernmost prefecture on the main island of Japan, where speech patterns tend toward the terse; according to one theory, this is because of cold temperatures. Kyushu is a southern island where temperatures are warm and speech habits are more easy-going.

searched the corners of the compound as their final destination came into full view.

At the center of a large tract of land traversed by neat rows of houses stood the long-awaited school, an almost solid wall of glass on the side facing south. The fields that once occupied the site had been leveled away without a trace. An American observer would not have found the compound remarkable, much less luxurious. But the solid houses planted sparsely over the landscape, the spacious bedrooms illuminated by lamps even in broad daylight, the young Japanese maids attending to the needs of American babies—all of this was clearly revealed at a glance, and impressed the weary visitors as a vignette of some heavenly dwelling place.

Michiko reflected that her command of a foreign language and her general level of education might set her far above most of the residents; nevertheless, it was she who had walked four miles for the privilege of visiting their school, she who had reveled secretly in the pathetic expectation of showing off her high-heeled shoes. Surrounded by this verdant park, she now saw herself as too small and destitute even to set foot in such a place.

"What's the point of our sitting in on their classes?" she overheard a colleague complain to Shibamoto. He was the one, she recalled, who had been so quick to urge Isa to go barefoot. "What can we hope to learn from classes held in a place like this? The only lesson we'll leave with is the one we've learned just getting here: we lost! These magnificent buildings that we're only allowed to peek at—they were built with our taxes. Doesn't it make you want to cry?"

Michiko turned away, ashamed that she had perhaps been noticed before with her hands pressed sorrowfully over her eyes. She felt equally awkward in her present pose, and so she moved a few steps apart from the group, bent over and, though it scarcely mattered anymore, put on her high heels. The first thing she saw as she raised her head again was Isa, shoes still dangling down from one hand, coming toward her across the playground—and standing motionless in the background, the beautiful figure of an American schoolmistress. Michiko wanted to change back into sneakers.

The long march on an empty stomach had reduced some of the group to sullen anger, others to a numb exhaustion. Their leader rose up to his full height, and with a few heaves of his broad shoulders began to harangue them. "You mustn't forget that you're here by special invitation. We in the administrative section worked hard to get it for you, and if anyone misbehaves we are the ones who'll be blamed—You there, what do you think you're doing?" As he spoke, Shibamoto's roving gaze was arrested by a man sitting on the ground with his back to the group. It was Isa. Shibamoto resumed in the same hectoring tone: "I must ask you not to sit down right in front of the school. You look like a beggar. When did you get back?"

"You see, sir, that's what I meant," Yamada interjected. "We have to put our best foot forward, bargain from strength. Otherwise we might as well not have come in the first place. Leave it to me."

Shibamoto cut him off with a vague "We'll see," and quickly moved on to the next item on the agenda. He took a sheaf of printed questionnaires from his briefcase and passed them out to the teachers. As they studied the form he explained that they were to use it to record in detail their impressions of the school; afterwards it would be collected and put on file for future reference.

"What can we possibly write down? What would it prove, anyway?" cried Michiko in a shrill voice. She was visibly overwrought.

"Never mind," Yamada interrupted again. "You can just put down what I have. I intend to comment very critically on the instructional objectives of this school, the aptitude of their teachers, and so forth. I'll show it around when I'm done, and everyone can use it as a model. You needn't worry about that. Instead you might give some thought to . . ."

"No, no, you've missed the point," said Michiko impatiently.

"Well, then, what is the problem?"

Michiko fell silent. There was no use trying to explain to the likes of Yamada. And Isa—what a timid little soul! But he did seem to have a way with women. She would have to get to the bottom of this business with the schoolmistress. For the moment Yamada and Isa were confused in her troubled thoughts.

Just then the iron gate in front of the school opened and a thirtyish, bespectacled man stood before them with a welcoming smile. He introduced himself to the group as Mr. Williams, the Principal. At his appearance the teachers ceased their idle chatter and prepared to begin their visit. Yamada barged through the gate ahead of the others, who hesitated and deferred to one another before following him in. Isa came last, dragging his feet, as the gate swung shut behind them.

Hardly any doubt remained in Isa's mind about Yamada's devious plan, which he had sniffed out from its inception, to face off with him in a demonstration class before the day was over. He was determined to silence Yamada on this subject and prevent the encounter at any cost. But so far no suitable defense had suggested itself, and he approached the potentially fateful classrooms with ever more halting steps.

The group advanced in double file so as not to interfere with the students passing to and fro. Yamada had already attached himself to Mr. Williams. After the Principal's every utterance he would raise his hand as if to call for attention, turn to the person behind him, and communicate his version of the remark. This would be relayed in some form or other from one teacher to the next until it reached the end of the line: a procedure arrived at spontaneously, whether as a throwback to the rigid military chain of command or by simple analogy with a bucket brigade. It took some time for the message to be transmitted to Michiko and Isa in the rear, and in the interval all but the most provocative implications were filtered out.

Mr. Williams's opening remarks, that is, Yamada's rendering of them, went as follows: "Since the school was to be built with Japanese funds, we had little choice but to go along with the specifications given to us by some Japanese architects. The results, as you can see for yourselves, were less than satisfactory. To begin with, the budget was barely twenty percent of what would be considered normal back in the States. In our country we place great emphasis on bright and cheerful surroundings, and this school certainly does not meet those standards. We have twenty students in a class here, which is three too many. The ideal is seven-*teen*. Now I understand that in your country there are seven-*ty* in a class. Imagine! Classes that size are really out of the question. They necessitate regimentation, and this inevitably leads to militarism."

Here Yamada's voice trailed off into silence as Mr. Williams's expression took on a sudden severity, accompanied by a pudgy finger pointed at

Yamada's forehead. When Yamada resumed interpreting, he spoke at first in tremulous tones.

The subject had changed to salaries, which, Mr. Williams assured them, were paid by the American government. The lowest salary level at the school, the one for beginning instructresses, was still about ten times the average wage of Japanese teachers, according to the figures he had heard. This was, it was true, a bit more than they would receive in comparable jobs at home; but things were a good deal more expensive in such a remote country; and if the discrepancy seemed excessive, it should be borne in mind that the standard of living which American teachers had to maintain was, after all, extremely high, so it was only natural that the basic salary be of a different order.

The only part of this speech to reach Isa's ear was the startling information, passed down the line with a collective sigh, that the teachers at this school got ten times as much money as they did. This so amazed Michiko that as she repeated it to Isa she had to lean on him to keep her balance. "We should have listened to our colleague there," she commented. "We should have just turned around and gone home."

"Right. That's so," said Isa.

"Did that woman do something about your feet?"

"Right. She did."

"What did you talk about?"

"Nothing."

"Look at those two over there—how disgusting!" Michiko muttered censoriously.

Isa looked in the direction she had indicated and focused on two students who stood holding hands in a corner of the corridor, their eyes closed in mutual infatuation. Miss Emily came up behind the couple and tapped them both gently on the back, not so much to chastise them, it appeared, as to alert them to the presence of visitors. Afterward she turned toward Michiko and smiled.

"It looks like paradise from the outside," said Michiko, "but there's no telling what goes on between these walls."

"Right. That's so."

Michiko did not know what to make of Isa's laconic responses. She looked at his frightened, rabbitlike eyes and recalled what Yamada had said about him. Then he broke his silence.

"Why must I go through this humiliating ordeal?"

"What ordeal? You mean having to go barefoot before?"

"No. I mean having to look at all this beauty."

"Beauty? From a certain point of view, I suppose."

"I'll tell you why. Simply because I'm a so-called English teacher."

"Oh? You don't like speaking English?"

"I d-d-detest it!"

Michiko was not surprised. There were a lot of men like that, the opposite type from Yamada, and Isa must be one of them.

Although the teachers had been told that they should each choose a class to visit and go their separate ways, they preferred to stick together. In the end Shibamoto divided them arbitrarily into three subgroups and dispatched them to different classrooms, with the veiled threat of force that was always present in his judo master's bearing. These smaller units soon congealed so that each proceeded as one, like flocks of peasants being herded around the capital.

Michiko hovered next to Isa. She could hardly forget the small favor she had yet to beg of him, after dwelling on it the length of that asphalt road. Moreover, it was reassuring to have him by her side—here, where almost anything might happen, and now, while she felt so despicably drab in the shadow of the foreign lady. Isa seemed to her the perfect companion for the occasion.

Meanwhile, Isa stayed as close as possible to Yamada, watching his every move, and fervently wishing that he might fall down some stairs and break his neck. He was even prepared, should the opportunity arise, to give him a little nudge. Failing that, in his present position he could at least intervene without delay if Yamada broached the subject of a demonstration class. And as one of his entourage, Isa was spared the necessity of pronouncing a single word of English, for Yamada had appropriated the role of spokesman for their party.

Isa and Michiko followed hard on Yamada's heels as together they entered the designated room, where they found a drawing class in session. Yamada soon retired to the supply closet to note down his observations. When he had finished he faced Michiko and whispered slyly: "Take a good look. With all their money and their fancy buildings, the children can't draw worth a damn."

There was a meek chorus of agreement from several colleagues who stood nearby, hanging on Yamada's every word. Michiko herself shared his opinion of the drawings, but she did not wish to be associated in any way with these people. They were the mean and cunning sort of Japanese; she and Isa were different, Michiko told herself, looking to Isa for confirmation. She caught him stooping over his shoes again: a new pair of sneakers which, she quickly deduced, must have come from that schoolmistress. They were much too big for him and he was trying to compensate by lacing them up tight. The moment Isa's eyes met hers, he blushed and turned the other way.

Michiko proposed that they have a closer look at the work now in progress. As they moved into the classroom and studied the drawings, they found themselves submerged in a waterless sea teeming with fish of various colors, shapes, and sizes. They were all unique, each one the product of a collaborative effort by a small group. Over by the window a few junior-high-school students of both sexes were sketching the thatched-roof cottages which appeared in the distance, beyond the confines of the American compound. They began to steal glances at the visitors over their shoulders, then one of the boys pointed at Shibamoto with his right hand while with his left he indicated a drawing of a seadevil. On closer inspection of other drawings, it was discovered that Yamada had been turned into a shark, Isa into a flying fish, suggested, perhaps, by his emaciated figure, and Michiko a goldfish. In the same fashion the whole party emerged within the next few moments as a school of highly distinctive fish.

As soon as they were back in the corridor, Yamada said to Shibamoto: "What kind of school are they running here, allowing such insulting behavior—and even toward a lady! I think we should submit a written protest. How about the rest of you? And you, Mrs. . . . ?"

"I didn't really mind it so much," said Michiko. "In fact, we sort of asked for it, with our down-and-out attitude."

"Down-and-out? I'm talking about a serious failing in their instructional objectives, a complete lack of discipline. That art teacher ought to be severely reprimanded. But why should I waste my breath! If you don't mind being turned into a goldfish, that's your business."

Not a glint of amusement alleviated Yamada's peevish expression as he finished berating Michiko and began to make further notations in his little book. "What did they do with you?" he asked Isa, looking up from his book. "Oh yes. It was a flying fish, and quite a masterpiece, too. They must have got the idea from the way you were flitting around in your bare feet."

Isa was at the moment too intent on his malevolent wishes to hear.

Isa stood at the door of the classroom in his borrowed sneakers and listened to the lady whose initials they bore teach English. Michiko had gone inside with the others, this time without trying to coax him into coming along. After a while the group filed back into the corridor one by one and clustered together to exchange comments in a half-whisper.

"You might almost say that our English is better than theirs," Yamada observed to Michiko in Japanese. "Weren't you amazed at all the mistakes in their grammar?"

"But the teacher is pretty, isn't she?"

"Hmm. It's like hiring a movie star to teach at a ridiculous salary."

"You were right about *him*—he really does hate English," said Michiko, switching languages as she again changed the subject.

"I know all that. I am also aware that he harbors some marice toward me."

Michiko acknowledged to herself that in referring to Isa as "him" and making her remark in English she had stilled the pangs of guilt which she would normally have felt in this betrayal of trust. And that, she reflected, was no doubt one reason for Isa's hatred of the foreign language: when you spoke it you stopped being yourself. It was too easy to be carried away by the titillation of the words, words not exactly your own. She knew she ought to get away from Yamada, the sooner the better.

When Michiko was back at Isa's side again she startled herself by blurting out, "If you hate speaking English so much, you must hate me too."

"It's different with women," said Isa.

"Women make good mimics. Is that what you mean?"

Maybe that *was* what he had meant, Isa could not be sure.

Without warning Michiko leaned over and whispered something in his ear. She had reverted to Japanese, to Isa's relief, but he could still make out only the general drift.

"You mean even you . . . ?" Isa blushed a deeper hue than Michiko, though she had brought the matter up.

"Have I embarrassed you again?" she asked.

It was perhaps in part the extraordinary scene now unfolding before their eyes that had driven her to divulge such a delicate matter, and so impetuously. They were now in the gymnasium, where, in preparation for tomorrow's basketball game with a neighboring school, a rally was being conducted by a spirited cheering section. A trio of girls in uniform, sixteen or seventeen years old, stood in front of the others calling out the names of the players with mounting fervor. When the shouting had risen to a high pitch of frenzied excitement, like a line of chorus girls they all began to lift up their skirts while the cheerleaders launched into cartwheels and somersaults.

"It's all set for the demonstration class this afternoon—you and me," said Yamada, who had appeared out of nowhere and taken Isa by surprise.

"I-I-I don't know what you're talking about. I have nothing to do with it."

"Well, you know now. Shibamoto decided on the two of us. I'll meet you after lunch, as soon as the hour for visiting classes is over. And don't try to run away. Shibamoto would not be pleased." Thrusting his jaw out toward Michiko, he added in an insinuating tone: "I'm sure you can get some coaching from her."

Yamada had in fact not the slightest desire to stand in front of a class next to Isa. The man was sure to bring disgrace on the whole profession. But in the middle of the rally he had caught sight of Michiko whispering in Isa's ear, then watched as Isa blushed and nodded in agreement. At that moment he had declared war.

Yamada went directly to the Principal and made his proposal with the same lunatic zeal he had shown to Shibamoto. Shibamoto stood by, wondering anxiously how the Principal would react to this bizarre request, which sounded less like a bid for a classroom demonstration than a demand for satisfaction by a man whose honor had been challenged. Yet, whether because like Shibamoto he saw no way out, or because he was soon to return to America and hoped it might yield a piece of Japanese bravado to regale his friends with, the Principal had accepted the proposal on the spot.

Yamada took leave of Isa and Michiko with a few curt instructions as to where they were to eat their lunch: on some benches in the schoolyard, about three hundred feet outside the gate—and nowhere else.

With quivering lips Isa stared vacantly after Yamada as he retreated across the gymnasium.

"Isa-san.[1] I'll take your place this afternoon," said Michiko.

"It's too late for that," Isa replied. "Either I knock him out, or I quit my job . . . or else I go ahead with the class and just stand there without saying a word."

Isa made as if to run after Yamada, but the sores on his feet seemed to be acting up again, and he had barely managed to limp forward a few steps when Michiko seized him by the hand and held him back.

"Wait a minute," she said. "Please don't forget the little favor I asked you a moment ago. If you'll let me have them now, I'll wash them right away."

Isa's immediate response was a blank look and an incessant blinking of his rabbit-eyes.

"You know, what we talked about before," Michiko prompted.

Isa finally understood what she wanted. All right, she could have them. But only after he had finished with them. Even at this juncture, on the brink of coming to blows with Yamada, he could not ignore his other concern, one from which he was never altogether free.

1. *San* is a title attached to names, corresponding to our Mr., Miss, Mrs., etc.

With sudden resolution Isa removed from his satchel a small bundle wrapped in newspaper and thrust it toward Michiko, all the while keeping his eyes on Yamada's vanishing figure. Michiko reached out in some confusion to take the coveted article from him—hardly ten seconds had passed since he had at last seemed to grasp her wish. But like an overeager relay runner, Isa had moved too soon, and he was off before the bundle was safely in her hands. Uneasy about the transaction to begin with, Michiko now blushed furiously, fumbled, and in the end lost her balance. Her high heels slid out from under her, and with a piercing shriek that filled the corridor she toppled over onto the floor. The bundle lay open where she had hurled it aside in her fall, revealing a pair of black chopsticks.

It remained a secret shared by Isa and Michiko alone that she had fallen while clutching at this homely artifact of their native land. As soon as Mr. Williams arrived on the scene, he loudly ordered the Japanese who had gathered around to disperse, whereupon up and down the corridor foreigners came rushing out of every other door. The Principal drove off this new crowd, leaving only a few women to help Michiko to the dispensary.[2]

Afterward, as he questioned Shibamoto about the accident, Mr. Williams kept adjusting his glasses in an irritable gesture that suggested he found it all very regrettable. What had Michiko and Isa been up to? he wanted to know. Yamada, having rejoined them, interpreted stiffly for Shibamoto to the effect that the man with the limp had been struggling to catch up with yours truly to request that he be allowed to substitute for his colleague in today's demonstration class; meanwhile, the lady, who cherished similar aspirations, had been strenuously attempting to dissuade her colleague from his determined course when she slipped and fell. "It all proceeded from their pedagogical dedication," Yamada concluded on Shibamoto's behalf, "and their devotion to the English language."

"Ah yes. The old kamikaze spirit," said the Principal.

The heavy irony was lost on Yamada, who took the remark as a compliment, and presented it as such to his superior. Shibamoto fluttered his eyelashes in silent modesty.

Seeing that his sally had been deflected by misinterpretation, Mr. Williams pushed back his glasses again and turned on them with his sternest expression. "From now on, there are two things which I must strictly forbid," he announced. "The first is for any Japanese instructor to conduct a class here, to engage in any attempts to do so, or in any way to involve himself in the educational process at this school. Secondly, in the future high heels will not be permitted on these premises. If there are any violations, we will have to terminate all further visits."

After spitting out these injunctions with an air of finality, the Principal strode rapidly down the corridor to the door of the dispensary. He showed no inclination to enter, merely surveying the situation from outside.

A long pause ensued during which Yamada neglected to translate Mr. Williams's last pronouncement. When he was summoned back to reality by a poke in the ribs from Shibamoto, he spun around and fled toward the exit, without so much as a word of explanation. Then, with Shibamoto in the lead, the rest of the group hurried after, as though suddenly reminded of some vital errand. Only Isa was left behind, alone once again.

2. An office in a school, hospital, or other institution where medicines and medical aid are dispensed.

BERNARD DADIÉ
born 1916

Bernard Dadié is one of the pioneers of modern African literature. In its application to his work, the term "pioneer" serves to acknowledge his achievement in the effort to create a new African literature out of the language inherited from the colonial experience—in this case, French. But it also registers his status as an innovative writer with a varied and accomplished body of work that includes six volumes of poetry, an autobiography, two travel books, and several plays and collections of short stories.

Bernard Binlin Dadié was born in 1916 at Assinie, a village near Abidjan, capital of Ivory Coast, at the time a colony of France. After attending the Catholic elementary school in the Grand Bassam, he left his native country to continue his education at the famous École William Ponty in Dakar, Senegal, a teacher-training college where the first generation of the French-speaking African elite was trained. His literary talents first manifested themselves at this institution, at which students were encouraged to write stories and plays based on the local customs of their communities of origin. The productions of the William Ponty students were to prove significant in the emergence of francophone African literature, especially in the development of French African theater.

At his graduation in 1936, Dadié was appointed to a research position at the Institut Français de l'Afrique Noire, the embryo of the University of Dakar (now Université Cheik Anta Diop), where he remained until his return to his native country in 1947. Over the next few years, Dadié occupied a variety of government posts before going into active politics, a move that confirmed his earlier activities as a militant in the anticolonial movement that was gathering impetus throughout Africa during the 1950s. After the independence of Ivory Coast in 1960, Dadié was named to a succession of ministerial positions, serving in particular as minister of culture for over a decade before his retirement in the mid-1980s.

Like Birago Diop and Léopold Sédar Senghor, Dadié sought to give expression in his work to an authentic African vision and sensibility. The oral tradition and, in particular, the communal heritage of the folktale, serving as the foundation of what one might call an African imagination, offered him a vital resource for a creative interpretation and revaluation of the continent's cultures, a central preoccupation of the French-speaking African writers and intellectuals associated with the Négritude movement. While it is undeniable that the tales collected in Dadié's volume, translated under the title *The Black Cloth*, derive a good part of their interest from this circumstance, his individual crafting of these tales lends to his adaptations of the folk material a literary quality that removes them from the sphere of documentary ethnography. His tales thus reflect a personal appropriation of a narrative genre that forms a mainstay of his cultural background.

The three tales reproduced here reflect this dual character of Dadié's approach to the tradition. *The Mirror of Dearth* demonstrates the use of animal characters in the folktales, often in interaction with human types, as vehicles for their didactic purpose. The protagonist here is Spider, a trickster figure who functions as the hero of a whole cycle of folktales in the Akan-speaking areas of West Africa, including parts of Ghana and Ivory Coast. But the folktale also accommodates purely human situations, as exemplified by the collection's title story. The motif of the innocent orphan and wicked stepmother that provides the keynote of *The Black Cloth* has been made familiar to many readers by the stories of Cinderella and of Snow White. But this motif takes on a special dimension here, inherent in the structural connection between the heroine's journey into the unknown and the testing of her will and endurance, leading in the conclusion to a epiphany that gives dramatic effect and trenchant meaning to her trial. For in its reminder of human mortality, this conclusion lends the tale an undoubted spiritual significance. *The Hunter and the Boa,* a classic example of the dilemma tale, reaches toward a similarly deeper significance in its interrogation of moral values and the nature of the good life. These features give such resonance to these tales that the stories can be seen to assume a reflective function.

As with Birago Diop, Dadié adheres closely to the narrative procedures of the folktale as conditioned by the aesthetics of oral presentation. His recourse to such devices as the interpolation of songs, with their standard refrains; repetition, sometimes serving to establish a leitmotif in the narrative development; and formulaic phrases, as well as to paratextual forms such as onomatopoeia and ideophone, reminds us that the active participation of the audience represents an integral element of the oral genre. This essential feature of the folktale is well illustrated in the conclusion to *The Hunter and the Boa* in which the narrator addresses the dilemma presented by the story directly to his audience. Dadié's personal style functions within this formal framework, sometimes even straining against it, as attested by aspects of his vocabulary. His introduction of terms foreign to the African environment—words such as "El Dorado" "barbed wire," "Castle"—calls attention to his location between two cultures. Moreover, his reference to "the fairy tale" in one of his stories not only provides evidence of his keen awareness of this factor of his personal situation, but also hints at a self-reflexive placing of the African genre in relation to the Western.

Despite his advanced age, Dadié is still active in African literary and cultural life in French-speaking Africa. It is a sign of his growing reputation beyond this area that his work has been brought to the attention of a wider English-speaking audience by the use of his poem *Dry Your Tears, Africa!* in the soundtrack of Steven Spielberg's film *Amistad*, the text having been set to music by composer/conductor John Williams.

Karen Hatch's introduction to her translation of *The Black Cloth* (1987) contains an excellent survey of Dadié's work in general and of the tales in particular. Marie S. Tollerson, *Mythology and Cosmology in the Narratives of Bernard Dadié and Birago Diop* (1984), is a scholarly work that can be consulted with profit. Bernth Lindfors, *Forms of Folklore in Africa* (1977), and Robert Pelton, *The Trickster in West Africa* (1980), are useful for general background to the tales.

The Mirror of Dearth[1]

This was a mirror never to look in; if you did, psst! all good things would fly away, disappear, evaporate. To attempt to look you had to be Spider: brave, courageous, and fearless like Spider; curious but stupid like Spider. Yes, once again it was Kacou Ananzè[2] who defied fate, but only after he had known dizzy spells and the blues, those attendant nightmares that hunger always drags behind her. This, after his stomach, bloated like a goat skin and as resonant as a well-warmed tom-tom, had permitted him to taste life's eternal joys, to contemplate the sullen pink of a sun tired of always chasing after an elusive moon; to swoon with joy because the evening breeze tickled the soles of his feet. That evening, the breeze had made herself so seductive, so captivating, had tickled the soles of his feet and blown on his neck and in his ears so much that he finally said to himself: "Why not look at myself in the mirror?"[3]

Ah! I can hear you cry out: "One really must be an idiot to go that far!" I

---

1. All three selections translated by Karen Hatch.   2. A dialectal variant of the standard Akan form, Kwaku Ananse, from which was derived the term "Nancy" stories, as they are known in the West Indies.
3. This scene serves not only to create suspense, but also to set the context for Spider's trial later in the story.

beg your pardon! And what about us? The rest of us who are always analyzing why we are happy, we who are always breaking open our playthings to see how they work—are we not in the same boat and just as curious? Besides, we must get it through our heads once and for all that one is not an idiot if he is called Kacou Ananzè. If he allows himself certain boldnesses, it is because he always has more than one trick in his head, more than one phrase on his tongue to help him out of a scrape. Ah no! You can't catch Kacou Ananzè like that! In order to get him, the elders would group themselves in ten, in twenty, even by the hundred . . . but despite the best of traps, he would always come out the victor. For when they thought they had him by the arm, they had hold of only one leg; and when they were convinced that they held him by the trunk of his body, there was only the trunk of a tree between their hands.[4]

Kacou Ananzè! He delights in difficult situations; he delights in obstacles that enhance his powers, unshackle his intelligence, and spark ingenuity.

There was a famine in the village then. For three successive years, the rains had failed to keep their rendezvous. No longer did even one dark cloud lose its way in the sky. Starved, did the clouds die on route? In anger, the sun broiled everything; and the wind, in order to woo her, never stopped carting sand.[5] The grasses no longer grew. Every day the dry earth would crackle, and then crackle some more. Not content to set fire to forests, the sun burned cottages. The trees, stripped bare, were pitiful to see. They resembled a woman whose head had been shaved, whose ornaments had been removed. The branches, the boughs, the twigs—one would have taken them for roots, tiny roots seeking to draw from the overheated air a nourishing sap they no longer found in the parched earth. The distress was general. One could not single out anyone in particular as the cause,[6] because this time everyone suffered from the famine. In the beginning, one had tried to pick a quarrel with the monkey, who claimed to be the king of kings. And to state his claim, he would wander around, saying to all who came along: "The kings sit in chairs made from the trunk of the tree that I climb on to take care of my needs. Who then is king?"

To retaliate, because the monkey was talking about him without naming him, man would go about telling each and everyone: "It's the monkey, the monkey who brings us all this misfortune. Because he always climbs trees to take care of his needs, this is what he has brought down on us."

But to go on then and pick a quarrel with the monkey in times like this, a time when the monkey was jumping around on the branches, imploring God. Really now! The man[7] could therefore find no one to listen to him. And once again, the animals made fun of him.[8]

Every day the famine became more brutal. Despite their elaborate ceremonies, the fetishists[9] were not the least bit successful in luring even the tiniest cloud to the country. Not even a wisp of fog. Famine gave her hand to death. She gave both hands, for so many died, so many.

Unable to escape the common plight, even Kacou Ananzè himself felt the

---

4. It is not usual to ascribe magical prowess to Spider, who relies for survival essentially on his powers of intelligence. It is of interest to note the parallel to Proteus in classical Western mythology. 5. Thus creating a dust bowl. 6. As with the plague in *Oedipus Rex*, natural calamities are invariably blamed in traditional societies on the malevolence or wrongdoing of individuals. 7. By extension, humanity. 8. In a reversal of situations that privileges animals over human beings. 9. Those who officiate at traditional ritual ceremonies.

pains of hunger: stomach cramps, dizzy spells, aches in his joints, buzzing in his ears, blurred vision. He felt weak all over. Every evening he wondered whether he would be able to get up the next day.

In order to keep going, he became a fisherman. He fished all the time. As to the art of fishing, no one could deny Ananzè's ability. He would throw out his line and pull in some sort of shellfish. But, as if to tease him, one of these thousand inhabitants of the water would nibble at the bait and drag the float to the bottom, only to let it go at the precise moment our fisherman was preparing to set the hook. Oh, those bandits, those bandits who refuse to let me take them! But he didn't get angry. What good would that have done? He had learned patience. The times demanded patience.

So Kacou Ananzè fished. Often he would spend the night on the bank, which was warm and free of mosquitoes. The water was receding onto its bed more and more each day, leaving everywhere a white sand, which, in the moonlight, seemed to be an immense shroud.[1] It was settling back onto its bed to fight against the dryness, against the sun that heated everything. They were all gone, all of them: the cascades, the eddies, the whirlpools, the waterfalls crowned with foam! The trees, pushed far back on the banks by the receding water, were, only a short time ago, magnificent as they leaned over the shimmering waves, leisurely gazing at their necklaces of liana vines, their curled headdresses, and their jewellike clusters of fruit. Let's not even mention the reeds and the mangroves. They all had disappeared: everything was dead, burned to cinders. Having divorced themselves from the forest, the waters flowed sadly, without song, without even the slightest whisper that one could hear at the feet of the trees when the water was still a friend of the forest.

The waters from the lagoons and rivers, all those blue, white, and black waters carrying along with them promenading duckweed,[2] water lilies, and tufts of reeds that turned round themselves, getting caught a moment here as if to give someone the news, leaving again suddenly, as if hurrying to reach the end of their voyage, all those waters with their flotillas[3] and twigs gathered up here and there along the way; those waters, in their struggle to survive, fought painfully against the thirsty, white-hot sun. And they would doze, barely flowing. You should see them, you should see those waters getting lower every day! Were they hungry too?

Kacou Ananzè continued to fish. Stubbornly he fished along the banks of the trickling water. The great rivers that once frightened men both by their length and depth, those rivers with their tumultuous courses, devouring men and domestic animals, all those rivers were now forced to beat a retreat, to double up on themselves in order to resist; and, in so doing, they had become mere threads, puddles. Sometimes a swallow would lose her way in this torrid country and drink of this water. Burned all the way to the core, she would rise up again with cries of despair and shoot straight into the sky as if to go and tell God: "People are dying! You must save them!"

In truth, the earth was losing people. Some wandered around with flat bellies, bellies so flat that one wondered if they still housed any insides.

And still, Kacou Ananzè fished. For a week now, the float had not budged.

---

1. An image in keeping with the grim atmosphere being depicted.   2. A kind of flowery plant that floats on water; a favorite food for ducks.   3. Like a fleet of boats gaily decked out for a ceremonial.

It had not even winked—as we say in our country—to warn Ananzè: "Look out! Take care! A victim is on the end of the line." The float was mute.

"Ah, now I understand! I wasn't sitting in my usual place."

He sat down in his usual place. The float still did not budge.

"Wait! I wasn't sitting like this. But how was I sitting?"

"I had my feet spread apart like this, my head to the right, and the sack on the left."

He took that position, but the float still did not budge.

"How stupid I am! I wasn't holding the line this way! There . . . that's how I was holding it when I caught those shellfish."

He held his line as he had before. And the float still did not budge.

"What kind of spell has been cast on me? Am I going to die of hunger too? Me? Kacou Ananzè? Die of hunger? Never! Has Death really taken a fancy to me? Has hunger really weighed on me?" He threw his line out again. And still the float did not budge. Kacou Ananzè began to feel dizzy; he saw things, and he heard voices. He chattered on alone so that he himself could then impose silence, as though other people were doing the talking. . . .

"What? What's happening? I ask you, is this true? The float! The float! Look at it! It's moving! It's going under! Do you see it?"

Wide-eyed, Kacou Ananzè stared at the float, which was making tiny waves around itself as it moved.

"Do I pull up now? How should I go about this to make sure that I bring up some little shellfish?"

The float disappeared into the water. Our fisherman got up, placed one leg here, one leg there, like that, held his breath, closed his eyes, bent over, and *fihô!*[4] brought in his line. Dangling at the end of it was a sheat-fish[5] no bigger than the little finger of a newborn baby. Kacou Ananzè threw himself on it, took it in his two hands, and began to dance. There it was, the little sheat-fish, no bigger than the little finger of a newborn baby, whispering to him and trembling all over: "Have mercy on me, Papa Ananzè."

"What did you say?"

"Put me back in the water, and you will be happy."

"I know that old song. I sing it often to certain people, to those suckers I take in."

"Believe me, you will be happy."

"Enough of this twaddle. I won't be happy until I feel you in my belly."

"Listen to me."

"Go ahead, speak."

"You must climb that silk-cotton tree[6] over there, all the way up to the twelfth branch."

"The shakiest one?"

"That very one. Let yourself fall down from there, and you will have all you desire."

"Why you're not stupid at all, are you, little sheat-fish no bigger than the little finger of a newborn baby? The very idea! Are you saying this to me? Me? The master of tricks? What Death couldn't do, you want to do? Never! Climb up that silk-cotton tree, let myself fall down and break my neck all

---

4. An ideophone, expressive of speed.   5. Also known as sheathfish, a freshwater fish, usually very large in size. Its small size here emphasizes its helplessness.   6. A massive tropical tree with large pods containing seeds surrounded by silks that yield the fiber kapok.

because I took the advice of a child like you? Come on now, are you discounting my age and intelligence? All the experience I've had?"

"Trust me."

The voice was so imploring, the tone so frank, that Kacou Ananzè attempted the venture. In two leaps he was at the foot of the silk-cotton tree; he climbed up. One would have said that thousands of arms were pushing him, pulling him, toward the twelfth branch. Despite the enormous thorns, the trunk seemed to him smooth, even soft. Left on the bank white with light, the little sheat-fish nodded to him. And he was no longer little, but big, very big.

Ananzè closed his eyes and *floup*, jumped, but in such a way that his head wouldn't go first. A broken neck, and it'd death; a broken arm or leg, and there's still life. Playing the skiff[7] rocked by the waves, he had scarcely left the twelfth branch when he found himself in the most marvelous and opulent city in the world, the busiest trading center on earth. Men were coming and going, buying, exchanging, negotiating, bartering, speculating, transporting, unloading, delivering, and all without the least bristle of argument and discussion that ignores courtesy, the first rule in this fairy-tale land. And there were palaces and colored lights everywhere, giving the city a truly magical look by day as well as by night. No matter where you looked the view was forever changing. As for prosperity, I need hardly tell you about it. The bright and happy faces of the citizens alone would tell you what an Eldorado this was. Each one of them was a walking picture of health. It was a fabulous city, not only in size and activity, but also in population. Kacou Ananzè was astonished, and he whispered to himself: "That little sheat-fish didn't trick me after all."

He had fallen in a field where just about everything grew. And he ate and ate. And he grew fat. His cheeks were like that! with creases and rolls of fat all over. In the midst of this plenty, he lost all notion of time.

Someone surprised him in his quiet retreat one day, and he found himself being conducted to the queen of this prodigious city. Kacou Ananzè behaved himself so well that he became prime minister of the kingdom.

The queen had said to him, however: "You may do anything in my kingdom, anything in my palaces, but what you must never do is look at yourself in that mirror over there."

"Very well," replied Kacou Ananzè.

His misfortunes began that day. "In that day they have given me everything, why shouldn't I look at myself in that mirror? This must be a magical mirror. Ah! this queen wants to see who's the smartest. What kind of behavior is that?"

And the mirror was over there, just like all the other mirrors.

"Well, if it's so plain to look at, it must mean that its powers are great."

The evening breeze never stopped tickling the soles of his feet, or blowing on his neck and in his ears. She caressed his whiskers and eyebrows. She so tickled the soles of his feet that . . . blew on his neck and in his ears so much that . . . Kacou Ananzè said to himself: "Why not look at myself in the mirror?"[8]

And so he did. But he immediately found himself once again at the edge of the river with the burning banks, the line in his hand, the float immobile.

---

7. A small boat.   8. This recapitulation of the initial theme takes us to the core of the story.

And he was hungry! so hungry! He threw out his line, and threw it out again. The float went under. Ananzè brought in the line. Hanging from the hook was a tiny sheat-fish no bigger than the little finger of a newborn baby. Our fisherman was very happy and carefully unhooked him. The sheat-fish said nothing.

"Well! Well! Here's my friend the sheat-fish. How are you?"

". . ."

"Don't you recognize me? Ah! yes, that's it . . . you like to do good in secret. . . . Just the same, I'll prove to you that you know me."

". . ."

"But it's me, Spider, Kacou Ananzè . . . Spider, from the other day! Don't you remember our last meeting? It was a morning like this one. . . . I had taken you out of the river, and you said to me. . . . How did you say it? Ah! . . . yes . . . 'Have mercy on me. . . . Trust me. . . . You will be happy. . . . Listen, you will have the good fortune. . . .'"

". . ."

"Must I broil you?"

"If you want."

"Come on now, what do you take me for? Would I broil my friend? That, I would never do! Do you want me to put you back in the water?"

"If you want to!"

"Are you going to tell me to climb up on the twelfth branch of that silk-cotton tree again? The last time, at your urging, I scrambled up to that twelfth branch, and from there, *floup!* I jumped. . . . Oh! how frightened I was at the beginning . . . but you, there on the bank, you nodded at me, you encouraged me in this feat. . . . Do you want us to start all over again?"

"If you want!"

"If I want! But that is what I want. Wait! Look, I'm going to climb up. I'm climbing."

It was truly painful climbing too. The huge thorns were like barbed wire and thwarted him at every step. Kacou Ananzè bled. Nevertheless, he reached the twelfth branch and played, once again, the skiff balanced by the swells. But feeling dizzy, Kacou Ananzè went crashing to the ground.

Fortunately, he did not die; his adventures would have ended, and we men would have little to tell each other during the evening hours. . . .

And like all lies,[9] it is through you that mine will be thrown out to sea, to roam the world over. . . .

The Black Cloth

Once upon a time there was a young girl who had lost her mother. She had lost her on the very day she came into the world.

Labor had lasted for a week. Several older women had kept running over. But the labor pains persisted.

The first cry of the baby girl coincided with the last sigh of the mother.[1]

The husband gave his wife a splendid funeral. Time passed, and the hus-

---

9. A formula that stresses the moral truth of the story, despite its imaginary basis.   1. The coincidence of the two events stresses the utter solitude of the heroine at very moment that she comes into the world.

band remarried. Little Aïwa's calvary[2] began on that day. There were no deprivations or insults that she did not suffer; no hard labor that she did not do! And yet she would smile all the time. Her smile irritated the stepmother who kept harassing her with snide remarks.

Little Aïwa was beautiful, truly beautiful, more beautiful than all the other girls in the village. And this too irritated the stepmother, who envied this glorious, captivating beauty.

The more she increased the insults, the humiliations, the forced labors, and the deprivations, the more Aïwa smiled, the more beautiful she became, the more she sang—and this little orphan girl sang wonderfully. But she was beaten because of her good humor, beaten because she was the first to rise and the last to go to bed. She would awaken before the roosters and go to bed only after the dogs themselves had gone to sleep.[3]

The stepmother no longer knew just what to do to get the better of this young girl. She looked to find a way: in the morning when she awakened, at noon when she ate, in the evening when she dozed. And these thoughts hurled beastlike sparks from her eyes. She searched for a way to end the young girl's smiling, to stop her singing, to dull her radiant beauty.

She searched for a way with such perseverance and such eagerness that, one morning, as she was leaving the hut, she said to the little orphan girl: "Wait up! go and wash this black cloth. Go wherever you like, but wash it so that it turns as white as chalk."

Aïwa picked up the black cloth that the stepmother had thrown at her feet and smiled. For her, the smile took the place of complaining, of moaning and crying, of sobbing.

And this magnificent smile which charmed everyone for miles around put fire in the heart of the stepmother. It sowed coals in the heart of the stepmother. And with all her claws showing, she fell on the little orphan girl who kept smiling.

Finally, Aïwa grabbed the piece of black linen and left. After having walked for a moon,[4] she arrived at the edge of a stream. She immersed the cloth in the water. It was not the least bit wet. And the water flowed along calmly, little fish and water lilies playing on its bed. On the banks, the frogs swelled their voices as if to frighten the little orphan girl who smiled. Aïwa once again immersed the cloth in the water, but the water refused to dampen it. She then resumed her journey, singing:

> "Mother, if you could see me on the road,
>   Aïwa-o! Aïwa![5]
> On the road that leads to the river,
>   Aïwa-o! Aïwa!
> The black cloth must become white,
> And the stream refuses to dampen it.
>   Aïwa-o! Aïwa!
> The water slips by like the day,
> The water slips by like happiness,
> O Mother, if you could see me on the road,
>   Aïwa-o! Aïwa!"

---

2. A long experience of suffering; derived from Calvary, the hilltop where Jesus Christ was crucified. 3. That is, at dawn, since the dogs serve as guards during the night. 4. The natural cycle of twenty-eight days, from one full moon to another—in other words, a month. 5. Sung in a tone of lament, the line would be taken up by the audience as a refrain.

She kept going. She walked for six more moons. Lying across the road in front of her was a huge silk-cotton tree; and in a hollow of the trunk there was some water, completely yellow but very clear water, water that slept beneath the breeze; and all around this water enormous ants with huge pincers stood guard. And these ants were talking to each other. And they were going and coming and crossing in front of each other, dispensing orders. Perched atop the main branch, which pointed a pale, dead finger toward the sky, was a huge vulture, whose wings obscured the sun for leagues and leagues. Its eyes threw out flames, like flashes of lightning; and its talons, like powerful aerial roots, dragged the ground. And it had one of those horrible beaks![6]

The little orphan girl immersed her black linen in this yellow and limpid water, but the water refused to dampen it.

"Mother, if you could see me on the road,
    Aïwa-o! Aïwa!
The road to the spring that will dampen the black cloth
    Aïwa-o! Aïwa!
The black cloth which the water from the silk-cotton tree refuses to
    dampen
    Aïwa-o! Aïwa!"

And she continued on her way, smiling always.

She walked for moons and moons, for so many moons that no one remembers the exact number any longer. She walked by day and by night, never stopping to rest, nourishing herself on fruits gathered alongside the road, drinking the dew deposited on the leaves.

She reached a village of chimpanzees and told them her story. The chimpanzees thumped their chests with their two hands, as a sign of indignation, but after a while they gave her permission to wash the black cloth in the spring that flowed through the village. But even the water from this spring—it too—refused to dampen the black cloth.

So the little orphan girl resumed her journey. She was now in a truly strange place. The road before her opened up only to close again behind her. Everything talked:[7] the trees, the birds, the insects, the earth, both the dead leaves and the dry leaves, the liana vines, and the fruit. And yet, there was no trace of a human being. She was knocked about and hollered at, little Aïwa was, as she walked and walked, only to realize that she had not budged since she had started walking. And then, all of a sudden, as if pushed along by some wonderful power, she leaped over distance upon distance, and found herself plunging still deeper into the forest where an agonizing silence reigned.

There was a clearing in front of her and, at the foot of a banana tree, a spring rose up out of the earth. She knelt down, smiling. The water quivered. And it was so clear that it reflected the sky, the clouds, and the trees.

Aïwa took some of this water and threw it onto the black cloth. The cloth became wet. Kneeling at the edge of the spring, she spent two moons washing the cloth, but it still remained black. She would look at her hands that were covered with blisters and then go back to work again.

6. An atmosphere of dread that lends dramatic force to the test of Aïwa's endurance.   7. In both a literal and a symbolic sense.

"Mother, come and see me!
    Aïwa-o! Aïwa!
Come and see me at the edge of the spring,
    Aïwa-o! Aïwa!
The black cloth must become as white as chalk,
    Aïwa-o! Aïwa!
Come and see my hands, come and see your daughter!
    Aïwa-o! Aïwa!

She had scarcely finished singing when there stood her mother holding a white cloth, a cloth whiter than chalk. She took the black cloth and, without saying a word, melted into the air.

When the stepmother saw the white cloth, she was stupefied; her eyes grew big. She shook, not from anger this time, but from fear; for she recognized one of the white cloths that was used to bury her husband's first wife.

But Aïwa just smiled. She always smiled.

And she is still smiling the smile that one finds time and again on the lips of young girls.

The Hunter and the Boa[1]

A very poor hunter had set his traps along the banks of a river.

None of the traps anywhere had caught even the tiniest animal. Not even a palm-rat, hurrying to scramble up a palm tree to get at the finely ripened fruit. And not even a single scatter-brained partridge who, always traveling with a group, frisked about in the clearings and undergrowth!

The hunter was, indeed, a very poor man. Therefore, he had gathered up all of his traps and had set them along the banks of the river; for even those that he had placed in trees had never caught a single bird. The birds would fly over in squadrons to the nearby trees, and perch on the bent wood of the traps to give their concert. And the traps would remain that way, as they listened to the music of the birds. The traps had, in fact, listened to the music for so long now that they lost all interest in catching anything anymore. And so, they always remained bent. Did they perhaps understand all that whispering, and wailing, and shrieking of the grief-stricken bush as it rebelled against the hunter? Against man?

The hunter then went to set his traps in the savanna. They caught nothing. He took them into the forest. The traps remained bent. He took them into the newly burned fields;[2] but the traps persisted in catching nothing. That is why he took them to the banks of the river, for it was there that all the animals came to drink. But the traps still caught nothing. The man was wondering where next to go when, one morning, he discovered that he had snared a boa. With spear raised, he was just about ready to finish it off when the boa said to him: "Don't kill me, Hunter."

---

1. The boa is a huge snake that swallows its victim whole.   2. In many parts of Africa, peasants set little fires to farmlands during the dry season to facilitate sowing. The process also helps to fertilize the land during the rainy season.

"Why shouldn't I kill you? Do you let us go free?"

"Hunter, have I ever done wrong to anyone in your family?"

"Well what about all those men the boas keep killing?"

"Release me, Hunter. I know that you're very, very poor. For months now your traps have caught nothing. If you want to be rich, the richest man in the whole world, then unhook me."

The hunter set down his spear. He hesitated a bit. A thousand ideas passed and repassed through his head, like whirlwinds in a hurricane. "If this boa were killed, skinned, cut up, and dried, why, it would mean a fortune! If I listen to his sugary proposals, unhook him, and let him escape, what part would he play in the bargain? And what if he turned on me after I let him go? A boa is a snake. And you must always watch out for snakes." He raised his spear once more and prepared to strike.

"No, don't kill me, Hunter. Release me, and you'll be the richest man in the world."

The waters flowed by. Along the banks and in among the mangrove trees, they told a thousand stories to the immovable land, a land that would never travel to another region, but one that would always be crouching there, over the water, admiring her mop of hair composed of trees and weeds that were crawling with all the lice in the world, swarming with every vermin in creation. Stirring loose thousands of twigs along the banks, the waters recounted their adventures to an attentive land, a land fascinated by the exciting news that the indiscreet and forever-gossiping waters had picked up while listening to the conversation between the hunter and the boa just so they could repeat it farther on, as they made their long journey. The small fry[3] pretended to quarrel over a piece of fruit, or an insect, and gave each other quick flicks with their tails. And one by one, the little waves made their way to the banks to deposit their cargo of twigs and to push their earlier loads farther up onto the land.

"You have your destiny right in your own two hands, Hunter. Whether you'll be rich or poor, happy or miserable, depends on you. Go ahead and choose."

"If I release you, will you harm me?"

"Since when have the bush animals behaved like you?"[4]

"It's just that. . . ."

"We animals attack straight out, face to face, and we're even more direct when it comes to rewarding our benefactors. We've never envied their good fortune. And we've never been jealous of the positions they may have won as a result. On the contrary, the happier they are, the prouder we are. We like to show our good-heartedness. . . ."

The rope was pulled so tightly around his throat that the boa's eyes grew red, and redder still, as the blood rushed into them; they were so red, in fact, that the hunter could no longer stare into them.

"Go ahead and choose, Hunter. Today your fate lies in your own two hands. You can be rich or poor, wretched or powerful."

The hunter set down his spear and released the boa, who said to him: "Follow me!"

And the man followed him into the forest. They traveled through the forest

---

3. The little fishes.   4. That is, like human beings, judged here to be faithless

of boas, and through the forest of genies, for there are other forest besides man's; and in those forests there were mountains, and rivers, and species quite different from those found in man's forest. And an undisturbed peace reigned throughout these regions. The flies when they swarmed made such beautiful music! And the breeze sang such charming melodies as it brushed against the leaves. Even the air that one breathed was so invigorating there. And a moss that was softer than cotton was to be found everywhere. . . .

They finally reached the boa's village. How many days, or moons, or years did the hunter remain there? He never could say. For when you spend a thousand years in that country, you think that you have only spent one! The fact remains, however, that when he left, the boa handed him two little gourds[5] and said: "Return home. As soon as you arrive, throw this gourd to the ground. Keep the other one, for thanks to it, you'll be able to understand the languages of all those who live on the earth."

The happy man took his leave, eager to have charge of his own fortune. He carefully pressed the two gourds to his breast, which was beating with joy. He was so afraid that the boa might change his mind and come back to get the gourds that he almost ran.

As soon as he arrived home, even before he put down his spear, he threw the first gourd to the ground. And what do you think he saw? You can imagine what. A castle just like those he had seen in the land of the genies. And all the wealth of the entire world was there inside.

Our hunter lived happily now. And sometimes he would whisper to himself: "Poverty can force you to make such big mistakes! If I had listened to my anxieties and hunger pains, and killed the boa, would I now have all these blessings?"

The hunter had a dog, and this dog was friends with another dog, one that was mangy[6] and without a master.

One noonday, right at mealtime, the mangy dog was sitting up there on his bottom, a bone between his paws, when he said to his friend: "Two moons from now we'll have a famine. Whoever wants to get rich should listen to me."

"And who's going to listen to you, my friend? You know very well that no one can understand our language. Would you like me to go into business?"

"If your master by chance. . . ."

"No, he doesn't understand."

"Be this as it may, if I had a master, I'd tell him to profit from the famine so that he could get rich."

"Get rich on another's misery?"

"But men do that anyway. It's the only way they know."

"Come on now!"

"But yes, I tell you they do!"

"You only make such remarks because you don't have a master."

"Me, with a master? What for? I don't need a guardian: I have myself."

"I have a good master who's been very generous ever since he returned from the boa's village."

"Even a good master is a crotchety master. You know that. I prefer the bush and freedom. I even prefer my mange."

5. Fruits of a vine, shaped like a pot and hollow. They come in all sizes and are commonly used as containers.   6. Miserable; affected by the mange—a skin inflammation, caused by a parasitic mite, that makes animals, especially dogs, lose the hair.

Profiting from the conversation that he had overheard, the hunter bought and stockpiled an entire year's harvest. The famine came. The hunter resold his provisions to everyone at a higher price and, in so doing, became even richer.

The mangy dog came back once more and said to his friend: "Did you see what your master did?"

"What did he do?"

"Didn't you see the prices he charged for his provisions? I keep telling you that in the world of men the misery of one makes the fortune of another. And one thing more. In a month's time, all the young girls of the village will die. The only ones who'll survive are those who move to the other side of the river."

"Survive what?"

"Hum!"

"You can tell me, my friend. We'll keep it to ourselves."

"The plague."

Once again the hunter overheard the conversation, and after he had arranged for a beautiful house to be built on the other side of the river, he moved his family there.

The plague set in with a vengeance and swept away all the young girls of the village.

After the devastation, the hunter moved his family back, and since he was the only one who had young girls, he became the father-in-law of all the young men of the village. And he became even more powerful.[7]

The mangy dog went back to his friend and said: "A fire will destroy the village. Your master's entire fortune will be the victim of its flames."

A fire did break out; it was terrible and pitiless. Only the aging hunter was able to save his goods, for he had heard the mangy dog's words.

"Your master understands our language."

"Men don't understand animals."

"Then you must be the one who tells him what I say each time I come."

"Why do you think I'm the one who tells him what you say? I've got a fine master; he's far better than any other man."

"Your master has managed to escape every hardship. That's good. But in a week's time there'll be a flood, a flood without precedent in this country. It'll be impossible to calculate the damage."

The hunter once more took the necessary precautions and suffered nothing from the calamity.

Both dogs began to worry. That man could understand their language, for sure!

Ten years went by. The village filled with people once more, and resumed its old ways. Memories of past hardships became dim and distant. Whenever someone mentioned them, a few thought they were talking about things that happened centuries ago. Death continued to claim a man here, a woman there. Let's not even mention the children. Death is a glutton, a permanent calamity. She lives in every hut, waits at every turn in the road, at every intersection, and hounds all men. She walks with the young girls who go to the springs for water; she follows the women who go to the fields in search of food; she accompanies the fisherman when he throws his nets, the hunter

---

7. All the young men in the village are his sons-in-law and by custom have to work for him.

when he scours the bush, the traveler. . . . She stays awake while the rest of the village sleeps. And she is still awake the next day.

Twenty years had passed since the day the hunter had released the boa.

One morning, the same mangy dog, now mangier than ever, went up to his friend and said: "Your master's going to die."

"What's that you say?"

"I'm saying that on this very day, precisely when the trees gather their shadows up under them, your master will die."

"And how can he be saved?"

"Only by returning the second gourd to the boa. But if he returns that gourd, misery will stalk him once more; he'll have to take up his spear and visit his traps again. He'll be even poorer than he was before. But he'll live for a long time yet. He must choose what he wants to do."

The man overheard the conversation. He was going to die. He watched the sun climb the sky and creep up to the tree tops; he watched it dwarf the shadows and move them over; he watched it pile them up little by little underneath the trees, and he wanted to imprison that sun. He went from the gourd to his wealth: to his gold, his diamonds, his rubies, all radiating dazzling streaks of light. In the rooms there, they seemed like mounds of glowing embers fanned by the wind. And it was then that he really became conscious of how well-off he was. And the higher the sun climbed, the more his wealth dug deep into his heart, clung there, and ingrained itself.

He ran to the gourd grabbed it, but put it down again.

His cheerful wives[8] were talking and laughing in the courtyard. The children were playing. He listened to their gay voices and his heart was moved.

The sun kept climbing. Glittering fluffs of kapock scattered their seeds and their featherlike flakes in the wind and were carried off. The flowers smelled sweet. Bees were humming in the blossoming trees; butterflies were darting about and birds were chirping. June bugs[9] perched there for a moment, then left.

As if to make fun of the hunter, the mangy dog kept saying over and over: "What's wrong with your master? Does he know that he's going to die?"

" . . . "

"He must know, for ever since I mentioned to you that he was going to die, he's totally changed his ways. We'll see if he has the courage to abandon his wealth and become poor again, if he chooses to scour the bush once more, with the spear on his shoulder. Let's make a bet."

"Why?"

"I, for one, contend that he won't have the courage to abandon his wealth. That he won't want to live without it. But life is so sweet. . . . Just look at the flowers, listen to their music, smell them. Could you give up life as easily as that? Misery lasts only a moment; we must remember that happiness is what endures: it's people living together in harmony, it's a sense of well-being that's felt everywhere. . . . Your master sees only his own little happiness. He thinks that his fortune taught him how to appreciate life. Look at him there, hovering over his wealth. The poor man."

And they both laughed, as the mangy dog kept on teasing and goading.[1]

---

8. Use of the plural reflects the practice of polygamy.   9. Scarab beetles.   1. The mangy dog is now aware that the hunter understands animal language.

The sun climbed higher; the shadows huddled beneath the trees; it was just about noontime, the fatal hour. The hunter kept hesitating; he paced back and forth, from the gourd to his wealth, from his wealth to the gourd. He still hesitated, and the sun kept climbing. It was almost noon.

If you were in his place, what would you do?

JUAN RULFO
1918–1986

Juan Rulfo's *Pedro Páramo* is a landmark novel in the modern literature of the Americas. Using a spare, everyday vocabulary and the colloquial speech of rural Mexico, Rulfo depicted the most intimate memories of the doomed townspeople of Comala in a style that would become known as magical realism. The story takes place during a crucial period in Mexican history: the years around the Revolution of 1910, with its struggles between rich and poor, clergy and laity, and large landowners and dispossessed Indians. The powerful realism of the novel's personal dramas activates a progressively larger framework, whether it be an allegory of Mexico's modern political history, or a mythic vision of individual lives taking part in an eternal struggle between life and death or good and evil. In communicating this picture of a society in turmoil, Rulfo used, for the first time in Latin American literature, the poetic prose and narrative techniques of twentieth-century modernism. For the novelist Carlos Fuentes, he represents an influential break with previous literary tradition comparable to that of William Faulkner. Gabriel García Márquez, who could recite *Pedro Páramo* from memory, compared Rulfo's taut scenes to the dramas of an earlier writer: for him, these pages are "just as lasting as those that we know by Sophocles."

Juan Rulfo was born on May 16, 1918, in a small town in Sayula, in the Mexican state of Jalisco, a rural region whose landscape and speech patterns he would reproduce in later fiction. His parents, Juan Nepomuceno Pérez and María Vizcaníno Arias, moved next year with their son to San Gabriel, a small but prosperous town in Jalisco. He entered elementary school there in 1924 but was sent with his brothers to finish primary school in Guadalajara in 1927. Rulfo did not have a peaceful childhood: his father was murdered in 1925, and civil war came to San Gabriel in 1926 in the form of the Cristero Revolt, a rebellion of conservative Catholics against the national government. Young Juan witnessed scenes of death and horror over the next two years, in San Gabriel and in Guadalajara, as the government suppressed the revolt. At the same time, he read widely in foreign novels that had been left in his grandmother's house for safekeeping by a local priest whose parish house was about to be turned into a barracks; he was particularly impressed by Knut Hamsun's *Hunger*.

After his mother's death in 1927, Rulfo's grandmother took custody of the children. He was sent as a boarder to the Luis Silva school for orphans in Guadalajara, where he finished his secondary education and registered at Guadalajara University in 1933. A student strike closed the institution, however, and Rulfo went in 1934 to live with an uncle in Mexico City, where he began to study law at National University. A year later, he was obliged to terminate his studies and take a job in the Office of Immigration, where, after hours, he began work on a novel, *Son of Affliction*. The manuscript was never published, however; Rulfo threw it away, explaining later that it was "a rather conventional novel, very highstrung, in which I tried to express certain solitary feelings." When World War II began in 1939, the Office of Immigration gave him the task of processing crew members from German and Italian ships that had been impounded by the Allies.

After the unsatisfactory attempt at a novel, Rulfo turned to writing short stories with the encouragement of a co-worker in Immigration, Efrén Hernéndez, who was already an established short-story writer. Hernéandez also introduced him to the editors of the periodical *America*, and Rulfo not only became part of its editorial board but co-founded, with two colleagues, another literary review, *Pan*. In 1945, he published one story in *America* and two others in *Pan*: the latter, *Macario* and *They Gave Us the Land,* became the first two stories in *The Burning Plain* (1953) and introduced themes that would recur throughout his work.

They Gave Us The Land narrates the discovery, by four peasants who have been awarded lots as part of national land reform, that the land allotted to them is not fertile soil by the river but a "crust of rocky ground" in an arid, scorching plain. Implicit in the background is the historical struggle over land in Mexico, dating to the system of property division under Spanish colonialism, when large landowners monopolized water to irrigate their estates and the Indian farmers (a rapidly diminishing population) struggled to survive on barren soil. Revolutions in 1810, 1855, and 1910 had attempted to redistribute land but were suppressed or frustrated. In 1921, the government of Álvaro Obregón and his successors began a concerted attempt at land reform that met with strong opposition from landowners, the military, foreign investors, and the clergy; several revolts ensued and were brutally crushed. Growing up in rural Jalisco, Rulfo had witnessed these struggles and the plight of the farmers at firsthand. He was also living in Mexico City in 1940, when a new government ended the social revolution and emphasized industrial growth and foreign investment over land reform and the situation of the Indians. Contemporary Mexico continues to struggle with the same social issues, as witnessed by the 1994 rebellion of the Indian population in Chiapas.

Rulfo does not emphasize historical issues for themselves, as his predecessors, novelists of the Mexican Revolution such as Mariano Azuela or Martín Guzmán, tend to do. Instead, he focuses on individual men and women as they cope with circumstances and lets the reader deduce the social context from its impact on their lives. In *They Gave Us the Land,* Rulfo re-creates his characters' hopelessness and confusion, and the barrenness of the land through which they walk, in a spare and objective style whose poetic effect derives from the characters' own angle of vision. The story's narrator, for example, comments that you see a buzzard occasionally, "flying fast, trying to get away as soon as possible from this hard white earth, where nothing moves and where you walk as if losing ground." Rulfo is not an "engaged" writer like his immediate predecessors (or like Pablo Neruda, in this volume), but his sympathy for the dispossessed is evident.

Rulfo's reputation as a fine short-story writer grew throughout the 1940s but did not produce much income. He married in 1947 and had four children, supporting himself and his family with office jobs that had nothing to do with literature. Between 1947 and 1954, he was a tire salesman with the Mexican branch of B. F. Goodrich Rubber Company. A series of grants between 1952 and 1954 gave him time to work on his writing, and he completed *The Burning Plain* (1953) and the manuscript of *Pedro Páramo* (1955). Diverse clerical positions followed, most of them in governmental offices or institutes, and in 1962 he became director of the editorial department at the National Institute for Indigenous Studies, a position he held until his death in 1986. He wrote a short novel, *The Golden Cockerel,* and a number of film and television scripts (collected in 1980 as *The Golden Cockerel and Other Texts for Cinema*). Film adaptations were made of various works: two short stories, *The Golden Cockerel* (1964) and *Pedro Páramo*, which was filmed both in 1966 and in 1976. Rulfo was also a fine photographer, and his photographs of Mexico's land and people were published not only as part of a national homage to him in 1980 (*Inframundo*), but separately after his death. His works were widely translated, and he advised young writers as co-director of the Mexican Writer's Center and was awarded the Mexican National Prize for Letters in 1970. A decade later, he was elected a member of Mexican Academy of Letters, and the Spanish government presented him with its Principe de Asturias award in 1983. Despite these various honors, Rulfo actually published relatively little over his lifetime. A perfectionist, he worked for many years on a new novel, *La Cordillera*, writing and revising, but he finally abandoned it and responded to a question by saying, "I am not a professional writer . . . I write when I feel like it." His international reputation stems from the extraordinary achievement of a few years: *The Burning Plain* and *Pedro Páramo*, which introduced a new narrative style that would become widely known under the name of magical realism. Rulfo died in Mexico City of a heart attack on January 7, 1986.

Pedro Páramo is both a novel of violence, murder, anguish, guilt, and frustrated love and a dreamlike narrative told through several perspectives—all of which belong to the dead. It is a story of return: Juan Preciado, the son of Pedro Páramo and his abandoned wife Dolores, returns to the town of Comala after his mother's death in order to find his father. Trudging along the rural roads, he keeps hearing his mother's voice describing the green and fertile countryside she loved, but when he arrives in Comala he discovers empty streets and a dusty wasteland under the blazing sun. Abundio, one of Pedro Páramo's many illegitimate sons, has guided him to the village while expressing his own hatred for the father he calls "living bile"; it is the same Abundio who, despairing over the death of his wife, kills Pedro Páramo at the end of the novel. "End," however, is a misleading word, for the reader finds halfway through that all the characters are dead (including Juan Preciado), that everything has already happened, and that the inhabitants of the town are living in a kind of purgatory that reenacts scenes from their former lives. Distinctions between life and death, or past and present, are blurred; characters know they are dead, but they relive crucial moment from their past—moments that usually involve the evil influence of the regional boss or *cacique*, Pedro Páramo. Pedro Páramo himself appears in this purgatory, either dramatized as the vicious exploiter of his neighbors for personal gain or in his own complex memories: his father's murder, his revenge, the killings and manipulations that made him rich and feared, his love for Susana San Juan, and his revenge on the town of Comala after she dies, insane, without ever having loved him.

Although dates are not mentioned, events in the story span a period from about 1880 (the recalled childhood of Pedro Páramo and Susana San Juan), through the Mexican Revolution (1910), to the Cristero Revolt in 1926, when Pedro Páramo dies. The individual tragedies that make up this bleak tale give a personal dimension to broader themes of social history: the oppression of the Indians by rich landowners and the devastation of the countryside during war. As *cacique*, Pedro Páramo is a local microcosm of the Latin American dictator, a subject so prevalent in modern Latin American novels that it has its own subgenre, "the novel of dictators." All the characters have some relation to him, and his evil influence permeates their lives: indeed, *Páramo* means *wasteland* in Spanish. Their struggles take on mythic qualities that are reinforced by biblical allusions to damnation and purgatory, and they convey, throughout, a sense of universal human anguish dominated by solitude, silence, and death.

The novel is composed of short juxtaposed scenes that create a narrative kaleidoscope, revealing little by little a pattern of interrelated personal histories. There is Miguel Páramo, Pedro's violent son, who kills and rapes with impunity until he is thrown from his horse and dies; Dorotea, obsessed with her imaginary baby, who provides Miguel with girls and is denied absolution by Father Rentería; Toribio Aldrete, murdered when he refuses to give his lands to Pedro Páramo; Fulgor Sedano, Pedro Páramo's foreman, who arranges Pedro Páramo's evil deeds and is killed by revolutionaries; Donis and his sister, an incestuous couple condemned by the bishop; Damasio "El Tilcuate," who conducts Pedro Páramo's infiltration and manipulation of revolutionary forces; Gerardo Trujillo, the corrupt lawyer who works for Pedro

Páramo but is disappointed at the end; Father Rentería, the guilt-stricken local priest who does the will of Pedro Páramo, is refused absolution by a neighboring priest and ends up joining the revolutionaries; and, above all, Susana San Juan, Pedro Páramo's deranged second wife, exploited and abused as a child, whose sensual memories of her deliriously happy short marriage to Florencio consume her after his death. At one point, Rulfo said that Susana was the central personage of the novel, and certainly Pedro Páramo's actions throughout are determined by his love for her. Yet the author also described the central personage as the village and explained that he conceived *Pedro Páramo* as a way to bring a dead town back to life after seeing his home town of San Gabriel in decay. Most likely, it is impossible and unnecessary to separate the different aspects: the very structure of the novel denies a single focus by changing narrative perspectives and juxtaposing fragments of individual stories whose inter-relationships emerge in the course of reading.

Pedro Páramo is known for its poetic prose and for introducing into Latin American literature modernist techniques such as the ruptured narrative, flashbacks, interior monologue, and rapidly shifting points of view. These shifts are not signaled by the narrative itself, but are indicated by blank spaces between sections. Rulfo referred to *Pedro Páramo* as a "structure made of silences, of hanging threads, of cut scenes, where everything occurs in a simultaneous time which is a not-time." For a while, it gives the appearance of a realistic novel, as Juan Preciado trudges along the dusty road in Abundio's company, but that realism starts to disintegrate when he encounters the ghostlike houses and inhabitants of Comala and enters the home of Eduviges Dyada. Suddenly, it is no longer Juan Preciado who speaks, and the scene shifts unannounced to Pedro Páramo's childhood memories of the privy and his daydreams about Susana San Juan. A few pages later, it shifts—abruptly and without explana-tion—to the middle of a conversation between Juan Preciado and his hostess: "Oh yes. I was nearly your mother." The passages do not have a formal beginning and end, nor are the monologuists quickly identified, as if to preserve the impression of alter-nating between different minds and moments of existence.

In this "no-time" distinctions between life and death are not clear. Eduviges seems alive when she greets Juan Preciado and gives him a room (a dead man's room) upon his arrival in Comala, but a later scene shows that she had committed suicide. Miguel Páramo keeps riding his horse and does not appear to know that he is dead. Juan Preciado's confusion and anxious interrogations ("Are you alive, Damiana?" and later, "Are you dead?") coexist with contradictory references to the life or death of different characters and prepare the reader's discovery, on page 2655, that Juan Preciado him-self is dead and is buried in the same grave as Dorotea. It soon becomes clear that everything reported up to then has been a series of interlocking memories, evoked, according to tradition, when rain wets the ground and awakens the dead in their graves. As the story unfolds, piece by piece, these memories cluster around a few crucial identities—Pedro Páramo, Susana San Juan, and Father Rentería, depicting thestagnant half-life of Comala and the tragic worldview for which Rulfo is known.

Luis Léal, *Juan Rulfo* (1983), is a useful biography and discussion of works up to 1982; it is the only book-length study in English. José Carlos González Boixo analyzes *Pedro Páramo* as part of a valuable essay on the figure of the local dictator, or *cacique,* "The Underlying Currents of 'Caciquismo' in the Narratives of Juan Rulfo," in *Struc-tures of Power: Essays on Twentieth-Century Spanish-American Fiction* (1996), edited by Peter Standish and Terry J. Peavler. A substantial interview with Rulfo appears in *Into the Mainstream: Conversations with Latin-American Writers* (1967). Wilma Else Detjens, *Home As Creation* (1993), examines the influence of early experience on the work of Rulfo, Gabriel García Márquez, and Augustin Yáñnez. *Inframundo: The Mex-ico of Juan Rulfo* (1983), is a striking book of Rulfo's photographs of Mexico that also contains tributes by a number of writers and pages by Rulfo on writing *Pedro Páramo.* Also useful is George D. Schade's introduction to his translation of *The Burning Plain and Other Stories* (1967).

PRONOUNCING GLOSSARY

The following list uses common English syllables and stress accents to provide rough equivalents of selected words whose pronunciation may be unfamiliar to the general reader.

Abundio Martínez: *ah-boon'-dee-oh mar-tee'-nez*

Bartolomé San Juan: *bar-tol-oh-may' san hwan*

Comala: *coh-mah'-lah*

Damiana Cisneros: *dah-mee-ah'-nah cees-nehr-os'*

Doña Eduviges Dyada: *dohn'-yah ay-doo-vee-hes dee-yah'-da*

Doña Inés: *dohn'-yah ee-nes'*

Don Fulgor Sedano: *don fool-gohr' say-dah'-noh*

El Tilcuate (Damasio): *el teel-kwah'-tay (dah-mah'-see-oh)*

Father Rentería: *ren-tay-ree'-ah*

Gerardo Trujillo: *hay-rar'-doh troo-hee'-hoh*

Juan Preciado: *hwahn pray-cee-ah'-doh*

Miguel Páramo: *mee-gel' pah'-rah-moh*

Pedro Páramo: *pay'-droh pah'-rah-moh*

Susana San Juan: *soo-sah'-nah sahn hwan*

Toribio Aldrete: *tor-ee'-bee-oh ahl-dray'-tay*

Pedro Páramo[1]

I came to Comala[2] because I had been told that my father, a man named Pedro Páramo, lived there. It was my mother who told me. And I had promised her that after she died I would go see him. I squeezed her hands as a sign I would do it. She was near death, and I would have promised her anything. "Don't fail to go see him," she had insisted. "Some call him one thing, some another. I'm sure he will want to know you." At the time all I could do was tell her I would do what she asked, and from promising so often I kept repeating the promise even after I had pulled my hands free of her death grip.

Still earlier she had told me:

"Don't ask him for anything. Just what's ours. What he should have given me but never did. . . . Make him pay, son, for all those years he put us out of his mind."

"I will, Mother."

I never meant to keep my promise. But before I knew it my head began to swim with dreams and my imagination took flight. Little by little I began to build a world around a hope centered on the man called Pedro Páramo, the man who had been my mother's husband. That was why I had come to Comala.

It was during the dog days, the season when the August wind blows hot, venomous with the rotten stench of saponaria[3] blossoms.

1. Translated by Margaret Sayers Peden. 2. I.e., "the place over the embers." Rulfo derives the town's name from *comal,* a dish used to heat tortillas over coals. 3. A low herbaceous plant with reddish blossoms.

The road rose and fell. *It rises or falls depending on whether you're coming or going. If you are leaving, it's uphill; but as you arrive it's downhill.*[4]

"What did you say that town down there is called?"

"Comala, señor."

"You're sure that's Comala?"

"I'm sure, señor."

"It's a sorry-looking place, what happened to it?"

"It's the times, señor."

I had expected to see the town of my mother's memories, of her nostalgia—nostalgia laced with sighs. She had lived her lifetime sighing about Comala, about going back. But she never had. Now I had come in her place. I was seeing things through her eyes, as she had seen them. She had given me her eyes to see. *Just as you pass the gate of Los Colimotes there's a beautiful view of a green plain tinged with the yellow of ripe corn. From there you can see Comala, turning the earth white, and lighting it at night.* Her voice was secret, muffled, as if she were talking to herself. . . . Mother.

"And why are you going to Comala, if you don't mind my asking?" I heard the man say.

"I've come to see my father," I replied.

"Umh!" he said.

And again silence.

We were making our way down the hill to the clip-clop of the burros' hooves. Their sleepy eyes were bulging from the August heat.

"You're going to get some welcome." Again I heard the voice of the man walking at my side. "They'll be happy to see someone after all the years no one's come this way."

After a while he added: "Whoever you are, they'll be glad to see you."

In the shimmering sunlight the plain was a transparent lake dissolving in mists that veiled a gray horizon. Farther in the distance, a range of mountains. And farther still, faint remoteness.

"And what does your father look like, if you don't mind my asking?"

"I never knew him," I told the man. "I only know his name is Pedro Páramo."

"Umh! that so?"

"Yes. At least that was the name I was told."

Yet again I heard the burro driver's "Umh!"

I had run into him at the crossroads called Los Encuentros.[5] I had been waiting there, and finally this man had appeared.

"Where are you going?" I asked.

"Down that way, señor."

"Do you know a place called Comala?"

"That's the very way I'm going."

So I followed him. I walked along behind, trying to keep up with him, until he seemed to remember I was following and slowed down a little. After that, we walked side by side, so close our shoulders were nearly touching.

"Pedro Páramo's my father, too," he said.

A flock of crows swept across the empty sky, shrilling "caw, caw, caw."

---

4. Italics indicate the voice of Juan Preciado's dead mother.   5. Literally, "Encounters."

Up- and downhill we went, but always descending. We had left the hot wind behind and were sinking into pure, airless heat. The stillness seemed to be waiting for something.

"It's hot here," I said.

"You might say. But this is nothing," my companion replied. "Try to take it easy. You'll feel it even more when we get to Comala. That town sits on the coals of the earth, at the very mouth of hell. They say that when people from there die and go to hell, they come back for a blanket."

"Do you know Pedro Páramo?" I asked.

I felt I could ask because I had seen a glimmer of goodwill in his eyes.

"Who is he?" I pressed him.

"Living bile," was his reply.

And he lowered his stick against the burros for no reason at all, because they had been far ahead of us, guided by the descending trail.

The picture of my mother I was carrying in my pocket felt hot against my heart, as if she herself were sweating. It was an old photograph, worn around the edges, but it was the only one I had ever seen of her. I had found it in the kitchen safe, inside a clay pot filled with herbs: dried lemon balm, castilla blossoms, sprigs of rue. I had kept it with me ever since. It was all I had. My mother always hated having her picture taken. She said photographs were a tool of witchcraft. And that may have been so, because hers was riddled with pinpricks, and at the location of the heart there was a hole you could stick your middle finger through.

I had brought the photograph with me, thinking it might help my father recognize who I was.

"Take a look," the burro driver said, stopping. "You see that rounded hill that looks like a hog bladder? Well, the Media Luna[6] lies right behind there. Now turn that way. You see the brow of that hill? Look hard. And now back this way. You see that ridge? The one so far you can't hardly see it? Well, all that's the Media Luna. From end to end. Like they say, as far as the eye can see. He owns ever' bit of that land. We're Pedro Páramo's sons, all right, but, for all that, our mothers brought us into the world on straw mats. And the real joke of it is that he's the one carried us to be baptized. That's how it was with you, wasn't it?"

"I don't remember."

"The hell you say!"

"What did you say?"

"I said, we're getting there, señor."

"Yes. I see it now. . . . What could it have been?"

"That was a *correcaminos*, señor. A roadrunner. That's what they call those birds around here."

"No. I meant I wonder what could have happened to the town? It looks so deserted, abandoned really. In fact, it looks like no one lives here at all."

"It doesn't just *look* like no one lives here. No one *does* live here."

"And Pedro Páramo?"

"Pedro Páramo died years ago."

---

6. Literally, half-moon; the name of Pedro Páramo's property. A hill and a ranch by that name are situated midway between San Gabriel and Zapotlán, Mexico.

It was the hour of the day when in every little village children come out to play in the streets, filling the afternoon with their cries. The time when dark walls still reflect pale yellow sunlight.

At least that was what I had seen in Sayula,[7] just yesterday at this hour. I'd seen the still air shattered by the flight of doves flapping their wings as if pulling themselves free of the day. They swooped and plummeted above the tile rooftops, while the children's screams whirled and seemed to turn blue in the dusk sky.

Now here I was in this hushed town. I could hear my footsteps on the cobbled paving stones. Hollow footsteps, echoing against walls stained red by the setting sun.

This was the hour I found myself walking down the main street. Nothing but abandoned houses, their empty doorways overgrown with weeds. What had the stranger told me they were called? "*La gobernadora*, señor. Creosote bush. A plague that takes over a person's house the minute he leaves. You'll see."

As I passed a street corner, I saw a woman wrapped in her rebozo;[8] she disappeared as if she had never existed. I started forward again, peering into the doorless houses. Again the woman in the rebozo crossed in front of me.

"Evening," she said.

I looked after her. I shouted: "Where will I find doña Eduviges?"

She pointed: "There. The house beside the bridge."

I took note that her voice had human overtones, that her mouth was filled with teeth and a tongue that worked as she spoke, and that her eyes were the eyes of people who inhabit the earth.

By now it was dark.

She turned to call good night. And though there were no children playing, no doves, no blue-shadowed roof tiles, I felt that the town was alive. And that if I heard only silence, it was because I was not yet accustomed to silence—maybe because my head was still filled with sounds and voices.

Yes, voices. And here, where the air was so rare, I heard them even stronger. They lay heavy inside me. I remembered what my mother had said: "*You will hear me better there. I will be closer to you. You will hear the voice of my memories stronger than the voice of my death—that is, if death ever had a voice.*" Mother. . . . So alive.

How I wished she were here, so I could say, "You were mistaken about the house. You told me the wrong place. You sent me 'south of nowhere,' to an abandoned village. Looking for someone who's no longer alive."

I found the house by the bridge by following the sound of the river. I lifted my hand to knock, but there was nothing there. My hand met only empty space, as if the wind had blown open the door. A woman stood there. She said, "Come in." And I went in.

So I stayed in Comala. The man with the burros had gone on his way. Before leaving, he'd said:

"I still have a way to go, yonder where you see that band of hills. My house is there. If you want to come, you will be welcome. For now, if you want to

---

7. The district in Jalisco where Rulfo was born.   8. A woman's shawl, about a yard and a half long, that goes over the shoulders and covers the bust.

stay here, then stay. You got nothing to lose by taking a look around, you may find someone who's still among the living."

I stayed. That was why I had come.

"Where can I find lodging?" I called, almost shouting now.

"Look up doña Eduviges, if she's still alive. Tell her I sent you."

"And what's your name?"

"Abundio," he called back. But he was too far for me to hear his last name.

"I am Eduviges Dyada. Come in."

It was as if she had been waiting for me. Everything was ready, she said, motioning for me to follow her through a long series of dark, seemingly empty, rooms. But no. As soon as my eyes grew used to the darkness and the thin thread of light following us, I saw shadows looming on either side, and sensed that we were walking down a narrow passageway opened between bulky shapes.

"What do you have here?" I asked.

"Odds and ends," she said. "My house is chock full of other people's things. As people went away, they chose my house to store their belongings, but not one of them has ever come back to claim them. The room I kept for you is here at the back. I keep it cleaned out in case anyone comes. So you're her son?"

"Whose son?" I asked.

"Doloritas's boy."

"Yes. But how did you know?"

"She told me you would be coming. Today, in fact. That you would be coming today."

"Who told you? My mother?"

"Yes. Your mother."

I did not know what to think. But Eduviges left me no time for thinking.

"This is your room," she said.

The room had no doors, except for the one we had entered. She lighted the candle, and I could see the room was completely empty.

"There's no place to sleep," I said.

"Don't worry about that. You must be tired from your journey, and weariness makes a good mattress. I'll fix you up a bed first thing in the morning. You can't expect me to have things ready on the spur of the moment. A person needs some warning, and I didn't get word from your mother until just now."

"My mother?" I said. "My mother is dead."

"So that was why her voice sounded so weak, like it had to travel a long distance to get here. Now I understand. And when did she die?"

"A week ago."

"Poor woman. She must've thought I'd forsaken her. We made each other a promise we'd die together. That we would go hand in hand, to lend each other courage on our last journey—in case we had need for something, or ran into trouble. We were the best of friends. Didn't she ever talk about me?"

"No, never."

"That's strange. Of course, we were just girls then. She was barely married. But we loved each other very much. Your mother was so pretty, so, well, *sweet*, that it made a person happy to love her. You *wanted* to love her. So, she got a head start on me, eh? Well, you can be sure I'll catch up with her.

No one knows better than I do how far heaven is, but I also know all the shortcuts. The secret is to die, God willing, when you want to, and not when He proposes. Or else to force Him to take you before your time. Forgive me for going on like this, talking to you as if we were old friends, but I do it because you're like my own son. Yes, I said it a thousand times: 'Dolores's boy should have been my son.' I'll tell you why sometime. All I want to say now is that I'll catch up with your mother along one of the roads to eternity."

I wondered if she were crazy. But by now I wasn't thinking at all. I felt I was in a faraway world and let myself be pulled along by the current. My body, which felt weaker and weaker, surrendered completely; it had slipped its ties and anyone who wanted could have wrung me out like a rag.

"I'm tired," I said.

"Come eat something before you sleep. A bite. Anything there is."

"I will. I'll come later."

Water dripping from the roof tiles was forming a hole in the sand of the patio.[9] Plink! plink! and then another plink! as drops struck a bobbing, dancing laurel leaf caught in a crack between the adobe bricks. The storm had passed. Now an intermittent breeze shook the branches of the pomegranate tree, loosing showers of heavy rain, spattering the ground with gleaming drops that dulled as they sank into the earth. The hens, still huddled on their roost, suddenly flapped their wings and strutted out to the patio, heads bobbing, pecking worms unearthed by the rain. As the clouds retreated the sun flashed on the rocks, spread an iridescent sheen, sucked water from the soil, shone on sparkling leaves stirred by the breeze.

"What's taking you so long in the privy, son?"

"Nothing, mamá."

"If you stay in there much longer, a snake will come and bite you."

"Yes, mamá."

I was thinking of you, Susana. Of the green hills. Of when we used to fly kites in the windy season. We could hear the sounds of life from the town below; we were high above on the hill, playing out string to the wind. "Help me, Susana." And soft hands would tighten on mine. "Let out more string."

The wind made us laugh; our eyes followed the string running through our fingers after the wind until with a faint pop! it broke, as if it had been snapped by the wings of a bird. And high overhead, the paper bird would tumble and somersault, trailing its rag tail, until it disappeared into the green earth.

Your lips were moist, as if kissed by the dew.

"I told you, son, come out of the privy now."

"Yes, mamá. I'm coming."

I was thinking of you. Of the times you were there looking at me with your aquamarine eyes.

He looked up and saw his mother in the doorway.

"What's taking you so long? What are you doing in there?"

"I'm thinking."

"Can't you do it somewhere else? It's not good for you to stay in the privy

9. Pedro Páramo's memories.

so long. Besides, you should be doing something. Why don't you go help your grandmother shell corn?"

"I'm going, mamá. I'm going."

"Grandmother, I've come to help you shell corn."

"We're through with that, but we still have to grind the chocolate. Where have you been? We were looking for you all during the storm."

"I was in the back patio."

"And what were you doing? Praying?"

"No, Grandmother. I was just watching it rain."

His grandmother looked at him with those yellow-gray eyes that seemed to see right through a person.

"Run clean the mill, then."

Hundreds of meters above the clouds, far, far above everything, you are hiding, Susana. Hiding in God's immensity, behind His Divine Providence where I cannot touch you or see you, and where my words cannot reach you.

"Grandmother, the mill's no good. The grinder's broken."

"That Micaela must have run corn through it. I can't break her of that habit, but it's too late now."

"Why don't we buy a new one? This one's so old it isn't any good anyway."

"That's the Lord's truth. But with all the money we spent to bury your grandfather, and the tithes we've paid to the church, we don't have anything left. Oh, well, we'll do without something else and buy a new one. Why don't you run see doña Inés Villalpando and ask her to carry us on her books until October. We'll pay her at harvest time."

"All right, Grandmother."

"And while you're at it, to kill two birds with one stone, ask her to lend us a sifter and some clippers. The way those weeds are growing, we'll soon have them coming out our ears. If I had my big house with all my stock pens, I wouldn't be complaining. But your grandfather took care of that when he moved here. Well, it must be God's will. Things seldom work out the way you want. Tell doña Inés that after harvest time we'll pay her everything we owe her."

"Yes, Grandmother."

Hummingbirds. It was the season. He heard the whirring of their wings in blossom-heavy jasmine.

He stopped by the shelf where the picture of the Sacred Heart stood, and found twenty-four centavos. He left the four single coins and took the veinte.[1]

As he was leaving, his mother stopped him:

"Where are you going?"

"Down to doña Inés Villalpando's, to buy a new mill. Ours broke."

"Ask her to give you a meter of black taffeta,[2] like this," and she handed him a piece. "And to put it on our account."

"All right, mamá."

"And on the way back, buy me some aspirin. You'll find some money in the flowerpot in the hall."

---

1. Twenty; i.e., the twenty-cent piece. *Sacred Heart*: a Catholic religious picture.   2. A heavy silk cloth.

He found a peso. He left the veinte and took the larger coin. "Now I have enough money for anything that comes along," he thought.

"Pedro!" people called to him. "Hey, Pedro!"

But he did not hear. He was far, far away.

During the night it began to rain again. For a long time, he lay listening to the gurgling of the water; then he must have slept, because when he awoke, he heard only a quiet drizzle. The windowpanes were misted over and raindrops were threading down like tears. . . . I watched the trickles glinting in the lightning flashes, and every breath I breathed, I sighed. And every thought I thought was of you, Susana.

The rain turned to wind. He heard ". . . the forgiveness of sins and the resurrection of the flesh. Amen." That was deeper in the house, where women were telling the last of their beads. They got up from their prayers, they penned up the chickens, they bolted the door, they turned out the light.

Now there was only the light of night, and rain hissing like the murmur of crickets.

"Why didn't you come say your Rosary? We were making a novena for your grandfather."

His mother was standing in the doorway, candle in hand. Her long, crooked shadow stretched toward the ceiling. The roof beams repeated it, in fragments.

"I feel sad," he said.

Then she turned away. She snuffed out the candle. As she closed the door, her sobs began; he could hear them for a long time, mixed with the sound of the rain.

The church clock tolled the hours, hour after hour, hour after hour, as if time had been telescoped.

"Oh, yes. I was nearly your mother. She never told you anything about it?"

"No. She only told me good things. I heard about you from the man with the train of burros. The man who led me here, the one named Abundio."

"He's a good man, Abundio. So, he still remembers me? I used to give him a little something for every traveler he sent to my house. It was a good deal for both of us. Now, sad to say, times have changed, and since the town has fallen on bad times, no one brings us any news. So he told you to come see me?"

"Yes, he said to look for you."

"I'm grateful to him for that. He was a good man, one you could trust. It was him that brought the mail, and he kept right on even after he went deaf. I remember the black day it happened. Everyone felt bad about it, because we all liked him. He brought letters to us and took ours away. He always told us how things were going on the other side of the world, and doubtless he told them how we were making out. He was a big talker. Well, not afterward. He stopped talking then. He said there wasn't much point in saying things he couldn't hear, things that evaporated in the air, things he couldn't get the taste of. It all happened when one of those big rockets we use to scare away water snakes went off too close to his head. From that day on, he never spoke, though he wasn't struck dumb. But one thing I tell you, it didn't make him any less a good person."

"The man I'm talking about heard fine."

"Then it can't have been him. Besides, Abundio died. I'm sure he's dead. So you see? It couldn't have been him."

"I guess you're right."

"Well, getting back to your mother. As I was telling you . . ."

As I listened to her drone on, I studied the woman before me. I thought she must have gone through some bad times. Her face was transparent, as if the blood had drained from it, and her hands were all shriveled, nothing but wrinkled claws. Her eyes were sunk out of sight. She was wearing an old-fashioned white dress with rows of ruffles, and around her neck, strung on a cord, she wore a medal of the María Santísima del Refugio with the words "Refuge of Sinners."

". . . This man I'm telling you about broke horses over at the Media Luna ranch; he said his name was Inocencio Osorio. Everyone knew him, though, by his nickname 'Cockleburr'; he could stick to a horse like a burr to a blanket. My compadre Pedro used to say that the man was born to break colts. The fact is, though, that he had another calling: conjuring. He conjured up dreams. That who he really was. And he put it over on your mother, like he did so many others. Including me. Once when I was feeling bad, he showed up and said, 'I've come to give you a treatment so's you'll feel better.' And what that meant was he would start out kneading and rubbing you: first your fingertips, then he'd stroke your hands, then your arms. First thing you knew he'd be working on your legs, rubbing hard, and soon you'd be feeling warm all over. And all the time he was rubbing and stroking he'd be telling you your fortune. He would fall into a trance and roll his eyes and conjure and curse, with spittle flying everywhere—you'd of thought he was a gypsy. Sometimes he would end up stark naked; he said we wanted it that way. And sometimes what he said came true. He shot at so many targets that once in a while he was bound to hit one.

"So what happened was that when your mother went to see this Osorio, he told her that she shouldn't lie with a man that night because the moon was wrong.

"Dolores came and told me everything, in a quandary about what to do. She said there was no two ways about it, she couldn't go to bed with Pedro Páramo that night. Her wedding night. And there I was, trying to convince her she shouldn't put any stock in that Osorio, who was nothing but a swindler and a liar.

"'I can't,' she told me. 'You go for me. He'll never catch on.'

"Of course I was a lot younger than she was. And not quite as dark-skinned. But you can't tell that in the dark.

"'It'll never work, Dolores. You have to go.'

"'Do me this one favor, and I'll pay you back a hundred times over.'

"In those days your mother had the shyest eyes. If there was something pretty about your mother, it was those eyes. They could really win you over.

"'You go in my place,' she kept saying.

"So I went.

"I took courage from the darkness, and from something else your mother didn't know, and that was that she wasn't the only one who liked Pedro Páramo.

"I crawled in bed with him. I was happy to; I wanted to. I cuddled right up against him, but all the celebrating had worn him out and he spent the whole night snoring. All he did was wedge his legs between mine.

"Before dawn, I got up and went to Dolores. I said to her: 'You go now. It's a new day.'

" 'What did he do to you?' she asked me.

" 'I'm still not sure,' I told her.

"You were born the next year, but I wasn't your mother, though you came within a hair of being mine.[3]

"Maybe your mother was ashamed to tell you about it."

Green pastures. Watching the horizon rise and fall as the wind swirled through the wheat, an afternoon rippling with curling lines of rain. The color of the earth, the smell of alfalfa and bread. A town that smelled like spilled honey . . .

"She always hated Pedro Páramo. 'Doloritas! Did you tell them to get my breakfast?' Your mother was up every morning before dawn. She would start the fire from the coals, and with the smell of the tinder the cats would wake up. Back and forth through the house, followed by her guard of cats. 'Doña Doloritas!'

"I wonder how many times your mother heard that call? 'Doña Doloritas, this is cold. It won't do.' How many times? And even though she was used to the worst of times, those shy eyes of hers grew hard."

Not to know any taste but the savor of orange blossoms in the warmth of summer.

"Then she began her sighing.

" 'Why are you sighing so, Doloritas?'

"I had gone with them that afternoon. We were in the middle of a field, watching the bevies of young thrushes. One solitary buzzard rocked lazily in the sky.

" 'Why are you sighing, Doloritas?'

" 'I wish I were a buzzard so I could fly to where my sister lives.'

" 'That's the last straw, doña Doloritas!' You'll see your sister, all right. Right now. We're going back to the house and you're going to pack your suitcases. That was the last straw!'

"And your mother went. 'I'll see you soon, don Pedro.'

" 'Good-*bye*, Doloritas!'

"And she never came back to the Media Luna. Some months later, I asked Pedro Páramo about her.

" 'She loved her sister more than she did me. I guess she's happy there. Besides, I was getting fed up with her. I have no intention of asking about her, if that's what's worrying you.'

" 'But how will they get along?'

" 'Let God look after them.' "

. . . Make him pay, Son, for all those years he put us out of his mind.

"And that's how it was until she advised me that you were coming to see me. We never heard from her again."

"A lot has happened since then," I told Eduviges. "We lived in Colima. We were taken in by my Aunt Gertrudis, who threw it in our faces every day that we were a burden. She used to ask my mother, 'Why don't you go back to your husband?'

---

3. Of being my son.

" 'Oh? Has he sent for me? I'm not going back unless he asks me to. I came because I wanted to see you. Because I loved you. That's why I came.'

" 'I know that. But it's time now for you to leave.'

" 'If it was up to me . . . ' "

I thought that Eduviges was listening to me. I noticed, though, that her head was tilted as if she were listening to some faraway sound. Then she said:

"When will you rest?"

The day you went away I knew I would never see you again. You were stained red by the late afternoon sun, by the dusk filling the sky with blood. You were smiling. You had often said of the town you were leaving behind, "I like it because of you; but I hate everything else about it—even having been born here." I thought, she will never come back; I will never see her again.

"What are you doing here at this hour? Aren't you working?"

"No, Grandmother. Rogelio asked me to mind his little boy. I'm just walking him around. I can't do both things—the kid and the telegraph. Meanwhile he's down at the poolroom drinking beer. On top of everything else, he doesn't pay me anything."

"You're not there to be paid. You're there to learn. Once you know something, then you can afford to make demands. For now, you're just an apprentice. Maybe one day you will be the boss. But for that you need patience and, above all, humility. If they want you to take the boy for a walk, do it, for heaven's sake. You must learn to be patient."

"Let others be patient, Grandmother. I'm not one for patience."

"You and your wild ideas! I'm afraid you have a hard row ahead of you, Pedro Páramo."

"What was that I just heard, doña Eduviges?"

She shook her head as if waking from a dream.

"That's Miguel Páramo's horse, galloping down the road to the Media Luna."

"Then someone's living there?"

"No, no one's living there."

"But . . . ?"

"It's only his horse, coming and going. They were never apart. It roams the countryside, looking for him, and it's always about this time it comes back. It may be that the poor creature can't live with its remorse. Even animals realize when they've done something bad, don't they?"

"I don't understand. I didn't hear anything that sounded like a horse."

"No?"

"No."

"Then it must be my sixth sense. A gift God gave me—or maybe a curse. All I know is that I've suffered because of it."

She said nothing for a while, but then added:

"It all began with Miguel Páramo. I was the only one knew everything that happened the night he died. I'd already gone to bed when I heard his horse galloping back toward the Media Luna. I was surprised, because Miguel never came home at that hour. It was always early morning before he got back. He went every night to be with his sweetheart over in a town called

Contla, a good distance from here. He left early and got back late. But that night he never returned. . . . You hear it now? Of course you can hear it. It's his horse coming home."

"I don't hear anything."

"Then it's just me. Well, like I was saying, the fact that he didn't come back wasn't the whole story. His horse had no more than gone by when I heard someone rapping at my window. Now you be the judge of whether it was my imagination. What I know is that something made me get up and go see who it was. And it was him. Miguel Páramo. I wasn't surprised to see him, because there was once a time when he spent every night at my house, sleeping with me—until he met that girl who drank his blood.

" 'What's happened,' I asked Miguel Páramo. 'Did she give you the gate?'

" 'No. She still loves me,' he said. 'The problem is that I couldn't locate her. I couldn't find my way to the town. There was a lot of mist or smoke or something. I do know that Contla isn't there anymore. I rode right past where it ought to be, according to my calculations, and there was nothing there. I've come to tell you about it, because I know you will understand. If I told anyone else in Comala they'd say I'm crazy—the way they always have.'

" 'No. Not crazy, Miguel. You must be dead. Remember, everyone told you that horse would be the death of you one day. Remember that, Miguel Páramo. Maybe you did do something crazy, but that's another matter now.'

" 'All I did was jump that new stone fence my father had built. I asked El Colorado to jump it so I wouldn't have to go all the way around, the way you have to now to get to the road. I know that I jumped it, and then kept on riding. But like I told you, everything was smoke, smoke, smoke.'

" 'Your father's going to be sick with grief in the morning,' I told him. 'I feel sorry for him. Now go, and rest in peace, Miguel. I thank you for coming to say good-bye.'

"And I closed the window. Before dawn, a ranch hand from the Media Luna came to tell me, 'The *patrón* is asking for you. Young Miguel is dead. Don Pedro wants your company.'

" 'I already knew,' I told him. 'Did they tell you to cry?'

" 'Yes. Don Fulgor told me to cry when I told you.'

" 'All right. You tell don Pedro that I'll be there. How long ago did they bring him back?'

" 'No more than half an hour. If it'd been sooner, maybe they could of saved him. Although the doctor who looked him over said he had been cold for some time. We learned about it when El Colorado came home with an empty saddle and made such a stir that no one could sleep. You know how him and that horse loved one another, and as for me, I think the animal is suffering more than don Pedro. He hasn't eaten or slept, and all he does is chase around in circles. Like he knows, you know? Like he feels all broken and chewed up inside.'

" 'Don't forget to close the door as you go.'

"And with that the hand from the Media Luna left."

"Have you ever heard the moan of a dead man?" she asked me.

"No, doña Eduviges."

"You're lucky."

Drops are falling steadily on the stone trough.[4] The air carries the sound of the clear water escaping the stone and falling into the storage urn. He is conscious of sounds: feet scraping the ground, back and forth, back and forth. The endless dripping. The urn overflows, spilling water onto the wet earth.

"Wake up," someone is saying.

He hears the sound of the voice. He tries to identify it, but he sinks back down and drowses again, crushed by the weight of sleep. Hands tug at the covers; he snuggles beneath their warmth, seeking peace.

"Wake up!" Again someone is calling.

That someone is shaking his shoulders. Making him sit up. He half opens his eyes. Again he hears the dripping of water falling from the stone into the brimming urn. And those shuffling footsteps . . . And weeping.

Then he heard the weeping. That was what woke him: a soft but penetrating weeping that because it was so delicate was able to slip through the mesh of sleep and reach the place where his fear lived.

Slowly he got out of bed; he saw a woman's face resting against a doorframe still darkened by night. The woman was sobbing.

"Why are you crying, mamá?" he asked; the minute his feet touched the floor he recognized his mother's face.

"Your father is dead," she said.

And then, as if her coiled grief had suddenly burst free, she turned and turned in a tight circle until hands grasped her shoulders and stopped the spiraling of her tortured body.

Through the door he could see the dawn. There were no stars. Only a leaden gray sky still untouched by the rays of the sun. A drab light that seemed more like the onset of night than the beginning of day.

Outside in the patio, the footsteps, like people wandering in circles. Muted sounds. And inside, the woman standing in the doorway, her body impeding the arrival of day: through her arms he glimpsed pieces of sky and, beneath her feet, trickles of light. A damp light, as if the floor beneath the woman were flooded with tears. And then the sobbing. Again the soft but penetrating weeping, and the grief contorting her body with pain.

"They've killed your father."

And you, Mother? Who killed you?

There is wind and sun, and there are clouds. High above, blue sky, and beyond that there may be songs; perhaps sweeter voices. . . . In a word, hope. There is hope for us, hope to ease our sorrows.

"But not for you, Miguel Páramo, for you died without forgiveness and you will never know God's grace."

Father Rentería walked around the corpse, reciting the mass for the dead. He hurried in order to finish quickly, and he left without offering the final benediction to the people who filled the church.

"Father, we want you to bless him!"

"No," he said, shaking his head emphatically. "I won't give my blessing. He was an evil man, and he shall not enter the Kingdom of Heaven. God will not smile on me if I intercede for him."

4. Pedro Páramo remembers his childhood.

As he spoke, he clasped his hands tightly, hoping to conceal their trembling. To no avail.

That corpse weighed heavily on the soul of everyone present. It lay on a dais in the center of the church, surrounded with new candles and flowers; a father stood there, alone, waiting for the mass to end.

Father Rentería walked past Pedro Páramo, trying not to brush against him. He raised the aspergillum gently, sprinkling holy water from the top of the coffin to the bottom, while a murmur issued from his lips that might have been a prayer. Then he knelt, and everyone knelt with him:

"Oh, God, have mercy on this Your servant."

"May he rest in peace, Amen," the voices chorused.

Then, as his rage was building anew, he saw that everyone was leaving the church, and that they were carrying out the body of Miguel Páramo.

Pedro Páramo approached him and knelt beside him:

"I know you hated him, Father. And with reason. Rumor has it that your brother was murdered by my son, and you believe that your niece Ana was raped by him. Then there were his insults, and his lack of respect. Those are all reasons anyone could understand. But forget all that now, Father. Weigh him and forgive him, as perhaps God has forgiven him."

He placed a handful of gold coins on the prie-dieu and got to his feet: "Take this as a gift for your church."

The church was empty now. Two men stood in the doorway, waiting for Pedro Páramo. He joined them, and together they followed the coffin that had been waiting for them, resting on the shoulders of four foremen from the Media Luna. Father Rentería picked up the coins, one by one, and walked to the altar.

"These are Yours," he said. "He can afford to buy salvation. Only you know whether this is the price. As for me, Lord, I throw myself at your feet to ask for the justice or injustice that any of us may ask . . . For my part, I hope you damn him to hell."

And he closed the chapel.

He walked to the sacristy, threw himself into a corner, and sat there weeping with grief and sorrow until his tears were exhausted.

"All right, Lord. You win," he said.

At suppertime, he drank his hot chocolate as he did every night. He felt calm.

"So, Anita. Do you know who was buried today?"

"No, Uncle."

"You remember Miguel Páramo?"

"Yes, Uncle."

"Well, that's who."

Ana hung her head.

"You *are* sure he was the one, aren't you?"

"I'm not positive, Uncle. No. I never saw his face. He surprised me at night, and it was dark."

"Then how did you know it was Miguel Páramo?"

"Because he said so: 'It's Miguel Páramo, Ana. Don't be afraid.' That was what he said."

"But you knew he was responsible for your father's death, didn't you?"

"Yes, Uncle."

"So what did you do to make him leave?"

"I didn't do anything."

The two sat without speaking. They could hear the warm breeze stirring in the myrtle leaves.

"He said that was why he had come: to say he was sorry and to ask me to forgive him. I lay still in my bed, and I told him, 'The window is open.' And he came in. The first thing he did was put his arms around me, as if that was his way of asking forgiveness for what he had done. And I smiled at him. I remembered what you had taught me: that we must never hate anyone. I smiled to let him know that, but then I realized that he couldn't see my smile because it was so black that I couldn't see him. I could only feel his body on top of me, and feel him beginning to do bad things to me.

"I thought he was going to kill me. That's what I believed, Uncle. Then I stopped thinking at all, so I would be dead before he killed me. But I guess he didn't dare.

"I knew he hadn't when I opened my eyes and saw the morning light shining in the open window. Up till then, I felt that I had in fact died."

"But you must have some way of being sure. His voice. Didn't you recognize him by his voice?"

"I didn't recognize him at all. All I knew about him was that he had killed my father. I had never seen him, and afterward I never saw him again. I couldn't have faced him, Uncle."

"But you knew who he was."

"Yes. And what he was. And I know that by now he must be in the deepest pit of hell. I prayed to all the saints with all my heart and soul."

"Don't be too sure of that, my child. Who knows how many people are praying for him! You are alone. One prayer against thousands. And among them, some much more intense than yours—like his father's."

He was about to say: "And anyway, I have pardoned him." But he only thought it. He did not want to add hurt to the girl's already broken spirit. Instead, he took her arm and said:

"Let us give thanks to the Lord our God, Who has taken him from this earth where he caused such harm; what does it matter if He lifted him to His Heaven?"

A horse galloped by the place where the main street crosses the road to Contla. No one saw it. Nevertheless, a woman waiting on the outskirts of the village told that she had seen the horse, and that its front legs were buckled as if about to roll head over hooves. She recognized it as Miguel Páramo's chestnut stallion. The thought had even crossed her mind that the animal was going to break its neck. Then she saw it regain its footing and without any interruption in stride race off with its head twisted back, as if frightened by something it had left behind.

That story reached the Media Luna on the night of the burial, as the men were resting after the long walk back from the cemetery.

They were talking, as people talk everywhere before turning in. "That death pained me in more ways than one," said Terencio Lubianes. "My shoulders are still sore."

"Mine, too," said his brother Ubillado. "And my bunions must have swelled an inch. All because the *patrón* wanted us to wear shoes. You'd have thought it was a holy day, right, Toribio?"

"What do you want me to say? I think it was none too soon he died."

In a few days there was more news from Contla. It came with the latest ox cart.

"They're saying that his spirit is wandering over there. They've seen it rapping at the window of a lady friend. It was just like him. Chaps and all."

"And do you think that don Pedro, with that disposition of his, would allow his son to keep calling on the women? I can just imagine what he'd say if he found out: 'All right,' he'd say. 'You're dead now. You keep to your grave. And leave the affairs to us.' And if he caught him wandering around, you can bet he'd put him back in the ground for good."

"You're right about that, Isaías. That old man doesn't put up with much."

The driver went on his way. "I'm just telling you what was told me."

Shooting stars. They fell as if the sky were raining fire.

"Look at that," said Terencio. "Please look at the show they're putting on up there."

"Must be celebrating Miguelito's arrival," Jesus put in.

"You don't think it's a bad omen?"

"Bad for who?"

"Maybe your sister's lonesome and wants him back."

"Who're you talking to?"

"To you."

"It's time to go, boys. We've traveled a long road today, and we have to be up early tomorrow."

And they faded into the night like shadows.

Shooting stars. One by one, the lights in Comala went out.

Then the sky took over the night.

Father Rentería tossed and turned in his bed, unable to sleep.

It's all my fault, he told himself. Everything that's happening. Because I'm afraid to offend the people who provide for me. It's true; I owe them my livelihood. I get nothing from the poor, and God knows prayers don't fill a stomach. That's how it's been up to now. And we're seeing the consequences. All my fault. I have betrayed those who love me and who have put their faith in me and come to me to intercede on their behalf with God. What has their faith won them? Heaven? Or the purification of their souls? And why purify their souls anyway, when at the last moment . . . I will never forget María Dyada's face when she came to ask me to save her sister Eduviges:

"She always served her fellowman. She gave them everything she had. She even gave them sons. All of them. And took the infants to their fathers to be recognized. But none of them wanted to. Then she told them, 'In that case, I'll be the father as well, even though fate chose me to be the mother.' Everyone took advantage of her hospitality and her good nature; she never wanted to offend, or set anyone against her."

"But she took her own life. She acted against the will of God."

"She had no choice. That was another thing she did out of the goodness of her heart."

"She fell short at the last hour," that's what I told María Dyada. "At the last minute. So many good acts stored up for her salvation, and then to lose them like that, all at once!"

"But she didn't lose them. She died of her sorrows. And sorrow . . . You once told us something about sorrow that I can't remember now. It was because of her sorrows she went away. And died choking on her own blood. I can still see how she looked. That face was the saddest face I have ever seen on a human."

"Perhaps with many prayers . . ."

"We're already saying many prayers, Father."

"I mean maybe, just perhaps, with Gregorian masses.[5] But for that we would need help, have to bring priests here. And that costs money."

And there before my eyes was the face of María Dyada, a poor woman still ripe with children.

"I don't have money. You know that, Father."

"Let's leave things as they are. Let us put our hope in God."

"Yes, Father."

Why did she look courageous in her resignation? And what would it have cost him to grant pardon when it was so easy to say a word or two—or a hundred if a hundred were needed to save a soul? What did he know of heaven and hell? And yet even an old priest buried in a nameless town knew who had deserved heaven. He knew the roll. He began to run through the list of saints in the Catholic pantheon, beginning with the saints for each day of the calendar: "Saint Nunilona, virgin and martyr; Anercio, bishop; Saints Salomé, widow, and Alodia-or-Elodia and Nulina, virgins; Córdula and Donato." And on down the line. He was drifting off to sleep when he sat up straight in his bed. "Here I am reciting the saints as if I were counting sheep."

He went outside and looked at the sky. It was raining stars. He was sorry, because he would rather have seen a tranquil sky. He heard roosters crowing. He felt the mantle of night covering the earth. The earth, "this vale of tears."[6]

"You're lucky, son. Very lucky," Eduviges Dyada told me.

It was very late by now. The lamp in the corner was beginning to grow dim; it flickered and went out.

I sensed that the woman rose, and I supposed she was leaving to get another lamp. I listened to her receding footsteps. I sat there, waiting.

After a while, when I realized that she was not coming back, I got up, too. I inched my way forward, groping in the darkness, until I reached my room. I lay down on the floor to wait for sleep to come.

I slept fitfully.

It was during one of those intervals that I heard the cry. It was a drawn-out cry, like the howl of a drunk. "Ay-y-y-y, life! I am too good for you!"

I sat bolt upright because it had sounded almost in my ear. It could have been in the street, but I had heard it here, sticking to the walls of my room. When I awoke, everything was silent: nothing but the sound of moths working and the murmur of silence.

No, there was no way to judge the depth of the silence that followed that scream. It was as if the earth existed in a vacuum. No sound: not even of my breathing or the beating of my heart. As if the very sound of consciousness had been stilled. And just when the pause ended and I was regaining my

---

5. In the Catholic Church, prayers said over thirty days for the soul of the dead.   6. The quotation with its biblical overtones is a literal translation into Spanish of a well-known phrase in *Three Old Saws*, short poems by Lucy Larcom (1824–93).

calm, the cry was repeated; I heard it for a long, long while. "You owe me something, even if it's nothing more than a hanged man's right to a last word."

Then the door was flung open.

"Is that you, doña Eduviges?" I called. "What's going on? Were you afraid?"

"My name isn't Eduviges. I am Damiana. I heard you were here and I've come to see you. I want you to come sleep at my house. You'll be able to rest there."

"Damiana Cisneros? Aren't you one of the women who lived at the Media Luna?"

"I do live there. That's why it took me so long to get here."

"My mother told me about a woman named Damiana who looked after me when I was born. Was that you?"

"Yes. I'm the one. I've known you since you first opened your eyes."

"I'll be glad to come. I can't get any rest here because of the yelling. Didn't you hear it? How they were murdering someone? Didn't you hear it just now?"

"It may be some echo trapped in here. A long time ago they hanged Toribio Aldrete in this room. Then they locked the door and left him to turn to leather. So he would never find rest. I don't know how you got in, when there isn't any key to open this door."

"It was doña Eduviges who opened it. She told me it was the only room she had available."

"Eduviges Dyada?"

"Yes, she was the one."

"Poor Eduviges. That must mean she's still wandering like a lost soul."

"I, Fulgor Sedano, fifty-four years of age, bachelor, administrator by profession and skilled in filing and prosecuting lawsuits, by the power invested in me and by my own authority, do claim and allege the following . . ."

That was what he had written when he filed the complaint against deeds committed by Toribio Aldrete. And he had ended: "The charge is falsifying boundaries."

"There's no one can call you less than a man, don Fulgor. I know you can hold your own. And not because of the power behind you, but on your own account."

He remembered. That was the first thing Aldrete had told him after they began drinking together, reputedly to celebrate the complaint:

"We'll wipe our asses with this paper, you and I, don Fulgor, because that's all it's good for. You know that. In other words, as far as you're concerned, you've done your part and cleared the air. Because you had me worried, which anyone might be. But now I know what it's all about, it makes me laugh. Falsify boundaries? *Me*? If he's that stupid, your *patrón*[7] should be red in the face."

He remembered. They had been at Eduviges's place. He had even asked her:

"Say, 'Viges. Can you let me have the corner room?"

"Whatever rooms you want, don Fulgor. If you want, take them all. Are your men going to spend the night?"

7. Boss.

"No, I just need one. Don't worry about us, go on to bed. Just leave us the key."

"Well, like I told you, don Fulgor," Toribio Aldrete had said. "There's no one can doubt your manhood, but I'm fuckin' well fed up with that shit-ass son of your *patrón*."

He remembered. It was the last thing he heard with all his wits about him. Later, he had acted like a coward, yelling, "Power behind me, you say? 'S'at right?"

He used the butt of his whip to knock at Pedro Páramo's door. He thought of the first time he had done that, two weeks earlier. He waited, as he had that first time. And again as he had then, he examined the black bow hanging above the door. But he did not comment again: "Well, how about that! They've hung one over the other. The first one's faded now, but the new one shines like silk, even though you can see it's just something they've dyed."

That first time he had waited so long that he'd begun to think maybe no one was home. He was just leaving when Pedro Páramo finally appeared.

"Come in, my friend."

It was the second time they had met. The first time only he had been aware of the meeting because it was right after little Pedro was born. And this time. You might almost say it was the first time. And here he was being treated like an equal. How about that! Fulgor followed with long strides, slapping his whip against his leg. He'll soon learn that I'm the man who knows what's what. He'll learn. And know why I've come.

"Sit down, Fulgor. We can speak at our ease here."

They were in the horse corral. Pedro Páramo made himself comfortable on a feed trough, and waited.

"Don't you want to sit down?"

"I prefer to stand, Pedro."

"As you like. But don't forget the don."

Who did the boy think he was to speak to him like that? Not even his father, don Lucas Páramo, had dared do that. So the very first thing, this kid, who had never stepped foot on the Media Luna or done a lick of work, was talking to him as if he were a hired hand. How about *that*!

"So, what shape is this operation in?"

Sedano felt this was his opportunity. "Now it's my turn," he thought.

"Not so good. There's nothing left. We've sold off the last head of cattle."

He began taking out papers to show Pedro Páramo how much he owed. And he was just ready to say, "We owe such and such," when he heard the boy ask:

"Who do we owe it *to*? I'm not interested in how much, just who to."

Fulgor ran down the list of names. And ended: "There's nowhere to get the money to pay. That's the crux of the problem."

"Why not?"

"Because your family ate it all up. They borrowed and borrowed without ever returning any of it. One day you have to pay the piper. I always used to say, 'One of these days they're going to have everything there is.' Well, that's what happened. Now, I know someone who might be interested in buying the land. They'll pay a good price. It will cover your outstanding debts, with a little left over. Though not very much."

"That 'someone' wouldn't be you?"

"What makes you think it's me?"

"I'm suspicious of my own shadow. Tomorrow morning we'll begin to set our affairs in order. We'll begin with the Preciado women. You say it's them we owe the most?"

"Yes. And them we've paid the least. Your father always left the Preciados to the last. I understand that one of the girls, Matilde, went to live in the city. I don't know whether it was Guadalajara or Colima. And that Lola, that is, doña Dolores, has been left in charge of everything. You know, of don Enmedio's ranch. She's the one we have to pay."

"Then tomorrow I want you to go and ask for Lola's hand."

"What makes you think she'd have me? I'm an old man."

"You'll ask her for *me*. After all, she's not without her charms. Tell her I'm very much in love with her. Ask her if she likes the idea. And on the way, ask Father Rentería to make the arrangements. How much money can you get together?"

"Not a centavo, don Pedro."

"Well, promise him something. Tell him the minute I have any money, I'll pay him. I'm pretty sure he won't stand in the way. Do it tomorrow. Early."

"And what about Aldrete?"

"What does Aldrete have to do with anything? You told me about the Preciado women, and the Fregosos and the Guzmáns. So what's this about Aldrete?"

"It's the matter of the boundaries. He's been putting up fences, and now he wants us to put up the last part in order to establish the property lines."

"Leave that for later. You're not to worry about fences. There're not going to be any fences. The land's not to be divided up. Think about that, Fulgor, but don't tell anyone just yet. For now, first thing, set it up with Lola. Sure you won't sit down?"

"I will, don Pedro. God's truth, I'm beginning to like working with you."

"You string Lola a line, and tell her I love her. That's important. It's true, Sedano, I do love her. Because of her eyes, you know? You do that first thing in the morning. And I'll relieve you of some of your administrative duties. You can leave the Media Luna to me."

I wonder where in hell the boy learned those tricks, Fulgor Sedano thought on his second trip to the Media Luna. I never expected anything from him. "He's worthless," my old *patrón* don Lucas used to say. "A born weakling." And I couldn't argue. "When I die, Fulgor, you look for another job." "I will, don Lucas." "I tell you, Fulgor, I tried sending him to the seminary, hoping that at least he would have enough to eat and could look after his mother when I'm no longer here. But he didn't even stick with that." "You deserve better, don Lucas." "Don't count on him for anything, not even to care for me when I'm old. He's turned out bad, Fulgor, and that's that." "That's a real shame, don Lucas."

And now this. If the Media Luna hadn't meant so much to him, he'd never have called on Miguel. He'd have left without contacting him. But he loved that land: the barren hills that had been worked year in and year out and still accepted the plow, giving more every year. . . . Beloved Media Luna . . . And each new addition, like Enmedio's land: "Come to me, sweetheart." He could see it, as easy as if it were already done. And what does a woman matter, after all. "Damn right!" he said, slapping the whip against his leg as he walked through the main door of the hacienda.

It had been easy enough to gull Dolores. Her eyes shone and her face showed her discomposure.

"Forgive me for blushing, don Fulgor. I can't believe don Pedro ever noticed me."

"He can't sleep for thinking about you."

"But he has so many to choose from. There are so many pretty girls in Comala. What will they say when they find out?"

"He thinks of no one but you, Dolores. Nobody but you."

"You give me the shivers, don Fulgor. I never dreamed . . ."

"It's because he's a man of so few words. Don Lucas Páramo, may he rest in peace, actually told him you weren't good enough for him. So out of obedience he kept his silence. But now his father's gone, there's nothing to stand in the way. It was his first decision—although I've been slow to carry it out because of all the things I had to do. We'll set the wedding for day after tomorrow. How does that suit you?"

"Isn't that awfully soon? I don't have anything ready. I'll need time to get my trousseau together. I'll want to write my sister. No, I'll send her a letter by messenger. But no matter what, I won't be ready before the eighth of April. Today is the first. Yes, the earliest would be the eighth. Ask him to wait just a few short days longer."

"He wishes it were this minute. If it's just a matter of your wedding dress, we'll provide that. Don Pedro's dear dead mother would want you to have hers. It's a family custom."

"But there's another reason I want those extra days. It's a woman's matter, you know. Oh! I'm so embarrassed to say this, don Fulgor. My face must be a hundred colors. But it's my time of the month. Oh, I'm so ashamed."

"What does that have to do with it? Marriage isn't a question of your time or not your time. It's a matter of loving each other. When you have that, nothing else matters."

"But you don't understand what I'm saying, don Fulgor."

"I understand. The wedding will be day after tomorrow."

And he left her with arms outstretched, begging for one week, just one week.

I mustn't forget to tell don Pedro—God, that Pedro's a sharp boy!—I mustn't forget to tell him, remember to tell the judge to put the property in joint ownership. Don't forget, now, Fulgor, to tell him first thing tomorrow.

Meanwhile, Dolores was running to the kitchen with a water jug to set water to boil. "I'll have to try to bring it on sooner. This very night. But whatever I do, it will still last three days. There's no way around it. But oh, I'm so happy. So happy! Thank you, God, for giving me don Pedro." And then she added. "Even if later he does get tired of me."

"I've asked her, and she's for it. The priest wants sixty pesos to overlook the matter of the banns. I told him he'd get it in due time. He says he needs it to fix the altar, and that his dining room table is on its last legs. I promised that we'd send him a new table. He says you never come to mass. I promised him you would. And since your grandmother died, he says, no one over here has tithed. I told him not to worry. He'll go along."

"You didn't ask for a little advance from Dolores?"

"No, *patrón*. I didn't dare. That's the truth. She was so happy I didn't want to dim her enthusiasm."

"What a baby you are."

A baby he says? Me, with all my fifty-five years? Look at him, just beginning to live, and me only a few steps from the grave. "I didn't want to spoil her happiness."

"In spite of everything, you're still a kid."

"Anything you say, *patrón*."

"Next week, I want you to go over to see Aldrete. Tell him to check his fences. He's on Media Luna land."

"He did a good job measuring the boundary lines. I can vouch for that."

"Well, tell him he made a mistake. That he didn't figure right. If necessary, tear down the fences."

"And the law?"

"What law, Fulgor? From now on, we're the law. Do you have any hard-asses working on the Media Luna?"

"Well, there's one or two."

"Send them over to do business with Aldrete. You draw up a complaint accusing him of squatting on our land, or whatever occurs to you. And remind him that Lucas Páramo is dead. And that from now on he'll be dealing with me."

There were only a few clouds in the still-blue sky. Higher up, air was stirring but down below it was still and hot.

Again he knocked with the butt of the whip, if only to assert his presence, since he knew by now that no one would open until Pedro Páramo fancied. Seeing the black bows above the door, he thought: Those ribbons look pretty; one for each.

At that moment the door opened, and he stepped inside.

"Come in, Fulgor. Did you take care of Toribio Aldrete?"

"That job's done, *patrón*."

"We still have the matter of the Fregosos. We'll let that ride. Right now I'm all wrapped up in my honeymoon."

"This town is filled with echoes. It's like they were trapped behind the walls, or beneath the cobblestones. When you walk you feel like someone's behind you, stepping in your footsteps. You hear rustlings. And people laughing. Laughter that sounds used up. And voices worn away by the years. Sounds like that. But I think the day will come when those sounds fade away."

That was what Damiana Cisneros was telling me as we walked through the town.

"There was a time when night after night I could hear the sounds of a fiesta. I could hear the noise clear out at the Media Luna. I would walk into town to see what the uproar was about, and this is what I would see: just what we're seeing now. Nothing. No one. The streets as empty as they are now.

"Then I didn't hear anything anymore. You know, you can get worn out celebrating. That's why I wasn't surprised when it ended.

"Yes," Damiana Cisneros repeated. "This town is filled with echoes. I'm not afraid anymore. I hear the dogs howling, and I let them howl. And on windy days I see the wind blowing leaves from the trees, when anyone can see that there aren't any trees here. There must have been once. Otherwise, where do the leaves come from?

"And the worst of all is when you hear people talking and the voices seem to be coming through a crack, and yet so clear you can recognize who's speaking. In fact, just now as I was coming here I happened upon a wake. I stopped to recite the Lord's Prayer. And while I was praying, one woman stepped away from the others and came toward me and said, 'Damiana! Pray for me, Damiana!'

"Her rebozo fell away from her face and I recognized my sister Sixtina.

" 'What are you doing here?' I asked her.

"Then she ran back and hid among the other women.

"In case you didn't know, my sister Sixtina died when I was twelve years old. She was the oldest. There were sixteen of us, so you can figure how long she's been dead. And look at her now, still wandering through this world. So don't be afraid if you hear newer echoes, Juan Preciado."

"Was it my mother who told you I was coming?" I asked.

"No. And by the way, whatever happened to your mother?"

"She died," I replied.

"Died? What of?"

"I don't really know. Sadness, maybe. She sighed a lot."

"That's bad. Every sigh is like a drop of your life being swallowed up. Well, so she's dead."

"Yes. I thought maybe you knew."

"Why would I know? I haven't heard a thing from her in years."

"Then how did you know about me?"

Damiana did not answer.

"Are you alive, Damiana? Tell me, Damiana!"

Suddenly I was alone in those empty streets. Through the windows of roofless houses you could see the tough stems of tall weeds. And meager thatch revealing crumbling adobe.

"Damiana!" I called. "Damiana Cisneros!"

The echo replied: ". . . ana . . . neros! . . . ana . . . neros!"

I heard dogs barking, as if I had roused them. I saw a man crossing the street.

"Hey, you!" I called.

"Hey, you!" came back my own voice.

And as if they were just around the next corner, I heard two women talking:

"Well, look who's coming toward us. Isn't that Filoteo Aréchiga?"

"The very one. Pretend you don't see him."

"Even better, let's leave. And if he walks after us, it means he wants something of one of us. Which one of us do you think he's following?"

"It must be you."

"Well, I figure it's you he wants."

"Oh, we don't have to run anymore. He stopped back on the corner."

"Then it wasn't either of us. You see?"

"But what if it had been? What then?"

"Don't get ideas."

"It's a good thing he didn't. Everyone says that he's the one who gets the girls for don Pedro. Which just missed being us."

"Is that right? Well, I don't want to have anything to do with that old man."

"We better go."

"Yes, let's. Let's go home."

Night. Long after midnight. And the voices:

"I'm telling you that if we have a good corn crop this year I'll be able to pay you. But if we lose it, well, you'll just have to wait."

"I'm not pushing you. You know I've been patient with you. But it's not your land. You've been working land that's not yours. So where are you going to get the money to pay me?"

"And who says the land isn't mine?"

"I heard you sold it to Pedro Páramo."

"I haven't been anywhere near him. The land's still mine."

"That's what you say. But everyone is saying it's his."

"Just let them say that to *me*."

"Look, Galileo, just between the two of us, in confidence, I like you a lot. After all, you're my sister's husband. And I never heard anyone say you don't treat her well. But don't try to tell me you didn't sell the land."

"I do tell you, I haven't sold it to anyone."

"Well, it belongs to Pedro Páramo. I know that's how he means it to be. Didn't don Fulgor come see you?"

"No."

"Then you can be sure he'll be here tomorrow. And if not tomorrow, some day soon."

"Then one of us will die, but he's not going to get his way on this."

"Rest in peace, Amen, dear brother-in-law. Just in case."

"I'll be around, you'll see. Don't worry about me. My mother tanned my hide enough to make me good and tough."

"Till tomorrow, then. Tell Felicitas that I won't be to dinner tonight. I wouldn't want to have to say later, 'I was with him the night before he died.' "

"We'll save something for you in case you change your mind at the last minute."

Receding footsteps sounded to the jingle of spurs.

"Tomorrow morning at dawn you're coming with me, Chona. I have the team hitched up."

"And what if my father has a fit and dies? As old as he is . . . I'd never forgive myself if something happened to him because of me. I'm the only one he has to see that he takes care of himself. There's no one else. Why are you in such a hurry to steal me from him? Wait just a little longer. It won't be long till he dies."

"That's what you told me last year. You even taunted me for not being willing to take a chance, and from what you said then, you were fed up with everything. I've harnessed the mules and they're ready. Are you coming with me?"

"Let me think about it."

"Chona! You don't know how much I want you. I can't stand it any longer, Chona. One way or another, you're coming with me."

"I need to think about it. Try to understand. We have to wait until he dies. It won't be long now. Then I'll go with you and we won't have to run away."

"You told me that, too, a year ago."

"And so?"

"Chona, I had to hire the mules. They're ready. They're just waiting for you. Let him get along on his own. You're pretty. You're young. Some old woman will come look after him. There's more than enough kind souls to go around."

"I can't."

"Yes you can."

"I can't. It hurts me, you know that. But he is my father."

"Then there's nothing more to say. I'll go see Juliana, she's crazy about me."

"Fine. I won't tell you not to."

"Then you don't want to see me tomorrow?"

"No. I don't ever want to see you again."

Sound. Voice. Murmurs. Distant singing:

> My sweetheart gave me a lace-bordered
> handkerchief to dry my tears . . .

High voices. As if it were women singing

I watched the carts creaking by. The slowly moving oxen. The crunching of stones beneath the wheels. The men, seeming to doze.

. . . Every morning early the town trembles from the passing carts. They come from everywhere, loaded with niter, ears of corn, and fodder. The wheels creak and groan until the windows rattle and wake the people inside. That's also the hour when the ovens are opened and you can smell the new-baked bread. Suddenly it will thunder. And rain. Maybe spring's on its way. You'll get used to the "suddenlys" there, my son.

Empty carts, churning the silence of the streets. Fading into the dark road of night. And shadows. The echo of shadows.

I thought of leaving. Up the hill I could sense the track I had followed when I came, like an open wound through the blackness of the mountains.

Then someone touched my shoulder.

"What are you doing here?"

"I came to look for . . ." I was going to say the name, but stopped. "I came to look for my father."

"Why don't you come in?"

I went in. Half the roof had fallen in on the house. The tiles lay on the ground. The roof on the ground. And in the other half were a man and a woman.

"Are you dead?" I asked them.

The woman smiled. The man's gaze was serious.

"He's drunk," the man said.

"He's just scared," said the woman.

There was an oil stove. A reed cot, and a crude chair where the woman's clothes were laid. Because she was naked, just as God had sent her into the world. And the man, too.

"We heard someone moaning and butting his head against our door. And there you were. What happened to you?"

"So many things have happened that all I want to do is sleep."

"That's what we were doing."

"Let's all sleep, then."

My memories began to fade with the light of dawn.

From time to time I heard the sound of words, and marked a difference. Because until then, I realized, the words I had heard had been silent. There had been no sound, I had sensed them. But silently, the way you hear words in your dreams.

"Who could he be?" the woman was asking.

"Who knows?" the man replied.

"I wonder what brought him here?"

"Who knows?"

"I think I heard him say something about his father."

"I heard him say that, too."

"You don't think he's lost? Remember when those people happened by who said they were lost? They were looking for a place called Los Confines, and you told them you didn't know where it was."

"Yes, I remember. But let me sleep. It's not dawn yet."

"But it will be before long. And I'm talking to you because I want you to wake up. You told me to remind you before dawn. That's why I'm doing it. Get up!"

"Why do you want me to get up?"

"I don't know why. You told me last night to wake you. You didn't tell me why."

"If that's your only reason, let me sleep. Didn't you hear what the man said when he came? To let him sleep. That was all he had to say."

It seemed as if the voices were moving away. Fading. Being choked off. No one was saying anything now. It was a dream.

But after a while, it began again:

"He moved. I'll bet he's about to wake up. And if he sees us here he'll ask questions."

"What questions can he ask?"

"Well. He'll have to say something, won't he?"

"Leave him alone. He must be very tired."

"You think so?"

"That's enough, woman."

"Look, he's moving. See how he's tossing? Like something inside him was jerking him around. I know, because that's happened to me."

"What's happened to you?"

"That."

"I don't know what you're talking about."

"I wouldn't mention it except that when I see him tossing in his sleep like that I remember what happened to me the first time you did it to me. How it hurt, and how bad I felt about doing it."

"What do you mean, 'it'?"

"How I felt right after you did it to me, and how, whether you like it or not, I knew it wasn't done right."

"Are you going to start that again? Why don't you go to sleep, and let me sleep, too."

"You asked me to remind you. That's what I'm doing. Dear God, I'm doing what you asked me to. Come on! It's almost time for you to get up."

"Leave me alone, woman."

The man seemed to sleep. The woman kept on scolding, but in a quiet voice:

"It must be after dawn by now, because I can see light. I can see that man from here, and if I can see him it's only because there's enough light to see. The sun will be up before long. I don't need to tell you that. What do you bet he's done something wrong. And we took him in. It doesn't matter that it was only for tonight; we hid him. And in the long run that will mean trouble for us . . . Look how restless he is, as if he can't get comfortable. I'll bet he has a heavy load on his soul."

It was growing lighter. Day was routing the shadows. Erasing them. The room where I lay was warm with the heat of sleeping bodies. I sensed the dawn light through my eyelids. I felt the light. I heard:

"He's thrashing around like he's damned. He has all the earmarks of an evil man. Get up, Donis! Look at him. Look how he's writhing there on the ground, twisting and turning. He's drooling. He must have killed a lot of people. And you didn't even see it."

"Poor devil. Go to sleep . . . and let us sleep!"

"And how can I sleep if I'm not sleepy?"

"Get up, then, and go somewhere you won't be pestering me!"

"I will. I'll go light the fire. And as I go I'll tell what's-his-name to come sleep here by you, here in my place."

"You tell him that."

"I can't. I'd be afraid to."

"Then go about your work and leave us alone."

"I'm going to."

"What are you waiting for?"

"I'm on my way."

I heard the woman get out of bed. Her bare feet thudded on the ground and she stepped over my head. I opened and closed my eyes.

When I opened them again, the sun was high in the sky. Beside me sat a clay jug of coffee. I tried to drink it. I took a few swallows.

"It's all we have. I'm sorry it's so little. We're so short of everything, so short . . . ."

It was a woman's voice.

"Don't worry on my account," I told her. "Don't worry about me. I'm used to it. How do I get out of here?"

"Where are you going?"

"Anywhere."

"There's dozens of roads. One goes to Contla, and there's another one comes from there. One leads straight to the mountains. I don't know where the one goes you can see from here," and she pointed past the hole in the roof, the place where the roof had fallen in. "That other one down there goes past the Media Luna. And there's still another that runs the length of the place; that's the longest."

"Then that may be the way I came."

"Where are you heading?"

"Toward Sayula."

"Imagine. I thought Sayula was that way. I always wanted to go there. They say there's lots of people there."

"About like other places."

"Think of that. And us all alone here. Dying to know even a little of life."

"Where did your husband go?"

"He isn't my husband. He's my brother, though he doesn't want anyone to know. Where did he go? I guess to look for a stray calf that's been wandering around here. At least that's what he told me."

"How long have you two been here?"

"Forever. We were born here."

"Then you must have known Dolores Preciado."

"Maybe *he* did, Donis. I know so little about people. I never go out. I've been right here for what seems forever. Well, maybe not that long. Just since he made me his woman. Ever since then, I've been closed up here, because I'm afraid to be seen. He doesn't want to believe it, but isn't it true I would give anyone a scare?" She walked to stand in the sunlight. "Look at my face!"

It was an ordinary face.

"What is it you want me to see?"

"Don't you see my sin? Don't you see those purplish spots? Like impetigo? I'm covered with them. And that's only on the outside; inside, I'm a sea of mud."

"But who's going to see you if there's no one here? I've been through the whole town and not seen anyone."

"You think you haven't, but there are still a few people around. Haven't you seen Filomeno? Or Dorotea or Melquiades or old Prudencio? And aren't Sóstenes and all of them still alive? What happens is that they stay close to home. I don't know what they do by day, but I know they spend their nights locked up indoors. Nights around here are filled with ghosts. You should see all the spirits walking through the streets. As soon as it's dark they begin to come out. No one likes to see them. There's so many of them and so few of us that we don't even make the effort to pray for them anymore, to help them out of their purgatory. We don't have enough prayers to go around. Maybe a few words of the Lord's Prayer for each one. But that's not going to do them any good. Then there are our sins on top of theirs. None of us still living is in God's grace. We can't lift up our eyes, because they're filled with shame. And shame doesn't help. At least that's what the Bishop said. He came through here some time ago giving confirmation, and I went to him and confessed everything:

" 'I can't pardon you,' he said.

" 'I'm filled with shame.'

" 'That isn't the answer.'

" 'Marry us!'

" 'Live apart!'

"I tried to tell him that life had joined us together, herded us like animals, forced us on each other. We were so alone here; we were the only two left. And somehow the village had to have people again. I told him now maybe there would be someone for him to confirm when he came back."

" 'Go your separate ways. There's no other way.'

" 'But how will we live?'

" 'Like anyone lives.'

"And he rode off on his mule, his face hard, without looking back, as if he was leaving an image of damnation behind him. He's never come back. And that's why this place is swarming with spirits: hordes of restless souls who died without forgiveness, and people would never have won forgiveness in any case—even less if they had to depend on us. He's coming. You hear?"

"Yes, I hear."

"It's him."

The door opened.

"Did you find the calf?" she asked.

"It took it in its head not to come, but I followed its tracks and I'll soon find where it is. Tonight I'll catch it."

"You're going to leave me alone at night?"

"I may have to."

"But I can't stand it. I need you here with me. That's the only time I feel comfortable. That time of night."

"But tonight I'm going after the calf."

"I just learned," I interrupted, "that you two are brother and sister."

"You just learned that? I've known it a lot longer than you. So don't be sticking your nose into it. We don't like people talking about us."

"I only mentioned it to show I understand. That's all."

"Understand what?"

The woman went to stand beside him, leaning against his shoulder, and repeated in turn:

"You understand what?"

"Nothing," I said. "I understand less by the minute." And added: "All I want is to go back where I came from. I should use what little light's left of the day."

"You'd better wait," he told me. "Wait till morning. It'll be dark soon, and all the roads are grown over. You might get lost. I'll start you off in the right direction tomorrow."

"All right."

Through the hole in the roof I watched the thrushes, those birds that flock at dusk before the darkness seals their way. Then, a few clouds already scattered by the wind that comes to carry off the day.

Later the evening star came out; then, still later, the moon.

The man and woman were not around. They had gone out through the patio and by the time they returned it was already dark. So they had no way of knowing what had happened while they were gone.

And this was what happened:

A woman came into the room from the street. She was ancient, and so thin she looked as if her hide had shrunk to her bones. She looked around the room with big round eyes. She may even have seen me. Perhaps she thought I was sleeping. She went straight to the bed and pulled a leather trunk from beneath it. She searched through it. Then she clutched some sheets beneath her arm and tiptoed out as if not to wake me.

I lay rigid, holding my breath, trying to look anywhere but at her. Finally I worked up the courage to twist my head and look in her direction, toward the place where the evening star had converged on the moon.

"Drink this," I heard.

I did not dare turn my head.

"Drink it! It will do you good. It's orange-blossom tea. I know you're scared because you're trembling. This will ease your fright."

I recognized the hands, and as I raised my eyes I recognized the face. The man, who was standing behind her, asked:

"Do you feel sick?"

"I don't know. I see things and people where you may not see anything. A woman was just here. You must have seen her leave."

"Come on," he said to his wife. "Leave him alone. He talks like a mystic."

"We should let him have the bed. Look how he's trembling. He must have a fever."

"Don't pay him any mind. People like him work themselves into a state to get attention. I knew one over at the Media Luna who called himself a divine. What he never 'divined' was that he was going to die as soon as the *patrón* 'divined' what a bungler he was. This one's just like him. They spend their lives going from town to town 'to see what the Good Lord has to offer,' but he'll not find anyone here to give him so much as a bite to eat. You see how he stopped trembling? He hears what we're saying."

It was as if time had turned backward. Once again I saw the star nestling close to the moon. Scattering clouds. Flocks of thrushes. And suddenly, bright afternoon light.

Walls were reflecting the afternoon sun. My footsteps sounded on the cobblestones. The burro driver was saying, "Look up doña Eduviges, if she's still alive!"

Then a dark room. A woman snoring by my side. I noticed that her breathing was uneven, as if she were dreaming, or as if she were awake and merely imitating the sounds of sleep. The cot was a platform of reeds covered with gunnysacks that smelled of piss, as if they'd never been aired in the sun. The pillow was a saddle pad wrapped around a log or a roll of wool so hard and sweaty it felt as solid as a rock.

I could feel a woman's naked legs against my knee, and her breath upon my face. I sat up in the bed, supporting myself on the adobe-hard pillow.

"You're not asleep?" she asked.

"I'm not sleepy. I slept all day long. Where's your brother?"

"He went off somewhere. You heard him say where he had to go. He may not come back tonight."

"So he went anyway? In spite of what you wanted?"

"Yes. And he may never come back. That's how they all do. 'I have to go down there; I have to go on out that way.' Until they've gone so far that it's easier not to come back. He's been trying and trying to leave, and I think this is the time. Maybe, though he didn't say so, he left me here for you to take care of. He saw his chance. The business of the stray was just an excuse. You'll see. He's not coming back."

I wanted to say, "I feel dizzy. I'm going out to get a little air." Instead, I said:

"Don't worry. He'll be back."

When I got out of bed, she said:

"I left something for you on the coals in the kitchen. It's not very much, but it will at least keep you from starving."

I found a piece of dried beef, and a few warm tortillas.

"That's all I could get," I heard her saying from the other room. "I traded my sister two clean sheets I've had since my mother died. I kept them under the bed. She must have come to get them. I didn't want to tell you in front of Donis, but she was the woman you saw . . . the one who gave you such a scare."

A black sky, filled with stars. And beside the moon the largest star of all.

"Don't you hear me?" I asked in a low voice.

And her voice replied: "Where are you?"

"I'm here, in your village. With your people. Don't you see me?"

"No, son. I don't see you."

Her voice seemed all-encompassing. It faded into distant space.

"I don't see you."

I went back to the room where the woman was sleeping and told her:

"I'll stay over here in my own corner. After all, the bed's as hard as the floor. If anything happens, let me know."

"Donis won't be back," she said. "I saw it in his eyes. He was waiting for someone to come so he could get away. Now you'll be the one to look after me. Won't you? Don't you want to take care of me? Come sleep here by my side."

"I'm fine where I am."

"You'd be better off up here in the bed. The ticks will eat you alive down there."

I got up and crawled in bed with her.

The heat woke me just before midnight. And the sweat. The woman's body was made of earth, layered in crusts of earth; it was crumbling, melting into a pool of mud. I felt myself swimming in the sweat streaming from her body, and I couldn't get enough air to breathe. I got out of bed. She was sleeping. From her mouth bubbled a sound very like a death rattle.

I went outside for air, but I could not escape the heat that followed wherever I went.

There was no air; only the dead, still night fired by the dog days of August.

Not a breath. I had to suck in the same air I exhaled, cupping it in my hands before it escaped. I felt it, in and out, less each time . . . until it was so thin it slipped through my fingers forever.

I mean, forever.

I have a memory of having seen something like foamy clouds swirling above my head, and then being washed by the foam and sinking into the thick clouds. That was the last thing I saw.

"Are you trying to make me believe you drowned, Juan Preciado? I found you in the town plaza, far from Donis's house, and he was there, too, telling me you were playing dead. Between us we dragged you into the shadow of the arches, already stiff as a board and all drawn up like a person who'd died of fright. If there hadn't been any air to breathe that night you're talking about, we wouldn't have had the strength to carry you, even less bury you. And, as you see, bury you we did."

"You're right, Doroteo. You say your name's Doroteo?"

"It doesn't matter. It's really Dorotea. But it doesn't matter."

"It's true, Dorotea. The murmuring killed me."

There you'll find the place I love most in the world. The place where I grew thin from dreaming. My village, rising from the plain. Shaded with trees and leaves like a piggy bank filled with memories. You'll see why a person would want to live there forever. Dawn, morning, midday, night: always the same, except for the changes in the air. The air changes the color of things there. And life whirs by as quiet as a murmur . . . the pure murmuring of life . . .

"Yes, Dorotea. The murmuring killed me.[8] I was trying to hold back my fear. But it kept building until I couldn't contain it any longer. And when I was face to face with the murmuring, the dam burst.

"I went to the plaza. You're right about that. I was drawn there by the sound of people; I thought there really were people. I wasn't in my right mind by then. I remember I got there by feeling my way along the walls as if I were walking with my hands. And the walls seemed to distill the voices, they seemed to be filtering through the cracks and crumbling mortar. I heard them. Human voices: not clear, but secretive voices that seemed to be whispering something to me as I passed, like a buzzing in my ears. I moved away from the walls and continued down the middle of the street. But I still heard them; they seemed to be keeping pace with me—ahead of me, or just behind me. Like I told you, I wasn't hot anymore. Just the opposite, I was cold. From the time I left the house of that woman who let me use her bed, the one— I told you—I'd seen dissolving in the liquid of her sweat, from that time on I'd felt cold. And the farther I walked, the colder I got, until my skin was all goose bumps. I wanted to turn back; I thought that if I went back I might find the warmth I'd left behind; but I realized after I walked a bit farther that the cold was coming from *me*, from my own blood. Then I realized I was afraid. I heard all the noise in the plaza, and I thought I'd find people there to help me get over my fear. That's how you came to find me in the plaza. So Donis came back after all? The woman was sure she'd never see him again."

"It was morning by the time we found you. I don't know where he came from. I didn't ask him."

"Well, anyway, I reached the plaza. I leaned against a pillar of the arcade. I saw that no one was there, even though I could still hear the murmuring of voices, like a crowd on market day. A steady sound with no words to it, like the sound of the wind through the branches of a tree at night when you

8. An earlier title for *Pedro Páramo* was *The Murmurs*.

can't see the tree or the branches but you hear the whispering. Like that. I couldn't take another step. I began to sense that whispering drawing nearer, circling around me, a constant buzzing like a swarm of bees, until finally I could hear the almost soundless words 'Pray for us.' I could hear that's what they were saying to me. At that moment, my soul turned to ice. That's why you found me dead."

"You'd have done better to stay home. Why did you come here?"

"I told you that at the very beginning. I came to find Pedro Páramo, who they say was my father. Hope brought me here."

"Hope? You pay dear for that. My illusions made me live longer than I should have. And that was the price I paid to find my son, who in a manner of speaking was just one more illusion. Because I never had a son. Now that I'm dead I've had time to think and understand. God never gave me so much as a nest to shelter my baby in. Only an endless lifetime of dragging myself from pillar to post, sad eyes casting sidelong glances, always looking past people, suspicious that this one or that one had hidden my baby from me. And it was all the fault of one bad dream. I had two: one of them I call the 'good dream,' and the other the 'bad dream.' The first was the one that made me dream I had a son to begin with. And as long as I lived, I always believed it was true. I could feel him in my arms, my sweet baby, with his little mouth and eyes and hands. For a long, long time I could feel his eyelids, and the beating of his heart, on my fingertips. Why wouldn't I think it was true? I carried him with me everywhere I went, wrapped in my rebozo, and then one day I lost him. In heaven they told me they'd made a mistake. That they'd given me a mother's heart but the womb of a whore. That was the other dream I had. I went up to heaven and peeked in to see whether I could recognize my son's face among the angels. Nothing. The faces were all the same, all made from the same mold. Then I asked. One of those saints came over to me and, without a word, sank his hand into my stomach, like he would have poked into a ball of wax. When he pulled out his hand he showed me something that looked like a nutshell. 'This proves what I'm demonstrating to you.'

"You know how strange they talk up there, but you can understand what they're saying. I wanted to tell them that it was just my stomach, all dried up from hunger and nothing to eat, but another one of those saints took me by the shoulders and pushed me to the door. 'Go rest a while more on earth, my daughter, and try to be good so that your time in purgatory will be shortened.'

"That was my 'bad dream,' and the one where I learned I never had a son. I learned it very late, after my body had already shriveled up and my backbone jutted up higher than the top of my head and I couldn't walk anymore. And to top it off, everyone was leaving the village; all the people set out for somewhere else and took their charity with them. I sat down to wait for death. After we found you, my bones determined to find their rest. 'No one will notice me,' I thought. 'I won't be a bother to anyone.' You see, I didn't even steal space from the earth. They buried me in the grave with you, and I fit right in the hollow of your arms. Here in this little space where I am now. The only thing is that probably I should have my arms around *you*. You hear? It's raining up there. Don't you hear the drumming of the rain?"

"I hear something like someone walking above us."

"You don't have to be afraid. No one can scare you now. Try to think nice thoughts, because we're going to be a long time here in the ground."

At dawn a heavy rain was falling over the earth. It thudded dully as it struck the soft loose dust of the furrows. A mockingbird swooped low across the field and wailed, imitating a child's plaint; a little farther it sang something that sounded like a sob of weariness and in the distance where the horizon had begun to clear, it hiccupped and then laughed, only to wail once more.

Fulgor Sedano breathed in the scent of fresh earth and looked out to see how the rain was penetrating the furrows. His little eyes were happy. He took three deep gulps, relishing the savor, and grinned till his teeth showed.

"Ahhhh!" he said "We're about to have another good year." And then added: "Come on down, rain. Come on down. Fall until you can't fall anymore! And then move on. Remember that we worked the ground just to pleasure you."

And he laughed aloud.

Returning from its survey of the fields, the mockingbird flew past him and wailed a heartrending wail.

The rain intensified until in the distance where it had begun to grow light the clouds closed in, and it seemed that the darkness that had been retreating was returning.

The huge gate of the Media Luna squealed as it swung open, wet from the moist wind. First two, then another two, then two more rode out, until two hundred men on horseback had scattered across the rainsoaked fields.

"We'll have to drive the Enmedio herd up past where Estagua used to be, and the Estagua cattle up to the Vilmayo hills," Fulgor Sedano ordered as the men rode by. "And hustle, the rain's really coming down!"

He said it so often that the last to leave heard only, "From here to there, and from there, farther on up."

Every man of them touched the brim of his hat to show that he had understood.

Almost immediately after the last man had left, Miguel Páramo galloped in at full tilt and without reining in his horse dismounted almost in Fulgor's face, leaving his mount to find its own way to the stall.

"Where've you been at this hour, boy?"

"Been doing a little milking."

"Milking who?"

"You can't guess?"

"Must have been that Dorotea. *La Cuarraca.*[9] She's the only one around here likes babies."

"You're a fool, Fulgor. But it's not your fault."

And without bothering to remove his spurs, Miguel went off to find someone to feed him breakfast.

In the kitchen Damiana Cisneros asked him the same question:

"Now where've you been, Miguel?"

"Oh, just around. Calling on the mothers of the region."

"I didn't mean to rile you, Miguel. How do you want your eggs."

"Could I have them with a special side dish?"

---

9. Lame woman.

"I'm being serious, Miguel."

"I know, Damiana. Don't worry. Listen. Do you know a woman named Dorotea? The one they call *La Cuarraca*?

"I do. And if you want to see her, you'll find her right outside. She gets up early every morning to come by here for her breakfast. She's the one who rolls up a bundle in her rebozo and sings to it, and calls it her baby. It must be that something terrible happened to her a long while back, but since she never talks, no one knows what it was. She lives on handouts."

"That damned Fulgor! I'm going to give him a lick that'll make his eyes whirl."

He sat and thought for a while, wondering how the woman might be of use to him. Then without further hesitation he went to the back kitchen door and called Dorotea:

"Come here a minute, I've got a proposition to make you," he said.

Who knows what deal he offered her; the fact is that when he came inside he was rubbing his hands.

"Bring on those eggs!" he yelled to Damiana. And added: "From now on, I want you to give that woman the same food you give me, and if it makes extra work, it's no problem of mine."

In the meantime, Fulgor Sedano had gone to check the amount of grain left in the bins. Since harvest was a long way off, he was worried about the shrinking supply. In fact, the crops were barely in the ground. "I have to see if we can get by." Then he added: "That boy! A ringer for his father, all right, but he's starting off too early. At this rate, I don't think he'll last. I forgot to tell him that yesterday someone came by and said he'd killed a man. If he keeps up like this . . ."

He sighed and tried to imagine where the ranch hands would be by now. But he was distracted by Miguel Páramo's young chestnut stallion, rubbing its muzzle against the corral fence. "He never even unsaddled his horse," he thought. "And he doesn't intend to. At least don Pedro is more reliable, and he has his quiet moments. He sure indulges Miguel, though. Yesterday when I told him what his son had done, he said, 'Just think of it as something I did, Fulgor. The boy couldn't have done a thing like that; he doesn't have the guts yet to kill a man. That takes balls this big.' And he held his hands apart as if he was measuring a squash. 'Anything he does, you can lay it on me.' "

"Miguel's going to give you a lot of headaches, don Pedro. He likes to wrangle."

"Give him his head. He's just a boy. How old is he now? Going on seventeen, Fulgor?"

"About that. I can remember when they brought him here; it seems like yesterday. But he's wild, and he lives so fast that sometimes it appears to me he's racing with time. He'll be the one to lose that game. You'll see."

"He's still a baby, Fulgor."

"Whatever you say, don Pedro; but that woman who came here yesterday, weeping and accusing your son of killing her husband, was not to be consoled. I know how to judge grief, don Pedro, and that woman was carrying a heavy load. I offered her a hundred and fifty bushels of maize to overlook the matter, but she wouldn't take it. Then I promised we'd make things right somehow. She still wasn't satisfied."

"What was it all about?"

"I don't know the people involved."

"There's nothing to worry about, Fulgor. Those people don't really count."

Fulgor went to the storage bins, where he could feel the warmth of the maize. He took a handful and examined it to see whether it had been infested with weevils. He measured the height in the bins. "It'll do," he said. "As soon as we have grass we won't have to feed grain anymore. So there's more than enough."

As he walked back he gazed at the overcast sky. "We'll have rain for a good while." And he forgot about everything else.

"The weather must be changing up there. My mother used to tell me how as soon as it began to rain everything was filled with light and with the green smell of growing things. She told me how the waves of clouds drifted in, how they emptied themselves upon the earth and transformed it, changing all the colors. My mother lived her childhood and her best years in this town, but couldn't even come here to die. And so she sent me in her place. It's strange, Dorotea, how I never saw the sky. At least it should have been the sky she knew."

"I don't know, Juan Preciado. After so many years of never lifting up my head, I forgot about the sky. And even if I had looked up, what good would it have done? The sky is so high and my eyes so clouded that I was happy just knowing where the ground was. Besides, I lost all interest after padre Rentería told me I would never know glory. Or even see it from a distance. . . . It was because of my sins, but he didn't have to tell me that. Life is hard enough as it is. The only thing that keeps you going is the hope that when you die you'll be lifted off this mortal coil; but when they close one door to you and the only one left open is the door to Hell, you're better off not being born. . . . For me, Juan Preciado, heaven is right here."

"And your soul? Where do you think it's gone?"

"It's probably wandering like so many others, looking for living people to pray for it. Maybe it hates me for the way I treated it, but I don't worry about that anymore. And now I don't have to listen to its whining about remorse. Because of it, the little I ate turned bitter in my mouth; it haunted my nights with black thoughts of the damned. When I sat down to die, my soul prayed for me to get up and drag on with my life, as if it still expected some miracle to cleanse me of my sins. I didn't even try. 'This is the end of the road,' I told it. 'I don't have the strength to go on.' And I opened my mouth to let it escape. And it went. I knew when I felt the little thread of blood that bound it to my heart drip into my hands."

They pounded at his door, but he didn't answer. He heard them knock at door after door, waking everyone around. Fulgor—he knew him by his footsteps—paused a moment as he hurried toward the main door, as if he meant to knock again. Then kept running.

Voices. Slow, scraping footsteps, like people carrying a heavy load.

Unidentifiable sounds.

His father's death came to his mind. It had been an early dawn like this, although that morning the door had been open and he had seen the gray of a dismal, ashen sky seeping through. And a woman had been leaning against the doorframe, trying to hold back her sobs. A mother he had forgotten, forgotten many times over, was telling him: "They've killed your father!" In a broken quavering voice held together only by the thread of her sobs.

He never liked to relive that memory because it brought others with it, as if a bulging sack of grain had burst and he was trying to keep the kernels from spilling out. The death of his father dragged other deaths with it, and in each of them was always the image of that shattered face: one eye mangled, the other staring vengefully. And another memory, and another, until that death was erased from memory and there was no longer anyone to remember it.

"Lay him down here. No, not like that. Put his head that way. You! What are you waiting for?"

All this in a low voice.

"Where's don Pedro?"

"He's sleeping. Don't wake him. Don't make any noise."

But there he stood, towering, watching them struggle with a large bundle wrapped in old gunnysacks and bound with hemp like a shroud.

"Who is it?" he asked.

Fulgor Sedano stepped forward and said:

"It's Miguel, don Pedro."

"What did they do to him?" he shouted.

He was expecting to hear "They killed him." And he felt the stirrings of rage forming hard lumps of rancor; instead he heard Fulgor Sedano's soft voice saying:

"No one did anything to him. He met his death alone."

Oil lamps lighted the night.

"His horse killed him," one man volunteered.

They laid him out on his bed; they turned back the mattress and exposed the bare boards, and arranged the body now free of the bonds they had used to carry it home. They crossed his hands over his chest and covered his face with a black cloth. "He looks bigger than he was," Fulgor thought to himself.

Pedro Páramo stood there, his face empty of expression, as if he were far away. Somewhere beyond his consciousness, his thoughts were racing, unformed, disconnected. At last he said:

"I'm beginning to pay. The sooner I begin, the sooner I'll be through."

He felt no sorrow.

When he spoke to the people gathered in the patio, to thank them for their presence, making his voice heard above the wailing of the women, he was not short either of breath or of words. Afterward, the only sound was that of the pawing of Miguel Páramo's chestnut stallion.

"Tomorrow," he ordered Fulgor Sedano, "get someone to put that animal down and take him out of his misery."

"Right, don Pedro. I understand. The poor beast must be suffering."

"That's my feeling, too, Fulgor. And as you go, tell those women not to make such a racket; they're making too much fuss over my loss. If it was their own, they wouldn't be so eager to mourn."

Years later Father Rentería would remember the night when his hard bed had kept him awake and driven him outside. It was the night Miguel Páramo died.

He had wandered through the lonely streets of Comala, his footsteps spooking the dogs sniffing through the garbage heaps. He walked as far as the river, where he stood gazing at how stars falling from the heavens were reflected in the quiet eddies. For several hours he struggled with his thoughts, casting them into the black waters of the river.

It had all begun, he thought, when Pedro Páramo, from the low thing he was, made something of himself. He flourished like a weed. And the worst of it is that I made it all possible. "I have sinned, padre. Yesterday I slept with Pedro Páramo." "I have sinned, padre. I bore Pedro Páramo's child." "I gave my daughter to Pedro Páramo, padre." I kept waiting for him to come and confess something, but he never did. And then he extended the reach of his evil through that son of his. The one he recognized—only God knows why. What I do know is that I placed that instrument in his hands.

He remembered vividly the day he had brought the child to Pedro Páramo, only hours old.

He had said to him:

"Don Pedro, the mother died as she gave birth to this baby. She said that he's yours. Here he is."

Pedro Páramo never even blinked; he merely said:

"Why don't you keep him, Father? Make a priest out of him."

"With the blood he carries in his veins, I don't want to take that responsibility."

"Do you really think he has bad blood?"

"I really do, don Pedro."

"I'll prove you wrong. Leave him here with me. I can find someone to take care of him."

"That's just what I had in mind. At least he'll eat if he's with you."

Tiny as he was, the infant was writhing like a viper.

"Damiana! Here's something for you to take care of. It's my son."

Later he had uncorked a bottle:

"This one's for the deceased, and for you."

"And for the child?"

"For him, too. Why not?"

He filled another glass and both of them drank to the child's future.

That was how it had been.

Carts began rumbling by toward the Media Luna. Father Rentería crouched low, hiding in the reeds along the river's edge. "What are you hiding from?" he asked himself.

"Adios, padre," he heard someone say.

He rose up and answered:

"Adios! May God bless you."

The lights in the village went out one by one. The river was glowing with luminous color.

"Padre, has the Angelus[1] rung yet?" asked one of the drivers.

"It must be much later than that," he replied. And he set off in the opposite direction, vowing not to be stopped.

"Where are you off to so early, padre?"

---

1. The bell for the Angelus, or morning prayers; church bells indicate the time of day for the country people.

"Where's the death, padre?"

"Did someone in Contla die, padre?"

He felt like answering, "I did. I'm the one who's dead." But he limited himself to a smile.

As he left the last houses behind, he walked faster.

It was late morning when he returned.

"Where have you been, Uncle," his niece Ana asked. "A lot of women have been here looking for you. They wanted to confess; tomorrow's the first Friday."

"Tell them to come back this evening."

He sat for a quiet moment on a bench in the hall, heavy with fatigue.

"How cool the air is, Ana."

"It's very warm, Uncle."

"I don't feel it."

The last thing he wanted to think about was that he had been in Contla, where he had made a general confession to a fellow priest who despite his pleas had refused him absolution.

"That man whose name you do not want to mention has destroyed your church, and you have allowed him to do it. What can I expect of you now, Father? How have you used God's might? I want to think that you're a good man and that you're held in high esteem because of that. But it's not enough to be good. Sin is not good. And to put an end to sin, you must be hard and merciless. I want to think that your parishioners are still believers, but it is not you who sustains their faith. They believe out of superstition and fear. I feel very close to you in your penury, and in the long hours you spend every day carrying out your duties. I personally know how difficult our task is in these miserable villages to which we have been banished; but that in itself gives me the right to tell you that we cannot serve only the few who give us a pittance in exchange for our souls. And with your soul in their hands, what chance do you have to be better than those who are better than you? No, Father, my hands are not sufficiently clean to grant you absolution. You will have to go elsewhere to find that."

"What do you mean? That I must look somewhere else if I want to confess?"

"Yes, you must. You cannot continue to consecrate others when you yourself are in sin."

"But what if they remove me from my ministry?"

"Maybe you deserve it. They will be the ones to judge."

"Couldn't you . . . ? Provisionally, I mean. . . . I must administer the last rites . . . give communion. So many are dying in my village, Father."

"Oh, my friend, let God judge the dead."

"Then you won't absolve me?"

And the priest in Contla had told him no.

Later the two of them had strolled through the azalea-shaded cloister of the parish patio. They sat beneath an arbor where grapes were ripening.

"They're bitter, Father," the priest anticipated Father Rentería's question. "We live in a land in which everything grows, thanks to God's providence; but everything that grows is bitter. That is our curse."

"You're right, Father. I've tried to grow grapes over in Comala. They don't bear. Only guavas and oranges: bitter oranges and bitter guavas. I've forgotten the taste of sweet fruit. Do you remember the China guavas we had in the seminary? The peaches? The tangerines that shed their skin at a touch? I brought seeds here. A few, just a small pouch. Afterward, I felt it would have been better to leave them where they were, since I only brought them here to die."

"And yet, Father, they say that the earth of Comala is good. What a shame the land is all in the hands of one man. Pedro Páramo *is* still the owner, isn't he?"

"That is God's will."

"I can't believe that the will of God has anything to do with it. You don't believe that, do you, Father?"

"At times I have doubted; but they believe it in Comala."

"And are you among the 'they'?"

"I am just a man prepared to humble himself, now while he has the impulse to do so."

Later, when they said their good-byes, Father Rentería had taken the priest's hands and kissed them. Now that he was home, and returned to reality, he did not want to think about the morning in Contla.

He rose from the bench and walked to the door.

"Where are you going, Uncle?"

His niece Ana, always present, always by his side, as if she sought his shadow to protect her from life.

"I'm going out to walk for a while, Ana. To blow off steam."

"Do you feel sick?"

"Not sick, Ana. Bad. I feel that's what I am. A bad man."

He walked to the Media Luna and offered his condolences to Pedro Páramo. Again he listened to his excuses for the charges made against his son. He let Pedro Páramo talk. None of it mattered, after all. On the other hand, he did decline his invitation to eat.

"I can't do that, don Pedro. I have to be at the church early because a long line of women are already waiting at the confessional. Another time."

He walked home, then toward evening went directly to the church, just as he was, bathed in dust and misery. He sat down to hear confessions.

The first woman in line was old Dorotea, who was always waiting for the church doors to open.

He smelled the odor of alcohol.

"What? Now you're drinking? How long have you been doing this?"

"I went to Miguelito's wake, padre. And I overdid it a little. They gave me so much to drink that I ended up acting like a clown."

"That's all you've ever done, Dorotea."

"But now I've come with my sins, padre. Sins to spare."

On many occasions he had told her, "Don't bother to confess, Dorotea; you'd be wasting my time. You couldn't commit a sin anymore, even if you tried. Leave that to others."

"I have now, padre. It's the truth."

"Tell me."

"Since it can't do him any harm now, I can tell you that I'm the one who used to get the girls for the deceased. For Miguelito Páramo."

Father Rentería, stalling for time to think, seemed to emerge from his fog as he asked, almost from habit:

"For how long?"

"Ever since he was a boy. From that time he had the measles."

"Repeat to me what you just said, Dorotea."

"Well, that I was the one who rounded up Miguelito's girls."

"You took them to him?"

"Sometimes I did. Other times I just made the arrangements. And with some, all I did was head him in the right direction. You know, the hour when they would be alone, and when he could catch them unawares."

"Were there many?"

He hadn't meant to ask, but the question came out by force of habit.

"I've lost count. Lots and lots."

"What do you think I should do with you, Dorotea? You be the judge. Can you pardon what you've done?"

"I can't, padre. But you can. That's why I'm here."

"How many times have you come to ask me to send you to Heaven when you die? You hoped to find your son there, didn't you, Dorotea? Well, you won't go to Heaven now. May God forgive you."

"Thank you, padre."

"Yes. And I forgive you in His name. You may go."

"Aren't you going to give me any penance?"

"You don't need it, Dorotea."

"Thank you, padre."

"Go with God."

He rapped on the window of the confessional to summon another of the women. And while he listened to "I have sinned," his head slumped forward as if he could no longer hold it up. Then came the dizzyness, the confusion, the slipping away as if in syrupy water, the whirling lights; the brilliance of the dying day was splintering into shards. And there was the taste of blood on his tongue. The "I have sinned" grew louder, was repeated again and again: "for now and forever more," "for now and forever more," "for now . . ."

"Quiet, woman," he said. "When did you last confess?"

"Two days ago, padre."

Yet she was back again. It was as if he were surrounded by misfortune. What are you doing here, he asked himself. Rest. Go rest. You are very tired.

He left the confessional and went straight to the sacristy. Without a glance for the people waiting, he said:

"Any of you who feel you are without sin may take Holy Communion tomorrow."

Behind him, as he left, he heard the murmuring.

I am lying in the same bed where my mother died so long ago,[2] on the same mattress, beneath the same black wool coverlet she wrapped us in to sleep. I slept beside her, her little girl, in the special place she made for me in her arms.

I think I can still feel the calm rhythm of her breathing; the palpitations and sighs that soothed my sleep. . . . I think I feel the pain of her death. . . . But that isn't true.

Here I lie, flat on my back, hoping to forget my loneliness by remembering

2. Susana San Juan recalls her childhood.

those times. Because I am not here just for a while. And I am not in my mother's bed but in a black box like the ones for burying the dead. Because I am dead.

I sense where I am, but I can think. . . .

I think about the limes ripening. About the February wind that used to snap the fern stalks before they dried up from neglect. The ripe limes that filled the overgrown patio with their fragrance.

The wind blew down from the mountains on February mornings. And the clouds gathered there waiting for the warm weather that would force them down into the valley. Meanwhile the sky was blue, and the light played on little whirlwinds sweeping across the earth, swirling the dust and lashing the branches of the orange trees.

The sparrows were twittering; they pecked at the wind-blown leaves, and twittered. They left their feathers among the thorny branches, and chased the butterflies, and twittered. It was that season.

February, when the mornings are filled with wind and sparrows and blue light. I remember. That is when my mother died.

I should have wailed. I should have wrung my hands until they were bleeding. That is how you would have wanted it. But in fact, wasn't that a joyful morning? The breeze was blowing in through the open door, tearing loose the ivy tendrils. Hair was beginning to grow on the mound between my legs, and my hands trembled hotly when I touched my breasts. Sparrows were playing. Wheat was swaying on the hillside. I was sad that she would never again see the wind playing in the jasmines; that her eyes were closed to the bright sunlight. But why should I weep?

Do you remember, Justina? You arranged chairs in a row in the corridor where the people who came to visit could wait their turn. They stood empty. My mother lay alone amid the candles; her face pale, her white teeth barely visible between purple lips frozen by the livid cold of death. Her eyelashes lay still; her heart was still. You and I prayed interminable prayers she could not hear, that you and I could not hear above the roar of the wind in the night. You ironed her black dress, starched her collar and the cuffs of her sleeves so her hands would look young crossed upon her dead breast—her exhausted, loving breast that had once fed me, that had cradled me and throbbed as she crooned me to sleep.

No one came to visit her. Better that way. Death is not to be parceled out as if it were a blessing. No one goes looking for sorrow.

Someone banged the door knocker. You went to the door.

"You go," I said. "I see people through a haze. Tell them to go away. Have they come for money for the Gregorian masses? She didn't leave any money. Tell them that, Justina. Will she have to stay in purgatory if they don't say those masses? Who are they to mete out justice, Justina? You think I'm crazy? That's fine."

And your chairs stood empty until we went to bury her, accompanied by the men we had hired, sweating under a stranger's weight, alien to our grief. They shoveled damp sand into the grave; they lowered the coffin, slowly, with the patience of their office, in the breeze that cooled them after their labors. Their eyes cold, indifferent. They said: "It'll be so much." And you paid them, the way you might buy something at the market, untying the corner of the tear-soaked handkerchief you'd wrung out again and again, the one that now contained the money for the burial. . . .

And when they had gone away, you knelt on the spot above her face and you kissed the ground, and you would have dug down toward her if I hadn't said: "Let's go, Justina. She isn't here now. There's nothing here but a dead body."

"Was that you talking, Dorotea?"

"Who, me? I was asleep for a while. Are you still afraid?"

"I heard someone talking. A woman's voice. I thought it was you."

"A woman's voice? You thought it was me? It must be that woman who talks to herself. The one in the large tomb. Doña Susanita. She's buried close to us. The damp must have got to her, and she's moving around in her sleep."

"Who is she?"

"Pedro Páramo's last wife. Some say she was crazy. Some say not. The truth is that she talked to herself even when she was alive."

"She must have died a long time ago."

"Oh, yes! A long time ago. What did you hear her say?"

"Something about her mother."

"But she didn't have a mother. . . ."

"Well, it was her mother she was talking about."

"Hmmm. At least, her mother wasn't with her when she came. Wait a minute. I remember now the mother was born here, and when she was getting along in years, they vanished. Yes, that's it. Her mother died of consumption. She was a strange woman who was always sick and never visited with anyone."

"That's what she was saying. That no one had come to visit her mother when she died."

"What did she mean? No wonder no one wanted to step inside her door, they were afraid of catching her disease. I wonder if the Indian woman remembers?"

"She was talking about that."

"When you hear her again, let me know. I'd like to know what she's saying."

"You hear? I think she's about to say something. I hear a kind of murmuring."

"No, that isn't her. That's farther away and in the other direction. And that's a man's voice. What happens with these corpses that have been dead a long time is that when the damp reaches them they begin to stir. They wake up."[3]

"The heavens are bountiful. God was with me that night. If not, who knows what might have happened. Because it was already night when I came to. . . ."

"You hear it better now?"

"Yes."

". . . I was covered with blood. And when I tried to get up my hands slipped in the puddles of blood in the rocks. It was *my* blood. Buckets of blood. But I wasn't dead. I knew that. I knew that don Pedro hadn't meant to kill me. Just give me a scare. He wanted to find out whether I'd been in Vilmayo that day two years before. On San Cristobal's day. At the wedding. What wedding? Which San Cristobal's? There I was slipping around in my own blood, and I asked him just that: 'What wedding, don Pedro? No! No, don Pedro. I wasn't

---

3. A popular belief in Spanish American countries.

there. I may have been near there, but only by chance. . . . ' He never meant to kill me. He left me lame—you can see that—and, sorry to say, without the use of my arm. But he didn't kill me. They say that ever since then I've had one wild eye. From the scare. I tell you, though, it made me more of a man. The heavens are bountiful. And don't you ever doubt it."

"Who was that?"

"How should I know? Any one of dozens. Pedro Páramo slaughtered so many folks after his father was murdered that he killed nearly everybody who attended that wedding. Don Lucas Páramo was supposed to give the bride away. And it was really by accident that he died, because it was the bridegroom someone had a grudge against. And since they never found out who fired the bullet that struck him down, Pedro Páramo wiped out the lot. It happened over there on Vilmayo ridge, where there used to be some houses you can't find any trace of now. . . . Listen. . . . Now that sounds like her. Your ears are younger. You listen. And then tell me what she says."

"I can't understand a thing. I don't think she's talking; just moaning."

"What's she moaning about?"

"Well, who knows."

"It must be about something. No one moans just to be moaning. Try harder."

"She's moaning. Just moaning. Maybe Pedro Páramo made her suffer."

"Don't you believe it. He loved her. I'm here to tell you that he never loved a woman like he loved that one. By the time they brought her to him, she was already suffering—maybe crazy. He loved her so much that after she died he spent the rest of his days slumped in a chair, staring down the road where they'd carried her to holy ground. He lost interest in everything. He let his lands lie fallow, and gave orders for the tools that worked it to be destroyed. Some say it was because he was worn out; others said it was despair. The one sure thing is that he threw everyone off his land and sat himself down in his chair to stare down that road.

"From that day on the fields lay untended. Abandoned. It was a sad thing to see what happened to the land, how plagues took over as soon as it lay idle. For miles around, people fell on hard times. Men packed up and left in search of a better living. I remember days when the only sound in Comala was good-byes; it seemed like a celebration every time we sent someone on his way. They went, you know, with every intention of coming back. They asked us to keep an eye on their belongings and their families. Later, some sent for their family but not their things. And then they seemed to forget about the village, and about us—and even about their belongings. I stayed because I didn't have anywhere to go. Some stayed waiting for Pedro Páramo to die, because he'd promised to leave them his land and his goods and they were living on that hope. But the years went by and he lived on, propped up like a scarecrow gazing out across the lands of the Media Luna.

"And not long before he died we had that Cristeros war, and the troops drained off the few men he had left. That was when I really began to starve, and things were never the same again.

"And all of it was don Pedro's doing, because of the turmoil of his soul. Just because his wife, that Susanita, had died. So you tell me whether he loved her."

It was Fulgor Sedano who told him:

"*Patrón*. You know who's back in town?"

"Who?"

"Bartolomé San Juan."

"How come?"

"That's what I asked myself. Wonder why he's come back?"

"Haven't you looked into it?"

"No. I wanted to tell you first. He didn't inquire about a house. He went straight to your old place. He got off his horse and moved in his suitcases, just as if you'd already rented it to him. He didn't seem to have any doubts."

"And what are you doing about it, Fulgor? Why haven't you found out what's going on? Isn't that what you're paid to do?"

"I was a little thrown off by what I just told you. But tomorrow I'll find out, if you think we should."

"Never mind about tomorrow. I'll look into the San Juans. Both of them came?"

"Yes. Him and his wife. But how did you know?"

"Wasn't it his daughter?"

"Well, the way he treats her, she seems more like his wife."

"Go home and go to bed, Fulgor."

"With your leave."

I waited thirty years for you to return, Susana. I wanted to have it all. Not just part of it, but everything there was to have, to the point that there would be nothing left for us to want, no desire but your wishes. How many times did I ask your father to come back here to live, telling him I needed him. I even tried deceit.

I offered to make him my administrator, anything, as long as I could see you again. And what did he answer? "No response," the messenger always said. "Señor don Bartolomé tears up your letters as soon as I hand them to him." But through that boy I learned that you had married, and before long I learned you were a widow and had gone back to keep your father company.

Then silence.

The messenger came and went, and each time he reported: "I can't find them, don Pedro. People say they've left Mascota. Some say they went in one direction, and some say another."

I told him: "Don't worry about the expense. Find them. They haven't been swallowed up by the earth."

And then one day he came and told me:

"I've been all through the mountains searching for the place where don Bartolomé San Juan might be hiding and at last I found him, a long way from here, holed up in a little hollow in the hills, living in a log hut on the site of the abandoned La Andromeda mines."

Strange winds were blowing then. There were reports of armed rebellion.[4] We heard rumors. Those were the winds that blew your father back here. Not for his own sake, he wrote in his letter, but your safety. He wanted to bring you back to civilization.

I felt that the heavens were parting. I wanted to run to meet you. To

4. The Mexican Revolution of 1910.

envelop you with happiness. To weep with joy. And weep I did, Susana, when I learned that at last you would return.

"Some villages have the smell of misfortune. You know them after one whiff of their stagnant air, stale and thin like everything old. This is one of those villages, Susana.

"Back there, where we just came from, at least you could enjoy watching things being born: clouds and birds and moss. You remember? Here there's nothing but that sour, yellowish odor that seems to seep up from the ground. This town is cursed, suffocated in misfortune.

"He wanted us to come back. He's given us his house. He's given us everything we need. But we don't have to be grateful to him. This is no blessing for us, because our salvation is not to be found here. I feel it.

"Do you know what Pedro Páramo wants? I never imagined that he was giving us all this for nothing. I was ready to give him the benefit of my toil, since we had to repay him somehow. I gave him all the details about La Andromeda, and convinced him that the mine had promise if we worked it methodically. You know what he said? 'I'm not interested in your mine, Bartolomé San Juan. The only thing of yours I want is your daughter. She's your crowning achievement.'

"He loves you, Susana. He says you used to play together when you were children. That he knows you. That you used to swim together in the river when you were young. I didn't know that. If I'd known I would have beat you senseless."

"I'm sure you would."

"Did I hear what you said? 'I'm sure you would'?"

"You heard me."

"So you're prepared to go to bed with him?"

"Yes, Bartolomé."

"Don't you know that he's married, and that he's had more women than you can count?"

"Yes, Bartolomé."

"And don't call me Bartolomé! I'm your father!"

Bartolomé San Juan, a dead miner. Susana San Juan, daughter of a miner killed in the Andromeda mines. He saw it clearly. "I must go there to die," he thought. Then he said:

"I've told him that although you're a widow, you are still living with your husband—or at least you act as if you are. I've tried to discourage him, but his gaze grows hard when I talk to him, and as soon as I mention your name, he closes his eyes. He is, I haven't a doubt of it, unmitigated evil. That's who Pedro Páramo is."

"And who am I?"

"You are my daughter. Mine. The daughter of Bartolomé San Juan."

Ideas began to form in Susana San Juan's mind, slowly at first; they retreated and then raced so fast she could only say:

"It isn't true. It isn't true."

"This world presses in on us from every side; it scatters fistfuls of our dust across the land and takes bits and pieces of us as if to water the earth with our blood. What did we do? Why have our souls rotted away? Your mother always said that at the very least we could count on God's mercy. Yet you deny it, Susana. Why do you deny me as your father? Are you mad?"

"Didn't you know?"

"*Are* you mad?"

"Of course I am, Bartolomé. Didn't you know?"

"You know of course, Fulgor, that she is the most beautiful woman on the face of the earth. I had come to believe I had lost her forever. I don't want to lose her again. You understand me, Fulgor? You tell her father to go explore his mines. And there . . . I imagine it wouldn't be too hard for an old man to disappear in a territory where no one ever ventures. Don't you agree?"

"Maybe so."

"We need it to be so. She must be left without family. We're called on to look after those in need. You agree with that, don't you?"

"I don't see any difficulty with that."

"Then get about it, Fulgor. Get on with it."

"And what if she finds out?"

"Who's going to tell her? Let's see, tell me. Just between the two of us, who's going to tell her?"

"No one, I guess."

"Forget the 'I guess.' Forget that as of now, and everything'll work out fine. Remember how much needs to be done at the Andromeda. Send the old man there to keep at it. To come and go as he pleases. But don't let him get the idea of taking his daughter. We'll look after her here. His work is there in the mines and his house is here anytime he wants it. Tell him that, Fulgor."

"I'd like to say once more that I like the way you do things, *patrón*. You seem to be getting your spirit back."

Rain is falling on the fields of the valley of Comala. A fine rain, rare in these lands that know only downpours. It is Sunday. The Indians have come down from Apango[5] with their rosaries of chamomile, their rosemary, their bunches of thyme. They have come without ocote pine, because the wood is wet, and without oak mulch, because it, too, is wet from the long rain. They spread their herbs on the ground beneath the arches of the arcade. And wait.

The rain falls steadily, stippling the puddles.

Rivers of water course among the furrows where the young maize is sprouting. The men have not come to the market today; they are busy breaching the rows so the water will find new channels and not carry off the young crop. They move in groups, navigating the flooded fields beneath the rain, breaking up soft clumps of soil with their spades, firming the shoots with their hands, trying to protect them so they will grow strong.

The Indians wait. They feel this is a ill-fated day. That may be why they are trembling beneath their soaking wet *gabanes*, their straw capes—not from cold, but fear. They stare at the fine rain and at the sky hoarding its clouds.

No one comes. The village seems uninhabited. A woman asks for a length of darning cotton, and a packet of sugar, and, if it is to be had, a sieve for

<hr />

5. Situated to the northwest of San Gabriel in Jalisco, a population of Mexican Indians speaking their own indigenous language.

straining cornmeal gruel. As the morning passes, the *gabanes* grow heavy with moisture. The Indians talk among themselves, they tell jokes, and laugh. The chamomile leaves glisten with a misting of rain. They think, "If only we'd brought a little pulque, it wouldn't matter; but the hearts of the magueys are swimming in a sea of water. Well, what can you do?"

Beneath her umbrella Justina Díaz makes her way down the straight road leading from the Media Luna, avoiding the streams of water gushing onto the sidewalks. As she passed the main entry to the church, she made the sign of the cross. She walked beneath the arches into the plaza. All the Indians turned to watch her. She felt their eyes upon her, as if she were under intense scrutiny. She stopped at the first display of herbs, bought ten centavos worth of rosemary, and then retraced her steps, followed by countless pairs of Indian eyes.

"Everything costs so much this time of year," she thought as she walked back toward the Media Luna. "This pitiful little bunch of rosemary for ten centavos. It's barely enough to give off a scent."

Toward dusk the Indians rolled up their wares. They walked into the rain with their heavy packs on their backs. They stopped by the church to pray to the Virgin, leaving a bunch of thyme as an offering. Then they set off toward Apango, on their way home. "Another day," they said. And they walked down the road telling jokes, and laughing.

Justina Díaz went into Susana San Juan's bedroom and set the rosemary on a small shelf. The closed curtains blocked out the light, so that she saw only shadows in the darkness; she merely guessed at what she was seeing. She supposed that Susana San Juan was asleep; she wished that she did nothing but sleep, and as she was sleeping now, Justina was content. But then she heard a sigh that seemed to come from a far corner of the darkened room.

"Justina!" someone called.

She looked around. She couldn't see anyone but she felt a hand on her shoulder and a breath against her ear. A secretive voice said, "Go away, Justina. Bundle up your things, and leave. We don't need you anymore."

"She needs me," she replied, standing straighter. "She's sick, and she needs me."

"Not anymore, Justina. I will stay here and take care of her."

"Is that you, don Bartolomé?" But she did not wait for the answer. She screamed a scream that reached the ears of men and women returning from the fields, a cry that caused them to say "That sounded like someone screaming, but it can't be human."

The rain deadens sounds. It can be heard when all other sound is stilled, flinging its icy drops, spinning the thread of life.

"What's the matter, Justina? Why did you scream?" Susana San Juan asked.

"I didn't scream, Susana. You must have been dreaming."

"I've told you, I never dream. You have no consideration. I scarcely slept a wink. You didn't put the cat out last night, and it kept me awake."

"It slept with me, between my legs. It got wet, and I felt sorry for it and let it stay in my bed; but it didn't make any noise."

"No, it didn't make any noise. But it spent the night like a circus cat, leaping from my feet to my head, and meowing softly as if it were hungry."

"I fed it well, and it never left my bed all night. You've been dreaming lies again, Susana."

"I tell you, it kept startling me all night with its leaping about. Your cat may be very affectionate, but I don't want it around when I'm sleeping."

"You're seeing things, Susana. That's what it is. When Pedro Páramo comes, I'm going to tell him that I can't put up with you any longer. I'll tell him I'm leaving. There are plenty of nice people who will give me work. Not all of them are crazy like you, or enjoy humiliating a person the way you do. Tomorrow morning I'm leaving; I'll take my cat and leave you in peace."

"You won't leave, you perverse and wicked Justina. You're not going any-where, because you will never find anyone who loves you the way I do."

"No, I won't leave, Susana. I won't leave. You know I will take care of you. Even though you make me swear I won't, I will always take care of you."

She had cared for Susana from the day she was born. She had held her in her arms. She had taught her to walk. To take those first steps that seemed eternal. She had watched her lips and eyes grow sweet as sugar candy. "Mint candy is blue. Yellow and blue. Green and blue. Stirred with spearmint and wintergreen." She nibbled at her chubby legs. She entertained her by offering her a breast to nurse that had no milk, that was only a toy. "Play with this," she told Susana. "Play with your own little toy." She could have hugged her to pieces.

Outside, rain was falling on the banana leaves and water in the puddles sounded as if it were boiling.

The sheets were cold and damp. The drainpipes gurgled and foamed, weary of laboring day and night, day and night. Water kept pouring down, stream-ing in diluvial burbling.

It was midnight; outside, the sound of the rain blotted out all other sounds.

Susana San Juan woke early. She sat up slowly, then got out of bed. Again she felt the weight in her feet, a heaviness rising up her body, trying to reach her head:

"Is that you, Bartolomé?"

She thought she heard the door squeak, as if someone were entering or leaving. And then only the rain, intermittent, cold, rolling down the banana leaves, boiling in its own ferment.

She slept again and did not wake until light was falling on red bricks beaded with moisture in the gray dawn of a new day. She called:

"Justina!"

Justina, throwing a shawl around her shoulders, appeared immediately, as if she had been right outside the door.

"What is is, Susana?"

"The cat. The cat's in here again."

"My poor Susana."

She laid her head on Susana's breast and hugged her until Susana lifted her head and asked "Why are you crying? I'll tell Pedro Páramo how good you are to me. I won't tell him anything about how your cat frightens me. Don't cry, Justina."

"Your father's dead, Susana. He died night before last. They came today to say there's nothing we can do; they've already buried him. It was too far to bring his body back here. You're all alone now, Susana."

"Then it was Father," Susana smiled. "So he came to tell me good-bye," she said. And smiled.

Many years earlier, when she was just a little girl, he had said one day:

"Climb down, Susana, and tell me what you see."

She was dangling from a rope that cut into her waist and rubbed her hands raw, but she didn't want to let go. That rope was the single thread connecting her to the outside world.

"I don't see anything, papá."

"Look hard, Susana. See if you don't see something."

And he shone the lamp on her.

"I don't see anything, papá."

"I'll lower you a little farther. Let me know when you're on the bottom."

She had entered through a small opening in some boards. She had walked over rotted, decaying, splintered planks covered with clayey soil.

"Go a little lower, Susana, and you'll find what I told you."

She bumped lower and lower, swaying in the darkness, with her feet swinging in empty space.

"Lower, Susana. A little lower. Tell me if you see anything."

And when she felt the ground beneath her feet she stood there dumb with fear. The lamplight circled above her and then focused on a spot beside her. The yell from above made her shiver.

"Hand me that, Susana!"

She picked up the skull in both hands, but when the light struck it fully, she dropped it.

"It's a dead man's skull," she said.

"You should find something else there beside it. Hand me whatever's there."

The skeleton broke into individual bones: the jawbone fell away as if it were sugar. She handed it up to him, piece after piece, down to the toes, which she handed him joint by joint. The skull had been first, the round ball that had disintegrated in her hands.

"Keep looking, Susana. For money. Round gold coins. Look everywhere, Susana."

And then she did not remember anything, until days later she came to in the ice: in the ice of her father's glare.

That was why she was laughing now.

"I knew it was you, Bartolomé."

And poor Justina, weeping on Susana's bosom, sat up to see what she was laughing about, and why her laughter had turned to wild guffaws.

Outside, it was still raining. The Indians had gone. It was Monday and the valley of Comala was drowning in rain.

The winds continued to blow, day after day. The winds that had brought the rain. The rain was over but the wind remained. There in the fields, tender leaves, dry now, lay flat against the furrows, escaping the wind. By day the wind was bearable; it worried the ivy and rattled the roof tiles; but by night it moaned, it moaned without ceasing. Canopies of clouds swept silently across the sky, so low they seemed to scrape the earth.

Susana San Juan heard the wind lashing against the closed window. She was lying with her arms crossed behind her head, thinking, listening to the night noises: how the night was buffeted by bursts of restless wind. Then the abrupt cessation.

Someone has opened the door. A rush of air blows out the lamp. She sees only darkness, and conscious thought is suspended. She hears faint rustlings. The next moment she hears the erratic beating of her heart. Through closed eyelids she senses the flame of light.

She does not open her eyes. Her hair spills across her face. The light fires drops of sweat on her upper lip. She asks:

"Is that you, Father?"

"Yes, I am your father, my child."

She peers through half-closed eyelids. Her hair seems to be cloaking a shadowy figure on the ceiling, its head looming above her face. Through the haze of her eyelashes a blurred figure takes form. A diffuse light burns in the place of its heart, a tiny heart pulsing like a flickering flame. "Your heart is dying of pain," Susana thinks. "I know that you've come to tell me Floren-cio is dead, but I already know that. Don't be sad about anything else; don't worry about me. I keep my grief hidden in a safe place. Don't let your heart go out!"

She got out of bed and dragged herself toward Father Rentería.

"Let me console you," he said, protecting the flame of the candle with his cupped hand, "console you with my own inconsolable sorrow."

Father Rentería watched as she approached him and encircled the lighted flame with her hands, and then she lowered her face to the burning wick until the smell of burning flesh forced him to jerk the candle away and blow out the flame.

Again in darkness, Susana ran to hide beneath the sheets.

Father Rentería said:

"I have come to comfort you, daughter."

"Then you may go, Father," she replied. "Don't come back. I don't need you."

And she listened to the retreating footsteps that had always left a sensation of cold and fear.

"Why do you come see me, when you are dead?"

Father Rentería closed the door and stepped out into the night air.

The wind continued to blow.

A man they called El Tartamudo came to the Media Luna and asked for Pedro Páramo.

"Why do you want to see him?"

"I want to t-talk with him."

"He isn't here."

"T-tell him, when he comes back, that it's about d-don Fulgor."

"I'll go look for him, but you may have to wait a while."

"T-tell him it's uh-urgent."

"I'll tell him."

El Tartamudo waited, without dismounting from his horse. After a while Pedro Páramo, whom El Tartamudo had never seen, came up and asked:

"What can I do for you?"

"I need to t-talk directly to the *patrón*."

"I am the *patrón*. What do you want?"

"W-well. Just this. They've m-murdered don Fulgor Sedano. I was w-with him. We'd ridden down to the spillways to find out whuh-why the water had dried up. And wh-while we were doing that a band of m-men came riding toward us. And o-one of them yelled 'I n-know him. He's the foreman of the M-Media Luna.'

"Th-they ignored me. But they t-told don Fulgor to get off his horse. They s-said they were r-revolutionaries. And th-that they wanted your land. 'T-take off!' they told don Fulgor. "R-run tell your *patrón* to be expecting us!' And he st-started off, sc-scared as hell. N-not too fast, because he's so fat; but he ran. They sh-shot him as he ran. He d-d-died with one foot in the air and one on the g-ground.

"I didn't m-move a hair. I waited for n-night, and here I am to t-tell you what happened."

"Well, what are you hanging around for? Get on your way. Go tell those men that I'm here anytime they want to see me. I'll deal with them. But first ride by La Consagración ranch. You know El Tilcuate?[6] He'll be there. Tell him I need to see him. And tell those men that I'll expect them at the first opportunity. What brand of revolutionaries are they?"

"I don't know. Th-that's what they c-called themselves."

"Tell El Tilcuate that I need him here *yesterday*."

"I w-will, *patrón*."

Pedro Páramo again closed the door to his office. He felt old and weary. He lost no time worrying about Fulgor, who'd been, after all, "more of the next world than this." He'd given all he had to give. He could be useful, though no more than any other man. "But those dumb bastards have never run into a boa constrictor like El Tilcuate," he thought.

And then his thoughts turned to Susana San Juan, always in her room sleeping, or if not sleeping, pretending to be. He had spent the whole night in her room, standing against the wall and observing her in the wan candle-light: sweaty face, hands fidgeting with the sheets and tugging at her pillow until it was in shreds.

Ever since he had brought her to live with him, every night had been like this, nights spent watching her suffering, her endless agitation. He asked himself how long it would go on.

He hoped not long. Nothing can last forever; there is no memory, however intense, that does not fade.

If only he knew what was tormenting her, what made her toss and turn in her sleeplessness until it seemed she was being torn apart inside.

He had thought he knew her. But even when he found he didn't, wasn't it enough to know that she was the person he loved most on this earth? And—and this was what mattered most—that because of her he would leave this earth illuminated by the image that erased all other memories.

But what world was Susana San Juan living in? That was one of the things Pedro Páramo would never know.

"The warm sand felt so good against my body. My eyes were closed, my arms flung wide and my legs open to the breeze from the sea. The sea there before me, stretching toward the horizon, leaving its foam on my feet as the waves washed in. . . ."

---

6. A large water snake that attacks human beings and eats other serpents.

"Now that's her talking, Juan Preciado. Don't forget to tell me what she says."

". . . It was early morning. The sea rose and fell. It slipped from its foam and raced away in clear green silent waves.

" 'I always swim naked in the sea,' I told him. And he followed me that first day, naked too, phosphorescent as he walked from the sea. There were no gulls; only those birds they call 'sword beaks,' that grunt as if they're snoring and disappear once the sun is up. He followed me the first day; he felt lonely, even though I was there.

" 'You might just as well be one of the birds,' he said. 'I like you better at night when we're lying on the same pillow beneath the same sheets in the darkness.'

"He went away.

"I went back. I would always go back. The sea bathes my ankles, and retreats; it bathes my knees, my thighs; it puts its gentle arm around my waist, circles my breasts, embraces my throat, presses my shoulders. Then I sink into it, my whole body. I give myself to its pulsing strength, to its gentle possession, holding nothing back.

" 'I love to swim in the sea,' I told him.

"But he didn't understand.

"And the next morning I was again in the sea, purifying myself. Giving myself to the waves."

As dusk fell, the men appeared. They were carrying carbines, and cartridge belts crisscrossed their chests. There were about twenty of them. Pedro Páramo invited them in to eat. Without removing their sombreros, or uttering a word, they sat down at the table and waited. The only sounds came as they drank their chocolate and ate repeated servings of tortillas and beans.

Pedro Páramo watched them. These were not faces he knew. El Tilcuate stood right behind him, in the shadows.

"Señores," said Pedro Páramo, when he saw they were through. "What else can I do for you?"

"You own all this?" one of them asked with a sweeping gesture.

But another man interrupted:

"I do the talking here!"

"All right. What can I do for you?" Pedro Páramo repeated.

"Like you see, we've taken up arms."

"And?"

"And nothing. That's it. Isn't that enough?"

"But why have you done it?"

"Well, because others have done the same. Didn't you know? Hang on a little till we get our instructions, and then we'll tell you why. For now, we're just here."

"I know why," another said. "And if you want, I'll tell you. We've rebelled against the government and against people like you because we're tired of putting up with you. Everyone in the government is a crook, and you and your kind are nothing but a bunch of lowdown bandits and slick thieves. And as for the governor himself, I won't say nothing, because what we have to say to him we'll say with bullets."

"How much do you need for your revolution?" Pedro Páramo asked. "Maybe I can help you."

"The señor is talking sense, Perseverancio. You shouldn't let your tongue run on like that. We need to get us a rich man to help outfit us, and who better than this señor here. Casildo, how much do we need?"

"Well, whatever the señor feels he can give us."

"What! This man wouldn't throw a crumb to a starving man. Now that we're here, we'd ought to grab our chance and take everything he's got, right down to the last scrap of food stuffed in his filthy mouth."

"Easy now, Perseverancio. You catch more flies with sugar than with vinegar. We can make a deal here. How much, Casildo?"

"Well, I figure off the top of my head that twenty thousand pesos wouldn't be too bad as a starter. What do the rest of you think? Now, who knows but what our señor here maybe could do a little more, seeing he's so willing to help us. So, let's say fifty thousand. How does that strike you?"

"I'll give you a hundred thousand," Pedro Páramo told them. "How many are there of you?"

"I'd say three hundred."

"All right. I'm going to lend you another three hundred men to beef up your contingent. Within a week you'll have both men and money at your disposal. I'm giving you the money; the men are just a loan. As soon as you're through with them, send them back here. Is that a bargain?

"You bet."

"So until a week from now, señores. It's been a pleasure to meet you."

"All right," said the last to leave. "But remember, if you don't live up to your word, you'll hear from Perseverancio, and that's me."

Pedro Páramo shook the man's hand as he left.

"Which one of them do you think is the leader?" he asked El Tilcuate after they'd gone.

"Well, I think maybe the one in the middle, the one with the big belly who never even looked up. I have a feeling he's the one. I'm not often wrong, don Pedro."

"You are this time, Damasio. *You're* the leader. Or would you rather not get tied up in this revolution?"

"Well, I have been a little slow getting to it. Considering how much I like a good scrap."

"You have an idea now what it's all about, so you don't need my advice. Get yourself three hundred men you can trust and sign up with these rebels. Tell them you're bringing the men I promised them. You'll know how to take care of the rest."

"And what do I tell them about the money? Do I hand that over, too?"

"I'll give you ten pesos for each man. Just enough for their most pressing needs. You tell them I'm keeping the rest here for them. That it isn't a good idea to haul so much money around in times like these. By the way, how would you like that little *rancho* over in Puerta de Piedra? Fine. It's yours, as of this minute. Take this note to my lawyer in Comala, old Gerardo Trujillo, and he'll put the property in your name then and there. How does that sound, Damasio?"

"No need to ask, *patrón*. Though I'd be happy to do this with or without the *rancho*—just for the hell of it. You know me. At any rate, I'm grateful to you. My old woman will have something to keep her busy while I'm off roaring around."

"And look, while you're at it, round up a few head of cattle. What that *rancho* needs is a little activity."

"Would you mind if I took Brahmas?"

"Choose any you want, your wife can look after them. Now, to get back to our business. Try not to get too far away from my land, so that when anyone comes they'll find men already here. And come by whenever you can, or when you have news."

"Be seeing you, *patrón*."

"What is it she's saying, Juan Preciado?"

"She's saying she used to hide her feet between his legs. Feet icy as cold stones, and that he warmed them, like bread baking in the oven. She says he nibbled her feet, saying they were like golden loaves from the oven. And that she slept cuddled close to him, inside his skin, lost in nothingness as she felt her flesh part like a furrow turned by a plow first burning, then warm and gentle, thrusting against her soft flesh, deeper, deeper, until she cried out. But she says his death hurt her much much more. That's what she said."

"Whose death does she mean?"

"Must have been someone who died before she did."

"But who could it have been?"

"I don't know. She says that the night he was late coming home, she felt sure he'd come back very late, maybe about dawn. She thought that because her poor cold feet felt as if they'd been wrapped in something, as if someone had covered them and warmed them. When she woke up she found that her feet were under the newspaper she had been reading while she was waiting for him; although the paper had fallen to the floor when she couldn't stay awake any longer, her feet were wrapped in it when they came to tell her he was dead."

"The box they buried her in must have split open, because I hear something like boards creaking."

"Yes, I hear it, too."

That night she had the dreams again. Why such intense remembering of so many things? Why not simply his death, instead of this tender music from the past?

"Florencio is dead, señora."

How big the man was! How tall! And how hard his voice was. Dry as the driest dirt. She couldn't see his body clearly; or had it become blurred in memory? As if rain were falling between them. What was it he had said? Florencio? What Florencio? Mine? Oh, why didn't I weep then and drown myself in tears to wash away my anguish? Oh, God! You are not in Your heaven! I asked You to protect him. To look after him. I asked that of You. But all You care about is souls. And what I want is his *body*. Naked and hot with love; boiling with desire; stroking my trembling breasts and arms. My transparent body suspended from his. My lustful body held and released by his strength. What shall I do now with my lips without his lips to cover them? What shall become of my poor lips?

While Susana San Juan tossed and turned, Pedro Páramo, standing by the door, watched her and counted the seconds of this long new dream. The oil in the lamp sputtered, and the flame flickered and grew weaker. Soon it would go out.

If only she were suffering pain, and not these relentless, interminable, exhausting dreams, he could find some way to comfort her. Those were Pedro Páramo's thoughts as he stood watching Susana San Juan, following her every movement. What would he do if she died like the flame of the pale light that allowed him to watch her?

He left the room, noiselessly closing the door behind him. Outside, the cool night air erased Susana San Juan's image from his mind.

Just before dawn, Susana awakened. She was sweating. She threw the heavy covers to the floor, and freed herself of the heat of the sheets. She was naked, cooled by the early morning air. She sighed, and then fell back to sleep.

That was how Father Rentería found her hours later; naked and sleeping.

"Have you heard, don Pedro? They got the best of El Tilcuate."

"I knew there was shooting last night, because I could hear the racket. But that's all I knew. Who told you this, Gerardo?"

"Some of the wounded made it to Comala. My wife helped bandage them. They said they'd been with Damasio, and that a lot of men died. Seems like they met up with some men who called themselves Villistas."[7]

"Good God, Gerardo! I see bad times ahead. What do you plan to do?"

"I'm leaving, don Pedro. For Sayula. I'll start over there."

"You lawyers have the advantage; you can take your fortune with you anywhere, as long as they don't knock you off."

"Don't you believe it, don Pedro. We have our problems. Besides, it hurts to leave people like you; all your courtesies will be sorely missed. It's fair to say that our world is constantly changing. Where would you like me to leave your papers?"

"Don't leave them. Take them with you. Or won't you be able to look after my affairs where you're going?"

"I appreciate your confidence, don Pedro. Truly I do. Although I venture to say that it won't be possible for me to continue. Certain irregularities . . . Let's say . . . information no one but you should have. Your papers could be put to bad use if they fell into the wrong hands. The surest thing would be to leave them with you."

"You're right, Gerardo. Leave them here. I'll burn them. With papers or without them, who's going to argue with me over my property."

"No one, I'm sure of that, don Pedro. No one. Now I must be going."

"Go with God, Gerardo."

"What did you say?"

"I said, may God be with you."

Gerardo Trujillo, lawyer, left very slowly. He was old, but not so old he had to walk so haltingly, so reluctantly. The truth was that he had expected a reward. He had served don Lucas—might he rest in peace—don Pedro's father; then, and up till now, don Pedro. Even Miguel, don Pedro's son. The truth was that he expected some recognition. A large, and welcome, return for his services. He had told his wife:

"I'm going over to tell don Pedro I'm leaving. I know he'll want to thank

---

7. Followers of Francisco (Pancho) Villa (1878–1923), the Mexican revolutionary leader.

me. Let me say that with the money he gives me we can establish ourselves in Sayula and live in comfort for the rest of our days."

But why is it that women always have doubts? What is it, anyway? Do they receive their information from on high? His wife had not been at all sure he would be rewarded.

"You'll have to work like a dog to keep your head above water. You won't get anything from him."

"Why do you say that?"

"I just know."

He was still walking toward the front door, listening for a sudden summons:

"Oh, Gerardo! I've been so preoccupied that I wasn't thinking straight. You know I owe you favors that can't be repaid with money. Here, take this: a small thank-you."

But the summons never came. He left through the front entrance and untied his horse from the hitching post. He mounted and slowly started back toward Comala, trying not to ride out of earshot, in case anyone called. When he realized that the Media Luna had faded from sight, he thought, "What a terrible comedown it would be to ask for a loan."

"Don Pedro. I've come back because I'm not happy with myself. I'd be pleased to continue to look after your affairs."

He was again sitting in Pedro Páramo's office, which he'd left less than a half hour before.

"Fine with me, Gerardo. Here are the papers, right where you left them."

"I'd also appreciate . . . My expenses . . . Moving . . . A small advance on my fees . . . And a little something extra, if that seems all right."

"Five hundred?"

"Couldn't we make it a little, well, just a little more?"

"Will a thousand do?"

"How about five?"

"Five what? Five thousand pesos? I don't have that much. You of all people know that everything I have is tied up. Land, cattle. You know that. Take a thousand. That's all you'll need."

Trujillo sat thinking. With his head on his chest. He heard pesos clinking on the desk where Pedro Páramo was counting the money. He was remembering don Lucas, who had always put off paying his fees. And don Pedro, who'd started with a clean slate. And his son Miguel. What a lot of trouble that boy had caused!

He had got him out of jail at least fifteen times, if not more. And there was the time he'd murdered that man. What was his name? Rentería, yes, that was it. They'd put a pistol in the corpse's hand. Miguelito'd been scared to death, though he'd laughed about it later. How much would just that one time have cost don Pedro if things had moved ahead to legal proceedings? And what about all the rapes, eh? Think of all the times he'd taken money from his own pocket to keep the girls quiet. "You should be thankful," he'd told them, "that you'll be having a fair-skinned baby."

"Here you are, Gerardo. Take good care of this, because money doesn't grow on trees."

And Trujillo, who was still deep in his meditations, replied, "Just like dead men don't spring up from their graves."

It was a long time till dawn. The sky was filled with fat stars, swollen from the long night. The moon had risen briefly and then slipped out of sight. It was one of those sad moons that no one looks at or pays attention to. It had hung there a while, misshapen, not shedding any light, and then gone to hide behind the hills.

From far away, shrouded in darkness, came the bellowing of bulls.

"Those creatures never sleep," said Damiana Cisneros. "They never sleep. They're like the Devil, who's always out looking for souls to spirit away."

She turned over in bed, putting her face close to the wall. That was when she heard the knocking.

She held her breath and opened her eyes. Again she heard three sharp taps, as if someone were rapping on the wall. Not right beside her, but farther away—although on the same wall.

"Heaven help us! It must have been San Pascual, tapping three times as warning to one of his faithful that his hour has come."

Since she hadn't made a novena for so long because of her rheumatism, she didn't worry; but she was afraid, and even more than afraid, curious.

She quietly got up from her cot and peered out the window.

The fields were black. Even so, she knew the landscape so well that she could see the large mass of Pedro Páramo's body swinging into the window of young Margarita.

"Oh, that don Pedro!" said Damiana. "He never gets over chasing the girls. What I don't understand is why he insists on doing things on the sly. If he'd just let me know, I would have told Margarita that the *patrón* had need of her tonight, and he wouldn't have had the bother of leaving his bed."

She closed the window when she heard the bulls still bellowing. She lay down on her cot and pulled the cover up over her ears, and then lay there thinking about what must be happening to young Margarita.

A little later she had to get up and strip off her nightgown, because the night seemed to have turned hot.

"Damiana!" she heard.

And she was a girl again.

"Open the door, Damiana!"

Her heart had leapt like a toad hopping beneath her ribs.

"But why, *patrón*?"

"Open up, Damiana!"

"But I'm fast asleep, *patrón*."

Then she had heard don Pedro stalking off down the long corridor, his heels clicking loudly, as they did when he was angry.

The next night, to avoid angering him again, she left the door ajar, and even went to bed naked to make things easy for him. But Pedro Páramo had never returned.

And so tonight, now that she was the head of all the Media Luna servants, and was old and had earned her respect, she still thought of that night when the *patrón* had called, "Open the door, Damiana!"

And she fell asleep thinking how happy young Margarita must be at this hour.

Later, she again heard knocking, but this time at the main door, as if someone were trying to beat it down with the butt of a gun.

A second time she opened the window and looked out into the night. She saw nothing, although it seemed to her the earth was steaming, as it does after a rain when the earth is roiling with worms. She could sense something rising, something like the heat of many men. She heard frogs croaking, and crickets: a quiet night in the rainy season. Then once again she heard the pounding at the door.

A lamp spilled its light on the faces of a band of men. Then it went out.

"These things have nothing to do with me," said Damiana Cisneros, and closed her window.

I heard you got your tail whipped, Damasio. Why did you let that happen?"

"You got the wrong story, *patrón*. Nothing happened to me. I didn't lose a man. I have seven hundred of my own, and a few tagalongs. What happened was that a few of the old-timers got bored with not seeing any action and started firing at a patrol of shave-heads who turned out to be a whole army. Those Villistas, you know."

"Where had they come from?"

"From the North, leveling everything they found in their path. It seems, as far as we can make out, that they're riding all through here getting the lay of the land. They're powerful. You can't take that from them."

"Well, why don't you join up with them? I've told you before we have to be on the side of whoever's winning."

"I've already done it."

"Then why are you here?"

"We need money, *patrón*. We're tired of eating nothing but meat. We don't have a taste for it anymore. And no one wants to give us credit. That's why we've come, hoping you can buy us provisions and we won't have to steal from anyone. If we were way off somewhere, we wouldn't mind 'borrowing' a little from the locals, but everyone around here is a relative, and we'd feel bad robbing them. It's money we need, to buy food, even if only a few tortillas and chilis. We're sick of meat."

"So now you're making demands on me, Damasio?"

"Oh, no, *patrón*. I'm speaking for the boys. I don't want nothing for myself."

"It speaks well for you that you're looking after your men, but go somewhere else to get what you need. I've already given you money. Be happy with what you've got. Now I don't want to offer this as advice, but haven't you thought of riding on Contla? Why do you think you're fighting a revolution? Only a dunce would be asking for handouts. You might as well go home and help your wife look after the hens. Go raid some town! You're risking your skin, so why the hell don't others do their part? Contla is crawling with rich men. Take a little out of their hides. Or maybe you think you're their nursemaid and have to look after their interests? No, Damasio. Show them that you're not just out for a good time. Rough them up a little, and the centavos will flow."

"I'll do like you say, *patrón*. I can always count on good advice from you."

"Well, make good use of it."

Pedro Páramo watched as the men rode away. He could hear horses trotting past, invisible in the darkness. Sweat and dust; trembling earth. When the light of fireflies again dotted the sky, he knew all the men had left. Only he remained, alone, like a sturdy tree beginning to rot inside.

He thought of Susana San Juan. He thought of the young girl he had just slept with. Of the small, frightened, trembling body, and the thudding of a heart that seemed about to leap from her chest. "You sweet little handful," he had said to her. And embraced her, trying to transform her into Susana San Juan. "A woman who is not of this world."

As dawn breaks, the day turns, stopping and starting. The rusty gears of the earth are almost audible: the vibration of this ancient earth overturning darkness.

"Is it true that night is filled with sins, Justina?"

"Yes, Susana."

"Really true?"

"It must be, Susana."

"And what do you think life is, Justina, if not sin? Don't you hear? Don't you hear how the earth is creaking?"

"No, Susana, I can't hear anything. My fate is not as grand as yours."

"You would be frightened. I'm telling you, you would be frightened if you heard what I hear."

Justina went on cleaning the room. Again and again she passed the rag over the wet floorboards. She cleaned up the water from the shattered vase. She picked up the flowers. She put the broken pieces into the pail.

"How many birds have you killed in your lifetime, Justina?"

"Many, Susana."

"And you never felt sad?"

"I did, Susana."

"Then, what are you waiting for to die?"

"I'm waiting for Death, Susana."

"If that's all, it will come. Don't worry."

Susana San Juan was sitting propped up against her pillows. Her uneasy eyes searching every corner. Her hands were clasped over her belly like a protective shell. A humming like wings sounded above her head. And the creaking of the pulley in the well. The sounds of people waking up.

"Do you believe in hell, Justina?"

"Yes, Susana. And in heaven, too."

"I only believe in hell," Susana said. And closed her eyes.

When Justina left the room, Susana San Juan fell asleep again, while outside the sun sparkled. Justina met Pedro Páramo in the hall.

"How is the señora?"

"Bad," she replied, ducking her head.

"Is she complaining?"

"No, señor. She doesn't complain about anything; but they say the dead never complain. The señora is lost to us all."

"Has Father Rentería been to see her?"

"He came last night to hear her confession. She should have taken Communion today but she must not be in a state of grace, because padre Rentería hasn't brought it. He said he'd be here early, but you see the sun's up and he hasn't come. She must not be in a state of grace."

"Whose grace?"

"God's grace, señor."

"Don't be silly, Justina."

"As you say, señor."

Pedro Páramo opened the door and stood beside it, letting a ray of light fall upon Susana San Juan. He saw eyes pressed tightly shut as if in pain; a moist, half-open mouth; sheets thrown back by insentient hands to reveal the nakedness of a body beginning to twist and turn in convulsions.

He rushed across the brief space separating him from the bed and covered the naked body writhing like a worm in more and more violent contortions. He spoke into her ear, "Susana!" He repeated, "Susana!"

The door opened and Father Rentería entered quietly, saying only:

"I've come to give you Communion, my child."

He waited until Pedro Páramo helped her sit up and arranged her pillows against the headboard. Susana San Juan, still half-asleep, held out her tongue and swallowed the Host. Then she said, "We had a glorious day, Florencio." And sank back down into the tomb of her sheets.

"You see that window, doña Fausta, there at the Media Luna where the light is always on?"

"No, Angeles. I don't see any window."

"That's because the room is dark now. Don't you think that means something bad is going on over there? There's been a light in that window for more than three years, night after night. People who've been there say that's the room of Pedro Páramo's wife, a poor crazy woman who's afraid of the dark. And look, now the light's out. Isn't that a bad sign?"

"Maybe she died. She's been real sick. They say she doesn't know people anymore, and that she talks to herself. It's a fitting punishment for Pedro Páramo, being married to that woman."

"Poor don Pedro."

"No, Fausta, he deserves it. That and more."

"See, the window is still dark."

"Just let the window be, and let's get home to bed. It's late for two old women like us to be out roaming the streets."

And the two women, who had left the church about eleven, disappeared beneath the arches of the arcade, watching the shadow of a man crossing the plaza in the direction of the Media Luna.

"Look, doña Fausta. Do you think that man over there is Doctor Valencia?"

"It looks like him, although I'm so blind I wouldn't recognize him if he was right in front of me."

"But you remember, he always wears those white pants and a black coat. I'll bet something bad is happening out at the Media Luna. Look how fast he's walking, as if he had a real reason to hurry."

"Which makes me think it really is serious. I feel like I ought to go by and tell padre Rentería to get out there; that poor woman shouldn't die without confessing."

"God forbid, Angeles. What a terrible thought. After all she's suffered in this world no one would want her to go without the last rites and then suffer forever in the next life. Although the psychics always say that crazy people don't need to confess, that even if they have sin in their soul, they're innocents. God only knows. . . . Look! Now the light's back on in the window. I hope everything turns out all right. If someone dies in that house imagine what would happen to all the work we've gone to to decorate the church for Christmas. As important as don Pedro is, our celebration would go right up in smoke."

"You always think of the worst, doña Fausta. You should do what I do: put everything in the hands of Divine Providence. Say an Ave Maria to the Virgin, and I'm sure nothing will go wrong between now and morning. And then, let God's will be done. After all, she can't be very happy in this life."

"Believe me, Angeles, I always take comfort from what you say. I can go to sleep with those good thoughts on my mind. They say that our sleeping thoughts go straight to Heaven. I hope mine make it that far. I'll see you tomorrow."

"Until tomorrow, Fausta."

The two old women slipped through the half-open doors of their homes. And the silence of the night again fell over the village.

"My mouth is filled with earth."

"Yes, Father."

"Don't say, 'Yes, Father.' Repeat with me the words I am saying."

"What are you going to say? You want me to confess again? Why again?"

"This isn't a confession, Susana. I've just come to talk with you. To prepare you for death."

"I'm going to die?"

"Yes, daughter."

"Then why don't you leave me in peace? I want to rest. Someone must have told you to come keep me awake. To stay with me until sleep is gone forever. Then what can I do to find him? Nothing, Father. Why don't you just go away and leave me alone?"

"I will leave you in peace, Susana. As you repeat the words I tell you, you will drift off, as if you were crooning yourself to sleep. And once you are asleep, no one will wake you. . . . You will never wake again."

"All right, Father. I will do what you say."

Father Rentería, seated on the edge of the bed, his hands on Susana San Juan's shoulders, his mouth almost touching her ear to keep from being overheard, formed each word in a secretive whisper: "My mouth is filled with earth." Then he paused. He looked to see whether her lips were moving. He saw her mouthing words, though no sound emerged:

"My mouth is filled with you, with your mouth. Your tightly closed lips, pressing hard, biting into mine. . . ."

She, too, paused. She looked at Father Rentería from the corner of her eye; he seemed far away, as if behind a misted glass.

Again she heard his voice, warm in her ear:

"I swallow foamy saliva; I chew clumps of dirt crawling with worms that knot in my throat and push against the roof of my mouth. . . . My mouth caves in, contorted, lacerated by gnawing, devouring teeth. My nose grows spongy. My eyeballs liquefy. My hair burns in a single bright blaze. . . ."

He was surprised by Susana San Juan's calm. He wished he could divine her thoughts and see her heart struggling to reject the images he was sowing within her. He looked into her eyes, and she returned his gaze. It seemed as if her twitching lips were forming a slight smile.

"There is more. The vision of God. The soft light of his infinite Heaven. The rejoicing of the cherubim and song of the seraphim. The joy in the eyes of God, which is the last, fleeting vision of those condemned to eternal suffering. Eternal suffering joined to earthly pain. The marrow of our bones becomes like live coals and the blood in our veins threads of fire, inflicting unbelievable agony that never abates, for it is fanned constantly by the wrath of God."

"He sheltered me in his arms. He gave me love."

Father Rentería glanced at the figures gathered around them, waiting for the last moment. Pedro Páramo waited by the door, with crossed arms; Doctor Valencia and other men stood beside him. Farther back in the shadows, a small group of women eager to begin the prayer for the dead.

He meant to rise. To anoint the dying woman with the holy oils and say, "I have finished." But no, he hadn't finished yet. He could not administer the sacraments to this woman without knowing the measure of her repentance.

He hesitated. Perhaps she had nothing to repent of. Maybe there was nothing for him to pardon. He bent over her once more and said in a low voice, shaking her by the shoulders:

"You are going into the presence of God. And He is cruel in His judgment of sinners."

Then he tried once more to speak into her ear, but she shook her head:

"Go away, Father. Don't bother yourself over me. I am at peace, and very sleepy."

A sob burst forth from one of the women hidden in the shadows.

Susana San Juan seemed to revive for a moment. She sat straight up in bed and said:

"Justina, please go somewhere else if you're going to cry!"

Then she felt as if her head had fallen upon her belly. She tried to lift it, to push aside the belly that was pressing into her eyes and cutting off her breath, but with each effort she sank deeper into the night.

"I . . . I saw doña Susanita die."

"What are you saying, Dorotea?"

"What I just told you."

Dawn. People were awakened by the pealing of bells. It was the morning of December eighth.[8] A gray morning. Not cold, but gray. The pealing began with the largest bell. The others chimed in. Some thought the bells were ringing for High Mass, and doors began to open wide. Not all the doors opened; some remained closed where the indolent still lay in bed waiting for the bells to advise them that morning had come. But the ringing lasted longer than it should have. And it was not only the bells of the large church, but those in Sangre de Cristo, in Cruz Verde, and the Santuario. Noon came, and the tolling continued. Night fell. And day and night the bells continued, all of them, stronger and louder, until the ringing blended into a deafening lament. People had to shout to hear what they were trying to say. "What could it be?" they asked each other.

After three days everyone was deaf. It was impossible to talk above the

---

8. The date of the Catholic celebration of the Immaculate Conception of Mary.

clanging that filled the air. But the bells kept ringing, ringing, some cracked, with a hollow sound like a clay pitcher.

"Doña Susana died."

"Died? Who?"

"The señora."

"Your señora?"

"Pedro Páramo's señora."

People began arriving from other places, drawn by the endless pealing. They came from Contla, as if on a pilgrimage. And even farther. A circus showed up, who knows from where, with a whirligig and flying chairs. And musicians. First they came as if they were onlookers, but after a while they settled in and even played concerts. And so, little by little, the event turned into a fiesta. Comala was bustling with people, boisterous and noisy, just like the feast days when it was nearly impossible to move through the village.

The bells fell silent, but the fiesta continued. There was no way to convince people that this was an occasion for mourning. Nor was there any way to get them to leave. Just the opposite, more kept arriving.

The Media Luna was lonely and silent. The servants walked around with bare feet, and spoke in low voices. Susana San Juan was buried, and few people in Comala even realized it. They were having a fair. There were cock-fights and music, lotteries, and the howls of drunken men. The light from the village reached as far as the Media Luna, like an aureole in the gray skies. Because those were grey days, melancholy days for the Media Luna. Don Pedro spoke to no one. He never left his room. He swore to wreak vengeance on Comala:

"I will cross my arms and Comala will die of hunger."

And that was what happened.

El Tilcuate continued to report:

"We're with Carranza now."

"Fine."

"Now we're riding with General Obregón."[9]

"Fine."

"They've declared peace. We're dismissed."

"Wait. Don't disband your men. This won't last long."

"Father Rentería's fighting now. Are we with him or against him?"

"No question. You're on the side of the government."

"But we're irregulars. They consider us rebels."

"Then take a rest."

"As fired up as I am?"

"Do what you want, then."

"I'm going to back that old priest. I like how they yell. Besides, that way a man can be sure of salvation."

"I don't care what you do."

Pedro Páramo was sitting in an old chair beside the main door of the Media Luna a little before the last shadow of night slipped away. He had been there,

---

9. General Álvaro Obregón, revolutionary leader and president of Mexico after Carranza (1920–24). Carranza: Venustiano Carranza, revolutionary leader and first president of the Mexican Republic (1917–1920).

alone, for about three hours. He didn't sleep anymore. He had forgotten what sleep was, or time. "We old folks don't sleep much, almost never. We may drowse, but our mind keeps working. That's the only thing I have left to do." Then he added, aloud: "It won't be long now. It won't be long."

And continued: "You've been gone a long time, Susana. The light is the same now as it was then; not as red, but that same pale light veiled in the white gauze of the mist. Like now. And it was just this hour. I was sitting here by the door, watching it dawn, watching as you went away following the path to Heaven; there, where the sky was beginning to glow with light, leaving me, growing fainter and fainter among the shadows of this earth.

"That was the last time I saw you. As you went by, you brushed the branches of the Paradise tree beside the path, sweeping away its last leaves with your passing. Then you disappeared. I called after you, 'Come back, Susana!' "

Pedro Páramo's lips kept moving, whispering words. Then as he pressed his lips together, he opened his eyes, where the pale light of dawn was reflected.

Day was beginning.

At the same hour, doña Inés, the mother of Gamaliel Villalpando, sweeping the street in front of her son's store, saw Abundio Martínez push the half-open door and go inside. He found Gamaliel asleep on the counter, his sombrero over his face as protection against the flies. Abundio waited a while for him to wake up. He waited until doña Inés, who had completed her chore of sweeping the street, came in and poked her son's ribs with the broomstick:

"You have a customer here! Get up!"

Gamaliel sat up, surly and grunting. His eyes were bloodshot from being up so late, and from waiting on drunks—in fact, getting drunk with them. Now, sitting on the counter, he cursed his mother, he cursed himself, and uninterruptedly cursed life, "which isn't worth shit." Then he lay back down with his hands stuffed between his legs, and fell asleep still mumbling curses:

"It's not my fault if drunks are still dragging their asses around at this hour."

"My poor boy. Forgive him, Abundio. The poor man spent the night waiting on some travelers; the more they drank the more quarrelsome they got. What brings you here so early in the morning?"

She was shouting as she spoke, because Abundio was so hard of hearing.

"Well, I need a bottle of liquor."

"Has Refugio fainted again?"

"No, she died on me, madre Villa. Just last night, about eleven. After I went and sold my burros. I even sold my burros, so I could get help to make her better."

"I can't hear what you're saying. What did you say? What are you telling me?"

"I said I spent the night sitting up with my dead wife, Refugio. She gave up the ghost last night."

"I knew I smelled a death. That's what I said to Gamaliel: 'I have a feeling that someone's died. I can smell it.' But he didn't pay me any mind. Trying to get along with those strangers, the poor man got drunk. You know how he is when he's like that; he thinks everything's funny, and doesn't pay any attention. But, let's see now. Have you invited anyone to the wake?"

"No one, madre Villa. That's why I need the liquor, to ease my sorrow."

"Do you want it straight?"

"Yes, madre Villa. To get drunk faster. And give it to me quick. I need it right now."

"I'll give you two pints for the price of one, because it's you. I want you to tell your poor dead wife that I always thought well of her, and for her to remember me when she gets to the pearly gates."

"I will, madre Villa."

"You tell her that before she gets cold."

"I'll tell her. I know she's counting on you to pray for her. She died grieving because there wasn't anyone to give her the last rites."

"What! Didn't you go for padre Rentería?"

"I did. But they told me he was in the hills."

"What hills?"

"Well, off there somewhere. You know there's a revolution."

"You mean he's in it, too? God have mercy on our souls, Abundio."

"What do we care about all that, madre Villa? It doesn't touch us. Pour me another. Sort of on the sly, like. After all, Gamaliel's asleep."

"Then don't you forget to ask Refugio to pray to God for me; I need all the help I can get."

"Don't worry. I'll tell her the minute I get home. I'll get her to promise. I'll tell she has to do it or else you'll be worrying your head about it."

"That's just what I want you to do. Because you know how women are. You have to see that they do what they promise."

Abundio Martínez set another twenty centavos on the counter.

"Now I'll take that other one, señora. And if your hand is a little liberal, well that's up to you. The one thing I promise is that I'll drink this one at home with the departed; there beside my Cuca."

"Get along then, before my son wakes up. He's pretty sour when he wakes up after a drunk. Get on home, and don't forget my message to your wife."

Abundio left the store sneezing. The liquor was pure fire, but since he'd been told that drinking it fast made you drunk faster, he gulped down swallow after swallow, fanning his mouth with his shirttail. He meant to go straight home, where Refugio was waiting, but he took a wrong turn and staggered up the street rather than down, following the road out of town.

"Damiana!" called Pedro Páramo. "Go see who that man is coming down the road."

Abundio stumbled on, head hanging, at times crawling on all fours. He felt as if the earth were tilting, that it was spinning, and flinging him off. He would make a grab for it, but just when he had a good hold, it would start spinning again . . . Until he found himself facing a man sitting outside his door.

"I need money to bury my wife," he said. "Can you help me?"

Damiana Cisneros prayed: "Deliver us, O God, from the snares of the Devil." And she thrust her hands toward Abundio, making the sign of the cross.

Abundio Martínez saw a frightened woman standing before him, making a cross; he shuddered. He was afraid that the Devil might have followed him there, and he looked back, expecting to see Satan in some terrible guise. When he saw nothing, he repeated:

"I've come to ask for a little charity to help bury my wife."

The sun was as high as his shoulder. A cool, early-morning sun, hazy in the blowing dust.

As if he were hiding from the sunlight, Pedro Páramo's face vanished beneath the shawl covering his shoulders, as Damiana's cries grew louder, cutting through the fields: "They're murdering don Pedro!"

Abundio Martínez could hear a woman screaming. He didn't know how to make her stop, and he couldn't find the thread of his thoughts. He was sure that the old woman's screams could be heard a long way away. Even his wife must be hearing them, because they were piercing his eardrums, even though he couldn't understand the words. He thought of his wife, laid out on her cot, all alone there in the patio of his house where he had carried her to lie in the cool air, hoping to slow the body from decomposing. His Cuca, who just yesterday had lain with him, live as life, frolicking like a filly, nipping and nuzzling him. The woman who had given him the son who had died almost as soon as he was born, because they said, she was in such bad health: a sore eye, the ague, a bad stomach, and who knows what all, according to the doctor who'd come at the last minute, after he'd sold his burros to pay for the price of his visit. And none of it had done any good . . . His Cuca, lying there in the night dew, her eyes fast shut, unable to see the dawn, this sun . . . any sun.

"Help me!" he said. "I need a little money."

But he couldn't hear his own words. The woman's screams deafened him.

Small black dots were moving along the road from Comala. Soon the dots turned into men, and then they were standing beside him. Damiana Cisneros had stopped screaming now. She had relaxed her cross. She had fallen to the ground, and her mouth was open as if she were yawning.

The men lifted her from the ground and carried her inside the house.

"Are you all right, *patrón*?" they asked.

Pedro Páramo's head appeared. He nodded.

They disarmed Abundio, who still held the bloody knife in his hand.

"Come with us," they said. "A fine mess you've got yourself into."

He followed them.

Before they got to the village he begged them to excuse him. He, walked to the side of the road and vomited something yellow as bile. Streams and streams, as if he had drunk ten liters of water. His head began to burn and his tongue felt thick.

"I'm drunk," he said.

He returned to where the men were waiting. He put his arms across their shoulders, and they dragged him back, his toes carving a furrow in the dust.

Behind them, still in his chair, Pedro Páramo watched the procession making its way back to the village. As he tried to lift his left hand, it dropped like lead to his knees, but he thought nothing of it. He was used to seeing some part of him die every day. He watched the leaves falling from the Paradise tree. "They all follow the same road. They all go away." Then he returned to where he had left his thoughts.

"Susana," he said. He closed his eyes. "I begged you to come back. . . .

"An enormous moon was shining over the world. I stared at you till I was nearly blind. At the moonlight pouring over your face. I never grew tired of looking at you, at the vision you were. Soft, caressed by the moonlight, your swollen, moist lips iridescent with stars, your body growing transparent in the night dew. Susana. Susana San Juan."

He tried to raise his hand to wipe the image clear, but it clung to his legs like a magnet. He tried to lift the other hand, but it slipped slowly down his side until it touched the floor, a crutch supporting his boneless shoulder.

"This is death," he thought.

The sun was tumbling over things, giving them form once again. The ruined, sterile earth lay before him. Heat scalded his body. His eyes scarcely moved; they leapt from memory to memory, blotting out the present. Suddenly his heart stopped, and it seemed as if time and the breath of life stopped with it.

"So there won't be another night," he thought.

Because he feared the nights that filled the darkness with phantoms. That locked him in with his ghosts. That was his fear.

"I know that within a few hours Abundio will come with his bloody hands to ask for the help I refused him. But I won't have hands to cover my eyes, to block him out. I will have to hear him, listen until his voice fades with the day, until his voice dies."

He felt a hand touch his shoulder, and straightened up, hardening himself.

"It's me, don Pedro," said Damiana. "Don't you want me to bring you your dinner?"

Pedro Páramo replied:

"I'm coming along. I'm coming."

He supported himself on Damiana Cisnero's arm and tried to walk. After a few steps he fell; inside, he was begging for help, but no words were audible. He fell to the ground with a thud, and lay there, collapsed like a pile of rocks.

ALEXANDER SOLZHENITSYN
born 1918

The reputation of Russian novelist Alexander Solzhenitsyn is divided almost equally between two complementary aspects: he continues the tradition of the realistic nineteenth-century novel (following the example of his compatriots Tolstoy and Dostoevsky), and he has assumed the role of moral conscience in a modern society where both East and West are fatally flawed. Expelled from the Soviet Union in 1974 and stripped of his citizenship until a new regime restored it in 1990, Solzhenitsyn proclaims the virtues of an older, religious way of life as the only salvation for a civilization that has been dehumanized by political oppression and materialist greed. Art and literature, he feels, are "endowed with the miraculous power to communicate" and thus make it possible for people to experience situations that they have not lived. This basis of common communication erases divisions and allows us to have "a single system of evaluation for evil deeds and for good ones." Solzhenitsyn tries to encompass both the historian's and the moralist's aims when he writes about the history of his own country in the twentieth century and paints a picture of human suffering and moral endurance under oppression. Like Thomas Mann, he includes a range of characters and diverse social types in novels that allude to larger social issues; unlike Mann, his tone is overtly moral and even didactic, especially in his later works. Solzhenitsyn is impelled to testify for all those who cannot speak: for the woman in *Cancer Ward* (1968), for example, who says "Where can I read about us? Will that be only in a hundred years?" His testimony ranges from the more personal account of a day in concentration camp (*One Day in the Life of Ivan Denisovich*, 1963) to broad historical panoramas such as *August 1914* (1971), which focuses on the defeat of the Russian Second Army in East Prussia during World War I, and *Gulag Archipelago* (1973–75), a description of the Soviet concentration camp system. Clearly he finds the form of the realistic novel—expanded, in *August 1914*, with documents and imitation film scripts—the most appropriate method for representing the truth of history. Solzhenitsyn has little patience with avant-garde literature, which, he says, "has been thought up by empty-headed people." Instead, he tries to render the essence of history by blending documented fact and narrative fiction in his creative works and, in recent years, by editing and publishing (in Russian) historical documents from pre-Revolutionary Russia.

He was born Alexander Isayevich Solzhenitsyn on December 11, 1918, in Kislovodsk, in the northern Caucasus. His father had died six months earlier, and his mother supported them in Rostov-on-Don by working as a typist. The family was extremely poor, and—although Solzhenitsyn would have preferred studying literature in Moscow—he was obliged upon graduation from high school to enroll in the local Department of Mathematics at Rostov University. The choice, he says, was a lucky one, for his double degree in mathematics and physics allowed him to spend four years of his prison camp sentence in a relatively privileged *sharashka*, or research institute, instead of at hard manual labor. During 1939–41 he also took correspondence courses from the Institute of History, Philosophy, and Literature in Moscow. When Solzhenitsyn graduated in 1941, in the middle of World War II, he was immediately inducted into the army, where he drove horse-drawn transport vehicles until he was sent to artillery school in 1942. That November he was put in charge of an artillery reconnaissance battery at the front, a position he held until his sudden arrest in February 1945.

The military censor had found passages in his letters to a friend that were—even under a pseudonym—visibly disrespectful of Stalin, and Solzhenitsyn was sentenced in July to eight years in the prison camps. From 1946 to 1950 he worked as a mathematician in research institutes staffed by prisoners (such as that described in *The First Circle*) but in 1950 was taken to a new kind of camp for political prisoners only, where he worked as a manual laborer. After his sentence was ostensibly over, an administrative order sent him into perpetual exile in southern Kazakhstan. Solzhenitsyn spent the years of exile teaching physics and mathematics in a rural school and wrote prose in secret. The tumor that had developed in his first labor camp grew worse, and in 1954 the author received treatment in a clinic in Tashkent (recalled in the novel *Cancer Ward*). He returned to exile in 1955 (the year he wrote *The First Circle*) and was not released until June 1956. Official rehabilitation came in 1957, and the author moved to Ryazan in European Soviet Union where he continued to teach physics and mathematics, while secretly writing fiction, until 1962. *Matryona's Home* and *One Day in the Life of Ivan Denisovich* were written during this period.

At the age of forty-two, Solzhenitsyn had written a great deal but published nothing. In 1961, however, it looked as though the climate of political censorship might change. Nikita Khrushchev had just publicly attacked the "cult of personality" and hero worship that had surrounded Stalin, and the poet and editor Alexander Tvardovsky called on writers to portray "truth," not the artificial picture of perfect Soviet society that Stalin preferred. Solzhenitsyn was encouraged to submit *One Day in the Life of Ivan Denisovich*, which appeared (with Khrushchev's approval) in the November 1962 issue of Tvardovsky's journal *Novy Mir*. In January 1963 Tvardovsky published the stories *Matryona's Home* and *Incident at Krechetovka Station* but—with the exception of two short stories and an article on style—Solzhenitsyn would not be allowed to publish anything more in his native land. Even the highly praised *One Day in the Life of Ivan Denisovich* was removed from candidacy for the Lenin Prize in 1963. Khrushchev himself was forced into retirement in October 1964, and the temporary loosening of censorship came to an end. The novel *The First Circle* (already accepted by *Novy Mir*) and two plays (*The Lovegirl and the Innocent*, written 1954; *Candle in the Wind*, written 1960) were prohibited during 1964–65, and *Cancer Ward*, after the type was already partially set, was refused publication permission by the Writers' Union in 1966. Solzhenitsyn protested both the censorship and the fact that the Writers' Union did not defend its members before official attacks, but instead he himself was expelled from the Writers' Union in 1969, after *The First Circle* and *Cancer Ward* had appeared in the West. The only means of publishing officially unacceptable works was to convey them abroad to a Western publishing house or to circulate them in *samizdat* ("self-publishing") form by circulating copies of typewritten manuscripts. Solzhenitsyn made arrangements to have his works published in the West and continued work on the larger historical novels: *The Gulag Archipelago*, which he had begun earlier, and *August 1914*, which he wrote in 1969–70. In 1970 he was awarded the Nobel Prize in literature, which he accepted in absentia because he was afraid that he would not be permitted to re-enter the Soviet Union once he left. After the publication abroad of the first volume of *The Gulag Archipelago*, however, he was arrested in February 1974 and expelled from the country. From 1974 to 1976 Solzhenitsyn lived in Zurich, and in 1976 he moved to the United States, where he lived in seclusion on a farm in Vermont. The expulsion remained in effect until the new president of the Soviet Union, Mikhail S. Gorbachev, offered in 1990 to restore Solzhenitsyn's citizenship as part of an attempt to rehabilitate artists and writers disgraced during previous regimes. Solzhenitsyn did not accept the offer, and later in the year he refused a prize awarded him by the Russian Republic for *The Gulag Archipelago*, noting that the book was not widely available in the Soviet Union and that the "phenomenon of the Gulag" had not been overcome. In September 1991, however, the old charge of treason was officially dropped, and the writer returned to Russia in May 1994 to widespread public acclaim. The novelist expected, and was expected, to be a prominent voice in contemporary Russian society—for a while, he even had a television program. His moral strictures and nostalgia for a simpler past, however, proved alien to a post-Soviet society intent on prosperity. Still a respected moral authority, Solzhenitsyn seems nowadays fated to speak from the margin.

Solzhenitsyn's first three novels have in common the themes of imprisonment, of personal suffering, and of the moral purity to be gained by those who endure and learn from their suffering. *One Day in the Life of Ivan Denisovich* is the story, told at a very basic level of hunger, cold, and brutally demanding work, of one fairly good day in the life of a prison camp inmate, the peasant Ivan Denisovich Shukhov. When the book appeared, it was the first public recognition of Stalin's prison camp system, and Solzhenitsyn's matter-of-fact narration of the prisoners' day-to-day struggle to survive and retain their humanity shocked readers in Russia and in the West. Shukhov is not a heroic figure, or even portrayed as particularly intelligent, but in his deprivation he has found a core of inner spiritual strength that might well be envied, Solzhenitsyn suggests, by those outside prison who compromise their principles, and accede to injustices, for fear of losing what they have.

The worlds of *Cancer Ward* and *The First Circle* are more privileged than that of *One Day in the Life of Ivan Denisovich*, but each retains the atmosphere of imprisonment and imminent death, and each composes a picture of society by juxtaposing characters with different backgrounds and different points of view. Solzhenitsyn calls this technique of juxtaposition "polyphonic" or many-voiced: he writes a "polyphonic novel with concrete details specifying the time and place of action. A novel without a central hero. . . . Each character becomes central when the action reverts to him." In *Cancer Ward*, thirteen patients representing different social and political classes are brought together in a ward at the cancer clinic in Tashkent; this microcosm of Soviet society is faced with sickness, suffering, death, and an authoritarian medical system that administers treatment without explaining it (or its side effects) to the patient. The ward becomes a metaphor for Soviet society, a metaphor given further dimensions when the inmates articulate their different values in response to a story by Tolstoy: "What Men Live By." The ultimate question is not collective but individual, says Kostoglotov: a man may be a member of a collective, "but only while he's alive. . . . He has to die alone."

The same emphasis on the testing of individual values occurs in *The First Circle,* a novel whose title refers to the least painful circle of Hell in Dante's *Inferno* and indicates here the *sharashka* or prisoner-staffed research section of the Mavrino Institute. The prisoners working in the *sharashka* are under pressure from their superiors (who are under pressure from Stalin) to produce spying devices, including a method for identifying voices on taped telephone calls, and an impregnable telephone coding system for Stalin. If they do not produce satisfactory work, they are sent back to almost-certain death in the labor camps (the lower circles of this Hell); if they do, they become part of the police state. No one is free, not even the dictator who is imprisoned by his own suspicions. The whole society of *The First Circle* is an Inferno, and only by sacrificing everything can one hope to retain spiritual freedom.

Solzhenitsyn turned next to a larger panoramic scope, where the authorial voice would dominate and interpret a mass of historical information. *August 1914* is the first volume of a planned trilogy inquiring into the course of modern Russian history: later volumes (of which a few chapters have appeared in journals and in the fictional portrait, *Lenin in Zurich*) are titled after revolutionary dates, *October 1916* and *March 1917. August 1914* describes the defeat of the Second Russian Army in East Prussia during World War I and—in a consciously fragmented style that moves from scene to scene, includes extracts of documents, newspapers, proverbs, and songs, and provides sections marked "Screen" that imitate film scripts—attempts to depict a broad social panorama with characters from all classes, thus recording a moment in history from an epic point of view.

The second broad panorama is *The Gulag Archipelago,* a three-volume, seven-section account of Stalin's widespread prison camp system. (*Gulag* stands for "Chief Administration of Corrective Labor Camps," camps that were scattered across the Soviet Union like islands in a sea [the archipelago].) Solzhenitsyn describes the horror of these camps in quasi-anecdotal form, using personal experience, oral testimony, excerpts of documents, written eyewitness reports, and altogether a massive collection of evidence accumulated inside *An Attempt at Artistic Investigation* (the subtitle). In this book, perhaps even more than in *August 1914,* there is a tension between the bare facts that Solzhenitsyn transmits and the spiritual interpretation of history into which they fit. The author is overtly present, commenting, guessing intuititively from context when particular facts are missing, and stressing in his own voice the theme that has pervaded all his work: the purification of the soul through suffering. The title of the fourth section, "The Soul and Barbed Wire," symbolizes the recurrent opposition of soul and imprisoning society that has become familiar to his readers.

Since Solzhenitsyn is such a dedicated anti-Communist and anti-Marxist, many Westerners have jumped to the conclusion that he is in favor of the Western democratic system. Such is not the case. He looks back to an earlier, more nationalist and spiritual authoritarianism represented for him by the image of Holy Russia: "For a thousand years Russia lived with an authoritarian order . . . that authoritarian order possessed a strong moral foundation . . . Christian Orthodoxy." In a speech given at Harvard in 1978, *A World Split Apart,* he criticized Western democracy's "herd instinct" and "need to accommodate mass standards," its emphasis on "well-being" and "constant desire to have still more things," its "spiritual exhaustion" in which "mediocrity triumphs under the guise of democratic restraints." Once again, he returns to the theme of purification by suffering that permeates his fiction: "We have been through a spiritual training far in advance of Western experience. The complex and deadly crush of life has produced stronger, deeper, and more interesting personalities than those generated by standardized Western well-being."

One of those strong and deep personalities is surely Matryona in *Matryona's Home*. Solzhenitsyn's story, which is probably modeled on the old Russian literary form of the saint's life, is a testimony to Matryona's absolute simplicity, her refusal to possess anything more than the basic necessities (she will not raise a pig to kill for food), her willingness to help others without promise of reward, and finally to let her greedy in-laws tear down part of her own home and cart it off. The narrator of the story, like Solzhenitsyn an ex-convict and mathematics teacher, has buried himself deep in the country to avoid signs of modern Soviet society and to find—if it still exists—an image of the Old Russia. The town of Talnovo itself is tainted, not just by the *kolkhoz* (collective farm) system, which ceases to consider Matryona part of the collective as soon as she becomes ill, but also by the laziness, selfishness, and predatory greed of its inhabitants. Yet there remains Matryona. Her life has been filled with disappointment and deprivation, and she remains an outsider in a materialist society that despises her lack of acquisitive instinct, but she seems to live in a dimension of spiritual contentment and love that is unknown to those around her. Only the narrator, who has learned to value essential qualities from his own experience in the concentration camps, is able finally to recognize her as "the righteous one," one of those whose spiritual merit seems alien to modern society, yet is needed to save society from divine retribution (Genesis 18.23–33).

Andrej Kodjak, *Alexander Solzhenitsyn* (1978), provides a biographical and critical introduction to Solzhenitsyn up to his deportation from the Soviet Union in 1974; it includes a discussion of Russian terms. Michael Scammell's detailed *Solzhenitsyn: A Biography* (1984) is complemented by D. M. Thomas, *Alexander Solzhenitsyn: A Century in His Life* (1998), which adds new information and a discussion of the writer's work after his return to Russia. Kathryn B. Feuer, ed., *Solzhenitsyn: A Collection of Critical Essays* (1976), and Harold Bloom, ed., *Alexander Solzhenitsyn* (2000), contain a range of essays on aspects and particular works, including *Matryona's Home*. John B. Dunlop, Richard S. Haugh, and Michael Nicholson, eds., *Solzhenitsyn in Exile: Critical Essays and Documentary Material* (1985), offer critical essays and discussions of Solzhenitsyn's reception in different countries. John Dunlop, Richard Haugh, Alexis Klimoff, eds., *Aleksandr Solzhenitsyn: Critical Essays and Documentary Materials* (1973), is a useful collection with a wide range of essays and reprinted texts, including a short autobiography by Solzhenitsyn and his Nobel Prize lecture.

PRONOUNCING GLOSSARY

The following list uses common English syllables and stress accents to provide rough equivalents of selected words whose pronunciation may be unfamiliar to the general reader.

Matryona Vasilyevna: *mah-treeoh'-na*   Vysokoye Polye: *vai-so'-koy pol'-ye*
vah-seel'-yev-na

Matryona's Home[1]

1

A hundred and fifteen miles from Moscow trains were still slowing down to a crawl a good six months after it happened. Passengers stood glued to the windows or went out to stand by the doors. Was the line under repair, or what? Would the train be late?

It was all right. Past the crossing the train picked up speed again and the passengers went back to their seats.

1. Translated by H. T. Willetts.

Only the engine drivers knew what it was all about.
The engine drivers and I.

In the summer of 1953 I was coming back from the hot and dusty desert, just following my nose—so long as it led me back to European Russia. Nobody waited or wanted me at my particular place, because I was a little matter of ten years overdue. I just wanted to get to the central belt, away from the great heat, close to the leafy muttering of forests. I wanted to efface myself, to lose myself in deepest Russia . . . if it was still anywhere to be found.

A year earlier I should have been lucky to get a job carrying a hod this side of the Urals.[2] They wouldn't have taken me as an electrician on a decent construction job. And I had an itch to teach. Those who knew told me that it was a waste of money buying a ticket, that I should have a journey for nothing.

But things were beginning to move.[3] When I went up the stairs of the N—— Regional Education Department and asked for the Personnel Section, I was surprised to find Personnel sitting behind a glass partition, like in a chemist's shop, instead of the usual black leather-padded door. I went timidly up to the window, bowed, and asked, "Please, do you need any mathematicians somewhere where the trains don't run? I should like to settle there for good."

They passed every dot and comma in my documents through a fine comb, went from one room to another, made telephone calls. It was something out of the ordinary for them too—people always wanted the towns, the bigger the better. And lo and behold, they found just the place for me—Vysokoe Polye. The very sound of it gladdened my heart.

Vysokoe Polye[4] did not belie its name. It stood on rising ground, with gentle hollows and other little hills around it. It was enclosed by an unbroken ring of forest. There was a pool behind a weir. Just the place where I wouldn't mind living and dying. I spent a long time sitting on a stump in a coppice and wishing with all my heart that I didn't need breakfast and dinner every day but could just stay here and listen to the branches brushing against the roof in the night, with not a wireless anywhere to be heard and the whole world silent.

Alas, nobody baked bread in Vysokoe Polye. There was nothing edible on sale. The whole village lugged its victuals in sacks from the big town.

I went back to the Personnel Section and raised my voice in prayer at the little window. At first they wouldn't even talk to me. But then they started going from one room to another, made a telephone call, scratched with their pens, and stamped on my orders the word "Torfoprodukt."

Torfoprodukt? Turgenev[5] never knew that you can put words like that together in Russian.

On the station building at Torfoprodukt, an antiquated temporary hut of gray wood, hung a stern notice, BOARD TRAINS ONLY FROM THE PASSENGERS' HALL. A further message had been scratched on the boards with a nail, *And*

---

2. Mountain chain separating European Russia from (Asiatic) Siberia.   3. Stalin's death, on March 5, 1953, brought a gradual relaxation of the Soviet state's repressive policies.   4. High meadow.   5. A master of Russian prose style (1818–1883), best known for the novel *Fathers and Sons* (1861) and for a series of sympathetic sketches of peasant life published as *A Sportsman's Sketches* (1882). *Torfoprodukt*: peat product; a new word made by combining two words of Germanic origin: *torf* ("peat") and *produkt*.

Without Tickets. And by the booking office, with the same melancholy wit, somebody had carved for all time the words, *No Tickets.* It was only later that I fully appreciated the meaning of these addenda. Getting to Torfopro-dukt was easy. But not getting away.

Here too, deep and trackless forests had once stood and were still standing after the Revolution. Then they were chopped down by the peat cutters and the neighboring kolkhoz.[6] Its chairman, Shashkov, had razed quite a few hectares of timber and sold it at a good profit down in the Odessa region.

The workers' settlement sprawled untidily among the peat bogs—monot-onous shacks from the thirties, and little houses with carved façades and glass verandas, put up in the fifties. But inside these houses I could see no partitions reaching up to the ceilings, so there was no hope of renting a room with four real walls.

Over the settlement hung smoke from the factory chimney. Little loco-motives ran this way and that along narrow-gauge railway lines, giving out more thick smoke and piercing whistles, pulling loads of dirty brown peat in slabs and briquettes. I could safely assume that in the evening a loudspeaker would be crying its heart out over the door of the club and there would be drunks roaming the streets and, sooner or later, sticking knives in each other.

This was what my dream about a quiet corner of Russia had brought me to—when I could have stayed where I was and lived in an adobe hut looking out on the desert, with a fresh breeze at night and only the starry dome of the sky overhead.

I couldn't sleep on the station bench, and as soon as it started getting light I went for another stroll round the settlement. This time I saw a tiny market-place. Only one woman stood there at that early hour, selling milk, and I took a bottle and started drinking it on the spot.

I was struck by the way she talked. Instead of a normal speaking voice, she used an ingratiating singsong, and her words were the ones I was longing to hear when I left Asia for this place.

"Drink, and God bless you. You must be a stranger round here?"

"And where are you from?" I asked, feeling more cheerful.

I learnt that the peat workings weren't the only thing, that over the railway lines there was a hill, and over the hill a village, that this village was Talnovo, and it had been there ages ago, when the "gipsy woman" lived in the big house and the wild woods stood all round. And farther on there was a whole countryside full of villages—Chaslitsy, Ovintsy, Spudni, Shevertni, Shesti-mirovo, deeper and deeper into the woods, farther and farther from the rail-way, up towards the lakes.

The names were like a soothing breeze to me. They held a promise of backwoods Russia. I asked my new acquaintance to take me to Talnovo after the market was over and find a house for me to lodge in.

It appeared that I was a lodger worth having: in addition to my rent, the school offered a truckload of peat for the winter to whoever took me. The woman's ingratiating smile gave way to a thoughtful frown. She had no room herself, because she and her husband were "keeping" her aged mother, so she took me first to one lot of relatives then to another. But there wasn't a separate room to be had and both places were crowded and noisy.

---

6. Collective farm.

We had come to a dammed-up stream that was short of water and had a little bridge over it. No other place in all the village took my fancy as this did: there were two or three willows, a lopsided house, ducks swimming on the pond, geese shaking themselves as they stepped out of the water.

"Well, perhaps we might just call on Matryona," said my guide, who was getting tired of me by now. "Only it isn't so neat and cozy-like in her house, neglects things she does. She's unwell."

Matryona's house stood quite near by. Its row of four windows looked out on the cold backs, the two slopes of the roof were covered with shingles, and a little attic window was decorated in the old Russian style. But the shingles were rotting, the beam ends of the house and the once mighty gates had turned gray with age, and there were gaps in the little shelter over the gate.

The small gate was fastened, but instead of knocking my companion just put her hand under and turned the catch, a simple device to prevent animals from straying. The yard was not covered, but there was a lot under the roof of the house. As you went through the outer door a short flight of steps rose to a roomy landing, which was open, to the roof high overhead. To the left, other steps led up to the top room, which was a separate structure with no stove, and yet another flight led down to the basement. To the right lay the house proper, with its attic and its cellar.

It had been built a long time ago, built sturdily, to house a big family, and now one lonely woman of nearly sixty lived in it.

When I went into the cottage she was lying on the Russian stove[7] under a heap of those indeterminate dingy rags which are so precious to a working man or woman.

The spacious room, and especially the big part near the windows, was full of rubber plants in pots and tubs standing on stools and benches. They peopled the householder's loneliness like a speechless but living crowd. They had been allowed to run wild, and they took up all the scanty light on the north side. In what was left of the light, and half-hidden by the stovepipe, the mistress of the house looked yellow and weak. You could see from her clouded eyes that illness had drained all the strength out of her.

While we talked she lay on the stove face downward, without a pillow, her head toward the door, and I stood looking up at her. She showed no pleasure at getting a lodger, just complained about the wicked disease she had. She was just getting over an attack; it didn't come upon her every month, but when it did, "It hangs on two or three days so as I shan't manage to get up and wait on you. I've room and to spare, you can live here if you like."

Then she went over the list of other housewives with whom I should be quieter and cozier and wanted me to make the round of them. But I had already seen that I was destined to settle in this dimly lit house with the tarnished mirror, in which you couldn't see yourself, and the two garish posters (one advertising books, the other about the harvest), bought for a ruble each to brighten up the walls.

Matryona Vasilyevna made me go off round the village again, and when I called on her the second time she kept trying to put me off, "We're not clever, we can't cook, I don't know how we shall suit. . . ." But this time she was on

---

7. A large stove built of masonry, used for both heating and cooking.

her feet when I got there, and I thought I saw a glimmer of pleasure in her eyes to see me back. We reached an agreement about the rent and the load of peat which the school would deliver.

Later on I found out that, year in year out, it was a long time since Matryona Vasilyevna had earned a single ruble. She didn't get a pension. Her relatives gave her very little help. In the kolkhoz she had worked not for money but for credits; the marks recording her labor days in her well-thumbed workbook.

So I moved in with Matryona Vasilyevna. We didn't divide the room. Her bed was in the corner between the door and the stove, and I unfolded my camp bed by one window and pushed Matryona's beloved rubber plants out of the light to make room for a little table by another. The village had electric light, laid on back in the twenties, from Shatury. The newspapers were writing about "Ilyich's little lamps," but the peasants talked wide-eyed about "Tsar Light."[8]

Some of the better-off people in the village might not have thought Matryona's house much of a home, but it kept us snug enough that autumn and winter. The roof still held the rain out, and the freezing winds could not blow the warmth of the stove away all at once, though it was cold by morning, especially when the wind blew on the shabby side.

In addition to Matryona and myself, a cat, some mice, and some cockroaches lived in the house.

The cat was no longer young, and was gammy-legged as well. Matryona had taken her in out of pity, and she had stayed. She walked on all four feet but with a heavy limp: one of her feet was sore and she favored it. When she jumped from the stove she didn't land with the soft sound a cat usually makes, but with a heavy thud as three of her feet struck the floor at once—such a heavy thud that until I got used to it, it gave me a start. This was because she stuck three feet out together to save the fourth.

It wasn't because the cat couldn't deal with them that there were mice in the cottage: she would pounce into the corner like lightning and come back with a mouse between her teeth. But the mice were usually out of reach because somebody, back in the good old days, had stuck embossed wallpaper of a greenish color on Matryona's walls, and not just one layer of it but five. The layers held together all right, but in many places the whole lot had come away from the wall, giving the room a sort of inner skin. Between the timber of the walls and the skin of wallpaper the mice had made themselves runs where they impudently scampered about, running at times right up to the ceiling. The cat followed their scamperings with angry eyes, but couldn't get at them.

Sometimes the cat ate cockroaches as well, but they made her sick. The only thing the cockroaches respected was the partition which screened the mouth of the Russian stove and the kitchen from the best part of the room.

They did not creep into the best room. But the kitchen at night swarmed with them, and if I went in late in the evening for a drink of water and switched on the light the whole floor, the big bench, and even the wall would

8. The newspapers reflect the new order. *Ilyich:* i.e., Vladimir Ilyich Lenin (1870–1924), leader of the 1917 Russian Revolution and first head of the new state. The peasants still think in terms of the emperor (*Tsar*, or czar).

be one rustling brown mass. From time to time I brought home some borax from the school laboratory and we mixed it with dough to poison them. There would be fewer cockroaches for a while, but Matryona was afraid that we might poison the cat as well. We stopped putting down poison and the cockroaches multiplied anew.

At night, when Matryona was already asleep and I was working at my table, the occasional rapid scamper of mice behind the wallpaper would be drowned in the sustained and ceaseless rustling of cockroaches behind the screen, like the sound of the sea in the distance. But I got used to it because there was nothing evil in it, nothing dishonest. Rustling was life to them.

I even got used to the crude beauty on the poster, forever reaching out from the wall to offer me Belinsky, Panferov,[9] and a pile of other books—but never saying a word. I got used to everything in Matryona's cottage.

Matryona got up at four or five o'clock in the morning. Her wall clock was twenty-seven years old and had been bought in the village shop. It was always fast, but Matryona didn't worry about that—just as long as it didn't lose and make her late in the morning. She switched on the light behind the kitchen screen and moving quietly, considerately, doing her best not to make a noise, she lit the stove, went to milk the goat (all the livestock she had was this one dirty-white goat with twisted horns), fetched water and boiled it in three iron pots: one for me, one for herself, and one for the goat. She fetched potatoes from the cellar, picking out the littlest for the goat, little ones for herself and egg-sized ones for me. There were no big ones, because her garden was sandy, had not been manured since the war, and she always planted with potatoes, potatoes, and potatoes again, so that it wouldn't grow big ones.

I scarcely heard her about her morning tasks. I slept late, woke up in the wintry daylight, stretched a bit, and stuck my head out from under my blanket and my sheepskin. These, together with the prisoner's jerkin round my legs and a sack stuffed with straw underneath me, kept me warm in bed even on nights when the cold wind rattled our wobbly windows from the north. When I heard the discreet noises on the other side of the screen I spoke to her, slowly and deliberately:

"Good morning, Matryona Vasilyevna!"

And every time the same good-natured words came to me from behind the screen. They began with a warm, throaty gurgle, the sort of sound grandmothers make in fairy tales.

"M-m-m . . . same to you too!"

And after a little while, "Your breakfast's ready for you now."

She didn't announce what was for breakfast, but it was easy to guess: taters in their jackets or tatty soup (as everybody in the village called it), or barley gruel (no other grain could be bought in Torfoprodukt that year, and even the barley you had to fight for, because it was the cheapest and people bought it up by the sack to fatten their pigs on it). It wasn't always salted as it should be, it was often slightly burnt, it furred the palate and the gums, and it gave me heartburn.

But Matryona wasn't to blame: there was no butter in Torfoprodukt either,

9. Fedor Ivanovich Panferov (1896–1960), socialist-realist writer popular in the 1920s, best known for his novel *The Iron Flood*. Vissarion Grigoryevich Belinsky (1811–1848), Russian literary critic who emphasized social and political ideas.

margarine was desperately short, and only mixed cooking fat was plentiful, and when I got to know it, I saw that the Russian stove was not convenient for cooking: the cook cannot see the pots and they are not heated evenly all round. I suppose the stove came down to our ancestors from the Stone Age, because you can stoke it up once before daylight, and food and water, mash and swill will keep warm in it all day long. And it keeps you warm while you sleep.

I ate everything that was cooked for me without demur, patiently putting aside anything uncalled-for that I came across: a hair, a bit of peat, a cockroach's leg. I hadn't the heart to find fault with Matryona. After all, she had warned me herself.

"We aren't clever, we can't cook—I don't know how we shall suit. . . ."

"Thank you," I said quite sincerely.

"What for? For what is your own?" she answered, disarming me with a radiant smile. And, with a guileless look of her faded blue eyes, she would ask, "And what shall I cook you for just now?"

For just now meant for supper. I ate twice a day, like at the front. What could I order for just now? It would have to be one of the same old things, taters or tater soup.

I resigned myself to it, because I had learned by now not to look for the meaning of life in food. More important to me was the smile on her roundish face, which I tried in vain to catch when at last I had earned enough to buy a camera. As soon as she saw the cold eye of the lens upon her, Matryona assumed a strained or else an exaggeratedly severe expression.

Just once I did manage to get a snap of her looking through the window into the street and smiling at something.

Matryona had a lot of worries that winter. Her neighbors put it into her head to try and get a pension. She was all alone in the world, and when she began to be seriously ill she had been dismissed from the kolkhoz as well. Injustices had piled up, one on top of another. She was ill, but was not regarded as a disabled person. She had worked for a quarter of a century in the kolkhoz, but it was a kolkhoz and not a factory, so she was not entitled to a pension for herself. She could only try and get one for her husband, for the loss of her breadwinner. But she had had no husband for twelve years now, not since the beginning of the war, and it wasn't easy to obtain all the particulars from different places about his length of service and how much he had earned. What a bother it was getting those forms through! Getting somebody to certify that he'd earned, say, three hundred rubles a month; that she lived alone and nobody helped her; what year she was born in. Then all this had to be taken to the Pension Office. And taken somewhere else to get all the mistakes corrected. And taken back again. Then you had to find out whether they would give you a pension.

To make it all more difficult the Pension Office was twelve miles east of Talnovo, the Rural Council Offices six miles to the west, the Factory District Council an hour's walk to the north. They made her run around from office to office for two months on end, to get an *i* dotted or a *t* crossed. Every trip took a day. She goes down to the Rural District Council—and the secretary isn't there today. Secretaries of rural councils often aren't here today. So come again tomorrow. Tomorrow the secretary is in, but he hasn't got his rubber stamp. So come again the next day. And the day after that back she goes yet again, because all her papers are pinned together and some cockeyed clerk has signed the wrong one.

"They shove me around, Ignatich," she used to complain to me after these fruitless excursions. "Worn out with it I am."

But she soon brightened up. I found that she had a sure means of putting herself in a good humor. She worked. She would grab a shovel and go off to pull potatoes. Or she would tuck a sack under her arm and go after peat. Or take a wicker basket and look for berries deep in the woods. When she'd been bending her back to bushes instead of office desks for a while, and her shoulders were aching from a heavy load, Matryona would come back cheerful, at peace with the world and smiling her nice smile.

"I'm on to a good thing now, Ignatich. I know where to go for it (peat she meant), a lovely place it is."

"But surely my peat is enough, Matryona Vasilyevna? There's a whole truckload of it."

"Pooh! Your peat! As much again, and then as much again, that might be enough. When the winter gets really stiff and the wind's battling at the windows, it blows the heat out of the house faster than you can make the stove up. Last year we got heaps and heaps of it. I'd have had three loads in by now. But they're out to catch us. They've summoned one woman from our village already."

That's how it was. The frightening breath of winter was already in the air. There were forests all round, and no fuel to be had anywhere. Excavators roared away in the bogs, but there was no peat on sale to the villagers. It was delivered, free, to the bosses and to the people round the bosses, and teachers, doctors, and workers got a load each. The people of Talnovo were not supposed to get any peat, and they weren't supposed to ask about it. The chairman of the kolkhoz walked about the village looking people in the eye while he gave his orders or stood chatting and talked about anything you liked except fuel. He was stocked up. Who said anything about winter coming?

So just as in the old days they used to steal the squire's wood, now they pinched peat from the trust. The women went in parties of five or ten so that they would be less frightened. They went in the daytime. The peat cut during the summer had been stacked up all over the place to dry. That's the good thing about peat, it can't be carted off as soon as it's cut. It lies around drying till autumn, or, if the roads are bad, till the snow starts falling. This was when the women used to come and take it. They could get six peats in a sack if it was damp, or ten if it was dry. A sackful weighed about half a hundredweight and it sometimes had to be carried over two miles. This was enough to make the stove up once. There were two hundred days in the winter. The Russian stove had to be lit in the mornings, and the "Dutch"[1] stove in the evenings.

"Why beat about the bush?" said Matryona angrily to someone invisible. "Since there've been no more horses, what you can't have around yourself you haven't got. My back never heals up. Winter you're pulling sledges, summer it's bundles on your back, it's God's truth I'm telling you."

The women went more than once in a day. On good days Matryona

---

1. Not a real tiled Dutch stove, but a cheap small stove (probably made from an oil barrel) that provided heat with less fuel than a big Russian stove.

brought six sacks home. She piled my peat up where it could be seen and hid her own under the passageway, boarding up the hole every night.

"If they don't just happen to think of it, the devils will never find it in their born days," said Matryona smiling and wiping the sweat from her brow.

What could the peat trust do? Its establishment didn't run to a watchman for every bog. I suppose they had to show a rich haul in their returns, and then write off so much for crumbling, so much washed away by the rain. Sometimes they would take it into their heads to put out patrols and try to catch the women as they came into the village. The women would drop their sacks and scatter. Or somebody would inform and there would be a house-to-house search. They would draw up a report on the stolen peat and threaten a court action. The women would stop fetching it for a while, but the approach of winter drove them out with sledges in the middle of the night.

When I had seen a little more of Matryona I noticed that, apart from cooking and looking after the house, she had quite a lot of other jobs to do every day. She kept all her jobs, and the proper times for them, in her head and always knew when she woke up in the morning how her day would be occupied. Apart from fetching peat and stumps which the tractors unearthed in the bogs, apart from the cranberries which she put to soak in big jars for the winter ("Give your teeth an edge, Ignatich," she used to say when she offered me some), apart from digging potatoes and all the coming and going to do with her pension, she had to get hay from somewhere for her one and only dirty-white goat.

"Why don't you keep a cow, Matryona?"

Matryona stood there in her grubby apron, by the opening in the kitchen screen, facing my table, and explained to me.

"Oh, Ignatich, there's enough milk from the goat for me. And if I started keeping a cow she'd eat me out of house and home in no time. You can't cut the grass by the railway track, because it belongs to the railway, and you can't cut any in the woods, because it belongs to the foresters, and they won't let me have any at the kolkhoz because I'm not a member any more, they reckon. And those who are members have to work there every day till the white flies swarm and make their own hay when there's snow on the ground—what's the good of grass like that? In the old days they used to be sweating to get the hay in at midsummer, between the end of June and the end of July, while the grass was sweet and juicy."

So it meant a lot of work for Matryona to gather enough hay for one skinny little goat. She took her sickle and a sack and went off early in the morning to places where she knew there was grass growing—round the edges of fields, on the roadside, on hummocks in the bog. When she had stuffed her sack with heavy fresh grass she dragged it home and spread it out in her yard to dry. From a sackful of grass she got one forkload of dry hay.

The farm had a new chairman, sent down from the town not long ago, and the first thing he did was to cut down the garden plots for those who were not fit to work. He left Matryona a third of an acre of sand—when there was over a thousand square yards just lying idle on the other side of the fence. Yet when they were short of working hands, when the women dug in their heels and wouldn't budge, the chairman's wife would come to see Matryona. She was from the town as well, a determined woman whose short gray coat and intimidating glare gave her a somewhat military appearance. She walked into the house without so much as a good morning and looked sternly at Matryona. Matryona was uneasy.

"Well now, Comrade Vasilyevna," said the chairman's wife, drawing out her words. "You will have to help the kolkhoz! You will have to go and help cart manure out tomorrow!"

A little smile of forgiveness wrinkled Matryona's face—as though she understood the embarrassment which the chairman's wife must feel at not being able to pay her for her work.

"Well—er," she droned. "I'm not well, of course, and I'm not attached to you any more . . . ," then she hurried to correct herself, "What time should I come then?"

"And bring your own fork!" the chairman's wife instructed her. Her stiff skirt crackled as she walked away.

"Think of that!" grumbled Matryona as the door closed. "Bring your own fork! They've got neither forks nor shovels at the kolkhoz. And I don't have a man who'll put a handle on for me!"

She went on thinking about it out loud all evening.

"What's the good of talking, Ignatich. I must help, of course. Only the way they work it's all a waste of time—don't know whether they're coming or going. The women stand propped up on their shovels and waiting for the factory whistle to blow twelve o'clock. Or else they get on to adding up who's earned what and who's turned up for work and who hasn't. Now what I call work, there isn't a sound out of anybody, only—oh dear, dear—dinner time's soon rolled round—what, getting dark already."

In the morning she went off with her fork.

But it wasn't just the kolkhoz—any distant relative, or just a neighbor, could come to Matryona of an evening and say, "Come and give me a hand tomorrow, Matryona. We'll finish pulling the potatoes."

Matryona couldn't say no. She gave up what she should be doing next and went to help her neighbor, and when she came back she would say without a trace of envy, "Ah, you should see the size of her potatoes, Ignatich! It was a joy to dig them up. I didn't want to leave the allotment, God's truth I didn't."

Needless to say, not a garden could be plowed without Matryona's help. The women of Talnovo had got it neatly worked out that it was a longer and harder job for one woman to dig her garden with a spade than for six of them to put themselves in harness and plow six gardens. So they sent for Matryona to help them.

"Well—did you pay her?" I asked sometimes.

"She won't take money. You have to try and hide it on her when she's not looking."

Matryona had yet another troublesome chore when her turn came to feed the herdsmen. One of them was a hefty deaf mute, the other a boy who was never without a cigaret in his drooling mouth. Matryona's turn came round only every six weeks, but it put her to great expense. She went to the shop to buy canned fish and was lavish with sugar and butter, things she never ate herself. It seems that the housewives showed off in this way, trying to outdo one another in feeding the herdsmen.

"You've got to be careful with tailors and herdsmen," Matryona explained.

"They'll spread your name all round the village if something doesn't suit them."

And every now and then attacks of serious illness broke in on this life that was already crammed with troubles. Matryona would be off her feet for a day or two, lying flat out on the stove. She didn't complain and didn't groan, but she hardly stirred either. On these days Masha, Matryona's closest friend from her earliest years, would come to look after the goat and light the stove. Matryona herself ate nothing, drank nothing, asked for nothing. To call in the doctor from the clinic at the settlement would have seemed strange in Talnovo and would have given the neighbors something to talk about—what does she think she is, a lady? They did call her in once, and she arrived in a real temper and told Matryona to come down to the clinic when she was on her feet again. Matryona went, although she didn't really want to; they took specimens and sent them off to the district hospital—and that's the last anybody heard about it. Matryona was partly to blame herself.

But there was work waiting to be done, and Matryona soon started getting up again, moving slowly at first and then as briskly as ever.

"You never saw me in the old days, Ignatich. I'd lift any sack you liked, I didn't think a hundredweight was too heavy. My father-in-law used to say, 'Matryona, you'll break your back.' And my brother-in-law didn't have to come and help me lift on the cart. Our horse was a warhorse, a big strong one."

"What do you mean, a warhorse?"

"They took ours for the war and gave us this one instead—he'd been wounded. But he turned out a bit spirited. Once he bolted with the sledge right into the lake, the men folk hopped out of the way, but I grabbed the bridle, as true as I'm here, and stopped him. Full of oats that horse was. They liked to feed their horses well in our village. If a horse feels his oats he doesn't know what heavy means."

But Matryona was a long way from being fearless. She was afraid of fire, afraid of "the lightning," and most of all she was for some reason afraid of trains.

"When I had to go to Cherusti,[2] the train came up from Nechaevka way with its great big eyes popping out and the rails humming away—put me in a regular fever. My knees started knocking. God's truth I'm telling you!" Matryona raised her shoulders as though she surprised herself.

"Maybe it's because they won't give people tickets, Matryona Vasilyevna?"

"At the window? They try to shove only first-class tickets on to you. And the train was starting to move. We dashed about all over the place, 'Give us tickets for pity's sake.' "

"The men folk had climbed on top of the carriages. Then we found a door that wasn't locked and shoved straight in without tickets—and all the carriages were empty, they were all empty, you could stretch out on the seat if you wanted to. Why they wouldn't give us tickets, the hardhearted parasites, I don't know. . . ."

2. About 100 miles east of Moscow and some 250 miles northwest of Nechaevka.

Still, before winter came, Matryona's affairs were in a better state than ever before. They started paying her at last a pension of eighty rubles. Besides this she got just over one hundred from the school and me.

Some of her neighbors began to be envious.

"Hm! Matryona can live forever now! If she had any more money, she wouldn't know what to do with it at her age."

Matryona had some new felt boots made. She bought a new jerkin. And she had an overcoat made out of the worn-out railwayman's greatcoat given to her by the engine driver from Cherusti who had married Kira, her foster daughter. The hump-backed village tailor put a padded lining under the cloth and it made a marvelous coat, such as Matryona had never worn before in all her sixty years.

In the middle of winter Matryona sewed two hundred rubles into the lining of this coat for her funeral. This made her quite cheerful.

"Now my mind's a bit easier, Ignatich."

December went by, January went by—and in those two months Matryona's illness held off. She started going over to Masha's house more often in the evening, to sit chewing sunflower seeds with her. She herself didn't invite guests in the evening out of consideration for my work. Once, on the feast of the Epiphany, I came back from school and found a party going on and was introduced to Matryona's three sisters, who called her "nan-nan" or "nanny" because she was the oldest. Until then not much had been heard of the sisters in our cottage—perhaps they were afraid that Matryona might ask them for help.

But one ominous event cast a shadow on the holiday for Matryona. She went to the church three miles away for the blessing of the water and put her pot down among the others. When the blessing was over, the women went rushing and jostling to get their pots back again. There were a lot of women in front of Matryona and when she got there her pot was missing, and no other vessel had been left behind. The pot had vanished as though the devil had run off with it.

Matryona went round the worshipers asking them, "Have any of you girls accidentally mistook somebody else's holy water? In a pot?"

Nobody owned up. There had been some boys there, and boys got up to mischief sometimes. Matryona came home sad.

No one could say that Matryona was a devout believer. If anything, she was a heathen, and her strongest beliefs were superstitious: you mustn't go into the garden on the fast of St. John or there would be no harvest next year. A blizzard meant that somebody had hanged himself. If you pinched your foot in the door, you could expect a guest. All the time I lived with her I didn't once see her say her prayers or even cross herself. But, whatever job she was doing, she began with a "God bless us," and she never failed to say "God bless you," when I set out for school. Perhaps she did say her prayers, but on the quiet, either because she was shy or because she didn't want to embarrass me. There were icons[3] on the walls. Ordinary days they were left in darkness, but for the vigil of a great feast, or on the morning of a holiday, Matryona would light the little lamp.

3. Religious images or portraits, usually painted on wood. A small lamp was set in front of the icons to illuminate them.

She had fewer sins on her conscience than her gammy-legged cat. The cat did kill mice.

Now that her life was running more smoothly, Matryona started listening more carefully to my radio. (I had, of course, installed a speaker, or as Matryona called it, a peeker.)[4]

When they announced on the radio that some new machine had been invented, I heard Matryona grumbling out in the kitchen, "New ones all the time, nothing but new ones. People don't want to work with the old ones any more, where are we going to store them all?"

There was a program about the seeding of clouds from airplanes. Matryona, listening up on the stove, shook her head, "Oh, dear, dear, dear, they'll do away with one of the two—summer or winter."

Once Shalyapin[5] was singing Russian folk songs. Matryona stood listening for a long time before she gave her emphatic verdict, "Queer singing, not our sort of singing."

"You can't mean that, Matryona Vasilyevna—just listen to him."

She listened a bit longer and pursed her lips, "No, it's wrong. It isn't our sort of tune, and he's tricky with his voice."

She made up for this another time. They were broadcasting some of Glinka's[6] songs. After half a dozen of these drawing-room ballads, Matryona suddenly came from behind the screen clutching her apron, with a flush on her face and a film of tears over her dim eyes.

"That's our sort of singing," she said in a whisper.

2

So Matryona and I got used to each other and took each other for granted. She never pestered me with questions about myself. I don't know whether she was lacking in normal female curiosity or just tactful, but she never once asked if I had been married. All the Talnovo women kept at her to find out about me. Her answer was, "You want to know—you ask him. All I know is he's from distant parts."

And when I got round to telling her that I had spent a lot of time in prison, she said nothing but just nodded, as though she had already suspected it.

And I thought of Matryona only as the helpless old woman she was now and didn't try to rake up her past, didn't even suspect that there was anything to be found there.

I knew that Matryona had got married before the Revolution and had come to live in the house I now shared with her, and she had gone "to the stove" immediately. (She had no mother-in-law and no older sister-in-law, so it was her job to put the pots in the oven on the very first morning of her married life.) I knew that she had had six children and that they had all died very young, so that there were never two of them alive at once. Then there was a sort of foster daughter, Kira. Matryona's husband had not come back from the last war. She received no notification of his death. Men from the village

---

4. The translator is imitating Solzhenitsyn's wordplay. In the original, the narrator calls the speaker *razvedka* ("scout," literal trans; a military term); Matryona calls it *rozetka* (an electric plug). 5. Feodor Ivanovich Shalyapin (or Chaliapin, 1873–1938), Russian operatic bass with an international reputation as a great singer and actor; he included popular Russian music in his song recitals. 6. Mikhail Ivanovich Glinka (1804–1857), Russian composer who was instrumental in developing a "Russian" style of music, including the two operas *A Life for the Czar* and *Ruslan and Ludmila*.

who had served in the same company said that he might have been taken prisoner, or he might have been killed and his body not found. In the eight years that had gone by since the war Matryona had decided that he was not alive. It was a good thing that she thought so. If he was still alive he was probably in Brazil or Australia and married again. The village of Talnovo and the Russian language would be fading from his memory.

One day when I got back from school, I found a guest in the house. A tall, dark man, with his hat on his lap, was sitting on a chair which Matryona had moved up to the Dutch stove in the middle of the room. His face was completely surrounded by bushy black hair with hardly a trace of gray in it. His thick black moustache ran into his full black beard, so that his mouth could hardly be seen. Black side-whiskers merged with the black locks which hung down from his crown, leaving only the tips of his ears visible; his broad black eyebrows met in a wide double span. But the front of his head as far as the crown was a spacious bald dome. His whole appearance made an impression of wisdom and dignity. He sat squarely on his chair, with his hands folded on his stick, and his stick resting vertically on the floor, in an attitude of patient expectation, and he obviously hadn't much to say to Matryona, who was busy behind the screen.

When I came in, he eased his majestic head round toward me and suddenly addressed me, "Schoolmaster, I can't see you very well. My son goes to your school. Grigoryev, Antoshka."

There was no need for him to say any more. However strongly inclined I felt to help this worthy old man, I knew and dismissed in advance all the pointless things he was going to say. Antoshka Grigoryev was a plump, red-faced lad in 8-D who looked like a cat that's swallowed the cream. He seemed to think that he came to school for a rest and sat at his desk with a lazy smile on his face. Needless to say, he never did his homework. But the worst of it was that he had been put up into the next class from year to year because our district, and indeed the whole region and the neighboring region were famous for the high percentage of passes they obtained; the school had to make an effort to keep its record up. So Antoshka had got it clear in his mind that however much the teachers threatened him they would promote him in the end, and there was no need for him to learn anything. He just laughed at us. There he sat in the eighth class, and he hadn't even mastered his decimals and didn't know one triangle from another. In the first two terms of the school year I had kept him firmly below the passing line and the same treatment awaited him in the third.

But now this half-blind old man, who should have been Antoshka's grandfather rather than his father, had come to humble himself before me—how could I tell him that the school had been deceiving him for years, and that I couldn't go on deceiving him, because I didn't want to ruin the whole class, to become a liar and a fake, to start despising my work and my profession.

For the time being I patiently explained that his son had been very slack, that he told lies at school and at home, that his record book must be checked frequently, and that we must both take him severely in hand.

"Severe as you like, Schoolmaster," he assured me, "I beat him every week now. And I've got a heavy hand."

While we were talking I remembered that Matryona had once interceded for Antoshka Grigoryev, but I hadn't asked what relation of hers he was and I had refused to do what she wanted. Matryona was standing in the kitchen doorway like a mute suppliant on this occasion too. When Faddey Miron-ovich left, saying that he would call on me to see how things were going, I asked her, "I can't make out what relation this Antoshka is to you, Matryona Vasilyevna."

"My brother-in-law's son," said Matryona shortly, and went out to milk the goat.

When I'd worked it out, I realized that this determined old man with the black hair was the brother of the missing husband.

The long evening went by, and Matryona didn't bring up the subject again. But late at night, when I had stopped thinking about the old man and was working in a silence broken only by the rustling of the cockroaches and the heavy tick of the wall-clock, Matryona suddenly spoke from her dark corner, "You know, Ignatich, I nearly married him once."

I had forgotten that Matryona was in the room. I hadn't heard a sound from her—and suddenly her voice came out of the darkness, as agitated as if the old man were still trying to win her.

I could see that Matryona had been thinking about nothing else all evening.

She got up from her wretched rag bed and walked slowly toward me, as though she were following her own words. I sat back in my chair and caught my first glimpse of a quite different Matryona.

There was no overhead light in our big room with its forest of rubber plants. The table lamp cast a ring of light round my exercise books, and when I tore my eyes from it the rest of the room seemed to be half-dark and faintly tinged with pink. I thought I could see the same pinkish glow in her usually sallow cheeks.

"He was the first one who came courting me, before Efim did—he was his brother—the older one—I was nineteen and Faddey was twenty-three. They lived in this very same house. Their house it was. Their father built it."

I looked round the room automatically. Instead of the old gray house rot-ting under the faded green skin of wallpaper where the mice had their play-ground, I suddenly saw new timbers, freshly trimmed, not yet discolored, and caught the cheerful smell of pine tar.

"Well, and what happened then?"

"That summer we went to sit in the woods together," she whispered. "There used to be a woods where the stable yard is now. They chopped it down. I was just going to marry him, Ignatich. Then the German war started. They took Faddey into the army."

She let fall these few words—and suddenly the blue and white and yellow July of the year 1914 burst into flower before my eyes: the sky still peaceful, the floating clouds, the people sweating to get the ripe corn in. I imagined them side by side, the black-haired Hercules with a scythe over his shoulder, and the red-faced girl clasping a sheaf. And there was singing out under the open sky, such songs as nobody can sing nowadays, with all the machines in the fields.

"He went to the war—and vanished. For three years I kept to myself and waited. Never a sign of life did he give."

Matryona's round face looked out at me from an elderly threadbare head-scarf. As she stood there in the gentle reflected light from my lamp, her face seemed to lose its slovenly workday wrinkles, and she was a scared young girl again with a frightening decision to make.

Yes . . . I could see it. The trees shed their leaves, the snow fell and melted. They plowed and sowed and reaped again. Again the trees shed their leaves, and the snow fell. There was a revolution. Then another revolution. And the whole world was turned upside down.

"Their mother died and Efim came to court me. 'You wanted to come to our house,' he says, 'so come.' He was a year younger than me, Efim was. It's a saying with us—sensible girls get married after Michaelmas, and silly ones at midsummer. They were shorthanded. I got married. . . . The wedding was on St. Peter's day, and then about St. Nicholas' day[7] in the winter he came back—Faddey, I mean, from being a prisoner in Hungary."

Matryona covered her eyes.

I said nothing.

She turned toward the door as though somebody were standing there. "He stood there at the door. What a scream I let out! I wanted to throw myself at his feet! . . . but I couldn't. 'If it wasn't my own brother,' he says, 'I'd take my ax to the both of you.' "

I shuddered. Matryona's despair, or her terror, conjured up a vivid picture of him standing in the dark doorway and raising his ax to her.

But she quieted down and went on with her story in a sing-song voice, leaning on a chairback, "Oh dear, dear me, the poor dear man! There were so many girls in the village—but he wouldn't marry. I'll look for one with the same name as you, a second Matryona, he said. And that's what he did— fetched himself a Matryona from Lipovka. They built themselves a house of their own and they're still living in it. You pass their place every day on your way to school."

So that was it. I realized that I had seen the other Matryona quite often. I didn't like her. She was always coming to my Matryona to complain about her husband—he beat her, he was stingy, he was working her to death. She would weep and weep, and her voice always had a tearful note in it. As it turned out, my Matryona had nothing to regret, with Faddey beating his Matryona every day of his life and being so tightfisted.

"Mine never beat me once," said Matryona of Efim. "He'd pitch into another man in the street, but me he never hit once. Well, there was one time—I quarreled with my sister-in-law and he cracked me on the forehead with a spoon. I jumped up from the table and shouted at them, 'Hope it sticks in your gullets, you idle lot of beggars, hope you choke!' I said. And off I went into the woods. He never touched me any more."

Faddey didn't seem to have any cause for regret either. The other Matryona had borne him six children (my Antoshka was one of them, the littlest, the runt) and they had all lived, whereas the children of Matryona and Efim had died, every one of them, before they reached the age of three months, without any illness.

"One daughter, Elena, was born and was alive when they washed her, and then she died right after. . . . My wedding was on St. Peter's day, and it was St. Peter's day I buried my sixth, Alexander."

The whole village decided that there was a curse on Matryona.

7. December 19 (December 6, old style). *Michaelmas:* October 12 (September 29, old style). *St. Peter's Day:* probably July 12 (June 29, old style), Sts. Peter and Paul's Day.

Matryona still nodded emphatic belief when she talked about it. "There was a *course*[8] on me. They took me to a woman who used to be a nun to get cured, she set me off coughing and waited for the *course* to jump out of me like a frog. Only nothing jumped out."

And the years had run by like running water. In 1941 they didn't take Faddey into the army because of his poor sight, but they took Efim. And what had happened to the elder brother in the First World War happened to the younger in the Second—he vanished without a trace. Only he never came back at all. The once noisy cottage was deserted, it grew old and rotten, and Matryona, all alone in the world, grew old in it.

So she begged from the other Matryona, the cruelly beaten Matryona, a child of her womb (or was it a drop of Faddey's blood?), the youngest daughter, Kira.

For ten years she brought the girl up in her own house, in place of the children who had not lived. Then, not long before I arrived, she had married her off to a young engine driver from Cherusti. The only help she got from anywhere came in dribs and drabs from Cherusti: a bit of sugar from time to time, or some of the fat when they killed a pig.

Sick and suffering, and feeling that death was not far off, Matryona had made known her will: the top room, which was a separate frame joined by tie beams to the rest of the house, should go to Kira when she died.[9] She said nothing about the house itself. Her three sisters had their eyes on it too.

That evening Matryona opened her heart to me. And, as often happens, no sooner were the hidden springs of her life revealed to me than I saw them in motion.

Kira arrived from Cherusti. Old Faddey was very worried. To get and keep a plot of land in Cherusti the young couple had to put up some sort of building. Matryona's top room would do very well. There was nothing else they could put up, because there was no timber to be had anywhere. It wasn't Kira herself so much, and it wasn't her husband, but old Faddey who was consumed with eagerness for them to get their hands on the plot at Cherusti.

He became a frequent visitor, laying down the law to Matryona and insisting that she should hand over the top room right away, before she died. On these occasions I saw a different Faddey. He was no longer an old man propped up by a stick, whom a push or a harsh word would bowl over. Although he was slightly bent by backache, he was still a fine figure; in his sixties he had kept the vigorous black hair of a young man; he was hot and urgent.

Matryona had not slept for two nights. It wasn't easy for her to make up her mind. She didn't grudge them the top room, which was standing there idle, any more than she ever grudged her labor or her belongings. And the top room was willed to Kira in any case. But the thought of breaking up the roof she had lived under for forty years was torture to her. Even I, a mere lodger, found it painful to think of them stripping away boards and wrenching out beams. For Matryona it was the end of everything.

But the people who were so insistent knew that she would let them break up her house before she died.

8. *Curse/course* reflects wordplay in the Russian original, where a similar misuse of language indicates Matryona's lack of formal education.   9. Lumber was scarce and valuable, and old houses were well built. Moving houses or sections of houses is still common in the country.

So Faddey and his sons and sons-in-law came along one February morning, the blows of five axes were heard and boards creaked and cracked as they were wrenched out. Faddey's eyes twinkled busily. Although his back wasn't quite straight yet, he scrambled nimbly up under the rafters and bustled about down below, shouting at his assistants. He and his father had built this house when he was a lad, a long time ago. The top room had been put up for him, the oldest son, to move into with his bride. And now he was furiously taking it apart, board by board, to carry it out of somebody else's yard.

After numbering the beam ends and the ceiling boards, they dismantled the top room and the storeroom underneath it. The living room and what was left of the landing they boarded up with a thin wall of deal. They did nothing about the cracks in the wall. It was plain to see that they were wreckers, not builders, and that they did not expect Matryona to be living there very long.

While the men were busy wrecking, the women were getting the drink ready for moving day—vodka would cost too much. Kira brought forty pounds of sugar from the Moscow region, and Matryona carried the sugar and some bottles to the distiller under cover of night.

The timbers were carried out and stacked in front of the gates, and the engine-driver son-in-law went off to Cherusti for the tractor.

But the very same day a blizzard, or "a blower," as Matryona once called it, began. It howled and whirled for two days and nights and buried the road under enormous drifts. Then, no sooner had they made the road passable and a couple of trucks had gone by, than it got suddenly warmer. Within a day everything was thawing out, damp mist hung in the air and rivulets gurgled as they burrowed into the snow, and you could get stuck up to the top of your jackboots.

Two weeks passed before the tractor could get at the dismantled top room. All this time Matryona went around like someone lost. What particularly upset her was that her three sisters came, with one voice called her a fool for giving the top room away, said they didn't want to see her any more, and went off. At about the same time the lame cat strayed and was seen no more. It was just one thing after another. This was another blow to Matryona.

At last the frost got a grip on the slushy road. A sunny day came along, and everybody felt more cheerful. Matryona had had a lucky dream the night before. In the morning she heard that I wanted to take a photograph of somebody at an old-fashioned handloom. (There were looms still standing in two cottages in the village; they wove coarse rugs on them.) She smiled shyly and said, "You just wait a day or two, Ignatich, I'll just send off the top room there and I'll put my loom up, I've still got it, you know, and then you can snap me. Honest to God!"

She was obviously attracted by the idea of posing in an old-fashioned setting. The red frosty sun tinged the window of the curtailed passageway with a faint pink, and this reflected light warmed Matryona's face. People who are at ease with their consciences always have nice faces.

Coming back from school before dusk I saw some movement near our house. A big new tractor-drawn sledge was already fully loaded, and there was no room for a lot of the timbers, so old Faddey's family and the helpers they had called in had nearly finished knocking together another homemade sledge. They were all working like madmen, in the frenzy that comes upon people when there is a smell of good money in the air or when they are looking forward to some treat. They were shouting at one another and arguing.

They could not agree on whether the sledges should be hauled separately or both together. One of Faddey's sons (the lame one) and the engine-driver son-in-law reasoned that the sledges couldn't both be taken at once because the tractor wouldn't be able to pull them. The man in charge of the tractor, a hefty fat-faced fellow who was very sure of himself, said hoarsely that he knew best, he was the driver, and he would take both at once. His motives were obvious: according to the agreement, the engine driver was paying him for the removal of the upper room, not for the number of trips he had to make. He could never have made two trips in a night—twenty-five kilometers each way, and one return journey. And by morning he had to get the tractor back in the garage from which he had sneaked it out for this job on the side.

Old Faddey was impatient to get the top room moved that day, and at a nod from him his lads gave in. To the stout sledge in front they hitched the one they had knocked together in such a hurry.

Matryona was running about among the men, fussing and helping them to heave the beams on the sledge. Suddenly I noticed that she was wearing my jacket and had dirtied the sleeves on the frozen mud round the beams. I was annoyed and told her so. That jacket held memories for me: it had kept me warm in the bad years.

This was the first time that I was ever angry with Matryona Vasilyevna.

Matryona was taken aback. "Oh dear, dear me," she said. "My poor head. I picked it up in a rush, you see, and never thought about it being yours. I'm sorry, Ignatich."

And she took it off and hung it up to dry.

The loading was finished, and all the men who had been working, about ten of them, clattered past my table and dived under the curtain into the kitchen. I could hear the muffled rattle of glasses and, from time to time, the clink of a bottle, the voices got louder and louder, the boasting more reckless. The biggest braggart was the tractor driver. The stink of hooch floated in to me. But they didn't go on drinking long. It was getting dark and they had to hurry. They began to leave. The tractor driver came out first, looking pleased with himself and fierce. The engine-driver son-in-law, Faddey's lame son, and one of his nephews were going to Cherusti. The others went off home. Faddey was flourishing his stick, trying to overtake somebody and put him right about something. The lame son paused at my table to light up and suddenly started telling me how he loved Aunt Matryona, and that he had got married not long ago, and his wife had just had a son. Then they shouted for him and he went out. The tractor set up a roar outside.

After all the others had gone, Matryona dashed out from behind the screen. She looked after them, anxiously shaking her head. She had put on her jacket and her headscarf. As she was going through the door, she said to me, "Why ever couldn't they hire two? If one tractor had cracked up, the other would have pulled them. What'll happen now, God only knows!"

She ran out after the others.

After the boozing and the arguments and all the coming and going, it was quieter than ever in the deserted cottage, and very chilly because the door had been opened so many times. I got into my jacket and sat down to mark exercise books. The noise of the tractor died away in the distance.

An hour went by. And another. And a third. Matryona still hadn't come back, but I wasn't surprised. When she had seen the sledge off, she must have gone round to her friend Masha.

Another hour went by. And yet another. Darkness, and with it a deep silence had descended on the village. I couldn't understand at the time why it was so quiet. Later, I found out that it was because all evening not a single train had gone along the line five hundred yards from the house. No sound was coming from my radio, and I noticed that the mice were wilder than ever. Their scampering and scratching and squeaking behind the wallpaper was getting noisier and more defiant all the time.

I woke up. It was one o'clock in the morning, and Matryona still hadn't come home.

Suddenly I heard several people talking loudly. They were still a long way off, but something told me that they were coming to our house. And sure enough, I heard soon afterward a heavy knock at the gate. A commanding voice, strange to me, yelled out an order to open up. I went out into the pitch darkness with a torch. The whole village was asleep, there was no light in the windows, and the snow had started melting in the last week so that it gave no reflected light. I turned the catch and let them in. Four men in greatcoats went on toward the house. It's a very unpleasant thing to be visited at night by noisy people in greatcoats.

When we got into the light though, I saw that two of them were wearing railway uniforms. The older of the two, a fat man with the same sort of face as the tractor driver, asked, "Where's the woman of the house?"

"I don't know."

"This is the place the tractor with a sledge came from?"

"This is it."

"Had they been drinking before they left?"

All four of them were looking around, screwing up their eyes in the dim light from the table lamp. I realized that they had either made an arrest or wanted to make one.

"What's happened then?"

"Answer the question!"

"But . . ."

"Were they drunk when they went?"

"Were they drinking here?"

Had there been a murder? Or hadn't they been able to move the top room? The men in greatcoats had me off balance. But one thing was certain: Matryona could do time for making hooch.

I stepped back to stand between them and the kitchen door. "I honestly didn't notice. I didn't see anything." (I really hadn't seen anything—only heard.) I made what was supposed to be a helpless gesture, drawing attention to the state of the cottage: a table lamp shining peacefully on books and exercises, a crowd of frightened rubber plants, the austere couch of a recluse, not a sign of debauchery.

They had already seen for themselves, to their annoyance, that there had been no drinking in that room. They turned to leave, telling each other this wasn't where the drinking had been then, but it would be a good thing to put in that it was. I saw them out and tried to discover what had happened. It was only at the gate that one of them growled. "They've all been cut to bits. Can't find all the pieces."

"That's a detail. The nine o'clock express nearly went off the rails. That would have been something." And they walked briskly away.

I went back to the hut in a daze. Who were "they"? What did "all of them" mean? And where was Matryona?

I moved the curtain aside and went into the kitchen. The stink of hooch rose and hit me. It was a deserted battlefield: a huddle of stools and benches, empty bottles lying around, one bottle half-full, glasses, the remains of pickled herring, onion, and sliced fat pork.

Everything was deathly still. Just cockroaches creeping unperturbed about the field of battle.

They had said something about the nine o'clock express. Why? Perhaps I should have shown them all this? I began to wonder whether I had done right. But what a damnable way to behave—keeping their explanations for official persons only.

Suddenly the small gate creaked. I hurried out on to the landing. "Matryona Vasilyevna?"

The yard door opened, and Matryona's friend Masha came in, swaying and wringing her hands. "Matryona—our Matryona, Ignatich—"

I sat her down, and through her tears she told me the story.

The approach to the crossing was a steep rise. There was no barrier. The tractor and the first sledge went over, but the towrope broke and the second sledge, the homemade one, got stuck on the crossing and started falling apart—the wood Faddey had given them to make the second sledge was no good. They towed the first sledge out of the way and went back for the second. They were fixing the towrope—the tractor driver and Faddey's lame son, and Matryona (heaven knows what brought her there) were with them, between the tractor and the sledge. What help did she think she could be to the men? She was forever meddling in men's work. Hadn't a bolting horse nearly tipped her into the lake once, through a hole in the ice? Why did she have to go to the damned crossing? She had handed over the top room and owed nothing to anybody. The engine driver kept a lookout in case the train from Cherusti rushed up on them. Its headlamps would be visible a long way off. But two engines coupled together came from the other direction, from our station, backing without lights. Why they were without lights nobody knows. When an engine is backing, coal dust blows into the driver's eyes from the tender and he can't see very well. The two engines flew into them and crushed the three people between the tractor and the sledge to pulp. The tractor was wrecked, the sledge was matchwood, the rails were buckled, and both engines turned over.

"But how was it they didn't hear the engines coming?"

"The tractor engine was making such a din."

"What about the bodies?"

"They won't let anybody in. They've roped them off."

"What was that somebody was telling me about the express?"

"The nine o'clock express goes through our station at a good clip and on to the crossing. But the two drivers weren't hurt when their engines crashed, they jumped out and ran back along the line waving their hands, and they managed to stop the train. The nephew was hurt by a beam as well. He's hiding at Klavka's now so that they won't know he was at the crossing. If they find out they'll drag him in as a witness. . . . 'Don't know lies up, and do know gets tied up.' Kira's husband didn't get a scratch. He tried to hang himself, they had to cut him down. It's all because of me, he says, my aunty's killed and my brother. Now he's gone and given himself up. But the madhouse is where he'll be going, not prison. Oh, Matryona, my dearest Matryona. . . ."

Matryona was gone. Someone close to me had been killed. And on her last day I had scolded her for wearing my jacket.

The lovingly drawn red and yellow woman in the book advertisement smiled happily on.

Old Masha sat there weeping a little longer. Then she got up to go. And suddenly she asked me, "Ignatich, you remember, Matryona had a gray shawl. She meant it to go to my Tanya when she died, didn't she?"

She looked at me hopefully in the half-darkness—surely I hadn't forgotten?

No, I remembered. "She said so, yes."

"Well, listen, maybe you could let me take it with me now. The family will be swarming in tomorrow and I'll never get it then." And she gave me another hopeful, imploring look. She had been Matryona's friend for half a century, the only one in the village who truly loved her.

No doubt she was right.

"Of course—take it."

She opened the chest, took out the shawl, tucked it under her coat, and went out.

The mice had gone mad. They were running furiously up and down the walls, and you could almost see the green wallpaper rippling and rolling over their backs.

In the morning I had to go to school. The time was three o'clock. The only thing to do was to lock up and go to bed.

Lock up, because Matryona would not be coming.

I lay down, leaving the light on. The mice were squeaking, almost moaning, racing and running. My mind was weary and wandering, and I couldn't rid myself of an uneasy feeling that an invisible Matryona was flitting about and saying good-bye to her home.

And suddenly I imagined Faddey standing there, young and black-haired, in the dark patch by the door, with his ax uplifted. "If it wasn't my own brother, I'd chop the both of you to bits."

The threat had lain around for forty years, like an old broad sword in a corner, and in the end it had struck its blow.

3

When it was light the women went to the crossing and brought back all that was left of Matryona on a hand sledge with a dirty sack over it. They threw off the sack to wash her. There was just a mess . . . no feet, only half a body, no left hand. One woman said, "The Lord has left her her right hand. She'll be able to say her prayers where she's going."

Then the whole crowd of rubber plants were carried out of the cottage—these plants that Matryona had loved so much that once when smoke woke her up in the night she didn't rush to save her house but to tip the plants onto the floor in case they were suffocated. The women swept the floor clean. They hung a wide towel of old homespun over Matryona's dim mirror. They took down the jolly posters. They moved my table out of the way. Under the icons, near the windows, they stood a rough unadorned coffin on a row of stools.

In the coffin lay Matryona. Her body, mangled and lifeless, was covered with a clean sheet. Her head was swathed in a white kerchief. Her face was almost undamaged, peaceful, more alive than dead.

The villagers came to pay their last respects. The women even brought their small children to take a look at the dead. And if anyone raised a lament, all the women, even those who had looked in out of idle curiosity, always joined in, wailing where they stood by the door or the wall, as though they were providing a choral accompaniment. The men stood stiff and silent with their caps off.

The formal lamentation had to be performed by the women of Matryona's family. I observed that the lament followed a coldly calculated, age-old ritual. The more distant relatives went up to the coffin for a short while and made low wailing noises over it. Those who considered themselves closer kin to the dead woman began their lament in the doorway and when they got as far as the coffin, bowed down and roared out their grief right in the face of the departed. Every lamenter made up her own melody. And expressed her own thoughts and feelings.

I realized that a lament for the dead is not just a lament, but a kind of politics. Matryona's three sisters swooped, took possession of the cottage, the goat, and the stove, locked up the chest, ripped the two hundred rubles for the funeral out of the coat lining, and drummed it into everybody who came that only they were near relatives. Their lament over the coffin went like this, "Oh, nanny, nanny! Oh nan-nan! All we had in the world was you! You could have lived in peace and quiet, you could. And we should always have been kind and loving to you. Now your top room's been the death of you. Finished you off, it has, the cursed thing! Oh, why did you have to take it down? Why didn't you listen to us?"

Thus the sisters' laments were indictments of Matryona's husband's family: they shouldn't have made her take the top room down. (There was an underlying meaning, too: you've taken the top room, all right, but we won't let you have the house itself!)

Matryona's husband's family, her sisters-in-law, Efim and Faddey's sisters, and the various nieces lamented like this, "Oh poor auntie, poor auntie! Why didn't you take better care of yourself! Now they're angry with us for sure. Our own dear Matryona you were, and it's your own fault! The top room is nothing to do with it. Oh why did you go where death was waiting for you? Nobody asked you to go there. And what a way to die! Oh why didn't you listen to us?" (Their answer to the others showed through these laments: we are not to blame for her death, and the house we'll talk about later.)

But the "second" Matryona, a coarse, broad-faced woman, the substitute Matryona whom Faddey had married so long ago for the sake of her name, got out of step with family policy, wailing and sobbing over the coffin in her simplicity, "Oh my poor dear sister! You won't be angry with me, will you now?

Oh-oh-oh! How we used to talk and talk, you and me! Forgive a poor miserable woman! You've gone to be with your dear mother, and you'll come for me some day, for sure! Oh-oh-oh-oh! . . ."

At every "oh-oh-oh" it was as though she were giving up the ghost. She writhed and gasped, with her breast against the side of the coffin. When her lament went beyond the ritual prescription, the women, as though acknowledging its success, all started saying, "Come away now, come away."

Matryona came away, but back she went again, sobbing with even greater abandon. Then an ancient woman came out of a corner, put her hand on Matryona's shoulder, and said, "There are two riddles in this world: how I was born, I don't remember, how I shall die, I don't know."

And Matryona fell silent at once, and all the others were silent, so that there was an unbroken hush.

But the old woman herself, who was much older than all the other old women there and didn't seem to belong to Matryona at all, after a while started wailing, "Oh, my poor sick Matryona! Oh my poor Vasilyevna! Oh what a weary thing it is to be seeing you into your grave!"

There was one who didn't follow the ritual, but wept straight-forwardly, in the fashion of our age, which has had plenty of practice at it. This was Matryona's unfortunate foster daughter, Kira, from Cherusti, for whom the top room had been taken down and moved. Her ringlets were pitifully out of curl. Her eyes looked red and bloodshot. She didn't notice that her headscarf was slipping off out in the frosty air and that her arm hadn't found the sleeve of her coat. She walked in a stupor from her foster mother's coffin in one house to her brother's in another. They were afraid she would lose her mind, because her husband had to go on trial as well.

It looked as if her husband was doubly at fault: not only had he been moving the top room, but as an engine driver, he knew the regulations about unprotected crossings and should have gone down to the station to warn them about the tractor. There were a thousand people on the Urals express that night, peacefully sleeping in the upper and lower berths of their dimly lit carriages, and all those lives were nearly cut short. All because of a few greedy people, wanting to get their hands on a plot of land, or not wanting to make a second trip with a tractor.

All because of the top room, which had been under a curse ever since Faddey's hands had started itching to take it down.

The tractor driver was already beyond human justice. And the railway authorities were also at fault, both because a busy crossing was unguarded and because the coupled engines were traveling without lights. That was why they had tried at first to blame it all on the drink, and then to keep the case out of court.

The rails and the track were so twisted and torn that for three days, while the coffins were still in the house, no trains ran—they were diverted onto another line. All Friday, Saturday, and Sunday, from the end of the investigation until the funeral, the work of repairing the line went on day and night. The repair gang was frozen, and they made fires to warm themselves and to light their work at night, using the boards and beams from the second sledge, which were there for the taking, scattered around the crossing.

The first sledge just stood there, undamaged and still loaded, a little way beyond the crossing.

One sledge, tantalizingly ready to be towed away, and the other perhaps still to be plucked from the flames—that was what harrowed the soul of black-bearded Faddey all day Friday and all day Saturday. His daughter was going out of her mind, his son-in-law had a criminal charge hanging over him, in his own house lay the son he had killed, and along the street the woman he had killed and whom he had once loved. But Faddey stood by the coffins, clutching his beard, only for a short time, and went away again. His high forehead was clouded by painful thoughts, but what he was thinking about was how to save the timbers of the top room from the flames and from Matryona's scheming sisters.

Going over the people of Talnovo in my mind, I realized that Faddey was not the only one like that.

Property, the people's property, or my property, is strangely called our "goods." If you lose your goods, people think you disgrace yourself and make yourself look foolish.

Faddey dashed about, never stopping to sit down, from the settlement to the station, from one official to another, there he stood with his bent back, leaning heavily on his stick, and begged them all to take pity on an old man and give him permission to recover the top room.

Somebody gave permission. And Faddey gathered together his surviving sons, sons-in-law, and nephews, got horses from the kolkhoz and from the other side of the wrecked crossing, by a roundabout way that led through three villages, brought the remnants of the top room home to his yard. He finished the job in the early hours of Sunday morning.

On Sunday afternoon they were buried. The two coffins met in the middle of the village, and the relatives argued about which of them should go first. Then they put them side by side on an open sledge, the aunt and the nephew, and carried the dead over the damp snow, with a gloomy February sky above, to the churchyard two villages away. There was an unkind wind, so the priest and the deacon waited inside the church and didn't come out to Talnovo to meet them.

A crowd of people walked slowly behind the coffins, singing in chorus. Outside the village they fell back.

When Sunday came the women were still fussing around the house. An old woman mumbled psalms by the coffin, Matryona's sisters flitted about, popping things into the oven, and the air round the mouth of the stove trembled with the heat of red-hot peats, those Matryona had carried in a sack from a distant bog. They were making unappetizing pies with poor flour.

When the funeral was over and it was already getting on toward evening, they gathered for the wake. Tables were put together to make a long one, which hid the place where the coffin had stood in the morning. To start with, they all stood round the table, and an old man, the husband of a sister-in-law, said the Lord's Prayer. Then they poured everybody a little honey and warm water,[1] just enough to cover the bottom of the bowl. We spooned it up without bread or anything, in memory of the dead. Then we ate something and drank vodka and the conversation became more animated. Before the jelly they all stood up and sang "Eternal remembrance" (they explained to me that it had to be sung before the jelly). There was more drinking. By now

---

1. Traditionally Russians have *kutiia,* a wheat pudding with honey and almonds, at funerals and memorial gatherings; the villagers are too poor to have the main ingredients and their honey and water are symbolic of the *kutiia.*

they were talking louder than ever, and not about Matryona at all. The sister-in-law's husband started boasting, "Did you notice, brother Christians, that they took the funeral service slowly today? That's because Father Mikhail noticed me. He knows I know the service. Other times, it's saints defend us, homeward wend us, and that's all."

At last the supper was over. They all rose again. They sang "Worthy Is She." Then again, with a triple repetition of "Eternal Remembrance."[2] But the voices were hoarse and out of tune, their faces drunken, and nobody put any feeling into this "eternal memory."

Then most of the guests went away, and only the near relatives were left. They pulled out their cigarets and lit up, there were jokes and laughter. There was some mention of Matryona's husband and his disappearance. The sister-in-law's husband, striking himself on the chest, assured me and the cobbler who was married to one of Matryona's sisters, "He was dead, Efim was dead! What could stop him coming back if he wasn't? If I knew they were going to hang me when I got to the old place, I'd come back just the same!"

The cobbler nodded in agreement. He was a deserter and had never left the old place. All through the war he was hiding in his mother's cellar.

The stern and silent old woman who was more ancient than all the ancients was staying the night and sat high up on the stove. She looked down in mute disapproval on the indecently animated youngsters of fifty and sixty.

But the unhappy foster daughter, who had grown up within these walls, went away behind the kitchen screen to cry.

Faddey didn't come to Matryona's wake—perhaps because he was holding a wake for his son. But twice in the next few days he walked angrily into the house for discussions with Matryona's sisters and the deserting cobbler.

The argument was about the house. Should it go to one of the sisters or to the foster daughter? They were on the verge of taking it to court, but they made peace because they realized that the court would hand over the house to neither side, but to the Rural District Council. A bargain was struck. One sister took the goat, the cobbler and his wife got the house, and to make up Faddey's share, since he had "nursed every bit of timber here in his arms," in addition to the top room which had already been carried away, they let him have the shed which had housed the goat and the whole of the inner fence between the yard and the garden.

Once again the insatiable old man got the better of sickness and pain and became young and active. Once again he gathered together his surviving sons and sons-in-law, they dismantled the shed and the fence, he hauled the timbers himself, sledge by sledge, and only toward the end did he have Antoshka of 8-D, who didn't slack this time, to help him.

They boarded Matryona's house up till the spring, and I moved in with one of her sisters-in-law, not far away. This sister-in-law on several occasions came out with some recollection of Matryona and made me see the dead woman in a new light. "Efim didn't love her. He used to say, 'I like to dress in an educated way, but she dresses any old way, like they do in the country.'

2. Dirges, religious hymns sung to honor the dead. The village still follows religious rituals in time of crisis and does not use the civil ceremony proposed by the Soviet government.

Well then, he thinks, if she doesn't want anything, he might as well drink whatever's to spare. One time I went with him to the town to work, and he got himself a madam there and never wanted to come back to Matryona."

Everything she said about Matryona was disapproving. She was slovenly, she made no effort to get a few things about her. She wasn't the saving kind. She didn't even keep a pig, because she didn't like fattening them up for some reason. And the silly woman helped other people without pay. (What brought Matryona to mind this time was that the garden needed plowing, and she couldn't find enough helpers to pull the plow.)

Matryona's sister-in-law admitted that she was warmhearted and straightforward, but pitied and despised her for it.

It was only then, after these disapproving comments from her sister-in-law, that a true likeness of Matryona formed before my eyes, and I understood her as I never had when I lived side by side with her.

Of course! Every house in the village kept a pig. But she didn't. What can be easier than fattening a greedy piglet that cares for nothing in the world but food! You warm his swill three times a day, you live for him—then you cut his throat and you have some fat.

But she had none.

She made no effort to get things round her. She didn't struggle and strain to buy things and then care for them more than life itself.

She didn't go all out after fine clothes. Clothes, that beautify what is ugly and evil.

She was misunderstood and abandoned even by her husband. She had lost six children, but not her sociable ways. She was a stranger to her sisters and sisters-in-law, a ridiculous creature who stupidly worked for others without pay. She didn't accumulate property against the day she died. A dirty-white goat, a gammy-legged cat, some rubber plants. . . .

We had all lived side by side with her and had never understood that she was the righteous one without whom, as the proverb says, no village can stand.[3]

Nor any city.

Nor our whole land.

3. See Genesis 18.23–33, the story of Sodom.

DORIS LESSING
born 1919

The clash between cultures, between attitudes within cultures, and between elements of one's own personality, as well as the attempt to integrate opposing elements into a higher level of consciousness, are all fundamental to Doris Lessing's work and are explored in a style that ranges from the detailed realism of her earliest stories to the fantasies and "inner-space fiction" of her novels of the 1970s. Lessing herself has lived in the midst of such conflicts: brought up in the British colony of Rhodesia, she has written harsh indictments of colonial society and its cruel blindness to black culture and rights; living in London, she has described political and social issues and the way they determine interpersonal relationships; as a woman pursuing independence and the right to shape her own identity, she has investigated the psychology of the self in both sexual and intellectual terms and pondered the relations of the individual to the community. Lessing's social realism, her description of the frustrated and incomplete relationships between human beings, and her yearning (especially evident in the later novels) for a higher plane of awareness in which there is perfect understanding recall D. H. Lawrence's criticism of society and his vision of perfect harmony in tune with nature. Yet there are important differences, including Lessing's refusal to accept the archetypal roles of the sexes that Lawrence found the key to natural harmony. Her own experience could not be content with such answers, and her stories and novels have never ceased to explore the layers of consciousness that make up individual identity and social interaction.

She was born Doris May Tayler in Persia (now Iran), on October 22, 1919. Her parents were British—her mother a nurse and her father a clerk in the Imperial Bank of Persia who had been crippled in World War I and whose horror-filled memories of the "war to end war" punctuate her recollections of childhood. In 1925 her father decided to start a new life in British Africa, where the colonial government of Rhodesia (now Zimbabwe) was offering economic incentives to encourage the immigration of white settlers. For ten shillings an acre, he bought three thousand acres of farming land in Mashonaland, a section of Southern Rhodesia that was the homeland of the Matabele tribe but from which the government had evicted most of the population. The farm never prospered. Lessing attended a convent school in the capital city of Salisbury (now Harare) until fourteen, but considers herself largely self-educated from her avid reading of classics of European and American literature. She especially loved the nineteenth-century novel, and Tolstoy, Dostoevsky, Stendhal, and the other great realists impressed her with their "climate of ethical judgement" in which she felt "the warmth, the compassion, the humanity, the love of people" that are so important in her own works. Gradually she became aware of the problems of racial injustice in her new home and of the fact that she was one of a privileged class of white immigrants who had displaced the previous owners of the land. As she later noted, she was "a member of the white minority, pitted against a black majority that was abominably treated and still is." Themes of this early awakening, which combines a strong attachment to the land itself with horror at racial inequities and the sterility of white civilization in Rhodesia, run through much of her work: in particular, her first novel *The Grass Is Singing* (1949) and the collected *African Stories* (1964). To Lessing, "literature should be committed" in the face of all forms of tyranny. She herself was politically active in Rhodesia and a member of the British Communist Party from 1952 until 1956, the year of the intervention in Hungary. Much of her writing describes the painful clash of two ideals—individual conscience and collective good—as they were embodied for Lessing in her experience of communism. Her political activism and descriptions of racial injustice made their mark, and in 1956 she was declared a prohibited alien in both Southern Rhodesia and South Africa.

While still in Rhodesia, Lessing worked in several office jobs in Salisbury and made two unsuccessful marriages (Lessing is the surname of her second husband). In 1949 she moved to England with the son of her second marriage and published *The Grass Is Singing*. It was an immediate success, and she was henceforth able to make her living as a writer. She began the five-volume series *Children of Violence* (1952–69), which follows the life of a symbolically named heroine, Martha Quest, whose career in many instances parallels Lessing's own. *Children of Violence* is the portrait of an age and two cultures, and it explores with Lessing's characteristic energy a series of moral and intellectual issues for the time: the (female) protagonist's pursuit of individual freedom and the right to achieve her own identity, parent-child relationships, race relations, the hopes and frustrations of political idealism, reason versus irrationality, the shaping influence of culture and historical events. It follows the form of the nineteenth-century *Bildungsroman*, or "education novel": Martha Quest moves toward greater understanding of the cultural forces acting on her, but it cannot be said that she controls the process of her development as consciously as will Lessing's later protagonists.

The Golden Notebook (1962), Lessing's most famous novel, makes a sharp break with the linear style of narrative found in Children of Violence and in the bildungsroman tradition. Once again, a protagonist (Anna Wulf) is struggling to build a unified identity from the multiple selves that constitute her fragmented personality. Linear narrative, however, cannot do justice to these many dimensions, or to the exploratory process by which Anna finally creates a free, integrated personality. "The point of that book was the relation of its parts to each other," said Lessing, and this relation (although framed by a conventional short novel called Free Women) is essentially that of an overlapping series of differently colored notebooks that contain Anna's different versions of her experience: black for Africa, red for politics, yellow for a fictionalized version with herself as a character named Ella, and blue for a factual diary. By analyzing her life from these different perspectives, Anna is able to understand and synthesize their interaction: to write, ultimately, the "Golden Notebook," which is "all of me in one book." A chronological account of the events would start with Anna's breakdown and inability to write and end with her regained equilibrium after a tangled love affair with a similarly split character, Saul Green. Such an account would miss the core of the book, however, or the process by which it all happens: Lessing's detailed description of a mind healing itself by recalling and assessing its relationships with other people, adjusting earlier views according to new insights, weighing (and sometimes rejecting) the explanations of psychoanalysis, comparing different ways of interpreting experience, and measuring the constantly changing whole against the test of each new encounter.

Although The Golden Notebook is now taken as one of the major novels of the twentieth century, it was seen at the time chiefly as a feminist manifesto—a one-sided appraisal that infuriated the author. To accusations of being "unfeminine" and a "man-hater" for putting into print emotions of female aggression, hostility, and resentment, she responded dryly, "apparently what many women were thinking, feeling, experiencing came as a great surprise." Yet, she notes, when at the same time novels and plays caustically attacked women as underminers and betrayers, "these attitudes in male writers were taken for granted, accepted as sound philosophical bases, as quite normal, certainly not as woman-hating, aggressive, or neurotic." Lessing's feminism is often a matter of establishing balances and an insistence on honesty of emotions and critical self-awareness in all her protagonists, whether male (The Temptation of Jack Orkney, 1963) or female (Anna Wulf).

The newly integrated "all of me" at the end of The Golden Notebook has broken beyond intellectualized understanding and reached "beyond the region where words could be made to have sense." In the "inner-space fiction" written during the 1970s and early 1980s, Lessing took up these themes of quasi-mystical insight: first with a schizophrenic hero whose cosmic imaginings are closer to psychic wholeness than his normal life (Briefing for a Descent into Hell, 1971), later in the dream-exploration of other "bizarre" dimensions beyond the "ordinary" living-room wall (Memoirs of a Survivor, 1974), and then in a science-fiction series, Canopus in Argos: Archives (1979–83), which describes the different protagonists' consciousness evolving under pressure to a higher plane of existence. These later books, as Lessing states, are influenced by Sufi mysticism with its insistence on detached perception and the evolution of consciousness and on learning as a process of discovering the right questions. The wordless moment of understanding that comes when the right question is asked may seem a long way from Lessing's first novels about race relations in Southern Rhodesia, or Martha Quest's awakening to emotional, intellectual, and political maturity. In each case, however, a process of listening to experience is required. The focus has not changed when she writes in the "Afterword" to the fourth Canopus novel: "It seems to me that we do not know nearly enough about ourselves." The attempt to know about ourselves, to grow through such knowledge, and to achieve harmony in this world or "in worlds or dimensions elsewhere" pervades her entire work.

Annoyed at criticism of her shift to science fiction, Lessing published two realistic novels under the name of Jane Somers: *The Diary of a Good Neighbor* (1983), a novel that gave graphic descriptions of the difficulties of aging and illness, and its sequel *If the Old Could . . .* (1984). Sales were respectable but not outstanding; and when both were reprinted in 1984 as *The Diaries of Jane Somers,* Lessing announced that she had published them under a pseudonym to test whether the critics who had disliked her new style would recognize the "realistic" Lessing under another name. They did not. Since then, she has produced realistic stories with a satirical or symbolic twist: *The Good Terrorist* (1985), a satire of naive British terrorists who arrange a homey atmosphere in a London squat while carrying out bombing raids, and *The Fifth Child* (1988), which recounts the gradual destruction of a London family by their "alien" and uncontrollably savage fifth child. Lectures reprinted in *Prisons We Choose to Live Inside* (1987) reject the savagery that has dominated human history and that persists in wars such as the Afghan resistance, which Lessing documents in *The Wind Blows Away Our Words* (1987). The writer's role, she asserts, is to be both committed and detached, clarifying issues and suggesting remedies for those who are caught up in "mass emotions and social conditions." As both novelist and non-fiction writer, Lessing upholds the concept of the writer as a moral figure, whether the "moralist" of the French tradition who awakens our conscience to ethical issues (Albert Camus), or the polemic voice sounded in novels and essays by Alexander Solzhenitsyn.

The Old Chief Mshlanga is one of Lessing's earliest African stories, written during the period from 1950 to 1958 when she wrote most of her African fiction and published in *This Was the Old Chief's Country* (1951). This collection, together with five novellas set in Africa in *Five* (1953) and her best-selling novel *The Grass Is Singing* (1949), established Lessing as an important interpreter of modern Africa—or rather, of the colonial experience in Africa. She herself draws the distinction between the African experience as it can be understood by African whites and as it is felt by the black Africans whose heritage has been forcibly displaced. Lessing writes in the preface to her 1973 *Collected African Stories:*

> It can be said of all white-dominated Africa that it was—and indeed still is—the Old Chief's Country. So all the stories I write of a certain kind, I think of as belonging under that heading: tales about white people, sometimes about black people, living in a landscape that not so very long ago was settled by black tribes, living in complex societies that the white people are only just beginning to study, let alone understand. . . .
>
> I am not able to write about what has been lost, which was and still is recorded orally. As a writer that is my biggest regret, as it is of all the white writers from Africa I have known. The tribal life that was broken seems now to have had more real dignity, more responsibility for what is important in people—their self-respect, more tolerance of individuality, than our way of living has. The breakup of that society, the time of chaos that followed it, is as dramatic a story as any; but if you are a white writer, it is a story that you are told by others.

The dispossession that underlies the plot of *The Old Chief Mshlanga* began with the economic infiltration of the country by white colonizers, soon formalized in Chartered Company policies that divided land into categories of "alienated" (owned by white settlers) and "unalienated" (occupied by natives, including the Reserves whose inhabitants paid a head tax). The official Land Apportionment Act of 1930 confirmed this arrangement by separating the territory into areas called Native and European. The figure of the Old Chief bridges past and present, a proud era fifty years earlier when his people owned the entire country and the diminished present in which they can be forcibly relocated on a Reserve after disagreeing with a white settler. Yet it is not the Old Chief who is the protagonist; significantly, his situation is pushed into the background until the middle of the story, when it intrudes on the consciousness of a young white settler girl. Only gradually does the "vein of richness" that he and his people represent come to light. By the end of the story the tribe has disappeared. The girl visits their village to find it disintegrating into the riotously fertile landscape, and the richness of their existence is preserved mainly as an obscure recognition in her mind.

Yet in spite of her comment that "there was nothing there," the girl's close description of the lush scene shows that her eyes have been opened to an African presence that initially she could not see. The gain, however, is one-sided: even now it cannot bring her closer to the experience of the tribespeople but is restricted to a feeling for the landscape. There is no advantage for the Old Chief: he and his people have disappeared into a symbolic essence, buried in a "richness" that inheres in the land even when it is turned over to a new settler—as it will be. Lessing's observant young girl has been changed by the encounter with the Old Chief, but hers is a bleak awakening that includes a sense of loss and indirect responsibility. Perhaps, one day, she will write about it.

Ruth Whittaker, *Doris Lessing* (1988), is a concise, informative discussion of Lessing's fiction to 1985; it includes biographical contexts and selective bibliography. Two volumes of Lessing's autobiography are published as *Under My Skin* (1995) and *Walking in the Shade: Volume Two of My Autobiography, 1949–1962* (1997). Michael Thorpe, *Doris Lessing's Africa* (1978), is a valuable historical and critical commentary on Lessing's writings about Africa. Claire Sprague and Virginia Tiger, *Critical Essays on Doris Lessing* (1986), offers diverse perspectives on the range of Lessing's work; numerous interviews on a range of subjects are collected in Doris May Lessing, *Putting Questions Differently: Interviews with Doris Lessing, 1964–1994* (1994). A good critical study of the novels is Roberta Rubenstein, *The Novelistic Vision of Doris Lessing* (1979). Perspectives on women and literature are the focus of Gayle Greene, *Doris Lessing: The Poetics of Change* (1994).

The Old Chief Mshlanga

They were good, the years of ranging the bush over her father's farm which, like every white farm, was largely unused, broken only occasionally by small patches of cultivation. In between, nothing but trees, the long sparse grass, thorn and cactus and gully, grass and outcrop and thorn. And a jutting piece of rock which had been thrust up from the warm soil of Africa unimaginable eras of time ago, washed into hollows and whorls by sun and wind that had travelled so many thousands of miles of space and bush, would hold the weight of a small girl whose eyes were sightless for anything but a pale willowed river, a pale gleaming castle—a small girl singing: "Out flew the web and floated wide, the mirror cracked from side to side . . ."[1]

Pushing her way through the green aisles of the mealie[2] stalks, the leaves arching like cathedrals veined with sunlight far overhead, with the packed red earth underfoot, a fine lace of red starred witchweed would summon up a black bent figure croaking premonitions: the Northern witch, bred of cold Northern forests, would stand before her among the mealie fields, and it was the mealie fields that faded and fled, leaving her among the gnarled roots of an oak, snow falling thick and soft and white, the woodcutter's fire glowing red welcome through crowding tree trunks.

---

1. The child is reciting lines 114–15 of Tennyson's *The Lady of Shalott*.   2. Maize; corn.

A white child, opening its eyes curiously on a sun-suffused landscape, a gaunt and violent landscape, might be supposed to accept it as her own, to make the msasa trees and the thorn trees as familiars, to feel her blood running free and responsive to the swing of the seasons.

This child could not see a msasa tree,[3] or the thorn, for what they were. Her books held tales of alien fairies, her rivers ran slow and peaceful, and she knew the shape of the leaves of an ash or an oak, the names of the little creatures that lived in English streams, when the words "the veld"[4] meant strangeness, though she could remember nothing else.

Because of this, for many years, it was the veld that seemed unreal; the sun was a foreign sun, and the wind spoke a strange language.

The black people on the farm were as remote as the trees and the rocks. They were an amorphous black mass, mingling and thinning and massing like tadpoles, faceless, who existed merely to serve, to say "Yes, Baas,"[5] take their money and go. They changed season by season, moving from one farm to the next, according to their outlandish needs, which one did not have to understand, coming from perhaps hundreds of miles north or east, passing on after a few months—where? Perhaps even as far away as the fabled gold mines of Johannesburg,[6] where the pay was so much better than the few shillings a month and the double handful of mealie meal twice a day which they earned in that part of Africa.

The child was taught to take them for granted: the servants in the house would come running a hundred yards to pick up a book if she dropped it. She was called "Nkosikaas"—Chieftainess, even by the black children her own age.

Later, when the farm grew too small to hold her curiosity, she carried a gun in the crook of her arm and wandered miles a day, from vlei to vlei, from *kopje*[7] to *kopje*, accompanied by two dogs: the dogs and the gun were an armour against fear. Because of them she never felt fear.

If a native came into sight along the kaffir[8] paths half a mile away, the dogs would flush him up a tree as if he were a bird. If he expostulated (in his uncouth language which was by itself ridiculous) that was cheek. If one was in a good mood, it could be a matter for laughter. Otherwise one passed on, hardly glancing at the angry man in the tree.

On the rare occasions when white children met together they could amuse themselves by hailing a passing native in order to make a buffoon of him; they could set the dogs on him and watch him run; they could tease a small black child as if he were a puppy—save that they would not throw stones and sticks at a dog without a sense of guilt.

Later still, certain questions presented themselves in the child's mind; and because the answers were not easy to accept, they were silenced by an even greater arrogance of manner.

It was even impossible to think of the black people who worked about the house as friends, for if she talked to one of them, her mother would come running anxiously: "Come away; you mustn't talk to natives."

It was this instilled consciousness of danger, of something unpleasant, that made it easy to laugh out loud, crudely, if a servant made a mistake in his

---

3. A large tree of central Africa, notable for the vivid colorings (pink through copper) of its spring foliage and for the fragrance of its white flowers.   4. Unenclosed country, open grassland.   5. Boss. 6. The largest city in the Union (now Republic) of South Africa.   7. A small hill (Afrikaans). *Vlei*: a shallow pool or swamp (Afrikaans).   8. A black African; usually used disparagingly.

English or if he failed to understand an order—there is a certain kind of laughter that is fear, afraid of itself.

One evening, when I was about fourteen, I was walking down the side of a mealie field that had been newly ploughed, so that the great red clods showed fresh and tumbling to the vlei beyond, like a choppy red sea; it was that hushed and listening hour, when the birds send long sad calls from tree to tree, and all the colours of earth and sky and leaf are deep and golden. I had my rifle in the curve of my arm, and the dogs were at my heels.

In front of me, perhaps a couple of hundred yards away, a group of three Africans came into sight around the side of a big antheap. I whistled the dogs close in to my skirts and let the gun swing in my hand, and advanced, waiting for them to move aside, off the path, in respect for my passing. But they came on steadily, and the dogs looked up at me for the command to chase. I was angry. It was "cheek"[9] for a native not to stand off a path, the moment he caught sight of you.

In front walked an old man, stooping his weight on to a stick, his hair grizzled white, a dark red blanket slung over his shoulders like a cloak. Behind him came two young men, carrying bundles of pots, assegais,[1] hatchets.

The group was not a usual one. They were not natives seeking work. These had an air of dignity, of quietly following their own purpose. It was the dignity that checked my tongue. I walked quietly on, talking softly to the growling dogs, till I was ten paces away. Then the old man stopped, drawing his blanket close.

"Morning, Nkosikaas," he said, using the customary greeting for any time of the day.

"Good morning," I said. "Where are you going?" My voice was a little truculent.

The old man spoke in his own language, then one of the young men stepped forward politely and said in careful English: "My Chief travels to see his brothers beyond the river."

A Chief! I thought, understanding the pride that made the old man stand before me like an equal—more than an equal, for he showed courtesy, and I showed none.

The old man spoke again, wearing dignity like an inherited garment, still standing ten paces off, flanked by his entourage, not looking at me (that would have been rude) but directing his eyes somewhere over my head at the trees.

"You are the little Nkosikaas from the farm of Baas Jordan?"

"That's right," I said.

"Perhaps your father does not remember," said the interpreter for the old man, "but there was an affair with some goats. I remember seeing you when you were . . ." The young man held his hand at knee level and smiled.

We all smiled.

"What is your name?" I asked.

"This is Chief Mshlanga," said the young man.

"I will tell my father that I met you," I said.

The old man said: "My greetings to your father, little Nkosikaas."

9. Impudence.   1. Spears.

"Good morning," I said politely, finding the politeness difficult, from lack of use.

"Morning, little Nkosikaas," said the old man, and stood aside to let me pass.

I went by, my gun hanging awkwardly, the dogs sniffing and growling, cheated of their favourite game of chasing natives like animals.

Not long afterwards I read in an old explorer's book the phrase: "Chief Mshlanga's country." It went like this: "Our destination was Chief Mshlanga's country, to the north of the river; and it was our desire to ask his permission to prospect for gold in his territory."

The phrase "ask his permission" was so extraordinary to a white child, brought up to consider all natives as things to use, that it revived those questions, which could not be suppressed: they fermented slowly in my mind.

On another occasion one of those old prospectors who still move over Africa looking for neglected reefs, with their hammers and tents, and pans for sifting gold from crushed rock, came to the farm and, in talking of the old days, used that phrase again: "This was the Old Chief's country," he said. "It stretched from those mountains over there way back to the river, hundreds of miles of country." That was his name for our district: "The Old Chief's Country"; he did not use our name for it—a new phrase which held no implication of usurped ownership.

As I read more books about the time when this part of Africa was opened up, not much more than fifty years before, I found Old Chief Mshlanga had been a famous man, known to all the explorers and prospectors. But then he had been young; or maybe it was his father or uncle they spoke of—I never found out.

During that year I met him several times in the part of the farm that was traversed by natives moving over the country. I learned that the path up the side of the big red field where the birds sang was the recognized highway for migrants. Perhaps I even haunted it in the hope of meeting him: being greeted by him, the exchange of courtesies, seemed to answer the questions that troubled me.

Soon I carried a gun in a different spirit; I used it for shooting food and not to give me confidence. And now the dogs learned better manners. When I saw a native approaching, we offered and took greetings; and slowly that other landscape in my mind faded, and my feet struck directly on the African soil, and I saw the shapes of tree and hill clearly, and the black people moved back, as it were, out of my life: it was as if I stood aside to watch a slow intimate dance of landscape and men, a very old dance, whose steps I could not learn.

But I thought: this is my heritage, too; I was bred here; it is my country as well as the black man's country; and there is plenty of room for all of us, without elbowing each other off the pavements and roads.

It seemed it was only necessary to let free that respect I felt when I was talking with old Chief Mshlanga, to let both black and white people meet gently, with tolerance for each other's differences: it seemed quite easy.

Then, one day, something new happened. Working in our house as servants were always three natives: cook, houseboy, garden boy. They used to change as the farm natives changed: staying for a few months, then moving on to a new job, or back home to their kraals.[2] They were thought of as "good" or "bad" natives; which meant: how did they behave as servants? Were they lazy, efficient, obedient, or disrespectful? If the family felt good-humoured, the phrase was: "What can you expect from raw black savages?" If we were angry, we said: "These damned niggers, we would be much better off without them."

One day, a white policeman was on his rounds of the district, and he said laughingly: "Did you know you have an important man in your kitchen?"

"What!" exclaimed my mother sharply. "What do you mean?"

"A Chief's son." The policeman seemed amused. "He'll boss the tribe when the old man dies."

"He'd better not put on a Chief's son act with me," said my mother.

When the policeman left, we looked with different eyes at our cook: he was a good worker, but he drank too much at week-ends—that was how we knew him.

He was a tall youth, with very black skin, like black polished metal, his tightly growing black hair parted white man's fashion at one side, with a metal comb from the store stuck into it; very polite, very distant, very quick to obey an order. Now that it had been pointed out, we said: "Of course, you can see. Blood always tells."

My mother became strict with him now she knew about his birth and prospects. Sometimes, when she lost her temper, she would say: "You aren't the Chief yet, you know." And he would answer her very quietly, his eyes on the ground: "Yes, Nkosikaas."

One afternoon he asked for a whole day off, instead of the customary half-day, to go home next Sunday.

"How can you go home in one day?"

"It will take me half an hour on my bicycle," he explained.

I watched the direction he took; and the next day I went off to look for this kraal; I understood he must be Chief Mshlanga's successor: there was no other kraal near enough our farm.

Beyond our boundaries on that side the country was new to me. I followed unfamiliar paths past *kopjes* that till now had been part of the jagged horizon, hazed with distance. This was Government land, which had never been cultivated by white men; at first I could not understand why it was that it appeared, in merely crossing the boundary, I had entered a completely fresh type of landscape. It was a wide green valley, where a small river sparkled, and vivid water-birds darted over the rushes. The grass was thick and soft to my calves, the trees stood tall and shapely.

I was used to our farm, whose hundreds of acres of harsh eroded soil bore trees that had been cut for the mine furnaces and had grown thin and twisted, where the cattle had dragged the grass flat, leaving innumerable criss-crossing trails that deepened each season into gullies, under the force of the rains.

This country had been left untouched, save for prospectors whose picks had struck a few sparks from the surface of the rocks as they wandered by; and for migrant natives whose passing had left, perhaps, a charred patch on the trunk of a tree where their evening fire had nestled.

---

2. Native villages; collections of huts surrounding a central space.

It was very silent: a hot morning with pigeons cooing throatily, the midday shadows lying dense and thick with clear yellow spaces of sunlight between and in all that wide green park-like valley, not a human soul but myself.

I was listening to the quick regular tapping of a woodpecker when slowly a chill feeling seemed to grow up from the small of my back to my shoulders, in a constricting spasm like a shudder, and at the roots of my hair a tingling sensation began and ran down over the surface of my flesh, leaving me goose-fleshed and cold, though I was damp with sweat. Fever? I thought; then uneasily, turned to look over my shoulder; and realized suddenly that this was fear. It was extraordinary, even humiliating. It was a new fear. For all the years I had walked by myself over this country I had never known a moment's uneasiness; in the beginning because I had been supported by a gun and the dogs, then because I had learnt an easy friendliness for the Africans I might encounter.

I had read of this feeling, how the bigness and silence of Africa, under the ancient sun, grows dense and takes shape in the mind, till even the birds seem to call menacingly, and a deadly spirit comes out of the trees and the rocks. You move warily, as if your very passing disturbs something old and evil, something dark and big and angry that might suddenly rear and strike from behind. You look at groves of entwined trees, and picture the animals that might be lurking there; you look at the river running slowly, dropping from level to level through the vlei, spreading into pools where at night the bucks come to drink, and the crocodiles rise and drag them by their soft noses into underwater caves. Fear possessed me. I found I was turning round and round, because of that shapeless menace behind me that might reach out and take me; I kept glancing at the files of *kopjes* which, seen from a different angle, seemed to change with every step so that even known landmarks, like a big mountain that had sentinelled my world since I first became conscious of it, showed an unfamiliar sunlit valley among its foothills. I did not know where I was. I was lost. Panic seized me. I found I was spinning round and round, staring anxiously at this tree and that, peering up at the sun which appeared to have moved into an eastern slant, shedding the sad yellow light of sunset. Hours must have passed! I looked at my watch and found that this state of meaningless terror had lasted perhaps ten minutes.

The point was that it was meaningless. I was not ten miles from home: I had only to take my way back along the valley to find myself at the fence; away among the foothills of the *kopjes* gleamed the roof of a neighbour's house, and a couple of hours' walking would reach it. This was the sort of fear that contracts the flesh of a dog at night and sets him howling at the full moon. It had nothing to do with what I thought or felt; and I was more disturbed by the fact that I could become its victim than of the physical sensation itself: I walked steadily on, quietened, in a divided mind, watching my own pricking nerves and apprehensive glances from side to side with a disgusted amusement. Deliberately I set myself to think of this village I was seeking, and what I should do when I entered it—if I could find it, which was doubtful, since I was walking aimlessly and it might be anywhere in the hundreds of thousands of acres of bush that stretched about me. With my mind on that village, I realized that a new sensation was added to the fear: loneliness. Now such a terror of isolation invaded me that I could hardly walk; and if it were not that I came over the crest of a small rise and saw a village below me, I should have turned and gone home. It was a cluster of thatched huts in a clearing among trees. There were neat patches of mealies and pumpkins and millet, and cattle grazed under some trees at a distance. Fowls scratched among the huts, dogs lay sleeping on the grass, and goats friezed a *kopje* that jutted up beyond a tributary of the river lying like an enclosing arm around the village.

As I came close I saw the huts were lovingly decorated with patterns of yellow and red and ochre mud on the walls; and the thatch was tied in place with plaits of straw.

This was not at all like our farm compound, a dirty and neglected place, a temporary home for migrants who had no roots in it.

And now I did not know what to do next. I called a small black boy, who was sitting on a lot playing a stringed gourd, quite naked except for the strings of blue beads round his neck, and said: "Tell the Chief I am here." The child stuck his thumb in his mouth and stared shyly back at me.

For minutes I shifted my feet on the edge of what seemed a deserted village, till at last the child scuttled off, and then some women came. They were draped in bright cloths, with brass glinting in their ears and on their arms. They also stared, silently; then turned to chatter among themselves.

I said again: "Can I see Chief Mshlanga?" I saw they caught the name; they did not understand what I wanted. I did not understand myself.

At last I walked through them and came past the huts and saw a clearing under a big shady tree, where a dozen old men sat crosslegged on the ground, talking. Chief Mshlanga was leaning back against the tree, holding a gourd in his hand, from which he had been drinking. When he saw me, not a muscle of his face moved, and I could see he was not pleased: perhaps he was afflicted with my own shyness, due to being unable to find the right forms of courtesy for the occasion. To meet me, on our own farm, was one thing; but I should not have come here. What had I expected? I could not join them socially: the thing was unheard of. Bad enough that I, a white girl, should be walking the veld alone as a white man might: and in this part of the bush where only Government officials had the right to move.

Again I stood, smiling foolishly, while behind me stood the groups of brightly clad, chattering women, their faces alert with curiosity and interest, and in front of me sat the old men, with old lined faces, their eyes guarded, aloof. It was a village of ancients and children and women. Even the two young men who kneeled beside the Chief were not those I had seen with him previously: the young men were all away working on the white men's farms and mines, and the Chief must depend on relatives who were temporarily on holiday for his attendants.

"The small white Nkosikaas is far from home," remarked the old man at last.

"Yes," I agreed, "it is far." I wanted to say: "I have come to pay you a friendly visit, Chief Mshlanga." I could not say it. I might now be feeling an urgent helpless desire to get to know these men and women as people, to be accepted by them as a friend, but the truth was I had set out in a spirit of curiosity: I had wanted to see the village that one day our cook, the reserved and obedient young man who got drunk on Sundays, would one day rule over.

"The child of Nkosi Jordan is welcome," said Chief Mshlanga.

"Thank you," I said, and could think of nothing more to say. There was a silence, while the flies rose and began to buzz around my head; and the wind shook a little in the thick green tree that spread its branches over the old men.

"Good morning," I said at last. "I have to return now to my home."

"Morning, little Nkosikaas," said Chief Mshlanga.

I walked away from the indifferent village, over the rise past the staring amber-eyed goats, down through the tall stately trees into the great rich green valley where the river meandered and the pigeons cooed tales of plenty and the woodpecker tapped softly.

The fear had gone; the loneliness had set into stiff-necked stoicism; there was now a queer hostility in the landscape, a cold, hard, sullen indomitability that walked with me, as strong as a wall, as intangible as smoke; it seemed to say to me: you walk here as a destroyer. I went slowly homewards, with an empty heart: I had learned that if one cannot call a country to heel like a dog, neither can one dismiss the past with a smile in an easy gush of feeling, saying: I could not help it, I am also a victim.

I only saw Chief Mshlanga once again.

One night my father's big red land was trampled down by small sharp hooves, and it was discovered that the culprits were goats from Chief Mshlanga's kraal. This had happened once before, years ago.

My father confiscated all the goats. Then he sent a message to the old Chief that if he wanted them he would have to pay for the damage.

He arrived at our house at the time of sunset one evening, looking very old and bent now, walking stiffly under his regally-draped blanket, leaning on a big stick. My father sat himself down in his big chair below the steps of the house; the old man squatted carefully on the ground before him, flanked by his two young men.

The palaver was long and painful, because of the bad English of the young man who interpreted, and because my father could not speak dialect, but only kitchen kaffir.

From my father's point of view, at least two hundred pounds' worth of damage had been done to the crop. He knew he could not get the money from the old man. He felt he was entitled to keep the goats. As for the old Chief, he kept repeating angrily: "Twenty goats! My people cannot lose twenty goats! We are not rich, like the Nkosi Jordan, to lose twenty goats at once."

My father did not think of himself as rich, but rather as very poor. He spoke quickly and angrily in return, saying that the damage done meant a great deal to him, and that he was entitled to the goats.

At last it grew so heated that the cook, the Chief's son, was called from the kitchen to be interpreter, and now my father spoke fluently in English, and our cook translated rapidly so that the old man could understand how very angry my father was. The young man spoke without emotion, in a mechanical way, his eyes lowered, but showing how he felt his position by a hostile uncomfortable set of the shoulders.

It was now in the late sunset, the sky a welter of colours, the birds singing their last songs, and the cattle, lowing peacefully, moving past us towards their sheds for the night. It was the hour when Africa is most beautiful; and here was this pathetic, ugly scene, doing no one any good.

At last my father stated finally: "I'm not going to argue about it. I am keeping the goats."

The old Chief flashed back in his own language: "That means that my people will go hungry when the dry season comes."

"Go to the police, then," said my father, and looked triumphant.

There was, of course, no more to be said.

The old man sat silent, his head bent, his hands dangling helplessly over his withered knees. Then he rose, the young men helping him, and he stood facing my father. He spoke once again, very stiffly; and turned away and went home to his village.

"What did he say?" asked my father of the young man, who laughed uncomfortably and would not meet his eyes.

"What did he say?" insisted my father.

Our cook stood straight and silent, his brows knotted together. Then he spoke. "My father says: All this land, this land you call yours, is his land, and belongs to our people."

Having made this statement, he walked off into the bush after his father, and we did not see him again.

Our next cook was a migrant from Nyasaland, with no expectations of greatness.

Next time the policeman came on his rounds he was told this story. He remarked: "That kraal has no right to be there; it should have been moved long ago. I don't know why no one has done anything about it. I'll have a chat with the Native Commissioner next week. I'm going over for tennis on Sunday, anyway."

Some time later we heard that Chief Mshlanga and his people had been moved two hundred miles east, to a proper Native Reserve; the Government land was going to be opened up for white settlement soon.

I went to see the village again, about a year afterwards. There was nothing there. Mounds of red mud, where the huts had been, had long swathes of rotting thatch over them, veined with the red galleries of the white ants. The pumpkin vines rioted everywhere, over the bushes, up the lower branches of trees so that the great golden balls rolled underfoot and dangled overhead: it was a festival of pumpkins. The bushes were crowding up, the new grass sprang vivid green.

The settler lucky enough to be allotted the lush warm valley (if he chose to cultivate this particular section) would find, suddenly, in the middle of a mealie field, the plants were growing fifteen feet tall, the weight of the cobs dragging at the stalks, and wonder what unsuspected vein of richness he had struck.

ZHANG AILING (EILEEN CHANG)
1920–1995

In many ways the case of Zhang Ailing embodies the complexities and strange historical twists of a national literature finding its place in a global community—in this case, the literature of a nation with an immense and intellectually vibrant diaspora. Often acclaimed as the best Chinese writer of the mid-twentieth century, Zhang Ailing's reputation was established by a member of that diaspora: C. T. Hsia, a Chinese professor with a doctorate in British history from Yale University teaching Chinese literature at Columbia University. Zhang's fame then spread to Taiwan and Hong Kong and at last to China itself. Although the literary work on which her fame rests was done in China and Hong Kong, Zhang Ailing herself lived more than half of her life in the United States, and her best-known novel, *The Rice-Sprout Song*, from her second residence in Hong Kong, was written first in English and then rewritten in Chinese.

Zhang Ailing was born into an old family of imperial officialdom, with an irascible, opium-smoking father and a mother who left to study in France when Zhang Ailing was a child; her family background combined the decadence and fierce independence of spirit of the Shanghai elite in the 1920s and 1930s. After her parents divorced, she was mistreated by her father and fled his house to live with her mother. When the war in China broke out, she left Shanghai to study at the University of Hong Kong; but after the fall of Hong Kong to the Japanese, she returned to Shanghai, where, under Japanese occupation, she wrote her most famous shorter works. Her marriage, albeit brief, to the collaborator Hu Lancheng and her own passive acceptance of Japanese rule made her suspect after the war, and her family background placed her in an even more uncomfortable position when the Communists took Shanghai and the People's Republic of China was established. In 1952 she went again to Hong Kong, where she had to put her talents at the service of the anticommunist passions of the era; there she wrote her two novels, both critical of the People's Republic: *The Rice-Sprout Song*, which enjoyed a modest success, and *Naked Earth*, which did not. In 1955 she left for the United States. After remarriage and the death of her second husband, she went to Berkeley as a researcher and at last to Los Angeles, where she lived her last days in bleak austerity.

Far more than her novels, her stories from the 1940s, collected as *Tales* (sometimes translated as *Romances*), form the core of her work. One of the best known, a long story later turned into a novella, *The Golden Cangue* tells of a woman who must choose between love and financial advantage; her choice of the latter eventually destroys her and all around her, including her children. In addition to the stories and novels, Zhang Ailing wrote essays and memoirs that are much admired; she also did scholarly work on *Story of the Stone* and an annotated translation of a late Qing novel in Wu dialect into Mandarin Chinese.

Chinese fiction of the first half of the century was often absorbed with the desolation of Chinese culture in the modern world; Zhang's works were no exception. But her enduring success may lie in the fact that underneath the particulars of a culture in ruins, she saw a humanity that transcended the historical moment. Her most compelling works display headstrong individuals struggling inside—or trying to escape— the constraints of the Chinese family system.

Perhaps no theme has preoccupied modern Chinese fiction as much as the Chinese family—its constraints, rivalries, and the way it can shape or break an individual. Although family was the central presence in the eighteenth-century novel *Story of the Stone*, in twentieth-century Chinese fiction it was often invested with an almost demonically destructive power. One cliché about Chinese society is that the individual is subordinated to the interests of the family. It is important to understand this concern in modern Chinese fiction not as a simple representation of the way things were—or now are—but rather as a powerful means to articulate the value of individual autonomy and freedom. A second point to keep in mind is that these are all elite families: this enclosed family world, whose young people "ought to" be free, is filled with servants apparently without constant ties to their own families and is penetrated by outsiders who often, like Liuyuan in *Love in a Fallen City*, make their own decisions.

Love in a Fallen City begins with the heroine Liusu trapped in the relationships of the Chinese family. In her late twenties, Liusu has been divorced for seven or eight years; her ex-husband has just died, and his family wants her back for ritual purposes, to play the role of the grieving widow in the funeral ceremony and perhaps to adopt a son to carry on her ex-husband's family line. Her own family, having spent all of her money, urges her to accept this sterile future. In China, as in much of the world until the nineteenth and early twentieth centuries, elite families did have the power to dispose of children in marriage; if in China that social fact is represented with enraged protest, that tells us more about Chinese values than the particular nature of the Chinese family as it differs from other cultures. Liusu wants the security of a marriage, but on her own terms, and she invites the attentions of a rich playboy, Liuyuan, who a matchmaker had arranged to meet her sister. Liusu dances with Liuyuan at their first meeting, and the couple continues to dance in a literal and figurative sense for much of the rest of the story.

Born and raised in England, Liuyuan has come back to China in search of an old China of his imagination. In Liusu he seems to find the very embodiment of the China he sought, and he wants her love, but on his own terms. Thereafter the two lovers are trapped in a dance of courtship, each with a calculated goal, with terms that require that the other "pay" first. Liusu, the daughter of a gambler, has staked her reputation by accepting Liuyuan's invitation to join him in Hong Kong seemingly as Liuyuan's mistress. She is unwilling to accept the financial insecurity of that position. The only power she retains is in withholding both her body and her heart. Liuyuan does love her, but he is no less calculating; he is a businessman, and it would be a bad investment to marry her until he knows that she loves him. Through an attentive courtship, Liuyuan traps Liusu—and she understands quite well that she is being trapped—for everyone comes to believe that she is his mistress. When she attempts to escape the trap and return to Shanghai and her family, she discovers just how well the trap has been set: to her family, she is a scandal, and she has no choice but to return to Hong Kong and become Liuyuan's mistress in fact as well as appearance.

The day after they first make love, Liuyuan tells Liusu that he must go to England on a business trip and sets her up in a house with a maid. Immediately after he takes his leave, the Japanese attack Hong Kong, and the house is damaged during the bombing. The couple is reunited the next day, and as they struggle to survive during the Japanese bombing of Hong Kong, they also find each other—"one moment of deep understanding, but this moment was enough to keep them happy together for a decade or so." Zhang Ailing's economy of happiness—how much time a moment of understanding can buy—is not entirely unlike the spiritual and financial negotiations of her protagonists.

At the end we return to the title, which, like much else in the story, is poised between a world of romance and the banality of the present. Any Chinese reader of the day would have understood the title not as *Love in a Fallen City*, but as "love for a beauty who could make a city fall." The Chinese term is *qingcheng*, understood most naturally as "[she who could] make a city fall." This term was the standard phrase for *femmes fatales*, those beauties so loved by ancient rulers that their passion resulted in the destruction of their kingdoms (Helen of Troy is an excellent example from the Western literary tradition). The lovers are not up to the grand promise of the title, and at last the story turns out to be only "love in a fallen city." At the end Liusu tries to read her own story in terms of the old theme of romance: the city had to fall to vindicate her.

This final moment embodies Zhang Ailing's peculiar sensibility. She has written a story in which large public events, though occurring without regard to the lovers, conclude the personal narrative and let the lovers finally understand each other, if only for a moment.

C. T. Hsia's *A History of Modern Chinese Fiction* (1961) contains the first study of Zhang Ailing's work. *The Rice-Sprout Song* (reprinted 1988) has an excellent introduction by David Der-Wei Wang.

PRONOUNCING GLOSSARY

The following list uses common English syllables to provide rough equivalents of selected words whose pronunciation may be unfamiliar to the general reader.

Bai: *by*

Baoluo: *baw-luo*

Guangzhou: *gwahng-joe*

Hu Lancheng: *hoo lahn-chung*

huqin: *who-chin*

Jiang: *jyahng*

Jinchan: *jin-chahn*

Jinzhi: *jin-jer*

Liusu: *lyoh-soo*

Liuyuan: *lyoh-yooan*

Qing: *ching*

Xu: *syew*

Zhang Ailing: *jahng ay-ling*

Zhao Xiangqing: *jao syahng-ching*

Zhu: *jew*

Love in a Fallen City[1]

Shanghai was "saving daylight", so all the clocks had been set forward one hour, but in the Bai residence they said, "We keep the old time." Their ten o'clock was other people's eleven o'clock. Their singing was behind the beat; they couldn't keep up with the *huqin*[2] of life.

The *huqin* wails in the night of a thousand burning lamps; the bow slides back and forth, pouring out a tale desolate beyond words—Oh, what's the point of asking?! A *huqin* story should be performed by a radiant entertainer, two long streaks of rouge pointing to her fine, jade-like nose as she sings, as she smiles, covering her mouth with her sleeve . . . But here it was just Fourth Master Bai[3] sitting by himself on a run-down balcony sunk in darkness, playing the *huqin*.

In the midst of his playing, the doorbell rang downstairs. For the Bai household, this was most unusual, since the old etiquette held that it wasn't proper to pay social calls after dark. If a visitor came at night, or a telegram arrived without warning, then either something of great import had transpired, or else somebody had died.

Fourth Master sat still and listened, but since Third Master, Third Mistress, and Fourth Mistress were shouting all at once as they came up the stairs he couldn't understand what was being said. Sitting in the drawing-room just off the balcony were Sixth Young Lady, Seventh Young Lady, and Eighth Young Lady, along with the Third and Fourth Masters' children, and

---

1. Translated by Karen Kingsbury. The pinyin system of transliteration has been used throughout.   2. A kind of fiddle (i.e., bowed lute), originally from Central Asia, popular in China.   3. Within a particular generation of a family, numbers were given according to relative seniority. Wives of male members of the household were ranked by their husband's level of seniority; thus, "First Mistress" is the wife of the eldest brother.

all of them quite anxious. From where Fourth Master sat on the darkened balcony, he could see everything in the well-lit room very clearly. So when the door opened, there was Third Master in his undershirt and shorts, standing on the door-sill with legs spraddled wide, reaching behind his thighs to slap at mosquitos, and calling out to Fourth Master: "Hey, Old Four, guess what!? That fellow that Sixth Sister divorced, well, it seems he's caught pneumonia and died!"

Fourth Master put down the *huqin*, walked into the room, and asked, "Who brought this news?"

"Mrs Xu," said Third Master. Then he turned to shoo his wife back with his fan. "Don't tag along, just chasing after excitement! Isn't Mrs Xu still downstairs? She's a big lady, doesn't like to climb stairs—you'd better go look after her."

Third Mistress left. Fourth Master puzzled it out. "Isn't the deceased a relative of Mrs Xu?"

"That's right," said Third Master. "It looks like they've made a point of getting Mrs Xu to bring us the news, which obviously implies something."

"They don't want Sixth Sister to go back for the funeral, do they?"

Third Master scratched his scalp with the handle of the fan. "Well, according to the rules, it would be only right . . ."

They both looked over at their Sixth Sister. Bai Liusu was sitting in the corner of the room calmly embroidering a slipper. During the close exchange between her brothers she hadn't had any opportunity to speak, but now she said, in a clear, light voice, "Get divorced and then act like the widow? That's enough to make people laugh till their teeth fall out!" She went on sewing the slipper just as if she hadn't a care in the world, but her palms grew clammy and her needle stuck—she couldn't draw it through anymore.

"Sixth Sister, now that's no way to talk," said Third Master. "Back then, he treated you badly, we know that. But now he's dead—surely you aren't going to go on holding it against him, are you? Those two concubines he left behind won't be content to remain widows for the rest of their lives, that's for sure. You just go back with your head held high and lead the mourning faithfully—who will dare to laugh at you? It's true you didn't have any children, but he has lots of nephews, and you can choose one of them to be his heir. Even though his family don't have much property left, they're still a big clan, so even if they only set you up to watch over his shrine, they won't let a mother and child starve."

Bai Liusu laughed sarcastically and said, "Third Brother's plans for me are very thorough indeed, but unfortunately it's a bit too late. The divorce went through some seven or eight years ago. According to you, those legal proceedings were just for show. But the law isn't something to fool around with!"

"Don't you try to scare us with the law," Third Master warned. "The law is one thing today and another tomorrow, but what I'm talking about is the law of family relations, and *that* never changes! As long as you live you belong to his family, and after you die your ghost will belong to them too! The tree may be a thousand feet tall, but the leaves always fall back to the same roots."

Liusu stood up. "Why didn't you say all this seven or eight years ago?!"

"I was afraid you'd be upset and think that we weren't willing to take you in."

Liusu gasped. "But now you're not afraid of upsetting me? Now that you've spent all my money, you're not afraid of upsetting me?!"

"I spent your money?!" Third Master confronted her full-face. "I spent your few paltry coins? You live in our house, and everything you eat and drink comes out of our pockets. Sure, in the past, it didn't much matter. Adding one more person then just meant putting one more pair of chopsticks on the table. But these days, well, just go and ask for yourself—what does rice cost now? I didn't mention money, but you had to bring it up!"

Fourth Mistress, who was standing behind Third Master, laughed. "They say you shouldn't talk about money with your own flesh and blood. Once you start the money-talk, there's quite a lot to say! I've been telling Fourth Master for quite a while now. I've been telling him, 'Old Four, you'd better warn Third Master. When you two are dealing in gold and stocks, you shouldn't use Sixth Sister's money. It will bring you bad luck! As soon as she married into her husband's family, he started losing all their money. Then she came back here, and now her family, as everyone can see, has lost all its money. A real bad-luck comet, that one!' "

Third Master said, "Fourth Mistress is right. If we hadn't let her into those stock deals, we never would have lost all our property!"

Liusu shook with anger. She clamped one half-embroidered slipper to her jaw, which quivered so much it seemed in danger of falling off.

Third Master continued, "I remember how you came home crying, making all that fuss about getting a divorce. Well, I'm a proud man, and when I saw that he had beaten you into such a state, I couldn't bear it, so I struck my chest and said, 'All right! I, the third son of the Bai family, may be poor, but my home must provide my sister's bowl of rice.' I just thought you young married folk always have a few fights, but nothing so serious that you wouldn't change your mind and be ready to go back after you've stayed at your parents' house for a few years. If I had known that you two really wanted to break things off, would I have helped you get a divorce?! Breaking up other people's marriages means losing one's own sons and grandsons in return. I, the third son of the Bai family, am a man with sons, and I am expecting their help in my old age."

Liusu had now reached the height of fury, but she simply laughed and said, "Yes, yes, everything is my fault. You're poverty-stricken? It's because I've eaten you out of house and home. You've lost your money? It must be that I've led you on. Your sons die? Of course it's because I've brought evil into your lives."

At this, Fourth Mistress grabbed her son's collar and rammed his head into Liusu, shouting, "Cursing the children now! After what you've said, if my son dies, I'll come looking for you!"

Liusu quickly dodged out of the way, then clasped Fourth Master and said, "Fourth Brother, look, just look, and be fair about it!"

Fourth Master said, "Now don't get so excited. If you have something to say then say it, and we'll take our time and consider things carefully. Third Brother is only trying to help you . . ." Liusu angrily let go of him, and headed straight for the inner bedroom.

No lamps were lit in the inner room. Peering through the red gauze bed-curtains in the darkness Liusu could dimly see her mother lying on the big redwood bed, slowly waving a round, white fan. Liusu walked over to the foot of the bed, and then her knees weakened and down she knelt, leaning against the bed. "Mother," she sobbed.

Old Mrs Bai's hearing was still good, so she hadn't missed anything that had been said in the outer room. She coughed, felt around next to her pillow for a small spittoon, spat into it, and only then began to speak. "Your Fourth Sister-in-law has a sharp tongue, but that doesn't mean that you should be like her. We have all have our own problems, you know. Your Fourth Sister-in-law is just naturally a strong-willed person and she's always managed the household. But your Fourth Brother is weak, and wastes himself on whoring, gambling, and such. It's bad enough that he's made himself ill, but then he took money from the household accounts, and that's why she's in disgrace. Now she has to let Third Sister-in-law take charge of things. This is all too much for her to take, so she's always out of sorts. Your Third Sister-in-law isn't the robust type and running this household really is not easy! You should bear all these things in mind, and try to make allowances."

Hearing the tone of her mother's words, the way that she played down the tension, Liusu felt quite disappointed. She just sat there in silence. Old Mrs Bai turned over to lie facing the wall, then said, "These past few years we've had to raise money any way we can. It used to be that we could sell off some land and get enough to get by on for a couple years, but that's not the case anymore. I'm old now, and when it's time for me to go, I'll have to go, and I won't be able to take care of the family. There's no party that doesn't end sometime. It should be clear to you that staying with me is not a long-term solution for you. It would be better to go back. Spend your time raising a child, bear your troubles for a dozen years or so, and your day to shine will come in the end."

As she was speaking, the door-curtain moved. "Who's there?" said Old Mrs Bai. Fourth Mistress poked her head in and said, "Mother, Mrs Xu is still downstairs waiting to talk to you about Seventh Sister's marriage."

"I'm just getting up," said Old Mrs Bai. "Let's have some light."

When the lamp had been lit, Fourth Mistress helped the old lady sit up, then waited on her as she got dressed and out of bed. "Has Mrs Xu found a suitable match?" the old lady asked.

"It all sounds very good, though he is a bit older."

Old Mrs Bai coughed. "This child Baoluo is already twenty-four this year, and she really weighs on my heart. I'm very concerned about her future, but people still criticize me and say I've neglected her because she's not my own daughter!"

Fourth Mistress helped the old lady toward the outer room. "Take out my new tea-leaves from over there and brew a bowl for Mrs Xu," said the old lady. "The Dragon-Well tea that Great Aunt brought back last year is in the green tin cannister, the Green Spring is in the tall cannister. Be sure to get it right."

Fourth Mistress nodded, then called out: "We're coming! Turn up the lamps!" There was a drumming of footsteps as a small throng of sturdy young servants came over to help an elderly maid carry the old lady down the stairs.

Fourth Mistress was alone in the outer room, rifling cabinets and trunks in search of the old lady's private stock of tea-leaves, when suddenly she cried out. "Oh, Seventh Sister! What hole did you climb out of?! Scared me half to death! Why, you disappeared on us just now!"

"I was sitting in the cool air out on the balcony," Baoluo murmured.

"Bashful, eh?" Fourth Mistress snickered. "I say, Seventh Sister, when you have in-laws, you should be a little careful. Don't feel that you can make trouble whenever you like. Is divorce such an easy thing, that you can get divorced anytime you want? If it were really that easy, why haven't I divorced your Fourth Brother, since he's never amounted to much! I too have my own family, it's not as if I don't have a place to run to. But in times like these I have to think of their needs too. I've got a conscience, and I have to think of them—can't weigh them down and drive them into poverty. I still have some sense of shame!"

Bai Liusu was kneeling forlornly by her mother's bed. When she heard these words, she crushed the embroidered slipper in her hand against her chest. The needle that was stuck in the slipper pierced her hand, but she didn't feel any pain. "I can't live in this house any longer," she whispered. "I just can't!" Her voice was faint and floating, like a trailing tendril of dust. She felt as if she were dreaming, tendrils streaming from her face and head. Falling forward in a daze, she thought she was clasping her mother's knees, and she started sobbing aloud. "Mother, Mother, please help me!" Her mother kept her face blank, and kept smiling without saying a word. Liusu wrapped her arms around her mother's legs, shaking her violently and crying, "Mother! Mother!"

In her daze, it was many years before: she was about ten years old, coming out of a theatre, and in the midst of a torrential downpour she was separated from her family. She stood alone on the sidewalk staring at people, the people staring back at her, and beyond the dripping-wet bus windows, on the other side of those featureless shields, there were endless numbers of strangers. They were all closed inside their own little worlds; she could break her head slamming against it but she'd never break through: it seemed she was trapped in a nightmare.

Suddenly she heard the sound of footsteps behind her, and guessed that her mother had returned. With a fierce effort she steadied herself, not saying anything. The mother she was praying to and the mother she really had were two different people.

Someone walked over to the bed and sat down, but when she spoke, it was in Mrs Xu's voice. Mrs Xu chided her, "Sixth Young Lady, don't be upset. Get up, get up, the weather is so hot . . ."

Bracing herself against the bed, Liusu struggled to her feet and said, "Auntie, I can't stay here anymore. I've known for a long time that others resented me, only they didn't say so out loud. But now that they've banged the drums and sounded the gongs and said so to my face, I've lost too much face to go on living here!"

Mrs Xu made Liusu sit down with her on the edge of the bed. "You're too good, no wonder people bully you," she said tenderly. "Your older brothers played the market with your money until they'd spent it all! They really ought to support you for the rest of your life."

Liusu rarely heard this kind of decency: she didn't ask whether it was sincere or not, she just let her heart well up and her tears rain down. "Why was I such a fool? All because of this little bit of money, now I have no way out of here."

Mrs Xu said, "Someone so young can always find a way to make a life for herself."

"If there were a way, I'd be long gone!" said Liusu. "I haven't studied much, and I can't lift and carry, so what kind of job can I get?"

"Looking for a job won't get you anywhere. But looking for a somebody, that's the way to go."

"No, I'm afraid not," said Liusu. "It's already ended for me."

"Such talk is only for the rich, for people who don't have to worry about what they'll eat or what they'll wear. Poor people, even if they want to, can't make an end to things. Even if you shave your head and become a nun, when you ask for alms you'll still have to deal with people—you can't just up and leave the human race!"

Liusu bowed her head, and didn't say anything.

Mrs Xu said, "If you had come to me about this a few years ago it would have been better."

"Yes, that's right," said Liusu. "I'm already twenty-eight."

"For a person with your qualities, twenty-eight doesn't matter. I'll keep you in mind. But I really should scold you—you've been divorced for seven or eight years now. If you'd made up your mind earlier you could have set yourself free and saved yourself so much grief!"

Liusu said, "Auntie, of course you know the situation. Would a family like mine ever let me go out and meet people? How could I count on them to find me a match? They wouldn't approve, and even if they did, I have two younger sisters who are still unmarried, and then there are Third and Fourth Brothers' daughters, all growing up fast. They can't even manage for the younger ones. Why would they do anything for me?"

"Speaking of your sister," Mrs Xu said, "I'm still waiting for their reply."

"Do things look good for Seventh Sister?" asked Liusu.

"I think we're getting close," said Mrs Xu. "I wanted to let the ladies talk it over among themselves, so I said I'd come up here to look in on you. I'd better be getting back now. Would you go down with me?"

Liusu had to help Mrs Xu down the stairs. The stairs were old, and Mrs Xu was large, so they creaked and squeaked all the way down together. Then they entered the drawing-room, and Liusu wanted to turn on the lights, but Mrs Xu said, "Don't bother, we can see well enough. The others are in the east wing. You come with me, and we'll all have a nice chat, and that way everything will be smoothed over. Otherwise, tomorrow at mealtime, when you can't avoid seeing them, it will be awkward and unpleasant."

Liusu couldn't bear to hear that word "mealtime". Her heart ached, and her throat went dry. Forcing a smile, she demurred. "Thank you very much, Auntie, but I'm not feeling very well right now—I really can't see anyone. I'm afraid I'd be so nervous that I'd say something disastrous, and that would be a terrible way to repay all your kindness."

Mrs Xu saw that Liusu was determined not to budge, and so she had to leave things where they stood, and go in by herself.

As soon as the door closed behind her, the drawing-room fell into shadow. Two squares of yellow light streamed in through the glass panes in the upper part of the door, and landed on the green tile floor. Through the gloom one could see a long stretch of book casings lining the walls, purplish sandalwood casings with neat, formal characters carved in green. On a neat little tea-table, under a glass dome, there was a cloisonné chiming clock. It was broken, and hadn't worked in years. Hanging on either side were two paper scrolls with a set of paired verses; the paper was crimson-red, embossed with gold "Longevity" characters over which the verses ran in big, black streaks. In the dim light, each word of the verses seemed to float in emptiness, far from the paper's surface. Liusu felt she was like those words, drifting and unconnected. The Bai household was like a fairyland: the single day that crept by here was a thousand years in the outside world. But if you spent a thousand years here, every day would be the same, all equally flat and dull.

She crossed her arms and clasped her neck with her hands. Seven, eight years—they'd gone by in the blink of an eye. Are you still young? Don't worry, in another few years you'll be old, youth isn't worth much here. They've got youth everywhere—the children born one after another, with their bright new eyes, their tender new mouths, their quick new wits. One after another the years went grinding by, the eyes were dulled, the minds were dulled, and then another round of children was born. Then the older ones melted into that dark welter of crimson and gold, where the little flecks of palest gold were the frightened eyes of those who had gone before.

Liusu cried out, covered her eyes, and fled, her feet beating a rapid retreat all the way up, up the stairs, to her own room. She turned on the lamp, set it next to the dressing-mirror, and studied her reflection. Good enough: she wasn't too old yet. She had the kind of slender figure that doesn't show age— a waist forever thin, and a budding, girlish bosom. Her face had always been as white as fine porcelain, but now had changed from porcelain to jade— semi-translucent jade with a tinge of pale green. Her cheeks had once been round, but now had grown thinner, making her small face even smaller and more attractive. She had a fairly narrow face, but her eyes—clear and lively, slightly coquettish eyes—were set well apart.

Out on the balcony, Fourth Master started playing the *huqin* again. Following the undulating tune, Liusu's head tilted to one side, and her hands and eyes started to gesture subtly. As she performed in the mirror, the *huqin* no longer sounded like a *huqin*, but like strings and flutes intoning a solemn court dance. She stepped toward the right a few paces, then turned again to the left. Her steps seemed to trace the lost rhythms of an ancient melody.

Suddenly, she smiled—a private, malevolent smile—and the music came to a discordant halt. Outside, the *huqin* still played, but it was telling tales of fealty and filial piety, chastity and righteousness: distant tales that had nothing to do with her.

Fourth Master had retreated to the balcony because he knew there was no place for him to speak in the family council that was taking place downstairs. After Mrs Xu had left, the Bai family had to thoroughly assess every aspect of her proposal. Mrs Xu planned to help Baoluo make a match with a Mr Fan, who had fairly close business ties with Mr Xu in the mining business, and so Mrs Xu knew his background and was sure that he was quite reliable. This Mr Fan's father was a well-known overseas Chinese who had properties scattered through Ceylon, Malaya, and other such places. Fan Liuyuan was now thirty-two years old, and both of his parents had passed away.

Everyone in the Bai family kept asking Mrs Xu why such an eligible man could still be single, and she told them that when Fan Liuyuan returned from England, a whole lot of mothers were dead set on pushing their daughters onto Mr Fan. They had schemed and squabbled, pulling every trick in the book and making a huge fuss over him. This had completely spoiled Mr Fan, who from then on thought women were just the mud under his feet. Due to his unusual childhood, he had always been a little odd anyway. His parents weren't officially married. His father met his mother in London, when he was making a tour of Europe. She was an overseas Chinese girl, a woman often seen at parties, and they got married secretly. Then Fan's wife got wind of this. Because they feared her revenge, the couple never dared return to China, and so Fan Liuyuan was raised in England. After his father died, Liuyuan wanted to be legally recognized as his father's heir. Despite the fact that the wife only had two daughters, there was still quite a bit of nastiness. Liuyuan was left all alone in England, and went through some hard times, but at last he got the right to inherit his father's wealth. The Fan family was still very hostile towards him, so he lived in Shanghai most of the time, never returning to the family home in Guangzhou unless it was absolutely necessary. Due to the emotional upsets he had suffered in his youth, bit by bit he became a playboy, gambling and feasting and visiting prostitutes. The only pleasure he denied himself was married bliss.

"A man like this is probably quite choosy," said Fourth Mistress. "Our Seventh Sister's mother was a concubine. I'm afraid he would look down on her. It would be a shame to lose so good a connection!"

"He too is the child of a secondary wife," said Third Master.

"But he's a very clever man," said Fourth Mistress. "Can our Number Seven, such a dolt, ever hope to catch him? My eldest daughter, however is very quick. Don't be fooled by looks—she is little, but she is smart! She knows how to behave."

"But there's such a difference in their ages," said Third Mistress.

Fourth Mistress snorted. "You just don't know! This kind of man likes them young. If my eldest won't do, there's always her younger sister."

Third Mistress laughed. "Your second daughter is twenty years younger than Mr Fan!"

Fourth Mistress quietly tugged at her sister-in-law's arm, a serious look on her face. "Third Sister, don't be so foolish! You're protecting Number Seven, but what is she to the Bai family? Having a different mother really makes a big difference. No one here should hope for any benefit after she gets married! What I'm saying is for the good of the family."

But Old Mrs Bai was consumed with anxiety lest the relatives should say she had wronged a motherless girl. She decided to pursue the proposal. Mrs Xu would arrange the meeting, and Baoluo would be introduced to Fan Liuyuan.

Mrs Xu, in a two-pronged attack, also scouted for Liusu. She found a Mr Jiang, who worked in the customs office. He had recently lost his wife, who left behind five children, and he was very anxious to remarry. Mrs Xu thought it best to take care of Baoluo first, and then make a match for Liusu, because Fan Liuyuan would soon be leaving for Singapore. The Bai household looked at Liusu's remarriage as some kind of joke, but since they wanted to get her out of the house they just ignored the whole thing, letting Mrs Xu manage it.

But for Baoluo they fell all over themselves, bustling about with great fanfare, turning the house upside down. The two were both daughters in the same house, but for the one there was a stir and fuss, and for the other cold silence. The difference was pretty hard to bear.

Old Mrs Bai was not satisfied until she had dressed Baoluo in every last stitch of the family's best finery. Third Mistress's daughter had received a length of silk as a birthday present from her godmother. Old Mrs Bai forced

Third Mistress to hand it over, and then she had it made into a cheongsam[4] for Baoluo. The old lady's private cache of fine goods consisted mostly of furs, and since furs couldn't be worn in the summertime, she had to pawn a sable jacket, then use the money to have several old pieces of jewelry redesigned. Of course Baoluo was also given pearl earrings, jade bracelets and emerald rings to wear. Everyone wanted to make sure she was fully adorned, a glittering beauty.

On the appointed day, Old Mrs Bai, Third Master, Third Mistress, Fourth Master, and Fourth Mistress all wanted to go along. Baoluo had learned, through round-about means, of Fourth Mistress' plot against her. She fumed in secret, determined not to let Fourth Mistress's daughters anywhere near her when she made her entrance. But since she couldn't very well say that she didn't want the girls there, she instead insisted that Liusu should go with her. After seven people had been crammed into the taxi-cab, there really wasn't room for any more, so Fourth Mistress' two daughters, Jinzhi and Jinchan, were left forlornly behind.

They left at five o'clock in the afternoon, and didn't return until eleven that evening. How could Jinzhi and Jinchan relax and go to sleep? They were wide-eyed with expectation when everyone came home, but no one had anything to say. Baoluo walked into Old Mrs Bai's room with a long face, stripped off all her jewels and ornaments, gave them back to the old lady, and went to her own room without saying a word. Jinzhi and Jinchan dragged their mother out to the balcony and begged to hear what had happened.

"I've never seen anything like you girls," Fourth Mistress snapped. "It's not you who are looking for a husband, so no need to get randy about it!"

Third Mistress followed them onto the balcony and said softly, "Don't say things she might take the wrong way."

Fourth Mistress turned to face Liusu's room and shouted, "I may be pointing at the mulberry but I'm cursing the locust-tree. And why shouldn't I curse her?! It's not as if she hadn't seen a man for a thousand years! So why does she, the minute she catches a whiff of one, just let herself go completely, panting and fainting and simply going crazy!"

Jinzhi and Jinchan were bewildered by their mother's outburst, but Third Mistress managed to calm her down, and then told the girls, "First we went to see a movie."

"See a movie?" Jinzhi was quite surprised.

"Pretty strange, all right," said Third Mistress. "The whole point of the meeting was for them to see each other, but sitting in the dark, you can't see anything. Later, Mrs Xu said this was all that Mr Fan's idea, as a way of playing a trick. He wanted to make her sit around for a couple hours, till the sweat made her make-up run, so he could get a better look. That's what Mrs Xu thinks. I think that Mr Fan never was serious about the whole thing. He wanted to go to a movie because he didn't want to talk to us. As soon as the movie was over, didn't he try to slip away?"

Fourth Mistress couldn't hold back. "What do you mean? The whole thing was going very well. If it hadn't been for that troublemaker we took with us, we would be halfway there by now!"

---

4. A sheathlike dress with a mandarin collar and slit skirt very popular in China during the 1920s and 1930s.

"Then what? Then what?!" Jinzhi and Jinchan frantically begged their aunt.

"Well, then Mrs Xu stopped Mr Fan and said we all should go and have something to eat. Mr Fan said it would be his treat."

Fourth Mistress clapped her hands together. "If we were going to eat, then we should have just gone to eat. It's obvious that Seventh Sister doesn't know how to dance, so what's the point of going to a dancing place and just sitting around? Really, this was Third Master's fault. He goes out, he knows the town, so when Mr Fan told the cab driver to go to a dancing place, he should have said something."

"So many restaurants in Shanghai," Third Mistress rose in defense. "How could he know which restaurants have dance-floors, and which don't? He doesn't have as much leisure as Fourth Master, he doesn't go around and find out such things!"

Jinzhi and Jinchan still wanted to hear the rest of the story, but Third Mistress had been challenged by Fourth Mistress so many times that she now lost interest. "So we went to eat, and then we came home."

"What kind of person is this Mr Fan?" Jinchan asked.

"How should I know?" said Third Mistress. "Altogether, I heard less than three whole sentences from him." She thought for a moment. "He dances pretty well, though."

Jinzhi let out a small gasp. "Who did he dance with?"

Fourth Mistress cut in. "Who else? It was your Sixth Aunt of course! Those of us from educated families aren't allowed to learn to dance. But your Sixth Sister learned all that from that no-good husband of hers. So shameless! Someone asks you to dance, can't you say you don't know how, just let it end there? There's no shame in not knowing how to dance. Look at your Third Aunt, or me, we're all from good families, we've been around long enough to see quite a few things, and we don't dance."

Third Mistress sighed. "One dance, you still could say this was out of courtesy to him. But to dance again, and again!"

When Jinzhi and Jinchan heard this, their jaws almost hit the floor.

Fourth Mistress turned in *that* direction again and started swearing. "You've got a heart smeared with pig fat! If you think by ruining you sister's chances, you can try your own luck, you'd better just forget it! He's turned down so many ladies, do you think he'd want a soiled flower like you?"

Liusu and Baoluo shared a room, and Baoluo had already gone to bed. Liusu squatted in the dark and lit a stick of mosquito incense. She had heard every word that was spoken out on the balcony, but this time she was perfectly calm. She struck the match and watched it burn, the little three-cornered pennant of flaming red flickering in its own draft, coming closer and closer toward her fingers. A little puff of the lips, and she blew it out, leaving only the glowing red pennant-pole. Then the pole twisted and shrank, curling into the grey shape of a fiend. She tossed the dead match into the incense burner.

She hadn't planned this night's events, but, in any case, she had given them quite a show. Did they think that she was already finished, her life over? It was still early in the game! She smiled. Baoluo must be cursing her silently, far more fiercely even than Fourth Mistress. But she knew that even though Baoluo hated her, there was also admiration and respect. It doesn't matter how great a woman is: if she can't get the love of a man, she can't get the respect of other women. Women are petty this way.

Did Fan Liuyuan really like her? That wasn't at all certain. All those things he'd said to her—she didn't believe a word of it. She could tell that he was used to lying to women, she'd have to be very careful. Family, family all around, but no one she could turn to—she had only herself. Her moon-white silk gauze cheongsam hung from the bed frame. Twisting to one side, she sat down on the floor, and buried her face in the long skirt. The green smoke of the mosquito incense floated up in steady puffs, and seeped into her brain. In her eyes, there was the gleam of tears.

A few days later, Mrs Xu came to the Bai household again. Fourth Mistress had already made her forecast: "After Sixth Sister got up to such antics, Seventh Sister's chances were ruined. How could Mrs Xu not be angry? And if Mrs Xu blamed Sixth Sister then would she still be willing to introduce people to her? This is called 'trying to steal a chicken, but losing both the bird and the bait'."[5]

And indeed Mrs Xu wasn't as enthused as she had been. First she beat around the bush awhile, explaining why she hadn't come by in the past few days. Her husband had some business to take care of in Hong Kong, and so, if all went well, they planned to go to Hong Kong, rent a house, and stay there a year or so. That was why she'd been so busy in the last few days, packing things up and getting ready to go with him. As for Baoluo's plans, Mr Fan had already left Shanghai, so they'd have to let that rest for a while. And it turned out that Liusu's potential match, Mr Jiang, according to what Mrs Xu had just learned, already had a mistress. Trying to break them up would be quite a lot of trouble. Mrs Xu felt that this kind of person really wasn't very reliable, so it would be better to give it up. When Third and Fourth Mistress heard this, they gave each other a meaningful look and smirked.

Mrs Xu wrinkled her brow and continued: "My husband has a lot of friends in Hong Kong, but the problem is that 'distant water can't put out a nearby fire'[6] . . . if Sixth Young Lady could go there for a bit, she would probably find lots of opportunities. In the past few years, so many Shanghai men have gone to Hong Kong that it is teeming with men of promise. Shanghai men, naturally enough, prefer to be with other Shanghainese, so young ladies from their hometown are, according to report, very popular. If Sixth Young Lady went, could there be any doubt that she'd find a good match? She could grab a handful and take her pick."

Everyone felt that Mrs Xu really had a way with words. A few days ago her grand plans for making a match had come to naught, leaving her high and dry, so she was making offhand excuses to cover her confusion. Old Mrs Bai sighed and said, "Going to Hong Kong, well, easier said than done! After all—"

To everyone's surprise, Mrs Xu cheerfully cut in. "If Sixth Young Lady wants to go, she can go as my guest. I agreed to help her, so I should see it through."

At this, everyone had to turn and blink at each other, and even Liusu was taken aback. She figured that Mrs Xu's volunteering to find her a match was the product of a moment's good-heartedness and real sympathy for her sit-

5. Folk wisdom.   6. Also folk wisdom.

uation. To run about fixing things up, setting up a dinner-party and inviting that Mr Jiang—this much good-heartedness was possible. But to pay her fare and expenses and take her to Hong Kong—that would be a financial loss. Why would Mrs Xu want to spend money on her for no good reason? There may be lots of good people in this world, but there aren't many idiots willing to be good where money is concerned. Mrs Xu must have a backer. Could it be a plot hatched by that Fan Liuyuan? Mrs Xu had said that her husband had close business ties with Fan, and she and her husband were probably quite eager to do things for him. Sacrificing some poor and lonely little relative in order to gain favour with him—this was quite probable.

While Liusu's mind was racing, Old Mrs Bai said, "Oh, this won't do. We can't let you—"

Mrs Xu laughed this off. "It's no problem. A little thing like this—of course I can manage it! Anyway, I want Sixth Young Lady to help me. I've got two children, and high blood-pressure, and I shouldn't let myself get too tired. If she travels with us, there will be someone to take care of things. I won't be too polite to her, I'll want her to help out quite a lot!"

Old Mrs Bai came up with a stream of polite answers on Liusu's behalf. Mrs Xu turned, and opened a direct attack. "Well, Sixth Young Lady, you really should agree to go with us. Even if you just think of it as sight-seeing it will be worth it!"

Liusu bowed her head, and said with a smile, "You're really too good to me."

She made a rapid calculation. There was no hope of getting that Mr Jiang, and even if someone made another match for her, it wouldn't be much different from Jiang, maybe not even that good. Liusu's father had been a famous gambler. For the sake of gambling, he'd ruined the family, losing their fortune and starting the descent into the ranks of poor, declining households. Liusu had never touched cards or dice, but she too liked to gamble. She decided to wager her future. If she lost, her reputation would be ruined, and she wouldn't even be allowed to play stepmother to five children. If she won, she would get the prize that everyone was watching with greedy tiger eyes—Fan Liuyuan—and all her stifled rancour would be washed away.

She agreed to Mrs Xu's plan, and Mrs Xu was to leave within the week. Liusu was very busy packing. Even though she didn't have much, and there really wasn't anything to pack, she had a lot to do for several days. She sold a few small things in order to have some clothes made. Mrs Xu, even in the middle of this rush, still found time to help her with advice. When the Bai household saw Mrs Xu being so kind to Liusu, they too started to take an interest in her. They were suspicious of her, but they also became more cautious, holding long whispered consultations behind her back instead of scolding her so spitefully to her face. Once in a while they even addressed her quite respectfully, thinking that if she really married a rich man in Hong Kong and returned home in glory, they'd better be on speaking terms with her. It wouldn't do to offend her.

The Xu family picked Liusu up in a car and took her with them to the ship. They were travelling on a Dutch ship, in a first-class cabin. But the ship was small, and pitched violently, so as soon as they had boarded, Mr and Mrs Xu collapsed into their berths. What with the adults retching and the children crying, Liusu really did wait on them for several days.

Not until the ship had finally reached the shore did she have a chance to go up on deck and look out at the sea. It was a fiery afternoon, and the most striking part of the view was the giant billboards that stretched along the pier, their reds, oranges, and pinks reflected in reverse in the lush green water. Below the water's surface, each bar and blot of clashing colour surged and plunged in murderous confusion. In this city of excesses, Liusu thought to herself, the smallest slip would lead to a painful fall. Her heart started to pound.

Suddenly someone rushed up from behind and grabbed her legs, almost knocking her down. Liusu gasped. Then she saw that it was one of the Xu children. She quickly steadied herself, and went back to help Mrs Xu. The dozen suitcases and two children simply refused to line up together; no sooner were the bags in order than a child went missing again. Exhausted by her labours, Liusu had no more time to watch the scenery.

After disembarking, they took two taxis to the Repulse Bay Hotel. The taxis drove out of the teeming city, rising and dipping across the hilly terrain. After a while, the road was flanked by cliffs of yellow or red soil, with ravines that revealed the dense green of the forest or the aquamarine of the sea. As they came closer to Repulse Bay, the cliffs and trees continued, but grew more gentle and inviting. Returning picnickers swept past them in flower-laden cars, the sound of scattered laughter fading in the wind.

When they arrived at the hotel entrance, they couldn't actually see the hotel. They got out of the car and went up a broad flight of stone steps. Not until they had reached the top, where an ornamental garden was laid out, did they see two yellow buildings farther up above. Mr Xu had already reserved their rooms, and so the hotel staff led them along a small gravel path, through the amber dimness of the lobby and hallway, then up to the second floor. They turned a corner, and there, through a doorway, was a small balcony, with flowering vines on a trellis and the sun's rays slanting across half the wall.

There were two people standing on the balcony and talking. One was a woman who stood with her back towards them, her long black hair hanging down to her ankles. She wore a twisted golden anklet over bare skin, and though you could not tell whether she was wearing backless slippers or not, above the anklet you could glimpse a pair of slim, Indian-style pants. She stood between them and a man, but he called out "Ah, Mrs Xu!" and came over to greet the couple, then also nodded, with a suppressed smile, toward Liusu.

Liusu saw that it was Fan Liuyuan, and though she had been expecting this, her heart began to pound again. The woman on the balcony disappeared. Liuyuan accompanied them up the stairs. As they walked, everyone kept saying how surprised and pleased they were, just as if, while travelling far from home, they had unexpectedly met an old friend.

Although Fan Liuyuan couldn't really be called handsome, he was attractive in a rugged sort of way. Mr and Mrs Xu led the porters who were carrying their luggage, and Liuyuan and Liusu walked ahead. "Mr Fan," inquired Liusu with a glint of a smile, "it seems you haven't gone to Singapore?"

"I've been waiting for you here," Liuyuan said lightly.

It had never occurred to Liusu that he would be so direct. She didn't inquire further, afraid that if he went on to say that it was he, not Mrs Xu, who had invited her to Hong Kong, she wouldn't know what to say. So she treated it as a joke, and replied with a smile.

Having learned that she was in room 130, Liuyuan stopped in front of a door and said, "Here it is." The porter unlocked the door. Liusu walked in, and was drawn straight to the window. It was as if the whole room were but a dark picture-frame around the big painting in the window. The roaring ocean-breakers spilled right onto the curtains, turning their edges blue.

"Just put the trunk in front of the wardrobe," Liuyuan said to the porter.

His voice sounded next to Liusu's ear, startling her. She turned and saw that the porter had gone, though the door had not been closed. Liuyuan leaned against the window, supporting himself with a hand stretched along the frame. Her line of vision thus blocked, he gazed at her with a smile. Liusu bowed her head.

Liuyuan laughed. "Did you realize? Your specialty is bowing the head."

Liusu raised her head. "What? I don't understand."

"Some people are good at talking, or at laughing, or at keeping house, but you're good at bowing your head."

"I'm no good at anything," said Liusu. "I'm utterly useless."

"It's the useless women who are the most formidable."

Liusu walked away laughing. "I'm not going to discuss this with you any more. I'm going next door to have a look around."

"Next door? My room or Mrs Xu's room?"

Liusu was again startled. "You're staying next door?"

Liuyuan had already swung the door open for her. "Sorry . . . my room's a mess, no visitors allowed."

He knocked at No. 131, and Mrs Xu opened the door to let them in. "Come and have tea with us. We have a sitting-room." Then she rang the bell to call for refreshments.

Mr Xu came out of the bedroom and said, "I telephoned my friend Mr Zhu, and he insists on throwing a party tonight to welcome us. He's invited us to the Hong Kong Hotel." He turned to Liuyuan. "Of course you're included."

"My, you've got a lot of energy," said Mrs Xu. "After all those days seasick on the boat, shouldn't we go to bed early? Let's not go out tonight."

"The Hong Kong Hotel has the most old-fashioned ballroom I've ever seen," said Liuyuan. "Everything about the place—building, lights, decor, orchestra—is very English and, forty or fifty years ago, was very up-to-date. But nowadays it's nothing to get excited about. There's nothing to see there, except maybe the odd little waiters. Even on a very hot day, they wear those Northern-style trousers, gathered tight at the ankles."

"Why?" asked Liusu.

"Chinese flavour!"

Mr Xu laughed. "Well, since we're here we might as well go and have a look. Sorry, you'll just have to keep us company!"

"I'm not sure I'm going, so don't wait for me."

Seeing how Liuyuan seemed really uninterested in going, while Mr Xu, who did not make a habit of frequenting ballrooms, was unusually excited, as if he truly wanted to introduce her to his friends, Liusu felt quite unsure about what was going on.

But when they got to the Hong Kong Hotel that night, the group that had gathered to welcome them was composed of old married couples. The few single men were all youths in their early twenties. While Liusu was dancing, Fan Liuyuan suddenly appeared and cut in on her partner. In the lychee-red light of the ballroom, she couldn't see his darkened face clearly, but she could tell that he was unusually withdrawn.

"Why so quiet?" she teased.

"Everything that can be said to a person's face, I've already said."

Liusu chuckled. "And just what is it that you have to say behind people's backs?"

"There are some kinds of foolishness that you don't want other people to hear, don't even want yourself to hear. Even hearing yourself say it makes you feel embarrassed. For instance, I love you, I will love you for the rest of my life."

Liusu turned away and chided him softly. "Such nonsense!"

"If I don't say anything, you complain because I'm too quiet, but if I talk, you complain that I talk too much."

"Listen," said Liusu. "Why didn't you want me to go dancing?"

"Most men like to lead good girls astray, then reform the bad girls and make them good again. I don't go around making so much work for myself. I think that if a woman is good, she should stay straight-forward and honest."

Liusu gave him a sideways glance. "You think you're different from others? It seems to me you're just as selfish."

"Selfish? How?"

To herself, she thought: "Your idea of the perfect woman is someone who is pure and high-minded but still very ready to flirt. The pure high-mindedness is toward others, but the flirting is towards you. If I were an entirely good woman, you never would have noticed me in the first place!"

She leaned her head to one side and said, "You want me to be good in front of others, but bad when I'm with you."

Liuyuan thought for a moment. "I don't understand."

Liusu explained again. "You want me to be bad to others and good only to you."

"Now you've turned it around again! You're just making me more confused."

He was silent for a while, then said, "What you're saying isn't so."

Liusu laughed. "Ah, so now you understand."

"I don't care if you're good or bad. I don't want you to change. It's not easy to find a real Chinese girl like you."

Liusu sighed softly. "I'm just old-fashioned, that's all."

"Real Chinese women are the most beautiful women in the world. They're never out of fashion."

"But for a modern man like you—"

"You say 'modern', but what you probably mean is Western-style. It's true that I'm not a real Chinese. It's just that in the past few years I've become a little more like a Chinese. But you know, a foreigner who's become Chinese also becomes reactionary, even more reactionary than an old-fashioned scholar from the last dynasty."

Liusu laughed. "You're reactionary, and I'm reactionary. And you've already said that the Hong Kong Hotel is the most old-fashioned ballroom ever . . ."

They both laughed, and just then the music ended. Liuyuan led her back to her seat, then told the others that "Miss Bai has a headache, so I will see her home."

This was entirely unexpected. Liusu had no time to think, but knew she didn't want to cross him. They didn't know each other well enough to argue openly. And so she let him help her with her coat, apologized to the others, and left with him.

Directly in their path was a group of Western gentlemen who, like stars around the moon, stood clustered around a woman. Liusu first noticed the woman's long black hair, which had been done up in two long braids and then coiled on top of her head. She was Indian, and though she was dressed Western-style she still had a very Oriental aura. Under a dark, sheer cape she wore a long, close-fitting gown, goldfish-red, that covered even her hands, leaving only her pearly fingernails exposed. The plunging neckline of her dress formed a narrow V, reaching to her waist; it was the latest fashion from Paris, called "Ligne du Ciel". Her complexion was rich and tawny, like a gold-plated Buddha statue, but in her dark eyes a devil lay in wait. A classically straight nose, if a bit too sharp and thin. And a small mouth with pink, full lips that almost seemed swollen.

Liuyuan stopped and made a slight bow in her direction. Liusu looked at the woman, and the hauteur of the woman's returning gaze put a thousand miles between them.

Liuyuan introduced them. "Miss Bai. Princess Saheiyini."

Liusu couldn't help but be impressed. Saheiyini reached out and touched Liusu's hand with her fingertips. "Is Miss Bai from Shanghai too?" She asked Liuyuan, who nodded. "She doesn't seem like someone from Shanghai," she said, with a smile.

"Then what does she seem like?" Liuyuan asked.

Saheiyini placed one finger alongside her cheek and thought for a moment, then brought her hands together, fingers pointing upwards, as if she wanted to say something but words had simply failed her. Then she shrugged her shoulders, laughed, and walked on into the ballroom. Liuyuan continued leading Liusu out of the hotel. Though Liusu couldn't understand much English, she had followed their expressions, so now she said with a smile, "I *am* a country bumpkin."

"As I said just now, you are a real Chinese. Of course that's a bit different from what she calls a Shanghainese."

They got in a taxi, and Liuyuan said, "Don't be bothered by the airs she puts on. She struts around saying that she is the daughter of Prince Krishna Kramupa, but that her mother lost the Prince's favour and was told to commit suicide, and so she too had to flee, and now must wander in exile, unable to return home. In fact, it's true that she can't go back to her own country, but nothing else in her story has been proven."

"Has she been to Shanghai?"

"She is very well-known in Shanghai. She came to Hong Kong with an Englishman. Did you see that old man standing behind her? He's the one who's keeping her these days."

"You men are always like this. When you're talking to her, you can't think of enough polite things to say, but behind her back you say she's worthless. I can just imagine what you say to others about me, daughter of a poor old Qing official, even lower-ranking than she is!"

Liuyuan laughed. "Who would dare speak of you two in the same breath?"

Pursing her lips, Liusu said, "Maybe that's because her name is too long. Can't get it all out in one breath."

"You needn't worry. Whatever sort of person you are, I'll treat you as just that sort of person. That's a promise."

Looking reassured, Liusu leaned against the car window. "Really?" she murmured. Indeed, he did not seem to be mocking her. She had discovered that when they were alone he behaved like a perfect gentleman. For some reason that she could not fathom, he was a model of self-control when no one else was around, but took liberties when they were with other people. She couldn't, for the moment, figure out whether this was just his peculiar personality, or whether he was up to something.

When they got to Repulse Bay, he helped her out of the taxi, then pointed to the dense copse alongside the road. "Do you see that tree? It's a southern variety. The English call it 'flame of the forest'."

"Is it red?" asked Liusu.

"Red, red, red!"

In the darkness, Liusu couldn't see the red, but she knew instinctively that it was the reddest red, red beyond belief. Great masses of little red flowers, nestled in a huge tree that reached up to the sky, a riotous welter that burned all the way up, staining the indigo sky with red. Leaning her head back, she gazed upwards.

"The Cantonese call it the 'shadow tree'," said Liuyuan. "Look at this leaf."

The leaf was as light as a fern; when a slight breeze made the delicate silhouette flutter, they seemed to hear a faint, almost melodic sound, like the tinkling of wind-chimes in the eaves.

"Let's walk over there a bit," said Liuyuan.

Liusu didn't say anything. But as he walked, she slowly followed. After all, it was still early, and lots of people went out for walks on the road—it would be all right. A little ways past the Repulse Bay Hotel, an overhead bridge arched through the air. On the far side of the bridge was a mountain slope; on the near side there was a grey brick retaining wall. Liuyuan leaned against the wall, and Liusu leaned too, looking up along the great height, a wall so high that its upper edge could not be seen. The wall was cool and rough, the colour of death. Against it her face looked different: red mouth, shining eyes, a face of flesh and blood and feeling.

"I don't know why," said Liuyuan, looking at her, "but this wall makes me think of the old sayings about the end of the world. Someday, when human civilization has been completely destroyed, when everything is burnt, burst, utterly collapsed and ruined, maybe this wall will still be here. If, at that time, we can meet at this wall, then maybe, Liusu, you will honestly care about me, and I will honestly care about you."

"You admit that you like to play games," Liusu huffed coyly, "but that doesn't mean you can drag me along with you! When have you caught me lying?"

"Fair enough," said Liuyuan with a snicker. "There's no one more open-hearted than you."

"That's enough . . . . stop patronizing me."

Liuyuan was silent for a long time. Then he sighed.

"Something you're unhappy about?" said Liusu.

"Lots."

"If someone as free as you are thinks that life is unfair, then someone like me ought just go and hang herself."

"I know you're not happy," said Liuyuan. "You've certainly seen more than enough of all these awful people, and awful things, all around us. But if you were seeing them for the first time, it would be even harder to bear, even harder to get used to. That's what it has been like for me. When I arrived in China I was already twenty-four. I had so many dreams about my homeland. You can imagine how disappointed I was. I couldn't stand the shock, and so I started to slip downwards. If . . . if you had known me before, then maybe you could forgive me for the way I am now."

Liusu tried to imagine what it would be like to see her Fourth Sister-in-law for the first time. Then she burst out: "That would still be better. When you see them for the first time, then no matter how awful, no matter how dirty they are, they—or it—is still outside of you. But if you live in it for a long time, how can you tell how much of it is them, and how much of it is you?"

Liuyuan fell silent. After a long pause he said, "Maybe you are right. Maybe what I'm saying is just an excuse, and I'm just fooling myself." Then he laughed suddenly. "Actually, I don't need any excuses! I like to have a good time—and I have plenty of money, plenty of time—do I need any other reason?!"

He thought it over, and again grew frustrated. He said to her, "I don't understand myself—but I want you to understand me! I want you to understand me!" He spoke like this, but in his heart he had already given up hope. Still he said stubbornly, plaintively: "I want you to understand me!"

Liusu was willing to try. Within certain limits, she was willing to try anything. She leaned her head towards him, and answered softly, "I do understand. I do." But while comforting him, she thought of her moonlit face. That delicate profile, her eyes, her brow, all of an irrational, ethereal beauty. She slowly bowed her head.

Liuyuan began chuckling. "That's right, don't forget," he said, in a new tone of voice. "Your specialty is bowing the head. But there are those who say that only teenage girls can bow the head well. If you're good at it, then it will become a habit. And when you've bowed the head for many years, you might get wrinkles on the neck."

Liusu turned away, but couldn't help raising her hand to feel the skin on her neck. "Don't worry," laughed Liuyuan, "of course you don't have any wrinkles. When you get back to your room, when no one else is around, you can unbutton your collar and check."

Liusu didn't reply, just turned and started walking. Liuyuan caught up to her. "I'll tell you why you'll keep your good looks. Saheiyini once said that she didn't dare get married because Indian women, once they start relaxing at home, sitting around all day, just get fat. I told her that Chinese women, when they sit around, won't even do so much as get fat—because even getting fat takes some kind of effort. So it turns out that laziness has its advantages!"

Liusu ignored him, and he was apologetic all the way back, making conversation and laughing very humbly. When she had got back to the hotel, she finally softened a bit, and they each went quietly to their respective rooms.

Liusu assessed the situation. It turned out that what Liuyuan cared about was spiritual love. She agreed entirely, since spiritual love always leads to marriage, while carnal love tends to stop at a certain level, with very little hope of marriage. There is only one little problem with spiritual love: in the course of falling in love, the man always says things that the woman doesn't understand. But that doesn't matter too much. In the end there is the getting-married, the house-buying, the furniture-arranging, the servant-hiring—and in all these things, the woman is much more adept than the man. Thinking of it this way, Liusu felt this evening's little misunderstanding wasn't anything to worry about.

The next morning, there wasn't a single peep from Mr and Mrs Xu's room, and so she realized that she must have slept late. She remembered that Mrs Xu had told her that in this hotel there was an extra charge for breakfast delivered to the room, not to mention the tip, and so she decided to save them a little money by going to the dining-hall. She washed and dressed, and had just walked out the door when a porter who had been waiting outside, upon seeing her, went immediately to knock at Liuyuan's room. Liuyuan appeared at once. "Let's go to breakfast together," he smiled.

As they were walking, he asked, "Mr and Mrs Xu haven't raised the bed-curtains yet?"

"They got tired out from having a good time last night!" returned Liusu. "I didn't hear them come in, so it must have been near dawn."

They chose a table on the verandah outside the dining-hall. Beyond the stone railing there was an enormous palm-tree, its feathery fronds trembling in the sun, like a fountain of light. Beneath the tree there was a pool of water with its own fountain, less magnificent by far.

"What are Mr and Mrs Xu going to do today?" asked Liuyuan.

"I think they're going to look at houses."

"Let them go look at houses, and we'll go have our own fun. Would you rather go to the beach, or into the city to look around?"

The afternoon before, Liusu had surveyed the beach scene through binoculars. Strapping youths and gorgeous girls. Very exciting but a little too boisterous. Preferring to err on the side of caution, she suggested that they go into town. So they caught one of the buses provided by the hotel and went into the city centre.

Liuyuan took her to the Great China to eat. When Liusu heard the waiters speaking Shanghainese, filling the air with her native tongue, she asked in surprise, "Is this a Shanghai restaurant?"

"Don't you feel homesick?" Liuyuan laughed.

"But . . . it seems a bit silly to make a special trip to Hong Kong just so we can eat Shanghai food."

"When I'm with you, I do a lot of silly things. Like take a tram round in circles, see a movie I've seen twice already . . ."

"Because you've caught silliness from me, right?"

"Take it to mean whatever you please."

When they had finished eating, Liuyuan raised his glass and drained the remaining tea, then lifted the glass high and stared into it.

"If there's something worth seeing, let me have a look," said Liusu.

"Hold it up to the light," said Liuyuan.

"The scene inside reminds me of the forests of Malaya."

When the glass was tilted, the green tea-leaves stuck to one side, forming irregular patterns; when the glass was held up to the light, the leaves looked like a flourishing plantain tree, while the tea-leaves that were piled along the bottom in a tangled swirl looked like knee-high grass and undergrowth. Liusu peered up into the glass, and Liuyuan leaned over, pointing all this out. Through the dusky green glass, Liusu suddenly saw him watching her with eyes that seemed to laugh and yet didn't laugh. She put the glass down and smiled.

"I'll take you to Malaya," Liuyuan said.

"What for?"

"To return to nature." He thought for a moment. "But there's just one problem—I can't imagine you running through the forest in a cheongsam. But neither can I imagine you not wearing a cheongsam."

Liusu's face stiffened. "Stop talking nonsense."

"But I'm serious. The first time I saw you, I thought that you shouldn't bare your arms in this kind of trendy tunic, but neither should you wear Western-style clothes. A Manchu-style dress might suit you better, but its lines are too severe."

"In the end, if a person is ugly, then no matter how she dresses it still won't look right!"

Liuyuan laughed. "You keep turning my words around! What I mean is that you're like someone from another world. You have all these little gestures, and a romantic aura, very much like a Peking opera singer."

Liusu raised her eyebrows. "An opera singer indeed!" she said sarcastically, "But of course it takes more than one to put on a show, and I've been forced into it. A person acts clever with me, and if I don't do the same, he takes me for a fool and insults me!"

When Liuyuan heard this, he was rather crest-fallen. He raised the empty glass, tried to drink from it, then put it down again and sighed. "Right," he said. "My fault. I'm used to throwing out lines, because everyone throws lines at me. But to you I have said one or two sincere things, and you can't tell."

"I'm not the worm in your innards—I can't read your mind."

"Right. My fault. But for your sake I really have done a lot. When I first met you in Shanghai, I thought that if you could get away from those people in your family, maybe you could be more natural. So I waited and waited till you came to Hong Kong . . . now, I want to take you to Malaya, to the forest of primitive peoples . . ." He laughed at himself, his voice hoarse and dry, and called for the check. When they had paid, he had already recovered his good spirits, and again took up his very courteous, very chivalrous manner.

He took her out every day, and they did everything there was to do . . . movies, Cantonese opera, casinos, the Gloucester Hotel, the Cecil Hotel, the Bluebird Coffee Bar, Indian silk shops, Szechuan food in Kowloon . . . and they went for walks at night, often until very late at night. She could hardly believe it, but he rarely so much as touched her hand. She was always very edgy, fearing that he would suddenly drop the pretense and launch a surprise attack. But day after day he kept to his gentlemanly ways; it was like facing a great enemy who remained perfectly passive. At first this made her feel quite unsteady, like missing a step when going down a flight of stairs, and her heart was very jumpy. But, after a while, she got used to it.

There was one incident, though, on the beach. By this time Liusu knew Liuyuan a little better, and so she felt that going to the beach would be all right. So they spent a morning there, and even sat together on the sand, but facing in opposite directions. Liusu squealed, saying that she'd been bitten by a mosquito.

"It isn't a mosquito," said Liuyuan. "It's a little insect called a sand fly. When it bites, it leaves a red mark, like a mole on your skin."

"There's too much sun," Liusu complained again.

"Let's sit out just a bit longer, and then we can go into one of those cabanas. I've already got one rented."

The thirsty sun sucked in the sea-water, rising and spitting in steady rhythm. It lapped up all the moisture in their bodies, so that they grew light and empty, like dry, golden leaves. Liusu started to feel that strange, light-headed happiness, but she couldn't keep from squealing, "Ouch! Mosquito!" She twisted around and slapped her own bare back.

"That's the hard way," said Liuyuan. "Here, I'll slap for you, and you slap for me."

So, in fact, Liusu did watch his back, and when she saw one she slapped. "Aiiya, it got away!" And Liuyuan watched her back. They started hitting and slapping, and then they broke into laughter. Suddenly, Liusu took offense, stood up, and walked back towards the hotel. This time Liuyuan didn't follow her. When she had reached the trees, and the stone path that ran between two rush-mat cabanas, Liusu stopped, shook the sand out of her short skirt, and looked back. Liuyuan was still there, stretched out in the sun, arms folded under his neck, a man who very clearly was just dreaming in the sun, turning again into a golden leaf. Liusu went into the hotel, and through binoculars she looked again from her window. Now there was a woman lying next to him, with braids coiled up on her head. Saheiyini could be burned to ashes and Liusu would still know who it was.

From this day on, Liuyuan spent all his time with Saheiyini. Apparently, he had decided to let Liusu cool her heels a bit. Liusu had gotten used to going out every day, and so now, suddenly left with nothing to do, and no good explanation to give Mr and Mrs Xu, she had to catch a cold and stay in her room for a few days. Fortunately, the gods were very considerate; they sent a nice, kind rain that made a further excuse, and so there was no need to go out.

One afternoon, Liusu came back to the hotel with her umbrella, having gone for a walk in the hotel's garden. It was getting dark, and she guessed that Mr and Mrs Xu would soon be back from house-hunting, so she sat on the verandah waiting for them. She opened her shiny oiled-paper umbrella and set it out on the railing, blocking her face from view. The umbrella was pink with stone-green lotus-leaves painted on it, and the raindrops slid down along the spines. It was raining hard. The sound of car tyres came scuffing through the rain, and a mixed crowd laughed and scrambled their way up to the hotel, with Fan Liuyuan in the lead. Saheiyini was leaning on his arm, but she was not a pretty sight—her bare legs were flecked with mud. She took off her big straw-hat, splashing the ground with water. Liuyuan caught sight of Liusu's umbrella, said a few words to Saheiyini at the foot of the stairs, and Saheiyini went up by herself. Liuyuan came over, and pulled out a handkerchief to wipe the rain from his face and clothes. Liusu had to greet him briefly. Liuyuan sat down and said, "I heard you haven't been feeling well?"

"Just a summer cold."

"This weather is so muggy. We've just been out on that Englishman's yacht to have a picnic, sailed out to Tsingyi Island."

So Liusu asked him about the scenery on Tsingyi Island. Just then, Saheiyini came back down in an Indian outfit, trailing a gosling-yellow shawl long enough to touch the floor and covered with embossed silver-thread flowers, each at least two inches in diameter. She, too, sat down by the railing, at a table far away, one arm stretched out along the back of her chair, silver polish glinting on her fingernails.

"Why don't you go over?" Liusu laughed at Liuyuan.

"There's someone with a controlling interest."

"How can that Englishman tell her what to do?"

"He can't control her, but you can control me."

Liusu puckered her lips. "Oooh! I could be the Governor of Hong Kong, or the city god, all the people under my control, and I wouldn't be able to control you!"

Liuyuan shook his head. "A woman who doesn't get jealous must be a bit abnormal."

Liusu let out a laugh. Then, after a short silence, "Why are you watching me?"

"I'm trying to see if you'll be nice to me from now on."

"Whether I'm nice to you or not, what difference could it make to you?"

Liuyuan clapped his hands together. "Ah! That's more like it! Now there's just a bit of venom in her voice!"

Liusu had to laugh. "I've never seen anyone like you, so intent on making people jealous!"

After that, they became friendly again, and they went to dinner together. On the surface, Liusu warmed to him a little more, but deep down she was quite depressed. Trying to make her jealous was a way of taunting her, trying to make her run, of her own accord, right into his arms. She'd kept him at a distance for so long now; if, at this point, she softened towards him, she'd be sacrificing herself for nothing. He wouldn't really feel obligated; he'd just think that she'd fallen for a trick. She would be dreaming if she thought he'd marry her after that . . . Clearly, he did want her, but he wasn't willing to marry her. But since her family, poor as they were, was still a respectable family, and they were all moving in the same social set, he didn't want to get a reputation as a seducer. That was why he put on that open and above-board manner. Now she knew that it was all faked innocence. He didn't want to be held responsible. If he left her, there was nothing she could complain about.

When Liusu had thought all this out, she couldn't help grinding her teeth in anger. Outwardly, she still went along with him as usual. Mrs Xu had already rented a house in Happy Valley, and planned to move in soon. Liusu would have like to go with them, but since she had already troubled them for more than a month, the idea of being their long-term guest was quite embarrassing. Staying at the hotel was also out of the question. She suffered the agony of indecision, not knowing whether to advance or retreat.

Then one night, when she had lain in bed for many hours, tossing and turning, finally drifting off a bit, the telephone by her bed suddenly rang. It was Liuyuan's voice saying, "I love you." And then he hung up. Her heart pounding, Liusu held the receiver in her hand and stared into space, then very lightly put it back in the cradle. No sooner had she hung up than it rang again. Again she raised the receiver, and Liuyuan said, "I forgot to ask—do you love me?"

Liusu coughed, and when she spoke her throat was still dry and raspy. "You must have known long ago," she said in a low voice, "Why else did I come to Hong Kong?"

Liuyuan sighed. "I knew, but even when truth is staring me in the face, I'm still not willing to believe. Liusu, you don't love me."

"Why do you say that?"

Liuyuan didn't say anything. Then, after a long while, "There's a verse in the *The Book of Songs*[7]—"

"I don't understand that sort of thing," Liusu cut in.

"I know you don't understand," Liuyuan said impatiently. "If you understood, I wouldn't need to explain! So listen: 'Life, death, separation—with thee there is happiness; thy hand in mine, we will grow old together.'[8]

"My Chinese isn't very good, and I don't know if I've got it right. I think this is a very mournful poem which says that life and death and parting are all enormous things, far beyond human control. Compared to the great forces in the world, people are very small, very weak. But still we say 'I will stay with you forever, we will never, in this lifetime, leave one another'—as if we really could decide these things!"

Liusu was silent for a while, but finally she burst out. "Why not go ahead and just say, flat-out, that you don't want to marry me, and leave it at that! Why beat about the bush, with all this talk of not being able to decide things?! Even for an old-fashioned person like me there is the saying 'The first marriage for the family, the second marriage for oneself.' If someone as free and unburdened as you are can't decide for himself, then who can decide for you?!"

"You don't love me, have you the power to decide a question such as this?" Liuyuan said coldly.

"If you really love me, why worry if I do?"

"I'm not such a fool that I'll pay to marry someone who doesn't care about me, just so that she can tell me what to do! That's too unfair. And it's unfair to you, too. Well, maybe you don't care. Basically, you think that marriage is long-term prostitution . . ."

Liusu didn't wait for him to finish. She slammed the receiver down, her whole face crimson with rage. How dare he talk to her like this?! How dare he?! She sat on the bed, the feverish darkness wrapped around her like a purple wool rug. Her body was covered with sweat, itching terribly, and her hair stuck to her neck and back, so irritating she could hardly bear it. She pressed her hands against her cheeks, and her palms were ice-cold.

The phone rang again. She didn't answer, just let it ring. "Brring . . . Brring . . ." The sound was unusually ear-piercing in the quiet room, in the quiet hotel, in the quiet Repulse Bay. Liusu suddenly realized that she couldn't wake up the whole Repulse Bay Hotel. First of all, there was Mrs Xu just next door . . . Trembling with fear, she picked the receiver up and laid it on the bedsheet. But the night was so still that even from a distance

---

7. That is, *Classic of Poetry* 31.   8. A more commonly accepted interpretation is: "In life as in death, here is my promise to thee: thy hand in mine, we will grow old together."

she could hear Liuyuan's perfectly calm voice saying, "Liusu, from your window, can you see the moon?"

She didn't know why, but suddenly she was sobbing. The moon shone bright and blurry through her tears, silver, with a slightly greenish tint. "In my window," said Liuyuan, "there is a flowering-vine that blocks half the view. Maybe it's a rose. Or maybe not." He didn't say anything more, but the phone stayed off the hook. After a very long while, Liusu began to wonder if he had dozed off, but finally there was a gentle little click. Her hand still shaking, Liusu took the receiver from where it lay on the bed and put it back in the cradle. She feared he would call a fourth time, but he didn't. It was all a dream—the more she thought about it, the more it seemed like a dream.

The next day, she didn't dare ask him about it, because he would be sure to tease her—"dreams are just your heart's desire". Was she really so infatuated with him, that even in her sleep she dreamed he called up to say "I love you"? There was no change in his attitude. They went out for the day, just as usual. Liusu suddenly noticed that there were lots of people who took them for husband and wife—the porters, the ladies and old ladies that she chatted with in the hotel—and they could hardly be blamed for this. She and Liuyuan had rooms right next to each other, they came in and went out side by side, they took late-night walks on the beach, totally unconcerned about what other people might think. A nanny wheeled a baby-carriage by, nodded to Liusu, and greeted her as "Mrs Fan". Liusu froze, unable to either smile or not smile. She could only look at Liuyuan from under her brows and say, in a low voice, "I wonder what they think."

"Don't worry about those who call you 'Mrs Fan'. But those who call you 'Miss Bai'—what must they think?"

The colour drained from Liusu's face. Liuyuan stroked his chin and laughed. "Since that's what people think anyway, why not do it?"

Liusu stared at him in shock, suddenly seeing how wicked this man was. Whenever they were in public, he made sure to give the impression of affectionate intimacy, so that she now had no way to prove that they had not slept together. She was riding the tiger now, no way to go back home, no way to go back to her family, no way out except to become his mistress. But if she relented towards him now, all her effort thus far would be wasted, with no hope of recovery. She wouldn't! Even if that's what everyone thought, he had taken advantage of her in name only. The real truth was that he had not gotten her. And since he hadn't, then maybe someday he would come back, offering better peace-treaty terms.

She made up her mind, and told Liuyuan that she wanted to go back to Shanghai. Liuyuan didn't try to keep her; instead he volunteered to see her home. "Oh, that's not necessary," said Liusu. "Aren't you going to Singapore?"

"I've already put it off this long, delaying a little longer won't matter. I've got things to do in Shanghai too."

Liusu knew that he was still playing the same hand, afraid that others wouldn't talk about them enough. The more that people had to talk about, the less she'd be able to defend herself, and Shanghai would become a very uncomfortable place for her. But Liusu reasoned that even if he didn't go back with her, she wouldn't be able to keep things from her family. She had braved damnation thus far, she might as well let him see her home.

When Mrs Xu saw that the pair that had seemed to be getting along so well suddenly wanted to break things off, she was surprised, to say the least. She asked each of them, and they both made excuses for the other, but of course Mrs Xu didn't believe a word they said.

On the ship, they had many chances to be together, but if Liuyuan could resist the moon in Repulse Bay, he could resist the moon on shipboard. He didn't say a single concrete thing to her. He seemed nonchalant, but Liusu could tell that it was the nonchalance of a man who is quite pleased with himself—he was sure she couldn't escape him now, sure he had her in the palm of his hand.

When they got to Shanghai, he took her to her house, but didn't get out of the taxi. The Bai household had heard the news long before, and were very well aware that Sixth Young Lady and Fan Liuyuan had cohabited in Hong Kong. Going off with a man for a whole month, then waltzing back as if nothing were the matter—this clearly was intended to bring disgrace to the Bai family.

Liusu had taken up with Fan Liuyuan—it had to be for his money. If she had gotten the money, she wouldn't have come home so very quietly; it was clear she hadn't gotten anything from him. Basically, a woman who was tricked by a man deserved to die, while a woman who tricked a man was a whore. If a woman tried to trick a man but failed, and instead was tricked by him, that was whoredom twice over. Kill her and you'd only dirty the knife.

Ordinarily, when anyone in the Bai family made a mistake the size of a sesame-seed, it got blown out of all proportion. Now that they had a truly sensational, enormous crime, they were so over-excited, stammering so hard, they couldn't get anything out. First they decided that "dirty laundry shouldn't be aired in public", so they spread out, and made all their friends and relatives swear to keep their mouths shut. Then they went back around to those friends and relatives, one by one, trying to find out if they knew, and if so, how much. In the end they decided it couldn't be kept quiet, so they cheerfully announced it, bringing it into the open, slapping their thighs, moaning and sighing about the whole thing. They spent the whole autumn managing all this, and so didn't get around to doing anything definite about Liusu herself.

Liusu knew very well when she went back that things would be even worse than before. The ties of affection and loyalty between her and this family had long ago been severed. Of course she considered looking for a job, anything to earn a bowl of rice. No matter how rough it was, it would still be better than living with a hostile family. But if she took some menial job, she would lose her social status. That status wasn't something you could eat, but losing it would be a pity. And she had not yet given up all hope concerning Fan Liuyuan. She could not sell herself cheap now, or else he would have a perfect excuse for refusing to marry her. And so she just had to hang on a little while longer.

Finally, at the end of November, Fan Liuyuan sent a telegram from Hong Kong. That telegram was eyeballed by everyone in the family before Old Mrs Bai called for Liusu, and put it in her hand. There were just a few laconic words: "PLEASE COME TO HK. BOAT TICKET ALREADY ARRANGED BY THOMAS COOK." Old Mrs Bai gave a long sigh. "Since he's sent for you, you should go!"

Was she so cheap? Tears dropped from her eyes. Crying made her lose all her self-control: she found she could not bear it any more. In one autumn, she had already aged two years—she couldn't afford to get old! And so she left home and went to Hong Kong for the second time. This time, she did not have any of her earlier eagerness for adventure. She had lost. Of course, everyone likes to be vanquished, but only within certain bounds. If she had been vanquished solely by Fan Liuyuan's charms, that would be one thing. But mixed with that was the pressure from her family—the most painful factor in her defeat.

Fan Liuyuan was waiting for her at the dock in a light, drizzling rain. He said that her green rain slicker looked like a bottle. "A medicine bottle," he explained. She thought he was teasing her because she had grown so frail, but then he said into her ear: "You're just the medicine I need." She blushed, and turned her eyes away.

He had reserved her old room for her. It was already 2 a.m. when they got back to the hotel. When she was in the bathroom, getting ready for bed, she turned the light off and then remembered that the bedroom light switch was by the bed. Fumbling in the dark, she stepped on a shoe and almost fell. She cursed herself for being so careless, leaving her shoes lying around, but then there was a laugh from the bed, "Don't be frightened! It's my shoe!"

Liusu stopped. "What are you doing here?"

"I always wanted to see the moon from your window. You can see it much better from this room than you can from that one."

So he *had* phoned her that night! It was not a dream! He loved her. What an awful, fiendish man! He loved her, and still he treated her like this! Her heart went cold. She turned away, walked over to the dressing-table. The faint light of the late November crescent moon, just a thin hook of white, was like frost on the window-pane. But the moon shone on the sea, was reflected from the sea through the window, and then its faint glow lit the mirror. Liusu slowly stripped her hairnet off, mussing her hair; the hairpins loosened and fell out, then clattered to the floor. She pulled the hair-net on again, holding the strings in her tight-pressed lips, and bent down, frowning, to pick the hairpins up one by one.

Liuyuan had already walked over behind her in his bare feet. He put one hand on her head, turned her face towards his, and kissed her mouth. The hairnet slipped down. This was the first time he had kissed her, but it didn't feel like the first time to either of them, because they both had imagined it so many times. They had had so many opportunities—the right place, the right mood—he had thought of it, and she had worried about the possibility. But they both were such clever people, making their plans so carefully that they had never dared to take the risk. Now that it suddenly was reality, they both were dazed. Liusu felt her head spin, and she fell against the mirror, her back pressed tightly against its icy surface. His mouth did not leave hers. He pushed her into the mirror, they seemed to fall down into it, into another shadowy world—freezing cold, searing hot, the flame of the forest burning all over their bodies.

The next day, he told her that he was going to England in a week. She asked him to take her with him, but he said it was not possible. He offered to rent a house for her in Hong Kong so she could wait for his return, which would be in a year or so. If she would rather live with her family in Shanghai, that would be fine too.

Of course she was not willing to go back to Shanghai. The more distance she could put between those people and herself, the better. Living alone in Hong Kong would be lonely, but she could bear that. The problem was whether or not the situation would change when he came back, and that all depended on him. Could a week's love hold his heart? But then, on the other hand, Liuyuan wasn't a man of stable affections; meeting and parting so quickly as this, he had no chance to get tired of her, so maybe it was best for her after all. A week is more worth remembering than a year. . . . Yet if he did come back looking for her, his heart full of warm memories, she might have changed! A woman near thirty can be unusually attractive, but she can also grow haggard in a moment. In the end, trying to hold onto a man without the surety of marriage is a difficult, painful, and tiring business, well nigh impossible. But what did it matter?! She had to admit that Liuyuan was quite delightful, and that he gave her a wonderful time, but what she wanted from him was financial security. On this point, she knew she could rest assured.

They took a house on Babington Road, up on a mountain slope. When the rooms had been painted, they hired a Cantonese maid called Ah Li. They had time to set up only the most basic furnishings, and then Liuyuan had to leave. Liusu could take her time setting up the rest. There wasn't any food in the house, so on the winter evening when she saw him off to the ship, they grabbed a few sandwiches in the ship's dining-hall. Because she was so dejected, Liusu had a few drinks, and then the sea-wind blew her around for a bit; by the time she got home, she was feeling a bit tipsy.

When she came in, Ah Li was in the kitchen heating water so she could wash her child's feet. Liusu went around the house, just walking and looking, and turning on all the lights as she went. The green paint on the sitting-room door and window was still wet. She touched it with her index finger, then pressed her sticky finger against the wall, leaving a green mark each time. Why not? Was it against the law? This was her house! She laughed, then went ahead and put a fresh green handprint on the dandelion-white of the plaster wall.

She sashayed into the next room. Empty rooms, one after another—pure empty space. She felt she could fly up to the ceiling. Walking around on those big empty floors was like being on the smooth, dust-free ceiling. The room was too empty, she had to fill it with light. But the light was too dim. She would have to remember to change the bulb tomorrow for a brighter one.

She went up the stairs. Emptiness was good, she was in such desperate need of peace and quiet. She was worn out. Trying to please Liuyuan was very hard work. He was an odd person to begin with, but then, since he had fallen in love with her, he had been even more odd towards her, easily displeased. It was good that he had gone, it would give her a chance to relax. Now, she did not want any people at all—hateful people, lovable people— she didn't want any of them. Ever since she was small, her world had been crammed to overflowing with people. Pushing, squeezing, trampling, hugging, hauling, old ones, young ones—there were people everywhere. Twenty-some people in a family, all in one house; you sat in a room clipping a fingernail, and there was someone watching you from the window. Now at last she had flown far away, to this unpeopled place. If she were officially Mrs Fan, she would have all sorts of responsibilities, she would not be able to get rid of people. But now she was just Fan Liuyuan's mistress, kept in the background. She should avoid people and people should avoid her.

But, good as it is to have peace and quiet, she had no interests except people. Her only little bit of knowledge and skill grew from this kind of ability. She could be a good daughter-in-law and a caring mother. But now she was a warrior without a battleground. How could she "mind the house" when there was nothing to mind? Raise children? Liuyuan didn't want children. Save on expenses, budget for the future? She did not even have to think about money. So how would she while away all this time? Play mahjong with Mrs Xu, watch operas? Then start flirting with actors, smoke opium, go the route of the concubine? She pulled herself up short and straightened her shoulders, clenching her clasped hands behind her back. It would not come to that! She was not that kind of person, she could control herself. But . . . could she keep herself from going mad? Six rooms, three up, three down, all ablaze with light. The newly waxed floors shone snow-bright. But no sign of anyone. One room after another, echoing emptiness. Liusu lay on the bed. She wanted to turn off the lights, but she could not move. Finally she heard Ah Li coming up the stairs in her wooden clogs, clomping back and forth, turning off the lights; bit by bit her overwrought mind unwound itself.

That was on 7 December, 1941. On 8 December, the bombing started. In between the explosions, the silvery winter mist slowly cleared, and on the mountain peaks, in the mountain valleys, all the people on the island looked toward the sea and said, "The war has started, the war has started." No one could believe it, but the war had started. Liusu was alone on Babington Road; what did she know about it? By the time Ah Li had gone around to all the neighbours to get the news, and woken her up in a panic, the fighting had begun in earnest. There was a science research station near Babington Road, with an anti-aircraft gun, and stray shells kept whizzing down with a sharp whistling sound, then dropped to earth with a "crump". The whistling noise split the air, tore up the nerves. The light blue sky was ripped into strips that drifted in the winter wind. Drifting also in the wind were countless nerve ends.

Liusu's rooms were empty, her heart was empty, and there wasn't any food in the house, so her belly was empty too. Emptiness sharpened everything, so she was especially hard hit by the attacks of fear. She tried to phone the Xu home in Happy Valley, but could not get through, since everyone who had a phone was calling around, trying to find out where the safest places were, so they would know where to go. That afternoon, Liusu finally got through, but the phone just kept ringing, no one coming to answer, which must mean that Mr and Mrs Xu had already fled to some safer place. Liusu didn't know what to do, and the shellfire got more intense. The nearby anti-aircraft gun became a target for the bombers. The planes circled overhead, droning like flies, like a dentist's drill boring painfully into the soul. Ah Li sat on the threshold of the sitting room hugging her crying child. She seemed dazed, rocking side to side, singing as though in a dream, comforting and patting her child. The whistling sounded again, and then the "crump" broke off one corner of the eaves, spilling down rubble. Ah Li screamed, jumped up, and rushed toward the door, still carrying her child. Liusu ran after her, and caught her at the front door. "Where are you going?"

"We can't stay here! I'm taking her to the sewer to hide!"

"You're crazy!" said Liusu. "You'll be killed out there!"

"Let me go! This child . . . she's my only one . . . can't let her die . . . got to go to the sewer to hide . . ."

Liusu held her back with all her might, but Ah Li pushed, and Liusu fell. Then Ah Li rushed out the door. Just as she reached the door, there was an earth-shattering boom, and the whole world went black, like a giant lid closing on some great, stupendous trunk. All the world's angst and anger was shut up inside.

Liusu thought that her life was over, but, astonishingly, she was still alive. She blinked, and saw the floor covered with glass shards and sunlight. She struggled to her feet, and went to look for Ah Li. Ah Li was still clutching her child, her head drooping, her forehead propped against the porch wall. She had been knocked into a stupor. Liusu pulled her back inside, and they heard the cries of people outside saying that a bomb had fallen next door and blown a huge crater in the garden. After this great boom and the closing of the lid, they still had no peace. The crumping sounds continued, like someone hammering nails on the lid, hammering on and on. It hammered from day to dark, and then from dark to day again.

Liusu thought of Liuyuan, and wondered if his ship had left the harbour, wondered if it had been sunk. But he seemed very vague to her, like someone in another world. The present and the past had nothing to do with each other, like a song played halfway through on the radio, then suddenly cut off by the crackling of static, interrupting the song. When the crackling stopped, the song would go on playing. But if the song were already finished, there would be nothing left to hear.

The next day, Liusu, Ah Li and her child shared the last biscuits from a tin. She was weak and exhausted, each crack of a screaming bomb slapping her hard in the face. From the street there came the lumbering sound of an army truck. It stopped at their door. The doorbell rang, and Liusu went to answer it. It was Liuyuan. She grabbed his hand, then clutched his arm, like Ah Li clutching her child, and fell forward, her head banging against the porch wall.

Liuyuan lifted her face with his other hand. "Frightened? Don't worry," he urged her. "Go and get your things together. We're going to Repulse Bay. Hurry now!"

Liusu ran back in and started rushing around, asking as she did, "Is it safe in Repulse Bay?"

"They say a navy can't land there. Anyway, the hotel has huge stocks of food, so there'll be something to eat."

"Your ship . . ."

"The ship never left. They took the first-class passengers to the Repulse Bay Hotel. I tried to come yesterday to fetch you, but I couldn't get a car, and the buses were completely full. Finally, today I managed to get this truck."

Liusu couldn't think clearly enough to pack her things, so she just grabbed a little bag and stuffed it full. Liuyuan gave Ah Li two months' salary and told her to watch the house. Then the two of them got into the truck, and laid face-down in the back, with a khaki-coloured awning over them. They rattled down the road, scraping the skin off their elbows and knees.

Liuyuan sighed. "This bombing blasted off the ends of an awful lot of stories!"

Liusu was filled with sorrow. Then, after a moment, she said, "If you were killed, my story would be over. But if I were killed, you'd still have a lot of story left!"

"Were you planning on being my faithful widow?"

They were both a little unnerved, and so for no reason at all they started laughing. Once they started they could not stop. When the laughing was over, they kept shaking all over.

The truck drove through the rain of bullets back to Repulse Bay. Army troops were stationed on the ground floor, so they stayed in their old room on the first floor. After they had settled in, they found out that all the stores of food were reserved for the troops. Besides the canned milk, beef, mutton, and fruit, there were sacks and sacks of bread, both bran and white. But the guests were given just two soda crackers, or two lumps of sugar, at each meal. Everyone was famished.

For a couple of days it was all quiet at Repulse Bay, but suddenly things changed, and the action heated up. There was nowhere to take cover on the first floor, so no one could stay there. They all went downstairs and stayed in the dining hall. The glass doors were opened wide, with sandbags piled up in front, and the British troops were firing cannon from there. When the gunboats out in the bay found out where the shooting was coming from, they returned fire. Shellfire was exchanged across the palm tree and the fountain. Liuyuan and Liusu, along with everyone else, pressed their backs against the wall.

That dark scene looked like an ancient Persian carpet, with all kinds of people woven into it—old lords, princesses, scholars and beauties. The carpet had been draped over a bamboo pole and was being beaten, dust flying in the wind. Blow after blow, it was beaten till those people had nowhere to hide, nowhere to go. The shells came lobbing this way, and they all ran over that way; the shells went flying that way, and they all ran over this way. Eventually the hall was reduced to a wreck, and one wall had collapsed, so they had nowhere to hide. They could only sit on the ground, awaiting their fate.

At this point, Liusu wished that Liuyuan were not with her. When a person seems to have two bodies, the danger is doubled. If she weren't hit, he still might be, and if he died, or were badly wounded, it would be worse than anything she could imagine. If she were wounded, then in order not to burden him she would have to force herself to die. Even if she died, it wouldn't be as clean and simple as dying when you are alone. She could tell that Liuyuan also felt this way; now she had only him, and he had only her.

The fighting ended. The men and women who had been trapped in the hotel slowly started walking to the city centre. They walked past yellow cliffs, then red cliffs, more red cliffs, then yellow cliffs again, almost wondering if they had got lost, and were going in circles. But no, they had not passed this gaping pit blasted in the road before, full of rock rubble.

Liuyuan and Liusu didn't say much. It used to be that whenever they took a short trip in a car, there was a dinner-party's worth of conversation, but now when they were walking several miles together, there was nothing to say. Once in a while one of them started a sentence, but the other knew exactly what the rest would be, so there was no need to go on.

"Look, on the beach," said Liuyuan.

"Yes."

The beach was full of tangled barbed-wire coils. Past the barbed-wire, the white seawater gurgled as it drank in and spat out the yellow sand. The clear winter sky was a faint blue. The flame of the forest was past its flowering season.

"That wall . . ." said Liusu.

"Haven't gone to see."

Liusu sighed. "Forget about it."

Liuyuan got hot from walking, took off his coat and slung it over his shoulder, but his back kept sweating.

Liusu said, "You're hot. Let me take it."

Previously, Liuyuan never would have agreed, but now he wasn't so chivalrous; he handed it to her.

As they walked on further, the mountains started to grow taller. Either it was the wind blowing in the trees, or it was the moving shadow of a cloud, but somehow the greenish yellow lower slopes slowly darkened. Looking more closely, you saw that it wasn't the wind, and it wasn't the clouds; it was the sun moving slowly over the mountaintop, plunging half the lower slopes into a giant blue shadow. Up on the mountain, smoke rose from some burning houses—white on the shaded slopes, black on the sun-lit slopes—but the sun just kept moving slowly over the mountaintop.

They got home, pushed open the half-closed door, and a little flock of pigeons took wing and fled. The hallway was full of dirt and pigeon droppings. Liusu went to the staircase, then cried out in surprise. The trunks she had bought and put in the rooms upstairs were strewn about wide open, and two of them had slid partway down to the ground floor, so that the stairs were buried in a flowing mass of satins and silks. Liusu bent down and picked up a brown wool-lined cheongsam. It was not hers. Sweat and dirt marks, cigarette burns, and the scent of cheap perfume. She found more women's things, old magazines and an open can of lychees, the juice dripping out on to her clothes. Had some troops been staying here? British troops who had women with them? It seemed they had left in a hurry. The poor local looters had not been here; if they had, these things would not have been left here. Liuyuan helped her call for Ah Li. The last grey-backed pigeon scurried past them, buzzed through the sunlit doorway, and flew off.

Ah Li was gone, who knew where. But even with the servant gone, the masters of the house had to go on living. They could not worry about the house yet, they had to think about food first. Scrambling around, they finally found a bag of rice, which they bought at a very high price. Fortunately the gas lines had not been cut, but there wasn't any running water. Taking a lead-lined bucket, Liuyuan went up the mountain to get some spring-water for cooking. In the following days, they spent all their time preparing meals and cleaning up the house. Liuyuan did all kinds of chores, sweeping, mopping, and helping Liusu wring out the heavy laundered sheets. Liusu was cooking for the first time, but the food she cooked actually had a Shanghainese flavour. Since Liuyuan was fond of Malayan food, she learned how to make satay and curried fish. Food became a major source of interest, but they had to be very careful about expenses. Liuyuan did not have a lot of Hong Kong dollars with him, so just as soon as they could get a boat, they would have to get back to Shanghai.

Anyway, Hong Kong after the disaster was not a place in which they wanted to stay for long. They were busy all day long just scraping for the basics. Then, at night, there were no lights, no sounds of people in that dead city; there was only the strong winter wind, wailing on and on in three long tones—oooh, aaah, eeei. When it stopped here, it started up there, like three grey dragons flying side by side in a straight line, long bodies trailing on and on, tails never coming into sight. Oooh, aaah, eeei—wailing until even the sky dragons had gone, and there was only a stream of empty air, a bridge of emptiness that crossed into the dark, crossed into the void of voids. Here, everything had ended. There were only some broken bits of levelled wall and, stumbling and fumbling about, a civilized man who had lost his memory; he seemed to be searching for something, but there was nothing left.

Liusu sat up hugging her quilt and listening to the mournful wind. She was sure that the grey brick wall near Repulse Bay was still standing straight and tall. The wind stopped there, like three grey dragons coiling on top of the wall, the moonlight glinting off their silver scales. She seemed to return in a dream, back to the base of that wall, where she met Liuyuan, finally and truly met him.

In this uncertain world, money, land, all the things that last forever, all are unreliable. She could rely only on this breath in her body, and this person sleeping next to her. Suddenly, she crawled over to him, hugging him through his quilt. He reached out from the bedding and grasped her hand. They looked and saw each other, saw each other entirely. It was only one moment of deep understanding, but this moment was enough to keep them happy together for a decade or so.

He was just a selfish man, and she was just a selfish woman. In this age of chaos and disorder, there is no place for individualists, but there is always room for an ordinary married couple.

One day, when they were out shopping for food, they ran into Princess Sahei-yini. Her face was rather sallow, and her loosened braids had been piled up in a fluffy top-knot. She was dressed in a long black cotton-wadded gown she had picked up who knows where, but on her feet she still wore a pair of fancy Indian slippers, colourfully embroidered and bejewelled. She shook their hands warmly, asked where they were living, and wanted very much to come and see their new house. Seeing the shelled oysters in Liusu's basket, she wanted to learn from her how to make steamed oyster soup. So Liuyuan invited her to come and have a simple meal, and she went back with them very happily. Her Englishman had been interned, and she was living now with an Indian police-man's family, people she knew well, people who had often done little things for her. She had not had a full meal in a long time. She called Liusu "Miss Bai".

"This is my wife," said Liuyuan. "You should congratulate us!"

"Really? When did you get married?"

Liuyuan shrugged and said, "We just put a notice in the Chinese news-paper. You know, wartime weddings are always a bit slapdash."

Liusu did not understand what they had said. Saheiyini kissed him, then kissed her. But the meal was very skimpy, and Liuyuan made sure that Sah-eiyini understood that they rarely had oyster soup. Saheiyini did not come back to their house.

When they went to the door to see their guest off, Liusu stood on the door-sill and Liuyuan stood behind. He closed her hands in his and said, "Well, when should we get married?"

When she heard this, Liusu could not say anything. She bowed her head, and then the tears began to fall.

"Now, now . . ." Liuyuan said, gripping her hands tightly. "We can go today to put a notice in the paper—unless of course you'd rather wait, and when we get back to Shanghai, throw a big bash, invite all the relatives . . ."

"Those people! Who'd want them?!" When she said this, she started laughing, then leaned back and let herself go, falling against his body. Liuyuan stroked his finger down her face and said, "First you cry, and then you laugh!"

They walked into town together. When they had got to a place where the road took a sharp turn, it suddenly fell away, revealing an empty space; all they saw was a pale grey, damp empty sky. Sticking out from a little iron gate was an enamel sign-plate that said "Dr Zhao Xiangqing, Dentist". The wind rattled the sign's iron clasp with a slight creaking sound, and behind the sign there was only that empty grey sky.

Liuyuan stopped walking and gazed for a while, sensing the terror in this ordinary scene, and shivered. "Now you must believe 'Death, life, separation . . .' How can we decide things? When the bombing was going on, just one little slip . . ."

Liusu chided him: "Even now you still say you haven't the power to decide?!"

"No, no, I'm not giving up half-way! What I mean is . . ." He looked at her face, then laughed. "OK, I won't try to say it!"

They went on walking, and Liuyuan said, "The gods must be behind this; we really did find out what love is!"

"You said a long time ago that you loved me."

"That doesn't count. We were too busy falling in love, how could we possibly find time to really love?"

When the marriage announcement was posted in the paper, Mr and Mrs Xu rushed over to offer their congratulations. Liusu was not altogether happy with them, since they had moved themselves to a safe place when the city was besieged, not worrying a bit whether she lived or died, but she had to smile and welcome them. Liuyuan got some wine and a few dishes for a belated celebration. Not much later, travel between Hong Kong and Shanghai opened up again, and so they went back to Shanghai.

Liusu went back to the Bai household just once, afraid that with so many people's busy mouths, something was sure to go wrong. But trouble could not be avoided: Fourth Mistress decided to divorce Fourth Master, and everyone blamed Liusu for this. Liusu had divorced and married again, with such astonishing success—no wonder that other people wanted to follow her example. Liusu crouched in the lamplight, lighting mosquito incense. When she thought of Fourth Mistress, she smiled.

Liuyuan did not try to tease her anymore, saving all his daring talk for other women. This was good, something to celebrate, since it meant he took her as family—his real, official wife—but Liusu was still somewhat saddened by it.

Hong Kong's defeat had given her victory. But in this unreasonable world, who can say which was the cause, and which the result? Who knows? Maybe it was in order to vindicate her that an entire city fell. Countless thousands of people dead, countless thousands of people suffering, and what followed was an earth-shaking revolution . . . Liusu did not feel that her place in history was anything remarkable. She just stood up smiling, and kicked the pan of mosquito-incense under the table.

The legendary beauties who felled cities and kingdoms were probably all like that.

There are legends everywhere, but they do not necessarily have such a happy ending. The *huqin* wails in the night of a thousand burning lamps; the bow slides back and forth, pouring out a tale desolate beyond words— oh! What's the point of asking?!

TADEUSZ BOROWSKI
1922–1951

Incarcerated in the extermination camps of Auschwitz-Birkenau and Dachau from the age of twenty to the age of twenty-two, a tormented suicide by gas at twenty-nine, Tadeusz Borowski wrote stories of life in the camps that have made him the foremost writer of the "literature of atrocity." The stories' brutal realism and matter-of-fact tone convey, as passionate declamations could never do, the mind-numbing horror of a situation in which systematic slaughter was the background for everyday life. The narrator of these stories, modeled on Borowski but also a composite figure, has become part of the concentration camp system, to survive. He assists the Kapos, or senior prisoners who organize the camp; has a job in the system; and carries a burden of guilt that cannot quite be suppressed by his adopted impersonal attitude. Borowski's stories shocked their postwar audience by their uncompromising honesty: here were no saintly victims and demoniacally evil executioners, but human beings going about the business of extermination or, reduced to near-animal level, cooperating in their own and others' destruction. Any belief in civilization, in common humanity, or in divine Providence is sorely tested; Borowski's bleak picture questions everything and does not pretend to offer encouragement. His fiction is still read for its powerful evocation of the death camps, for its analysis of human relationships under pressure, and for an agonizing portrayal of individuals forced to choose between physical or spiritual survival.

Tadeusz Borowski was born on November 12, 1922, in the Polish city of Żytomierz, part of the then-Soviet Ukraine. When he was three years old, his father was sent to a labor camp in Siberia as a suspected dissident; four years later, his mother was deported as well, and Tadeusz and his twelve-year-old brother were separated. He was raised by an aunt and educated in a Soviet school until a prisoner exchange in 1932 brought his father home; his mother's release in 1934 reunited the family. Money was scarce, however, and the young boy was sent away to a Franciscan boarding school where he could be educated inexpensively. Much later, he commented that he had never had a family life: "either my father was sitting in Murmansk or my mother was in Siberia, or I was in a boarding school, on my own or in a camp." World War II began when he was still sixteen, and—since the Nazis did not permit higher education for Poles—Borowski continued his studies at Warsaw University in illegal underground classes. Unlike his fellow students, he refused to join political groups and did not become involved in the resistance; he wanted merely to write poetry, continue his literary studies, and write a master's thesis on the poetry of Leopold Staff. Polish publications were illegal, however, and his first poetry collection, *Wherever the Earth* (1942)—run off in 165 copies on a clandestine mimeograph machine— was enough to condemn him. *Wherever the Earth* prefigures the bleak perspective of the concentration camp stories: prophesying the end of the human race, it sees the world as a gigantic labor camp and the sky as a "low, steel lid" or "a factory ceiling" (an oppressive image he may have adapted from Baudelaire's *Spleen LXXXI*). Borowski and his fiancée, Maria Rundo, were arrested in late February 1943 and sent to Auschwitz two months later. In the meantime, he was able to see from his cell window both the Jewish uprising in the Warsaw ghetto and the ghetto's fiery destruction by Nazi soldiers.

Borowski's camp experiences are reproduced in the 1948 story collection *Farewell to Maria*, from which *Ladies and Gentlemen, to the Gas Chamber* is taken. Arriving in Auschwitz, he was put to hard labor with the other prisoners; but after a bout with pneumonia, he learned to survive by taking a position as an orderly in the Auschwitz hospital—which was not just a clinic but a place where prisoners were used as experimental subjects. Maria had been sent to the women's barracks at the same camp, and he wrote her daily letters that were smuggled in. The story *Auschwitz, Our Home* contains a series of such letters and conveys, in addition to reassurances of his love, the writer's succeeding moods of hope, anger, cynicism, and despair ("We remain as numb as trees when they are being cut down"). Love lyrics written to Maria in 1942, published by his friends in 1944, display the sensuous softness of dream and contrast sharply with the camp stories' harsh illumination.

> I'm dreamy today. Noise from the street,
> the sky-curtain's rustlings, every
> sound comes in like the horizon's smoke
> through a mist.
> . . . It's how at night
> I take your hair in my hand, let its
> waves flow through my palm and
> stay quiet, full of you,
> as sleep is quiet now in me.
> (trans. Addison Bross)

The narrator's dispassionate tone in the stories, as he describes senseless cruelty and mass murder, individual scenes of desperation, or the eccentric emotions of people about to die, continue to shock many readers. Borowski is certainly describing a world of antiheroes, those who survive by accommodating themselves to things as they are and avoiding acts of heroism. His second collection of stories, *World of Stone* (1948), uses the same tone to describe life in the repatriation camps (he spent two years in such camps before being sent home) and the writer's disgust at the false normalcy of postwar society. Yet his impersonality is chiefly a shield; vulnerable, he finds a way to cope with overwhelming events by holding them at a distance. Borowski is recording events for future testimony, and he writes to his fiancée, "I do not know whether we shall survive, but I like to think that one day we shall have the courage to tell the world the whole truth and call it by its proper name." At the end of *The World of Stone*, his ambition is "to grasp the true significance of the events, things, and people I have seen. For I intend to write."

Upon his return to Poland after the war, Borowski's searing talent was recognized; the stories *Ladies and Gentlemen, to the Gas Chamber* and *A Day at Harmensee* (a subcamp of Auschwitz) had been published, and he became a prominent writer. He married Maria and was courted by Poland's Stalinist government. At the government's urging, he wrote journalism and weekly stories that followed political lines and employed a newly strident tone. The Cold War had begun, and Borowski was persuaded that he had joined a popular revolution that would prevent any more horrors like Auschwitz. He went so far as to do intelligence work in Berlin for the Polish secret police in 1949. The revelation of Soviet prison camps, however, and political purges in Poland, gradually disillusioned him: once more, he was part of a concentration camp system and complicit with the oppressors. He committed suicide by gas on July 3, 1951.

Ladies and Gentlemen, to the Gas Chamber was written in Munich, at a repatriation camp where Borowski was sent after his release from Dachau (many Birkenau prisoners were transferred as the Allied armies moved farther into Germany). Narrated in an impersonal tone by one of the prisoners, the story describes the extermination camp of Birkenau, the second and largest of three concentration camps at Auschwitz

(Polish: *Oświęcim*), an enclosed world of hierarchical authority and desperate struggles to survive. Food, shoes, shirts, underwear: this vital currency of the camp is obtained when new prisoners are stripped of their belongings as they arrive in railway cattle cars. The story could equally well have been titled *A Day with Canada*, for it follows the narrator's first trip to the railroad station with the labor battalion "Canada." The trip will salvage goods from a train bringing fifteen thousand Polish Jews, former inhabitants of the cities Sosnowiec and Będzin. By the end of the day, most of the travelers will be burning in the crematorium, and the camp will live for a few more days on the loot from "a good, rich transport."

Borowski suggests the systematic dehumanization of the camps from the beginning: people are equated with lice, and they mill around by naked thousands in blocked-off sections. Lice and people are poisoned with the same gas, sealed tightly into the camp or expelled from a section by the delousing process. People will later be equated with sick horses (the converted stables retain their old signs), lumber and concrete trucked in from the railroad station, and insects whose jaws work away on moldy pieces of bread. Constantly supervised, subject to arbitrary rules and punishment, malnourished and pushed to exhaustion, their identities reduced to numbers tattooed on the arm, the prisoners live in the shadow of a hierarchical authority that is to be feared and placated. Paradoxically, their common vulnerability leads to alienation and rage at their fellow victims rather than at the executioners. The Nazis have foreseen everything, explains his friend Henri, including the fact that helplessness needs to vent itself on someone weaker. The only way to cope is to distance oneself from what is happening, to become a cog in the machine so that one does not really experience what is happening—to suspend, for the moment, one's humanity.

Borowski emphasizes the range of cultures and languages brought together in Birkenau, and that variety is contrasted with the rigid narrowness of their jailers. French, Russian, and German phrases appear in this Polish-language story, as well as the camp "Esperanto" spoken by the Greeks. Separate scenes focus on the suffering of individual men, women, and children; and the narrator mentions the chaotic, multi-colored appearance of the crowds in their rags and variously striped uniforms. Over and against this cultural multiplicity is set the narrowly homogeneous model of the Nazi authorities: a lock-step "one mass, one will," bred from "Aryan" genes and trained in obedience to the Führer. The soldier with his blond hair and blue eyes, or the blonde woman commandant who wears her hair in a "Nordic" knot, offer images of the proposed master race. The SS officers are sleek, clean-shaven, and well-fed; they dress in identical uniforms with silver insignia, shiny boots, whips and revolvers, and briefcases to keep records in order. It is a picture of prosperity and efficient organization, all the more chilling in its pretense of normalcy and civilized behavior. The same officer who urges prisoners ("Gentlemen") to be orderly and show goodwill suddenly whips a woman stooping to pick up a handbag. Sharp contrasts emphasize the hollowness of their civilized image: a group of officers shake hands and share news from home and family pictures while the train of deportees rolls into the station; an officer fumbles with a balky cigarette lighter as he orders the labor detail to remove infants' corpses from the cattle car; another officer superciliously refers to a desperate woman who tries to escape being condemned with her child as an "unnatural mother."

It is the narrator's first experience with the Canada salvage team, and he expects that his carefully cultivated impersonality will work as well here as it has in the camp. This day will test his defenses, however, and his ability to survive through willful alienation. For a while, he registers events intellectually, noting the dimensions of the camp and crematoria. Soon, however, unforeseen emotional challenges arise and his control becomes shaky.

Words of sympathy from a condemned woman strike home: his vision blurs, and he asks Henri, "Are we good people?" It is only the first in a series of shocks, however, culminating when an apparently dead body grasps his hand. Vomiting from the cumulative horror, the narrator finds that the two dimensions he has tried to keep apart have temporarily fused—and he retreats once more to a dream of alienation. The narrator's utter defeat and despair are underlined when the returning labor battalion moves aside for an SS detachment singing lustily about conquering the world. Borowski's story was written after the Nazi downfall, but for the moment the picture is one of a spiritual desolation that not only illustrates a shameful moment in modern history but raises questions about what it means to be civilized, or even "human."

Brief discussions of Borowski are found in Czeslaw Milosz, *The History of Polish Literature* (1969); and from a different perspective, Sidra DeKoven Ezrahi, *By Words Alone: The Holocaust in Literature* (1980). Jan Kott, "Introduction" to *This Way for the Gas, Ladies and Gentlemen* (1967), and Jan Walc, "When the Earth Is No Longer a Dream and Cannot Be Dreamed through to the End," *Polish Review* (1987), combine biography and literary analysis. Selections from the poetry are available in *Selected Poems* (1990), trans. Tadeusz Pióro with Larry Rafferty, and "Five Poems by Tadeusz Borowski," *Polish Review* (1983), trans. Addison Bross. Also pertinent are the *Historical Atlas of the Holocaust* (1996) and psychiatrist Bruno Bettelheim's analysis of different responses to genocide in *Surviving the Holocaust* (1986).

PRONOUNCING GLOSSARY

The following list uses common English syllables and stress accents to provide rough equivalents of selected words whose pronunciation may be unfamiliar to the general reader.

Auschwitz: *ow'-shvits*

Birkenau: *beer'-ken-ow*

Katowice: *kah-toh-veet'-se*

Sosnowiecz-Będzin: *sos-nawv'-yets ben-jin*

Tadeusz Borowski: *tah-day'-yoosh bor-off'-skee*

Ladies and Gentlemen, to the Gas Chamber[1]

The whole camp[2] went about naked. True, we had already passed through the delousing process and received our clothing back from the tanks filled with a dilution of cyclone[3] in water which so excellently poisoned lice in clothing and people in gas chambers—and only the blocks separated from us by trestles had not yet been issued clothing, nonetheless both the former and the latter went about naked: the heat was terrific. The camp was sealed up tight. Not a prisoner, not a louse could venture beyond its gates. The work of the commandos[4] had stopped. Thousands of naked people milled about all day on the roads and roll-call grounds; they siestaed under walls and on the roofs. People slept on bare boards, for the straw mattresses and blankets were being disinfected. The FKL[5] could be seen from the last blocks; delousing was going on there, too. Twenty-eight thousand women had been stripped and turned out of the blocks; they could be seen right now scrambling on the meadows, roads and roll-call grounds.

The morning is spent in waiting for dinner, contents of food parcels are being eaten, friends visited. The hours pass slowly as they do in extreme heat. Even the usual recreation is lacking: the wide roads to the crematoria are empty. There have been no transports for some days. Part of "Canada"[6]

---

1. Translated by Jadwiga Zwolska.   2. Auschwitz II, or Birkenau, the largest of the Nazi extermination camps, established in October 1941 near the town of Birkenau, Poland. Its death toll is usually estimated between 1 million and 2.5 million people.   3. Cyclone-B, the extermination gas.   4. Labor battalions. 5. Frauen Konzentration Lager: Women's concentration camp (German).   6. The name given to the camp stores (as well as prisoners working there) where valuables and clothing taken from prisoners were sorted for dispatch to Germany. Like the nation of Canada, the store symbolized wealth and prosperity to the camp inmates.

has been liquidated and assigned to a commando. Being well-fed and rested they chanced on the hardest one: the Harmensee.[7] For envious justice rules in the camp: when a mighty one falls, his friends make every effort that he may fall as low as possible. Canada, our Canada, is not like Fiedler's,[8] fragrant with resin, only with French perfume, but fewer tall pines probably grow there than the number of diamonds and coins—collected from all Europe—cached here.

Several of us are sitting right now on a top bunk swinging our legs in a carefree manner. We take out white, extravagantly baked bread: crumbly, falling to pieces, a little provoking in taste, but, for all that, bread that had not been moulding for weeks. Bread sent from Warsaw.[9] Barely a week ago, my mother had it in her hands. Good God . . .

We get out bacon and onions, open a tin of condensed milk. Huge, dripping with sweat, Henri yearns aloud for French wine brought by the transports from Strasbourg, from the vicinities of Paris, from Marseilles[1] . . .

"Listen, *mon ami*,[2] when we go on the loading platform again, I'll bring you real champagne. You've never drunk it, have you?"

"No. But you won't be able to smuggle it across the gate, so don't string me along. You'd better 'organize' a pair of shoes—you know, perforated leather, with a double sole.[3] And I'm not mentioning a sports shirt, you've promised me one long ago."

"Patience, patience. When the transports come I'll bring you everything. We'll go on the loading platform again."

"What if there won't be any more transports for the smokestack?"[4] I threw in maliciously. "You see how things eased up in the camp: unlimited food parcels, flogging not allowed. You've written home, haven't you? . . . People say all sorts of things about the regulations, you yourself do a lot of gabbing. Anyhow, damn it, they'll run out of people."

"Don't talk nonsense," says the plump Marseillaise, his face spiritual like a Cosway[5] miniature (he's my friend, and yet I don't know his name). His mouth filled with a sardine sandwich, he repeated, "don't talk nonsense," swallowing with difficulty ('it went down, damn it,') "don't talk nonsense, they can't run out of people or we'd all be finished in the camp. We all live on what they bring."

"Well, not all. We have food parcels . . ."

"You have, and a pal of yours has, and tens of your pals have them. You Poles have them, and not all of you at that. But we, the Jews, the Russkis? and what then? If we, the transport 'organization,' had nothing to eat, would you be eating these food parcels of yours so calmly? We wouldn't let you."

"You'd let us, or you'd die of starvation like the Greeks. Whoever in the camp has food, has power."

"You've got them and we've got them, so why quarrel?"

That is true, no use quarreling. You have them and I have them, we eat together, sleep in one bunk. Henri cuts the bread, makes a tomato salad. It has a marvellous taste with the mustard from the camp canteen.

---

7. One of the subcamps outside Birkenau itself.　8. Arkady Fiedler, Polish writer of travel books, one of which was about Canada.　9. Capital of Poland; most of its Jewish residents were executed by the Nazis.　1. A large French port on the Mediterranean Sea. Strasbourg is a city in northeast France. 2. My friend (French).　3. A Hungarian style.　4. The crematorium.　5. Richard Cosway (1740–1821), an English miniaturist, or painter of miniature portraits that could be kept in a locket.

Under us, in the block, naked, sweating people mill about. They move here and there in the passages between the bunks, alongside the huge, ingeniously built stove, amidst the improvements which change the stables (there is still a sign on the door saying that *verseuchte Pferde*[6]—infected horses, should be sent to such and such a place) into a cozy home for more than half a thousand men. They nest on the lower bunks by eights and nines: stinking of sweat and excrement, their cheeks emaciated, they lie naked and bony. Under me, on the very bottom bunk—a rabbi; he has covered his head[7] with a bit of rag torn from the blanket and is reading a Hebrew prayer book (there's plenty of that kind of reading here . . .) in a loud and monotonous lament.

"Maybe we could shut him up? He yells as though he had caught God by the feet."

"I don't feel like getting down from the bunk. Let him yell; he'll go all the quicker to the smokestack."

"Religion is the opium of the people.[8] I like to smoke opium," the Marseillaise to my left, who is a communist and a *rentier*,[9] adds sententiously.

"If they did not believe in God and in a life beyond they'd have wrecked the crematorium long ago."

"And why don't you do it?"

The sense of the question is metaphoric, however, the Marseillaise replies, "Idiot," stuffs his mouth with a tomato and gestures as though he would say something, but he munches and keeps silent. We just finished stuffing ourselves when a bigger hubbub started near the door of the block: the Mussulmen[1] jumped back and scurried off among the bunks. A messenger ran into the block leader's cubbyhole. After a moment the block leader emerged[2] majestically.

"Canada! Fall in! Snappy now! A transport's coming!"

"Good God," shouted Henri, leaping down from the bunk.

The Marseillaise choked on the tomato, grabbed his coat, shouted *"raus"*[3] to those who sat below him, and in a moment they were already in the doorway. Everything seethed on the other bunks. Canada was going to the loading platform.

"Henri, shoes!" I shouted as a farewell. "*Keine Angst*,"[4] he shouted back, already outside.

I packed up the food and tied the satchel with string. In it, cheek by jowl with Portuguese sardines, lay onions and tomatoes from my father's garden in Warsaw, and the bacon from the "Bacutil" in Lublin (from my brother) mingled with genuine candied fruit from Salonika.[5] I tied it all up, pulled my trousers on and climbed down from the bunk.

"*Platz!*"[6] I shouted, shouldering my way through the Greeks. They drew aside. In the door I came upon Henri.

"*Allez, allez, vite, vite!*"

---

6. Infected horses (German).   7. Jews are expected to keep their heads covered while at prayer.   8. A quotation from the German political philosopher Karl Marx (1818–1883).   9. Someone with unearned income, a stockholder (French).   1. Or Muslim; people who had given up, considered the camp pariahs. 2. A Kapo, or senior prisoner in charge of a group of prisoners.   3. Outside (German).   4. Don't panic (German).   5. Major port city in northeast Greece. Lublin is a city in eastern Poland. *Bacutil*: A meat-products company with branches in many Polish cities.   6. Make room (German).

"*Was ist los?*"[7]

"Do you want to go to the loading platform with us?"

"Can do."

"Then hurry, take your coat. They're a few men short, I spoke to the kapo," and he pushed me out of the block.

We lined up, someone wrote down our numbers, someone at the head shouted: "march, march" and we ran up to the gates accompanied by the babel of the multitude already being driven back to the block with thongs. It was not everyone that could go to the loading platform . . . Good-byes said, we are already at the gate.

"*Links, zwei, drei, vier! Mützen ab!*"[8] Straightened up, with arms held stiffly at hips, we pass through the gate with a brisk, springy step—almost gracefully. Holding a huge tablet in his hand, a sleepy SS[9]-man counts drowsily, separating with his finger in the air every five men.

"*Hundert!*"[1] he shouted when the last five had passed him.

"*Stimmt!*"[2] a hoarse voice calls back from the head.

We march rapidly, almost at a run. Many outposts: youngsters with automatics. We pass all the sectors of Camp II B: the untenanted *Lager*[3] C, Czech and quarantine, and plunge deep among the apple and pear trees of the military hospital; amidst the exotic verdure, as though out of the moon, strangely exuberant these few sunny days, we pass in an arc some sort of wooden sheds, pass the big *Postenkette* lines and in a run reach the highway—we are there. A few score metres more, and among the trees—the loading platform.

It was an idyllic platform, as is usual with rural stations lost in remote areas. A square, bordered with the green of tall trees, was strewn with gravel. A tiny wooden shack squatted down at one side of the road, uglier and more jerry-built than the ugliest and flimsiest station shack. Farther away lay great stacks of rails, railway sleepers, piles of deal boards, parts of wooden sheds, bricks, stones and concrete well-rings. It is here that goods are unloaded for Birkenau: material for the expansion of the camp and people for the gas chambers. An ordinary work day: trucks drive up, take lumber, cement, people . . .

Guards take their places on the rails, on the lumber, under the green shade of the Silesian[4] chestnuts, they surround the loading platform with a tight circle. They wipe perspiration from their foreheads and drink from their canteens. The heat is terrific, the sun stands motionless in the zenith. "Fall out!" We sit in patches of shade under the stacked rails. The hungry Greeks (a few of them have managed, the devil knows how, to slip out with us) ferret among the rails; someone finds a tin of food, mouldy buns, an unfinished tin of sardines. They eat.

"*Schweinedreck*,"[5] a tall, young guard with abundant blond hair and

---

7. What's the matter? (German). *Allez, allez, vite!*: Come on, come on, quickly, quickly! (French).
8. Left, two, three, four! Caps off! (German).   9. Abbreviation for *Schutzstaffel* (Protective echelon, German), the Nazi police system that began as Hitler's private guard and grew, by 1939, to a powerful 250,000-member military and political organization that administered all state security functions. The SS was divided into many bureaucratic units, one of which, the Death's Head Battalions, managed the concentration camps. Selected for physical perfection and (Aryan) racial purity, SS members wore black or gray-green uniforms decorated with silver insignia.   1. A hundred! (German).   2. Right! (German).
3. Camp (German).   4. Probably local chestnuts. Silesia, in central Europe, was partitioned between Poland, Czechoslovakia, and Germany after World War I; Germany occupied Polish Silesia in 1939.
5. Dirty pigs (German).

dreamy blue eyes, spits at them. "After all, you'll have so much grub in a moment that you won't be able to gobble it all. You'll have your fill for a long time." He adjusts his automatic and wipes his face with a handkerchief.

"Swine," we confirm in unison.

"Hey you, fatty," the guard's shoe touches lightly the back of Henri's neck. "*Pass mal auf*,[6] want a drink?"

"I'm thirsty, but I've no marks," the Frenchman replies in a business-like manner.

"Too bad."

"But, *Herr*[7] Guard, doesn't my word mean anything any more? Hasn't *Herr* Guard done business with me? How much?"

"A hundred. A deal?"

"A deal."

We drink the insipid and tasteless water on tick against the money and people not yet here.

"Look here, you," the Frenchman says throwing away the empty bottle which crashes somewhere away on the rails, "take no money, for there may be a search. And, anyway, what the hell d'you need money for, you've got enough to eat. Don't take a suit either, for that's suspicious, and might look like a get-away. Take a shirt, but only a silk one and with a collar. Underneath, a gym vest. And if you find anything to drink, don't call me. I can take care of myself. And look out you don't get walloped."

"Do they whip you?"

"That's normal. One has to have eyes in the back. *Arschaugen*."[8]

All around us sit the Greeks; like huge, inhuman insects they move their jaws greedily and voraciously devour mouldy chunks of bread. They are uneasy because they do not know what they're going to do. They are alarmed by the lumber and the rails. They don't like lifting heavy loads.

"*Was wir arbeiten?*"[9] they ask.

"*Nix. Transport kommen, alles Krematorium, compris?*"[1]

"*Alles verstehen*," they reply in the crematorium Esperanto.[2] They calm down; they won't have to load the rails on trucks or carry the lumber.

In the meantime the loading platform has become more and more noisy and crowded. The foremen are dividing up the groups, assigning some to opening and unloading the railway cars that are to arrive; others they assign to the wooden steps and explain to them how to work properly. These were wide, portable steps like those to mount a rostrum. Roaring motorcycles arrived bringing non-commissioned SS officers, hefty, well fed men in glossy top-boots, with bespangled silver insignia, their faces churly and shiny. Some arrived with brief cases, others had flexible reed canes. This gave them an official and efficient air. They entered the canteen—for that miserable shack was their canteen where in summer they drank mineral water, *Sudetenquelle*,[3] and in winter warmed themselves with hot wine.

---

6. See here (German).   7. Mister (German).   8. Eyes in your ass (German, literal trans.). 9. What are we working on? (German).   1. Nothing. Transport coming, everything crematorium, understood? (German; *compris* is French).   2. An artificial language created in 1887 by L. L. Zamenhof to simplify communication between different nationalities. *Alles verstehen*: Everything understood. 3. Water from the Sudetenland or Sudeten Mountains; a narrow strip of land on the northern and western borders of the Czech Republic. The Sudeten was annexed by Hitler in 1938.

They greeted one another in stately fashion: the arm stretched out in the Roman manner[4] and then, cordially shaking hands, they smiled warmly at one another, talked about letters, news from home, their children; they showed one another photographs. Some of them promenaded in the square with dignity, the gravel crunched, the boots crunched, the silver distinctions gleamed on the collars and the bamboo canes swished impatiently.

The throng in vari-coloured camp stripes lay in the narrow strips of shade under the rails, breathed heavily and unevenly, chattered in their own tongue, gazed lazily and indifferently at the majestic people in the green uniforms, at the green of the trees—near and unattainable, at the spires of a distant church from which a belated Angelus[5] was just being rung.

"The transport's coming," said someone, and all of them rose expectantly. The freight cars were coming around the bend, the locomotive driving from behind. The brakeman standing on the tender, leaned out, waved his arm and whistled. The locomotive whistled screechingly in reply, panted, and the train chugged slowly along the station. In the small, barred windows could be seen human faces, pale and crumpled, dishevelled as though they had not had enough sleep; terrified women, and men who, strange to say, had hair. They passed slowly and looked at the station in silence. And then, inside the cars there began a seething and a pounding on the wooden walls.

"Water! Air!" rose dull, despairing shrieks.

Human faces leaned out of windows, mouths desperately gasped for air. Having drawn a few gulps of air the people left the windows and others stormed their places and then also disappeared. The screams and the rattling grew louder and louder.

A man in a green uniform more bespangled with silver than that of the others, frowned with disgust. He puffed on his cigarette, then threw it away with a sudden motion, transferred his brief case from his right to his left hand and beckoned to a guard. The latter slowly removed his automatic from his shoulder, took aim and fired a round at the railway cars. Silence fell. In the meantime trucks backed up to the train, stools were placed at the back of each, and the camp workers took positions expertly at the cars. The giant with the brief case made a sign with his hand.

"Whoever takes gold or anything else but food will be shot as a thief of *Reich*property. Understood? *Verstanden?*"

"*Jawohl!*"[6] came the shout, discordant but expressing good will.

"*Also loos!*[7] To work!"

The bolts clattered, the freight cars were opened. A wave of fresh air rushed inside, stunning people as though with monoxide gas. Packed to the limit, overwhelmed by a fantastic amount of luggage: suitcases, satchels, gladstone bags, rucksacks and bundles of every description (for they were bringing everything that had constituted their former life and was to start their future) they were squeezed into terribly cramped quarters, fainting from the heat, being suffocated and smothering others. Now they had clustered around the open door, panting like fish thrown on sand.

"Attention! Get down with your luggage. Take everything. Place all your

---

4. The official "Heil Hitler!" (Hail Hitler!) salute, with the straight right arm abruptly raised in imitation of ancient Roman military salutes. Adolf Hitler was chancellor of Germany under Nazism (1933–45). 5. A call to prayer, rung three times a day in the Catholic Church. *Green uniforms*: i.e., the regular gray-green army uniforms. 6. Yes! (German). *Verstanden*: understand? (German). 7. Then get going!

duds in a pile near the car. Hand over your coats. It's summer. March to the left. Understand?"

"Sir, what's going to happen to us?"—uneasy, nerves quivering, they are already jumping down onto the gravel.

"Where are you from?"

"Sosnowiec, Będzin.[8] Sir, what'll happen?" They stubbornly repeat the questions, gazing fervently into strange, tired eyes.

"I don't know, I don't understand Polish."

There is the law of the camp that people going to their death must be deceived to the last moment. It is the only permissible form of pity. The heat is sweltering. The sun has reached its zenith, the burnished sky trembles, the air shimmers; the wind, which blows through us intermittently, is merely hot, moist air. Lips are already cracked, the mouth savours the salty taste of blood. The body is weak and stiff from lying long in the sun. To drink, oh, to drink!

Like a stupefied, blind river that seeks a new bed, the motley throng, heavily laden, pours out of the car. But before they regain consciousness after being stunned by the fresh air and the smell of verdure, their baggage is torn from their hands, coats pulled off them, handbags snatched from the women's hands, sunshades taken away.

"But, mister, that's my sunshade, I can't . . ."

"*Verboten*,"[9] a guard barks through his teeth, hissing loud. In the back stands an SS-man: calm, self-possessed, expert.

"*Meine Herrschaften*,[1] don't throw your things about like that. You must show a little good will." He speaks kindly, and the thin cane bends with the nervous movement of his hands.

"Yes, sir, yes, sir," they reply in unison passing by, and walk at a brisker pace alongside the train cars. A woman bends down and quickly picks up a handbag. The cane swished, the woman cried out, stumbled and fell under the feet of the crowd. A child running behind her squeaked: "*Mamele!*"— just a tousled little girl . . .

The heap of things grows: suitcases, bundles, rucksaks, travel rugs, clothes, and handbags which open in falling and spill rainbow-coloured banknotes, gold, watches; in front of the car doors there rise piles of bread, collections of jars with multi-coloured jams and marmalades; pyramids of hams and sausages swell out, sugar spills on the gravel. Trucks packed with people drive away with an infernal racket amidst the lamentations and the shrieks of women wailing for their children separated from them, while the men, in stupefied silence, suddenly remain alone. They are the ones who went to the right: the young and healthy, they will go to the camp. They will not escape gassing, but first they will be put to work.

The trucks drive away and return continuously like some monstrous assembly line. The Red-Cross[2] ambulance goes back and forth ceaselessly. The huge, blood-red cross on the radiator cover melts in the sun. The Red-Cross ambulance travels tirelessly: it is precisely this car that carries that gas, the gas which will poison these people.

8. Two cities in Katowice province (southern Poland). Będzin was also the site of a concentration camp, and more than ten thousand of its inhabitants were exterminated. 9. Forbidden (German). 1. Gentlemen (German). 2. Ordinary trucks were painted with Red Cross insignia to quiet incoming prisoners by suggesting that they would receive humane treatment and medical care.

Those from "Canada" who are near the steps have not a moment's rest: they separate the people for gassing from those who go to the camp; they push the former on to the steps and pack them in the trucks: sixty, more or less, to a truck.

A young, clean-shaven gentleman, an SS-man, stands at the side with a notebook in his hand; each truck means a check mark—when sixteen trucks pass, it means a thousand, more or less. The gentleman is poised and accurate. No truck will leave without his knowledge and his check mark. *Ordnung muss sein.*[3] The check marks swell into thousands, the thousands swell into whole transports of which brief mention is made: "From Salonika," "from Strasbourg," "from Rotterdam."[4] Today's transport will be referred to as "from Będzin." But it will receive the permanent name of "Będzin–Sosnowiec." Those who will go to the work camp from this transport will receive numbers 131–132. Thousands, of course, but abbreviated they will be referred to just like that: 131–132.

The transports grow with the passing of weeks, months, years. When the war is over, the cremated will be counted. There will be four and a half million of them. The bloodiest battle of the war, the greatest victory of Germany united in solidarity. *Ein Reich, ein Volk, ein Führer*[5] and—four crematoria. But in Oświęcim there will be sixteen crematoria capable of incinerating fifty thousand bodies daily. The camp is being expanded until its electrified wire fence will reach the Vistula;[6] it will be inhabited by 300,000 people in camp stripes, it will be called *Verbrecher-Stadt*—the City of Criminals. No, they will not run short of people. Jews will be cremated, Poles will be cremated, Russians will be cremated; people will come from the West and from the South, from the continent and from islands. People in prison stripes will come, they will rebuild ruined German towns, plough the fallow soil and when they weaken from pitiless toil, from an eternal *Bewegung!*[7] *Bewegung!* the doors of the gas chambers will open. The chambers will be improved, more economical, more cleverly camouflaged. They will be like those in Dresden about which legends were already rife.

The cars are already empty. A thin, pock-marked SS-man calmly glances inside, nods his head with disgust, encompasses us with his glance and points inside:

"*Rein.*[8] Clean it out!"

We jump inside. Babies, naked monsters with huge heads and bloated bellies, lie scattered about in corners amidst human excrement and lost watches. They are carried out like chickens: a few of them making a handful.

"Don't take them to the truck. Let the women have them," says the SS-man lighting a cigarette. His lighter has stuck, he is extremely busy with it.

"For God's sake, take these babies," I burst out, for the women run away from me in terror, drawing in their heads between lifted shoulders.

The name of God is strangely unnecessary, for the women with the children go to the trucks, all of them—there is no exception. We all know what that means and look at one another with hate and horror.

"What's that, you don't want them?" The pock-marked SS-man asked as though surprised and reproachful, and starts to ready his revolver.

3. Order in everything (German).   4. Large port city in the Netherlands.   5. One State, One People, One Leader! (the slogan of Nazi Germany).   6. A river running through central Poland.   7. Hurry up! (German).   8. Clean it (German).

"No need to shoot, I'll take them."

A grey-haired, tall lady took the infants from me and for a while looked straight into my eyes.

"You poor child," she whispered smiling. Stumbling on the gravel she walked away.

I leaned on the side of a railway car. I was extremely tired. Someone is tugging my arm.

"*En avant*,[9] under the rails, come on!"

I gaze: the face flickers before my eyes, it melts—it huge and transparent—it becomes confused with the trees, immobile and strangely black, with the pouring throngs . . . I blink my eyes sharply: Henri.

"Look here, Henri, are we good people?"

"Why ask stupid questions?"

"You see, my friend, an unreasonable rage at these people wells up in me that I must be here on their account. I am not in the least sorry for them, that they're going to the gas chambers. May the ground open under them all. I'd throw myself on them with my fists. This must be pathological, I can't understand it."

"Oh, no, quite the contrary, it's normal, foreseen and taken into account. You are tired with this unloading business, you're rebellious, and rage can best be vented on someone weaker. It's even desirable that you should vent it. That's common sense, *compris?*" says the Frenchman somewhat ironically, placing himself comfortably under the rails. "Look at the Greeks, they know how to make the best of it. They gobble up everything they lay their hands on; I saw one of them finish a whole jar of jam."

"Cattle. Half of them will die tomorrow of the trots."

"Cattle? You, too, were hungry."

"Cattle," I repeat obstinately. I close my eyes, hear the shrieks, feel the trembling of the ground and the humid air on my lips. My throat is completely dry.

The flow of people is endless, the trucks growl like enraged dogs. Corpses are brought out of the cars before my eyes; trampled children, cripples laid out with the corpses, and crowds, crowds . . . Railway cars are brought alongside the loading platform, the piles of rags, suitcases and rucksacks grow, people get out, look at the sun, breathe, beg for water, enter the trucks, drive away. Again cars are rolled up, again people . . . I feel the pictures become confused within me, I don't know if all this is really happening, or if I'm dreaming. I suddenly see the green of trees rocking with an entire street, with a motley crowd: but yes, it's the Avenue![1] My head is whirring. I feel that in a moment I will vomit.

Henri tugs at my arm.

"Don't sleep, we're going to load the stuff."

There are no more people. Stirring up huge clouds of dust, the last trucks move along the highway in the distance, the train has left, the SS-men walk stiff-necked on the emptied loading platform, the silver on their collars sparkling. Their boots gleam, their bloated red faces shine. There is a woman among them. Only now do I realize that she been here all the time, this

---

9. Forward (French).   1. A famous boulevard in the center of Warsaw that used to be the Polish king's route from the current Old Town to outside the city.

dried-up, bosomless, bony woman. Sparse, colourless hair combed smoothly back and tied in a "Nordic"[2] knot, her hands in the pockets of her wide trouser-skirt. She strides from one end of the loading platform to the other, a rat-like, rancorous smile on her dry lips. She hates feminine beauty with the hatred of a repulsive woman aware of her repulsiveness. Yes, I have seen her many times and well remember her; she's the commandant of the FKL; she has come to look over her acquisitions, for some of the women have been stood aside and will walk to the camp. Our boys, hairdressers from Zaune,[3] will shave their heads completely and will have no end of fun at the sight of their humiliation, so alien to camp life.

So we load the stuff. We drag the heavy valises, spacious, well stocked, and with an effort throw them on the truck. There they are stacked, rammed down, crammed; anything that can be cut is carved up with a knife for the pleasure of it and in search of alcohol and perfume; the latter is poured right over oneself. One of the valises opens up: clothing, shirts, books tumble out . . . I grab a bundle, it is heavy, I open it: gold, two good handfuls—watch cases, bracelets, rings, necklaces, diamonds . . .

"Gib her,"[4]—an SS-man says calmly, holding up an open brief case full of gold and coloured foreign banknotes. He closes it, gives it to an officer, takes another empty one and stands on guard at another truck. The gold will go to the Reich.[5]

Heat, sweltering heat. The air stands like an immobile, white-hot column. Throats are parched, every spoken word causes pain. Oh, for a drink! We work feverishly: faster and faster, if only to get into shade, if only to rest. We finish loading, the last trucks leave; we pick up every bit of paper lying on the railway track, dig out of the fine gravel the alien rubbish of the transport, "so that no trace of that filth is left," and at the moment when the last truck disappears beyond the trees and we finally go towards the rails to rest and drink (maybe the Frenchman will again buy it from the guard?), the whistle of the railway man is heard from beyond the bend. Slowly, extremely slowly cars roll up, the locomotive whistles back screechingly, from the windows human faces look out, pale and crumpled and flattened like paper cut-outs, their eyes huge and feverish. The trucks are here already, and the calm gentleman with his notebook; the SS-men with brief cases for the gold and money come out of the canteen. We open the cars.

No, self-control is no longer possible. Valises are brutally jerked out of people's hands, overcoats torn off. "Go on, go on, move on!" They go, they pass on. Men, women, children. Some of them know . . .

Here is a woman walking quickly, hurrying imperceptibly but feverishly. A small child only a few years old, with the rosy, chubby face of a cherub, runs after her; it cannot catch up with her and holds out its little arms crying: "Mummy, mummy!"

"You, woman, pick up the child!"

"It isn't mine, sir, it isn't mine!" the woman shouts hysterically and, covering her face with her hands, runs away. She wants to hide, she wants to catch up with the other women who will not go by truck, who will walk, who will live. She is young, healthy and pretty, she wants to live.

But the child follows her, complaining loudly:

---

2. A northern (especially Scandinavian) style, encouraged by the Nazis to establish an image of Teutonic racial purity.   3. The "sauna" barracks, in front of Canada, where prisoners were bathed, shaved, and deloused.   4. Give it to me (German).   5. The German state.

"Mummy, mummy, don't run away!"

"It isn't mine, no, it isn't!"

Finally, Andrei, a sailor from Sevastopol,[6] caught up with her. His eyes were bleary from vodka and the heat. He caught up with her, knocked her off her feet with one wide swing of his arm, grabbed her by the hair when she was falling and put her on her feet her again. His face is livid with rage.

"Oh, you, *yebi tvoyu mat' blad' jevreyskaya!*[7] So you'd run away from your child! I'll fix you, you whore!" He caught her round her waist, choked down her shriek with a huge paw and with a swing threw her like a heavy sack of grain on the truck.

"That's for you! Take it, you bitch!" and threw the child at her feet.

"*Gut gemacht,* that's how unnatural mothers should be punished," said the SS-man who stood at the truck. "*Gut, gut Russki.*"[8]

"Shut up!" Andrei growled through his teeth and walked up to the railway cars. He drew out a canteen hidden under a pile of rags, unscrewed it, put it to his mouth and then to mine. Raw alcohol. It burns the throat. A roar in the head, my legs wobble under me, my gorge rises.

Suddenly, from this tide of humanity which, like a river driven by an invisible force, blindly pushes on toward the trucks, a girl emerged, jumped lightly from the car onto the gravel, and looked about her with a searching glance like one surprised at something.

Thick blond hair has spilled in a soft wave on her shoulders; she tossed it back impatiently. She instinctively passed her hands over her blouse, furtively adjusted her skirt. She stood like that for a moment. Finally, she tore her eyes away from the crowd and her gaze moved over our faces as though searching for someone. Unconsciously I sought to catch her glance, until our eyes met.

"Listen, tell me, where are they taking us?"

I looked at her. Here, before me, stood a girl with beautiful blond hair, wonderful breasts in an organdy summer blouse, her look wise and mature. Here she stood looking straight into my face and waited. Here, the gas chamber: mass death, loathsome and revolting. Here, the camp: a shaved head, quilted Soviet trousers in all that heat, the obnoxious, sickly odour of dirty, overheated feminine body; the animal hunger, inhuman toil, and the same gas chamber, only the death still more disgusting, more revolting, more horrible. Whoever has once entered here will never again pass the sentry post, not even as a handful of ashes, will never return to his former life.

"Why did she ever bring it here, they'll take it away from her," I thought automatically, seeing on her wrist a wonderful watch on a fine, gold bracelet. Tuśka had one like it, but hers was on a narrow, black ribbon.

"Listen, answer me."

I remained silent. She set her mouth.

"I already know," she said with a shade of haughty contempt in her voice, throwing her head back; boldly she walked up to the trucks. Someone wanted to stop her, but she boldly moved him aside and ran up the steps into the nearly filled truck. In the distance I saw only the thick, blond hair tousled by the speed.

I went into cars, carried out the infants, threw out the luggage. I touched

---

6. A Soviet (now Russian) port on the Black Sea. 7. An untranslatable, extremely vulgar Russian expression. 8. Good, good, Russki (German). *Gut gemacht:* well done (German).

corpses but could not overcome the wild terror welling up within me. I ran away from them but they lay everywhere: placed side by side on the gravel, on the edge of the concrete platform, in the cars. Babies, repulsive, naked women, men twisted by convulsions. I ran away as far as I could. Someone caned me across the back, out of the corner of my eye I notice a cursing SS-man, I slip away from him and mix with the stripe-clad "Canada." Finally, I again crawl under the rails. The sun has gone down over the horizon and bathes the loading platform with its bloody, waning light. The shadows of the trees grow monstrously long; in the silence that settles on nature with the coming of evening, human cries soar skywards ever louder, ever more insistently.

It was only from here, from under the rails, that the entire inferno seething on the platform can be seen. Here is a couple fallen on the ground, locked in a desperate embrace. He has dug his fingers convulsively into her flesh and caught her dress in his teeth. She is shrieking hysterically, swearing, blaspheming until, trampled down by a boot, she gurgles and is still. Torn apart like pieces of wood, they are driven like animals into a truck. Here, four men from "Canada" strain under the weight of a corpse: a huge, swollen old woman: they swear and sweat with the effort, kick out of the way stray children who get underfoot all over the platform and howl horribly like dogs. They catch the children by the neck, by the head and arms and throw them in a pile on the trucks. Those four cannot manage to lift the woman to the truck, they call others and with a collective heave push the mountain of flesh on the floor of the truck. Huge, bloated, swollen corpses are carried from the whole ramp. Thrown among these are cripples, paralyzed, smothered and unconscious people. The mountain of corpses seethes, whines and howls. The driver starts the motor and drives away.

"Halt, halt!" the SS-man shrieks from a distance. "Stop, stop, damn you!"

They are dragging an old man in a full dress suit with an armband on his sleeve. His head is knocked about on the gravel and the stones, he groans and laments incessantly and monotonously: "*Ich will mit dem Herrn Kommendanten sprechen,* I want to speak to the commandant." He repeats this with senile doggedness all the way. Thrown into the truck, trampled down by someone's foot, smothered, he continues to rattle: "*Ich will mit dem . . .*"

"Calm down, man!" calls out a young SS-man to him, laughing boisterously, "in half an hour you will speak to the supreme commandant! Only don't forget to say '*Heil Hitler*' to him."

Others carry a little girl who has only one leg, they hold her by the arms and that leg. Tears stream down her cheeks, and she whimpers pitifully: "Gentlemen, it hurts, it hurts . . ." They throw her on the truck with the corpses. She will be cremated alive with them.

Night falls, cool and starlit. We lie on the rails. It is immensely quiet. On tall posts anemic lamps throw out circles of light into the impenetrable darkness. A step into it and a man disappears irretrievably. But the eyes of the guards watch carefully. The automatics are ready to fire.

"Have you changed your shoes?" Henri asks me.

"No."

"Why not?"

"Man, I've had enough, completely enough."

"So soon, after the first transport? Just think, I . . . since Christmas, probably a million people have passed through my hands. The transports from around Paris are the worst ones, a man always comes upon acquaintances."

"And what do you tell them?"

"That they're going to have a bath and then we'll meet in the camp, And what would you say?"

I remain silent. We drink coffee spiked with alcohol; someone opens a tin of cocoa, mixes it with sugar. This is ladled up with the hand; the cocoa pastes up the mouth. Again coffee, again alcohol.

"What are we waiting for, Henri?"

"There'll be another transport. But no one knows."

"If there's another, I'm not going to unload it. I can't do it."

"It's got hold of you, yes? A fine 'Canada!' " Henri smiles benevolently and disappears in the dark. He returns shortly.

"Very well. But be careful that the SS-man doesn't catch you. You'll stay here all the time. And I'll fix you up with a pair of shoes."

"Don't bother me with the shoes."

I am sleepy. It is deep night.

Again *antreten*, again a transport. Cars emerge from the dark, pass the strip of light and again disappear in the gloom. The loading platform is small but the circle of light is still smaller. We will unload the cars as they come, one by one. Trucks growl somewhere, they back up to the steps, spectrally black, their reflectors light up the trees. *Wasser! Luft!*[9] The same all over again, a late showing of the same film: they discharge a volley from their automatics; the railway cars calm down. Only a little girl has leaned down to her waist from the little window of the car and losing her balance fell to the gravel. For a while she lay stunned, finally got up and started walking around in a circle, faster and faster, waving her arms stiffly as if at calisthenics, drawing her breath in noisily, and monotonously and howling shrilly. Suffocating—she has gone mad. She set the nerves on edge, so an SS-man ran up to her and kicked her with a hobbled boot in the small of the back; she fell. He pressed her down with his foot, took his revolver out and fired once and then again; she lay, kicking the ground with her feet until she stiffened. The cars begin to be opened.

I was again at the cars. A warm, sweetish odour gushed out. The car is filled to half its height with a mound of humanity: immobile, horribly tangled up but still steaming.

"*Ausladen!*"[1] sounded the voice of the SS-man who emerged out of the dark. On his breast hung a portable reflector. He lighted up the inside of the car.

"Why are you standing so stupidly? Unload!" and he swished his cane across my back. I grabbed the arm of a corpse, his hand closed convulsively around mine. I jerked away with a shriek and ran off. My heart pounded, my gorge rose. Nausea suddenly doubled me up. Crouching under the car I vomited. Staggering, I stole away under the stack of rails.

I lay on the kind, cool iron and dreamed of returning to the camp, about my bunk on which there is no straw mattress, about a bit of sleep among comrades who will not go to the gas chambers in the night. All at once the camp seemed like some haven of quiet; others are constantly dying and some-

---

9. Water! Air! (German).   1. Unload! (German).

how one is still alive, has something to eat, strength to work, has a fatherland, a home, a girl . . .

The lights twinkle spectrally, the wave of humanity flows endlessly—turbid, feverish, stupefied. It seems to these people that they are beginning a new life in the camp and they prepare themselves psychologically for a hard struggle for existence. They do not know that they will immediately die and that the gold, the money, the diamonds which they providently conceal in the folds and seams of their clothing, in the heels of their shoes, in recesses of their bodies, will no longer be needed by them. Efficient, business-like people will rummage in their intestines, pull gold from under the tongue, diamonds from the placenta and the rectum. They will pull out their gold teeth and send them in tightly nailed-up cases to Berlin.[2]

The black figures of the SS-men walk about calm and proficient. The gentleman with the notebook in hand puts down the last check marks, adds up the figures; fifteen thousand.

Many, many trucks have driven off to the crematorium.

They are finishing up. The corpses spread on the ramp will be taken by the last truck, the luggage is all loaded. "Canada," loaded with bread, jams, sugar, smelling of perfume and clean underwear, lines up to march away. The "kapo" finishes packing the tea cauldron with gold, silk, and coffee. That's for the guards at the gates, they will let the commando pass without a search. For a few days the camp will live off that transport: eat its hams and its sausages, its preserved and fresh fruit, drink its brandies and liqueurs, wear its underwear, trade in its gold and luggage. Much will be taken out of the camp by civilians to Silesia, to Cracow and points beyond. They will bring cigarettes, eggs, vodka and letters from home.

For a few days the camp will speak about the "Sosnowiec-Będzin" transport. It was a good, rich transport.

When we return to the camp, the stars begin to pale, the sky becomes more and more transparent, rises higher up above us: the night clears. It foretells a fine, hot day.

Mighty columns of smoke rise up from the crematoria and merge into a huge, black river which rolls very slowly across the sky over Birkenau and disappears beyond the forests in the direction of Trzebinia.[3] The Sosnowiec transport is already being cremated.

We pass an SS detachment marching with machine guns to change the guard. They walk in step, shoulder to shoulder, one mass, one will.

"*Und morgen die ganze Welt . . .*"[4] they sing lustily.

"*Rechts ran!*[5] To the right march!" comes the order from up front. We move out of their way.

---

2. The capital of Germany.   3. A town west of Auschwitz, near Krakow.   4. And tomorrow the whole world (German); the last line of the Nazi song "The Rotten Bones Are Shaking," written by Hans Baumann. The previous line reads "for today Germany belongs to us."   5. To the right, get going! (German).

ALAIN ROBBE-GRILLET
born 1922

More than anyone else, Alain Robbe-Grillet represents in his novels, *ciné-romans* (film-novels), and theoretical statements the rejection of the nineteenth-century realistic tradition and the exploration of a new "mental realism." Terms such as *antinovel* and *new novel,* early applied to his works, reflect both the turning away from older models (like Balzac and Flaubert) and the notion that a new experiment with form is under way. Not that it is completely new; clearly there are links to other twentieth-century works in the modernist tradition. Robbe-Grillet himself mentions the influence of Kafka, Camus, and Faulkner (as well as *Alice in Wonderland*), and other readers will note parallel experimentation in Pirandello, Woolf, Beckett, and Joyce. Moreover, Robbe-Grillet calls on some of the same sources of fascination as his nineteenth-century predecessors. He may not use a linear plot, but he writes ambiguous, circular detective stories where erotic and violent crimes *seem* to have been committed. He may refuse to portray a consistently developing character, but his minute descriptions of objects and gestures impel the reader to imagine an underlying psychology and to speculate on the meaning of the observer's repetition and distortion of details.

Nonetheless, with Robbe-Grillet, we move to a particular phenomenon of mid-twentieth-century literature and a prime example of what has been called the postmodernist tradition. To the breakdown of conventional storytelling models familiar from literary modernism, he adds an insistence on the artificiality of all writing and representation. Reader are faced with cumulative uncertainty: with a self-contained "text" in which there is no stable narrative voice or "authorized" explanation. Here is not the abstractly intellectual puzzle of Borges but an often terrifying evocation of a sensuous reality that will not stay in place. This literature has become a "game" (as it is for Borges), but it is a deadly game. Playing with erotic and murderous images, with the treacherous undercurrents of an apparently familiar reality, Robbe-Grillet fascinates and sometimes repels his readers. At the same time that he reminds us that we cannot know what we see and that we share the world with a host of objects different from ourselves, he entices us to figure out the meaning of events—only to reestablish, at every turn, the absolute subjectivity of our most "objective" perceptions. We cannot be disengaged from Robbe-Grillet's descriptions, because they make a direct appeal to our senses; they manipulate our awareness of physical experience. Throughout his career, Robbe-Grillet has explored the limits of representation with a collagelike technique that remains more true to life, he feels, than the planned coherence of a conventionally "realistic" novel.

Robbe-Grillet was born in Brittany, in northwestern France, to a family of scientists and engineers. His early training was not at all literary: in 1939 and 1941 the future writer took baccalaureate degrees in mathematics and natural science, and in 1946 (his career interrupted by forced labor in a German factory) a further degree from the National Agronomy Institute. He began work with the National Institute of Statistics and published an article on livestock possibilities before deciding to work part-time in his sister's biology laboratory and write a novel. This novel, *A Regicide,* was completed in 1949 but not published until 1978, well after Robbe-Grillet had become a successful novelist. In the meantime he took a position with an agricultural institute that sent him to Martinique, in the West Indies, to supervise banana plantations. Falling ill in 1951, Robbe-Grillet took advantage of the leisure time in the hospital and on the voyage home to write his second novel, *The Erasers,* which was immediately accepted and appeared in 1953.

The Erasers is a puzzling detective story involving confused identities, an abortive assassination carried out exactly twenty-four hours later by the muddled detective sent to investigate the original attempt, repeated allusions to the Oedipus myth, changing perspectives, and an overwhelming copiousness of detail about the most mundane natural objects. The novel became famous for its meticulous description of a tomato wedge cataloged with such scientific precision that it took on an objective existence of its own and implicitly challenged the human-centered orientation of a perspective that would see it only as part of a salad. "The flesh on the periphery, compact and uniform, of a fine chemical red, is evenly thick between a strip of shiny skin and the compartment where the seeds are lined up, yellow, well sized, held in place by a thin layer of greenish jelly alongside a swelling of the heart. This latter, of a faded and slightly grainy pink, begins, on the side of the depression below, in a cluster of white veins, one of which extends up to the seeds—in, perhaps, a somewhat uncertain manner." While minutely detailed descriptions are not new in literature, this catalog of physical properties had additional significance for its readers because it correlated so well with the notion, in contemporary phenomenological or existential philosophy, that we should recognize that things have their own existence separate from ourselves, their own "being-in-the-world."

The Erasers received the Fénéon Prize in 1954, but was not widely known; it was not until the scandal caused by The Voyeur (1955) that Robbe-Grillet reached a wide audience. Although The Voyeur was awarded the Critics' Prize in 1955, the jury was split between those who believed that it was not a "novel" at all (and was immoral and insane to boot) and those who admired its formal innovations. Mathias, the "voyeur" of the title, is a traveling watch salesman who may or may not have murdered a young girl during a sales trip on an island. The reader must piece together a version of what happened from a fragmented time span during which Mathias neglects to describe certain crucial hours, from actions and anxieties that suggest a guilty conscience, from a schizophrenic crisis when the crime is described in a café, and from obsessive erotic imaginings that may be just that—imaginings—or may be traces of the crime.

With the controversy over The Voyeur, Robbe-Grillet and his new mode of writing became the focus of critical debate in France. In Objective Literature, the influential critic Roland Barthes proposed that Robbe-Grillet had discovered a truer "neutral" writing by focusing on objects instead of repeating traditional socially inspired interpretations of reality. In 1955 Robbe-Grillet began a series of articles on modern literature, which he collected in 1963 as For a New Novel. The term new novel became popular; and although not all those described as "new novelists" wrote in the same way, they all rejected the traditional novel's assumption of a core of meaning—with a logically developing plot and psychologically consistent characters—that claimed to reflect a similar core of meaning in society. His next two novels, Jealousy (1957) and In the Labyrinth(1959), as well as the separate short pieces collected in Snapshots (1962), exploit the ideas developed in these articles, seeking patterns of potential meaning behind extended, objective description. In 1959 he temporarily abandoned novels to experiment with films, writing the script for Last Year at Marienbad (1961, filmed by Alain Resnais) and writing and directing The Immortal One (1963). Films, like novels, allowed Robbe-Grillet to manipulate visions of reality as he insistently focused on surfaces and shapes, presented different versions of the same scene, composed a sound track that contradicted or commented on photographed action and—in recent works—challenged his own imagination by including unexpected incidents that occurred on location. Robbe-Grillet published the scenarios of Last Year at Marienbad and The Immortal One, and a more documentary account of The Progressing Slippages of Pleasure (1974), as ciné-romans, which represent his pluralistic, decentered view of reality in audiovisual as well as verbal form.

Novels up to and including In the Labyrinth could still be interpreted as the subterranean story of a single protagonist. Later novels eliminated that anchoring center to display the presence of many centers—each a competing version of reality. Here emphasis is on the writer's freedom to create different and even mutually contradictory worlds and on the readers' freedom to choose and arrange their own version of events. Some passages do not really fit into any of the story lines; the action progresses according to the suggestions of wordplay or verbal echoes; the same narrative persona may appear grammatically as "he" or "she"; or books are composed in collage fashion. Robbe-Grillet has been taught in the classroom for many years as a master of formal experimentation and only recently challenged on the quarantined atmosphere and obsessive sadism of his work. Women, for example, are repeatedly victimized, and terror and death are constant themes. Uncomfortable, perhaps, at this change in critical perspective, he has justified sadistic fantasies in his work partly as reflecting popular themes in a correspondingly sadistic and dehumanized world and partly as the therapeutic expression of his own obsessions (therapeutic for Robbe-Grillet because they are brought to a conscious level and thereby subject to change).

Therapeutic or not, there is no mistaking the basic images of Robbe-Grillet's world or the disturbing angles from which they are presented. *The Secret Room,* reprinted here from *Snapshots,* arranges in an artistic homage to the Symbolist painter Gustave Moreau (1826–1898) many of Robbe-Grillet's most obsessive images: the spreading bloodstain; the young woman stretched out erotically in chains and stabbed under the left breast; the ascending staircase; the different points of view directed down on the victim; the mysterious, anonymous criminal; and even the S shape of smoke coiling upward from the incense burner. The scene is bound to shock for its overt sadism, for the artistic savoring of human sacrifice, and for the erotic pleasure it suggests in female victimization. It would not be appropriate to ignore or repress this response, for the subject matter is not neutral or intended as such. Robbe-Grillet has presented an additional challenge, however, by insisting on the stylized *unreality* of the scene and by displacing the reader's attention to the technical triumph in which verbal art emulates a painterly style. The text imitates the Oriental luxury and morbid eroticism of a famous painter so convincingly that one could almost name the artist even without the dedication. Yet this verbal art goes beyond its painterly model when Robbe-Grillet adds to it the passage of time, thus bringing a strange life to the subject seen paradoxically both as a finished canvas and as recreated stages of the same murderous event. It is a bizarre and disturbing scene, made to unsettle readers who try to reconcile its various aspects: its manipulation of stereotypes of the victimized woman, the horror of the helpless sacrifice, and an alienated perspective that is attributed to art but at the same time suggests sadistic impersonality.

Ilona Leki, *Alain Robbe-Grillet* (1983), is a good biography and survey of Robbe-Grillet's work in historical context, discussing each work up to 1983, with a last chapter on the films. The author's introductory essays in Alain Robbe-Grillet, *Two Novels* (1993, 1965), discuss his descriptive strategies. Bruce Morrissette, *The Novels of Robbe-Grillet* (1975), provides a valuable critical study that takes the works and films before 1975 in chronological order. Morrissette, *Novel and Film: Essays in Two Genres* (1985), makes Robbe-Grillet the chief example in a discussion of modern cinematic vision. Ben Stoltzfus, *Alain Robbe-Grillet and the New French Novel* (1964), is an early introduction to Robbe-Grillet in the context of existentialism and the emerging new novel form. Raylene L. Ramsay, *Robbe-Grillet and Modernity: Science, Sexuality, and Subversion* (1992), interrogates contemporary culture and the thematics of sexual violence. Roch Charles Smith, *Understanding Alain Robbe-Grillet* (2000), is an analytic overview of Robbe-Grillet's work from the early narratives (such as *Snapshots*) to the latest novels and films; it includes a chronology to 1998 and an annotated bibliography.

PRONOUNCING GLOSSARY

The following list uses common English syllables and stress accents to provide rough equivalents of selected words whose pronunciation may be unfamiliar to the general reader.

Alain Robbe-Grillet: *ah-lanh' rob—gree-   yay'*   Gustave Moreau: *gyew-stahv' mor-oh'*

The Secret Room[1]

To Gustave Moreau[2]

The first thing to be seen is a red stain, of a deep, dark, shiny red, with almost black shadows. It is in the form of an irregular rosette, sharply outlined, extending in several directions in wide outflows of unequal length, dividing and dwindling afterward into single sinuous streaks. The whole stands out against a smooth, pale surface, round in shape, at once dull and pearly, a hemisphere joined by gentle curves to an expanse of the same pale color—white darkened by the shadowy quality of the place: a dungeon, a sunken room, or a cathedral—glowing with a diffused brilliance in the semidarkness.

Farther back, the space is filled with the cylindrical trunks of columns, repeated with progressive vagueness in their retreat toward the beginning of a vast stone stairway, turning slightly as it rises, growing narrower and narrower as it approaches the high vaults where it disappears.

The whole setting is empty, stairway and colonnades. Alone, in the foreground, the stretched-out body gleams feebly, marked with the red stain—a white body whose full, supple flesh can be sensed, fragile, no doubt, and vulnerable. Alongside the bloody hemisphere another identical round form, this one intact, is seen at almost the same angle of view; but the haloed point at its summit, of darker tint, is in this case quite recognizable, whereas the other one is entirely destroyed, or at least covered by the wound.

In the background, near the top of the stairway, a black silhouette is seen fleeing, a man wrapped in a long, floating cape, ascending the last steps without turning around, his deed accomplished. A thin smoke rises in twisting scrolls from a sort of incense burner placed on a high stand of ironwork with a silvery glint. Nearby lies the milkwhite body, with wide streaks of blood running from the left breast, along the flank and on the hip.

It is a fully rounded woman's body, but not heavy, completely nude, lying on its back, the bust raised up somewhat by thick cushions thrown down on the floor, which is covered with Oriental rugs. The waist is very narrow, the neck long and thin, curved to one side, the head thrown back into a darker area where, even so, the facial features may be discerned, the partly opened mouth, the wide-staring eyes, shining with a fixed brilliance, and the mass of long, black hair spread out in a complicated wavy disorder over a heavily folded cloth, of velvet perhaps, on which also rest the arm and shoulder.

It is a uniformly colored velvet of dark purple, or which seems so in this lighting. But purple, brown, blue also seem to dominate in the colors of the cushions—only a small portion of which is hidden beneath the velvet cloth, and which protrude noticeably, lower down, beneath the bust and waist—as well as in the Oriental patterns of the rugs on the floor. Farther on, these same colors are picked up again in the stone of the paving and the columns, and vaulted archways, the stairs, and the less discernible surfaces that disappear into the farthest reaches of the room.

The dimensions of this room are difficult to determine exactly; the body of the young sacrificial victim seems at first glance to occupy a substantial portion of it, but the vast size of the stairway leading down to it would imply

---

1. Translated by Bruce Morrissette.   2. French Symbolist painter (1826–1898), known for exotic, luminous scenes with subtly erotic and morbid overtones, such as *The Death of Darius* and *Dance of Salome*.

rather that this is not the whole room, whose considerable space must in reality extend all around, right and left, as it does toward the faraway browns and blues among the columns standing in line, in every direction, perhaps toward other sofas, thick carpets, piles of cushions and fabrics, other tortured bodies, other incense burners.

It is also difficult to say where the light comes from. No clue, on the columns or on the floor, suggests the direction of the rays. Nor is any window or torch visible. The milkwhite body itself seems to light the scene, with its full breasts, the curve of its thighs, the rounded belly, the full buttocks, the stretched-out legs, widely spread, and the black tuft of the exposed sex, provocative, proffered, useless now.

The man has already moved several steps back. He is now on the first steps of the stairs, ready to go up. The bottom steps are wide and deep, like the steps leading up to some great building, a temple or theater; they grow smaller as they ascend, and at the same time describe a wide, helical curve, so gradually that the stairway has not yet made a half-turn by the time it disappears near the top of the vaults, reduced then to a steep, narrow flight of steps without handrail, vaguely outlined, moreover, in the thickening darkness beyond.

But the man does not look in this direction, where his movement nonetheless carries him; his left foot on the second step and his right foot already touching the third, with his knee bent, he has turned around to look at the spectacle for one last time. The long, floating cape thrown hastily over his shoulders, clasped in one hand at his waist, has been whirled around by the rapid circular motion that has just caused his head and chest to turn in the opposite direction, and a corner of the cloth remains suspended in the air as if blown by a gust of wind; this corner, twisting around upon itself in the form of a loose S, reveals the red silk lining with its gold embroidery.

The man's features are impassive, but tense, as if in expectation—or perhaps fear—of some sudden event, or surveying with one last glance the total immobility of the scene. Though he is looking backward, his whole body is turned slightly forward, as if he were continuing up the stairs. His right arm—not the one holding the edge of the cape—is bent sharply toward the left, toward a point in space where the balustrade should be, if this stairway had one, an interrupted gesture, almost incomprehensible, unless it arose from an instinctive movement to grasp the absent support.

As to the direction of his glance, it is certainly aimed at the body of the victim lying on the cushions, its extended members stretched out in the form of a cross, its bust raised up, its head thrown back. But the face is perhaps hidden from the man's eyes by one of the columns, standing at the foot of the stairs. The young woman's right hand touches the floor just at the foot of this column. The fragile wrist is encircled by an iron bracelet. The arm is almost in darkness, only the hand receiving enough light to make the thin, outspread fingers clearly visible against the circular protrusion at the base of the stone column. A black metal chain running around the column passes through a ring affixed to the bracelet, binding the wrist tightly to the column.

At the top of the arm a rounded shoulder, raised up by the cushions, also stands out well lighted, as well as the neck, the throat, and the other shoulder, the armpit with its soft hair, the left arm likewise pulled back with its wrist bound in the same manner to the base of another column, in the extreme foreground; here the iron bracelet and the chain are fully displayed, represented with perfect clarity down to the slightest details.

The same is true, still in the foreground but at the other side, for a similar chain, but not quite as thick, wound directly around the ankle, running twice around the column and terminating in a heavy iron embedded in the floor. About a yard farther back, or perhaps slightly farther, the right foot is identically chained. But it is the left foot, and its chain, that are the most minutely depicted.

The foot is small, delicate, finely modeled. In several places the chain has broken the skin, causing noticeable if not extensive depressions in the flesh. The chain links are oval, thick, the size of an eye. The ring in the floor resembles those used to attach horses; it lies almost touching the stone pavement to which it is riveted by a massive iron peg. A few inches away is the edge of a rug; it is grossly wrinkled at this point, doubtless as a result of the convulsive, but necessarily very restricted, movements of the victim attempting to struggle.

The man is still standing about a yard away, half leaning over her. He looks at her face, seen upside down, her dark eyes made larger by their surrounding eyeshadow, her mouth wide open as if screaming. The man's posture allows his face to be seen only in a vague profile, but one senses in it a violent exaltation, despite the rigid attitude, the silence, the immobility. His back is slightly arched. His left hand, the only one visible, holds up at some distance from the body a piece of cloth, some dark-colored piece of clothing, which drags on the carpet, and which must be the long cape with its gold-embroidered lining.

This immense silhouette hides most of the bare flesh over which the red stain, spreading from the globe of the breast, runs in long rivulets that branch out, growing narrower, upon the pale background of the bust and the flank. One thread has reached the armpit and runs in an almost straight, thin line along the arm; others have run down toward the waist and traced out, along one side of the belly, the hip, the top of the thigh, a more random network already starting to congeal. Three or four tiny veins have reached the hollow between the legs, meeting in a sinuous line, touching the point of the V formed by the outspread legs, and disappearing into the black tuft.

Look, now the flesh is still intact: the black tuft and the white belly, the soft curve of the hips, the narrow waist, and, higher up, the pearly breasts rising and falling in time with the rapid breathing, whose rhythm grows more accelerated. The man, close to her, one knee on the floor, leans farther over. The head, with its long, curly hair, which alone is free to move somewhat, turns from side to side, struggling; finally the woman's mouth twists open, while the flesh is torn open, the blood spurts out over the tender skin, stretched tight, the carefully shadowed eyes grow abnormally large, the mouth opens wider, the head twists violently, one last time, from right to left, then more gently, to fall back finally and become still, amid the mass of black hair spread out on the velvet.

Afterward, the whole setting is empty, the enormous room with its purple shadows and its stone columns proliferating in all directions, the monumental staircase with no handrail that twists upward, growing narrower and vaguer as it rises into the darkness, toward the top of the vaults where it disappears.

Near the body, whose wound has stiffened, whose brilliance is already growing dim, the thin smoke from the incense burner traces complicated scrolls in the still air: first a coil turned horizontally to the left, which then straightens out and rises slightly, then returns to the axis of its point of origin, which it crosses as it moves to the right, then turns back in the first direction, only to wind back again, thus forming an irregular sinusoidal[3] curve, more and more flattened out, and rising, vertically, toward the top of the canvas.

3. S-shaped.

YEHUDA AMICHAI
1924–2000

Yehuda Amichai belongs to the first generation of Israeli poets to be fully naturalized into both the language and the landscape of modern Israel. This generation, which came of age with the establishment of the state in 1948, includes such remarkable poets as Nathan Zach, Dalia Ravikovitch, T. Carmi, and Dan Pagis. As a very diverse group, they brought to fruition the dream of preceding generations of Israeli poets, including H. N. Bialik and Saul Tchernikovsky, to create a poetic idiom that was completely at home with the colloquial rhythms and idiomatic expressions of modern Hebrew. The challenge of this task is a function of the unique history of that language. Hebrew was a spoken language only up to the close of the biblical period in the sixth century B.C. For the next 2,500 years, beginning with the exile of the Jews to Babylonia and their long dispersion from the land of Israel and continuing to the present day—a period known as the Diaspora—Hebrew ceased to be a spoken language. During the Diaspora, Hebrew was principally a vehicle for the sacred and the liturgical writings, for biblical and Talmudic discourse, and for official communication, while local Jewish dialects like Yiddish and Ladino served the more immediate function of the vernacular. The movement to modernize medieval Hebrew began in the eighteenth century, and by the late nineteenth century modern Hebrew had established itself as a vigorous literary language. But it was not revived as a spoken language and adapted to the daily needs of ordinary secular life until the early twentieth century, when European Jews emigrated to Palestine with the intention of ending the Diaspora. As an essential element of reestablishing a Jewish state in Palestine, they set about reviving Hebrew as a modern, spoken language.

The long separation of biblical Hebrew from daily life meant that it had not undergone the changes in pronunciation, grammar, syntax, and vocabulary that gradually change living languages over the years. As a result, modern Hebrew is just one step away from the biblical and preserves archaic forms of the language far more fully and immediately than modern Greek and Italian, for instance, preserve classical Greek and Latin. The poets who emerged out of Israel's war for independence in 1948, known collectively as the "Palmach generation," and those who followed them have faced the challenge of reconciling the highly charged spiritual resonance of the biblical language with the worldly concerns of contemporary Israeli society. Amichai, perhaps more than any other contemporary poet, contributed not only to liberating the language of modern Israeli poetry from the great burden of its history but, by juxtaposing the monumental and the ordinary, to appropriating the language of the epic struggles of Israel for the mundane realities of the twentieth century.

At times there is a deceptive simplicity about Amichai's lyrics. They seem to address such ordinary moments, such casual encounters. And yet in their simplicity they capture the many, resonating layers of the language and the insistent and contradictory realities of contemporary Israeli life. His language is despairing, gently ironic, playful and passionate by turns, moving easily between a child's artlessness and the brusque directness of a war-hardened veteran. The scope of his poetry is enormous, but what he brings to each poem is a freshness of vision and metaphors that are rich in unexpected and illuminating juxtapositions—Rachel's tomb and Herzl's tomb, drying laundry and entrenched enmities, stones and undelivered messages, a lost child and a lost kid, the weariness of the poet who sees soldiers carried home from the hills like so much small change. These metaphors that thrust the deeply historical into the arms of the grittily immediate inspired critics to compare Amichai not with his contemporaries but with Donne and Shakespeare.

Amichai's form of choice was the short lyric, but he composed at least one memorable narrative poem, *The Travels of the Last Benjamin of Tudela,* and he often linked a number of shorter poems into cycles on a single theme, as in the wrenching *Seven Laments for the War Dead* or the romantic *Six Poems for Tamar.* Many of his best poems are love poems, addressed to a woman or to Jerusalem—not as alternatives but as embedded in each others' essence. His poetry evokes with stunning immediacy that ancient city that other peoples and religions besides the Jews know as sacred and claim as home. Jerusalem is "an eternal heart, burning red," the place that must be remembered when all else is forgotten. Until 1967, it was a city divided only by a wall, across which intimate but hostile neighbors could watch each others' laundry drying.

This comfortableness with the language and landscape of Israel may appear surprising in light of the fact that Amichai was born in Würzberg, Germany, and only came to Israel with his family in 1936, when he was twelve. He had grown up in an Orthodox Jewish home and studied Hebrew since early childhood, however, and like so many other immigrants, he made the transition to modern Hebrew with relative ease. Despite the enforced move from Germany, in his poetry he speaks of his childhood as a time of happiness and peace now lost. His adult life began during the turbulent struggle to establish the Jewish state. He served with the Jewish Brigade in World War II and saw active duty as an infantryman with the Palmach during the Israeli War of Independence and with the Israeli army in 1956 and 1973.

After completing his studies at Hebrew University, Amichai became a secondary school teacher of Hebrew literature and the Bible, but his career as a teacher soon took second place to his career as a poet. He had begun writing poetry in 1949 and published his first collection of poems, *Now and in Other Days,* in 1955. With his second collection, *Two Hopes Away* (1958), he established himself as a major poet. From the late 1950s until his death in 2000, Amichai published more than nine more volumes of poetry as well as novels—including the one translated as *Not of This Time, Not of This Place* (1968)—short stories, and plays.

Each volume of Amichai's poetry has sold nearly fifteen thousand copies, and that in a country with a population of only three million. His poems are included in school anthologies and recited on public occasions. In the introduction to *The Selected Poetry of Yehuda Amichai,* Chana Bloch relates an anecdote that gives a more telling sense of the widespread popularity his works enjoy: "Some Israeli students were called up in the 1973 Yom Kippur War. As soon as they were notified, they went back to their rooms at the university, and each packed his gear, a rifle, and a book of Yehuda Amichai's poems." And this, as she points out, despite the fact that his work "isn't patriotic in the ordinary sense of the word, it doesn't cry death to the enemy, and it offers no simple consolation for killing and dying." Amichai was first brought to the attention of British and American readers by Ted Hughes, who published his work first in the journal *Modern Poetry in Translation* and collaborated with Amichai in translating a volume of selections from his early poetry, *Amen* (1977). Eight volumes of his poetry have appeared in English translation, and there are numerous translations into other languages as well.

Glenda Abramson, *The Writing of Yehuda Amichai: A Thematic Approach* (1989), provides a comprehensive overview of Amichai's work. A good sampling of his reviews can be found in *Contemporary Literary Criticism* (vols. 9, 22, and 57) and *Contemporary Authors* (vols. 85–88). Joseph Cohen, *Voices of Israel* (1990), includes a long essay on Amichai as well as an extended interview. Articles by Glenda Abramson, Naomi B. Sokoloff, and Nili Scharf Gold appear in "Amichai at Sixty" (1984), a special issue of *Prooftexts*.

PRONOUNCING GLOSSARY

The following list uses common English syllables and stress accents to provide rough equivalents of selected words whose pronunciation may be unfamiliar to the general reader.

Herzl: *hertz'-ul*

Ladino: *luh-dee'-no*

Palmach: *pall'-muhk*

Tudela: *too-del'uh*

Yehuda Amichai: *yuh-hoo'-duh a'-mi-kai*

If I Forget Thee, Jerusalem[1]

If I forget thee, Jerusalem,
Then let my right be forgotten.[2]
Let my right be forgotten, and my left remember.
Let my left remember, and your right close
And your mouth open near the gate.   5

I shall remember Jerusalem
And forget the forest—my love will remember,
Will open her hair, will close my window,
Will forget my right,
Will forget my left.   10

If the west wind does not come
I'll never forgive the walls,
Or the sea, or myself.
Should my right forget,
My left shall forgive,   15
I shall forget all water,
I shall forget my mother.

If I forget thee, Jerusalem,
Let my blood be forgotten.
I shall touch your forehead,   20
Forget my own,
My voice change
For the second and last time
To the most terrible of voices—
Or silence.   25

---

1. Translated by Assia Gutmann. The title is from Psalm 137:5.   2. Compare Psalm 137.5: "If I forget thee, O Jerusalem, let my right hand forget its cunning."

Of Three or Four in a Room[3]

Of three or four in a room
there is always one who stands beside the window.
He must see the evil among thorns
and the fires on the hill.
And how people who went out of their houses whole   5
are given back in the evening like small change.

Of three or four in a room
there is always one who stands beside the window,
his dark hair above his thoughts.
Behind him, words.   10
And in front of him, voices wandering without a knapsack,
hearts without provisions, prophecies without water,
large stones that have been returned
and stay sealed, like letters that have no
address and no one to receive them.   15

Sleep in Jerusalem[1]

While a chosen people[2]
become a nation like all the nations,
building its houses, paving its highways,
breaking open its earth for pipes and water,
we lie inside, in the low house,   5
late offspring of this old landscape.
The ceiling is vaulted above us with love
and the breath of our mouth
is as it was given us
and as we shall give it back.   10

Sleep is where there are stones.
In Jerusalem there is sleep. The radio
brings day-tunes from a land
where there is day.
And words that here are bitter,   15
like last year's almond on a tree,
are sung in a far country, and sweet.

And like a fire
in the hollowed trunk of an olive tree
an eternal heart is burning red   20
not far from the two sleepers.

3. Translated by Stephen Mitchell.   1. Translated by Harold Schimmel.   2. According to the Old
Testament, God chose Abraham's descendants, the Jews, as the people through whom he would reveal
himself.

God Has Pity on Kindergarten Children[3]

God has pity on kindergarten children.
He has less pity on school children.
And on grownups he has no pity at all,
he leaves them alone,
and sometimes they must crawl on all fours   5
in the burning sand
to reach the first-aid station
covered with blood.

But perhaps he will watch over true lovers
and have mercy on them and shelter them   10
like a tree over the old man
sleeping on a public bench.

Perhaps we too will give them
the last rare coins of compassion
that Mother handed down to us,   15
so that their happiness will protect us
now and in other days.

Jerusalem[1]

On a roof in the Old City[2]
laundry hanging in the late afternoon sunlight:
the white sheet of a woman who is my enemy,
the towel of a man who is my enemy,
to wipe off the sweat of his brow.   5

In the sky of the Old City
a kite.
At the other end of the string,
a child
I can't see   10
because of the wall.

We have put up many flags,
they have put up many flags.
To make us think that they're happy.
To make them think that we're happy.   15

---

3. Translated by Stephen Mitchell.   1. Translated by Stephen Mitchell.   2. The oldest, walled portion of Jerusalem, around which the new city has been built.

Tourists[1]

1

So condolence visits is what they're here for,
sitting around at the Holocaust Memorial, putting on a serious face
at the Wailing Wall,[2]
laughing behind heavy curtains in hotel rooms.

They get themselves photographed with the important dead   5
at Rachel's Tomb and Herzl's Tomb, and up on Ammunition Hill.[3]
They weep at the beautiful prowess of our boys,
lust after our tough girls
and hang up their underwear
to dry quickly   10
in cool blue bathrooms.

2

Once I was sitting on the steps near the gate at David's[4] Citadel and I
put down my two heavy baskets beside me. A group of tourists stood
there around their guide, and I became their point of reference. "You
see that man over there with the baskets? A little to the right of his head
there's an arch from the Roman period. A little to the right of his head."
"But he's moving, he's moving!" I said to myself: Redemption will come
only when they are told, "Do you see that arch over there from the
Roman period? It doesn't matter, but near it, a little to the left and then
down a bit, there's a man who has just bought fruit and vegetables for
his family."

An Arab Shepherd Is Searching for His Goat on Mount Zion[1]

An Arab shepherd is searching for his goat on Mount Zion
and on the opposite mountain I am searching
for my little boy.
An Arab shepherd and a Jewish father
both in their temporary failure.   5
Our voices meet above the Sultan's Pool[2]
in the valley between us. Neither of us wants
the child or the goat to get caught in the wheels
of the terrible *Had Gadya*[3] machine.

Afterward we found them among the bushes   10
and our voices came back inside us, laughing and crying.

---

1. Translated by Chana Bloch.   2. A remnant of the western wall of the second temple in Jerusalem; a
site of pilgrimage, lamentation, and prayer for Jews.   3. The site of a major battle in Israel's War of
Independence. Rachel was the second wife of Jacob and mother of Joseph and Benjamin. Theodor Herzl
(1860–1904), Hungarian-born founder of Zionism.   4. King David (died ca. 962 B.C.), who slew Goliath
and became the second king of Judah and Israel (after Saul); reputed author of many psalms.   1. Translated by Chana Bloch. The fortress of Jerusalem is built on Mt. Zion.   2. Translation of the Hebrew
name for a pool located in the valley just outside the walls of the Old City of Jerusalem.   3. One kid
(Hebrew); alludes to a Passover song in which "the kid that Daddy bought is eaten by a cat that is bitten
by a dog," and so on.

Searching for a goat or a son
has always been the beginning
of a new religion in these mountains.

North of San Francisco[1]

Here the soft hills touch the ocean
like one eternity touching another
and the cows grazing on them
ignore us, like angels.
Even the scent of ripe melon in the cellar   5
is a prophecy of peace.

The darkness doesn't war against the light,
it carries us forward
to another light, and the only pain
is the pain of not staying.   10

In my land, called holy,
they won't let eternity be:
they've divided it into little religions,
zoned it for God-zones,
broken it into fragments of history,   15
sharp and wounding unto death.
And they've turned the tranquil distances
into a nearness twitching with the pain of the present.

On the beach at Bolinas,[2] at the foot of the wooden steps,
I saw some girls lying face-down in the sand   20
naked and unashamed, drunk
on the kingdom everlasting,
their souls like doors
closing and opening,
closing and opening inside them   25
to the rhythm of the surf.

I Passed a House[1]

I passed a house where I once lived:
A man and a woman are still together in the whispers.
Many years have passed with the silent buzz
of staircase bulbs—on, off, on.

The keyholes are like small delicate wounds   5
through which all the blood has oozed out
and inside people are pale as death.

1. Translated by Chana Bloch.   2. A small town north of San Francisco.   1. Translated by Yehuda
Amichai and Ted Hughes.

I want to stand once more as in my
first love, leaning on the doorpost
embracing you all night long, standing.   10
When we left at early dusk the house
started to crumble and collapse
and since then the town
and since then the whole world.

I want once more to have this longing   15
until dark-red burn marks show on the skin.

I want once more to be written
in the book of life, to be written
anew every day
until the writing hand hurts.   20

CLARICE LISPECTOR
1925–1977

Reaching for an apple in the dark, claims Brazilian modernist Clarice Lispector, demonstrates the limits of our knowledge: here, we know only that the object is an apple
and little more. Its color and ripeness remain hidden in obscurity, tantalizingly *there*
and *not there* at the same time. Characters in Lispector's novels and short stories are
similarly open to mystery; they live on a plane of immediate experience and bodily
sensations that has little to do with the daylight world, where everything is already
named and placed within a cognitive or social system. When these characters encounter a conflict between their own experience and social norms, a few try to reinvent
their lives. Most do not change, and their example defamiliarizes, for the reader, the
conventional patterns of everyday life. Lispector's protagonists are often women, and
she readily explores the existence of those whose position on the margins of society
suggest an alternative vision. A pivotal figure in modern Brazilian literature, she
employs a simple vocabulary but an unusual syntax in Portuguese, and makes
extended use of interior monologues to evoke the immediacy of subjective consciousness. Lispector is internationally known for her descriptions of psychological states
of mind and for a language whose elliptical allusions suggest the power of unspoken
circumstances in shaping human identity.

She was born in December 1925 in Tchetchelik, a small town in Ukraine, as her
parents—Russian Jewish immigrants—made the long trip to a new home in Brazil.
The family arrived in Brazil when she was two months old and later settled in Recife,
capital of the northeastern state of Pernambuco, where Lispector received her early
schooling. A precocious child, she began composing short stories at seven and a play
about love (in three acts and four pages) at nine. These were happy years, but the
family was poor and they moved to Rio de Janeiro, then the capital of Brazil, in hopes
of bettering their circumstances. Lispector was by then a voracious reader and had
already decided to become a writer; she was particularly impressed by the novelists
Fyodor Dostoevsky and Hermann Hesse, and the short-story writer Katherine Mansfield. In 1937, the budding author finished secondary school and published her first
story. Entering law school in 1941, she also took a job working as editor and interviewer at the news agency Agência Nacional. Here she met many young writers as
well as the established novelist Lúcio Cardoso, who advised her and took an interest

in her work. The law degree she received in 1944 served as general education rather than as preparation for a career, for in 1942 she had become the first woman reporter at *A Noite*, a major newspaper whose diverse assignments enriched her understanding of people and society and gave her new impetus for writing. Around this time, perhaps influenced by her work as a reporter, she began to develop a unique system of writing that would remain with her throughout her career and impart a specific, recognizable stamp to her fiction. Lispector wrote down notes during the day, and then—instead of abandoning them as preliminary jottings for a another, different work—developed and refined them until they became integral parts of the final text. Her first novel, *Close to the Savage Heart* (the title taken from a line in Joyce's *Portrait of the Artist as a Young Man*), published in 1944, won her the Graça Aranha Prize and a reputation as an important and innovative young Brazilian writer. She was nineteen years old.

Over the next fifteen years, she traveled widely with her husband, a diplomat whom she had married when they were both in law school. They lived in Italy, Switzerland, and England before moving to the United States and Washington, D.C., in 1952. During this period, she published two novels, *The Chandelier* (1946) and *The Besieged City* (1949), and her first short-story collection, *Some Stories* (1952). All display the same preoccupation with her characters' psychological states and with questions of authentic being (the latter theme strengthened when she read the existentialist fiction of French philosopher Jean-Paul Sartre in 1946). Seven years after her arrival in Washington, Lispector separated from her husband and returned to Rio with her two young sons; she would stay there for the rest of her life.

She had not published anything during the long stay in Washington but kept writing notes in her characteristic manner. Once again in Rio, she made use of those notes to compose her best-known short-story collection, *Family Ties* (1960), which won the Jabuti Prize and from which our selection is taken, and a novel with existential and symbolic themes, *Apple in the Dark* (1961), which won the Cármen Dolores Barbosa Prize. Both books were praised for the innovative use of syntax to capture states of mind; the novel, in addition, formally links philosophical inquiry to the exploration of language and thus foreshadows themes in later works. Martim, the protagonist of *Apple in the Dark*, flees after trying to murder his wife; seeking freedom, he interrogates his sense of self, the nature of existence, and finally language's ability to convey knowledge of existence. At first he abandons his individual identity and sinks into pure being: "like a plant he was aware of himself and of the world—with that same delicate tension with which a weed is a plant down to its last extremities"; and later, "Absurdity enveloped the man, logical, magnificent, horrible, perfect—darkness enveloped him." By the end of the novel, Martim has reached a kind of knowledge that goes beyond rational categories, and is symbolized by the image of an apple in the dark: his groping fingers recognize it for an apple, but the dark also prevents him from knowing it completely. "Martim no longer asked for the name of things. It was enough for him to recognize them in the dark" and to know that their daylight names are false.

Lispector published novels, short stories, chronicles (nonfiction pieces), and children's tales during the fifteen years before her death. She further developed the existential themes of *Apple in the Dark* in a short novel, *The Passion According to G. H.* (1964), this time eschewing dialogue and adopting the point of view of a woman, G. H., who starts her voyage to self-discovery by meditating on the body of a cockroach she has just crushed. The unnamed female protagonist of another novel, the lyrical *Stream of Life* (1973), works through similar questions of personal identity, reality, and language in a long introspective letter addressed to her lover. Lispector's third collection of short stories, *The Foreign Legion*, appeared in 1964 and included, for the first time, chronicles and remarks about her own writing. Other novels and collections followed, of which the best known are the novel *The Hour of the Star* (1977; adapted for film in 1986) and the stories and chronicles included in *The Cross Way of the Flesh* (1974) and *Where Were You at Night?* (1974). Two years before her death, she published two collections of nonfiction pieces and interviews, *Sound of Body* and *Vision of Splendor,* the latter containing various essays that discuss literature and her own writing.

In 1967, at the request of her fourteen-year-old son, she began writing children's tales. Fables that include chickens, rabbits, and her pet dog Ulisse as narrator, these tales are written for adult readers as well as children and seem to comment on the military dictatorship that took over the government in 1964. Thus, *The Mystery of the Thinking Rabbit* (1967) describes a pet rabbit who, escaping from his cage, acquires a taste for freedom and thereupon becomes a thinking rabbit; and *Almost True* (1978) tells of the animals' revolt against a tyrannical and unproductive fig tree that takes away their food and civil rights. Although Lispector's fictional world is generally focused on interior struggles rather than external or political realities, she raises social issues in various chronicles and newspaper columns, and demonstrated in the 1960s and 1970s in support of political and artistic freedoms. In fact, as she commented in 1975, "I feel myself 'engaged.' Everything I write is connected, at least inside of me, to the reality in which we live." Her last novel, *The Hour of the Star,* attempts to make this connection between internal and external reality more visible. On the one hand, it pushes even further the exploration of writing and knowledge, for the fictional narrator, Rodrigo S.M., is writing about writing this same novel and treats both his reader ("you") and his characters as real people. On the other hand, Rodrigo S.M. has chosen to write about the inner life of a poor, exploited typist named Macabea, and concurrently about a real social problem: the miserable life of poverty-stricken immigrants to the city from northeastern Brazil. The National Cultural Foundation honored Lispector in 1976 for her contributions to Brazilian literature; by then her work had been translated into French, German, and English, and her reputation as a major modernist writer was established in many other countries as well. She died of cancer on December 9, 1977.

Lispector is best known as a writer of intense, tightly structured short stories that portray the external world through a character's innermost thoughts and feelings, and that explore sensual perceptions to gain an intuitive knowledge beyond words. In this respect, she has often been compared with Virginia Woolf, although other aspects of their writing (for example, Lispector's emphasis on the body and on extended meta-physical speculation) distinguish the two writers from each other. The Brazilian author's unique contribution to literary modernism may well lie in her ability to draw connections between bodily sensations, the limits of language, and a sustained inquiry into being—and to make these connections the unifying structure of her work. Her fluid, lyrical style has been called a "feminine writing" insofar as it explores the rela-tionship of immediate bodily experience to language and concepts of being. The term "feminine writing" is not restricted to women, however; instead, it implies an explor-atory, sensuously self-reflexive style that challenges the narrowness of dominant ways of looking at the world. When narration is reduced to the most basic bodily sensations, its refusal of further literary and social constructions disrupts both conventional mod-els of prose fiction and the evaluative hierarchies of organized society.

Daydreams of a Drunk Woman is such a disruptive tale. The title disposes of the protagonist in a few words: she is an alcoholic, and she imagines things. (The *rapariga* [young woman] of the original title suggests, in addition, that she is promiscuous and possibly of poor immigrant stock; the term means "young woman" in Portugal, but is less used in Brazilian Portuguese, where it often connotes promiscuity.) These descriptions are confirmed in the course of the story, which, over two and a half days, shows the woman sleeping all day in bed, fantasizing a romantic encounter, imagining doing housework (always postponed), getting drunk at home and in a restaurant, and flying into alcoholic rages and self-pity. The situation does not change, and the end finds her exclaiming, in a self-indulgent, humorous accusation, "you slut!"

Yet the story reveals a great deal more about this woman. Sequences of brilliant images and obliquely conveyed information suggest other dimensions to her life: the reasons for her misery and repressed rage, the choices that she has made to become secure and protected, and, by indirection, the flaws in a society that encourages such pathetic careers. From the beginning, when she stares at her reflection in the triple mirror and sees "the intersected breasts of several women," her identity appears fragmented, a self-image either in pieces or swollen and unreachable. Repeatedly congratulating herself on being "protected like everyone who had attained a position in life," and viciously criticizing a more fashionable woman in the restaurant, she reveals that she has reached this position, and escaped poverty, by using her body to marry a man she neither loves nor respects. A repressed understanding of what she has done surfaces in obsessive themes of sexual encounters, social position, security and protection, escape from misery, and, above all, her "pretty and plump" body, which metamorphoses, in her drunken vision, into something grotesquely large and out of control. While in the restaurant, dizzy with too much wine, she is upset when basic distinctions between people and things begin to blur: "the soup tureen on the one hand, the waiter on the other—became strangely linked by their true nature." Moreover, if categories blur, the absolute separation between creatures tragically does not, "as if the one might never be able to converse with the other." The existential dilemma that the drunk woman experiences and half-understands emerges from Lispector's prose along with a devastatingly detailed picture of the woman in all her day-to-day delusions, unhappiness, and destructive relationships.

Earl E. Fitz, *Clarice Lispector* (1985), is a valuable introduction to her life and work, and contains an annotated bibliography. A section on Lispector is included *The Voyage In: Fictions of Female Development*, edited by Elizabeth Abel, Marianne Hirsch, and Elizabeth Longland (1983). Hélène Cixous, *Reading with Clarice Lispector*, edited, translated, and introduced by Verena Andermatt Conley (1990), discusses Lispector's style with reference to three stories and three novels. Recent studies include Marta Peixoto, *Passionate Fictions: Gender, Narrative, and Violence in Clarice Lispector* (1994), and Maria José Somerlate Barbosa, *Clarice Lispector: Spinning the Webs of Passion* (1997).

PRONOUNCING GLOSSARY

The following list uses common English syllables and stress accents to provide rough equivalents of selected words whose pronunciation may be unfamiliar to the general reader.

Jacarepaguá: *zhah-kah-reh-pah-gwah'*

Maria Quiteria: *mah-ree'-ah kee-tehr'-yah*

Mem de Sá: *mayn de sah*

Minho: *meen'-yoh*

Riachuelo: *hree-ah-shoo-ay'-loh*

Tiradentes: *chee-rah-dayn'-chees*

The Daydreams of a Drunk Woman[1]

It seemed to her that the trolley cars were about to cross through the room as they caused her reflected image to tremble. She was combing her hair at her leisure in front of the dressing table with its three mirrors, and her strong white arms shivered in the coolness of the evening. Her eyes did not look away as the mirrors trembled, sometimes dark, sometimes luminous. Outside, from a window above, something heavy and hollow fell to the ground. Had her husband and the little ones been at home, the idea would already have occurred to her that they were to blame. Her eyes did not take them-

---

1. Translated by Giovanni Pontiero.

selves off her image, her comb worked pensively, and her open dressing gown revealed in the mirrors the intersected breasts of several women.

"Evening News" shouted the newsboy to the mild breeze in Riachuelo Street,[2] and something trembled as if foretold. She threw her comb down on the dressing table and sang dreamily: "Who saw the little spar-row . . . it passed by the window . . . and flew beyond Minho!"[3]—but, suddenly becoming irritated, she shut up abruptly like a fan.

She lay down and fanned herself impatiently with a newspaper that rustled in the room. She clutched the bedsheet, inhaling its odor as she crushed its starched embroidery with her red-lacquered nails. Then, almost smiling, she started to fan herself once more. Oh my!—she sighed as she began to smile. She beheld the picture of her bright smile, the smile of a woman who was still young, and she continued to smile to herself, closing her eyes and fanning herself still more vigorously. Oh my!—she would come fluttering in from the street like a butterfly.

"Hey there! Guess who came to see me today?" she mused as a feasible and interesting topic of conversation. "No idea, tell me," those eyes asked her with a gallant smile, those sad eyes set in one of those pale faces that make one feel so uncomfortable. "Maria Quiteria, my dear!" she replied coquettishly with her hand on her hip. "And who, might we ask, would she be?" they insisted gallantly, but now without any expression. "You!" she broke off, slightly annoyed. How boring!

Oh what a succulent room! Here she was, fanning herself in Brazil. The sun, trapped in the blinds, shimmered on the wall like the strings of a guitar. Riachuelo Street shook under the gasping weight of the trolley cars which came from Mem de Sá Street. Curious and impatient, she listened to the vibrations of the china cabinet in the drawing room. Impatiently she rolled over to lie face downward, and, sensuously stretching the toes of her dainty feet, she awaited her next thought with open eyes. "Whosoever found, searched," she said to herself in the form of a rhymed refrain, which always ended up by sounding like some maxim. Until eventually she fell asleep with her mouth wide open, her saliva staining the pillow.

She only woke up when her husband came into the room the moment he returned from work. She did not want to eat any dinner nor to abandon her dreams, and she went back to sleep: let him content himself with the leftovers from lunch.

And now that the kids were at the country house of their aunts in Jacarepaguá,[4] she took advantage of their absence in order to begin the day as she pleased: restless and frivolous in her bed . . . one of those whims perhaps. Her husband appeared before her, having already dressed, and she did not even know what he had prepared for his breakfast. She avoided examining his suit to see whether it needed brushing . . . little did she care if this was his day for attending to his business in the city. But when he bent over to kiss her, her capriciousness crackled like a dry leaf.

"Don't paw me!"

<hr/>

2. A street in Rio de Janeiro that intersects with Mem de Sá Street. Riachuelo is the name of a large department store; Mem de Sá was a sixteenth-century Portuguese governor-general of Brazil and the founder of Rio de Janeiro.   3. A river in northwest Portugal.   4. A quiet neighborhood in Rio de Janeiro with a beach where families would gather to picnic.

"What the devil's the matter with you?" the man asked her in amazement, as he immediately set about attempting some more effective caress.

Obstinate, she would not have known what to reply, and she felt so touchy and aloof that she did not even know where to find a suitable reply. She suddenly lost her temper. "Go to hell! . . . prowling round me like some old tomcat."

He seemed to think more clearly and said, firmly, "You're ill, my girl."

She accepted his remark, surprised, and vaguely flattered.

She remained in bed the whole day long listening to the silence of the house without the scurrying of the kids, without her husband who would have his meals in the city today. Her anger was tenuous and ardent. She only got up to go to the bathroom, from which she returned haughty and offended.

The morning turned into a long enormous afternoon, which then turned into a shallow night, which innocently dawned throughout the entire house.

She was still in bed, peaceful and casual. She was in love. . . . She was anticipating her love for the man whom she would love one day. Who knows, this sometimes happened, and without any guilt or injury for either partner. Lying in bed thinking and thinking, and almost laughing as one does over some gossip. Thinking and thinking. About what? As if she knew. So she just stayed there.

The next minute she would get up, angry. But in the weakness of that first instant she felt dizzy and fragile in the room which swam round and round until she managed to grope her way back to bed, amazed that it might be true. "Hey, girl, don't you go getting sick on me!" she muttered suspiciously. She raised her hand to her forehead to see if there was any fever.

That night, until she fell asleep, her mind became more and more delirious—for how many minutes?—until she flopped over, fast asleep, to snore beside her husband.

She awoke late, the potatoes waiting to be peeled, the kids expected home that same evening from their visit to the country. "God, I've lost my self-respect, I have! My day for washing and darning socks. . . . What a lazy bitch you've turned out to be!" she scolded herself, inquisitive and pleased . . . shopping to be done, fish to remember, already so late on a hectic sunny morning.

But on Saturday night they went to the tavern in Tiradentes Square[5] at the invitation of a rich businessman, she with her new dress which didn't have any fancy trimmings but was made of good material, a dress that would last her a lifetime. On Saturday night, drunk in Tiradentes Square, inebriated but with her husband at her side to give her support, and being very polite in front of the other man who was so much more refined and rich—striving to make conversation, for she was no provincial ninny and she had already experienced life in the capital. But so drunk that she could no longer stand.

And if her husband was not drunk it was only because he did not want to show disrespect for the businessman, and, full of solicitude and humility, he left the swaggering to the other fellow. His manner suited such an elegant occasion, but it gave her such an urge to laugh! She despised him beyond

5. A square in Rio de Janeiro named after the Brazilian revolutionary patriot; he was executed by the Portuguese in 1792.

words! She looked at her husband stuffed into his new suit and found him so ridiculous . . . so drunk that she could no longer stand, but without losing her self-respect as a woman. And the green wine[6] from her native Portugal slowly being drained from her glass.

When she got drunk, as if she had eaten a heavy Sunday lunch, all things which by their true nature are separate from each other—the smell of oil on the one hand, of a male on the other; the soup tureen on the one hand, the waiter on the other—became strangely linked by their true nature and the whole thing was nothing short of disgraceful . . . shocking!

And if her eyes appeared brilliant and cold, if her movements faltered clumsily until she succeeded in reaching the toothpick holder, beneath the surface she really felt so far quite at ease . . . there was that full cloud to transport her without effort. Her puffy lips, her teeth white, and her body swollen with wine. And the vanity of feeling drunk, making her show such disdain for everything, making her feel swollen and rotund like a large cow.

Naturally she talked, since she lacked neither the ability to converse nor topics to discuss. But the words that a woman uttered when drunk were like being pregnant—mere words on her lips which had nothing to do with the secret core that seemed like a pregnancy. God, how queer she felt! Saturday night, her every-day soul lost, and how satisfying to lose it, and to remind her of former days, only her small, ill-kempt hands—and here she was now with her elbows resting on the white and red checked tablecloth like a gambling table, deeply launched upon a degrading and revolting existence. And what about her laughter? . . . this outburst of laughter which mysteriously emerged from her full white throat, in response to the polite manners of the businessman, an outburst of laughter coming from the depths of that sleep, and from the depths of that security of someone who has a body. Her white flesh was as sweet as lobster, the legs of a live lobster wriggling slowly in the air . . . that urge to be sick in order to plunge that sweetness into something really awful . . . and that perversity of someone who has a body.

She talked and listened with curiosity to what she herself was about to reply to the well-to-do businessman who had so kindly invited them out to dinner and paid for their meal. Intrigued and amazed, she heard what she was on the point of replying, and what she might say in her present state would serve as an augury for the future. She was no longer a lobster, but a harsher sign—that of the scorpion. After all, she had been born in November.

A beacon that sweeps through the dawn while one is asleep, such was her drunkenness which floated slowly through the air.

At the same time, she was conscious of such feelings! Such feelings! When she gazed upon that picture which was so beautifully painted in the restaurant, she was immediately overcome by an artistic sensibility. No one would get it out of her head that she had really been born for greater things. She had always been one for works of art.

But such sensibility! And not merely excited by the picture of grapes and pears and dead fish with shining scales. Her sensibility irritated her without causing her pain, like a broken fingernail. And if she wanted, she could allow herself the luxury of becoming even more sensitive, she could go still further,

---

6. *Vinho Verde*, literally "green wine," is a soft wine produced in Portugal and often drunk cold before meals.

because she was protected by a situation, protected like everyone who had attained a position in life. Like someone saved from misfortune. I'm so miserable, dear God! If she wished, she could even pour more wine into her glass, and, protected by the position which she had attained in life, become even more drunk just so long as she did not lose her self-respect. And so, even more drunk, she peered round the room, and how she despised the barren people in that restaurant. Not a real man among them. How sad it really all seemed. How she despised the barren people in that restaurant, while she was plump and heavy and generous to the full. And everything in the restaurant seemed so remote, the one thing distant from the other, as if the one might never be able to converse with the other. Each existing for itself, and God existing there for everyone.

Her eyes once more settled on that female whom she had instantly detested the moment she had entered the room. Upon arriving, she had spotted her seated at a table accompanied by a man and all dolled up in a hat and jewelry, glittering like a false coin, all coy and refined. What a fine hat she was wearing! . . . Bet you anything she isn't even married for all that pious look on her face . . . and that fine hat stuck on her head. A fat lot of good her hypocrisy would do her, and she had better watch out in case her airs and graces proved her undoing! The more sanctimonious they were, the bigger frauds they turned out to be. And as for the waiter, he was a great nitwit, serving her, full of gestures and finesse, while the sallow man with her pretended not to notice. And that pious ninny so pleased with herself in that hat and so modest about her slim waistline, and I'll bet she couldn't even bear her man a child. All right, it was none of her business, but from the moment she arrived she felt the urge to give that blonde prude of a woman playing the grand lady in her hat a few good slaps on the face. She didn't even have any shape, and she was flat-chested. And no doubt, for all her fine hats, she was nothing more than a fishwife trying to pass herself off as a duchess.

Oh, how humiliated she felt at having come to the bar without a hat, and her head now felt bare. And that madam with her affectations, playing the refined lady! I know what you need, my beauty, you and your sallow boy friend! And if you think I envy you with your flat chest, let me assure you that I don't give a damn for you and your hats. Shameless sluts like you are only asking for a good hard slap on the face.

In her holy rage, she stretched out a shaky hand and reached for a toothpick.

But finally, the difficulty of arriving home disappeared; she now bestirred herself amidst the familiar reality of her room, now seated on the edge of the bed, a slipper dangling from one foot.

And, as she had half closed her blurred eyes, everything took on the appearance of flesh, the foot of the bed, the window, the suit her husband had thrown off, and everything became rather painful. Meanwhile, she was becoming larger, more unsteady, swollen and gigantic. If only she could get closer to herself, she would find she was even larger. Each of her arms could be explored by someone who didn't even recognize that they were dealing with an arm, and someone could plunge into each eye and swim around without knowing that it was an eye. And all around her everything was a bit painful. Things of the flesh stricken by nervous twinges. The chilly air had caught her as she had come out of the restaurant.

She was sitting up in bed, resigned and sceptical. And this was nothing yet, God only knew—she was perfectly aware that this was nothing yet. At this moment things were happening to her that would only hurt later and in earnest. When restored to her normal size, her anesthetized body would start to wake up, throbbing, and she would begin to pay for those big meals and drinks. Then, since this would really end up by happening, I might as well open my eyes right now (which she did) and then everything looked smaller and clearer, without her feeling any pain. Everything, deep down, was the same, only smaller and more familiar. She was sitting quite upright in bed, her stomach so full, absorbed and resigned, with the delicacy of one who sits waiting until her partner awakens. "You gorge yourself and I pay the piper," she said sadly, looking at the dainty white toes of her feet. She looked around her, patient and obedient. Ah, words, nothing but words, the objects in the room lined up in the order of words, to form those confused and irksome phrases that he who knows how will read. Boredom . . . such awful boredom. . . . How sickening! How very annoying! When all is said and done, heaven help me—God knows best. What was one to do? How can I describe this thing inside me? Anyhow, God knows best. And to think that she had enjoyed herself so much last night . . . and to think of how nice it all was—a restaurant to her liking—and how she had been seated elegantly at table. At table! The world would exclaim. But she made no reply, drawing herself erect with a bad-tempered click of her tongue . . . irritated . . . "Don't come to me with your endearments" . . . disenchanted, resigned, satiated, married, content, vaguely nauseated.

It was at this moment that she became deaf: one of her senses was missing. She clapped the palm of her hand over her ear, which only made things worse . . . suddenly filling her eardrum with the whirr of an elevator . . . life suddenly becoming loud and magnified in its smallest movements. One of two things: either she was deaf or hearing all too well. She reacted against this new suggestion with a sensation of spite and annoyance, with a sigh of resigned satiety. "Drop dead," she said gently . . . defeated.

"And when in the restaurant . . ." she suddenly recalled when she had been in the restaurant her husband's protector had pressed his foot against hers beneath the table, and above the table his face was watching her. By coincidence or intentionally? The rascal. A fellow, to be frank, who was not unattractive. She shrugged her shoulders.

And when above the roundness of her low-cut dress—right in the middle of Tiradentes Square! she thought, shaking her head incredulously—that fly had settled on her bare bosom. What cheek!

Certain things were good because they were almost nauseating . . . the noise like that of an elevator in her blood, while her husband lay snoring at her side . . . her chubby little children sleeping in the other room, the little villains. Ah, what's wrong with me! she wondered desperately. Have I eaten too much? Heavens above! What *is* wrong with me?

It was unhappiness.

Her toes playing with her slipper . . . the floor not too clean at that spot. "What a slovenly, lazy bitch you've become."

Not tomorrow, because her legs would not be too steady, but the day after tomorrow that house of hers would be a sight worth seeing: she would give it a scouring with soap and water which would get rid of all the dirt! "You mark my words," she threatened in her rage. Ah, she was feeling so well, so strong, as if she still had milk in those firm breasts. When her husband's friend saw her so pretty and plump he had immediately felt respect for her. And when she started to get embarrassed she did not know which way to look. Such misery! What was one to do? Seated on the edge of the bed, blinking in resignation. How well one could see the moon on these summer nights. She leaned over slightly, indifferent and resigned. The moon! How clearly one could see it. The moon high and yellow gliding through the sky, poor thing. Gliding, gliding . . . high up, high up. The moon! Then her vulgarity exploded in a sudden outburst of affection; "you slut", she cried out, laughing.

INGEBORG BACHMANN
1926–1973

Ingeborg Bachmann's reputation as one of the most significant postwar writers in the German language is almost overshadowed by her image as an interpreter of women's experience and a critic of fascism. Winning early fame as a brilliant young poet whose vivid yet philosophical lyrics brought her prize after prize, she abandoned poetry in mid-career to write fiction that would say what "needed to be said" and speak for those who could not speak for themselves. Women in particular became the protagonists of her later work. Bachmann described the complex and frequently unrecognized forces that shape women's social experience and constitute "ways of death" as often as ways of life. Her powerful intellect and gift for precise description fused with a lyric tendency and strong ethical concerns to create a remarkable body of work that has been translated into twenty-two languages and continues to influence contemporary writers.

Bachmann was born on June 25, 1926, in Klagenfurt, a city in southern Austria close to the Italian and Yugoslavian borders. She was the oldest of three children; her father was a teacher and later a school principal, and her mother's family operated a knitwear firm. Although she lived outside Austria for most of her adult life, moving permanently to Rome in 1963, much of her work is dominated by the image of a spiritual "Austria" whose fluctuating borders and multiethnic heritage create a unique view of the world. Several languages are spoken in her home province of Carinthia, and the valley in which she lived had two names, German and Slovene. Austria itself, although politically powerless, was the former center of the multinational Hapsburg Empire and still participated in many cultures. The notion of physical and psychological boundaries permeates all levels of her writing, along with glimpses of an ideal freedom to move beyond artificial frontiers. Bachmann's own experience of political borders was sharpened when the Nazis marched into Klagenfurt in 1938. She was twelve years old, and that moment, she said, marked the end of her childhood. Attending schools in Klagenfurt throughout the war, she graduated in 1944 and studied briefly in Innsbruck and Graz before entering the University of Vienna in 1946.

Bachmann's first story, *The Ferryboat,* was published in 1946; other stories and her first poems appeared over the next few years. While earning recognition as a creative writer, she also pursued a degree in philosophy with minors in psychology and German literature. She prized the analytical philosophy of the Vienna School (proscribed under Hitler) and rejected the "German irrationalism" represented by existential philosopher Martin Heidegger (1889–1976). Her doctoral dissertation (1950) was openly critical in analyzing the reception of Heidegger's philosophy. Three years later she published a major appreciative essay on the Viennese linguistic philosopher Ludwig Wittgenstein (1889–1951). What fascinated her about Wittgenstein was *"his despairing attempt to chart the limits of linguistic expression"* (emphasis in original), an attempt that is paralleled in her own poetry and fiction.

In the years following her doctorate, Bachmann traveled to Paris and London; gave poetry readings; held a series of jobs, ranging from scriptwriter to newspaper correspondent; and began to write in different genres. She worked briefly in the office of the American occupation authorities in Vienna and was a member of the broadcasting group Red/White/Red between 1951 and 1953. For Red/White/Red she wrote a number of radio plays, including adaptations of works by Thomas Wolfe and Louis MacNeice. Her translation of MacNeice's radio script *The Dark Tower* was produced with music by British composer Benjamin Britten, and Bachmann's interest in mixed genres continued after she left Red/White/Red. Her second radio play, *The Cicadas,* was produced in 1954 with music by composer Hans Werner Henze, who later set several of her poems to music. Bachmann collaborated with Henze on other occasions and wrote the libretti for two of his operas as well as a ballet scenario. During the 1950s, she also wrote a novel, *City without a Name,* only to have it rejected by five publishers. Her early reputation was clearly based on the poetry, and recognition came quickly for her extraordinary combination of striking natural images and abstract argument. Addressing the constellation Ursa Major, she began "Great Bear, come down, shaggy night, / cloud-coated beast with the old eyes, star eyes. / Through the thickets your paws break / shimmering with their claws, / star claws." Her first volume, *Mortgaged Time,* appeared in 1953, and in the same year she received the prestigious annual prize awarded by Group 47 (a group of Austrian writers who banded together in 1947 in an effort to establish new directions for German literature). A second collection, *Invocation of the Great Bear,* was published in 1956, by which time she had moved to Rome, published poems in the international poetry journal *Botteghe oscure,* received a second prize, and been the subject of a cover story in the popular German magazine *Der Spiegel.*

Bachmann's work took a sharp turn in the 1960s, so that critics have often spoken of the "two Bachmanns," the first a more hermetic writer aiming at formal beauty, and the second a socially engaged writer of prose who once proclaimed: "I no longer try to make each sentence a work of art. The only thing that matters is what needs to be said." While there is a visible change in emphasis from poetry to prose (her last poem, *No More Delicacies,* was written in 1964 as she began the novel sequence *Ways of Death*), Bachmann's later fiction makes great use of lyrical elements. Unlike Alexander Solzhenitsyn or Naguib Mahfouz, she never attempted to emulate the linear style of the nineteenth-century realist novel. The prose writers who interest her are those who take a modernist perspective on problems of identity, communication, and narrative discourse: Marcel Proust, Italo Svevo (1861–1928), James Joyce, Franz Kafka, Robert Musil (1880–1942), William Faulkner, and Samuel Beckett, all of whom she discussed at length in her 1959–60 lectures *Questions of Contemporary Poetry* at the University of Frankfurt. She related their exploratory style to the problem of the self in modern society, a focus that she adapted to her own circumstances in later work.

Even during the 1950s Bachmann had been concerned with political issues. As "R. K." in Rome, she wrote political articles for a West German newspaper from 1954 to 1955, and she later joined a committee that opposed equipping the German army with atomic weapons. In the 1960s, she wrote a public letter to Simon Wiesenthal that protested reducing the statute of limitations for Nazi war crimes, and she later marched and signed declarations against the Vietnam War. She used her influence with a major publisher to block a translation of Anna Akhmatova's poems by a former leader of the Hitler Youth (she had met Akhmatova in Rome). The change in her writing was not a sudden affirmation of social responsibility, therefore, but a new way of understanding how her writing could be an instrument of social change. Stories such as *Youth in an Austrian Town* and *Among Murderers and Madmen*, from her prize-winning collection, *The Thirtieth Year* (1961), already depicted the historical context of German fascism. Their style, however, is relatively picturesque, their conflicts inner and individual, and their situations symbolic or extraordinary. One story in the collection is narrated by a water nymph; in another, a trial judge breaks down when attempting to ascertain the truth about a defendant who has the same name.

Shifting to broader social themes, Bachmann concentrated on women's experience. Instead of choosing unusual situations, she lingered over the implications of everyday scenes, describing the daily life of Austrian women who were, individually and collectively, victims of a patriarchal society. Readers accustomed to Bachmann's elegantly precise poetry were disconcerted by the presence, in the story collection *Three Paths to the Lake* (1972), of a prosaic "women's literature" that presented not only mundane topics but also rambling narrators and a diffuse awareness. Yet Bachmann's skill was still evident in the way she orchestrated inner references into a structure of cumulative significance, or employed an apparently undisciplined stream of consciousness to reveal repressed thoughts and thought patterns in women who had never been allowed to develop their own voice and identity.

There is a strong link between the writer's earlier preoccupation with fascism and her later studies of women. Fascism must begin somewhere, she said, before it becomes a political movement and an agent of mass destruction. She located the principles of fascism—the oppression of the weak and a sadistic desire for dominance and control—uncomfortably close to home, in the subordination of women by men. "Fascism is the first thing in the relationship between a man and a woman," she declared in an interview. Such repression permeates society in many forms. Bachmann's character Franziska Jordan (the victimized wife of her unfinished novel, *The Franza Case*) compares her situation to that of aborigines or preindustrial cultures in modern society: "I am a Papuan woman." In this view, the social structures of a patriarchal society gather all control into a central point dominated by white men, who in turn reinforce their power by pushing to the margins any other cultural or psychological identity. These newly marginalized figures, moreover, are kept in their place by being defined as childlike and primitive. Discouraged from developing a voice of their own, unable to put their experience into words, they lose control of their identity. Like modern philosophers of language and psychoanalysts, Bachmann realized that language is crucial to a sense of self. Experience that cannot be expressed is unrecognizable and soon *unspeakable*. The moral task of a writer, she felt, was to find the right words for that experience. By bringing the unspeakable into the light of consciousness, Bachmann hoped to operate a change in social consciousness itself.

She envisaged a novel cycle, *Ways of Death*, that would illuminate women's experience through the linked stories of individual figures appearing and reappearing in major or minor roles. Two projected novels, *The Franza Case* and *Requiem for Fanny Goldmann*, remained unfinished and have been published only as posthumous fragments. In 1966, however, Bachmann gave readings from a novel that would be published as *Malina* (1971), a challenging modernist work that includes a variety of forms and techniques: fairy tale, letters, dream sequences, dramatic dialogue, and finally the inexplicable disappearance of the narrator from a story that previously depended on her. The violent dreams in the second chapter, including a vision of Malina's father as a Nazi murderer, and a "cemetery of murdered daughters," give symbolic expression to Bachmann's horror of fascism as a consistent pattern of violence directed first against individual women and leading to mass destruction.

The Franza Case presents similar themes even more directly. Franziska Jordan (who also appears in *The Barking*) is married to the respected Viennese psychiatrist Leo Jordan, a man with sadistic tendencies and a fascination with Nazism. Franziska ("Franza") is his third wife, and he is systematically driving her mad as he did the others. He destroys her sanity by leaving notes on her "case" around the house for her to find, and in a desperate attempt to save herself she flees the clinic in which she had been placed and travels to Egypt with her brother. In the purity of a desert setting remote from the Viennese society where Dr. Jordan rules, she hopes to understand "who I am, where I come from, what is wrong with me, and what I am looking for in this waste"—in short, to reconstruct her violated identity. She never has a chance to recover from the damage inflicted by Dr. Jordan's psychological torture, for violence catches up with her again when she is attacked and raped. After Franziska's death, her brother Martin returns home alive but unable to explain what has happened. The cumulative effect is of a series of little murders, different in scale from the genocide of World War II but remarkably similar in the exercise of power to control, to suppress, and to kill.

Bachmann was still working on *Ways of Death* when she herself died in Rome on October 17, 1973, three weeks after the night her apartment caught fire and she was badly burned. Her second collection of stories, *Three Paths to the Lake*, had appeared the previous year, with characters and themes growing directly out of *Ways of Death*. In the spring of 1973 she had traveled to Poland to give a series of readings, during which time she also visited the concentration camps at Auschwitz and Birkenau. The camps were a reminder of the destructive arrogance of power and of a fascist mentality whose presence and cost she made it her task to describe.

The Barking, taken from *Three Paths to the Lake,* chronicles another aspect of *The Franza Case.* The major figure is Leo Jordan's mother, now old and in failing health, who is befriended by her daughter-in-law Franziska. In a series of conversations, the topic of which is invariably the brilliant Leo, the two women inadvertently bring to light his real selfishness and cruelty. Old Frau Jordan is unable to admit her fear and dislike of Leo and has lived a devoted lie all her life. Rather than recognize the truth emerging from these conversations, she escapes into hallucinations of barking dogs. The barking that barricades her from her son and removes "the fear of an entire lifetime" merely suggests rebellion, and yet it does recall the resentment voiced earlier by her pet dog, Nuri, who was given away because he barked at Dr. Jordan.

Franziska, in contrast, becomes more critical of Leo's behavior even though she also cannot bring herself to blame him openly. Her relationship with Leo disintegrates during the course of the story, although we are never told exactly why. There is no indication here of the systematic attempt to drive Franziska mad that governs *The Franza Case,* but certainly the picture of a homophobic, control-obsessed psychiatrist who belittles human relationships and specializes in concentration camp psychoses implies, for Bachmann, an essentially Nazi mentality. Much of the story's strength lies in its subtly *indirect* depiction of this mentality and its simultaneous analysis of the roots of power. Leo Jordan is described obliquely, through the eyes of his dependent mother and wife. He instills fear in them and controls their lives, but this control also depends on their willingness to obliterate their own personalities to appease him. Bachmann leaves open the possibility of other modes of being: Frau Jordan's truly maternal relationship with another child, Kiki; Franziska's care for her mother-in-law; and Franziska's brother's generosity in paying the taxi bills his dead sister had incurred for Frau Jordan. The fate of the story's two main characters, however, bleakly illustrates Bachmann's conviction that the oppressive power relationships of fascism begin at an insidiously personal level, in the relationships of men and women, and in a systematic disrespect for human individuality.

Karen Achberger, *Understanding Ingeborg Bachmann* (1995), is a good overview of Bachmann's work; it includes a short biography and bibliographic references. Introductions by Mark Anderson to Bachmann's *In the Storm of Roses: Selected Poems* (1986) and *Three Paths to the Lake: Stories* (1989) provide an excellent short overview of the writer's poetry and prose. Gudrun Brokoph-Mauch, *Thunder Rumbling at My Heels: Tracing Ingeborg Bachmann* (1997), may also be consulted. Juliet Wigmore, "Ingeborg Bachmann" in Keith Bullivant, ed., *The Modern German Novel* (1987), discusses *Malina* and the *Ways of Death* cycle. Inta Ezergailis, *Women Writers—The Divided Self* (1982), has chapters on Bachmann and Doris Lessing, among others. A special issue of *Modern Austrian Literature* (1979) devoted to Austrian women writers contains several essays on Bachmann.

PRONOUNCING GLOSSARY

The following list uses common English syllables and stress accents to provide rough equivalents of selected words whose pronunciation may be unfamiliar to the general reader.

Bachmann: *bakh'-mahn* Frau: *frow*

Franziska: *frahn-tsis'-kah* Johannes: *yoh-hah'-nes*

The Barking[1]

Old Frau[2] Jordan had been called "old Frau Jordan" for the past three decades because there had been first one and now another young Frau Jordan, and although she did live in Hietzing,[3] she had only a one-room apartment in a dilapidated villa, with a tiny kitchen and no more than half a tub in the bathroom. From her distinguished son Leo, the professor, she received 1,000 schillings[4] per month, and somehow she managed to make do, although those 1,000 schillings had depreciated so much over the last twenty years that she was just barely able to pay an older woman, a certain Frau Agnes, who "looked in" on her twice a week, to tidy up a little, just "the bare minimum." She even saved some of the money for birthday and Christmas presents for her son and grandson from her son's first marriage, whom the first young wife sent over punctually every Christmas to pick up his present. Leo on the other hand was too busy to notice, and since he had become famous and his local prestige had blossomed into international renown, he was busier than ever. Things only changed when the latest young Frau Jordan began to visit the old woman as often as she could, a really nice, likable girl, as the old woman soon admitted to herself, but at each visit she said only: But Franziska, it's not right, you shouldn't come so often, it's such a waste. You two surely have enough expenses as it is, but Leo is just such a good son!

  Franziska always brought something with her, delicacies and sherry, some pastries, because she had guessed that the old woman liked to take a sip now and then and, moreover, attached great importance to having something in the house "for the company." After all, Leo might drop by, and he mustn't notice how much she was missing and that all day long she wondered how to allocate her money and how much she could put aside for presents. Her apartment was meticulously clean, but gave off a faint "old-woman" smell which she was not aware of and which put Leo Jordan to flight, apart from the fact that he had no time to lose and no idea what to talk about with his eighty-five-year-old mother. Sometimes, seldom, he had been amused—that much Franziska knew—namely, when he was having a relationship with a married woman, because then old Frau Jordan had gone without sleep and made strange, convoluted allusions, trembling for his safety: she believed

---

1. Translated by Mary Fran Gilbert. 2. Mrs. (German). 3. A suburb west of Vienna, Austria.
4. The basic Austrian unit of currency.

that the married men whose wives Leo Jordan was living with were dangerous and jealous and bloodthirsty, and she wasn't able to calm down until he married Franziska, who did not have a jealous husband lurking in the bushes but was young and cheerful, an orphan, admittedly not from an educated family, but at least with a brother who had gone to college. Families of the educated classes and educated men in general carried great weight with Frau Jordan, although she didn't do much socializing; she only heard about things. But her son had the right to marry into an educated family. The old woman and Franziska talked almost exclusively about Leo, because he was the only productive topic the two of them had, and Franziska was shown the photo album over and over again, Leo in a stroller, Leo at the beach, and Leo through the years, taking hikes, pasting stamps in his collection, and so on until his military service.

The Leo she came to know through the old woman was a completely different Leo from the man she had married, and when the two women sat drinking their sherry the old woman would say: He was a complicated child, a strange boy, actually you could tell all along that he was destined for great things.

For a while Franziska was happy to hear these assertions, that Leo was so good to his mother and had always done everything conceivable to help her, but then she noticed that something was wrong, and with dismay she realized—the old woman was afraid of her son. It began with the old woman saying, sometimes hastily and parenthetically (she believed it to be a clever tactic that Franziska would never see through because she was blinded by admiration for her husband): But please don't mention a word of it to Leo, you know how concerned he is, it might upset him, whatever you do, please don't tell him that something is wrong with my knee, it's such a little thing, he might get upset about it.

Although Franziska had since learned that Leo never got upset at all, certainly not because of his mother, and only listened to her reports with half an ear, she suppressed this first realization. Unfortunately she had already told him about the knee but swore to the old woman she wouldn't say a word. Leo had reacted with annoyance and then, to placate her, had explained that he really couldn't drive out to Hietzing because of such a trifle. Just tell her— he rattled off some medical terminology—she should buy this and that and do and walk as little as possible. Franziska bought the medication without further comment and claimed in Hietzing that she had secretly spoken with one of her husband's assistants without mentioning any names and that he had given her this advice, although she was at a loss as to how to keep the old woman in bed without the help of a nurse. But she no longer had enough courage to approach Leo about it, because a nurse cost money, and now she was caught in the middle. On the one hand Frau Jordan didn't want anything to do with it, and on the other Leo Jordan—albeit for completely different reasons—simply didn't want to hear about it. When Frau Jordan's knee was swollen, Franziska lied to her husband several times; she drove quickly to Hietzing, allegedly to the hairdresser's, and straightened up the little apartment, bringing all sorts of things with her. She purchased a radio but was uneasy afterward: Leo was bound to notice the expenditure, so she quickly transferred the money back and broke into the meager savings she had set aside for some sort of emergency which would hopefully never arise and could only be a minor emergency at any rate. She and her brother had divided what little remained after the death of their entire family, with the exception of a cottage in southern Carinthia[5] which was slowly falling into disrepair. In the end she called a general practitioner in the neighborhood and asked him to treat the old woman for a while, paying him out of her own savings. More importantly, she didn't dare reveal to the doctor who she was and who the old woman was, because that would only have hurt Leo's reputation, and protecting Leo's reputation was also in Franziska's best interest. But the old woman thought much more selflessly: there was no way she could ask her famous son to go so far as to come and take a look at her knee. She had used a cane before on occasion, but after this knee problem she really needed it, so Franziska sometimes drove her to town. Shopping with the old woman was a somewhat laborious undertaking: once she had only needed a comb, but there were no combs like the ones "in her day," and although the old woman was polite, standing in the store with erect dignity, she annoyed the little saleswoman by eyeing the price tags suspiciously, unable to refrain from telling Franziska in a clearly audible whisper that the prices here were outrageous, they'd better go somewhere else. The saleswoman, who was in no position to judge how important buying this comb was to the old woman, replied rudely that they wouldn't find this comb cheaper anywhere in town. Franziska launched into embarrassed negotiations with the mother, took the comb the old woman wanted but looked on as costing a fortune and quickly paid for it, saying: Just consider it a Christmas present from us, a present in advance. Prices have really gone up horrendously everywhere. The old woman didn't say a word, she sensed her defeat, but still, if prices really were so outrageous—a comb like this used to cost two schillings and nowadays it cost sixty—well then there wasn't much left for her to understand in this world.

After a while the topic "the good son" had been exhausted and Franziska repeatedly steered the conversation to the old woman herself, because the only thing she knew was that Leo's father had died young of a heart attack or stroke, quite suddenly, on a staircase, and that must have been a long time ago, because if you stopped to figure it out this woman had been a widow for almost half a century. First she had worked for years to raise her only child, and then she was suddenly an old woman nobody cared about anymore. She never spoke about her marriage, only in connection with Leo who had had a very difficult life, without a father, and she was so preoccupied with Leo that she failed to see the parallel to Franziska, who had lost both her parents when she was young. Her son was the only one who could have had a difficult time, and then it turned out that it hadn't been so bad after all, because a distant cousin had paid for his education, a certain Johannes about whom Franziska had heard very little, merely a few derogatory, critical references to some eternal—now aging—loafer who was swimming in money and supposedly led a life of idleness with all its ridiculous affectations. He dabbled a little in art, collected Chinese lacquerware, and was just another one of those freeloaders found in every family. Franziska knew also that he was homosexual, but she was really amazed how someone like Leo, whose very profession obliged him to uphold a neutral and scientific attitude toward

---

5. A southwestern province of Austria.

homosexuality and phenomena of a quite different magnitude, could go on and on about this cousin as though he had somehow, through his own negligence, fallen prey to works of art, homosexuality, and an inheritance to boot, but at that time Franziska still admired her husband too much to be more than irritated and hurt. With relief she heard from the old woman, in discussing those hard times, that Leo was infinitely grateful and had been a big help to this Johannes, who was then in the throes of a number of personal crises—which were better left untold. The old woman hesitated and then added, because she was, after all, sitting opposite the wife of a psychiatrist: I think you should know that Johannes is sexual.

Franziska controlled herself and suppressed a laugh, it was surely the most daring revelation the old woman had roused herself to in years, but with Franziska she was opening up more and more. She told her how Leo had often given Johannes advice, naturally free of charge, but Johannes was a hopeless case, and if a person didn't have the willpower to change it was understandable that he would be at his wits' end, and from what she heard, Johannes just kept on with it, the same as always. Franziska carefully translated this naive story into reality and understood even less why Leo talked about this cousin in such a disparaging and malicious way. At that time the obvious reason escaped her, namely, that Leo was reluctant to be reminded of his mother and his former wives and lovers who were nothing to him but a conspiracy of creditors from whom he could escape only by belittling them to himself and others. His tirades about his first wife were similar: she had been the epitome of everything diabolical, unappreciative and spiteful, traits that had not been revealed in depth until the divorce when her aristocratic father had hired a lawyer for her to secure some of the money for the child, money she'd given him when he was a young doctor and hard times had struck again. It was an alarmingly large sum to Franziska but, as she was told, one could expect nothing less from the "baroness," as Leo ironically called her, because the family had always treated him like an upstart, without having the slighest idea who was dwelling in their midst. It amused him to note that the "baroness" had never remarried and lived in total seclusion. After him she hadn't been able to find another fool—young and gullible and poor, as he had been—who would have married such a deserving Fräulein. She had understood nothing about his work, absolutely nothing, and although she behaved fairly in respect to the agreement about their son, sending him for regular visits and teaching him to respect his father, she obviously did it for no other reason than to prove to the world how generous she was.

The brilliant doctor's rise to fame along the thorny path of suffering had already become Franziska's religion at that time, and again and again she reproached herself with the image of him making his way, against indescribable odds and despite the obstacle that dreadful marriage posed, all the way to the top. And the cross he was forced to bear because of his mother, the financial and moral burden, was no light one for him, but that at least Franziska could take off his shoulders. Although it otherwise might not have occurred to her to spend her free hours with an old woman the time became something special when she thought of Leo: a helping hand, evidence of her love for him, allowing him to devote his undivided attention to his work.

Leo was just too good to her, he told her that she was overdoing it, the

way she took care of his mother, a telephone call now and again would have
sufficed. For the past few years the old woman had had a telephone which
she feared more than loved: she didn't like to talk on the phone and always
shouted into the mouthpiece and couldn't hear what the other party said,
and besides that, the phone was too expensive, but of course Franziska wasn't
to mention that to Leo. Once the old woman—prompted by Franziska and
a second glass of sherry—did in fact begin to talk about the old days, the
very old days, and it turned out that she wasn't from an educated family, her
father had knit gloves and socks in a small factory in Lower Austria and she
had been the oldest of eight children, but then she'd had a wonderful time
when she took up employment with a Greek family, immensely rich people
with a little boy, the most beautiful child she had ever laid eyes on, and she
was his nursemaid. Being a nursemaid was a really good job, nothing degrading about it, and the Greek's young wife had had servants aplenty, oh yes,
she'd had a real stroke of luck, such a good position had been hard to find
back then. The child's name was Kiki, at least everyone had called him Kiki.
When the old woman began talking about Kiki more and more frequently,
remembering every detail—what Kiki had said, how cute and affectionate
he was, the walks they'd taken together—her eyes lit up as they never did
when she spoke of her own child. Kiki had simply been a little angel, never
naughty, she stressed, never naughty at all, and the separation must have
been terrible, they hadn't told Kiki that the Fräulein was leaving, and she
had cried all night long, and once, years later, she had tried to find out what
had become of the family. First she'd heard that they were traveling, then
that they were back in Greece, and now she had no idea whatsoever what
had happened to Kiki, who must be over sixty by now, yes, over sixty she said
pensively, and she had been forced to leave because the Greek family had
planned their first major trip and couldn't take her along, and when they left
the young wife had given her a wonderful present. The old woman stood up
and rummaged in a jewelry box, then showed her the brooch from Kiki's
mother, it was the real thing, with diamonds, but she still asked herself today
if they hadn't let her go because the wife had noticed that Kiki was more
attached to her than to his own mother, she could understand that all right,
but it had been the hardest blow of all, and she had never completely recovered from it. Franziska regarded the brooch thoughtfully; perhaps it really
was quite valuable, she didn't know much about jewelry, but she was beginning to realize something else: this Kiki must have meant more to the old
woman than Leo. She often hesitated to talk about Leo's childhood, or she
began only to break off in fright saying abruptly: It was just childish nonsense, you know boys are so hard to raise, he didn't do it on purpose, he was
just having such a bad time and it was all I could do to make ends meet. But
you get everything back a hundredfold when a child has grown up and made
his own way and become so famous, he takes after his father more than me,
you know.

Franziska carefully handed back the brooch, and once again the old
woman started in fear. Please Franziska, don't mention a word of this to Leo,
it could annoy him. I have my plans, you know, if I get sick I could sell it so
that I won't become even more of a burden to him. Franziska embraced the
old woman with a hug that was both timid and fierce. Don't ever do that,
promise me you'll never sell this brooch. You're not a burden to us at all!

On the way home she made one detour after the other, in a state of inner turmoil, this poor woman shouldn't sell her brooch while she and Leo spent money freely, went on trips, entertained. She kept debating what she should say to Leo, but a first, faint alarm sounded inside her, because even though the old woman had her quirks and exaggerated things, she must be right about something, and so in the end she didn't say a word about it at home and only reported cheerfully that his mother was doing very well. But before they left for a conference in London she arranged a contract with a garage which ran a private taxi service, made a downpayment, and said to the old woman: An idea has occurred to us, because you shouldn't walk too far by yourself. Just call a taxi when you want to go out, it hardly costs a thing, it's just a favor from an old patient, but don't say anything about it, especially not to Leo, you know how he is, he doesn't like it when you thank him and everything, and you just ride to town when you need something, and have the taxi wait, but always have Herr Pineider take you, the young one. He doesn't know that his father was one of Leo's patients though, that comes under professional secrecy, you know, I was, just there and talked to him, and you have to promise me, for Leo's sake, that you'll take the taxi, it would ease our minds. In the beginning, the old woman made little use of the taxi, and Franziska scolded her for it when she returned from England; her leg had worsened and the old woman had naturally done all her shopping on foot, once even going so far as to take the streetcar into town because one could hardly get anything in Hietzing, and Franziska said firmly, as if to a stubborn child: This is definitely not to happen again.

They exhausted one topic after another: Kiki, the life of a young nursemaid in Vienna before the First World War and before her marriage, and sometimes it was only Franziska who talked, especially when she had just returned from a trip with Leo, a brilliant talk he'd delivered at the conference, and that he had given her this offprint for his mother. The old woman labored through the title with an effort: "The Significance of Endogenous and Exogenous Factors in Connection with the Occurrence of Paranoid and Depressive Psychoses in Former Concentration Camp Inmates and Refugees." Franziska assured her it was merely the groundwork for a much larger study he was working on, and he was even letting her help him with it. It would probably become the most significant and the first really important book in the field. A work of incalculable impact.

The old woman was strangely mute, surely she didn't understand the implications of these studies, maybe nothing at all of what her son was doing. Then she said, surprisingly: I hope he won't make too many enemies with it, here in Vienna, and then there's that other thing . . .

Franziska grew agitated: But that's exactly the point, that would be a very good thing, it's a provocation, too, and Leo isn't afraid of anyone, for him it's the only thing that counts, that has a purpose far beyond its scientific significance.

Yes, of course, the old woman said quickly, and he knows how to defend himself, and if you're famous you always have enemies. I was just thinking about Johannes, but that's so long ago now. Did you know that he was in a concentration camp for a year and a half before the war ended? Franziska was surprised, she hadn't known, but she failed to see the connection. The old woman didn't want to say any more but then continued: It meant a certain amount of danger for Leo, having a relative who, well, you know what I mean. Yes, of course, said Franziska, still somewhat confused; sometimes the old woman had such a roundabout way of saying things without really saying them, and she couldn't make head or tail of it, although suddenly she was bursting with pride that a member of Leo's family had been through something so terrible and that Leo, in his tactful, modest way, had never said anything about it to her, not even about the danger he must have faced as a young doctor. That afternoon the old woman didn't want to go on talking; she merely asked disjointedly: Do you hear it, too?

What?

The dogs, the old woman said. There were never so many dogs in Hietzing, I've heard them barking again, and they bark at night, too. Frau Schönthal next door has a poodle now. It doesn't bark much though, it's such a nice dog, I see her almost every day when I go shopping, but we only say hello, her husband doesn't have much of an education.

Franziska drove home as quickly as she could; this time she wanted to ask Leo if there was anything to the fact that his mother had suddenly begun talking about dogs, if it was an alarming symptom, maybe it had something to do with her age. She had also noticed that the old woman had been upset once about ten schillings which had been lying on the table and then disappeared when Frau Agnes left, all this excitement about ten missing schillings, certainly she had only imagined it anyway, weren't those all signs of the process of aging? It couldn't possibly have been the cleaning woman, she was what people in certain circles—that is, in better circles—called a "God-fearing" woman who came more out of pity than for the money, which she didn't need anyway—she did it as a favor and nothing more. And old Frau Jordan's pitiful presents—an ancient, threadbare purse or some other useless paraphernalia—would hardly have induced Frau Agnes to come; she had realized long ago that she had nothing to expect from the old woman or from her son, and she knew nothing of Franziska's enthusiastic plans for improving the situation; Franziska had chided the old woman as though she were a child, because she didn't want to lose this valuable help over a bout of senile obstinacy and an unfounded suspicion.

More and more often she found the old woman at the window when she arrived, and they no longer sat together when Franziska came to drink sherry and nibble on pastries. The business with the dogs continued, although at the same time her hearing problem grew worse, and Franziska was at a loss. Something had to be done, and Leo, whom she bothered with none of this, was not going to avoid devoting some attention to his mother one of these days. Only then things started becoming complicated between Leo and herself, and she discovered that he had so intimidated her that she was afraid of him. But at least once, in a fit of her old courage, she overcame her inexplicable fear and suggested at dinner: Why don't we invite your mother to come and stay with us, we have enough room, and then our Rosi could always be with her and you would never have to worry, besides, she's so quiet and undemanding, she would never disturb you, and certainly not me, I'm suggesting it for your sake because I know how much you worry. Leo was in a good mood that evening and secretly happy about something. She didn't realize what it was but had decided to make use of the opportunity, and he answered, laughing: What an idea, you have no feel for the situation, my dear, you can't uproot an elderly person after a while, it would only depress her and she needs her freedom, she's a strong woman who has lived alone for decades. You don't know her the way I do, she would die of fright here, just from the kind of people who come over. She'd probably debate for hours on end whether to use the bathroom, out of fear that one of us just might want to use it. Come on, my little Franziska, please don't make such a face, I think your impulse is touching and admirable, but that wonderful idea of yours would be the death of her. Believe me, it's just that I happen to know more about these things.

But this business with the dogs . . . ? Franziska began to stutter, she hadn't wanted to talk about it and would gladly have immediately taken back what she'd said. She was no longer capable of putting her apprehension into words.

What, her husband asked in a completely different tone of voice, she doesn't still want a mutt, does she? I don't understand, Franziska answered. Why should she—you don't mean she wants to have a dog, do you?

Of course I do, and I'm more than glad that this childish interlude has blown over so quickly, at her age she just couldn't handle a dog, she should take care of herself, that's more important to me, a dog is such a nuisance, she has no idea what they would mean, with her advancing senility. She never said anything about it, Franziska replied half-heartedly, I don't think she wants a dog. I wanted to say something entirely different, but it's not important, sorry. Would you like a cognac, are you going to work later, should I type anything for you?

At her next visit Franziska didn't know how to persuade the old woman, who was always on the alert, to give her answers she needed to know. She approached the subject in a roundabout way, remarking casually: Incidentally, I saw Frau Schönthal's dog today, really a cute dog, I like poodles a lot, actually all animals, because I grew up in the country, you know, we always had dogs, I mean my grandparents and everyone in the village, and cats, too, of course. Wouldn't it be good for you to have a dog or a cat, now that you have trouble reading. I mean, certainly that kind of thing passes, but I for one would absolutely love to have a dog. But you know, in the city it's just a bother and not really fair to the dog, but here in Hietzing, where it can frisk around in the yard and you can go for walks . . .

The old woman exclaimed in agitation: A dog, no, no, I don't want a dog! Franziska realized she had done something wrong, but felt at the same time that she hadn't offended the old woman as she might have had she suggested a parrot or canaries: it must have been something else entirely that had put her in such a state of agitation. After a while the old woman said very quietly: Nuri was a really nice dog, and I got along well with him, that was, let me think, it must have been five years ago, but then I had to give him away, to a home or a place where they resell them. Leo doesn't like dogs. No, what am I saying, it was different, there was something in that dog I can't really understand, he couldn't stand Leo, he always jumped at him and barked madly whenever Leo made the slightest move toward the door, and then once he almost bit him, and Leo was so indignant, of course that's understandable, when a dog is that wild, but he was never like that otherwise, not even with strangers, and then naturally I gave him away. I couldn't let Leo be barked at and bitten by Nuri, no, that would have been too much, Leo should be able to feel at home when he visits me and not have to get angry about some poorly trained dog.

Franziska thought that, although there was no longer a dog who jumped at him and disliked him, Leo came seldom enough as it was, and even less often since Franziska came instead. How long had it been anyway since his last visit? Once the three of them had gone for a short ride along the Weinstrasse and into the Helenenthal and lunched at an inn with his mother; otherwise Franziska always came alone.

Be sure not to say anything to Leo, though, that business with Nuri really hurt his feelings, he's very sensitive, you know, and to this day I can't forgive myself for being so selfish as to want to have Nuri, but old people are very selfish, dear Franziska, you can't understand that yet, you're still so young and good, but when you're very old you get all these selfish desires, and you can't just let yourself give in to them. What would have become of me if Leo hadn't taken care of me, his father died all of a sudden like that and there was no time to make any arrangements, and there wasn't any money, either, my husband was a little careless, no, not a spendthrift, but he had a hard time of it and didn't have much of a knack with money, Leo doesn't take after him in that respect. In those days I could still work, the boy was a reason to keep going, and I was still young, but what would I do nowadays? My one fear has always been having to go to an old people's home, but Leo would never stand for that, and if I didn't have this apartment I'd have to go to some home, and I guess a dog isn't worth all that. Franziska listened to her, clenched up inside, and she said to herself: So that's it, that's it, she gave her dog away for his sake. And she asked herself: What kind of people are we?—because she was incapable of thinking: What kind of a man is my husband!—we're just so cruel, and she thinks she's selfish, and all the time we have everything we want! In order to hide her tears she quickly unpacked a small package from Meinl, little things, and acted as though she hadn't understood. Oh, by the way, I'm so scatterbrained today, I've only brought you the tea and coffee and a little smoked salmon and Russian salad. Actually it doesn't go together all that well, but I was really flustered at the store because Leo is leaving and one of the manuscripts isn't finished yet. But he'll give you a call tonight, and he'll be back in a week anyway.

He needs a break, the old woman said, see to it that he gets one if you can, you two haven't had any vacation at all yet this year. Franziska said brightly: That's a good idea, I'll convince him some way or another, I just need to think of a strategy, but thanks a lot, that's really a good piece of advice, he's constantly overworked, you know, and at some point I have to make him slow down.

What Franziska did not know was that this was her last visit to the old woman and she no longer needed the strategy, because other things came to pass, events of such hurricane force that she almost forgot the old woman and a great many other things as well.

In her fear, the old woman didn't ask her son on the phone why Franziska had stopped coming. She was worried, but her son sounded cheerful and unconcerned, and once he even came over and stayed for twenty minutes. He didn't touch the pastries, he didn't finish the sherry and he didn't talk about Franziska, but he did talk quite a bit about himself, and that made her ecstatic because it had been such a long time since he had spoken about himself. So he was leaving on vacation now, he needed a break, but the word "Mexico" gave the old woman a mild shock, wasn't that the place where they had scorpions and revolutions and savages and earthquakes, but he laughed reassuringly, kissed her and promised to write. He sent a few postcards, which she read religiously. Franziska hadn't added her regards. Once Franziska called her from Carinthia. Really, the money these young people throw out the window! Franziska had only called to ask if everything was okay. Then they talked about Leo, but the old woman kept shouting at the most inappropriate times: It's getting too expensive, child, but Franziska kept talking, yes, she had finally succeeded, he was finally taking a break, and she had had to go to her brother's, there was something to settle here, that was why she hadn't been able to accompany Leo. Family matters in Carinthia. Because of the house. Then the old woman received a strange envelope with a few lines from Franziska. She didn't say anything, just sent her regards and wrote that she would like her to have this photo she had taken herself, the photograph was of Leo, apparently on the Semmering Pass,[6] laughing in a snowy landscape in front of a large hotel. The old woman decided not to say anything to Leo; he wouldn't have asked her anyway. She hid the photograph under the brooch in her jewelry box.

She could no longer read books and was bored by the radio; newspapers were all she wanted, and Frau Agnes got them for her. It took her hours to decipher them, she read the obituaries and always felt a certain satisfaction when someone younger than herself had passed away. Well, look at that, Professor Haderer too, he could hardly have been more than seventy. Frau Schönthal's mother had died, too, of cancer, she wasn't even sixty-five. The old woman stiffly offered her condolences in the grocery store and didn't even look at the poodle, and then she went home and stood at the window. She slept more than old people are said to sleep, but she often awoke, only to hear the dogs again. She was startled whenever the cleaning woman came: since Franziska's visits had ended, it bothered her when anyone came over, and she had the impression that she was changing. Now she actually was frightened of suddenly collapsing in the street or losing control of herself when she had to go to town for something, and so she obediently called young Herr Pineider, who drove her around. And she became accustomed to this small precaution for her own safety. She completely lost her sense of time, and when Leo once came by to see her, deeply tanned, she no longer knew if he was returning from Mexico or when he had been there at all. But she was careful not to ask, and gathered from something he said that he had just arrived from Ischia,[7] back from a trip to Italy. Confused, she said: Good, good. That was good for you. And while he was telling her something the dogs began to bark, several of them, all at once, very near, and she was so completely encircled by the barking and a very gentle, gentle terror that she was no longer afraid of her son. The fear of an entire lifetime suddenly left her.

When he said on his way out: Next time I'll bring Elfi over, you have to meet her one of these days! she had no idea what he was talking about. Wasn't he married to Franziska anymore, how long had it been, how many wives was that now anyway, she could no longer remember how long he had lived with Franziska and when, and she said: Go ahead and bring her over. Fine. Whatever is best for you. The barking was so close now that for an

---

6. In the Alps in southern Austria, known as a tourist resort and center for winter sports.   7. An island vacation spot north of the Bay of Naples.

instant she was certain that Nuri was with her again and would jump at him and bark. She wished he would finally leave, she wanted to be alone. She thanked him out of habit, just in case, and he asked in astonishment: Whatever for? Now I really did go and forget to bring you my book after all. A phenomenal success. I'll have it sent.

Well then, thank you so much my child. Send it over, but unfortunately your dumb old mother can hardly read anymore and doesn't understand much anyway.

She let him embrace her and found herself alone again surrounded by the barking. It came from every garden and house in Hietzing, an invasion of the beasts had begun, the dogs came closer, barking to her, and she stood erect, as always, no longer dreaming of the time with Kiki and the Greeks, no longer thinking of the day when the last ten schillings had disappeared and Leo had lied to her. Instead she redoubled her efforts to hide things better, wishing she could throw them away, especially the brooch and the photograph, so that Leo wouldn't find anything after she died. But she couldn't think of a good hiding place, maybe the bucket with the scraps, but she trusted Frau Agnes less and less, too, because she would have had to give her the rubbish, and she suspected that the woman would rummage through it and find the brooch. Once she said, a little too harshly: At least you could give the bones and the leftovers to the dogs.

The cleaning woman looked at her in amazement and asked: What dogs? To the dogs, of course, insisted the old woman in an imperious tone, I want the dogs to have them!

She was a suspicious looking creature, a thief. She probably took the bones home with her.

To the dogs, I said. Can't you understand me, are you deaf or something? No wonder, at your age.

Then the barking diminished, and she thought: someone has chased the dogs off or given them away, because now it was no longer that same powerful, recurrent, barking. The fainter the barking, the more adamant she became: she was only biding her time until the louder barking resumed. One had to be able to wait, and she could wait. All at once it was no longer a barking sound, although there was no doubt it came from the dogs in the neighborhood. It wasn't a growling either, just now and again the great, wild, triumphant howling of a single dog, then a whimpering, the faint barking of all the others fading into the distance.

One day nearly two years after the death of his sister Franziska, Dr. Martin Ranner received a bill from a company by the name of Pineider for taxi services listed separately by date, for which Frau Franziska Jordan had made a downpayment and signed a contract. But because only very few trips had been made while Franziska was alive and the majority after her death he called the company for an explanation of this mysterious bill. Although the explanation actually explained very little, he had no desire to call his former brother-in-law or ever see him again, so he paid the fares, in installments, for a woman he had never known and never had anything to do with. He came to the conclusion that the old Frau Jordan must have passed away some time ago; the company had let several months go by since her last trip, perhaps out of reverence, before asserting its claims.

MAHASWETA DEVI

born 1926

Author of more than a hundred books, including novels, plays, and collections of short stories, Mahasweta Devi is the leading contemporary writer in Bengali, the language of the state of West Bengal in eastern India, and of neighboring Bangladesh as well. Translations of her work into other Indian languages and into English have brought her national and international recognition. One of several modern Bengali writers committed to social and political critique from a leftist perspective, Mahasweta (the *Devi* in her name is a term of respect attached to a woman's name in Bengali) writes about peasants, outcastes, women, tribal peoples who live in the forest regions of India, and other marginalized groups struggling to survive and resisting their exploitation by dominant groups. Her fiction and plays are distinguished by a powerful, direct, unsentimental style and by the subtlety and sensitivity with which she approaches the themes of struggle, resistance, and empowerment.

Bengali fiction from the 1930s onward reflects the growing radicalization of various segments of Bengali society, including the rapidly growing middle class and the urban poor. Since the 1920s, when sharecroppers revolted against landlords and the British colonial government, Bengal has been the arena of a series of peasant uprisings and unrest among the masses. The region was devastated by a man-made famine in 1943. When India was partitioned in 1947, the eastern portion of Bengal (the former East Bengal) became East Pakistan, a part of the newly formed nation of Pakistan, which had been conceived as a homeland for the Muslim populations of the Indian subcontinent. As a result, the whole of Bengal was torn apart by Hindu-Muslim communal riots and the massive displacement of populations. Exploited as much in independent India as in the colonial era, the Munda and other tribal peoples in Bengal and the neighboring state of Bihar rose in revolt, and in the 1960s urban students participated in peasant and tribal struggles in a movement known as the Naxalbari movement (after the village where it began), only to be brutally suppressed by the Bengal state government. Yet another upheaval was caused by East Pakistan's proclamation of independence from Pakistan as the new nation of Bangladesh in 1970. Mahasweta and other major Bengali writers, such as Manik Bandyopadhyay (1908–1956), and Hasan Azizul Huq (born 1938), have responded to these events with fiction that shifted the focus of modern Bengali literature from the lives of the educated, urban middle class to the politics of the exploitation of the underclasses.

Mahasweta Devi was born into a family of distinguished and politically engaged artists and intellectuals in Dhaka (Dacca) in the former East Bengal (now Bangladesh). After graduating in 1946 from Santiniketan, the famous alternative school established by Rabindranath Tagore, she devoted several years to political activism in rural Bengal, in collaboration with her first husband. During this time she held a variety of jobs, including teaching. Throughout, Mahasweta wrote mainly fiction but also columns and articles for journals. In 1963, after receiving a master's degree in English literature at Calcutta University, she became a professor of English at a Calcutta college.

Although Mahasweta's early work was motivated by a concern for social justice, it was not until the Naxalbari student-peasant uprisings of the 1960s that the lives of tribal peoples and peasants became the primary focus of her fiction. At this time she adopted a pattern of activism that she still maintains, participating in, observing, and recording the struggles of oppressed groups in Bengal. Her experience with the Naxalbari movement resulted in *Hajar Churasir Ma* (Number 1084's Mother, 1973), a nationally acclaimed novel indicting organized violence on the part of the state. In *Aranyer Adhikar* (Rights over the Forest, 1977), perhaps the most famous of her novels, she turned to the history of the Munda tribal revolt in Bengal and Bihar in the nineteenth century. Since 1984, when she gave up her academic position, she has devoted her time entirely to grassroots work among tribals and outcastes in rural

Bengal and Bihar and also edits a quarterly journal, the main contributors to which are people from these marginalized communities.

In *Breast-Giver* (*Stanadayini*, 1980) Mahasweta focuses not so much on the resistance of the oppressed as on the dynamics of oppression itself. Theoretically a member of the highest of the Hindu castes, the brahmin Kangalicharan is a helpless victim of the rich patriarch Haldarbabu's clan. Forced to become the wage earner of the household, Kangalicharan's wife, Jashoda, becomes a wet-nurse for the Haldar family, who retain her services until she becomes useless to them. Mahasweta's narrative is aimed at exposing the relentless collusion of patriarchal and capitalist ideologies in the exploitation of the disadvantaged. Themselves victims, the women of the Haldar household are Jashoda's chief exploiters. The status of wage earner not only fails to release Jashoda from the expectations of wifehood and motherhood but saddles her with the ultimately self-destructive task of being "mother of the world." Nevertheless, neither victimization nor its awareness fully robs Jashoda and Kangalicharan of their sense of agency and power.

Like the funeral wailer and the medicine woman in Mahasweta's short story *Dhowli* or the landless tribal laborer in *Draupadi,* Jashoda, the principal character in *Breast-Giver,* is a working woman or, as the narrator puts it, "*professional* mother." As translator Gayatri Spivak has pointed out, in the story's title the author deliberately foregrounds the centrality of the female body in Jashoda's transactions with her clients—she is not just a "wet-nurse," a provider of milk, but a "breast-giver," a distinction further underscored by the grim ironies that unfold in the narrative of her career. The story offers new avenues for examining the points at which gender and class oppression intersect.

Breast-Giver is representative of Mahasweta's fiction, in which the deceptive surface of linear, seemingly realistic narrative is constantly undercut by mythic and satirical inflections. Not only is Jashoda the breast-giver named for Yashoda, the mother of the beloved cowherd-child-god Krishna, but in the course of the narrative the professional mother merges with other Indian icons of motherhood—sacred cows, the Lion-seated goddess, "mother India" herself. The story is open to competing, yet not mutually exclusive, analyses, in terms of Marxist and feminist economic and social theory, myth, or political allegory. While the many layers of meaning in *Breast-Giver* are accessible even in translation, much of the power of the original derives from Mahasweta's distinctive style and voice. In this story, as in the author's other works, classical Hindu myths connect with quotations from Shakespeare and Marx, and slang, dialect, literary Bengali, and English blend together. The result is a powerful language that in many respects resembles modern Bengali usage, yet remains a unique creation of the author.

In addition to her excellent translations of *Breast-Giver* and *Draupadi,* Gayatri Chakravorty Spivak, *In Other Worlds: Essays in Cultural Politics* (1988), offers an analysis of Mahasweta Devi's stories from theoretical perspectives in gender and Third World studies. Compare Spivak's translation with that of Ella Dutta, *The Wet Nurse,* in Kali for Women, ed., *Truth Tales: Contemporary Stories Written by Women Writers of India* (1986). Several of Mahasweta's stories can be found in Kalpana Bardhan, *Of Women, Outcastes, Peasants, and Rebels* (1990), an anthology of translations of short fiction by the major modern Bengali writers on the themes of oppression and resistance, with reference to issues of gender and class.

PRONOUNCING GLOSSARY

The following list uses common English syllables and stress accents to provide rough equivalents of selected words whose pronunciation may be unfamiliar to the general reader.

Arun: *o-roon'*

Basini: *bah'-shee-nee*

Basanti: *bah'-shon-tee*

Beleghata: *bay'-lay-gah'-tah*

Dakshineswar: *dok'-khi-naysh'-wuhr*

Haldarkartha: *huhl'-duhr-kuhr-tah*

Harisal: *ho-ree'-shahl*

Jagaddhatri: *jo-god-dah'-tree*

Jashoda: *jo'-shoh-dah*

Kangalicharan Patitundo: *kahn-gah'-
lee-chuh-ruhn po'-tee-toon'-do*

Kayastha: *kah-yuhs'-tuh*

Mahasweta Devi: *muh-hah'-shway-tah
day'-vee*

Maniktala-Bagmari: *mah-neek'-to-lah—
bahg'-mah-ree*

Nabin: *no'-been*

Naxalbari: *nuhk'-shuhl-bah'-ree*

Neno: *nay'-noh*

Padmarani: *puhd'-mah-rah-nee*

Sarala: *suh'-ro-lah*

Saratchandra: *shuh-ruht-chuhnd'-ruh*

Savitri: *shah-beet'-ree*

stanadayini: *sto'-no-dah'-ye-nee*

Tarakeswar: *tah'-ruh-kaysh-shor*

Breast-Giver[1]

1

My aunties they lived in the woods, in the forest their home
they did make.
Never did Aunt say here's a sweet dear, eat, sweetie,
here's a piece of cake.

Jashoda doesn't remember if her aunt was kind or unkind. It is as if she
were Kangalicharan's wife from birth, the mother of twenty children, living
or dead, counted on her fingers. Jashoda doesn't remember at all when there
was no child in her womb, when she didn't feel faint in the morning, when
Kangali's body didn't *drill* her body like a geologist in a darkness lit only by
an oil-lamp. She never had the time to calculate if she could or could not
bear motherhood. Motherhood was always her way of living and keeping alive
her world of countless beings. Jashoda was a mother by profession, *professional mother*. Jashoda was not an *amateur* mama like the daughters and
wives of the master's house. The world belongs to the professional. In this
city, this kingdom, the amateur beggar-pickpocket-hooker has no place. Even
the mongrel on the path or sidewalk, the greedy crow at the garbage don't
make room for the upstart *amateur*. Jashoda had taken motherhood as her
profession.

The responsibility was Mr. Haldar's new son-in-law's Studebaker and the
sudden desire of the youngest son of the Haldar-house to be a driver. When
the boy suddenly got a whim in mind or body, he could not rest unless he
had satisfied it instantly. These sudden whims reared up in the loneliness of
the afternoon and kept him at slave labor like the khalifa of Bagdad.[2] What
he had done so far on that account did not oblige Jashoda to choose motherhood as a profession.

One afternoon the boy, driven by lust, attacked the cook and the cook,
since her body was heavy with rice, stolen fishheads, and turnip greens, and

---

1. Translated by Gayatri Chakravorty Spivak. Spivak has italicized English words that appeared in the
original Bengali text.   2. Or caliph ("ruler") of Baghdad; according to legend, he kept a djinn ("spirit")
who would do his bidding.

her body languid with sloth, lay back, saying, "Yah, do what you like." Thus did the incubus of Bagdad get off the boy's shoulders and he wept repentant tears, mumbling, "Auntie, don't tell." The cook—saying, "What's there to tell?"—went quickly to sleep. She never told anything. She was sufficiently proud that her body had attracted the boy. But the thief thinks of the loot. The boy got worried at the improper supply of fish and fries in his dish. He considered that he'd be fucked if the cook gave him away. Therefore on another afternoon, driven by the Bagdad djinn, he stole his mother's ring, slipped it into the cook's pillowcase, raised a hue and cry, and got the cook kicked out. Another afternoon he lifted the radio set from his father's room and sold it. It was difficult for his parents to find the connection between the hour of the afternoon and the boy's behavior, since his father had created him in the deepest night by the astrological calendar[3] and the tradition of the Haldars of Harisal. In fact you enter the sixteenth century as you enter the gates of this house. To this day you take your wife by the astrological almanac. But these matters are mere blind alleys. Motherhood did not become Jashoda's profession for these afternoon-whims.

One afternoon, leaving the owner of the shop, Kangalicharan was return-ing home with a handful of stolen samosas and sweets under his dhoti.[4] Thus he returns daily. He and Jashoda eat rice. Their three offspring return before dark and eat stale samosas and sweets. Kangalicharan stirs the seething vat of milk in the sweet shop and cooks and feeds "food cooked by a good Brah-min" to those pilgrims at the Lionseated goddess's[5] temple who are proud that they are not themselves "fake Brahmins by sleight of hand." Daily he lifts a bit of flour and such and makes life easier. When he puts food in his belly in the afternoon he feels a filial inclination toward Jashoda, and he goes to sleep after handling her capacious bosom. Coming home in the afternoon, Kangalicharan was thinking of his imminent pleasure and tasting paradise at the thought of his wife's large round breasts. He was picturing himself as a farsighted son of man as he thought that marrying a fresh young thing, not working her overmuch, and feeding her well led to pleasure in the afternoon. At such a moment the Haldar son, complete with Studebaker, swerving by Kangalicharan, ran over his feet and shins.

Instantly a crowd gathered. It was an accident in front of the house after all, "otherwise I'd have drawn blood," screamed Nabin, the pilgrim-guide. He guides the pilgrims to the Mother goddess of Shakti-power,[6] his temper is hot in the afternoon sun. Hearing him roar, all the Haldars who were at home came out. The Haldar chief started thrashing his son, roaring, "You'll kill a Brahmin,[7] you bastard, you unthinking bull?" The youngest son-in-law breathed relief as he saw that his Studebaker was not much damaged and, to prove that he was better human material than the money-rich, *culture-poor* in-laws, he said in a voice as fine as the finest muslin, "Shall we let the man die? Shouldn't we take him to the hospital?"—Kangali's boss was also

---

3. In traditional Indian belief, the position of the stars and planets at the time of conception and birth is one of the forces that shape the individual's personality and life.   4. Untailored cloth worn as a garment for the lower body by Indian men. *Samosas*: savory, hot snacks.   5. Durga, a martial goddess who rides a lion; her worship is popular throughout Bengal. *"Food cooked by a good Brahmin"*: In Hindu communities, food cooked by brahmins, who are highest in the caste hierarchy because of their ritually pure status, is considered to be beneficial.   6. The goddess, worshiped as the mother of the universe, is said to be a personification of Shakti, the energy of the cosmos.   7. A member of the priestly elite castes. Killing a brahmin is the worst offence a Hindu can commit.

in the crowd at the temple and, seeing the samosas and sweets flung on the roadway was about to say, "Eh Brahmin!! Stealing food?" Now he held his tongue and said, "Do that *sir*." The youngest son-in-law and the Haldar-chief took Kangalicharan quickly to the hospital. The master felt deeply grieved. During the Second War, when he helped the anti-Fascist struggle of the Allies by buying and selling scrap iron—then Kangali was a mere lad. Reverence for Brahmins crawled in Mr. Haldar's veins. If he couldn't get chatterjeebabu in the morning he would touch the feet of Kangali, young enough to be his son, and put a pinch of dust from his chapped feet on his own tongue.[8] Kangali and Jashoda came to his house on feast days and Jashoda was sent a gift of cloth and vermillion when his daughters-in-law were pregnant.[9] Now he said to Kangali—"Kangali! don't worry son. You won't suffer as long as I'm around." Now it was that he thought that Kangali's feet, being turned to ground meat, he would not be able to taste their dust. He was most unhappy at the thought and he started weeping as he said, "What has the son of a bitch done." He said to the doctor at the hospital, "Do what you can! Don't worry about cash."

But the doctors could not bring the feet back. Kangali returned as a lame Brahmin. Haldarbabu had a pair of crutches made. The very day Kangali returned home on crutches, he learned that food had come to Jashoda from the Haldar house every day. Nabin was third in rank among the pilgrim-guides. He could only claim thirteen percent of the goddess's food[1] and so had an inferiority complex. Inspired by seeing Rama-Krishna[2] in the movies a couple of times, he called the goddess "my crazy one" and by the book of the Kali-worshippers kept his consciousness immersed in local spirits. He said to Kangali, "I put flowers on the crazy one's feet in your name. She said I have a share in Kangali's house, he will get out of the hospital by that fact." Speaking of this to Jashoda, Kangali said, "What? When I wasn't there, you were getting it off with Nabin?" Jashoda then grabbed Kangali's suspicious head between the two hemispheres of the globe and said, "Two maid servants from the big house slept here every day to guard me. Would I look at Nabin? Am I not your faithful wife?"

In fact Kangali heard of his wife's flaming devotion at the big house as well. Jashoda had fasted at the mother's temple, had gone through a female ritual, and had travelled to the outskirts to pray at the feet of the local guru.[3] Finally the Lionseated came to her in a dream as a midwife carrying a *bag* and said, "Don't worry. Your man will return." Kangali was most overwhelmed by this. Haldarbabu said, "See, Kangali? The bastard unbelievers say, the Mother gives a dream, why togged as a midwife? I say, she creates as mother, and preserves as midwife."

Then Kangali said, "Sir! How shall I work at the sweetshop any longer. I

8. Younger men and women show respect to older persons and to those of higher social rank by touching their feet and (symbolically) placing dust from the feet on their own heads or lips. *Chatterjeebabu*: "Chatterjee" is a brahmin family name; "babu" is a term of respect used for men of high castes or rank. 9. Married brahmin women are given gifts of cloth and vermilion (red cosmetic) powder, symbols of good luck, in return for the blessings that they are thought to be capable of giving pregnant women. 1. Temple priests divide up the food offerings pilgrims and devotees bring to the temple. 2. A renowned Bengali mystic and spiritual teacher (1836–1886), who was a priest and worshiper of the fierce and enigmatic goddess Kali, to whom goats are sacrificed. Some Kali worshipers engage in esoteric ritual practices, including breaking the Hindu ritual taboo against consuming alcohol. 3. Chaste women are thought to be capable of saving their husband's lives by the power they accumulate through fasting and performing other rituals of austerity and devotion.

can't stir the vat with my kerutches.[4] You are god. You are feeding so many people in so many ways. I am not begging. Find me a job."

Haldarbabu said, "Yes Kangali! I've kept you a spot. I'll make you a shop in the corner of my porch. The Lionseated is across the way! Pilgrims come and go. Put up a shop of dry sweets.[5] Now there's a wedding in the house. It's my bastard seventh son's wedding. As long as there's no shop, I'll send you food."

Hearing this, Kangali's mind took wing like a rainbug in the rainy season. He came home and told Jashoda, "Remember Kalidasa's pome? You eat because there isn't, wouldn't have got if there was? That's my lot, chuck. Master says he'll put up a shop after his son's wedding. Until then he'll send us food. Would this have happened if I had legs? All is Mother's will, dear!"[6]

Everyone is properly amazed that in this fallen age[7] the wishes and wills of the Lionseated, herself found by a dream-command a hundred and fifty years ago, are circulating around Kangalicharan Patitundo. Haldarbabu's change of heart is also Mother's will. He lives in independent India, the India that makes no distinctions among people, kingdoms, languages, varieties of Brahmins, varieties of Kayasthas[8] and so on. But he made his cash in the British era, when *Divide and Rule*[9] was the policy. Haldarbabu's mentality was constructed then. Therefore he doesn't trust anyone—not a Panjabi-Oriya-Bihari-Gujarati-Marathi-Muslim.[1] At the sight of an unfortunate Bihari child or a starvation-ridden Oriya beggar his flab-protected heart, located under a forty-two inch Gopal brand vest, does not itch with the rash of kindness. He is a successful son of Harisal. When he sees a West Bengali fly he says, "Tchah! at home even the flies were fat—in the bloody West[2] everything is pinched-skinny." All the temple people are struck that such a man is filling with the milk of human-kindness toward the West Bengali Kangalicharan. For some time this news is the general talk. Haldarbabu is such a patriot that, if his nephews or grandsons read the lives of the nation's leaders in their schoolbook, he says to his employees, "Nonsense! why do they make 'em read the lives of characters from Dhaka, Mymansingh, Jashore?[3] Harisal is made of the bone of the martyr god. One day it will emerge that the *Vedas* and the *Upanishads* were also written in Harisal."[4] Now his employees tell him, "You have had a *change of heart,* so much kindness for a West Bengali, you'll see there is divine *purpose* behind this." The Boss is delighted. He laughs loudly and says, "There's no East or West for a Brahmin. If there's

---

4. Crutches.   5. That is, not dipped in syrup, used as offerings for the goddess.   6. Kangali misquotes a Sanskrit verse attributed to Kālidāsa (ca. 4th century A.D.), the eminent classical poet of the Gupta era. 7. Hindus believe that the current era is one of deterioration, the fourth and last phase in the pattern of fourfold cosmic era cycles (*yuga*), by means of which time is measured in the Hindu tradition.   8. A high-ranking north Indian caste of administrators and educators.   9. Refers to the British colonial government's policy of dealing with Hindu and Muslim communities as separate constituencies. Mahasweta satirizes the rhetoric of politicians who claim that the independent nation of India has achieved equality for all its members, regardless of differences in language, regional affiliation, economic class, or caste. 1. Parody of a line in the Indian national anthem (written by the Bengali author Rabindranath Tagore), in which various regions of (preindependence) India are named: "Punjab-Sindh-Gujarat-Maratha-Dravida-Utkala-Vanga."   2. Harisal is in the eastern part of Bengal, in what was formerly East Bengal, later East Pakistan, and now Bangladesh. The British colonial government partitioned the older state of Bengal into a western and an eastern section in 1905.   3. In eastern Bengal.   4. Haldar asserts the superiority of Harisal, revealing the extent of his provincialism in the claim that the Vedas and the Upanisads, the oldest Sanskrit sacred texts of the Hindus, were probably written in Harisal (contrary to the scholarly opinion that the Vedas were composed by the Indo-Aryans who lived in northwestern India).

a sacred thread[5] around his neck you have to give him respect even when he's taking a shit."

Thus all around blow the sweet winds of sympathy-compassion-kindness. For a few days, whenever Nabin tries to think of the Lionseated, the heavy-breasted, languid-hipped body of Jashoda floats in his mind's eye. A slow rise spreads in his body at the thought that perhaps she is appearing in his dream as Jashoda just as she appeared in Jashoda's as a midwife. The fifty percent pilgrim-guide says to him, "Male and female both get this disease. Bind the root of a white forget-me-not in your ear when you take a piss."

Nabin doesn't agree. One day he tells Kangali, "As the Mother's[6] son I won't make a racket with Shakti-power. But I've thought of a plan. There's no problem with making a Hare Krishna racket.[7] I tell you, get a Gopal in your dream. My Aunt brought a stony Gopal from Puri.[8] I give it to you. You announce that you got it in a dream. You'll see there'll be a to-do in no time, money will roll in. Start for money, later you'll get devoted to Gopal."

Kangali says, "Shame, brother! Should one joke with gods?"

"Ah get lost," Nabin scolds. Later it appears that Kangali would have done well to listen to Nabin. For Haldarbabu suddenly dies of heart failure. Shakespeare's welkin[9] breaks on Kangali and Jashoda's head.

2

Haldarbabu truly left Kangali in the lurch. Those wishes of the Lionseated that were manifesting themselves around Kangali via-media Haldarbabu disappeared into the blue like the burning promises given by a political party before the elections and became magically invisible like the heroine of a fantasy. A European witch's bodkin pricks the colored balloon of Kangali and Jashoda's dreams and the pair falls in deep trouble. At home, Gopal, Nepal, and Radharani whine interminably for food and abuse their mother. It is very natural for children to cry so for grub. Ever since Kangalicharan's loss of feet they'd eaten the fancy food of the Haldar household. Kangali also longs for food and is shouted at for trying to put his head in Jashoda's chest in the way of Gopal, the Divine Son.[1] Jashoda is fully an Indian woman, whose unreasonable, unreasoning, and unintelligent devotion to her husband and love for her children, whose unnatural renunciation and forgiveness have been kept alive in the popular consciousness by all Indian women from Sati-Savitri-Sita[2] through Nirupa Roy and Chand Osmani.[3] The creeps of the world understand by seeing such women that the old Indian tradition is still flowing free—they understand that it was with such women in mind that the following aphorisms have been composed—"a female's life hangs on like a turtle's"—"her heart breaks but no word is uttered"—"the woman will burn,

5. A symbol of brahmin caste identity, received at the time of religious initiation.   6. That is, the mother goddess.   7. A reference to the worldwide Hare Krishna cult, an offshoot of the traditional worship of the Hindu god Krishna in India.   8. A pilgrimage center and the site of the great temple of Jagannath, a form of Krishna. Stony Gopal: an image of Krishna made of stone.   9. Sky (archaic).   1. In the manner of the infant Krishna sucking at his mother Jashoda's breast.   2. Or Sati ("the chaste wife"), the goddess Parvati, who sacrificed her life for the sake of her husband Siva's honor; thus her name is a word denoting all chaste wives. In the Mahābhārata epic, the devoted effort of Savitri saves her husband, Satyavan, from death. Sita is the devoted, self-sacrificing wife of Rama, the hero of the Rāmāyaṇa epic. 3. Actresses in popular Hindi films made in Bombay in the 1940s and 1950s.

her ashes will fly[4] / Only then will we sing her / praise on high." Frankly, Jashoda never once wants to blame her husband for the present misfortune. Her mother-love wells up for Kangali as much as for the children. She wants to become the earth and feed her crippled husband and helpless children with a fulsome harvest. Sages did not write of this motherly feeling of Jashoda's for her husband. They explained female and male as Nature and the Human Principle.[5] But this they did in the days of yore—when they entered this *peninsula* from another land.[6] Such is the power of the Indian soil that all women turn into mothers here and all men remain immersed in the spirit of holy childhood. Each man the Holy Child and each woman the Divine Mother. Even those who deny this and wish to slap *current posters* to the effect of the *"eternal she"*—"Mona Lisa"—"La passionaria"—"Simone de Beauvoir," et cetera, over the old ones and look at women that way are, after all, Indian cubs. It is notable that the educated Babus desire all this from women outside the home. When they cross the threshold they want the Divine Mother in the words and conduct of the revolutionary ladies. The *process* is most complicated. Because he understood this the heroines of Saratchandra[7] always fed the hero an extra mouthful of rice. The apparent simplicity of Saratchandra's and other similar writers' writings is actually very complex and to be thought of in the evening, peacefully after a glass of wood-apple[8] juice. There is too much influence of fun and games in the lives of the people who traffic in studies and intellectualism in West Bengal and therefore they should stress the wood-apple correspondingly. We have no idea of the loss we are sustaining because we do not stress the wood-apple-type-herbal remedies correspondingly.

However, it's incorrect to cultivate the habit of repeated incursions into *byelanes* as we tell Jashoda's life story. The reader's patience, unlike the cracks in Calcutta[9] streets, will not widen by the decade. The real thing is that Jashoda was in a cleft stick. Of course they ate their fill during the Master's funeral days, but after everything was over Jashoda clasped Radharani to her bosom and went over to the big house. Her aim was to speak to the Mistress and ask for the cook's job in the vegetarian kitchen.[1]

The Mistress really grieved for the Master. But the lawyer let her know that the Master had left her the proprietorship of this house and the right to the rice warehouse. Girding herself with those assurances, she has once again taken the rudder of the family empire. She had really felt the loss of fish and fish-head.[2] Now she sees that the best butter, the best milk sweets from the best shops, heavy cream, and the best variety of bananas can also keep the body going somehow. The Mistress lights up her easychair. A six-months' babe in her lap, her grandson. So far six sons have married. Since

---

4. A reference to the custom of Sati (see also n. 2, above), in which virtuous widows were encouraged to burn themselves on the funeral pyres of their husbands (Hindus cremate their dead). Sati was officially banned in 1829 under British rule.   **5.** In several major schools of Indian philosophy Nature and the Human Principle are conceived as female and male in sexual relationship.   **6.** Reference to the coming of the Indo-Aryan tribes into India from west and central Asia, a theory advanced by Western scholars in the 19th and 20th centuries.   **7.** Saratchandra Chatterjee (1876–1938), the master of the sentimental middle-class novel in Bengali fiction.   **8.** A fruit that is used for its medicinal properties, especially as a laxative.   **9.** Established by the British East India Company in the 17th century, it was the capital of British India. It is now the capital of the state of West Bengal and the center of Bengali culture.   **1.** In Bengal, traditional Hindu women become strict vegetarians after the death of their husbands as a sign of austerity.   **2.** Fish is an important part of the Bengali diet.

the almanac approves of the taking of a wife almost every month of the year, the birth rooms in a row on the ground floor of the Mistress's house are hardly ever empty. The *lady doctor* and Sarala the midwife never leave the house. The Mistress has six daughters. They too breed every year and a half. So there is a constant *epidemic* of blanket-quilt-feeding spoon-bottle-oilcloth-*Johnson's baby powder*-bathing basin.

The Mistress was out of her mind trying to feed the boy. As if relieved to see Jashoda she said, "You come like a god! Give her some milk, dear, I beg you. His mother's sick—such a brat, he won't touch a bottle." Jashoda immediately suckled the boy and pacified him. At the Mistress's special request Jashoda stayed in the house until nine p.m. and suckled the Mistress's grandson again and again. The Cook filled a big bowl with rice and curry for her own household. Jashoda said as she suckled the boy, "Mother! The Master said many things. He is gone, so I don't think of them. But Mother! Your Brahmin-son does not have his two feet. I don't think for myself. But thinking of my husband and sons I say, give me any kind of job. Perhaps you'll let me cook in your household?"

"Let me see dear! Let me think and see." The Mistress is not as sold on Brahmins as the Master was. She does not accept fully that Kangali lost his feet because of her son's afternoon whims. It was written for Kangali as well, otherwise why was he walking down the road in the blazing sun grinning from ear to ear? She looks in charmed envy at Jashoda's *mammal projections* and says, "The good lord sent you down as the legendary Cow of Fulfillment.[3] Pull the teat and milk flows! The ones I've brought to my house, haven't a quarter of this milk in their nipples!"

Jashoda says, "How true Mother! Gopal was weaned when he was three. This one hadn't come to my belly yet. Still it was like a flood of milk. Where does it come from, Mother? I have no good food, no pampering!"

This produced a lot of talk among the women at night and the menfolk got to hear it too at night. The second son, whose wife was sick and whose son drank Jashoda's milk, was particularly uxorious. The difference between him and his brothers was that the brothers created progeny as soon as the almanac gave a good day, with love or lack of love, with irritation or thinking of the accounts at the works. The second son impregnates his wife at the same *frequency*, but behind it lies deep love. The wife is often pregnant, that is an act of God. But the second son is also interested in that the wife remains beautiful at the same time. He thinks a lot about how to *combine* multiple pregnancies and beauty, but he cannot fathom it. But today, hearing from his wife about Jashoda's surplus milk, the second son said all of a sudden, "Way found."

"Way to what?"

"Uh, the way to save you pain."

"How? I'll be out of pain when you burn me. Can a year-breeder's[4] health mend?"

"It will, it will, I've got a divine engine in my hands! You'll breed yearly *and* keep your body."

The couple discussed. The husband entered his Mother's room in the

3. The magical cow of Hindu legend, said to be able to fulfill all wishes.   4. A woman who gets pregnant every year.

morning and spoke in heavy whispers. At first the Mistress hemmed and hawed, but then she thought to herself and realized that the proposal was worth a million rupees. Daughters-in-law *will* be mothers. When they are mothers, they will suckle their children. Since they will be mothers as long as it's possible—progressive suckling will ruin their shape. Then if the sons look outside, or harass the maidservants, she won't have a voice to object. Going out because they can't get it at home—this is just. If Jashoda becomes the infants' suckling-mother, her daily meals, clothes on feast days, and some monthly pay will be enough. The Mistress is constantly occupied with women's rituals. There Jashoda can act as the fruitful Brahmin wife.[5] Since Jashoda's misfortune is due to her son, that sin too will be lightened.

Jashoda received a portfolio when she heard her proposal. She thought of her breasts as most precious objects. At night when Kangalicharan started to give her a feel she said, "Look. I'm going to pull our weight with these. Take good care how you use them." Kangalicharan hemmed and hawed that night, of course, but his Gopal frame of mind disappeared instantly when he saw the amount of grains—oil—vegetables coming from the big house. He was illuminated by the spirit of Brahma the Creator[6] and explained to Jashoda, "You'll have milk in your breasts only if you have a child in your belly. Now you'll have to think of that and suffer. You are a faithful wife, a goddess. You will yourself be pregnant, be filled with a child, rear it at your breast, isn't this why Mother came to you as a midwife?"

Jashoda realized the justice of these words and said, with tears in her eyes, "You are husband, you are guru. If I forget and say no, correct me. Where after all is the pain? Didn't Mistress-Mother breed thirteen? Does it hurt a tree to bear fruit?"

So this rule held. Kangalicharan became a professional father. Jashoda was by *profession* Mother. In fact to look at Jashoda now even the skeptic is convinced of the profundity of that song of the path of devotion.[7] The song is as follows:

> Is a Mother so cheaply made?
> Not just by dropping a babe!

Around the paved courtyard on the ground floor of the Haldar house over a dozen auspicious milch cows live in some state in large rooms. Two Biharis look after them as Mother Cows.[8] There are mountains of rind-bran-hay-grass-molasses. Mrs. Haldar believes that the more the cow eats, the more milk she gives. Jashoda's place in the house is now above the Mother Cows. The Mistress's sons become incarnate Brahma and create progeny. Jashoda preserves the progeny.

Mrs. Haldar kept a strict watch on the free flow of her supply of milk. She called Kangalicharan to her presence and said, "Now then, my Brahmin son? You used to stir the vat at the shop, now take up the cooking at home and give her a rest. Two of her own, three here, how can she cook at day's end after suckling five?"

Kangalicharan's intellectual eye was thus opened. Downstairs the two

---

Biharis gave him a bit of chewing tobacco and said, "Mistress Mother said right. We serve the Cow Mother as well—your woman is the Mother of the World."

From now on Kangalicharan took charge of the cooking at home. Made the children his assistants. Gradually he became an expert in cooking plantain curry, lentil soup, and pickled fish, and by constantly feeding Nabin a head-curry with the head of the goat dedicated to the Lionseated he tamed that ferocious cannabis-artist and drunkard.[9] As a result Nabin inserted Kangali into the temple of Shiva the King.[1] Jashoda, eating well-prepared rice and curry every day, became as inflated as the *bank account* of a Public Works Department *officer*. In addition, Mistress-Mother gave her milk gratis. When Jashoda became pregnant, she would send her preserves, conserves, hot and sweet balls.

Thus even the skeptics were persuaded that the Lionseated had appeared to Jashoda as a midwife for this very reason. Otherwise who has ever heard or seen such things as constant pregnancies, giving birth, giving milk like a cow, without a thought, to others' children? Nabin too lost his bad thoughts. Devotional feelings came to him by themselves. Whenever he saw Jashoda he called out "Mother! Mother! Dear Mother!" Faith in the greatness of the Lionseated was rekindled in the area and in the air of the neighborhood blew the *electrifying* influence of goddess-glory.

Everyone's devotion to Jashoda became so strong that at weddings, showers, namings, and sacred-threadings they invited her and gave her the position of chief fruitful woman. They looked with a comparable eye on Nepal-Gopal-Neno-Boncha-Patal etc. because they were Jashoda's children, and as each grew up, he got a sacred thread and started catching pilgrims for the temple. Kangali did not have to find husbands for Radharani, Altarani, Padmarani and such daughters. Nabin found them husbands with exemplary dispatch and the faithful mother's faithful daughters went off each to run the household of her own Shiva! Jashoda's worth went up in the Haldar house. The husbands are pleased because the wives' knees no longer knock when they riffle the almanac. Since their children are being reared on Jashoda's milk, they can be the Holy Child in bed at will. The wives no longer have an excuse to say "no." The wives are happy. They can keep their figures. They can wear blouses and bras of "European cut." After keeping the fast of Shiva's night by watching all-night picture shows they are no longer obliged to breast-feed their babies. All this was possible because of Jashoda. As a result Jashoda became vocal and, constantly suckling the infants, she opined as she sat in the Mistress's room, "A woman breeds, so here medicine, there bloodpeshur,[2] here doctor's visits. Showoffs! Look at me! I've become a year-breeder! So is my body failing, or is my milk drying? Makes your skin crawl? I hear they are drying their milk with injishuns.[3] Never heard of such things!"

The fathers and uncles of the current young men of the Haldar house used to whistle at the maidservants as soon as hair grew on their upper lips. The young ones were reared by the Milk-Mother's milk, so they looked upon the maid and the cook, their Milk-Mother's friends, as mothers too and started

9. That is, he tamed Nabin with the power of the goddess inherent in the flesh of the goat that was ritually sacrificed to her. Nabin's consumption of alcohol and cannabis (marijuana) is part of his esoteric regimen of Kali worship.   1. One of the three great gods of the Hindu pantheon; he is also said to be the spouse of Kali.   2. Blood pressure.   3. Injections.

walking around the girls' school. The maids said, "Joshi! You came as The Goddess! You made the air of this house change!" So one day as the youngest son was squatting to watch Jashoda's milking, she said, "There dear, my Lucky! All this because you swiped him in the leg! Whose wish was it then?" "The Lionseated's," said Haldar junior.

He wanted to know how Kangalicharan could be Brahma without feet?[4] This encroached on divine area, and he forgot the question.

All is the Lionseated's will!

3

Kangali's shins were cut in the fifties, and our narrative has reached the present. In twenty-five years, sorry in thirty, Jashoda has been confined twenty times. The maternities toward the end were profitless, for a new wind entered the Haldar house somehow. Let's finish the business of the twenty-five or thirty years. At the beginning of the narrative Jashoda was the mother of three sons. Then she became gravid[5] seventeen times. Mrs. Haldar died. She dearly wished that one of her daughters-in-law should have the same good fortune as her mother-in-law. In the family the custom was to have a second wedding if a couple could produce twenty children. But the daughters-in-law called a halt at twelve-thirteen-fourteen. By evil counsel they were able to explain to their husbands and make arrangements at the hospital. All this was the bad result of the new wind. Wise men have never allowed a new wind to enter the house. I've heard from my grandmother that a certain gentleman would come to her house to read the liberal journal *Saturday Letter*. He would never let the tome enter his home. "The moment wife, or mother, or sister reads that paper," he would say, "she'll say 'I'm a woman! Not a mother, not a sister, not a wife.'" If asked what the result would be, he'd say, "They would wear shoes while they cooked." It is a perennial rule that the power of the new wind disturbs the peace of the women's quarter.

It was always the sixteenth century in the Haldar household. But at the sudden significant rise in the *membership* of the house the sons started building new houses and splitting. The most objectionable thing was that in the matter of motherhood, the old lady's granddaughters-in-law had breathed a completely different air before they crossed her threshold. In vain did the Mistress say that there was plenty of money, plenty to eat. The old man had dreamed of filling half Calcutta with Haldars. The granddaughters-in-law were unwilling. Defying the old lady's tongue, they took off to their husbands' places of work. At about this time, the pilgrim-guides of the Lionseated had a tremendous fight and some unknown person or persons turned the image of the goddess around. The Mistress's heart broke at the thought that the Mother had turned her back. In pain she ate an unreasonable quantity of jackfruit in full summer and died shitting and vomiting.

4

Death liberated the Mistress, but the sting of staying alive is worse than death. Jashoda was genuinely sorry at the Mistress's death. When an elderly

---

4. Haldar junior's curiosity is in regard to Kangali's sexual and procreative capabilities.   5. Pregnant.

person dies in the neighborhood, it's Basini who can weep most elaborately. She is an old maidservant of the house. But Jashoda's meal ticket was offered up with the Mistress. She astounded everyone by weeping even more elaborately.

"Oh blessed Mother!," Basini wept. "Widowed, when you lost your crown, you became the Master and protected everyone! Whose sins sent you away Mother! Ma, when I said, don't eat so much jackfruit, you didn't listen to me at all Mother!"

Jashoda let Basini get her breath and lamented in that pause, "Why should you stay, Mother! You are blessed, why should you stay in this sinful world! The daughters-in-law have moved the throne! When the tree says I won't bear, alas it's a sin! Could you bear so much sin, Mother! Then did the Lionseated turn her back, Mother! You knew the abode of good works had become the abode of sin, it was not for you Mother! Your heart left when the Master left Mother! You held your body only because you thought of the family. O mistresses, o daughters-in-law! take a vermillion print of her footstep! Fortune will be tied to the door if you keep that print! If you touch your forehead to it every morning, pain and disease will stay out!"[6]

Jashoda walked weeping behind the corpse to the burning ghat[7] and said on return, "I saw with my own eyes a chariot descend from heaven, take Mistress-Mother from the pyre, and go on up."

After the funeral days were over, the eldest daughter-in-law said to Jashoda, "Brahmin sister! the family is breaking up. Second and Third are moving to the house in Beleghata. Fourth and Fifth are departing to Maniktala-Bagmari. Youngest will depart to our Dakshineswar house."[8]

"Who stays here?"

"I will. But I'll let the downstairs. Now must the family be folded up. You reared everyone on your milk, food was sent every day. The last child was weaned, still Mother sent you food for eight years. She did what pleased her. Her children said nothing. But it's no longer possible."

"What'll happen to me, elder daughter-in-law-sister?"

"If you cook for my household, your board is taken care of. But what'll you do with yours?"

"What?"

"It's for you to say. You are the mother of twelve living children! The daughters are married. I hear the sons call pilgrims, eat temple food, stretch out in the courtyard. Your Brahmin-husband has set himself up in the Shiva temple, I hear. What do you need?"

Jashoda wiped her eyes. "Well! Let me speak to the Brahmin."

Kangalicharan's temple had really caught on. "What will you do in my temple?" he asked.

"What does Naren's niece do?"

"She looks after the temple household and cooks. You haven't been cooking at home for a long time. Will you be able to push the temple traffic?"

"No meals from the big house. Did that enter your thieving head? What'll you eat?"

"You don't have to worry," said Nabin.

---

6. Jashoda invokes the power of a Sati (see n. 2, p. 2830).   7. The cremation ground, usually situated near a river or other body of water.   8. Areas in the city of Calcutta.

"Why did I have to worry for so long? You're bringing it in at the temple, aren't you? You've saved everything and eaten the food that sucked my body."

"Who sat and cooked?"

"The man brings, the woman cooks and serves. My lot is inside out. Then you ate my food, now you'll give me food. Fair's fair."

Kangali said on the beat, "Where did you bring in the food? Could you have gotten the Haldar house? Their door opened for *you* because *my* legs were cut off. The Master had wanted to set *me* up in business. Forgotten everything, you cunt?"

"Who's the cunt, you or me? Living off a wife's carcass, you call that a man?"

The two fought tooth and nail and cursed each other to the death. Finally Kangali said, "I don't want to see your face again. Buzz off!"

"All right."

Jashoda too left angry. In the meantime the various pilgrim-guide factions conspired to turn the image's face forward, otherwise disaster was imminent. As a result, penance rituals were being celebrated with great ceremony at the temple. Jashoda went to throw herself at the goddess's feet. Her aging, milkless, capacious breasts are breaking in pain. Let the Lionseated understand her pain and tell her the way.

Jashoda lay three days in the courtyard. Perhaps the Lionseated has also breathed the new wind. She did not appear in a dream. Moreover, when, after her three days' fast, Jashoda went back shaking to her place, her youngest came by. "Dad will stay at the temple. He's told Naba and I to ring the bells. We'll get money and holy food every day."

"I see! Where's dad?"

"Lying down. Golapi-auntie is scratching the prickly heat on his back. Asked us to buy candy with some money. So we came to tell you."

Jashoda understood that her usefulness had ended not only in the Haldar house but also for Kangali. She broke her fast in name and went to Nabin to complain. It was Nabin who had dragged the Lionseated's image the other way. After he had settled the dispute with the other pilgrim-guides re the overhead income from the goddess Basanti ritual, the goddess Jagaddhatri ritual, and the autumn Durgapuja,[9] it was he who had once again pushed and pulled the image the right way. He'd poured some liquor into his aching throat, had smoked a bit of cannabis, and was now addressing the local electoral candidate: "No offerings for the Mother from you! Her glory is back. Now we'll see how you win!"

Nabin is the proof of all the miracles that can happen if, even in this decade, one stays under the temple's power. He had turned the goddess's head himself and had himself believed that the Mother was averse because the pilgrim-guides were not organizing like all the want-votes groups. Now, after he had turned the goddess's head he had the idea that the Mother had turned on her own.

Jashoda said, "What are you babbling?"

Nabin said, "I'm speaking of Mother's glory."

Jashoda said, "You think I don't know that you turned the image's head yourself?"

9. Goddesses, who are also seen as aspects or forms of the great mother goddess.

Nabin said, "Shut up, Joshi. God gave me ability, and intelligence, and only then could the thing be done through me."

"Mother's glory has disappeared when you put your hands on her."

"Glory disappeared! If so, how come, the fan is turning, and you are sitting under the fan? Was there ever an elettiri[1] fan on the porch ceiling?"

"I accept. But tell me, why did you burn my luck? What did I ever do to you?"

"Why? Kangali isn't dead."

"Why wait for death? He's more than dead to me."

"What's up?"

Jashoda wiped her eyes and said in a heavy voice, "I've carried so many, I was the regular milk-mother at the Master's house. You know everything. I've never left the straight and narrow."

"But of course. You are a portion of the Mother."

"But Mother remains in divine fulfillment. Her 'portion' is about to die for want of food. Haldar-house has lifted its hand from me."

"Why did you have to fight with Kangali? Can a man bear to be insulted on grounds of being supported?"

"Why did you have to plant your niece there?"

"That was divine play. Golapi used to throw herself in the temple. Little by little Kangali came to understand that he was the god's companion-incarnate and she *his* companion."

"Companion indeed! I can get my husband from her clutches with one blow of a broom!"

Nabin said, "No! that can't be any more. Kangali is a man in his prime, how can he be pleased with you any more? Besides, Golapi's brother is a real hoodlum, and he is guarding her. Asked *me* to *get out*. If I smoke ten pipes, he smokes twenty. Kicked me in the midriff. I went to speak for you. Kangali said, don't talk to me about her. Doesn't know her man, knows her master's house. The master's house is her household god, let her go there."

"I will."

Then Jashoda returned home, half-crazed by the injustice of the world. But her heart couldn't abide the empty room. Whether it suckled or not, it's hard to sleep without a child at the breast. Motherhood is a great addiction. The addiction doesn't break even when the milk is dry. Forlorn Jashoda went to the Haldaress. She said, "I'll cook and serve, if you want to pay me, if not, not. You must let me stay here. That sonofabitch is living at the temple. What disloyal sons! They are stuck there too. For whom shall I hold my room?"

"So stay. You suckled the children, *and* you're a Brahmin. So stay. But sister, it'll be hard for you. You'll stay in Basini's room with the others. You mustn't fight with anyone. The master is not in a good mood. His temper is rotten because his third son went to Bombay and married a local girl. He'll be angry if there's noise."

Jashoda's good fortune was her ability to bear children. All this misfortune happened to her as soon as that vanished. Now is the downward time for Jashoda, the milk-filled faithful wife who was the object of the reverence of the local houses devoted to the Holy Mother. It is human nature to feel an

1. Electric.

inappropriate vanity as one rises, yet not to feel the *surrender* of "let me learn to bite the dust since I'm down" as one falls. As a result one makes demands for worthless things in the old way and gets kicked by the weak.

The same thing happened to Jashoda. Basini's crowd used to wash her feet and drink the water. Now Basini said easily, "You'll wash your own dishes. Are you my master, that I'll wash your dishes. You are the master's servant as much as I am."

As Jashoda roared, "Do you know who I am?" she heard the eldest daughter-in-law scold, "This is what I feared. Mother gave her a swelled head. Look here, Brahmin sister! I didn't call you, you begged to stay, don't break the peace."

Jashoda understood that now no one would attend to a word she said. She cooked and served in silence and in the late afternoon she went to the temple porch and started to weep. She couldn't even have a good cry. She heard the music for the evening worship at the temple of Shiva. She wiped her eyes and got up. She said to herself, "Now save me, Mother! Must I finally sit by the roadside with a tin cup? Is that what you want?"

The days would have passed in cooking at the Haldar-house and complaining to the Mother. But that was not enough for Jashoda. Jashoda's body seemed to keel over. Jashoda doesn't understand why nothing pleases her. Everything seems confused inside her head. When she sits down to cook she thinks she's the milk-mother of this house. She is going home in a showy sari with a free meal in her hand. Her breasts feel empty, as if wasted. She had never thought she wouldn't have a child's mouth at her nipple.

Joshi became bemused. She serves nearly all the rice and curry, but forgets to eat. Sometimes she speaks to Shiva the King, "If Mother can't do it, you take me away. I can't pull any more."

Finally it was the sons of the eldest daughter-in-law who said, "Mother! Is the milk-mother sick? She acts strange."

The eldest daughter-in-law said, "Let's see."

The eldest son said, "Look here? She's a Brahmin's daughter, if anything happens to her, it'll be a sin for us."

The eldest daughter-in-law went to ask. Jashoda had started the rice and then lain down in the kitchen on the spread edge of her sari.[2] The eldest daughter-in-law, looking at her bare body, said, "Brahmin sister! Why does the top of your left tit look so red? God! flaming red!"

"Who knows? It's like a stone pushing inside. Very hard, like a rock."

"What is it?"

"Who knows? I suckled so many, perhaps that's why?"

"Nonsense! One gets breast-stones or pus-in-the-tit if there's milk. Your youngest is ten."

"That one is gone. The one before survived. That one died at birth. Just as well. This sinful world!"

"Well the doctor comes tomorrow to look at my grandson. I'll ask. Doesn't look good to me."

Jashoda said with her eyes closed, "Like a stone tit, with a stone inside. At first the hard ball moved about, now it doesn't move, doesn't budge."

---

2. Indian woman's garment made of a long unconstructed length of fabric. It is draped around the body, with one end hanging free over the shoulder.

"Let's show the doctor."

"No, sister daughter-in-law, I can't show my body to a male doctor."

At night when the doctor came the eldest daughter-in-law asked him in her son's presence. She said, "No pain, no burning, but she is keeling over."

The doctor said, "Go ask if the *nipple* has shrunk, if the armpit is swollen like a seed."

Hearing "swollen like a seed," the eldest daughter-in-law thought, "How crude!" Then she did her field investigations and said, "She says all that you've said has been happening for some time."

"How old?"

"If you take the eldest son's age she'll be about about fifty-five."

The doctor said, "I'll give medicine."

Going out, he said to the eldest son, "I hear your *Cook* has a problem with her *breast*. I think you should take her to the *cancer hospital*. I didn't see her. But from what I heard it could be *cancer* of the *mammary gland.*"

Only the other day the eldest son lived in the sixteenth century. He has arrived at the twentieth century very recently. Of his thirteen offspring he has arranged the marriages of the daughters, and the sons have grown up and are growing up at their own speed and in their own way. But even now his grey cells are covered in the darkness of the eighteenth- and the pre-Bengal-Renaissance[3] nineteenth centuries. He still does not take smallpox vaccination and says, "Only the lower classes get smallpox. I don't need to be vaccinated. An upper-caste family, respectful of gods and Brahmins, does not contract that disease."

He pooh-poohed the idea of cancer and said, "Yah! Cancer indeed! That easy! You misheard, all she needs is an ointment. I can't send a Brahmin's daughter to a hospital just on your word."

Jashoda herself also said, "I can't go to hospital. Ask me to croak instead. I didn't go to hospital to breed, and I'll go now? That corpse-burning devil returned a cripple because he went to hospital!"

The elder daughter-in-law said, "I'll get you a herbal ointment. This ointment will surely soothe. The hidden boil will show its tip and burst."

The herbal ointment was a complete failure. Slowly Jashoda gave up eating and lost her strength. She couldn't keep her sari on the left side. Sometimes she felt burning, sometimes pain. Finally the skin broke in many places and sores appeared. Jashoda took to her bed.

Seeing the hang of it, the eldest son was afraid, if at his house a Brahmin died! He called Jashoda's sons and spoke to them harshly, "It's your mother, she fed you so long, and now she is about to die! Take her with you! She has everyone and she should die in a Kayastha[4] household?"

Kangali cried a lot when he heard this story. He came to Jashoda's almost-dark room and said, "Wife! You are a blessed auspicious faithful woman! After I spurned you, within two years the temple dishes were stolen, I suffered from boils in my back, and that snake Golapi tricked Napla, broke the safe, stole everything and opened a shop in Tarakeswar. Come, I'll keep you in state."

Jashoda said, "Light the lamp."

---

3. The great flowering of cultural activity in Bengal (late 18th and the 19th centuries). 4. An elite caste, second only to brahmins.

Kangali lit the lamp.

Jashoda showed him her bare left breast, thick with running sores and said, "See these sores? Do you know how these sores smell? What will you do with me now? Why did you come to take me?"

"The Master called."

"Then the Master doesn't want to keep me."—Jashoda sighed and said, "There is no solution about me. What can you do with me?"

"Whatever, I'll take you tomorrow. Today I clean the room. Tomorrow for sure."

"Are the boys well? Noblay and Gaur used to come, they too have stopped."

"All the bastards are selfish. Sons of my spunk after all. As inhuman as I."

"You'll come tomorrow?"

"Yes—yes—yes."

Jashoda smiled suddenly. A heart-splitting nostalgia-provoking smile.

Jashoda said, "Dear, remember?"

"What, wife?"

"How you played with these tits? You couldn't sleep otherwise? My lap was never empty, if this one left my nipple, there was that one, and then the boys of the Master's house. How I could, I wonder now!"

"I remember everything, wife!"

In this instant Kangali's words are true. Seeing Jashoda's broken, thin, suffering form even Kangali's selfish body and instincts and belly-centered consciousness remembered the past and suffered some empathy. He held Jashoda's hand and said, "You have fever?"

"I get feverish all the time. I think by the strength of the sores."

"Where does this rotten stink come from?"

"From these sores."

Jashoda spoke with her eyes closed. Then she said, "Bring the holy doctor. He cured Gopal's *typhoid* with *homeopathy*."

"I'll call him. I'll take you tomorrow."

Kangali left. That he went out, the tapping of his crutches, Jashoda couldn't hear. With her eyes shut, with the idea that Kangali was in the room, she said spiritlessly, "If you suckle you're a mother, all lies! Nepal and Gopal don't look at me, and the Master's boys don't spare a peek to ask how I'm doing." The sores on her breast kept mocking her with a hundred mouths, a hundred eyes. Jashoda opened her eyes and said, "Do you hear?"

Then she realized that Kangali had left.

In the night she sent Basini for *Lifebuoy* soap[5] and at dawn she went to take a bath with the soap. Stink, what a stink! If the body of a dead cat or dog rots in the garbage can you get a smell like this. Jashoda had forever scrubbed her breasts carefully with soap and oil, for the master's sons had put the nipples in their mouth. Why did those breasts betray her in the end? Her skin burns with the sting of soap. Still Jashoda washed herself with soap. Her head was ringing, everything seemed dark. There was fire in Jashoda's body, in her head. The black floor was very cool. Jashoda spread her sari and lay down. She could not bear the weight of her breast standing up.

As Jashoda lay down, she lost sense and consciousness with fever. Kangali came at the proper time: but seeing Jashoda he lost his grip. Finally Nabin

---

5. A brand of antibacterial soap.

came and rasped, "Are these people human? She reared all the boys with her milk and they don't call a doctor? I'll call Hari the doctor."

Haribabu took one look at her and said, "Hospital."

Hospitals don't admit people who are so sick. At the efforts and recommendations of the eldest son, Jashoda was admitted.

"What's the matter? O Doctorbabu, what's the problem?"—Kangali asked, weeping like a boy.

"Cancer."

"You can get cancer in a tit?"

"Otherwise how did she get it?"

"Her own twenty, thirty boys at the Master's house—she had a lot of milk—"

"What did you say? How many did she *feed?*"

"About fifty for sure."

"Fif-ty!"

"Yes sir."

"She had twenty children?"

"Yes sir."

"*God!*"

"Sir!"

"What?"

"Is it because she suckled so many—?"

"One can't say why someone gets cancer, one can't say. But when people breast-feed too much—didn't you realize earlier? It didn't get to this in a day?"

"She wasn't with me, sir. We quarreled—"

"I see."

"How do you see her? Will she get well?"

"Get well! See how long she lasts. You've brought her in the last stages. No one survives this stage."

Kangali left weeping. In the late afternoon, harassed by Kangali's lamentations, the eldest son's second son went to the doctor. He was minimally anxious about Jashoda—but his father nagged him and he was financially dependent on his father.

The doctor explained everything to him. It happened not in a day, but over a long time. Why? No one could tell. How does one perceive breast cancer? A hard lump inside the breast toward the top can be removed. Then gradually the lump inside becomes large, hard, and like a congealed pressure. The skin is expected to turn orange, as is expected a shrinking of the nipple. The gland in the armpit can be inflamed. When there is *ulceration,* that is to say sores, one can call it the final stages. Fever? From the point of view of seriousness it falls in the second or third category. If there is something like a sore in the body, there can be fever. That is *secondary.*

The second son was confused with all this specialist talk. He said, "Will she live?"

"No."

"How long will she suffer?"

"I don't think too long."

"When there's nothing to be done, how will you treat her?"

"*Painkiller, sedative, antibiotic* for the fever. Her body is very, very *down.*"

"She stopped eating."

"You didn't take her to a doctor?"

"Yes."

"Didn't he tell you?"

"Yes."

"What did he say?"

"That it might be cancer. Asked us to take her to the hospital. She didn't agree."

"Why would she? She'd die!"

The second son came home and said, "When Arun-doctor said she had *cancer,* she might have survived if treated then."

His mother said, "If you know that much then why didn't you take her? Did I stop you?"

Somewhere in the minds of the second son and his mother an unknown sense of guilt and remorse came up like bubbles in dirty and stagnant water and vanished instantly.

Guilt said—she lived with us, we never took a look at her, when did the disease catch her, we didn't take it seriously at all. She was a silly person, reared so many of us, we didn't look after her. Now, with everyone around her she's dying in hospital, so many children, husband living, when she clung to us, then we had ——! What an alive body she had, milk leaped out of her, we never thought she would have this disease.

The disappearance of guilt said—who can undo Fate? It was written that she'd die of *cancer*—who'd stop it? It would have been wrong if she had died here—her husband and sons would have asked, how did she die? We have been saved from that wrongdoing. No one can say anything.

The eldest son assured them, "Now Arun-doctor says no one survives *cancer.* The cancer that Brahmin-sister has can lead to cutting of the tit, removing the uterus, even after that people die of *cancer.* See, Father gave us a lot of reverence toward Brahmins—we are alive by father's grace. If Brahmin-sister had died in our house, we would have had to perform the penance-ritual."

Patients much less sick than Jashoda die much sooner. Jashoda astonished the doctors by hanging on for about a month in hospital. At first Kangali, Nabin, and the boys did indeed come and go, but Jashoda remained the same, comatose, cooking with fever, spellbound. The sores on her breast gaped more and more and the breast now looks like an open wound. It is covered by a piece of thin *gauze* soaked in *antiseptic lotion,* but the sharp smell of putrefying flesh is circulating silently in the room's air like incense-smoke. This brought an ebb in the enthusiasm of Kangali and the other visitors. The doctor said as well, "Is she not responding? All for the better. It's hard to bear without consciousness, can anyone bear such death-throes consciously?"

"Does she know that we come and go?"

"Hard to say."

"Does she eat."

"Through tubes."

"Do people live this way?"

"Now you're very ——"

The doctor understood that he was unreasonably angry because Jashoda was in this condition. He was angry with Jashoda, with Kangali, with women who don't take the signs of breast-cancer *seriously* enough and finally die in this dreadful and hellish pain. Cancer constantly defeats patient and doctor. One patient's cancer means the patient's death and the defeat of science, and of course of the doctor. One can medicate against the secondary symptom, if eating stops one can *drip glucose* and feed the body, if the lungs become incapable of breathing there is *oxygen*—but the advance of *cancer*, its expansion, spread, and killing, remain unchecked. The word *cancer* is a general signifier, by which in the different parts of the body is meant different *malignant growths*. Its characteristic properties are to destroy the infected area of the body, to spread by *metastasis*, to return after *removal*, to create *toximeia*.

Kangali came out without a proper answer to his question. Returning to the temple, he said to Nabin and his sons, "There's no use going any more. She doesn't know us, doesn't open her eyes, doesn't realize anything. The doctor is doing what he can."

Nabin said, "If she dies?"

"They have the *telephone number* of the old Master's eldest son, they'll call."

"Suppose she wants to see you. Kangali, your wife is a blessed auspicious faithful woman! Who would say the mother of so many. To see her body— but she didn't bend, didn't look elsewhere."

Talking thus, Nabin became gloomily silent. In fact, since he'd seen Jashoda's infested breasts, many a philosophic thought and sexological argument have been slowly circling Nabin's drug-and-booze-addled dim head like great rutting snakes emptied of venom. For example, I lusted after her? This is the end of that intoxicating bosom? Ho! Man's body's a zero. To be crazy for that is to be crazy.

Kangali didn't like all this talk. His mind had already *rejected* Jashoda. When he saw Jashoda in the Haldar-house he was truly affected and even after her admission into hospital he was passionately anxious. But now that feeling is growing cold. The moment the doctor said Jashoda wouldn't last, he put her out of mind almost painlessly. His sons are his sons. Their mother had become a distant person for a long time. Mother meant hair in a huge topknot, blindingly white clothes, a strong personality. The person lying in the hospital is someone else, not Mother.

Breast *cancer* makes the *brain comatose*, this was a solution for Jashoda.

Jashoda understood that she had come to hospital, she was in the hospital, and that this desensitizing sleep was a medicated sleep. In her weak, infected, dazed brain she thought, has some son of the Haldar-house become a doctor? No doubt he sucked her milk and is now repaying the milk-debt? But those boys entered the family business as soon as they left high school! However, why don't the people who are helping her so much free her from the stinking presence of her chest? What a smell, what treachery? Knowing these breasts to be the rice-winner, she had constantly conceived to keep them filled with milk. The breast's job is to hold milk. She kept her breast clean with perfumed soap, she never wore a top, even in youth, because her breasts were so heavy.

When the *sedation* lessens, Jashoda screams, "Ah! Ah! Ah!"—and looks for the *nurse* and the doctor with passionate bloodshot eyes. When the doctor comes, she mutters with hurt feelings, "You grew so big on my milk, and now you're hurting me so?"

The doctor says, "She sees her milk-sons all over the world."

Again injection and sleepy numbness. Pain, tremendous pain, the cancer is spreading *at the expense of the human host*. Gradually Jashoda's left breast bursts and becomes like the *crater* of a volcano. The smell of putrefaction makes approach difficult.

Finally one night, Jashoda understood that her feet and hands were getting cold. She understood that death was coming. Jashoda couldn't open her eyes, but she understood that some people were looking at her hand. A needle pricked her arm. Painful breathing inside. Has to be. Who is looking? Are these her own people? The people whom she suckled because she carried them, or those she suckled for a living? Jashoda thought, after all, she had suckled the world, could she then die alone? The doctor who sees her every day, the person who will cover her face with a sheet, will put her on a cart, will lower her at the burning ghat, the untouchable[6] who will put her in the furnace, are all her milk-sons. One must become Jashoda[7] if one suckles the world. One has to die friendless, with no one left to put a bit of water in the mouth. Yet someone was supposed to be there at the end. Who was it? It was who? Who was it?

Jashoda died at 11 p.m.

The Haldar-house was called on the phone. The phone didn't ring. The Haldars *disconnected* their phone at night.

Jashoda Devi, Hindu female, lay in the hospital morgue in the usual way, went to the burning ghat in a van, and was burnt. She was cremated by an untouchable.

Jashoda was God manifest, others do and did whatever she thought. Jashoda's death was also the death of God. When a mortal masquerades as God here below, she is forsaken by all and she must always die alone.

6. Outcastes who handle corpses at the cremation ground. They are considered untouchable because of their contact with ritually polluting objects and substances.   7. Here mother of the divine child Krishna and hence mother of the world.

GABRIEL GARCÍA MÁRQUEZ
born 1928

One of the great novelists and prose stylists for more than four decades, Gabriel García Márquez possesses both the technical virtuosity of the French "new novelists" and the breadth and historical scope of the traditional realistic writer. His most famous work, *One Hundred Years of Solitude* (1967), is also the best-known novel from the amazing literary explosion of the 1960s and 1970s called the Latin American "Boom," and embodies the mixture of fantasy and realism called "magical realism." In this novel and related stories, he follows the rise and fall of the Buendía family fortunes in a mythical town called Macondo, and sketches at the same time an echoing, intricate pattern of social, cultural, and psychological themes that become a symbolic picture of Latin American society. Not all of García Márquez's works are about Macondo, but the same themes and images reappear throughout: the contrast of dreamlike and everyday reality and the "magical" aspect of fictional creation, mythic overtones often rooted in local folklore, the representation of broader social and psychological conflicts through regional tales, the essential solitude of individuals facing love and death in a society of which they never quite seem a part. García Márquez is a political novelist in that many of his fictional situations are openly drawn from conditions in Latin American history, so that local readers will recognize current history in the change from prosperity to misery in Macondo that accompanies the presence and withdrawal of the banana company, the massacre of striking banana workers by government forces in 1928, the extreme separation of rich and poor, and the grotesquely oppressive power of political dictators pictured most recently in *The Autumn of the Patriarch* (1975). Yet his fiction achieves its impact not because of its base in real events but because these events are transformed and interpreted inside an artistic vision that—experimenting with many forms—creates a fictional universe all its own.

García Márquez was born in the small town of Aracataca in the "banana zone" of Colombia on March 6, 1928, to Gabriel Eligio García and Maria Márquez Iguarán. The first of twelve children, he was raised by his maternal grandparents until his grandfather died in 1936. He attributes his love of fantasy to his grandmother, who would tell him fantastic tales whenever she did not want to answer his questions. The recurring image of an old military man battered by circumstances (the grandfather of *Leaf Storm*, 1955; the protagonist of *No One Writes to the Colonel*, 1958; and in his younger days, Colonel Aureliano Buendía of *One Hundred Years of Solitude*) likewise recalls his grandfather, a retired colonel who had served on the Liberal side of a civil war at the beginning of the century. A scholarship student at the National Colegio in Zipaquirá, García Márquez received his bachelor's degree in 1946 and studied law at universities in Bogotá and Cartagena from 1947 to 1950. In 1947 he published his first story, *The Third Resignation*, a Kafkaesque tale of a man who continued to grow and retain consciousness in his coffin for seventeen years after his death. García Márquez had worked as a journalist while studying law, and in 1950 he abandoned his legal studies for journalism in order to have more time as a writer. His first novel, *Leaf Storm*, was published in 1955 and—in its use of interior monologue and juxtaposition of different perspectives—shows the strong influence of Faulkner. He would soon abandon the more subjective Faulknerian style for an objective manner derived both from his experience in journalism and from Ernest Hemingway. In *Leaf Storm*, we may perceive reality through the mind of a ten-year-old boy: "The heat won't let you breathe in the closed room. You can hear the sun buzzing in the streets, but that's all. The air is stagnant, like concrete; you get the feeling that it could get all twisted like a sheet of steel." In his next novel, *No One Writes to the Colonel*, an impersonal narrator catalogues the actions of the colonel about to make coffee: "He removed the pot from the fire, poured half the water onto the earthen floor, and scraped the inside of the can with a knife until the last scrapings of the ground coffee, mixed with bits of rust, fell into the pot."

In 1954 García Márquez had joined the newspaper *El Espectador* (The Spectator) in Bogotá; a report he wrote in 1955 that indirectly revealed corruption in the navy irritated the Rojas Pinilla dictatorship, and the paper was shut down. Working in Paris as *El Espectador*'s foreign correspondent when he learned that his job had been abolished, he lived in extreme poverty for the next year while beginning *The Evil Hour* (1962) and *No One Writes to the Colonel*. In 1957, after traveling in Eastern Europe, he returned to Latin America. Here he worked for several different newspapers in Venezuela, and later for the international press agency, Prensa Latina, in Cuba and New York, and for the Mexican periodicals *La Familia* and *Sucesos* (a sensationalist magazine) before beginning to write film scripts in 1963. A collection of short stories, *Big Mama's Funeral*, was published in 1962, along with the first edition of *The Evil Hour*, which, printed in Spain, was later repudiated by the author because of tampering by proofreaders. In 1965 the various themes and characters he had been developing throughout his earlier novels and short stories came together as the fully developed concept of a new book, and García Márquez shut himself up in his study for a year and a half to write *One Hundred Years of Solitude.* Published in 1967, the novel was a best-seller, immediately translated into numerous (now twenty-five) languages; it received prizes in Italy and France in 1969, and—when published in English in 1970—was chosen by American critics as one of the dozen best books of the year.

Layers of meaning accumulate around a core story in *One Hundred Years,* as the history of the doomed Buendía family takes on different and intertwined shades of significance. The family is cursed from the moment that its founder, José Arcadio Buendía, kills a friend who had insulted him and consummates an incestuous marriage; he then sets out in search of the sea and stops to settle in Macondo. Throughout a hundred years of family history in the nineteenth and twentieth centuries, the Buendías are soldiers, scholars, merchants, explorers, revolutionaries, inventors, lovers, ascetics, labor organizers, and above all stubborn individuals. Yet these individuals are caught up in, and defined by, a larger family history of which they sometimes appear only interrelated, component parts: names echo one another, and parallel situations evoke a feeling of half-recognition inside a mirrorlike pattern of structural oppositions. The Buendía story is set in history but also exists on a mythic level: Remedios the Beauty is lifted up into heaven clutching her sheets when she dies, and when José Arcadio is killed, blood runs from his ear down the street all the way to his mother in her kitchen. The last Buendía is born with the sign of the curse—a pig's tail—and dies eaten by ants at the end. Yet this is not really the end, for in the very last pages, after his son's death and as a whirlwind gathers to destroy Macondo, Aureliano Babilonia reads the manuscript left by the dead magician Melquíades. At last able to decipher a text that could not be read until one hundred years had passed, Aureliano Babilonia finds that this text is the story of his own family; thus he is learning about his own existence, predicted and described a century ago. "It was the history of the family, written by Melquíades, down to the most trivial details, one hundred years ahead of time. He had written it in Sanskrit, which was his mother tongue, and he had encoded the even lines in the private cipher of the Emperor Augustus and the odd ones in a Lacedemonian military code." Behind García Márquez there is yet another author—Melquíades—who has written *One Hundred Years of Solitude,* a novel whose complexity and self-contained referentiality recall the circular fictions of Borges.

The magical realism of *One Hundred Years of Solitude* depends on the juxtaposition of real and fantastic worlds, and it elicits a series of interpretations whose variety can be emulated only by interpretations of Kafka. For some readers, the novel is an allegory of the human condition and its fall from innocence; for others, it recounts the destructive, alienating influence on Latin American society of the aggressive individualism in Western culture; for others, it depicts essential human loneliness and the failure to communicate—even in love; for still others, it is a "total fiction" peculiarly valid for intricate repetitive patterns that refer to folklore and real life but finally create only a fictional universe. Each interpretation draws on the novel's blurring of real and unreal worlds, so that historical facts become the basis for fiction and fictional manipulation liberates our perspective on reality—a typically modernist method of using the imagination to encourage historical change.

After *One Hundred Years of Solitude,* García Márquez found new ways to combine magical-realist techniques and social commentary. In 1972, he published a collection of seven stories, *The Incredible and Sad Story of Innocent Eréndira and Her Heartless Grandmother,* which contains the story printed here, *Death Constant Beyond Love.* From the title story, in which Eréndira's monstrously fat, tattooed, green-blooded grandmother is finally murdered after prostituting her grandchild to the entire countryside to repay a debt, to symbolic fantasies such as *A Very Old Man with Enormous Wings* (in which a castaway angel is exhibited in a chicken coop until his feathers grow back and he can fly away), the author presents tales in which the substance is incredible but the details themselves are highly realistic. The winged man smells bad and his wings are infested with parasites; the farm truck in which Eréndira tries to escape with her lover has an old motor and cannot outrun the military patrol summoned by her grandmother. The mixture of fantasy and realism is not easily interpretable in a single symbolic sense: Eréndira's prostitution may be political and cultural as well as personal, and larger social relationships may be symbolized in the town's attitude toward the angel. Throughout, the narrative line can easily be followed but also interpreted in several ways.

Increasingly preoccupied with contemporary political events, he next published *The Autumn of the Patriarch*, an intricate study of the idea of dictatorship embodied in reactions to a first, false death of the patriarch (his double was assassinated instead), and a second, apparently real death, on which new authorities are already gathering to divide up the power. García Márquez is aiming at more than a specific political situation: he points to a habit of mind, a social lethargy in which there is no apparent connection between the passive acceptance of life as it always has been and the manipulation of society by a succession of dictators. In his next novel, *Chronicle of a Death Foretold* (1981), he describes the same inertia in a small town where everyday life continues its ordinary gossipy routine around two life-shattering events: the rejection of Angela Vicario by her new husband when he finds she is not a virgin, and her brothers' murder of the local dandy whom she names (probably falsely) as her seducer. Against the background of a whole society's passive complicity in a murder that everyone knows will happen, it is death and love that are the two overriding realities.

In recent years—questioning the effectiveness of literature to remedy the social ills he so often describes—García Márquez has been more and more active politically, speaking out for revolutionary governments in Latin America and organizing assistance for political prisoners. Living in Mexico City, he continues to write, including a number of stories that are still unpublished and an account of Cuba under the U.S. blockade. He received the Nobel Prize in literature in 1982.

The story printed here, *Death Constant Beyond Love* (1970), also has a political background although its protagonist, Senator Onésimo Sánchez, is seen chiefly as he struggles with his elemental problem of death. He is no hero: in *Innocent Eréndira* he writes a letter vouching for the grandmother's morality, and in this story he is clearly a corrupt politician who accepts bribes and stays in power by helping the local property owners avoid reform. His electoral train is a traveling circus with carnival wagons, fireworks, a readymade audience of hired Indians, and a cardboard village with imitation brick houses and a painted ocean liner to offer the illusion of future prosperity; he uses carefully placed gifts to encourage support and a feeling of dependence.

Yet the background of poverty and corruption, the entertaining spectacle of the senator's "fictional world," and the political campaign itself fade into insignificance before broader themes of life and death. Forty-two, happily married, in full control of his own and others' lives as a successful politician in midcareer, he is made to feel suddenly helpless, vulnerable, and alone when told that all this will stop and he will be dead "forever" by next Christmas. Theoretically, he knows that death is inevitable and nature cannot be defeated. He has read the Stoic philosopher Marcus Aurelius (A.D. 121–180) and even refers to the *Meditations*, which recommends the cheerful acceptance of natural order (including death and oblivion), criticizes the delusions of those "who have tenaciously stuck to life," and stresses both the tranquil "ordering of the mind" and the idea that human beings are all "fellow-citizens" of a shared "political community." The example of the philosopher is not mere chance: Marcus Aurelius was also a political figure, a Roman emperor who wrote his *Meditations* as personal guidelines in a time of plague and political unrest.

The senator does gain some Stoic insight into the illusions of his career: he notices how similar are the dusty village and the worn cardboard facade that represents its hopes, and he is fed up with what he recognizes to be background maneuverings that keep him in power by prolonging the exploitation of the poor. But he also loses sympathy for the barefoot Indians standing in the square, and his newly alienated perspective is not accompanied by the Stoic injunction to maintain a just and ordered mind and to accept everything that happens as necessary and good. In this crisis, the senator is reduced to a basic and instinctual existence, expressed in García Márquez's recurrent themes of solitude, love, and death. The beautiful Laura provides an opportunity for him to sublimate his fear of death in erotic passion (inextricably intertwined, according to Freud). His choice means scandal and the destruction of his political career, but by now Onésimo Sánchez has felt the emptiness of his earlier activities and is engaged in a struggle to cheat death.

He does not succeed, of course, and dies weeping with rage that death separates him from Laura Farina. *Death Constant Beyond Love* has reversed the ambitious claim of a famous sonnet by the Spanish Golden Age writer Quevedo (1580–1645), according to which there is "Love Constant Beyond Death." Such love is an illusion, for it is death that awaits us beyond everything else. García Márquez repeatedly plays on these oppositions and inversions when he describes the real village and the cardboard version created by false political promises, the paper birds that magically take on life and fly out to sea, the paper butterfly that seems to fly and lands on the wall, the bribery money that flaps around like butterflies, the grotesquely padlocked chastity belt that Laura Farina wears, and even the initial opposition between the senator's living rose (symbol of womanhood and love) and the roseless town (named "The Viceroy's Rosebush") where he encounters his destiny. His destiny is to be liberated from some illusions but not all: his final delusion is to try to hide from death in erotic love. The senator's defeat at the end, which is clearly emphasized as a defeat, suggests that his response was a futile retreat, and—at the same time that it evokes pity for his loneliness, terror, and rage—puts in question what that response should be.

Regina Janes, *Gabriel García Márquez, Revolutions in Wonderland* (1981), is an excellent early study on García Márquez in a Latin American context. Other useful introductions to the writer and his work are George P. McMurray, *Gabriel García Márquez* (1977); Robin W. Fiddian, *García Márquez* (1995); and Joan Mellen, *Gabriel García Márquez* (2000). See also Isabel Rodriguez-Vergara, *Haunting Demons: Critical Essays on the Works of Gabriel García Márquez* (1998). The summer 1972 issue of *Books Abroad* is dedicated to García Márquez. Harley D. Oberhelman, ed., *Gabriel García Márquez: A Study of the Short Fiction* (1991), includes a bibliography.

Death Constant Beyond Love[1]

Senator Onésimo Sánchez had six months and eleven days to go before his death when he found the woman of his life. He met her in Rosal del Virrey,[2] an illusory village which by night was the furtive wharf for smugglers' ships, and on the other hand, in broad daylight looked like the most useless inlet on the desert, facing a sea that was arid and without direction and so far from everything no one would have suspected that someone capable of changing the destiny of anyone lived there. Even its name was a kind of joke, because the only rose in that village was being worn by Senator Onésimo Sánchez himself on the same afternoon when he met Laura Farina.

It was an unavoidable stop in the electoral campaign he made every four years. The carnival wagons had arrived in the morning. Then came the trucks

1. Translated by Gregory Rabassa.   2. The Rosebush of the Viceroy (governor).

with the rented Indians[3] who were carried into the towns in order to enlarge the crowds at public ceremonies. A short time before eleven o'clock, along with the music and rockets and jeeps of the retinue, the ministerial automobile, the color of strawberry soda, arrived. Senator Onésimo Sánchez was placid and weatherless inside the air-conditioned car, but as soon as he opened the door he was shaken by a gust of fire and his shirt of pure silk was soaked in a kind of light-colored soup and he felt many years older and more alone than ever. In real life he had just turned forty-two, had been graduated from Göttingen[4] with honors as a metallurgical engineer, and was an avid reader, although without much reward, of badly translated Latin classics. He was married to a radiant German woman who had given him five children and they were all happy in their home, he the happiest of all until they told him, three months before, that he would be dead forever by next Christmas.

While the preparations for the public rally were being completed, the senator managed to have an hour alone in the house they had set aside for him to rest in. Before he lay down he put in a glass of drinking water the rose he had kept alive all across the desert, lunched on the diet cereals that he took with him so as to avoid the repeated portions of fried goat that were waiting for him during the rest of the day, and he took several analgesic pills before the time prescribed so that he would have the remedy ahead of the pain. Then he put the electric fan close to the hammock and stretched out naked for fifteen minutes in the shadow of the rose, making a great effort at mental distraction so as not to think about death while he dozed. Except for the doctors, no one knew that he had been sentenced to a fixed term, for he had decided to endure his secret all alone, with no change in his life, not because of pride but out of shame.[5]

He felt in full control of his will when he appeared in public again at three in the afternoon, rested and clean, wearing a pair of coarse linen slacks and a floral shirt, and with his soul sustained by the anti-pain pills. Nevertheless, the erosion of death was much more pernicious than he had supposed, for as he went up onto the platform he felt a strange disdain for those who were fighting for the good luck to shake his hand, and he didn't feel sorry as he had at other times for the groups of barefoot Indians who could scarcely bear the hot saltpeter coals of the sterile little square. He silenced the applause with a wave of his hand, almost with rage, and he began to speak without gestures, his eyes fixed on the sea, which was sighing with heat. His measured, deep voice had the quality of calm water, but the speech that had been memorized and ground out so many times had not occurred to him in the nature of telling the truth, but, rather, as the opposite of a fatalistic pronouncement by Marcus Aurelius in the fourth book of his *Meditations*.

"We are here for the purpose of defeating nature," he began, against all his convictions. "We will no longer be foundlings in our own country, orphans of God in a realm of thirst and bad climate, exiles in our own land. We will be different people, ladies and gentlemen, we will be a great and happy people."

There was a pattern to his circus. As he spoke his aides threw clusters of

---

3. People descended from the original inhabitants of the continent; generally poorer and less privileged than those descended from Spanish or Portuguese colonists.   4. A well-known German university.
5. "Death is such as generation is, a mystery of nature . . . altogether not a thing of which any man should be ashamed" (Marcus Aurelius, *Meditations* 4.5).

paper birds into the air and the artificial creatures took on life, flew about the platform of planks, and went out to sea. At the same time, other men took some prop trees with felt leaves out of the wagons and planted them in the saltpeter soil behind the crowd. They finished by setting up a cardboard façade with make-believe houses of red brick that had glass windows, and with it they covered the miserable real-life shacks.

The senator prolonged his speech with two quotations in Latin in order to give the farce more time. He promised rainmaking machines, portable breeders for table animals, the oils of happiness which would make vegetables grow in the saltpeter and clumps of pansies in the window boxes. When he saw that his fictional world was all set up, he pointed to it. "That's the way it will be for us, ladies and gentlemen," he shouted. "Look! That's the way it will be for us."

The audience turned around. An ocean liner made of painted paper was passing behind the houses and it was taller than the tallest houses in the artificial city. Only the senator himself noticed that since it had been set up and taken down and carried from one place to another the superimposed cardboard town had been eaten away by the terrible climate and that it was almost as poor and dusty as Rosal del Virrey.

For the first time in twelve years, Nelson Farina didn't go to greet the senator. He listened to the speech from his hammock amidst the remains of his siesta, under the cool bower of a house of unplaned boards which he had built with the same pharmacist's hands with which he had drawn and quartered his first wife. He had escaped from Devil's Island[6] and appeared in Rosal del Virrey on a ship loaded with innocent macaws, with a beautiful and blasphemous black woman he had found in Paramaribo[7] and by whom he had a daughter. The woman died of natural causes a short while later and she didn't suffer the fate of the other, whose pieces had fertilized her own cauliflower patch, but was buried whole and with her Dutch name in the local cemetery. The daughter had inherited her color and her figure along with her father's yellow and astonished eyes, and he had good reason to imagine that he was rearing the most beautiful woman in the world.

Ever since he had met Senator Onésimo Sánchez during his first electoral campaign, Nelson Farina had begged for his help in getting a false identity card which would place him beyond the reach of the law. The senator, in a friendly but firm way, had refused. Nelson Farina never gave up, and for several years, every time he found the chance, he would repeat his request with a different recourse. But this time he stayed in his hammock, condemned to rot alive in that burning den of buccaneers. When he heard the final applause, he lifted his head, and looking over the boards of the fence, he saw the back side of the farce: the props for the buildings, the framework of the trees, the hidden illusionists who were pushing the ocean liner along. He spat without rancor.

"*Merde*," he said. "*C'est le Blacamán de la politique.*"[8]

After the speech, as was customary, the senator took a walk through the streets of the town in the midst of the music and the rockets and was besieged

---

6. A former French penal colony off the coast of French Guiana in northern South America.   7. Capital of Suriname (formerly Dutch Guiana) and a large port.   8. Shit. He's the Blacamán of politics (French). Blacamán is a charlatan and huckster who appears in several stories, including *Blacamán the Good, Vendor of Miracles.*

by the townspeople, who told him their troubles. The senator listened to them good-naturedly and he always found some way to console everybody without having to do them any difficult favors. A woman up on the roof of a house with her six youngest children managed to make herself heard over the uproar and the fireworks.

"I'm not asking for much, Senator," she said. "Just a donkey to haul water from Hanged Man's Well."

The senator noticed the six thin children. "What became of your husband?" he asked.

"He went to find his fortune on the island of Aruba,"[9] the woman answered good-humoredly, "and what he found was a foreign woman, the kind that put diamonds on their teeth."

The answer brought on a roar of laughter.

"All right," the senator decided, "you'll get your donkey."

A short while later an aide of his brought a good pack donkey to the woman's house and on the rump it had a campaign slogan written in indelible paint so that no one would ever forget that it was a gift from the senator.

Along the short stretch of street he made other, smaller gestures, and he even gave a spoonful of medicine to a sick man who had had his bed brought to the door of his house so he could see him pass. At the last corner, through the boards of the fence, he saw Nelson Farina in his hammock, looking ashen and gloomy, but nonetheless the senator greeted him, with no show of affection.

"Hello, how are you?"

Nelson Farina turned in his hammock and soaked him in the sad amber of his look.

"*Moi, vous savez,*"[1] he said.

His daughter came out into the yard when she heard the greeting. She was wearing a cheap, faded Guajiro Indian[2] robe, her head was decorated with colored bows, and her face was painted as protection against the sun, but even in that state of disrepair it was possible to imagine that there had never been another so beautiful in the whole world. The senator was left breathless. "I'll be damned!" he breathed in surprise. "The Lord does the craziest things!"

That night Nelson Farina dressed his daughter up in her best clothes and sent her to the senator. Two guards armed with rifles who were nodding from the heat in the borrowed house ordered her to wait on the only chair in the vestibule.

The senator was in the next room meeting with the important people of Rosal del Virrey, whom he had gathered together in order to sing for them the truths he had left out of his speeches. They looked so much like all the ones he always met in all the towns in the desert that even the senator himself was sick and tired of that perpetual nightly session. His shirt was soaked with sweat and he was trying to dry it on his body with the hot breeze from an electric fan that was buzzing like a horse fly in the heavy heat of the room.

"We, of course, can't eat paper birds," he said. "You and I know that the

9. Off the coast of Venezuela, famous as a tourist resort. 1. Oh well, as for me, you know (French).
2. Inhabitant of the rural Guajira Peninsula of northern Colombia. The figure of Laura Farina is thus connected with the rustic poor, with earthy reality (*farina* means "flour"), and with erotic inspiration. (*Laura* was the beloved celebrated by the Italian Renaissance poet Francis Petrarch, 1304–1374.)

day there are trees and flowers in this heap of goat dung, the day there are shad instead of worms in the water holes, that day neither you nor I will have anything to do here, do I make myself clear?"

No one answered. While he was speaking, the senator had torn a sheet off the calendar and fashioned a paper butterfly out of it with his hands. He tossed it with no particular aim into the air current coming from the fan and the butterfly flew about the room and then went out through the half-open door. The senator went on speaking with a control aided by the complicity of death.

"Therefore," he said, "I don't have to repeat to you what you already know too well: that my reelection is a better piece of business for you than it is for me, because I'm fed up with stagnant water and Indian sweat, while you people, on the other hand, make your living from it."

Laura Farina saw the paper butterfly come out. Only she saw it because the guards in the vestibule had fallen asleep on the steps, hugging their rifles. After a few turns, the large lithographed butterfly unfolded completely, flattened against the wall, and remained stuck there. Laura Farina tried to pull it off with her nails. One of the guards, who woke up with the applause from the next room, noticed her vain attempt.

"It won't come off," he said sleepily. "It's painted on the wall."

Laura Farina sat down again when the men began to come out of the meeting. The senator stood in the doorway of the room with his hand on the latch, and he only noticed Laura Farina when the vestibule was empty.

"What are you doing here?"

"*C'est de la part de mon père*,"[3] she said.

The senator understood. He scrutinized the sleeping guards, then he scrutinized Laura Farina, whose unusual beauty was even more demanding than his pain, and he resolved then that death had made his decision for him.

"Come in," he told her.

Laura Farina was struck dumb standing in the doorway to the room: thousands of bank notes were floating in the air, flapping like the butterfly. But the senator turned off the fan and the bills were left without air and alighted on the objects in the room.

"You see," he said, smiling, "even shit can fly."

Laura Farina sat down on a schoolboy's stool. Her skin was smooth and firm, with the same color and the same solar density as crude oil, her hair was the mane of a young mare, and her huge eyes were brighter than the light. The senator followed the thread of her look and finally found the rose, which had been tarnished by the saltpeter.

"It's a rose," he said.

"Yes," she said with a trace of perplexity. "I learned what they were in Riohacha."[4]

The senator sat down on an army cot, talking about roses as he unbuttoned his shirt. On the side where he imagined his heart to be inside his chest he had a corsair's tattoo of a heart pierced by an arrow. He threw the soaked shirt to the floor and asked Laura Farina to help him off with his boots.

She knelt down facing the cot. The senator continued to scrutinize her,

3. My father sent me (French).   4. A port on the Guajira Peninsula.

thoughtfully, and while he was untying the laces he wondered which one of them would end up with the bad luck of that encounter.

"You're just a child," he said.

"Don't you believe it," she said. "I'll be nineteen in April."

The senator became interested.

"What day?"

"The eleventh," she said.

The senator felt better. "We're both Aries,"[5] he said. And smiling, he added:

"It's the sign of solitude."

Laura Farina wasn't paying attention because she didn't know what to do with the boots. The senator, for his part, didn't know what to do with Laura Farina, because he wasn't used to sudden love affairs and, besides, he knew that the one at hand had its origins in indignity. Just to have some time to think, he held Laura Farina tightly between his knees, embraced her about the waist, and lay down on his back on the cot. Then he realized that she was naked under her dress, for her body gave off the dark fragrance of an animal of the woods, but her heart was frightened and her skin disturbed by a glacial sweat.

"No one loves us," he sighed.

Laura Farina tried to say something, but there was only enough air for her to breathe. He laid her down beside him to help her, he put out the light and the room was in the shadow of the rose. She abandoned herself to the mercies of her fate. The senator caressed her slowly, seeking her with his hand, barely touching her, but where he expected to find her, he came across something iron that was in the way.

"What have you got there?"

"A padlock,"[6] she said.

"What in hell!" the senator said furiously and asked what he knew only too well. "Where's the key?"

Laura Farina gave a breath of relief.

"My papa has it," she answered. "He told me to tell you to send one of your people to get it and to send along with him a written promise that you'll straighten out his situation."

The senator grew tense. "Frog[7] bastard," he murmured indignantly. Then he closed his eyes in order to relax and he met himself in the darkness. *Remember,* he remembered, *that whether it's you or someone else, it won't be long before you'll be dead and it won't be long before your name won't even be left.*[8]

He waited for the shudder to pass.

"Tell me one thing," he asked then. "What have you heard about me?"

"Do you want the honest-to-God truth?"

"The honest-to-God truth."

"Well," Laura Farina ventured, "they say you're worse than the rest because you're different."

The senator didn't get upset. He remained silent for a long time with his

5. The first sign in the zodiac; people born between March 21 and April 19 are said to be under the sign of Aries.   6. She is wearing a chastity belt, a medieval device worn by women to prevent sexual intercourse.   7. Epithet for "French."   8. A direct translation of a sentence from Marcus Aurelius's *Meditations* (4.6).

eyes closed, and when he opened them again he seemed to have returned from his most hidden instincts.

"Oh, what the hell," he decided. "Tell your son of a bitch of a father that I'll straighten out his situation."

"If you want, I can go get the key myself," Laura Farina said.

The senator held her back.

"Forget about the key," he said, "and sleep awhile with me. It's good to be with someone when you're so alone."

Then she laid his head on her shoulder with her eyes fixed on the rose. The senator held her about the waist, sank his face into woods-animal armpit, and gave in to terror. Six months and eleven days later he would die in that same position, debased and repudiated because of the public scandal with Laura Farina and weeping with rage at dying without her.

CHINUA ACHEBE
born 1930

The best-known African writer today is the Nigerian Chinua Achebe, whose first novel, *Things Fall Apart*, exploded the colonialist image of Africans as childlike people living in a primitive society. Achebe's novels, stories, poetry, and essays have made him a respected and prophetic figure in Africa. In Western countries, where he has traveled, taught, and lectured widely, he is admired as a major writer who has given an entirely new direction to the English-language novel. Achebe has created not only the African postcolonial novel with its new themes and characters but also a complex narrative point of view that questions cultural images—including its own—with a subtle irony and compassion born from bicultural experience. His vantage point is different from that of Doris Lessing or Albert Camus, two authors whose work is also concerned with African experience: Achebe writes, as he says, "from the inside." For him as for many other writers in this volume, literature is important because it liberates the human imagination; it "begins as an adventure in self-discovery and ends in wisdom and human conscience."

Chinua Achebe was born in the town of Ogidi, an Igbo-speaking town of Eastern Nigeria, on November 16, 1930. He was the fifth of six children in the family of Isaiah Okafor Achebe, a teacher for the Church Missionary Society, and his wife, Janet. Achebe's parents christened him Albert after Prince Albert, husband of Queen Victoria. When he entered the university the author rejected his British name in favor of his indigenous name Chinua, which abbreviates Chinualumogu, or "My spirit come fight for me." Achebe's novels offer a picture of Igbo society with its fierce egalitarianism and "town meeting" debates. Two cultures coexisted in Ogidi: on the one hand, African social customs and traditional religion, and on the other, British colonial authority and Christianity. Instead of being torn between the two, Achebe found himself curious about both ways of life and fascinated with the dual perspective that came from living "at the crossroads of cultures."

He attended Church schools in Ogidi where instruction was carried out in English after the first two years. Achebe read the various books in his father's library, most of them primers or Church related, but he also listened eagerly to his mother and sister when they told traditional Igbo stories. Entering a prestigious government college (secondary school) in Umuahia, he immediately took advantage of its well-stocked

library. Achebe later commented on the crucial importance of books in creating writers and committed readers, noting that private secondary schools had few if any books
and that almost all the first generation of Nigerian writers—including himself and
Wole Soyinka (born 1934)—had gone to a government college.

After graduating in 1948, Achebe entered University College, Ibadan, on a scholarship to study medicine. In the following year he changed to a program in liberal
arts that combined English, history, and religious studies. Research in the last two
fields deepened his knowledge of Nigerian history and culture; the assigned literary
texts, however, brought into sharp focus the distorted image of African culture offered
by British colonial literature. Reading Joyce Cary's *Mister Johnson* (1939), a novel
recommended for its depiction of life in Nigeria, he was shocked to find Nigerians
described as violent savages with passionate instincts and simple minds: "and so I
thought if this was famous, then perhaps someone ought to try and look at this from
the inside." He began writing while at the university, contributing articles and
sketches to several campus papers and publishing four stories in the *University Herald,* a magazine whose editor he became in his third year.

Upon receiving his B.A. in 1953, Achebe joined the Nigerian Broadcasting Service,
working in the Talks Section and traveling to London in 1956 to attend the British
Broadcasting Corporation Staff School. Promotions came quickly; he was named
head of the Talks Section in 1957, controller of the Eastern Region Stations in 1959,
and in 1961 director of External Services in charge of the Voice of Nigeria. The radio
position was more than a merely administrative post, for Achebe and his colleagues
were working to create a sense of shared national identity through broadcasting
national news and information about Nigerian culture. Ever since the end of World
War II, Nigeria had been torn by intellectual and political rivalries that overlaid the
common struggle for independence (achieved in 1960). The three major ethno-
linguistic groups—Yoruba, Hausa-Fulani, and Igbo (once spelled Ibo)—were increasingly locked in economic and political rivalry at the same time they were fighting to
erase the vestiges of British colonial rule. These problems eventually boiled over in
the Nigerian Civil War (1967–70). The persistence of political corruption is depicted
in *A Man of the People* (1966) and *Anthills of the Savannah* (1987).

Achebe is convinced of the writer's social responsibility, and he draws frequent
contrasts between the European "art for art's sake" tradition and an African belief in
the indivisibility of art and society. His favorite example is the Owerri Igbo custom of
mbari, a communal art project in which villagers selected by the priest of the earth
goddess Ala live in a forest clearing for a year or more, working under the direction
of master artists to prepare a temple of images in the goddess's honor. This creative
communal enterprise and its culminating festival are diametrically opposed, he says,
to the European custom of secluding art objects in museums or private collections.
Instead, *mbari* celebrates art as a cultural process, affirming that "art belongs to all
and is a 'function' of society." Achebe's own practice as novelist, poet, essayist, founder and editor of two journals, lecturer, and active representative of African letters
exemplifies this commitment to the community.

His first novel, *Things Fall Apart* (1958), was a conscious attempt to counteract
the distortions of Cary's *Mister Johnson* by describing the richness and complexity of
traditional African society before the colonial and missionary invasion. It was important, Achebe said, to "teach my readers that their past—with all its imperfections—
was not one long night of savagery from which the first Europeans acting on God's
behalf delivered them." The novel was recognized immediately as an extraordinary
work of literature in English. It also became the first classic work of modern African
fiction, translated into nine languages, and Achebe became for many readers and
writers the teacher of a whole generation. In 1959 he received the Margaret Wrong
Memorial Prize, and in 1960—after the publication of a sequel, *No Longer at Ease*—
he received the Nigerian National Trophy for literature. His later novels continue to
examine the individual and cultural dilemmas of Nigerian society, although their

background varies from the traditional religious society of *Arrow of God* (1964) to thinly disguised accounts of contemporary political strife.

Achebe's reputation as the "father of the African novel in English" does not depend solely on his accounts of Nigerian society. In contrast with writers such as Ngugi wa Thiong'o (b. 1938), who insist that the contemporary African writer has a moral obligation to write in one of the tribal languages, Achebe maintains his right to compose in the English he has used since his school days. His literary language is an English skillfully blended with Igbo vocabulary, proverbs, images, and speech patterns to create a new voice embodying the linguistic pluralism of modern African experience. By including standard English, Igbo, and pidgin in different contexts, Achebe demonstrates the existence of a diverse society that is otherwise concealed behind language barriers—a culture, he suggests, that escaped colonial officials who wrote about African character without ever understanding the language. He also thereby acknowledges that his primary African audience is composed of younger, schooled readers who are relatively fluent in English.

It is hard to overestimate the influence of Nigerian politics on Achebe's life after 1966. In January, a military coup d'état led by young Igbo officers overthrew the government; six months later, a second coup led by non-Igbo officers took power. Ethnic rivalries intensified: thousands of Igbos were killed and driven out of the north. Achebe and his family fled the capital of Lagos when soldiers were sent to find him, and the novelist became a senior research fellow at the University of Nigeria, Nsukka (in Eastern Nigeria). In May 1967 the eastern region, mainly populated by Igbo-speakers, seceded as the new nation of Biafra. From then on until the defeat of Biafra in January 1970, a bloody civil war was waged with high civilian casualties and widespread starvation. Achebe traveled in Europe, North America, and Africa to win support for Biafra, proclaiming that "no government, black or white, has the right to stigmatize and destroy groups of its own citizens without undermining the basis of its own existence." A group of his poems about the war won the Commonwealth Poetry Prize in 1972, the same year that he published a volume of short stories, *Girls at War*, and left Nigeria to take up a three-year position at the University of Massachusetts at Amherst. Returning to Nsukka as professor of literature in 1976, Achebe continued to participate in his country's political life. He published an attack on the corrupt leadership in *The Trouble with Nigeria* (1983) and—drawing on circumstances surrounding a fifth military coup in 1985—produced his fifth novel, *Anthills of the Savannah*, in 1987. Although it reiterates Achebe's familiar indictment of ruthless politicians, alienated intellectuals, and those who accept dictatorship as a route to reform, this novel offers hope for the future through a return to the people and a symbolic child born at the end: a girl child with a boy's name, "May the Path Never Close." Badly hurt in a car accident the year after *Anthills* was published, Achebe slowly recovered and returned to writing and teaching at Bard College. By the end of the century, he had published three more volumes, including interviews collected as *Conversations with Chinua Achebe* (1997) and another book of essays, *Home and Exile* (2000).

A predominant theme in Achebe's novels and essays is the notion of balance or interdependence: balance between earth and sky, individual and community, man and woman, or different perspectives on the same situation. Igbo thought is fundamentally dualistic, the novelist explains: "Wherever Something stands, Something Else will stand beside it. Nothing is absolute." Extremes carry the seeds of destruction. Indeed, destruction follows in Achebe's novels whenever balance is disturbed: when Okonkwo in *Things Fall Apart* represses any signs of "female" softness; when the priest Ezeulu in *Arrow of God* is imprisoned and refuses to authorize the feast of the New Yam, without which his people cannot plant their crops; and when, in later books, the lust for power and possessions blinds Nigerian leaders to the needs of the people.

The fundamental image of this balance is contained in the Igbo concept of *chi*, which recurs throughout Achebe's work. *Chi* is a personal deity, a fragment of the supreme being unique for each individual. A person's *chi,* says Achebe, may be visualized "as his other identity in spirit-land—his *spirit being* complementing his terrestrial *human being.*" It is both all-powerful and subject to persuasion: "When a man says yes his *chi* says yes also," but at the same time "a man does not challenge his *chi* to a wrestling match." *Chi* is simultaneously destiny and an internal commitment that cannot be denied, a religious concept and also a picture of psychic harmony. Both aspects are linked throughout Achebe's novels, beginning with *Things Fall Apart.* In killing Ikemefuna, whom he loves and who calls him father, Okonkwo sins not only against the earth goddess, protector of family relations, but also against his inmost feelings and thus against his *chi.* If Okonkwo's destiny (*chi*) is marked by bad luck, one reason may be that—driven by fear of resembling his father—he struggles to repress part of his personality (*chi*), with predictably ill results. In the final assessment, no one can fully explain *chi:* it is mysteriously uncertain, the element of fate over which we have no real control.

Things Fall Apart is both Okonkwo's tragedy and that of his society. The title (taken from William Butler Yeats's *The Second Coming*) introduces a narrative in which a complex and dignified traditional society disintegrates before foreign invaders who assault its political, economic, and religious institutions. The setting is eastern Nigeria around the turn of the century in the clan of Umuofia, which is composed of nine interrelated villages. One of these villages, Iguedo, is the home of the protagonist Okonkwo, an ambitious and powerful man who is driven by the memory of his father's failure and weakness.

During the first two-thirds of the book, Achebe paints the picture of a rich and coherent society, establishing an image of traditional African culture into which the final chapters' missionaries, court messengers, and district commissioner intrude as alien and disruptive elements. In sharp contrast to the simplified vision of African life given by European novelists Joyce Cary, Joseph Conrad, or Graham Greene, he explores the complex feelings and interpersonal relationships of diverse villagers seen as men, women, parents, children, friends, neighbors, or priests of the local deities. The intricate patterns of Umuofia's economic and social customs also emerge, belying European images of African "primitive" simplicity. No one who has read about Obierika's intricate marriage negotiations, the etiquette of *kola* hospitality, the religious "week of peace," Ezeudu's elaborate funeral rites, the domestic arbitration conducted by the *egwugwu* court, the female kinship customs linking families and villages, or indeed Umuofia's entire set of taboos and punishments will find this a simple society. The title system itself, which plays such a large part in the novel, is an ingenious social strategy for redistributing wealth throughout the community. The four honorific *ozo* titles (*Ozo, Idemili, Omalo,* and *Erulu*), through which a man enters the spiritual community of his ancestors and achieves increasing levels of prestige, are acquired in festivities during which the candidate divests himself of excess material wealth. There is a dignity and purpose to this society despite inner tensions that—as Achebe shows—create pain as well as vulnerability to attack from outside. The moderate Obierika disapproves of killing Ikemefuna and begins to question the practice of throwing away twins; one of the first converts to Christianity is a woman who gave birth to several sets of twins, all of whom were exposed (left in the wild) at birth. The general subordination of women is another source of tensions that have taken longer to surface. Whatever its cultural differences from European society, however, this is a highly organized and complex society that offers a great deal of continuity and coherence to its members.

Igbo names, like names throughout black Africa, consist of whole phrases or sentences. Some names are dictated by circumstance (referring to the day of birth, for example) and some (the "given" name selected by the child's father, for example) reflect the family situation or a child's expected destiny. Adults may earn additional titles of honor. Achebe uses the connotations of personal names to reinforce important themes in *Things Fall Apart*. Okonkwo's father's character as a lazy, artistic, and improvident man is suggested by the name Unoka, signifying "the home is supreme." Okonkwo's son Nwoye, who has inherited his grandfather's peace-loving nature and artistic qualities, is named after the second day of the Igbo week (*Oye*); unlike Okonkwo, Nwoye lacks a prefix specifying adulthood or even gender, for *Nwa* means "child." Ikemefuna, who is condemned to death by the Oracle and will be killed by his adoptive father, is named "My strength should not be dissipated." Although all names have significance, only those with some relevance to the story will be annotated in this edition.

Okonkwo's character and career suggest epic dimensions. He is on the one hand a hero of enormous energy and determination, "one of the greatest men in Umuofia" as his friend Obierika says, but his particular mode of greatness also causes his downfall. Like Achilles in Homer's *Iliad*, Okonkwo clings to traditionally respected values of pride and warlike aggression, and he will die to preserve those values. His unwillingness to change sets him apart from the community and eventually isolates him from the clan with its emphasis on group decisions. Okonkwo is a passionate man who counts on physical strength, hard work, and courage to make his way. Humiliated by his father's laziness, shameful death, and lack of title, compelled early to support the entire family, he struggles desperately to root out any sign of inherited "feminine" weakness in himself or his son Nwoye. By cultivating strength and valor, he finds a way to surpass his father and become one of the village leaders. Okonkwo is not without tender feelings: he loves his wife Ekwefi; his daughter, Ezinma; and the youth Ikemefuna who is given to him to foster. When he cuts down Ikemefuna so as not to appear weak, he is shattered for days thereafter. Nonetheless, his obsession with fierce masculinity and his open disrespect for "womanly" qualities of gentleness, compassion, and peace separate him not only from other members of his clan such as the more balanced Obierika but also from the earth goddess herself. This imbalance leads to disaster.

A recent and full biography is Ezenwa Ohaeto, *Chinua Achebe: A Biography* (1997). C. L. Innes, *Chinua Achebe* (1990), is a comprehensive study of Achebe's work through 1988 that emphasizes his literary techniques and Africanization of the novel. Simon Gikandi, *Reading Chinua Achebe: Language and Ideology in Fiction* (1991), is also recommended. Robert M. Wren, *Achebe's World: The Historical and Cultural Context of the Novels of Chinua Achebe* (1980), provides historical background and cultural context for Achebe's novels and includes glossary and bibliography. Studies of *Things Fall Apart* include Kate Turkington, *Chinua Achebe: Things Fall Apart* (1977), a concise introductory study; Steven H. Gale, *Chinua Achebe's Things Fall Apart* (1998); and the nine essays in Solomon Ogbede Iyasere, ed., *Understanding Things Fall Apart: Selected Essays and Criticism* (1998). C. L. Innes and Bernth Lindfors, eds., *Critical Perspectives on Chinua Achebe* (1978), collect twenty-one essays on Achebe's work (almost exclusively the novels) through 1973. G. D. Killam, *The Writings of Chinua Achebe* (1977), is a commentary on Achebe's work through the mid-1970s, concentrating on the first four novels. Also of interest is Chinua Achebe, *Conversations with Chinua Achebe* (1997), ed. Bernth Lindfors.

PRONOUNCING GLOSSARY

The following list uses common English syllables and stress accents to provide rough equivalents of selected words whose pronunciation may be unfamiliar to the general reader. Most of the names in *Things Fall Apart* are pronounced basically as they would be in English (for example, Okonkwo as *oh-kon'-kwo*), except that Igbo (like other African languages and Chinese) is a tonal language and also uses high or low tones for individual syllables.

Chielo: *chee'-ay-loh*

Chinua Achebe: *chin'-oo-ah ah-chay'-*
    bay

egwugwu: *eg-woog'-woo*

Erulu: *air-oo'-loo*

Ezeani: *ez-ah'-nee*

Ezeugo: *e'-zoo-goh*

Idemili: *ee-day-mee'lee*

Igbo: *ee'-boh*

Ikemefuna: *ee-kay-may'-foo-na*

mbari: *mbah'-ree*

Ndulue: *in'-doo-loo'-eh*

Nwakibie: *nwa'-kee-ee'-bee-yay*

Nwayieke: *nwah'-ee-eh'-kay*

Umuofia: *oo'-moo-off'-yah*

Things Fall Apart

Turning and turning in the widening gyre
The falcon cannot hear the falconer;
Things fall apart; the centre cannot hold;
Mere anarchy is loosed upon the world . . .
—W. B. Yeats, "The Second Coming"

Part One

1

Okonkwo was well known throughout the nine villages and even beyond. His fame rested on solid personal achievements. As a young man of eighteen he had brought honor to his village by throwing Amalinze the Cat. Amalinze was the great wrestler who for seven years was unbeaten, from Umuofia[1] to Mbaino.[2] He was called the Cat because his back would never touch the earth. It was this man that Okonkwo threw in a fight which the old men agreed was one of the fiercest since the founder of their town engaged a spirit of the wild for seven days and seven nights.

The drums beat and the flutes sang and the spectators held their breath. Amalinze was a wily craftsman, but Okonkwo was as slippery as a fish in water. Every nerve and every muscle stood out on their arms, on their backs and their thighs, and one almost heard them stretching to breaking point. In the end Okonkwo threw the Cat.

That was many years ago, twenty years or more, and during this time Okonkwo's fame had grown like a bush-fire in the harmattan.[3] He was tall and huge, and his bushy eyebrows and wide nose gave him a very severe look. He breathed heavily, and it was said that, when he slept, his wives and children in their houses could hear him breathe. When he walked, his heels hardly touched the ground and he seemed to walk on springs, as if he was going to pounce on somebody. And he did pounce on people quite often. He had a slight stammer and whenever he was angry and could not get his words out quickly enough, he would use his fists. He had no patience with unsuccessful men. He had had no patience with his father.

Unoka,[4] for that was his father's name, had died ten years ago. In his day he was lazy and improvident and was quite incapable of thinking about tomorrow. If any money came his way, and it seldom did, he immediately

---

1. Man [*oko*] born on Nkwo Day; the name also suggests stubborn male pride. *Okonkwo:* "Four settlements."   2. Four settlements. Umuofia means children of the forest (literal trans.); but *ofia* ("forest") also means "bush" or land untouched by European influence.   3. A dusty wind from the Sahara.   4. Home is supreme.

bought gourds of palm-wine, called round his neighbors and made merry. He always said that whenever he saw a dead man's mouth he saw the folly of not eating what one had in one's lifetime. Unoka was, of course, a debtor, and he owed every neighbor some money, from a few cowries[5] to quite substantial amounts.

He was tall but very thin and had a slight stoop. He wore a haggard and mournful look except when he was drinking or playing on his flute. He was very good on his flute, and his happiest moments were the two or three moons after the harvest when the village musicians brought down their instruments, hung above the fireplace. Unoka would play with them, his face beaming with blessedness and peace. Sometimes another village would ask Unoka's band and their dancing *egwugwu*[6] to come and stay with them and teach them their tunes. They would go to such hosts for as long as three or four markets,[7] making music and feasting. Unoka loved the good fare and the good fellowship, and he loved this season of the year, when the rains had stopped and the sun rose every morning with dazzling beauty. And it was not too hot either, because the cold and dry harmattan wind was blowing down from the north. Some years the harmattan was very severe and a dense haze hung on the atmosphere. Old men and children would then sit round log fires, warming their bodies. Unoka loved it all, and he loved the first kites[8] that returned with the dry season, and the children who sang songs of welcome to them. He would remember his own childhood, how he had often wandered around looking for a kite sailing leisurely against the blue sky. As soon as he found one he would sing with his whole being, welcoming it back from its long, long journey, and asking it if it had brought home any lengths of cloth.

That was years ago, when he was young. Unoka, the grown-up, was a failure. He was poor and his wife and children had barely enough to eat. People laughed at him because he was a loafer, and they swore never to lend him any more money because he never paid back. But Unoka was such a man that he always succeeded in borrowing more, and piling up his debts.

One day a neighbor called Okoye[9] came in to see him. He was reclining on a mud bed in his hut playing on the flute. He immediately rose and shook hands with Okoye, who then unrolled the goatskin which he carried under his arm, and sat down. Unoka went into an inner room and soon returned with a small wooden disc containing a kola nut, some alligator pepper and a lump of white chalk.[1]

"I have kola," he announced when he sat down, and passed the disc over to his guest.

"Thank you. He who brings kola brings life. But I think you ought to break it," replied Okoye, passing back the disc.

"No, it is for you, I think," and they argued like this for a few moments

<hr />

5. Glossy half-inch-long tan-and-white shells, collected in strings and used as money. A bag of twenty-four thousand cowries weighed about sixty pounds and, at the time of the story, was worth approximately one British pound.   6. Here, masked performers as part of musical entertainment.   7. Counting one important market day a week, roughly two English weeks. The Igbo week has four days: Eke, Oye, Afo, and Nkwo. Eke is a rest day and the main market day; Afo, a half day on the farm; and Oye and Nkwo, full work days.   8. A kind of hawk.   9. Man born on Oye Day; a generic "Everyman" name.   1. Signifies coolness and peace and is offered in rituals of hospitality so that the guest may draw his personal emblem on the floor. *Kola nut:* a bitter, caffeine-rich nut that is broken and eaten ceremonially; it indicates life or vitality. *Alligator pepper:* black pepper, known as the "pepper for kola" to distinguish it from cooking pepper, or chilies.

before Unoka accepted the honor of breaking the kola. Okoye, meanwhile, took the lump of chalk, drew some lines on the floor, and then painted his big toe.[2]

As he broke the kola, Unoka prayed to their ancestors for life and health, and for protection against their enemies. When they had eaten they talked about many things: about the heavy rains which were drowning the yams, about the next ancestral feast and about the impending war with the village of Mbaino. Unoka was never happy when it came to wars. He was in fact a coward and could not bear the sight of blood. And so he changed the subject and talked about music, and his face beamed. He could hear in his mind's ear the blood-stirring and intricate rhythms of the *ekwe* and the *udu* and the *ogene*,[3] and he could hear his own flute weaving in and out of them, decorating them with a colorful and plaintive tune. The total effect was gay and brisk, but if one picked out the flute as it went up and down and then broke up into short snatches, one saw that there was sorrow and grief there.

Okoye was also a musician. He played on the *ogene*. But he was not a failure like Unoka. He had a large barn full of yams and he had three wives. And now he was going to take the Idemili title,[4] the third highest in the land. It was a very expensive ceremony and he was gathering all his resources together. That was in fact the reason why he had come to see Unoka. He cleared his throat and began:

"Thank you for the kola. You may have heard of the title I intend to take shortly."

Having spoken plainly so far, Okoye said the next half a dozen sentences in proverbs. Among the Ibo the art of conversation is regarded very highly, and proverbs are the palm-oil with which words are eaten. Okoye was a great talker and he spoke for a long time, skirting round the subject and then hitting it finally. In short, he was asking Unoka to return the two hundred cowries he had borrowed from him more than two years before. As soon as Unoka understood what his friend was driving at, he burst out laughing. He laughed loud and long and his voice rang out clear as the *ogene*, and tears stood in his eyes. His visitor was amazed, and sat speechless. At the end, Unoka was able to give an answer between fresh outbursts of mirth.

"Look at that wall," he said, pointing at the far wall of his hut, which was rubbed with red earth so that it shone. "Look at those lines of chalk;" and Okoye saw groups of short perpendicular lines drawn in chalk. There were five groups, and the smallest group had ten lines. Unoka had a sense of the dramatic and so he allowed a pause, in which he took a pinch of snuff and sneezed noisily, and then he continued: "Each group there represents a debt to someone, and each stroke is one hundred cowries. You see, I owe that man a thousand cowries. But he has not come to wake me up in the morning for it. I shall pay you, but not today. Our elders say that the sun will shine on those who stand before it shines on those who kneel under them. I shall pay my big debts first." And he took another pinch of snuff, as if that was paying the big debts first. Okoye rolled his goatskin and departed.

2. If the guest has taken the first title, he marks his big toe. Higher titles require different facial markings.
3. A bell-shaped gong made from two pieces of sheet iron. *Ekwe:* a wooden drum, about three feet long, that produces high and low tones (as does the Igbo language). *Udu:* a clay pot with a hole to one side of the neck opening; various resonant tones are produced when the hole is struck with one hand while the other hand covers or uncovers the top.   4. A title of honor named after the river god Idemili, to whom the python is sacred. *Barn:* not a building, but a walled enclosure for the yam stacks (frames on which individual yams are tied, shaded with palm leaves, and exposed to circulating air).

When Unoka died he had taken no title at all and he was heavily in debt. Any wonder then that his son Okonkwo was ashamed of him? Fortunately, among these people a man was judged according to his worth and not according to the worth of his father. Okonkwo was clearly cut out for great things. He was still young but he had won fame as the greatest wrestler in the nine villages. He was a wealthy farmer and had two barns full of yams, and had just married his third wife. To crown it all he had taken two titles and had shown incredible prowess in two inter-tribal wars. And so although Okonkwo was still young, he was already one of the greatest men of his time. Age was respected among his people, but achievement was revered. As the elders said, if a child washed his hands he could eat with kings. Okonkwo had clearly washed his hands and so he ate with kings and elders. And that was how he came to look after the doomed lad who was sacrificed to the village of Umuofia by their neighbors to avoid war and bloodshed. The ill-fated lad was called Ikemefuna.[5]

2

Okonkwo had just blown out the palm-oil lamp and stretched himself on his bamboo bed when he heard the *ogene* of the town crier piercing the still night air. *Gome, gome, gome, gome,* boomed the hollow metal. Then the crier gave his message, and at the end of it beat his instrument again. And this was the message. Every man of Umuofia was asked to gather at the market place tomorrow morning. Okonkwo wondered what was amiss, for he knew certainly that something was amiss. He had discerned a clear overtone of tragedy in the crier's voice, and even now he could still hear it as it grew dimmer and dimmer in the distance.

The night was very quiet. It was always quiet except on moonlight nights. Darkness held a vague terror for these people, even the bravest among them. Children were warned not to whistle at night for fear of evil spirits. Dangerous animals became even more sinister and uncanny in the dark. A snake was never called by its name at night, because it would hear. It was called a string. And so on this particular night as the crier's voice was gradually swallowed up in the distance, silence returned to the world, a vibrant silence made more intense by the universal trill of a million million forest insects.

On a moonlight night it would be different. The happy voices of children playing in open fields would then be heard. And perhaps those not so young would be playing in pairs in less open places, and old men and women would remember their youth. As the Ibo say: "When the moon is shining the cripple becomes hungry for a walk."

But this particular night was dark and silent. And in all the nine villages of Umuofia a town crier with his *ogene* asked every man to be present tomorrow morning. Okonkwo on his bamboo bed tried to figure out the nature of the emergency—war with a neighboring clan? That seemed the most likely reason, and he was not afraid of war. He was a man of action, a man of war. Unlike his father he could stand the look of blood. In Umuofia's latest war he was the first to bring home a human head. That was his fifth head; and he was not an old man yet. On great occasions such as the funeral of a village celebrity he drank his palm-wine from his first human head.

5. My strength should not be dissipated.

In the morning the market place was full. There must have been about ten thousand men there, all talking in low voices. At last Ogbuefi Ezeugo stood up in the midst of them and bellowed four times, "Umuofia kwenu,"[6] and on each occasion he faced a different direction and seemed to push the air with a clenched fist. And ten thousand men answered "Yaa!" each time. Then there was perfect silence. Ogbuefi Ezeugo was a powerful orator and was always chosen to speak on such occasions. He moved his hand over his white head and stroked his white beard. He then adjusted his cloth, which was passed under his right armpit and tied above his left shoulder.

"Umuofia kwenu," he bellowed a fifth time, and the crowd yelled in answer. And then suddenly like one possessed he shot out his left hand and pointed in the direction of Mbaino, and said through gleaming white teeth firmly clenched: "Those sons of wild animals have dared to murder a daughter of Umuofia." He threw his head down and gnashed his teeth, and allowed a murmur of suppressed anger to sweep the crowd. When he began again, the anger on his face was gone and in its place a sort of smile hovered, more terrible and more sinister than the anger. And in a clear unemotional voice he told Umuofia how their daughter had gone to market at Mbaino and had been killed. That woman, said Ezeugo, was the wife of Ogbuefi Udo,[7] and he pointed to a man who sat near him with a bowed head. The crowd then shouted with anger and thirst for blood.

Many others spoke, and at the end it was decided to follow the normal course of action. An ultimatum was immediately dispatched to Mbaino asking them to choose between war on the one hand, and on the other the offer of a young man and a virgin as compensation.

Umuofia was feared by all its neighbors. It was powerful in war and in magic, and its priests and medicine men were feared in all the surrounding country. Its most potent war-medicine was as old as the clan itself. Nobody knew how old. But on one point there was general agreement—the active principle in that medicine had been an old woman with one leg. In fact, the medicine itself was called *agadi-nwayi*, or old woman. It had its shrine in the center of Umuofia, in a cleared spot. And if anybody was so foolhardy as to pass by the shrine after dusk he was sure to see the old woman hopping about.

And so the neighboring clans who naturally knew of these things feared Umuofia, and would not go to war against it without first trying a peaceful settlement. And in fairness to Umuofia it should be recorded that it never went to war unless its case was clear and just and was accepted as such by its Oracle—the Oracle of the Hills and the Caves. And there were indeed occasions when the Oracle had forbidden Umuofia to wage a war. If the clan had disobeyed the Oracle they would surely have been beaten, because their dreaded *agadi-nwayi* would never fight what the Ibo call *a fight of blame.*

But the war that now threatened was a just war. Even the enemy clan knew that. And so when Okonkwo of Umuofia arrived at Mbaino as the proud and imperious emissary of war, he was treated with great honor and respect, and two days later he returned home with a lad of fifteen and a young virgin.

6. United Umuofia! An orator's call on the audience to respond as a group. *Ogbuefi*: cow killer (literal trans.); indicates someone who has taken a high title (e.g., the Idemili title) for which the celebration ceremony requires the slaughter of a cow. *Ezeugo*: a name denoting a priest or high initiate, someone who wears the eagle feather.   7. Peace.

The lad's name was Ikemefuna, whose sad story is still told in Umuofia unto this day.

The elders, or *ndichie*, met to hear a report of Okonkwo's mission. At the end they decided, as everybody knew they would, that the girl should go to Ogbuefi Udo to replace his murdered wife. As for the boy, he belonged to the clan as a whole, and there was no hurry to decide his fate. Okonkwo was, therefore, asked on behalf of the clan to look after him in the interim. And so for three years Ikemefuna lived in Okonkwo's household.

Okonkwo ruled his household with a heavy hand. His wives, especially the youngest, lived in perpetual fear of his fiery temper, and so did his little children. Perhaps down in his heart Okonkwo was not a cruel man. But his whole life was dominated by fear, the fear of failure and of weakness. It was deeper and more intimate than the fear of evil and capricious gods and of magic, the fear of the forest, and of the forces of nature, malevolent, red in tooth and claw. Okonkwo's fear was greater than these. It was not external but lay deep within himself. It was the fear of himself, lest he should be found to resemble his father. Even as a little boy he had resented his father's failure and weakness, and even now he still remembered how he had suffered when a playmate had told him that his father was *agbala*. That was how Okonkwo first came to know that *agbala* was not only another name for a woman, it could also mean a man who had taken no title. And so Okonkwo was ruled by one passion—to hate everything that his father Unoka had loved. One of those things was gentleness and another was idleness.

During the planting season Okonkwo worked daily on his farms from cock-crow until the chickens went to roost. He was a very strong man and rarely felt fatigue. But his wives and young children were not as strong, and so they suffered. But they dared not complain openly. Okonkwo's first son, Nwoye,[8] was then twelve years old but was already causing his father great anxiety for his incipient laziness. At any rate, that was how it looked to his father, and he sought to correct him by constant nagging and beating. And so Nwoye was developing into a sad-faced youth.

Okonkwo's prosperity was visible in his household. He had a large compound enclosed by a thick wall of red earth. His own hut, or *obi*, stood immediately behind the only gate in the red walls. Each of his three wives had her own hut, which together formed a half moon behind the *obi*. The barn was built against one end of the red walls, and long stacks of yam stood out prosperously in it. At the opposite end of the compound was a shed for the goats, and each wife built a small attachment to her hut for the hens. Near the barn was a small house, the "medicine house" or shrine where Okonkwo kept the wooden symbols of his personal god and of his ancestral spirits. He worshiped them with sacrifices of kola nut, food and palm-wine, and offered prayers to them on behalf of himself, his three wives and eight children.

So when the daughter of Umuofia was killed in Mbaino, Ikemefuna came into Okonkwo's household. When Okonkwo brought him home that day he called his most senior wife and handed him over to her.

---

8. Child born on Oye Day.

"He belongs to the clan," he told her. "So look after him."

"Is he staying long with us?" she asked.

"Do what you are told, woman," Okonkwo thundered, and stammered. "When did you become one of the *ndichie* of Umuofia?"

And so Nwoye's mother took Ikemefuna to her hut and asked no more questions.

As for the boy himself, he was terribly afraid. He could not understand what was happening to him or what he had done. How could he know that his father had taken a hand in killing a daughter of Umuofia? All he knew was that a few men had arrived at their house, conversing with his father in low tones, and at the end he had been taken out and handed over to a stranger. His mother had wept bitterly, but he had been too surprised to weep. And so the stranger had brought him, and a girl, a long, long way from home, through lonely forest paths. He did not know who the girl was, and he never saw her again.

3

Okonkwo did not have the start in life which many young men usually had. He did not inherit a barn from his father. There was no barn to inherit. The story was told in Umuofia, of how his father, Unoka, had gone to consult the Oracle of the Hills and the Caves to find out why he always had a miserable harvest.

The Oracle was called Agbala,[9] and people came from far and near to consult it. They came when misfortune dogged their steps or when they had a dispute with their neighbors. They came to discover what the future held for them or to consult the spirits of their departed fathers.

The way into the shrine was a round hole at the side of a hill, just a little bigger than the round opening into a henhouse. Worshipers and those who came to seek knowledge from the god crawled on their belly through the hole and found themselves in a dark, endless space in the presence of Agbala. No one had ever beheld Agbala, except his priestess. But no one who had ever crawled into his awful shrine had come out without the fear of his power. His priestess stood by the sacred fire which she built in the heart of the cave and proclaimed the will of the god. The fire did not burn with a flame. The glowing logs only served to light up vaguely the dark figure of the priestess.

Sometimes a man came to consult the spirit of his dead father or relative. It was said that when such a spirit appeared, the man saw it vaguely in the darkness, but never heard its voice. Some people even said that they had heard the spirits flying and flapping their wings against the roof of the cave.

Many years ago when Okonkwo was still a boy his father, Unoka, had gone to consult Agbala. The priestess in those days was a woman called Chika.[1] She was full of the power of her god, and she was greatly feared. Unoka stood before her and began his story.

"Every year," he said sadly, "before I put any crop in the earth, I sacrifice a cock to Ani, the owner of all land. It is the law of our fathers. I also kill a

---

9. The Oracle is masculine, but his priestess, or Voice, is feminine.   1. Sky is supreme.

cock at the shrine of Ifejioku, the god of yams. I clear the bush and set fire
to it when it is dry. I sow the yams when the first rain has fallen, and stake
them when the young tendrils appear. I weed—"

"Hold your peace!" screamed the priestess, her voice terrible as it echoed
through the dark void. "You have offended neither the gods nor your fathers.
And when a man is at peace with his gods and his ancestors, his harvest will
be good or bad according to the strength of his arm. You, Unoka, are known
in all the clan for the weakness of your machete and your hoe. When your
neighbors go out with their ax to cut down virgin forests, you sow your yams
on exhausted farms that take no labor to clear. They cross seven rivers to
make their farms; you stay at home and offer sacrifices to a reluctant soil.
Go home and work like a man."

Unoka was an ill-fated man. He had a bad *chi* or personal god, and evil
fortune followed him to the grave, or rather to his death, for he had no grave.
He died of the swelling which was an abomination to the earth goddess.
When a man was afflicted with swelling in the stomach and the limbs he
was not allowed to die in the house. He was carried to the Evil Forest and
left there to die. There was the story of a very stubborn man who staggered
back to his house and had to be carried again to the forest and tied to a tree.
The sickness was an abomination to the earth, and so the victim could not
be buried in her bowels. He died and rotted away above the earth, and was
not given the first or the second burial. Such was Unoka's fate. When they
carried him away, he took with him his flute.

With a father like Unoka, Okonkwo did not have the start in life which
many young men had. He neither inherited a barn nor a title, nor even a
young wife. But in spite of these disadvantages, he had begun even in his
father's lifetime to lay the foundations of a prosperous future. It was slow
and painful. But he threw himself into it like one possessed. And indeed he
was possessed by the fear of his father's contemptible life and shameful
death.

There was a wealthy man in Okonkwo's village who had three huge barns,
nine wives and thirty children. His name was Nwakibie[2] and he had taken
the highest but one title which a man could take in the clan. It was for this
man that Okonkwo worked to earn his first seed yams.

He took a pot of palm-wine and a cock to Nwakibie. Two elderly neighbors
were sent for, and Nwakibie's two grown-up sons were also present in his
obi. He presented a kola nut and an alligator pepper, which were passed
round for all to see and then returned to him. He broke the nut saying: "We
shall all live. We pray for life, children, a good harvest and happiness. You
will have what is good for you and I will have what is good for me. Let the
kite perch and let the eagle perch too. If one says no to the other, let his
wing break."

After the kola nut had been eaten Okonkwo brought his palm-wine from
the corner of the hut where it had been placed and stood it in the center of
the group. He addressed Nwakibie, calling him "Our father."

"*Nna ayi*," he said. "I have brought you this little kola. As our people say,

2. The child surpasses his neighbors.

a man who pays respect to the great paves the way for his own greatness. I have come to pay you my respects and also to ask a favor. But let us drink the wine first."

Everybody thanked Okonkwo and the neighbors brought out their drinking horns from the goatskin bags they carried. Nwakibie brought down his own horn, which was fastened to the rafters. The younger of his sons, who was also the youngest man in the group, moved to the center, raised the pot on his left knee and began to pour out the wine. The first cup went to Okonkwo, who must taste his wine before anyone else.[3] Then the group drank, beginning with the eldest man. When everyone had drunk two or three horns, Nwakibie sent for his wives. Some of them were not at home and only four came in.

"Is Anasi not in?" he asked them. They said she was coming. Anasi was the first[4] wife and the others could not drink before her, and so they stood waiting.

Anasi was a middle-aged woman, tall and strongly built. There was authority in her bearing and she looked every inch the ruler of the womenfolk in a large and prosperous family. She wore the anklet of her husband's titles, which the first wife alone could wear.

She walked up to her husband and accepted the horn from him. She then went down on one knee, drank a little and handed back the horn. She rose, called him by his name and went back to her hut. The other wives drank in the same way, in their proper order, and went away.

The men then continued their drinking and talking. Ogbuefi Idigo was talking about the palm-wine tapper, Obiako, who suddenly gave up his trade.

"There must be something behind it," he said, wiping the foam of wine from his mustache with the back of his left hand. "There must be a reason for it. A toad does not run in the daytime for nothing."

"Some people say the Oracle warned him that he would fall off a palm tree and kill himself," said Akukalia.

"Obiako has always been a strange one," said Nwakibie. "I have heard that many years ago, when his father had not been dead very long, he had gone to consult the Oracle. The Oracle said to him, 'Your dead father wants you to sacrifice a goat to him.' Do you know what he told the Oracle? He said, 'Ask my dead father if he ever had a fowl when he was alive.'" Everybody laughed heartily except Okonkwo, who laughed uneasily because, as the saying goes, an old woman is always uneasy when dry bones are mentioned in a proverb. Okonkwo remembered his own father.

At last the young man who was pouring out the wine held up half a horn of the thick, white dregs and said, "What we are eating is finished." "We have seen it," the others replied. "Who will drink the dregs?" he asked. "Whoever has a job in hand," said Idigo, looking at Nwakibie's elder son Igwelo with a malicious twinkle in his eye.

Everyone agreed that Igwelo should drink the dregs. He accepted the half-full horn from his brother and drank it. As Idigo had said, Igwelo had a job in hand because he had married his first wife a month or two before. The

---

3. A ceremonial gesture; one who gives wine tastes it first to show that it is not poisoned.   4. First or favorite wife—not always the same.

thick dregs of palm-wine were supposed to be good for men who were going in to their wives.

After the wine had been drunk Okonkwo laid his difficulties before Nwakibie.

"I have come to you for help," he said. "Perhaps you can already guess what it is. I have cleared a farm but have no yams to sow. I know what it is to ask a man to trust another with his yams, especially these days when young men are afraid of hard work. I am not afraid of work. The lizard that jumped from the high iroko tree to the ground said he would praise himself if no one else did. I began to fend for myself at an age when most people still suck at their mothers' breasts. If you give me some yam seeds I shall not fail you."

Nwakibie cleared his throat. "It pleases me to see a young man like you these days when our youth has gone so soft. Many young men have come to me to ask for yams but I have refused because I knew they would just dump them in the earth and leave them to be choked by weeds. When I say no to them they think I am hard-hearted. But it is not so. Eneke the bird[5] says that since men have learned to shoot without missing, he has learned to fly without perching. I have learned to be stingy with my yams. But I can trust you. I know it as I look at you. As our fathers said, you can tell a ripe corn by its look. I shall give you twice four hundred yams. Go ahead and prepare your farm."

Okonkwo thanked him again and again and went home feeling happy. He knew that Nwakibie would not refuse him, but he had not expected he would be so generous. He had not hoped to get more than four hundred seeds. He would now have to make a bigger farm. He hoped to get another four hundred yams from one of his father's friends at Isiuzo.[6]

Sharecropping was a very slow way of building up a barn of one's own. After all the toil one only got a third of the harvest. But for a young man whose father had no yams, there was no other way. And what made it worse in Okonkwo's case was that he had to support his mother and two sisters from his meager harvest. And supporting his mother also meant supporting his father. She could not be expected to cook and eat while her husband starved. And so at a very early age when he was striving desperately to build a barn through sharecropping Okonkwo was also fending for his father's house. It was like pouring grains of corn into a bag full of holes. His mother and sisters worked hard enough, but they grew women's crops, like coco-yams, beans and cassava. Yam, the king of crops, was a man's crop.[7]

The year that Okonkwo took eight hundred seed-yams from Nwakibie was the worst year in living memory. Nothing happened at its proper time; it was either too early or too late. It seemed as if the world had gone mad. The first rains were late, and, when they came, lasted only a brief moment. The blazing sun returned, more fierce than it had ever been known, and scorched all the green that had appeared with the rains. The earth burned like hot coals and roasted all the yams that had been sown. Like all good farmers, Okonkwo

---

5. Proverbial.   6. Head of the road; a small town.   7. Yams, a staple food in Western Africa, were a sacred crop generally cultivated only by men and eaten either roasted or boiled. *Coco-yams* (a brown root also called taro) and *cassava* (or manioc, which is refined in various ways to remove natural cyanide) were low-status root vegetables, prepared for eating by boiling and pounding.

had begun to sow with the first rains. He had sown four hundred seeds when the rains dried up and the heat returned. He watched the sky all day for signs of rain clouds and lay awake all night. In the morning he went back to his farm and saw the withering tendrils. He had tried to protect them from the smoldering earth by making rings of thick sisal leaves around them. But by the end of the day the sisal rings were burned dry and gray. He changed them every day, and prayed that the rain might fall in the night. But the drought continued for eight market weeks and the yams were killed.

Some farmers had not planted their yams yet. They were the lazy easygoing ones who always put off clearing their farms as long as they could. This year they were the wise ones. They sympathized with their neighbors with much shaking of the head, but inwardly they were happy for what they took to be their own foresight.

Okonkwo planted what was left of his seed-yams when the rains finally returned. He had one consolation. The yams he had sown before the drought were his own, the harvest of the previous year. He still had the eight hundred from Nwakibie and the four hundred from his father's friend. So he would make a fresh start.

But the year had gone mad. Rain fell as it had never fallen before. For days and nights together it poured down in violent torrents, and washed away the yam heaps. Trees were uprooted and deep gorges appeared everywhere. Then the rain became less violent. But it went from day to day without a pause. The spell of sunshine which always came in the middle of the wet season did not appear. The yams put on luxuriant green leaves, but every farmer knew that without sunshine the tubers would not grow.

That year the harvest was sad, like a funeral, and many farmers wept as they dug up the miserable and rotting yams. One man tied his cloth to a tree branch and hanged himself.

Okonkwo remembered that tragic year with a cold shiver throughout the rest of his life. It always surprised him when he thought of it later that he did not sink under the load of despair. He knew that he was a fierce fighter, but that year had been enough to break the heart of a lion.

"Since I survived that year," he always said, "I shall survive anything." He put it down to his inflexible will.

His father, Unoka, who was then an ailing man, had said to him during that terrible harvest month: "Do not despair. I know you will not despair. You have a manly and a proud heart. A proud heart can survive a general failure because such a failure does not prick its pride. It is more difficult and more bitter when a man fails *alone*."

Unoka was like that in his last days. His love of talk had grown with age and sickness. It tried Okonkwo's patience beyond words.

4

"Looking at a king's mouth," said an old man, "one would think he never sucked at his mother's breast." He was talking about Okonkwo, who had risen so suddenly from great poverty and misfortune to be one of the lords of the clan. The old man bore no ill will towards Okonkwo. Indeed he respected him for his industry and success. But he was struck, as most people were, by Okonkwo's brusqueness in dealing with less successful men. Only a week ago a man had contradicted him at a kindred meeting which they held to discuss the next ancestral feast. Without looking at the man Okonkwo had said: "This meeting is for men." The man who had contradicted him had no titles. That was why he had called him a woman. Okonkwo knew how to kill a man's spirit.

Everybody at the kindred meeting took sides with Osugo[8] when Okonkwo called him a woman. The oldest man present said sternly that those whose palm-kernels were cracked for them by a benevolent spirit should not forget to be humble. Okonkwo said he was sorry for what he had said, and the meeting continued.

But it was really not true that Okonkwo's palm-kernels had been cracked for him by a benevolent spirit. He had cracked them himself. Anyone who knew his grim struggle against poverty and misfortune could not say he had been lucky. If ever a man deserved his success, that man was Okonkwo. At an early age he had achieved fame as the greatest wrestler in all the land. That was not luck. At the most one could say that his *chi* or personal god was good. But the Ibo people have a proverb that when a man says yes his *chi* says yes also. Okonkwo said yes very strongly; so his *chi* agreed. And not only his *chi* but his clan too, because it judged a man by the work of his hands. That was why Okonkwo had been chosen by the nine villages to carry a message of war to their enemies unless they agreed to give up a young man and a virgin to atone for the murder of Udo's wife. And such was the deep fear that their enemies had for Umuofia that they treated Okonkwo like a king and brought him a virgin who was given to Udo as wife, and the lad Ikemefuna.

The elders of the clan had decided that Ikemefuna should be in Okonkwo's care for a while. But no one thought it would be as long as three years. They seemed to forget all about him as soon as they had taken the decision.

At first Ikemefuna was very much afraid. Once or twice he tried to run away, but he did not know where to begin. He thought of his mother and his three-year-old sister and wept bitterly. Nwoye's mother was very kind to him and treated him as one of her own children. But all he said was: "When shall I go home?" When Okonkwo heard that he would not eat any food he came into the hut with a big stick in his hand and stood over him while he swallowed his yams, trembling. A few moments later he went behind the hut and began to vomit painfully. Nwoye's mother went to him and placed her hands on his chest and on his back. He was ill for three market weeks, and when he recovered he seemed to have overcome his great fear and sadness.

He was by nature a very lively boy and he gradually became popular in Okonkwo's household, especially with the children. Okonkwo's son, Nwoye, who was two years younger, became quite inseparable from him because he seemed to know everything. He could fashion out flutes from bamboo stems and even from the elephant grass. He knew the names of all the birds and could set clever traps for the little bush rodents. And he knew which trees made the strongest bows.

Even Okonkwo himself became very fond of the boy—inwardly of course. Okonkwo never showed any emotion openly, unless it be the emotion of anger. To show affection was a sign of weakness; the only thing worth dem-

8. Low-status [*osu*] person.

onstrating was strength. He therefore treated Ikemefuna as he treated everybody else—with a heavy hand. But there was no doubt that he liked the boy.
Sometimes when he went to big village meetings or communal ancestral
feasts he allowed Ikemefuna to accompany him, like a son, carrying his stool
and his goatskin bag. And, indeed, Ikemefuna called him father.

Ikemefuna came to Umuofia at the end of the carefree season between harvest and planting. In fact he recovered from his illness only a few days before
the Week of Peace began. And that was also the year Okonkwo broke the
peace, and was punished, as was the custom, by Ezeani, the priest of the
earth goddess.

Okonkwo was provoked to justifiable anger by his youngest wife, who went
to plait her hair at her friend's house and did not return early enough to cook
the afternoon meal. Okonkwo did not know at first that she was not at home.
After waiting in vain for her dish he went to her hut to see what she was
doing. There was nobody in the hut and the fireplace was cold.

"Where is Ojiugo?" he asked his second wife, who came out of her hut to
draw water from a gigantic pot in the shade of a small tree in the middle of
the compound.

"She has gone to plait her hair."

Okonkwo bit his lips as anger welled up within him.

"Where are her children? Did she take them?" he asked with unusual
coolness and restraint.

"They are here," answered his first wife, Nwoye's mother. Okonkwo bent
down and looked into her hut. Ojiugo's children were eating with the children of his first wife.

"Did she ask you to feed them before she went?"

"Yes," lied Nwoye's mother, trying to minimize Ojiugo's thoughtlessness.

Okonkwo knew she was not speaking the truth. He walked back to his *obi*
to await Ojiugo's return. And when she returned he beat her very heavily. In
his anger he had forgotten that it was the Week of Peace. His first two wives
ran out in great alarm pleading with him that it was the sacred week. But
Okonkwo was not the man to stop beating somebody half-way through, not
even for fear of a goddess.

Okonkwo's neighbors heard his wife crying and sent their voices over the
compound walls to ask what was the matter. Some of them came over to see
for themselves. It was unheard of to beat somebody during the sacred week.

Before it was dusk Ezeani, who was the priest of the earth goddess, Ani,
called on Okonkwo in his *obi*. Okonkwo brought out kola nut and placed it
before the priest.

"Take away your kola nut. I shall not eat in the house of a man who has
no respect for our gods and ancestors."

Okonkwo tried to explain to him what his wife had done, but Ezeani
seemed to pay no attention. He held a short staff in his hand which he
brought down on the floor to emphasize his points.

"Listen to me," he said when Okonkwo had spoken. "You are not a stranger
in Umuofia. You know as well as I do that our forefathers ordained that
before we plant any crops in the earth we should observe a week in which a
man does not say a harsh word to his neighbor. We live in peace with our
fellows to honor our great goddess of the earth without whose blessing our

crops will not grow. You have committed a great evil." He brought down his staff heavily on the floor. "Your wife was at fault, but even if you came into your *obi* and found her lover on top of her, you would still have committed a great evil to beat her." His staff came down again. "The evil you have done can ruin the whole clan. The earth goddess whom you have insulted may refuse to give us her increase, and we shall all perish." His tone now changed from anger to command. "You will bring to the shrine of Ani tomorrow one she-goat, one hen, a length of cloth and a hundred cowries." He rose and left the hut.

Okonkwo did as the priest said. He also took with him a pot of palm-wine. Inwardly, he was repentant. But he was not the man to go about telling his neighbors that he was in error. And so people said he had no respect for the gods of the clan. His enemies said his good fortune had gone to his head. They called him the little bird *nza*[9] who so far forgot himself after a heavy meal that he challenged his *chi*.

No work was done during the Week of Peace. People called on their neighbors and drank palm-wine. This year they talked of nothing else but the *nso-ani*[1] which Okonkwo had committed. It was the first time for many years that a man had broken the sacred peace. Even the oldest men could only remember one or two other occasions somewhere in the dim past.

Ogbuefi Ezeudu, who was the oldest man in the village, was telling two other men who came to visit him that the punishment for breaking the Peace of Ani had become very mild in their clan.

"It has not always been so," he said. "My father told me that he had been told that in the past a man who broke the peace was dragged on the ground through the village until he died. But after a while this custom was stopped because it spoiled the peace which it was meant to preserve."

"Somebody told me yesterday," said one of the younger men, "that in some clans it is an abomination for a man to die during the Week of Peace."

"It is indeed true," said Ogbuefi Ezeudu. "They have that custom in Obo-doani.[2] If a man dies at this time he is not buried but cast into the Evil Forest. It is a bad custom which these people observe because they lack understanding. They throw away large numbers of men and women without burial. And what is the result? Their clan is full of the evil spirits of these unburied dead, hungry to do harm to the living."

After the Week of Peace every man and his family began to clear the bush to make new farms. The cut bush was left to dry and fire was then set to it. As the smoke rose into the sky kites appeared from different directions and hovered over the burning field in silent valediction. The rainy season was approaching when they would go away until the dry season returned.

Okonkwo spent the next few days preparing his seed-yams. He looked at each yam carefully to see whether it was good for sowing. Sometimes he decided that a yam was too big to be sown as one seed and he split it deftly along its length with his sharp knife. His eldest son, Nwoye, and Ikemefuna helped him by fetching the yams in long baskets from the barn and in counting the prepared seeds in groups of four hundred. Sometimes Okonkwo gave

9. The one that talks back (literal trans.); a small aggressive bird. In the story, it is easily defeated (alternatively, caught by a hawk) when it becomes enough to challenge its personal god. 1. Sin, abomination against the Earth goddess Ani. 2. The town of the land (literal trans.); i.e., Anytown, Nigeria.

them a few yams each to prepare. But he always found fault with their effort, and he said so with much threatening.

"Do you think you are cutting up yams for cooking?" he asked Nwoye. "If you split another yam of this size, I shall break your jaw. You think you are still a child. I began to own a farm at your age. And you," he said to Ikemefuna, "do you not grow yams where you come from?"

Inwardly Okonkwo knew that the boys were still too young to understand fully the difficult art of preparing seed-yams. But he thought that one could not begin too early. Yam stood for manliness, and he who could feed his family on yams from one harvest to another was a very great man indeed. Okonkwo wanted his son to be a great farmer and a great man. He would stamp out the disquieting signs of laziness which he thought he already saw in him.

"I will not have a son who cannot hold up his head in the gathering of the clan. I would sooner strangle him with my own hands. And if you stand staring at me like that," he swore, "Amadiora[3] will break your head for you!"

Some days later, when the land had been moistened by two or three heavy rains, Okonkwo and his family went to the farm with baskets of seed-yams, their hoes and machetes, and the planting began. They made single mounds of earth in straight lines all over the field and sowed the yams in them.

Yam, the king of crops, was a very exacting king. For three or four moons it demanded hard work and constant attention from cock-crow till the chickens went back to roost. The young tendrils were protected from earth-heat with rings of sisal leaves. As the rains became heavier the women planted maize, melons and beans between the yam mounds. The yams were then staked, first with little sticks and later with tall and big tree branches. The women weeded the farm three times at definite periods in the life of the yams, neither early nor late.

And now the rains had really come, so heavy and persistent that even the village rain-maker no longer claimed to be able to intervene. He could not stop the rain now, just as he would not attempt to start it in the heart of the dry season, without serious danger to his own health. The personal dynamism required to counter the forces of these extremes of weather would be far too great for the human frame.

And so nature was not interfered with in the middle of the rainy season. Sometimes it poured down in such thick sheets of water that earth and sky seemed merged in one gray wetness. It was then uncertain whether the low rumbling of Amadiora's thunder came from above or below. At such times, in each of the countless thatched huts of Umuofia, children sat around their mother's cooking fire telling stories, or with their father in his *obi* warming themselves from a log fire, roasting and eating maize. It was a brief resting period between the exacting and arduous planting season and the equally exacting but light-hearted month of harvests.

Ikemefuna had begun to feel like a member of Okonkwo's family. He still thought about his mother and his three-year-old sister, and he had moments of sadness and depression. But he and Nwoye had become so deeply attached

---

3. God of thunder and lightning.

to each other that such moments became less frequent and less poignant. Ikemefuna had an endless stock of folk tales. Even those which Nwoye knew already were told with a new freshness and the local flavor of a different clan. Nwoye remembered this period very vividly till the end of his life. He even remembered how he had laughed when Ikemefuna told him that the proper name for a corn cob with only a few scattered grains was *eze-agadi-nwayi,* or the teeth of an old woman. Nwoye's mind had gone immediately to Nwayieke, who lived near the udala tree.[4] She had about three teeth and was always smoking her pipe.

Gradually the rains became lighter and less frequent, and earth and sky once again became separate. The rain fell in thin, slanting showers through sunshine and quiet breeze. Children no longer stayed indoors but ran about singing:

> The rain is falling, the sun is shining,
> Alone Nnadi[5] is cooking and eating.

Nwoye always wondered who Nnadi was and why he should live all by himself, cooking and eating. In the end he decided that Nnadi must live in that land of Ikemefuna's favorite story where the ant holds his court in splendor and the sands dance forever.

5

The Feast of the New Yam was approaching and Umuofia was in a festival mood. It was an occasion for giving thanks to Ani, the earth goddess and the source of all fertility. Ani played a greater part in the life of the people than any other deity. She was the ultimate judge of morality and conduct. And what was more, she was in close communion with the departed fathers of the clan whose bodies had been committed to earth.

The Feast of the New Yam was held every year before the harvest began, to honor the earth goddess and the ancestral spirits of the clan. New yams could not be eaten until some had first been offered to these powers. Men and women, young and old, looked forward to the New Yam Festival because it began the season of plenty—the new year. On the last night before the festival, yams of the old year were all disposed of by those who still had them. The new year must begin with tasty, fresh yams and not the shriveled and fibrous crops of the previous year. All cooking pots, calabashes and wooden bowls were thoroughly washed, especially the wooden mortar in which yam was pounded. Yam foo-foo[6] and vegetable soup was the chief food in the celebration. So much of it was cooked that, no matter how heavily the family ate or how many friends and relatives they invited from neighboring villages, there was always a large quantity of food left over at the end of the day. The story was always told of a wealthy man who set before his guests a mound of foo-foo so high that those who sat on one side could not see what was happening on the other, and it was not until late in the evening that one of them saw for the first time his in-law who had arrived during the course of

---

4. African star apple tree. *Nwayieke:* Woman born on Eke Day.   5. Father is there or Father exists. 6. A mashed, edible base that is shaped into balls with the fingers and then indented for cupping and eating soup.

the meal and had fallen to on the opposite side. It was only then that they exchanged greetings and shook hands over what was left of the food.

The New Yam Festival was thus an occasion for joy throughout Umuofia. And every man whose arm was strong, as the Ibo people say, was expected to invite large numbers of guests from far and wide. Okonkwo always asked his wives' relations, and since he now had three wives his guests would make a fairly big crowd.

But somehow Okonkwo could never become as enthusiastic over feasts as most people. He was a good eater and he could drink one or two fairly big gourds of palm-wine. But he was always uncomfortable sitting around for days waiting for a feast or getting over it. He would be very much happier working on his farm.

The festival was now only three days away. Okonkwo's wives had scrubbed the walls and the huts with red earth until they reflected light. They had then drawn patterns on them in white, yellow and dark green. They then set about painting themselves with cam wood and drawing beautiful black patterns on their stomachs and on their backs. The children were also decorated, especially their hair, which was shaved in beautiful patterns. The three women talked excitedly about the relations who had been invited, and the children reveled in the thought of being spoiled by these visitors from the motherland. Ikemefuna was equally excited. The New Yam Festival seemed to him to be a much bigger event here than in his own village, a place which was already becoming remote and vague in his imagination.

And then the storm burst. Okonkwo, who had been walking about aimlessly in his compound in suppressed anger, suddenly found an outlet.

"Who killed this banana tree?" he asked.

A hush fell on the compound immediately.

"Who killed this tree? Or are you all deaf and dumb?"

As a matter of fact the tree was very much alive. Okonkwo's second wife had merely cut a few leaves off it to wrap some food, and she said so. Without further argument Okonkwo gave her a sound beating and left her and her only daughter weeping. Neither of the other wives dared to interfere beyond an occasional and tentative, "It is enough, Okonkwo," pleaded from a reasonable distance.

His anger thus satisfied, Okonkwo decided to go out hunting. He had an old rusty gun made by a clever blacksmith who had come to live in Umuofia long ago. But although Okonkwo was a great man whose prowess was universally acknowledged, he was not a hunter. In fact he had not killed a rat with his gun. And so when he called Ikemefuna to fetch his gun, the wife who had just been beaten murmured something about guns that never shot. Unfortunately for her, Okonkwo heard it and ran madly into his room for the loaded gun, ran out again and aimed at her as she clambered over the dwarf wall of the barn. He pressed the trigger and there was a loud report accompanied by the wail of his wives and children. He threw down the gun and jumped into the barn, and there lay the woman, very much shaken and frightened but quite unhurt. He heaved a heavy sigh and went away with the gun.

In spite of this incident the New Yam Festival was celebrated with great joy in Okonkwo's household. Early that morning as he offered a sacrifice of new yam and palm-oil to his ancestors he asked them to protect him, his children and their mothers in the new year.

As the day wore on his in-laws arrived from three surrounding villages, and each party brought with them a huge pot of palm-wine. And there was eating and drinking till night, when Okonkwo's in-laws began to leave for their homes.

The second day of the new year was the day of the great wrestling match between Okonkwo's village and their neighbors. It was difficult to say which the people enjoyed more—the feasting and fellowship of the first day or the wrestling contest of the second. But there was one woman who had no doubt whatever in her mind. She was Okonkwo's second wife, Ekwefi, whom he nearly shot. There was no festival in all the seasons of the year which gave her as much pleasure as the wrestling match. Many years ago when she was the village beauty Okonkwo had won her heart by throwing the Cat in the greatest contest within living memory. She did not marry him then because he was too poor to pay her bride-price. But a few years later she ran away from her husband and came to live with Okonkwo. All this happened many years ago. Now Ekwefi[7] was a woman of forty-five who had suffered a great deal in her time. But her love of wrestling contests was still as strong as it was thirty years ago.

It was not yet noon on the second day of the New Yam Festival. Ekwefi and her only daughter, Ezinma,[8] sat near the fireplace waiting for the water in the pot to boil. The fowl Ekwefi had just killed was in the wooden mortar. The water began to boil, and in one deft movement she lifted the pot from the fire and poured the boiling water over the fowl. She put back the empty pot on the circular pad in the corner, and looked at her palms, which were black with soot. Ezinma was always surprised that her mother could lift a pot from the fire with her bare hands.

"Ekwefi," she said, "is it true that when people are grown up, fire does not burn them?" Ezinma, unlike most children, called her mother by her name.

"Yes," replied Ekwefi, too busy to argue. Her daughter was only ten years old but she was wiser than her years.

"But Nwoye's mother dropped her pot of hot soup the other day and it broke on the floor."

Ekwefi turned the hen over in the mortar and began to pluck the feathers.

"Ekwefi," said Ezinma, who had joined in plucking the feathers, "my eyelid is twitching."

"It means you are going to cry," said her mother.

"No," Ezinma said, "it is this eyelid, the top one."

"That means you will see something."

"What will I see?" she asked.

"How can I know?" Ekwefi wanted her to work it out herself.

"Oho," said Ezinma at last. "I know what it is—the wrestling match."

At last the hen was plucked clean. Ekwefi tried to pull out the horny beak but it was too hard. She turned round on her low stool and put the beak in the fire for a few moments. She pulled again and it came off.

"Ekwefi!" a voice called from one of the other huts. It was Nwoye's mother, Okonkwo's first wife.

"Is that me?" Ekwefi called back. That was the way people answered calls

---

7. An abbreviation of "Do you have a cow?"; the cow being a symbol of wealth. Okonkwo would presumably have repaid Ekwefi's bride-price to her first husband.   8. True beauty (literal trans.), or goodness.

from outside. They never answered yes for fear it might be an evil spirit calling.

"Will you give Ezinma some fire to bring to me?" Her own children and Ikemefuna had gone to the stream.

Ekwefi put a few live coals into a piece of broken pot and Ezinma carried it across the clean swept compound to Nwoye's mother.

"Thank you, Nma," she said. She was peeling new yams, and in a basket beside her were green vegetables and beans.

"Let me make the fire for you," Ezinma offered.

"Thank you, Ezigbo," she said. She often called her Ezigbo, which means "the good one."

Ezinma went outside and brought some sticks from a huge bundle of firewood. She broke them into little pieces across the sole of her foot and began to build a fire, blowing it with her breath.

"You will blow your eyes out," said Nwoye's mother, looking up from the yams she was peeling. "Use the fan." She stood up and pulled out the fan which was fastened into one of the rafters. As soon as she got up, the troublesome nanny goat, which had been dutifully eating yam peelings, dug her teeth into the real thing, scooped out two mouthfuls and fled from the hut to chew the cud in the goats' shed. Nwoye's mother swore at her and settled down again to her peeling. Ezinma's fire was now sending up thick clouds of smoke. She went on fanning it until it burst into flames. Nwoye's mother thanked her and she went back to her mother's hut.

Just then the distant beating of drums began to reach them. It came from the direction of the *ilo,* the village playground. Every village had its own *ilo* which was as old as the village itself and where all the great ceremonies and dances took place. The drums beat the unmistakable wrestling dance— quick, light and gay, and it came floating on the wind.

Okonkwo cleared his throat and moved his feet to the beat of the drums. It filled him with fire as it had always done from his youth. He trembled with the desire to conquer and subdue. It was like the desire for a woman.

"We shall be late for the wrestling," said Ezinma to her mother.

"They will not begin until the sun goes down."

"But they are beating the drums."

"Yes. The drums begin at noon but the wrestling waits until the sun begins to sink. Go and see if your father has brought out yams for the afternoon."

"He has. Nwoye's mother is already cooking."

"Go and bring our own, then. We must cook quickly or we shall be late for the wrestling."

Ezinma ran in the direction of the barn and brought back two yams from the dwarf wall.

Ekwefi peeled the yams quickly. The troublesome nanny goat sniffed about, eating the peelings. She cut the yams into small pieces and began to prepare a pottage, using some of the chicken.

At that moment they heard someone crying just outside their compound. It was very much like Obiageli,[9] Nwoye's sister.

"Is that not Obiageli weeping?" Ekwefi called across the yard to Nwoye's mother.

"Yes," she replied. "She must have broken her waterpot."

---

9. Born to eat (born into prosperity).

The weeping was now quite close and soon the children filed in, carrying on their heads various sizes of pots suitable to their years. Ikemefuna came first with the biggest pot, closely followed by Nwoye and his two younger brothers. Obiageli brought up the rear, her face streaming with tears. In her hand was the cloth pad on which the pot should have rested on her head.

"What happened?" her mother asked, and Obiageli told her mournful story. Her mother consoled her and promised to buy her another pot.

Nwoye's younger brothers were about to tell their mother the true story of the accident when Ikemefuna looked at them sternly and they held their peace. The fact was that Obiageli had been making *inyanga*[1] with her pot. She had balanced it on her head, folded her arms in front of her and began to sway her waist like a grown-up young lady. When the pot fell down and broke she burst out laughing. She only began to weep when they got near the iroko tree outside their compound.

The drums were still beating, persistent and unchanging. Their sound was no longer a separate thing from the living village. It was like the pulsation of its heart. It throbbed in the air, in the sunshine, and even in the trees, and filled the village with excitement.

Ekwefi ladled her husband's share of the pottage into a bowl and covered it. Ezinma took it to him in his *obi*.

Okonkwo was sitting on a goatskin already eating his first wife's meal. Obiageli, who had brought it from her mother's hut, sat on the floor waiting for him to finish. Ezinma placed her mother's dish before him and sat with Obiageli.

"Sit like a woman!" Okonkwo shouted at her. Ezinma brought her two legs together and stretched them in front of her.

"Father, will you go to see the wrestling?" Ezinma asked after a suitable interval.

"Yes," he answered. "Will you go?"

"Yes." And after a pause she said: "Can I bring your chair for you?"

"No, that is a boy's job." Okonkwo was specially fond of Ezinma. She looked very much like her mother, who was once the village beauty. But his fondness only showed on very rare occasions.

"Obiageli broke her pot today," Ezinma said.

"Yes, she has told me about it," Okonkwo said between mouthfuls.

"Father," said Obiageli, "people should not talk when they are eating or pepper may go down the wrong way."

"That is very true. Do you hear that, Ezinma? You are older than Obiageli but she has more sense."

He uncovered his second wife's dish and began to eat from it. Obiageli took the first dish and returned to her mother's hut. And then Nkechi came in, bringing the third dish. Nkechi was the daughter of Okonkwo's third wife.

In the distance the drums continued to beat.

6

The whole village turned out on the *ilo*, men, women and children. They stood round in a huge circle leaving the center of the playground free. The elders and grandees of the village sat on their own stools brought there by

1. Showing off.

their young sons or slaves. Okonkwo was among them. All others stood except those who came early enough to secure places on the few stands which had been built by placing smooth logs on forked pillars.

The wrestlers were not there yet and the drummers held the field. They too sat just in front of the huge circle of spectators, facing the elders. Behind them was the big and ancient silk-cotton tree which was sacred. Spirits of good children lived in that tree waiting to be born. On ordinary days young women who desired children came to sit under its shade.

There were seven drums and they were arranged according to their sizes in a long wooden basket. Three men beat them with sticks, working fever-ishly from one drum to another. They were possessed by the spirit of the drums.

The young men who kept order on these occasions dashed about, consult-ing among themselves and with the leaders of the two wrestling teams, who were still outside the circle, behind the crowd. Once in a while two young men carrying palm fronds ran round the circle and kept the crowd back by beating the ground in front of them or, if they were stubborn, their legs and feet.

At last the two teams danced into the circle and the crowd roared and clapped. The drums rose to a frenzy. The people surged forward. The young men who kept order flew around, waving their palm fronds. Old men nodded to the beat of the drums and remembered the days when they wrestled to its intoxicating rhythm.

The contest began with boys of fifteen or sixteen. There were only three such boys in each team. They were not the real wrestlers; they merely set the scene. Within a short time the first two bouts were over. But the third created a big sensation even among the elders who did not usually show their excitement so openly. It was as quick as the other two, perhaps even quicker. But very few people had ever seen that kind of wrestling before. As soon as the two boys closed in, one of them did something which no one could describe because it had been as quick as a flash. And the other boy was flat on his back. The crowd roared and clapped and for a while drowned the frenzied drums. Okonkwo sprang to his feet and quickly sat down again. Three young men from the victorious boy's team ran forward, carried him shoulder high and danced through the cheering crowd. Everybody soon knew who the boy was. His name was Maduka, the son of Obierika.[2]

The drummers stopped for a brief rest before the real matches. Their bodies shone with sweat, and they took up fans and began to fan themselves. They also drank water from small pots and ate kola nuts. They became ordi-nary human beings again, talking and laughing among themselves and with others who stood near them. The air, which had been stretched taut with excitement, relaxed again. It was as if water had been poured on the tight-ened skin of a drum. Many people looked around, perhaps for the first time, and saw those who stood or sat next to them.

"I did not know it was you," Ekwefi said to the woman who had stood shoulder to shoulder with her since the beginning of the matches.

"I do not blame you," said the woman. "I have never seen such a large crowd of people. Is it true that Okonkwo nearly killed you with his gun?"

2. The heart eats [enjoys] more.

"It is true indeed, my dear friend. I cannot yet find a mouth with which to tell the story."

"Your *chi* is very much awake, my friend. And how is my daughter, Ezinma?"

"She has been very well for some time now. Perhaps she has come to stay."

"I think she has. How old is she now?"

"She is about ten years old."

"I think she will stay. They usually stay if they do not die before the age of six."

"I pray she stays," said Ekwefi with a heavy sigh.

The woman with whom she talked was called Chielo.[3] She was the priestess of Agbala, the Oracle of the Hills and the Caves. In ordinary life Chielo was a widow with two children. She was very friendly with Ekwefi and they shared a common shed in the market. She was particularly fond of Ekwefi's only daughter, Ezinma, whom she called "my daughter." Quite often she bought beancakes and gave Ekwefi some to take home to Ezinma. Anyone seeing Chielo in ordinary life would hardly believe she was the same person who prophesied when the spirit of Agbala was upon her. The drummers took up their sticks and the air shivered and grew tense like a tightened bow.

The two teams were ranged facing each other across the clear space. A young man from one team danced across the center to the other side and pointed at whomever he wanted to fight. They danced back to the center together and then closed in.

There were twelve men on each side and the challenge went from one side to the other. Two judges walked around the wrestlers and when they thought they were equally matched, stopped them. Five matches ended in this way. But the really exciting moments were when a man was thrown. The huge voice of the crowd then rose to the sky and in every direction. It was even heard in the surrounding villages.

The last match was between the leaders of the teams. They were among the best wrestlers in all the nine villages. The crowd wondered who would throw the other this year. Some said Okafo was the better man; others said he was not the equal of Ikezue.[4] Last year neither of them had thrown the other even though the judges had allowed the contest to go on longer than was the custom. They had the same style and one saw the other's plans beforehand. It might happen again this year.

Dusk was already approaching when their contest began. The drums went mad and the crowds also. They surged forward as the two young men danced into the circle. The palm fronds were helpless in keeping them back.

Ikezue held out his right hand. Okafo seized it, and they closed in. It was a fierce contest. Ikezue strove to dig in his right heel behind Okafo so as to pitch him backwards in the clever *ege* style. But the one knew what the other was thinking. The crowd had surrounded and swallowed up the drummers, whose frantic rhythm was no longer a mere disembodied sound but the very heartbeat of the people.

The wrestlers were now almost still in each other's grip. The muscles on their arms and their thighs and on their backs stood out and twitched. It

---

3. Chi who plants.   4. Strength is complete (a boastful name).

looked like an equal match. The two judges were already moving forward to separate them when Ikezue, now desperate, went down quickly on one knee in an attempt to fling his man backwards over his head. It was a sad miscalculation. Quick as the lightning of Amadiora, Okafo raised his right leg and swung it over his rival's head. The crowd burst into a thunderous roar. Okafo was swept off his feet by his supporters and carried home shoulder high. They sang his praise and the young women clapped their hands:

> Who will wrestle for our village?
> Okafo will wrestle for our village.
> Has he thrown a hundred men?
> He has thrown four hundred men.
> Has he thrown a hundred Cats?
> He has thrown four hundred Cats.
> Then send him word to fight for us.

7

For three years Ikemefuna lived in Okonkwo's household and the elders of Umuofia seemed to have forgotten about him. He grew rapidly like a yam tendril in the rainy season, and was full of the sap of life. He had become wholly absorbed into his new family. He was like an elder brother to Nwoye, and from the very first seemed to have kindled a new fire in the younger boy. He made him feel grown-up; and they no longer spent the evenings in mother's hut while she cooked, but now sat with Okonkwo in his *obi*, or watched him as he tapped his palm tree for the evening wine. Nothing pleased Nwoye now more than to be sent for by his mother or another of his father's wives to do one of those difficult and masculine tasks in the home, like splitting wood, or pounding food. On receiving such a message through a younger brother or sister, Nwoye would feign annoyance and grumble aloud about women and their troubles.

Okonkwo was inwardly pleased at his son's development, and he knew it was due to Ikemefuna. He wanted Nwoye to grow into a tough young man capable of ruling his father's household when he was dead and gone to join the ancestors. He wanted him to be a prosperous man, having enough in his barn to feed the ancestors with regular sacrifices. And so he was always happy when he heard him grumbling about women. That showed that in time he would be able to control his women-folk. No matter how prosperous a man was, if he was unable to rule his women and his children (and especially his women) he was not really a man. He was like the man in the song who had ten and one wives and not enough soup for his foo-foo.

So Okonkwo encouraged the boys to sit with him in his *obi*, and he told them stories of the land—masculine stories of violence and bloodshed. Nwoye knew that it was right to be masculine and to be violent, but somehow he still preferred the stories that his mother used to tell, and which she no doubt still told to her younger children—stories of the tortoise and his wily ways, and of the bird *eneke-nti-oba*[5] who challenged the whole world to a wrestling contest and was finally thrown by the cat. He remembered the story

---

5. The swallow with the ear of a crocodile [who is deaf] (literal trans.); a bird who proverbially flies without perching.

she often told of the quarrel between Earth and Sky long ago, and how Sky
withheld rain for seven years, until crops withered and the dead could not be
buried because the hoes broke on the stony Earth. At last Vulture was sent
to plead with Sky, and to soften his heart with a song of the suffering of the
sons of men. Whenever Nwoye's mother sang this song he felt carried away
to the distant scene in the sky where Vulture, Earth's emissary, sang for
mercy. At last Sky was moved to pity, and he gave to Vulture rain wrapped in
leaves of coco-yam. But as he flew home his long talon pierced the leaves and
the rain fell as it had never fallen before. And so heavily did it rain on Vulture
that he did not return to deliver his message but flew to a distant land, from
where he had espied a fire. And when he got there he found it was a man
making a sacrifice. He warmed himself in the fire and ate the entrails.

   That was the kind of story that Nwoye loved. But he now knew that they
were for foolish women and children, and he knew that his father wanted
him to be a man. And so he feigned that he no longer cared for women's
stories. And when he did this he saw that his father was pleased, and no
longer rebuked him or beat him. So Nwoye and Ikemefuna would listen to
Okonkwo's stories about tribal wars, or how, years ago, he had stalked his
victim, overpowered him and obtained his first human head. And as he told
them of the past they sat in darkness or the dim glow of logs, waiting for the
women to finish their cooking. When they finished, each brought her bowl
of foo-foo and bowl of soup to her husband. An oil lamp was lit and Okonkwo
tasted from each bowl, and then passed two shares to Nwoye and Ikemefuna.

   In this way the moons and the seasons passed. And then the locusts came.
It had not happened for many a long year. The elders said locusts came once
in a generation, reappeared every year for seven years and then disappeared
for another lifetime. They went back to their caves in a distant land, where
they were guarded by a race of stunted men. And then after another lifetime
these men opened the caves again and the locusts came to Umuofia.

   They came in the cold harmattan season after the harvests had been gathered, and ate up all the wild grass in the fields.

   Okonkwo and the two boys were working on the red outer walls of the
compound. This was one of the lighter tasks of the after-harvest season. A
new cover of thick palm branches and palm leaves was set on the walls to
protect them from the next rainy season. Okonkwo worked on the outside
of the wall and the boys worked from within. There were little holes from
one side to the other in the upper levels of the wall, and through these
Okonkwo passed the rope, or *tie-tie*,[6] to the boys and they passed it round
the wooden stays and then back to him; and in this way the cover was
strengthened on the wall.

   The women had gone to the bush to collect firewood, and the little children
to visit their playmates in the neighboring compounds. The harmattan was
in the air and seemed to distill a hazy feeling of sleep on the world. Okonkwo
and the boys worked in complete silence, which was only broken when a
new palm frond was lifted on to the wall or when a busy hen moved dry
leaves about in her ceaseless search for food.

   And then quite suddenly a shadow fell on the world, and the sun seemed
hidden behind a thick cloud. Okonkwo looked up from his work and won-

---

6. A creeper used as a rope to lash sections in building (pidgin English from "to tie").

dered if it was going to rain at such an unlikely time of the year. But almost immediately a shout of joy broke out in all directions, and Umuofia, which had dozed in the noon-day haze, broke into life and activity.

"Locusts are descending," was joyfully chanted everywhere, and men, women and children left their work or their play and ran into the open to see the unfamiliar sight. The locusts had not come for many, many years, and only the old people had seen them before.

At first, a fairly small swarm came. They were the harbingers sent to survey the land. And then appeared on the horizon a slowly moving mass like a boundless sheet of black cloud drifting towards Umuofia. Soon it covered half the sky, and the solid mass was now broken by tiny eyes of light like shining star dust. It was a tremendous sight, full of power and beauty.

Everyone was now about, talking excitedly and praying that the locusts should camp in Umuofia for the night. For although locusts had not visited Umuofia for many years, everybody knew by instinct that they were very good to eat. And at last the locusts did descend. They settled on every tree and on every blade of grass; they settled on the roofs and covered the bare ground. Mighty tree branches broke away under them, and the whole country became the brown-earth color of the vast, hungry swarm.

Many people went out with baskets trying to catch them, but the elders counseled patience till nightfall. And they were right. The locusts settled in the bushes for the night and their wings became wet with dew. Then all Umuofia turned out in spite of the cold harmattan, and everyone filled his bags and pots with locusts. The next morning they were roasted in clay pots and then spread in the sun until they became dry and brittle. And for many days this rare food was eaten with solid palm-oil.

Okonkwo sat in his *obi* crunching happily with Ikemefuna and Nwoye, and drinking palm-wine copiously, when Ogbuefi Ezeudu came in. Ezeudu was the oldest man in this quarter of Umuofia. He had been a great and fearless warrior in his time, and was now accorded great respect in all the clan. He refused to join in the meal, and asked Okonkwo to have a word with him outside. And so they walked out together, the old man supporting himself with his stick. When they were out of earshot, he said to Okonkwo:

"That boy calls you father. Do not bear a hand in his death." Okonkwo was surprised, and was about to say something when the old man continued: "Yes, Umuofia has decided to kill him. The Oracle of the Hills and the Caves has pronounced it. They will take him outside Umuofia as is the custom, and kill him there. But I want you to have nothing to do with it. He calls you his father."

The next day a group of elders from all the nine villages of Umuofia came to Okonkwo's house early in the morning, and before they began to speak in low tones Nwoye and Ikemefuna were sent out. They did not stay very long, but when they went away Okonkwo sat still for a very long time supporting his chin in his palms. Later in the day he called Ikemefuna and told him that he was to be taken home the next day. Nwoye overheard it and burst into tears, whereupon his father beat him heavily. As for Ikemefuna, he was at a loss. His own home had gradually become very faint and distant. He still missed his mother and his sister and would be very glad to see them. But somehow he knew he was not going to see them. He remembered once when men had talked in low tones with his father; and it seemed now as if it was happening all over again.

Later, Nwoye went to his mother's hut and told her that Ikemefuna was going home. She immediately dropped her pestle with which she was grinding pepper, folded her arms across her breast and sighed, "Poor child."

The next day, the men returned with a pot of wine. They were all fully dressed as if they were going to a big clan meeting or to pay a visit to a neighboring village. They passed their cloths under the right arm-pit, and hung their goatskin bags and sheathed machetes over their left shoulders. Okonkwo got ready quickly and the party set out with Ikemefuna carrying the pot of wine. A deathly silence descended on Okonkwo's compound. Even the very little children seemed to know. Throughout that day Nwoye sat in his mother's hut and tears stood in his eyes.

At the beginning of their journey the men of Umuofia talked and laughed about the locusts, about their women, and about some effeminate men who had refused to come with them. But as they drew near to the outskirts of Umuofia silence fell upon them too.

The sun rose slowly to the center of the sky, and the dry, sandy footway began to throw up the heat that lay buried in it. Some birds chirruped in the forests around. The men trod dry leaves on the sand. All else was silent. Then from the distance came the faint beating of the *ekwe*. It rose and faded with the wind—a peaceful dance from a distant clan.

"It is an *ozo* dance,"[7] the men said among themselves. But no one was sure where it was coming from. Some said Ezimili, others Abame or Aninta. They argued for a short while and fell into silence again, and the elusive dance rose and fell with the wind. Somewhere a man was taking one of the titles of his clan, with music and dancing and a great feast.

The footway had now become a narrow line in the heart of the forest. The short trees and sparse undergrowth which surrounded the men's village began to give way to giant trees and climbers which perhaps had stood from the beginning of things, untouched by the ax and the bush-fire. The sun breaking through their leaves and branches threw a pattern of light and shade on the sandy footway.

Ikemefuna heard a whisper close behind him and turned round sharply. The man who had whispered now called out aloud, urging the others to hurry up.

"We still have a long way to go," he said. Then he and another man went before Ikemefuna and set a faster pace.

Thus the men of Umuofia pursued their way, armed with sheathed machetes, and Ikemefuna, carrying a pot of palm-wine on his head, walked in their midst. Although he had felt uneasy at first, he was not afraid now. Okonkwo walked behind him. He could hardly imagine that Okonkwo was not his real father. He had never been fond of his real father, and at the end of three years he had become very distant indeed. But his mother and his three-year-old sister . . . of course she would not be three now, but six. Would he recognize her now? She must have grown quite big. How his mother would weep for joy, and thank Okonkwo for having looked after him so well and for bringing him back. She would want to hear everything that had happened to him in all these years. Could he remember them all? He would tell her about Nwoye and his mother, and about the locusts. . . . Then quite suddenly a thought came upon him. His mother might be dead. He

***

7. Part of the *ozo* rituals, the spiritual ceremonies that accompanied the taking of titles.

tried in vain to force the thought out of his mind. Then he tried to settle the matter the way he used to settle such matters when he was a little boy. He still remembered the song:

> Eze elina, elina!
> > Sala
> Eze ilikwa ya
> Ikwaba akwa oligholi
> Ebe Danda nechi eze
> Ebe Uzuzu nete egwu
> > Sala[8]

He sang it in his mind, and walked to its beat. If the song ended on his right foot, his mother was alive. If it ended on his left, she was dead. No, not dead, but ill. It ended on the right. She was alive and well. He sang the song again, and it ended on the left. But the second time did not count. The first voice gets to Chukwu, or God's house. That was a favorite saying of children. Ikemefuna felt like a child once more. It must be the thought of going home to his mother.

One of the men behind him cleared his throat. Ikemefuna looked back, and the man growled at him to go on and not stand looking back. The way he said it sent cold fear down Ikemefuna's back. His hands trembled vaguely on the black pot he carried. Why had Okonkwo withdrawn to the rear? Ikemefuna felt his legs melting under him. And he was afraid to look back.

As the man who had cleared his throat drew up and raised his machete, Okonkwo looked away. He heard the blow. The pot fell and broke in the sand. He heard Ikemefuna cry, "My father, they have killed me!" as he ran towards him. Dazed with fear, Okonkwo drew his machete and cut him down. He was afraid of being thought weak.

As soon as his father walked in, that night, Nwoye knew that Ikemefuna had been killed, and something seemed to give way inside him, like the snapping of a tightened bow. He did not cry. He just hung limp. He had had the same kind of feeling not long ago, during the last harvest season. Every child loved the harvest season. Those who were big enough to carry even a few yams in a tiny basket went with grown-ups to the farm. And if they could not help in digging up the yams, they could gather firewood together for roasting the ones that would be eaten there on the farm. This roasted yam soaked in red palm-oil and eaten in the open farm was sweeter than any meal at home. It was after such a day at the farm during the last harvest that Nwoye had felt for the first time a snapping inside him like the one he now felt. They were returning home with baskets of yams from a distant farm across the stream when they heard the voice of an infant crying in the thick forest. A sudden hush had fallen on the women, who had been talking, and they had quickened their steps. Nwoye had heard that twins were put in earthenware pots and thrown away in the forest, but he had never yet come across them. A vague chill had descended on him and his head had seemed to swell, like a solitary walker at night who passes an evil spirit on the way.

8. King don't eat, don't eat / Sala / King if you eat it / You will weep for the abomination / Where Danda installs a king / Where Uzuzu dances / Sala. *Sala:* meaningless refrain. *Danda:* the ant. *Uzuzu:* sand. Ikemefuna reassures himself by singing his favorite song about the country where the "sands dance forever" (see p. 2875).

Then something had given way inside him. It descended on him again, this feeling, when his father walked in, that night after killing Ikemefuna.

8

Okonkwo did not taste any food for two days after the death of Ikemefuna. He drank palm-wine from morning till night, and his eyes were red and fierce like the eyes of a rat when it was caught by the tail and dashed against the floor. He called his son, Nwoye, to sit with him in his *obi*. But the boy was afraid of him and slipped out of the hut as soon as he noticed him dozing.

He did not sleep at night. He tried not to think about Ikemefuna, but the more he tried the more he thought about him. Once he got up from bed and walked about his compound. But he was so weak that his legs could hardly carry him. He felt like a drunken giant walking with the limbs of a mosquito. Now and then a cold shiver descended on his head and spread down his body.

On the third day he asked his second wife, Ekwefi, to roast plantains for him. She prepared it the way he liked—with slices of oil-bean and fish.

"You have not eaten for two days," said his daughter Ezinma when she brought the food to him. "So you must finish this." She sat down and stretched her legs in front of her. Okonkwo ate the food absent-mindedly. 'She should have been a boy,' he thought as he looked at his ten-year-old daughter. He passed her a piece of fish.

"Go and bring me some cold water," he said. Ezinma rushed out of the hut, chewing the fish, and soon returned with a bowl of cool water from the earthen pot in her mother's hut.

Okonkwo took the bowl from her and gulped the water down. He ate a few more pieces of plantain and pushed the dish aside.

"Bring me my bag," he asked, and Ezinma brought his goatskin bag from the far end of the hut. He searched in it for his snuff-bottle. It was a deep bag and took almost the whole length of his arm. It contained other things apart from his snuff-bottle. There was a drinking horn in it, and also a drinking gourd, and they knocked against each other as he searched. When he brought out the snuff-bottle he tapped it a few times against his knee-cap before taking out some snuff on the palm of his left hand. Then he remembered that he had not taken out his snuff-spoon. He searched his bag again and brought out a small, flat, ivory spoon, with which he carried the brown snuff to his nostrils.

Ezinma took the dish in one hand and the empty water bowl in the other and went back to her mother's hut. "She should have been a boy," Okonkwo said to himself again. His mind went back to Ikemefuna and he shivered. If only he could find some work to do he would be able to forget. But it was the season of rest between the harvest and the next planting season. The only work that men did at this time was covering the walls of their compound with new palm fronds. And Okonkwo had already done that. He had finished it on the very day the locusts came, when he had worked on one side of the wall and Ikemefuna and Nwoye on the other.

"When did you become a shivering old woman," Okonkwo asked himself, "you, who are known in all the nine villages for your valor in war? How can a man who has killed five men in battle fall to pieces because he has added a boy to their number? Okonkwo, you have become a woman indeed."

He sprang to his feet, hung his goatskin bag on his shoulder and went to visit his friend, Obierika.

Obierika was sitting outside under the shade of an orange tree making thatches from leaves of the raffia-palm. He exchanged greetings with Okonkwo and led the way into his *obi*.

"I was coming over to see you as soon as I finished that thatch," he said, rubbing off the grains of sand that clung to his thighs.

"Is it well?" Okonkwo asked.

"Yes," replied Obierika. "My daughter's suitor is coming today and I hope we will clinch the matter of the bride-price. I want you to be there."

Just then Obierika's son, Maduka, came into the *obi* from outside, greeted Okonkwo and turned towards the compound.

"Come and shake hands with me," Okonkwo said to the lad. "Your wrestling the other day gave me much happiness." The boy smiled, shook hands with Okonkwo and went into the compound.

"He will do great things," Okonkwo said. "If I had a son like him I should be happy. I am worried about Nwoye. A bowl of pounded yams can throw him in a wrestling match. His two younger brothers are more promising. But I can tell you, Obierika, that my children do not resemble me. Where are the young suckers that will grow when the old banana tree dies? If Ezinma had been a boy I would have been happier. She has the right spirit."

"You worry yourself for nothing," said Obierika. "The children are still very young."

"Nwoye is old enough to impregnate a woman. At his age I was already fending for myself. No, my friend, he is not too young. A chick that will grow into a cock can be spotted the very day it hatches. I have done my best to make Nwoye grow into a man, but there is too much of his mother in him."

"Too much of his grandfather," Obierika thought, but he did not say it. The same thought also came to Okonkwo's mind. But he had long learned how to lay that ghost. Whenever the thought of his father's weakness and failure troubled him he expelled it by thinking about his own strength and success. And so he did now. His mind went to his latest show of manliness.

"I cannot understand why you refused to come with us to kill that boy," he asked Obierika.

"Because I did not want to," Obierika replied sharply. "I had something better to do."

"You sound as if you question the authority and the decision of the Oracle, who said he should die."

"I do not. Why should I? But the Oracle did not ask me to carry out its decision."

"But someone had to do it. If we were all afraid of blood, it would not be done. And what do you think the Oracle would do then?"

"You know very well, Okonkwo, that I am not afraid of blood; and if anyone tells you that I am, he is telling a lie. And let me tell you one thing, my friend. If I were you I would have stayed at home. What you have done will not please the Earth. It is the kind of action for which the goddess wipes out whole families."

"The Earth cannot punish me for obeying her messenger," Okonkwo said. "A child's fingers are not scalded by a piece of hot yam which its mother puts into its palm."

"That is true," Obierika agreed. "But if the Oracle said that my son should be killed I would neither dispute it nor be the one to do it."

They would have gone on arguing had Ofoedu[9] not come in just then. It was clear from his twinkling eyes that he had important news. But it would be impolite to rush him. Obierika offered him a lobe of the kola nut he had broken with Okonkwo. Ofoedu ate slowly and talked about the locusts. When he finished his kola nut he said:

"The things that happen these days are very strange."

"What has happened?" asked Okonkwo.

"Do you know Ogbuefi Ndulue?"[1] Ofoedu asked.

"Ogbuefi Ndulue of Ire village," Okonkwo and Obierika said together.

"He died this morning," said Ofoedu.

"That is not strange. He was the oldest man in Ire," said Obierika.

"You are right," Ofoedu agreed. "But you ought to ask why the drum has not beaten to tell Umuofia of his death."

"Why?" asked Obierika and Okonkwo together.

"That is the strange part of it. You know his first wife who walks with a stick?"

"Yes. She is called Ozoemena."[2]

"That is so," said Ofoedu. "Ozoemena was, as you know, too old to attend Ndulue during his illness. His younger wives did that. When he died this morning, one of these women went to Ozoemena's hut and told her. She rose from her mat, took her stick and walked over to the *obi*. She knelt on her knees and hands at the threshold and called her husband, who was laid on a mat. 'Ogbuefi Ndulue,' she called, three times, and went back to her hut. When the youngest wife went to call her again to be present at the washing of the body, she found her lying on the mat, dead."

"That is very strange, indeed," said Okonkwo. "They will put off Ndulue's funeral until his wife has been buried."[3]

"That is why the drum has not been beaten to tell Umuofia."

"It was always said that Ndulue and Ozoemena had one mind," said Obierika. "I remember when I was a young boy there was a song about them. He could not do anything without telling her."

"I did not know that," said Okonkwo. "I thought he was a strong man in his youth."

"He was indeed," said Ofoedu.

Okonkwo shook his head doubtfully.

"He led Umuofia to war in those days," said Obierika.

Okonkwo was beginning to feel like his old self again. All that he required was something to occupy his mind. If he had killed Ikemefuna during the busy planting season or harvesting it would not have been so bad; his mind would have been centered on his work. Okonkwo was not a man of thought but of action. But in absence of work, talking was the next best.

Soon after Ofoedu left, Okonkwo took up his goatskin bag to go.

"I must go home to tap my palm trees for the afternoon," he said.

"Who taps your tall trees for you?" asked Obierika.

---

9. The ancestors are our guide.   1. Life has arrived.   2. Another bad thing will not happen.   3. A wife dying shortly after her husband was sometimes considered guilty of his death, so the village preserves appearances by burying Ozoemena before announcing Ogbuefi Ndulue's death.

"Umezulike," replied Okonkwo.

"Sometimes I wish I had not taken the *ozo* title," said Obierika. "It wounds my heart to see these young men killing palm trees in the name of tapping."

"It is so indeed," Okonkwo agreed. "But the law of the land must be obeyed."

"I don't know how we got that law," said Obierika. "In many other clans a man of title is not forbidden to climb the palm tree. Here we say he cannot climb the tall tree but he can tap the short ones standing on the ground. It is like Dimaragana, who would not lend his knife for cutting up dogmeat because the dog was taboo to him, but offered to use his teeth."

"I think it is good that our clan holds the *ozo* title in high esteem," said Okonkwo. "In those other clans you speak of, *ozo* is so low that every beggar takes it."

"I was only speaking in jest," said Obierika. "In Abame and Aninta the title is worth less than two cowries. Every man wears the thread of title on his ankle, and does not lose it even if he steals."

"They have indeed soiled the name of *ozo*," said Okonkwo as he rose to go.

"It will not be very long now before my in-laws come," said Obierika.

"I shall return very soon," said Okonkwo, looking at the position of the sun.

There were seven men in Obierika's hut when Okonkwo returned. The suitor was a young man of about twenty-five, and with him were his father and uncle. On Obierika's side were his two elder brothers and Maduka, his sixteen-year-old son.

"Ask Akueke's mother to send us some kola nuts," said Obierika to his son. Maduka vanished into the compound like lightning. The conversation at once centered on him, and everybody agreed that he was as sharp as a razor.

"I sometimes think he is too sharp," said Obierika, somewhat indulgently. "He hardly ever walks. He is always in a hurry. If you are sending him on an errand he flies away before he has heard half of the message."

"You were very much like that yourself," said his eldest brother. "As our people say, 'When mother-cow is chewing grass its young ones watch its mouth.' Maduka has been watching your mouth."

As he was speaking the boy returned, followed by Akueke,[4] his half-sister, carrying a wooden dish with three kola nuts and alligator pepper. She gave the dish to her father's eldest brother and then shook hands, very shyly, with her suitor and his relatives. She was about sixteen and just ripe for marriage. Her suitor and his relatives surveyed her young body with expert eyes as if to assure themselves that she was beautiful and ripe.

She wore a coiffure which was done up into a crest in the middle of the head. Cam wood was rubbed lightly into her skin, and all over her body were black patterns drawn with *uli*.[5] She wore a black necklace which hung down in three coils just above her full, succulent breasts. On her arms were red and yellow bangles, and on her waist four or five rows of *jigida*, or waist beads.

---

4. Wealth of Eke (a divinity). Similar names built on *ako* ("wealth") connote riches and are associated with the idea of women as a form of exchangeable material wealth.   5. A liquid made from crushed seeds, which caused the skin to pucker temporarily. It was used to create black tattoolike decorations. *Cam wood*: a shrub. The powdered red heartwood of the shrub was used as a cosmetic dye.

When she had shaken hands, or rather held out her hand to be shaken, she returned to her mother's hut to help with the cooking.

"Remove your *jigida* first," her mother warned as she moved near the fire-place to bring the pestle resting against the wall. "Every day I tell you that *jigida* and fire are not friends. But you will never hear. You grew your ears for decoration, not for hearing. One of these days your *jigida* will catch fire on your waist, and then you will know."

Akueke moved to the other end of the hut and began to remove the waist-beads. It had to be done slowly and carefully, taking each string separately, else it would break and the thousand tiny rings would have to be strung together again. She rubbed each string downwards with her palms until it passed the buttocks and slipped down to the floor around her feet.

The men in the *obi* had already begun to drink the palm-wine which Akueke's suitor had brought. It was a very good wine and powerful, for in spite of the palm fruit hung across the mouth of the pot to restrain the lively liquor, white foam rose and spilled over.

"That wine is the work of a good tapper," said Okonkwo.

The young suitor, whose name was Ibe, smiled broadly and said to his father: "Do you hear that?" He then said to the others: "He will never admit that I am a good tapper."

"He tapped three of my best palm trees to death," said his father, Ukegbu.

"That was about five years ago," said Ibe, who had begun to pour out the wine, "before I learned how to tap." He filled the first horn and gave to his father. Then he poured out for the others. Okonkwo brought out his big horn from the goatskin bag, blew into it to remove any dust that might be there, and gave it to Ibe to fill.

As the men drank, they talked about everything except the thing for which they had gathered. It was only after the pot had been emptied that the suitor's father cleared his voice and announced the object of their visit.

Obierika then presented to him a small bundle of short broomsticks. Ukegbu counted them.

"They are thirty?" he asked.

Obierika nodded in agreement.

"We are at last getting somewhere," Ukegbu said, and then turning to his brother and his son he said: "Let us go out and whisper together." The three rose and went outside. When they returned Ukegbu handed the bundle of sticks back to Obierika. He counted them; instead of thirty there were now only fifteen. He passed them over to his eldest brother, Machi, who also counted them and said:

"We had not thought to go below thirty. But as the dog said, 'If I fall down for you and you fall down for me, it is play.' Marriage should be a play and not a fight; so we are falling down again." He then added ten sticks to the fifteen and gave the bundle to Ukegbu.

In this way Akuke's bride-price was finally settled at twenty bags of cowries. It was already dusk when the two parties came to this agreement.

"Go and tell Akueke's mother that we have finished," Obierika said to his son, Maduka. Almost immediately the women came in with a big bowl of foo-foo. Obierika's second wife followed with a pot of soup, and Maduka brought in a pot of palm-wine.

As the men ate and drank palm-wine they talked about the customs of their neighbors.

"It was only this morning," said Obierika, "that Okonkwo and I were talking about Abame and Aninta, where titled men climb trees and pound foo-foo for their wives."

"All their customs are upside-down. They do not decide bride-price as we do, with sticks. They haggle and bargain as if they were buying a goat or a cow in the market."

"That is very bad," said Obierika's eldest brother. "But what is good in one place is bad in another place. In Umunso they do not bargain at all, not even with broomsticks. The suitor just goes on bringing bags of cowries until his in-laws tell him to stop. It is a bad custom because it always leads to a quarrel."

"The world is large," said Okonkwo. "I have even heard that in some tribes a man's children belong to his wife and her family."

"That cannot be," said Machi. "You might as well say that the woman lies on top of the man when they are making the children."

"It is like the story of white men who, they say, are white like this piece of chalk," said Obierika. He held up a piece of chalk, which every man kept in his *obi* and with which his guests drew lines on the floor before they ate kola nuts. "And these white men, they say, have no toes."[6]

"And have you never seen them?" asked Machi.

"Have you?" asked Obierika.

"One of them passes here frequently," said Machi. "His name is Amadi."

Those who knew Amadi laughed. He was a leper, and the polite name for leprosy was "the white skin."

<h3 style="text-align:center">9</h3>

For the first time in three nights, Okonkwo slept. He woke up once in the middle of the night and his mind went back to the past three days without making him feel uneasy. He began to wonder why he had felt uneasy at all. It was like a man wondering in broad daylight why a dream had appeared so terrible to him at night. He stretched himself and scratched his thigh where a mosquito had bitten him as he slept. Another one was wailing near his right ear. He slapped the ear and hoped he had killed it. Why do they always go for one's ears? When he was a child his mother had told him a story about it. But it was as silly as all women's stories. Mosquito, she had said, had asked Ear to marry him, whereupon Ear fell on the floor in uncontrollable laughter. "How much longer do you think you will live?" she asked. "You are already a skeleton." Mosquito went away humiliated, and any time he passed her way he told Ear that he was still alive.

Okonkwo turned on his side and went back to sleep. He was roused in the morning by someone banging on his door.

"Who is that?" he growled. He knew it must be Ekwefi. Of his three wives Ekwefi was the only one who would have the audacity to bang on his door.

"Ezinma is dying," came her voice, and all the tragedy and sorrow of her life were packed in those words.

Okonkwo sprang from his bed, pushed back the bolt on his door and ran into Ekwefi's hut.

6. They wear shoes.

Ezinma lay shivering on a mat beside a huge fire that her mother had kept burning all night.

"It is *iba*,"[7] said Okonkwo as he took his machete and went into the bush to collect the leaves and grasses and barks of trees that went into making the medicine for *iba*.

Ekwefi knelt beside the sick child, occasionally feeling with her palm the wet, burning forehead.

Ezinma was an only child and the center of her mother's world. Very often it was Ezinma who decided what food her mother should prepare. Ekwefi even gave her such delicacies as eggs, which children were rarely allowed to eat because such food tempted them to steal. One day as Ezinma was eating an egg Okonkwo had come in unexpectedly from his hut. He was greatly shocked and swore to beat Ekwefi if she dared to give the child eggs again. But it was impossible to refuse Ezinma anything. After her father's rebuke she developed an even keener appetite for eggs. And she enjoyed above all the secrecy in which she now ate them. Her mother always took her into their bedroom and shut the door.

Ezinma did not call her mother *Nne* like all children. She called her by her name, Ekwefi, as her father and other grown-up people did. The relationship between them was not only that of mother and child. There was something in it like the companionship of equals, which was strengthened by such little conspiracies as eating eggs in the bedroom.

Ekwefi had suffered a good deal in her life. She had borne ten children and nine of them had died in infancy, usually before the age of three. As she buried one child after another her sorrow gave way to despair and then to grim resignation. The birth of her children, which should be a woman's crowning glory, became for Ekwefi mere physical agony devoid of promise. The naming ceremony after seven market weeks became an empty ritual. Her deepening despair found expression in the names she gave her children. One of them was a pathetic cry, Onwumbiko—"Death, I implore you." But Death took no notice; Onwumbiko died in his fifteenth month. The next child was a girl, Ozoemena—"May it not happen again." She died in her eleventh month, and two others after her. Ekwefi then became defiant and called her next child Onwuma—"Death may please himself." And he did.

After the death of Ekwefi's second child, Okonkwo had gone to a medicine man, who was also a diviner of the Afa Oracle,[8] to inquire what was amiss. This man told him that the child was an *ogbanje*, one of those wicked children who, when they died, entered their mothers' wombs to be born again.

"When your wife becomes pregnant again," he said, "let her not sleep in her hut. Let her go and stay with her people. In that way she will elude her wicked tormentor and break its evil cycle of birth and death."

Ekwefi did as she was asked. As soon as she became pregnant she went to live with her old mother in another village. It was there that her third child was born and circumcised on the eighth day. She did not return to Okonkwo's compound until three days before the naming ceremony. The child was called Onwumbiko.

Onwumbiko was not given proper burial when he died. Okonkwo had

---

7. A fever accompanied by jaundice, probably caused by malaria.   8. One who communicates with the clients' ancestors by reading patterns made by objects (e.g., seeds, teeth, shells) thrown on a flat surface.

called on another medicine man who was famous in the clan for his great knowledge about *ogbanje* children. His name was Okagbue Uyanwa. Okagbue was a very striking figure, tall, with a full beard and a bald head. He was light in complexion and his eyes were red and fiery. He always gnashed his teeth as he listened to those who came to consult him. He asked Okonkwo a few questions about the dead child. All the neighbors and relations who had come to mourn gathered round them.

"On what market-day was it born?" he asked.

"*Oye*," replied Okonkwo.

"And it died this morning?"

Okonkwo said yes, and only then realized for the first time that the child had died on the same market-day as it had been born. The neighbors and relations also saw the coincidence and said among themselves that it was very significant.

"Where do you sleep with your wife, in your *obi* or in her own hut?" asked the medicine man.

"In her hut."

"In future call her into your *obi*."

The medicine man then ordered that there should be no mourning for the dead child. He brought out a sharp razor from the goatskin bag slung from his left shoulder and began to mutilate the child. Then he took it away to bury in the Evil Forest, holding it by the ankle and dragging it on the ground behind him. After such treatment it would think twice before coming again, unless it was one of the stubborn ones who returned, carrying the stamp of their mutilation—a missing finger or perhaps a dark line where the medicine man's razor had cut them.

By the time Onwumbiko died Ekwefi had become a very bitter woman. Her husband's first wife had already had three sons, all strong and healthy. When she had borne her third son in succession, Okonkwo had gathered a goat for her, as was the custom. Ekwefi had nothing but good wishes for her. But she had grown so bitter about her own *chi* that she could not rejoice with others over their good fortune. And so, on the day that Nwoye's mother celebrated the birth of her three sons with feasting and music, Ekwefi was the only person in the happy company who went about with a cloud on her brow. Her husband's wife took this for malevolence, as husbands' wives were wont to. How could she know that Ekwefi's bitterness did not flow outwards to others but inwards into her own soul; that she did not blame others for their good fortune but her own evil *chi* who denied her any?

At last Ezinma was born, and although ailing she seemed determined to live. At first Ekwefi accepted her, as she had accepted others—with listless resignation. But when she lived on to her fourth, fifth and sixth years, love returned once more to her mother, and, with love, anxiety. She determined to nurse her child to health, and she put all her being into it. She was rewarded by occasional spells of health during which Ezinma bubbled with energy like fresh palm-wine. At such times she seemed beyond danger. But all of a sudden she would go down again. Everybody knew she was an *ogbanje*. These sudden bouts of sickness and health were typical of her kind. But she had lived so long that perhaps she had decided to stay. Some of them did become tired of their evil rounds of birth and death, or took pity on their mothers, and stayed. Ekwefi believed deep inside her that Ezinma had come to stay. She believed because it was that faith alone that gave her own life any kind of meaning. And this faith had been strengthened when a year or so ago a medicine man had dug up Ezinma's *iyi-uwa*. Everyone knew then that she would live because her bond with the world of *ogbanje* had been broken. Ekwefi was reassured. But such was her anxiety for her daughter that she could not rid herself completely of her fear. And although she believed that the *iyi-uwa* which had been dug up was genuine, she could not ignore the fact that some really evil children sometimes misled people into digging up a specious one.

But Ezinma's *iyi-uwa* had looked real enough. It was a smooth pebble wrapped in a dirty rag. The man who dug it up was the same Okagbue who was famous in all the clan for his knowledge in these matters. Ezinma had not wanted to cooperate with him at first. But that was only to be expected. No *ogbanje* would yield her secrets easily, and most of them never did because they died too young—before they could be asked questions.

"Where did you bury your *iyi-uwa*?" Okagbue had asked Ezinma. She was nine then and was just recovering from a serious illness.

"What is *iyi-uwa*?" she asked in return.

"You know what it is. You buried it in the ground somewhere so that you can die and return again to torment your mother."

Ezinma looked at her mother, whose eyes, sad and pleading, were fixed on her.

"Answer the question at once," roared Okonkwo, who stood beside her. All the family were there and some of the neighbors too.

"Leave her to me," the medicine man told Okonkwo in a cool, confident voice. He turned again to Ezinma. "Where did you bury your *iyi-uwa*?"

"Where they bury children," she replied, and the quiet spectators murmured to themselves.

"Come along then and show me the spot," said the medicine man.

The crowd set out with Ezinma leading the way and Okagbue following closely behind her. Okonkwo came next and Ekwefi followed him. When she came to the main road, Ezinma turned left as if she was going to the stream.

"But you said it was where they bury children?" asked the medicine man.

"No," said Ezinma, whose feeling of importance was manifest in her sprightly walk. She sometimes broke into a run and stopped again suddenly. The crowd followed her silently. Women and children returning from the stream with pots of water on their heads wondered what was happening until they saw Okagbue and guessed that it must be something to do with *ogbanje*. And they all knew Ekwefi and her daughter very well.

When she got to the big udala tree Ezinma turned left into the bush, and the crowd followed her. Because of her size she made her way through trees and creepers more quickly then her followers. The bush was alive with the tread of feet on dry leaves and sticks and the moving aside of tree branches. Ezinma went deeper and deeper and the crowd went with her. Then she suddenly turned round and began to walk back to the road. Everybody stood to let her pass and then filed after her.

"If you bring us all this way for nothing I shall beat sense into you," Okonkwo threatened.

"I have told you to let her alone. I know how to deal with them," said Okagbue.

Ezinma led the way back to the road, looked left and right and turned right. And so they arrived home again.

"Where did you bury your *iyi-uwa*?" asked Okagbue when Ezinma finally stopped outside her father's *obi*. Okagbue's voice was unchanged. It was quiet and confident.

"It is near that orange tree," Ezinma said.

"And why did you not say so, you wicked daughter of Akalogoli?" Okonkwo swore furiously. The medicine man ignored him.

"Come and show me the exact spot," he said quietly to Ezinma.

"It is here," she said when they got to the tree.

"Point at the spot with your finger," said Okagbue.

"It is here," said Ezinma touching the ground with her finger. Okonkwo stood by, rumbling like thunder in the rainy season.

"Bring me a hoe," said Okagbue.

When Ekwefi brought the hoe, he had already put aside his goatskin bag and his big cloth and was in his underwear, a long and thin strip of cloth wound round the waist like a belt and then passed between the legs to be fastened to the belt behind. He immediately set to work digging a pit where Ezinma had indicated. The neighbors sat around watching the pit becoming deeper and deeper. The dark top soil soon gave way to the bright red earth with which women scrubbed the floors and walls of huts. Okagbue worked tirelessly and in silence, his back shining with perspiration. Okonkwo stood by the pit. He asked Okagbue to come up and rest while he took a hand. But Okagbue said he was not tired yet.

Ekwefi went into her hut to cook yams. Her husband had brought out more yams than usual because the medicine man had to be fed. Ezinma went with her and helped in preparing the vegetables.

"There is too much green vegetable," she said.

"Don't you see the pot is full of yams?" Ekwefi asked. "And you know how leaves become smaller after cooking."

"Yes," said Ezinma, "that was why the snake-lizard killed his mother."

"Very true," said Ekwefi.

"He gave his mother seven baskets of vegetables to cook and in the end there were only three. And so he killed her," said Ezinma.

"That is not the end of the story."

"Oho," said Ezinma. "I remember now. He brought another seven baskets and cooked them himself. And there were again only three. So he killed himself too."

Outside the *obi* Okagbue and Okonkwo were digging the pit to find where Ezinma had buried her *iyi-uwa*. Neighbors sat around, watching. The pit was now so deep that they no longer saw the digger. They only saw the red earth he threw up mounting higher and higher. Okonkwo's son, Nwoye, stood near the edge of the pit because he wanted to take in all that happened.

Okagbue had again taken over the digging from Okonkwo. He worked, as usual, in silence. The neighbors and Okonkwo's wives were now talking. The children had lost interest and were playing.

Suddenly Okagbue sprang to the surface with the agility of a leopard.

"It is very near now," he said. "I have felt it."

There was immediate excitement and those who were sitting jumped to their feet.

"Call your wife and child," he said to Okonkwo. But Ekwefi and Ezinma had heard the noise and run out to see what it was.

Okagbue went back into the pit, which was now surrounded by spectators. After a few more hoe-fuls of earth he struck the *iyi-uwa*. He raised it carefully with the hoe and threw it to the surface. Some women ran away in fear when it was thrown. But they soon returned and everyone was gazing at the rag from a reasonable distance. Okagbue emerged and without saying a word or even looking at the spectators he went to his goatskin bag, took out two leaves and began to chew them. When he had swallowed them, he took up the rag with his left hand and began to untie it. And then the smooth, shiny pebble fell out. He picked it up.

"Is this yours?" he asked Ezinma.

"Yes," she replied. All the women shouted with joy because Ekwefi's troubles were at last ended.

All this had happened more than a year ago and Ezinma had not been ill since. And then suddenly she had begun to shiver in the night. Ekwefi brought her to the fireplace, spread her mat on the floor and built a fire. But she had got worse and worse. As she knelt by her, feeling with her palm the wet, burning forehead, she prayed a thousand times. Although her husband's wives were saying that it was nothing more than *iba*, she did not hear them.

Okonkwo returned from the bush carrying on his left shoulder a large bundle of grasses and leaves, roots and barks of medicinal trees and shrubs. He went into Ekwefi's hut, put down his load and sat down.

"Get me a pot," he said, "and leave the child alone."

Ekwefi went to bring the pot and Okonkwo selected the best from his bundle, in their due proportions, and cut them up. He put them in the pot and Ekwefi poured in some water.

"Is that enough?" she asked when she had poured in about half of the water in the bowl.

"A little more . . . I said a *little*. Are you deaf?" Okonkwo roared at her.

She set the pot on the fire and Okonkwo took up his machete to return to his *obi*.

"You must watch the pot carefully," he said as he went, "and don't allow it to boil over. If it does its power will be gone." He went away to his hut and Ekwefi began to tend the medicine pot almost as if it was itself a sick child. Her eyes went constantly from Ezinma to the boiling pot and back to Ezinma.

Okonkwo returned when he felt the medicine had cooked long enough. He looked it over and said it was done.

"Bring me a low stool for Ezinma," he said, "and a thick mat."

He took down the pot from the fire and placed it in front of the stool. He then roused Ezinma and placed her on the stool, astride the steaming pot. The thick mat was thrown over both. Ezinma struggled to escape from the choking and overpowering steam, but she was held down. She started to cry.

When the mat was at last removed she was drenched in perspiration. Ekwefi mopped her with a piece of cloth and she lay down on a dry mat and was soon asleep.

10

Large crowds began to gather on the village *ilo* as soon as the edge had worn off the sun's heat and it was no longer painful on the body. Most communal ceremonies took place at that time of the day, so that even when it was said that a ceremony would begin "after the midday meal" everyone understood that it would begin a long time later, when the sun's heat had softened.

It was clear from the way the crowd stood or sat that the ceremony was for men. There were many women, but they looked on from the fringe like outsiders. The titled men and elders sat on their stools waiting for the trials to begin. In front of them was a row of stools on which nobody sat. There were nine of them. Two little groups of people stood at a respectable distance beyond the stools. They faced the elders. There were three men in one group and three men and one woman in the other. The woman was Mgbafo and the three men with her were her brothers. In the other group were her husband, Uzowulu, and his relatives. Mgbafo and her brothers were as still as statues into whose faces the artist has molded defiance. Uzowulu and his relatives, on the other hand, were whispering together. It looked like whispering, but they were really talking at the top of their voices. Everybody in the crowd was talking. It was like the market. From a distance the noise was a deep rumble carried by the wind.

An iron gong sounded, setting up a wave of expectation in the crowd. Everyone looked in the direction of the *egwugwu*[9] house. *Gome, gome, gome* went the gong, and a powerful flute blew a high-pitched blast. Then came the voices of the *egwugwu,* guttural and awesome. The wave struck the women and children and there was a backward stampede. But it was momentary. They were already far enough where they stood and there was room for running away if any of the *egwugwu* should go towards them.

The drum sounded again and the flute blew. The *egwugwu* house was now a pandemonium of quavering voices: *Aru oyim de de de dei!*[1] filled the air as the spirits of the ancestors, just emerged from the earth, greeted themselves in their esoteric language. The *egwugwu* house into which they emerged faced the forest, away from the crowd, who saw only its back with the many-colored patterns and drawings done by specially chosen women at regular intervals. These women never saw the inside of the hut. No woman ever did. They scrubbed and painted the outside walls under the supervision of men. If they imagined what was inside, they kept their imagination to themselves. No woman ever asked questions about the most powerful and the most secret cult in the clan.

Aru oyim de de de dei! flew around the dark, closed hut like tongues of fire. The ancestral spirits of the clan were abroad. The metal gong beat continuously now and the flute, shrill and powerful, floated on the chaos.

And then the *egwugwu* appeared. The women and children sent up a great shout and took to their heels. It was instinctive. A woman fled as soon as an *egwugwu* came in sight. And when, as on that day, nine of the greatest masked spirits in the clan came out together it was a terrifying spec-

9. Here the term refers to the village's highest spiritual and judicial authority, prominent men who, after putting on elaborate ceremonial costumes, embody the village's ancestral spirits.   1. Body of my friend, greetings!

tacle. Even Mgbafo took to her heels and had to be restrained by her brothers.

Each of the nine *egwugwu* represented a village of the clan. Their leader was called Evil Forest. Smoke poured out of his head.

The nine villages of Umuofia had grown out of the nine sons of the first father of the clan. Evil Forest represented the village of Umueru, or the children of Eru, who was the eldest of the nine sons.

"*Umuofia kwenu!*" shouted the leading *egwugwu*, pushing the air with his raffia arms. The elders of the clan replied, "*Yaa!*"

"*Umuofia kwenu!*"

"*Yaa!*"

"*Umuofia kwenu!*"

"*Yaa!*"

Evil Forest then thrust the pointed end of his rattling staff into the earth. And it began to shake and rattle, like something agitating with a metallic life. He took the first of the empty stools and the eight other *egwugwu* began to sit in order of seniority after him.

Okonkwo's wives, and perhaps other women as well, might have noticed that the second *egwugwu* had the springy walk of Okonkwo. And they might also have noticed that Okonkwo was not among the titled men and elders who sat behind the row of *egwugwu*. But if they thought these things they kept them within themselves. The *egwugwu* with the springy walk was one of the dead fathers of the clan. He looked terrible with the smoked raffia body, a huge wooden face painted white except for the round hollow eyes and the charred teeth that were as big as a man's fingers. On his head were two powerful horns.

When all the *egwugwu* had sat down and the sound of the many tiny bells and rattles on their bodies had subsided, Evil Forest addressed the two groups of people facing them.

"Uzowulu's body, I salute you," he said. Spirits always addressed humans as "bodies." Uzowulu bent down and touched the earth with his right hand as a sign of submission.

"Our father, my hand has touched the ground," he said.

"Uzowulu's body, do you know me?" asked the spirit.

"How can I know you, father? You are beyond our knowledge."

Evil Forest then turned to the other group and addressed the eldest of the three brothers.

"The body of Odukwe, I greet you," he said, and Odukwe bent down and touched the earth. The hearing then began.

Uzowulu stepped forward and presented his case.

"That woman standing there is my wife, Mgbafo. I married her with my money and my yams. I do not owe my in-laws anything. I owe them no yams. I owe them no coco-yams. One morning three of them came to my house, beat me up and took my wife and children away. This happened in the rainy season. I have waited in vain for my wife to return. At last I went to my in-laws and said to them, 'You have taken back your sister. I did not send her away. You yourselves took her. The law of the clan is that you should return her bride-price.' But my wife's brothers said they had nothing to tell me. So I have brought the matter to the fathers of the clan. My case is finished. I salute you."

"Your words are good," said the leader of the *egwugwu*. "Let us hear Odukwe. His words may also be good."

Odukwe was short and thickset. He stepped forward, saluted the spirits and began his story.

"My in-law has told you that we went to his house, beat him up and took our sister and her children away. All that is true. He told you that he came to take back her bride-price and we refused to give it him. That also is true. My in-law, Uzowulu, is a beast. My sister lived with him for nine years. During those years no single day passed in the sky without his beating the woman. We have tried to settle their quarrels time without number and on each occasion Uzowulu was guilty—"

"It is a lie!" Uzowulu shouted.

"Two years ago," continued Odukwe, "when she was pregnant, he beat her until she miscarried."

"It is a lie. She miscarried after she had gone to sleep with her lover."

"Uzowulu's body, I salute you," said Evil Forest, silencing him. "What kind of lover sleeps with a pregnant woman?" There was a loud murmur of approbation from the crowd. Odukwe continued:

"Last year when my sister was recovering from an illness, he beat her again so that if the neighbors had not gone in to save her she would have been killed. We heard of it, and did as you have been told. The law of Umuofia is that if a woman runs away from her husband her bride-price is returned. But in this case she ran away to save her life. Her two children belong to Uzowulu. We do not dispute it, but they are too young to leave their mother. If, in the other hand, Uzowulu should recover from his madness and come in the proper way to beg his wife to return she will do so on the understanding that if he ever beats her again we shall cut off his genitals for him."

The crowd roared with laughter. Evil Forest rose to his feet and order was immediately restored. A steady cloud of smoke rose from his head. He sat down again and called two witnesses. They were both Uzowulu's neighbors, and they agreed about the beating. Evil Forest then stood up, pulled out his staff and thrust it into the earth again. He ran a few steps in the direction of the women; they all fled in terror, only to return to their places almost immediately. The nine *egwugwu* then went away to consult together in their house. They were silent for a long time. Then the metal gong sounded and the flute was blown. The *egwugwu* had emerged once again from their underground home. They saluted one another and then reappeared on the *ilo*.

"*Umuofia kwenu!*" roared Evil Forest, facing the elders and grandees of the clan.

"*Yaa!*" replied the thunderous crowd; then silence descended from the sky and swallowed the noise.

Evil Forest began to speak and all the while he spoke everyone was silent. The eight other *egwugwu* were as still as statues.

"We have heard both sides of the case," said Evil Forest. "Our duty is not to blame this man or to praise that, but to settle the dispute." He turned to Uzowulu's group and allowed a short pause.

"Uzowulu's body, I salute you," he said.

"Our father, my hand has touched the ground," replied Uzowulu, touching the earth.

"Uzowulu's body, do you know me?"

"How can I know you, father? You are beyond our knowledge," Uzowulu replied.

"I am Evil Forest. I kill a man on the day that his life is sweetest to him."

"That is true," replied Uzowulu.

"Go to your in-laws with a pot of wine and beg your wife to return to you. It is not bravery when a man fights with a woman." He turned to Odukwe, and allowed a brief pause.

"Odukwe's body, I greet you," he said.

"My hand is on the ground," replied Odukwe.

"Do you know me?"

"No man can know you," replied Odukwe.

"I am Evil Forest, I am Dry-meat-that-fills-the-mouth, I am Fire-that-burns-without-faggots. If your in-law brings wine to you, let your sister go with him. I salute you." He pulled his staff from the hard earth and thrust it back.

"*Umuofia kwenu!*" he roared, and the crowd answered.

"I don't know why such a trifle should come before the *egwugwu*," said one elder to another.

"Don't you know what kind of man Uzowulu is? He will not listen to any other decision," replied the other.

As they spoke two other groups of people had replaced the first before the *egwugwu*, and a great land case began.

11

The night was impenetrably dark. The moon had been rising later and later every night until now it was seen only at dawn. And whenever the moon forsook evening and rose at cock-crow the nights were as black as charcoal.

Ezinma and her mother sat on a mat on the floor after their supper of yam foo-foo and bitter-leaf soup. A palm-oil lamp gave out yellowish light. Without it, it would have been impossible to eat; one could not have known where one's mouth was in the darkness of that night. There was an oil lamp in all the four huts on Okonkwo's compound, and each hut seen from the others looked like a soft eye of yellow half-light set in the solid massiveness of night.

The world was silent except for the shrill cry of insects, which was part of the night, and the sound of wooden mortar and pestle as Nwayieke pounded her foo-foo. Nwayieke lived four compounds away, and she was notorious for her late cooking. Every woman in the neighborhood knew the sound of Nwayieke's mortar and pestle. It was also part of the night.

Okonkwo had eaten from his wives' dishes and was now reclining with his back against the wall. He searched his bag and brought out his snuff-bottle. He turned it on to his left palm, but nothing came out. He hit the bottle against his knee to shake up the tobacco. That was always the trouble with Okeke's snuff. It very quickly went damp, and there was too much saltpeter in it. Okonkwo had not bought snuff from him for a long time. Idigo was the man who knew how to grind good snuff. But he had recently fallen ill.

Low voices, broken now and again by singing, reached Okonkwo from his wives' huts as each woman and her children told folk stories. Ekwefi and her daughter, Ezinma, sat on a mat on the floor. It was Ekwefi's turn to tell a story.

"Once upon a time," she began, "all the birds were invited to a feast in the sky. They were very happy and began to prepare themselves for the great day. They painted their bodies with red cam wood and drew beautiful patterns on them with *uli*.

"Tortoise saw all these preparations and soon discovered what it all meant. Nothing that happened in the world of the animals ever escaped his notice; he was full of cunning. As soon as he heard of the great feast in the sky his throat began to itch at the very thought. There was a famine in those days and Tortoise had not eaten a good meal for two moons. His body rattled like a piece of dry stick in his empty shell. So he began to plan how he would go to the sky."

"But he had no wings," said Ezinma.

"Be patient," replied her mother. "That is the story. Tortoise had no wings, but he went to the birds and asked to be allowed to go with them.

" 'We know you too well,' said the birds when they had heard him. 'You are full of cunning and you are ungrateful. If we allow you to come with us you will soon begin your mischief.'

" 'You do not know me,' said Tortoise. 'I am a changed man. I have learned that a man who makes trouble for others is also making it for himself.'

"Tortoise had a sweet tongue, and within a short time all the birds agreed that he was a changed man, and they each gave him a feather, with which he made two wings.

"At last the great day came and Tortoise was the first to arrive at the meeting place. When all the birds had gathered together, they set off in a body. Tortoise was very happy and voluble as he flew among the birds, and he was soon chosen as the man to speak for the party because he was a great orator.

" 'There is one important thing which we must not forget,' he said as they flew on their way. 'When people are invited to a great feast like this, they take new names for the occasion. Our hosts in the sky will expect us to honor this age-old custom.'

"None of the birds had heard of this custom but they knew that Tortoise, in spite of his failings in other directions, was a widely traveled man who knew the customs of different peoples. And so they each took a new name. When they had all taken, Tortoise also took one. He was to be called *All of you.*

"At last the party arrived in the sky and their hosts were very happy to see them. Tortoise stood up in his many-colored plumage and thanked them for their invitation. His speech was so eloquent that all the birds were glad they had brought him, and nodded their heads in approval of all he said. Their hosts took him as the king of the birds, especially as he looked somewhat different from the others.

"After kola nuts had been presented and eaten, the people of the sky set before their guests the most delectable dishes Tortoise had ever seen or dreamed of. The soup was brought out hot from the fire and in the very pot in which it had been cooked. It was full of meat and fish. Tortoise began to sniff aloud. There was pounded yam and also yam pottage cooked with palm-oil and fresh fish. There were also pots of palm-wine. When everything had been set before the guests, one of the people of the sky came forward and tasted a little from each pot. He then invited the birds to eat. But Tortoise jumped to his feet and asked: 'For whom have you prepared this feast?'

" 'For all of you,' replied the man.

"Tortoise turned to the birds and said: 'You remember that my name is *All of you*. The custom here is to serve the spokesman first and the others later. They will serve you when I have eaten.'

"He began to eat and the birds grumbled angrily. The people of the sky thought it must be their custom to leave all the food for their king. And so Tortoise ate the best part of the food and then drank two pots of palm-wine, so that he was full of food and drink and his body filled out in his shell.

"The birds gathered round to eat what was left and to peck at the bones he had thrown all about the floor. Some of them were too angry to eat. They chose to fly home on an empty stomach. But before they left each took back the feather he had lent to Tortoise. And there he stood in his hard shell full of food and wine but without any wings to fly home. He asked the birds to take a message for his wife, but they all refused. In the end Parrot, who had felt more angry than the others, suddenly changed his mind and agreed to take the message.

" 'Tell my wife,' said Tortoise, 'to bring out all the soft things in my house and cover the compound with them so that I can jump down from the sky without very great danger.'

"Parrot promised to deliver the message, and then flew away. But when he reached Tortoise's house he told his wife to bring out all the hard things in the house. And so she brought out her husband's hoes, machetes, spears, guns and even his cannon. Tortoise looked down from the sky and saw his wife bringing things out, but it was too far to see what they were. When all seemed ready he let himself go. He fell and fell and fell until he began to fear that he would never stop falling. And then like the sound of his cannon he crashed on the compound."

"Did he die?" asked Ezinma.

"No," replied Ekwefi. "His shell broke into pieces. But there was a great medicine man in the neighborhood. Tortoise's wife sent for him and he gathered all the bits of shell and stuck them together. That is why Tortoise's shell is not smooth."

"There is no song in the story," Ezinma pointed out.

"No," said Ekwefi. "I shall think of another one with a song. But it is your turn now."

"Once upon a time," Ezinma began, "Tortoise and Cat went to wrestle against Yams—no, that is not the beginning. Once upon a time there was a great famine in the land of animals. Everybody was lean except Cat, who was fat and whose body shone as if oil was rubbed on it . . ."

She broke off because at that very moment a loud and high-pitched voice broke the outer silence of the night. It was Chielo, the priestess of Agbala, prophesying. There was nothing new in that. Once in a while Chielo was possessed by the spirit of her god and she began to prophesy. But tonight she was addressing her prophecy and greetings to Okonkwo, and so everyone in his family listened. The folk stories stopped.

"*Agbala do-o-o-o! Agbala ekeneo-o-o-o,*"[2] came the voice like a sharp knife cutting through the night. "*Okonkwo! Agbala ekene gio-o-o-o! Agbala cholu ifu ada ya Ezinmao-o-o-o!*"[3]

---

2. Agbala wants something! Agbala greets.   3. Agbala greets you! Agbala wants to see his daughter Ezinma!

At the mention of Ezinma's name Ekwefi jerked her head sharply like an animal that had sniffed death in the air. Her heart jumped painfully within her.

The priestess had now reached Okonkwo's compound and was talking with him outside his hut. She was saying again and again that Agbala wanted to see his daughter, Ezinma. Okonkwo pleaded with her to come back in the morning because Ezinma was now asleep. But Chielo ignored what he was trying to say and went on shouting that Agbala wanted to see his daughter. Her voice was as clear as metal, and Okonkwo's women and children heard from their huts all that she said. Okonkwo was still pleading that the girl had been ill of late and was asleep. Ekwefi quickly took her to their bedroom and placed her on their high bamboo bed.

The priestess screamed. "Beware, Okonkwo!" she warned. "Beware of exchanging words with Agbala. Does a man speak when a god speaks? Beware!"

She walked through Okonkwo's hut into the circular compound and went straight toward Ekwefi's hut. Okonkwo came after her.

"Ekwefi," she called, "Agbala greets you. Where is my daughter, Ezinma? Agbala wants to see her."

Ekwefi came out from her hut carrying her oil lamp in her left hand. There was a light wind blowing, so she cupped her right hand to shelter the flame. Nwoye's mother, also carrying an oil lamp, emerged from her hut. The children stood in the darkness outside their hut watching the strange event. Okonkwo's youngest wife also came out and joined the others.

"Where does Agbala want to see her?" Ekwefi asked.

"Where else but in his house in the hills and the caves?" replied the priestess.

"I will come with you, too," Ekwefi said firmly.

"*Tufia-a!*"[4] the priestess cursed, her voice cracking like the angry bark of thunder in the dry season. "How dare you, woman, to go before the mighty Agbala of your own accord? Beware, woman, lest he strike you in his anger. Bring me my daughter."

Ekwefi went into her hut and came out again with Ezinma.

"Come, my daughter," said the priestess. "I shall carry you on my back. A baby on its mother's back does not know that the way is long."

Ezinma began to cry. She was used to Chielo calling her "my daughter." But it was a different Chielo she now saw in the yellow half-light.

"Don't cry, my daughter," said the priestess, "lest Agbala be angry with you."

"Don't cry," said Ekwefi, "she will bring you back very soon. I shall give you some fish to eat." She went into the hut again and brought down the smoke-black basket in which she kept her dried fish and other ingredients for cooking soup. She broke a piece in two and gave it to Ezinma, who clung to her.

"Don't be afraid," said Ekwefi, stroking her head, which was shaved in places, leaving a regular pattern of hair. They went outside again. The priestess bent down on one knee and Ezinma climbed on her back, her left palm closed on her fish and her eyes gleaming with tears.

---

4. A curse in words meaning "spitting" or "clearing out," often accompanied by spitting.

"*Agbala do-o-o-o! Agbala ekeneo-o-o-o!* . . ." Chielo began once again to chant greetings to her god. She turned round sharply and walked through Okonkwo's hut, bending very low at the eaves. Ezinma was crying loudly now, calling on her mother. The two voices disappeared into the thick darkness.

A strange and sudden weakness descended on Ekwefi as she stood gazing in the direction of the voices like a hen whose only chick has been carried away by a kite. Ezinma's voice soon faded away and only Chielo was heard moving farther and farther into the distance.

"Why do you stand there as though she had been kidnapped?" asked Okonkwo as he went back to his hut.

"She will bring her back soon," Nwoye's mother said.

But Ekwefi did not hear these consolations. She stood for a while, and then, all of a sudden, made up her mind. She hurried through Okonkwo's hut and went outside. "Where are you going?" he asked.

"I am following Chielo," she replied and disappeared in the darkness. Okonkwo cleared his throat, and brought out his snuff-bottle from the goat-skin bag by his side.

The priestess's voice was already growing faint in the distance. Ekwefi hurried to the main footpath and turned left in the direction of the voice. Her eyes were useless to her in the darkness. But she picked her way easily on the sandy footpath hedged on either side by branches and damp leaves. She began to run, holding her breasts with her hands to stop them flapping noisily against her body. She hit her left foot against an outcropped root, and terror seized her. It was an ill omen. She ran faster. But Chielo's voice was still a long way away. Had she been running too? How could she go so fast with Ezinma on her back? Although the night was cool, Ekwefi was beginning to feel hot from her running. She continually ran into the luxuriant weeds and creepers that walled in the path. Once she tripped up and fell. Only then did she realize, with a start, that Chielo had stopped her chanting. Her heart beat violently and she stood still. Then Chielo's renewed outburst came from only a few paces ahead. But Ekwefi could not see her. She shut her eyes for a while and opened them again in an effort to see. But it was useless. She could not see beyond her nose.

There were no stars in the sky because there was a rain-cloud. Fireflies went about with their tiny green lamps, which only made the darkness more profound. Between Chielo's outbursts the night was alive with the shrill tremor of forest insects woven into the darkness.

"*Agbala do-o-o-o! . . . Agbala ekeneo-o-o-o! . . .*" Ekwefi trudged behind, neither getting too near nor keeping too far back. She thought they must be going towards the sacred cave. Now that she walked slowly she had time to think. What would she do when they got to the cave? She would not dare to enter. She would wait at the mouth, all alone in that fearful place. She thought of all the terrors of the night. She remembered that night, long ago, when she had seen *Ogbu-agali-odu*, one of those evil essences loosed upon the world by the potent "medicines" which the tribe had made in the distant past against its enemies but had now forgotten how to control. Ekwefi had been returning from the stream with her mother on a dark night like this when they saw its glow as it flew in their direction. They had thrown down their water-pots and lain by the roadside expecting the sinister light to descend on them and kill them. That was the only time Ekwefi ever saw *Ogbu-agali-odu*. But although it had happened so long ago, her blood still ran cold whenever she remembered that night.

The priestess's voice came at longer intervals now, but its vigor was undiminished. The air was cool and damp with dew. Ezinma sneezed. Ekwefi muttered, "Life to you." At the same time the priestess also said, "Life to you, my daughter." Ezinma's voice from the darkness warmed her mother's heart. She trudged slowly along.

And then the priestess screamed. "Somebody is walking behind me!" she said. "Whether you are spirit or man, may Agbala shave your head with a blunt razor! May he twist your neck until you see your heels!"

Ekwefi stood rooted to the spot. One mind said to her: "Woman, go home before Agbala does you harm." But she could not. She stood until Chielo had increased the distance between them and she began to follow again. She had already walked so long that she began to feel a slight numbness in the limbs and in the head. Then it occurred to her that they could not have been heading for the cave. They must have by-passed it long ago; they must be going towards Umuachi, the farthest village in the clan. Chielo's voice now came after long intervals.

It seemed to Ekwefi that the night had become a little lighter. The cloud had lifted and a few stars were out. The moon must be preparing to rise, its sullenness over. When the moon rose late in the night, people said it was refusing food, as a sullen husband refuses his wife's food when they have quarrelled.

"*Agbala do-o-o-o! Umuachi! Agbala ekene unuo-o-o!*" It was just as Ekwefi had thought. The priestess was now saluting the village of Umuachi. It was unbelievable, the distance they had covered. As they emerged into the open village from the narrow forest track the darkness was softened and it became possible to see the vague shape of trees. Ekwefi screwed her eyes up in an effort to see her daughter and the priestess, but whenever she thought she saw their shape it immediately dissolved like a melting lump of darkness. She walked numbly along.

Chielo's voice was now rising continuously, as when she first set out. Ekwefi had a feeling of spacious openness, and she guessed they must be on the village *ilo*, or playground. And she realized too with something like a jerk that Chielo was no longer moving forward. She was, in fact, returning. Ekwefi quickly moved away from her line of retreat. Chielo passed by, and they began to go back the way they had come.

It was a long and weary journey and Ekwefi felt like a sleepwalker most of the way. The moon was definitely rising, and although it had not yet appeared on the sky its light had already melted down the darkness. Ekwefi could now discern the figure of the priestess and her burden. She slowed down her pace so as to increase the distance between them. She was afraid of what might happen if Chielo suddenly turned round and saw her.

She had prayed for the moon to rise. But now she found the half-light of the incipient moon more terrifying than darkness. The world was now peopled with vague, fantastic figures that dissolved under her steady gaze and then formed again in new shapes. At one stage Ekwefi was so afraid that she nearly called out to Chielo for companionship and human sympathy. What she had seen was the shape of a man climbing a palm tree, his head pointing to the earth and his legs skywards. But at that very moment Chielo's voice rose again in her possessed chanting, and Ekwefi recoiled, because there was no humanity there. It was not the same Chielo who sat with her in the market and sometimes bought bean-cakes for Ezinma, whom she called her daughter. It was a different woman—the priestess of Agbala, the Oracle of the Hills and Caves. Ekwefi trudged along between two fears. The sound of her benumbed steps seemed to come from some other person walking behind her. Her arms were folded across her bare breasts. Dew fell heavily and the air was cold. She could no longer think, not even about the terrors of night. She just jogged along in a half-sleep, only waking to full life when Chielo sang.

At last they took a turning and began to head for the caves. From then on, Chielo never ceased in her chanting. She greeted her god in a multitude of names—the owner of the future, the messenger of earth, the god who cut a man down when his life was sweetest to him. Ekwefi was also awakened and her benumbed fears revived.

The moon was now up and she could see Chielo and Ezinma clearly. How a woman could carry a child of that size so easily and for so long was a miracle. But Ekwefi was not thinking about that. Chielo was not a woman that night.

"Agbala do-o-o-o! Agbala ekeneo-o-o-o! Chi negbu madu ubosi ndu ya nato ya uto daluo-o-o! . . ."[5]

Ekwefi could already see the hills looming in the moonlight. They formed a circular ring with a break at one point through which the foot-track led to the center of the circle.

As soon as the priestess stepped into this ring of hills her voice was not only doubled in strength but was thrown back on all sides. It was indeed the shrine of a great god. Ekwefi picked her way carefully and quietly. She was already beginning to doubt the wisdom of her coming. Nothing would happen to Ezinma, she thought. And if anything happened to her could she stop it? She would not dare to enter the underground caves. Her coming was quite useless, she thought.

As these things went through her mind she did not realize how close they were to the cave mouth. And so when the priestess with Ezinma on her back disappeared through a hole hardly big enough to pass a hen, Ekwefi broke into a run as though to stop them. As she stood gazing at the circular darkness which had swallowed them, tears gushed from her eyes, and she swore within her that if she heard Ezinma cry she would rush into the cave to defend her against all the gods in the world. She would die with her.

Having sworn that oath, she sat down on a stony ledge and waited. Her fear had vanished. She could hear the priestess's voice, all its metal taken out of it by the vast emptiness of the cave. She buried her face in her lap and waited.

She did not know how long she waited. It must have been a very long time.

5. Agbala wants something! Agbala greets . . . God who kills a man on the day his life is so pleasant he give thanks!

Her back was turned on the footpath that led out of the hills. She must have heard a noise behind her and turned round sharply. A man stood there with a machete in his hand. Ekwefi uttered a scream and sprang to her feet.

"Don't be foolish," said Okonkwo's voice. "I thought you were going into the shrine with Chielo," he mocked.

Ekwefi did not answer. Tears of gratitude filled her eyes. She knew her daughter was safe.

"Go home and sleep," said Okonkwo. "I shall wait here."

"I shall wait too. It is almost dawn. The first cock has crowed."

As they stood there together, Ekwefi's mind went back to the days when they were young. She had married Anene because Okonkwo was too poor then to marry. Two years after her marriage to Anene she could bear it no longer and she ran away to Okonkwo. It had been early in the morning. The moon was shining. She was going to the stream to fetch water. Okonkwo's house was on the way to the stream. She went in and knocked at his door and he came out. Even in those days he was not a man of many words. He just carried her into his bed and in the darkness began to feel around her waist for the loose end of her cloth.

12

On the following morning the entire neighborhood wore a festive air because Okonkwo's friend, Obierika, was celebrating his daughter's *uri*. It was the day on which her suitor (having already paid the greater part of her bride-price) would bring palm-wine not only to her parents and immediate relatives but to the wide and extensive group of kinsmen called *umunna*. Everybody had been invited—men, women and children. But it was really a woman's ceremony and the central figures were the bride and her mother.

As soon as day broke, breakfast was hastily eaten and women and children began to gather at Obierika's compound to help the bride's mother in her difficult but happy task of cooking for a whole village.

Okonkwo's family was astir like any other family in the neighborhood. Nwoye's mother and Okonkwo's youngest wife were ready to set out for Obierika's compound with all their children. Nwoye's mother carried a basket of coco-yams, a cake of salt and smoked fish which she would present to Obierika's wife. Okonkwo's youngest wife, Ojiugo, also had a basket of plantains and coco-yams and a small pot of palm-oil. Their children carried pots of water.

Ekwefi was tired and sleepy from the exhausting experiences of the previous night. It was not very long since they had returned. The priestess, with Ezinma sleeping on her back, had crawled out of the shrine on her belly like a snake. She had not as much as looked at Okonkwo and Ekwefi or shown any surprise at finding them at the mouth of the cave. She looked straight ahead of her and walked back to the village. Okonkwo and his wife followed at a respectful distance. They thought the priestess might be going to her house, but she went to Okonkwo's compound, passed through his *obi* and into Ekwefi's hut and walked into her bedroom. She placed Ezinma carefully on the bed and went away without saying a word to anybody.

Ezinma was still sleeping when everyone else was astir, and Ekwefi asked Nwoye's mother and Ojiugo to explain to Obierika's wife that she would be late. She had got ready her basket of coco-yams and fish, but she must wait for Ezinma to wake.

"You need some sleep yourself," said Nwoye's mother. "You look very tired."

As they spoke Ezinma emerged from the hut, rubbing her eyes and stretching her spare frame. She saw the other children with their water-pots and remembered that they were going to fetch water for Obierika's wife. She went back to the hut and brought her pot.

"Have you slept enough?" asked her mother.

"Yes," she replied, "Let us go."

"Not before you have had your breakfast," said Ekwefi. And she went into her hut to warm the vegetable soup she had cooked last night.

"We shall be going," said Nwoye's mother. "I will tell Obierika's wife that you are coming later." And so they all went to help Obierika's wife—Nwoye's mother with her four children and Ojiugo with her two.

As they trooped through Okonkwo's *obi* he asked: "Who will prepare my afternoon meal?"

"I shall return to do it," said Ojiugo.

Okonkwo was also feeling tired, and sleepy, for although nobody else knew it, he had not slept at all last night. He had felt very anxious but did not show it. When Ekwefi had followed the priestess, he had allowed what he regarded as a reasonable and manly interval to pass and then gone with his machete to the shrine, where he thought they must be. It was only when he had got there that it had occurred to him that the priestess might have chosen to go round the villages first. Okonkwo had returned home and sat waiting. When he thought he had waited long enough he again returned to the shrine. But the Hills and the Caves were as silent as death. It was only on his fourth trip that he had found Ekwefi, and by then he had become gravely worried.

Obierika's compound was as busy as an anthill. Temporary cooking tripods were erected on every available space by bringing together three blocks of sun-dried earth and making a fire in their midst. Cooking pots went up and down the tripods, and foo-foo was pounded in a hundred wooden mortars. Some of the women cooked the yams and the cassava, and others prepared vegetable soup. Young men pounded the foo-foo or split firewood. The children made endless trips to the stream.

Three young men helped Obierika to slaughter the two goats with which the soup was made. They were very fat goats, but the fattest of all was tethered to a peg near the wall of the compound. It was as big as a small cow. Obierika had sent one of his relatives all the way to Umuike to buy that goat. It was the one he would present alive to his in-laws.

"The market of Umuike is a wonderful place," said the young man who had been sent by Obierika to buy the giant goat. "There are so many people on it that if you threw up a grain of sand it would not find a way to fall to earth again."

"It is the result of a great medicine," said Obierika. "The people of Umuike wanted their market to grow and swallow up the markets of their neighbors. So they made a powerful medicine. Every market day, before the first cock-crow, this medicine stands on the market ground in the shape of an old woman with a fan. With this magic fan she beckons to the market all the neighboring clans. She beckons in front of her and behind her, to her right and to her left."

"And so everybody comes," said another man, "honest men and thieves. They can steal your cloth from off your waist in that market."

"Yes," said Obierika. "I warned Nwankwo to keep a sharp eye and a sharp ear. There was once a man who went to sell a goat. He led it on a thick rope which he tied round his wrist. But as he walked through the market he realized that people were pointing at him as they do to a madman. He could not understand it until he looked back and saw that what he led at the end of the tether was not a goat but a heavy log of wood."

"Do you think a thief can do that kind of thing single-handed?" asked Nwankwo.

"No," said Obierika. "They use medicine."

When they had cut the goats' throats and collected the blood in a bowl, they held them over an open fire to burn off the hair, and the smell of burning hair blended with the smell of cooking. Then they washed them and cut them up for the women who prepared the soup.

All this anthill activity was going smoothly when a sudden interruption came. It was a cry in the distance: *Oji odu achu ijiji-o-o!* (*The one that uses its tail to drive flies away!*) Every woman immediately abandoned whatever she was doing and rushed out in the direction of the cry.

"We cannot all rush out like that, leaving what we are cooking to burn in the fire," shouted Chielo, the priestess. "Three or four of us should stay behind."

"It is true," said another woman. "We will allow three or four women to stay behind."

Five women stayed behind to look after the cooking-pots, and all the rest rushed away to see the cow that had been let loose. When they saw it they drove it back to its owner, who at once paid the heavy fine which the village imposed on anyone whose cow was let loose on his neighbors' crops. When the women had exacted the penalty they checked among themselves to see if any woman had failed to come out when the cry had been raised.

"Where is Mgbogo?" asked one of them.

"She is ill in bed," said Mgbogo's next-door neighbor. "She has *iba.*"

"The only other person is Udenkwo," said another woman, "and her child is not twenty-eight days yet."

Those women whom Obierika's wife had not asked to help her with the cooking returned to their homes, and the rest went back, in a body, to Obierika's compound.

"Whose cow was it?" asked the women who had been allowed to stay behind.

"It was my husband's," said Ezelagbo. "One of the young children had opened the gate of the cowshed."

Early in the afternoon the first two pots of palm-wine arrived from Obierika's in-laws. They were duly presented to the women, who drank a cup or two each, to help them in their cooking. Some of it also went to the bride and her attendant maidens, who were putting the last delicate touches of razor to her coiffure and cam wood on her smooth skin.

When the heat of the sun began to soften, Obierika's son, Maduka, took a long broom and swept the ground in front of his father's *obi*. And as if they had been waiting for that, Obierika's relatives and friends began to arrive, every man with his goatskin bag hung on one shoulder and a rolled goatskin mat under his arm. Some of them were accompanied by their sons bearing carved wooden stools. Okonkwo was one of them. They sat in a half-circle and began to talk of many things. It would not be long before the suitors came.

Okonkwo brought out his snuff-bottle and offered it to Ogbuefi Ezenwa, who sat next to him. Ezenwa[6] took it, tapped it on his kneecap, rubbed his left palm on his body to dry it before tipping a little snuff into it. His actions were deliberate, and he spoke as he performed them:

"I hope our in-laws will bring many pots of wine. Although they come from a village that is known for being closefisted, they ought to know that Akueke is the bride for a king."

"They dare not bring fewer than thirty pots," said Okonkwo. "I shall tell them my mind if they do."

At that moment Obierika's son, Maduka, led out the giant goat from the inner compound, for his father's relatives to see. They all admired it and said that that was the way things should be done. The goat was then led back to the inner compound.

Very soon after, the in-laws began to arrive. Young men and boys in single file, each carrying a pot of wine, came first. Obierika's relatives counted the pots as they came. Twenty, twenty-five. There was a long break, and the hosts looked at each other as if to say, "I told you." Then more pots came. Thirty, thirty-five, forty, forty-five. The hosts nodded in approval and seemed to say, "Now they are behaving like men." Altogether there were fifty pots of wine. After the pot-bearers came Ibe, the suitor, and the elders of his family. They sat in a half-moon, thus completing a circle with their hosts. The pots of wine stood in their midst. Then the bride, her mother and a half a dozen other women and girls emerged from the inner compound, and went round the circle shaking hands with all. The bride's mother led the way, followed by the bride and the other women. The married women wore their best cloths and the girls wore red and black waist-beads and anklets of brass.

When the women retired, Obierika presented kola nuts to his in-laws. His eldest brother broke the first one. "Life to all of us," he said as he broke it. "And let there be friendship between your family and ours."

The crowd answered: "*Ee-e-e!*"

"We are giving you our daughter today. She will be a good wife to you. She will bear you nine sons like the mother of our town."

"*Ee-e-e!*"

The oldest man in the camp of the visitors replied: "It will be good for you and it will be good for us."

"*Ee-e-e!*"

"This is not the first time my people have come to marry your daughter. My mother was one of you."

"*Ee-e-e!*"

"And this will not be the last, because you understand us and we understand you. You are a great family."

6. King from childhood (strong praise).

"*Ee-e-e!*"

"Prosperous men and great warriors." He looked in the direction of Okonkwo. "Your daughter will bear us sons like you."

"*Ee-e-e!*"

The kola was eaten and the drinking of palm-wine began. Groups of four or five men sat round with a pot in their midst. As the evening wore on, food was presented to the guests. There were huge bowls of foo-foo and steaming pots of soup. There were also pots of yam pottage. It was a great feast.

As night fell, burning torches were set on wooden tripods and the young men raised a song. The elders sat in a big circle and the singers went round singing each man's praise as they came before him. They had something to say for every man. Some were great farmers, some were orators who spoke for the clan; Okonkwo was the greatest wrestler and warrior alive. When they had gone round the circle they settled down in the center, and girls came from the inner compound to dance. At first the bride was not among them. But when she finally appeared holding a cock in her right hand, a loud cheer rose from the crowd. All the other dancers made way for her. She presented the cock to the musicians and began to dance. Her brass anklets rattled as she danced and her body gleamed with cam wood in the soft yellow light. The musicians with their wood, clay and metal instruments went from song to song. And they were all gay. They sang the latest song in the village:

> If I hold her hand
> She says, "Don't touch!"
> If I hold her foot
> She says, "Don't touch!"
> But when I hold her waist-beads
> She pretends not to know.

The night was already far spent when the guests rose to go, taking their bride home to spend seven market weeks with her suitor's family. They sang songs as they went, and on their way they paid short courtesy visits to prominent men like Okonkwo, before they finally left for their village. Okonkwo made a present of two cocks to them.

13

Go-di-di-go-go-di-go. Di-go-go-di-go. It was the *ekwe* talking to the clan. One of the things every man learned was the language of the hollowed-out wooden instrument. Diim! Diim! Diim! boomed the cannon at intervals.

The first cock had not crowed, and Umuofia was still swallowed up in sleep and silence when the *ekwe* began to talk, and the cannon shattered the silence. Men stirred on their bamboo beds and listened anxiously. Somebody was dead. The cannon seemed to rend the sky. Di-go-go-di-go-di-di-go-go floated in the message-laden night air. The faint and distant wailing of women settled like a sediment of sorrow on the earth. Now and again a full-chested lamentation rose above the wailing whenever a man came into the place of death. He raised his voice once or twice in manly sorrow and then sat down with the other men listening to the endless wailing of the women and the esoteric language of the *ekwe*. Now and again the cannon boomed.

The wailing of the women would not be heard beyond the village, but the *ekwe* carried the news to all the nine villages and even beyond. It began by naming the clan: *Umuofia obodo dike*, "the land of the brave." *Umuofia obodo dike! Umuofia obodo dike!* It said this over and over again, and as it dwelt on it, anxiety mounted in every heart that heaved on a bamboo bed that night. Then it went nearer and named the village: "*Iguedo*[7] of the yellow grinding-stone!" It was Okonkwo's village. Again and again Iguedo was called and men waited breathlessly in all the nine villages. At last the man was named and people sighed "E-u-u, Ezeudu is dead." A cold shiver ran down Okonkwo's back as he remembered the last time the old man had visited him. "That boy calls you father," he had said. "Bear no hand in his death."

Ezeudu was a great man, and so all the clan was at his funeral. The ancient drums of death beat, guns and cannon were fired, and men dashed about in frenzy, cutting down every tree or animal they saw, jumping over walls and dancing on the roof. It was a warrior's funeral, and from morning till night warriors came and went in their age groups. They all wore smoked raffia skirts and their bodies were painted with chalk and charcoal. Now and again an ancestral spirit or *egwugwu* appeared from the underworld, speaking in a tremulous, unearthly voice and completely covered in raffia. Some of them were very violent, and there had been a mad rush for shelter earlier in the day when one appeared with a sharp machete and was only prevented from doing serious harm by two men who restrained him with the help of a strong rope tied round his waist. Sometimes he turned round and chased those men, and they ran for their lives. But they always returned to the long rope he trailed behind. He sang, in a terrifying voice, that Ekwensu, or Evil Spirit, had entered his eye.

But the most dreaded of all was yet to come. He was always alone and was shaped like a coffin. A sickly odor hung in the air wherever he went, and flies went with him. Even the greatest medicine men took shelter when he was near. Many years ago another *egwugwu* had dared to stand his ground before him and had been transfixed to the spot for two days. This one had only one hand and it carried a basket full of water.

But some of the *egwugwu* were quite harmless. One of them was so old and infirm that he leaned heavily on a stick. He walked unsteadily to the place where the corpse was laid, gazed at it a while and went away again—to the underworld.

The land of the living was not far removed from the domain of the ancestors. There was coming and going between them, especially at festivals and also when an old man died, because an old man was very close to the ancestors. A man's life from birth to death was a series of transition rites which brought him nearer and nearer to his ancestors.

Ezeudu had been the oldest man in his village, and at his death there were only three men in the whole clan who were older, and four or five others in his own age group. Whenever one of these ancient men appeared in the crowd to dance unsteadily the funeral steps of the tribe, younger men gave way and the tumult subsided.

7. The yellow grindstone.

It was a great funeral, such as befitted a noble warrior. As the evening drew near, the shouting and the firing of guns, the beating of drums and the brandishing and clanging of machetes increased.

Ezeudu had taken three titles in his life. It was a rare achievement. There were only four titles in the clan, and only one or two men in any generation ever achieved the fourth and highest. When they did, they became the lords of the land. Because he had taken titles, Ezeudu was to be buried after dark with only a glowing brand to light the sacred ceremony.

But before this quiet and final rite, the tumult increased tenfold. Drums beat violently and men leaped up and down in frenzy. Guns were fired on all sides and sparks flew out as machetes clanged together in warriors' salutes. The air was full of dust and the smell of gunpowder. It was then that the one-handed spirit came, carrying a basket full of water. People made way for him on all sides and the noise subsided. Even the smell of gunpowder was swallowed in the sickly smell that now filled the air. He danced a few steps to the funeral drums and then went to see the corpse.

"Ezeudu!" he called in his guttural voice. "If you had been poor in your last life I would have asked you to be rich when you come again. But you were rich. If you had been a coward, I would have asked you to bring courage. But you were a fearless warrior. If you had died young, I would have asked you to get life. But you lived long. So I shall ask you to come again the way you came before. If your death was the death of nature, go in peace. But if a man caused it, do not allow him a moment's rest." He danced a few more steps and went away.

The drums and the dancing began again and reached fever-heat. Darkness was around the corner, and the burial was near. Guns fired the last salute and the cannon rent the sky. And then from the center of the delirious fury came a cry of agony and shouts of horror. It was as if a spell had been cast. All was silent. In the center of the crowd a boy lay in a pool of blood. It was the dead man's sixteen-year-old son, who with his brothers and half-brothers had been dancing the traditional farewell to their father. Okonkwo's gun had exploded and a piece of iron had pierced the boy's heart.

The confusion that followed was without parallel in the tradition of Umuofia. Violent deaths were frequent, but nothing like this had ever happened.

The only course open to Okonkwo was to flee from the clan. It was a crime against the earth goddess to kill a clansman, and a man who committed it must flee from the land. The crime was of two kinds, male and female. Okonkwo had committed the female, because it had been inadvertent. He could return to the clan after seven years.

That night he collected his most valuable belongings into head-loads. His wives wept bitterly and their children wept with them without knowing why. Obierika and half a dozen other friends came to help and to console him. They each made nine or ten trips carrying Okonkwo's yams to store in Obierika's barn. And before the cock crowed Okonkwo and his family were fleeing to his motherland. It was a little village called Mbanta,[8] just beyond the borders of Mbaino.

As soon as the day broke, a large crowd of men from Ezeudu's quarter

8. Small town.

stormed Okonkwo's compound, dressed in garbs of war. They set fire to his houses, demolished his red walls, killed his animals and destroyed his barn. It was the justice of the earth goddess, and they were merely her messengers. They had no hatred in their hearts against Okonkwo. His greatest friend, Obierika, was among them. They were merely cleansing the land which Okonkwo had polluted with the blood of a clansman.

Obierika was a man who thought about things. When the will of the goddess had been done, he sat down in his *obi* and mourned his friend's calamity. Why should a man suffer so grievously for an offense he had committed inadvertently? But although he thought for a long time he found no answer. He was merely led into greater complexities. He remembered his wife's twin children, whom he had thrown away. What crime had they committed? The Earth had decreed that they were an offense on the land and must be destroyed. And if the clan did not exact punishment for an offense against the great goddess, her wrath was loosed on all the land and not just on the offender. As the elders said, if one finger brought oil it soiled the others.

Part Two

14

Okonkwo was well received by his mother's kinsmen in Mbanta. The old man who received him was his mother's younger brother, who was now the eldest surviving member of that family. His name was Uchendu,[9] and it was he who had received Okonkwo's mother twenty and ten years before when she had been brought home from Umuofia to be buried with her people. Okonkwo was only a boy then and Uchendu still remembered him crying the traditional farewell: "Mother, mother, mother is going."

That was many years ago. Today Okonkwo was not bringing his mother home to be buried with her people. He was taking his family of three wives and their children to seek refuge in his motherland. As soon as Uchendu saw him with his sad and weary company he guessed what had happened, and asked no questions. It was not until the following day that Okonkwo told him the full story. The old man listened silently to the end and then said with some relief: "It is a female *ochu*."[1] And he arranged the requisite rites and sacrifices.

Okonkwo was given a plot of ground on which to build his compound, and two or three pieces of land on which to farm during the coming planting season. With the help of his mother's kinsmen he built himself an *obi* and three huts for his wives. He then installed his personal god and the symbols of his departed fathers. Each of Uchendu's five sons contributed three hundred seed-yams to enable their cousin to plant a farm, for as soon as the first rain came farming would begin.

At last the rain came. It was sudden and tremendous. For two or three moons the sun had been gathering strength till it seemed to breathe a breath of fire on the earth. All the grass had long been scorched brown, and the sands felt like live coals to the feet. Evergreen trees wore a dusty coat of

9. The thought created by life.   1. Murder, manslaughter.

brown. The birds were silenced in the forests, and the world lay panting under the live, vibrating heat. And then came the clap of thunder. It was an angry, metallic and thirsty clap, unlike the deep and liquid rumbling of the rainy season. A mighty wind arose and filled the air with dust. Palm trees swayed as the wind combed their leaves into flying crests like strange and fantastic coiffure.

When the rain finally came, it was in large, solid drops of frozen water which the people called "the nuts of the water of heaven." They were hard and painful on the body as they fell, yet young people ran about happily picking up the cold nuts and throwing them into their mouths to melt.

The earth quickly came to life and the birds in the forests fluttered around and chirped merrily. A vague scent of life and green vegetation was diffused in the air. As the rain began to fall more soberly and in smaller liquid drops, children sought for shelter, and all were happy, refreshed and thankful.

Okonkwo and his family worked very hard to plant a new farm. But it was like beginning life anew without the vigor and enthusiasm of youth, like learning to become left-handed in old age. Work no longer had for him the pleasure it used to have, and when there was no work to do he sat in a silent half-sleep.

His life had been ruled by a great passion—to become one of the lords of the clan. That had been his life-spring. And he had all but achieved it. Then everything had been broken. He had been cast out of his clan like a fish onto a dry, sandy beach, panting. Clearly his personal god or *chi* was not made for great things. A man could not rise beyond the destiny of his *chi*. The saying of the elders was not true—that if a man said yea his *chi* also affirmed. Here was a man whose *chi* said nay despite his own affirmation.

The old man, Uchendu, saw clearly that Okonkwo had yielded to despair and he was greatly troubled. He would speak to him after the *isa-ifi*[2] ceremony.

The youngest of Uchendu's five sons, Amikwu, was marrying a new wife. The bride-price had been paid and all but the last ceremony had been performed. Amikwu and his people had taken palm-wine to the bride's kinsmen about two moons before Okonkwo's arrival in Mbanta. And so it was time for the final ceremony of confession.

The daughters of the family were all there, some of them having come a long way from their homes in distant villages. Uchendu's eldest daughter had come from Obodo, nearly half a day's journey away. The daughters of Uchendu's brothers were also there. It was a full gathering of *umuada*,[3] in the same way as they would meet if a death occurred in the family. There were twenty-two of them.

They sat in a big circle on the ground and the bride sat in the center with a hen in her right hand. Uchendu sat by her, holding the ancestral staff of the family. All the other men stood outside the circle, watching. Their wives watched also. It was evening and the sun was setting.

Uchendu's eldest daughter, Njide, asked the questions.

"Remember that if you do not answer truthfully you will suffer or even die

2. A ceremony to ascertain that a wife (here, a promised bride) had been faithful to her husband during a separation.   3. The daughters, who, according to Igbo custom, married outside the clan, perform a special initiation upon returning home for important gatherings.

at childbirth," she began. "How many men have lain with you since my brother first expressed the desire to marry you?"

"None," she answered simply.

"Answer truthfully," urged the other women.

"None?" asked Njide.

"None," she answered.

"Swear on this staff of my fathers," said Uchendu.

"I swear," said the bride.

Uchendu took the hen from her, slit its throat with a sharp knife and allowed some of the blood to fall on his ancestral staff.

From that day Amikwu took the young bride to his hut and she became his wife. The daughters of the family did not return to their homes immediately but spent two or three days with their kinsmen.

On the second day Uchendu called together his sons and daughters and his nephew, Okonkwo. The men brought their goatskin mats, with which they sat on the floor, and the women sat on a sisal mat spread on a raised bank of earth. Uchendu pulled gently at his gray beard and gnashed his teeth. Then he began to speak, quietly and deliberately, picking his words with great care:

"It is Okonkwo that I primarily wish to speak to," he began. "But I want all of you to note what I am going to say. I am an old man and you are all children. I know more about the world than any of you. If there is any one among you who thinks he knows more let him speak up." He paused, but no one spoke.

"Why is Okonkwo with us today? This is not his clan. We are only his mother's kinsmen. He does not belong here. He is an exile, condemned for seven years to live in a strange land. And so he is bowed with grief. But there is just one question I would like to ask him. Can you tell me, Okonkwo, why it is that one of the commonest names we give our children is Nneka, or "Mother is Supreme?" We all know that a man is the head of the family and his wives do his bidding. A child belongs to its father and his family and not to its mother and her family. A man belongs to his fatherland and not to his motherland. And yet we say Nneka—'Mother is Supreme.' Why is that?"

There was silence. "I want Okonkwo to answer me," said Uchendu.

"I do not know the answer," Okonkwo replied.

"You do not know the answer? So you see that you are a child. You have many wives and many children—more children than I have. You are a great man in your clan. But you are still a child, *my* child. Listen to me and I shall tell you. But there is one more question I shall ask you. Why is it that when a woman dies she is taken home to be buried with her own kinsmen? She is not buried with her husband's kinsmen. Why is that? Your mother was brought home to me and buried with my people. Why was that?"

Okonkwo shook his head.

"He does not know that either," said Uchendu, "and yet he is full of sorrow because he has come to live in his motherland for a few years." He laughed a mirthless laughter, and turned to his sons and daughters. "What about you? Can you answer my question?"

They all shook their heads.

"Then listen to me," he said and cleared his throat. "It's true that a child belongs to its father. But when a father beats his child, it seeks sympathy in its mother's hut. A man belongs to his fatherland when things are good and life is sweet. But when there is sorrow and bitterness he finds refuge in his motherland. Your mother is there to protect you. She is buried there. And that is why we say that mother is supreme. Is it right that you, Okonkwo, should bring to your mother a heavy face and refuse to be comforted? Be careful or you may displease the dead. Your duty is to comfort your wives and children and take them back to your fatherland after seven years. But if you allow sorrow to weigh you down and kill you, they will all die in exile." He paused for a long while. "These are now your kinsmen." He waved at his sons and daughters. "You think you are the greatest sufferer in the world? Do you know that men are sometimes banished for life? Do you know that men sometimes lose all their yams and even their children? I had six wives once. I have none now except that young girl who knows not her right from her left. Do you know how many children I have buried—children I begot in my youth and strength? Twenty-two. I did not hang myself, and I am still alive. If you think you are the greatest sufferer in the world ask my daughter, Akueni, how many twins she has borne and thrown away. Have you not heard the song they sing when a woman dies?

> For whom is it well, for whom is it well?
> There is no one for whom it is well.

"I have no more to say to you."

15

It was in the second year of Okonkwo's exile that his friend, Obierika, came to visit him. He brought with him two young men, each of them carrying a heavy bag on his head. Okonkwo helped them put down their loads. It was clear that the bags were full of cowries.

Okonkwo was very happy to receive his friend. His wives and children were very happy too, and so were his cousins and their wives when he sent for them and told them who his guest was.

"You must take him to salute our father," said one of the cousins.

"Yes," replied Okonkwo. "We are going directly." But before they went he whispered something to his first wife. She nodded, and soon the children were chasing one of their cocks.

Uchendu had been told by one of his grandchildren that three strangers had come to Okonkwo's house. He was therefore waiting to receive them. He held out his hands to them when they came into his *obi*, and after they had shaken hands he asked Okonkwo who they were.

"This is Obierika, my great friend. I have already spoken to you about him."

"Yes," said the old man, turning to Obierika. "My son has told me about you, and I am happy you have come to see us. I knew your father, Iweka. He was a great man. He had many friends here and came to see them quite often. Those were good days when a man had friends in distant clans. Your generation does not know that. You stay at home, afraid of your next-door neighbor. Even a man's motherland is strange to him nowadays." He looked at Okonkwo. "I am an old man and I like to talk. That is all I am good for now." He got up painfully, went into an inner room and came back with a kola nut.

"Who are the young men with you?" he asked as he sat down again on his goatskin. Okonkwo told him.

"Ah," he said. "Welcome, my sons." He presented the kola nut to them, and when they had seen it and thanked him, he broke it and they ate.

"Go into that room," he said to Okonkwo, pointing with his finger. "You will find a pot of wine there."

Okonkwo brought the wine and they began to drink. It was a day old, and very strong.

"Yes," said Uchendu after a long silence. "People traveled more in those days. There is not a single clan in these parts that I do not know very well. Aninta, Umuazu, Ikeocha, Elumelu, Abame—I know them all."

"Have you heard," asked Obierika, "that Abame is no more?"

"How is that?" asked Uchendu and Okonkwo together.

"Abame has been wiped out," said Obierika. "It is a strange and terrible story. If I had not seen the few survivors with my own eyes and heard their story with my own ears, I would not have believed. Was it not on an Eke day that they fled into Umuofia?" he asked his two companions, and they nodded their heads.

"Three moons ago," said Obierika, "on an Eke market day a little band of fugitives came into our town. Most of them were sons of our land whose mothers had been buried with us. But there were some too who came because they had friends in our town, and others who could think of nowhere else open to escape. And so they fled into Umuofia with a woeful story." He drank his palm-wine, and Okonkwo filled his horn again. He continued:

"During the last planting season a white man had appeared in their clan."

"An albino," suggested Okonkwo.

"He was not an albino. He was quite different." He sipped his wine. "And he was riding an iron horse.[4] The first people who saw him ran away, but he stood beckoning to them. In the end the fearless ones went near and even touched him. The elders consulted their Oracle and it told them that the strange man would break their clan and spread destruction among them." Obierika again drank a little of his wine. "And so they killed the white man and tied his iron horse to their sacred tree because it looked as if it would run away to call the man's friends. I forgot to tell you another thing which the Oracle said. It said that other white men were on their way. They were locusts, it said, and that first man was their harbinger sent to explore the terrain. And so they killed him."

"What did the white man say before they killed him?" asked Uchendu.

"He said nothing," answered one of Obierika's companions.

"He said something, only they did not understand him," said Obierika. "He seemed to speak through his nose."

"One of the men told me," said Obierika's other companion, "that he repeated over and over again a word that resembled Mbaino. Perhaps he had been going to Mbaino and had lost his way."

"Anyway," resumed Obierika, "they killed him and tied up his iron horse. This was before the planting season began. For a long time nothing happened. The rains had come and yams had been sown. The iron horse was still tied to the sacred silk-cotton tree. And then one morning three white

4. Bicycle.

men led by a band of ordinary men like us came to the clan. They saw the iron horse and went away again. Most of the men and women of Abame had gone to their farms. Only a few of them saw these white men and their followers. For many market weeks nothing else happened. They have a big market in Abame on every other Afo day and, as you know, the whole clan gathers there. That was the day it happened. The three white men and a very large number of other men surrounded the market. They must have used a powerful medicine to make themselves invisible until the market was full. And they began to shoot. Everybody was killed, except the old and the sick who were at home and a handful of men and women whose *chi* were wide awake and brought them out of that market."[5] He paused.

"Their clan is now completely empty. Even the sacred fish in their mysterious lake have fled and the lake has turned the color of blood. A great evil has come upon their land as the Oracle had warned."

There was a long silence. Uchendu ground his teeth together audibly. Then he burst out:

"Never kill a man who says nothing. Those men of Abame were fools. What did they know about the man?" He ground his teeth again and told a story to illustrate his point. "Mother Kite once sent her daughter to bring food. She went, and brought back a duckling. 'You have done very well,' said Mother Kite to her daughter, 'but tell me, what did the mother of this duckling say when you swooped and carried its child away?' 'It said nothing,' replied the young kite. It just walked away.' 'You must return the duckling,' said Mother Kite. 'There is something ominous behind the silence.' And so Daughter Kite returned the duckling and took a chick instead. 'What did the mother of this chick do?' asked the old kite. 'It cried and raved and cursed me,' said the young kite. 'Then we can eat the chick,' said her mother. 'There is nothing to fear from someone who shouts.' Those men of Abame were fools."

"They were fools," said Okonkwo after a pause. "They had been warned that danger was ahead. They should have armed themselves with their guns and their machetes even when they went to market."

"They have paid for their foolishness," said Obierika. "But I am greatly afraid. We have heard stories about white men who made the powerful guns and the strong drinks and took slaves away across the seas, but no one thought the stories were true."

"There is no story that is not true," said Uchendu. "The world has no end, and what is good among one people is an abomination with others. We have albinos among us. Do you not think that they came to our clan by mistake, that they have strayed from their way to a land where everybody is like them?"

Okonkwo's first wife soon finished her cooking and set before their guests a big meal of pounded yams and bitter-leaf soup. Okonkwo's son, Nwoye, brought in a pot of sweet wine tapped from the raffia palm.

"You are a big man now," Obierika said to Nwoye. "Your friend Anene asked me to greet you."

"Is he well?" asked Nwoye.

---

5. Achebe bases his account on a similar incident in 1905 when British troops massacred the town of Ahiara in reprisal for the death of a missionary.

"We are all well," said Obierika.

Ezinma brought them a bowl of water with which to wash their hands. After that they began to eat and to drink the wine.

"When did you set out from home?" asked Okonkwo.

"We had meant to set out from my house before cock-crow," said Obierika. "But Nweke did not appear until it was quite light. Never make an early morning appointment with a man who has just married a new wife." They all laughed.

"Has Nweke married a wife?" asked Okonkwo.

"He has married Okadigbo's second daughter," said Obierika.

"That is very good," said Okonkwo. "I do not blame you for not hearing the cock crow."

When they had eaten, Obierika pointed at the two heavy bags.

"That is the money from your yams," he said. "I sold the big ones as soon as you left. Later on I sold some of the seed-yams and gave out others to sharecroppers. I shall do that every year until you return. But I thought you would need the money now and so I brought it. Who knows what may happen tomorrow? Perhaps green men will come to our clan and shoot us."

"God will not permit it," said Okonkwo. "I do not know how to thank you."

"I can tell you," said Obierika. "Kill one of your sons for me."

"That will not be enough," said Okonkwo.

"Then kill yourself," said Obierika.

"Forgive me," said Okonkwo, smiling. "I shall not talk about thanking you any more."

16

When nearly two years later Obierika paid another visit to his friend in exile the circumstances were less happy. The missionaries had come to Umuofia. They had built their church there, won a handful of converts and were already sending evangelists to the surrounding towns and villages. That was a source of great sorrow to the leaders of the clan; but many of them believed that the strange faith and the white man's god would not last. None of his converts was a man whose word was heeded in the assembly of the people. None of them was a man of title. They were mostly the kind of people that were called *efulefu*, worthless, empty men. The imagery of an *efulefu* in the language of the clan was a man who sold his machete and wore the sheath to battle. Chielo, the priestess of Agbala, called the converts the excrement of the clan, and the new faith was a mad dog that had come to eat it up.

What moved Obierika to visit Okonkwo was the sudden appearance of the latter's son, Nwoye, among the missionaries in Umuofia.

"What are you doing here?" Obierika had asked when after many difficulties the missionaries had allowed him to speak to the boy.

"I am one of them," replied Nwoye.

"How is your father?" Obierika asked, not knowing what else to say.

"I don't know. He is not my father," said Nwoye, unhappily.

And so Obierika went to Mbanta to see his friend. And he found that Okonkwo did not wish to speak about Nwoye. It was only from Nwoye's mother that he heard scraps of the story.

The arrival of the missionaries had caused a considerable stir in the village of Mbanta. There were six of them and one was a white man. Every man and woman came out to see the white man. Stories about these strange men had grown since one of them had been killed in Abame and his iron horse tied to the sacred silk-cotton tree. And so everybody came to see the white man. It was the time of the year when everybody was at home. The harvest was over.

When they had all gathered, the white man began to speak to them. He spoke through an interpreter who was an Ibo man, though his dialect was different and harsh to the ears of Mbanta. Many people laughed at his dialect and the way he used words strangely. Instead of saying "myself" he always said "my buttocks."[6] But he was a man of commanding presence and the clansmen listened to him. He said he was one of them, as they could see from his color and his language. The other four black men were also their brothers, although one of them did not speak Ibo. The white man was also their brother because they were all sons of God. And he told them about this new God, the Creator of all the world and all the men and women. He told them that they worshipped false gods, gods of wood and stone. A deep murmur went through the crowd when he said this. He told them that the true God lived on high and that all men when they died went before Him for judgment. Evil men and all the heathen who in their blindness bowed to wood and stone were thrown into a fire that burned like palm-oil. But good men who worshipped the true God lived forever in His happy kingdom. "We have been sent by this great God to ask you to leave your wicked ways and false gods and turn to Him so that you may be saved when you die," he said.

"Your buttocks understand our language," said someone light-heartedly and the crowd laughed.

"What did he say?" the white man asked his interpreter. But before he could answer, another man asked a question: "Where is the white man's horse?" he asked. The Ibo evangelists consulted among themselves and decided that the man probably meant bicycle. They told the white man and he smiled benevolently.

"Tell them," he said, "that I shall bring many iron horses when we have settled down among them. Some of them will even ride the iron horse themselves." This was interpreted to them but very few of them heard. They were talking excitedly among themselves because the white man had said he was going to live among them. They had not thought about that.

At this point an old man said he had a question. "Which is this god of yours," he asked, "the goddess of the earth, the god of the sky, Amadiora of the thunderbolt, or what?"

The interpreter spoke to the white man and he immediately gave his answer. "All the gods you have named are not gods at all. They are gods of deceit who tell you to kill your fellows and destroy innocent children. There is only one true God and He has the earth, the sky, you and me and all of us."

"If we leave our gods and follow your god," asked another man, "who will protect us from the anger of our neglected gods and ancestors?"

"Your gods are not alive and cannot do you any harm," replied the white man. "They are pieces of wood and stone."

When this was interpreted to the men of Mbanta they broke into derisive

6. The Igbo language has high and low tones so that the same word may have different meanings according to its pronunciation. Here, Achebe is probably referring to a famous pair of near-homonyms: *íké* ("strength") and *íkè* ("buttocks").

laughter. These men must be mad, they said to themselves. How else could they say that Ani and Amadiora were harmless? And Idemili and Ogwugwu too? And some of them began to go away.

Then the missionaries burst into song. It was one of those gay and rollicking tunes of evangelism which had the power of plucking at silent and dusty chords in the heart of an Ibo man. The interpreter explained each verse to the audience, some of whom now stood enthralled. It was a story of brothers who lived in darkness and in fear, ignorant of the love of God. It told of one sheep out on the hills, away from the gates of God and from the tender shepherd's care.

After the singing the interpreter spoke about the Son of God whose name was Jesu Kristi. Okonkwo, who only stayed in the hope that it might come to chasing the men out of the village or whipping them, now said:

"You told us with your own mouth that there was only one god. Now you talk about his son. He must have a wife, then." The crowd agreed.

"I did not say He had a wife," said the interpreter, somewhat lamely.

"Your buttocks said he had a son," said the joker. "So he must have a wife and all of them must have buttocks."

The missionary ignored him and went on to talk about the Holy Trinity. At the end of it Okonkwo was fully convinced that the man was mad. He shrugged his shoulders and went away to tap his afternoon palm-wine.

But there was a young lad who had been captivated. His name was Nwoye, Okonkwo's first son. It was not the mad logic of the Trinity that captivated him. He did not understand it. It was the poetry of the new religion, something felt in the marrow. The hymn about brothers who sat in darkness and in fear seemed to answer a vague and persistent question that haunted his young soul—the question of the twins crying in the bush and the question of Ikemefuna who was killed. He felt a relief within as the hymn poured into his parched soul. The words of the hymn were like the drops of frozen rain melting on the dry palate of the panting earth. Nwoye's callow mind was greatly puzzled.

17

The missionaries spent their first four or five nights in the marketplace, and went into the village in the morning to preach the gospel. They asked who the king of the village was, but the villagers told them that there was no king. "We have men of high title and the chief priests and the elders," they said.

It was not very easy getting the men of high title and the elders together after the excitement of the first day. But the missionaries persevered, and in the end they were received by the rulers of Mbanta. They asked for a plot of land to build their church.

Every clan and village had its "evil forest." In it were buried all those who died of the really evil diseases, like leprosy and smallpox. It was also the dumping ground for the potent fetishes of great medicine men when they died. An "evil forest" was, therefore, alive with sinister forces and powers of darkness. It was such a forest that the rulers of Mbanta gave to the missionaries. They did not really want them in their clan, and so they made them that offer which nobody in his right senses would accept.

"They want a piece of land to build their shrine," said Uchendu to his peers when they consulted among themselves. "We shall give them a piece of land." He paused, and there was a murmur of surprise and disagreement. "Let us give them a portion of the Evil Forest. They boast about victory over death. Let us give them a real battlefield in which to show their victory." They laughed and agreed, and sent for the missionaries, whom they had asked to leave them for a while so that they might "whisper together." They offered them as much of the Evil Forest as they cared to take. And to their greatest amazement the missionaries thanked them and burst into song.

"They do not understand," said some of the elders. "But they will understand when they go to their plot of land tomorrow morning." And they dispersed.

The next morning the crazy men actually began to clear a part of the forest and to build their house. The inhabitants of Mbanta expected them all to be dead within four days. The first day passed and the second and third and fourth, and none of them died. Everyone was puzzled. And then it became known that the white man's fetish had unbelievable power. It was said that he wore glasses on his eyes so that he could see and talk to evil spirits. Not long after, he won his first three converts.

Although Nwoye had been attracted to the new faith from the very first day, he kept it secret. He dared not go too near the missionaries for fear of his father. But whenever they came to preach in the open marketplace or the village playground, Nwoye was there. And he was already beginning to know some of the simple stories they told.

"We have now built a church," said Mr. Kiaga, the interpreter, who was now in charge of the infant congregation. The white man had gone back to Umuofia, where he built his headquarters and from where he paid regular visits to Mr. Kiaga's congregation at Mbanta.

"We have now built a church," said Mr. Kiaga, "and we want you all to come in every seventh day to worship the true God."

On the following Sunday, Nwoye passed and repassed the little red-earth and thatch building without summoning enough courage to enter. He heard the voice of singing and although it came from a handful of men it was loud and confident. Their church stood on a circular clearing that looked like the open mouth of the Evil Forest. Was it waiting to snap its teeth together? After passing and repassing by the church, Nwoye returned home.

It was well known among the people of Mbanta that their gods and ancestors were sometimes long-suffering and would deliberately allow a man to go on defying them. But even in such cases they set their limit at seven market weeks or twenty-eight days. Beyond that limit no man was suffered to go. And so excitement mounted in the village as the seventh week approached since the impudent missionaries built their church in the Evil Forest. The villagers were so certain about the doom that awaited these men that one or two converts thought it wise to suspend their allegiance to the new faith.

At last the day came by which all the missionaries should have died. But they were still alive, building a new red-earth and thatch house for their teacher, Mr. Kiaga. That week they won a handful more converts. And for the first time they had a woman. Her name was Nneka, the wife of Amadi, who was a prosperous farmer. She was very heavy with child.

Nneka had had four previous pregnancies and childbirths. But each time she had borne twins, and they had been immediately thrown away. Her husband and his family were already becoming highly critical of such a woman and were not unduly perturbed when they found she had fled to join the Christians. It was a good riddance.

One morning Okonkwo's cousin, Amikwu, was passing by the church on his way from the neighboring village, when he saw Nwoye among the Christians. He was greatly surprised, and when he got home he went straight to Okonkwo's hut and told him what he had seen. The women began to talk excitedly, but Okonkwo sat unmoved.

It was late afternoon before Nwoye returned. He went into the *obi* and saluted his father, but he did not answer. Nwoye turned round to walk into the inner compound when his father, suddenly overcome with fury, sprang to his feet and gripped him by the neck.

"Where have you been?" he stammered.

Nwoye struggled to free himself from the choking grip.

"Answer me," roared Okonkwo, "before I kill you!" He seized a heavy stick that lay on the dwarf wall and hit him two or three savage blows.

"Answer me!" he roared again. Nwoye stood looking at him and did not say a word. The women were screaming outside, afraid to go in.

"Leave that boy at once!" said a voice in the outer compound. It was Okonkwo's uncle, Uchendu. "Are you mad?"

Okonkwo did not answer. But he left hold of Nwoye, who walked away and never returned.

He went back to the church and told Mr. Kiaga that he had decided to go to Umuofia where the white missionary had set up a school to teach young Christians to read and write.

Mr. Kiaga's joy was very great. "Blessed is he who forsakes his father and his mother for my sake," he intoned. "Those that hear my words are my father and my mother."

Nwoye did not fully understand. But he was happy to leave his father. He would return later to his mother and his brothers and sisters and convert them to the new faith.

As Okonkwo sat in his hut that night, gazing into a log fire, he thought over the matter. A sudden fury rose within him and he felt a strong desire to take up his machete, go to the church and wipe out the entire vile and miscreant gang. But on further thought he told himself that Nwoye was not worth fighting for. Why, he cried in his heart, should he, Okonkwo, of all people, be cursed with such a son? He saw clearly in it the finger of his personal god or *chi*. For how else could he explain his great misfortune and exile and now his despicable son's behavior? Now that he had time to think of it, his son's crime stood out in its stark enormity. To abandon the gods of one's father and go about with a lot of effeminate men clucking like old hens was the very depth of abomination. Suppose when he died all his male children decided to follow Nwoye's steps and abandon their ancestors? Okonkwo felt a cold shudder run through him at the terrible prospects, like the prospect of annihilation. He saw himself and his fathers crowding round their ancestral shrine waiting in vain for worship and sacrifice and finding nothing but ashes of bygone days, and his children the while praying to the white man's god. If such a thing were ever to happen, he, Okonkwo, would wipe them off the face of the earth.

Okonkwo was popularly called the "Roaring Flame." As he looked into the log fire he recalled the name. He was a flaming fire. How then could he have begotten a son like Nwoye, degenerate and effeminate? Perhaps he was not his son. No! he could not be. His wife had played him false. He would teach her! But Nwoye resembled his grandfather, Unoka, who was Okonkwo's father. He pushed the thought out of his mind. He, Okonkwo, was called a flaming fire. How could he have begotten a woman for a son? At Nwoye's age Okonkwo had already become famous throughout Umuofia for his wrestling and his fearlessness.

He sighed heavily, and as if in sympathy the smoldering log also sighed. And immediately Okonkwo's eyes were opened and he saw the whole matter clearly. Living fire begets cold, impotent ash. He sighed again, deeply.

18

The young church in Mbanta had a few crises early in its life. At first the clan had assumed that it would not survive. But it had gone on living and gradually becoming stronger. The clan was worried, but not overmuch. If a gang of *efulefu* decided to live in the Evil Forest it was their own affair. When one came to think of it, the Evil Forest was a fit home for such undesirable people. It was true they were rescuing twins from the bush, but they never brought them into the village. As far as the villagers were concerned, the twins still remained where they had been thrown away. Surely the earth goddess would not visit the sins of the missionaries on the innocent villagers?

But on one occasion the missionaries had tried to overstep the bounds. Three converts had gone into the village and boasted openly that all the gods were dead and impotent and that they were prepared to defy them by burning all their shrines.

"Go and burn your mothers' genitals," said one of the priests. The men were seized and beaten until they streamed with blood. After that nothing happened for a long time between the church and the clan.

But stories were already gaining ground that the white man had not only brought a religion but also a government. It was said that they had built a place of judgment in Umuofia to protect the followers of their religion. It was even said that they had hanged one man who killed a missionary.

Although such stories were now often told they looked like fairy-tales in Mbanta and did not as yet affect the relationship between the new church and the clan. There was no question of killing a missionary here, for Mr. Kiaga, despite his madness, was quite harmless. As for his converts, no one could kill them without having to flee from the clan, for in spite of their worthlessness they still belonged to the clan. And so nobody gave serious thought to the stories about the white man's government or the consequences of killing the Christians. If they became more troublesome than they already were they would simply be driven out of the clan.

And the little church was at that moment too deeply absorbed in its own troubles to annoy the clan. It all began over the question of admitting outcasts.

These outcasts, or *osu*, seeing that the new religion welcomed twins and such abominations, thought that it was possible that they would also be received. And so one Sunday two of them went into the church. There was an immediate stir; but so great was the work the new religion had done among the converts that they did not immediately leave the church when the outcasts came in. Those who found themselves nearest to them merely moved to another seat. It was a miracle. But it only lasted till the end of the service. The whole church raised a protest and was about to drive these people out, when Mr. Kiaga stopped them and began to explain.

"Before God," he said, "there is no slave or free. We are all children of God and we must receive these our brothers."

"You do not understand," said one of the converts. "What will the heathen say of us when they hear that we receive *osu* into our midst? They will laugh."

"Let them laugh," said Mr. Kiaga. "God will laugh at them on the judgment day. Why do the nations rage and the peoples imagine a vain thing? He that sitteth in the heavens shall laugh. The Lord shall have them in derision."

"You do not understand," the convert maintained. "You are our teacher, and you can teach us the things of the new faith. But this is a matter which we know." And he told him what an *osu* was.

He was a person dedicated to a god, a thing set apart—a taboo for ever, and his children after him. He could neither marry nor be married by the free-born. He was in fact an outcast, living in a special area of the village, close to the Great Shrine. Wherever he went he carried with him the mark of his forbidden caste—long, tangled and dirty hair. A razor was taboo to him. An *osu* could not attend an assembly of the free-born, and they, in turn, could not shelter under his roof. He could not take any of the four titles of the clan, and when he died he was buried by his kind in the Evil Forest. How could such a man be a follower of Christ?

"He needs Christ more than you and I," said Mr. Kiaga.

"Then I shall go back to the clan," said the convert. And he went. Mr. Kiaga stood firm, and it was his firmness that saved the young church. The wavering converts drew inspiration and confidence from his unshakable faith. He ordered the outcasts to shave off their long, tangled hair. At first they were afraid they might die.

"Unless you shave off the mark of your heathen belief I will not admit you into the church," said Mr. Kiaga. "You fear that you will die. Why should that be? How are you different from other men who shave their hair? The same God created you and them. But they have cast you out like lepers. It is against the will of God, who has promised everlasting life to all who believe in His holy name. The heathen say you will die if you do this or that, and you are afraid. They also said I would die if I built my church on this ground. Am I dead? They said I would die if I took care of twins. I am still alive. The heathen speak nothing but falsehood. Only the word of our God is true."

The two outcasts shaved off their hair, and soon they were the strongest adherents of the new faith. And what was more, nearly all the *osu* in Mbanta followed their example. It was in fact one of them who in his zeal brought the church into serious conflict with the clan a year later by killing the sacred python, the emanation of the god of water.

The royal python was the most revered animal in Mbanta and all the surrounding clans. It was addressed as "Our Father," and was allowed to go wherever it chose, even into people's beds. It ate rats in the house and sometimes swallowed hens' eggs. If a clansman killed a royal python accidentally, he made sacrifices of atonement and performed an expensive burial ceremony such as was done for a great man. No punishment was prescribed for a man who killed the python knowingly. Nobody thought that such a thing could ever happen.

Perhaps it never did happen. That was the way the clan at first looked at it. No one had actually seen the man do it. The story had arisen among the Christians themselves.

But, all the same, the rulers and elders of Mbanta assembled to decide on their action. Many of them spoke at great length and in fury. The spirit of wars was upon them. Okonkwo, who had begun to play a part in the affairs of his motherland, said that until the abominable gang was chased out of the village with whips there would be no peace.

But there were many others who saw the situation differently, and it was their counsel that prevailed in the end.

"It is not our custom to fight for our gods," said one of them. "Let us not presume to do so now. If a man kills the sacred python in the secrecy of his hut, the matter lies between him and the god. We did not see it. If we put ourselves between the god and his victim we may receive blows intended for the offender. When a man blasphemes, what do we do? Do we go and stop his mouth? No. We put our fingers into our ears to stop us hearing. That is a wise action."

"Let us not reason like cowards," said Okonkwo. "If a man comes into my hut and defecates on the floor, what do I do? Do I shut my eyes? No! I take a stick and break his head. That is what a man does. These people are daily pouring filth over us, and Okeke says we should pretend not to see." Okonkwo made a sound full of disgust. This was a womanly clan, he thought. Such a thing could never happen in his fatherland, Umuofia.

"Okonkwo has spoken the truth," said another man. "We should do something. But let us ostracize these men. We would then not be held accountable for their abominations."

Everybody in the assembly spoke, and in the end it was decided to ostracize the Christians. Okonkwo ground his teeth in disgust.

That night a bell-man went through the length and breadth of Mbanta proclaiming that the adherents of the new faith were thenceforth excluded from the life and privileges of the clan.

The Christians had grown in number and were now a small community of men, women and children, self-assured and confident. Mr. Brown, the white missionary, paid regular visits to them. "When I think that it is only eighteen months since the Seed was first sown among you," he said, "I marvel at what the Lord hath wrought."

It was Wednesday in Holy Week and Mr. Kiaga had asked the women to bring red earth and white chalk and water to scrub the church for Easter; and the women had formed themselves into three groups for this purpose. They set out early that morning, some of them with their water-pots to the stream, another group with hoes and baskets to the village red-earth pit, and the others to the chalk quarry.

Mr. Kiaga was praying in the church when he heard the women talking excitedly. He rounded off his prayer and went to see what it was all about. The women had come to the church with empty water-pots. They said that some young men had chased them away from the stream with whips. Soon after, the women who had gone for red earth returned with empty baskets.

Some of them had been heavily whipped. The chalk women also returned to tell a similar story.

"What does it all mean?" asked Mr. Kiaga, who was greatly perplexed.

"The village has outlawed us," said one of the women. "The bell-man announced it last night. But it is not our custom to debar anyone from the stream or the quarry."

Another woman said, "They want to ruin us. They will not allow us into the markets. They have said so."

Mr. Kiaga was going to send into the village for his men-converts when he saw them coming on their own. Of course they had all heard the bellman, but they had never in all their lives heard of women being debarred from the stream.

"Come along," they said to the women. "We will go with you to meet those cowards." Some of them had big sticks and some even machetes.

But Mr. Kiaga restrained them. He wanted first to know why they had been outlawed.

"They say that Okoli killed the sacred python," said one man.

"It is false," said another. "Okoli told me himself that it was false."

Okoli was not there to answer. He had fallen ill on the previous night. Before the day was over he was dead. His death showed that the gods were still able to fight their own battles. The clan saw no reason then for molesting the Christians.

19

The last big rains of the year were falling. It was the time for treading red earth with which to build walls. It was not done earlier because the rains were too heavy and would have washed away the heap of trodden earth; and it could not be done later because harvesting would soon set in, and after that the dry season.

It was going to be Okonkwo's last harvest in Mbanta. The seven wasted and weary years were at last dragging to a close. Although he had prospered in his motherland Okonkwo knew that he would have prospered even more in Umuofia, in the land of his fathers where men were bold and warlike. In these seven years he would have climbed to the utmost heights. And so he regretted every day of his exile. His mother's kinsmen had been very kind to him, and he was grateful. But that did not alter the facts. He had called the first child born to him in exile Nneka—"Mother is Supreme"—out of politeness to his mother's kinsmen. But two years later when a son was born he called him Nwofia—"Begotten in the Wilderness."

As soon as he entered his last year in exile Okonkwo sent money to Obierika to build him two huts in his old compound where he and his family would live until he built more huts and the outside wall of his compound. He could not ask another man to build his own *obi* for him, nor the walls of his compound. Those things a man built for himself or inherited from his father.

As the last heavy rains of the year began to fall, Obierika sent word that the two huts had been built and Okonkwo began to prepare for his return, after the rains. He would have liked to return earlier and build his compound that year before the rains stopped, but in doing so he would have taken something from the full penalty of seven years. And that could not be. So he waited impatiently for the dry season to come.

It came slowly. The rain became lighter and lighter until it fell in slanting showers. Sometimes the sun shone through the rain and a light breeze blew. It was a gay and airy kind of rain. The rainbow began to appear, and sometimes two rainbows, like a mother and her daughter, the one young and beautiful, and the other an old and faint shadow. The rainbow was called the python of the sky.

Okonkwo called his three wives and told them to get things together for a great feast. "I must thank my mother's kinsmen before I go," he said.

Ekwefi still had some cassava left on her farm from the previous year. Neither of the other wives had. It was not that they had been lazy, but that they had many children to feed. It was therefore understood that Ekwefi would provide cassava for the feast. Nwoye's mother and Ojiugo would provide the other things like smoked fish, palm-oil and pepper for the soup. Okonkwo would take care of meat and yams.

Ekwefi rose early on the following morning and went to her farm with her daughter, Ezinma, and Ojiugo's daughter, Obiageli, to harvest cassava tubers. Each of them carried a long cane basket, a machete for cutting down the soft cassava stem, and a little hoe for digging out the tuber. Fortunately, a light rain had fallen during the night and the soil would not be very hard.

"It will not take us long to harvest as much as we like," said Ekwefi.

"But the leaves will be wet," said Ezinma. Her basket was balanced on her head, and her arms folded across her breasts. She felt cold. "I dislike cold water dropping on my back. We should have waited for the sun to rise and dry the leaves."

Obiageli called her "Salt" because she said that she disliked water. "Are you afraid you may dissolve?"

The harvesting was easy, as Ekwefi had said. Ezinma shook every tree violently with a long stick before she bent down to cut the stem and dig out the tuber. Sometimes it was not necessary to dig. They just pulled the stump, and earth rose, roots snapped below, and the tuber was pulled out.

When they had harvested a sizable heap they carried it down in two trips to the stream, where every woman had a shallow well for fermenting her cassava.

"It should be ready in four days or even three," said Obiageli. "They are young tubers."

"They are not all that young," said Ekwefi. "I planted the farm nearly two years ago. It is a poor soil and that is why the tubers are so small."

Okonkwo never did things by halves. When his wife Ekwefi protested that two goats were sufficient for the feast he told her that it was not her affair.

"I am calling a feast because I have the wherewithal. I cannot live on the bank of a river and wash my hands with spittle. My mother's people have been good to me and I must show my gratitude."

And so three goats were slaughtered and a number of fowls. It was like a wedding feast. There was foo-foo and yam pottage, egusi[7] soup and bitter-leaf soup and pots and pots of palm-wine.

7. Melon seed, which is roasted, ground, and cooked in soup.

All the *umunna*[8] were invited to the feast, all the descendants of Okolo, who had lived about two hundred years before. The oldest member of this extensive family was Okonkwo's uncle, Uchendu. The kola nut was given him to break, and he prayed to the ancestors. He asked them for health and children. "We do not ask for wealth because he that has health and children will also have wealth. We do not pray to have more money but to have more kinsmen. We are better than animals because we have kinsmen. An animal rubs its itching flank against a tree, a man asks his kinsman to scratch him." He prayed especially for Okonkwo and his family. He then broke the kola nut and threw one of the lobes on the ground for the ancestors.

As the broken kola nuts were passed round, Okonkwo's wives and children and those who came to help them with the cooking began to bring out the food. His sons brought out the pots of palm-wine. There was so much food and drink that many kinsmen whistled in surprise. When all was laid out, Okonkwo rose to speak.

"I beg you to accept this little kola," he said. "It is not to pay you back for all you did for me in these seven years. A child cannot pay for its mother's milk. I have only called you together because it is good for kinsmen to meet."

Yam pottage was served first because it was lighter than foo-foo and because yam always came first. Then the foo-foo was served. Some kinsmen ate it with egusi soup and others with bitter-leaf soup. The meat was then shared so that every member of the *umunna* had a portion. Every man rose in order of years and took a share. Even the few kinsmen who had not been able to come had their shares taken out for them in due term.

As the palm-wine was drunk one of the oldest members of the *umunna* rose to thank Okonkwo:

"If I say that we did not expect such a big feast I will be suggesting that we did not know how open-handed our son, Okonkwo, is. We all know him, and we expected a big feast. But it turned out to be even bigger than we expected. Thank you. May all you took out return again tenfold. It is good in these days when the younger generation consider themselves wiser than their sires to see a man doing things in the grand, old way. A man who calls his kinsmen to a feast does not do so to save them from starving. They all have food in their own homes. When we gather together in the moonlit village ground it is not because of the moon. Every man can see it in his own compound. We come together because it is good for kinsmen to do so. You may ask why I am saying all this. I say it because I fear for the younger generation, for you people." He waved his arm where most of the young men sat. "As for me, I have only a short while to live, and so have Uchendu and Unachukwu and Emefo. But I fear for you young people because you do not understand how strong is the bond of kinship. You do not know what it is to speak with one voice. And what is the result? An abominable religion has settled among you. A man can now leave his father and his brothers. He can curse the gods of his fathers and his ancestors, like a hunter's dog that suddenly goes mad and turns on his master. I fear for you; I fear for the clan." He turned again to Okonkwo and said, "Thank you for calling us together."

8. Children of the father (literal trans.); the clan (male).

Part Three

20

Seven years was a long time to be away from one's clan. A man's place was not always there, waiting for him. As soon as he left, someone else rose and filled it. The clan was like a lizard; if it lost its tail it soon grew another.

Okonkwo knew these things. He knew that he had lost his place among the nine masked spirits who administered justice in the clan. He had lost the chance to lead his warlike clan against the new religion, which, he was told, had gained ground. He had lost the years in which he might have taken the highest titles in the clan. But some of these losses were not irreparable. He was determined that his return should be marked by his people. He would return with a flourish, and regain the seven wasted years.

Even in his first year in exile he had begun to plan for his return. The first thing he would do would be to rebuild his compound on a more magnificent scale. He would build a bigger barn than he had had before and he would build huts for two new wives. Then he would show his wealth by initiating his sons into the *ozo* society. Only the really great men in the clan were able to do this. Okonkwo saw clearly the high esteem in which he would be held, and he saw himself taking the highest title in the land.

As the years of exile passed one by one it seemed to him that his *chi* might now be making amends for the past disaster. His yams grew abundantly, not only in his motherland but also in Umuofia, where his friend gave them out year by year to sharecroppers.

Then the tragedy of his first son had occurred. At first it appeared as if it might prove too great for his spirit. But it was a resilient spirit, and in the end Okonkwo overcame his sorrow. He had five other sons and he would bring them up in the way of the clan.

He sent for the five sons and they came and sat in his *obi*. The youngest of them was four years old.

"You have all seen the great abomination of your brother. Now he is no longer my son or your brother. I will only have a son who is a man, who will hold his head up among my people. If any one of you prefers to be a woman, let him follow Nwoye now while I am alive so that I can curse him. If you turn against me when I am dead I will visit you and break your neck."

Okonkwo was very lucky in his daughters. He never stopped regretting that Ezinma was a girl. Of all his children she alone understood his every mood. A bond of sympathy had grown between them as the years had passed.

Ezinma grew up in her father's exile and became one of the most beautiful girls in Mbanta. She was called Crystal of Beauty, as her mother had been called in her youth. The young ailing girl who had caused her mother so much heartache had been transformed, almost overnight, into a healthy, buoyant maiden. She had, it was true, her moments of depression when she would snap at everybody like an angry dog. These moods descended on her suddenly and for no apparent reason. But they were very rare and short-lived. As long as they lasted, she could bear no other person but her father.

Many young men and prosperous middle-aged men of Mbanta came to marry her. But she refused them all, because her father had called her one evening and said to her: "There are many good and prosperous people here, but I shall be happy if you marry in Umuofia when we return home."

That was all he had said. But Ezinma had seen clearly all the thought and hidden meaning behind the few words. And she had agreed.

"Your half-sister, Obiageli, will not understand me," Okonkwo said. "But you can explain to her."

Although they were almost the same age, Ezinma wielded a strong influence over her half-sister. She explained to her why they should not marry yet, and she agreed also. And so the two of them refused every offer of marriage in Mbanta.

"I wish she were a boy," Okonkwo thought within himself. She understood things so perfectly. Who else among his children could have read his thoughts so well? With two beautiful grown-up daughters his return to Umuofia would attract considerable attention. His future sons-in-law would be men of authority in the clan. The poor and unknown would not dare to come forth.

Umuofia had indeed changed during the seven years Okonkwo had been in exile. The church had come and led many astray. Not only the low-born and the outcast but sometimes a worthy man had joined it. Such a man was Ogbuefi Ugonna,[9] who had taken two titles, and who like a madman had cut the anklet of his titles and cast it away to join the Christians. The white missionary was very proud of him and he was one of the first men in Umuofia to receive the sacrament of Holy Communion, or Holy Feast as it was called in Ibo. Ogbuefi Ugonna had thought of the Feast in terms of eating and drinking, only more holy than the village variety. He had therefore put his drinking-horn into his goatskin bag for the occasion.

But apart from the church, the white men had also brought a government. They had built a court where the District Commissioner judged cases in ignorance. He had court messengers who brought men to him for trial. Many of these messengers came from Umuru on the bank of the Great River, where the white men first came many years before and where they had built the center of their religion and trade and government. These court messengers were greatly hated in Umuofia because they were foreigners and also arrogant and high-handed. They were called kotma,[1] and because of their ash-colored shorts they earned the additional name of Ashy-Buttocks. They guarded the prison, which was full of men who had offended against the white man's law. Some of these prisoners had thrown away their twins and some had molested the Christians. They were beaten in the prison by the kotma and made to work every morning clearing the government compound and fetching wood for the white Commissioner and the court messengers. Some of these prisoners were men of title who should be above such mean occupation. They were grieved by the indignity and mourned for their neglected farms. As they cut grass in the morning the younger men sang in time with the strokes of their machetes:

9. Father's honor (with the eagle feather).   1. Court messenger (pidgin English).

Kotma of the ash buttocks,
He is fit to be a slave.
The white man has no sense,
He is fit to be a slave.

The court messengers did not like to be called Ashy-Buttocks, and they beat the men. But the song spread in Umuofia.

Okonkwo's head was bowed in sadness as Obierika told him these things.

"Perhaps I have been away too long," Okonkwo said, almost to himself. "But I cannot understand these things you tell me. What is it that has happened to our people? Why have they lost the power to fight?"

"Have you not heard how the white man wiped out Abame?" asked Obierika.

"I have heard," said Okonkwo. "But I have also heard that Abame people were weak and foolish. Why did they not fight back? Had they no guns and machetes? We would be cowards to compare ourselves with the men of Abame. Their fathers had never dared to stand before our ancestors. We must fight these men and drive them from the land."

"It is already too late," said Obierika sadly. "Our own men and our sons have joined the ranks of the stranger. They have joined his religion and they help to uphold his government. If we should try to drive out the white men in Umuofia we should find it easy. There are only two of them. But what of our own people who are following their way and have been given power? They would go to Umuru and bring the soldiers, and we would be like Abame." He paused for a long time and then said: "I told you on my last visit to Mbanta how they hanged Aneto."

"What has happened to that piece of land in dispute?" asked Okonkwo.

"The white man's court has decided that it should belong to Nnama's family, who had given much money to the white man's messengers and interpreter."

"Does the white man understand our custom about land?"

"How can he when he does not even speak our tongue? But he says that our customs are bad; and our own brothers who have taken up his religion also say that our customs are bad. How do you think we can fight when our own brothers have turned against us? The white man is very clever. He came quietly and peaceably with his religion. We were amused at his foolishness and allowed him to stay. Now he has won our brothers, and our clan can no longer act like one. He has put a knife on the things that held us together and we have fallen apart."

"How did they get hold of Aneto to hang him?" asked Okonkwo.

"When he killed Oduche in the fight over the land, he fled to Aninta to escape the wrath of the earth. This was about eight days after the fight, because Oduche had not died immediately from his wounds. It was on the seventh day that he died. But everybody knew that he was going to die and Aneto got his belongings together in readiness to flee. But the Christians had told the white man about the accident, and he sent his *kotma* to catch Aneto. He was imprisoned with all the leaders of his family. In the end Oduche died and Aneto was taken to Umuru and hanged. The other people were released, but even now they have not found the mouth with which to tell of their suffering."

The two men sat in silence for a long while afterwards.

21

There were many men and women in Umuofia who did not feel as strongly as Okonkwo about the new dispensation. The white man had indeed brought a lunatic religion, but he had also built a trading store and for the first time palm-oil and kernel[2] became things of great price, and much money flowed into Umuofia.

And even in the matter of religion there was a growing feeling that there might be something in it after all, something vaguely akin to method in the overwhelming madness.

This growing feeling was due to Mr. Brown, the white missionary, who was very firm in restraining his flock from provoking the wrath of the clan. One member in particular was very difficult to restrain. His name was Enoch and his father was the priest of the snake cult. The story went around that Enoch had killed and eaten the sacred python, and that his father had cursed him.

Mr. Brown preached against such excess of zeal. Everything was possible, he told his energetic flock, but everything was not expedient. And so Mr. Brown came to be respected even by the clan, because he trod softly on its faith. He made friends with some of the great men of the clan and on one of his frequent visits to the neighboring villages he had been presented with a carved elephant tusk, which was a sign of dignity and rank. One of the great men in that village was called Akunna[3] and he had given one of his sons to be taught the white man's knowledge in Mr. Brown's school.

Whenever Mr. Brown went to that village he spent long hours with Akunna in his *obi* talking through an interpreter about religion. Neither of them succeeded in converting the other but they learned more about their different beliefs.

"You say that there is one supreme God who made heaven and earth," said Akunna on one of Mr. Brown's visits. "We also believe in Him and call Him Chukwu. He made all the world and the other gods."

"There are no other gods," said Mr. Brown. "Chukwu is the only God and all others are false. You carve a piece of wood—like that one" (he pointed at the rafters from which Akunna's carved *Ikenga*[4] hung), "and you call it a god. But it is still a piece of wood."

"Yes," said Akunna. "It is indeed a piece of wood. The tree from which it came was made by Chukwu, as indeed all minor gods were. But He made them for His messengers so that we could approach Him through them. It is like yourself. You are the head of your church."

"No," protested Mr. Brown. "The head of my church is God Himself."

"I know," said Akunna, "but there must be a head in this world among men. Somebody like yourself must be the head here."

"The head of my church in that sense is in England."

"That is exactly what I am saying. The head of your church is in your country. He has sent you here as his messenger. And you have also appointed

---

2. The red fleshy husk of the palm nut is crushed manually to produce cooking oil, leaving a fibrous residue along with hard kernels. The Europeans bought both the red oil and the kernels, from which they could extract a very fine oil by using machines.   3. Father's wealth.   4. A carved wooden figure with the horns of a ram that symbolized the strength of a man's right hand. Every adult male kept an *Ikenga* in his personal shrine.

your own messengers and servants. Or let me take another example, the District Commissioner. He is sent by your king."

"They have a queen," said the interpreter on his own account.

"Your queen sends her messenger, the District Commissioner. He finds that he cannot do the work alone and so he appoints *kotma* to help him. It is the same with God, or Chukwu. He appoints the smaller gods to help Him because His work is too great for one person."

"You should not think of Him as a person," said Mr. Brown. "It is because you do so that you imagine He must need helpers. And the worst thing about it is that you give all the worship to the false gods you have created."

"That is not so. We make sacrifices to the little gods, but when they fail and there is no one else to turn to we go to Chukwu. It is right to do so. We approach a great man through his servants. But when his servants fail to help us, then we go to the last source of hope. We appear to pay greater attention to the little gods but that is not so. We worry them more because we are afraid to worry their Master. Our fathers knew that Chukwu was the Overlord and that is why many of them gave their children the name Chuk-wuka—"Chukwu is Supreme.""

"You said one interesting thing," said Mr. Brown. "You are afraid of Chukwu. In my religion Chukwu is a loving Father and need not be feared by those who do His will."

"But we must fear Him when we are not doing His will," said Akunna. "And who is to tell His will? It is too great to be known."

In this way Mr. Brown learned a good deal about the religion of the clan and he came to the conclusion that a frontal attack on it would not succeed. And so he built a school and a little hospital in Umuofia. He went from family to family begging people to send their children to his school. But at first they only sent their slaves or sometimes their lazy children. Mr. Brown begged and argued and prophesied. He said that the leaders of the land in the future would be men and women who had learned to read and write. If Umuofia failed to send her children to the school, strangers would come from other places to rule them. They could already see that happening in the Native Court, where the D.C. was surrounded by strangers who spoke his tongue. Most of these strangers came from the distant town of Umuru on the bank of the Great River where the white man first went.

In the end Mr. Brown's arguments began to have an effect. More people came to learn in his school, and he encouraged them with gifts of singlets[5] and towels. They were not all young, these people who came to learn. Some of them were thirty years old or more. They worked on their farms in the morning and went to school in the afternoon. And it was not long before the people began to say that the white man's medicine was quick in working. Mr. Brown's school produced quick results. A few months in it were enough to make one a court messenger or even a court clerk. Those who stayed longer became teachers; and from Umuofia laborers went forth into the Lord's vineyard. New churches were established in the surrounding villages and a few schools with them. From the very beginning religion and education went hand in hand.

Mr. Brown's mission grew from strength to strength, and because of its

---

5. Undershirts, T-shirts.

link with the new administration it earned a new social prestige. But Mr. Brown himself was breaking down in health. At first he ignored the warning signs. But in the end he had to leave his flock, sad and broken.

It was in the first rainy season after Okonkwo's return to Umuofia that Mr. Brown left for home. As soon as he had learned of Okonkwo's return five months earlier, the missionary had immediately paid him a visit. He had just sent Okonkwo's son, Nwoye, who was now called Isaac,[6] to the new training college for teachers in Umuru. And he had hoped that Okonkwo would be happy to hear of it. But Okonkwo had driven him away with the threat that if he came into his compound again, he would be carried out of it.

Okonkwo's return to his native land was not as memorable as he had wished. It was true his two beautiful daughters aroused great interest among suitors and marriage negotiations were soon in progress, but, beyond that, Umuofia did not appear to have taken any special notice of the warrior's return. The clan had undergone such profound change during his exile that it was barely recognizable. The new religion and government and the trading stores were very much in the people's eyes and minds. There were still many who saw these new institutions as evil, but even they talked and thought about little else, and certainly not about Okonkwo's return.

And it was the wrong year too. If Okonkwo had immediately initiated his two sons into the *ozo* society as he had planned he would have caused a stir. But the initiation rite was performed once in three years in Umuofia, and he had to wait for nearly two years for the next round of ceremonies.

Okonkwo was deeply grieved. And it was not just a personal grief. He mourned for the clan, which he saw breaking up and falling apart, and he mourned for the warlike men of Umuofia, who had so unaccountably become soft like women.

22

Mr. Brown's successor was the Reverend James Smith, and he was a different kind of man. He condemned openly Mr. Brown's policy of compromise and accommodation. He saw things as black and white. And black was evil. He saw the world as a battlefield in which the children of light were locked in mortal conflict with the sons of darkness. He spoke in his sermons about sheep and goats and about wheat and tares. He believed in slaying the prophets of Baal.

Mr. Smith was greatly distressed by the ignorance which many of his flock showed even in such things as the Trinity and the Sacraments. It only showed that they were seeds sown on a rocky soil. Mr. Brown had thought of nothing but numbers. He should have known that the kingdom of God did not depend on large crowds. Our Lord Himself stressed the importance of fewness. Narrow is the way and few the number. To fill the Lord's holy temple with an idolatrous crowd clamoring for signs was a folly of everlasting consequence. Our Lord used the whip only once in His life—to drive the crowd away from His church.

Within a few weeks of his arrival in Umuofia Mr. Smith suspended a young

---

6. Son of Abraham, offered to God as a sacrifice (Genesis 22).

woman from the church for pouring new wine into old bottles. This woman had allowed her heathen husband to mutilate her dead child. The child had been declared an *ogbanje,* plaguing its mother by dying and entering her womb to be born again. Four times this child had run its evil round. And so it was mutilated to discourage it from returning.

Mr. Smith was filled with wrath when he heard of this. He disbelieved the story which even some of the most faithful confirmed, the story of really evil children who were not deterred by mutilation, but came back with all the scars. He replied that such stories were spread in the world by the Devil to lead men astray. Those who believed such stories were unworthy of the Lord's table.

There was a saying in Umuofia that as a man danced so the drums were beaten for him. Mr. Smith danced a furious step and so the drums went mad. The over-zealous converts who had smarted under Mr. Brown's restraining hand now flourished in full favor. One of them was Enoch, the son of the snake-priest who was believed to have killed and eaten the sacred python. Enoch's devotion to the new faith had seemed so much greater than Mr. Brown's that the villagers called him the outsider who wept louder than the bereaved.

Enoch was short and slight of build, and always seemed in great haste. His feet were short and broad, and when he stood or walked his heels came together and his feet opened outwards as if they had quarreled and meant to go in different directions. Such was the excessive energy bottled up in Enoch's small body that it was always erupting in quarrels and fights. On Sundays he always imagined that the sermon was preached for the benefit of his enemies. And if he happened to sit near one of them he would occasionally turn to give him a meaningful look, as if to say, "I told you so." It was Enoch who touched off the great conflict between church and clan in Umuofia which had been gathering since Mr. Brown left.

It happened during the annual ceremony which was held in honor of the earth deity. At such times the ancestors of the clan who had been committed to Mother Earth at their death emerged again as *egwugwu* through tiny ant-holes.

One of the greatest crimes a man could commit was to unmask an *egwugwu* in public, or to say or do anything which might reduce its immortal prestige in the eyes of the uninitiated. And this was what Enoch did.

The annual worship of the earth goddess fell on a Sunday, and the masked spirits were abroad. The Christian women who had been to church could not therefore go home. Some of their men had gone out to beg the *egwugwu* to retire for a short while for the women to pass. They agreed and were already retiring, when Enoch boasted aloud that they would not dare to touch a Christian. Whereupon they all came back and one of them gave Enoch a good stroke of the cane, which was always carried. Enoch fell on him and tore off his mask. The other *egwugwu* immediately surrounded their dese-crated companion, to shield him from the profane gaze of women and chil-dren, and led him away. Enoch had killed an ancestral spirit, and Umuofia was thrown into confusion.

That night the Mother of the Spirits walked the length and breadth of the clan, weeping for her murdered son. It was a terrible night. Not even the oldest man in Umuofia had ever heard such a strange and fearful sound, and it was never to be heard again. It seemed as if the very soul of the tribe wept for a great evil that was coming—its own death.

On the next day all the masked *egwugwu* of Umuofia assembled in the marketplace. They came from all the quarters of the clan and even from the neighboring villages. The dreaded Otakagu came from Imo, and Ekwensu, dangling a white cock, arrived from Uli. It was a terrible gathering. The eerie voices of countless spirits, the bells that clattered behind some of them, and the clash of machetes as they ran forwards and backwards and saluted one another, sent tremors of fear into every heart. For the first time in living memory the sacred bull-roarer was heard in broad daylight.

From the marketplace the furious band made for Enoch's compound. Some of the elders of the clan went with them, wearing heavy protections of charms and amulets. These were men whose arms were strong in *ogwu*, or medicine. As for the ordinary men and women, they listened from the safety of their huts.

The leaders of the Christians had met together at Mr. Smith's parsonage on the previous night. As they deliberated they could hear the Mother of Spirits wailing for her son. The chilling sound affected Mr. Smith, and for the first time he seemed to be afraid.

"What are they planning to do?" he asked. No one knew, because such a thing had never happened before. Mr. Smith would have sent for the District Commissioner and his court messengers, but they had gone on tour on the previous day.

"One thing is clear," said Mr. Smith. "We cannot offer physical resistance to them. Our strength lies in the Lord." They knelt down together and prayed to God for delivery.

"O Lord, save Thy people," cried Mr. Smith.

"And bless Thine inheritance," replied the men.

They decided that Enoch should be hidden in the parsonage for a day or two. Enoch himself was greatly disappointed when he heard this, for he had hoped that a holy war was imminent; and there were a few other Christians who thought like him. But wisdom prevailed in the camp of the faithful and many lives were thus saved.

The band of *egwugwu* moved like a furious whirlwind to Enoch's compound and with machete and fire reduced it to a desolate heap. And from there they made for the church, intoxicated with destruction.

Mr. Smith was in his church when he heard the masked spirits coming. He walked quietly to the door which commanded the approach to the church compound, and stood there. But when the first three or four *egwugwu* appeared on the church compound he nearly bolted. He overcame this impulse and instead of running away he went down the two steps that led up to the church and walked towards the approaching spirits.

They surged forward, and a long stretch of the bamboo fence with which the church compound was surrounded gave way before them. Discordant bells clanged, machetes clashed and the air was full of dust and weird sounds. Mr. Smith heard a sound of footsteps behind him. He turned round and saw Okeke, his interpreter. Okeke had not been on the best of terms with his master since he had strongly condemned Enoch's behavior at the meeting of the leaders of the church during the night. Okeke had gone as far as to say that Enoch should not be hidden in the parsonage, because he would only draw the wrath of the clan on the pastor. Mr. Smith had rebuked him in very strong language, and had not sought his advice that morning. But now, as he came up and stood by him confronting the angry spirits, Mr. Smith looked at him and smiled. It was a wan smile, but there was deep gratitude there.

For a brief moment the onrush of the *egwugwu* was checked by the unexpected composure of the two men. But it was only a momentary check, like the tense silence between blasts of thunder. The second onrush was greater than the first. It swallowed up the two men. Then an unmistakable voice rose above the tumult and there was immediate silence. Space was made around the two men, and Ajofia began to speak.

Ajofia was the leading *egwugwu* of Umuofia. He was the head and spokesman of the nine ancestors who administered justice in the clan. His voice was unmistakable and so he was able to bring immediate peace to the agitated spirits. He then addressed Mr. Smith, and as he spoke clouds of smoke rose from his head.

"The body of the white man, I salute you," he said, using the language in which immortals spoke to men.

"The body of the white man, do you know me?" he asked.

Mr. Smith looked at his interpreter, but Okeke, who was a native of distant Umuru, was also at a loss.

Ajofia laughed in his guttural voice. It was like the laugh of rusty metal. "They are strangers," he said, "and they are ignorant. But let that pass." He turned round to his comrades and saluted them, calling them the fathers of Umuofia. He dug his rattling spear into the ground and it shook with metallic life. Then he turned once more to the missionary and his interpreter.

"Tell the white man that we will not do him any harm," he said to the interpreter. "Tell him to go back to his house and leave us alone. We liked his brother who was with us before. He was foolish, but we liked him, and for his sake we shall not harm his brother. But this shrine which he built must be destroyed. We shall no longer allow it in our midst. It has bred untold abominations and we have come to put an end to it." He turned to his comrades. "Fathers of Umuofia, I salute you"; and they replied with one guttural voice. He turned again to the missionary. "You can stay with us if you like our ways. You can worship your own god. It is good that a man should worship the gods and the spirits of his fathers. Go back to your house so that you may not be hurt. Our anger is great but we have held it down so that we can talk to you."

Mr. Smith said to his interpreter: "Tell them to go away from here. This is the house of God and I will not live to see it desecrated."

Okeke interpreted wisely to the spirits and leaders of Umuofia: "The white man says he is happy you have come to him with your grievances, like friends. He will be happy if you leave the matter in his hands."

"We cannot leave the matter in his hands because he does not understand our customs, just as we do not understand his. We say he is foolish because he does not know our ways, and perhaps he says we are foolish because we do not know his. Let him go away."

Mr. Smith stood his ground. But he could not save his church. When the *egwugwu* went away the red-earth church which Mr. Brown had built was a pile of earth and ashes. And for the moment the spirit of the clan was pacified.

23

For the first time in many years Okonkwo had a feeling that was akin to happiness. The times which had altered so unaccountably during his exile seemed to be coming round again. The clan which had turned false on him appeared to be making amends.

He had spoken violently to his clansmen when they had met in the marketplace to decide on their action. And they had listened to him with respect. It was like the good old days again, when a warrior was a warrior. Although they had not agreed to kill the missionary or drive away the Christians, they had agreed to do something substantial. And they had done it. Okonkwo was almost happy again.

For two days after the destruction of the church, nothing happened. Every man in Umuofia went about armed with a gun or a machete. They would not be caught unawares, like the men of Abame.

Then the District Commissioner returned from his tour. Mr. Smith went immediately to him and they had a long discussion. The men of Umuofia did not take any notice of this, and if they did, they thought it was not important. The missionary often went to see his brother white man. There was nothing strange in that.

Three days later the District Commissioner sent his sweet-tongued messenger to the leaders of Umuofia asking them to meet him in his headquarters. That also was not strange. He often asked them to hold such palavers, as he called them. Okonkwo was among the six leaders he invited.

Okonkwo warned the others to be fully armed. "An Umuofia man does not refuse a call," he said. "He may refuse to do what he is asked; he does not refuse to be asked. But the times have changed, and we must be fully prepared."

And so the six men went to see the District Commissioner, armed with their machetes. They did not carry guns, for that would be unseemly. They were led into the courthouse where the District Commissioner sat. He received them politely. They unslung their goatskin bags and their sheathed machetes, put them on the floor, and sat down.

"I have asked you to come," began the Commissioner, "because of what happened during my absence. I have been told a few things but I cannot believe them until I have heard your own side. Let us talk about it like friends and find a way of ensuring that it does not happen again."

Ogbuefi Ekwueme[7] rose to his feet and began to tell the story.

"Wait a minute," said the Commissioner. "I want to bring in my men so that they too can hear your grievances and take warning. Many of them come from distant places and although they speak your tongue they are ignorant of your customs. James! Go and bring in the men." His interpreter left the courtroom and soon returned with twelve men. They sat together with the men of Umuofia, and Ogbuefi Ekwueme began to tell the story of how Enoch murdered an *egwugwu*.

It happened so quickly that the six men did not see it coming. There was only a brief scuffle, too brief even to allow the drawing of a sheathed machete. The six men were handcuffed and led into the guardroom.

"We shall not do you any harm," said the District Commissioner to them

7. A person who does what he says (a praise name).

later, "if only you agree to cooperate with us. We have brought a peaceful administration to you and your people so that you may be happy. If any man ill-treats you we shall come to your rescue. But we will not allow you to ill-treat others. We have a court of law where we judge cases and administer justice just as it is done in my own country under a great queen. I have brought you here because you joined together to molest others, to burn people's houses and their place of worship. That must not happen in the dominion of our queen, the most powerful ruler in the world. I have decided that you will pay a fine of two hundred bags of cowries. You will be released as soon as you agree to this and undertake to collect that fine from your people. What do you say to that?"

The six men remained sullen and silent and the Commissioner left them for a while. He told the court messengers, when he left the guardroom, to treat the men with respect because they were the leaders of Umuofia. They said, "Yes, sir," and saluted.

As soon as the District Commissioner left, the head messenger, who was also the prisoners' barber, took down his razor and shaved off all the hair on the men's heads. They were still handcuffed, and they just sat and moped.

"Who is the chief among you?" the court messengers asked in jest. "We see that every pauper wears the anklet of title in Umuofia. Does it cost as much as ten cowries?"

The six men ate nothing throughout that day and the next. They were not even given any water to drink, and they could not go out to urinate or go into the bush when they were pressed. At night the messengers came in to taunt them and to knock their shaven heads together.

Even when the men were left alone they found no words to speak to one another. It was only on the third day, when they could no longer bear the hunger and the insults, that they began to talk about giving in.

"We should have killed the white man if you had listened to me," Okonkwo snarled.

"We could have been in Umuru now waiting to be hanged," someone said to him.

"Who wants to kill the white man?" asked a messenger who had just rushed in. Nobody spoke.

"You are not satisfied with your crime, but you must kill the white man on top of it." He carried a strong stick, and he hit each man a few blows on the head and back. Okonkwo was choked with hate.

As soon as the six men were locked up, court messengers went into Umuofia to tell the people that their leaders would not be released unless they paid a fine of two hundred and fifty bags of cowries.

"Unless you pay the fine immediately," said their head-man, "we will take your leaders to Umuru before the big white man, and hang them."

This story spread quickly through the villages, and was added to as it went. Some said that the men had already been taken to Umuru and would be hanged on the following day. Some said that their families would also be hanged. Others said that soldiers were already on their way to shoot the people of Umuofia as they had done in Abame.

It was the time of the full moon. But that night the voice of children was not heard. The village *ilo* where they always gathered for a moon-play was empty. The women of Iguedo did not meet in their secret enclosure to learn a new dance to be displayed later to the village. Young men who were always abroad in the moonlight kept to their huts that night. Their manly voices were not heard on the village paths as they went to visit their friends and lovers. Umuofia was like a startled animal with ears erect, sniffing the silent, ominous air and not knowing which way to run.

The silence was broken by the village crier beating his sonorous *ogene*. He called every man in Umuofia, from the Akakanma age group upwards, to a meeting in the marketplace after the morning meal. He went from one end of the village to the other and walked all its breadth. He did not leave out any of the main footpaths.

Okonkwo's compound was like a deserted homestead. It was as if cold water had been poured on it. His family was all there, but everyone spoke in whispers. His daughter Ezinma had broken her twenty-eight-day visit to the family of her future husband, and returned home when she heard that her father had been imprisoned, and was going to be hanged. As soon as she got home she went to Obierika to ask what the men of Umuofia were going to do about it. But Obierika had not been home since morning. His wives thought he had gone to a secret meeting. Ezinma was satisfied that something was being done.

On the morning after the village crier's appeal the men of Umuofia met in the marketplace and decided to collect without delay two hundred and fifty bags of cowries to appease the white man. They did not know that fifty bags would go to the court messengers, who had increased the fine for that purpose.

24

Okonkwo and his fellow prisoners were set free as soon as the fine was paid. The District Commissioner spoke to them again about the great queen, and about peace and good government. But the men did not listen. They just sat and looked at him and at his interpreter. In the end they were given back their bags and sheathed machetes and told to go home. They rose and left the courthouse. They neither spoke to anyone nor among themselves.

The courthouse, like the church, was built a little way outside the village. The footpath that linked them was a very busy one because it also led to the stream, beyond the court. It was open and sandy. Footpaths were open and sandy in the dry season. But when the rains came the bush grew thick on either side and closed in on the path. It was now dry season.

As they made their way to the village the six men met women and children going to the stream with their waterpots. But the men wore such heavy and fearsome looks that the women and children did not say "*nno*" or "welcome" to them, but edged out of the way to let them pass. In the village little groups of men joined them until they became a sizable company. They walked silently. As each of the six men got to his compound, he turned in, taking some of the crowd with him. The village was astir in a silent, suppressed way.

Ezinma had prepared some food for her father as soon as news spread that the six men would be released. She took it to him in his *obi*. He ate absent-mindedly. He had no appetite; he only ate to please her. His male relations and friends had gathered in his *obi*, and Obierika was urging him to eat. Nobody else spoke, but they noticed the long stripes on Okonkwo's back where the warder's whip had cut into his flesh.

The village crier was abroad again in the night. He beat his iron gong and announced that another meeting would be held in the morning. Everyone knew that Umuofia was at last going to speak its mind about the things that were happening.

Okonkwo slept very little that night. The bitterness in his heart was now mixed with a kind of childlike excitement. Before he had gone to bed he had brought down his war dress, which he had not touched since his return from exile. He had shaken out his smoked raffia skirt and examined his tall feather head-gear and his shield. They were all satisfactory, he had thought.

As he lay on his bamboo bed he thought about the treatment he had received in the white man's court, and he swore vengeance. If Umuofia decided on war, all would be well. But if they chose to be cowards he would go out and avenge himself. He thought about wars in the past. The noblest, he thought, was the war against Isike. In those days Okudo[8] was still alive. Okudo sang a war song in a way that no other man could. He was not a fighter, but his voice turned every man into a lion.

"Worthy men are no more," Okonkwo sighed as he remembered those days. "Isike will never forget how we slaughtered them in that war. We killed twelve of their men and they killed only two of ours. Before the end of the fourth market week they were suing for peace. Those were days when men were men."

As he thought of these things he heard the sound of the iron gong in the distance. He listened carefully, and could just hear the crier's voice. But it was very faint. He turned on his bed and his back hurt him. He ground his teeth. The crier was drawing nearer and nearer until he passed by Okonkwo's compound.

"The greatest obstacle in Umuofia," Okonkwo thought bitterly, "is that coward, Egonwanne.[9] His sweet tongue can change fire into cold ash. When he speaks he moves our men to impotence. If they had ignored his womanish wisdom five years ago, we would not have come to this." He ground his teeth. "Tomorrow he will tell them that our fathers never fought a 'war of blame.' If they listen to him I shall leave them and plan my own revenge."

The crier's voice had once more become faint, and the distance had taken the harsh edge off his iron gong. Okonkwo turned from one side to the other and derived a kind of pleasure from the pain his back gave him. "Let Egonwanne talk about a 'war of blame' tomorrow and I shall show him my back and head." He ground his teeth.

The marketplace began to fill as soon as the sun rose. Obierika was waiting in his *obi* when Okonkwo came along and called him. He hung his goatskin bag and his sheathed machete on his shoulder and went out to join him. Obierika's hut was close to the road and he saw every man who passed to the marketplace. He had exchanged greetings with many who had already passed that morning.

8. Great eagle feather (a praise name).   9. Wealth of a sibling.

When Okonkwo and Obierika got to the meeting place there were already so many people that if one threw up a grain of sand it would not find its way to the earth again. And many more people were coming from every quarter of the nine villages. It warmed Okonkwo's heart to see such strength of numbers. But he was looking for one man in particular, the man whose tongue he dreaded and despised so much.

"Can you see him?" he asked Obierika.

"Who?"

"Egonwanne," he said, his eyes roving from one corner of the huge market-place to the other. Most of the men sat on wooden stools they had brought with them.

"No," said Obierika, casting his eyes over the crowd. "Yes, there he is, under the silk-cotton tree. Are you afraid he would convince us not to fight?"

"Afraid? I do not care what he does to *you*. I despise him and those who listen to him. I shall fight alone if I choose."

They spoke at the top of their voices because everybody was talking, and it was like the sound of a great market.

"I shall wait till he has spoken," Okonkwo thought. "Then I shall speak."

"But how do you know he will speak against war?" Obierika asked after a while.

"Because I know he is a coward," said Okonkwo. Obierika did not hear the rest of what he said because at that moment somebody touched his shoulder from behind and he turned round to shake hands and exchange greetings with five or six friends. Okonkwo did not turn round even though he knew the voices. He was in no mood to exchange greetings. But one of the men touched him and asked about the people of his compound.

"They are well," he replied without interest.

The first man to speak to Umuofia that morning was Okika, one of the six who had been imprisoned. Okika was a great man and an orator. But he did not have the booming voice which a first speaker must use to establish silence in the assembly of the clan. Onyeka[1] had such a voice; and so he was asked to salute Umuofia before Okika began to speak.

"*Umuofia kwenu!*" he bellowed, raising his left arm and pushing the air with his open hand.

"*Yaa!*" roared Umuofia.

"*Umuofia kwenu!*" he bellowed again, and again and again, facing a new direction each time. And the crowd answered, "*Yaa!*"

There was immediate silence as though cold water had been poured on a roaring flame.

Okika sprang to his feet and also saluted his clansmen four times. Then he began to speak:

"You all know why we are here, when we ought to be building our barns or mending our huts, when we should be putting our compounds in order. My father used to say to me: 'Whenever you see a toad jumping in broad daylight, then know that something is after its life.' When I saw you all pouring into this meeting from all the quarters of our clan so early in the morning, I knew that something was after our life." He paused for a brief moment and then began again:

---

1. "Who surpasses [God]?" (a rhetorical question).

"All our gods are weeping. Idemili is weeping, Ogwugwu is weeping, Agbala is weeping, and all the others. Our dead fathers are weeping because of the shameful sacrilege they are suffering and the abomination we have all seen with our eyes." He stopped again to steady his trembling voice.

"This is a great gathering. No clan can boast of greater numbers or greater valor. But are we all here? I ask you: Are all the sons of Umuofia with us here?" A deep murmur swept through the crowd.

"They are not," he said. "They have broken the clan and gone their several ways. We who are here this morning have remained true to our fathers, but our brothers have deserted us and joined a stranger to soil their fatherland. If we fight the stranger we shall hit our brothers and perhaps shed the blood of a clansman. But we must do it. Our fathers never dreamed of such a thing, they never killed their brothers. But a white man never came to them. So we must do what our fathers would never have done. Eneke the bird was asked why he was always on the wing and he replied: 'Men have learned to shoot without missing their mark and I have learned to fly without perching on a twig.' We must root out this evil. And if our brothers take the side of evil we must root them out too. And we must do it *now*. We must bail this water now that it is only ankle-deep. . . ."

At this point there was a sudden stir in the crowd and every eye was turned in one direction. There was a sharp bend in the road that led from the marketplace to the white man's court, and to the stream beyond it. And so no one had seen the approach of the five court messengers until they had come round the bend, a few paces from the edge of the crowd. Okonkwo was sitting at the edge.

He sprang to his feet as soon as he saw who it was. He confronted the head messenger, trembling with hate, unable to utter a word. The man was fearless and stood his ground, his four men lined up behind him.

In that brief moment the world seemed to stand still, waiting. There was utter silence. The men of Umuofia were merged into the mute backcloth of trees and giant creepers, waiting.

The spell was broken by the head messenger. "Let me pass!" he ordered.

"What do you want here?"

"The white man whose power you know too well has ordered this meeting to stop."

In a flash Okonkwo drew his machete. The messenger crouched to avoid the blow. It was useless. Okonkwo's machete descended twice and the man's head lay beside his uniformed body.

The waiting backcloth jumped into tumultuous life and the meeting was stopped. Okonkwo stood looking at the dead man. He knew that Umuofia would not go to war. He knew because they had let the other messengers escape. They had broken into tumult instead of action. He discerned fright in that tumult. He heard voices asking: "Why did he do it?"

He wiped his machete on the sand and went away.

25

When the District Commissioner arrived at Okonkwo's compound at the head of an armed band of soldiers and court messengers he found a small crowd of men sitting wearily in the *obi*. He commanded them to come outside, and they obeyed without a murmur.

"Which among you is called Okonkwo?" he asked through his interpreter.

"He is not here," replied Obierika.

"Where is he?"

"He is not here!"

The Commissioner became angry and red in the face. He warned the men that unless they produced Okonkwo forthwith he would lock them all up. The men murmured among themselves, and Obierika spoke again.

"We can take you where he is, and perhaps your men will help us."

The Commissioner did not understand what Obierika meant when he said, "Perhaps your men will help us." One of the most infuriating habits of these people was their love of superfluous words, he thought.

Obierika with five or six others led the way. The Commissioner and his men followed, their firearms held at the ready. He had warned Obierika that if he and his men played any monkey tricks they would be shot. And so they went.

There was a small bush behind Okonkwo's compound. The only opening into this bush from the compound was a little round hole in the red-earth wall through which fowls went in and out in their endless search for food. The hole would not let a man through. It was to this bush that Obierika led the Commissioner and his men. They skirted round the compound, keeping close to the wall. The only sound they made was with their feet as they crushed dry leaves.

Then they came to the tree from which Okonkwo's body was dangling, and they stopped dead.

"Perhaps your men can help us bring him down and bury him," said Obierika. "We have sent for strangers from another village to do it for us, but they may be a long time coming."

The District Commissioner changed instantaneously. The resolute administrator in him gave way to the student of primitive customs.

"Why can't you take him down yourselves?" he asked.

"It is against our custom," said one of the men. "It is an abomination for a man to take his own life. It is an offense against the Earth, and a man who commits it will not be buried by his clansmen. His body is evil, and only strangers may touch it. That is why we ask your people to bring him down, because you are strangers."

"Will you bury him like any other man?" asked the Commissioner.

"We cannot bury him. Only strangers can. We shall pay your men to do it. When he has been buried we will then do our duty by him. We shall make sacrifices to cleanse the desecrated land."

Obierika, who had been gazing steadily at his friend's dangling body, turned suddenly to the District Commissioner and said ferociously: "That man was one of the greatest men in Umuofia. You drove him to kill himself; and now he will be buried like a dog. . . ." He could not say any more. His voice trembled and choked his words.

"Shut up!" shouted one of the messengers, quite unnecessarily.

"Take down the body," the Commissioner ordered his chief messenger, "and bring it and all these people to the court."

"Yes, sah," the messenger said, saluting.

The Commissioner went away, taking three or four of the soldiers with him. In the many years in which he had toiled to bring civilization to different parts of Africa he had learned a number of things. One of them was that a

District Commissioner must never attend to such undignified details as cutting a hanged man from the tree. Such attention would give the natives a poor opinion of him. In the book which he planned to write he would stress that point. As he walked back to the court he thought about that book. Every day brought him some new material. The story of this man who had killed a messenger and hanged himself would make interesting reading. One could almost write a whole chapter on him. Perhaps not a whole chapter but a reasonable paragraph, at any rate. There was so much else to include, and one must be firm in cutting out details. He had already chosen the title of the book, after much thought: *The Pacification of the Primitive Tribes of the Lower Niger.*

DEREK WALCOTT
born 1930

From the beginning of his career at the age of eighteen, Derek Walcott has situated his work firmly within the broad perspective of Afro-Caribbean experience as it derives from and relates to what constitute for him its main areas of reference: Europe, Africa, and the Americas. For although the Asian connection forms part of the social and cultural configuration of the Caribbean, his work as a writer engages principally these three areas as they determine his self-awareness as a West Indian of mixed African and European ancestry. His poetry, plays, and essays invariably have, as their point of departure, the state of tension created by the contradictory pressures that a complex racial and cultural situation exerts upon his sensibility. An early poem, *A Far Cry from Africa,* from the volume *In a Green Night* (1962), alludes to events in Africa during the violent uprising in Kenya against British colonialism and gives poignant expression, in lines that have often been quoted, to the conflicting allegiances entailed by his situation:

> I who am poisoned with the blood of both
> Where shall I turn, divided to the vein?
> I who have cursed
> The drunken officer of British rule, how choose
> Between this Africa and the English tongue I love?
> Betray them both or give back what they give?
> How can I face such slaughter and be cool?
> How can I turn from Africa and live?

Despite its rhetorical excess, the passage conveys a note of intense personal anguish proceeding from Walcott's sense of a wider cultural and spiritual predicament, whose implications extend to every sphere of life and consciousness in West Indian society.

Walcott's entire imaginative work is marked by a dual impulse: it registers both the Afro-Caribbean quest for an established sense of place and of community and, at the same time, the compulsion to move toward wider horizons presented to the Caribbean personality and imagination by the background of historical events and cultural encounters of which the West Indies have been a living theater. Walcott's expression is thus posited on the idea of a creative potential inherent in the Caribbean situation by virtue of the possibilities it offers of shaping a distinctive mode of being, in which disparate impulses are integrated into a new wholeness, one that provides an enduring psychological and moral foundation for an original relation to the world.

Derek Walcott was born, along with his twin brother, Roderick, in Castries, the capital of the island of St. Lucia, on January 23, 1930. Shortly after their first birthday, their father, who was a government functionary and a talented artist, suddenly died, and the two boys were brought up by their mother, a schoolteacher who later became headmistress of the Methodist elementary school where they began their education. Both inherited their father's creative gift, Derek primarily in language, Roderick in the pictorial arts, and they remained intellectual and artistic companions until Roderick's death in 1999. Their mother provided an environment in which their talents could be nurtured, an essential factor in Walcott's development as a poet that he acknowledges in the tribute to her memory in the title poem of the collection *The Bounty* (1997): "let the ants teach me again with the long line of words / my business and duty, the lesson you taught your sons / to write of the light's bounty on familiar things."

But despite the sustenance he drew from his family and encouragement for his creative bent received from other members of the St. Lucian community, Walcott's sentiment of being an orphan (in both a literal and cultural sense) could not be fully assuaged. He acquired early on a sense of his singularity from the fact that he was of pronounced mixed parentage in a predominantly black society as well as being a Protestant and member of the educated middle class in a peasant and Catholic community. Moreover, although he was brought up to speak standard English as his first language, his exposure to the local French creole—both languages the result of the island's successive occupations, first by the French and then by the English—reinforced his sense of his ambiguous relation to the communal life around him. But far from unsettling Walcott, these factors of personal history become in his work a source of strength. For the special quality of stance and tone in his writings springs from his having to work through the varied implications of his peculiar marginality within his own society and in the wider world—as a West Indian, product of a colonial history—toward the inauguration, in symbolic terms, of a new and integral self.

This trajectory of Walcott's themes has been implicit in his writing from the outset. His precocity manifested itself while he was a student at St. Mary's College in Castries, where he began writing poems and plays. By the time he left school, he had already published two volumes, 25 *Poems* (1948) and *Epitaph for the Young* (1949), both of which drew from Frank Collymore, the "dean" of West Indian letters at the time, an enthusiastic essay drawing attention his promise. Walcott also wrote at this time a historical play, *Henri Christophe* (1950), devoted to the tragic career of one of the principal actors in the Haitian revolution, a play that was considered accomplished enough to be read on the BBC Caribbean Service. Going up that same year to the University College of the West Indies in Kingston, Jamaica, to read English, French, and Latin, he brought with him a reputation as a young writer destined for a brilliant future.

The university years in Jamaica were crucial for Walcott's subsequent development. They enabled him to acquire an expanded view of the Caribbean as an area unified by a common experience and a common legacy of history. Equally important, his literary studies familiarized him with the great works of Western literature and led him to appreciate their role in a cultural heritage integral to his own status as a product of the European imperial adventure. This wider range became apparent in his next volume, *Poems* (1953), which demonstrates the efforts of a young writer still dependent on recognized literary models—the influence of T. S. Eliot is especially pronounced in the idiom and imagery—and undergoing a strenuous apprenticeship to his craft as a preliminary to finding his true voice. After his graduation in 1953, Walcott taught school for a while in Kingston, while also doing occasional work in journalism, before moving to Port of Spain, Trinidad, where he became a feature writer for a major local newspaper, the *Sunday Guardian*. In 1957, he was awarded a Rockefeller Fellowship to study theater at New York University. His encounter with the problems of race during his American sojourn gave further definition to his self-

awareness as a West Indian; the experience confirmed for him the inescapable connection between race and history with which black people in the New World have to
contend. On his return two years later to Port of Spain, he founded the Trinidad
Theatre Workshop, to which he devoted his energies for nearly two decades.

The publication in England of *In a Green Night* (1962) brought Walcott's work to
the attention of an international public and established his reputation beyond the
Caribbean region. The poems in the volume are marked by a striking eloquence of
diction and a rich tapestry of imagery. They center on his multiple heritage as a West
Indian and indicate besides a determined wrestling with form: "I seek / As climate
seeks its style to write / Verse crisp as sand, clear as sunlight / Cold as the curled
wave, ordinary / As a tumbler of island water." With this volume, Walcott consciously
assumes the weight of English literary tradition by translating its references and
resources into a new poetic register determined by his Caribbean experience and
sensibility. The poem *As John to Patmos* rehearses the religious and cultural references
that form part of his affective and intellectual inheritance and thus enter directly into
his vocation as a poet devoted to his island home yet open to the world. *Ruins of a
Great House* announces the all-embracing theme of his location in history: the ambiguous note on which its recall of plantation culture is rung springs from the black
poet's sense of historical grievance, but the echo in the title of Wordsworth's *Ruined
Cottage* lends the poem a certain romantic resonance that moves its theme beyond
the "tribal sorrow" of a race to a meditation on time.

It is in *The Castaway* (1969), his next volume, that Walcott attained full maturity
as a poet. A cluster of poems devoted to the figure of Robinson Crusoe brings into
prominence the presiding idea of the volume: its celebration of the heroic or creative
individual in the shaping of history. *Crusoe's Journal* lends a poetic grandeur to the
figure of the castaway, the lonely and bold adventurer who assumes the burden of
pathfinder, creating a new reality—and, indeed, a new world—out of the unpromising
materials at hand. In consonance with this special valuation of the castaway figure,
Walcott situates the poet as the node of consciousness in the larger community. The
theme is pursued again in *The Gulf* (1969), which turns on the poet's need to cultivate
his singularity as a condition for the shaping of a redeeming vision for his people.
The title poem extends the local reference, dwelling on privileged insight his isolation
offers the poet into the human condition.

This preoccupation with the poetic vocation leads to the extended self-scrutiny in
Another Life (1973), an autobiography in verse tracing Walcott's artistic development
and the growth of his mind as he encounters the wider world of events and individuals.
The figure of Odysseus is evoked to depict the process of this growth as a journey
into his own ambiguous self: "My sign was water / tears, and the sea / my sign was
Janus / I saw with twin heads / and everything I say is contradicted." The ambiguity
that Walcott dwells upon here becomes, however, an enabling factor, for it compels
him, in his specific Caribbean context, to an urgent creative purpose: "we were the
light of the world! / We were blest with a virginal unpainted world / with Adam's task
of giving things their name." His next volume, *Sea Grapes* (1976), is devoted largely
to reflections on the Caribbean poet's calling as proclaimed in these lines. He does
not lose sight, however, of the ironies involved in the relation between poet and
community, as attested by the theme of the artist as doomed hero, already broached
in an early poem, *Epitaph for Youth,* and elaborated anew in the homage to a fellow
poet, Federico García Lorca, built into his evocation of the city of Granada in *The
Bounty* (1997).

With *The Star-Apple Kingdom* (1977), Walcott brought to the fore the political and
social themes that served in the previous volumes as the broad canvas to his meditations on the self in relation to history. The opening poem, *The Schooner Flight,*
uses the journey motif to chart, through the adventure of Shabine (the personna
whose monologue the poem records), the decline of the Caribbean archipelago
through time, beginning with the violation of its primal purity by Columbus. It evokes
the subsequent nightmare of the Middle Passage and the harsh experience of slavery,

followed by the humiliations of colonial domination and the uncertainties of the islands' present freedom: "and I, Shabine, saw / when these slums of empire was paradise." The opening poem sets the pathetic tone of the entire volume, which is a long and anxious questioning of the destiny of the Caribbean, now being corrupted by tourism and commerce ("this chain store of islands."). *The Sea Is History*, in the same volume, gives further clarity to the historical consciousness that informs his themes. In this as in other poems, history is relived by the poet, both through a recall of its broad configurations indicated by its marking episodes, and through a reenactment of its very movement as human drama. Poetry thus serves as an imaginative exploration of this history that also involves an interrogation of its meaning for the Caribbean people.

The broader context of this interrogation emerges more fully in *The Fortunate Traveller* (1981), where Walcott's perception of the racial divide between the affluent North and the impoverished South dictates the ironic posture indicated by the title. Walcott continues here, on a more personal note, the reflection on the social and political condition of America begun in *Elegy* (in the collection *The Gulf*), so that the new volume can be read as a poetic diary of his encounter with North America. In the poem *North and South*, Walcott evokes America in its quotidian ordinariness, but against a background of a landscape that has served as the theater for a historical drama of immense proportions and tragic human implications. The epic scale of the evocation barely intimated in the poem is given a succinct and powerful statement in *Sea Cranes* and is developed in the work that has come to be regarded as Walcott's masterpiece, *Omeros*.

All Walcott's poetry flows into *Omeros*, which is best grasped as the imaginative summation of human history as seen from his Caribbean perspective. Its retrospective vision assumes an especial emotional value for the poet for whom, as he says, "Art is History's nostalgia." In an expansive recollection of his previous themes, *Omeros* sums up the West Indian experience through the adventures of Achille, a humble St. Lucian fisherman, whose travels take him to the points of compass of the West Indian consciousness. Homer's great epics, the *Iliad* and the *Odyssey*, serve as obvious as references for the work, and the figure of Homer himself, in his modern Greek rendering of "Omeros," is evoked in a key passage of the poem in which he is represented as the quintessential exile. Moreover, Walcott's recourse to the image of the blind poet, of which Demokodos in Homer's *Odyssey* is the original model, reproduced in the character of Seven Seas in *Omeros* and that of Billy Blue in Walcott's *The Odyssey*, reinforce these references anticipated in earlier work but newly sustained by the scale of *Omeros*. The poem also employs some of the standard tropes of the classical epic, such as descent into the underworld and conflict and contest. Above all, the conflation of the poet's persona with Homer's hero lends a truly epic dimension and mythical significance to his quest for meaning in history.

Despite these connections, *Omeros* is not by any means a mere rehash of Homer, with whose works there are few direct correlations in terms of content. Although the poem contains stretches of narration, they do not build up into a dramatic progression of events such as we find in the conventional epic. The rivalry between Achille and another local fisherman, Hector, over Helen (who is hardly idealized in the poem and remains, for all her beauty, an ordinary village woman) is presented as part of a strictly mundane local history that features other actors such as the white settler couple, Major Plunkett and his wife, Maud, as well as minor characters who move in and out of the narrative. Thus, the poem does not unfold in a linear fashion in the development of a plot, but represents rather a vast kaleidoscope, a series of tableaux presenting scenes, always evoked in striking visual terms, episodes that bear a relation to Caribbean experience, and incidents in the collective life of the folk, all woven around the figure of its major protagonist, and the whole framed by personal reminiscences and reflections that ground the poet's reconstruction of collective memory.

Achilles' descent into the underworld recounted in Chapter VIII can be seen in this light to extend the significance of the sea as the arena and graveyard of history to suggest a plumbing of the Caribbean unconscious, a reaching into the deep impulses embedded by centuries of a turbulent history. This plunge into a violent past has an obvious connection with the poet's recollection, in Chapter XXXV, of the Native Americans' experience and condition, the pathos of a "tribal sorrow" that originates in the tragic confrontation with the white race.

Walcott's exploration of the African element in Caribbean life, dramatized in Chapter XXV in the dream sequence that takes Achille back to the ancestral homeland, also arises from his preoccupation with the collective memory and its relation to identity. The theme is developed in the dialogue between Achille and his mythic progenitor, Afolabe, in terms that are less ambivalent than Walcott's previous handling of the African question in Dream on Monkey Mountain. In Omeros, the reconnection with Africa occurs through a recognition of the cultural continuum that links the West Indians to the continent of their forbears and becomes instrumental in the process of self-acceptance essential to the West Indians' repossession of their island home.

The journey motif links Walcott's Omeros with the work of other West Indian poets such as St. John Perse, Aimé Césaire, and Kamau Brathwaite. The motif underlies Walcott's meditations on the work of the painter Camille Pissarro in his latest collection, Tiepolo's Hound (1999), attesting again to a restlessness rendered native to the Caribbean spirit by its living environment, dominated by the vast expanse of sea and sky by which it is encircled. It conditions a charged naturalism that forms a powerful undercurrent to Walcott's evocations and that occasionally surfaces, as in these lines:

> O Sun, the one eye of heaven, O Force, O Light,
> my heart kneels to you, my shadow has never changed
> since the salt-fresh mornings of encircling delight
>
> across whose cities the wings of the frigate ranged
> freer than any republic, gliding with ancient
> ease! I praise you not for my eyes. That other sight.

Omeros is Walcott's triumphant affirmation of the vitality of the Caribbean soul. The poem illustrates the poet's genius in its full scope, his gift of language by which he gives sensuous embodiment to that other life of the intellect and of the imagination that he intimates in his autobiographical poem. The award in 1992 of the Nobel Prize for literature came as a fitting recognition of a work as rich in its abundance and variety as in its human import.

Walcott's collection of essays, What the Twilight Says (1998), is an indispensable compendium of his social and aesthetic ideas. Robert Hamner, Derek Walcott (1978, rev. 1993), is a comprehensive and accessible full-length study of the writer's work; John Thieme, Derek Walcott (1999), is more up to date and provides commentaries on the key poems in Walcott's various collections and on the dramatic works. Lloyd Brown, West Indian Poetry (1978, repr. London 1984), contains a helpful chapter on Walcott's poetry in the context of the development of West Indian poetry in English. Edward Baugh, Derek Walcott: Memory as Vision (1978), provides an extended exegesis on Another Life; Rei Terada, Derek Walcott's Poetry: American Mimicry (1992), examines Walcott's creative integration within his poetry of influences from various sources. Bruce King, Derek Walcott and West Indian Drama (1995), is a history of the Trinidad Theatre Workshop and a study of the development of Walcott's dramatic art; the work is complemented by the same author's Derek Walcott: A Caribbean Life (2000), the first major biography of the writer. Robert Hamner, Epic of the Dispossessed (1997), provides a detailed discussion of Omeros that considers its adaptation of epic idiom to the experience and life dilemmas of the common folk. The Art of Derek Walcott, edited by Stewart Brown (1991), and Critical Perspectives on Derek Walcott, edited by Robert Hamner (1993), are collective volumes, that, though somewhat dated, can still be recommended for their coverage of Walcott's work up to their respective dates of their publication.

PRONOUNCING GLOSSARY

The following list uses common English syllables and stress accents to provide rough equivalents of selected words whose pronunciation may be unfamiliar to the general reader.

Achille: *ah-shee'l*   Choiseul: *shwah-zeuhl'*

Afolabe: *ah-foh-lah'-be*   Laurier-cannelle: *loh-reeay'-cah-nel'*

Bois-campêche: *bwah-cahm-pesh'*   Ville de Paris: *veel deu pah-ree'*

Bois-flot: *bwah-floh'*

As John to Patmos

As John to Patmos,[1] among the rocks and the blue, live air, hounded
His heart to peace, as here surrounded
By the strewn-silver on waves, the wood's crude hair, the rounded
Breasts of the milky bays,[2] palms, flocks, the green and dead

Leaves, the sun's brass coin on my cheek, where   5
Canoes brace the sun's strength, as John, in that bleak air,
So am I welcomed richer by these blue scapes, Greek there,[3]
So I shall voyage no more from home; may I speak here.

This island is heaven—away from the dustblown blood of cities;
See the curve of bay, watch the straggling flower, pretty is   10
The wing'd sound of trees, the sparse-powdered[4] sky, when lit is
The night. For beauty has surrounded
Its black children, and freed them of homeless ditties.[5]

As John to Patmos, in each love-leaping air,
O slave, soldier, worker under red trees sleeping,[6] hear   15
What I swear now, as John did:
To praise lovelong, the living and the brown dead.[7]

Ruins of a Great House[1]

> though our longest sun sets at right declensions and
> makes but winter arches, it cannot be long before we
> lie down in darkness, and have our light in ashes . . .
> —BROWNE, *Urn Burial*[2]

Stones only, the disjecta membra[3] of this Great House,
Whose moth-like girls are mixed with candledust,
Remain to file the lizard's dragonish claws.[4]

1. The Evangelist John the Divine's name is associated with the Greek island of Patmos, where he was banished for several years and wrote the Book of Revelation.   2. Low hills (in French patois, *mornes*) rising on the gently sloping landscape against the background of the sea, a feature of many of the smaller Caribbean islands.   3. Walcott establishes a parallel between Patmos and the poet's own island home of St. Lucia.   4. Almost cloudless.   5. I.e., Negro spirituals, songs of exile.   6. The poet's self-dedication addressed to his fellow countrymen.   7. The total "organic" community.   1. The principal building around which life in the slave plantation revolved. As in the American South, many of the great houses in the Caribbean were constructed on a grand scale, modeled on classical Greek architectural style (cf. line 13, below).   2. Thomas Browne (1605–1682) was an English physician and essayist, best known for his book *Religio Medici*. The epigram here is taken from *Urn Burial* (1658), a work that dwells on the passing of time and on human mortality.   3. Disjointed limbs (Latin).   4. The dragon is often represented as a great lizard.

The mouths of those gate cherubs[5] shriek with stain;
Axle and coach wheel silted under the muck   5
Of cattle droppings
        Three crows[6] flap for the trees
And settle, creaking the eucalyptus boughs.
A smell of dead limes quickens in the nose
The leprosy of empire.[7]   10
        "Farewell, green fields,
        Farewell, ye happy groves!"[8]
Marble like Greece, like Faulkner's South in stone,[9]
Deciduous[1] beauty prospered and is gone,
But where the lawn breaks in a rash of trees   15
A spade below dead leaves will ring the bone
Of some dead animal or human thing
Fallen from evil days, from evil times.

It seems that the original crops were limes
Grown in the silt that clogs the river's skirt;   20
The imperious rakes[2] are gone, their bright girls gone,
The river flows, obliterating hurt.[3]
I climbed a wall with the grille ironwork
Of exiled craftsmen protecting that great house
From guilt,[4] perhaps, but not from the worm's rent[5]   25
Nor from the padded cavalry of the mouse.
And when a wind shook in the limes I heard
What Kipling[6] heard, the death of a great empire, the abuse
Of ignorance by Bible and by sword.[7]

A green lawn, broken by low walls of stone,   30
Dipped to the rivulet, and pacing, I thought next
Of men like Hawkins, Walter Raleigh, Drake,[8]
Ancestral murderers and poets, more perplexed
In memory now by every ulcerous crime.
The world's green age then was a rotting lime   35
Whose stench became the charnel galleon's text.
The rot remains with us, the men are gone.
But, as dead ash is lifted in a wind
That fans the blackening ember of the mind,
My eyes burned from the ashen prose of Donne.[9]   40

---

5. Gates that display little angels with chubby cheeks and wings.   6. Birds of ill omen.   7. Slavery as moral blight.   8. The quotation is from Blake's poem *Night*.   9. William Faulkner (1897–1962), considered by many to be the greatest writer of the American South.   1. Said of trees that shed their leaves in the winter. The idea here is that the splendor of the great house and the lifestyle associated with it seemed destined to last forever.   2. Young men in the slave-owning community who lived wild and riotous lives.   3. Symbolizing the impersonal flow of time.   4. Presumably of slavery.   5. I.e., inevitable decay and death, a tribute to time.   6. Rudyard Kipling (1865–1936), English writer born in India. He is often remembered for the slogan he coined, "the white man's burden," to justify European colonial domination of nonwhite races.   7. The two means by which native populations were conquered.   8. *Hawkins, Raleigh*, and *Drake* were considered heroes of English imperial history. John Hawkins was a noted early slaver; Walter Raleigh was a favorite of Queen Elizabeth I of England, who knighted him for his exploration in America on behalf of the crown; Francis Drake was also knighted for his daring acts of piracy directed against Spanish merchant ships.   9. John Donne (1572–1631) was dean of St. Paul's Cathedral in London and the leading figure among the Renaissance English poets known as "the Metaphysicals." The reference here is to Donne's sermons, specifically Meditation 17, which contains the sentence "Ask not for whom the bell tolls, it tolls for thee," a reminder of human mortality—hence, "ashen prose." The quotations in lines 45 and 51 are from the same sermon; they express the theme of our common humanity, summed up by the famous phrase "No Man is an island" that occurs elsewhere in the sermon.

Ablaze with rage I thought,
Some slave is rotting in this manorial lake,
But still the coal of my compassion fought
That Albion[1] too was once
A colony like ours, "part of the continent, piece of the main,"   45
Nook-shotten, rook o'erblown, deranged
By foaming channels and the vain expense
Of bitter faction
     All in compassion ends
So differently from what the heart arranged: 50
"as well as if a manor of thy friend's . . ."

The Almond Trees[1]

There's nothing here
this early;
cold sand
cold churning ocean, the Atlantic,
no visible history,[2]   5

except this stand
of twisted, coppery, sea-almond trees[3]
their shining postures surely
bent as metal, and one

foam-haired, salt-grizzled fisherman,   10
his mongrel growling, whirling on the stick
he pitches him; its spinning rays
'no visible history'
until their lengthened shapes amaze the sun.

By noon,   15
this further shore of Africa[4] is strewn
with the forked limbs of girls toasting their flesh
in scarves, sunglasses, Pompeian bikinis,[5]

brown daphnes,[6] laurels, they'll all have
like their originals, their sacred grove,   20
this frieze
of twisted, coppery, sea-almond trees.

---

1. Poetic name for England. 1. The tropical almond (also known as the Indian almond) is a tree that bears a fleshy fruit with a kernel that has some resemblance to the temperate variety. It denotes here a sense of place, the poet's rootedness in the resilience and enduring quality of his people. 2. I.e., one marked by monuments and a sense of achievement. This negative view of the Caribbean was first put forward by the English historian James Anthony Froude (1818–1894) and later echoed by the Caribbean novelist V. S. Naipaul (born 1932). The reprise of the phrase as a quotation eight lines further draws attention to these sources. 3. The trees have assimilated to the fauna and flora as elements of a common landscape of experience. The idea, restated in line 33, governs the poem's theme and imagery. 4. The Caribbean as an extension of Africa in terms of climate, natural environment, ethnic composition, and, ultimately, forms of cultural expression. 5. The scantily clad girls evoke the liberal lifestyle for which the ancient Roman city of Pompeii was famous. Pompeii was destroyed in A.D. 63 by volcanic lava from the eruption of the Mount Vesuvius. 6. The immediate reference is to the laurel tree. It also refers to the Greek myth of the nymph Daphne, who was turned into a laurel while fleeing from Apollo.

The fierce acetylene[7] air
has singed
their writing trunks with rust, the same   25
hues as a foundered, peeling barge.
It'll sear a pale skin copper with its flame.

The sand's white-hot ash underheel,
but their aged limbs have got their brazen sheen
from fire. Their bodies fiercely shine!   30
They're cured,
they endured their furnace.[8]

Aged trees and oiled limbs share a common colour!

Welded in one flame,
huddling naked, stripped of their name,   35
for Greek or Roman tags,[9] they were lashed
raw by wind, washed
out with salt and fire-dried,
bitterly nourished where their branches died,

their leaves' broad dialect[1] a coarse,   40
enduring sound
they shared together.

Not as some running hamadryad's[2] cries
rooted, broke slowly into leaf
her nipples peaking to smooth, wooden boles   45

Their grief[3]
howls seaward through charred, ravaged holes.

One sunburnt body now acknowledges
that past and its own metamorphosis
as, moving from the sun, she kneels to spread   50
her wrap within the beat arms of this grove
that grieves in silence,[4] like parental love.[5]

Crusoe's Journal

I looked now upon the world as a thing remote, which I
had nothing to do with, no expectation from, and, indeed,
no desires about. In a word, I had nothing indeed
to do with it, nor was ever like to have; so I thought

---

7. A gas-fired flame used to soften metal.   8. I.e., the furnace of history. The black people are represented as having gone through a trial by fire, becoming tempered like steel.   9. Slaves were often given classical names by their owners.   1. The language and expressive culture of a new, distinctive community that has emerged from a common history.   2. A *hamadryad* is a nymph who lives in a tree.   3. The pathos of the slave experience.   4. I.e., that grieves not so much in resignation as in forgiveness.   5. A love marked by tolerance and understanding.

it looked as we may perhaps look upon it hereafter,
viz., as a place I had lived in but was come out
of it; and well might I say, as Father Abraham
to Dives, "Between me and thee is a great gulf fixed."
—ROBINSON CRUSOE[1]

Once we have driven past Mundo Nuevo[2] trace
     safely to this beach house
perched between ocean and green, churning forest
     the intellect appraises
objects surely, even the bare necessities   5
     of style are turned to use,
like those plain iron tools he salvages
     from shipwreck,[3] hewing a prose
as odorous as raw wood to the adze;[4]
     out of such timbers   10
came our first book, our profane Genesis[5]
     whose Adam speaks that prose
which, blessing some sea-rock, startles itself
     with poetry's surprise,
in a green world, one without metaphors;   15
     like Christofer[6] he bears
in speech mnemonic[7] as a missionary's
     the Word to savages,
its shape an earthen, water-bearing vessel's
     whose sprinkling alters us   20
into good Fridays[8] who recite His praise,
     parroting our master's
style and voice, we make his language ours,
     converted cannibals
we learn with him to eat the flesh of Christ[9]   25

All shapes, all objects multiplied from his,
     our ocean's Proteus,[1]
in childhood, his derelict's old age
     was like a god's. (Now pass
in memory, in serene parenthesis,   30
     the cliff-deep leeward coast
of my own island filing past the noise
     of stuttering canvas,[2]
some noon-struck village, Choiseul, Canaries,[3]
     crouched crocodile canoes,   35

---

1. The epigram from Daniel Defoe's (1660–1731) novel captures the Western frame of mind, a rational approach that establishes a rigorous separation between consciousness and the world of experience.   2. A route in Trinidad that leads to the house that Walcott is describing.   3. Apart from the reference to the Crusoe story, this is also a metaphor for the historical experience of slavery.   4. Sharp tool like a small ax used for carving wood.   5. The first book of the Judeo-Christian Bible containing the story of the world's creation and of Adam, the first man who was entrusted by God to name the objects of the world. 6. I.e., Christopher Columbus (1451–1506), acknowledged as the first European to encounter the New World.   7. Aiding memory.   8. Defoe's hero, Robinson Crusoe, gave the name Friday to the indigenous man he captured and made his manservant on the island. Note the punning allusion to the Christian observation of the Crucifixion of Christ.   9. In the Catholic doctrine of transubstantiation, the bread eaten at the Sacrament of Communion was deemed to be the body of Christ.   1. The Greek sea god who had the power of changing into various forms.   2. The Caribbean landscape envisioned as a work of art.   3. Villages in St. Lucia.

a savage settlement from Henty's novels,
    Marryat or R.L.S.[4]
with one boy signalling at the sea's edge,
    though what he cried is lost.)
So time, that makes us objects, multiplies   40
    our natural loneliness.

For the hermetic skill,[5] that from earth's clays
    shapes something without use,
and, separate from itself, lives somewhere else,[6]
    sharing with every beach   45
a longing for those gulls that cloud the cays[7]
    with raw, mimetic cries,
never surrenders wholly, for it knows
    it needs another's praise
like hoar, half-cracked Ben Gunn,[8] until it cries   50
    at last, "O happy desert!"
and learns again the self-creating peace
    of islands. So from this house
that faces nothing but the sea, his journals
    assume a household use;   55
we learn to shape from them, where nothing was
    the language of a race,[9]
and since the intellect demands its mask
    that sun-cracked, bearded face[1]
provides us with the wish to dramatize   60
    ourselves at nature's cost,
to attempt a beard, to squint through the sea-haze,
    posing as naturalists,
drunks, castaways, beachcombers, all of us
    yearn for those fantasies   65
of innocence,[2] for our faith's arrested phase
    when the clear voice
startled itself saying "water, heaven, Christ,"
    hoarding such heresies[3] as
God's loneliness moves in His smallest creatures.   70

---

4. The works of the writers *Henty, Marryat,* and *R.L.S.* were staples of colonial education throughout the former British empire. George Alfred Henty (1832–1902) was a prolific writer of children's stories; Captain Frederick Marryat (1792–1848) was an officer of the British navy who wrote a series of sea novels, of which the best known is *Mr Midshipman Easy;* Robert Louis Stevenson (1850–1894) is renowned for his classic novel of adventure *Treasure Island.*   5. Poetry, which is sometimes regarded as a form of prophecy or divination. As an art form, it has no practical purpose ("without use") since its aesthetic significance is an end in itself.   6. In another dimension.   7. Inlets into the sea.   8. A character in R. L. Stevenson's *Treasure Island.* He had been marooned on the island and was found by the party of treasure seekers. 9. Like Crusoe, the inhabitants of the Caribbean have created a new culture out of the debris of their historical experience.   1. The physical outward aspect expressive of an inward attitude of stern resolution.   2. As of Eden, of new beginnings.   3. The pantheism given expression in the final line.

Verandah

[for Ronald Bryden][1]

Grey apparitions[2] at verandah ends
like smoke,[3] divisible, but one
your age is ashes, its coherence gone,

Planters[4] whose tears were marketable gum,[5] whose voices
scratch the twilight like dried fronds   5
edged with reflection,

Colonels, hard as the commonwealth's greenheart,
middlemen, usurers whose art
kept an empire in the red,[6]

Upholders of Victoria's china seas[7]
lapping embossed around a drinking mug,   10
bully-boy roarers[8] of the empire club,

To the tarantara of the bugler, the sunset furled
round the last post,
the "flamingo colours"[9] of a fading world,

A ghost steps from you, my grandfather's ghost![1]
Uprooted from some rainy English shire,   15
you sought your Roman

End in suicide by fire.[2]
Your mixed son gathered your charred blackened bones
in a child's coffin.

And buried them himself on a strange coast.   20
Sire,
why do I raise you up? Because

Your house has voices, your burnt house
shrills with unguessed, lovely inheritors,[3]
your genealogical roof tree, fallen, survives,   25
like seasoned timber through green, little lives.

---

1. As literary editor of the Royal Shakespeare Company, he commissioned Walcott's *The Joker of Seville*.
2. Ghosts of the imperial past.   3. Insubstantial.   4. The term for white settlers in the West Indies
who owned sugar plantations worked by slaves.   5. A pun on "medicinible gum" from Shakespeare's
Othello, 5.2.360.   6. An allusion to the violent repression of colonized populations by the various imperial
agents mentioned in the stanza.   7. Possibly an allusion to the attempt by the British to annex China
and to the Opium Wars of 1839–1842 that resulted. *Victoria*: queen of England from 1837 to 1901.
8. Pun on bullroarers, indigenous instruments that make a frightening sound.   9. The pageantry of
empire exemplified by the ceremonial lowering of the flag at sunset to the sound of the bugle, a ritual that,
ironically, anticipates the decline of empire ("fading world").   1. The poet is of English ancestry on his
father's side.   2. In contrast to the Roman habit of falling on one's sword.   3. The black and mulatto
children are the unlikely continuators of the white grandfather's ancestral line, which they rejuvenate
("green, little lives," line 26).

I ripen towards your twilight, sir, that dream
where I am singed in that sea-crossing, steam
towards that vaporous world, whose souls,

Like pressured trees, brought diamonds out of coals.[4]   30
The sparks pitched from your burning house are stars.
I am the man my father loved and was.

I climb the stair
and stretch a darkening hand to greet those friends[5]
who share with you the last inheritance   35
of earth, our shrine and pardoner,

grey, ghostly loungers at verandah ends.

Elegy[1]

Our hammock swung between Americas,[2]
we miss you, Liberty. Che's
bullet-riddled body falls,[3]
and those who cried, the Republic must first die
to be reborn, are dead,   5
the freeborn citizen's ballot in the head.[4]
Still, everybody wants to go to bed
with Miss America.[5] And, if there's no bread,
let them eat cherry pie,[6]

But the old choice of running, howling, wounded   10
wolf-deep in her woods,
while the white papers snow on
genocide is gone;
no face can hide
its public, private pain,   15
wincing, already statued.[7]

Some splintered arrowhead lodged in her brain
sets the black singer howling in his bear trap,

4. Of the same chemical composition and evolving into diamonds under intense pressure over time.
5. Portraits of those who have passed away and now form part of the general life of the earth ("our shrine,"
line 36).   1. Since the date of composition at the end of the poem indicates that it was written shortly
after the assassination of Robert Kennedy in 1968, the poem can be taken as an elegy to him, even though
he is not mentioned in it.   2. A reference to the Caribbean, which is between North and South America.
3. Ernesto (Che) Guevara (1928–1967) was a companion of Fidel Castro who was killed by government
forces in Colombia, where he had gone to lead a revolutionary movement.   4. The bullet rather than the
ballot as a political weapon; a commentary on the peculiar strain of violence in American life.   5. The
winner of the popular annual beauty pageant, she is considered the ideal American beauty. Walcott uses
the pageant as a symbol of popular culture in the United States.   6. Ironic echo, in pointedly American
terms, of the French queen Marie Antoinette's celebrated phrase "Let them eat cake" in response to the
clamor that arose from the populace for bread during the French Revolution. The expression has since
been taken as a reflection of the insensitiveness of the privileged to the plight of the poor.   7. Open to
public gaze.

shines young eyes with the brightness of the mad,
tires the old with her residual sadness;   20
and yearly lilacs in her dooryards bloom,⁹
and the cherry orchard's surf
blinds Washington¹ and whispers
to the assassin in his furnished room²
of an ideal America, whose flickering screens   25
show, in slow herds, the ghosts of the Cheyennes³
scuffling across the staked and wired plains
with whispering, rag-bound feet,

while the farm couple framed in their Gothic door⁴
like Calvin's saints,⁵ waspish, pragmatic, poor,   30
gripping the devil's pitchfork
stare rigidly towards the immortal wheat.

6 June 1968

The Sea Is History

Where are your monuments, your battles, martyrs?
Where is your tribal memory? Sirs,
in that gray vault. The sea. The sea
has locked them up. The sea is History.

First, there was the heaving oil,   5
heavy as chaos;
then, like a light at the end of a tunnel,

the lantern of a caravel,
and that was Genesis.
Then there were the packed cries,   10
the shit, the moaning:

Exodus.¹
Bone soldered by coral to bone,
mosaics
mantled by the benediction of the shark's shadow,   15

9. An allusion to the opening lines of the famous elegy by Walt Whitman (1819–1892) to U.S. president Abraham Lincoln (1809–1865), assassinated shortly after the end of the Civil War. 1. A reference to the white flowers of the cherry orchards in Washington, D.C., which burst into bloom early in the spring. 2. Suggesting the assassin is untroubled by his crime. 3. A Native American nation that was forced to migrate from Minnesota to the Platte River. 4. A reference to *American Gothic* (1930), a painting by Iowa Regionalist Grant Wood (1892–1942) that shows in sharp, cold detail a severe-looking farm couple standing in front of their barn, she looking slightly sideways at him, he looking directly at the viewer. 5. Puritans, followers of John Calvin (1509–1564), the Protestant reformer whose doctrine of predestination is considered by other Christian sects too rigid and dogmatic. The passage relies for its meaning on this view of the doctrine. 1. Into exile in the New World, as opposed to the exodus of the Jews, under the leadership of Moses, out of bondage in Egypt.

that was the Ark of the Covenant.[2]
Then came from the plucked wires
of sunlight on the sea floor

the plangent[3] harps of the Babylonian bondage,[4]
as the white cowries[5] clustered like manacles   20
on the drowned women,

and those were the ivory bracelets
of the Song of Solomon,[6]
but the ocean kept turning blank pages

looking for History.   25
Then came the men with eyes heavy as anchors
who sank without tombs,

brigands who barbecued cattle,
leaving their charred ribs like palm leaves on the shore,
then the foaming, rabid maw   30

of the tidal wave swallowing Port Royal,[7]
and that was Jonah,[8]
but where is your Renaissance?

Sir, it is locked in them sea sands
out there past the reef's moiling shelf,[9]   35
where the men-o'-war floated down;

strop[1] on these goggles, I'll guide you there myself.
It's all subtle and submarine,
through colonnades of coral,

past the gothic windows of sea fans   40
to where the crusty grouper,[2] onyx[3]-eyed,
blinks, weighted by its jewels, like a bald queen;

and these groined caves with barnacles
pitted like stone
are our cathedrals,   45

and the furnace before the hurricanes:
Gomorrah.[4] Bones ground by windmills
into marl[5] and cornmeal,

2. Noah, whose ark survived the Flood, was given the rainbow as a sign of assurance that the earth would never again be destroyed by water.   3. Pouring out in waves of sound.   4. Which occurred between the fall of Jerusalem in 586 B.C. and the restoration of worship there by the decree of Cyrus the Great in 538 B.C.   5. Seashells that used to serve as currency in pre-colonial West Africa. They were also used in divination.   6. A book in the Old Testament that is a collection of love poems; it is generally thought to be an allegory of God's love for Israel.   7. The former capital of Jamaica, destroyed in 1692 by an earthquake, during which most of the city sank into the sea.   8. In the Old Testament, the man who lived in the belly of a whale for three days and nights before being disgorged alive.   9. *Shelf* here suggests the continental shelf, the relatively shallow stretch of coastal land ending in a sharp dip to the deep seabed. *Moiling:* turbulent.   1. Strap (dialect).   2. A species of fish.   3. A highly valued gem, usually jet black.   4. A city often associated with Sodom, both synonymous with sin.   5. Finely ground sand.

and that was Lamentations[6]—
that was just Lamentations,   50
it was not History;

then came, like scum on the river's drying lip,
the brown reeds of villages
mantling[7] and congealing into towns,

and at evening, the midges[8] choirs,   55
and above them, the spires
lancing the side of God[9]

as His son set, and that was the New Testament.

Then came the white sisters clapping
to the waves' progress,   60
and that was Emancipation[1]—

jubilation, O jubilation—
vanishing swiftly
as the sea's lace dries in the sun,

but that was not History,   65
that was only faith,
and then each rock broke into its own nation;[2]

then came the synod of flies,
then came the secretarial heron,
then came the bullfrog bellowing for a vote,   70

fireflies with bright ideas
and bats like jetting ambassadors
and the mantis,[3] like khaki police,

and the furred caterpillars of judges[4]
examining each case closely,   75
and then in the dark ears of ferns

and in the salt chuckle of rocks
with their sea pools, there was the sound
like a rumor without any echo

of History, really beginning.   80

---

6. Songs in the Old Testament by the prophet Jeremiah, lamenting the fall of Jerusalem.   7. A reference to Shakespeare's *The Tempest*, where *mantling* apparently describes the scummy covering of the shore.
8. Small insects, chirping in chorus.   9. An allusion to the Roman soldier's piercing the side of the
crucified Jesus to ascertain whether he was dead or not (see "His son set" in the following line).
1. Which, in the British West Indies, occurred in 1834.   2. A reference to the breakup of the West
Indian Federation in 1962. The next two stanzas describe the ensuing confusion in the political life of the
West Indies.   3. The characteristic posture of the praying mantis is generally interpreted as a demonstration of hypocrisy.   4. A reference to the dress of judges in formal sessions.

North and South

Now, at the rising of Venus[1]—the steady star
that survives translation, if one can call this lamp
the planet that pierces us over indigo islands—
despite the critical sand flies, I accept my function
as a colonial upstart at the end of an empire,   5
a single, circling, homeless satellite.
I can listen to its guttural death rattle in the shoal
of the legions' withdrawing roar, from the raj,[2]
from the Reich,[3] and see the full moon again
like a white flag rising over Fort Charlotte,[4]   10
and sunset slowly collapsing like the flag.[5]

It's good that everything's gone, except their language,[6]
which is everything. And it may be a childish revenge
at the presumption of empires to hear the worm
gnawing their solemn columns into coral,   15
to snorkel over Atlantis,[7] to see, through a mask,
Sidon up to its windows in sand, Tyre, Alexandria,[8]
with their wavering seaweed spires through a glass-bottom boat,
and to buy porous fragments of the Parthenon[9]
from a fisherman in Tobago,[1] but the fear exists,   20
Delenda est Carthago[2] on the rose horizon,[3]

and the side streets of Manhattan are sown with salt,[4]
as those in the North all wait for that white glare
of the white rose of inferno,[5] all the world's capitals.
Here, in Manhattan, I lead a tight life   25
and a cold one, my soles stiffen with ice
even through woollen socks; in the fenced back yard,
trees with clenched teeth endure the wind of February,
and I have some friends under its iron ground.
Even when spring comes with its rain of nails,   30
with its soiled ice oozing into black puddles,
the world will be one season older but no wiser.

Fragments of paper swirl round the bronze general
of Sheridan Square,[6] syllables of Nordic tongues
(as an Obeah priestess[7] sprinkles flour on the doorstep   35

---

1. The morning star, the brightest in the solar system.   2. Term for British rule in India.   3. German word for "empire," associated with Adolf Hitler's Third Reich and his ambition to found a 2,000-year rule of the German people over the rest of the world.   4. On the West Indian island of St. Vincent.   5. The flag is lowered at sunset.   6. I.e., English, valued by the poet as a positive inheritance of British colonial rule.   7. In Greek mythology, a fabled island situated in the Atlantic Ocean off the southwestern coast of Spain.   8. *Sidon, Tyre,* and *Alexandria* were great centers of ancient civilization.   9. The temple of Athena built in the fifth century B.C. on the summit of the Acropolis in Athens.   1. An English-speaking Caribbean island federated with Trinidad, just to its north.   2. "Carthage must be destroyed," words attributed to the Roman Senator Marcus Porcius Cato (234–149 B.C.), who was so obsessed with the threat of this African state to Rome that he used the phrase to conclude every speech he gave in the Roman Senate.   3. Homeric epithet for dawn.   4. The salt is used to melt the snow in winter, but there is a suggestion of sterility.   5. A species of the begonia flower that comes into full bloom in the spring.   6. The statue of General Philip Sheridan in Christopher Park, in Greenwich Village, New York, not far from the square named after him. Sheridan (1831–1888) was a Union general during the Civil War (see line 41) and later became commander in chief of the U.S. Army.   7. African-derived religion in the West Indies.

to ward off evil, so Carthage was sown with salt);
the flakes are falling like a common language
on my nose and lips, and rime forms on the mouth
of a shivering exile from his African province;
a blizzard of moths whirls around the extinguished lamp   40
of the Union general, sugary insects crunched underfoot.

You move along dark afternoons where death
entered a taxi and sat next to a friend,
or passed another a razor, or whispered "Pardon"
in a check-clothed restaurant behind her cough—   45
I am thinking of an exile farther than any country.
And, in this heart of darkness,[8] I cannot believe
they are now talking over palings by the doddering
banana fences,[9] or that seas can be warm.

How far I am from those cacophonous seaports   50
built round the single exclamation of one statue
of Victoria Regina![1] There vultures shift on the roof
of the red iron market, whose patois[2]
is brittle as slate, a gray stone flecked with quartz.
I prefer the salt freshness of that ignorance,   55
as language crusts and blackens on the pots
of this cooked culture, coming from a raw one;
and these days in bookstores I stand paralyzed

by the rows of shelves along whose wooden branches
the free-verse nightingales are trilling "Read me! Read me!"   60
in various metres of asthmatic pain;
or I shiver before the bellowing behemoths
with the snow still falling in white words on Eighth Street,
those burly minds that barrelled through contradictions
like a boar through bracken, or an old tarpon[3]   65
bristling with broken hooks, or an old stag
spanielled[4] by critics to a crag at twilight,

the exclamation of its antlers like a hat rack
on which they hang their theses. I am tired of words,
and literature is an old couch stuffed with fleas,   70
of culture stuffed in the taxidermist's hides.
I think of Europe as a gutter of autumn leaves
choked like the thoughts in an old woman's throat.
But she was home to some consul in snow-white ducks[5]
doing out his service in the African provinces,   75
who wrote letters like this one home and feared malaria
as I mistrust the dark snow, who saw the lances of rain

---

8. An image of Africa used in Joseph Conrad's novel of the same name. It implies alienation in a foreign land and applies here to the poet's despondent mood in New York in winter.   9. These separate the homesteads in the poet's native island. He feels so removed from its human atmosphere and landscape— its warmth—that it now seems to him unimaginable.   1. Queen Victoria, proclaimed empress of India in 1877, came to embody the British empire during her long reign.   2. A French term for a local dialect. It refers here to the form of French pidgin spoken in St. Lucia.   3. A large fish found in the warm waters of the Caribbean. Since it is difficult to catch, it is considered a rare prize among game fishermen and -women.   4. The critics are like spaniels, fawning and obsequious.   5. Trousers of light white flannel worn by colonial officers in the tropics.

marching like a Roman legion over the fens.
So, once again, when life has turned into exile,
and nothing consoles, not books, work, music, or a woman,   80
and I am tired of trampling the brown grass,
whose name I don't know, down an alley of stone,
and I must turn back to the road, its winter traffic,
and others sure in the dark of their direction,
I lie under a blanket on a cold couch,   85
feeling the flu in my bones like a lantern.

Under the blue sky of winter in Virginia
the brick chimneys flute white smoke through skeletal lindens,[6]
as a spaniel churns up a pyre of blood-rusted leaves;[7]
there is no memorial here to their Treblinka[8]—   90
as a van delivers from the ovens loaves
as warm as flesh, its brakes jaggedly screech
like the square wheel of a swastika.[9] The mania
of history veils even the clearest air,
the sickly-sweet taste of ash, of something burning.   95

And when one encounters the slow coil of an accent,[1]
reflexes step aside as if for a snake,
with the paranoid anxiety of the victim.
The ghosts of white-robed horsemen[2] float through the trees,
the galloping hysterical abhorrence of my race—   100
like any child of the Diaspora,[3] I remember this
even as the flakes whiten Sheridan's shoulders,
and I remember once looking at my aunt's face,
the wintry blue eyes, the rusty hair, and thinking

maybe we are part Jewish, and felt a vein   105
run through this earth and clench itself like a fist
around an ancient root, and wanted the privilege
to be yet another of the races they fear and hate
instead of one of the haters and the afraid.
Above the spiny woods, dun[4] grass, skeletal trees,   110
the chimney serenely fluting something from Schubert[5]—
like the wraith of smoke that comes from someone burning—
veins the air with an outcry that I cannot help.

The winter branches are mined with buds,
the fields of March will detonate the crocus,[6]   115
the olive[7] battalions of the summer woods

---

6. Also known as basswood, this tree has romantic associations.   7. Note the grim associations of the imagery.   8. A Nazi concentration camp in Poland where many people—especially Jews—perished. The five lines that follow develop the theme of the Holocaust introduced by this reference.   9. Symbol of the Nazis in the form of a Greek cross, the end of its arms extended at right angles all going in the same direction.   1. That is, the Southern accent, which sets off a cautious reflex in the poet due to its association with hatred for black people.   2. Members of the Ku Klux Klan. They would terrorize black people by, among other things, lynching them by hanging them on trees.   3. An ethnic or national community separated from its original homeland.   4. Light brown in color.   5. Franz Schubert (1797–1828) was a German Romantic composer. Overseers at the Nazi death camps often played classical music while Jews were gassed and their bodies cremated.   6. The crocus puts out its white flowers in late winter and very early spring.   7. Here, a reference to the olive drab uniforms worn by the U.S. Army.

will shout orders back to the wind. To the soldier's mind
the season's passage round the pole is martial,
the massacres of autumn sheeted in snow, as
winter turns white as a veterans hospital.   120
Something quivers in the blood beyond control—
something deeper than our transient fevers.

But in Virginia's woods there is also an old man
dressed like a tramp in an old Union greatcoat,
walking to the music of rustling leaves, and when   125
I collect my change from a small-town pharmacy,
the cashier's fingertips still wince from my hand
as if it would singe hers—well, yes, *je suis un singe*,[8]
I am one of that tribe of frenetic or melancholy
primates who made your music[9] for many more moons   130
than all the silver quarters in the till.

Sea Cranes[1]

"Only in a world where there are cranes and horses,"
wrote Robert Graves,[2] "can poetry survive."
Or adept goats on crags. Epic
follows the plough, metre the ring of the anvil;
prophecy divines the figurations of storks,[3] and awe   5
the arc of the stallion's neck.[4]

The flame has left the charred wick of the cypress;
the light will catch these islands in their turn.[5]

Magnificent frigates inaugurate the dusk
that flashes through the whisking tails of horses,   10
the stony fields they graze.
From the hammered anvil of the promontory
the spray settles in stars.[6]

Generous ocean,[7] turn the wanderer
from his salt sheets, the prodigal   15
drawn to the deep troughs of the swine-black porpoise.[8]

Wrench his heart's wheel and set his forehead here.[9]

---

8. "I am a monkey" (French).   9. Of poetry, nobler than the ring of coins in the shopkeeper's till.
1. Tall wading birds with white plumage and long legs.   2. Graves (1895–1985), an English writer who
first gained attention as a poet, also wrote an autobiography, nonfiction, essays, and a series of historical
novels based in antiquity. He is the author of the two-volume *The Greek Myths*, in which he not only retells
the tales of the Greek gods and heroes, but reinterprets them.   3. Ancient diviners claimed to be able
to read the future from the entrails of birds.   4. Apart from its beauty, the stallion is a symbol of elemental
force.   5. The islands destined for glory.   6. The sea spray linking earth and sky.   7. In the sense
of being large, copious, and bountiful.   8. A small, gregarious toothed whale with black skin and white
underbelly.   9. That is, facing homeward.

OMEROS

From Book One

From Chapter I

II

Achille looked up at the hole[1] the laurel had left.
He saw the hole silently healing with the foam
of a cloud like a breaker. Then he saw the swift[2]

crossing the cloud-surf, a small thing, far from its home,
confused by the waves of blue hills. A thorn vine gripped   5
his heel. He tugged it free. Around him, other ships

were shaping from the saw. With his cutlass he made
a swift sign of the cross, his thumb touching his lips
while the height rang with axes. He swayed back the blade,

and hacked the limbs from the dead god,[3] knot after knot,   10
wrenching the severed veins from the trunk as he prayed:
"Tree! You can be a canoe! Or else you cannot!"

The bearded elders endured the decimation
of their tribe without uttering a syllable
of the language they had uttered as one nation,[4]   15

the speech taught their saplings: from the towering babble
of the cedar to green vowels of *bois-campêche*.
The *bois-flot* held its tongue with the *laurier-cannelle*,[5]

the red-skinned logwood endured the thorns in its flesh,
while the Aruacs' patois[6] crackled in the smell   20
of a resinous bonfire that turned the leaves brown

with curling tongues, then ash, and their language was lost.
Like barbarians striding columns they have brought down,
the fishermen shouted. The gods were down at last.

Like pygmies they hacked the trunks of wrinkled giants   25
for paddles and oars. They were working with the same
concentration as an army of fire-ants.[7]

But vexed by the smoke for defaming their forest,
blow-darts of mosquitoes kept needling Achille's trunk.
He frotted white rum on both forearms that, at least,   30

---

1. The opening stanza describes the ritual felling of a laurel tree from which a dugout canoe is to be made. This refers to the hole in the ground where the tree had stood. The section that follows describes the making of the canoe.   2. A small, plainly colored bird, related to the swallow, that serves as a guide to the wandering hero.   3. The laurel tree, venerated as nature.   4. The flora as part of the total living environment.   5. *Bois-campêche, bois-flot, laurier-cannelle:* French for logwood, timber, and laurel, respectively.   6. Dialect. *Aruacs:* the original inhabitants of the Caribbean; also Arawaks.   7. Omnivorous ants with powerful stingers in their tails.

those that he flattened to asterisks would die drunk.
They went for his eyes. They circled them with attacks
that made him weep blindly. Then the host retreated

to high bamboo like the archers of Aruacs
running from the muskets of cracking logs,[8] routed   35
by the fire's banner and the remorseless axe

hacking the branches. The men bound the big logs first
with new hemp[9] and, like ants, trundled them to a cliff
to plunge through tall nettles.[1] The logs gathered that thirst

for the sea which their own vined bodies were born with.   40
Now the trunks in eagerness to become canoes
ploughed into breakers of bushes, making raw holes

of boulders, feeling not death inside them, but use—
to roof the sea, to be hulls. Then, on the beach, coals[2]
were set in their hollows that were chipped with an adze.   45

A flat-bed truck had carried their rope-bound bodies.
The charcoals, smouldering, cored the dugouts for days
till heat widened the wood enough for ribbed gunwales.[3]

Under his tapping chisel Achille felt their hollows
exhaling to touch the sea, lunging towards the haze   50
of bird-printed islets, the beaks of their parted bows.

Then everything fit. The pirogues[4] crouched on the sand
like hounds with sprigs in their teeth. The priest
sprinkled them with a bell, then he made the swift's sign.[5]

When he smiled at Achille's canoe, *In God We Troust*,[6]   55
Achille said: "Leave it! Is God' spelling and mine."
After Mass one sunrise the canoes entered the troughs[7]

of the surpliced[8] shallows, and their nodding prows
agreed with the waves to forget their lives as trees;
one would serve Hector and another, Achilles.   60

From *Chapter VIII*

I

In the islet's museum there is a twisted
wine-bottle, crusted with fool's gold[1] from the iron-
cold depth below the redoubt. It has been listed

8. Log houses from which white men shot at the Aruacs.   9. The vine is excellent for making ropes.
1. A plant that stings.   2. They are used to fire the hollowed-out logs.   3. That is, the heat expanded
the wood so that metal strips could be inserted to reinforce the sides of the boat.   4. French for dugout
canoes.   5. The swift's wings are shaped like a cross.   6. The boat's name. The phrase "In God We
Troust" is found on American money.   7. Sea channels.   8. The canoes make a lacelike pattern on the
water, resembling the surplice worn by Catholic priests at Mass.   1. Pyrite or, by extension, any pyritic
material that resembles gold.

variously by experts; one, that a galleon
blown by a hurricane out of Cartagena,[2]   5
this far east, had bled a trail of gold bullion

and wine from its hold (a view held by many a
diver lowering himself); the other was nonsense
and far too simple: that the gold-crusted bottle

came from a flagship in the Battle of the Saints,[3]   10
but the glass was so crusted it was hard to tell.
Still, the myth widened its rings every century:[4]

that the *Ville de Paris*[5] sank there, not a galleon
crammed with imperial coin, and for her sentry,
an octopus-cyclops,[6] its one eye like the moon.   15

Deep as a diver's faith but never discovered,
their trust in the relic converted the village,
who came to believe that circling frigates hovered

over the relic, that gulls attacked them in rage.
They kept their faith when the experts' ended in doubt.   20
The galleon's shadow rode over the ruled page

where Achille, rough weather coming, counted his debt
by the wick of his kerosene lamp; the dark ship
divided his dreams, while the moon's octopus eye

climbed from the palms that lifted their tentacles' shape.   25
It glared like a shilling.[7] Everything was money.
Money will change her, he thought. Is this bad living

that make her come wicked. He had mocked the belief
in a wrecked ship out there. Now he began diving
in a small shallop[8] beyond the line of the reef,   30

with spear-gun[9] and lobster-pot.[1] He had to make sure
no sail would surprise him, feathering the oars back
without clicking the oarlocks. He fed the anchor

carefully overside. He tied the cinder-block
to one heel with a slip-knot[2] for faster descent,   35
then slipped the waterproof bag around his shoulders

---

2. I.e., Cartagena, a seaport on the northwest coast of Colombia.   3. Naval battle fought off the coast of Martinique on April 12, 1782, between the French fleet commanded by Admiral de Grasset and a British fleet under Admiral Sir George Bridges Rodney. The French were routed, their fleet annihilated.   4. Like rings on a tree as it ages.   5. The flagship of the French fleet.   6. Here Walcott conflates an octopus— a mollusk that has eight arms, each with two rows of suckers—with Greek mythology's Cyclops, a one-eyed giant who, in Homer's *Odyssey*, holds Odysseus and his men captive until they escape by blinding him. 7. An English coin worth one-twentieth of a pound. Its use was discontinued when Britain adopted the decimal currency in 1969.   8. A small boat (from French *chaloupe*).   9. A gun that has a forked end on which fish are speared.   1. A basket for trapping lobsters.   2. A knot that moves along the rope on which it is tied.

for a money-pouch. She go get every red cent,
he swore, crossing himself as he dived. Wedged in boulders
down there was salvation and change. The concrete, tied

to his heel, pulled him down faster than a lead-   40
weighted, canvas-bound carcass, the stone heart inside
his chest added its poundage. What if love was dead

inside her already? What good lay in pouring
silver coins on a belly that had warmed him once?
This weighed him down even more, so he kept falling   45

for fathoms towards his fortune: moidores, doubloons,[3]
while the slow-curling fingers of weeds kept calling;
he felt the cold of the drowned entering his loins.

II

Why was he down here, from their coral palaces.
pope-headed turtles asked him, waving their paddles[4]   50
crusted with rings, nudged by curious porpoises

with black friendly skins. Why? asked the glass sea-horses,[5]
curling like questions. What on earth had he come for,
when he had a good life up there? The sea-mosses[6]

shook their beards angrily, like submarine cedars,   55
while he trod the dark water. Wasn't love worth more
than the coins of light pouring from the galleon's doors?

In the corals' bone kingdom his skin calcifies.[7]
In that wavering garden huge fans on hinges
swayed, while fingers of seaweed pocketed the eyes[8]   60

of coins with the profiles of Iberian kings;[9]
here the sea-floor was mud, not corrugating sand
that showed you its ribs; here, the mutating fishes

had goggling eye-bulbs; in that world without sound,
they sucked the white coral, draining it like leeches,   65
and what looked like boulders sprung the pincers of crabs.

This was not a world meant for the living, he thought.
The dead didn't need money, like him, but perhaps
they hated surrendering things their hands had brought.

The shreds of the ocean's floor passed him from corpses   70
that had perished in the crossing, their hair like weeds,
their bones were long coral fingers, bubbles of eyes

---

3. These are Portuguese and Spanish gold coins, respectively.   4. The turtles propel themselves using their flippers as paddles.   5. Small bony fishes that have a horse-shaped head and the body of a fish with a curved tail (hence "curling like questions").   6. Any of certain frondlike red algae that look like moss (and hence "shook their beards").   7. Hardens.   8. Here, covered completely.   9. Relating to Iberia, the peninsula made up of Spain and Portugal.

watched him, a brain-coral[1] gurgled their words,
and every bubble englobed a biography,
no less than the wine-bottle's mouth, but for Achille,   75

treading the mulch floor of the Caribbean Sea,
no coins were enough to repay its deep evil.
The ransom of centuries shone through the mossy doors

that the moon-blind Cyclops counted, every tendril
raked in the guineas[2] it tested with its soft jaws.   80
Light paved the ceiling with silver with every swell.

Then he saw the galleon. Her swaying cabin-doors
fanned vaults of silvery mackerel. He caught the glint
of their coin-packed scales,[3] then the tentacle-shadows

whose motion was a miser's harvesting his mint.   85
He loosened the block[4] and shot up. Next day, her stealth
increased, her tentacles calling, until the wreck

vanished with all hope of Helen. Once more the whelk[5]
was his coin, his bank the sea-conch's.[6] Now, every day
he was clear-headed as the sea, wrenching lace fans   90

from the forbidden reef, or tailing a sting-ray[7]
floating like a crucifix when it sensed his lance,
and saving the conch-shells he himself had drowned.

And though he lost faith[8] in any fictional ship,
an anchor still forked his brow whenever he frowned,   95
for she was a spectre now, in her ribbed shape,

he did not know where she was. She'd never be found.
He thought of the white skulls rolling out there like dice
rolled by the hand of the swell, their luck was like his;

he saw drowned Portuguese captains, their coral eyes   100
entered by minnows,[9] as he hauled the lobster-pot,
bearded with moss, in the cold shade of the redoubt.[1]

---

1. A reef coral with its surface covered by ridges and furrows.   2. English coins, supposedly struck from gold from the Guinea coast in West Africa.   3. The fishes' scales are like silver coins.   4. Concrete (referred to in lines 39–42).   5. A large marine snail with a spiral shell.   6. A large spiral-shelled marine mollusk. Its shell resonates when blown into; runaway slaves often sent messages to each other this way.   7. A ray with a flat body and whiplike tail with spines near its base capable of inflicting severe wounds.   8. See line 16, above.   9. Tiny fish.   1. A small, usually temporary fort.

From Book Three

Chapter XXV

I

Mangroves,[1] their ankles in water, walked with the canoe.
The swift, racing its browner shadow, screeched, then veered
into a dark inlet. It was the last sound Achille knew

from the other world. He feathered the paddle,[2] steered
away from the groping mangroves, whose muddy shelves   5
slipped warted crocodiles,[3] slitting the pods of their eyes;

then the horned river-horses[4] rolling over themselves
could capsize the keel. It was like the African movies
he had yelped at in childhood. The endless river unreeled

those images that flickered into real mirages: 10
naked mangroves walking beside him, knotted logs
wriggling into the water, the wet, yawning boulders

of oven-mouthed hippopotami. A skeletal[5] warrior
stood up straight in the stern and guided his shoulders,
clamped his neck in cold iron,[6] and altered the oar.   15

Achille wanted to scream, he wanted the brown water
to harden into a road, but the river widened ahead
and closed behind him. He heard screeching laughter

in a swaying tree, as monkeys swung from the rafter
of their tree-house, and the bared sound rotted the sky   20
like their teeth. For hours the river gave the same show

for nothing, the canoe's mouth muttered its lie.
The deepest terror was the mud. The mud with no shadow
like the clear sand. Then the river coiled into a bend.

He saw the first signs of men, tall sapling fishing-stakes;   25
he came into his own beginning and his end,
for the swiftness of a second is all that memory takes.

Now the strange, inimical river surrenders its stealth
to the sunlight. And a light inside him wakes,[7]   30
skipping centuries, ocean and river, and Time itself.

And God said to Achille, "Look, I giving you permission
to come home. Is I send the sea-swift as a pilot,
the swift whose wings is the sign of my crucifixion.

---

1. Tropical trees that grow in lagoons and waterways.   2. Turned the oar so that it was horizontal when lifted from the water at the end of a stroke. This reduces air resistance.   3. The skin of the crocodiles seems to be covered with hardened protuberances.   4. I.e., hippopotami.   5. Here, ghostly, which is appropriate to the character of the passage as a dream sequence.   6. Reminiscent of the chains with which slaves were bound.   7. I.e., awakens ancestral memory.

And thou shalt have no God should in case you forgot
my commandments." And Achille felt the homesick shame   35
and pain of his Africa. His heart and his bare head

were bursting as he tried to remember the name
of the river- and the tree-god in which he steered,
whose hollow body carried him to the settlement ahead.

II

He remembered this sunburnt river with its spindly
stakes and the peaked huts platformed above the spindles
where thin, naked figures as he rowed past looked unkindly

or kindly in their silence. The silence an old fence kindles
in a boy's heart. They walked with his homecoming
canoe past bonfires in a scorched clearing near the edge   45

of the soft-lipped shallows whose noise hurt his drumming
heart as the pirogue slid its raw, painted wedge
towards the crazed sticks of a vine-fastened pier.

The river was sloughing[8] its old skin like a snake
in wrinkling sunshine; the sun resumed its empire   50
over this branch of the Congo; the prow found its stake

in the river and nuzzled it the way that a piglet
finds its favourite dug[9] in the sweet-grunting sow,
and now each cheek ran with its own clear rivulet

of tears, as Achille, weeping, fastened the bow   55
of the dugout, wiped his eyes with one dry palm,
and felt a hard hand help him up the shaking pier.

Half of me was with him. One half with the midshipman
by a Dutch canal.[1] But now, neither was happier
or unhappier than the other. An old man put an arm   60

around Achille, and the crowd, chattering, followed both.
They touched his trousers, his undershirt, their hands
scrabbling[2] the texture, as a kitten does with cloth,

till they stood before an open hut. The sun stands
with expectant silence. The river stops talking,   65
the way silence sometimes suddenly turns off a market.

The wind squatted low in the grass. A man kept walking
steadily towards him, and he knew by that walk it
was himself in his father, the white teeth, the widening hands.

---

8. Shedding.   9. The nipple of a pig from which the young suck milk.   1. Spoken in the author's own
voice, this passage expresses the split in Walcott's heritage—half African, half Dutch.   2. Scraping.

III

He sought his own features in those of their life-giver,   70
and saw two worlds mirrored there: the hair was surf
curling round a sea-rock, the forehead a frowning river,

as they swirled in the estuary of a bewildered love,
and Time stood between them. The only interpreter
of their lips' joined babble, the river with the foam,   75

and the chuckles of water under the sticks of the pier,
where the tribe stood like sticks themselves, reversed
by reflection.[3] Then they walked up to the settlement,

and it seemed, as they chattered, everything was rehearsed
for ages before this. He could predict the intent   80
of his father's gestures; he was moving with the dead.

Women paused at their work, then smiled at the warrior
returning from his battle with smoke,[4] from the kingdom
where he had been captured, they cried and were happy.

Then the fishermen sat near a large tree under whose dome   85
stones sat in a circle. His father said:

        "Afo-la-be,"[5]
touching his own heart.
       "In the place you have come from

what do they call you?"
      Time translates.   90
          Tapping his chest,
the son answers:
     "Achille." The tribe rustles, "Achille."
Then, like cedars at sunrise, the mutterings settle.

     AFOLABE
Achille. What does the name mean? I have forgotten the one   95
that I gave you. But it was, it seems, many years ago.
What does it mean?

     ACHILLE
   Well, I too have forgotten.

Everything was forgotten. You also. I do not know.
The deaf sea has changed around every name that you gave   100
us; trees, men, we yearn for a sound that is missing.

     AFOLABE
A name means something.[6] The qualities desired in a son,
and even a girl-child; so even the shadows who called
you expected one virtue, since every name is a blessing,

---

3. Mirrored upside down in the river. 4. Of an ordeal, in the dim past. 5. A Yoruba name meaning "born with honor." 6. African names always have a meaning of great social significance.

since I am remembering the hope I had for you as a child.   105
Unless the sound means nothing. Then you would be nothing.
Did they think you were nothing in that other kingdom?[7]

ACHILLE

I do not know what the name means. It means something,
maybe. What's the difference? In the world I come from
we accept the sounds we were given. Men, trees, water.   110

AFOLABE

And therefore, Achille, if I pointed and I said, There
is the name of that man, that tree, and this father,
would every sound be a shadow that crossed your ear,

without the shape of a man or a tree? What would it be?
(And just as branches sway in the dusk from their fear   115
of amnesia,[8] of oblivion, the tribe began to grieve.)

ACHILLE

What would it be? I can only tell you what I believe,
or had to believe. It was prediction, and memory,
to bear myself back, to be carried here by a swift,

or the shadow of a swift making its cross on water,   120
with the same sign I was blessed with[9] with the gift
of this sound whose meaning I still do not care to know.

AFOLABE

No man loses his shadow except it is in the night,
and even then his shadow is hidden, not lost. At the glow
of sunrise, he stands on his own in that light.   125

When he walks down to the river with the other fishermen
his shadow stretches in the morning, and yawns, but you,
if you're content with not knowing what our names mean,

then I am not Afolabe, your father, and you look through
my body as the light looks through a leaf. I am not here   130
or a shadow. And you, nameless son, are only the ghost

of a name. Why did I never miss you until you returned?
Why haven't I missed you, my son, until you were lost?
Are you the smoke from a fire that never burned?

There was no answer to this, as in life.[1] Achille nodded,   135
the tears glazing his eyes, where the past was reflected
as well as the future. The white foam lowered its head.

---

7. I.e., the New World.   8. Loss of memory.   9. Baptized as a Christian, with possibly a pun on the
French *blessé*, "wounded."   1. Which is filled with unresolved questions.

From *Chapter XXVI*

I

In a language as brown[1] and leisurely as the river,
they muttered about a future Achille already knew
but which he could not reveal even to his breath-giver

or in the council of elders. But he learned to chew
in the ritual of the kola nut,[2] drain gourds of palm-wine,[3]   5
to listen to the moan of the tribe's triumphal sorrow

in a white-eyed storyteller[4] to a balaphon's whine,[5]
who perished in what battle, who was swift with the arrow,
who mated with a crocodile,[6] who entered a river-horse

and lived in its belly, who was the thunder's favourite,   10
who the serpent-god[7] conducted miles off his course
for some blasphemous offence and how he would pay for it

by forgetting his parents, his tribe, and his own spirit
for an albino god,[8] and how that warrior was scarred
for innumerable moons so badly that he would disinherit   15

himself. And every night the seed-eyed, tree-wrinkled[9] bard,
the crooked tree who carried the genealogical leaves[1]
of the tribe in his cave-throated moaning,

traced the interlacing branches of their river-rooted lives
as intricately as the mangrove roots. Until morning   20
he sang, till the river was the only one to hear it.

Achille did not go down to the fishing stakes one dawn,
but left the hut door open, the hut he had been given
for himself and any woman he chose as his companion,

and he climbed a track of huge yams, to find that heaven   25
of soaring trees, that sacred circle of clear ground
where the gods assembled. He stood in the clearing

and recited the gods' names. The trees within hearing
ignored his incantation. He heard only the cool sound
of the river. He saw a tree-hole, raw in the uprooted ground.[2]   30

*   *   *

---

1. Muddy, alluvial, and therefore fertile.   2. The bitter, caffeine-laden seed of the kola tree; it is chewed
on ceremonial occasions.   3. The natural sap of the tropical palm, which, when drawn, ferments and
becomes alcoholic.   4. The bard, or griot, whose function was to preserve the community's history (see
lines 16–20).   5. An African instrument with flat wooden keys like the xylophone that is played to accompany the griot's narrative.   6. In myths, heroes were often said to descend from mixed parentage of
humans and animals; in other instances, certain animals are held to be ancestors or relatives of members
of the tribe and thus function as their totem.   7. The cult of the serpent is central to many African
religions and to their derivatives in the New World.   8. Lacking in pigment, white, and therefore an
alien god.   9. Gaunt, like an old tree.   1. I.e., the leaves of the family tree.   2. See n. 1, p. 2968.

III

He walked the ribbed sand under the flat keels of whales,
under the translucent belly of the snaking current,
the tiny shadows of tankers passed over him like snails

as he breathed water, a walking fish in its element.   35
He floated in stride, his own shadow over his eyes
like a grazing shark, through vast meadows of coral,

over barnacled[3] cannons whose hulks sprouted anemones[4]
like Philoctete's shin; he walked for three hundred years
in the silken wake like a ribbon of the galleons,

their bubbles fading like the transparent men-o'-wars   40
with their lilac dangling tendrils, bursting like aeons,[5]
like phosphorous galaxies; he saw the huge cemeteries

of bone and the huge crossbows of the rusted anchors,
and groves of coral with hands as massive as trees
like calcified ferns and the greening gold ingots of bars   45

whose value had outlasted that of the privateers.[6]
Then, one afternoon, the ocean lowered and clarified
its ceiling, its emerald net, and after three centuries

of walking, he thought he could hear the distant quarrel
of breaker with shore; then his head broke clear,[7] and   50
his neck; then he could see his own shadow in the coral

grove, ribbed and rippling with light on the clear sand,
as his fins spread their toes, and he saw the leaf
of his own canoe far out, the life he had left behind

and the white line of surf around low Barrel of Beef[8]   55
with its dead lantern. The salt glare left him blind
for a minute, then the shoreline returned in relief.[9]

He woke to the sound of sunlight scratching at the door
of the hut, and he smelt not salt but the sluggish odour
of river. Fingers of light rethatched the roof's straw.   60

On the day of his feast they wore the same plantain trash
like Philoctete at Christmas. A bannered mitre[1]
of bamboo was placed on his head, a calabash

---

3. A barnacle is a type of marine crustacean with feathery appendages for gathering food; as adults, they affix themselves permanently to objects.   4. A reference to sea anemones, marine coelenterates whose form, bright colors, and clusters of tentacles resemble flowers.   5. Vast stretches of time.   6. Armed ships and their crew commissioned by governments to attack enemy ships on the open sea.   7. As he resurfaced.   8. A rocky site off the coast of St. Lucia, a prominent landmark on the island.   9. In the double sense of being sharply outlined and of bringing a sense of relief.   1. A ritual headress, but more usually applied to the liturgical headress worn by bishops and abbots.

mask, and skirts that made him both woman and fighter.
That was how they danced at home, to fifes and tambours,   65
the same berries round their necks and the small mirrors

flashing from their stuffed breasts. One of the warriors
mounted on stilts walked like lightning over the thatch
of the peaked village. Achille saw the same dances

that the mitred warriors did with their bamboo stick   70
as they scuttered around him, lifting, dipping their lances
like divining rods turning the earth to music,

the same chac-chac and ra-ra,[2] the drumming the same,
and the chant of the seed-eyed prophet to the same
response from the blurring ankles. The same, the same.[3]   75

From Book Four

From *Chapter XXXV*

I

"Somewhere over there," said my guide, "the Trail of Tears
started." I leant towards the crystalline creek. Pines
shaded it. Then I made myself hear the water's

language around the rocks in its clear-running lines
and its small shelving falls with their eddies, "Choctaws,"   5
"Creeks," "Choctaws,"[1] and I thought of the Greek revival

carried past the names of towns with columned porches,
and how Greek it was, the necessary evil
of slavery, in the catalogue of Georgia's

marble past, the Jeffersonian ideal[2] in   10
plantations with its Hectors and Achilleses,
its foam in the dogwood's spray, past towns named Helen,

Athens, Sparta, Troy. The slave shacks, the rolling peace
of the wave-rolling meadows, oak, pine, and pecan,
and a creek like this one. From the window I saw   15

the bundles of women moving in ragged bands
like those on the wharf,[3] headed for Oklahoma;
then I saw Seven Seas,[4] a rattle in his hands.

---

2. Dance forms in the Caribbean. *Ra-ra* is derived from a Yoruba genre of chanted poetry.   3. Walcott registers the protagonist's recognition of his cultural connection to Africa.   1. Native American nations expelled from their original homes and forced to march to reservations in Oklahoma (see line 17).   2. "Life, liberty and the pursuit of happiness," belied by the institution of slavery.   3. Captured Africans waiting to be shipped to America. This passage establishes a parallel between the fate of Native Americans and that of African slaves.   4. A blind poet and singer in St. Lucia who features prominently in Walcott's play *The Odyssey*, a stage adaptation of Homer's epic.

A huge thunderhead[5] was unclenching its bruised fist
over the county. Shadows escaped through the pines   20
and the pecan groves and hounds[6] were closing in fast

deep into Georgia, where history happens
to be the baying echoes of brutality,
and terror in the oaks along red country roads,

or the gibbet[7] branches of a silk-cotton tree   25
from which Afolabes hung like bats. Hooded clouds[8]
guarded the town squares with their calendar churches,

whose white, peaked belfries asserted that pastoral
of brooks with leisurely accents. On their verges,
like islands reflected on windscreens, Negro shacks   30

moved like a running wound, like the rusty anchor
that scabbed Philoctete's shin,[9] I imagined the backs
moving through the foam of pods, one arm for an oar,

one for the gunny sack.[1] Brown streams tinkled in chains.
Bridges arched their spines. Led into their green pasture,[2]   35
horses sagely grazed or galloped the plantations.

II

"Life is so fragile. It trembles like the aspens.[3]
All its shadows are seasonal, including pain.
In drizzling dusk the rain enters the lindens

with its white lances, then lindens enclose the rain.   40
So that day isn't far when they will say, 'Indians
bowed under those branches, which tribe is not certain.'

Nor am I certain I lived. I breathed what the farm
exhaled. Its soils, its seasons. The swayed goldenrod,
the corn where summer hid me, pollen on my arm,   45

sweat tickling my armpits. The Plains were fierce as God
and wide as His mind. I enjoyed diminishing,
I exalted in insignificance after

the alleys of Boston, in the unfinishing
chores of the farm, alone. Once, from the barn's rafter   50
a swift or a swallow shot out, taking with it

5. A large mass of dark cumulus clouds presaging a thunderstorm.   6. Dogs were used to recapture
runaway slaves, they were also set upon black protesters during the civil rights movement.   7. Gallows.
The reference here is to the lynching in the Deep South of blacks, usually by hanging.   8. The Ku Klux
Klan.   9. The companion of Achille in his Caribbean home and, like him, a fisherman.   1. A bag made
from coarse, heavy material.   2. Conveying an impression of blessed peace, but deceptive.   3. A type
of poplar tree whose leaves flutter in the slightest breeze. The speaker here is Catherine Weldon, a historical
figure that Walcott has woven into the poem.

my son's brown, whirring soul,[4] and I knew that its aim
was heaven. More and more we learn to do without
those we still love. With my father it was the same.

The bounty of God pursued me over the Plains   55
of the Dakotas, the pheasants, the quick-volleyed
arrows of finches; smoke bound me to the Indians

from morning to sunset when I have watched its veiled
rising, because I am a widow, barbarous
and sun-cured in the face, I loved them ever since   60

I worked as a hand in Colonel Cody's[5] circus,
under a great canvas larger than all their tents,
when they were paid to ride round in howling circles,

with a dime for their glory, and boys screamed in fright
at the galloping braves. Now the aspens encloseb   65
the lances of rain, and the wet leaves shake with light."

*   *   *

From Book Six

From *Chapter LII*

II

Provinces, Protectorates, Colonies, Dominions,
Governors-General, black Knights, ostrich-plumed[1] Viceroys,
deserts, jungles, hill-stations, all an empire's zones,

lay spilled from a small tea-chest; felt-footed houseboys
on fern-soft verandahs, hearty Toby-jugged[2] Chiefs   5
of Police, Girl-Guide Commissioners, Secretaries,

poppies on cenotaphs,[3] green-spined Remembrance wreaths,
cornets, kettledrums, gum-chewing dromedaries[4]
under Lawrence,[5] parasols, palm-striped pavilions,

dhows[6] and feluccas,[7] native-draped paddle-ferries   10
on tea-brown rivers, statue-rehearsing lions,
sandstorms seaming their eyes, horizontal monsoons,

---

4. Perhaps a reference to an aspect of Native American beliefs.   **5.** I.e., William F. Cody, also called
Buffalo Bill (1846–1917), who founded a circus and a traveling show that featured Native Americans in
various humiliating roles. "A dime for their glory" (line 64) is an ironic comment on this.   **1.** The ceremonial uniform of British colonial governors was topped by a cap with ostrich feathers.   **2.** A Toby jug
is a small vessel—a mug, for instance—shaped like a fat man wearing a cocked hat.   **3.** Flowers atop
tombs or monuments.   **4.** Camels, which constantly chew their cud.   **5.** A reference to T. E. Lawrence
(1888–1935), also known as Lawrence of Arabia, who served as liaison officer between the British forces
and Arab guerrillas fighting against Turkish rule during the First World War.   **6.** Arab sailboats.
7. Small, fast sailing vessels common to the Mediterranean. They are equipped with both masts and oars.

rank odour of a sea-chest, mimosa memories
touched by a finger, lead soldiers, clopping Dragoons.[8]
Breadfruit hands on a wall. The statues close their eyes.   15

Mosquito nets, palm-fronds, scrolled Royal Carriages,
dacoits,[9] gun-bearers,[1] snarling apes on Gibraltar,[2]
sermons to sweat-soaked kerchiefs, the Rock of Ages[3]

pumped by a Zouave[4] band, lilies light the altar,
soldiers and doxies[5] by a splashing esplanade,   20
waves turning their sheet music, the yellowing teeth

of the parlour piano, *Airs from Erin*[6] played
to the whistling kettle, and on the teapot's head
the cozy's bearskin shako,[7] biscuits break with grief,

gold-braid laburnums,[8] lilac whiff of lavender,
columned poplars marching to Mafeking's relief.[9]   25
Naughty seaside cards, the sepia surrender

of Gordon[1] on the mantel, the steps of Khartoum,
The World's Classics[2] condensed, Clive[3] as brown as India
bathers in Benares,[4] an empire in costume.

His will be done, O Maud, His kingdom come,   30
as the sunflower turns,[5] and the white eyes widen
in the ebony faces, the sloe-eyes, the bent smoke

where a pig totters across a village midden[6]
over the sunset's shambles, Rangoon to Malta,[7]
the regimental button of the evening star.   35

Solace of laudanum, menstrual cramps, the runnings,
tinkles in the jordan, at dusk the zebra shade
of louvres on the quilt, the maps spread their warnings

and the tribal odour of the second chambermaid.
And every fortnight, ten sharp on Sunday mornings,   40
shouts and wheeling patterns from our Cadet Brigade.[8]

---

8. Heavily armed cavalry unit.   9. A gang of robbers of (Hindi).   1. Armored vehicles.   2. A reference to the Barbary macaques that live in Gibraltar, a British enclave at the southern tip of Spain, long a tourist attraction.   3. A well-known Judeo-Christian hymn.   4. The Zouaves were Algerian infantry units in the French and American Confederate armies.   5. Prostitutes.   6. Ireland.   7. The tea cozy, a cushioned cover draped over a teapot to keep the contents warm, resembles a *shako*, a stiff military hat with a high crown, in this case made from bearskin.   8. A shrub with bright yellow flowers (i.e., "gold-braid").   9. A town in South Africa relieved by British forces after a long siege by Afrikaners during the Boer War.   1. Charles Gordon (1833–1885), British governor-general in the Sudan who was killed on the steps of his residence at Khartoum during an uprising by the local population.   2. A famous collection of great literature published by Oxford University Press.   3. Robert Clive (1725–1774), an agent of the East India Company considered to have secured India for the British by thwarting the French and by defeating the local Bengali ruler at the Battle of Plassey in 1757.   4. Holy Hindu city situated on the northern bank of the Ganges in India and associated with Buddha.   5. Fragment of an Irish song beginning "Believe me if all those endearing young charms."   6. Rubbish heap.   7. Rangoon is a city in Myanmar (formerly Burma), a former British colony; Malta, an island in the Mediterranean off the Italian coast, was also a British colony.   8. A company of schoolboys selected and groomed to be future officers in the colonial army.

All spilt from a tea-chest, a studded souvenir,
props for an opera, Victoria Regina,[9]
for a bolster-plump Queen the pillbox sentries stamp,

piss, straw and saddle-soap, heaume[1] and crimson feather,   45
post-red double-deckers,[2] spit-and-polished leather,
and iron dolphins leaping round an Embankment[3] lamp.

*   *   *

From Book Seven

From *Chapter LXIV*

I

I sang[1] of quiet Achille, Afolabe's son,
who never ascended in an elevator,
who had no passport, since the horizon needs none,

never begged nor borrowed, was nobody's waiter,
whose end, when it comes, will be a death by water   5
(which is not for this book, which will remain unknown

and unread by him). I sang the only slaughter
that brought him delight, and that from necessity—
of fish, sang the channels of his back[2] in the sun.

I sang our wide country, the Caribbean Sea.   10
Who hated shoes, whose soles were as cracked as a stone,
who was gentle with ropes, who had one suit alone,

whom no man dared insult and who insulted no one,
whose grin was a white breaker cresting, but whose frown
was a growing thunderhead, whose fist of iron   15

would do me a greater honour if it held on
to my casket's oarlocks[3] than mine lifting his own
when both anchors are lowered in the one island,

but now the idyll dies, the goblet is broken,
and rainwater trickles down the brown cheek of a jar   20
from the clay of Choiseul. So much left unspoken

by my chirping nib![4] And my earth-door lies ajar.
I lie wrapped in a flour-sack sail. The clods thud
on my rope-lowered canoe. Rasping shovels scrape

9. I.e., Queen Victoria (Latin); the insignia of Queen Victoria on English coins.   1. Helmet worn by armored men in the Middle Ages.   2. London buses.   3. Area in London where the Houses of Parliament and the main government offices are located.   1. The invocation, usually placed at the beginning of an epic poem, is here put at the end and expressed in the past tense.   2. The ripples of muscles, denoting strength. The human frame represented as a furrowed landscape.   3. At the poet's own funeral.
4. The point of a pen dipped in ink often makes a rasping noise on the paper.

2984 / Derek Walcott

a dry rain of dirt on its hold, but turn your head   25
when the sea-almond rattles or the rust-leaved grape
from the shells of my unpharaonic pyramid[5]

towards paper shredded by the wind and scattered
like white gulls that separate their names from the foam
and nod to a fisherman[6] with his khaki dog   30

that the skitters from the wave-crash, then frown at his form
for one swift second. In its earth-trough, my pirogue
with its brass-handled oarlocks is sailing. Not from

but with them, with Hector, with Maud[7] in the rhythm
of her beds[8] trowelled over, with a swirling log   35
lifting its mossed head from the swell; let the deep hymn

of the Caribbean continue my epilogue;
may waves remove their shawls as my mourners walk home
to their rusted villages, good shoes in one hand,

passing a boy who walked through the ignorant foam,   40
and saw a sail going out or else coming in,
and watched asterisks of rain[9] puckering the sand.

*   *   *

Granada[1]

Red earth and raw, the olive clumps olive and silver
in the thud of wind like a cape[2] shaping the car,
the tormented olives smaller than you thought they were,
as a sadness, not incalculable but measured,
its distance diminishing in the humming coil of the road   5
widens astonishing Granada. This is how to read
Spain, backwards, like memory, like Arabic,[3] mountains
and predicted cypresses confirming that the only tense
is the past, where a sin lies that is all of Spain's.
It writhes in the olive's trunk, it gapes in the ochre   10
echo of a stone hillside, like a well's dry mouth: "Lorca."[4]
The black olives of his eyes, the bread dipped in its saucer.
A man in a torn white shirt with its wine-stains,

---

5. Modest, without the monumental grandeur of Egypt's pyramids.   6. I.e., Philoctete.   7. The wife of an English colonial officer, Major Plunkett, whose adventures, intertwined with the life of the St. Lucians, are narrated in earlier passages of the poem. *Hector*: rival of Achille who was killed in a car accident. 8. A reference to the flowerbeds tended by Maud. The image evokes her final resting place in the earth. 9. Which is life-giving.   1. A city in southern Spain founded by the Moors in the 8th century. Its fall in 1492 to the combined forces of the Christian monarchs Isabel of Castille and Ferdinand of Aragon marked the end of Arab presence in Spain. The Alhambra palace and its gardens, completed under the Arabs in the 14th century, provide testimony of the height that Moorish civilization reached in that city. 2. An allusion to the cape worn by Spanish bullfighters.   3. Arabic is read from right to left.   4. Federico García Lorca (1898–1936), Spanish poet, was born near Granada. He was assassinated by conservative forces during the Spanish civil war.

a black suit, and leather soles stumbling on the stones.
You cannot stand outside, apart from it, and the other ones   15
on the open hill, the staccato of carbine-fire,
of the dancer's heels, the O of the flamenco[5] singer
and the mouth of the guitar; they are there in Goya,[6]
the clown that dies, eyes open, in *The Third of May*
where the heart of Spain is. Why Spain will always suffer.   20
Why do they return from this distance, this far away
from the cypresses, the mountains, the olives turning silver?

5. The music that accompanies the vigorous, rhythmical dances of the Andalusian Gypsies. It is usually played on the guitar and involves the clicking of heels and castanets. The "O" in line 17 represents the exclamation "Olé!" often heard at flamenco performances.   6. Francisco José de Goya y Lucientes (1746–1828), Spanish painter whose mature works are renowned for their innovative realistic style. *The Third of May*, one of his best-known paintings, depicts the massacre of a group of unarmed men at the hands of uniformed soldiers.

KAMAU BRATHWAITE
born 1930

When Kamau Brathwaite's *Rights of Passage* appeared in 1967, it was hailed as a landmark in West Indian literature. Its fame derived from its powerful and original statement of African-Caribbean experience presented in its full historical stretch: from the distant African past, through the era of slavery, to the contemporary circumstances of the Caribbean population. The volume also announced a major new voice in Caribbean poetry written in English, bringing into the language a distinctive idiom marked by the inflexions and rhythms of West Indian speech and the forms of black music both in the West Indies and in North America. The connection between Brathwaite's sustained exploration of the situation of black people in the New World and the formal innovations he adopted to convey its tensions becomes evident in the alternation of lyrical passages with expressive breaks in voice and rhythm that render palpable the discontinuities within black historical experience. But although the poems are dominated by a sense of predicament arising from a troubled history, the final note of the volume is, paradoxically, affirmative:

> Sharp thorn
> against toe
> hard rock
>
> under heel
> feet stretched
> into stride
> made you a man
>
> again.

These lines sound the keynote of Brathwaite's poetry, which is at once a narrative of his people's confrontation with adversity and a formulation of their resolve to endure and prosper. For him, the history of Africans in the New World, and especially in the Caribbean, may have been one of pain and loss, but it initiated a process of self-re-creation in a new environment. That this endeavor has been animated largely by a sense of a racial and cultural connection to the ancestral homeland, whose presence in the islands is manifested in the life and spirituality of the common people, indicates for him a deep current of authentic being that runs beneath the prevailing social arrangements in the Caribbean and contradicts the claims of the official culture, reflecting Western values, to represent the ideal of African-Caribbean self-expression. For not only has the African substratum offered black West Indians strategies of survival in the past, but also it contains the promise of their revitalization in the present. Brathwaite's sentiments on this question, voiced in *Timehri* (1974), are a matter of public record:

> In the Caribbean, whether it be African or Amerindian, the recognition of an ancestral relationship with the folk or aboriginal culture involves the artist in a journey into the past and hinterland which is at the same time a movement of possession into the present and future. Through this movement of possession we become ourselves, truly our own creators, discovering word for object, image for word.

The conviction underlying this statement may be the driving force of Brathwaite's writings. It grew out of the circumstances of a singular career that has enabled him, as a West Indian separated from his African background, to recover this background and to appreciate its continued vitality in his native West Indies. Born Lawson Edward Brathwaite in 1930 in Barbados, an island whose landscape recalls the English countryside in the summer but has a predominantly black population, Brathwaite grew up in Bridgetown, the capital, where he received his primary education. He went on to Harrison College, an elite school in the secluded heart of the island, where he was put through the standard colonial curriculum, with its Western orientation. Upon passing the terminal examinations with distinction, he was awarded a scholarship to Cambridge University and left for England in 1950. Brathwaite has explained that, although his literary interests were already formed when he entered the university, he majored in history because he sought to understand the past that had shaped him as a West Indian. Though Brathwaite's studies at Cambridge could hardly provide him with ready answers to his questions, they laid the foundation for the imaginative and moral grasp of history from which the themes of his poetry would proceed. After graduation in 1953, he spent another year studying for a teacher's certificate; following a tradition of West Indians in the British colonial service, he left for the Gold Coast (now Ghana) to take up a position as education officer.

Brathwaite arrived in the Gold Coast at a turning point in modern African history. This was the era of decolonization, and the territory, which had been at the forefront of the nationalist movement in Africa, was in a state of transition from colony to independent nation. As with nationalism everywhere, the claims for political autonomy in Africa were legitimized by a cultural affirmation that sought to reverse the demoralizing effects of colonial ideology. Cultural nationalism in the Gold Coast itself had been forwarded since the early years of the century by a group of indigenous scholars. One of the most prominent among these was the historian J. B. Danquah, who recalled in his works African achievements and in particular revived the creation myths of the Akan-speaking people, who inhabit the central and southeastern parts of Ghana and the neighboring Ivory Coast. Another scholar, the jurist John Mensah-Sarbah, stressed the sacredness of customary law in traditional society and its continuing relevance to communal life. Brathwaite became acquainted with the works of these and other scholars who challenged the presuppositions of colonial rule. Of immediate interest for him as a poet was the work of Kwabena Nketia, whose researches into Akan music and oral poetry drew attention to their formal complexity and their function in the renewal of the collective consciousness around a cluster of consecrated symbols. The influence of the new scholarship gave impulse to an impressive cultural revival, of which the Ashanti Empire became the principal focus, its prestige undimmed despite its subjugation by the British, and its public rituals, centered on its famous golden stool, the object of devoted and regular observance. The revival fostered throughout the country a resurgence of spirit, encapsulated in the term *African personality*, which served as rallying cry for the recovery of the continent's dignity. Thus, at the accession to independence in 1957 under Kwame Nkrumah, the colony took the name *Ghana*, in a conscious gesture to reclaim the historical legacy associated with the West African medieval empire of that name.

During Brathwaite's eight-year sojourn in Ghana, he familiarized himself with the oral tradition and cultural practices of the Akan, with whom his postings afforded him prolonged contact. The experience revealed to him an indigenous African civilization to which he could relate, as an essential component of his own West Indian inheritance. Above all, the enlivening effect exerted by this kind of reaffirmation on a people of the black race became a determining factor in the cultural reappraisal he later offered to his West Indian compatriots. Appointed in 1960 to the textbook department of the Ministry of Education, he began to write children's books adapted to local conditions and based on indigenous lore, and completed a play, *Odale's Choice*, which was later produced by the Trinidad Theatre Workshop. On his return to the West Indies in 1962, Brathwaite was appointed a tutor in the Department of Extra-Mural Studies of the University of the West Indies at its branch in St. Lucia. The following year, he moved, as lecturer in history, to the Mona campus of the university, in Kingston, Jamaica. His poems began to appear in various journals, notably *Bim*, the venerable literary journal that has played a signal role in the development of English-speaking West Indian literature. These early poems were later revised and published in *Rights of Passage*, which was soon followed by *Masks* (1968) and *Islands* (1969). The organic unity of the three volumes compelled their republication in 1973 as a single volume, under the general title *The Arrivants: A New World Trilogy*.

Meanwhile, Brathwaite had obtained a Ph.D. in 1968 from the University of Sussex; his dissertation was titled *The Development of Creole Society in Jamaica, 1771–1820* and was published in 1973. His academic career had been developing alongside his literary activities, and when he founded the cultural journal *Savacou* in 1970, his reputation was considerable, established through not only his poetry but also his lectures and essays, the most important of which have now been collected in *Roots* (1993). These reflect the scope and intensity of the intellectual and cultural crusade he had embarked on to enlist what he saw as the restorative potential of folk culture, especially in its African dimension, for Caribbean self-knowledge. He was also active in promoting younger English-speaking Caribbean writers through a series of anthologies devoted to their work. He rose to become professor of social and cultural history at the University of the West Indies, a post he held until retirement in 1991. After taking up a series of visiting positions in American universities, he returned to full-time academic life in 1993 as professor of comparative literature at New York University, where his colleague the African novelist Ngugi wa Thiongo gave him the African name by which he is now known. The recipient of numerous awards and fellowships, including the Guggenheim, Brathwaite was named the winner in 1994 of the highly regarded Neustadt Prize.

The three volumes of *The Arrivants* owe their unity to the poet's effort to formulate responses to the issues raised by the black presence in the Americas. The triadic structure, formed by the cycle of home, departure, and return, is already fully contained in *Rights of Passage*. In this first volume, the motif of the journey that governs the thematic progression of the sequence is established: the poems compose a kaleidoscope of impressions of the black condition in America, framed between a reenactment, in the prelude, of the epochal moments of African destiny and the poet's meditation, in the epilogue, on their terminal phase for him and his people in the West Indies. The succeeding volumes expand the themes broached in the first, *Masks* with particular reference to the historical drama of the black race in Africa, and *Islands* with respect to its implications for the Caribbean.

Rights of Passage marks the point of departure of the adventure recorded in the sequence. The tragic sense of history that runs through the volume is articulated in the annunciatory poem, *New World A-Coming*:

> Click lock
> you fire-
> lock fore-
> arm fire-
> arm flashed
> fire and our firm
> fleshed, flame
> warm, fly
> bitten warriors
> fell. . . . .
>
> Fire
> falls walls, fashions
> these fire-
> locks darker than iron,
> and we filed down the path
> locked in a new
> clinked silence of iron.

The aftermath of this catastrophe from which black experience flows constitutes the burden of the volume. It is made up of a series of tableaux that detail the historical predicament of the black race, forced by conquest and enslavement from its original homeland into exile in the Americas. The individual portraits and vignettes of daily experience and the shifting modulations of tone exemplify the modes of accommodation of black people to their situation in America. The variations on the journey motif by which this presentation is developed become associated with jazz, which suggests a constantly improvised existence and a rootlessness:

> Never seen
> a man
> travel more
> seen more lands
> than this poor
> path-
> less harbourless
> spade.

The quest for an integrated consciousness felt in *Rights of Passage* translates for the poet into a dream of home and prompts his pilgrimage, of which *Masks* is a record, to the historical and cultural sources of the self, symbolized by Africa. Brathwaite revisits in this volume a history both collective and personal—hence the antiphonal structure of the volume, which places in thematic and expressive relation the two voices of the poet's mode of address: that of the institutional memory of African oral tradition, and that of the poet himself as he seeks entry into the stream of history the tradition commemorates.

Brathwaite brings into play in *Masks* the full force of his historical imagination. His reconstruction in *Pathfinders*, the opening section of the volume, of an Akan story of Exodus draws on the Akan myth of origin but invests the account of their tribulations with the quality of felt experience. The section retraces the forced departure of the Akan from their original abode near the Red Sea and their migration westward across the Nile Valley through the Sahara and then south to the West African forest. In the next section, *Limits* (printed here), the poet relives their struggle with nature, compounded by human perversities, to fashion a distinctive mode of life. The title of this section designates the area of Akan historical being, bounded by desert and sea, and denotes the overlapping of time and space in the unfolding of history. The sea emerges in the final poem, *White River,* as a symbol of the boundlessness of time and of the provisional nature of all human arrangements. More pointedly, as the determining element of the encounter between Africa and Europe, the sea becomes a figure of the ironies of history as they have affected the Akan. The sea thus comes to have meaning for the poet not only as the gateway to exile but also as the path of return, for it links his island abode to the ancestral homeland and offers him, after centuries of separation, the possibility of a reintegration into the ancestral culture.

Masks commemorates origins, but it does not present a mythical or sentimental vision of Africa. The particularity of its evocations indicates an understanding of the complex factors that have gone into the African experience and bind it to human experience everywhere.

The Arrivants was followed by *Other Exiles* (1975), a transitional volume between the first trilogy and Brathwaite's second, consisting of *Mother Poems* (1977), *Sun Poem* (1982), and *X/Self* (1987). The second trilogy, whose central reference is the poet's native Barbados, brings a new intensity to the fusion of large social and moral concerns with an ancestralism that underwrites the poet's vision of hope for his people. The vigor Brathwaite attains in these three volumes confirms the deeply rooted power of inspiration in all his poetry.

Gordon Rohlehr, *Pathfinder: Black Awakening in "The Arrivants" of Edward Kamau Brathwaite* (1981), is a detailed study of the first trilogy. Maureen Warner-Lewis, *Edward Kamau Brathwaite's "Masks": Essays and Annotations* (1992), is an indispensable guide to the cultural background and references of the second volume of the trilogy; the introductory essay provides an excellent analysis of Brathwaite's themes and of his poetic technique. Lloyd W. Brown, *West Indian Poetry* (1984), covers the poetry up to *The Arrivants;* Nathaniel Mackey, *Discrepant Engagement* (1993), and J. Edward Chamberlin, *Come Back to Me My Language* (1993), contain extensive discussions of Brathwaite's entire work to date.

PRONOUNCING GLOSSARY

The following list uses common English syllables to provide rough equivalents of selected words whose pronunciation may be unfamiliar to the general reader.

Akuapim: *ah-kwah-peem*

Akuse: *ah-koo-say*

Ananse: *ah-nahn-see*

Golokwati: *goh-loh-kwah-tee*

Kaneshie: *kah-neh-shee*

Koforidua: *koh-foh-ree-jwah*

Kpandu: *kpahn-doo*

Krachi: *krah-chee*

nkyekyere: *en-cheh-chreh*

Nsuta: *en-soo-tah*

Pong: *kpawng*

Shai: *shah-ee* (or *shy*)

Techiman: *teh-chee-mahn*

Limits

I

The Forest

1

Like walls the forest stops us.
Over the ford at Yeji[1] it was waiting:
tangled squat mahogany outriders[2] and then the dense, the
dark green tops, bright   5
shining standing trunks:
wawa, dahoma, esa and
odum;[3] the doom
of the thick stretching green.
Leaves gathered darkness; no   10
pathway showed the way.
The trunks grew tall and
taller, dark and darker; earth
now damp, fern cool, moss
soft. We hacked our way   15
through root and tendril, climber
shoot and yellow clinger. This
was the pistil[4] journey into moistened gloom. Dews
dripped, lights twink-   20
led, crickets chirped and still
the dark was silence, still
the dark was home. We
scorched, we raked, we
settled; cleared path,   25
cut clearing, burnt the dry rot
out of withered wood to make this farm.
And at night, so that no harm
would come from dark still heavy on us,
made this fire: fire-   30
flies[5] from sticks, from cinders; and we
sang:
in praise of those who journey
those who find the way

those who clear the path   35
those who go on before us

to prepare the way.

---

1. A town, on the river Volta in eastern Ghana, marking the transition from open savannah to forest.
2. These tropical trees are described as *outriders* because they are few and scattered, merely dotting the
sparse vegetation; but they announce the onset of denser vegetation.   3. Species of tropical trees.
4. The straight stem in the center of the flower from which the fruit develops.   5. That is, sparks from
the burning wood.

We sang of warmth and fires,
bodies touching, eyes of embers,[6] watching.

Where are the open spaces now   40
clear sky, the stars, horizons' distances?

We sang of warmth and fires,
bodies safe and touching.

                          2

But the lips remember
temples, gods and pharaohs,[7]   45

gold, silver ware; imagination
rose on wide unfolded wings.

But here in the dark,
we rest:

time to forget   50
the kings;

time to forget
the gods.

That fat man
with the fire-   55

light's grease
that dances

on his belly—
belly button

bunged[8]—is he   60
the king

or glutton?
He lives

on human
blood[9]   65

and dies
in human

blood;
our empire's

past of stone   70
and skulls

---

6. That is, bloodshot with lack of sleep. A reference to guards posted to watch over the village and, more broadly, to the anxieties of its inhabitants.   **7.** Rulers of ancient Egypt.   **8.** Closed up.   **9.** Literally, in the sense of human sacrifice, and metaphorically, in the sense of the heavy burden of toil the ancient rulers imposed on the masses, exemplified by the death of the slaves who were forced to construct the royal tombs.

demands it.
And Ra,[1]

the sun
god's gold, 75

demanded blood
to make it

sacred.
Time to forget

these kings. 80
Time to forget

these gods.
The jewelled sun

has splintered
on these leaves. 85

The moon-
light rusts.

Only the frogs wear jewels
here; the cricket's chirp is

emerald; the praying mantis' 90
topaz pleases; and termites'

tunnel eyes illuminate the dark.
No sphinx[2] eyes close and dream

us of our destiny; the desert
drifting certainties outside us. 95

Here leaf eyes shift, twigs
creak, buds flutter, the stick

becomes a snake;[3] uncertainties adrift
within us.

3

So praise the new eyes, 100
leaves' butterflies, flies'
sympathy; the dark trees
understand.

Raise the mantis face, my
brother; mother tree, your 105
rough bark mocks me
but we understand.

1. The sun god of ancient Egyptian mythology.   2. Mythical beast of ancient Egyptian and Greek mythology.   3. An aspect of African belief that expresses general fear of the forest, where apparently harmless objects can change their nature and become dangerous.

For night of leaves and leaves
of stars and stars' winked darkness
is a new world of discovered here;   110
new world of time and time's uncertainty.

                              4

So that with new warm arms the forest holds us.
From this womb'd heaven comes the new curled god
with goblin old man's grinning, flat face smiling,
crouched like a frog with monkey hands and   115
insect fingers. This we will carve and carry
with our cooking pots, wood mud and wattle;[4]
symbol sickness fetish for our sickness.
For man eats god,[5] eats life, eats world, eats wickedness.
This we now know, this we digest and hold;   120
this gives us bone and sinews, saliva grease and sweat;
this we can shit. And that no doubt will ever hit
us, the worm's mischance defeat us, dark roots
of time move in our way to trip us; look, we dance.

                             II

                          Adowa[6]

          No whirl of the flute
          here;
          bamboo shoots
          flar-
          ing the dryness;[7]   5
          no high yodel steel
          in the brightness;

          into the shift of the darkness,
          mud-flowered heel[8]
          stamping the softness, dare   10
          we now the fanged roots'
          whisper and lisp of our fear's
          darkness, tender and mute?

          But slow-
          ly our daring un-   15
          curls the mute
          fear; hands
          whisper and twist

---

4. A reference to traditional houses, which were made of woven branches and leaves that were plastered with mud.   5. An Africanism meaning that human beings require spiritual sustenance. The same construction is employed to describe other human propensities.   6. A ceremonial dance of the Ashantis. 7. A reference to the flute's thin sound in the desert air, as opposed to the deeper sound of drums, more appropriate to the forest, which accompany the *adowa* dance.   8. An extremely compressed image, suggesting the life-enhancing effect of the dance. (Compare the closing lines of Senghor's *Prayer to the Masks*, p. 2509.)

into move-
ment;[9] butt-
ocks shift   20
stones of inertia;
rhythms a-
rise in the darkness;
we dance   25

and we dance
on the firm
earth; cer-
tainties, farms,
tendrils un-   30
locking; wrong's
chirping lightning

no longer harms
us; birds echo
what the earth   35
learns; and the earth
with its mud, fat
and stones, burns
in the tun-
nelling drum[1]   40
of our hot
timeless
morning,
explo-
ding dimensions   45
of song.

III

Techiman[2]

1

The path through gloom, dark
drip-

ping through star-
wet leaves' crevices,

will not soon   5
turn to light, set

like a square window; will not let
in the free sail of night's moon

---

9. The *adowa* dance involves elaborate hand gestures, each one with a different meaning.   **1.** In visual terms, the towering, elongated shape of the drum and, suggested by onomatopoeia, its deep affective impact. **2.** A trading center in Ashantiland, in central Ghana. The poem recounts a journey by the poet along the old slave route from the interior of the country to the coast and superimposes impressions of the present on memories of the past.

that voyages the Arab's roomy
heaven.[3]   10

Here green's net sticks
wet, clings soft sweet comfort cunning[4]

like Ananse's[5] tune-
less, once Onyame's,[6] trap of doom.

2

But the way lost   15
is a way to be found
again;

the moist
stones, warm
pebbles of rain,   20

move into tossed
leaves of darkness; round
my mud hut I hear again

the cry of the lost
swallows, horizons' halloos, found-   25
ationless voices, voyages . . .

Techiman drizzles in sun-
light; Peki[7] peeps
out of the valley; fun-
loving Nsuta[8] sleeps   30

in the misty, water-
well'd dawn. Burn
Koforidua,[9] holy tree
blasted by lightning;[1] turn

in your sleep, sleepers   35
at Krachi;[2] the almond leaves
scratching your rocks, rock
you awake for new journeys; stop-

ping at Golokwati, Kpandu and Pong[3]
for rest, salt and water;   40
then onward to Teshie,
Labadi, Kaneshie[4] . . .

Time's walking river is long.

3. The clear, expansive sky over the desert, populated mainly by Arabs; also hints at Arab enslavement of
Africans.   4. The anxieties of the forest.   5. The Spider, who features as a trickster figure in a cycle
of Akan folktales, re-created in the Caribbean as "Nancy stories."   6. The name for the supreme deity
in the Akan language.   7. Peki Blengo, a town in eastern Ghana.   8. A town in central Ghana, known
for its music.   9. An important junction that links two major roads from Accra, the capital of the modern
state of Ghana, on the Atlantic coast, to Kumasi, the capital of the precolonial Ashanti Empire.   1. A
reference to a historical disaster.   2. Kete Krachi, a town on the Volta, a river in eastern Ghana, which
divides the Akan- and Ewe-speaking areas.   3. Or Kpong. Golokwati and Kpandu are towns along the
Volta.   4. Villages on the Atlantic coast that have become suburbs of Accra, capital of Ghana.

IV

The White River[5]

1

From the Akuapim[6] ridge unrolled a new land.
Hands on the hoe
knew new grasses:

nkyekyere and lemon;[7]   5
and the bold knocking demon
of darkness was tamed on the Akropong rocks.[8]
Light rounded to flesh

at Aburi;[9] and the hills
of the Ga lands: Akuse   10
and Shai:[1] were like islands
burning to green in the water of pastures;[2]

plains drowned in the shallow
drifting of cloud. Crowds
flocked to the Volta, darker   15
at Ada;[3] and over we ferried

to the hard, sandy gold of Keta.[4]
Here at last was the rager,[5]
the growler, wet breather,
life giver, white curly smoker,   20

time's river, rushing forever: round pebbles, carved musical
shells; wet ropes in the tide,
tugging moon's motion;

wet sails in the salt; winds drying   25
the sand into powder; drying
fish, glittered silver;
guinea cock's[6] eyes of their scales in the dark
wood of boats: forest trees fallen and scooped
with tongue's fire;[7] canoes reaping danger;   30
sharp shark's teeth's death-whiteness ready;
at the slow sloping ledge of our village; time's water's

edge; the white river.[8]

---

5. The White Volta, the upper (northern) arm of the Volta River.   6. A region inhabited by a subgroup of the Akan, the Akwapim-Twi, on a ridge north of the coastal plain on which Accra is situated.   7. Varieties of grass: "guinea grass" and "lemongrass."   8. In many myths, the founding of communities is ascribed to a hero who has to subdue a supernatural being or force.   9. The principal town of the Akwapims.   1. A town, at the southern edge of the Akwapim ridge, overlooking the coastal plain, inhabited by the Ga-speaking people.   2. Akuse is a town in the Shai hills, adjacent to Akwapim.   3. At the mouth of the Volta; the itinerary described in the poem, previously north to south, has now shifted eastward.   4. A coastal town, famous for fishing, in the Ewe-speaking area, on the eastern side of the Volta.   5. The Atlantic ocean.   6. A species of wild fowl.   7. Canoes are hollowed out of giant trees with fire.   8. Here, the Atlantic Ocean. Time's water's edge: divides the New World blacks' historical experience in Africa from that in America.

2

This was at last the last;
this was the limit of motion;   35
voyages ended;
time stopped where its movement began;

horizons returned inaccessible.
Here at last was the limit;
the minutes of pebbles drop-   40
ping into the hourless pool.

Hands reached into water;
gods nudged us like fish;
black bottomless whales that we worshipped.
O new world of want, who will build the new ways,   45

the new ships?[9]

9. Ships from Europe, ushering in a new dispensation and new problems demanding new solutions; ultimately, these ships will lead to captivity and the exile of slavery in the New World.

NAWAL EL SAADAWI
born 1931

In her autobiography *A Daughter of Isis* (1999), Nawal El Saadawi states that she
realized early in her life how the very fact of their gender constitutes for women in
the Arab-Islamic world in which she grew up an almost insuperable limiting factor to
their life chances. "I had been born a female in a world that wanted only males," she
writes. Elsewhere in the same book, she sums up the essential predicament of women
in this world, as determined by religion and social convention: "When I was six years
old, I learnt these three words by heart and they were like one sentence: 'God, calamity, marriage.' " Her work challenges the patriarchal conception of the nature and
role of women in the general culture of her world, a conception that governs attitudes
and social practice, and imposes on women an immense burden of existence. It is her
acute awareness of the damaging impact of this burden and her strong sense of
solidarity with her fellow females that have sustained her abundant output—novels,
short stories, autobiography, essays, and addresses as well as scientific treatises and
sociological studies—in an active career that has spanned some fifty years.
  Nawal El Saadawi was born in 1931 in Kafir Tahla, a village in the delta region of
Egypt, into a well-to-do middle-class family with strong connections to the ruling elite
of the country. Her father was a highly placed government functionary, her mother
descended from the traditional aristocracy. They saw to it that all their nine children
received an education all the way to university level. Nawal El Saadawi herself studied
medicine at the University of Cairo and, after her graduation in 1955, practiced as a
psychiatrist before being appointed in 1958 to the Ministry of Health, where she rose
to become director of public health. However, she was dismissed from her post in
1972 after the publication of her book *Woman and Sex*, which aroused the displeasure
of the Egyptian authorities for its frank treatment of a subject that was considered
taboo. This was the beginning of her long struggle for her individual right of expres-

sion and of her crusade for female emancipation in Egypt specifically and the Arab world generally.

After losing her government position, she devoted herself to research on women; she also worked for a year with the United Nations. In 1981, she was imprisoned during the campaign of repression directed against intellectuals by the Sadat regime, an experience that inspired her novel *The Fall of the Imam*. Upon her release in 1982, she founded the Arab Women's Solidarity Association (AWSA), a nongovernmental organization dedicated to informed discussion of women's problems. The association was dissolved by the government in 1991 and its assets confiscated. Nawal El Saadawi sued the government, but, despite support from a distinguished panel of lawyers, she could not prevail against the forces ranged against her. Because she had also incurred the wrath of Islamic fundamentalists and ran a real risk of being assassinated, she went into exile in 1992. She was writer-in-residence at Duke University in North Carolina between 1993 and 1994.

Nawal El Saadawi is probably best known for her novel *Woman at Point Zero*, a reliving of the experience of a female prisoner condemned to death for killing a pimp who preys on her during her life as a prostitute in the city after her flight from the village in order to escape a forced marriage and the constricted existence it promised. The psychological and moral dilemmas highlighted by the novel and the arresting simplicity of its narrative style have ensured the continuing success of the work. In other novels such as *God Dies by the Nile* and *The Innocence of the Devil*, Nawal El Saadawi develops plot and situation while exploring customs and religious beliefs as they affect women in her society. The former novel is an uncompromising examination of the brutalization these women often have to endure, and the violent responses the depredations of the men are liable to engender even in the most unlikely of circumstances. The latter novel, in which the action takes place in a mental institution, dramatizes the psychic disruptions generated by Islamic orthodoxy, which is invoked to rationalize the unfeeling conduct of men toward women in her society. In their bleak depiction of the female predicament, both novels seek to document, albeit in fictional form, the vicissitudes in the lives of her women, denied fulfillment by forces beyond their control.

The short story *In Camera*, taken from the collection entitled *Death of an Ex-Minister*, is a representative sample of her work. Its ironic title highlights the reversal of situations in which the public trial of the heroine is transformed into a closed session at which judge himself becomes the accused. The triviality of the legal discourse in the final episode of the story extends the critique of the entire ideological apparatus that underwrites the social system and state machinery in the fictional kingdom portrayed in the story. Its political theme is developed at the explicit level of its narrative of the trial and through the irreverence of the portrayal, notably the animal imagery employed to represent the king and the agents of the state in his service.

The story's emphasis, however, is placed firmly on the ordeal of the female protagonist, on trial for an act of defiance against the system. Her physical violation and mental agony are reconstructed through the series of flashbacks that constitute the frames by which the story's atmosphere is built up. The bonds between her and her parents, the values she shares with them as well as the gulf that also separates her from them, are interwoven with the vivid enactment of their anxieties as they all sit through her trial. The subtle modulations of narrative voice and alternating of points of view enable the reader to participate in the mental life of the characters in the closed world of a private tragedy that the story portrays, against the background of a desolate public order.

Nawal El Saadawi's focus on the female condition in the Arab-Islamic world is joined to a vision of artistic creativity as dissidence—the refusal of traditional patterns and the assertion of new possibilities. In a lecture delivered at Oxford in 1995, she emphasized the link between changing the world and changing perceptions:

> Every struggle has its own unique theory inseparable from action. Creativity means uniqueness: innovation. Discovering new ways of thinking and acting, of creating a system based on more and more justice, freedom, love, and compassion. If you are creative, you must be dissident.

This statement places her preoccupation with the oppression of women in her society within the broad human perspective that gives it resonance beyond its immediate reference to a particularized historical moment and sociocultural context. It also clarifies the essential relationship that she perceives between the imaginative function and the fabric of experience as it shapes the lives of individuals. For her, this relationship is necessarily defined by a determined and constant calling into question of an unacceptable destiny. The act of writing represents here a gesture of refusal, an effort to break the silence that surrounds the culture of abuse and repression of which her women are victims, by uncovering the inner spaces of female consciousness. Nawal El Saadawi's work thus illustrates in its concrete references and vindicates the claims of the imagination to represent a heightened awareness of experience as a mode of meeting its moral challenges.

Several articles in journals and collective volumes offer views and assessments of aspects of Nawal El Saadawi's work, but Fedwa Malti-Douglas, *Men, Women and God(s): Nawal El Saadawi and Arab Feminist Poetics* (1995), is the only study so far devoted to a systematic account and critical interpretation of the entire corpus in the light of its social and cultural background.

PRONOUNCING GLOSSARY

The following list uses common English syllables and stress accents to provide rough equivalents of selected words whose pronunciation may be unfamiliar to the general reader.

Leila Al-Fargani: *lay'-ee'-lah el-fahr'-gah-'knee*

Nawal El Saadawi: *nah'-wahl el sah'-dah'-we*

In Camera[1]

The first thing she felt was a blinding light. She saw nothing. The light was painful, even though her eyes were still shut. The cold air hit her face and bare neck, crept down to her chest and stomach and then fell lower to the weeping wound, where it turned into a sharp blow. She put one hand over her eyes to protect them from the light, whilst with the other she covered her neck, clenching her thighs against the sudden pain. Her lips too were clenched tight against a pain the like of which her body had never known, like the sting of a needle in her eyes and breasts and armpits and lower abdomen. From sleeping so long while standing and standing so long while sleeping, she no longer knew what position her body was in, whether vertical or horizontal, dangling in the air by her feet or standing on her head in water.

The moment they sat her down and she felt the seat on which she was sitting with the palms of her hands, the muscles of her face relaxed and resumed their human form. A shudder of sudden and intense pleasure shook her from inside when her body took up a sitting position on the wooden seat and her lips curled into a feeble smile as she said to herself: Now I know what pleasure it is to sit!

1. Translated by Shirley Eber. *In camera*: the judicial term for "closed session." The oppressive atmosphere of the trial scene is immediately conveyed by the title.

The light was still strong and her eyes still could not see, but her eyes were beginning to catch the sound of voices and murmurings. She lifted her hand off her eyes and gradually began to open them. Blurred human silhouettes moved before her on some elevated construction. She suddenly felt frightened, for human forms frightened her more than any others. Those long, rapid and agile bodies, legs inside trousers and feet inside shoes. Everything had been done in the dark with the utmost speed and agility. She could not cry or scream. Her tongue, her eyes, her mouth, her nose, all the parts of her body, were constrained. Her body was no longer hers but was like that of a small calf struck by the heels of boots. A rough stick entered between her thighs to tear at her insides. Then she was kicked into a dark corner where she remained curled up until the following day. By the third day, she still had not returned to normal but remained like a small animal incapable of uttering the simple words: My God! She said to herself: Do animals, like humans, know of the existence of something called God?

Her eyes began to make out bodies sitting on that elevated place, above each head a body, smooth heads without hair, in the light as red as monkeys' rumps. They must all be males, for however old a woman grew, her head could never look like a monkey's rump. She strained to see more clearly. In the centre was a fat man wearing something like a black robe, his mouth open; in his hand something like a hammer. It reminded her of the village magician, when her eyes and those of all the other children had been mesmerized by the hand which turned a stick into a snake or into fire. The hammer squirmed in his hand like a viper and in her ears a sharp voice resounded: The Court! To herself she said: He must be the judge. It was the first time in her life she'd seen a judge or been inside a court. She'd heard the word 'court' for the first time as a child. She'd heard her aunt tell her mother: The judge did not believe me and told me to strip so he could see where I'd been beaten. I told him that I would not strip in front of a strange man, so he rejected my claim and ordered me to return to my husband. Her aunt had cried and at that time she had not understood why the judge had told her aunt to strip. I wonder if the judge will ask me to strip and what he will say when he sees that wound, she said to herself.

Gradually, her eyes were growing used to the light. She began to see the judge's face more clearly. His face was as red as his head, his eyes as round and bulging as a frog's, moving slowly here and there, his nose as curved as a hawk's beak, beneath it a yellow moustache as thick as a bundle of dry grass, which quivered above the opening of a mouth as taut as wire and permanently gaping like a mousetrap.

She did not understand why his mouth stayed open. Was he talking all the time or breathing through it? His shiny bald head moved continually with a nodding movement. It moved upwards a little and then backwards, entering into something pointed; then it moved downwards and forwards, so that his chin entered his neck opening. She could not yet see what was behind him, but when he raised his head and moved it backwards, she saw it enter something pointed which looked like the cap of a shoe. She focused her vision and saw that it really was a shoe, drawn on the wall above the judge's head. Above the shoe she saw taut legs inside a pair of trousers of expensive leather or leopard skin or snakeskin and a jacket, also taut, over a pair of shoulders. Above the shoulders appeared the face she'd seen thousands of times in the papers, eyes staring into space filled with more stupidity than simplicity, the nose as straight as though evened out by a hammer, the mouth pursed to betray that artificial sincerity which all rulers and kings master when they sit before a camera. Although his mouth was pinched in arrogance and sincerity, his cheeks were slack, beneath them a cynical and comical smile containing chronic corruption and childish petulance.

She had been a child in primary school the first time she saw a picture of the king. The face was fleshy, the eyes narrow, the lips thin and clenched in impudent arrogance. She recalled her father's voice saying: he was decadent and adulterous. But they were all the same. When they stood in front of a camera, they thought they were god.

Although she could still feel her body sitting on the wooden seat, she began to have doubts. How could they allow her to sit all this time? Sitting like this was so very relaxing. She could sit, leaving her body in a sitting position, and enjoy that astounding ability which humans have. For the first time she understood that the human body differed from that of an animal in one important way—sitting. No animal could sit the way she could. If it did, what would it do with its four legs? She remembered a scene that had made her laugh as a child, of a calf which had tried to sit on its backside and had ended up on its back. Her lips curled in a futile attempt to open her mouth and say something or smile. But her mouth remained stuck, like a horizontal line splitting the lower part of her face into two. Could she open her mouth a little to spit? But her throat, her mouth, her neck, her chest, everything, was dry, all except for that gaping wound between her thighs.

She pressed her legs together tighter to close off the wound and the pain and to enjoy the pleasure of sitting on a seat. She could have stayed in that position for ever, or until she died, had she not suddenly heard a voice calling her name: Leila Al-Fargani.

Her numbed senses awoke and her ears pricked up to the sound of that strange name: Leila Al-Fargani. As though it wasn't her name. She hadn't heard it for ages. It was the name of a young woman named Leila, a young woman who had worn young woman's clothes, had seen the sun and walked on two feet like other human beings. She had been that woman a very long time ago, but since then she hadn't worn a young woman's clothes nor seen the sun nor walked on two feet. For a long time she'd been a small animal inside a dark and remote cave and when they addressed her, they only used animal names.

Her eyes were still trying to see clearly. The judge's head had grown clearer and moved more, but it was still either inside the cap of the shoe whenever he raised it or was inside his collar whenever he lowered it. The picture hanging behind him had also become clearer. The shiny pointed shoes, the suit as tight as a horseman's, the face held taut on the outside by artificial muscles full of composure and stupidity, on the inside depraved and contentious.

The power of her sight was no longer as it had been, but she could still see ugliness clearly. She saw the deformed face and remembered her father's words: They only reach the seat of power, my girl, when they are morally deformed and internally corrupt.

And what inner corruption! She had seen their real corruption for herself. She wished at that moment they would give her pen and paper so that she could draw that corruption. But would her fingers still be capable of holding a pen or of moving it across a piece of paper? Would she still have at least two fingers which could hold a pen? What could she do if they cut off one of those two fingers? Could she hold a pen with one finger? Could a person walk on one leg? It was one of those questions her father used to repeat. But she hated the questions of the impotent and said to herself: I will split the finger and press the pen into it, just as Isis split the leg of Osiris.[2] She remembered that old story, still saw the split leg pouring with blood. What a long nightmare she was living! How she wanted her mother's hand to shake her so she could open her eyes and wake up. She used to be so happy when, as a child, she opened her eyes and realized that the monster which had tried to rip her body to pieces was nothing but a dream, or a nightmare as her mother used to call it. Each time she had opened her eyes, she was very happy to discover that the monster had vanished, that it was only a dream. But now she opened her eyes and the monster did not go away. She opened her eyes and the monster stayed on her body. Her terror was so great that she closed her eyes again to sleep, to make believe that it was a nightmare. But she opened her eyes and knew it was no dream. And she remembered everything.

The first thing she remembered was her mother's scream in the silence of the night. She was sleeping in her mother's arms, like a child of six even though she was an adult and in her twenties. But her mother had said: You'll sleep in my arms so that even if they come in the middle of the night, I will know it and I'll hold on to you with all my might and if they take you they'll have to take me as well.

Nothing was as painful to her as seeing her mother's face move further and further away until it disappeared. Her face, her eyes, her hair, were so pale. She would rather have died than see her mother's face so haggard. To herself she said: Can you forgive me, Mother, for causing you so much pain? Her mother always used to say to her: What's politics got to do with you? You're not a man. Girls of your age think only about marriage. She hadn't replied when her mother had said: Politics is a dirty game which only ineffectual men play.

The voices had now become clearer. The picture also looked clearer, even though the fog was still thick. Was it winter and the hall roofless, or was it summer and they were smoking in a windowless room? She could see another man sitting not far from the judge. His head, like the judge's, was smooth and red but, unlike the judge's, it was not completely under the shoe. He was sitting to one side and above his head hung another picture in which there was something like a flag or a small multicoloured banner. And for the first time, her ears made out some intelligible sentences:

Imagine, ladies and gentlemen. This student, who is not yet twenty years old, refers to Him, whom God protect to lead this noble nation all his life, as 'stupid'.

The word 'stupid' fell like a stone in a sea of awesome silence, making a sound like the crash of a rock in water or the blow of a hand against something solid, like a slap or the clap of one hand against another.

Was someone clapping? She pricked up her ears to catch the sound. Was

2. Isis and Osiris were a royal couple in Egyptian mythology. In the celebrated story of the couple, Isis wandered the land in search of the body of her murdered husband (who was also her brother), whose body had been thrown into the Nile in a golden casket. She recovered the body, into which she was able to breathe life and from which she conceived a son. However, the body was discovered by his murderer, who tore it into pieces, leaving Isis to collect the limbs and other parts, into which she again breathed life. Osiris soon died again and descended into the underworld, where he reigned over the dead.

it applause? Or a burst of laughter, like a cackle? Then that terrifying silence pervaded the courtroom once again, a long silence in which she could hear the beating of her heart. The sound of laughter or of applause echoed in her ears. She asked herself who could be applauding at so serious a moment as when the mighty one was being described as stupid, and aloud too.

Her body was still stuck to the wooden seat, clinging on to it, frightened it would suddenly be taken away. The wound in her lower abdomen was still weeping. But she was able to move her head and half opened her eyes to search for the source of that applause. Suddenly she discovered that the hall was full of heads crammed together in rows, all of them undoubtedly human. Some of the heads appeared to have a lot of hair, as if they were those of women or girls. Some of them were small, as if those of children. One head seemed to be like that of her younger sister. Her body trembled for a moment on the seat as her eyes searched around. Had she come alone or with her father and mother? Were they looking at her now? How did she look? Could they recognize her face or her body?

She turned her head to look. Although her vision had grown weak, she could just make out her mother. She could pick out her mother's face from among thousands of faces even with her eyes closed. Could her mother really be here in the hall? Her heartbeats grew audible and anxiety grew inside her. Anxiety often gripped her and she felt that something terrible had happened to her mother. One night, fear had overcome her when she was curled up like a small animal and she'd told herself: She must have died and I will not see her when I get out. But the following day, she had seen her mother when she came to visit. She'd come, safe and sound. She was happy and said: Don't die, Mother, before I get out and can make up for all the pain I've caused you.

The sound was now clear in her ears. It wasn't just one clap but a whole series of them. The heads in the hall were moving here and there. The judge was still sitting, his smooth head beneath the shoe. The hammer in his hand was moving impatiently, banging rapidly on the wooden table. But the clapping did not stop. The judge rose to his feet so that his head was in the centre of the stomach in the picture. His lower lip trembled as he shouted out words of rebuke which she couldn't hear in all the uproar.

Then silence descended for a period. She was still trying to see, her hands by her side holding on to the seat, clinging on to it, pressing it as if she wanted to confirm that it was really beneath her or that she was really sitting on it. She knew she was awake and not asleep with her eyes closed. Before, when she opened her eyes, the monster would disappear and she'd be happy that it was only a dream. But now she was no longer capable of being happy and had become frightened of opening her eyes.

The noise in the hall had died down and the heads moved as they had done before. All except one head. It was neither smooth nor red. It was covered in a thick mop of white hair and was fixed and immobile. The eyes also did not move and were open, dry and fixed on that small body piled on top of the wooden seat. Her hands were clasped over her chest, her heart under her hand beating fast, her breath panting as if she were running to the end of the track and could no longer breath. Her voice broke as she said to herself: My God! Her eyes turn in my direction but she doesn't see me. What have they done to her eyes? Or is she fighting sleep? God of Heaven and Earth, how could you let them do all that? How, my daughter, did you stand so much pain? How did I stand it together with you? I always felt that you, my daughter, were capable of anything, of moving mountains or of crumbling rocks, even though your body is small and weak like mine. But when your tiny feet used to kick the walls of my stomach, I'd say to myself: God, what strength and power there is inside my body? Your movements were strong while you were still a foetus and shook me from inside, like a volcano shakes the earth. And yet I knew that you were as small as I was, your bones as delicate as your father's, as tall and slim as your grandmother, your feet as large as the feet of prophets.[3] When I gave birth to you, your grandmother pursed her lips in sorrow and said: A girl and ugly too! A double catastrophe! I tensed my stomach muscles to close off my womb to the pain and the blood and, breathing with difficulty, for your birth had been hard and I suffered as though I'd given birth to a mountain, I said to her: She's more precious to me than the whole world! I held you to my breast and slept deeply. Can I, my daughter, again enjoy another moment of deep sleep whilst you are inside me or at least near to me so that I can reach out to touch you? Or whilst you are in your room next to mine so that I can tiptoe in to see you whilst you sleep? The blanket always used to fall off you as you slept, so I'd lift it and cover you. Anxiety would waken me every night and make me creep into your room. What was that anxiety and at what moment did it happen? Was it the moment the cover fell off your body? I could always feel you, even if you had gone away and were out of my sight. Even if they were to bury you under the earth or build a solid wall of mud or iron around you, I would still feel a draught of air on your body as though it were on mine. I sometimes wonder whether I ever really gave birth to you or if you are still inside me. How else could I feel the air when it touches you and hunger when it grips you. Your pain is mine, like fire burning in my breast and stomach. God of Heaven and Earth, how did your body and mine stand it? But I couldn't have stood it were it not for the joy of you being my daughter, of having given birth to you. And you can raise your head high above the mountains of filth. For three thousand and twenty-five hours (I've counted them one by one), they left you with the vomit and pus and the weeping wound in your stomach. I remember the look in your eyes when you told me, the bars between us: If only the weeping were red blood. But it's not red. It's white and has the smell of death. What was it I said to you that day? I don't know, but I said something. I said that the smell becomes normal when we get used to it and live with it every day. I could not look into your emaciated face, but I heard you say: It's not a smell, mother, like other smells which enter through the nose or mouth. It's more like liquid air or steam turned to viscid[4] water or molten lead flowing into every opening of the body. I don't know, mother, if it is burning hot or icy cold. I clasped my hands to my breast, then grasped your slender hand through the bars, saying: When heat became like cold, my daughter, then everything is bearable. But as soon as I left you, I felt my heart swell and swell until it filled my chest and pressed on my lungs so I could no longer breathe. I felt I was choking and tilted my head skywards to force air into my lungs. But the sky that day was void of air and the sun over

3. The passage conjures up an image of devoted pupils sitting at the feet of the prophets.   4. Sticky.

my head was molten lead like the fire of hell. The eyes of the guards stung me and their uncouth voices piled up inside me. If the earth had transformed into the face of one of them, I'd have spat and spat and spat on it until my throat and chest dried up. Yes, my daughter, brace the muscles of your back and raise your head and turn it in my direction, for I'm sitting near you. You may have heard them when they applauded you. Did you hear them? I saw you move your head towards us. Did you see us? Me and your father and little sister? We all applauded with them. Did you see us?

Her eyes were still trying to penetrate the thick fog. The judge was still standing, his head smooth and red, his lower lip trembling with rapid words. To his right and to his left, she saw smooth red heads begin to move away from that elevated table. The judge's head and the others vanished, although the picture on the wall remained where it was. The face and the eyes were the same as they had been, but now one eye appeared to her to be smaller, as though half-closed or winking at her, that common gesture that a man makes to a woman when he wants to flirt with her. Her body trembled in surprise. Was it possible that he was winking at her? Was it possible for his eyes in the picture to move? Could objects move? Or was she sick and hallucinating? She felt the seat under her palm and raised her hand to touch her body. A fierce heat emanated from it, like a searing flame, a fire within her chest. She wanted to open her mouth and say: Please, a glass of water. But her lips were stuck together, a horizontal line as taut as wire. Her eyes too were stuck on the picture, while the eye in the picture continued to wink at her. Why was it winking at her? Was it flirting with her? She had only discovered that winking was a form of greeting when, two years previously, she'd seen a file of foreign tourists walking in the street. She'd been on her way to the university. Whenever she looked at the faces of one of the men or women, an eye would suddenly wink at her strangely. She had been shocked and hadn't understood how a woman could flirt with her in such a way. Only later had she understood that it was an American form of greeting.

The podium was still empty, without the judge and the smooth heads around him. Silence prevailed. The heads in the hall were still close together in rows and her eyes still roamed in search of a mop of white hair, a pair of black eyes which she could see with eyes closed. But there were so many heads close together she could only see a mound of black and white, circles or squares or oblongs. Her nose began to move as if she were sniffing, for she knew her mother's smell and could distinguish it from thousands of others. It was the smell of milk when she was a child at the breast or the smell of the morning when it rises or the night when it sleeps or the rain on wet earth or the sun above the bed or hot soup in a bowl. She said to herself: Is it possible that you're not here, Mother? And Father, have you come?

The fog before her eyes was still thick. Her head continued to move in the direction of the rows of crammed heads. The black and white circles were interlocked in tireless movement. Only one circle of black hair was immobile above a wide brown forehead, two firm eyes in a pale slender face and a small body piled on to a chair behind bars. His large gaunt hands gripped his knees, pressing on them from the pain. But the moment he heard the applause, he took his hands off his knees and brought them together to clap. His hands did not return to his knees, the pain in his legs no longer tangible. His heart beat loudly in time to his clapping which shook his slender body on the seat. His eyes began to scour the faces and eyes, and his lips parted a little as though he were about to shout: I'm her father, I'm Al-Fargani who fathered her and whose name she bears. My God, how all the pain in my body vanished in one go with the burst of applause. What if I were to stand up now and reveal my identity to them? This moment is unique and I must not lose it. Men like us live and die for one moment such as this, for others to recognize us, to applaud us, for us to become heroes with eyes looking at us and fingers pointing at us. I have suffered the pain and torture with her, day after day, hour after hour, and now I have the right to enjoy some of the reward and share in her heroism.

He shifted his body slightly on his seat as if he were about to stand up. But he remained seated, though his head still moved. His eyes glanced from face to face, as if he wanted someone to recognize him. The angry voice of the judge and the sharp rapid blows of his hammer on the table broke into the applause. Presently the judge and those with him withdrew to the conference chambers. Silence again descended on the hall, a long and awesome silence, during which some faint whispers reached his ears: They'll cook up the case in the conference chamber . . . That's common pratice . . . Justice and law don't exist here . . . In a while they'll declare the public hearing closed . . . She must be a heroine to have stayed alive until now . . . Imagine that young girl who is sitting in the dock causing the government so much alarm . . . Do you know how they tortured her? Ten men raped her, one after the other. They trampled on her honour and on her father's honour. Her poor father! Do you know him! They say he's ill in bed. Maybe he can't face people after his honour was violated!

At that moment he raised his hands to cover his ears so as not to hear, to press on his head so that it sunk into his chest, pushing it more and more to merge his body into the seat or underneath it or under the ground. He wanted to vanish so that no one would see or know him. His name was not Al-Fargani, not Assharqawi, not Azziftawi, not anything. He had neither name nor existence. What is left of a man whose honour is violated? He had told her bitterly: Politics, my girl, is not for women and girls. But she had not listened to him. If she had been a man, he would not be suffering now the way he was. None of those dogs would have been able to violate his honour and dignity. Death was preferable for him and for her now.[5]

Silence still reigned over the hall. The judge and his entourage had not yet reappeared. Her eyes kept trying to see, searching out one face amongst the faces, for eyes she recognized, for a mop of white hair the colour of children's milk. But all she could see were black and white circles and squares intermingled and constantly moving. Is it possible you're not here, Mother? Is Father still ill? Her nose too continued to move here and there, searching for a familiar smell, the smell of a warm breast full of milk, the smell of the sun and of drizzle on grass. But her nose was unable to pick up the smell. All it could pick up was the smell of her body crumpled on the seat and the weeping wound between her thighs. It was a smell of pus and blood and the

5. According to the Arab-Islamic code of honor, decreed and upheld by men.

putrid stench of the breath and sweat of ten men, the marks of whose nails were still on her body, with their uncouth voices, their saliva and the sound of their snorting. One of them, lying on top of her, had said: This is the way we torture you women—by depriving you of the most valuable thing you possess. Her body under him was as cold as a corpse but she had managed to open her mouth and say to him: You fool! The most valuable thing I possess is not between my legs. You're all stupid. And the most stupid among you is the one who leads you.

She craned her neck to raise her head and penetrate the fog with her weak eyes. The many heads were still crammed together and her eyes still strained. If only she could have seen her mother for a moment, or her father or little sister, she would have told them something strange. She would have told them that they had stopped using that method of torture when they discovered that it didn't torture her. They began to search for other methods.

In the conference chamber next to the hall, the judge and his aides were meeting, deliberating the case. What should they do now that the public had applauded the accused? The judge began to face accusations in his turn:

—We're not accusing you, Your Honour, but you did embarrass us all. As the saying goes: 'The road to hell is paved with good intentions'! You did what you thought was right, but you only managed to make things worse. How could you say, Your Honour, about Him, whom God protect to lead this noble nation all his life, that he is stupid?

—God forbid, sir! I didn't say that, I said that *she* said he was stupid.

—Don't you know the saying, 'What the ear doesn't hear, the heart doesn't grieve over'? You declared in public that he's stupid.

—I didn't say it, sir. I merely repeated what the accused said to make the accusation stick. That's precisely what my job is.

—Yes, that's your job, Your Honour. We know that. But you should have been smarter and wiser than that.

—I don't understand.

—Didn't you hear how the people applauded her?

—Is that my fault?

—Don't you know why they applauded?

—No, I don't.

—Because you said in public what is said in private and it was more like confirming a fact than proving an accusation.

—What else could I have done, sir?

—You could have said that she cursed the mighty one without saying exactly *what* she said.

—And if I'd been asked what kind of curse it was?

—Nobody would have asked you. And besides, you volunteered the answer before anyone asked, as though you'd seized the opportunity to say aloud and in her words, what you yourself wanted to say or perhaps what you do say to yourself in secret.

—Me? How can you accuse me in this way? I was simply performing my duty as I should. Nobody can accuse me of anything. Perhaps I was foolish, but you cannot accuse me of bad faith.

—But foolishness can sometimes be worse than bad faith. You must know that foolishness is the worst label you can stick on a man. And as far as he's concerned, better that he be a swindler, a liar, a miser, a trickster, even a thief or a traitor, rather than foolish. Foolishness means that he doesn't think, that he's mindless, that he's an animal. That's the worst thing you can call an ordinary man. And all the more so if he's a ruler. You don't know rulers, Your Honour, but I know them well. Each of them fancies his brain to be better than any other man's. And it's not just a matter of fantasy, but of blind belief, like the belief in God. For the sake of this illusion, he can kill thousands.[6]

—I didn't know that, sir. How can I get out of this predicament?

—I don't know why you began with the description 'stupid', Your Honour. If you'd read everything she said, you'd have found that she used other less ugly terms to describe him.

—Such as what, sir? Please, use your experience to help me choose some of them. I don't want to leave here accused, after coming in this morning to raise an accusation.

—Such descriptions cannot be voiced in public. The session must be closed. Even a less ugly description will find an echo in the heart of the people if openly declared. That's what closed sessions are for, Your Honour. Many matters escape you and it seems you have little experience in law.

A few minutes later, utter silence descended on the hall. The courtroom was completely emptied. As for her, they took her back to where she'd been before.

---

6. An overt critique of the murderous inclinations fostered by religious fanaticism.

ALICE MUNRO
born 1931

"I don't take up a story and follow it as if it were a road, taking me somewhere, with views and neat diversions along the way," writes Alice Munro in her essay *What Is Real?* "I go into it and move back and forth and settle here and there, and stay in it for a while." This description of Munro the reader applies equally to Munro the writer. Munro's stories join the familiar to the enigmatic in a style that, like Virginia Woolf's, savors the nuances and subtleties of human relationships. Combining this writerly style with a keen attention to physical and psychological detail that places her in the realist tradition of Tolstoy and Chekhov, Munro's short fiction is marked by compassion and the awareness of multiple points of view. Whether focused on fox farming, high school dances, chance sexual encounters, marriage and divorce, or discovery and self-discovery, Munro's vision frequently centers on the lives of girls and women and on their introspective responses to the world around them. This writing is less concerned with "getting somewhere" than with settling here and there to reveal the mystery and complexity of seemingly simple day-to-day realities.

Born Alice Anne Laidlaw in the Scots-Irish community of Wingham, Ontario, Munro began writing stories in her teens—tales of romance and adventure far removed from her rural Canadian home. Her parents, Robert Eric Laidlaw and Ann Chamney Laidlaw, struggled throughout their marriage to make ends meet—fox farming during the Depression, selling wares door to door, raising turkeys—but no venture was successful enough to lift the family out of poverty. In 1949, Munro enrolled at the University of Western Ontario, leaving school in 1951 to marry James Munro and moving with him to Vancouver, British Columbia. While raising three daughters and managing a bookshop there during the 1950s and 1960s, Munro honed her story-telling skills. When, in 1968, *Dance of the Happy Shades* (from which the story printed here is taken) introduced her to the reading public, the response was overwhelming. Praised by critics, recipient also of the prestigious Governor General's Award for fiction (the first of three), she had found a place for herself in the world of professional writers. In 1972 she published *Lives of Girls and Women*, a novel composed of a series of linked stories, all recounting the emergence of the character Del Jordan from her confined childhood to a career and an adult identity far transcending the borders of her hometown of Jubilee. This was followed in 1974 by a third book of stories: *Something I've Been Meaning to Tell You*. Munro's first marriage ended in divorce in 1976, after which she remarried and moved to the central Canadian town of Clin-ton, Ontario. Since then, she has published seven other collections of short fiction: *Who Do You Think You Are?: Stories* (1978; published outside Canada as *The Beggar Maid*, 1979), *The Moons of Jupiter* (1982), *The Progress of Love* (1986), *Friend of My Youth* (1990), *Open Secrets* (1994), a cumulative *Selected Stories* in 1996, and a new volume, *The Love of a Good Woman* (1998), which received the Giller Prize. She continues to receive prizes and awards.

The vagaries of life in rural Canada figure prominently in Munro's writing, and because of this, some critics have labeled her a "regionalist." Her characters often inhabit small fictional towns similar to the Wingham of her youth, and the area of *Walker Brothers Cowboy* recalls just such a region in southwestern Ontario. Yet the worlds of human relationships that they create for themselves are more expansive and universal than the term *regionalist* implies. In this, she resembles James Joyce in *Dubliners*, William Faulkner writing about his mythic Yoknapatawpha County, and writers of the modern American South for whom she feels a marked affinity: Flannery O'Connor, Eudora Welty, Carson McCullers, and Walker Percy. Munro too focuses on interconnected lives in small communities and on the puzzles and discoveries of growing up. Her most memorable characters—Del Jordan of *Lives of Girls and Women*, and Rose of the story cycle *The Beggar Maid*—though distinct in their cir-cumstances and personalities, share a breadth of vision and an openness to life's inconstancies that makes them seem larger and more significant than their surround-ings. Through their eyes, we see a world not of heroic resolutions and tragic ends or of a linear progression from "here" to "there" but rather of moments and of details; of disappointments and small victories; and above all, of the inevitable swoop and sway between intimacy and alienation. What we see most powerfully is the masks we all wear, "the faces we put on to meet the faces that we meet" (to paraphrase T. S. Eliot). Munro's characters disguise themselves from themselves and from others, but seek at the same time to be unmasked, discovered, and more fully human. Describing her fondness for the short-story form, Munro says: "I like looking at people's lives over a number of years, without continuity. Like catching them in snapshots. And I like the way people relate, or don't relate, to the people they were earlier." Like Munro's later work, *Walker Brothers Cowboy* catches a snapshot of the relationship between a character's present and past lives. The same story also illustrates the way the writer manipulates the boundaries between autobiography and fiction, basing her stories in personal experience but also radically changing historical facts. Thus there actually was a Nora who loved dancing and clothes with flowered prints; and Nora did give a dance lesson to the nine-year-old Alice Laidlaw, whose father was a traveling salesman; and Alice was impressed by Nora's vitality and joy. The romantic nostalgia that is so crucial to *Walker Brothers Cowboy*, however, is complete fiction; according to Munro, Nora would have been fifteen when her father married at twenty-five. Using memory, introspection, and a supreme gift for adapting reality to her ends, Munro the storyteller creates characters who struggle to understand and accept the vicissi-tudes of human relationships and, correspondingly, of life itself.

One of Munro's best-known stories, *Walker Brothers Cowboy* is the first story of her first collection, *Dance of the Happy Shades* (1968), and it already reveals the mixture of realistic observation and overtones of mystery that permeate her work. The small towns with their cracking sidewalks, the isolated farmhouses, the pricks of sunlight that come through a straw hat: such details not only confirm the solid reality of these scenes but also establish an atmosphere of awareness and discovery that will be important later on. Here, two children accompany their father, a door-to-door salesman, on a sales trip around the back country roads of southwest Ontario. The narrator, a solitary young girl, reports the day's events in a matter-of-fact tone, sketching in the process a picture of the family and its everyday existence. Their disappointed, plaintive, somewhat snobbish mother strives to maintain appearances and cannot resign herself to having come down in the world; their father copes cheerfully, telling the children stories as they walk by the lake or making up funny songs as they drive from place to place; the narrator and her younger brother, usually required to stay in their yard, find the sales trip a chance for adventure. It is a settled existence, with small frictions and disappointments but no surprises. An unscheduled trip to Nora's home, however, opens up other dimensions by hinting at an unforgotten romance in their father's past. The contrasts between the cheerless mother and Nora—full of warmth and vitality—are quietly implied, and the father's unaccustomed silence as they drive back home suggests emotional undercurrents that were previously invisible. The narrator's life—once so familiar and ordinary—has been changed into a different kind of landscape: "into something you will never know, with all kinds of weathers, and distances you cannot imagine."

Catherine S. Ross, *Alice Munro: A Double Life* (1991), is a compact, readable biography that highlights the sources of Munro's writing; it includes a bibliography, photographs, maps, and interview comments about Nora. E. D. Blodgett, *Alice Munro* (1988), and Coral Ann Howells, *Alice Munro* (1998), introduce the writer and her work. Robert Thacker, ed., *The Rest of the Story: Critical Essays on Alice Munro* (1999), assembles eleven essays, including a discussion of Munro's correspondence with her literary agent; J. R. Struthers, "Alice Munro and the American South" in John Moss, ed., *The Canadian Novel: Here and Now* (1983), is also recommended. Louis MacKendrick, ed., *Probable Fictions: Alice Munro's Narrative Acts* (1983), is an excellent survey of critical essays and of interviews with the author herself. For more on Munro's approach to gender issues and male/female relationships, see Beverly Rasporich, *Dance of the Sexes: Art and Gender in the Fiction of Alice Munro* (1990). Sheila Munro brings a personal perspective to *Lives of Mothers and Daughters: Growing Up with Alice Munro* (2001).

Walker Brothers Cowboy[1]

After supper my father says, "Want to go down and see if the Lake's still there?" We leave my mother sewing under the dining-room light, making clothes for me against the opening of school. She has ripped up for this purpose an old suit and an old plaid wool dress of hers, and she has to cut and match very cleverly and also make me stand and turn for endless fittings, sweaty, itching from the hot wool, ungrateful. We leave my brother in bed in the little screened porch at the end of the front veranda, and sometimes he kneels on his bed and presses his face against the screen and calls mournfully, "Bring me an ice-cream cone!" but I call back, "You will be asleep," and do not even turn my head.

---

1. A traveling salesman for a Canadian door-to-door sales company that is probably modeled on the still-operating Watkins Products firm.

Then my father and I walk gradually down a long, shabby sort of street, with Silverwoods Ice Cream signs standing on the sidewalk, outside tiny, lighted stores. This is in Tuppertown, an old town on Lake Huron,[2] an old grain port. The street is shaded, in some places, by maple trees whose roots have cracked and heaved the sidewalk and spread out like crocodiles into the bare yards. People are sitting out, men in shirtsleeves and undershirts and women in aprons—not people we know but if anybody looks ready to nod and say, "Warm night," my father will nod too and say something the same. Children are still playing. I don't know them either because my mother keeps my brother and me in our own yard, saying he is too young to leave it and I have to mind him. I am not so sad to watch their evening games because the games themselves are ragged, dissolving. Children, of their own will, draw apart, separate into islands of two or one under the heavy trees, occupying themselves in such solitary ways as I do all day, planting pebbles in the dirt or writing in it with a stick.

Presently we leave these yards and houses behind; we pass a factory with boarded-up windows, a lumberyard whose high wooden gates are locked for the night. Then the town falls away in a defeated jumble of sheds and small junkyards, the sidewalk gives up and we are walking on a sandy path with burdocks, plantains, humble nameless weeds all around. We enter a vacant lot, a kind of park really, for it is kept clear of junk and there is one bench with a slat missing on the back, a place to sit and look at the water. Which is generally gray in the evening, under a lightly overcast sky, no sunsets, the horizon dim. A very quiet, washing noise on the stones of the beach. Further along, towards the main part of town, there is a stretch of sand, a water slide, floats bobbing around the safe swimming area, a lifeguard's rickety throne. Also a long dark-green building, like a roofed veranda, called the Pavilion, full of farmers and their wives, in stiff good clothes, on Sundays. That is the part of the town we used to know when we lived at Dungannon and came here three or four times a summer, to the Lake. That, and the docks where we would go and look at the grain boats, ancient, rusty, wallowing, making us wonder how they got past the breakwater let alone to Fort William.

Tramps hang around the docks and occasionally on these evenings wander up the dwindling beach and climb the shifting, precarious path boys have made, hanging on to dry bushes, and say something to my father which, being frightened of tramps, I am too alarmed to catch. My father says he is a bit hard up himself. "I'll roll you a cigarette if it's any use to you," he says, and he shakes tobacco out carefully on one of the thin butterfly papers, flicks it with his tongue, seals it and hands it to the tramp, who takes it and walks away. My father also rolls and lights and smokes one cigarette of his own.

He tells me how the Great Lakes came to be. All where Lake Huron is now, he says, used to be flat land, a wide flat plain. Then came the ice, creeping down from the North, pushing deep into the low places. Like *that*— and he shows me his hand with his spread fingers pressing the rock-hard

2. One of the Great Lakes, bordering on Ontario (Canada) and eastern Michigan. Place names are both real and invented. Real places mentioned in the story include Sunshine, a small town close to Munro's childhood home in Wingham; Dungannon, a small town close to Goderich; Fort William, which merged with Port Arthur in 1970 to become the city of Thunder Bay; and Brantford, a city in southeastern Ontario. Other place names, like Tuppertown, Turnaround, and Boylesbridge, are adapted or fictitious.

ground where we are sitting. His fingers make hardly any impression at all and he says, "Well, the old ice cap had a lot more power behind it than this hand has." And then the ice went back, shrank back towards the North Pole where it came from, and left its fingers of ice in the deep places it had gouged, and ice turned to lakes and there they were today. They were *new,* as time went. I try to see that plain before me, dinosaurs walking on it, but I am not able even to imagine the shore of the Lake when the Indians were there, before Tuppertown. The tiny share we have of time appalls me, though my father seems to regard it with tranquillity. Even my father, who sometimes seems to me to have been at home in the world as long as it has lasted, has really lived on this earth only a little longer than I have, in terms of all the time there has been to live in. He has not known a time, any more than I, when automobiles and electric lights did not at least exist. He was not alive when this century started. I will be barely alive—old, old—when it ends. I do not like to think of it. I wish the Lake to be always just a lake, with the safe-swimming floats marking it, and the breakwater and the lights of Tuppertown.

My father has a job, selling for Walker Brothers. This is a firm that sells almost entirely in the country, the back country. Sunshine, Boylesbridge, Turnaround—that is all his territory. Not Dungannon where we used to live, Dungannon is too near town and my mother is grateful for that. He sells cough medicine, iron tonic, corn plasters, laxatives, pills for female disorders, mouthwash, shampoo, liniment, salves, lemon and orange and raspberry concentrate for making refreshing drinks, vanilla, food coloring, black and green tea, ginger, cloves, and other spices, rat poison. He has a song about it, with these two lines:

> And have all liniments and oils,
> For everything from corns to boils. . . .

Not a very funny song, in my mother's opinion. A peddler's song, and that is what he is, a peddler knocking at backwoods kitchens. Up until last winter we had our own business, a fox farm. My father raised silver foxes and sold their pelts to the people who make them into capes and coats and muffs. Prices fell, my father hung on hoping they would get better next year, and they fell again, and he hung on one more year and one more and finally it was not possible to hang on anymore, we owed everything to the feed company. I have heard my mother explain this, several times, to Mrs. Oliphant, who is the only neighbor she talks to. (Mrs. Oliphant also has come down in the world, being a schoolteacher who married the janitor.) We poured all we had into it, my mother says, and we came out with nothing. Many people could say the same thing, these days, but my mother has no time for the national calamity, only ours. Fate has flung us onto a street of poor people (it does not matter that we were poor before; that was a different sort of poverty), and the only way to take this, as she sees it, is with dignity, with bitterness, with no reconciliation. No bathroom with a claw-footed tub and a flush toilet is going to comfort her, nor water on tap and sidewalks past the house and milk in bottles, not even the two movie theatres and the Venus Restaurant and Woolworths so marvellous it has live birds singing in its fan-cooled corners and fish as tiny as fingernails, as bright as moons, swimming in its green tanks. My mother does not care.

In the afternoons she often walks to Simon's Grocery and takes me with her to help carry things. She wears a good dress, navy blue with little flowers, sheer, worn over a navy-blue slip. Also a summer hat of white straw, pushed down on the side of the head, and white shoes I have just whitened on a newspaper on the back steps. I have my hair freshly done in long damp curls which the dry air will fortunately soon loosen, a stiff large hair ribbon on top of my head. This is entirely different from going out after supper with my father. We have not walked past two houses before I feel we have become objects of universal ridicule. Even the dirty words chalked on the sidewalk are laughing at us. My mother does not seem to notice. She walks serenely like a lady shopping, like a *lady* shopping, past the housewives in loose belt-less dresses torn under the arms. With me her creation, wretched curls and flaunting hair bow, scrubbed knees and white socks—all I do not want to be. I loathe even my name when she says it in public, in a voice so high, proud, and ringing, deliberately different from the voice of any other mother on the street.

My mother will sometimes carry home, for a treat, a brick of ice cream— pale Neapolitan; and because we have no refrigerator in our house we wake my brother and eat it at once in the dining room, always darkened by the wall of the house next door. I spoon it up tenderly, leaving the chocolate till last, hoping to have some still to eat when my brother's dish is empty. My mother tries then to imitate the conversations we used to have at Dungannon, going back to our earliest, most leisurely days before my brother was born, when she would give me a little tea and a lot of milk in a cup like hers and we would sit out on the step facing the pump, the lilac tree, the fox pens beyond. She is not able to keep from mentioning those days. "Do you remember when we put you in your sled and Major pulled you?" (Major our dog, that we had to leave with neighbors when we moved.) "Do you remember your sandbox outside the kitchen window?" I pretend to remember far less than I do, wary of being trapped into sympathy or any unwanted emotion.

My mother has headaches. She often has to lie down. She lies on my brother's narrow bed in the little screened porch, shaded by heavy branches. "I look up at that tree and I think I am at home," she says.

"What you need," my father tells her, "is some fresh air and a drive in the country." He means for her to go with him, on his Walker Brothers route.

That is not my mother's idea of a drive in the country.

"Can I come?"

"Your mother might want you for trying on clothes."

"I'm beyond sewing this afternoon," my mother says.

"I'll take her then. Take both of them, give you a rest."

What is there about us that people need to be given a rest from? Never mind. I am glad enough to find my brother and make him go to the toilet and get us both into the car, our knees unscrubbed, my hair unringleted. My father brings from the house his two heavy brown suitcases, full of bottles, and sets them on the back seat. He wears a white shirt, brilliant in the sunlight, a tie, light trousers belonging to his summer suit (his other suit is black, for funerals, and belonged to my uncle before he died), and a creamy straw hat. His salesman's outfit, with pencils clipped in the shirt pocket. He goes back once again, probably to say goodbye to my mother, to ask her if she is sure she doesn't want to come, and hear her say, "No. No thanks, I'm better just to lie here with my eyes closed." Then we are backing out of the driveway with the rising hope of adventure, just the little hope that takes you over the bump into the street, the hot air starting to move, turning into a breeze, the houses growing less and less familiar as we follow the shortcut my father knows, the quick way out of town. Yet what is there waiting for us all afternoon but hot hours in stricken farmyards, perhaps a stop at a country store and three ice-cream cones or bottles of pop, and my father singing? The one he made up about himself has a title—"The Walker Brothers Cowboy"—and it starts out like this:

> Old Ned Fields, he now is dead,
> So I am ridin' the route instead. . . .

Who is Ned Fields? The man he has replaced, surely, and if so he really is dead; yet my father's voice is mournful-jolly, making his death some kind of nonsense, a comic calamity. "Wisht I was back on the Rio Grande,[3] plungin' through the dusky sand." My father sings most of the time while driving the car. Even now, heading out of town, crossing the bridge and taking the sharp turn onto the highway, he is humming something, mumbling a bit of a song to himself, just tuning up, really, getting ready to improvise, for out along the highway we pass the Baptist Camp, the Vacation Bible Camp, and he lets loose:

> Where are the Baptists, where are the Bapists,
>   where are all the Baptists today?
> They're down in the water, in Lake Huron water,
>   with their sins all a-gittin' washed away."

My brother takes this for straight truth and gets up on his knees trying to see down to the Lake. "I don't see any Baptists," he says accusingly. "Neither do I, son," says my father. "I told you, they're down in the Lake."

No roads paved when we left the highway. We have to roll up the windows because of dust. The land is flat, scorched, empty. Bush lots at the back of the farms hold shade, black pine-shade like pools nobody can ever get to. We bump up a long lane and at the end of it what could look more unwelcoming, more deserted than the tall unpainted farmhouse with grass growing uncut right up to the front door, green blinds down, and a door upstairs opening on nothing but air? Many houses have this door, and I have never yet been able to find out why. I ask my father and he says they are for walking in your sleep. *What?* Well, if you happen to be walking in your sleep and you want to step outside. I am offended, seeing too late that he is joking, as usual, but my brother says sturdily, "If they did that they would break their necks."

The 1930s. How much this kind of farmhouse, this kind of afternoon seem to me to belong to that one decade in time, just as my father's hat does, his bright flared tie, our car with its wide running board (an Essex, and long past its prime). Cars somewhat like it, many older, none dustier, sit in the farmyards. Some are past running and have their doors pulled off, their seats removed for use on porches. No living things to be seen, chickens or cattle. Except dogs. There are dogs lying in any kind of shade they can find, dreaming, their lean sides rising and sinking rapidly. They get up when my father

---

3. A large river that begins in Colorado and flows south, becoming the border between Mexico and the United States.

opens the car door, he has to speak to them. "Nice boy, there's a boy, nice old boy." They quiet down, go back to their shade. He should know how to quiet animals, he has held desperate foxes with tongs around their necks. One gentling voice for the dogs and another, rousing, cheerful, for calling at doors. "Hello there, missus, it's the Walker Brothers man and what are you out of today?" A door opens, he disappears. Forbidden to follow, forbidden even to leave the car, we can just wait and wonder what he says. Sometimes trying to make my mother laugh, he pretends to be himself in a farm kitchen, spreading out his sample case. "Now then, missus, are you troubled with parasitic life? Your children's scalps, I mean. All those crawly little things we're too polite to mention that show up on the heads of the best of families? Soap alone is useless, kerosene is not too nice a perfume, but I have here—" Or else, "Believe me, sitting and driving all day the way I do I *know* the value of these fine pills. Natural relief. A problem common to old folks too, once their days of activity are over—How about you, Grandma?" He would wave the imaginary box of pills under my mother's nose and she would laugh finally, unwillingly. "He doesn't say that really, does he?" I said, and she said no of course not, he was too much of a gentleman.

One yard after another, then, the old cars, the pumps, dogs, views of gray barns and falling-down sheds and unturning windmills. The men, if they are working in the fields, are not in any fields that we can see. The children are far away, following dry creek beds or looking for blackberries, or else they are hidden in the house, spying at us through cracks in the blinds. The car seat has grown slick with our sweat. I dare my brother to sound the horn, wanting to do it myself but not wanting to get the blame. He knows better. We play I Spy, but it is hard to find many colors. Gray for the barns and sheds and toilets and houses, brown for the yard and fields, black or brown for the dogs. The rusting cars show rainbow patches, in which I strain to pick out purple or green; likewise I peer at doors for shreds of old peeling paint, maroon or yellow. We can't play with letters, which would be better, because my brother is too young to spell. The game disintegrates anyway. He claims my colors are not fair, and wants extra turns.

In one house no door opens, though the car is in the yard. My father knocks and whistles, calls, "Hullo there ! Walker Brothers man!" but there is not a stir of reply anywhere. This house has no porch, just a bare, slanting slab of cement on which my father stands. He turns around, searching the barnyard, the barn whose mow must be empty because you can see the sky through it, and finally he bends to pick up his suitcases. Just then a window is opened upstairs, a white pot appears on the sill, is tilted over and its contents splash down the outside wall. The window is not directly above my father's head, so only a stray splash would catch him. He picks up his suitcases with no particular hurry and walks, no longer whistling, to the car. "Do you know what that was?" I say to my brother. "*Pee.*" He laughs and laughs.

My father rolls and lights a cigarette before he starts the car. The window has been slammed down, the blind drawn, we never did see a hand or face. "Pee, pee," sings my brother ecstatically. "Somebody dumped down pee!" "Just don't tell your mother that," my father says. "She isn't liable to see the joke." "Is it in your song?" my brother wants to know. My father says no but he will see what he can do to work it in.

I notice in a little while that we are not turning in any more lanes, though it does not seem to me that we are headed home. "Is this the way to Sunshine?" I ask my father, and he answers, "No, ma'am, it's not." "Are we still in your territory?" He shakes his head. "We're going *fast*," my brother says approvingly, and in fact we are bouncing along through dry puddle-holes so that all the bottles in the suitcases clink together and gurgle promisingly.

Another lane, a house, also unpainted, dried to silver in the sun.

"I thought we were out of your territory."

"We are."

"Then what are we going in here for?"

"You'll see."

In front of the house a short, sturdy woman is picking up washing, which had been spread on the grass to bleach and dry. When the car stops she stares at it hard for a moment, bends to pick up a couple more towels to add to the bundle under her arm, comes across to us and says in a flat voice, neither welcoming nor unfriendly, "Have you lost your way?"

My father takes his time getting out of the car. "I don't think so," he says. "I'm the Walker Brothers man."

"George Golley is our Walker Brothers man," the woman says, "and he was out here no more than a week ago. Oh, my Lord God," she says harshly, "it's you."

"It was, the last time I looked in the mirror," my father says.

The woman gathers all the towels in front of her and holds on to them tightly, pushing them against her stomach as if it hurt. "Of all the people I never thought to see. And telling me you were the Walker Brothers man."

"I'm sorry if you were looking forward to George Golley," my father says humbly.

"And look at me, I was prepared to clean the henhouse. You'll think that's just an excuse but it's true. I don't go round looking like this every day." She is wearing a farmer's straw hat, through which pricks of sunlight penetrate and float on her face, a loose, dirty print smock, and canvas shoes. "Who are those in the car, Ben? They're not yours?"

"Well, I hope and believe they are," my father says, and tells our names and ages. "Come on, you can get out. This is Nora, Miss Cronin. Nora, you better tell me, is it still Miss, or have you got a husband hiding in the woodshed?"

"If I had a husband that's not where I'd keep him, Ben," she says, and they both laugh, her laugh abrupt and somewhat angry. "You'll think I got no manners, as well as being dressed like a tramp," she says. "Come on in out of the sun. It's cool in the house."

We go across the yard ("Excuse me taking you in this way but I don't think the front door has been opened since Papa's funeral, I'm afraid the hinges might drop off"), up the porch steps, into the kitchen, which really is cool, high-ceilinged, the blinds of course down, a simple, clean, threadbare room with waxed worn linoleum, potted geraniums, drinking-pail and dipper, a round table with scrubbed oilcloth. In spite of the cleanness, the wiped and swept surfaces, there is a faint sour smell—maybe of the dishrag or the tin dipper or the oilcloth, or the old lady, because there is one, sitting in an easy chair under the clock shelf. She turns her head slightly in our direction and says, "Nora? Is that company?"

"Blind," says Nora in a quick explaining voice to my father. Then, "You won't guess who it is, Momma. Hear his voice."

My father goes to the front of her chair and bends and says hopefully, "Afternoon, Mrs. Cronin."

"Ben Jordan," says the old lady with no surprise. "You haven't been to see us in the longest time. Have you been out of the country?"

My father and Nora look at each other.

"He's married, Momma," says Nora cheerfully and aggressively. "Married and got two children and here they are." She pulls us forward, makes each of us touch the old lady's dry, cool hand while she says our names in turn. Blind! This is the first blind person I have ever seen close up. Her eyes are closed, the eyelids sunk away down, showing no shape of the eyeball, just hollows. From one hollow comes a drop of silver liquid, a medicine, or a miraculous tear.

"Let me get into a decent dress," Nora says. "Talk to Momma. It's a treat for her. We hardly ever see company, do we, Momma?"

"Not many makes it out this road," says the old lady placidly. "And the ones that used to be around here, our old neighbors, some of them have pulled out."

"True everywhere," my father says.

"Where's your wife then?"

"Home. She's not too fond of the hot weather, makes her feel poorly."

"Well." This is a habit of country people, old people, to say "well," meaning, "Is that so?" with a little extra politeness and concern.

Nora's dress, when she appears again—stepping heavily on Cuban heels down the stairs in the hall—is flowered more lavishly than anything my mother owns, green and yellow on brown, some sort of floating sheer crêpe, leaving her arms bare. Her arms are heavy, and every bit of her skin you can see is covered with little dark freckles like measles. Her hair is short, black, coarse and curly, her teeth very white and strong. "It's the first time I knew there was such a thing as green poppies," my father says, looking at her dress.

"You would be surprised all the things you never knew," says Nora, sending a smell of cologne far and wide when she moves and displaying a change of voice to go with the dress, something more sociable and youthful. "They're not poppies anyway, they're just flowers. You go and pump me some good cold water and I'll make these children a drink." She gets down from the cupboard a bottle of Walker Brothers Orange syrup.

"You telling me you were the Walker Brothers man!"

"It's the truth, Nora. You go and look at my sample cases in the car if you don't believe me. I got the territory directly south of here."

"Walker Brothers? Is that a fact? You selling for Walker Brothers?"

"Yes, ma'am."

"We always heard you were raising foxes over Dungannon way."

"That's what I was doing, but I kind of run out of luck in that business."

"So where're you living? How long've you been out selling?"

"We moved into Tuppertown. I been at it, oh, two, three months. It keeps the wolf from the door. Keeps him as far away as the back fence."

Nora laughs. "Well, I guess you count yourself lucky to have the work. Isabel's husband in Brantford, he was out of work the longest time. I thought if he didn't find something soon I was going to have them all land in here to feed, and I tell you I was hardly looking forward to it. It's all I can manage with me and Momma."

"Isabel married," my father says. "Muriel married too?"

"No, she's teaching school out West. She hasn't been home for five years.
I guess she finds something better to do with her holidays. I would if I was
her." She gets some snapshots out of the table drawer and starts showing
him. "That's Isabel's oldest boy, starting school. That's the baby sitting in her
carriage. Isabel and her husband. Muriel. That's her roommate with her.
That's a fellow she used to go around with, and his car. He was working in
a bank out there. That's her school, it has eight rooms. She teaches Grade
Five." My father shakes his head. "I can't think of her any way but when she
was going to school, so shy I used to pick her up on the road—I'd be on my
way to see you—and she would not say one word, not even to agree it was a
nice day."

"She's got over that."

"Who are you talking about?" says the old lady.

"Muriel. I said she's got over being shy."

"She was here last summer."

"No, Momma, that was Isabel. Isabel and her family were here last summer. Muriel's out West."

"I meant Isabel."

Shortly after this the old lady falls asleep, her head on the side, her mouth
open. "Excuse her manners," Nora says. "It's old age." She fixes an afghan
over her mother and says we can all go into the front room where our talking
won't disturb her.

"You two," my father says. "Do you want to go outside and amuse
yourselves?"

Amuse ourselves how? Anyway, I want to stay. The front room is more
interesting than the kitchen, though barer. There is a gramophone and a
pump organ and a picture on the wall of Mary, Jesus' mother—I know that
much—in shades of bright blue and pink with a spiked band of light around
her head. I know that such pictures are found only in the homes of Roman
Catholics and so Nora must be one. We have never known any Roman Catholics at all well, never well enough to visit in their houses. I think of what
my grandmother and my Aunt Tena, over in Dungannon, used to always say
to indicate that somebody was a Catholic. *So-and-so digs with the wrong foot,*
they would say. *She digs with the wrong foot.* That was what they would say
about Nora.[4]

Nora takes a bottle, half full, out of the top of the organ and pours some
of what is in it into the two glasses that she and my father have emptied of
the orange drink.

"Keep it in case of sickness?" my father says.

"Not on your life," says Nora. "I'm never sick. I just keep it because I keep
it. One bottle does me a fair time, though, because I don't care for drinking
alone. Here's luck!" She and my father drink and I know what it is. Whisky.
One of the things my mother has told me in our talks together is that my
father never drinks whisky. But I see he does. He drinks whisky and he talks
of people whose names I have never heard before. But after a while he turns
to a familiar incident. He tells about the chamberpot that was emptied out
the window. "Picture me there," he says, "hollering my heartiest. *Oh, lady,
it's your Walker Brothers man, anybody home?*" He does himself hollering,

---

4. Protestant-Catholic feuds were transplanted to southern Ontario by Irish settlers.

grinning absurdly, waiting, looking up in pleased expectation, and then—oh, ducking, covering his head with his arms, looking as if he begged for mercy (when he never did anything like that, I was watching), and Nora laughs, almost as hard as my brother did at the time.

"That isn't true! That's not a word true!"

"Oh, indeed it is, ma'am. We have our heroes in the ranks of Walker Brothers. I'm glad you think it's funny," he says sombrely.

I ask him shyly, "Sing the song."

"What song? Have you turned into a singer on top of everything else?"

Embarrassed, my father says, "Oh, just this song I made up while I was driving around, it gives me something to do, making up rhymes."

But after some urging he does sing it, looking at Nora with a droll, apologetic expression, and she laughs so much that in places he has to stop and wait for her to get over laughing so he can go on, because she makes him laugh too. Then he does various parts of his salesman's spiel. Nora when she laughs squeezes her large bosom under her folded arms. "You're crazy," she says. "That's all you are." She sees my brother peering into the gramophone and she jumps up and goes over to him. "Here's us sitting enjoying ourselves and not giving you a thought, isn't it terrible?" she says. "You want me to put a record on, don't you? You want to hear a nice record? Can you dance? I bet your sister can, can't she?"

I say no. "A big girl like you and so good-looking and can't dance!" says Nora. "It's high time you learned. I bet you'd make a lovely dancer. Here, I'm going to put on a piece I used to dance to and even your daddy did, in his dancing days. You didn't know your daddy was a dancer, did you? Well, he is a talented man, your daddy!"

She puts down the lid and takes hold of me unexpectedly around the waist, picks up my other hand, and starts making me go backwards. "This is the way, now, this is how they dance. Follow me. This foot, see. One and one-two. One and one-two. That's fine, that's lovely, don't look at your feet! Follow me, that's right, see how easy? You're going to be a lovely dancer! One and one-two. One and one-two. Ben, see your daughter dancing!" *Whispering while you cuddle near me, Whispering so no one can hear me* . . . [5]

Round and round the linoleum, me proud, intent, Nora laughing and moving with great buoyancy, wrapping me in her strange gaiety, her smell of whisky, cologne, and sweat. Under the arms her dress is damp, and little drops form along her upper lip, hang in the soft black hairs at the corners of her mouth. She whirls me around in front of my father—causing me to stumble, for I am by no means so swift a pupil as she pretends—and lets me go, breathless.

"Dance with me, Ben."

"I'm the world's worst dancer, Nora, and you know it."

"I certainly never thought so."

"You would now."

She stands in front of him, arms hanging loose and hopeful, her breasts, which a moment ago embarrassed me with their warmth and bulk, rising and

---

5. From the popular song "Whispering," words and music by John Schonberger, Vincent Rose, and Richard Coburn. The original 1920 recording by Paul Whiteman's band was one of the first records to sell a million copies.

falling under her loose flowered dress, her face shining with the exercise, and delight.

"Ben."

My father drops his head and says quietly, "Not me, Nora."

So she can only go and take the record off. "I can drink alone but I can't dance alone," she says. "Unless I am a whole lot crazier than I think I am."

"Nora," says my father, smiling. "You're not crazy."

"Stay for supper."

"Oh, no. We couldn't put you to the trouble."

"It's no trouble. I'd be glad of it."

"And their mother would worry. She'd think I'd turned us over in a ditch."

"Oh, well. Yes."

"We've taken a lot of your time now."

"Time," says Nora bitterly. "Will you come by ever again?"

"I will if I can," says my father.

"Bring the children. Bring your wife."

"Yes, I will," says my father. "I will if I can."

When she follows us to the car he says, "You come to see us too, Nora. We're right on Grove Street, left-hand side going in, that's north, and two doors this side—east—of Baker Street."

Nora does not repeat these directions. She stands close to the car in her soft, brilliant dress. She touches the fender, making an unintelligible mark in the dust there.

On the way home my father does not buy any ice cream or pop, but he does go into a country store and get a package of licorice, which he shares with us. She digs with the wrong foot, I think, and the words seem sad to me as never before, dark, perverse. My father does not say anything to me about not mentioning things at home, but I know, just from the thoughtfulness, the pause when he passes the licorice, that there are things not to be mentioned. The whisky, maybe the dancing. No worry about my brother, he does not notice enough. At most he might remember the blind lady, the picture of Mary.

"Sing," my brother commands my father, but my father says gravely, "I don't know, I seem to be fresh out of songs. You watch the road and let me know if you see any rabbits."

So my father drives and my brother watches the road for rabbits and I feel my father's life flowing back from our car in the last of the afternoon, darkening and turning strange, like a landscape that has an enchantment on it, making it kindly, ordinary and familiar while you are looking at it, but changing it, once your back is turned, into something you will never know, with all kinds of weathers, and distances you cannot imagine.

When we get closer to Tuppertown the sky becomes gently overcast, as always, nearly always, on summer evenings by the Lake.

WOLE SOYINKA
born 1934

The governing theme of Wole Soyinka's work is the dualism of life and consciousness in modern Africa. His entire output, now considerable, occupies itself with the conditions of the African community in transition. Transition, for Soyinka, carries more than a historical and social meaning. It is charged with a metaphysical significance that derives from his perception of humanity in general, while referring to the transformations of modes of life, sensibility, and thought which have taken place in contemporary Africa as Western modernities impinge on indigenous life. Soyinka's work can be read both as a meditation on the profound disruptions in the collective psyche produced by this process and as an imaginative effort to repair the collapse of the old order with a new founding myth, a myth derived from his Yoruba inheritance and embodying his vision of a new, distinctively African moral and spiritual awareness.

Soyinka's acute sense of African dualism owes much to his personal life and background. He was born on July 13, 1934, in Abeokuta, western Nigeria, the second child in a family that had strong ties to the traditional Yoruba ruling class as well as to the new educated elite produced by Christian missionary activity. Soyinka's remarkable reconstruction, in *Isarà* (1989), of his father's youth, education, and teaching career in the missionary school was undertaken primarily as a gesture of filial devotion but is important too in its recall of the formation of an articulate Yoruba intelligentsia, whose nationalist aspirations and modernizing zeal have been largely responsible for the making of modern Nigeria. The book thus evokes the social history that underlies his own development and provides an extended perspective on what was to become the immediate context of his own work. Soyinka has also recounted his early life in *Aké: The Years of Childhood* (1981).

Soyinka began his education in 1938, at the parsonage school at Aké, where his father was headmaster. He entered Abeokuta Grammar School in 1944 for his secondary education but after a year transferred to Government College, an elite boarding school at Ibadan, some sixty miles north of his native city. In 1952, he enrolled at University College, Ibadan, which had recently been founded and was then affiliated with the University of London. His earliest writing was done while there, for a student journal, which had been started and edited by Chinua Achebe, who had preceded him as a student at the university. After two years at Ibadan, Soyinka left for England and entered the University of Leeds to study English literature. The Shakespeare scholar G. Wilson Knight has often been cited as a major influence on Soyinka during his years at Leeds, but mention must also be made of Arnold Kettle, who taught English at Leeds and whose Marxist readings of literature as a product of the play of social forces Soyinka could hardly ignore.

Graduating in 1957, Soyinka moved to London, where he was for a while a schoolteacher before becoming attached, as a playreader, to the Royal Court Theatre in 1959. The central role played by this theater company in the great postwar revival of British drama, through its productions of the work of Samuel Beckett, John Osborne, and Arnold Wesker, exposed Soyinka to the most innovative endeavor in English theater during this period. Also influential was the work of John Synge and Sean O'Casey, whose plays disclosed the poetry of Irish speech and endowed with symbolism the communal experience of the Irish people. And so were the efforts of T. S. Eliot and, in a less serious vein, of Christopher Fry, to revive English verse drama. Their plays may well have suggested to Soyinka the dramatic potential of Yoruba, his own native tongue. The theater of ideas, as developed by George Bernard Shaw, the dominant figure in British theater at this time, and by the German playwright Bertolt Brecht, also made an impression on Soyinka. Brecht's plays in particular, by combining dialogue with mime and song, must have recalled to Soyinka the multiform character of the performance traditions of his native culture.

The convergence of these many influences is evident in Soyinka's two early plays, *The Lion and the Jewel* and *The Swamp Dwellers*, first performed in 1959 as a double bill at Ibadan University Arts Theatre by the student drama group. With these works, Soyinka inaugurated a new era in Nigerian drama, bringing a sophisticated dramaturgy to bear on issues of relevance to his audience: in a light-hearted commentary on cultural ambiguity in *The Lion and the Jewel* and in the stark atmosphere of *The Swamp Dwellers*, a brooding reflection on the degradation of spiritual symbols in the service of power.

Early in 1960, Soyinka returned to Nigeria to the department of English at Ibadan, whose chair, Molly Mahood, had arranged for him a Rockefeller grant to research traditional drama in west Africa. This was on the eve of Nigerian independence, and he responded to the country's mood of anticipation by writing *A Dance of the Forests*, performed by the "1960 Masks," a theatrical group he had put together for the occasion. This play contains Soyinka's first major statement on issues of national life. Its sardonic vision of history as an interminable procession of human stupidities is intended not merely to counter the exaggerated claims, based on a romantic vision of the past, of a triumphant nationalism, but also to serve as a moral challenge to the new nation. For Soyinka begins to define here his conception of the creative artist as one who, despite his own human contradictions, must serve as an agent of moral insight and renewal for the people. The forest setting and the active presence of spirit characters both recall and enlarge the allegorical implications of traditional Yoruba folktales.

Over the next two years, Soyinka traveled extensively in west Africa observing indigenous drama and absorbing the performance styles of the popular Yoruba traveling theater, which flourished alongside the university-based drama in English that his own work was helping to revitalize. His research became apparent in his next play, *The Strong Breed*, which draws on the conventions of traditional theater ritual in treating a theme of heroic sacrifice in the service of communal redemption. Appointed lecturer in English at the University of Ife in 1962, Soyinka formed the "Orisun Theatre," a semiprofessional company that he trained and directed in a wide range of plays. His own were already appearing in print, helping to establish his reputation beyond Nigeria. In 1965 his first novel, *The Interpreters*, was published; it portrayed, within a densely symbolic narrative framework, a group of young Nigerian intellectuals futilely trying to give purpose to their lives and to chart a moral course for their society. His next play, *The Road* (1965), provides a realistic depiction of the desperate conditions of the underprivileged class in Nigerian society, underlining at the same time a broader theme of the transience of life. In the play, Soyinka draws heavily on Yoruba religious belief and cultic practices to portray life as a series of transitional states of being, a mystical progress through the cosmic realm. The play introduces one of Soyinka's most memorable characters, "Professor," an ambiguous figure, half quack, half visionary, whose morbid obsession with death provides its metaphysical focus; his quest for "the word" involves, ultimately, an intense engagement with the mystery of life.

In October 1965, Soyinka found himself drawn into a political storm that had been gathering in Nigeria for more than a year. Arrested for allegedly holding up a state radio station and broadcasting a seditious message, he was acquitted at his trial for lack of evidence. In January 1966, a military coup toppled the government, and the country was plunged into a national crisis. Soyinka had meanwhile moved to Lagos, where he had been appointed head of the department of English at the university. *Kongi's Harvest*, written during this period and produced at the Dakar Arts Festival in May 1966, gives a political focus to the social anxieties expressed in his earlier work. It represents his personal contribution to the debate on political and socioeconomic organization in postindependence Africa, but his dramatic handling of the issue extends beyond the ideological framework of the debate. The politics of the modern dictator Kongi is seen to be not only a violation of human decency but a poisoning of the wellsprings of communal existence. We begin to form an idea of what these values are from the poetically charged speeches of King Danlola, a traditional ruler who is Kongi's antithesis. The same values receive a more intense formulation in *Idanre and Other Poems* (1967), Soyinka's first collection of poems.

Civil war broke out in Nigeria in July 1967. Arrested a month later by the federal authorities for collaborating with the rebel regime of Biafra, Soyinka was held without trial until October 1969. His prison experience gave new urgency to his moral concerns. As he writes in *The Man Died* (1972), a moving account of his detention and a searing indictment of the military regime, "The man dies in all who keep silent in the face of tyranny." These years of crisis and war account for the somber mood that runs through the play *Madmen and Specialists* (1970), with its absurdist emphasis on evil as a force in the universe, and the novel *Season of Anomy* (1973), dominated by visions of carnage and waste. However, the poems in *A Shuttle in the Crypt* (1971), a lyrical record of Soyinka's moods and feelings while in solitary confinement, provide evidence of his effort, through writing, to shore up his mind and, through meditation, to achieve a new insight into human experience: "Thought is hallowed in the lean oil / of Solitude."

After a brief tenure as director of the School of Drama at Ibadan, Soyinka went into exile in 1971, living mostly in England. On a commission from the British National Theatre, he wrote *The Bacchae of Euripides* (1973), a highly personal and verbally exuberant adaptation of the Greek classic. The life-affirming impulses associated with the cult of Dionysus are summoned against an overbearing King Pentheus, representative of a repressive order. Soyinka spent the 1973–74 academic year as a visiting fellow at Churchill College, Cambridge; while there, he delivered a series of lectures later published as *Myth, Literature and the African World* (1976). The volume contains his celebrated essay *The Fourth Stage*, an exposition of the Yoruba concept of tragedy. For Soyinka, the forms of ritual in his culture display an anguished disconnection from the "fourth stage," a state of transition to a new and fuller state of being that completes the continuum formed by the living, the dead, and the unborn. Here Ogun, the Yoruba god of iron, becomes central. As the first to accomplish this transition on behalf of humanity, he is venerated as the first artist, and the ritual commemoration in traditional Yoruba drama of his accomplishment replicates it symbolically to bridge a metaphysical gulf in the culture.

Soyinka's essay must be considered not so much a factual account of Yoruba myth as a statement of what he takes to be its spirit. *Death and the King's Horseman*, his next play, illustrates the function of myth as Soyinka sees it, a function linked to his theory of a tragic human incompleteness that seeks completeness in ritual. The play is based on an actual event—a British colonial officer's intervention to prevent the ritual suicide, following the king of Oyo's death, of his "horseman," a minor chief whose privileges were conditional on his accompanying his king to the afterworld. In deriving the theme from this historical incident, Soyinka shifts focus from its anecdotal and ethnographic interest to the response of human beings to death. It is, however, essential to consider both aspects, for they reflect the dualism played out in the play. The opening scene offers us a view of Yoruba collective ethos as Soyinka intends us to understand it. The market setting registers the fusion of economic, social, and religious life in Yoruba culture, rehearsing, on an eminently festive note, the people's belief system. The prominent role of Iyaloja in the scene affirms the centrality of the female principle in this belief system, founded as it is on the idea of a constant flow of life through the entire realm of being. In this light, the "Not I" episode becomes crucial. Elesin's apparently joyous assumption of his tragic burden prepares the psychological ground for his later failure of will. His reiterations of responsibility for the integrity of his world take on more and more the character of protests and thus betray an ambivalence toward his culture's strategy for confronting death. The opening scene displays the original coherence of the Yoruba world, together with a suggestion of its latent tensions. Essential for this effect are the resources of the Yoruba oral tradition, for much of the verbal exchange between the characters, and especially between Elesin and his praise singer, is an adaptation of consecrated forms of Yoruba oral poetry, proverbs, and lineage praise names (*oriki orile*) which situate the individual within a network of social relations and obligations.

The intensity of this opening scene contrasts with the deliberate flatness of the second, which exhibits the colonial world as an inverted image of its Yoruba counterpart. The conventions of drawing room theater appropriately frame Pilkings's insensitive attitude to Yoruba ritual, demonstrated in his choice of traditional Yoruba dress as costume for a vulgar masked ball. Amusa's announcement of Elesin's impending suicide leads to the collision of the colonial and indigenous worlds dramatized in scene 3. The massing of the women in this scene and their sexual taunting of Amusa, the emasculated colonial subject, are highlighted by the action that takes place off stage—Elesin's union with his new bride and the symbolic meaning attached to it, the creation of new life.

With the return onstage of Elesin, the play moves to its highpoint as he steps into the realm of transition, suspended between life and death. The ritual quality of this scene is registered in the language, as the praise singer's trance-inducing words allude more and more to the incantations employed by healers and diviners. The arrest of Elesin breaks the spell of the praise singer's words, and the play begins a downward course toward a tragic resolution. Olunde's conversation with Jane Pilkings in scene 4, in which he vindicates the Yoruba position on ritual suicide with a view of sacrifice as a cultural and moral imperative, anticipates his own gesture to save the family honor and reestablish the social and spiritual bonds broken by what he sees as his father's betrayal of a sacred trust. Dominant in the final scene is the figure of Iyaloja, who now assumes the role of Earth Mother. Her pronouncement at the end accords with the vision of humanity that she has all along embodied, one that subsumes the individual in the comprehensive vision of universal life that Yoruba myth enunciates.

Death and the King's Horseman is Soyinka's masterpiece; in it, the verbal resourcefulness and mastery of theatrical effects evident in his earlier plays come together to produce a work whose evocative power ensures its appeal both as a mode of reconnection to a living tradition and as an exploration of a universal human dilemma. In an obvious reference to the play, the citation for the award to Soyinka of the Nobel Prize in Literature in 1986 describes his work as depicting "the drama of existence." By the time Soyinka retired from the University of Ife in 1985, he had become an international figure, and his plays have been produced all over the world. Besides the Nobel Prize, he has received many honors, including the French Legion of Honor, and the range and diversity of his work have ensured his reputation as one of the most versatile and accomplished of contemporary writers.

Derek White, *Wole Soyinka* (1993), is a comprehensive and up-to-date study of Soyinka's work; but Eldred Jones, *The Writing of Wole Soyinka* (1973), can be consulted with profit, as can Gerald Moore, *Wole Soyinka* (1971). For an extended discussion of *Death and the King's Horseman* in the context of Soyinka's system of ideas, see Biodun Jeyifo, *Wole Soyinka: A Voice of Africa* (1990). These studies are complemented by James Gibbs, ed., *Critical Perspectives on Wole Soyinka* (1980), and James Gibbs and Bernth Lindfors, eds., *Research on Wole Soyinka* (1993), both collections of essays on various aspects of Soyinka's work and career.

PRONOUNCING GLOSSARY

The following list uses common English syllables to provide rough equivalents of selected words whose pronunciation may be unfamiliar to the general reader.

agbada: *ah-gbah-dah*

Alafin: *ah-lah-feeng*

Apinke: *ah-kpeeng-keh*

egungun: *ay-goong-goong*

Elegbara: *eh-leh-gbah-rah*

Elesin Oba: *eh-leh-sheeng aw-bah*

Esu: *ay-shoo*

gbedu: *gbeh-doo*

Ifawomi: *ee-fah-woh-mee*

Ilesi: *ee-lay-see*

Iyaloja: *ee-yah-law-jah*

Olohun-iyo: *oh-loh-hoong—yaw*

Olunde: *oh-loong-day*

opele: *aw-kpeh-leh*

osugbo: *oh-shoo-gboh*

Oya: *aw-yah*

sanyan: *song-yong*

sigidi: *shee-gee-dee*

Wuraola: *woo-rah-aw-lah*

Death and the King's Horseman

CAST

PRAISE-SINGER

ELESIN, *Horseman of the King*

IYALOJA, *"Mother" of the market*

SIMON PILKINGS, *District Officer*

JANE PILKINGS, *his wife*

SERJEANT AMUSA

JOSEPH, *houseboy to the Pilkingses*

BRIDE

H. R. H. THE PRINCE

THE RESIDENT

AIDE-DE-CAMP

OLUNDE, *eldest son of Elesin*

DRUMMERS, WOMEN, YOUNG GIRLS,

   DANCERS *at the Ball*

Scene One

A passage through a market in its closing stages. The stalls are being emptied, mats folded. A few WOMEN *pass through on their way home, loaded with baskets. On a cloth-stand, bolts of cloth are taken down, display pieces folded and piled on a tray.* ELESIN OBA *enters along a passage before the market, pursued by his* DRUMMERS *and* PRAISE-SINGERS. *He is a man of enormous vitality, speaks, dances and sings with that infectious enjoyment of life which accompanies all his actions.*

PRAISE-SINGER: Elesin o! Elesin Oba! Howu![1] What tryst is this the cockerel goes to keep with such haste that he must leave his tail behind?

ELESIN: [*Slows down a bit, laughing.*] A tryst where the cockerel needs no adornment.

PRAISE-SINGER: O-oh, you hear that my companions? That's the way the world goes. Because the man approaches a brand new bride he forgets the long faithful mother of his children.

ELESIN: When the horse sniffs the stable does he not strain at the bridle? The market is the long-suffering home of my spirit and the women are packing up to go. That Esu[2]-harrassed day slipped into the stewpot while we feasted. We ate it up with the rest of the meat. I have neglected my women.

PRAISE-SINGER: We know all that. Still it's no reason for shedding your tail on this day of all days. I know the women will cover you in damask and

---

1. An exclamation of surprise.   2. The god of fate in the Yoruba pantheon; also a trickster figure.

alari[3] but when the wind blows cold from behind, that's when the fowl knows his true friends.

ELESIN: Olohun-iyo![4]

PRAISE-SINGER: Are you sure there will be one like me on the other side?

ELESIN: Olohun-iyo!

PRAISE-SINGER: Far be it for me to belittle the dwellers of that place but, a man is either born to his art or he isn't. And I don't know for certain that you'll meet my father, so who is going to sing these deeds in accents that will pierce the deafness of the ancient ones. I have prepared my going— just tell me: Olohun-iyo, I need you on this journey and I shall be behind you.

ELESIN: You're like a jealous wife. Stay close to me, but only on this side. My fame, my honour are legacies to the living; stay behind and let the world sip its honey from your lips.

PRAISE-SINGER: Your name will be like the sweet berry a child places under his tongue to sweeten the passage of food. The world will never spit it out.

ELESIN: Come then. This market is my roost. When I come among the women I am a chicken with a hundred mothers. I become a monarch whose palace is built with tenderness and beauty.

PRAISE-SINGER: They love to spoil you but beware. The hands of women also weaken the unwary.

ELESIN: This night I'll lay my head upon their lap and go to sleep. This night I'll touch feet with their feet in a dance that is no longer of this earth. But the smell of their flesh, their sweat, the smell of indigo[5] on their cloth, this is the last air I wish to breathe as I go to meet my great forebears.

PRAISE-SINGER: In their time the world was never tilted from its groove, it shall not be in yours.

ELESIN: The gods have said No.

PRAISE-SINGER: In their time the great wars came and went, the little wars came and went; the white slavers came and went, they took away the heart of our race, they bore away the mind and muscle of our race. The city fell and was rebuilt; the city fell and our people trudged through mountain and forest to find a new home but Elesin Oba do you hear me?

ELESIN: I hear your voice Olohun-iyo.

PRAISE-SINGER: Our world was never wrenched from its true course.

ELESIN: The gods have said No.

PRAISE-SINGER: There is only one home to the life of a river-mussel; there is only one home to the life of a tortoise; there is only one shell to the soul of man; there is only one world to the spirit of our race. If that world leaves its course and smashes on boulders of the great void, whose world will give us shelter?

ELESIN: It did not in the time of my forebears, it shall not in mine.

PRAISE-SINGER: The cockerel must not be seen without his feathers.

ELESIN: Nor will the Not-I bird be much longer without his nest.

PRAISE-SINGER: [*Stopped in his lyric stride.*] The Not-I bird, Elesin?

---

3. A rich woven cloth, brightly coloured [Author's note].   4. "Sweet voice": affectionate nickname for the praise-singer.   5. A deep blue dye.

ELESIN: I said, the Not-I bird.

PRAISE-SINGER: All respect to our elders but, is there really such a bird?

ELESIN: What! Could it be that he failed to knock on your door?

PRAISE-SINGER: [*Smiling.*] Elesin's riddles are not merely the nut in the kernel that breaks human teeth; he also buries the kernel in hot embers and dares a man's fingers to draw it out.

ELESIN: I am sure he called on you, Olohun-iyo. Did you hide in the loft and push out the servant to tell him you were out?

[ELESIN *executes a brief, half-taunting dance. The* DRUMMER *moves in and draws a rhythm out of his steps.* ELESIN *dances towards the market-place as he chants the story of the Not-I bird, his voice changing dexterously to mimic his characters. He performs like a born raconteur,*[6] *infecting his retinue with his humour and energy. More* WOMEN *arrive during his recital, including* IYALOJA.]

Death came calling
Who does not know his rasp of reeds?
A twilight whisper in the leaves before
The great araba[7] falls? Did you hear it?
Not I! swears the farmer. He snaps
His fingers round his head,[8] abandons
A hard-worn harvest and begins
A rapid dialogue with his legs.

"Not I," shouts the fearless hunter, "but—
It's getting dark, and this night-lamp
Has leaked out all its oil. I think
It's best to go home and resume my hunt
Another day." But now he pauses, suddenly
Lets out a wail: "Oh foolish mouth, calling
Down a curse on your own head! Your lamp
Has leaked out all its oil, has it?"
Forwards or backwards now he dare not move.
To search for leaves and make etutu[9]
On that spot? Or race home to the safety
Of his hearth? Ten market-days have passed
My friends, and still he's rooted there
Rigid as the plinth of Orayan[1]

The mouth of the courtesan barely
Opened wide enough to take a ha'penny robo[2]
When she wailed: "Not I." All dressed she was
To call upon my friend the Chief Tax Officer.
But now she sends her go between instead:
"Tell him I'm ill: my period[3] has come suddenly
But not—I hope—my time."

Why is the pupil crying?
His hapless head was made to taste

6. A storyteller.   7. A tall and majestic tropical tree.   8. The gesture for warding off evil.   9. Rites of propitiation, often involving a sacrifice.   1. The mythical founder of Ife, the sacred city of the Yoruba people. *Plinth:* a tall stone column planted into the earth at Ife, reputed to have been the staff of Oranyan. 2. A delicacy made from crushed melon seeds, fried in tiny balls [Author's note].   3. That is, she is menstruating.

The knuckles of my friend the Mallam:[4]
"If you were then reciting the Koran
Would you have ears for idle noises
Darkening the trees, you child of ill omen?"
He shuts down school before its time
Runs home and rings himself with amulets.
And take my good kinsman Ifawomi.[5]
His hands were like a carver's, strong
And true. I saw them
Tremble like wet wings of a fowl.
One day he cast his time-smoothed opele[6]
Across the divination board. And all because
The supplliant looked him in the eye and asked,
"Did you hear that whisper in the leaves?"
"Not I," was his reply; "perhaps I'm growing deaf—
Good-day." And Ifa spoke no more that day
The priest locked fast his doors,
Sealed up his leaking roof—but wait!
This sudden care was not for Fawomi
But for Osenyin,[7] a courier-bird of Ifa's
Heart of wisdom. I did not know a kite
Was hovering in the sky
And Ifa now a twittering chicken in
The brood of Fawomi the Mother Hen.[8]

Ah, but I must not forget my evening
Courier from the abundant palm, whose groan
Became Not I, as he constipated down
A wayside bush. He wonders if Elegbara[9]
Has tricked his buttocks to discharge
Against a sacred grove. Hear him
Mutter spells to ward off penalties
For an abomination he did not intend.
If any here
Stumbles on a gourd of wine, fermenting
Near the road, and nearby hears a stream
Of spells issuing from a crouching form.
Brother to a *sigidi*,[1] bring home my wine,
Tell my tapper I have ejected
Fear from home and farm. Assure him,
All is well.

PRAISE-SINGER: In your time we do not doubt the peace of farmstead and
home, the peace of road and hearth, we do not doubt the peace of the
forest.

ELESIN: There was fear in the forest too.
            Not-I was lately heard even in the lair
            Of beasts. The hyena cackled loud. Not I,

4. A teacher in a koranic school.   5. A name (later shortened to Fawomi) that designates a devotee of
Ifa, the god of divination, referred to further in the passage.   6. A string of beads used in Ifa divination
[Author's note].   7. The tutelary deity of Yoruba traditional healers.   8. That is, reduced in status,
humiliated. Even a god as powerful as Ifa can be cowed by death.   9. Another name for Esu.   1. A
malevolent spirit.

           The civet twitched his fiery tail and glared:
           Not I. Not-I became the answering name
           Of the restless bird,[2] that little one
           Whom Death found nesting in the leaves
           When whisper of his coming ran
           Before him on the wind. Not-I
           Has long abandoned home. This same dawn
           I heard him twitter in the gods' abode.
           Ah, companions of this living world
           What a thing this is, that even those
           We call immortal
           Should fear to die.

IYALOJA: But you, husband of multitudes?
ELESIN: I, when that Not-I bird perched
           Upon my roof, bade him seek his nest again.
           Safe, without care or fear. I unrolled
           My welcome mat for him to see. Not-I
           Flew happily away, you'll hear his voice
           No more in this lifetime—You all know
           What I am.

PRAISE-SINGER: That rock which turns its open lodes
           Into the path of lightning. A gay
           Thoroughbred whose stride disdains
           To falter though an adder[3] reared
           Suddenly in his path.

ELESIN: My rein is loosened.
           I am master of my Fate. When the hour comes
           Watch me dance along the narrowing path
           Glazed by the soles of my great precursors.
           My soul is eager. I shall not turn aside.

WOMEN: You will not delay?
ELESIN: Where the storm pleases, and when, it directs
           The giants of the forest. When friendship summons
           Is when the true comrade goes.

WOMEN: Nothing will hold you back?
ELESIN: Nothing. What! Has no one told you yet
           I go to keep my friend and master company.
           Who says the mouth does not believe in
           "No, I have chewed all that before?" I say I have.
           The world is not a constant honey-pot.
           Where I found little I made do with little.
           Where there was plenty I gorged myself.
           My master's hands and mine have always
           Dipped together and, home or sacred feast,
           The bowl was beaten bronze, the meats
           So succulent our teeth accused us of neglect.
           We shared the choicest of the season's
           Harvest of yams. How my friend would read

---

2. Most likely the canary, which, when caged, is constantly making short, rapid movements.   3. Or puff-adder, an extremely poisonous snake.

	Desire in my eyes before I knew the cause—
	However rare, however precious, it was mine.
WOMEN:	The town, the very land was yours.
ELESIN:	The world was mine. Our joint hands
	Raised housepots[4] of trust that withstood
	The siege of envy and the termites of time.
	But the twilight hour brings bats and rodents—
	Shall I yield them cause to foul the rafters?
PRAISE-SINGER:	Elesin Oba! Are you not that man who
	Looked out of doors that stormy day
	The god of luck[5] limped by, drenched
	To the very lice that held
	His rags together? You took pity upon
	His sores and wished him fortune.
	Fortune was footloose this dawn, he replied,
	Till you trapped him in a heartfelt wish
	That now returns to you. Elesin Oba!
	I say you are that man who
	Chanced upon the calabash of honour
	You thought it was palm wine[6] and
	Drained its contents to the final drop.
ELESIN:	Life has an end. A life that will outlive
	Fame and friendship begs another name.
	What elder takes his tongue to his plate,
	Licks it clean of every crumb?[7] He will encounter
	Silence when he calls on children to fulfill
	The smallest errand! Life is honour.
	It ends when honour ends.
WOMEN:	We know you for a man of honour.

ELESIN: Stop! Enough of that!

WOMEN: [*Puzzled, they whisper among themselves, turning mostly to* IYA-LOJA.] What is it? Did we say something to give offence? Have we slighted him in some way?

ELESIN: Enough of that sound I say. Let me hear no more in that vein. I've heard enough.

IYALOJA: We must have said something wrong. [*Comes forward a little.*] Elesin Oba, we ask forgiveness before you speak.

ELESIN: I am bitterly offended.

IYALOJA: Our unworthiness has betrayed us. All we can do is ask your forgiveness. Correct us like a kind father.

ELESIN: This day of all days . . .

IYALOJA: It does not bear thinking. If we offend you now we have mortified the gods. We offend heaven itself. Father of us all, tell us where we went astray. [*She kneels, the other* WOMEN *follow.*]

ELESIN:	Are you not ashamed? Even a tear-veiled
	Eye preserves its function of sight.
	Because my mind was raised to horizons

---

4. Used for storing the household's water.   **5.** Esu, who is represented as lame.   **6.** The sweet sap of the palm oil tree, which ferments naturally to become a potent drink. *Calabash:* container made from the fruit of a vine.   **7.** Elders are expected to deny themselves for the young.

Even the boldest man lowers his gaze
In thinking of, must my body here
Be taken for a vagrant's?

IYALOJA: Horseman of the King, I am more baffled than ever.

PRAISE-SINGER: The strictest father unbends his brow when the child is penitent, Elesin. When time is short, we do not spend it prolonging the riddle. Their shoulders are bowed with the weight of fear lest they have marred your day beyond repair. Speak now in plain words and let us pursue the ailment to the home of remedies.

ELESIN: Words are cheap. "We know you for
A man of honour." Well tell me, is this how
A man of honour should be seen?
Are these not the same clothes in which
I came among you a full half-hour ago?
[*He roars with laughter and the* WOMEN, *relieved, rise and rush into stalls to fetch rich clothes.*]

WOMEN: The gods are kind. A fault soon remedied is soon forgiven. Elesin Oba, even as we match our words with deed, let your heart forgive us completely.

ELESIN: You who are breath and giver of my being
How shall I dare refuse you forgiveness
Even if the offence was real.

IYALOJA: [*Dancing round him. Sings.*]
He forgives us. He forgives us.
What a fearful thing it is when
The voyager sets forth
But a curse remains behind.

WOMEN: For a while we truly feared
Our hands had wrenched the world adrift
In emptiness.

IYALOJA: Richly, richly, robe him richly
The cloth of honour is alari
Sanyan[8] is the band of friendship
Boa-skin makes slippers of esteem.

WOMEN: For a while we truly feared
Our hands had wrenched the world adrift
In emptiness.

PRAISE-SINGER: He who must, must voyage forth
The world will not roll backwards
It is he who must, with one
Great gesture overtake the world.

WOMEN: For a while we truly feared
Our hands had wrenched the world
In emptiness.

PRAISE-SINGER: The gourd[9] you bear is not for shirking.
The gourd is not for setting down
At the first crossroad or wayside grove.
Only one river may know its contents.

---

8. Richly decorated woven cloth.   9. Used for carrying water.

WOMEN: We shall all meet at the great market
          We shall all meet at the great market
          He who goes early takes the best bargains
          But we shall meet, and resume our banter.

[ELESIN *stands resplendent in rich clothes, cap, shawl, etc. His sash is of a bright red alari cloth. The* WOMEN *dance round him. Suddenly, his attention is caught by an object off-stage.*]

ELESIN: The world I know is good.
WOMEN: We know you'll leave it so.
ELESIN: The world I know is the bounty
          Of hives after bees have swarmed.
          No goodness teems with such open hands
          Even in the dreams of deities.
WOMEN: And we know you'll leave it so.
ELESIN: I was born to keep it so. A hive
          Is never known to wander. An anthill
          Does not desert its roots. We cannot see
          The still great womb of the world—
          No man beholds his mother's womb—
          Yet who denies it's there? Coiled
          To the navel of the world is that
          Endless cord that links us all
          To the great origin. If I lose my way
          The trailing cord will bring me to the roots.
WOMEN: The world is in your hands.

[*The earlier distraction, a beautiful young girl, comes along the passage through which* ELESIN *first made his entry.*]

ELESIN: I embrace it. And let me tell you, women—
          I like this farewell that the world designed,
          Unless my eyes deceive me, unless
          We are already parted, the world and I,
          And all that breeds desire is lodged
          Among our tireless ancestors. Tell me friends,
          Am I still earthed in that beloved market
          Of my youth? Or could it be my will
          Has outleapt the conscious act and I have come
          Among the great departed?

PRAISE-SINGER: Elesin Oba why do your eyes roll like a bush-rat who sees his fate like his father's spirit, mirrored in the eye of a snake? And all those questions! You're standing on the same earth you've always stood upon. This voice you hear is mine, Oluhun-iyo, not that of an acolyte in heaven.

ELESIN: How can that be? In all my life
          As Horseman of the King, the juiciest
          Fruit on every tree was mine. I saw,
          I touched, I wooed, rarely was the answer No.
          The honour of my place, the veneration I
          Received in the eye of man or woman
          Prospered my suit and
          Played havoc with my sleeping hours.

And they tell me my eyes were a hawk
In perpetual hunger. Split an iroko tree[1]
In two, hide a woman's beauty in its heartwood
And seal it up again—Elesin, journeying by,
Would make his camp beside that tree
Of all the shades in the forest.

PRAISE-SINGER: Who would deny your reputation, snake-on-the-loose in dark passages of the market! Bed-bug who wages war on the mat and receives the thanks of the vanquished! When caught with his bride's own sister he protested—but I was only prostrating myself to her as becomes a grateful in-law. Hunter who carries his powder-horn on the hips and fires crouching or standing! Warrior who never makes that excuse of the whining coward—but how can I go to battle without my trousers?—trouserless or shirtless it's all one to him. Oka[2]-rearing-from-a-camouflage-of-leaves, before he strikes the victim is already prone! Once they told me, Howu, a stallion does not feed on the grass beneath him; he replied, true, but surely he can roll on it!

WOMEN: Ba-a-a-ba O![3]

PRAISE-SINGER: Ah, but listen yet. You know there is the leaf-knibbling grub and there is the cola-chewing beetle; the leaf-nibbling grub lives on the leaf, the cola-chewing beetle lives in the colanut. Don't we know what our man feeds on when we find him cocooned in a woman's wrapper?

ELESIN: Enough, enough, you all have cause
To know me well. But, if you say this earth
Is still the same as gave birth to those songs,
Tell me who was that goddess through whose lips
I saw the ivory pebbles of Oya's[4] river-bed.
Iyaloja, who is she? I saw her enter
Your stall; all your daughters I know well.
No, not even Ogun[5]-of-the-farm toiling
Dawn till dusk on his tuber patch
Not even Ogun with the finest hoe he ever
Forged at the anvil could have shaped
That rise of buttocks, not though he had
The richest earth between his fingers.
Her wrapper was no disguise
For thighs whose ripples shamed the river's
Coils around the hills of Ilesi.[6] Her eyes
Were new-laid eggs glowing in the dark.
Her skin . . .

IYALOJA: Elesin Oba . . .

ELESIN: What! Where do you all say I am?

IYALOJA: Still among the living.

ELESIN: And that radiance which so suddenly
Lit up this market I could boast
I knew so well?

IYALOJA: Has one step already in her husband's home. She is betrothed.

1. A tropical hardwood tree; it is a large tree with abundant foliage.   2. The python, a huge snake that swallows its victims whole.   3. A form of salute to an elder male.   4. A Yoruba goddess said to live in the river Niger.   5. The Yoruba god of iron and of war (equivalent in some ways to Mars).   6. A town.

ELESIN: [*Irritated.*] Why do you tell me that?
    [IYALOJA *falls silent. The* WOMEN *shuffle uneasily.*]

IYALOJA: Not because we dare give you offence Elesin. Today is your day
and the whole world is yours. Still, even those who leave town to make
a new dwelling elsewhere like to be remembered by what they leave
behind.

ELESIN: Who does not seek to be remembered?
    Memory is Master of Death, the chink
    In his armour of conceit. I shall leave
    That which makes my going the sheerest
    Dream of an afternoon. Should voyagers
    Not travel light? Let the considerate traveller
    Shed, of his excessive load, all
    That may benefit the living.

WOMEN: [*Relieved.*] Ah Elesin Oba, we knew you for a man of honour.

ELESIN: Then honour me. I deserve a bed of honour to lie upon.

IYALOJA: The best is yours. We know you for a man of honour. You are not
one who eats and leaves nothing on his plate for children. Did you not
say it yourself? Not one who blights the happiness of others for a
moment's pleasure.

ELESIN: Who speaks of pleasure? O women, listen!
    Pleasure palls. Our acts should have meaning.
    The sap of the plantain[7] never dries.
    You have seen the young shoot swelling
    Even as the parent stalks begins to wither.
    Women, let my going be likened to
    The twilight hour of the plantain.

WOMEN: What does he mean Iyaloja? This language is the language of our
elders, we do not fully grasp it.

IYALOJA: I dare not understand you yet Elesin.

ELESIN: All you who stand before the spirit that dares
    The opening of the last door of passage,
    Dare to rid my going of regrets! My wish
    Transcends the blotting out of thought
    In one mere moment's tremor of the senses.
    Do me credit. And do me honour.
    I am girded for the route beyond
    Burdens of waste and longing.
    Then let me travel light. Let
    Seed that will not serve the stomach
    On the way remain behind. Let it take root
    In the earth of my choice, in this earth
    I leave behind.

IYALOJA: [*Turns to* WOMEN.] The voice I hear is already touched by the
waiting fingers of our departed. I dare not refuse.

WOMAN: But Iyaloja . . .

IYALOJA: The matter is no longer in our hands.

WOMAN: But she is betrothed to your own son. Tell him.

IYALOJA: My son's wish is mine. I did the asking for him, the loss can be

7. A plant related to the banana. It constantly regenerates itself from its young shoots ("suckers").

remedied. But who will remedy the blight of closed hands on the day
when all should be openness and light? Tell him, you say! You wish that
I burden him with knowledge that will sour his wish and lay regrets on
the last moments of his mind. You pray to him who is your intercessor
to the world—don't set this world adrift in your own time; would you
rather it was my hand whose sacrilege wrenched it loose?

WOMAN: Not many men will brave the curse of a dispossessed husband.

IYALOJA: Only the curses of the departed are to be feared. The claims of
one whose foot is on the threshold of their abode surpasses even the
claims of blood. It is impiety even to place hindrances in their ways.

ELESIN: What do my mothers[8] say? Shall I step
            Burdened into the unknown?

IYALOJA: Not we, but the very earth says No. The sap in the plantain does
not dry. Let grain that will not feed the voyager at his passage drop here
and take root as he steps beyond this earth and us. Oh you who fill the
home from hearth to threshold with the voices of children, you who now
bestride the hidden gulf and pause to draw the right foot across and into
the resting-home of the great forebears, it is good that your loins be
drained into the earth we know, that your last strength be ploughed back
into the womb that gave you being.

PRAISE-SINGER: Iyaloja, mother of multitudes in the teeming market of the
world, how your wisdom transfigures you!

IYALOJA: [*Smiling broadly, completely reconciled.*] Elesin, even at the narrow end of the passage I know you will look back and sigh a last regret
for the flesh that flashed past your spirit in flight. You always had a
restless eye. Your choice has my blessing. [*To the* WOMEN.] Take the
good news to our daughter and make her ready. [*Some* WOMEN *go off.*]

ELESIN: Your eyes were clouded at first.

IYALOJA: Not for long. It is those who stand at the gateway of the great
change to whose cry we must pay heed. And then, think of this—it makes
the mind tremble. The fruit of such a union is rare. It will be neither of
this world nor of the next. Nor of the one behind us. As if the timelessness
of the ancestor world and the unborn have joined spirits to wring an
issue of the elusive being of passage . . . Elesin!

ELESIN: I am here. What is it?

IYALOJA: Did you hear all I said just now?

ELESIN: Yes.

IYALOJA: The living must eat and drink. When the moment comes, don't
turn the food to rodents' droppings in their mouth. Don't let them taste
the ashes of the world when they step out at dawn to breathe the morning
dew.

ELESIN: This doubt is unworthy of you Iyaloja.

IYALOJA: Eating the awusa nut is not so difficult as drinking water
afterwards.[9]

ELESIN: The waters of the bitter stream are honey to a man
            Whose tongue has savoured all.

IYALOJA: No one knows when the ants desert their home; they leave the

---

8. Here, a term of affection.   9. The awasa nut eaten alone has a pleasant taste, but it turns bitter in
the mouth if water is drunk just after.

mound intact. The swallow is never seen to peck holes in its nest when it is time to move with the season. There are always throngs of humanity behind the leave-taker. The rain should not come through the roof for them, the wind must not blow through the walls at night.

ELESIN: I refuse to take offence.

IYALOJA: You wish to travel light. Well, the earth is yours. But be sure the seed you leave in it attracts no curse.

ELESIN: You really mistake my person Iyaloja.

IYALOJA: I said nothing. Now we must go prepare your bridal chamber. Then these same hands will lay your shrouds.

ELESIN: [*Exasperated.*] Must you be so blunt? [*Recovers.*] Well, weave your shrouds, but let the fingers of my bride seal my eyelids with earth and wash my body.

IYALOJA: Prepare yourself Elesin.

[*She gets up to leave. At that moment the* WOMEN *return, leading the* BRIDE. ELESIN's *face glows with pleasure. He flicks the sleeves of his agbada*[1] *with renewed confidence and steps forward to meet the group. As the girl kneels before* IYALOJA, *lights fade out on the scene.*]

Scene Two

The verandah of the District Officer's bungalow. A tango is playing from an old hand-cranked gramophone and, glimpsed through the wide windows and doors which open onto the forestage verandah are the shapes of SIMON PILKINGS *and his wife,* JANE, *tangoing in and out of shadows in the living room. They are wearing what is immediately apparent as some form of fancy-dress. The dance goes on for some moments and then the figure of a "Native Administration"* POLICEMAN *emerges and climbs up the steps onto the verandah. He peeps through and observes the dancing couple, reacting with what is obviously a long-standing bewilderment. He stiffens suddenly, his expression changes to one of disbelief and horror. In his excitement he upsets a flower-pot and attracts the attention of the couple. They stop dancing.*

PILKINGS: Is there anyone out there?

JANE: I'll turn off the gramophone.

PILKINGS: [*Approaching the verandah.*] I'm sure I heard something fall over. [*The* CONSTABLE *retreats slowly, open-mouthed as* PILKINGS *approaches the verandah.*] Oh it's you Amusa. Why didn't you just knock instead of knocking things over?

AMUSA: [*Stammers badly and points a shaky finger at his dress.*] Mista Pirinkin . . . Mista Pirinkin . . .

PILKINGS: What is the matter with you?

JANE: [*Emerging.*] Who is it dear? Oh, Amusa . . .

PILKINGS: Yes it's Amusa, and acting most strangely.

AMUSA: [*His attention now transferred to* MRS. PILKINGS.] Mammadam[2] . . . you too!

1. A long flowing robe.   2. A confused stammer of the word *madam*.

PILKINGS: What the hell is the matter with you man!

JANE: Your costume darling. Our fancy dress.

PILKINGS: Oh hell, I'd forgotten all about that. [*Lifts the face mask over his head showing his face. His wife follows suit.*]

JANE: I think you've shocked his big pagan heart bless him.

PILKINGS: Nonsense, he's a Moslem. Come on Amusa, you don't believe in all that nonsense do you? I thought you were a good Moslem.

AMUSA: Mista Pirinkin, I beg you sir, what you think you do with that dress? It belong to dead cult, not for human being.

PILKINGS: Oh Amusa, what a let down you are. I swear by you at the club you know—thank God for Amusa, he doesn't believe in any mumbo-jumbo. And now look at you!

AMUSA: Mista Pirinkin, I beg you, take it off. Is not good for man like you to touch that cloth.

PILKINGS: Well, I've got it on. And what's more Jane and I have bet on it we're taking first prize at the ball. Now, if you can just pull yourself together and tell me what you wanted to see me about . . .

AMUSA: Sir, I cannot talk this matter to you in that dress. I no fit.

PILKINGS: What's that rubbish again?

JANE: He is dead earnest too Simon. I think you'll have to handle this delicately.

PILKINGS: Delicately my. . . ! Look here Amusa, I think this little joke has gone far enough hm? Let's have some sense. You seem to forget that you are a police officer in the service of His Majesty's Government. I order you to report your business at once or face disciplinary action.

AMUSA: Sir, it is a matter of death. How can man talk against death to person in uniform of death? Is like talking against government to person in uniform of police. Please sir, I go and come back.

PILKINGS: [*Roars.*] Now! [AMUSA *switches his gaze to the ceiling suddenly, remains mute.*]

JANE: Oh Amusa, what is there to be scared of in the costume? You saw it confiscated last month from those *egungun*[3] men who were creating trouble in town. You helped arrest the cult leaders yourself—if the juju[4] didn't harm you at the time how could it possibly harm you now? And merely by looking at it?

AMUSA: [*Without looking down.*] Madam, I arrest the ringleaders who make trouble but me I no touch *egungun*. That *egungun* inself,[5] I no touch. And I no abuse 'am. I arrest ringleader but I treat *egungun* with respect.

PILKINGS: It's hopeless. We'll merely end up missing the best part of the ball. When they get this way there is nothing you can do. It's simply hammering against a brick wall. Write your report or whatever it is on that pad Amusa and take yourself out of here. Come on Jane. We only upset his delicate sensibilities by remaining here.

[AMUSA *waits for them to leave, then writes in the notebook, somewhat laboriously. Drumming from the direction of the town wells up.* AMUSA *listens, makes a movement as if he wants to recall* PILKINGS *but changes his mind. Completes his note and goes. A few moments later* PILKINGS *emerges, picks up the pad and reads.*]

3. Ancestral masks.   4. Charms and the occult power they possess.   5. Itself (pidgin English).

Jane!

JANE: [*From the bedroom.*] Coming darling. Nearly ready.

PILKINGS: Never mind being ready, just listen to this.

JANE: What is it?

PILKINGS: Amusa's report. Listen. "I have to report that it come to my information that one prominent chief, namely, the Elesin Oba, is to commit death tonight as a result of native custom. Because this is criminal offence I await further instruction at charge office. Sergeant Amusa."

[JANE *comes out onto the verandah while he is reading.*]

JANE: Did I hear you say commit death?

PILKINGS: Obviously he means murder.

JANE: You mean a ritual murder?

PILKINGS: Must be. You think you've stamped it all out but it's always lurking under the surface somewhere.

JANE: Oh. Does it mean we are not getting to the ball at all?

PILKINGS: No-o. I'll have the man arrested. Everyone remotely involved. In any case there may be nothing to it. Just rumours.

JANE: Really? I thought you found Amusa's rumours generally reliable.

PILKINGS: That's true enough. But who knows what may have been giving him the scare lately. Look at his conduct tonight.

JANE: [*Laughing.*] You have to admit he had his own peculiar logic. [*Deepens her voice.*] How can man talk against death to person in uniform of death? [*Laughs.*] Anyway, you can't go into the police station dressed like that.

PILKINGS: I'll send Joseph with instructions. Damn it, what a confounded nuisance!

JANE: But don't you think you should talk first to the man, Simon?

PILKINGS: Do you want to go to the ball or not?

JANE: Darling, why are you getting rattled? I was only trying to be intelligent. It seems hardly fair just to lock up a man—and a chief at that—simply on the er . . . what is the legal word again? uncorroborated word of a sergeant.

PILKINGS: Well, that's easily decided. Joseph!

JOSEPH: [*From within.*] Yes master.

PILKINGS: You're quite right of course, I am getting rattled. Probably the effect of those bloody drums. Do you hear how they go on and on?

JANE: I wondered when you'd notice. Do you suppose it has something to do with this affair?

PILKINGS: Who knows? They always find an excuse for making a noise . . . [*Thoughtfully.*] Even so . . .

JANE: Yes Simon?

PILKINGS: It's different Jane. I don't think I've heard this particular— sound—before. Something unsettling about it.

JANE: I thought all bush drumming sounded the same.

PILKINGS: Don't tease me now Jane. This may be serious.

JANE: I'm sorry. [*Gets up and throws her arms around his neck. Kisses him. The houseboy enters, retreats and knocks.*]

PILKINGS: [*Wearily.*] Oh, come in Joseph! I don't know where you pick up all these elephantine notions of tact. Come over here.

JOSEPH: Sir?

PILKINGS: Joseph, are you a Christian or not?

JOSEPH: Yessir.

PILKINGS: Does seeing me in this outfit bother you?

JOSEPH: No sir, it has no power.

PILKINGS: Thank God for some sanity at last. Now Joseph, answer me on the honour of a Christian—what is supposed to be going on in town tonight?

JOSEPH: Tonight sir? You mean the chief who is going to kill himself?

PILKINGS: What?

JANE: What do you mean, kill himself?

PILKINGS: You do mean he is going to kill somebody don't you?

JOSEPH: No master. He will not kill anybody and no one will kill him. He will simply die.

JANE: But why Joseph?

JOSEPH: It is native law and custom. The King die last month. Tonight is his burial. But before they can bury him, the Elesin must die so as to accompany him to heaven.

PILKINGS: I seem to be fated to clash more often with that man than with any of the other chiefs.

JOSEPH: He is the King's Chief Horseman.

PILKINGS: [In a resigned way.] I know.

JANE: Simon, what's the matter?

PILKINGS: It would have to be him!

JANE: Who is he?

PILKINGS: Don't you remember? He's that chief with whom I had a scrap some three or four years ago. I helped his son get to a medical school in England, remember? He fought tooth and nail to prevent it.

JANE: Oh now I remember. He was that very sensitive young man. What was his name again?

PILKINGS: Olunde.[6] Haven't replied to his last letter come to think of it. The old pagan wanted him to stay and carry on some family tradition or the other. Honestly I couldn't understand the fuss he made. I literally had to help the boy escape from close confinement and load him onto the next boat. A most intelligent boy, really bright.

JANE: I rather thought he was much too sensitive you know. The kind of person you feel should be a poet munching rose petals in Bloomsbury.[7]

PILKINGS: Well, he's going to make a first-class doctor. His mind is set on that. And as long as he wants my help he is welcome to it.

JANE: [After a pause.] Simon.

PILKINGS: Yes?

JANE: This boy, he was the eldest son wasn't he?

PILKINGS: I'm not sure. Who could tell with that old ram?

JANE: Do you know, Joseph?

JOSEPH: Oh yes madam. He was the eldest son. That's why Elesin cursed master good and proper. The eldest son is not supposed to travel away from the land.

JANE: [Giggling.] Is that true Simon? Did he really curse you good and proper?

PILKINGS: By all accounts I should be dead by now.

---

6. "My lord or deliverer has come"; a contraction of Olumide.   7. An area in central London associated with a brilliant group of writers in the years between the world wars; Virginia Woolf was the principal figure among them.

JOSEPH: Oh no, master is white man. And good Christian. Black man juju can't touch master.

JANE: If he was his eldest, it means that he would be the Elesin to the next king. It's a family thing isn't it Joseph?

JOSEPH: Yes madam. And if this Elesin had died before the King, his eldest son must take his place.

JANE: That would explain why the old chief was so mad you took the boy away.

PILKINGS: Well it makes me all the more happy I did.

JANE: I wonder if he knew.

PILKINGS: Who? Oh, you mean Olunde?

JANE: Yes. Was that why he was so determined to get away? I wouldn't stay if I knew I was trapped in such a horrible custom.

PILKINGS: [*Thoughtfully.*] No, I don't think he knew. At least he gave no indication. But you couldn't really tell with him. He was rather close you know, quite unlike most of them. Didn't give much away, not even to me.

JANE: Aren't they all rather close, Simon?

PILKINGS: These natives here? Good gracious. They'll open their mouths and yap with you about their family secrets before you can stop them. Only the other day . . .

JANE: But Simon, do they really give anything away? I mean, anything that really counts. This affair for instance, we didn't know they still practised that custom did we?

PILKINGS: Ye-e-es, I suppose you're right there. Sly, devious bastards.

JOSEPH: [*Stiffly.*] Can I go now master? I have to clean the kitchen.

PILKINGS: What? Oh, you can go. Forgot you were still here.

[JOSEPH *goes.*]

JANE: Simon, you really must watch your language. Bastard isn't just a simple swear-word in these parts, you know.

PILKINGS: Look, just when did you become a social anthropologist, that's what I'd like to know.

JANE: I'm not claiming to know anything. I just happen to have overheard quarrels among the servants. That's how I know they consider it a smear.

PILKINGS: I thought the extended family system took care of all that. Elastic family, no bastards.

JANE: [*Shrugs.*] Have it your own way.

[*Awkward silence. The drumming increases in volume.* JANE *gets up suddenly, restless.*]

That drumming Simon, do you think it might really be connected with this ritual? It's been going on all evening.

PILKINGS: Let's ask our native guide. Joseph! Just a minute Joseph. [JOSEPH *re-enters.*] What's the drumming about?

JOSEPH: I don't know master.

PILKINGS: What do you mean you don't know? It's only two years since your conversion. Don't tell me all that holy water nonsense also wiped out your tribal memory.

JOSEPH: [*Visibly shocked.*] Master!

JANE: Now you've done it.

PILKINGS: What have I done now?

JANE: Never mind. Listen Joseph, just tell me this. Is that drumming connected with dying or anything of that nature?

JOSEPH: Madam, this is what I am trying to say: I am not sure. It sounds like the death of a great chief and then, it sounds like the wedding of a great chief. It really mix me up.

PILKINGS: Oh get back to the kitchen. A fat lot of help you are.

JOSEPH: Yes master. [*Goes.*]

JANE: Simon . . .

PILKINGS: All right, all right. I'm in no mood for preaching.

JANE: It isn't my preaching you have to worry about, it's the preaching of the missionaries who preceded you here. When they make converts they really convert them. Calling holy water nonsense to our Joseph is really like insulting the Virgin Mary before a Roman Catholic. He's going to hand in his notice tomorrow you mark my word.

PILKINGS: Now you're being ridiculous.

JANE: Am I? What are you willing to bet that tomorrow we are going to be without a steward-boy? Did you see his face?

PILKINGS: I am more concerned about whether or not we will be one native chief short by tomorrow. Christ! Just listen to those drums. [*He strides up and down, undecided.*]

JANE: [*Getting up.*] I'll change and make up some supper.

PILKINGS: What's that?

JANE: Simon, it's obvious we have to miss this ball.

PILKINGS: Nonsense. It's the first bit of real fun the European club has managed to organise for over a year, I'm damned if I'm going to miss it. And it is a rather special occasion. Doesn't happen every day.

JANE: You know this business has to be stopped Simon. And you are the only man who can do it.

PILKINGS: I don't have to stop anything. If they want to throw themselves off the top of a cliff or poison themselves for the sake of some barbaric custom what is that to me? If it were ritual murder or something like that I'd be duty-bound to do something. I can't keep an eye on all the potential suicides in this province. And as for that man—believe me it's good riddance.

JANE: [*Laughs.*] I know you better than that Simon. You are going to have to do something to stop it—after you've finished blustering.

PILKINGS: [*Shouts after her.*] And suppose after all it's only a wedding? I'd look a proper fool if I interrupted a chief on his honeymoon, wouldn't I? [*Resumes his angry stride, slows down.*] Ah well, who can tell what those chiefs actually do on their honeymoon anyway? [*He takes up the pad and scribbles rapidly on it.*] Joseph! Joseph! Joseph! [*Some moments later* JOSEPH *puts in a sulky appearance.*] Did you hear me call you? Why the hell didn't you answer?

JOSEPH: I didn't hear master.

PILKINGS: You didn't hear me! How come you are here then?

JOSEPH: [*Stubbornly.*] I didn't hear master.

PILKINGS: [*Controls himself with an effort.*] We'll talk about it in the morning. I want you to take this note directly to Sergeant Amusa. You'll find him at the charge office. Get on your bicycle and race there with it. I expect you back in twenty minutes exactly. Twenty minutes, is that clear?

JOSEPH: Yes master [*Going.*]

PILKINGS: Oh er . . . Joseph.

JOSEPH: Yes master?

PILKINGS: [*Between gritted teeth.*] Er . . . forget what I said just now. The holy water is not nonsense. *I* was talking nonsense.

JOSEPH: Yes master [*Goes.*]

JANE: [*Pokes her head round the door.*] Have you found him?

PILKINGS: Found who?

JANE: Joseph. Weren't you shouting for him?

PILKINGS: Oh yes, he turned up finally.

JANE: You sounded desperate. What was it all about?

PILKINGS: Oh nothing. I just wanted to apologise to him. Assure him that the holy water isn't really nonsense.

JANE: Oh? And how did he take it?

PILKINGS: Who the hell gives a damn! I had a sudden vision of our Very Reverend Macfarlane[8] drafting another letter of complaint to the Resident about my unchristian language towards his parishioners.

JANE: Oh I think he's given up on you by now.

PILKINGS: Don't be too sure. And anyway, I wanted to make sure Joseph didn't "lose" my note on the way. He looked sufficiently full of the holy crusade to do some such thing.

JANE: If you've finished exaggerating, come and have something to eat.

PILKINGS: No, put it all away. We can still get to the ball.

JANE: Simon . . .

PILKINGS: Get your costume back on. Nothing to worry about. I've instructed Amusa to arrest the man and lock him up.

JANE: But that station is hardly secure Simon. He'll soon get his friends to help him escape.

PILKINGS: A-ah, that's where I have out-thought you. I'm not having him put in the station cell. Amusa will bring him right here and lock him up in my study. And he'll stay with him till we get back. No one will dare come here to incite him to anything.

JANE: How clever of you darling. I'll get ready.

PILKINGS: Hey.

JANE: Yes darling.

PILKINGS: I have a surprise for you. I was going to keep it until we actually got to the ball.

JANE: What is it?

PILKINGS: You know the Prince is on a tour of the colonies don't you? Well, he docked in the capital only this morning but he is already at the Residency. He is going to grace the ball with his presence later tonight.

JANE: Simon! Not really.

PILKINGS: Yes he is. He's been invited to give away the prizes and he has agreed. You must admit old Engleton is the best Club Secretary we ever had. Quick off the mark that lad.

JANE: But how thrilling.

PILKINGS: The other provincials are going to be damned envious.

JANE: I wonder what he'll come as.

---

8. Irish priests were predominant in Catholic missionary activity in Nigeria.

PILKINGS: Oh I don't know. As a coat-of-arms perhaps. Anyway it won't be anything to touch this.

JANE: Well that's lucky. If we are to be presented I won't have to start looking for a pair of gloves. It's all sewn on.[9]

PILKINGS: [*Laughing.*] Quite right. Trust a woman to think of that. Come on, let's get going.

JANE: [*Rushing off.*] Won't be a second. [*Stops.*] Now I see why you've been so edgy all evening. I thought you weren't handling this affair with your usual brilliance—to begin with, that is.

PILKINGS: [*His mood is much improved.*] Shut up woman and get your things on.

JANE: All right boss, coming.

> [PILKINGS *suddenly begins to hum the tango to which they were dancing before. Starts to execute a few practice steps. Lights fade.*]

Scene Three

A swelling, agitated hum of women's voices rises immediately in the background. The lights come on and we see the frontage of a converted cloth stall in the market. The floor leading up to the entrance is covered in rich velvets and woven cloth. The WOMEN *come on stage, borne backwards by the determined progress of Sergeant* AMUSA *and his two* CONSTABLES *who already have their batons out and use them as a pressure against the* WOMEN. *At the edge of the cloth-covered floor however the* WOMEN *take a determined stand and block all further progress of the* MEN. *They begin to tease them mercilessly.*

AMUSA: I am tell you women for last time to commot my road.[1] I am here on official business.

WOMAN: Official business you white man's eunuch? Official business is taking place where you want to go and it's a business you wouldn't understand.

WOMAN: [*Makes a quick tug at the* CONSTABLE's *baton.*] That doesn't fool anyone you know. It's the one you carry under your government knickers that counts. [*She bends low as if to peep under the baggy shorts. The embarrassed* CONSTABLE *quickly puts his knees together. The* WOMEN *roar.*]

WOMAN: You mean there is nothing there at all?

WOMAN: Oh there was something. You know that handbell which the white-man uses to summon his servants. . . ?

AMUSA: [*He manages to preserve some dignity throughout.*] I hope you women know that interfering with officer in execution of his duty is criminal offence.

WOMAN: Interfere? He says we're interfering with him. You foolish man we're telling you there's nothing to interfere with.

AMUSA: I am order you now to clear the road.

WOMAN: What road? The one your father built?

---

9. The masquerade costume is designed to cover the entire body of the wearer, to conceal his or her identity.　1. Get out of my way.

WOMAN: You are a policeman not so? Then you know what they call tres-passing in court. Or—[*pointing to the cloth-lined steps*]—do you think that kind of road is built for every kind of feet.

WOMAN: Go back and tell the white man who sent you to come himself.

AMUSA: If I go I will come back with reinforcement. And we will all return carrying weapons.

WOMAN: Oh, now I understand. Before they can put on those knickers the white man first cuts off their weapons.

WOMAN: What a cheek! You mean you come here to show power to women and you don't even have a weapon.

AMUSA: [*Shouting above the laughter.*] For the last time I warn you women to clear the road.

WOMAN: To where?

AMUSA: To that hut. I know he dey dere.

WOMAN: Who?

AMUSA: The chief who call himself Elesin Oba.

WOMAN: You ignorant man. It is not he who calls himself Elesin Oba, it is his blood that says it. As it called out to his father before him and will to his son after him. And that is in spite of everything your white man can do.

WOMAN: Is it not the same ocean that washes this land and the white man's land? Tell your white man he can hide our son away as long as he likes. When the time comes for him, the same ocean will bring him back.

AMUSA: The government say dat kin' ting[2] must stop.

WOMAN: Who will stop it? You? Tonight our husband and father will prove himself greater than the laws of strangers.

AMUSA: I tell you nobody go prove anyting tonight or anytime. Is ignorant and criminal to prove dat kin' prove.

IYALOJA: [*Entering from the hut. She is accompanied by a group of young girls who have been attending the* BRIDE.] What is it Amusa? Why do you come here to disturb the happiness of others.

AMUSA: Madame Iyaloja, I glad you come. You know me, I no like trouble but duty is duty. I am here to arrest Elesin for criminal intent. Tell these women to stop obstructing me in the performance of my duty.

IYALOJA: And you? What gives you the right to obstruct our leader of men in the performance of his duty.

AMUSA: What kin' duty be dat one Iyaloja.

IYALOJA: What kin' duty? What kin' duty does a man have to his new bride?

AMUSA: [*Bewildered, looks at the women and at the entrance to the hut.*] Iyaloja, is it wedding you call dis kin' ting?

IYALOJA: You have wives haven't you? Whatever the white man has done to you he hasn't stopped you having wives. And if he has, at least he is married. If you don't know what a marriage is, go and ask him to tell you.

AMUSA: This no to wedding.[3]

IYALOJA: And ask him at the same time what he would have done if anyone had come to disturb him on his wedding night.

AMUSA: Iyaloja, I say dis no to wedding.

---

2. That kind of thing.   3. This is not a wedding.

IYALOJA: You want to look inside the bridal chamber? You want to see for yourself how a man cuts the virgin knot?

AMUSA: Madam . . .

WOMAN: Perhaps his wives are still waiting for him to learn.

AMUSA: Iyaloja, make you tell dese women make den no insult me again. If I hear dat kin' insult once more . . .

GIRL: [Pushing her way through.] You will do what?

GIRL: He's out of his mind. It's our mothers you're talking to, do you know that? Not to any illiterate villager you can bully and terrorise. How dare you intrude here anyway?

GIRL: What a cheek, what impertinence!

GIRL: You've treated them too gently. Now let them see what it is to tamper with the mothers of this market.

GIRL: Your betters dare not enter the market when the women say no!

GIRL: Haven't you learnt that yet, you jester in khaki and starch?

IYALOJA: Daughters . . .

GIRL: No no Iyaloja, leave us to deal with him. He no longer knows his mother, we'll teach him.

[With a sudden movement they snatch the batons of the two CON-STABLES. They begin to hem them in.]

GIRL: What next? We have your batons? What next? What are you going to do?

[With equally swift movements they knock off their hats.]

GIRL: Move if you dare. We have your hats, what will you do about it? Didn't the white man teach you to take off your hats before women?

IYALOJA: It's a wedding night. It's a night of joy for us. Peace . . .

GIRL: Not for him. Who asked him here?

GIRL: Does he dare go to the Residency without an invitation?

GIRL: Not even where the servants eat the left-overs.

GIRLS: [In turn. In an "English" accent.] Well well it's Mister Amusa. Were you invited? [Play acting to one another. The older WOMEN encourage them with their titters.]

—Your invitation card please?

—Who are you? Have we been introduced?

—And who did you say you were?

—Sorry, I didn't quite catch your name.

—May I take your hat?

—If you insist. May I take yours? [Exchanging the POLICEMEN's hats.]

—How very kind of you.

—Not at all. Won't you sit down?

—After you.

—Oh no.

—I insist.

—You're most gracious.

—And how do you find the place?

—The natives are all right.

—Friendly?

—Tractable.

—Not a teeny-weeny bit restless?

—Well, a teeny-weeny bit restless.

—One might even say, difficult?
—Indeed one might be tempted to say, difficult.
—But you do manage to cope?
—Yes indeed I do. I have a rather faithful ox called Amusa.
—He's loyal?
—Absolutely.
—Lay down his life for you what?
—Without a moment's thought.
—Had one like that once. Trust him with my life.
—Mostly of course they are liars.
—Never known a native to tell the truth.
—Does it get rather close around here?
—It's mild for this time of the year.
—But the rains may still come.
—They are late this year aren't they?
—They are keeping African time.[4]
—Ha ha ha ha
—Ha ha ha ha
—The humidity is what gets me.
—It used to be whisky
—Ha ha ha ha
—Ha ha ha ha
—What's your handicap old chap?
—Is there racing by golly?
—Splendid golf course, you'll like it.
—I'm beginning to like it already.
—And a European club, exclusive.
—You've kept the flag flying.
—We do our best for the old country.
—It's a pleasure to serve.
—Another whisky old chap?
—You are indeed too too kind.
—Not at all sir. Where is that boy? [*With a sudden bellow.*] Sergeant!
AMUSA: [*Snaps to attention.*] Yessir!
          [*The* WOMEN *collapse with laughter.*]
GIRL: Take your men out of here.
AMUSA: [*Realising the trick, he rages from loss of face.*] I'm give you
    warning . . .
GIRL: All right then. Off with his knickers! [*They surge slowly forward.*]
IYALOJA: Daughters, please.
AMUSA: [*Squaring himself for defence.*] The first woman wey touch me . . .
IYALOJA: My children, I beg of you . . .
GIRL: Then tell him to leave this market. This is the home of our mothers.
    We don't want the eater of white left-overs at the feast their hands have
    prepared.
IYALOJA: You heard them Amusa. You had better go.
GIRL: Now!

---

4. A standard colonial prejudice was that Africans lack a sense of time.

AMUSA: [*Commencing his retreat.*] We dey go now, but make you no say we
no warn you.[5]

GIRLS: Now!

GIRL: Before we read the riot act—you should know all about that.

AMUSA: Make we go. [*They depart, more precipitately.*]

[*The* WOMEN *strike their palms across in the gesture of wonder.*]

WOMEN: Do they teach you all that at school?

WOMAN: And to think I nearly kept Apinke[6] away from the place.

WOMAN: Did you hear them? Did you see how they mimicked the white
man?

WOMAN: The voices exactly. Hey, there are wonders in this world!

IYALOJA: Well, our elders have said it: Dada[7] may be weak, but he has a
younger sibling who is truly fearless.

WOMAN: The next time the white man shows his face in this market I will
set Wuraola[8] on his tail.

[*A* WOMAN *bursts into song and dance of euphoria—"Tani l'awa o
l'ogbeja? Kayi! A l'ogbeja. Omo Kekere l'ogbeja."*[9] *The rest of the*
WOMEN *join in, some placing the* GIRLS *on their back like infants,
others dancing round them. The dance becomes general, mounting
in excitement.* ELESIN *appears, in wrapper only. In his hands a white
velvet cloth folded loosely as if it held some delicate object. He cries
out.*]

ELESIN: Oh you mothers of beautiful brides! [*The dancing stops. They turn
and see him, and the object in his hands.* IYALOJA *approaches and gently
takes the cloth from him.*] Take it. It is no mere virgin stain, but the union
of life and the seeds of passage. My vital flow, the last from this flesh is
intermingled with the promise of future life. All is prepared. Listen! [*A
steady drum beat from the distance.*] Yes. It is nearly time. The King's dog
has been killed. The King's favourite horse is about to follow his master.
My brother chiefs know their task and perform it well. [*He listens again.*]

[*The* BRIDE *emerges, stands shyly by the door. He turns to her.*]

Our marriage is not yet wholly fulfilled. When earth and passage wed,
the consummation is complete only when there are grains of earth on
the eyelids of passage. Stay by me till then. My faithful drummers, do
me your last service. This is where I have chosen to do my leave-taking,
in this heart of life, this hive which contains the swarm of the world in
its small compass. This is where I have known love and laughter away
from the palace. Even the richest food cloys when eaten days on end; in
the market, nothing ever cloys. Listen. [*They listen to the drums.*] They
have begun to seek out the heart of the King's favourite horse. Soon it
will ride in its bolt of raffia[1] with the dog at its feet. Together they will
ride on the shoulders of the King's grooms through the pulse centres of
the town. They know it is here I shall await them. I have told them. [*His
eyes appear to cloud. He passes his hand over them as if to clear his sight.
He gives a faint smile.*] It promises well; just then I felt my spirit's eager-

---

5. Don't say that we didn't warn you.   **6.** "One Who Is Equally Cherished by All"; the name of one of
the girls.   **7.** A child born with tangled hair.   **8.** "Dear as Gold"; a woman's name.   **9.** Who says we
haven't a defender? Silence! We have our defenders. Little children are our champions [Author's transla-
tion].   **1.** The stem of this shrub is used for the decorative skirt worn in many African dances.

ness. The kite makes for wide spaces and the wind creeps up behind its tail; can the kite say less than—thank you, the quicker the better? But wait a while my spirit. Wait. Wait for the coming of the courier of the King. Do you know friends, the horse is born to this one destiny, to bear the burden that is man upon its back. Except for this night, this night alone when the spotless stallion will ride in triumph on the back of man. In the time of my father I witnessed the strange sight. Perhaps tonight also I shall see it for the last time. If they arrive before the drums beat for me, I shall tell him to let the Alafin[2] know I follow swiftly. If they come after the drums have sounded, why then, all is well for I have gone ahead. Our spirits shall fall in step along the great passage. [*He listens to the drums. He seems again to be falling into a state of semi-hypnosis; his eyes scan the sky but it is in a kind of daze. His voice is a little breathless.*] The moon has fed, a glow from its full stomach fills the sky and air, but I cannot tell where is that gateway through which I must pass. My faithful friends, let our feet touch together this last time, lead me into the other market with sounds that cover my skin with down yet make my limbs strike earth like a thoroughbred. Dear mothers, let me dance into the passage even as I have lived beneath your roofs. [*He comes down progressively among them. They make way for him, the drummers playing. His dance is one of solemn, regal motions, each gesture of the body is made with a solemn finality. The* WOMEN *join him, their steps a some-what more fluid version of his. Beneath the* PRAISE-SINGER's *exhortations the* WOMEN *dirge "Ale le le, awo mi lo."*]

PRAISE-SINGER: Elesin Alafin, can you hear my voice?
ELESIN: Faintly, my friend, faintly.
PRAISE-SINGER: Elesin Alafin, can you hear my call?
ELESIN: Faintly my king, faintly.
PRAISE-SINGER: Is your memory sound Elesin?
           Shall my voice be a blade of grass and
           Tickle the armpit of the past?
ELESIN: My memory needs no prodding but
           What do you wish to say to me?
PRAISE-SINGER: Only what has been spoken. Only what concerns
           The dying wish of the father of all.
ELESIN: It is buried like seed-yam in my mind
           This is the season of quick rains, the harvest
           Is this moment due for gathering.
PRAISE-SINGER: If you cannot come, I said, swear
           You'll tell my favourite horse. I shall
           Ride on through the gates alone.
ELESIN: Elesin's message will be read
           Only when his loyal heart no longer beats.
PRAISE-SINGER: If you cannot come Elesin, tell my dog.
           I cannot stay the keeper too long
           At the gate.
ELESIN: A dog does not outrun the hand
           That feeds it meat. A horse that throws its rider

---

2. "Owner of the Palace" (literal trans.); the title of the king of Oyo.

Slows down to a stop. Elesin Alafin
Trusts no beasts with messages between
A king and his companion.

PRAISE-SINGER: If you get lost my dog will track
The hidden path to me.

ELESIN: The seven-way crossroads confuses
Only the stranger. The Horseman of the King
Was born in the recesses of the house.

PRAISE-SINGER: I know the wickedness of men. If there is
Weight on the loose end of your sash, such weight
As no mere man can shift; if your sash is earthed
By evil minds who mean to part us at the last . . .

ELESIN: My sash is of the deep purple *alari*;
It is no tethering-rope. The elephant
Trails no tethering-rope; that king
Is not yet crowned who will peg an elephant—
Not even you my friend and King.

PRAISE-SINGER: And yet this fear will not depart from me
The darkness of this new abode is deep—
Will your human eyes suffice?

ELESIN: In a night which falls before our eyes
However deep, we do not miss our way.

PRAISE-SINGER: Shall I now not acknowledge I have stood
Where wonders met their end? The elephant deserves
Better than that we say "I have caught
A glimpse of something."[3] If we see the tamer
Of the forest let us say plainly, we have seen
An elephant.

ELESIN: [*His voice is drowsy.*]
I have freed myself of earth and now
It's getting dark. Strange voices guide my feet.

PRAISE-SINGER: The river is never so high that the eyes
Of a fish are covered. The night is not so dark
That the albino fails to find his way.[4] A child
Returning homewards craves no leading by the hand.
Gracefully does the mask[5] regain his grove at the end of
the day . . .
Gracefully. Gracefully does the mask dance
Homeward at the end of the day, gracefully . . .

[ELESIN's *trance appears to be deepening, his steps heavier.*]

IYALOJA: It is the death of war that kills the valiant,
Death of water is how the swimmer goes
It is the death of markets that kills the trader
And death of indecision takes the idle away
The trade of the cutlass blunts its edge
And the beautiful die the death of beauty.
It takes an Elesin to die the death of death . . .
Only Elesin . . . dies the unknowable death of death . . .

3. A Yoruba saying, meaning that an outstanding person or deed must be granted proper recognition.
4. Many albinos have poor eyesight. 5. Of the *egungun* masquerade.

Gracefully, gracefully does the horseman regain
The stables at the end of day, gracefully . . .
PRAISE-SINGER: How shall I tell what my eyes have seen? The Horseman
gallops on before the courier, how shall I tell what my eyes have seen?
He says a dog may be confused by new scents of beings he never dreamt
of, so he must precede the dog to heaven. He says a horse may stumble
on strange boulders and be lamed, so he races on before the horse to
heaven. It is best, he says, to trust no messenger who may falter at the
outer gate, oh how shall I tell what my ears have heard? But do you hear
me still Elesin, do you hear your faithful one?
[ELESIN *in his motions appears to feel for a direction of sound, subtly,
but he only sinks deeper into his trance dance.*]
Elesin Alafin, I no longer sense your flesh. The drums are changing now
but you have gone far ahead of the world. It is not yet noon in heaven;
let those who claim it is begin their own journey home. So why must you
rush like an impatient bride: why do you race to desert your Olohun-iyo?
[ELESIN *is now sunk fully deep in his trance, there is no longer sign
of any awareness of his surroundings.*]
Does the deep voice of *gbedu*[6] cover you then, like the passage of royal
elephants? Those drums that brook no rivals, have they blocked the passage to your ears that my voice passes into wind, a mere leaf floating in
the night? Is your flesh lightened Elesin, is that lump of earth I slid
between your slippers to keep you longer slowly sifting from your feet?
Are the drums on the other side now tuning skin to skin with ours in
osugbo?[7] Are there sounds there I cannot hear, do footsteps surround
you which pound the earth like *gbedu*, roll like thunder round the dome
of the world? Is the darkness gathering in your head Elesin? Is there now
a streak of light at the end of the passage, a light I dare not look upon?
Does it reveal whose voices we often heard, whose touches we often felt,
whose wisdoms come suddenly into the mind when the wisest have
shaken their heads and murmured: It cannot be done? Elesin Alafin,
don't think I do not know why your lips are heavy, why your limbs are
drowsy as palm oil in the cold of harmattan.[8] I would call you back but
when the elephant heads for the jungle, the tail is too small a handhold
for the hunter that would pull him back. The sun that heads for the sea
no longer heeds the prayers of the farmer. When the river begins to taste
the salt of the ocean, we no longer know what deity to call on, the river-
god or Olokun.[9] No arrow flies back to the string, the child does not
return through the same passage that gave it birth. Elesin Oba, can you
hear me at all? Your eyelids are glazed like a courtesan's, is it that you
see the dark groom and master of life? And will you see my father? Will
you tell him that I stayed with you to the last? Will my voice ring in your
ears awhile, will you remember Olohun-iyo even if the music on the other
side surpasses his mortal craft? But will they know you over there? Have
they eyes to gauge your worth, have they the heart to love you, will they

---

6. Drums. Their deep resonance is caused by the hardwood from which they are made. 7. The secret
executive cult of the Yoruba; its meeting place [Author's note]. 8. A sharp, dry wind from the Sahara
that blows over western Africa in December. The wind brings dust and noticeably cools the air. Palm oil
congeals in cold weather and is thus said to sleep. Compare the American "slow as molasses in January."
9. Goddess of the sea.

know what thoroughbred prances towards them in caparisons[1] of honour? If they do not Elesin, if any there cuts your yam with a small knife, or pours you wine in a small calabash, turn back and return to welcoming hands. If the world were not greater than the wishes of Olohun-iyo, I would not let you go . . .

> [*He appears to break down.* ELESIN *dances on, completely in a trance. The dirge wells up louder and stronger.* ELESIN's *dance does not lose its elasticity but his gestures become, if possible, even more weighty. Lights fade slowly on the scene.*]

Scene Four

A Masque. The front side of the stage is part of a wide corridor around the great hall of the Residency extending beyond vision into the rear and wings. It is redolent of the tawdry decadence of a far-flung but key imperial frontier. The COUPLES *in a variety of fancy-dress are ranged around the walls, gazing in the same direction. The guest-of-honour is about to make an appearance. A portion of the local police brass band with its white* CONDUCTOR *is just visible. At last, the entrance of* ROYALTY. *The band plays "Rule Britannia," badly, beginning long before he is visible. The couples bow and curtsey as he passes by them. Both he and his companions are dressed in seventeenth century European costume. Following behind are the* RESIDENT *and his* PARTNER *similarly attired. As they gain the end of the hall where the orchestra dais begins the music comes to an end. The* PRINCE *bows to the guests. The* BAND *strikes up a Viennese waltz and the* PRINCE *formally opens the floor. Several bars later the* RESIDENT *and his companion follow suit. Others follow in appropriate pecking order. The orchestra's waltz rendition is not of the highest musical standard.*

Some time later the PRINCE *dances again into view and is settled into a corner by the* RESIDENT *who then proceeds to select* COUPLES *as they dance past for introduction, sometimes threading his way through the dancers to tap the lucky* COUPLE *on the shoulder. Desperate efforts from many to ensure that they are recognised in spite of perhaps, their costume. The ritual of introductions soon takes in* PILKINGS *and his* WIFE. *The* PRINCE *is quite fascinated by their costume and they demonstrate the adaptations they have made to it, pulling down the mask to demonstrate how the* egungun *normally appears, then showing the various press-button controls they have innovated for the face flaps, the sleeves, etc. They demonstrate the dance steps and the guttural sounds made by the* egungun, *harrass other dancers in the hall,* MRS. PILKINGS *playing the "restrainer"[2] to* PILKINGS' *manic darts. Everyone is highly entertained, the Royal Party especially who lead the applause.*

At this point a liveried FOOTMAN *comes in with a note on a salver and is intercepted almost absent-mindedly by the* RESIDENT *who takes the note and reads it. After polite coughs he succeeds in excusing the* PILKINGS *from the* PRINCE *and takes them aside. The* PRINCE *considerately offers the* RESIDENT's WIFE *his hand and dancing is resumed.*

---

1. Rich ceremonial cloth draped over the saddle of a horse.   2. Masqueraders sometimes become possessed and go berserk; ropes are, therefore, tied to their waists and held by *restrainers*.

On their way out the RESIDENT *gives an order to his* AIDE-DE-CAMP. *They come into the side corridor where the* RESIDENT *hands the note to* PILKINGS.

RESIDENT: As you see it says "emergency" on the outside. I took the liberty of opening it because His Highness was obviously enjoying the entertainment. I didn't want to interrupt unless really necessary.

PILKINGS: Yes, yes of course, sir.

RESIDENT: Is it really as bad as it says? What's it all about?

PILKINGS: Some strange custom they have, sir. It seems because the King is dead some important chief has to commit suicide.

RESIDENT: The King? Isn't it the same one who died nearly a month ago?

PILKINGS: Yes, sir.

RESIDENT: Haven't they buried him yet?

PILKINGS: They take their time about these things, sir. The pre-burial ceremonies last nearly thirty days. It seems tonight is the final night.

RESIDENT: But what has it got to do with the market women? Why are they rioting? We've waived that troublesome tax haven't we?

PILKINGS: We don't quite know that they are exactly rioting yet, sir. Sergeant Amusa is sometimes prone to exaggerations.

RESIDENT: He sounds desperate enough. That comes out even in his rather quaint grammar. Where is the man anyway? I asked my aide-de-camp to bring him here.

PILKINGS: They are probably looking in the wrong verandah. I'll fetch him myself.

RESIDENT: No no you stay here. Let your wife go and look for them. Do you mind my dear. . . ?

JANE: Certainly not, your Excellency. [*Goes.*]

RESIDENT: You should have kept me informed, Pilkings. You realise how disastrous it would have been if things had erupted while His Highness was here.

PILKINGS: I wasn't aware of the whole business until tonight, sir.

RESIDENT: Nose to the ground Pilkings, nose to the ground. If we all let these little things slip past us where would the empire be eh? Tell me that. Where would we all be?

PILKINGS: [*Low voice.*] Sleeping peacefully at home I bet.

RESIDENT: What did you say, Pilkings?

PILKINGS: It won't happen again, sir.

RESIDENT: It mustn't, Pilkings. It mustn't. Where is that damned sergeant? I ought to get back to His Highness as quickly as possible and offer him some plausible explanation for my rather abrupt conduct. Can you think of one, Pilkings?

PILKINGS: You could tell him the truth, sir.

RESIDENT: I could? No no no no Pilkings, that would never do. What! Go and tell him there is a riot just two miles away from him? This is supposed to be a secure colony of His Majesty, Pilkings.

PILKINGS: Yes, sir.

RESIDENT: Ah, there they are. No, these are not our native police. Are these the ring-leaders of the riot?

PILKINGS: Sir, these are my police officers.

RESIDENT: Oh, I beg your pardon officers. You do look a little . . . I say, isn't there something missing in their uniform? I think they used to have some rather colourful sashes. If I remember rightly I recommended them myself in my young days in the service. A bit of colour always appeals to the natives, yes, I remember putting that in my report. Well well well, where are we? Make your report man.

PILKINGS: [*Moves close to* AMUSA, *between his teeth.*] And let's have no more superstitious nonsense from you Amusa or I'll throw you in the guard-room for a month and feed you pork![3]

RESIDENT: What's that? What has pork to do with it?

PILKINGS: Sir, I was just warning him to be brief. I'm sure you are most anxious to hear his report.

RESIDENT: Yes yes yes of course. Come on man, speak up. Hey, didn't we give them some colourful fez[4] hats with all those wavy things, yes, pink tassells . . .

PILKINGS: Sir, I think if he was permitted to make his report we might find that he lost his hat in the riot.

RESIDENT: Ah yes indeed. I'd better tell His Highness that. Lost his hat in the riot, ha ha. He'll probably say well, as long as he didn't lose his head. [*Chuckles to himself.*] Don't forget to send me a report first thing in the morning young Pilkings.

PILKINGS: No, sir.

RESIDENT: And whatever you do, don't let things get out of hand. Keep a cool head and—nose to the ground Pilkings. [*Wanders off in the general direction of the hall.*]

PILKINGS: Yes, sir.

AIDE-DE-CAMP: Would you be needing me, sir?

PILKINGS: No thanks, Bob. I think His Excellency's need of you is greater than ours.

AIDE-DE-CAMP: We have a detachment of soldiers from the capital, sir. They accompanied His Highness up here.

PILKINGS: I doubt if it will come to that but, thanks, I'll bear it in mind. Oh, could you send an orderly with my cloak.

AIDE-DE-CAMP: Very good, sir. [*Goes.*]

PILKINGS: Now, sergeant.

AMUSA: Sir . . . [*Makes an effort, stops dead. Eyes to the ceiling.*]

PILKINGS: Oh, not again.

AMUSA: I cannot against death to dead cult. This dress get power of dead.

PILKINGS: All right, let's go. You are relieved of all further duty Amusa. Report to me first thing in the morning.

JANE: Shall I come, Simon?

PILKINGS: No, there's no need for that. If I can get back later I will. Otherwise get Bob to bring you home.

JANE: Be careful Simon . . . I mean, be clever.

PILKINGS: Sure I will. You two, come with me. [*As he turns to go, the clock in the Residency begins to chime.* PILKINGS *looks at his watch then turns, horror-stricken, to stare at his wife. The same thought clearly occurs to her. He swallows hard. An* ORDERLY *brings his cloak.*] It's midnight. I had no idea it was that late.

---

3. Muslims are prohibited from eating pork.   4. Red caps worn by African officials in the colonial service.

JANE: But surely . . . they don't count the hours the way we do. The moon, or something . . .

PILKINGS: I am . . . not so sure.

> [*He turns and breaks into a sudden run. The two* CONSTABLES *follow, also at a run.* AMUSA, *who has kept his eyes on the ceiling throughout waits until the last of the footsteps has faded out of hearing. He salutes suddenly, but without once looking in the direction of the* WOMAN.]

AMUSA: Goodnight, madam.

JANE: Oh. [*She hesitates.*] Amusa . . . [*He goes off without seeming to have heard.*] Poor Simon . . . [*A figure emerges from the shadows, a young black* MAN *dressed in a sober western suit. He peeps into the hall, trying to make out the figures of the dancers.*]

> Who is that?

OLUNDE: [*Emerges into the light.*] I didn't mean to startle you madam. I am looking for the District Officer.

JANE: Wait a minute . . . don't I know you? Yes, you are Olunde, the young man who . . .

OLUNDE: Mrs. Pilkings! How fortunate. I came here to look for your husband.

JANE: Olunde! Let's look at you. What a fine young man you've become. Grand but solemn. Good God, when did you return? Simon never said a word. But you do look well Olunde. Really!

OLUNDE: You are . . . well, you look quite well yourself Mrs. Pilkings. From what little I can see of you.

JANE: Oh, this. It's caused quite a stir I assure you, and not all of it very pleasant. You are not shocked I hope?

OLUNDE: Why should I be? But don't you find it rather hot in there? Your skin must find it difficult to breathe.

JANE: Well, it is a little hot I must confess, but it's all in a good cause.

OLUNDE: What cause Mrs. Pilkings?

JANE: All this. The ball. And His Highness being here in person and all that.

OLUNDE: [*Mildly.*] And that is the good cause for which you desecrate an ancestral mask?

JANE: Oh, so you are shocked after all. How disappointing.

OLUNDE: No I am not shocked, Mrs. Pilkings. You forget that I have now spent four years among your people. I discovered that you have no respect for what you do not understand.

JANE: Oh. So you've returned with a chip on your shoulder. That's a pity Olunde. I am sorry.

> [*An uncomfortable silence follows.*]

> I take it then that you did not find your stay in England altogether edifying.

OLUNDE: I don't say that. I found your people quite admirable in many ways, their conduct and courage in this war[5] for instance.

JANE: Ah yes, the war. Here of course it is all rather remote. From time to time we have a black-out drill just to remind us that there is a war on. And the rare convoy passes through on its way somewhere or on manoeu-

---

5. That is, World War II.

vres. Mind you there is the occasional bit of excitement like that ship that was blown up in the harbour.[6]

OLUNDE: Here? Do you mean through enemy action?

JANE: Oh no, the war hasn't come that close. The captain did it himself. I don't quite understand it really. Simon tried to explain. The ship had to be blown up because it had become dangerous to the other ships, even to the city itself. Hundreds of the coastal population would have died.

OLUNDE: Maybe it was loaded with ammunition and had caught fire. Or some of those lethal gases they've been experimenting on.

JANE: Something like that. The captain blew himself up with it. Deliberately. Simon said someone had to remain on board to light the fuse.

OLUNDE: It must have been a very short fuse.

JANE: [Shrugs.] I don't know much about it. Only that there was no other way to save lives. No time to devise anything else. The captain took the decision and carried it out.

OLUNDE: Yes . . . I quite believe it. I met men like that in England.

JANE: Oh just look at me! Fancy welcoming you back with such morbid news. Stale too. It was at least six months ago.

OLUNDE: I don't find it morbid at all. I find it rather inspiring. It is an affirmative commentary on life.

JANE: What is?

OLUNDE: That captain's self-sacrifice.

JANE: Nonsense. Life should never be thrown deliberately away.

OLUNDE: And the innocent people around the harbour?

JANE: Oh, how does one know? The whole thing was probably exaggerated anyway.

OLUNDE: That was a risk the captain couldn't take. But please Mrs. Pilkings, do you think you could find your husband for me? I have to talk to him.

JANE: Simon? [As she recollects for the first time the full significance of OLUNDE's presence.] Simon is . . . there is a little problem in town. He was sent for. But . . . when did you arrive? Does Simon know you're here?

OLUNDE: [Suddenly earnest.] I need your help Mrs. Pilkings. I've always found you somewhat more understanding than your husband. Please find him for me and when you do, you must help me talk to him.

JANE: I'm afraid I don't quite . . . follow you. Have you seen my husband already?

OLUNDE: I went to your house. Your houseboy told me you were here. [He smiles.] He even told me how I would recognise you and Mr. Pilkings.

JANE: Then you must know what my husband is trying to do for you.

OLUNDE: For me?

JANE: For you. For your people. And to think he didn't even know you were coming back! But how do you happen to be here? Only this evening we were talking about you. We thought you were still four thousand miles away.

OLUNDE: I was sent a cable.

JANE: A cable? Who did? Simon? The business of your father didn't begin till tonight.

OLUNDE: A relation sent it weeks ago, and it said nothing about my father.

6. A reference to an incident that occurred in Lagos, the capital of Nigeria, in 1944.

All it said was, Our King is dead. But I knew I had to return home at once so as to bury my father. I understood that.

JANE: Well, thank God you don't have to go through that agony. Simon is going to stop it.

OLUNDE: That's why I want to see him. He's wasting his time. And since he has been so helpful to me I don't want him to incur the enmity of our people. Especially over nothing.

JANE: [Sits down open mouthed.] You . . . you Olunde!

OLUNDE: Mrs. Pilkings, I came home to bury my father. As soon as I heard the news I booked my passage home. In fact we were fortunate. We travelled in the same convoy as your Prince, so we had excellent protection.

JANE: But you don't think your father is also entitled to whatever protection is available to him?

OLUNDE: How can I make you understand? He has protection. No one can undertake what he does tonight without the deepest protection the mind can conceive. What can you offer him in place of his peace of mind, in place of the honour and veneration of his own people? What would you think of your Prince if he refused to accept the risk of losing his life on this voyage? This . . . showing the flag tour of colonial possessions.

JANE: I see. So it isn't just medicine you studied in England.

OLUNDE: Yet another error into which your people fall. You believe that everything which appears to make sense was learnt from you.

JANE: Not so fast Olunde. You have learnt to argue I can tell that, but I never said you made sense. However clearly you try to put it, it is still a barbaric custom. It is even worse—it's feudal! The king dies and a chieftan must be buried with him. How feudalistic can you get!

OLUNDE: [Waves his hand towards the background. The PRINCE is dancing past again—to a different step—and all the guests are bowing and curtseying as he passes.] And this? Even in the midst of a devastating war, look at that. What name would you give to that?

JANE: Therapy, British style. The preservation of sanity in the midst of chaos.

OLUNDE: Others would call it decadence. However, it doesn't really interest me. You white races know how to survive; I've seen proof of that. By all logical and natural laws this war should end with all the white races wiping out one another, wiping out their so-called civilisation for all time and reverting to a state of primitivism the like of which has so far only existed in your imagination when you thought of us. I thought all that at the beginning. Then I slowly realised that your greatest art is the art of survival. But at least have the humility to let others survive in their own way.

JANE: Through ritual suicide?

OLUNDE: Is that worse than mass suicide? Mrs. Pilkings, what do you call what those young men are sent to do by their generals in this war? Of course you have also mastered the art of calling things by names which don't remotely describe them.

JANE: You talk! You people with your long-winded, roundabout way of making conversation.

OLUNDE: Mrs. Pilkings, whatever we do, we never suggest that a thing is the opposite of what it really is. In your newsreels I heard defeats, thorough, murderous defeats described as strategic victories. No wait, it wasn't just on your newsreels. Don't forget I was attached to hospitals all the time. Hordes of your wounded passed through those wards. I spoke to them. I spent long evenings by their bedsides while they spoke terrible truths of the realities of that war. I know now how history is made.

JANE: But surely, in a war of this nature, for the morale of the nation you must expect . . .

OLUNDE: That a disaster beyond human reckoning be spoken of as a triumph? No. I mean, is there no mourning in the home of the bereaved that such blasphemy is permitted?

JANE: [*After a moment's pause.*] Perhaps I can understand you now. The time we picked for you was not really one for seeing us at our best.

OLUNDE: Don't think it was just the war. Before that even started I had plenty of time to study your people. I saw nothing, finally, that gave you the right to pass judgement on other peoples and their ways. Nothing at all.

JANE: [*Hesitantly.*] Was it the . . . colour thing? I know there is some discrimination.

OLUNDE: Don't make it so simple, Mrs. Pilkings. You make it sound as if when I left, I took nothing at all with me.

JANE: Yes . . . and to tell the truth, only this evening, Simon and I agreed that we never really knew what you left with.

OLUNDE: Neither did I. But I found out over there. I am grateful to your country for that. And I will never give it up.

JANE: Olunde, please . . . promise me something. Whatever you do, don't throw away what you have started to do. You want to be a doctor. My husband and I believe you will make an excellent one, sympathetic and competent. Don't let anything make you throw away your training.

OLUNDE: [*Genuinely surprised.*] Of course not. What a strange idea. I intend to return and complete my training. Once the burial of my father is over.

JANE: Oh, please. . . !

OLUNDE: Listen! Come outside. You can't hear anything against that music.

JANE: What is it?

OLUNDE: The drums. Can you hear the drums? Listen.

[*The drums come over, still distant but more distinct. There is a change of rhythm, it rises to a crescendo and then, suddenly, it is cut off. After a silence, a new beat begins, slow and resonant.*]

There it's all over.

JANE: You mean he's . . .

OLUNDE: Yes, Mrs. Pilkings, my father is dead. His will power has always been enormous; I know he is dead.

JANE: [*Screams.*] How can you be so callous! So unfeeling! You announce your father's own death like a surgeon looking down on some strange . . . stranger's body! You're just a savage like all the rest.

AIDE-DE-CAMP: [*Rushing out.*] Mrs. Pilkings. Mrs. Pilkings. [*She breaks down, sobbing.*] Are you all right, Mrs. Pilkings?

OLUNDE: She'll be all right. [*Turns to go.*]

AIDE-DE-CAMP: Who are you? And who the hell asked your opinion?

OLUNDE: You're quite right, nobody. [*Going.*]

AIDE-DE-CAMP: What the hell! Did you hear me ask you who you were?

OLUNDE: I have business to attend to.

AIDE-DE-CAMP: I'll give you business in a moment you impudent nigger. Answer my question!

OLUNDE: I have a funeral to arrange. Excuse me. [*Going.*]

AIDE-DE-CAMP: I said stop! Orderly!

JANE: No, no, don't do that. I'm all right. And for heaven's sake don't act so foolishly. He's a family friend.

AIDE-DE-CAMP: Well he'd better learn to answer civil questions when he's asked them. These natives put a suit on and they get high opinions of themselves.

OLUNDE: Can I go now?

JANE: No no don't go. I must talk to you. I'm sorry about what I said.

OLUNDE: It's nothing, Mrs. Pilkings. And I'm really anxious to go. I couldn't see my father before, it's forbidden for me, his heir and successor to set eyes on him from the moment of the king's death. But now . . . I would like to touch his body while it is still warm.

JANE: You will. I promise I shan't keep you long. Only, I couldn't possibly let you go like that. Bob, please excuse us.

AIDE-DE-CAMP: If you're sure . . .

JANE: Of course I'm sure. Something happened to upset me just then, but I'm all right now. Really.

[*The* AIDE DE CAMP *goes, somewhat reluctantly.*]

OLUNDE: I mustn't stay long.

JANE: Please, I promise not to keep you. It's just that . . . oh you saw yourself what happens to one in this place. The Resident's man thought he was being helpful, that's the way we all react. But I can't go in among that crowd just now and if I stay by myself somebody will come looking for me. Please, just say something for a few moments and then you can go. Just so I can recover myself.

OLUNDE: What do you want me to say?

JANE: Your calm acceptance for instance, can you explain that? It was so unnatural. I don't understand that at all. I feel a need to understand all I can.

OLUNDE: But you explained it yourself. My medical training perhaps. I have seen death too often. And the soldiers who returned from the front, they died on our hands all the time.

JANE: No. It has to be more than that. I feel it has to do with the many things we don't really grasp about your people. At least you can explain.

OLUNDE: All these things are part of it. And anyway, my father has been dead in my mind for nearly a month. Ever since I learnt of the King's death. I've lived with my bereavement so long now that I cannot think of him alive. On that journey on the boat, I kept my mind on my duties as the one who must perform the rites over his body. I went through it all again and again in my mind as he himself had taught me. I didn't want to do anything wrong, something which might jeopardise the welfare of my people.

JANE: But he had disowned you. When you left he swore publicly you were no longer his son.

OLUNDE: I told you, he was a man of tremendous will. Sometimes that's another way of saying stubborn. But among our people, you don't disown a child just like that. Even if I had died before him I would still be buried like his eldest son. But it's time for me to go.

JANE: Thank you. I feel calmer. Don't let me keep you from your duties.

OLUNDE: Goodnight, Mrs. Pilkings.

JANE: Welcome home.

[*She holds out her hand. As he takes it footsteps are heard approaching the drive. A short while later a woman's sobbing is also heard.*]

PILKINGS: [*Off.*] Keep them here till I get back. [*He strides into view, reacts at the sight of* OLUNDE *but turns to his wife.*] Thank goodness you're still here.

JANE: Simon, what happened?

PILKINGS: Later Jane, please. Is Bob still here?

JANE: Yes, I think so. I'm sure he must be.

PILKINGS: Try and get him out here as quickly as you can. Tell him it's urgent.

JANE: Of course. Oh Simon, you remember . . .

PILKINGS: Yes yes. I can see who it is. Get Bob out here. [*She runs off.*] At first I thought I was seeing a ghost.

OLUNDE: Mr. Pilkings, I appreciate what you tried to do. I want you to believe that. I can tell you it would have been a terrible calamity if you'd succeeded.

PILKINGS: [*Opens his mouth several times, shuts it.*] You . . . said what?

OLUNDE: A calamity for us, the entire people.

PILKINGS: [*Sighs.*] I see. Hm.

OLUNDE: And now I must go. I must see him before he turns cold.

PILKINGS: Oh ah . . . em . . . but this is a shock to see you. I mean er thinking all this while you were in England and thanking God for that.

OLUNDE: I came on the mail boat. We travelled in the Prince's convoy.

PILKINGS: Ah yes, a ah, hm . . . er well . . .

OLUNDE: Goodnight. I can see you are shocked by the whole business. But you must know by now there are things you cannot understand—or help.

PILKINGS: Yes. Just a minute. There are armed policemen that way and they have instructions to let no one pass. I suggest you wait a little. I'll er . . . give you an escort.

OLUNDE: That's very kind of you. But do you think it could be quickly arranged.

PILKINGS: Of course. In fact, yes, what I'll do is send Bob over with some men to the er . . . place. You can go with them. Here he comes now. Excuse me a minute.

AIDE-DE-CAMP: Anything wrong sir?

PILKINGS: [*Takes him to one side.*] Listen Bob, that cellar in the disused annexe of the Residency, you know, where the slaves were stored before being taken down to the coast . . .

AIDE-DE-CAMP: Oh yes, we use it as a storeroom for broken furniture.

PILKINGS: But it's still got the bars on it?

AIDE-DE-CAMP: Oh yes, they are quite intact.

PILKINGS: Get the keys please. I'll explain later. And I want a strong guard over the Residency tonight.

AIDE-DE-CAMP: We have that already. The detachment from the coast . . .

PILKINGS: No, I don't want them at the gates of the Residency. I want you to deploy them at the bottom of the hill, a long way from the main hall so they can deal with any situation long before the sound carries to the house.

AIDE-DE-CAMP: Yes of course.

PILKINGS: I don't want His Highness alarmed.

AIDE-DE-CAMP: You think the riot will spread here?

PILKINGS: It's unlikely but I don't want to take a chance. I made them believe I was going to lock the man up in my house, which was what I had planned to do in the first place. They are probably assailing it by now. I took a roundabout route here so I don't think there is any danger at all. At least not before dawn. Nobody is to leave the premises of course—the native employees I mean. They'll soon smell something is up and they can't keep their mouths shut.

AIDE-DE-CAMP: I'll give instructions at once.

PILKINGS: I'll take the prisoner down myself. Two policemen will stay with him throughout the night. Inside the cell.

AIDE-DE-CAMP: Right sir. [Salutes and goes off at the double.]

PILKINGS: Jane. Bob is coming back in a moment with a detachment. Until he gets back please stay with Olunde. [He makes an extra warning gesture with his eyes.]

OLUNDE: Please, Mr. Pilkings . . .

PILKINGS: I hate to be stuffy old son, but we have a crisis on our hands. It has to do with your father's affair if you must know. And it happens also at a time when we have His Highness here. I am responsible for security so you'll simply have to do as I say. I hope that's understood.

[Marches off quickly, in the direction from which he made his first appearance.]

OLUNDE: What's going on? All this can't be just because he failed to stop my father killing himself.

JANE: I honestly don't know. Could it have sparked off a riot?

OLUNDE: No. If he'd succeeded that would be more likely to start the riot. Perhaps there were other factors involved. Was there a chieftancy dispute?

JANE: None that I know of.

ELESIN: [An animal bellow from off.] Leave me alone! Is it not enough that you have covered me in shame! White man, take your hand from my body!

[OLUNDE stands frozen to the spot. JANE understanding at last, tries to move him.]

JANE: Let's go in. It's getting chilly out here.

PILKINGS: [Off.] Carry him.

ELESIN: Give me back the name you have taken away from me you ghost from the land of the nameless!

PILKINGS: Carry him! I can't have a disturbance here. Quickly! stuff up his mouth.

JANE: Oh God! Let's go in. Please Olunde.

[OLUNDE does not move.]

ELESIN: Take your albino's hand from me you . . .

[Sounds of a struggle. His voice chokes as he is gagged.]

OLUNDE: [*Quietly.*] That was my father's voice.

JANE: Oh you poor orphan, what have you come home to?
> [*There is a sudden explosion of rage from off-stage and powerful steps come running up the drive.*]

PILKINGS: You bloody fools, after him!
> [*Immediately* ELESIN, *in handcuffs, comes pounding in the direction of* JANE *and* OLUNDE, *followed some moments afterwards by* PILK-INGS *and the* CONSTABLES. ELESIN, *confronted by the seeming statue of his son, stops dead.* OLUNDE *stares above his head into the distance. The* CONSTABLES *try to grab him.* JANE *screams at them.*]

JANE: Leave him alone! Simon, tell them to leave him alone.

PILKINGS: All right, stand aside you. [*Shrugs.*] Maybe just as well. It might help to calm him down.
> [*For several moments they hold the same position.* ELESIN *moves a step forward, almost as if he's still in doubt.*]

ELESIN: Olunde? [*He moves his head, inspecting him from side to side.*] Olunde! [*He collapses slowly at* OLUNDE'S *feet.*] Oh son, don't let the sight of your father turn you blind!

OLUNDE: [*He moves for the first time since he heard his voice, brings his head slowly down to look on him.*] I have no father, eater of left-overs.
> [*He walks slowly down the way his father had run. Light fades out on* ELESIN, *sobbing into the ground.*]

Scene Five

A wide iron barred gate stretches almost the whole width of the cell in which ELESIN *is imprisoned. His wrists are encased in thick iron bracelets, chained together; he stands against the bars, looking out. Seated on the ground to one side on the outside is his recent* BRIDE, *her eyes bent perpetually to the ground. Figures of the two* GUARDS *can be seen deeper inside the cell, alert to every movement* ELESIN *makes.* PILKINGS *now in a police officer's uniform enters noiselessly, observes him a while. Then he coughs ostentatiously and approaches. Leans against the bars near a corner, his back to* ELESIN. *He is obviously trying to fall in mood with him. Some moments' silence.*

PILKINGS: You seem fascinated by the moon.

ELESIN: [*After a pause.*] Yes, ghostly one. Your twin-brother up there engages my thoughts.

PILKINGS: It is a beautiful night.

ELESIN: Is that so?

PILKINGS: The light on the leaves, the peace of the night . . .

ELESIN: The night is not at peace, District Officer.

PILKINGS: No? I would have said it was. You know, quiet . .

ELESIN: And does quiet mean peace for you?

PILKINGS: Well, nearly the same thing. Naturally there is a subtle difference . . .

ELESIN: The night is not at peace, ghostly one. The world is not at peace. You have shattered the peace of the world for ever. There is no sleep in the world tonight.

PILKINGS: It is still a good bargain if the world should lose one night's sleep as the price of saving a man's life.

ELESIN: You did not save my life, District Officer. You destroyed it.

PILKINGS: Now come on . . .

ELESIN: And not merely my life but the lives of many. The end of the night's work is not over. Neither this year nor the next will see it. If I wished you well, I would pray that you do not stay long enough on our land to see the disaster you have brought upon us.

PILKINGS: Well, I did my duty as I saw it. I have no regrets.

ELESIN: No. The Regrets of life always come later.

[*Some moments' pause.*]

You are waiting for dawn, white man. I hear you saying to yourself: only so many hours until dawn and then the danger is over. All I must do is to keep him alive tonight. You don't quite understand it all but you know that tonight is when what ought to be must be brought about. I shall ease your mind even more, ghostly one. It is not an entire night but a moment of the night, and that moment is past. The moon was my messenger and guide. When it reached a certain gateway in the sky, it touched that moment for which my whole life has been spent in blessings. Even I do not know the gateway. I have stood here and scanned the sky for a glimpse of that door but, I cannot see it. Human eyes are useless for a search of this nature. But in the house of *osugbo,* those who keep watch through the spirit recognised the moment, they sent word to me through the voice of our sacred drums to prepare myself. I heard them and I shed all thoughts of earth. I began to follow the moon to the abode of the gods . . . servant of the white king, that was when you entered my chosen place of departure on feet of desecration.

PILKINGS: I'm sorry, but we all see our duty differently.

ELESIN: I no longer blame you. You stole from me my first-born, sent him to your country so you could turn him into something in your own image. Did you plan it all beforehand? There are moments when it seems part of a larger plan. He who must follow my footsteps is taken from me, sent across the ocean. Then, in my turn, I am stopped from fulfilling my destiny. Did you think it all out before, this plan to push our world from its course and sever the cord that links us to the great origin?

PILKINGS: You don't really believe that. Anyway, if that was my intention with your son, I appear to have failed.

ELESIN: You did not fail in the main, ghostly one. We know the roof covers the rafters, the cloth covers blemishes; who would have known that the white skin covered our future, preventing us from seeing the death our enemies had prepared for us. The world is set adrift and its inhabitants are lost. Around them, there is nothing but emptiness.

PILKINGS: Your son does not take so gloomy a view.

ELESIN: Are you dreaming now, white man? Were you not present at my reunion of shame? Did you not see when the world reversed itself and the father fell before his son, asking forgiveness?

PILKINGS: That was in the heat of the moment. I spoke to him and . . . if you want to know, he wishes he could cut out his tongue for uttering the words he did.

ELESIN: No. What he said must never be unsaid. The contempt of my own

son rescued something of my shame at your hands. You have stopped
me in my duty but I know now that I did give birth to a son. Once I
mistrusted him for seeking the companionship of those my spirit knew
as enemies of our race. Now I understand. One should seek to obtain
the secrets of his enemies. He will avenge my shame, white one. His
spirit will destroy you and yours.

PILKINGS: That kind of talk is hardly called for. If you don't want my
consolation . . .

ELESIN: No white man, I do not want your consolation.

PILKINGS: As you wish. Your son anyway, sends his consolation. He asks
your forgiveness. When I asked him not to despise you his reply was: I
cannot judge him, and if I cannot judge him, I cannot despise him. He
wants to come to you and say goodbye and to receive your blessing.

ELESIN: Goodbye? Is he returning to your land?

PILKINGS: Don't you think that's the most sensible thing for him to do? I
advised him to leave at once, before dawn, and he agrees that is the right
course of action.

ELESIN: Yes, it is best. And even if I did not think so, I have lost the father's
place of honour. My voice is broken.

PILKINGS: Your son honours you. If he didn't he would not ask your blessing.

ELESIN: No. Even a thoroughbred is not without pity for the turf he strikes
with his hoof. When is he coming?

PILKINGS: As soon as the town is a little quieter. I advised it.

ELESIN: Yes, white man, I am sure you advised it. You advise all our lives
although on the authority of what gods, I do not know.

PILKINGS: [*Opens his mouth to reply, then appears to change his mind. Turns
to go. Hesitates and stops again.*] Before I leave you, may I ask just one
thing of you?

ELESIN: I am listening.

PILKINGS: I wish to ask you to search the quiet of your heart and tell me—do
you not find great contradictions in the wisdom of your own race?

ELESIN: Make yourself clear, white one.

PILKINGS: I have lived among you long enough to learn a saying or two.
One came to my mind tonight when I stepped into the market and saw
what was going on. You were surrounded by those who egged you on
with song and praises. I thought, are these not the same people who say:
the elder grimly approaches heaven and you ask him to bear your greetings yonder; do you really think he makes the journey willingly? After
that, I did not hesitate.

    [*A pause. ELESIN sighs. Before he can speak a sound of running feet
is heard.*]

JANE: [*Off.*] Simon! Simon!

PILKINGS: What on earth. . . ! [*Runs off.*]

    [ELESIN *turns to his new wife, gazes on her for some moments.*]

ELESIN: My young bride, did you hear the ghostly one? You sit and sob in
your silent heart but say nothing to all this. First I blamed the white man,
then I blamed my gods for deserting me. Now I feel I want to blame you
for the mystery of the sapping of my will. But blame is a strange peace
offering for a man to bring a world he has deeply wronged, and to its
innocent dwellers. Oh little mother, I have taken countless women in

my life but you were more than a desire of the flesh. I needed you as the abyss across which my body must be drawn, I filled it with earth and dropped my seed in it at the moment of preparedness for my crossing. You were the final gift of the living to their emissary to the land of the ancestors, and perhaps your warmth and youth brought new insights of this world to me and turned my feet leaden on this side of the abyss. For I confess to you, daughter, my weakness came not merely from the abomination of the white man who came violently into my fading presence, there was also a weight of longing on my earth-held limbs. I would have shaken it off, already my foot had begun to lift but then, the white ghost entered and all was defiled.

[*Approaching voices of* PILKINGS *and his wife.*]

JANE: Oh Simon, you will let her in won't you?

PILKINGS: I really wish you'd stop interfering.

[*They come into view.* JANE *is in a dressing gown.* PILKINGS *is holding a note to which he refers from time to time.*]

JANE: Good gracious, I didn't initiate this. I was sleeping quietly, or trying to anyway, when the servant brought it. It's not my fault if one can't sleep undisturbed even in the Residency.

PILKINGS: He'd have done the same thing if we were sleeping at home so don't sidetrack the issue. He knows he can get round you or he wouldn't send you the petition in the first place.

JANE: Be fair Simon. After all he was thinking of your own interests. He is grateful you know, you seem to forget that. He feels he owes you something.

PILKINGS: I just wish they'd leave this man alone tonight, that's all.

JANE: Trust him Simon. He's pledged his word it will all go peacefully.

PILKINGS: Yes, and that's the other thing. I don't like being threatened.

JANE: Threatened? [*Takes the note.*] I didn't spot any threat.

PILKINGS: It's there. Veiled, but it's there. The only way to prevent serious rioting tomorrow—what a cheek!

JANE: I don't think he's threatening you Simon.

PILKINGS: He's picked up the idiom all right. Wouldn't surprise me if he's been mixing with commies or anarchists over there. The phrasing sounds too good to be true. Damn! If only the Prince hadn't picked this time for his visit.

JANE: Well, even so Simon, what have you got to lose? You don't want a riot on your hands, not with the Prince here.

PILKINGS: [*Going up to* ELESIN.] Let's see what he has to say. Chief Elesin, there is yet another person who wants to see you. As she is not a next-of-kin I don't really feel obliged to let her in. But your son sent a note with her, so it's up to you.

ELESIN: I know who that must be. So she found out your hiding place. Well, it was not difficult. My stench of shame is so strong, it requires no hunter's dog to follow it.

PILKINGS: If you don't want to see her, just say so and I'll send her packing.

ELESIN: Why should I not want to see her? Let her come. I have no more holes in my rag of shame. All is laid bare.

PILKINGS: I'll bring her in. [*Goes off.*]

JANE: [*Hesitates, then goes to* ELESIN.] Please, try and understand. Everything my husband did was for the best.

ELESIN: [*He gives her a long strange stare, as if he is trying to understand who she is.*] You are the wife of the District Officer?

JANE: Yes. My name, is Jane.

ELESIN: That is my wife sitting down there. You notice how still and silent she sits? My business is with your husband.

[PILKINGS *returns with* IYALOJA.]

PILKINGS: Here she is. Now first I want your word of honour that you will try nothing foolish.

ELESIN: Honour? White one, did you say you wanted my word of honour?

PILKINGS: I know you to be an honourable man. Give me your word of honour you will receive nothing from her.

ELESIN: But I am sure you have searched her clothing as you would never dare touch your own mother. And there are these two lizards[7] of yours who roll their eyes even when I scratch.

PILKINGS: And I shall be sitting on that tree trunk watching even how you blink. Just the same I want your word that you will not let her pass anything to you.

ELESIN: You have my honour already. It is locked up in that desk in which you will put away your report of this night's events. Even the honour of my people you have taken already; it is tied together with those papers of treachery[8] which make you masters in this land.

PILKINGS: All right. I am trying to make things easy but if you must bring in politics we'll have to do it the hard way. Madam, I want you to remain along this line and move no nearer to the cell door. Guards! [*They spring to attention.*] If she moves beyond this point, blow your whistle. Come on Jane. [*They go off.*]

IYALOJA: How boldly the lizard struts before the pigeon when it was the eagle itself he promised us he would confront.

ELESIN: I don't ask you to take pity on me Iyaloja. You have a message for me or you would not have come. Even if it is the curses of the world, I shall listen.

IYALOJA: You made so bold with the servant of the white king who took your side against death. I must tell your brother chiefs when I return how bravely you waged war against him. Especially with words.

ELESIN: I more than deserve your scorn.

IYALOJA: [*With sudden anger.*] I warned you, if you must leave a seed behind, be sure it is not tainted with the curses of the world. Who are you to open a new life when you dared not open the door to a new existence? I say who are you to make so bold? [*The* BRIDE *sobs and* IYALOJA *notices her. Her contempt noticeably increases as she turns back to* ELESIN.] Oh you self-vaunted stem of the plantain, how hollow it all proves. The pith is gone in the parent stem, so how will it prove with the new shoot? How will it go with that earth that bears it? Who are you to bring this abomination on us!

ELESIN: My powers deserted me. My charms, my spells, even my voice lacked strength when I made to summon the powers that would lead me over the last measure of earth into the land of the fleshless. You saw it, Iyaloja. You saw me struggle to retrieve my will from the power of the

---

7. That is, the guards.   8. The treaties of annexation forced by the British on African traditional rulers, who often did not understand their implications.

stranger whose shadow fell across the doorway and left me floundering and blundering in a maze I had never before encountered. My senses were numbed when the touch of cold iron came upon my wrists. I could do nothing to save myself.

IYALOJA: You have betrayed us. We fed you sweetmeats such as we hoped awaited you on the other side. But you said No, I must eat the world's left-overs. We said you were the hunter who brought the quarry down; to you belonged the vital portions of the game. No, you said, I am the hunter's dog and I shall eat the entrails of the game and the faeces of the hunter. We said you were the hunter returning home in triumph, a slain buffalo pressing down on his neck; you said wait, I first must turn up this cricket hole with my toes. We said yours was the doorway at which we first spy the tapper when he comes down from the tree, yours was the blessing of the twilight wine, the purl[9] that brings night spirits out of doors to steal their portion before the light of day. We said yours was the body of wine whose burden shakes the tapper like a sudden gust on his perch. You said, No, I am content to lick the dregs from each calabash when the drinkers are done. We said, the dew on earth's surface was for you to wash your feet along the slopes of honour. You said No, I shall step in the vomit of cats and the droppings of mice; I shall fight them for the left-overs of the world.

ELESIN: Enough Iyaloja, enough.

IYALOJA: We called you leader and oh, how you led us on. What we have no intention of eating should not be held to the nose.[1]

ELESIN: Enough, enough. My shame is heavy enough.

IYALOJA: Wait. I came with a burden.

ELESIN: You have more than discharged it.

IYALOJA: I wish I could pity you.

ELESIN: I need neither pity nor the pity of the world. I need understanding. Even I need to understand. You were present at my defeat. You were part of the beginnings. You brought about the renewal of my tie to earth, you helped in the binding of the cord.

IYALOJA: I gave you warning. The river which fills up before our eyes does not sweep us away in its flood.

ELESIN: What were warnings beside the moist contact of living earth between my fingers? What were warnings beside the renewal of famished embers lodged eternally in the heart of man. But even that, even if it overwhelmed one with a thousandfold temptations to linger a little while, a man could overcome it. It is when the alien hand pollutes the source of will, when a stranger's force of violence shatters the mind's calm resolution, this is when a man is made to commit the awful treachery of relief, commit in his thought the unspeakable blasphemy of seeing the hand of the gods in this alien rupture of his world. I know it was this thought that killed me, sapped my powers and turned me into an infant in the hands of unnamable strangers. I made to utter my spells anew but my tongue merely rattled in my mouth. I fingered hidden charms and the contact was damp; there was no spark left to sever the life-strings

---

9. The frothy head of the palm wine. *Tapper:* one who climbs to the very top of the palm tree for its wine. The profession is a highly specialized one. *Cricket hole:* hunting crickets is a favorite game of Yoruba boys.
1. Considered uncouth by Yorubas.

that should stretch from every fingertip. My will was squelched in the spittle of an alien race, and all because I had committed this blasphemy of thought—that there might be the hand of the gods in a stranger's intervention.

IYALOJA: Explain it how you will, I hope it brings you peace of mind. The bush rat fled his rightful cause, reached the market and set up a lamentation. "Please save me!"—are these fitting words to hear from an ancestral mask? "There's a wild beast at my heels" is not becoming language from a hunter.

ELESIN: May the world forgive me.

IYALOJA: I came with a burden I said. It approaches the gates which are so well guarded by those jackals whose spittle will from this day be on your food and drink. But first, tell me, you who were once Elesin Oba, tell me, you who know so well the cycle of the plantain: is it the parent shoot which withers to give sap to the younger or, does your wisdom see it running the other way?

ELESIN: I don't see your meaning Iyaloja?

IYALOJA: Did I ask you for a meaning? I asked a question. Whose trunk withers to give sap to the other? The parent shoot or the younger?

ELESIN: The parent.

IYALOJA: Ah. So you do know that. There are sights in this world which say different Elesin. There are some who choose to reverse the cycle of our being. Oh you emptied bark that the world once saluted for a pith-laden being, shall I tell you what the gods have claimed of you?

[*In her agitation she steps beyond the line indicated by* PILKINGS *and the air is rent by piercing whistles. The two* GUARDS *also leap forward and place safe-guarding hands on* ELESIN. IYALOJA *stops, astonished.* PILKINGS *comes racing in, followed by* JANE.]

PILKINGS: What is it? Did they try something?

GUARD: She stepped beyond the line.

ELESIN: [*In a broken voice.*] Let her alone. She meant no harm.

IYALOJA: Oh Elesin, see what you've become. Once you had no need to open your mouth in explanation because evil-smelling goats, itchy of hand and foot had lost their senses. And it was a brave man indeed who dared lay hands on you because Iyaloja stepped from one side of the earth onto another. Now look at the spectacle of your life. I grieve for you.

PILKINGS: I think you'd better leave. I doubt you have done him much good by coming here. I shall make sure you are not allowed to see him again. In any case we are moving him to a different place before dawn, so don't bother to come back.

IYALOJA: We foresaw that. Hence the burden I trudged here to lay beside your gates.

PILKINGS: What was that you said?

IYALOJA: Didn't our son explain? Ask that one. He knows what it is. At least we hope the man we once knew as Elesin remembers the lesser oaths he need not break.

PILKINGS: Do you know what she is talking about?

ELESIN: Go to the gates, ghostly one. Whatever you find there, bring it to me.

3068 / WOLE SOYINKA

IYALOJA: Not yet. It drags behind me on the slow, weary feet of women. Slow as it is Elesin, it has long overtaken you. It rides ahead of your laggard will.

PILKINGS: What is she saying now? Christ! Must your people forever speak in riddles?

ELESIN: It will come white man, it will come. Tell your men at the gates to let it through.

PILKINGS: [*Dubiously.*] I'll have to see what it is.

IYALOJA: You will. [*Passionately.*] But this is one oath he cannot shirk. White one, you have a king here, a visitor from your land. We know of his presence here. Tell me, were he to die would you leave his spirit roaming restlessly on the surface of earth? Would you bury him here among those you consider less than human? In your land have you no ceremonies of the dead?

PILKINGS: Yes. But we don't make our chiefs commit suicide to keep him company.

IYALOJA: Child, I have not come to help your understanding. [*Points to* ELESIN.] This is the man whose weakened understanding holds us in bondage to you. But ask him if you wish. He knows the meaning of a king's passage; he was not born yesterday. He knows the peril to the race when our dead father, who goes as intermediary, waits and waits and knows he is betrayed. He knows when the narrow gate was opened and he knows it will not stay for laggards who drag their feet in dung and vomit, whose lips are reeking of the left-overs of lesser men. He knows he has condemned our king to wander in the void of evil with beings who are enemies of life.

PILKINGS: Yes er . . . but look here . . .

IYALOJA: What we ask is little enough. Let him release our King so he can ride on homewards alone. The messenger is on his way on the backs of women. Let him send word through the heart that is folded up within the bolt. It is the least of all his oaths, it is the easiest fulfilled.

[*The* AIDE-DE-CAMP *runs in.*]

PILKINGS: Bob?

AIDE-DE-CAMP: Sir, there's a group of women chanting up the hill.

PILKINGS: [*Rounding on* IYALOJA.] If you people want trouble . . .

JANE: Simon, I think that's what Olunde referred to in his letter.

PILKINGS: He knows damned well I can't have a crowd here! Damn it, I explained the delicacy of my position to him. I think it's about time I got him out of town. Bob, send a car and two or three soldiers to bring him in. I think the sooner he takes his leave of his father and gets out the better.

IYALOJA: Save your labour white one. If it is the father of your prisoner you want, Olunde, he who until this night we knew as Elesin's son, he comes soon himself to take his leave. He has sent the women ahead, so let them in.

[PILKINGS *remains undecided.*]

AIDE-DE-CAMP: What do we do about the invasion? We can still stop them far from here.

PILKINGS: What do they look like?

AIDE-DE-CAMP: They're not many. And they seem quite peaceful.

PILKINGS: No men?

AIDE-DE-CAMP: Mm, two or three at the most.

JANE: Honestly, Simon, I'd trust Olunde. I don't think he'll deceive you about their intentions.

PILKINGS: He'd better not. All right then, let them in Bob. Warn them to control themselves. Then hurry Olunde here. Make sure he brings his baggage because I'm not returning him into town.

AIDE-DE-CAMP: Very good, sir. [Goes.]

PILKINGS: [To IYALOJA.] I hope you understand that if anything goes wrong it will be on your head. My men have orders to shoot at the first sign of trouble.

IYALOJA: To prevent one death you will actually make other deaths? Ah, great is the wisdom of the white race. But have no fear. Your Prince will sleep peacefully. So at long last will ours. We will disturb you no further, servant of the white king. Just let Elesin fulfil his oath and we will retire home and pay homage to our King.

JANE: I believe her Simon, don't you?

PILKINGS: Maybe.

ELESIN: Have no fear ghostly one. I have a message to send my King and then you have nothing more to fear.

IYALOJA: Olunde would have done it. The chiefs asked him to speak the words but he said no, not while you lived.

ELESIN: Even from the depths to which my spirit has sunk, I find some joy that this little has been left to me.

[The WOMEN enter, intoning the dirge "Ale le le" and swaying from side to side. On their shoulders is borne a longish object roughly like a cylindrical bolt, covered in cloth. They set it down on the spot where IYALOJA had stood earlier, and form a semi-circle round it. The PRAISE SINGER and DRUMMER stand on the inside of the semi-circle but the drum is not used at all. The DRUMMER intones under the PRAISE SINGER's invocations.]

PILKINGS: [As they enter.] What is that?

IYALOJA: The burden you have made white one, but we bring it in peace.

PILKINGS: I said what is it?

ELESIN: White man, you must let me out. I have a duty to perform.

PILKINGS: I most certainly will not.

ELESIN: There lies the courier of my King. Let me out so I can perform what is demanded of me.

PILKINGS: You'll do what you need to do from inside there or not at all. I've gone as far as I intend to with this business.

ELESIN: The worshipper who lights a candle in your church to bear a message to his god bows his head and speaks in a whisper to the flame. Have I not seen it ghostly one? His voice does not ring out to the world. Mine are no words for anyone's ears. They are not words even for the bearers of this load. They are words I must speak secretly, even as my father whispered them in my ears and I in the ears of my first-born. I cannot shout them to the wind and the open night sky.

JANE: Simon . . .

PILKINGS: Don't interfere. Please!

IYALOJA: They have slain the favourite horse of the king and slain his dog.

They have borne them from pulse to pulse centre of the land receiving prayers for their king. But the rider has chosen to stay behind. Is it too much to ask that he speak his heart to heart of the waiting courier? [PILKINGS *turns his back on her.*] So be it. Elesin Oba, you see how even the mere leavings are denied you. [*She gestures to the* PRAISE SINGER.]

PRAISE SINGER: Elesin Oba! I call you by that name only this last time. Remember when I said, if you cannot come, tell my horse. [*Pause.*] What? I cannot hear you? I said, if you cannot come, whisper in the ears of my horse. Is your tongue severed from the roots? Elesin? I can hear no response. I said, if there are boulders you cannot climb, mount my horse's back, this spotless black stallion, he'll bring you over them. [*Pauses.*] Elesin Oba, once you had a tongue that darted like a drummer's stick. I said, if you get lost my dog will track a path to me. My memory fails me but I think you replied: My feet have found the path, Alafin.

[*The dirge rises and falls.*]

I said at the last, if evil hands hold you back, just tell my horse there is weight on the hem of your smock. I dare not wait too long.

[*The dirge rises and falls.*]

There lies the swiftest ever messenger of a king, so set me free with the errand of your heart. There lie the head and heart of the favourite of the gods, whisper in his ears. Oh my companion, if you had followed when you should, we would not say that the horse preceded its rider. If you had followed when it was time, we would not say the dog has raced beyond and left his master behind. If you had raised your will to cut the thread of life at the summons of the drums, we would not say your mere shadow fell across the gateway and took its owner's place at the banquet. But the hunter, laden with slain buffalo, stayed to root in the cricket's hole with his toes. What now is left? If there is a dearth of bats, the pigeon must serve us for the offering.[2] Speak the words over your shadow which must now serve in your place.

ELESIN: I cannot approach. Take off the cloth. I shall speak my message from heart to heart of silence.

IYALOJA: [*Moves forward and removes the covering.*] Your courier Elesin, cast your eyes on the favoured companion of the King.

[*Rolled up in the mat, his head and feet showing at either end, is the body of* OLUNDE.]

There lies the honour of your household and of our race. Because he could not bear to let honour fly out of doors, he stopped it with his life. The son has proved the father Elesin, and there is nothing left in your mouth to gnash but infant gums.

PRAISE SINGER: Elesin, we placed the reins of the world in your hands yet you watched it plunge over the edge of the bitter precipice. You sat with folded arms while evil strangers tilted the world from its course and crashed it beyond the edge of emptiness—you muttered, there is little that one man can do, you left us floundering in a blind future. Your heir has taken the burden on himself. What the end will be, we are not gods to tell. But this young shoot has poured its sap into the parent stalk, and we know this is not the way of life. Our world is tumbling in the void of strangers, Elesin.

2. Sacrifice.

[ELESIN *has stood rock-still, his knuckles taut on the bars, his eyes glued to the body of his son. The stillness seizes and paralyses everyone, including* PILKINGS *who has turned to look. Suddenly* ELESIN *flings one arm round his neck, once, and with the loop of the chain, strangles himself in a swift, decisive pull. The* GUARDS *rush forward to stop him but they are only in time to let his body down.* PILKINGS *has leapt to the door at the same time and struggles with the lock. He rushes within, fumbles with the handcuffs and unlocks them, raises the body to a sitting position while he tries to give resuscitation. The* WOMEN *continue their dirge, unmoved by the sudden event.*]

IYALOJA: Why do you strain yourself? Why do you labour at tasks for which no one, not even the man lying there would give you thanks? He is gone at last into the passage but oh, how late it all is. His son will feast on the meat and throw him bones. The passage is clogged with droppings from the King's stallion; he will arrive all stained in dung.

PILKINGS: [*In a tired voice.*] Was this what you wanted?

IYALOJA: No child, it is what you brought to be, you who play with strangers' lives, who even usurp the vestments of our dead, yet believe that the stain of death will not cling to you. The gods demanded only the old expired plantain but you cut down the sap-laden shoot to feed your pride. There is your board, filled to overflowing. Feast on it. [*She screams at him suddenly, seeing that* PILKINGS *is about to close* ELESIN's *staring eyes.*] Let him alone! However sunk he was in debt he is no pauper's carrion abandoned on the road. Since when have strangers donned clothes of indigo[3] before the bereaved cries out his loss?

[*She turns to the* BRIDE *who has remained motionless throughout.*] Child.

[*The girl takes up a little earth, walks calmly into the cell and closes* ELESIN's *eyes. She then pours some earth over each eyelid and comes out again.*]

Now forget the dead, forget even the living. Turn your mind only to the unborn.

[*She goes off, accompanied by the* BRIDE. *The dirge rises in volume and the* WOMEN *continue their sway. Lights fade to a black-out.*]

3. Worn for mourning.

A. B. YEHOSHUA
born 1936

A. B. Yehoshua is a master of symbolic narratives that move easily between the fantastic and the grittily real and that give life to questions of psychological depth and subtlety. His earliest stories have an abstract and allegorical quality, set in no particular time or place, and are peopled with vivid but stereotypical characters. But as he has matured as a writer Yehoshua has grounded his stories with increasing sureness in a specific social and political reality, and his characters have taken on a psychological depth and richness as well. Yehoshua is also a profoundly political writer, and, indeed, the clarity and force with which his narratives explore and illuminate current political realities in Israel have meant that critics are as likely to address the political and social implications of his works as their literary merits. He is best known in the West for his novels and short stories, but he has written plays as well. Yehoshua is also an outspoken advocate of peace and a vigorous advocate of reformulating the terms *Jew, Israeli,* and *Zionist* to lessen the tension between Israel and its Arab citizens. In addition to his writing, Yehoshua has pursued an active career as a professor of literature at Haifa University. He shares with Amos Oz the distinction of being one of the two most highly regarded prose writers in Israel today.

Yehoshua was born in Jerusalem in 1936 and raised and educated in the British Mandate Palestine of the 1940s, remote from the agonies of European Jewry in World War II. His parents both belonged to the Sephardic (Oriental) Jewish community. His father, Ja'acov, a noted Orientalist scholar, had also been born in Jerusalem. Ja'acov's mother belonged to a family that had lived in Jerusalem for generations, and his father, who had come to Jerusalem from Salonika in Greece as a baby, later became chief judge of the Sephardic court. Yehoshua's mother was one of the younger children of a wealthy Moroccan merchant who, after the death of his wife in 1932, chose to leave his home and business to move to Palestine for personal and spiritual reasons. Yehoshua's deep Sephardic roots recur as a central theme in his mature fiction. For him the Sephardic community's history in Palestine and Israel provides an instructive alternative to that of the Ashkenazi (European) Jewish community's, a counternarrative to the master narrative that has dominated efforts to establish and define an Israeli national identity.

The great watershed in the modern history of Israel was, of course, the 1948 War for Independence, which brought about the establishment of the Jewish state in what had formerly been Palestine. The successful conclusion of the long campaign by European Zionists to establish a permanent Jewish homeland in the land of their historical origin and the gathering in of the Jewish communities of the Diaspora ended the first cycle of modern Israeli history. The Diaspora was the period of Jewish history from the dispersal of the Jewish tribes outside of Israel in the sixth century B.C. to the foundation of Israel. Success is often followed by disenchantment, however, and these victories had been won at a terrible cost. The intractable problems inherent in building a new society in a new state had been put aside while the struggle before them now demanded attention. (How were they to integrate the many diverse communities that had been gathered into the new state? What was to be done with the hostile Arabs now living among them? Now that the fundamental goal of establishing a state had been achieved, what new goal could unite and energize the nation?)

The new generation of poets and writers that came into its own in the late 1950s abandoned the collectivist ideological sentiment of the generation of the War of Independence. They sought new topics, new characters, and an escape from ideology itself. The new hero, in Yehoshua's words, "was a marginal, perverted and somewhat estranged character." His works, perhaps, most fully embodied this new literary genre in which freeing the hero from ideology also freed him from clearly defined boundaries of place and time and blurred the borders between the realistic and the surreal.

Yehoshua had begun writing humorous and fantastic sketches in high school and continued to do so while serving in the parachute corps and attending Hebrew University, where he majored in literature. His first short story, *Death of the Old Man,* which appeared in 1957, is a first-person narrative in which a strong-willed old woman decides that a very old but exceptionally vital man who lives in her apartment house has lived too long. Since he refuses to die on his own, she decides to dispose of him by performing a funeral and burying him alive and enlists the aid of the other tenants to carry out her bizarre scheme. This story provides the title of his first collection of stories, which was published in 1962. The other stories in this collection also combine elements of the unusual, the unexpected, and the bizarre with sudden eruptions of violent and self-destructive energies, and they take place in a vague region outside of time or place. The stories in his second collection, *Facing the Forests* (1968), contain these same elements as well, but the characters begin to take on a psychological depth and they exist in real, identifiable contexts.

All the characters of the story *Facing the Forests* appear as types, not individuals, and this tells us at once that it is an allegory. However, there are jokers in this deck. The student, for example, is an anomaly, a bright student who inexplicably fails to live up to his promise. He is aimless and indifferent to the symbols that define his culture, both the concrete (the national forest with its shiny memorial plaques) and the abstract (the energetic striving that permits his contemporaries to advance while he lags behind). The Arab is also another anomaly, a non-Jew in a Jewish state, who is further excluded from membership in any sense by his ignorance of Hebrew. He can, in fact, speak no language since his tongue has been cut out.

Yehoshua has constructed the symbols and characters of his story to suit the facts of modern Israeli history, but in doing so he is drawing on a narrative that has an archetypal resonance. On the one hand there is the impotent intellectual who has grown disaffected with the values and concerns of his own culture and with his intellect itself. Words, the stock-in-trade of an intellectual, no longer have any meaning for him. On the other, there is the disenfranchised and inarticulate "native" who lives to right an old wrong done to him and his people by the master culture of which the intellectual is a part. He either lacks the words to make his grievances known or cannot compel his oppressors to hear them. The nihilism of the intellectual leads him to collude, consciously or unconsciously, in the violence of the disenfranchised native.

What sets Yehoshua's story apart from more conventional treatments of this basic narrative is his refusal to celebrate this alliance. The plight of the Arab is presented with sympathy but not advocacy, and the intellectual who colludes with him and betrays his own culture is an unappealing figure who has not actively espoused the Arab's cause so much as drifted under its spell out of a feeling of general malaise. The violent solution of the Arab is also no solution at all. He has destroyed the forest, but his village has not been reborn as a result. He himself will now be imprisoned, and his daughter will become a ward of the state. Finally, the student seems to have learned nothing from the experience himself.

Where the story is remarkably prescient is in its implicit warning that a failure to address these buried problems can lead to a terrible and violent despair, a despair in which even self-destructive acts become preferable to continued inaction. Israelis, Yehoshua implies, cannot afford to ignore the rights of the Arabs whom they have displaced, for the price of that neglect will be a terrible and costly conflagration.

Yehoshua's first novel, *The Lover* (1977), is written as a series of individual narratives by the principal characters, a technique that Yehoshua learned from the works of Faulkner like *As I Lay Dying* and which he has used subsequently in *A Late Divorce* (1983) and, most strikingly perhaps, in *Mr. Mani* (1992), where the monologues take the form of dialogues in which we hear the voice of only one speaker. In *The Lover*, set during the Yom Kippur War (1973), the characters have individual and distinctive personalities, they live in modern Haifa, and they tell their tales in a straightforward, realistic style. Yet it is a work built on bizarre paradoxes: a husband who seeks lovers for both his wife and his daughter with obsessive zeal, an Arab who longs to assimilate to Hebrew culture, a Sephardic Israeli soldier who first emigrates from Israel and then, on his return, both deserts from the army and takes refuge in an ultra-Orthodox Ashkenazic community. As the Israeli critic Gershon Shaked points out, these social paradoxes reflect the existential dilemmas of identity that underlie contemporary Israeli society. Moreover, in this novel Yehoshua initiates his Sephardic counternarrative in the character of Veducha, a Sephardic grandmother, whose life and character embody the principal elements of that narrative. Surely the most fully developed exploration of this theme is his novel, *Mr. Mani,* a work of stylistic brilliance and artistic originality that traces the evolution of one Sephardic family through five generations.

Although Yehoshua's work received substantial and favorable critical attention from the very first, with the publication of *The Lover,* which appeared in English translation only a year later, he began to receive international recognition as well. This recognition has grown with each of his subsequent works so that he is now one of the handful of Israeli writers who, like Amos Oz and Yehuda Amichai, enjoy a wide readership outside of Israel as well as within it. His works have been translated into many languages, and among other honors, he was awarded the Brenner Prize in 1983; the Alterman Prize in 1986; the Bialik Prize in 1989; and for *Mr. Mani* (1992), the Israeli award for the best work of literature to appear in the preceding two years.

A substantial majority of Yehoshua's writings have been translated into English: *Three Days and a Child* (1970), the collection from which the story printed here was taken; *Early in the Summer of 1970* (1977), a novella; two plays, *A Night in May and Last Treatment* (1974) and *Until Winter* (1974); and a second short story collection. All his novels have been translated: *The Lover* (1978), *A Late Divorce* (1983), *Five Seasons* (1989), and *Mr. Mani* (1992). A book of political essays, *Between Right and Right* (1981), has also been published in English.

There are no book-length studies of Yehoshua in English as yet, but his works are reviewed in major American journals. Robert Alter, *Modern Hebrew Literature* (1975), an anthology with extensive introductions, contains a detailed analysis of *Facing the Forests.*

PRONOUNCING GLOSSARY

The following list uses common English syllables and stress accents to provide rough equivalents of selected words whose pronunciation may be unfamiliar to the general reader.

Ashkenazi: *ash'-kuh-nah'-zee*   Veducha: *vuh-dew'-chuh*

Diaspora: *dee-ass'-puh-ruh*   Yehoshua: *ye-hoh-shoo'-uh*

Sephardic: *suh-far'-dik*

Facing the Forests[1]

I

Another winter lost in fog. As usual he did nothing; postponed examinations, left papers unwritten. He had completed all his courses long ago, attended all the lectures, and the string of signatures on his tattered student card testified that all had performed their duty toward him, silently disappeared, and left the rest of the task in his own limp hands. But words weary him; his own, let alone the words of others. He drifts from one rented room to another, rootless, jobless. But for an occasional job tutoring backward children he would starve to death. Here he is approaching thirty and a bald spot crowns his wilting head. His defective eyesight blurs many things. His dreams at night are dull. They are uneventful; a yellow waste, where a few stunted trees may spring up in a moment of grace, and a naked woman. At student revels he is already looked at with faint ridicule. The speed with which he gets drunk is a regular part of the program. He never misses a party. They need him still. His limp figure is extremely popular and there is no one like him for bridging gaps between people. His erstwhile fellow students have graduated since and may be seen carrying bulging briefcases, on

1. Translated by Miriam Arad.

their way to work every morning of the week. Sometimes, at noon, returning from their offices, they may encounter him in the street with his just-awake eyes: a gray moth in search of its first meal. They, having heard of his dissipations, promptly pronounce the unanimous, half-pitying, half-exasperated decree: "Solitude!"

Solitude is what he needs. For he is not without talent nor does he lack brains. He needs to strengthen his willpower.

He, as a rule, will drop his arms by his sides in a gesture of pious despair, back up against the nearest available wall, languidly cross his legs and plead in a whisper:

"But where? Go on, tell me, where?"

For look, he himself craves solitude. He plainly needs to renew his acquaintance with words, to try and concentrate on the material that threatens ever to wear him down. But then he would have to enter prison. He knows himself (a sickly smile): if there should be the tiniest crack of escape through, he would make it a tunnel at once. No, please, no favors. Either—or.

Some content themselves with this feeble excuse, shrug their shoulders wryly, and go their way. But his real friends, those whose wives he loves as well, two budding lecturers who remember him from days gone by, remember him favorably for the two or three amazingly original ideas that he had dropped at random during his student days—friends who are concerned for his future—these two are well aware that the coming spring is that much more dangerous to him, that his desultory affairs with women will but draw zeal from the blue skies. Is it any wonder, then, if one fine day they will catch hold of him in the street, their eyes sparkling. "Well, your lordship, we've found the solution to your lordship's problem at last." And he will be quick to show an expectant eagerness, though cunning enough to leave himself ample means of retreat.

"What?"

The function of forest scout. A fire-watcher. Yes, it's something new. A dream of a job, a plum. Utter, profound solitude. There he will be able to scrape together his crumbled existence.

Where did they get the idea?

From the papers, yes, from a casual skimming of the daily papers.

He is astonished, laughs inordinately, hysterically almost. What now? What's the idea? Forests . . . What forests? Since when do we have forests in this country? What do they mean?

But they refuse to smile. For once they are determined. Before he has time to digest their words they have burned the bridges over which he had meant to escape, as usual. "You said, either—or. Here is your solution."

He glances at his watch, pretending haste. Will not a single spark light up in him then? For he, too, loathes himself, doesn't he?

II

And so, when spring has set the windows ajar, he arrives early one morning at the Afforestation Department. A sunny office, a clerk, a typist, several typists. He enters quickly, armed with impressive recommendations, heralded by telephone calls. The man in charge of the forests, a worthy character edging his way to old age, is faintly amused (his position permits him as much), grins to himself. Much ado about nothing, about such a marginal job. Hence he is curious about the caller, even considers rising to receive him. The plain patch of barrenness atop the head of the candidate adds to his stature. The fellow inspires surely trust, is surely meant for better things.

"Are you certain that this is what you want? The observation post is a grim place. Only really primitive people can bear such solitude. What is it you wish to write? Your doctorate?"

No, sad to say, he is still at the elementary stages of his study.

Yes, he has wasted much time.

No, he has no family.

Yes, with glasses, his vision is sound.

Gently the old manager explains, that in accordance with a certain semi-official agreement, this work is reserved for social cases only and not for how-shall-I-put-it, romantics, ha-ha, intellectuals in search of solitude . . . However, he is prepared, just this once, to make an exception and include an intellectual among the wretched assortment of his workers. Yes, he is himself getting sick of the diverse social cases, the invalids, the cripples, the cranks. A fire breaks out, and these fellows will do nothing but stand and stare panic-stricken at the flames till the fire brigade arrives. Whenever he is forced to send out one such unstable character he stays awake nights thinking what if in an obscure rage, against society or whatever, the fire-watcher should himself set the forest on fire. He feels certain that he, the man in front of him here, though occupied with affairs of the mind, will be sufficiently alert to his duty to abandon his books and fight the fire. Yes, it is a question of moral values.

Sorry, the old man has forgotten what it is his candidate wishes to write? A doctorate?

Once more he apologizes. He is still, sad to say, at the elementary stages of his study. Yes, he has wasted much time. Indeed, he has no family.

A young secretary is called in.

Then he is invited to sign an inoffensive little contract for six months: spring, summer (ah, summer is dangerous!), and half the autumn. Discipline, responsibility, vigilance, conditions of dismissal. A hush descends while he runs his eyes cursorily over the document. Manager and secretary are ready with a pen, but he prefers to sign with his own. He signs several copies. First salary due on April the fifth. Now he eases himself into his chair, unable to rise, tired still. He is not used to waking so early. Meanwhile he tries to establish some sort of contact, display an interest. He inquires about the size of the forests, the height of the trees. To tell the truth—he runs on expansively, in a sort of dangerous drowsiness—the fact is that he has never yet seen a real forest in this country. An occasional ancient grove, yes, but he hardly believes (ha-ha-ha) that the Authorities in charge of Afforestation have anything to do with that. Yes, he keeps hearing over the radio about forests being planted to honor this, that, and the other personage. Though apparently one cannot actually see them yet . . . The trees grow slowly . . . don't gain height . . . Actually he understands . . . this arid soil . . . In other countries, now . . .

At last he falters. Naturally he realizes, has realized from the start, that he has made a bad blunder, has sensed it from the laughter trembling in the girl's eyes, from the shocked fury coloring the face of the manager who is edging his way to old age. The candidate has, to use a tangible image, taken a careless step and trampled a tender spot in the heart of the man in charge of forests, who is fixing him now in a harsh stare and delivering a monologue for his benefit.

What does he mean by small trees? He has obviously failed to use his eyes. Of course there are forests. Real forests. Jungles, no; but forests, yes, indeed. If he will pardon the question: What does he know about what happens in this country anyway? For even when he travels through it on a bus he won't bother to take his head out of his book. It's laughable, really, these flat allegations. He, the old man, has come across this kind of talk from young people, but the candidate is rather past that age. If he, the manager, had the time to spare, he could show him maps. But soon he will see for himself. There are forests in the Hills of Judea, in Galilee, Samaria, and elsewhere. Perhaps the candidate's eyesight is weak, after all. Perhaps he needs a stronger pair of spectacles. The manager would like to ask the candidate to take spare spectacles with him. He would rather not have any more trouble. Good-bye.

Where are they sending him?

A few days later he is back. This time he is received not by the manager, but by an underling. He is being sent to one of the larger forests. He won't be alone there but with a laborer, an Arab. They feel certain he has no prejudices. Good-bye. Ah yes, departure is on Sunday.

III

Things happen fast. He severs connections and they appear to come loose with surprising ease. He vacates his room and his landlady is glad of it, for some reason. He spends the last nights with one of his learned friends, who sets to work at once to prepare a study schedule for him. While his zealous friend is busy in one room cramming books into a suitcase, the prospective fire-watcher fondles the beloved wife in another. He is pensive, his hands gentle, there is something of joy in his expectations of the morrow. What shall he study? His friends suggest the Crusades. Yes, that would be just right for him. Everyone specializes in a certain subject. He may yet prove to be a little researcher all in his own right, just so long as he won't fritter his time away. He ought to bring some startling scientific theory back from the forests. His friends will take care of the facts later.

But in the morning, when the lorry[2] of the Afforestation Department comes to fetch him out of his shattered sleep, he suddenly imagines that all this has been set in motion just to get rid of him; and, shivering in the cold morning air, he can but console himself with the thought that this adventure will go the way of all others and be drowned in somnolence. Is it any wonder that Jerusalem, high on its hills, Jerusalem, which is left behind now, is fading like a dream? He abandons himself to the jolts and pitches of the lorry. The laborers with their hoes and baskets sit huddled away from him in the back of the car. They sense that he belongs to another world. The bald patch and the glasses are an indication, one of many.

2. Truck.

Traveling half a day.

The lorry leaves the highway and travels over long, alien dirt roads, among nameless immigrant settlements. Laborers alight, others take their place. Everyone receives instructions from the driver, who is the one in command around here. We are going south, are we? Wide country meeting a spring-blue sky. The ground is damp still and clods of earth drop off the lorry's tires. It is late in the morning when he discovers the first trees scattered among rocks. Young slender pines, tiny, light green. "Then I was right," he tells himself with a smile. But farther on the trees grow taller. Now the light bursts and splinters. Long shadows steal aboard the lorry like stowaways. People keep changing and only the driver, the passenger and his suitcases stay put. The forests grow denser, no more bare patches now. Pines, always, and only the one species, obstinately, unvaryingly. He is tired, dusty, hungry, has long ago lost all sense of direction. The sun is playing tricks, twisting around him. He does not see where he is going, only what he is leaving behind. At three o'clock the lorry is emptied of laborers and only he is left. For a long time the lorry climbs over a rugged track. He is cross, his mouth feels dry. In despair he tries to pull a book out of one suitcase, but then the lorry stops. The driver gets off, bangs the door, comes around to him and says:

"This is it. Your predecessor's already made off—yesterday. Your instructions are all up there. You at least can read, for a change."

Laboriously he hauls himself and his two suitcases down. An odd, charming, stone house stands on a hill. Pines of all sizes surround it. He is at a high altitude here, though he cannot yet see everything from where he is. Silence, a silence of trees. The driver stretches his legs, looks around, breathes the air, then suddenly he nods good-bye and climbs back into his cab and switches the engine on.

He who must stay behind is seized with regret. Despair. What now? Just a minute! He doesn't understand. He rushes at the car, beats his fists against the door, whispers furiously at the surprised driver.

"But food . . . what about food?"

It appears that the Arab takes care of everything.

IV

Alone he trudges uphill, a suitcase in each hand. Gradually the world comes into view. The front door stands open and he enters a large room, the ground floor. Semidarkness, dilapidated objects on the floor, food remnants, traces of a child. The despair mounts in him. He lets go of the suitcases and climbs absently to the second floor. The view strikes him with awe. Five hills covered with a dense green growth—pines. A silvery blue horizon with a distant sea. He is instantly excited, on fire, forgetting everything. He is even prepared to change his opinion of the Afforestation Department.

A telephone, binoculars, a sheet covered with instructions. A large desk and an armchair beside it. He settles himself into the chair and reads the instructions five times over, from beginning to end. Then he pulls out his pen and makes a few stylistic corrections. He glances fondly at the black instrument. He is in high spirits. He considers calling up one of his friends in town, to say something tender to one of his aging ladyloves. He might announce his safe arrival, describe the view perhaps. Never has he had a public telephone at his disposal yet. He lifts the receiver to his ear. An endless purring. He is not familiar with the proceedings. He tries dialing. In vain. The purr remains steady. At last he dials zero, like a sober citizen expecting a sober reply.

The telephone breaks its silence.

The Fire Brigade comes on with a startled "What's happened?" Real alarm at the other side. (Where, where, confound it!) Before he has said a word, questions rain down on him. How large is the fire? What direction the wind? They are coming at once. He tries to put in a word, stutters, and already they are starting a car over there. Panic grips him. He jumps up, the receiver tight in his hand. He breaks out in a cold sweat. With the last remnant of words in his power he explains everything. No. There is no fire. There is nothing. Only getting acquainted. He has just arrived. Wanted to get through to town. His name is so-and-so. That is all.

A hush at the other side. The voice changes. This must be their chief now. Pleased to meet you, Sir, we've taken down your name. Have you read all the instructions? Personal calls are quite out of the question. Anyway, you've only just arrived, haven't you? Or is there some urgent need? Your wife? Your children?

No, he has no family.

Well, then, why the panic? Lonely? He'll get used to it. Please don't disturb again in the future. Good-bye.

The ring closes in on him a little. Pink streaks on the horizon. He is tired, hungry. He has risen early, and he is utterly unused to that. This high, commanding view makes him dizzy. The silence. He picks up the binoculars with a limp hand and raises them to his eyes. The world leaps close, blurred. Pines lunge at him upright. He adjusts the forest, the hills, the sea horizon to the quality of his eyes. He amuses himself a bit, then lets go of the binoculars and eases himself into the chair. He has a clear conception of his new job now. Just watching. His eyes grow heavy. He dozes, sleeps perhaps.

Suddenly he wakes—a red light is burning on his glasses. He is bewildered, scared, his senses heavy. The forest has caught fire, apparently, and he has missed it. He jumps up, his heart wildly beating, grabs the telephone, the binoculars, and then it occurs to him that it is the sun, only the sun setting beyond the trees. He is facing west. Now he knows. Slowly he drops back into the chair. His heart contracts with something like terror, like emptiness. He imagines himself deserted in this place, forgotten. His glasses mist over and he takes them off and wipes them.

When dusk falls, he hears steps.

V

An Arab and a little girl are approaching the house. Swiftly he rises to his feet. They notice him, look up and stop in their tracks—startled by the soft, scholarly figure. He bows his head. They walk on but their steps are hesitant now. He goes down to them.

The Arab turns out to be old and mute. His tongue was cut out during the war. By one of them or one of us? Does it matter? Who knows what the last words were that stuck in his throat? In the dark room, its windows ablaze with the last light, the fire-watcher shakes a heavy hand, bends to pat the child, who flinches, terrified. The ring of loneliness closes in on him. The Arab puts on lights. The fire-watcher will sleep upstairs.

The first evening, and a gnawing sadness. The weak yellow light of the bulbs is depressing. For the time being, he draws comfort only from the wide view, from the soft blue of the sea in the distance and the sun writhing in it. He sits cramped on his chair and watches the big forests entrusted to his eyes. He imagines that the fire may break out at any moment. After a long delay, the Arab brings up his supper. An odd taste, a mixture of tastes. But he devours everything, leaves not a morsel. His eyes rove hungrily between the plate and the thick woods. Suddenly, while chewing, he discovers a few faraway lights—villages. He broods a while about women, then takes off his clothes, opens the suitcase that does not hold books, and takes out his things. It seems a long time since he left town. He wraps himself in blankets, lies facing the forests. A cool breeze caresses him. What sort of sleep will come to one here? The Arab brings him a cup of coffee to help him stay awake. The fire-watcher would like to talk to him about something; perhaps about the view, or about the poor lighting perhaps. He has words left in him still from the city. But the Arab does not understand Hebrew. The fire-watcher smiles wearily in thanks. Something about his bald crown, the glint of his glasses, seems to daunt the Arab.

It is half-past nine—the beginning of night. Cicadas strike up. He struggles against sleep engulfing him. His eyes close and his conscience tortures him. The binoculars dangle from their strap around his neck, and from time to time he picks them up, lifts them to his eyes blinded with sleep, glasses clicking against glass. He opens his eyes in a stare and finds himself in the forest, among pines, hunting for flames. Darkness.

How long does it take for a forest to burn down? Perhaps he will only look every hour, every two hours. Even if the forest should start to burn, he would still manage to raise the alarm in time to save the rest. The murmur downstairs has died down. The Arab and his child are asleep. And he is up here, light-headed, tired after his journey, between three walls and a void gaping to the sea. He must not roll over onto his other side. He nods, and his sleep is pervaded by the fear of fire, fire stealing upon him unaware. At midnight he transfers himself from bed to chair; it is safer that way. His head droops heavily onto the desk, his spine aches, he is crying out for sleep, full of regret, alone against the dark empire swaying before him. Till at last the black hours of the first night pass; till out of the corner of his eye he sees the morning grow among the hills.

Only fatigue makes him stay on after the first night. The days and nights following after revolve as on a screen, a misty, dreamlike screen lit up once every twenty-four hours by the radiant glow of the setting sun. It is not himself but a stranger who wanders those first days between the two stories of the house, the binoculars slung across his chest, absently chewing on the food left him by the unseen Arab. The heavy responsibility that has suddenly fallen upon his shoulders bewilders him. Hardest of all is the silence. Even with himself he hardly manages to exchange a word. Will he be able to open a book here? The view amazes and enchants him still and he cannot have enough of it. After ten days of anguish he is himself again. In one brief glance he can embrace all the five hills now. He has learned to sleep with his eyes open. A new accomplishment; rather interesting, one must admit.

VI

At last the other suitcase, the one with the books, gets opened, with a slight delay of but a fortnight or so. The delay does not worry him in the least, for aren't the spring, the summer, and half the autumn still before him? The first day is devoted to sorting the books, spelling out titles, thumbing the pages. One can't deny that there is some pleasure in handling the fat, fragrant, annotated volumes. The texts are in English, the quotations all in Latin. Strange phrases from alien worlds. He worries a little. His subject—"The Crusades." From the human, that is to say, the ecclesiastical aspect. He has not gone into particulars yet. "Crusades," he whispers softly to himself and feels joy rising in him at the word, the sound. He feels certain that there is some dark issue buried within the subject and that it will startle him, startle other issues in him. And it will be just out of this drowsiness that envelops his mind like a permanent cloud that the matter will be revealed to him.

The following day is spent on pictures. The books are rich in illustrations. Odd, funny ones. Monks, cardinals; a few blurred kings, thin knights, tiny, villainous Jews. Curious landscapes, maps. He studies them, compares, dozes. On the hard road to the abstract he wishes to linger a while with the concrete. That night he is kept from his studies by a gnat. Next morning he tells himself: Oh, wondrous time, how fast it flies upon these lonely summits. He opens the first book on the first page, reads the author's preface, his grateful acknowledgment. He reads other prefaces, various acknowledgments, publication data. He checks a few dates. At noon his mind is distracted from the books by an imaginary flame flashing among the trees. He remains tense for hours, excited, searching with the binoculars, his hand on the telephone. At last, toward evening, he discovers that it is only the red dress of the Arab's little daughter who is skipping among the trees. The following day, when he is all set to decipher the first page, his father turns up suddenly with a suitcase in his hand.

"What's happened?" the father asks anxiously.

"Nothing . . . Nothing's happened . . ."

"But what made you become a forester then?"

"A bit of solitude . . ."

"Solitude . . ." he marvels. "You want solitude?"

The father bends over the open book, removes his heavy glasses and peers closely at the text. "The Crusades," he murmurs. "Is that what you're engaged in?"

"Yes."

"Aren't I disturbing you in your work? I haven't come to disturb you . . . I have a few days' leave."

"No, you're not disturbing me."

"Magnificent view."

"Yes, magnificent."

"You're thinner."

"Could be."

"Couldn't you study in the libraries?"

Apparently not. Silence. The father sniffs around the room like a little hedgehog. At noon he asks his son:

"Do you think it is lonely here? That you'll find solitude?"

"Yes, what's to disturb me?"

"I'm not going to disturb you."

"Of course not. What makes you think that?"

"I'll go away soon."

"No, don't go. Please stay."

The father stays a week.

In the evening the father tries to become friendly with the Arab and his child. A few words of Arabic have stuck in his memory from the days of his youth, and he will seize any occasion to fill them with meaning. But his pronunciation is unintelligible to the Arab, who only nods his head dully.

They sit together, not speaking. The son cannot read a single line with the father there, even though the father keeps muttering: "Don't bother about me. I'll keep myself in the background." At night the father sleeps on the bed and the fire-watcher stretches himself out on the floor. Sometimes the father wakes in the night to find his son awake. "Perhaps we could take turns," he says. "You go to sleep on the bed and I'll watch the forest." But the son knows that his father will see not a forest but a blurred stain. He won't notice the fire till it singes his clothes. In the daytime they change places—the son lies on the bed and the father sits by the desk and tries to read the book, which lies open still. How he would like to strike up a conversation with his son, stir up some discussion. For example, he fails to understand why his son won't deal with the Jews, the Jewish aspect of the Crusades. For isn't mass suicide a wonderful and terrible thing?[3] The son gives him a kindly grin, a noncommittal reply, and silence. During the last days of his visit the father occupies himself with the dumb Arab. A host of questions bubbles up in him. Who is the man? Where is he from? Who cut his tongue out? Why? Look, he has seen hatred in the man's eyes. A creature like that may yet set the forest on fire some day. Why not?

On his last day the father is given the binoculars to play with.

Suitcase in hand, back bent, he shakes his son's hand. Then—tears in the eyes of the little father.

"I've been disturbing you, I know I have . . ."

In vain does the son protest, in vain mumble about the oceans of time still before him—about half the spring, the whole long summer, half the distant autumn.

From his elevated seat he watches his lost, blind father fumbling for the back of the lorry. The driver is rude and impatient with him. When the lorry moves off, the father waves good-bye to the forest by mistake. He has lost his bearings.

VII

For a week he crawls from line to line over the difficult text. After every sentence he raises his head to look at the forest. He is still awaiting a fire. The air grows hot. A haze shimmers above the sea horizon. When the Arab returns at dusk his garments are damp with sweat, the child's gestures are

---

3. The father's allusion may be to a dark chapter in the history of the Crusades. In the late 11th century, German crusaders attacked and slaughtered Jewish communities in Germany before continuing on to Palestine. In many instances Jews committed suicide to escape torture or forced conversion.

tired. Anyway you look at it, he himself is lucky. At such a time to be here, high above any town. Ostensibly, he is working all the time, but observing could hardly be called work, could it? The temperature rises day by day. He wonders whether it is still spring, or whether perhaps the summer has crept upon the world already. One can gather nothing from the forest, which shows no change, except thorns fading to yellow among the trees perhaps. His hearing has grown acute. The sound of trees whispers incessantly in his ears. His eyes shine with the sun's gaining strength, his senses grown keen. In a way he is becoming attached to the forest. Even his dreams are growing richer in trees. The women sprout leaves.

His text is difficult, the words distant. It has turned out to be only the preface to a preface. Yet, thorough as he is, he does not skip a single passage. He translates every word, then rewrites the translation in rhyme. Simple, easy rhymes, in order that the words should merge in his mind, should not escape into the silence.

No wonder that by Friday he can count but three pages read, out of the thousands. "Played out," he whispers to himself and trails his fingertips over the desk. Perhaps he'll take a rest? A pensive air comes over the green empire before him each Sabbath eve and makes his heart contract. Though he believes neither in God nor in all his angels, there is a sacredness that brings a lump to his throat.

He combs his beard in honor of the holy day. Yes, there is a new beard growing here along with the pines. He brings some order into the chaos of his room, picks a page off the floor. What is this? The instruction sheet. Full of interest, he reads it once more and discovers a forgotten instruction, or one added by his own hand, perhaps.

"Let the forest scout go out from time to time for a short walk among the trees, in order to sharpen his senses."

His first steps in the forest are like a baby's. He circles the observation post, hugging its walls as though afraid to leave them. Yet the trees attract him like magic. Little by little he ventures among the hills, deeper and deeper. If he should smell burning, he will run back.

But this isn't a forest yet, only the hope and promise of one. Here and there the sun appears through the foliage and a traveler among the trees is dappled with flickers of light. This isn't a rustling forest but a very small one, like a graveyard. A forest of solitudes. The pines stand erect, slim, serious; like a company of new recruits awaiting their commander. The ranging fire-watcher is pleased by the play of light and shadow. With every step he crushes dry pine needles underfoot. Softly, endlessly, the pines shed their needles; pines arrayed in a garment of mingling life and death.

The rounded human moving among trees whose yearning is so straight, so fierce. His body aches a bit, the ache of cramped limbs stretching; his legs are heavy. Suddenly he catches sight of the telephone line. A yellowish wire smelling of mold. Well, so this is his contact with the world. He starts tracing the yellow wire, searching for its origin, is charmed by its pointless twists and loops between the trees. They must have let some joker unwind the drum over the hills.

Suddenly he hears voices. He wavers, stops, then sees the little clearing in the woods. The Arab is seated on a pile of rocks, his hoe by his side. The child is talking to him excitedly, describing something with animated gestures. The scout tiptoes nearer, as lightly as his bulk will permit. They are instantly aware of him, sniff his alien being, and fall silent. The Arab jumps up, stands by his hoe as though hiding something. He faces them, wordless. It is the Sabbath eve today, isn't it, and there is a yearning in his heart. He stands and stares, for all the world like a supervisor bothered by some obscure triviality. The soft breeze caresses his eyes. If he did not fear for his status, he would hum them a little tune, perhaps. He smiles absently, his eyes stray and slowly he withdraws, with as much dignity as he can muster.

The two remain behind, petrified. The child's joy has shriveled halfway through her interrupted story, the Arab starts weeding the thorns at his feet. But the scout has retreated already, gone forth into the empire. He has been wandering in the woods for all of an hour now and is still making new dis- coveries. The names of donors, for example. It had never occurred to him that this wouldn't be just some anonymous forest but one with a name, and not just one name either. Many rocks bear copper plates, brilliantly bur- nished. He stoops, takes off his glasses, reads: Louis Schwartz of Chicago; the King of Burundi and his People. Flickers of light play over the letters. The names cling to him, like the falling pine needles that slip into his pocket. How odd! The tired memory tries to refresh itself with these faceless names. Name after name is absorbed by him as he walks, and by the time he reaches the observation post he can already hold a little rehearsal. He recites the sorted names, a vacuous smile on his face.

Friday night.

A wave of sadness wells within him. His mind happens to be perfectly lucid at the moment. We'll clear out on Sunday he whispers suddenly, and starts humming a snatch of song; inaudibly at first, the sound humming inside him, but soon trilling and rising high to the darkening sky. A hidden abyss behind him echoes in reply. The light drips, drips. Strings of light tear the sunset across and he shouts song at it, shrills recklessly, wanton with solitude. He starts one song, stops, plunges into another without change of key. His eyes fill with tears. The dark stifles his throat at last, suddenly he hears himself and falls silent.

Peace returns to the forest. Remnants of light linger. Five minutes pass and then the Arab and the girl emerge from the cover of the underbrush and hurry to the house with bent heads.

The Sabbath passes in a wonderful tranquillity. He is utterly calm. He has begun counting the trees for a change. Sunday he is on the verge of escaping but then the lorry brings him his salary, a part of the job he had forgotten. He is amazed, gushes his thanks to the mocking driver. So there's a prize in the whispering world, is there?

He returns to the books.

VIII

Hot summer. Yes, but we have forgotten the birds. Presumably the obser- vation post stands on an ancient crossroads of bird trajectories. How else to explain the mad flocks swooping in from the forest to beat their wings against the walls, drop on the bed, dive at the books, shed gray feathers and green dung, shatter the dull air with their restlessness—and vanish on their cir- cuitous flight to the sea. A change has come over him. Sunburned, yes, but

there is more to it than that. The heat wells up in him, frightens him. A dry
flow of desert wind may rouse the forest to suicide; hence he redoubles his
vigilance, presses the binoculars hard against his eyes and subjects the forest
in his care to a strict survey. How far has he come? Some slight twenty pages
are behind him, thousands still before. What does he remember? A few
words, the tail end of a theory, the atmosphere on the eve of the Crusades.
The nights are peaceful. He could have studied, could have concentrated,
were it not for the gnats. Night after night he extinguishes the lights and sits
in darkness. The words have dropped away from him like husks. Cicadas.
Choruses of jackals. A bat wings heavily across the gloom. Rustlings.

Hikers start arriving in the forest. Lone hikers some of them, but mostly
they come in groups. He follows them through the binoculars. Various interesting ages. Like ants they swarm over the forest, pour in among the trees,
calling out to each other, laughing; then they cast off their rucksacks all at
once, unburden themselves of as many clothes as possible and hang them
up on branches, and promptly come over to the house.

Water is what they want. Water!

He comes down to them, striking them with wonder. The bald head among
the green pines, the heavy glasses. Indeed, everything indicates an original
character.

He stands by the water tap, firm and upright, and slakes their thirst. Everyone begs permission to go upstairs for a look at the view. He consents, joyfully. They crowd into his little room and utter the stock formula of admiring
exclamations. He smiles as though he had created it all. Above everything,
they are surprised by the sea. They had never imagined one could see the
sea from here. Yet how soon they grow bored! One glance, a cry of admiration, and they grow restless already and eager to be away. They peep at his
notes, at the heavy books, and descend the staircase brimming with veneration for him and his view. The group leaders ask him to give some account
of the place, but there is no account to give. Everything is still artificial here.
There is nothing here, not even some archaeology for amateurs, nothing but
a few donors inscribed on rocks. Would they be interested in the names?
Well, for instance . . .

They laugh.

The girls look at him kindly. No, he isn't handsome. But might he not
become engraved on one of their hearts?

They light campfires.

They wish to cook their food, or to warm themselves. A virtuous alarm
strikes him. Tiny flames leap up in the forest, a bluish smoke starts blowing
gaily about the treetops. A fire? Yes and no. He stays glued, through his
binoculars, to the lively figures.

Toward evening he goes to explore his flickering, merrymaking empire. He
wishes to sound a warning. Softly, soundlessly he draws near the campfires,
the figures wreathed in flames. He approaches them unnoticed, and they are
startled when they discover him beside them. Dozens of young eyes look up
at him together. The leaders rise at once.

"Yes? What do you want?"

"The fire. Be careful! One spark, and the forest may burn down."

They are quick to assure him. Laying their hands on their young hearts
they give him their solemn promise to watch with all the eyes shining in a

row before him. They will keep within bounds, of course they will, what does he think?

He draws aside. Appeased? Yes and no. There, among the shadows, in the twilight of the fire, he lingers and lets his eyes rove. The girls and their bare, creamy legs, slender does. The flames crackle and sing, softly, gently. He clenches his fists in pain. If only he could warm his hands a little.

"Like to join us?" they ask politely. His vertical presence is faintly embarrassing.

No, thanks. He can't. He is busy. His studies. They have seen the books, haven't they? Now there is nothing for it but to withdraw with measured tread. But as soon as he has vanished from their view he flings himself behind the trees, hides among the needle branches. He looks at the fire from afar, at the girls, till everything fades, and blankets are spread for sleep. Giggles, girls' affected shrieks, leaders' rebukes. Before he can begin to think, select one out of the many figures, it will be dawn. Silence is still best. At midnight he feels his way through the trees, back to the observation post. He sits in his place, waiting. One of the figures may be working its way in the darkness toward him. But no, nothing. They are tired, sleeping already.

And the same next day, and all the days following.

Early in the morning he will open his book and hear wild song in the distance. He does not raise his eyes from the page but his hand strays to the binoculars. A dappled silence. Flashes of light through branches. His eyes are faithful to the written page, but his thoughts have gone whoring already. From the corner of his eye he follows the procession threading through the forest—sorting, checking ages, colors, joys of youth. There is something of abandon about them from afar, like a procession of Crusaders; except that these women are bare. He trembles, choking suddenly. He removes his glasses and beats his head against the books. Half an hour later they arrive. Asking for water to drink and the view to look at, as usual. They have heard about the wonderful view to be seen from up here. Perhaps they have heard about the scholar as well, but they say nothing. The group leaders take them, a batch at a time, into his room turned public property. No sooner have they scattered about the forest than the campfires leap up, as though that were their prime necessity. In the evening he rushes over the five hills, from fire to fire, impelled by his duty to warn them or by an obscure desire to reveal himself. He never joins any of the circles though. He prefers to hide in the thicket. Their singing throbs in his heart, and even more than that—the whisperings. Warm summer nights—something constantly seeping through the leaves.

Gradually the groups of hikers blend. One excursion leaves, another arrives. By the time he has managed to learn a few outstanding names, their owners are gone and the sounds alone survive among the branches. Languor comes over him. No longer does he trouble to caution against fire. On the contrary. He would welcome a little conflagration, a little local tumult. The hikers, however, are extremely responsible. They, themselves, take care to stamp out every dying ember. Their leaders come in advance to set his mind at rest.

The birds know how much he has neglected his studies; the birds whom he watches constantly lest they approach his desk. A month has passed since last he turned a page and he is stuck squirming between two words. He says:

let the heat abate, the hikers be gone—then I shall race over the lines. If only he could skip the words and get to the essence. From time to time he scribbles in his notebook. Stray thoughts, speculations, musings, outlines of assumptions. Not much. A sentence a day. He would like to gain a hold upon it all indirectly. Yet he is doubtful whether he has gained a hold even upon the forest in front of his eyes. Look, here the Arab and the girl are disappearing among the trees and he cannot find them. Toward evening they emerge from an unforeseen direction as though the forest had conceived them even now. They tread the soil softly. They avoid people, choose roundabout ways. He smiles at them both but they recoil.

Friday. The forest is overrun, choking with people. They come on foot and by car, crowds disgorged by the faraway cities. Where is his solitude now? He sprawls on his chair like a dethroned king whose empire has slipped from his hands. Twilight lingers on the treetops. Sabbath eve. His ears alone can catch, beyond the uproar of voices, beyond the rustling, the thin cry of the weary soil ceaselessly crushed by the teeth of young roots. A hikers' delegation comes to see him. They just want to ask him a question. They have argued, laid wagers, and he shall be their arbiter. Where exactly is this Arab village that is marked on the map? It ought to be somewhere around here, an abandoned Arab village. Here, they even know its name, something like . . . actually, it must be right here, right in the forest. . . . Does he know anything about it perhaps? They're simply curious.

The fire-watcher gives them a tired look. "A village?" he repeats with a polite, indulgent smile at their folly. No, there is no village here. The map must be wrong, the surveyor's hand must have shaken.

But in the small hours of the night, somewhere between a doze and a slumber, in the face of the whispering, burgeoning forest, the name floats back into his mind of a sudden and he is seized with restlessness. He descends to the ground floor, feels his way in the dark to the bed of the Arab, who lies asleep covered with rags. Roughly he wakes him and whispers the name of the village. The Arab does not understand. His eyes are consumed with weariness. The fire-watcher's accent must be at fault. He tries again, therefore, repeats the name over and over and the Arab listens and suddenly he understands. An expression of surprise, of wonder and eagerness, suffuses all his wrinkles. He jumps up, stands there in his hairy nakedness and flings up a heavy arm in the direction of the window, pointing fervently, hopelessly, at the forest.

The fire-watcher thanks him and departs, leaving the big naked figure in the middle of the room. When he wakes tomorrow, the Arab will think he has dreamed it.

IX

Ceremonies. A season of ceremonies. The forest turns all ceremonial. The trees stand bowed, heavy with honor, they take on meaning, they belong. White ribbons are strung to delimit new domains. Luxurious buses struggle over the rocky roads, a procession of shining automobiles before and behind. Sometimes they are preceded by a motorcycle mounted by an excited policeman. Unwieldy personages alight, shambling like black bears. The women flutter around them. Little by little they assemble, crush out cigarettes with their black shoes and fall silent—paying homage to the memory of themselves. The fire-watcher, too, participates in the ceremony, from afar, he and his binoculars. A storm of obedient applause breaks out, a gleam of scissors, a flash of photographers, ribbons sag. A plaque is unveiled, a new little truth is revealed to the world. A brief tour of the conquered wood, and then the distinguished gathering dissolves into its various vehicles and sallies forth.

Where is the light gone?

In the evening, when the fire-watcher comes down to the drooping ribbons, to the grateful trees, he will find nothing but a pale inscription saying, for example: "Donated by the Sackson children in honor of Daddy Sackson of Baltimore, a fond tribute to his paternity. End of Summer Nineteen Hundred and . . ."

Sometimes the fire-watcher, observing from his heights, will notice one of the party who is darting troubled looks about him, raising his eyes at the trees as though searching for something. It takes many ceremonies before the fire-watcher's wandering mind will grasp that this is none other than the old man in charge of Afforestation, who comes and repeats himself, dressed always in the same clothes, at every ceremony.

Once he goes down to him.

The old man is walking among his distinguished foreign party, is jesting with them haltingly in their language. The fire-watcher comes out of the trees and plants himself in front of him for the inevitable encounter. The distinguished party stops, startled. An uneasy silence falls over them. The ladies shrink back.

"What do you want?" demands the old man masterfully.

The fire-watcher gives a weak smile.

"Don't you know me? I'm the watchman. That is to say, the fire-watcher . . . employee of yours . . ."

"Ah!" fist beating against aged forehead, "I didn't recognize you, was alarmed, these tatters have changed your appearance so, this heavy beard. Well, young man, and how's the solitude?"

"Solitude?" he wonders.

The old man presents him to the party.

"A scholar . . ."

They smile, troubled, meet his hand with their fingertips, move on. They do not have complete faith in his cleanliness. The old man, on the other hand, looks at him affectionately. A thought crosses his mind and he stays behind a moment.

"Well, so there are forests," he grins with good-natured irony.

"Yes," admits the scout honestly. "Forests, yes . . . but . . ."

"But what?"

"But fires, no."

"Fires?" the old man wonders, bending toward him.

"Yes, fires. I spend whole days here sitting and wondering. Such a quiet summer."

"Well, why not? Actually, there hasn't been a fire here for several years now. To tell you the truth, I don't think there has ever been a fire at all in this forest. Nature itself is harnessed to our great enterprise here, ha-ha."

"And I was under the impression . . ."

"That what?"

"That fires broke out here every other day. By way of illustration, at least. This whole machinery waiting on the alert, is it all for nothing? The fire engines . . . telephone lines . . . the manpower . . . for months my eyes have been strained with waiting."

"Waiting? Ha-ha, what a joke!"

The old one hurries along. The drivers are switching on their engines. That is all he needs, to be left overnight in this arboreal silence. Before he goes he would just like to know the watchman's opinion of the dumb Arab. The lorry driver has got the idea into his head that the fellow is laying in a stock of kerosene. . . .

The watchman is stirred. "Kerosene?"

"Daresay it's some fancy of that malicious driver. This Arab is a placid kind of fellow, isn't he?"

"Wonderfully placid," agrees the fire-watcher eagerly. Then he walks a few steps around the old man and whispers confidentially: "Isn't he a local?"

"A local?"

"Because our forest is growing over, well, over a ruined village. . . ."

"A village?"

"A small village."

"A small village? Ah—" (Something is coming back to him anyway.) "Yes, there used to be some sort of a farmstead here. But that is a thing of the past."

Of the past, yes, certainly. What else . . . ?

X

One day's program as an example.

Not having slept at night, he does not wake up in the morning. Light springs up between his fingers. What date is today? There is no telling. Prisoners score lines on the walls of their cell, but he is not in prison. He has come of his own free will, and so he will go. He could lift the receiver and find out the date from the firemen bent over their fire engines, waiting in some unknown beyond, but he does not want to scare them yet.

He goes down to the tap and sprinkles a few drops of water over his beard to freshen it up. Then he climbs back to his room, snatches up the binoculars and holds a pre-breakfast inspection. Excitement grips him. The forest filled with smoke? No, the binoculars are to blame. He wipes the lenses with a corner of his grimy shirt. The forest clears up at once, disappointingly. None of the trees has done any real growing overnight.

He goes down again. He picks up the dry loaf of bread and cuts himself a rough slice. He chews rapidly, his eyes roving over a torn strip of newspaper in which tomatoes are wrapped. It is not, God forbid, out of a hunger for news, but to keep his eyes in training lest they forget the shape of the printed letter. He returns to his observation post, his mouth struggling with an enormous half-rotten tomato. He sucks, swallows, gets smeared with the red, trickling sap. At last he throws a sizable remnant away. Silence. He dozes a bit, wakes, looks for a long time at the treetops. The day stretches out ahead of him. Softly he draws near the books.

Where are we? How many pages read? Better not count them or he will fall prey to despair; for the time being he is serene, and why spoil it. It isn't a question of quantity, is it? And he remembers what he has read up to now perfectly well, forward and backward. The words wave and whirl within him. For the time being, therefore, for the past few weeks, that is, he has been devoting his zeal to one single sheet of paper. A picture? Rather, a map. A map of the area. He will display it on this wall here for the benefit of his successors, that they may remember him. Look, he has signed his name already, signed it to begin with, lest he forget.

What is he drawing? Trees. But not only trees. Hills too, a blue horizon too. He is improving day by day. If he had colored crayons he could have added some birds as well; at least, say, those native to the area. What interests him in particular is the village buried beneath the trees. That is to say, it hasn't always been as silent here. His curiosity is of a strictly scientific nature. What was it the old man had said? "A scholar." He strokes the beard and his hand lingers, disentangles a few hairs matted with filth. What time is it? Early still. He reads a line about the attitude of the Pope to the German emperor and falls asleep. He wakes with a start. He lights a cigarette, tosses the burning match out into the forest, but the match goes out in mid-air. He flings the cigarette butt among the trees and it drops on a stone and burns itself out in solitude.

He gets up, paces about restlessly. What time is it? Early still.

He goes in search of the Arab, to say good morning. He must impress his own vigilant existence upon the man, lest he be murdered some morning between one nap and another. Ever since the fire-watcher has spoken the name of the vanished village in his ears, the Arab has become suspicious, as though he were being watched all the time. The fire-watcher strides rapidly between the pines. How light his footstep has grown during the long summer months. His soundless appearance startles the two.

"Shalom,"[4] he says.

They reply in two voices. The child—a voice that has sweetness in it, the Arab—a harsh grunt. The fire-watcher smiles to himself and hurries on as though he were extremely busy. Chiseled stones lie scattered among the trees, outlines of buildings, ruins and relics. He searches for marks left by humans. Every day he comes and disturbs a few stones, looking for traces.

A man and a woman are lying here entwined, like statues toppled from their base. Their terror when the bearded head bends silently over them! Smile at them and run, you! A couple slipped away from a group-hike, no doubt.

What is he looking for? Relics of thoughts that have flitted here, words that have completed their mission. But what will he find one fine day, say even the day that we have taken for a sample? Small tins filled with kerosene. How wonderful! The zeal with which someone has filled tin after tin here and covered them up with the girl's old dress. He stoops over the treasure, the still liquid on whose surface dead pine needles drift. His reflection floats back at him together with the faint smell.

Blissfully he returns to the house, opens a tin of meat and bolts its contents to the last sliver. He wipes his mouth and spits far out among the branch-filled air. He turns two pages of a book and reads the Cardinal's reply to a Jew's epistle. Funny, these twists and turns of the Latin, but what a threat

---

4. "Peace" (Hebrew, literal trans.); hello.

is conveyed by them. He falls asleep, wakes, realizes he has nearly missed an important ceremony on the easternmost hill. From now on the binoculars stay glued to his eyes and he mingles with the distinguished crowd from afar. He can even make out the movements of the speakers' lips; he will fill in the missing sound himself. But then the flames of the sunset catch his eye and divert his attention, and with a daily returning excitement he becomes absorbed in the splendor, the terrible splendor.

Afterward he wipes the dust off the silent telephone. To give him his due—he bestows meticulous care on the equipment that belongs to the Afforestation Department, whereas his own equipment is already falling apart. The loose buttons shed among the trees, the frayed shirt, the ragged trousers.

A private outing of joyriders arrives with loud fanfare to spend the night in the forest. Wearily he chews his supper. Nightfall brings the old familiar sadness.

The Arab and his daughter go to bed. Darkness. The first giggle that emerges from the trees is a slap in his listening face. He turns over a few dark pages, swats a gnat, whistles.

Night. He does not fall asleep.

XI

Then it is the end of summer. The forest is emptying. And with the first autumn wind, who is blown to him like a withered leaf? His aging mistress, the wife of the friend who sent him here. Clad in a summer frock she comes, a wide-brimmed straw hat on her head. Then she is clicking her high heels around his room, rummaging through his drawers, bending over the books, peering through the papers. She had gone for a brief vacation by herself somewhere in this neighborhood and had remembered him. How is it when a man sits solitary, facing the forest, night after night? She had wanted to surprise him. Well, and what has he come up with? A fresh Crusade perhaps? She is awfully curious. Her husband speaks well of him too. In this solitude, among the trees, says the husband, he may yet flower into greatness.

The fire-watcher is moved. Without a word, he points at the map on the wall. She trips over to look, does not understand. Actually she is interested in texts. What has he written? She is very tired. Such a time till she found this place and she's more dead than alive. The view is pretty, yes, but the place looks awfully neglected. Who lives downstairs? The Arab? Is that so! She met him on the way, tried to ask him something and suddenly—the shock! Dumb, his severed tongue. But the Afforestation Department—hats off to them. Who would have imagined such forests growing in this country! He has changed, though. Grown fatter? This new beard of his is just awful. Why doesn't he say something?

She sinks down on the bed.

Then he rises, approaches her with that quiet which is in his blood now. He removes her hat, crouches at her feet, unbuckles her shoes. He is trembling with desire, choking.

She is shocked. She draws back her bare tired feet at once with something of terror, perhaps with relief. But he has let go already, stands holding the binoculars and looks at the forest, looks long, peering through the trees, waiting for fire. Slowly he turns to her, the binoculars at his eyes, turns the lenses upon her mischievously, sees the tiny wrinkles whittled in her face, the sweat drops, her fatigue. She smiles at him as in an old photograph. But when the moment drags, her smile turns into protest. She draws herself together crossly, holds up a hand.

"Hey, you! Stop it!"

Only toward sunset does he finally manage to undress her. The binoculars are still on his chest, pressed between their bodies. From time to time he coolly interrupts his kisses and caresses, raises the binoculars to his eyes and inspects the forest.

"Duty," he whispers apologetically, smiling oddly to the naked, embarrassed woman. Everything mingles with the glory of the crimson sun—the distant blue of the sea, the still trees, the blood on his cracked lips, the despair, the futility, the loneliness of the act. Accidentally her hand touches the bald crown and flinches.

When the Arab returns, it is all over. She is lying in the tangle of her clothes, drowsy. A beautiful night has descended on the world. He sits by his desk, what else should he do? The dark transforms her into a silhouette. The forest bewitches her. Suddenly she rouses herself. The soft voice of the little Arab girl sends a shiver through her. What is she doing here? She dresses rapidly, buttons, buckles. Her voice floats on the darkness.

Actually, she has come out of pity. No one had thought he would persist so long. When does he sleep anyway? She has been sent here to deliver him, deliver him from this solitude. His silence rouses suspicions. Her husband and his friends have suddenly begun to wonder, have become afraid, ha-ha, afraid that he may be nursing some secret, some novel idea, that he may outshine them all with some brilliant research.

A sudden dark breeze bursts into the room through the gap where there is no wall, whirls around for a little and dies out in the two corners. He is kindled. His eyes glow.

"Pity? No, unnecessary. When do I sleep? Always . . . though different from the city sleep. Leave here now, just like that? Too late. I haven't finished counting the trees yet. Novel ideas? Maybe, though not what they imagine . . . not exactly scientific . . . Rather, human . . ."

Does she wish him to accompany her on her way back through the forest, or perhaps would she go by herself?

She jumps up.

They cut diagonally across the hills. He walks in front, she drags behind, staggering over the rocks in her high heels, hurt and humiliated. Though thickset, his feet are light and he slips through the foliage swift as a snake, never turning his head. She struggles with the branches whipping back behind him. The moonlight reveals them on their silent trip. What do you say now, my autumn love? Have I gone completely out of my mind? But that was to be expected, wasn't it? Out of my round of pleasures, you have cast me into solitude. Trees have taken the place of words for me, forests the place of books. That is all. Eternal autumn, fall, needles falling endlessly on my eyes. I am still awaiting a conflagration.

Wordless they reach the black highway. Her heels click on the asphalt with a last fury. Now he looks at her. Her face is scratched, her arms blood-stained. How assertively the forest leaves its mark. She contains the thin cry rising in her. Her silence grants her dignity. After some minutes a sleek car driven by a lone gray-templed man halts at her waving hand. She joins him in the car without a parting word. She will yet crumble between his fingers on the long road.

He turns in his tracks. After a few paces, the Arab pops up in front of him. He is breathing heavily, his face is dull. And what do you have to say, mister? From where have you sprung now? The Arab holds out her forgotten hat, the straw hat. The fire-watcher smiles his thanks, spreads his arms in a gesture of nothing we can do, she's gone. But how amazing, this attention. Nothing will escape the man's eye. He takes the hat from the Arab and pitches it on top of his own head, gives him a slight bow and the other is immediately alarmed. His face is alert, watching. Together, in silence, they return to the forest, their empire, theirs alone. The fire-watcher strides ahead and the Arab tramples on his footsteps. A few clouds, a light breeze. Moonlight pours over the branches and makes them transparent. He leads the Arab over roads that are the same roads always. Barefoot he walks, the Arab, and so quietly. Round and round he is led, roundabout and to his hideout, amid chiseled stones and silence. The Arab's steps falter. His footfalls lag, die, and come alive again. A deathly cold grips the fire-watcher's heart, his hands freeze. He kneels on the rustling earth. Who will give him back all the empty hours? The forest is dark and empty. No one there. Not one campfire. Just now, when he would dip his hands in fire, warm them a little. He heaps up some brown needles, takes a match, lights it, and the match goes out at once. He takes another and cups his hands around it, strikes, and this one too flares up and dies. The air is damp and treacherous. He rises. The Arab watches him, a gleam of lunatic hope in his eyes. Softly the fire-watcher walks around the pile of stones to the sorry little hideout, picks up a tin of clear liquid and empties it over the heap of pine needles, tosses in a burning match and leaps up with the surging flame—singed, happy. At last he, too, is lit up a little. Stunned, the Arab goes down on his knees. The fire-watcher spreads his palms over the flame and the Arab does likewise. Their bodies press in on the fire, which has already reached its highest pitch. He might leave the flame now and go and bathe in the sea. Time, time wasting here among the trees, will do his work for him. He muses, his mind distracted. The fire shows signs of languishing, little by little it dies at his feet. The Arab's face takes on a look of bitter disappointment. The bonfire fades. Last sparks are stamped out meticulously. Thus far it was only a lesson. The wandering mind of the fire-watcher trembles between compromises. He rises wearily and leaves. The Arab slouches in his wake.

Who is sitting on the chair behind the book-laden desk? The child. Her eyes are wide open, drinking in the dark. The Arab has put her there to replace the roving fire-watcher. It's an idea.

XII

Strange days follow. We would say: autumn—but that means nothing yet. The needles seem to fall faster, the sun grows weaker, clouds come to stay, and a new wind. His mind is slipping, growing unhinged. The ceremonies are over. The donors have gone back to their countries, the hikers to their work, pupils to their study. His own books lie jumbled in a glow of dust. He is neglecting his duties, has left his chair, his desk, his faithful binoculars, and has begun roving endlessly about the forest, by day and by night; a broken twig in his hand, he slashes at the young tree trunks as he walks, as though marking them. Suddenly he slumps down, rests his head against a shining copper plaque, removes his glasses and peers through the blurring foliage, searches the gray sky. Something like a wail, suddenly. Foul fantasies. Then he collects himself once more, jumps up to wander through the wood, among the thistles and rocks. The idea has taken hold in his dim consciousness that he is being called insistently to an encounter at the edge of the forest, at its other end. But when he plunges out of the forest and arrives there, whether it be at night or at noon or in the early dawn, he finds nothing but a yellow waste, a strange valley, a kind of cursed dream. And he will stand there for a long time, facing the empty, treeless silence and feeling that the encounter is taking place, is being successful even though it happens wordlessly. He has spent a whole spring and a long summer never once properly sleeping, and what wonder is it if these last days should be like a trance.

He has lost all hope of fire. Fire has no hold over this forest. He can therefore afford to stay among the trees, not facing them. In order to soothe his conscience he sits the girl in his chair. It has taken less than a minute to teach her the Hebrew word for "fire." How she has grown during his stay here! She is like a noble mare now with marvelous eyes. Unexpectedly her limbs have ripened, her filth become a woman's smell. At first her old father had been forced to chain her to the chair, or she would have escaped. Yes, the old Arab has grown very attached to the negligent fire-watcher, follows him wherever he goes. Ever since the night when the two of them hugged the little bonfire the Arab, too, has grown languid. He has abandoned his eternal hoe. The grass is turning yellow under his feet, the thistles multiply. The fire-watcher will be lying on the ground and see the dusky face thrusting at him through the branches. As a rule he ignores the Arab, continues lying with his eyes on the sky. But sometimes he calls him and the man comes and kneels by his side, his heavy eyes wild with terror and hope. Perhaps, he, too, will fail to convey anything and it will all remain dark.

The fire-watcher talks to him therefore, quietly, reasonably, in a positively didactic manner. He tells him about the Crusades, and the other bends his head and absorbs the hard, alien words as one absorbing a melody. He tells him about the fervor, about the cruelty, about Jews committing suicide, about the Children's Crusade; things he has picked up from the books, the unfounded theories he has framed himself. His voice is warm, alive with imagination. The Arab listens with mounting tension and is filled with hate. When they return at twilight, lit by a soft autumnal glow, the fire-watcher will lead the Arab to the tree-engulfed house and will linger a moment. Then the Arab explains something with hurried, confused gestures, wiggling his severed tongue, tossing his head. He wishes to say that this is his house and that there used to be a village here as well and that they have simply hidden it all, buried it in the big forest.

The fire-watcher looks on at this pantomime and his heart fills with joy. What is it that rouses such passion in the Arab? Apparently his wives have been murdered here as well. A dark affair, no doubt. Gradually he moves away, pretending not to understand. Did there used to be a village here? He sees nothing but trees.

More and more the Arab clings to him. They sit there, the three of them like a family, in the room on the second floor. The fire-watcher sprawling on the bed, the child chained to the chair, the Arab crouching on the floor. Together they wait for the fire that does not come. The forest is dark and strong, a slow-growing world. These are his last days. His contract is drawing to an end. From time to time he gets up and throws one of the books back into the suitcase, startling the old Arab.

The nights are growing longer. Hot desert winds and raindrops mingle, soft shimmers of lightning flash over the sea. The last day is come. Tomorrow he will leave this place. He has discharged his duty faithfully. It isn't his fault that no fires have broken out. All the books are packed in the suitcase, scraps of paper litter the floor. The Arab has disappeared, has been missing since yesterday. The child is miserable. From time to time she raises her voice in a thin, ancient lament. The fire-watcher is growing worried. At noon the Arab turns up suddenly. The child runs toward him but he takes no notice of her. He turns to the abdicating fire-watcher instead, grabs him between two powerful hands and—feeble and soft as he is and suffering from a slight cold—impels him toward the edge of the observation post and explains whatever he can explain to him with no tongue. Perhaps he wishes to throw the abdicating fire-watcher down two stories and into the forest. Perhaps he believes that only he, the fire-watcher, can understand him. His eyes are burning. But the fire-watcher is serene, unresponsive; he shades his eyes with his palm, shrugs his shoulders, gives a meaningless little smile. What else is left him?

He collects his clothes and bundles them into the other suitcase.

Toward evening the Arab disappears again. The child has gone to look for him and has come back empty-handed. Gently the hours drift by. A single drop of rain. The fire-watcher prepares supper and sets it before the child, but she cannot bring herself to eat. Like a little animal she scurries off once more into the forest to hunt for her father and returns in despair, by herself. Toward midnight she falls asleep at last. He undresses her and carries the shabby figure to the bed, covers it with the torn blanket. What a lonely woman she will grow up to be. He muses. Something is flowing between his fingers, something like compassion. He lingers awhile. Then he returns to his observation post, sits on his chair, sleepy. Where will he be tomorrow? How about saying good-bye to the Fire Brigade? He picks up the receiver. Silence. The line is dead. Not a purr, not a gurgle. The sacred hush has invaded the wire as well.

He smiles contentedly. In the dark forest spread out before him, the Arab is moving about like a silent dagger. He sits watching the world as one may watch a great play before the rising of the curtain. A little excitement, a little drowsing in one's seat. Midnight performance.

Then, suddenly—fire. Fire, unforeseen, leaping out of the corner. A long graceful flame. One tree is burning, a tree wrapped in prayer. For a long moment one tree is going through its hour of judgment and surrendering its spirit. He lifts the receiver. Yes, the line is dead. He is leaving here tomorrow.

The loneliness of a single flame in a big forest. He is beginning to worry whether the ground may not be too wet and the thistles too few, and the show be over after one flame. His eyes are closing. His drowsiness is greatest now, at this most wonderful of moments. He rises and starts pacing nervously through the room in order to walk off his fatigue. A short while passes and then a smile spreads over his face. He starts counting the flames. The Arab is setting the forest on fire at its four corners, then takes a firebrand and rushes through the trees like an evil spirit, setting fire to the rest. The thoroughness with which he goes about his task amazes the fire-watcher. He goes down to look at the child. She is asleep. Back to the observation post— the forest is burning. He ought to run and raise the alarm, call for help. But his movements are so tranquil, his limbs leaden. Downstairs again. He adjusts the blanket over the child, pushes a lock of hair out of her eyes, goes back up, and a blast of hot air blows in his face. A great light out there. Five whole hills ablaze. Flames surge as in a frenzy high over the trees, roar at the lighted sky. Pines split and crash. Wild excitement sweeps him, rapture. He is happy. Where is the Arab now? The Arab speaks to him out of the fire, wishes to say everything, everything and at once. Will he understand?

Suddenly he is aware of another presence in the room. Swiftly he turns his head and sees the girl, half-naked, eyes staring, the light of the fire playing over her face. He smiles and she weeps.

Intense heat wells up from the leisurely burning forest. The first excitement has passed. The fire is turning from a vision into a fact. Flames are mobilizing from all the four winds to come and visit the observation post. He ought to take his two suitcases and disappear. But he only takes the child. The lights of the neighboring settlements have become so pitiful, so plain. They are no doubt sure, over there, that the fight against the fire is in full swing here already. Who would imagine that the fire is still being nourished here, brooded over? Hours will go by before the village watchmen come to wake the sleepers. The nights are cold already and people not disposed to throw off their blankets. He seizes the trembling child by the hand, goes down and begins his retreat. The road is lit up far into the distance. Behind his back the fire, and in his face—a red, mad, burning moon that floats in the sky as though it wished to see the blaze as well. His head feels heavy, the road stretches ahead. They drag along, dipping in light and in darkness. In the lanes the trees whisper, agitated, waiting. A fearful rumor has reached them.

The observation post can be seen from afar, entirely lit up. The earth is casting off its shackles. After a long walk the trees start thinning out at last, they grow smaller, then disappear. He arrives at the yellow waste, the valley, his dream. A few dry, twisted trees, desert trees, alien and salty; trees that have sprung up parched, over which the fire has no hold. He sits the barefoot girl on the ground, slumps beside her. His exhaustion erupts within him and covers them both.

With sleeping eyes he sees the shining fire engines arrive at last, summoned by another. They, too, know that all is lost. In a dream the Arab appears—tired, disheveled, black with soot, his face ravaged—takes the child and vanishes. The fire-watcher falls asleep, really asleep.

XIII

At dawn, shivering and damp, he emerges from the cover of the rocks, polishes his glasses and once more he is the little scholar who has some kind of future before him. Five, bare, black hills, and slender wisps of blue-gray

smoke rising from them. The observation post juts out over the bare landscape like a great demon grinning with white windows. For a moment it
seems as though the forest had never burned down but had simply pulled
up its roots and gone off on a journey, far off on a journey, far off to the sea,
for instance, which has suddenly come into view. The air is chilly. He adjusts
his rumpled clothes, does up the last surviving button, rubs his hands to
warm them, then treads softly among the smoking embers, light of foot. The
first rays of the sun hit his bald patch. There is a sadness in this sudden
nudity, the sadness of wars lost, blood shed in vain. Stately clouds sail in the
cold sky. Soon the first rain will fall. He hears sounds of people everywhere.
Utter destruction. Soot, a tangle of charred timber, its wounds still smoldering, and a residue of living branches unvisited by fire. Wherever he sets
foot a thousand sparks fly. The commemorative plaques alone have survived;
more than that, they have gained luster after their baptism of fire. There they
lie, golden in the sun: Louis Schwartz of Chicago, the King of Burundi and
his People.

He enters the burned building, climbs the singed stairs. Everything is still
glowing hot. It is as though he were making his way through hell. He arrives
at his room. The fire has visited it in his absence and held its riot of horror
and glee. Shall we start with the books burned to ashes? Or the contorted
telephone? Or perhaps the binoculars fused to a lump? The map of the area
has miraculously survived, is only blackened a bit at the edges. Gay fire
kittens are still frolicking in the pillow and blankets. He turns his gaze to the
fire-smoking hills, frowns—there, out of the smoke and haze, the ruined
village appears before his eyes; born anew in its basic outlines as an abstract
drawing, as all things past and buried. He smiles to himself, a thin smile.
Then abruptly it dies on his face. Directly under him, in the bluish abyss at
the foot of the building, he sees the one in charge of forests who is edging
his way to old age, wrapped in an old windbreaker, his face blue with cold.
How has this one sprung up here, all of a sudden?

The old one throws his gray head back and sends up a look full of hatred.
Looking down upon the man from his high post, his own eyes would be
faintly contemptuous in any case. For a few seconds they stay thus, their
eyes fixed on each other; at last the fire-watcher gives his employer a fatuous
smile of recognition and slowly starts coming down to him. The old man
approaches him with quick, mad steps. He would tear him to pieces if he
could. He is near collapse with fury and pain. In a choking voice he demands
the whole story, at once.

But there is no story, is there? There just isn't anything to tell. All there
is, is: Suddenly the fire sprang up. I lifted the receiver—the line was dead.
That's it. The child had to be saved.

The rest is obvious. Yes, the fire-watcher feels for the forest too. He has
grown extremely attached to it during the spring, the summer, and half the
autumn. So attached, in fact, that (to tell the truth, for once) he hasn't
managed to learn a single line, actually.

He feels that the old man would like to sink to the ground and beat his
head against some rock, would tear out the last of his white hair. The late
fire-watcher is surprised. Because the forests are insured, aren't they (at least
they ought to be, in his humble and practical opinion), and the fire won't be
deducted from the budget of the old man's department, will it? Right now

(this morning has found him amazingly clearheaded), he would very much like to be told about other forest fires. He is willing to bet that they were quite puny ones.

Except that now, ghostlike through the smoke, the firemen appear, accompanied by some fat and perspiring policemen. Soon he is surrounded by uniforms. Some of the men drop to the ground with exhaustion. Though the fire has not been completely tracked down as yet, they have already unearthed a startling piece of intelligence.

It has been arson.

Yes, arson. The smell of morning dew comes mingled with a smell of kerosene.

The old man is shattered.

"Arson?" he turns to the fire-watcher.

But the other smiles gently.

The investigation is launched at once. First the firemen, who are supposed to write a report. They draw the fire-watcher aside, take out large sheets of paper, ornate ballpoints, and then it appears that they have difficulty with the language, with phrasing and spelling. They are embarrassed. Tactfully he helps them, spells out words, formulates their sentences for them. They are very grateful.

"What have *you* lost in the fire?" they inquire sympathetically.

"Oh, nothing of importance. Some clothes and a few textbooks. Nothing to worry about."

By the time they are through, it is far into the morning. The Arab and the child appear from nowhere, led by two policemen. If he will be careful not to let his glance encounter those burning eyes, he may possibly sleep in peace in the nights to come. Two tough-looking sergeants improvise a kind of emergency interrogation cell among the rocks, place him on a stone and start cross-examining him. For hours they persist, and that surprises him—the plodding tenacity, the diligence, page upon written page. A veritable research is being compiled before his eyes. The sun climbs to its zenith. He is hungry, thirsty. His interrogators chew enormous sandwiches and do not offer him a crumb. His glasses mist with sweat. A queer autumn day. Inside the building, they are conducting a simultaneous interrogation of the Arab, in Arabic, eked out with gestures. Only the questions are audible.

The old forest manager dodges back and forth between the two interrogations, adding questions of his own, noting down replies. The interrogators have their subject with his back against the rock, they repeat the same questions over and over. A foul stench rises from the burned forest, as though a huge carcass were rotting away all around them. The interrogation gains momentum. A big bore. What did he see? What did he hear? What did he do? It's insulting, this insistence upon the tangible—as though that were the main point, as though there weren't some idea involved here.

About noon his questioners change, two new ones appear and start the whole process over again. The subject is dripping with sweat. How humiliating, to be interrogated thus baldly on scorched earth, on rocks, after a sleepless night. The tedium of it. The fire-watcher spits, grows angry, loses his temper. He removes his glasses and his senses go numb. He starts contradicting himself. At three o'clock he breaks in their hands, is prepared to suggest the Arab as a possible clue.

This, of course, is what they have been waiting for. They suspected the Arab all along. Promptly they handcuff him, and then all at once everything is rapidly wound up. The police drivers start their cars. The Arab is bundled into one of them and there is a gratified expression in his eyes now, a sense of achievement. The child clings to him desperately. Autumn clouds, autumn sadness, everything is flat. Stupid. Suddenly he walks over to the forest manager and boldly demands that something be done for the child. The other makes no reply. His old eyes wander over the lost forest as though in parting. This old one is going mad as well, his senses are growing confused. He stares at the fire-watcher with vacant eyes as though he, too, had lost the words, as though he understood nothing. The fire-watcher repeats his demand in a loud voice. The old man steps nearer.

"What?" he mumbles in a feeble voice, his eyes watery. Suddenly he throws himself at the fire-watcher, attacks him with shriveled fists, hits out at him. With difficulty, the firemen pull him back. To be sure, he blames only this one here. Yes, this one with the books, with the dim glasses, with that smug cynicism of his.

The policemen extricate the fire-watcher and whisk him into one of their cars. They treat him roughly, something of the old man's hostility has stuck to them. Before he has time to say good-bye to the place where he has spent nearly six months he is being borne away at a mad pace toward town. They dump him on one of the side streets. He enters the first restaurant he comes to and gorges himself to bursting point. Afterward he paces the streets, bearded, dirty, sunburned—a savage. The first dusty rain has already smirched the pavements.

At night, in some shabby hotel room, he is free to have a proper sleep, to sleep free from obligations for the first time, just sleep without any further dimensions. Except that he will not fall asleep, will only go on drowsing. Green forests will spring up before his troubled eyes. He may yet smart with sorrow and yearning, may feel constricted because he is shut in by four walls, not three.

And so it will be the day after, and perhaps all the days to come. The solitude has proved a success. True, his notes have been burned along with the books, but if anyone thinks that he does not remember—he does.

Yet he has become a stranger now in his so-familiar town. He seems to have forgotten already. A new generation is breaking into the circles. His waggish friends meet him, slap him on the back, and with ugly grins say, "We hear your forest burned down!" As we said, he is still young. But his real friends have given him up in despair. He drops in on them, winter nights, shivering with cold—wet dog begging for fire and light—and they scowl and ask:

"Well, what now?"

ANITA DESAI
born 1937

Author of ten novels and two collections of short stories, Anita Desai is a distinguished writer and a leading figure among Indian writers in English. Indian fiction in English came into its own in the 1930s with the novels of R. K. Narayan, Mulk Raj Anand, and Raja Rao. Desai belongs to a later generation, but she began writing well before the upsurge of significant fiction in English by writers of Indian origin, starting with the publication of Salman Rushdie's *Midnight's Children* (1980). Born of a Bengali father and German mother in Mussoorie in north India, Desai was educated in Delhi and started writing fiction at the age of ten. Her first novel, *Cry, the Peacock*, was published in 1963. *Fire on the Mountain* (1977) won India's Sahitya Akademi (Academy of Letters) Award as well as Britain's Royal Society of Literature's Winifred Holtby Memorial Prize. *Clear Light of Day* (1980) and *In Custody* (1984) were nominated for the Booker Prize in Britain. Desai has lived in Bombay and Delhi, and has taught at various colleges in the United States. She currently teaches at the Massachusetts Institute of Technology.

Desai excels in illuminating the inner lives of individuals in the setting of the Indian family. Her concern with female experience distinguishes her earlier novels from those of her Indian contemporaries writing in English, while her focus on the urban middle class as well as her emphasis on interiority set her apart from Mahasweta Devi (p. 2824) and other writers in Indian languages who also deal with women's lives. In her more recent novels, Desai has turned her attention to male protagonists and more public themes. The short stories, especially those in *Games at Twilight* (1977), Desai's first collection, offer vignettes of the lives of a wide variety of characters, affirming at the same time the author's preoccupation with interior perspectives.

A major theme in Desai's earlier novels is the power of the Indian family to stifle individual aspirations for emotional and personal fulfillment, a power that is devastatingly played out in the lives of middle-class women. Maya, the young protagonist in *Cry, the Peacock*, is ultimately broken by the relentless pressure of the emotional demands made of her and her failure to make her husband understand her. In *Where Shall We Go This Summer* (1975), confronted by an unexpected pregnancy, Sita, the protagonist, realizes both the crushing effect of family duty and motherhood on her personal aspirations, and her powerlessness to take charge of her life. *Fire on the Mountain* is the narrative of Nanda Kaul, who tries to "live alone" in the ultimate sense, by cutting herself off from family responsibilities and connections. Nanda is violently forced back into the web of family by her need to relate to her great-granddaughter Raka, who is sent to live with her.

Clear Light of Day, Desai's sixth novel, is in many ways her most fully realized work. Here, in a bold departure from her earlier novels, she effectively establishes the interconnection between family and nation and between the private and public lives of her characters. The narrative centers on the process by which, during a summer visit from her sister Tara, Bim (short for Bimla) Das, a college professor who lives with her retarded brother, Baba, in the crumbling family home in Old Delhi, comes to terms with her complex relationship with her siblings and their shared past. The family past is intertwined with the tragic events surrounding the partition of India into the new nations of India and Pakistan; in the nonlinear narrative, events of the present alternate with the momentous events of the summer of 1947, refracted mainly through the consciousness of Bim and Tara. At first, the meeting of the siblings brings back memories of the family as the setting for illness, emotional oppression, alienation, and death. But in contrast to other Desai heroines, Bim, who is sensitive yet robust and dynamic, is able to draw on her familial past and her love for her siblings as a source of inner strength.

In *In Custody* (1984) and *Baumgartner's Bombay* (1988, winner of the 1989 *Ha-*

dassah prize), Desai ventures in new directions. *In Custody* traces the development of an unlikely friendship between Deven, a small-town college lecturer, and his hero, the decadent poet Nur Shahjehanabadi. Pitched perfectly in tragicomic tones, the novel illuminates the inner life of a man of romantic sensibility who is mired in the dullness of middle-class life as well as the decaying world of Urdu poetry that fires his imagination and makes the aging poet his hero. *Baumgartner's Bombay* is a brilliant evocation of the tragic world of Hugo Baumgartner, a German Jewish refugee who lives in Bombay. In her two most recent novels, *Journey to Ithaca* (1995) and *Fasting, Feasting* (1999), Desai places her intimate explorations of individuals, families, and relationships on the broad canvas of intercultural encounter. The feeling for the lives and sensibilities of marginalized figures, characteristic of Desai's earlier novels, is evident in the later novels as well, manifested as a focus on the ordinary person trying to find self-expression in a bewilderingly complex and often hostile world.

Desai's considerable gifts as a novelist include a keen observation, a richly evocative style, and a quietly compelling voice. Her finely crafted prose beautifully captures the flavor of particular times and places—Old Delhi, the city of the Mughal emperors, and the endless summers of childhood (*Clear Light of Day*), the city of Calcutta (*Voices in the City*, 1965), the landscape of the hills of Himachal Pradesh in north India (*Fire on the Mountain*). These gifts and the thematic concerns of the novels carry over into the short stories as well. The protagonists of the short stories, like those of the novels, are ordinary men and women caught between the mundane drabness of their lives and the sense of forces beyond their control that govern their lives. In the briefer compass of the short story, however, Desai often focuses on a minor epiphany, a fleeting moment of awareness.

The Rooftop Dwellers, the short story presented here, appears in Desai's recent collection *Diamond Dust* (2000). Young Moyna, the protagonist, has left the comfort and security of her provincial home and overprotective family, and has arrived in Delhi, determined to live the independent life of a working woman in the city. The story traces her initiation into the world of Delhi's "rooftop dwellers," working men and women who live in rented rooms called *barsati* on the roof terraces of Delhi homes, originally built for shelter from rain when sleeping alfresco in the summer. In following Moyna's complex dealings with her landlords, the Bhallas, with her job and her colleagues at a literary magazine, and with life in Delhi, we are initiated into the worlds within worlds of the average person in a rapidly globalizing city in modern India.

Longer than the average story in *Games at Twilight*, *The Rooftop Dwellers* is also different in tone, approach, and characterization. Moyna lacks the brooding intensity of Desai's other heroines, nor does she have the charisma or special gifts of a Bimala Das or a Nanda Kaul. On the other hand, she earns our admiration for her sheer determination and for the flair with which she negotiates the new situations she encounters: interacting with the Bhallas and their servant, entertaining foreign young men, seeking advertisements for *Books*. Indeed, Moyna's sense of the joy of living—perfectly embodied in the epiphany of the rooftop pipal tree—makes her immensely likable.

Desai's powers of observation are evident in the many finely drawn vignettes of middle-class life in *The Rooftop Dwellers*—the Bhallas gathered round their television set to the watch the *Mahabharata* epic, Gurmail Singh and his autorickshaw, Moyna's colleague Tara's changes of ideology, or the new colleague Mohan as a connoisseur of samosas. Desai's comic gift, which enlivens *Clear Light of Day* and which is fully developed in *In Custody*, once again comes to the fore in this short story, and the tone seems just right for the delineation of an enthusiastic, if ordinary, young woman's adventures in the big city. The view from Moyna's rooftop room is as exciting as any in the world.

William Walsh, *Indian Literature in English* (1990), Meenakshi Mukherjee, *The Twice-Born Fiction* (1971), and M. K. Naik, *A History of Indian English Literature*

(1982), are good introductions to Indian literature in English. Studies of Anita Desai's fiction include Ramesh K. Srivastava, *Perspectives on Anita Desai* (1984), Jasbir Jain, *Stairs to the Attic: The Novels of Anita Desai* (1987), and Sunaina Singha, *The Novels of Margaret Atwood and Anita Desai: A Comparative Study in Feminist Perspectives* (1994). In "Codes in Conflict: Post-Independence Alienation in Anita Desai's Early Novels," *Journal of Gender Studies* 5, no. 3 (1996): 317–328, Josna Rege examines the relationship between women and the postcolonial nation in Desai's early work.

PRONOUNCING GLOSSARY

The following list uses common English syllables and stress accents to provide rough equivalents of selected words whose pronunciation may be unfamiliar to the general reader.

barsati: *buhr-sah'-tee* Mahabharata: *muh-hah-bah'-ruh-tuh*

beti: *bay'-tee* pipal: *pee'-puhl*

Bhalla: *buhl'-lah* Ramayana: *rah-mah'-yuh-nuh*

Bharat: *bah'-rut* samosa: *suh-moh'-sah*

chapati: *chuh-pah'-tee*

The Rooftop Dwellers[1]

Paying off the autorickshaw[2] driver, she stepped down cautiously, clutching her handbag to her. The colony was much further out than she had expected—they had travelled through bazaars and commercial centres and suburbs she had not known existed—but the name given on the gate matched the one in her purse. She went up to it and rattled the latch to announce her arrival. Immediately a dog began to yap and she could tell by its shrillness that it was one of those small dogs that readily sink their tiny teeth into one's ankle or rip through the edge of one's sari.[3] There were also screams from several children. Yet no one came to open the gate for her and finally she let herself in, hoping the dog was chained or indoors. Certainly there was no one in the tiny garden which consisted of a patch of lawn and a tap in front of the yellow stucco villa. All the commotion appeared to be going on indoors and she walked up to the front door—actually at the side of the house—and rang the bell, clearing her throat like a saleswoman preparing to sell a line in knitting patterns or home-made jams.

She was finally admitted by a very small servant boy in striped cotton pyjamas and a torn grey vest, and taken to meet the family. They were seated on a large bed in the centre of a room with walls painted an electric blue, all watching a show on a gigantic television set. It was an extremely loud, extremely dramatic scene showing a confrontation between a ranting hero, a weeping heroine and a benignly smiling saint, and the whole family was watching open-mouthed, reluctant to turn their attention away from it. But when their dog darted out from under the bed at her, she screamed and the servant boy flapped his duster and cried, 'No, Candy! Get down, Candy!' they had no alternative but to turn to her, resentfully.

---

1. From *Diamond Dust: Stories* (2000). **2.** Three-wheeled motorized vehicle used for transportation, like a taxi. **3.** Traditional woman's garment in India. It is a long, single piece of cloth draped around the body.

'You have come just at *Mahabharata*[4] time,' the woman crosslegged on the bed reproached her.

'Sit down, sit down, beti.[5] You can watch it with us,' the man said more agreeably, waving at an open corner on the bed, and since they had all transferred their attention back to the screen, she was forced to perch on it, fearfully holding her ankles up in the air so as not to be nipped by Candy, who had been driven back under the bed and hid there, growling. The two children stared at her for a bit, impassively, then went back to picking their noses and following the episode of the *Mahabharata* that the whole city of Delhi[6] watched, along with the rest of the country, on Sunday evenings—everyone, except for her.

There had been too much happening in her life to leave room for watching television and keeping up with the soap operas and mythological sagas. In any case, there was no television set in the women's hostel where she had a room. There was nothing in it except what was absolutely essential: the dining room on the ground floor with its long tables, its benches, its metal plates and utensils, and the kitchen with its hatch through which the food appeared in metal pots; and upstairs the rows of rooms, eight feet by ten, each equipped with a wooden bedframe, and a shelf nailed to the wall. She had had to purchase a plastic bucket to take to the bathroom at the end of the corridor so she could bathe under the standing tap—not high enough to work as a shower—and had arranged her toilet articles on the shelf and left her clothes in her tin trunk which she covered with a pink tablecloth and sat on when she did not want to sit on her bed, or when one of the other women in the hostel came to visit her and climbed onto her bed to have a chat.

The minimalism of these living arrangements was both a novelty and a shock to her. She came from a home where the accommodation of objects, their comfortable clutter and convenience, could be taken for granted. Nothing had been expensive or elaborate but there had been plenty of whatever there was, accumulated over many years: rugs, chairs, cushions, clothes, dishes, in rooms, verandas,[7] odd corners and spaces. So for the first two weeks she felt she was trapped in a cell; whenever she shut the door, she was swallowed by the cell, its prisoner. If she left the door ajar, every girl going past would look in, scream, 'Oh, Moy-na!' and come in to talk, tell her of the latest atrocity committed by the matron or of the unbelievably rotten food being served downstairs, and also of their jobs, their bosses, their colleagues, and homes and families. Some were divorcees, some widows, and some supported large families, all of which led to an endless fund of stories to be told. In order to get any sleep, she would have to shut the door and pretend not to be in. Then she began to wonder if she was in herself.

But such was her determination to make her new life as a working woman in the metropolis succeed, and such was her unexpected, unforeseen capacity for adjustment, that after a month or so the minimalism became no longer privation and a challenge but simply a way of life. She even found herself stopping at her neighbours' open doors on her way back from the office, to say, 'D'you know what they're cooking for our dinner downstairs?' and laugh-

---

4. Ancient Indian epic narrating the war between the Pāṇḍava and Kaurava princes. It was serialized on Indian television in the 1980s.   5. "Daughter" (Hindi); a term used by older people to address young women.   6. Capital of India.   7. Roofed porch or balcony extending along the exterior of a building.

ing when the others groaned, invariably, 'Pumpkin!' because that was all there ever was, or else to give the warning, 'Matron's *mad*! I heard her screaming at Leila—she found out about her iron. Hide yours, quick!' It became a habit, instead of a subject of complaint, to carry her bucket down to the bathroom when she wanted to bathe, and bring it back to her room so it wouldn't be stolen: thefts were common, unfortunately. Even the tap, and water, began to seem like luxuries, bonuses not to be taken for granted in that hostel.

After a breakfast of tea, bread and fried eggs, she went out to stand at the bus stop with the other women, all of whom caught the Ladies' Special that came around at nine o'clock and carried them to their work places as telephone operators, typists, desk receptionists, nurses, teachers, airline hostesses and bank tellers, without the menace of crazed young men groping at them or pressing into them as if magnetised, or even delivering vicious pinches before leaping off the bus and running for their lives. Some women had had to develop defensive strategies. Lily, known to be 'bold', instructed others to carry a sharp pin concealed in their fists and use that to prod anyone who came too close. 'I've made big men cry,' she boasted proudly, but most women in the hostel preferred to pay the extra rupee or two to travel on the Ladies' Special instead of the regular DTS.[8] Like tap water, it was a luxury, a bonus, which had their gratitude.

Moyna's descriptions of these strategies of living earned her the admiration of her family and friends back at home to whom she described them, but trouble began for her just as she was settling into this new, challenging way of life. She came across the hostel cook kicking viciously at the skeletal yellow kitten that had crept in from outside in the hope of one of life's unexpected bonuses—a drop of milk left in someone's tumbler, or a scrap from the garbage bin. Instinctively she lowered her hand and called it to her—she came from a home that was shelter to an assortment of cats, dogs, birds, some maimed, some pregnant, some dying. She shared her bread and fried egg with the kitten, and soon it started weaving in and out of her sari folds, then followed her up the stairs and darted into her room. This was novelty indeed: having someone to share the cell with her. It was curious how instantly the room ceased to be a prison. The kitten settled onto the pink tablecloth on the trunk and began to lick itself clean, delicately raising one leg at a time into the air and making a thorough toilet, as if it were preparing to be fit for such luxurious accommodation. Later, that night, she woke to find it had sprung from the trunk to her bed. Knowing it probably had fleas, she tried to kick it off, but it clung on and started to purr, as if to persuade her of its accomplishments. Purring, it lay against her leg and lulled her back to sleep.

One day the matron was inspecting during the day, when they were all away, for such forbidden items as irons and hot plates, and came out holding the kitten by the scruff of his neck. Moyna pleaded innocence and swore she did not know how he had got into her room. But when she was caught red-handed, emptying the milk jug into a saucer for Mao under the table, the matron slapped her with the eviction notice. Had Moyna not read the rule: No Pets Allowed?

8. Delhi Transport Service.

Instinctively, she knew not to mention Mao to this family. Somehow that would have to be sorted out, if she took the room they had to offer. But, glancing round at their faces in the flickering light from the television set, she began to feel uncertain if she would take it. At her office, Tara, who was experienced in these matters, had told her, 'You don't have to take the first room you see, Moyna. You can look around and *choose*.' But Moyna had already 'looked around' and while, by comparison with the cell in the women's hostel, all the rooms had seemed princely, shamingly it was she who had been turned down by one prospective landlord or landlady after the other. She had been scrutinised with such suspicion, questioned with such hostility, that she realised that no matter what they stated in their advertisements, they had nothing but fear and loathing for the single working woman, and the greatest dread of allowing one into their safe, decent homes. Moyna wondered how she could convey such an impression of sin and wantonness. She dressed in a clean, starched cotton sari every day, and even though her hair was cut short, it was simply pinned back behind her ears, not curled or dyed. And surely her job in the office of a literary journal was innocent enough? But they narrowed their eyes, saw her as too young, too pretty, too unattached, too much an *instrument* of danger, and dismissed her as a candidate for their barsatis.[9] These rooms had once been built on Delhi's flat rooftops so that families who slept out on their roofs on summer nights could draw in their beds in case of a sudden dust storm or thunder shower. But now that Delhi was far too unsafe for sleeping alfresco, these barsatis were being rented out to working spinsters or bachelors at a delightful profit.

Suddenly convinced that she would not, after all, want to occupy this unwelcoming family's barsati, Moyna lowered her feet to the floor gingerly and tried to rise and murmur an excuse. 'I have to be at the hostel before nine,' she said when the episode of the *Mahabharata* ended with a great display of fiery arrows being shot into the sky and a whirling disc beheading the villain. The landlord gestured to the children to turn off the set and, turning to Moyna, he shouted to the servant boy to bring her a drink. 'What will you have, beti? Chai,[1] lassi,[2] lemonade?'

'No, thank you, no, thank you,' she murmured, seeing the landlady's steely eyes on her, willing her to refuse, but the servant boy came out with a thick glass of tepid water for her anyway. While she sipped it, the inquisition began, interrupted frequently by the children who alternately demanded their dinner or another show on television and by the dog who emerged from under the bed and sniffed at her suspiciously. Moyna kept her eyes lowered to watch for Candy and perhaps they saw that as becoming modesty or demureness because, to her surprise, the landlady said, 'You want to see the room? Ramu, Ramu—eh, Ramu! Get the key to the barsati and open it up.'

And there, on the flat rooftop of the plain yellow stucco villa in a colony Moyna had never heard of before on the outskirts of New Delhi, there to her astonishment was a palace, a veritable palace amongst barsatis. The rooftop, which covered the entire area of the villa, seemed to her immense, larger than any space she had occupied since her arrival in Delhi, and it was

9. A room built on the roof terraces of Delhi houses for shelter from the rain when sleeping alfresco in the summer.   1. Tea.   2. Buttermilk drink.

clear, empty space under an empty sky, with a view of all the other rooftops stretching out on every side, giving Moyna, as she stood there, a sense of being the empress of all she surveyed. Of course it would bake under her feet in the heat of summer but—and this was the crowning glory—a pipal[3] tree that grew in the small walled courtyard at the back of the house rose up over the barsati itself, sheltering it from the sun with a canopy of silvery, rustling leaves, spreading out its branches and murmuring, Moyna felt certain, a gracious welcome.

After that auspicious view, what could it matter if the barsati itself was merely a square walled cube, that it had not been cleaned in so long that its single window had turned opaque with dust, and spider-webs hung in swags from every corner, that the bed was nothing but a string cot, the cheapest kind of charpai? What did it matter that the single cupboard against the wall had doors that did not seem to meet but sagged on their hinges and could never be locked, that the 'kitchen' was only a blackened kerosene stove atop a wooden table that also served as desk and dining table, that the 'bathroom' was a closet-sized attached enclosure, open to the sky, with a very stained and yellowed squatter-type toilet and a single stand-pipe? Already Moyna's mind was racing with visions of what she could transform the place into. Why, its very bareness gave her the freedom to indulge her wildest dreams and fancies.

Then her look fell upon the servant boy who stood waiting by the door that opened onto the staircase, twirling the key round his finger and smirking, and she became aware that she herself had a smile across her face and that her hands were clasped to her throat in a most foolish fashion. Immediately she dropped them, adjusted her expression to one of severity, and followed him down the stairs.

The landlord and landlady, now risen from the bed and waiting for her on the veranda, looking as alike as twins with their corpulence, their drooping chins and expressions of benign self-satisfaction, appeared confident of her answer: it was only what could be expected after seeing what they were offering. She would of course sign a year's lease which could be terminated whenever they chose, pay three months' deposit, plus the first month's rent right now, immediately, 'and we will welcome you to our house as our own beti,' they assured her magnanimously. 'From now on, you need worry about nothing. Your parents need have no worries about you. We will be your parents.'

Tara came over from the office with her husband Ritwick to help her to move in. Moyna had only one tin trunk, a bedding roll and now her kitten in a basket, but they insisted she would not be able to move on her own, and Ritwick growled that he wanted to meet the Bhallas 'to make sure'. The Bhallas were seated on a wicker sofa in the veranda when they arrived, and watched them carry every item up the stairs with openly inquisitive stares. It seemed to Moyna that it was not Ritwick who was sizing them up so much as that they were sizing *him* up. Certainly they questioned him closely, when Moyna introduced him to them, regarding his parentage, ancestral home, present occupation and relation to Tara and Moyna before allowing him to

3. A variety of fig tree (*Ficus religiosa*) related to the Indian banyan tree and sacred to Buddhists and Hindus.

set one foot on the stairs. But once they arrived on the rooftop, Ritwick looked into every crack and crevice with a suspicion to equal theirs. Then he asked, 'Where's the water tank?'

'What water tank?'

'*Your* water tank. Where is your water supply coming from?'

'I don't know. Where *does* it come from? The pipes, I suppose.'

He strode to the bathroom and turned on the tap. It spun around weakly, gurgled in a complaining tone, and sputtered into silence. There was no water. Moyna stood in the doorway, stricken. 'Water shortage,' she explained. 'You know Delhi has a water shortage, Ritwick.'

'Not if you have a storage tank. Everyone has a storage tank—or several. The Bhallas will have one downstairs, but you need a booster pump and your own tank up here so water can be pumped up from the one below.'

'Oh.'

He looked at her with the kind of exasperation her own brothers turned on her when she failed to understand what they were doing under the bonnet of the car or with electric gadgets at home. She came from a family so competent that she had never needed to be competent herself.

'Did you ask the Bhallas about it?'

'About what?'

'The storage tank. The booster pump.'

'No,' she admitted.

He strode off towards the staircase with every show of determination to enquire immediately. She ran after him, crying, 'Oh, Ritwick, I'll ask them—I'll ask them—later, when I go down.'

Tara came out of the barsati. 'D'you have curtains?'

'What for?'

'Because if you wipe the windowpanes clean, your neighbors can look right in.'

'No, they can't! There's the tree—don't you see my beautiful tree? It's like a screen.'

'Come in and see.'

Tara had wiped the windowpanes clean, and a young man with a face like a pat of butter and with a small moustache twitching over his pursed lips was standing on his rooftop and gazing at them with unconcealed curiosity and, it could easily be made out since the distance was small, some admiration.

'Oh, Tara, why did you go and clean that?' Moyna cried. 'No, I don't have a curtain. Where would I get a curtain from?'

'Get me a bedsheet then,' Tara commanded, 'and help me put it up at once.'

'But the tree—' Moyna tried again, and went out to see why it had not lowered a branch where it was needed. The tree shaded the entire barsati (and Ritwick admitted it would keep off the sun which would otherwise make a tandoori oven[4] of it) but it was tall and provided no screen against the other rooftops and the rooftop dwellers who suddenly all seemed to be standing outside their barsati doors, surveying this newcomer to their level of elevation. Moyna suddenly realised she had joined a community.

'When I came yesterday, I saw no one,' she mumbled, abashed.

---

4. Special oven used in north India for baking chicken, bread, and meat.

'Well, you can introduce yourself to all of them now,' Ritwick said, 'and just hope none of them are thieves or murderers because if they are—' he looked grim and gestured—'all they need is one jump from their ledge to yours.'

'Don't, Ritwick,' Tara said sharply. 'Why are you trying to frighten poor Moyna?'

'All I'm saying is Moyna'd better stay indoors and keep her door locked.'

'But I was going to drag my bed out and sleep under the stars!'

'Are you *crazy?*' both Tara and Ritwick said together, and Tara added, 'D'you want your picture in the evening news, with a headline: "Single Woman robbed and murdered in barsati"?' They looked at her sternly to see if their words had had the requisite effect, and Tara added, 'Now let's go to the market and get you all the things you need. Like one great big lock and key.'

When they returned from the market with cleaning fluids, brooms, scrubbing materials, provisions for 'the kitchen'—and the lock and key—Ritwick confronted the landlady who had in the meantime shampooed her hair and now sat on the veranda, to dry it in the sun.

'Excuse me,' he said, not very politely. 'Can you please show Moyna where the switch is for the booster pump?'

'What switch? What booster pump?' She parted her hair and peered out from under it with some hostility.

'Is there no booster pump to send water up to the barsati?'

'Water up to the barsati?' she repeated, as if he were mad. 'Why? Why? What is wrong?'

'There's no water in the tap. She'll need water, won't she?'

'She will get water,' declared Mrs Bhalla, drawing herself up and tossing her head so that the grey strands flew, 'when municipality is sending water.[5] Municipality water is coming at five o'clock every morning and five o'clock every evening. The barsati will be getting water whenever municipality sends.'

'At five in the morning and five in the evening?' shouted Ritwick. 'You need a storage tank so water will collect.'

'Collect? Why she cannot collect in a bucket?' Mrs Bhalla shouted back. 'She has no bucket?' she added insultingly.

Tara and Moyna were standing with their purchases in their arms, ready to bolt upstairs, but Ritwick yelled, 'Yes, she *has* bucket, but how can she collect at five in the morning and five in the evening?'

'What is wrong?' Mrs Bhalla screamed back. 'We are all collecting—why she cannot collect also?'

'Because she will be sleeping at five in the morning and at work at five in the evening!'

Mrs Bhalla turned away from him and looked at her tenant with an expression that made clear what she thought of any young woman who would be asleep at five in the morning and 'at work' at five in the evening. She clearly had an equally low opinion of sleep and work, at least where her young tenant was concerned. Ritwick was shouting, 'Storage tank—booster pump—' when

---

5. The frequent use of the present continuous tense is a trait of some forms of Indian English. Mrs. Bhalla is probably speaking English. In cosmopolitan cities such as Delhi, Indians often communicate with each other in English.

Moyna fled upstairs, dropping matchboxes and kitchen dusters along the way. When Tara followed her up, she found her sitting on her bed in tears, howling, 'And I've signed the lease for one year and paid for three months in advance!'

Moyna's way of life changed completely. It had to be adjusted to that of the Bhallas. She left her tap turned on when she went to bed—which she did earlier and earlier—so she could be woken by the sound of water gushing into the plastic bucket at five in the morning and get up to fill every pot, pan and kettle she had acquired before turning it off. All around her she could hear her fellow rooftop dwellers performing the same exercise—as well as bathing and washing clothes in the starlight before the water ran out. She went back to bed and lay there, panting, trying to get back to sleep, but by six o'clock all the birds that roosted in the pipal tree were awake and scream- ing and running on their little clawed feet across the corrugated iron roof, then lining up along the ledge of the rooftop to flutter their wings, crow, squawk and chirp their ode to dawn. It was just as well that they made it impossible for her to fall asleep again because at six she had to go downstairs and walk to the market where Mother Dairy would have opened its booth and all the colony residents would be lining up with their milk cans to have them filled. She stood there with all the servant boys and maidservants, sleepy-eyed, for the sake of having her milk pail filled for Mao, and then carried it back carefully through the dust, in her slippers, trying not to spill any.

No Ladies' Special serviced this colony, and Tara had warned her against attempting to travel to work on an ordinary DTS bus. 'You don't know what men in Delhi do to women,' she said darkly. 'This isn't Bombay or Calcutta, you know.'

Moyna had heard this warning in the women's hostel but asked, 'What d'you mean?'

'In Calcutta all men call women Mother or Sister and never touch them. In Bombay, if any man did, the woman would give him a tight slap and drag him by his hair to the police station. But in Delhi—these Jats[6] . . .', she shuddered, adding, 'Don't you even *try*.'

So Moyna walked back to the marketplace after breakfast, to the auto- rickshaw stand in front of Mother Dairy, and spent a sizeable part of her income on taking one to work. She clearly made a woebegone figure while waiting, and a kindly Sikh[7] who rode his autorickshaw as if it were a sturdy ox, his slippered feet planted on either side of the gearbox, the end of his turban flying, and a garland of tinsel twinkling over the dashboard where he had pasted a photograph of his two children and an oleograph of Guru Go- bind Singh,[8] took pity on her. 'Beti, every day you go to work at the same time, to the same place. I will take you, for a monthly rate. It will be cheaper for you.' So Gurmail Singh became her private chauffeur, so to speak, and Moyna rode to work bouncing on the narrow backseat, her sari held over her nose to keep out the dust and oil and diesel fumes from all the office-bound traffic through which he expertly threaded his way. Quite often he was wait-

---

6. A north Indian cultivator caste.   7. Follower of the Sikh religion, founded in Punjab by Guru Nanak (1469–1538).   8. Guru Gobind Singh (1666–1708), the tenth guru (preceptor) of the Sikhs, instituted a number of changes in Sikh religious practice.

ing for her outside the office at six o'clock to take her home. 'I live in that colony myself, so it is no trouble to me,' he told her. 'If I have no other customer, I can take you, why not?' In a short while she got to know his entire family—his mother who cooked the best dhal[9] in the land, and the finest corn bread and mustard greens, his daughter who was the smartest student in her class—class two, he told Moyna—and his son who had only just started going to school but was unfortunately not showing the same keen interest in his studies as his sister. 'I tell him, "Do you want to go back to the village and herd buffaloes?" But he doesn't care, his heart is only in play. When it is school-time, he cries. And his mother cries with him.'

'Gurmail Singh thinks it is the school that is bad. Bluebells, it's called,' Moyna reported at the office. 'He wants to get him into a good convent school, like St Mary's, but you need pull for that.' She sighed, lacking any.

'Moyna, can't you talk about anything but the Bhallas and Gurmail Singh and his family?' Tara asked one day, stubbing out her cigarette in an ashtray on her desk.

Moyna was startled: she had not realised she was growing so obsessive about these people, so prominent in her life, so uninteresting to her colleagues. But didn't Tara talk about Ritwick's position in the university, and about her own son and his trials at school, or the hardships of having to live with her widowed mother-in-law for lack of their own house? 'What d'you want to talk about then?' she asked, a little hurt.

'Look, we have to bring out the magazine, don't we?' Tara said, smoking furiously. 'And it isn't getting easier, it just gets harder all the time to get people to read a journal about *books*. Bose Sahib[1] hardly comes to see what is going on here—' she complained.

'What is going on?' asked Raj Kumar, the peon, bringing them two mugs of coffee from the shop downstairs. 'I am here, running everything for you. Why do you need Bose Sahib?'

'Oh, Raj Kumar,' Tara sighed, putting out her cigarette and accepting the rich, frothing coffee from him. 'What will you do to make *Books* sell?'

Tara was the first person Ajoy Bose had employed when he started his literary review, *Books*, after coming to Delhi as a member of parliament from Calcutta. He had missed the literary life of that city so acutely, and had been so appalled by the absence of any equivalent in New Delhi, that he had decided to publish a small journal of book reviews to inform readers on what was being published, what might be read, a service no other magazine seemed to provide, obsessed as they all were with politics or the cinema, the only two subjects that appeared to bring people in the capital to life. Having first met Ritwick at the Jawaharlal Nehru University[2] during a conference on Karl Marx and Twentieth Century Bengali Literature,[3] and through him Tara, he had engaged her as the Managing Editor. The office was installed in two rooms above a coffee and sweet shop in Bengali Market. It was Tara's first paid job—she had been working in non-government organisations[4] simply to escape from home and her mother-in-law—and she was extremely

---

9. Stewlike dish made of lentils.   1. "Lord," "master," an Urdu term of respect, often used to indicate aristocracy.   2. A well-known university in Delhi, named after India's first prime minister, Jawaharlal Nehru (1899–1964).   3. West Bengal, the state where Bengali is spoken, has been strongly influenced by Marxism and has had a Communist political majority.   4. Since the 1980s, Indian women have formed and participated in grass-roots, feminist, and activist nongovernmental organizations.

proud of these two modest rooms that she had furnished with cane mats and bamboo screens. Bose Sahib had magnanimously installed a desert cooler and a water cooler to keep life bearable in the summer heat. Together they had interviewed Raj Kumar, and found him literate enough to run their errands at the post office and bank. Then Tara had interviewed all the candidates who had applied for the post of assistant, and chosen Moyna. Moyna had no work experience at all, having only just taken her degree, in English literature, at a provincial university. She managed somehow to convey her need to escape from family and home, and Tara felt both maternal and proprietorial towards her, while Moyna immensely admired her style, the way she smoked cigarettes and drank her coffee black and spoke to both Raj Kumar and Bose Sahib as equals, and she hoped ardently to emulate her, one day.

Of course the only reason she had been allowed by her family to come to Delhi and take the job was that it was of a literary nature, and her father had known Bose Sahib at the university. They approved of all she told them in her weekly letters and, Moyna often thought while opening parcels of books that had arrived from the publishers or upon receiving stacks of printed copies of their journal fresh from the press, how proud they would be if they could see her, their youngest, and how incredulous . . .

Now here was Tara claiming that sales were so poor as to be shameful, and that if no one came to its rescue, the journal would fold. 'Just look at our list of subscribers,' Tara said disgustedly, tossing it over the desk to Moyna. 'It's the same list Bose Sahib drew up when we began—we haven't added one new subscriber in the last year!'

'Oh, Tara, my father is now a subscriber,' Moyna reminded her nervously, but Tara glared at her so she felt compelled to study the list seriously. It was actually quite interesting: apart from the names of a few of Bose Sahib's fellow members of parliament, and a scattering of college libraries, the rest of the list was made up of a circle so far-flung as to read like a list of the rural districts of India. She could not restrain a certain admiration. 'Srimati Shakuntala Pradhan in PO Barmana, Dist. Bilaspur, HP, and Sri Rajat Khanna in Dist. Birbhum, 24 Parganas, W. Bengal[5] . . . Tara, just think of all the places the journal *does* get to! We ought to have a map on the wall—'

Raj Kumar, who was listening while washing out the coffee mugs in the corner with the water cooler which stood in a perennial puddle, called out heartily, 'Yes, and I am posting it from Gole Market Post Office to the whole of Bharat![6] Without me, no one is getting *Books!*'

Moyna turned to throw him a look of mutual congratulation but Tara said, 'Shut up, Raj Kumar. If we can't find new names for our list, we'll lose the special rate the post office gives journals.'

'Send to bogus names, then, and bogus addresses!' Raj Kumar returned smartly.

Now Tara turned to stare at him. 'How do you know so much about such bogus tricks?'

He did not quite give her a wink but, as he polished the mugs with a filthy rag, he began to hum the latest hit tune from the Bombay cinema which was the great love of his life and the bane of the two women's.

'The next time Bose Sahib comes, we'll really have to have a serious dis-

---

5. That is, West Bengal. *Dist.*: district. *H.P.*: Himachal Pradesh (name of a state).   6. India.

cussion,' Tara said. The truth was that her son Bunty had received such a bad report from school that it was clear he would need tutoring in maths[7] as well as Hindi,[8] and that would mean paying two private tutors on top of the school fees which were by no means negligible—and the matter of Ritwick's promotion had still not been brought up for consideration. She lit another cigarette nervously.

Bose only came to visit them when parliament opened for its summer session. He, too, had much on his mind—in his case, of a political nature—and *Books* was not a priority for him. But when he was met on the appointed day at the door by two such anxious young women, and saw the coffee and the Gluco biscuits spread out on Tara's desk in preparation for his announced visit, he realised this was not to be a casual visit but a business conference. He cleared his throat and sat down to listen to their problems with all the air of an MP[9] faced with his constituents.

'So, we have to have a sales drive, eh?' he said after listening to Tara spell out the present precarious state of the journal.

'Yes, but before we have that, we have to have an overhaul,' Tara told him authoritatively. 'For instance, Bose Sahib, the name *Books* just has to go. I told you straightaway it is the most boring, unattractive name you could think up—'

'What do you mean? What do you mean?' he spluttered, tobacco flakes spilling from his fingers as he tamped them into his pipe. 'What can be more *attractive* than *Books*? What can be less *boring* than *Books*?' He seemed appalled by her philistinism.

'Oh, that's just for *you*.' Tara was not in the least put out by the accusation in his mild face or his eyes blinking behind the thick glasses in their black frames. 'What about people browsing in a shop, seeing all these magazines with pin-ups and headlines? Are they going to *glance* at a journal with a plain yellow cover like a school note book, with just the word *Books* on it?'

'Why not? Why not?' he spluttered, still agitated.

'Perhaps we could choose a new title?' Moyna suggested, rubbing her fingers along the scratches on the desk, nervously.

The two women had already discussed the matter between them, and now spilled out their suggestions: *The Book Bag, The Book Shelf* . . . well, perhaps those weren't so much more exciting than plain *Books* but what about, what about—*Pen and Ink? The Pen Nib? Pen and Paper? Press and Paper?*

It seemed to make Bose Sahib think that new blood was required on the staff because his reaction to their session was to send them, a month later, a new employee he had taken on, a young man newly graduated from the university of Hoshiarpur who would aid Tara and Moyna in all their office chores. He would deal with the press, see the paper through the press, supervise its distribution, visit bookshops and persuade them to display the journal more prominently, and allow Tara and Moyna to take on extra work such as hunting for new subscribers and advertisers.

Tara and Moyna were not at all sure if they liked the new arrangement or if they really wanted anyone else on the staff. As for Raj Kumar, he was absolutely sure he did not. No warm reception had been planned for the

7. Mathematics.   8. The language of a majority of north Indians, and the official language of India, in addition to English.   9. Member of Parliament.

graduate from Hoshiarpur University (in the opinion of Tara and Moyna, there could be no institution of learning on a lower rung of the ladder) but when young Mohan appeared, they had been disarmed. By his woebegone looks and low voice they learned he no more wanted to be there than they wanted to have him there, that he had merely been talked into it by his professor, an old friend of Bose Sahib's. He himself was very sad to leave Hoshiarpur where his mother and four sisters provided him with a life of comfort. The very thought of those comforts made his eyes dewy when he told Tara and Moyna of the food he ate at home, the grilled chops, the egg curries, the biryanis[1] and home-made pickles. Moreover, if it was necessary to begin a life of labour so young—he had only graduated three months ago and hardly felt prepared for the working life—then he had hoped for something else.

'What *would* you have liked to do, Mohan?' Moyna asked him sympathetically (she was not at all certain if she was cut out for a career at *Books* either).

'Travel and Tourism,' he announced without hesitation. 'One friend of mine, he is in Travel and Tourism and he is having a fine time—going to airport, receiving foreign tourists, taking them to five-star hotels in rented cars, with chauffeurs—and receiving tips. Fine time he is having, and much money also, in tips.'

Moyna felt so sorry for the sad contrast provided by *Books* that she asked Raj Kumar to fetch some samosas[2] for them to have with their tea. Mohan slurped his up from a saucer, and when Raj Kumar returned with the samosas in an oily newspaper packet, he snapped up two without hesitation. Moyna wondered if he was living in a barsati: she thought she saw signs that he did. Wiping his fingers on Raj Kumar's all-purpose duster, Mohan remarked, 'Not so good as my sister makes.'

Tara thought Moyna could go out in search of advertisements, but when Moyna looked terror-struck and helpless, and cried, 'Oh, but I don't even know Delhi, Tara,' she got up, saying resignedly, 'All right, we'll do the rounds together, just this once,' and gave Raj Kumar and Mohan a string of instructions before leaving the office. Putting on her dark glasses, slinging her handbag over her shoulder, and hailing an autorickshaw that was idling outside the coffee shop, Tara looked distinctly cheerful at the prospect.

Moyna could not see what there was to be cheerful about: the publishing houses they visited were all in the back lanes of Darya Ganj and Kashmere Gate, far from salubrious to her way of thinking, particularly on a steaming afternoon in late summer, and the publishers they met all seemed oppressed by the weather, slumped in their offices listlessly, under slowly revolving fans—if the electricity had not broken down altogether, in which case they would be plunged in gloom, in dim candlelight—and they seemed far from interested in increasing sales of their wares by advertising in *Books*. 'We have been advertising,' one reminded them brusquely, 'for more than two years, and we are seeing no increase in sales. Who is reading *Books*? Nobody is reading.' Tara looked extremely offended and swept out with great dignity after reminding him that he had yet to pay for the advertisements he had

1. A spicy north Indian rice dish, with marinated meat or vegetables. 2. Savory fried snacks.

placed. Moyna followed her, quietly impressed if uncertain as to whether she could bring off a confrontation so satisfactorily.

They had a little better luck with the bookshops in Connaught Place and Khan Market which were not nearly so depressing and were often run by pleasant proprietors who sent out for Campa Cola and Fanta for them, and at times even agreed to place a few advertisements of their best-selling thrillers. The bookshop for the publications of the USSR—mostly cheerful and cheap translations of Russian folk tales and fables in bright colours for children—proved particularly supportive. A charming Russian gentleman gave them a free calendar and a brochure listing the film, dance and music programmes at Tolstoy Bhavan. Encouraged, Tara suggested they visit the British Council next. 'But do they publish books?' Moyna asked. She was dusty, hot and very tired by now. Tara thought that irrelevant—they could advertise their library, couldn't they?

Actually, they could not, and did not, but the young man they spoke to, who had been summoned out of his office to deal with them, was so apologetic about the refusal that they gave him a copy of the latest edition of *Books* gratis. He looked overcome, pushing back a lock of his fair hair from his forehead and gazing at the magazine as if it were a work of art. 'Oh,' he said, several times, 'how perfectly splendid. Perfectly splendid, really.' Tara straightened her shoulders and gave Moyna significant look before rising to her feet and making her departure. Moyna followed her reluctantly: the lobby of the British Council library had the best air-conditioning they had run into all day. After that—and the discreet lighting, the carpeting, the soft rustle of newspapers, the attractive look of detective novels and romantic fiction on the shelves—they returned to their office in Bengali Market with a sense of resignation. They did not really expect any results.

But there was Tara at the top of the stairs to the rooftop, pounding on the door and shouting, 'Moyna! Moyna, open up, Moyna!'

Moyna had just been preparing for a bath. It was not entirely uncommon for Tara and Ritwick to drop in on her unannounced if they had managed to persuade Ritwick's mother to mind their little son for a bit, and since she had still not managed to get a telephone installed, there was no way they could warn her. 'Wait a minute,' she called, and slipped back into her clothes before going barefoot across the roof to open the door to them.

Tara was standing there, laughing and in great spirits, not with Ritwick at all but, to Moyna's unconcealed astonishment, with the fair young man from the British Council, who stood a few steps lower down, looking more embarrassed even than before, and clutching in his hands a bottle filled with some dark liquid. Moyna stared.

'Oh, open the door, Moyna, and let us in. I know you don't have a phone so how could I warn you? Adrian rang me up about an advertisement and I asked him to come over, but you know how the Dragon Lady is in such a temper with me these days, so I brought him here instead.'

'Oh,' said Moyna doubtfully, thinking of her own Dragon Lady downstairs. '*Won't* you let us in?'

Moyna stood aside and then led them towards her barsati. She really could not have company in there—Tara ought to know that. Feeling both vexed and embarrassed, she stood in front of the door now, frowning, and finally said, 'I'll bring out some chairs,' and left them waiting again. To her annoyance, Adrian followed her in to help pull out some chairs, first placing the bottle on the table and saying, 'I brought you some—um—wine. I thought—um—we could have a drink together. Um.'

'And I told him you would at least have peanuts—' Tara shouted from outside.

What could she mean—peanuts? What peanuts? Moyna frowned. After the chairs, there was the bother with glasses. What made Tara think she might have wine glasses? All she could find were two tumblers and a mug—and certainly there were no peanuts. In fact, she had just finished the last bit of bread with her dinner, there was not so much as a piece of toast to offer. But once they were seated on the rooftop, with the wine poured out, and had had a sip of that, Moyna looked up to see that the sky still had a pink flush to it, that it was not entirely dark, that the first stars were beginning to emerge from the day's dust and grime and glare, that the pipal tree was beginning to rustle like a shower of rain in the first breath of air that evening, and suddenly she felt her spirits break free and lift. Here she was, entertaining friends on 'her terrace' on a starry evening, just as she had imagined an adult working woman in the metropolis might do, just as she had imagined *she* would do—and now it was happening. She looked at Adrian, his six narrow feet of height somehow folded onto a small upright chair, and said with incredulity, 'This is nice!' He thought she meant the wine and hurried to refill her glass, blinking happily behind his spectacles.

It was not only she who thought it was nice. Tara seemed liberated by coming away from her mother-in-law's house where she had to live because of Ritwick's stalled promotion at the university. Adrian seemed enchanted by everything his eye encountered on the rooftop—the parrots streaking in to settle in the branches of the pipal tree for the night, the neighbourliness of the other roof dwellers, several of whom had lined up along their ledges to watch (discreetly or not so discreetly) Moyna's first social gathering. Mao the cat jumped upon Adrian's knee and sat there as if on a tall perch with his eyes narrowed to slits, and by the time the bottle of wine was emptied, they had begun to talk much more loudly and laugh more than they were aware. Tara had an endless fund of mother-in-law stories, as Moyna already knew, but Adrian was gratifyingly astounded by them. When Tara told them of the first time Ritwick had brought her to meet his mother and how the first thing she said to Tara was, 'Aré, why are you wearing this pale colour? It does not suit you at all, it makes your complexion muddy,' or of how she would insist Tara wear her wedding jewellery to work 'otherwise people will think you are a widow', Adrian became wide-eyed and gulped, 'She *said* that? You mean she has licence to say what she *likes* to you?' Tara, greatly encouraged, began to exaggerate—as Moyna could tell—and her stories grew wilder and funnier, reducing even Adrian to laughter. The neighbours spied on them, scandalised, hidden now by night's darkness, but they were unaware how their voices carried downstairs as well, and what a degree of grim disapproval was mounting there. When they descended the stairs, Moyna accompanying them with the key to unlock the front gate for them, they found Mr and Mrs Bhalla pacing up and down the small driveway, grey-faced with censure. They had let Candy out from under their bed and now she flew at them, yipping with small snaps of her teeth, till she was curtly called back by Mr Bhalla.

Their looks made Moyna wonder if it was really so late, had they been kept awake? She put on an apologetic look but Tara, on the contrary, threw back her head and said loudly, 'OK, Moyna, good night—see you tomorrow!' and swept out of the gate. Adrian followed her hastily, carefully keeping out of range of Candy's snapping jaws.

Moyna was certain she would have to face the Bhallas' wrath as she turned around, but they drew back and stared at her in silence as she walked up the stairs and vanished.

Although they did not bring it up directly, after that whenever Moyna encountered them, on her way to work or back, they never failed to refer obliquely to that evening. 'You are having more guests tonight?' they would ask when they saw her returning with the shopping she had done along the way. 'No? You seem to be having many friends,' they went on, prodding her to say more. She shook her head, hurrying. 'No? Then why not come and watch TV tonight? *Ramayana*[3] is showing at seven p.m. Very fine film, *Ramayana*. You should join us,' they commanded, as if testing her true colours. She shook her head, making her excuses. 'Oh, then you are going out? With your friends?' they deliberately misunderstood, taunting her. The children, Sweetie and Pinky, giggled behind their fingers.

'Tara, please don't bring Adrian again,' Moyna begged. 'I don't know what my landlord thinks about me. He seems to think I'm some *hostess* or *entertainer*, the way he and his wife go on.'

'Oh, tell them to go to hell,' Tara snapped. 'As if renting their bloody barsati means you can't have any social life.'

'Social life with girls would be all right, but not with *men*, and not with *foreign* men.'

'Really, Moyna,' Tara stared at her and shrugged, 'when are you going to grow up?' Her mother-in-law had clearly had a lot to say about Tara's going out without Ritwick the other evening; Tara showed all the signs of having had a fine row.

'I *am* grown up! I live in a barsati! I don't want to be thrown out of it, that's all.'

Mohan looked up from the omelette he was eating. He had no cooking facilities where he roomed, and the first thing he did on entering the office in the morning was to send Raj Kumar to fetch him a bun omelette which he seemed to greatly enjoy. Wiping up the last streak of grease with the remains of the bun, he said, 'Barsati living is no good for girls. Why not women's hostel?'

She need not have worried about Adrian visiting her again: the look the landlord had given him, plus Candy's warning nips, proved quite enough of a disincentive. The next male to create a problem for Moyna was Mao, now a strapping young tom ready to test his charms in the wider world. No longer willing to stay where she put him, he liked to strut about the barsati roof, or leap up onto the ledge and slowly perform his toilet there where he could be seen, occasionally lifting his head to snarl at a sparrow that mocked and taunted him from a safe distance in the pipal tree, or blink when he became aware of someone watching, possibly admiring him. Moyna feared she would

---

3. Ancient Indian epic narrating the life and deeds of Prince Rāma and his wife Sītā.

not be able to keep him concealed for long. Already the Bhalla children, Sweetie and Pinky, suspecting his existence, would come up the stairs and peep under the door to catch a glimpse of him, cry, 'Tiger! Tiger!' if they did, and come running pell-mell down the stairs again. They had clearly said something to their mother who would watch Moyna return from the market clutching a wet paper bag reeking of fish and call out, 'Oh, I see you are fond of eating fish!' and had also noted that Moyna took in an unlikely quantity of milk. 'So much milk you are drinking,' she had commented early one morning, seeing Moyna return with her filled pail. 'Very good habit—drinking milk,' she added, contriving to make Moyna understand that this was an indirect comment on the evil of drinking wine. 'Or you are making curd?[4] Kheer pudding,[5] then? No? You don't know how to make kheer pudding?'

The next signal Mao gave was an audible one: a strange, unexpected, long drawn-out wail in the night that woke Moyna and made her shoot out of bed, ready to leap to the door. Mao himself was nowhere to be seen; he generally slipped in and out of the window which had a missing pane that Mr Bhalla had never thought to replace and now proved a convenience. Looking through it, Moyna saw, as in a dream, a feline bacchanalia in full swing on the rooftop. How had all these female felines found their way to the barsati—and to Mao? Moyna rushed out in her nightgown to make sure the door was locked. It was. Was there a drainpipe they might have climbed? There couldn't be or Mao would have discovered it long ago. As she stood wondering, the cats crept into a corner discreetly screened by a box or two, and as she watched, the pipal tree gave a shiver. The pipal tree—of course! She stared at its massive trunk, pale in the moonlight, and the sinuous branches and twigs silvery and ashiver, and spied another insomniac—her neighbour, a few feet away, his moony face cupped in his hands as he leaned upon the ledge and gazed yearningly at her. He was close enough to speak to her but, instead, he first sighed and then began to hum. It sounded like the tune of a disgusting song to Moyna's ears, a lewd, suggestive song, an outrageous affront of a song:

> 'O, a girl is like a flame,
> O, a girl can start a fire—'

Moyna darted back into her room and slammed the door. Its echoes rang out and for a while there was a shocked silence. But, a little later, the cats crept out to caterwaul again and all Moyna could do was wrap a pillow round her head and moan.

Although she did her best to avoid the Bhallas next morning—and usually when she left for work they were in the dining room, from which tantalising whiffs of fried dough, curried eggs and creamy tea floated out—today Mrs Bhalla was lying in wait, having her scalp massaged at that very hour. She looked up from under the tent of greying hair spread out on her shoulders and fixed her eye on the rapidly fleeing Moyna. 'Come here!' she cried. 'I'm late!' shouted Moyna from the gate. 'What is that animal on your roof?' shrieked Mrs. Bhalla, throwing off the ministering fingers of the old crone she had engaged for the service. 'Animal?' called Moyna from the other side of the gate, 'What animal?' and jumped across the ditch to the dusty road

---

4. Yogurt.   5. Pudding made with milk, sugar, and rice or other grains.

where Gurmail Singh waited for her, his autorickshaw put-putting reassuringly.

Catastrophe struck from an unexpected quarter. Returning from work the same day, Moyna climbed slowly up the stairs with a bag of fish she had stopped to buy, unlocked the door to the rooftop and went in, sighing with relief at having gained the open barsati, at seeing the pipal tree dark against the mauve and pink evening sky, wondering if there was enough water in the bucket for a wash. She let herself into her room and set about putting away her sling bag, her market bag, slipping out of her slippers, shedding the day like a worn garment, sweaty and dusty. Mao was not around but he rarely was now that he had discovered the route of the pipal tree: there was nothing she could do but hope Candy would not be waiting at the foot of it. She decided to switch on some music instead, reached out—and saw the blank space beside her bed where she kept her radio and tape recorder. It was not there.

Her first foolish reaction was to blame Mao. Could he have taken it? Then she whirled around, thinking she might have placed it elsewhere last night, or this morning, and forgotten. It was not on the kitchen table, and there was no other surface where it could be. Looking around for some corner where it might have hidden itself, she began to notice other objects were missing: her alarm clock, the little box containing the tapes, even the tin-framed mirror she had hung on the wall. What else? Flinging open the cupboard that would not lock, she began to cry as she groped on the shelves, trying to count her saris. Wiping her face with her hand, she banged it shut and ran down the stairs to the Bhallas.

They were all seated crosslegged on the bed, chins cupped in their hands, deeply absorbed in the latest episode of their favourite American soap opera (the mythological epics were aired only on Sundays, to guarantee maximum viewership). Sweetie and Pinky refused to turn their attention away from *I Love Lucy* but the elder Bhallas sensed Moyna's hysteria, turned off the TV, listened to her tearful outburst, then burst themselves, with fulsome indignation. What was she insinuating? Was she accusing *them?* Did she think *they* would go up to her barsati and haul away her miserable goods—*they*, with all these goods of their own around them . . .

Now Moyna had to deny their accusation, assure them she had never harboured such an idea, only wanted to know if they had any idea *who* it could be. *Who?* they thundered, how would they know *who?* What with Moyna's unsavoury circle of friends coming and going at all hours of the day and night, how could they tell which one had found his way to her barsati? Had they seen anyone? she begged. *Seen* anyone? Seen *who?* they roared. At this point, she wailed, 'Please call the police!' which incensed them further. They nearly exploded—even Candy, Sweetie and Pinky shrank back. Police? On their property? What was Moyna suggesting? Was she out of her mind? If the police visited their house, their immaculate, impeccable house of decency, purity and family values, what would their neighbors think, or say? Never had such a thing happened in their home, their locality, their community—till *she* had come along and brought into their midst this evil, this sin . . .

Moyna retreated. She shut the door upon the Bhallas, who were standing at the foot of the stairs and shaking their fists and shouting loud enough for all the neighbors to hear. Then she sat down on a chair under the tree, feeling as if all her strength were gone; she could not even stand. Mao reappeared, wrapping himself around and around her legs, finally leaping onto her lap and kneading it with his paws, loudly purring. She held him, sure he was telling her something, saying comforting, consoling things, and sat there till it was dark, listening to him and the pipal tree that shivered and rustled, the birds subsiding into its branches, eventually falling silent. More than any other sensation, it was homesickness she felt: she was trying to suppress the most childish urge to run and hide her head in her mother's lap, feel her mother stroking her hair. She was also suppressing the urge to write a long letter home, describing everything as it really was. She told herself it would be unforgivable to cause her parents concern. As it was, they had never felt comfortable about her living alone in the big city; every letter from them voiced their anxiety, begging her to keep her doors securely locked, never go out after dark and take good care of her health. She also knew she was trying to hold onto her pride, as she sat there, stroking and stroking Mao.

Still, Moyna knew she had to do something, and planned to tell Tara immediately. But next morning Tara had arranged to hold a 'conference', as she liked to call such a gathering, with their usual cast of reviewers. Most of them were Ritwick's friends and colleagues from the Jawaharlal Nehru University, with a sprinkling of 'outsiders' from Delhi University and the lesser colleges. This was not a regular meeting but somehow, by some kind of natural osmosis that no one quite understood, the hard core of their critics who reviewed regularly for *Books* happened to have a free morning and came to meet Tara and Moyna at the Coffee House in Connaught Place where they took up a long table in one corner. This was the occasion, greatly enjoyed by all, when the young lecturers and readers pleaded for the books they were desperate to have, the latest academic treatises published by the university presses at Oxford and Cambridge, Harvard and Yale, at impossible prices, and Tara and Moyna magnanimously dispensed them with the understanding that the reviewers could expect little reward other than the prized books themselves. In return, the eager young men in their handspun shirts, shaggy beards and dusty sandals plied them with small earthen mugs of coffee and all the delicacies the Coffee House had to offer—dosa, idli, vada,[6] whatever they liked—and which harried waiters flapping dishcloths and tin trays around brought to them in regular relays. There were also some professional critics, usually older men, some really quite old, worn and grey from years of piecing together a living by writing, who looked over the books with a more practised and cynical eye and quickly reached for whatever would take the least time to read and fetch the most at the second-hand bookshops on the pavement outside.

But the customary bonhomie of the occasion which recalled their carefree student days—O careless youth!—was unexpectedly disrupted that morning by Moyna's state of agitation which she could not conceal, leading to an open confession under questioning from Tara. Theft, landlords, police—all were appalled and looked at Moyna in horror.

6. South Indian savory snacks.

'Bloody lumpen proletariat!'[7] raged the young man who always contrived to sit directly across from Moyna in order to gaze at her when he was not looking out for a book he could attack and demolish. 'Should be taught a lesson. Think they rule the world, huh? Have to be shown—'

'By whom? The polizia? Those stooges—'

This enraged the young gallant. 'If not, I'll make them. Come on, Moyna, I'll go to the police if the landlord won't—'

Moyna grew alarmed. She had here all the reaction she could have asked for but was not at all sure if she wanted to go any further, that is, go to the police about it. She had come to the office that morning hoping Tara or Raj Kumar or Mohan might offer to go with her, or at least offer sympathy and advice. Then she had found Tara bustling about, arranging to leave the office to Raj Kumar and go to the Coffee House with Moyna and a pile of books, while Raj Kumar settled down to telephone all his friends and Mohan was poring over a postcard from his sisters about a prospective bride they had found for him. She had had to hold back the matter till it had burst from her when someone merely asked, 'How's life, Moyna?' which in turn had lead to this show of outrage and gallantry.

A few minutes later Ritwick dropped in on the conference, hoping to pick up a book on medieval trade routes through the Arabian Sea that Tara had promised to keep for him. On hearing of Moyna's calamity, he insisted on accompanying her and Karan to the police station. 'Is there a justice system or is there not?' he demanded, glaring at all around the table with its coffee cups, its trays and plates of greasy fried food. 'I need to know!'

At the police station, the officer in charge sat at his desk looking uncomfortable in a khaki uniform that did not fit and had to be nudged, tugged and scratched into place constantly. Several lesser officials stood around with their nightsticks, and stared at Moyna with open mouths while the two men did all the talking. Moyna was glad not to have to speak but she did have to sign the yellow charge sheet that the officer filled out with slow deliberation, then handed to her. When she had done that, he rose from his chair and commanded his underlings to follow him to the Bhalla household.

At the gate, Moyna's courage failed. She looked around wildly in the hope of seeing Gurmail Singh with his autorickshaw ready to put-put her away from the scene, but of course he was not there and Ritwick and Karan between them silently compelled her to open the gate and lead the party in.

Only Mrs Bhalla was at home at that hour; the servant boy vanished from sight as soon as the police made their appearance. Nevertheless, the scene was awful. Or so it seemed to Moyna although, in retrospect, perhaps not as awful as it might have been. It was true that Mrs Bhalla stood at the foot of the stairs, screaming imprecations against tenants who made false accusations and brought disgrace to the homes that sheltered them, but the police merely marched past her and up the stairs, stalked around the barsati, twisting their moustaches like comic-book or cartoon cops, pointing out the sights to each other with an amused, even bemused air—Mao stretched out on the bed, blinking lazily at the intruders, the neighbours peering over the walls and ledges with open curiosity, Moyna's toilet goods arranged on the windowsill—and examined the full height and length of the pipal tree, then

7. Marginalized or degraded section of the working class.

climbed down the stairs, and vanished. 'Complaint has been filed,' they told the indignant Ritwick and Karan. 'Investigation has been completed.'

When Moyna queued up at the Mother Dairy with her milk can next morning, she found herself standing next to a young woman she had often noticed there but never spoken to: she seemed to be a foreigner, with light brown hair pulled back and tied in a long pigtail down her back, wearing the cheapest of cotton saris and rubber slippers. Now the young woman spoke to her, unexpectedly. 'I have heard,' she said haltingly, 'you have had—theft?' Moyna nodded, and hardly dared reply, knowing everyone in the line was listening. Many did turn around at the word 'theft'. 'I too,' said the young woman sympathetically. 'I see you on roof. I, too,' she said, and after they had had their milk cans filled, they walked back together along the dusty verge of the road, and Simona told Moyna how she had employed a boy who had regularly burgled her barsati of anything she bought for it. 'But didn't you dismiss him?' Moyna asked, thinking that even she would have had the wits to do that. 'Of course,' Simona replied, 'after first time! But he had key for my barsati, came back and thieved again, and again. Now I have nothing left, nothing,' she added, with a joyful smile. 'And the police—?' 'Oh, they caught him—again, and again. But always they had to let him go because he said he was twelve years old! Too young for gaol.'[8] Simona shrugged. 'Still he is twelve. He does not grow any older. So he can be thief for longer.'

This gave Moyna so much food for thought that she walked along in silence, and almost forgot to ask Simona her name or address. When she did, it turned out that Simona was one of her neighbours, only too discreet to hang over her ledge and spy on Moyna like the others. Now she promised to wave and call when she saw Moyna out on her rooftop. 'You have most beautiful tree,' she said on parting, and Moyna glowed till it struck her it could be the reason why she stayed on with the Bhallas, and if that would not be considered foolishness by anyone but Simona.

The next day Tara and Ritwick came to visit. They stalked around the rooftop, peering through every possible loophole through which the burglar might re-enter. The trouble was that he probably had a key to the door and could let himself in whenever Moyna left: it was unlikely he risked climbing the great tree in the backyard.

'This place is just not secure, Moyna. You've got to ask your landlord to make it secure. Fence in the entire outer wall—'

'Ask Mr Bhalla?' Moyna croaked.

Lately whenever Moyna passed through the Bhalla home she felt she needed protective clothing. Mr Bhalla's jowls seemed set in a permanent scowl like a thunder cloud (the fact that he rarely shaved and his jaws were always blue added to the illusion) while Mrs Bhalla would plant herself in a central location, her eyes following Moyna down to the gate or up the stairs as if she suspected Moyna herself of the theft. Her mutterings implied as much—'These girls, these days, think they can go to work, live alone—huh! Can't even take care of their own belongings!' Did she actually say these

8. Jail.

words, or was Moyna imagining them? She felt them creep over her back, across her neck, like spiders settling there.

As for their servant boy, after her conversation with Simona, Moyna was certain she sensed an extra insouciance to his manner. He had always watched her with open, unconcealed curiosity, but now she felt he gave his hips an insulting swing, twitched his filthy kitchen duster over his shoulder with a flick, and pursed his lips to whistle a bar from some Bombay film tune although that was surely not fitting in a servant boy, even if employed in a household like the Bhallas'. When she passed the open kitchen door one day and he cocked an eyebrow at her and sang:

> 'With blouse cut low, with hair cut short,
> This memsahib[9] so fine—'

she decided to complain to the Bhallas, but discovered she had chosen a bad moment: that very morning, while she was at work, Mao had slithered down the tree trunk to the Bhallas' compound and been pounced upon by Candy, with Sweetie and Pinky in hot pursuit. Mao had somehow escaped from all three, but Moyna's secret of owning what the Bhallas insultingly called a 'billa', a tom, had been uncovered. Rising to her feet, Mrs Bhalla launched into a tirade about lying tenants who neglected to inform their landlords of their pets that would never have been permitted into their own pristine homes. Moyna, already incensed by the servant boy's behaviour and now by his employers', stood her ground stoutly and replied, 'Then do you want me to leave?' half hoping the reply would free her of them. But Mrs Bhalla retreated promptly—she knew to a whisker's breadth how far she could go as a landlady—claiming she could hear the telephone ringing. That evening she sent Pinky and Sweetie upstairs to ask if Moyna would like to come down and watch a rerun of the old film classic Awaara[1] with them. Moyna told them she had a cold.

It was not untrue. The change of season had affected Moyna as it had practically every other citizen of Delhi. Still listless from the heat during the day, at night she found herself shivering under her cotton quilt in the barsati: the windowpane had never been replaced and allowed a chill blast of wintry air in.

She was sniffling over her desk at the office one morning with her head in her hands, trying to correct proofs, only half-listening to Tara complain of her mother-in-law's unreasonable and ungenerous reaction to Tara and Ritwick's staying out at the cinema late last night, when a visitor appeared at the door, demanding to see the editor. Tara's tirade was cut short, she hastily tossed her nail file into a drawer, pulled a page of proofs from Moyna's desk, and lifted an editorial expression to a man whose face appeared to be made entirely out of bristling hair and gleaming teeth, although he did wear thick, black-framed glasses and a silk scarf as well, tucked into the v-neck of a purple sweater.

'What can I do for you?' Tara had barely asked when she began to regret it.

---

9. "Mistress, Madam" (literally, "Madam master"), a respectful term used for addressing women by people of lower status such as servants. 1. Vagabond, very popular Hindi film of 1951, starring screen idols Raj Kapoor and Nargis.

The visitor was the author of a collection of short stories in Hindi that had been reviewed by Karan in the last issue. He had a copy of it rolled up in his hand. He spread it out before them, asking if they, as editors, had paid attention to what they were printing in a journal that at one time had had a distinguished reputation but now was nothing but a rag in the filthy hands of reviewers like the one who signed himself KK. Did they know who he was talking about?

Moyna got up and came across to glance at the review together with Tara, out of a sense of loyalty to her and an awareness of threat, as the author of the short stories jabbed his finger at one line, then another—'so devoid of imagination that Sri[2] Awasthi has had to borrow from sources such as *The Sound of Music* and—' 'in language that would get a sixth standard student in trouble with his teacher—' 'situations so absurd that he can hardly expect his readers to take them any more seriously than the nightly soap opera on TV—' 'characters cut out of cardboard and pasted onto the page with Sri Awasthi's stunning lack of subtlety—'

Tara recovered her poise before Moyna could. Snatching the journal out of the visitor's hands, she held it out of his reach. 'We choose our reviewers for their standing in the academic world. Every one of them is an authority on—'

'Authority? What authority? This dog—he claims he is an authority on Hindi literature?' ranted the man, snatching the journal back from Tara. 'It is a scandal—such a standard of reviewing is a scandal. It must not go unnoticed—or unpunished. Where is this man? I would like to see him. I should like to know—'

'If you have any complaint, you can make it in writing,' Tara told him. She was, Moyna could see, as good a fighter as she had always claimed.

'Make it in writing? If I make it, will you publish it? If I put in writing what I think of your journal, your name will be—'

'Mr Awashti,' Tara said, using his name as if she remembered it with difficulty, and managing to mispronounce it, 'there is no need to be so insulting.'

'If that is so, then why have I been insulted? I am a member of Sahitya Akademi.[3] I am author of forty volumes of short stories, one of autobiography, seven books of travel, and also of essays. I am award-winning. I am invited by universities in foreign countries. My name is known in all Hindi-speaking areas—'

Mohan suddenly strode in; he had been standing in the doorway with Raj Kumar but now entered the room to stand beside Tara and Moyna. He was enjoying this; it was the first drama to take place in the office. Plucking the journal out of Mr Awasthi's hands, he tossed it on the desk with a contemptuous gesture. 'The editor is not responsible for the reviewer's views,' he announced, which it had not occurred to the two women to say.

This was not very original but Mr Awasthi's face turned a dangerously purple colour, not unlike the sweater he wore. But now Mohan had him by the elbow and was guiding him out of the door. Tara and Moyna fell back into their chairs, pushing their hair away from their flushed faces. Tara, lighting a cigarette with shaking hands, said, 'Did you *hear* Mohan? Did you *see* how he got him out?'

2. Corresponds to "Mr." 3. The Indian national academy of letters.

That visit proved to be a prelude to an entire winter in which the battle raged. Mr Awasthi's rebuttal was printed in the next issue, followed by Karan's still more scurrilous response—he worked in an attack on the Hindi-speaking 'cow belt'[4] which proved a starting point for a whole new series of entertaining insults—and their days at the office were enlivened by visits from, either one or other, each intent on getting the 'editor's ear' (in the case of Karan, it was mostly the Assistant Editor's ear he tried to get). Even Bose Sahib wrote from Calcutta and implored Tara to close the correspondence on the matter (he thought mention of the 'cow belt' particularly deplorable and unparliamentary). He added some disquieting remarks that Tara relayed to Moyna gloomily. 'He says the journal is still in the red, and he may not be able to go on publishing it if it fails to make money. Never thought Bose Sahib would consider *Books* as if it were a commercial enterprise. Ritwick says it is clear capitalism has killed Marxism in Calcutta[5] if even Bose Sahib talks like an industrialist.'

'Oh Tara,' Moyna said in dismay. It was not just that Bose Sahib was something of an icon in their circle but it also shook her confidence in her ability to be a career woman in Delhi. What would happen if she lost her job? What if she did not find another employer? Would she lose her barsati? And return to her parents' home? Back where she started from? She began to sniffle.

Her cold, which had been growing worse for weeks, burgeoned into full-scale flu. After going downstairs to send Gurmail Singh away in his autorickshaw, she went back to bed, pulling the quilt over her ears. Mao, sympathetic or, perhaps, delighted at this development, crept in beside her. She drifted in and out of sleep, and her sleep was always crowded with thoughts of office life. Behind closed lids, she continued to see the journal's columns before her, requiring her to proofread:

> Sir—Sri Ritwick Misra has reviewed Sri Nirad Chaudhuri's biography of Max Müller[6] without proving his credentials for doing so. Has Sri Misra any knowledge of Max Müller's native tongue? Has Sri Chaudhuri? If not, can we believe all the necessary documents have been studied without which no scholar can trust, etc., Yrs truly, B. Chattopadhyay, Asansol, W. Bengal.

> Sir—May I compliment you on your discovery of a true genius, i.e. Srimati[7] Devika Bijliani, whose poem, *Lover, lover*, is a work of poetic excellence. I hope you will continue to publish the work of this lovable poetess. Kindly convey my humble respects to her. Also publish photograph of same in next issue. Yrs truly, A. Reddy, Begumpet, Hyderabad, A.P.[8]

It was in this state that Raj Kumar found her when he came in with a message from Tara saying, 'Why won't you get yourself a phone, Moyna, and

---

4. So called because of the predominantly rural and agrarian character of this region of north India.
5. Capital of West Bengal and the center of Bengali literature and culture.   6. An eminent British Sanskrit scholar and Orientalist (1823–1900). Nirad C. Chaudhuri (1897–1999), the author of *Scholar Extraordinary: The Life of Professor the Rt. Hon. Friedrich Max Müller, P.C.* (1974).   7. Corresponds to "Mrs." or "Ms."   8. Andhra Pradesh, the name of a state in southeast India.

tell us when you're not coming to work? Just when the new issue is ready to go to press—' and ending 'Shall I bring over a doctor this evening?'

Moyna was not sure what to do with Raj Kumar but was grateful for his obvious concern and felt she could not send him straight back to the office. 'Can I make you a cup of tea, Raj Kumar?' she asked hoarsely. 'I'll have some, too.'

Raj Kumar perched on the edge of her straight-backed chair. He planted his hands on his knees, and studied every object in the room with the same deep interest while Moyna boiled water in a pan and got out the earthen mugs to make tea.

'No TV?' he asked finally.

She shook her head and put a few biscuits on a plate to offer him. He ate one with great solemnity, as if considering its qualities, then asked, 'Who is doing the cooking?' She admitted she did her own, wondering who he imagined would perform such chores for her. 'Ah, that is why you are never bringing lunch from home,' he said, with pity. She agreed it was. He of course had a wife to fill a tiffin[9] container's three or four compartments to bursting with freshly cooked, still warm food. He asked for more details of her domestic existence. As Moyna told him of her regimen of rising to store water at five, then queueing for milk at six, and the shopping she did at the market on her way home with the essential stop at the fish shop for Mao's diet, Raj Kumar's eyes widened. He was too polite to say anything but when he had finished his tea and biscuits and rose to go, he said in a voice of true concern, 'Please lock door safely. Not safe to live alone like this.' She assured him she would.

At the door he turned to say, 'Also, you should purchase TV set,' with great earnestness. 'TV set is good company,' he explained, 'like friend.'

Going back to bed after shutting and locking the door behind him, she did feel friendless—but not convinced that she wanted a TV in place of one. And no sooner had she closed her eyes than the lines of print began to unroll again:

> Sir—It is a great disappointment that you continue to harbour a reviewer such as KK who has a clear bias against one of the great languages of our motherland. Because he is reviewing for an English-language journal in the capital, does he think he has the right to spurn the literature composed in the vernacular? This attitude is as despicable as the sight of seeing mother's milk rejected for sake of foreign liquor. Yrs truly, C. Bhanot, Pataliputra Colony, Bihar.

> Sir—The monthly arrival of *Books* is greatly looked forward to by my immediate family. I regret that you choose to include in it such filth as Srimati Devika Bijliani's poem, *Lover, lover*. This is not what we expect to find in decent family magazine. Kindly refrain from publishing offensive matter of sexual nature and return to former family status. Yrs truly, D. Ramanathan, Trivandrum, Kerala.

Simona, not having seen Moyna in the milk queue for days, came to visit. She brought with her a gift that touched Moyna deeply—fish tails and heads

---

9. *Tiffin* denotes snacks or foods eaten with afternoon tea or between meals; but a tiffin carrier with compartments is used for carrying a complete lunch.

wrapped in newspaper for Mao's dinner. Simona explained, 'I saw you are not getting milk so I know that cat is not getting fish.' She sat crosslegged on Moyna's bed, tucking her cotton sari around her shoulders, and told Moyna that she herself had been sick—'for many, many days. Months, perhaps. Hep-a-ti-tis. You have Hep-a-ti-tis?' 'Oh no,' Moyna denied it vigorously, 'only flu,' and was afraid to think now that she might lie alone in the barsati for so long, sick, away from home. 'And you are so far from home,' she said to Simona with sudden sympathy, and wondered what could keep the young woman here, ageing before her eyes into a pale, drawn invalid. But Simona put on her rapt expression, one that often overtook her even in the most inconvenient places—passing the garbage heap behind the marketplace, for instance, or seeing a beggar approach—and told Moyna joyfully, 'This is my home. It is where my guru lives, you see.' Moyna cowered under her quilt: she did not feel strong enough for such revelations. 'Please make yourself tea,' she croaked, and broke into a paroxysm of coughs.

Having received a letter in which Moyna mentioned that she had flu, Moyna's mother arrived. Moyna was actually on her way to recovery by then and many of the remedies her mother brought with her, the special teas and balms and syrups, were no longer needed, but evidently much else was. Putting her hand into the containers on Moyna's kitchen shelf, her mother was shocked to find less than a handful of rice, of lentils. 'You are starving!' she exclaimed, as horrified at herself as her daughter, 'and we did not know!' 'Do I look as if I'm starving?' Moyna asked, but she could not stop her mother from shopping and cooking and storing food in a storm of energy and activity in the barsati, which was now bathed in mild sunlight and at its most livable in Delhi's pleasant winter.

Mrs Bhalla downstairs roused herself too, and began to cook and send treats upstairs, either with the servant boy or with Pinky or Sweetie, little jars of pickles she had put up, or metal trays with sweets she had made, dissolving in pools of oil and reeking of rose water, or covered pots containing specialities known only to Mrs Bhalla and the village that was once her home.

'How kind she is,' Moyna's mother exclaimed, accepting these gifts. 'How lucky you are to have found such a landlady, Moyna.'

Nothing Moyna told her could completely alter her mother's impression. 'She's just trying to fool you,' she cried. 'She *wants* you to think she's a nice person.'

She glowered at Mrs Bhalla whenever she passed her on the veranda, but Mrs Bhalla now called out to her with great sweetness, 'How is your mother, Moyna? Please ask her to come and visit me.'

'I don't know why you both like each other so much,' Moyna said darkly, on conveying this message.

'We are both mothers, that is why,' her mother replied with what Moyna now found an indigestible sweetness. It was this motherliness she had missed and longed for but now she found it superfluous. Her barsati no longer looked as it had in the days of penury, austerity and minimalism. Her mother had bought curtains, cushions, filled every available space with kitchen gadgets, foods, whatever comfort she could think of. Now Moyna found she was no longer used to comfort, that it annoyed and irritated her. Picking up Mao and a book, she would retreat to the rooftop while her mother bustled about in the crowded room, clattering and humming and enjoying herself. She leaned over the ledge and stared moodily into the quaking leaves of the pipal tree and the hazy winter light that filtered through. Downstairs, in the Bhallas' brightly lit kitchen, she could see the Bhallas' servant boy, rolling out chapatis[1] for their dinner. He had music on to entertain him while he worked, and Moyna listened too. She was enjoying its somewhat melancholy and dirge-like tone when she started in recognition: was that not Joan Baez singing? And was it not one of her own tapes? She stiffened and bent over the ledge, trying to look past the pipal leaves to get a clearer picture of what was on the kitchen counter below. But she did not really need to look, she could hear clearly enough, and it made her roll her hands into fists and pound on the ledge with frustration.

While her instinct was to run and tell her mother, then run down and inform Mrs Bhalla and demand her belongings back, she found herself silent. Letting her mother pile a spinach curry and lentils on her plate at dinner, she kept quiet: she knew it would be unwise to tell her mother that she lived amongst thieves. How then could she declare to her that she intended to remain here with them, not return to family and home, comfort and care?

'What are you thinking, Moyna?' her mother asked impatiently. 'Why don't you eat?'

Fortunately, her mother could not stay long. Unfortunately, when Moyna returned with relief to her own routine, she found Tara at the office consumed by the same housemaking fervour. This was not at all customary where Tara was concerned. Tara had taken the job at *Books* to escape from housewifeliness, as her mother-in-law so cannily suspected—and now she confounded Moyna by talking incessantly of real estate, bank loans, co-ops . . . true, not housekeeping matters exactly, but just as boring to Moyna who had plunged into the next issue which had yet another blistering attack by Karan on the Hindi author's newest offering. Tara was hardly around to see to it; she was either on the telephone, earnestly discussing finances with Ritwick, or, with her handbag slung over her shoulder and her dark glasses on, was off to visit yet another co-op.

'Why are you doing this?' Moyna protested. 'You *have* a nice house to live in. I mean,' she added hastily, seeing Tara's expression, 'I know it's the Dragon Lady's, but still, it *is* nice and you don't pay for it—' She refrained from mentioning the free babysitting service it provided.

'You don't understand. You're too young. At our age, we need our own place,' Tara explained loftily.

In her concern for this nest for the future, Tara seemed strangely unaffected by the letter they received from Bose Sahib, announcing his decision to close the magazine. He was planning to start another, he added, this time about development projects in rural areas—were Tara and Moyna interested in working for it? Tara would not even consider it: she was settling into this nest she had found, she was not going to go touring the hinterland, she would turn down the offer. Moyna was pale with dismay and disbelief; she begged Tara not to speak so loudly, to come down to the sweet shop below where

---

1. Flat unleavened bread, a staple of north Indian cuisine.

they could discuss it over a cup of tea without Mohan and Raj Kumar over-hearing. 'It will be such a shock to them,' she explained to Tara. But Tara did not see any cause for shock: 'Mohan is looking for a job in hotels anyway, or a travel agency,' she said. 'What?' asked Moyna. Why had she not been told the world of *Books* was coming unravelled around her? Had she been so immersed in the wretched business of barsati living to ignore far more important matters? What about all the book reviewers and their supply of foreign books being cut short? She sat at the small tin-topped table with Tara, not able to swallow her tea, and pleaded with her to reconsider. 'But why?' Tara asked, her eyes looking into the distance where her dream house waited for her like a mirage in the desert outside Delhi. 'I'm not married to *Books*, or to Bose Sahib. Let them go to hell. I'm not going to go around looking at weaving centres and dairy farms for Bose Sahib!'

Moyna bit her lip. It was certainly not what she had come to Delhi for, nor was it what she had expected to do with her life. But she had grown used to the two-roomed office with its bamboo shutters, Raj Kumar sitting in a corner and tying up book parcels, Mohan enjoying his bun omelette and samosas at his desk. She had even grown used, if that was what resignation could be called, to the barsati, although when the year's lease was up, she would be free to rent another: there were almost as many barsatis in Delhi as there were top-floor flats. She turned the teaspoon over and over in her hands, considering all the possibilities, weighing the pros and cons, till Tara snatched it out of her hand. 'Stop fidgeting, Moyna. Just *decide*,' she snapped, tossing back her hair with all the authority of someone who had done just that.

It was too difficult, too weighty a decision to be made in a moment, over a cup of tea. Moyna went back and forth between the office and the barsati, sick with anxiety. Only occasionally and momentarily could she forget the problem: when Gurmail Singh told her with pride that his daughter had passed the entrance test to the Loreto Convent, ensuring a fine future for her and leaving him only to worry about his less promising son; or when she received an invitation to a film show at the British Council to be followed by a reception, placing her on a rung above those who went there only for the air conditioning and the newspapers. Then she would fall to brooding again and sit crosslegged on her bed, stroking Mao and turning the matter over in her mind.

It was when she was in such a state that a letter arrived from her mother. She opened it listlessly, knowing in advance what it would contain—advice on how to run her household, how to cook a specially strengthening stew, an offer of monetary help, pleas to return home, her father's message that she should consider studying for a higher degree before embarking on a career—and she glanced at it cursorily: her mother did not understand even now the attraction of living, alone, in Delhi, and could think of it only as a poor substitute for living at home.

But at the bottom of this letter, her mother had added, craftily:

> Our neighbours have invited us to a welcome party next week; their son Arun is returning from the United States. He has taken a degree in geology and is expected to find a suitable job in the field. I am sure he

would be pleased to meet you again. If you are planning a visit soon, we shall ask him over for a meal. I know his family is very keen[2] . . .

Mao gave a leap off the bed as Moyna flung herself backwards, at the same time throwing the letter into the air with a shout of laughter. She rolled her head about on the pillow, spluttering, 'Oh, Mama—re-a-ll-y, Mama!' Mao had not seen such behaviour in a long time. He sat by the door and watched her, his paws primly together, his tail wrapped around him, disapproving. It was clear he thought she had gone crazy. Even he, with his fine senses, could not know that the letter made up Moyna's mind for her. She was free, she was determined, she had made her decision, and she sat up, laughing.

In the kitchen below, the Bhallas' servant boy turned up the music and sang along with it.

---

2. Indian marriages are usually arranged by the parents. Moyna's mother suggests the possibility of a match between Moyna and the young man mentioned in the letter.

LORNA GOODISON
born 1947

Lorna Goodison's work belongs to a hitherto neglected but impressive tradition of feminine endeavor and expression in the Caribbean, a tradition that is only now receiving attention in the historical accounts and literary representations of the region. The note of intense engagement that Goodison brings to her interpretation of Caribbean life provides a reminder that women have been not merely bearers of the race—the role in which they are often cast in the largely male-oriented literature—but also closely involved in the making of Caribbean history. The heroic legacy of Caribbean women has come to be exemplified by the slave rebel "Maroon Nanny," who has been accorded the status of national hero in Jamaica and whom Goodison celebrates in a dramatic monologue that concludes with this vibrant, prophetic statement:

> I was sent, tell that to history
>
> When your sorrow obscures the skies
> other women like me will rise.

But apart from the involvement of exceptional female figures in Caribbean history, women have functioned even more fundamentally as the principal repositories of the collective memory. The tales and legends in the oral tradition, transmitted from generation to generation since the time of slavery, compose a comprehensive narrative of collective survival distinctive to the Caribbean people. The compulsion to uncover the unbroken continuity of this experience has led to a reappraisal of the formative role of women in Caribbean life. Thus writers, in particular women writers, have begun to bring into new prominence this essential component of Caribbean history. Perhaps the most striking example of this orientation is the central role played by the character Telumée Miracle in the novel by the Guadeloupean author Simone Schwarz-Bart, *The Bridge of Beyond*. The trend can be observed even earlier in the English-speaking Caribbean, notably in the poetry of Louise Bennet, written in the Jamaican dialect, or patois; more recently, it can be seen in the work of Caribbean writers such as Olive Senior, Pamela Mordecai, Maryse Condé, Merle Hodge, and Jamaica Kincaid.

Goodison's work represents a significant contribution to this movement. In two of her best-known poems, she assumes the legacy bequeathed to the present generation by the long line of Caribbean women whose devotion and tenacity have nurtured the Caribbean people in body and spirit. *For My Mother* is a poem of filial devotion and appreciation, but its wider relevance as homage to the resourcefulness displayed by her mother and other women like her is unmistakable from its tone. Goodison's homage in that poem assumes a symbolic resonance in the final lines of the title poem of her second volume, *I Am Becoming My Mother* (1986):

> My mother raises rare blooms
> and waters them with tea
> her birth waters sang like rivers
> my mother is now me

The movement here toward a defining moment of personal identification shows Goodison situating herself within the historical procession of indomitable Caribbean women. "Guinea Woman," the archetype of the Caribbean grandmother celebrated in Goodison's poem of that title, becomes emblematic of the matriarchal culture, with origins in Africa, which her poetry seeks to endow with imaginative significance. Goodison thus places her individual voice in what she calls in another poem "a singing chain of ancient names."

Goodison was born on August 1, 1947, in Kingston, Jamaica, to a family of modest means. After her primary and secondary education, she entered the Jamaica School of Art to study painting and sculpture, continuing to the Arts Students' League in New York for further training. This beginning as artist has left a mark on her poetry, which often alludes directly to the visual arts and incorporates a strong visual element in its imagery. Goodison has continued to paint, and her art works have been exhibited in the West Indies, Britain, and the United States; she has also illustrated many books, including all her own volumes. She was for a while a teacher and has also held visiting positions at several American universities. Now resident in Jamaica, she is frequently in demand for her powerful readings of her own poetry.

Goodison's first volume, *Tamarind Seasons* (1980), published in Jamaica, revolves around the daily realities of the common people's depressed condition. This theme underlies much of her work and is further developed in her second volume, *I Am Becoming My Mother,* which won the Commonwealth Prize for poetry for the Caribbean region and brought her international attention. *Heartease* (1988) expands considerably the scope of her two previous volumes not only in its greater emphasis on social issues but also in its more developed lyrical register and mystical orientation. Goodison has also published a collection of short stories, *Baby Mother and the King of Swords* (1990), which explores the social geography of feminine experience in Jamaica.

Although Goodison has turned increasingly to social themes, her work conveys a wholehearted acceptance of the gift of life. This accounts for the vigor of her expression, a feature of her work that is deliberately cultivated in the self-portraits she offers in several poems, most notably in *Songs of Release:* "I stand with palms open, salute the sun / The old ways over. / I new born one." The open disposition to experience these lines bespeak is evident in *New York Is a Subway Stop,* where she revels in the spectacle that the city offers. The youthful exuberance displayed in this poem translates her "layered love of simplest ways," which is transposed into a heroic key in *To Us, All Flowers Are Roses,* a poem of remembrance in which the geographical features of Jamaica function both as signposts of history and as metaphors of the national consciousness.

Goodison's imaginative investment in her world provides the framework for the celebration in her poetry of everyday existence in the Caribbean. From vignettes charged with social meaning, such as *Kenscoff,* to the more extended "reportage" of social mores in such poems as *Wedding in Hanover* and *Bridge Views,* she is attentive to the varied texture of lived experience. Her vision ranges from the centers of power in her male-dominated society, which she regards with an ironic interest, to the margins inhabited by the dispossessed, in whom she discerns the true pulse of the communal sensibility. Goodison's confident embrace of life is most apparent in her handling of the theme of love. The discreet eroticism of *Letter to My Love* illustrates her vision of sexual love as natural self-expression and as a gift of the self. Her profound reverence for the integrity of personal relationships is expressed in *Love Song of Cane in Three Parts:* "Something happens when we love. In some ways it is outside telling."

The theme of maternity links her love poetry, with its emphasis on individual fulfillment, to her representations of the communal experience. *Songs for My Son* demonstrates her conception of a maternity that goes beyond the conventional view of woman as perpetuator of the race ("her life's work begun") to a more personal valuation of her offspring, who not only represent an extension of her self but connect her with another individual ("the connection three way") and, beyond him, with an organic community of blood and values. At the same time, the child's existence puts the mother's private history in immediate touch with social fact, a connection clarified in *My Will,* in which the poet bequeathes to her son "the gift of song" and in a telling colloquial turn continues:

> eat each day's salt and bread
> with praise
> and may you never know hungry.

Goodison's attention to her world attests to the deep sincerity of her social commitment. However, her critical consciousness, sharply focused on the female condition, is sustained at the price of a tension between her vital enthusiasms and her moral response to the harsh realities of the real world. This tension is evident in such poems as *This Is a Hymn* and *My Last Poem;* in both, her documentation of material and moral discomfort yields to an optimism that seems contrived. Nonetheless her characterization of the plight of Caribbean women remains sharp, even in the unstressed pathos of this portrait in *Tamarind Season:*

> The soft welcome within
> needs protecting
> so she grows wasp-waited.
> again
> wasp-waited
>
> The welcome turns sour
> she finds a woman's tongue
> and clacks curses at the wind
> for taking advantage
>
> box her about this way
> and that is the reason
>
> wait is the reason
> Tamarind Season.

In this and other poems centered on the female condition, Goodison displays an understanding of her subjects' anxieties and sympathy for their daily miseries. This generous impulse does not imply ambivalence, for she is capable of sounding the occasional note of revolt, as in the conclusion of *Judges:* "I'm lining up these words / holding them behind the barrier of my teeth / biding my time as only a woman can / I have a poem for you, judge man." Perhaps the poem that best sums up the tension in her work is *We Are the Women,* a vindication of the stoicism that enables the Caribbean woman to wrest some form of triumph over an immemorial adversity:

"We've made peace / with want / if it doesnt kill us / we'll live with it." At the same time, she perceives the disabling effect of a self-sacrifice that impedes change:

> We've buried our hope
> too long
> as the anchor to our navel strings
> we are rooting at
> the burying sport
> we are uncovering our hope.

Ultimately, Goodison's poetry proposes a redeeming vision of art. Her acute sense of her vocation informs the lyricism of *I Shall Light a Candle of Understanding*, a poem that is both a powerful expression of spiritual commitment and, in its measured simplicity, a triumph of form. Her achievement both in this poem and in her work as a whole points to the moral purpose she ascribes to her artistic mission: "this voice is to heal / To speak of possibility."

The most comprehensive discussion of Goodison's work is contained in Edward Baugh's two essays, "Lorna Goodison in the Context of Feminist Criticism" and "Goodison on the Road to Heartease," both in the *Journal of West Indian Literature*, 1986 and 1990 respectively. J. Edward Chamberlin, *Come Back to Me, My Language* (1993), also contains a lengthy and enthusiastic appraisal of Goodison's poetry. Carole Boyce Davis and Elaine Savory Fido, eds., *Out of the Kumbla: Caribbean Women and Literature* (1990), offers an essential general introduction to Caribbean women's literature; in her chapter "Textures of Third World Reality in the Poetry of Four Caribbean Women," Elaine Savory Fido considers the relationship between Goodison's poetry and its social reference. The volume also contains Rhonda Cobham's survey, "Women in Jamaican Literature: 1900–1950." Carolyn Cooper, *Noises in the Blood* (1993), is a rewarding study of Jamaican popular culture in its social context and is thus useful as background to Goodison's poetry.

PRONOUNCING GLOSSARY

The following list uses common English syllables to provide rough equivalents of selected words whose pronunciation may be unfamiliar to the general reader.

Accompong: *ah-cawm-pong*   Kumina: *koo-mee-nah*

Ashanti: *ah-shan-tee*   Nyamekopon: *en-yah-me-caw-pong*

Catadupa: *kah-tah-doo-pah*

To Us, All Flowers Are Roses

> Accompong is Ashanti, root, Nyamekopon[1]
> appropriate name Accompong, meaning
> warrior or lone one. Accompong,
> home to bushmasters, bushmasters being
> maroons,[2] maroons dwell in dense places   5
> deep mountainous well sealed
> strangers unwelcome. Me No Send You No Come.[3]

---

1. The Supreme Being (Ashanti). Accompong is a town in the hilly region of western Jamaica, founded by escaped slaves. Most of the proper nouns in this poem are places in Jamaica. *Ashanti:* an ethnic group in the central region of present-day Ghana; also their language.   2. Escaped slaves. Because of their long isolation, maroon communities preserved intact their genetic stock and way of life inherited from their African ancestors.   3. Jamaican English for "strangers unwelcome."

I love so the names of this place
how they spring brilliant like "roses"
(to us all flowers are roses) engage you   10
in flirtation. What is their meaning? pronunciation?
a strong young breeze that just takes
these names like blossoms and waltzes
them around, turn and wheel them on the tongue.

There are angels in St. Catherine somewhere.   15
Arawak[4] is a post office in St. Ann.
And if the Spaniards hear of this
will they come again in Caravelles[5]
to a post office (in suits of mail)
to enquire after any remaining Arawaks?   20
Nice people, so gentle, peaceful, and hospitable.

There is everywhere here.[6]
There is Alps and Lapland and Berlin.
Armagh, Carrick Fergus, Malvern[7]
Rhine and Calabar,[8] Askenish   25
where freed slaves went to claim
what was left of the Africa within,
staging secret woodland ceremonies.

Such ceremonies! such dancing, ai Kumina![9]
drum sound at Barking Lodge where we hear   30
a cargo of slaves landed free, because
somebody signed a paper[1] even as they
rode as cargo shackled on the high seas.
So they landed here, were unchained, went free.
So in some places there is almost pure Africa.   35

Some of it is lost, though, swept away forever,
maybe at Lethe[2] in Hanover, Lethe springs
from the Greek, a river which is the river
of Oblivion. There is Mount Peace here
and Tranquility and Content. May Pen   40
Dundee Pen, Bamboo Pen and for me,
Faith's Pen, therefore will I write.

There is Blackness here which is sugar land
and they say is named for the ebony[3] of the soil.
At a wedding there once the groom wore cobalt blue   45
and young bride, cloud white, at Blackness.
But there is blood, red blood in the fields
of our lives, blood the bright banner flowing
over the order of cane and our history.

The Hope River in hot times goes under   50
but pulses underground strong enough to rise

4. Named after the native Carib inhabitants of Jamaica.   5. Spanish sailing ships.   6. A reference to
the extraordinary genetic mixture of different peoples in the Caribbean.   7. Towns in Ireland, from which
part of the Jamaican population emigrated.   8. A coastal town in eastern Nigeria, which served as a slave
depot.   9. An African-derived ritual and the dance form associated with it.   1. The Abolition Decree
of August 1, 1934.   2. Note the play on the classical connotation of this place name—that is, the river
of forgetfulness in the underworld of Greek mythology (lines 38–39).   3. Darkness or richness.

again and swell to new deep, when the May rains
fall for certain. There was a surfeit once
of Swine in Fat Hog quarter and somehow
Chateau Vert slipped on the Twi[4] of our tongue   55
and fell to rise up again as "Shotover."

They hung Paul Bogle's[5] body at sea
so there is blood too in the sea, especially
at Bloody Bay where they punctured balloons
of great grey whales. There is Egypt here   60
at Catadupa, a name they spoke first softly
to the white falling cataracts of the Nile.
There is Amity and Friendship and Harmony Hall

Stonehenge, ... Sevens, Duppy Gate, Wait a Bit,
Wild Horses, Tan and See, Time and Patience,   65
Unity. It is Holy here, Mount Moses
dew falls upon Mount Nebo, south of Jordan,
Mount Nebo, rises here too hola Mount Zion high.
Paradise is found here, from Pisgah we look out
and Wait a Bit Wild Horses, Tan and See Time and Patience.   70

Unity, for the wounded a Doctor's Cave
and at Phoenix Park from Burnt Ground new rising.
Good Hope, the mornings dawn crystalline
at Cape Clear. It is good for brethren
and sistren to dwell together in Unity   75
on Mount Pleasant. Doctor Breezes issue from the side
of the sea across parishes[6] named for saints.

Rivers can be tied together in eights.
Mountains are Lapis Lazuli or Sapphire[7]
impossibly blue and rivers wag their waters   80
or flow Black or White or of Milk.
And the waters of the Fish River do contain
and will yield up good eating fish. O heart
when some night you cannot sleep

for wondering why you have been charged   85
to keep some things of which you cannot speak,
think what release will mean, when your name
is changed to Tranquility. I was born at Lineen—
Jubilee!—on the anniversary of Emancipation Day.[8]
I recite these names in a rosary, speak them   90
when I pray, for Heartease, my Mecca, aye Jamaica.

---

4. Another name for the Ashanti language.   5. In October 1865 he led the Morant Bay Rebellion, a
weeklong uprising against British authorities in Jamaica. Within the week he was captured and executed.
6. Administration areas, similar to counties.   7. Blue gemstones; a reference to the Blue Mountains of
Jamaica.   8. See n. 1, p. 3133.

Guinea[1] Woman

Great grandmother
was a guinea woman
wide eyes turning
the corners of her face
could see behind her,   5
her cheeks dusted with
a fine rash of jet-bead warts
that itched when the rain set up.

Great grandmother's waistline
the span of a headman's hand,   10
slender and tall like a cane stalk
with a guinea woman's antelope-quick walk
and when she paused,
her gaze would look to sea[2]
her profile fine like some obverse impression   15
on a guinea coin from royal memory.[3]

It seems her fate was anchored
in the unfathomable sea
for great grandmother caught the eye of a sailor
whose ship sailed without him from Lucea harbor.   20
Great grandmother's royal scent of
cinnamon and scallions
drew the sailor up the straits of Africa,
the evidence my blue-eyed grandmother
the first Mulatta,[4]   25
taken into backra's[5] household
and covered with his name.
They forbade great grandmother's
guinea woman presence.
They washed away her scent of   30
cinnamon and scallions,
controlled the child's antelope walk,
and called her uprisings rebellions.

But, great grandmother,
I see your features blood dark   35
appearing
in the children of each new
breeding.
The high yellow brown
is darkening down.   40
Listen, children,
it's great grandmother's turn.

---

1. A general term for the West African coast.   2. That is, to Africa. In Caribbean folk belief, the souls
of slaves who died went back to Africa.   3. A reference to both the idea of the great-grandmother's noble
ancestry and the coin struck for the British royal family from pure gold obtained from mines in West Africa.
4. Person of mixed blood (Spanish, feminine form).   5. White man, master (Jamaican).

"I Shall Light a Candle of Understanding in Thine Heart Which Shall Not Be Put Out"

—Esdras[1]

I shall light.
First debts to pay and fences to mend,
lay to rest the wounded past, foes disguised as friends.

I shall light a candle of understanding

Cease the training of impossible hedges round this life   5
for as fast as you sow them, serendipity's thickets will appear and
outgrow them.

I shall light a candle of understanding in thine heart.

All things in their place then, in this many-chambered heart.
For each thing a place and for HIM a place apart.   10

I shall light a candle of understanding in thine heart
which shall not be put out.

By the hand that lit the candle.
By the never to be extinguished flame.
By the candle-wax which wind-worried drips   15
into candle wings luminous and rare.
By the illumination of that candle
exit, death and fear and doubt,
here love and possibility
within a lit heart, shining out.   20

Heartease II[1]

In what looked like the blackout[2] last week
a meteorite burst from the breast of the sky
smoking like a censer, it spelled out in
incandescent calligraphy
a message for all who had deep eyes.   5

If you did not see it I'll tell you what
it said:
Cultivate the search-mi-heart[3] and
acres of sincerity grass and turn your
face towards Heartease.   10

Set out a wash pan and catch mercy rain[4]
forget bout drought, catch the mercy rain,
bathe and catch a light from this meteoric flame
and sit down cleansed, to tell a rosary of your
ancestor's names,   15

---

1. The title is taken from Esdras II, 14.25—an apocryphal book in the Bible.   1. Heartease is a Jamaican place name.   2. A reference to the frequent power outages, common in developing countries.
3. Introspection.   4. In homes without plumbing, rainwater is collected for storage and later use.

a singing chain of ancient names to bind them tight
all who work evil downward through the night.

> And toward morning the sun come and tell you
> "sleep, I'll mark your place with this azure / rose ribbon
> taken from the hidden locks of the dawn   20
> sleep in the day and you will dream when you sleep
> the second surah[5] of this message."

And who hear, do all that and sleep in the darkened day and
dream as them sleep, how the one whose hand draw the veil,
(for it was not a blackout) the one who fling the meteor   25
was in a celestial vexation
saying, Imagine, how I put you here so in this most favored place
and look how you take it and less count it.[6]
Look how you root up my rarest blooms,
look how you take my flower bed dem turn tombs,   30
look how you eye red from looking over a next one yard
from envying everything him have.
Like him concrete-stressed-cast-iron-lawn
and him man-made-robot-made-by-man-to-replace-man,
you want to know how far this thing gone?   35
Some calling Siberia a nice open land.
At this point it look like him was too grieved to go on
him had to drink some dew water from the throat
of a glass-petaled flower.
And when his wrath was dampened he spoke again: 40

I have many names and one is merciful . . .
So in that name I have decided that the veil I draw
will be lifted, when you look to the condition of
your part of this yard.[7]
When you stop draw blood cross the promise line in the   45
young people's palms.
When the scribes cleanse their hands and rise to write
new psalms.
When you sight up why outta the whole human race
is you of all people I choose to dwell in this place.   50
So who hear send me here to tell you say
we do not know bout the intentions of a next one
but we catching mercy rain in zinc and tub pan
and in addition
to the search-mi-heart   55
the sincerity seeds
and the pilgrimage to Heartease
we planting some one-love
undivided ever-living healing trees
and next week if you want to come, welcome   60
for we going to set up again
to extend the singing rosary of our ancestors' names
till the veil is rent from the eyes of the sky

5. A chapter in the Koran, the Muslim holy book.   6. That is, do not appreciate it.   7. A neighborhood
composed of adjoining households.

of everyone
forever and ever   65
illumination.

The Pictures of My New Day

The pictures of my new day
will now be colored, drawn,
by the tempera of first light
stored for me by a thoughtful dawn
who knew of my love for late sleeping.   5

Now, more than love on earth,
the untamed imaginings rooted under
my hair,
more than the sanded varnished scars
jeweled now I wear,   10
more than the silver life sign of survival
and the paid penance of poems,
this light.
It flared up one evening, a Sunday
towards seven.   15
I swear it descended a living shaft
of brightest light
lit from within by light.
And as if sighting the woman's love
of show   20
not content with the perfection of itself
perfect pole running floor to ceiling
to floor[1]
it spawned and spiraled from itself
ribbons and banners of light, more light.   25
I have seen it.

Heartease New England 1987

I see a bird trapped
under the iron girders of the Ashmont station[1] overpass.
It is trying to measure the distance between columns
with its given wing span, and it fails
for being alone and not having a wing span wide enough.   5
I am told that birds travel faster over greater distances
when they move in chevron formation[2]
a group of birds could measure the width of the Ashmont
station overpass . . . I know how the bird feels.

---

1. Possible reference to the central pole (*poteau mitan*) in Haitian cult houses, around which vodun (voo-
doo) rituals are celebrated.   1. In Boston.   2. That is, in a V-formation, which apparently facilitates
communication within the group.

I have come to see the backyards of the richest lands   10
on earth, their basements, their backrooms,
I have seen the poor asleep in carcasses of rooms.
Those who sleep together are fortunate
not to be one of the ultimate dispossessed
the truly homeless are usually alone   15
and tend to wakefulness.
In the fall I search for signs
a pattern in the New England flaming trees
"What is my mission? Speak, leaves"
(for all journeys have hidden missions).   20
The trees before dying, only flame brighter
maybe that is the answer, live glowing while you can.

That is the only answer, except one evening in November
I see an African in Harvard Square.
He is telling himself a story as he walks   25
in telling it, he takes all the parts
and I see that he has taken himself home.
And I have stories too, until I tell them
I will not find release, that is my mission.
Some nights though, anxiety assails me   30
a shroud spinning in the snow.
They say it's the affliction of this age,
it appears unasked, an unwelcome companion
who always wants you
to sit down and die with him   35
when for your own good you should keep going.
I know how the bird trying to measure the overpass
feels.
I too can never quite get the measure of this world's structure
somewhere I belong to community, there   40
I am part of a grouping of many souls and galaxies
I am part of something ever evolving, familiar, and most mighty
I reaffirm this knowing one evening, a Wednesday
as I go up Shephard Street.[3] Someone is playing
Bob Marley[4] and the notes are levitating   45
across the Garden Street end of the street.
They appear first as notes and then feather into birds
pointing their wings, arranging themselves for traveling
long distances.
And birds are the soul's symbol, so I see   50
that I am only a sojourner here but I came as friend
came to record and sing and then, depart.
For my mission this last life is certainly this
to be the sojourner poet caroling for peace
calling lost souls to the way of Heartease.   55

---

3. In Cambridge, Massachusetts, where Harvard University is located.   4. Popular Jamaican musician
(1945–1981), who helped to make reggae music world famous.

Mother the Great Stones Got to Move

Mother, one stone is wedged across the hole in our history
and sealed with blood wax.
In this hole is our side of the story, exact figures,
headcounts, burial artifacts, documents, lists, maps
showing our way up through the stars; lockets of brass   5
containing all textures of hair clippings.
It is the half that has never been told, some of us
must tell it.

Mother, there is the stone on the hearts of some women and men
something like an onyx, cabochon-cut[1]   10
which hung on the wearer seeds bad dreams. Speaking for the small
dreamers of this earth, plagued with nightmares, yearning
for healing dreams
we want that stone to move.

Upon an evening like this, mother, when one year is making way   15
for another, in a ceremony attended by a show of silver stars,[2]
mothers see the moon, milk-fed, herself a nursing mother
and we think of our children and the stones upon their future
and we want these stones to move.

For the year going out came in fat at first   20
but towards the harvest it grew lean.
And many mouth corners gathered white[3]
and another kind of poison, powdered white
was brought in to replace what was green.
And death sells it with one hand   25
and with the other death palms a gun
then death gets death's picture
in the papers asking,
"where does all this death come from?"
Mother, stones are pillows   30
for the homeless sleep on concrete sheets.
Stone flavors soap, stone is now meat,
the hard-hearted giving our children
stones to eat.

Mother, the great stones over mankind got to move.   35
It's been ten thousand years we've been watching them now
from various points in the universe.
From the time of our birth as points of light
in the eternal coiled workings of the cosmos.
Roll away stone of poisoned powders come   40
to blot out the hope of our young.
Move stone of sacrificial lives we breed
to feed to tribalistic economic machines.
From across the pathway to mount morning

---

1. That is, cut in a round, convex shape. *Onyx:* a translucent quartz stone, usually black or red.
2. Fireworks to celebrate the new year.   3. From undernourishment and hunger.

site of the rose quartz fountain　　　　　　　　　45
brimming anise[4] and star water
bright fragrant for our children's future.
Mother these great stones got to move.

4. A licorice-tasting herb used in drinks and medicines.

LESLIE MARMON SILKO
born 1948

Novelist, poet, memoirist, and writer of short fiction, Leslie Marmon Silko, within the confines of a single work, can comfortably alternate between prose and poetry in a manner reminiscent of the traditional Native American narrators from whom she descends. Among her primary concerns as an artist are the continuity of native tradition and the power of ancient forces to govern modern life. The people of whom she writes draw vitality from the mysterious personifications that represent the land; and reciprocally, the land maintains, or regains, its freshness through prescribed contact with its human tenants. Conflict, illness, and despair are traced to a disharmony between people and nature, sometimes recognizable in the form of witchcraft. Such trouble is as old as time itself and perhaps ineradicable. For healing to take place, at least temporarily, the disharmony and its perpetrators must be removed. It follows that modern evils are neither caused nor cured by Western civilization. The West simply does not have that power. Control, then, rests in the hands of those who harness the energies of native thought. The techniques involve ritual and, especially, storytelling. Since the latter implies a mixture of humor and detachment, it is understandable that Silko's work, for all its seriousness and its lyricism, is marked by a touch of irreverence. She is well acquainted with the proverbial trickster, Coyote, and has demonstrated that she herself is an accomplished live teller of Coyote tales. But storytelling holds more than amusement. "I will tell you something about stories," protests an unnamed voice in one of her novels. "They aren't just entertainment. Don't be fooled."

Storytelling has deep roots. But if a story is to be viable it must be constantly reshaped; and Silko is an unabashed reshaper. Her view of tradition as an ever-shifting body of knowledge, responsive to new influences even if deeply planted, is objectively correct, yet it may also be said to emerge from her personal background. She has written:

> My family are the Marmons at Old Laguna on the Laguna Pueblo Reservation where I grew up. We are mixed bloods—Laguna, Mexican, white—but the way we live is like Marmons, and if you are from Laguna Pueblo you will understand what I mean. All those languages, all those ways of living are combined, and we live somewhere on the fringes of all three. But I don't apologize for this any more—not to whites, not to full bloods—our origin is unlike any other. My poetry, my storytelling rise out this source.

She has also written: "I grew up at Laguna Pueblo. I am of mixed-breed ancestry, but what I know is Laguna. This place I am from is everything I am as a writer and human being."

Situated on a knoll above the San José River, forty miles west of the Rio Grande, Laguna Pueblo, like its near neighbor Acoma, is one of the Keresan-speaking communities of northern New Mexico. In existence at its present site since the 1400s, it has absorbed migrants from other Keresan towns and from among the Zuni, Hopi, and Navajo. In the 1860s and 1870s, two surveyors from Ohio, first Walter Marmon and, a little later, his brother, Robert, both government employees, settled in Laguna and married Laguna women. The Marmons wrote a constitution for Laguna, modeled after the U.S. Constitution, and each served a term as governor of the pueblo, an office never before held by a nonnative. The second of the two Marmons to arrive in Laguna, Robert Gunn Marmon, was the great-grandfather of Leslie Marmon Silko.

Born in Albuquerque on March 5, 1948, Silko spent her early years at Laguna, attending Laguna Day School until fifth grade, when she was transferred to Manzano Day School, a small private school in Albuquerque. Between 1964 and 1969 she attended the University of New Mexico (where she earned a B.A. in English), married, and gave birth to the first of her two sons, Cazimir Silko. During these years she published her first story, *Tony's Story*, a provocative tale of witchery and renewal that foreshadowed her masterwork, *Ceremony*, which would not appear for another decade.

Following graduation, she stayed on at the university and taught courses in creative writing and oral literature. After giving birth to her second son, Robert William Chapman, she studied for three semesters in the university's American Indian Law Program, with the intention of filing native land claims. In 1971 a National Endowment for the Arts Discovery Grant changed her mind about law school, and she quit to devote herself to writing. Seven of her stories, including *Yellow Woman*, were published in 1974 in a collection edited by Kenneth Rosen—*The Man to Send Rain Clouds: Contemporary Stories by American Indians*. It was from this that her reputation began to build.

The novel *Ceremony*, her first large-scale work, appeared in 1977. Widely hailed, it propelled her into the front rank of a growing legion of indigenous writers in the United States whose combined activity would now be recognized as a Native American renaissance. This group's success in winning critical attention and a broad audience would be comparable to the earlier "boom" in Latin American letters that had brought acclaim to such writers as Jorge Luis Borges and Gabriel García Márquez. The Kiowa novelist N. Scott Momaday, whose *House Made of Dawn* had won the Pulitzer Prize in 1969, was already being viewed as the father of the new movement; and the prolific, talented Louise Erdrich, of Chippewa descent, would eventually be accorded its greatest commercial success. But it was Silko—and *Ceremony*—that enabled the movement to come of age.

Though of average length, *Ceremony* is an extremely complex novel; it has two casts of characters, one predominantly male and human, the other female-dominated and intimately connected to the landscape. It is a story of illness and healing, witchery and exorcism, drought and revivification, with political overtones that acknowledge the influence of nonnative society without permitting this to overwhelm or even direct the inner core of native experience. *Ceremony* is a love story but of a special Native American kind that connects the human and nonhuman worlds, transferring power from nature to culture. With a sure grasp of its material, the novel rolls to its conclusion, sweeping up smaller, parablelike stories along the way, creating a many-chambered vehicle that energizes subplots as well as the larger story.

On the strength of *Ceremony*, Silko in 1981 was awarded a MacArthur Fellowship. That same year she brought out a second large work, *Storyteller*, combining previously published poems and short stories (including *Yellow Woman*) with new material in an arrangement one critic has called an autobiography. It is at least partly that, partly a tribute to Laguna, and partly a showcase in which her earlier work, contextualized, takes on a deeper significance.

Another result of *Ceremony* had been the opportunity to teach at the University of Arizona in Tucson. But with the MacArthur grant Silko was able to withdraw from teaching and (while continuing to live in Tucson) concentrate on an ambitious new writing project. Virtually silent for ten years, as rumors of a major new novel kept building, Silko in due course brought forth *The Almanac of the Dead* (1991). An ocean of story, spreading far beyond Laguna Pueblo to embrace all of North America, including Mexico, Silko's largest work documents the imagined history of an American apocalypse. Inspired by prophetic texts ranging from the Maya Books of Chilam Balam to the songs of the Plains Ghost Dance, native people in league with the spirits of their ancestors conspire to heal the American land and rid it of alien influence. As the various stories converge and the millennium draws near, an irresistible army led by twin heroes, newly emerged from ancient Native American tradition, marches northward out of Mexico to reclaim the continent. In the words of one critic the novel is a "wild, jarring, graphic, mordant, prodigious book" with "genius in the sheer, tireless variousness of its interconnecting tales."

Over the years, as Silko's work has expanded and deepened, one of her shortest and earliest pieces, *Yellow Woman,* has continued to grow in esteem. Often reprinted, it became the subject of a volume of critical essays published in 1993. In traditional Laguna lore Yellow Woman is either the heroine or a minor character in a wide range of tales. Occasionally Yellow Woman is mentioned together with her three sisters, Blue Woman, Red Woman, and White Woman, thus completing the four colors of corn. But although she may originally have been a corn spirit, she eventually became a kind of Everywoman. In fact, a traditional Laguna prayer-song, recited at the naming ceremony for a newborn daughter, begins, "Yellow Woman is born, Yellow Woman is born." In narrative lore, however, Yellow Woman most frequently appears in tales of abduction, where she is said to have been captured by a strange man at a stream while she is fetching water. Her captor, who carries her off to another world, is sometimes a kachina, or ancestral spirit; and when at last she returns to her home she is imbued with new power that proves of value for her people. In Silko's version, these traditional elements are constantly in the foreground. Or are they merely in the background? The story's ambiguity, frequently commented on by critics, is the source of its fascination.

Melody Graulich, ed., *"Yellow Woman": Leslie Marmon Silko* (1993), is a collection of pertinent critical essays. The story itself is profitably read, or reread, in Silko's *Storyteller* (1981), where it appears in context with several of her other short pieces on the Yellow Woman theme. *Yellow Woman* and other works are treated in Louise K. Barnett and James L. Thorson, eds., *Leslie Marmon Silko: A Collection of Critical Essays* (1999). Peter G. Beidler, noting that Silko was only twenty when she wrote *Yellow Woman,* includes eight short undergraduate essays on the subject in his article "Silko's Originality in 'Yellow Woman,'" *Studies in American Indian Literatures* (summer 1996): 61–84. For traditional texts on Yellow Woman and other figures in Laguna mythology, the best source is Franz Boas, *Keresan Texts* (1928); the stories in Boas's volume were obtained in 1919–21 from several Laguna informants, including Leslie Silko's great-grandfather, Robert Marmon.

PRONOUNCING GLOSSARY

The following list uses common English syllables and stress accents to provide rough equivalents of selected words whose pronunciation may be unfamiliar to the general reader.

kachina: *kuh-chee'-nuh*   Keres: *kay'-ruhs*

ka'tsina: *kuht-see'-nuh*

Yellow Woman

My thigh clung to his with dampness, and I watched the sun rising up through the tamaracks and willows. The small brown water birds came to the river and hopped across the mud, leaving brown scratches in the alkali-white crust. They bathed in the river silently. I could hear the water, almost at our feet where the narrow fast channel bubbled and washed green ragged moss and fern leaves. I looked at him beside me, rolled in the red blanket on the white river sand. I cleaned the sand out of the cracks between my toes, squinting because the sun was above the willow trees. I looked at him for the last time, sleeping on the white river sand.

I felt hungry and followed the river south the way we had come the afternoon before, following our footprints that were already blurred by lizard tracks and bug trails. The horses were still lying down, and the black one whinnied when he saw me but he did not get up—maybe it was because the corral was made out of thick cedar branches and the horses had not yet felt the sun like I had. I tried to look beyond the pale red mesas to the pueblo. I knew it was there, even if I could not see it, on the sandrock hill above the river, the same river that moved past me now and had reflected the moon last night.

The horse felt warm underneath me. He shook his head and pawed the sand. The bay whinnied and leaned against the gate trying to follow, and I remembered him asleep in the red blanket beside the river. I slid off the horse and tied him close to the other horse, I walked north with the river again, and the white sand broke loose in footprints over footprints.

"Wake up."

He moved in the blanket and turned his face to me with his eyes still closed. I knelt down to touch him.

"I'm leaving."

He smiled now, eyes still closed. "You are coming with me, remember?" He sat up now with his bare dark chest and belly in the sun.

"Where?"

"To my place."

"And will I come back?"

He pulled his pants on. I walked away from him, feeling him behind me and smelling the willows.

"Yellow Woman," he said.

I turned to face him. "Who are you?" I asked.

He laughed and knelt on the low, sandy bank, washing his face in the river. "Last night you guessed my name, and you knew why I had come."

I stared past him at the shallow moving water and tried to remember the night, but I could only see the moon in the water and remember his warmth around me.

"But I only said that you were him and that I was Yellow Woman—I'm not really her—I have my own name and I come from the pueblo on the other side of the mesa. Your name is Silva and you are a stranger I met by the river yesterday afternoon."

He laughed softly. "What happened yesterday has nothing to do with what you will do today, Yellow Woman."

"I know—that's what I'm saying—the old stories about the ka'tsina[1] spirit and Yellow Woman can't mean us."

My old grandpa liked to tell those stories best. There is one about Badger

---

1. Kachina, an ancestral spirit.

and Coyote who went hunting and were gone all day, and when the sun was going down they found a house. There was a girl living there alone, and she had light hair and eyes and she told them that they could sleep with her. Coyote wanted to be with her all night so he sent Badger into a prairie-dog hole, telling him he thought he saw something in it. As soon as Badger crawled in, Coyote blocked up the entrance with rocks and hurried back to Yellow Woman.

"Come here," he said gently.

He touched my neck and I moved close to him to feel his breathing and to hear his heart. I was wondering if Yellow Woman had known who she was—if she knew that she would become part of the stories. Maybe she'd had another name that her husband and relatives called her so that only the ka'tsina from the north and the storytellers would know her as Yellow Woman. But I didn't go on; I felt him all around me, pushing me down into the white river sand.

Yellow Woman went away with the spirit from the north and lived with him and his relatives. She was gone for a long time, but then one day she came back and she brought twin boys.

"Do you know the story?"

"What story?" He smiled and pulled me close to him as he said this. I was afraid lying there on the red blanket. All I could know was the way he felt, warm, damp, his body beside me. This is the way it happens in the stories, I was thinking, with no thought beyond the moment she meets the ka'tsina spirit and they go.

"I don't have to go. What they tell in stories was real only then, back in time immemorial, like they say."

He stood up and pointed at my clothes tangled in the blanket. "Let's go," he said.

I walked beside him, breathing hard because he walked fast, his hand around my wrist. I had stopped trying to pull away from him, because his hand felt cool and the sun was high, drying the river bed into alkali. I will see someone, eventually I will see someone, and then I will be certain that he is only a man—some man from nearby—and I will be sure that I am not Yellow Woman. Because she is from out of time past and I live now and I've been to school and there are highways and pickup trucks that Yellow Woman never saw.

It was an easy ride north on horseback. I watched the change from the cottonwood trees along the river to the junipers that brushed past us in the foothills, and finally there were only piñons, and when I looked up at the rim of the mountain plateau I could see pine trees growing on the edge. Once I stopped to look down, but the pale sandstone had disappeared and the river was gone and the dark lava hills were all around. He touched my hand, not speaking, but always singing softly a mountain song and looking into my eyes.

I felt hungry and wondered what they were doing at home now—my mother, my grandmother, my husband, and the baby. Cooking breakfast, saying, "Where did she go?—maybe kidnapped." And Al going to the tribal police with the details: "She went walking along the river."

The house was made with black lava rock and red mud. It was high above the spreading miles of arroyos and long mesas. I smelled a mountain smell of pitch and buck brush. I stood there beside the black horse, looking down on the small, dim country we had passed, and I shivered.

"Yellow Woman, come inside where it's warm."

He lit a fire in the stove. It was an old stove with a round belly and an enamel coffeepot on top. There was only the stove, some faded Navajo blankets, and a bedroll and cardboard box. The floor was made of smooth adobe plaster, and there was one small window facing east. He pointed at the box.

"There's some potatoes and the frying pan." He sat on the floor with his arms around his knees pulling them close to his chest and he watched me fry the potatoes. I didn't mind him watching me because he was always watching me—he had been watching me since I came upon him sitting on the river bank trimming leaves from a willow twig with his knife. We ate from the pan and he wiped the grease from his fingers on his Levi's.

"Have you brought women here before?" He smiled and kept chewing, so I said, "Do you always use the same tricks?"

"What tricks?" He looked at me like he didn't understand.

"The story about being a ka'tsina from the mountains. The story about Yellow Woman."

Silva was silent; his face was calm.

"I don't believe it. Those stories couldn't happen now," I said.

He shook his head and said softly, "But someday they will talk about us, and they will say, 'Those two lived long ago when things like that happened.' "

He stood up and went out. I ate the rest of the potatoes and thought about things—about the noise the stove was making and the sound of the mountain wind outside. I remembered yesterday and the day before, and then I went outside.

I walked past the corral to the edge where the narrow trail cut through the black rim rock. I was standing in the sky with nothing around me but the wind that came down from the blue mountain peak behind me. I could see faint mountain images in the distance miles across the vast spread of mesas and valleys and plains. I wondered who was over there to feel the mountain wind on those sheer blue edges—who walks on the pine needles in those blue mountains.

"Can you see the pueblo?" Silva was standing behind me.

I shook my head. "We're too far away."

"From here I can see the world." He stepped out on the edge. "The Navajo reservation begins over there." He pointed to the east. "The Pueblo boundaries are over here." He looked below us to the south, where the narrow trail seemed to come from. "The Texans have their ranches over there, starting with that valley, the Concho Valley. The Mexicans run some cattle over there too."

"Do you ever work for them?"

"I steal from them," Silva answered. The sun was dropping behind us and the shadows were filling the land below. I turned away from the edge that dropped forever into the valleys below.

"I'm cold," I said, "I'm going inside." I started wondering about this man who could speak the Pueblo language so well but who lived on a mountain and rustled cattle. I decided that this man Silva must be Navajo, because Pueblo men didn't do things like that.

"You must be a Navajo."

Silva shook his head gently. "Little Yellow Woman," he said, "you never give up, do you? I have told you who I am. The Navajo people know me, too." He knelt down and unrolled the bedroll and spread the extra blankets out on a piece of canvas. The sun was down, and the only light in the house came from outside—the dim orange light from sundown.

I stood there and waited for him to crawl under the blankets.

"What are you waiting for?" he said, and I lay down beside him. He undressed me slowly like the night before beside the river—kissing my face gently and running his hands up and down my belly and legs. He took off my pants and then he laughed.

"Why are you laughing?"

"You are breathing so hard."

I pulled away from him and turned my back to him.

He pulled me around and pinned me down with his arms and chest. "You don't understand, do you, little Yellow Woman? You will do what I want."

And again he was all around me with his skin slippery against mine, and I was afraid because I understood that his strength could hurt me. I lay underneath him and I knew that he could destroy me. But later, while he slept beside me, I touched his face and I had a feeling—the kind of feeling for him that overcame me that morning along the river. I kissed him on the forehead and he reached out for me.

When I woke up in the morning he was gone. It gave me a strange feeling because for a long time I sat there on the blankets and looked around the little house for some object of his—some proof that he had been there or maybe that he was coming back. Only the blankets and the cardboard box remained. The .30-30 that had been leaning in the corner was gone, and so was the knife I had used the night before. He was gone, and I had my chance to go now. But first I had to eat, because I knew it would be a long walk home.

I found some dried apricots in the cardboard box, and I sat down on a rock at the edge of the plateau rim. There was no wind and the sun warmed me. I was surrounded by silence. I drowsed with apricots in my mouth, and I didn't believe that there were highways or railroads or cattle to steal.

When I woke up, I stared down at my feet in the black mountain dirt. Little black ants were swarming over the pine needles around my foot. They must have smelled the apricots. I thought about my family far below me. They would be wondering about me, because this had never happened to me before. The tribal police would file a report. But if old Grandpa weren't dead he would tell them what happened—he would laugh and say, "Stolen by a ka'tsina, a mountain spirit. She'll come home—they usually do." There are enough of them to handle things. My mother and grandmother will raise the baby like they raised me. Al will find someone else, and they will go on like before, except that there will be a story about the day I disappeared while I was walking along the river. Silva had come for me; he said he had. I did not decide to go. I just went. Moonflowers blossom in the sand hills before dawn, just as I followed him. That's what I was thinking as I wandered along the trail through the pine trees.

It was noon when I got back. When I saw the stone house I remembered that I had meant to go home. But that didn't seem important any more, maybe because there were little blue flowers growing in the meadow behind the stone house and the gray squirrels were playing in the pines next to the house. The horses were standing in the corral, and there was a beef carcass hanging on the shady side of a big pine in front of the house. Flies buzzed around the clotted blood that hung from the carcass. Silva was washing his hands in a bucket full of water. He must have heard me coming because he spoke to me without turning to face me.

"I've been waiting for you."

"I went walking in the big pine trees."

I looked into the bucket full of bloody water with brown-and-white animal hairs floating in it. Silva stood there letting his hand drip, examining me intently.

"Are you coming with me?"

"Where?" I asked him.

"To sell the meat in Marquez."

"If you're sure it's O.K."

"I wouldn't ask you if it wasn't," he answered.

He sloshed the water around in the bucket before he dumped it out and set the bucket upside down near the door. I followed him to the corral and watched him saddle the horses. Even beside the horses he looked tall, and I asked him again if he wasn't Navajo. He didn't say anything; he just shook his head and kept cinching up the saddle.

"But Navajos are tall."

"Get on the horse," he said, "and let's go."

The last thing he did before we started down the steep trail was to grab the .30-30 from the corner. He slid the rifle into the scabbard that hung from his saddle.

"Do they ever try to catch you?" I asked.

"They don't know who I am."

"Then why did you bring the rifle?"

"Because we are going to Marquez where the Mexicans live."

The trail leveled out on a narrow ridge that was steep on both sides like an animal spine. On one side I could see where the trail went around the rocky gray hills and disappeared into the southeast where the pale sandrock mesas stood in the distance near my home. On the other side was a trail that went west, and as I looked far into the distance I thought I saw the little town. But Silva said no, that I was looking in the wrong place, that I just thought I saw houses. After that I quit looking off into the distance; it was hot and the wildflowers were closing up their deep-yellow petals. Only the waxy cactus flowers bloomed in the bright sun, and I saw every color that a cactus blossom can be; the white ones and the red ones were still buds, but the purple and the yellow were blossoms, open full and the most beautiful of all.

Silva saw him before I did. The white man was riding a big gray horse, coming up the trail towards us. He was traveling fast and the gray horse's feet sent rocks rolling off the trail into the dry tumbleweeds. Silva motioned for me to stop and we watched the white man. He didn't see us right away, but finally his horse whinnied at our horses and he stopped. He looked at us briefly before he lapped the gray horse across the three hundred yards that separated us. He stopped his horse in front of Silva, and his young fat face was shadowed by the brim of his hat. He didn't look mad, but his small, pale eyes moved from the blood-soaked gunny sacks hanging from my saddle to Silva's face and then back to my face.

"Where did you get the fresh meat?" the white man asked.

"I've been hunting," Silva said, and when he shifted his weight in the saddle the leather creaked.

"The hell you have, Indian. You've been rustling cattle. We've been looking for the thief for a long time."

The rancher was fat, and sweat began to soak through his white cowboy shirt and the wet cloth stuck to the thick rolls of belly fat. He almost seemed to be panting from the exertion of talking, and he smelled rancid, maybe because Silva scared him.

Silva turned to me and smiled. "Go back up the mountain, Yellow Woman."

The white man got angry when he heard Silva speak in a language he couldn't understand. "Don't try anything, Indian. Just keep riding to Marquez. We'll call the state police from there."

The rancher must have been unarmed because he was very frightened and if he had a gun he would have pulled it out then. I turned my horse around and the rancher yelled, "Stop!" I looked at Silva for an instant and there was something ancient and dark—something I could feel in my stomach—in his eyes, and when I glanced at his hand I saw his finger on the trigger of the .30-30 that was still in the saddle scabbard. I slapped my horse across the flank and the sacks of raw meat swung against my knees as the horse leaped up the trail. It was hard to keep my balance, and once I thought I felt the saddle slipping backward; it was because of this that I could not look back.

I didn't stop until I reached the ridge where the trail forked. The horse was breathing deep gasps and there was a dark film of sweat on its neck. I looked down in the direction I had come from, but I couldn't see the place. I waited. The wind came up and pushed warm air past me. I looked up at the sky, pale blue and full of thin clouds and fading vapor trails left by jets.

I think four shots were fired—I remember hearing four hollow explosions that reminded me of deer hunting. There could have been more shots after that, but I couldn't have heard them because my horse was running again and the loose rocks were making too much noise as they scattered around his feet.

Horses have a hard time running downhill, but I went that way instead of uphill to the mountain because I thought it was safer. I felt better with the horse running southeast past the round gray hills that were covered with cedar trees and black lava rock. When I got to the plain in the distance I could see the dark green patches of tamaracks that grew along the river; and beyond the river I could see the beginning of the pale sandrock mesas. I stopped the horse and looked back to see if anyone was coming; then I got off the horse and turned the horse around, wondering if it would go back to its corral under the pines on the mountain. It looked back at me for a moment and then plucked a mouthful of green tumbleweeds before it trotted back up the trail with its ears pointed forward, carrying its head daintily to one side to avoid stepping on the dragging reins. When the horse disappeared over the last hill, the gunny sacks full of meat were still swinging and bouncing.

I walked toward the river on a wood-hauler's road that I knew would eventually lead to the paved road. I was thinking about waiting beside the road for someone to drive by, but by the time I got to the pavement I had decided it wasn't very far to walk if I followed the river back the way Silva and I had come.

The river water tasted good, and I sat in the shade under a cluster of silvery willows. I thought about Silva, and I felt sad at leaving him; still, there was something strange about him, and I tried to figure it out all the way back home.

I came back to the place on the river bank where he had been sitting the first time I saw him. The green willow leaves that he had trimmed from the branch were still lying there, wilted in the sand. I saw the leaves and I wanted to go back to him—to kiss him and to touch him—but the mountains were too far away now. And I told myself, because I believe it, he will come back sometime and be waiting again by the river.

I followed the path up from the river into the village. The sun was getting low, and I could smell supper cooking when I got to the screen door of my house. I could hear their voices inside—my mother was telling my grandmother how to fix the Jell-O and my husband, Al, was playing with the baby. I decided to tell them that some Navajo had kidnaped me, but I was sorry that old Grandpa wasn't alive to hear my story because it was the Yellow Woman stories he liked to tell best.

A Note on Translation

Reading literature in translation is a pleasure on which it is fruitless to frown. The purist may insist that we ought always read in the original languages, and we know ideally that this is true. But it is a counsel of perfection, quite impractical even for the purist, since no one in a lifetime can master all the languages whose literatures it would be a joy to explore. Master languages as fast as we may, we shall always have to read to some extent in translation, and this means we must be alert to what we are about: if in reading a work of literature in translation we are not reading the "original," what precisely are we reading? This is a question of great complexity, to which justice cannot be done in a brief note, but the following sketch of some of the considerations may be helpful.

One of the memorable scenes of ancient literature is the meeting of Hector and Andromache in Book VI of Homer's *Iliad*. Hector, leader and mainstay of the armies defending Troy, is implored by his wife Andromache to withdraw within the city walls and carry on the defense from there, where his life will not be constantly at hazard. In Homer's text her opening words to him are these: δαιμόνιε, φθίσει σε τὸ σὸν μένος (daimonie, phthisei se to son menos). How should they be translated into English?

Here is how they have actually been translated into English by capable translators, at various periods, in verse and prose:

1. George Chapman, 1598:

> O noblest in desire,
> Thy mind, inflamed with others' good, will set thy self on fire.

2. John Dryden, 1693:

> Thy dauntless heart (which I foresee too late),
> Too daring man, will urge thee to thy fate.

3. Alexander Pope, 1715:

> Too daring Prince! . . .
> For sure such courage length of life denies,
> And thou must fall, thy virtue's sacrifice.

4. William Cowper, 1791:

> Thy own great courage will cut short thy days,
> My noble Hector. . .

5. Lang, Leaf, and Myers, 1883 (prose):

> Dear my lord, this thy hardihood will undo thee. . . .

6. A. T. Murray, 1924 (prose):

> Ah, my husband, this prowess of thine will be thy doom. . . .

7. E. V. Rieu, 1950 (prose):

"Hector," she said, "you are possessed. This bravery of yours will be your end."

8. I. A. Richards, 1950 (prose):

"Strange man," she said, "your courage will be your destruction."

9. Richmond Lattimore, 1951:

Dearest,
Your own great strength will be your death. . . .

10. Robert Fitzgerald, 1979:

O my wild one, your bravery will be
Your own undoing!

11. Robert Fagles, 1990:

reckless one,
Your own fiery courage will destroy you!

From these strikingly different renderings of the same six words, certain facts about the nature of translation begin to emerge. We notice, for one thing, that Homer's word μένος (menos) is diversified by the translators into "mind," "dauntless heart," "such courage," "great courage," "hardihood," "prowess," "bravery," "courage," "great strength," "bravery," and "fiery courage." The word has in fact all these possibilities. Used of things, it normally means "force"; of animals, "fierceness" or "brute strength" or (in the case of horses) "mettle"; of men and women, "passion" or "spirit" or even "purpose." Homer's application of it in the present case points our attention equally— whatever particular sense we may imagine Andromache to have uppermost—to Hector's force, strength, fierceness in battle, spirited heart and mind. But since English has no matching term of like inclusiveness, the passage as the translators give it to us reflects this lack and we find one attribute singled out to the exclusion of the rest.

Here then is the first and most crucial fact about any work of literature read in translation. It cannot escape the linguistic characteristics of the language into which it is turned: the grammatical, syntactical, lexical, and phonetic boundaries that constitute collectively the individuality or "genius" of that language. A Greek play or a Russian novel in English will be governed first of all by the resources of the English language, resources that are certain to be in every instance very different, as the efforts with μένος show, from those of the original.

Turning from μένος to δαιμόνιε (daimonie) in Homer's clause, we encounter a second crucial fact about translations. Nobody knows exactly what shade of meaning δαιμόνιε had for Homer. In later writers the word normally suggests divinity, something miraculous, wondrous; but in Homer it appears as a vocative of address for both chieftain and commoner, man and wife. The coloring one gives it must therefore be determined either by the way one thinks a Greek wife of Homer's era might actually address her husband (a subject on which we have no information whatever) or in the way one thinks it suitable for a hero's wife to address her husband in an epic poem, that is to say, a highly stylized and formal work. In general, the translators of our century will be seen to have abandoned formality to stress the intimacy; the wifeliness; and, especially in Lattimore's case, a certain chiding tenderness, in Andromache's appeal: (6) "Ah, my husband," (7) "Hector" (with perhaps a hint, in "you are possessed," of the alarmed distaste with which wives have so often viewed their husbands' bellicose moods), (8) "Strange man," (9) "Dearest," (10) "O my wild one" (mixing an almost motherly admiration with reproach and concern), and (11) "reckless one." On the other hand, the older translators have obviously removed Andromache to an epic or heroic distance from her beloved, whence she sees and kindles to his selfless courage, acknowledging, even in the moment of pleading with him to be otherwise, his moral grandeur and the tragic destiny this too certainly implies: (1) "O noblest in desire, . . . inflamed by others' good"; (2) "Thy dauntless heart (which I foresee too late), / Too daring man"; (3) "Too daring Prince! . . . / And thou must fall, thy virtue's sacrifice"; (4) "My noble Hector." Even the less specific "Dear my lord" of Lang, Leaf, and Myers looks in the same direction because of its echo of the speech of countless Shakespearean men and women who have shared this powerful moral sense: "Dear my lord, make me acquainted with your cause of grief"; "Perseverance, dear my lord, keeps honor bright"; etc.

The fact about translation that emerges from all this is that just as the translated work reflects the individuality of the language it is turned into, so it reflects the individuality of the age in which it is made, and the age will permeate it everywhere like yeast in dough. We think of one kind of permeation when we think of the governing verse forms and attitudes toward verse at a given epoch. In Chapman's time, experiments seeking an "heroic" verse form for English were widespread, and accordingly he tries a "fourteener" couplet (two rhymed lines of seven stresses each) in his *Iliad* and a pentameter couplet in his *Odyssey*. When Dryden and Pope wrote, a closed pentameter couplet had become established as the heroic form par excellence. By Cowper's day, thanks largely to the prestige of *Paradise Lost,* the couplet had gone out of fashion for narrative poetry in favor of blank verse. Our age, inclining to prose and in verse to proselike informalities and relaxations, has, predictably, produced half a dozen excellent prose translations of the *Iliad* but only three in verse (by Fagles, Lattimore, and Fitzgerald), all relying on rhythms that are much of the time closer to the verse of William Carlos Williams and some of the prose of novelists like Faulkner than to the swift firm tread of Homer's Greek. For if it is true that what we translate from a given work is what, wearing the spectacles of our time, we see in it, it is also true that we see in it what we have the power to translate.

Of course, there are other effects of the translator's epoch on a translation besides those exercised by contemporary taste in verse and verse forms. Chapman writes in a great age of poetic metaphor and, therefore, almost instinctively translates his understanding of Homer's verb $\phi\theta\iota\sigma\epsilon\iota$ (phthisei, "to cause to wane, consume, waste, pine") into metaphorical terms of flame, presenting his Hector to us as a man of burning generosity who will be consumed by his very ardor. This is a conception rooted in large part in the psychology of the Elizabethans, who had the habit of speaking of the soul as "fire," of one of the four temperaments as "fiery," of even the more material bodily processes, like digestion, as if they were carried on by the heat of fire ("concoction," "decoction"). It is rooted too in that characteristic Renaissance élan so unforgettably expressed in characters such as Tamburlaine and Dr. Faustus, the former of whom exclaims to the stars above:

> . . . I, the chiefest lamp of all the earth,
> First rising in the East with mild aspect,
> But fixèd now in the meridian line,
> Will send up fire to your turning spheres,
> And cause the sun to borrow light of you. . . .

Pope and Dryden, by contrast, write to audiences for whom strong metaphor has become suspect. They therefore reject the fire image (which we must recall is not present in the Greek) in favor of a form of speech more congenial to their age, the *sententia* or aphorism, and give it extra vitality by making it the scene of a miniature drama: in Dryden's case, the hero's dauntless heart "urges" him (in the double sense of physical as well as moral pressure) to his fate; in Pope's, the hero's courage, like a judge, "denies" continuance of life, with the consequence that he "falls"—and here Pope's second line suggests analogy to the sacrificial animal—the victim of his own essential nature, of what he is.

To pose even more graphically the pressures that a translator's period brings, consider the following lines from Hector's reply to Andromache's appeal that he withdraw, first in Chapman's Elizabethan version, then in Lattimore's twentieth-century one:

Chapman, 1598:

> The spirit I did first breathe
> Did never teach me that—much less since the contempt of death
> Was settled in me, and my mind knew what a Worthy was,
> Whose office is to lead in fight and give no danger pass
> Without improvement. In this fire must Hector's trial shine.
> Here must his country, father, friends be in him made divine.

Lattimore, 1951:

> and the spirit will not let me, since I have learned to be valiant
> and to fight always among the foremost ranks of the Trojans,
> winning for my own self great glory, and for my father.

If one may exaggerate to make a necessary point, the world of Henry V and Othello suddenly gives way here to our own, a world whose discomfort with any form of heroic self-assertion is remarkably mirrored in the burial of Homer's key terms (*spirit, valiant, fight, foremost, glory*)—five out of twenty-two words in the original, five out of thirty-six in the translation—in a cushioning huddle of harmless sounds.

Besides the two factors so far mentioned (language and period) as affecting the character of a translation, there is inevitably a third—the translator, with a particular degree of talent; a personal way of regarding the work to be translated; a special hierarchy of values, moral, aesthetic, metaphysical (which may or may not be summed up in a "worldview"); and a unique style or lack of it. But this influence all readers are likely to bear in mind, and it needs no laboring here. That, for example, two translators of Hamlet, one a Freudian, the other a Jungian, will produce impressively different translations is obvious from the fact that when Freudian and Jungian argue about the play in English they often seem to have different plays in mind.

We can now return to the question from which we started. After all allowances have been made for language, age, and individual translator, is anything of the original left? What, in short, does the reader of translations read? Let it be said at once that in utility prose—prose whose function is mainly referential—the reader who reads a translation reads everything that matters. "Nicht Rauchen," "Défense de Fumer," and "No Smoking," posted in a railway car, make their point, and the differences between them in sound and form have no significance for us in that context. Since the prose of a treatise and of most fiction is preponderantly referential, we rightly feel, when we have paid close attention to Cervantes or Montaigne or Machiavelli or Tolstoy in a good English translation, that we have had roughly the same experience as a native Spaniard, Frenchman, Italian, or Russian. But *roughly* is the correct word; for good prose points iconically *to* itself as well as referentially beyond itself, and everything that it points to in itself in the original (rhythms, sounds, idioms, wordplay, etc.) must alter radically in being translated. The best analogy is to imagine a Van Gogh painting reproduced in the medium of tempera, etching, or engraving: the "picture" remains, but the intricate interanimation of volumes with colorings with brushstrokes has disappeared.

When we move on to poetry, even in its longer narrative and dramatic forms—plays like *Oedipus*, poems like the *Iliad* or the *Divine Comedy*—our situation as English readers worsens appreciably, as the many unlike versions of Andromache's appeal to Hector make very clear. But, again, only appreciably. True, this is the point at which the fact that a translation is *always* an interpretation explodes irresistibly on our attention; but if it is the best translation of its time, like John Ciardi's translation of the *Divine Comedy* for our time, the result will be not only a sensitive interpretation but also a work with intrinsic interest in its own right—at very best, a true work of art, a new poem. In these longer works, moreover, even if the translation is uninspired, many distinctive structural features—plot, setting, characters, meetings, partings, confrontations, and specific episodes generally—survive virtually unchanged. Hence even in translation it remains both possible and instructive to compare, say, concepts of the heroic or attitudes toward women or uses of religious ritual among civilizations as various as those reflected in the *Iliad,* the *Mahābhārata, Beowulf,* and the epic of *Son-Jara.* It is only when the shorter, primarily lyrical forms of poetry are presented that the reader of translations faces insuperable disadvantage. In these forms, the referential aspect of language has a tendency to disappear into, or, more often, draw its real meaning and accreditation from, the iconic aspect. Let us look for just a moment at a brief poem by Federico García Lorca and its English translation (by Stephen Spender and J. L. Gili):

> ¡*Alto pinar!*
> *Cuatro palomas por el aire van.*
>
> *Cuatro palomas*
> *vuelan y tornan.*
> *Llevan heridas*
> *sus cuatro sombras.*
>
> ¡*Bajo pinar!*
> *Cuatro palomas en la tierra están.*
>
> Above the pine trees:
> Four pigeons go through the air.
>
> Four pigeons
> fly and turn round.
> They carry wounded
> their four shadows.
>
> Below the pine trees:
> Four pigeons lie on the earth.

In this translation the referential sense of the English words follows with remarkable exactness the referential sense of the Spanish words they replace. But the life of Lorca's poem does not lie in that sense. It lies in such matters as the abruptness, like an intake of breath at a sudden revelation, of the two exclamatory lines (1 and 7), which then exhale musically in images of flight and death; or as the echoings of *palomas* in *heridas* and *sombras,* bringing together (as in fact the hunter's gun has done) these unrelated nouns and the unrelated experiences they stand for in a sequence that seems, momentarily, to have all the logic of a tragic action, in which *doves* become *wounds* become *shadows,* or as the external and internal rhyming among the five verbs, as though all motion must (as in fact it must) end with *están.*

Since none of this can be brought over into another tongue (least of all Lorca's rhythms), the translator must decide between leaving a reader to wonder why Lorca is a poet to be bothered about at all and making a new but true poem, whose merit will almost certainly be in inverse ratio to its likeness to the original. Samuel Johnson made such a poem in translating Horace's famous *Diffugere nives,* and so did A. E. Housman. If we juxtapose the last two stanzas of each translation, and the corresponding Latin, we can see at a glance that each has the consistency and inner life of a genuine poem and that neither of them (even if we consider only what is obvious to the eye, the line-lengths) is very close to Horace:

> *Cum semel occideris, et de te splendida Minos*
> *fecerit arbitria,*

> non, Torquate, genus, non te facundia, non te
>   restituet pietas.
>
> Infernis neque enim tenebris Diana pudicum
>   liberat Hippolytum
> nec Lethaea valet Theseus abrumpere caro
>   vincula Pirithoo.

Johnson:

> Not you, Torquatus, boast of Rome,
> When Minos once has fixed your doom,
> Or eloquence, or splendid birth,
> Or virtue, shall restore to earth.
> Hippolytus, unjustly slain,
> Diana calls to life in vain;
> Nor can the might of Theseus rend
> The chains of hell that hold his friend.

Housman:

> When thou descendest once the shades among,
>   The stern assize and equal judgment o'er,
> Not thy long lineage nor thy golden tongue,
>   No, nor thy righteousness, shall friend thee more.
>
> Night holds Hippolytus the pure of stain,
>   Diana steads him nothing, he must stay;
> And Theseus leaves Pirithous in the chain
>   The love of comrades cannot take away.

The truth of the matter is that when the translator of short poems chooses to be literal, most or all of the poetry is lost; and when the translator succeeds in forging a new poetry, most or all of the original author is lost. Since there is no way out of this dilemma, we have always been sparing, in this anthology, in our use of short poems in translation.

In this Second Edition, we have adjusted our policy to take account of the two great non-Western literatures in which the short lyric or "song" has been the principal and by far most cherished expression of the national genius. During much of its history from earliest times, the Japanese imagination has cheerfully exercised itself, with all the delicacy and grace of an Olympic figure skater, inside a rigorous verse pattern of five lines and thirty-one syllables: the *tanka*. Chinese poetry, while somewhat more liberal to itself in line length, has been equally fertile in the fine art of compression and has only occasionally, even in its earliest, most experimental phase, indulged in verse lines of more than seven characters, often just four, or in poems of more than fifty lines, usually fewer than twenty. What makes the Chinese and Japanese lyric more difficult than most other lyrics to translate satisfactorily into English is that these compressions combine with a flexibility of syntax (Japanese) or a degree of freedom from it (Chinese) not available in our language. They also combine with a poetic sensibility that shrinks from exposition in favor of sequences and juxtapositions of images: images grasped and recorded in, or *as if in*, a moment of pure perception unencumbered by the explanatory linkages, background scenarios, and other forms of contextualization that the Western mind is instinctively driven to establish.

Whole books, almost whole libraries, have been written recently on the contrast of East and West in worldviews and value systems as well as on the need of each for the other if there is ever to be a community of understanding adequate to the realities both face. Put baldly, much too simply, and without the many exceptions and qualifications that rightly spring to mind, it may be said that a central and characteristic Western impulse, from the Greeks on down, has been to see the world around us as something to be *acted on*: weighed, measured, managed, used, even (when economic interests prevail over all others) fouled. Likewise, put oversimply, it may be said that a central and characteristic Eastern counterpart to this over many centuries (witness Taoism, Buddhism, and Hinduism, among others) has been to see that same world as something to be *received*: contemplated, touched, tasted, smelled, heard, and most especially, immersed in until observer and observed are one. To paint a bamboo, a stone, a butterfly, a person—so runs a classical Chinese admonition for painters— you must *become* that bamboo, that stone, that butterfly, that person, then paint from the inside. No one need be ashamed of being poor, says Confucius, putting a similar emphasis on *receiving* experience, "only of not being cultivated in the perception of beauty."

The problem that these differences in linguistic freedom and philosophical outlook pose for the English translator of classical Chinese and Japanese poetry may be glimpsed, even if not fully grasped, by considering for a moment in some detail a typical Japanese *tanka* (*Kokinshu*, 9) and a typical Chinese "song" (*Book of Songs*, 23). In its own language but transliterated in the Latin alphabet of the West, the *tanka* looks like this:

> *kasumi tachi*
> *ko no me mo haru no*
> *yuki fureba*
> *hana naki sato mo*
> *hana zo chirikeru*

In a literal word-by-word translation (so far as this is possible in Japanese, since the language uses many particles without English equivalents and without dictionary meaning in modifying and qualifying functions—for example, *no, mo,* and *no* in line 2), the poem looks like this:

> haze rises
> tree-buds swell
> when snow falls
> village(s) without flower(s)
> flower(s) fall(s)

The three best-known English renderings of this *tanka* look like this:

1. Helen Craig McCullough:

> When snow comes in spring—
> fair season of layered haze
> and burgeoning buds—
> flowers fall in villages
> where flowers have yet to bloom.

2. Laurel Rasplica Rodd and Mary Catherine Henkenius:

> When the warm mists veil
> all the buds swell while yet the
> spring snows drift downward
> even in the hibernal
> village crystal blossoms fall.

3. Robert H. Brower and Earl Miner:

> With the spreading mists
> The tree buds swell in early spring
> And wet snow petals fall—

> So even my flowerless country village
> Already lies beneath its fallen flowers.

The reader will notice at once how much the three translators have felt it desirable or necessary to add, alter, rearrange, and explain. In McCullough's version the time of year is affirmed twice, both as "spring" and as "fair season of . . . haze"; the haze is now "layered"; the five coordinate perceptions of the original (haze, swelling buds, a snowfall, villages without flowers, flowers drifting down) have been structured into a single sentence with one main verb and two subordinate clauses spelling out "when" and "where"; and the original poem's climax, in a scene of drifting petallike snow-flakes, has been shifted to a bleak scenery of absence: "flowers have yet to bloom." The final stress, in other words, is not on the fulfilled moment in which snow flowers replace the cherry blossoms, but on the cherry blossoms not yet arrived.

Similar additions and explanations occur in Rodd and Henkenius's version. This time the mist is "warm" and "veil[s] all" to clarify its connection with "buds." Though implicit already in "warm" and "burgeoning," spring is invoked again in "spring snows," and the snows are given confirmation in the following line by the insistently Latinate "hibernal," chosen, we may reasonably guess, along with "veil," "all," "swell," "while," "crystal," and "fall" to replace some of the chiming internal rhyme in the Japanese: *ko, no, mo, no, sato, mo, zo.* To leave no *i* undotted, "crystal" is imported to assure us that the falling "blossoms" of line 5 are really snowflakes, and the scene of flowerlessness that in the original (line 4) accounts for a special joy in the "flowering" of the snowflakes (line 5) vanishes without trace.

Brower and Miner's also fills in the causative links between "spreading mists" and swelling buds; makes sure that we do not fail to see the falling snow in flower terms ("wet snow petals"), thus losing, alas, the element of surprise, even magic, in the transfor-mation of snowflakes into flowers that the original poem holds in store in its last two lines; and tells us (somewhat redundantly) that villages are a "country" phenomenon and (somewhat surprisingly) that this one is the speaker's home. In this version, as in the original and Rodd and Henkenius's, the poem closes with the snow scene, but here it is a one-time affair and "already" complete (lines 4 and 5), not a recurrent phenome-non that may appear under certain conditions anywhere at any time.

Some of the differences in these translations arise inevitably from different trade-offs, as in the first version, where the final vision of falling snow blossoms is let go presumably to achieve the lovely lilting echo and rhetorical turn of "flowers fall in villages / where flowers have yet to bloom." Or as in Rodd and Henkenius's version, where preoccupations with internal rhyme have obviously influenced word choices, not always for the better. Or as in all three versions, where different efforts to remind the reader of the wordplay on *haru* (in the Japanese poem both a noun meaning "spring" and a verb meaning "swell") have had dissimilar but perhaps equally indif-ferent results. Meantime, the immense force compacted into that small word in the original as both noun and verb, season of springtime and principal of growth, cause and effect (and thus in a sense the whole mighty process of earth's renewal, in which an interruption by snow only foretells a greater loveliness to come) fizzles away unfelt. A few differences do seem to arise from insufficient command of the nerves and sinews of English poetry, but most spring from the staggering difficulties of respond-ing in any uniform way to the minimal clues proffered by the original text. The five perceptions—haze, buds, snowfall, flowerless villages, flowers falling—do not as they stand in the Japanese or any literal translation quite compose for readers accustomed to Western poetic traditions an adequate poetic whole. This is plainly seen in the irresistible urge each of the translators has felt to catch up the individual perceptions, as English tends to require, in a tighter overall grammatical and syntactical structure than the original insists on. In this way they provide a clarifying network of principal and subordinate, time when, place where, and cause why. Yet the inevitable result is a disassembling, a spinning out, spelling out, thinning out of what in the Japanese is an as yet unraveled imagistic excitement, creating (or memorializing) in the poet's mind, and then in the mind of the Japanese readers, the original thrill of consciousness when these images, complete with the magical transformation of snow into the longed-for cherry blossoms, first flashed on the inward eye.

What is comforting for us who must read this and other Japanese poems in translation is that each of the versions given here retains in some form or other all or most of the five images intact. What is less comforting is that the simplicity and suddenness, the explosion in the mind, have been diffused and defused.

When we turn to the Chinese song, we find similarly contesting forces at work. In one respect, the Chinese language comes over into English more readily than Japanese, being like English comparatively uninflected and heavily dependent on word order for its meanings. But in other respects, since Chinese like Japanese lacks distinctions of gender, of singular and plural, of *a* and *the,* and in the classical mode in which the poems in this anthology are composed, also of tenses, the pressure of the English translator to rearrange, straighten out, and fill in to "make sense" for his or her readers remains strong.

Let us examine song no. 23 of the *Shijing.* In its own Chinese characters, it looks like this:

野有死麕

林有樸樕　死鹿　白茅純束　有女如玉
吉士誘之。　野有死麕　白茅包之。有女懷春
舒而脱脱兮　無
感我帨兮　無使
龙也吠。

Eleven lines in all, each line having four characters as its norm, the poem seemingly takes shape around an implicit parallel between a doe in the forest, possibly killed by stealth and hidden under long grass or rushes (though on this point as on all others the poem refuses to take us wholly into confidence), and a young girl possibly "ruined" (as she certainly would have been in the post-Confucian society in which the *Shijing* was prized and circulated, though here again the poem keeps its own counsel) by loss of her virginity before marriage.

In its bare bones, with each character given an approximate English equivalent, a translation might look like this:

```
wild(s)    is       dead       deer
white      grass(es) wrap/cover (it).
is         girl      feel       spring.
fine       man       tempt      (her).
woods      is(are)   bush(es),  underbrush.   5
wild(s)    is        dead       deer.
white      grass(es) bind       bundle.
is         girl      like       jade.
slow       _____     slow       slow.
not        move      my         sash.         10
not        cause     dog        bark.
```

Lines 1 to 4, it seems plain, propose the parallel of slain doe and girl, whatever that parallel may be intended to mean. Lines 5 to 8 restate the parallel, adding that the girl is as beautiful as jade and (apparently) that the doe lies where the "wild" gives way to smaller growth. If we allow ourselves to account for the repetition (here again is a Western mind-set in search of explanatory clues) by supposing that lines 1 to 4 signal at some subliminal level the initiation of the seduction and lines 5 to 8, again subliminally, its progress or possibly its completion, lines 9 to 11 fall easily into place as a miniature drama enacting in direct speech the man's advances and the girl's gradually crumbling resistance. They also imply, it seems, that the seduction takes place not in the forest, as we might have been led to suppose by lines 1 to 8, but in a dwelling with a vigilant guard dog.

Interpreted just far enough to accommodate English syntax, the poem reads as follows:

1. Wai-lim Yip:

> In the wilds, a dead doe.
> White reeds to wrap it.
> A girl, spring-touched.
> A fine man to seduce her.
> In the woods, bushes. 5
> In the wilds, a dead deer.
> White reeds in bundles.
> A girl like jade.
> Slowly. Take it easy.
> Don't feel my sash! 10
> Don't make the dog bark!

Interpreted a stage further in a format some have thought better suited to English poetic traditions, the poem reads:

2. Arthur Waley:

> In the wilds there is a dead doe,
> With white rushes we cover her.
> There was a lady longing for spring,
> A fair knight seduced her.
>
> In the woods there is a clump of oaks, 5
> And in the wilds a dead deer
> With white rushes well bound.
> There was a lady fair as jade.
>
> "Heigh, not so hasty, not so rough.
> "Heigh, do not touch my handkerchief. 10
> "Take care or the dog will bark."

Like the original and the literal translation, this version leaves the relationship between the doe's death and the girl's seduction unspecified and problematic. It holds the doe story in present tenses, assigning the girl story to the past. Still, much has been changed to give the English poem an explanatory scenario. The particular past assigned to the girl story, indeterminate in the Chinese original, is here fixed as the age of knights and ladies; and the seduction itself, which in the Chinese hovers as an eternal possibility within the timeless situation of man and maid ("A fine man *to* seduce her"), is established as completed long ago: "A fair knight seduced her." A teasing oddity in this version is the mysterious "we" who "cover" the slain doe, never to be heard from again.

Take interpretation toward its outer limits and we reach what is perhaps best called a "variation" on this theme:

3. Ezra Pound:

> Lies a dead doe on yonder plain
> whom white grass covers,
> A melancholy maid in spring

> is luck
>> for   5
>> lovers
> Where the scrub elm skirts the wood
> be it not in white mat bound,
> As a jewel flawless found
>> dead as a doe is maidenhood.   10
> Hark!
> Unhand my girdle knot.
>> Stay, stay, stay
>> or the dog
>> may   15
>> bark.

Here too the present is pushed back to a past by the language the translator uses: not a specific past, as with the era of knights and ladies, but any past in which contemporary speech still features such (to us) archaic formalisms as "Unhand" or "Hark," and in which the term "maid" still signifies a virgin and in which virginity is prized to an extent that equates its loss with the doe's loss of life. But these evocations of time past are so effectively countered by the obtrusively present tense throughout (lines 1, 2, 4, 7, 8, 10, 11, 12, 13, and 15) that the freewheeling "variation" remains in this important respect closer to the spirit of the original than Waley's translation. On the other hand, it departs from the original and the two other versions by brushing aside the reticence that they carefully preserve as to the precise implications of the girl-deer parallel, choosing instead to place the seduction in the explanatory framework of the oldest story in the world: the way of a man with a maid in the springtime of life.

What both these examples make plain is that the Chinese and Japanese lyric, however contrasting in some ways, have in common at their center a complex of highly charged images generating something very like a magnetic field of potential meanings that cannot be got at in English without bleeding away much of the voltage. In view of this, the best practical advice for those of us who must read these marvelous poems in English translations is to focus intently on these images and ask ourselves what there is in them or in their effect on each other that produces the electricity. To that extent, we can compensate for a part of our losses, learn something positive about the immense explosive powers of imagery, and rest easy in the secure knowledge that translation even in the mode of the short poem brings us (despite losses) closer to the work itself than not reading it at all. "To a thousand cavils," said Samuel Johnson, "one answer is sufficient; the purpose of a writer is to be read, and the criticism which would destroy the power of pleasing must be blown aside." Johnson was defending Pope's Homer for those marks of its own time and place that make it the great interpretation it is, but Johnson's exhilarating common sense applies equally to the problem we are considering here. Literature is to be read, and the criticism that would destroy the reader's power to make some form of contact with much of the world's great writing must indeed be blown aside.

MAYNARD MACK

Sources

Brower, Robert H., and Earl Miner. *Japanese Court Poetry.* Stanford: Stanford University Press, 1961.

The Classic Anthology Defined by Confucius. Tr. Ezra Pound. New Directions, 1954.

Kokinshū: A Collection of Poems Ancient and Modern. Tr. Laurel Rasplica Rodd and Mary Catherine Henkenius. Princeton: Princeton University Press, 1984.
Kokin Wakashū: The First Imperial Anthology of Japanese Poetry. Tr. and ed. Helen Craig McCullough. Stanford: Stanford University Press, 1985.
Legge, James. *The Chinese Classics*. Hong Kong: Hong Kong University Press, 1960.
Waley, Arthur. *170 Chinese Poems*. New York, 1919.

Index